GW00691539

THE MACMILLAN
CONCISE
ENCYCLOPEDIA

THE MACMILLAN
CONCISE
ENCYCLOPEDIA

MACMILLAN

Notes

1. *Chinese translations*
This encyclopedia follows official Chinese practice in using the pinyin system of transliterating Chinese names. Thus, almost all articles appear under the pinyin transliteration of the subjects name. However, the transliteration of the name in the Wade-Giles system (formerly the system most commonly used in the English-speaking world) will also be found in its alphabetical place, where the reader will be cross referred to the pinyin name under which the article appears. The Wade-Giles equivalent (unless the Wade-Giles and pinyin transliterations are almost identical) and, when it exists, the conventional western name is given in brackets following the pinyin name. A small number of names are so well known in their Wade-Giles or conventional western forms that it has become usual to retain these very familiar spellings. They are Canton, Chiang Dai-shek, China, Chou En-Lai, Inner Mongolia, Mao Tse-tung, Peking, Sun Yat-sen, Tibet, Yangzte River, Yellow River.

2. *Population figures*
For towns and cities the population figures given refer, wherever possible, to the town or city proper rather than the urban agglomeration of which it forms part.

KINGS AND QUEENS OF ENGLAND

A

Aachen (French name: Aix-la-Chapelle) 50 46N 06 06E A spa city in W West Germany, in North Rhine-Westphalia near the Belgian and Dutch borders. It is an important industrial centre with iron and steel and textile industries. *History*: it was the N capital of Charlemagne's empire and many Holy Roman Emperors were crowned in the cathedral (founded in 796 AD). It was annexed by France in 1801 and passed to Prussia (1815). Extensively damaged during World War II, it was the first major German city captured by the Allies (1944). Population (1986): 238 600.

Aalborg. *See* Ålborg.

aardvark (Afrikaans: earth pig) A nocturnal African mammal, *Orycteropus afer*, also called ant bear. It is about 1.5 m long, lives in grassland, and has a long snout, large ears, and a thick tail. Its strong claws are used to dig burrows and tear open the mounds of termites, which are picked up with its long sticky tongue. The aardvark is the only member of its order (*Tubulidentata*).

Aarhus. *See* Århus.

AARDVARK *This strange animal feeds entirely on termites and ants.*

abacus A calculating device consisting of balls strung on wires or rods set in a frame, probably of Babylonian origin. Its use declined in Europe with the introduction of Arabic numerals in about the 10th century AD.

Abadan 30 20N 48 15E A city in SW Iran, on an island in the Shatt (river) al-Arab. Much of Iran's oil is brought here by pipeline for refining or exporting. Population (1985 est): 294 068.

abalone A marine gastropod mollusc belonging to the widely distributed family *Haliotidae*, of rocky coasts, also called ear shell or ormer. Up to 30 cm long, their dishlike shells have a row of holes along the outer edge through which deoxygenated water and waste products are expelled from the body. The large foot is considered a delicacy and the shells are used as mother-of-pearl for ornaments.

Abbevillian A culture of the Lower Palaeolithic in Europe. It is characterized by crude stone hand axes made by hammering flakes off a flint with another stone. Named after Abbeville in France, the Abbevillian also appears in Britain but in Africa similar early hand axes are designated Acheulian.

Abbey Theatre A Dublin theatre opened in 1904. Annie Horniman (1860–1937), a friend of W. B. Yeats, initiated the building of the theatre as a home for the Irish National Dramatic Society, a company founded by the actors Frank Fay (1870–1931) and his brother W. G. Fay (1872–1947). The Abbey Theatre gained an international reputation as a repertory theatre dedicated to performing mainly plays by Irish playwrights on Irish subjects. The original playhouse burnt down in 1951, but a new theatre was built and opened in 1966.

abdomen In mammals (including man), the region of the body extending from the lower surface of the diaphragm to the pelvis. The abdomen contains the intestines, liver, pancreas, kidneys, gall bladder, and—in females—the ovaries and womb. In arthropods, the abdomen is the posterior section of the body, which is usually segmented.

Abdullah (1882–1951) Emir of Transjordan (1921–46) and first King of Jordan (1946–51). He fought in the Arab revolt against Turkish rule during World War I. He was assassinated in 1951.

Abelard, Peter (1079–1142) French philosopher. His ill-fated marriage with Heloïse, niece of a canon of Paris, ended when Abelard was castrated by thugs hired by the canon (1118). He retired to a monastery and she became a nun. A quarrelsome disputant, Abelard was perpetually in trouble with the church authorities; his *Sic et Non* (*For and Against*), for example, outraged opponents by listing points on which acknowledged authorities differed. *See also* scholasticism.

Abercrombie, Sir (Leslie) Patrick (1879–1957) British town planner and architect, best known for his detailed schemes for London, *The County of London Plan* (1943) and *The Greater London Plan* (1944). Later plans include those for Edinburgh, Hull, and the West Midlands. He was professor at Liverpool University (1915–35) and London University (1935–46).

Aberdeen 57 10N 2 04W A city, port, and former county of NE Scotland, the administrative centre of Grampian Region situated on the North Sea coast between the mouths of the Rivers Don and Dee. Aberdeen is an old cathedral city with a university dating from 1494 (King's College). Fishing has always been important, as has the working of local granite; the "Granite City" provided stone for London's cobbled streets in the 18th century. Other industries include shipbuilding, paper making, textiles, chemicals, and engineering. Aberdeen's proximity to North Sea oil has transformed it into an important service centre for the oil industry. Population (1985 est): 215 246.

Aberdeen Angus A breed of polled (naturally hornless) beef cattle, originating from NE Scotland. Short, stocky, and usually black (some have red coats), they are hardy and adapt well to different climates. Angus bulls are commonly mated with dairy breeds to produce a polled beef cross.

Aberdeen terrier. *See* Scottish terrier.

aberration **1.** A defect in a lens or mirror that causes blurring or distortion of the image. **Spherical aberration** is caused by rays from the outside of the lens or mirror being brought to a focus at a different point from those nearer to the centre. In **chromatic aberration**, different colours are focused at different points, since the refractive index of glass varies with the wavelength. *See also* astigmatism. **2.** An apparent displacement in the position of a star or other heavenly body due to the motion of the observer with the earth in its orbit round the sun.

Aberystwyth 52 25N 4 05W A town and resort in Wales, in Dyfed on Cardigan Bay. A college of the University of Wales was established in 1872 and the National Library of Wales, in 1911. Population (1981): 15 000.

Abidjan 5 19N 4 00W The former capital of Côte d'Ivoire, off the Gulf of Guinea. A small village until developed by the French in the 1920's, it was the capital in 1934. It is now an important port, linked to the sea by the Vridi Canal. Population (1984): 1 850 000.

Abominable Snowman A creature, also called Yeti (Tibetan: Snowman), that is believed to live at high altitudes in the Himalayas. There have been no authenticated sightings, but gigantic footprints in the snow have been photographed (which may have other natural causes).

ABORIGINES *A piece of aboriginal art painted on a rock wall in the Kimberley area of Australia.*

Aborigines The dark-skinned hunters and gatherers who inhabited Australia before European settlement. They were a diverse people culturally but, in general, material culture was rudimentary, while kinship organization and terminology were complex. Aboriginal mythology was generally rich and elaborate and included accounts of creation during the primordial dawn, which they call "Dream Time." There are roughly 136 000 people of Aboriginal descent in Australia. The small proportion who maintain a nomadic way of life are threatened by encroachments upon their lands. A movement to protect Aborigines' rights has gathered momentum and in 1971 the first Aborigine MP was elected.

abortion The expulsion or removal of a fetus from the womb before it is capable of independent survival. In the UK a fetus is not legally viable until 28 weeks old, but there are moves to reduce this to 24 weeks. (Expulsion of a dead fetus at any later time is called a stillbirth.) Abortion may be natural, i.e. spontaneous (a miscarriage), or induced for therapeutic or social reasons. In the UK it is illegal to induce an abortion unless it is carried out under the terms of the Abortion Act (1968): two doctors must agree that termination of the pregnancy is necessary (e.g. to prevent the birth of a severely deformed or abnormal child or to preserve the health of the mother) and the operation must be performed in approved premises. Methods used include dilatation and curettage, suction using a vacuum aspirator, and the administration of certain drugs.

Aboukir, Battle of (25 July, 1799) The battle in which Napoleon defeated the Ottoman Turks during his occupation of Egypt. The 7000-strong French army defeated the unruly Turkish force of 18 000.

Abraham, Plains of A plateau in E Canada, on the W edge of Quebec citadel. Here Gen James Wolfe defeated the French under Gen Montcalm (13 September, 1759), leading to British control over Canada.

Abruzzi (*or* Abruzzo) A region in E central Italy. It consists of the Apennines in the W and a coastal region in the E. Agriculture is limited, producing mainly cereals. Manufacturing industry is primarily for local needs but there is a large fishing fleet. Area: 10 794 sq km (4167 sq mi). Population (1985 est): 1 254 129. Capital: L'Aquila.

absolute magnitude. *See* magnitude.

absolute zero The lowest temperature that can theoretically be attained. It is equal to $-273.15°C$ or 0 K. In practice, absolute zero can never be reached, although temperatures of a few thousandths of a degree above absolute zero have been achieved. *See* cryogenics.

absorption. *See* adsorption.

abstract art A nonobjective and nonrepresentational form of art. Tendencies to abstraction can be found in almost any age or school of art, particularly oriental and decorative art. However, the widespread use of photography in the 20th century to create a permanent visual record of people, places, events, etc., made the strictly representational function of painting much less important. This shift of emphasis released artists from the confines of realism, enabling them to explore the wider fields of abstraction. In about 1910 Wassily Kandinsky (1866–1944) produced the first abstract watercolour, heralding the free expression of such artists as Jackson Pollock; in contrast, cubism led to the geometric abstract style of such painters as Piet Mondrian and Kasimir Malevich (1878–1935). A particular characteristic of abstract sculpture is the use of new materials, such as plastic, glass, and steel. *See also* action painting; constructivism; minimal art; Op art.

abstract expressionism. *See* action painting.

Abu Dhabi. *See* United Arab Emirates.

Abuja 9 10N 7 06E A city in Nigeria, named as the future capital in 1982. Agriculture is the most important activity with some local manufacturing.

Abu Simbel A monumental rock-cut temple complex constructed about 1250 BC by Pharaoh Ramses II in Nubia. Four colossal statues of Ramses, each 20 m (66 ft) high, at the entrance were raised to escape inundation by Lake Nasser (1968).

ABU SIMBEL *A Nubian masterpiece.*

Abydos An ancient city in Upper Egypt, founded before 3000 BC and continuously occupied until Roman times. It was a principal centre of Osiris worship. The most impressive remaining structure is Seti I's Great Temple (c. 1300 BC), with shrines for six deities and the god pharaoh. The Table of Abydos, a king list carved on its walls, provides information about earlier pharaohs.

abyssal zone The ocean depths lying below 1000 m. It is the zone of greatest ocean depth, lying seawards of the continental slope (*see* continental shelf). Since no light penetrates to these depths, they contain relatively little marine life and the temperature never rises above 4°C. The ocean depths below 6000 m, the deep-sea trenches, may be classified separately as the **hadal zone**.

Abyssinia. *See* Ethiopia.

Abyssinian cat A breed of short-haired cat, many individuals of which are descendants of one exported to the UK from Abyssinia in the 19th century. They have slender bodies and wedge-shaped heads with large ears. The reddish-brown coat has black or brown markings and the eyes are green, yellow, or hazel. The Red Abyssinian is a rich copper-red.

Acacia A genus of tropical and subtropical trees and shrubs (over 700 species), particularly abundant in Australia (*see* wattle). Acacias have clusters of yellow or white flowers, produce long flattened pods, and usually have compound leaves consisting of many small leaflets. In some species the leaflets do not develop and the leaf-stalks assume their function, being broad and flattened. These species are often very spiny. Acacias yield a number of useful products: gums (including gum arabic), tannins, dyes, and woods suitable for furniture. Many are grown as ornamental plants. Family: *Leguminosae*.

Académie Française The French literary academy founded by Cardinal de Richelieu in 1634 (incorporated 1635) to preserve the French literary heritage. Its membership is limited at any one time to 40 "immortals," who have included Corneille, Racine, and Voltaire. It is continuously engaged in the revision of the official French dictionary.

Academy, Greek The college founded (c. 385 BC) near Athens by Plato, which continued in various guises until its dissolution by Justinian in 529 AD. It is famed mainly for contributions to philosophy and science.

Academy of Motion Picture Arts and Sciences An organization founded in Hollywood in 1927 to raise the artistic and technical standards of the film industry. It is responsible for the annual presentation of the Academy Awards, popularly known as Oscars, for excellence in acting, writing, directing, and other aspects of film production.

Acanthus A genus of perennial herbaceous plants (about 50 species), mostly native to the Mediterranean region: *A. mollis* and *A. spinosus* are the species most commonly planted in temperate gardens. Growing to a height of 1–1.5 m, they have tough, often spiny, leaves and spikes of purple and white flowers. The fruit—a capsule—explodes to disperse the seeds. Family: *Acanthaceae*.

acanthus A decorative element of classical architecture. It is mainly found on the capitals of Corinthian and Composite columns, comprising heavy carvings of stylized leaves.

a cappella (Italian: in the church style) A marking on a piece of music for several voices, indicating that it is to be sung unaccompanied.

Acapulco 16 51N 99 56W A seaside resort in S Mexico, on the Pacific Ocean. Known as the Riviera of Mexico, it has fine sandy beaches and many hotels. Population (1985): 638 000.

ACAS (advisory, conciliation and arbitration service) A public body set up by parliament in 1975 to work with trade unions and employers to settle disputes and promote methods of collective bargaining.

acceleration The rate of change of a body's velocity. Linear acceleration is the rate of change of linear velocity. It is measured in such units as metres per second per second. Angular acceleration is the rate of change of angular velocity and is measured in such units as radians per second per second.

acceleration of free fall (g) Formerly called acceleration due to gravity; the acceleration of a falling body when air resistance is neglected. Caused by gravitational attraction between the body and the earth, it varies slightly at different points on the earth's surface. Its standard value is 9.806 metres per second per second.

accelerators Large machines used for accelerating beams of charged particles (electrons, protons, etc.) to very high speeds primarily for research in particle physics. The particles are accelerated by electric fields either in a straight line, as in the linear accelerator, or in a circle, as in the cyclotron, synchrotron, and synchrocyclotron. The beam is confined to its path by magnetic fields. Particle accelerators are used by directing a beam of particles at a stationary target or, for greater energy, by colliding two beams of particles together. Accelerators are also used to create artificial isotopes and in radiotherapy. The first accelerator was a linear accelerator, produced in 1932 by Cockcroft and Watson.

accessory In law, a person who incites another to commit a crime but is not present when the crime is committed is an accessory before the fact. (An abettor is distinguished from an accessory before the fact by being present at the commission of a crime.) A person who assists another whom he knows has committed a crime is an accessory after the fact.

DENMARK 94 68%
NORWAY 194 93%
323 84% SWEDEN
779 32%
NETHERLANDS 152 76% E.GERMANY
GREAT BRITAIN 654 20%
935 29% POLAND
CZECHOSLOVAKIA
BELGIUM 147 57%
685 41%
FRANCE 781 55%
ITALY 781 55% W. GERMANY
103 89% SWITZERLAND
851 23%
2062 81% AUSTRIA

384 58% Average annual deposits of sulphur in 1984 ('000 tonnes)
Percentage received from other countries

ACID RAIN *Sulphur deposits in Europe.*

accomplice In law, a person concerned with one or more other persons in committing a crime, either as its actual perpetrator or as an abettor or accessory.

accordion A portable musical instrument invented in Berlin in 1822. A member of the reed-organ family, the accordion is a boxlike instrument in which bellows force air through reeds mounted in end panels. In the modern **piano accordion** a small piano-like keyboard supplies the melody, while buttons operated by the other hand produce chords.

Accra 5 32N 0 12W The capital of Ghana, a port on the Gulf of Guinea. It is built on the site of three 17th-century trading fortresses founded by the English, Dutch, and Danish. It became the capital of the Gold Coast in 1877. Following the opening of a railway to the agricultural hinterland (1923) it developed rapidly into the commercial centre of Ghana. The University of Ghana was founded in 1948 at Legon, just outside Accra. Population (1984): 964 879.

accumulator A cell or battery that can be recharged by passing a current through it in the direction opposite to that of the discharge current. The most common example is the lead-acid accumulator used in motor vehicles. This consists, when charged, of a positive lead dioxide electrode and a negative spongy lead electrode, both immersed in sulphuric acid with a relative density of 1.20–1.28. During discharge lead sulphate forms on the electrodes and the acid density falls.
Nickel-iron (NiFe) accumulators with an electrolyte of 20% potassium hydroxide are also used. Interest in electric cars has stimulated accumulator development in recent years. While lead accumulators will deliver up 8×10^4 joules per kilogram, the newer zinc-air accumulator can produce five times this energy density.

acetylcholine A chemical that transmits impulses between the ends of two adjacent nerves and is confined largely to the parasympathetic nervous system. Acetylcholine is released on stimulation of the nerve and diffuses across the gap of the synapse to stimulate the adjacent nerve. It is rapidly converted to an inactive form by the enzyme cholinesterase, permitting the passage of a further impulse.

acetylene (*or* ethyne; C_2H_2) A colourless toxic inflammable gas formed by the action of water on calcium carbide. It is widely used as a starting material for many organic compounds. Because of its high flame temperature (about 3300°C) it is used in oxy-acetylene welding. *See also* alkynes.

achene A small dry fruit having a single seed that is attached to the fruit wall at one point only. The fruit does not open at maturity (i.e. the fruit is indehiscent) and the seed is thus retained until germination. Lettuce fruits are examples of achenes.

Acheron A river in N Greece, in Greek mythology the chief river of the underworld. In Dante, it is the river across which the souls of the dead are ferried to hell by Charon.

Acheulian A culture of the Lower Palaeolithic. It is characterized by hand axes made by hammering flakes off a flint with a hammer of wood, antler, or bone, producing a more regular and effective tool than the Abbevillian hand axe. Named after St Acheul near Amiens (N France), the Acheulian occurs widely in Eurasia and also in Africa, where it apparently originated and survived longest (until about 58 000 years ago). Acheulian sites provide the earliest evidence of man's use of fire and are often associated with *Homo erectus* remains (*see* Homo).

Achilles In Greek mythology, the greatest Greek warrior in the Trojan War. The son of Peleus, King of Thessaly, and Thetis, a sea nymph, he was dipped by his mother in the River Styx as a child, which made his whole body invulnerable except for the heel by which she had held him. After a quarrel with Agamemnon he ceased fighting until the death of his friend Patroclus at the hand of Hector. Achilles then slew Hector and was himself later killed by Paris, who shot a poisoned arrow into his heel.

acid rain Rain that contains sulphuric and nitric acids as a result of the absorption of sulphur dioxide and nitrogen oxides in the atmosphere. It is contended that the effects can include destruction of fish, crops, and trees, as well as damage to buildings. Attempts to control the presence of these oxides, especially from industrial and vehicle emissions, have been hampered by absence of international agreement.

acids and bases Acids are chemical compounds containing hydrogen that can be replaced by a metal atom to produce a salt. They have a sour taste and turn litmus red. When dissolved in water they dissociate into ions. Hydrochloric acid (HCl), for instance, gives chloride ions and hydrogen ions: $HCl + H_2O \rightarrow Cl^- + H^+ + H_2O$. The hydrogen ion is associated with a water molecule, a combination referred to as a hydroxonium ion (H_3O^+).
Bases are compounds that react with acids to form salts and water. Bases that dissolve in water, known as **alkalis**, produce hydroxide ions (OH^-). Many are metal hydroxides, such as sodium hydroxide (NaOH). The neutralization of an acid by a base in solution is a reaction in which hydrogen and hydroxide ions combine to give water. The concept of an acid has been extended to include any compound that can donate a proton and a base as a proton acceptor. This (the Brönsted-Lowry theory) can be applied to reactions in nonaqueous solvents. A further extension of the terms (Lewis theory) defines an acid as an acceptor of an unshared electron pair and a base as a pair donor. *See also* pH.

Aconcagua, Mount (Spanish name: Cerro Aconcagua) 32 40S 70 02W A mountain in W Argentina, in the Andes, regarded as being the highest point in the W hemisphere. It is of volcanic origin. Height: 6960 m (22 835 ft).

aconite A European herbaceous plant, *Aconitum napellus*, also known as monkshood. Growing to a height of 1 m, its flowers are usually purplish-blue and hood-shaped; the bulbous roots yield poisonous alkaloids, including aconitine, which have been used in medicine as narcotics and analgesics. Winter aconite is a related plant, *Eranthis hyemalis*, with yellow flowers. Family: *Ranunculaceae* (buttercup family).

acornworm A wormlike marine invertebrate animal, 5–180 cm long, that burrows in soft sand or mud. A filter feeder, it has an acorn-shaped head with the mouth at the base. Chief genera: *Balanoglossus, Saccoglossus*; phylum: *Hemichordata*.

ACOUSTICS *An engineer tests a talk-writer computer in a soundproof laboratory.*

acoustics The branch of physics concerned with the production, propagation, reception, properties, and uses of sound. It has several subdivisions. The most important, architectural acoustics, is concerned with the design of public auditoriums so that sounds can be heard in all parts of them with the maximum clarity and the minimum distortion. Ultrasonics is the study of very high frequency sound. The structure and function of sound sources, such as loudspeakers, and sound receptors, such as microphones, also form part of acoustics. Other fields include speech communication and the design of machines that can understand spoken instructions.

acquired characteristic. *See* Lamarckism.

acquittal In law, the clearing of an accused person of the charge against him, usually by court verdict. In England there must be a verdict of "not guilty"; in Scotland the verdict may be either "not guilty" or "not proven." Acquittal prevents a person from being prosecuted for the same offence again. Anyone charged as an accessory to a crime is automatically acquitted if the principal is acquitted.

acropolis (Greek: high town) In ancient Greek towns, the isolated rocky plateau on which stood the religious and administrative nucleus of the town and which served as a citadel in time of war. The most famous is the Acropolis of Athens, which is still adorned by remains of buildings erected by Cimon, Themisto-

cles, and Pericles after the sack of Athens by the Persians (480 BC). These buildings include the Propylaea, Parthenon, Erectheum, and the reconstructed temple of Athena Nike.

acrylics Synthetic materials produced by polymerization of acrylonitrile (vinyl cyanide; CH_2:CHCN). Acrylic resins are used in paints and plastics, the most common being Perspex. Acrylic fibre is widely used in textiles, mainly for knitwear, furnishing fabrics, and carpets.

Actaeon A mythological Greek hunter, son of the god Aristaeus and Autonoe, daughter of Cadmus, King of Thebes. Ovid, in his *Metamorphoses*, relates how Actaeon accidentally caught sight of the goddess Artemis bathing naked and was turned by her into a stag and killed by his own hounds.

ACTH (adrenocorticotrophic hormone) A peptide hormone, secreted by the anterior lobe of the pituitary gland, that stimulates the cortex of the adrenal glands to produce three types of corticosteroid hormones. Secretion of ACTH is stimulated by physical stress and is regulated by secretions of the hypothalamus of the brain.

actinides A group of related chemical elements in the periodic table ranging from actinium (atomic number 89) to lawrencium (atomic number 103). They are radioactive and include a number of transuranic elements. Chemically, they resemble the lanthanides.

actinium (Ac) A highly radioactive metal that occurs naturally in uranium minerals. It is the first of the actinide series of elements and is chemically similar to the lanthanide elements. It was discovered in 1899 by A. L. Debierne (1874–1949). The **actinium series** of radioactive decay is headed by uranium-235, which undergoes a series of alpha and beta decays ending with the stable isotope lead-207. At no 89; at wt (227); mp 1050°C; half-life of ^{227}Ac 21.6 yrs.

action painting A modern style, also called abstract expressionism, in which paint is sprayed, splashed, or dribbled over a large canvas to form an unpremeditated and usually abstract design. Jackson Pollock invented it in 1947 to give free rein to his own emotions. Together with colour-field painting, action painting was the dominant style in the USA in the 1950s and made New York, for the first time, the most advanced centre of modern art.

Actium, Battle of (31 BC) The decisive land and sea battle that ended the civil war in ancient Rome. Octavian, later Augustus (the first Roman emperor), defeated the forces of Mark Antony and Cleopatra.

act of God In law, an occurrence due to a sudden violent natural cause, such as a storm, which could not reasonably have been guarded against and loss from which could not have been avoided or predicted.

Act of Parliament. *See* parliament.

Actors' Studio An actors' workshop founded in New York in 1947 by Elia Kazan and others. Under its director Lee Strasberg (1901–82), who joined it in 1950, it became famous for its emphasis on "method" acting, which was developed from the theories of Stanislavsky. Film actors influenced by it include Marlon Brando, Rod Steiger (1925–   ), and James Dean.

actuary A mathematician employed by an insurance company to calculate the premiums payable on policies. The calculations are based on statistically determined risks and eventualities (e.g. sickness, life expectancy). In the UK qualifications are awarded by the Institute of Actuaries through examination.

acupuncture A traditional Chinese system of healing in which thin metal needles are inserted into selected

ACUPUNCTURE *Widely practised in China.*

points in the body. The needles are stimulated either by manual rotation or electrically. Acupuncture is used in the Far East to relieve pain and in China as an anaesthetic for surgical operations. The traditional explanation of its effectiveness, dating back to 2500 BC, relates to balancing the opposing life forces yin and yang. Recent research in the West suggests that the needles may activate deep sensory nerves, which cause the pituitary and midbrain to release endorphins (natural pain killers; *see* encephalins).

Adam, Robert (1728–92) British architect and interior designer, born in Kirkcaldy, Fifeshire, the son of the Palladian architect **William Adam** (1689–1748). He evolved a unique style that blended the rococo and neoclassicism, although he occasionally used gothic forms. After visiting Italy (1755–58), Robert, often in collaboration with his brother **James Adam** (1732–94), built many country houses, notably Kenwood House (1768), the interior of Syon House (1769), and Osterley Park (1780). His building of town houses in London, such as Apsley House (1775), led him into severe financial difficulties. In his last years in Edinburgh he produced much of his finest work, for instance Charlotte Square (1791).

Adams, John (1735–1826) US statesman; first vice president (1789–97) and second president of the USA (1797–1801). During the American Revolution he successfully mobilized European support for the North American cause. His term as president was troubled by disputes with his vice president, Thomas Jefferson, over US policy towards Revolutionary France. Adams was defeated by Jefferson in the election of 1800. His son **John Quincy Adams** (1767–1848) was sixth president of the USA (1825–29). As secretary of state (1817–25) he was largely responsible for the Monroe Doctrine (1823). His term as president was made difficult by the opposition of Andrew Jackson, who defeated Adams in the presidential election in 1828. From 1831 Adams served in the House of Representatives, where he campaigned vigorously against slavery.

adaptive radiation The process by which a uniform population of animals or plants evolves into a number of different forms. The original population increases in size and spreads to occupy different habitats. It forms several subpopulations, each adapted to the particular conditions of its habitat. In time–and if the subpopulations differ sufficiently–a number of new species will be formed from the original stock. The Australian marsupials evolved in this way into burrowers, fliers, carnivores, herbivores, and many other different forms.

adder A widely distributed European viper, *Vipera berus*, about 80 cm long, common in heathland areas. It is usually greyish with a broad black zigzag line along its back and black spots on its sides. Although venomous, its bite is rarely fatal. It is one of the three species of snakes found in Britain. The name adder is also given to a highly venomous Australian snake (death adder) of the cobra family and to some harmless North American snakes. *See also* puff adder.

Addington, ' Henry, 1st Viscount Sidmouth (1757–1844) British statesman; prime minister (1801–04), replacing Pitt the Younger. Addington was attacked for his management of the Napoleonic Wars and resigned. As home secretary (1812–21) he has been held responsible for the Peterloo Massacre.

Addis Ababa 9 02N 38 43E The capital of Ethiopia, on a central plateau 2440 m (8000 ft) above sea level. It became the new capital of Ethiopia in 1889 and was capital of Italian East Africa (1936–41). It is the country's administrative centre and chief market place and its major industries produce cement, tobacco, textiles, and shoes. A railway line links the city with the port of Djibouti on the Gulf of Aden. It is also an important pan-African centre with the headquarters of the Organization of African Unity and the UN Economic Commission for Africa. The National University was established in 1961. Population (1984): 1 412 575.

Addison's disease A rare disease of the adrenal glands, first described by the British physician Thomas Addison (1793–1860), characterized by a reduced secretion of corticosteroid hormones. This leads to weakness, intestinal upsets, darkening of the skin, low blood pressure, and collapse. Formerly fatal, Addison's disease can now be readily treated with synthetic steroids.

additive process. *See* colour.

Adelaide 34 56S 138 36E The capital of South Australia, on the Torrens River. Founded in 1837, the city was laid out in wide straight streets. Extensive parklands remain, separating the city from its suburbs. It is an important commercial centre with a harbour at Port Adelaide. Industries include the manufacture of cars and textiles, oil refining, and electronics. Population (1986): 993 100.

Aden 12 50N 45 03E The capital of South Yemen, on the **Gulf of Aden**, an arm of the Indian Ocean connecting the main body with the Red Sea. Taken by the British in 1839, Aden was an important coaling station on the route to India through the Suez Canal (opened 1869). It became part of the Federation of Saudi Arabia in 1963 and was the scene of fighting between rival nationalist groups until 1968, when it became the capital of the independent republic of South Yemen. Economic activity centres on the port and an oil refinery. Population (1984): 318 000.

Adenauer, Konrad (1876–1967) German statesman. He was a successful Rhineland politician until the Nazi government forced him out of public life (1934) and imprisoned him (1934, 1944). In 1946 Adenauer re-emerged as chairman of the Christian Democratic Union (CDU) and became the first chancellor (1949–63) of the Federal Republic of Germany. He presided over Germany's economic miracle and did much to restore its international prestige.

adenoids Two masses of tissue situated at the back of the nose. They consist of lymphatic tissue, which destroys disease-causing microbes in the throat. In children they are normally large, and when associated with recurrent throat infections or persistent breathing through the mouth are usually removed surgically. This operation is often combined with tonsillectomy (removal of the tonsils) as the tonsils tend to be infected at the same time.

adenosine triphosphate. *See* ATP.

adiabatic process Any process in which heat neither enters nor leaves a system. Usually, such a process changes the temperature of the system. An example is the sudden compression of a gas, causing its temperature to rise. The compression is assumed to take place so quickly that the gas loses none of its acquired heat.

adjutant stork A large carrion-eating stork, *Leptotilos dubius*, occurring in Asia and similar to the related marabou. It has a white plumage with dark-grey back, wings, and tail, a short neck, and a heavy pointed bill. Its head and neck are naked and a bald pouch hangs from the throat. Order: *Ciconiiformes*.

Adler, Alfred (1870–1937) Austrian psychiatrist who introduced the concept of the inferiority complex. Initially an associate of Sigmund Freud, Adler's views diverged from Freud's and by 1911 he had founded his own school. Adler viewed each individual as a unique entity striving to compensate for feelings of inferiority resulting from physical or social disabilities (*The Neurotic Constitution*, 1912) and regarded sex as an opportunity to express dominance. In 1921, he opened the first of his child-guidance clinics in Vienna.

ADJUTANT STORK *Standing about 1.5 m tall, they feed on animal carcasses.*

Admiral's Cup A biennial sailing competition (instituted in 1957) held by the Royal Ocean Racing Club in the English Channel. Three yachts represent each nation and the competition comprises five races (the fifth race was added in 1977), including the Fastnet Cup.

Admiralty Court. *See* maritime law.

Admiralty Islands A group of about 40 islands in the SW Pacific Ocean, in Papua New Guinea in the Bismarck Archipelago. Copra and pearls are exported. The main island is Manus with the chief town, Lorengau. Area: about 2000 sq km (800 sq mi). Population (1980): 25 844.

Adonis In Greek mythology, a youth from Cyprus, loved by Aphrodite for his great beauty. Zeus decreed that his time should be divided between Aphrodite on earth, Persephone, queen of the underworld, and himself. He was celebrated in many festivals, his death and resurrection representing seasonal change.

adoption The process enabling a natural parent's legal rights and duties towards an unmarried minor to be transferred to another adult. The Adoption Act (1976), controls the work of adoption societies, the rights of the natural parents, and the adopted child's right to know his original name. Birth control, abortion, and the acceptance of one-parent families has decreased the number of children available for adoption in recent years. However, greater publicity has been given to finding adoptive homes for children with special needs, e.g. older children, children of mixed race, and the physically or mentally handicapped.

adrenal glands Two small pyramid-shaped endocrine glands in man and other mammals, one at the upper end of each of the kidneys. Each gland has an outer cortex, controlled by hormones secreted by the pituitary gland, and an inner medulla producing adrenaline and noradrenaline, controlled directly by the nervous system. The cortex secretes three classes of steroid hormones that regulate the balance of salts and water, the use of carbohydrates, and the activity of the sex glands (*see* corticosteroids). *See also* Addison's disease; Cushing's disease.

adrenaline (*or* epinephrine) A hormone secreted by the medulla of the adrenal glands. A catecholamine derived from the amino acid tyrosine, adrenaline increases heart rate, raises blood pressure, and increases the level of blood glucose. Its release is triggered by stress in preparation by the body for "fight or flight." Adrenaline is also secreted by nerve endings of the sympathetic nervous system. *See also* noradrenaline.

adrenocorticotrophic hormone. *See* ACTH.

Adrian IV (Nicholas Breakspear; c. 1100–59) Pope (1154–59). The only English pope, also known as Hadrian IV, he was unanimously elected after a career of papal service, leading the mission to the Scandinavian churches (1152). His claim that the Holy Roman Empire was held by papal grant occasioned a major quarrel with Emperor Frederick Barbarossa.

Adriatic Sea A northern arm of the Mediterranean Sea, extending between Italy and Yugoslavia for about 750 km (466 mi). Its principal ports are Brindisi, Bari, Venice, Trieste, and Rijeka. The Italian and Yugoslav coasts are strikingly different: the one flat and sandy, the other rocky and irregular with many offshore islands.

adsorption The production of a layer of atoms or molecules of a substance on a solid or liquid surface. The adsorbed atoms or molecules may be strongly held by chemical bonds (**chemisorption**), in which case the adsorbed layer is usually only one molecule thick. Adsorption may also occur through weaker physical forces (**physisorption**), often giving rise to several molecular layers. In contrast, **absorption** involves material penetrating into the bulk of a solid or liquid.

adultery   Voluntary sexual intercourse between a married person and someone who is not that person's husband or wife. In many countries, including some US states, adultery is a crime; under some systems, such as Islamic law, it may carry the death penalty. Generally, however, it is only a ground for divorce or judicial separation, as in English law, where it is considered proof of the "irretrievable breakdown" of a marriage.

Advent (from Latin: *adventus*, coming)   The first season of the church year, leading up to Christmas. It begins on the Sunday nearest St Andrew's Day (30 Nov). From the 6th century it has been observed as a solemn preparation for celebrating Christ's birth and for his Second Coming.

adventists   Several Protestant Christian denominations that stress a belief in the imminent Second Coming of Christ. In the USA adventism began in 1831 with the millenarian preaching of William Miller (1782–1849), who predicted the Second Coming for 1843–44, but postponed the date when his prediction proved false. In the UK a similar movement was founded in 1832 as the Catholic Apostolic Church. There have been many adventist movements, the Seventh-Day Adventists being the main church today.

advocate   In Scotland and in some countries, such as France, having a legal system based on Roman law, a person whose profession is to plead the cases of others in a court of justice. The English equivalent is a barrister. In Scotland, the **Lord Advocate** is the chief law officer of the Crown, generally equivalent to the attorney general in England.

Aegean Sea   A section of the NE Mediterranean Sea, lying between Greece and Turkey and containing many islands, including the Cyclades, Dodecanese, and N Sporades.

Aeneas   A legendary Trojan leader, son of Anchises and Aphrodite, and hero of Virgil's *Aeneid*. After the Greek victory in the Trojan War, he sailed away from burning Troy with his family and other survivors and was shipwrecked near Carthage. He fell in love with Dido but abandoned her to continue his divinely ordained voyage to Italy, where he founded what was to become Rome.

Aeolus   The Greek god of the winds and ruler of Aeolia. In Homer's *Odyssey* he gave Odysseus a bag containing contrary winds; Odysseus' companions untied it, causing his ship to be blown back to Aeolia. An **aeolian harp**, a wooden resonating box strung with gut string produces chordal sounds that vary according to the wind pressure, when hung in the open air.

aerial (*or* antenna)   An electrical conductor that transmits and receives radio or other electromagnetic waves. An oscillating electromagnetic field, caused by waves from a distant source, induces an oscillating current in the receiving aerial. A transmitting aerial works by the same process in reverse. A modern aerial for UHF (ultra-high frequency) and VHF (very high frequency) consists of a dipole formed from two metal rods, each approximately one-quarter of the operating wavelength. In the **Yagi aerial** named after H. Yagi (1886–1976), a reflector rod is set behind the dipole and several director rods are placed in front of it. This provides a more directional array than the simple dipole and is widely used as a receiving and transmitting aerial for television.

aerobics   A method of keeping fit by exercising to stimulate the heart and lungs to work faster, thereby increasing the volume of oxygen available to the body. It involves repetitive and sustained use of the muscles and claims to reduce the resting pulse rate and increase the efficiency of the heart. The system was started in the USA by Dr Ken Cooper for the US forces in the 1970s and subsequently adapted by Jackie Sorensen as a dance and exercise form.

aerodynamics   The study of the behaviour and flow of air around objects. As air is a viscous fluid any object moving through it experiences a drag. Aerodynamics is important in the design of vehicles travelling at more than 50 km per hour (31 mph), buildings and bridges, engines, furnaces, as well as aircraft (*see* aeronautics) and missiles.

forces acting on aircraft

cross-section of aerofoil

AERONAUTICS   *The forces acting on an aircraft. The aerofoil cross-section shows how the lift, which keeps it in the air, results from the passage of the aerofoil through the air, causing a lower pressure above it and a higher pressure below it.*

aeronautics   The science and history (*see also* aircraft) of flight. An object flying through air is subject to four basic forces: its own weight (vertically downwards as a result of gravity), lift (to counterbalance its weight and keep it in the air), thrust (to force it through the air), and drag (resulting from friction between the body and the air). Birds and insects use their wings to provide both lift and thrust; man, in his heavier-than-air fixed-wing craft, uses an aerofoil to provide the lift and an internal-combustion engine (propeller or jet) to provide the thrust (*see also* aircraft; gliders). Helicopters use rotating aerofoils to provide lift, while rockets use no lift surfaces; the jet of expanding gas providing both lift and thrust. The use of aerofoils as lift surfaces depends on Bernoulli's theorem, according to which the total energy of a flowing fluid remains constant; thus, if the velocity of the fluid increases, its pressure decreases in proportion. An aerofoil is a wing so shaped that (at subsonic speeds) air is accelerated over its rounded leading edge and curved upper surface, causing a reduced pressure above it. A smaller reduction in air velocity on its underside causes a slightly increased pressure below it. The combination of these pressure differences provides the lift. The design of practical aircraft wings has to take into account a number of complex factors, including turbulence in the airflow. At supersonic speeds these forces are somewhat altered (*see* sound barrier) and the aerofoil has to be more sweptback and more streamlined. *See also* airships; balloons.

aerosol A colloidal suspension of particles of liquid or solid in a gaseous medium. Fog, mist, and smoke are common natural examples. By means of pressurized packages, aerosols can be produced from a huge range of substances, including insecticides, paints, hairsprays, etc. In these, the substance is mixed with an easily liquefied gas (often a chlorofluorocarbon, CFC), which acts as a propellant when the pressure is released. Because there is evidence that CFCs cause damage to the ozone layer, safer propellants are being sought.

Aeschylus (c. 525–456 BC) Greek tragic dramatist, the first of the great trio of Athenian tragedians that included Sophocles and Euripides. He wrote over 80 plays, of which only 7 survive: *The Persians* (472), *Seven against Thebes* (467), the *Oresteia* trilogy (*Agamemnon, Libation Bearers*, and *Eumenides*; 458), *Suppliant Women* and *Prometheus Bound*. His introduction of a second actor, allowing dialogue and action independent of the chorus, and his innovations in costume and scenery, transformed the conventions of drama.

Aesop The supposed author of a collection of Greek fables, said by Herodotus to be a slave from Samos who lived in the 6th century BC. Originating in popular folklore, the fables are anecdotal stories whose animal characters are used to illustrate a moral point. The Roman poet Phaedrus popularized them in the 1st century AD, and the French poet La Fontaine wrote more sophisticated versions in the 17th century.

Aesthetic movement A British literary and artistic movement of the late 19th century, summarized in the slogan "art for art's sake." Reacting against the ugliness of industrialism and against contemporary utilitarian social philosophies, its followers sought to create beauty for its own sake, self-consciously divorcing art from life. They included Swinburne, William Morris, and others, culminating in the work of Oscar Wilde, Aubrey Beardsley, and the other contributors to the periodical *The Yellow Book* (1894–97).

Afars and the Issas, French territory of the. *See* Djibouti, Republic of.

Afghan hound A breed of large dog having long legs, large drooping ears, and a very long silky coat, which may be of any colour. The Afghan probably originated in ancient Egypt and was later used in Afghanistan to hunt leopards and gazelles. Height: 68–73 cm (dogs); 61–66 cm (bitches).

Afghanistan, Republic of A state in central Asia. The country is mountainous, the Hindu Kush range rising over 6000 m (20 000 ft). The only lower lying areas are along the River Amu Darya (ancient name: Oxus) in the N and the delta of the River Helmand in the SW. The population consists of mixed ethnic groups, the largest being the Pathans and the Tadzhiks. *Economy*: largely agricultural, primarily stock raising (especially of fat-

tailed sheep). There has been industrial development in recent years, especially since the discovery of natural gas in the N. Building of asphalt roads has been carried out with US and Soviet help. There is still no substantial railway system. Main exports include Persian lambskins, fruit, cotton, wool, carpets, and natural gas (to the Soviet Union). *History*: before the opening up of international sea routes in the 15th century Afghanistan was an important centre on the overland routes across central Asia. For centuries under the rule of different powers, including the Mongol Genghis Khan in the 13th century, it became an independent kingdom in 1747. During the 19th century Afghanistan became involved in the struggle between Britain and Russia for influence in central Asia. After two wars with Britain (1839–42 and 1878–80) it became a buffer state between British India and Russia, with Britain controlling its foreign policy. Independence was achieved in 1921 under Amanollah Khan (1892–1960) after the third Afghan War. In 1926 Amanollah declared himself king. He was deposed in 1929 by a brigand chief, Habibullah, who was in turn defeated by Nader Khan. When the latter was assassinated in 1933 he was succeeded by his son, King Zahir. Since World War II there has been friction with Pakistan over the question of an independent Pathan state in Pakistan. In 1973 the monarchy was overthrown by Mohammed Daud, a cousin of King Zahir, and in 1977 a republic was set up with Daud as president. In 1978 he was killed in a military coup and a new government under Nur Mohammed Taraki (1917–79) was set up by the Marxist People's Democratic Party. In 1979, Babrak Karmal came to power with Soviet aid; he was succeeded in 1986 by Mohammad Najibullah (1947–   ). Soviet military occupation of Afghanistan provoked worldwide condemnation. After nine years of fighting against Mujahidin guerrillas, in which 20 000 Soviet troops died, Soviet forces withdrew in 1989. Since then, continued attempts by the Mujahidin to overthrow the government and establish an Islamic state have been frustrated by lack of firm leadership and interfaction fighting. Joint official languages: Pushtu and Dari Persian. Official currency: afghani of 100 puls. Area: 657 500 sq km (250 000 sq mi). Population (1988 est): 9 000 000. Capital: Kabul.

Africa The second largest continent in the world. A notable feature of the NE is the Great Rift Valley, which contains an extensive system of freshwater lakes as well as the continent's highest point, Mount Kilimanjaro. The principal rivers are the Nile, Niger, Zaïre, and Zambezi. Africa's climate and vegetation vary considerably from the arid desert of the Sahara to the tropical rainforest of the Congo basin. The inhabitants of Africa are principally of Negroid origin, although the originators of the Berber language group remain dominant in N Africa and the Sahara and there are a few Cushitespeaking peoples in the NE. *History*: Africa's long history has been substantiated by Louis Leakey's finds of hominoid man at Olduvai Gorge. The earliest African civilization was established in Egypt in about 3400 BC. From the 7th century AD Arab influence was strong and Islam spread with the trans-Saharan and East African coastal trade. Several African kingdoms and empires emerged during this period, notably the Sudanese empires of Ghana, Mali, and Songhai. From the 15th century European exploration and exploitation began, initiated by the Portuguese. Slaves, ivory, and gold were exported from Africa from the 17th to the late 19th centuries. From 1880 to 1912 most of Africa was partitioned by the European powers, which imposed political boundaries upon the continent that bore no relationship to former political and social organizations; this resulted in long-standing problems (*see also* South Africa, Republic of). In the 1950s there was movement towards independence and Africa now consists of independent nations. Area: about 30 300 000 sq km (11 700 000 sq mi). Population (1984 est): 537 000 000.

African languages   A geographical classification of the heterogeneous languages spoken in the African continent. The Hamito-Semitic group extends across N Africa from Mauretania to Somalia. The Nilo-Saharan group is spoken in many dialects in central Africa, and the Niger-Congo languages, many of them Bantu languages, cover most of the area S of the Sahara. In S Africa the Khoisan languages survive. There are up to a thousand indigenous languages of the continent as well as the European languages (English, Afrikaans, French, Portuguese) imported by colonizers. Malagasy, a language of Austronesian origin, is spoken in Madagascar. Swahili is an important lingua franca in East Africa. Certain African languages are unique in using click sounds in their phonology; predominance of certain consonantal groups (kp, gb, mb, nd) is also common in Africa.

African violet   A flowering plant, *Saintpaulia ionantha*, native to tropical East Africa. The plants have rosettes of hairy, often deeply ridged, leaves, bear clusters of pink, blue, purple, or white flowers, and grow to a height of 10–15 cm. Many varieties and hybrids have been developed as ornamentals. Family: *Gesneriaceae*.

Afrikaans.   *See* Afrikaner.

Afrikaner   A South African of Dutch or Huguenot descent. The Afrikaners comprise about 60% of the Republic's White population. Formerly called "Boers" (farmers), they have undergone considerable urbanization since the 1930s. In the 18th and 19th centuries they led a seminomadic life, resisting governmental control from Cape Town. Their two independent states, the South African Republic and the Orange Free State, came under British rule after the second Boer War. Their language, **Afrikaans**, derives, but is distinct, from Dutch and together with English has been an official language of South Africa since 1925. *See also* Great Trek.

Afro-Asiatic languages.   *See* Hamito-Semitic languages.

Agadir   30 30N 9 40W A port in SW Morocco, on the Atlantic coast. An earthquake in 1960 destroyed much of the town and killed about 12 000 people. Population (1984): 62 300.

Aga Khan IV   (1936–   ) Imam (leader) of the Ismaili sect of Muslims (1957–   ), succeeding his grandfather Aga Khan III. He married (1969) an Englishwoman, Sarah Croker Poole.

agama   A common African broad-headed lizard belonging to the family *Agamidae* (50 species). 30–45 cm long, agamas have a thick body and a tapering tail and feed on insects. The common agama (*Agama agama*) is variously coloured: dominant males have a brick-red head, blue body and legs, and banded tail; other males are duller coloured, like the females.

Agamemnon   King of Mycenae and commander of the Greek army in the Trojan War. His quarrel with

Achilles is the main theme of Homer's *Iliad*. After his return from Troy with Cassandra, the captured daughter of King Priam, he was murdered by his wife Clytemnestra and her lover Aegisthus.

agaric   A fungus belonging to a large family (*Agaricaceae*) found throughout the world. The group includes many edible mushrooms, such as the white mushroom (*Agaricus bisporus*) and field mushroom (*A. campestris*), as well as the poisonous death cap. The visible part of the fungus consists of a stipe (stalk) bearing a cap with gills on the undersurface. Class: *Basidiomycetes*. *See also* fly agaric; mushroom.

agate   A banded or concentrically patterned form of chalcedony. The banding is due to intermittent deposition in rock cavities and the colours, ranging from white, milky blue, yellow, and brown to red, are due to traces of mineral or organic colouring matter. Being hard, it is used for mortars for grinding, and also for ornamental purposes.

Agave   A genus of plants (about 300 species) of the S USA and tropical America, many of which are widely grown for ornament. Agaves have a basal tuft of thick fleshy, sometimes toothed, leaves and a cluster of flowers that—in some species—grows on a tall stalk (up to 12 m high). Growth is slow—it may be 60 or more years before flowers are produced; after flowering the plant dies. Several species are commercially important as a source of fibre, especially sisal; the fermented juice of others is used as an alcoholic drink (pulque) or distilled to produce spirits (*see* tequila). Family: *Agavaceae* (or *Amaryllidaceae*).

agglomerate   A rock composed of a mixture of coarse angular fragments and finer-grained material formed by volcanic explosions; it is usually found in or near the volcanic vent.

AGRICULTURAL REVOLUTION   *Thomas Coke bred sheep that transformed yields of both wool and meat.*

Agincourt, Battle of   (25 October, 1415) The battle that took place during the Hundred Years' War at Agincourt (now in the Pas-de-Calais), in which the French were defeated by an English army led by Henry V. The decisive English victory, which owed much to their outstanding archers, was achieved with not more than 1600 dead; the French may have lost as many as 6000 men.

Agora   A central feature of ancient Greek town planning. Similar to the Roman forum, the primary function of the agora was as the town market. In addition, however, it also became the main social and political meeting place. Together with the acropolis, it normally contained the most important buildings of the town.

agoraphobia. *See* phobia.

agouti A rabbit-sized rodent belonging to a genus (*Dasyprocta*; 13 species) of Central and South American forests. Agoutis have long legs, small ears, and a very short hairless tail. The hair on the rump is often long and brightly coloured and can be erected when the animal is alarmed. Family: *Dasyproctidae* (agoutis and pacas); suborder: *Hystricomorpha*.

Agra 27 09N 78 00E A city in India, in Uttar Pradesh on the River Jumna. Former capital of the Mogul Empire (1566–69 and 1601–58), it fell to the British in 1803 and from 1835 until 1862 was capital of the North-West Provinces. Notable buildings include the celebrated Taj Mahal. Population (1981 est): 747 318.

Agricola, Gnaeus Julius (40–93 AD) Roman governor of Britain and father-in-law of his biographer Tacitus. Sent to govern Britain in 78, after holding previous legionary posts there, he followed a policy of romanization, exploration, and expansion before his recall in 84.

agricultural revolution The name given to the changes in agriculture in Britain that took place mainly in the 18th century. The open-field system of strip farming was replaced by larger enclosed fields, hedged and ditched, in which improved agricultural methods and new implements could be used (*see* Tull, Jethro); the quality of cattle and sheep was improved by scientific stock breeding. This resulted in a greater production of food for the growing industrial population (*see* industrial revolution), although it meant hardship for those farmers who were displaced by enclosure.

agriculture The study of farming. Settled farming probably dates back to the 10th millennium BC, when in many regions of the world it began to replace man's activities as a hunter and gatherer of food. The domestication of cattle, goats, sheep, and pigs together with the cropping of wheat, barley, rice, etc., enabled settled communities to evolve and primitive civilizations to flourish in such regions as the fertile river basins of the Tigris, Euphrates, and Nile.

Until the end of the 19th century farming was based on energy derived from man and his draught animals. Some parts of the world still use such traditional methods; however, during the 20th century, especially in developed countries, the tractor has become the primary energy source. In this century, too, there has been great success in improving breeds of plants and animals, improving soil fertility (*see* fertilizers), increasing mechanization, and control of plant and animal pests, measures that have enormously increased the quantity and quality of food produced. These measures are now being applied in the developing world, where they are bringing about the Green Revolution that is needed to feed the world's growing population. However, reconciling maximum food production and conservation of the environment is one of the principal tasks of the UN Food and Agriculture Organization. *See also* arable farming; livestock farming.

Agrigento 37 19N 13 35E A seaport in Italy, in S Sicily. Founded about 580 BC, it has famous ancient temples and is the birthplace of the philosopher Empedocles.

Sulphur mining is the main occupation. Population (1981): 51 931.

agronomy The management of land, especially for the production of arable crops. Agronomy involves the determination of the nature of a soil and how its fertility may be improved by such processes as drainage, irrigation, the application of natural and artificial fertilizers, and husbandry techniques (e.g. crop rotation). Equally important is the breeding of crop plants that are suited to a particular soil.

Aguascalientes 21 51N 102 18W A city in central Mexico. A commercial centre, its industries include ceramics production, tanning, and railway engineering. There are medicinal hot springs nearby. Population (1980): 359 454.

Ahmadabad (*or* Ahmedabad) 23 03N 72 40E An industrial city in central India, in Gujarat. Founded in 1411, it is a major rail and textile centre (established 1859–61). Its university was established in 1949. Population (1981 est): 2 548 057.

ai. *See* sloth.

Aidan, St (c. 600–51 AD) Irish monk and bishop. A monk at Iona until his consecration as bishop of Northumbria in 635, he founded the monastery at Lindisfarne (*see* Holy Island), the centre of his extensive missionary activity in N England. His life is described by Bede in his *Ecclesiastical History*. Feast day: 31 Aug.

AIDS (*acquired immune deficiency syndrome*) A viral disease characterized by a decrease of certain T-lymphocytes, resulting in a breakdown of the immune system and increased susceptibility to other diseases. The causative agent, the human immunodeficiency virus (HIV), is transmitted in blood, semen, vaginal fluid, and breast milk; a high proportion of HIV-positive people (virus carriers) may develop symptoms of disease. About 203 000 cases were reported worldwide in 1989, about half of which were fatal. AIDS is found most frequently in homosexual males and intravenous drug users, but the virus can also be transmitted by sexual intercourse and transfusions of infected blood (all of which is now tested). Such drugs as azidovudine (or AZT) so far merely alleviate the symptoms and do not yet offer a cure.

aikido A Japanese martial art, primarily for self-defence by means of dodging an attacker and leading him in the direction in which his momentum takes him before subduing him without injury.

Ailanthus. *See* tree of heaven.

air. *See* atmosphere.

aircraft Any machine capable of flying. Aircraft fall into two categories: lighter-than-air machines (*see* airships; balloons) and heavier-than-air machines. The latter include helicopters and fixed-wing aircraft, first gliders and then powered aeroplanes. 19th-century experience of gliding, especially by Otto Lilienthal (1849–96) in Germany, provided the Wright Brothers with the information they needed to build their first powered aircraft in 1907. The power source was provided by the Otto-Daimler internal-combustion engine. In 1909 the Frenchman Louis Blériot flew across the English Channel. By the beginning of World War I, aircraft were sufficiently advanced to be used for reconnaissance and their usefulness as bombers soon became evident. Fast manoeuvrable fighters to shoot down the slower heavily laden bombers were an obvious subsequent development. By the end of the war aerial combat was established as an integral part of modern warfare.

Wright Brothers' Flyer *The first powered flight at Kitty Hawk, North Carolina, USA, on 17 December, 1903 lasted 12 seconds.*

Blériot XI *Louis Blériot's 30-minute flight from Calais to Dover on 25 July, 1909 was the first cross-Channel flight.*

Handley Page 42E Hannibal *In 1928 the British airline, Imperial Airways, bought eight HP42 aircraft. The 24-seater Hannibal had a top speed of 100 mph (160 km/hr).*

Douglas DC3 *Introduced in 1936, it was widely used in World War II as the Dakota transport. Its Pratt and Whitney 1200 hp engines gave it a maximum speed of 200 mph (320 km/hr).*

Vickers Viscount *Introduced into service in 1950, it was the first successful turboprop airliner. Powered by four Rolls-Royce Dart engines, it carried 60 passengers.*

De Havilland Comet I *The first jet airliner, it went into service in 1952. Crashes due to metal fatigue caused its withdrawal and in 1958 it was replaced by the Comet IV.*

Boeing 747 *Nicknamed the "jumbo jet" this widebodied jetliner, which can carry up to 500 passengers, has been in service with many airlines since 1970.*

Concorde *The first supersonic airliner, it was built by the French and British in cooperation. Powered by four Rolls-Royce Olympus engines, it came into service in 1976.*

AIRCRAFT (MILITARY)

Sopwith Camel *A highly manoeuvrable fighter, first delivered in 1917. Its 130 hp Clerget engine gave it a top speed of 113 mph (181 km/hr).*

Handley Page 0/400 *The largest World War I bomber. Its twin 360 hp engines enabled it to carry 2000 lbs (907 kg) of bombs.*

Supermarine Spitfire *British fighter. Originally powered by a Rolls-Royce Merlin engine, it later had the Griffon engine, giving it a top speed of 450 mph (724 km/hr).*

Messerschmitt 109 *German fighter, designed in 1935. The latest version (the 109G) had an 1800 hp engine enabling it to fly at 430 mph (692 km/hr).*

Boeing B-29 Superfortress *This enormous US bomber entered the war in 1943 and was used to drop the atom bombs on Japan.*

General Dynamics F-111 *US fighter and fighter-bomber, the first warplane to have swing wings (1967). It is powered by a Pratt and Whitney TF30 turbo fan.*

Hawker Siddeley Harrier *British VTOL aircraft developed in 1969. Two movable nozzles direct the thrust of its engine downwards for vertical take-off.*

Northrop B2 stealth bomber *US Bomber, publicly revealed in 1989. The most expensive warplane ever developed, costing £350 million each, its revolutionary 'flying wing' design is alleged to make it invisible to enemy radar.*

After the war air circuses and flying clubs using World War I aircraft sprang up all over the world, popularizing the concept of flying and heralding the age of civil aviation. In 1924 Imperial Airways was formed in the UK, using Handley Page airliners, and during the 1930s a worldwide network of commercial routes developed. The Atlantic was first flown nonstop from New York to Paris in 1927 by Charles Lindbergh and by 1939 there was a transatlantic flying-boat service, using Class C Short flying boats with in-flight refuelling.

By the outbreak of World War II aircraft of all kinds were poised for aerial combat. During the course of the war many British bombers (including Wellingtons, Blenheims, Halifaxes, and Lancasters) were in service against the German Heinkel 111, Dornier 17, and Junkers 88. Dominant British fighters were the Supermarine Spitfire and the Hawker Hurricane, the latter being slightly slower than the main German fighter, the Messerschmitt Me Bf109. The British jet-powered Gloster Meteor entered service in 1944, as did the German Messerschmitt Me 262 jet.

By the end of war the practicality of the jet engine had been established and it has dominated aircraft design ever since. However, the first postwar generation of civil aircraft used the jet engine to drive propellers (e.g. the Vickers Viscount), the first true jet to enter passenger service being the ill-fated British Comet. The highly successful Boeing 707 (with its four engines in pods suspended below the wings) followed in 1954.

The first aircraft to break the sound barrier were military and nearly all modern warplanes are supersonic and armed with missiles. Examples include the British Hawker Hunter and Avro Vulcan; the US McDonnell Douglas Phantom, Convair Hustler, and General Dynamics Swingwing F111; the French Mirage; and the Soviet MiGs. The first supersonic passenger aircraft (SST) to fly was the Soviet Tupolev Tu-144 in 1968. This was followed a year later by the Anglo-French Concorde, which is now in worldwide service. However, long- and medium-range passenger services are likely to be dominated for most of the remainder of this century by the wide-bodied (jumbo) jets, such as the Boeing 747 and the European Airbus. *See also* aeronautics.

aircraft carrier A naval vessel with a large flat deck for launching and landing warplanes. The first flight from the deck of a ship was made in 1910, and the first true aircraft carrier, HMS *Argus*, was completed for the Royal Navy in 1918, too late for action in World War I. Carriers played a dominant role in World War II, being especially effective in the war against the Japanese. After World War II carriers came to be regarded chiefly as tactical units, although they saw considerable action in the Korean and Vietnam Wars. The USS *Enterprise*, the first nuclear-powered carrier (1961), displaced 76 000 tonnes and steamed more than 432 000 km (270 000 mi) before requiring refuelling. Because of the increased range of aircraft, the enormous cost of carriers, and their vulnerability to sophisticated missiles, few are likely to be built in the future. HMS *Ark Royal*, the UK's last aircraft carrier, was withdrawn from service in 1979, but a new *Ark Royal* was commissioned in 1985.

air-cushion vehicle. *See* Hovercraft.

Airedale terrier The largest breed of terrier, originating in Yorkshire. It has a long squarish muzzle, a short tail, and a tan-coloured wiry coat with a black saddle region. A powerful and intelligent dog, the Airedale has

been used as a guard dog, for hunting, and as a police dog. Height: 58–61 cm (dogs); 56–58 cm (bitches).

airships Dirigible balloons that obtain their thrust from a propeller. The first airship to fly was a French steam-powered machine, designed in 1852 by H. Giffard; however, the first practical airship was the electrically powered *La France* (1884), built by Renard and Krebs. By 1900 the initiative in airships had passed to Germany, with the machines of Count Ferdinand von Zeppelin (1838–1917) leading the field. Between 1910 and 1914 Zeppelins were in extensive passenger service, carrying some 35 000 passengers, without mishap. In World War I these machines were used by the Germans to bomb England. Thereafter, a series of disasters destroyed the credibility of hydrogen-filled airships. The British *R101* caught fire at Beauvais in 1930, the US *Shenandoah* and the *Akron* were lost in 1933, and the German *Hindenberg* was destroyed in 1937. However, the availability of the nonflammable gas helium has created a mild revival of interest in recent years.

Aix-en-Provence (Latin name: Aquae Sextiae) 43 31N 5 27E A city in S France, in the Bouches-du-Rhône department. The capital of Provence in the middle ages, it has a gothic cathedral and a university (1409). Cézanne was born here. An agricultural centre, it trades in olive oil and fruit. Population (1982 est): 124 550.

Aix-la-Chapelle. *See* Aachen.

Ajaccio 41 51N 8 43E The capital of Corsica, a port on the Gulf of Ajaccio. Napoleon I was born here. Tourism is important. Population (1982 est): 55 279.

Ajax A legendary Greek hero, son of Telamon, King of Salamis. Described in Homer's *Iliad* as great in stature and in courage, he fought Hector in single combat. He became insane with rage after being defeated by Odysseus in the contest for the armour of the dead Achilles. Sophocles' play *Ajax* depicts the hero recovering his sanity, only to be driven by shame to suicide.

Akihito (1933–) Emperor of Japan (1989–). Educated at Oxford, he succeeded his father Hirohito.

Alabama A state in the SE USA, on the Gulf of Mexico. Except for the forested uplands in the NE it consists of an undulating plain, drained by the Alabama and Tombigbee Rivers. The iron and steel industry around the state's largest city, Birmingham, is the most important. Mobile is an important seaport. Cotton production in the central Black Belt has decreased since the boll weevil blight (1915) but remains a principal crop along with peanuts, soya beans, wheat, and maize; the raising of cattle and poultry is also important. *History*: first explored by the Spanish in the 16th century, it passed to the British (1763) following disputes with the Spanish and French. In 1783 it came under US control and with an area to the S added in the Louisiana Purchase (1803) became a state in 1819. New settlers established large cotton plantations based on slave labour and following secession from the Union (1861), the state sent most of its White male population to fight against the N. Area: 133 677 sq km (51 609 sq mi). Population (1986 est): 4 053 000. Capital: Montgomery.

alabaster A pure fine-grained form of gypsum. It is white or delicately shaded and often translucent and attractively veined. It has long been worked ornamentally, for carvings, etc., but weathers too easily for external use. The alabaster of Volterra, Tuscany, is well known.

Alain-Fournier (Henri-Alban Fournier; 1886–1914) French novelist. The son of a country schoolmaster, he became a literary journalist in Paris and was killed in World War I. The mood of his one completed novel, *Le Grand Meaulnes* (1913), is nostalgic and almost mystical; set in the French countryside of his childhood, it describes a young man's search for a girl he has glimpsed only briefly.

Alamo, the A mission in the USA, in San Antonio, Texas. During the Texas revolution it was defended from 24 Feb until 6 March, 1836, by less than 200 Texan volunteers (including the legendary Davy Crockett), who were all massacred during the onslaught of 4000 Mexican troops led by Santa Anna. Six weeks later a victory at San Jacinto secured Texan independence.

Alaska The largest state in the USA, occupying the extreme NW corner of the North American continent. It is a mountainous volcanic area, rising over 6000 m (20 000 ft) to Mount McKinley, the highest peak in North America. The numerous rivers include the Yukon flowing W into the Bering Sea. Oil production (discovered 1950) is the major industry and there are rich supplies of natural gas. Coal, gold, and copper are mined. Fishing, especially salmon, and forestry are also major industries. Agricultural development is hindered by the short growing season and severe climate. *History*: first settled by Russians following voyages by the Dane, Vitus Bering (1728, 1741), it was under the trade control of the Russian American company until 1867 when it was purchased by the USA. A number of gold rushes in the late 19th century helped to swell the sparse population. It became the 49th state in 1959. A 2437 km (1523 mi)-road from Dawson Creek, Canada to Fairbanks, Alaska, called the **Alaska Highway** was built for defence against Japan (1942). Area: 1 518 800 sq km (586 412 sq mi). Population (1986 est): 534 000. Capital: Juneau.

albacore A fast-swimming tuna fish, *Thunnus alalunga*, found in warm seas. Up to 1 m long, it has very long pectoral fins. It is the chief source of tuna for canning.

Alban, St (3rd century AD) The first English martyr. A pagan soldier, he protected a Christian priest and was converted by him. On admitting this to the Roman authorities, he was scourged and beheaded on a site subsequently dedicated to him as the Abbey of St Albans. Feast day: 22 or 17 June. Emblem: a stag.

Albania, People's Socialist Republic of (Albanian name: Shqiperia) A country in SE Europe, occupying part of the Balkan Peninsula on the Adriatic Sea. It consists of a mountainous interior, rising to over 2700 m (9000 ft), with extensive forests and fertile coastal lowlands. The people belong to two main groups, the Ghegs (N of the River Shkumbi) and the Tosks (S). *Economy*: mainly agricultural, organized into state farms and collectives, although industrial development is increasing. There have been recent attempts to develop the rich mineral resources as well as the rich natural-gas deposits. Main exports include crude oil, bitumen, chrome ore, copper wire, tobacco, fruit, and vegetables. *History*: became independent in 1912 after more than four centuries of Turkish rule. Following a civil war, in which Italy intervened, Albania became a republic in 1925 and a monarchy in 1928, when its president, Ahmed Beg Zogu (1895–1961), was proclaimed as King Zog. After occupation by Italy and Germany during World War II, another republic was set up in 1946, with a communist-controlled assembly. It aligned itself with the Soviet Union but after the death of Stalin relations between the two countries weakened and in 1961 diplomatic relations were broken off. Meanwhile Albania, alone of the East European communist states, maintained close relations with China. It began to emerge from decades of isolation in the 1980s. Enver Hoxha (1908–85), as first party secretary, was executive leader from 1946 to 1985. Head of state: Ramiz Alia (1925–). Official language: Albanian. Currency: lek of 100 qintars. Area: 28 748 sq km (11 101 sq mi). Population (1988): 3 080 000. Capital: Tirana. Main port: Durrës.

Albany 42 40N 73 49W A city in the USA, the capital of New York state on the Hudson River. Founded in 1614 by the Dutch, it is one of North America's oldest cities. Economic growth accelerated with the building of the Erie Canal (1825) and today its main manufactures are electrical goods, textiles, dental goods, chemicals, and building materials. Population (1980): 101 727.

albatross A large seabird belonging to a family (*Diomedeidae;* 14 species) that occurs mainly in southern oceans. It has a stout hooked bill; usually a white or brown plumage, often with darker markings on the back, wings, or tail; and very long narrow wings (the wandering albatross, *Diomedea exulans*, has the largest wingspan of any bird, reaching up to 3.5 m). Albatrosses can glide for hours over the open sea, feeding on squids and cuttlefish; they come ashore only to breed. Order: *Procellariiformes* (see petrel).

albedo A measure of the reflecting power of a nonluminous object, such as a planet or natural satellite or a surface feature on such a body. It is the ratio of the amount of light reflected in all directions from the object to the amount of incident light. Clouds, snow, and ice have high albedos while volcanic rocks have very low albedos.

Albee, Edward (1928–) US dramatist. His early one-act plays, notably *Zoo Story* (1958) and *The Death of Bessie Smith* (1960), analyse contemporary social tensions using techniques of the Theatre of the Absurd. His first three-act play, *Who's Afraid of Virginia Woolf?* (1962), which dramatizes the love-hate relationship of an academic couple, was very successful. Later plays include *A Delicate Balance* (1967, Pulitzer Prize) and *Seascape* (1975).

ALBATROSS

Albéniz, Isaac Manuel Francisco (1860–1909) Spanish composer and pianist. A child prodigy, he frequently ran away from home, giving recitals in North and South America and Europe. He began serious composition after studying with d'Indy and Dukas in Paris. His works include operas, songs, and *Iberia* (1906–09), a collection of 12 piano pieces.

Albert I (1875–1934) King of the Belgians (1909–34). As commander in chief of the Belgian army, Albert led his country's heroic but unsuccessful resistance to the German invasion (1914) and contributed to the Allied victory in World War I. After the war he did much to encourage industrial reconstruction and currency reform.

Albert, Prince (1819–61) Prince Consort of the United Kingdom and younger son of Ernest I, Duke of Saxe-Coburg-Gotha. In 1840 he married his cousin Queen Victoria and became her chief adviser. Although he was initially unpopular, his devotion to duty and his active patronage of the arts, science, and industry eventually won him respect. He is perhaps best remembered for his organization of the Great Exhibition (1851). He died of typhoid.

Alberta A province of W Canada, mostly on the Great Plains. It consists mainly of a plateau, rising to the foothills of the Rocky Mountains in the SW. The undulating S prairie and parkland further N support profitable ranches and grain farms. Alberta is Canada's largest oil and gas producer, possesses vast coalfields, and includes the Athabasca tar sands, one of the world's largest oil reserves (at present untapped). *History*: first explored in the 18th century, Alberta became Canadian territory in 1869. The arrival of the railway from E Canada (1883) facilitated agricultural settlement, and Alberta became a province in 1905. Area: 644 389 sq km (248 799 sq mi). Population (1986): 2 365 825. Capital: Edmonton.

Albert Canal A canal in Belgium, completed in 1939. It links the River Meuse at Liège with the River Scheldt at Antwerp. Length: 130 km (80 mi).

albinism An inherited disorder in which tyrosinase, one of the enzymes required for the formation of the pigment melanin, is absent. Albinos have abnormally pale skin, fair hair, and pink or light-blue irises. The condition can be eased by the use of spectacles to treat the lens abnormalities common in albinos and by protection of the skin and eyes from direct sunlight. Albinism, which can affect all human races, is also seen in animals.

Albinoni, Tomaso (1671–1750) Italian composer and court musician to the Duke of Mantua. His works, which influenced J. S. Bach, include 50 operas, a violin concerto, and two oboe concertos. The *Adagio* for organ and strings often attributed to Albinoni was in fact composed by his Italian biographer Remo Giazotto (1910–   ) and incorporates a fragment of a bass part by Albinoni.

Ålborg (*or* Aalborg) 57 03N 09 56E A city and seaport in Denmark, in N Jutland. Founded in 1342 AD, it has a gothic cathedral and a 16th-century castle. A university was established in 1974. Its industries include shipbuilding, cement manufacture, and textiles. Population (1983 est): 154 755.

albumins A class of proteins that are soluble in both water and dilute aqueous salt solutions. Serum albumins are constituents of blood; α-lactalbumin is found in milk; and ovalbumin is part of egg white. Preparations of albumins are used in therapeutic transfusions.

Albuquerque 35 05N 106 38W A city in the USA, in New Mexico on the Rio Grande. The state's largest city, it is situated in a rich agricultural area and food canning and the manufacture of livestock products are its principal industries. It is the home of the University of New Mexico (1892). Population (1986 est): 366 750.

Alcatraz An island in the USA, in W California in San Francisco Bay. It was the site of a notorious maximum security prison from 1934 until 1962.

ALCHEMY *Detail from a 16th-century engraving after a painting by Breughel the Elder.*

alchemy A pseudoscience combining practical chemistry with mystical views of the universe. Originating independently in China and Egypt, probably before the 3rd century BC, alchemy remained a legitimate branch of science and philosophy in Asia, Europe, and the Islamic lands for over 1500 years. It had three principal goals: the elixir of life (to ensure immortality), the panacea (or universal medicine), and the means of transmuting base metals into gold (*see* philosopher's stone). In China, Taoism, which highly esteemed long life, fostered alchemical experimentation in search of the elixir. In Europe, concentration upon gold-making brought alchemy into disrepute.

Alcibiades (c. 450–404 BC) Athenian general and politician. Brought up by Pericles, he was the pupil and lover of Socrates. Alcibiades encouraged Athenian imperialism during the Peloponnesian War (431–404) until, accused of desecrating monuments in Athens, he defected to Sparta (415). He regained Athenian favour (410) and was a successful commander until defeat, the fault of a subordinate, forced him into exile (406). He was murdered in Phrygia.

Alcmaeon In Greek mythology, the son of Amphiarus, one of the Seven Against Thebes, and Eriphyle. He killed his mother to avenge the death of Amphiarus, and was pursued by the Furies. His first wife was Arsinoë, daughter of King Pegeus of Psophis, but on his wanderings he married the daughter of the river god Achelous, and was pursued and killed by Pegeus and his sons. His own sons later avenged his death by killing Pegeus.

Alcock, Sir John (William) (1892–1919) British aviator. He served with the Royal Naval Air Service in

World War I and in 1919, accompanied by **(Sir) Arthur Brown** (1886–1948), was the first to fly the Atlantic Ocean. They flew a Vickers-Vimy from St John's, Newfoundland, to Clifden, Co Galway, in 16 hours 27 minutes. A few months later Alcock was killed in a flying accident.

Alcoholics Anonymous A voluntary organization started in the USA in 1934 to help alcoholics. Members, who must genuinely want to stop drinking, help one another on the basis of group therapy by sharing their experiences of alcoholism. There are local autonomous groups in over 90 countries, including the UK, which has more than 950 groups. An associated organization, **AL-ANON**, provides support for the close relatives of alcoholics.

alcoholism An illness caused by physical and psychological dependence on alcohol. Alcoholism causes mood changes, deterioration in personal standards, and periods of memory loss. Continued heavy consumption will eventually lead to cirrhosis of the liver, heart disease, and damage to the nerves. Sudden withdrawal may produce tremor, delusions, and hallucinations. Treatment, which is lengthy and difficult, includes initial alcohol withdrawal (with appropriate sedation) accompanied and followed by adequate psychological support. Drugs such as disulfiram (Antabuse), which cause vomiting after drinking alcohol, may assist the treatment. *See* Alcoholics Anonymous.

alcohols The class of organic compounds that includes ethanol (ethyl alcohol; C_2H_5OH) and methanol (methyl alcohol; CH_3OH). Ethanol is the common alcohol found in intoxicating drinks and is often called simply "alcohol." Alcohols contain at least one hydroxyl group and have the general formula ROH, where R is a hydrocarbon group. They react with acids to give esters and water. Primary alcohols oxidize to form aldehydes and secondary alcohols to form ketones.

alcohol strength The measurement of the percentage volume of ethanol (ethyl alcohol) in alcoholic drinks in order to calculate government duty on them. In the USA, 100° proof is 50% alcohol by volume. Until January, 1980, the UK used a similar system for spirits, but with 57.06%, measured at 15°C, as the standard (100° proof), pure alcohol being 175° proof. France and Italy formerly used the Gay-Lussac scale, which simply states the percentage volume of alcohol, measured at 15°C. The **OMIL** (International Organization of Legal Metrology) system, now used throughout the EC, is based on percentage volume of alcohol at 20°C. Thus a bottle of spirits labelled in the EC "35% vol" is approximately equivalent to 61° proof in the former UK system or 70° proof in the US system.

Alcott, Louisa May (1832–88) US novelist. Her first book, *Flower Fables* (1854), was written when she was 16 to raise money for her family. *Hospital Sketches* (1863) recounted her experiences as a nurse in the Civil War. *Little Women* (1868–69), her most famous book, was largely autobiographical. Other works include *An Old-Fashioned Girl* (1870), *Little Men* (1871), and *Jo's Boys* (1886).

Aldeburgh 52 9N 1 35E A small resort in SE England in Suffolk. Once an important port, it is now famous for its annual music festival established in 1948 by Benjamin Britten, who lived here. It is the birthplace of the poet, George Crabbe, and Dr Elizabeth Garrett Ander-

son (1836–1917) was elected the first woman mayor in England here in 1908. Population (1985 est): 3000.

aldehydes A class of organic chemicals that contain the -CHO group. They are prepared by the oxidation of alcohols and are themselves oxidized to form carboxylic acids. Common aldehydes are formaldehyde and acetaldehyde.

alder A tree or shrub belonging to a genus (*Alnus*; about 30 species) of the N hemisphere. The leaves are roundish and toothed; the flowers grow as separate male and female catkins on the same tree. The fruit is a woody cone containing small winged nuts. The black alder (*A. glutinosa*), about 20 m high, is found in wet places throughout Europe and Asia and in N Africa. Its timber is used in general turnery. Family: *Betulaceae* (birch family).

alderfly An insect, also known as a fish fly, having two pairs of delicate finely veined wings and long antennae. Up to 50 mm long (including the wings), alderflies live near fresh water, feeding on smaller insects and laying their eggs on reeds. The larvae, which are also carnivorous, live in the water and crawl out.to pupate in burrows in the soil. Family: *Sialidae*; order: *Neuroptera* (lacewings, etc.).

alderman In the UK, senior members of the major local authorities, normally elected by the directly elected members, until the Local Government Act (1972) abolished the office as an active rank except in the City of London. The term derives from the Anglo-Saxon local official—the ealdorman. In the USA, many cities call their local-government officers aldermen but their powers vary from city to city.

Aldermaston 51 23N 1 09W A village in S England, in Berkshire. It is associated with protest marches (1958–63) organized by the Campaign for Nuclear Disarmament and is the site of the Atomic Weapons Research Establishment. Population (1987 est): 2157.

Alderney (French name: Aurigny) 49 43N 2 12W The third largest of the Channel Islands, separated from France by the dangerous Race of Alderney channel. Its economy is based on dairy farming and tourism. Area: 8 sq km (3 sq mi). Population (1981 est): 2086. Chief town: St Anne.

Aldershot 51 15N 0 47W A town in S England, in Hampshire. It is the chief garrison town and army training centre in the UK. Population (1985 est): 38 000.

Aldrin, Jr, Edwin Eugene (1930–) US astronaut, the second man to walk on the moon. Known as "Buzz", he was an air force pilot during the Korean War before becoming an astronaut in 1963. He undertook a 5½-hour spacewalk in 1966 and was lunar module pilot (under Neil Armstrong) in Apollo 11 when it made the first moon landing in 1969.

ale. *See* beer.

Aleppo (Arabic name: Halab) 36 14N 37 10E A town in NW Syria. The Crusaders tried in vain to capture it, and from 1516 to 1919 Aleppo was part of the Ottoman Empire. After World War II, it was incorporated into independent Syria. It is now an industrial centre and the terminus of a pipeline from Iraq; its university was founded in 1960. Population (1982 est): 985 413.

Aleutian Islands A chain of volcanic Alaskan islands lying between the Bering Sea and the Pacific Ocean, divided politically between the Soviet Union and the USA. The chief settlements are on Unalaska. Russian exploitation of supplies after 1741 greatly reduced the population, but fishing and seal, otter, and fox hunting are now regulated. There are strategic US military stations on the islands and underground nuclear tests have been made (since 1971).

Alexander I (c. 1077–1124) King of the Scots (1107–24), who ruled the highlands while his brother and successor David ruled the lowlands. He was noted for his reform of the Scottish church and his foundation of the monastery of Scone (1114). He aided Henry I of England's campaign against Wales (1114).

Alexander II (1198–1249) King of the Scots (1214–49). Hoping to regain the northern counties of England, he supported the unsuccessful Barons' War (1215–17) against King John. In 1221 he married Joan, the sister of Henry III of England, and gave up his claims to English territory in 1237, when the present border between England and Scotland was fixed.

ALEXANDER (III) THE GREAT *A detail of a mosaic at Pompeii showing Alexander on his horse Bucephalus.*

Alexander (III) the Great (356–323 BC) King of Macedon (336–323), who between 334 and his death conquered most of the world known to antiquity. Alexander, who was a pupil of Aristotle, inherited a plan to invade Persia from his father Philip II; having secured his position in Macedon and Greece, he put this plan into action. In 333 he defeated the Persian king Darius III at Issus; in 332 he reduced Tyre in his greatest victory. Alexander then proceeded to conquer Egypt and Babylon (331). Moving on to Media and then east into central Asia, he finally embarked on the Indian expedition (327–325). He crossed the River Indus and conquered the Punjab. Forced to turn back by his reluctant army, he died at Babylon shortly after the marathon return journey.

Alexander III (1241–86) King of the Scots (1249–86). He married (1251) Margaret, daughter of Henry III of England. Under his leadership, the Scots defeated the Norwegians at the battle of Largs (1263) and by the Treaty of Perth (1266) gained the Isle of Man and the Hebrides from Norway.

Alexander of Tunis, Harold, 1st Earl (1891–1969) British field marshal. After distinguished service in World War I, Alexander held command in India. In World War II he commanded the evacuation of British forces from Dunkirk and was the last man to leave France. He became commander in chief in the Middle East (1942) and then, as Eisenhower's deputy, directed the offensive that defeated the Germans in N Africa (1943). He ended the war as Allied supreme commander in the Mediterranean and was subsequently governor general of Canada (1946–52) and Conservative minister of defence (1952–54).

Alexandra (1844–1925) A Danish princess who married (1863) Edward VII of the United Kingdom, when he was the Prince of Wales. In 1902 she founded Queen Alexandra's Imperial (now Royal) Army Nursing Corps and in 1912 she instituted the Alexandra Rose Day in aid of hospitals.

Alexandra (1872–1918) The wife from 1894 of Nicholas II of Russia. A German princess and granddaughter of Queen Victoria, Alexandra fell under the evil influence of Rasputin. His disastrous domination of her government while Nicholas was supreme commander of the Russian forces in World War I precipitated the Russian Revolution and the execution of Alexandra and her family by the Bolsheviks.

Alexandria (Arabic name: al-Iskandariyah) 31 13N 22 55E' The chief seaport and second largest, city in Egypt, between Lake Mareotis and the Mediterranean Sea. It handles most of Egypt's trade and the chief export is cotton; industries include oil refining and cotton ginning. *History*: founded in 332 BC by Alexander the Great, partly on the island of Pharos, which was linked to the mainland by a mole, it remained the Egyptian capital for over a thousand years. It was a Greek and Jewish cultural centre with a famous library founded by Ptolemy I Soter in the 3rd century BC and largely destroyed by fire in 97 BC. In 30 BC Alexandria fell to the Romans, becoming their most important regional capital. It declined following the discovery of the Cape of Good Hope passage and the removal of the capital to Cairo. It was bombarded by the British in 1882, Pompey's Pillar being one of the few ancient monuments to escape destruction. Two obelisks that also survived, Cleopatra's Needles, were removed and one is now in London, the other in New York. Population (1985): 2 821 000.

alfalfa A perennial flowering plant, *Medicago sativa*, also called lucerne. Growing to a height of 1 m, it resembles clover, having clusters of small purple flowers. Native to Europe, it is widely grown as forage for cattle and because of its ability to fix nitrogen. Family: *Leguminosae*.

Alfred the Great (849–99) King of Wessex (871–99). He prevented the Danish conquest of England, defeating them at Edington (878) after a campaign of guerrilla warfare based at Athelney. The legend of the king, travelling incognito, burning the peasant housewife's cakes, and being severely reprimanded by her, possibly refers to this unsettled period of his life. After his victory he allowed the Danes to keep their conquests in Mercia and East Anglia provided that Guthrum, their king, was converted to Christianity. Alfred built a navy of warships to defend the south coast against further Danish invasions (885–86; 892–96) and protected Wessex with a chain of fortifications. He took London (886), thus gaining control of all England save the Danish areas.

algae A vast group of simple plants (about 25 000 species) that contain the green pigment chlorophyll (and can therefore carry out photosynthesis) but have no true stems, roots, or leaves (*see* Thallophyta). They range from single-celled organisms to the giant seaweeds.

Most algae are aquatic, although some live in damp places on land—on rocks, trees, or in soils. A few are parasitic or associate with other organisms (*see* lichens). Reproduction is extremely variable and may involve asexual means, such as cell division, fragmentation, or spore production, and/or sexual means by gamete production. The more advanced algae often alternate between sexual and asexual phases. Algae provide a valuable food source for aquatic herbivorous animals and many are used as fertilizers and in industry. There are generally considered to be six divisions of algae, including the green, yellow-green, brown, and red algae; blue-green algae are now classified as bacteria.

Algarve The most southerly province of Portugal, bordering on Spain and the Atlantic Ocean. It became a Moorish kingdom in 1140 and was the last stronghold of the Moors in Portugal, being reconquered in 1249. Sparsely populated inland, its fertile coastal belt is densely populated and produces chiefly maize, figs, almonds, and olives; fishing is also important. Tourism is a flourishing industry. Area: 5071 sq km (1957 sq mi). Population (1981): 328 605. Chief town: Faro.

algebra The branch of mathematics that uses symbols to represent unknown quantities. The first treatise on the subject was written by Diophantus of Alexandria in the 3rd century AD and the name derives from the Arabic *al-jabr*, a term used by the mathematician al-Khwarizmi to denote the addition of equal quantities to both sides of an equation and later adopted as the name for the whole subject. Algebra was used in ancient Babylon, Egypt, and India and brought to Europe by the Arabs. In classical algebra symbols, such as x and y, represent ordinary numbers and the central part of the subject is the study of algebraic equations. Modern, or abstract, algebra is concerned with any system of quantities that obey a particular set of general rules and relationships.

Algeciras 36 08N 5 27W A port in S Spain, in Andalusia on the Bay of Gibraltar. Founded in 713 AD, it was destroyed by Alfonso XI of Castile (1311–50; reigned 1312–50) in 1344. The present town was rebuilt in 1760. In 1906 it was the site of the Algeciras Conference, a meeting of European powers to solve their dispute over Morocco. Its exports include oranges and cork. Population (1981): 86 042.

Algeria, Democratic and Popular Republic of A country in N Africa, on the Mediterranean Sea. It consists chiefly of the N Sahara Desert, with the Atlas Mountains in the N and small fertile areas near the coast. The inhabitants, who live almost entirely in the N, are mainly Arabs and Berbers. *Economy*: mainly agricultural although industrialization has proceeded rapidly since independence, financed by the discovery of oil (the main export) and natural gas in the desert areas. *History*: a former province of the Roman Empire, Algeria was subjugated in the 7th century by the Arabs, who introduced Islam. Overrun by Turks in the 16th century, it became a pirate state in the 18th century under the domination of *deys*, independent rulers who preyed on Mediterranean shipping. Algeria was annexed by the French in the 19th century and in 1881 the N section became part of Metropolitan France. A war of independence, waged by the Front de Libération nationale (FLN), lasted from 1954 to 1962 when independence was granted by de Gaulle, following referenda held in both Algeria and France. A republic was set up under Ahmed Ben

Bella but was overthrown in 1965 by a Council of Revolution. Col Houari Boumédienne (1925–78) became president; following Boumédienne's death, Col Benjedid Chadli (1929–) became the new president. After riots, a multi-party system was introduced in 1989. Prime minister: Mouloud Hamrouche. Official language: Arabic; French is also widely spoken. Official religion: Islam. Currency: dinar of 100 centimes. Area: 2 381 745 sq km (919 595 sq mi). Population (1988 est): 23 546 000. Capital and main port: Algiers.

Algiers (Arabic name: al-Jaza'ir; French name: Alger) 36 45N 3 05E The capital of Algeria, an important port in the N of the Mediterranean Sea. Its main exports include wine, citrus fruits, and iron ore. The University of Algiers was founded in 1879 and the University of Science and Technology in 1974. *History*: originally founded by the Phoenicians, it was re-established by the Arabs in the 10th century. Overrun by Turks in the 16th century, it became a base for Barbary pirates until taken by the French in 1830. During World War II it was the headquarters of the Allied forces in N Africa and for a time the seat of the French government-in-exile. Population (1988): 1 721 607.

algin (sodium alginate) A slimy substance extracted from seaweed. It is used as a thickener in such foods as ice cream and in industrial compounds.

Algol (*algo*rithmic *l*anguage) A computer-programming language. Algol is a high-level language, i.e. statements made in it resemble English and algebraic formulae rather than a computer notation. *See* program.

Algonkian A group of North American Indian languages, including Cree, Cheyenne, Blackfoot, and others, spoken by tribes living to the S and E of Hudson Bay and in the eastern woodland zone. The Algonkian tribes lived by hunting and fishing and roamed widely in small family groups and bands.

ALHAMBRA *The Court of the Lions features the horseshoe arches characteristic of Moorish architecture.*

Alhambra A castle on a hilly terrace outside Granada (Spain), built between 1238 and 1358. It was the last stronghold of the Muslim kings of Granada. Combining citadel and palace, it is an outstanding example of Moorish architecture, with magnificent courts and gardens. The name derives from Arabic *al-hamra*, the red, an allusion to the red stucco used on the walls.

Ali (c. 600–67) The cousin of Mohammed and his son-in-law by marriage to Fatimah. Born at Mecca, he was the second, or perhaps the first, person to embrace Islam. He became the fourth caliph in 656, but faced much opposition and was murdered in 661 at Kufa, Iraq. His tomb is venerated at Najaf. According to Shiite Muslims, Ali was the only legitimate successor of Mohammed and only his descendants are recognized as imams.

Ali, Muhammad (Cassius Marcellus Clay; 1942–) US boxer. A gold medallist in the 1960 Olympic Games, he became professional world heavyweight champion (1964). On becoming a Black Muslim he changed his name and was soon afterwards stripped of his title for three years because of his refusal to join the US army. Defeated (1971) by Joe Frazier, he again became champion in 1974 by defeating George Foreman, losing the title briefly in 1978 to Leon Spinks. His defeat of Spinks later that year made him the only boxer to become world champion three times. In 1980 he was defeated by Larry Holmes in his bid to regain the world title. He is renowned for his extrovert personality but suffers from Parkinson's disease as a result of blows to the brain.

Alicante 38 21N 0 29W A port in SE Spain, in Valencia on the Mediterranean Sea. Exports include wine, olive oil, and fruits. Industries include oil refining, textiles, chemicals, soap, and tobacco. It is a popular tourist resort. Population (1981): 251 387.

Aligarh 27 42N 78 25E A city in N India, in Uttar Pradesh. An agricultural trading centre, it is the site of the notable Aligarh Muslim University (founded as a college in 1875). Population (1981 est): 320 861.

aliphatic compounds Organic chemical compounds that are not aromatic. They include the alkanes, alkenes, and alkynes as well as some cyclic compounds (cycloalkanes).

alkali. See acids and bases.

alkali metals The elements forming group I of the periodic table: lithium, sodium, potassium, rubidium, caesium, and francium. All are soft, silvery-white metals with low densities, melting points, and boiling points. In chemical reactions they tend to form positive ions and have a valence of 1. They are highly reactive. The oxides and hydroxides are alkalis.

alkaline-earth metals The elements forming group II of the periodic table: beryllium, magnesium, calcium, strontium, barium, and radium. They are similar to the alkali metals in appearance and chemistry, but are harder, have higher melting and boiling points, and are somewhat less reactive. They have a valence of 2. The **alkaline earths** are the oxides of these metals.

alkaloids A group of nitrogen-containing basic compounds that are produced by plants and have diverse effects on the body. Many alkaloids are used as medicinal drugs, including quinine, reserpine, morphine, scopolamine, and atropine. Others, such as strychnine and coniine (from hemlock) are poisons. Caffeine, nicotine, and LSD are also alkaloids.

alkanes (or paraffins) A series of hydrocarbons, which contain only single bonds between the carbon atoms. They have the general formula C_nH_{2n+2}. The first four members of the series methane (CH_4), ethane (C_2H_6), propane (C_3H_8), and butane (C_4H_{10}) are gases, higher members are liquids or waxes. They are obtained from natural gas or oil and they and their substitution products have many uses.

alkanet A herbaceous plant of the genus *Anchusa*, native to Eurasia but widely grown for ornament (*A. azurea* is a common garden plant). It may reach a height of 50–120 cm, with clusters of small blue or white flowers and narrow or oval leaves. Family: *Boraginaceae*. A similar and related plant, *Pentaglottis sempervirens*, is also called alkanet.

alkenes (or olefins) Hydrocarbons that contain at least one carbon–carbon double bond in their molecules. The simplest types, with one double bond, have the general formula C_nH_{2n}; ethylene (or ethene, C_2H_4) is the first member of this series. The alkenes are more reactive than the alkanes, undergoing addition and polymerization reactions. They are obtained by cracking petroleum and their main use is as starting materials in industrial chemistry.

Al Khalil. See Hebron.

al-Khwarizmi, Muhammed Ibn Musa (c. 780–c. 850 AD) Arabic mathematician, who introduced the Hindu decimal system and the use of zero into Arabic mathematics. He also extended the work of Diophantus on algebraic equations in a book the title of which included the word *al-jabr* ("transposition"), from which the modern word "algebra" is derived.

alkynes (or acetylenes) Hydrocarbons that contain at least one carbon–carbon triple bond in their molecules. The simplest types, with one triple bond, have the general formula C_nH_{2n-2}; acetylene (or ethyne, C_2H_2) is the first member of this series. The alkynes, like the alkenes, undergo addition and polymerization reactions. They are extremely reactive, tending to explode under pressure, and are difficult to use in large quantities.

Allah (Arabic, probably from *al-ilah*: the god) The Islamic name of God. Allah was worshipped in pre-Islamic Arabia as early as the 3rd century BC. In Mecca he was given special rank as "the god," but lesser tribal gods continued to be worshipped alongside him until Mohammed proclaimed Allah as the one omnipotent and omniscient God, the same God as worshipped by Jews and Christians. He is eternal, the creator of the universe, the judge of men, merciful and compassionate. His word is embodied in the Koran.

Allahabad 25 57N 81 50E A city in N India, in Uttar Pradesh at the confluence of the Rivers Ganges and Jumna. It is principally an administrative and educational centre; its university was established in 1887. There is an annual religious festival and a much larger one every 12 years. A former centre of the independence movement, it was the home of the Nehru family. Population (1981 est): 650 070.

allegory A verse or prose narrative in which characters and events in the plot refer to a deeper, usually moral, meaning. It is an ancient and universal form, similar to but usually longer than the fable and the parable. Examples of allegory include the French *Roman de la rose* (13th century), Bunyan's *The Pilgrim's Progress* (1678), Swift's *Gulliver's Travels* (1726), and Orwell's *Animal Farm* (1945).

allele Any one of the various alternative forms of a gene that can occur at the same site on a chromosome. In *Drosophila* fruit flies, for example, several alternative eye colours are possible depending on which of the various alleles of the gene for eye colour is present in the individual.

Allen, Ethan (1739–89) American soldier, who pursued the independence from New York and New Hampshire of the Green Mountain region (now Vermont). Between 1770 and 1775 he commanded the Green Mountain Boys, who helped to capture Fort Ticonderoga (1775), the first American victory in the American Revolution. He was imprisoned by the British (1775–78) and died shortly before Vermont achieved statehood in 1789.

WOODY ALLEN

Allen, Woody (Allen Stewart Konigsberg; 1935–) US film actor and director. His films include *Play It Again, Sam* (1972), *Annie Hall* (1977), *Manhattan* (1979), *The Purple Rose of Cairo* (1985), *Hannah and Her Sisters* (1986), and *Another Woman* (1989).

Allenby, Edmund Henry Hynman, 1st Viscount (1861–1936) British field marshal. After experience in the Boer War, he commanded the Third Army in France in World War I. In 1917, appointed commander in chief of the Egyptian Expeditionary Force against the Turks in Palestine, he captured (9 Dec) Jerusalem (as a "Christmas present" for the British people) and then went on to devastate the Turks at Megiddo (1918). He ended his career as high commissioner in Egypt (1919–25).

Allende (Gossens), Salvador (1908–73) Chilean statesman; president of Chile (1970–73), the first Marxist to come to power through free elections. A founder of the Chilean Socialist Party, Allende governed a coalition of left-wing parties. His nationalization policies created much opposition and he was overthrown and killed by a military coup.

allergy An abnormal reaction by the body that is provoked by certain substances, including pollen, dust, certain foods and drugs, fur, moulds, etc. Normally all foreign substances (antigens) entering the body are destroyed by antibodies. Allergic people, however, become hypersensitive to certain antigens (called allergens), so that whenever they are subsequently encountered they stimulate not only the normal antibody reaction but also the specific symptoms of the allergy. Allergic conditions include hay fever, some forms of asthma and dermatitis, and urticaria. Treatment includes the use of antihistamines, corticosteroids, and desensitization.

alligator A large broad-snouted reptile belonging to the genus *Alligator* (2 species). Each side of the jaw contains 17–22 teeth, which are all covered when the mouth is closed. The American alligator (*A. mississippiensis*) is mainly black and lives in rivers of the SE USA, reaching a length of 5–6 m; the rare Chinese alligator (*A. sinensis*) of the Yangtze River is smaller. They dig burrows in which they hibernate during cold weather. Order: *Crocodilia* (*see* crocodile).

Allium A genus of herbaceous plants (about 450 species), including the onion, shallot, garlic, leek, chive, etc. They have bulbs, those of several species being widely used in temperate regions for food and flavouring, and in many the flowers are replaced by small bulbs (bulbils), by means of which the plants can be propagated. Family: *Liliaceae* (or *Alliaceae* according to some authorities).

Allosaurus A large bipedal dinosaur of the Jurassic and Cretaceous periods (200–65 million years ago). Up to 11 m long, it had large strong hind limbs, a well-developed tail, small forelegs, and thick protective knobs of bone over the eyes. Although fairly slow, it hunted prey, possibly in groups, and was equipped with sharp claws, powerful jaws, and sharp pointed teeth. Order: *Saurischia*.

alloy A blend of a metal with other metals or nonmetals. The first alloy was probably bronze, which was used in Europe in about 2000 BC. Steel and brass are the most widely used alloys. Alloys of aluminium are also common, especially in the aircraft industry. Alloys may consist of intermetallic compounds, solid solutions, heterogenous mixtures, or any combination of these forms. In general, intermetallic compounds tend to be hard and brittle: iron carbide, which strengthens iron to form steel is an example. Solid solutions, on the other hand, are usually soft and ductile: cartridge-case brass is a typical example. Most alloys melt over a range of temperatures unlike a pure metal, which has a specific melting point. **Eutectic alloys** consist of solid solutions having the lowest melting point of all the possible mixtures of the components. They are used in fuses and other safety mechanisms.

All Saints' Day A Christian feast commemorating all saints, whether known or unknown. In the Eastern Churches it has always been observed on the first Sunday after Pentecost. In the West its date varied until fixed as 1 Nov by Gregory III. *See also* Hallowe'en.

All Souls' Day A Christian feast in the Western Church commemorating all Christians who have died (the "faithful departed"). It is observed on 2 Nov. Requiem masses, containing the *Dies Irae*, are celebrated.

allspice (*or* pimento) A widely used aromatic spice, so named because it combines the flavours of several different spices. It is derived from the powdered dried unripe berries of an evergreen tree, *Pimenta dioca*, which is native to Central America and the West Indies and grows to a height of 9 m. Family: *Myrtaceae*.

Alma Ata 43 19N 76 55E (name until 1921: Verny) A city in the S Soviet Union, the capital of the Kazakh SSR. Situated in the foothills of the Trans-Alay Alatau (mountains), its industries include food and tobacco processing, and it has a thriving film industry. Population (1987): 1 108 000.

Almagest. *See* Ptolemy.

almanac A calendar of the months and days of the year containing astronomical and other miscellaneous data. It usually includes information about eclipses, phases of the moon, positions of the planets, times of sunset and sunrise and of high and low tides, as well as religious and secular holidays. Modern almanacs include official government publications listing national statistics.

almond A tree, *Prunus amygdalus*, native to SW Asia but widely grown in warm regions for its nuts. The edible nuts are produced by a variety called sweet almond; the nuts of the bitter almond yield aromatic almond oil, used as a flavouring. Almond trees grow to a height of 7 m; they have attractive pink flowers and are grown for ornament in cooler regions. Family: *Rosaceae*. *See also* Prunus.

Aloe A genus of succulent herbaceous plants (about 200 species), all native to Africa. A stem is usually absent, the toothed fleshy leaves forming a basal rosette, up to 40 cm in diameter. The flowers are red or yellow and some species are ornamental (e.g. *A. variegata*); the juice of some species, especially *A. vera*, is used as a purgative (bitter aloes). Family: *Liliaceae*.

alpaca A shaggy-coated hoofed mammal, *Lama pacos*, traditionally domesticated and bred in the South American Andes. Its dark fine high-quality fleece reaches nearly to the ground from its shoulder height of 90 cm and is shorn every two years, each animal yielding about 3 kg. Alpacas thrive at high altitudes, keeping to damp grassy plateaus. Family: *Camelidae* (camels).

alphabets Writing systems in which each symbol represents a speech sound (*see* phonetics). Many pictographic writing systems developed as far as ideography and even syllabaries, but the breakthrough to true alphabetic phonetic writing took place, it seems, only on the E shores of the Mediterranean around 2000 BC. From this Semitic alphabet all the major alphabets in use today—Roman, Greek, Cyrillic, Hebrew, Arabic, and Devanagari—are ultimately derived. *See also* International Phonetic Alphabet.

alpha particle The nucleus of a helium-4 atom, consisting of two protons and two neutrons. It is extremely stable and is emitted by some radioactive nuclei in the process known as **alpha decay**, a process that reduces the mass number of the nucleus by four and its atomic number by two. An example is the decay of uranium-238 into thorium-234.

Alphege, St (954–1012) Archbishop of Canterbury and martyr. He became Bishop of Winchester in 984 and was appointed Archbishop of Canterbury in 1006. He was captured by the Danes in 1011 and murdered because he refused to save himself at the expense of his tenants. Feast day: 19 April.

alphorn A musical instrument used in Switzerland for calling cattle. Made of wood, it is commonly 2 m long or more. Its mouthpiece is similar to that of a cornet. Being valveless, it plays only harmonics.

Alps The highest mountain range in Europe. It extends some 800 km (497 mi) in an arc roughly E–W through France, Switzerland, Italy, and Austria, and rises to 4807 m (15 771 ft) at Mont Blanc near the W end. Several major rivers rise here, including the Rhône, Rhine, Drava, and Po. The snowline varies between 2400 m and 3000 m (7874 ft and 9843 ft) and many of the lower slopes are used as pasture in summer, while in winter the Alps are Europe's major skiing area. There are several road and rail routes across the chain, including a number of tunnels. *See also* Maritime Alps.

Alsace (German name: Elsass) A planning region and former province in NE France, separated from West Germany by the River Rhine. It is a fertile agricultural area and has important potassium deposits. *History*: it was often a scene of conflict between France and Germany. Under Roman occupation from the 1st century AD, it became a Frankish duchy in the 5th century and was part of the Holy Roman Empire from the 10th to the 17th centuries. The French gained control of Alsace in 1648, after the Thirty Years' War, but it was lost to Germany in 1871, after the Franco-Prussian War, and linked with Lorraine to form the German imperial territory of **Alsace-Lorraine**. This existed until it reverted to France in 1919. It came under German control again in World War II and was restored to France in 1945. Area: 8310 sq km (3208 sq mi). Population (1986 est): 1 599 800.

Phoenician	Early Hebrew	Early Aramaic	Early Greek	Classical Greek	Etruscan	Early Latin	Classical Latin	Russian-Cyrillic	Modern Roman
				A	A	A	A	А	A
				B		B	B	Б	B
				Γ		<	C	Г	C
				Δ			D	Д	D
				E		E	E	Е	E
						F	F	Ф	F
				Γ			G	Г	G
				H		H	H	И	H
				I	I	I	I	I	I
									J
				K		K	K	К	K
				Λ		L	L	Л	L
				M		M	M	М	M
				N		N	N	Н	N
				O		O	O	О	O
				Π			P	П	P
						Q	Q		Q
				P		R	R	Р	R
				Σ		S	S	С	S
				T		T	T	Т	T
				Y		V	V	У	U
				Y		V	V		V
				Y					W
				Ξ		X	X		X
						Y	Y		Y
				Z		Z	Z	3	Z

ALPHABETS *The letters of the modern Roman alphabet have developed from the ancient Phoenician syllabary. This script in its Aramaic form was also the ultimate source of the Arabic alphabet and probably of the Brahmi alphabet, from which the many scripts of modern India are derived. The Cyrillic alphabet was derived directly from the Greek, whereas the Roman came through Etruscan and Latin.*

Alsatian dog. *See* German shepherd dog.

Altamira Upper Palaeolithic cave site in N Spain, recognized in 1879, noted for the 150 magnificent paintings of animals on the cave's ceiling. Bison, painted in red ochre with black manganese manes, tails, and hooves, are the chief species depicted. *See also* Magdalenian.

alternating current (ac) Electrical current that periodically reverses its direction. It is the form of current that is produced when a coil of wire rotates in a magnetic field and, as this is the way in which current is produced in power stations by electric generators, it is the form of current most widely used. The electromotive force (emf), E, produced by a generator is equal to $E'\sin \omega t$, where E' is the maximum emf, ω is the angular velocity of rotation, and t is the time. Thus the current has the form of a sine wave, with a frequency $\omega/2\pi$. *See also* electricity supply.

alternation of generations A phenomenon occurring in the life cycles of many plants and some animals (particularly coelenterates) in which there is an alternation between two distinct forms (generations), which differ from each other in structure, reproduction, and also often in habit. In plants the generation reproducing sexually is the gametophyte and the asexual generation is the sporophyte. Either phase may be predominant in a particular species; for example, the gametophyte is dominant in mosses and the sporophyte in flowering plants. In coelenterates sedentary asexual polyps alternate with free-living sexual medusae.

ALTERNATIVE ENERGY *A 300 kW aerogenerator in use in Scotland.*

alternative energy The use of natural energy from the environment. Most countries now rely heavily on fossil fuels (oil, coal, and natural gas) and nuclear power for their energy needs. However, reserves of fossil fuels are declining, although dates for their total exhaustion vary. They also contribute to the greenhouse effect by emitting carbon dioxide into the atmosphere. The estimates of recoverable uranium reserves are also uncertain

and there is opposition to the development of nuclear reactors, mainly on the grounds of safety and environmental hazard from waste disposal. Fusion reactors are still very much in the experimental stage. Although nuclear power is still regarded as the main option, renewable energy sources, including solar power, wind power, and tidal power are therefore being seriously investigated in the UK. Hydroelectric power is already in use and has limited potential for further expansion. Geothermal power, wave power, and biomass energy are also being actively explored. It is estimated that 20–25% of the UK's energy requirements could be met by renewable sources by 2025. *See also* biomass energy; geothermal energy; hydroelectric power; solar power; tidal power; wave power; wind power.

alternative medicine Systems of treatment of physical and mental illness used as alternatives to those of orthodox medicine. Known also as fringe, natural, and unorthodox medicine, it includes such specialties as osteopathy, homeopathy, acupuncture, and hypnosis, which are recognized and practised by some qualified doctors. Other branches include chiropractic, naturopathy, herbalism, dietary treatments, the laying on of hands, and self-healing (e.g. by yoga, biofeedback, etc.). *See also* holistic medicine.

Althing The parliament of Iceland, the oldest in the world, founded in about 930 AD. Since independence in 1944 it has been the country's sovereign legislature. It has 60 members in two houses of equal power.

altimeter A device for measuring altitude in one of two ways. A **pressure altimeter** consists of an aneroid barometer calibrated in metres (or feet) above sea level. A **radio altimeter** consists of a device that measures the time taken for a radio or radar signal to reach the ground and return.

altitude The angular distance of an astronomical body above or below an observer's horizon. It reaches a maximum of 90° when the body is directly overhead. It is used with the angular distance **azimuth**, measured eastwards along the horizon from the direction of N, to specify the position of an astronomical body on the celestial sphere.

alto A high adult male singing voice produced by falsetto. Range: that of the countertenor and contralto.

altocumulus cloud (Ac) A medium type of cloud appearing as globular masses in bands across the sky.

altostratus cloud (As) A medium type of cloud appearing as a greyish sheet, sometimes thin enough for the sun to be seen through it. It usually heralds rain.

aluminium (Al) A light silvery-white metal first isolated by Wöhler in 1827. It is the most abundant metal in the earth's crust and the main source is bauxite, an impure hydrated oxide. The metal is extracted by electrolysis of the oxide dissolved in a flux of low melting point with the mineral cryolite. Its most important uses depend on its lightness (relative density 2.70), ductility, and good electrical conductivity. It is used in electrical power cables, kitchen utensils, and many industrial applications. Pure aluminium is soft, but its alloys with copper, magnesium, and other elements have considerable strength. This combined with their low densities makes such alloys important in aircraft construction. Compounds include alum ($K_2SO_4.Al_2(SO_4)_3.24H_2O$) and the oxide alumina (Al_2O_3), which occurs naturally as corundum and ruby and is used as an abrasive, a gem, and in lasers. The hydroxide ($Al(OH)_3$) is used in glass manufacture and as an antacid in medicine. At no 13; at wt 26.9815; mp 660.4°C; bp 1800°C.

alveolus. *See* lungs.

Alyssum A genus of low-growing herbaceous plants (about 150 species), mostly native to S Europe but widely grown in gardens. Alyssums have small flowers grouped in terminal clusters. Varieties of sweet alyssum (*A. maritimum*), 10–15 cm high, have white or pink flowers and are grown as annuals. Perennial alyssums include *A. saxatile*, which grows to 30 cm high and has yellow flowers. Family: *Cruciferae*.

Alzheimer's disease (*or* presenile dementia) A degenerative disease that affects nerve cells of the brain. It causes speech disturbances, progressive loss of mental faculties, and other symptoms of senility though it may occur in middle age. Its cause is uncertain but it is thought that either a virus or a genetic disorder may be responsible. Named after the German neurologist Alois Alzheimer (1864–1915).

Amaranthus A genus of herbaceous plants (50–60 species) native to tropical and subtropical regions but now widely distributed (as pigweed). The small petalless flowers grow in long drooping spikes. Several species are grown for ornament, including *A. caudatus* (love-lies-bleeding), 60–100 cm tall with dark-red flowers, *A. tricolor* (Joseph's coat), with purple flowers and red, yellow, and green leaves. Family: *Amaranthaceae*.

amaryllis A perennial herbaceous plant, *Amaryllis belladonna*, also called belladonna lily, native to South Africa but widely cultivated for ornament. Growing from bulbs, it has strap-shaped leaves and a 45 cm long stem bearing 5–12 funnel-shaped sweet-scented flowers, usually rose-pink. Family: *Amaryllidaceae*.

Amati A family of violin makers in Cremona, Italy. **Andrea Amati** (c. 1520–c. 1578) developed the design that became the standard modern violin. His sons **Antonio Amati** (?1550–1638) and **Girolamo Amati** (1551–1635) worked as a team. Girolamo's son **Nicolò Amati** (1596–1684) was the family's greatest craftsman and taught Andrea Guarneri (d. 1698) and Stradivari.

Amazon, River (Portuguese name: Rio Amazônas) The largest river system and the second longest river in the world. Rising as the Río Marañón in the Andes, in Peru, it flows generally W-E to enter the Atlantic Ocean in NE Brazil. Its drainage basin extends over much of Brazil, parts of Venezuela, Columbia, Ecuador, Peru, and Bólivia. It is covered by a mantle of tropical rain forest (selva) and is navigable to oceangoing vessels as far as Iquitos, 3700 km (2300 mi) upstream. Destruction of much of the forest caused international concern in the 1980s. Length: 6440 km (4000 mi). Drainage basin area: about 5 827 500 sq km (2 250 000 sq mi).

Amazons (Greek: breastless ones) A mythical nation of female warriors who were believed by the ancient Greeks to live in Pontus, near the Black Sea. Trained for war and hunting, the Amazons got their name from their habit of removing the right breast to facilitate the drawing of bows. They intervened in the Trojan War against the Greeks, but Achilles killed their queen, Penthesilea. They also invaded Attica but were defeated by Theseus, who took their queen Hippolyte captive.

amber A translucent or opaque yellow fossil resin exuded by coniferous trees; insects and leaves are often preserved in the mineral, having been trapped on the sticky surface prior to hardening. It is found predominantly in Tertiary deposits around the S Baltic coast. It is used for beads, ornaments, and amber varnish.

ambergris A waxy substance found in the intestines of sperm whales. Mainly cholesterol, with fatty oils and steroids, it has a musky scent. It is used in making perfumes.

amboyna A tropical Asian tree, *Pterocarpus indicus*, that reaches a height of about 9 m and yields reddish beautifully grained wood used for furniture. Family: *Leguminosae*.

America. *See* United States of America.

American eagle. *See* bald eagle.

American football. *See* football.

American Indians A diverse group of peoples of North, Central, and South America and the Caribbean Islands. In many respects they resemble the Mongoloid peoples of Asia, which has led to their classification as a subtype of the Mongoloid race. However, their physical diversity, and the possession of certain features not common among Mongoloids, suggests other origins. Their ancestors probably migrated to the Americas from Asia via Alaska between 10 000 and 20 000 years ago. They have coarse dark straight hair, yellowish-brown skins, and sparse body hair. They speak a variety of languages and culturally range from primitive hunters and gatherers to the creators of the Aztec, Maya, and Inca civilizations.

AMERICAN INDIANS *A Bolivian-Indian woman and her child, direct descendants of the Incas.*

American Revolution (*or* American War of Independence; 1775–83) The conflict in which the 13 colonies of North America gained independence from Britain. American resentment at Britain's authoritative rule focused in the mid-18th century on taxation. Protests against such legislation as the Stamp Act (1765) and Townshend Acts (1767) culminated in the Boston Tea Party (1773), to which Britain responded with the punitive Intolerable Acts (1774). The first Continental Congress was summoned at Philadelphia and, after attempts by both sides at negotiation had failed, the first shots of the war were fired at Lexington and Concord (April, 1775). In the autumn the Americans invaded Canada, taking Montreal and besieging Quebec until forced to withdraw to Ticonderoga in Spring, 1776. On 4 July the second Continental Congress issued the Declaration of Independence. Gen Howe landed on Long Island in August and defeated the newly appointed American commander in chief, Washington, near White Plains. At the beginning of January, 1777, however, Washington dealt a counterblow at Princeton before settling in winter quarters. Britain's strategy in 1777 was based on a plan for Burgoyne to march S from Canada and join forces with Howe at the Hudson River. Burgoyne duly arrived at the Hudson (Aug) but Howe had left New York by sea, landed at Chesapeake Bay, and defeated Washington at the Brandywine, taking Philadelphia (Sept). Burgoyne, meanwhile, was forced to surrender his army at Saratoga, a defeat that proved a turning point by bringing France into the war on the American side. In 1778 the British began an offensive in the S. Howe's successor, Clinton, took Charleston, South Carolina, and Cornwallis defeated Gates at Camden (1780). In early 1781 the British lost badly at Cowpens (17 Jan) but won, with heavy casualties, the battle of Guilford Court House (15 March). Cornwallis now moved into Virginia, establishing a base at Yorktown. There besieged by a Franco-American force under the Comte de Rochambeau (1725–1807) and Washington, on 19 October Cornwallis surrendered. Ultimate American victory was now assured although conflict continued, chiefly at sea. The British navy had been threatened throughout by American privateers and the activities of such commanders as John Paul Jones, but the main threat at sea came from America's European allies—the French, Spanish (from 1779), and Dutch (from 1780), who gained control of the English Channel and threatened invasion. Rodney's success (1782) in the West Indies enabled Britain to regain control of the Atlantic. In 1783 Britain acknowledged American independence in the Treaty of Paris.

America's Cup A sailing race held periodically off Newport, Rhode Island (USA) and elsewhere, in which US yachts are challenged for a cup won by the US *America* off the Isle of Wight in 1851. The USA retained the cup until 1983, when it was won by the Australian entry *Australia II*. The 1987 result was disputed.

americium (Am) The fourth transuranic element, synthesized (1944) by G. T. Seaborg and others by addition of neutrons to plutonium followed by β-decay. It forms the oxide (AmO_2) and such trihalides as $AmCl_3$; it is strongly radioactive. At no 95; at wt (243); mp 994°C.

amethyst A gemstone comprising a purple variety of quartz. Its colour is due to impurities, particularly iron oxide. The best crystals are found in Brazil and the Urals. It is used for jewellery. Birthstone for February.

Amiens 49 54N 2 18E A city in NE France, the capital of the Somme department situated on the River Somme. Known as Samarobriva in pre-Roman times, it was the ancient capital of Picardy. The **Peace of Amiens** (1802), which marked a respite in the Revolutionary and Napoleonic Wars, was signed here. Its fine gothic cathedral survived the damage of both World Wars. An important railway junction, Amiens' industries include textiles, tyres, and chemicals. Population (1982 est): 136 358.

Amin Dada, Idi (c. 1925–) Ugandan politician; president (1971–79). He rose rapidly in the army, becoming commander in 1966. He overthrew Milton Obote (1925–) to become president and in 1972 ordered the expulsion of 80 000 non-Ugandan Asians. He and his government were notorious for their brutality;

Amin was overthrown in a Tanzanian-backed coup after which he went into exile.

amines A class of basic organic compounds derived from ammonia (NH_3), in which one (primary amines), two (secondary amines), or three (tertiary amines) of the hydrogen atoms are replaced by organic groups. *See also* amino acids.

amino acids A group of organic acids characterized by having at least one carboxyl group (–COOH) and at least one amino group (–NH_2). About 20 different amino acids comprise the basic constituents of proteins, the arrangement and types of amino acids determining the structure and hence the function of the protein molecule. Certain essential amino acids cannot be manufactured by the body and must be supplied in the diet. In man these are: arginine, histidine, isoleucine, leucine, lysine, methionine, phenylalanine, threonine, tryptophan, and valine.

Amis, Kingsley (1922–) British novelist and poet, one of the *Angry Young Men. Educated at Oxford, he taught at Swansea and Cambridge universities and in the USA. His first novel, *Lucky Jim* (1954), was a popular success. Later novels include *I Want It Now* (1968), *Ending Up* (1974), *Jake's Thing* (1978), *Stanley and the Women* (1984), *The Old Devils* (1986), which won the 1986 Booker Prize, and *The Green Man* (1988). He published several volumes of poetry, contributed to the verse anthology *New Lines* (1956), and edited the *Oxford Book of Light Verse* (1978). His son **Martin Amis** (1949–) is the author of such books as *The Rachel Papers* (1974), *Money* (1984), and *London Fields* (1989).

Amman 31 57N 35 56E The capital of Jordan. Amman was the capital of the biblical Ammonites, and there are some Greek and Roman remains. Under the British mandate in Palestine, the town grew from a small village, and in 1946 it became the capital of independent Jordan. The city has had large influxes of refugees following fighting in the Arab-Israeli Wars (1948, 1967, and 1973); in 1970 tension resulting from the refugee presence led to fighting on the streets of Amman between Jordanian forces and Palestinians. The university was founded in 1962. Amman is now an important communications centre, with some manufacturing industry. Population (1984): 777 500.

ammeter An instrument for measuring electric current. The two most common types are the moving-coil and the moving-iron ammeters. The moving-coil ammeter is more sensitive but will only measure direct current. The moving-iron ammeter will measure both alternating and direct current but is less sensitive and its scale is nonlinear. Some modern instruments are electronic and have a digital display.

ammonia (NH_3) A colourless toxic basic gas used for the manufacture of fertilizers, nitric acid, explosives, and synthetic fibres. It is made by the Haber process.

ammonite A cephalopod mollusc belonging to the subclass *Ammonoidea* (over 600 genera), abundant during the late Palaeozoic and Mesozoic eras, becoming extinct 100 million years ago. Their fossilized remains have either straight or coiled shells, some up to 200 cm in diameter, containing many chambers, which provided buoyancy for the free-swimming animal.

Ammonites An ancient Semitic tribe who were descended from Ben-ammi, the son of Lot, and lived E of Jordan. They worshipped the god Moloch and often warred against the Israelites.

amnesia Loss of memory resulting from such causes as head injuries, drugs, hysteria, senility, or psychological illness. The memory loss may be for events before the injury or disease (**retrograde amnesia**) or for events after it (**anterograde amnesia**). In some cases specific areas of the brain show pathological changes. Treatment is related to the cause.

Amnesty International An organization, founded by Peter Benenson in the UK in 1961, aiming to defend freedom of speech, opinion, and religion in all parts of the world. It campaigns for the release of "prisoners of conscience," against torture, and for human rights and is concerned for the welfare of refugees. It has some 100 000 members in 75 countries and is funded by voluntary contributions. It won the Nobel Peace Prize in 1977.

amniocentesis The removal for examination of a small quantity of the fluid (amniotic fluid) that surrounds an unborn baby in the mother's womb. The specimen may be taken by needle through the abdominal wall or, later in pregnancy, the opening of the womb. Tests on the amniotic fluid may reveal the presence of certain diseases or congenital disorders in the baby (e.g. Down's syndrome or spina bifida). If serious abnormality is detected, the possibility of abortion can be considered. Amniocentesis is offered to women of any age when there is a family history of congenital disease and is routinely offered to all women over 35 years of age.

Amoeba A genus of free-living microscopic animals (*Protozoa*). They occur widely in soil and water and their flexible cells assume various shapes. The common amoeba (*A. proteus*) may be up to 0.5 mm long. Amoebas move by extending their cytoplasm into lobes (pseudopodia), which also engulf food particles and liquids. They reproduce by binary fission and under adverse conditions form protective cysts. Some related forms are parasitic, including *Entamoeba histolytica*, which causes amoebic dysentery in man. Class: *Sarcodina*.

Amorites Semitic nomads of Palestine and Syria, who invaded the centres of civilization of Mesopotamia during the late 3rd millennium and 2nd millennium BC. They occupied Babylonia, assimilated its culture and established numerous small kingdoms. Many Babylonian kings, including Hammurabi, were of Amorite stock.

amount of substance A quantity proportional to the number of particles, such as atoms or ions, in a sample. The constant of proportionality is Avogadro's number. Amount of substance is measured in moles.

ampere (A) The SI unit of electric current equal to the current that when passed through two parallel infinitely long conductors placed 1 metre apart in a vacuum produces a force between them of 2×10^{-7} newton per metre of length. This 1948 definition replaced all former definitions including that of the international ampere based on the rate of deposition of silver from a solution of silver nitrate. Named after A. M. Ampère.

Ampère, André Marie (1775–1836) French physicist, who was a professor at Bourg and later in Paris. He introduced the important distinctions between electrostatics and electric currents and between current and voltage, demonstrated that current-carrying wires exert a force on each other, and gave an explanation of magnetism in terms of electric currents. **Ampère's law** states that the strength of the magnetic field at any point produced by a current (I) flowing through a conductor of length l is proportional to Il/d^2 where d is the distance between the point and the conductor. The unit of electric current is named after him.

amphetamine A stimulant drug that produces a feeling of alertness and wellbeing, increases muscular activity, and reduces fatigue and appetite. Because of the risk of addiction, particularly when combined with barbiturates ("purple hearts"), amphetamine is now rarely prescribed. It is occasionally used to treat obesity and narcolepsy (a tendency to fall asleep at any time). Trade name: Benzedrine.

amphibian An animal belonging to the class *Amphibia*, which contains over 2500 species of frogs, toads, newts, salamanders, and caecilians. Adult amphibians breathe through lungs and have adapted to a wide range of habitats; however they require damp surroundings in order to minimize loss of body fluids through their thin, moist and usually scaleless skin. Generally amphibians lay their eggs in ponds or rivers, often migrating long distances to do so. The eggs hatch into aquatic tadpole larvae that breathe using gills and develop into adults by a complete bodily transformation known as metamorphosis.

amphiboles A group of rock-forming minerals, mostly complex hydrous ferromagnesian silicates. Horneblende and tremolite are examples. Amphiboles are common in igneous and metamorphic rocks and often occur in fibrous or acicular forms, including some forms of asbestos.

amphioxus A small slender fishlike animal, also called lancelet, which belongs to the subphylum *Cephalochordata* (about 30 species). Up to 5 cm long, they occur in shallow coastal waters, living mostly in burrows with the front end protruding. Food particles are filtered from the water, which enters the mouth and leaves through gill slits, there is a supportive rodlike notochord and a nerve cord running the length of the body. Amphioxus is thought to resemble the primitive ancestors of other chordate animals, including vertebrates. Genera: *Branchiostoma*; *Asymmetron*. *See also* Chordata.

AMRITSAR *The Golden Temple, centre of the Sikh religion.*

amphitheatre An elliptical or circular building with tiers of seats surrounding an arena, designed by the Romans as a setting for gladiatorial and wild-beast shows, etc. The earliest stone amphitheatre is that at Pompeii

(c. 70 BC). The largest is the Colosseum in Rome but there are also impressive remains of amphitheatres in Arles, Nîmes, Capua, Verona, and in Sicily and N Africa.

Amphitrite The Greek goddess of the sea. Poseidon chose her to be his wife when he saw her dancing with her sister Nereids. She rejected him and fled to the island of Naxos, but he sent a dolphin to reclaim her. She bore him three sons, Triton, Rhodos, and Benthesicyma.

amplifier An electronic device for intensifying an electrical signal in an alternating-current circuit, with an external steady voltage supply. Originally built with thermionic valves, but now almost exclusively with transistors, amplifiers are designed to multiply the input (current, voltage, or power) by a specific factor, known as the gain. Often an amplifier consists of several stages, the output from one stage becoming the input to the next stage.

amplitude modulation. *See* modulation.

Amritsar 31 35N 74 56E A city in NW India, in Punjab. Founded in 1577 by the fourth guru of the Sikhs, Ram Das, it has become the centre of the Sikh faith. It was the scene of a massacre (1919), in which hundreds of Indian nationalists were killed when fired upon by troops under British control. In 1984 about 1000 people died when the Sikh shrine, the Golden Temple, was fortified by Sikh extremists and stormed by the Indian army. The assassination of Mrs Gandhi later in the year was a reprisal for this event. A commercial, cultural, and communications centre, it manufactures textiles and silk. Population (1981 est): 594 844.

Amsterdam 52 21N 4 54E The official capital of the Netherlands, in North Holland province on the Rivers Amstel and IJ. The government seat is at The Hague. Linked to the North Sea by canal (1876), it is a major seaport. It is also an important financial and industrial centre, possessing a renowned diamond cutting and polishing trade. Industries include shipbuilding, dairy produce, tobacco, and brewing. The city is mostly built on piles and linked with a radial system of canals and approximately 1000 bridges. *History*: chartered in 1300, it joined the Hanseatic League in 1369. It became the capital in 1808. Population (1989): 691 837.

Amu Darya, River A river in central Asia. Rising in the Pamirs, it flows mainly NW through the Hindu Kush and the Turkmen and Uzbek SSRs to join the Aral Sea through a large delta. It forms part of the border between Afghanistan and the Soviet Union and it is important for irrigation. It is navigable for over 1450 km (800 mi). Length: 2400 km (1500 mi).

Amundsen, Roald (1872–1928) Norwegian explorer, the first person to reach the South Pole. In 1897 he became first mate on the *Belgica*, which was engaged in Antarctic exploration. After sailing the Northwest Passage in the *Gjöa* (1903–06) he abandoned his plan to reach the North Pole on hearing of Peary's success (1909). He himself beat Scott to the South Pole in 1911. In 1926 he flew a dirigible over the North Pole with Umberto Nobile (1885–1928). Amundsen died while searching for Nobile following the latter's dirigible crash in the Arctic Ocean. A small section of the S Pacific Ocean, bordering on Ellsworth Land in Antarctica, is called **Amundsen Sea** after him.

Anabaptists (from Greek: rebaptizers) Any of various radical religious groups originating in several continental countries during the Reformation. They were called Anabaptists because they rejected infant baptism in favour of baptizing adults when they professed their faith. Persecuted by Roman Catholics and Protestants, they were accused of fanaticism, heresy, and immorality. They believed in pacifism, common ownership of goods, and millenarianism, and held radical political views. Their modern descendants, such as the Mennonites, number more than 500 000.

anabolic steroids. *See* androgens.

anabolism. *See* metabolism.

anaconda A nonvenomous South American constrictor snake, *Eunectes murinus*. Up to 10 m long, it is typically dark green with oval black spots and lives in swamps and rivers, feeding on fish and small caymans and also hunting deer, peccaries, and birds along the water's edge.

anaemia A reduction in the number of red cells or the quantity of red pigment (*see* haemoglobin) in the blood. It may be due to loss of blood, for example after an accident or operation or from chronic bleeding of a peptic ulcer, or lack of iron, which is necessary for the production of haemoglobin. **Haemolytic anaemias** are caused by increased destruction of the red blood cells, as may occur in certain blood diseases (e.g. sickle-cell disease and thalassaemia) and malaria or because of the presence of toxic chemicals. Anaemia can also result from the defective production of red cells, such as occurs in **pernicious anaemia** (when it is due to deficiency of vitamin B_{12}).

anaesthesia A state of insensitivity to pain. Anaesthesia occurs in certain diseases of the nervous system, but is induced artificially for surgical operations. Alcohol and opium derivatives have been used as anaesthetics for centuries, but it was not until the 1840s that the first anaesthetic gases—ether, nitrous oxide, and chloroform—were used to induce **general anaesthesia** (total unconsciousness). This procedure now involves premedication (including administration of sedatives) to prepare the patient for surgery, followed by induction of anaesthesia by injecting a short-acting barbiturate (usually sodium thiopentone). Anaesthesia is maintained by inhalation of an anaesthetic gas (e.g. halothane). **Local anaesthesia** is usually used for dental surgery and also for other minor operations. Procaine and lignocaine are widely used local anaesthetics. **Spinal anaesthesia** (epidural or subarachnoid) produces loss of sensation in a particular part of the body by injecting a local anaesthetic into the space round the spinal cord. It may be used, for example, during childbirth.

Anaheim 33 50N 117 56W A city in the USA, in S California near Los Angeles. It is a major tourist centre, containing the famous Disneyland opened in 1955. Population (1986): 240 730.

analgesics A class of drugs that relieve pain. **Narcotic analgesics**, such as morphine, are powerful pain killers that act directly on the brain. Some anaesthetics also have analgesic properties. Aspirin and paracetemol are examples of **antipyretic analgesics**, which also reduce fever. These drugs are not addictive but are less potent than the narcotics.

analog computer. *See* computer.

analytic geometry The study of geometrical relations by algebraic methods. Geometrical figures are placed in a coordinate system, each point in the figure being represented by its coordinates, which satisfy an algebraic equation. Also known as coordinate geometry or Cartesian geometry, after its inventor René Descartes.

anaphylaxis A form of allergy that follows the inter-action of the foreign substance (allergen) with antibody that is bound to the surface of certain cells (mast cells). This leads to the release of bradykinin, histamine, and other chemicals, which cause the symptoms. Symptoms are either local (such as asthma) or general (shock and collapse). The latter usually follows injection of the al-lergen (such as penicillin) and is a medical emergency; it is treated with injections of corticosteroids and adrena-line.

anarchism A political theory advocating abolition of the state and all governmental authority. Most anar-chists believe that voluntary cooperation between indi-viduals and groups is not only a fairer and more moral way of organizing society but is also more effective and orderly. Anarchism aims at maximizing personal free-dom and holds that societies in which freedom is limited by coercion and authority are inherently unstable. As an influential political force, anarchism was defeated in Russia by communism but persisted in Europe, especial-ly in Spain until the end of the Civil War (1939).

ANASTASIA *Nicholas II's children in 1910; (from the left) Anastasia, Olga, Alexis, Maria, and Tatiana.*

Anastasia (1901–?1918) The youngest daughter of Nicholas II of Russia. Although she was believed to have been executed after the Russian Revolution, a Mrs Anna Anderson (d. 1984) claimed from 1920 that she was Anastasia. In 1961 her claim was officially rejected.

Anatolia. *See* Asia Minor.

anatomy The study of the structure of living organ-isms. Early studies of human anatomy were made by the Greek physician Galen, in the 2nd century AD, but it was not until the 16th century that the prejudice against dis-secting human cadavers was overcome and anatomists –notably Vesalius–made valuable contributions to the science. In the 17th century William Harvey discovered the circulation of blood and the development of the mi-croscope enabled advances in the detailed structure of the body to be made by such microscopists as Malpighi, Leeuwenhoek, and Swammerdam. In the 20th century anatomy received a valuable tool with the development of the electron microscope, which greatly extended the investigation of microscopic structure. Specialized

branches of anatomy include embryology (the study of development), histology (tissues), and cytology (cells).

Anaxagoras (c. 500–428 BC) Greek philosopher, born at Clazomenae (Asia Minor). In about 480 he moved to Athens, but because of his influence on Peri-cles, he was eventually (450) banished on a trumped-up charge of impiety. He believed that the physical universe was made up of an infinite number of substances and that matter was infinitely divisible. He was also the first to explain solar eclipses.

Anaximander (c. 610–c. 546 BC) Greek philosopher, born in Miletus (Asia Minor). He was one of the earliest thinkers to develop a systematic philosophical view of the physical universe. He held that it came from some-thing unlimited, not just one particular kind of matter, and maintained that the earth lay unsupported at the centre of the universe. He also had an evolutionary view of the origin of life, holding that it arose in the sea, and that man evolved from some more primitive species.

anchovy A small herring-like fish belonging to the tropical and warm-temperate family *Engraulidae* (100 species). 10–25 cm long, anchovies have a large mouth extending behind the eye, a small lower jaw, and a point-ed snout. They live in large shoals, chiefly in coastal wa-ters, and are widely fished for food, bait, and animal feeds.

Anchusa. *See* alkanet.

ancient lights In English law, the right of an owner of a building to have uninterrupted light through a win-dow. The passage of light through a window is protected against obstruction if it has been enjoyed without inter-ruption for at least 20 years.

Ancona 43 37N 13 31E A seaport in central Italy, the capital of Marche on the Adriatic Sea. It dates from 1500 BC, when it was founded by the Dorians. Its industries are connected with shipbuilding, engineering, and sugar refining. Population (1986): 104 409. -

Andalusia (Spanish name: Andalucía) The southern-most region of Spain, bordering on the Atlantic Ocean and Mediterranean Sea. It occupies chiefly the river ba-sin of the Guadalquivir and is one of Spain's most fertile regions producing citrus fruit, olives, and wine. Under Roman control after the 2nd century BC, the region was named Andalusia (after its 5th-century Vandal settlers) by the Muslims, who invaded the region in the early 8th century; much evidence of the Muslim occupation re-mains. In the 15th century Castile finally recovered Andulusia from the Muslims. After the Moriscos (Chris-tians of Moorish descent) were expelled in 1609 the re-gion's prosperity diminished. It is popular with tourists, who are attracted by the great Moorish buildings found especially in Córdoba, Seville, and Granada.

Andaman and Nicobar Islands A Union Territory of India, comprising two island groups in the E Bay of Bengal. The Andaman forests support plywood and match industries. Coconuts, rubber, and coffee are also important. The Nicobar Islands 120 km (75 mi) S of the Andaman Islands, produce coconuts, areca nuts, and fish. Area: 8293 sq km (3215 sq mi). Population (1981): 188 254. Capital: Port Blair.

Andersen, Hans Christian (1805–75) Danish au-thor, famous for his fairy tales. The son of a shoemaker, he attempted to become an actor in Copenhagen. A benefactor enabled him to attend the university there in 1828; he subsequently travelled widely in Europe and wrote novels, plays, and travel books. His international reputation, however, was earned by the 168 fairy tales that he wrote between 1835 and 1872. These include such classics as "The Snow Queen," "The Little Mermaid," and "The Ugly Duckling."

ANDES   *Mount Huayna Potosi (6093 m; 19 991 ft) in Bolivia.*

Andes (Spanish name: Cordillera de los Andes) A mountain system in W South America. It extends N for about 7250 km (4500 mi) from Cape Horn to the Isthmus of Panama, reaching 6960 m (22 835 ft) at Mount Aconcagua and separating a narrow coastal belt from the rest of the continent. Comprising a series of parallel mountain ranges, it is chiefly of volcanic origin and contains several active volcanoes, including Cotopaxi; earthquakes are common phenomena. It is rich in mineral wealth; the chief metals extracted include gold, silver, platinum, mercury, copper, and lead.

Andhra Pradesh A state in E central India, on the Bay of Bengal. The coastal plain rises westwards over the Eastern Ghats into the Deccan plateau. Rice, sugar cane, cotton, tobacco, and pulses are farmed. Large forests provide teak, bamboo, and fruit trees. Manganese, iron ore, mica, and coal are mined. A few industries exist, such as textile, machinery, and shipbuilding, which has been developed with cheap hydroelectricity. Area: 275 281 sq km (106 258 sq mi). Population (1981 est): 53 550 000. Capital: Hyderabad. Chief seaport: Vishakhapatnam.

Andorra, Principality of (Catalan name: Valls d'Andorra; French name: Les Vallées d'Andorre) A small principality in the E Pyrenees, between France and Spain. It is mountainous with peaks reaching heights of almost 3000 m (about 9500 ft). *Economy*: tourism and agriculture (wheat, potatoes, livestock raising, and tobacco) are the principal industries. *History*: in 1278 it was placed under the joint overlordship of the Bishop of Urgel in Spain and the Comte de Foix in France. The latter's rights passed in the 16th century to the French Crown and are now held by the president. Andorra pays dues in alternate years of 960 francs to France and 460 pesetas to the bishopric respectively. Andorra is a tax haven and immigration has been substantial in recent years. Official language: Catalan; French and Spanish are also spoken. Official currencies: French and Spanish currencies are both in use. Area:

465 sq km (179 sq mi). Population (1988): 42 712. Capital: Andorra la Vella.

Andrea del Sarto (Andrea d'Agnolo; 1486–1530) A leading Florentine Renaissance painter, whose work, through its influence on his pupils Jacopo da Pontormo (1494–1557), Giovanni Battista Rosso (1494–1540), and Giorgio Vasari (1511–74), became a starting point for Tuscan mannerism. Andrea spent most of his life in Florence, producing frescoes in the Scalzi and the SS Annunziata. Among his most important paintings are several representing the Holy Family, some portraits, and the *Madonna of the Harpies* (1517; Uffizi).

Andrew, St In the New Testament, one of the 12 Apostles. Originally a fisherman with his brother Simon Peter, he was a disciple of John the Baptist before following Jesus. Apparently crucified, he is the patron saint of Scotland and Russia. Feast day: 30 Nov.

Androcles The hero of a story by Aulus Gellius (?125–?165 AD). Androcles was an escaped slave who removed a thorn from the paw of a lion. The lion later recognized the recaptured slave in the arena and spared him; both were freed.

androgens A group of steroid hormones that influence the development and function of the male reproductive system and determine male secondary sexual characteristics, such as the growth of body hair and deepening of the voice at puberty. The major androgens are testosterone and androsterone, produced by the testes in higher animals and man and also in small amounts by the adrenal glands and ovaries in mammals. Natural and synthetic androgens are used in medicine to treat conditions caused by androgen deficiency. Some androgens promote the growth of muscle and bone. These –the **anabolic steroids**–have been used for body-building in debilitated patients and athletes.

Andropov (name from 1946 until 1958: Shcherbakov; name from 1958 to 1984: Rybinsk) 58 01N 38 52E A port in the W central Soviet Union, on the River Volga. It is situated below the **Rybinsk Reservoir**, an artificial lake of 5200 sq km (2000 sq mi) created in 1941. Population (1987): 254 000.

Andropov, Yuri Vladimirovich (1914–84) Soviet statesman; general secretary of the Soviet Communist Party (1982–84) and president of the Soviet Union (1983–84). He was ambassador to Hungary (1953–57) and headed the KGB (1967–82). In 1984 the city of Rybinsk was renamed Andropov in his honour.

androsterone. *See* androgens.

Aneirin (6th century AD) Welsh poet. His poem "Y Gododdin," preserved in the manuscript *Book of Aneirin* (c. 1250), celebrates the heroes of an expedition sent from Edinburgh to recapture Catterick from the Saxons. Out of 300 warriors only one survived.

Anemone A genus of herbaceous perennial plants (about 150 species) mostly native to N temperate regions. The leaves are segmented and the flowers lack true petals. The Eurasian wood anemone (*A. nemorosa*), 10–15 cm high, has white flowers. Many species are cultivated as ornamentals for their brightly coloured flowers, including the poppy and Japanese anemones (*A. coronaria* and *A. japonica*). Family: *Ranunculaceae*.

aneroid barometer. *See* barometer.

aneurysm A swelling in the wall of an artery, due to a weakness in the wall. The most common cause in the western world is now atherosclerosis. Aneurysms may rupture, causing fatal haemorrhage. Treatment consists of surgical removal of the aneurysm and its replacement with a graft.

angelfish 1. A fish of the tropical marine family *Chaetodontidae*, having a narrow oval laterally compressed body, a small mouth, and often an elongated snout. Up to 70 cm long, angelfish are solitary, living around coral reefs. They are usually patterned in a variety of brilliant colours. 2. A South American cichlid fish of the genus *Pterophyllum*, especially *P. scalare*, which is valued as an aquarium fish.

Angelica A genus of tall perennial herbs (about 70 species) distributed in the N hemisphere and New Zealand. They grow up to 2 m tall and have umbrella-like clusters of white or greenish flowers. The Eurasian species *A. archangelica* yields an oil used in liqueur and perfume making, and its stems are candied to make the confectionary angelica. *A. sylvestris* (wild angelica) is native to Europe and Asia and introduced in Canada. Family: *Umbelliferae*.

Angelico, Fra (Guido di Pietro; c. 1400–55) Italian painter of the early Renaissance, born in Vicchio (Tuscany). In the early 1420s he became a Dominican monk in Fiesole. His order transferred in 1436 to St Mark's Convent, Florence, where he painted several frescoes, including a famous *Annunciation*. From 1445 to about 1450 he painted fresco cycles in the Vatican but only the *Scenes from the Lives of SS Stephen and Lawrence* has survived. He was an exclusively religious painter, whose spiritual serenity is reflected both in his art and his "angelic" nature (hence his popular name).

angina pectoris Chest pain caused by a reduction in the supply of blood to the heart due to narrowing of the coronary blood vessels supplying the heart. It is usually associated with atherosclerosis, is brought on by exercise, and can herald a heart attack. Treatment includes rest and administration of glyceryl trinitrate and drugs to reduce blood pressure.

angiosperm Any flowering plant. Angiosperms comprise a vast group of diverse leafy green plants (about 250 000 species) in which the seeds are formed within an ovary, which becomes the fruit. They are thought to have evolved from the cone-bearing gymnosperms in the Jurassic period (about 180 million years ago), rapidly radiating and becoming the dominant plants in the mid-Cretaceous (about 100 million years ago). They include many trees and shrubs but most are herbaceous. The 300 families are grouped into two classes: the monocotyledons and dicotyledons.

anglerfish A marine fish, also called goosefish, belonging to the order *Lophiiformes*. Anglerfish are generally small and have flat bodies, large heads, and wide mouths. The first ray of the spiny dorsal fin is modified to form a "fishing line" ending with a fleshy flap of skin —the "bait," which is often luminous in deepsea species. Fish, invertebrates, and even seabirds are lured and snapped up by the huge mouth.

Angles A Germanic tribe originating from the Angeln district of Schleswig, which together with the Saxons and Jutes invaded and conquered most of England during the 5th century AD. England is named after them.

Anglesey (Welsh name: Ynys Môn; Latin name: Mona) A low-lying island off the NW coast of Wales, linked to the mainland by road and rail bridges over the Menai Strait. Now part of Gwynedd, it formed a separate county until local government reorganization in

1974. The chief agricultural activity is sheep rearing. Area: 705 sq km (272 sq mi). Population (1984 est): 68 500. Chief town: Beaumaris.

Anglican Communion The fellowship of episcopal Churches in communion with the see of Canterbury. Until 1786, when the consecration of bishops for foreign sees was legalized, it consisted of the Churches of England, Ireland, and Wales and the Episcopal Church of Scotland. In 1787 the Protestant Episcopal Church of the USA was founded and thereafter Anglican dioceses were formed in all parts of the British Empire and elsewhere. The member churches are fully autonomous, comprising about 350 dioceses; they meet for consultation at the Lambeth Conferences. Total membership is estimated at 65 million.

Anglo-Catholicism A movement within the Anglican Communion that stresses the continuity of the Church of England with Catholic Christianity. The main impetus of modern Anglo-Catholicism was provided by the Oxford Movement. Anglo-Catholics emphasize the historic episcopate, the sacramental life of the Church, and traditional Catholic practices with regard to the celebration of the Eucharist, vestments, etc.

ANGLO-SAXONS *Detail of a page from the Lindisfarne Gospels painted c. 700 AD.*

Anglo-Saxons The Germanic conquerors of Britain during the 5th century AD (*see* Angles; Saxons; Jutes). They first established a number of separate kingdoms, principally Northumbria, Mercia, and Wessex, but eventually England was unified under an Anglo-Saxon dynasty. Kings ruled with the assistance of a witan or council of wise men. Popular government and justice at the local level took the form of hundred courts. They were converted to Christianity as a result of the mission of St Augustine of Canterbury. The Anglo-Saxons developed a rich art and literature. Their language is also known as Old English. *See also* English.

Angola, People's Republic of A country in SW Africa, on the Atlantic Ocean. The Cabinda district lies to the N of the River Congo and is separated from the rest of the country by a section of Zaïre. The country consists of a narrow coastal plain and a broad dissected plateau that reaches heights of over 2000 m (6500 ft). The inhabitants are almost all Negroes (mainly of Bantu origin) with small numbers of mixed race. *Economy*: agriculture is run on a cooperative basis and the main crops are sugar cane and coffee. Angola is rich in mineral resources and diamonds have long been an important source of revenue. There is considerable oil production, especially offshore from Cabinda, and hydroelectricity is being harnessed. Main exports include oil, coffee, diamonds, and iron ore. *History*: discovered and settled by the Portuguese in the late 15th century, the area remained a Portuguese colony (apart from a brief period of Dutch occupation from 1641 to 1648) until 1951 when it became an overseas province of Portugal. During the 1950s and 1960s there was a rise in nationalism and in 1974 Portugal agreed to independence but, owing to lack of internal unity, civil war broke out. The various groups took over different parts of the country and in November, 1975, Portugal granted independence to the "Angolan people" rather than to any one group. The People's Republic of Angola was declared by the MPLA (Popular Movement for the Liberation of Angola), with its capital in Luanda, supported by the Soviet Union and Cuba. Eventually, with further help from Cuba, the MPLA gained control over other factions in 1976 but opposition from the National Front for the Liberation of Angola (FNLA) and the National Union for the Total Independence of Angola (UNITA) continued. South African and Cuban troops began to leave in 1988. President: Dr José dos Santos. Official language: Portuguese. Official currency: kwanza of 100 lwei. Area: 1 246 700 sq km (481 351 sq mi). Population (1988): 8 960 000. Capital and main port: Luanda.

Angora goat A breed of goat, originating in Turkey, whose long silky hair is regularly sheared and used commercially to make mohair. Mohair is now also obtained from several other goat breeds derived from the Angora.

Angora rabbit A breed of domesticated rabbit, originating in France in the 17th century, of which there are now both English and French varieties. The long wool, which is usually white but can be black or blue, is periodically shorn and spun for use in clothing manufacture (**Angora wool**).

angostura A bitters made from distilled herbs and plants. Angostura bitters originated in Ciudad Bolívar (formerly Angostura) in Venezuela as a tonic and febrifuge but its manufacture was transferred to Trinidad in 1975. A few drops are added to gin to make a pink gin.

Angry Young Men A group of British novelists and dramatists in the 1950s whose attitudes included dissatisfaction with postwar British society and disrespect for the so-called "Establishment". Many of them came from working-class or lower-middle-class backgrounds. The phrase "angry young man" was first applied to the dramatist John Osborne. Associated with this group were the novelists Kingsley Amis, John Wain (1925–), and John Braine (1922–86), the dramatist Arnold Wesker, and the critic Colin Wilson (1931–).

angstrom A unit of wavelength equal to 10^{-10} m (one tenth of a nanometre), named after A. J. Ångström.

Ångström, Anders Jonas (1814–74) Swedish physicist and astronomer. He was a founder of spectroscopy, his work on solar spectra leading to the discovery (1862) of hydrogen in the sun.

Anguilla 18 14N 63 05W A West Indian island in the E Caribbean Sea, in the Leeward Islands. Formerly part of the UK Associated State of St Kitts-Nevis-Anguilla, it became a separate British dependency in 1980. Its economy is based on stock raising, salt production, boatbuilding, and fishing. Area: 90 sq km (35 sq mi). Population (1985 est): 7000. *See also* St Kitts-Nevis.

angular velocity. *See* velocity.

Anhui (*or* Anhwei) A province in E China. The Yangtze River in the S and the Huai River in the N are linked by ancient waterways, which provide transport and irrigation. Main products are tea, rice, soya beans, silk, and steel. Area: 13 986 sq km (54 000 sq mi). Population (1985): 51 030 000. Capital: Hefei.

Anhwei. *See* Anhui.

animal A living organism belonging to the kingdom *Animalia*. Animals are typically mobile and feed on plants, other animals, or their remains. Their body cells lack the rigid cellulose wall of plant cells and they require specialized tissues, such as bone, for protection and support. Because of their activity, animals have specialized organs for sensing the nature of their environment; information from the sense organs is transmitted and coordinated by means of a nervous system. There are over one million species of animals, grouped into about 30 phyla. *See also* life; taxonomy.

animal behaviour. *See* ethology.

animal rights movement A campaign conducted by several organizations in protest against cruelty to and exploitation of animals. Targets of the movement, which developed in the 1970s, include zoos, animal research centres, foxhunts, and retailers of animal products. Some groups, such as the League Against Cruel Sports, favour parliamentary action, while others, such as the Animal Liberation Front, condone criminal acts, including damage to property.

anise An annual Mediterranean herb, *Pimpinella anisum*, growing to a height of up to 75 cm and having umbrella-like clusters of small yellow-white flowers. It is cultivated in subtropical areas for its liquorice-flavoured seeds (aniseed), which are used in cookery and yield an oil used to flavour drinks, etc. Family: *Umbelliferae*.

Ankara 39 55N 32 50E The capital of Turkey, in the W central region of the country. Conquered by Alexander the Great in the 4th century BC, it later came within the Roman and Byzantine Empires. It was attacked by Persians and Arabs, and in the 11th century it was defeated by the Turks. It became the capital of modern Turkey in 1923; it has three universities. Population (1985): 2 251 533.

ankylosaur A heavily armoured dinosaur of the late Cretaceous period, which ended 65 million years ago. Ankylosaurs were low and flat and their backs were covered with hard protective bony plates. *Euoplocephalus* (or *Ankylosaurus*) reached a length of 5 m, weighed 3 tonnes, and its plated tail ended in a large bony knob. Order: *Ornithischia*.

Annaba (former name: Bône) 36 57N 7 39E A large port in E Algeria, on the Mediterranean Sea. An early centre of Christianity, it held the bishopric of St Augustine (396–430 AD). In 1832 it was captured by the French. Mineral exports are important, particularly phosphates and iron ore. Industries include flour milling and iron and steel processing. Population (1980 est): 284 000.

Annapurna, Mount 28 34N 83 50E A massif in NW central Nepal, in the Himalayas. Its highest peak **Annapurna I**, at 8078 m (26 504 ft), was first climbed in 1950 by a French team.

Anne (1665–1714) Queen of England and Scotland (Great Britain from 1707) and Ireland (1702–14). Anne, the last Stuart monarch, was the daughter of the Roman Catholic James II but was herself brought up as a Protestant. Following the overthrow (1688) of James, she supported the accession of her Protestant brother-in-law, William III, whose heiress she became. She married (1683) Prince George of Denmark (1653–1708) and was pregnant 18 times by him; none of her five children born alive survived childhood. Anne therefore agreed to the Act of Settlement (1701), which provided for the Hanoverian succession after her death.

PRINCESS ANNE *Visiting a gipsy site in London as president of the Save the Children Fund.*

Anne (Elizabeth Alice Louise) (1950–) Princess of the United Kingdom, who became Princess Royal in 1987. The only daughter of Elizabeth II, she is seventh in line of succession to the throne. In 1973 she married Mark Phillips (1948–), having a son Peter (1977–) and a daughter Zara (1981–) before their separation in 1989. An accomplished horsewoman, she is president of the Save the Children Fund.

annealing. *See* heat treatment.

annelid worm An invertebrate animal belonging to a phylum (*Annelida*) of about 9000 species, widely distributed in salt water, fresh water, and on land. The body is characteristically a muscular cylinder divided into many fluid-filled segments. Annelids are divided into three classes: the Polychaeta, or bristleworms (*see* ragworm; lugworm; fanworm); the Oligochaeta (*see* earthworm; tubifex), and the Hirudinea (*see* leech).

Anne of Bohemia (1366–94) The first wife (from 1382) of Richard II of England and daughter of Emperor Charles IV. Her household extravagance was a cause of dissension between Richard and parliament.

Anne of Cleves (1515–57) The fourth wife of Henry VIII of England. The marriage (January, 1540) was ar-

ranged to effect an alliance with German Protestant rulers but Henry found Anne unattractive and quickly divorced her (July, 1540).

Anne of Denmark (1574–1619) The wife (from 1589) of James I of England and VI of Scotland. She spent heavily on building and court entertainments (appearing herself in Ben Jonson's masques) and was suspected of Roman Catholic sympathies.

Annigoni, Pietro (1910–88) Italian painter. One of the most famous 20th-century artists to use the techniques of the Old Masters, Annigoni worked chiefly in tempera and fresco. He is best known for his portraits of President Kennedy (1961) and Queen Elizabeth II (1955 and 1970). In later years he devoted himself to a fresco cycle of the life of Christ in the Church of S Michele Arcangelo, in Ponte Buggianese, near Florence.

annihilation The conversion of a particle and its antiparticle into electromagnetic radiation (annihilation radiation) as a result of a collision. The energy of the radiation is equivalent to the combined mass of the two particles. *See also* antimatter.

annual rings (*or* growth rings) A pattern of rings visible in a cross section of a tree trunk, produced by different rates of wood growth: the wood produced in spring consists of large cells corresponding to vigorous growth; autumn wood has small cells as growth slows down, and in winter growth ceases. The number of rings gives an estimate of the age of the tree. *See also* dendrochronology.

annuals Plants that complete their life cycle—from germination, flowering, and seed production to death—within one year. Many annuals are used for bedding plants (e.g. marigolds) and flower extensively in the summer months. *Compare* perennials.

annuity A form of pension in which an insurance company makes a series of periodic payments to a person (annuitant) or his or her dependents over a number of years (term), in return for either a lump sum or regular instalments. An immediate annuity begins at once and a deferred annuity after a fixed period. An annuity certain is for a specific number of years. A life annuity is paid from a certain age until death. A perpetuity continues indefinitely.

annulment The process establishing that a marriage is not legally valid, as opposed to divorce, which ends a valid marriage. An invalid marriage is considered void, never to have existed. A marriage is void if, for example, the husband or wife is insane, too young, or already married. When the husband or wife is unable or unwilling to consummate the marriage, it may be declared void if either partner wishes it.

Annunciation In the Bible, the announcement by the angel Gabriel to the Virgin Mary of her conception of Christ (Luke 1.26–38). The feast, in full called the Annunciation of the Blessed Virgin Mary, or Lady Day, is celebrated on 25 March.

anode The positive electrode of an electrolytic cell, valve, etc. It is the electrode by which the electrons leave the system. *Compare* cathode.

anodizing A process in which a light metal or alloy, usually aluminium, is covered with a protective layer by oxidation in an electrolytic cell. Usually the cell contains chromic acid; the metal treated is the anode of the cell. A porous layer of oxide is formed, which can be dyed to give a coloured finish.

Anopheles A widespread genus of mosquitoes (about 350 species), the females of which are important as vectors of the malarial parasite *Plasmodium*. The best-known malaria carrier is *A. maculipennis*. Some species transmit filariasis and encephalitis. Unlike other mosquitoes the larvae lack a siphon and lie flat on the surface of the water.

anorexia nervosa A psychological illness in which the patient, usually an adolescent girl, refuses food over a long period. It often starts with dieting to lose weight, which becomes obsessional: the patient becomes emaciated and may—without treatment—starve to death. The psychological causes are complex, often involving disturbances in family relationships. Hospitalization may be required for the treatment, which involves intensive nursing, sedation, and psychotherapy.

Anouilh, Jean (1910–87) French dramatist. His first play, *The Ermine*, was performed in 1932. He achieved his first success in 1937 with *Traveller without Luggage*. His plays include reworkings of Greek myths (*Antigone*, 1944), social comedies (*Ring Round the Moon*, 1950), and historical dramas (*Becket*, 1959).

Anschluss (German: union; 1938) The union of Austria with Germany. Following the forced resignation of the Austrian chancellor Kurt von Schuschnigg (1897–1977), Nazi forces entered Austria and Schuschnigg was imprisoned. *Anschluss* was declared and ratified by a plebiscite.

Anselm of Canterbury, St (c. 1033–1109) Italian theologian and philosopher, Archbishop of Canterbury, and Doctor of the Church. Appointed to the see of Canterbury in 1093, Anselm defended church rights against William II Rufus until he went into exile to Rome in 1097. Recalled by Henry I in 1100, he eventually reached an uneasy compromise with him. He is the leading early scholastic philosopher and is perhaps best known for his formulation of the ontological argument for the existence of God, which states that if God is "that than which nothing greater can be conceived," then the existence of God is necessary, for it is possible to conceive of a greater entity than a nonexistent God. Feast day: 21 April. Emblem: a ship.

ant An insect belonging to the family *Formicidae* (over 10 000 species). Ants occur in almost all terrestrial habitats, are 0.05–25 cm long, and show a high degree of social organization. A colony consists of wingless sterile female workers and a smaller number of fertile males and females that are generally the progeny of a single queen. The young males and females fly from the nest to mate, after which the males die and the young queens found new colonies. Ant societies range from simple groups of a few individuals to large complex nests comprising millions of ants and sometimes involving a second species taken as slaves to work in the colony. Some ants have stings; others secrete burning acids (such as formic acid) as a defence. Order: *Hymenoptera*.

Antakya. *See* Antioch.

Antananarivo (former name: Tananarive) 18 52S 47 30E The capital of Madagascar. It was occupied by the French in 1895. A cultural centre, it has a university (1961) and two cathedrals. Industries include tobacco and leather goods. Population (1982 est): 600 000.

Antarctica The most southerly continent, surrounding the South Pole. An almost circular ice-covered plateau, it is indented by the Weddell and Ross Seas and

ANTARCTICA *Under the Antarctic Treaty (1959) all political claims were halted and freedom of scientific research in the continent was ensured.*

contains about 90% of the world's ice. The continent's climate is the severest in the world and although it lacks vegetation it has abundant wildlife including whales, seals, and penguins. Scientific stations were established during the International Geophysical Year (1957–58). Some nations (*see* Australian Antarctic Territory; British Antarctic Territory; Norwegian Antarctic Territory; Ross Dependency) have political claims to territory in Antarctica. Argentina and Chile have also laid claims, as yet unrecognized, to portions of British Antarctic Territory (*see also* Antarctic Treaty). *History*: in his voyage of 1772–75 Capt James Cook circumnavigated the continent. Many explorations took place during the 19th century culminating in the race for the South Pole. This was reached first by Roald Amundsen of the Norwegian Antarctic Expedition on 14 December, 1911, and a month later by Scott of the British Expedition, which perished on the return journey. Area: about 14 200 000 sq km (5 500 000 sq mi).

Antarctic Ocean The sections of the S Atlantic, Pacific, and Indian Oceans around Antarctica. Except in the height of summer (late Feb to early March), it is covered by drifting pack ice.

Antarctic Treaty (1959) An agreement, signed by Argentina, Australia, Belgium, Chile, France, Japan, New Zealand, Norway, South Africa, the Soviet Union, the UK, and the USA, to maintain the Antarctic as a demilitarized zone for 30 years.

ant bear. *See* aardvark.

anteater A long-tailed animal belonging to a family (*Myrmecophagidae*; 3 species) occurring in tropical South America. It is toothless and has a narrow snout with a long sticky tongue used to pick up ants and termites after tearing open their nests with its powerful claws. The giant anteater (*Myrmecophaga tridactyla*) reaches 1.8 m in length and has grey and black fur and a bushy tail. The other species are smaller arboreal animals with prehensile tails (*see* tamandua). Order: *Edentata*. The name anteater is given to several other unrelated animals that feed on ants or termites: the pangolins (scaly anteaters), echidnas (spiny anteaters), and aardvark.

Antelami, Benedetto (active 1177–1233) Italian sculptor. He developed a style that marked the transition between the romanesque and the gothic. His best-known works are the reliefs on the doors of the baptistry at Parma, of which he was probably also the architect.

antelope A fast-running hoofed mammal belonging to the family *Bovidae* and occurring chiefly in Africa but occasionally in Asia. The shoulder height varies from 25 cm in the royal antelope to 180 cm in the eland. All male antelopes and some females have horns. *See also* dik-dik; duiker; gazelle; gnu; kudu; waterbuck.

antenna (zoology) The sensory feeler of insects, crustaceans, and many other arthropods, one or two pairs of which are attached to the head. They are usually jointed threadlike structures containing receptors of sound, smell, touch, and temperature.

anther. *See* stamen.

anthracite. *See* coal.

anthrax A contagious disease of many animals, including farm livestock, that can be transmitted to man. Caused by the bacterium *Bacillus anthracis*, it is usually contracted by eating contaminated food. Onset is often sudden with a rise in temperature, staggering, respiratory distress, convulsions, and death. In horses and pigs a subacute form may occur, with progressive swelling of the throat and neck resulting in laboured breathing and choking. In many countries the authorities must be notified of any outbreaks. Treatment is with antibiotics and prevention is by vaccination of herds. Man may develop localized swellings after handling infected carcasses or acquire a pneumonia from inhaling the bacterial spores (woolsorters' disease).

anthropoid ape A tailless primate belonging to the family *Pongidae*, includes the gibbons, chimpanzees, orang-utans, and gorillas. *See* ape.

anthropology The scientific study of man in his physical and social aspects. It includes archaeology, linguistics, cultural or social anthropology, and physical anthropology. Physical anthropology is concerned with the origins and evolution of man through the examination of his fossil remains, and the study and classification of the races (*see also* anthropometry). Cultural anthropology is concerned with the evolution of human society and culture, including language, and with the systematic comparison of social, linguistic, technical, and behavioural diversity.

anthropometry The science concerned with the measurement of the human body, particularly with respect to the variation that exists between different populations and races. Anthropometry ranges from the measurement of structural characteristics, such as height, cranial capacity, etc., to the analysis of chemical constituents of the body, such as blood groups. By comparing fossil and present-day measurements anthropometry has also helped to reveal the sequence of events that has occurred during the evolution of man (*see* anthropology).

antiballistic missiles High-speed nuclear weapons used to attack hostile ballistic missiles. Operated by ground-based radar and computers, they rely for their final attack on their own guidance systems, destroying the target by radiation from their warheads. Short-range versions with low-yield warheads (e.g. US *Sprint*) are designed to seek and destroy targets within the earth's atmosphere; long-range missiles with high-yield warheads operate in space (e.g. US *Spartan*, Soviet *Galosh*).

ANTHROPOID APE *A gorilla.*

antibiotics Drugs derived from microorganisms or synthetically to treat infections caused by bacteria or fungi. Bacteriocidal antibiotics, such as penicillin, kill bacteria, whereas bacteriostatic antibiotics, such as tetracycline and chloramphenicol, simply halt their growth. Examples of antifungal antibiotics are nystatin and griseofulvin. Possible adverse effects of antibiotic treatment include allergic reactions and the development of resistant strains of bacteria, which may set up a secondary infection. Nevertheless, the widespread use of antibiotics since World War II has enabled bacterial and fungal diseases to be controlled.

antibody A protein produced by certain white blood cells (lymphocytes) that reacts specifically with and neutralizes a foreign protein (e.g. a bacterium), which is known as the **antigen**. Antibody production is stimulated by contact with the antigen: subsequent exposure to the antigen produces a greater antibody response, which provides the basis of immunity. Antibodies contribute to the body's resistance to infection and are responsible for the rejection of foreign tissue or organ transplants.

anticline An arch-shaped fold or upfold in folded rock strata, the oldest rocks occurring at the core. In areas of complex folding an upfold may have its youngest rocks at the core, the resulting structure being termed an antiform. *Compare* syncline.

anticoagulants Drugs, such as heparin and warfarin, that interfere with blood clotting. They are used when there has been, or there is a risk of, clots forming in the blood vessels, as after thrombosis of the leg veins.

anticyclone (*or* high) An area of atmospheric pressure higher than the surrounding air with one or more isobars of approximately circular form around its centre. Winds, generally light, circulate around the high pressure centre in a clockwise direction in the N hemisphere and anticlockwise in the S hemisphere. Calm settled weather is usually synonymous with anticyclones in temperate latitudes.

antidepressants A class of drugs used to relieve depression. The most widely used are the tricyclic antidepressants, which include amitriptyline and imipramine, and the tetracyclic antidepressants. The MAO inhibitors prevent the action of the enzyme monoamine oxidase in breaking down adrenaline and related compounds that affect mood. These antidepressants may have serious side effects and are therefore restricted to the treatment of severe psychological disorders.

BATTLE OF ANTIETAM *One of the earliest war photographs, taken by Mathew Brady (1823–96).*

Antietam, Battle of (17 September, 1862) A decisive engagement in the US Civil War, which prevented the Confederate capture of Washington, DC. In the last of a series of battles, the advance of the Confederate general Robert E. Lee, was checked at Antietam by the Federal general George B. McClellan (1826–85). The South lost about 10 000 men but McClellan allowed Lee to withdraw into Virginia.

antigen. *See* antibody.

Antigone In Greek mythology, the daughter of Oedipus and Jocasta, whose story forms the basis of Sophocles' tragedy *Antigone*. When her father was banished from Thebes she accompanied him into exile in Colonus. Her brothers Eteocles and Polyneices had agreed to reign alternately in Thebes, but Eteocles' refusal to yield the crown led to their killing each other. Despite the Theban senate's decree prohibiting the burial of Polyneices, Antigone performed the funeral rites for her brother. She was consequently ordered to be buried alive by Creon, ruler of Thebes, and hanged herself.

Antigua and Barbuda A West Indian country in the E Caribbean Sea, comprising the islands of Antigua,

Barbuda, and Redonda. Tourism is the chief source of revenue; sugar and cotton production are also important. *History*: Antigua was discovered by Columbus (1493) and colonized by British settlers in 1632. It formed an associated state within the British Commonwealth from 1967 until gaining independence in 1981. It is a member of CARICOM. Prime minister: Vere C. Bird. Area: 440 sq km (170 sq mi). Population (1986 est): 81 500. Capital: St John's.

antihistamines Drugs that interfere with the action of histamine, a chemical produced by the body that is responsible for the symptoms of an allergic reaction. Antihistamines are therefore used to treat hay fever, nettle rash, and other allergies. Some antihistamines (e.g. dramamine) are used to prevent travel sickness and others are effective sedatives (drowsiness is a common side effect of many antihistamines).

Antilles The islands of the West Indies, excluding the Bahamas. The group is divided into the Greater Antilles and the Lesser Antilles.

antimatter Hypothetical matter in which the constituent atoms consist of antiparticles. For every elementary particle (*see* particle physics) there exists an antiparticle that is identical except for certain of its properties, such as electric charge and isospin number, which are of equal magnitude but opposite in sign. An atom of antimatter would contain a nucleus of antiprotons and antineutrons surrounded by positrons (antielectrons). *See also* annihilation.

antimony (Sb) A metallic element, probably known in antiquity. It occurs in nature as the element and more commonly in the sulphide stibnite (Sb_2S_3). The element exists in two forms: the normal metallic form, which is brittle bluish-white and flaky, and an amorphous grey form. It forms the oxide (Sb_2O_3) by burning in air and the volatile hydride, stibine (SbH_3), which like many antimony compounds is toxic. Pure antimony is used in making semiconductors; other uses include addition to lead to increase its hardness in battery plates and as oxides or sulphides in paints, glasses, and ceramics. At no 51; at wt 121.75; mp 630.7°C; bp 1750°C.

Antioch (modern Turkish name: Antakya) 36 12N 36 10E A town in central S Turkey, near the coast and the Syrian border. Founded in 301 BC, it had a large early Christian community, and there are notable Roman mosaics in the Archaeological Museum. Population (1980): 94 942.

antiparticle. *See* antimatter.

antipope Those raised to the papacy in opposition to a lawfully elected pope. Hippolitus, the first of some 40 antipopes, was created in the early 3rd century. During the later Roman Empire and the middle ages most antipopes represented rival factions supporting different political or doctrinal claims. In the 11th and 12th centuries some 14 antipopes were chosen by the Holy Roman Emperors, who resented the Church's growing independence from lay control. From 1378, following the Great Schism, the popes remaining in Avignon under French control were styled antipopes. The Council of Pisa (1409) elected a new pope to end the Schism, but he too was regarded as an antipope until unity was restored at the Council of Constance (1515). There have been no antipopes since the mid-15th century.

Antirrhinum A genus of chiefly Mediterranean and W North American herbaceous plants (about 40 species). The most widely cultivated species is the ornamental snapdragon (*A. majus*), 30–80 cm high with brightly coloured two-lipped tubular flowers adapted to pollination by large bees. Family: *Scrophulariaceae*.

antitoxin An antibody produced against a toxin. Antitoxins can be isolated from inoculated healthy animals and used to treat or prevent specific infections; for example, an antitoxin against tetanus is obtained from the plasma of animals inoculated against tetanus.

antitrust acts US legislation to control monopolies and preserve a competitive market. The Sherman Antitrust Act (1890), the first of several measures, prohibited contracts "in restraint of trade." Interpreted narrowly at first, these laws were strengthened by successive legislation (including the Clayton Act 1914 and the Antimerger Act 1950) prohibiting or restricting interlocking directorships, price fixing, and takeovers. In the UK, the less stringent Fair Trading Act (1973) performs similar functions.

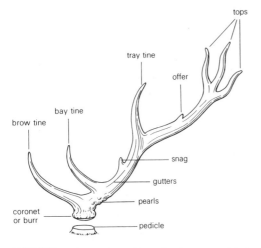

ANTLERS *The number of branches increases with the age of the stag. This antler has 6 branches; a stag with a head of 12 branches is called a royal.*

antlers The paired bony structures growing from the heads of deer, generally confined to males. In temperate regions the antlers begin to grow in early summer: they are at first covered with velvety skin, which is later shed. Used for fighting and display, the antlers are shed each year at the end of the mating season. Deer grow their first set of antlers, which are usually straight spikes, at the age of 1–2 years. The number of points is increased in successive years.

antlion An insect belonging to a family (*Myrmeleontidae*) in which the adults resemble dragonflies and live only long enough to mate and lay eggs. The predatory larva lives 1–3 years, generally at the bottom of a conical pit in loose sand: any insect that falls into the pit is snapped up with its large jaws, which protrude from the sand. Order: *Neuroptera*.

Antonescu, Ion (1882–1946) Romanian general and politician. A pro-Nazi, he became prime minister (1940), replacing Carol II's government with a totalitarian regime. In 1941 he commanded the army in Bessarabia. He was executed for war crimes.

Antonine Wall A Roman frontier defence work 58.5 km (36.5 mi) long, linking the Firths of Forth and Clyde in S Scotland and still surviving in places. It was built about 142 AD by Lollius Urbicus, governor of Britain, for the emperor Antoninus Pius, and abandoned in 196 AD. A military road linked 29 small forts along a turf wall 3 m (10 ft) high and 4.3 m (14 ft) wide, behind a substantial ditch. *See also* Hadrian's Wall.

Antoninus Pius (86–161 AD) Roman emperor (138–61). Antoninus was admitted by Emperor Hadrian to his advisory council and adopted as his successor in 138. His reign was generally prosperous; minor campaigns were fought abroad and noted legal reforms were introduced; the Antonine Wall was built during his reign. He was deified after his death.

Antonioni, Michelangelo (1912–) Italian film maker. Born into a bourgeois provincial family, in 1939 he moved to Rome to work for the magazine *Cinema*. His first films were *Gente del Po* (1943–47) and *Cronaca di un amore* (1950). Later films include *L'avventura* (1959), *La notte* (1961), *Blow-Up* (1966), *Zabriskie Point* (1970), and *The Passenger* (1975).

Antwerp (Flemish name: Antwerpen; French name: Anvers) 51 13N 4 25E A city in Belgium, on the River Scheldt. Antwerp is one of the largest seaports in the world and has important shipbuilding and ship-repairing industries. Other industries include oil refining, diamond cutting, textiles, and electronics. It possesses many fine buildings, including the 14th-century gothic cathedral and the 16th-century Butchers' Hall. There is a large Flemish-speaking population. *History*: the leading commercial centre of western Europe in the 16th century, its decline began with religious strife and its sacking by Spaniards (1576); this was further hastened by the closure of the River Scheldt (1648). The revival of its economy began when Belgium purchased the shipping rights of the river from the Netherlands. Population (1989 est): 474 000.

Anura An order of amphibians (over 2000 species) comprising the frogs and toads. Anurans are specialized for jumping, having a short backbone, no tail, and large hind legs. The eggs hatch into tadpoles, which undergo metamorphosis. This order is also called the *Salientia*.

anus. *See* intestine.

ANZAC The Australian and New Zealand Army Corps, which served in World War I in Europe and the Middle East. On ANZAC Day, 25 April (the day of the ANZAC landing in Gallipoli in 1915), the dead of both World Wars are remembered.

aorta. *See* artery; heart.

aoudad A tawny-coloured sheep, *Ammotragus lervia*, also called Barbary sheep, that is the only wild sheep in Africa. Aoudads live in dry rocky northern regions and obtain water mainly from vegetation and dew. They stand 102 cm at the shoulder and have outward-curving horns and long hair hanging from the neck and chest.

Aouita, Saïd (1960–) Moroccan middle-distance runner. In 1987 he became the holder of world records in the 2000 m, 5000 m, and 1500 m events.

Apache A North American Indian people with six major divisions: the Jicarillos, Mescaleros, Chiricahuas, and Western Apache of the S Plains and SW region of the USA; and the Lipan and Kiowa-Apache living further to the east. Their language is of Athabascan type. They were feared raiders, who frequently attacked the villages of Pueblo Indians and Spanish settlements. In addition to hunting, some groups practised farming. Normally tribal unity was slight but in the late 19th century, under the leadership of chiefs, such as Geronimo and Victorio, they would form groups to attack the Americans. There are today about 10 000 Apaches on reservations.

APACHE   *Geronimo (1829-1909), the Apache chief, photographed in 1895.*

apartheid (Afrikaans: apartness)   The policy of separate development of the White and non-White populations in South Africa. Apartheid, which was introduced by the Afrikaner National Party in 1948, aims to divide South Africa into separate regions for Whites and Blacks. The White minority that governs South Africa has been criticized for this policy and in 1961 South Africa was forced to withdraw from the British Commonwealth. In 1985 non-Whites won limited constitutional rights and interracial marriage was allowed. Increased internal unrest, combined with sporting and financial pressure from outside, led to further concessions.

apatite   The commonest phosphorous mineral, of composition $Ca_5(PO_4)_3(OH,F,Cl)$. It is found as an accessory mineral in many igneous rocks and is used in the production of fertilizers. The enamel of teeth is composed almost entirely of apatite (*see also* fluoridation) and the chief inorganic constituent of bone is hydroxy-apatite, $Ca_{10}(PO_4)_6(OH)_2$.

Apatosaurus   A huge herbivorous dinosaur, formerly called *Brontosaurus*, of the late Jurassic period, which ended about 135 million years ago. Up to 21 m long and weighing up to 30 tonnes, it had massive pillar-like legs, a long neck and tail, and spent most of its time in swamps, coming ashore to lay eggs. With its nostrils placed high on its head, it was able to stand almost fully submerged. Order: *Saurischia*.

ape   A highly intelligent tailless primate belonging to the family *Pongidae* (11 species), found in central Africa and S Asia. There are two subfamilies: the arboreal *Hylobatinae* (*see* gibbon; siamang) and the ground-dwelling *Ponginae* (*see* chimpanzee; orang-utan; gorilla), also called great apes. Forest apes are often solitary but ground-dwelling apes live in complex societies and all have highly developed means of communication. Some tailless primates of other families are also called apes.

Apennines (Italian name: Appennini)   A mountain range in Italy. It extends about 1050 km (652 mi) down the Italian peninsula from the Maritime Alps in the NW to the Strait of Messina in the S. The range is not generally very high but it affords few easy crossing points; the highest peak is Monte Corno at 2914 m (9560 ft). The Apennines are volcanic in the S (*see* Vesuvius).

aphelion   The point in the orbit of a body around the sun at which the body is furthest from the sun. The earth is at aphelion on 3 July. *Compare* perihelion.

aphid   An insect, also called a plant louse, belonging to a family (*Aphidae*) of important plant pests. Small, soft, and often wingless, aphids have long thin antennae and weak legs and are usually green (greenfly), red, or brown. There are two thin tubes projecting from the abdomen from which honeydew is secreted. Aphids feed on plant sap, piercing plant tissues with sharp beaklike mouthparts, causing leaf curl, retardation of growth, and often forming galls. Order: *Hemiptera*.

aphrodisiac   A drug that increases sexual desire or sexual performance. No true aphrodiasic has yet been discovered and most preparations act (if at all) by suggestion. Some drugs (such as alcohol and morphine) produce a general euphoria and reduce inhibitions but usually have an adverse effect on sexual performance. Local irritants, such as cantharides (Spanish fly), can prolong an erection at the cost of considerable discomfort.

Aphrodite   In Greek mythology, the goddess of love, called Venus by the Romans. According to Homer she was the daughter of Dione and Zeus; Hesiod says that she was born from the foam after Uranus had been castrated and his genitals thrown into the sea. She was the wife of Hephaestus but had an affair with Ares. Paris' choice of her as the most beautiful of the three goddesses at the wedding feast of Peleus and Thetis (the others were Hera and Athena) caused the Trojan War. Revered throughout Greece as the personification of spiritual love, she also embodied sensual lust.

apocalypse (Greek: revelation)   In the New Testament, the Revelation of St John the Divine. The term is also used of various noncanonical writings, such as the *Book of Enoch*, and of parts of the Old Testament books of *Isaiah*, *Ezekiel*, and *Daniel*. These are all examples of "apocalyptic literature." Full of symbolism and imagery, they describe visions of a great new era that will suddenly supersede the present age of suffering.

Apocrypha (Greek: hidden things)   Twelve books taken over by the early Christian Church from the Greek version of the Old Testament but not forming part of the Hebrew Bible. They originated in the Hellenistic Judaism of Alexandria but were not accepted as canonical by orthodox Jews. In the Vulgate, most of them are printed with the Old Testament but they are omitted or printed as a separate section in Protestant versions of the Bible. They are: I Esdras, Tobit, Judith, the Rest of Esther, the Wisdom of Solomon, Ecclesiasticus, Baruch with the Epistle of Jeremy, the Song of the Three Holy Children, the History of Susanna, Bel and the Dragon, the Prayer of Manasses, and I and II Maccabees.

apogee   The point in the orbit of the moon or of an artificial satellite around the earth at which the body is furthest from the earth. *Compare* perigee.

Apollo   A Greek god of many aspects, symbol of light, of reason, and of male beauty. He is also associated with medicine, prophecy, music and poetry, the care of animals and crops, morality, and the maintenance of society. He and his sister Artemis were the children of Zeus by Leto. He established his oracle at Delphi after killing Python, its dragon guardian.

APOLLO MOON PROGRAMME *"Buzz" Aldrin on the moon in July 1969.*

Apollo moon programme The US programme to land men on the moon by 1970, announced by President Kennedy in 1961. The programme was directed by NASA. A Saturn V rocket launched the Apollo spacecraft towards the moon and, once the craft was in lunar orbit, the lunar module descended to the moon's surface carrying two astronauts. The third astronaut remained in the orbiting craft. At the end of the surface mission the lunar module's descent stage was left on the moon while its ascent stage was shot into lunar orbit and docked with the orbiting craft. Following the transfer of the two astronauts, the ascent stage was jettisoned and the spacecraft returned to earth. The astronauts travelled to and from the moon in the command module, the rocket engines for in-flight manoeuvres, fuel cells, etc., being carried in the separate service module, which was jettisoned prior to re-entering the earth's atmosphere.

The first six Apollo missions were unmanned test flights, the next four being manned. Apollo 11 made the first manned lunar landing in July, 1969. Of the six ensuing missions, all, except Apollo 13, were highly successful.

Apostles In the New Testament, the 12 men chosen by Jesus as his disciples who, after his death, were to spread his teaching throughout the Roman world. Originally they were: Andrew, Bartholomew (*or* Nathaniel), James son of Alphaeus, James son of Zebedee, John, Jude (*or* Thaddeus), Judas Iscariot, Matthew (*or* Levi), Philip, Simon Peter, Simon the Zealot, and Thomas. Af-

ter his suicide Judas Iscariot was replaced by Matthias. St Paul is also included among the Apostles because of his claim to having seen Jesus after the resurrection.

Apostles' Creed A Christian profession of faith in three sections concerning God the Father, Jesus Christ, and the Holy Spirit. Widely used in the Western Churches, it is of uncertain date but its present title first occurs in a letter of St Ambrose of about 390 AD.

apostolic succession A Christian doctrine held by the Roman Catholic and Orthodox Churches and by some Anglicans. Its upholders claim that the Apostles appointed the first bishops and that there is thus a continuous line of succession from the Apostles to the present ministries of these Churches along which the power and authority given by Christ to the former have passed to the latter.

Appalachian Mountains A mountain range in the USA. It extends NE–SW from the Mohawk River to Alabama, separating the Mississippi-Missouri lowlands from the Atlantic coastal plain. It consists of a series of mountain ranges and plateaus, including the Allegheny Mountains, the Catskill Mountains, and the White Mountains of New Hampshire. Its highest point is Mount Mitchell, at 2038 m (6684 ft). Coalmining is important and iron ore is also extracted. It also contains the **Appalachian Trail**, the longest continuous footpath in the world.

apparent magnitude. *See* magnitude.

appeal In law, the review of a court decision by a higher court, usually at the request of one of the parties to the case. The decisions of some administrative or professional bodies may also be appealed against in the courts. Appeals in common law systems are usually based on alleged errors of law in the original trial, but may sometimes also be based on errors of fact. *See also* courts of law.

appendicitis Inflammation of the appendix, which is most common in childhood and adolescence. Surgical removal of an infected appendix is often required to prevent its rupture and subsequent peritonitis.

appendix (*or* vermiform appendix) A thin blind-ended tube, 7–10 cm long, that opens from the end of the large intestine. It has no known function in man and is prone to infection (*see* appendicitis). In herbivorous animals (e.g. rabbits and cows) the appendix is large and functions in the digestion of vegetable matter.

Appian Way The road, built about 312 BC by the statesman Appius Claudius, between Rome and Capua. It was the first in the strategic network of Roman roads. A short stretch is still visible near Rome.

apple A deciduous tree or shrub of the genus *Malus* (about 35 species), native to N temperate regions and widely cultivated for their rounded fleshy fruits (pomes). Several species have been cultivated, especially *M. pumila* of W Asia, with the development of numerous varieties of dessert, cooking, and cider apples. Shoots of the required variety are grafted onto selected rootstocks. Apples are also used for soft drinks and as a source of pectin. Family: *Rosaceae*. *See also* crab apple.

Appleton layer. *See* ionosphere.

apricot A tree, *Prunus armenica*, native to China and widely grown in warm temperate countries, especially Spain, for its fruits. It is 6–9 m tall and has white five-petalled flowers and toothed heart-shaped leaves. The hairy-skinned orange-yellow fruits have sweet flesh and smooth stones. Family: *Rosaceae*.

Apulia (*or* Puglia) A region in SE Italy, on the Adriatic Sea. It consists of lowlands in the N and S (the "heel" of Italy) and a hilly central area. Wheat, tobacco, vegetables, olives, figs, vines, and almonds are the main products. Manufacturing is being developed, particularly at Taranto. Area: 19 347 sq km (7470 sq mi). Population (1982 est): 3 908 484. Capital: Bari.

Aqaba 29 32N 35 00E A port in Jordan, on the **Gulf of Aqaba**, a narrow inlet at the NE end of the Red Sea. Aqaba was the Roman stronghold of Aelana. Being Jordan's only port, it has been considerably expanded to export phosphates. Population (1983 est): 40 000.

aquamarine A pale blue or green variety of beryl. Many fine specimens of this gemstone come from Brazil, Madagascar, and California.

AQUEDUCT *The* Pont du Gard *built by the Romans in 19 BC across the River Gard in Provence (France).*

aqueduct A narrow bridge, channel, or conduit designed to enable water to flow at a steady rate over an irregular natural terrain, such as a valley. Aqueducts were built by the Greeks, but the technique was developed by the Romans. Impressive Roman examples still survive at Nîmes, Segovia, and Rome.

Aquilegia A genus of perennial herbaceous plants (1000 species) of temperate regions, commonly known as columbines. Their showy flowers have petals with long honey-secreting spurs. A favorite garden flower, aquilegias have been cultivated since the 16th century. Many modern garden hybrids are derived from the European columbine (*A. vulgaris*), 40–100 cm high with purple to white flowers. Family: *Ranunculaceae*.

Aquinas, St Thomas (c. 1225–74) Italian Dominican theologian, scholastic philosopher, and Doctor of the Church, known as *Doctor Angelicus*. Born near Naples, the son of Count Landulf of Aquino, he was educated at the Benedictine school at Monte Cassino and at the University of Naples. Joining the Dominican Order in 1244 in spite of parental opposition, he became a pupil of Albertus Magnus in Paris (1245) and followed him to Cologne in 1248. He was a theological adviser to the papal Curia between 1259 and 1269 and then taught at Paris until 1272, when he was appointed a professor at Naples. He was canonized in 1323. His two most influential works are the *Summa contra gentiles* (1259–64), written for the use of missionaries, and the uncompleted *Summa theologica* (1266–73), the first systematic work on Latin theology. Feast day: 7 March.

Aquino, Cory (Corazón Aquino; 1933–) Philippine stateswoman; president (1986–). She became a popular political leader after the assassination of her husband **Benigno S. Aquino** (1933–83) and head of state when the corrupt Marcos regime came to an end.

Aquitaine (Latin name: Aquitania) A planning region in SW France, bordering on the Bay of Biscay. Formerly an administrative region in Roman Gaul, it extended from the Pyrenees N to the River Loire. It became an independent duchy under the Merovingians (7th century). The marriages of Eleanor of Aquitaine to Louis VII of France and then to Henry II of England resulted in rival French-English claims to the territory (*see* Hundred Years' War). Area: 41 408 sq km (15 984 sq mi). Population (1986 est): 2 718 200.

Arab horse An ancient breed of horse originally bred by the Bedouins in Arabia. It is usually grey, chestnut, or bay with a long silky mane and tail, a wedge-shaped head, and an arched neck. The Arab is prized as a riding horse because of its speed, hardiness, and docile temperament. Height: 1.42–1.52 m (14–15 hands).

Arabia A peninsula in the Middle East, forming the SW tip of Asia and bordered by the Red Sea, the Gulf of Aden, the Gulf of Oman, and the Persian Gulf. It consists of Saudi Arabia, North and South Yemen, Oman, the United Arab Emirates, Qatar, Bahrain, and Kuwait. *History*: as remains of irrigation systems show, S Arabia was the site of technologically advanced ancient civilizations. It was conquered briefly by the Persians in 575 AD and later unified from Mecca by Islam in the 7th century, when the previously warring Arab tribes turned their attention to the conquest of N Africa, SW Asia, and S Europe. From the 16th century until World War I the Ottoman Turks held nominal control over much of the peninsula, challenged chiefly by the Wahhabiyah. From the mid-19th century until the late 1960s the UK was the chief foreign presence.

Arabian Desert 1. A desert chiefly in Saudi Arabia. Area: about 2 300 000 sq km (887 844 sq mi). 2. A desert in E Egypt between the River Nile and the Red Sea.

Arabian Sea A section of the NW Indian Ocean between Arabia and India. Connected to the Mediterranean Sea by the Red Sea and the Suez Canal, it forms a major shipping route.

Arabic A member of the Semitic group of languages. It is written from right to left. Arabic is the mother-tongue of some 110 million people inhabiting SW Asia (the Middle East) and the countries of N Africa. Arabic can be roughly classified into three parts: (a) Classical Arabic, the language of the Koran and the great Arab writers and poets; (b) Modern Literary, or Standard, Arabic, the language of the press and broadcasting; and (c) the colloquial dialects (vernaculars), which differ in a greater or lesser degree from country to country.

Arabic numerals The number symbols 0, 1, 2, 3, 4, 5, 6, 7, 8, 9. They are believed to have originated in India and were introduced into Europe by the Arabs in about the 10th century AD. *Compare* Roman numerals.

Arab-Israeli Wars. *See* Israel, State of.

Arab League An organization formed to promote Arab unity and cooperation. Formed in Cairo in 1945, it consisted of those Arab countries that were then independent; others joined on attaining independence. A secretariat was established in Cairo. The League has had some success in the scientific and cultural field but in politics has been split between its conservative and progressive members. In 1979, following the Egyptian-Israeli peace treaty, Egypt was expelled from the League, which was relocated in Tunis. Egypt was readmitted in 1989.

arable farming The cultivation of plants for food, fibres, vegetable oils, etc. Arable farming is often carried out in conjunction with livestock farming, enabling the farmer to grow his own animal feeds and to make use of animal manures as fertilizers. Grass is the chief feed for ruminant livestock and a major arable crop. Apart from grazing, grass is cut and conserved for winter food.

Cereal crops are a principal source of food and animal feedstuffs. The major cereals are wheat, barley, rice, and maize with oats, millet, sorghum, and rye cultivated to a lesser extent. Wheat may be sown either in autumn or spring and is harvested in late summer.

Beans are grown as a major source of vegetable protein, the most important being soyabean, produced chiefly in China and the USA. They are harvested mechanically using a specially adapted combine harvester. Harvesting root crops, such as potatoes and sugar beet, requires specialized machines that excavate the crop and remove soil. Crops grown for their oil content include sunflower, groundnut, linseed, cottonseed, and rape. Modern pesticides and fertilizers, together with innovations in mechanization, irrigation, and plant breeding have resulted in dramatic increases in crop yields, bringing about a Green Revolution, especially in developing countries.

ARABS *Bedouin woman making butter by the traditional method.*

Arabs A Semitic people originally inhabiting the Arabian peninsula. They are roughly divided into two cultural groups: the nomadic Bedouin tribes and the settled communities of the towns and oases. Wealth from oil has recently led to industrialization and westernization in the towns, but Islam remains a strong conservative force in social customs, particularly in women's role in society. The Arabs appeared as a power in world history early in the 7th century AD, with the rise of Islam, and they carried their language (*see* Arabic), religion, and culture as far as Spain in the W and Indonesia in the E.

Arachne In Greek mythology, a girl from Lydia who defeated Athena in a tapestry-weaving contest. The jealous goddess destroyed all Arachne's work; she attempted to hang herself, but Athena changed her into a spider.

arachnid An invertebrate animal belonging to an order (*Arachnida*; 65 000 species) of chiefly terrestrial arthropods, including the spiders, scorpions, harvestmen, ticks, and mites. An arachnid's body is divided into two parts: a combined head and thorax (cephalothorax) and an abdomen. The cephalothorax bears four pairs of legs and two pairs of head appendages, one of which consists of strong pincer-like claws. Arachnids are mostly carnivorous; many secrete poison from specialized glands to kill prey or enemies. Others are parasites, some of which are carriers of disease. Arachnids usually lay eggs, which hatch into immature adults.

Arafat, Yassir (1929–) Palestinian leader. In the 1950s he was one of the founders of al-Fatah and in 1968 became president of the Palestine Liberation Organization.

Aragon A region and medieval kingdom in NE Spain, of which Ramoir I (d. 1063) was the first king (1035–63). A series of conquests during the 11th and 12th centuries brought the Aragonese rule over much of N Spain. Union with Catalonia was secured by marriage in 1140. Later expansion gave the Aragonese Sicily (1282) and Sardinia (1320) and culminated in the conquest by Alfonso the Magnanimous (1385–1458) of the kingdom of Naples (1442). In 1469 Ferdinand the Catholic (1452–1516), heir to the Aragonese throne, married Isabella the Catholic (1451–1504) of Castile and on his accession in 1479 the two kingdoms were united.

Arakan A state in W Burma, extending along the Bay of Bengal and flanked by the Arakan Yoma, a mountain range rising over 3000 m (1000 ft). The principal economic activity is the cultivation of rice. The majority of the inhabitants are of Burmese descent but there is a large minority of Bengali Muslims in the N. *History*: a powerful kingdom in the 15th century, it was absorbed into Burma (1783) before passing to Britain (1826–1948). The activities of secessionist movements led to its change of status (from a division to a state) in 1975. Area: 36 762 sq km (14 191 sq mi). Population (1983): 2 045 891. Capital: Sittwe.

Aral Sea The fourth largest lake in the world, in the SW Soviet Union in the Kazakh and Uzbek SSRs. It receives the Rivers Amu Darya and Syr Darya and has no outlets. Its maximum depth varies by 10%. Area: about 66 000 sq km (25 477 sq mi).

Aramaic A western branch of the Semitic group of languages. Its 22-character alphabet is the ancestor of both Hebrew and Arabic alphabets. Aramaic became extensively used during the late Babylonian empire and was the official language of the Persian Empire under Darius I. It replaced Hebrew as the language of the Jews from about the time of the Exile in 605 BC until after the rise of Islam.

Ararat, Mount (Turkish name: Ağrı Dağı) 39 44N 44 15E A mountain in E Turkey, near the Soviet and Iranian borders. It is volcanic in origin and isolated but for a secondary peak 12 km (7 mi) away. Traditionally, Noah's ark came to rest here after the flood (Genesis 8.4). Height: 5165 m (16 946 ft).

Araucaria A genus of coniferous trees (about 15 species), native to Australasia and South America (it is named after a district of Chile). They have whorled horizontal branches covered with scale leaves, and male and female flowers usually grow on separate trees. The genus includes the ornamental monkey puzzle and several trees yielding useful timber, including the Norfolk Island pine (*A. heterophylla*); the hoop pine (*A. cunninghamii*) and the bunya bunya (*A. bidwillii*), both from E Australia; and the parana pine (*A. angustifolia*), of Brazil. Family: *Araucariaceae*.

Arawak Indians of the Greater Antilles and northern and western areas of the Amazon basin. Their languages are the most widespread of the South American Indian languages and include Goajiro in Colombia, Campa and Machiguenga in Peru, and Mojo and Bauré in Bolivia. They are sedentary farmers growing manioc and maize. Prior to the Spanish conquests they were divided into numerous hereditary chiefdoms. They were never a warlike people and in the Caribbean area Carib tribes frequently raided Arawak groups and enslaved Arawak women. The tribal gods were the spirits of chiefs represented by a hierarchy of idols called zemis, which were housed in temples.

arbor vitae A coniferous tree of the genus *Thuja* (6 species), native to North America and E Asia. They have scalelike leaves, which densely cover the flattened stems, and small scaly cones, 1–1.8 cm long. The Chinese arbor vitae or cedar (*T. orientalis*), which grows to a height of 30 m, is a popular ornamental tree; the giant arbor vitae, or western red cedar (*T. plicata*), of W North America, grows to a height of 40 m and yields a valuable timber. Family: *Cupressaceae*.

Arbutus A genus of evergreen trees and shrubs (about 20 species) distributed in Central and North America and W Europe. The small white or pinkish flowers are borne in terminal clusters and the berries are fleshy and reddish. The leaves are tough, dark green, toothed, and shiny above. The strawberry tree (*A. unedo*) of SW Europe is widely grown as an ornamental, reaching a height of 9 m. Family: *Ericaceae*.

Arcadia A mountainous region of ancient Greece, in the central Pelopponesus, that was identified in the literature of Greece, Rome, and the Renaissance (e.g. in Sidney's *Arcadia*) as an earthly paradise. It is a modern department.

Arc de Triomphe A ceremonial arch standing at the centre of the Étoile at the top of the Champs Elysées in Paris. It was commissioned to celebrate the victories of Napoleon I and built between 1806 and 1836 to the designs of Jean Chalgrin (1739–1811).

archaeology The scientific study of the material remains of man's past. Archaeology may be supplemented by written records, where they exist, but its techniques are principally concerned with nonliterary evidence for man's social and cultural development. Modern archaeology has numerous specialized branches—classical, industrial, underwater, etc. Before the 19th century, digging was carried out to plunder precious objects from ruins. Scientific excavation followed the realization that often more could be learnt from the surroundings in which objects are discovered than from the objects themselves. Essential techniques include stratigraphy, based on the principle that in any sequence of deposits the uppermost is latest and the lowest earliest, and typology, the study of changes in forms (e.g. of pottery). Methods of dating include radiometric dating, palaeomagnetism, thermoluminescence, varve dating, and dendrochronology.

Archaeopteryx A genus of extinct primitive birds, fossils of which date from the Jurassic period (160–120 million years ago). It had many reptilian features, such as numerous teeth, a long bony tail, and claws on the hand, but was fully feathered and is believed to be the ancestor of modern birds. *Archaeopteryx* lived in dense forests, climbing trees using its claws and gliding down in search of food.

Archangel (Russian name: Arkhangelsk) 64 32N 40 40E A port in the NW Soviet Union, in the RSFSR on the River Dvina, 50 km (30 mi) from the White Sea. Founded in 1584, it was Russia's leading port until the early 18th century. The Soviet Union's largest timber-exporting port, it has timber-processing and shipbuilding industries and also supports a fishing fleet. Population (1987): 416 000.

archery A sport in which generally a specified number of arrows are shot at a target over a prescribed distance. The modern bow developed from the medieval longbow, but the skill of shooting arrows from a bow dates back 30 millenniums. **Target archery** consists of shooting at a target of standard size marked with five or ten scoring zones. Different competitions require different permutations of distances and numbers of arrows. **Field archery** consists of shooting at large animal figures with superimposed scoring rings. In **clout shooting** arrows are shot into the air to fall on a target marked on the ground, while in **flight shooting** the purpose is to achieve the maximum distance. Archery is an amateur sport, governed internationally by the Fédération internationale de Tir à l'Arc (founded 1931).

ARC DE TRIOMPHE

Archimedes (c. 287–c. 212 BC) Greek mathematician and inventor, regarded as the greatest scientist of classical times. Archimedes was born in Syracuse, Sicily, and studied in Alexandria, afterwards returning to Syracuse, where he remained for the rest of his life. He is best known for his discovery of Archimedes' principle, supposedly in response to the King of Syracuse asking him to determine whether a gold crown had been adulterated with silver. Legend has it that he made his discovery while taking a bath and ran through the streets of Syracuse shouting "Eureka!" **Archimedes' principle** states that when a body is partly or wholly immersed in a fluid its apparent loss of weight is equal to the weight of the liquid displaced. He is also credited with the invention of **Archimedes' screw**, a device for raising water consisting of an inclined helical screw rotated about a central axis in a trough of water, although the device was probably already known to the Egyptians. He was killed by a soldier during the Roman invasion of Syracuse.

architecture The art of designing and constructing buildings that are both functionally and aesthetically satisfying. Factors principally influencing an architect are: the use to which the building will be put; the materials obtainable; the resources available in money and labour; and contemporary artistic taste. The earliest civilizations built on a monumental scale for their gods or the deified dead (*see* pyramids; ziggurat). Secular architecture reflected the needs of local rulers for security, comfort, and—very important—display. The Greeks were the first to develop the concepts of proportion and harmony that still influence western architectural theory. Roman engineers greatly extended flexibility of design by their use of arches and domes. Medieval European architecture reached its zenith in the gothic cathedral but the Renaissance brought a resurgence of interest in the principles of classical architecture. This was followed by a gothic revival at the beginning of the 19th century. In the 20th century technical advances in the use of prestressed concrete opened the way to modern architecture; while the necessities of engineering increasingly determine a building's appearance, the best modern architects demonstrate that architecture can still survive as an art form.

Arctic Circle The area around the North Pole enclosed by the parallel of latitude 66°32′N. It includes parts of Greenland, the Soviet Union, the USA, Canada, and Scandinavia and extensive areas of ice-covered ocean, notably the Arctic Ocean. The population consists mainly of Eskimos, who live by hunting. *History*: during the 16th century exploration of the Arctic by the Dutch and English began in the search for a Northeast or Northwest Passage to the Far East. In 1725–42 the Russian Imperial Navy carried out exploration. In 1879 a US expedition under G. W. De Long (1844–81) became trapped in the ice while attempting to reach the North Pole and its ship was crushed. Wreckage found off the coast of Greenland having drifted across the Arctic Ocean suggested that a sea route through the ice was possible. The Norwegian Fridtjof Nansen in the *Fram* drifted for nearly two years (1893–95) through the ice and proved that the North Pole was within an ice-covered sea. Robert E. Peary was the first to reach the North Pole (1909). Since then extensive mapping and geological and meteorological studies have been carried out; the Soviet Union has been particularly active and, like the USA, has established several drifting scientific stations.

Arctic fox A small fox, *Alopex lagopus*, found throughout tundra regions. It feeds on birds and small mammals, especially lemmings and Arctic hares, and grows a dense woolly coat of fur in winter. There are two colour varieties: the white fox, which has a white winter coat and a brown summer coat; and the blue fox, which is dark grey in summer and pale grey in winter. Arctic foxes have been farmed commercially for their fur.

Arctic Ocean The world's smallest ocean, almost completely enclosed by North America, Eurasia, and Greenland. Explored since the 17th century, it is covered by ice.

Ardennes A chain of hills in W Europe. It extends through N Luxembourg, S Belgium, and NE France at an average height of about 500 m (1640 ft), forming the watershed between the Rivers Meuse and Moselle.

are (a) A unit of area in the metric system equal to 100 square metres. The hectare is more frequently used than the are.

Areca. *See* betel.

Ares The Greek god of war, identified by the Romans with Mars. Son of Zeus and Hera, his popularity never rivalled that of the other Olympian gods. He loved Aphrodite, by whom he had three offspring, Deimos, Phobos, and Harmonia.

Argentina, Republic of The second largest country in South America. It consists chiefly of subtropical plains and forests (the Gran Chaco) in the N, the fertile temperate pampas in the centre, the Andes in the W, and the semidesert Patagonian plateau in the S. The inhabitants are almost all of European origin, mainly Italian and Spanish, with a very small and dwindling Indian population. *Economy*: chiefly agricultural with stock rearing, especially cattle. The main industries have traditionally been meat processing and packing but there has been recent growth in oil refining, plastics, textiles, and chemicals. Natural-gas deposits have been intensively developed and Argentina is practically self-sufficient in oil. There are plans to increase the use of hydroelectric power and nuclear energy is also being developed. *History*: colonized by the Spanish from 1515 onwards. During this period the native Indian inhabitants put up a fierce resistance but by the 19th century they had almost been wiped out. The country gained its independence in 1816, under José de San Martín, and a new constitution in 1853 marked the end of civil war and unrest. Since the late 19th century Argentina has been ruled mostly by military dictatorships. Most prominent among the rulers since World War II has been Lt Gen Juán Perón, who came to power in 1946. Following the death (1952) of his popular wife, Eva, he was overthrown in a military revolution (1955). In 1973, following the election of one of his supporters, Dr Hector Campóra, he returned to power but died the following year. He was succeeded by his second wife, Isabel, but as the economic situation continued to deteriorate, allegations of corruption were made against her government. In 1976 Lt Gen Jorge Rafael Videla (1925–   ) came to power at the head of a

ARGENTINA *Cattle ranching, with gauchos, is still an important industry.*

ARCHITECTURE

the orders of classical architecture

Doric   Tuscan   Ionic   Corinthian   Composite

plan   plan   plan   plan   plan

entablature

capital

shaft

base

some terms in classical architecture

pediment

acroterion   tympanum   cornice

cornice

entablature

frieze

architrave   triglyph   metope

capital   echinus   abacus

column

shaft

flutes

drum

entasis (curvature of shaft)

stylobate

some terms in gothic architecture

foil   string course

cusp   extrados

cinquefoil   mouldings

intrados

spandrel

voussoir

corbel

spring of arch

capital

column (pier)

detached shaft

base

three-man junta and strong measures were introduced to combat the violence and unrest. Lt Gen Roberto Viola succeeded Videla as president in 1981 but was later removed from office by the military junta, led by Gen Leopoldo Galtieri, who subsequently became president in December, 1981. On 2 April, 1982, Argentina launched an invasion of the Falkland Islands (which it calls the Islas Malvinas) to which it laid claim but following armed conflict with a task force sent by the UK was forced to surrender on 14 June, 1982; a defeat that forced Galtieri's resignation and later imprisonment. Gen Reynaldo Bignone replaced him until Raúl Alfonsín (1926–) was elected president in 1983. He was succeeded by Carlos Saúl Menem (1931–) in 1989. Official language: Spanish. Official religion: Roman Catholic. Official currency: austral of 100 centavos. Area: 2 777 815 sq km (1 072 515 sq mi). Population (1986 est): 31 060 000. Capital and main port: Buenos Aires.

argon (Ar) A noble gas that occurs in the atmosphere (0.94%). It was first isolated in 1894 by Rayleigh and Ramsay, by the distillation of liquid air. Because it is chemically inert, it is used to fill fluorescent lamps and as an inert gas blanket for welding reactive metals. At no 18; at wt 39.948; mp $-189.2°C$; bp $-185.7°C$.

Argonauts In Greek mythology, the 50-man crew of Jason's ship *Argo*, on the quest of the Golden Fleece. Accounts of its composition vary, but all agree that it included the shipbuilder Argo, the tireless helmsman Tiphys, the keen-sighted Lynceus, Heracles and his follower Hylas, and even Orpheus and the Dioscuri, Castor and Pollux. The Argonauts encountered such perils as the Sirens, the Harpies, the Symplegades (moving rocks that crushed ships) and the bronze giant Talos.

Argos 37 38N 22 43E A town in the NE Peloponnese (S Greece). Belonging in Homeric times to a follower of Agamemnon, Argos gave its name to the surrounding district (the Argolid). Eclipsed by nearby Sparta after the 6th century BC, Argos remained neutral or the ineffective ally of Athens during the 5th century. Considerable remains of the city survive.

Århus (*or* Aarhus) 56 10N 10 13E A seaport in Denmark, in E Jutland. One of the oldest cities in Denmark, it has a gothic cathedral and a university (1928). Its industries include electronic goods, machinery, and textiles. Population (1987): 255 932.

aria (Italian: air) A solo song with instrumental accompaniment, usually in an opera or oratorio. The name was also used of instrumental pieces but its meaning became restricted with the development of the three part *aria da capo* by Monteverdi, Scarlatti, and Handel. Attacked by reformers, such as Gluck and Wagner, the aria form is little used in modern opera.

Ariadne In Greek legend, the daughter of Minos, King of Crete, and Pasiphaë. She helped Theseus to kill the Minotaur and escape from its labyrinth. He abandoned her on the island of Naxos, where she was found by Dionysus, who married her.

Ariane. *See* European Space Agency.

Arias Sánchez, Oscar (1941–) Costa Rican statesman; president (1986–90). His Central American peace plan was intended to end regional conflicts by 1988 but has had only limited success. He won the Nobel Peace Prize in 1987.

Ariel A computerized system used by institutional investors (e.g. pension funds) in the UK to buy and sell equity shares by negotiating directly with each other through a television network. The acceptance houses set it up in 1974 to enable subscribers to save on stock-exchange commission. It is based on *Instinct*, a similar system used in the USA.

Aristarchus of Samos (c. 310–230 BC) Greek astronomer, who maintained that the earth rotates upon its axis and orbits the sun. He made the first attempts to estimate trigonometrically the size and distance from the earth of the sun and the moon.

Aristophanes (c. 450–c. 385 BC) Greek comic dramatist. He wrote about 40 plays, of which 11 survive: *The Acharnians* (425), *The Knights* (424), *The Clouds* (423), *The Wasps* (422), *The Peace* (421), *The Birds* (414), *Lysistrata* (411), *Thesmophoriazusae* (410), *The Frogs* (405), *Women in Parliament* (393), and *Plutus* (388). His plots were satirical fantasies on contemporary topics.

Aristotle (384–322 BC) Greek philosopher and scientist. His father was court physician in Macedonia. Aristotle joined Plato's Academy at Athens (367–347) but, failing to become head of the Academy at Plato's death, he accepted the protection of Hermeias, ruler of Atarneus in Asia Minor, and married his patron's niece. About 343 Philip of Macedon appointed Aristotle tutor to his son Alexander, then aged 13. After Alexander's accession in 336, Aristotle founded the Lyceum at Athens (a research community with library and museum). When Alexander died in 323 BC, anti-Macedonian reaction forced Aristotle to withdraw to Chalcis, where he died. Aristotle wrote over 400 books; those that survive (about one-quarter), edited by Andronicus of Rhodes about 40 BC, are apparently memoranda for his students' use, not intended for general publication.

arithmetic The branch of mathematics that deals with elementary theories of numbers, measurement, and computation. The fundamental operations of arithmetic are addition, subtraction, multiplication, and division. Addition and multiplication are assumed to obey the associative law, the commutative law, and the distributive law. Other operations in arithmetic include extracting roots, raising a number to a power, and taking logarithms. Arithmetic is also concerned with fractions and the various number systems, such as the decimal system and the binary system.

arithmetic progression (*or* arithmetic sequence) A sequence of numbers in which successive terms have a constant difference, for example, 1, 4, 7, 10, 13 . . . .

Arizona A state in the SW USA. It falls into two natural regions: in the NE part of the Colorado Plateau, an area of dry plains and escarpments, and in the S and W is an area of desert basins and gentle valleys, drained by the Gila and Salt Rivers. The Colorado River flows through the Grand Canyon in the NW of the state. In such an arid region inadequate water supplies have long been a problem and a number of major irrigation projects have been built. Most of the population lives in urban settlements in the S and W. Manufacturing (electrical, communications, aeronautical, and aluminium products) is the major industry. The state produces over half of the USA's copper as well as gold, silver, oil, and timber. Tourism is an important source of revenue. The main crops are cotton, vegetables, and citrus fruits; livestock is also important. It has the largest Indian population in the USA; the main tribes are the Navajo, Hopi, and Apache. *History*: inhabited by Indians as early as 25 000 BC, the area was explored by the Spanish in the 16th century. Following the Mexican War, Arizona, then part of New Mexico, was ceded to the USA (1848).

It was swept by Apache wars until 1877 and became a state in 1912. Area: 295 023 sq km (113 909 sq mi). Population (1986 est): 3 317 000. Capital: Phoenix.

Arkansas A state in the S central USA, lying W of the Mississippi River. It consists chiefly of the largely forested uplands of the N and W, descending to the Mississippi alluvial plain in the E and the West Gulf coastal plain in the S. The **Arkansas River** (2335 mi; 1450 mi) bisects the state from W to E. The state is no longer primarily agricultural although the Mississippi Plain provides fertile land; soya beans and rice have replaced cotton as the major crop. There are major lumbering, petroleum, and gas developments around Smackover and El Dorado and coal deposits in the Arkansas River Valley. The state produces 90% of US bauxite. Manufactures include electronic equipment and wood products. *History*: explored by the Spanish and French in the 16th and 17th centuries, it formed part of the Louisiana Purchase by the USA in 1803. It became a state in 1836, seceded from the Union in 1861, and was readmitted in 1868. Area: 137 539 sq km (53 104 sq mi). Population (1986 est): 2 372 000. Capital: Little Rock.

Ark of the Covenant In the Old Testament, the sacred chest of the Israelites that contained the tablets of the law (the Ten Commandments) and was symbolic of God's presence and the covenant made between God and Israel. Made of acacia wood, inlaid, and covered with gold, it was eventually placed in the Temple of Jerusalem. It probably disappeared during the Babylonian exile.

Arkwright, Sir Richard (1732–92) British inventor and industrialist, who invented a spinning frame powered by water, the so-called water frame (patented in 1769). Arkwright subsequently mechanized other spinning processes and his mills were vandalized by spinners put out of work by the incipient factory system.

Arlberg Pass A mountain pass in W Austria, in the Alps, linking Vorarlberg with the Tirol by road. A railway tunnel (completed 1884) cuts through the mountain for a distance of over 10 km (6 mi). Height: 1802 m (5910 ft).

Arlington National Cemetery The largest cemetery in the USA, comprising 170 hectares (420 acres). Since 1864 it has been the burial ground of Americans killed in action and of eminent public servants.

Armada, Spanish The fleet of 130 ships sent by Philip II of Spain in 1588 to invade England. After indecisive encounters with the English fleet led by Howard of Effingham, under whom Sir John Hawkins held command, the Armada anchored off Calais only to be dispersed by English fireships during the night of 28 July. A major engagement off Gravelines followed, in which the Armada was defeated. It suffered further losses in storms as it escaped round Scotland and Ireland, arriving in Spain with 86 ships. The defeat was a major blow to Spain, which had claimed divine authority for its crusade against Protestant England. *See also* Drake, Sir Francis.

armadillo A mammal belonging to the family *Dasypodidae* (12 species), widespread in open country in the southern USA and South America. Armadillos have a covering of jointed bands or horny plates that enables them to roll themselves into a ball for protection. They have long-clawed toes for burrowing, simple peglike teeth, and feed on insects and other invertebrates. Armadillos range in size from the giant armadillo (*Priodontes giganteus*), about 120 cm long, to the rare pink

fairy armadillo (*Chlamyphorus truncatus*), 12 cm long. Order: *Edentata*.

Armageddon. *See* Megiddo.

Armenians A people of NE Turkey and SW Russia speaking an Indo-European language. Approximately 1.5 million live in Turkey, Europe, and America and 3 million in the Armenian Soviet Socialist Republic, with smaller numbers in the Georgian and Azerbaidzhan SSRs. Their culture is ancient, with a literature written in an alphabet derived from Greek and Syriac script. Their language is the only representative of a distinct branch of the Indo-European family. They call themselves Hay and their land Hayastan. They mainly belong to the Armenian Church, founded by St Gregory the Illuminator (c. 240–332) about 300 AD. During the 19th and 20th centuries they suffered massacres at the hands of the Ottoman Turks.

ARMADA *Detail of a contemporary painting of the English Fleet in pursuit.*

Armenian Soviet Socialist Republic A densely populated and mountainous republic in the S Soviet Union. Industry includes food processing, metallurgy, and chemicals. The rich mineral deposits include copper, lead, and zinc. The raising of livestock is the chief agricultural activity. *History*: the region formed the E part of the historic area inhabited by the Armenians. It was acquired by Russia in 1828. The Russian province declared its independence in 1918 but it subsequently formed part of the Transcaucasian Soviet Federated Republic. It became a separate republic in 1936. In 1988 25 000 people died in an earthquake. There have also been violent ethnic disturbances over the disputed Nagorno-Karabakh territory. Area: 29 800 sq km (11 490 sq mi). Population (1988): 3 360 000. Capital: Yerevan.

armour Defensive equipment used as a protection in warfare. Body armour (helmet, breastplate, greaves) was used in Bronze Age Greece. The Romans evolved heavier armour for both men and horses. In the early Middle Ages chainmail was widely used but after about 1300 plate armour, often sumptuously decorated and encasing the whole body, was worn by knights on horseback. Gunpowder gradually rendered most body armour obsolete. See p. 46.

Armstrong, Louis (1900–71) US Black jazz trumpeter and singer, known as "Satchmo." Born in New Orleans, he learned to play the cornet in his youth. His career took him to Chicago, where he made many recordings (some of them with Earl Hines), which earned him a worldwide reputation. He played with several large orchestras as a soloist and toured Europe in 1932. His gravelly singing voice and superb trumpet playing were featured in many films.

ARMOUR *The skill of the European armourer reached its height in the late 15th and early 16th centuries, when suits of plate armour were made to cover the entire body.*

Armstrong, Neil Alden (1930–) US astronaut, the first man to walk on the moon. A navy pilot during the Korean War, he worked for NASA, (1955–71) and became an astronaut in 1962. He was commander of Apollo 11 (1969). As he stepped onto the moon he said "That's one small step for a man, one giant leap for mankind."

Arnhem 52 00N 5 53E A city in the E Netherlands, the capital of Gelderland province. In World War II a large airborne landing of British troops attempted to secure a bridgehead over the River Rhine here to facilitate an Allied invasion of Germany. The attempt failed with heavy casualties in the ensuing battle (17–27 September, 1944). A railway junction, its industries include engineering and pharmaceuticals. Population (1987): 127 671.

Arno, River A river in central Italy. Rising in the Apennines, it flows mainly W through Florence and Pisa to the Ligurian Sea. It burst its banks in 1966 causing disastrous floods in Florence. Length: 240 km (150 mi).

Arnold, Thomas (1795–1842) British educator. Appointed headmaster of Rugby (1828), Arnold reformed

the school and instituted the prefectorial system, which came to characterize English public schools. Arnold's piety was infectious, and Rugby became noted for "muscular Christianity." *Tom Brown's Schooldays* provides a record of Arnold's achievement. His son **Matthew Arnold** (1822–88) was a poet and critic. He worked as a government inspector of schools from 1851 to 1886. His critical works include *Essays in Criticism* (1865; 1888) and *Culture and Anarchy* (1869), in which he advocated literary and cultural values as an antidote to the progressive materialism of Victorian society. His poetry included "Dover Beach" (1867), "The Scholar Gypsy" (1853), and "Sohrab and Rustum" (1853).

aromatic compound A type of cyclic organic chemical compound that includes benzene and its derivatives. On conventional theories of valence these compounds appear to be unsaturated (i.e. contain double bonds). However, benzene and similar compounds are much less reactive than the alkenes, tending to undergo substitution reactions rather than addition reactions. The explanation for the stability of the benzene ring lies in a model in which the carbon atoms are joined by single bonds and the extra six valence electrons are free to move around the ring in a delocalized orbital. Aromatic compounds were originally distinguished from aliphatic compounds because of the distinctive properties of benzene compounds, many of which have a fragrant odour.

Arp, Jean (Hans) (1887–1966) French sculptor and poet. He was one of the founders of the dada movement (1916) and later associated with the surrealist movement in Paris. Arp experimented with collages of torn coloured papers, designed according to chance, and produced numerous painted wood reliefs. In about 1930 he began his abstract sculptures suggesting organic rather than geometric forms. His wife and occasional collaborator was the artist Sophie Tauber (1889–1943).

arquebus. *See* musket.

arrest The forcible detention of a person to compel obedience to the law. In England, a person may be arrested on a magistrate's warrant to answer to a criminal charge, or for a civil offence, such as contempt of court. He may also be arrested if he commits, or is clearly about to commit, a crime. In theory any citizen can make an arrest and is bound to do so if a felony or breach of the peace is committed in his presence, but in practice most valid arrests are made by the police or other law-enforcement officers, who are empowered to make arrests without warrants.

arrowroot A herbaceous perennial plant, *Maranta arundinacea*, native to Guyana but widely cultivated in the West Indies for the fine starch that is extracted from its underground fleshy tubers and used in cooking. The plant is about 1.5 m high and has short-stalked white flowers and broad-bladed leaves with long narrow sheaths. Family: *Marantaceae*.

Arrow War. *See* Opium Wars.

ars antiqua (Latin: old art) A style of European music of the 13th century. It was particularly associated with composers of the Parisian school, such as Pérotin (c. 1155–c. 1202) and Léonin (late 12th century), and characterized by the use of complex forms of organum. It was succeeded by *ars nova*.

arsenic (As) A brittle semimetal that occurs in nature in a variety of forms: native, as the sulphides realgar ($As_2 S_2$) and orpiment ($As_2 S_3$), as sulpharsenides, such as arsenopyrite ($FeSAs$), and as arsenates. The element occurs in several forms and was known to the ancients. Pure arsenic has important uses as a dopant in the semiconductor industry. Arsenic and its common compounds are extremely poisonous. Compounds include the white oxide (As_2O_3), the gaseous hydride arsine (AsH_3), and arsenates, some of which are used as insecticides. At no 33; at wt 74.9216; mp 817°C (28 atm); sublimes 613°C.

ars nova (Latin: new art) A style of European music of the 14th century, which succeeded *ars antiqua*. The name was taken from the title of a treatise by Philippe de Vitry (1291–1361), which set out new principles for the composition of motets and for the notation of complex rhythms.

arson At common law, maliciously setting fire to something, including buildings, vehicles, etc. As a distinct offence, arson was abolished in English law by the Criminal Damage Act (1971), which is the statute covering all types of criminal damage (the destruction or damage of property belonging to another). Criminal damage committed by fire is still, however, charged as arson.

ART DECO *Typical bronze and ivory figures with their clean sharp lines.*

Art Deco The style of design predominant in the decorative arts of the 1920s and 1930s. The name derives from the 1925 Exposition Internationale des Arts Décoratifs in Paris. In deliberate contrast to Art Nouveau, Art Deco was characterized by emphatic geometrical lines and shapes, vibrant colour schemes, and the use of man-made substances, such as plastic. Influenced by the Bauhaus, Art Deco included among its practitioners René Lalique (1860–1945) and Romaine de Tirtoff Erté (1892–   ). It was debased by shoddy mass production, but interest in it rekindled late in the 1960s.

Artemis In Greek mythology, the daughter of Zeus and Leto and twin sister of Apollo. Settled in Arcadia, she and her band of Oceanids and nymphs spent their time hunting. Love was banned, and Artemis rigorously punished all transgressors. Actaeon was killed for watching her bathe and Orion for touching her. Despite this severity she was protectress of both animal and human young. Ephesus was the most famous centre of her worship. She was associated with the moon and identified by the Romans with Diana. *Compare* Hecate.

Artemis, Temple of One of the Seven Wonders of the World, built at Ephesus in 356 BC. The deity worshipped here was the many-breasted fertility goddess called Diana of the Ephesians in Acts 19.28, rather than the classical Artemis.

arteriosclerosis The loss of elasticity in the walls of arteries. It covers various conditions of the arteries and arterioles (small arteries) associated with the ageing process. It is also used as a synonym for atherosclerosis.

artery A thick-walled blood vessel that carries oxygen-rich blood away from the heart to supply all the tissues and organs of the body. The largest is the aorta, which leads directly from the heart and descends into the abdomen, giving rise to all the other arteries of the body. In middle age the lining of the arteries commonly becomes thickened by atherosclerosis, which may lead to various diseases caused by obstruction of blood flow (e.g. strokes, heart attacks). *See also* blood pressure.

artesian well A well sunk into an aquifer (a water-saturated rock stratum) that is confined between two layers of impermeable rock and through which water flows upwards under pressure. The aquifer reaches the surface and receives rainfall where the water table is higher than the site of the well, resulting in a head of pressure.

arthritis Inflammation of one or more joints, causing pain, swelling, and restriction of movement. Many different diseases can cause arthritis, the most important of which are osteoarthritis, rheumatoid arthritis, and gout. **Rheumatoid arthritis**, which is more common in women, usually affects the hands and feet and often also the hips, knees, and shoulders. The synovial membrane lining the joint becomes inflamed, resulting in damage to the cartilage over the joint with consequent pain and deformity. An autoimmune disease (*see* autoimmunity), it is diagnosed by a blood test (the blood contains the rheumatoid factor) and X-rays. Treatment is usually based on analgesic and anti-inflammatory drugs; some patients benefit from gold salts and steroids, while severe cases may require surgical replacement of the affected joint(s).

arthropod An invertebrate animal belonging to the largest and most diverse phylum (*Arthropoda*) of the animal kingdom, containing about a million species (i.e. 75% of all known species). There are about 12 classes, the most important of which are the arachnids, crustaceans, insects, centipedes, and millipedes. An arthropod has a segmented body with a hard outer skeleton (cuticle) made of chitin, which is shed periodically to allow the body to grow. Jointed appendages are modified for swimming, walking, feeding, respiration, reproduction, etc. Young arthropods often go through metamorphosis to reach the adult form. Many are harmful—as pests, parasites, or vectors of disease—but others are beneficial to man, as pollinators, food sources, predators of pests, and decomposers of organic wastes.

Arthurian legend The medieval romances concerning the legendary British king Arthur and his knights. Arthur first emerges as a figure of romance in the *Historia Regum Britanniae* of Geoffrey of Monmouth. In the legend, he is the son of Uther Pendragon, was born at Tintagel in Cornwall, became king of Britain at 15, and won a number of famous victories. He married Guinevere and held court at Caerleon in Wales (or, in some versions, at Camelot, which may have been near South Cadbury, Somerset). Involved in a war at Rome, he left his kingdom in the charge of his nephew Modred, who betrayed him and abducted Guinevere. Arthur returned to Britain and defeated Modred but was himself wounded. He was taken to the Isle of Avalon (the Celtic paradise, associated with Glastonbury) to be healed. Succeeding writers added new episodes: the Anglo-Norman poet Wace (c. 1100–c. 1175) introduced the knightly fellowship of the Round Table, Layamon (early 13th century) added magical elements, and Chrétien de Troyes focused on the quest of the Holy Grail. Other characters were the magician Merlin and the sorceress Morgan le Fay (Arthur's sister). Sir Thomas Malory's *Morte d'Arthur* (c. 1470) was the culmination of the medieval tradition, although Tennyson's *Idylls of the King* (from 1842) and T. H. White's *The Once and Future King* (1958) are later versions.

artichoke A perennial thistle-like herbaceous plant, *Cynara scolemus*, also known as globe artichoke, native to central and W Mediterranean regions and widely grown in warm temperate areas for its nutty-tasting immature flower heads. The hairy indented straplike leaves, 1 m long, arise each year from the base of the short annual stems, which carry branched flower stalks bearing purplish flowers. Family: *Compositae. See also* Jerusalem artichoke.

Articles of Confederation The first constitution of the USA (written 1776–77, adopted 1781), which was replaced by the Constitution of 1789. The leaders of the American Revolution feared the abuses of a centralized government and adopted a federal system that guaranteed each state its "sovereignty, freedom, and independence." The Continental Congress could not levy taxes but could wage war and borrow and issue money.

artificial insemination The artificial introduction of semen into the vagina of a female at or shortly after ovulation. Although practised in the 14th century by Arab horse breeders, the techniques were developed largely for livestock in the Soviet Union during the early 20th century. Semen collected from a single male can be stored at low temperatures for months before being used to fertilize many females. This has resulted in dramatic breed improvements and the control of venereal disease. Artificial insemination is also used in human medicine; for an infertile husband, semen is obtained from an anonymous donor (artificial insemination donor–AID). Semen may be provided by the husband in cases of impotence (artificial insemination husband–AIH). When the wife is infertile the husband's semen may be used to artificially inseminate a surrogate mother. This woman gives birth to the child, usually for money, and must then be prepared to relinquish all claims on it to the natural father and his wife. Commercial surrogacy is growing in the USA, but in the UK the Surrogacy Arrangements Act (1985) prohibits commercial agencies from engaging women as surrogate mothers. *See also* test-tube baby.

artificial intelligence (AI) The design of computer programs to perform tasks that involve intelligence when carried out by human beings. Tasks performed by AI include playing games, learning, understanding natural language and speech, formulating plans, proving theorems, and visual perception. Perceptual tasks involve unconscious computation in humans, which is hard to simulate. AI programs sometimes simulate human behaviour by building computer models of cognitive processes, but in most cases they aim to do the task set or do it better than it has been done before.

artificial kidney. *See* dialysis.

artificial respiration The restoration of the flow of air into and out of the lungs when the patient's own breathing movements have ceased, for example after drowning, poisoning, etc. Mouth-to-mouth respiration –the "kiss of life"–involves a person breathing out into the patient's mouth: carbon dioxide in this exhaled air acts as a stimulus for the natural breathing reflexes. In hospitals artificial respiration by a respirator is sometimes provided during surgery, severe pneumonias, and after head injuries.

artillery Firearms with a calibre in excess of 20 mm, used to bombard enemy positions, provide cover, etc. Early guns were classed by projectile weight, e.g. 12-pounder. Modern weapons are identified by calibre: light (below 120 mm), medium (121–160 mm), heavy (161–210 mm), and super or very heavy (above 211 mm). Gun projectiles have flat trajectories, while mortars and howitzers have high trajectories, with correspondingly short ranges. Artillery rockets deliver more explosive further, without needing heavy launchers. Modern electronic equipment enables artillery fire to score a direct hit with near certainty on any visible target; as this also applies to the guns themselves artillery is now usually remote controlled.

Artiodactyla An order of hoofed mammals (150 species), distributed worldwide except for Australasia and Antarctica. Artiodactyls are terrestrial herbivores having two or four toes on each foot and often bearing horns. The group is divided into three suborders: *Suiformes* (pigs, peccaries, and hippopotamuses); *Tylopoda* (camels and llamas); and *Ruminantia* (*see* ruminant), which comprises deer, cattle, antelopes, giraffes, pronghorns, and chevrotains. *Compare* Perissodactyla.

ART NOUVEAU *Flowing lines and graceful drapery typify the style in these bronze figures.*

Art Nouveau A decorative style pervading all visual art forms in Britain, France, Germany (Jugendstil), Austria (Sezessionstil), Belgium, Spain, and the USA in the 1890s and early 1900s. It is characterized by designs of naturalistic foliage and shapes linked by undulating lines. In Britain it is associated with the Arts and Crafts movement of William Morris, the designs of Charles Rennie Mackintosh (1868–1928), and the graphic work of Aubrey Beardsley. On the Continent leading examples are the Parisian metro designs of Hector Guimard

(1867–1942), the extravagant Barcelona flats and hotels of Antonio Gaudí (1852–1926), and the Belgian stores and houses of Victor Horta (1861–1947).

Arts and Crafts movement An English 19th-century aesthetic movement derived from William Morris and his Pre-Raphaelite associates, whose firm was founded (1861) to produce handmade furnishings. The movement revived the principles of medieval craftsmanship and respect for materials. It culminated in the establishment of the Century Guild for Craftsmen (1882) and the Arts and Crafts Exhibition Society (1888). It helped to create the emerging Art Nouveau style.

Aruba 12 30N 70 00W A West Indian island, in the Netherlands Antilles from which it became independent in 1986. Oil refining is important. Area: 193 sq km (75 sq mi). Population (1985 est): 61 000. Chief town: Oranjestad.

arum (*or* arum lily) A plant of the tropical African genus *Zantedeschia* (8 species), especially *Z. aethiopica*, widely grown as an ornamental. It has arrow-shaped leaves and a flower head of tiny yellow flowers surrounded by a white funnel-shaped bract (spathe). *Araceae*. The European genus *Arum*, of the same family, contains the cuckoopint. The related bog arum, or wild calla (*Calla palustris*), grows in swamps of N temperate and subarctic regions. It has heart-shaped leaves and small flowers enveloped in a white spathe.

Arunachal Pradesh (name until 1972: North-East Frontier Agency) A state in NE India, stretching N from the Brahmaputra Valley to the Himalayas. There it shares a disputed border with Tibet, from which Chinese troops have twice invaded since 1945. It became the 24th state of India in 1986. Mostly rainforest, it is inhabited by hill tribes. Area: 81 426 sq km (31 430 sq mi). Population (1981 est): 631 839. Capital: Itanagar.

Arundel 50 51N 0 34W A market town in SE England, in West Sussex on the River Arun. Its 11th-century castle (mainly rebuilt in the 19th century) is the seat of the Dukes of Norfolk. Other notable buildings include the 19th-century cathedral. Population (1981): 2235.

Aryans Peoples speaking Indo-European, Indo-Iranian, or Indo-Aryan languages. It has been claimed that all the Indo-European peoples originated from an Aryan people who dispersed from a common homeland into Europe and N India. Indo-Aryan-speaking peoples invaded and settled in N India in the second millennium BC. They were tribal herdsmen who became farmers. The earliest literature of India, the Vedas, written in Sanskrit, contains details of Aryan ritual practices.

ASA rating The American Standards Association measure of the sensitivity or speed of photographic film. A film rated at 200 is twice as fast (i.e. needs half the exposure time) as 100 ASA film. General-purpose films have speeds between 50 and 160 ASA. High-speed films for poor light are rated between 200 and 1000 ASA.

asbestos A fibrous form of certain silicate minerals, particularly the amphiboles anthophyllite, tremolite, riebeckite, and actinolite, or a fibrous form of serpentine, called chrysotile. Blue asbestos is crocidolite, a fibrous riebeckite. Asbestos is heat-resistant, chemically inert, and has a high electrical resistance; it is much used in industry. The fibres are spun and woven or made into blocks. The main producers are Canada, the Soviet Union, and Brazil. *See also* asbestosis.

asbestosis A lung disease caused by the inhalation of asbestos fibres. It is an occupational disease to which those exposed to large amounts of the mineral are particularly prone: tighter factory health controls have greatly reduced its incidence. It affects the air sacs of the lungs, which become thickened and scarred, causing breathlessness: patients are liable to develop lung cancer.

Ascension 7 57S 14 22W A rocky island in the S Atlantic Ocean, a dependency of St Helena. It has little vegetation and was uninhabited until 1815. A British telecommunications centre, it is also a US air base and space research station. Area: 88 sq km (35 sq mi). Population (1985): 1708. Chief settlement: Georgetown.

Ascension In the Christian calendar, the day on which it is believed Christ ascended into Heaven (*see* Acts 1.4–11). Since the 4th century it has been celebrated 40 days after Easter.

Asclepius (*or* Aesculapius) In Greek mythology, a son of Apollo and the god of medicine. He was instructed by the centaur Chiron in hunting and medicine. When he restored Hippolytus to life as a favour to Artemis, Zeus became angry and struck him dead with a thunderbolt. The sick, believing in Asclepius's power to cure them through dreams, came to sleep in his temples, the chief of which were at Epidaurus and on the island of Cos.

Ascomycetes A large class of fungi (about 15 000 species), known as sac fungi because their spores are formed in a saclike structure (called an ascus). The nonreproductive part of these fungi is often a microscopical meshwork of cells. The group includes the truffles, yeasts, *Penicillium*, and *Aspergillus*.

ascorbic acid. *See* vitamin C.

Ascot 51 25N 0 41W A village in S England, in Berkshire. The construction of its famous racecourse was ordered by Queen Anne in 1711. Traditionally the sovereign opens the Royal Ascot meeting in June, driving in an open carriage round the course from nearby Windsor Castle. Population (1983 est): 13 234, with Sunningdale.

ASDIC. *See* echo sounding.

ash A tree of the genus *Fraxinus* (about 50 species), native to the N hemisphere. Many species yield a pale-yellow wood of commercial importance and others are widely grown as ornamentals. Reaching a height of 30 m, ashes have compound leaves made up of pairs of oval or lance-shaped leaflets, small inconspicuous flowers, and winged fruits ("ash keys"). Most species are deciduous, including the European ash (*F. excelsior*). Family: *Oleaceae* (olive family). *See also* mountain ash.

Ashcroft, Dame Peggy (1907–) British actress. She made her debut at the Birmingham Repertory Theatre in 1926. Her most notable performances include Juliet in 1935, Hedda Gabler in 1954, and more recent roles in plays by Pinter and Beckett. She won an Oscar for her performance in the film *A Passage to India* (1984).

Ashdown, Paddy (Jeremy John Dunham A.; 1941–) British politician, leader of the Social and Liberal Democratic Party (1988–). He entered parliament in 1983 after service in the Commandos and the Special Boat Section.

Ashes A mock trophy awarded to the winning team in cricket Test matches between England and Australia. It originated with the first Australian victory (1882), when an obituary for English cricket in the *Sporting Times* ended with the words: "The body will be cremated and the ashes taken to Australia." In 1883 the victorious English captain was presented with an urn (now kept in the pavilion at Lord's cricket ground) containing the ashes of the stumps used in the match. See p. 50.

```
In Affectionate Remembrance
            OF
ENGLISH CRICKET,
  WHICH DIED AT THE OVAL
            ON
  29th AUGUST, 1882,
Deeply lamented by a large circle of sorrowing
    friends and acquaintances.
    ─────────
         R. I. P.
    ─────────
N.B.—The body will be cremated and the
      ashes taken to Australia.
```

ASHES *The original advertisement that appeared as a joke in the* Sporting Times *in August, 1882.*

Ashkenazim Jews of German or Eastern European origin, as opposed to Sephardim. They have a distinct tradition of pronouncing Hebrew, as well as other customs, and until this century they mostly spoke Yiddish. The first Ashkenazy synagogue in London was founded in 1690.

Ashkenazy, Vladimir (1937–) Russian pianist and conductor. He won the 1955 Warsaw Chopin Competition and was joint winner of the 1962 Tchaikovsky Competition. In 1973 he settled in Iceland.

Ashmolean Museum A museum in Oxford, housing paintings and archaeological collections. The collection was donated to Oxford University in 1675 by Elias Ashmole (1617–92) and put on public display in 1683. Now in the neoclassical building (1845) of Charles Robert Cockerell (1788–1863), its highlights include Italian Renaissance paintings and English 19th-century works.

Ashton, Sir Frederick (William Mallandaine) (1904–88) British ballet dancer and choreographer, born in Ecuador. He joined the Sadler's Wells Ballet in 1935, became an associate director in 1952, and was director of the Royal Ballet from 1963 to 1970. His works include *Cinderella* (1948), *Ondine* (1958), *La Fille mal gardée* (1960), and many ballets choreographed for Margot Fonteyn.

Ashur The oldest Assyrian capital (modern Qalat Sharqat) on the River Tigris in Iraq. Named after its guardian sun-god, Ashur became capital of the rising Assyrian empire (14th century BC) to which it gave its name. With its later cocapitals Nimrud and Nineveh it was destroyed in 612 BC. First excavated in 1903, Ashur's ruins include major temples and a ziggurat.

Ash Wednesday In the Christian calendar, the first day of Lent, which is so named from the custom, probably dating from the 8th century, of marking the foreheads of the congregation with ashes as a sign of penitence.

Asia The largest continent in the world, it occupies about one-third of the dry land. Extending W to the Ural Mountains, it is separated from the continent of Africa by the Red Sea and bounded on the N by the Arctic Ocean. It includes the islands of Indonesia, Japan, the Philippines, and Taiwan. It contains the world's highest point (Mount Everest) and also its lowest (the Dead Sea). Its great central mass of mountains and plateaus has historically formed a major barrier between N and S Asia. Vast alluvial plains border the major rivers, including the Rivers Ganges, Mekong, and Ob and the Yangtze and Yellow Rivers. Containing about half of the world's total population, it is the most populous continent. There are three main population groups: Negroid (in the Philippines), Mongoloid (including the Chinese, Japanese, and Koreans), and Caucasoid (including the Arabs, Afghans, and Pakistanis). Other groups, including the Malays, are a mixture of these main races. All the world's major religions originated in Asia, including Christianity, Judaism, Hinduism (with the largest following), Buddhism, Islam, Confucianism (in China), and Shintoism (in Japan). Agriculture is the chief occupation, employing about two-thirds of the total population. Asia also has important mineral resources, notably the oil and natural-gas deposits of the Arab states. Area: 44 391 162 sq km (17 139 445 sq mi). Population (1984 est): 2 778 000 000.

Asia Minor (*or* Anatolia) The westernmost part of Asia between the Black Sea and the Mediterranean Sea approximating to present-day Turkey. For much of the second millennium BC, Asia Minor was the centre of the Hittite empire. After the Hittites' collapse (12th century BC) central and W Asia Minor were dominated by Phrygia, which reached its zenith in the 8th century, when the Assyrian Empire conquered SE Asia Minor. Phrygia fell to Lydia in the 6th century but in 546 Cyrus the Great established Achaemenian control over Asia Minor. In 333 it was conquered by Alexander the Great and after his death, during the Hellenistic age, the S was contested by the Seleucids and the Ptolemies. Asia Minor came under Roman control in the 2nd and 1st centuries BC, forming part of the Roman Empire and then the Eastern Roman (subsequently Byzantine) Empire. Conquered by the Seljuq Turks in the 11th century AD and overrun by the Mongols in the 13th, Asia Minor was incorporated in the Ottoman Empire during the 14th and 15th centuries.

Asmara (*or* Asmera) 15 20N 38 49E A city in N Ethiopia, the capital of Eritrea province. The population still includes many Italians, Eritrea having been an Italian colony from 1890 until Allied occupation (1941). Industries include meat processing, distilling, and clothes manufacture. Population (1984): 275 385.

asp An aggressive European viper, *Vipera aspis*, that lives in dry habitats. About 60 cm long, it is grey-brown to coppery brown with dark bars or zigzags, grey, yellowish, or blackish underparts, and a yellow patch under the tail tip. The snout is upturned into a small spike. The asp that killed Cleopatra was probably the Egyptian cobra (*Naja haje*).

Asparagus A genus of herbaceous plants (about 300 species), with creeping underground stems (rhizomes), found throughout the Old World. *A. officinalis* is widely cultivated in temperate and subtropical regions for its young edible shoots. Several African species are ornamental: *A. plumosus*, known as **asparagus fern**, produces attractive feathery sprays of branchlets. Family: *Liliaceae*.

aspen One of several poplar trees having slender flattened leafstalks, so that the leaves tremble in the faintest breeze. The European aspen (*Populus tremula*), which grows to a height of 25 m has rounded toothed leaves. Its soft white wood is used for matches and paper pulp.

ASP The Death of Cleopatra, *a favourite subject for 19th-century engravers.*

asphalt A black highly viscous or solid hydrocarbon compound, used in road construction and the manufacture of roofing materials. It is obtained from the distillation of certain crude oils and from surface deposits (asphalt lakes), which occur naturally after the lighter fractions of a crude oil reservoir have evaporated.

asphodel A white- or yellow-flowered lily-like plant of the mostly Mediterranean genera *Asphodelus* and *Asphodeline*. In Greek mythology, the asphodel said to grow in the Elysian fields was *Asphodeline lutea*, which has yellow flowers. The asphodel of the early English and French poets was probably the daffodil. The bog asphodel (*Narthecium ossifragum*), of NW Europe, grows in swampy regions. It grows to a height of 30 cm and has a head of small yellow flowers. Family: *Liliaceae*.

Aspidistra A genus of herbaceous plants (8 species) native to E Asia. *A. elatior* is commonly grown as a hardy pot plant for its long ornamental leaves. It may produce purple bell-shaped flowers. Family: *Liliaceae*.

aspirin Acetylsalicylic acid: a drug widely used to treat mild pain, such as headache and toothache. It also relieves inflammation and is therefore helpful in the treatment of rheumatoid arthritis, and it reduces fever and can help to prevent coronary thrombosis and strokes. In some people aspirin may cause bleeding from the stomach and it is no longer used for children. *See also* analgesics.

Asquith, Herbert Henry, 1st Earl of Oxford and (1852–1928) British statesman and Liberal prime minister (1908–16). Asquith's government introduced important social reforms, including noncontributory old-age pensions (1908 budget) and the National Insurance Act (1911); it ended the veto power of the House of Lords with the 1911 Parliament Act. After the outbreak of World War I Asquith headed a Liberal-Conservative coalition government (1915–16). He remained leader of the Liberal Party until 1926. His second wife **Margot Asquith** (1865–1945) wrote an outspoken *Autobiography* (1922). His children by his first marriage included **Lady Violet Bonham-Carter, Baroness Asquith** (1887–1969),

who was president of the Liberal Party Organization (1944–45). His children by his second marriage included **Anthony Asquith** (1902–68), director of such films as *Shooting Stars* (1928), *The Winslow Boy* (1948), and *The Millionairess* (1961).

ass A small fast-running mammal belonging to the genus *Equus* (horses), native to Africa and Asia. Asses are about 200 cm long, weighing up to 250 kg, and have characteristically long ears. The Asiatic wild ass (*E. hemionus*) has a grey or tan hide, a dark bristly mane, and a dark stripe along the back. The African wild ass (*E. asinus*) is the ancestor of the domestic donkey. *See also* mule.

Assad, Hafiz al- (1928–) Syrian statesman; president (1971–). In 1966, following the coup in Syria by the radical Ba'athists, he became minister of defence. In 1970 he led a coup by the military wing of the Ba'ath party and was elected president the following year.

Assam A state in NE India, mostly in the Brahmaputra Valley beyond Bangladesh. High rainfall supports tea, Assam's economic mainstay. Rice, jute, sugar cane, and cotton are also grown. Assam produces half of India's oil, as well as coal. *History*: a flourishing region by 1000 BC, Assam received later migrants from China and Burma. Burmese invasions led Britain to assume control (1826). In World War II Assam played a strategic role in the Allied advance into Burma. Area: 78 523 sq km (30 310 sq mi). Population (1981): 19 902 826. Capital: Dispur.

Assassins (Arabic: hashish eaters) A sect of the Ismaili. In Persia and Syria in the 12th and 13th centuries they were notorious for their practice of stabbing opponents, especially Muslims. It was commonly believed that the stabbings were carried out while they were under the influence of hashish, hence their name.

Assisi 43 04N 12 37E A town in central Italy, in Umbria. It is the birthplace of St Francis of Assisi, who founded the Franciscan Order in 1209, and is the site of a Franciscan convent, which has two gothic churches containing frescoes by Giotto. Population (1989 est): 24 567.

Association football. *See* football.

associative law The mathematical rule, obeyed by addition and multiplication in ordinary arithmetic, that the order in which successive identical operations are performed does not affect the result: for addition $a + (b + c) = (a + b) + c$; for multiplication $a(bc) = (ab)c$

Assyrian Empire An ancient kingdom on the Upper Tigris (now N Iraq), where the Assyrians (named after their god Ashur) settled in about 2500 BC, forming a dependency of Babylon. Ashur-uballit I (c. 1365–c. 1330) laid the foundations of the Empire, which was extended by Tiglath-pileser I (1120–1074), who conquered the city of Babylon. A new era of aggressive expansion was initiated by Ashurnasirpal II (883–859). The Assyrian domain was extended to Syria and Palestine under Shalmaneser III (858–824) and Assyrian ascendancy reached its zenith under Tiglath-pileser III (745–727). Nineveh, the capital, fell to Media and Babylon in 612.

Astaire, Fred (Frederick Austerlitz; 1899–1987) US dancer and film star. He began his career as a music-hall dancer. His best-known films are the 1930s musicals in which he partnered Ginger Rogers. These include *Top Hat* (1935), *Follow the Fleet* (1936), and *Shall We Dance*

FRED ASTAIRE *With Ginger Rogers in the 1930s.*

(1937). His later costars included Judy Garland, Leslie Caron, and Audrey Hepburn.

astatine (At) A short-lived radioactive halogen. Its longest-lived isotope, ^{210}At, has a half-life of 8.3 hours. Small amounts exist in nature as a result of uranium and thorium decay. At no 85; at wt (210); mp 302°C; bp 337°C.

Aster A genus of perennial herbaceous plants (about 500 species), many species of which are commonly known as Michaelmas daisies. Native to N temperate regions, they are widely grown as garden plants. Usually 60–100 cm tall, they have flowers with blue, red, or white rays and a central yellow disc. *A. amellus* and *A. aeris* are common ornamental species. Family: *Compositae.*

asteroid. See minor planet.

asthma A disorder in which breathlessness and wheezing are aggravated by certain stimuli, which cause the bronchi to become constricted. Bronchial asthma may be an allergic reaction (*see* allergy), it may occur secondarily to respiratory infection, or it may be brought on by exertion, certain drugs, or strong emotion. The most common treatment is by means of bronchodilator drugs, usually in the form of aerosol inhalers; severe attacks require corticosteroid inhalers. Cardiac asthma is associated with some forms of heart disease and requires a different treatment.

astigmatism A form of aberration that can occur in mirrors and lenses (including the eye). It results when the curvature is different in two mutually perpendicular planes; rays in one plane may then be in focus while rays in the other are out of focus. It is corrected in the eye by the use of cylindrical lenses.

Astor, Nancy Witcher, Viscountess (1879–1964) British politician, who was the first woman MP to sit in the House of Commons (1919–45). An American by birth, she championed the causes of women's rights and education, representing the constituency that was formerly that of her husband **Waldorf, 2nd Viscount Astor** (1879–1952). An MP from 1910 to 1919, Astor was proprietor (1919–45) of the *Observer* newspaper.

Astrakhan 46 22N 48 04E A port in the Soviet Union, in the SE RSFSR on the River Volga. The city was an important trading centre, declining after the Revolu-

tion. Astrakhan fur, from the Karakul lamb of central Asia, was first brought to Russia by Astrakhan traders. More than half the population is employed in fishing or allied occupations. Population (1987): 509 000.

astrology The study of the positions of the heavenly bodies in relation to their presumed influence upon human affairs. Astrology originated in Babylonia and then passed to Greece, India, China, and the Islamic lands. In medieval Europe astrologers had a respected role in public and personal life. Astrology is based upon an elaborate system of hypothetical relationships: each "house" (*see* zodiac), for instance, imparts a particular character to those born under its influence and the sun, moon, and principal planets in various positions predispose people to good or ill. The two branches of astrology are "natural" (concerned mainly with observations and theory) and "judicial" (foretelling events by means of a horoscope). *See also* birthstone.

astronomer royal An eminent British astronomer appointed by the sovereign on the advice of the prime minister. Until 1971 the astronomer royal was also head of the Royal Observatory (formerly at Greenwich, then at Herstmonceux, and at Cambridge from 1990). The first holder was John Flamsteed, appointed in 1675 when the Observatory was founded. The present holder is Prof. E. Graham Smith.

astronomical unit (AU) A unit of length equal to the mean distance between the earth and the sun (1.495 × 10^{11} metres, 92.9 × 10^6 miles).

ASTRONOMY *The Isaac Newton Telescope, moved to the Canary Islands in 1979.*

astronomy The study of celestial bodies. One of the most ancient of the sciences, naked-eye astronomy flourished in China, Babylonia, Egypt, and classical Greece (*see* Aristarchus of Samos; Hipparchus; Ptolemaic system). After the decline of ancient Greek culture, interest in astronomy was the preserve of the Arabs for many centuries. European interest in the heavens, transmitted from the Arabs through Spain, reawakened in the 16th century with the work of Copernicus and Tycho Brahe, who were able to separate the science of astronomy from astrology. But it was not until 1609 that Galileo's refracting telescope enabled the sky to be investigated in any detail; in 1671 Newton devised the more effective reflecting telescope. These devices provided the means for the development of astrometry and celestial mechanics. In the 19th century, the use of spectroscopy (*see* spectrum) provided the basis for the new sciences of astrophysics and astrochemistry.

Until the 1930s all observations of the heavens were made by observing the light that passed through the atmosphere. Jansky's discovery (1932) that radio waves are emitted by celestial bodies marked the beginnings of radio astronomy.

The advent of high-altitude balloons and rockets and then artificial satellites orbiting above the atmosphere has enabled the radiation from space that is absorbed by the atmosphere—gamma rays, X-rays, ultraviolet, and most wavelengths of infrared radiation—to provide information, for example, on the birth of stars and the more violent cosmic phenomena. In addition planetary probes, such as the two Voyager craft, have greatly increased our knowledge of many members of the solar system.

astrophysics The study of the physical and chemical processes and characteristics associated with celestial objects. It is based on theories developed in astronomy, physics, and chemistry and on observations of the radiation emitted by the objects. Originally only studies at optical and then at radio and infrared wavelengths were made, but with the recent advent of rockets and artificial satellites, sources of X-rays, gamma rays, and ultraviolet radiation can also be observed. *See also* cosmology.

Asunción 25 15S 57 40W The capital of Paraguay, an important port in the S on the River Paraguay. Founded in 1536, it was for a time the centre of the Spanish settlements in the area. The National University was founded in 1890 and the Catholic University in 1960. Industries include flour milling, food processing, and textiles. Population (1984): 729 307.

Aswan (*or* Assuan; Greek name: Syene) 24 05N 32 56E A city in S Egypt, on the River Nile. Some ruins of the ancient city of Syene remain. Nearby quarries supplied granite for many Egyptian monuments. The **Aswan High Dam** and earlier **Aswan Dam** are also nearby and have stimulated growth within the city. The High Dam was begun in 1960 and financed by the Soviet Union; it was completed in 1970. It is about 5 km (3 mi) long and 100 m (328 ft) high; its reservoir, **Lake Nasser**, extends for about 560 km (350 mi) behind the dam. Since its construction the famous annual Nile floods have been controlled and water is available for irrigation and for hydroelectric power. Ancient Nubian monuments (notably the Abu Simbel and Philae temples) that were threatened with permanent flooding were moved to new sites. About 7 km (4 mi) downstream is the earlier **Aswan Dam** (completed 1902); 2 km (1.2 mi) long and 54 m (177 ft) high, this provides irrigation water. Population (1985): 182 700.

Asyut (*or* Assiut; ancient name: Lycopolis) 27 14N 31 07S The largest city in Upper Egypt, on the River Nile. It is an important commercial centre and is renowned for its handicrafts and its textile industries. Below the city the Asyut barrage provides water for irrigation. It has a university (1957). Population (1985): 274 400.

Atacama Desert (Spanish name: Desierto de Atacama) A cool arid area in N central Chile, extending for about 1100 km (700 mi) S from the Peruvian border. It consists chiefly of a series of salt basins and is one of the driest areas in the world. There are valuable deposits of copper and it is a major source of nitrates. Area: about 80 290 sq km (31 000 sq mi).

Atalanta A swift-footed huntress of Greek mythology. Hippomenes (or Meilanion), on her promise to marry any man who could outrun her, raced with her. Furnished with three of the Hesperides' golden apples by Aphrodite, which he dropped to distract her, he won the race and married her.

Atatürk, Kemal (Mustafa Kemal; 1881–1938) Turkish statesman, who was the chief founder of modern Turkey; president (1923–38). Born in Salonika, he entered the army and distinguished himself in World War I. After the war he opposed the humiliating Treaty of Versailles and as president of the provisional government organized the defeat of the Greek invasion of Asia Minor (1920). In 1922 the Ottoman sultan was deposed and Mustafa Kemal became the first president of Turkey. From then until his death he worked to make Turkey a modern secular state. He took the surname Atatürk (Father of the Turks) in 1934.

Athanasian Creed A Christian profession of faith traditionally attributed to St Athanasius (296–373 AD) but probably dating from the 5th century. Its central statements concern the doctrines of the Trinity and of the Incarnation. Once popular in the Western Churches, it is now little used.

Athelney, Isle of A small area in Somerset, near the confluence of the Rivers Tone and Parrett. It was formerly an island, isolated by marshes. Alfred the Great built a small fortification here in 878 as a base for his campaign against the Danes.

Athelstan (d. 939) King of England (925–39), succeeding his father Edward the Elder; he was crowned King of Mercia in 924. He defeated a Scottish invasion force in 937 and is also known for six extant legal codes.

Athena (*or* Pallas Athena) The virgin Greek goddess of war and of wisdom, the protectress of Athens which is named after her. Born from the head of Zeus, fully armed with a javelin, she was his favourite child. In the Trojan War she constantly aided the Greeks. She also helped Heracles in his labours and guided Perseus on his expedition against the Gorgons. She is identified with the Roman Minerva.

Athens (Modern Greek name: Athínai) 37 59N 23 42E The capital of Greece, situated on a plain in the SE of the country. It is the administrative, cultural, and economic centre of the country and adjoins its port and industrial sector, Piraeus. Athens combines the ancient and the modern, with only one or two small Byzantine and neo-Byzantine churches surviving to testify to the period between Roman times and the early 19th century. The many remains of ancient Athens are focused on the Acropolis. Crowned by the Parthenon, it also contains the Ionic Erechtheum, the Propylaea (a gateway), and the tiny temple of Athena Nike. To the NW, the recently restored Agora (market), contains the Theseum (5th century BC), probably the best-preserved ancient temple. To the N and E lies modern Athens. *History*: there is evidence of settlements dating back to the 3rd millennium BC. Athens probably enjoyed its first rise to fame under Pisistratus and his sons in the 6th century BC. Around 506 Cleisthenes established a democracy for the free men of Athens. During the following century it became the leading Greek city state, defeating the Persians with the aid of its powerful navy (*see* Greek-Persian Wars). The Long Walls, connecting the city to Piraeus, and the Parthenon date from this period. Under Pericles, it reached a peak of intellectual brilliance with the philosophy of Socrates and the drama of Aeschylus, Sophocles, and Euripides. Defeated by Sparta in the Peloponnesian War (431–404), it recovered slowly, regaining its intellectual supremacy with such figures as Plato, Aristotle, and Aristophanes. Defeated by Philip of Macedon in 338 BC, it came under the rule of Rome in the 2nd century BC. Owing to the influence of Hellenic culture on the Romans it continued to prosper and, despite being overrun by Germanic tribes in the 4th century AD, maintained its academic standing until the closure of the schools of philosophy by Justinian in 529. The city fell to the Crusaders in 1204 and was under Turkish occupation from 1456 until 1833, when it became the capital of the newly independent kingdom of Greece. Population (1981): 885 136.

atherosclerosis (*or* atheroma) Patchy thickening of the lining of arteries caused by the deposition of fatty material and fibrous tissue. This tends to obstruct the blood flow and predisposes to thrombosis, which may lead to a heart attack or a stroke. In the western world atherosclerosis is common in adults: its cause is believed to be associated with a diet high in animal fats (*see* cholesterol), cigarette smoking, and obesity.

ATHLETICS *Fatima Whitbread throwing the javelin (1986).*

athletics Sports that involve running, walking, throwing, and jumping competitions. They are divided into track and field events. At international level the track events include races over 100 m, 200 m, 400 m, 800 m, 1500 m, 5000 m, and 10 000 m; the 110 m and 400 m hurdles (*see* hurdling); the 4 × 100 and 4 × 400 m relay races; the 3000 m steeplechase; the marathon; and the 20 km walk (*see* walking). The standard field events are high jump, long jump, triple jump, pole vault, shot put, discus throw, hammer throw, and javelin throw. In addition there are the decathlon (for men), the modern pentathlon, and the pentathlon (for women). The governing body is the International Amateur Athletic Federation.

Athos, Mount 1. 40 10N 24 19E A mountain in NE Greece, at the end of Aktí, the easternmost promontory of Chalcidice. Height: 2033 m (6670 ft). **2.** An autonomous Greek Orthodox monastic republic occupying the

mountain. Area: 80 sq km (31 sq mi). Population (1971 est): 1713.

Atlanta 33 45N 84 23W A city in the USA, the capital of Georgia, situated at the foot of the Appalachian Mountains. Founded in 1837 and partly destroyed by Gen Sherman in 1864, it is now the industrial, administrative, transportation, and cultural centre of the SE USA. Population (1986): 421 910.

Atlantic, Battle of the. *See* World War II.

Atlantic Ocean The world's second largest ocean, extending between Antarctica, America, Europe, and Africa. Its major currents include the Gulf Stream crossing it W – E. Its floor is rich in minerals, oil and gas now being exploited. The Mid-Atlantic Ridge rises above sea level as islands, such as the Azores. The youngest ocean, the Atlantic was formed when the continents now surrounding it split apart 200 million years ago.

Atlantis In Greek legend, a large island civilization in the Atlantic beyond the Pillars of Hercules (Straits of Gibraltar), which, according to Plato's dialogues the *Timaeus* and *Critias*, was destroyed by earthquake. The story, transmitted to the Greeks by the Egyptians, may refer to a cataclysmic volcanic eruption (c. 1450 BC) on the island of Thera in the Cyclades N of Crete.

Atlas In Greek mythology, the brother of Prometheus and son of the Titan Iapetus and the nymph Clymene. As a punishment for his part in the revolt of the Titans against the Olympians he was forced to hold up the pillars separating heaven from earth. From the 16th century this was commonly depicted in the frontispieces of books of maps, which thus came to be called atlases.

Atlas Mountains A mountain system in NW Africa, extending generally NE from the Atlantic coast of Morocco to Tunisia. It consists of several mountain chains and plateaus and rises to 4165 m (13 664 ft) at Mount Toubkal in the Moroccan Great Atlas range.

atman (Sanskrit: breath, soul) A fundamental concept of Hinduism, signifying the individual soul or the eternal essential self. When the body dies the *atman* is continuously reincarnated until final spiritual release is achieved. In the later Upanishads, and in the Hindu philosophical schools of Samkhya and orthodox Vedanta, the function of *atman* and its relation to Brahman is the central issue.

atmosphere (meteorology) The gaseous envelope surrounding the earth or any other celestial body. The earth's atmosphere is composed of nitrogen (78.08%), oxygen (20.95%), argon (0.93%), and carbon dioxide (0.03%), together with small proportions of other gases and variable amounts of water vapour. In the lowest layer of the earth's atmosphere, the **troposphere**, air temperature decreases as height increases. The thickness of this layer varies from about 7 km (4.5 mi) to about 16 km (9.9 mi) at the equator. It is here that most meteorological phenomena occur. In the **stratosphere**, which goes up to about 50 km (31 mi), temperature is fairly constant because the sun's radiation counteracts the effect of decreasing density. Above this is the ionosphere. The outermost layer, from about 400 km (248 mi), is called the **exosphere**. From 100 km (62 mi) upwards the oxygen dissociates into atoms. There is little nitrogen above 150 km (93 mi). The atmosphere protects the earth from excessive radiation and cosmic particles and is important in maintaining the heat balance of the earth. *See also* ozone.

atmosphere (unit) A unit of pressure equal to 101 325 pascals or 760 mm of mercury.

atmospheric pressure The pressure exerted by the atmosphere. It decreases with altitude and, at ground level, varies around 760 millimetres of mercury, 101 325 pascals, or 1013.25 millibars.

atom. *See* atomic theory.

atomic bomb. *See* nuclear weapons.

atomic clock A highly accurate clock based on the frequency at which certain atoms or molecules vibrate between two states. For example, the nitrogen atom in the ammonia molecule vibrates through the plane of the three hydrogen atoms and back again with a frequency of 23 870 hertz. In the ammonia clock, a quartz-crystal oscillator feeds energy into ammonia gas at this frequency. The ammonia only absorbs energy at this frequency, enabling a feedback circuit to control the frequency of the oscillator. The caesium clock depends on the energy difference between states of the caesium nucleus in a magnetic field.

atomic energy. *See* nuclear energy.

Atomic Energy Authority A UK body established in 1954 to research into and develop nuclear energy. Its principal research establishments are situated at Harwell and Culham, both in Oxfordshire.

Atomic Energy Commission A US agency established in 1946 to control the production of nuclear weapons and atomic energy.

atomic mass unit (amu) A unit of mass equal to one-twelfth of the mass of an atom of carbon-12 ($1.660\ 33 \times 10^{-27}$ kg). Atomic weights (relative atomic masses) are based on this unit. The unit is also called the dalton (after John Dalton).

atomic number (Z) The number of protons in a nucleus of an atom. It determines the position of the element in the periodic table and, in a neutral atom, is equal to the number of electrons surrounding the nucleus. It is also known as proton number.

atomic theory The theory that an atom is the smallest particle of an element that can take part in a chemical reaction. Democritus is credited with first conceiving the idea, which was, however, vigorously attacked by Aristotle. The concept fell from favour until the early 19th century, when John Dalton used it to explain how ele-

ments combine in simple proportions. The structure of the atom was first investigated by Lord Rutherford, who discovered that it consisted of a heavy positively charged core (the nucleus) surrounded by electrons. Niels Bohr elaborated on this model (the Bohr atom) but the modern concept of the atom was not finally elucidated until the advent of Schrödinger's wave mechanics.

Almost all of the atom's mass is concentrated in the nucleus, which consists of positively charged protons and neutral neutrons of almost equal mass (the mass of the electron is only 1/1836 that of the proton). The number of electrons in a neutral atom is equal to the number of protons in the nucleus, as the charge on the proton is equal but opposite to that of the electron. The electrons can be thought of as existing in a series of shells around the nucleus, each shell corresponding to a particular energy level. The chemical behaviour of an atom is largely determined by the number of electrons in its outermost shell, as atoms are most stable when they have no partly filled shells, a state often achieved by chemical combination. *See also* particle physics; chemical bond.

atomic weight The ratio of the average mass of the atoms in a given sample to one-twelfth the mass of a carbon-12 atom. The modern, more correct, name is relative atomic mass.

atonality The use in music of all 12 notes of the scale in such a way as to avoid tonality. Atonality arose from the increasing chromaticism of the music of the late 19th century. *See also* serialism.

ATP (adenosine triphosphate) An energy-rich compound (a nucleotide) with an important role in the metabolism of living organisms. On its formation from ADP (adenosine diphosphate) in the mitochondria of cells, ATP incorporates a large amount of energy that, on release, is used by cells to manufacture proteins, carbohydrates, etc., and to provide energy for muscle contraction and other dynamic processes.

atropine An alkaloid, extracted from deadly nightshade, that acts on certain nerves of the autonomic nervous system. It is used during anaesthesia to decrease lung secretions, which lowers the risk of postoperative chest infections. It also dilates the pupil and speeds up the heart rate.

There is no simple way to illustrate an atom:

by the 19th century it was regarded as a minute solid billiard ball;

with the work of Rutherford between 1906 and 1914 and Bohr in 1913 it was depicted as a miniature solar system with a central nucleus and orbiting electron;

Sommerfeld's refinements of quantum theory in 1916 led to a model with precessing elliptical orbits and spinning electrons;

by 1926 Schrödinger's wave mechanics had been published, based on de Broglie's dual wave – particle concept of electrons. The atom is now regarded as a nucleus surrounded by a "haze" of probabilities that electrons will occur in certain positions.

ATOMIC THEORY

Atropos. *See* Fates.

Attenborough, Sir Richard (1923–) British film actor, director, and producer. A versatile character actor, he appeared in such films as *Loot* (1969) and *10 Rillington Place* (1971). As director, his films include *A Bridge Too Far* (1977), *Gandhi* (1982), *A Chorus Line* (1985), and *Cry Freedom* (1987). His brother **Sir David Attenborough** (1926–) is a naturalist and broadcaster, whose television series include *Zoo Quest* (1954), *Life on Earth* (1978), and *The Living Planet* (1983).

Attica A region of ancient E central Greece. According to Greek legend the 12 towns of Attica were united by Theseus into a single state, which was dominated by Athens by the 5th century BC.

Attila (c. 406–53) King of the Huns (434–53), known as the Scourge of God. After murdering his brother and coruler, Bleda, he extended his possessions in central Europe and attacked (441–43) the eastern frontier of the Roman Empire. In 451 he invaded Gaul and suffered his only defeat, at the battle of the Catalaunian Plains. His campaigns in Italy (452) caused much destruction. The pope paid him to spare Rome and Attila died shortly afterwards.

Attlee, Clement (Richard), 1st Earl (1883–1967) British statesman; Labour prime minister (1945–51). A barrister by profession, Attlee taught at the London School of Economics (1913–23). He was elected MP for Limehouse in 1922 and was leader of the Labour Party (1935–55) and deputy prime minister of the wartime coalition government (1942–45). As the first postwar prime minister he introduced the welfare state, nationalized major industries, and granted independence to India.

attorney general The chief law officer of the Crown in England and Wales and its representative in the courts. He is legal adviser to the government and the House of Commons, of which he is always a member and to which he is answerable, and is head of the English bar. He advises on the drafting of Acts of Parliament. With his subordinate, the director of public prosecutions, he prosecutes crimes in the sovereign's name.

aubergine A spiny herbaceous plant, *Solanum melongena*, native to S Asia and also known as eggplant. It is commonly grown in warmer regions for its fruit, a large white, yellow, or purple berry that is eaten as a vegetable. The plant grows to a height of 60–100 cm. Family: *Solanaceae*.

Aubrietia (*or* Aubrieta) A genus of trailing herbaceous perennial flowering plants (about 15 species), native to mountainous areas of E Europe and W Asia. *A. deltoidea* is commonly grown in rock gardens, bearing small purple, red, or pink flowers. Family: *Cruciferae*.

Auckland 36 55S 174 47E The largest city and port in New Zealand, on North Island. Founded in 1840, it was the capital of New Zealand until 1865. The University of Auckland was established in 1882 and there are two cathedrals (Roman Catholic and Anglican). The city is connected with the mainly residential North Shore by the Auckland Harbour Bridge (1959). Auckland is a major industrial centre with engineering, food processing, shipbuilding, and chemical industries. Population (1987): 889 200.

Auden, W(ystan) H(ugh) (1907–73) British poet. His early volumes, beginning with *Poems* (1930) and *Look, Stranger!* (1936), established him as a leading left-wing poet of the 1930s. He also wrote verse dramas in

W. H. AUDEN *Seen at Christ Church, Oxford.*

collaboration with Christopher Isherwood, with whom he went to the USA in 1939. He became a US citizen in 1946, returning to England while he was professor of poetry at Oxford (1956–61). He wrote several opera libretti, notably for Stravinsky's *The Rake's Progress* (1951).

audio frequency A frequency in the range 20 to 20 000 hertz, i.e. the range of frequencies to which the human ear is sensitive.

audiovisual education Education carried out with the help of audio (sound) or visual techniques. There are a whole range of audiovisual aids, including television, tape and video recorders, teaching machines, overhead projectors, and the long-established wallcharts and blackboards. Although audiovisual education has been used throughout history, its systematic application developed in the 20th century. Research has shown that, when properly used, it increases both the student's interest and his recall of the material presented. Since 1958 the US Congress has provided aid for educational broadcasting. In the UK, the BBC and the independent television companies run an extensive educational service. *See also* Open University.

Aughrim, Battle of (12 July, 1691) The final defeat of the main army of the former King James II of England by the army of William III in Ireland. It was the most disastrous battle in Irish history, with 7000 Jacobite dead. It is still celebrated, together with the battle of the Boyne, by Ulster Unionists on its anniversary (*see also* Orange Order).

Augsburg 48 21N 10 54E A city in S West Germany, in Bavaria at the confluence of the Rivers Wertach and Lech. It is a major industrial centre; its manufactures include textiles, chemicals, cars, aircraft, and printing machinery. Many of its historic buildings, including the 10th-century cathedral, survived the bombardment of World War II. *History*: founded by the Romans in 15 BC, it became an important banking and commercial centre in the 15th and 16th centuries. An imperial free city from 1276, it was the seat of the notable diets of 1530 (*see* Augsburg Confession) and 1555, which issued the religious compromise establishing the coexistence of Catholicism and Lutheranism, known as the **Peace of Augsburg**. Population (1986): 245 600.

Augsburg Confession The main and distinctive confession of faith of the Lutheran Churches. Drawn up in its original form by Melancthon and approved by Luther, it was presented to the imperial diet that Emperor Charles V had summoned at Augsburg in 1530 to judge Luther's controversial preaching.

Augustine of Canterbury, St (died c. 604) Italian churchman, the first Archbishop of Canterbury. Chosen by Pope Gregory I to evangelize England in 596, he converted Ethelbert I of Kent and successfully established Canterbury as the primatial see. Feast day: 26 or 27 May.

Augustine of Hippo, St (354–430 AD) North African theologian; Father and Doctor of the Church, born at Tagaste. After studying at Carthage, he became a Manichaean, but under the influence of St Ambrose, Bishop of Milan, he converted to Christianity in 386. On his return to Africa, he lived as a monk until he was ordained at Hippo in 391. He became Bishop of Hippo in 396 and died there during a Vandal siege. His *The City of God*, a defence of Christianity in 22 books, and his spiritual autobiography, *The Confessions*, are the most important books written by an early Father of the Church. **Augustinians** are members of religious orders that follow the Rule of St Augustine, especially the orders of the Augustinian (*or* Austin) Canons, founded in the 11th century, and the Augustinian Hermits (*or* Austin Friars), founded in the 13th century. Feast day: 28 Aug.

Augustus (*or* Octavian; 63 BC–14 AD) The first Roman emperor, who restored the greatness of the Roman world following the disintegration of the Republic. Born Gaius Octavius, he was the great-nephew and adopted son of Julius Caesar. After Caesar's assassination in 44, Augustus (now Gaius Julius Caesar Octavianus; *or* Octavian) came to an agreement with Mark Antony and in 43 they formed the second Triumvirate with Lepidus. Lepidus was forced to retire in 36 and Augustus' relations with Mark Antony failed to withstand Antony's abandonment of his wife Octavia (Augustus' sister) for Cleopatra. Antony's defeat at Actium in 31 allowed Augustus to establish his personal supremacy at the head of an autocratic government known as the principate. In 27 he was proclaimed Augustus (sacred).
With the military assistance of Agrippa, and later of his own stepson Tiberius, he secured and then expanded the Empire. In 4 AD he named Tiberius his heir. Augustus was deified after his death.

auk A stout-bodied seabird belonging to a family (*Alcidae*; 22 species) occurring in the N hemisphere and having a black and white plumage and short pointed wings. The family includes puffins, razorbills, guillemots, and the extinct flightless great auk (*Pinguinus impennis*). Order: *Charadriiformes* (gulls, plovers, etc.).

aurora A display of diffuse changing coloured light seen high in the earth's atmosphere, often taking the form of red or green streamers. Aurorae occur predominantly in polar regions when energetic charged particles from the sun become trapped in the earth's magnetic field. The rapidly moving particles interact with atoms and molecules in the upper atmosphere and cause them to emit light.

Auschwitz. *See* Oświęcim.

Austen, Jane (1775–1817) British novelist. She was the daughter of a clergyman and lived an outwardly uneventful life with her family in the south of England, settling in Chawton in Hampshire in 1809. Her six major

JANE AUSTEN *The only portrait of her from life, which was done by her sister Cassandra.*

novels are *Sense and Sensibility* (1811), *Pride and Prejudice* (1813), *Mansfield Park* (1814), *Emma* (1815–16), *Northanger Abbey* (1818), and *Persuasion* (1818).

austenite A form of steel that exists when the metal is heated to about 1000°C, in which the carbon exists as a solid solution in the iron. Austenitic steels retain this structure at room temperature because of the presence of an alloying element, such as manganese. Austenite is nonmagnetic and has a high ductility. Named after Sir William C. Roberts-Austen (1843–1902).

Austerlitz, Battle of (2 December, 1805) The battle in which Napoleon's 68 000–strong army outmanoeuvred and defeated almost 90 000 Russians and Austrians led by Mikhail Kutuzov (1745–1813). It took place near Austerlitz (now Slavkov u Brna, Czechoslovakia). Napoleon's great victory forced the Austrians to make peace with France by the Treaty of Pressburg and the Russian army to return to Russia.

Australia, Commonwealth of A country in the S Pacific, comprising the whole of the smallest continent and the island of Tasmania to the SE. External territories include Norfolk Island, Christmas Island, the Cocos (Keeling) Islands, and the Australian Antarctic Territory. Much of the country has a hot dry climate and a large part of the vast central plains are desert or semidesert. The most fertile areas are in the E, along the coastal plains, and in the extreme SW. The Great Barrier Reef lies off the tropical NE coast and the highest mountains, rising over 2000 m (7000 ft), are in the Great Dividing Range, which runs parallel to the E coast. The Murray River and its tributaries in the SE form the main river system. The inhabitants are very largely of European, especially British, origin but there are about 100 000 Aborigines and people of mixed race living in the interior. Since World War II the population has increased dramatically, largely as a result of immigration. *Economy*: agriculture continues to make a substantial contribution to the economy, the main crops being cereals, sugar cane, and fruit. Livestock, particularly sheep and cattle, is also important. Since the 1960s, however, there has been marked growth in iron and steel products. Mining is now of vital importance, especially the extraction of coal, iron, bauxite, uranium, copper, lead, and zinc; about 70% of oil for home consumption is now produced in Australia. The main exports are wool, meat, cereals, sugar, iron ore, and nonferrous ores. *History*: the country was inhabited by the Aborigines, immigrants from SE Asia, for approximately 20 000 years before the arrival of the Europeans, beginning with the Portuguese in the 16th century and the Dutch in the early 17th century. In 1770 Captain Cook claimed the fertile E coast for Britain, which was first used as a penal colony. After the introduction of the merino sheep, however, civilian settlements were established further to the N and W towards the interior, eventually reaching the far side of the Blue Mountains in 1813. Colonies were developed in Tasmania, Western Australia, Victoria, South Australia, and Queensland. By 1829 the whole continent was a British dependency. The discovery of gold in Victoria in 1851 attracted large numbers of immigrants and from this period the colonies struggled for greater independence. In 1901 the six colonies were federated to form the Commonwealth, becoming an independent dominion of the British Empire. In 1911 the Australian Capital Territory (the site for the federal capital) and the Northern Territory were added to the Commonwealth. Since World War II closer economic ties have been developed with Japan. In 1978 the Northern Territory achieved self-government although the federal government retained control over uranium. Australia is a member of the British Commonwealth. Constitutional links with the UK were ended in 1986. Prime minister: Robert Hawke. Official language: English. Official currency: Australian dollar of 100 cents. Area: 7 686 884 sq km (2 967 283 sq mi). Population (1988 est): 16 500 000. Capital: Canberra. Main port: Sydney.

Australian Alps A mountain range in SE Australia. Part of the Great Dividing Range, it extends from E Victoria into SE New South Wales and contains the Snowy Mountains and Mount Kosciusko, Australia's highest mountain. It is a popular winter-sports area.

Australian Antarctic Territory The area of Antarctica claimed by Australia. It includes all the land lying S of latitude 60°S and between longitudes 45°E and 160°E, excluding Terre Adélie. Several research stations are sited here.

Australian Capital Territory An administrative division of SE Australia. It was created in 1911 from the Limestone Plains region of New South Wales as a site for Canberra, the capital of Australia. Jervis Bay was transferred to the territory in 1915 for development as a seaport. It is the site of the Australian Academy of Science, the Royal Military College, and the Royal Australian Naval College (at Jervis Bay). Area: 2432 sq km (939 sq mi). Population (1985): 253 085.

Australian Rules. *See* football.

Australopithecus A genus of fossil manlike higher primates of the late Pliocene and Pleistocene eras of S and E Africa. Although small in brain size, their cranial and skeletal structures were more like those of modern man than of apes. They walked erect, were vegetarians, and used primitive tools. They are now thought not to have been the direct ancestors of modern man, having diverged from the *Homo* evolutionary line some 4 million years ago. There were several species, including *A. afarensis* and *A. robustus*, which probably coexisted with early forms of man. Significant fossil finds of *Australopithecus* have been made by Louis and Richard Leakey at Olduvai and Lake Turkana. *See* Homo.

AUSTRIA *The city of Salzburg, the birthplace of Mozart.*

Austria, Republic of (German name: Österreich) A country in central Europe, on the N side of the Alps. A large part of the country is mountainous but the E area consists of lower hills and plains, with the River Danube flowing through the NE. Most of the inhabitants are German but there are minorities of Croats, Slovenes, and others. *Economy*: although agriculture and forestry are important, there is considerable heavy industry, based particularly on iron and steel. Hydroelectric power is a valuable source of energy. Main exports include iron and steel, machinery, paper and paper products, wood, and textiles. *History*: Austria has a long history going back to the Celtic settlements of the early Iron Age. The area was part of the Roman Empire from 15 BC until the 5th century AD when it was overrun by Germanic tribes. In succeeding centuries it was occupied in turn by Slavs and Magyars from whom it was taken in 955 by the Holy Roman Emperor Otto I. He conferred it upon Leopold of Babenberg, who founded the first Austrian dynasty. In 1282 the Habsburgs acquired Austria, which was to become the core of their vast empire. In 1526 Bohemia and Hungary were united under the Austrian Crown. The Austrian Empire continued to hold a predominant position in Europe until the middle of the 19th century when its power was lessened by successive defeats, especially in the Austro-Prussian War. In 1867 the Habsburgs formed the Dual Monarchy of Austria-Hungary, under the Emperor Francis Joseph. During his reign there was considerable unrest, especially among the Slavs; the assassination of the Archduke Francis Ferdinand by Serbian nationalists in 1914 was the immediate cause of World War I. In 1918 Austria became a republic. In spite of efforts on the part of the chancellor Schuschnigg to maintain independence, it was annexed by Nazi Germany in 1938 (*see* Anschluss). After World War II it was occupied jointly by the Allies, regaining its independence as a republic in 1955. Chancellor Fred Sinowatz was succeeded by Franz Vranitsky in 1986. In 1989 Austria applied to join the EC. President: Kurt Waldheim. Official language: German. Currency: schilling of 100 groschen. Area: 85 853 sq km (32 375 sq mi). Population (1986): 7 564 000. Capital: Vienna.

Austria-Hungary, Dual Monarchy of The Habsburg monarchy from 1867 to 1918, established in response to the militant demands of Hungarian nationalism. The empire of Austria and the kingdom of Hungary each had its own laws, parliament, and ministries but were united by the monarch (Emperors Francis Joseph and then Charles), minister for foreign affairs and minister for war, and by the biannual meetings of delegations of representatives of each parliament. The Dual Monarchy disappeared in 1918 with the proclamation of an Austrian republic.

Austrian Succession, War of the (1740–48) The war between Austria and Prussia, in which Britain supported Austria and France and Spain were allied to Prussia. It was brought about by the disputed succession of Maria Theresa to the Austrian lands. Hostilities were begun by Frederick the Great of Prussia, who annexed the Austrian province of Silesia in 1740. The war was ended by the Treaty of Aix-la-Chapelle, at which Prussia obtained the greater share of Silesia.

Austro-Prussian War (*or* Seven Weeks' War; 1866) A war between German states led respectively by Austria and Prussia. The Prussian victory was an important landmark in Bismarck's strategy for uniting Germany under Prussian leadership.

Authorized Version. *See* King James Version.

autism A rare and severe mental illness that starts in early childhood. Autistic children do not form normal personal relationships but they can become emotionally attached to things. They do not communicate normally, often cannot form abstract concepts, and they are very upset by tiny changes in their familiar surroundings. Most, but not all, are mentally retarded. Autism can be caused by brain damage and can also be inherited. Lengthy specialized education is usually necessary for autistic children.

auto-da-fé (Portuguese: act of faith) The public ceremony at which persons convicted of crimes by the Inquisition in Portugal, Spain, and their colonies were sentenced. Punishment of victims, including the burning of heretics, was the responsibility of the secular authorities. The first *auto-da-fé* was held in Seville in 1481 and the last, in Mexico in 1815.

autogiro An aircraft with large horizontal freely rotating blades to obtain lift. It differs from the helicopter in that a propeller provides forward motion, which in turn causes the rotation of the unmotorized horizontal blades.

autoimmunity A condition in which the body produces antibodies (called autoantibodies) that damage or destroy its own tissues. This produces symptoms of various **autoimmune diseases**, the majority of which are poorly understood. Rheumatoid arthritis is caused by the production of autoantibodies against joint tissue; the disease can be diagnosed by the detection of these antibodies in the serum. A more general production of autoantibodies causes systemic lupus erythematosis, which can affect most tissues in the body.

automation The use of electronic devices controlled by computer in mechanical processes that would otherwise be controlled by human operators. It has made considerable impact on production engineering in such fields as steel and chemical manufacture. Telecommunications (automatic telephone exchanges), transport (navigation, railway signals), and mining also employ automated systems.

autopsy (necropsy *or* postmortem) The dissection and examination of a dead body. An autopsy is performed when the cause of death is uncertain: it may provide further information on a poorly understood disease or evidence of criminal involvement. Except for sudden death or death due to obscure causes, permission for autopsy must be granted by the relatives.

autumnal equinox. *See* equinox.

autumn crocus A herbaceous perennial European plant, *Colchicum autumnale*, also called meadow saffron. It has narrow strap-shaped leaves, up to 30 cm long, and a single purple-blue crocus-like flower, which appears in autumn after the leaves have died. The drug colchicine, extracted from the corms, is used in the treatment of gout and in genetic research. Some plants of the genus are cultivated for ornament. Family: *Liliaceae*. *Compare* Crocus.

Auvergne A planning region and former province in S central France. Its name derives from the Averni, who strongly resisted Roman control of the area. Crossed by the volcanic Auvergne Mountains that rise to over 1800 m (6000 ft), it has many mineral springs and some level fertile districts. It is predominantly agricultural and is noted for the growing of wheat and grapes and the rearing of cattle; cheese and wine are also produced. Area: 25 988 sq km (10 032 sq mi). Population (1986 est): 1 334 400.

auxin An organic substance, produced within a plant, that stimulates, inhibits, or modifies growth of the plant. Auxins are sometimes known as plant hormones. The main auxin is indoleacetic acid (IAA). Auxins are responsible for a variety of effects, for example shoot curvature, leaf fall, and fruit growth. Synthetic auxins, such as 2,4-dichlorophenoxyacetic acid (2,4-D), are used as weedkillers for broad-leaved weeds.

Avalon. *See* Arthurian legend.

AVEBURY   *Part of a stone circle.*

Avebury 51 27N 1 51W A village in S England, in Wiltshire, on the site of a large complex of Neolithic and early Bronze Age stone circles, banks, and ditches. The principal circle, with its ditch and outer bank, encloses over 12 hectares (30 acres); within it are two smaller ones. Nearby is Silbury Hill.

avens A perennial herbaceous plant of the genus *Geum* (about 40 species), native to temperate and Arctic regions. Most species rarely exceed 60 cm in height. Their flowers, 2–3 cm long, are white, yellow, orange, or red, either solitary or in clusters. *G. coccineum* is a common ornamental. Family: *Rosaceae*.

Averroes (Ibn Rushd; 1126–98) Muslim philosopher and a judge in Córdoba and Seville. Averroes' main works were his commentaries on Aristotle, which greatly influenced the philosophy of medieval Christianity. He defended philosophy as the highest form of enquiry, holding that faith and reason are separate ways of arriving at the truth.

aversion therapy A form of conditioning used to treat some kinds of undesirable behaviour, such as sexual deviation, alcoholism, and drug addiction. An unpleasant stimulus (e.g. an electric shock) is associated with a stimulus related to the problem behaviour (e.g. the taste of alcohol). *See also* behaviour therapy.

Avesta The sacred scriptures of Zoroastrianism. Written in Old Iranian, the five books of the *Avesta* contain prayers (probably by Zoroaster himself) hymns, ritual and liturgical instruction, and the main body of Zoroastrian law. Its surviving form dates from about the 6th century AD.

Avignon 43 56N 4 48E A town in SE France, the capital of the Vaucluse department on the River Rhône. The papacy, under French control, was removed to Avignon (1309–77; *see* Avignon papacy) and there were subsequently rival popes at Rome and Avignon until 1417 (*see* Great Schism). Famous landmarks include the 14th-century papal palace and the 12th-century bridge, of which only four arches remain. A popular tourist centre, Avignon trades in wine and has chemical, soap, and cement industries. Population (1983): 88 650.

Avignon papacy (1309–77) The period during which the popes resided in Avignon (France) rather than Rome. The papal court was established in Avignon by Clement V, who, like his six successors in Avignon, was French. English and German criticism of French dominance over the papacy eventually forced its return to Rome under Gregory XI. Shortly afterwards the division in the Church known as the Great Schism occurred, largely in response to the increased power acquired by the cardinals during the Avignon papacy (*see also* antipope).

avocado A tree, *Persea americana*, up to 18 m tall, native to Mexico and Central America but now extensively cultivated in Florida, California, and South Africa for its fruit. These fruits—**avocado pears**—may reach a weight of 2 kg: they have a green to dark-purple skin, a fatty flesh rich in fat, protein, and vitamins A and B, and a single hard seed.

avocet A wading bird of the genus *Recurvirostra*, having long slender legs and a long thin upcurved bill used to skim the surface of mud or water in search of small invertebrates. The Eurasian avocet (*R. avosetta*), 50 cm long, has a black-and-white plumage and is protected in Britain. Family: *Recurvirostridae*; order: *Charadriiformes* (gulls, plovers, etc.).

Avogadro, Amedeo, Conte di Quaregna e Ceretto (1776–1856) Italian physicist, who became professor of physics at the University of Turin. He developed Gay-Lussac's hypothesis that equal volumes of gases contain equal numbers of particles, establishing the difference between atoms and molecules. Because he made this vital distinction the theory is now known as **Avogadro's hypothesis**. His name is also commemorated in the **Avogadro number** (*or* the Avogadro constant), the number of molecules in one mole of substance (it has the value

$6.022\,52 \times 10^{23}$ mol^{-1}). Avogadro's work was not acknowledged until Cannizzaro brought it to public notice in 1854.

Avon A county of SW England, bordering on the Severn estuary. It was formed in 1974 from parts of NE Somerset and SW Gloucestershire. It consists mainly of low-lying basin, rising to the Cotswold Hills in the NE and the Mendip Hills in the S. The River Avon flows W into the Severn estuary. Dairy farming is the chief agricultural activity. Industry, including engineering, printing, paper making, packaging, and aircraft manufacture, is concentrated in the Bristol area. Avonmouth is a major port. There is a thriving tourist industry, notably at Weston-super-Mare and Bath. Area: 1337 sq km (516 sq mi). Population (1988 est): 954 300. Administrative centre: Bristol.

Avon, (Robert) Anthony Eden, 1st Earl of (1897–1977) British statesman; Conservative prime minister (1955–57). Foreign secretary from 1935 to 1938, he resigned in opposition to Neville Chamberlain's policy of appeasement. At the beginning of World War II he was secretary for war and then (1940–45; 1951–55) foreign secretary. He succeeded Churchill as prime minister and following Nasser's nationalization (1956) of the Suez Canal and an Israeli attack on Egypt, joined France in an offensive against Egypt. Egypt retained control of Suez and Eden was much criticized: he resigned shortly afterwards. He became Earl of Avon in 1961.

Avon, River The name of several rivers in the UK, including: **1.** A river in central England, flowing SW from Northamptonshire to the River Severn at Tewkesbury. Length: 154 km (96 mi). **2.** A river in SW England, flowing S and W from Gloucestershire to the Severn estuary at Avonmouth. Length: 120 km (75 mi). **3.** A river in S England, flowing S from Wiltshire to the English Channel. Length: 96 km (60 mi).

Axis Powers The coalition of Germany, Italy, and Japan that opposed the Allied Powers in World War II. It originated in agreements going back to 1936 and it culminated in the Tripartite Pact (1940).

axolotl A salamander, *Ambystoma mexicanum*, occurring in Mexican lakes. It reaches a length of 25 cm, has a long tail and weak limbs, and is typically dark brown. Axolotls retain their larval characteristics permanently, reproducing in this state, although under certain conditions they may develop into adults. Family: *Ambystomatidae*.

Ayatollah Ruholla Khomeini. *See* Khomeini, Ayatollah Ruholla.

Ayckbourn, Alan (1939–) British dramatist. After working in provincial repertory theatre, he gained his first London success with *Relatively Speaking* (1967). His later comedies include *Absurd Person Singular* (1973), the trilogy *The Norman Conquests* (1974), *Season's Greetings* (1984), and *Man of the Moment* (1988), all characterized by detailed observation of middle-class life. He directs a repertory theatre in Scarborough.

Ayer, Sir Alfred (Jules) (1910–89) British philosopher; Wykeham Professor of Logic at Oxford (1959–78). Ayer's major contribution to British philosophy was his bringing to England the teachings of the Vienna Circle, in particular the doctrine of logical positivism, which he expounded in *Language, Truth and Logic* (1936). His later books include *The Foundations of*

Empirical Knowledge (1940), *The Problem of Knowledge* (1956), and an autobiography *Part of My Life* (1977).

AYERS ROCK

Ayers Rock The largest monolith in the world, in Australia, in SW Northern Territory. It consists of a vast red rock, 335 m (1099 ft) high and 10 km (6.25 mi) in circumference. Its colour varies according to atmospheric changes and the position of the sun.

Aylesbury 51 50N 0 50W A market town in S central England, the administrative centre for Buckinghamshire. Lying in an agricultural area it has food-processing industries as well as printing, engineering, and various light industries. Population (1985 est): 50 000.

Aylward, Gladys (1903–70) British missionary. From 1930 she worked as an independent missionary in China. Her life story was the subject of a popular film, *The Inn of the Sixth Happiness* (1958), in which she was played by Ingrid Bergman.

Ayrshire cattle A breed of red or brown and white cattle originating in Ayrshire, SW Scotland. A hardy breed, Ayrshires are primarily producers of good quality milk, used especially in cheese making. Many herds have been replaced by the higher yielding Friesians.

Ayub Khan, Mohammad (1907–74) Pakistani statesman; president (1958–69). After a distinguished military career he became defence minister in 1954. Following President Iskander Mirza's coup d'état in 1958 Ayub Khan became chief martial law administrator and then ousted Mirza to become president. He negotiated (1966) the ceasefire agreement with Shastri following the India-Pakistan war of 1965. He was forced to resign following civil unrest in East Pakistan.

azalea A deciduous shrub of the genus *Rhododendron*. (Most horticulturalists prefer to restrict the term rhododendron to the large evergreen species.) Growing to a height of up to 2 m, azaleas are native to North America and S Asia but are widely cultivated as ornamentals. The attractive flowers are funnel-shaped (about 6 cm in diameter) and of various colours. Family: *Ericaceae*.

Azerbaidzhan Soviet Socialist Republic A constituent republic in the S Soviet Union on the Caspian Sea. Most of the population are Shiite Muslims. Oil and gas are the most important industries. *History*: the region was acquired by Russia from Persia in the early 19th century, proclaimed its independence in 1918, but subsequently formed part of the Transcaucasian Soviet Federated Socialist Republic; it became a separate republic in 1936. In the late 1980s there were riots over Armenian claims to Nagorno-Karabakh and demands for easier access to Iran. Area: 86 600 sq km (33 430 sq mi). Population (1987 est): 6 800 000. Capital: Baku.

azimuth. *See* altitude.

Azores (Portuguese name: Açôres) 38 30N 28 00W Three groups of volcanic islands in the N Atlantic Ocean, in Portugal. The chief islands include São Miguel, Terceira, Faial, and Flores. Settled by the Portuguese in the 15th century, they were previously, uninhabited. Naval fighting between the English and Spanish took place here in the 16th and 17th centuries. The site of US air bases, they produce fruit, tobacco, and wine. Area: 2300 sq km (888 sq mi). Population (1986 est): 253 500. Capital: Ponta Delgada, on São Miguel.

AZTECS *The calendar stone in the National Museum of Anthropology, Mexico City.*

Aztecs A Nahuatl-speaking people who ruled an empire in central and S Mexico before their defeat by Hernán Cortés in the 16th century. They had an advanced, elaborate, and rich civilization centred on their capital Tenochtitlán and other cities. They constructed large palaces and temples in which they worshipped many gods, especially Huitzilopochtli to whom they sacrificed human victims, captives of warfare, by ripping out their hearts while they still lived. Authority and influence were vested in a class of chiefs and priests and in the kings, the last of whom was Montezuma.

B

Ba'ath Party An Arab political party, influential in many Middle Eastern countries, notably Syria and Iraq, that urges the creation of a united socialist Arab nation. The Ba'athists supported the formation of the United Arab Republic (1958–61) and rose to power in Iraq and Syria in 1963.

Babbage, Charles (1792–1871) British mathematician and inventor. In an attempt to produce more accurate mathematical tables, Babbage conceived the idea of a mechanical computer that could store information. Although he never completed the machine, it was the forerunner of the modern computer.

babbler A small songbird belonging to a family (*Timaliidae*; 280 species) occurring in Old World regions, particularly in SE Asia. Babblers have short rounded wings, a long tail, strong legs and bill, and a noisy babbling cry. The plumage is often brightly coloured, although some species are plain brown. Babblers live in wooded regions, searching the undergrowth in groups for insects and berries.

Babel, Isaac Emmanullovich (1894–1941) Russian short-story writer. Of Jewish descent, he served in the imperial army, but fought for the Bolsheviks in 1917. His *Odessa Tales* were published in 1916 in a journal edited by Gorki. *Red Cavalry* (1926) was a series of sketches based on his experience in the war against Poland. He died in a Siberian prison camp, a victim of Stalin's purges, but was posthumously rehabilitated in the 1950s.

Babi faith A religion founded in 1844 by Mirza 'Ali Mohammed (1819–50), who became known as the Bab (the Gate). It was the immediate precursor of the Baha'i faith.

baboon A large Old World monkey belonging to the genus *Papio* (5 species), of African and Asian grassland. Baboons are 95–185 cm long including the tail (45–70 cm) and have a shaggy mane and a long doglike face with large teeth. They feed on insects, small vertebrates, and vegetable matter. They live in well-organized troops containing 40–150 individuals arranged in a social hierarchy according to age and sex.

Babylon The capital of ancient Babylonia, strategically positioned on the River Euphrates S of modern Baghdad. Its first period of prominence was about 2150 to 1740 BC, under a dynasty of which Hammurabi was the most illustrious member. Subsequently, rising Assyrian power threatened Babylonian independence, though some Babylonians, such as Nebuchadnezzar I (reigned c. 1146–1123), temporarily reversed the trend. Sacked in 689 BC by the king of Assyria, Sennacherib (d. 681 BC), Babylon was rebuilt from 625 BC onwards, especially during the reign (c. 605–562) of Nebuchadnezzar II. The remains of this city that were excavated (1899–1917) by the German archaeologist Robert Koldewey (1855–1925). In 539 BC Babylon surrendered to Cyrus the Great of Persia (d. 529 BC); by 275 BC it was virtually depopulated. *See also* Hanging Gardens; ziggurat.

Babylonia The area of Mesopotamia on the alluvial plain on the lower reaches of the River Euphrates, which was controlled by ancient Babylon. Before about 2000 BC approximately the same area was known as Sumer, of which Ur was the capital.

BABYLON *A boundary stone dating back to the 10th century BC (British Museum).*

Bacchanalia The Roman form of the Hellenistic mystery rites in honour of Bacchus (*see* Dionysus). The cult reached Rome from S Italy in the 2nd century BC. Originally involving only women, Bacchic worship included ecstatic rituals and secret orgies. In 186 BC a decree of the Senate prohibited Bacchanalia in Rome.

Bacchus. *See* Dionysus.

Bach, Johann Sebastian (1685–1750) German composer and keyboard player, the greatest member of a large musical family. He became a chorister in Lüneburg and in 1703 a violinist at the Weimar court, later becoming organist there. In 1707 he married his cousin Maria Barbara Bach (1684–1720); after her death he married Anna Magdalena Wilcken (1701–60). He became kapellmeister at the court of Prince Leopold of Anhalt at Köthen in 1717 and finally cantor of St Thomas' Church, Leipzig, in 1723. Among his greatest works are the *St John Passion* (1723), the *St Matthew Passion* (1729), and the *Mass in B minor* (1733–38), as well as over 200 cantatas. His compositions for orchestra include violin and harpsichord concertos and the *Brandenburg Concertos* (1721). For the harpsichord and clavichord he composed a collection of 48 preludes and fugues entitled the *Well-Tempered Clavier* (Part I, 1722; Part II, 1744) and the *Goldberg Variations* (1742). Bach's music did not become widely known until Mendelssohn revived it.

Of Bach's 20 children, 3 sons became famous musicians. His eldest son **Wilhelm Friedemann Bach** (1710–84) studied in Leipzig and became church organist in Dresden (1733–46) and subsequently in Halle (1746–64). He ended his life in poverty, leaving cantatas, concertos, and symphonies.

His third son **Karl Philipp Emanuel Bach** (1714–88) became musician to Frederick the Great in Berlin and subsequently director of the principal church in Hamburg in succession to Telemann. He developed a new monophonic style of composition in his symphonies, concertos, and keyboard music that became the basis of the classical style.

J. S. Bach's 11th son **Johann Christian Bach** (1735–82), called the English (or London) Bach, studied in Berlin and after holding posts in Italy became music master to the British royal family. He composed 13 operas, as well as concertos, church music, and piano pieces.

bacillus Any rod-shaped bacterium, specifically a bacteria of the genus *Bacillus*: spore-forming species including parasites of plants and animals. *B. anthracis* was first shown to cause anthrax in livestock by Robert Koch (1843–1910).

backgammon A board game for two players that was known in ancient Mesopotamia, Greece, and Rome and in medieval England (as "the tables"). Each player has 15 pieces, which are moved round the 24 chevrons (points) marked on the board, the number of points moved being indicated by the throws of two dice. From their starting positions the players move in opposite directions. Each tries to bring all his pieces into the last quarter (his home board), after which he can remove them from the board Simultaneously he must block his opponent's moves. A chevron is occupied (point is made) when a player has two or more pieces on it, i.e. his opponent cannot land on it. A single piece on a point is a blot, i.e. vulnerable to the opponent's taking it and forcing it to travel round the board again.

background radiation Low-intensity radiation naturally present on the earth. It results either from the bombardment of the earth by cosmic rays or from naturally occurring radioactive substances in the earth's crust.

backswimmer A water bug, belonging to the worldwide family *Notonectidae* (nearly 200 species), that swims on its back, using a pair of oarlike legs for propulsion. Backswimmers can fly but are normally found in fresh water, preying voraciously on insects, tadpoles, and small fish. They must return to the surface periodically to replenish their air store.

Bacon, Francis (1909–   ) British painter, born in Dublin of English parentage. Self-taught, he was assured a place in British art with his *Three Studies* (of figures for the base of a *Crucifixion*). Another of his well-known paintings is *Study after Velázquez* (1951), a version of Velázquez's portrait of pope Innocent X.

Bacon, Francis, 1st Baron Verulam, Viscount St Albans (1561–1626) English lawyer and philosopher. He was called to the Bar in 1582 and became an MP in 1584. Under James I (reigned 1603–25) Bacon became attorney general (1613) and Lord Chancellor (1618). In 1621, however, he was found guilty of bribery and corruption, fined £40,000, and banished from office.

In 1597 he published his first group of *Essays*; further such discourses appeared in 1625. *The Advancement of Learning* (1605) presented a new classification of sciences and was expanded in the *De augmentis scientiarum* of 1623. In *Novum organum scientiarum* (1620) he advocated the scientific method of induction. His other works include a *History of Henry VII* (1622) and the *New Atlantis* (1626), which describes his ideal state.

Bacon, Roger (c. 1214–c. 1292) English monk, scholar, and scientist, called Doctor Mirabilis for his diverse skills and learning. In three books written for Pope Clement IV he attempted to systematize the current state of knowledge; other works prophesied aeroplanes, microscopes, steam engines, and telescopes; he also detected errors in the Julian calendar and has been credited with the invention of gunpowder and of the magnifying glass.

bacteria Microscopic single-celled organisms found wherever life is possible. Generally 0.0001–0.005 mm long, they may be spherical (coccus), rodlike (*see* bacillus), or spiral-shaped (spirillum) and often occur in chains or clusters of cells. True bacteria have a rigid cell wall, which may be surrounded by a slimy capsule, and they often have long whiplike flagella for locomotion and short hairlike pili used in a form of sexual reproduction. A few bacteria can grow on simple inorganic substrates using carbon dioxide from the atmosphere to manufacture their own nutrients, but the majority require a source of organic carbon and other nutrients for growth. Some bacteria can reproduce every 15 minutes, leading to rapid population growth.

The most important role of bacteria is in decomposing dead plant and animal tissues and releasing their constituents to the soil (*see* carbon cycle). Nitrogen-fixing bacteria in the soil or sea convert atmospheric nitrogen gas to nitrites and nitrates, which can then be used by plants (*see* nitrogen cycle). Cheese making and fermentation reactions depend on bacteria. Bacteria also play an important part in animal digestion, especially in ruminants. However, certain (pathogenic) species may cause disease while others, such as *Salmonella*, can cause food poisoning.

bacteriophage (*or* phage) A virus that infects a bacterium. 25–800 nanometres in size, phages may be spherical, filamentous, or tadpole-shaped with a head and tail. They consist of a protein coat surrounding a core of nucleic acid (either DNA or RNA) that is inserted into the bacterium. The viral genes then use the protein-synthesis apparatus of the bacterium to produce new phages, which are released from the cell, usually causing its destruction.

Baden-Powell, Robert Stephenson Smyth, 1st Baron (1857–1941) British general and founder of the Boy Scouts (*see* Scout Association). He achieved fame through his defence of Mafeking in the Boer War (1899–1900). Utilizing the experience of character training he had gained overseas, he founded the Boy Scouts in 1908 and, with his sister Agnes, the Girl Guides in 1910.

Baden-Württemberg A *Land* in SW West Germany, bordering on France and Switzerland, formed by an amalgamation of three former *Länder* (1952). Area: 35 751 sq km (13 800 sq mi). Population (1986): 9 295 100. Capital: Stuttgart.

Bader, Sir Douglas (1910–82) British fighter pilot. After losing his legs in a flying accident (1931), Bader argued himself back into the RAF at the start of World War II. Becoming a national hero, he was finally shot down and imprisoned by the Germans, who only prevented his escape by depriving him of his artificial legs. In 1976 he was knighted for his work for the disabled.

badger A nocturnal burrowing mammal of the weasel family (*Mustelidae*). The largest of the eight species is the gregarious Eurasian badger (*Meles meles*), about 90 cm long, with short strong legs, long coarse greyish hair on the body, and a black and white striped head. It lives in a complex of burrows (a set) and feeds on insects, rodents, worms, berries, etc.

Bad Godesberg. *See* Godesberg.

BADMINTON *The dimensions of the court. The top of the net at the centre is 5 ft (1.5 m) above the floor.*

badminton An indoor court game for two or four players, played with rackets and a shuttlecock of nylon or cork and feathers. It originated in about 1870, probably from battledore and shuttlecock and may have first been played in the park of Badminton House, in the village of Badminton (Avon). It is a volleying game (the shuttles do not bounce) and points are scored only by the serving side. If the serving side fails to make a good return the service changes (in doubles games both partners serve before their opponents). A game is usually played to 15 points (women's singles go to 11 points).

Baekeland, Leo Hendrik (1863–1944) US industrial chemist, born in Belgium. He invented Bakelite (*see* urea-formaldehyde resins), the first synthetic thermosetting plastic, while searching for a synthetic substitute for shellac.

Baez, Joan (1941–   ) US folksinger, whose performance at the 1959 Newport Festival led to a series of successful recordings of folksongs and later of contemporary protest songs. An active pacifist, she opposed the Vietnam War.

Baffin Island The largest island of the Canadian Arctic, in Franklin district lying N of Hudson Strait, named after William Baffin (c. 1584–1622). It is separated from Greenland by a Strait forming **Baffin Bay** (in the N) and Davis Strait. Mountainous with many glaciers and snowfields, its sparse population is concentrated in Frobisher Bay. Area: 476 068 sq km (183 810 sq mi).

Baghdad 33 20N 44 26E The capital of Iraq, on the River Tigris near the centre of the country. Built by the caliph Mansur in the 8th century, it was a centre of commerce, learning, and religion until sacked by the Mongols in 1258. It became the capital of independent Iraq (1927) and has three universities (1947, 1957, and 1963). Population (1982 est): 4 038 430.

Baghdad Pact A treaty between Turkey, Iraq, Iran, Pakistan, and the UK. Signed in 1955, its goals were military, economic, and social cooperation in the Middle East. When Iraq withdrew from it in 1959, its headquarters moved to Ankara from Baghdad and it was renamed the Central Treaty Organization.

bagpipes A reed-pipe instrument of ancient origin, found in many countries. Air is forced into a windbag either by the mouth (Scottish bagpipes) or by a bellows (Northumbrian pipes). By pressing the bag under his arm the player pushes air into the sounding pipes, which consist of one to three drones (each sounding a single note) and a chanter pipe. Bagpipes are regarded as the national instrument of Scotland, having been introduced to the British Isles in the 13th century.

Baha'i faith A religion founded in Persia in 1863 by Mirza Husain 'Ali (1817–92), who was known as Baha' Allah (Glory of God). He proclaimed himself to be the Promised One whose coming was foretold by the Bab (*see* Babi faith). His eldest son and then his great-grandson led the Baha'is after his death until 1957. Since 1963 the faith has been governed by the Universal House of Justice, a council at Haifa, Israel, elected by national spiritual assemblies. The basic tenet of the faith is that God reveals himself to man through prophets who appear at various stages in history and the most recent of these is Baha' Allah. The faith has now spread to the West despite persecution in Iran.

Bahamas, Commonwealth of the A state consisting of about 700 islands and innumerable cays in the West Indies, off the SE coast of Florida. The principal islands, which are mainly low lying, include New Providence (with the capital Nassau), Grand Bahama, Abaco, Eleuthera, Andros, and Watling Island (San Salvador). The majority of the population is of African descent. *Economy*: tourism accounts for over 50% of revenue and employment. Efforts are now being made to develop agriculture and fisheries; foreign investment is encouraged by the tax position, 90% of companies being foreign-owned. Main exports include cement, petroleum products, chemicals, and fish. *History*: in 1492 Columbus made his first landing in the W hemisphere on the island of San Salvador. The first European occupation comprised an English religious settlement in the mid-17th century, and the islands became a British crown colony in 1717. In 1973 it attained full independence within the Commonwealth. Prime minister: Lynden Oscar Pindling (1930–   ). Official language: English. Official currency: Bahamian dollar of 100 cents. Area: 13 864 sq km (5353 sq mi). Population (1986): 235 000. Capital and main port: Nassau.

Bahia. *See* Salvador.

Bahrain, State of An independent sheikdom in the Arabian Gulf, occupying a low-lying archipelago between Saudi Arabia and the Qatar Peninsula. The two main islands, Bahrain and Al-Muharraq, are connected by a causeway and there are also plans for a causeway to Saudi Arabia. The inhabitants are mainly Arabs. *Economy*: almost totally dependent upon oil. A large refinery processes local oil and much larger amounts coming from Saudi Arabia by pipeline. Efforts are being made to develop other industry with some success. *History*: the islands were under Portuguese rule from 1521 until 1602, and during parts of the 17th century Iran had control, eventually being expelled by the Khalifa family, who have ruled the area for most of the time since. It was a British protected state from 1861 until 1971 when full independence was declared by the emir, Sheik Isa ibn Sulman al-Khalifa (1933–   ). Bahrain became a member of OPEC in 1970. Official language: Arabic; English is also widely spoken. Official religion: Islam. Official currency: Bahrain dinar of 1000 fils. Area: 660 sq km (255 sq mi). Population (1987): 416 275. Capital and main port: Manama.

bail The release by a court of an imprisoned person, usually while awaiting trial, into the keeping of people who agree to ensure his reappearance at a particular date and time. If these people, called "sureties," then fail to produce him, they forfeit whatever sum of money the court has set for bail. The person bailed must also stand as surety for himself; if thought trustworthy, he may be bailed without other sureties, "in his own recognizance."

Bainbridge, Beryl (1934–) British novelist and playwright. Born in Liverpool, she has written such novels as *The Dressmaker* (1973), *The Bottle Factory Outing* (1974), *Injury Time* (1977), and *Filthy Lucre* (1986). Her plays include *Somewhere More Central* (1981).

JOHN LOGIE BAIRD *The inventor of television.*

Baird, John Logie (1888–1946) British electrical engineer, who invented an early television system. In 1924 he first succeeded in transmitting the outline of shapes, although his 240-line system was not adopted by the BBC. Baird also worked on radar and fibre optics.

Baker, Kenneth (1935–) British Conservative politician; secretary of state for the environment (1985–86) and for education and science (1986–89). In 1989 he became chairman of the Conservative party.

Bakhtaran (name until 1987: Kermanshar) 34 19N 47 04E A town in W Iran, with a largely Kurdish population. Population (1986): 565 544.

Bakhtyari An Islamic tribe of W Iran of some 400 000 members speaking the Luri dialect of Persian. About one-third are still nomadic herdsman living in tents. They migrate 150 miles from their winter pastures on the plains to the summer pastures in the mountains.

baking powder A mixture, usually of sodium bicarbonate and tartaric acid or cream of tartar, used in baking. It generates carbon dioxide on heating or wetting, thus making the dough rise.

Baku 40 22N 49 53E A port in the S Soviet Union, the capital of Azerbaidzhan SSR on the Caspian Sea. Its ancient buildings include mosques and a 17th-century palace. It is the oldest centre of Soviet oil production. Population (1987): 1 741 000.

Bala, Lake (Welsh name: Llyn Tegid) The largest natural lake in Wales, in E Gwynedd. The town of Bala lies at its N end. Length: 6 km (4 mi).

Balaclava, Battle of (25 October, 1854) An indecisive battle between Russian and British-Turkish forces in the Crimean War. It was made famous by Tennyson's poem "Charge of the Light Brigade", notorious for the heavy British casualties caused by misunderstanding between Lord Raglan, the British commander in chief, and Lord Lucan (1800–88), the cavalry commander. The courageous Light Brigade charged Russian artillery in a narrow valley and of its 673 men, 113 were killed.

balalaika A Russian plucked instrument of the guitar family, having a long fretted fingerboard, a triangular body, and three wire strings that are plucked with a plectrum. Small versions are held like a guitar and the larger ones balanced on the floor like a double bass.

balance A sensitive device for comparing two masses, consisting of a beam pivoted at its centre (usually on an agate knife edge) with pans hanging from each of its ends. The material of unknown mass is placed in one pan and standard weights are placed in the other. A pointer indicates when the beam is horizontal and the whole device is enclosed in a glass case to avoid draughts and temperature changes. A standard balance will weigh to the nearest 0.0001 g, while extremely sensitive **microbalances** can be used to weigh objects with a mass of only 1 microgram.

balance of payments The difference between a country's income and its expenditure abroad. The current account records the country's balance-of-trade earnings or deficit on visible goods and invisible earnings on such items as insurance, transport, tourism, and some kinds of government spending. The capital account records all long- and short-term capital flows. If the sum of the current and capital accounts shows a deficit there will be a net loss of foreign exchange.

balance of power The principle seeking to ensure that no nation or group of nations becomes too dominant. Practised by Greek city states, the principle was adopted in Europe in the alliance system of 15th-century Italy and by the Congress of Vienna at the start of the 19th century. In the 20th century the League of Nations and the UN have both tried to establish international harmony, but the concept has been largely replaced by the nuclear deterrent.

balance of trade The difference in money between the value of a country's imports and its exports. Together with the invisibles account and capital transfers it makes up the balance of payments. The balance of trade can be in deficit without necessarily meaning that the balance of payments will also be in deficit.

Balanchine, George (Georgy Melitonovich Balanchivadze; 1904–83) US ballet dancer and choreographer, born in Russia. He worked for Diaghilev's Ballets Russes in Europe from 1924 and went to the USA in 1933, becoming artistic director of the New York City Ballet. His ballets include *Firebird* (1950) and *Don Quixote* (1965).

Balaton, Lake A lake in W Hungary, the largest in central Europe. There are vineyards and holiday resorts on its shore and its outlet is a canal leading to a tributary of the River Danube. Area: 598 sq km (231 sq mi).

bald eagle A large sea eagle, *Haliaetus leucocephalus*, also called the American eagle; it is the national emblem of the USA and an endangered species. It is dark brown with a white head and tail and has a prominent curved beak and unfeathered legs. See p. 66.

Baldwin, James Arthur (1924–87) US Black novelist, essayist, and dramatist. His first novel, *Go Tell It on* the *Mountain* (1953), is based on his experience of poverty and religion in Harlem, New York City, where he was born. He lived in Paris from 1948 to 1957, when he returned to the USA as an active civil-rights campaigner. His works include novels, such as *Giovanni's Room* (1956) and *Just Above My Head* (1979), two plays, and collections of essays.

BALD EAGLE

Baldwin of Bewdley, Stanley, 1st Earl (1867–1947) British statesman, who was Conservative prime minister (1923–24, 1924–29, 1935–37), when he dealt with the General Strike (1926) and Edward VIII's abdication (1936). Baldwin was criticized for condoning Italy's conquest of Ethiopia and his reluctance to rearm in the face of Germany's military build-up.

Balearic Islands An archipelago in the W Mediterranean Sea comprising a Spanish province. It includes the chief islands of Majorca, Minorca, Ibiza, and Formentera, together with several islets. The islands were conquered by Aragon from the Moors in the 14th century. Area: 5014 sq km (1936 sq mi). Population (1982): 669 101. Capital: Palma, on Majorca.

Balfour Declaration (1917) The decision of the British Government, made known in a letter of 2 Nov from the British foreign secretary, Arthur Balfour (1848–1930), to Lionel, Baron Rothschild (1868–1937), the chairman of the British Zionist Federation, to support the establishment of a national Jewish home in Palestine. Arab aspirations in Palestine, however, prevented the British Government from fulfilling the promise of the Declaration, which was abandoned in 1939.

Bali An Indonesian island off E Java. Mountainous and volcanic, it has southern fertile plains that produce chiefly rice. *History*: Hindu since the 7th century AD, Bali resisted the 16th–17th century spread of Islam through Indonesia. Dutch rule began in 1908. In the 1965–67 Indonesian purge of communists 40 000 people were killed. Area: 5558 sq km (2146 sq mi). Population (1980): 2 469 930. Chief town: Denpasar.

Balkan Mountains (Bulgarian name: Stara Planina) A mountain range extending 500 km (311 mi) E–W for the entire width of central Bulgaria. It rises to 2376 m (7795 ft) at Botev Peak.

Balkans An area in SE Europe consisting of present-day Greece, Albania, Yugoslavia, Bulgaria, part of Romania, and the European part of Turkey. Part of the Roman empire from the 2nd century BC and of the Eastern Roman (Byzantine) Empire from the 5th century AD, the Balkans were ruled by the Ottoman Turks from the 15th to the 19th century, when independence was granted (*see also* Balkan Wars). All the Balkan states, except Greece, became communist after World War II.

Balkan Wars (1912–13) In the first Balkan War (1912–13) the Balkan League (Bulgaria, Serbia, Greece, and Montenegro) defeated Turkey. In the concluding Treaty of London, Turkey lost all its European possessions except E Thrace. In the second Balkan War (1913) the victors fought over their acquisitions in Macedonia, from most of which Bulgaria was excluded by the Treaty of Bucharest; Turkey regained Thrace.

Ballesteros, Severiano (1957–) Spanish golfer. His first major win was the Dutch Open Championship (1976). Subsequent victories included three British Open Championships (1979, 1984, and 1988), and the Barcelona Open Championship (1985).

ballet A dramatic art in which dancing and mime, accompanied by music, combine to tell a story or evoke a mood. Ballet originated in the formal dances of French court entertainments, notably under Louis XIV. In the 18th century ballet established itself in the public theatre but still as an adjunct to opera or other forms of drama. Dancing on the tips of the toes (*sur les pointes*) was introduced early in the 19th century, which saw the heyday of romantic ballet. Modern ballet arose in the early 20th century when Fokine and Diaghilev (*see also* Ballets Russes) combined the polished technique of the imperial Russian dancers with the naturalism advocated by the American Isadora Duncan. Since World War II innovative choreographers have created new ballets inspired by folk dance, jazz, and even gymnastics.

Ballets Russes A Russian ballet company (1909–29) founded in Paris by Diaghilev. It gave the West its first opportunity to see Russian imperial dancers and fostered the most avantgarde talents of the period, greatly influencing the subsequent development of ballet. Its choreographers included Fokine, Massine, Balanchine, and Nijinsky, who was also one of its principal dancers. Ravel and Stravinsky composed music for several of its ballets.

Balliol, John (c. 1250–1314) King of the Scots (1292–96), chosen by Edward I of England, arbitrator in the contest for the throne. In 1295 he rebelled against English domination and was defeated by Edward at Dunbar (1296) and deposed. His son **Edward Balliol** (d. 1364) became King of the Scots in 1332, after invading Scotland, supported by Edward III of England. An uprising against Balliol was put down by Edward (1333), who retained the Scottish lowlands, but internal opposition forced Balliol's abdication in 1356.

ballistic missiles Rocket-powered nuclear missiles that are propelled to desired altitudes and then follow an unpowered trajectory. Their accuracy is calculated as a probability (e.g. 45–60%) of landing within a stated radius about their target (Circular Error of Probability). Intercontinental ballistic missiles (ICBMs) are capable of reaching any point on the surface of the earth. Both the USA and the Soviet Union possess large numbers of these, some of which (MIRVs—multiple independently targeted re-entry vehicles) have up to ten separate warheads. *See also* antiballistic missiles.

ball lightning   A luminous moving sphere, several centimetres in diameter, occurring just above the ground on rare occasions during thunderstorms. It hisses, has a distinct odour, and may be either red, orange, or yellow. It lasts for only a few seconds and then either dies away or explodes. The phenomenon is not fully understood but one theory suggests that it consists of plasma.

BALLOONS   *A hot-air balloon.*

balloons   Lighter-than-air craft, consisting of a bag of gas that displaces a volume of air of greater mass than the total mass of the balloon and its contents. The first successful balloon flight, man's first aerial voyage, was made in 1783 by the Montgolfier brothers' hot-air balloon; it flew 9 km across Paris. Two years later a hydrogen balloon designed by J. A. C. Charles, flew across the Channel. The use of balloons in war began with Napoleon's observation balloons in 1794, after which they continued to play a sporadic but largely ineffectual part, until their extensive use in both World Wars in the form of barrage balloons. The sport of **ballooning** has enjoyed a revival in recent years, using a hot-air balloon carrying its own propane air heater. The height record for a manned balloon is 30 480 m (D. Simons, US Air Force, 1957). The first crossing of the Atlantic Ocean by helium balloon was achieved in 1978.

balm   A fragrant-leaved herbaceous plant of, or related to, the genus *Melissa*, native to the Old World. Lemon balm, or balm gentle (*M. officinalis*), is widely grown in temperate regions and used for flavouring foods and in perfumes. The European bastard balm (*Melittis melissophylum*) is more strongly scented. Others species include bee balm (*Monarda didyma*) and horse balm (*Collinsonia canadensis*). Family: *Labiatae*.

Balmoral Castle   The principal country residence of the British monarch in Scotland, situated in SW Aberdeenshire by the River Dee. It was bought by the royal family in 1848 and rebuilt in the 1850s.

balsa   An evergreen tree, *Ochroma pyramidale*, native to Central and South America, also called corkwood. About 12 m tall, it is the source of an extremely light pale-coloured wood, which is widely used for corks, canoes, floats, etc. Family: *Bombacaceae*.

balsam   An aromatic resinous substance derived from the Central American leguminous tree *Myroxylon peneirae*, grown in El Salvador. It is used in medicine and perfumes.

Baltic Sea   A section of the Atlantic Ocean in N Europe, bounded by Denmark, Norway, Sweden, Finland, the Soviet Union, Poland, East and West Germany. To the W, it leads into the Little Belt, the Great Belt, and the Sound, and to the E, the Gulfs of Bothnia, Finland, and Riga. It has very low salinity since it receives rivers draining almost one-fifth of Europe and it can freeze sufficiently to hinder navigation.

Baltic states   The territories on the SE coast of the Baltic Sea that comprise the present-day Latvian, Lithuanian, and Estonian SSRs of the Soviet Union, which between World Wars I and II were independent states.

Baltimore   39 25N 76 40W A city in the USA, in Maryland at the mouth of the Patapsco River. Established in 1729, it was named after the first Baron Baltimore who founded Maryland. It was the starting point of the USA's first railway (1827). Baltimore contains a number of universities; in the 1980s considerable rebuilding in the port area has revitalized the city. Industries include steel, food processing, oil refining, and chemicals. Population (1986): 752 800.

Baluchistan   A province in W Pakistan, on the Arabian Sea and the Iranian and Afghani borders. Mostly rough arid highlands, it is inhabited by pastoral Pathans, Baluchs, and other peoples. The NW deserts are practically uninhabited but the coastal plain and E lowlands support cereals and herbs. *History*: on trade routes from India to the Middle East, Baluchistan has flourished since ancient times. It usually enjoyed autonomy until Britain won control (19th century). In 1947 it became part of Pakistan. Area: 347 190 sq km (134 050 sq mi). Population (1985 est): 4 908 000. Capital: Quetta.

Balzac, Honoré de   (1799–1850) French novelist. A lawyer's clerk, he wrote popular novels under pseudonyms. In 1828, bankruptcy forced him to turn to writing; *Les Chouans* (1829) was his first successful novel, and in the next 20 years he added over 40 novels to the cycle *La Comédie humaine*. In these novels, which included *Eugénie Grandet* (1833), *Le Père Goriot* (1834), and *La Cousine Bette* (1846), he developed new techniques of realism.

Bamako   12 40N 7 59W The capital of Mali, a port in the S on the River Niger. A centre of Muslim learning under the medieval Mali Empire, it had dwindled to a small village by the end of the 19th century. It became the capital of the French Sudan in 1905. Population (1981): 620 000.

bamboo   A treelike plant of the tribe *Bambuseae*, native to tropical and subtropical regions, particularly SE Asia. From an underground stem (rhizome) arise hollow woody jointed stems, which may reach a height of 40 m in some species. These are used for building, etc., while the young shoots are eaten. Family: *Gramineae* (grasses).

Banaba. *See* Ocean Island.

banana A palmlike plant of the Old World tropical genus *Musa*, especially *M. paradisiaca sapientum*. The "trunk," up to 9 m high, is composed of the overlapping bases of the leaves, which are often 3 m or more long. The tip of the flowering stem bears male flowers; clusters of female flowers, further up the stem, develop into seedless fruits, up to 30 cm long, without being fertilized. (All cultivated bananas are sterile hybrids: the plants are propagated from suckers arising from the underground rhizome.) Varieties called plantains are cooked and eaten when still green in Africa and the Caribbean. Family: *Musaceae*.

Bandar Seri Begawan (former name: Brunei Town) 4 56N 114 58E The capital of Brunei, a port in the NE near the mouth of the Brunei River. Population (1984): 54 000.

bandicoot A ratlike marsupial mammal of a family (*Peramelidae*; 20 species) occurring in Australia (including Tasmania) and New Guinea. About the size of rabbits, bandicoots are mainly carnivorous, eating insects, worms, and grubs.

Bandung 6 57S 107 34E A city in Indonesia, in W Java. Its chief industries are chemicals, quinine, plastics, metal processing, and textiles. It has two universities and a nuclear research centre (1964). Population (1981): 1 400 000.

Bangalore 12 58N 77 35E A city in S India, the capital of Karnataka. Founded in the 16th century, it fell to the British in 1791. Its modern industries include aircraft assembly, machine tools, and electronics. Population (1983): 2 914 000.

Bangkok (Thai name: Krung Threp) 13 44N 100 30E The capital and main port of Thailand, in the SW near the mouth of the River Chao Phraya. It became a royal city and the capital in 1782. Distinctive features of the city are its canal system and the many Buddhist temples. It is the centre of most of the country's industry and commerce and it has eight universities. Population (1986): 5 446 708.

Bangladesh, People's Republic of A country in the Indian subcontinent in the delta of the Rivers Ganges and Brahmaputra. *Economy*: Its large population, mostly Bengali, is largely occupied in agriculture, rice being by far the most important crop. Bangladesh produces 50% of the world's raw jute, its main export. Fishing, is also important. Most industry is now nationalized. *History*: the area formed part of the kingdom of Bengal, and its conquest by the Afghans in the 12th century led to the growth of the Islamic religion. It was part of British India from 1857 until 1947 when it became a province of Pakistan (East Pakistan). Discontent under a government centred in West Pakistan led to the outbreak of civil war in 1971, Indian forces coming to the aid of the Bengalis. In 1972 East Pakistan achieved independence as Bangladesh and Sheikh Mujibur Rahman (1920–75) became prime minster. In 1974 floods and famine led to political unrest and terrorism and in 1975 Mujib assumed absolute power before being assassinated in a military coup. Gen Ziaur Rahman assumed power in 1976 and was elected president in 1978 in the first presidential election; he was assassinated in 1981. The military, led by Lt Gen Hussain Mohammed Ershad, took power in March, 1982, and in 1983 Ershad became

BANGKOK *Chakri Building in the Grand Palace.*

president. There were further severe floods in 1987 and 1988. Bangladesh became a member of the Commonwealth in 1972. Official language: Bengali. Official religion: Islam. Official currency: taka of 100 paisa. Area: 142 797 sq km (55 126 sq mi). Population (1987): 104 100 000. Capital: Dhaka. Main port: Chittagong.

Bangui 4 23N 19 20E The capital of the Central African Republic, a port in the SW on the Ubangi River. Founded in 1889, the port handles goods for both the Central African Republic and Chad; its main exports are cotton and coffee. Population (1984): 473 817.

Banjul (name until 1973: Bathurst) 13 20N 16 38W The capital of The Gambia, a port in the W at the mouth of the River Gambia, founded by the British in 1816. Population (1983): 44 188.

Bank of England The British central bank, which was nationalized in 1946. It was originally incorporated in 1694, being set up by a group of London merchants to lend money to William III. Since the mid-19th century it has been the only bank authorized to issue banknotes. The Bank is responsible for financing the national debt and holding the country's gold reserves.

bankruptcy The legal process by which the property of a person who cannot pay his debts is distributed among his creditors. In England bankruptcy was originally a branch of the criminal law aimed at preventing fraudulent traders evading their creditors, but since the reign of Queen Anne the law has also sought to protect the bankrupt by ending his obligation to repay most of his past debts. The Bankruptcy Act (1914) and the Insolvency Acts (1976, 1986) stipulate the circumstances in which a person may be made bankrupt, what portion of his property is to be distributed, and the creditors who are to be paid in priority to others. Liquidation is the equivalent process applicable to a company.

Bannister, Sir Roger (Gilbert) (1929–) British doctor and middle-distance runner, who on 6 May, 1954, was the first man to run a mile in under 4 minutes (3 minutes 59.4 seconds).

Bannockburn 56 06N 3 55W A village in Scotland, in the Central Region. 1.5 km (1 mi) NW is Scotland's most famous battlefield, where in 1314 Robert the

Bruce, King of the Scots, routed the English under Edward II, who had come to relieve the besieged Stirling Castle. Population (1981): 6068.

Banting, Sir Frederick Grant (1891–1941) Canadian physiologist, who, with C. H. Best, discovered a technique for the successful isolation of the hormone insulin from pancreatic tissue in 1921, enabling diabetes to be treated. Banting was awarded a Nobel Prize (1923).

Bantu A large subgroup of African languages of the Niger-Congo group spoken over the whole of the S half of Africa by about 60 million people. It includes Zulu, Xhosa, and Kongo; perhaps the most widely known representative is Swahili, the language of Tanzania and lingua franca of E Africa.

BANTU HOMELANDS   *The areas designated as Black African territories in South Africa are dispersed over the E and N parts of the Republic.*

Bantu Homelands (*or* Bantustans) The areas of South Africa designated for the Black populations, comprising just over 13% of the land area. Acts of parliament in 1913 and 1936 controlled the extent of African lands and prohibited Blacks from holding land in White areas. Limited self-government was to be granted to these areas; the Transkei was the first to receive this (1963); it was granted full independence in 1976. Bantustan policy has been opposed by African leaders (in particular Chief Buthelezi) and many of the territories have resisted self-government, regarding it as a poor substitute for majority rule in South Africa.

banyan A tropical Asian tree, *Ficus benghalensis*, related to the fig and reaching a height of 30 m. Supporting aerial roots, which grow down to penetrate the soil, subsequently give rise to thorny branches of their own. Family: *Moraceae*.

baobab A tropical African tree, *Adansonia digitata*, with a tapering conical trunk (the base of which may exceed 10 m in diameter) reaching a height of 18 m and bearing branches at its apex. The fruits contain an edible pulp surrounded by a tough woody capsule and the bark yields a fibre of local importance. Family: *Bombacaceae*.

baptism A ceremony of initiation, occurring in many religions, involving the use of water as a symbol of purification from sin. In the Christian Church, it is a sacrament performed in the name of the Father, the Son, and the Holy Spirit. Both the Baptists and the modern descendants of the Anabaptists practise adult baptism, but most other Churches prefer infant baptism.

Baptists Protestant Christians who baptize, by immersion, only those old enough consciously to accept the Christian faith. "General Baptist" Churches, owed their origin in 1612 to John Smyth (c. 1554–1612) and Thomas Helwys (c. 1550–c. 1616), while "Particular Baptist" Churches, founded in 1633 by Calvinists, believed that salvation was only for a particular few. Both movements merged into the Baptist Union in 1891. The first Baptist Church in America was established at Providence, Rhode Island, by Roger Williams in 1639.

Baqqarah A cattle-herding Arab people of Chad and the Sudan. As a result of intermarriage with other local peoples they have dark skins and speak a distinct dialect of Arabic. They migrate seasonally between northern wet-season grazing lands and southern dry-season river areas.

bar A unit of pressure equal to 10^5 pascals (0.987 atmosphere). The commonly used unit is the millibar (one-thousandth of a bar).

Barbados An island state in the West Indies, E of the Windward Islands. Most of the population is of African descent. *Economy*: sugar cane is the main crop, and tourism is important. The discovery of offshore oil and natural gas has assisted the growth of small industries. *History*: a British colony from 1627 until 1966, it became independent within the Commonwealth. Prime minister: Erskine Sandiford (1937–   ). Official language: English. Official currency: Barbados dollar of 100 cents. Area: 430 sq km (166 sq mi). Population (1987 est): 256 000. Capital and main port: Bridgetown.

Barbary A region in N Africa stretching from Egypt to the Atlantic Ocean that is named after the Berbers. In antiquity it consisted of Mauritania, Numidia, Africa, Propria, and Cyrenaica. It was successively conquered by the Romans, Vandals, Arabs, Turks, Spaniards, French, and Italians. Between the 16th and 18th centuries, Barbary was notorious for its pirates, who caused havoc in the Mediterranean.

Barbary ape A large monkey, *Macaca sylvana*, also called magot, the only macaque found in N Africa. Barbary apes are tailless and roam in bands over the forest floor, feeding on seeds, leaves, insects, etc.

barbel A long slender freshwater fish, belonging to the genus *Barbus*, that is related to carp and occurs in clear fresh waters of Asia, Africa, and Europe. It has four fleshy threadlike appendages (barbels) near its mouth, which detect prey while exploring the river bed. *B. barbus* of Europe is usually 30–50 cm long.

Barber, Samuel (1910–81) US composer. Two of his works, the opera *Vanessa* (1958) and the piano concerto

(1963), won Pulitzer Prizes. His output includes chamber music, choral works, symphonies, and concertos. His best-known work is the *Adagio for Strings*, an arrangement of the slow movement of his string quartet (1936).

Barbirolli, Sir John (1899–1970) British conductor of Franco-Italian parents. Originally a cellist he subsequently became conductor of several major orchestras in Britain and the USA. From 1949 until his death he was principal conductor of the Hallé Orchestra, Manchester.

barbiturates A class of drugs that act by depressing the activity of the brain. Short-acting barbiturates, such as thiopentone, are used to induce anaesthesia. Medium-acting barbiturates, such as pentobarbitone, are used as sleeping tablets. Small doses of long-acting barbiturates, such as phenobarbitone, are used for day-time sedation and to control epilepsy. As barbiturates are habit-forming their use is now severely limited.

BARENBOIM *Conducting the Orchestre de Paris.*

Barcelona 41 25N 2 10E A city in NE Spain, in Catalonia on the Mediterranean Sea. Manufactures include locomotives, aircraft, textiles, and electrical equipment. The focus of Catalan art and literature, it has many educational establishments including the University founded in 1430. *History*: founded by the Carthaginians, it was taken by the Moors in 713 AD and by Charlemagne in 801 AD. In 1137 Catalonia and Aragón united and Barcelona became the capital, rivalling Genoa and Venice as a leading European port. During the 19th century it became important through its cotton industry. It was the seat of the Catalan autonomous government and later of the Republican government, during the Spanish Civil War (1936–39). In 1939 Barcelona fell to Gen Franco. The 1992 Olympics are to be held here. Population (1981): 1 754 900.

Bardeen, John (1908–) US physicist, who shared the 1956 Nobel Prize for his part in the invention of the transistor (with W. B. Shockley and W. H. Brattain) while working at the Bell Telephone Laboratories in 1948. He also shared the 1972 Nobel Prize for his work on the theory of superconductivity (with L. N. Cooper and J. R. Schrieffer).

Bardot, Brigitte (1934–) French film actress. Her films include *And God Created Woman* (1956), *Vie privée* (1961), *Viva Maria* (1965), and *Shalako* (1968). She became probably the best-known sex symbol of the 1960s.

Barebones Parliament The assembly, also known as the parliament of saints, called by Oliver Cromwell in July, 1653. It consisted mainly of merchants and lesser gentry, "godly men" nominated by the congregations, and was named after one of them, Praisegod Barebone (c. 1596–1679).

Barenboim, Daniel (1942–) Israeli pianist and conductor, who studied in Salzburg, Paris, and Rome. He made his debut in London in 1955. In 1967 he married the cellist **Jacqueline du Pré** (1945–87), with whom he gave recitals. Barenboim conducted the Orchestre de Paris from 1975 to 1989, and then became music director of the Chicago Symphony Orchestra.

Barents Sea A section of the Arctic Ocean between Eurasia and Svalbard. It covers part of the Eurasian continental shelf and is rich in fish. It is named after the Dutch navigator Willem Barents (1550–97).

baritone A deep adult male singing voice, lower than tenor and higher than bass. Range: G at the bottom of the bass stave to G two octaves above.

barium (Ba) A silvery reactive metal that resembles calcium in its behaviour. It was discovered in 1808 by Sir Humphry Davy and occurs naturally as barytes ($BaSO_4$) and witherite ($BaCO_3$). The sulphate is used as a white pigment in paint and, because of its opacity to X-rays, is used in X-ray diagnosis. All soluble barium compounds are toxic, the carbonate being used as rat poison. At no 56; at wt 137.34; mp 725°C.

bark The dead outer layer of the stems and roots of woody plants, which protects the inner tissues. Antiseptic deposits, such as tannins, give the colour. Bark may include layers of insulating cork, which is responsible for the characteristic ridges and patterns on some tree trunks. Small breathing pores (called lenticels) in the bark are conspicuous in many of the smooth-barked trees. Bark is a source of cinnamon, quinine, and various other products.

bark beetle A hard cylindrical beetle, also called an engraver beetle, belonging to a family (*Scolytidae*; 7000 species) of wood borers. It is usually less than 6 mm long, coloured red-brown or black, and causes considerable damage to trees. It burrows underneath the bark to lay eggs that develop into burrowing larvae: the elaborate patterns of tunnels produced are generally characteristic of the species. Certain species also transmit diseases (*see* elm bark beetle) and can be serious economic pests.

Barkly Tableland An area of Australia, extending SE of the Gulf of Carpentaria, in Northern Territory, into Queensland. It consists of undulating uplands on which beef cattle are raised. Area: about 130 000 sq km (50 000 sq mi).

Bar Kokhba (Simeon bar Kosiba; d. 135 AD) Jewish freedom fighter. In 132 he launched a revolt against Roman rule and attempted to set up an independent Jewish state. He was hailed as Messiah by some but was killed when his last stronghold, Betar, fell.

barley A cereal grass of the genus *Hordeum*, especially *H. vulgare*, which produces its grain in four rows; *H. distichon* (two-rowed barley); and *H. hexadistichon* (six-rowed barley). Over 165 million tonnes of grain are harvested annually. It is used in the brewing industry, as an animal feed, and to produce pearl barley.

Bar Mitzvah (Hebrew: son of the commandment) The ceremony marking the initiation of a Jewish boy into the adult community at the age of 13.

Barnabas, St In the New Testament (Acts), a Christian Apostle of the 1st century. After going with St Paul to evangelize Cyprus (his birthplace), he clashed with him and they parted company. He is regarded as the founder of the Cypriot Church. Feast day: 11 June.

barnacle A marine crustacean belonging to the subclass *Cirripedia* (1000 species). Some members of the group are parasitic, but the typical (nonparasitic) barnacles live attached to rocks, ships, etc., and filter food particles from the water with long feathery appendages, which protrude from the calcareous shell. Goose barnacles (e.g. *Lepas anatifera*) are attached by means of a stalk; others, including the acorn barnacle (*Balanus*), are unstalked. Barnacles are hermaphrodite; their larvae are free-swimming, but later settle and become fixed to a surface by means of a cement-like substance secreted by their antennae.

Barnard, Christiaan Neethling (1922–) South African surgeon, who (in 1967 at the Groote Schuur Hospital in Cape Town) performed the world's first successful heart transplant operation. He retired in 1983.

Barnardo, Thomas John (1845–1905) British doctor and philanthropist. In 1867 Barnardo founded the first of his famous homes at Stepney, London, to care for destitute children. Over a hundred homes exist in the UK, with others in Australia and New Zealand.

barn owl An owl belonging to a family (*Tytonidae*; 9 species) with a worldwide distribution. Barn owls have heart-shaped faces, long feathered legs, and usually a reddish plumage with pale underparts. The common barn owl (*Tyto alba*), 30–45 cm long, nests in old barns and hunts for small rodents.

Barnsley 53 34N 1 28W A town in N England, in South Yorkshire on the River Dearne. Principally a coalmining centre, Barnsley's other industries include glass manufacture, engineering, etc. It has a large mining and technical college. Population (1981): 73 646.

Barnum, Phineas Taylor (1810–91) US showman. His presentation of natural curiosities from 1842 attracted unprecedented crowds. His circus merged with that of J. A. Bailey (1847–1906) to become the Barnum and Bailey Circus in 1881.

Baroda. *See* Vadodara.

barometer An instrument for measuring atmospheric pressure. In the mercury barometer, atmospheric pressure forces mercury from a reservoir into a vertical evacuated glass tube marked with a scale. The height of the mercury column is directly proportional to the atmospheric pressure. In the aneroid barometer, variations in the atmospheric pressure on the lid of an evacuated metal box cause a pointer to move round a dial. The aneroid barometer is less sensitive than the mercury barometer but it is smaller and more convenient to use.

Barons' Wars 1. (1215–17) The civil war between King John of England and his barons. John's failure to honour the Magna Carta led the barons to offer the English Crown to the future Louis VIII of France, who invaded England. John's death and the reissue of Magna Carta (1216) removed many baronial grievances but war continued until the barons' defeat at Lincoln and Sandwich (1217). 2. (1264–67) The civil war between Henry III of England and his barons led by Simon de Montfort, following Henry's repudiation of the Provisions of Oxford. He was captured at the battle of Lewes (1264) and England was controlled by de Montfort until his death

at Evesham (1265). Hostilities continued until the royalist capture of the Isle of Ely in 1267.

baroque In architecture, a style dominant in European Roman Catholic countries in the 17th and early

BAROQUE *Rubens'* Samson and Delilah *(detail), a typical baroque painting.*

18th centuries. Beginning in Italy as a reaction against classicism, it was characterized by curved and broken lines, ornate decoration (which led to the rococo), and elaborate spatial effects. English architects, such as Wren and Vanbrugh, were influenced by it.

In art, the baroque was a style that developed from Italian mannerism.

In music, the compositions of the 17th and early 18th centuries, from Monteverdi to Bach, are frequently called baroque music.

Barotse. *See* Lozi.

Barquisimeto 10 03N 69 18W A city in NW Venezuela. It is the commercial centre of a coffee-growing area and has a university (1963). Population (1984 est): 459 000.

barracuda A shoaling fish of the family *Sphyraenidae* (about 20 species), found in all tropical seas and caught for food and sport. Its body is up to 1.8 m long and bears two dorsal fins. Barracudas feed voraciously on other fish and the larger species are considered dangerous to man. Order: *Perciformes.*

Barranquilla 11 00N 74 50W An important port in NW Colombia, on the Río Magdalena near its mouth on the Caribbean Sea. Its manufactures include textiles, vegetable oils, and chemicals. It has two universities (1941, 1967). Population (1985): 920 695.

Barren Grounds (*or* Lands) The largely uninhabited permafrost plain of N Canada, stretching from about 59°N to the Arctic Ocean and from Hudson Bay to the

Mackenzie Valley. Caribou and other animals live on the short grasses and other flowering plants.

Barrie, Sir James (Matthew) (1860–1937) British dramatist and novelist. The son of a Scots weaver, he came to London as a freelance writer in 1885. After two successful novels about Scottish rural life he wrote mostly for the theatre. His best-known plays are *The Admirable Crichton* (1902), *Peter Pan* (1904), which has also remained a popular children's book, and *Dear Brutus* (1917).

BARROW *A Neolithic long barrow (3000–1600 BC) at West Kennet.*

barrow A prehistoric burial mound, also called a tumulus or cairn. From about 2000 BC earth barrows, concealing stone or timber passages and burial chambers, were built all over Europe for the interment of warrior chiefs. Long (i.e. rectangular or trapezoidal) barrows, such as at West Kennet (S England), were used for Neolithic multiple burials. Round barrows were more usual in Bronze Age cultures. Barrows continued in use in Iron Age Europe, and as late as the 7th century AD.

Barry, Sir Charles (1795–1860) British architect. Barry worked in both classical and gothic styles. In 1836 he won the competition to rebuild the Houses of Parliament (*see* Palace of Westminster), which, assisted by Augustus Pugin (1812–52), he designed in the gothic manner. He also designed the Reform Club (1837) in London.

Barrymore, Lionel (1878–1954) US actor. He is remembered for his performances in the first series of *Dr Kildare* films. His sister **Ethel Barrymore** (1879–1959) acted with Sir Henry Irving in London, and later became a leading stage actress in the USA. Their brother **John Barrymore** (1882–1942) was also an actor. His greatest stage success was his performance of Hamlet in 1922. As a film star during his later career he was famous for such films as *Grand Hotel* (1932) and *Moby Dick* (1930). He was also renowned for his tempestuous private life.

Bartholdi, Frédéric August (1834–1904) French sculptor, famous for the Lion of Belfort, commemorating the gallant defence of Belfort during the Franco-Prussian War (1870–71), and the Statue of Liberty.

Bartók, Béla (1881–1945) Hungarian composer. Bartók studied and taught at the Budapest Academy of Music, where he and Zoltán Kodály (1882–1967) undertook research into Hungarian folksong. In 1940 he

went to live in the USA, where he died in poverty. A virtuoso pianist, he composed three piano concertos, *Mikrokosmos* (1926–37), and other piano works. His stage works include the opera *Duke Bluebeard's Castle* (1911) and the ballet *The Miraculous Mandarin* (1919). In his six string quartets and *Music for Strings, Percussion, and Celesta* (1936) he explored unusual sonorities. His most popular work is the *Concerto for Orchestra* (1943).

Bartolommeo, Fra (Baccio della Porta; c. 1472–1517) Florentine Renaissance painter. After training under Cosimo Rosselli (1439–1507), he became a supporter of Savonarola, whose death moved him to join the Dominican monastery of S Marco (1500) and abandon painting until 1504. His works include *St Mark* and the *Pietà* (both Palazzo Pitti, Florence).

baryon A collective term for nucleons and other elementary particles that have a proton or neutron in their decay products. All baryons have a quantum number called the baryon number, which is equal to $+1$ and is always conserved in an interaction. *See* particle physics.

Baryshnikov, Mikhail (Nikolayevich) (1948–) Soviet-born ballet dancer. A leading dancer with the Kirov Ballet (1967–74), he defected to the West in 1974 joining the American Ballet Theatre (ABT) (1974–78) and becoming its artistic director (1980–90). His films include *White Nights* (1986).

basalt A volcanic rock of basic composition, typically dark, heavy, and fine textured. Three broad groups of basalt are recognized: alkali basalt, high-alumina basalt, and tholeiite. Basalt constitutes over 90% of volcanic rocks.

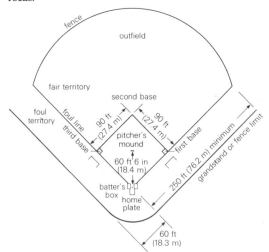

BASEBALL *The dimensions of the field.*

baseball A nine-a-side bat-and-ball game that evolved from rounders, played mainly in the USA, Japan, and Latin America. The object for each team while batting is to score as many runs as possible and while fielding to prevent the other team from doing so. A team bats until three players are out; one turn at bat for both teams constitutes an inning, of which there are usually nine in a game. The pitcher, standing at the pitcher's mound, throws the ball to the batter, standing at home plate, who tries to hit it into fair territory and run. He scores a home run by making a complete circuit of the bases (first, second, third, and home). A player may be struck out (if he misses the ball or hits it into foul territory in each of three attempts), caught out, tagged out (if he or the base he is running towards is touched by a player with the ball), or put out by being hit by a batted ball while running.

Basel. *See* Basle.

bases. *See* acids and bases.

Basic A computer language developed in the USA in the 1960s. Designed principally for use by inexperienced programmers, it is one of the easiest languages to learn and is widely used, in more recent versions, in personal computers.

Basic English A simplified form of the English language, which uses a vocabulary of 850 common English words. It was developed in the late 1920s by the linguist C. K. Ogden (1889–1957), who intended it to be a simply learnt method of international communication and a rival to Esperanto.

Basidiomycetes A large class of fungi (about 13 000 species) that includes many mushrooms, the bracket fungi, puffballs, etc., as well as important microscopic forms, such as the parasitic rusts and smuts of crops. They reproduce by basidia, which are typically club-shaped and produce spores at the tips of stalklike projections.

Basie, Count (William B.; 1904–84) US Black jazz pianist and band leader. He became famous for his distinctive "big band" style and recorded many albums, including *Atomic Mr. Basie* and *Straight Ahead*.

basil An annual herbaceous plant of the Indian genus *Ocimum*, cultivated as a pot herb. Sweet basil (*O. basilicum*), up to 30 cm high, has toothed leaves and small white or bluish flowers. Family: *Labiatae*.

Basildon 51 34N 0 25E A town in SE England, in Essex. Created as a new town in 1949 from several townships, its industries include engineering, printing, and tobacco. Population (1985 est): 160 000.

basilica 1. A Roman public meeting hall. In imperial times, many had a layout similar to the Basilica of Maxentius in Rome: rectangular ground plan, colonnaded aisles, entrance porch (narthex), and windows in the upper storey (clerestory). 2. A Christian church based on a similar plan (e.g. S Giovanni in Laterano in Rome).

basilisk 1. An arboreal lizard belonging to the tropical American genus *Basiliscus*. Up to 60 cm long, it has a narrow body, a long whiplike tail, and a flat lobe protruding from the back of its head. It has long hind legs with lobed toes fringed with scales, enabling it to run over the surface of water. 2. A legendary snakelike serpent of ancient Greece and Rome whose glance was believed to be fatal to all living things except the weasel.

Basingstoke 51 16N 1 05W A town in S England, in Hampshire. Its manufactures include agricultural machinery, scientific instruments, and leather goods. It is also developing as a warehousing and distribution centre for southern England. Population (1984 est): 80 000.

basketball A five-a-side court game invented in the USA (1891) by James Naismith (1861–1939). The object is to toss or put an inflated ball into the opponents' basket, a net mounted 3.05 m (10 ft) above the floor on a backboard. Players use only their hands, passing the ball or dribbling it by bouncing, and they may not run with it. A professional game has 4 12-minute quarters. Five

BASKETBALL *The dimensions of the court.*

substitutes are allowed to each side. The premier professional basketball league is the National Basketball Association in the USA (founded in 1949).

basking shark A large shark belonging to the family *Cetorhinidae*. Up to 15 m long, they are grey-brown or blackish and inhabit cold and temperate regions of the Atlantic, Pacific, and Indian Oceans. Basking sharks usually occur in shoals near the surface and float or swim slowly, feeding on plankton.

Basle (French name: Bâle; German name Basel) 47 33N 7 36E The second largest city in Switzerland, on the river Rhine where the French, German, and Swiss borders meet. A Roman fort originally occupied the site. Industries include chemical, pharmaceuticals, and engineering. The Bank for International Settlements was established here in 1929. Population (1985): 174 600.

Basle, Council of A general council of the Roman Catholic Church summoned by Pope Martin V in 1431 to consider the heretical Hussites and the nature of papal power. Martin's successor, moved it to Ferrara. However, a minority of councillors remained at Basle, electing the antipope, Felix V, in 1439. He resigned in 1449 and the council was brought to an end.

Basque A non-Indo-European language spoken by some 500 000 Basque people of the W Pyrenean areas of Spain and France. The Basques are strongly Roman Catholic and traditionally enjoyed a degree of regional autonomy, forming an independent government (1936–37) at the time of the Spanish Civil War. Nationalism remains a significant force and the Basque Separatist movement is still active. Since 1968 guerrilla tactics have been adopted by the ETA (*Euskadi ta Azkatasuna*) and the French-based *Enbata* groups.

Basra 30 30N 47 50E A town in SE Iraq, on the Shatt (river) al-Arab. It is linked by rail and river steamer to Baghdad; the modern port (Al Ma'qil) was constructed by the British during World War I. Population (1985 est): 616 700.

bass (fish) One of several perchlike bony fish of the order *Perciformes*. The majority belong to the family *Serranidae* (*see* sea bass), which includes the common European bass (*Dicentrarchus labrax*). This can grow up to 1 m long and has a grey or blue back with a white or yellowish belly. North American freshwater bass belong to the family *Centrarchidae*.

bass (music) **1.** The deepest adult male singing voice. Range: E below the bass stave to E two octaves above. **2.** The lowest voice or instrumental part of a piece of music.

Bassano, Jacopo (Jacopo *or* Giacomo da Ponte; c. 1517–92) Italian painter of the Venetian school, born in Bassano, the son of a painter. He was one of the earliest painters of rustic life, in both secular, e.g. *Pastoral* (Lugano), and religious scenes, e.g. *Adoration of the Kings* (National Gallery, Edinburgh).

basset hound A breed of dog originating in France. It has a long body with very short legs and a narrow face with drooping ears and a mournful expression. They were formerly popular hunting dogs. Height: 33–38 cm.

bassoon A musical instrument of the woodwind family. Its conically bored tube is about 2.5 m (8 ft) long and is bent back on itself. It has a metal crook into which a double reed is inserted. Its extensive compass (about three and a half octaves above B flat below the bass stave) allows it a melodic as well as a bass role.

Bass Strait A channel separating the mainland of Australia from Tasmania. It has valuable oil and natural gas deposits. Length: 290 km (180 mi). Maximum width: 240 km (150 mi).

BASTILLE *The murder of its last commander during the storming of the fortress.*

Bastille A fortress in Paris. It was built in about 1370 to protect the wall around Paris against English attack and became a state prison under Cardinal de Richelieu. The storming of the Bastille on 14 July, 1789, is regarded as the beginning of the French Revolution.

Basutoland. *See* Lesotho, Kingdom of.

bat A flying mammal belonging to the order *Chiroptera* (981 species), distributed in most temperate and tropical regions. There are two suborders: the fruit bats (*Megachiroptera*; 150 species) and the insect-eating bats (*Microchiroptera*; 831 species). Bats may also feed on pollen, nectar, blood, and small animals. The wings are extensions of skin that are supported between the forelimb, with its very long fingers, the hind limbs, and the tail. Insectivorous bats use echolocation for navigation and catching prey whereas fruit bats have eyes adapted for night vision.

Bataan A mountainous forested peninsula in the Philippines, in W Luzon W of Manila Bay. In a famous action during World War II, US-Filipino forces resisted the Japanese invasion for almost three months here (1942); after their capture, thousands died on a forced Death March. Length: about 48 km (30 mi).

bateleur An African snake eagle, *Terathopius ecaudatus*, having very long wings and a short tail. It flies vast distances, preying on reptiles, mammals, and carrion, which it seizes with its short rough powerful toes.

Bateson, William (1861–1926) British biologist, whose experiments on inheritance helped found the science of genetics. His results (1905–08) corroborated the findings of Gregor Mendel published in 1865 although he refused to accept the chromosome theory proposed by T. H. Morgan.

Bath 51 23N 2 22W A city in SW England, in Avon on the River Avon. It was an early Roman centre known as Aquae Sulis because of its hot natural springs. The Roman baths have survived and are considered the best Roman remains in the UK. Bath became fashionable as a spa town in the 18th century when many of the finest buildings were built, including the Royal Crescent and the Assembly Rooms. Bath Abbey, mainly 16th-century, lies in the town centre. Population (1981): 79 965.

Bath, Order of the A British order of knighthood, formed by George I in 1725 as a successor to the Knights of the Bath, traditionally founded by Henry IV in 1399. It comprises the sovereign, knights and dames grand cross (GCB), knights and dames commanders (KCB), and companions (CB). Its name is derived from the bathing ceremony that formed the principal rite of admission to the original order.

Bathurst. *See* Banjul.

batik Cloth, traditionally cotton, dyed by a special method. An ancient Indonesian craft, batik involves the repeated application of melted wax, later removed, to protect parts of the material from the dye.

Baton Rouge 30 30N 91 10W A city in the USA, the capital of Louisiana situated on the Mississippi River. It is a major deepwater port with oil and sugar refineries. Population (1980): 241 483.

Battenberg. *See* Mountbatten of Burma, Louis, 1st Earl.

battered baby syndrome Injuries inflicted on babies or young children by their parents. Battering commonly takes the form of facial bruises, cigarette burns, head injuries (often with brain damage), and fractured bones. The parents are often emotionally disturbed or have themselves suffered from physical abuse in infancy. A care order is often necessary to safeguard a child from further abuse.

Battle 50 55N 0 29E A town in S England, in East Sussex. It was the scene of the battle of Hastings (1066) in which Harold II was defeated by William the Conqueror, who built Battle Abbey to commemorate his victory. Population (1981): 5141.

Baudelaire, Charles (1821–67) French poet. He inherited his father's fortune in 1842 and lived extravagantly until what was left of the capital was placed in trust by his family (1844). In 1852 he discovered Edgar Allan Poe, publishing several translations of his works (1856–65). His only volume of poetry, *Les Fleurs du mal* (1857, revised 1861), contained several erotic poems, which led to his being convicted for obscenity. He became paralysed as a result of venereal disease and died in Paris soon after.

Baudouin I (1930–   ) King of the Belgians (1951–   ), succeeding his father Leopold III. He was interned by the Nazis in World War II. In 1960 he married Fabiola de Mora y Aragón (1928–   ).

BAUHAUS *The building designed by Gropius at Dessau.*

Bauhaus A German school of design founded in 1919 at Weimar and closed by the Nazis in 1933. From 1925 to 1932 it was housed at Dessau in a building designed by Gropius (its director until 1928), itself a work of great influence. The Bauhaus sought to produce a practical synthesis of all the arts and to develop a style appropriate for the industrial 20th century. *See also* Kandinsky; Klee.

bauxite The chief ore of aluminium. It is a residual deposit formed by the weathering of aluminium-rich rocks (mainly syenites) under tropical conditions and consists mainly of hydrated aluminium oxide.

Bavaria (German name: Bayern) The largest *Land* of West Germany, bordering on Austria, Czechoslovakia, and East Germany. Predominantly agricultural, the main crops are rye, wheat, and barley. *History*: a duchy and later a kingdom ruled by the Wittelsbachs from 1180 to 1918, it then became a republic. Area: 70 547 sq km (29 232 sq mi). Population (1986): 10 993 400. Capital: Munich.

Bax, Sir Arnold Edward Trevor (1883–1953) British composer. His tone poems, such as *Tintagel* (1917) and *The Garden of Fand* (1916), and his seven symphonies remain his most popular works. He was Master of the King's Music from 1941 until his death.

bay A Mediterranean evergreen tree, *Laurus nobilis*. It can reach a height of 20 m, has aromatic dark-green lance-shaped leaves, small yellowish flowers, and blackish berries. The leaves are used to season food. Family: *Lauraceae* (*see* laurel).

Bayeux 49 16N 0 42W A town in NW France, in the Calvados department on the River Aure. Its museum houses the famous Bayeux tapestry and there is a fine

13th-century cathedral. Industries include dairy foods and plastics. Population (1982 est): 15 237.

Bayeux tapestry An 11th-century embroidered linen strip, 69 m (231 ft) long, which depicts the Norman conquest of England (1066). The tapestry was reputedly commissioned for Bayeux cathedral by its bishop, Odo, the half-brother of William the Conqueror, whose wife Matilda is traditionally credited with its making. Experts have concluded, however, that it was made in England.

Bay of Pigs (Spanish name: Bahia de los Cochinos) A bay on the SW coast of Cuba where on 17 April, 1961, about 1200 Cuban exiles attempted to invade the country. Hoping to overthrow Fidel Castro, and supported by the US Central Intelligence Agency, the invasion was unsuccessful largely because it lacked sufficient US military backing.

bayonet A blade that may be attached to the muzzle of a firearm. The bayonet, which is thought to have originated in the early 17th century in Bayonne (France), replaced the pike. Bayonets were used in both World Wars.

Bayreuth 49 27N 11 35E A town in SE West Germany, in Bavaria. It is famous as the home of Richard Wagner, who designed its Festival Theatre (1872–76), where his operas are performed annually. Population (1984 est): 71 800.

bazooka Originally a 2.36 inch (60 mm) antitank rocket launcher fired from the shoulder and used by the US army in World War II. The term was later applied to all similar weapons. The name came from a tubular wind instrument made famous by Bob Burns, an American comedian.

BBC. *See* British Broadcasting Corporation.

BCG (*bacille Calmette Guérin*) A vaccine consisting of a weakened form of the tuberculosis bacterium, which is injected to give partial protection against tuberculosis. A successful vaccination produces a lump at the injection site.

Beaconsfield, Benjamin Disraeli, 1st Earl of. *See* Disraeli, Benjamin.

beagle A long-established breed of dog originating in the UK. It has a deep chest, strong shoulders, and drooping ears. Beagles have long been used as hunting hounds; more recently, they have become popular household pets. Height: 33–40 cm.

bean The seed or fruit of certain herbs, shrubs, or trees of the family *Leguminosae*. *See* broad bean; carob; French bean; haricot bean; Lima bean; mung bean; runner bean; soya bean.

bear A large heavy mammal belonging to a family (*Ursidae*; 7 species) found in Europe, Asia, and America. Bears have a shaggy coat and a short tail and walk flat on the soles of their broad feet. They can stand erect and most of them are vegetarian. Newly born bears are very small (about the size of rats), blind, and toothless. Order: *Carnivora*. *See* black bear; brown bear; polar bear; spectacled bear; sun bear.

bearbaiting A blood sport formerly popular in Britain and Europe. A bear, sometimes blinded, was chained to a stake in a bear pit or bear garden and dogs were let loose to attack it. **Bullbaiting** used bulls in a similar way. Both bearbaiting and bullbaiting were made illegal in the UK in 1835.

bearded tit. *See* reedling.

bearded vulture. *See* lammergeier.

BEARDSLEY *Detail from an illustration for Wilde's* Salome.

Beardsley, Aubrey Vincent (1872–98) British illustrator of the periodicals *The Yellow Book* and *The Savoy* and of several books, including Wilde's *Salome* and Pope's *Rape of the Lock*, he achieved notoriety with his grotesque and erotic imagery. His curved lines, characteristic of Art Nouveau, contrast with dense areas of black ink.

Beas, River A river in NW India, flowing mainly W from the Himalayas to the River Sutlej. It forms part of the Punjab irrigation scheme. Length: 470 km (290 mi).

beating the bounds A traditional ceremony that takes place in several English towns and villages on Ascension Day. Primarily a religious event, it evolved during the reign of Elizabeth I, and is derived from the earlier ceremonies of Rogationtide. A priest leads those present round the parish boundaries offering prayers for the harvest while young boys beat the boundary stones with sticks. An equivalent Scottish ceremony is called riding the marches.

Beatitudes In the New Testament, the eight blessings with which Jesus opened the Sermon on the Mount (Matthew 5.3–12). They describe such Christian virtues as meekness, mercy, and purity of heart (e.g. "Blessed are the meek: for they shall inherit the earth."). The word derives from the Latin of the Vulgate, *beati sunt* (blessed are).

Beatles A British rock group, which achieved worldwide popularity during the 1960s. The Beatles appeared at the Cavern Club in Liverpool in 1962 and subsequently recorded "Love Me Do" and "She Loves You," which became top of the Hit Parade in 1963. By this time the group consisted of George Harrison, John Lennon, Paul McCartney, and Ringo Starr; they toured the USA suc-

cessfully, made two films, and were awarded MBEs in 1965. In 1970 they disbanded to pursue separate careers.

Beat movement US literary and social movement of the 1950s that sought personal liberation through art, drugs, sex, and any other "consciousness-expanding" means. The movement centred on the artistic communities of Greenwich Village in New York and of San Francisco and Los Angeles. Among its prominent writers were William Burroughs (1914–), Allen Ginsberg (1926–), and Jack Kerouac (1922–69).

Beaton, Sir Cecil (Walter Hardy) (1904–80) British photographer. From the 1920s onwards he became famous for his society portraits, many taken for *Vanity Fair* and *Vogue* magazines. After World War II he turned also to scenery and costume designs, notably for *My Fair Lady*.

Beatrix (1938–) Queen of the Netherlands since the abdication (1980) of her mother Queen Juliana. Her marriage (1966) to the West German Claus von Amsberg (1926–) caused some controversy.

beats Variations in the intensity of sound when two tones of nearly equal frequency are heard. The effect is similar to that of interference. At certain times, the amplitudes of the waves reinforce each other and, at intermediate times, they tend to cancel each other out. The frequency of the beats is equal to the difference in the frequencies of the two notes.

Beatty, David, 1st Earl (1871–1936) British admiral. In World War I, Beatty took part in the destruction of three German cruisers in Heligoland Bight (1914) and the sinking of the *Blücher* near Dogger Bank (1915). He also fought in the battle of Jutland (1916). As commander of the Grand Fleet, he received the German naval surrender in 1918.

Beaufort scale A scale of wind speed devised in 1805 by Admiral Sir Francis Beaufort (1774–1857).

Beaufort Sea The section of the Arctic Ocean N of North America, between the Chukchi Sea and the Canadian archipelago. It is often covered by floating ice.

Beaumarchais, Pierre-Augustin Caron de (1732–99) French dramatist. Son of a watchmaker, he became rich and famous with *The Barber of Seville* (1775) and *The Marriage of Figaro* (1778), which inspired operas by Rossini and Mozart. Constantly involved in lawsuits, he wrote *Mémoires* (1773–75) in self-defence.

Beaumaris 53 16N 4 05W A resort in North Wales, in Gwynedd, situated on the island of Anglesey. It is a yachting centre with a moated castle (1295). Population (1981): 2046.

Beaune 47 02N 4 50E A town in E central France, in the Côte-d'Or department. The centre for the wine trade of Burgundy, it has a wine museum. Population (1982 est): 21 127.

Beauvais 49 26N 2 05E A market town in N France, in the Oise department. Its fine cathedral (begun 1227) was damaged during World War II and the factory in which the famous Gobelin tapestries had been made since the 17th century was completely destroyed. Population (1982 est): 54 147.

Beauvoir, Simone de (1908–86) French novelist and essayist. The constant companion of Jean-Paul Sartre, whom she met at the Sorbonne in 1929, her novels include *The Blood of Others* (1948), *The Mandarins* (1956), *The Coming of Age* (1973), and *All Said and Done* (1975).

Beaufort number	description of wind	wind speed	
		knots	metres per second
0	calm	<1	0.0– 0.2
1	light air	1– 3	0.3– 1.5
2	light breeze	4– 6	1.6– 3.3
3	gentle breeze	7–10	3.4– 5.4
4	moderate breeze	11–16	5.5– 7.9
5	fresh breeze	17–21	8.0–10.7
6	strong breeze	22–27	10.8–13.8
7	near gale	28–33	13.9–17.1
8	gale	34–40	17.2–20.7
9	strong gale	41–47	20.8–24.4
10	storm	48–55	24.5–28.4
11	violent storm	56–63	28.5–32.6
12	hurricane	≥64	≥32.7

BEAUFORT SCALE

beaver A large aquatic rodent, *Castor fiber*, of Europe, Asia, and North America. Over 1 m long and weighing up to 40 kg, beavers have a dark sleek waterproof coat and a broad flat tail used for balance and swimming. They build a "lodge" of sticks and mud using their large incisor teeth to cut wood. During the summer they feed on vegetation. Family: *Castoridae*.

Beaverbrook, Max(well) Aitken, 1st Baron (1879–1964) British newspaper proprietor and politician, born in Canada. In 1919 he bought a majority interest in the *Daily Express*, in 1921 he founded the *Sunday Express*, and in 1929 bought the *Evening Standard* (London). In World War I he served in Lloyd George's War Cabinet as minister of information (1918) and in Churchill's World War II Cabinet as minister of aircraft production (1940–41).

bebop. *See* bop.

Bechet, Sidney (1897–1959) US Black jazz clarinetist and soprano saxophone player. He achieved wide recognition after a tour of Europe in 1919, subsequently worked with Duke Ellington, and after World War II lived in Paris.

Bechuanaland. *See* Botswana, Republic of.

BORIS BECKER

Becker, Boris (1967–) West German tennis player. In 1985, aged 17, he became the youngest player ever to win the men's singles at Wimbledon, which he also won in 1986 and 1989.

Becket, St Thomas (c. 1118–70) English churchman. The son of a London merchant, Becket became chancellor to Henry II in 1154 and archbishop of Canterbury in 1162. After quarrelling with Henry he refused to swear allegiance to the Constitutions of Clarendon and was exiled to France (1164–70). Subsequent attempts to resolve the dispute failed and on 29 December, 1170 he was murdered in Canterbury Cathedral at Henry's instigation. He was canonized in 1173.

Beckett, Samuel (1906–89) Irish novelist, dramatist, and poet. After studying at Trinity College, Dublin he settled in Paris in 1937. He wrote in both French and English. His plays, which include *Waiting for Godot* (1954), and his prose works, such as *Malone Dies* (1956) and *How It Is* (1964), treat human existence with a nihilism tempered by desperate humour. His later works, such as *Breath* (1972) and *Not I* (1973), are notably brief and concentrated. He won the Nobel Prize in 1969.

becquerel (Bq) The SI unit of activity (radioactivity) equal to the number of atoms of a radioactive substance that disintegrate in one second. Named after Antoine Henri Becquerel.

Becquerel, (Antoine) Henri (1852–1908) French physicist, who was professor at the Conservatoire des Arts et Métiers in Paris. He discovered radioactivity (1896) by chance, on finding that invisible rays from uranium salts could affect a photographic plate even through a light-proof wrapper. For his fundamental research on these radiations, Becquerel shared the Nobel Prize (1903) with his associates Pierre and Marie Curie.

bedbug A flat wingless insect, about 5 mm long, belonging to a family (*Cimicidae*; 30 species) of bloodsucking parasites. In temperate regions *Cimex lectularius* is the species that most commonly attacks man, hiding by day in bedding, furniture, etc., and becoming active at night. Order: *Hemiptera* (bugs).

Bedchamber Crisis (1839) The issue in British politics over Queen Victoria's ladies of the bedchamber. After the resignation of Lord Melbourne, a Whig, Peel attempted to form a Tory ministry and requested that Victoria dismiss her Whig ladies. She refused and Melbourne remained in office until his government fell in

1841, when Victoria consented to the dismissal of·three ladies.

Bede, St (c. 673–735 AD) English historian, known as the Venerable Bede. After 682 he lived at the monastery of Jarrow in Northumberland. His *Ecclesiastical History of the English People* (c. 731), written in Latin and later translated into English is an important source for Anglo-Saxon history (5th–8th centuries). He was the author of many grammatical, scientific, and historical works. Feast day: 27 May.

Bedford 52 08N 0 29W A town in S England, the administrative centre of Bedfordshire on the River Ouse. John Bunyan was born nearby and spent 12 years in Bedford gaol. Manufactures include Diesel engines, transistors, and metal tubes. Population (1983 est): 89 200.

Bedford Level. *See* Fens, the.

Bedfordshire A county in the South Midlands of England. It is chiefly low lying, rising to the Chiltern Hills in the SW, and is drained by the Great Ouse River. Agricultural products include wheat and vegetables. The chief industries are centred on Luton, Dunstable, and Bedford. Area: 1235 sq km (477 sq mi). Population (1986 est): 521 000. Administrative centre: Bedford.

Bedlington terrier A breed of dog originating in Bedlington, N England, in the early 19th century. It has long legs and a long narrow face and is a popular sporting dog locally. The thick coat may be blue or sandy. Height: about 40 cm.

Bedouin The nomadic Arab tribes of the Syrian and Arabian deserts. Their economy is based on camels, sheep, and goats. Courageous fighters, the Bedouin played an active role in the early Arab conquests, but are now under pressure to take up a settled existence.

bee A four-winged insect (10–30 mm long) belonging to the worldwide superfamily *Apoidea* (about 12 000 species). Bees feed on pollen and nectar and are important pollinators. The ovipositor is used to sting attackers and in some species is barbed, remaining in the wound. Most solitary bees nest in soil, hollow trees, or wall cavities. Some, however, tunnel into wood (the carpenter bee) or construct nests using earth (*see* mason bee) or leaves (*see* leafcutter bee). The female lays one or more eggs in a nest that is then sealed. The social bees (families *Apidae* and *Halictidae*) live in communities organized into castes—workers (infertile females), drones (males, developed from unfertilized eggs), and a queen (a fertile female). Colonies are established in trees, walls, or cliffs (*see also* honeybee). Order: *Hymenoptera*.

beech A tree of the genus *Fagus* (10 species), native to N temperate regions, occasionally reaching a height of 40 m. Beeches have smooth grey bark. The leaves are oval, pointed, and toothed, the flowers are unisexual and inconspicuous, and the fruits are nutlike seeds enclosed in husks (beechnuts or mast). The common beech of Europe and Asia is *Fagus sylvatica*, the timber of which is used for furniture and flooring. Family: *Fagaceae*.

In the S hemisphere beeches are represented by a related genus (*Notofagus*; 14 species) and differ in being evergreen and having separate trees bearing male or female flowers.

Beecham, Sir Thomas (1879–1961) British conductor. He used his inherited fortune for the advancement of English musical life. He championed the works of Richard Strauss, Sibelius, and particularly Delius, whose friend and biographer he became. He founded the London Philharmonic Orchestra (1932) and the Royal Philharmonic Orchestra (1947).

bee-eater A brightly coloured bird belonging to a family (*Meropidae*; 24 species) occurring mainly in tropical Old World regions. Bee-eaters have pointed wings, long central tail feathers, a slender curved bill, and, commonly, a black eye stripe. They nest in burrows and feed in flight, chiefly on bees and wasps. Order: *Coraciiformes* (hornbills, kingfishers, etc.).

beekeeping (*or* apiculture) The rearing of colonies of honeybees in hives, usually for their honey or beeswax. Sheets of wax in wooden frames (starter combs) are hung inside the hive. Onto these the bees build wax cells that they fill with honey and seal. When a frame is full it is removed, the honey is extracted, and the comb is re-used. A colony makes about 32 kg of honey in a summer, but 14 kg of this is needed by the bees for food during the winter; following a bad summer they must be fed sugar syrup. About 10 000–20 000 bees survive the winter; during the spring, when a colony has increased to over 50 000, a large group is likely to leave the hive (i.e. it swarms). The beekeeper collects the swarm and puts it into an empty hive.

beer and brewing Beer is an alcoholic drink made from fermented malt flavoured with hops. Brewing is the process of making beer. Barley, or other grain, is first malted by being allowed to germinate, the resulting malt being dried (kilned), ground, and heated with water (mashed). Starch in the grain is converted into soluble carbohydrates by enzymes in the malt. The resulting liquid wort is boiled with hops to concentrate the wort and utilize the bitter flavour of the hops. The wort is then filtered and cooled ready for fermentation. Yeast is added and the carbohydrates in the wort are converted into alchohol. The liquid is drained and stored. Beer was drunk in ancient Egypt and has been enjoyed in a great many countries ever since. **Ale** was originally a stronger drink than beer, brewed without hops. The terms are now interchangeable, although ale is sometimes reserved for stronger brews fermented at higher temperatures. **Mild** beer is made with fewer hops than **bitter** and a darker malt is used to impart colour. **Lager** is traditionally a light beer matured over a long period at low temperature. **Stout** is made from a blend of roasted barley and malts.

Beersheba 31 15N 34 47E A town in S Israel, the largest in the Negev. In World War I it was the scene of a British victory over the Turks. Population (1986): 115 000.

beeswax A substance produced by bees to build honeycombs. It is collected by heating the honeycomb in water (after removing the honey) so that the floating wax can be separated after solidification on cooling. Beeswax (melting point 61–69°C) is used in high-quality polishes, etc.

beet A herbaceous plant, *Beta vulgaris*, native to Europe and the Mediterranean region. Several varieties are widely cultivated in temperate areas, the most important of which is the sugar beet. The taproot of the red or garden beet yields beetroot, while the mangel-wurzel (*B. vulgaris vulgaris*) is an important fodder. Family: *Chenopodiaceae*.

Beethoven, Ludwig van (1770–1827) German composer, born in Bonn. His father, a court musician, attempted to exploit him as a child prodigy. He settled in

LUDWIG VAN BEETHOVEN   *This portrait (detail) is considered to be one of the best likenesses of him.*

Vienna in 1792 after studying there with Haydn. At the age of 30 he began to go deaf, an experience that increased his loneliness and eccentricity, but did not stop him composing. About 600 of Beethoven's works survive, among them 9 symphonies, 5 piano concertos, 1 violin concerto, 16 string quartets, 10 violin and piano sonatas, 32 piano sonatas, 2 ballets, 2 masses, the opera *Fidelio* (1805–14), and about 200 song settings. His last most intense works include the *Missa Solemnis* (1818–23), the ninth symphony (1817–23), and the innovative late string quartets.

beetle   An insect belonging to the largest order (*Coleoptera*; about 278 000 species) of the animal kingdom. The forewings are specialized as hard structures (called elytra), which cover the functional hindwings when these are not in use. The elytra and the thick cuticle provide protection against predation and desiccation and enable aquatic species to trap a store of air.
Many beetles are serious pests of crops, timber, textiles, etc.; others are useful by preying on insect pests or by speeding up the process of decomposition. *See also* weevil.

Beeton, Isabella Mary   (1836–65) British writer, author of one of the most famous English cookery books, *The Book of Household Management* (1861), first published in a women's magazine founded by her husband.

beetroot.   *See* beet.

Begin, Menachem   (1913–) Israeli statesman; prime minister (1977–83). Born in Russia, he commanded Jewish forces in Palestine from 1942. In 1948 he founded the Freedom (Herut) Movement and in 1973 became joint chairman of the Unity Party. In 1979 he negotiated the Camp David peace treaty with Sadat, for which they shared the Nobel Peace Prize.

Begonia   A genus of generally succulent herbaceous plants (about 1000 species) native to the tropics. They are widely grown as ornamental plants for their brightly coloured flowers. The underground parts are long lived and may be tuberous, fibrous, or rhizomatous. Family: *Begoniaceae*.

Behan, Brendan   (1923–64) Irish playwright. His first play, *The Quare Fellow* (1954), and his autobiography, *Borstal Boy* (1958), were based on his years of detention and imprisonment for Irish Republican Army

(IRA) activities. His best-known play was *The Hostage* (1957).

behaviourism   A school of psychology, founded in the USA by J. B. Watson (1878–1958) in the early 20th century, in which the emphasis is on describing and predicting observable behaviour. The approach was successful in describing how animals learnt tasks in the laboratory but has been limited in its ability to account for such complex processes as emotion, language, and interpersonal relationships. Behaviour therapy was developed from behaviourism.

behaviour therapy   A method of treating psychological problems by assuming that they are the result of faulty learning. It was developed mainly by H. Eysenck from behaviourism. Sometimes conditioning is used to teach new behaviour, such as better ways of relating to other people, or to eliminate undesirable behaviour, such as excessive drinking (*see* aversion therapy). It includes treatment for phobias, in which repeated exposure to the feared object or situation gradually reduces the subject's fear of it.

Beiderbecke, Bix   (Leon Bismarck B.; 1903–31) US jazz cornetist and pianist. He played with Louis Armstrong and in the band of Paul Whiteman (1891–1967), becoming a jazz legend because of his great originality and his early death from alcoholism.

Beijing.   *See* Peking.

BEIRUT   *Violence between religious factions inflicts death on a life that has barely begun.*

Beirut   33 52N 35 30E The capital of the Lebanon, on the E Mediterranean. After centuries of Turkish domination, it was held by the French from World War I until 1941, when it became the capital of the newly independent Lebanon. It was badly damaged in the civil war (1975–76) and in 1982 when Israeli forces besieged the city and forced the Palestine Liberation Organization to leave. It was subsequently the scene of violent clashes between religious factions and between Syrian and Christian troops. Population (1989 est): 1 500 000.

Belau, Republic of   (name until 1981: Palau *or* Pelew) A group of islands in the W Pacific Ocean, within the UN Trust Territory of the Pacific Islands. Self-government was achieved in 1981. President: N. Etpison.

Area: 476 sq km (184 sq mi). Population (1987 est): 15 000.

bel canto (Italian: fine singing) A delicate and lyrical style of singing that was developed in Italian opera during the 17th and 18th centuries and reached its peak in the 19th century.

Belém 1 27S 48 29W A port in N Brazil, the capital of Pará state on the Rio do Pará. It exports products from the Amazon basin including nuts, jute, and rubber. Population (1980 est): 758 117.

Belfast 54 40N 5 50W The capital of Northern Ireland, a seaport situated where the River Lagan enters Belfast Lough. The principal buildings, include the City Hall (1906) and Parliament Buildings (1932) at Stormont. *History*: large-scale growth of Belfast came with the expansion of the linen-making and shipbuilding industries in the 19th century; it became a city in 1888. The Parliament of Northern Ireland sat in the city from 1921 to 1972. Recently conflict between Protestant and Roman Catholic communities has intensified, each becoming increasingly concentrated in ghettoes. This has led to an exacerbation of the housing problem, which is now one of the worst in Europe. The British army has maintained a presence in Belfast since August, 1969. Population (1985): 300 000.

Belgae The Germanic tribes occupying NE Gaul in ancient Roman times. Julius Caesar, who named them, defeated them in 57 BC but they continued their opposition to the Romans from SE Britain.

Belgian Congo. *See* Zaïre, Republic of.

Belgium, Kingdom of (French name: Belgique; Flemish name: België) A country in NW Europe, on the North Sea. It is generally low lying except for the Ardennes in the SE. The main rivers are the Scheldt and the Meuse, which are linked by an extensive network of inland waterways. The population is divided between the French and the Flemish, with other small minorities. *Economy*: highly industrialized, with coal and iron resources supporting considerable heavy industry. Agriculture and food processing are important. In 1921 a customs union was formed with Luxembourg and in 1948 both joined with the Netherlands to form the Benelux Economic Union. Belgium is also a member of the EC and almost two-thirds of its trade is with other members. *History*: the area was part of the Roman Empire until about the end of the 2nd century AD, when it was invaded by Germanic tribes. In medieval times the cities of Ghent, Bruges, and Ypres rose to virtual independence and economic prosperity through the wool industry. In view of its strategic position, Belgium had considerable importance in the balance of power in Europe over the centuries and after being occupied by France during the Napoleonic Wars, it was joined to the Netherlands in 1815. Following an uprising, it became independent in 1830, and the National Congress elected Prince Leopold of Saxe-Coburg as King of the Belgians in 1831. In spite of efforts to remain neutral it was attacked and occupied by Germany in both World Wars. When the Germans invaded in 1940, King Leopold III surrendered immediately but the government struggled on in exile in London. In 1950 the king was persuaded to abdicate in favour of his son, Baudouin. The main political problem since World War II has been tension between the French-speaking Walloons in the S and the Flemish-speaking community in the N. In 1989 a new federal constitution divided Belgium into the autonomous regions of Flanders, Wallonia, and Brussels. Prime minister: Dr Wilfried Martens (1936–). Official languages: French, Flemish, Dutch, and German. Official currency: Belgian franc of 100 centimes. Area: 30 513 sq km (11 778 sq mi). Population (1988 est): 9 888 000. Capital: Brussels. Main port: Antwerp.

Belgrade (Serbo-Croat name: Beograd) 44 50N 20 30E The capital of Yugoslavia and of Serbia, situated in the NE at the confluence of the Rivers Danube and Sava. It became the Serbian capital in the early 15th century. It later suffered Turkish and Austrian occupations but again became capital of Serbia in the late 19th century and of Yugoslavia after World War I. It was occupied by the Germans in World War II and has expanded considerably. Population (1981): 1 407 073.

Belize (name until 1973: British Honduras) A country in Central America between Mexico and Guatemala. The country is generally low lying, rising to the Maya Mountains in the SW. The population is of African, Spanish-American, and Mayan Indian descent, with other small minorities. *Economy*: mainly agricultural; the combined value of sugar and citrus exports have exceeded that of timber since the early 1960s. *History*: once an important Mayan settlement, Belize was discovered by Columbus in 1502 but the first European occupation was an independent settlement of British woodcutters, which held out against the Spanish throughout the 17th century; in 1862 it became a British colony under Jamaica, becoming an independent colony in 1884; it attained self-government in 1964. Claims, based on early Spanish treaties, were made to it by Guatemala but it was granted full independence in 1981. Prime minister: George Price. Official language: English; Spanish is also widely spoken. Official currency: Belize dollar of 100 cents. Area: 22 963 sq km (8867 sq mi). Population (1986 est): 171 000. Capital: Belmopan.

Belize City 17 29N 88 10W The chief port of Belize, on the Caribbean coast. It was formerly capital of Belize but following a severe hurricane (1961), Belmopan, which became capital in 1970, was constructed inland. The main exports are timber, coconuts, and maize. Population (1980): 39 887.

Bell, Alexander Graham (1847–1922) Scottish sci-

ALEXANDER GRAHAM BELL *Inaugurating the New York–Chicago telephone line in 1892.*

entist and inventor. He went to Canada in 1870 and to the USA in 1873, where he became professor of vocal physiology at Boston University. Bell's work in telegraphy and telephony led to the invention of the telephone, which he patented in 1876, demonstrated at American exhibitions, and had in commercial use by 1877.

belladonna. *See* deadly nightshade.

belladonna lily. *See* amaryllis.

Bellerophon In Greek mythology, the grandson of Sisyphus and son of Glaucus, King of Corinth. Sent by Iobates, King of Lycia, to kill the Chimera, he was able to carry out his task by flying above the dragon on Pegasus, a winged horse.

Bellini, Jacopo (c. 1400–c. 1470) Venetian painter, who was a pupil of Gentile da Fabriano. Although his few surviving paintings retain the decorative conventions of Byzantine and Gothic art, his two sketchbooks (British Museum and Louvre) reveal a remarkable understanding of perspective. They influenced his son-in-law Andrea Mantegna and his two sons, who both trained under him. The eldest, **Gentile Bellini** (c. 1429–1507), is best known for his portraits and procession scenes. *The Procession in St Mark's Square* (Accademia, Venice) depicts his native city with realism. Gentile's brother **Giovanni Bellini** (c. 1430–1516) was an important influence on Venetian art, especially through his pupils Titian and Giorgione. His paintings included several altarpieces, such as *Madonna and Saints* (S Zaccaria, Venice) and portraits, such as *Doge Loredano* (National Gallery, London).

Bellini, Vincenzo (1801–35) Italian opera composer. Of his 11 operas, *La somnambula* and *Norma* (both 1831) and *I Puritani* (1835) remain popular, although the coloratura roles require singers of outstanding ability.

Belloc, (Joseph-Pierre) Hilaire (1870–1953) British poet and essayist. Born in France, he served as a Liberal MP from 1906 to 1910. His works include light verse, such as *Cautionary Tales* (1907), essays, biographies, and satirical novels, often illustrated by his friend G. K. Chesterton. An energetic Roman Catholic apologist, he vigorously opposed the socialism of G. B. Shaw and H. G. Wells.

Bellow, Saul (1915–) Canadian-born US novelist, the son of poor Russian Jewish immigrants. His first novel, *Dangling Man* (1944), was influenced by existentialism. His later novels, such as *Mr Sammler's Planet* (1970), *Humboldt's Gift* (1975), *The Dean's December* (1982), and *More Die of Heartbreak* (1987), are ironic and reflective studies of harassed Jewish intellectuals in an urban chaos. He won the Nobel Prize in 1976.

Bell Rock (*or* Inchcape Rock) 56 26N 2 24W A reef off the NE coast of Scotland, in the North Sea. A lighthouse designed by Robert Stevenson, grandfather of Robert Louis Stevenson, was built here (1807–11).

Belmopan 17 12N 88 00W The capital of Belize, on the River Belize about 80 km (50 mi) inland from Belize City, which it succeeded as capital in 1970 after the latter was damaged by a hurricane in 1961. Population (1989 est): 3700.

Belo Horizonte 19 54S 43 54W A city in SE Brazil, in Minas Gerais state. Founded in 1897, it was Brazil's first planned city. Distinctive architecture includes Oscar Niemayer's Chapel of São Francisco. The chief industries include cotton textiles, meat processing, and iron and steel. Population (1980 est): 1 442 483.

Belorussian Soviet Socialist Republic (Belorussia *or* White Russia) A constituent republic in the W central Soviet Union. The majority of its inhabitants are Belorussians, an Eastern Slav people. Belorussia has the largest petrochemical complex in Europe. Formed in 1919, it was devastated in World War II. It has a separate seat in the UN. Area: 207 600 sq km (80 134 sq mi). Population (1987): 10 100 000. Capital: Minsk.

HILAIRE BELLOC *With G. B. Shaw (left) and G. K. Chesterton (right) at a debate chaired by Belloc in 1927.*

beluga 1. A giant sturgeon, *Huso huso*, up to 8.4 m long, that occurs in the Caspian and Black Seas and the River Volga of E Europe. It is a highly prolific egg producer and the source of the best caviar. 2. *See* white whale.

Bendigo 36 48S 144 21E A city in Australia, in central Victoria. It grew rapidly following a gold discovery in 1851 and is now a commercial centre with the third largest livestock market in Australia. Population (1986): 62 380.

bends. *See* decompression sickness.

Benedictines The monks and nuns belonging to the Roman Catholic Order of St Benedict (OSB), a union of independent abbeys, which follow the Rule of St Benedict of Nursia (c. 480–c. 550). They were responsible for preserving the learning of antiquity after the fall of the Roman Empire. The liqueur Bénédictine is named after the order and is made at Fécamp, France.

benefit of clergy The development in England of the 12th-century canon law that criminous clerks (criminal clerics) should not be tried by both ecclesiastical and secular courts. Henry II established that all clerics had the right to be tried solely in ecclesiastical courts. These could not inflict capital punishment. This privilege was much abused in the middle ages and although limited during the Reformation it was not finally abolished until the early 19th century.

Benelux The customs union formed by *Bel*gium, the *Net*herlands, and *Lux*embourg in 1948. It was the first free-trade market in Europe. All three countries are now members of the EC, which has similar aims.

Beneš, Edvard (1884–1948) Czechoslovak statesman. In 1918 Beneš helped Tomáš Masaryk to found Czechoslovakia and became foreign minister, playing an important role in the League of Nations. In 1935 he became president but spent World War II as president of a provisional government in London, returning to Czechoslovakia in 1945. He resigned the presidency in 1948, when Czechoslovakia became a communist state.

Bengal A region of the Indian subcontinent, in the NE on the Bay of Bengal around the Ganges and Brahmaputra deltas; it is divided between India and Bangladesh. *History*: the centre of Buddhist (8th–12th centuries), Hindu (11th–13th centuries), and Islamic dynasties, Bengal became the base for British expansion through India. It was partitioned between India and Pakistan at independence (1947).

Bengal, Bay of The shallow NE limb of the Indian Ocean, between the Indian subcontinent on the W and Burma and the Andaman and Nicobar Islands on the E. Shipping and coastal life are dominated by the NE winter monsoon and the SW summer monsoon.

Bengali An Indo-Aryan language spoken by 80 million people in Bangladesh and West Bengal (India). The literary form of the language uses many Sanskrit words. There is a distinct colloquial form.

Benghazi (*or* Banghazi; Italian name: Bengasi) 32 07N 20 05E The second largest city in Libya, on the Gulf of Sidra. Severely damaged during World War II, it has experienced recent growth with the development of local oilfields. Population (1981): 368 000.

Ben-Gurion, David (David Gruen; 1886–1973) Israeli statesman, known as the Father of the Nation. He was Israel's first prime minister (1948–53, 1955–63). In 1917 he joined the British Army's Jewish Legion to free Palestine from Ottoman control (achieved in 1918) and to establish a Jewish home in Palestine, promised in the Balfour Declaration. In 1920 he founded the General Federation of Labour (the Histadrut) and in 1930, the Israeli Workers' Party (Mapai). He led the Zionist effort to establish a Jewish state, finally achieved in 1948. After resigning the prime ministership in 1963, he was leader of the opposition party, the Rafi, until his retirement in 1970.

Benin, People's Republic of (name until 1975: Dahomey) A country in West Africa, on the Gulf of Guinea. Flat forests and swamps in the S rise to plateaus in the centre and to mountains in the N. The population is mainly Fon and Yoruba in the N and Somba and Bariba in the S. *Economy*: chiefly agricultural, cotton has been introduced in the N and coffee in the S, and these provide the main exports. Offshore oil has been found and hydroelectric schemes are being planned in conjunction with Togo. Most industry has been nationalized. *History*: the powerful Aja kingdom of Dahomey was a centre of the slave trade in the 17th century but was conquered by the French in 1893 and became part of French West Africa. Dahomey attained self-government in 1958 and became an independent republic within the French Community in 1960. A series of military coups ensued, in the last of which (1972) Brig Gen Mathieu Kerékou (1933–) seized power. In 1974 he established a Marxist-Leninist state and in 1984 was re-elected as president. Official language: French. Official currency: CFA (Communauté financière africaine) franc of 100 centimes. Area: 112 600 sq km (43 464 sq mi). Population (1987 est): 4 153 000. Capital: Porto Novo. Main port: Cotonou.

Benin City 6 19N 5 41E A city in Nigeria. It is an important centre for the rubber industry and also exports palm oil. Population (1984): 231 976.

Benn, Anthony (Neil) Wedgwood (1925–) British Labour politician, a leader of the party's left wing. The 2nd Viscount Stansgate from 1960, he renounced his peerage in 1963, the first person to do so under the Peerage Act (1963). He was minister of technology (1966–70), for industry (1974–75), and for energy (1975–79). He lost his parliamentary seat in the 1983 general election but won a by-election at Chesterfield in 1984.

Bennett, (Enoch) Arnold (1837–1931) British novelist. The son of a solicitor in Newcastle-under-Lyme, he published his first novel, *A Man from the North*, in 1898 and lived in Paris from 1902 to 1912. His best-known novels are about life in the Potteries area of Staffordshire, where he grew up. They include *Anna of the Five Towns* (1902), *The Old Wives' Tale* (1908), and *Clayhanger* (1910).

Bennett, Richard Rodney (1936–) British composer known primarily for his atmospheric scores for such films as *Far from the Madding Crowd* (1967), *Murder on the Orient Express* (1974), and *Yanks* (1980), and for his five major operas, including *The Mines of Sulphur* (1963) and *Victory* (1970).

Ben Nevis 56 48N 5 00W The highest mountain in the British Isles, in the Highland Region of Scotland, in the Grampians. Height: 1343 m (4406 ft).

JEREMY BENTHAM *The preserved body, with wax head, kept at University College, London, in accordance with his wishes.*

Bentham, Jeremy (1748–1832) British philosopher, pioneer of utilitarianism. From a wealthy middle-class background, studied law, but preferred theory to practice and in 1776 published *A Fragment on Government*. In 1789 *Principles of Morals and Legislation* presented utilitarianism. He retired to the country in 1814 and wrote copiously on politics and ethics until his death.

Bentley, Edmund Clerihew (1875–1956) British writer. A close friend of G. K. Chesterton, he wrote a classic detective novel, *Trent's Last Case* (1913). He invented the clerihew, a humorous verse form: Sir Christopher Wren Said, "I am going to dine with some men. If anybody calls Say I am designing St Paul's."

bentwood furniture Furniture constructed by a mass-production process invented by a Viennese designer Michael Thonet (1796–1871). It involved steaming beechwood rods and laminated board until they could be bent into the desired shapes. The shaped sections were transported unassembled and screwed together at the destination. Typical chairs, coat stands, etc., are curved in rococo style.

Benue, River A river in West Africa. Rising in N Cameroon, it flows W across Nigeria to join the River Niger at Lokoja. Length: 1400 km (870 mi).

Benxi (*or* Pen-ki) 41 21N 123 45E A city in NE China, in Liaoning province. It is a centre of iron and steel production. Population (1982): 669 000.

Benz, Karl (Friedrich) (1844–1929) German engineer and car manufacturer. In 1885 he built the first car to be driven by an internal-combustion engine. The Benz Company merged with Daimler in 1926 to form Daimler-Benz, the makers of Mercedes-Benz cars.

Benzedrine. *See* amphetamine.

benzene (*or* benzol; C_6H_6) A colourless highly flammable liqud. It is the simplest aromatic compound, its molecules consisting of a ring of six carbon atoms each with a hydrogen atom attached. Benzene is obtained from oil and from coal tar. It is widely used in the chemical industry.

benzodiazepines A class of tranquillizing drugs that act by depressing specific areas of the brain. Benzodiazepines, such as diazepam (Valium) and chlordiazepoxide (Librium), are used as sedatives. Nitrazepam (Mogadon) is used as a sleeping pill (a hypnotic). Both nitrazepam and diazepam are habit forming.

Beowulf An Anglo-Saxon epic poem preserved in a late 10th-century manuscript. Probably composed in the 8th century by a Christian poet sympathetic to pagan ideals, it alludes to historical events of early 6th-century Scandinavia. In the first part the hero, Beowulf, kills the marauding monster, Grendel; in the second part, Beowulf, now king of the Swedish tribe of Geats, slays a dragon and seizes its hoard of treasure.

Berberis A widely distributed genus of deciduous or evergreen spiny shrubs (over 400 species). The small yellow or orange flowers usually grow in clusters and the fruits are red or blue berries. Berberis is implicated in a rust disease of wheat and is therefore outlawed in some areas. Family: *Berberidaceae*.

Berbers A Muslim people occupying parts of N Africa (Morocco, Algeria, Tunisia, and adjacent regions) and speaking a non-Semitic language. Prior to the introduction of Arabic speech in the 7th century AD, Berber languages were spoken over the whole of the area and are still spoken by an estimated ten million people; Morocco is still predominantly Berber in population. The Berbers played an important role in the Islamic conquest of the Iberian peninsula in the 8th century.

Berenson, Bernard (1865–1959) US art historian, whose works set new standards of criticism. Inspired by the beauty of Italy, where he spent much time, he wrote the definitive *Italian Painters of the Renaissance* (1894–1907) and *Drawings of the Florentine Painters* (1903).

Berg, Alban (1885–1935) Austrian composer. A friend and pupil of Schoenberg, he adopted atonality and used serialism. His greatest works are the operas *Wozzeck* (1915–21) and *Lulu* (1928–35), the intensely personal *Lyric Suite* (for string quartet; 1925–26), and a violin concerto (1935).

bergamot A tree, *Citrus bergamia*, closely related to the orange. An essence (oil of bergamot) extracted from the rind of its fruit is used in perfumery. The name is also given to two plants of the mint family (*Labiatae*): *Mentha citrata*, which yields an extract similar to oil of bergamot, and *Monarda citriodora* (lemon bergamot) sometimes used in a tealike beverage.

Bergen 60 23N 5 20E A seaport and second largest city in Norway, situated in the SW. Founded about 1070 AD, it became the chief commercial city and the country's capital (12th–13th centuries). It had connections with Hanseatic merchants (14th–18th centuries). It was rebuilt after damage by fire in 1702, 1855, and 1916 and by bombing during World War II. It exports fish products and base metals. Population (1989): 209 000.

Bergenia A genus of herbaceous perennial plants (6 species), native to central and E Asia but often cultivated for their attractive foliage and early-blooming pink or white flowers. Family: *Saxifragaceae*.

Bergius, Friedrich (1884–1949) German chemist, who shared the 1931 Nobel Prize with C. Bosch for inventing a process for making motor fuels from coal or petroleum residues by treating them with hydrogen under high pressure and temperature (1913). This process was used extensively by Germany in World War II.

INGRID BERGMAN *With Humphrey Bogart in* Casablanca *(1942).*

Bergman, Ingmar (1918–) Swedish film and stage director. His films include *The Seventh Seal* (1956), *Wild Strawberries* (1957), *Persona* (1966), *Scenes from a Marriage* (1974), *Autumn Sonata* (1978), and *Fanny and Alexander* (1982).

Bergman, Ingrid (1915–82) Swedish actress. She went to Hollywood in 1939 and became an international film star, appearing in such films as *Casablanca* (1942), *Gaslight* (1944), and numerous other major films, her last being *Autumn Sonata* (1978).

Bergson, Henri (1859–1941) French philosopher and psychologist, one of the greatest thinkers of his time. To reconcile free will and determinism, Bergson distinguishes between consciousness, an indivisible flow of cumulative states in which (free) will operates, and the external physical world where causality reigns. His works include *Matière et mémoire* (1896) and *L'Evolution créatrice* (1907). He won the Nobel Prize for Literature in 1927.

Beria, Lavrenti Pavlovich (1899–1953) Soviet politician. Head of the Soviet secret police from 1938, Beria became a member of the politburo (now the presidium) in 1946. After Stalin's death in 1953, he was involved in a power struggle with Malenkov and Khrushchev. He was accused of conspiracy, tried secretly, and executed.

beriberi A disease caused by deficiency of vitamin B_1 (thiamine), common in areas where the staple diet is polished rice (thiamine occurs mainly in the rice husks). Dry beriberi affects the peripheral nerves, causing muscular weakness and pain. Wet beriberi is probably the result of combined protein malnutrition and thiamine deficiency: it causes accumulation of fluid and swelling of the limbs, leading eventually to heart failure. Treatment consists of providing a diet with adequate thiamine and vitamin supplements.

Bering Sea A section of the N Pacific Ocean between the Soviet Union, Alaska, and the Aleutian Islands. Navigation is difficult, with storms and a partial ice covering in winter. The NE continental shelf contains oil and gas, as yet unexploited.

Bering Strait A narrow shallow channel between Asia and North America, connecting the Bering Sea with the Arctic Ocean. During the Ice Age it bridged the continents when the sea level fell.

Beriosova, Svetlana (1932–) Russian ballet dancer. In 1952 she joined the British Sadler's Wells company, becoming prima ballerina (1955–75).

Berkeley, George (1685–1753) Irish bishop and idealist philosopher. In *A New Theory of Vision* (1709), *Principles of Human Knowledge* (1710), and *Three Dialogues between Hylas and Philonous* (1713), he argued that the material world exists only in being perceived by the mind.

Berkeley, Sir Lennox Randal Francis (1903–89) British composer. He studied under Nadia Boulanger and taught at the Royal Academy of Music from 1946 to 1968. Berkeley's compositions include the *Serenade for Strings* (1939), *Four Poems of St Teresa* for contralto and strings (1947), and the fourth symphony (1978).

berkelium (Bk) A synthetic transuranic element synthesized by Seaborg at the University of California at Berkeley in 1949. The longest-lived isotope (^{249}Bk) has a half-life of 314 days. At no 97; at wt (247).

Berkshire A county of S England. It consists mainly of lowlands rising to the Berkshire Downs in the N. It is predominantly agricultural; industries include paints, plastics, and pharmaceutical goods at Slough and light engineering and horticulture at Reading; the Atomic Research Establishment is at Aldermaston. Area: 1256 sq km (485 sq mi). Population (1986 est): 734 100. Administrative centre: Reading.

Berlin 52 31N 13 20E A city in N Germany, on the River Spree, divided since 1948 into East Berlin, now capital of the German Democratic Republic (East Germany), and West Berlin, part of the Federal Republic of Germany (West Germany). *History*: founded in the 13th

BERLIN *The Brandenburg Gate with crowds of East and West Germans standing on the Wall after it was breached in November 1989.*

century, it was an important member of the Hanseatic League. Its independence was reduced by the Hohenzollern Electors of Brandenburg from the 15th century, but it became their capital and grew in importance with their increasing power, becoming the capital of Prussia in the 18th century and of the German Empire in 1871. Badly damaged in World War II, it was occupied by the four major powers after the defeat of Germany. In 1948 Berlin became two separate administrative units: Soviet-controlled East Berlin and West Berlin, formed from the US, UK, and French zones. The Soviet Union blockaded the city for almost a year (*see* Berlin airlift). In 1961 the Berlin wall was built to curb the flow of refugees from E to W. Demolition of the wall began in 1989. **East Berlin** The capital of East Germany. Area: 403 sq km (156 sq mi). Population (1986): 1 223 309. **West Berlin** The largest city and a *Land* of West Germany, forming an enclave within East Germany. Area: 480 sq km (188 sq mi). Population (1986): 1 867 700.

Berlin, Congress of (1878) A meeting of European powers, which revised the Treaty of San Stefano that had ended the 1877–78 Russo-Turkish War. The Congress limited Russian naval expansion, permitted Austria-Hungary to occupy Bosnia-Hercegovina, and gained Turkish recognition of the independence of Serbia, Romania, and Montenegro.

Berlin, Sir Isaiah (1909–) British philosopher and historian, who was also a diplomat in Washington and Moscow. His works include *The Inevitability of History* (1954), *The Age of Enlightenment* (1956), and *Two Concepts of Liberty* (1959).

Berlin airlift (1948–49) An operation by the Allies to supply isolated West Berlin with the necessities of life after the Soviet Union cut off all rail, road, and water links with the city in an attempt to force the Allies to abandon their rights there. The airlift continued until the blockade was lifted as a result of an embargo on exports from the E European states.

Berlioz, (Louis) Hector (1803–69) French Romantic composer and conductor. His first successful work, the *Symphonie Fantastique* (1830–31), was influenced by his love for his future wife, the Irish actress, Harriet Smithson (1800–54). His dramatic symphony *Harold in Italy* (1834) and choral symphony *Romeo and Juliet*

(1839) were popular successes. The oratorio *The Childhood of Christ* (1850–54) was his last major success, for his two-part opera *The Trojans* (1856–59) was not performed complete in his lifetime. He was the author of a famous treatise on orchestration and a volume of memoirs.

Bermejo, Río   A river of S central South America. Rising in S Bolivia, it flows SE into Argentina to join the River Paraguay. Length: 1046 km (650 mi).

Bermuda   A British crown colony, comprising some 300 coral islands (of which 20 are inhabited), in the W Atlantic Ocean. The largest island is Bermuda (*or* Great Bermuda), while smaller ones include Somerset, Ireland, and St George. Approximately three-quarters of the population is Black. *Economy*: tourism and agriculture are the main activities. *History*: visited by the Spanish navigator Juan de Bermudez in 1515, the islands were first settled in 1609 by British colonists shipwrecked there on the way to Virginia. They became the responsibility of the British Crown in 1684 and became self-governing in 1968 but demands for independence have grown; the governor was assassinated in 1973 and there was serious rioting in December, 1977. Governor: Viscount Dunrossil (1926–   ). Official language: English. Official currency: Bermuda dollar of 100 cents. Area: 53 sq km (20 sq mi). Population (1986): 59 000. Capital: Hamilton.

Bermuda Triangle   The most notorious of several geographic regions, all lying roughly between 30° and 40° of latitude, in which numerous ships and aircraft have vanished without trace. The Triangle covers about 3 900 000 sq km (1 500 000 sq mi) between Bermuda, Florida, and Puerto Rico. No generally satisfactory explanation of these disappearances has been advanced, but the powerful currents may explain the lack of wreckage.

Bern (French name: Berne)   46 57N 95 58W The capital of Switzerland, on the River Aare. Founded as a military post in the 12th century, it joined the Swiss Confederation in 1353 and became the capital in 1848. It has considerable industry and contains the headquarters of several international organizations. Population (1985): 138 600.

Bernadette of Lourdes, St   (1844–79) French peasant girl, who in 1858 claimed to have had 18 visions of the Virgin Mary at a grotto near Lourdes. At 20 she became a nun. She was canonized in 1933 and her shrine is a place of pilgrimage. Feast day: 18 Feb or 16 April.

Bernadotte, Jean Baptiste Jules   (c. 1763–1844) French marshal, who was King of Sweden (1818–44) as Charles XIV John, founding the present Swedish royal house. Rising from the ranks he became a marshal under Napoleon with whose support he was adopted as heir by the dying Charles XIII of Sweden. Turning against Napoleon, Bernadotte contributed to his defeat at Leipzig (1813). In 1814 he forced Denmark to cede Norway to the Swedish monarchy.

Berne Convention   An international copyright agreement of 1866. Its main provision guarantees copyright in all signatory countries of any work copyrighted in any one of them. The USA is still not a signatory.

Bernese Oberland (*or* Bernese Alps)   A section of the Alps in SW Switzerland, 105 km (65 mi) long, between the Rivers Rhône and Aare. Its mountain peaks include the Eiger and the Finsteraarhorn and it is a popular area for mountain climbing.

SARAH BERNHARDT   *In the role of Hamlet at the Adelphi Theatre, London (1889).*

Bernhardt, Sarah   (Sarah Henriette Rosine Bernard; 1844–1923) French actress. Plays in which she gave worldwide performances include *Phèdre* (1879), *La Dame aux camélias*, and *L'Aiglon* by Edmond Rostand. She was also manager of several theatres in Paris and opened the old Théâtre des Nations as the Théâtre Sarah Bernhardt.

Bernina, Piz   46 23N 9 54E A mountain in SE Switzerland, in the Alps near St Moritz. Height: 4049 m (13 284 ft).

Bernini, Gian Lorenzo   (1598–1680) Italian baroque sculptor and architect, born in Naples, the son of a sculptor. His first major sculptures were for Cardinal Scipione Borghese and included *Apollo and Daphne* (1622–24; Borghese Gallery, Rome). Encouraged by Urban VIII, he extended his talents into architecture, major works being the baldachin over the tomb of St Peter (1624–33) and the piazza and colonnade (1656–67) of St Peter's, Rome. Later sculptures included fountains for Roman piazzas and such portrait busts as *Louis XIV* (1665; Versailles).

Bernoulli's principle   The principle of conservation of energy applied to fluid flow. If the effects of friction are neglected the total energy of the flow at any point in a pipe is equal to the sum of the kinetic energy due to the flow velocity, the gravitational potential energy due to height, and the energy of pressure in the fluid itself. Bernoulli's theorem states that the sum of these three components is constant throughout a flow system. Named after Daniel Bernoulli (1700–82).

Bernstein, Leonard   (1918–   ) US conductor, composer, and pianist. From 1958 to 1969 he was musical director and conductor of the New York Philharmonic Orchestra. His compositions, including symphonies, choral works, and songs, often contain jazz and folk elements. His musicals, such as *On the Town* (1944) and *West Side Story* (1957), have been widely popular.

Berruguete, Pedro   (c. 1450–c. 1504)   Castillian Renaissance painter. In the 1470s he worked in Italy at the court of Urbino, where he painted *Federigo da Montefeltro and his Son* (Urbino). On returning to Spain (1482) he painted frescoes for Toledo cathedral and altarpieces for the Dominican order in Avila. His son **Alonso Berruguete** (c. 1489–1561) was a mannerist painter and sculptor, who worked in Italy (c. 1504–c. 1517) and became court painter to Emperor Charles V (1518).

berry Loosely, any small succulent fruit. Botanically, a berry is a simple fruit with a thin skin and pulpy flesh containing many loose seeds: the tomato and grape are examples. Blackberries and raspberries are not strictly berries, but collections of small drupes.

berserkers (Old Norse: bear-shirts) In Scandinavian mythology, savage warriors whose frenzy in battle transformed them from men into wolves or bears and gave them immunity from harm by the sword or fire—hence the phrase "to go berserk." They were devotees of Odin and, in early Scandinavian history, warriors called berserkers were often employed as bodyguards to nobles.

Berthollet, Claude Louis, Comte (1748–1822) French chemist and physician. He introduced bleaching by chlorine; he also showed that ammonia consists of hydrogen and nitrogen. Berthollet, working with Lavoisier, developed a new chemical nomenclature. He travelled to Egypt as scientific adviser to Napoleon, who made him a senator and a count.

Bertolucci, Bernardo (1940–) Italian film director. Many of his films are strongly influenced by Marxist ideology, notably *Before the Revolution* (1965) and the epic *1900* (1977). He achieved his greatest commercial success with the controversial *Last Tango in Paris* (1972) and with *The Last Emperor* (1988).

beryl A mineral consisting of beryllium alumino-silicate, found principally in granites and granite pegmatites. It occurs as crystals up to one metre in length and is white, pale blue, or green. Aquamarine and emerald are gem varieties.

beryllium (Be) A light (relative density 2.34) alkaline-earth metal that was discovered in 1828 by F. Wöhler and A. Bussy (1794–1882) independently. Its salts are highly toxic and require careful handling. It occurs in nature in such minerals as beryl and phenacite (Be_2SiO_4). It is transparent to X-rays and is used as windows on X-ray tubes. Alloys with copper are extensively used and the oxide (BeO), having a high melting point (2530°C), is used as a ceramic. At no 4; at wt 9.0122; mp 1278°C; bp 2450°C.

Berzelius, Jöns Jakob, Baron (1779–1848) Swedish chemist, whose main work was the discovery of atomic compositions of chemical compounds. He discovered the elements selenium (1817), silicon (1824), and thorium (1828) and determined the atomic and molecular weights of more than 2000 elements and compounds. He introduced the current notation for chemical formulae and the use of oxygen as a reference standard for atomic weights.

Bes The Egyptian god of recreation, also associated with children and childbirth. Images of the god, represented as a grotesque dwarf with a tail, were kept in homes as protection against evil.

Besançon 47 14N 6 02E A town in E France, the capital of the Doubs department on the River Doubs. It is the French watchmaking centre and produces cars and textiles. Population (1983): 120 000.

Bessarabia A region in the SW Soviet Union, largely in the Moldavian and Ukrainian SSRs and with a predominantly Moldavian population. The main activity is agriculture and food processing. *History*: the region was colonized by the Greeks and later fell successively to the Romans, Huns, Magyars, Mongols, and Turks, passing to Russia in 1812. In 1918 Bessarabia declared its independence, later voting for union with Romania. In 1940 Romania ceded Bessarabia to the Soviet Union. Area: about 44 300 sq km (17 100 sq mi).

Bessemer process A steelmaking process invented by Sir Henry Bessemer (1813–98) in 1855. A long cylindrical vessel (Bessemer converter) is charged with molten pig iron; air, introduced through holes in the bottom of the converter, is blown through the iron to oxidize the carbon, silicon, and manganese impurities. Phosphorus is removed by reaction with the converter's basic refractory lining. Carbon, in the form of spiegel, is then added to give steel of the required carbon content. It has now been largely replaced by the basic-oxygen process.

Best, Charles Herbert (1899–1978) US physiologist, who, as an undergraduate research assistant to Banting, helped to isolate the hormone insulin.

BESTIARY *An illustration of a mule from a bestiary of c. 1240.*

bestiary A medieval treatise containing short accounts of different species of animal, both real and imaginary. Based on ancient Greek and Latin sources, bestiaries were often fancifully illustrated but were generally wildly inaccurate in their natural history.

beta blocker A drug, such as propranolol, that prevents certain nerve endings (beta receptors) of the sympathetic nervous system from being stimulated, thus reducing heart activity. Developed by Sir James Black, they are used to treat angina and hypertension.

beta decay A radioactive process in which a neutron within a nucleus decays by the weak interaction into a proton, an electron (beta particle), and an antineutrino; alternatively, a proton may decay into a neutron, a positron, and a neutrino. Since the nuclear charge changes by one in both cases, the nucleus is converted into the nucleus of another element.

betatron A type of particle accelerator used for producing very high energy electrons. The electrons are accelerated round a circular path in an evacuated torus-shaped chamber, by means of a large pulsed magnetic field. Electron energies up to 300 MeV are possible.

betel A mixture of the boiled dried seeds (**betel nuts**) of the areca, or betel palm (*Areca catechu*), and the leaves of the betel pepper (*Piper betle*), which produces copious salivation when chewed with lime—common in India.

Betelgeuse An immense remote yet conspicuous red supergiant, over 500 light years distant, that is the second brightest star in the constellation Orion. It is a variable star with its magnitude ranging, usually, from 0.3 to 0.9 over a period of about 5.8 years.

Bethe, Hans Albrecht (1906–   ) US physicist, born in Germany, who worked on the atom bomb during World War II. He received the 1967 Nobel Prize for his work on quantum electrodynamics.

Bethlehem 31 42N 35 12E A town on the West Bank of the River Jordan, near Jerusalem. The Church of the Nativity was built in 326 over the grotto that is the presumed birthplace of Jesus Christ. Population (1984): 20 000.

Betjeman, Sir John (1906–84) British poet. He published his first book of poetry in 1933. His verse autobiography, *Summoned by Bells* (1960), reflected the nostalgia and gentle social satire characteristic of his other poems. He took a keen interest in Victorian and Edwardian architecture. He was poet laureate from 1972.

betony A widespread perennial herb, *Stachys officinalis* (or *Betonica officinalis*), up to 30 cm high. It has round-toothed leaves and a dense head of reddish-purple tubular flowers. The leaves may be used for tea and for herbal tobacco. Family: *Labiatae*.

Betti, Ugo (1892–1953) Italian dramatist. A lawyer, Betti's plays, notably *Corruption in the Palace of Justice* (1944) and *The Fugitive* (1953), concern justice and social responsibility.

Betty Trask Award An annual prize of £12,500 for authors under 35 awarded for a first novel "of a romantic or traditional, rather than experimental, nature." It was set up in 1984 by a legacy of the writer Betty Trask.

Bevan, Aneurin (1897–1960) British Labour politician, A brilliant orator, Nye Bevan clashed with the Labour Party in 1939 over its ambivalence towards Hitler. He edited the socialist *Tribune* from 1940 to 1945. As minister of health (1945–51), he was the architect of the National Health Service. He was also minister of labour in 1951. His wife **Jenny, Baroness Lee** (1904–88), a Labour MP (1929–31, 1945–70), was minister for the arts (1967–70).

Beveridge, William Henry Beveridge, 1st Baron (1879–1963) British economist, writer, and academic. Beveridge became an authority on unemployment. His best-known work was the *Report on Social Insurance and Allied Services* (1942), the so-called **Beveridge Report**, which created the welfare state.

Bevin, Ernest (1881–1951) British politician and trade-union leader. Bevin formed, and was general secretary (1921–40) of, the Transport and General Workers' Union and in 1937 became chairman of the TUC. In 1940 he became minister of labour, serving in Churchill's war cabinet. He was foreign secretary (1945–51) in the postwar Labour Government, when he helped to form NATO.

bezique A card game, usually for two players, that became popular in France about 1860. Two packs of 32 cards are used (standard packs with the cards from two to six removed). Each player is dealt eight cards; the next card indicates the trump suit and the rest form the stockpile. The object is to score points by collecting melds (certain combinations of cards) and to take tricks containing brisques (aces and tens). Play continues until one player's score reaches 1000 or 1500.

BHAGAVADGITA   *Arjuna and Krishna (left).*

Bhagavadgita (Sanskrit: Song of the Lord)   Hindu poem probably composed about 300 BC, forming part of the epic *Mahabharata*. It blends a number of Hindu philosophies. Arjuna, one of the five Pandava brothers, is compelled to battle with his kinsmen, the Kauravas; he is persuaded by Krishna, acting as his charioteer, of the virtue of selflessly performing the duties of caste.

Bhavachakra (Sanskrit: wheel of becoming)   In Buddhism, an image of the cyclical nature of earthly existence, in the form of a wheel held by the demon of impermanence. At the centre, turning the wheel, are greed, hatred, and delusion, depicted as a cockerel, snake, and pig, biting each other's tails. Around the rim, the 12 stages in the cycle of life are symbolically expressed.

Bhopal 23 17N 77 28E A city in India, the capital of Madhya Pradesh. Notable buildings include the unfinished Taj-ul-Masjid, the largest mosque in India. Bhopal's varied manufactures include vehicle parts and cotton textiles. In 1984 over 2000 people died after poisonous isocyanate gas escaped from the US-owned Union Carbide factory. Population (1981): 672 000.

Bhoskhara II (1114–c. 1185) Indian mathematician, who was the first to use the decimal system in a written work, invented the + and – convention, and used letters to represent unknown quantities as in modern algebra.

Bhutan, Kingdom of (Bhutanese name: Druk-yul)   A small country in the E Himalayas, between India and Tibet. It is entirely mountainous, rising over 7300 m (21 900 ft) in the N. Over half the population are of Tibetan origin, known as Bhutias, with minorities of Nepalese in the S and Indians in the E. *Economy*: mainly agricultural; forests cover almost 70% of the land and hydroelectricity is being developed. A new postal system was inaugurated in 1972 and since then postage stamps have been a valuable source of foreign currency. *History*: in 1865 part of S Bhutan was annexed by the British and a treaty was concluded in which Britain agreed to pay an annual subsidy. In 1910 Britain agreed not to interfere in Bhutan's internal affairs and in 1910 Sir Ugyen Wangchuk was elected the first hereditary maharaja (now referred to as king). In 1969 the absolute monarchy was replaced by a "democratic monarchy" and power is now divided between the king, the Council of Ministers, the National Assembly, and the monastic head of Bhutan's lamas. Head of state: King Jigme Singye Wangchuk (1955–). Official language: Dzongkha Bhutanese. Official currency: ngultrum of 100 chetrums. Area: 46 600 sq km (18 000 sq mi). Population (1985): 1 286 000. Capital: Thimphu.

Bhutto, Zulfikar Ali (1928–79) Pakistani statesman; president (1971–73) and then prime minister (1973– 77). He formed the Pakistan People's Party in 1967 and became president after the secession of East Pakistan (Bangladesh). Ousted by a military coup, he was defeated in the subsequent election and executed for conspiring to murder an opponent. His daughter **Benazir Bhutto** (1953–) lived in Britain (1984–86) before returning to Pakistan as leader of her father's party. She became prime minister in 1988, being the first female leader of a Muslim country.

Biafra The Ibo secessionist eastern region of the Federal Republic of Nigeria (1967–70). In an attempt to protect their interests the Ibo people declared unilateral independence under Lieut Col Odumegwu Ojukwu (1933–). The federal government under Gen Yakuba Gowon (1934–) refused to recognize the new state and attacked it. The Ibo were decimated.

Białystok 53 09N 23 10E A city in NE Poland. It grew mainly under the Branicki family in the 18th century. In World War II the Germans killed half the population and destroyed the industry but cloth manufacture has been revived. Population (1985): 245 000.

biathlon 1. An athletic event first included in the Winter Olympic Games in 1960; competitors ski 20 km (12.5 mi) with rifles and ammunition and at each of four points along the course take five shots at 150 m (164 yd). 2. An athletic event consisting of running 4000 m (2.5 mi) and swimming 300 m (328 yd), introduced in 1968 by the Modern Pentathlon Association of Great Britain as a preparation for the full modern pentathlon.

Bible (Greek *biblia*, books) The collected books of the Old Testament, the New Testament, and the Apocrypha. The canon of the Hebrew Old Testament was definitively established by the rabbinical council of Jamnia (90–100 AD), although most of the books had acquired authority much earlier. The New Testament canon was also established gradually but had essentially its present form by the 3rd century AD. To Christians it represented the complete fulfilment of the prophecies of the Old Testament. Both Jews and Christians originally regarded their scriptures as divinely inspired, hence correct in every particular. All Christians agreed, until relatively recently, on the literal truth of the contents, a belief slowly eroded by the development of science from the 17th century onwards. Despite the attempts to condemn scientific findings when these appeared to conflict with scripture, as in the case of Galileo, the scientific method was soon applied to the study of the Bible itself. The oldest extant complete manuscript of the Old Testament dates from the 11th century AD, but there are much earlier versions of parts of the text, for example the Pentateuch (*see also* Dead Sea Scrolls). The earliest fragments of the New Testament date from the 2nd century AD; thereafter there are an extremely large number of manuscripts of quite early date. *Translations*: the first translation of the Bible is the Latin Vulgate of St Jerome. Major English versions are: the version prefaced by Wycliffe (1382–88), the last manuscript Bible written before the introduction of printing; the New Testament (1525) by Tyndale; the Bible of Miles Coverdale; the Great Bible

(1539), supervised by Coverdale under the patronage of Thomas Cromwell; the Geneva (*or* Breeches) Bible; the Bishops' Bible (1568); the Douai Bible; the King James (*or* Authorized) Version; the *Revised Version* (1881–95); the *Revised Standard Version* (1946–57); and *The New English Bible* (1961–70).

Bibliothèque Nationale The national library of France in Paris, containing around seven million volumes. It is based on the royal libraries of Charles the Wise (1364–80) and his successors. From 1537 it received a copy of every book published in France.

bicycles Light two-wheeled vehicles, the wheels of which are moved by cranks attached to pedals operated by the rider. Bicycles developed in the 19th century from a two-wheeled hobby-horse, known as the dandy-horse or celeripede. Around 1840 a Scotsman, Kirkpatrick Macmillan, applied the dandy-horse principle to models with pedals. The first true bicycles, with rotary cranks on their front wheels, went into production in Paris in 1865. Nicknamed "boneshakers," they popularized cycling as a pastime. To increase efficiency the front wheel was gradually made larger, resulting in the 20-year vogue of the ordinary (*or* pennyfarthing) bicycle. This was superseded by the so-called safety bicycle (1876), which had a chain and sprocket drive to the rear wheel and was essentially the same as the modern bicycle. Pneumatic rubber tyres (1889), a freewheeling mechanism (1894), and variable gears (1899) were later refinements. The first race was held in France in 1868.

Biddle, John (1615–62) English religious leader, founder of Unitarianism (*see* Unitarians). While a schoolmaster he wrote his *Twelve Arguments* against the deity of the Holy Ghost, for which he was imprisoned in 1645. Although his adherents began to meet openly from 1652, he was arrested and banished under Cromwell and finally died in prison in London.

Biedermeier style A style of furniture and painting that flourished in Austria, Germany, and Scandinavia from about 1816 to about 1848. It was satirically named after the fictional Gottlieb Biedermeier, created by the poet Ludwig Eichrocht (1827–92) to characterize bourgeois bad taste. Biedermeier furniture utilized French Empire style design for modern functional purposes. Biedermeier paintings aimed at extreme naturalism in outdoor scenes and intimacy in interiors and portraits.

Bielefeld 52 02N 8 32E A city in N West Germany, in North Rhine-Westphalia. Its linen mills were the first in Germany to be mechanized (1851). Silks, clothing, and machinery are also manufactured here. Population (1986): 299 200.

bigamy The offence of marrying a person while being married to another. Defences include an honest and reasonable belief in the death of the original marriage partner, or that the first marriage was invalid. Although a person would not be guilty of bigamy in such cases, the second marriage will still be invalid.

Big Bang. *See* stock exchange.

big-bang theory A cosmological theory (*see* cosmology), first proposed in the 1920s, that all the matter and radiation in the universe originated in an immense explosion about 10 to 20 thousand million years ago. As the universe so created expanded, the initially high temperature decreased, enabling hydrogen and helium to form. This matter eventually interacted to form galaxies. The theory also predicts that the radiation formed shortly after the explosion should by now have cooled to about three kelvin. This is indeed the temperature of the isotropic microwave background radiation, detected in 1965 and now considered strong evidence for the big-bang theory.

Big Ben The 14-ton bell in the clock tower of the Palace of Westminster (London), named after Sir Benjamin Hall (1802–67), commissioner of works when the clock was installed (1859). Both the clock and the tower itself are also known by this name.

bighorn A mountain sheep, *Ovis canadensis*, of North America. There is considerable variation within the species, ranging from the small Nelson's bighorn to the largest Rocky Mountain bighorns, which stand 100 cm at the shoulder.

Bihar A state in N India, bordering on Nepal. The densely populated rural Ganges plain in the N produces rice, sugar cane, pulses, and vegetables. The S Chota Nagpur plateau yields minerals, including much of the world's mica. *History*: the centre of N Indian civilization from 1500 BC, it was the scene of the early development of Buddhism and Jainism. Area: 173 876 sq km (67 116 sq mi). Population (1981): 69 823 154. Capital: Patna.

Bikaner 28 01N 73 22E A city in India, in Rajasthan. The former centre of a princely state, its fort (1571–1611) houses a fine collection of Sanskrit and Persian manuscripts. Bikaner is famous for the manufacture of carpets, shawls, and blankets. Population (1981): 280 000.

Bikini Atoll 11 35N 165 20E An atoll in the central Pacific Ocean in the Marshall Islands. It was the site of US atomic and hydrogen bomb tests (some underwater) from 1946 to 1958.

Biko, Steven. *See* Black Consciousness.

Bilbao 43 15N 2 56W A port in N Spain, the largest city in the Basque Provinces on the River Nervión. One of Spain's chief ports, its exports include iron ore, lead, and wine. Population (1981): 433 030.

bilberry A deciduous shrub, *Vaccinium myrtillus*, 30–60 cm high, also known as blaeberry, huckleberry, and whortleberry. It is found on acid moors and mountains in N Europe and N Asia. The green angular stems bear small pointed leaves that turn red in autumn. The globular pink flowers develop into blue berries, which

may be eaten raw or cooked. Family: *Ericaceae* (heath family).

bile A greenish alkaline fluid secreted by the liver and stored in the gall bladder. Contraction of the gall bladder, which is triggered by a hormone released from the duodenum in the presence of food, causes the bile to be expelled through the common bile duct into the intestine. Bile is composed of a mixture of bile salts (which emulsifies fatty foods for digestion) and bilirubin (a breakdown product of the blood pigment haemoglobin).

bilharziasis. *See* schistosomiasis.

billiards A game for two players using cues and balls on a table. In **English billiards** the table measures 12 × 6 ft (3.6 × 1.8 m) and has six pockets (holes round the edges of the table); points are scored using three balls 2 in (5.2 cm) in diameter. The white and the white-with-a-spot balls are cue balls, one for each player. A cannon, in which the cue ball strikes both the other balls, scores two points; a winning hazard, in which the cue ball pockets another ball, scores two points (white) or three (red); a losing hazard, in which the cue ball is pocketed after striking another ball, scores two points (off white) or three (off red). A turn (*or* break) lasts until the player fails to score. **Carom billiards** is played on a smaller table with no pockets and scoring is by cannons (*or* caroms). **Bar billiards** is played on a small table with a timing device and holes in the surface, into which balls are potted off each other until the time runs out. *See also* snooker.

Billingsgate A fish market in London, situated since the 16th century on the N bank of the River Thames by London Bridge. In 1982 was moved to its present location on the Isle of Dogs. The market porters are known for their heavy leather hats on which they balance boxes of fish.

Bill of Rights **1.** (1689) An act of parliament that incorporated the Declaration of Rights, the conditions on which the English throne was offered to William and Mary (*see* Glorious Revolution). It curtailed the royal prerogative. MPs were to be freely elected and guaranteed freedom of speech. Roman Catholics were barred from the throne. **2.** (1791) The first ten amendments to the US Constitution, described by Jefferson as "what the people are entitled to against every

BIG BEN *In 1858 it took 16 horses to pull the bell to the Palace of Westminster.*

government on earth." They include freedom of press, speech, and religion and the right to a fair and public trial.

binary star Two stars moving around each other under mutual gravitational attraction. Possibly 50% of stars are members of binary or other multiple systems. The components of a **visual binary** can be distinguished by telescope whereas a **spectroscopic binary** can only be detected by spectroscope measurements, the components usually being very close. In an **eclipsing binary** the orbital plane is so orientated that one component passes alternately in front of and then behind the other, causing the combined brightness to fluctuate. In a **close binary** the two components are close enough to exchange gaseous matter and can even share gas.

binary system A number system that uses only two digits 0 and 1. Numbers are expressed in powers of 2 instead of powers of 10, as in the decimal system. In binary notation, 2 is written as 10, 3 as 11, 4 as 100, 5 as 101, and so on. Computers calculate in binary notation, the two digits corresponding to two switching positions (e.g. on or off) in the logic circuits.

binding energy The energy released when protons and neutrons bind together to form an atomic nucleus. The mass of a nucleus is always less than the sum of the masses of the constituent protons and neutrons. The missing mass is converted into the binding energy according to Einstein's law $E = mc^2$.

bindweed A widely distributed climbing plant of the temperate and subtropical genera *Convolvulus* and *Calystegia*. Bindweeds twine their stems around other plants for support and can be persistent weeds. The leaves are large and arrow-shaped and the conspicuous white, pink, or yellow flowers are funnel-shaped. Family: *Convolvulaceae*.

bingo (former names: tombola; housy-housy) A gambling game that developed in the 1880s from the children's game of lotto. Each player buys a card containing lines of random numbers (from 1 to 75 in the USA and usually from 1 to 90 in the UK). As numbers are called out, the players cover corresponding squares on their cards with counters; the first person to complete a line or the card wins. It became popular in the UK following a relaxation of the gaming laws during the 1960s, many local cinemas being converted into bingo halls.

binoculars A portable optical instrument used for magnifying distant objects. It consists of two telescopes fixed side by side, one for each eye, inside which there are a number of lenses for magnifying and focusing the image and usually prisms for altering the direction of the light and thus increasing the effective length of the telescope.

binomial nomenclature A system devised by Linnaeus in the 18th century for the scientific naming of plants and animals, each species being identified by two Latin names—the name of the genus (written with an initial capital letter) followed by the name of the species. The specific name may be followed by the author's name, usually abbreviated. Thus the wolf is *Canis lupus* L (for Linnaeus).

binomial theorem The theorem, discovered by Newton in 1676, that the quantity $(a + n)^n$, where n is an integer, can be expanded in a series: $(a + b)^n = a^n b^n$ where, for example, 3! (called factorial three) is $3 \times 2 \times 1$.

binturong A mammal, *Arctictis binturong*, of SE Asia, closely related to the palm civets. It has a dark-grey shaggy coat, tufted ears, short legs, and a bushy prehensile tail (60 cm long). Binturongs live in trees and feed mainly on fruit and other vegetation.

biochemistry The scientific study of the chemical composition and reactions of living organisms. Central to biochemistry is metabolism and the determination of the complex sequence of reactions involved in the digestion of food, the utilization of energy, the manufacture of new tissues, etc. Biochemists are also concerned with the role of genes, hormones, and enzymes in initiating and controlling metabolic reactions.

biodegradable substances Materials that can be broken down by such processes as decomposition by fungi and bacteria—and can therefore be reused by living organisms. Substances that are **nonbiodegradable**, such as plastics, persist in the environment, pollution.

bioengineering (*or* biomechanics) The application of biological and engineering principles to the design and manufacture of equipment for use in conjunction with biological systems. Examples include artificial limbs, heart pacemakers, life-support systems for astronauts, etc.

biogas *See* alternative energy.

biological control The control of pests by the use of living organisms. The controlling agent is usually a predator, parasite, or disease of the pest organism. For example, the virus disease myxomatosis was introduced into Australia and Britain to control the rabbit population. Recent methods of controlling insect pests include the release of sterile males to mate among the population. Biological control avoids the environmental pollution of chemical pesticides.

BIOLOGICAL WARFARE *Nuclear, bacteriological, and chemical warfare (NBC) suits.*

biological warfare The use of disease-causing microorganisms as weapons. In World War I, the Germans infected Allied cavalry horses with bacteria causing glanders. Although biological warfare is now officially banned by the major powers, research continues in developing new strains of such organisms as the plague bacterium (*Pasteurella pestis*) and the smallpox virus. The organisms are required to be highly virulent and could be delivered in the warhead of a missile. Alternatively, they could be added to water or food supplies in a covert operation.

bioluminescence The production of light by living organisms, including certain bacteria, fungi, and animals (e.g. fireflies and glowworms). In some the luminescence is due to symbiotic light-producing bacteria. The light is emitted by the compound luciferin when it is oxidized: the reaction is catalysed by an enzyme, luciferase.

biomass The total weight (mass) of all living organisms (or of all members of a particular species) found in a given area. Biomass is expressed as mass per unit area.

biomass energy Energy obtained from the methane (biogas) generated by sewage or farm, industrial, and household organic waste, from specially cultivated organisms, or from crops, such as trees and sugar cane. Known collectively as **biofuels**, these alternative energy sources already supply some 4% of US fuel requirements. Research into such products is being actively pursued.

biome A geographical region that is characterized by a predominant type of vegetation and associated fauna. Examples include grassland, desert, tropical forest, etc.

bionics The study of living systems in order to design man-made systems based on similar principles. It assumes that most living creatures have adapted in the best possible way to their environments. The applications of bionics include the design of a ship's propellor modelled on a fish's tail.

biophysics The scientific discipline concerned with the explanation of biological phenomena in terms of the laws of physics. Biophysics emerged in the 1940s with the work of such scientists as Max Perutz and John Kendrew, who applied the phenomenon of X-ray diffraction to determine the structure of biological molecules. More recent topics include the nature of the nervous impulse and the operation of sense organs.

biopsy The removal of a sample of living tissue from the body for microscopic examination. Biopsies are used to assist in the diagnosis of diseases, including cancer, jaundice and anaemia.

biosphere The zone of the earth and its atmosphere that is occupied by living organisms.

biotin. *See* vitamin B complex.

birch A deciduous tree or shrub of the genus *Betula* (40 species), of the N hemisphere. Birches grow up to 25 m and have smooth grey bark, that peels off in strips. The glossy leaves are usually triangular, with toothed edges. The flowers are male and female catkins producing tiny winged nuts. Birch wood, especially that of the Eurasian silver birch (*B. pendula*), is used for turned articles. Family: *Betulaceae*.

bird A warm-blooded animal belonging to the class *Aves* (about 8600 species), adapted for flight by having fore limbs modified as wings and a body covering of feathers. Other adaptations include a light skeleton with hollow bones and a large breastbone providing attachment for the powerful flight muscles. The jaws are elongated into a horny bill (teeth are absent or reduced). Birds have good eyesight and colour vision and most are active by day. Many communicate by song (*see* songbird) and some undergo seasonal migrations.

Birds are of great economic importance to man. The eggs and flesh of many provide food (game or poultry). Wildfowl and game birds are hunted for sport, and the feathers of some birds provide ornamental plumes, etc.

Other species are pests, for example by damaging crops. Modern birds include both flying and flightless species (ratites); they are grouped into 28 orders, the largest of which is the *Passeriformes* (*see* passerine bird). *See also* ornithology.

bird of paradise A bird, 30–65 cm long, belonging to a family (*Paradisaeidae*; 40 species) occurring in New Guinea and neighbouring islands. The male is usually brightly coloured, with long tail feathers and ornamental plumes, and performs an acrobatic display to attract the dull-coloured female. Their feathers are much prized and were formerly exported for use in ladies' hats.

bird of prey A bird that hunts other animals for food, also called raptor. Birds of prey are divided into the nocturnal hunters, comprising the owls (order *Strigiformes*), and those that hunt by day, comprising the eagles, falcons, hawks, secretary bird, and the vultures (order *Falconiformes*). Live prey is normally taken but the vultures specialize in feeding on carrion. Birds of prey are characterized by their strong hooked bills for tearing flesh, clawed talons, and powerful flight with a high-speed dive onto prey.

bird's nest fern An Old World tropical fern, *Asplenium nidus*, that has a dense rosette of upward-pointing leaves, 60–120 cm long, with a central hollow forming a nest in which humus collects. The plant is grown for ornament. Family: *Aspleniaceae*.

bireme. *See* ships.

Birkbeck, George (1776–1841) British educationalist. As professor of natural philosophy at the Andersonian Institute, Glasgow, Birkbeck lectured unpaid to working men. With Brougham, Bentham, Cobbett, and others, he founded the London Mechanics' Institute (1824). This became affiliated to London University as Birkbeck College.

Birkenhead 53 24N 3 02W A port and engineering centre in NW England, in Merseyside, linked with Liverpool by road and rail tunnels. Population (1981): 123 907.

Birkenhead, F(rederick) E(dwin) Smith, 1st Earl of (1872–1930) British Conservative politician. A barrister, Birkenhead entered parliament in 1906. As attorney general (1915–19) he was famous for his prosecution of Sir Roger Casement and while lord chancellor (1919–22) he introduced major land-law reforms. He was secretary for India (1924–28).

Birmingham 52 30N 1 50W A city in central England, in the West Midlands. Britain's second largest city, it is a centre of engineering and metalworking. A cultural centre, it possesses two universities, Aston University (1966) and Birmingham University (1900), an art gallery (1874–81), a symphony orchestra, a ballet company, and a repertory theatre founded in 1913. Among postwar developments are a shopping complex centred on the Bull Ring (to be redeveloped in the 1990s), where a market has been held since ancient times, and The National Exhibition Centre (1976) at Bickenhill. *History*: an Anglo-Saxon settlement, its development dates largely from the industrial revolution although its metalworking tradition is much older. It was severely bombed during World War II. Population (1985): 1 008 000.

Birmingham 33 30N 86 55W A city in the USA, in Alabama. Settled in 1813, it is the state's largest city and the main industrial centre of the South. It has an important iron and steel industry. Population (1986): 277 510.

Biró, Laszlo (1900–85) Hungarian inventor, who in 1938 patented the ballpoint pen containing quick-drying ink. Such pens are now commonly known as biros.

birthstone In astrology, a gemstone associated with a particular date of birth. The wearing of one's birthstone as a lucky charm originated in the ancient belief that certain gems had supernatural powers. The modern list of birthstones is usually: January–garnet; February –amethyst; March–bloodstone; April–diamond; May –emerald; June–pearl; July–ruby; August–sardonyx; September–sapphire; October–opal; November–topaz; December–turquoise.

Birtwistle, Sir Harrison (1934–) British avant-garde composer. His compositions include the operas *Punch and Judy* (1966–67), and *The Mask of Orpheus* (1984), the chamber ensemble *Medusa* (1969–70), *An Imaginary Landscape* (for orchestra; 1971), and *Endless Parade* (for trumpet and orchestra; 1987).

Biscay, Bay of (French name: Golfe de Gascogne; Spanish name: Golfo de Vizcaya) An inlet of the Atlantic Ocean, off the coast of W France and N Spain. It is comparatively deep and subject to rough seas. Width: about 320 km (199 mi).

bisexuality. *See* homosexuality.

Bismarck, Otto Eduard Leopold, Prince von (1815–98) Prussian statesman; first chancellor of the German Empire (1871–90). A conservative, known as the Iron Chancellor, Bismarck came to prominence after the collapse of the Revolution of 1848. After victory in the Franco-Prussian War (1870–71) William I of Prussia accepted the imperial crown and Bismarck became chancellor of the new German Empire. He came into conflict (the Kulturkampf) with the Roman Catholic Church and, abroad, presided over the Congress of Berlin (1878) and formed the Triple Alliance with Austria and Italy. Losing the support of William II, Bismarck resigned in 1890 over the abolition of antisocialist laws.

Bismarck Archipelago A group of volcanic islands in the SW Pacific Ocean, in Papua New Guinea. It includes New Britain, New Ireland, and the Admiralty Islands. Area: 49 658 sq km (19 173 sq mi). Population (1980 est): 314 308.

bismuth (Bi) A dense white brittle metal, similar in properties to tin and lead. It is obtained as a by-product of lead, copper, tin, silver, and gold refining and also occurs naturally as the pure metal, the sulphide (Bi_2S_3), and the oxide (Bi_2O_3). It has unusual properties for a metal, having low thermal and electrical conductivity, and decreasing in volume on melting. With tin and cadmium it is used to make low-melting alloys in fire prevention systems. At no 83; at wt 208.9808; mp 271.3°C; bp 1560°C.

bison A massive hoofed mammal belonging to the genus *Bison* (2 species). The North American bison (*B. bison*) was once abundant on the plains but is now found only on reserves. Over 150 cm at the shoulder and weighing up to 1000 kg, it has a shaggy mane and low-slung head with incurved horns. The smaller European bison (*B. bonasus*), also called wisent, is now found only in zoos. Family: *Bovidae*.

Bissau 11 50N 15 37N The capital and chief port of Guinea-Bissau, on the Geba estuary. Founded by the Portuguese in 1687, it was capital of Portuguese Guinea (1941–74). Population (1979): 109 486.

bit A *binary digit*. The basic unit of information in information theory and computer memory stores. It is the amount of information needed to specify one of two alternatives, i.e. to distinguish between 1 and 0 in the binary notation.

BITTERN *Well hidden deep in the reedbed, the bittern's nest may be 1 m across.*

bittern A bird belonging to the subfamily *Botaurinae*, occurring throughout the world in swamps and reedbeds. The European bittern (*Botaurus stellaris*) is a solitary bird, 70 cm long, with a yellow-brown dark-streaked plumage that provides camouflage. The little bittern (*Ixobrychus minutus*) is 34 cm long with buffish-white wing patches. Family: *Ardeidae* (herons, etc.).

bittersweet A perennial plant, the woody nightshade.

bitumen The tarry residue left after distillation of oil, lignite, or coal, consisting almost entirely of a mixture of carbon with large hydrocarbon molecules. Its principal uses are in roadmaking and binding cement.

bivalve A mollusc belonging to the class *Bivalvia* (also called *Lamellibranchia* and *Pelecypoda*; about 10 000 species). Bivalves are characterized by having two hinged shell plates (valves) and include clams, mussels, oysters, and scallops. Bivalves inhabit both salt and fresh water. Most bivalves are of separate sexes but some are hermaphrodite. Some hermaphrodite bivalves, including *Ostrea* oysters, incubate the fertilized eggs.

Bizet, Georges (Alexandre César Léopold B.; 1838– 75) French composer. In 1855 he produced his first major work, the symphony in C major. Among his best works are the music to Alphonse Daudet's play *L'Arlésienne* (1872) and the opera *Carmen* (1873–74).

Black, Sir James (Whyte) (1924–) British biochemist. His discovery of beta blockers and his work on drugs for peptic ulcers and other uses won him a Nobel Prize (1988).

Black and Tans The soldiers recruited by the British Government to fight the IRA in Ireland in 1920–21. Their name derives from their uniform, khaki with black caps and belts. They acted with great severity and were hated by the Irish.

black bear The native bear of North American forests, *Ursus* (or *Euarctos*) *americanus*. American black bears grow to a weight of 150 kg; they climb well and eat berries, pine cones, and grass as well as small animals.

The name is also used for the Himalayan black, or moon, bear, *Selenarctos thibetanus*, which inhabits forests of central and E Asia and has a white V-shaped mark on its chest.

BLACK AND TANS   *The Royal Irish Constabulary in 1921; they were hated by the Irish.*

black beetle. *See* cockroach.

blackberry (*or* bramble) A prickly scrambling shrub, *Rubus fruticosus* (an aggregate species), occurring throughout Europe. The stems, up to 5 m long, root wherever they touch the ground. The dark-green leaves usually consist of five oval toothed leaflets and the pinkish-white flowers are borne in terminal clusters. The fruits, each of which consists of an aggregate of several small berries, are eaten raw or cooked. Family: *Rosaceae.*

blackbird A songbird, *Turdus merula*, that is one of the commonest European birds, particularly in urban areas. The male, about 25 cm long, is black with a bright-yellow bill and eye ring; the larger female is dark brown with a dark bill. Blackbirds feed chiefly on worms and other invertebrates but will also eat scraps. Family: *Turdidae* (thrushes).

black body A theoretical body that absorbs all the electromagnetic radiation falling upon it. When heated it emits radiation (black-body radiation) having a continuous distribution of wavelengths with a maximum at a particular wavelength, which depends only on the temperature of the body.

Blackburn 53 45N 2 29W A town in NW England, in Lancashire on the Leeds–Liverpool Canal. Traditionally a cotton-weaving town, its chief industry now is engineering. Population (1981): 88 236.

blackcap A European warbler, *Sylvia atricapillus*. About 14 cm long, it has an olive-brown plumage with paler underparts and a darker cap (black in the male and reddish-brown in the female). Blackcaps feed chiefly on insects but—before migrating—they eat fruit to build up energy reserves.

Black Consciousness The recognition by minority Black communities throughout the world of their identity, history, and culture, as distinct from that of Whites. Political and social movements contributing to the development in the USA have included the National Association for the Advancement of Coloured People, and the later Black Muslims. In South Africa the Black Consciousness Movement was led by **Steven Biko** (d. 1977),

whose death from extensive injuries while in police detention provoked worldwide concern.

Black Country, the An industrial area of central England. Situated N of Birmingham, it corresponds roughly to the S Staffordshire coalfield. It gained its name from the grime produced by intense industrialization in the 19th century.

blackcurrant A shrub, *Ribes nigrum*, native to most of Europe and N Asia and widely cultivated. The stems and three-lobed leaves emit a characteristic smell. The drooping clusters of greenish bell-shaped flowers develop into edible black berries. Family: *Grossulariaceae* (gooseberry family).

BLACK DEATH   *Victims being buried (1349).*

Black Death The worst outbreak of plague, principally bubonic but also pneumonic and septicaemic, of the medieval period. Orginating in the Far East, it spread through Europe and England in May, 1348. Estimates of mortality rates vary from 20% to more than 50%. The outbreak had a profound effect not only on demographic trends but,also upon rural society and the economy as a whole. Further outbreaks followed in the 1350s and 1370s.

black earth. *See* chernozem.

blackfly Any black aphid, especially the bean aphid (*Aphis fabae*). Bean aphids occur in masses on beans, spinach, dock, etc., in summer months. They overwinter as fertilized eggs in *Euonymus, Viburnum,* and *Philadelphus* trees.

black grouse A Eurasian grouse, *Lyrurus tetrix*, of moorlands. The male (also called blackcock), 50 cm long, has a glossy black plumage and a lyre-shaped tail; the female is reddish brown. Both have conspicuous red wattles above the eyes.

black hole A celestial "object" that has undergone such total gravitational collapse that no light can escape from it. Once a collapsing object's radius has shrunk below a critical value (the Schwarzschild radius) it becomes a black hole; for a star, this radius is about 10 km or less. The surface having this radius is called the event horizon of the black hole. The object will continue to contract until compressed to an infinite density at a single central point—a singularity. Black holes of 10^6 to 10^9 solar masses are now thought to exist at the centres of certain galaxies, possibly including our own, and to be the powerful sources of energy in quasars.

Black Hole of Calcutta A small cell (5.5 m × 4.5 m) in which over one hundred British soldiers were allegedly confined overnight in 1756, less than 25 men surviving. The outrage was perpetrated by the Nawab of Bengal, who, objecting to the fortification of Calcutta by the East India Company, defeated the British garrison.

blackjack A card game based on pontoon played in casinos. The croupier deals two cards face up to each punter and 1 to himself; blackjack consists of a 10 and an ace, and pays 3 to 2, unless the dealer also makes blackjack on his second card (in which case no money changes hands).

black mass A blasphemous parody of the Roman Catholic mass, celebrated by satanists in honour of the devil. A naked woman is usually present at or on the altar and participants take hallucinatory drugs.

Black Mountains A mountain range in SE Wales, in Powys, mainly in the Brecon Beacons National Park. It rises to 811 m (2660 ft) at Wann Fach.

Black Muslims Members of the Nation of Islam movement founded in Detroit (USA) in 1930 by W. D. Fard, believed by Black Muslims to be the Saviour. After the disappearance of Fard in 1933, the movement was led by Elijah Muhammad (1897–1975); Malcolm X was a leading member until 1964. It aims to establish a new Black Islamic state and follows many Muslim practices.

Blackpool 53 50N 3 03W A resort in NW England, on the Lancashire coast, famous for its 160 m (520 ft) high Tower (modelled on the Eiffel Tower), Pleasure Beach, and illuminations. Population (1987): 144 100.

Black Prince, Edward the. *See* Edward, the Black Prince.

Black Rod An official of the House of Lords, first appointed in 1522, having been called usher of the Order of the Garter since 1350. He maintains order in the House and when the monarch delivers a speech, summons members of the Commons by knocking on their door with his black rod.

Black Sea An inland sea bounded by Bulgaria, Romania, the Soviet Union, and Turkey; it is connected to the Mediterranean Sea via the Bosporus in the SW and to the sea of Azov in the N. Its salinity is kept low principally by the influx of fresh water from the Rivers Danube and Dnepr.

black swan The only Australian swan, *Cygnus atratus*. Almost 1 m in length, both sexes have a pure black plumage, red bill, and a trumpeting call.

blackthorn (*or* sloe) A thorny shrub, *Prunus spinos*, forming dense thickets, up to 4 m high, in many parts of Europe and Asia. The clusters of white flowers usually appear before the leaves, which are oval and toothed. The bitter-tasting blue-black stone fruits are used to flavour sloe gin. Family: *Rosaceae*.

black widow A venomous spider, also called button or redback spider, that belongs to a genus (*Latrodectus*; about 6 species) found in tropical and subtropical regions. The female of *L. mactans*, the most common North American species, has a shiny black body, 25 mm long, with red markings on the abdomen. (The male is about 6 mm long and usually killed and eaten by the female after mating.) The bite is serious but rarely fatal. Family: *Theridiidae*.

bladder In anatomy, any hollow organ containing fluid, especially the urinary bladder, into which urine drains from the kidneys.

bladderwort A plant of the widely distributed genus *Utricularia* (about 200 species, many tropical). Most bladderworts are submerged aquatic plants with finely divided leaves bearing small bladders, which trap tiny aquatic animals by a trapdoor mechanism triggered by sensitive hairs. The two-lipped tubular flowers protrude above the water. Family: *Lentibulariaceae*.

Blake, Robert (1599–1657) English admiral. A Parliamentarian in the Civil War, Blake became one of Cromwell's most successful commanders and in 1650 destroyed Prince Rupert's Royalist fleet. In the first Dutch War, Blake was largely responsible for the English victory and sank 16 Spanish ships at Santa Cruz off Tenerife (1657). He died while returning to Plymouth.

WILLIAM BLAKE *Detail of an illustration from* The Book of Job, *engraved in 1823–25.*

Blake, William (1757–1827) British visionary poet, painter, and engraver. His poems, the texts of which he engraved and illustrated, include *Songs of Innocence* (1789), *Songs of Experience* (1794), various "Prophetic Books," *Milton* (1808), and *Jerusalem* (1820). His watercolours for *The Book of Job* (1826) and Dante's *Divine Comedy* (1827) were inspired by his visions and engravings after Michelangelo. Although unrecognized by his generation, except by a few friends, he was a precursor of Romanticism.

Blantyre (*or* Blantyre-Limbe) 15 46S 35 00E The largest city in Malawi, in the Shire Highlands. In 1956 it was linked with the nearby town of Limbe, a major railway centre, and is Malawi's chief industrial centre. Population (1985 est): 355 200.

Blarney 51 56N 8 34W A village in the Republic of Ireland, in Co Cork. Blarney Castle contains the famous Blarney Stone, which is kissed to receive the gift of "blarney" or smooth talk. Population (1985 est): 1500.

blast furnace A furnace used in the smelting of ore. In steel making, iron ore, coke, and limestone are poured in at the top of a vertical furnace and a blast of hot air is blown in at the bottom to burn the coke. Molten iron is drawn off at the bottom. A glassy waste, called slag, is also produced.

bleaching The whitening, lightening, or removing of colour by chemical treatment or exposure to sunlight. Most bleaching agents are oxidizing agents, which convert a pigment into an oxidized colourless form. Examples are hydrogen peroxide, bleaching powder, and hypochlorites. In some processes reducing agents, such as sulphur dioxide, are used.

bleaching powder (*or* chloride of lime) A whitish powder containing calcium hypochlorite ($Ca(OCl)_2$), calcium chloride ($CaCl_2$), calcium hydroxide ($Ca(OH)_2$), and water. It reacts with dilute acids to produce chlorine, which acts as a bleaching agent.

bleeding heart An ornamental plant of the genus *Dicentra*, especially *D. spectabilis* from Siberia and Japan and *D. eximia* from North America. They are perennials with arching stems, up to 90 cm long, bearing strings of large rose-red heart-shaped flowers with whitish tips. Family: *Fumariaceae*.

Blenheim, Battle of (13 August, 1704) The battle won by the Duke of Marlborough and Prince Eugene of Savoy (1663–1736) against the French army in the War of the Spanish Succession. It was fought at Blenheim (now Blindheim) on the Danube River and Blenheim Palace was built for Marlborough by a grateful parliament.

Blenheim Palace The baroque palace built between 1705 and 1725 at Woodstock, Oxfordshire (England), as a gift from Queen Anne to the Duke of Marlborough for his victories over the French, especially at the Battle of Blenheim. Designed by Vanbrugh, the gardens were laid out by Capability Brown.

blenny A small fish belonging to a family (*Bleniidae*; about 300 species) found among rocks in shallow waters of tropical and temperate seas. Blennies have an elongated scaleless body with a blunt nose. Many have small tentacles on their heads. The name is also used for several other fish of the order *Perciformes*.

Blériot, Louis (1872–1936) French aviator. Beginning his career as a motorcar engineer he was the first to fly the English Channel (1909), from Calais to Dover, in a monoplane. He later became a manufacturer of aircraft.

blewits An edible mushroom, *Tricholoma* (or *Lepista*) *saevum*, occurring mainly in open pastures. It has a bluish-grey stalk and a flat clay-coloured cap, 6–12 cm in diameter. The wood blewits (*T. nudum*) has a lilac or purple cap and is usually found beneath trees. Family: *Tricholomataceae*.

Bligh, William (1754–1817) British admiral. He accompanied Cook on his second voyage round the world and in 1787 was sent to Tahiti on the *Bounty* to collect specimens of the breadfruit tree. Setting sail for home, his crew mutinied, leaving Bligh and 18 officers aboard a small boat without maps. He eventually reached safety. In 1805 he was made governor of New South Wales.

blight A severe disease of plants caused by pests, fungi, or other agents. Symptoms commonly include spotting followed by wilting and death. The notorious potato blight that devastated Ireland in the mid-19th century was caused by the fungus *Phytophthora infestans*.

blindworm. *See* slowworm.

Bliss, Sir Arthur Edward Drummond (1891–1975) British composer. Director of music at the BBC (1942–44), Bliss was knighted in 1950 and was Master of the Queen's Music (1953–75). His works include *A Colour Symphony* (1922), music for the film *The Shape of Things to Come* (1935), the opera *The Olympians* (1948–49), and a cello concerto (1970).

blister beetle A brightly coloured beetle, about 10–15 mm long, belonging to a widely distributed family (*Meloidae*; about 2000 species), which also includes the oil beetles. The larvae are parasitic upon other insects, while the adults generally feed on plants. Their secretion of cantharidin, a powerful blistering agent, has led to the medicinal use of various species, especially Spanish fly.

Blitzkrieg (German: lightning war) A military tactic aiming to disorganize enemy forces by suprise attacks using tanks and aerial bombardment. It was extensively used by the Germans in World War II. The **Blitz** refers to the intensive German air raids on London during the battle of Britain in World War II.

Bloch, Ernest (1880–1959) Swiss-born composer of Jewish descent who moved to the USA in 1916. His opera *Macbeth* (1903–09), a rhapsody for cello and orchestra entitled *Schelomo* (1916), *Concerto Grosso* (1925), and *Sacred Service* (1930–33) incorporate Jewish musical elements.

Bloch, Felix (1905–83) US physicist, born in Zurich, who moved to the USA when Hitler came to power. He developed the nuclear magnetic resonance technique for which he shared the Nobel Prize (1952) with E. M. Purcell. During World War II he worked on development of the atomic bomb. In 1954 he became the first director of CERN.

Bloemfontein 29 07S 26 14E The judicial capital of South Africa and the capital of the Orange Free State. Founded in 1846, it is an important agricultural centre and new gold mines have been opened nearby. Population (1985): 204 000.

Blondin, Charles (Jean-François Gravelet; 1824–97) French acrobat and tightrope walker. In 1859 he walked across a tightrope suspended over Niagara Falls and later repeated the feat several times. See p. 96.

blood The red body fluid consisting of a watery plasma in which are suspended various blood cells—the red cells (*see* erythrocyte) and several kinds of white cells (*see* leucocyte). The platelets are small particles involved in blood clotting. Blood acts as a medium for transporting oxygen, carbon dioxide, digested food, hormones, waste materials, salts, and many other substances to and from the tissues. An average adult has about 70 millilitres of blood per kilogram of body weight (i.e. about 5 litres in an average man). Blood is present in all animals with a circulatory system: its functions are similar to that of human blood although its composition varies. *See also* blood clotting; blood groups; circulation of the blood.

blood clotting The mechanism by which blood is converted from a liquid to a solid state to prevent loss of blood after injury. The process involves chemical reactions between soluble proteins (clotting factors) in the blood in the presence of platelets, resulting in the formation of a fibrous protein (fibrin), which forms the basis of the blood clot. *See also* thrombosis.

CHARLES BLONDIN *Crossing the Niagara Falls on a tight-rope in 1859.*

blood fluke A parasitic flatworm of the genus *Schistosoma* (3 species), which causes the disease schistosomiasis in many parts of the world. The flukes are carried by freshwater snails and enter their human hosts to inhabit blood vessels, feeding on blood and causing severe debilitation. *See also* fluke.

blood groups The different types of blood, classified on the basis of the presence of certain proteins (*see* antibody) on the surface of the red cells, which is genetically determined. The major grouping is the ABO system, discovered in 1900 by Karl Landsteiner (1868–1943). It consists of four groups: A, B, AB, and O. Group A cells carry the A antigen and the plasma contains antibodies against B antigen (anti-B antibodies); the converse applies to group B blood. Transfusion of blood between these groups causes destruction of the donor blood cells (*see* blood transfusion). Group O blood contains neither antigen and can therefore be used in transfusions to people of groups A and B. Group AB blood contains neither anti-A nor anti-B antibody: people of this blood group can accept both A and B blood during transfusion. *See also* rhesus factor.

bloodhound An ancient breed of dog with a keen sense of smell, originating around the Mediterranean and used for tracking. It has a sturdy frame and a large head with long drooping ears and wrinkled skin around the eyes. Height: 63–69 cm (dogs); 58–64 cm (bitches).

blood pressure The pressure that blood exerts on the walls of the arteries, due to the pumping action of the heart. Blood pressure is at its lowest between heartbeats (i.e. at diastole) and at its highest when the ventricles of the heart are contracting (i.e. systole). It is recorded, using a sphygmomanometer, as the height in millimetres of a column of mercury (mmHg). Blood pressure varies but a healthy adult might have a systolic pressure of about 120 mmHg and a diastolic pressure of 80 mmHg, expressed as 120/80. *See also* hypertension.

blood sports Sports in which a quarry is hunted and killed or a spectacle is made of an animal being killed. In the UK most of the blood sports in the latter category

have been made illegal—bull and bear baiting since 1835, cockfighting since 1849, and badger baiting since 1973. Bullfighting, however, continues in Spain, while foxhunting, staghunting, beagling, and coursing still continue in the UK, although the League against Cruel Sports has been fighting to make them illegal.

bloodstone A mineral of a green colour speckled with red. It is a variety of chalcedony. Birthstone for March.

blood transfusion Usually the transfer of blood from a **blood bank** to a person who has suffered extensive loss of blood; for example, during surgery or following an accident. Some people (e.g. Jehovah's Witnesses) object to transfusion on religious grounds. The blood is stored in the bank at 4°C and should be used within 3–4 weeks. The blood group of the recipient must match that of the donor.

Bloody Assizes. *See* Jeffreys of Wem, George, 1st Baron.

Bloomsbury group A group of English writers and artists active in the 1910s and 1920s who met in private houses in Bloomsbury, London. The group included the writers Virginia Woolf, E. M. Forster, and Lytton Strachey, the art critics Clive Bell (1881–1964) and Roger Fry, and the economist J. M. Keynes. Most of them had studied at Cambridge University and were influenced by G. E. Moore's *Principia Ethica* (1903).

blowfly A large buzzing fly belonging to the family *Calliphoridae*. Some blowflies lay their eggs in human food, but more commonly the larvae develop in decaying organic material. The larvae of certain species (e.g. of the American genus *Cochliomyia* are serious pests of sheep and cattle. Chief genera: *Calliphora* (bluebottles), *Lucilia* (greenbottles).

bluebell One of several plants having bell-shaped blue flowers. In England the bluebell is *Endymion nonscriptus*, up to 50 cm high, which overwinters as a bulb. Family: *Liliaceae*. In Scotland the name is applied to the harebell.

bluebottle. *See* blowfly.

blue fox. *See* Arctic fox.

blue-green algae Organisms formerly classified as algae (division *Cyanophyta*) but now reclassified as bacteria (cyanobacteria). They contain a blue pigment (phycocyanin), in addition to the green chlorophyll. Reproduction is asexual. They occur on moist surfaces and in the soil, where they contribute to nitrogen fixation. Aquatic blue-green algae are a constituent of plankton.

blue gum *See* Eucalyptus.

Blue Mountains A mountain range in Australia, in New South Wales. Part of the Great Dividing Range, it reaches 1180 m (3871 ft) at Bird Rock and contains the Blue Mountains National Park.

Blue Riband of the Atlantic An award for the fastest seaborne crossing of the Atlantic. First awarded in 1838, the title has been held by many famous passenger liners, notably the *Queen Mary* (1938–52) and the *United States* (from 1952), which won it with a time of 3 days, 10 hours, and 40 minutes. In 1986 Richard Branson's *Virgin Atlantic Challenger II* power boat reduced this to 3 days, 8 hours, 31 minutes.

blues A type of US folk music that evolved from the Negro spirituals and work songs of the 1860s. The first published blues were "Memphis Blues" (1912) by W. C. Handy (1873–1958) and Jelly Roll Morton's "Jelly Roll Blues" (1915). The blues influenced the development of jazz and rock music and stimulated composers, such as George Gershwin, who wrote the orchestral *Rhapsody in Blue* (1924). Famous blues singers include Bessie Smith.

bluetit A European tit, *Parus caeruleus*, with a blue crown and wings, a yellow breast, and white face. Bluetits feed chiefly on insect larvae.

bluets A tufted herb of the genus *Houstonia* (about 25 species), native to North America and widely grown in rock gardens. The small funnel-shaped flowers are borne singly or in clusters. Some species provide ground cover in shade. Family: *Rubiaceae* (madder family).

BOBSLEDDING *A four-man bob competing in the European championships.*

blue whale The largest living whale, *Balaenoptera musculus*, growing to over 30 m and weighing over 150 tonnes. They are nearing extinction due to overhunting. Family: *Balaenopteridae* (*see* rorqual).

Blunt, Anthony. *See* Maclean, Donald.

Blyth, Chay (Charles Blyth; 1940–) British yachtsman. After service in the armed forces (1958–67), he circumnavigated the world: westwards in 1970–71 (solo) and eastwards in 1973–74 (with a crew). In 1984 he was rescued off Chile when his yacht sank.

Blyton, Enid (1897–1968) British writer of children's books. She introduced her famous character Noddy in 1949 and wrote over 600 books for children.

boa A snake belonging to the subfamily *Boinae* (40–60 species) of the constrictor family and occurring in Old and New World regions. 20–760 cm long, boas are usually green or yellowish with a camouflaging pattern. They kill their prey by biting and then constricting. The boa constrictor (*Boa constrictor*), occurring from Mexico to Argentina, is about 3.5 m long.

Boadicea (Latin name: Boudicca; d. 61 AD) Queen of the Iceni. Her husband Prasutagus ruled in what is now Norfolk (England). At his death in 61, Roman officials maltreated Boadicea and her daughters. She led the Iceni into rebellion, sacking Colchester, London, and St Albans. The Roman governor Suetonius Paulinus defeated the rebels at or near Fenny Stratford. Boadicea committed suicide.

boar, wild A Eurasian wild pig, *Sus scrofa*, once common in European forests. Up to 1.5 m long and 1 m high at the shoulder, they have a rough greyish bristly coat. The ancestors of domestic pigs, males have four tusks.

boatbill A nocturnal heron, *Cochlearius cochlearius*, occurring in tropical American swamps. It is about 50 cm tall and has a grey plumage. It closely resembles the night heron but has a broad hook-tipped bill.

Boat Race An annual rowing race on the River Thames between Oxford and Cambridge Universities, first held in 1829 at Henley. The present course of 6.8 km (4.25 mi) from Putney to Mortlake was established in 1845. By 1989 Cambridge had won 69 races and Oxford 65, with one dead heat (1877).

bobcat A short-tailed cat *Felis rufa*, resembling a lynx, found in North America. About 90 cm long, it is brown with greyish markings and has large ears.

bobsledding The sport of racing bobsleds (also called bobsleighs or bobs), which was developed by British sportsmen at St Moritz (Switzerland) in the late 19th century. A bobsled is a steel-bodied toboggan with two pairs of runners, the front pair steerable, and a rear brake, holding two or four people. The bobsleds slide down a narrow chute some 1500 m (1640 yd) long with high walls, reaching speeds of over 130 km per hour (81 mph).

Boccaccio, Giovanni (1313–75) Italian writer and poet. Son of a merchant of Florence, he wrote *Filocolo*, a prose romance, *Filostrato*, which supplied the plot of Chaucer's *Troilus and Criseyde*, and *Teseida*, the source of Chaucer's *Knight's Tale*. Between 1348 and 1353 he composed the *Decameron*, a collection of a hundred stories told by a party escaping from plague-stricken Florence in 1348. In later life he chiefly wrote scholarly works in Latin and lectured on Dante's *Divine Comedy*.

Bodensee. *See* Constance, Lake.

Bodhisattva In Mahayana Buddhism, the title of a person who is to become a Buddha; also the Buddha (Gautama) before his enlightenment. The Bodhisattva ideal is that of the individual who seeks enlightenment not for himself alone but for all beings.

Bodleian Library The major library of Oxford University, first established in 1409 and restored and enlarged by Sir Thomas Bodley from 1598 to 1602. Since 1610 it has been entitled to receive a free copy of every book published in Britain; it contains well over 2.5 million volumes.

Boeotia A region of central Greece, N and W of Attica. Its rich central plains are surrounded by hills and mountains. The dozen or so city states that shared the territory formed a federal state dominated by Thebes in 446 BC.

Boer Wars (*or* South African Wars) The wars fought against the British by the Boers or Afrikaners of South Africa. In the first (1880–81) the Boers of the Transvaal under Kruger rebelled against British rule. After inflicting a massive defeat on the British garrison at Majuba Hill, the Transvaal regained its independence under the Pretoria Convention. In the second Boer War (1899–1902) the Boer forces were initially successful, besieging Ladysmith, Mafeking, and Kimberley. They suffered reverses during 1900 but were able to hold off the British under Kitchener and F. S. Roberts (1832–1914). The British devastated the countryside, rounded up Boer women and children, of whom some 20 000 died in concentration camps, and finally defeated the Boers, who lost their independence in the Peace of Vereeniging (1902). See p. 98.

Boethius, Anicius Manlius Severinus (c. 480–524 AD) Roman statesman and philosopher. A pa-

BOER WARS *A unit of the Boer army at Newcastle, Natal.*

trician, he became chief minister under Theoderic. His championing of Roman traditions earned Theoderic's displeasure, and Boethius was imprisoned, tortured, and eventually executed. His translations of Aristotle and treatises on music and mathematics were standard texts in medieval Europe but his most famous work is *The Consolation of Philosophy*, written while he was in prison.

Bogarde, Dirk (Derek van den Bogaerde; 1921–   ) British film actor of Dutch descent. His major performances were *The Damned* (1969), *Death in Venice* (1970), and *Providence* (1978). He is also the author of the autobiographical *A Postilion Struck by Lightning* (1977), *Snakes and Ladders* (1978), and *An Orderly Man* (1983) as well as the novels *A Gentle Occupation* (1980) and *Voices in the Garden* (1981).

Bogart, Humphrey (1899–1957) US film actor. His films include *Casablanca* (1942), *To Have and Have Not* (1944), in which Lauren Bacall (1924–   ), whom he subsequently married, made her screen debut, *The Big Sleep* (1946), and *The African Queen* (1951).

Bogotá, Santa Fé de 4 38N 74 15W The capital of Colombia, on a fertile central plateau of the E Andes at an altitude of 2640 m (8600 ft). Founded by the Spanish in the early 16th century on the site of the conquered Indian settlement of Bacatá, it became the capital of the viceroyalty of New Grenada. Population (1985): 4 185 174.

Bohemia (Czech name: Čechy; German name: Böhmen) An area and former province (1918–49) of W Czechoslovakia. It consists chiefly of a plateau enclosed by mountains. It is the most industrialized part of Czechoslovakia; agriculture and mining are also important. *History*: Bohemia derives its name from the Boii (the first known inhabitants), who were displaced by the Czechs (1st-5th centuries AD). Bohemia became part of the greater Moravian empire in the 9th century. It achieved the height of its power following the acquisitions of the Přemyslid Otakar II (1230–78; reigned 1253–78). The Přemyslid dynasty came to an end with the assassination of Wencelas III (1289–1306; reigned 1305–06) and John of Luxembourg was subsequently elected king (1310). The golden age of Bohemia was established by his son Charles I (Emperor Charles IV).

Bohr, Niels Henrik David (1885–1962) Danish physicist, who worked with J. J. Thomson at Cambridge and Rutherford at Manchester. He made an immense contribution to atomic theory by combining Rutherford's nuclear model with Planck's quantum theory. The model of the atom (the Bohr atom), in which a central nucleus is surrounded by electrons confined to circular orbits corresponding to fixed energy levels, was modified by Sommerfeld but is the basis for modern atomic theory. Bohr also invented the concept of complementarity to combine the particle and wave aspects of subatomic particles. Bohr later worked at Los Alamos on the bomb, after escaping from German-occupied Denmark. A fervent advocate of atomic energy for peaceful uses, he organized the first Atoms for Peace Conference in 1955.

boiling point The temperature at which the vapour pressure of a liquid is equal to the atmospheric pressure, usually given at standard atmospheric pressure (101 325 pascals).

Boise 43 38N 116 12W A city in the USA, the capital and largest city of Idaho. The centre of a gold rush in 1862, it has timber, food-processing, and agricultural industries. Population (1984 est): 107 188.

Boletus A genus of mushrooms (about 50 species). The undersurface of the cap bears a series of vertical tubes (instead of gills), in which the spores are formed. Most grow near trees and they are generally edible or harmless (*see* cèpe), except Satan's boletus (*B. satanas*), which is poisonous. It has a short stalk and a grey cap 10–20 cm in diameter. Family: *Boletaceae*; class: *Basidiomycetes*.

Boleyn, Anne (c. 1507–36) The second wife (from 1533) of Henry VIII and the mother of Elizabeth I. When Henry tired of her she was accused of treason through committing adultery and executed.

Bolingbroke, Henry St John, 1st Viscount (1678–1751) English statesman and philosopher. A Tory MP, he became secretary of war (1704–08). As a supporter of the Jacobites, he fled to France after his dismissal (1714) by George I, where he helped to organize the Fifteen Rebellion. He also wrote *Reflections upon Exile* and *Reflections Concerning Innate Moral Principles*. Returning to England in 1725, he became the opponent of

Robert Walpole. In 1735 he returned to France. He also wrote *The Idea of a Patriot King* (1749).

Bolívar, Simón (1783–1830) South American soldier, known as the Liberator. The son of a wealthy Venezuelan creole family, his travels in Europe instilled a lasting admiration for the ideas of the Enlightenment. He returned to Latin America in 1807 and devoted the rest of his life to its liberation from Spain. In 1813 he seized Caracas but after defeat in 1814 went into exile until 1817. His victory at the battle of Boyacá (1819) achieved the liberation of New Granada (renamed Colombia). Bolívar became its president and, after liberating Venezuela and Quito (Ecuador) in 1821, organized a federation of the three newly independent states. Latin America was finally freed of the Spanish by campaigns in Peru, Upper Peru taking the name Bolivia in his honour. His dream of a united Andean republic was thwarted by political bickering.

Bolivia, Republic of An inland country in South America consisting of low plains in the N and E, crossed by the Madre de Dios, Bené, and Mamoré river systems; in the W, ranges of the Andes rise to over 6400 m (21 000 ft) and the Altiplano, a plateau averaging about 3900 m (13 000 ft), contains Lakes Titicaca and Poopó. Bolivia has some of the world's highest inhabited regions, most of the population, of mixed Indian and Spanish descent, living at altitudes of over 3000 m (10 000 ft): *Economy*: tinmining remains the principal industry. Other minerals include zinc, lead, antimony, and copper. The main crops are sugar cane, potatoes, maize, rice, and wheat. Illegal trade in cocaine also thrives. *History*: ruins near Tiahuanaco indicate a pre-Inca civilization (the Aymaras) going back to the 10th century. The area later became part of the Inca Empire and was conquered by the Spanish in the 16th century, when it became known as Upper Peru. The discovery of tin and silver led to great prosperity. In 1776 it became part of the viceroyalty of Buenos Aires. After a long war it gained its independence with the help of Simón Bolívar in 1825 and became a republic with Antonio José de Sucre (1795–1830) as first president. During the remainder of the century struggles with neighbouring countries cost Bolivia much territory. Political unrest and violent changes of government have continued into the 20th century and in 1971 a military coup brought Gen Hugo Banzer Suárez to power; he was overthrown in a coup in 1978. By 1985 Bolivia had the highest rate of inflation in the world and massive foreign debts, while disputes with Peru and Chile continue over access to the Pacific coast. President: Jaime Paz Zamora. Official languages: Spanish, Quechua, and Aymara. Official currency: boliviano of 1 000 000 pesos. Area: 1 098 580 sq km (424 160 sq mi). Population (1987 est): 6 730 000. Capital: La Paz (legal capital: Sucre).

boll weevil A brownish weevil, *Anthonomus grandis*, also called cotton boll weevil. Originally a native of the New World tropics, it is now a major insect pest of cotton crops in the W hemisphere. The female lays a single egg within each cotton boll, which thus fails to develop.

Bologna 44 30N 11 20E A city in N Italy, the capital of Emilia-Romagna. The site dates from Etruscan times, but it did not become a free city until the middle ages; the Emperor Charles V was crowned here in 1530. Regarded as Italy's gastronomic centre, its industries include engineering and food processing. Population (1986): 432 406.

Bologna, Giovanni da. *See* Giambologna.

Bolsheviks One of the two factions into which the Russian Social Democratic Workers' Party split in 1903 in London (the other was the Mensheviks). The Bolsheviks, which means those in the majority, were led by Lenin, who believed that the revolution must be guided by a single centralized party of professional revolutionaries. The Bolsheviks came to power in the Russian Revolution (1917).

BOLSHOI BALLET   *The corps de ballet in* Giselle.

Bolshoi Ballet The principal Russian ballet company, based at the Bolshoi Theatre in Moscow. It originated from a dancing class established by the Moscow orphanage in the late 18th century and moved into its present premises in 1856 after fire had destroyed the first Bolshoi Theatre. It first appeared in London in 1956 and has since become one of the world's leading ballet companies.

Bolt, Robert Oxton (1924–) British dramatist. His plays include *A Man for All Seasons* (1960), a study of Sir Thomas More. He has written screenplays for *Lawrence of Arabia* and other films directed by David Lean.

Bolton 53 35W 2 26W A town in NW England, in Greater Manchester. Traditionally a cotton-spinning town, Bolton also manufactures textile machinery and chemicals. Population (1985): 261 000.

bombardier beetle A blue-grey and orange beetle, about 9 mm long, belonging to a widely distributed genus (*Brachinus*) of ground beetles. It emits puffs of an irritant secretion from the anal glands. Similar beetles of the genus *Pherosophus* occur in Africa and Asia.

Bombay 18 56N 72 51E A city in India, the capital of Maharashtra and the country's main seaport on the W coast. The city occupies a group of islands united by a system of causeways. Its natural harbour, 11 km (7 mi) wide, is the focus of most of India's international trade. The Tata hydroelectric system powers much of Bombay's industry, which includes cotton textiles, food processing, and oil refining. The population is mainly Hindu but there are large Muslim, Christian, and Jewish minorities. *History*: ceded to the Portuguese in 1534, it passed to Charles II of England in 1661 and to the British East India Company in 1668. The railways, the opening of the Suez Canal, and land reclamation led to expansion in the 19th century. Population (1981): 8 227 000.

Bombay duck A fish, *Harpodon nehereus*, found in the estuaries of N India, where it is widely used for food. It has a grey or brown body, about 40 cm long, with small dark speckles and large fins. Order: *Myctophiformes*.

Bon The pre-Buddhist religion of Tibet, characterized by the belief in a supreme sky god. Elaborate ritual, including animal or even human sacrifice, abounded; religious practice was presided over by a class of shamans (*see* shamanism), priest-magicians who could influence the spirits by means of white or black magic.

bone A rigid tissue that forms most of the skeleton of higher animals and man. Most bones have a central cavity filled with marrow. Bone is composed of a matrix of fibres of the protein collagen, responsible for their strength, and bone salts, chiefly calcium salts (*see* apatite). This tissue is formed by activity of bone cells (osteoblasts), which become enclosed in the matrix when they have ceased to function. Bone formation starts during embryonic life. Most bones (including the long bones) develop from cartilage and the process is complete at birth. Membrane bones (e.g. the skull bones) are formed directly in connective tissue, the process being completed after birth (hence the gap (called a fontanelle) in a newborn baby's skull).

Bône. *See* Annaba.

bone-black (*or* animal charcoal) Charcoal obtained by heating bones. It is about one-tenth carbon, the rest being calcium and magnesium phosphates and other salts. Bone-black is used as an absorbent, for example in removing colouring, refining sugar, etc.

bongo An antelope, *Boocerus euryceros*, of African forests. About 120 cm high at the shoulder, bongos are red-brown with white body stripes and markings on the head. The male has spiralled horns up to 100 cm long. Bulls are solitary; cows and calves live in small herds.

Bonhoeffer, Dietrich (1906–45) German pastor and theologian. He opposed the pro-Nazi part of the Lutheran church; during the war he became involved with anti-Hitler conspirators. He was arrested in 1943, sent to Buchenwald concentration camp, and finally hanged. His *Letters and Papers from Prison* (1953) and theological writings are still widely read.

Bonington, Chris (Christian John Storey B.; 1934–) British mountaineer, author, and photographer. He is famous especially for the first British ascent of the N face of the Eiger (1962) and his ascent of Everest in 1985.

bonito A swift marine food and game fish, belonging to the worldwide genus *Sarda*, which is related to mackerel and tuna. About 75 cm long, bonitos are greenish above, with dark longitudinal stripes.

Bonn 50 43N 7 07E The capital of the Federal Republic of Germany (West Germany), in North Rhine-Westphalia on the River Rhine. The old part of the town contains the cathedral (12th–13th centuries) and Beethoven's birthplace (now a museum). *History*: settled by the Romans, it was destroyed by the Normans (9th century), and was the seat of the Electors of Cologne (13th to 16th centuries). It passed from France to Prussia in 1815 and became federal capital in 1949. Population (1986): 290 000.

Bonnard, Pierre (1867–1947) French painter. Originally a lawyer, he attracted attention with his litho-

graphs, *Aspects of the Life of Paris* (1895), and illustrations for Verlaine's book *Parallèlement* (1900). After 1900 his paintings of interiors, landscapes, and bathing women were treated increasingly with dazzling colour and light.

Bonneville Salt Flats (*or* Bonneville Flats) A barren salt plain in the USA, in NW Utah, forming part of the Great Salt Lake Desert. Several land speed records have been established here.

Bonnie Prince Charlie. *See* Charles Edward Stuart, the Young Pretender.

BONSAI *An example from the Bonsai Museum in Heidelberg.*

bonsai An ordinary shrub or tree, such as a conifer or flowering cherry, that is developed as a miniature (up to about 60 cm high). The technique was first practised in China over 700 years ago. It was later perfected by the Japanese and has now spread to the W hemisphere. Both branches and roots of potted cuttings are trained and pruned. The trees may take ten years to acquire an aged appearance, and some live 300–400 years.

bony fish Any fish belonging to the class *Osteichthyes* (or *Pisces*), which includes the majority of food and game fishes (*see* teleost). They have bony skeletons and their gills are covered by a structure called an operculum. Many species use a swim bladder for buoyancy control and even for breathing air (*see* lungfish). Fertilization of the eggs occurs outside the body. Subclasses: *Actinopterygii; Sarcopterygii*.

booby A large tropical seabird belonging to the family *Sulidae* (gannets, etc.; 9 species) characterized by a large head, a long tapering bill, and a wedge-shaped tail. Boobies are 65–85 cm long and typically have a white plumage with brown markings. Boobies dive into the sea to catch fish.

bookbinding The practice of sewing or gluing together the pages of a book and securing them between protective covers (boards) joined across the back (spine) by a flexible hinge. In the middle ages wooden boards were common and elaborate examples were encrusted with precious metals and gems. The advent of printing encouraged diversification in the types of material used for binding, with leather and vellum becoming paramount. Gold tooling reached a peak of elaboration in the 17th and 18th centuries. The spread of literacy caused a demand for still cheaper binding materials; cloth bindings

(1822), and in the 20th century paper and plastics, have catered for this need.

Modern books are bound by machinery, the bindings being similar to hand bindings except in paperbacks, which are simply glued together.

Booker Prize An annual prize of £20,000 for a work of British fiction. It was set up in 1968 by the British engineering company Booker McConnell, in conjunction with the Publishers' Association. Since 1971 it has been administered by the Book Trust (formerly the National Book League). Recent winners include Penelope Lively (1987), Peter Carey (1988), and Kazuo Ishiguro (1989).

Book of the Dead A collection of ancient Egyptian texts dating from the 16th century BC. They consist of charms and spells written on papyrus and placed inside mummy cases for use by the dead in the afterlife.

bookworm Any insect that damages books by gnawing the bindings and boring holes in the paper. Bookworms therefore include silverfish, booklice (order *Psocoptera*), moth and beetle larvae, etc.

Boole, George (1815–64) British mathematician, who applied the methods of algebra to logic. By replacing logical operations by symbols, Boole showed that the operations could be manipulated to give logically consistent results. His method, known as Boolean algebra or symbolic logic, led to mathematics being given a logically consistent foundation. The subject was further developed by G. Frege, A. B. W. Russell, and A. N. Whitehead.

boomerang A curved hand-thrown wooden missile used by Australian Aborigines to kill game or as a weapon of war. The angled shape and the spin given to the missile when thrown enables them to return to the thrower if they miss their target. Up to 75 cm (30 in) long, they can be effective to a distance of 45 m (50 yd).

boomslang A venomous green snake, *Dispholidus typus*, occurring in Africa and reaching 1.8 m in length. It feeds on birds and chameleons, often holding its body erect and motionless before striking. Its venom can cause fatal haemorrhaging in man. Family: *Colubridae*.

Booth, William (1829–1912) British preacher and founder of the Salvation Army. He was born in Nottingham and became an itinerant Methodist preacher. He established a mission in Whitechapel in 1865. The reluctance of established churches to accept his slum converts led to the foundation of the Salvation Army (1877).

Boothia Peninsula A peninsula of N Canada projecting into the Arctic Ocean.

Bootle 53 28N 3 00W A town in NW England, on the River Mersey adjacent to N Liverpool. Bootle's docks are extensive. Population (1981): 62 463.

bop (or bebop) A type of jazz that originated in the USA in the 1940s as a reaction against swing. Bop emphasized the art of melodic improvisation but was also characterized by harmonic and rhythmic experimentation. In New York City, Dizzy Gillespie and Charlie "Bird" Parker established small bop bands that required the audience to listen rather than dance.

Bophutha Tswana, Republic of A small country in South Africa, consisting of several separate landlocked areas. The majority of the population is Tswana. *Economy*: chiefly agriculture, especially livestock. Large numbers of people still work and live in South Africa. Mineral resources include chrome, platinum, asbestos, and iron. *History*: in 1972 it became the first Bantu Home-

land to receive self-government under the Bantu Homelands Constitution Act (1971). It was granted independence in 1977, but this is recognized only by South Africa. President and prime minister: Chief L. L. M. Mangope (1923–). Official currency: South African rand. Area: 38 261 sq km (14 769 sq mi). Population (1984 est): 1 420 000, of whom 65% lived in South Africa. Capital: Montshiwa.

borage A widely grown annual Mediterranean herb, *Borago officinalis*. Up to 60 cm high, with terminal clusters of small blue flowers with backward-pointing petals, borage is used in herbal remedies, beverages, etc. Family: *Boraginaceae*.

boranes Compounds of boron and hydrogen. The simplest is diborane B_2H_6, which is made by reacting sodium borohydride ($NaBH_4$) with sulphuric acid.

Bordeaux (Latin name: Burdigala) 44 50N 0 34W A city in SW France, the capital of the Gironde department on the River Garonne. It is a major seaport and wine centre. Industries include shipbuilding, engineering, and oil and sugar refining. *History*: an important centre under the Romans, it became the capital of Aquitania (*see* Aquitaine) but declined following the collapse of the Roman Empire. It flourished once again under English rule (1154–1453), becoming a centre of the Fronde in the 17th century and of the Girondins during the French Revolution. It was the seat of the French government for a brief period in 1914 and again in 1940. Population (1983): 221 500.

Borders Region An administrative region in SE Scotland, bordering on England. It was created under local government reorganization in 1975 from the counties of Berwick, Roxburgh, Peebles, Selkirk, and the SW part of Midlothian. The region consists chiefly of uplands descending E to the Merse lowlands. It is predominantly agricultural. Area: 4672 sq km (1804 sq mi). Population (1988 est): 102 592. Administrative centre: Newtown St Boswells.

border terrier A breed of working dog originating in the border region of England and Scotland. It has a deep narrow body, triangular forward-falling ears, and a short strong muzzle. Weight: 6–7 kg (dogs); 5–6 kg (bitches).

bore A tidal flood wave occurring in certain estuaries and travelling upstream several kilometres at great speed. It occurs when the spring flood tide brings sea water into an estuary more quickly than it can travel up the river.

Borghese An Italian family that originated in Siena and rose to fame in Rome in 1605 after **Camillo Borghese** (1552–1621) became Pope Paul V. His adopted nephew **Scipione Caffarelli** (1576–1633), sponsored Bernini in the building of the Villa Borghese (now an art gallery) in Rome.

Borgia, Cesare (c. 1475–1507) Duke of the Romagna and captain general of the armies of the Church. The illegitimate son of Pope Alexander VI, Borgia became Archbishop of Valencia and a cardinal. He surrendered his cardinalship to marry the sister of the King of Navarre and to become captain general of the Church. He won the Romagna in three campaigns (1499–1502) but was forced to relinquish it after Alexander's death (1502). He escaped from imprisonment and died in the employ of the Navarrese king. His sister **Lucrezia Borgia** (1480–1519) was married three times by her father Alexander VI to further his political aims. Her third husband

Alfonso (1486–1534) became Duke of Este and she presided over a distinguished court at Ferrara.

Boris III (1894–1943) King of Bulgaria (1918–1943). Boris ruled as a dictator from 1938 and supported the Axis Powers in World War II. He apparently died of a heart attack but may have been assassinated.

Bormann, Martin (1900–45) German Nazi leader, who became Hitler's personal secretary in 1942. He was sentenced to death in absentia at Nuremberg. In 1973 it was established that he had committed suicide in May, 1945.

Born, Max (1882–1970) British physicist, born in Germany. He shared the 1954 Nobel Prize with W. Bothe for his work in statistical mechanics. With Heisenberg he developed matrix mechanics. Born was professor of natural philosophy at Edinburgh University from 1936 to 1953.

Borneo A mountainous island SE of Peninsular Malaysia, in the Greater Sunda Islands. During the 19th century Borneo was settled and partitioned by the Dutch and British. It now consists of the Indonesian territory of Kalimantan, the Malaysian states of Sabah and Sarawak, and the British-protected sultanate of Brunei. The chief population groups are the coastal Malays and indigenous Dyaks. It possesses valuable resources of oil, coal, and gold. Area: 750 000 sq km (290 000 sq mi).

Bornholm 55 02N 15 00E A Danish island in the Baltic Sea, SE of Sweden. Dairy farming and pottery are the main activities. Area: 588 sq km (227 sq mi). Population (1987): 46 839. Chief town: Rønne.

BOROBUDUR *During restoration of the buildings the statues depicting Buddha were removed from the walls.*

Borobudur A huge Buddhist stupa (shrine) in central Java, built about 800 AD and abandoned, unfinished, about 1000. It has five square terraces of diminishing size, one on top of the other, on the vertical surfaces of which is carved a relief depicting the Buddha's life. On top, three circular terraces support 72 stupas. Restored (1973–83) at a cost of £20 million, it was badly damaged in a terrorist attack in 1985.

Borodin, Aleksandr Porfirevich (1833–87) Russian composer, one of the Five. A professor of chemistry, he produced two symphonies (1867 and 1876), the tone poem *In the Steppes of Central Asia* (1880), three string quartets, and the opera *Prince Igor* (completed by Rimsky-Korsakov and Glazunov in 1890).

boron (B) A nonmetallic element isolated (1808) by Sir Humphry Davy. It has two forms: an impure brownish amorphous powder and pure brown crystals. The main source, kernite ($Na_2B_4O_7.4H_2O$), is mined in California. Boron is used in semiconductors and in hardened steel. The isotope boron-10 absorbs neutrons: boron carbide (B_4C) and boron alloys are used in the control rods and shielding of nuclear reactors. Borax ($Na_2B_4O_7.10H_2O$), is used in glass manufacture. At no 5; at wt 10.81; mp 2300°C.

borough A unit of local government originating in Anglo-Saxon England. In the UK, county boroughs were set up by the Local Government Act (1888) but were wound up by the Local Government Act (1972). Boroughs remain the units of local government in London (outside the City). The title borough may be granted by royal charter for ceremonial purposes.

Borrowdale A scenic valley in NW England, in Cumbria extending southwards from Derwentwater towards Scafell.

Borstal system An English penal system established by the Prevention of Crime Act (1908) for the rehabilitation of offenders aged between 15 and 21. The name derives from the prison at Borstal near Rochester, Kent, where the system was introduced. It was abolished by the Criminal Justice Act (1982).

borzoi A breed of large dog originating in Russia, also called Russian wolfhound, and used originally for hunting wolves. A swift runner, it has a long silky coat. Height: about 70 cm.

Bosch, Carl (1874–1940) German chemist, who developed the Haber process for the conversion of atmospheric nitrogen into ammonia, so that it could be used industrially. This Haber-Bosch process has been widely used to make nitrates for explosives and fertilizers.

Bosch, Hieronymus (Jerome van Aeken; c. 1450–c. 1516) Dutch painter. He was born in 's Hertogenbosch (hence his name), where from 1486 he belonged to the Roman Catholic Brotherhood of Our Lady. The often inexplicable symbolism of his half-animal half-human creatures and devils was inspired by contemporary proverbs. Among his major works are *The Haywain* (El Escorial) and *Garden of Earthly Delights* (Prado).

Bosnia and Hercegovina (Serbo-Croat name: Bosna i Hercegovina) A constituent republic of Yugoslavia. It is primarily agricultural. *History*: part of ancient Illyria, the region was inhabited by Slavs from the 7th century AD onwards. Bosnia became a separate political entity in the 10th century but later came under the control of Hungary. It became an independent kingdom in the late 14th century and annexed Hercegovina but fell to the Turks in 1463. In 1908 it was annexed to Austria-Hungary; Serbian opposition to this led to the assassination of Archduke Francis Ferdinand, precipitating World War I. Area: 51 129 sq km (19 737 sq mi). Population (1985): 4 310 000. Capital: Sarajevo.

boson A class of elementary particles with integral spin. Bosons obey Bose-Einstein statistics and include all the mesons and the photon. *See* particle physics.

Bosporus (Turkish name: Karadeniz Boğazi) A strait separating Europe and Asia and connecting the Black Sea with the Sea of Marmara. It is spanned by one of the world's longest suspension bridges. Length: about 30 km (19 mi). Width: about 0.6–4 km (0.4–2.5 mi).

Boston 42 20N 71 05W A city in the USA, the capital of Massachusetts. It is an important port and financial centre. Boston is a major cultural and educational centre. It is the site of Boston University (1869), Northeastern University (1898), and Boston Latin School (established in 1635 and one of the country's first free secondary schools). Harvard Medical School is also situated here. *History*: founded in 1630 by Puritan Englishmen, it became a centre of opposition to the British prior to the American Revolution (*see* Boston Tea Party). It was a leading force in the antislavery movement during the 1830s. Population (1986): 573 600.

BOSTON TEA PARTY   *A contemporary engraving.*

Boston Tea Party (1773) An expression of colonial hostility towards Britain before the American Revolution. A group of American radicals objecting to the import of cheap tea, enforced by the Tea Act to rid the East India Company of its surplus stocks, threw a cargo of tea into Boston harbour. Britain retaliated with the Intolerable Acts. *See also* Stamp Act.

Boston terrier A breed of dog originating in the USA from crosses between bulldogs and terriers. It is compactly built with a short square muzzle and a short tail. Height: about 38 cm.

Boswell, James (1740–95) Scottish writer, the biographer of Samuel Johnson. Son of an Edinburgh advocate, he first met Johnson in 1763. He travelled widely on the Continent from 1764 to 1766, meeting Voltaire and Rousseau. The biography, published in 1791, was widely acclaimed.

Bosworth Field, Battle of (22 August, 1485) The battle fought near Market Bosworth, Leicestershire, in which Henry Tudor defeated Richard III, thereby ending the Wars of the Roses. Richard was killed in the battle and Henry became the first Tudor monarch, as Henry VII.

botany The scientific study of plants. Scientific botany dates from the 4th century BC, with the studies of the ancient Greeks–notably Theophrastus and Dioscorides. The basic principles of modern plant classification were laid down by John Ray at the end of the 17th century, and by the middle of the 18th century Linnaeus had published his works on the naming and classification of plants, which established the principles of taxonomy still in use. The invention of the microscope in the 16th century enabled detailed studies of plant structure, culminating in Schleiden's theory of the cellular nature of plants in the 1830s. The 18th century saw important advances in plant physiology with the discovery of photosynthesis. During the 19th century the origin of plant species was elucidated in Charles Darwin's theory of evolution and Gregor Mendel established the mechanisms of inheritance. Botany in the 20th century has been revolutionized by advances in physiology, biochemistry, and breeding techniques.

Botany Bay An inlet of the Tasman Sea, in SE Australia. It was the site of Capt Cook's first landing in Australia (1770), is now surrounded by the suburbs of Sydney. Area: about 42 sq km (16 sq mi).

bot fly A hairy beelike fly belonging to the families *Gasterophilidae* (horse bot flies), *Calliphoridae* (e.g. the deer bot fly), or *Oestridae* (e.g. the sheep bot fly). The larvae are parasitic in mammals, often living within nasal cavities or the digestive tract to cause irritation and vertigo. When mature the larvae pass out with the faeces. *Compare* warble fly.

Botha, Pieter Willem (1916–) South African statesman; prime minister (1978–84) and president (1984–89). Although a vehement supporter of apartheid, he presided over the new constitution of 1984, which allowed some non-Whites limited political power.

IAN BOTHAM

Botham, Ian Terence (1955–) British cricketer. A brilliant all-rounder, he played for Somerset (1973–86), Worcestershire (1987–), Queensland (1987–88), and England (1977–), captaining the side (1980–81). He held a record number of test wickets (until 1988) and has scored over 3000 runs in Test matches.

Bothnia, Gulf of A shallow section of the Baltiç Sea, between Sweden and Finland. It remains frozen for about five months of the year. Area: about 117 000 sq km (45 200 sq mi).

Bothwell, James Hepburn, 4th Earl of (c. 1535–78) The third husband of Mary, Queen of Scots. He was almost certainly responsible for the murder of her second husband Darnley in 1567. Following their defeat at Carberry Hill, Bothwell escaped to Denmark, where he died, insane, in captivity.

bo tree An Indian tree, *Ficus religiosa*, up to 30 m high, also called the peepul or pipal. It has heart-shaped leaves and globular purple fruits. Related to the fig, the bo tree is sacred to Buddhists, as Buddha sat beneath one when he attained enlightenment. Family: *Moraceae* (mulberry family).

Botswana, Republic of (former name until 1966: Bechuanaland) A country in the centre of S Africa, lying between the Rivers Zambezi and Molopo. It is largely an arid plateau, with the Kalahari Desert in the S and W. The River Okavango in the N is important for irrigation. The majority of the population, consisting mainly of the Bantu-speaking Tswana group, lives along the E border. The original inhabitants, the Bushmen, are now a small minority. *Economy*: chiefly agricultural. In 1975 land ownership was reformed and minerals, including coal and diamonds discovered in the 1960s, are being developed. *History*: the area became the British Protectorate of Bechuanaland in 1885 and was annexed to the Cape Colony in 1895. It later became a British High Commission Territory, gaining internal self-government in 1965 and full independence in 1966 as the Republic of Botswana within the Commonwealth. Until 1980 it was under the democratic rule of Sir Seretse Khama (1921–80). Head of state: Dr Quette Masire. Official language: English; the main African language is Tswana. Official currency: pula of 100 thebe. Area: 575 000 sq km (222 000 sq mi). Population (1986 est): 1 131 700. Capital: Gaborone.

Botticelli, Sandro (Alessandro di Mariano Filipepi; c. 1445–1510) Florentine Renaissance painter, called by his brother's nickname, meaning "little barrel." His chief patrons were the Medici, for whom he produced illustrations for Dante's *Divine Comedy* and allegorical paintings, such as *Primavera*, *Birth of Venus* (both Uffizi), and *Mars and Venus* (National Gallery, London). In 1481–82 he worked on frescoes for the Sistine Chapel, in the Vatican.

bottlebrush An evergreen Australian shrub or tree of the genus *Callistemon* (25 species). Growing to a height of about 6 m, it has stiff narrow leaves, 5 cm long. The flower heads consist mainly of bunches of fluffy red or yellow stamens, resembling bottle brushes. The fruits are woody. Family: *Myrtaceae*.

bottlenose A dolphin, *Tursiops truncatus*, grey-blue and growing to 4 m. They are a shallow-water species, popular in dolphinariums and for research into the social behaviour of whales.

botulism A rare and serious form of food poisoning from foods containing the toxin produced by the bacterium *Clostridium botulinum*. The toxin can affect the cardiac and respiratory centres of the brain and may result in death. The bacterium thrives in improperly preserved foods but is invariably destroyed in cooking.

Bouaké 7 42N 5 00W A city in central Côte d'Ivoire. It is an important trade centre, linked to Abidjan. Population: (1982 est): 640 000.

Boucher, François (1703–70) French rococo painter. Born in Paris, the son of a lacemaker, he was chiefly influenced by Watteau. He worked for Louis XV, and Madame de Pompadour, whom he painted (National Gallery of Scotland). He became director of both the Gobelins tapestry factory (1755) and the French Academy (1765).

Boudicca. *See* Boadicea.

Boudin, Eugène (1824–98) French painter and forerunner of impressionism, born in Honfleur. He painted his coastal scenes in the open air.

Bougainville A volcanic forested island in the SW Pacific Ocean, the largest in the Solomon Islands archipelago and a province of Papua New Guinea. Copra, cocoa, timber, and tortoise shell are exported. Area: about 10 360 sq km (4000 sq mi). Population (1980): 109 000. Chief town: Kieta.

Bougainvillea A genus of tropical South American shrubs (18 species) climbing by means of hooked thorns. The shrubs bear numerous showy "flowers" for most of the year. The coloured parts are actually large bracts, which surround the small inconspicuous flowers. Family: *Nyctaginaceae*.

Boulanger, Nadia (Juliette) (1887–1979) French composer, teacher, and conductor. Lennox Berkeley and Aaron Copland were among her pupils. Her works include the cantata *La Sirène* (1908; awarded the Prix de Rome), and the opera *La Ville morte* (1911).

Boulez, Pierre (1925–) French composer and conductor, a pupil of Messiaen, he was influenced by Schoenberg, Webern, and Cage. He has used serialism in such works as *Structures I and II* (for two pianos; 1951–52 and 1956–61) and has set poems by René Char and Mallarmé.

Boulle, André Charles (*or* Buhl; 1642–1732) French cabinetmaker in the service of Louis XIV. Boullework (*or* buhlwork), is a style of marquetry using brass, tortoiseshell, etc., inlaid on ebony.

Boulogne-sur-Mer 50 43N 1 37E A port and resort in N France, in the Pas-de-Calais. It was severely damaged in World War II. It is the country's main fishing port and has a ferry service to England. Population (1983): 48 500.

Boult, Sir Adrian (Cedric) (1889–1983) British conductor of the BBC Symphony Orchestra (1930–49) and the London Philharmonic Orchestra (1949–57). He was knighted in 1937. He was associated particularly with the works of Elgar, Holst, and Vaughan Williams.

Bourbons A European dynasty that originated in Bourbonnais (now Allier, central France). It acquired ducal status in 1272, when Agnès Bourbon married the sixth son of Louis IX. The first Bourbon king of France was Henry IV (reigned 1589–1610) and Bourbons continued to rule until the French Revolution (1792). The present pretender to the French throne is Henry, Count of Paris (1908–).
The Bourbon Louis XIV's grandson became (1700) Philip V of Spain, where the Bourbons ruled almost continuously until the abdication of Alfonso XIII in 1931. His grandson Juan Carlos was restored to the Spanish throne in 1975. In Naples and Sicily Bourbons ruled between 1734 and 1860.

BOURBONS　*Henry IV, first Bourbon king of France (detail).*

Bourges (Latin name: Avaricum)　47 05N 2 23E A city in central France, the capital of the Cher department. An important town of Aquitaine, it became the capital of Berry in the 12th century and the centre of power following the battle of Agincourt (1415). Population (1983): 76 500.

Bourguiba, Habib (1902–　) Tunisian statesman; president (1957–87). A leading figure in the struggle for Tunisian independence, he spent ten years between 1934 and 1955 in French prisons. After independence in 1956 he became president, and in 1975 became life president; he was deposed in a bloodless coup.

Bournemouth　50 43N 1 54W A resort in S England, in Dorset. It has a symphony orchestra, conducted by Uri Segal (1944–　). Population (1985 est): 145 000.

Bovidae　A family of hoofed ruminant mammals (about 128 species), comprising antelopes, cattle, sheep, and goats. Several species have been domesticated for meat, milk, hides, and wool. Order: *Artiodactyla*.

Bow, Clara　(1905–65) US film actress. She personified the 1920s in such films as *Mantrap* (1926) and *It* (1927), becoming known as the "It" girl. She retired in the 1930s, being unsuccessful in sound films.

Bowdler, Thomas　(1754–1825) British doctor and editor. His *Family Shakespeare* (1818) expurgated all words "which cannot with propriety be read aloud in a family." He similarly "bowdlerized" Gibbon's *Decline and Fall of the Roman Empire* (1826).

bowerbird　A songbird belonging to a family (*Ptilonorhynchidae*; 18 species) found in Australasian forests. 22–35 cm long, it is related to the bird of paradise. Males court females by building dome-shaped bowers with twigs, moss, etc., often decorating them with feathers and shells.

Bowie, David　(David Jones; 1947–　) British pop singer. His albums include *Ziggy Stardust* (1972), *Heroes* (1977), *Let's Dance* (1983), and *Tin Machine* (1989). He has also acted in films, notably *The Man Who Fell to Earth* (1976), *Absolute Beginners* (1986), and *Labyrinth* (1986).

bowling (*or* tenpin bowling)　A game in which two players compete by attempting to knock down standing pins with rolling balls. The ten pins, 38.1 cm (15 in) high and each weighing about 1.5 kg (3.5 lb), are placed in a triangle (frame) 18.29 m (20 yd) distant at the end of a wooden lane. The balls, which have a thumb hole and two finger holes, have a maximum circumference of 68.5 cm (27 in) and a maximum weight of 7.26 kg (16 lb). Ten frames comprise a game.

bowls　A game in which biased bowls ("woods") are rolled towards a smaller one (the "jack"). **Flat green bowls** is played on a level grass surface 40–44 yd (36.6–40.2 m) square. Matches are usually played between two sides of four, each player using two bowls; a contest consists of three to six simultaneous matches. The jack is rolled onto the green by the first player and is followed by the other bowls in turn, the object being to position them as near the jack as possible. **Crown green bowls** is played, mainly in N England, on a green 30–60 yd (27.4–54.9 m) square and sloping up to a central area raised 6–12 in (15–30 cm). Matches are usually singles lasting until one player reaches a score of 21.

box　A small evergreen tree, *Buxus sempervirens*, up to 9 m high. The leaves are small and glossy and being slow growing, box is widely grown as hedges for topiary. Family: *Buxaceae*.

boxer　A breed of working dog originating in Germany. It has a powerful frame with long straight legs and a broad muzzle. Height: 56–61 cm (dogs); 53–58 cm (bitches).

BOXER RISING　*A cartoon showing Europeans fleeing from the members of a Chinese secret society.*

Boxer Rising　(1900) A rebellion in China so called because the rebels belonged to a secret society named the Fists of Righteous Harmony. They opposed the western presence in China and, wearing yellow sashes, marched on Peking, killing and pillaging as they went. The rebellion was eventually suppressed by an international force.

boxing　Fist-fighting between men wearing gloves in a roped-off ring. Organized boxing in modern times began in 18th-century England. The modern boxing rules, which established the use of gloves, are the **Queensberry Rules**, drawn up under the patronage of the Marquess of Queensberry (1844–1900) and published in 1867. In professional boxing the ring is 14 × 20 ft (4 × 6 m) square. The weight limits for professional boxers are: flyweight, 112 lb (50.8 kg); bantamweight, 118 lb (53.5 kg); featherweight, 126 lb (57.2 kg); lightweight, 135 lb (61.2 kg); light welterweight, 140 lb (63.5 kg); welterweight, 147 lb (66.7 kg); light middleweight, 154 lb (69.8 kg); middleweight, 160 lb (72.6 kg); light heavyweight, 175 lb (79.4 kg); heavyweight, unlimited. A bout consists of up to 15 3-minute rounds, separated by 1-minute intervals. A fight may be decided on points (marks awarded by the judges after each round), by disqualification, or by knockout (defined as being unable to rise within ten seconds). World titles are offered by the World Boxing Council, the World Boxing Association, and the International Boxing Federation. Great medical concern has recently been expressed regarding the danger to health of this sport.

box turtle A terrestrial turtle belonging to the North American genus *Terrapene* (6 species). Up to 18 cm long, they have a high-domed carapace and a hinged plastron, which allows the shell to form a protective box. Family: *Emydidae*.

Boycott, Geoffrey (1940–) British cricketer who played for Yorkshire (1962–86; captain 1970–78) and England (1964–74, 1977–81). An outstanding opening batsman, he made 150 centuries in first-class cricket.

Boyer, Charles (1899–1978) French film actor. He went to Hollywood in 1929 and played romantic lovers in such films as *Mayerling* (1937) and *Love Affair* (1939).

Boyle, Robert (1627–91) Irish scientist. His *The Skeptical Chymist* (1661) distinguished between elements, compounds, and mixtures and dismissed the Aristotelian concept of the four elements. His work on gases led to Boyle's law (1663).

Boyle's law At constant temperature, the pressure of unit mass of a gas is inversely proportional to its volume. This law is only approximately true for real gases. A gas that obeys Boyle's law exactly is called an ideal gas. Named after Robert Boyle.

Boyne, Battle of the (1 July, 1690) The victory of William III of England over the former King James II in Ireland. The battle was fought at the River Boyne, N of Dublin, where James hoped to halt the Williamites' advance southwards. The battles of the Boyne and of Aughrim are still celebrated by Ulster Unionists on the latter's anniversary, 12 July.

Boyoma Falls (former name: Stanley Falls) A series of seven cataracts in NE central Zaïre, on a 100-km (62-mi) stretch of the River Lualuba, where it becomes the Zaïre River.

Boy Scouts. *See* Scout Association.

Brachiopoda A phylum of primitive marine invertebrate animals (about 250 species) called lamp shells because of their resemblance to Roman oil lamps. The body is protected by two shell valves, usually attached to the sea bed by a fleshy stalk (peduncle). Eggs and sperm are discharged into the sea and produce free-swimming larvae.

bracken (*or* brake) A widely distributed fern, *Pteridium aquilinum*. Its black underground rhizome creeps extensively, producing aerial fronds, up to 5 m high, with stalks bearing triangular blades made up of branches of paired leaflets. Spore capsules occur in brownish clusters (sori) under the leaflets. Family: *Dennstaedtiaceae*.

Bracknell 51 26N 0 46W A town in SE England, in Berkshire. Developed as a new town since 1949, industries include engineering, electronics, clothing, and furniture manufacture. The Meteorological Office is here. Population (1985 est): 51 552.

bract A modified leaf, often small and scalelike, found at the base of a flower or inflorescence (flower cluster). Occasionally bracts are large and brightly col-

oured, resembling petals, as in the poinsettias. Smaller bracts (bracteoles) may be found on the flower stalk.

Bradbury, Malcolm Stanley (1932–) British novelist and critic, who established his reputation with *The History Man* (1975). Other comic novels include *Eating People is Wrong* (1959), *Rates of Exchange* (1983), and *Cuts* (1988).

Bradbury, Ray (1920–) US science-fiction writer. His novels include *The Illustrated Man* (1951), *Fahrenheit 451* (1953), and *Death is a Lonely Business* (1986). His many collections of stories include *The Golden Apples of the Sun* (1953).

Bradford 53 48N 1 45W A city in N England, in West Yorkshire near Leeds. It is the foremost wool textile town in the UK. In 1985 56 people died when a timber grandstand at Bradford City's football ground caught fire. Population (1989): 466 000.

Bradley, Omar Nelson (1893–1981) US general. In World War II, he commanded in North Africa and Sicily (1945) and the First US Army in France (1944). In 1948 he became army chief of staff and was then the first chairman of the joint chiefs of staff (1949–53).

Bradman, Sir Donald George (1908–) Australian cricketer, who was the most successful batsman of his era (1928–48). He scored 117 centuries in 338 first-class innings and in Test matches averaged 99.94 runs. His best score was 452 not out (1929–30). As Australian captain (1936–48) he never lost a series.

BRAEMAR *Tossing the caber at the Highland games.*

Braemar 57 01N 2 34W A village in NE Scotland, in Grampian Region on Clunie Water (a tributary of the River Dee). It hosts the annual Highland games.

Bragança (*or* Braganza) The ruling dynasty of Portugal from 1640 to 1910 and of Brazil from 1822 to 1889. The family was descended from Alfonso, illegitimate son of John I (1357–1433; reigned 1385–1433) and 1st Duke of Bragança. The first Bragança king was John IV (1604–56; reigned 1640–56) and the last was Manuel II (1889–1932; reigned 1908–10), after whose deposition Portugal became a republic. When Brazil became independent (1822), it was ruled by two members of the family, Pedro I (1798–1834; reigned 1822–31) and Pedro II (1825–91; reigned 1831–89), before becoming a republic (1889).

Bragg, Sir William Henry (1862–1942) British physicist, who worked in Australia from 1886 to 1908. His early research is described in *Studies in Radioactivity* (1912). With his son **Sir (William) Lawrence Bragg** (1890–1971) he discovered the law of X-ray diffraction that bears their name. Together they wrote *X-rays and Crystal Structure* (1915) and were jointly awarded the Nobel Prize for 1915.

Bragg's law If two parallel X-rays of wavelength λ are reflected by adjacent planes, distance *d* apart, in a crystal lattice and the rays then constructively interfere, then $2d\sin\theta = n\lambda$, where *n* is an integer and *θ* the angle between the X-rays and the planes. *θ* is called the Bragg angle. If *n* is half-integral, then destructive interference is observed. Named after Sir William and Sir Lawrence Bragg.

Brahe, Tycho (1546–1601) Danish astronomer, who made accurate astronomical instruments enabling him to revise existing astronomical tables. As a result of observing a nova in 1572, King Frederick II had two observatories built for him, where he worked from 1580 to 1597. A supporter of Copernicus' theory that the planets revolve round the sun, he believed the earth to be immovable. After Frederick's death, he moved to Prague, where Kepler became his student. After Tycho's death, Kepler used his teacher's observations to test his laws of planetary motion.

Brahma The creator god of later Vedic religion. Arising from the cosmic Golden Egg, he brings into existence the cyclical process of the creation and destruction of the world. His four heads and arms represent the four Vedas, castes, and yugas (ages of the world). Brahma represents the creative aspect of supreme deity in the trimurti triad but since the 7th century his worship has been superseded by that of Siva and Vishnu.

Brahman (Hinduism) In the Upanishads, the changeless source of the phenomenal universe, seen as an all-pervading infinite Being, who is both the basis of existence and the state of one who has achieved release (*see* atman). Brahman originally meant "the sacred Word," and was the exclusive domain of the literate priestly caste. In its extended significance it came to be the proper spiritual object of that class alone. See Brahmanism.

Brahman (cattle). *See* zebu.

Brahmanas Commentaries on the Vedas, written in Sanskrit between about 1000 and 600 BC. They are major sources of Indian philosophy, theology, and myth.

Brahmanism An early speculative rather than devotional form of Hinduism, derived from the Vedas and characterized by the veneration of an elite priestly caste, who, as the privileged keepers of religious knowledge embodied the sacred word. *See also* Brahman.

Brahmaputra River A river in S Asia. Rising in SW Tibet as the Tsangpo, it flows generally E across the Himalayas before turning S into the Assam Valley of NE India as the Dihang. From here, as the Brahmaputra, it flows WSW across NE India to join the River Ganges N of Gaolundo Ghat. Length: 2900 km (1800 mi).

brahmin (*or* brahman) The first of the four major Hindu castes, that of the priests, they alone are able to perform the most important religious tasks, to study and recite the scriptures. Since in India spiritual and secular knowledge are virtually inseparable, brahmins frequently wield considerable intellectual and political power. After India achieved independence in 1947, opposition to brahminical elitism strengthened, but this has not yet significantly weakened their sacerdotal role.

Brahms, Johannes (1833–97) German composer, born in Hamburg. Brahms moved to Vienna in 1863 and later became musical director of the Gesellschaft der Musikfreunde (Society of Friends of Music; 1872–75). His main orchestral works comprise four symphonies, two piano concertos, a violin concerto, and a concerto for violin and cello. His choral works include *A German Requiem* (1868) and the *Alto Rhapsody* (1869). He wrote a large quantity of chamber music and composed much piano music and many songs.

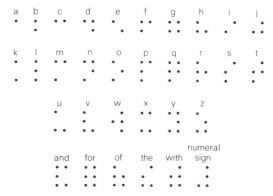

BRAILLE *The alphabet.*

Braille, Louis (1809–52) French teacher, who, blinded by an accident at the age of three, published a system of writing that allows the blind to read by touch. Modern Braille consists of 63 characters, each of which is made up of one to six embossed dots.

brain The nervous tissue that lies within the skull and is ensheathed by three membranes (meninges). It is the organ of the mind and it controls many bodily activities. The hindmost part of the brain, joining the spinal cord, is the medulla oblongata: this ascends to the pons, which joins the midbrain. These parts, together called the brainstem, control breathing and heartbeat and regulate the level of consciousness. They also convey information to and from the cerebrum. The cerebellum, connected to the brainstem, ensures the coordination of movements. The upper end of the brainstem is connected to the most highly developed part of the brain—the cerebrum. This consists of two cerebral hemispheres joined by a tract of nerve fibres. Its surface is intricately folded and is made up of an outer layer of nerve cell bodies (grey matter) and an inner mass of nerve fibres (white matter). The cerebrum is largely responsible for understanding language, thought, and the voluntary control of movements. The hemispheres differ in function: one hemisphere controls the dominant side of the body (normally the left hemisphere in right-handed people) and that hemisphere controls speech. The nondominant hemisphere specializes in analysing how things are arranged in space. Deep within the cerebrum and brainstem lie cavities (ventricles) filled with cerebrospinal fluid. The brain of vertebrate animals is similar but less highly developed than the human brain; in lower animals a collection of ganglia (nerve cell bodies) functions as the brain. See p. 108.

striped bass   grass snake   pigeon   cat

chimpanzee

man

BRAIN   *The brains of these representative vertebrates (drawn to the same scale) show a progressive increase in the size and complexity of the cerebrum. In man this development is such that the cerebrum covers or encloses all the other parts of the brain.*

bramble.   *See* blackberry.

brambling   A finch, *Fringilla montifringilla*, 14.5 cm long, that breeds in Asia and N Europe and migrates south in winter. It has a brown-speckled plumage with white wing bars and orange underparts but in winter the male has a black head and back.

Bran   A legendary Celtic god-king of Britain, whose story is told in the *Mabinogion*. A giant, who once waded across the Irish sea, his severed head lived on for some 80 years, giving good advice beore being finally buried in London to protect Britain from invasion. It was dug up by King Arthur, who believed that the protection was better served by the valour of individuals.

Branchiopoda   A subclass of small, mostly freshwater crustaceans (over 800 species). They include the fairy shrimps, tadpole shrimps, water fleas, and clam shrimps, all bearing flat fringed appendages used for locomotion, respiration, and filter feeding. Parthenogenesis is common.

Brancusi, Constantin   (1876–1957)   Romanian sculptor, he moved to Paris in 1904. His stone and metal sculptures, such as the *Sleeping Muse* series beginning in 1906 and the *Birds* variations (1912–40), possess an abstract simplicity. In contrast, his wood sculptures, such as the *Prodigal Son* (1915), utilize angular forms inspired by African art.

Brandenburg   52 24N 12 31E A city in East Germany, on the River Havel. It was the former capital of the province of Brandenburg and has been largely rebuilt since World War II. Population (1983): 95 052.

Brandenburg   A former state corresponding to the present-day districts of Magdeburg, Potsdam, Neu-brandenburg, and Frankfurt of East Germany and to part of W Poland. The region was conquered by the Germans between the 10th and 12th centuries and in 1157 Albert (I) the Bear became margrave, and then elector, of Brandenburg. Under Frederick William, the Great Elector (1640–88), Brandenburg gained suzerainty of Prussia and became a leading German power. In 1701 the Elector of Brandenburg became Frederick I of Prussia.

Brandenburg Gate   A ceremonial gateway, now in East Berlin, built (1789) in the neoclassical style by the architect C. G. Langhans (1732–1808). Situated at the W end of Unter den Linden, it became the symbol of the modernized city.

Brando, Marlon   (1924–   ) US film actor, influenced by the "method" of the New York Actors' Studio in the 1950s. His films include *A Streetcar Named Desire* (1951), *On the Waterfront* (1954), *The Godfather* (1972), and *Apocalypse Now* (1979).

Brandt, Willy   (1913–   ) West German statesman; chancellor (1969–74). In Norway from 1933, he was a leader of the resistance movement against the Nazis throughout World War II. A member of the Social Democratic Party from 1931, he was its chairman (1964–87). As chancellor he negotiated treaties with Russia, Poland, and East Germany and in 1971 was awarded the Nobel Peace Prize. He resigned the chancellorship when it was revealed that one of his aides was an East German spy.

brandy   A spirit distilled from fermented grape juice (wine) or other fruit juices. The best types of wine brandy are matured in oak casks and named after the Cognac and Armagnac districts of France. Marc (French) or grappa (Italian) brandy is made from the refermented grape pips, skins, and stems left after pressing for wine. VSOP–very superior old pale–brandy is usually 20–25 years old.

Brandywine, Battle of the   (11 September, 1777) A battle during the American Revolution. Sir William Howe (1729–1814), advancing on Philadelphia, encircled Gen George Washington's troops in an attempt to cut off the city. Howe crossed the Brandywine Creek, defeated Washington's surprised troops, and subsequently occupied Philadelphia.

Braque, Georges   (1882–1963) French painter, who with Picasso developed cubism. Notable among Braque's innovations were the use of lettering in compositions, e.g. *The Portuguese* (1911; Basle), mixing paint with sand to produce interesting textures, and papiers collés (paper pasted on canvases).

Brasília   16 0S 48 10W The capital and a federal district of Brazil, situated on the central plateau. It was inaugurated in 1960, the chief designer being Lúcio Costa and the principal architect, Oscar Niemeyer (1907–   ). Its fine modern buildings include the National Congress Building and the cathedral. Population (1980): 411 305.

brass   An alloy of copper and zinc. Brasses containing less than 36% zinc are ductile when cold, those with more than 36% zinc are harder. It does not rust but exposure to sea water causes dezincification (leaching out of the zinc). This is partially prevented by the addition of tin (1%) in Naval Brass, sometimes with about 0.05% of arsenic.

Brassica   A genus of mainly annual or biennial herbs (about 40 species), with erect clusters of four-petalled yellow flowers. The genus includes many important vegetables, including broccoli, Brussels sprout, cabbage, cauliflower, kale, rape, swede, and turnip.

brass instruments   Wind instruments made of brass. The French horn, trumpet, trombone, and tuba are used in orchestras; brass bands also include bugles and cornets. Brass instruments have either a cup-shaped or cone-shaped mouthpiece, the shape of which influences the tone quality, as does the type of bore, which may be conical (horn) or cylindrical (trumpet). A brass instrument plays the harmonic series natural to its length; additional series are made available by the use of crooks, slides, or valves.

Bratby, John   (1928–   ) British painter and writer. Known for his domestic interiors his paintings for the film of Joyce Carey's novel *The Horse's Mouth* (1944; filmed 1958) became widely known.

Bratislava   (German name: Pressburg; Hungarian name: Pozsony) 48 10N 17 10E The third largest city in Czechoslovakia, the capital of the Slovak Republic on the River Danube. It was the capital of Hungary (1526–1784). Notable buildings include the gothic cathedral (13th century), where many of the kings of Hungary were crowned. Oil from the Soviet Union is refined here. Population (1986): 417 000.

Brattain, Walter Houser   (1902–   ) US physicist, who shared the 1956 Nobel Prize for his part in the invention of the transistor (with W. B. Shockley and John Bardeen).

Braun, Eva   (1910–45) The mistress and finally the wife of Adolf Hitler. Their relationship probably began in 1933 and they were married shortly before their suicides on 30 April, 1945.

Braunschweig.   *See* Brunswick.

Brazil, Federative Republic of (Portuguese name: Brasil)   A country comprising almost half the area of South America. The N of the country is dominated by the Amazon basin with its tropical rain forests. The land rises to the Guiana Highlands in the N and the Brazilian Highlands in the S, with large tracts of grassland in between. The population is largely of European descent, with a small and dwindling Indian minority. *Economy*: mainly an agricultural country, the chief crops are sugar cane, manioc, maize, rice, and beans. Formerly the world's largest producer of coffee, Brazil overproduced, which led to a decline in its position. Livestock breeding has also increased and Brazil is now ahead of Argentina as a cattle producer. The fishing industry has been nationalized and in 1971 territorial waters were extended to 320 km (200 mi). Brazil is exceptionally rich in mineral resources; the iron-ore reserves are estimated to be the largest in the world. Recently large deposits of phosphates have been discovered there, as well as uranium, manganese, gold, and copper. 90% of power comes from hydroelectric sources. There is now an agreement with West Germany, based on Brazil's uranium deposits, to build eight nuclear power stations. Oil production only provides a fraction of Brazil's domestic needs although new offshore fields have been found near Campos. *History*: claimed by the Portuguese in 1500, it became a Portuguese settlement. During the Napoleonic Wars the Portuguese court was transferred to Brazil and in 1815 it was made a kingdom. In 1822 independence was declared by Pedro I (1798–1834), son of John VI of Portugal, with a constitution that proclaimed him emperor. In 1889 his son Pedro II (1825–91) was deposed and Brazil became a republic. From 1930 to 1945 it was ruled by the benevolent dictator Getúlio Vargas (1883–1954). Less stable governments followed; in 1964 Gen Humberto Castelo Branco (1900–67) came to power in a military coup. In 1967 Marshal Artur da Costa e Silva (1902–69) was elected president, being replaced in 1969 by a junta comprising the three heads of the armed forces. Elections were held in 1985; when president elect Tancredo Neves (1910–85) died before taking office, vice-president José Sarney (1930–   ) assumed power. Following further elections he was succeeded by Fernando Collor dé Mello (1949–   ) in 1990. Destruction of the Amazon rain forests caused worldwide concern in the late 1980s. Official language: Portuguese. Official currency: cruzado of 1000 cruzeiros. Area: 8 511 965 sq km (3 286 000 sq mi). Population (1987): 141 459 000. Capital: Brasília. Main port: Rio de Janeiro. See p. 110.

Brazil nut   The seed of a tall forest tree, *Bertholletia excelsa*, up to 45 m high, native to tropical South America. The tree produces fluffy flowers that develop into woody fruits, each containing 12–24 seeds (the nuts). Family: *Lecythidaceae*.

brazilwood   An evergreen tree, *Caesalpinia brasiliensis*, of tropical South America. The leaves are bipinnate and the orange flowers develop into seed pods. The tree yields a very hard wood used for cabinetwork. Family: *Leguminosae*.

brazing.   *See* solder.

Brazzaville   4 07W 15 15E The capital of the People's Republic of Congo, situated on the Zaïre River opposite Kinshasa (Zaïre). Founded in the 1880s, it became capital of French Equatorial Africa in 1910. During World

BRAZIL *The capital from 1763 to 1960, Rio de Janeiro is dominated by the giant Christ overlooking the Sugar Loaf Mountain.*

War II it was the centre of the Free French forces in Africa. It became capital of the newly independent Republic of Congo in 1960. Population (1980 est): 310 500.

breadfruit The starchy fruit of a tropical tree *Artocarpus communis*. When roasted it forms a staple part of the diet in the Pacific islands. The tree grows to a height of 30 m and has shiny divided leaves. The large round fruits have a thick rind and develop from long female catkins. Family: *Moraceae*.

bream One of several teleost fishes, especially *Abramis brama*, a food and game fish related to carp that occurs in European lakes and slow-moving rivers. Its deep body, 30–70 cm long, is bluish grey or brown above and silvery below. *See also* sea bream.

Bream, Julian Alexander (1933–) British guitarist and lutenist, whose repertoire includes arrangements of baroque and Renaissance pieces as well as works written for him by Britten and Henze.

breathalyzer A roadside test used by the police to estimate the amount of alcohol in the breath, which reflects the level of alcohol in the blood. In the UK a suspected driver blows through a tube containing potassium dichromate crystals into a balloon. When the ballon is inflated (i.e. sufficient breath has been examined), if the colour change extends beyond a line marked on the tube, the driver has an alcohol level in excess of the legal limit (80 mg per litre of blood). He is then taken to a police station to have a blood or urine test in the presence of a doctor. Electronic devices largely replaced the traditional breathalyzer during the 1980s.

breccia A sedimentary rock consisting of relatively large (over 2 mm in diameter) angular fragments of pre-existing rocks. Scree material cemented together forms one kind of breccia.

Brecht, Bertolt (1898–1956) German dramatist and poet. He first studied medicine and was converted to Marxism in 1928. *Die Dreigroschenoper* was an adaptation of John Gay's *The Beggar's Opera*, with music by Kurt Weil. In 1933 he moved to Scandinavia and the USA (1941–47). During these years he wrote *Galileo* (1938), *Mother Courage* (1939) and *The Caucasian Chalk Circle* (1949). In 1949 he returned to East Berlin and founded his famous Berliner Ensemble Company.

Breda 51 35N 4 46E A town in the SW Netherlands, in North Brabant province. Occupied several times, its capture by the Spanish in 1625 is depicted in Velázquez' famous painting, *The Surrender of Breda*. Population (1987): 119 427.

Breeches Bible. *See* Geneva Bible.

breeder reactor. *See* fast reactor.

Brehon Laws A collection of ancient Irish laws, dating back to the 8th century, which constitute one of the most important sources for the history of contemporary Irish society. The Brehon was an official who pronounced upon the law. The Laws describe conditions of tenure and transfer of land and fixes penalties and fines for criminal acts.

Bremen 53 05N 8 48E The second largest port in West Germany, capital of the *Land* of Bremen. Its industries include shipbuilding, oil refining, and food processing. Population (1986): 524 700.

Bremen The smallest *Land* of West Germany, comprising the cities of Bremen and Bremerhaven enclosed by the *Land* of Lower Saxony. Area: 404 sq km (156 sq mi). Population (1986): 657 500.

Bremerhaven 53 33N 8 35E A city in N West Germany, in Bremen on the Weser estuary. It is a major fishing, freight, and passenger port. Population (1986): 132 800.

bremmstrahlung Electromagnetic radiation emitted by a charged particle when it is decelerated on passing close to a nucleus. The effect is most often observed with electrons since they are light and therefore easily decelerated. Cosmic rays dissipate their energy as bremmstrahlung on entering the earth's atmosphere.

Brendan, St (484–c. 578 AD) Irish abbot. He is traditionally credited with founding the monastery at Clonfert (Cluain Fearta), Co Galway. The Latin *Navigation of St Brendan* (c. 1050) recounts his voyage to "northern and western islands." Feast day: 16 May.

Bren gun A gas-operated light machine gun with interchangeable barrels first built at *Br*no, Czechoslovakia (1933), and later manufactured at *En*field, UK (1935). Widely used in World War II, it was accurate and reliable and used 0.303 calibre ammunition.

Brenner Pass 47 02N 11 32E The lowest of the chief passes in the Alps, on the Austrian-Italian border. Important since Roman times, it links Innsbruck (Austria) with Verona (Italy).

Brescia 45 33N 10 13E A city in Italy, in Lombardy. It has Roman remains, 9th-century and 17th-century cathedrals, and a 12th-century palace. Population (1986): 199 286.

Breslau. *See* Wrocław.

Bresson, Robert (1907–   ) French film director. In most of his austere films concerning moral and religious dilemmas he uses unknown actors. His films include *Le Journal d'un curé de campagne* (1950), *Mouchette* (1967), and *Lancelot du lac* (1974).

Brest (name until 1921: Brest-Litovsk; Polish name: Brześć nad Bu-giem) 52 08N 23 40E A port in the W Soviet Union, in the Belorussian SSR. It is a major industrial centre. Population (1987): 238 000.

Brest 48 23N 4 30W A port and naval base in NW France, in the Finistère department on the Atlantic Ocean. A German U-boat base in World War II, it was almost entirely destroyed by Allied bombing. Industries include fishing, chemicals, and clothing. Population (1983): 166 500.

Brethren Members of the Protestant Brethren Churches. The largest, called the Church of the Brethren, was founded in Germany in the early 18th century. Persecution forced its members to emigrate to America, where they became known as "Tunkers," "Dunkers," or "German Baptists." They believe in temperance and pacifism and practise adult baptism by triple immersion.

Brétigny, Treaty of (1360) The treaty that concluded the first phase of the Hundred Years' War. Never fully effective, it promised a ransom of £500,000 for John II of France (1319–64; reigned 1350–64; captured at Poitiers in 1356) and granted territories, including Aquitaine, to Edward III of England. In return, Edward was to renounce his claim to the French throne.

Breton A Celtic language of the Brythonic group with four distinct dialects spoken in Brittany by about one million people. Originally introduced by immigrants from SW England, it is related to Cornish and Welsh but has been strongly influenced by French. It has a literature that dates from the 15th century.

Bretton Woods Conference (1944) A conference held at Bretton Woods, New Hampshire (USA), at which the USA, UK, and Canada established a system of international financial rules, which led to the setting up of the International Monetary Fund (IMF) and the International Bank for Reconstruction and Development (World Bank). Each country agreed to maintain its currency within 1% of a value fixed for gold and to back the IMF in bridging any temporary payments imbalances. The system collapsed in 1971, following the US Government's suspension of convertibility from dollars to gold.

brewing. *See* beer and brewing.

Brewster's law Light reflected from a solid surface is plane polarized, with maximum polarization occurring when the tangent of the angle of incidence is equal to the refractive index. Named after Sir David Brewster (1781–1868), Scottish physicist.

Brezhnev, Leonid Ilich (1906–82) Soviet statesman; secretary of the Soviet Communist Party (1964–82) and president of the Soviet Union (1977–82). Brezhnev, a metallurgist, was a political leader in the Red Army during World War II. He and Kosygin forced Khrushchev to resign in 1964.

briar A shrubby rambling rose with arching prickly stems, found in hedgerows and scrub in many parts of Europe. The principal species are *Rosa rubiginosa*, *R. micrantha*, *R. agrestis*, and *R. elliptica*. *See also* sweet briar.

Briar is also the name of a shrubby white heath (*Erica arborea*), the roots of which are used for making briar pipes.

bribery and corruption The giving of a gift to a person in a position of trust, to induce him to act contrary to his duty. If such a gift is secretly given it is presumed to be corrupt. Bribery of public servants is illegal according to the Public Bodies Corrupt Practices Act (1889). Obtaining a title or similar honour by bribery is a crime according to the Honours (Prevention of Abuses) Act (1925). Bribery in connection with parliamentary and other elections is a corrupt practice forbidden by the Parliamentary Elections Act (1868) and the Representation of the People Act (1949).

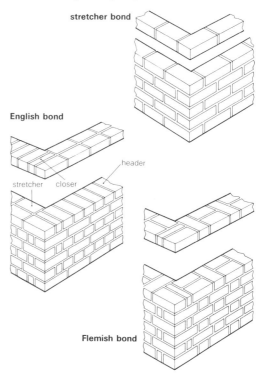

BRICKS *The factors of cost, strength, and decorative effect influence a bricklayer's choice of bond for a particular task.*

bricks A traditional building material in the form of a rectangular block usually measuring 225 × 112 × 75 mm. They are normally made from clay and baked or fired in a kiln at about 900°C. Water is driven off, organic matter becomes oxidized, and some of the clay minerals fuse and fill the gaps between the clay particles. Iron oxide gives the brick its reddish colour. London stock bricks are yellowish on account of the sand and alumina they contain. Bricks are laid in various patterns, known as bonds.

Bride, St. *See* Bridget, St.

bridge A card game deriving from whist. **Straight bridge** was first played in Britain about 1880; having overtaken whist in popularity, about 1911 it was displaced by its descendant, **auction bridge**, in which the opposing pairs of partners competed to decide the trump suit. By 1929 **contract bridge**, which had developed in the USA, was popularized by Ely Culbertson (1891–1955). Two pairs of partners bid to name the trump suit (or to play without a trump suit) and "contract" to win a specified number of tricks above the six tricks of the "book." A game consists of 100 points, with each spade or heart trick counting 30, each diamond or club 20, and for a bid in no trumps 40 for the first trick and 30 for subsequent tricks. Only the tricks contracted for in the bidding are counted towards game; extra points are awarded separately for "honours" (ace to ten of trumps), overtricks, and for slams (when the partners have bid for and won all the tricks or all but one trick in a hand). Penalty points are awarded to the opponents for undertricks. The side winning two games consecutively or two games out of three wins the rubber, which counts as either 500 or 700 extra points.

Bridge, Frank (1879–1941) British composer. Bridge studied composition with Stanford and his orchestral suite *The Sea* (1910–11) earned him early popularity. His later works, such as the third string quartet (1926) and *Oration* (for cello and orchestra; 1930), are in a highly individual modern idiom. He was the teacher of Benjamin Britten.

Bridge of Sighs (Italian name: Ponte dei Sospiri) A covered bridge in Venice (Italy) linking the Doge's Palace with the state prison. Its name derives from the sighs of the prisoners who were conducted over it.

Bridges, Robert Seymour (1844–1930) British poet, who worked as a doctor until 1882. Several volumes of lyrics preceded the long philosophical poem, *The Testament of Beauty* (1929). He also produced an edition of the poems of his friend Gerard Manley Hopkins. He was made poet laureate in 1913.

Bridget, St (St Bride *or* St Brigit; died c. 523 AD) Irish abbess and second patron saint of Ireland. She is believed to have founded the first Irish convent, at Kildare. Feast day: 1 Feb.

Bridgetown 14 05N 59 35W The capital of Barbados, a port in the SW on Carlisle Bay, founded in 1628. Population (1983 est): 7466.

Bridgewater Canal A waterway constructed in 1761–76 by James Brindley (1716–72) from Worsley to Manchester (later extended to Liverpool) for transporting coal. The first British canal, it is constructed on an aqueduct across the Irwell Valley.

Bridie, James (Osborne Henry Mavor; 1888–1951) British dramatist. His plays, which were never popular outside the UK, include *Tobias and the Angel* (1930) and *The Anatomist* (1931). He was the founder of the Glasgow Citizens' Theatre.

Brie An area in N France, between the Rivers Seine and Marne. Predominantly agricultural, it produces wheat and sugar beet and is noted for its cheese. Area: 6500 sq km (2510 sq mi).

Bright, Richard (1789–1858) British physician, who described many disorders, particularly the group of symptoms, including oedema (retention of body fluid),

that he showed to be due to kidney disease. This is sometimes called **Bright's disease** (*see* nephritis).

Brighton 50 50N 0 10W A resort in S England, on the East Sussex coast. Originally a fishing village, its growth

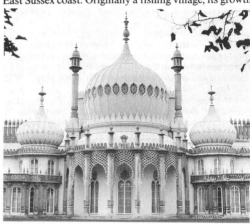

BRIGHTON *The Royal Pavilion, John Nash's oriental fantasy redesigned for George IV.*

began with the development of sea bathing in the 1750s and the patronage of the Prince Regent (later George IV), who had the Royal Pavilion redesigned by John Nash in oriental style. Other notable features include the Lanes (famous for their antique shops) and the boating marina (completed in 1979). Population (1981): 146 134.

Brigit A Celtic goddess of fire, fertility, and culture. Elements of her cult were passed into the traditions surrounding St Bridget, notably the burning of a sacred fire by her shrine.

brill An edible flatfish, *Scophthalmus rhombus*, related to turbot, that occurs in European coastal waters. Its smooth body is sandy with light and dark spots above.

brimstone A lemon-yellow butterfly, *Gonopteryx rhamni*, found in Europe, N Africa, and parts of Asia. Adults hibernate, flying early in spring. The next generation emerges in June or later, the caterpillars feeding on buckthorn. Family: *Pieridae*.

Brindley, James (1716–72) British canal builder. He designed and built some 588 km of canals, including the Bridgewater Canal for the Duke of Bridgewater in 1759 to transport coal from Worsley to Manchester, without ever using diagrams or calculations.

Brisbane 27 30S 153 00E The third largest city in Australia, the capital and chief port of Queensland. Exports include wool, meat, mineral sands, and wheat. Notable buildings include Parliament House (1869), the Observatory (1829) built by convicts, and the Queen Elizabeth II Stadium built for the 1982 Commonwealth Games. *History*: originally a penal colony, the settlement was opened to colonists in 1842. Population (1983 est): 1 138 400.

bristlecone pine A pine tree, *Pinus aristata*, native to mountainous regions of Colorado, Arizona, and New Mexico. Up to 15 m tall. Bristlecone pines are among the longest-lived trees: some trees have reached an age of 5000 years and have been used to date archaeological sites (*see* dendrochronology).

bristletail   A slender wingless insect, 5–20 mm long, that has two or three long tail bristles and belongs to the orders *Thysanura* (three-pronged bristletails) or *Diplura* (two-pronged bristletails). Most bristletails live in damp sheltered places and feed on plant detritus (*see also* silverfish; firebrat).

Bristol   51 27N 2 35W A port and industrial city in SW England, the administrative centre of Avon. A major port in the 17th and 18th centuries, trading mostly with the Americas (and prospering greatly from the slave trade), its docks at Avonmouth and Portishead (including the modern Portbury dock) are still active. Nearby is the Avon Gorge, spanned by Brunel's Clifton Suspension Bridge (1832–64). Population (1985): 394 000.

Bristol Channel   An inlet of the Atlantic Ocean in the UK, between South Wales and SW England. It forms an extension of the Severn Estuary and has the greatest tidal range in England. Length: about 137 km (85 mi).

Britain, Battle of.   *See* World War II.

Britannia metal   An alloy of tin (80–90%) with variable amounts of antimony and copper. It was formerly used for tableware.

British Academy   A learned society formed in 1901 to provide British representation of the humanities at the International Association of Academies. Incorporated in 1902, it promotes the study of languages and literatures, history, archaeology, philosophy, religion, law, economics, and the visual arts.

British Antarctic Territory   A British colony established in 1962 that consists of the South Orkney and South Shetland islands and a part of the Antarctic. It is used as a base for the British Antarctic Survey stations.

British Broadcasting Corporation (BBC)   A broadcasting authority in the UK. The BBC was first set up as a private company in 1922 and was incorporated as a public body under royal charter in 1927; it is responsible to parliament and is politically neutral and independent. It runs two national television stations, four national radio stations, and a number of local radio stations. It relies on revenue from television licences as it is not permitted to carry advertising. The BBC provides external services in 38 languages.

British citizenship   A new form of citizenship introduced on 1 January 1983 by the British Nationality Act (1981). It is acquired by birth in the UK to a parent who is either a British citizen or a settled resident there, by descent, by registration, or by naturalization. With two other new forms, British Dependent Territories citizenship and British Overseas citizenship, it replaced the composite citizenship of the UK and Colonies created by the British Nationality Act (1948).

British Columbia   The westernmost province of Canada, on the Pacific Ocean. It is bounded by the Rocky Mountains in the E and the Coast Range in the W. The main rivers (the Fraser, Kootenay, Thompson, and Columbia) and their tributaries are swift flowing and there are many lakes and waterfalls. Forests cover over 55% of the surface. There are rich mineral resources; gold, silver, lead, zinc, copper, coal, and oil are all produced. Only a small area is farmed, and half the population lives in the Lower Mainland. *History*: the area was visited by Captain Cook (1778) and a British colony established on Vancouver Island (1849) spread to the mainland when gold was discovered (1858). Entry into Canada (1871) and the transcontinental railway (1885)

encouraged development. Area: 930 528 sq km (359 277 sq mi). Population (1986): 2 883 367. Capital: Victoria.

British Council   An institution set up in 1934 and incorporated by royal charter in 1940. The Council's chief aims are to promote a knowledge of the UK abroad, to promote the teaching of English, and to foster cooperation between the developing countries and the UK.

British Council of Churches   A body, set up in 1947, of representatives of the major Churches in Britain and Ireland except the Roman Catholic Church (although this sends observers to meetings). The recommendations it makes to member Churches are designed to effect unity. It founded Christian Aid and is an Associate Council of the World Council of Churches.

British Dependent Territories   Overseas territories for which constitutional responsibility rests with the Foreign and Commonwealth Office. There are currently 15 such territories.

British Guiana.   *See* Guyana, Cooperative Republic of.

British Honduras.   *See* Belize.

British Indian Ocean Territory   A British colony established in 1965 consisting of the Chagos Archipelago, the largest island of which is Diego Garcia, claimed by Mauritius. Aldabra, Farquhar, and Desroches were returned to the Seychelles in 1976. The islands are at present leased to companies that run copra plantations. Population (1982 est): 3000.

British Legion.   *See* Royal British Legion.

British Library   The national library, founded in 1753 and housed in the British Museum, to which George II presented the royal library in 1757. It contains over 18 million volumes. New premises are being prepared.

BRITISH MUSEUM   *The Elgin Marbles (north frieze) c. 440 BC.*

British Museum   The national museum founded in 1753 to house the private collection of Sir Hans Sloane, it now occupies Sir Robert Smirke's neoclassical building (1847) in Bloomsbury, London. Its collections are unique and include Egyptian mummies, the Elgin Marbles, and the Rosetta Stone. Its reading room is available only to ticket holders. The natural history exhibits were transferred to a building (designed by Alfred Waterhouse (1830–1905) and built 1873–80) in South Kensington, known as the Natural History Museum.

British Open Championship An annual golf tournament inaugurated at Prestwick in 1860 and held successively on different British courses. It is one of the major championship tournaments for both amateurs and professionals.

British Standards Institution (BSI) An institution founded in 1901 (renamed in 1931). Its function is to establish minimum standards of quality for various products and to avoid duplication of design, sizes, and patterns. Products that conform to BSI standards bear the Kite mark as a symbol of quality. The BSI collaborates with the International Organization for Standardization.

British thermal unit (btu) A unit of energy equal to the amount of heat required to raise the temperature of 1 lb of water through 1°F. It is equal to 1055.06 joules (251.997 calories).

Britons The indigenous inhabitants of Britain before the Anglo-Saxon settlements. They spoke languages of the Brythonic branch of the Celtic language family. At the Roman conquest (1st century AD) Britain was divided into tribal kingdoms with a common Celtic culture (*see* La Tène).

Brittany (Breton name: Breiz; French name: Bretagne) A planning region and former province in NW France. It consists of a peninsula between the Bay of Biscay and English Channel. It was part of ancient Armorica and in 56 BC was conquered by Julius Caesar. During the 5th–6th centuries AD Celts from Britain migrated here to escape the Anglo-Saxon invasion. Finally incorporated into France in 1532, it has retained its own distinctive culture. Area: 27 184 sq km (10 494 sq mi). Population (1986 est): 2 764 200.

Britten, (Edward) Benjamin, Baron (1913–76) British composer. A pupil of Frank Bridge, he spent the years 1939–42 in the USA and subsequently founded the English Opera Group (1947) and the Aldeburgh Festival (1948). He wrote many leading roles in his operas for his lifelong friend, the tenor Sir Peter Pears. Among Britten's compositions are the operas *Peter Grimes* (1945), *Billy Budd* (1951), and *Death in Venice* (1973); the orchestral works *Variations on a Theme by Frank Bridge* (1937) and the *Cello Symphony* (1964); choral works, such as the *Spring Symphony* (1949) and *A War Requiem* (1962); and many chamber works.

brittle star A marine invertebrate animal, also called sand star or serpent star, belonging to a class (*Ophiuroidea*) of echinoderms. It has a small disclike body bearing five long fragile arms, used for locomotion.

Brno (German name: Brünn) 49 12N 16 40E The second largest city in Czechoslovakia, formerly the capital of the province of Moravia. A fortified town in the middle ages, it contains the Spilberk fortress, an Austrian political prison (1621–1857). The botanist Gregor Mendel devised his fundamental principles of heredity here (1865). Brno is now an important industrial centre. Population (1986): 385 000.

broad bean An annual plant, *Vicia faba*, 60–150 cm tall, with a ribbed stem and compound grey-green leaves. The flowers have white petals and dark-purple blotches. The large pod has a woolly lining surrounding large flat edible beans, for which the plant is cultivated. *See also* bean.

broadbill A brightly coloured passerine bird belonging to a family (*Eurylaimidae*; 14 species) of tropical African and Asian forests. It is about 12 cm long with a large head, partly joined toes, and a very broad short bill. Most species are insectivorous.

Broads, the A low-lying area mainly in Norfolk but extending into Suffolk. It consists of shallow lakes, believed to have originated as medieval peat diggings, linked to the Rivers Bure and Yare and their tributaries. They now provide boating and fishing facilities.

Broadway A major street in New York City along and near which are sited most of the leading commercial theatres.

broccoli A cultivated variety of wild cabbage (*Brassica oleracea*) with a stout upright stem and a loose cluster of flower heads at the top. Sprouting broccoli has purple or white flowers. Calabrese or green sprouting broccoli is an Italian variety, often with fused parallel stems. Both are eaten as vegetables. *See also* Brassica.

broch A circular dry-stone defensive structure built in N Scotland and adjacent islands, probably in the period 100 BC to 100 AD. The six-storey-high broch at Mousa (Shetland) is a famous example.

bromine (Br) A dense reddish-brown liquid element, discovered by A. J. Balard (1802–76) in 1826. It is extracted from sea water and other natural brines by electrolysis or by displacement with chlorine. The liquid element is volatile and its vapour has a pungent smell reminiscent of chlorine with severe irritating effects. Compounds include silver bromide (AgBr), used in photography. At no 35; at wt 79.904; mp −7.2°C; bp 58.78°C.

bronchi. *See* lungs.

bronchitis Inflammation of the bronchi. Acute bronchitis is often due to a virus infection. Chronic bronchitis is common in middle-aged men in the UK, being aggravated by cigarette smoking. Irritation of the mucus-secreting glands in the bronchi results in a persistent cough, with the production of large amounts of sputum. The patient is breathless and liable to chest infections. Treatment consists of the prompt management of any chest infection.

Brontë sisters Three British novelists, daughters of the rector of Haworth, an isolated village in Yorkshire. After attending a local boarding school, **Charlotte Brontë** (1816–55) and **Emily Brontë** (1818–48) rejoined their sister **Anne Brontë** (1820–49) at home. Their early writings chronicled the imaginary kingdoms of Angria and Gondal. All the sisters worked for brief periods as governesses and teachers to help pay off the debts of their alcoholic artist brother, **Patrick Branwell Brontë** (1817–48). In 1846 the sisters published *Poems by Currer, Ellis, and Acton Bell* and in 1847, under the same pseudonyms, the novels *Jane Eyre* (by Charlotte), *Wuthering Heights* (by Emily), and *Agnes Grey* (by Anne). In 1848 Emily died of tuberculosis, as did Anne in 1849. Charlotte published *Shirley* (1849) and *Villette* (1853). She married her father's curate in 1854 and died in pregnancy a year later.

Brontosaurus. *See* Apatosaurus.

Brontotherium A genus of extinct North American hoofed mammals—titanotheres—that lived during the Oligocene epoch (between 38 and 26 million years ago). Standing 2.5 m at the shoulder, *Brontotherium* had a large skull with a pair of bony horns.

bronze An alloy of copper and (4–11%) tin. Because it melts between 900°C and 1000°C, about the temperature of an ordinary wood fire, it was one of the first metals to be used for making weapons and utensils, being known around 2000 BC in Britain. It is harder than pure copper. *See also* gun metal.

BRONTËS *Detail from a portrait (c. 1834) by Branwell; (from left) Anne, Emily, and Charlotte.*

Bronze Age The cultural phase during which metallurgical technology, based first on copper (in the Chalcolithic period) and then on bronze, replaced the stone technology of the Neolithic period. In Eurasia the development of international trade, literacy, the plough, and the wheel took place during this phase, which began at varying dates according to locality (the earliest being about 6500 BC in Anatolia); it gave way to the Iron Age in about 1000 BC. In Africa, iron, discovered about 800 BC, replaced stone without an intervening Bronze Age. In the Americas, copper, discovered about 100 AD, was followed rapidly by iron.

Bronzino, Il (Agnolo di Cosimo; 1503–72) Florentine mannerist painter (*see* mannerism). His religious and allegorical works, such as *Venus, Cupid, and Folly* (National Gallery, London), were influenced by Michelangelo. As court painter to Cosimo I de' Medici he painted many portraits, including *Eleanor of Toledo and Her Son Giovanni* (Uffizi), a characteristic work.

Brooke, Rupert (Chawner) (1887–1915) British poet. His scholarship, charm, and good looks gained him many influential friends in literary circles. He received a naval commission in 1914 but died of blood poisoning on a hospital ship in the Aegean, without having seen action. The idealistic patriotism of his wartime poetry, *1914 and Other Poems* (1915), made him a national hero.

broom A deciduous shrub, *Sarothamnus scoparius* (or *Cytisus scoparius*), 60–200 cm high, with shiny green five-angled stems and small pointed compound leaves. The bright-yellow flowers are clustered at the ends of the twigs. Broom is found in heaths and woodland glades in Europe. It is poisonous to livestock but is often grown as an ornamental. Family: *Leguminosae*.

Brouwer, Adriaen (c. 1605–38) Flemish painter, who worked in Holland, initially as a pupil of Hals, and later in Antwerp. He excelled in small paintings of brawling and drunken peasants.

Brown, Sir Arthur. *See* Alcock, Sir John.

Brown, Capability (Lancelot B.; 1716–83) British landscape gardener, who carried on the work of William Kent. Abandoning the formal continental style, Brown's gardens, as for example at Blenheim Palace (1765), sought to create a stylized imitation of nature, establishing an English style of park. He was also an architect, designing houses and garden buildings. His nickname arose because he frequently told his patrons that their grounds had "capabilities" for landscaping. See p. 116.

Brown, Ford Madox (1821–93) British painter, born in Calais. Influenced by the Pre-Raphaelites, he painted chiefly historical themes, although his most famous paintings, *Work* (Manchester) and *The Last of England* (Birmingham), are of contemporary subjects.

Brown, John (1800–59) US abolitionist, who raided the Federal Arsenal at Harpers Ferry, Virginia, in an attempt to establish a slave refuge and a base for promoting slave uprisings. He was captured and executed for treason; he is the hero of the song "John Brown's Body."

Brown, Robert (1773–1858) Scottish botanist, who in 1831 first recognized the nucleus as a fundamental constituent of cells. Four years earlier, while observing a solution of pollen grains in water under a microscope, he discovered the continuous random movement of the grains, now known as the **Brownian movement**. Although Brown was unable to exlain it, it is now known to be due to collisions between the atoms and molecules of the fluid with the particles.

brown algae Algae of the division *Phaeophyta* (1500 species), which contain a brown pigment (fucoxanthin) in addition to and sometimes masking the green chlorophyll. Brown algae include all the larger seaweeds, such as wracks and kelps. Many show an alternation of generations.

brown bear A large shaggy mostly brown bear, *Ursus arctos*, of the N hemisphere. There are many local races and subspecies—the reputedly ferocious grizzly bear (*U. arctos horribilis*), of N Canada and Alaska, reaches a length of 2.5 m and a weight of 550 kg; the Alaskan Kodiac bear—a giant grizzly—is the largest living land carnivore, reaching a length of 2.8 m and a weight of 760 kg.

Browning, Robert (1812–89) British poet. The son of a bank clerk, he wrote several verse dramas and dramatic monologues, including the famous "My Last Duchess" (1842). The poem cycle *The Ring and the Book* was his last major work. His wife **Elizabeth Barrett Browning** (1806–61) was also a poet. A spinal injury when she was 15 made her a lifelong semi-invalid. She met Robert Browning in 1845 and in 1846 she defied her domineering father and eloped with Browning to Italy. Here she wrote her most famous work, *Sonnets from the Portuguese* (1850). She later became involved in Italian politics, the abolition of slavery, and spiritualism.

Browning Automatic Rifle (BAR) A gas-operated automatic rifle designed in 1917 by John Moses Browning (1855–1926). The standard automatic weapon in the US army until the Korean War, it weighed over 8.6 kg (19 lbs).

Brownshirts The colloquial name for the Nazi Sturmabteilung (SA; stormtroopers). They were founded in 1921 and reorganized by Ernst Röhm (1887–1934) in 1930. Squads of thugs, who eliminated the Nazis' opponents, they numbered two million by 1933. In 1934 Hitler eliminated Röhm himself and reduced their power. *See also* SS.

Brubeck, Dave (1920–) US jazz pianist, who studied composition with Darius Milhaud and Arnold

CAPABILITY BROWN   *Petworth Park in Sussex laid out by Brown.*

Schoenberg. Brubeck formed a quartet in 1951. One of his most famous pieces is "Take Five."

Bruce, Robert.   *See* Robert (I) the Bruce.

brucellosis (*or* undulant fever)   An infectious disease of farm animals caused by the bacterium *Brucella abortus*. Symptoms include fever weakness, cough, joint pain, and sometimes swelling of the lymph nodes. Tetracycline usually cures the disease, which can be contracted by man from contaminated milk.

Bruch, Max   (1838–1920) German composer, best known for his first violin concerto (1868) and *Kol Nidrei* (1880) for cello and orchestra, based on a Jewish hymn.

Brücke, Die (German: The Bridge)   A German organization founded in 1905 to promote modern art. Its members, notably Kirchner, were influenced, like their French contemporaries, the fauves (*see* fauvism), by Van Gogh, Gauguin, Munch, and primitive art. Although the group broke up in 1913, their crudely painted, vibrantly coloured works had a lasting influence on the graphic arts. *See also* expressionism.

Bruckner, Anton   (1824–96) Austrian composer. A professor at the Vienna conservatoire (1871–91), he was granted a pension and apartments in the Belvedere palace in Vienna in 1891, where he worked on his ninth (unfinished) symphony (1887–96). His symphonies had a mixed reception during his lifetime and were frequently performed in shortened versions. Bruckner also composed choral and chamber music and a *Te Deum* (1881–84).

Brueghel the Elder, Pieter (*or* Bruegel; 1525–69) Flemish painter, popularly called Peasant Brueghel, whose patrons included Cardinal de Granvelle (1517–86). Influenced by Bosch in such works as the macabre *Triumph of Death* (Prado), in 1563 he settled in Brussels, where he executed his best-known works, e.g. *Peasant Wedding* (Kunsthistorisches Museum, Vienna), and a landscape series entitled the *Labours of the Months*. Many of his paintings were copied by his eldest son **Pieter Brueghel the Younger** (?1564–?1638). His younger son **Jan Brueghel the Elder** (1568–1625) is noted for his flower and landscape paintings.

Bruges (Flemish name: Brugge) 51 13N 3 14E A town in NW Belgium. It was the capital of Flanders in the 12th century and during the 13th and 14th centuries it became the centre of the Hanseatic League. It has many fine gothic buildings, including the 14th-century cathedral, the Church of Notre Dame and the Market Hall (13th–15th centuries) with its famous belfry. It is linked by canal to many European ports. Population (1987 est): 117 755.

Brummell, George Bryan   (1778–1840) British dandy, known as Beau Brummell. He was a prominent member of fashionable society and a close friend of the Prince Regent, later George IV. After becoming bankrupt he fled to France and died in an asylum.

Brunei, State of   A small sultanate in NW Borneo, consisting of two separate areas, bounded by the Malaysian state of Sarawak. The people are mainly Malays, while about a quarter of the population are Chinese or other minorities. *Economy*: dominated by oil since the discovery of the Seria oilfield in 1929 and the later offshore oilfields. A deepwater port and a natural-gas liquefaction plant have recently been built. Agriculture is being encouraged. *History*: a powerful state in the 16th century controlling the whole of Borneo, it became a British protected state in 1888. In 1962 there was a revolt, against the proposal to join the Federation of Malaysia, and since then the sultan has ruled by decree. In 1967 Hassanal Bolkia Mu'izuddin Waddaulah (1946–) succeeded his father as sultan. Internal self-government was achieved in 1971 and full independence in 1983. Offical language: Malay; Chinese and English are also widely spoken. Official religion: Islam. Official currency: Brunei dollar of 100 cents. Area: 5800 sq km (2226 sq mi). Population (1983 est): 209 000. Capital and main port: Bandar Seri Begawan.

Brunel, Isambard Kingdom   (1806–59) British engineer, whose most famous works were the Clifton suspension bridge (1864) and his ships the *Great Western* (1837), the *Great Britain* (1843), and the *Great Eastern* (1858). Much of his work was done for the Great Western Railway, for which he built over 1600 km of track. His father **Sir Marc Isambard Brunel** (1769–1849) was also an engineer. Born in France, he worked in New York after fleeing the French Revolution. He moved to England in 1799, where he became famous for his tunnelling shield, which allowed tunnels to be dug below water. His tunnel under the River Thames from

ISAMBARD KINGDOM BRUNEL *Standing in front of the launching chains of "The Great Eastern" in 1857.*

Rotherhithe to Wapping took from 1825 to 1842 to complete.

Brunelleschi, Filippo (1377–1446) Italian Renaissance architect, who began his career as a goldsmith. His taste for classical architecture is demonstrated by his most famous construction, the dome of Florence cathedral (1430s). The Ospedale degli Innocenti (1419–26) is often regarded as the first architectural expression of the Renaissance.

Brunhild (*or* Brynhild) A heroine of Norse and Germanic legend. In the *Volsungasaga* she is the daughter of Odin, doomed to sleep on a fire-encircled rock until wakened by a mortal (*see* Siegfried). In the *Nibelungenlied* she is the queen of Issland.

Brünn. *See* Brno.

Bruno, Frank(lyn Roy) (1961–) British boxer. In 1985 he became European heavyweight champion. He unsuccessfully challenged Tim Witherspoon (1986) and Mike Tyson (1989) for the world championship title.

Brunswick (German name: Braunschweig) 52 15N 10 30E A city in NE West Germany, in Lower Saxony on the River Oker. It was the capital of the former duchy of Brunswick. Notable buildings include the castle and the romanesque cathedral (both 12th-century), the old town hall (14th-15th centuries), and the ducal palace (1768–69). Population (1989): 254 851.

brush turkey A megapode bird, *Alectura lathami*, occurring in rain forests of New Guinea and E Australia. It is 65–70 cm long with a black plumage and builds a huge nest of fermenting plant material.

Brussels (French name: Bruxelles) 50 51N 4 22E The capital of Belgium, situated on the River Senne. The headquarters of the EC and NATO, it has many fine buildings including the 15th-century gothic town hall, the 13th-century Maison du Roi, the 18th-century Palais de la Nation (parliament building), and the Royal Palace. *History*: settled by the French in the 7th century AD, it developed into a centre of the wool industry in the 13th century. It became the capital of the Spanish Netherlands in the 15th century and later of the Austrian S Netherlands. In 1830 it was chosen as capital of the new kingdom of Belgium. Population (1987 est): 973 499.

Brussels sprout A variety of wild cabbage, *Brassica oleracea* var. *gemmifera*, cultivated for its large edible buds. The stout shoots, up to 80 cm high, have curly leaves arranged spirally up the stem; the large buds grow in the angle between the leaf bases and the stem. *See also* Brassica.

Brutus, Marcus Junius (?85–42 BC) Roman soldier, who supported Pompey against Caesar in the civil war, was pardoned by Caesar and made governor of Cisalpine Gaul (46). He subsequently joined the conspiracy to murder Caesar (44) and committed suicide after his defeat by Antony at Philippi (42).

bryony Either of two unrelated Eurasian plants. **Black bryony** (*Tamus communis*) is a herbaceous climber with heart-shaped leaves. The bell-shaped yellow flowers are borne in separate male and female spikes. The fruits are scarlet berries, and the plant overwinters as a tuber. Family: *Dioscoreaceae* (yam family). **White bryony** (*Bryonia dioica*) is a perennial climbing herb. The hairy stem arises from a large rootstock and the leaves are palmately lobed. Greenish male and female flowers occur on separate plants and produce poisonous scarlet berries. Family: *Cucurbitaceae* (gourd family).

bryophyte A small flowerless green plant of the division *Bryophyta* (about 25 000 species), comprising the liverworts and mosses. The plant body is either differentiated into stems and leaves or is a flat branching structure (thallus). Bryophytes lack true vascular (conducting) tissues and roots (the rootlike rhizoids serve mainly for anchorage). They show alternation of generations: the plant itself is the sexual (gametophyte) phase, which bears male and female sex organs (antheridia and archegonia, respectively). Fertilization of an egg cell results in the development of a spore capsule–the asexual (sporophyte) phase–which remains attached to the gametophyte. The spores germinate to form new plants.

Bryozoa (*or* Ectoprocta) A phylum of aquatic colonial invertebrate animals (about 6000 species), called moss animals, found chiefly in seas as matlike encrustations on rocks. A colony consists of individuals, each up to 3 mm long and with a chitinous or gelatinous case and a ring of ciliated tentacles around the mouth. These waft food particles into the U-shaped digestive tract.

Brythonic languages. *See* Celtic languages.

bubonic plague. *See* plague.

Buchan, John, 1st Baron Tweedsmuir (1875–1940) British novelist. *Prester John* (1910) was the first of a series of vigorous adventure novels that included *The Thirty-Nine Steps* (1915). Director of Information during World War 1, he was made governor general of Canada in 1935.

Bucharest (Romanian name: Bucureşti) 44 25N 26 07E The capital of Romania, in the SE on a tributary of the Danube. *History*: a fortress was built in the 15th century and it became capital of Walachia in 1659. Bucharest became capital of Romania in 1862. It was badly damaged by German bombing in World War II. Population (1980 est): 1 861 007.

Buckingham, George Villiers, 1st Duke of (1592–1628) He replaced Robert Carr, Earl of Somerset, in the favour of James I of England (1615), becoming Earl of Buckingham (1617), Lord High Admiral (1619), and Duke of Buckingham (1623). His attempt to negotiate the marriage of Prince Charles to the daughter of the Spanish king failed (1623); he was assassinated after his unsuccessful expedition to relieve the Huguenots at La

Rochelle (1627). His son **George Villiers, 2nd Duke of Buckingham** (1628–87) was a member of the Cabal group of ministers under Charles II. After his father's death he was brought up in the royal family, with whom he went into exile after the royalist defeat in the Civil War (1651). He became a privy councillor at the Restoration. Also a playwright, he wrote the satirical *The Rehearsal* (1671).

Buckingham Palace The London residence of the British monarch. It was built about 1705 for the Duke of Buckingham, becoming a royal residence in 1761. It was completely redesigned by Nash for George IV, although its main façade was not added until 1913.

Buckinghamshire A county of England, bordering on Greater London. Under local government reorganization in 1974 it lost part of the S, including Slough, to Berkshire. The land rises gently N from the River Thames to the Chiltern Hills before descending to the fertile Vale of Aylesbury. It is mainly agricultural; industry includes the manufacture of furniture at High Wycombe, based on the extensive beech woods. Area: 1878 sq km (725 sq mi). Population (1986 est): 612 900. Administrative centre: Aylesbury.

buckthorn A small thorny deciduous tree or shrub of the genus *Rhamnus* (about 13 species), widespread in the N hemisphere. The leaves are oval and the small green flowers produce blue-black berries. The alder buckthorn (*Frangula alnus*) is a similar and related shrub that lacks thorns. Family: *Rhamnaceae*.

buckwheat A herbaceous plant of the genus *Fagopyrum*, especially *F. esculentum*. Up to 60 cm tall, they have arrow-shaped leaves and clusters of densely packed small pink or white flowers. Buckwheats are native to Asia but widely cultivated for their seed, used as a cereal substitute. Family: *Polygonaceae* (dock family).

Budapest 47 33N 19 03E The capital of Hungary, situated in the N of the country on the River Danube. Most of Hungary's industry is sited here. *History*: from the 14th century the fortress of Buda, on the W bank of the Danube, was the seat of the Magyar kings. After occupation by the Turks, it came under Habsburg rule in the 17th century. In 1872 it united with Pest, on the E bank, to form the city that became the capital of Hungary in 1918. In 1956 it was the scene of a popular rising, suppressed by Soviet troops. Population (1985 est): 2 089 000.

Budd, Zola (1966–) South African athlete, who received British nationality in 1984 and competed for Britain in the 1984 Olympic Games. She set new world records for the 5000 metres (14 mins 48.07 secs) in 1985 and for the 3000 metres (8 mins 39.66 secs) in 1986 but retired in 1988 over her South African links.

Buddh Gaya (*or* Bodh Gaya) 24 42N 85 00E A village in India, in Bihar, in which Gautama Buddha attained enlightenment under the sacred bo tree. Population (1981): 15 724.

Buddhism The nontheistic religion system founded in NE India in the 6th century BC by Gautama Siddhartha (the Buddha). His followers seek to emulate his example of perfect morality, wisdom, and compassion, culminating in a transformation of consciousness known as enlightenment. The apparent substantiality of all objects, including the self, is illusion; everything mundane is impermanent and ultimately unsatisfying. The central beliefs of Buddhism are based on the Buddha's Four Noble Truths, the last of which is the Eightfold Path by which enlightenment may be attained and the individual self annihilated in nirvana. Buddhism is not dogmatic, but has developed into many schools (*see* Mahayana; Zen Buddhism). It has more than 500 million followers in Sri Lanka, Nepal, Japan, and elsewhere.

Buddleia A widespread genus of trees and shrubs (about 100 species). The small four-petalled flowers are usually clustered in dense heads; the fruit is a capsule or berry. Many species are grown as ornamentals, especially *B. davidii* (butterfly bush) 4–5 m high, the long purple flower heads of which attract butterflies; and *B. globosa*, which has round orange flower heads. Family: *Buddleiaceae*.

budgerigar A small parakeet, *Melopsitticus undulatus*, occurring in large flocks in Australia. It is 19 cm long and has a green and yellow plumage. Since its introduction to Britain in 1840 it has become a popular cagebird. Selective breeding has produced birds of many colours.

Buenaventura 3 54N 77 02W A port in W Colombia, on the Pacific Ocean. Exports include coffee and sugar

BUCKINGHAM PALACE *John Nash's building with the Marble Arch in its original position (painted 1846).*

from the Cauca Valley and gold and platinum from the Chocó district. Population (1984 est): 122 500.

Buenos Aires 34 50S 58 37W The capital of Argentina situated on the Río de la Plata estuary. The financial, commercial, and industrial centre of the country, its chief exports are beef and wool. It possesses a national library and a famous opera house (the Teatro Colón). *History*: founded in 1580, after Indian attacks on earlier settlements, it became capital of the newly created viceroyalty of the Río de la Plata in 1776 and of the new Republic of Argentina in 1880. In the late 19th and early 20th centuries its population was greatly swelled by European immigrants. Population (1980 est): 2 922 800.

buffalo A large African hoofed mammal, *Syncerus caffer*, also called Cape buffalo. Weighing over 700 kg and measuring 110–150 cm at the shoulder, buffaloes have massive curved horns and a smooth black coat. They live in large herds in grassy areas where both tree cover and water are available. Family: *Bovidae*. Compare bison; water buffalo.

Buffalo 42 52N 78 55W A city in the USA, in New York state on Lake Erie and the Niagara River. It is linked to New York City by the New York State Barge Canal (formerly Erie Canal). Population (1986): 324 820.

Buffalo Bill. *See* Cody, William F(rederick).

bug A common name for any insect-like animal. Specifically, the term refers to insects of the order *Hemiptera* (the true bugs), especially the bedbug and insects of the suborder *Heteroptera* (plant bugs, water bugs, etc.).

Bug, River 1. (*or* Western Bug) A river in E central Europe, rising in the Soviet Union and flowing NW as part of the border between the Soviet Union and Poland to the River Vistula. Length: 724 km (450 mi). 2. (*or* Southern Bug) A river in the SW Soviet Union, rising in the W Ukraine and flowing SE to the Dnieper estuary on the Black Sea. Length: 853 km (530 mi).

Buganda A former kingdom in East Africa, now comprising an administrative region of Uganda bordering on Lake Victoria.

bugle A high-pitched brass instrument with a wide conical tube, a cup-shaped mouthpiece, and a small bell. It lacks valves and so can only play a single harmonic series (usually having the fundamental of C). Formerly much used for military signalling, it is now used on ceremonial occasions.

Bukhari, al- (810–70 AD) Muslim scholar. After extensive travels, he collected more than 600 000 traditional records (the Hadith) of the prophet Mohammed. The resulting collection is revered by Muslims as second in authority only to the Koran.

Bukharin, Nikolai Ivanovich (1888–1938) Soviet politician. In exile after 1911, Bukharin edited the socialist newspaper *Novy Mir*, in New York. He returned to Russia during the Revolution and became editor of the newspaper *Pravda*. He was chairman of the Comintern until dismissed by Stalin in 1929. He helped draft the 1936 constitution but died in Stalin's purges.

Bukovina (*or* Bucovina) An area in E Europe, in the NE Carpathian Mountains. As part of the principality of Moldavia, it fell to the Turks in 1512 and was ceded to Austria in 1775. Occupied by the Romanians in 1918, the N part was ceded to the Soviet Union (1940), later becoming part of the Ukrainian SSR. S Bukovina remained a Romanian province until it was abolished in 1952.

Bulawayo 20 10S 28 43E The second largest city in Zimbabwe. It was founded in 1894 by the British, near to Lobengula, the centre of the Ndebele tribe. The city is the country's chief industrial centre. Population (1982): 414 800.

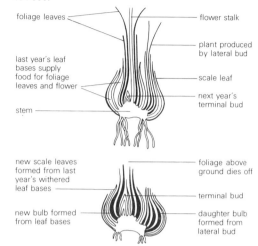

BULB *A section through a daffodil bulb in spring (above) and summer (below) to show growth cycle.*

bulb A modified underground stem of certain perennial herbaceous plants, for example onions and tulips, that serves as an overwintering organ. Food is stored in overlapping fleshy leaves or leaf bases, borne on a very short stem, and is used to produce one or more plants the following season.

Bulganin, Nikolai Aleksandrovich (1895–1975) Soviet statesman; prime minister (1955–58). Bulganin became (1944) a member of Stalin's war cabinet and in 1947, defence minister. As prime minister, Bulganin participated in the attempt to oust Khrushchev in 1957 and was subsequently dismissed.

Bulgaria, People's Republic of A country in SE Europe, in the E Balkans on the Black Sea. The low-lying Danube basin in the N rises to the Balkan Mountains in the centre; further S the Rhodope Mountains reach heights of almost 3000 m (10 000 ft). The inhabitants are mainly Bulgars, with minorities of Macedonians, Turks, and Gipsies. *Economy*: industrialization has proceeded rapidly since World War II with a centrally planned economy. Coal, iron, and other minerals are mined and hydroelectricity and nuclear energy contribute to power supplies. Oil and natural gas have been found offshore in the Black Sea. Agriculture has been mechanized and organized on a cooperative basis. Bulgaria is a member of COMECON. *History*: following the invasion of the Bulgars in the 7th century AD and their gradual adoption of the culture of the conquered Slavs, Bulgaria became a significant power in SE Europe. Under Turkish rule in 1396, the Bulgars retained their national identity over the centuries until becoming independent in 1908. Bulgaria aligned itself with Germany in both World Wars. In 1944 it was occupied by the Soviet Union; power was seized by the left-wing Fatherland Front, which formed a pro-Soviet government that declared war on Germany. In 1946 a People's Republic was proclaimed. In 1989 mass unrest led to the ending of the Communist Party's monopoly of power. Head of State: Petur Mladenov (1936–). Official language: Bulgarian. Official currency: lev of 100 stotinki. Area: 110 912 sq km (42 823 sq mi). Population (1987): 8 949 600. Capital: Sofia. Main port: Varna.

Bulgarian A language belonging to the South Slavonic group spoken by eight million people in Bulgaria, Greece, Romania, and areas of the Soviet Union. It differs from other Slavonic languages in lacking declensions for nouns and shares grammatical features with other non-Slavonic Balkan languages. The literature written in Bulgarian dates from the establishment of Christianity (9th century).

Bulge, Battle of the. *See* World War II.

bulk modulus. *See* elastic modulus.

bull (from Latin: *bulla*, seal) Originally, the seal attached to papal edicts it later referred to the documents themselves, now only to important missives. Issued to assert doctrine, they are named by their opening phrase, for example *Pastor Aeternus* (Eternal Father; 1870).

bulldog A breed of dog originating in England, where it was used in bull- and bearbaiting. It has a compact rounded body with short sturdy legs and a short tail. The relatively large head has an undershot jaw and loose folds of skin. Weight: 25 kg (dogs); 23 kg (bitches).

bullfighting The national spectator sport of Spain, it is also popular in parts of France and Latin America; mounted bullfighting, in which the bulls are not killed, is practised in Portugal. At a Spanish *corrida de toros* (bullfight) three matadors kill two bulls each. Following the initial ceremonial procession the first bull enters the ring. Preliminary passes are made by the *banderilleros* (assistants) with their capes to attract the bull's attention. The matador then makes his first series of passes with his cape, controlling the bull's charge. During the next stage, the matadors make the bull charge at a mounted picador, who uses a lance to stab the bull's neck, so that it lowers its head. This procedure is repeated up to three times. During the following stage the neck muscle is further weakened by pairs of barbed sticks (*banderillas*) thrust into it by the *banderilleros*. In the final stage the matador performs a series of passes with his *muleta* (a small red cape folded over a stick) to weaken the bull until he can sever its aorta with his sword.

bullfinch A woodland finch, *Pyrrhula pyrrhula*, of N Eurasia. It is about 14 cm long and has a grey back, a pinkish breast, and black head. Bullfinches strip trees and shrubs and are often regarded as pests.

bullfrog A large frog, *Rana catesbiana*, of North America. Dull green with a slightly warty skin, bullfrogs grow to about 20 cm. Females are larger than males. Other large frogs—*Pyxicephalus adspersus* in Africa and *Rana tigrina* in India—are also called bullfrogs.

bull mastiff A breed of dog resulting from crosses between bulldogs and mastiffs. It is sturdily built with a short broad muzzle and folds of skin surrounding the face. The short coat is red-brown. Height: 63–68 cm (dogs); 61–66 cm (bitches).

Bull Run, Battles of (*or* Battles of Manassas) Two battles in the US Civil War fought in NE Virginia. Both were Confederate victories. In the first (21 July, 1861), Federal forces failed to prevent the unification of Confederate forces under Gen P. G. T. Beauregard (1818– 93) and Gen Joseph E. Johnstone (1807–91) at

Manassas Junction near a stream named Bull Run. The second (29–30 August, 1862) followed an unsuccessful Federal attempt to capture Gordonsville, the Confederate capital. The 70 000 Federal troops, awaiting reinforcements were attacked by Stonewall Jackson and forced to retreat to Washington.

bull terrier A breed of dog originating in the UK from crosses between bulldogs and terriers. It is strongly built with a courageous temperament. Height: 48–56 cm. (Miniature bull terriers must not exceed 36 cm in height.)

bulrush A widely distributed perennial herbaceous plant, *Scirpus lacustris*, growing in ponds, rivers, etc. 1–3 m high, it has cylindrical leafless stems bearing branched clusters of small reddish-brown flowers. Family: *Cyperaceae* (sedges, etc.). The name is also applied to the reedmace; the biblical bulrush is the papyrus.

bumblebee A social bee belonging to a genus (*Bombus*) found mainly in temperate regions. Bumblebees, 15–25 mm long, are usually black with yellow or orange bands. They live in colonies containing 100–400 workers in the summer. Their life cycle is like that of the honeybee, although only young fertilized queens survive the winter. Solitary parasitic bumblebees belong to the genus *Psithyrus*. Family: *Apidae*.

Bunker Hill, Battle of (17 June, 1775) A battle of the American Revolution actually fought on Breed's Hill (next to Bunker Hill) in Charlestown, near Boston. The Americans defended the strategic hill from two British attacks but Sir William Howe (1729–1814) displaced them at the third attempt.

Bunsen, Robert Wilhelm (1811–99) German chemist. He did not invent the Bunsen burner although he did popularize it. In collaboration with Kirchhoff, Bunsen developed the technique of spectroscopy, using a Bunsen burner to heat the substance. In 1860 they used the technique to discover the elements rubidium and caesium.

Bunsen burner A gas burner for laboratory use, popularized by R. Bunsen. It consists of a vertical metal tube with a variable air inlet at the bottom, adjustment of which enables the flame to be controlled.

bunting A sparrow-like bird belonging to a subfamily (*Emberizinae*) of the finches. Buntings are 12–20 cm long and usually have a brownish or greyish plumage. The subfamily includes the yellowhammer and the snow bunting.

Buñuel, Luis (1900–83) Spanish film director whose films, made mainly in France and Mexico, include *Un Chien andalou* (1928), *Viridiana* (1961), and *That Obscure Object of Desire* (1977).

bunya bunya. *See* Araucaria.

Bunyan, John (1628–88) British writer. Son of a tinker, he fought in the parliamentary army during the Civil War. After being converted to religion, he became the leader of a group of Baptists in Bedford and in 1660 he was imprisoned for preaching without a licence. During his 12 years in prison he wrote his spiritual autobiography, *Grace Abounding* (1666), and began his imaginative allegory *The Pilgrim's Progress* (1678).

burbot A food fish, *Lota lota*, related to the ling. Up to 1.1 m long, it lives on the bottom in cold fresh waters, feeding on other fish.

Burgas 42 30N 29 29E A city in E Bulgaria, on the Black Sea. Its industries include fishing, mining, and oil refining. Population (1985): 182 570.

JOHN BUNYAN *A portrait (detail) painted, a few years before his death, by Thomas Sadler.*

Burgenland A federal state in E Austria, bordering on Hungary. It was ceded to Austria by Hungary following World War I. It is predominantly agricultural. Area: 3965 sq km (1531 sq mi). Population (1986): 267 279. Capital: Eisenstadt.

Burgess, Anthony (John Burgess Wilson; 1917–) British novelist and former teacher of English literature. His novels include *A Clockwork Orange* (1962), *Inside Mr Enderby* (1963), *Nothing like the Sun* (1964), *Napoleon Symphony* (1974), *Earthly Powers* (1980), *The Kingdom of the Wicked* (1985), and *Any Old Iron* (1989).

Burgess, Guy. *See* Maclean, Donald.

Burghley, William Cecil, Lord (1520–98) English statesman; close adviser to Elizabeth I. He served both Somerset and Northumberland under Edward VI and outwardly espoused Roman Catholicism under Mary I. His pragmatism is evident in Elizabeth's religious settlement (*see* Reformation). He influenced Elizabeth's pro-Protestant foreign policy and helped to prepare for the Spanish invasion (*see* Armada, Spanish). He secured the execution of Mary, Queen of Scots. He was succeeded as royal adviser by his son **Robert Cecil, 1st Earl of Salisbury** (c. 1563–1612), who negotiated the accession of James VI of Scotland to the English throne as James I (1603). As lord treasurer (1608–12), he was James' chief adviser.

Burgos 42 21N 3 41W A city in N Spain, in Old Castile. Its cathedral (13th–16th centuries) contains the remains of the legendary hero El Cid. Population (1981): 156 449.

Burgundy A region in France, E of the Rivers Rhône and Saône. A Scandinavian people occupied the region in the 4th century AD, establishing a kingdom that was conquered by the Franks in 534. The NW part of the region became a duchy in the 9th century, passing to the French Crown in the mid-14th century.

Buridan, Jean (c. 1297–c. 1358) French philosopher. He is associated with "Buridan's ass," an animal that has free will but starves through being unable to choose between equally attractive piles of hay.

Burke, Edmund (1729–97) British political philosopher. An MP from 1765, he became a Rockingham Whig. He attacked George III's exalted view of the monarch's political role in the pamphlet *Thoughts on the Cause of the Present Discontents* (1770) and blamed the unrest in the American colonies on British misgovernment. An opponent of democracy on the grounds that it brought demagogues to the fore, he advocated responsible aristocratic government and also emphasized the dangers of large schemes of speculative reform. Both these ideas were expounded in his condemnation of the French Revolution (*Reflections on the Revolution in France*, 1790). He also wrote *A Philosophical Enquiry into the Origin of Our Ideas of the Sublime and Beautiful* (1757).

Burkina Faso (name until 1984: Upper Volta) A landlocked country in West Africa. It consists mainly of a low-lying plateau, crossed by the headwaters of the River Volta. The population is almost entirely African, the largest groups being the Mossi and Fulani. *Economy*: chiefly agricultural. Production of crops is being increased by improved water supplies. Some minerals, including manganese, have been found. *History*: the area was occupied by powerful Mossi states from the 14th century. It became part of the French protectorate of Soudan in 1898 and in 1919 the separate protectorate of Upper Volta was formed. In 1932 it was divided between Niger, Ivory Coast, and Soudan but was reconstituted in 1947. In 1958 Upper Volta became an autonomous republic, gaining full independence in 1960. A military coup in 1966 brought Lt Col (later Gen) Sangoulé Lamizana (1916–) to power; he was overthrown in a coup in 1980. In 1983, after another military coup, Capt Thomas Sankara assumed power; he died in 1987 in a coup led by Capt Blaise Compaoré, who promised a return to democracy. Official language: French. Official currency: CFA (Communauté financière africaine) franc of 100 centimes. Area: 274 002 sq km (105 764 sq mi). Population (1987 est): 8 334 000. Capital: Ouagadougou.

Burma, Socialist Republic of the Union of (Burmese name from 1989: Myanmar, Union of) A country in SE Asia, on the Bay of Bengal. A narrow plain running N–S, rises to the Arakan Mountains and the Chin Hills in the W and the Shan Plateau in the E. The majority of the population, concentrated in the delta of the River Irrawaddy, is Burmese but there are several minorities, including the Shan, Karen, Chachin, and Chin peoples. *Economy*: primarily agricultural, the main crop is rice; in 1976 the government set up cooperative farming, mainly on virgin land. Almost half the land is under forest. There is some mining, especially of lead and zinc, and all industry is nationalized. Foreign trade is carried out through government trading organizations, the main exports being rice, rubber, jute, and timber. *History*: by the 13th century the Burmese had a civilization based on Hinayana Buddhism. Following defeat by the Mongols in 1287, the area was ruled by the Shans and the Mons. The rule of the Burmese Alaungpaya in the 18th century began a period of increased prosperity. After successive wars it came under British rule in 1885 as part of British India. In 1937 it attained a measure of self-government and was separated from India. In World War II it was occupied by Japan and fought first with the Japanese but later against them with the British. In 1948 it became a republic outside the Commonwealth. In 1962 its parliamentary democracy was overthrown in a military coup by Gen U Ne Win (1911–), who formed a one-party socialist republic in 1974. Following U Ne Win's resignation in 1981 Gen San Yu (1919–) was elected president; in 1988 Gen Sein Lwin held power for just 18 days before being replaced by President Maung Maung, who was himself replaced by Gen Saw Maung within weeks. Martial law was then imposed. Official language: Burmese. Official currency: kyat of 100 pyas. Area: 678 000 sq km (261 789 sq mi). Population (1987 est): 37 850 000. Capital and main port: Rangoon.

Burmese A language of the Tibeto-Burman branch of Sino-Tibetan, spoken by 20 million people in Burma, where it is the official language. Written in an alphabet derived from the Pali script of India, Burmese literature dates from the 11th century AD.

Burmese cat A breed of short-haired cat originating from an Asian hybrid imported into the USA in 1933. The Burmese has a small head with large ears and greenish-yellow eyes and usually a dark-brown or silver coat.

Burne-Jones, Sir Edward Coley (1833–98) British Pre-Raphaelite painter and designer. After meeting Rossetti (1856) he abandoned his studies at Oxford, for an art career. Typical of his romantic paintings is *King Cophetua and the Beggar Maid* (Tate Gallery). More influential were his designs for stained glass and tapestries, often for the firm of William Morris.

burnet A slender perennial herb of the genera *Sanguisorba* (about 3 species) and *Poterium* (about 25 species), of N temperate regions. 500–1000 cm high, they have pinnate toothed leaves and oval heads of crimson or greenish petal-less flowers. Family: *Rosaceae*.

Burnet, Sir Frank Macfarlane (1899–) Australian physician, who discovered the phenomenon of acquired immunological tolerance to foreign tissue transplants, for which he shared a Nobel Prize (1960) with Sir Peter Medawar. He received the OM in 1957.

Burnley 53 48N 2 14W A town in N England, in Lancashire in the Calder Valley. It developed as a cotton-weaving town. Population (1989 est): 85 400.

Burns, Robert (1759–96) Scottish poet. Son of a poor farmer in Ayrshire, Burns became the Scottish national poet. *Poems, Chiefly in the Scottish Dialect* (1786) won him immediate fame; from 1786 until 1788 he was lionized by Edinburgh society. His return to farming was a failure and from 1789 he worked for the excise service. His poems range from love lyrics to broad humour, as in "Tam o'Shanter" (1788), and scathing satire,

as in "The Twa Dogs" (1786). He also collected and wrote numerous songs.

Bursa 40 12N 29 04E A town in NW Turkey. It was the capital of the Ottoman Turks for most of the 14th century and contains notable mosques and sultans' tombs. Population (1985): 614 133.

Burton, Richard (Richard Jenkins; 1925–84) British actor, born in Wales. He first achieved success in Shakespearean roles, but from the 1950s acted mainly in films. These included *Look Back in Anger* (1959), *Becket* (1964), and *Who's Afraid of Virginia Woolf?* (1966). His two marriages to Elizabeth Taylor were highly publicized.

Burton-upon-Trent 52 49N 1 36W A town in central England, in E Staffordshire on the River Trent. Formerly a cotton-spinning town, its brewing tradition dates back to brewing by the Benedictine monks of Burton Abbey (founded 1002). Population (1983): 57 725.

Burundi, Republic of A small inland country in central Africa, bordering on Lake Tanganyika. It consists chiefly of high plateau along the Nile-Congo dividing range, descending to the Great Rift Valley in the W. Most of the population belongs to the Hutu, a Bantu tribe, but the rulers are Tutsi and there are other tribal minorities. *Economy*: mainly subsistence agriculture; coffee is the main export and tea is also being developed. Minerals have been found although industry still provides only a small proportion of the revenue. *History*: the area became part of German East Africa in 1890 and from 1919 it was administered by Belgium, first under League of Nations mandate and then as a UN trust territory. It became independent in 1962. In 1966 the hereditary Mwami Mwambutsa IV was deposed by his son, who was enthroned as Mwami Ntare V. In the same year, following a military coup, Capt (later Lt Gen) Michel Micombero (1940–83) set up a republic with himself as president. In 1972 he assumed absolute powers and fighting broke out in which thousands were killed. In 1976 Micombero was overthrown in a coup and Jean-Baptiste Bagaza (1946–) became president. He was overthrown in 1987 by Maj Pierre Buyoya. Official languages: French and Kirundi. Official currency: Burundi franc of 100 centimes. Area: 27 834 sq km

BURNE-JONES *Detail from the* Legend of the Briar Rose *series.*

(10 759 sq mi). Population (1987 est): 4 927 000. Capital: Bujumbura.

burying beetle A strong beetle, also called a sexton beetle, belonging to a genus (*Necrophorus*) occurring in N temperate regions. 1.5–35 mm long, many have black and orange markings. They feed and lay their eggs on the dead bodies of small animals, which they first bury. Family: *Silphidae* (carrion beetles).

Bury St Edmunds 52 15N 0 43E A market town in E England, in Suffolk. Its ruined abbey was built as a shrine to St Edmund, last King of East Anglia (martyred in 870 AD). Population (1989 est): 32 000.

Bush, George (Herbert Walker) (1924–   ) US statesman; Republican president (1989–   ). Ambassador to the UN (1971–72), he was director of the CIA (1976–77) and vice president (1981–88) under Ronald Reagan before winning the presidency against Democrat Michael Dukakis (1933–   ).

bushbaby A small nocturnal prosimian primate of the genus *Galago* (4 species), of African forests. They are 27–80 cm long including the tail (15–40 cm). Common bushbabies (*G. senegalensis*) have soft dense greyish fur and a long bushy tail. They live in small groups. Family: *Lorisidae*.

bushel A unit of capacity (dry or liquid) equal to 8 gallons or 2219.36 cubic inches in the UK and 2150.42 cubic inches in the USA.

Bushido The code of the Japanese samurai class. It originated in about the 13th century, although the term was not used until the 17th. Obedience to one's lord and fearlessness were its main virtues; in the 13th–14th centuries it was influenced by Zen Buddhism and in the 17th–19th centuries, by Confucianism. In the mid-19th century it became the basis of Japanese emperor worship and nationalism. *See also* martial arts.

Bushman. *See* Khoisan.

bushmaster A pit viper, *Lachesis muta*, occurring in scrub and forests of Central and South America. The longest venomous snake (its venom can be fatal) of the New World, it reaches a length of 1.8 m and is brownish pink with dark diamond-shaped blotches.

bushrangers Outlaws in the Australian outback in the late-18th and 19th centuries. They robbed farmsteads and stagecoaches, murdered, and plundered, but while some were ruthless, others shared their gains with the poor. The most famous is probably Ned Kelly.

bustard A large omnivorous bird belonging to a family (*Otididae*; 22 species) occurring in grasslands of the Old World and having long legs adapted for running. Bustards have a long stout neck, broad wings, and a grey or brown mottled plumage. The great bustard (*Otis tarda*), 120 cm long and weighing 14 kg, is the largest European land bird. Order: *Gruiformes* (cranes, rails, etc.).

butadiene ($H_2C{:}CHHC{:}CH_2$) A colourless flammable gas made from butanes and butenes. It is used in making synthetic rubbers.

butane (C_4H_{10}) A colourless flammable gaseous alkane. It is used in the manufacture of synthetic rubber and, in its pressurized liquefied form, as a fuel.

butcherbird. *See* shrike.

Bute A Scottish island in the Firth of Clyde, in Strathclyde Region separated from the mainland by the Kyles of Bute. The island serves Glasgow as a holiday resort. Area: 121 sq km (47 sq mi). Population (1981): 7733. Chief town: Rothesay.

Butler, Samuel (1835–1902) British novelist. Son of a clergyman, he rejected his family and religion in 1859 to emigrate to New Zealand. In 1864 he returned wealthy and turned to literature. *Erewhon* (1872), which made him famous, satirizes Victorian ideals. The autobiographical *The Way of All Flesh* (1903) recounts his liberation from his family background.

butte A small steep-sided mass of rock left upstanding after the erosion of a mesa. It usually consists of a resistant rock capping that protects the underlying rock from erosion.

BUSHRANGERS *A contemporary engraving of Ned Kelly in home-made armour; his final battle (1880).*

butterflies and moths Insects belonging to the order *Lepidoptera* (about 100 000 species), distributed worldwide. The adults have two pairs of scale-covered wings, which are often highly coloured and patterned; the wingspan ranges from 4 mm to up to 300 mm. They all undergo a complete metamorphosis comprising a four-stage life cycle: egg, larva (*see* caterpillar), pupa (chrysalis), and adult (imago). The caterpillars feed mainly on plants, in some cases becoming serious crop pests; the adults feed mainly on nectar and other plant juices using a long tubular proboscis and may aid plant pollination in the process. Butterflies generally are active by day and rest with their wings vertical; moths, which are mainly nocturnal, generally rest with their wings horizontal. Antennae, which are smooth and club-shaped in butterflies and plumed or feathery in moths.

butterfly bush. *See* Buddleia.

Buttermere, Lake A lake in NW England, in Cumbria in the Lake District. Length: 2 km (1.25 mi).

butterwort A carnivorous plant of the genus *Pinguicula* (about 30 species), found in the N hemisphere and South America. 12–15 cm high, they have a rosette of yellow-green leaves covered with sticky glands, on which insects are trapped, and a single funnel-shaped violet or pink flower. Family: *Lentibulariaceae*.

button quail A small ground-dwelling bird belonging to a family (*Turnicidae*; 15 species) found in warm Old World grassland regions. Button quails are 13–19 cm long with a brown streaked plumage, short wings, and a slender bill. The female courts the male, who incubates the eggs and tends the young. Order: *Gruiformes* (cranes, rails, etc.).

Buxtehude, Dietrich (1637–1707) Danish composer. He settled in Germany in 1668 as organist at the Marienkirche, Lübeck. J. S. Bach walked 200 miles to Lübeck to hear Buxtehude's music. One of the most influential of the North German organists, he composed much sacred organ music.

Buxton 53 17N 1 55W A spa in the Peak District of Derbyshire on the River Wye. Its mineral waters were first used by the Romans. During the 1970s Buxton Opera House, built in 1903 and formerly used only as a theatre and cinema, was restored to its original condition. Population (1981): 20 797.

buzzard A hawk belonging to a widespread genus (*Buteo*) characterized by broad wings, a rounded tail, and brown plumage. Buzzards hunt for small mammals, reptiles, etc., and soar gracefully. The common Eurasian buzzard (*B. buteo*), 55 cm long, occurs in a number of races; the migratory rough-legged buzzard (*B. lagopus*) is distinguished by its feathered legs.

buzz bomb. *See* V-1.

Byblos 34 08N 35 38E A Phoenician city state on the E Mediterranean coast, now Jubeil (Lebanon). Egyptian records from the 14th to the 10th centuries BC attest a thriving trade with Byblos. Under Greek and Roman rule Byblos dwindled in importance but remained a centre of orgiastic worship of Astarte (*see* Aphrodite). *See also* Tyre.

Byng, John (1704–57) British admiral who, in 1756, failed to relieve Minorca, then under attack by the French, and retreated to Gibraltar. He was made a scapegoat and shot for failing to do his duty–or, in Voltaire's satirical view, as a warning to his colleagues ("pour encourager les autres").

Byrd, William (?1543–1623) English composer, who, in spite of being a Roman Catholic, became organist of Lincoln Cathedral and subsequently of the Chapel Royal (1572). His compositions include Catholic masses and motets, Anglican services, anthems, and keyboard music.

LORD BYRON *Portrait (detail) by Thomas Phillips (1770–1845).*

Byron, George Gordon, Lord (1788–1824) British poet. Born with deformed ankles and a clubfoot, he was lionized by London society, after the publication of *Childe Harolde's Pilgrimage* (1812). He was bisexual and among many love affairs had an incestuous relationship with his half-sister Augusta Leigh. His marriage (1815) to Annabella Milbanke lasted one year. Byron then left England to stay near Geneva with Shelley. In Italy in 1818 he began writing the satire *Don Juan*. He died in Greece while training troops at Missolonghi, involved in the Greek struggle for independence.

Byzantine Empire. *See* Eastern Roman Empire.

Byzantium. *See* İstanbul.

C

Cabal Five ministers of Charles II of England who dominated politics from 1667 to about 1674. They were Sir Thomas Clifford (1630–73), Lord Ashley (later 1st Earl of Shaftesbury), the 2nd Duke of Buckingham, the Earl of Arlington (1618–85), and the Earl of Lauderdale (1616–82).

cabbage A flowering plant, *Brassica oleracea* var. *capitata*, widely cultivated as a vegetable. The short stem bears a round heart, up to 25 cm in diameter, of tightly compressed leaves. Many varieties have been developed for cooking, salads, and pickling. All cabbages and many other brassicas are derived from the wild cabbage (*B. oleracea*), a perennial herb native to coastal regions of W Europe. Family: *Cruciferae*.

cabbage white butterfly A white butterfly belonging to the genus *Pieris*, whose caterpillars eat cabbages and related vegetables. The species are the large white (*P. brassicae*), the green-veined white (*P. napi*), and the small white (*P. rapae*).

cabinet A committee of the executive heads of government. In the UK the cabinet originated in the 16th-century cabinet council, a committee of the Privy Council. Cabinet power was enhanced by William III's recognition that his ministers should be selected from the political group prominent in parliament and by the emergence in the 18th century of the prime minister. By the end of the 19th century the principle of collective cabinet responsibility to parliament had been established. Cabinets now consist of some 20 leading ministers, from either house of parliament, whom the prime minister has appointed to head executive departments.

cable TV A system of television broadcasting in which signals are transmitted by cables instead of by radio waves. Developed in 1949 to improve reception in areas in which aerials were unsatisfactory, cable TV was first widely adopted in the USA in the 1970s. The first cable TV systems were installed in the UK in selected areas in the 1980s, offering possibilities of home banking, shopping, and information.

Cabot, John (Italian name: Giovanni Caboto; c. 1450–c. 1499) Italian explorer. He settled in England in about 1484 and under Henry VII's patronage discovered Cape Breton Island (which he thought to be Asia) in 1497. He set out on a second voyage in 1498 and appears to have died at sea. His son **Sebastian Cabot** (c. 1476–1557) was a cartographer to Henry VIII. In Spanish service he explored the coast of South America (1525–28).

cacao. *See* cocoa and chocolate.

cachalot. *See* sperm whale.

CACTUS *The giant tree cactus,* Carnegiea gigantea *(or* Cereus giganteus*) of Arizona.*

cactus A flowering plant belonging to the family *Cactaceae* (over 2000 species). These perennial herbs and shrubs grow chiefly in the drier regions of tropical America and the West Indies. Plant size and shape varies widely; the larger species may grow to a height of 10 m or more. Cacti show pronounced modifications to prevent water loss–their leaves or shoots are reduced to spines, they have thick waxy outer layers, and many possess succulent water-storing stems. The flowers, borne singly, are large and brightly coloured.

caddis fly A mothlike insect, also called sedge fly, belonging to the worldwide order *Trichoptera* (about 5000 species). Caddis flies–1.5–40 mm long, with long antennae–are found in cool damp places and feed on nectar. The omnivorous larvae (called caddis worms) live in flowing fresh water, often in portable cases constructed from sand, stones, pieces of leaf, etc.

Cader Idris A mountain ridge in NW Wales, in Gwynedd, in Snowdonia National Park. It rises to 892 m (2927 ft) at Pen-y-Gader.

Cádiz 36 32N 6 18W A city and seaport in SW Spain, in Andalusia on the Gulf of Cádiz. It was founded by Phoenician merchants (c. 1100 BC). Following the discovery of America it prospered as a base for the Spanish treasure fleet; the harbour was burned by Sir Francis Drake in 1587. Population (1981): 157 766.

cadmium (Cd) A soft dense metal, discovered in 1817 by Friedrich Strohmeyer (1776–1835). Cadmium occurs naturally as the mineral greenockite (CdS) and in zinc, copper, and lead sulphide ores. It is chemically similar to lead and is a component of low-melting-point alloys. It is used in the control rods of nuclear reactors, in light meters, television-tube phosphors, batteries, solders, and in special low-friction alloys for bearings. At no 48; at wt 112.40; mp 320.9°C; bp 765°C.

Caen 49 11N 0 22W A city and port in NW France, the capital of the Calvados department on the River Orne. Situated at the centre of an agricultural and horse-breeding area, Caen has iron, silk, and leather industries. Population (1982 est): 117 119.

Caerleon 51 37N 2 57W A town in South Wales, in S Gwent on the River Usk. A Roman legionary fortress (Isca) was built here (c. 75 AD). Its amphitheatre is the best preserved in Britain. Caerleon is also associated with Arthurian legend. Population (1981): 6711.

Caernarfon (English name: Caernarvon) 53 08N 4 16W A town in North Wales, the administrative centre of Gwynedd on the Menai Strait. Caernarfon is a tourist centre, market town, and small port. Its castle (built by Edward I in 1284) is the likely birthplace of Edward II, the first Prince of Wales, and was the scene of the investiture of Prince Charles as Prince of Wales in 1969. Population (1981): 9506.

Caerphilly 51 35N 3 14W A market town in South Wales, in Mid Glamorgan. Situated in a coalmining area, it is best known for Caerphilly cheese (originally made here) and its castle, the largest in Wales. Population (1981): 42 736.

Caesar, (Galus) Julius (100–44 BC) Roman general and statesman, whose career marked the end of the Roman Republic. Caesar, born of a patrician family, allied himself with the popular party by his marriage in 84 to Cinna's daughter Cornelia. After her death in 68, he married Pompeia, whom he divorced in 62, and in 59 he married Calpurnia.

During the 60s Caesar ascended the political ladder, joining Pompey and Crassus in the first Triumvirate (60) and becoming consul (59) and then governor of Gaul. Caesar's subjugation of Gaul (58–50), and his brief campaigns in Britain (55, 54), confirmed his military reputation and made him a popular hero. When the Triumvirate ended (50) the Senate, with Pompey's support, asked Caesar to resign his armies. He refused and, crossing the River Rubicon into Italy (49), initiated the civil war. Caesar defeated Pompey at Pharsalus (48) and spent the following winter in Alexandria with Cleopatra, who became his lover. He later defeated the remnants of Pompey's party at Thapsus (46) and Munda (45), after which he returned to Rome as dictator. On the Ides of March (15 March, 44), Caesar was assassinated in the Senate House by republicans, including Brutus and Cassius, who feared his monarchical aspirations.

Caesar wrote outstanding accounts of his campaigns in Gaul (*De bello gallico*) and the civil war (*De bello civili*).

Caesarean section A surgical operation in which a baby is delivered through an incision made in the abdominal wall and the womb, so called because Julius Caesar was said to have been born in this way. Caesarean section is employed when a baby cannot be delivered through the vagina; for instance, because it is abnormally positioned in the womb or is too large to pass through the birth canal.

caesium (Cs) The most reactive and electropositive alkali metal. It was discovered by Bunsen and Kirchhoff in 1860 and occurs naturally in the mica lepidolite and as pollucite, $(Cs,K)AlSi_2O_6 \cdot nH_2O$. It is used in photoelectric cells. At no 55; at wt 132.905; mp 28.40°C; bp 690°C.

caffeine (*or* theine; $C_8H_{10}O_2N_4$) The substance in coffee and tea that acts as a stimulant. In its pure form it is white and crystalline.

Cage, John (1912–) Avantgarde US composer. His works include *4 minutes 33 seconds* (1954), silence in three movements for any instrument(s), *Apartment Building 1776* (1976), and *Thirty Pieces for Five Orchestras* (1981).

Cagney, James (1899–1986) US actor. He began making films in the 1930s, after working in vaudeville, and became famous for his portrayals of tough gangsters. His films include *Public Enemy* (1931) and *The Roaring Twenties* (1939).

Caicos Islands. *See* Turks and Caicos Islands.

Cainozoic era. *See* Cenozoic era.

cairn. *See* barrow.

Cairngorm Mountains A mountain range in NE Scotland, in Grampian Region, forming a N extension of the Grampians. Its highests peaks include Ben Macdhui at 1309 m (4296 ft) and Braeriach at 1296 m (4252 ft). The area is popular for winter sports, centred on Aviemore.

cairn terrier A breed of small dog originating in the Scottish Highlands, where it was used to flush game from cover (such as stone cairns). It has a long outer coat and a short soft undercoat; the colour varies from red, sandy, or grey to almost black. Height: about 25 cm.

CAIRO *The mosque of El Azhar was founded in 970 AD. It is the earliest surviving Fatimid building.*

Cairo (Arabic name: El Qahira) 80 01N 31 14E The capital of Egypt, situated in the N of the country on the E bank of the River Nile. It is the largest city in Africa. Its many mosques include the Mosque of Omar (643 AD), Cairo's earliest remaining Arabic building. Population (1985): 6 205 000. *See also* Giza, El.

caisson disease. *See* decompression sickness.

calabash A tree, *Crescentia cujete*, 7.5–15 m tall, native to tropical America (particularly Brazil). Funnel-shaped flowers are borne on the old stems and produce gourdlike fruits, up to 50 cm long. These fruits have woody outer layers and, after removal of the inner pulp, are used as pots, cooking utensils, etc. Family: *Bignoniaceae.*

Calabria A mountainous region occupying the southern "toe" of Italy. Crotone is the main industrial centre. Area: 15 080 sq km (5822 sq mi). Population (1985 est): 2 139 301. Capital: Catanzaro.

Calais 50 57N 1 52E A port in N France, in the Pas-de-Calais department. It lies on the shortest sea route to England. Calais produces lace, tulle, and other textiles. *History*: besieged and captured by the English under Edward III in 1346, Calais remained in English hands until 1558. Population (1982 est): 76 935.

calamine An ore of zinc. In English usage it refers to zinc carbonate (smithsonite) and in the USA it refers to zinc silicate (hemimorphite). A skin lotion of the same name contains zinc oxide.

Calceolaria A genus of perennial herbs and shrubs (300–400 species) native to temperate South America. The plants grow to a height of 30–70 cm and bear brightly coloured slipper-shaped flowers. Some species and hybrids are grown as ornamentals. Family: *Scrophulariaceae.*

calcite A common rock-forming mineral consisting of crystalline calcium carbonate. It is usually colourless or white. It occurs in igneous, metamorphic, and sedimentary rocks. *See also* limestone.

calcium (Ca) A reactive metal, first isolated by Sir Humphry Davy in 1808. It occurs in nature as calcite $(CaCO_3)$, fluorite (CaF_2), and gypsum $(CaSO_4 \cdot 2H_2O)$ and is an essential constituent of shells, bones, and teeth. The element is extracted by electrolysis of the molten chloride $(CaCl_2)$. At no 20; at wt 40.08; mp 839 ± 2°C; bp 1484°C.

calculus The mathematical techniques, developed by Newton and Leibniz, that are based on the concept of infinitely small changes in continuously varying quantities. For example, calculus is used to define the velocity of a moving body as the rate of change of its position at any instant. Velocity (v) is said to be the derivative of position (x) with respect to time (t); in calculus it is written $v = dx/dt$. In this notation dt is a vanishingly small time interval and dx is the distance the body travels in this time. If x is a known function of t, values for v at any time can be obtained by calculating the derivative of (differentiating) this function with respect to time. Similarly, the derivative of the velocity (or the second derivative of position) at any instant gives its acceleration (a), i.e. $d^2x/dt^2 = dv/dt = a$.

The **differential calculus** is the system of rules for making such calculations. On a graph, the derivative of a function is the gradient of the curve at any point. The **integral calculus** is concerned with the same process in reverse. If velocity is a continuously varying function of time, the change in position over a measurable time interval is calculated by summing the products of v and dt for each of the infinitessimally small intervals of time (dt) that make up the measurable interval. As with differential calculus, the extraction of integrals follows general rules. On a graph, the area between the curve of a function and the horizontal axis is the integral of the function over the specified interval.

Calcutta 22 35N 88 21E A city in India, the capital of West Bengal on the River Hooghly. It is a major industrial centre and the most important seaport on the E coast of India. Jute manufacturing dominates the industrial sector, while engineering, cotton textiles, and chemicals are also important. The city itself is part of a conurbation that has a combined population of over seven million people, many of whom live in appalling conditions. By way of contrast, the city centre contains many imposing buildings, situated around Fort William (a British building dating from 1758). Calcutta was founded in 1692 as a trading post for the British East India Company. *See also* Black Hole of Calcutta). Population (1981 est): 9 165 650.

Caldwell, Erskine (1903–87) US novelist. After taking a wide variety of jobs he gained international fame with his novels *Tobacco Road* (1932) and *God's Little Acre* (1933). His blend of social criticism, comedy, and sex, is most forcefully expressed in his journalism, notably in *You Have Seen Their Faces* (1937) and *In Search of Bisco* (1965). Other works include *Stories of Life: North and South* (1983).

Caledonian Canal A system of lochs and canals in Scotland, linking the North Sea with the Irish Sea, via the Great Glen. Engineered by Thomas Telford, it was opened to navigation in 1822. Today it is used mainly by small craft. Length: about 100 km (60 mi).

CALENDAR *Part of a 12th-century calendar, including some of the signs of the zodiac.*

calendar Any of a variety of systems for the reckoning of time over an extended period. Calendars are usually based on the earth's orbital period around the sun (a year), although in some systems the moon's orbital period around the earth (a month) is used. Since the seasons recur after each tropical year (which contains 365.2422 days), the length of the calendar year, averaged over many years, should correspond as closely as possible to that of the tropical year. This is achieved by using leap years, which contain one more day than the usual calendar year.

In 46 BC, Julius Caesar established the so-called **Julian calendar** in which a period of three years, each of 365 days, was followed by a leap year of 366 days. The aver-

age length of the year was therefore 365.25 days. Since this was over 11 minutes longer than the tropical year, an extra day appeared about every 128 years. This discrepancy was amended by the **Gregorian calendar**, which was introduced in Roman Catholic countries in 1582 by Pope Gregory XIII, was made law in Britain and its colonies in 1752, and is now in almost worldwide use. Leap years are restricted to century years divisible by 400 (e.g. 1600 and 2000) and any other year divisible by four. This reduces the average length of the calendar year to a much more acceptable 365.2425 days.

Calgary 51 05N 114 05W A city in W Canada, in Alberta. It is the centre of Canada's petroleum industry and the distribution and farming centre of S Alberta. The Calgary Stampede, a famous rodeo, is celebrated annually. Population (1986): 636 104.

calico A simple woven cotton fabric that originated as a printed fabric from Calicut, India. Strong and serviceable with a wide range of textures, it is used mainly for dresses and domestic purposes.

California The third largest state in the USA, on the W coast. It consists of a narrow coastal plain rising to the Coast Range, with the fertile central valleys of the Sacramento and San Joaquin Rivers, deserts in the S, and the Sierra Nevada Mountains in the E. It is the most populous and prosperous state in the USA; the predominantly urban population is concentrated along the coast. Oil is exploited along with natural gas, cement, sand and gravel, and borate. Aircraft and ship construction are important industries, as well as general construction and food processing; wine production is especially important. The state also produces grapes, tomatoes, cotton, sugar beet, strawberries, citrus fruits, hay, beef cattle, and turkeys. *History*: first discovered by the Spanish (1542) it remained under their control until it was ceded to the USA (1848). In the same year gold was discovered, leading to a rapid increase in the number of immigrants. California became a state in 1850. Area: 411 013 sq km (158 693 sq mi). Population (1987 est): 27 662 900. Capital: Sacramento.

californium (Cf) A synthetic transuranic element first isolated in 1950. Californium-252 is an intense neutron emitter. It is used as a neutron source in instruments for determining moisture contents and discovering precious metals. At no 98; at wt (251).

Caligula (Gaius Caesar; 12–41 AD) Roman emperor (37–41), son of Germanicus Caesar and Agrippina the Elder. Succeeding Tiberius, he initially enjoyed great popularity but his subsequent tyrannical and extravagant behaviour brought allegations of madness, from both contemporaries and historians, and he was assassinated.

calisaya. *See* Cinchona.

calla. *See* arum.

Callaghan, (Leonard) James, Baron (1912–) British statesman; Labour prime minister (1976–79). He entered parliament in 1945 and was chancellor of the exchequer (1964–67), resigning in protest against Harold Wilson's devaluation of the pound, and then home secretary (1967–70) and foreign secretary (1974–76). He became prime minister when Wilson resigned and was defeated in the 1979 election, but remained party leader until 1980.

Callas, Maria (Maria Kalogeropoulos; 1923–77) US-born soprano of Greek parentage. She possessed a brilliant coloratura voice and fine acting ability. From 1950 she was prima donna of La Scala, Milan.

Calliope In Greek legend, goddess of epic poetry and the chief of the nine Muses. She was loved by Apollo; her children included Hymen, Ialemus, and Orpheus.

Callisto. *See* Galilean satellites.

calorie A unit of heat now being replaced by the joule. Formerly defined as the amount of heat required to raise the temperature of 1 gram of water through 1°C, the calorie is now defined as 4.1868 joules. The kilocalorie or Calorie (with a capital "C") is equal to 1000 calories and was formerly used to express the energy value of foods.

Calvary A hill beyond the walls of Jerusalem where Christ was crucified. The Hebrew name is Golgotha (a skull). Its precise location is unknown but traditionally it has been taken as the spot, now within the Church of the Holy Sepulchre, where St Helena discovered a supposed relic of the Cross in 327 AD.

Calvin, John (1509–64) French Protestant reformer, founder of Calvinism. He studied law and theology and in the early 1530s openly sided with Protestantism. Settling in Basle in 1536, he published the first edition of his influential *Institutes*. During a visit to Geneva in 1536 he met the Protestant reformer, Guillaume Farel (1489–1565), who persuaded him to stay. Their efforts to organize the Reformation in the city resulted in their exile (1538). Calvin then preached in Strasbourg, but was invited back to Geneva in 1541, remaining there as its virtual dictator until his death.

Calvinism The Christian teaching of John Calvin, much of it published in his work *The Institutes*. On it are based the doctrines of most of the reformed Churches that are not Lutheran, including the state Churches of Holland and Scotland (*see* Presbyterianism), various Nonconformist Churches, and some Churches in North America and Germany. Calvin's systematic writings stress the transcendant power of God and man's total depravity outside God's redeeming grace. Like Luther, Calvin believed that faith must be based on Scripture alone, that justification (that is, righteousness in God's eyes) could only be achieved through faith, and that men lacked free will. Unlike Luther, he believed that some people, the elect, were predestined for salvation and the rest for damnation and also that the church should control the state.

calx. *See* phlogiston theory.

calypso orchid A rare and highly prized perennial orchid, *Calypso bulbosa*, also known as the fairy slipper orchid, native to cold N temperate regions. 8–10 cm high, it has a solitary pink flower with brown, purple, and yellow markings and a single crinkled dark-green leaf.

Camargue, la The Rhône delta area in S France, between the river channels of the Grand Rhône and the Petit Rhône. Once chiefly marshy, much land reclamation has occurred and cattle, especially bulls for the bullring, and horses are reared. Rice is also grown here. Area: about 560 sq km (215 sq mi).

Camberwell beauty A nymphalid butterfly, *Nymphalis antiopa*, occurring in temperate Eurasia and in North America, where it is called mourning cloak because of its sombre coloration: purple wings with cream edges. The adults hibernate and the caterpillars feed on various trees.

cambium A layer of cells in woody plants that is re-

sponsible for producing additional xylem and phloem tissue, bringing about an increase in girth. The cambium also produces bark and protective callus tissue after injury. *See also* meristem.

LA CAMARGUE *The distinctive white horses bred here.*

Cambodia (former name : Kampuchea) A country in SE Asia, in the Indochina Peninsula on the Gulf of Thailand. It consists mainly of an alluvial plain drained by the River Mekong and enclosed by mountains. Most of the inhabitants are Khmers, with small minorities of Vietnamese and Chinese. *Economy*: predominantly agricultural, the staple crop being rice. Production has been severely reduced by the recent political upheavals and there is little industry. Cambodia is rich in forests, and phosphates, gemstones, and gold are produced; there are also known quantities of unexploited iron ore and manganese. There is an abundance of freshwater fish. Exports include rubber and dried fish. *History*: the kingdom of Funan (1st–6th centuries AD) was conquered by the Buddhist Khmers. Following the collapse of their empire in the 15th century, Cambodia was prey to attack from the Thais and Vietnamese until 1863, when it became a French protectorate. In 1887 it became part of the Union of Indochina. In 1949 it achieved self-government as a member of the French Union, gaining full independence in 1953. Under Prince Sihanouk Cambodia was used as a base by North Vietnamese (communist) forces (*see* Vietnam War) and, following the failure of his attempts to negotiate their withdrawal, he was deposed (1970) by Gen Lon Nol (1913–85), who was supported by the USA. Shortly afterwards US and South Vietnamese troops invaded the renamed Khmer Republic to support Lon Nol against the communist Khmer Rouge guerrillas. In the ensuing civil war the Khmer Rouge was finally victorious in 1974, introducing a new constitution in 1975. The Khmer Rouge Government, led by Pol Pot (1925–), attempted to reshape the country's economy on cooperative lines by driving the Cambodians out of the towns, depriving them of their property, and killing some three million of the aged, sick, or dissenting. Although Pol Pot's regime maintained an uneasy relationship with the Chinese, they failed to come to its aid when the Vietnamese invaded the country on 25 December, 1978. Pol Pot was overthrown and a People's Revolutionary Council was set up under the pro-Vietnamese Heng Samrin (1935–). The retreating Khmer Rouge burnt existing rice stocks and devastated the land leaving behind them a trail of famine and disease. Continued fighting between the Khmer Rouge and Vietnam on the Cambodia–Thai border and in Thai territory incensed Thailand. Vietnamese forces finally withdrew in 1989, after which the Khmer Rouge stepped up military action against the government. Prime minister: Hun Sen (1951–). Official language: Khmer; French is widely spoken. Official currency: riel of 100 sen. Area: 181 000 sq km (71 000 sq mi). Population (1985 est): 6 232 000. Capital and main port: Phnom Penh.

Cambrian Mountains A mountain system in Wales, extending N–S and including Snowdonia, Plynlimon, and the Black Mountains.

Cambrian period The earliest geological period of the Palaeozoic era. It began about 590 million years ago and lasted at least 70 million years, lying between the Precambrian and Ordovician periods. Rocks of this period are the first to contain an abundance of fossils, including primitive representatives of most invertebrates living today. Trilobites were very abundant, as well as brachiopods and gastropods. The Cambrian period is divided into Lower, Middle, and Upper.

Cambridge 52 12N 0 07E A city in E England, the administrative centre of Cambridgeshire on the River Cam (*or* Granta), a tributary of the Great Ouse. The city is dominated by its university (*see* Cambridge, University of). Cambridge has electronics and printing industries and manufactures scientific instruments. It is also an important market centre for East Anglia. Its many historic university buildings, its famous Backs (lawns sloping down to the river), and Bridge of Sighs make it a popular tourist centre. Population (1988): 103 000.

Cambridge 42 22N 71 06W A city in the USA, in Massachusetts on the Charles River opposite Boston. A famous educational centre, it is the site of Harvard University (1636) and the Massachusetts Institute of Technology (MIT). Industries include printing and publishing. Population (1980): 95 322.

Cambridge, University of One of the oldest universities in Europe. It is organized as a federation of colleges (*see* Oxford, University of), the oldest of which, Peterhouse, dates from 1284. Kings College was founded in 1441 and its chapel (built 1446–1515 in the perpendicular gothic style) is a distinctive landmark. The largest college, Trinity, was founded by Henry VIII in 1546. The first college for women, Girton, opened in 1869 (although it was not initially located at Cambridge).

Cambridgeshire A county of E England. Since 1974 it has included the former counties of Huntingdon and Peterborough, Cambridgeshire and the Isle of Ely (combined in 1965), as well as parts of W Suffolk. It consists chiefly of low-lying fenland, crossed by the Rivers Ouse and Nene. It is predominantly agricultural, the main products being cereals, fruit, and vegetables. Area: 3409 sq km (1316 sq mi). Population (1989): 652 740. Administrative centre: Cambridge.

camel A hoofed mammal belonging to the genus *Camelus* (2 species). Camels are now almost entirely domesticated and are used for riding, as pack animals, and as a source of milk, meat, wool, and hides. The one-humped Arabian camel (*C. dromedarius*) is about 2 m

high at the shoulder and generally brown in colour. The dromedary is a long-legged breed of Arabian camel, developed for racing and riding. The heavier two-humped Bactrian camel (*C. bactrianus*) is native to central Asian steppes, where wild herds still exist.

Adapted to living in sandy deserts, camels can close their nostrils, have heavy protective eyelashes, hairy ear openings, and horny knee pads for kneeling. Although unable to store water, camels can replace rapidly the water that is lost from the body, drinking up to 60 litres of water at a time. Fat is stored in the hump, which shrinks when food is scarce. Family: *Camelidae*; order: *Artiodactyla*.

Camellia A genus of evergreen shrubs and trees (80–100 species) native to India, China, and Japan. Several species are widely grown as ornamentals. The best known, *C. japonica*, grows to a height of 9 m and has attractive glossy oval leaves. The popular double-flowered varieties have overlapping petals ranging from white to pink and red. The genus also includes the tea plant. Family: *Theaceae*.

CAMELOT *A 19th-century rendering by Gustave Doré in his illustrations of Tennyson's* Idylls.

Camelot The legendary capital of King Arthur's kingdom (*see* Arthurian legend). Cadbury Camp, near Yeovil, and Winchester are among the places identified with it.

Camembert 48 52N 0 10E A village in NW France, in the Orme department. Camembert is famous for the creamy cheese named after it.

camera, photographic A device for producing a photographic image. Basically, a camera consists of a light-tight box containing a lens and light-sensitive film or plate. The light image coming through the lens is brought into focus on the film by adjusting the distance between the film and the lens. A picture is taken by opening the shutter over the lens for a certain period to expose the film. The exposure time is determined by the shutter speed. The diameter of the opening (aperture) in front of the lens is measured by its f-number. Shutter speed and lens aperture determine the light available to record the image on the film.

camera, television A camera for the instantaneous transmission of moving pictures. The scene to be televised is focused onto a screen in the electronic camera tube. This optical image is scanned in horizontal lines, fast enough to appear as a continuous moving picture to the human eye; in most cameras, the image is scanned 25 to 30 times per second. The intensity of light at each point of the image is converted to an electrical signal, which is amplified before being transmitted together with the sound and synchronization signals. *See also* television.

Cameroon, Republic of (French name: République du Cameroun)   A country in West Africa, on the Gulf of Guinea. Hot swampy coastal plains rise to forested plateaus in the centre and to the Adamwa Highlands in the N. The main river is the Sanaga. The population consists of over a hundred different ethnic groups, the most numerous being the Bamileke. *Economy*: chiefly subsistence agriculture with varied crops; the main cash crop is coffee. Hydroelectricity is used for aluminium smelting, which is the chief industry. Oil was discovered in 1973 and provides half the country's revenue. *History*: in 1884 the German protectorate of Kamerun was established and after World War I it was divided into the French and British Cameroons, which were governed from 1922 under League of Nations mandate and from 1946 as UN trust territories. The French Cameroons attained self-government in 1957 and became independent as the Federal Republic of the Cameroon in 1960. After a plebiscite in the British Cameroons in 1961, the S joined Cameroon and the N joined Nigeria. President: Paul Biya (1933–   ). Official languages: French and English. Official currency: CFA (Communauté financière africaine) franc of 100 centimes. Area: 475 442 sq km (183 530 sq mi). Population (1986 est): 9 880 000. Capital: Yaoundé. Main port: Doula.

camomile (*or* chamomile)   A perennial scented European herb, *Anthemis nobilis* (or *Chamaemelum nobile*). The spreading much-branched stems (10–30 cm in length) carry long-stalked daisy-like flowers. An infusion of the flowers (camomile tea) is used as a tonic. Family: *Compositae* (daisy family).

Campaign for Nuclear Disarmament (CND)   An organization formed in 1958 to campaign for Britain's nuclear disarmament. In the late 1950s and early 1960s, led by Canon John Collins (1905–82) and Bertrand Russell, it organized large demonstrations, including the Aldermaston marches. It revived in the early 1980s amid new fears of nuclear war. General secretary: Meg Beresford.

Campanula   A genus of annual and perennial herbaceous plants (about 300 species), often known as bellflowers, native to N temperate zones (particularly the Mediterranean region) and tropical mountains. 15–120 cm high, they bear spikes of blue, pink, or white bell-shaped flowers. The fruit is a capsule. Some species (including Canterbury bell) are grown as ornamentals. Family: *Campanulaceae*.

Campbell, Sir Malcolm (1885–1949) British motor engineer, who broke the land-speed record nine times between 1924 and 1935 and the water-speed record three times between 1937 and 1939. He was the first man to exceed 483 km per hour (300 mph; 1935). His son **Donald Malcolm Campbell** (1921–67) also set land-and water-speed records, including 648.7 km per hour (403.1 mph) for a wheel-driven car at Lake Eyre (1964). He was killed in an attempt to break his own water-speed record on Coniston Water. The speed at which he crashed, 527.9 km per hour (328 mph), was the unofficial record

for several years. His daughter **Gina Campbell** (1948–   ) broke the women's water-speed record in 1984.

Campbell, Mrs Patrick (Beatrice Stella Tanner; 1865–1940) British actress. Her stage successes included plays by Shakespeare and Ibsen. She created the role of Eliza Doolittle in *Pygmalion* by her friend George Bernard Shaw.

Campbell-Bannerman, Sir Henry (1836–1908) British statesman; Liberal prime minister (1905–08). Campbell-Bannerman's government granted the Transvaal and Orange River Colony responsible government and passed the Trades Disputes Act (1906), which gave trades unionists greater freedom to strike. Resigning shortly before his death, he left his successor Asquith a strong and united Liberal Party.

Camp David   The retreat in the Appalachian Mountains, Maryland, of the president of the USA. It was here that Anwar Sadat and Menachem Begin agreed in September, 1978, to a framework for establishing peace in the Middle East. This agreement, mediated by President Jimmy Carter, laid the foundations for the peace treaty between Israel and Egypt signed in March, 1979.

Camus, Albert (1913–60) French novelist, an exponent of existentialism. Born in poverty in Algiers, he won a school scholarship and studied philosophy at university. During World War II he edited *Combat*, a journal of the French Resistance. Camus published several collections of essays and plays, and three novels, notably *The Outsider* (1942), *The Plague* (1947), and *The Rebel* (1953). In 1957 he won the Nobel Prize.

Canaan   An area roughly corresponding to modern Israel, W Jordan, and S Syria, known from the Bible as the land promised by God to the Israelites before the Exodus.

Canada   A country occupying the entire northern half of the North American continent (except for Alaska). More than half of Canada consists of the Canadian Shield, at the centre of which lies the Hudson Bay lowlands. The Western Cordillera, which is partly made up of the Coast Mountains and the Rocky Mountains, runs parallel to the Pacific coast and contains Mount Logan, Canada's highest peak. Between the Rocky Mountains and the Canadian Shield lie the Interior Lowlands (consisting of prairies, plains, and the Mackenzie Lowlands). The SE region of Canada is dominated by the St Lawrence River and the Great Lakes and is the most densely populated area in the country. The population is mainly of British and French descent but there are several substantial minorities, including Germans, Italians, Ukrainians, and Dutch as well as the original inhabitants, the Indians and Eskimos. *Economy*: both agriculture and industry are highly developed and the numerous manufacturing industries (concentrated mainly in Ontario and Quebec) include paper, iron and steel, motor vehicles, and food processing. As well as iron ore, the rich mineral resources include asbestos, nickel, zinc, molybdenum, uranium, silver, and gold. Oil production has increased considerably since the discovery of large oilfields in Alberta and natural gas is also produced. Agriculture is important, with cereals in the Prairie Provinces and considerable fruit growing in British Columbia and Ontario. There is a valuable fishing industry; forestry has long been important to Canada's economy and the other traditional industry, the fur trade, continues. Main exports include oil, wheat, wood pulp, and paper. *History*: there is evidence of Viking settlement in the NE of Canada around 1000 AD. In 1497 John Cabot reached Newfoundland and Nova Scotia, the first being claimed for England in 1583. In 1534 Jacques Cartier explored the Gulf of St Lawrence and in 1608 Champlain established the first permanent settlement at Quebec. Known as New France, this became a royal province in 1663. Later in the 17th century, when the Iroquois defeated the Huron indians, the French colony was almost completely destroyed. The fur trade was of extreme importance to all settlers and in 1670 the English set up the Hudson's Bay Company. By 1696 the French and English were in open conflict: in 1713 the Treaty of Utrecht gave Acadia (former French colony centred on present-day Nova Scotia), Newfoundland, and Hudson Bay to Britain and after the Seven Years' War, during which Gen Wolfe defeated the French under Gen Montcalm (1759), Canada was ceded to Britain by the Treaty of Paris (1763). In the late 18th century the United Empire Loyalists, fleeing from the American Revolution, settled in Canada. The ensuing racial tension led to the division of Quebec into French-speaking Lower Canada and English-speaking Upper Canada (1791), which were reunited again in 1841. By the British North America Act (1867) a confederation of Lower Canada (Quebec), Upper Canada (Ontario), Nova Scotia, and New Brunswick was established. In 1869 Rupert's Land was bought from the Hudson's Bay Company and the province of Manitoba was created from it in the following year. In 1871 British Columbia and in 1873 Prince Edward Island joined the confederation. Alberta and Saskatchewan were created from the NW Territories in 1905. Canada's constitutional independence was defined by the Statute of Westminster in 1931. In 1982 a new constitution for Canada was signed by Elizabeth II (although Quebec has not accepted it). Official languages: English and French. Official currency: Canadian dollar of 100 cents. Area: 9 976 169 sq km (3 851 809 sq mi). Population (1987): 25 963 000. Capital: Ottawa. Main port: Montreal.

Canada balsam A transparent resin obtained from fir trees. It is used as an adhesive in optical instruments because its refractive index is similar to that of glass.

Canada goose A large goose, *Branta canadensis*, that breeds in Canada and Alaska, migrating in flocks to the southern USA for the winter. It is 60–100 cm long and has a black head and neck, white throat, dark-brown back, and pale underparts. The Canada goose has been introduced to parts of Europe as a sporting bird.

Canadian Shield. *See* shield.

Canaletto (Antonio Canal; 1697–1768) Venetian painter, famous for his views of Venice. He trained under his father, a theatrical-scenery painter, before visiting Rome (1719–20), where he designed opera sets. His popularity with English collectors led to a stay in England (1746–55), where he painted views of London. His early work, painted in the open air, was considerably freer than his later much more architectural painting, for which he used mechanical drawing instruments.

canals Man-made open water channels. They are divided into two categories: conveyance canals and navigation canals. The former carry water for irrigation, power, or drainage; the latter, to facilitate transportation, often connect two natural waterways. Canals have been dug from ancient times. The Grand Canal in China, started in 109 BC, was 1000 km (620 mi) long by the 8th century and carried 1.8 million tonnes of freight per annum. Some modern ship canals achieve spectacular reductions in voyage distances, especially the Suez Canal (completed in 1869) and the Panama Canal (1914). Others of considerable local importance include the Corinth Canal (1893), the Kiel Canal (1895), and the St Lawrence Seaway (1959) connecting the Great Lakes.

canary A small songbird, *Serinus canarius*, native to the Canary Islands, Madeira, and the Azores. Wild canaries have an olive-green plumage with yellow to grey underparts streaked with black. Popular as cagebirds since the 15th century, they have been selectively bred both for their musical song and attractive plumage—usually pure yellow but sometimes white or striped and occasionally with ornamental plumes. Subfamily: *Carduelinae*; family: *Fringillidae* (finches).

Canary Islands (Spanish name: Islas Canarias) A group of Spanish islands in the Atlantic Ocean, close to NW Africa. Since 1927 they have constituted two provinces named after their capitals of Las Palmas (including the islands of Fuerteventura, Gran Canaria, and Lanzarote) and Santa Cruz de Tenerife (including the

CANALETTO *A view of London from Somerset House (1750).*

islands of Ferro, Gomera, La Palma, and Tenerife). The islands became Spanish possessions in the 15th century. The islands are of volcanic formation and, with the help of irrigation, fruit such as bananas and tomatoes are grown for export. Tourism is also a major source of revenue. Total area: 7270 sq km (2807 sq mi). Population (1986 est): 1 442 500.

Canaveral, Cape (name from 1963 until 1973: Cape Kennedy) A barrier island in the USA, in E central Florida separated from the mainland by lagoons. It is the site of operations by NASA at the Kennedy Space Center.

Canberra 35 15S 149 10E The capital of Australia, in the Australian Capital Territory on the Molonglo River. Formally inaugurated in 1927, the establishment of the National University in 1946 and the growth of government departments have led to sizeable increases in population. Population (1986 est): 285 800.

cancer A group of diseases caused by the abnormal and uncontrolled division of cells to form tumours that invade and destroy the tissues in which they arise. Such tumours are described as malignant: their cells spread through the bloodstream or lymphatic system or across body cavities to set up secondary tumours at other sites in the body (this spread is called metastasis). The cause of cancer remains uncertain, although it is known that exposure to certain substances (*see* carcinogen) will produce it. Cancer can arise in almost any tissue: in the western world the breasts, colon, lungs, bronchi, prostate gland, and stomach are common sites. Carcinomas are cancers arising in epithelium; less common but more malignant are sarcomas–cancers of connective tissue (bone, cartilage, muscle, etc.). Leukaemia is a form of sarcoma affecting the bone marrow and other blood-forming tissues. Treatment, which varies with the type of cancer, includes cytotoxic drugs, radiotherapy, and surgery.

Cancer (Latin: Crab) An inconspicuous constellation in the N sky, lying on the zodiac between Leo and Gemini. It contains the star cluster Praesepe.

candela (cd) The SI unit of luminous intensity equal to the intensity in a given direction of a source emitting radiation at 540×10^{12} Hz with a radiant intensity of $1/683$ W sr^{-1}.

Candia. *See* Iráklion.

candidiasis An infection caused by a species of yeast (*Candida albicans*). Popularly known as thrush, it affects the mouth and vagina most frequently; it may develop after treatment with certain antibiotics and with diseases (e.g. leukaemia) and drugs (e.g. steroids) that reduce the natural immunity of the body. The infection is cleared readily by such fungicides as nystatin.

Candlemas The Christian feast of the Purification of the Virgin Mary and the Presentation of Christ in the Temple (Luke 2.22–38), which is observed on 2 Feb. It is so called because of the distribution of candles, symbolizing Christ's appearance as the "light of the world."

cane The stem of certain large grasses and of some palms. In some species it is hollow and jointed, e.g. reeds (*Phragmites* species), bamboo (*Bambusa* species), and sugar cane; in others it is solid, e.g. rattan and Malacca (*Calamus* species) used for making furniture, walking sticks, etc.

Canea (Greek name: Khaniá) 35 31N 24 01E The capital of Crete, on the Gulf of Khaniá. The island's main port, it exports leather, olives, olive oil, and fruit.

Population (1981): 47 804.

Canidae The dog family: a family of mammals belonging to the order *Carnivora*. It includes the dogs, wolves, jackals, coyote, and foxes.

cannabis The resin (hashish) or crushed leaves and flowers (marihuana, "grass," or "pot") obtained from certain species of hemp. The drug is eaten or inhaled and produces a variety of effects on the mind. These include euphoria, distortion of time sense, and increased awareness of sight, sound, and memory. Occasionally feelings of anxiety and apprehension are experienced. The long-term effects of cannabis use are obscure but may affect memory and cause progression to "hard" drugs. *See also* hallucinogens.

Cannae, Battle of (216 BC) The battle, fought at the village of Cannae in Apulia (SE Italy), in which Hannibal and the Carthaginians killed almost 50 000 Romans. It is the worst Roman defeat on record.

Cannes 43 33N 7 00E A resort in S France, in the Alpes-Maritimes department on the French Riviera. Its development as a fashionable resort dates from 1834, when the British statesman Lord Brougham (1778–1868) built a villa here. It has numerous hotels, sports facilities, boulevards, and casinos; an annual film festival is held here. Population (1982 est): 72 787.

cannibalism The practice of eating human flesh, either as food or for ritual or magical purposes. In ritual cannibalism certain parts of a defeated enemy may be eaten in order to absorb his strength and courage or to prevent his spirit taking revenge. In other cases (endo-cannibalism) it forms part of rituals performed at the death of a kinsman. The word is derived from the Arawak term for the Carib Indians among whom it was common. Ritual cannibalism was practised also by the New Zealand Maoris, the Fijian islanders, in Polynesia, in parts of Africa, in New Guinea, and among some North American Indian peoples.

Canning, George (1770–1827) British statesman; foreign secretary (1807–09, 1822–27) and Tory prime minister (1827). An MP from 1793, he held office under Pitt and contributed (1797–98) to the weekly *Anti-Jacobin*, which opposed the French Revolution. He became foreign secretary in 1807 but resigned in 1809 in opposition to the management of the Napoleonic Wars by the secretary for war, Castlereagh. He again became foreign secretary after Castlereagh's suicide before briefly becoming prime minister. His son **Charles John, Earl Canning** (1812–62) was governor general of India (1856–62).

cannon An early form of artillery firearm used primarily until 1670 as a siege gun. A 14th-century invention (by the German monk, Berthold Schwarz), early cannon were made of wrought-iron rods welded together, covered in lead, and wrapped with iron bands. Cast guns were made in England after 1500. Modern cannons include guns, mortars, and howitzers.

canonization In the Christian Church, the conferring of the status of saint on a dead person. In the Roman Catholic Church this is done by a formal declaration of the pope after a long investigation. Beatification, by which the Church permits the veneration of a person, with the title "Blessed," within a particular diocese, order, or other limited area, precedes canonization and depends on evidence of the person's exceptional virtue and authentic miracles. The Church then puts the case for the canonization and appoints someone, the *Promotor*

Fidei (Latin: promoter of the faith, popularly known as the devil's advocate), to oppose it, and completes the process after proof of further miracles.

canon law The laws of Christian Churches, particularly the Roman Catholic, Anglican, and Orthodox Churches. They include regulations governing the clergy, the ecclesiastical courts, matters of worship and doctrine, and so on. In the 12th century Gratian (died c. 1179) produced his *Decretum*, a collection of rules that the Roman Catholic Church recognized as authoritative. The *Decretum* in turn formed part of a later collection, the Corpus Juris Canonici, which in 1917 was revised to form the Codex Juris Canonici, the present Roman Catholic code of law. The ecclesiastical law of the Church of England was mainly contained in the early-17th-century *Book of Canons*, but new laws were introduced in the 1960s.

Cantabrian Mountains (Spanish name: Cordillera Cantábrica) A mountain range in N Spain extending E–W along the Atlantic coast and rising to 2648 m (8868 ft).

CANTERBURY *A 13th-century representation, from a Latin psalter, of the murder of Thomas Becket.*

Canterbury 51 17N 1 05E A city in SE England, in Kent on the River Stour. The cathedral (11th–15th centuries), where Thomas Becket was martyred in 1170, is the seat of the Archbishop and Primate of the Anglican Church. The University of Kent (1960) overlooks the city. Population (1984): 39 000.

Canterbury, Archbishop of The chief bishop of the Anglican Communion of churches, called Primate of All England. The first of the line was St Augustine of Canterbury. He takes precedence after the royal princes and before the Lord Chancellor and the other peers and signs himself with his Christian name and the Latin abbreviation of Canterbury, for example "Robert Cantuar." The present incumbent is Robert Alexander Kennedy Runcie (1921– ; 102nd Archbishop 1980–).

Canterbury bell An annual or biennial flowering plant, *Campanula medium*, native to S Europe and frequently grown as a garden ornamental. The plant grows to a height of 75 cm and bears spikes of pink, rose, lavender, blue, or white bell-shaped flowers, each 5 cm or more long. Family: *Campanulaceae*.

Canterbury Plains A low-lying area of New Zea-land, on E central South Island bordering on the Pacific Ocean. It is the most densely populated area of South Island and is important agriculturally, especially for fat-lamb raising and the production of cereals, fodder crops, and vegetables. Area: about 10 000 sq km (4000 sq mi). Chief town: Christchurch.

Canton (Chinese names: Guangzhou *or* Kuang-chou) 23 08N 113 20E A port in S China, the capital of Guangdong province on the Zhu Jiang (Pearl River) delta. Densely populated, it is the commercial and industrial centre of S China; industries include steel, shipbuilding, paper, textiles, and the manufacture of machinery and chemicals. Population (1986): 3 290 000.

Cantonese. *See* Chinese.

Cantor, Georg (1845–1918) Russian mathematician, born in St Petersburg. Cantor's family moved in 1856 to Germany, where he spent the rest of his life. He was the first mathematician to set the concept of infinity on a rigorous mathematical foundation. His ideas created great controversy and were viciously attacked, by Leopold Kronecker (1823–91) in particular. He broke down in 1884 under the strain and died in a mental asylum.

Canute II (*or* Cnut; c. 994–1035) Danish King of England after defeating Edmund Ironside (1016). He became King of Denmark (1019) and of Norway (1028). He defended England from Viking attacks (1017, 1026, 1028) and subjected Malcolm II of Scotland (1028). According to legend, he proved to flatterers the limits of his powers by demonstrating his inability to induce the waves to recede.

canyon A deep steep-sided gorge found mainly in arid and semiarid areas, the depth of which considerably exceeds its width. Canyons are often formed by rapidly eroding rivers down-cutting into soft rock in arid areas. The lack of rainfall hinders weathering and maintains the steep slopes; where hard- and soft-rock bands occur, a stepped formation results. The largest and best-known canyon is the Grand Canyon (USA).

Capablanca y Graupera, José Raúl (1888–1942) Cuban chess player, who was world champion from 1921 to 1927.

capacitance The ability of an electrical component (a capacitor or formerly a condenser) to store charge. It is measured in farads and defined as the ratio of the stored charge in coulombs to the voltage drop across the component. Capacitance is one of the factors that control the frequency response of circuits and components to alternating currents.

Cape Breton Island An island in SE Canada, in Nova Scotia, separated from the mainland by the Strait of Canso. It was ceded to Britain by the French (1763). Area: 10 280 sq km (3975 sq mi). Population (1981): 170 088.

Cape Coast 5 10N 1 13W A town in central Ghana, on the Gulf of Guinea. It was the capital of the British colony of the Gold Coast until 1874. Population (1982 est): 72 142.

Cape Cod A sandy peninsula in the USA, in Massachusetts between Cape Cod Bay and the Atlantic Ocean. A popular summer resort area, it also produces cranberries and asparagus. Length: 105 km (65 mi).

Cape Horn (Spanish name: Cabo de Hornes) The most southerly point in South America, at the S end of Horn Island, Chile. It is notorious for its stormy weather.

Cape of Good Hope A headland in South Africa, in the SW extremity of Cape Province. It was discovered (1488) by Dias, who named it the Cape of Storms.

Cape Province (official name: Cape of Good Hope Province; Afrikaans name: Kaapprovinsie) The largest province in South Africa, in the extreme S of the African continent. It consists chiefly of plateaus separated by mountain ranges. The SW produces most of South Africa's fruit and vegetables for export and has many vineyards; sheep and cattle rearing is extensive and wheat and alfalfa are grown. Diamonds and copper are the chief minerals, others being asbestos, manganese, and iron ore. *History*: first settled by the Dutch (1652), it was ceded to Britain in 1814, becoming known as the Cape Colony. The discovery of diamonds in Griqualand West led to its annexation to the Cape Colony (1871). In 1910 the colony became a province in the Union of South Africa. Area: 646 332 sq km (400 762 sq mi). Population (1986): 4 901 261. Capital: Cape Town.

caper A bramble-like spiny shrub, *Capparis spinosa*, native to drier regions of S Europe. The pickled flower buds are the capers used in flavouring. The fruit is a berry. Family: *Capparidaceae*.

CAPERCAILLIE *A male in its elaborate courtship display.*

capercaillie The largest European grouse, *Tetrao urogallus*, of Eurasian coniferous forests, where it feeds on pine buds and needles. The male, almost 100 cm long, is black with a blue-green gloss and red wattles above the eyes. The smaller female is brown with black and white markings.

Cape Town (Afrikaans name: Kaapstad) 33 56S 18 28E The legislative capital of South Africa and capital of Cape Province, on the Atlantic Ocean. Founded by Jan van Riebeeck in 1652 as a supply post for the Dutch East India Company, it is the oldest White settlement in South Africa. Cape Town is a major port and is an important commercial and industrial city besides being a popular holiday centre. Its industries include oil refining, chemicals, motor vehicles, and textiles. Population (1980): 213 830.

Cape Verde, Republic of (Portuguese name: Cabo Verde) A country occupying an archipelago in the N Atlantic Ocean, off the coast of West Africa. It consists of ten islands and five islets, most of which are mountainous. The majority of the population is of mixed Afri-

can and European descent. *Economy*: mainly subsistence agriculture. Fish and fish products are the main exports. *History*: the Cape Verde Islands were settled by the Portuguese in the mid-15th century, becoming a Portuguese colony in the 19th century and gaining full independence in 1975. Official language: Portuguese. Official currency: Cape Verdean escudo of 100 centavos. Area: 4033 sq km (1557 sq mi). Population (1988 est): 331 000. Capital: Praia. Main port: Mindelo.

Cape York Peninsula The most northerly part of Australia, in Queensland, situated between the Gulf of Carpentaria and the Coral Sea.

capital An element of architecture used to join a column to the part of the building it supports. In classical architecture there are five orders of columns with strictly defined types of capital, of varying degrees of ornateness, for each (*see* orders of architecture). In romanesque and gothic architecture, the rules became less strict and the type of capital used depended mainly on the skill and taste of the masons involved. Thus the capital could vary from the plain (called a cushion capital) to the highly ornate, with carvings of foliage, people, and animals.

capital-gains tax A UK tax, introduced in 1965, on the profit arising from the disposal of an asset by sale or gift (and until 1971 by death). It applies to stocks and shares (except some government stocks), to dwellings that are not the owner's only residence, and to all other saleable assets with some exceptions (e.g. cars, assets sold for less than £3,000). It does not apply to gains from gambling or life-assurance policies. The rate of tax is the taxpayer's marginal rate of income tax (25% or 40%) on the gain, but the first £5,000 of a person's gains in any year are exempt.

capitalism An economic and political system that developed following the industrial revolution. Essential features of the system are uncontrolled free markets, based on the profit motive, and unrestricted ownership of the means of production (capital). If the system is allowed to develop without restriction it has certain undesirable attributes (*see* laissez-faire). This has led western countries to restrict capitalism by the establishment of mixed economies, characterized by substantial government regulation. Communist countries have followed the doctrines of Karl Marx (*see* Marxism), which favours the central direction of the economy by the government.

capital punishment The punishment of a convicted criminal by execution. In 18th-century Britain over 200 offences carried the death penalty, including such crimes as petty theft and forgery. In 1868 public executions were abolished and by the Homicide Act (1957) only certain kinds of murder remained punishable by death (murder committed in the course or furtherance of theft, in resisting arrest, etc.). In 1965 the death penalty was abolished for all crimes except treason, violent piracy, and (until 1971) arson in royal dockyards. Several US states revived it in 1976.

Capodimonte porcelain A valuable soft-paste porcelain made (1743–59) near Naples at a factory started by Charles IV of Naples. Typical pieces were peasant figures and vessels and services modelled like local sea shells and seaweeds.

Capone, Al (1899–1947) US gangster, born in Italy, who dominated the Chicago underworld of organized crime in the late 1920s. He was imprisoned in 1931 for income-tax evasion.

AL CAPONE *Playing cards with his guard (right) on the way to prison in 1931.*

Capra, Frank (1897–) US film director, born in Italy. His best-known films include several popular sentimental comedies, notably *It Happened One Night* (1934), *Arsenic and Old Lace* (1942), and *It's a Wonderful Life* (1946).

Capri, Island of (Latin name: Capreae) An Italian island at the SW entrance to the Bay of Naples. Its mild climate, fine scenery, and beaches have made it a popular resort since Roman times. The Blue Grotto, a cavern accessible only by sea, is a notable feature. Area: about 13 sq km (5 sq mi). Population (1981 est): 7489.

Capricorn (astrology). *See* zodiac.

Capsicum A genus of annual and perennial flowering plants (about 50 species), native to Central and South America. The fruits (berries) of some species, particularly the various cultivated varieties of *C. annuum* and *C. frutescens*, are the chillies and peppers used in cookery. Large fruits (up to about 10 cm long) are the sweet peppers, which have a mild taste and are used in salads or cooked as a vegetable. They are usually green but may be red (the red varieties—paprika—can be ground to produce a spice). Smaller berries (about 2 cm long) are the hot-tasting red peppers (or chillies); when dried and ground these form cayenne pepper. Dwarf varieties are grown for ornament. Family: *Solanaceae*.

capsule In botany, a type of dry fruit that releases its seeds at maturity through pores, teeth, or slits: an example is the poppy capsule. The term also refers to the spore-producing structures of mosses and liverworts and the slimy envelope surrounding some bacterial cells. In zoology, it is the layer of connective tissue surrounding some organs, for example the kidney.

capuchin monkey A long-tailed monkey belonging to the genus *Cebus* (4 species), of South America. Capuchins are 70–90 cm long including the tail (40–50 cm) and live in large troops in the treetops, feeding chiefly on fruit but also eating insects, birds, and eggs. Family: *Cebidae*.

Capuchins A Roman Catholic order of friars founded in 1525. They are reformed Franciscans, named after the pointed cowl (capuche) they wear in emulation of St Francis. Opposed by the established Franciscans, they were almost suppressed in 1542, but survived to become

an important force during the Counter-Reformation, being recognized in 1619 as one of the three independent branches of the Franciscan order.

capybara The largest living rodent, *Hydrochoerus hydrochaeris*. Resembling giant guinea-pigs, up to 1.25 m long and 50 cm high, capybaras graze on river banks in Central and South America, living in groups of up to 20 individuals. They have short coarse yellowish-brown hair and partially webbed feet (they are expert swimmers). The capybara is the only member of its family (*Hydrochoeridae*).

car A self-propelled road vehicle. The search for a means of replacing the horse as a means of transport began seriously at the beginning of the 18th century, when Newcomen and Watt had shown that steam could be harnessed to produce power. Joseph Cugnot (1725–1804) in 1770 used a steam engine to drive a gun tractor and in 1808 Richard Trevithick built a working steam carriage. But neither these vehicles nor the many other steam carriages of the first half of the 19th century were more than cumbersome novelties. An effective horseless carriage needed a smaller more efficient power source. This was eventually provided by two German engineers, Nikolaus Otto and Gottlieb Daimler, who in 1876 patented the Otto-cycle internal-combustion engine. In 1885, another German, Karl Benz, used a 3 hp version of this engine to power a tricycle capable of 15 mph (20 km per hour). By 1890 both Daimler and Benz were selling motorized dog carts and in France, during the closing decade of the 19th century, Panhard, Comte Albert de Dion, Georges Bouton, and Peugeot were all selling cars. In the USA, Henry Ford built his first car in 1896. In the UK, however, the development of the motor car from the early steam carriages was hampered by nervous legislation introduced in 1865, which insisted that they must be preceded on the roads by a man carrying a red flag. This law was not repealed until 1896. Some ten years later Henry Royce, dissatisfied with the quality of imported cars, decided to build his own. In partnership with C. S. Rolls, he sold his first Rolls-Royce Silver Ghost in 1907.

By the start of World War I, some 130 000 cars were registered in the UK. Motoring was still the preserve of the rich, however. In the early 1920s a family Ford, Austin, Citroën, Morris, or Renault cost about £500. It was not until 1925, when Ford brought the price of his Model T down to $290 in the USA and £185 in the UK, that motoring became more widely accessible. During the 1930s the price of cars steadily declined until at the beginning of World War II a British-made Ford 8 or Austin 7 could be bought for about £100. But the real mass market did not develop until after World War II, since when a model has to sell a million vehicles to be a commercial success.

Caracas 10 35N 66 56W The capital of Venezuela, situated near the N coast and linked by road to its port, La Guaira. It was founded by the Spanish as Santiago de León de Caracas in the 16th century. It is the birthplace of Simón Bolívar. Population (1987): 1 246 677.

carat **1.** A unit of weight for precious stones, formerly defined as 4 grains (Troy), but now equal to 0.200 grams. **2.** A measure of the fineness of gold equal to the number of parts of gold by weight in 24 parts of the alloy. Thus 18-carat gold contains 18/24ths pure gold.

Caratacus (*or* Caractacus; 1st century AD) King of the Catuvellauni; son of Cunobelinus (Cymbeline).

Benz 8hp *1600 of these "horseless carriages" were sold between 1898 and 1900. Described as the first reliable car offered to the public, its twin-cyclinder 1570 cc engine gave it a top speed of 18 mph (29 km/hr).*

Rolls-Royce Silver Ghost *First built in 1907 (and continuing in production until 1927) it quickly established itself as "the best car in the world." Its 7-litre 6-cylinder engine gave it a top speed of 65 mph (105 km/hr).*

Ford Model T *15 million of this first mass-produced car (nicknamed the "Tin Lizzie") were made between 1908 and 1927. Its 4-cylinder, 2898 cc engine gave it a top speed of 40 mph (64 km/hr).*

Bugatti Royale *Made to compete with the Rolls-Royce, this 13-litre 8-cylinder car cost over £5000 in 1927 – too much for even its intended royal customers. Six were sold. In 1987 one survivor was sold for £5.5 M.*

Volkswagen *Nicknamed "the Beetle," this 1937 German design by Ferdinand Porsche was still selling in the 1970s, making it the best selling car ever made. Its air-cooled slow-revving rear engine increased from 1131 to 1600 cc over the years.*

MG TC *This post-war British sports car (1946-55) was little changed from the TA model first built in 1937. The TC had a 1250 cc engine.*

Buick *This 1949 US car represented a release from wartime restrictions and set the trend for a generation of large American cars.*

Mini *The best selling British car ever made. Designed by Alec Issigonis, the Mini was introduced in 1959 and is still selling. Its frontwheel drive, transverse engine, and 10-inch wheels make it an extremely roomy car for its size.*

Citroen BX *This 1987 French 1900 cc diesel-powered model has a top speed of 103 mph (166 km/hr) and claims a fuel consumption of 61.4 mpg at 56 mph (90 km/hr). It also features Citroen's self-levelling hydropneumatic suspension.*

Caratacus organized resistance to the Roman invasion of 43 AD. Defeated, he fled first to Wales then to the north British queen, Cartimandua, who betrayed him. He was pardoned by Emperor Claudius but died in exile.

Caravaggio (Michelangelo Merisi; 1573–1610) An influential Italian baroque painter, whose nickname derives from his birthplace. In Rome he painted scenes of the life of St Matthew in S Luigi dei Francesi. He also executed numerous altarpieces, some of which, e.g. *Death of the Virgin* (Louvre), were condemned for depicting sacred personages as coarse peasants. Caravaggio is noted for his dramatic contrasts of light and shade in such paintings as *Supper at Emmaus* (National Gallery, London).

caraway A perennial flowering plant, *Carum carvi*, native to N temperate regions from Europe to the Himalayas. The much-branched stem grows to a height of 25–60 cm and terminates in clusters of small white flowers. The fruit is an oblong capsule containing the familiar caraway seeds, used in cookery. Family: *Umbelliferae*.

carbohydrate One of a large group of chemical compounds containing the elements carbon, hydrogen, and oxygen and having the general formula $C_x(H_2O)_x$. Green plants manufacture carbohydrates—such as sugars and starch—during photosynthesis and their cell walls consist largely of carbohydrates—predominantly cellulose. Hence plant carbohydrates are the primary source of food energy for animals. Glycogen is a carbohydrate energy reserve found in animals, while chitin is a structural carbohydrate occurring in arthropods (and also in fungi). Chemically, carbohydrates can be classified according to the number of sugar units they contain —one (*see* monosaccharide), several (oligosaccharides), or many (*see* polysaccharide).

carbolic acid. *See* phenols.

carbon (C) A chemical element that is unique in terms of the huge number and variety of its compounds. The element occurs naturally in two forms: graphite, which is a soft greyish-black mineral, and diamond, the hardest substance known. Charcoal and coke are also composed of carbon. The extensive and varied chemistry of carbon results from its ability to form single, double, and triple bonds with itself and other elements and to form chains and rings. At no 6; at wt 12.011; sublimes at 3367 ± 25°C.

carbon cycle (biology) The process by which carbon (in the form of carbon dioxide) in the atmosphere is taken up by plants during photosynthesis and transferred from one organism to the next in a food chain, i.e. the plants are eaten by herbivorous animals that are themselves eaten by carnivores. At various stages carbon is returned to the environment with the release of carbon dioxide at respiration and through decay.

carbon dioxide (CO_2) A colourless odourless noncombustible gas. It is present (about 0.03% by volume) in air, being produced by combustion of carbon compounds and by respiration. Industrially, CO_2 is made from chalk or limestone and is used as a coolant in nuclear reactors, as a refrigerant, in fire extinguishers, and in "fizzy" drinks.

Carboniferous period A geological period of the Palaeozoic era occurring about 370–280 million years ago between the Devonian and Permian periods. During the period land plants increased prolifically and led to the formation of the world's major coal deposits. Amphibians became more common and by the end of the period some reptiles had evolved. The Carboniferous is divided into Lower and Upper (Mississippian and Pennsylvanian). Limestone deposits were widespread in the Lower Carboniferous; millstone grits and the Coal Measures (alternating beds of coal, sandstone, shale, and clay), in the Upper.

carbon monoxide (CO) A colourless odourless flammable gas. It is produced by the incomplete combustion of carbon compounds (e.g. coke or natural gas). CO is highly toxic, combining with red blood cells and preventing them from carrying oxygen. It is present in the exhaust fumes of internal-combustion engines.

carborundum A dark crystalline compound (silicon carbide) manufactured by heating silica (sand) with carbon (coke). It is used as an abrasive and as a refractory material.

carboxylic acids. *See* fatty acid.

carburettor The device in a petrol engine that vaporizes the fuel and mixes it with air in the correct proportions. The carburettor also contains a choke to make the petrol-air mixture richer (i.e. contain more petrol and less air) for cold starting, a throttle valve (which controls the speed of the engine) and an air filter. In some petrol engines the carburettor is replaced by a fuel-injection system.

carcinogen An agent that causes cancer. Carcinogens can be chemicals, radiation, and some viruses. Chemical carcinogens include tar (such as that produced by cigarette smoking), aniline, and azo dyes. Large doses of radiation and the polyoma virus are known to cause cancer, particularly leukaemia.

carcinoma. *See* cancer.

cardamon A perennial herb, *Elettaria cardamomum*, native to India. 1.5–3 m tall, it has large leaves, green and purple veined flowers, and small capsules filled with hard angular seeds. The spice cardamon consists of whole or ground dried fruit or seeds. It is cultivated in India, Sri Lanka, and Guatemala. Family: *Zingiberaceae* (ginger family).

Cardiff (Welsh name: Caerdydd) 51 30N 3 13W The capital of Wales and the administrative centre of South Glamorgan and Mid Glamorgan, situated at the mouth of the River Taff. Its port still handles general cargo but employment in the city is now largely dependent on service occupations. At the centre of the city lies the Norman castle, rebuilt by the 3rd Marquess of Bute in the 1870s. University College, Cardiff (founded 1883), the University of Wales Registry (1893), the University of Wales Institute of Science and Technology (UWIST), the Welsh National School of Medicine, and the National Museum of Wales are all located in the city. Cardiff Arms Park is the home of Welsh rugby. *History*: originally a small Roman fort, the site was reoccupied by the Normans, who built the stone castle keep. It received its first royal charter in 1581. Cardiff's modern prosperity was based on coal from the valleys to the N of the city; by 1913 it was the largest coal-exporting port in the world. Trade declined rapidly, however, after World War I. Cardiff was chosen as the capital of Wales in 1955. Population (1983): 279 800.

Cardigan, James Thomas Brudenell, 7th Earl of (1797–1868) British cavalry officer. In 1854, during the Crimean War, he led the fatal charge of the Light Brigade at Balaclava, made famous by Tennyson. The

EARL OF CARDIGAN

woollen garment known as a cardigan was named after him.

cardinals, college of (*or* Sacred College) The body of the highest dignitaries next to the pope in the Roman Catholic Church. Originating in the advisory roles played by the parish priests and deacons of the city of Rome, the present membership of 125 was established under John XXIII and Paul VI. Cardinals from all over the world are nominated and elected by the pope, who invests them with the flat broad-brimmed red hat symbolic of their rank. They assist the pope as a privy council, conducting the temporal affairs of the Church, advising on questions of doctrine, etc.; they elect the pope from among their own number.

cargo cults Religious cults found chiefly in Melanesia since the late 19th century. Their adherents believe that a new paradise will be heralded mainly by the arrival of a supernatural cargo of goods brought by spirits, who are variously viewed as gods, ancestors, or White foreigners.

Carib An American Indian people of the Lesser Antilles and northern South America, after whom the Caribbean was named. The maritime island Caribs were warriors and cannibals, who before the advent of the Spaniards expelled the Arawak Indians from the Lesser Antilles, enslaving the women and killing and eating the men. As a consequence, in these islands men spoke Carib and women, Arawak. The mainland Caribs were less aggressive and their culture was adapted to the tropical forest region.

Caribbean Sea A section of the Atlantic Ocean, between the West Indies, E Central America. Area: 2 718 200 sq km (1 049 500 sq mi). Maximum depth: 7686 m (25 216 ft).

caribou. *See* reindeer.

caries Cavities in the teeth caused by bacterial erosion of the enamel and dentine. The bacteria feed on sugar from the diet: the sugar and bacteria become attached to the teeth to form a layer called plaque, and acid formed by bacterial breakdown of the sugar causes the damage of caries. *See also* fluoridation.

Carlisle 54 54N 2 55W A city in NW England, the administrative centre of Cumbria on the River Eden. Once a Roman military centre (Luguvallum) and important

fortress in the border wars with the Scots, it has a 12th-century cathedral and a castle (11th-13th centuries). Industries include flour milling, biscuit making, textiles, and agricultural engineering. Population (1981 est): 71 503.

Carlow (Irish name: Ceatharlach) A county in the E Republic of Ireland, in Leinster. Chiefly low lying, it rises to mountains in the E. Agriculture is intensive producing barley, wheat, and sugar beet. Area: 896 sq km (346 sq mi). Population (1986): 40 948. County town: Carlow.

Carlyle, Thomas (1795–1881) Scottish historian and essayist. *Sartor Resartus*, a blend of fiction, philosophy, and autobiography, was published in 1836 and was followed by his major work, *The French Revolution*, in 1837. This and later works express his view of history as shaped by the "Hero," or inspired individual.

Carmelites A Roman Catholic religious order founded around the mid-12th century by St Berthold (died c. 1195), who established a monastery at Mount Carmel in what is now N Israel. With the collapse of the Crusader kingdoms, the order moved to Europe. The original strict rule was relaxed in some respects. In 1452 an order of Carmelite nuns was instituted. In the 16th century the order was reformed by St Teresa of Avila and emphasized the cultivation of the contemplative life.

Carnap, Rudolf (1891–1970) German-born logical positivist philosopher. A founder of the Vienna Circle, he was professor of philosophy successively at universities in Vienna, Prague, Chicago, and Los Angeles. He worked on formal logic and its applications to science and epistemology, believing that the analysis and clarification of knowledge should be the purpose of philosophy. By developing logical syntax and semantics, he tried to construct a formal language for the empirical sciences to eliminate confusion, ambiguity, and similar obstacles to knowledge.

carnation A large-flowered cultivated form of the clove pink (*Dianthus caryophyllus*). These perennials grow to heights of 40–60 cm, have tufts of dense grass-like foliage, and double flowers in white, yellow, orange, pink, red, or lavender. Hardy border carnations are suitable for outdoor cultivation, while the perpetual flowering varieties should be grown under glass. Flowers of carnations (and pinks) are noted for their clovelike fragrance. Family: *Caryophyllaceae*. *See also* Dianthus.

Carnivora An order of mammals adapted for hunting and eating flesh. Carnivores have strong jaws, with sharp incisor teeth and pointed canine teeth; some of the cheek (molar) teeth, called carnassials, act as shears to chop up meat. They are the major predators and most species are terrestrial, stalking or pouncing on their prey. The 252 species are divided into seven families: *Canidae* (dogs); *Ursidae* (*see* bear); *Procyonidae* (*see* raccoon; panda); *Mustelidae* (weasels, skunks, etc.); *Viverridae* (genets, mongooses, etc.); and *Felidae* (cats).

carnivorous plant A plant that obtains at least some of its nutrients by the digestion of insects and other small animals. Carnivorous, or insectivorous, plants show remarkable structural adaptations for their mode of life. Butterworts and sundews trap and digest insects by means of the sticky secretions produced by glands in the leaves. The Venus flytrap traps its prey between bilobed hinged leaves with marginal teeth. Another common method of capture and digestion is by means of

CARNIVOROUS PLANT *A dragonfly caught in a Venus flytrap.*

liquid-filled "pitchers" into which the insects fall (*see* pitcher plant).

carob The horn-shaped edible fruit pod of the carob tree, *Ceratonia siliqua*, an evergreen native to the Mediterranean region. The pods, sometimes known as algaroba or St John's bread, contain a sugary pulp and are used for fodder. The seeds are believed to have been the original carats of jewellers. Carob is also widely used as a substitute for chocolate. Family: *Leguminosae*.

Carolina. *See* North Carolina; South Carolina.

Caroline of Ansbach (1683–1737) The wife of George II of Great Britain and a strong supporter of Sir Robert Walpole. She was appointed regent during George's absences abroad.

Caroline of Brunswick (1768–1821) The wife of George IV of the United Kingdom. After their separation (1796), he forbade her to see their child Charlotte. When George became king (1820), his attempt to divorce Caroline failed owing to popular support for her but she was excluded from the coronation (1821).

carotenoids A group of yellow, orange, or red pigments manufactured by bacteria, fungi, and plants and essential in the diet of animals. There are two groups —carotenes (including beta-carotene, a precursor of vitamin A) and xanthophylls. Carotenoid pigments are important for display and camouflage colouring in both plants and animals and also as eye pigments.

carp An omnivorous freshwater fish, *Cyprinus carpio*, native to Asia but widely introduced elsewhere and raised for food. It has an elongated body, usually about 35 cm long, with large scales, greenish or brownish above and paler below, four barbels on the upper lip, and a long dorsal fin. Related fish include the Crucian carp and golden carp (*see* goldfish). Family: *Cyprinidae* (about 2000 species); order: *Cypriniformes*.

Carpaccio, Vittore (c. 1460–c. 1525) Venetian painter, noted for his paintings of his native city and his narrative cycles. His works, influenced by Gentile and Giovanni Bellini, include a cycle of *Scenes from the Life of St Ursula* and *The Miracle of the Cross* (Accademia, Venice).

Carpathian Mountains A mountain range in Czechoslovakia, Poland, Hungary, the Soviet Union, and Romania. They form a rough semicircle about 1450 km (90 mi) long (including the Transylvanian Alps, which are also known as the **Southern Carpathians**) between Bratislava and the Iron Gate, both on the River Danube. The highest peak is Mount Gerlachovka, at 2663 m (8737 ft), in NE Czechoslovakia.

carpel The female organ of a flower, consisting of the stigma, style, and ovary. After fertilization, each carpel may ripen to produce a fruit containing one or more seeds. *See also* pistil.

Carpentaria, Gulf of A shallow inlet of the Arafura Sea, in N Australia situated between Arnhem Land and Cape York Peninsula. Area: about 287 500 sq km (11 000 sq mi).

Carrantuohill 52 00N 9 45W The highest mountain in Ireland, in Co Kerry, in Macgillicuddy's Reeks. Height: 1041 m (3414 ft).

carrion crow An omnivorous Eurasian crow, *Corvus corone corone*, about 46 cm long with a pure-black plumage and a harsh croaking call. It is a notorious egg thief, unpopular with gamekeepers.

LEWIS CARROLL *Detail from a self-portrait.*

Carroll, Lewis (Charles Lutwidge Dodgson; 1832–98) British writer and mathematician. He lectured in mathematics at Oxford University from 1855 to 1881. The children's classic, *Alice's Adventures in Wonderland* (1865), was written for the young Alice Liddell, the daughter of the head of his Oxford College. It and the sequel, *Through the Looking-Glass* (1872), combine elements of fantasy, logic, and nonsense and have had a lasting appeal to adults as well as children. He also wrote nonsense verse, notably *The Hunting of the Snark* (1876).

carrot A biennial flowering plant, *Daucus carota*, found in grassy places in temperate regions from Europe to India. The stem grows to a height of 30–100 cm and bears a head of small white flowers. *Daucus carota sativus* is the cultivated carrot. This is grown as an annual, and produces an orange thick fleshy edible root. Many varieties of the cultivated carrot have been developed, with roots 15–25 cm in length and 2–5 cm in diameter. Family: *Umbelliferae*.

Carte, Richard D'Oyly. *See* D'Oyly Carte, Richard.

Carter, Jimmy (James Earl C.; 1924–) US statesman; Democratic president (1977–81). Carter left his family peanut farming and warehousing business in

Georgia for politics and was governor of Georgia from 1970 to 1974. He is best known for bringing about the peace treaty between Egypt and Israel (1979).

Cartesian coordinates. *See* coordinate systems.

Carthage (Punic name: *Kart-Hadasht*, New City) An ancient city of N Africa, near modern Tunis. Traditionally founded 814 BC by Dido and exiles from Tyre, Carthage rapidly became leader of the Phoenician trading cities of N Africa, waging intermittent war with the Greeks of Marseilles and Sicily. From 264 BC Carthage fought the three Punic Wars with Rome, her former ally, and was totally destroyed (146 BC). Refounded by Julius Caesar (45 BC), Carthage became, in turn, the commercial, cultural, and administrative capital of Roman Africa, the capital of the Vandal kingdom (439–533 AD), and a Byzantine outpost, until destroyed by the Muslims in 697 AD.

Carthusians A contemplative Roman Catholic religious order founded in 1084 by St Bruno and taking its name from the location of the first community, La Grande Chartreuse, near Grenoble. Although originally without a written rule, the Carthusians observed a rigorous life of fasting and solitude and were vowed to silence. The French monks are noted for the liqueur Chartreuse, which they make.

Cartier, Jacques (1491–1557) French navigator. In 1534, under the patronage of Francis I, he sailed in search of the Northwest Passage and explored the coast of N Canada and Newfoundland. The next year he sailed up the St Lawrence as far as what became Montreal but failed to found a colony there. His discoveries were important to French claims in Canada in the 17th century.

Cartier-Bresson, Henri (1908–) French photographer and pioneer of photojournalism. His often poignant photographs, collected in such books as *The Decisive Moment* (1952) and *Europeans* (1955), concentrate on ordinary people and their fleeting expressions and gestures. As a film maker, he collaborated with Jean Renoir in the late 1930s and returned to this medium in the 1960s.

cartilage A flexible supportive tissue consisting chiefly of a polysaccharide–chondroitin sulphate–in which elastic or collagen fibres may be embedded. Cartilage lines the bone ends at joints and also provides the skeleton of the nose, external ear, and parts of the throat (larynx) and airways of the respiratory tract. A tough cartilage forms the intervertebral discs between the bones of the spine. During development a large amount of bone is formed from pre-existing cartilage.

cartilaginous fish Any fish belonging to the class *Chondrichthyes*, comprising the sharks, rays, and chimaeras. They have a cartilaginous skeleton, usually a ventrally situated mouth, and exposed gill slits. The males have pelvic fins modified to form copulatory organs (claspers) and fertilization occurs inside the female's body. Some species deposit their eggs on the sea bed while in others the eggs are retained and develop internally resulting in the birth of live young.

Cartwright, Edmund (1743–1823) British inventor and industrialist. In 1785 he invented a power loom and then set up a factory in Doncaster for weaving and spinning yarn. Four years later he invented a machine for combing wool. In 1793 his business failed but parliament recognized his achievements in 1809 with an award of £10,000.

caryatid A carved column in the shape of a draped female figure that first appeared in Greek architecture around 500 BC. The most notable caryatids to have survived are on the Erechtheum on the Acropolis of Athens. Caryatids were infrequent in Roman architecture but enjoyed a limited revival in 19th-century classicism.

Casablanca (Arabic name: Dar-el-Beida) 33 39N 7 35W A port in Morocco, on the Atlantic coast. First established by the Portuguese (1515), it was taken by the French in 1907. During World War II it was the scene of the Casablanca Conference (1943), a summit meeting between Franklin D. Roosevelt and Sir Winston Churchill. The largest and most important city in Morocco, its major industries include textiles, electronics, chemicals, cement, and food processing. Fishing and tourism are also important. Population (1984): 2 600 000.

Casals, Pablo (Pau C.; 1876–1973) Spanish cellist, conductor, and composer. Casals revolutionized the style and technique of cello playing and excelled as an interpreter of Bach's six suites for unaccompanied cello and of the cello concertos of Dvořák, Elgar, and Schumann.

Casanova, Giovanni Giacomo, Chevalier de Seingalt (1725–98) Italian adventurer. He lived in many European cities, working at different times as a violinist, a spy, and a librarian. His adventures, which included a dramatic escape from prison in Venice in 1756 and many romantic liaisons, are recorded in his memoirs, of which the first complete edition was published in 1960.

Cascade Range A volcanic mountain range in North America. It extends N–S, nearly parallel to the Pacific coast, between the Fraser River in British Columbia (Canada) and N California (USA), where it becomes continuous with the Sierra Nevada. It reaches 4392 m (14 408 ft) at Mount Rainier.

casein The major protein present in milk. Casein is easily digested and contains a good balance of essential amino acids, making it–in dietary terms–a high-quality protein. Cheese consists largely of insoluble para-casein, formed from casein by the action of enzymes. Casein is also used industrially to make thermoplastics (e.g. knife handles), paints, and adhesives.

cashew A tree, *Anacardium occidentale*, native to tropical America and cultivated widely in the tropics. It grows to a height of about 12 m and has sweet-scented red flowers. The fruit is a kidney-shaped nut that develops at the end of a hanging pear-shaped receptacle. The edible kernel–the cashew nut–is extracted after the fruit is roasted. Family: *Anacardiaceae*.

cashmere A warm soft wool-like fabric made from the undercoat of the Kashmir goat, produced mainly in China, Mongolia, and Iran. Originally used in shawls from Kashmir, it is an expensive fabric as each goat produces only small quantities of fine soft hair and processing is costly. Imitations are common and any soft woollen textile, natural or synthetic, is frequently called cashmere.

Caspian Sea The largest inland sea in the world, bounded by Iran and the Soviet Union and fed chiefly by the River Volga. Its surface is 28.5 m (93.5 ft) below sea level and is generally becoming lower due to irrigation and increased evaporation from the Volga. The chief ports are Astrakhan and Baku, both in the Soviet Union. Sturgeon and seals are caught here and oil and gas extracted. Area: about 370 000 sq km (142 827 sq mi).

Cassandra A legendary Trojan prophetess, daughter of King Priam of Troy. After she had refused to submit to Apollo's advances, he condemned her prophecies to eternal disbelief. When Troy fell she was taken by Agamemnon, with whom she was later murdered.

CASSAVA   *Harvesting the roots in Madagascar.*

cassava A shrubby flowering plant, *Manihot esculentus* (or *M. utilissimus*), also known as manioc, native to tropical America. Many varieties of this species—divided into two groups, sweet and bitter cassavas—are cultivated in the tropics for their edible starchy tuberous roots. These can be processed into tapioca, ground to produce manioc or cassava meal (Brazilian arrowroot), used as animal fodder, or cooked and eaten as a vegetable. Family: *Euphorbiaceae* (spurge family).

cassia The aromatic bark of a Chinese tree, *Cinnamomum cassia*, used as a substitute for cinnamon. The dried unripe fruits (cassia buds) are also used as a spice. Family: *Lauraceae*.

Cassia A genus of trees, shrubs, and herbs (500–600 species) of tropical and warm regions of Asia, Africa, and America. The laxative drug senna is extracted from the dried leaves and pods (fruits) of many cultivated species. The fruit of *C. fistula* (cassia pods or purging cassia) is also used as a laxative. Some species are grown as ornamentals. Family: *Leguminosae*.

cassiopeium. *See* lutetium.

cassiterite The only commercial ore of tin, consisting of stannic oxide. It is found in association with acid igneous rocks and as alluvial deposits. It is brown or black.

Cassius Longinus, Gaius (d. 42 BC) Roman general. Cassius supported Pompey until Pompey's defeat by Julius Caesar at Pharsalus. He was then pardoned by Caesar but joined the conspiracy to assassinate him in 44. Outlawed, Cassius committed suicide after defeat in the battle of Philippi.

Casson, Sir Hugh (Maxwell) (1910–) British architect. A planning adviser to many war-damaged areas in England after World War II, he became director of architecture for the Festival of Britain in 1948. His books on architecture include *Victorian Architecture* (1948).

cassowary A large flightless bird belonging to a family (*Casuariidae*; 3 species) occurring in rain forests of Australia and New Guinea. The largest cassowary (*Casuarius casuarius*) is 150 cm tall and has a black plumage, two red throat wattles, and a blue head with a protective bony helmet. Cassowaries have long powerful legs, each having a long sharp claw, and feed on seeds and berries. Order: *Casuariiformes*.

Castagno, Andrea del (Andrea di Bartolo de Simone; c. 1421–57) Italian Renaissance painter, who was born near Castagno but settled in Florence. His major frescoes depict the *Last Supper* and the *Passion* (Sta Apollonia, Florence). Later works, showing the influence of Donatello, include the equestrian portrait of *Niccolò da Tolentino* (Duomo, Florence).

castes The elements of a system of social stratification in which social boundaries are very definite. A pure caste system consists of a hierarchy of hereditary endogamous occupational groups, in which positions are fixed and mobility from one caste to another is prevented by ritual systems. The classical Hindu caste system (Sanskrit word: varna) of India provides the cardinal example. Traditionally there are four main caste divisions: brahmins (priests), ksatriyas (warriors), vaisyas (merchants), and sundras (serfs). Outside these groups are the "outcastes" or "untouchables".

Castile A former kingdom in central Spain. Originally a district at the foot of the Cantabrian Mountains, Castile expanded in the 9th and 10th centuries, becoming a united country. In 1035 it became a kingdom and in 1230 was united with the kingdom of León, a union dominated by Castile. In 1479 Spain was virtually united following the marriage of Isabella of Castile to Ferdinand the Catholic and Castile became the political, administrative, cultural, and linguistic centre of Spain.

cast iron A form of impure iron containing between 2.5% and 4.5% of carbon by weight. The high carbon content makes it relatively hard and brittle and it tends to crack under tension. Cast iron is made by casting pig iron and adjusting its composition to improve the strength. It is used for complicated shapes.

castle A fortified defensive building. Its name deriving from Latin *castellum*, a small fortified place, the castle underwent many changes in its history to counteract the development of increasingly powerful weapons. In the early middle ages a castle consisted of a simple building on a mound of earth surrounded by a wooden fence (the motte and bailey castle), a design later copied in stone. The simplest stone castle, such as the White Tower in London, is called a keep or donjon. Later designs became more complicated, involving extensive outworks of battlemented towers and walls (curtain walls), for example Caernarfon Castle in Wales. See p. 142.

Castlereagh, Robert Stewart, Viscount (1769–1822) British statesman, born in Ulster; foreign secretary (1812–22). An MP in the Irish parliament (1780), he became Viscount Castlereagh in 1796, when his father Robert Stewart (1739–1821) became 1st Marquess of Londonderry. Appointed chief secretary for Ireland in 1798, he resigned in 1801, when George III rejected Catholic Emancipation. His policies as secretary for war (1807–09) were attacked by Canning, with whom Castlereagh fought a duel. As foreign secretary he played an important role at the Congress of Vienna (1814–15).

shell keep   concentric castle   artillery fort

CASTLE *The early medieval shell keep gave way to the massive fortifications of the 14th and 15th centuries, which were in turn superseded by the artillery fort with its low walls and sweeping lines of fire.*

Castor and Pollux Twin heroes of classical mythology, also known as the Dioscuri. Pollux was immortal, the son of Zeus and Leda; Castor was mortal, the son of Tyndareus and Leda. When Castor died, Pollux asked Zeus to allow them to remain unseparated. Transformed into the Gemini constellation, they were the patrons of mariners.

castor oil A pale yellow viscous oil extracted from the seeds of the castor-oil plant. It is used as a laxative and is also a raw material for the manufacture of resins, plastics, and lubricants.

castor-oil plant A flowering plant, *Ricinus communis*, up to 12 m high, native to tropical Africa and Asia. It is cultivated widely, in the tropics for its seeds, from which castor oil is extracted, and in temperate regions as an ornamental shrub with attractive fanlike leaves (ornamental forms are seldom taller than 2 m). Family: *Euphorbiaceae* (spurge family).

castration Removal of the testes (orchidectomy) or ovaries (oophorectomy). In medicine, castration may be performed in cases of cancer of the testes: it always produces sterility but—unless done before puberty—need not cause impotence. Castration is widely used in livestock management to increase meat production or docility.

Castro (Ruz), Fidel (1926–) Cuban statesman; president of Cuba (1976–). The son of a wealthy sugar planter, Castro became an opponent of the dictator Fulgencio Batista (1901–73). On 26 July, 1953, he led an unsuccessful attack on the Moncada barracks and was imprisoned until 1955. In 1956 he invaded Cuba from Mexico with a small armed band and after a long guerrilla war he defeated government troops. He entered Havana on 1 January, 1959. Castro established a socialist government, which the USA attempted to subvert. As a result, Cuba became heavily dependent on the Soviet Union. *See also* Bay of Pigs.

cat A carnivorous mammal belonging to the family *Felidae* (36 species). Most cats have sheathed claws and sharp canine teeth to kill their prey, which consists of mammals, birds, and fish. Their acute vision (especially in poor light), sense of smell, and hearing are adaptations for hunting stealthily, often at night. With no natural enemies, the kittens (or cubs) are born blind and toothless and learn hunting techniques through play. The wide range of different breeds of domestic cat (*Felis catus*), including Persian, Siamese, and Abyssinian, are thought to have been developed from the African wildcat, or cafer cat (*F. lybica*) and possibly the European

wildcat. Wild species range in size from the tiger to the tiny South African black-footed cat (*F. nigripes*), which is smaller than the average domestic cat.

catabolism. *See* metabolism.

CATACOMBS *The Capuchin Catacombs in Sicily, dating from the 16th century.*

catacombs Subterranean cemeteries, especially those containing early Christian graves. The earliest and biggest catacombs are in Rome, particularly those of St Calixtus and St Sebastian along the Appian Way. Most catacombs consist of narrow passages into the walls of which the burial niches were cut. With the acceptance of Christianity they fell into disuse, although some remained as centres of pilgrimage.

Catalan A Romance language spoken by about five million people in Catalonia and the Balearic Islands in Spain, Andorra, and the Roussillon region of France. It is closely related to Spanish and to the Occitan language of France.

catalepsy A condition associated with certain abnormal mental states, including schizophrenia and hysteria, in which the patient, usually female, remains motionless, often with the limbs in fixed positions, for a variable length of time.

Catalonia (Spanish name: Cataluña; Catalan name: Catalunya) A mainly mountainous region of NE Spain, on the Mediterranean Sea. Agriculture is important, the main crops being cereals, olives, and grapes. It is the most highly industrialized region in Spain. *History*: united with Aragon in 1137 and Castile in 1497, Catalonia has nevertheless maintained a strong separatist tradition. In 1932 an autonomous government was established and this lasted throughout the Civil War (1936–39), in which Catalonia was on the Republican side. The Catalan government was restored provisionally in 1977. Area: 31 932 sq km (12 329 sq mi). Population (1986 est): 6 057 200. Capital: Barcelona.

catalysis The acceleration of a chemical reaction by a substance (catalyst) that is not itself consumed in the reaction. The catalyst allows the reaction to proceed via a different lower-energy pathway. Since the reverse reaction is also accelerated, catalysis does not shift the chemical equilibrium, it merely speeds its attainment. Catalysis is used extensively in industrial chemical processes. In living organisms enzymes are catalysts for biochemical reactions.

catamaran A modern sailing vessel with two identical hulls, rigidly fastened parallel to one another, and, usually, a single mast with a triangular mainsail and jib. Because of their buoyancy, the hulls of a catamaran offer very little resistance to the water, making it extremely fast. The modern catamaran is based on a native canoe-like vessel of the SW Pacific, which in some forms was basically a raft with a sail.

cataract (ophthalmology) Opacities in the lens of the eye resulting in blurred vision and caused by the deposition of small crystals or changes in the composition of the lens substance. The former condition increases with age; such cataracts are a common cause of blindness in the elderly. Certain diseases, such as poorly controlled diabetes mellitus, can also lead to cataracts. Cataracts are usually treated by surgical removal of the lens and the use of appropriate spectacles. In some cases a plastic lens may be implanted to replace the one removed.

catecholamines Amine derivatives of catechol. They include adrenaline, noradrenaline, and dopamine, which act as neurotransmitters and hormones. Depletion of dopamine in the basal ganglia of the brain is associated with parkinsonism.

categorical imperative The fundamental moral law in Kant's ethical theory: an act is moral only if the principle on which it is justified is universally applicable.

catenary The curve obtained by suspending a string between two points. If the middle of the string, the lowest point, is at height a above a reference level, then the height, y, at distance x along the string from the middle is given by: $y = \frac{1}{2}a\,(e^{x/a} + e^{-x/a})$.

caterpillar The larva of butterflies and moths. Soft-bodied and wingless, all caterpillars have a head and 13 body segments with 3 pairs of true thoracic legs and 5 pairs of abdominal prolegs, which aid in locomotion. The mouthparts are adapted for chewing leaves or feeding on sap. Some species are serious crop pests. Caterpillars exhibit a wide variety of camouflaging colours and shapes. Some produce irritating or poisonous secretions.

Catesby, Robert. *See* Fawkes, Guy.

catfish A bony fish of the order *Siluriformes* (about 2500 species), with a stout scaleless body, 4–450 cm long, a broad flat head, and long whisker-like barbels. Freshwater catfish (family *Ictaluridae*), sometimes called bullheads, occur worldwide; marine catfish (family *Ariidae*) inhabit tropical and coastal waters and are generally bottom-dwelling scavengers used as food, game, and aquarium fish. The name is also used for

marine fish of the family *Anarhichadidae* (order *Perciformes*).

cathedral The principal church of an ecclesiastical area (diocese), governed by a bishop or an archbishop. The name comes from Latin *cathedra*, bishop's seat. Generally larger and more magnificent than other churches, cathedrals, such as St Peter's Basilica, Rome, St Paul's Cathedral, London, and Notre-Dame de Paris, contain some of their country's finest works of art.

CATHERINE THE GREAT

Catherine (II) the Great (1729–96) Empress of Russia (1762–96), who gained the throne in a coup in which her unpopular husband, Emperor Peter III (1728–62; reigned 1762), was murdered. Catherine's reign marked the expansion of Russian territory as a result of her successful wars against the Turks (1768–74, 1787–92) and the partition of Poland (1772, 1793, 1795). Influenced by the ideas of the Enlightenment, she had to abandon her scheme to emancipate the serfs in the face of opposition from their masters. Of her many lovers, only Potemkin exerted a durable influence on government.

Catherine de' Medici (1519–89) Regent of France (1560–63) during the minority of her second son, Charles IX, and virtual ruler until his death (1574). The daughter of Lorenzo de' Medici, Duke of Urbino, she married Henry II of France in 1533. Intent on upholding royal authority during the Wars of Religion, she advocated tolerance for the Huguenots but later supported the Catholics. She was largely responsible for the St Bartholomew's Day Massacre. Her influence waned during the reign of her third son Henry III.

Catherine of Aragon (1485–1536) The first wife (1509–33) of Henry VIII of England and the mother of Mary I. Failing to bear him a son, she was divorced by Henry, who argued that their marriage was invalid because Catherine was the widow of his brother Arthur. The pope's refusal to accept their divorce provoked the English Reformation.

Catherine of Braganza (1638–1705) The wife (from 1662) of Charles II of England. A Portuguese princess and a devout Roman Catholic, her unpopularity was intensified by her failure to produce an heir to the throne.

cathode The negative electrode of an electrolytic cell, valve, etc. It is the electrode by which the electrons enter the system. *Compare* anode.

cathode-ray oscilloscope (CRO) An instrument that displays electrical quantities on the screen of a cathode-ray tube. It can be used to show the variation of a signal strength with time or with another electrical quantity. The CRO is used extensively in electronics laboratories and in other scientific work.

cathode-ray tube (CRT) A vacuum tube that converts electrical signals into visible form by projecting a beam of electrons onto a fluorescent screen. It is an essential component of the television receiver and the cathode-ray oscilloscope (CRO). The electron beam is produced by an electron gun, and deflected horizontally and vertically by an arrangement of plates and magnets, which move it back and forth across the screen and focus it by creating an electromagnetic field, the strength of which varies according to input signals. In a television tube the beam intensity varies to form the light and dark regions of the picture.

Catholic emancipation A campaign in Britain and Ireland to secure full civil and political rights for Roman Catholics. In the late 18th century several relief acts were passed but parliamentary representation was still denied. The opposition of the Tory establishment and the monarchy continued until O'Connell's efforts achieved the Catholic Emancipation Act of 1829.

Cato the Elder (Marcus Porcius C.; 234–149 BC) Roman statesman, who wrote the first history of Rome. A moral and political conservative, Cato as censor (184) legislated against luxury and sponsored improvements in public works.

Cato the Younger (Marcus Porcius C.; 95–46 BC) Roman politician; the great-grandson of Cato the Elder and an opponent of Julius Caesar. Caesar, with Pompey and Crassus, created the first Triumvirate (60) in part to neutralize Cato's opposition to their political ambitions. Forced to support Pompey in the civil war in an attempt to save the Republic, Cato escaped after Pompey's death to Utica, in Africa. There, on hearing of Caesar's victory at Thapsus, he committed suicide.

cat's-tail. *See* reedmace.

cattle Ruminant mammals belonging to the genus *Bos* (7 species), also called oxen, native to Eurasia and Africa. Modern domestic cattle (*B. taurus*), which are probably descended from such ancestors as the auroch, vary in body shape, size, and colour according to breed but are generally 90–110 cm high at the shoulder and weigh 400–900 kg. Cattle are used for milk and meat production and for draught purposes (*see* livestock farming). Family: *Bovidae*. *See also* gaur; yak.

Catullus, Valerius (c. 84–c. 54 BC) Roman poet. Born in Verona, he became the leading member of a group of young innovatory poets in Rome. 116 poems survive, of which the most famous are the 25 lyrics addressed to a married woman named Lesbia.

Caucasian languages. *See* Northeast Caucasian; Northwest Caucasian; South Caucasian.

Caucasoid A race or group of races and peoples originally inhabiting Europe, North Africa, and the Near East. They are characterized by skin pigmentation ranging from very pale to dark brown, straight to curly hair, narrow high-bridged noses, plentiful body hair, and a high frequency of Rh-negative blood type.

Caucasus Mountains (Russian name: Kavkaz) Two mountain ranges in the SW Soviet Union extending NW–SE between the Black Sea and the Caspian Sea and separated by the River Kura: the **Great Caucasus**, some 1000 km (621 mi) long, to the N and the **Little Caucasus**, about half that length, along the Turkish border. Their highest point is Mount Elbrus.

cauliflower A variety of wild cabbage, *Brassica oleracea* var. *botrytis*, cultivated as a vegetable. The short stem bears a round white heart, up to 25 cm in diameter, of tightly compressed flower buds surrounded by green leaves. *See also* Brassica.

Cavalier poets A group of English poets connected with the court of Charles I (1625–49), including Richard Lovelace and Robert Herrick. Their love lyrics and poems about war and honour were characterized by a sophisticated elegance.

Cavaliers The royalist party during the English Civil War. After the Restoration of the monarchy (1660) the name was kept by the court party and was given to the parliament that sat from 1661 to 1679. The cavaliers were distinguished by their elaborate dress, with lace ruffles, feathers, and velvet, in contrast to the sober attire of the Roundheads.

Cavan (Irish name: Cabhán) A county in the NE Republic of Ireland, in Ulster. It is generally hilly, drained chiefly by the River Erne, with lakes and drumlins. Agriculture is the mainstay of the economy producing oats, potatoes, and dairy products. Some small industries exist in the towns. Area: 1890 sq km (730 sq mi). Population (1986): 53 881. County town: Cavan.

Cavell, Edith (1865–1915) British nurse. From 1907 she worked at a training institute for nurses in Brussels. She was executed by the Germans in 1915 for helping Allied soldiers escape from German-occupied Belgium. Before she died she is reputed to have said "I realize that patriotism is not enough. I must have no hatred or bitterness towards anyone."

CAVES *Fingal's Cave in the Hebrides, Scotland.*

Cavendish, Henry (1731–1810) British physicist; grandson of the Duke of Devonshire, from whom he inherited a fortune. He discovered hydrogen and investigated its properties. He also identified the gases in the atmosphere and showed that water is a compound. The first to measure accurately the universal gravitational constant, he used it to calculate the mass of the earth.

caves Underground hollows, usually opening directly onto the ground surface or connected with it by a passage. In limestone regions, where most caves occur, many constitute part of a system of natural underground drainage and are connected by subterranean streams. These caves are excavated by the slow solution of limestone by slightly acidic rain water percolating through its joints. The other main type of cave is that eroded from the base of a cliff by the sea. Such caves are located at some point of weakness in an otherwise resistant rock, such as a fault plane or bed of softer material. Fingal's Cave in the Scottish Hebrides is a spectacular cavern in columnar basalt, the sea forming its floor.

caviare A delicacy, eaten as an hors d'oeuvre, which consists of sturgeon's roe, salted and freed from all fat. It is a Russian speciality. The roe of the beluga is considered the best, although caviare is also obtained from other types of sturgeon. Real caviare is extremely expensive, but a substitute made from lumpfish roe is relatively inexpensive.

Cavour, Camillo Benso di, Count (1810–61) Italian statesman; the architect of Italian unification. In 1852 he formed his first government under Victor Emmanuel II of Sardinia-Piedmont. Cavour accepted an alliance with France and Britain during the Crimean War and negotiated a further alliance with France at Plombières in 1859 to oust Austria from Italy. He resigned when France came to terms with Austria but became prime minister again in 1860, negotiating the union of Sardinia-Piedmont with Parma, Modena, Tuscany, and the Romagna. By 1861 he had achieved the establishment of a united Italy.

cavy A small South American rodent belonging to the genus *Cavia* (6 species); the ancestor of the domestic guinea pig. Cavies are mainly nocturnal and live in groups in scrub and grassland, digging burrows and feeding on vegetation and seeds. Family: *Caviidae*.

Cawnpore. *See* Kanpur.

Caxton, William (c. 1422–91) The first English printer. A cloth merchant, Caxton lived in Bruges from 1446 until 1470, when he moved to Cologne. There he learned the technique of printing and in 1474 set up a press that produced the first printed book in English, *Recuyell of the Historyes of Troye* (1475). On returning to England (1476), he set up a press at Westminster, where he printed a long and varied list, including Chaucer's *Canterbury Tales* (1478) and an encyclopedia that was the first illustrated English book, *The Myrrour of the Worlde* (1481).

Cayenne 4 55N 52 18W The capital and main Atlantic port of French Guiana, in the NW of the Île de Cayenne. Founded by the French in 1643, it served as a French penal settlement (1854–1938). Cayenne pepper derives its name from a plant grown in the area. Population (1982): 38 091.

cayman (*or* caiman) An amphibious reptile occurring in rivers of Central and South America. 1.2–4.5 m long, it feeds on fish, birds, and insects. Genera: *Caiman* (2 species), *Melanosuchus* (1 species), *Paleosuchus* (2 species); subfamily: *Alligatorinae* (alligators and caimans); order: *Crocodilia* (*see* crocodile).

Cayman Islands A British colony in the Caribbean Sea, consisting of three low-lying coral islands (Grand Cayman, Little Cayman, and Cayman Brac) lying about 320 km (200 mi) NW of Jamaica. The population is mainly of mixed African and European descent. The Cayman Islands are a tax haven and tourist centre. The main exports are turtle shell, dried turtle meat, and tropical fish. *History*: discovered in 1503 by Columbus, who named them Las Tortugas because of the abundance of turtles. Formerly attached to Jamaica, they gained a certain measure of self-government in 1959 and became a separate British colony in 1962. Official language: English. Official currency: Jamaican dollar of 100 cents. Area: 260 sq km (100 sq mi). Population (1987 est): 22 900. Capital and main port: Georgetown.

CBE. *See* Order of the British Empire.

CBI. *See* Confederation of British Industry.

Ceanannus Mór. *See* Kells.

cedar A conifer of the genus *Cedrus* (4 species), native to the Mediterranean region and the Himalayas and widely planted for ornament and timber. Cedars usually grow to a height of 40 m. Their stiff needle-like leaves grow in tufts of 10–40 on short spurs and their cones are erect and barrel-shaped, 5–14 cm long. The best-known species are the deodar; the Atlas cedar (*C. atlantica*), from the Atlas mountains; and the cedar of Lebanon (*C. libani*), of the E Mediterranean. Family: *Pinaceae*.

Ceefax. *See* teletext.

Celebes. *See* Sulawesi.

celeriac A variety of cultivated celery, *Apium graveolens* var. *rapaceum*, also known as turnip-rooted or knob celery, grown for its globular edible root. The root, up to 15 cm in diameter, has a celery-like flavour.

celery The cultivated form of wild celery, or smallage (*Apium graveolens*), a biennial herb native to grassy coastal areas from Europe to India and Africa. Many varieties of cultivated celery have been developed for their edible leafstalks (up to 30 cm in length), which may

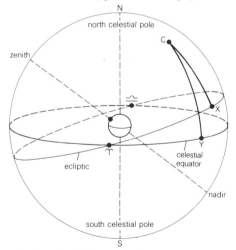

♈	first point of Aries; vernal equinox
♎	first point of Libra; autumnal equinox
C	celestial object
♈Y	right ascension of C (in hours anticlockwise from ♈)
♈X	celestial longitude of C (in degrees anticlockwise from ♈)
YC	declination of C
XC	celestial latitude of C

CELESTIAL SPHERE

be pink, yellow, or green. Traditionally, the green varieties are blanched to tenderize the tissues. The wild plant has an erect grooved stem, 30–60 cm long, bearing whorls of clusters of small greenish-white flowers. Family: *Umbelliferae*.

celesta A small keyboard instrument the quiet bell-like tone of which is produced by hammers striking steel plates hung over wooden resonators. Invented about 1880, it was used by Tchaikovsky in his ballet *Casse-Noisette*.

celestial mechanics The study of the motions of celestial bodies subject to mutual gravitational interaction through the application of the laws of gravitation and of mechanics.

celestial sphere The large imaginary sphere at the centre of which lies the earth and on the inner surface of which can be projected the stars and other celestial bodies. The directions of these bodies, as seen from earth, are measured in terms of their angular distances from certain points and circles on the celestial sphere. These circles include the ecliptic, the observer's horizon, and the **celestial equator**, where the earth's equatorial plane meets the celestial sphere. The reference points include the equinoxes, the zenith, and the **celestial poles**, where the earth's axis meets the celestial sphere. The earth's daily rotation causes an apparent and opposite rotation of the celestial sphere. See p. 145.

cell The basic unit of living matter, which performs the vital processes of producing energy, synthesizing new molecules from raw materials, division, and self-replication. All plants and animals are composed of

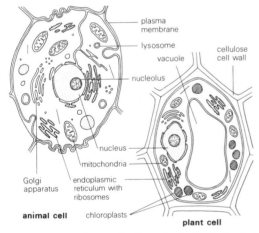

plasma membrane
lysosome
vacuole
cellulose cell wall
nucleolus
nucleus
mitochondria
Golgi apparatus
endoplasmic reticulum with ribosomes
animal cell chloroplasts
plant cell

CELL *Plant and animal cells are basically similar but plant cells are supported by cellulose cell walls and contain the green pigment chlorophyll within chloroplasts. Plant cells often also have large fluid-filled vacuoles, which help to control turgidity of the cell.*

cells, the average size of which ranges from 0.01 to 0.1 mm; the simplest organisms (bacteria, protozoa, etc.) consist only of a single cell. The fundamental importance of cells was first recognized by Schleiden and Schwann in 1838–39. A cell consists essentially of a mass of protoplasm bounded by a membrane. All cells except those of bacteria and blue-green algae and mammalian red blood cells possess a nucleus, containing the

genetic material, and cytoplasm, within which are structures (organelles) specialized for different metabolic functions (*see* Golgi apparatus; lysosome; mitochondria; ribosome). The cells of the body that are not involved in reproduction (somatic cells) divide by mitosis to produce daughter cells identical to themselves. The reproductive cells divide by meiosis to produce gametes, each containing half the number of chromosomes of the somatic cells. The difference between plant and animal cells is the presence in the former of a rigid cellulose cell wall and chlorophyll (*see* chloroplast).

Cellini, Benvenuto (1500–71) Florentine goldsmith and sculptor, famous for his autobiography (1558–62). Cellini worked chiefly as a medallist and craftsman for the papacy in Rome, the Medici in Florence, and Francis I in France. The famous gold saltcellar (Kunsthistorisches Museum, Vienna) was made for Francis. His *Perseus* (Loggia dei Lanzi, Florence) attests to his skills as a sculptor.

cello (full name: violoncello) A musical instrument of the violin family, held between the knees and supported at its lower end by an adjustable pin. It has an extensive range above its lowest note (C two octaves below middle C). Its four strings are tuned C, G, D, A. It emerged as a solo instrument in the 18th and 19th centuries.

cellular network A radiotelephone network for mobile subscribers that connects them to the main telephone system. It consists of a number of adjacent cells, each containing a transmit/receive station connected to the main telephone network and reached by the mobile subscriber using a battery-operated portable radiotelephone. As subscribers move from one geographical cell to another (e.g. by car), they are automatically switched to receive signals from the new area.

celluloid A highly flammable thermoplastic material made from cellulose nitrate and camphor. It became the first commercially made plastic (about 100 years ago).

cellulose $(C_6H_{10}O_5)_n$ A carbohydrate that is an important constituent of the cell walls of plants and consists of linked glucose units. Industrially, it is made from wood pulp and is used to manufacture rayon and cellulose-acetate plastics. Cellulose is important in the human diet since it forms part of dietary fibre.

cellulose nitrate (*or* nitrocellulose) A substance made by treating cellulose with a mixture of nitric acid and sulphuric acid. It is used as an explosive (gun cotton) and rocket propellant.

Celsius scale A temperature scale devised by Anders Celsius (1701–44), who originally designated zero as the boiling point of water and 100° as the freezing point. The scale was later reversed. Until 1948 it was known as the centigrade scale.

Celtic languages A branch of the Indo-European language family formerly widespread in W Europe. It is divided into two subgroups: Gaulish and Insular Celtic. The Gaulish languages are now extinct, being superseded in early medieval times by Romance, Germanic, and other languages. Insular Celtic can be further divided into Goidelic (including Manx and Gaelic) and Brythonic (including Welsh, Cornish, and Breton).

Celtic Sea The part of the Atlantic Ocean between Ireland, Wales, and SW England.

Celts A people who occupied a large part of Iron Age Europe. They were known to the Greeks as Keltoi and to the Romans as Gauls. There were numerous Celtic tribes and chiefdoms sharing a culture that can be traced back to the Bronze Age of central Europe (c. 1200 BC). *See also* Druids.

cement A powdered mixture of calcium silicates and aluminates. On mixing with water it undergoes complex hydration processes and sets into a hard solid mass. **Portland cement** and similar materials are made by heating limestone with clay and grinding the product. Portland cement was invented by a British stonemason, Joseph Aspdin (1799–1855), and named after the stone quarried at Portland, Dorset, which it resembles. It is used extensively in mortars and in concrete.

cenotaph Any memorial to the dead that does not contain a body. The cenotaph by Lutyens in Whitehall, London, commemorates the dead of both world wars. *See also* Remembrance Sunday.

Cenozoic era (*or* Cainozoic era) The geological era beginning about 65 million years ago and following the Mesozoic era. It is usually taken to include both the Tertiary and Quaternary periods. During this era the mammals flourished, after the extinction of most of the reptiles dominant in the Mesozoic; the Cenozoic is sometimes known as the age of mammals. Birds and flowering plants also flourished.

CENTAUR *Legendary Greek creatures.*

centaur In Greek legend, one of a race of wild creatures, half-human and half-horse, living in the mountains of Thessaly and descended from Ixion, King of the Lapiths. They were defeated by the Lapiths in a battle resulting from their characteristically unruly behaviour at the wedding of Ixion's son. *See also* Chiron.

centigrade scale. *See* Celsius scale.

centipede An arthropod belonging to the worldwide class *Chilopoda* (about 2800 species). It has long antennae and a slender flattened body of 15–181 segments. The first segment bears a pair of poison claws and nearly all the remaining segments bear a single pair of legs (*compare* millipede). The tropical order *Scolopendrida* contain the largest species, up to 280 mm long. Centipedes are found under stones, logs, and leaf litter during the day and at night prey on earthworms, insects, and sometimes small vertebrates. They lay eggs or produce live young.

Central African Federation. *See* Rhodesia and Nyasaland, Federation of.

Central African Republic (name from 1976 until 1979: Central African Empire) A country in central Africa, consisting mainly of a plateau lying at about 900 m (3000 ft). The dense forests in the S are drained by the River Ubangi, an important channel of communication. Most of the population belongs to the Banda and Baya tribes. *Economy*: chiefly subsistence agriculture, although diamonds have been successfully mined in recent years and there is now a state uranium mine. The main exports are cotton and coffee. *History*: as Ubangi-Shari it was one of the four territories of French Equatorial Africa and from 1958 had internal self-government as a member of the French Community. It became independent in 1960 as the Central African Republic. Official language: French; Sango is the national language. Official currency: CFA (Communauté financière africaine) franc of 100 centimes. Area: 625 000 sq km (241 250 sq mi). Population (1987 est): 2 775 000. Capital: Bangui.

Central America An isthmus of S North America, extending from the Isthmus of Tehuantepec to the NW border of Colombia and comprising an area of 596 000 sq km (230 000 sq mi). It consists of Belize, Costa Rica, El Salvador, Guatemala, Honduras, Nicaragua, and Panama, together with four Mexican states.

Central Criminal Court The Crown Court having jurisdiction to try all offences committed in the City of London and Greater London. The recorder of London and common serjeant are permanent judges of the court and all judges of the Queen's Bench Division also officiate on a rota system. The court is known as the Old Bailey.

Central Intelligence Agency (CIA) A US government department established in 1947 to coordinate US intelligence operations. It is not permitted to operate within the USA.

central nervous system. *See* nervous system.

Central Region An administrative region in central Scotland, created under local government reorganization in 1975 from the counties of Clackmannan, most of Stirling, S Perth, and part of West Lothian. It consists of the lowland plain of the Rivers Forth and Teith rising to uplands in the N and S. Agriculture includes cattle and dairy farming in the W and arable and livestock farming in the E. Industry is important with coalmining around Fallin and oil refining. Tourism is a thriving industry, especially around the Trossachs in the N of the region. Area: 2518 sq km (971 sq mi). Population (1986 est): 271 819. Administrative centre: Stirling.

centre of gravity A fixed point through which the resultant gravitational force on a body always passes no matter what its orientation.

centrifugal force. *See* centripetal force.

centripetal force A force that acts on a moving body causing it to move in a curved path. An object is constrained to move in a circle by a centripetal force directed towards the centre. It has an acceleration towards the centre of v^2/r, where v is the objects' velocity and r the radius of the circle. The centripetal force is necessary to overcome the object's tendency to move in a straight line and appears to be balanced by an equal **centrifugal force** directed radially outwards.

ceorl The free peasant (as distinct from the slave) of Anglo-Saxon England. The economic pressures of the Danish invasions and the Norman conquest contributed to the ceorl's declining status and eventual absorption amongst the unfree villeins. Thus "churl" has come to mean an uncouth person.

cèpe An edible mushroom, *Boletus edulis*. Common in temperate woodlands from August to November, it has a stout whitish or brown stalk and a hemispherical cap, brown to white in colour and 6–20 cm in diameter.

cephalopod A mollusc belonging to the class *Cephalopoda* (about 600 species), which includes octopuses, squids, and cuttlefishes. The most advanced of the molluscs, cephalopods are carnivorous and mostly free swimming, with a ring of tentacles around the mouth, well-developed eyes, and shells that are reduced and often absent. They are found in both shallow and deepwater marine habitats. In cephalopods the sexes are usually separate and fertilization is internal, often preceded by courtship behaviour.

Cepheid variable A highly luminous supergiant star the brightness of which varies very regularly in a period (1–70 days) that depends on the luminosity of the star. By measuring the period and the average apparent magnitude of a Cepheid, its distance can be determined. *See also* variable stars. Cepheids occur in ours and other galaxies and are a major means of measuring distances of galaxies up to about 20 million light years away.

ceramics Any nonmetallic inorganic material that is made by heat treatment into useful articles. The main categories are heavy articles made of baked clay, such as bricks and tiles, refractories to withstand high temperatures, such as furnace linings, sintered articles, such as abrasives, and domestic products made from earthenware, stoneware, or porcelain.

Cerberus In Greek legend, the monstrous dog who guarded the entrance to the underworld, usually portrayed as having three heads and a dragon's neck and tail. The final task of Heracles was to overpower this monster.

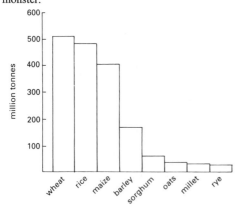

CEREALS *World production of cereals (1988).*

cereals Cultivated grasses selected for their high yields of grain, which constitutes a major item in the diet of man and livestock. Wheat, rice, and maize are the most important cereals, but barley, oats, rye, and millet are also widely cultivated. *See also* arable farming.

cerebellum. *See* brain.

cerebral palsy Damage to the developing brain resulting in uncoordinated movements and muscular weakness and paralysis (the affected child is called a spastic). The brain damage may be caused by injury during birth, insufficient oxygen before, during, or immediately after birth, or a viral infection of the brain. In some cases intelligence is affected. Treatment includes physiotherapy to improve movement and special education; speech therapy may also be needed.

cerebrospinal fluid The fluid that surrounds the brain and spinal cord. It is produced by special blood vessels inside the cerebrum and is reabsorbed by special bunches of veins. It acts as a shock absorber and support for the central nervous system. A normal adult has 130 ml of clear fluid; samples of it are taken for diagnostic tests for diseases of the nervous system.

cerebrum. *See* brain.

Ceres (astronomy) The largest minor planet, 1003 km in diameter, and the first to be discovered (in 1801 by Piazzi). It orbits at between 2.55 and 2.98 astronomical units from the sun, with a period of 4.6 years.

Ceres (mythology). *See* Demeter.

cerium (Ce) The most abundant lanthanide element, discovered in 1803 by Berzelius and others. It occurs naturally in several minerals including monazite, $(Ce,La,Th)PO_4$, and allanite, a complex aluminosilicate. It is used as a catalyst in self-cleaning ovens, in gas mantles, as a polishing agent. At no 58; at wt 140.12; mp 799°C; bp 3426°C.

CERN (Organisation (previously Conseil) européenne pour la Recherche nucléaire) A W European organization founded in 1954 to carry out nuclear research. Its headquarters are in Geneva and its staff are recruited from CERN's 12 member countries. It built and runs a 28GeV proton synchrotron accelerator, with an intersecting storage ring system, which is 300 m (328 yd) in diameter.

Cervantes, Miguel de (1547–1616) Spanish novelist. In 1569 he went to Italy and fought at the battle of Lepanto in 1571. Returning to Spain in 1575, he was captured by pirates and imprisoned for five years. After 1580 he held several minor jobs in the civil service while writing a pastoral novel, *La Galatea* (1585), and several plays. *Don Quixote* (Part I, 1605; Part II, 1615), his revolutionary picaresque novel about a self-deluding knight errant and his cunning squire, Sancho Panza, won him fame throughout Europe but little financial reward.

cetane number A quality rating for Diesel fuel, similar to the octane number for petrol. Two reference fuel compounds, cetane and alpha-methylnaphthalene, are given the numbers 100 and 0 respectively. Mixtures of these two have intermediate numbers and other Diesel fuels are compared with them in a standard engine. Most Diesel engines can run on fuel that has a cetane number of 40 or 50.

Ceylon. *See* Sri Lanka, Democratic Socialist Republic of.

Cézanne, Paul (1839–1906) French postimpressionist painter, born in Aix-en-Provence, the son of a banker. After studying law for two years, he was encouraged by his childhood friend Emile Zola to settle in Paris (1861). His crude and often erotic early paintings failed, however, to find favour. In 1872, while working with Pissarro in Pontoise, he turned to impressionism, a period represented by *The Suicide's House* (Louvre) but he soon rejected its flickering effects of light and movement in favour of more stability and solidity. His views influenced the development of cubism. Living mainly in Provence, he painted portraits, e.g. *The Card Players* (Louvre), still lifes, landscapes, especially of Mont St Victoire and L'Éstaque, and a series of *Bathers*.

CFCs. *See* fluorocarbons.

CÉZANNE   *Detail from* The Card Players *(Louvre).*

c.g.s. system   A metric system of units based on the centimetre, gram, and second.   It includes dynes, ergs, and both electrostatic and electromagnetic units. It has been replaced for scientific purposes by SI units.

Chablis   47 49N 3 48E A village in central France, in the Yonne department. Chablis is famous for the white wine named after it.

Chabrol, Claude   (1930–) French film director. He was a leading member of the New Wave group of French directors in the late 1950s. His films, many of which are influenced by Alfred Hitchcock and use tense murder plots to illuminate bourgeois social relationships, include *Les Biches* (1968), *Le Boucher* (1969), *Coq au Vin* (1985), and *Une Affaire des Femmes* (1988).

Chaco.   *See* Gran Chaco.

Chad, Republic of (French name: Tchad) A country covering an extensive area in N central Africa, consisting mainly of poor semidesert. The land rises from Lake Chad in the SW to the Tibesti Mountains in the N, reaching heights of about 3400 m (11 000 ft). The majority of the rather sparse population (concentrated in the S) is Sara, a Bantu people; most of the nomadic peoples of the N are Muslims. *Economy*: mainly subsistence agriculture with livestock and fishing. The main exports are cotton and meat. *History*: one of the four territories of French Equatorial Africa, it had internal self-government as a member of the French Community from 1958, gaining independence in 1960. Since 1963 there has been considerable rebellion and unrest in the N. From 1983 to 1987 there was heavy fighting between the government and Libyan-backed rebels. Official language: French. Official currency: CFA (Communauté financière africaine) franc of 100 centimes. Area: 1 284 000 sq km (495 624 sq mi). Population (1987 est): 5 241 000. Capital: N'djamena (formerly Fort Lamy).

Chadwick, Sir James   (1891–1974) British physicist, who worked at Cambridge with Rutherford and went on to discover the neutron in 1932. Physicists had previously suspected the existence of neutrons but had been unable to detect them: by analysing the radiation emitted by beryllium when bombarded with alpha particles, Chadwick was able to show that it consisted of neutrons. He was awarded the 1935 Nobel Prize.

chafer   A herbivorous beetle belonging to the family *Scarabaeidae* (*see* scarab beetle). Chafers cause much damage to trees and crops by eating the foliage and flowers; the larvae, which live in the soil, attack the roots. Chief genera: *Melolontha* (*see* cockchafer), *Cetonia* (rose chafers), and *Phyllopertha* (garden chafers).

chaffinch   A finch, *Fringilla coelebs*, about 15 cm long, that is common in woods and parks in Europe, W Asia, and N Africa. The male chaffinch has a chestnut back, pinkish breast, greyish-blue crown and nape, and two conspicuous white wing bars. The female has a duller plumage with an olive-green back. Chaffinches are often migratory and have a lively song.

Chagall, Marc   (1887–1985) Russian-born painter and printmaker of Jewish parentage. After studying in St Petersburg (1907–10), he visited Paris (1910). There he painted some of his best-known works, recalling Russian village life, such as *Me and the Village* (1911; New York). His childlike figures and objects, distorted in scale and often floating upside down in space, influenced the surrealists. Moving to France (1922), he illustrated Gogol's *Dead Souls* and La Fontaine's *Fables*. During World War II he lived in the USA, where he designed ballet sets and costumes and subsequently worked on mosaics and tapestries for the Israeli Knesset building (1966).

Chagos Islands.   *See* British Indian Ocean Territory.

chain   1. A measure of length equal to 66 feet. 2. A measuring device used in surveying. A Gunter's chain is 66 feet long (consisting of 100 links), whereas an Engineer's chain is 100 feet long (also 100 links).

Chain, Sir Ernst Boris   (1906–79) British biochemist, born in Germany, who–with Lord Florey–isolated and purified penicillin and performed the first clinical trials. Coming to England in 1933, Chain worked first at Cambridge and then at Oxford with Florey. For their work, Chain, Florey, and Sir Alexander Fleming (the discoverer of penicillin) were awarded a Nobel Prize (1945).

chain reaction   A series of reactions in which the product of each reaction sets off further reactions. In a nuclear chain reaction each nuclear fission is induced by a neutron ejected by a previous fission. For example, the fission of a uranium-235 nucleus produces either two or three neutrons each of which can induce the fission of another uranium-235 nucleus. Chain reactions are used as a source of energy in nuclear reactors and nuclear weapons. *See also* critical mass.

chaise   A light two- or four-wheeled carriage drawn by one, two, or four horses. A chaise usually had a collapsible hood (calash). "Chaise" could also apply to a curricle or phaeton.

chalcedony   A cryptocrystalline (submicroscopically grained) sometimes fibrous silica mineral. The numerous varieties include carnelian (red); agate, onyx, and sardonyx (banded); jasper (red or brown); and chert and flint (opaque grey or black). The last two occur in limestones; others occur mainly in veins and amygdales.

Chalcidice   (Modern Greek name: Khalkidhiki) A peninsula in NE Greece. It ends in three promontories, the northernmost of which contains Mount Athos. There are fertile low-lying areas but it is mostly wooded and mountainous. It is named after Chalcis, the capital of the Greek island of Euboea, which originally established a colony here. Area: 2945 sq km (1149 sq mi).

chalcopyrite The principal ore of copper, sometimes called copper pyrites, of composition $CuFeS_2$. It is brassy yellow with a greenish black streak and occurs mainly in veins associated with the upper part of an acid igneous intrusion.

Chaldea (*or* Chaldaea) The region of S Babylonia where the new Babylonian empire was established by Nabopolassar (d. 605 BC) in 625 in the last years of the Assyrian empire. At its height under Nebuchadnezzar II (reigned 604–562), the Chaldean empire, centred on the rebuilt city of Babylon, dominated the Middle East for about 70 years until overthrown by the Achaemenians in 539.

chalk A sedimentary rock that is a pure-white fine-grained variety of limestone (calcium carbonate). Coccoliths (the calcareous remains of extinct unicellular organisms) are the main constituents of chalk although other invertebrate remains are included. Chalk is very characteristic of the Upper Cretaceous period in W Europe and the Chalk is sometimes used synonymously with the Upper Cretaceous. Nodules of flint are often found in chalk; these are formed from the remains of siliceous organisms, dissolved and redeposited.

chamberlain An officer appointed by a monarch, nobleman, or corporation to perform ceremonial duties. The chamberlains of medieval England were financial officers and were figures of great political importance in the 12th century. The chamberlain was succeeded by the Lord Chamberlain, who is responsible for the administration of the royal household. Until 1968 he also licensed plays for public performance.

NEVILLE CHAMBERLAIN *Returning from Germany with the Munich Agreement (1938).*

Chamberlain, Joseph (1836–1914) British politician. He was mayor of Birmingham (1873–76), and became a Liberal MP in 1876. In 1886 he split the Liberal Party because of Gladstone's support of Irish Home Rule. In 1895 he became colonial secretary in the Conservative Government. His reputation was enhanced by his policies in the Boer War but his commitment to imperial preference in tariff rates caused a split in the Conservative ranks, which led to his resignation (1903) and contributed to electoral defeat in 1906. His eldest son **Sir (Joseph) Austen Chamberlain** (1863–1937) became a Liberal-Unionist MP in 1892. He was chancellor of the exchequer (1919–21) and then foreign secretary (1924–

29), when he negotiated the Locarno Pact and won a Nobel Peace Prize (1925). Joseph's son by his second marriage, **(Arthur) Neville Chamberlain** (1869–1940), was a Conservative MP and prime minister of the National Government (1937–40), when he advocated a policy of appeasement towards the fascist powers. He recognized Italy's conquest of Ethiopia and kept out of the Spanish Civil War. To avoid a European war he visited Hitler three times in 1938, coming to the Munich Agreement, which recognized Germany's possession of the Sudetenland. He returned to Britain claiming to have brought "peace for our time" but was forced by Hitler's invasion of Czechoslovakia to abandon appeasement. He declared war after Hitler's attack on Poland but his ineffective direction of the war led to his resignation in May, 1940.

chamber music Music written to be played in the intimacy of a room rather than in a large hall, church, or theatre. In the baroque period chamber sonatas were distinguished from church sonatas and in the late 18th century Haydn, Mozart, and Beethoven established the piano trio (violin, cello, and piano), the duo sonata (one instrument and piano), and the string quartet (two violins, viola, and cello) as the main chamber music forms. Chamber music has been written for other combinations of players, including the woodwind quintet (oboe, flute, clarinet, horn, and bassoon), the clarinet quintet (clarinet and string quartet), and the piano quintet (piano and string quartet).

chameleon An arboreal lizard belonging to the Old World family *Chamaeleontidae* (84 species) and characterized by its ability to change its skin colour. 17–25 cm long, chameleons have a narrow body, an extensile tongue for capturing insects, and bulging eyes that can move independently. Some species have a helmet-shaped head or conspicuous horns. They may be green, yellow, cream, or dark brown, often with spots, and change colour by concentration or dispersion of pigment in skin cells. Genera: *Brookesia*, *Chamaeleo*.

chamois An agile hoofed mammal, *Rupicapra rupicapra*, of mountainous regions in Europe and SW Asia. Chamois grow to about 75 cm high at the shoulder and have distinctive narrow upright horns with backward-pointing hooked tips. Their tawny coat becomes darker and longer in winter. Their hide was formerly used for chamois (or shammy) leather. Family: *Bovidae*.

chamomile. *See* camomile.

champagne A wine, usually sparkling, produced in the districts around Reims and Epernay, NE France. Champagne is usually made from black (*pinot noir*) and white (*pinot chardonnay*) grapes. After fermentation sugar and yeast are added to the still wine, which, when bottled, undergoes a secondary fermentation, which produces the sparkle. A dosage of sugar syrup determines whether it will be sweet (*sec*) or dry (*brut*) champagne.

Champagne A former province in NE France, now incorporated in the planning region of **Champagne-Ardenne**. Ruled by counts during the middle ages, it became important for its trade fairs and at the end of the 17th century began to produce the sparkling champagne for which it is famous.

Chancery, Court of In English law, the court in which the system of equity developed. It developed in the 15th century as the personal court of the king's chief law officer, the Lord Chancellor, in which he dealt with

CHANNEL TUNNEL *Due for completion in 1993, the tunnel (consisting of two running tunnels linked by a service tunnel) will provide 100 mph rail shuttles with a peak 10–12 minute frequency. The 35 minute journey will halve the train journey time between London and Paris. Terminals will be built at Folkestone and Coquelles with new road and rail links (see map).*

cases for which the common law could not provide a remedy. It dealt with such matters as partnerships, the administration of estates, and the execution of trusts. In 1875 it was merged with the Supreme Court of Judicature; it survives as the Chancery Division of the High Court.

Chandigarh 30 43N 76 47E A Union Territory and modern (1953) city in NW India, on the Haryana–Punjab border. The joint capital of both states, it was planned by Le Corbusier in 30 rectangular sectors for housing, government, and industry. Punjab University was established here in 1947. Area: 114 sq km (44 sq mi). Population (1981 est): 451 610.

Chandler, Raymond (1888–1959) US novelist. Educated at Dulwich College, England, he returned to the USA and worked in business before starting to write detective stories in the 1930s. The detective Philip Marlowe features in all his nine novels, which include *The Big Sleep* (1939), *Farewell My Lovely* (1940), and *The Long Goodbye* (1954).

change ringing The sounding of a peal of church bells (which contains from 5 to 12 bells) in a fixed order. Each bell is rung by a single individual. The changes are prescribed by numerical order, e.g. 12345, 21345, 23145.

Chang Jiang. *See* Yangtze River.

Channel Islands (French name: Îles Normandes) A group of islands in the English Channel, off the coast of NW France. The chief islands comprise Jersey (the largest), Guernsey, Alderney, and Sark. Since the Norman conquest (1066) they have been a dependency of the British Crown. During World War II they were the only British territory to come under German occupation. Tourism is of major economic importance but the islands are also noted for their early agricultural produce. This includes flowers, fruit, potatoes, and tomatoes; the Jersey and Guernsey breeds of cattle are world famous. Area: 194 sq km (75 sq mi). Population (1986): 144 494.

Channel tunnel (*or* Chunnel) A proposed tunnel linking Britain with France. First suggested to Napoleon in 1802, digging was actually started by two private companies in each country in 1882. A press outcry in Britain forced the government to intervene on security grounds and the scheme was abandoned in 1883. In 1964 the two governments revived the project, simultaneously considering plans for a Channel bridge. The tunnel was agreed upon and in the early 1970s work again started, to be abandoned on economic grounds in 1974. Work upon a high-speed rail tunnel began in 1987.

chanterelle An edible mushroom, *Cantharellus cibarius*, occurring in temperate woodlands. It is funnel-shaped and yellow with the gills clearly visible and measures 3–10 cm across the cap. The flesh is a delicacy. Family: *Cantharellaceae*; class: *Basidiomycetes*.

Chantilly 49 12N 2 28E A town in France, in the Oise department near the Forest of Chantilly. Once renowned for its lace making, Chantilly is famous for its racecourse and the Grand Château's art collection. Population (1982 est): 10 208.

Chaos In earliest Greek mythology, the goddess representing the primeval emptiness from which evolved Night, Erebus (darkness), Tartarus (the underworld), and Eros (desire).

chaparral A scrub form of vegetation occurring in S California (USA) and NW Mexico. It consists chiefly of sclerophyllous broad-leaved evergreen shrubs and bushes and is related to the Mediterranean maquis.

Chaplin, Charlie (Sir Charles C.; 1889–1977) US film actor, born in Britain. He was recruited by the Keystone Studio while touring the USA with Fred Karno's pantomine company in 1913. He gained immediate popular and financial success with his portrayals of the tramp, a sensitive but pathetic figure dressed in baggy trousers and a bowler hat, and from 1918 he wrote and directed his own films. These included *The Gold Rush* (1924), *City Lights* (1931), and, following the introduction of sound, *Modern Times* (1936) and *The Great Dictator* (1940). Accused of having communist sympathies, he left the USA in 1952 to live in Switzerland. He was awarded an Oscar in 1973 and was knighted in 1976.

char A food and game fish belonging to the genus *Salvelinus*, related to trout, especially *S. alpinus*, found in Arctic coastal waters and fresh waters of Europe and North America. Its torpedo-shaped body, about 30 cm long, is olive-green to moss-green with yellow spots above and silvery or bright red below.

Chardin, Jean-Baptiste-Siméon (1699–1779) French painter of still lifes and domestic interiors after the Dutch tradition of Vermeer, noted for the simplicity of his paintings, e.g. *The Housewife* (Louvre) and *The Young Schoolmistress* (National Gallery, London).

Charente, River A river in W central France. Rising in the Haute-Vienne department, it flows mainly W to the Bay of Biscay. Length: 362 km (225 mi).

Chari, River (*or* R. Shari) A river in N central Africa. Rising in the N Central African Republic, it flows N to Lake Chad. Length: 2250 km (1400 mi).

Charing Cross A district in the Greater London borough of the city of Westminster. The last of 12 crosses, marking the resting places of Queen Eleanor's coffin on its journey to Westminster Abbey, was erected here (1290) by Edward I.

Charlemagne (c. 742–814) King of the Franks (771–814) and the first postclassical western emperor (800–14). The son of Pepin the Short, he conquered the Saxon tribes (772–81) and became King of Lombardy (773). In 778 he campaigned in NE Spain, where at Roncesvalles his paladin Roland was killed. In 800, having conquered most of western Christendom, he was crowned emperor of the West by Pope Leo III.

Charles (Philip Arthur George) (1948–) Prince of Wales and heir-apparent to the throne of the United Kingdom as the eldest son of Elizabeth II. After studying at Trinity College, Cambridge (1967–70), he served in the RAF and the Royal Navy before undertaking more public duties. He is known for his controversial views on modern architecture and his concern for the environment. In 1981 he married Lady Diana Spencer (1961–). Their first child, Prince William Arthur Philip Louis of Wales, was born in 1982 and their second, Prince Henry Charles Albert David, in 1984.

Charles I (1600–49) King of England, Scotland, and Ireland (1625–49), succeeding his father James I. Charles' disputes with parliament led ultimately to his execution (*see* Civil War, English). His first three parliaments (1625; 1626; 1628–29) were dominated by Puritan members, who attempted to make its award of financial grants to the king dependent on his agreement to its demands. Charles resorted to levying taxes without parliamentary consent and ruled without parliament from 1629 to 1640. His government became increasingly unpopular and his attempt to impose Laud's Anglican prayer book on Presbyterian Scotland led to the Bishops' Wars (1639–40). The financial demands of the Wars forced Charles to summon parliament again but the so-called Short Parliament (April–May 1640) proved so critical that he soon dissolved it. The Long Parliament, summoned in November following Charles' defeat by the Scots, demanded far-reaching reforms. Charles attempted to arrest five members of the House of Commons and in April 1642 the Civil War broke out. After his defeat at Naseby (1645), his cause was lost and he surrendered to the Scots at Newark in 1646. Charles was tried at Westminster Hall, found guilty of treason, and beheaded (30 January, 1649).

Charles (II) the Bald (823–77) Holy Roman Emperor (875–77) and, as Charles I, King of France (843–77). After the death of his father Louis I, civil war broke out between Charles and his three older brothers. By 843 Charles had procured by the Treaty of Verdun the nucleus of what was to become France.

Charles II (1630–85) King of England, Scotland, and Ireland (1660–85). He fought with his father, Charles I, in the Civil War and, after his father's execution (1649), was crowned by the Scots. Defeated by Cromwell (1651), he was forced into exile. After the fall of the Protectorate (1659), George Monck negotiated the Restoration of the monarchy and Charles became king after promising a general pardon and liberty of conscience in the Declaration of Breda. In 1662 he married Catherine of Braganza. At first dependent on the Earl of Clarendon (1609–74), Charles was forced to dismiss his adviser (1667) after the failure of the Dutch War of 1665–67 and replaced him with a group of ministers known as the Cabal. His Roman Catholic sympathies became clear with his Declaration of Indulgence (1672), which an-

nulled the penal laws against Dissenters and Roman Catholics. Parliament responded with the Test Act (1673) excluding Dissenters and Roman Catholics from office, which together with the unpopular Dutch War of 1672–74 served to destroy the Cabal. Fear of Roman Catholicism exacerbated by Catherine's childlessness, came to a head with the Popish Plot (1678), which fabricated a Catholic plot to murder Charles and place his Roman Catholic brother and heir, later James II, on the throne. Charles resisted subsequent parliamentary attempts to exclude James from the succession and from 1681 ruled without parliament. On his deathbed he acknowledged his Roman Catholicism.

CHARLES *The Prince and Princess of Wales on a skiing holiday.*

Charles (V) the Wise (1337–80) King of France (1364–80) during the Hundred Years' War with England. As regent (1356–60) for his father John II, Charles suppressed the peasants' revolt known as the Jacquerie (1358). Between 1369 and 1375 he regained most of the territory lost to England by the disastrous Treaty of Brétigny (1360).

Charles V (1500–58) Holy Roman Emperor (1519–56). Charles inherited Burgundy and the Netherlands (1506) from his father Philip of Burgundy (1478–1506); he became King of Spain and Naples (1516) on the death of his maternal grandfather Ferdinand II of Aragon and Holy Roman Emperor on the death of his paternal grandfather Maximilian I. Charles' vast possessions provoked intermittent warfare with Francis I of France (1494–1547; reigned 1515–47): in 1525, having defeated Francis at Pavia, Charles briefly took the French king prisoner and in 1527, in response to an alliance between France, the papacy, Venice, and Milan, Charles' troops sacked Rome. Their contest for European hegemony ended inconclusively with the Treaty of Crépy (1544).

Charles' reign saw the emergence of the Reformation and in 1521 he presided over the Diet of Worms, which condemned Luther. His subsequent attempts to conciliate the Protestants failed and in 1546 Charles took up arms against the Protestant Schmalkaldic League, defeating it at Mühlberg (1547). In 1551, however, two

German Protestant rulers allied with Henry II of France and Charles was forced to accept Protestant demands. Exhausted by the great problems of his Empire, Charles retired to a Spanish monastery, dividing his possessions between his son, who became Philip II of Spain, and his brother, Emperor Ferdinand I (1503–64).

Charles (VI) the Well-Beloved (1368–1422) King of France (1380–1422). Charles suffered attacks of insanity from 1392 and the ensuing conflict for the regency led to civil war between the Armagnacs and the Burgundians. In 1415 Henry V of England invaded France and defeated the French at Agincourt. After further campaigns Henry married (1420) Charles' daughter Catherine of Valois (1401–37) and was named as regent of France and Charles' heir.

Charles VI (1685–1740) Holy Roman Emperor (1711–40), who issued the Pragmatic Sanction (1713) to secure the succession of his daughter Maria Theresa to his Austrian possessions. His claim (1700) to the Spanish throne gave rise to the War of the Spanish Succession (1701–14), in which he was unsuccessful. In 1716–18 and 1736–39 he fought the Turks; he lost the War of the Polish Succession (1733–38).

Charles VII (1403–61) King of France (1422–61). He suffered losses to the invading English and their Burgundian allies until 1429 when, with Joan of Arc, he liberated Orleans. By 1453, he had driven the English from all of France, except Calais. He instituted reforms to strengthen the monarchy but his last years were troubled by the intrigues of the dauphin. *See also* Hundred Years' War.

Charles VII (1697–1745) Holy Roman Emperor (1742–45) during the War of the Austrian Succession. The Elector of Bavaria (1726–45), Charles joined the alliance against Maria Theresa when she claimed the Austrian inheritance. He was elected emperor in opposition to Maria Theresa's husband Francis (subsequently Emperor Francis I).

Charles IX (1550–74) King of France (1560–74) during the Wars of Religion. His mother Catherine de' Medici dominated his reign and was largely responsible for the Saint Bartholomew's Day Massacre of Huguenots that Charles ordered in 1572.

Charles X (1757–1836) King of France (1824–30). Charles lived abroad after the French revolution, returning at the Bourbon restoration (1815), when he became leader of the ultraroyalist party. His reactionary rule led to his overthrow (1830) and he fled to England.

Charles Edward Stuart, the Young Pretender (1720–88) The son of the Old Pretender, James Edward Stuart. Romantically known as Bonnie Prince Charlie, in 1745 he landed in Scotland, rallied his Jacobite supporters and marched S to claim the English throne. Lack of support forced his withdrawal again to Scotland. Defeated in battle at Culloden (1746), he escaped to exile in Europe.

Charles's law For a gas at constant pressure, its volume is directly proportional to its absolute temperature. The law is not strictly obeyed but is closely approximated in gases above their critical state. An alternative statement of the law is that gases expand by 1/273 of their volume at 0°C for every 1°C rise in temperature. Named after Jacques Charles (1746–1823).

Charleston 38 23N 81 40W A city in the USA, the capital of West Virginia. It was the home (1788–95) of Daniel Boone. Industries include chemicals, glass, and paints. Population (1985 est): 59 371.

Charleston 32 48N 79 58W A city in the USA, in South Carolina near the Atlantic coast. Founded in 1670, it was here that the US Civil War started with the bombardment of Fort Sumter by Confederate troops in 1861. A major port, its manufactures include fertilizer, paper, and steel. It was badly damaged by Hurricane Hugo in 1989. Population (1986): 68 900.

CHARLESTON   *Dancing in the 1920s, from a cartoon in* Punch.

Charleston A ballroom dance of the 1920s named after Charleston, South Carolina, where it had been a popular Black dance in the early 1900s. It became a national craze following the Black musical *Runnin' Wild* (1923) with its 4/4 time, syncopated rhythms, and twisting toe-in steps.

Charleston, Battles of Two battles of the American Revolution fought at Charleston, South Carolina. In the first (1776) the Americans repulsed the British, whose invasion of the South was thus delayed. In the second the Americans surrendered (12 May, 1780) Charleston after a 45-day siege.

Charlton, Bobby (Robert C.; 1937–) British Association footballer, who played for Manchester United (1956–73). He also played for England 106 times and scored a record 49 goals; he was a member of the England team that won the 1966 World Cup. His brother **Jackie Charlton** (John C.; 1935–) was also an Association footballer, who played for Leeds United and England.

charm A property of matter, expressed as a quantum number, postulated to account for the unusually long lifetime of the psi particle (discovered in 1974). According to this hypothesis a quark (*see* particle physics) exists having the property called charm. Charm is believed to be conserved in strong interactions and in electromagnetic interactions.

Charon In Greek legend, the ferryman who carried the souls of the dead over the Rivers Styx and Acheron to the underworld. Only the correctly buried dead were taken. A coin placed in the mouth of the corpse was his payment.

Chartism A British working–class movement for political reform, centring on the London Working Men's Association (LWMA). Founded in June, 1836 by William Lovett (1800–77), the LWMA drew up a People's Charter (1838) of six points: universal male suffrage, the secret ballot, equal electoral districts, abolition of the property qualifications for MPs, payment of MPs, and annual general elections. The Chartists quickly gained support throughout the country and presented their Charter with 1.2 million signatures to parliament (1839). It was rejected, as were their two later petitions (1842, 1848). Chartism lost support in the 1840s because of lack of organization, rivalry between its leaders, Lovett and Feargus O'Connor (1794–1855), and reviving trade and greater prosperity. The movement was spent by the end of the decade.

Chartres 48 27N 1 30E A town in N central France, the capital of the Eure-et-Loire department on the River Eure. The gothic cathedral (begun c. 1194) is famous, especially for its 13th-century stained glass. Chartres is the principal market town of the Beauce region. Population (1982 est): 39 243.

Charybdis *See* Scylla and Charybdis.

chat A songbird belonging to the thrush family. True chats include stonechats, whinchats, wheatears, and redstarts although the name is also given to certain Australian wrens (family *Muscicapidae*) and to American wood warblers (family *Parulidae*).

Chatham 51 23N 0 32E A town in SE England, in Kent on the Medway estuary. Its naval base, dating from Tudor times, closed in 1984. Population (1981): 61 909.

Chatham, 1st Earl of. *See* Pitt the Elder, William.

Chaucer, Geoffrey (c. 1342–1400) English poet. Chaucer made various journeys to Europe as a soldier and diplomat, held positions in the customs service, and received pensions from Richard II and Henry IV. His poems *The Book of the Duchess* and *The Parliament of Fowls* derive from the French tradition of the allegorical dream poem. Chaucer also parodied Dante's *Divine Comedy* in *The House of Fame* and used Boccaccio's poem *Il filostrato* as the basis for *Troilus and Criseyde*. His best-known work is *The Canterbury Tales*, a collection of stories told by a group of pilgrims travelling from London to Canterbury. The tales range from the tragedy of *The Knight's Tale* to the bawdiness of *The Miller's Tale*.

Cheddar 51 17N 2 46W A village in SW England, in Somerset, famous for its cheese and for the caves and rare limestone flora of the **Cheddar Gorge**, a pass through the Mendip Hills. Population (1983): 3994.

cheese A dairy product made from separated milk solids (curd). Curd is made by coagulating milk with rennet or some other enzyme and removing the liquid (whey). It is then salted, pressed into blocks, and left to mature. Cheese is a rich source of protein and calcium. It contains fat but little carbohydrate since most of it is left in the whey.

cheetah A large cat, *Acinonyx jubatus*, of Africa and SW Asia, also called hunting leopard. It has a reddish-yellow coat with black spots and grows to about 2 m in length. Cheetahs have nonretractable claws and rough pads and they hunt by running down prey. They are the fastest mammals, sprinting at up to 110 km per hour (70 mph).

Chekhov, Anton Pavlovich (1860–1904) Russian dramatist and short-story writer. He first studied medicine at Moscow University and developed as a serious writer after graduating in 1884. Suffering from tubercu-

losis, he bought a farm at Melikhovo in 1892 and, after a haemorrhage in 1897, lived at Yalta in the Crimea. His first play, *The Seagull* (1896), failed at first but succeeded triumphantly when revived in 1898 by Stanislavsky's Moscow Art Theatre. His major plays—*Uncle Vanya* (1897), *The Three Sisters* (1901), and *The Cherry Orchard* (1904)—were written for this company, and in 1901 he married one of the actresses, Olga Knipper.

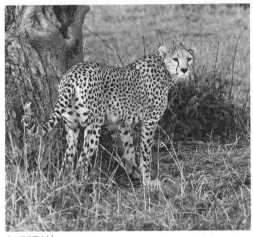

CHEETAH

Chelonia An order of reptiles (600 species) comprising the aquatic turtles and terrapins and the terrestrial tortoises, widely distributed in warm and temperate regions. They have a protective shell consisting of an upper carapace and a lower plastron joined together at the sides with openings for the head, tail, and limbs. The neck is long and mobile and can be withdrawn into the shell.

Chelsea A residential district in the Greater London borough of Kensington and Chelsea, on the N bank of the River Thames. It is noted for the Chelsea Royal Hospital for old soldiers (Chelsea Pensioners), designed by Wren and completed in 1692. It has a long history of literary and artistic associations.

Chelsea porcelain A pioneer soft-paste porcelain made at Chelsea (London) between 1743 and 1785. From early sparsely decorated figures and small dishes the factory improved to become one of the most important in contemporary Europe. *See also* Derby ware.

Cheltenham 51 54N 2 04W A town in SW England, in Gloucestershire. A fashionable spa town in the 18th century, it is famous for its schools (Cheltenham College, a boys' public school, and Cheltenham Ladies' College) and racecourse. Population (1988): 86 400.

chemical bond The force that holds the atoms together in a molecule or the ions together in a crystalline solid. In general, atoms combine to form molecules and ions combine to form crystals in order to increase their stability by sharing or transferring outer electrons in such a way that the stable noble-gas configuration results (*see* atomic theory). In **covalent bonds**, atoms are held together by sharing pairs of electrons in their outer shells. In the **electrovalent** (*or* ionic) **bond** an outer electron is transferred from one atom to another so that ions are formed. The electrostatic force between the ions holds the molecule or crystal together. **Coordinate** (*or* dative) **bonds** are covalent bonds in which both electrons are donated by the same atom.

chemical engineering The design, maintenance, and operation of equipment used in industrial chemical processes. Chemical engineers study both chemistry and engineering subjects. In the UK the profession is controlled by the Institution of Chemical Engineers.

chemical reaction A process in which one or more chemical substances change to other substances, either spontaneously or as a result of heat, irradiation, etc. Chemical reaction involves rearrangement of electrons between reacting species to form different molecules.

chemical warfare The use of toxic substances to kill or disable personnel, pollute food or water supplies, or make any other military use of chemicals, for example smoke screens, etc. (explosives are excluded). Chlorine, phosgene, and mustard gas were used in World War I but are ineffective against modern protection. They were not used in World War II but were subsequently employed in the Gulf War. Poisons have now been developed to penetrate the skin, circumventing gas masks. Chemical weapons vary in potency, ranging from the relatively humane tear gas to the lethal nerve gases.

chemisorption. *See* adsorption.

chemistry The scientific study of matter, especially the changes and interactions it can undergo. Chemistry can be said to have originated with Aristotle's four-element (earth, air, fire, water) analysis of matter. This view persisted unchallenged from the 4th century BC, through some 2000 years of alchemy, until it was finally demolished by Robert Boyle in his *Skeptical Chymist* (1661). The modern concept of an element was provided by Boyle, who also correctly distinguished between elements, compounds, and mixtures. The elucidation of the structure of compounds in terms of the elements they contain was developed by such 18th-century chemists as Cavendish, Priestley, and Lavoisier. Berzelius' law of constant proportions and Dalton's atomic theory, produced at the beginning of the 19th century, established chemistry on a quantitative basis. However, it was not until the beginning of the 20th century that the work of J. J. Thomson and Rutherford (*see* atomic theory) had established the structure of the atom, enabling the electronic theory of valence to emerge. This theory made sense of the work of Newlands and Mendeleyev in ordering the elements into the structure of the periodic table. **Inorganic chemistry** is concerned with the study of all these elements (except carbon) and their compounds and interactions. **Organic chemistry** is the study of the enormous number of compounds of carbon. **Physical chemistry** is concerned with the application of physics to a quantitative assessment of the structures and properties of compounds and the laws that control chemical reactions.

Chemnitz. *See* Karl-Marx-Stadt.

chemoreception The reception by an organism of chemical stimuli. In man and other air-breathing vertebrates, chemicals ingested in food, etc., are sensed by taste buds on the tongue and walls of the mouth, while airborne chemicals are detected by smell (olfactory) receptors in the lining of the nasal passages (*see also* pheromone). Both smell and taste organs are present in fish, worms and other lower animals have only a general sensitivity to chemicals over the body surface. Chemoreception is used by animals for locating and identifying other organisms, food sources, and scent marks and trails.

chemotherapy The treatment of disease by means of drugs. The term was originally coined by Paul Ehrlich, for the synthetic chemicals used to treat infectious diseases (e.g. salvarsan for syphilis), but it was later expanded to include antibiotics. Today chemotherapy commonly refers to the chemical treatment of cancer —by means of cytotoxic and other drugs, which inhibit the action of cancer cells—as distinct from treatment with X-rays (*see* radiotherapy).

Chequers (*or* Chequers Court) A country house in S England, in Buckinghamshire near Princes Risborough. Dating from 1565, it was given to the nation by Arthur Hamilton, 1st Viscount Lee of Fareham (1868–1947), and has been the official country residence of British prime ministers since 1921, when it was occupied by David Lloyd George.

Cherbourg 49 38N 1 37W A seaport in NW France, in the Manche department on the Cotentin Peninsula. Cherbourg has civil and military docks and large shipbuilding yards. In the heyday of ocean liners Cherbourg was an important transatlantic port; the cross-channel service to Southampton remains important. Population (1982 est): 30 112.

Cherenkov, Pavel Alekseievich (1904–) Soviet physicist, who discovered **Cherenkov radiation** in 1934. This radiation consists of blue-white light emitted by the atoms of a medium through which a high-energy charged particle is passing at a speed in excess of the speed of light in that medium. Three years later the effect was explained by James Franck (1882–1964) and Igor Tamm (1895–1971). The three physicists shared the 1958 Nobel Prize for their work.

Chernenko, Konstantin Ustinovich (1911–85) Soviet statesman; secretary of the Soviet Communist Party and president of the Soviet Union (1984–85). A protégé of Brezhnev, he made few reforms in his short period in office.

CHERNOBYL   *The scene of a terrifying nuclear accident (1986).*

Chernobyl 51 17N 30 15E A town in the SW Soviet Union, in the Ukrainian SSR. In 1986 the nuclear reactor here exploded, causing the deaths of 31 people at the time (a further 219 died later) and the release of a radioactive cloud. Mass evacuation of people living near the reactor followed and restrictions were placed upon food imports from E Europe: the reactor itself was subsequently entombed in concrete. The accident led to widespread reviews of the safety in the nuclear industry. *See* nuclear power.

chernozem (*or* black earth)   A type of soil that is characteristic of the grasslands of the continental interiors. There is a dark surface layer rich in alkaline humus, underlain by calcium carbonate concretions. Chernozems are agriculturally among the richest soils in the world.

Cherokee   A North American Indian people of the hill country of E Tennessee and North Carolina, speaking an Iroquoian language. They lived in farming towns of 30 to 60 log cabins.

cherry   A tree or shrub of the genus *Prunus*, of N temperate regions, having small rounded juicy fruits surrounding a hard stone containing a seed. Cherry trees produce clusters of white or pinkish flowers in spring, and some varieties are grown only for ornament. Cherries cultivated for their fruits are of two main types —sour and sweet. Sour cherries have been developed from *P. cerasus*, a widespread shrubby tree growing to 7 m. Morello—the best variety—has dark-red fruits used in jams and liqueurs. Sweet dessert cherries arose from the gean (*P. avium*), native to Eurasia and N Africa. Found in woods and hedges, it grows to 25 m. Fruits of cultivated forms vary from pale yellow to dark red. Hybrids between *P. cerasus* and *P. avium* are used for cooking.

cherubim and seraphim   Supernatural beings who are the two highest orders of angels in the celestial hierarchy. The seraphim are described by Isaiah (Isaiah 6.2–7) as six-winged attendants upon God's throne. The cherubim, who are traditionally depicted as winged heads, appear in the Bible as guardians of the divine presence; for instance, they bar the approaches to the Garden of Eden after the Fall (Genesis 3.24).

chervil   An annual herb, *Anthriscus cerefolium*, 30–50 cm high, grown for its leaves, used for salads and seasonings. Its white flowers grow in umbrella-like clusters. A native of central, E, and S Europe, it now grows on hedgebanks and waste ground throughout Europe, the Americas, N Africa, and New Zealand. Family: *Umbelliferae*.

Cherwell, Viscount   *See* Lindemann, Frederick Alexander, 1st Viscount Cherwell.

Chesapeake Bay   The largest inlet on the USA's Atlantic coast, bordering on Virginia and Maryland. Length: approximately 320 km (200 mi).

Cheshire   A county in NW England, bordering on Wales. It consists chiefly of the low-lying Cheshire Plain rising to the Pennines in the E. It is predominantly agricultural, dairy farming being especially important. In the local government reorganization in 1974 the northern industrial part of the Wirral Peninsula, including Birkenhead, became part of Merseyside and the areas in the NE, including Stockport, passed to Greater Manchester. Remaining industries include chemicals, based on the Cheshire salt fields, and textiles. Area: 2322 sq km (897 sq mi). Population (1988 est): 955 800. Administrative centre: Chester.

Cheshire, (Geoffrey) Leonard, Group Capt (1917–) British philanthropist. In the RAF during World War II, he won the Victoria Cross. His horror at the atomic bombing of Nagasaki led him to devote himself to the relief of suffering. He founded the Cheshire Foundation Homes for the incurably sick, of which

there are 222 in 44 countries. He married (1959) **Sue, Baroness Ryder** (1923–), who founded the Sue Ryder Foundation for the Sick and Disabled of All Age Groups. In 1989 he launched the World War Memorial Fund for Disaster Relief.

Chesil Beach (*or* Chesil Bank)   50 36N 2 32W A shingle spit in S England, on the Dorset coast, extending 14 km (9 mi) from Portland to Abbotsbury.

chess   A board game for two players, each of whom controls 16 pieces. The pieces are moved according to strict rules, the object of the game being to force the opponent's king into a position from which it cannot escape. A player attempts to weaken his opponent's position by capturing his pieces (other than the king). The game is immensely complicated and there is a vast literature devoted to its tactics and strategy. Chess pieces dating back to the 2nd century demonstrate the game's antiquity. Well known to 5th-century Hindus, it seems to have reached Europe, via Persia and Arabia, in the 10th century. The rules of the game have hardly changed since the 16th century, although the identities of some of the pieces have. Since 1922 the rules have been controlled by the Fédération internationale des Échecs (FIDE), which also organizes world championships.

Chester   53 12N 2 54W A city in NW England, the administrative centre of Cheshire on the River Dee. It was a Roman fortress (Deva) and a medieval walled city and port (the walls remain intact and there are many half-timbered buildings). The Rows are two-tiered arcades of shops with covered balustrades. Its cathedral dates from the 11th century. Chester is a commercial and railway centre, with clothing and metallurgical industries. Population (1988): 58 500.

Chesterfield   53 15N 1 25W A town in N central England, in Derbyshire. Its 14th-century parish church has a famous crooked spire. Chesterfield's industries include engineering, iron founding, chemicals, glass, and pottery. Population (1981): 70 546.

Chesterton, G(ilbert) K(eith) (1874–1936) British essayist, novelist, and poet. His detective stories featuring a Roman Catholic priest and beginning with *The Innocence of Father Brown* (1911) were highly successful. With Hilaire Belloc, who he met in 1900, he was an opponent of the socialism of G. B. Shaw and H. G. Wells. Chesterton was converted to Roman Catholicism in 1922, and thereafter most of his work was devoted to religious subjects, for example *St Francis of Assisi* (1923). He published more than 100 volumes, including the critical studies *Dickens* (1906) and *The Victorian Age in Literature* (1913) as well as the fictional works *The Napoleon of Notting Hill* (1904), *The Club of Queer Trades*, (1905), and *The Man Who Was Thursday* (1908).

chestnut   A tree, *Castanea sativa*, also called sweet or Spanish chestnut, bearing large brown edible nuts inside prickly burs. Native to Europe and N Africa and widely introduced, it grows to a height of 30 m. The leaves—10–25 cm long—are toothed and pointed and the flowers grow in yellow catkins, 10–12 cm long. The North American chestnut (*C. dentata*)—once one of the largest common trees of eastern areas—has been largely destroyed by the chestnut blight fungus. Family: *Fagaceae* (beech family). *Compare* horse chestnut.

Chevalier, Maurice (1888–1972) French singer and actor. Starting as an entertainer in Parisian revues, he went to Hollywood in the 1930s and starred in many successful musical films. These included *Love Me To-*

CHESS

castle (rook) bishop king knight castle (rook)

knight queen bishop

black pawns

white pawns

castle (rook) bishop king knight

knight queen bishop castle (rook)

The chessboard ready for play. A white square is always on the player's right. The queen always starts on a square of her own colour.

BLACK

	a	b	c	d	e	f	g	h	
8	QR1 / QR8	QN1 / QN8	QB1 / QB8	Q1 / Q8	K1 / K8	KB1 / KB8	KN1 / KN8	KR1 / KR8	8
7	QR2 / QR7	QN2 / QN7	QB2 / QB7	Q2 / Q7	K2 / K7	KB2 / KB7	KN2 / KN7	KR2 / KR7	7
6	QR3 / QR6	QN3 / QN6	QB3 / QB6	Q3 / Q6	K3 / K6	KB3 / KB6	KN3 / KN6	KR3 / KR6	6
5	QR4 / QR5	QN4 / QN5	QB4 / QB5	Q4 / Q5	K4 / K5	KB4 / KB5	KN4 / KN5	KR4 / KR5	5
4	QR5 / QR4	QN5 / QN4	QB5 / QB4	Q5 / Q4	K5 / K4	KB5 / KB4	KN5 / KN4	KR5 / KR4	4
3	QR6 / QR3	QN6 / QN3	QB6 / QB3	Q6 / Q3	K6 / K3	KB6 / KB3	KN6 / KN3	KR6 / KR3	3
2	QR7 / QR2	QN7 / QN2	QB7 / QB2	Q7 / Q2	K7 / K2	KB7 / KB2	KN7 / KN2	KR7 / KR2	2
1	QR8 / QR1	QN8 / QN1	QB8 / QB1	Q8 / Q1	K8 / K1	KB8 / KB1	KN8 / KN1	KR8 / KR1	1
	a	b	c	d	e	f	g	h	

WHITE

Chess notations. In the algebraic notation each square is referred to by a file letter a–h and a rank number 1–8. In the descriptive notation the files bear the names of the piece on the first rank. The ranks are counted 1–8 away from the player.

The king, weak and vulnerable, moves only one square at a time (in any direction). The name of the game is a corruption of the Persian word for king–shah.

The queen, the most powerful piece, moves any distance in any direction. Originally known as the counsellor, its present name and moves were adopted in the 15th century.

The castle or rook moves any distance vertically or horizontally. Originally represented as a chariot (Arabic: rukh), it is known in many languages as a castle or tower (French: tour).

The knight, the only piece to jump over other pieces, moves one square horizontally and two vertically or two horizontally and one vertically. Usually represented by a horse's head, it is sometimes known as the horse (as it was in the Arabic version).

The bishop moves in any direction diagonally. In the Hindu and Arabic games the piece was called an elephant. In the European games the piece has acquired a variety of identities: a bishop in English, a jester (fou) in French, a runner (Laufer) in German, but still an elephant (slon) in Russian.

The pawn moves forward one square (or two on its first move). In Arabic it was called a foot-soldier, the English word deriving from the Latin pes, pedis. In some European languages the piece is called a peasant (e.g. German: Bauer).

night (1932), *Love in the Afternoon* (1957), and *Gigi* (1958).

Cheviot Hills A range of hills in the UK. They extend along the border between Scotland and England, mainly in Northumberland, reaching 816 m (2677 ft) at The Cheviot.

chevrotain A small hoofed mammal of the family *Tragulidae*. Asiatic chevrotains (genus *Tragulus*; 3–6 species), also called mouse deer, of SE Asia, measure 20–33 cm at the shoulder and resemble small deer. Their brownish coats have white underparts; some species have white stripes or spots on the body. They are not true deer, lacking antlers and having a three-chambered stomach; males have enlarged upper canine teeth that form tusks. The African water chevrotain (*Hyemoschus aquaticus*) is very similar.

Cheyenne An Algonkian-speaking North American Indian people of the Plains region. They orginally lived in what is now Minnesota but intertribal wars forced the abandonment of their agriculturalist life in favour of the nomadic buffalo-hunting culture of the Plains. The northern branch was present at the battle of the Little Bighorn (1876).

Cheyenne 41 08N 104 50W A city in the USA, the capital and largest city of Wyoming. It is an agricultural trading centre. Population (1980): 40 207.

Chiang Ch'ing. *See* Jiang Qing.

Chiang Ching-kuo. *See* Chiang Kai-shek.

Chiang Kai-shek (*or* Jiang Jie Shi; 1887–1975) Nationalist Chinese soldier and statesman. He took part in the overthrow of the Qing dynasty in 1911 and in 1925 became leader of the Guomindang (Nationalist People's Party). Originally allied with the communists (*see* China), the Nationalists began fighting the communists in 1927; following Japan's defeat in World War II civil war again broke out. Chiang was forced to flee to Taiwan in 1949, where he established the Republic of China. His son Jiang Jing Guo (*or* Chiang Ching-kuo; 1910–88), prime minister (1971–78) and president (1978–88), studied in the Soviet Union and married a Russian. On returning to China in 1937, he joined the Guomindang, fleeing with his father to Taiwan in 1949.

chiaroscuro (Italian: light-dark) The overall pattern of light and shade in a picture. Controlled chiaroscuro was an important element of Renaissance composition, while strong contrasts of light and shade were a main feature of baroque painting. Chiaroscuro is displayed to supreme effect in etchings by Rembrandt and Whistler.

Chicago 41 50N 87 45N A city and major port in the USA, in Illinois on Lake Michigan. The third largest city in the country, its manufactures include iron and steel, textiles, and chemicals and there are large grain mills and meat-packing plants, although many of the stockyards are now closing as this industry moves further W. The first of its towering skyscrapers was built in 1887 and the Sears Tower (1974) is the world's tallest office building, 443 m (1454 ft) high. *History*: founded in 1803 near the site of Fort Dearborn, it became a city in 1837 and expanded rapidly with the construction of the railways. In 1871 it was almost completely destroyed by a disastrous fire, in which several hundred people were killed. Chicago was subsequently rebuilt in stone and steel. During the Prohibition years (1919–33), Chicago was notorious for its gangster activities, especially those of Al Capone. Population (1986): 3 009 530.

Chichén Itzá A Maya city in N Yucatán (Mexico) that was the political and religious centre of a wide area under Toltec influence from the late 10th to the 13th centuries. Remains include El Castillo (a pyramidal temple mound), an astronomical observatory, and a cenote (natural well), from which gold, jade, and other sacrificial objects have been recovered.

Chichester 50 50N 0 48W A market town in SW England, the administrative centre of West Sussex. Chichester has Roman remains, including its street plan. Its cathedral dates from the 11th century. Other notable buildings include a 16th-century octagonal market cross and the Festival Theatre (1962). Population (1981): 24 189.

CHICHÉN ITZA *El Castillo, the pyramidal temple mound.*

chickenpox A common very infectious virus disease. It is usually contracted in childhood and one attack normally gives an immunity that lasts for life. At the end of the incubation period (about a fortnight) the patient develops a fever and an irritating rash. Small raised spots appear on the chest and spread—in the next few days —over the body, face, and limbs. The spots become sore reddened blisters, which then dry and flake off, usually in less than a week. The patient is infectious until the last blister has flaked off. *See also* shingles.

chick pea An annual plant, *Cicer arietinum*, up to 40 cm high, with whitish flowers and edible pealike seeds. It is the chief pulse crop of India, where the cooked seeds are called dhal. Probably native to W Asia, it has long been cultivated in S Europe. Family: *Leguminosae*.

chicory A perennial herb, *Cichorium intybus*, 30–120 cm high, with bright-blue flowers. The dried ground roots yield chicory, a coffee additive, while the blanched leaves are used in salads. A native of Eurasia and N Africa, it is widely cultivated elsewhere. Family: *Compositae*. *See also* endive.

Ch'ien-lung. *See* Qian Long.

chiffchaff A woodland warbler, *Phylloscopus collybita*, about 10 cm long, with a grey-green plumage and whitish underparts. It occurs in Europe and W Asia during the summer and winters in S Europe and Africa. It resembles the willow warbler but can usually be distinguished by its "chiff-chaff" call.

chigger. *See* harvest mite.

Chihuahua A breed of dog originating from an ancient Mexican breed and developed in the USA. Its coat is variable in colour and either smooth and glossy or long and soft. Height: about 13 cm.

child abuse The physical or sexual abuse of children, usually by a relative (sometimes a parent). In the 1980s the extent of sexual abuse of minors in the UK caused great concern. Overreaction in 1987 in Cleveland by two doctors, who sent over 200 children into care on grounds of alleged abuse, was the subject of a public inquiry, which was highly critical of the doctors. Physical abuse is also a growing problem (*see* battered baby syndrome). Several charities have been set up to attempt to alleviate these problems.

Children's Crusade (1212) A bizarre episode of the Crusades, in which some 50 000 children set out from France and Germany to capture Jerusalem. None reached their destination, most being sold as slaves.

Chile, Republic of A country in South America, extending in a narrow strip along the W coast of the S half of the continent. There are many islands off the coast, some of which (including Easter Island) are well out into the Pacific Ocean. Chile also includes half of the island of Tierra del Fuego and has claims to part of Antarctica. The country is dominated by the Andes, which are separated from a lower coastal range by a central valley. The majority of the population is of mixed Spanish and Indian descent. *Economy*: based chiefly on the export of minerals, found principally in the N. Chile is one of the world's largest producers and exporters of copper, while the production of iron ore now exceeds that of nitrates. Coal is also mined in quantity and oil was found in the S in 1945. Production of natural gas is more than enough for domestic needs. The main crops are wheat, sugar beet, potatoes, and maize. Fruit and forest production is growing in importance and there are government attempts to promote the dairy industry. *History*: when Magellan, the first European to set eyes on what became Chile, sailed through (1520) the strait named after him, S Chile was occupied by Araucanian Indians. A Spanish colony was founded at Santiago in 1541 and Chile was attached to the viceroyalty of Peru. The revolt against Spain began in 1810, when a provisional republic was declared, but victory over the Spaniards was achieved only in 1817 with the military help of the Argentine liberator José de San Martin. In 1818 the Republic of Chile was established under Bernardo O'Higgins. President Salvador Allende was overthrown by Gen Pinochet in 1973. Pinochet was defeated in elections in 1988 and Patricio Aylwin won the presidential elections in 1989. Official language: Spanish. Official currency: Chilean peso of 100 centavos. Area: 741 767 sq km (286 397 sq mi). Population (1987): 12 416 000. Capital: Santiago. Main port: Valparaiso.

chilli A tropical American shrubby plant, *Capsicum frutescens*, also called red pepper, bearing elongated hot-tasting red fruits, 2–3 cm long. They are used in cooking and as an ingredient of curry powder and tabasco sauce. Family: *Solanaceae*.

Chiltern Hills A chalk escarpment in S central England. It extends NE from the Goring Gap in the Thames Valley, reaching 255 m (852 ft) at Coombe Hill.

Chiltern Hundreds Since the mid-18th century, if an MP wishes to resign (which he may not do directly), he applies for a stewardship of the Chiltern Hundreds, which disqualifies him from membership of the Commons.

chimaera (*or* chimera) An organism that is composed of cells of two genetically different types. Plants with variegated leaves are chimaeras resulting from a mutation in a cell in the growing region (apical meristem). Plant chimaeras can also be produced by grafting, being known as graft hybrids.

Chimborazo, Mount 1 29S 78 52W An extinct volcano in the Andes, the highest point in Ecuador. Height: 6267 m (20 681 ft).

Chimera A legendary Greek fire-breathing monster with a lion's head, a goat's body, and a serpent's tail. After ravaging Lycia she was killed by Bellerophon.

chimpanzee An ape, *Pan troglodytes*, of West African forests. Chimpanzees are 100–170 cm tall when standing erect and live in small groups, mostly on the ground, feeding chiefly on fruit and leaves but occasionally eating meat. They communicate by facial expressions and calls and possess considerable intelligence.

Ch'in. *See* Qin.

CHINA *Concerned with its population the government advertises the merits of the one-child family.*

China, People's Republic of A country in E Asia, covering vast areas of land ranging from the low-lying and densely populated plains of the NE to the high peaks of the Tibetan Plateau in the W. China proper falls into three natural regions, formed around the three main rivers: the Yellow River in the N, the Yangtze in the centre, and the Xi Jiang in the S. Over 90% of the inhabitants are Han Chinese. *Economy*: mainly dependent upon agriculture, which is now socialized through a system of communes, although there are still some very small private holdings. The emphasis is on foodcrops, rice in the S, wheat and millet in the N, as well as livestock, especially pigs. Cotton is grown in the N and tea in the S. Coal is extensively mined and is the major source of power. China has been self-sufficient in oil since 1973 and small amounts of natural gas are also produced. Iron ore is the most important mineral deposit and China is the main world producer of tungsten ore. Other minerals include antimony, lead, bauxite, and manganese. Exports include farm produce, textiles, and minerals. *History*: China is one of the world's oldest civilizations, with a history of organized society going back over nearly four millenniums. The first important recorded dynasty was the Shang in the valley of the Yellow River (18th–12th centuries BC). From the 12th to the 3rd centuries BC the Zhou spread S and E. Under the Qin, in the 3rd century BC, a unified empire came into being and the first Great Wall was built. The rule of the Han dynasty, from the 3rd century BC to the early 3rd century AD, saw spectacular advances in technology and manufacturing but its decline was followed by centuries of struggle between different parts of the empire. With the Tang dynasty (7th–10th centuries) China was once again reunited and reached the high point of its civilization. It was followed by the Song (10th–13th centuries), the Mongol (13th–14th centuries), the Ming (14th–17th centuries), and the Qing, which lasted until 1912. From the 16th century Europeans came to China and set up trading posts despite opposition from the Qing. British efforts to open up the country to free trade led to the Opium War in 1839 and to the opening of treaty ports (and also to the cession of Hong Kong). Later other trade concessions were made to several European countries and Chinese opposition to these moves included the Taiping Rebellion (1851–64) and the antiforeign Boxer Rebellion (1899–1900). In 1911 a revolution under the leadership of Sun Yat-sen ousted the Qing and a republic was set up. The 1920s saw the rise of the Guomindang (Nationalist People's Party) under Gen Chiang Kai-shek and the foundation of the Chinese Communist Party in 1921. In 1926 relations between them broke down and a struggle began that, in effect, continued until after World War II. In the 1930s threats from Japan culminated in open attack and the occupation of parts of the country, which lasted until the end of World War II. This put a temporary halt to internal party struggles, but in 1949 the Guomindang was defeated by the communists and a People's Republic was set up by Mao Tse-tung. Chiang Kai-shek retreated to Taiwan, where he set up the Republic of China. During the early years of the communist regime relations with the Soviet Union were close but they later deteriorated. In 1966 Mao Tse-tung launched the Great Proletarian Cultural Revolution, designed to eradicate "revisionism" and to prevent the rise of a ruling class. Both Mao Tse-tung and the prime minister, Chou En-lai, died in 1976 and were succeeded by the moderate Hua Guo Feng (1921–). Attempts by a "radical" faction (known as the Gang of Four and including Mao's widow Jiang Qing) to gain power were thwarted by the arrest of its members. During the 1970s Deng Xiao Ping (1904–) became the dominant force in government. Following a period of liberalization, the government authorized the massacre of thousands of protesting students in Peking in 1989 and a return to repressive policies. Since 1971 China has had a seat at the UN. President: Yang Shangkun. General Secretary: Jiang Zemin. Prime minister: Li Peng. Official language: Mandarin Chinese. Official currency: yuan of 10 chiao and 100 fen. Area: 9 597 000 sq km (3 704 440 sq mi). Population (1988): 1 072 200 000. Capital: Peking. Main port: Shanghai.

china clay A mineral deposit consisting mainly of kaolin, a hydrous aluminium silicate. Kaolin is produced by weathering or by hydrothermal processes acting on the feldspars in granite. It is used for making high-grade ceramic products and in many industrial processes.

chinchilla A rodent belonging to the genus *Chinchilla* (2 species), widely bred for its valuable long soft blue-grey fur. Measuring 30–50 cm long, wild chinchillas are found high in the Andes, living among rocks and feeding at night on vegetation.   South American captive

chinchillas are mostly short-tailed (*C. brevicaudata*) while in North America the long-tailed species (*C. laniger*) is bred. Family: *Chinchillidae*.

Chinchilla cat A breed of long-haired cat. Chinchillas have a compact body with short legs and a broad head with a snub nose and small tufted ears. The white fur is tipped with black on the back, flanks, head, ears, and tail, giving it a silvery lustre. The eyes are emerald or blue-green.

Chinchilla rabbit A breed of domesticated rabbit originating in France in the early 20th century. Although its thick bluish coat does not resemble that of the South American chinchilla, it has been bred for its pelts.

Chindits The 77th Indian Brigade, organized by Orde Wingate in 1943 in Burma as a "long-range penetration" infantry division. A guerrilla force, the Chindits were so called after the mythological Burmese temple guardian, the *chinthe*, and because they operated beyond the River Chindwin. Initially successful in severing Japanese lines of communication they were later in danger of being encircled and were forced to return to India in groups.

Chindwin, River A river in N Burma, flowing S to join the Irrawaddy River near Myingyan. Length: 1046 km (650 mi).

Chinese A language or group of languages of the Sino-Tibetan family spoken in E Asia. The many distinct forms or dialects of Chinese, which include Mandarin, Min, Kan, Hakka, Hsiang, Wu, and Cantonese (or Yüeh), are mutually unintelligible. In China there have been attempts recently to standardize the language, using Mandarin as a basis. Chinese is a tonal language, many words, otherwise identical, having quite distinct meanings according to intonation. Words are usually monosyllabic and do not change their form to indicate part of speech. The language is written in logographic characters or symbols of pictorial origin (*see* ideographic writing systems), which enables them to be understood by speakers of any Chinese dialect. There are as many as 40 000 of these of which 10 000 are in common use. Literacy requires knowledge of about 2000 of them. For transliteration purposes, Pinyin (phonetic spelling) is superseding the older Wade-Giles system, which does not attempt as close a phonetic description of the language. Pinyin is used in this book.

Chinese lantern plant A hardy ornamental, *Physalis alkekengi*, also called bladder cherry or winter cherry. A native of S and central Europe, it grows to a height of 20–60 cm. The edible fruit is enclosed in a reddish inflated calyx resembling a lantern. Family: *Solanaceae*.

Chinese water deer A very small deer, *Hydropotes inermis*, most common along the banks of the Yangtze River in China. Only 50 cm high at the shoulder, with a pale-brown coat and short tail, it has no antlers; the male's upper canine teeth are elongated into tusks.

Ch'ing. *See* Qing.

chinoiserie Decorative art and architecture that incorporated Chinese motifs into European fantasy designs and was popular in the late 17th and 18th centuries. The fashion was inspired by importation into Europe of Chinese porcelain, lacquer, etc., in the 17th century. Instances of chinoiserie in England include the willow pattern, combining Chinese elements into a new design; the interior of the Brighton Royal Pavilion is an architectural example.

Chinook A North American Indian people of the NW Pacific coast of the USA. The Chinook language forms part of a division of the Penutian language family. The Chinook were salmon fishers and traders, their location along the lower Columbia River being ideally suited for exchanging goods with peoples to the N and S and in the interior. Chinook Jargon, a combination of Chinook, Nootka, and other Indian languages mixed with English and French words, became the trading language of the entire W coast of America.

chipmunk A ground squirrel belonging to the genus *Tamias* (18 species), of North America and Asian forests. Chipmunks are 15–30 cm long and have a black and white striped back and strong feet and claws for digging. They live in burrows and, in the winter, do not hibernate but feed on a store of nuts and dried fruit carried under ground in their large cheek pouches.

CHIPPENDALE   *An ornate double chair.*

Chippendale, Thomas (1718–79) British cabinet-maker, famous for his elegant furniture designs, especially his chairs. His illustrated collection of rococo furniture designs, *The Gentleman and Cabinet Maker's Director* (1754), was the first comprehensive furniture catalogue and was widely influential in England and America, although his later neoclassical styles are considered the finest. His son, also **Thomas Chippendale** (died c. 1822), continued the business.

Chippewa. *See* Ojibwa.

Chiron In Greek legend, a centaur, son of Cronos and the sea nymph Philyra. Unlike his fellow centaurs, he was revered for his wisdom and knowledge of medicine. After being accidentally wounded by Heracles he bequeathed his immortality to Prometheus and was transformed into the constellation Sagittarius.

chiropractic A fringe medical specialty based on the assumption that most diseases originate from disorders of the nervous system, particularly as a result of compression of the nerve roots as they emerge from the spine. A chiropractor attempts to relieve symptoms by manipulating the spine with his hands.

Chiroptera. *See* bat.

Chittagong 22 20N 91 48E A city and major port in Bangladesh, on the Indian Ocean. The focal point of road, rail, and air routes, it is the second most important industrial centre in the country. Population (1986): 1 750 000.

chive A small hardy perennial plant, *Allium schoenoprasum*, native to Europe. It has small white elongated bulbs and produces clumps of thin tubular leaves and dense attractive spherical heads of bluish or lilac flowers on long stalks. The leaves are used for seasoning and garnishing foods. Family: *Liliaceae*.

chloramphenicol An antibiotic usually reserved for severe bacterial infections. It is particularly useful in the treatment of typhoid fever and some forms of pneumonia and meningitis. In rare cases chloramphenicol causes serious blood disorders.

chlordiazepoxide. *See* benzodiazepines.

chlorine (Cl) A greenish poisonous halogen gas, discovered in 1774 by C. W. Scheele. It is found in nature only in compounds, especially common salt (NaCl), sylvite (KCl), and carnallite ($KMgCl_3.6H_2O$). Chlorine is liberated by the electrolysis of brine. It irritates the respiratory system and was used as a poisonous gas in World War I. Chlorine gas is reactive and combines directly with most elements. Its oxidizing properties make it useful for disinfecting drinking water and swimming pools. It is used in the manufacture of many compounds. At no 17; at wt 35.453; mp −100.98°C; bp −34.6°C.

chlorofluorocarbons (CFCs). *See* fluorocarbons.

chloroform (*or* trichloromethane; $CHCl_3$) A colourless volatile liquid. It is made by reacting bleaching powder with acetone, acetaldehyde, or ethanol. Its main use is now in the manufacture of fluorocarbons but it is also used as a solvent and as an anaesthetic.

chlorophyll A green pigment present in organisms capable of photosynthesis. Higher plants possess chlorophylls *a* and *b*, located in chloroplasts; chlorophyll *c* is found in some primitive marine plants, and bacteriochlorophyll occurs in photosynthetic bacteria. The chlorophylls absorb red and blue light, trapping light energy for photosynthesis.

chloroplast A structure within a plant cell in which the process of photosynthesis takes place. It is bounded by a membrane and contains the green pigment chlorophyll. Chloroplasts vary greatly in shape and number within a cell. The greatest concentration occurs in the palisade mesophyll tissue of the leaves—the main photosynthesizing region.

chloroquine A drug used to prevent and treat malaria. It acts by preventing the digestion of haemoglobin (the red pigment of blood) by the malaria parasite. Chloroquine is also used in the treatment of rheumatoid arthritis and related diseases.

chocolate. *See* cocoa and chocolate.

cholera An acute infection of the intestine caused by the bacterium *Vibrio cholerae*, which is transmitted in drinking water contaminated by faeces of a patient. Epidemics of cholera occur in regions where sanitation is poor. After an incubation period of 1–5 days, cholera causes severe vomiting and diarrhoea, which—untreated—leads to dehydration that can be fatal. Treatment consists of replacement of fluid and salts by intravenous injections. Vaccinations against cholera provide only temporary immunity.

cholesterol A compound derived from steroids and found in many animal tissues. Cholesterol is manufactured by the liver and other tissues and its derivatives form constituents of cell membranes, bile, blood, and gallstones. High levels of cholesterol in the blood have been associated with an increased risk of heart disease, as a result of fatty deposits in the walls of arteries. *See also* atherosclerosis.

FRÉDÉRIC CHOPIN *Playing at a salon given by Prince Antoine Radziwill in 1829.*

Chomsky, Noam (1928–) US linguist, under whose influence the aims and methods of general linguistic theory and especially of grammar were radically revised. *Syntactic Structures* (1957) and *Aspects of the Theory of Syntax* (1965) develop the idea of transformations by which a sentence may be generated from an underlying "deep structure."

Chopin, Frédéric (François) (1810–49) Polish composer and pianist of French descent. He studied in Warsaw but later settled in Paris, where he lived with the novelist George Sand from 1838 to 1847. A fervent nationalist, much of his music was influenced by Polish folk music. He developed a highly characteristic style of writing for the piano, for which he composed 2 concertos, 3 sonatas, 24 preludes, and many waltzes, nocturnes, polonaises, and studies. He also wrote a cello sonata, a piano trio, and songs.

Chordata A phylum of animals that comprises the primitive protochordates and the vertebrates (*see* Vertebrata). They are distinguished from other animals by three features: a hollow dorsal nerve cord; a rodlike notochord that forms the basis of the internal skeleton; and paired gill slits in the wall of the pharynx behind the head, although in higher chordates these are apparent only in early embryonic stages.

chorea Involuntary jerky movements caused by disease of the brain. Huntington's chorea is a hereditary disease causing mental deterioration. Sydenham's chorea, formerly known as St Vitus's dance, is often associated with rheumatic fever in children. It can be treated with sedatives.

choreography The art of composing ballet and other theatrical dances. Choreography originally referred only to a dance notation, the lack of which has made precise reconstruction of many ballets difficult. The most comprehensive system for recording dance steps is that devised by the Hungarian dancer Rudolph Laban (1829–1958), known as Labanotation. The choreographer is usually a professional dancer, who selects, arranges into sequences, and teaches the dancers each step of the ballet.

Chota Nagpur. *See* Bihar.

Chou. *See* Zhou.

Chou En-lai (*or* Zhou En Lai; 1898–1976) Chinese communist statesman; prime minister (1949–76) and foreign minister (1949–58). Chou studied in Japan, France, and Germany. He led workers in the 1927 general strike in Shanghai, after which he escaped Guomindang (Nationalist) assassins and fled to Nanchang, where he helped to organize an uprising. In 1932 he became political commissar to the Red Army and during the Sino-Japanese War (1937–45) his reputation as a negotiator grew. After the establishment in 1949 of the People's Republic of China, he gained worldwide prominence as a diplomat and at home was largely responsible for establishing communist China's bureaucracy. Regarded as a moderate he exercised a stabilizing influence on his extremist colleagues.

chough A large black songbird, *Pyrrhocorax pyrrhocorax*, about 37 cm long, with red legs and a long red down-curved bill. It occurs in the Alps, Spain, and a few sea cliffs around Britain where it can be seen giving displays of aerial acrobatics. The yellow-billed Alpine chough (*P. graculus*) occurs at high altitudes in European mountains. Family: *Corvidae* (crows).

chow chow A breed of dog originating in China more than 200 years ago. The chow has a compact body and –unusually–a blue-black tongue. The thick coat forms a mane around the neck and shoulders and the tail is held well over the back. Height: 46–51 cm.

Chrétien de Troyes (12th century AD) French poet, author of the earliest romances dealing with the Arthurian legend. He was a native of Champagne and a member of the court of Marie, countess of Champagne, to whom his romance *Lancelot* was dedicated. Little else is known of his life. His romances include *Erec*, *Cligés*, *Yvain*, and *Perceval* (or *Conte del Graal*), in which the Holy Grail appears in a literary work for the first time.

Christadelphians A religious movement founded in Brooklyn, New York, in 1848 by John Thomas (1805–71), an English immigrant. The sect rejects much orthodox Christian teaching, including the Trinity, the existence of Christ prior to the Incarnation, and the immortality of the soul.

Christchurch 43 33S 172 40E A city in New Zealand, on E South Island. Founded in 1850, it has a gothic-style cathedral (completed in 1901) and many fine parks. Industries are primarily associated with the rich agriculture of the Canterbury Plains; these include meat processing, tanning, chemicals, and flour milling. Population (1987): 333 200.

Christian Aid A British organization founded in 1949 by the British Council of Churches to direct the use of donations made to assist the Third World. Christian Aid, which makes no distinctions as to race, religion, or politics, supports development programmes in agriculture, health, and education, giving relief aid in emergencies.

Christian Democrats Political parties having programmes based on Christian principles and generally of a conservative nature. In West Germany the **Christlich-Demokratische Union** (Christian Democratic Union; CDU), founded in 1945 held power, in alliance with the Christlich-Soziale Union (Christian Social Union; CSU), from 1948 to 1969 under Konrad Adenauer. The CDU/CSU alliance is now led by Theo Waigel. In Italy the **Democrazia Cristiana** (Christian Democratic

Party; DC), founded in 1943 as the successor to the Partito Popolare Italiano (Italian Popular Party), has dominated government since 1945. Other Christian Democratic parties are found in Austria, Belgium, France, Norway, and Spain.

Christianity The religious faith based on the teachings of Jesus Christ, which had its origin in Judaism. Its believers hold that Jesus is the Messiah prophesied in the Old Testament. It began as a movement within Judaism, and one of the first disputes among the early Christians was the right of the Gentiles to be admitted to the faith. Chiefly through the missionary activities of St Paul, the Apostle of the Gentiles, Christianity spread rapidly through the Roman Empire, despite persecutions under Nero and later emperors. Christian belief was at first taught by the Apostles by word of mouth; however, the need for a written record of Jesus' life and teaching was soon fulfilled by the Gospels. The definition of Christian belief and the authority of bishops and scriptures was well developed when Constantine became emperor (312). A series of general councils, the first held in 325 at Nicaea, defined orthodox Christian belief. Constantine's establishment of his new capital, Constantinople, led to a growing polarization between the Eastern Orthodox Church and the Western Roman Catholic Church. Despite the collapse of the Western Empire, Western Christianity, under the Bishop of Rome who claimed authority as St Peter's successor, spread vigorously. The Orthodox Church, not so rigorously centralized, became increasingly isolated, and with the development of doctrinal differences the two Churches drifted apart. The date of the formal separation is generally regarded as 1054. The Western Church by the end of the first millennium was rapidly gaining power, the papacy reaching the zenith of its influence in the 13th century under Pope Innocent III. In the later middle ages increasing nationalism and the assertion of power by temporal rulers weakened the united structure of the papacy and Holy Roman Empire. With the attack on central authority came a greater boldness in dissident criticism of the Church, such as that of John Wycliffe in England.

By the 16th century the Church no longer had the power to override national interests; in this weakened state it was unable to resist the inevitable fragmentation caused by the Reformation. Some reformers, such as the followers of Martin Luther and the English Church, were comparatively conservative, while the Calvinists, centred in Geneva, were considerably more radical. Coinciding with the exploration of the globe, the Reformation and the Roman Catholic response to it, the Counter-Reformation, in fact stimulated the spread of Christianity throughout the world, giving rise to the many different Christian denominations and communions of the modern world. The total number of Christians has been estimated at more than 944 million, or approximately 24% of the world population.

Christian Science A religious movement founded by Mary Baker Eddy. After being healed of various illnesses in 1862 by P. P. Quimby (d. 1866), a mesmerist, she formulated a set of principles of faith healing based on Christ's healing powers, which she claimed to have discovered and which she expounded in *Science and Health* (1875). The First Church of Christ, Scientist, opened in Boston, Massachusetts, in 1879. The movement spread to Europe with the establishment of 3500 branches by 1980. The principles of the movement are based on denial of the reality of the material world and healing through spiritual control.

AGATHA CHRISTIE

Christie, Dame Agatha (1890–1976) British author of detective fiction and playwright. She introduced her most famous character, the Belgian detective Hercule Poirot, in *The Mysterious Affair at Styles* (1920); he met his end in *Curtain* (1975). Later detective novels include *The Murder of Roger Ackroyd* (1926), *Murder on the Orient Express* (1934), and *Death on the Nile* (1937). In all, she wrote over 50 popular detective stories, creating other well-known fictional detectives, including Miss Jane Marple. Several stories have been filmed, and her play *The Mousetrap* has had an unparalleled long run in London since its opening in 1952.

Christmas The Feast of the Nativity of Christ. In the West it has been celebrated on 25 Dec since 336 AD, partly in order to replace the pagan sun worship on the same date. In the East, both the Nativity and Epiphany were originally celebrated on 6 Jan, but by the end of the 4th century 25 Dec was almost universally accepted, although the Armenian Church still celebrates Christmas on 6 Jan. Many of the popular customs associated with Christmas can be traced back to pagan origins.

Christmas Island An island in the Indian Ocean, SW of Java. It became a territory of the Commonwealth of Australia in 1958. The only commercial activity is phosphate mining. Area: 135 sq km (52 sq mi). Population (1986 est): 2000.

Christmas Island (*or* Kiritimati) A large coral atoll in the W central Pacific Ocean, in Kiribati in the Line Islands. British and US nuclear tests were held here between 1957 and 1962. It has coconut plantations. Area: 359 sq km (139 sq mi). Population (1985): 1737.

Christmas rose A perennial herbaceous plant, *Helleborus niger*, about 35 cm tall, native to central and S Europe and Asia Minor. Grown in gardens for its attractive white or pink winter-flowering blossoms, it prefers rich moist shady sites. The poisonous rhizomes are irritant to the skin when fresh. Dried, they have been used medicinally. Family: *Ranunculaceae*.

Christopher, St (3rd century AD) Christian martyr of Syria. According to legend, he carried a child across a river where he was working as a ferryman. The child grew heavier and he learned that it was in fact Christ and he was thus carrying the weight of the world. He is the patron saint of travellers. Feast day: 25 July.

chromium (Cr)   A hard grey transition metal, discovered in 1798 by Louis Nicolas Vauquelin (1763–1829). It occurs in nature principally as chromite ($FeCr_2O_4$), which is mined in the Soviet Union, Zimbabwe, and elsewhere. The metal is extracted by reducing the oxide (Cr_2O_3) with aluminium. The principal uses of chromium are in electroplating steel and in making alloys with iron. All chromium compounds are coloured and the most widely used, other than the oxide, are chromates (for example K_2CrO_4) and dichromates ($K_2Cr_2O_7$), which are used as oxidizing agents and in the dyeing industry. At no 24; at wt 51.996; mp 1857 ± 20°C; bp 2482°C.

chromosome   One of the threadlike structures that carry the genetic information (*see* gene) of living organisms and are found in the nuclei of their cells. Chromosomes consist of a central axis of DNA with associated RNA and proteins. Before cell division, the long filamentous threads contract and thicken and each chromosome can be seen as two identical threads (chromatids) joined at the centromere. The chromatids later separate to become the daughter chromosomes (*see* mitosis). Chromosome number is characteristic of a species. For example, a normal human body cell has 46 chromosomes comprising 22 matched pairs (called autosomes) and two sex chromosomes. A human sperm or egg cell has half this number of chromosomes (*see* meiosis). Abnormal numbers or parts of chromosomes often lead to abnormalities in the individual concerned. Down's syndrome (mongolism) in man is caused by the presence of an extra number 21 chromosome.

chromosphere   The layer of a star's atmosphere that lies between the photosphere and the corona. It is very much less dense than the photosphere. The sun's chromosphere is a few thousand kilometres thick; the temperature increases rapidly from about 4000°C near the photosphere to about 500 000°C at the base of the corona, with the atmosphere becoming increasingly rarified with height. The solar chromosphere cannot be seen without special equipment, except at a total solar eclipse.

chronicle plays   Plays that dramatize historical events in order to convey general moral lessons. The successors to the medieval morality plays, they were popular in England during the Elizabethan era. Examples are Marlowe's *Edward II* (first produced in 1592) and Shakespeare's *King John* (c. 1596). Many of the plots were taken from Holinshed's *Chronicles* (1578).

Chronicles, Books of   Two Old Testament books covering the history of Judah from the Creation to the end of the Babylonian exile (538 BC). They were probably written in the 4th century BC and originally formed a continuous history with the books of Ezra and Nehemiah. After opening with genealogies from Adam, they describe the reigns of David and Solomon and the succeeding Kings of Judah. Special emphasis is given to the building of the Temple at Jerusalem.

chrysalis   The pupa of most insects of the order Lepidoptera. *See also* butterflies and moths.

Chrysanthemum   A genus of herbaceous plants and shrubs (about 200 species) native to Eurasia, Africa, and North America. The wild ancestors of the horticultural chrysanthemums are not known, but probably more

than one species—almost certainly of Japanese and Chinese origin—was involved. The showy forms are widely and easily cultivated, having colourful single or double long-lasting flower heads. The different varieties may bloom at any time from early spring to autumn. Family: *Compositae*. *See also* pyrethrum.

chub   One of several freshwater fish related to carp, found in Europe and North America. The European chub (*Leucixus cephalus*) has a plump elongated body, usually 30–40 cm long, and is dark blue or green above and silvery below. Certain unrelated freshwater fish of the genus *Leucichthys* (order: *Salmoniformes*) are also called chub.

Churchill, Lord Randolph Henry Spencer   (1849–95) British Conservative politician; third son of the 7th Duke of Marlborough and the father of Sir Winston Churchill. He entered parliament in 1874 and led the group of Tory Democrats known as the Fourth Party. After serving as secretary for India (1885–86), he was briefly chancellor of the exchequer, when his budget was not accepted by the prime minister, Lord Salisbury, because Churchill wished to reduce funds allocated to the armed forces. He married (1874) Jeanette (Jennie) Jerome (1854–1921), an American.

SIR WINSTON CHURCHILL   *Touring Berlin during a visit in July 1945.*

Churchill, Sir Winston (Leonard Spencer) (1874–1965) British statesman and author. The son of Lord Randolph Churchill, he was a direct descendant of the 1st Duke of Marlborough. Churchill served in the army and as a war correspondent in the second Boer War before becoming a Conservative MP in 1900. In 1904 he joined the Liberals and subsequently served as president of the Board of Trade (1908–10), home secretary (1910–11), and first lord of the admiralty (1911–15). In 1915, during World War I, he rejoined the army and served in France. In 1917 he became minister of munitions, supporting the development of the tank. Churchill lost his parliamentary seat in 1922 but was re-elected as a constitutionalist in 1924, becoming chancellor of the exchequer in Baldwin's government. From 1929 he was out of office until the outbreak of World War II, when he became first lord of the admiralty and then, in 1940, prime minister of a coalition government. During World War II, his remarkable oratory and outstanding qualities as a leader made him a symbol of British resistance to tyranny throughout the free world. He was largely responsible for Britain's victorious alliance with the Soviet Union and the USA (1941) but came to view Soviet communism as a future threat, speaking later of an "iron curtain" drawn across Europe. Churchill's coalition government was defeated in 1945 but he returned as Conservative prime minister in 1951, serving until his resignation in 1955.

His writings include *The Second World War* (1948–54) and *A History of the English-Speaking Peoples* (1956–58); he won the 1953 Nobel Prize for Literature.

Churchill Falls A waterfall in E Canada in W Labrador on the Churchill River. Height: 75 m (245 ft); 316 m (1038 ft) including rapids.

Churchill River A river in W Canada, flowing from NW Saskatchewan E and NE through Manitoba to Hudson Bay. Length: 1610 km (1000 mi).

Church of England The established church in England, which embodies Protestant elements but also claims continuity with the English Church as established by St Augustine, the first Archbishop of Canterbury. Christianity was probably introduced in Britain during the Roman occupation in the 2nd century AD. Prior to the mission of St Augustine (597), the native Church was dominated by Celtic missionaries from Ireland and Scotland. Conflicts between the indigenous Celtic Church and Rome were resolved in favour of Roman usage at the Synod of Whitby (664), and thereafter the English Church remained under papal authority until the Reformation. Under Henry VIII, papal supremacy was rejected and the king was acknowledged Supreme Head of the Church, but there were otherwise no doctrinal changes. The two bases of Anglican doctrine and worship were formulated in the succeeding reigns: the Book of Common Prayer, introduced in the reign of Edward VI, and the Thirty-Nine Articles, published under Elizabeth I, whose excommunication (1570) by the pope completed the break with Rome. The Church was disestablished during the Commonwealth but re-established by Charles II. By the 19th century three parties had developed within the Church and these continue to the present: the Low Church or Evangelical group, which emphasizes the Protestant tradition; the High Church group (*see* Anglo-Catholicism); and a Liberal group stressing adaptation to modern ideas. The two provinces of the Church are the archbishoprics of Canterbury (*see* Canterbury, Archbishop of) and York (*see* York, Archbishop of), each of which is further divided into bishoprics. Ecclesiastical affairs are supervised by the General Synod (established 1970 to replace the Church Assembly), composed of bishops, clergy, and laity; its decisions are subject to parliamentary approval. In 1987 the Synod agreed in principle to the ordination of women and discussed union with the Catholic church. Church property and endowments are administered by the Church Commissioners for England (established 1948). *See also* Anglican Communion; holy orders; Lambeth Conferences; latitudinarianism.

Church of Scotland The Established Church in Scotland. The Scottish Church's secession from Rome was effected in 1560, largely under the influence of John Knox. The argument over Church government between Episcopalians and Presbyterians continued until the reign of William of Orange, who established the Presbyterian Church in 1690. During the 18th century, disputes arose between traditional Evangelicals and Moderates,

and this, together with the question of patronage, led to secessions. During the 19th and 20th centuries many of these divisions were healed, especially following abolition of patronage in 1874.

CIA. *See* Central Intelligence Agency.

cicada An insect belonging to the mainly tropical family *Cicadidae* (over 2000 species). Cicadas are 20–50 mm long and have large membranous wings. Males produce loud noises by vibrating two membranes at the base of the abdomen (stridulation). Cicadas usually inhabit trees and the females lay eggs in the wood. The nymphs drop to the ground and burrow to feed on plant juices from roots. After 1–17 years they emerge as adults. Order: *Hemiptera*.

cicely A perennial herbaceous plant, *Myrrhis odorata*, also called sweet cicely. 60–100 cm high, it has umbrella-like clusters of white flowers and a strong aromatic smell. Cicely is native to Europe and also occurs in Chile (where it was probably introduced). Formerly widely used as a vegetable, it is still used for seasoning. Family: *Umbelliferae*.

Cicero, Marcus Tullius (106–43 BC) Roman orator and statesman. Elected consul in 63 BC, his execution of the Catiline conspirators without trial lost him support and he was exiled in 58 BC for 18 months. During the civil war he supported Pompey against Caesar. After the assassination of Caesar in 44 BC he made a series of attacks on Antony, the *Philippics*, for which he was later arrested and killed. The greatest of Roman orators, he also wrote treatises on rhetoric and philosophical works influenced by Greek political theory.

cichlid A freshwater fish of the family *Cichlidae* (over 6000 species), found in tropical regions, especially Africa. Cichlids have a brightly coloured deep body, up to 30 cm long, and a single long dorsal fin; they feed on plants or animals. Many are popular aquarium fish. Order: *Perciformes*.

CID. *See* Criminal Investigation Department.

cider An alcoholic drink made from fermented apple juice. In England cider is made predominantly in the West Country, from apples grown specifically for cider making. Sweet cider has a large amount of unfermented sugar, dry cider little sugar, and rough cider is dry cider with some acetic acid.

Ciliata A class of microscopic single-celled animals (*see* Protozoa) having two nuclei and tracts of hairlike cilia over the cell surface, used for feeding and swimming. Most are free-swimming (e.g. Paramecium) but some are attached to the substrate by a stalk (*see* Stentor; Vorticella). Most ciliates feed on organic detritus, other protozoans, etc., but some are parasitic, especially on fish and other aquatic animals.

Cimon (died c. 450 BC) Athenian general and politician. He opposed Themistocles' policy of enmity towards the Spartans, believing Persia was the common Greek enemy, and in about 466 he scored a great victory against the Persians. His opponents, including Pericles, caused him to be ostracized (461) but after his return to Athens, Cimon negotiated a truce with Sparta (c. 450) and died fighting the Persians in Cyprus.

Cinchona A genus of trees (40 species) of the South American Andes, now cultivated elsewhere in the tropics, especially India. One of the most important species is calisaya (*C. calisaya*). The bark yields powerful medicinal drugs, including cinchonidine, quinine, and cinchona (useful for coughs and sore throats). Cultivation, which is generally by coppicing, has lost importance since the development of similar synthetic drugs lacking side-effects. Family: *Rubiaceae*.

Cincinnati 39 10N 84 30W A city in the USA, in SW Ohio on the Ohio River. Founded in 1788, it developed as a meat-packing centre in the 19th century. Today it is an important inland port and major manufacturing centre. Population (1986): 369 750.

CINEMA An early poster advertises the Lumière Cinématographe.

cinema The art form and industry of films. The first motion picture exhibited to a public audience was made in 1895 by the French brothers Louis and Auguste Lumière, whose equipment was developed from the inventions of Thomas Edison, and the first commercial success was the American film *The Great Train Robbery* (1903). Influential pioneers of the silent cinema in the USA were D. W. Griffith, Mack Sennett, and Charlie Chaplin. In Europe, technological developments were creatively exploited by such directors as F. W. Murnau (1889–1931) in Germany and Eisenstein in Russia. The end of the era of silent films was signalled by the success of Al Jolson's *The Jazz Singer* (1927), which had a synchronized musical score; colour film, introduced in the 1930s, added further popular appeal. Between 1930 and 1945 the cinema industry in the USA became essentially an entertainment factory, controlled by the giant Hollywood studios MGM and Paramount. The decline in cinema audiences from the late 1940s because of the rival attraction of television caused the break-up of the Hollywood system, and since World War II the most significant developments in the cinema have been achieved by directors elsewhere. Prominent British directors included Carol Reed, David Lean, Alfred Hitchcock, Richard Attenborough, and Ken Russell; directors elsewhere include Fellini, Antonioni, Bergman, Buñuel, Coppola, Kurosawa, Polanski, and Ray.

cineraria A herbaceous perennial pot plant developed from *Senecio cruentus* of the Canary Islands. There are numerous horticultural varieties, noted for their handsome, sometimes brilliantly coloured, daisy-like flowers. Family: *Compositae*.

Cinna, Lucius Cornelius (d. 84 BC) Roman politician. Expelled from Rome by his opponent Sulla (87), Cinna returned with Marius and captured Rome. He tried to restrain Marius' brutal revenge on their opponents and as consul (86–84) restored order. He was killed in a mutiny shortly before Sulla's return to Italy.

cinnabar (moth) A moth, *Callimorpha jacobaeae*, of Europe and Asia. Both the adults—scarlet and black—and the caterpillars—striped black and yellow—taste bad: their warning coloration discourages predators. The caterpillars feed on ragwort and have been used to control this weed. Superfamily: *Caradrinoidea* (noctuids, tiger moths, etc.).

cinnabar (ore) A mineral consisting of mercury sulphide, the chief ore of mercury. It is bright red and occurs in veins and impregnations associated with volcanic rocks. Spain, the Soviet Union, Italy, and Mexico are the main producers.

cinnamon An evergreen tree, *Cinnamomum zeylanicum*, 7–10 m high, native to Sri Lanka and cultivated widely in the tropics. It is coppiced, the bark of the twigs being peeled off and rolled up to form the spice. Family: *Lauraceae*.

Cinque Ports An association of five English ports (Sandwich, Dover, Hythe, New Romney, Hastings) in Kent and Sussex formed during the 11th century to defend the Channel coast. After the Norman conquest they were granted considerable privileges in return for providing the nucleus of the navy. Winchelsea and Rye were added to their number and many other towns in the southeast became associate members. The Lord Warden of the Cinque Ports survives as an honorary office.

Circe Legendary Greek sorceress, who had the power to transform men into beasts. Odysseus, who visited her island of Aeaea on his voyage from Troy, was protected by the herb moly, and forced her to restore his men to human form.

circle A curve defined as the locus of all the points lying in a plane at a certain distance, called the radius, from a fixed point, called the centre. Its diameter is any straight line joining two points on the circle and passing through the centre. The ratio of the distance around any circle (the circumference) to its diameter is equal to the number π (*see* pi). The area of a circle, radius r, is πr^2.

circulation of the blood The passage of blood through the heart and the network of arteries and veins associated with it. By supplying the tissues with blood, the circulatory system effects the transport of oxygen, nutrients, etc., and the removal of waste products. Oxygen-rich blood is pumped out of the heart into the aorta and then, via the arteries, to all the tissues of the body. Here oxygen is removed, and deoxygenated blood returns, through the veins, to the heart. This blood is then pumped to the lungs, where it is reoxygenated, and returned to the heart to repeat the circuit. The circulation of the blood was first discovered by William Harvey in 1628.

circumcision The removal of all or part of the foreskin. In many primitive societies circumcision usually forms part of a ceremony initiating youths into adulthood. Among some Islamic peoples it is performed just before marriage; Jewish babies are circumcised in a religious ceremony when they are eight days old. Its origin is unknown but it has hygienic advantages, especially in hot climates, and cancer of the penis occurs infrequently among circumcised men. It is also carried out for medical reasons in certain circumstances. Female circumcision (the removal of the clitoris) is also practised among some primitive peoples.

Cirencester 51 44N 1 59W A market town in SW England, in Gloucestershire. In Roman times it was the second largest town in Britain (Corinium) and it was an important wool centre in the middle ages. The Royal Agricultural College is situated here. Population (1981): 15 622.

cirque (*or* corrie) A rounded rock basin with steep sides, often containing a lake or cirque glacier. Common in glaciated mountain ranges, cirques form through freeze-thaw action on the headwall and basin floor together with abrasion by slipping ice and debris.

cirrhosis Destruction of the cells of the liver followed by their replacement with fibrous tissue, which eventually produces symptoms of liver failure (e.g. jaundice, swelling of the legs and abdomen, and vomiting of blood). Cirrhosis may be caused by alcoholism, hepatitis, obstruction of the bile duct, and heart failure, but often the cause is not known. Treatment is determined by the underlying condition.

cirrocumulus cloud (Cc) A high cloud with a mottled appearance composed of ice crystals; it is sometimes known as "mackerel sky."

cirrostratus cloud (Cs) A high thin veil of cloud composed of ice crystals, visible as a halo around the sun or moon.

cirrus cloud (Ci) A high detached cloud occurring in the troposphere above 6000 m (20 000 ft), composed of ice crystals and appearing wispy and fibrous. It is usually associated with fair weather.

CIRQUE *An example on the Isle of Skye, Hebrides.*

Cistercians An order of Roman Catholic monks founded by St Robert of Molesme (c. 1027–1111) as a stricter offshoot of the Benedictine order. The mother house at Cîteaux, France, from whence the order took its name, was founded in 1098. In the 17th century the order underwent a reform resulting in two groups: the monks of the Strict Observance, as opposed to the Common Observance, are known as Trappists.

Citizens' Advice Bureaux, National Association of (CAB) A British organization with some 900 branches throughout the UK that provides free and confidential advice to anyone on any subject. Their trained staff is equipped to advise on such matters as the social and health services, housing, and legal-aid schemes, as well as on personal matters.

citizens' band radio (CB) A short-distance two-way radio link, commonly installed in motor vehicles. These systems became popular in Britain in the 1970s although they were illegal; many CB clubs were formed and a special CB slang evolved. After a CB channel was authorized in 1981, interest in this activity declined.

citric acid An organic compound that occurs in plant and animal tissues and is involved in the series of metabolic reaction called the Krebs cycle. A commercial preparation of citric acid is used as a flavouring agent in foods.

citron A citrus tree, *Citrus medica*, 2–3 m high. Originally from the Far East, it was introduced into the Mediterranean region in about 300 BC; this remains the main centre of commercial cultivation. The rough yellowish sour fruits are used to make candied peel, produced by soaking in brine and preserving in sugar.

citronella A grass, *Cymbopogon nardus*, cultivated in tropical regions of Africa and Asia and introduced into tropical America. It forms dense tufts and contains geraniol or citronella oil, used in cosmetics and insect repellents.

Citrus The largest and most important genus of tropical and subtropical fruits (10 species), originating in SE Asia. All the species are small evergreen trees or shrubs with simple glossy leaves and five-petalled, usually white, flowers. The juicy fruits are rich in vitamin C, citric acid, and pectin (used in jam making). The most important are the orange, lemon, lime, grapefruit, citron, bergamot, and tangerine. Family: *Rutaceae*.

city states Independent municipalities, each comprising a town and its surrounding countryside, characteristic of ancient Greece. There were several hundreds of city states, of which Athens was the largest.

Ciudad Juárez 31 42N 106 29W A city in N Mexico, on the Rio Grande. Its importance is due to its location on the US border and as a marketing centre for cotton. Population (1980): 567 365.

civet A solitary nocturnal mammal belonging to the family *Viverridae*. The African civet (*Viverra civetta*) is cat-like, about 1.2 m long with coarse greyish spotted fur. Mainly carnivorous, civets also eat fruit and roots. The secretion of their anal glands is used in perfumes as a fixative, making other scents last longer. *See also* palm civet.

civil engineering The branch of engineering that deals with the design and construction of buildings and public structures, such as roads, railways, dams, canals, etc. The term was first used in 1750 by John Smeaton (1724–92) to distinguish himself from military engineers, although the practice went back to ancient times.

civil law The body of law governing the rights of private individuals and their relationships with each other rather than with the state. It is also called private law, as distinguished from public law and criminal law. The term is also used of the European legal systems derived from Roman law, which are different from common law systems in important respects. For example, in civil law court decisions have no legal force in the decision of similar cases. English-speaking countries generally use common law, although the law of Scotland is more closely related to civil law.

civil list In the UK, the sum given annually from the Consolidated Fund to the monarch and his or her consort and children (except the Prince of Wales, who receives the revenues of the Duchy of Cornwall) to meet their expenses. The list was introduced in 1689, became law in 1697, and in 1830 all government expenses were removed from it. Originally parliament voted at the monarch's accession a fixed sum to be paid annually but it may now be increased by Treasury order. **Civil list pensions**, charged to the Consolidated Fund but not forming part of the civil list, are awarded by the monarch on the advice of the prime minister to distinguished persons.

civil rights The individual's rights to liberty, equality of treatment, education, etc., under the law and safeguarded by the state. In countries with a written constitution, such as the USA, they form part of the constitution. In England there have been a number of unsuccessful attempts to codify these rights, which are still only protected by the general law. *See also* Bill of Rights; human rights.

ENGLISH CIVIL WAR *Charles I at the Battle of Naseby – a major defeat for the royalists.*

Civil War, English (1642–51) The war between Charles I and parliament, which led to the execution of the king (1649) and the establishment of Oliver Cromwell's Protectorate (1653). The Civil War was the outcome of a conflict between king and parliament that had steadily worsened during the reigns of James I (1603–25) and Charles. The struggle for power culminated in the events of the Long Parliament (summoned in 1640). War was precipitated by Charles' rejection of parliament's Nineteen Propositions in June, 1642, and on 22 Aug he raised his standard at Nottingham. The first battle, at Edgehill, ended indecisively but during 1643 the royalists (*or* Cavaliers) gained ground in the N and W. The parliamentarian (*see* Roundheads) negotiation of the Solemn League and Covenant with the Scots led to its victory at Marston Moor (1644); the formation of the New Model Army brought about the decisive defeat of Charles at Naseby (1645). In 1646 Charles surrendered to the Scots at Newark and the first Civil War was brought to an end. He was handed over to parliament in January, 1647, but was seized by the army in June. He escaped to the Isle of Wight and in December reopened negotiations with the Scots. The second Civil War ensued (1648), with royalist uprisings in Wales and Kent, ending with Cromwell's defeat of the Scots at Preston in

August. In the following year, Charles was tried and executed and the Commonwealth was established by the Rump Parliament. The Civil War was concluded by Cromwell's subjection of Ireland (1649–50), his defeat of Charles' heir (later Charles II) at Dunbar (1650), and his victory against the Scots at Worcester in 1651.

Civil War, US (1861–65) The conflict between the Federal government of the USA and the 11 Confederate States in the South. The war arose from the conflict of interest between the predominantly agricultural slave-owning South and the industrialized North. The election of a president, Abraham Lincoln, opposed to slavery precipitated the secession of the southern states under Jefferson Davis, and war broke out when the Confederates opened fire on Fort Sumter, South Carolina, which the Federal government had refused to evacuate. The opening campaigns in Virginia culminated in the Confederate victory at the first battle of Bull Run (July). Early in 1862 the Confederate Stonewall Jackson conducted a brilliant campaign in the Shenandoah Valley but on 4 May the Federal Army of the Potomac under George B. McClellan captured Yorktown and defeated Robert E. Lee's force in the Seven Days' battles (25 June–1 July). The Confederates retaliated in August by scoring a victory at the second battle of Bull Run and Lee pushed N into Maryland. Defeated at Antietam (Sept), the Confederates were then victorious at Fredericksburg (Dec). In Tennessee, meanwhile, the Confederate success at Shiloh (6–7 April) was followed by a reverse at Stones River (31 Dec–2 Jan). In 1863, following his victory at Chancellorsville, Virginia (1–5 May), Lee began his second invasion of the N, only to be defeated at Gettysburg (July). In the W, Federal troops under Ulysses S. Grant besieged Vicksburg, Mississippi, which fell on 4 July, and, after defeat at Chickamauga (19–20 Sept), won the victory of Chatanooga (23–25 Nov). In 1864 Grant, by now the Federal general in chief, advanced against Lee, whom he encountered inconclusively at Cold Harbor (June). Sherman, who held the Federal command in the W, took Atlanta (Sept) before making his historic March to the Sea. After capturing Savannah in September, Sherman moved N through the Carolinas and on 9 April, 1865, Lee surrendered at Appomatox Court House. By 2 June the Federal victory was complete.

Clair, René (René Chomette; 1898–1981) French film director. Both his early silent comedies and his pioneering sound films, such as *Sous les toits de Paris* (1930), were distinguished by his gifts for humour and fantasy. During World War II he worked in Hollywood, and his later films included *Les Belles de nuit* (1952).

clairvoyance. *See* extrasensory perception.

clam A bivalve mollusc with two equal shells and a muscular burrowing foot. Burrowing clams live buried in sand and mud, mainly in shallow coastal waters; they feed by taking in water through a tube (siphon) extended into the water. The largest burrowing clam is the geoduck (*Panopea generosa*), weighing up to 5 kg, while the giant clam (*Tridacna gigas*) can exceed 250 kg.

clan A group tracing actual or putative descent in either the male or female line from a common ancestor. Clans are frequently important divisions in primitive societies, as in the pre-18th-century Scottish Highlands. The Scottish clans, until their suppression following the Jacobite rebellions of 1715 and 1745, controlled distinctive territories and were frequently rivals. The members of a clan wore characteristic clothing (*see* Highland dress) and often bore the name of its founder preceded by Mac (son of), e.g. MacDonald. The clan chiefs are still officially recognized, both in Scotland and Ireland.

Clare (Irish name: Chláir) A county in the W Republic of Ireland, in Munster situated between Galway Bay and the Shannon estuary. It consists of a low-lying central plain rising E to mountains and W to the limestone area of the Burren. Agriculture is the chief occupation with cattle rearing and dairy farming. Area: 3188 sq km (1231 sq mi). Population (1986): 91 343. County town: Ennis.

Clare, John (1793–1864) British poet, the self-educated son of a farm labourer in Northamptonshire. His first book, *Poems Descriptive of Rural Life and Scenery* (1820), brought him fame and patronage in London. Three further volumes, including his best-known work, *The Shepherd's Calendar* (1827), were less successful, and he lived in great poverty. In 1837 he became insane and in 1841 was confined to a lunatic asylum in Northampton, where he wrote some of his best poems.

Clarendon, Edward Hyde, 1st Earl of (1609–74) English statesman and historian. He served as the king's chancellor of the exchequer during the English Civil war and went into exile in 1646, settling eventually with the future Charles II in France. At the Restoration (1660) he became Lord Chancellor and gave his name to the Clarendon Code of anti-Nonconformist legislation. His daughter Anne married the future James II. Criticized for the sale of Dunkirk to France (1662) and for his handling of the second Dutch War (1664–67), the Cabal brought about his fall. Forced again into exile, he completed his monumental *History of the Rebellion and Civil Wars in England* (1702–04).

Clare of Assisi, St (1194–1253) Italian nun, founder of the "Poor Clares." Influenced by the teaching of St Francis of Assisi, she gave up all her possessions and followed him. St Francis established a community of women with Clare as abbess in 1215. They lived in absolute poverty without even communal property. She was canonized in 1255. Because of an incident in which she saw mass celebrated at a distance, she was proclaimed patron saint of television in 1958. Feast day: 12 Aug.

clarinet A woodwind instrument with a single reed and a cylindrical bore. It is a transposing instrument existing in several sizes and generally has a fundamental of A or B flat; it has a range of three and a half octaves. The clarinet did not become a regular member of the orchestra until the late 18th century. The **bass clarinet** is pitched an octave lower than the B flat clarinet.

classicism The aesthetic qualities that were embodied in the visual arts and literature of ancient Greece and Rome and served as ideals for various later European artistic movements. Qualities associated with the concept include harmony and balance of form, clarity of expression, and emotional restraint. The Italian Renaissance of the 15th and 16th centuries was the first and most general attempt to revive these qualities in the arts. Its achievements in art and architecture provided standards the emulation of which was the goal of artists throughout Europe during the next two centuries. In literature, Renaissance interpretations of Aristotle's *Poetics* influenced writers throughout Europe in the 17th and 18th centuries, notably in the reigns of Louis XIV (1643–1715) in France and Anne (1702–14) in England. Towards the end of the 18th century there was a general reaction against rigid neoclassicist doctrines.

CLAVICHORD *An instrument made in 1630 by Johannes Ruckers of Antwerp.*

Classics In flat racing in England, five annual races (*see* Derby; Oaks; One Thousand Guineas; St Leger; Two Thousand Guineas) for three-year-old horses only.

Claudius I (10 BC–54 AD) Roman emperor (41–54). Claudius owed his accession to the chaos that followed the murder of his nephew Emperor Caligula. His rule was generally efficient: he extended the Empire, taking part in the invasion of Britain (43), but his susceptibility to the influence of freed men and of his third wife Valeria Messalina alienated the Senate. Agrippina the Younger, his niece and fourth wife, was suspected of his murder. Claudius had been taught by Livy and he himself wrote histories.

Clausewitz, Karl von (1780–1831) Prussian general and military theorist. In 1812 Clausewitz negotiated the Treaty of Tauroggen, which set in motion the joint Prussian, Russian, and British war effort against Napoleon. Of his many military works the posthumously published *Vom Kriege* is the most famous and had a profound influence up to World War I.

Clausius, Rudolf Julius Emanuel (1822–88) German physicist, who in 1854 formulated the concept of entropy and used it in a statement of the second law of thermodynamics. He also contributed to the development of the kinetic theory of gases and suggested that electrolysis involved the dissociation of molecules into charged particles.

claustrophobia. *See* phobia.

clavichord A keyboard instrument, popular from the 15th to the 18th centuries. Its delicate tone is produced by small brass plates fixed to the end of each key, which strike the strings. It is strung lengthways and has a range of about four octaves.

clavicle The collar bone. There are two clavicles, each running from the upper end of the breastbone to form a joint with the shoulder blade. They brace the shoulders and help to support the arms.

clay A sedimentary deposit that has plastic properties when wet and hardens and cracks when dry. It consists of fine rock particles (less than 0.004 mm in diameter), formed from the decomposition of other rocks. The principal minerals present in clays (the clay minerals) are hydrous silicates, mainly of aluminium and magnesium.

Clay, Cassius. *See* Ali, Muhammad.

clay-pigeon shooting. *See* shooting.

cleavage The repeated division of a fertilized egg cell (zygote) to produce a ball of cells that forms the blastula. In egg cells with little yolk, such as those of frogs and mammals, the entire cell divides: this is termed holoblastic cleavage. Meroblastic cleavage occurs in yolky egg cells, such as those of birds, when only the yolk-free region divides.

clef (French: key) The symbol placed at the beginning of a musical stave to indicate the pitch of the notes. The treble clef, a decorative G, indicates that the second line up of the stave is the G above middle C; the bass clef, an archaic F, indicates that the fourth line up is the F below middle C. The C clef can be set on any of the lines of the stave to establish it as middle C; the alto clef (used for viola music) has the C on the middle line; the tenor clef (used for cello music) has the C on the fourth line up.

cleft palate An abnormality caused by failure of the left and right halves of the palate to fuse during embryonic development. It leaves the nasal and oral cavities in continuity and it may be associated with a harelip. The cleft can be repaired surgically at 16 to 18 months of age.

Clematis A genus of herbaceous or woody plants (about 250 species), mainly climbing perennials, widely distributed in temperate regions. There are many horticultural varieties, grown for their showy flowers. Some species from which popular garden varieties have been developed are *C. alpina*, *C. montana*, and *C. patens* Family: *Ranunculaceae*.

Clemenceau, Georges (1841–1929) French statesman; prime minister (1906–09, 1917–20). A member of the chamber of deputies from 1876 to 1893, when he became known as the Tiger for his attacks on other politicians, he subsequently devoted much of his energies to polemical journalism. During the prewar years he urged military preparation against Germany and then attacked the World War I government for defeatism until becoming prime minister for the second time, when he led France to victory.

Cleopatra VII (69–30 BC) Queen of Egypt (51–48, 47–30), famous as the mistress of Julius Caesar and then of Mark Antony. Cleopatra was coruler with her brother Ptolemy XIII (61–48), who ousted her in 48. Restored by Caesar, she accompanied him to Rome and gave birth to (allegedly) his son Caesarion. After Caesar's murder, Cleopatra returned to Egypt and in 41 she met Antony. In 37 he abandoned his wife Octavia and lived with Cleopatra, who bore him three sons. In 31 Antony's brother-in-law Octavian defeated Antony and Cleopatra at Actium and in 30 they both committed suicide.

Cleopatra's Needles A pair of ancient Egyptian obelisks carved in the reign of Thutmose III (c. 1475 BC) at Heliopolis. They were moved by Augustus Caesar to Alexandria in 12 BC. They were moved again in 1878, one being set up on the Victoria Embankment, London, the other in Central Park, New York.

Cleveland 41 30N 81 41W A city in the USA, in Ohio on Lake Erie. It is a major Great Lakes port and the largest city in Ohio. One of the country's leading iron and steel centres, its other industries include oil refining, food processing, and the manufacture of motor vehicles. Population (1986): 535 830.

Cleveland A county in NE England, bordering on the North Sea. It was created in 1974 from parts of SE Durham and NE Yorkshire. It consists chiefly of lowlands rising to the Cleveland Hills in the S. The main river, the Tees, flows NE. Industry is important and includes chemicals, iron and steel, and engineering. Area: 583 sq km (255 sq mi). Population (1986 est): 557 600. Administrative centre: Middlesbrough.

CLEOPATRA'S NEEDLE *About to be erected on the Embankment in 1878.*

Cleveland, Stephen Grover (1837–1908) US statesman; Democratic president (1885–89, 1893–97). In his first term as president he tried to stamp out graft and excessive tariff protection. His second term was troubled by a financial crisis and labour strife.

Cleveland Bay A breed of horse developed in the Cleveland region of N Yorkshire, England (now a separate county), and always reddish brown (bay) with black mane, tail, and legs. Formerly a pack and coach horse, Clevelands are now used mainly for crossing with Thoroughbreds to produce showjumpers. Height: 1.57–1.68 m (15½–16½ hands).

click beetle A long narrow flat beetle, also called skipjack beetle, belonging to a large and worldwide family (*Elateridae*; 8000 species). If upturned it is able to right itself by springing into the air, making a clicking sound in the process. The larvae, known as wireworms, are serious pests of root crops. Species of the genus *Pyrophorus* are luminous, resembling firefly beetles.

climate The long-term weather conditions prevalent in an area. Climate is determined by three main factors. The first is latitude and the tilt of the earth's axis, which determines the amount of solar radiation received by an area. Second, the distribution of land and sea will affect climate as the land heats and cools far more rapidly than the sea. Ocean currents will also modify a region's climate (*see* Gulf Stream). The third factor is the altitude and topography of an area; temperature will fall with increased altitude and hills and mountain barriers force clouds to rise and produce rainfall.

clipper ship A fast sailing vessel developed in the 19th century for international commerce, so called because it clipped short the time required for a given passage. Clipper ships were designed more for speed than for their cargo capacity, which was relatively limited.

clitoris. *See* penis.

Clive of Plassey, Robert, Baron (1725–74) British soldier and colonial administrator, who established British supremacy in India. He joined the East India Com-

CLIPPER SHIP   *The* Cutty Sark *in full sail.*

pany in 1743 and made his name by capturing Arcot (1751). In 1757 he recaptured Calcutta from the Nawab of Bengal, whom he then defeated at Plassey. This assured the East India Company control of Bengal, of which Clive was virtual ruler until 1760, when he returned to England. He was appointed governor and commander in chief of Bengal in 1764, remaining in office until 1767. He was subsequently named in an inquiry into the East India Company's affairs, was vindicated (1773), but committed suicide shortly afterwards.

cloaca   The posterior chamber of the body in all vertebrate animals except the placental mammals, into which the digestive, urinary, and genital tracts open. Faeces, urine, and eggs or sperm are discharged through its vent.

clock   A device for measuring the passage of time. Clockwork has two essential components: an energy store (a raised weight or a coiled spring) and an escapement that regulates the release of energy from the store. The earliest recorded escapement was in a giant Chinese astronomical clock (c. 1090 AD). Early European clocks (called turret clocks from their usual position in church towers) were crude ironwork with verge escapements, driven by falling weights and recording time by striking on the hour, but the 14th-century Italian family of Dondi introduced dials on their sophisticated astronomical mechanisms. The innovation of mainsprings about 1500 enabled portable clocks (*see also* watch) to be made. Refinements in the 17th century were the anchor escapement (1671) and the application of pendulums to clockwork (*see* Huygens). An important advance in the 18th century was the development of an accurate marine chronometer, used by navigators to determine position. Scientific advances in the 20th century have led to the development of clocks regulated by the natural vibrations of atoms (*see* atomic clock).

clone   A population of organisms produced from a single parent cell by asexual division—for example by vegetative reproduction in plants or parthenogenesis in animals. The individuals of a clone are genetically identical. Some lower animals have been successfully cloned by inserting the nucleus of a somatic (body) cell of the animal to be cloned into an egg cell from which its own nucleus has been removed.

closed shop   A place of work in which all employees are required to be members of one or more specified trade unions. Closed shops are usually sanctioned by the employer, whose collective bargaining position may be made simpler if the union (or unions) can speak for the whole workforce.

clothes moth   A small tineid moth whose larvae feed on clothes, carpets, blankets, etc. There are a number of species of widespread distribution. Adults generally have a wingspan of 12–25 mm and are pale grey-brown in colour. They prefer dark places. Pesticides, dry cleaning, and man-made fibres have reduced their damaging effects.

Clotho.   *See* Fates.

cloud   A mass of minute water droplets or ice crystals, or a combination of both, produced by the condensation of water vapour in the atmosphere. When conditions are favourable the droplets grow and precipitation may occur. Various classifications of clouds exist but the one internationally agreed upon and most extensively used by meteorologists is based on cloud appearance and height and comprises ten principal forms. The high clouds, normally above 5000 m (16 000 ft) are cirrus (Ci), cirrostratus (Cs), and cirrocumulus (Cc). The medium clouds at 2000–5000 m (6500–16 000 ft) comprise altocumulus (Ac) and altostratus (As). Below this level the low clouds are stratus (St), stratocumulus (Sc), and nimbostratus (Ns). Some clouds grow vertically and cannot be classified solely by height; these are chiefly cumulus (Cu) and cumulonimbus.

cloud chamber   A device, invented by C. T. R. Wilson, used for studying the properties of ionizing particles. It contains a chamber containing a vapour that can be made supersaturated. When an ionizing particle passes through the chamber drops of liquid condense along its trail, thus making the trail visible.

clouded leopard   A large nocturnal forest cat, *Neofelis nebulosa*, of SE Asia, Borneo, Sumatra, and Java. It is 120–190 cm long including its tail (60–90 cm) and has a greyish or yellowish coat with black markings.

clove   An evergreen Indonesian tree, *Eugenia caryophyllata*, growing to a height of 12 m. The dried flower buds are used as spice. The whole tree is aromatic, clove oil being distilled from the buds, stalks, and leaves for use in medicine and as artificial vanilla. Family: *Myrtaceae*.

clover An annual or perennial plant of the genus *Trifolium* (about 290 species), which also includes the trefoils. Clovers, which occur mainly in N temperate regions, have leaves divided into three leaflets and dense heads of flowers. They are valuable as fódder plants and for their nitrogen-fixing ability. Alsike (*T. hybridum*), red clover (*T. pratense*), and crimson clover (*T. incarnatum*) are three widely grown and naturalized species. Family: *Leguminosae*.

clubmoss A perennial mosslike plant, also called ground pine, belonging to a genus (*Lycopodium*; about 200 species) of pteridophytes, found mainly in tropical and subtropical forests and mountainous regions. It has a creeping stem with wiry branches, densely covered with green, yellowish, or greyish needle-like leaves. The spore capsules occur at the base of special leaves (sporophylls), which are often arranged in conelike clusters (strobili). Family: *Lycopodiaceae*; class: *Lycopsida*.

Cluny 46 25N 4 39E A town in E France, in the Saône-et-Loire department. Its famous Benedictine abbey (founded 910 AD) became the centre of the Cluniac order, a reformed Benedictine order that was widely influential in Europe (c. 950–c. 1130). Population (1982 est): 4734.

cluster of galaxies A group of galaxies that are physically associated by mutual gravitational effects. Most galaxies are members of a cluster: our own Galaxy belongs to the Local Group. The densest clusters contain a thousand or more galaxies. Adjacent clusters are loosely grouped into **superclusters**.

clutch A device enabling two rotating shafts to be coupled and uncoupled. Positive clutches have square or spiral jaws to transmit torque without slipping. They can be used where slow speeds and light loads are involved, but normally both shafts have to be at rest for engagement. Friction clutches provide a period of slipping while the shafts are being engaged, and they do not have to be stopped for engagement. The torque is transmitted by friction between attachments to each shaft: in a plate clutch the attachments are flat discs, which press against each other; in a hydraulic clutch they are radial vanes immersed in a fluid.

Clutha River A river in New Zealand, the longest river in South Island. It flows generally S from Lake Wanaka, in the Southern Alps, to enter the Pacific Ocean near Kaitangata. Length: 340 km (210 mi).

Clwyd A county of NE Wales, bordering on the Irish Sea and the Dee estuary. It was created under local government reorganization in 1974 from Flintshire, most of Denbighshire, and E Merionethshire. It is mainly hilly with fertile valleys. Tourism is important. Area: 2425 sq km (936 sq mi). Population (1986 est): 399 600. Administrative centre: Mold.

Clyde, River A river in W Scotland. Rising in SE Strathclyde Region, it flows NW through Glasgow and Clydebank to enter the Atlantic Ocean at the Firth of Clyde. Length: 170 km (106 mi).

Clydebank 55 54N 4 24W A town in W central Scotland, in Strathclyde Region on the River Clyde. Shipbuilding was formerly the most important industrial activity. Population (1987 est): 30 060.

Clydesdale A breed of draught horse developed in the Clydesdale region of Scotland in the 18th century. It

has a compact body with strong legs and feet and may be bay, brown, black, or chestnut. Height: about 1.75 m (17 hands).

Clytemnestra In Greek legend, the daughter of Tyndareus, King of Sparta, and Leda, and wife of Agamemnon. She and her lover Aegisthus killed Agamemnon after the Trojan War and she herself was killed by her son Orestes.

CND *See* Campaign for Nuclear Disarmament.

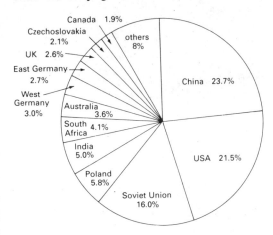

COAL *World production of coal (1988).*

coal A carbonaceous mineral deposit used as a fuel and raw material for the chemical industry. Coal results from the compaction and heating of partially decomposed fossil vegetable matter. During the coalification process the plant remains are changed progressively from a peatlike material into lignite (brown coal), sub-bituminous and bituminous coal, semianthracite, and anthracite. During this process the percentage of carbon present increases and the moisture and volatile content decreases; anthracite is about 90% carbon. These coals are known as the humic coals. The sapropelic coals (cannel coal and boghead coal) are derived from finely divided vegetable matter (algae, spores, and fungal material). Most coal was formed in the Carboniferous period, although some of the younger coals, for example lignite, date from Mesozoic and Tertiary times.

Coal has been mined in Britain since Roman times but on a small scale until the industrial revolution. In about 1800 coal was being carbonized on a commercial scale for the first time, the resulting coal gas being used for gas lighting and the coke for smelting iron ore. By the middle of the 19th century, interest in the by-products (coal tar, ammonia, and pitch) was awakening. The chemistry of the constituents of coal tar developed into the study of organic chemistry, and the use of aromatic compounds from coal tar led to the development of the dyestuffs and explosives industries. In the 20th century these products also became the foundation of the plastics industry. During the 1920s and 1930s processes were also developed (mainly in Germany) for converting coal into oil –providing Germany with valuable quantities of oil during World War II. Subsequently, natural gas has largely replaced coal gas and petrochemicals (*see* oil) have to a considerable extent replaced coal tar as sources of organic raw materials.

coal gas A gas consisting mainly of hydrogen (50%) and methane (30%), with some carbon monoxide (8%) and other gases. It is made by destructive distillation of coal, a process that involves heating it to 1000°C. Coal gas was formerly supplied to homes for heating and cooking, but it has now been largely replaced, in the UK, by natural gas from the North Sea.

Coal Measures. *See* Carboniferous period.

coastguard A paranaval force formed by some countries during the 19th century to hinder smuggling. In Britain it now deals principally with lifesaving and maritime safety through a network of coast-watching stations and provides a meteorological service.

Coast Mountains A mountain range of W Canada, extending from the US border 1600 km (1000 mi) N into Alaska. Very rugged, it rises steeply from the Pacific coast. It includes Canada's largest mountain mass and a long glacier belt. Mount Waddington at 3978 m (13 260 ft) is the highest point.

cobalt (Co) A transition metal similar to iron and noted for its deep-blue colour when reacted in ceramics. It was discovered by G. Brandt (1694–1768) in 1735 and occurs naturally as cobaltite (CoAsS) and in copper, nickel, iron, silver, and lead ores. Cobalt is mined chiefly in Zaïre and Canada. It is used as an alloy in the manufacture of cutting steels and magnets. The isotope ^{60}Co is a strong gamma-emitter produced in nuclear reactors and used in radiotherapy (the **cobalt bomb**) and in industry. At no 27; at wt 58.9332; mp 1495°C; bp 2870°C.

Cobbett, William (1763–1835) British journalist, who championed the cause of the underprivileged. After army service in Canada he accused his officers of corruption and was forced to flee Britain (1792), returning in 1800. He was imprisoned (1810–12) for attacking the flogging of militiamen and in 1817 was again forced to flee to the USA. Returning to Britain in 1819, he began in 1821 the country tours described in his *Rural Rides* (1830).

Coblenz. *See* Koblenz.

cob nut. *See* hazel.

Cobol (*common business oriented language*) A computer-programming language used mainly for business applications.

cobra A highly venomous snake occurring in warm regions of Africa and Asia and able to expand its neck ribs to form a hood. The king cobra (*Ophiophagus hannah*) of S Asia is over 3.6 m long, making it the largest venomous snake; it preys chiefly on other snakes. The common Indian cobra (*Naja naja*), used by snake charmers, is 1.7 m long and frequently enters houses at night in search of rats. Family: *Elapidae* (cobras, mambas, coral snakes).

coca A Peruvian tree, *Erythroxylon coca*, cultivated in Java, South America, and Sri Lanka for its leaves, which —when dried—yield cocaine. Coca leaves have been chewed for centuries in South America for their effect in relieving fatigue and hunger; prolonged use can cause addiction and mental and physical damage. Family: *Erythroxylaceae*.

cocaine An alkaloid ($C_{17}H_{21}O_4N$) derived from coca leaves and also made synthetically. The first drug to be used as a local anaesthetic, it has largely been replaced by safer drugs for this purpose (e.g. procaine) although it is still used in pain-killing mixtures for treating people with terminal illnesses (e.g. cancer). Cocaine is an addictive stimulant: it is taken for the euphoria produced by its action on the brain. *See also* anaesthesia.

COBRA   *Indian cobra and snake charmer.*

cochineal A natural red dye obtained from the dried bodies of certain female scale insects, especially *Dactylopius coccus* of Mexico. It has now been largely replaced by synthetic dyes, but continues to be used for colouring foodstuffs and cosmetics.

cochlea. *See* ear.

cockatiel A small Australian cockatoo, *Nymphicus hollandicus*, of interior grasslands. It is 32 cm long and has a grey plumage with white wing patches, a yellow head and crest, and reddish ear patches.

cockatoo A parrot belonging to a genus (*Cacatua*; 17 species) ranging throughout Australia, Malaysia, and the Philippines. Cockatoos are usually white, often with a pink or yellow blush, although some species are black; all have a long erectile crest and a large hooked bill used to crack open nuts and extract grubs from wood.

cockchafer A European beetle, *Melolontha melolontha*, also called maybug, that is very destructive to plants (*see* chafer). Up to 35 mm long, it is black with reddish-brown legs and wing cases and has a loud buzzing flight. The larvae—which cause the most damage, particularly to cereals and grasses—are also called white grubs or rookworms.

Cockcroft, Sir John Douglas (1897–1967) British physicist, who shared the 1951 Nobel Prize with Ernest Walton for their development of the first particle accelerator in 1932, was used for accelerating protons to split an atomic nucleus (of lithium) for the first time. In World War II he worked on the atom bomb and in 1946 became director of the Atomic Energy Research Establishment at Harwell.

Cockerell, Sir Christopher Sydney (1910–) British engineer and inventor of the hovercraft. After working on radar in World War II, he concentrated upon hydrodynamics. He filed his first patent for an air-cushion vehicle in 1955. The first practical hovercraft, the SR.N1, was launched in 1959.

cocker spaniel A breed of gundog, thought to be of Spanish origin. It is compact with short legs, a short tail, and a square muzzle. The long flat silky coat is usually black, red, or cream, either plain or in mottled combinations. Height: 39–41 cm (dogs); 38 cm (bitches).

cockfighting A blood sport in which two or more gamecocks fight against each other, often to the death. Illegal in Britain since 1849, it is still widespread in certain parts of the world. The cocks are equipped with steel or bone spurs on their legs and set against each other in a cockpit.

cockle A bivalve mollusc of the family *Cardiidae* (about 250 species). The ribbed shell valves, 1–23 cm in diameter, are rounded, producing a relatively globular bivalve. Cockles burrow in sand or mud, straining food particles from water drawn in through their protruding siphons. The European cockle (*Cardium* (or *Cerastoderma*) *edule*) is edible.

cockroach A nocturnal insect belonging to the mainly tropical family *Blattidae* (3500 species). It has a black or brown flat body, 12–50 mm long, with long antennae and leathery forewings. Cockroaches seldom fly; they feed on plant and animal materials and can be household pests. A widely distributed species is the common cockroach, or black beetle (*Blatta orientalis*). Order: *Dictyoptera*.

cocoa and chocolate Foods derived from the seeds of the cacao tree (*Theobroma cacao*), native to tropical America and cultivated mainly in West Africa. The tree is pruned and woody pods, 23–30 cm long, grow directly from its trunk. The pods contain seeds (cocoa, or cacao, beans) embedded in a whitish pulp, which are scraped out, fermented, and dried before export. Manufacturing is carried out mainly in the importing countries, where the beans are shelled, roasted, and ground. From them cocoa powder and chocolate are made. Cocoa butter, a fat retained in chocolate but removed from cocoa powder, is a rich source of food energy. Family: *Sterculiaceae*.

coconut The fruit of the coconut palm, *Cocos nucifera*; one of the most important tropical crops. The tree has a slender trunk, up to 25 m high, which bears a crown of giant feather-like leaves. The coconuts take a year to ripen and have a thick fibrous husk surrounding a single-seeded nut. The hollow core contains coconut milk; the white kernel is eaten raw or dried to yield copra, from which coconut oil is extracted for use in soaps, synthetic rubbers, and edible oils. The residual coconut cake is used as a livestock feed and the coarse husk fibre (coir) is used for matting, etc.

Cocos Islands (*or* Keeling Islands) Two Australian coral atolls in the E Indian Ocean. They were visited by Charles Darwin (1836). First settled in 1826, they were under Australian administration from 1955 and became part of Northern Territory in 1984. Copra is produced and there is an important meteorological station. Area: 13 sq km (5 sq mi). Population (1986): 616.

Cocteau, Jean (1889–1963) Versatile French poet and artist. He made his name with the novel *Les Enfants terribles* (1929) and sketches written for Diaghilev's ballet company, such as *Parade* (1917). In World War I he served as an ambulance driver and became acquainted with Picasso, Modigliani, and other leading painters and writers. His creative work includes poetry (*L'Ange Heurtebise*, 1925), plays (*Orphée*, 1926), novels, films (*Le Sang d'un poète*, 1929; and his own *Les Enfants terribles*, 1950), and graphic work in various media.

cod A carnivorous fish, *Gadus morhua*, that lives near the bottom in temperate N Atlantic waters and is commercially fished for food and liver oil. Its elongated body, up to 1.8 m long, is generally dark grey with spots and has three dorsal fins, two anal fins, and a whisker-like barbel on its lower jaw. *G. macrocephalus* is a similar N Pacific species. Family: *Gadidae* (haddock, ling, pollack, whiting, etc.); order: *Gadiformes*.

codeine An analgesic drug used to relieve mild pain. It is a derivative of morphine but less toxic and less likely to become addictive. The combination of aspirin and codeine is a stronger pain killer than either of the two drugs used separately. Codeine combined with a chalky substance, such as kaolin, is an effective treatment for diarrhoea. It depresses the cough centre of the brain and is therefore often added to cough mixtures.

Code Napoléon The systematic collection of the civil law of France. Drafted by a commission set up by Napoleon I when he was first consul, the code—properly called the *Code Civil*—was brought into force in 1804. It and the other codes subsequently produced under Napoleon's administration remain the basis of present French law and served as a model for civil law codes elsewhere.

Cody, William F(rederick) (1846–1917) US showman, known as Buffalo Bill. An army scout and Pony Express rider, he gained his nickname from his success in supplying the men working on the Union (later Kansas) Pacific Railway with buffalo—killing 4280 in eight months (1867–68). In 1883 he began touring the USA and Europe with his Wild West Show.

SEBASTIAN COE *Winning the Olympic 1500 metres (1980).*

Coe, Sebastian (1956–) British middle-distance runner. A gold medallist in the 1500 m race at the 1980 and 1984 Olympics, he held world records at distances of 800 m, 1000 m, and the mile.

coelacanth A bony fish of the suborder *Coelacanthini*. Once thought to have been extinct for 60 million years, several living representatives have been found since the discovery, in 1938, of *Latimeria chalumnae* off the coast of SE Africa. It has a heavy body, up to 1.5 m long, with a short head and limblike fins, and crawls on the bottom, feeding on other fish. Order: *Crossopterygii*.

coelenterate An aquatic invertebrate animal of the phylum *Coelenterata* (or *Cnidaria*; about 9000 species), including Hydra, jellyfish, sea anemones, corals, etc. There are two different generations of the life cycle (*see* polyp; medusa) and either or both may occur. The body cavity has a single opening (mouth) and stinging cells (nematocysts) are used for defence or catching prey.

coeliac disease A disease in which the small intestine is abnormally sensitive to gliadin (a component of the protein gluten, found in wheat). It results in abnormalities in the cells of the intestine, which cannot digest or absorb food. The symptoms include diarrhoea, stunted growth, and general malaise, the condition is treated by a gluten-free diet.

coelom The body cavity of many animals. In mammals (including man) the embryonic coelom is divided into three cavities, which become occupied by the lung, heart, and intestines. In the fully developed mammal the coelom is reduced to the virtually nonexistent spaces between the membranes lining the heart (the pericardium), the lungs (the pleura), and the intestines (the peritoneum).

coenzyme A nonprotein substance that forms a complex with certain enzymes and is essential for the proper functioning of these enzymes. Coenzymes include nucleotide derivatives (e.g. ATP and NAD), coenzyme A (important in the Krebs cycle), and vitamins of the B complex.

coffee The seeds (called beans) of certain tropical evergreen trees of the genus *Coffea*, which yield a stimulating drink. *C. arabica* is the most widely grown coffee tree, producing the best quality beans. *C. canephora* is more disease resistant, longer living, and can be grown at lower altitudes. *C. liberica*, of still lower quality, is grown in Malaysia and Guyana. The coffee beans are usually fermented, then sun dried before export. The main coffee-producing areas are South and Central America, Jamaica, East Africa, and Mysore in India. Family: *Rubiaceae*.

Cognac 45 42N 0 19W A town in W France, in the Charente department. Under French law, the name Cognac may only be applied to brandy produced in a certain area around the town. Population (1982 est): 20 995.

coherent radiation Electromagnetic radiation in which different waves have a constant phase difference. Light from most sources is not coherent because it is emitted in random bursts. *See also* laser.

coke A fuel consisting mainly of carbon. It is made by heating coal in the absence of air and is produced as a by-product of coal gas. Coke is used in blast furnaces and other industrial processes as well as for domestic heating.

cola. *See* kola.

Colchester 51 54N 0 54E A market town in SE England, in Essex on the River Colne. Founded by Cymbeline (Cunobelinus) in about 10 AD, Colchester was an important Roman town (Camulodunum), the Roman walls remain in part and there is a Norman castle. Essex University (1961) is nearby. Colchester's industries include engineering and printing. Population (1981 est): 81 945.

colchicine. *See* autumn crocus.

Cold Harbor, Battles of Two battles in the US Civil War fought near Richmond, Virginia, the Confederate capital. In the first (27 June, 1862) the Confederate general, Robert E. Lee defeated the Federal forces under George B. McClellan (1826–85), both sides suffering heavy losses. In the second (3–12 June, 1864), the Federal advance on Richmond under Ulysses S. Grant was temporarily halted when he encountered Lee's entrenched forces.

Colditz 51 08N 12 49E A town in East Germany, on the River Mulde. It is famous for its castle, built by Augustus II on a cliff above the town, which was used as a top-security prisoner-of-war camp during World War II. Many escapes were attempted, some of which were successful.

Coldstream 55 39N 2 15W A town in SE Scotland, on the English border. The Coldstream Guards were formed here in 1660. Like Gretna Green, it was a refuge for eloping couples. Population (1984): 1677.

Cold War The hostility between the USA and the Soviet Union, and their respective allies, following World War II. The term was first used in 1947 by the US politician Bernard Baruch (1870–1965). Fear of nuclear war prevented a military confrontation, and the Cold War was fought on economic, political, and ideological fronts. At its most virulent in the 1950s, it had given way by the 1970s to the movement towards detente.

Coleoptera. *See* beetle.

SAMUEL TAYLOR COLERIDGE *Detail from a portrait painted in 1795 by P. Vandyke.*

Coleridge, Samuel Taylor (1772–1834) British poet and critic. In 1795 he met William Wordsworth and their joint publication of *Lyrical Ballads* (first edition 1798) marked a decisive break with 18th-century poetry. His finest poems, such as *Kubla Khan* (1797) and *The Rime of the Ancient Mariner* (1797–98), were written at this time, but his personal life was troubled by his marriage, his poverty, and his increasing opium addiction. His subsequent creative energies were committed to journalism, lectures, and the writing of the critical and metaphysical *Biographia Literaria* (1817).

Coleridge-Taylor, Samuel (1875–1912) British composer, the son of a doctor from Sierra Leone and a British mother. Educated at the Royal College of Music, he is best known for the trilogy *Song of Hiawatha* (for solo voices, chorus, and orchestra; 1898–1900).

Colet, John (c. 1466–1519) English theologian and humanist. After his ordination, he lectured at Oxford, collaborating with Thomas More and Erasmus, prior to his appointment as dean of St Paul's Cathedral. He founded St Paul's School in 1509. He was a fierce opponent of Church corruption and published numerous theological works.

Coleus A genus of herbaceous or shrubby plants (150 species) originating in the Old World tropics. Many cultivated varieties of the species *C. blumei* are grown for their variegated leaves of a diversity of colours. Family: *Labiatae.*

colitis Inflammation of the large intestine (the colon), causing abdominal pain and diarrhoea (sometimes with the passage of blood). Colitis can be caused by bacterial infection (e.g. dysentery) or by Crohn's disease. In ulcerative colitis the colon becomes ulcerated. The latter condition, which fluctuates in severity, is treated with corticosteroids or sulphásalazine (a sulphonamide drug). Surgery may be required for severe cases.

collagen A structural protein that is the main component of the white fibres of connective tissue. Inelastic but with great tensile strength, it is found in tendons and ligaments and also in skin, bone, and cartilage.

collar bone. *See* clavicle.

collective farms Agricultural cooperatives found especially in communist countries. Collectivization was first instituted in the Soviet Union by Stalin. The farms and equipment belong to the state, which decides what is to be grown and in what quantities, but farmworkers, who live in surrounding villages, pay rent for their homes and are permitted to have their own garden plots and livestock; profits are shared in collective farms while in state farms workers receive wages. Collectivization was introduced into China in 1955. There, communes correspond to the Soviet collective farms, which are also found in Israel (*see* kibbutz).

collective unconscious In Jungian psychology, a body of images and ideas that are inherited and shared by all humans, rather than acquired by the individual. These ideas are called archetypes and Jung believed them to be detected in the myths, dreams, and mental disturbances of mankind.

College of Arms (*or* Heralds' College) An English heraldic society, comprising three kings of arms, six heralds, and four pursuivants of arms. Its origins lie in the royal officers of arms, who received a charter from Richard III in 1484. The College was reincorporated in 1555. Its functions include the settling of rights to bear arms, which the kings may grant by letters patent.

collie A breed of dog originating in Scotland and widely used as a sheepdog. It has a streamlined body and a pointed muzzle. The rough-coated collie has a long dense coat and bushy tail; the smooth-coated variety has a shorter smooth coat and the bearded collie has a long coat with a shaggy beard. Collies are grey, fawn, or sandy, with or without white markings. Height: 56–61 cm (dogs); 51–56 cm (bitches).

Collingwood, Cuthbert, 1st Baron (1750–1810) British admiral. He joined the navy at the age of 11 and fought outstandingly at the battles of the Glorious First of June (1794) and Cape St Vincent (1797) during the Revolutionary and Napoleonic Wars. After Nelson's death at Trafalgar (1805) he succeeded to his command and was eventually buried alongside him in St Paul's Cathedral.

colloid A system in which a disperse phase is present in a dispersion medium in the form of particles 10^{-9} to 10^{-6} m in length, rather than as single molecules or ions. If the disperse phase is solid and the dispersion medium is liquid the colloid is known as a **sol** (examples include

milk and glue). If both are liquid the colloid is known as an **emulsion** (e.g. mayonnaise). A colloidal suspension in which the particles of the disperse phase link together, with the dispersion medium circulating through the meshwork, is called a **gel** (e.g. a photographic emulsion). *See also* aerosol.

Colloids contain charged particles. In lyophilic (solvent-loving) colloids, stability is achieved by attraction between the particles and the molecules of the dispersion medium. Lyophobic (solvent-hating) colloids usually consist of large inorganic particles (e.g. clays, metals, etc.). They maintain stability by repulsion between similarly charged aggregates. They often precipitate on the addition of a salt.

Cologne (German name: Köln) 50 56N 06 57E A city in W West Germany on the River Rhine. It is the site of a university (1388) and the largest gothic cathedral in N Europe (founded 1248). The cathedral and the old gothic town hall were among the buildings reconstructed after World War II. *History*: founded by the Romans, it became the capital of the northern empire in 258 AD and later the seat of Frankish kings. In 1798 it was annexed by France, passing to Prussia in 1815. Population (1980 est): 976 800.

Colombia, Republic of A country in NW South America, on the Pacific Ocean and the Caribbean Sea. The majority of the population is of mixed Spanish and Indian descent. *Economy*: the chief product is coffee, which accounts for over half the total exports. There is also widespread trafficking in and processing of cocaine. The country is rich in mineral resources; gold, silver, copper, lead, and mercury are mined and Colombia is one of the world's richest sources of platinum and emeralds. There are also large reserves of oil, coal, and natural gas. *History*: inhabited by Indians before the Spanish colonization of the 16th century. In 1819 Simón Bolívar secured the independence of Greater Colombia, which included what are now Panama, Venezuela, and Ecuador as well as Colombia. This lasted until 1830 when Venezuela and Ecuador broke away; Panama became independent in 1903. Official language: Spanish. Official religion: Roman Catholic. Official currency: Colombian peso of 100 centavos. Area: 1 138 914 sq km (456 535 sq mi). Population (1981 est): 27 800 000. Capital: Bogotá. Main port: Barranquilla.

Colombo 6 55N 79 52E The capital and main port of Sri Lanka, on the W coast at the mouth of the River Kelani. Colombo has one of the largest artificial harbours in the world. Population (1981): 585 776.

Colombo Plan An agreement, signed in Colombo (Ceylon) in 1951, designed to foster economic development in the countries of S and SE Asia. It now has 27 members—21 countries within the region and Australia, Canada, Japan, New Zealand, the UK, and the USA.

colon. *See* intestine.

colophony. *See* rosin.

Colorado One of the Mountain States in the W central USA. Most of the population lives and works in a transition zone, the Colorado Piedmont, between the Rocky Mountains in the W and the Great Plains of the E. Manufacturing is the most important sector of the economy, especially the production of machinery, chemicals, military equipment, and food products. Colorado also produces molybdenum, coal, and oil. Tourism, especially winter sports, is of growing importance. *History*: explored by the Spanish, part of Colorado was acquired by the USA in the Louisiana Purchase (1803) and part from Mexico in 1848. Following the discovery of gold (1859), it became a territory in 1861 and a state in 1876. Area: 269 998 sq km (104 247 sq mi). Population (1986 est): 3 267 118. Capital: Denver.

Colorado potato beetle A brown and yellow striped leaf beetle, *Leptinotarsa decemlineata*, about 10 mm long. Both the adults and larvae eat potato leaves: the larvae also attack the tubers. It is native to W North America but has spread eastwards, throughout Europe, to become a serious pest of potato crops everywhere.

Colorado River A river in the W USA, rising in the Rocky Mountains and flowing SW through Colorado, Utah, and Arizona (where it passes through the Grand Canyon) to the Gulf of California in Mexico. It is extensively used for irrigation and as a source of hydroelectric power. Length: 2320 km (1440 mi).

COLOSSEUM *It could be flooded to enable mock naval battles to be staged.*

Colosseum An amphitheatre in Rome. One of the most impressive of all Roman remains, the Colosseum was begun (c. 70 AD) by the emperor Vespasian. It is an elliptical building, four storeys high, 188 m (617 ft) long, and 156 m (512 ft) wide. It could seat 47 000 people and was used mainly for gladiatorial and wild-beast fights.

Colossians, Epistle of Paul to the A New Testament book written by the Apostle Paul about 60 AD to the church in Colossae in W Asia Minor. Its theme is that the Christian faith is sufficient and that speculative philosophy diverts attention from this truth.

Colossus of Rhodes A gigantic statue of the sun god Helios by the harbour of Rhodes. Cast in bronze by Chares of Lindos about 280 BC and standing about 31 m (100 ft) tall, it was counted among the Seven Wonders of the World. An earthquake destroyed it 50 years after its completion.

colour The sensation produced when light of different wavelengths falls on the human eye. Although it is actually continuous, the visible spectrum is usually split into seven major colours: red, orange, yellow, green, blue, indigo, and violet, in order of decreasing wavelength (from about 6.5×10^{-7} m for red light to 4.2×10^{-7} m for violet). A mixture of all these colours in equal proportions gives white light; other colours are produced by varying the proportions or omitting com-

ponents. Coloured pigments, dyes, and filters selectively absorb certain wavelengths, transmitting or reflecting the rest. Thus a red book illuminated by white light absorbs all the components of white light except red, which is reflected. This is a subtractive process, since the final colour is that remaining after absorption of the others. Combining coloured lights, on the other hand, is an additive process. A mixture of the whole spectrum gives white light, as will a mixture of lights of three primary colours.

colour blindness The inability to distinguish certain colours. There are various forms, the most common of which is red-green colour blindness (the inability to distinguish red and green). Colour blindness is usually an inherited and incurable condition. Because it is a recessive trait carried on the X chromosome it is far more common in men than women (about 8% of males of Caucasian origin are colour blind). Very occasionally colour blindness may be due to disease of the retina.

colour television. *See* television.

Colt revolver A revolver with a five-shot cylinder rotated and locked in line with the single barrel by cocking the weapon. Invented by the US engineer Samuel Colt (1814–62) in 1835, it became the .45 calibre Frontier Peacemaker (1873) and the standard .45 US army and navy revolver, remaining in service until 1945.

colugo An arboreal mammal belonging to the genus *Cyanocephalus* and order *Dermoptera* (2 species), also called flying lemur, found in Asia, Borneo, and the Philippines. About 60 cm long, colugos have a membrane of skin, extending from the chin via the fore and hind limbs to the tail, with which they can glide up to 70 m. Colugos feed on leaves and fruit.

Columba, St (c. 521–597 AD) Irish missionary and abbot. Ordained in 551, he founded churches and monasteries in Ireland before setting up a monastery on Iona. From here, Scotland was evangelized. Feast day: 9 June.

Columbia 34 00N 81 00W A city in the USA, the capital of South Carolina. An important commercial centre, its industries include textiles, plastics, and machinery. Fort Jackson (a major US Army post) is adjacent to the city. Population (1986): 93 020.

Columbia River A river in North America, flowing SW from British Columbia, through Washington State, to the Pacific Ocean at Oregon. It is an important source of hydroelectric power and forms the only deepwater harbour N of San Francisco. Length: 1930 km (1200 mi).

columbine. *See* Aquilegia.

columbium. *See* niobium.

Columbus 39 59N 83 03W A city in the USA, the capital of Ohio on the Scioto River. A major industrial and commercial centre of a rich agricultural area, its manufactures include aircraft, machinery, and footwear. Population (1980): 564 871.

Columbus, Christopher (1451–1506) Italian navigator, who discovered America. He was born in Genoa, became a pirate, and in 1476 was shipwrecked off the coast of Portugal, where he settled. He conceived the idea of reaching the East by sailing westwards but his plan was rejected by the Portuguese king (John the Perfect) and Columbus approached (1486) the Spanish monarchs Ferdinand and Isabella. He eventually won their patronage and on 3 August, 1492, set sail in the *Santa Maria*, accompanied by the *Pinta* and the *Niña*. On 12 Oct he landed on either Watling Island (now San

CHRISTOPHER COLUMBUS *Landing in the Americas; from a 15th-century book.*

Salvador Island) or Samana Cay (both in the Bahamas) and in Nov visited Hispaniola. On his second voyage (1493–96) he discovered Guadeloupe, Puerto Rico, and Jamaica. His third voyage (1498–1500) achieved the discovery of Trinidad and the mainland of South America but ended in disaster: in 1499, following a revolt against his command, a Spanish governor was dispatched to relieve Columbus, who was sent back in chains to Spain. On his arrival, however, he was released and compensated and shortly afterwards set off on his last voyage (1502–04). From this he returned ill and disheartened, dying not long afterwards in Valladolid.

column. *See* orders of architecture.

Comanche A North American Indian people of the southern Plains. They speak a language of the Uto-Aztecan group, closely related to Shoshone. They moved to this area from Wyoming in the 18th century. Horse breeders and fierce warriors, they often attacked white settlers in Texas until they agreed to settle in Oklahoma in 1867.

combustion A chemical reaction in which a substance combines with oxygen, producing heat and light. The oxidation reactions in combustion are generally chain reactions involving free radicals, the principal overall reactions being the oxidation of carbon to carbon dioxide and the oxidation of hydrogen to water $(C + 2H_2 + 2O_2 \rightarrow CO_2 + 2H_2O)$.

COMECON. *See* Council for Mutual Economic Assistance.

Comédie-Française The French national theatre, founded in 1680 and reconstituted in 1803 by Napoleon. It is organized as a cooperative society, owned by its members. Despite its strong emphasis on tradition, it has produced many of France's most original actors.

comet A small body that moves, usually in a very elongated orbit, around the sun. A typical comet consists of a small nucleus of ice and dust surrounded by an immense tenuous luminous cloud of gas and dust, the coma. Tails of gas and of dust only appear when a comet is near the sun; they point away from the sun and may be millions of kilometres long. **Short-period comets** (such as Halley's comet) have orbital periods of less than 150 years. The remainder have much longer periods, some exceeding 10 000 years, and move in approximately par-

abolic orbits. A comet eventually decays to produce a stream of meteoroids around its orbit.

comfrey A perennial herbaceous plant, *Symphytum officinale*, also called boneset. Up to 100 cm high, it has drooping creamy or purplish flowers. Native to Europe and temperate Asia and formerly used medicinally, it is now grown as a garden flower, as are the related plants *S. grandiflorum* (yellow flowers) and *S. peregrinum* (blue and pink flowers). Family: *Boraginaceae*.

Comintern. *See* International.

commedia dell'arte An Italian form of popular theatre that flourished throughout Europe from the 16th to the 18th centuries. It was performed by professional actors whose comic and often vulgar improvisations were based on a set of stock situations, usually concerning romantic intrigues, and stereotyped characters. These included the clown Harlequin, the cuckold Pantaloon, and the lover Inamorato.

commensalism A relationship between two individuals of different species in which one (the commensal) lives in, on, or with the other (the host), from which it derives food, shelter, support, or transport. The association neither harms nor benefits the host. An example is provided by certain barnacles, which live attached to whales. *See also* symbiosis.

commercial banks Institutions that offer a deposit, transfer, and loan service to companies and private individuals. In the UK, the commercial banks (or high-street banks) are public limited companies (joint-stock banks), which emerged from World War I as the big five: Barclays Bank, Lloyds Bank, Midland Bank, National Provincial Bank, and Westminster Bank (in 1968 the last two merged to form the National Westminster Bank). Others include the Royal Bank of Scotland and the Trustee Savings Bank.

COMMEDIA DELL'ARTE *Comic actors satirizing human folly.*

Common Agricultural Policy (CAP) The agricultural policy adopted by members of the EC. The aims of the policy are to ensure reasonable living standards for farmers and to secure regular supplies and reasonable prices for consumers. CAP involves the distribution of grants and a price-support system. Target prices are agreed and if market prices fall below these targets the EC engages in support buying to keep the price up to an intervention price level. The system is criticized because it tends to produce embarrassing surpluses (the butter, beef, and wine "mountains") and because there is in principle no limit to the support that may be given. The imposition of production quotas on milk and other items in the 1980s caused widespread protests.

common law The part of the law of England and of most English-speaking countries that was originally unwritten and based on the common customs of the country. Its growth was the result of the principle of judicial precedent, by which an earlier judgment or decision was binding in deciding a similar case. Such decisions can only be overruled by statute or by a higher court. It is not the result of legislation and is therefore distinguished from the statute law established by Acts of Parliament. It is also distinguished from equity, administered by the Court of Chancery, and from the civil law of most European countries.

Common Market. *See* European Community.

Common Prayer, Book of The official liturgy of the Church of England. After the Reformation, Thomas Cranmer and others began to formulate an order of worship in English. The first Prayer Book was published under Edward VI in 1549; criticism led to a more Protestant revision in 1552. The Roman Catholic Queen Mary abolished the Prayer Book, and from the accession of Elizabeth I to the end of the Civil War, it was reinstated, further revised, and again abolished, this time by the Puritans. The version of 1662, established by the Act of Uniformity, is still in use; a revised version was authorized in 1928. The 1980 *Alternative Service Book*, in modern English, is preferred by the Church of England.

Commons, House of. *See* parliament.

Commonwealth (1649–53) The period in English history between the execution of Charles I and the Protectorate; the term is sometimes used synonymously with Interregnum to refer to the entire period between the execution of Charles I and the Restoration in 1660.

Commonwealth (British) A loose association of 49 independent nations once subject to the imperial government of the UK (*see* Empire, British). The Commonwealth of Nations was established by the Statute of Westminster (1931), which was based on the principles, enunciated at the 1926 Imperial Conference, of member states' autonomy, equality, and common allegiance to the Crown; its name was modified to the Commonwealth after World War II. Its member states are Antigua and Barbuda, Australia, the Bahamas, Bangladesh, Barbados, Belize, Botswana, Brunei, Canada, Cyprus, Dominica, The Gambia, Ghana, Grenada, Guyana, India, Jamaica, Kenya, Kiribati, Lesotho, Malawi, Malaysia, Malta, Mauritius, New Zealand, Nigeria, Pakistan, Papua New Guinea, St Kitts-Nevis, St Lucia, Seychelles, Sierra Leone, Singapore, Solomon Islands, Sri Lanka, Swaziland, Tanzania, Tonga, Trinidad and Tobago, Uganda, the UK, Vanuatu, Western Samoa, Zambia, and Zimbabwe; Nauru, Tuvalu, Maldives, and St Vincent and the Grenadines are special members and are not represented at the meetings of Commonwealth heads of government; there are in addition a number of associated states and dependent territories. Commonwealth heads of government meet every two years.

communications satellite An unmanned artificial satellite by which long-distance television broadcasting, telephone communications, and computer data links are achieved. High-frequency radio signals are sent from one transmitting station to the satellite, where they are amplified and retransmitted to one or more receiving stations.

The first active satellite was the US Telstar 1, launched in 1962. Telstar and other early satellites were in relatively low elliptical orbits and were only visible for a short portion of their orbit. A communications satellite is now usually placed in a geostationary orbit. This is a circular orbit lying about 36 000 km above the earth's equator. The satellite completes such an orbit in the same time (24 hours) as the earth rotates on its axis and thus to a ground-based radio station appears to remain nearly stationary in the sky. Three or more satellites, suitably placed around the equatorial orbit, can provide worldwide communications links.

Various organizations, serving commercial, private, or government interests, have been set up to provide worldwide communications; notably **Intelsat** (International Telecommunications Satellite Organization), which was founded in 1964 and now has over 100 member countries.

communism A movement based on the principle of communal ownership of all property. More specifically, it is associated with *The Communist Manifesto* (1848) of Marx and Engels according to which the capitalist profit-based system of private ownership is replaced by a communist society in which the means of production are communally owned. This process, initiated by the revolutionary overthrow of the bourgeoisie (*see* Marxism), passes through a transitional period marked by the dictatorship of the proletariat (*see* Leninism) and the preparatory stage of socialism.

In the second half of the 19th century Marxist theories motivated several social democratic parties in Europe, although their policies later developed along the lines of reforming capitalism (hence the epithet "reformist") rather than overthrowing it. The exception was the Russian Social Democratic Labour Party, which finally demolished the Tsar's regime in the Revolution of November, 1917. In 1918 this party changed its name to the Communist Party of the Soviet Union, thus establishing the distinction between communism and socialism. After the success of the Russian Revolution many socialist parties in other countries became communist parties, owing allegiance of varying degrees to the Soviet Communist Party (*see* International). In 1944–46 communist regimes were set up with the aid of the Soviet army in several E European countries, including Poland, Hungary, and Czechoslovakia, these repressive regimes finally fell in 1989 in a wave of mass unrest. In 1949 the communists in China, again with Soviet support, overthrew the Nationalists and inaugurated the People's Republic of China. The Soviet Communist Party voted to end its exclusive right to power in 1990. Since the early 1970s the term **Eurocommunism** has been used to refer to the policies of communist parties in W Europe. Such parties are electorally significant in France and Italy. The Communist Party of Great Britain (founded in 1920) claims some 7500 members.

Communism Peak (Russian name: Pik Kommunizma) 38 59N 72 01E The highest mountain in the Soviet Union, in the Pamirs in the S near the Afghan and Chinese borders. Height: 7495 m (24 589 ft).

community In ecology, an interdependent group of living organisms that occupies a particular habitat. The plants and animals of a community are closely associated with each other in various ecological relationships: for example, they depend on one another for food (*see* food chain). The size and composition of the community depend on the habitat and climate; it may show seasonal changes. During ecological succession, the structure of a community constantly changes until the stable climax community is established. *See also* ecology.

community service A form of sentence introduced in the UK by the Criminal Justice Act (1972). It requires an offender to work for a prescribed number of hours on behalf of the community instead of being imprisoned or fined. In the UK the offender must be aged 17 or over, have given his consent, and have committed no violence.

Como 45 48N 09 05E A city and resort in N Italy, in Lombardy on Lake Como. Known as Comum in Roman times, it is the birthplace of the elder and younger Pliny. It has a 15th-century marble cathedral and a gothic town hall. Como is an important tourist centre and has several industries, including the famous silk factories. Population (1981 est): 95 183.

Comoros, Federal Islamic Republic of the A country consisting of a group of islands in the Indian Ocean, between the Madagascar and the African mainland. The main islands are Grand Comoro, Anjouan, and Mohéli and exclude the island of Mayotte, which has remained French. The population is of mixed African and Arab descent. *Economy*: almost entirely agricultural. Sugar cane was formerly the main crop but others, such as vanilla and perfume plants, are now increasing in importance. *History*: became a French colony in the 19th century. At first joined to Madagascar, the Comoros became a separate French overseas territory in 1947. In a referendum in 1974 the majority voted in favour of independence, except for the island of Mayotte, which voted to remain French. In 1976 the independence of the three islands was recognized by France. From 1979 to 1989 effective control lay with the mercenary leader Bob Denard; he was ousted by the French after the assassination of President Abdallah in 1989. Head of state: Said Djohar. Official languages: French and Arabic; Swahili is also used commercially. Official currency: CFA franc of 100 centimes. Area: 1862 sq km (719 sq mi). Population (1987 est): 422 500. Capital and main port: Moroni.

compact disc. *See* recording of sound.

Companions of Honour, Order of the (CH) British order of chivalry, instituted in 1917. It comprises the sovereign and not more than 65 men and women who have made conspicuous contributions to the nation.

compass A device for determining the direction of magnetic north. The magnetic compass, which has been in use as an aid to navigation probably since the 2nd century BC, consists of a magnetic needle balanced on a point, allowing it to pivot freely. The S end of the magnet indicates magnetic N. Magnetic compasses are subject to interference from nearby ferrous metal objects and fittings, and compasses must be adjusted to compensate for distortion. Compensation must also be made, in the reading of a compass, for magnetic N not being in the same direction as geographic N in most longitudes. A more sophisticated kind of compass, used on larger vessels and in aircraft, is the **gyrocompass**, which employs the effect of the earth's rotation on the orientation of a spinning object's axis of rotation.

compass plant A perennial herbaceous plant, *Silphium laciniatum*, of the North American prairie. Its oval leaves are orientated N–S to avoid the intense midday radiation. 1–2 m high, it is sometimes cultivated and is also known as turpentine plant, from the substances that ooze from the stem. Family: *Compositae*.

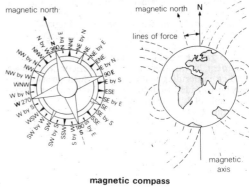

magnetic north

magnetic north

lines of force

magnetic axis

magnetic compass

weight

earth's rotation

west

A

B

east

equator

north pole

precession of gyroscope axis caused by weight

gyroscope axis

gyro case

weight

gyrocompass

COMPASS *In the magnetic compass, the needle lines up with the earth's magnetic field. In the gyrocompass a spinning gyroscope is suspended on three mutually perpendicular frames. The axis of spin of a free gyroscope shifts round as the earth rotates: as the axis of the gyrocompass moves from the horizontal at position A to position B, a weight pulls it downwards. The gyroscopic effect causes the axis to shift round at right angles to the gravitational force (precess) and describe a circle around the N-S direction. With damping the gyroscope axis settles down pointing N.*

Compiègne 49 25N 2 50E A town and resort in N France, in the Oise department on the River Oise. Joan of Arc was captured here by the English in 1430. A railway coach in the forest of Compiègne was the scene of the signing of the Armistice (1918) ending World War I and of the agreement made between the Pétain government and Hitler in 1940. Population (1983): 37 250.

complex numbers Quantities that consist of a real number and an imaginary number. They may be written in the form $a + ib$, where a and b are real numbers and $i = \sqrt{-1}$. Two complex numbers can be added and subtracted: for example $(a + ib) + (c + id) = (a + c) + i(b + d)$. They may also be multiplied and divided into each other. A complex number $a + ib$ may be thought of as a pair of ordered numbers (a,b) similar to a pair of Cartesian coordinates (x,y). Then (a,b) can be regarded as a point on a plane called the complex plane or Argand diagram in which the real axis is taken as horizontal and the imaginary axis is vertical.

Compositae The largest family of flowering plants (about 900 genera and 14 000 species). They vary from small herbs to trees and are found worldwide. The tiny flowers are grouped into heads that resemble a single large flower. The individual florets may be similar, as in thistles, or of two types (disc and ray flowers), as in daisies. Many composites are cultivated as ornamentals (e.g. chrysanthemums and dahlias); others are agricultural weeds (daisies, dandelions, etc.) and some are edible (such as lettuce).

Composite order. *See* orders of architecture.

comprehensive schools Secondary schools attended by children of all abilities. In the UK the widespread introduction of comprehensive schools was started in 1965 by the Labour Government and by 1977 some 70% of the secondary-school population attended comprehensives. By 1986 this had risen to 85.4%, with only 3% in grammar schools.

Compton, Arthur Holly (1892–1962) US physicist, who in 1923 discovered the **Compton effect** (increase in wavelength of electromagnetic radiation when scattered by free electrons). He could only explain the effect by assuming that the radiation consisted of photons, then still a novel idea. He shared the 1927 Nobel Prize with C. T. R. Wilson.

Compton-Burnett, Dame Ivy (1892–1969) British novelist. *Pastors and Masters* (1925) was the first of a series of 17 novels set in a stylized Victorian-Edwardian upper-class world. The series includes *Brothers and Sisters* (1929), *Manservant and Maidservant* (1947), and *Mother and Son* (1955).

COMPUTER *Now an essential part of the school environment.*

computer A device for processing information at high speeds, by electronic methods. The principles behind the modern computer were conceived by Charles Babbage in the 19th century. The first practical machines were built in Britain and the USA during World War II. Postwar developments in information theory and the invention of the transistor made possible the computer revolution of the next 20 years. Since the 1970s, advances in integrated circuits using silicon chips have led to the development of minicomputers and then microcomputers.

A **digital computer** processes information in the form of groups of binary numbers (*see* bit), which are represented by the on and off positions of electronic switches. The sequence of operations it performs on this information is controlled by a program, and the suite of programs that enables a computer to perform useful functions is called its software. The physical equipment, or hardware, of a computer generally has three main components: the central processing unit (CPU), main memory, and peripheral devices that enable information to be fed into the machine, display it in a readable form, or act as auxiliary memory. Input, formerly by punched tape or cards, is now by keyboard at a visual display unit (VDU) or by methods of automatic data capture, such as optical character recognition (OCR). Output is by printout on paper, VDU, or magnetic disc or tape. New developments, such as the use of compact discs as large permanent memories and the development of CPUs that work much faster by using optical rather than electrical impulses, promise to increase the power of computers. The transputer, which harnesses several microprocessors in parallel, seems to offer microcomputer users the computing speed of large mainframe computers.

An **analog computer** is a device that deals with continuously varying physical quantities, such as current or voltage. They are used mainly for simulation or monitoring and controlling continuous processes in industry and scientific research. Sometimes they act as peripheral devices for a digital computer (a combination known as a **hybrid computer**).

computer virus An unauthorized computer program that exploits weaknesses in a computer's operating system to insert itself into the system; it then propagates itself to other machines via networks or disks. It interferes with the machine's operation, and in some cases destroys data held on the machine.

Comte, Auguste (1798–1857) French philosopher. Often said to be the founder of sociology, he coined and defined the term, although work of a sociological nature had been done long before his time. He is best remembered for his positivism (the view that society could be studied scientifically by natural-science methods and was subject to general laws). His principal work is *Cours de philosophie positive* (6 vols, 1830–42).

Conakry (*or* Konakry) 9 25N 13 56W The capital of Guinea, a port in the SW on Tombo Island, which is linked to the mainland by a causeway. It was founded by the French in 1884 and became capital of French Guinea in 1893. Population (1980 est): 575 000.

concerto A musical composition for one or more solo instruments and orchestra, usually in three movements (a sonata form movement, a slow movement, and a rondo finale). In the late 18th century Mozart perfected the form in his piano concertos; subsequent concertos have been written in a number of different styles.

conch A heavy-shelled marine snail of the family *Strombidae* (about 80 species). Conch shells have a triangular outer whorl with a broad lip and can be 2–35 cm long. Indo-Pacific spider conchs (genus *Lambis*) have long horns around the aperture of their shell.

Concord 42 28N 71 17W A city in the USA, in Massachusetts on the Concord River. The first battle of the American Revolution occurred here on 19 April, 1775. Population (1985): 15 636.

Concorde. *See* aircraft.

concrete A building material that was used by the Romans but in its modern form came into use after the invention of Portland cement in 1824. Concrete consists of a mixture of a cement, usually Portland cement, and an aggregate of sand, gravel, and broken stones. Water is added to this mixture and complex hydration reactions cause the cement to harden around the aggregate. The material can be reinforced with steel bars (usually up to 50 mm in diameter) to increase its tensile strength. **Reinforced concrete** was invented in France in about 1850. In **prestressed concrete** the concrete is maintained in a state of compression by stretching the steel reinforcing wires (usually 6 mm in diameter) and keeping them in a state of tension after the concrete has set around them. Prestressed concrete is now widely used as a structural material as it has a reduced tendency to bend under load.

condensation 1. A change of physical state from a gas or vapour to a liquid. Thus as a gas is cooled below a certain temperature it may (depending on the pressure) condense to the liquid. Condensation occurs in buildings when warm moist air comes in contact with cold surfaces, such as windows and uninsulated walls. 2. A type of organic chemical reaction in which two molecules combine to form a larger molecule with elimination of a smaller molecule, such as water or methanol.

conditioned reflex A reflex response that is evoked by a stimulus other than that which normally produces it. A classic example is provided by Pavlov's experiments with dogs. The normal stimulus causing salivation (i.e. food) was paired with a different stimulus (a ringing bell) so often that eventually the bell by itself caused the dogs to salivate. A conditioned reflex gradually disappears if the stimulus is presented repeatedly; this process is called extinction. *See also* conditioning.

conditioning The process of modifying behaviour by changing the stimuli (and therefore responses) associated with it. Classical conditioning occurs when a response is associated with a stimulus by pairing the stimulus with an event that causes the response by reflex (*see* conditioned reflex). Operant conditioning is brought about by either rewarding or punishing an action by the subject, which thus either encourages or discourages the behaviour (*see also* aversion therapy). Behaviourism uses both forms of conditioning to explain how people learn.

condor A huge South American vulture, *Vultur gryphus*, found high in the Andes. It is black with a white ruff, bare pink head and neck, and has a wingspan of 3 m. It feeds chiefly on carrion but also takes lambs and young deer. The very rare Californian condor (*Gymnogyps californianus*) is smaller with a bare yellow head and red neck.

conduction 1. (thermal) The transfer of heat from a region of high temperature to one of lower temperature, without the transfer of matter. It occurs as a result of the transfer of kinetic energy by collisions between atoms and molecules in gases, liquids, and nonmetallic solids. In metals, which are the best thermal and electrical conductors, the energy is transferred by collisions between the free electrons that move through the crystal lattice and the ions of the lattice. 2. (electrical) The passage of an electric current through a substance. In metals, the best conductors, it results from the passage of free electrons moving in one direction under the influence of an electric field. In an electrolyte it is due to the passage of positive ions in one direction and negative ions in the

other. In gases it is due to positive ions flowing in one direction and electrons in the other. In semiconductors it results from the passage of electrons in one direction and positive holes in the other.

cone (botany) The structure, also called a strobilus, that bears the reproductive organs (sporophylls) in some pteridophytes (club mosses, horsetails, etc.) and the gymnosperms (conifers and related plants). In conifers both male and female cones are produced: the familiar woody cones of pines, larches, etc., are female strobili, made up of overlapping woody structures called bract scales, which bear the sporophylls in their axils.

Coney Island 40 35N 73 59W A resort in the USA, in New York City on the S shore of Long Island. With its amusement parks, fine beach, and the New York Aquarium it attracts many tourists.

Confederate States The 11 southern states of the USA that seceded from the Union (1860–61), precipitating the US Civil War: South Carolina, Georgia, Texas, Virginia, Arkansas, Tennessee, North Carolina, Mississippi, Florida, Alabama, and Louisiana.

Confederation of British Industry (CBI) The employers' federation in the UK. The CBI represents the employers in tripartite talks with the government and the Trades Union Congress on prices and incomes policies and formulates industry's views on economic and fiscal matters.

confirmation A Christian rite generally held to complete the initiation of a member into the Church. In the Eastern Orthodox Church, it is administered by a priest immediately after baptism and followed by Holy Communion; in the West, it is conferred by a bishop–in the Roman Catholic Church not before the seventh birthday and customarily at the age of 11 or 12, and in the Anglican Churches after the child has been able to learn the catechism.

Confucius (Kong Zi *or* K'ung-fu-tzu; c. 551–479 BC) Chinese philosopher, the founder of Confucianism. As a minor official, he gathered numerous disciples, mainly young gentlemen who wished to enter government service. Promoted to ministerial rank, he became famous for his just and effective policies, but on the ruler's refusing to heed his advice, he resigned (c. 496). The teaching of **Confucianism** is contained in five books. Retaining the concept of a divine will (*ming*), Confucianism emphasizes man's duty to his fellows. It was the official religion of China until the 1960s.

conglomerates Sedimentary rocks consisting of rounded fragments of former rocks cemented together, usually in sand. These fragments are over 2 mm in diameter and generally consist of hard material, such as quartzite or granite. Some conglomerates are used for crushed stone for road making and other purposes.

Congo, People's Republic of the (name until 1960: Middle Congo) A country in W central Africa, bordering on the Zaïre River. The uplands give way to plains in the NE. The population is composed chiefly of Bantu tribes. *Economy*: largely agricultural, the main cash crops being sugar cane, palm oil, cocoa, and tobacco. Minerals include lead, zinc, and gold, and oil was discovered in 1969. *History*: in the 15th century the Portuguese established trading relations with the Congo kingdom. In the 19th century the exploration of the Frenchman Pierre de Brazza (1852–1905) led to the establishment of the colony of Middle Congo, which in 1910 became one of the four territories of French Equatorial Africa. In 1958 it attained internal self-government as a member of the French Community and in 1960 became independent. Official language: French. Official currency: CFA (Communauté financière africaine) franc of 100 centimes. Area: 342 000 sq km (132 018 sq mi). Population (1987): 2 180 000. Capital: Brazzaville. Main port: Pointe-Noire.

Congo, Republic of.   *See* Zaïre, Republic of.

Congo River.   *See* Zaïre River.

Congregationalism   In Christianity, a form of church government in which centralized authority is rejected and each congregation is democratically autonomous. Congregationalist groups were active at the time of the Reformation, and in England the Independents, as they were known, were prominent during the Commonwealth, having played an important part in the opposition to Charles I. Congregationalism spread to America, where it flourished. In England, the United Reformed Church was founded in 1972 by the union of the Congregationalists with the Presbyterians.

Congress   The legislature of the USA instituted by the constitution (1789) and comprising the Senate, the upper house, and the House of Representatives, the lower house. The Senate serves as a check on the larger House of Representatives, with which it has equal legislative responsibility as well as further powers to ratify treaties and confirm appointments. Each state in the Union is equally represented by two senators. There are 435 seats in the House of Representatives, which are allocated among the states according to population.

Congreve, William   (1670–1729) British dramatist. Educated in Ireland, he returned to England in 1688 to study law but under the patronage of Dryden entered the literary world instead. The comedies *Love for Love* (1695) and *The Way of the World* (1700) are his best-known plays, although his contemporaries most admired his tragedy *The Mourning Bride* (1697).

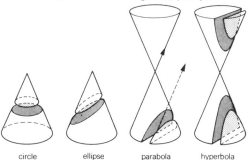

circle   ellipse   parabola   hyperbola

CONIC SECTION   *The circle, ellipse, parabola, and hyperbola are produced by slicing through the cone.*

conic sections   Geometrical figures produced by the intersection of a plane and a cone. If the plane cuts the cone at right angles to its axis the figure is a circle. If the plane is tilted slightly an ellipse is formed. If the plane is tilted further, until it lies parallel to the side of the cone, the figure is a parabola. Tilted more, the figure becomes a hyperbola. In the case of a hyperbola, the plane also intersects another cone the vertex of which touches the vertex of the first cone, the axes of the two cones being parallel. Consequently a hyperbola has two branches.

conifer   A gymnosperm tree of the widely distributed order *Coniferales* (400–500 species), most abundant in the colder temperate zones, especially in the north; elsewhere they are usually found at high altitudes. Nearly all conifers are evergreen (larches are exceptions), with simple needle-like or scalelike leaves. The reproductive organs are typically borne in separate male and female cones, usually on the same tree, and produce winged seeds that are dispersed by wind (the yew and juniper are exceptions).
The principal families are the *Pinaceae* (pines, cedars, spruces, firs, larches, hemlocks, etc.); *Cupressaceae* (cypresses, junipers, arbor vitae, etc.); *Taxodiaceae* (sequoias, swamp cypress, etc.); *Taxaceae* (yews); and *Araucariaceae* (monkey puzzle, etc.).

Coniston Water   A lake in NW England, in Cumbria in the Lake District. World water-speed records were established here by Sir Malcolm Campbell (1939) and his son Donald Campbell (1959). Length: 8 km (5 mi).

conjugation   The process by which exchange of genetic material occurs in certain lower organisms by means of a connection between the cytoplasm of the two "mating" individuals. In ciliate protozoa and certain algae it is a type of sexual reproduction, the gametes (or gametic nuclei) passing through a cytoplasmic bridge (protozoa) or a conjugation tube (algae). In bacteria the connection between "male" and "female" cells is by means of special hairs (pili) or cell-to-cell bridges.

conjunction   An alignment of two celestial bodies in the solar system, usually the sun and a planet, that occurs when the angular distance between them as seen from earth (i.e. the angle planet-earth-sun) becomes zero.

conjunctivitis   Inflammation of the conjunctiva–the membrane that covers the surface of the eye and lines the eyelids. Popularly known as pinkeye, it is marked by itching, redness, and watering of the eye. It may be caused by allergy to drugs or pollen; bacterial infection; or mechanical irritation.

Connacht (*or* Connaught)   A province and ancient kingdom of the NW Republic of Ireland. It consists of the counties of Galway, Leitrim, Mayo, Roscommon, and Sligo. Area: 17 122 sq km (6611 sq mi). Population (1986): 430 726.

Connaught.   *See* Connacht.

Connecticut   A state in the NE USA, in New England. It is one of the most densely populated states in the USA. Manufacturing is important. Yale University at New Haven is the most famous of its large number of universities and colleges. *History*: one of the original 13 colonies in the USA, it was first explored by the Dutch in the early 17th century. The first settlement was by English colonists from the Massachusetts Bay Colony (1633–35). Area: 12 973 sq km (5009 sq mi). Population (1983 est): 3 138 000. Capital: Hartford.

connective tissue   The tissue that supports, binds, or separates the specialized tissues and organs of the body. Connective tissue consists of a semifluid ground substance of polysaccharide and protein in which are embedded white collagen fibres, yellow elastic fibres, and various cells (including fibroblasts, which produce the ground substance and the fibres). The amount of collagen determines the toughness of the tissue. Specialized connective tissue includes fatty tissue, blood, bone, and cartilage.

Connemara An area in the W Republic of Ireland, in Co Galway bordering on the Atlantic Ocean. It contains many lakes, peat bogs, and the Twelve Bens, a group of quartzite mountains.

conquistador (Spanish: conqueror) One of the men who conquered the Indians of Central and South America for Spain in the first half of the 16th century. Few in number, the conquistadores were driven by a fanatical desire to find fame and gold and to serve the Roman Catholic Church. The most famous were Hernán Cortés and Francisco Pizarro.

Conrad, Joseph (Teodor Josef Konrad Watęcz Korzeniowski; 1857–1924) Polish-born British novelist, who knew no English before he was 20. Orphaned at the age of 11, he went to Marseilles in 1874, where he became a sailor. Conrad published his first novel, *Almayer's Folly*, in 1895. His seagoing experiences influenced both the themes of his fiction and his own moral outlook. His major novels include *Lord Jim* (1900), *Nostromo* (1904), *The Secret Agent* (1907), and *Under Western Eyes* (1911).

Conservative Party A UK political party that grew out of the Tory party in the 1830s under the leadership of Sir Robert Peel. His repeal of the Corn Laws (1846) caused a split in the party, with the Peelites later joining the Liberal Party. Under the leadership of Disraeli the Conservatives acquired a distinct philosophy that combined identification with the monarchy, the British Empire, and the Church of England with social reform. Under Salisbury and then Balfour the party was almost continuously in power from 1886 to 1905 and again, under Bonar Law, Baldwin, Neville Chamberlain, and Churchill, from 1922 to 1945, being the dominant party in the coalitions of 1931–35 and 1940–45. It was again in office from 1951 to 1964, led successively by Churchill, Eden (*see* Avon, Anthony Eden, Earl of), Macmillan, and Home, from 1970 to 1974 under Heath, and from 1979 under Thatcher. The party is now firmly committed to the furtherance of private enterprise and individualism rather than nationalization.

Consols. *See* gilt-edged security.

Constable, John (1776–1837) British landscape painter. After working for his father, he trained in London at the Royal Academy schools. He painted the Suffolk countryside, Hampstead Heath, and Salisbury Cathedral with a particular concern for changing weather conditions, exemplified in *The Leaping Horse* (1825; Royal Academy) and *Dedham Vale* (1828; National Gallery, Edinburgh). His *Haywain* (National Gallery, London) influenced Delacroix.

Constance, Council of (1414–18) The 16th ecumenical council of the Roman Catholic Church, which ended the Great Schism by electing Pope Martin V (1417). It decreed that the authority of a general council was superior to that of the pope.

Constance, Lake (German name: Bodensee) A lake on the River Rhine in West Germany, Switzerland, and Austria. Area: 531 sq km (205 sq mi).

constantan An alloy of 55% copper and 45% nickel. It is used in electrical equipment, such as resistors and thermocouples, because it has a high electrical resistance that does not change with temperature.

Constantine the Great (?285–337 AD) Roman emperor in the West (312–24) and sole emperor (324–37). The son of Constantius (c. 250–306), Roman emperor in the West (305–06), Constantine was acclaimed as his father's successor by his troops at York but did not secure his position until he defeated his rival Maxentius (d. 312). He became sole emperor after defeating the Eastern emperor Licinius (c. 270–325; reigned 311–24). Constantine was the first Roman emperor to adopt Christianity. In 313 he issued the Edict of Milan, which established toleration of Christians, and in 325 summoned the Council of Nicaea, the first general council of the Church. He was baptized on his deathbed.

CONSTABLE   *Self-portrait in pencil and watercolour.*

Constantinople. *See* Istanbul.

constellations The 88 areas into which the N and S hemispheres of the sky are now divided, using established boundaries. Each star, galaxy, or other celestial body lies within, or sometimes overlaps, the boundaries of one of the constellations and is often named in terms of this constellation. They originally had no fixed limits but were groups of stars forming a distinctive pattern outlining a mythological hero, animal, etc.

constitution The principles according to which a country is governed. The UK has an unwritten constitution comprising some statutes, much common law, and a good deal of custom. In many countries, the constitution is written. The **US constitution** was drawn up in 1787, ratified in 1788, and came into effect in 1789. It contains 7 articles and 27 amendments of which 10 constitute the Bill of Rights (1791). It defines the separation of powers, designed as a system of checks and balances, between the legislature, the executive, and the judiciary. Amendments subsequent to the Bill of Rights include the abolition of slavery (13), universal suffrage (15), and prohibition of liquor (18).

constrictor A snake belonging to the family *Boidae* (70 species) occurring chiefly in tropical regions. Constrictors are nonvenomous and kill their prey by coiling their thick muscular body around it and squeezing until it suffocates. They often have claws, which are vestigial limbs. The family comprises two subfamilies, *Boinae* (*see* boa) and *Pythoninae* (*see* python).

constructivism A movement in abstract sculpture, architecture, and design, which was launched in Russia by the *Realist Manifesto* (1920) of the brothers Naum Gabo (1890–1977) and Antoine Pevsner (1886–1962) with the aim of freeing contemporary art from political and social overtones. The chief principles of constructivism were functionalism, the articulation of space, and the use of modern materials, such as plastic and steel.

consuls The two magistrates who held supreme civil and military authority under the Roman Republic. They were elected annually by the Comitia Centuriata and presided over the Senate. Under the Empire they were nominated by the emperor and held office for only two to four months, the posts becoming honorary.

contact lenses A removable form of lens worn directly against the eye to replace spectacles for long or short sight or to protect the eye in some disorders of the outer transparent layer (cornea). Modern plastic contact lenses are hard (corneal), gas-permeable (allowing oxygen to permeate the cornea), or soft (hydrophilic).

contempt of court An act or omission that tends to undermine the authority of a court or that is likely to prejudice a fair trial. Examples are insulting a presiding judge or failing to comply with a court order; magistrates are not empowered to commit for contempt. The publication of matters *sub judice*, that is matters on which the court is to decide, is also a contempt. A person found in contempt is liable to a fine or imprisonment.

continent One of the major land masses of the earth: Asia, Africa, North America, South America, Europe, Australia, and Antarctica.

continental divide A major watershed separating the drainage basins of a continent. In North America a continental divide extends N–S along the Rocky Mountains dividing the rivers flowing E from those flowing W.

continental drift The theory, first set out in 1912 by Alfred Wegener, that the continents are not fixed in position but drift slowly (*see also* plate tectonics). Wegener's work was based on similarities in geological structures, flora and fauna, and coastal outlines; in recent years geophysical data, particularly from geomagnetic studies, have provided firmer evidence. It is believed that about 200 million years ago a supercontinent (termed Pangaea) began to break up (*see* Gondwanaland; Laurasia) and the fragments drifted apart until the continents reached their present positions. It is probable that continents have been joining together and breaking up throughout the earth's history.

continental shelf The area of sea floor adjacent to the continents, dipping gently from the shoreline to a depth of about 200 m. At this depth, the shelf edge, the continental slope begins, dipping more steeply to the ocean bottom. Shelves tend to be wider off low-lying regions than mountainous regions; the average width is about 70 km.

contraception The prevention of unwanted pregnancy, also known as birth control and family planning. The rhythm method and coitus interruptus are the most simple but least reliable. In the former intercourse is avoided around the middle of the menstrual cycle, when ovulation is most likely to occur; in the latter the penis is withdrawn before ejaculation. Barrier methods include the condom (or sheath), which is worn over the penis, and the diaphragm, which is fitted over the cervix of the womb and should be used with a spermicidal jelly. A far more reliable technique is the intra-uterine device (IUD) –a loop or coil, often impregnated with copper, that is inserted into the womb. Its method of action is not known. Some women, however, are unable to use an IUD as it causes side effects (heavy menstrual bleeding or recurrent infection). Since the 1960s, the most efficient means of preventing pregnancy has been by taking hormonal pills (*see* oral contraceptive), but this, too, may produce side effects and is unsuitable for some women. A long-term contraceptive method is the injection, at three-monthly intervals, of a synthetic hormone (progestogen), but this has recently been linked with the subsequent birth of disabled children and its use is controversial. Recently developed methods include the use of a soft polythene sponge impregnated with spermicide, which is inserted into the vagina and gives 24-hour protection, and a morning-after pill for women. *See also* sterilization.

contract In law, an enforceable promise or bargain, usually written but sometimes oral. A simple promise for which nothing is given in exchange is not a contract and is only enforceable at law as a deed. Something of value, called "consideration," must be exchanged in return for the promise; the value must be real but need not be equivalent. Breach of contract, meaning failure to fulfil its conditions, may result in the offender being sued for damages by the other party.

CONTINENTAL DRIFT *Computer graphics show America and Africa 50, 100, and 150 million years ago.*

contralto The deepest female singing voice. Range: F below middle C to D an octave and a sixth above.

convection The transfer of heat within a fluid by means of motion of the fluid. Convection may be natural or forced. In natural convection, the fluid flows by virtue of the warmer part being less dense than the cooler part. Thus the warmer fluid rises and the colder fluid sinks under the influence of gravity. In forced convection, some external cause, such as a fan, drives colder fluid into a warmer one, or vice versa.

convergence (*or* convergent evolution) The development in unrelated animals of similarities resulting from adaption to the same way of life. Thus whales (mammals) and fish, both aquatic, have evolved similar features independently.

Convocations of Canterbury and York The assemblies of the clergy of the two provinces of the Church of England. Dating from at least the 8th century, they were originally assemblies of bishops only. They later divided into two houses, an upper house composed of diocesan bishops and a lower house composed of certain lower clergy. The extent of their powers fluctuated, but essentially they exercised the right to tax themselves and managed to keep this prerogative until after the Restoration. From 1717 to 1852, however, they were prevented from dealing with questions of business and held only formal meetings. In 1969 many of their powers were assumed by the General Synod of the Church of England.

Convolvulus A widely distributed genus of annual or perennial twining plants (about 250 species). The flowers are funnel or bell-shaped and attractive. The Eurasian bindweed (*C. arvensis*) is a noxious weed with deep persistent roots and rapidly growing stems. Some species, such as *C. althaeoides*, are cultivated in gardens. Some have medicinal (purgative) properties. Family: *Convolvulaceae*.

Conway (Welsh name: Aberconwy) 53 18N 3 52W A market town and resort in North Wales, in Gwynedd on the estuary of the River Conway. It has a famous 13th-century castle. Population (1981): 12 969.

cony. *See* hyrax; pika.

Cook, Captain James (1728–79) British navigator and cartographer. He joined the Royal Navy (1755) and served in the Seven Years' War (1756–63), during which he surveyed the St Lawrence River. His observations on the eclipse of the sun in 1766 were presented to the Royal Society, which gave him command of an expedition to Tahiti to observe the transit of the planet Venus across the sun and to discover Terra Australis, a presumed southern continent. The expedition set sail in the *Endeavour* in 1768 and, Venus observed, Cook went on to discover and chart New Zealand and the E coast of Australia, returning to England in 1771. His second voyage (1772–75), in the *Resolution*, accompanied by the *Adventure*, achieved the circumnavigation of the Antarctic. He charted Easter Island and discovered New Caledonia, the South Sandwich Islands, and South Georgia Island. On his return he was made a captain and received the Royal Society's Copley Medal for his dietary work (on avoiding scurvy). On his third voyage (1776–79) he was killed by Hawaiians.

Cook, Mount (Maori name: Aorangi) 43 37S 170 08E The highest mountain in New Zealand, in South Island in the Southern Alps. Height: 3764 m (12 349 ft).

Cook Islands A group of scattered islands in the SE Pacific Ocean, a New Zealand dependency. The chief islands are Rarotonga, Atiu, and Aitutaki. Fruit, copra, and mother-of-pearl are exported. Area: 241 sq km (93 sq mi). Population (1981): 17 754. Capital: Avarua.

coolabar A tree, *Eucalyptus microtheca*, growing to 25 m, common inland in W Australia. The wood is grey near the outside, deep red within. Also called jinbul, moolar, blackbox, and dwarf box, it is used for building. Family: *Myrtaceae*. *See also* Eucalyptus.

Coolidge, John Calvin (1872–1933) US statesman; Republican president (1923–29). His presidency followed the scandals of the administration (1921–23) of Warren Harding (1865–1923) but Coolidge's own honesty was never questioned. He supported US business at home and abroad, but did little to curb the speculation on the stock market that ended in the 1929 financial crash.

Cooper, Gary (Frank James C.; 1901–61) US film actor. He is best known for his portrayals of tough but sensitive heroes in Hollywood westerns. These include *The Virginian* (1929), *The Westerner* (1940), and *High Noon* (1952).

cooperative societies Societies set up to manufacture, buy, or sell produce, either without profit or with profits distributed to members or shareholders as dividends. The cooperative movement was inspired by the British philanthropist Robert Owen in the early 19th century and was seen as an alternative to the hardship that seemed to be caused by competition. Cooperative societies in agriculture, in which machinery is shared and produce is marketed jointly, are common in both the advanced and developing countries. In the UK the largest cooperative is the Cooperative Wholesale Society (CWS).

coordinate systems Geometrical systems that locate points in space by a set of numbers.
In **Cartesian coordinates**, devised by René Descartes, a point is located by its distance from intersecting axes. In a plane (two dimensions) there are two axes and in space (three dimensions) there are three. Usually the axes are at right angles to each other and are known as rectangular axes, but oblique axes can also be used.
Polar coordinates denote position by distance and direction. A fixed point, called the origin, and a fixed line, called the polar axis, are taken as the references. For any point, the polar coordinates are the length, r, of the radius of the circle centred at the origin and passing through the point, and the angle, θ, between this radius and the polar axis. In three dimensions, **spherical polar coordinates** are used. The radius of a sphere centred at the origin and the two angles it makes with the polar axis define the point.

coot An aquatic rail of the genus *Fulica* (9 species). Coots have broadly lobed toes, diving deeply to feed on invertebrates and aquatic plants. The European coot (*F. atra*) occurs throughout the Old World and is 37 cm long with black plumage and a white bill and frontal shield.

Copenhagen (Danish name: København) 55 40N 12 35E The capital and chief port of Denmark, on the E coast of Sjælland. Notable buildings include the 17th-century Charlottenborg Palace (now the Royal Academy of Arts) and Christiansborg Palace (now the parliamentary and government buildings). *History*: already a human settlement in the year 900 AD, it became capital of Denmark in 1443. It was attacked by the Hanseatic League in the middle ages and by Sweden in the 17th century. In 1801 the Danish fleet was destroyed by Nelson at the battle of Copenhagen. In 1728, and again in 1795, it was badly damaged by fire. Occupied by the Germans in World War II, it became the centre of a strong resistance movement. Population (1987): 622 275.

cartesian coordinates

two-dimensional   three-dimensional

polar coordinates

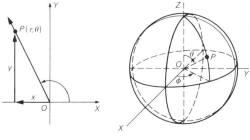

two-dimensional   three-dimensional

COORDINATE SYSTEMS *In two-dimensional Cartesian coordinates a point P is located by giving its x- and y- coordinates, in this case 4 and −3 (always given in this order, as shown). In three-dimensional Cartesian coordinates P is located in terms of three axes. In polar coordinates P is located by a radius r and an angle θ. In three dimensions a second angle, φ, is required. In the diagrams Cartesian coordinates are superimposed on the polar coordinates.*

Copepoda A subclass of crustaceans (7500 species), mostly 0.5–2 mm long, that have long antennae, a single median eye, and no carapace. There are 11 pairs of appendages on the head and thorax and forked tail filaments (furca). Copepods occur in abundance in fresh and salt water, forming a constituent of plankton. Most feed on microscopic plants or animals but some are parasitic on fish, other crustaceans, etc.

Copernicus, Nicolaus (1473–1543) Polish astronomer, formulator of the modern heliocentric theory of the solar system. After studying mathematics and music at Cracow and Bologna, Copernicus became interested in the problem of calculating planetary positions, since existing tables were out of date. He noticed that by using a system in which the earth revolved round the sun, instead of Ptolemy's geocentric system, these calculations would be much easier to make. Realizing that these ideas were at variance with the Church's view that the earth was at the centre of the universe, Copernicus only circulated them to a few friends. The full text of his book *De revolutionibus orbium coelestium* was published in 1543.

Copland, Aaron (1900–) US composer, a pupil of Nadia Boulanger. He has been active as a teacher, pianist, and champion of contemporary music. He is best known for his compositions in a popular style, such as the ballets *Billy the Kid* (1938) and *Rodeo* (1942). His other works employ a variety of styles and include a piano concerto (1927) in a jazz idiom, a *Piano Fantasy* (1950), and the tone poem *Inscape* (1967).

copper (Cu) A reddish-brown metal, known from prehistoric times and named after the island of Cyprus, which was the principal source in Roman times. It occurs naturally as the native element, the sulphide chalcopyrite ($CuFeS_2$), the carbonate malachite ($CuCO_3.Cu(OH)_2$), and other minerals. It is mined in Zambia, Zaïre, Chile, Australia, New Guinea, and elsewhere. Copper is extracted by smelting and electrolysis. It is malleable, ductile, and is important because of its good electrical (second only to silver) and thermal conductivity. Copper is widely used in the electrical industry and in the form of copper pipes in plumbing. It is contained in coins, and in the alloys brass and bronze. At no 29; at wt 63.546; mp 1083°C; bp 2595°C.

copra. *See* coconut.

Coptic Church The largest Christian Church in Egypt. The Copts trace the history of their Church to St Mark. As a result of its Monophysite beliefs, which were condemned at the Council of Chalcedon (451), the Coptic Church became somewhat isolated from other Christian bodies. The Muslim conquest of Egypt in 642, together with language and cultural differences, widened the division. The Church suffered some persecution under Arab dominion. In 1741 a number of Copts entered the Roman Catholic communion, becoming the Uniat Coptic Church. Alexandria held an eminent position in the early Church and remains the seat of the Coptic patriarch, who presides over the Church with 12 diocesan bishops. The Copts are in communion with the Armenian and Syrian (Orthodox) Churches.

copyright law The law protecting the exclusive right of anyone who creates or publishes original literary, dramatic, and artistic works to reproduce them and to exploit them. The protection in England lasts for 50 years after the death of the owner of the copyright. In contrast to a patent, copyright cannot exist in an idea, but only in its expression.

coracle An ancient boat, usually round, made of wickerwork or laths over which a waterproofed animal skin has been stretched. Coracles were used in Ireland and in Wales and other parts of W Britain.

coral A sedentary marine animal belonging to a class (*Anthozoa*) of coelenterates. They are found in all oceans, feeding mainly on small animals. Reproduction can be asexual (by budding) or sexual, the eggs being fertilized in the water.
The stony (*or* true) corals (order *Madreporaria*; about 1000 species) secrete a rigid external skeleton made of almost pure calcium carbonate. **Coral reefs** are slowly produced by succeeding generations of stony corals, occurring in dense colonies, chiefly at depths of less than 50 m and at temperatures above 20°C. Within this zone symbiotic algae (zooxanthellae) stimulate the growth of coral skeletons.

Coral Sea A section of the SW Pacific Ocean off NE Australia. It contains the Great Barrier Reef.

coral snake A New World burrowing venomous snake that preys on other snakes. The main genus,

Micrurus (40 species), ranges from the S USA to Argentina; most species are ringed with red, black, and yellow or white. Old World coral snakes are similar and found in SE Asia (genus *Calliophis*) and Africa (genus *Elaps*). Family: *Elapidae* (cobras, mambas, coral snakes).

The rear-fanged false coral snakes have similar patterning but belong to the family *Colubridae* (grass snakes, etc.).

COR ANGLAIS

cor anglais A double-reeded musical instrument, the alto member of the oboe family. It is a transposing instrument, the notes sounding a fifth lower than written. It has a range of two and a half octaves from the E below middle C.

Corbusier, Le. *See* Le Corbusier.

Cordaitales An order of extinct gymnosperm trees that—with *Calamites*—formed vast forests during the Carboniferous and Permian periods (370–240 million years ago). The trees probably grew up to 30 m high, with strap-shaped leaves, up to 1 m long.

cordgrass. *See* Spartina.

Córdoba 37 53N 4 46W A city in S Spain, in Andalusia on the River Guadalquivir. It became the capital of Moorish Spain in 756 AD and by the 10th century was Europe's largest cultural centre. Its immense Moorish cathedral (8th–10th centuries) was originally a mosque. Population (1981): 284 737.

Corfu (Latin name: Coreyra; Modern Greek name: Kérkira *or* Kérkyra) A Greek island in the NE Ionian Sea. It has belonged to many powers, including Venice (1386–1797) and Britain (1815–64). The local produce includes olives, figs, and citrus fruit, and tourism is important. Area: 641 sq km (250 sq mi). Population (1971): 92 933. Chief town: Corfu.

corgi One of two breeds of working dog originating in SW Wales. The Cardigan Welsh corgi has a long tail, rounded ears, and a shortish coat, which may be reddish brown, streaked brown, or black and tan; the Pembroke Welsh corgi has a short tail, pointed ears, and a finer coat of red, sable, fawn, or black and tan. Height: 30 cm (Cardigan); 25–30 cm (Pembroke).

coriander An annual plant, *Coriander sativum*, 20–70 cm high, with small pink or white flowers. Probably native to the Mediterranean, it is cultivated for its spicy seeds. Family: *Umbelliferae*.

Corinth (Greek name: Kórinthos) 37 56N 22 55E A port in S Greece. *History*: a settlement before 3000 BC, it became the second largest and richest of the Greek city states after Athens, rivalry between the two culminating in the Peloponnesian War. Destroyed by the Romans in 146 BC, Corinth was later revived as a Roman colony (44 BC). Population (1981): 22 495.

Corinthian order. *See* orders of architecture.

Corinthians, Epistles of Paul to the Two New Testament books written by the apostle Paul to the Christian Church at Corinth in about 57 AD. In the first he answers questions on practical and doctrinal issues, for example marriage and celibacy, the resurrection of the dead, and the Eucharist. In the second he defends himself against his opponents at Corinth.

Coriolis force A force required to account for the motion of a body as seen by an observer in a rotating frame of reference. For example, a shell shot from a gun at the centre of a rotating table appears to an outside observer to travel in a straight line. To an observer on the table it appears to have a curved path. The Coriolis force is required to account for this apparent tangential acceleration. Named after the French physicist Gaspard de Coriolis (1792–1843).

cork Tissue that forms the outer layer of bark in woody plants. The cork oak (*Quercus suber*) is cultivated in Portugal and SW Spain as the source of commercial cork. The cork is stripped from the tree every 8–10 years and is used for bungs, fishing floats, wall coverings, etc.

Cork (Irish name: Corcaigh) The largest county in the Republic of Ireland. Mountains in the W extend eastwards intersected by valleys, notably that of the River Blackwater. Its many coastal inlets include Bantry Bay and Cork Harbour. Agriculture and fishing are important. Its many castles include Blarney Castle, famous for the Blarney Stone. Area: 7459 sq km (2880 sq mi). Population (1986): 279 427. County town: Cork.

CÓRDOBA *Moorish arches in the cathedral, a former mosque.*

Cork (Irish name: Corcaigh) 51 54N 8 28W The second largest city in the Republic of Ireland and county town of Co Cork. The settlement grew up around a monastery (founded in about the 6th century AD) and has many notable buildings, especially its cathedrals and St Ann's Shaldon Church. It is an important industrial and trading centre with a fine harbour. Population (1986): 133 196.

corkwood. *See* balsa.

corm A fleshy underground stem base of certain perennial herbaceous plants that acts as an overwintering structure. Growth the following season occurs by one or more buds: if two or more plants are produced the corm is acting as an organ of vegetative reproduction.

cormorant A slender long-necked waterbird belonging to a family (*Phalacrocoracidae*; 30 species) and found on most coasts and some inland waters. 50–100 cm in length, cormorants are typically glossy black and have webbed feet and a long hook-tipped bill. Order: *Pelecaniformes* (gannets, pelicans, etc.).

corncrake A migratory bird, *Crex crex*, also called landrail, that breeds in Eurasian grasslands, wintering in S Africa and Asia. It is 26 cm long with a streaked brown plumage and a rasping call. Family: *Rallidae* (rails).

cornea The transparent outer layer of the eyeball. Corneal grafts have been used successfully; since the cornea has no blood supply the graft cannot be rejected by blood-borne antibodies.

cornet A trumpet-like valved brass instrument, with cup-shaped mouthpiece and conical bore. Pitched in B flat, it has a range of two and a half octaves from the E below middle C.

cornflower An annual, sometimes overwintering, herbaceous plant, *Centaurea cyanus*, growing to about 75 cm high; a cereal crop weed. Flower heads are bright blue with a purplish centre. Family: *Compositae*.

Cornish A Celtic language of the Brythonic group, formerly spoken in Cornwall and Devon, that became extinct in about 1800.

Corn Laws The British laws that regulated (1360–1846) the import and export of corn to guarantee farmers' incomes. These laws were bitterly resented by the working classes, because they kept the price of bread high, and by the manufacturers, who argued that little money was left for the purchase of manufactured goods. Opposition to the Corn Laws was led by the Anti-Corn Law League led by Richard Cobden (1804–65) and John Bright (1811–89). In 1846 Sir Robert Peel's government repealed them.

corn poppy An annual, or sometimes biennial, poppy, *Papaver rhoeas*, with scarlet flowers. Also called field poppy, it is widespread as a weed and grows to a height of 50 cm.

cornucopia A decorative motif from Greek antiquity denoting abundance and wealth. It consists of a goat's horn filled with fruit and flowers.

Cornwall (Celtic name: Kernow) The most southwesterly county of England, including the Isles of Scilly. It consists mainly of rugged hills rising to Bodmin Moor in the E. Tourism is a chief source of income. Agriculture is important but tinmining, important since early times, has declined. Area: 3546 sq km (1369 sq mi). Population (1986 est): 448 200. Administrative centre: Truro.

Cornwall, Duchy of A private estate of some 130 000 acres, mostly in Cornwall, Devon, and Somerset, belonging to the eldest son of the sovereign, who becomes Duke of Cornwall at birth or from the moment his parent is crowned.

corona The outer layer of a star's atmosphere. The sun's corona has two main components. The **inner corona** lies above the chromosphere and consists of rapidly moving electrons. Its temperature reaches about 2 000 000°C some 75 000 km above the visible solar surface (the photosphere). The **outer corona** extends for millions of kilometres and consists of comparatively slow-moving dust particles. *See also* solar wind.

coronary heart disease The most common form of heart disease in the western world. It is caused by atherosclerosis of the coronary arteries, which reduces the blood flow to the heart. This may precipitate the formation of a blood clot in these arteries—**coronary thrombosis**. The patient experiences sudden pain in the chest (*see* angina pectoris) and the result may be a heart attack (*see* myocardial infarction). Associated with smoking, lack of exercise, high-fat diets, hypertension, and middle age, it is commoner in men.

coroner In England and Wales, an officer of the Crown appointed for life by a county council from among suitably qualified barristers, solicitors, or qualified medical practitioners. The main duty of a coroner is to inquire into the death of anyone who dies by an act of violence, in suspicious circumstances, or in prison. He is often assisted by a jury of 7 to 11 people. A jury verdict of manslaughter or murder is equivalent to an indictment, and the coroner can commit the accused for trial. A coroner also inquires into cases of treasure trove. In Scotland, the coroner's duties are carried out by the procurator fiscal.

Corot, Jean Baptiste Camille (1796–1875) French landscape painter. Although he exhibited at the Paris Salon from 1827, he did not achieve critical acclaim until the 1850s, with his poetical misty landscapes populated by nymphs. More popular today are his open-air sketches, small landscapes, and figure studies.

corporation tax A tax levied on the profits of a company on an annual basis. In the UK, the rate of tax is announced by the chancellor of the exchequer in his budget.

Corpus Christi, Feast of (Latin: body of Christ) A Christian feast honouring the institution of the Eucharist, observed in the West on the second Thursday after Whit Sunday. The chief rite of the feast is the procession of the Blessed Sacrament. It is not generally observed by Protestant Churches.

CORNUCOPIA

Corpus Juris Civilis. *See* Roman law.

Correggio (Antonio Allegri; c. 1494–1534) Italian Renaissance painter, born at Correggio, near Modena. He worked chiefly in Parma, where he decorated the Camera di S Paolo, the domed vaulting of S Giovanni Evangelista, and the cathedral with frescoes that anticipate the baroque.

Corsica (French name: Corse) An island in the Mediterranean Sea, a region of France. It is mountainous and largely covered with *maquis*, a dense scrub type of vegetation. Agriculture is relatively undeveloped, producing citrus fruits, olives, vegetables, and tobacco; sheep and goats are extensively reared and tourism is a major source of income. *History*: under Genoese control from the 14th century, it was sold to France in 1768. During World War II it came under Italian occupation but was liberated by the French in 1943. Area: 8680 sq km (3367 sq mi). Population (1984): 244 600. Capital: Ajaccio.

CORTÉS   *A fanciful 19th-century view of Cortés and his conquistadores fighting the Aztecs.*

Cortés, Hernán (1485–1547) Spanish conquistador. In Hispaniola and Cuba from 1504, he led a small expedition to Mexico in 1519 and reached Tenochtitlán, the capital of the Aztec Empire. In Cortés' absence the Aztecs launched an attack on Tenochtitlán, forcing the Spaniards' retreat—the *noche triste* (night of sorrows). Cortés eventually rebuilt his forces and destroyed Tenochtitlán (1521) and the Aztec Empire, founding New Spain. After further expeditions he died in poverty in Spain.

cortex The outer tissues of an animal or plant organ. In plants the cortex is situated between the epidermis and vascular (conducting) tissues of stems and roots. Its cell walls may contain corky and woody materials or silica, providing strength, and also stored food, usually starch. In animals the outer tissue of the adrenal gland, the cerebrum, and the kidney is called the cortex.

corticosteroids Steroid hormones secreted by the cortex of the adrenal glands (the term also includes synthetic drugs with similar properties). The glucocorticoids (e.g. cortisone, prednisolone, and dexamethasone) affect carbohydrate metabolism. As anti-inflammatory drugs, they are used to treat allergic conditions, inflammatory disorders, and autoimmune diseases. They are also used to treat some cancers. The mineralocorticoids (e.g. aldosterone, fludrocortisone) control salt and water balance in the body.

corundum A mineral consisting mainly of aluminium oxide, the accessory minerals giving rise to a variety of colours. Sapphire is a blue variety containing iron and titanium; ruby contains chromium. The nongem varieties are used as abrasives (corundum is the second hardest mineral to diamond).

Corunna. *See* La Coruña.

corvette A small highly manoeuvrable lightly armed warship. They were used mainly for antisubmarine escort duty during World War II by the Royal Navy. In the days of sail, the corvette, smaller than a frigate, was a sloop rigged as a ship. Those that remained after World War II were renamed antisubmarine frigates in 1959.

Cos (Modern Greek name: Kos) A Greek island in the Dodecanese. It was a member of the Delian League and the home of Hippocrates. It produces chiefly fruit but also silk and tobacco. Cos lettuce originally came from here. Area: 282 sq km (109 sq mi). Population (1981): 20 350.

cosmic rays A continuous stream of very high-energy particles that bombard the earth from space. The primary radiation consists of protons and light nuclei with smaller numbers of neutral particles, such as photons and neutrinos. These particles collide with atomic nuclei in the earth's atmosphere producing large numbers of elementary particles, known as secondary radiation. One primary particle may produce a large number of secondary particles on colliding with a nucleus. This effect is called a shower. Some cosmic rays are believed to originate from the sun, others from outside the solar system.

cosmology The study of the origin, evolution, and structure of the universe. A great variety of cosmological models have been put forward through the ages. Two simple but incorrect common-sense models are the flat earth draped by a canopy of stars and the earth-centred (geocentric) universe, the Ptolemaic system. More accurate theories emerged as instruments were developed to study the heavens (*see* astronomy). Most assume that there are no preferred places in the universe: all directions appear indistinguishable to an observer and this isotropy exists about every point in space (the cosmological principle). *See* big-bang theory.

Cossacks A people of S and SW Russia descended from independent Tatar groups and escaped serfs from Poland, Lithuania, and Muscovy. They established a number of independent self-governing communities, which were given special privileges by Russian or Polish rulers in return for military service. Known for their horsemanship, the Cossacks slowly lost their autonomy as Russia expanded in the 17th and 18th centuries and there were occasional rebellions. Many fled Russia after the Revolution (1918–21) and collectivization subsumed remaining Cossack communities.

Costa Rica, Republic of A country in the Central American isthmus between Nicaragua and Panama. It includes the island of Cocos, 483 km (186 mi) to the SW. The Caribbean lowlands rise to a central plateau area, with volcanic peaks reaching 3819 m (12 529 ft). The inhabitants are mainly of Spanish and mixed descent, with a dwindling Indian population. *Economy*: chiefly agricultural, the main crops being coffee, bananas, and sugar (the principal export). Almost 75% of the land is forested with valuable woods, such as mahogany, rosewood, and cedar. Mineral resources include gold, haematite ore, and sulphur. *History*: discovered by Columbus in 1502, it became a Spanish colony in the 15th century and the native Indian population was practically wiped out. It was part of the captaincy general of Guatemala until gaining independence in 1821. From 1824 until 1838 it formed part of the Central American Federation. President: Rafael Angel Calderón. Official language: Spanish. Official religion: Roman Catholic. Official currency: colon of 100 centimos. Area: 50 900 sq km (19 653 sq mi). Population (1986): 2 714 000. Capital: San José. Main ports: Limón (on the Caribbean) and Puntarenas (on the Pacific).

cot death The death of a baby, usually occurring overnight in its cot, from an unidentifiable cause. Some 20% of infant mortality in the UK is accounted for in this way. The causes may include virus infections or allergic reactions.

Côte d'Ivoire, Republic of (name until 1986: Ivory Coast) A country in West Africa, on the Gulf of Guinea. Swamps and tropical forests give way to savanna to the N. The diverse African population includes Baule, Bete, Senufo, and Malinke. *Economy:* chiefly agricultural, livestock being important as well as crops, including maize, yams, and other tropical plants. The main crop is coffee. Mineral resources are on the whole sparse. *History:* explored by the Portuguese in the late 15th century, the area was disputed by several European trading nations, becoming a French colony in 1893. It became part of French West Africa in 1904 and an overseas territory in 1946. It possessed internal self-government as a member of the French Community from 1958 and became fully independent in 1960. President: Félix Houphouët-Boigny. Official language: French. Official currency: CFA (Communauté financière africaine) franc of 100 centimes. Area: 322 463 sq km (124 470 sq mi). Population (1986): 10 595 000. Capital: Yamoussoukro. Main port: Abidjan.

Cotoneaster A genus of shrubs and small trees (about 50 species) of N temperate regions of the Old World. Some species are evergreen. *C. horizontalis* is a popular ground and wall cover; *C. hybrida pendula* is a weeping standard. Family: *Rosaceae*.

Cotonou 6 24N 2 31E The chief city in Benin, on the Gulf of Guinea. A deepwater port, it is the nation's main commercial and financial centre. Population (1982 est): 487 020.

Cotopaxi 0 40S 78 28W The world's highest active volcano, in N central Ecuador, in the Andes. Height: 5896 m (19 457 ft).

Cotswold Hills A range of limestone hills in SW central England, mainly in Gloucestershire. It is noted for its picturesque towns and villages.

cotton A herbaceous plant of the genus *Gossypium* (20 or 67 species, according to the classification system), native to tropical and subtropical regions. Several species are cultivated for the whitish outer fibres of their seeds. Usually 1–2 m high, cotton plants bear whitish flowers and produce seed pods (bolls), which burst when filled with the soft masses of fibres. The bolls are harvested mechanically and the fibres separated from the seeds (ginning) and cleaned and aligned (carding), ready for spinning into yarn. Cotton forms a light durable cloth used in a wide range of garments, furnishings, and other products. The seeds are crushed to yield cottonseed oil, used in margarines, cooking oils, soaps, etc., and the

residual meal is used as a livestock feed. Family: *Malvaceae*.

cotyledon The seed leaf of seed-bearing plants (gymnosperms and angiosperms): a food store within seeds providing the embryo plant with sufficient energy to germinate. Flowering plants with one cotyledon are classified as monocotyledons; those with two as dicotyledons. *See* germination.

couch grass A grass, *Agropyron repens*, also known as quack grass or twitch, native to Europe and naturalized in other N temperate regions. 30–120 cm high, it is a serious weed of arable crops.

cougar A red-brown cat, *Felis concolor*, of North and South America, also called puma, mountain lion, and catamount. It is 1.5–3 m long including its tail (50–80 cm), with long hind legs enabling a powerful leap. It feeds on a variety of animals.

coulomb (C) The SI unit of electric charge equal to the quantity of electricity transferred by a current of one ampere in one second. Named after Charles de Coulomb (1736–1806), French physicist.

Coulomb's law. *See* electric charge.

Council for Mutual Economic Assistance (COMECON) An economic association of communist countries founded in 1949. Its members are the Soviet Union, Bulgaria, Czechoslovakia, East Germany, Hungary, Mongolia, Poland, Romania, and Cuba; Albania ceased to participate in 1961.

Council of Europe An association of European states, founded in 1949, that is pledged to uphold parliamentary democracy and to promote the economic and social progress of its members. Its seat is in Strasbourg.

COUNTERPOINT   *An example of counterpoint from J. S. Bach's Fantasia in C minor.*

counterpoint The art of combining two or more melodic lines simultaneously in music. The word derives from the Latin *punctus contra punctum*, point against point (i.e. note against note). The use of counterpoint continued beyond the end of the polyphonic period (*see* polyphony). Composers continue to make use of it today; contrapuntal techniques have been used by Stravinsky, Hindemith, Tippett, and others.

Counter-Reformation A movement within the Roman Catholic Church dedicated to combating the effects of the Protestant Reformation. Extending from the middle of the 16th to about the middle of the 17th century, it witnessed the emergence of the Jesuits, the Council of Trent, the extension of the Inquisition, and a revival of Catholic spirituality.

countertenor A natural high male singing voice, higher than tenor, common in England in the 17th and 18th centuries. It is distinguished from the male alto voice, which is produced by falsetto, but has the same range.

country and western A type of US popular music that evolved from the hillbilly ballads of the Appalachian Mountains and the cowboy songs of the West. The singer is accompanied by the guitar and other stringed instruments. Influenced by other styles of popular music, country and western has its own offshoots, such as bluegrass.

county A geographical unit of local government. In the UK counties are long established: the name was applied by the Normans to the Anglo-Saxon shire. The Local Government Act (1972; effective 1974) amalgamated some old counties and established new ones and placed a variety of public services in the hands of elected county councils. Metropolitan county councils were abolished in 1986. The Local Government (Scotland) Act (1973) created nine new regions and three island areas. Northern Ireland has 6 counties but administration is carried out by 26 district councils.

Couperin, François (1668–1733) French composer, called le Grand, the most famous member of a family that produced five generations of musicians. He was organist to Louis XIV and at St Gervais and is best known for his harpsichord music.

courgette A variety of marrow, also called zucchini, eaten when small and immature (up to 15 cm long). Mature courgettes resemble ordinary marrows.

coursing A blood sport dating back to at least 1500 BC, in which game (now usually hare) is pursued by hounds (usually greyhounds) that hunt by sight rather than scent. A meeting takes place on an open field and is presided over by a mounted umpire. Hounds are judged on points for their speed up to the quarry, for overtaking each other, and for forcing the quarry to turn. The British coursing season is from September to March and its main event is the Waterloo Cup, staged in February at Altcar, Lancashire.

court-martial A court, consisting of commissioned officers in the army, navy, or air force, convened to try a member of any of these services for an offence against military discipline or against ordinary law. An appeal court was established in 1951 and is now governed by the Courts-Martial (Appeals) Act (1968). An offender is not immune from trial by ordinary courts, but they must take into account any punishment to which he was sentenced by the court-martial.

Courtrai (Flemish name: Kortrijk) 50 50N 03 17E A town in Belgium, on the River Lys. It was the site of the battle of the Spurs (1297), in which the French army was defeated by the burghers of Bruges and Ghent. Population (1985): 76 110.

COURTS OF LAW

courts of law Assemblies in which the law is administered. In England and Wales civil law (*see also* common law; equity) is administered by the County Courts and the High Court of Justice and criminal law is administered by the Magistrates' Courts and the Crown Court.

Appeals from the civil law courts lie to the civil division of the Court of Appeal and those from the criminal law courts lie from Magistrate's Courts to the Crown Court and from the Crown Court to the criminal division of the Court of Appeal. Two or more judges of the High Court, when sitting together, may constitute a Divisional Court, which hears appeals on points of law from Magistrates' Courts, Crown Courts, and certain tribunals. The Divisional Court can either (1) order the lower court to continue its hearing of the case in point while directing how the law should be applied or (2) allow or dismiss the appeal itself, if all the facts of the case have already been heard and decided by the lower court. The House of Lords is the Supreme Court of Appeal in both criminal and civil cases. The High Court of Justice and the Court of Appeal together with the Crown Court form the Supreme Court of Judicature.

The County Courts have jurisdiction over most civil law actions, subject to financial limitations (e.g. £5000 for claims in contract or tort). As well as these, all divorce petitions start in the County Courts but are transferred to the High Court if defended. The High Court of Justice comprises the Chancery, Queen's Bench (including the Admiralty Court (*see* maritime law) and the Commercial Court), and Family Divisions.

A criminal case comes first before a Magistrates' Court (*see* justice of the peace), which has jurisdiction in less serious cases (e.g. traffic offences) but commits more serious cases for trial at the Crown Court. The Crown Court, which was created in 1971 to replace the Courts of Assize and Courts of Quarter Session, is organized in six circuits (Midland and Oxford, North Eastern, Northern, South Eastern, Wales and Chester, and Western). A Crown Court sits in London as the Central Criminal Court (Old Bailey). *See also* judge.

In Scotland the supreme court for civil cases is the Court of Session, established in 1532, and the supreme court for criminal cases is the High Court of Judiciary. Appeals from the former lie to the House of Lords and from the latter to a tribunal of three judges of the High Court of Justiciary. *See also* Crown Prosecution Service.

Cousteau, Jacques Yves (1910–) French naval officer and underwater explorer. He shared in the invention of the aqualung (1943) and invented a way of using television under water. In 1945 he founded the Undersea Research Group of the French navy at Marseilles and in 1950 became commander of the oceanographic research vessel *Calypso*. He is famous for such films as *The Silent World* (1953) and *The Living Sea* (1963) and for his environmental campaigns.

covenant A binding agreement between two parties whereby each promises to do something for the other (*see also* deed). In the Old Testament, the covenant between God and Israel forms the basis of the Jewish religion. In return for obedience to the Law (the Ten Commandments) as delivered to Moses, the Israelites were privileged as God's chosen people.

Covenanters Scottish Presbyterians who in the 16th and 17th centuries covenanted to defend their church. The National Covenant of 1638 was signed by thousands of Scottish Presbyterians after Charles I's attempt to introduce the English Prayer Book, this opposition culminating in the Bishops' Wars. In the English Civil War the Covenanters joined the parliamentarians in 1643 in return for the promise of church reform (the Solemn League and Covenant). After the Restoration

(1660) they were persecuted until the re-establishment of Presbyterianism in Scotland after the Glorious Revolution (1688).

COVENT GARDEN   *Charles Fowler's market building (1830) redeveloped in the 1970s.*

Covent Garden   The principal English opera house, officially named the Royal Opera House. The first theatre on the site was opened in 1732, and the present building dates from the 1850s; it is currently the home of both the Royal Opera and the Royal Ballet Company. It takes its name from a square (originally a convent garden) onto which it backs, which was laid out in 1631 by Inigo Jones. For many years London's fruit and vegetable market occupied the square but in 1973 it moved to Nine Elms (Wandsworth) and the square was redeveloped as a shopping precinct. Since 1987 the Old Flower Market has housed the Theatre Museum.

Coventry   52 25N 1 30W A city in central England, in the West Midlands. Heavily bombed during World War II, the city centre was almost entirely rebuilt. Its famous cathedral, designed by Sir Basil Spence, was opened in 1962 and retains the ruins of the old cathedral, which was bombed in 1940. Population (1984 est): 314 100.

Coward, Sir Noel   (1899–1973) British dramatist, composer, and actor. He first established his reputation with *The Vortex* (1924), a domestic drama, but his best-known plays are elegant comedies of manners, such as *Hay Fever* (1925) and *Blithe Spirit* (1941). He also contributed to revues, musicals, and films, notably *In Which We Serve* (1942) and *Brief Encounter* (1946). His best-known songs include "Mad Dogs and Englishmen".

Cowes   50 45N 1 18W A town in S England, situated on the Isle of Wight. It is a resort and yachting centre. Population (1981): 19 663.

cowpea   An annual African plant, *Vigna unguiculata*, widely grown for food in tropical areas. There are two forms: a short erect one grown in Africa and America, whose seeds are used dried, and a tall climbing one grown in SE Asia, whose long pods are eaten when young. Family: *Leguminosae*.

Cowper, William   (1731–1800) British poet. With John Newton he published *Olney Hymns* in 1779. "John Gilpin's Ride" (1783), a comic ballad, and "The Task" (1785), a long poem on rural themes, were both very successful. He was mentally unstable throughout his life, and frequently attempted suicide.

cowpox   A contagious virus disease of cattle that can be contracted by man. Edward Jenner used fluid from cowpox blisters to produce the first effective smallpox vaccine.

cowrie   A gastropod mollusc of the family *Cypraeidae* (about 160 species), mostly found in warm seas. 1–15 cm long, cowries have glossy shells with inrolled lips and feed at night on small animals. The shell of the tropical money cowrie (*Cypraea moneta*), about 3 cm long, is used as a form of currency in Africa and India.

cowslip   A perennial spring-flowering Eurasian herb, *Primula veris*, growing to a height of 20 cm. It has bright-yellow flowers and is found from lowland meadows to alpine pastures. Family: *Primulaceae* (primrose family).

coyote   A wild dog, *Canis latrans*, of Central and North American grassland, also called prairie wolf. Coyotes are about 120 cm long, including the bushy tail (30 cm), and have yellowish fur. They hunt alone or in packs and take food ranging from insects to small deer.

coypu   A South American aquatic rodent, *Myocaster coypus*. About 60 cm long (excluding a long hairless tail), it has thick brown fur and webbed hind feet. The under-fur of the belly is known as nutria, and coypus are farmed for fur. Family: *Capromyidae*.

crab   A crustacean belonging to the tribes *Brachyura* (true crabs; about 4500 species) or *Anomura* (about 1300 species). True crabs have a wide flat body covered by a hard carapace. There is a large pair of pincers and four pairs of legs used for walking (typically sideways) or swimming. They are carnivores or scavengers and most species are marine. Order: *Decapoda*.

crab apple   A tree, *Malus sylvestris*, 2–10 m high: one of the species from which cultivated apples have been developed. A native of Europe and Asia, it is sometimes grown as an ornamental. Family: *Rosaceae*.

Crabbe, George   (1754–1832) British poet, doctor, and cleric, born in Aldeburgh, Suffolk, scene of many of his poems. *The Village* (1783) was a brutally realistic portrayal of rural life. This theme he took up again in the verse tales of *The Borough* (1810) and *Tales of the Hall* (1819).

Crab nebula   A turbulent expanding mass of gas, lying about 6000 light years distant in the constellation Taurus. It is the remnant of a supernova that was observed in 1054. Within the nebula lies the **Crab pulsar**. This optical pulsar rotates with a period of only 0.033 seconds.

Cracow.   *See* Kraków.

Craig, Edward Henry Gordon.   *See* Terry, Ellen.

crake   A small shy bird belonging to the rail family, commonly found in marshes and swamps. The Eurasian spotted crake (*Porzana porzana*) is 23 cm long and has a red ring at the base of the bill.

Cram, Steve (1960–   )   British middle-distance runner. He won the world championship 1500 m title in 1983 and set several new world records.

Cranach the Elder, Lucas   (Lucas Müller; 1472–1553) German artist. Because of his portraits of Reformation leaders including his friend Luther, he is sometimes called the Reformation painter. He is also noted for his stylized but sensuous nudes, e.g. *Adam and Eve* (Courtauld Institute, London).

cranberry   A low evergreen shrub of the genus *Vaccinium*, bearing red edible berries and growing in acidic boggy areas. *V. oxycoccus* occurs in Europe, N Asia, and North America. *V. macrocarpon* of North America has larger fruits (about 1.5 cm across). Family: *Ericaceae* (heath family).

THOMAS CRANMER *Detail of a portrait (1546).*

crane (bird) A long-legged bird belonging to a family (*Gruidae*; 14 species) occurring in Old World regions and North America. Up to 140 cm tall with a wingspan of over 200 cm, cranes vary from grey to white with black wingtips; some species are crested. They feed on grain, shoots, and small animals; northern species are migratory. Order: *Gruiformes* (rails, etc.). *See also* demoiselle; whooping crane.

cranefly A harmless fly, also called daddy longlegs, belonging to the family *Tipulidae*. Craneflies are 6–75 mm long with long delicate legs and wings. The larvae generally occur in water or rotting vegetation. However some—the leatherjackets—are plant pests.

cranesbill A herbaceous plant of the genus *Geranium* (about 400 species), widely distributed, and usually having pink or purple flowers. They take their name from the long slender beaklike carpels. The meadow cranesbill (*G. pratense*), a perennial up to 60 cm high, has violet-blue flowers. Family: *Geraniaceae*.

Cranmer, Thomas (1489–1556) Anglican reformer and martyr. He was consecrated Archbishop of Canterbury in 1532, following his support of Henry VIII in the king's divorce dispute with the pope. He is especially remembered for his contributions to the Prayer Books of 1549 and 1552. Under Queen Mary he was tried as a heretic and burned at the stake.

Crassus, Marcus Licinius (c. 115–53 BC) Roman politician, nicknamed *Dives* (wealthy). Crassus suppressed Spartacus' revolt (71) and joined Pompey and Caesar in the first Triumvirate (60). He was killed during an invasion of Parthia.

crayfish A freshwater crustacean, also called crawfish and crawdad, belonging to the superfamily *Nephropidea*. It has a small lobster-like body, 25–75 mm long, and feeds on plant and animal material. Some species are edible. Order: *Decapoda*.

Crécy, Battle of (26 August, 1346) The first land battle of the Hundred Years' War, fought in N France, in which the English, led by Edward III, defeated the French under Philip VI.

Cree An Algonkian-speaking North American Indian people. They lived by hunting and trapping in small wandering bands. One group, known as Plains Cree, moved into the Plains and adopted the buffalo-hunting culture of this region often raiding for horses.

creeds In Christianity, formal summaries of the principal items of belief, recited as part of the eucharistic service in many Churches. The two most widely used are the Apostles' Creed (probably 3rd century AD) and the Nicene Creed, probably a revision by the Council of Constantinople (381) of the creed promulgated at the Council of Nicaea (325). The Athanasian Creed, probably dating from the 5th century, is used in the Anglican catechism.

Creek A Muskogean-speaking North American Indian people divided into the Muskogee of Georgia and the Hitchiti of Alabama. They were cultivators and hunters and tattooed their bodies heavily. A confederacy of Creek towns fought the encroaching whites in the 18th and early 19th centuries. On their defeat in the 1830s they were removed to Oklahoma.

Cremona 45 08N 10 01E A town in N Italy, in Lombardy. It has a 12th-century cathedral and a 13th-century palace. From the 16th to the 18th centuries it was famous for the manufacture of violins. Population (1981 est): 80 758.

creole 1. Originally a White person born in Spanish America during the colonial period (16th to 18th centuries). 2. A person of mixed blood living in the Caribbean area or in Latin America, extending to encompass a descendant of various other groups. 3. A patois based on French, English, or Dutch and spoken especially in the West Indies as a mother tongue.

creosote A substance produced by distilling tar. The creosote used for preserving wood is obtained from coal tar and is a brownish mixture of aromatic hydrocarbons and phenols. Creosote made from wood tar is a mixture of phenols and is used in pharmacy.

cresol (or methylphenol; $CH_3C_6H_4OH$) A liquid aromatic compound obtained from coal tar. It has three isomers, a mixture of which is used as a disinfectant.

BATTLE OF CRÉCY *A formal view, with the long bow prominent.*

cress A plant of the mustard family (*Cruciferae*) the leaves of which are used in salads, especially garden cress, or peppergrass (*Lepidium sativum*). The seedlings are eaten, often with those of white mustard (*Sinapis al-*

ba). The European winter, or land, cress (*Barbarea verna*) grows to a height of 100 cm.

Cretaceous period   A geological period of the Mesozoic era, between about 135 and 65 million years ago, divided into the Lower and Upper Cretaceous. The dinosaurs and other giant reptiles, as well as the ammonites and many other invertebrates, became extinct at the end of the Cretaceous.

Crete (Modern Greek name: Kríti)   The largest of the Greek islands, in the E Mediterranean Sea. It is generally mountainous, rising over 2400 m (7874 ft). The economy is based primarily on agriculture and tourism. *History*: colonized probably in the 6th millennium BC from Asia Minor, Crete achieved extensive maritime power during the Middle Minoan period (c. 2000–c. 1700 BC). Relics include the palace at Knossos and clay tablets bearing two different scripts known as Linear A and Linear B. Politically insignificant in the history of classical Greece, it fell to Rome (67 BC), Byzantium (395 AD), and the Muslims (826). In 1204 it was sold to the Venetians, who gave both the island and Iráklion the name Candia. It fell to Turkey in 1669 and was officially incorporated into Greece in 1913. Area: 8332 sq km (3217 sq mi). Population (1981): 502 165. Capital: Khaniá.

cretinism   The condition resulting from a deficiency of thyroid hormone, which is present from birth. Affected children are mentally retarded dwarfs with coarse skin and facial features. Cretinism is treated with injections of thyroxine.

Crewe   53 05N 2 27W   A town in NW England, in Cheshire. Crewe developed as an important railway junction with railway engineering and workshops. Population (1981): 47 759.

Crick, Francis Harry Compton (1916–) British biophysicist, who (with James D. Watson) proposed a model for the molecular structure of DNA (1953). Following this breakthrough, Crick helped to determine the mechanism of protein synthesis. He shared a Nobel Prize (1962) with Watson and Maurice Wilkins.

cricket (sport)   An 11-a-side bat-and-ball team game, in which the object is to score the most runs. It originated in England among shepherds using their crooks as bats; its rules were laid down in 1744 and the game is played almost exclusively in the UK and its former empire. Presided over by two umpires, it is played on a grass pitch 22 yd (20.12 m) long having at each end a wicket of three stumps surmounted by two bails. The cork and twine ball, encased in leather, is 8.8–9 in (22.4–22.9 cm) in circumference and weighs 5.5–5.75 oz (155.9–163 g). The members of one team take turns to bat in pairs, one defending each wicket; the batsmen's objective is to score runs by hitting the ball and exchanging ends before the ball is returned to the pitch. Each player bats until he is bowled, caught, stumped, run out, or judged lbw (leg before wicket). The members of the other team field, some taking turns to bowl the ball. After every over of six balls (sometimes eight in Australia) the bowler changes, the new bowler bowling from the other wicket. A match consists of one or two innings and may last for a few hours or up to six days, depending on the type of competition. International cricket is played mainly in Test matches between England, Australia, the West Indies, New Zealand, India, Pakistan, and Sri Lanka. In England first-class cricket chiefly involves the 17 professional first-class county teams. *See also* Ashes; Marylebone Cricket Club.

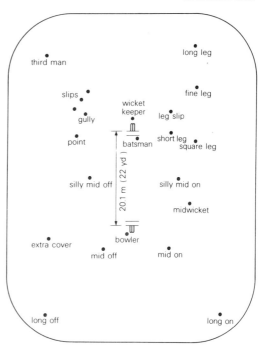

CRICKET   *The pitch, showing the usual fielding positions (for a right-handed batsman).*

cricket (zoology)   An insect, resembling a grasshopper but with longer antennae, belonging to one of several families of the order *Orthoptera*. The males stridulate (i.e. make a chirping noise) by rubbing the front wings together. True crickets (family *Gryllidae*; 2400 species) have black or brown flattened bodies, 3–50 mm long, with long tail appendages (cerci) and short forewings (they do not fly). The females have long needle-like ovipositors for depositing eggs in soil or crevices. True crickets are omnivorous.

Crimea (Russian name: Krym)   A peninsula and autonomous region (*oblast*) in the SW Soviet Union. It is mainly flat but rises to 1545 m (5069 ft) in the S. Iron ore is mined here and wheat, tobacco, and wine are produced. *History*: colonized by Greeks in the 6th century BC, the Crimea was invaded by Goths, Huns, and others and in 1239 was made a khanate by Tatars. This was overthrown by Turks in 1475, and the area was annexed by Russia in 1783. Area: about 27 000 sq km (10 423 sq mi). Population (1983): 2 277 000. *See also* Crimean War.

Crimean War   (1853–56) The war between Russia, on one side, and Britain, France, the Ottoman (Turkish) Empire, and (from 1855) Sardinia-Piedmont, on the other. Caused by Russia's expansionist ambitions in the Balkans, the war culminated in the year-long siege of Sevastopol and the battles of Balaclava and Inkerman. The Russians eventually evacuated the port in September, 1855 and peace was formally concluded at Paris (1856). Over 250 000 men were lost by each side, many from disease in the appalling hospitals of the Crimea. The British Government dispatched Florence Nightin-

CRIMEAN WAR *French and British soldiers during the siege of Sevastopol (1855).*

gale to inspect those at Scutari, where her work had a considerable effect in improving conditions.

Criminal Investigation Department (CID)   The investigative department of police forces in the UK. A CID was created at Scotland Yard in 1878, based on the detective branch that had been in existence since 1842. All UK police forces now have their own CIDs, all recruits to which must first have served as uniformed officers.

criminal law   The body of law determining the acts and circumstances that amount to a crime (a wrong against society prohibited by law) and the punishment for crimes. Criminal law derives in England chiefly from common law, although statute law has contributed significantly to its development. Most crimes entail both an act (*actus reus*) and a mental element (*mens rea*). However, there is a growing number of crimes in which no mental element is necessary (called crimes of strict liability), such as most motoring offences. Insanity, infancy (children under the age of ten), or duress (an act committed under threat of death or serious personal injury) may excuse a crime, but ignorance of the law does not if, in cases involving a mental element, the offender intends the result of his acts.
In England all criminal cases appear first before a Magistrates' Court and may then be committed to the Crown Court (*see* courts of law).

crinoid   A marine invertebrate animal belonging to a class (*Crinoidea*; about 700 species) of echinoderms. It has a small cup-shaped body covered with calcareous plates and with five radiating pairs of feathery flexible arms surrounding the mouth at the top. Sea lilies are fixed to the sea bottom, coral reefs, etc., by a stalk. Feather stars, e.g. *Antedon*, are free-swimming. Crinoids occur mainly in deep waters and feed on microscopic plankton and detritus. The larvae are sedentary.

Crippen, Hawley Harvey   (1862–1910) US murderer. He poisoned his wife in London and then attempted to escape to the USA with his mistress. He was arrested on board ship (following one of the first uses of shore to ship radio) and returned to England, where he was hanged.

critical mass   The mass of fissile substance that is just capable of sustaining a chain reaction within it. Below the critical mass, too many of the particles that might have induced a reaction escape.

critical-path analysis   A planning method based on the use of a schematic representation of the network of activities and events involved in a project. A critical path is a sequence of activities in which the key parameters, usually time and cost, cannot be increased without endangering the whole project. The method is commonly used in large construction projects.

critical state   The state of a gas at its critical temperature, pressure, and volume. The critical temperature is the temperature above which a gas cannot be liquefied by increased pressure alone. The vapour pressure of the gas at this temperature is the critical pressure and its volume, the critical volume. In the critical state the density of the vapour is equal to the density of the liquid.

Crivelli, Carlo   (c. 1430–95) Venetian painter, set apart from the Venetian school by his linear style and the decorative detail that appears in such paintings as *The Annunciation* (National Gallery, London).

Croatia (Serbo-Croat name: Hrvatska)   A constituent republic of NW Yugoslavia. It is chiefly mountainous, descending to plains in the NE. It is primarily agricultural, producing cereals, potatoes, tobacco, fruit, and livestock. *History*: settled by the Croats in the 7th century AD, the region was successively controlled by Hungary, Turkey, and Austria until the formation of the kingdom of the Serbs, Croats, and Slovenes (later Yugoslavia) in 1918. Following occupation by the Axis Powers in World War II, Croatia was proclaimed an independent state (1941). In 1945 Croatia rejoined Yugoslavia. Area: 56 538 sq km (22 050 sq mi). Population (1986 est): 4 665 000. Capital: Zagreb.

Croatian.   *See* Serbo-Croat.

Croce, Benedetto   (1866–1952) Italian philosopher. His system is expounded in *Philosophy of Mind* (1900–10). The only reality is mental and this reality is divided into theoretical and practical. Theoretical reality comprises intuition (art and aesthetics) and conception (philosophy or history). Practical reality comprises individual will (political and economic activity) and universal will (morality).

Crockett, Davy   (1786–1836) US frontiersman. As a colonel in the Tennessee militia and member of Congress he fought for Texas in its struggle for independence from Mexico and was killed at the Alamo.

crocodile   A reptile belonging to either of two genera, *Crocodylus* or *Osteolaemus*, and distinguished from alligators and caymans by having a more pointed snout and fewer teeth, the fourth tooth of the lower jaw remaining visible when the mouth is closed. Crocodiles occur chiefly in tropical fresh waters although the estuarine crocodile (*C. porosus*), which reaches a length of 6 m, occurs in coastal waters of SE Asia and Australia. Crocodiles belong to the order *Crocodilia* (about 20 species). Crocodilians are amphibious mainly nocturnal carnivores and rivers, where they prey chiefly on fish but also on water birds and land animals. They have long powerful jaws and a covering of protective bony plates; the ears and nostrils can be closed by valves when under water. The female builds a nest of mud or vegetation in which over a hundred shelled eggs may be laid.

crocodile bird   An African riverbank courser, *Pluvianus aegyptius*, that feeds on parasites picked from crocodiles. It is 23 cm long and is black with white markings.

Crocus A genus of low-growing plants (75 species), native to Mediterranean regions and widely planted in gardens. Spring-flowering species include *C. vernus*, with white, blue, or purple flowers, and *C. aureus*, with deep-yellow flowers. *C. speciosus* is a purple autumn-flowering species. An Asian species (*C. sativus*) is the source of saffron. Family: *Iridaceae*. *Compare* autumn crocus.

Croesus (died c. 546 BC) The last king of Lydia (c. 560–c. 546 BC), famous for his wealth. He conquered the Greek cities on the coast of Asia Minor but was defeated by the Persian king Cyrus (II) the Great (d. 529) in 546. According to legend, Croesus was saved by Apollo from execution by Cyrus.

Crohn's disease An inflammatory disorder of the intestinal tract named after the US physician B. B. Crohn (1884–1983), occurs most commonly between the ages of 20 and 40 years; symptoms include abdominal pain and diarrhoea. Its cause is not known but it may be a form of autoimmunity. Patients are treated with drugs; some cases require surgery.

Cro-Magnon A prehistoric race of men. Skeletal remains were found (1868) at Cro-Magnon SW France and similar bones of tall broad-faced individuals have been found at other European sites. They first appeared about 35 000 years ago. The Cro-Magnon hunted reindeer, bison, and wild horse and produced the earliest known examples of cave art (*see* Lascaux). *See also* Homo.

Crompton, Samuel (1753–1827) British inventor of the spinning mule (1779). It was able to produce yarn of a higher quality and at a greater speed than had previously been possible. Crompton sold his idea for very little money but in 1812 he was awarded a parliamentary grant of £5,000.

OLIVER CROMWELL *Dismissing the Rump of the Long Parliament (1653).*

Cromwell, Oliver (1599–1658) English soldier and statesman; Lord Protector of England (1653–58). Cromwell was MP for Huntingdon in the parliament of 1628–29 and a critic of Charles I in the Long Parliament, summoned in 1640. After the outbreak of the Civil War he raised a troop of cavalry, the nucleus of his Ironsides (formed 1643), and fought at Edgehill (1642). He held command at Marston Moor (1644) and was instrumental in the formation of the New Model Army under Fairfax, which with Cromwell as second in command decisively defeated Charles at Naseby (1645). Cromwell acted as mediator between the king, parliament, and the New Model Army but his conciliatory attitude hardened after Charles' flight to the Isle of Wight; when the second Civil War ended in Charles' defeat (1648), Cromwell signed the king's death warrant. After the establishment of the Commonwealth he ruthlessly subjected Ireland (1649–50) and defeated Charles' heir at Dunbar (1650) and Worcester (1651). In 1653 he expelled the Rump of the Long Parliament and following the failure of the Barebones Parliament (formed in 1653 and named after one of its members, Praisegod Barebones), he accepted the Instrument of Government, which established the Protectorate. As Lord Protector, Cromwell established Puritanism but permitted religious toleration. His attempt to decentralize government by dividing England into ten districts was short lived. His foreign policy was dictated by religious and commercial considerations: he ended the first Dutch War, allied with France against Spain (gaining Dunkirk), and conquered Jamaica (1655). He refused parliament's offer of the crown in 1657. He was succeeded as Lord Protector by his son **Richard Cromwell** (1626–1712), who was forced to abdicate in 1659.

Cromwell, Thomas, Earl of Essex (c. 1485–1540) English statesman, who drafted the legislation that made the English Church independent of Rome (*see* Reformation). He entered Wolsey's service in 1514, became an MP in 1529 and chancellor of the exchequer in 1533. He gained Henry's divorce from Catherine of Aragon by a series of Acts that made the king head of the English Church. Between 1536 and 1540 he organized the dissolution of the monasteries, after which his negotiation of Henry's disastrous marriage to Anne of Cleves led to his execution for treason.

Cronin, A(rchibald) J(oseph) (1896–1981) British novelist. He practised medicine until he published his successful first novel, *Hatter's Castle* (1931). His later novels include *The Citadel* (1937) and *The Judas Tree* (1961). The radio and television series *Dr Finlay's Casebook* was based on his medical stories.

Cronus A Greek deity, the youngest of the Titans. He ruled the universe after castrating his father Uranus. He swallowed all the children he fathered by his sister Rhea except Zeus, for whom a stone was substituted. Zeus was reared secretly in Crete and eventually overthrew Cronus.

Crookes, Sir William (1832–1919) British physicist, who showed that cathode rays consisted of charged particles rather than electromagnetic radiation, since they were deflected by a magnetic field. He invented the Crookes radiometer and Crookes glass, containing cerium, to protect the eyes of the industrial workers. He also discovered the element thalium.

croquet A ball-and-mallet game that probably developed from *paille-maille*, a French game played certainly by the 13th century. It is played on a grass lawn, ideally 35 × 28 yd (32 × 25.6 m), with an arrangement of six hoops and one peg. Two to four players attempt to follow a prescribed course through the hoops, each using a distinctively coloured ball, the winner being the first to hit the peg with his ball. If a player's ball hits (roquets) another ball, the player may croquet this ball by placing his own ball next to it and striking his own ball so that the opponent's ball is also moved; the object is to advance his own ball towards the peg and to drive his opponent's ball off course. After passing through a hoop or scoring a roquet a player has another turn.

Crosby, Bing (Harry Lillis C.; 1904–77) US popular singer. He achieved worldwide fame during the 1930s and 1940s with such hits as *White Christmas* (1942). He starred in many films, often with Bob Hope, and also in his own radio and television shows.

crossbill A finch of the genus *Loxia* (3 species), 14.5–17 cm long, whose unique cross-tipped bill is specialized for extracting seeds from unopened cones. The common crossbill (*L. curvirostra*) of Eurasia and North America feeds on spruce seeds. The male is red and the female grey-green. The parrot crossbill (*L. pytyopsittacus*) feeds on pine seeds.

crossbow A short bow mounted on a stock, used in Europe throughout the middle ages. Crossbows were composite, made of wood, horn, tendons, and by the early 15th century of steel (called an arbalest). They were drawn by hand, a belt hook, or a winch. The bolt or *quarrel* was short, iron-tipped, fletched with wood, leather, or brass, and capable of penetrating armour. Slower and less accurate than the longbow, it could be fired from behind cover. It is now used for sport.

ankh   Greek   Latin   tau

St Andrew's   Celtic   papal   Maltese

CROSSES *As a Christian symbol the cross was popularized by Constantine the Great and came into wide use in the 4th century.*

crosses As a symbol, the cross is found in the art of several ancient cultures. One of the earliest Egyptian hieroglyphs is the cruciform ankh (*crux ansata*), the symbol of life. The primary association of the cross is with Christianity. It had several forms, conventionally distinguished by their Latin names: a simple upright stake (*crux simplex*); a stake with a transverse beam towards the top (*crux immissa*), which is known as the Latin cross and is the common form in the Western Church; a stake topped by a transverse beam (*crux commissa*), also known as the tau cross or cross of St Anthony; and an X-shaped structure (*crux decussata*), known as the cross of St Andrew. In European art and Western Churches, the crucifixion is usually depicted with a Latin cross. The Greek cross or cross of St George has vertical and horizontal arms of equal length and is the traditional form in use in Orthodox Churches. The cross has influenced in-

numerable aspects of religious ritual, including the cruciform plan of churches. As a charge in heraldry, it is given various elaborated forms; a familiar example is the Maltese cross, the insignia of the Hospitallers and, in Britain, of the St John Ambulance Association.

Crossopterygii An order of bony fish, most of which are now extinct. The suborder *Rhipidistia* were predatory freshwater fishes of the Devonian and Carboniferous periods (about 400–280 million years ago), some of which evolved into the amphibians. The suborder *Coelacanthini* contains *Latimeria*, the only surviving member of the order (*see* coelacanth). Subclass: *Sarcopterygii*.

Croton A genus of tropical trees and shrubs (750 species) many of which are of economic importance. *C. tiglium* of SE Asia produces croton oil, a powerful laxative now considered unsafe. The bark of *C. cascarilla* and *C. eluteria*, trees of the Bahamas, produces cascarilla, used in tonics. *C. lacciferum* India and Sri Lanka provides a lac used in varnishes. Several Brazilian species produce dragon's-blood resin. Family: *Euphorbiaceae* (spurge family).

croup An acute infection of the respiratory tract, usually caused by viruses, resulting in inflammation and obstruction of the larynx (voice box). Croup occurs most commonly in children under five years of age; symptoms include difficulty in breathing. Treatment consists of steam inhalations and sedatives; severe cases may require surgery.

crow A large songbird of the widely distributed family *Corvidae* (102 species). 30–65 cm long, crows typically have a black or brightly coloured plumage and a stout bill. Their food includes carrion and they have a distinctive call. The typical crows are the carrion, hooded, and American crows but the family also includes the rooks, ravens, choughs, jays, and jackdaws.

crown colony A territory that is under the direct legislative control of the UK. Most crown colonies have now been granted independence: the most important one remaining is Hong Kong.

Crown Court. *See* courts of law.

crown jewels Royal insignia and regalia and the personal jewellery inherited or acquired by a sovereign. The British Crown Jewels, now kept in the Tower of London, were mainly amassed after the Restoration, the earlier set having been destroyed under Cromwell. Those used for coronations include a replica of St Edward's crown, the Sword of State, the Orb, and the Sceptre. Those used for other state occasions include the Imperial State Crown and another Sword of State.

Crown land Land that belongs to the UK monarch and is managed by the Crown Estate Commissioners. The profits from the land do not go to the monarch, as all revenues were surrendered by George III in 1760 in exchange for the income provided by the civil list.

crown of thorns 1. A Madagascan shrub, *Euphorbia splendens*, often cultivated for ornament. Up to 100 cm high, it has spiny stems and clusters of small flowers. See Euphorbia. 2. A spiny vigorous shrub, *Zizyphus spina-christi*. It is widespread in the Mediterranean region and is said to be the source of Christ's crown of thorns. Family: *Rhamnaceae* (buckthorn family).

crown-of-thorns starfish A reddish starfish, *Acanthaster planci*, that has a spiny body, up to 45 cm across, with 12–19 arms. With the decimation of its chief predator—the Pacific triton (*Charonia tritonis*)—by shell collectors, it has spread throughout the South Pacific.

Crown Prosecution Service An independent prosecuting body established in England and Wales in 1986 to decide whether a case should be pursued in the courts. It deals with cases brought by the police (excluding traffic offences) and is headed by the Director of Public Prosecutions.

Cruciferae A family of plants (about 1900 species), mainly annual or perennial herbs, abundant in N temperate regions. The flowers are four-petalled and cross-shaped. Many crucifers are of economic importance as food plants, cattle food, ornamentals, and weeds. Some, such as cabbage and other brassicas, have been grown since ancient times.

GEORGE CRUIKSHANK   *Detail of an illustration for Oliver Twist.*

Cruikshank, George (1792–1872) British painter and illustrator. He illustrated such books as Dickens' *Oliver Twist* and Ainsworth's *Tower of London*. His etchings of *The Bottle* and painting of *The Worship of Bacchus* (Tate Gallery) are moralizing sermons on alcoholism.

cruiser A fast heavily armed warship, smaller than a battleship but larger than a destroyer and designed for a larger cruising radius. Cruisers with increased firepower, nuclear power, and greater versatility have replaced most of the battleships in the world's major navies.

Crusades The military expeditions organized in western Christendom primarily to recover the Holy Places of Palestine from Muslim occupation. The first Crusade (1095–99) was launched under the aegis of the papacy. Jerusalem was captured and the Crusader states of the Kingdom of Jerusalem, the County of Edessa, Antioch, and Tripoli were created. The fall (1144) of Edessa inspired the unsuccessful second Crusade (1147–48) and the capture of Jerusalem by Saladin in 1187 led to the inconclusive third Crusade (1189–92), led by Philip II Augustus of France, Emperor Frederick I Barbarossa, and Richard (I) the Lionheart of England. The fourth Crusade (1202–04) was diverted from its initial objective, Egypt, and sacked Constantinople (1204). The four Crusades of the 13th century failed to recover lost ground and Acre, the last foothold of the West in Palestine, was lost in 1291. *See also* Children's Crusade.

crustacean An arthropod of the class *Crustacea* (over 35 000 species), which includes the barnacles, wood-

louse, shrimps, lobsters, crabs, etc. The head bears two pairs of antennae and three pairs of jaws; the head and thorax together are usually covered by a chitinous carapace. There are numerous pairs of forked appendages, which are modified for different functions. Crustaceans are predominantly aquatic, breathing by means of gills. A few, such as the fish louse, are parasitic on fish, whales, and other aquatic animals. The larvae are mainly free-swimming and pass through several stages (*see* metamorphosis) to reach the adult form.

cryogenics The production, effects, and uses of very low temperatures, usually meaning from −150°C down to absolute zero. The most common method of producing cryogenic temperatures is to use adiabatic processes. Cryogenic effects include changes in electrical properties, such as superconductivity, and changes in mechanical properties, such as superfluidity (*see* superfluid). Cryogenics has been applied to food preservation, life-support systems in space, and liquid propellants.

Crystal Palace A building designed by Joseph Paxton (1801–65) to house the Great Exhibition of 1851. The Crystal Palace, which had an area of 69 892 sq m (772 289 sq ft), was built in Hyde Park, London, of prefabricated glass and iron. It was later reassembled at Sydenham in SE London but burnt down in 1936.

crystals Solids that have a regular geometrical shape because the constituent atoms, ions, or molecules are arranged in an ordered repeating pattern, known as a crystal lattice. There are seven crystal systems, into which all crystals are classified. Crystal structures are studied by a variety of techniques, including X-ray diffraction and electron microscopy. **Crystallography** is concerned with the structure and properties of crystals. Noncrystalline solids, such as glass, are said to be amorphous.

ctenophore A marine invertebrate animal, also called comb jelly, sea gooseberry, and sea walnut, belonging to the phylum *Ctenophora* (about 80 species). Its transparent gelatinous body is usually rounded and bears eight rows of ciliated comblike plates, used for locomotion. Ctenophores often occur in swarms in coastal waters, feeding on planktonic animals.

Cuba, Republic of A country in the Caribbean Sea, off the S coast of Florida. It consists of two main islands, Cuba and the Isla de Pinos, together with over 1500 small islands and keys. On the island of Cuba fertile plains rise to mountains in the centre and SE and hills in the NW. The population is mainly of European origin, with large African and mixed minorities. *Economy*: state controlled, it is dependent upon its sugar crop. Tobacco is another important export crop and meat production is important in the domestic economy. Mineral resources include nickel (the second largest export). Largely dependent upon the Soviet Union for oil, Cuba has undertaken oil exploration. *History*: discovered by Columbus in 1492, it was a Spanish colony (except in 1762–63, when it was occupied by the British) until 1898, when Spain withdrew following war with the USA. After three years of US occupation Cuba became a republic (1901) but the USA continued to intervene in Cuba's affairs until 1934. In 1940 Fulgencio Batista (1901–73) took Cuba into World War II on the Allied side. His corrupt dictatorship was overthrown in Castro's second socialist revolt (1959), after which relations with the USA became increasingly strained and Cuba moved closer in its international relations to the Soviet Union. In 1961 an invasion of Cuban exiles with US support was defeated at the Bay of Pigs and in 1962 the Soviet installation of missile bases in Cuba resulted in a US naval blockade. The crisis was resolved when the Soviet Union agreed to remove the bases. In recent years Cuban troops have been involved in revolutionary conflicts in both Africa and the Caribbean. Head of government and first secretary of the Cuban Communist Party: Fidel Castro Ruz. Official language: Spanish. Official currency: Cuban peso of 100 centavos. Area 148 124 sq km (46 736 sq mi). Population (1988 est): 10 462 000. Capital and main port: Havana.

CUCKOO *A tiny hedge sparrow (right) feeds the usurping cuckoo.*

cubism A style of painting and sculpture, originating in the works of Picasso and Braque in about 1907. It started as an intellectual investigation of how a solid form can be represented in two dimensions without resorting to illusionism. Volume was suggested by the fusion of multiple viewpoints of an object, which was presented as a complex of geometrical shapes. The subject matter of early cubism was invariably everyday objects of simple form, many being suggested by the work of Cézanne. After 1911 the development of cubism led to the introduction of collage and a more decorative approach. Cubism was the principal catalytic influence on the evolution of abstract art.

cuckoo A bird belonging to a family (*Cuculidae*; 127 species) occurring worldwide and ranging from 16–70 cm in length. The European cuckoo (*Cuculus canorus*), grey with white barring, belongs to a subfamily of parasitic cuckoos (*Cuculinae*; 47 species); these lay their eggs in the nests of other birds, which rear their young. Order: *Cuculiformes* (cuckoos and turacos).

cuckoopint A perennial herbaceous European plant, *Arum maculatum*, also called lords-and-ladies. 30–50 cm tall, it has a cylindrical cluster of tiny flowers, which protrudes from a funnel-shaped bract (spathe). The flowers give rise to poisonous red berries. Family: *Araceae*.

cuckoo-spit insect. *See* froghopper.

cucumber An annual vine, *Cucumis sativus*, widely cultivated since ancient times. The long green juicy fruits, up to 60 cm long, are eaten raw, cooked, or pickled (*see* gherkin). Family: *Cucurbitaceae* (gourd family).

Cuernavaca 18 57N 99 15W A city and resort in S central Mexico. It is the site of Cortés' palace, a Franciscan cathedral (1529), and a university (1939). Many writers, artists, and film stars have resided here. Population (1980): 232 355.

cuisine minceur A recently developed style of gourmet cookery in which the traditional generous use of butter, cream, and other rich ingredients is minimized. Cuisine minceur was elaborated by the French chef Michel Guérard (1933–) in the 1970s at his restaurant at Eugénie-les-Bains in SW France.

Cullinan diamond An exceptional diamond weighing 3106 metric carats (c. 621 g) when found in the Premier Mine, South Africa, in 1905. It was cut into 9 major and 96 small stones. The two largest (Star of Africa and Cullinan II) are set in the British royal regalia.

Culloden Moor A moor in N Scotland, in the Highland Region near Inverness. In 1746 it was the scene of the last land battle to be fought in Britain, in which the Young Pretender, Charles Edward Stuart, was defeated by the Duke of Cumberland, thus ending the Jacobite cause in Britain.

Culpeper, Nicholas (1616–54) English herbalist, physician, and astrologer. In 1649 he published an unauthorized translation of the official London Pharmacopoeia. This was followed by his famous and equally popular *Complete Herbal* (1653).

Cultural Revolution, Great Proletarian (1966–68) A political rather than cultural movement launched in China by Mao 'Tse-tung in opposition to bureaucracy and to reinvigorate revolutionary attitudes. Many leading officials were dismissed, the formal educational system was abolished, and reforms to foster correct political views were introduced. Many universities were closed and young people, mobilized as Red Guards, attacked Party officials and destroyed cultural objects.

Cumberland A former county of NW England, now part of the new county of Cumbria.

Cumbria A county in NW England, bordering on the Irish Sea. It was created in 1974 from Westmorland, Cumberland, and parts of NW Lancashire and NW Yorkshire. It consists of the Lake District, enclosed by coastal lowlands and the Pennine uplands. Agricultural activity includes sheep, dairy, and arable farming. New industries are replacing the traditional ones of coal, iron, and steel. Atomic energy establishments exist at Sellafield and Calder Hall. Area: 6809 sq km (2628 sq mi). Population (1986 est): 486 600. Administrative centre: Carlisle.

cumin An annual herb, *Cuminum cyminum*, up to 30 cm high with small whitish flowers and bristly fruits. Native to the Mediterranean, it has long been cultivated in Europe, India, and China for its bitter fruits, which are used in curry powders, to flavour liqueurs, etc. Family: *Umbelliferae*.

cumulus cloud (Cu) A low type of cloud of convective origin having a heaped appearance and developing vertically from a flat base. **Cumulonimbus cloud** is heavy and dense, extending vertically to about 6000 m (20 000 ft), and is associated with thunderstorms. Its upper part often spreads out to form an anvil shape.

cuneiform The oldest writing system of which records survive, used to represent a number of ancient Near Eastern languages. The name derives from the wedge-shaped marks (Latin *cuneus*, a wedge) made by the imprint of a stylus in soft clay. Originally pictographic, by the 3rd millennium BC cuneiform pictures had become stylized in the form of groups of wedge-shaped imprints, many representing the sounds of sylla-

pictographs		cuneiform		
c. 3500 BC	c. 3000	c. 2800	c. 800	
				mountain
				fish
				barley grain

CUNEIFORM *The wedge-shaped strokes of cuneiform writing developed gradually from pictographs.*

bles. Probably devised by the Sumerians not later than 3100 BC, cuneiform spread to other language groups in the area. By 100 BC, however, it had largely been superseded by the North Semitic script that was used to represent the Aramaic language.

Cunobelinus (*or* Cymbeline; died c. 42 AD) British ruler (c. 10–c. 42) of the Catuvellauni tribe. Their lands embraced much of SE England after they overcame the Trinovantes. He founded Colchester (c. 10).

Cupid The Roman god of love, identified with the Greek Eros, and lover of Psyche. He is usually portrayed as a winged boy shooting arrows of love.

cupronickel A corrosion-resistant alloy of 75% copper and 25% nickel (by weight). In the UK the Coinage Act (1946) substituted cupronickel coinage for silver alloy; the four cupronickel coins now in circulation are the 5p, 10p, 20p, and 50p pieces.

Curaçao A West Indian island, the largest in the Netherlands Antilles. Discovered in 1499, it was settled by the Spanish before being colonized by the Dutch in 1634. The refining of oil from Venezuela is of major importance; other industries include the production of Curaçao liqueur and calcium-phosphate mining. Area: 444 sq km (173 sq mi). Population (1983): 165 011. Chief town: Willemstad.

curare A resinous substance obtained from South American trees of the genera *Strychnos* and *Chondodendron*, used as an arrow poison by South American Indians. Curare blocks the action of acetylcholine and causes muscular contraction; curare-like compounds (e.g. tubocurarine) are injected during general anaesthesia to relax muscles.

Curia, Roman. *See* Roman Curia.

Curia Regis The King's Court of early medieval Europe. It fulfilled all the functions of royal government —and from its specialist departments developed the public government offices, such as, in England, the Chancery and the Exchequer, as well as the courts of law and parliament.

curie (Ci) A unit of radioactivity equal to the amount of an isotope that decays at the rate of 3.7×10^{10} disintegrations per second. Named after Pierre Curie.

Curie, Marie (1867–1934) Polish chemist, renowned for her research into radioactivity. Born Marya Skłodowska, she emigrated to France and married (1895) **Pierre Curie** (1859–1906), a French physicist. Marie Curie noticed in 1898 that one particular uranium ore emitted an anomalously large amount of radiation. Realizing that the radiation was caused by a new ele-

ment, she and her husband spent four years isolating one gram of radium salt from eight tons of the ore. The Curies, together with Henri Becquerel, were awarded the 1903 Nobel Prize for Physics and, for her discovery of radium and polonium, she won the 1911 Nobel Prize for Chemistry. Pierre Curie discovered the piezoelectric effect (1880) and showed that ferromagnetism reverts to paramagnetism (*see* magnetism) above a certain temperature, now known as the Curie point (1895). He was killed in a road accident; she died as a result of the radiation to which she had been exposed. Their daughter **Irène Joliot-Curie** (1896–1956) married the French physicist **Frédéric Joliot** (1900–59) in 1926. They were the first to produce radioactivity artificially. For this work they were awarded the Nobel Prize for Chemistry in 1935.

curium (Cm) An artificial transuranic element discovered by Seaborg and others in 1944 and named after Marie and Pierre Curie. All 13 isotopes are radioactive and some intensely so. Curium is a silvery reactive metal. Its compounds include the oxides (CmO_2, Cm_2O_3) and halides (CmF_3, $CmCl_3$). At no 96; at wt (247); mp $1340 \pm 40\,°C$.

curlew A streaked brown or grey bird belonging to the genus *Numenius* (8 species). Curlews have a long neck and long curved bill. They breed in inland subarctic regions and migrate south in winter to marshes and mudflats, feeding on worms and crabs. The common Eurasian curlew (*N. arquata*) is almost 60 cm long and ranges from Britain to central Asia. Family: *Scolopacidae* (snipe, sandpipers, etc.).

curling A target game played on ice with stones fitted with handles, played since at least the early 16th century and strongly associated with Scotland. Two teams of four players take it in turns to slide two curling stones, each up to 36 m (39 yd), along the ice towards the "house," a series of concentric circles at the end of the rink. A team scores one point for each stone finishing nearer the centre of the house than any of its opponents'. Team-mates are allowed to sweep the ice ahead of a moving stone to remove impediments and influence its course.

MARIE CURIE *Working with her husband, Pierre, in their laboratory in 1903.*

currant 1. One of several species of shrubs belonging to the genus *Ribes*. Some are cultivated for their fruit, for example blackcurrant and redcurrant, and others, such as the flowering currant, are grown as ornamentals. Family: *Grossulariaceae*. **2.** The dried berry of a small seedless grape, grown in the Mediterranean region and used in cooking.

currawong An Australasian songbird of the genus *Strepera* (6 species). About 50 cm long, currawongs are usually black, sometimes with white markings, and have a long hook-tipped bill. They feed on insects, small mammals, and birds and frequently destroy fruit crops. Family: *Cracticidae* (Australian magpies).

cuscus A cat-sized marsupial mammal belonging to the genus *Phalanger*, found in forests of NE Australia, New Guinea, and nearby islands. Cuscuses have a prehensile tail and climb slowly around trees at night, eating mainly leaves and fruit but sometimes catching lizards or birds. Family: *Phalangeridae* (*see* phalanger).

Cushing's disease A disorder resulting from excess corticosteroid hormones in the body, named after H. W. Cushing (1869–1939). The symptoms include obesity, loss of minerals from the bones, and reddening of the face and neck; it may be associated with the symptoms of diabetes mellitus and high blood pressure. It may be caused by a tumour of the pituitary gland or the adrenal gland or by prolonged therapy with high doses of corticosteroids: the treatment is determined by the cause.

custard apple A small tree of the genus *Annona* so called because of the custard-like flavour of its fruits. The common custard apple (*A. reticulata*), 5–8 m high and widely grown in the West Indies, produces reddish many-seeded fruits, 8–12 cm in diameter. Family: *Annonaceae*.

Custer, George A(rmstrong) (1839–76) US cavalry general. After earning distinction in the Civil War, he commanded the Seventh Cavalry during the western campaigns against the Indians. Sent to round up Sioux and Cheyenne forces under Chief Sitting Bull in S Dakota's Black Hills in 1876, he and his force of about 260 were massacred at the Little Bighorn (Custer's Last Stand).

cuttlefish A cephalopod mollusc belonging to the family *Sepiidae* (about 100 species), of temperate coastal waters. 2.5–90 cm long, the body is supported by an internal calcareous shell—the cuttlebone—which gives buoyancy. When alarmed, the animal emits an inky fluid.

cutworm The larva of a noctuid moth belonging to the widely distributed genus *Agrotis*. Cutworms destroy crops by biting through the stems, often at ground level.

Cuyp, Aelbert Jacobsz (1620–91) Dutch landscape painter. He was born in Dordrecht, the son of **Jacob Gerritsz Cuyp** (1594–1651), a portrait and landscape painter. Aelbert's paintings are distinguished by their glow of golden light, one fine example being *Herdsmen with Cows by a River* (National Gallery, London).

Cuzco 13 32S 71 57W A city in S Peru, in the Andes 3416 m (11 207 ft) above sea level. It was the capital of the Inca Empire prior to the Spanish conquest in 1533; Inca ruins include the Temple of the Sun. Population (1981 est): 181 604.

cyanide process The extraction of gold from its ores by chemical treatment with potassium cyanide. The ore is crushed to a fine powder and mixed with a weak solution of cyanide in water. Once the gold is dissolved by

the cyanide the metallic gold is separated out by chemically displacing it from the compound with zinc.

GENERAL CUSTER *A photograph taken c. 1865.*

cyanocobalamin. *See* vitamin B complex.

Cybele An Asiatic earth goddess identified by the Greeks with Rhea. The centre of her worship was Phrygia, whence her cult spread to Athens and later to Rome. She represented the powers of nature and was a protectress of wild animals. Her priests were eunuchs known as Corybantes.

cybernetics The study of communication and control between men, machines, and organizations. The name was derived from the Greek word meaning "steersman" by Norbert Wiener, who pioneered the subject. It is an aspect of bionics, in which the human ability to adapt to changing circumstances and to make decisions is simulated in the design of computer-controlled systems. Cybernetics has also been used as a link between the physical and life sciences, for instance in using information theory to explain how messages are transmitted in nervous systems and in genetic processes.

cycad A gymnosperm plant belonging to the order *Cycadales* (about 100 species), native to warm and tropical regions. They resemble small palms, having short stout stems with a crown of frondlike leaves. Reproductive organs are in the form of separate male and female cones borne on different trees. The stems of some species yield a type of sago.

Cyclades (Modern Greek name: Kikládhes) A group of some 220 Greek islands in the S Aegean Sea, including Ándros, Delos, Íos, Míkonos, Melos, Náxos (the largest), Páros, and Syros. Total area: 2578 sq km (995 sq mi). Population (1981): 88 458. Capital: Hermopolis (on Syros).

Cyclamen A genus of perennial plants (15 species) native from the European Mediterranean to Iran and widely cultivated. The pot varieties are grown from *C. persicum*. The garden cyclamens include dwarf varieties, 5–8 cm high. All cyclamens produce corms but most can be grown from seed. They have drooping flowers with red, pink, or white reflexed petals. Family: *Primulaceae*.

cyclone An area of relatively low atmospheric pressure with a series of closed isobars around its centre. In the N hemisphere wind circulates in an anticlockwise direction around its centre, in the S hemisphere it is clockwise. Except in the tropics, cyclones are now usually referred to as depressions or lows. Tropical cyclones include hurricanes and typhoons.

Cyclops (zoology) A genus (44 species) of very small freshwater crustaceans of the subclass *Copepoda*, so named because of their single median eye. In Africa and Asia they transmit the parasitic Guinea worm larvae to man if accidentally swallowed.

cyclostome An eel-like jawless aquatic vertebrate of the class *Cyclostomata*, which includes the lamprey and hagfish. Cyclostomes have a long cylindrical body with fins arranged singly (*compare* fish), a cartilaginous skeleton, and a sucking mouth with numerous horny teeth. They occur mainly in temperate fresh waters and salt waters and many are parasitic on fish. Subphylum: *Agnatha*.

CYCLOTRON   *The charged particles are accelerated in the two D-shaped conductors* (D_1 *and* D_2), *which are supported in the magnetic field* B.

cyclotron A type of particle accelerator in which charged particles are accelerated in an outward spiral path inside two hollow D-shaped conductors (called dees) placed back to back. The maximum energy of the particles is about 25 MeV. *See also* synchrocyclotron.

Cymbeline. *See* Cunobelinus.

Cymbidium A genus of tropical and subtropical orchids (40–70 species), native to Asia and Australia. Most species have pseudobulbs and sprays of 6–20 flowers on each flower stalk. Cymbidiums are among the most popular orchids in cultivation today.

Cynics The followers of the Greek moral philosopher Diogenes of Sinope, who were active from the early 3rd century BC. They were outspoken critics of accepted social values and often lived unconventional lives. Positive freedom could be attained by self-realization, but often it was the negative side of the Cynics' beliefs that was emphasized. Their distinction between natural and artificial values strongly influenced other ancient philosophies.

cypress A conifer of the genus *Cupressus* (true cypresses; 20 species), native to S Europe, E Asia, and North America and widely planted for ornament and timber. Cypresses have tiny scalelike leaves and rounded cones, 1–4 cm in diameter. The Italian or funeral cypress (*C. sempervirens*), of the Mediterranean region,

is 25–45 m high. Family: *Cupressaceae*. Related trees of the genus *Chamaecyparis* (6 species), of North America and SE Asia, are known as false cypresses. *See also* swamp cypress.

Cyprus, Republic of (Greek name: Kypros; Turkish name: Kıbrıs) An island state in the E Mediterranean Sea. A central plain rises to the Kyrenia Range in the N, and in the SW the Troödos Massif rises over 1800 m (6000 ft). Most of the population is Greek or Turkish, the former being in the majority. *Economy*: mainly agricultural. Mineral resources include iron pyrites, asbestos, chromite, and copper ores. Tourism is also important. There is now an intensive development programme in the Turkish sector, largely based on agriculture, with the aim of creating a self-sufficient economy. Exports include wine, citrus fruits, potatoes, and metals. *History*: there was already a Greek colony on Cyprus almost 4000 years ago. It was conquered by Egypt in the 6th century BC and later formed part of the Persian, Macedonian, Roman, Byzantine, and Arab empires. In 1193 it became a Frankish kingdom and in 1489 a Venetian dependency. In 1571 it was conquered by the Turks and this occupation lasted until 1878 when it came under British administration. In the 1930s Greek Cypriots began advocating Enosis (Union with Greece), and in 1955 a Greek Cypriot organization (*see* EOKA), led by Archbishop Makarios and Gen Grivas, began guerrilla warfare against the British. Cyprus became a republic in 1960 and a member of the Commonwealth in 1961. There were fierce clashes between the Greek and Turkish communities in the 1960s and in 1964 a UN peacekeeping force was sent to the island. Following a Greek-supported military coup in 1974, in which Makarios was temporarily overthrown, Turkey invaded the island leading to its virtual partition. In 1975 the Turks set up the Turkish Federated State of Cyprus in the N, with Rauf Denktash as president. George Vassiliou (1931–   ) was elected president of the S in 1988. Reunification talks foundered in 1989. Official languages: Greek and Turkish; English is also widely spoken. Official currency: Cyprus pound of 1000 mils. Area: 9251 sq km (3572 sq mi). Population (1988 est): 689 000. Capital: Nicosia. Main port: Limassol.

Cyrano de Bergerac, Savinien (1619–55) French writer and dramatist. He wrote a comedy, *Le Pédant joué* (1654), tragedies, and two satirical romances (published posthumously). He was noted for his comically long nose as well as his chivalrous nature.

Cyrenaica A region of E Libya, inhabited mainly by tribesmen of the Senussi. From early times Cyrenaica was colonized or conquered by Greeks, Egyptians, Romans, Vandals, Arabs, Turks, and Italians successively. The scene of many battles in World War II, it was united with Libya in 1951.

Cyrillic alphabet The alphabet used for Russian, Belorussian, Ukrainian, Bulgarian, Serbian, and various other languages of the Soviet Union. It was developed from a Greek alphabet of the 9th century AD and is traditionally attributed to the Greek brothers, St Cyril (c. 827–69 AD) and St Methodius (c. 825–49 AD). It originally consisted of 43 letters, but modern versions have reduced this number to about 30.

cystic fibrosis A hereditary disease affecting the mucus-secreting and sweat glands. Symptoms, which appear in early childhood, are due to the production of thick mucus, which obstructs the pancreatic duct, intestinal glands, and bronchi. Patients suffer from malnutrition and recurrent chest infections. Treatment includes antibiotics, physiotherapy, a low-fat high-protein diet, and the administration of pancreatic enzymes.

cytokinins A group of plant growth-stimulating compounds derived from purines. Synthetic cytokinins are used commercially in the storage of vegetables.

cytology The study of the structure and function of cells. It began with the development of techniques for the study of materials under the light microscope, which enabled the nucleus and other organelles to be observed. This led to the identification of chromosomes. More recent developments have included the use of phase-contrast and electron microscopy, and the use of such techniques as cell separation and analysis, autoradiography, and tissue culture. Cytological tests provide the basis for diagnosis of many diseases, including cancer.

cytoplasm. *See* cell.

cytotoxic drugs Drugs used to kill cancer cells. These drugs have led to improvements in the treatment of some cancers (e.g. leukaemia) but often cause severe side effects, including damage to bone marrow.

Czech A West Slavonic language spoken by nine million people in W Czechoslovakia. It is the official language of this area and is written in the Latin alphabet in a standardized form based on the dialect of Prague.

Czechoslovakia, Socialist Republic of A landlocked country in central Europe. It is mainly wooded and mountainous. The population is about two-thirds Czech and almost a third Slovak. *Economy*: industry is entirely nationalized and since 1961 the emphasis has shifted from heavy to light industry. Agriculture is organized in collectives and state farms and the principal crops include sugar beet, wheat, potatoes, and barley. Forestry is also important. *History*: Czechoslovakia was created, under Tomáš Masaryk and Edvard Beneš, in 1918 following the collapse of the Austrian Empire. The new state was however unable to withstand the expansionist ambitions of Hitler's Germany, which had taken control of all Czechoslovakia by 1939. Following the war Ruthenia was ceded to the Soviet Union, and some three million Germans were expelled from Czechoslovakia. By 1948 the Communist Party was in power and Czechoslovakia was closely allied with the Soviet Union. In 1968 a liberalization programme initiated by Dubček provoked a Soviet invasion. In 1989 pressure for liberal reform culminated in the replacement of Gustáv Husák by Milos Jakes as president. After Jakes failed to expedite reform the Communist regime fell and Václav Havel became president of a new socialist government. Official languages: Czech and Slovak. Official currency: koruna of 100 halérů. Area: 127 877 sq km (49 365 sq mi). Population (1988 est): 15 723 000. Capital: Prague.

Częstochowa 50 49N 19 07E A city in S Poland. It has a monastery that was defended against the Swedes in the Thirty Years' War. Population (1985): 247 000.

D

dab One of several flatfish of the family *Pleuronectidae*, especially the genus *Limanda* found in N Atlantic and N Pacific waters. The European *L. limanda* is an important food fish.

dabbling duck A duck that feeds near the surface of water, rarely diving and frequently feeding on land. With relatively small feet and legs set well forward, dabbling ducks walk efficiently on land; they include the mallard, pintail, shoveler, teal, and wigeon. Drakes are usually brightly coloured and generally have a distinctive patch on the wing. *Compare* diving duck.

dabchick A small grebe, *Tachybaptus ruficollis*, common in quiet inland waters of Europe, S Asia, and Africa. It has a dark-brown back, pale underparts, and a bright chestnut breast, neck, and cheeks. It feeds on small fish and aquatic invertebrates.

Dacca. *See* Dhaka.

dace A slender lively fish belonging to the family *Cyprinidae*, which includes chub, roach, minnow, etc. The European dace (*Leuciscus leuciscus*) is up to 30 cm long, silvery coloured, and lives in schools in fast-flowing streams and rivers, eating both plant and animal material.

Dachau 48 15N 11 26E A town in SE West Germany, in Bavaria. It was the site of a Nazi concentration camp (1933–45). Population (1984 est): 33 200.

dachshund A breed of dog originating in Germany, where they were developed to pursue badgers to earth. There are two size varieties–standard and miniature –and three coat types–long-haired, smooth-haired, and wire-haired. Dachshunds are usually brownish or black and tan.

dada A European art and literary movement, beginning in Zürich in 1916 and aimed at deflating the status of the art-object. Since it had no coherent style, much of its ideology was more effectively transmitted in poetry periodicals, such as *L'Intransigeant* in France. Manufactured objects were favoured both in graphic art and sculpture. Their violent effect is shown in the collages of Arp, Ernst, and Schwitters and the ready-mades of Duchamp, who exported dada to the USA. Although dada petered out in the early 1920s, surrealism absorbed many of its characteristics.

Dadd, Richard (1817–86) British painter of detailed and complex works, mainly of biblical scenes, fairy life, and mythology. His best work was produced in an asylum, to which he was committed after killing his father.

daddy longlegs. *See* cranefly.

Daedalus A legendary Greek craftsman and sculptor, said to have built the labyrinth for King Minos of Crete. Minos imprisoned him but he created wings for himself and his son Icarus and flew away; **Icarus** was killed when the sun melted his wings but Daedalus reached Sicily safely.

daffodil A perennial European plant, *Narcissus pseudonarcissus*, widely grown as a garden bulb. It has narrow leaves and yellow flowers, each with a trumpet-shaped central crown surrounded by six segments. Family: *Amaryllidaceae*.

DAGUERRE *A daguerreotype of the inventor (c. 1845).*

Daguerre, Louis-Jacques-Mandé (1789–1851) French inventor of the first practicable photographic process (the daguerreotype). Working initially with Joseph Niepce (1765–1833), who had produced the first permanent photographic image (the heliograph), Daguerre succeeded during the 1830s in producing a photograph by focusing light onto a copper plate that had been coated with a silver salt. Daguerreotypes were widely made in the mid-19th century.

Dahlia A genus of herbaceous perennial tropical American plants (12 species), originally cultivated as a food crop for their tubers but now grown mainly for ornament. The brightly coloured flowers may be single or double and are of two main types. The varieties known as flat heads and pompoms are derived from *D. pinnata*; cactus-type flowers with pointed petals are varieties of *D. juarezii*. Family: *Compositae*.

Dahomey. *See* Benin, People's Republic of.

Dáil Éireann The representative assembly of the Republic of Ireland. It is the more important house in the National Parliament, the other house being the Seanad Éireann (the Senate). There are 144 members elected by proportional representation, at least once every 5 years. The president (the nominal head of state) summons and dissolves the Dáil on the advice of the prime minister.

Daimler, Gottlieb (Wilhelm) (1834–1900) German inventor, who contributed to the development of the internal-combustion engine. Daimler started to build his own engines in 1883, which were soon sufficiently light and efficient to power machines; in 1890 he founded a company to manufacture motor cars.

Dairen. *See* Lüda.

dairy products Foods and other products derived from the processing of milk. Separation of milk by centrifugation yields skimmed milk and cream. Churning the cream disrupts the fat globules, removes water, and produces butter, containing over 80% fat, and buttermilk. Cream is retailed in various stages of concentration, for example single cream and double cream; other less concentrated milk include evaporated milk (containing about 65% water) and condensed milk (about 26% water). Yogurt (*or* yoghurt) is produced by inocu-

lating whole milk with bacteria, principally of the genera *Streptococcus* and *Lactobacillus*. The acid they produce during incubation coagulates the milk. Whey is a by-product of cheese manufacture. *See also* milk.

daisy A herbaceous plant of the genus *Bellis* (15 species), native to Eurasia, with flower heads consisting of small central yellow disc florets surrounded by white or purple petal-like ray florets. The entire head is surrounded by bracts (leaflike structures). Many species are garden ornamentals, some with double-flowered varieties. The common wild Eurasian daisy is *B. perennis*, a perennial up to 6 cm high, common in grasslands and lawns. Family: *Compositae*.

Dakar 14 45N 17 08W The capital and main port of Senegal, on Cape Verde peninsula, and the country's main industrial centre. Population (1984): 671 000.

Dakota. *See* North Dakota; South Dakota.

Dalai Lama The title of the spiritual and political ruler of Tibet and head of the Gelukpa Buddhist school. The title, originating in the 14th century, signifies the incarnation of the Bodhisattva of compassion. Chosen by oracles after the death of the previous incumbent, the Dalai Lama is regarded as infallible. The 14th Dalai Lama went into exile in India in 1959. He won the Nobel Peace Prize in 1989.

Dali, Salvador (1904–89) Spanish surrealist painter. He joined the Paris surrealists (1929) and, inspired by Freudian theories of the unconscious, painted startling dream images with photographic realism during self-induced hallucinatory states. While living in New York (1940–55), he turned to religious subjects and became a Roman Catholic.

SALVADOR DALI *A surrealist photograph of the artist.*

Dalian. *See* Lüda.

Dallas 32 47N 96 48W A city in the USA, in NE Texas on the Trinity River. The discovery of oil in E Texas during the 1930s accelerated the city's growth, which was further enhanced by the introduction of the aircraft and electronics industries during World War II. Today Dallas is the state's second largest city and the financial and commercial centre of the SW. Population (1986): 1 003 520.

Dalmatia A coastal belt in W Yugoslavia, mainly in Croatia bordering on the Adriatic Sea. It is penetrated by a narrow corridor giving Bosnia and Hercegovina access to the sea. Predominantly mountainous with an indented coastline and many offshore islands, it has a thriving tourist industry. Wine production is important. The chief towns are Zadar, Split, and Dubrovnik.

Dalmatian dog   A breed named after Dalmatia, from where they were exported to the UK. Dalmatians are strongly built and were formerly used as carriage dogs. The short sleek coat has a pure white background with black or liver (brown) spots.

dalton.   *See* atomic mass unit.

Dalton, John   (1766–1844) British chemist and originator of the modern atomic theory of matter. His earliest researches led to Dalton's law of partial pressures. He believed that gases consist of particles, extending his theory in 1803 to suggest that all matter is particulate.

JOHN DALTON   *A caricature (c. 1840).*

Dalton's law of partial pressures   The total pressure exerted by a certain volume of a gaseous mixture is equal to the sum of the pressures (called partial pressures) exerted by each gas, if it alone occupied the same volume. Named after John Dalton.

dam   A barrier across a river. Dams are used for diverting the flow of water; raising the water level for navigation purposes; storing water for irrigation, industrial use, or water control; and providing a high-pressure source of water for hydroelectric power. Gravity dams, usually made of concrete, have a flat vertical face upstream. They are no longer used for the largest dams. Arch dams consist of curved concrete structures presenting their convex faces upstream.

Daman and Diu   A Union Territory in W India, formerly (until 1987) part of Goa, Daman, and Diu. Diu is an island off the coast of Gujarat. Area: 456 sq km (176 sq mi). Population (1981): 1 082 117. Chief town: Daman.

Damascus   33 30N 36 19E The capital of Syria, in the SE of the country close to the Lebanese border. Under Ottoman rule from 1516 until 1918, Damascus was taken by the French (1920) and became capital of independent Syria in 1941. Population (1987): 1 292 000.

damask rose   An Asian rose, *Rosa damascena*, about 1.5 m high, with spicy-scented pink and white flowers. It is the main source of attar of roses—used in perfumery.

Damocles   Legendary courtier of Dionysius I of Syracuse in the 9th century BC. Dionysius seated him at a banquet beneath a sword suspended by a single hair, thus illustrating the insecurity of human life, irrespective of wealth or power.

damselfly   A slender delicate insect belonging to the suborder *Zygoptera*, closely related to the dragonflies. It has similar habits but is smaller.

damson   The edible plumlike stone fruit of *Prunus damascena*, a slender twisted tree found across the N hemisphere. It has small white flowers that develop into purple fruits. Family: *Rosaceae. See also* plum.

Dan, tribe of   One of the 12 tribes of Israel. It claimed descent from Dan, the son of Jacob by his concubine Bilhah. Its territory lay N of the Sea of Galilee and its city of Dan was situated at the northernmost point of the Hebrew settlement.

Danae   In Greek legend, the daughter of Acrisius, King of Argos. He imprisoned her because an oracle said he would be killed by her child; Zeus visited her, however, and she gave birth to Perseus. Acrisius cast mother and son out to sea but Polydectes, King of Seriphos, rescued them.

Da Nang   (former name: Tourane)   16 04N 108 14E A port in S central Vietnam, on the South China Sea. It was the site of a major US airbase during the Vietnam War. Population (latest est): 318 655.

dandelion   A weedy perennial herbaceous plant of the worldwide genus *Taraxacum*, with a basal rosette of jagged toothed leaves and a solitary flower head of bright-yellow florets. The seeds have parachutes of fine white hairs and are dispersed by wind. The common dandelion (*T. officinale*) is found throughout the N hemisphere. Family: *Compositae.*

Dandie Dinmont terrier   A dog breed having a long body, short legs, and long drooping ears. Its long coat is a mixture of hard and soft hairs and can be either grey, black, or brown.

dandruff   Dry scaling of the scalp, which occurs in everybody to some degree. It is presumed to be due to an infection and may sometimes become more serious, extending to the face.

Danelaw   The area of Anglo-Saxon England E of Watling Street from the River Tees to the River Thames

DAM   *Aerial view of the Hoover Dam across the Colorado River.*

within which Danish laws and customs prevailed from the late 9th to the late 11th centuries.

Daniel (6th century BC) An Old Testament prophet and Jewish exile in Babylon. **The Book of Daniel** is usually credited to him, the first six chapters telling of various mainly supernatural episodes involving Daniel and his companions under Kings Nebuchadnezzar and Belshazzar.

Daniell cell An electric cell whose positive pole consists of copper immersed in a solution of copper sulphate and whose negative pole consists of zinc in a solution of sulphuric acid or zinc sulphate. It has an almost constant emf of 1.08 volts. Named after J. F. Daniell (1790–1845), British chemist.

Danish The official language of Denmark, spoken by about five million people. It belongs to the East Scandinavian branch of the North Germanic languages. Closely related to other Scandinavian languages, it is the most altered form of the common ancestral tongue.

DANTE *Detail from an illustration by Gustave Doré for an edition of* The Divine Comedy (Hell).

Dante Alighieri (1265–1321) Italian poet. Born into a noble Guelf family of Florence (*see* Guelfs and Ghibellines), his involvement in the political struggle between the Black Guelfs and the White Guelfs led to his exile (c. 1301) from Florence. Dante's major works include the autobiographical love poem *La vita nuova* (c. 1292), the epic poem *The Divine Comedy* (c. 1307), and two influential treatises on the value of vernacular Italian as a literary language.

Danube, River The second longest river in Europe after the River Volga. Rising in the Black Forest in West Germany, it flows mainly ESE across central and SE Europe to enter the Black Sea in Romania. Immensely important commercially, it is linked by the River Altmühl with canals to the Rivers Main and Rhine. Major cities along its course include Vienna, Budapest, and Belgrade. Length: 2850 km (1770 mi).

Danzig. *See* Gdańsk.

Daphne (botany) A genus of evergreen and deciduous shrubs (70 species) of the Old World, including many important ornamentals. The leaves are arranged spirally up the stem. The small, often fragrant, bell-shaped flowers occur in clusters. The genus includes the deciduous mezereon (*D. mezereum*), with reddish-purple flowers and red berries, and the evergreen spurge laurel (*D.*

laureola), with greenish flowers and black berries. These shrubs are native to Eurasia. Family: *Thymeleaceae*.

Daphne (Greek mythology) A mountain nymph who rejected Apollo and, to escape him, was transformed by Gaea into a laurel tree. Apollo made the laurel a symbol of honour and victory.

Daphnia. *See* water flea.

Daphnis In Greek legend, a Sicilian shepherd who was punished with blindness for infidelity in love. He consoled himself with songs and was thus revered as the inventor of pastoral poetry and song.

Da Ponte, Lorenzo (1749–1838) Italian author, originally a priest. Banished from Italy in 1779, he settled in Vienna and there wrote the libretti for Mozart's operas *The Marriage of Figaro* (1786), *Don Giovanni* (1787), and *Così fan tutte* (1790). In 1805 he went to the USA.

Dardanelles (Ancient name: Hellespont) A strait separating European and Asian Turkey and connecting the Sea of Marmara with the Aegean Sea. It was the scene of an unsuccessful campaign in World War I. Length: 60 km (37 mi); width: 1.5–6.5 km (1–4 mi).

Dar es Salaam 6 48S 39 12E The capital and main port of Tanzania, on the Indian Ocean. Founded in 1862, it was capital of German East Africa (1891–1916) and of Tanganyika (1916–64). It is an important commercial and industrial centre. Population (1985): 1 394 000.

Darjeeling 27 02N 88 20E A town in India, in West Bengal near the Himalayas. It is a tourist resort and a major tea-growing centre. Population (1981): 57 603.

darkling beetle A black or dark brown flightless beetle belonging to a widely distributed family (*Tenebrionidae*; 15 000 species), particularly common in warm regions. Nearly all are scavengers, feeding on decaying vegetation, dung, fungi, or stored grains and cereals. Mealworms (larvae of *Tenebrio molitor*) are common pests of flour mills, etc., and are also reared commercially as food for birds and fish.

Darling, Grace (1815–42) British heroine, daughter of a lighthouse keeper on the Northumberland coast. In 1838 she helped her father rescue five people from a ship (*Forfarshire*) that had struck the rocks during a storm.

Darling River A river in E Australia, rising in the Great Dividing Range and flowing generally SW across New South Wales before joining the Murray River at Wentworth. Length: 2740 km (1702 mi).

Darlington 54 31N 1 34W A town in NE England, in Durham. The Stockton–Darlington freight railway (1825) was the world's first railway. Darlington has engineering and construction industries. Population (1989): 99 200.

Darmstadt 49 52N 08 39E A city in central West Germany, in Hessen. It has a 16th-century palace. Population (1987): 133 600.

Darnley, Henry Stuart, Lord (1545–67) The second husband of Mary, Queen of Scots, and father of James I of England. He married Mary, his cousin, in 1565. He was involved in the murder of her secretary David Riccio (1566) and was himself murdered, probably by Bothwell.

darter A slender elongated bird belonging to a family (*Anhingidae*; 4 species) occurring in tropical and subtropical inland waters. Darters are about 88 cm long and black or brown with white markings; males have plumes on the head and neck. They have thin pointed bills for catching fish underwater and are excellent fliers. Order: *Pelecaniformes* (gannets, pelicans, etc.).

Dartford 51 27N 0 14E A town in SE England, in Kent linked with Purfleet (Essex) by the Dartford Tunnel (opened in 1963) under the River Thames. Population (1983 est): 77 315.

Dartmoor A moorland area of England, in SW Devon. A national park since 1951, it consists of a rolling granite upland rising to tors, the highest of which is High Willhays at 621 m (2039 ft). Its many historic remains include stone circles and Bronze Age and Iron Age settlements. A major tourist attraction, it is also used extensively as a military training area. Area: 945 sq km (365 sq mi).

Dartmouth 50 21N 3 35W A port and resort in SW England, in Devon on the Dart estuary. The Royal Naval College (1905) is situated here. Population (1981): 6298.

Darwin 12 23S 130 44E A city in Australia, the capital and chief port of the Northern Territory. It had to be largely rebuilt after a cyclone in 1974. Population (1986): 66 131.

CHARLES DARWIN

Darwin, Charles Robert (1809–1882) British naturalist, who originated the concept that living things evolve by means of natural selection. Following attempts to study medicine and theology, Darwin's interest in natural history led him to sail with HMS *Beagle* on an expedition to South America and the Pacific (1831–36). As ship's naturalist, Darwin made exhaustive observations of the geology and natural history of the region. Following the voyage, Darwin analysed his observations and formed them into a coherent view of nature. In 1859 he published his findings in *Origin of Species by Means of Natural Selection* (*see* Darwinism). His views aroused bitter controversy because they conflicted with the account of the Creation in the Bible. This culminated in the debate at Oxford in 1860 between Darwin's supporters, led by T. H. Huxley, and Bishop Samuel Wilberforce. Huxley's arguments won the day. In *The Descent of Man* (1871), Darwin applied his theories to mankind, and—slowly—this fundamental principle of biology gained widespread acceptance. His grandfather **Erasmus Darwin** (1731–1802) was a successful physician

noted for his radical views, especially on biology. Among his ideas were speculations about the nature of evolution that anticipated later theories, particularly those of Lamarck.

Darwinism The theory of evolution based on the work of Charles Darwin. Darwin drew his conclusions from the following observations: (1) in any population the organisms show individual variations; (2) the size of the population remains constant although more offspring are produced than are necessary to maintain it. He concluded that the forces acting on the population —competition, disease, climate, etc.—resulted in the survival of those best fitted to the environment, a process he called **natural selection**. The survivors would breed, thus passing on their inheritable advantageous variations to their offspring. With time—in a gradually changing environment—this process would result in a change in the whole population and ultimately the evolution of new species.

Darwin's theory has now been reinforced and modified by subsequent discoveries in genetics, which among other things have revealed the source of the variation on which it is based (mostly genetic mutations). The modern version of his theory is known as **neo-Darwinism**.

dasyure A small carnivorous marsupial mammal belonging to a family (*Dasyuridae*; 45 species) occurring in Australia and New Guinea. Dasyures are nocturnal and good climbers. See also Tasmanian devil.

data processing The organization, transmission, and storage of information. The operations almost always involve computers. In batch processing, data is grouped and coded before processing. In on-line processing each user feeds data into the system continuously. Many systems incorporate both of these forms of processing for different types of work. Most large organizations now use data-processing techniques extensively. The Data Protection Act (1984) came into force in November 1985 and seeks to protect the freedom of the individual.

date A palm tree, *Phoenix dactylifera*, native to N Africa and SW Asia and cultivated from Morocco to India for its sugar-rich fruits. Male and female flowers grow on separate trees, the female flowers developing into large clusters of single-seeded berries. The trunk of the tree yields a timber and the leaves are used for basketry, weaving, etc.

dating. *See* helium dating; potassium-argon dating; radiocarbon dating; rubidium-strontium dating; uranium-lead dating.

Daumier, Honoré (1808–79) French caricaturist, painter, and sculptor. He produced numerous documentary lithographs, such as *Rue Transnonain*. After 1835 he worked for *Charivari*, satirizing the legal and medical professions and other social and political targets. His paintings include *The Third Class Railway Carriage*.

dauphin From 1350 until 1830 the title of the heirs to the French Crown. It was the personal name, and later became the title, of the rulers of a former province of SE France, the Dauphiné, which was purchased by the future Charles V in 1350. After becoming king (1364), he granted the Dauphiné and its accompanying title to his son, thus establishing a precedent.

David (d. 962 BC) King of Israel (c. 1000–962). David was anointed by Samuel as the successor of Saul, the first King of Israel. He became a close friend of Saul's son, Jonathan, but his successes against the Philistines, including the slaying of Goliath, aroused Saul's jealousy and he became an outlaw. After the death of Saul and Jonathan, David was proclaimed King of Hebron and then of all Israel. He conquered Jerusalem, making it the nation's political and religious centre, finally defeated the Philistines, and united the tribes of Israel. His reign was troubled by the revolt of his son Absalom, who was eventually defeated and killed. David was succeeded by Solomon, his son by Bathsheba. According to the Jewish prophets, the Messiah must be a descendant of David.

David I (1084–1153) King of the Scots (1124–53). He recognized Matilda as successor to Henry I of England, and invaded N England (1138) after Stephen had seized the throne. Stephen defeated him in the battle of the Standard (1138), near Northallerton. David founded or refounded over a dozen monasteries.

David, St (or St Dewi; c. 520–600 AD) The patron saint of Wales and first abbot of Menevia (now St David's). He was also a missionary and the founder of many churches in Wales. Feast day: 1 March.

David ap Gruffudd (d. 1283) The brother of Llywelyn ap Gruffudd, after whose death (1282) David claimed the title Prince of Wales. He was executed by Edward I for leading the Welsh in rebellion against him.

Davies, Sir Peter Maxwell (1934–) British composer and director of the chamber ensemble The Fires of London. Some of his works are based on medieval music but employ modern compositional techniques. His output includes *Eight Songs for a Mad King* (1969) and four symphonies.

da Vinci, Leonardo. *See* Leonardo da Vinci.

Davis, Bette (Ruth Elizabeth D.; 1908–89) US film actress. From the 1930s to the 1950s she gave intense and dramatic performances in such films as *Jezebel* (1938), *Dark Victory* (1939), and *All About Eve* (1950). In later years she played elderly eccentric or neurotic women.

Davis, Sir Colin (1927–) British conductor. During a distinguished career he has conducted the BBC Scottish Symphony Orchestra, the BBC Symphony Orchestra, and the orchestras of the Metropolitan Opera, New York, and the Royal Opera, Covent Garden.

Davis, John (or J. Davys; c. 1550–1605) English navigator. He went on three voyages in search of the Northwest Passage (1585, 1586, 1587), passing through the strait named after him to Baffin Bay. In 1592, seeking the Magellan Strait, he discovered the Falkland Islands.

Davis, Miles (1926–) US jazz trumpeter and composer, one of the originators of cool jazz. His albums include *Miles Ahead* and the innovatory *Kind of Blue*.

Davis, Steve (1957–) British snooker player. He won the world professional championship in 1981, 1983, 1984, 1987, 1988, and 1989.

Davis Cup An international tennis competition that was instituted in 1900 for teams of men. The USA and Australia have won it most often.

Davos (Romansh name: Tarau) 46 47N 9 50E A mountain resort and winter-sports centre in E Switzerland. Population (1988 est): 13 000.

Davy, Sir Humphry (1778–1829) British chemist and inventor of the miner's safety lamp (1815), known as the Davy lamp. Davy began his career by discovering the value of nitrous oxide as an anaesthetic. For this work he was invited to join the Royal Institution in London, where his most important work was the discovery of

many new metallic elements—potassium in 1807 and sodium, calcium, barium, magnesium and strontium in 1808. He employed the young Michael Faraday as his assistant at the Royal Institution.

STEVE DAVIS

Day Lewis, C(ecil) (1904–72) British poet and critic. He was a leading left-wing poet of the 1930s but his later verse was more purely lyrical. He was appointed poet laureate in 1968. As "Nicholas Blake" he wrote a series of sophisticated detective stories.

day lily A herbaceous plant of the genus *Hemerocallis*, native to Europe and Asia and cultivated as garden flowers. They have long narrow leaves and clusters of orange or yellow lily-like flowers, which wither after a short time. Family: *Liliaceae*.

DBE. *See* Order of the British Empire.

DDT (dichlorophenyltrichloroethane) An organochlorine compound formerly widely used as a contact insecticide. It is active against many insects, including mosquitoes, flies, fleas, and bedbugs. However, many have become resistant to DDT, which is a very stable compound and accumulates not only in their tissues but also in the tissues of the animals that prey on them, causing toxic effects. Its use is banned in the UK.

deadly nightshade (or belladonna) A branching perennial herb, *Atropa belladonna*, native to Eurasia. It has solitary purple or greenish bell-shaped flowers. The shiny black berries taste sweet but contain a deadly poison. The plant is a source of a variety of alkaloids, especially hyoscyamine and atropine. Family: *Solanaceae. See also* nightshade.

Dead Sea A lake in E Israel and W Jordan. It is fed by the River Jordan and, having no outlet, is highly saline and supports no life. Area: 1050 sq km (401 sq mi).

Dead Sea Scrolls A group of Hebrew and Aramaic manuscript scrolls found in caves in the area of Khirbat Qumran, NW of the Dead Sea. The first were discovered in 1947; the rest were recovered as late as the 1950s. The 500 different documents, dating from 250 BC to 70 AD, seem to have formed the library of a Jewish, perhaps Essene, community that existed from about 125 BC to the Jewish revolt in 66–70 AD, when the scrolls were hidden for safekeeping. They include texts of many Old Testament books, commentaries, prayers, psalms, and material peculiar to the community. They are particularly valuable as evidence of the accuracy of previously known Old Testament texts.

Dean, Forest of An ancient royal forest in W England, in Gloucestershire between the Rivers Severn and Wye.

Dean, James (James Byron; 1931–55) US film actor who trained at the Actors' Studio, and became a cult hero for his generation. His films were *East of Eden* (1954), *Rebel without a Cause* (1955), and *Giant* (1955), released following his death in a car crash.

death The permanent cessation of all bodily functions in an organism. Until recently a person was medically pronounced dead when his heartbeat and breathing movements ceased, but since the advent of mechanical ventilators the heart beat may be maintained long after "natural" breathing has stopped as a result of irreversible brain damage. Death is therefore now defined on the basis of brain function: when the parts of the brain that control respiration and other vital reflexes have ceased to function the patient is said to be brain dead, i.e. truly dead, although his heart may continue to beat for some time with the aid of mechanical life-support systems.

DEATH CAP *A very dangerous mushroom.*

death cap A highly poisonous mushroom, *Amanita phalloides*, fairly common in and near deciduous woodlands. Its cap is usually pale greenish yellow. The stalk is white or greenish white, with a baglike sheath (volva) at its base.

death's-head moth A hawk moth, *Acherontia atropos*, with a wingspan of 125 mm, found in Europe, Africa, and Asia. Its thoracic markings resemble a skull and crossbones.

Death Valley A desert area in the USA, in SE California, and the hottest and driest part of North America. The flora and fauna that survive the harsh conditions are of interest to scientists. In 1933 it was declared a national monument.

deathwatch beetle A widely distributed wood-boring beetle, *Xestobium rufovillosum*, about 7 mm long, that can cause immense damage to old buildings and furniture. It lays its eggs in small crevices in the wood and the larvae tunnel in, eventually reducing it to powder. The pupae often make knocking sounds by repeatedly striking their heads against the walls of their burrows. Family: *Anobiidae*.

debenture stock A document setting out the terms of a fixed-interest loan to a company. A **secured debenture** is secured against a specified asset belonging to the company (fixed charge) or against all the company's assets (floating charge). An **unsecured debenture** has no such security, but if it cannot be paid back on the repayment date, debenture holders can force the company into liquidation and they then take priority over other shareholders in having their capital repaid. An **irredeemable debenture** is never repaid, being bought only for the interest it earns.

de Broglie, Louis Victor, 7th Duc (1892–1987) French physicist, who won the 1929 Nobel Prize for his theory that elementary particles have associated waves, known as **de Broglie waves**. The theory was confirmed by the subsequent observation of electron diffraction and forms the basis of the branch of quantum mechanics known as wave mechanics.

Debussy, Claude (Achille) (1862–1918) French composer. He spent most of his life in Paris and is regarded as the originator of musical impressionism. His most famous works include *Prélude à l'après-midi d'un faune* (for orchestra; 1892–94), the opera *Pelléas et Mélisande* (1892–1902), *La Mer* (three symphonic sketches; 1903–05), a string quartet, and a sonata for flute, viola, and harp.

Decadents A group of late-19th-century French symbolist poets and their contemporaries in England. They aimed to create a literature liberated from all moral and social responsibilities. Poets linked with the movement included Rimbaud, Verlaine, and Mallarmé in France, and Arthur Symons and Oscar Wilde in England. *See also* Aesthetic movement.

Decapoda A worldwide order of crustaceans (over 8500 species), with five pairs of thoracic appendages —anterior pincers and four pairs of walking legs. They include the shrimps and prawns (suborder: *Natantia*, "swimming forms") and lobsters, crayfish, and crabs (suborder: *Reptantia*, "walking forms").

decathlon An athletic competition for men, consisting of ten events over two days. On the first are 100 m sprint, long jump, shot put, high jump, and 400 m sprint; on the second are 110 m hurdles, discus throw, pole vault, javelin throw, and 1500 m run. Competitors score for performances in each event, the winner gaining the highest total.

Decembrists. *See* Dekabrists.

decibel (dB) A unit used to compare two power levels on a logarithmic scale. Two power levels P and P_0 differ by n decibels when $n = 10 \log_{10} P/P_0$. The unit is often used to express a sound intensity in which case P_0 is usually taken as the intensity of the lowest audible note of the same frequency as P.

deciduous plants. *See* evergreen plants.

decimal system The number system in common use, having a base 10 and thus using ten separate numerals. It also involves the use of a decimal point to express numbers less than one, as in 0.25. The decimal system was invented by the Hindus and adopted by the Arabs in the 9th century (*see also* mathematics). The use of decimal fractions originated in Italy in the 12th century but use of the decimal point did not occur until the early 18th century. Decimalization of currency systems was introduced by France after the Revolution and followed by most other European and American countries, except for Britain, which did not decimalize until 1971. *See also* metric system.

Declaration of Independence (4 July, 1776) The declaration, adopted by the 13 colonies of North America, that announced their independence from Great Britain. Written by Thomas Jefferson between 11 June and 2 July and revised before adoption, the Declaration is both specific (in its enumeration of grievances) and general (in its statement of principles of governance) and is one of the most influential proclamations in the western political tradition.

Declaratory Act. *See* Stamp Act.

declination. *See* magnetic declination; right ascension.

decompression sickness (*or* caisson disease) An occupational hazard of pilots and underwater divers caused by too rapid a return to normal atmospheric pressure. At high pressures large amounts of gas can be carried in the blood. A rapid return to normal pressure causes nitrogen (the main component of inhaled air) to form bubbles in the blood; this interrupts the blood supply to the tissues, producing joint pain (the bends), general discomfort, and respiratory problems (the chokes). Decompression sickness is prevented by a slow return to atmospheric pressure; it is treated by placing the patient in a hyperbaric chamber.

Decorated The style of gothic architecture predominant in England between 1300 and 1370. In contrast to the geometric restraint of its predecessor, Early English, Decorated is characterized by complex flowing patterns, especially in window tracery. Roof vaults were intricately ribbed and the ogee or double curved arch with elaborate ornamentation became common.

Dee, River The name of three rivers in the UK. **1.** A river in NE Scotland, flowing E to the North Sea at Aberdeen. Length: 140 km (87 mi). **2.** A river in North Wales and NW England, rising in Gwynedd and flowing E and N through Llangollen and Chester to the Irish Sea. Length: 112 km (70 mi). **3.** A river in S Scotland, flowing S to the Solway Firth. Length: 80 km (50 mi).

deed In law, a document in writing, signed, sealed, and delivered, transferring a right over property (titledeed) or creating an obligation on its maker. To be binding it need not fulfil conditions applicable to a contract. A deed may be between two parties, to establish mutual obligations, or it may involve one party only (deed poll).

deer A ruminant mammal of the family *Cervidae* (41 species), occurring mainly in the N hemisphere, although a few are found in South America and N Africa and they have been introduced to SE Asia and Australasia. Nearly all deer have bony antlers that are shed and replaced every year. Deer range in size from the elk to the small South American pudu. Most deer live in herds but some, such as the muntjac, are solitary.

deerhound A long-established British breed of dog, formerly used for hunting deer. It has a deep-chested long body with long legs and a long tapering head with small ears. The wiry coat is usually blue-grey but may be shades of brown or fawn.

defamation In law, a false and derogatory statement about another person that tends to lower him in the estimation of right-thinking members of the community generally. It is libel if made in a permanent form (e.g. in newspapers, broadcasts) and slander if made in a transient form, by spoken words or gestures. The remedy for both types of defamation is by civil proceedings, although libel may also be a crime if its publication is calculated to provoke a breach of the peace. Not only the originator of a libel but everyone who has subsequently repeated or published it may be sued by the person libelled. Action for libel cannot be brought against "privileged" proceedings or statements such as judicial and parliamentary proceedings. A statement judged to be a fair comment on a matter of public interest is also not actionable as defamation.

deficit financing The fiscal policy of stimulating the economy by government spending in excess of revenue by borrowing to finance the resultant deficit. Deficit financing was advocated by the British economist J. M. Keynes and became normal practice after World War II (*see* national debt).

deflation A government action to slow down the economy, with the aim of easing inflation or cutting down on imports and thus helping the balance of payments. Both monetary policy (credit "squeeze") and fiscal policy (increasing taxes, cutting government spending) can be used to deflate the economy.

Defoe, Daniel (1660–1731) British novelist, economist, and journalist. His early career as a merchant ended in bankruptcy in 1692. He worked as a journalist and informer for both Whigs and Tories and suffered imprisonment (1702) for one of his pamphlets. From 1704 to 1713 he wrote most of the thrice-weekly *Review* himself. His famous novels were written late in his career, *Robinson Crusoe* in 1719 and *Moll Flanders* and *Colonel Jack* in 1722.

defoliant A chemical applied to foliage in order to cause premature shedding of leaves. Defoliants are used to aid mechanical harvesting of cotton and for other peaceful uses. They are also employed in chemical warfare.

Degas, (Hilaire Germain) Edgar (1834–1917) French painter and sculptor. His early works were portraits and history paintings. From the mid-1860s he turned to painting contemporary scenes, particularly of ballet and racecourses, characterized by informal poses and unusual angles. His pastels of women at their toilet shocked his contemporaries but are among his finest works. He exhibited frequently with the impressionists but was little influenced by their style.

de Gaulle, Charles André Joseph Marie (1890–1970) French general and statesman who was an outstanding international figure in the mid-20th century; president (1958–69). An advocate of mechanized warfare during the 1930s, he was promoted early in World War II to general (1940). He opposed the Franco-German armistice, becoming leader of the Free French in London and a symbol of French patriotism. De Gaulle resented his dependence on Britain and the USA and the antagonism between them was to continue after the war. In 1958 he was summoned from retirement to deal with the crisis in Algeria, where French settlers, fearing the establishment of Algerian independence, were in revolt. He became president of the new Fifth Republic in 1959 and moved towards the achievement of Algerian independence. Successful by 1962, he subsequently pursued his vision of a Europe of nationally self-conscious states, free of US influence. He thus opposed the postwar multinational organizations, refusing to sign the Nuclear Test-Ban Treaty (1963) and withdrawing France from the military structure of NATO (1966). He was also pas-

DE GAULLE *During the celebrations of the liberation of Paris (1944).*

sionately opposed to UK membership of the EEC. At home his position was greatly weakened by the student and industrial unrest of May, 1968, and in 1969 he resigned. His policies, however, have endured in the right-wing Gaullist movement in French politics.

De Havilland, Sir Geoffrey (1882–1965) British aircraft designer and manufacturer, who produced some of the first jet-propelled aircraft. During both World Wars he designed several military aircraft, including the Mosquito of World War II.

dehydration A potentially serious condition resulting from excessive loss of water from the body. The water that is continuously lost from the body in urine, sweat, expired air, and faeces must be replaced by drinking. Dehydration may result from insufficient intake of water or from excessive loss in fever, vomiting, diarrhoea, or from the skin in hot climates. It may lead, if not treated, to shock and death.

deism A system of belief in God that, in contrast to theism, discounts revealed religion, especially Christianity, and takes God as the philosophical first cause. More specifically, deism was a rationalistic anti-Christian movement in England in the late 17th and early 18th centuries that criticized and rebutted the Scriptures after the manner of Locke's empiricism. Deism, often tending towards atheism, had more influence on German and French thinkers, including Voltaire, than in England.

Dekabrists (*or* Decembrists) Members of an unsuccessful anti-Tsarist revolt in December, 1825, following the death of Alexander I. They were members of various clandestine organizations formed after the Napoleonic Wars by discontented former military officers.

de Klerk, F(rederik) W(illem) (1937–) South African statesman; president (1989–). Having served in several ministerial posts, he succeeded P. W. Botha as president.

Delacroix, Eugène (1798–1863) French Romantic painter, influenced by Théodore Géricault (1791–1824), Rubens, and Constable. His richly coloured paintings were often inspired by incidents in Dante, Shakespeare, and Byron, and by contemporary events, e.g. *Massacre at Chios* (1824), based on a Turkish atrocity in Greece.

de la Mare, Walter (1873–1956) British poet, novelist, and anthologist, whose work is imbued with an atmosphere of mystery and magic. Among his best-known works are the poem "The Listeners" (1912), the fantastic novel *Memoirs of a Midget* (1921), and the anthologies *Come Hither* (1923) and *Love* (1943).

Delaunay, Robert (1885–1941) The earliest French painter of completely abstract compositions. His first major works represented the Eiffel Tower (1910–11) in cubist style but in his series of *Discs* (1912–13) he pioneered orphism (which he called *simultaneisme*), a style in which colour alone was the subject matter.

Delaware The second smallest state in the USA. It occupies part of the low-lying ground of the Atlantic coastal plain with higher ground in the NW, where most of the state's population and industry is concentrated. It is one of the most industrialized states; Wilmington contains the administrative centres of several large chemical companies. Motor vehicles, synthetic rubber, textiles, and food products are also produced. *History*: the Dutch established a settlement (1631) but it was the Swedes who founded the first permanent settlement Fort Christiana (now Wilmington) in 1638. Delaware was subsequently captured by the Dutch (1655) and the English (1664). It became part of Pennsylvania in 1682 and shared a governor with that colony until 1776. It was the first of the original 13 states of the USA. Area: 5328 sq km (2057 sq mi). Population (1986 est): 633 000. Capital: Dover.

Delft 52 01N 4 21E A town in the W Netherlands, in South Holland province. Since the late 16th century it has been famous for its pottery and porcelain known as delftware. Population (1987): 87 736.

NEW DELHI *Lutyens' President's House (1912–30).*

Delhi 28 40N 77 14E The capital of India, situated midway between the Ganges and Indus Valleys on the W bank of the River Jumna. It consists of the old city (Old Delhi), which was built in 1639 on the site of former cities of Delhi that date from the 15th century BC, and New Delhi, which replaced Calcutta as the capital of British India in 1912. Both the old and new cities together with the surrounding area comprise the Union Territory of Delhi, an administrative unit of some 1418 sq km (553 sq mi). The massive Red Fort of Old Delhi contains the Imperial Palace (1638–48) of Shah Jahan, and the Jami Masjid (Principal Mosque). New Delhi, with its spacious tree-lined streets and imposing government buildings, was designed chiefly by Sir Edwin Lutyens. Population (1981): 5 714 000.

Delian League A confederacy of Greek city states formed in 478 BC during the Greek-Persian Wars under the leadership of Athens. Members met on the sacred island of Delos. After the peace between Greece and Persia (c. 450) Athens regarded its allies as subjects. The League was disbanded after Athens' defeat (404) in the Peloponnesian War but was revived in defence against Sparta in 378, lasting until the defeat (338) of Athens and Thebes at Chaeronea.

Delibes, Leo (1836–91) French composer. He wrote a number of operas and operettas but his best-known works are the ballets *Coppélia* (1870) and *Sylvia* (1876).

deliquescence The process in which some crystalline substances, such as calcium chloride ($CaCl_2$), absorb water from the atmosphere to such an extent that they dissolve; this is extreme hygroscopic (water-attracting) behaviour. Deliquescent substances are used in several industries to provide dry atmospheres.

delirium An acute state of mental disturbance in which the patient has hallucinations and delusions and is incoherent, agitated, and restless. It is most commonly associated with a high fever, particularly in children. It also occurs in association with alcoholic poisoning and with alcohol withdrawal, when it is called **delirium tremens**. It can also be caused by intoxication with other drugs.

Delius, Frederick (1862–1934) British composer of German descent. Largely self-taught, he was influenced by Debussy and Grieg. His works include *Paris, the Song of a Great City* (1899), *Appalachia* (for orchestra and chorus; 1902), *On Hearing the First Cuckoo in Spring* (1912), and *North Country Sketches* (1913–14). Delius became blind in 1925 but continued to compose with the help of his amanuensis, Eric Fenby (1906–87).

Della Robbia, Luca (1400–82) Florentine Renaissance sculptor. Working first in marble, Luca produced the relief *Cantoria* (1431–38) for the Duomo, Florence. Subsequently he specialized in enamelled terracotta sculptures, the glazing process being his own invention. Their production was carried on by his nephew and sons.

Delos (Modern Greek name: Dhílos) 37 23N 25 15E A Greek island in the S Aegean Sea, one of the Cyclades. It was of great importance in antiquity (*see* Delian League), and many ancient temples and other buildings have been excavated. Area: 3 sq km (1 sq mi).

Delphi A village in central Greece. In antiquity, it was the principal sanctuary and oracle of Apollo. The oracle's advice about religion, morality, commerce, and colonial projects, interpreted from the trance utterances of a priestess, was widely sought by individuals and the Greek states. As traditional beliefs declined after the 4th century BC the oracle lost influence. It was closed by the Christian emperor, Theodosius (390 AD).

Delphinium A genus of annual or perennial herbs (250 species), also called larkspur, with tall spikes of deep-blue flowers. Delphiniums, native to the N hemisphere, are popular garden plants. Cultivated varieties have single or double flowers in shades of blue, pink, purple, or white. Family: *Ranunculaceae*.

delta A large fan-shaped accumulation of sediment deposited at the mouth of a river, where it discharges into a sea or lake. It forms when the river's flow is slowed down on meeting the comparatively static sea or lake,

resulting in a reduction of the river's load-bearing capacity. Clay particles also coagulate on meeting salt water and are deposited. The river is increasingly divided by the deposition into channels. Being fertile, deltas (such as the Nile Delta) are often extensively cultivated but are also prone to flooding.

Demeter A Greek corn goddess and mother goddess, sister of Zeus. She was worshipped at Eleusis, whose people helped her in her search for her daughter Persephone, abducted to the underworld. In gratitude she instructed them in agriculture and religion. She was identified with the Roman goddess Ceres.

de Mille, Cecil B(lount) (1881–1959) US film producer and director. His best-known films were epic productions involving spectacular crowd scenes and special effects. Many of these were based on biblical themes, notably *The Ten Commandments* (1923; remade 1956), *The King of Kings* (1927), and *Samson and Delilah* (1949).

democracy A form of government in which people either rule themselves, as in ancient Athens, or elect representatives to rule in their interests, as in most modern democracies. Elections, to be democratic, must be held regularly, be secret, and provide a choice of candidates; the elected assembly must also be free to legislate and to criticize government policy. Modern democratic ideas stem from 18th-century utilitarianism. Current debate centres on the theory that modern democratic government is by a political elite, which although voted into power invites little participation by the electorate.

Democratic Party One of the two major political parties in the USA (*compare* Republican Party). Originating in Jefferson's Republican Democrats in 1792, it became the Democratic Party during the presidency (1829–37) of Andrew Jackson. In 1860, just before the Civil War, the Democrats split over the issue of slavery into northern and southern factions and the party, dominated by southern Democrats, was eclipsed until regaining northern support in the 1880s. With F. D. Roosevelt's New Deal programme in the 1930s, the Democrats again became identified as a progressive party. Notable Democratic presidents include Woodrow Wilson, F. D. Roosevelt, and J. F. Kennedy.

Democritus (c. 460–370 BC), Greek philosopher and scientist. His atomism, developed from Leucippus, considered that all matter consists of minute particles—atoms—the multifarious arrangement of which accounts for different properties of matter apparent to our senses. Democritus wrote also on cosmology, biology, perception, music, and ethics.

demography A branch of the social sciences concerned with the statistical study of the sizes, distribution, and composition of human populations. It includes analysis of birth, death, and marriage rates for whole populations or groups within them. Demography overlaps with economics, mathematics, geography, and genetics.

demoiselle A crane, *Anthropoides virgo*, of dry grassy regions of central Europe and Asia. It is grey with a black head and neck, long black breast feathers, and long white plumes behind each eye.

Demosthenes (384–322 BC) Athenian orator and statesman. He attacked Philip of Macedon's imperial ambitions in Greece in a series of orations called the *Philippics* (351, 344, 341) and promoted an Athenian alliance with Thebes against Philip. This was defeated by

Philip at Chaeronea (338), whereby Macedonian supremacy in Greece was assured. After the death of Philip's son, Alexander the Great (323), Demosthenes again encouraged a Greek revolt. Condemned to death by Alexander's successors, Demosthenes fled Athens and committed suicide.

demotic script A form of Egyptian hieroglyphic writing. Pictorial hieroglyphics became less realistic and increasingly cursive from about 2500 BC until in the 7th century BC they developed into the cursive script called demotic. This continued in common use until the 5th century AD. *See also* Rosetta Stone.

dendrochronology (*or* tree-ring dating) An archaeological dating technique based on the annual rings of trees. Variations in ring widths have been shown to correspond to rainfall and temperature variations and thus very old tree trunks can give a record of past climates. Any construction incorporating timber can be dated by comparing the timber-ring patterns with a specimen of known age.

dendrology. *See* tree.

DENTISTRY *A child learning oral hygiene.*

denim A coarse twill-woven cloth, named after the French fabric *serge de Nîmes*. It is made of cotton, often with an admixture of nylon, and usually dyed blue. Originally popular for work garments, denim became fashionable for jeans and other casual clothes in the 1970s.

Denis, St (3rd century) The patron saint of France. Of Italian birth, he was sent to Gaul as a missionary and there became the first Bishop of Paris. He was martyred under the Emperor Valerian. His shrine is in the Benedictine abbey at St Denis near Paris. Feast Day: 9 Oct.

Denmark, Kingdom of (Danish name: Danmark) A country in N Europe, between the Baltic and the North Seas. It consists of the N section of the Jutland peninsula and about a hundred inhabited islands. Greenland and the Faroe Islands are also part of the Danish kingdom. The country is almost entirely flat. *Economy*: agriculture is important both for the home and export markets. Since World War II, however, industry has predominated, with engineering, chemicals, brewing, fishing, and food processing. Furniture, textiles, porcelain, metal goods, and glass are valued for their high-quality design. Exports include meat and meat products, dairy produce, cereals, fish, machinery, and metals. *History*: Viking

kingdoms occupied the area from the 8th to the 10th century, when Denmark became a united Christian monarchy under Harald Bluetooth. His grandson, Canute, ruled over Denmark, Norway, and England, forming the Danish Empire, which was dissolved soon after his death. In 1363 Norway again came under the Danish Crown by royal marriage. In 1397 Denmark and Norway joined with Sweden to form the Kalmar Union, which lasted until 1523. The Peace of Copenhagen (1660) concluded a long period of conflict between Denmark and Sweden. It then became an absolute monarchy until 1849, when a more liberal government was formed. Having supported Napoleon in the Napoleonic Wars, Denmark was compelled to cede Norway to Sweden by the Treaty of Kiel (1814). During World War II Denmark was occupied by Germany but a resistance movement aided the Allied victory. Iceland, which had previously been united with Denmark, became independent in 1944. A new constitution was formed in 1953, with a single-chamber parliament (elected by proportional representation) and executive power in the hands of the monarch through his ministers. In 1973 Denmark joined the EC. Head of state: Queen Margrethe II (1940–   ). Prime minister: Poul Schlüter (1929–   ). Official language: Danish. Official religion: Evangelical Lutheran. Official currency: krone of 100 øre. Area: 43 074 sq km (16 631 sq mi). Population (1988 est): 5 082 000. Capital and main port: Copenhagen.

density The mass of unit volume of a substance. In SI units it is measured in kilograms per cubic metre; water has a density of 1000 kg m^{-3} at 4°C. **Relative density** (formerly called "specific gravity") is the density of a substance divided by the density of water at 4°C. The density of a gas (vapour density) is often expressed as the mass of unit volume of the gas divided by the mass of the same volume of hydrogen at standard temperature and pressure.

dentistry The branch of medical science concerned with the care of the teeth, gums, and mouth. Restorative dentistry is concerned with the repair of teeth damaged by caries and the replacement of teeth lost through injury or extraction. Orthodontics deals with the correction of badly positioned teeth, usually by means of braces or other appliances but sometimes by surgery on the jaw. Periodontics includes the care of the gums and other structures supporting the teeth and the treatment of periodontal disease. Oral surgery deals with the extraction of teeth and the surgical repair of fractures or abnormalities of the jaws and facial bones. Preventive dentistry is concerned with preventing tooth decay and gum disease by such measures as education in oral hygiene and fluoridation of the public water supply.

Denver 39 45N 105 00W A city in the USA, the capital of Colorado on the South Platte River. Founded in 1858 during the Colorado gold rush, Denver is the financial, administrative, and industrial centre for a large agricultural area. Population (1986): 505 000.

deodar A tall cedar, *Cedrus deodara*, native to the Himalayas, where it forms vast forests, and widely planted for ornament in temperate regions and for timber in S Europe. It has young branches that droop down and large barrel-shaped cones.

deoxyribonucleic acid. *See* DNA.

depreciation The loss in value of capital goods as a result of wear and tear, obsolescence, etc. For example, a machine that costs £10,000 and is expected to last ten years depreciates at the rate of £1,000 a year. To keep its stock of capital goods, therefore, a firm must set aside a certain sum each year to account for depreciation. The life of a machine may be difficult to assess: changes in taste or technological developments may shorten the useful life of a machine.

DEPRESSION *Wall street during the Crash in 1929.*

depression (economics) A period during the trade cycle in which demand is low compared to industry's capacity to satisfy it. Profits, and therefore confidence and investment, are also correspondingly low. A depression is also characterized by high unemployment, as occurred in the 1930s (*see* Depression). Governments since World War II have adopted deficit financing policies to counter depressions, but the combination of depression and inflation in the 1970s led to widespread adoption of monetarism. A depression is also called a slump.

depression (meteorology) A cyclone in the midlatitudes; also called a low or a disturbance. Frequently accompanied by fronts, depressions move towards the NE in the N hemisphere and towards the SE in the S hemisphere. They are characterized by unsettled weather and are the main source of rainfall in the lowland areas of the midlatitudes.

depression (psychiatry) Severe and persistent misery. It can be a normal reaction to distressing events, such as bereavement (reactive depression). Sometimes, however, it is out of all proportion to the situation or may have no apparent external cause (endogenous depression): it can then be a sign of mental illness. In manic-depressive psychosis the depression is severe and leads the sufferer to despairing and guilty beliefs; sleep, appetite, and concentration can all be disturbed. In depressive neurosis the symptoms are less extreme but may still lead to suicide. Treatment with antidepressant drugs is often effective and psychotherapy is helpful. Severe cases may need electroconvulsive therapy.

Depression The period, also called the Slump, during the early 1930s, when worldwide economic collapse precipitated commercial failure and mass unemployment. Starting in the USA in 1929, when share prices fell so disastrously that thousands were made bankrupt, the Depression caused international repercussions. Overseas trade almost ceased, industrial production dropped, millions in industrialized countries were unemployed,

and agricultural countries were impoverished. Roosevelt's New Deal (1934) brought Americans hope of recovery, but Britain, despite abandoning free trade to protect its industries, never regained its commercial pre-eminence. In Germany the Depression contributed to the rise of Hitler's Nazi movement.

De Quincey, Thomas (1785–1859) British essayist and critic. He lived largely by journalism, writing numerous essays on diverse subjects. His autobiographical *Confessions of an English Opium Eater* first appeared in 1822.

Derain, André (1880–1954) French postimpressionist painter. In his bold designs and vibrant colours, particularly in his Thames paintings (1905–06), he was initially a leading exponent of fauvism, but after 1907 he came under the influence of Cézanne and painted in a cubist manner. He later reverted to a traditional style after an intensive study of the Old Masters. He produced some notable scenery and costume designs for Diaghilev's Ballets Russes.

Derby A flat race for three-year-old horses, run over 2.4 km (1.5 mi) at Epsom in early June. The most prestigious of the English Classics, it was instituted (1780) by the 12th Earl of Derby.

Derby 52 55N 1 30W A city in central England, in Derbyshire on the River Derwent. Its growth as a manufacturing centre began in the late 17th century. Today Derby is an important engineering centre (with Rolls-Royce aero engines) and has large railway workshops. Fine porcelain (*see* Derby ware), electrical equipment, paints, and textiles are manufactured. Population (1985 est): 215 000.

Derbyshire A county in N central England consisting of lowlands in the SE rising to the uplands of the Peak District in the NW. The main rivers are the Derwent, Trent, Dove, and Rother. Sheep and dairy farming is important with industrial activity centred on the coalfield in the E and SW. Area: 2631 sq km (1016 sq mi). Population (1986 est): 916 800. Administrative centre: Matlock.

Derby ware Porcelain first produced by William Duesbury (1725–86) at Derby in the 1750s. Early manufactures resemble Chelsea porcelain and Duesbury later bought the Chelsea works (1770). Utility products were decorated in bold blue, red, and gilt "Japan" patterns, but important portrait and fictional figures were also made in quantity. Products of the factory between 1786 and 1811 are called Crown Derby.

dermatology. *See* skin.

dernier A unit of weight, used to measure the fineness of woven materials, equal to 1 gram per 9000 metres.

Derwent, River The name of several rivers in England, including: **1.** A river in N central England, flowing SE from N Derbyshire to the River Trent. Length: 96 km (60 mi). **2.** A river in N England, flowing S from the North York Moors to join the River Ouse between Selby and Goole. Length: 92 km (57 mi). **3.** A river in NW England, flowing N and W from the Borrowdale Fells in Cumbria to the Irish Sea. Length: 54 km (34 mi).

Derwent Water A lake in NW England, in Cumbria in the Lake District. Area: about 8 sq km (3 sq mi).

desalination The removal of salt from brine to produce fresh water. Desalination is used to irrigate arid regions in which sea water is available, especially if solar power can be used as an energy source. Methods commonly employed are evaporation of the sea water, the condensed vapour forming relatively pure water, and freezing of the sea water, which produces pure ice. Freezing requires less energy than evaporation but the process is slower and technically more difficult.

Descartes, René (1596–1650) French philosopher and mathematician. After a Jesuit education he spent nine years in travel and military service before turning to study, primarily in Holland. Descartes' *Discourse on Method* (1637) introduced his technique of methodical doubt, which he developed in his greatest work the *Meditations* (1641). Asking "How and what do I know?" he arrived by a process of reduction at his famous statement "Cogito ergo sum" ("I think, therefore I am"). From this he proved to his own satisfaction God's existence (he was a sincere and lifelong Roman Catholic) and hence the existence of everything else. The importance of this approach lies in making epistemology the gateway to knowledge. Equally influential was his dualism: he considered that the world was composed of two different kinds of substance—mind, the essence of human beings, and matter—but never satisfactorily answered the problem of how mind and matter can interact. Descartes also contributed to the foundations of geometry (*see* coordinate systems) and optics. He held that mathematics was the supreme science in that the whole phenomenal world could be interpreted in terms of mathematical laws.

desert A virtually barren area of land where precipitation is minimal and sporadic, limiting vegetation growth. The mean annual rainfall is usually taken as being below 250 mm (10 in) for desert conditions to exist. Deserts may occur in areas of high atmospheric pressure, such as the Sahara, or near the W coast of continents cooled by cold ocean currents (e.g. the Atacama and Kalahari Deserts). They are also found in continental interiors where mountain barriers restrict precipitation, such as the Gobi Desert. Many deserts are characterized by stony scrublands with occasional resistant rock uplands and some areas of shifting sand dunes. The wind is an important agent of erosion and the rain, falling as violent downpours, is capable of moving large amounts of debris.

desertification The process by which arid or semiarid areas become deserts through human action or climatic change. Removal of the topsoil, by artificial means or erosion by wind, water, or desiccation, results in a reduction in the ground's water-storage capacity, which can cause crops to fail and famine. Overintensive farming and the cutting of trees for firewood helped to create the Dust Bowl in the USA and have caused deserts in Africa and SW Asia to advance by several kilometres each year. Solutions are now based on effective management of surface cover and climate.

desert rat. *See* jerboa.

De Sica, Vittorio (1901–74) Italian film director. His postwar films, in which he treated contemporary social themes with compassion and political awareness, included *Shoeshine* (1946), *Bicycle Thieves* (1948), and *Umberto D* (1952).

desman A small aquatic mammal belonging to the family *Talpidae* (moles). They have webbed hind feet, live in burrows in river banks, and feed on invertebrates and fish.

Des Moines 41 35N 93 35W A city in the USA, the capital of Iowa. Founded in 1843, it is an important industrial and commercial centre. Population (1980): 371 800.

DESERTIFICATION *Overgrazing can have disasterous results.*

destroyer A fast heavily armed naval vessel that is smaller than a cruiser, has a displacement of about 3000 tonnes, and is 110–150 m (330–450 ft) long. Destroyers are not armoured. Because of their speed, armament, and versatility, they are employed in antisubmarine warfare, in convoy work, and in "hunter-killer" attack groups consisting of one carrier and five or six destroyers.

detached retina A condition in which the retina—a layer of specialized light-sensitive cells at the back of the eye—becomes separated from the layer beneath it. It happens slowly and painlessly and the patient loses part of his vision. It is caused by injury to the eye or inflammation in the eye and is most common in very shortsighted people. Detached retina is treated surgically, sometimes using a laser beam to weld the retina in place.

detergents Chemicals used for cleansing. Although the term includes soaps it is usually applied in a more restricted sense to synthetic surfactants. Such detergents have large molecules, typically composed of a hydrocarbon oil-soluble part and a water-soluble part. These compounds are thus able to promote the solution of oil, grease, etc., in water. Household detergents may also contain water softeners, bleaches, and fabric brighteners.

determinism The philosophical theory that every event has a cause and that all events are determined by causal physical laws. According to one view every event could be causally explained and could be predicted if the conditions are not too complex for analysis. Applied to human actions, determinism appears to conflict with the concept of free will. If even desires, intentions, and motives are determined and if actions are, in principle, predictable, this contradicts the idea that actions are freely chosen, and hence the concept of moral responsibility. However, some philosophers believe that determinism and free will are compatible and that a person acts freely if his desires are the cause of his actions. *See also* predestination.

Detroit 42 23N 83 05W A city and port in the USA, in Michigan on the Detroit River. Founded in 1701, it is the fifth largest city in the USA. It is dominated by the motor-vehicle industry. Population (1986): 1 086 220.

deuterium (D; *or* heavy hydrogen ^{2}H) An isotope of hydrogen having a nucleus consisting of one proton and one neutron. It occurs naturally in hydrogen (0.0156%) and is used as a radioactive tracer. Heavy water (deuterium oxide; D_2O) is used in nuclear reactors as a moderator. *See also* thermonuclear reactor. At no 1; at wt 2.014.

Deuteronomy The fifth book of the Old Testament. It is a series of addresses by Moses to the Israelites immediately before the occupation of the Promised Land of Canaan (Palestine). After repeating the Ten Commandments, he exhorts the people to live differently from the surrounding nations and gives a code of religious and civil laws to be observed in Canaan.

De Valera, Eamon (1882–1975) Irish statesman; prime minister (1932–48, 1951–54, 1957–59) and president (1959–73). A commandant in the 1916 Easter Rising, he nevertheless escaped execution and in 1917 was elected to the British parliament and became the president of Sinn Féin. From 1919 to 1922 he was president of the newly declared Irish Republic but rejected the terms of the Anglo-Irish treaty of 1921 (*see* Home Rule). In 1926 he founded Fianna Fáil.

de Valois, Dame Ninette (Edris Stannus; 1898–) British ballet dancer and choreographer, born in Ireland. During the 1920s she worked with Diaghilev's Ballets Russes. In 1931 she founded the Sadler's Wells Ballet, the company that became the Royal Ballet in 1956 and that she directed until 1963.

devaluation A downward change in the value of one country's currency in terms of other currencies. A country that devalues makes its exports cheaper and its imports more expensive; thus devaluation should help correct a balance-of-payments deficit by increasing the volume of exports and decreasing the volume of imports. The measure is not always effective: the increased import bill may be larger than the increase in receipts from exports. Under the Bretton Woods fixed-rate system (*see* Bretton Woods Conference) devaluations only occurred occasionally but were large and destabilizing. In the floating-rate system that replaced it, the value of a currency in terms of others is determined by supply and demand with a minimum of government interference, so producing gradual devaluations.

developing countries Countries that do not have sophisticated industries and consequently have a low per capita income. They include almost all the countries in Africa, Asia, and South America. Their economies are characterized by abundant cheap unskilled labour and a scarcity of capital for investment. There is a marked difference in incomes between industrial and developing nations (the "north–south split"). Some 70% of the world's population lives in developing countries in largely agricultural economies from which poverty, hunger, disease, and illiteracy have not been eliminated. Many of these economies rely shakily on one main crop, which in years of crop failure, poor world demand, or low market prices can cause severe hardship.

Devil. *See* Lucifer.

devil ray. *See* manta ray.

devil's coach horse A large carnivorous rove beetle, *Staphylinus olens*, that occurs in gardens of W Europe.

devolution The delegation of political powers from a central government to regional governments, as occured

in the UK with the establishment of the Stormont parliament in Northern Ireland. Growing nationalist sentiment in Scotland and Wales led to the introduction of two devolution bills in the House of Commons in 1976; in March, 1979, referenda were held in these countries on the bills' final provisions. In Wales there was an absolute majority against the devolution plans; in Scotland an insufficiently large majority favoured them.

Devon A county of SW England, bordering on the Atlantic Ocean in the N and the English Channel in the S. It consists mainly of the mid-Devon plain, rising to Dartmoor in the SW and Exmoor in the NE. The chief rivers are the Dart, Exe, and Tamar. Tourism and agriculture are important while industry is concentrated around Exeter and Plymouth, a major naval base. Area: 6712 sq km (2591 sq mi). Population (1988): 1 021 100. Administrative centre: Exeter.

Devonian period A geological period of the Upper Palaeozoic era between the Silurian and Carboniferous periods, about 415 to 370 million years ago. It is divided into seven stages, based on invertebrate fossil remains, such as corals, brachiopods, ammonoids, and crinoids. The rocks containing these fossils were marine deposits but the Devonian period also shows extensive continental deposits (Old Red Sandstone). Fossils from these rocks include fish, land plants, and freshwater molluscs.

dew The condensation of moisture, which forms on the ground or on objects near the ground, especially at night. It occurs when the air near the ground cools to the **dew point**, at which it becomes saturated and the water vapour present condenses into water droplets.

Dewar flask A flask, used to store a substance at constant temperature. It has double glass walls, the space between the walls being evacuated to prevent heat loss by conduction. The inside wall is silvered to prevent heat loss by radiation and the flask is tightly stoppered to prevent heat loss by convection or evaporation. Also known as the Thermos or vacuum flask, it was invented by the Scottish scientist Sir James Dewar (1842–1923).

Dewey, John (1859–1952) US philosopher and educationalist. A pragmatist, Dewey believed thinking arises where practical problems arise.

Dewey Decimal Classification An international system for classifying the books in a library, originated in 1873 by the US librarian Melvil Dewey (1851–1931). Books are divided according to subject matter into ten groups, each group having a hundred numbers; principle subdivisions within each group are divided by ten, and with the use of decimal numbers further subdivisions can be generated without limit.

dextrose. *See* glucose.

Dhaka (name until 1984: Dacca) 23 42N 90 22E The capital of Bangladesh, situated in the SE of the country, on the Burhi Ganga River. It is a riverport and commercial and industrial centre. The capital of the Bengal province of the Mogul Empire in the 17th century, it came under British rule in the 18th century and upon independence in 1947 was made capital of East Pakistan. Population (1984 est): 3 600 000.

diabetes One of several diseases with a common symptom—the production of large quantities of urine. The term usually refers to **diabetes mellitus** (*or* sugar diabetes), in which the body is unable to utilize sugars to produce energy due to a deficiency of the pancreatic hormone insulin. Symptoms include thirst, weight loss, and a high level of glucose in the urine and in the blood (hyperglycaemia). Treatment is based on a carefully controlled diet, often with insulin injections or pills to reduce the amount of sugar in the blood. **Diabetes insipidus** is a rare disease due to a deficiency of the pituitary hormone vasopressin, which regulates water balance in the body. The patient produces large quantities of watery urine and is always thirsty. It is treated with doses of the hormone.

DIAGHILEV *Seen here with the French writer Jean Cocteau (left).*

Diaghilev, Sergei (Pavlovich) (1872–1929) Russian ballet impresario. The outstanding success of his season of Russian ballet (1909) resulted in the organization of a permanent company (1911), known as the Ballets Russes, which Diaghilev directed until his death.

dialect The language of a particular district or group of people. The distinction between language and dialect is not clear cut. As a general rule any two dialects of a language may be expected to be mutually comprehensible. Dialects develop as a result of geographical separation: slightly differing versions of one original language develop in different places within a generation or so of the time of separation. Social factors also affect dialect development. In English, for example, the medieval dialect of London has developed into a socially prestigious class dialect spoken in most parts of Britain (*see* received pronunciation).

dialectical materialism The official philosophy of Marxism, derived by Marx and Engels from a combination of contemporary (1850) science and Hegel's idealism. As philosophy dialectical materialism is obscure and apparently unrelated to Marxist political theory. However, **historical materialism**, expounded in the *Communist Manifesto*, is a coherent account of history on an economic basis: for every system of production there is an appropriate organization of class and property. While economic forces continually develop production systems, the class and property structure remains unchanged, causing tension between economic forces and social relations, which continues until the ultimate rational socialist society evolves.

dialysis A process, discovered by Thomas Graham (1804–69), for separating mixtures of fluids by diffusion through a semipermeable membrane. Different substances in a solution diffuse at different rates. The passage of large particles is almost completely blocked by a semipermeable membrane, whereas salt solutions pass through easily. The technique of dialysis is used in artificial kidney machines, or dialysers, which take over the function of diseased kidneys by filtering waste material from the blood but leaving behind proteins, blood cells, and other large particles.

diamond The hardest known mineral, comprising a cubic variety of crystalline carbon, formed under intense heat and pressure. Diamonds are mined in S Africa, Siberia, and Namibia; over 80% are used industrially, mainly for cutting and grinding tools, the others being used as gems. The largest diamond yet discovered is the Cullinan diamond. Many industrial diamonds are produced synthetically from graphite subjected to very high temperatures and pressures.

Diana The Roman goddess identified with the Greek Artemis, associated with women and childbirth and with the moon. She is usually represented as a virgin huntress armed with bow and arrows.

Dianthus A genus of annual and perennial herbs (300 species), mainly from Europe and Asia, having flower stems (often branched) with swollen joints and showy white, pink, or red flowers. Common species include *D. barbatus* (*see* sweet william), *D. caryophyllus* (*see* carnation), and *D. plumarius* (*see* pink). Family: *Caryophyllaceae.*

diaphragm 1. In anatomy, a dome-shaped sheet of muscle that separates the thorax (chest cavity) from the abdomen. The diaphragm is attached to the spine, lower ribs, and breastbone and contains a large opening through which the oesophagus (gullet) passes. It plays an important role in producing breathing movements (*see* respiration). 2. *See* contraception.

diarrhoea The frequent passing of liquid stools. It is a symptom, not a disease; causes include anxiety, infection or inflammation of the intestines, impaired absorption of food, and side effects of drugs. It can be eased by the use of drugs but proper treatment must aim at eliminating the cause.

diaspora (Greek: dispersion) The collective term for Jewish communities outside the land of Israel. Beginning with the Babylonian exile (6th century BC), Jews spread to most parts of the world, while continuing to regard Israel as their homeland. The most important centres of the diaspora were, in antiquity, Babylonia and Egypt; in the middle ages, Spain and France; and in early modern times, E Europe. In the late 19th century there was a massive exodus of Jews from Russia and Poland, and the Nazi holocaust destroyed many old European communities. The main centre is now the USA, with some six million Jews.

diastole. *See* blood pressure; heart.

diatoms Microscopic yellow-green algae of the class *Bacillariophyceae* (about 16 000 species), occurring abundantly as single cells or colonies in fresh water and oceans (forming an important constituent of plankton) and also in soil. They have silicon-rich cell walls (called frustules), often beautifully sculptured, composed of two halves that fit together. Fossilized frustules form a porous rock called diatomaceous earth (*or* kieselguhr), used in filters, insulators, abrasives, etc.

diazepam. *See* benzodiazepines.

Dicentra A genus of annual and perennial herbaceous plants (about 300 species) from North America and E Asia. They have divided compound leaves and sprays of hanging flowers that are flattened sideways. Many species are ornamentals (*see* bleeding heart. Family: *Fumariaceae*.

Dickens, Charles (1812–70) British novelist. He began his writing career by contributing to popular magazines, achieving sudden fame with *The Pickwick Papers* (1837), which he followed with *Oliver Twist* (1838) and *Nicholas Nickleby* (1839) and the very successful *Old Curiosity Shop* (1840–41); like all his novels, these first appeared in monthly instalments. *David Copperfield* (1849–50) was a strongly autobiographical work, portraying Dickens' father as the feckless Mr Micawber. His later novels, from *Bleak House* (1853) to the incomplete *Edwin Drood* (1870), were increasingly pessimistic in tone; *Great Expectations* (1860–61) and *Our Mutual Friend* (1864–65), in their depiction of the destructive powers of money and ambition, develop most fully Dickens' radical view of society.

dicotyledons The larger of the two main groups of flowering plants, which includes hardwood trees, shrubs, and many herbaceous plants (*compare* monocotyledons). Dicots are characterized by having two seed leaves (cotyledons) in the embryo. Typically the flower parts are arranged in fours or fives (or multiples of these) and the leaves have a netlike pattern of veins. *See also* angiosperm.

dictionaries. *See* lexicography.

Diderot, Denis (1713–84) French philosopher and writer. With Voltaire, Diderot helped create the Enlightenment, mainly through the *Encyclopédie*, which he edited after 1750 (*see* Encyclopedists).

Dido In Greek legend, the daughter of a king of Tyre, who fled to Africa when her husband was murdered; there she founded Carthage. According to legend she burnt herself to death on a funeral pyre to avoid marriage to Iarvas of Numidia; in Virgil's *Aeneid* she killed herself after being abandoned by her lover Aeneas.

DIDEROT *Detail of an illustration of a forge, taken from his* Encyclopédie.

dielectric A substance that acts as an electrical insulator and can sustain an electric field. When a voltage is applied across a perfect dielectric there is no energy loss

and the electric field strength changes simultaneously with voltage. In the real dielectrics, such as air, ceramics, or wax, which are used in capacitors, there is always a small energy loss.

MARLENE DIETRICH *In* The Blue Angel *(1930).*

Dien Bien Phu, Battle of (March–May, 1954) The decisive battle of the Indochina war, in NE Vietnam, in which Vietnamese forces defeated the French. It coincided with the Geneva Conference, which ended French control of Indochina.

Dieppe 49 55N 1 05E A port and resort in N France, in the Seine-Maritime department on the English Channel. Population (1983): 39 500.

Diesel engine. *See* internal-combustion engine.

diet, imperial. *See* Reichstag.

dietetics The study of the principles of nutrition and their application to the selection of appropriate diets both to maintain health and as part of the treatment of certain diseases. A balanced diet should contain foods with adequate amounts of all the nutrients—carbohydrates, fats, proteins, minerals, and vitamins—as well as foods with a high content of dietary fibre. An important aspect of the work of dieticians is to work out the special diets that are required for various diseases.

Dietrich, Marlene (Maria Magdalene von Losch; 1904–) German film actress and singer. Her image of sultry beauty was developed by the Austrian-born director Josef von Sternberg in such films as *The Blue Angel* (1930), *Blonde Venus* (1932), and *Shanghai Express* (1932).

diffraction The spreading or bending of light waves as they pass the edge of an object or pass through an aperture. The diffracted waves subsequently interfere with each other producing regions of alternately high and low intensity. This phenomenon can be observed in the irregular boundary of a shadow of an object cast on a screen by a small light source. A similar effect occurs with sound waves. *See also* interference.

diffusion 1. The mixing of different fluids, or the distribution of a substance from a region of high concentration to one of lower concentration, by means of the random thermal motion of its constituents. The rates at which gases diffuse are inversely proportional to their densities (Graham's law). Diffusion also occurs between certain solids; for example gold will slowly diffuse into lead. **2.** The scattering of a beam of radiation on reflection from a rough surface or on transmission through certain media. When diffusion occurs the laws of reflection and refraction are not obeyed.

digestion The process by which food is converted into substances that can be absorbed by the intestine. The process begins in the mouth, where the food is chewed and mixed with saliva, and continues with the action of digestive enzymes secreted by the stomach, duodenum, and pancreas. Rhythmic contractions of the muscular layer of the intestinal wall (called peristalsis) ensures a constant mixing of enzymes and food and the propulsion of food along the intestine. The products of digestion include amino acids, various sugars (such as lactose, maltose, and glucose), and fat molecules; these are absorbed by the intestine and conveyed to the bloodstream.

digital computer. *See* computer.

digitalis A crude drug prepared from the dried leaves of foxglove plants. Digitalis is purified to digoxin, digitoxin, and lanatoside C. These drugs are used to improve the action of a failing or inefficient heart and to reduce a dangerously fast heart rate. Side effects of digitalis compounds include nausea, vomiting, and pulse irregularities.

digital mapping The production of a map using a system in which the details of the map are stored in computerized form. The points and lines that make up a map are converted, or digitized, into computer data; this information is then stored on magnetic tapes. Subsequent reproduction may be of the whole map or of a selected part; it may be at a different scale and/or on a transformed projection. A print of the map can be produced or it may be displayed on a visual display unit. Changes can be simply made without the whole map having to be redrawn. In the UK the Ordnance Survey began converting its large-scale maps to digital data in 1973; by 1985 25 000 of the 1:1250 and 1:2500 scale maps had been converted.

digital recording. *See* recording of sound.

Dijon 47 20N 5 02E A city in France, the capital of the Côte-d'Or department on the Burgundy Canal. The former capital of Burgundy, it is the site of the palace of the Dukes of Burgundy and has a cathedral (13th–14th centuries). It is famous for its mustard. Population (1983): 150 500.

dik-dik A small African antelope belonging to the genus *Madoqua* (7 species), found in the undergrowth of forested areas. Dik-diks are generally solitary and only the males have horns.

dilatation and curettage (D and C) An operation in which the neck (cervix) of the womb is dilatated (widened) and the lining of the womb is scraped out. D and C may be performed for a variety of reasons, including the removal of any residual membranes after a miscarriage, removal of cysts or tumours, removal of a specimen of tissue for examination in the diagnosis of various gynaecological disorders, and for termination of a pregnancy (*see* abortion).

dill A widely cultivated annual or biennial European herb, *Anethum graveolens*, 60 cm high. The smooth stem bears feathery leaves and umbrella-like clusters of small yellow flowers, which produce small hard flat fruits. The young leaves and fruits are used to flavour soups, cakes,

salads, fish, and pickled cucumbers. Family: *Umbelliferae*.

D'Indy, Vincent (1851–1931) French composer, the pupil and biographer of Franck and the cofounder of the Paris Schola Cantorum (1894). He was greatly influenced by Wagner and wrote a number of large-scale orchestral compositions, as well as operas and chamber music. His most famous work is the *Symphony on a French Mountaineer's Song* (for piano and orchestra; 1886).

DINGO

dingo An Australian wild dog, *Canis familiaris* (formerly *C. dingo*), introduced from Asia. It has a tan-coloured coat. It is nocturnal and generally solitary.

Dinka A Nilotic people of the Nile basin region of the Sudan. Warlike and independent, the Dinka move with their cattle from dry-season pastures by the rivers to wet-season settlements, where they grow millet. There are many independent tribes.

dinosaur An extinct reptile that was the dominant terrestrial animal during the Jurassic and Cretaceous periods (200–65 million years ago). Dinosaurs first appeared about 225 million years ago, ranging in size from about 60 cm to such mighty creatures as *Diplodocus*, which reached 27 m in length. There were two orders: the *Saurischia*, which were mostly carnivores and included the bipedal *Allosaurus* and *Tyrannosaurus*; and the *Ornithischia*, which were all herbivores and included the bipedal *Iguanodon*, the horned *Triceratops*, and *Stegosaurus*. Why both orders died out at the end of the Cretaceous period along with other reptiles, such as ichthyosaurs, pterosaurs, and plesiosaurs, is still not certain. Dinosaurs had large bodies with heavy bones and protective armour and were probably unable to adapt to climatic changes and the effects of a rise in the sea level, which flooded their coastal habitats.

Diocletian(us), Gaius Aurelius Valerius (245–313 AD) Roman emperor (284–305). He rose to prominence in the army, to which he owed his accession. In 293 he established the tetrarchy to govern the Empire more effectively in a time of civil strife: the Empire was divided into East and West, with each ruled by an emperor and his associate. Diocletian ruled in the East with Galerius, abdicating in 305.

diode. *See* semiconductor diode; thermionic valve.

Diogenes Laertius (3rd century AD) Greek compiler of the opinions and biographical details of classical philosophers, including the Presocratics. The historical authenticity of his biographical material, for example about the life of Epicurus, is doubtful.

Diogenes of Sinope (412–322 BC) The founder of the philosophical sect of the Cynics. Diogenes claimed, in contrast to almost all Greek thinkers, total freedom and self-sufficiency for the individual. Unlike modern anarchists, he saw no need for violent rebellion to assert his independence, which he thought he already had. His disregard for social conventions made him the subject of many stories.

Dionysus (*or* Bacchus) The Greek god of wine, originally a vegetation god. He was the son of Semele (daughter of Cadmus) by Zeus. A common theme of many Dionysian legends is a people's refusal to accept his divinity and his subsequent retribution.

dioptre A unit used to measure the power of a lens equal to the reciprocal of its focal length in metres. The power of a converging lens is taken to be positive and that of a diverging lens as negative.

Dior, Christian (1905–57) French fashion designer, who first became known with his 1947 collection, which introduced the New Look, characterized by fitted bodices and long full skirts. His later designs included the H-line and the A-line.

Dioscuri. *See* Castor and Pollux.

diphtheria An acute bacterial infection primarily affecting the nose, throat, or larynx. Virtually eliminated from most western nations by extensive immunization, it formerly caused the death of many children. It is still found in Africa and India. Diphtheria produces a membrane across the throat that chokes the child. Alternatively death may be caused by poisons damaging the heart. The disease can be cured using penicillin and antitoxin.

Diplodocus An amphibious dinosaur of the Jurassic period (200–136 million years ago) and the largest terrestrial vertebrate ever to exist, reaching a length of 27 m. It had a narrow body with massive pillar-like legs, a long neck with a tiny head, and a long tail. It fed on soft vegetation in swamps and shallow lakes. Order: *Saurischia*.

dipper An aquatic songbird of the family *Cinclidae* (4 species) of Eurasia and America. Dippers are found near fast-flowing mountain streams, diving into the water to search for insects and small fish. The Eurasian white-breasted dipper (*Cinclus cinclus*) is about 17 cm long and has a dense dark-brown plumage with a white breast.

Diptera An order of insects comprising the two-winged, or true, flies. *See* fly.

Dirac, Paul Adrien Maurice (1902–84) British physicist. In 1928 he introduced a general formulation of quantum theory. Two years later he incorporated relativity into quantum theory and produced an equation that predicted the existence of antiparticles. He shared the 1933 Nobel Prize with Schrödinger.

direction finder Equipment for locating the source of a radio signal, such as a ship at sea. It consists of one or more directive aerials (usually in the form of a loop), designed to detect signals from a specific direction, and a receiver. Frequencies normally used are between 0.1 and 2 megahertz. Radar is a form of direction finding

based on picking up reflections of a transmitted signal.

discount houses Financial institutions in the UK that discount bills of exchange and buy and sell treasury bills, activities that they finance by borrowing short-term funds (money at call) from the commercial banks and other financial institutions. The discount houses take up the whole of the treasury bill issue each week, and in return the Bank of England acts as lender of last resort to the discount houses.

discus throw A field event in athletics. The circular discus is made of wood and metal, the men's weighing 2 kg (4.4 lb) and the women's 1 kg (2.2 lb). It is thrown as far as possible with one hand from within a circle 2.5 m (8.2 ft) in diameter.

disinfectant A substance or process that kills germs or prevents them multiplying. Carbolic acid (phenol) was introduced for this purpose in medicine in the 1870s by Joseph Lister. It is still used, as are many of its derivatives, in cleaning materials and, in weaker solutions, in skin disinfectants. Chlorine and such compounds as sodium hypochlorite kill bacteria and also some viruses. Other chemical disinfectants include chlorinated phenols, hydrogen peroxide (H_2O_2), iodine (I_2), and formaldehyde (HCHO). Dry heating to 140°C for about 3 hours will kill all disease-causing germs. Boiling water and ultraviolet light are also effective disinfectants.

WALT DISNEY

Disney, Walt (1901–66) US film producer and animator. His most famous cartoon character, Mickey Mouse, was designed in 1928. His films include full-length cartoon features, such as *Snow White and the Seven Dwarfs* (1938), *Pinocchio* (1939), and *Bambi* (1943), nature documentaries, and adventure films, such as *Treasure Island* (1950) and *Mary Poppins* (1964). His *Fantasia* (1940) used colourful visual images and cartoons to accompany several pieces of classical music. He opened Disneyland, an amusement park, in California in 1955. Walt Disney World in Florida was opened in 1971; another park was opened in Tokyo in 1983.

Disraeli, Benjamin, 1st Earl of Beaconsfield (1804–81) British statesman; Conservative prime minister (1868, 1874–80). Becoming an MP in 1837, Disraeli was critical of Peel's Conservative Government (1841–46) and opposed the repeal of the Corn Laws. He was three times chancellor of the exchequer in Derby's governments (1852, 1858–59, 1866–68): he was largely responsible for the 1867 Reform Act. He succeeded Derby in February, 1868, but lost office in the autumn election, to the Liberals under Gladstone. Under Disraeli's second term of leadership the Conservative Party came to be clearly identified with policies that upheld the monarchy, Empire, and Church of England, while sponsoring social reform. In 1875 he bought Britain a major stake in the Suez Canal and in 1876 secured passage of a bill that conferred the title Empress of India on Queen Victoria. A flamboyant and witty parliamentarian, Disraeli earned the respect and friendship of the queen. Also a writer, Disraeli's novels include *Vivien Grey* (1826), *Coningsby, or the New Generation* (1844), and *Sybil, or the Two Nations* (1845).

distillation A method of purifying or separating the components of a liquid by boiling or evaporating the liquid and condensing the vapour. It is used for separating either liquids from solids or a mixture of liquids whose components have different boiling points. The latter is known as fractional distillation. Distillation is employed in petroleum refineries to separate the various hydrocarbons, in the production of alcoholic spirits, and in extracting pure water from sea water.

District of Columbia A federal district of the E USA, coextensive with the federal capital, Washington. Area: 178 sq km (69 sq mi).

dittany A perennial European herbaceous plant, *Dictamnus albus*, also known as the gas plant. A strong-scented gland-covered plant, it gives off an aromatic oil. Dittany produces a drooping spike of white or pink flowers. Family: *Rutaceae*. The name is also applied to several other plants.

Diu. *See* Daman and Diu.

diuretics A large class of drugs that increase the excretion of urine by the kidneys. Diuretics are used in the treatment of diseases in which fluid accumulates in the tissues. These illnesses include heart failure, kidney failure, and some liver diseases (such as cirrhosis). Diuretics may also be used in the treatment of high blood pressure.

diver A large aquatic bird belonging to a family (*Gaviidae*; 3 species) occurring in the N hemisphere, also called loon. Divers breed on lakes and ponds and spend the winter in temperate coastal waters. They have small pointed wings and black and white plumage and they dive deeply, feeding on fish, frogs, and aquatic insects. Order: *Gaviiformes*.

dividend A share in the profits of a company paid to shareholders. The rate of dividend is declared at the company's annual general meeting and will reflect the preceding year's profit. It is usually expressed as a percentage of the par value of the share (e.g. a 5% dividend on a 20p share would pay 1p per share). The dividend yield of the share is the income it produces expressed as a percentage of its current value (e.g. a 5% dividend on a 20p share that has a current value of 35p is $20/35 \times 5 = 2.86\%$). Dividends are usually paid twice yearly, an interim dividend and a final dividend.

divine right of kings A political doctrine claiming that monarchs are responsible only to God and that their subjects owe them unquestioning obedience. The theory originated in the middle ages and was most fully developed in the 16th and 17th centuries, especially in England under the Stuart kings and in France under Louis XIV.

diving duck A duck that dives to the bottom of lakes or rivers to feed, aided by a dense high-domed skull. Diving ducks, which include the goldeneye, pochard, and scaup, usually have a drab plumage, thick neck, narrow wings, and large feet; the legs are set far back and they walk awkwardly on land. *Compare* dabbling duck.

Divisional Court. *See* courts of law.

divorce The legal process by which a marriage is ended. Until the Matrimonial Causes Act (1857), which established a Divorce Court, divorce in England was possible only by special Act of Parliament. Jurisdiction is now vested in the High Court and county courts (*see* courts of law). Since 1971, the only ground for divorce has been that the marriage has irretrievably broken down. The party who applies for the divorce (the petitioner) must show that the other party (the respondent) has (1) committed adultery, (2) behaved in such a way as the petitioner cannot reasonably be expected to live with him or her, (3) deserted the petitioner for two years, (4) lived separate and apart from the petitioner for two years and consents to the divorce, or (5) lived separate and apart from the petitioner for five years. Unless agreed between the parties, the court determines who is to have custody of the children under 16 and what financial arrangements should be made between the parties.

DIWALI *Preparations for the festival.*

Diwali An important Hindu religious festival held during October or November. It honours Lakshmi, the goddess of wealth (or in Bengal, Kali). There is feasting, gambling, and lighting of lamps in honour of Rama. Jains commemorate at this time the death of their saint Mahavira.

Dixieland A type of jazz played by White musicians in imitation of the traditional New Orleans style. It emerged in the early 20th century but declined during the swing and bebop eras.

Djakarta. *See* Jakarta.

Djibouti, Republic of (name until 1977: the French Territory of the Afars and the Issas) A small country in NE Africa, on the Gulf of Aden at its entrance to the Red Sea. It consists chiefly of an arid rocky coastal plain rising to a plateau inland. The main population groups are Somalis (chiefly Issas) and Afars, with Arabic and

European minorities. *Economy*: the port of Djibouti (a free port since 1949) is the country's economic focus handling an important transshipment trade. The port is linked by rail to Ethiopia and handles about half of that country's trade. *History*: French involvement, centred on the port, began in the mid-19th century. It was made a French colony known as French Somaliland in 1896 and proclaimed an overseas territory in 1967. It became independent in 1977 as Djibouti with Hassan Gouled Aptidon (1916–) as its first president. The country suffered from the war between Ethiopia and Somalia through the disruption of trade. Official languages: Hamitic languages of Somali. Official currency: Djibouti franc of 100 centimes. Area: 21 783 sq km (8409 sq mi). Population (1987): 470 000. Capital and chief port: Djibouti.

DNA (*or* deoxyribonucleic acid) A nucleic acid that is the chief constituent of the chromosomes, carrying genetic information, in the form of genes, necessary for the organization and functioning of living cells.

The molecular structure of DNA, proposed by J. D. Watson and F. H. Crick in 1953, consists of a double helix of two strands coiled around each other. Each strand is made up of alternating pentose sugar (deoxyribose) and phosphate groups, with an organic base attached to each pentose group. There are four possible bases: adenine (A), guanine (G), cytosine (C), and thymine (T). The bases on each strand are joined by hydrogen bonds and are always paired in the same way: A always binds with T and G with C. During replication, the strands of the helix separate and each provides a template for the synthesis of a new complementary strand, thus producing two identical copies of the original helix. This special property for accurate self-replication enables DNA to duplicate the genes of an organism during the cell divisions of growth (*see* mitosis) and the production of germ cells for the next generation (*see* meiosis).

Dnepr, River (*or* R. Dnieper) A river in the W Soviet Union. Rising in the Valdai Hills, NE of Smolensk, it flows mainly SE through the RSFSR and the Belorussian and Ukrainian SSRs to enter the Black Sea. It is the third longest river in Europe. Length: 2286 km (1420 mi).

Dnepropetrovsk (name from 1787 until 1796 and from 1802 until 1826: Ekaterinoslav) 48 29N 35 00E A city in the SW Soviet Union, in the Ukrainian SSR on the River Dnepr. It is one of the country's largest industrial cities, producing especially iron and steel, and it is also a transportation centre. Population (1987): 1 182 000.

Dnestr, River (*or* R. Dniester) A river in the SW Soviet Union. It flows mainly SE from the Carpathian Mountains, through the Ukrainian and Moldavian SSRs, to the Black Sea near Odessa. Length: 1411 km (877 mi).

Dobermann pinscher A breed of dog developed by Louis Dobermann in Germany in the late 19th century. It has a powerful streamlined body with a very short tail and a long muzzle. The short smooth coat is black, brown, or blue-grey with tan markings. Dobermanns are widely used as police, guard, and guide dogs.

dock A plant (usually perennial) of the genus *Rumex*, of temperate regions. It has a deep stout root and large lance-shaped leaves. The small greenish flowers borne in small clusters produce small nutlets, often surrounded by the reddish papery remains of the petals. Dock leaves

are the traditional antidote to nettle stings. Family: *Polygonaceae*. *See also* sorrel.

Dodecanese A group of some 20 Greek islands and islets in the SE Aegean Sea, including Cos, Rhodes (the largest), and Pátmos. They were taken from Turkey by Italy in 1912 and passed to Greece in 1947. Total area: 2719 sq km (1050 sq mi). Population (1981): 145 071. Capital: Rhodes.

Dodgson, Charles Lutwidge. *See* Carroll, Lewis.

dodo A large clumsy flightless bird, *Raphus cucullatus*, that lived on Mauritius but was extinct by 1681. It had a grey-blue plumage, tiny wings, a tuft of curly white tail feathers, and a large head with a massive hooked bill. Family: *Raphidae*; order: *Columbiformes* (pigeons, etc.).

Dodoma 6 10S 35 40E A town in E central Tanzania. It replaced Dar es Salaam as the capital in 1983. Population (latest est): 45 703.

dog A carnivorous mammal belonging to the family *Canidae*. Ancestors of the modern domestic dog (*Canis familiaris*), probably derived from wolves or jackals, were first domesticated over 10 000 years ago. Wild dogs generally live and hunt in packs, relying on speed and cooperation to secure their prey. They are specialized hunters with long legs, sharp teeth, strong jaws, and acute hearing and smell.

The intelligence and social nature of dogs have led to their selective breeding by man for a variety of purposes, principally as sporting dogs, working dogs, and ornamental breeds for household pets. There are up to 400 modern breeds and in the UK, standards for over 100 recognized breeds are established by the Kennel Club, founded in 1873.

doge The title of the chief magistrate of Venice from about 697 AD to the fall of the Venetian Empire in 1797. The doge was elected for life and wielded considerable power until 1172 when his authority was restricted by the creation of a supreme Great Council of 480 members. Further constitutional checks made the doge little more than a figurehead. The present richly decorated **Doge's Palace** originated in the early 14th century.

dogfish A small shark belonging to one of a number of families. *Scyliorhinus stellaris* and *S. canicula* are brown-spotted dogfish commonly found in Mediterranean and British coastal waters. They are edible and purchased as "rock salmon."

Dogger Bank A vast sandbank in the central North Sea, 17–36 m (55–120 ft) below water. It is a major fishing ground.

dog rose A shrubby rose, *Rosa canina*, with arching stems that grows in woods, hedges, and roadsides of Europe, North Africa, and SW Asia.

dogwood A shrub or small tree of the genus *Cornus* (about 45 species), mostly of the N hemisphere. It has oval pointed leaves with prominent curved veins and dense clusters of four-petalled flowers. The fruit is a berry. The common European dogwood (*C. sanguinea*) has white flowers, blood-red shoots and autumn leaves, and black berries. Family: *Cornaceae*.

Doha 25 15N 51 36E The capital of Qatar, on the E coast. Population (1983 est): 190 000.

Dohnányi, Ernö (Ernst von D.; 1877–1960) Hungarian composer and pianist. He spent his last years in the USA. He was greatly influenced by Brahms, who praised his early works. Unlike his contemporaries, Bartók and Kodály, Dohnányi remained uninfluenced by Hungarian folksong. His best-known composition is

DOG

sporting breeds

pointer

cocker spaniel

golden retriever

red setter

hounds

dachshund

borzoi

basset

Rhodesian ridgeback

working breeds

corgi

rough-coated collie

Old English sheepdog

German shepherd

terriers

bull terrier

cairn terrier

Airedale

smooth-haired fox terrier

Sealyham

toy breeds

Chihuahua

Pekingese

toy poodle

pug

Yorkshire terrier

non-sporting breeds

Boston

chow chow

schipperke

Dalmatian

the *Variations on a Nursery Theme* (for piano and orchestra; 1913), based on the tune known in England as "Baa Baa Black Sheep."

Dolby system An electronic device for reducing the hiss in sound reproduction, particularly in tape recorders. It was invented by Ray Dolby (1933–). The Dolby system selectively boosts the higher frequencies in the sound signal before recording it, to drown out the constant hiss produced by the tape, and attenuates them when playing back. It operates only when the music is quiet enough for the hiss to be heard. This avoids both distortion that occurs if lower frequencies are boosted to the same level and distortion from boosting already loud higher frequencies.

doldrums The equatorial belt within which the trade-wind zones converge. Winds are light and variable but the strong upward movement of air caused by the convergence produces frequent thunderstorms, heavy rains, and squalls.

dolerite A dark-coloured hypabyssal igneous rock, the medium-grained equivalent of gabbros. It contains calcic plagioclase feldspar and augite.

Dollfuss, Engelbert (1892–1934) Austrian statesman; chancellor (1932–34). His chancellorship was increasingly strained by his inability to control the Austrian Nazis or to cooperate with the Social Democrats. He was assassinated in July during an abortive attempt by the Nazis to seize power.

dolmen (Breton: table stone) A prehistoric tomb made of huge stone slabs set upright and supporting a stone roof. Widely distributed in Neolithic Europe, dolmens were often covered by a barrow.

Dolmetsch, Arnold (1858–1940) British musician and instrument maker. He pioneered the rediscovery of early music and its performance on contemporary instruments in its original style.

dolomite A mineral consisting of calcium magnesium carbonate, $CaMg(CO_3)_2$, colourless or white or grey in colour. Rocks containing over 15% magnesium carbonate are called dolomites, those containing less are magnesian limestones, and those containing both dolomite and calcite are dolomitic limestones. Dolomite occurs as a primary sediment, in metalliferous veins and in limestones altered by the process of dolomitization, by which the calcium carbonate is wholly or partly converted to dolomite by magnesium-rich sea water, or by magnesium-rich solutions permeating joints in the rock.

Dolomites (Italian name: Alpi Dolomitiche) A section of the Alps in NE Italy. Composed of dolomitic limestone, they are characterized by their steep-sided rocky peaks.

dolphin **1.** A toothed whale of the family *Delphinidae* (about 50 species). Agile and streamlined and up to 4.5 m long, dolphins live in large groups and feed mainly on fish. They are intelligent creatures with well-developed abilities for social communication and echolocation. The common dolphin (*Delphinus delphus*), which grows to 2.1 m, is blue-black with a white belly and striped body. *See also* bottlenose; porpoise. **2.** A large fast-moving marine fish of the family *Coryphaenidae* (2 species) that resembles the cetaceous dolphin. Order: *Perciformes*. See p. 226.

Domenico Veneziano (active c. 1438–1461) Italian painter of the early Renaissance, probably born in Venice. He settled in Florence, where he painted his famous *St Lucy Altarpiece* (central panel; Uffizi).

Dome of the Rock The great mosque in Jerusalem, built in 691 AD by the Umayyad caliph, 'Abd al-Malik. It is named after the rock (sacred also to the Jews) over which it was built and stands within the enclosure of the destroyed Jewish Temple of Jerusalem. It is the third most holy place of Islam, after Mecca and Medina.

Domesday Book (1086) The survey of England ordered by William I to assess the extent of his own possessions and the value for taxation purposes of the estates of his tenants in chief. Parts of N and NW England and some towns, including London and Winchester, were omitted. Royal commissioners collected, shire by shire, details about each manor, naming its present owner and its owner under Edward the Confessor, changes in its size since Edward's reign, the numbers of its inhabitants and the services or rents they owed, and the numbers of its ploughteams, mills, and fisheries. The survey, in two volumes, is now in the Public Record Office.

Domingo, Placido (1941–) Spanish tenor, educated in Mexico. He sings a wide range of roles but specializes in Puccini and Verdi, starring in film versions of *La Traviata* (1983) and *Otello* (1986).

Dominica, Commonwealth of An island country in the West Indies, the largest of the Windward Islands. It is of volcanic origin and very mountainous. The population is mainly of African descent. *Economy*: chiefly agricultural. *History*: discovered by Columbus in 1493, it was alternately French then British during the 18th century before finally becoming British in 1783. It became internally self-governing in 1967 and an independent republic within the British Commonwealth in November, 1978. President: Clarence A. Seignoret. Prime minister: Mary Eugenia Charles. Official language: English. Official currency: East Caribbean dollar of 100 cents. Area: 728 sq km (289 sq mi). Population (1987): 94 191. Capital: Roseau.

Dominican Republic A largely mountainous country in the Caribbean Sea, occupying the E two-thirds of the island of Hispaniola (Haiti occupies the W third). The population is mainly of mixed African and European descent. *Economy*: chiefly agricultural. Mining and light industry are being developed. *History*: becoming a

DOME OF THE ROCK *Built on the temple mount in Jerusalem.*

Spanish colony following the island's discovery in 1492 by Columbus, the E was ceded, 1795–1809, to the French, who had colonized the W. The E gained independence from Spain in 1821. It was held by Haiti from 1822 until 1844, when the Dominican Republic was founded. Political and economic instability led to US occupation (1916–22) and the establishment (1930) of Trujillo's 30-year dictatorship. Following Trujillo's assassination the elected president, Juan Bosch, was deposed (1963) in a military coup. President: Joaquín Balaguer. Official language: Spanish. Official currency: Dominican Republic peso of 100 centavos. Area: 48 442 sq km (18 700 sq mi). Population (1987): 6 708 000. Capital and main port: Santo Domingo.

Dominicans (Latin *Ordo Praedicatorum*: Order of Preachers) A Roman Catholic order of friars, also known as Black Friars, Friar Preachers, or (in France) Jacobins, founded by St Dominic (c. 1170–1221) and formally organized at Bologna in 1220–21. Their purpose was preaching and teaching, the individual friars leading mendicant lives much of the time. Among their great scholars was St Thomas Aquinas. They were prominent defenders of orthodoxy in the Inquisition. There are also two orders of Dominican nuns.

DOLPHIN *A performing bottlenose dolphin in a dolphinarium.*

Don, River A river in the SW Soviet Union, flowing mainly S to the Sea of Azov. A canal links it to the River Volga. Length: 1981 km (1224 mi).

Donatello (Donato de Nicolo di Betti Bardi; c. 1386–1466) Florentine sculptor. A pioneer of the Renaissance style, Donatello first broke with tradition in his marble sculptures, which are modelled as lifelike rather than idealized figures. Simultaneously he developed a new form of relief sculpture in which he created perspective. Working also in bronze from the early 1420s, he produced *David* (c. 1430–35; Florence), the influential equestrian monument in Padua known as the *Gattamelata* (1447–53), and the high altar for S Antonio, Padua (1446–50).

Donbass. *See* Donets Basin.

Doncaster 53 32N 1 07W An industrial town in N England, in South Yorkshire, with railway workshops and coalmining. Population (1981): 81 610.

Donegal (Irish name: Dún Na Ngall) A county in the N Republic of Ireland, in Ulster bordering on the Atlan-

tic Ocean. Chiefly mountainous, it has a rugged indented coastline. Area: 4830 sq km (1865 sq mi). Population (1986): 129 428. County town: Lifford.

Donets Basin (*or* Donbass) An industrial region in the SW Soviet Union, in the Ukrainian SSR. It is the major coal-producing and steel-manufacturing area in the country, the major city being Donetsk. Area: about 25 900 sq km (10 000 sq mi).

Dong Hai. *See* East China Sea.

Dönitz, Karl (1891–1980) German admiral. A U-boat commander in World War I, in World War II he developed the "pack" system of submarine attack. In 1943 he became grand admiral and then commander in chief of the German navy. He was appointed chancellor after Hitler's death and was imprisoned (1946–56) for war crimes.

Donizetti, Gaetano (1797–1848) Italian composer of operas. His 75 stage works rely more on coloratura display, the popular characteristic of his age, than on intrinsic dramatic effect. They include *Lucia di Lammermoor* (1835) and *Daughter of the Regiment* (1840).

Don Juan The great aristocratic libertine of European literature. In Tirso de Molina's play *El burlador de Sevilla* (1630) he kills the father of his latest victim; he mockingly invites the old man's statue to dinner, and it drags him off to hell. This plot is retained in subsequent versions, most notably Molière's *Don Juan* (1665) and Mozart's *Don Giovanni* (1787). In satirical treatments by Byron (*Don Juan*, 1819–24) and G. B. Shaw (*Man and Superman*, 1903) Juan is more hunted than hunter.

donkey A domesticated ass more commonly used for pack and draught work than for riding. *See also* mule.

Donleavy, J(ames) P(atrick) (1926–) Irish-American novelist. *The Ginger Man* (1956) was followed by further comic novels including *The Onion Eaters* (1971) and *Are You Listening Rabbi Löw?* (1987).

Donne, John (1572–1631) English metaphysical poet. Failing to gain secular advancement, despite having several influential patrons, he became an Anglican priest in 1615 and was appointed Dean of St Paul's in 1621. His poetry combines passionate feeling for God, woman, and humanity with brilliant intellectual wit. Almost all of it, even religious works, such as *La Corona* (1607), was written before 1615.

dopamine *See* catecholamines.

Doppler effect The apparent change in the frequency of a wave caused by relative motion between the source and the observer. When the source and the observer are approaching each other, the apparent frequency of the wave increases; when one is travelling away from the other, the apparent frequency decreases. An example is the change in pitch of a train whistle as the train passes through a station. The effect can also be observed as a shifting of the wavelength of light from a receding star towards the red end of the spectrum; this is known as the redshift. Named after Christian Doppler (1803–53), Austrian physicist.

Dorchester 50 43N 2 26W A market town in S England, the administrative centre for Dorset on the River Frome. Population (1985): 14 000.

Dordogne, River A river in SW France. Rising in the Auvergne Mountains, it flows SW and W to enter the Gironde estuary NNE of Bordeaux. It is important for hydroelectric power and has famous vineyards along its lower course. Length: 472 km (293 mi).

GUSTAVE DORÉ *Detail of an early photograph (c. 1860) by O. G. Rejlander.*

Doré, (Paul) Gustave (Louis Christophe) (1832–83) French illustrator, painter, and sculptor, born in Strasbourg. He established his wide and lasting popularity in the 1850s with his illustrations of Rabelais' books and Balzac's *Contes drôlatiques*. These were followed by illustrations to Dante, Cervantes, Tennyson, etc., showing his taste for the grotesque and dramatic. His realistic scenes of poverty in *London* influenced Van Gogh.

Dorians Iron Age Greek conquerors of the S Aegean region (c. 1100–1000 BC). Moving southward from Epirus and SW Macedonia, they displaced the Achaeans and brought about the final collapse of the Bronze Age Mycenaean civilization. They settled chiefly in the Peloponnese.

Doric order. *See* orders of architecture.

dormancy A period of reduced metabolic activity during which a plant or animal or a reproductive body (e.g. seeds or spores) can survive unfavourable environmental conditions. The onset may be triggered by, for example, changes in temperature, daylength (photoperiodism), and availability of water, oxygen, and carbon dioxide. The dormant phase of a life cycle is represented as spores in bacteria and fungi, cysts in protozoans and some invertebrates, and seeds, buds, and bulbs or similar organs in plants. *See also* hibernation.

dormouse A climbing rodent belonging to the family *Gliridae* (about 10 species) of Eurasia and Africa. The common dormouse (*Muscardinus avellanarius*) is reddish, about 6 cm long with a 5-cm bushy tail. It feeds at night on nuts, berries, and seeds, hibernating during winter.

Dorset A county of SW England, bordering on the English Channel. It consists chiefly of lowlands, crossed by ranges of hills. The chief rivers are the Frome and the Stour. Agriculture is predominant, especially livestock farming. Tourism is important, notably in Bournemouth and Weymouth. Many towns are associated with the writings of Thomas Hardy. Area: 2634 sq km (1017 sq mi). Population (1986 est): 638 200. Administrative centre: Dorchester.

Dortmund 51 32N 07 27E A city in NW West Germany, in North Rhine-Westphalia in the Ruhr. A port on the Dortmund–Ems Canal and a major industrial centre. Population (1986): 569 800.

Dortmund–Ems Canal A major canal in West Germany. Opened in 1899, it links the Ruhr industrial area with the North Sea near Emden. Length: about 270 km (168 mi).

dory. *See* John Dory.

Dos Passos, John (1896–1970) US novelist. He served as an ambulance driver in World War I and worked as a war correspondent in Spain, Mexico, and the Near East. His major work, the trilogy *U.S.A.*–comprising *The Forty-Second Parallel* (1930), *1919* (1932), and *The Big Money* (1936)–uses experimental techniques in its radical interpretation of American history from 1900 until the Depression.

Dostoievski, Fedor Mikhailovich (1821–81) Russian novelist. He lived in W Europe from 1867 to 1871, plagued by his epilepsy and compulsive gambling. He returned to Russia in 1871 and became relatively prosperous, stable, and conservative. His major novels, in which he explored moral and political themes with merciless psychological realism, are *Crime and Punishment* (1866), *The Idiot* (1868–69), *The Possessed* (1869–72), and *The Brothers Karamazov* (1879–80).

dotterel A small Eurasian plover, *Eudromias morinellus*, that nests in tundra regions and migrates to the Mediterranean and SW Asia for the winter. It has a broad white eye stripe and a grey breast separated by a narrow white band from its russet belly.

Douai Bible The Roman Catholic version of the Bible in English, translated from the Vulgate by Roman Catholic scholars from Oxford, who had fled to Europe during the reign of Elizabeth I and who were members of the English College at Douai. The New Testament was published at Reims in 1582 and the Old Testament at Douai in 1609–10. Its language influenced the translators of the King James Version.

Douala 4 04N 9 43E The largest city in Cameroon, on the River Wouri estuary. A deepwater port and the chief export point of the country, it is also a major West African industrial centre. Population (1985): 852 700.

DOUBLE BASS *Charlie Mingus, the renowned jazz double bass player.*

double bass The lowest-pitched musical instrument of the violin family. Unlike the violin, viola, and cello, its four strings are tuned in fourths (E, A, D, G). It has a range of over three octaves, from the E an octave below the bass stave. The double bass is a member of the symphony orchestra; it is also played in jazz and dance bands, usually by plucking the strings.

Douglas 54 09N 4 29W The capital of the Isle of Man, on the E coast. It is a port and resort, its buildings including the House of Keys (parliament house), the Manx Museum, and a casino. Population (1981 est): 64 679.

Douglas fir A conifer, *Pseudotsuga menziesii*, native to W North America and cultivated widely both for ornament and for its high-quality timber, used for construction, poles, masts, etc. 60–90 m high, it has flexible blunt-tipped needles and cylindrical cones. Family: *Pinaceae*.

Douglas-Home, Sir Alec. *See* Home of the Hirsel, Alec Douglas-Home, Baron.

Doulton English pottery works, originally at Lambeth (London), specializing in salt-glazed stoneware. Brown stoneware vessels with relief moulded portrait and landscape ornament were typical of the period to 1850. From 1856 unique studio pottery in coloured glazes was produced, using wood-fired kilns.

Dounreay The site in N Scotland, on the N coast of the Highland Region, of the world's first experimental fast-breeder reactor.

Douro, River (Spanish name: Duero) A river in SW Europe. Flowing W from N central Spain, it forms part of the border between Spain and Portugal before entering the Atlantic Ocean at Oporto. Length: 895 km (556 mi).

dove. *See* pigeon.

Dover 51 08N 1 19E A port in SE England, in Kent on the Strait of Dover. An ancient Cinque Port, it is the UK's chief ferry and Hovercraft port for the Continent. Population (1981): 32 843.

Dowding, Hugh Caswall Tremenheere, 1st Baron (1882–1970) British air chief marshal, who was head of the RAF Fighter Command in 1940. His strategic and tactical genius in coordinating early warning radar, pilots, and equipment played a major role in winning the battle of Britain.

Dow-Jones Index A weighted average of the prices on the New York Stock Exchange of 30 industrial shares, computed each working day by Dow Jones and Co. First devised in 1897 using only 12 shares, it is the principal indicator of movements in share prices in the USA.

Dowland, John (1563–1626) English composer and lutenist. He specialized in writing songs with lute accompaniment.

Downing Street A London street adjoining Whitehall. No 10 is the official residence of the prime minister; the chancellor of the exchequer resides at No 11. It was named after the English statesman Sir George Downing (1623–84).

Downs, North and South Two roughly parallel ranges of chalk hills in SE England, separated by the Weald. The North Downs extend W–E between Guildford, in Surrey, and Dover, in Kent. The South Downs extend generally SE from Winchester, in Hampshire, to Beachy Head. The Downs have traditionally been sheep-farming areas.

Down's syndrome A genetic disease in which a baby has one extra chromosome; it is named after J. L. H. Down (1828–96), English physician. Affected children are mentally retarded and their faces resemble those of orientals, which is why they were formerly called mongols and the disease mongolism. They are usually cheerful and with special education can live relatively normal lives in a family. Down's syndrome is more commonly seen in babies of mothers over 40; it can be detected during pregnancy (*see* amniocentesis).

CONAN DOYLE *Sherlock Holmes, the famous English detective, with his companion Dr John H. Watson (left).*

Doyle, Sir Arthur Conan (1859–1930) Scottish author, creator of the detective Sherlock Holmes. Conan Doyle graduated in medicine but soon turned to writing. Holmes, inspired by the diagnostic methods of an Edinburgh lecturer, first appeared in the novel *A Study in Scarlet* (1887), narrated, as are nearly all the short stories and novels about him, by Dr John H. Watson. Conan Doyle also created the coarsely brilliant Professor Challenger in *The Lost World* (1912) but he valued most highly his historical novels, such as *The White Company* (1890).

D'Oyly Carte, Richard (1844–1901) British theatre impresario and manager. He produced most of the comic operas of Gilbert and Sullivan. He opened the Savoy Theatre, London, in 1881 to house these productions.

Drabble, Margaret (1939–) British novelist. Her novels concern the moral and emotional problems of women in contemporary society. They include *The Millstone* (1965), *The Needle's Eye* (1972), *The Radiant Way* (1988), and *A Natural Curiosity* (1989).

Draco (7th century BC) Athenian lawgiver. His legal system was so harshly punitive that "draconian" has since been used to describe any rigorous or cruel law. Draco's code prescribed the death penalty by the state for most offences, taking retribution out of the hands of private citizens.

Draco. *See* flying lizard.

Dracula, Count The central character of Bram Stoker's gothic novel *Dracula* (1897) and of many horror films, a Transylvanian vampire. The name, meaning "demon," was applied to Vlad IV the Impaler, a 15th-century Walachian prince who was the prototype of the fictional character.

dragonfly A strong agile brightly coloured insect belonging to the widely distributed suborder *Anisoptera* (about 4500 species). It has a long body, large eyes, and transparent veined wings (spanning up to 180 mm).

Both the adults and freshwater nymphs (naiads) are active carnivores and control many insect pests, such as mosquitoes, flies, and gnats. Order: *Odonata*.

dragoon   European mounted soldier of the 16th and 17th centuries who could fight as a light cavalryman (*see also* hussars) or as an infantryman. Named after the muzzle-loading carbine they carried, they were originally used as an arm of the infantry. By the 18th century most light cavalrymen were called dragoons (or carabiniers).

drag racing   1. A form of motor racing that originated in the USA. It is held in heats of two cars on a straight strip a quarter of a mile (402 m) long. Using a standing start, races depend heavily on acceleration. Speeds have exceeded 400 km per hour (250 mph) in specially constructed light powerful vehicles. 2. A form of motorcycle racing organized in the same way.

Drake, Sir Francis   (1540–96) English navigator and admiral. Drake's first important voyages were trading expeditions to Guinea and the West Indies and in 1567 he accompanied Sir John Hawkins (a relative) to the Gulf of Mexico. In 1572 he embarked on a plundering expedition, destroying towns on the Isthmus of Panama and capturing considerable quantities of booty. In 1578 he became the first Englishman to navigate the Straits of Magellan intending, with Elizabeth I's consent, to raid the Pacific coast. Alone out of five ships, his *Golden Hind* sailed N but unable to find a way back to the Atlantic Ocean crossed the Pacific Ocean, returning home in 1580 via the Cape of Good Hope. Drake crowned his career by helping to defeat the Spanish Armada at Gravelines (1588).

Drakensberg Mountains   (*or* Quathlamba) The chief mountain range in S Africa, extending from Cape Province (South Africa) along the E border of Lesotho to Swaziland, reaching 3482 m (11 425 ft) at Thaba Ntlenyana.

draughts (US name: checkers)   A board game for two players, developed in 12th-century Europe from an ancient Egyptian game. Each player has 12 disc-shaped pieces which are placed on the 12 black squares at the opposite ends of a chessboard. The pieces move only on the black squares and black always starts. One piece per turn is moved diagonally forwards onto a vacant adjacent square. If the next square is occupied by one of the opponent's pieces but the square beyond that is vacant, the playing piece must jump onto the vacant square, removing the opponent's piece from the board. A further jump must be made from there if possible (in the same turn). If a piece reaches the opposing back line it becomes a "king" (a second piece is placed on top of it) and it may then move forwards or backwards. The winner is the player who takes or immobilizes all his opponent's pieces.

Dravidian languages   A large language family of up to 20 languages spoken mainly in S India. The major languages of the family are Tamil, Kanarese (*or* Kannada), Telugu, Malayalam, and Tulu. These are all spoken in a continuous area in India, and Tamil is also spoken in Sri Lanka.

Dresden   51 5N 13 41E A city in SE East Germany, on the River Elbe, the former capital of Saxony. One of the world's most beautiful cities prior to its devastation by bombs in 1945, it has since been rebuilt. Dresden is a centre of culture, light industry, and market gardening. Population (1986): 519 737.

Dresden porcelain.   *See* Meissen porcelain.

dressage   The training of a riding (*or* carriage) horse to make it calm, supple, and responsive to its rider (*or*

DRESSAGE   *Horse and rider in elegant harmony.*

driver). Originally a training for military charges, the present, more humane, methods developed in the 18th century. The most advanced stage is *haute école* equitation in which a horse is taught to perform intricate leaps and movements. Dressage competitions consist of a sequence of complex prescribed movements.

Dreyfus, Alfred   (1859–1935) French Jewish army officer. Unjustly accused of revealing state secrets to the German military attaché in Paris, in 1894 Dreyfus, the victim of antisemitism, was deported for life to the penal colony on Devil's Island (off the coast of French Guiana). His case was reopened in 1898, becoming the focus of conflict between royalist, nationalist, and militarist elements on the one hand and socialist, republican, and anticlerical factions on the other. Following a retrial in 1899, Dreyfus was pardoned but not completely cleared until 1906.

dromedary.   *See* camel.

drone.   *See* bee.

dropsy.   *See* oedema.

Drosera.   *See* sundew.

Drosophila   A genus of small fruit flies (about 1000 species). Most species feed on fermenting materials, such as rotting or damaged fruit. Some species, especially *D. melanogaster*, have been used extensively in laboratory studies of heredity and evolution because of the large chromosomes in their salivary glands and their short life cycle. Family: *Drosophilidae*.

drugs   Compounds that alter the physiological state of living organisms (including man). Medicinal drugs are widely used for the treatment, prevention, and diagnosis of disease. The wide range of drugs available for this purpose includes the anaesthetics (*see* anaesthesia), analgesics, antibiotics, cytotoxic drugs, diuretics, hormonal drugs, and tranquillizers.

Some drugs are taken solely for the pleasurable effects they produce. Many such drugs are addictive (*see* narcotics). Rigorous controls exist to restrict their use but illegal trade in them continues. These dangerous drugs include opium and its derivatives and synthetic substitutes, many stimulants (cocaine, amphetamine, etc.), and some sedatives.

Druids Ancient Celtic priests who were also revered as teachers and judges. They worshipped nature gods, believed in the immortality of the soul and reincarnation, and also taught astronomy. Their central religious rite involved the sacred oak tree. They sacrificed humans, usually criminals, on behalf of those near to death. In Gaul and Britain they were wiped out by the Romans, their last stand being in Anglesey (61 AD), but in Ireland they survived until the arrival of Christian missionaries.

drumlin A small streamlined hill, formed through glaciation and composed of glacial till or drift, sometimes with a rock core. Drumlins usually occur in groups or swarms (sometimes called basket-of-eggs topography), their long axes parallel to the direction of ice flow. They are common features in Co Down, Northern Ireland.

drupe A stone fruit, such as a cherry, plum, or peach. The fruit wall (pericarp) develops into three layers: an outer skin (epicarp), succulent flesh (mesocarp), and a stone (endocarp) containing the seed.

Drury Lane Theatre The oldest theatre in London, first opened in 1663. The present building dates from 1813. It has housed every form of dramatic production. Its early managers included David Garrick and R. B. Sheridan, and it has strong associations with the actors Edmund Kean and Sir Henry Irving.

Druses (*or* Druzes) Adherents of a religious sect living mainly in Syria, the Lebanon, and Israel. Druses are not generally accepted as Muslims. Their scriptures are based on the Bible, the Koran, and on Sufi writings.

Dryden, John (1631–1700) British poet and critic. He welcomed the Restoration of the monarchy and wrote several successful plays for the recently reopened theatres, for example *Marriage à la Mode* (1673) and *All for Love* (1677). He also wrote brilliant verse satires, notably *Absalom and Achitophel* (1681) and *MacFlecknoe* (1682).

dry rot The decay of timber caused by cellulose-digesting fungi, especially *Serpula lacrymans*. Spores are liable to germinate in timber having a moisture content of over 20% and the fungus appears as a whitish mass on the surface. The timber becomes cracked and crumbly and the infection may spread to adjoining dry timbers. Treatment is by removal of infected timbers and application of fungicide to the remaining parts. *Compare* wet rot.

Dubai. *See* United Arab Emirates.

Du Barry, Marie Jeanne Bécu, Comtesse (?1743–93) The last mistress of Louis XV of France from 1768 until his death (1774), when she was banished from court. She was guillotined during the French Revolution.

Dublin (Irish name: Baile Átha Cliath) 53 20N 6 15W The capital of the Republic of Ireland, on Dublin Bay. An important commercial and cultural centre, it is also the largest manufacturing centre and the largest port in the Republic. Its industries include whiskey distilling, brewing, clothing, glass, and food processing. It is noted for its wide streets and 18th-century Georgian squares. The Easter Rising of 1916 took place here. Population (1986): 502 337.

Dublin (Irish name: Baile Atha Cliath) A county in the E Republic of Ireland, in Leinster bordering on the Irish Sea. Chiefly low lying, it rises in the S to the Wick-

low Mountains and is drained by the River Liffey. Area: 922 sq km (356 sq mi). Population (1986): 1 020 796. County town: Dublin.

Dubrovnik (Italian name: Ragusa) 42 40N 18 07E A port and tourist resort in S Yugoslavia, in Croatia on the Adriatic coast. Population (1985): 35 000.

Duccio di Buoninsegna (c. 1255–c. 1318) Italian painter, founder of the Sienese school.

Duchamp, Marcel (1887–1968) French artist. His first success was *Nude Descending a Staircase* (1912; Philadelphia), influenced by cubism and futurism. This was followed by his controversial ready-made objects, for example a urinal, first exhibited in New York. He lived in New York after 1915 and became leader of its dada art movement. His best-known work is the glass and wire picture of *The Bride Stripped Bare by Her Bachelors, Even* (1915–23; Philadelphia).

duck A small short-necked waterbird belonging to the family *Anatidae* (ducks, geese, and swans), occurring in salt and fresh waters throughout the world except Antarctica. Ducks are adapted for swimming and diving, having a dense waterproofed outer plumage with a thick underlayer of down. The blunt spatulate bill is covered with a sensitive membrane and has internal horny plates for sifting food from water. The 200 species of duck are mostly gregarious; many are migratory and strong fliers. Ducks feed either at the surface of the water (*see* dabbling duck) or dive to forage in deeper water (*see* diving duck). Order: *Anseriformes* (ducks and geese).

DUCK-BILLED PLATYPUS *A unique egg-laying mammal.*

duck-billed platypus An aquatic monotreme mammal, *Ornithorhynchus anatinus*, of Australia and Tasmania. Platypuses have webbed feet and a broad flat toothless beak. The female lays two eggs and after incubation suckles the tiny young. Family: *Ornithorhynchidae*.

Duero, River. *See* Douro, River.

Dufay, Guillaume (c. 1400–74) Burgundian composer and priest. One of the outstanding composers of the middle ages, he wrote masses, motets, magnificats, and French and Italian chansons. He was also a famous teacher.

Dufy, Raoul (1877–1953) French painter. His early influences were impressionism and then fauvism. He later developed an individual style in lively racecourse and regatta scenes, notable for the way forms are drawn sketchily over areas of thinly applied colour.

dugong A marine herbivorous mammal, *Dugong dugon*, of the Indo-Pacific region. Dugongs, also known as sea cows, have blue-grey rough skin and a bristly snout; the males have short tusks. Their forelimbs are flippers and they lack hind limbs, having a flukelike tail for swimming. Family: *Dugongidae*; order: *Sirenia*.

duiker A small nocturnal African antelope belonging to the subfamily *Cephalophinae* (17 species), inhabiting bush or forest. Both sexes usually have smooth backward-pointing horns and often a distinct stripe along the back.

dulcimer A musical instrument consisting of a shallow resonating box with strings stretched over two moveable bridges. It is played with two small hammers and is much used in European and Asian folk music.

dulse An edible purplish-red seaweed, *Rhodymenia palmata*, found on N Atlantic coasts. A red alga, it has flat leathery lobed fronds.

Dumas, Alexandre (1802–70) French novelist and dramatist, often called Dumas *père*. He is noted for his historical romances, including *The Count of Monte Cristo* (1844–45), *The Three Musketeers* (1844), and *The Black Tulip* (1850).

His son **Alexandre Dumas** (1824–95), a dramatist, was often called Dumas *fils*. His best-known work is the novel *La Dame aux camélias* (1848), the basis of a play and Verdi's opera *La Traviata*.

Du Maurier, George (Louis Palmella Busson) (1834–96) British caricaturist and novelist, born in Paris, who contributed caricatures to *Punch* and other magazines. His novel *Trilby* (1894), remembered for its sinister hypnotist Svengali, is based on his life as an art student in Paris. The best-known works of his grand-daughter **Dame Daphne Du Maurier** (1907–89) are romances, usually set in Cornwall. They include *Rebecca* (1938) and *The Flight of the Falcon* (1965).

Dumfries and Galloway Region An administrative region in SW Scotland, bordering on the Solway Firth. It was formed in 1975 from the counties of Dumfries, Kirkudbright, and Wigtown. It consists of uplands and moors in the N descending to coastal lowlands in the S and has an indented coastline. The region is predominantly agricultural. Area: 6369 sq km (2460 sq mi). Population (1986 est): 146 770. Administrative centre: Dumfries.

Duncan I (d. 1040) King of the Scots (1034–40). His claim to the throne was challenged by Macbeth, by whom he was murdered.

Duncan, Isadora (1878–1927) US dancer. She lived mostly in Europe, where she gained a reputation for both her innovative modern interpretive dancing and her flamboyant lifestyle.

Dundee 56 28N 3 00W A city and port in E Scotland, the administrative centre of Tayside Region on the Firth of Tay. It is known chiefly for the manufacture of jute goods and also provides supplies and services for the North Sea oil industry. Population (1988): 174 255.

Dunedin 45 52S 170 30E A port in New Zealand, in SE South Island at the head of Otago Harbour. Founded by Scottish Presbyterians in 1848, it has two cathedrals (Anglican and Roman Catholic) and the University of Otago (the oldest in the country, founded in 1869). Population (1989): 116 000.

ISADORA DUNCAN   *A photograph taken c. 1922.*

Dunfermline 56 04N 3 29W A town in E Scotland, in Fife Region on the Firth of Forth. Several Scottish kings, including Robert the Bruce, are buried in the 11th-century abbey. Population (1981): 52 057.

dung beetle A scarab beetle, usually small and dark, that has the habit of rolling dung into balls, which serve as a food source for both the adults and larvae.

Dungeness 50 55N 0 58E A shingle headland in SE England, in Kent extending into the English Channel. Two nuclear power stations and an automatic lighthouse are located here.

Dunkirk (French name: Dunkerque) 51 02N 2 23E A port in N France, in the Nord department on the Strait of Dover. During World War II Allied troops were successfully evacuated from its beaches (1940) following the fall of France. Dunkirk is a rapidly growing industrial centre and has an oil refinery and naval shipbuilding yards. Population (1983): 83 760.

Dun Laoghaire 53 17N 6 08W A port in the E Republic of Ireland, in Co Dublin. It is the terminus of a ferry service from Holyhead, Wales. Population (1981): 54 496.

dunlin A common sandpiper, *Calidris alpina*, that breeds in far northern regions, ranging south to N Britain. It has a bill with a curved tip and a black and russet plumage that changes to grey in winter.

Dunlop, John Boyd (1840–1921) Scottish inventor, who is credited with inventing the pneumatic tyre (1887). Dunlop began to produce his tyres commercially in 1890. Initially for bicycles, they later contributed greatly to the development of motor cars.

dunnock A shy inconspicuous songbird, *Prunella modularis*, also called hedge sparrow. About 14 cm long, the dunnock has a dull-brown plumage with a greyish throat and breast. It has a fine sharp bill and feeds on insects. Family: *Prunellidae* (accentors).

Duns Scotus, John (c. 1260–1308) Scottish-born Franciscan philosopher, who, with Roger Bacon and William of Ockham, carried on controversy against Aquinas. Contradicting Aquinas, Duns Scotus held that what makes one thing distinct from another is its form, or essence, that is its essential properties rather than its accidental properties, as the latter may be removed or changed without altering its identity. Although nicknamed the Subtle Doctor by contemporaries, Duns Scotus suffered Renaissance ridicule, his name giving rise to the derisive label "dunce."

Dunstan, St (924–88 AD) English churchman and monastic reformer. Appointed Abbot of Glastonbury in 943, he rebuilt its monastery and revived English monasticism. The chief minister under·Kings Eadred and Edgar, he became Bishop of Worcester (957), Bishop of London (959), and Archbishop of Canterbury (960). Feast day: 19 May.

duodenal ulcer. *See* peptic ulcer.

duodenum. *See* intestine.

Durban 29 53S 31 00E The main seaport in South Africa and the largest city in Natal, on the Indian Ocean. Population (1985): 982 075.

ALBRECHT DÜRER *A self-portrait (detail) painted in 1498 (Prado, Madrid).*

Dürer, Albrecht (1471–1528) German Renaissance painter, engraver, draughtsman, and woodcut designer. He was influenced by Italian artists during a visit to Italy but his woodcuts of the *Apocalypse* (1498) are still gothic in style. In about 1500, he became preoccupied with the study of human proportions. Paintings of this period include the *Self-Portrait* as Christ (1500) and *Adoration of the Magi* (1504). He executed his most famous engravings, including *Knight, Death, and the Devil*, in the period 1512–19.

Durham 54 47N 1 34W A city in NE England, the administrative centre of Co Durham on the River Wear. It has a Norman cathedral and an 11th-century castle. Population (1986): 39 600.

Durham A county in NE England, bordering on the North Sea. It consists chiefly of undulating lowlands, rising W to the uplands of the Pennines and is drained by the Rivers Wear and Tees. Agriculture includes sheep and dairy farming. Coalmining, formerly of major importance, is concentrated in the E. Area: 2436 sq km (964 sq mi). Population (1986 est): 599 600. Administrative centre: Durham.

durmast A Eurasian oak, *Quercus petraea*, up to 40 m tall. It has long-stalked oval leaves with rounded lobes and hairy undersides and unstalked conical acorns (hence its other name—sessile oak). Its durable wood is used for furniture, construction work, and boat building and the bark for tanning.

Durrell, Lawrence George (1912–   ) British novelist and poet. His best-known work is *The Alexandria Quartet*, comprising *Justine* (1957), *Balthazar* (1958), *Mountolive* (1958), and *Clea* (1960). His later work includes *The Avignon Quintet* (1974–85). His brother **Gerald Malcolm Durrell** (1925–   ) is a naturalist and popular writer, famous for such books as *My Family and Other Animals* (1956).

durum. *See* wheat.

Düsseldorf 51 13N 6 47E A city in NW West Germany, capital of North Rhine-Westphalia on the River Rhine. A port and major commercial and industrial centre of the Ruhr, its main industry is iron and steel. Population (1986): 561 200.

Dust Bowl, the An area in the USA, extending across W Kansas, Oklahoma, and Texas, and into Colorado and New Mexico. During the 1930s droughts and overfarming caused topsoil erosion.

Dutch The national language of the Netherlands, belonging to the West Germanic language group. In Belgium it is one of the two official languages and is known as Flemish (*or* Vlaams). It is derived from Low Franconian, the speech of the Salic Franks, who settled in this area, and has numerous local variants.

Dutch East Indies. *See* Indonesia.

Dutch elm disease A serious disease, first described in the Netherlands in 1919, that reached epidemic proportions in Britain in the 1970s, killing millions of elm trees. The fungus responsible, *Ceratocystus ulmi*, blocks the vessels that carry water to the leaves, which wilt and eventually die. The disease is carried by bark beetles. Protective measures can be taken but are too expensive for widespread use.

Dutch Guiana. *See* Suriname.

Duvalier, François (1907–71) Haitian politician, known as Papa Doc; president (1957–71). He used his secret police, the Tonton Macoutes, to eliminate all opposition and exploited Negro nationalism and voodoo practices to maintain popular sympathy. In 1964 he became president for life, a post in which his son **Jean-Claude Duvalier** (1951–   ), known as Baby Doc, succeeded him, but had to flee to France after an uprising in 1986.

Dvořák, Antonín (1841–1904) Czech composer. He wrote his famous ninth symphony, entitled "From the New World", while director of the National Conservatory in New York, 1892–95. Besides the symphonies he wrote concertos for piano, violin, and cello, orchestral tone poems, chamber music, piano music, and songs. His Czech nationalism is particularly evident in his famous *Slavonic Dances* for piano duet (1878–86).

dyeing The process of permanently changing the colour of a material. Natural dyes, such as madder and indigo, have been known since 3000 BC. Mauveine, the first synthetic dye, was discovered in 1856 by W. H. Perkin. Most modern commercial dyes are made from aromatic hydrocarbons extracted from coal tar and oil. To dye fibres or textiles, the material is immersed in a solution containing the dye, so that the dye molecules adhere to the surface of the fibres. The solvent is usually water but occasionally other solvents are used. An inorganic chemical, known as a mordant, may be added to make the dye less soluble once it has adhered to the fibre. Dyes used without a mordant are called **direct dyes. Vat**

dyes are insoluble in water, but are applied in reduced soluble form and then reoxidized. These are used particularly in cellulosic fibres. *See also* pigments.

DYNAMITE   *800 lb in 777 charges reduced this 32-storey São Paulo (Brazil) block of flats to rubble.*

Dyfed   The largest county of Wales, in the SW bordering on the Irish Sea. It was created in 1974 from the former counties of Cardiganshire, Carmarthenshire, and Pembrokeshire. It consists mainly of undulating uplands and coastal plains (extensive in the S). Although predominantly agricultural, new industries are being introduced to the long-established coalmining and steel manufacturing areas in the SE and a major oil refining area has developed at Milford Haven. Area: 5765 sq km (2227 sq mi). Population (1986 est): 339 000. Administrative centre: Carmarthen.

Dylan, Bob   (Robert Allen Zimmerman; 1941–) US singer and songwriter. An outstanding lyricist, he spoke for the protest movement of the 1960s with such folk albums as *The Times They Are A-changin'* (1964); later albums include *Desire* (1975) and *Oh Mercy* (1989).

dynamics.   *See* mechanics.

dynamite   An explosive plastic solid consisting of 75% nitroglycerine and 25% kieselguhr, a porous form of silicon dioxide (SiO_2). It was invented in 1866 by Nobel. Nitroglycerine alone is very sensitive to shock. The kieselguhr makes it safe to handle. Dynamite is used for blasting, particularly under water.

dynamo.   *See* electric generator.

dyne   The unit of force in the c.g.s. system equal to the force that will impart to a mass of one gram an acceleration of one centimetre per second per second.

dysentery   An infection of the large bowel causing painful diarrhoea that often contains blood and mucus. It may be caused either by bacteria of the genus *Shigella* or by amoebae. It can occur wherever there is poor sanitation, but amoebic dysentery is much more common in tropical countries. Treatment for bacillary dysentery is usually by administration of fluids to prevent dehydration, but for amoebic dysentery drugs to kill the amoebae are also given.

dyslexia   Difficulty in learning to write, spell, and read. It is commonly discovered at school. Dyslexic children are usually of normal intelligence and with special teaching can improve greatly. In some cases the cause is genetic.

dysprosium   (Dy)   A lanthanide element discovered in 1886. It forms the oxide (Dy_2O_3) and halides (for example DyF_3) and can be separated from the other lanthanides by ion-exchange techniques. At no 66; at wt 162.50; mp 1412°C; bp 2335°C.

E

Eadred   (d. 955) King of England (946–55), who reconquered Northumbria by expelling Eric Bloodaxe (954), its Norwegian king.

Eadwig   (*or* Edwy; d. 959) King of England from 955 to 957, when he lost Mercia and Northumbria.

eagle   A large broad-winged bird of prey occurring throughout the world, mostly in remote mountainous regions. Eagles have a large hooked bill and strong feet with large curved talons and are typically dull brown. With a wingspan of 1.3–2.4 m, they can soar for long periods searching for food. Family: *Accipitridae* (hawks and eagles). *See also* bald eagle; golden eagle.

ealdorman   The chief royal official of the Anglo-Saxon shire. Almost always of noble rank, he presided over the shire court, executed royal orders, and raised the shire military levy. Ealdormen later became the hereditary earls, and the sheriffs succeeded to their duties.

ear   The organ of hearing and balance in vertebrate animals (including man). The human ear is divided into external, middle, and inner parts. Sound waves are transmitted through the auditory meatus and cause the eardrum (tympanic membrane) to vibrate. These vibrations are transmitted through the three small bones (ossicles) of the middle ear to the fenestra ovalis, which leads to the inner ear. A duct (the Eustachian tube) connects the middle ear to the back of the throat (pharynx), enabling the release of pressure that builds up in the middle ear. The cochlea—a spiral organ of the inner ear—contains special cells that convert the sound vibrations into nerve impulses, which are transmitted to the hearing centres of the brain via the cochlear nerve. The inner ear also contains the organs of balance: three semicircular canals, each of which registers movement in a different plane. The semicircular canals and cochlea are filled

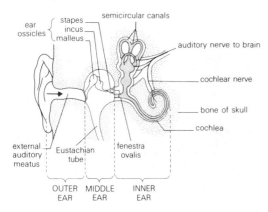

EAR *A vertical section through the human ear shows its internal structure; the middle and inner ears are embedded in the bone of the skull. The arrow indicates the direction of sound waves entering the ear.*

with fluid and are known together as the labyrinth of the ear.

Earhart, Amelia (1898–1937) US aviator, who was the first woman to fly solo across the Atlantic (1932) and Pacific (1935) Oceans. She died on an attempted flight around the world.

Early English The style of gothic architecture predominant in England in the 13th century. It is characterized by narrow pointed windows and arches, in contrast to the rounded features of the preceding period.

earth The third planet from the sun, at an average distance of 149.6 million km (93 million mi) from it. Its diameter at the equator is 12 756 km (7926 mi), slightly less at the Poles; its shape is therefore a flattened sphere. It completes an orbit of the sun in 365.26 days, and makes one rotation on its axis every 23.93 hours.
The earth is believed to be about 4600 million years old. Geologists divide this time into eras, periods, and epochs (*see* geological time scale). The earth consists of an inner core of solid iron, surrounded by an outer core of molten iron. Surrounding this is the solid mantle, inner and outer, which is separated from the crust by the Mohorovičić Discontinuity. The crust consists of basaltic oceanic crust surmounted by less dense granitic continental crust, which forms the continents. The crust varies in thickness from 5 km under the oceans to 60 km under mountain ranges. The composition of the crust is approximately 47% oxygen, 28% silicon, 8% aluminium, 4.5% iron, 3.5% calcium, 2.5% each sodium and potassium, and 2.2% magnesium. All other elements are present to an extent of less than 1% each. 70.8% of the earth's surface is ocean. The greatest ocean depth is over 11 000 m (36 000 ft), in the Marianas Trench; the greatest height of land is 8848 m (29 028 ft), at Mount Everest.

earthquake A series of shocks felt at the earth's surface, ranging from mild tremblings to violent oscillations, resulting from the fracturing of brittle rocks within the earth's crust and upper mantle. The magnitude of an earthquake depends on the amount of energy liberated in the seismic waves at the focus, where the overstrained rocks fracture. The Richter scale is used for comparing earthquake magnitudes. The majority of earthquakes occur in certain well-defined seismic zones, corresponding with the junction of lithospheric plates (*see* plate tectonics); these include the circum-Pacific belt, the Alpine-Himalayan belt, and the midocean ridges.

earthworm A terrestrial annelid worm belonging to a class (*Oligochaeta*) found all over the world. Earthworms feed on rotting vegetation, pulling the dead leaves down into their burrows and improving the fertility of the soil. The body consists of about 100 segments, each with four pairs of bristles for gripping the surface as the worm moves.

earwig A nocturnal usually herbivorous insect belonging to an order (*Dermaptera*; about 1100 species) found in Europe and warm regions. It has a dark slender body and a pair of pincers (cerci) at the end of the abdomen. At rest, the membranous semicircular hindwings are covered by short leathery forewings.

Eastbourne 51 00N 0 44W A resort in S England, on the East Sussex coast near Beachy Head, where the South Downs reach the sea. Population (1981): 77 608.

East China Sea (Chinese name: Dong Hai) A shallow section of the W Pacific Ocean, between China, South Korea, the Ryukyu Islands, and Taiwan. A monsoon area, it is rich in fish.

Easter The feast of the resurrection of Christ. Associated by the early Church with the Jewish Passover, the date of celebrating Easter was a matter of controversy. At the Council of Nicaea in 325 AD, it was agreed that it would be linked to the full moon on or following the vernal equinox and might thus fall on any Sunday between 22 March and 25 April. *See also* Good Friday; Lent.

EASTER ISLAND *The vast stone statues, of which there are over 600 on the island, occupy stone terraces.*

Easter Island (*or* Rapanui) 27 05S 109 20W A Chilean island of volcanic origin in the S Pacific Ocean. It is famed for its tall stone sculptures. The population is of Polynesian stock. Area: 166 sq km (64 sq mi). Population (1982 est): 1867. Chief settlement: Hanga-Roa.

Eastern Roman Empire (*or* Byzantine Empire) The Roman territories E of the Balkans separated from the western Roman Empire by Diocletian in 293 AD. An eastern emperor and magistrates coexisted with their western counterparts at Rome. Under Constantine the Great the Empire became Christian. Constantinople (previously Byzantium; now Istanbul) was inaugurated as the "New Rome" in 330 AD. The Eastern Empire survived until the fall of Constantinople to the Ottoman Turks in 1453.

Easter Rising (1916) An armed insurrection primarily in Dublin against the British Government. Patrick Pearse, a leader of the Irish Republican Brotherhood, and James Connolly with his Citizen Army, a total of 2000 men, occupied strategic positions in the city and proclaimed the establishment of the Irish Republic. Serious street fighting ensued with the government employing artillery. The insurgents had to surrender unconditionally and some 15 of the leaders were subsequently executed.

East Germany. *See* Germany.

East India Company **1.** (British) A commercial company that was incorporated in 1600 to trade in East Indian spices and came to wield considerable political power in British India. Its dominance in India was established at the expense of the French East India Company (founded 1664) by Robert Clive's victories in the Seven Years' War (1756–63). For the next decade the Company controlled government, its powers then being restricted by a series of Government of India Acts. The Company ceased to exist in 1873. **2.** (Dutch) A commercial company founded in 1602 to foster Dutch trade in the East Indies. By the late 17th century, it concentrated almost exclusively on the administration of Java.

Eastman, George (1854–1932) US inventor of the Kodak camera (1888) and founder of the Eastman Kodak Company (1892). In 1884 he patented a photographic film consisting of a paper base on which the necessary chemicals were fixed rather than being applied to photographic plates when required; the paper base was replaced by celluloid in 1889. In 1928 he developed a process for colour photography.

East River A river in the E USA, a tidal strait and navigable waterway flowing through New York City and connecting New York Harbour with Long Island Sound. Length: 26 km (16 mi).

East Sussex A county of SE England, formerly part of Sussex, bordering on the English Channel. It consists mainly of undulating land with the South Downs, drained by the River Ouse, in the S. It is predominantly agricultural. Coastal resorts include Brighton and Eastbourne. Area: 1795 sq km (693 sq mi). Population (1986 est): 689 700. Administrative centre: Lewes.

ebony The valuable heartwood of several tropical evergreen trees of the genus *Diospyros*. Ebony is very hard, dark, and heavy. It is used for cabinetwork, inlaying, etc. The most important species of trees are *D. ebenum* from India and Sri Lanka and *D. reticulata* from Mauritius. Family: *Ebenaceae*.

Eboracum (*or* Eburacum). *See* York.

EC. *See* Economic Community.

echidna A monotreme mammal belonging to the family *Tachyglossidae* (5 species), of Australia and New Guinea. The Australian echidna (*Tachyglossus aculeatus*), or spiny anteater, is about 45 cm long, with very long spines among its fur, and digs for ants, picking them up with its long sticky tongue. The single egg is incubated in a pouch on the female's belly. The young echidna is suckled at a teat in the pouch.

Echidna In Greek legend, a monster, half woman and half serpent. By the monster Typhon she gave birth to many other legendary monsters, including Chimera,

Cerberus, Orthus, Scylla, the Sphinx, and the dragons of the Hesperides and of Colchis.

echinoderm A marine invertebrate animal of the phylum *Echinodermata* (over 6000 species), including starfish, sea urchins, crinoids, sea cucumbers, etc. Echinoderms usually have a skin-covered skeleton of calcareous plates, often bearing spines. They use hydrostatic pressure to extend numerous small saclike organs (tube feet) used in locomotion, respiration, feeding, etc. Echinoderms generally occur on the sea floor.

Echo In Greek legend, a nymph deprived of speech by Hera and able to repeat only the final words of others. Her hopeless love for Narcissus caused her to fade away until only her voice remained.

echolocation A method by which certain animals can sense and locate surrounding objects by emitting sounds and detecting the echo. Insectivorous bats detect the echo by means of large ears or folds of the nostril, and are able to locate their prey when hunting on the wing. Toothed whales and porpoises emit brief intense clicks, enabling them to discriminate very small objects.

echo sounding The use of sound waves to measure the depth of the sea below a vessel or to detect other vessels or obstacles. The device used consists of a source of ultrasonic pulses and an electronic circuit to measure the time taken for the pulse to reach the target and its echo to return to the transducer. The device was developed originally by the Allied Submarine Detection Investigation Committee (ASDIC) in 1920 and was formerly known by this acronym. The name was changed to sonar (*so*und *na*vigation and *r*anging) in 1963.

eclipse The passage of all or part of an astronomical body into the shadow of another. A **lunar eclipse** occurs when the moon can enter the earth's shadow at full moon. The gradual obscuration of the moon's surface is seen wherever the moon is above the horizon. A **solar eclipse**, which is strictly an occultation, occurs at new moon, but only when the moon passes directly in front of the sun. The moon's shadow falls on and moves rapidly across the earth. Observers in the outer shadow region (the penumbra) will see a **partial eclipse**, with only part of the sun hidden. Observers in the dark inner (umbral) region of the shadow will see a **total eclipse**, in which the sun's disc is completely but briefly obscured; the corona can, however, be seen. If the moon is too far away totally to cover the sun, an **annular eclipse** is observed, in which a rim of light is visible around the eclipsed sun.

ecliptic The great circle in which the plane of the earth's orbit around the sun meets the celestial sphere. It marks the apparent path of the sun across the celestial sphere, as seen from earth over the course of a year.

ecology The scientific study of organisms in their natural environment. Modern ecology is concerned with the relationships of different species with each other and with the environment (habitat). A community of organisms and their habitat is called an ecosystem. Ecologists can calculate the productivity of various ecosystems in terms of energy, with important applications in agriculture. In addition, the effects of man's intervention on natural ecosystems can be predicted, enabling the effective conservation of wildlife and management of game and fish.

econometrics The application of statistical techniques to economics. Econometrics is used in the testing of the validity of economic theories. Usually a mathematical model of a specific theory is developed and tested against observations of the real world; if the theory is not refuted as a result, the model can then be used to make forecasts.

economics   A social science concerned with the production of goods and services, their distribution, exchange, and consumption. **Microeconomics** is concerned with the problems facing individuals and firms, while **macroeconomics** is concerned with the economy of a country and regulation of the economy by governments. In the western democracies problems centre upon the control of inflation, unemployment, and the balance of payments, as well as the encouragement of economic growth. *See also* monetarism.

ecosystem. *See* ecology.

ectopic pregnancy   Pregnancy occurring elsewhere than in the womb, most commonly in a Fallopian tube. It may lead to abortion or, more seriously, to rupture of the tube, with pain, bleeding, and shock. The usual treatment is surgical removal of the fetus and tube.

ECU.   *See* European Monetary System.

Ecuador, Republic of   A country in NW South America, lying on the Equator, from which it takes its name. It includes the Galápagos Islands. It consists chiefly of a coastal plain in the W, separated from the tropical jungles and rivers of the Amazon basin by the Andes (containing several active volcanoes). There are frequent earthquakes. The population is largely of Indian and mixed race, with minorities of European and African descent. *Economy*: mainly agricultural, with the main cash crops (bananas, coffee, and cocoa) grown in the lower coastal areas. Much of the country is forested and valuable hardwoods are produced. Fishing is important, especially shrimps. Ecuador is now South America's second largest oil producer. *History*: the Andean kingdom of Quito had already been conquered by the Incas when the Spanish established a colony in 1532. It gained independence in 1821 and in 1822 joined Gran Colombia under Bolívar. In 1830 it became the independent republic of Ecuador. In 1961 the president, Velasco Ibarra (1893–   ), was overthrown in a left-wing military coup and exiled. After several years of unsettled government he was again elected president. In 1970 he assumed dictatorial powers and in 1972 was deposed by a military regime. This regime was replaced by a three-man junta in 1976; a democratic constitution was introduced in 1979. Head of state: President Rodrigo Borja Cevallos. Official language: Spanish; the main Indian language is Quechua. Official currency: sucre of 100 centavos. Area: 270 670 sq km (104 505 sq mi). Population (1986): 9 640 000. Capital: Quito. Main port: Guayaquil.

eczema   Inflammation of the skin, resulting from contact with irritant or allergy-provoking substances, infections, drugs, or radiation, or without obvious cause.

Eddy, Mary Baker   (1821–1910) US religious leader, founder of Christian Science. Frequently ill as a young woman, Mrs Eddy was much influenced by the faith healer Phineas Parkhurst Quimby (1802–66). She published her beliefs in *Science and Health* (1875) and in 1879 founded the Church of Christ, Scientist, in Boston.

eddy current   An electric current induced in a conductor that experiences a changing magnetic field. In electric generators, motors, and transformers, energy is lost by unwanted eddy currents, either producing heat or opposing motion; these currents are reduced by laminating the iron cores to increase their resistance. Eddy

currents are useful in some applications, such as eddy-current heating and mechanical damping.

Eddystone Rocks   50 10N 4 16W A dangerous group of rocks off the coast of SW England, in the English Channel. The lighthouse built by John Smeaton (1759) was the first in which dovetail-jointed stones were used; it was replaced in 1882.

edelweiss   A common perennial alpine plant, *Leontopodium alpinum*, from Europe and South America, often grown in rock gardens. About 15 cm high, it has woolly leaves and tiny yellow flowers surrounded by whitish felted bracts. Family: *Compositae* (daisy family).

Eden, Anthony.   *See* Avon, (Robert) Anthony, 1st Earl of.

Edgar   (c. 943–75) The first king of a united England (959–75). He allowed his Danish subjects to retain Danish laws. Edgar promoted a monastic revival, encouraged trade by reforming the currency, and improved naval defence.

Edgar the Aetheling   (c. 1050–c. 1130) The grandson of Edmund II Ironside, his title Aetheling means royal prince. His claim to the English throne was rejected in 1066 owing to his minority and ill health. In 1068 and 1069 he led revolts against William I but came to terms with him in 1074.

Edinburgh   55 57N 3 13W The capital of Scotland and administrative centre of the Lothian Region, situated in the E centre of the country on the S shore of the Firth of Forth. In the old town, atop steep basalt cliffs that rise above the city, stands the castle. The Royal Mile extends E from the castle rock to the Palace of Holyrood House (begun c. 1500). The other famous thoroughfare in the city is Princes Street. The new town contains fine Georgian architecture situated around a network of broad streets, squares, and circuses. *History*: strategically important in medieval times in the wars between England and Scotland, Edinburgh emerged as the national capital in the 15th century. After James VI of Scotland (James I of England) moved his court to London in 1605 Edinburgh suffered a decline, but by the mid-18th century it was a centre of learning. The annual Edinburgh International Festival was founded in 1947. Population (1988 est): 433 480.

Edison, Thomas Alva   (1847–1931) US inventor,

THOMAS EDISON   *In his laboratory.*

owning a large research laboratory in Menlo Park, New Jersey. His most famous invention, the electric light bulb, was constructed in 1879. By 1881 Edison had built a generating station and was supplying electricity to over 80 customers. Among his other 1300 inventions were the gramophone, motion pictures, and improvements to Bell's telephone. He also discovered thermionic emission, enabling J. A. Fleming to produce the first thermionic valve.

Edmonton 53 34N 113 25W A city in W Canada, the capital of Alberta on the North Saskatchewan River. Population (1986): 785 465.

Edmund I (921–46) King of England (939–46), who expelled the Norse king Olaf from Northumbria (944).

Edmund II Ironside (c. 981–1016) The son of Ethelred II of England, his struggle with Canute for the vacant throne ended in Edmund's defeat at Ashingdon (1016). However, Canute agreed on the partition of England with Edmund, but after Edmund's sudden death Canute secured the whole kingdom.

Edward I (1239–1307) King of England (1272–1307), succeeding his father Henry III. He married (1254) Eleanor of Castile. He encouraged parliamentary institutions at the expense of feudalism and subdued Wales, on which he imposed the English system of administration. He later tried to assert his authority over Scotland and died while on his way to fight Robert Bruce (*see* Robert I).

Edward II (1284–1327) King of England (1307–27), succeeding his father Edward I. He became the first English Prince of Wales (1301). He married (1308) Isabella of France (1292–1358). His reign was troubled by his extravagance, his military disasters in Scotland, notably at Bannockburn (1314), and the unpopularity of his favourites, Piers Gaveston (d. 1312) and Hugh le Despenser (1262–1326). Isabella and her lover Roger de Mortimer murdered him.

Edward III (1312–77) King of England (1327–77), succeeding his father Edward II. He assumed effective power in 1330 after imprisoning his mother Isabella of France (1292–1358) and executing her lover Roger de Mortimer. Thereafter his reign was dominated by military adventures, his victories in Scotland encouraging him to plan (1363) the union of England and Scotland. Through his mother he claimed the French throne, thus starting (1337) the Hundred Years' War. His son John of Gaunt dominated the government during his last years.

Edward IV (1442–83) King of England (1461–70, 1471–83) during the Wars of the Roses. He married (1464) Elizabeth Woodville. The Yorkist leader, he was crowned after defeating the Lancastrians at Mortimer's Cross and Towton (1461). He was forced from the throne (1470) by the Earl of Warwick but regained it after defeating the Lancastrians at Tewkesbury (1471).

Edward V (1470–?1483) King of England (1483), succeeding his father Edward IV. His uncle, the Duke of Gloucester, imprisoned Edward and his brother Richard in the Tower of London, deposed Edward after a reign of only three months, and had himself crowned as Richard III. The two boys, known as the Princes in the Tower, were probably murdered in 1483.

Edward VI (1537–53) King of England (1547–53) and the son of Henry VIII, whom he succeeded, and Jane Seymour. Effective power was held by the protector, the Duke of Somerset, until 1550, when the Duke of Northumberland seized power. Edward became a fer-

vent Protestant and during his reign the Reformation in England made substantial progress.

Edward VII (1841–1910) King of the United Kingdom (1901–10), succeeding his mother Queen Victoria. He married (1863) Alexandra of Denmark. As Prince of Wales his indiscretions caused Victoria to exclude him from all affairs of state. A popular king, he ably represented Britain abroad.

EDWARD VIII   *As the Duke of Windsor, with the Duchess (Mrs Simpson) on their wedding day.*

Edward VIII (1894–1972) King of the United Kingdom (1936), succeeding his father George V. He abdicated on 11 December, 1936, because of objections to his liaison with the twice-divorced Mrs Wallis Simpson (1896–1986), whom he married in France in 1937. He became Duke of Windsor and was appointed governor of the Bahamas during World War II. He subsequently lived in France, where he remained until his death.

Edward, the Black Prince (1330–76) Prince of Wales and the eldest son of Edward III. His nickname may refer to the black armour he was said to have worn at Crécy (1346). He won victories against France in the Hundred Years' War and ruled Aquitaine from 1360 until ousted (1371).

Edward the Confessor (c. 1003–66) King of England (1042–66), nicknamed for his piety and his foundation of a new Westminster Abbey (consecrated 1065). His early reign was dominated by rivalry between his Norman favourites and his father-in-law Earl Godwin (d. 1053). After 1053 the Godwins were in the ascendant. Edward's childlessness led ultimately to the Norman conquest. He was canonized in 1161.

Edward the Elder (d. 924) King of England (899–924), succeeding his father Alfred the Great. He defeated the Danes (918), taking East Anglia, and also conquered Mercia (918) and Northumbria (920).

Edward the Martyr (c. 963–78) King of England (975–78), succeeding his father Edgar. He was murdered at Corfe Castle. He was canonized in 1001.

Edwin (c. 585–633) King of Northumbria (616–33), who became overlord of all English kingdoms S of the Humber, except for Kent. His marriage to Ethelburh, a Christian, led to his conversion and that of his people to Christianity (627). He was killed in battle against Penda of Mercia.

Edwy. *See* Eadwig.

EEC. *See* European Community.

eel A snakelike bony fish of the worldwide order *Anguilliformes* (or *Apodes*; over 500 species) having, usually, a scaleless body, no pelvic fins, and long dorsal and anal fins. Most species are marine, occurring mainly in shallow waters and feeding on other fish. The freshwater eels (family *Anguillidae*) migrate to the sea to breed—the Sargasso Sea in the case of European and American species—and the young eels (elvers) return to rivers and streams. *See also* electric eel.

eelgrass A perennial herbaceous marine plant of the genus *Zostera*, especially *Z. marina*, which grows in muddy intertidal flats and estuaries on the coasts of Europe and North America and is one of the few flowering plants to tolerate sea water. It has creeping underground stems (rhizomes), which help to stabilize mudbanks, and broad dark-green grasslike leaves. Family: *Zosteraceae*.

eelworm A very small nematode worm parasitic on plants, causing damage to agricultural crops. The larvae, on hatching, penetrate plant roots, which may react by forming root galls around them. Chief genera: *Anguina*, *Ditylenchus*, *Heterodera*.

EFTA. *See* European Free Trade Association.

egg (*or* ovum) The female reproductive cell (*see* gamete), which—when fertilized by a male gamete (sperm) —develops into a new individual of the same species. Animal eggs are surrounded by nutritive material (yolk) and—usually—one or more protective membranes, for example a jelly coat in amphibian eggs, the shell and other layers in birds' eggs. The amount of yolk varies, being greater in the eggs of egg-laying animals since the developing embryo depends on the yolk for nourishment: in mammals the egg is nourished from the maternal circulation and thus has little yolk. *See also* ovary.

eggplant. *See* aubergine.

eglantine. *See* sweet briar.

ego In psychoanalysis, the part of the mind that is closely in touch with the demands of external reality and operates rationally. It includes some motives (such as hunger and ambition), the individual's learned responses, and his (or her) conscious thought. It has to reconcile the conflicting demands of the id, the super-ego, and the outside world.

egret A white bird belonging to the heron subfamily. The great white egret (*Egretta alba*) has long silky ornamental plumes in the breeding season. The smaller cattle egret (*Aroleola ibis*) is 50 cm long and follows large grazing animals.

Egypt, Arab Republic of A country in NE Africa, extending into SW Asia. Most of the country consists of desert—the Sinai Peninsula, the Eastern Desert (a vast upland area), and the Western Desert (an extensive low plateau), while most of the population is concentrated along the fertile Nile Valley. *Economy*: the introduction of modern irrigation schemes, such as the Aswan High Dam, has led to an increase in the production of cotton, the chief cash crop, as well as a more diversified agricultural sector. There has been considerable expansion of the industrial sector since the 1950s, especially heavy industries. Oil was discovered in 1909 and in recent years production has greatly increased. Natural gas is also being exploited. Egypt's many historical and archaeological remains make tourism important. *History*: ancient Egyptian history is traditionally divided into 30 dynasties, beginning in about 3100 BC with the union of Upper

and Lower Egypt by Menes and ending in 343 BC with the death of the last Egyptian king, or pharaoh, Nectanebo II. The dynasties are grouped into the Old Kingdom (3rd–6th dynasties; c. 2686–c. 2160), the First Intermediate Period (7th–11th dynasties; c. 2160–c. 2040), the Middle Kingdom (12th dynasty; c. 2040–c. 1786), the Second Intermediate Period (13th–17th dynasties; c. 1786–c. 1567), and the New Kingdom (18th–20th dynasties; c. 1570–1085). During the New Kingdom there were territorial expansion and, later, trouble with the Sea Peoples; the 20th dynasty also saw the priests' power rise at the kings' expense. The outcome of Egypt's decline under the 21st–25th dynasties (1085–664) was the Assyrian invasion under Esarhaddon (671) and the 26th dynasty (664–525) was brought to an end by the Persian Achaemenians. Achaemenian rule was interrupted by the native 28th, 29th, and 30th dynasties (404–343) and was finally ended by Alexander the Great of Macedon, who obtained Egypt in 332.

On Alexander's death Egypt was acquired by the Macedonian Ptolemy I Soter. The Ptolemies ruled until the suicide of Cleopatra VII in 30 BC, when Egypt passed under Roman rule. In 395 AD, Egypt became part of the Byzantine (Eastern Roman) Empire. The Arabs conquered Egypt in 642 and it was then governed by representatives of the caliphate of Baghdad, under whom Islam was introduced. After 868 it gained virtual autonomy under a series of ruling dynasties. The last of these, the Fatimids, were overthrown by Saladin, who restored Egypt to the caliphate in 1171. It was ruled by the Mamelukes from 1250 until 1517, when it was conquered by the Ottoman Turks. The Turks governed Egypt through a viceroy but by the early 18th century power was largely in the hands of the Mameluke elite. In 1798 Napoleon established a French protectorate over Egypt, which in 1801 was overthrown by the British and Ottomans. Mehemet 'Ali was brought to power as viceroy in 1805, and in 1840 he was recognized by the Ottomans as hereditary ruler. British and French interests in Egypt intensified in the mid-19th century and in 1869 the opening of the Suez Canal enhanced Egypt's international significance. From 1882 the British dominated Egyptian government in spite of nominal Ottoman suzerainty. In 1914, on the outbreak of World War I, Egypt became a British protectorate until independence under King Fu'ad I was granted in 1922. In 1936 his son Farouk signed a treaty of alliance with Britain, which retained rights in the Suez Canal zone, and in World War II Egypt joined the Allies. The immediate postwar period saw the first Arab-Israeli War (1948–49) and a military coup (1952) that overthrew the monarchy (1953) and brought Nasser to power (1954). Nasser's nationalization of the Suez Canal in 1956 precipitated an invasion by Israeli and Anglo-French forces, which were compelled by the UN to withdraw. In 1958 Egypt, Syria, and subsequently North Yemen formed the United Arab Republic, a name retained by Egypt, in spite of Syria's withdrawal in 1961, until its present designation was adopted in 1971. Conflict with Israel erupted again in 1967, when in the Six Day War Egypt lost the Sinai peninsula, which was partly regained in the fourth war (1973). In 1970 Nasser was succeeded by Sadat, who in 1972 brought Egypt's close relationship with the Soviet Union to an end. In 1979, under US influence, Egypt and Israel signed a peace treaty. Increasing opposition to Sadat's policies culminated in his assassination by Islamic extremists in 1981. He was succeeded as president by Hosni Mubarak (1929–). Official language: Arabic. Official religion: Islam. Official currency: Egyptian pound of 100 piastres. Area: 1 000 000 sq km (386 198 sq mi). Population (1986): 50 000 000. Capital: Cairo. Main port: Alexandria.

Ehrlich, Paul (1854–1915) German bacteriologist. Ehrlich did much to develop the understanding of acquired immunity to disease in animals and, with Emil Behring (1854–1917), he prepared a serum against diphtheria. In 1910 he announced the discovery of an arsenical compound (Salvarsan) effective in treating syphilis. Ehrlich shared a Nobel Prize (1908) with I. I. Metchnikov (1845–1916).

eider A large sea duck, *Somateria mollissima*, of far northern sea coasts. About 55 cm long, males are mostly white with a black crown, belly, and tail; females are mottled dark brown. The soft breast feathers of the female are the source of eiderdown.

Eiffel Tower A metal tower in Paris, built for the 1889 Centennial Exposition by the French engineer Alexandre-Gustave Eiffel (1832–1923). The 300 m (984 ft) tower was the highest building in the world until 1930.

Eiger 46 34N 8 01E A mountain in central S Switzerland, in the Bernese Oberland. Its difficult N face was first climbed successfully in 1938. Height: 3970 m (12 697 ft).

Eightfold Path (*or* The Noble Eightfold Path) In Buddhism the fourth of the Four Noble Truths, which summarizes the eight ways that lead the Buddhist to enlightenment. They are: right understanding, right resolve, right speech, right action, right livelihood, right effort, right mindfulness, and right meditation. The Path is an integrated spiritual attitude.

Eilat (Elat *or* Elath) 29 33N 34 57E A resort and port in extreme S Israel, on the Gulf of Aqaba. The modern city was founded in 1949. Population (1982 est): 19 500.

Eindhoven 51 26N 5 30E A town in the S Netherlands, in North Brabant province. Population (1987): 190 962.

ALBERT EINSTEIN

Einstein, Albert (1879–1955) German physicist. Einstein was an undistinguished scholar, interested only in theoretical physics. In 1901 he obtained a post at the

Patent Office in Berne, Switzerland. While working there, he continued his researches and in 1905 published four highly original papers. One gave a mathematical explanation of the Brownian movement in molecular terms, the second explained the photoelectric effect in terms of photons, the third announced his special theory of relativity, and the fourth related mass to energy. In 1915 he extended the theory of relativity to the general case. He received the 1921 Nobel Prize for Physics. Einstein was lecturing in California when Hitler came to power in 1933. Being Jewish, Einstein decided to remain in the USA and spent the rest of his life at the Institute for Advanced Study in Princeton, unsuccessfully seeking a unified field theory. He became a US citizen in 1940. Originally a pacifist, Einstein was persuaded in 1939 to write to President Roosevelt warning him that an atom bomb could now be made and that Germany might make one first. He took no part in its manufacture, and became an active postwar advocate of nuclear disarmament.

einsteinium (Es) An artificial transuranic element discovered by Ghiorso and others in 1952 and named after Albert Einstein. It behaves chemically as a trivalent actinide. Its 11 isotopes are all radioactive, the longest-lived having a half-life of 276 days. At no 99; at wt (254).

Éire. *See* Ireland, Republic of.

Eisenhower, Dwight D(avid) (1890–1969) US general and statesman; Republican president (1953–61). In World War II he was commander of US troops in Europe (1942), of Allied forces in N Africa and Italy (1942–43), and then supreme commander of Allied forces in Europe (1943). He helped to plan and commanded the forces in the D-Day invasion of Normandy. In 1951 he became supreme commander of NATO. A popular president, "Ike" initiated social welfare programmes. His administration spanned the Cold War years and was marred by the anticommunist agitation of Joseph McCarthy. The **Eisenhower Doctrine** (1957) offered economic and military help to Middle Eastern nations against communist advances.

Eisenstein, Sergei (1898–1948) Russian film director. His films, which include *Battleship Potemkin* (1925), *Alexander Nevsky* (1938), and *Ivan the Terrible* (1942–46), used advanced editing and montage techniques.

eisteddfod A Welsh assembly in which bards and minstrels compete for prizes in literature, music, and drama. Originating in medieval times, the tradition later declined but was revived as the chief national cultural festival during the 19th century.

Ekaterinburg. *See* Sverdlovsk.

Ekaterinodar. *See* Krasnodar.

Ekaterinoslav. *See* Dnepropetrovsk.

eland A large horned antelope belonging to the genus *Taurotragus* (2 species), of African plains. The common eland (*T. oryx*) is light brown with thin vertical white stripes towards the shoulders. The Derby eland (*T. derbianus*) has a black neck with a white band at the base. Both species have a black-tufted tail and dewlap.

elastic modulus The ratio of the stress on a body obeying Hooke's law to the strain produced. The strain may be a change in length (Young's Modulus) or a change in volume (bulk modulus).

elastomer A polymer with elastic properties, i.e. one that can be deformed and will revert to its original shape. Rubber, a natural elastomer, still has many applications, especially for heavy-duty tyres. However,

synthetic elastomers of styrene-butadiene, polybuta-
diene, polyisoprene, silicones, etc., are now far more
widely used.

Elat (*or* Elath). *See* Eilat.

Elba An Italian island in the Tyrrhenian Sea. Napoleon I was exiled here (1814–15) following his abdication.
Area: 223 sq km (86 sq mi). Population (1981): 27 309.

Elbe, River (Czech name: Labe) A river in central Europe, flowing mainly NW from N Czechoslovakia,
through East and West Germany to the North Sea at
Hamburg. It is connected by various canal systems to
the Rivers Weser and Rhine as well as to the River Oder.
Length: 1165 km (724 mi).

El Cid (Rodrigo Díaz de Vivar; c. 1040–99) Spanish
warrior, immortalized in the epic poem *Cantar del mio
Cid*. A vassal of Alfonso VI of Castile, he was exiled by
the king in 1079 and became a soldier of fortune, fighting for both Spaniard and Moor. Always loyal to his
king, he was returned to favour and became protector
and then ruler of Valencia.

elder A shrub or tree of the genus *Sambucus* (40 species), found in temperate and subtropical areas. The
cream-coloured flowers, grouped into flat-topped clusters, can be used in tea or wine. The red or black berries,
rich in vitamin C, are used in wine, jams, and jellies. The
common European elder is *S. nigra*. Family: *Caprifoliaceae*.

ELDORADO *Francisco Pizarro sought the legendary
"golden land".*

Eldorado (Spanish: the golden one) An Indian ruler
in Colombia who, according to legend, ritually coated
himself in gold dust before bathing in a lake. The name
was later applied to a region of fabulous wealth the existence of which this legend suggested. The conquest of
South America in the 16th century was hastened by expeditions seeking Eldorado, notably those of Francisco
Pizarro (1539) and Jiménez de Quesada (1569–72).

Eleanor of Aquitaine (c. 1122–1204) The wife
(1137–52) of Louis VII of France and, after the annulment of their marriage, the wife (1154–89) of Henry II
of England. Henry imprisoned her (1174–89) for complicity in their sons' rebellion against him. After Henry's
death she helped to secure their peaceful accession as
Richard I (1189) and John (1199).

Eleanor of Castile (1246–90) The wife (from 1254)
of Edward I of England. Edward erected the **Eleanor**

Crosses (e.g. Charing Cross) wherever her body rested
on its way from Nottinghamshire, where she died, to her
funeral in London.

electoral college An indirect electoral system used
in the US for electing the president and vice president.
Each state chooses by popular vote a number of electors
to send to an electoral college. This number is equal to
its number of representatives in the House of Representatives plus its two senators. All the electors chosen by a
state pledge themselves to vote for the presidential candidate with the highest popular vote in the state. Thus
the majority of the elected president is enhanced in the
college, giving an increased influence to the more populous states.

Electra In Greek legend, the daughter of Agamemnon
and Clytemnestra. She helped her brother Orestes escape after the murder of Agamemnon and later helped
him to kill Clytemnestra and her lover Aegisthus.

Electra complex. *See* Oedipus complex.

electric car A car driven by one or more electric motors, which are powered by batteries. Diminishing oil
reserves and the pollution problems associated with the
internal-combustion engine have intensified the search
for an effective electric car. However, no electric car can
yet compete with a petrol-driven car, as some seven tonnes of conventional lead accumulators are required to
provide an energy store equivalent to five gallons of petrol, although milk floats have been in use since the
1930s. Two lines of research are therefore being pursued: improving accumulators and making workable fuel cells. Several commuter cars using special lead accumulators have been produced, with top speeds around
30 mph (44 km per hour). The hybrid electric car carries
its own petrol-engine-driven generator for use outside
towns.

electric charge A property of certain elementary
particles (*see* particle physics) that causes them to undergo electromagnetic interactions. The magnitude of the
charge is always the same and is equal to 1.6021×10^{-19}
coulomb (although quarks have a fractional
charge). Charge is of two kinds, arbitrarily called positive and negative. Like charges repel each other and unlike charges attract each other. The force (F) between
charges q_1 and q_2 is given by Coulomb's law, $F = q_1 q_2 / 4\pi\varepsilon_0 d^2$, where ε_0 is the electric constant and d is
the distance between charges. On a large scale, charge is
always due to an excess or deficiency of electrons compared to the number of protons in the nuclei of a
substance.

electric constant (ε_0) A constant that appears in
Coulomb's law (*see* electric charge). Its value is
8.854×10^{-12} farad per metre. It is also known as the
absolute permittivity of free space. *Compare* magnetic
constant.

electric eel An eel-like freshwater fish, *Electrophorus
electricus*, that occurs in NE South America. Up to 3 m
long, it swims by undulating its long anal fin and has
electric organs—modified muscle tissue—in the tail,
which produce electric shocks capable of killing prey
and of stunning a man. Family: *Electrophoridae*; order:
Cypriniformes.

electric field The pattern of the lines of force that
surround an electric charge. The field strength at any
point is inversely proportional to the square of the distance of that point from the charge (Coulomb's law).
Any other charge placed in this field experiences a force

proportional to the field strength and to the magnitude of the introduced charge. The force is attractive if the charges are opposite and repulsive if they are alike.

electric generator A device for converting mechanical energy into electricity, usually by electromagnetic induction. A simple electromagnetic generator, or dynamo, consists of a conducting coil rotated in a magnetic field. Current induced in this coil is fed to an external circuit by slip rings in an alternating-current generator (called an alternator) or by a commutator, which rectifies the current, in a direct-current generator.

Most of the electricity from power stations is produced by alternators as three-phase alternating current, i.e. there are three windings on each generator, producing three separate output voltages. For transmission there are three conductor wires with a common neutral wire. This three-phase system optimizes generator design and minimizes transmission losses. Generally, all three phases are supplied to large factories but the supply is split to single phase for homes, shops, and offices.

electricity The phenomena that arise as a result of electric charge. Electricity has two forms: static electricity, which depends on stationary charges, and current electricity, which consists of a flow of charges, specifically electrons. Current electricity was first demonstrated by Volta in 1800 and investigated by Ampère during the next 25 years. Oersted's discovery (1820) that a magnetic needle was deflected by an electric current inspired Faraday to a deep investigation of the relationship between electricity and magnetism, which led him to the discovery of electromagnetic induction, the electric generator, and the electric motor. The theory of electromagnetism was elucidated by Clerk Maxwell in the mid-1850s.

electricity supply The system that generates (see power station), transmits, and distributes the electric power in an industrialized society. Power stations are interconnected by transmission lines to form a grid. Grid-control centres continuously monitor the load

Modern life depends on electricity in so many ways, yet it is not known exactly what it is.

carbon atom

− ve + ve

electron proton

Atoms consist of electrons, protons, and neutrons. The electrons cluster round the central nucleus of protons and neutrons.

Electrons have a negative electric charge — protons are positively charged. The charges are equal but opposite.

Similar charges repel each other, opposite charges attract each other. These are the forces harnessed to make electricity.

helium atom

current flow ⟶

An electrical current consists of a flow of electrons in one direction. But in many atoms, such as helium, they are tightly bound to the nucleus. To flow as a current electrons have to be free.

In a metal wire some of the electrons are free to move about between the metal ions (atoms that have lost an electron). Normally they move about at random and no current flows.

When the majority of electrons flow in one direction this is an electric current. 1 ampere is equivalent to a flow of 6×10^{18} electrons per second.

There are two main methods of making electrons flow to generate a current.

coil of wire

N

field

S

current

magnet

rotating slip rings

carbon brush

2e

zinc electrode

copper electrode

H_2SO_4 + 2 Zn

2e SO_4^{2-} $2Zn^+$

H_2

⟶ $2H^+$ + 2e ⟶ 2H

dilute sulphuric acid (H_2SO_4)

One method is to subject them to a changing magnetic field—this is the principle of the dynamo. If a coil of wire is rotated between the poles of a magnet, the electrons are forced round the coil. This is the power-station method; coal or oil is burned to raise steam to drive a turbine, which rotates the coils.

The other way is to make use of a chemical reaction in an electric cell to dissociate the electrons from their atoms and molecules. The separated charges then flow in opposite directions as a result of the forces between them. This is how a battery works. The sulphuric acid dissolves the zinc electrode producing 2 electrons, a sulphate ion (SO_4^{2-}), 2 zinc ions (Zn^+), and 2 hydrogen ions (H^+).

from factories, offices, homes, etc., and match it with the best combination of available generating capacity, maintaining the supply at a constant voltage and frequency. Base-load stations run continuously. These are usually the larger or cheaper-to-run nuclear and coal-fired stations. Less economic or smaller stations that are easier to start up and shut down are brought in to supply the peak demand. The grid voltage is reduced at substations for area distribution and further reduced at local substations to the UK domestic supply voltage of 240 volts.

electric motor   A device that converts electrical energy into mechanical energy usually for driving machinery.

Electric motors depend on the principle that a current-carrying conductor in a magnetic field experiences a force and that when two electromagnets are placed close together the two magnetic fields force them apart. The simplest type of motor uses this principle to turn a single coil of wire (the armature or rotor) between the poles of a permanent magnet. Practical motors use a stationary winding (stator) in place of a permanent magnet. Most motors work on an alternating-current (ac) supply. In the induction motor, current is fed to the stator, which induces a current in the rotor; interaction between the magnetic field of the stator and the induced rotor current causes the rotor to rotate. In the synchronous ac motor, current is also fed to the rotor (through slip rings) and the rate of rotation is proportional to the supply frequency. In a dc motor current is fed to the rotor through a commutator.   *See also* linear motor.

electric ray   A fish, also called torpedo ray, belonging to a family (*Torpedinidae*) found mainly in shallow waters of warm and temperate regions. Electric organs —modified muscle tissue—on each side of the disclike head produce electric shocks used in defence and food capture. Order: *Batoidea* (*see* ray).

electrocardiography   Examination of the electrical activity of the heart. Impulses generated by the contraction of the heart muscle are transmitted through electrodes attached to the skin to a recording apparatus (electrocardiograph). The recording itself, called an electrocardiogram (ECG), indicates the rhythm of the heart and aids in the diagnosis of heart disease.

electroconvulsive therapy   (ECT)   A treatment for mental disorders, such as endogenous depression, in which an electric current is passed through the brain in order to cause a convulsion. The convulsion is greatly reduced by giving an anaesthetic and drugs to relax the muscles.

electroencephalography   The measurement of the electrical activity of the brain and the recording of the brain waves in the form of a tracing—an electroencephalogram (EEG). Brain waves were first recorded from electrodes on the scalp in 1926. Electroencephalography is now used widely to diagnose diseases of the brain and to study brain function.

electroluminescence.   *See* luminescence.

electrolysis   The chemical decomposition of a substance by passing an electric current through it. If a voltage is applied across two electrodes placed in a liquid (electrolyte) containing ions, the positive ions will drift towards the negative electrode (cathode) and the negative ions towards the positive electrode (anode). At the electrodes, the ions may give up their charge and form

molecules. Alternatively, the atoms of the electrode may ionize and pass into solution. Electrolysis is used to electroplate metals and in the manufacture of a number of chemicals, such as sodium and chlorine.

electromagnet.   *See* magnet.

electromagnetic field   A concept describing electric and magnetic forces that, like gravitational forces, act without physical contact (action at a distance). The interaction of electricity and magnetism was first investigated experimentally in the 19th century. Faraday explained the electromagnetic interaction in terms of magnetic lines of force, forming a field of force, which is distorted by the presence of a current-carrying conductor or by another magnet. James Clerk Maxwell developed the mathematical theory that electricity and magnetism are different manifestations of the same phenomenon (the electromagnetic field), magnetism being the result of relative motion of electric fields.

electromagnetic induction   The production of voltage in an electrical conductor when it is in a changing magnetic field or if it moves in relation to a steady magnetic field. The direction of the induced electromotive force opposes the change or motion causing it. Since a current-carrying conductor itself induces a magnetic field, if the current changes, **self-inductance** occurs, opposing the current change. **Mutual inductance** occurs in two adjacent conductors carrying changing currents.

electromagnetic interaction   An interaction that occurs between those elementary particles that possess an electric charge. The interaction can be visualized as the exchange of virtual photons (*see* virtual particle) between the interacting particles. The electromagnetic interaction is 200 times weaker than the strong interaction but 10^{10} times stronger than the weak interaction. *See also* particle physics.

electromagnetic radiation   Transverse waves consisting of electric and magnetic fields vibrating perpendicularly to each other and to the direction of propagation. In free space the waves are propagated at a velocity of 2.9979×10^8 metres per second, known as the velocity of light (symbol: c). Their wavelength, λ, and frequency, f, are related by the equation $\lambda f = c$. Those with the highest frequencies are known as gamma radiation; then in descending order of frequency the **electromagnetic spectrum** includes X-rays, ultraviolet radiation, visible light, infrared radiation, microwaves, and radio waves. Electromagnetic radiation exhibits typical wave properties, such as refraction, diffraction, interference, and polarization. However, it has a dual nature in that it can also be regarded as a stream of massless elementary particles called photons.

electromotive force   (emf)   The electrical potential difference or voltage between two points in an electric circuit. It causes the movement of charge that constitutes an electric current.

electron   A stable negatively charged elementary particle with mass $9.109\,56 \times 10^{-31}$ kilogram and spin $\frac{1}{2}$. Electrons are responsible for almost all commonly observed electrical and magnetic effects and, since they orbit the nucleus in atoms, are also responsible for most chemical processes. A **free electron** is one that has become detached from an atom. An electric current passing through a metal or low-pressure gas consists of a flow of free electrons; a current of 1 ampere is equivalent to a flow of 6×10^{18} electrons per second.

electronics The study of devices that control and utilize the movement of electrons and other charged particles. Originating with the invention of thermionic valves, it expanded rapidly during World War II to include radar, missile guidance systems, and computers. The replacement of bulky thermionic valves by semiconductor components, such as transistors, and later by integrated circuits has resulted in much more compact and reliable equipment. The social impact of electronics has been immense, leading for example to the development of television, communications satellites, and the computerization of office and factory systems.

electronic tagging A method of monitoring the movements of persons convicted of certain offences as an alternative to prison. The offender wears a microchip device emitting a signal to a transmitter attached to a telephone. If the offender moves out of a 75-metre (250-ft) range, the telephone sends a message to a controlling computer.

electron microscope A type of microscope in which a beam of electrons is focused by means of magnetic and electrostatic lenses onto a specimen and scattered by it to produce an image. Typically an electron microscope can resolve two points 10^{-9} metre apart and produce magnifications of up to a million.

electronvolt (eV) A unit of energy equal to the increase in the energy of an electron when it passes through a rise in potential of one volt. $1 \, eV = 1.6 \times 10^{-19}$ joule.

electroplating The process of depositing a layer of one metal on another by making the object to be plated the cathode in an electrolytic bath (*see* electrolysis). Metals used for electroplating include silver (*see* silverplate), gold, chromium, cadmium, copper, zinc, and nickel; they usually form the anode in the bath.

elementary particles. *See* particle physics.

elements Substances that cannot be broken down into simpler fragments by chemical means. A sample of an element contains atoms that are chemically virtually identical, since they have the same atomic number and thus the same number of electrons around the nucleus. Samples of a given element may consist of a mixture of isotopes. Over 100 elements are known, of which about 90 occur naturally, the rest having been synthesized in nuclear reactions. *See also* periodic table.

elephant A mammal of the order *Proboscidea*: the African elephant (*Loxodonta africana*) or the Indian elephant (*Elephas maximus*). (The extinct mammoths also belonged to this order.) Elephants have a tough brownish-grey skin and a muscular prehensile proboscis (trunk)—an extension of the nose and upper lip used to convey food (vegetation) and water to the mouth. The upper incisor teeth are continually growing ivory tusks. Elephants live in herds. The African elephant is the largest land mammal, standing 3–4 m high at the shoulder. The smaller Indian elephant—intelligent and readily trained—is used for transport and heavy work. See p. 244.

elephantiasis A chronic infection caused by nematode worms, called filariae. The worms block the lymphatic channels causing swelling of the legs and scrotum (or vulva). Elephantiasis occurs only in the tropics.

elephant seal A large seal belonging to the genus *Mirounga* (2 species). The male Antarctic elephant seal (*M. leonina*) grows to over 6 m; females are about half that size. The slightly smaller northern elephant seal (*M. angustirostris*) lives off the W coast of North America.

Eleusinian Mysteries An esoteric religious cult in ancient Greece, with its centre at Eleusis. It originated before 600 BC in an agrarian fertility cult, and the main deities worshipped were Demeter and Persephone.

Elgar, Sir Edward (1857–1934) British composer. A professional violinist, Elgar wrote choral works, two symphonies, concertos for violin and cello, and chamber music. His most famous works are the *Dream of Gerontius* (1900), the *Enigma Variations* (1899), and the *Pomp and Circumstance* marches (1901–30).

Elgin Marbles Ancient Greek marble sculptures, mostly a frieze from the Parthenon, sold to the British Museum in 1816 by Lord Elgin for £35,000. He acquired them from the Turks occupying Athens, who were using the Parthenon for target practice. The British government has not yielded to Greek agitation for their return.

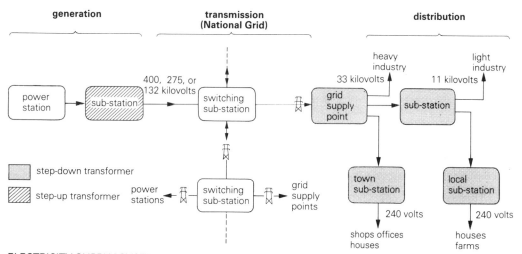

ELECTRICITY SUPPLY SYSTEM *A schematic diagram of the UK system.*

African elephant

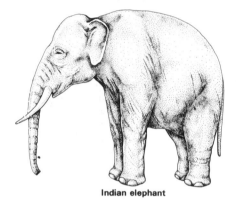

Indian elephant

ELEPHANT *The African elephant can be distinguished from the smaller Indian species by its larger ears, flatter forehead, smooth skin, and concave back.*

El Greco (Domenikos Theotokopoulos; 1541–1614) Painter of Greek parentage, born in Crete, who worked mainly in Spain. He trained in Venice under Titian in the 1560s and in 1577 moved to Spain, settling in Toledo. His early Spanish works were Venetian in inspiration, but his later paintings of saints and his masterpiece, *The Burial of Count Orgaz* (1586–88), are characterized by strident colours and dramatically elongated figures.

Elijah An Old Testament prophet, possibly 9th century BC. He attacked the cult of Baal among the Israelites (1 Kings 18) and successfully maintained the monotheistic worship of Jehovah.

Eliot, George (Mary Ann Evans; 1819–80) British woman novelist, noted for her depiction of provincial English society. She wrote the novels *Adam Bede* (1859), *The Mill on the Floss* (1860), *Silas Marner* (1861), the pioneering and influential *Middlemarch* (1871–72), and *Daniel Deronda* (1876).

Eliot, T(homas) S(tearns) (1888–1965) Anglo-American poet, critic, and dramatist, born in Missouri. His first volume of poetry was the innovatory *Prufrock and Other Observations* (1917). *The Waste Land* (1922) and *Four Quartets* (1935–41) are other major poetic achievements. In 1927 he became an Anglo-Catholic and a British subject. From 1922 to 1939 he edited *The*

Criterion, a critical review, and wrote a considerable amount of influential literary criticism. His verse dramas include *Murder in the Cathedral* (1935), *The Cocktail Party* (1949), and *The Elder Statesman* (1958). He was awarded the Nobel Prize in 1948.

Elizabeth I (1533–1603) Queen of England and Ireland (1558–1603), daughter of Henry VIII and Anne Boleyn. Her mother's execution and Elizabeth's imprisonment by Mary I made her cautious and suspicious but her devotion to England made her one of its greatest monarchs. Her religious compromise (1559–63) established Protestantism in England (*see* Reformation). England won a great naval victory in 1588 by destroying the Spanish Armada. Elizabeth never married and was called the Virgin Queen.

Elizabeth II (1926–) Queen of the United Kingdom (1952–), noted for her scrupulous fulfilment of the roles of constitutional monarch and head of the Commonwealth. She married Prince Philip in 1947; their four children are Prince Charles, Princess Anne, the Duke of York, and Prince Edward (1964–).

Elizabeth the Queen Mother (1900–) The widow of George VI, and mother of Elizabeth II and Princess Margaret. Formerly Lady Elizabeth Bowes-Lyon, she married in 1923.

elk The largest deer, *Alces alces*, found in forests of N Eurasia and also in N North America, where it is called a moose. Up to 2 m high at the shoulder, elks have a broad curved muzzle and a short neck with a heavy dewlap. The coat is grey-brown and males grow large palmate antlers. They feed on leaves and water plants and form herds in winter.

Ellice Islands. *See* Tuvalu.

Ellington, Duke (Edward Kennedy E.; 1899–1974) US Black jazz composer, band leader, and pianist. In New York he established a group of musicians that remained the core of his band for 30 years. The worldwide success of "Mood Indigo" in 1930 led to European tours and annual concerts in Carnegie Hall. Ellington concentrated on composing large-scale works for jazz orchestra.

ellipse A closed curve having the shape of an elongated circle. The sum of the distances from any point on the circumference to each of two fixed points, known as the

GEORGE ELIOT *A sketch done in 1865 by F. W. Burton.*

foci, is a constant. The ellipse is one of a family of curves known as conic sections.

ELIZABETH THE QUEEN MOTHER *Norman Parkinson's photograph celebrating her 80th birthday.*

Ellis, (Henry) Havelock (1859–1939) British psychologist and essayist, noted for his studies of human sexual behaviour. His major work, *Studies in the Psychology of Sex* (7 vols, 1897–1928), was among the first to deal frankly with sexual problems and met with legal opposition.

elm A tree of the genus *Ulmus* (about 30 species), widely distributed in N temperate regions. Up to 40 m high, elms have oval pointed toothed leaves, clusters of small reddish flowers, and rounded or heart-shaped winged nuts. Elms are widely planted for shade and ornament and for their strong durable timber, but the number in Europe and North America has been greatly reduced by Dutch elm disease. Species include the English elm (*U. procera*), the Eurasian wych elm (*U. glabra*), and the American elm (*U. americana*). Family: *Ulmaceae*.

elm bark beetle A wood-boring beetle that tunnels under the bark of elm trees and carries the fungus *Ceratostomella ulni*, which causes Dutch elm disease. Family: *Scolytidae* (*see* bark beetle).

El Salvador, Republic of A country in Central America, on the Pacific Ocean. Narrow coastal lowlands rise to a fertile plateau, which is enclosed by volcanic mountains. Most of the population is of mixed European and Indian descent. *Economy*: mainly agricultural, coffee and cotton being the main commercial crops. Most of the cultivated land is controlled by a few families. *History*: the Aztec population was conquered by the Spaniards in 1526 and after the overthrow of Spanish rule the region formed part of the Central American Federation (1823–38). In 1841 it became an independent republic. Tension arising from the emigration of Salvadoreans to Honduras culminated in war in 1965 and again in 1969. In 1978–79 internal unrest occurred in response to the repressive regime of Gen Carlos Humberto Romero (1924–   ). Romero was deposed in 1979 and a junta took control but the violence continued, including the assassination in 1980 of the archbishop of San Salvador, Oscar Romero; in 1989 rebels briefly occupied parts of the capital, San Salvador, itself. In

1984 José Napoléon Duarte was elected president; he was succeeded by Alfredo Cristiani in 1989. El Salvador is a member of the OAS. Official language: Spanish. Official religion: Roman Catholic. Official currency: colón of 100 centavos. Area 21 393 sq km (8236 sq mi). Population (1985 est): 5 480 000. Capital: San Salvador. Main port: Acajutla.

Elsinore. *See* Helsingór.

Ely 52 24N 0 16E A city in E England, in Cambridgeshire on the River Ouse. The Isle of Ely is an area of higher ground surrounded by fenland. Ely's 12th-century cathedral dominates the fen landscape. Population (1983 est): 11 030.

Elysium (*or* Elysian Fields) In Greek mythology, the fields on the banks of the River Oceanus where those favoured by the gods live in eternal happiness. In Roman mythology Elysium is part of the underworld.

Emancipation Proclamation (1863) The edict issued by President Abraham Lincoln that freed slaves in the rebellious southern states of the USA. Its provisions were extended and confirmed by the 13th Amendment, which abolished slavery throughout the nation (1865).

embolism The sudden blocking of an artery by a clot or other material that has come from another part of the body via the bloodstream. A clot most commonly forms in the leg and pieces break away and lodge in the arteries of the lung—a **pulmonary embolism**. A clot may sometimes come from the heart and lodge in the brain, causing a stroke. *See also* thrombosis.

embryo An animal or plant in the earliest stages of its development. In vertebrate animals the embryonic stage lasts from the first division of the fertilized egg until the young animal either hatches from the egg or is expelled from the womb at birth. A human embryo is called a fetus from the eighth week of pregnancy. In invertebrate animals the embryo is generally called a larva. In plants, the embryo lies within the seed. **Embryology** is the study of the development of embryos. See p. 246.

emerald A green variety of beryl, highly valued as a gemstone. It occurs mainly in metamorphic rocks, the finest specimens coming from Muzo, Colombia.

Emerson, Ralph Waldo (1803–82) US essayist and poet, a leading transcendentalist. He published *Nature*, his transcendentalist creed, in 1836 and expressed his optimistic humanism in *Representative Men* (1850) and *The Conduct of Life* (1860).

emery A granular greyish-black rock composed of corundum with magnetite, hematite, or spinel. It occurs mainly in metamorphic rocks or sediments and is used as an abrasive.

Emmental (*or* Emmenthal) The valley of the upper River Emme, in W central Switzerland. It is famous for its cheese.

Empedocles (c. 490–430 BC) Sicilian Greek philosopher. He founded the doctrine that earth, air, fire, and water make up the world, and that love and strife (attraction and antipathy) govern their distribution.

emperor penguin A large penguin, *Aptenodytes forsteri*. 1.2 m tall, it is the largest seabird and has a blue-grey plumage with a black head and throat, a white belly, and orange patches on the neck.

emphysema A progressive disease of the lungs characterized by destruction of lung tissue and distension of the air spaces. It is most commonly caused by cigarette smoking and is often accompanied by chronic bronchitis. Patients become very breathless on exertion.

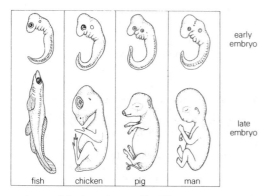

various vertebrate embryos *The different species are hard to distinguish in the early stages of development; later they develop individual characteristics.*

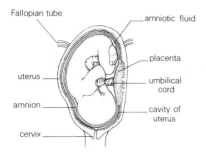

human embryo *A few weeks before birth this fetus is practically fully formed.*

EMBRYO

Empire, British Britain's overseas possessions from the 16th to early 20th centuries. Although originating in the discovery of Cape Breton Island (1497), permanent settlements in North America were not established until the early 17th century, when colonists, some escaping religious persecution, were granted charters by the Crown to settle Virginia, Maryland, and New England. The American colonies were lost in 1783 (*see* American Revolution). In Canada the English came into conflict with the French and only established control in the Seven Years' War (1756–63) from which they also emerged victorious in India. Robert Clive's victory at Plassey (1757) assured British, rather than French, dominance in India and the East India Company continued to govern until 1857, when its authority was replaced by the Crown's.

The Napoleonic Wars in the early 19th century brought possessions in the West Indies (Trinidad, Tobago, St Lucia) as well as Mauritius, Ceylon, and, in Africa, the Cape. Substantial possessions in Africa were not obtained until the late 18th century with the acquisition of what are now Sierra Leone, Ghana, and Nigeria. The 19th-century colonial expansion in Africa was fired by missionary zeal, which motivated such explorers as Livingstone, as well as commercial activities. The late 19th century saw the establishment of British dominance in Egypt and the Sudan but in South Africa it was undermined by Afrikaner hostility.

Colonies in Australia were initially penal settlements: New South Wales was settled in 1778, Tasmania in 1803, and Queensland in 1824. New Zealand was controlled by the British from 1840 and the 19th century also achieved the acquisition of Hong Kong (1841) and Burma (1886).

The colonies were supervised from 1801 by the Colonial Office, and were generally (*compare* crown colony) self-governing. In the mid-19th century, the self-governing colonies in Canada, Australia, New Zealand, and South Africa received responsible government, whereby governors were advised by local ministers. In 1907 Canada, Australia, and New Zealand (and in 1910 South Africa), by now federated, were termed dominions. In 1931 the Commonwealth of Nations was established, giving the dominions autonomy, and in the following decades Britain's other colonies gradually achieved full independence.

Empire style The neoclassical style in the decorative arts developing during the Napoleonic empire (1804–14). It was inspired by classical Greek, Roman, and Egyptian models and reflected contemporary interest in archaeology (e.g. Pompeii). Dark woods, such as rosewood, were favoured, sparsely ornamented with ormolu. Shapes tended to be plain but caryatids were used as supports. The grandiose **Second Empire style** was the official architectural style of the French Government under Emperor Napoleon III (1852–70).

Employment Training. *See* Training Agency.

Empson, Sir William (1906–84) British poet and critic, author of *Seven Types of Ambiguity* (1930). His poetry was published in *Poems* (1935) and *The Gathering Storm* (1940).

EMS. *See* European Monetary System.

emu A large flightless long-legged Australian bird, *Dromaius novaehollandiae*, found in open plains and forests. It has a dark-brown hairlike plumage with a naked blue spot on each side of the neck, and can run at high speeds.

emulsion. *See* colloid.

enamel A glaze that is fused onto the surface of metal. Enamelled gold jewellery dating back to the 13th century BC has been found, and various methods of enamelling have developed since then. Generally, a clear flux made from melted sand, soda potash, and red lead is stained with a metal oxide and left to harden. The resultant enamel cakes are ground and spread on the metal object, which is then placed in a furnace to fuse the enamel with the metal. Painted enamels are applied after the ground enamel has been fired and are not, therefore, true enamels. Painted enamelwork is particularly associated with Limoges (15th and 16th centuries) and England (18th century).

encephalins (*or* enkephalins) Short peptide molecules, found in parts of the brain and spinal cord, that are thought to relieve pain. These and similar compounds are called **endorphins**. In the spinal cord encephalins are believed to inhibit painful sensations by reacting with specific receptor sites on the sensory nerve endings. In the brain their function is less certain but may be associated with mood. The pain-relieving effects of acupuncture may be due to the release of the body's encephalins.

encephalitis Inflammation of the brain. It usually occurs as a result of a virus infection, but can be caused by malaria, fungi, or parasites (rarely by bacteria). The patient is often drowsy and fevered and has a bad headache. There is no specific treatment for viral encephalitis but the patient usually recovers.

Encke's comet A comet that has a period of only 3.3 years (decreasing by 2.5 hours/revolution) and has been very closely studied during its numerous apparitions. Its period was first established by the German astronomer J. F. Encke (1791–1865).

encyclical, papal A decree of the pope addressed to the whole Roman Catholic Church. *Humanae Vitae* (1968), for example, was issued by Paul VI and expressed the teaching of the Church on contraception.

Encyclopedists The French intellectuals who contributed to Diderot's monumental *Encyclopédie*, published in 28 volumes between 1751 and 1772. Five more volumes were published in 1776–77. Over 200 scholarly experts, including such leading figures of the Enlightenment as Voltaire and Rousseau, contributed articles. By their appeal to reason rather than faith the Encyclopedists threatened the authority of church and state.

endangered species A plant or animal species that is in danger of extinction. Some 25 000 plant species and 4500 animal species are currently endangered, mostly through destruction of natural habitats, pollution, and hunting and trapping. During the 20th century the number of endangered species has grown dramatically, and in 1948 the International Union for the Conservation of Nature and Natural Resources (IUCN) was founded to devise measures to protect them. The IUCN publishes the Red Data Book, which lists all known endangered species. Trade in endangered species is regulated by CITES – the Convention on International Trade in Endangered Species. This has been signed by 96 countries, including the UK. *See also* World Wide Fund for Nature.

chimpanzee	Mediterranean monk seal
mountain gorilla	†peregrine falcon
Spanish lynx	Californian condor
†European otter	leatherback turtle
black rhinoceros	green turtle
Indian elephant	Nile crocodile
Père David's deer	Chinese alligator
golden marmoset	common sturgeon
blue whale	longhorn beetle
dugong	large copper butterfly

†Endangered in the UK and protected under the Wildlife and Countryside Act (1981).

ENDANGERED SPECIES *Some animal examples.*

endive An annual or biennial plant, *Cichorium endivia*, probably native to S Asia and N China and cultivated widely. It has a rosette of shiny leaves, either curled and narrow (var. *crispa*), used for salads, or broad (*latifolia*), used for cooking. Family: *Compositae*. *See also* chicory.

endocrine glands Ductless glands that produce and secrete hormones into the bloodstream. Most are regulated by hormones from the pituitary gland, which is itself controlled by neurohormones secreted by the hypothalamus. Other endocrine glands include the thyroid, adrenal, and parathyroid glands, parts of the pancreas (the islets of Langerhans), and the ovaries and testes. The study of the endocrine glands in health and disease is called **endocrinology**.

endorphins. *See* encephalins.

Endymion In Greek legend, a beautiful youth who was put into an everlasting sleep by Selene, goddess of the moon, so that she could enjoy his beauty forever.

ENERGY *Primary sources (1988) : (a) UK; (b) World.*

energy A property of a system that enables it to do work, i.e. to move the point of application of a force. The several forms of energy can be converted into each other under appropriate conditions. Kinetic energy is energy of motion, whereas potential energy is stored energy, for example the energy stored in a body by virtue of its position in a gravitational or electric field. Other forms of energy include heat (the kinetic energy of the atoms and molecules in a body), chemical energy (the potential energy stored in the chemical bonds between atoms in a substance), nuclear energy (the potential energy stored in the atomic nucleus), and radiant energy (the energy associated with electromagnetic waves). As a consequence of the special theory of relativity, mass has also to be regarded as a form of energy. Energy is measured in joules (SI units), calories or ergs (c.g.s. units), kilowatt-hours or British thermal units (Imperial units).

Energy sources: the combustion of wood and fossil fuels (asphalt, coal, oil, natural gas) is a process, long known to man, in which chemical energy is converted into heat energy. The industrial revolution and the later advent of motorized transport brought explosive increases in the demand for energy and consequently for fossil fuels. These demands have steadily increased during the 20th century. There is now great concern over the extent of the remaining reserves of fossil fuels. Nuclear fission reactors (*see* nuclear energy), a source independent of fossil fuels, now provide some 7% of the world's energy needs and alternative energy sources are being explored. Thermonuclear reactors may be the main energy source in the next century.

energy band A concept used to explain the electrical properties of solids, particularly semiconductors. It is a band of allowed energies for electrons in a solid. The distribution of the bands in a solid determines the conducting properties of the solid.

Engels, Friedrich (1820–95) German socialist and chief collaborator of Karl Marx. He was able to introduce Marx to English economic conditions and the British working-class movement. Among other works he wrote the *Condition of the Working Class in England in 1844* (1845). After Marx's death, he edited the last volume of *Das Kapital* (1885).

engineering The systematic application of scientific knowledge to the design, creation, and use of structures and machines. Civil engineering arose from the study and design of such static structures as bridges, dams, buildings, etc., whereas mechanical engineering is concerned with dynamical systems, such as machinery and engines. Other important branches of engineering are electrical engineering, aeronautical engineering, and chemical engineering.

England The largest political division in the United Kingdom. With Wales to the W and Scotland to the N, it is separated from the mainland of Europe by the North Sea and the English Channel and from Ireland by the Irish Sea. It consists of two main zones: the lowlands, which extend across the Midlands, the SE, East Anglia, and the Fens, and the highlands of the Pennines and the Lake District in the N and the granite uplands of Dartmoor and Exmoor in the SW. The chief rivers are the Thames and the Severn. The centre of government and administration of the UK, England is also the wealthiest and most populous of the UK countries. *Economy*: the development of industry has been a major contributor to England's wealth. The recent exploitation of North Sea oil and gas continues to make an important contribution to the economy. The main English coalfields are situated in the East Midlands, Yorkshire, and Northumberland and Durham. Despite the expansion of industries based on advanced technology, together with the reorganization and modernization of older industries, the decline of heavy industry (including shipbuilding), traditionally concentrated in the North and Merseyside, has led to high levels of unemployment in these areas. Agriculture has increased in productivity. Dairy farming is dominant in the W, while livestock rearing (especially sheep and cattle) is important in the hilly areas of the N and SW. The major crops, mainly from the E and SE, are cereals, potatoes, and sugar beet. *History*: there is much archaeological evidence of prehistoric settlement in England but historical records begin with the Roman occupation, from 43 AD until the early 5th century. Christianity was introduced in the 4th century, and conquests between the 3rd and 7th centuries by Angles, Saxons, and Jutes led to the establishment of independent kingdoms (*see* Mercia; Northumbria; Wessex), which were united in the 9th century under the leadership of Wessex. By the late 800s the Danes had established themselves in the area that came to be known as the Danelaw and from 1016 to 1042 the English were ruled successively by the Danish kings Canute and Hardecanute. The Norman conquest (1066) ended the Anglo-Saxon period of English history and established a new dynasty of Norman kings. In 1455 the rival claims of the Houses of Lancaster and York precipitated the Wars of the Roses, which lasted until Richard III's defeat at Bosworth (1485) by Henry Tudor. The 16th century saw the establishment of Protestantism in England (*see* Reformation), the formal union of England and Wales (*see* Union, Acts· of), and, under Elizabeth I, a significant development·in overseas exploration and trade. The Tudors were succeeded by the Stuarts in 1603, when James VI of Scotland ascended the English throne as James I. The unpopularity of James and his son Charles I, especially with parliament, brought about the Civil War, which ended with Charles' execution (1649) and the establishment of republican government. The Stuart Restoration (1660) followed the fall of Oliver Crom-

well's Protectorate but the authoritarian and pro-Catholic policies of James II brought about his deposition in 1688 and the succession of William of Orange and his Stuart wife Mary. The crisis of the Glorious Revolution saw the emergence of the rival political groups known as Whigs (later Liberals) and Tories. The Tories' association with the Jacobites, who in 1714 threatened the Hanoverian succession (*see* Settlement, Act of), led to their political isolation. The 18th century saw union with Scotland (1707) and the loss of the American colonies (1783; *see* American Revolution). Following union with Ireland in 1801, England, Wales, Scotland, and Ireland became the United Kingdom of Great Britain and Ireland. With the industrial revolution the UK evolved from an agricultural to an industrial economy; during the long reign of Victoria there was agitation for an extension of the franchise (*see* Reform Acts) and a shift in political influence from the landowners to the urban middle class. The growing power of the trade unions led to the formation in 1900 of the Labour Party. The 19th century also saw the heyday of the British Empire and the beginning of colonial rivalry with Germany, which was a significant factor in the outbreak of World War I. The interwar years were dominated by the Depression and the growing threat of fascism, which culminated in World War II. 1945 saw the return of a Labour government, which began a programme of nationalization. From 1951 to 1964 government was in the hands of the Conservatives but Labour was then returned (until 1970 and then again from 1974 to 1979). From 1979 the Conservative government of Margaret Thatcher presided over extensive privatization and an economic recovery. Successive governments have failed to deal with the crisis in Northern Ireland. Area: 130 360 sq km (50 332 sq mi). Population (1986 est): 47 254 500. Capital: London.

English A West Germanic language spoken originally in Britain but now also in the USA, Canada, New Zealand, Australia, and many other parts of the world. It is the world's most widely known and used language. Its history may be divided into three periods. In the Old English period (c. 450–1100 AD), four dialects were spoken: Northumbrian, Mercian, Kentish, and West Saxon. The last became the standard form. Middle English refers to the period from 1100 to 1500, when five dialects were spoken: Northern (developed from Northumbrian), West and East Midlands (diverging from Mercian), South Western (from West Saxon) and South Eastern (from Kentish). Each developed in characteristic ways but in general the influence of French after the Norman conquest brought new vocabulary and sound patterns. Modern English covers the period from 1500 and was much influenced by the speech of London. Its vocabulary is about half Germanic and half Romance with many other borrowings.

English Channel (French name: La Manche) An arm of the Atlantic Ocean in NW Europe, between England and France. It is one of the busiest shipping lanes in the world. *See also* Channel tunnel.

English National Opera (ENO) The name adopted by the Sadler's Wells Opera Company in 1974, five years after the company moved from the Sadler's Wells Theatre to the London Coliseum. The company presents most of its operas in English. Its musical directors have included Sir Charles Mackerras (1970–78), Sir Charles Groves (1978–79), and Mark Elder (director 1979–   ).

ENGRAVING   *Detail of Dürer's* St Jerome in his Study.

engraving   A method of producing a reproductive plate by chiselling, carving, or biting the design onto a metal or wood plate. Intaglio engraving denotes such methods as etching, mezzotint, and soft- or hard-ground engraving, in which the printed impression pulls ink from inside the carved grooves. By contrast, relief engraving denotes methods, such as woodcut, in which the carved-away areas are not inked. Intaglio engraving allows for extreme delicacy and detail; relief engraving is often exploited for illustrations, where force and clarity are needed.

Enlightenment (*or* Age of Reason)   An 18th-century philosophical movement that sought to replace orthodox authoritarian beliefs with rational scientific inquiry. During the 17th century, as scientific knowledge increased, such scholars as Newton, Locke, Pascal, and Descartes questioned accepted beliefs, and criticism of established society and assumptions spread throughout Europe. In France the Philosophes (e.g. Voltaire) attacked established religion and the Enlightenment beliefs in individual liberty and equality were embodied in the work of Voltaire, Rousseau, and other Encyclopedists. The movement came to an end with the French Revolution.

entellus.   *See* langur.

entomology   The study of insects. Modern entomology dates from the 17th century, when the introduction of microscopy enabled fine details of insect anatomy to be described. Attention is now focused on insect pests, since knowledge of them is of prime importance in their control.

entropy   A measure of the disorder of a system, used in thermodynamics. Thus a solid has less entropy than a liquid since the constituent particles in a solid are in a more ordered state. The change in entropy of a reversible system is equal to the energy absorbed by the system divided by the thermodynamic temperature at which the change takes place. The entropy of a closed system never decreases during a thermodynamic process.

enzymes   A group of proteins that act as biological catalysts, i.e. they speed up (or slow down) the rate of chemical reactions in living organisms. Enzymes are manufactured by cells according to the genetic code carried by the chromosomes; because each enzyme cataly-

ses a specific reaction, it is the enzymes that determine the function of the cell. Control of metabolism is largely exerted through regulation of enzyme production and activity.

Eocene epoch.   *See* Tertiary period.

eohippus   An extinct (Eocene) ancestor of the horse. About 28 cm tall, it was a browsing forest dweller and had four toes on the forefoot and three on the hindfoot.

ephemeris (Greek: diary)   A reference manual, usually published annually, that is used in astronomical observation and navigation. It lists the predicted positions of the sun, moon, and planets in the forthcoming year and also gives times of eclipses, stellar positions, and other similar information.

Ephesians, Epistle of Paul to the   A New Testament book that originated as a circular letter from the Apostle Paul to churches in Asia Minor. Written about 60 AD, it deals with a number of religious and moral points and stresses the equality of Jewish and Gentile Christians.

Ephesus   An ancient Greek city and trading centre on the Ionian coast of Asia Minor. It maintained its prosperity under the Persians and Alexander the Great and in Roman times was rivalled only by Alexandria as a commercial centre. It was sacked by the Goths in 262 AD. *See also* Artemis, Temple of.

Epicureanism   A school of philosophy founded by Epicurus around 300 BC in Athens. He taught that the highest good was pleasure and the avoidance of pain, based on tranquillity of mind and conscience. Many seeking a licence for the pursuit of pleasure have styled themselves Epicureans.

Epicurus   (341–270 BC)   Greek philosopher and founder of the school of Epicureanism. His surviving works are few and fragmentary but his philosophy, especially his atomism, was expounded by Lucretius.

EPIDAURUS   *The theatre, built in the 4th century* BC, *is still in use.*

Epidaurus   A city state of ancient Greece, situated across the Saronic Gulf from Athens. Its sanctuary of Asclepius was famous in antiquity for its medical cures. The 4th-century BC theatre (part of the temple complex) is sufficiently preserved to be still used for plays.

epidemiology   The science that investigates the incidence and causative factors of diseases that are associated with a particular environment or way of life. Epidemiologists have enlarged their studies from the classical epidemics of communicable diseases, such as smallpox and cholera, to include noncommunicable diseases, such as cancer.

epidermis The outermost layer of cells in animals and plants. In higher animals (including mammals) it forms the outer layer of the skin.

epididymis. *See* testis.

epidural. *See* anaesthesia.

epiglottis A leaf-shaped flap of cartilage at the root of the tongue that prevents food and fluid from entering the windpipe during swallowing.

epilepsy A disease characterized by fits or sudden loss of consciousness: sufferers include Dostoievski, Van Gogh, Julius Caesar, and Byron. In grand mal epilepsy the patient suddenly becomes stiff, loses consciousness, and has convulsions for a few minutes. Petit mal is a mild form seen only in children, who suddenly lose consciousness for a few seconds but usually do not fall down. All forms are treated with anticonvulsant drugs.

epinephrine. *See* adrenaline.

Epiphany (*or* Twelfth Day) A Christian feast celebrated on 6 Jan. In Eastern Orthodox Churches it commemorates the baptism of Jesus. Introduced to the West in the 4th century, it developed as a celebration of the coming of the Magi to Bethlehem, representing the manifestation (Greek: *epiphaneia*) of Christ to the Gentiles. **Twelfth Night** is the night preceding Epiphany and traditionally devoted to festivities and entertainments.

epiphyte A plant that grows on another plant for support. Epiphytes are not parasites: some obtain nourishment from decaying plant remains and many solve the problem of obtaining water by developing such structures as aerial roots.

epistemology The philosophical discipline that considers the nature, basis, and limits of knowledge. It is one of the three main branches of modern philosophy and is considered fundamental to all philosophical and scientific enquiry.

Epistles The 21 books of the New Testament that were written as letters, mostly by Paul (13). The remainder are attributed to James, Peter (2), John (3), Jude, and an unknown author. In the liturgy of many Christian Churches, the Epistle is the name of the first of two passages of Scripture (usually taken from the New Testament Epistles) recited at the celebration of the Eucharist, the second being the Gospel.

epoch. *See* geological time scale.

epoxy resin A type of synthetic resin containing the –O– atom (epoxy group). They are viscous liquids but set to hard clear solids on the addition of curing agents. Epoxy resins are extensively used as adhesives, the resin and the curing agent being mixed immediately before use.

Epstein, Sir Jacob (1880–1959) British sculptor of US birth. Working in London after 1905, he achieved notoriety with some of his sculptures. After 1912 he briefly experimented with avantgarde sculpture and continued to provoke public criticism with such sculptures as *Genesis* (1931). However, his bronze portrait busts of Einstein (1933), T. S. Eliot, and Vaughan Williams (1950) were more favourably received. His last works included *Christ in Majesty* (1957) for Llandaff Ca-

EPSTEIN   *Plaster cast of a bust of T. S. Eliot.*

thedral and *St Michael and the Devil* (1958) for Coventry Cathedral.

equator The great circle around the earth at latitude 0°, lying midway between the poles in a plane at right angles to the earth's axis. It is 40 076 km (24 902 mi) long and divides the N from the S hemisphere.

Equatorial Guinea, Republic of A small country in W central Africa, on the Gulf of Guinea. It consists of two main parts: mainland Río Muni and the island of Bioko (formerly Macías Nguema), as well as the island of Pagalu (formerly Annobón) to the SW and several smaller islands. The inhabitants are mainly Fang, Fernandinos, and the indigenous Bubi (descendants of slaves from West Africa), who inhabit Bioko. *Economy*: chiefly agricultural. *History*: formerly a Spanish colony, the area became two Spanish provinces in 1959 and gained independence in 1968. In 1975 expulsion of Nigerian immigrant workers had an adverse effect on the economy. In 1979 the life president Francisco Macías Nguema (1924–79) was overthrown and executed in a coup led by Lt Col Teodoro Obiang Nguema Mbasogo. Official language: Spanish. Official currency: CFA (Communauté financière africaine) franc of 100 centimes. Area: 28 051 sq km (10 831 sq mi). Population (1987 est): 384 000. Capital and main port: Malabo.

equinox Either of the two points at which the ecliptic intersects the celestial equator (*see* celestial sphere). The ecliptic represents the apparent annual path of the sun around the celestial sphere. The sun crosses the celestial equator from S to N at the **vernal** (*or* spring) **equinox**, usually on 21 March. It crosses from N to S at the **autumnal equinox**, usually on 23 Sept. At the equinoxes night and day are of almost equal duration.

equity In law, the body of rules developed by the Court of Chancery to achieve a fair result in cases in which the application of common law would fail to do so. The rules of equity developed separately from but by the same method (judicial precedent) as the common law. The two systems were amalgamated in 1875 with the establishment of the High Court of Justice. Now all courts administer both law and equity, the rules of equity prevailing if in conflict with the common law. *See also* courts of law.

era. *See* geological time scale.

Erasmus, Desiderius (1466–1536) Christian humanist and writer, born at Rotterdam. A highly influential Renaissance thinker, he studied and taught all over Europe. He produced many original works and compilations, including *Encomium Moriae* (*Praise of Folly*; 1509), written for Thomas More. He also produced the first translation of the Greek New Testament.

erbium (Er) A lanthanide element that forms an oxide (Eb_2O_3) and halides (e.g. $EbCl_3$). It is added to phosphors, glasses, and alloys. At no 68; at wt 167.26; mp 1529°C; bp 2510°C.

Erevan. *See* Yerevan.

Erfurt 50 59N 11 00E A city in SW East Germany, on the River Gera. One of the oldest German cities, it became a member of the Hanseatic League in the 15th century and was of great commercial importance in the 16th century. Population (1986): 216 646.

erg The unit of energy in the c.g.s. system equal to the work done when a force of one dyne acts through a distance of one centimetre. 1 erg = 10^{-7} joule.

ergocalciferol. *See* vitamin D.

ergonomics The study of the psychological and physical factors that can be used to improve the design of both machines and systems for human use.

ergot A disease caused by the fungus *Claviceps purpurea*, which affects cereals and grasses, especially rye. In affected plants a hard black fungal body develops in place of the grain. Consumption of bread made with diseased grain produces the symptoms of **ergotism**: gangrene of the fingers and toes or convulsions.

Erica. *See* heath.

Erie, Lake The fourth largest of the Great Lakes in North America, between Canada and the USA. Linked with Lake Ontario via the Welland Ship Canal, it forms part of the St Lawrence Seaway system. It is closed to navigation during winter due to freezing. Area: 25 718 sq km (9930 sq mi).

Erinyes In Greek legend, three spirits of vengeance who lived in the underworld and ruthlessly pursued all evildoers. In Roman legend they were known as the Furies.

Eris A Greek goddess personifying strife. She threw a golden apple inscribed "To the Fairest" among the gods. Aphrodite, Hera, and Athena each claimed the apple. Paris, who had to decide, chose Aphrodite because she offered him in return the most beautiful woman as his wife. This myth, the Judgment of Paris, explains the origin of the Trojan War.

Eritrea A province in Ethiopia, bordering on the Red Sea. It consists of a narrow coastal plain rising inland to the Ethiopian plateau. Locusts and water shortage limit agricultural production. Its integration with Ethiopia in 1962 gave rise to political discontent. During the 1970s this developed into a bloody civil war, which continued into the 1980s, between the rebels and the Ethiopian government.

ERNIE. *See* premium bond.

Ernst, Max (1891–1976) German artist. He was a founder in 1919 of the Cologne dada movement. He excelled in collage, particularly of cut-out illustrations, and became a leading practitioner of surrealism in Paris. In 1941 he moved to the USA.

Eros (mythology) The Greek god of love, the son of Aphrodite by Zeus, Hermes, or Ares. He was usually portrayed as a winged youth armed with bow and arrows. He was identified with the Roman Cupid.

Erse. *See* Gaelic.

erythrocyte (*or* red blood cell) A disc-shaped blood cell, about 0.007 mm in diameter, that lacks a nucleus and contains haemoglobin, which combines reversibly with oxygen and is the means by which blood transports oxygen from the lungs to the tissues. A deficiency of red blood cells (below about 4.5 million per mm^3 of blood) or haemoglobin is called anaemia.

escape velocity The initial velocity required by a projectile to enable it, without any further source of power, to escape from the gravitational field of a celestial body. It depends on the mass and diameter of the celestial body. For the earth the escape velocity is 11 200 metres per second.

Escaut, River. *See* Scheldt, River.

eschatology (Greek *eschatos*: last) The part of Christian theology concerned with the last things, often summarized as death, judgment, heaven, and hell. It refers to the ultimate fate of both the individual and of human society. Eschatological writing in Old and New Testaments is linked with the expectation of a coming Messiah.

Escoffier, Auguste (1846–1935) French chef. He gained an international reputation while supervising the kitchens at the Savoy and the Carlton hotels in London.

Escorial, El A royal palace, mausoleum, and monastery near Madrid. Built for Philip II between 1563 and 1584, it is an austere, square, granite building. It houses a magnificent collection of books and paintings.

Esdras, Books of Two books of the Apocrypha purporting to be by Ezra.

Esfahan. *See* Isfahan.

Eskimo A Mongoloid people of the Arctic region of North America and Greenland. The men are traditionally hunters of seals, whales, walrus, and caribou, using harpoons. Fishing is also important. Their clothes are made of animal skins. Some construct semisubterranean sod shelters or use snow-covered skin tents, others use igloos.

Eskimo-Aleut languages A language group, sometimes included in the classification of American Indian languages. It consists of two distinct languages: Eskimo, spoken in Greenland and in many dialects along the N coast of Canada, and Aleut, spoken in the Aleutian Islands.

ESP. *See* extrasensory perception.

Esperanto An artificial language invented by a Polish philologist, L. L. Zamenhof (1859–1917), in 1887. Intended as a universal medium of communication, it is spoken by over 100 000 people. Grammatically it is entirely regular, its pronunciation is consistent with its spelling, and as well as grammatical rules it has the potential for the formation of new words.

Essen 51 27N 6 57E A city in W West Germany, in North Rhine-Westphalia near the River Ruhr. It has a 9th-century cathedral. It is the administrative centre of the Ruhr. Population (1986): 617 700.

Essenes An ancient Jewish sect active between the 2nd century BC and the 2nd century AD in Palestine. The Dead Sea Scrolls may be relics of an Essene community. *See* Qumran.

essential oils Substances with a characteristic scent produced by the glands of aromatic plants. They are used in perfumes, food flavourings, and medicines. Examples include attar of roses, lavender oil, and clove oil.

Essex A county of E England, bordering on the North Sea and Greater London. It is mainly low lying rising gently towards the chalk uplands of the NW. Agriculture is important. Industry is located mainly in the SW. Southend-on-Sea and Clacton are coastal resorts and Harwich is a major ferry port. Area: 3674 sq km (1419 sq mi). Population (1986 est): 1 512 100. Administrative centre: Chelmsford.

Essex, Robert Devereux, 2nd Earl of (?1566–1601) English soldier and courtier to Elizabeth I. He was appointed Master of the Horse (1587) after distinguishing himself against Spain. He commanded an expedition (1591–92) sent to aid Henry IV of France and in 1593 became a privy councillor; he took part in the sack of Cádiz (1596). He was dismissed (1600) after failing to suppress an Irish rebellion and in 1601 raised a riot in London, for which he was executed.

estate An interest in land, which in England may be held in one of two ways: (1) freehold tenure, in which the right over land (all of which belongs to the Crown) is for a period that is neither fixed nor liable to determination by another and for the use of which no payment in kind or money is due to another, except for such taxes as rates; (2) leasehold tenure, in which a tenant holds an estate from a landlord for a fixed period.

VILLA D'ESTE *Tivoli (near Rome).*

Este An Italian princely family of Lombard origin, which under **Obizzo II** (1264–93) gained control of Ferrara, Modena, and Reggio. His successors maintained control of these three regions in spite of papal opposition and were a dominant force in Italian Renaissance politics and culture until Ferrara was incorporated into the papal states in 1598. The **Villa d'Este**, at Tivoli, near Rome, was designed (1550) for Cardinal Ippolito II d'Este (1509–72).

esters Organic compounds produced by the reaction of an alcohol with an acid, with the elimination of water. Common organic esters are formed from carboxylic acids and have the general formula R.CO.OR'. The lighter ones often have a pleasant smell and taste and are widely used in perfumes and flavourings.

Esther An Old Testament woman who became the queen of the Persian King Ahasuerus. **The Book of Esther** recounts how Esther used her influence to frustrate a plot to massacre Persian Jews, commemorated in the Jewish feast of Purim.

Estonian A language of the Baltic-Finnic branch of the Finno-Ugric division of the Uralic language family. It is spoken by the Estonians and is related to Finnish.

Estonian Soviet Socialist Republic (*or* Estonia) A constituent republic in the NW Soviet Union. Estonia has many lakes and includes numerous islands in the Baltic Sea. Some 70% of the population are Estonians. Estonia was ceded to Russia in 1721. Rebellions in the 19th century culminated in a declaration of independence (1918), which was recognized by Soviet Russia in 1920. It was assigned to the Soviet Union by the Nazi-Soviet Pact (1939) and became an SSR in 1940. It was occupied by Germany in World War II. Its status is not accepted by the USA. The independence movement grew stronger in the 1980s. Area: 45 100 sq km (17 410 sq mi). Population (1987): 1 556 000. Capital: Tallinn.

etching A method of making prints from a metal plate covered with an acid-resistant ground, on which a design is drawn with a needle. The plate is then placed in acid, the exposed lines being eaten away. These recessed lines retain ink and the design is transferred to paper.

ethane (C_2H_6) A colourless gas, the second member of the alkane series. It occurs in natural gas.

ethanol (*or* ethyl alcohol; C_2H_5OH) A colourless flammable liquid that is the active constituent of alcoholic drinks. It is prepared by fermentation or by the catalytic hydration of ethylene. It is used as a solvent, a raw material for producing other chemicals, and a fuel.

Ethelbert (c. 552–616 AD) King of Kent, who became overlord of all England south of the Humber. Encouraging the conversion of his people to Christianity, he received Augustine's mission from Rome. He wrote the first extant English code of laws.

Ethelred I (d. 871 AD) King of England (866–71), in whose reign the Vikings launched a full-scale invasion of England. Ethelred died after his victory at Ashdown, leaving his brother Alfred the Great to fight on.

Ethelred the Unready (968–1016) King of England (978–1016). In the face of Danish raids, he was forced to pay huge tributes (Danegeld) to the enemy. He was driven into exile by King Sweyn of Denmark in 1013 but returned after Sweyn's death (1014).

ether Any member of the group of organic compounds with the general formula R–O–R', which are formed by the condensation of two alcohols. Diethyl ether, $C_2H_5OC_2H_5$, often known simply as ether, is a volatile liquid and is used as an anaesthetic and solvent.

ethics The science of morality, also called moral philosophy. It is one of the three main branches of modern philosophy and seeks to discover a consistent principle by which human actions and character can be judged. Until about a century ago, ethics aimed to guide men's conduct. Now it is more descriptive, attempting to discover how moral decisions are actually made. In utilitarianism the good of society is the criterion and this is the implicit basis of present-day commercial, legal, and social ethics, but conscience remains the guide of most individuals. *See also* hedonism; rationalism.

Ethiopia, People's Democratic Republic of (former name: Abyssinia) A country in NE Africa, on the Red Sea. It consists of deserts in the SE and NE and a central plateau, crossed by river valleys (including that of the

Blue Nile) and by mountain ranges. The population consists of many ethnic groups, including the Galla and Amhara. *Economy*: Ethiopia remains one of the poorest countries in the world and agriculture is chiefly at subsistence level. The situation has been worsened in recent years by serious crop failures, causing famines. All land was nationalized in 1975 and much of it is now farmed cooperatively. *History*: Ethiopia has a long history, legend claiming the descent of its rulers from Solomon and the Queen of Sheba. From the 2nd to the 9th century AD there was considerable prosperity and expansion; in the 4th century Ethiopia became the first Christian country in Africa. This period was followed by centuries of struggles (especially with the Muslims) and of internal divisions. Only in the 19th century was the country reunited. In 1896 Italian attempts to conquer Ethiopia were defeated but in 1935 Italy (under Mussolini) invaded. In 1936 Addis Ababa fell and the emperor, Haile Selassie, fled to England. Ethiopia then formed part of Italian East Africa (with Eritrea and Italian Somaliland). In 1941 the Allies liberated Ethiopia and Haile Selassie returned to the throne. Eritrea again became part of Ethiopia, becoming fully integrated in 1962. Haile Selassie was deposed in 1974 and a provisional military government came to power. After the execution of members of the ruling military council in 1977, the government became known as the Derg (Provisional Military Administrative Council) with Mengistu Haile Mariam (1937–) as president. During this unsettled period liberation movements in Eritrea and the Somali-speaking Ogaden area increased their armed struggle against the government. By the end of 1977 Somali troops had occupied most of the Ogaden region but with Soviet and Cuban help, Ethiopia regained control of the area. A government offensive against Eritrean secessionists in 1978 was successful but a similar offensive in 1982 resulted in heavy Derg losses. Droughts affecting the whole Horn of Africa in 1982, 1984, 1987, and 1989 led to famine and forced resettlement from the N to the fertile west. Massive foreign aid was hampered by internal strife and disorganization. *See also* Falashas. Official language: Amharic; English is widely spoken. Official religion: Ethiopian Orthodox (Coptic). Official currency: birr of 100 cents. Area: 1 000 000 sq km (386 000 sq mi). Population (1986 est): 46 000 000. Capital: Addis Ababa. Main port: Massawa.

ethnology   The comparative study and theory of contemporary cultures. In most current usages it is synonymous with cultural anthropology. Ethnography is the descriptive study of culture.

ethology   The study of animal behaviour, founded in Europe in the 1930s by the work of Konrad Lorenz and Niko Tinbergen (1907–), who studied animals in their natural states. Ethologists are concerned with how animals respond to signals or stimuli (whether from other animals, from their own bodies, or from the environment in which they live), how they sense these signals, and what their response means to other animals and to themselves. They demonstrate the interactions between the inherited (instinctive) aspects of behaviour and those determined by experience (learning).

ethyl alcohol.   *See* ethanol.

ethylene (*or* ethene; C_2H_4)   A colourless flammable gaseous alkene. It is made by cracking petroleum and is used to make polythene (polyethylene).

Etna, Mount   37 45N 15 00E A volcano in E Sicily. The first recorded eruption was in 476 BC and significant eruptions this century have occurred in 1928, 1949, and 1971. Height: 3263 m (10 705 ft).

Eton   51 31 N 0 37 W A town in SE England, in Berkshire opposite Windsor on the River Thames. Eton College, the famous public school, was founded by Henry VI in 1440. Population (1983 est): 3473.

ETRUSCANS   *Fresco from an Etruscan tomb showing two wrestlers.*

Etruscans   The ancient inhabitants of Etruria (now Tuscany) in central Italy N of Rome. From the 8th to the 5th centuries BC their cities, forming a loose political confederacy, dominated their neighbours but after 396 they were rapidly absorbed by the Romans. The Etruscans had extensive trading links. Their origins are mysterious. Their language was non-Indo-European but is still untranslated.

etymology   The study of the history of words, in which words are traced back to their earliest recorded forms, or even beyond these to hypothetical reconstructed forms. Most English words are derived either from Proto-Germanic (*see* Germanic languages) or from Latin and French. Many learned English words were taken from Greek or made up from Greek elements, while in the past 200 years English has come to borrow words from languages in every part of the world.

Eucalyptus   A genus of tropical and subtropical evergreen trees (about 600 species) native to Australia but widely cultivated elsewhere. Eucalypts–also known as gum trees–are among the tallest trees in the world, 90– 100 m high. The blue-grey bark is smooth and often peeling and the mature leaves are long and narrow. Fast-growing and drought-resistant, eucalypts are important sources of timber. The best known species are the blue gum and the red gum. All parts of the trees contain essential oils. Family: *Myrtaceae* (myrtle family).

Eucharist (Greek *eucharistia*: thanksgiving)   The chief sacrament and central act of worship of the Christian Churches. Also known as Holy Communion, the Lord's Supper, and the Mass, its institution is described in the three Synoptic Gospels. At the last meal of Christ and the apostles, bread and wine were blessed by Christ and shared, representing his death on the cross and the subsequent redemption of mankind.

Euclid (c. 300 BC) Greek mathematician, famous for his book entitled *Elements* in which he derived all that was known of geometry from a few simple axioms. The geometry that obeys Euclid's axioms is known as Euclidean geometry, all other kinds being called non-Euclidean.

eugenics The science that studies the inheritable factors that determine the physical and mental qualities of the human race, with the aim of improving the quality of life for future generations. It is concerned primarily with the detection and—where possible—elimination of such genetic diseases as Down's syndrome with the aid of prenatal diagnosis.

Eugénie (1826–1920) The influential wife (1853–73) of Napoleon III of France, several times acting as his regent. After the fall of the Empire (1870) she retired to England.

Euglena A genus of single-celled microorganisms found chiefly in fresh water. They are spindle-shaped, with a flexible cell wall and a gullet from which protrudes a long whiplike flagellum, used for locomotion. They are regarded by some authorities as algae and by others as protozoans.

Eulenspiegel, Till A German peasant folk hero, a crafty and often savage joker whose exploits inspired numerous folktales and many literary and musical works, notably the epic poem (1928) by Gerhart Hauptmann (1862–1946) and the tone poem by Richard Strauss.

Eumenides (Greek: the kindly ones) In Greek legend, spirits identical with the Erinyes. After Orestes was acquitted by the Areopagus of his mother's murder, the pursuing Erinyes became known as the Eumenides.

Euonymus A genus of widely distributed trees, shrubs, and woody climbers (176 species), often grown as ornamentals for their attractive foliage and fruits, which are surrounded by a bright-pink or orange fleshy coat. Family: *Celastraceae*.

euphonium Brass instrument with a wide conical bore, a cup-shaped mouthpiece, four valves, and a range of about three and a half octaves above the B flat below middle C.

Euphorbia A worldwide genus of herbs and small trees (1600 species), having clusters of small flowers each surrounded by conspicuous petal-like bracts. The genus includes some ornamental shrubs such as poinsettia. The herbaceous euphorbias are known as spurges. Family: *Euphorbiaceae*.

Euphrates, River A river in SW Asia, rising in E Turkey and flowing SE through Syria into Iraq. 190 km (118 mi) from the Persian Gulf, it joins the River Tigris to form the Shatt al-Arab. It flows past the historic sites of Babylon, Ur, Nippur, and Sippara. Length: 2700 km (1678 mi).

EURATOM. *See* European Atomic Energy Community.

Eureka project A European advanced technology cooperation programme. Originally proposed by the French government as an alternative to the US Strategic Defence Initiative, the project was launched in 1985; its 18 European member-nations aim to find peaceful applications for joint research.

Eureka Stockade (1854) A miners' rebellion in Victoria (Australia) against oppressive government legislation. The miners of Ballarat stockaded themselves into the Eureka goldfield. They were easily routed by government forces and about 25 miners and 5 troopers were killed.

eurhythmics A system of teaching music by developing the student's physical response to rhythm. Devised by Émile Jaques-Dalcroze (1865–1950) in about 1905, it has been used in physical education and ballet and modern dance training.

Euripides (c. 480–406 BC) Greek dramatist, the third (after Aeschylus and Sophocles) of the three major writers of Attic tragedy. Of approximately 90 plays, 19 survive, including the tragedies *Medea* (431), *Hippolytus* (428), *Electra* (415), *The Trojan Women* (415), *The Bacchae* (405), and *Iphigenia at Aulis* (405). His technical innovations included naturalistic dialogue and a diminution of the role of the chorus. He also explored feminine psychology.

Europa (Greek mythology) The daughter of King Agenor of Tyre. Carried to Crete by Zeus in the form of a bull, she bore him three sons: Minos, Rhadamanthus, and Sarpedon.

Europe A continent bordering on the Arctic Ocean (N), the Atlantic Ocean (W), and the Mediterranean Sea (S); the Ural Mountains, the River Ural, and the Caspian Sea form its E boundary. Europe is the second smallest continent but has exerted a disproportionate influence on the rest of the world. Its coastline is much indented with several peninsulas (e.g. Scandinavia, Italy) and offshore islands (e.g. the British Isles, Iceland). A central plain, extending from the Ural Mountains to the Atlantic Ocean and divided by uplands and the English Channel, comprises two-thirds of the continent. It rises in the S to a series of mountain systems (e.g. the Pyrenees, Alps, Apennines, Carpathian Mountains), and in the N to the mountainous region of Scandinavia and Scotland. The chief rivers flow from the Valdai Hills (e.g Volga, Don, Dnieper) or the Alps (e.g. Danube, Rhine, Rhône, Po). Its four **climatic zones** are characterized by mild winters, cool summers, and rain all the year round (NW); mild winters, hot summers, and chiefly spring and autumn rain (Mediterranean); cold winters, warm summers, and chiefly summer rain (Central Europe); and very cold winters (E Europe). **Vegetation zones** comprise, from N to S: tundra; a coniferous forest belt; a deciduous forest belt; and the mainly evergreen and scrub vegetation of the Mediterranean. Steppe and semidesert characterize the SE. Forest once covered some 80% of Europe but intense agriculture since the middle ages and industrialization since the 19th century have reduced it to 30% of the land mass. Europe possesses important mineral resources. Coalfields, especially in the UK, Germany, France, Belgium, and the Soviet Union, continue to be an important source of power, and oil and natural-gas reserves are found in the Soviet Union, Romania, Albania, and beneath the North Sea. Iron-ore deposits are found on a large scale only in the Soviet Union, which also has reserves of nickel, tin, and manganese, but nonmetallic minerals occur widely. Europe's high-density population is concentrated on its industrial regions. Most of the unusually large number of national groups in Europe speak an Indo-European language. The European peoples may be subdivided into racial types (e.g. Nordic, Germanic, Alpine, and Mediterranean) but extensive intermixing has occurred. Christianity, in its various forms, is the dominant religion. Europe's medieval and modern history is that of its diverse nations, conflicts between which culminated in the 20th century in the two World Wars. The postwar period has witnessed a split between the communist countries of E Europe, dominated by the Soviet Union, and the countries of W Europe, which have sought to resolve their rivalries by means of economic and political union (*see* European Community). Area: about 10 400 000 sq km (4 000 000 sq mi). Population (1985): 492 000 000.

European Atomic Energy Community (EUR-ATOM) An international organization founded in 1958 to promote peaceful uses of atomic energy in Europe. In 1967 it merged with the European Coal and Steel Community and the EEC.

European Community (EC) An organization of W European states created—as the European Economic Community (EEC) or Common Market—by the Treaty of Rome (1957) to foster economic cooperation and common development with the eventual aim of economic, and a measure of political, unity. Agreements have been reached on the removal of customs tariffs between members, the setting of a Common Customs Tariff (now the Common External Tariff) for imports from non-member states, and the abolition of barriers to free movement of labour, services, and capital between member states. Remaining trade barriers are to be dropped in 1992. The original six signatories were Belgium, France, Italy, Luxembourg, the Netherlands, and West Germany. In 1973 the UK, Denmark, and the Republic of Ireland became members; Greece joined in 1981 and Spain and Portugal in 1986. In 1985 Greenland left, having attained home rule from Denmark. In 1967 the merger of the European Atomic Energy Community and the European Coal and Steel Community with the EEC was initiated. The Common Agricultural Policy (CAP) was implemented in 1962 (modified in 1968) and the Common Fisheries Policy in 1983. The European Monetary Union aims to achieve full monetary union. European passports were introduced in the UK in 1988. The Commission of the European Communities is in Brussels and consists of one member or two appointed by each member country; its president is elected for a four-year term. The Commission acts as an advisory body to, and is responsible for implementing policy decided upon by, the Council of Ministers. The new Commission formed in 1985 is headed by Jacques Delors (1926–). Also in Brussels, the Council comprises ministers from the governments of the member countries. The heads of government meet triannually as the European Council. The European Parliament at Strasbourg or Luxembourg comments on the Commission's legislative proposals; it must be consulted on the annual budgets and may dismiss the Commission. Members are (since 1979) elected by direct vote in the member countries and sit as political groups in the Parliament.

European Free Trade Association (EFTA) An association of six states (Austria, Finland, Iceland, Norway, Sweden, and Switzerland) founded in 1960 to foster free trade between members. In 1984 free trade was established between the EC and EFTA.

European Monetary System (EMS) A monetary system created by the European Community in 1979 to promote monetary stability in Europe. Participating member states (the UK remains outside the system) limit fluctuations in their exchange rates through the Exchange Rate Mechanism (ERM) and link their currencies to the European Currency Unit (ECU), the value of which is based on a 'basket' of domestic currencies.

European Space Agency (ESA) An organization responsible for Europe's space programme, formed in 1975 from the merger of the European Space Research Organization (founded 1962) and the European Launcher Development Organization. There are at present 11 full-member nations, including the UK. ESA satellites are launched by the ESA launcher **Ariane**, the first successful launching of which took place in 1979.

europium (Eu) A lanthanide element, used in television-tube phosphors. At no 63; at wt 151.96; mp 822°C; bp 1597°C.

Eurydice In Greek legend, a dryad, the wife of Orpheus. She died of a snake bite. Orpheus descended to the underworld to recover her but lost her forever when he

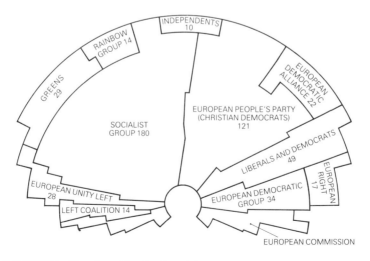

EUROPEAN COMMUNITY   *The plan of the chamber of the European Parliament.*

violated the condition of her release and turned to look at her before emerging.

euthanasia (Greek: easy death) The taking of life to relieve suffering from painful and incurable diseases. It is illegal. Voluntary euthanasia includes both active steps for taking life (e.g. administration of drugs) and the withholding of life-supporting treatment (passive euthanasia). With compulsory euthanasia the patient—for example, a severely deformed baby—is unable to express his own wishes and the responsibility for deciding to terminate life rests on society or a person acting on authority. Many societies exist to promote the cause of voluntary euthanasia.

eutrophication The overfertilization of lakes, due chiefly to pollution by sewage, runoff from the land, and industrial wastes (inorganic nitrates and phosphates). These compounds act as nutrients, stimulating algal growth. The oxygen content in the water is reduced, so killing animals with a high oxygen requirement.

Evans, Sir Arthur John (1851–1941) British archaeologist. His life's work was the excavation in Crete of Knossos (1899–1935). In *The Palace of Minos* (1921–36) he firmly established the chronology and main features of Minoan civilization.

Evans, Dame Edith (1888–1976) British stage and film actress. Her long career included many celebrated performances in Shakespearean roles and in classic comedies such as *The Rivals* and *The Importance of Being Earnest*.

Evelyn, John (1620–1706) English author, best known for his *Diary*, a detailed personal record of the years 1641–1706.

evening primrose A herbaceous plant of the genus *Oenothera* (100 species), 90–100 cm tall, native to the Americas but widespread in Europe. The fragrant yellow flowers open in the evening.

MOUNT EVEREST *Edmund Hillary and Sherpa Tenzing on their way to the summit in 1953.*

Everest, Mount 27 59N 86 56E The highest mountain in the world, on the Nepal–Tibet border in the Himalayas. Climbing attempts started in 1920 and the 12th expedition, led by Col John Hunt (1910–), was the first to succeed: (Sir) Edmund Hillary and Sherpa Tenzing Norgay reached the summit on 29 May, 1953. Height: 8848 m (29 028 ft), established 1955.

evergreen plants Plants the foliage of which is retained throughout the year. The leaves, which are tough and waxy, are produced and shed at different times all the year round, individual leaves often remaining on the tree for several years. Most conifers and many tropical broad-leaved trees are evergreen. **Deciduous plants** produce softer leaves, which are all shed before winter, leaving only the woody parts and protected buds exposed.

Evert, Chris(tine) (1954–) US tennis player who was Wimbledon singles champion in 1974, 1976 and 1981. She won the US singles title 1975–78, 1980, and 1982. She was formerly married to the British tennis player John Lloyd.

evolution In biology, the gradual and continuous process by which the first and most primitive of living organisms have developed into the diversity of plant and animal life known today. Until the 18th century it was generally believed that each group of organisms was separately and divinely created. Work by Linnaeus and Buffon indicated that this was incorrect.
The first theory of evolution was published by Lamarck, in 1809 (*see* Lamarckism). His idea of the inheritance of acquired characteristics lacked definite proof, although it has had its supporters. A more satisfactory theory was put forward by Charles Darwin and A. R. Wallace in 1858: they proposed that new species arose by a process of natural selection acting on individual inheritable variations in a population (*see* Darwinism). Later work has proved that these heritable changes result from spontaneous genetic mutations, and Darwin's theory—with some modifications—is now generally accepted.

Excalibur King Arthur's magic sword. In one legend Arthur succeeds, where others had failed, in drawing it from a stone, thereby proving his claim to the English throne. In another he receives it from the Lady of the Lake, to whom it is thrown back at his death. *See also* Arthurian legend.

excitation In physics, the raising of a system from its lowest energy level (the ground state) to a higher energy level (the excited state). The term is usually confined to atoms, molecules, ions, and nuclei and is most frequently caused by the absorption of a photon. In an atom or ion the photon is absorbed by an electron.

excommunication The exclusion of a Christian from the community of the Church for misconduct. In the early Church, exclusion from the sacraments was frequently used as a means of censure, and in the middle ages the papacy used it to apply political pressure against sovereigns. It is still used by the Roman Catholic Church as a form of discipline.

Exeter 50 43N 3 31W A city in SW England, the administrative centre of Devon on the River Exe. It has a 13th-century cathedral and an ancient Guildhall. Population (1983 est): 101 800.

existentialism A philosophical movement that rejects metaphysics and concentrates on the individual's existence in the world. The forerunner of existentialism was Kierkegaard, whose pragmatic psychologically realistic philosophy of existence was adapted by French intellectuals, especially Sartre, after World War II. Sartre's existentialism allows individuals freedom in a nihilistic universe. But a man is responsible for his effect on others, though only *his* existence is real to him and he is ultimately his own judge.

Exmoor A high moorland and national park of SW England, extending from NE Devon into W Somerset, reaching 520 m (1707 ft) at Dunkery Beacon. It now supports heather, bracken, and grass and is grazed by the small hardy Exmoor ponies, wild red deer, and sheep. Parts are now being ploughed. Area: 686 sq km (265 sq mi).

EXISTENTIALISM *Jean-Paul Sartre, a leading exponent.*

Exodus (Greek: going out) The second book of the Bible, traditionally ascribed to Moses, and probably compiled between the 9th and 4th centuries BC, relating events that may have occured in the 15th century BC. It recounts the events culminating in the departure of the Israelites from Egypt, where they had lived as slaves since the time of Joseph, and their arrival at Mount Sinai, where the Ten Commandments are given to Moses.

exorcism The religious practice of driving out evil spirits by means of prayers and other ritual acts. It is a common rite in a number of religions. In Christianity it refers specifically to the prayers, etc., used to expel evil spirits that supposedly possess a person. Although still available in some Churches, the rite may only be performed by a priest with a bishop's permission.

exosphere. *See* atmosphere.

expanding universe The theory that the universe is expanding was first confirmed by Edwin Hubble (1889–1953) in 1929 following observations that the light from distant galaxies is subject to a redshift, which arises from the recession of the galaxies from us (and from each other). The expansion can be explained by the big-bang theory. *See also* Hubble constant.

explosives Substances that can be made to produce a large volume of gas very suddenly. The energy of the expanding gases may be used for a number of industrial or military purposes. Most explosives used are **chemical explosives**. These include TNT, nitroglycerin, dynamite, and gelignite. Modern high explosives are often in the form of water gels, which are plastic, water resistant, and easy to handle safely. In **nuclear explosives**, there is an almost instantaneous release of nuclear energy, which is used for bombs and occasionally for mining.

exposure meter A device for measuring the intensity of light falling on a photographic camera, used to determine the film exposure time and lens f-number needed to suit the lighting conditions. The aperture and shutter speed can then be set manually or sometimes automatically.

expressionism A movement in modern art covering a variety of schools, the common aim of which was to convey the crude force of human emotion. The chief exponents were Die Brücke and Der Blaue Reiter groups in Germany.

extortion In law, a misdemeanour committed by someone holding a public office who, under the guise of his office, wrongfully takes from another money or any valuable thing not due to him. It was abolished in England by the Theft Act (1968) and is now mainly covered by blackmail.

extrasensory perception (ESP) Acquisition of information not accessible through normal perceptual processes. Three phenomena are usually classified under this heading: clairvoyance (knowledge of distant events and concealed objects), telepathy (thought transference between people), and precognition (knowledge of future events). Evidence for all three tends to be anecdotal.

extrusive rock. *See* igneous rock.

eye The organ of sight. The human eyes lie within two bony sockets in the skull and are attached by six muscles, which produce eye movements. At the front of the eye the white fibrous outer layer (sclera) is replaced by the transparent cornea. A delicate membrane (the conjunctiva) covers the white of the eye and lines the eyelids. Light entering the eye is refracted by the cornea and passes through the watery aqueous humour and pupil to the lens. The pigmented iris controls the amount of light entering the eye. The shape of the lens can be adjusted by means of the ciliary muscles so that an image is focused through the jelly-like vitreous humour onto the retina. Contraction of the ciliary muscles causes the lens to become flattened for focusing distant objects; relaxation of the muscles increases the curvature of the lens for focusing near objects. Light-sensitive cells in the retina send impulses to the brain via the optic nerve. *See also* longsightedness; ophthalmology; shortsightedness.

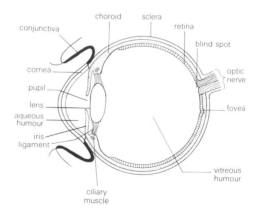

EYE *The structure of the human eye is revealed in this section. The blind spot, where the optic nerve leaves the eye, contains no visual cells and is therefore insensitive to light. The fovea is the area of acutest vision.*

Eyre, Lake A shallow salt lake of NE South Australia. It is normally dry except during the rainy season when heavy rains are fed into the lake. Area: about 9100 sq km (3500 sq mi).

F

FABERGÉ   *A golden Easter egg containing a replica of the tsar's coronation coach.*

Fabergé, Peter Carl (1846–1920) Russian goldsmith and jeweller. He designed elegant *objets d'art* and was patronized by European royalty. He was especially famous for the jewelled Easter eggs containing gifts.

Fabian Society A society, named after Fabius Maximus, formed in London in 1884 for the purpose of peacefully promoting socialist ideas and establishing a socialist state in Britain. Members included George Bernard Shaw and Sidney and Beatrice Webb. The Fabians were active in the establishment of the Labour Party.

Fabius Maximus, Quintus (d. 203 BC) Roman general of the second Punic War. Appointed dictator after Hannibal's defeat of the Romans at Trasimene in 217, Fabius adopted a policy of attrition, harassing Hannibal but avoiding pitched battles. Hannibal's victory at Cannae in 216 proved the wisdom of Fabius' tactics.

facsimile transmission. *See* fax.

factoring The commercial practice of buying trade debts and collecting them on behalf of clients. A manufacturer can sell debts owed by slow-paying customers to a factor, who will usually pay 80% of the debt immediately and the balance (less a service charge) when the debt has been collected. This service is often combined (for an extra charge) with credit insurance, enabling the debt to be guaranteed even if the debtor fails.

Factory Acts A series of UK parliamentary Acts that regulate conditions of work in factories. A response to the appalling conditions resulting from the industrial revolution, the early Factory Acts (1802, 1819, 1833) were primarily concerned with the employment of children. Ashley (later Lord Shaftesbury), leader of the ten-hour movement, was largely responsible for the Acts of 1844 and 1847, the achievements of which were consolidated in subsequent 19th-century legislation. The safety, health, and welfare of factory workers is now regulated

by the Factories Act (1961), which is increasingly being replaced by the Health and Safety at Work Act (1974).

Faeroe Islands (*or* Faroe Islands)   A Danish group of 22 self-governing islands in the N Atlantic Ocean, between the Shetland Islands and Iceland, the chief ones being Strømø, Østerø, and Vaagø. Fishing and fish processing is important. Area: 1400 sq km (540 sq mi). Population (1988 est): 46 000. Capital: Thorshavn, on Strømø.

Fahd bin Abdul Aziz (1923–   ) King of Saudi Arabia (1982–   ). He succeeded his half-brother Khalid Ibn Abdul Aziz.

Fahrenheit scale A temperature scale in which the temperature of melting ice is taken as 32 degrees and the temperature of boiling water, as 212 degrees. Named after the German physicist Gabriel Daniel Fahrenheit (1686–1736).

faience Several kinds of tin-glazed earthenware made in France. Strictly, *faience* is French shorthand for *porcellana di Faenza*, a species of maiolica made in Faenza, Italy, and the technique of coating fragile porous earthenware with impervious hard white opaque tin glaze derives from maiolica. Italian potters were using the method in France in the 16th century. Centres of production during the 17th and 18th centuries were Lyons, Marseilles, Moustiers, Nevers, and Rouen.

Fairbanks, Douglas (Julius Ullman; 1883–1939) US film actor. With D. W. Griffith, Charlie Chaplin, and his wife Mary Pickford he founded United Artists Corporation in 1919. His films, in which he played handsome athletic heroes, include *The Mark of Zorro* (1920) and *The Black Pirate* (1926). His son **Douglas Fairbanks Jr** (1909–   ) was also a film actor, playing similar roles, such as *The Prisoner of Zenda* (1937).

Fair Isle 59 32N 1 38W A sparsely inhabited island in the North Sea, off the N coast of Scotland between the Orkney and Shetland Islands. It is famous for its knitted goods with intricate patterns. Area: 16.5 sq km (6 sq mi).

fairy penguin The smallest of the penguins, *Eudyptula minor*, about 30 cm tall. It is the only penguin commonly occurring on Australian coasts.

Faisal I (1885–1933) King of Iraq (1921–33). He played an important part in the Arab revolt during World War I. After the war he was briefly King of Syria before the French occupation (1920). In 1921 the British installed him as king in mandatory Iraq.

Faisal Ibn Abdul Aziz (1905–75) King of Saudi Arabia (1964–75). He became the real ruler of Saudi Arabia in 1958, although his brother Saud (1902–69) was still nominally king until abdicating in 1964. His reign saw economic development and the increased international importance of Saudi Arabia as an oil-producing country. He was assassinated by his nephew.

faith healing (*or* spiritual healing)   The curing of illness or disability by supernatural means. The temple of Asclepius at Epidaurus was a famous faith-healing centre in antiquity. Christ is credited with several miraculous cures. The need for healing within the framework of the organized churches was recognized by Archbishop

William Temple, who founded the Council for Health and Healing in 1944. Some charismatic healers apparently achieve cures unaccountable to science.

Falabella The smallest breed of pony, developed by the Falabella family in Argentina using Shetland pony stock. Height: 38–76 cm.

Falange Española The Spanish Fascist party, created in 1933 by José António Primo de Rivera (1870–1936). The Falange wanted to regenerate Spain by means of revolution but rejected socialism. In 1937 Franco merged the Falange with the various Nationalist parties to create the National Movement, which became Spain's only legal party after the Civil War.

Falashas An Ethiopian tribe, who practise an early form of Judaism. In early 1985 the Israelis organized a secret airlift of over 7000 Falashas to Israel from famine-stricken Ethiopia.

falcon A ground-nesting bird of prey belonging to a widely distributed family (*Falconidae*; 58 species). Falcons are characterized by long pointed wings and a notched hooked bill. True falcons belong to the genus *Falco;* they kill small birds in flight with their claws or seize small mammals from the ground. Order: *Falconiformes* (falcons, hawks, etc.). *See also* gyrfalcon; kestrel; merlin; peregrine.

FALCONRY *Illustration from a treatise on falconry (1248) by Frederick II.*

falconry (*or* hawking) The sport of hunting small animals or birds with falcons, other hawks, or sometimes eagles. It was practised in Asia from the 8th century BC and was very popular in Europe from late medieval times to the 17th century. Traditionally the birds are either taken as fledglings (eyasses) or caught as one-year-old birds (passagers) or fully mature birds (haggards), but because many hunting birds are now protected species, they are often bred in captivity. They are then trained to sit hooded on the gloved fist and, by the use of a lure (an imitation bird with meat attached), to hunt and kill (but not retrieve).

Falkland Islands (Argentine name: Islas Malvinas) An island group and British crown colony in the S Atlantic Ocean: the main islands are East and West Falkland; its dependencies to the SE are South Georgia and the South Sandwich group. The population is almost entirely of British origin. Sheep farming is the main occu-

pation on the islands' rough moorland. *History*: the first landing was by Capt John Strong in 1690. In the early 19th century the islands became a British colony. Argentina has long made claims to the group and on 2 April, 1982, invaded the islands. Attempts at a diplomatic settlement failed and a task force sent by the UK recaptured South Georgia on 25 April and the Falkland Islands themselves on 14 June, after considerable loss of life on both sides. Argentina refused to declare a cessation of hostilities until 1989 and the British government refused to discuss a transfer of sovereignty. Area: 12 173 sq km (4700 sq mi). Population (1986): 1916. Capital: Stanley.

Falla, Manuel de (1876–1946) Spanish nationalist composer. His music was heavily influenced by Spanish folksong and he is best known for his ballet scores *Love the Magician* (1915) and *The Three-Cornered Hat* (1919), *Nights in the Gardens of Spain* (for piano and orchestra; 1909–15), and a concerto for harpsichord and chamber ensemble.

Fallopian tubes. *See* ovary.

fallout Radioactive particles deposited from the atmosphere after a nuclear explosion. Large particles are deposited within a radius of a few hundred kilometres during the first few hours after the explosion. This is known as local fallout. Tropospheric fallout may occur anywhere along the same line of latitude as the explosion during the first week after the explosion. Particles drawn high into the atmosphere can cause stratospheric fallout for several years.

fallow deer A deer, *Dama dama*, native to Mediterranean forests but widely kept in parks and woodlands. About 90 cm high at the shoulder, fallow deer are fawn with white spots in summer, becoming greyish in winter; males have flattened antlers with numerous points.

Famagusta 35 07N 33 57E A port in Cyprus, on the E coast. Founded in the 3rd century BC, it did not develop until the 13th century AD, when Christians fled here from Palestine. Many residents left in 1974 on the Turkish invasion of N Cyprus. Population (1985): 19 428.

family planning. *See* contraception.

Fang A Bantu people of West Africa comprising tribes in N Gabon, Equatorial Guinea, and S Cameroon.

Fangio, Juan Manuel (1911–) Argentinian motor-racing driver, who was world champion a record five times (1951, 1954–57).

fanworm A marine annelid worm belonging to the family *Sabellidae*, also called peacock or feather-duster worm. Fanworms build a parchment-like tube, up to 45 cm long, from which protrudes a feathery crown of tentacles that trap food particles and absorb oxygen. Class: *Polychaeta*.

FAO. *See* Food and Agriculture Organization.

farad (F) The SI unit of electrical capacitance equal to the capacitance of a parallel-plate capacitor with a potential difference of one volt across its plates when the capacitor is charged with one coulomb, i.e. 1 F = 1 CV^{-1}. Named after Michael Faraday.

Faraday, Michael (1791–1867) British chemist and physicist. In 1813 he became assistant to Sir Humphry Davy at the Royal Institution, eventually succeeding Davy there as professor of chemistry (1833). His major work was on electricity and electrochemistry. After discovering the process of electrolysis (1832) he went on to work out the laws that control it (*see* Faraday's laws of electrolysis). In electricity, he discovered the connection between electricity and magnetism and, independently of Joseph Henry (1797–1878), first showed that electromagnetic induction was possible. He used induction to produce the first electrical generator (1831) and also the first transformer.

Faraday constant The quantity of electricity equivalent to 1 mole of electrons, i.e. the product of Avogadro's number and the electronic charge. It has the value 96 487 coulombs per mole.

Faraday's laws of electrolysis Two laws formulated by M. Faraday in 1813–14. (1) The mass of a substance produced by an electrolytic reaction varies directly with the amount of electricity passed through the cell. (2) The masses of substances produced by a given amount of electricity are proportional to the equivalent masses of the substances.

farce A dramatic genre intended only to amuse its audience, less sophisticated and less intellectual than pure comedy and usually including peculiar situations, improbable coincidences, and ridiculous exaggerations of character and physical action. Some of the best farces were written in the late 19th century, notably those of Feydeau and Labiche in France and Pinero and W. S. Gilbert in England.

Fargo, William. *See* Wells, Henry.

Farnborough 51 17N 0 46W A town in S England, in Hampshire. The Royal Aircraft Establishment, the UK's chief aeronautical research centre, is situated here and there are annual air displays. Population (1982 est): 42 496.

FARNE ISLANDS *These islands provide breeding grounds for grey seals.*

Farne Islands (*or* The Staples) 55 38N 1 36W A group of about 30 islets and rocks in NE England, off the Northumberland coast. St Cuthbert lived on Inner Farne. In 1838 a heroic rescue by Grace Darling took place from Longstone Island lighthouse.

Faroe Islands. *See* Faeroe Islands.

Farouk I (1920–65) The last king of Egypt (1936–52). His inability to prevent British intervention in Egyptian affairs, and defeat in the first Arab-Israeli War (1948–49), led to his overthrow.

Fasciola. *See* liver fluke.

fascism A 20th-century political movement that first became an organized movement in Italy in 1919 under Mussolini. Social and economic backwardness, fear of

communist revolution, and frustrated national ambitions enabled Mussolini's Blackshirts to come to power in 1922. Fascism rejected ideas of individual liberty and equality, emphasized national or racial superiority, and concentrated authority on a dictatorial cult figure. In Germany Hitler added antisemitism to fascist militarism and anticommunism. World War II destroyed Mussolini's and Hitler's dictatorships and fascism won little support in other countries, except in Spain, where Franco's regime survived almost 40 years.

Fassbinder, Rainer Werner (1946–82) German film director who produced a rapid succession of bleak realistic films on contemporary social themes. These include *The Bitter Tears of Petra von Kant* (1972), *Fear Eats the Soul* (1974), *Despair* (1978), and *The Marriage of Maria Braun* (1979).

fast reactor A nuclear reactor (*see* nuclear energy) in which natural uranium enriched with uranium-235 or plutonium-239 is used without a moderator, the chain reaction being sustained by fast neutrons. In these reactors the core is surrounded by a blanket of natural uranium into which neutrons escape. These neutrons collide with U-238 nuclei to form U-239 nuclei, which decay to the fissionable isotope Pu-239. By suitable design, more Pu-239 can be produced in the blanket than is required to enrich the fuel in the core. These reactors are therefore called **breeder reactors**. They are 50 times more economical in uranium usage than thermal reactors. The temperature is so high that a liquid metal (usually sodium) has to be used as coolant.

Fatah, al- (Arabic: the victory) A Palestinian organization, also known as the Palestine National Liberation Movement, established in the late 1950s. Led by Yassir Arafat, al-Fatah began guerrilla warfare against Israel in the mid-1960s. By the early 1980s, the organization had split into factions pro and anti Arafat.

Fates In Greek mythology, three goddesses who determine human destinies. The daughters of Zeus and Themis, they are: Lachesis, who assigns a person's position at birth; Clotho, who spins out the thread of his existence; and Atropos, who cuts the thread at death.

fathom A unit used to express depths of water, equal to six feet.

Fatimah (d. 632) The daughter of Mohammed. She married Ali and was the mother of his sons, Hasan and Husayn, from whom most of the Shiite imams were descended. The Fatimid caliphs claimed descent from her.

fats and oils Lipid substances formed by the combination of glycerol with fatty acids. Fats occur widely in animals and plants as an energy store and as insulating material. Vegetable fats and oils are used in making soaps, margarines, cooking oils, paints, and lubricants. Animal fats are used in foods, soaps, and candles. Oils are distinguished from fats by being liquid at 20°C, whereas fats are solid. Mineral oils are hydrocarbons rather than lipids (*see* oil).

fatty acid (*or* carboxylic acid) An organic acid that comprises one or more carboxyl groups (–COOH) attached to an alkyl group. Fatty acids combine with glycerol to form glycerides, the main constituents of fats and oils. Animal fats tend to be hard because they contain a high proportion of saturated fatty acids; soft fats, such as vegetable and fish oils, contain greater proportions of unsaturated and polyunsaturated fatty acids (containing one or more double bonds). The risk of heart disease associated with dietary fat is thought to be reduced if the fat consumed is rich in polyunsaturated fatty acids. Certain essential fatty acids are required in the diet.

Faulkner, William (1897–1962) US novelist. *Sartoris* (1929) was the first of his stories set in the fictitious Yoknapatawpha County, based on his native northern Mississippi. His major novels include *The Sound and the Fury* (1929) and *Absalom, Absalom!* (1936). He was awarded the Nobel Prize in 1949.

fault A fracture plane in the rocks of the earth's crust, the rocks on each side being displaced relative to one another, either vertically, horizontally, or obliquely. Faulting occurs as a result of accumulated strain in the rocks, usually at plate margins (*see* plate tectonics). A rift valley is a downward vertical displacement between parallel faults.

Fauré, Gabriel (Urbain) (1845–1924) French composer and organist. His works include the well-known *Requiem* (1886–87), incidental music for Maeterlinck's play *Pelléas and Mélisande* (1898), the opera *Pénélope* (1913), the orchestral *Pavane* (1887), songs, such as those in the cycle *La Bonne Chanson* (1891–92), and much piano music and chamber music.

Faust A legendary medieval German scholar and magician who sold his soul to the Devil in exchange for knowledge and power. He has has inspired numerous literary works, notably by Marlowe (1592), Goethe (1808, 1832), and Thomas Mann (1947), as well as musical works, including operas by Gounod and Arrigo Boito (1842–1918). The character of Faust has varied from that of Marlowe's power-seeking magician to that of Goethe's rationalist philosopher.

fauvism A movement in French painting at the turn of the 19th century, characterized by the aggressive use of strong colours. Under the leadership of Matisse, the fauves included Dufy, Braque, Rouault, and Vlaminck.

GUY FAWKES *With some of the other conspirators.*

Fawkes, Guy (1570–1606) English conspirator. A convert to Roman Catholicism, he became involved in the Gunpowder Plot, led by Robert Catesby (1573–1605), to blow up James I and parliament. The conspirators were informed upon and Fawkes was discovered (5 November, 1605) with the gunpowder in a cellar of the Palace of Westminister. Catesby was killed while resisting arrest and Fawkes was executed. Nov 5 continues

to be celebrated with fireworks and the burning on a bonfire of effigies of Fawkes (so-called "guys").

fax (*or* facsimile transmission) A method of sending images (text or pictures) by a telecommunications link. Most fax transmissions are sent through the normal telephone network. The document is scanned optically to break it into a pattern of dots, which are transmitted as electrical pulses. The receiving device reconstructs the image from this information and prints it out on light-sensitive paper.

FBI. *See* Federal Bureau of Investigation.

feather star. *See* crinoid.

Federal Bureau of Investigation (FBI) The organization within the US Department of Justice that carries out investigations into possible breaches of federal law, especially those related to security. Founded as the Bureau of Investigation in 1908, it became the FBI in 1935; under J. Edgar Hoover (director 1924–72) it developed considerable autonomy. It campaigned against organized crime in the 1930s and participated in the anticommunist activities of Joseph McCarthy in the 1950s.

Fédération internationale de Football association (FIFA) The world governing body of association football, formed in Paris in 1904. Based in Zurich, it has over 140 members. It runs the World Cup competition.

feedback In electronics and communications theory, the process of returning to the input of a device a fraction of the output signal. **Negative feedback**, in which the feedback opposes and therefore reduces the input, is often used in amplifier circuits. It compensates for noise and distortion in the output signal, although it also reduces the overall amplification. **Positive feedback** reinforces the input signal. If it becomes too high, the circuit oscillates and the output becomes independent of the input. This is the cause of the singing noise heard in a public-address system when the microphone picks up feedback from the loudspeakers.
The principle of negative feedback also operates in biological systems, especially in controlling some biochemical reactions: the product of the reaction inhibits further activity of the enzyme catalysing it.

feldspars The most important group of rock-forming minerals and the major constituents of igneous rocks. There are four components of feldspars: anorthite (calcium plagioclase, $CaAl_2Si_2O_8$); albite (sodium plagioclase, $NaAlSi_3O_8$); orthoclase (potassium feldspar, $KAlSi_3O_8$); and celsian (barium feldspar, $BaAl_2Si_2O_8$).

Felixstowe 51 58N 1 20E A resort in E England, in Suffolk on the North Sea. It has developed rapidly as a container port. Population (1985 est): 20 858.

Fellini, Federico (1920–) Italian film director. His films, many characterized by autobiographical elements, include *La strada* (1954), *8½* (1963), *Roma* (1972), *Amarcord* (1974), *Casanova* (1976), *La città delle donne* (1980), *E la nave va* (1983), and *Intervista* (1987).

feminism. *See* women's movement.

fencing The art of combat with a sword, of which there are three main forms in sport: foil, épée, and sabre. Bouts are fought on a *piste*, or marked-out area. The winner is the first to score five hits (for men) or four (for women) in a time limit of six minutes (for men) or five (for women), the form of the hit varying between the three weapons. See p. 262.

Fenians Members of a secret Irish-American revolutionary society, the Irish Republican Brotherhood (IRB), formed in 1858 by James Stephens (1825–1901).

The IRB's influence continued into the 20th century, when it was superseded by the IRA.

Parts of a sword

Foil   *The foil weighs a maximum of 500 g. Its blade is quadrangular and very flexible.*

Épée   *The épée weighs a maximum of 770 g. Its blade is triangular and stiffer than that of the foil.*

Sabre   *The sabre weighs a maximum of 500 g. Its blade is a flattened V-shape.*

FENCING

fennec   A nocturnal desert fox, *Fennecus zerda*, of Africa and the Middle East, which is sandy-coloured and has large pointed ears.

fennel   A strong-smelling perennial herb, *Foeniculum vulgare*, native to S Europe and cultivated throughout temperate Eurasia. The feathery dark-green leaves and the greenish seeds (which taste of aniseed) are used to flavour food. Florence, or sweet, fennel (*F. dulce*) is cultivated for its bulblike leafstalks, which may be eaten cooked as a vegetable or raw in salads. Family: *Umbelliferae*.

Fens, the   A low-lying highly fertile area in E England, W and S of the Wash extending across parts of Cambridgeshire, Lincolnshire, Norfolk, and Suffolk. Once waterlogged, the first drainage attempt was made by the Romans. This was resumed during the 17th century by the Duke of Bedford. The Fens are now virtually all drained.

fenugreek   An annual herb, *Trigonella foenum-graecum*, native to the Mediterranean but widely cultivated. The brownish seeds are used to flavour curry and chutney. Family: *Leguminosae*.

Ferdinand (V and II) the Catholic   (1452–1516) King of Castile as Ferdinand V (1474–1504) and of Aragon as Ferdinand II (1479–1516). He ruled Castile jointly with his wife Isabella I of Castile and after her death was regent for their daughter Joanna the Mad. Ferdinand's accession to the Aragonese throne effected the union of Castile and Aragon, to which Granada, taken from the Moors in 1492, was added. The introduction of the Inquisition (1480) and the expulsion of the Jews (1492) aimed to strengthen both church and monarchy, to which Ferdinand's reforms in Aragon contributed.

Ferdinand VII   (1784–1833) King of Spain (1808, 1814–33). In 1808 Ferdinand was forced by Napoleon to abdicate but returned to the throne in 1814. His repressive policies caused a liberal uprising (1820) and the establishment of a liberal government until 1823, when it was ousted with French help.

Feriae   The sacred festival days of ancient Rome, usually marked by a public holiday, feasts, prayers, and sacrifices to the gods.

Fermat, Pierre de   (1601–65) French mathematician who founded number theory and, with Blaise Pascal, probability theory.

fermentation   The process by which microorganisms and tissues respire in the absence of oxygen (i.e. anaerobically). It can cause the decomposition of organic materials. The fermentation of carbohydrates by yeasts to form alcohol is the basis of making wines and beers and the production of industrial alcohol. Other types of fermentation produce lactic acid, as in the souring of milk by bacteria.

Fermi, Enrico   (1901–54) US physicist, born in Italy. His early work in Italy was concerned with the mathematical statistics of nuclear particles. For his work on the bombardment of uranium by thermal neutrons he was awarded the 1938 Nobel Prize. He moved in 1938 to the USA. He achieved the first controlled nuclear chain reaction and later played a central role in the development of the atom bomb at Los Alamos. He bitterly opposed Teller in the development of the hydrogen bomb.

fermium   (Fm) An artificial transuranic element, named after Fermi and found in debris from the 1952 hydrogen-bomb explosion. The most stable isotope, ^{257}Fm, has a half-life of 80 days. At no 100; at wt (257).

fern   A perennial leafy pteridophyte plant of the class *Pteropsida* (or *Filicinae* according to some classification schemes; about 9000–15 000 species), most abundant in shady damp tropical regions but also widely distributed elsewhere. The life cycle shows alternation of generations. The fern plant itself is the asexual (sporophyte) generation, which has a creeping underground stem (rhizome) bearing roots and aerial fronds, which reach a height of 25 m in the tree ferns. The fronds are featherlike and usually divided one or more times into leaflets. Asexual spores are produced in spore capsules, which usually occur in clusters on the underside of the leaflets. The spores develop into the inconspicuous sexual (gametophyte) generation—a tiny heart-shaped plant (called a prothallus) producing egg and sperm cells. The fertilized egg cell develops into a new sporophyte plant, which grows up from the prothallus.

ferret   A domesticated form of polecat, *Mustela putorius*, that is slightly smaller than the European polecat and lighter in colour (sometimes albino). They are used to drive rats and rabbits from their burrows.

ferrimagnetism   A form of magnetism occurring in certain antiferromagnetic materials. The behaviour is weakly ferromagnetic below the Néel temperature and paramagnetic above it.

ferrite   1. A compound of iron with the general chemical formula MFe_2O_4, where M is a metal. Most ferrites are ferromagnetic or ferrimagnetic ceramic materials and they are used in transformers and computer memories. **2.** Iron in its body-centred cubic crystal structure, either pure or as a constituent of steel.

ferromagnetism The property of a material that enables it to become a permanent magnet, i.e. ferromagnetic materials when placed in a magnetic field develop a very strong internal field and retain some of it when the external field is removed. The most common ferromagnetic substances are iron, cobalt, nickel, and alloys of these metals. Ferromagnetism, like paramagnetism, is caused by the unbalanced spin of atomic electrons, which produces the effect of a tiny magnet. In ferromagnetic substances, the application of an external field causes groups of these tiny magnets, called domains, to become aligned; many of them remain aligned when the field is removed. Above a certain temperature, called the Curie point, thermal agitation destroys the domain structure and the substance becomes paramagnetic.

Fertile Crescent A strip of land in the Middle East roughly comprising the lower Nile Valley, the E Mediterranean coast, Syria, and Mesopotamia. Formerly enjoying a wetter climate, it was the cradle of civilization, with sites showing evidence of settled communities from at least 9000 BC.

fertility drugs Drugs given to infertile women to stimulate the release of an egg cell from the ovary. The best known are the gonadotrophins—hormones normally released by the pituitary gland to control activity of the ovary.

fertilization The union of a male and a female gamete, involving the fusion of hereditary material: it is the essential process of sexual reproduction. The resulting cell, called a zygote, undergoes division (*see* cleavage), growth, and development to form a new individual, in which half the chromosomes (and therefore the genes) are of paternal origin and half of maternal origin. In **self-fertilization** both gametes are produced by the same individual; in **cross-fertilization** they derive from different individuals (these terms are applied particularly to the processes in flowering plants). In most aquatic animals the gametes are expelled into the water and fertilization is external; in most terrestrial animals the sperms are introduced into the body of the female, where fertilization takes place.

fertilizers Substances added to soils to maintain or improve soil fertility. Natural farmyard manures have long been used as a source of plant nutrients and humus, which maintains the physical structure of the soil. Other traditional fertilizers have included bone meal, dried blood, and other animal products. Modern artificial fertilizers have provided the means for dramatic increases in crop yields. The major plant nutrients required are nitrogen (chiefly provided as ammonium nitrate derived from fixation of atmospheric nitrogen), phosphate (derived from naturally occurring rock phosphate), and potassium (from mined potash deposits). Artificial fertilizers have been of immense benefit in helping to feed a rapidly expanding human population, although excessive application can lead to pollution of rivers. Awareness of these risks has led to renewed interest in organic farming, using natural fertilizers.

Fès (*or* Fez) 34 05N 5 00W A city in N Morocco. In the 14th century the Islamic city reached its peak as a major centre for commerce and learning. It remains important for Arabic and Islamic teaching and has two mosques; the Qarawiyin Mosque is the oldest in Africa and contains a university (859 AD). Population (1982): 448 823.

fescue A grass of the genus *Festuca* (about 100 species), native to temperate and cold regions of the N hemisphere. It grows in tufts. Meadow fescue (*F. pratensis*) is sown as a pasture grass and used for livestock fodder; sheep's fescue (*F. ovina*) grows on mountains and in dry and exposed soil. Red or creeping fescue (*F. rubra*) is common in grass mixtures for lawns.

fetishism **1.** In anthropology, the practice of using charms magically, found among W African tribes and, hence, in the West Indies. Sir Edward Tylor (1832–1917) reserved the term for the idea of spirits embodied in or associated with material objects. **2.** In psychiatry, the abnormal condition in which sexual satisfaction is obtained by handling or otherwise using nongenital objects (fetishes). The fetish may be an article of clothing, rubber objects, leather, etc.

fetus (*or* foetus) The developing baby in the womb from the beginning of the ninth week of pregnancy until birth. The fetus is protected by a series of membranes enclosing a fluid (amniotic fluid), which can be extracted and used for diagnostic purposes. The fetus is connected through the umbilical cord and placenta to the mother's bloodstream.

feudalism The type of land tenure, characteristic of medieval Europe, in which property was held by a vassal of a lord in return for military service and a pledge of homage. Feudalism originated in the 8th and 9th centuries. It led to a fragmentation of authority, which was reflected in the rapid growth of feudal armies, often engaged in private wars, the development of the castle as an administrative and military centre, and the growth of private justice administered by local lords rather than by a central authority. From the 12th century these implications of feudal tenure were challenged by the growing power of western rulers, especially in England, where it was abolished in 1661. Their governments increasingly depended on a royal bureaucracy and an army of mercenaries rather than the feudal bands. The growth of towns, outside the feudal framework, also contributed to the decline of feudalism.

Feydeau, Georges (1862–1921) French playwright, famous for his many farces, written between 1881 and 1916. They include *The Lady from Maxim's* (1889), *Hotel Paradiso* (1894), and *A Flea in Her Ear* (1907).

Feynman, Richard Phillips (1918–88) US physicist, who shared the 1965 Nobel Prize with Julian Schwinger (1918–) and Shinitiro Tomonaga (1906–79) for their development of quantum electrodynamics.

Fez. *See* Fès.

Fianna Fáil (Irish: Soldiers of Destiny) Irish political party, founded in 1926 by Eamon De Valera from moderate Sinn Féin members. The ruling party in the years 1932–48, 1951–54, 1957–73, 1977–81, 1982, and from 1987, its leaders have been De Valera (until 1959), Sean Lemass (until 1966), Jack Lynch (until 1979), and Charles Haughey.

fibre (*or* dietary fibre) The constituent of the human diet that is not digested. It consists of the cell walls of plants, i.e. cellulose, lignin, hemicellulose, and pectic substances. Significant amounts are present in wholewheat cereals and flour, root vegetables, nuts, and fruit: highly refined foods, such as sugar, have a low fibre content. Dietary fibre is considered helpful in preventing constipation, diverticular disease, obesity, diabetes mellitus, and colonic cancer.

fibreglass (glass fibre *or* spun glass) Material made from glass drawn into fine threads. Glass fibre has excellent heat- and fire-resistant properties and is a good electrical insulator. It is spun and woven into curtain material; made into glass wool for heat, electrical, and sound insulation; woven into coarse mats for filters; and used in reinforcing moulded plastics for boats, car bodies, etc.

fibre optics The use of thin flexible glass fibres for transmitting light. Each fibre, which may be used singly or in bunches, has a high refractive index. The light inside the fibre is totally internally reflected and travels through the fibre with little loss of intensity. The fibres are highly polished and coated with a substance of lower refractive index to reduce dispersion further. Glass fibres are used in communications and for examining otherwise inaccessible places, for example in medical diagnosis and in specialized industrial processes.

fibres Threadlike substances of animal, vegetable, or man-made origin. Wool and silk are the most widely used animal fibres. Vegetable fibres include cotton, flax, hemp, jute, and sisal. Man-made fibres fall into two categories: **modified natural fibres**, including rayon made from wood cellulose, and **synthetic fibres**, most of which are made by the polymerization of petrochemicals. They include polyesters, nylon, and acrylics. Carbon fibres, fibreglass, and asbestos are formed from inorganic substances.

fiddler crab A small burrowing crab, 25–30 mm long, belonging to the genus *Uca* (about 65 species). The brightly coloured male has an enlarged claw. Fiddler crabs are found on salt marshes and sandy beaches of tropical and temperate regions.

field In physics, a region of space in which a body possessing certain properties can exert a force on similar bodies, when they are not in contact. For example, a body having mass exerts an attractive force on all other massive bodies as a result of its gravitational field. Similarly, an electrically charged body exerts a force (attractive or repulsive, depending on polarity) on other charged bodies and a magnetized body will have a magnetic field around it. A field is often represented by lines of force to indicate the direction in which the force acts at that point.

Field, John (1782–1837) Irish pianist and composer, who settled in St Petersburg. Field composed much piano music and created the piano "nocturne"; his music influenced Chopin.

field emission The emission of electrons from the surface of certain materials when they are subjected to a very high electric field (typically fields of about 10^{10} volts per metre). The effect is utilized in the **field-emission microscope**, in which a magnified image of a surface is obtained by subjecting it to a high electric field and observing the distribution of emitted electrons on a cathode-ray screen.

Fielding, Henry (1707–54) British novelist and dramatist. He wrote about 25 plays, mostly satirical and topical comedies, between 1728 and 1737. His major novels include *Joseph Andrews* (1742), the ironical *Jonathan Wild* (1743), and *Tom Jones* (1749).

fieldmouse A small nocturnal long-tailed mouse, *Apodemus sylvaticus*, of Europe, Asia, and N Africa. About 9 cm long, with an 8-cm tail, it has a rich brown coat with white underparts. Fieldmice feed on seeds and grain and can become a pest.

Field of the Cloth of Gold (1520) The meeting near Calais of Henry VIII of England and Francis I of France. Francis hoped for English support against Emperor Charles V, with whom, however, Henry subsequently formed an alliance.

Fields, Gracie (Dame Grace Stansfield; 1898–1979) British popular entertainer. She began her career as a music-hall singer and comedian and made several films during the 1930s. During World War II she gave many concerts for the troops; she lived in Capri.

Fields, W. C. (William Claude Dukenfield; 1880–1946) US film actor. In *The Bank Dick* (1940), *My Little Chickadee* (1940), and other films, he exploited his genuine eccentricity and intolerance of sentimentality.

FIFA. *See* Fédération internationale de Football association.

fife A small transverse flute, pitched in B flat and used in military fife-and-drum bands.

Fife Region An administrative region in E Scotland, bordering on the North Sea, coextensive with the former county of Fife. It consists of a lowland peninsula located between the Firths of Forth and Tay. Agriculture is most important in the N with industry concentrated in the S. Area: 1305 sq km (504 sq mi). Population (1986 est): 348 825. Administrative centre: Glenrothes.

Fifteen Rebellion. *See* Jacobites.

fig A spreading tree or shrub, *Ficus carica*, probably native to W Asia but widely cultivated in warm temperate and subtropical regions. The large dark-green leathery leaves are usually deeply lobed. The tiny flowers are borne inside a fleshy pear-shaped structure, which develops into the edible fig after fertilization of the flowers. Figs—eaten fresh, dried, or preserved—are rich in sugar and iron and have laxative properties. Family: *Moraceae* (mulberry family).

fighting fish One of several labyrinth fishes, especially of the genus *Betta*, found in SE Asia and the Malay Archipelago and named for the aggression shown by the males towards each other and to immature females. The Siamese fighting fish (*B. splendens*) is about 6.5 cm long and greenish or brown in colour.

fig marigold A plant of the genus *Mesembryanthemum* (about 200 species), found in warm regions, especially South Africa, and widely cultivated as ornamentals. Fig marigolds are spreading herbs or shrubs, often succulent, with large brilliantly coloured daisy-like flowers and figlike fruits. Family: *Aizoaceae*.

Fiji, Republic of A country in the S Pacific Ocean. It consists of over 800 islands, only 106 of which are inhabited; the largest are Viti Levu and Vanua Levu. Most of the population are Indians and Fijians with some Europeans, Chinese, and other Pacific islanders. *Economy*: chiefly agricultural, sugar cane being the main cash crop. *History*: discovered by Abel Tasman in 1643, the islands were visited by Capt Cook in 1774 and ceded to Britain in 1874. Fiji became independent within the British Commonwealth in 1970. It left the Commonwealth in 1987 after two military coups and the declaration of a republic. President: Ratu Sir Penaia Ganilau. Official language: English. Official currency: Fiji dollar of 100 cents. Area: 18 272 sq km (7055 sq mi). Population (1987): 726 000. Capital: Suva.

filaria A parasitic nematode worm, mainly of central Africa, Asia, and the SW Pacific. The species *Wucherer-*

FIELD OF THE CLOTH OF GOLD   *Detail of a painting showing Henry VIII's arrival.*

ia bancrofti and *Brugia malayi* cause the disease **filariasis**. The tiny larval worm enters the body in the saliva of a biting mosquito or mite. It then grows up to 8 cm long in lymph and blood vessels, causing swelling and pain (*see* elephantiasis).

film   A thin flexible strip of cellulose acetate, or similar transparent plastic, coated with a light-sensitive emulsion. A black-and-white photographic emulsion usually consists of gelatin containing tiny suspended crystals of silver halide (usually bromide or chloride). After the film has been exposed to light in a camera the exposed crystals are easily reduced to metallic silver when treated with the chemicals in the developer. This produces black deposits of fine particles of metallic silver on the parts of the film upon which the light has fallen, giving a reversed (or negative) image. Bathing the film in sodium thiosulphate (hypo) or other fixers renders the unchanged silver halides soluble, enabling them to be washed away with water. The sensitivity (speed) of film is usually quoted as an ASA rating, which determines the amount of light required to form a given amount of metallic silver. *See also* photography.

films.   *See* cinema.

filter   A device that allows one substance to pass through it but not others. For example, a filter is used to remove solid particles from a liquid or gas by passing the mixture through a porous substance, such as paper or fibreglass, the holes in which are fine enough to prevent the passage of the particles. Such filters are used in some air-conditioning units, for water purification, etc. In optics, coloured glass filters are used to select light with a certain range of wavelengths. In electronics, filters are circuits used to allow alternating currents of a certain frequency range to pass, while currents with frequencies outside the range are stopped.

finch   A songbird belonging to a family (*Fringillidae*; 176 species) occurring in most regions of the world except Australia. Finches have hard conical bills used to crack open seeds, although they also feed on buds and fruit. There are two subfamilies: the *Fringillinae*, including the finer-billed chaffinch and brambling of the Old World, and the *Carduelinae*, comprising the heavier-billed species found in both the Old World and North America. *Compare* weaverfinch.

Fine Gael   (Irish: Tribe of Gaels)   Irish political party, formed in 1933. It was the senior member of ruling coalitions in Ireland (1948–51, 1954–57, 1973–77, 1981–Jan 1982, Dec 1982–87), led successively by John Costello, Liam Cosgrave, Dr Garret Fitzgerald, and, since 1987, Alan Dukes.

arch   whorl   loop

FINGERPRINT   *Loops are the commonest form of pattern (c. 65%), followed by whorls (c. 30%), and then arches (c. 5%).*

fingerprint   The impression made by the pattern of ridges on the palmar side of the end joint of the fingers and thumbs. The taking of a person's fingerprints, which are virtually unique, for the purpose of identifying habitual criminals was introduced into the UK in 1901, largely as a result of the work of Sir William Herschel (1833–1917) and Sir Edward Henry (1859–1931). The print is taken by rolling the fingers and thumbs in ink and then rolling them on paper. Fingerprints left at the scene of a crime may be taken by photography. Scotland Yard has a library of over two million prints of known criminals and the FBI in the USA has more than 70 million. Classification relies on a numerical value given to a print, which identifies the finger and the pattern of ridges. *See also* genetic fingerprinting.

Finisterre, Cape   42 52N 9 16W   The most westerly point in Spain, on the Atlantic coast.

Finland, Republic of   (Finnish name: Suomi)   A country in N Europe, with S and W coastlines on the Baltic Sea. It includes the Åland Islands, situated at the mouth of the Gulf of Bothnia. The land is generally low lying. Over 10% of the area consists of lakes, which, together with rivers and canals, provide an extensive network of inland waterways. The majority of the population are Finns, with minorities of Swedes, Lapps, and Russians. *Economy*: agriculture is highly mechanized and, together with cereals, dairy produce is of particular importance. Over 70% of the land is under forest, providing ample resources for the timber and pulp and paper industries. Hydroelectricity provides the main source of power. *History*: prehistorically the Finnic peoples migrated into Finland, gradually driving the Lapps northwards. Conquered by Sweden in the 12th century AD, Finland had a considerable degree of independence, becoming a grand duchy in the 16th century. In the 18th century the SE was occupied by Russia and in 1809 the rest of the country was ceded to Russia, becoming an autonomous grand duchy. It became independent in 1917, following the Russian Revolution, and a republic two years later. In 1939 it was invaded by Soviet forces and in 1940, and again in 1944, was forced to cede certain territories to the Soviet Union. A treaty of friendship between the two countries, first signed in 1948, continues in force. President: Dr Mauno Henrik Koivisto (1923–). Official languages: Finnish and Swedish. Official currency: markka of 100 pennia. Area: 305 475 sq km (117 913 sq mi). Population (1987): 4 942 000. Capital and main port: Helsinki.

Finney, Albert (1936–) British actor. Following his early successful performances in plays by modern dramatists he made several films, notably *Saturday Night and Sunday Morning* (1960), *The Dresser* (1983), and *Orphans* (1987).

Finnic A group of languages of the Finno-Ugric branch of the Uralic family. Finnic includes Finnish, Estonian, and Lapp.

Finno-Ugric languages A large group of languages of the Uralic family, spoken by more than 20 million people in dispersed communities in Scandinavia, E Europe, and W Asia. Thought to have diverged about five millennia ago, the Finnic and Ugric languages can be further divided into the following major groups: Ugric (Hungarian and Ob-Ugric) and Finnic (Finnish, Estonian, Lapp, Mari, Permic, and a number of other languages). Periodically and to varying degrees, neighbouring languages have exercised an influence on the vocabularies of the Finno-Ugric languages. Many Turkic forms, for example, have been absorbed into the Hungarian language.

fins Organs of locomotion and balance in fish and some other aquatic animals. The fins of fish are supported by bony or cartilaginous fin rays and are either median or paired. The median fins include the tail (or caudal) fin, typically used for propulsion (in conjunction with the muscular body) and the dorsal and anal fins, used for balancing. The paired pectoral fins, just behind the gills, and pelvic fins, further back, are used for steering (although in rays the large pectorals provide motive force).

Fiordland The largest national park of New Zealand, in SW South Island. It is a mountainous region with glacial lakes and fjords, including Lakes Manapouri and Te Anau, and Milford Sound. Area: about 11 400 sq km (4401 sq mi).

fir A coniferous tree of the genus *Abies* (about 50 species). Mostly native to N temperate regions, these trees are also called silver firs, as many species have leaves with a silvery undersurface. Firs have blunt-tipped needles and erect stout woody cones; they are important softwood trees (*see* timber). The European silver fir (*A. alba*), which forms pure forests in the mountains of central Europe, is widely grown for its timber: it reaches a height of 50 m. Another widely planted timber tree is the grand, or giant, fir (*A. grandis*), which grows up to 90 m in its native W North America. Family: *Pinaceae*.

firebrat A primitive wingless insect, *Thermobia domestica*: a three-pronged bristletail that is abundant in buildings all over the world. It prefers warm moist places, such as around stoves, furnaces, and bakery ovens, where it feeds on starchy or sugary materials.

fireclay A soft unbedded clay often occurring beneath coalseams; it is possibly fossil soil or earth in which swamp plants grew. Fireclays consist mainly of aluminium oxide and silica, being deficient in iron and alkalis; kaolin is the principal clay mineral. They are used as refractory materials.

firefly A nocturnal beetle belonging to a family (*Lampyridae*; 2000 species) common in tropical and temperate regions. Fireflies emit a greenish light—often as short rhythmic flashes—from organs on the abdomen (*see* bioluminescence). Many have conspicuous orange or yellow markings. The wingless females and larvae are called glowworms.

Firenze. *See* Florence.

Fire of London (2–5 September, 1666) The fire that started in a baker's shop in Pudding Lane and destroyed four-fifths of the City. More than 13 000 buildings, including the medieval St Paul's Cathedral, were razed to the ground. Sir Christopher Wren played a major part in the subsequent rebuilding. The **Monument**, which he designed in 1671, stands close to Pudding Lane to commemorate the Fire.

firethorn. *See* Pyracantha.

fireworks Combustible devices, used for signals, flares, and displays. Gunpowder rockets and fire crackers were first used in ancient China for military purposes and celebrations and in Europe from the middle ages. The basic explosive, usually gunpowder, is coloured by the addition of metallic salts: sodium salts for yellow, barium for green, strontium for red, and copper for blue. Metal filings are added for sparks and aniline dyes provide coloured smokes.

firn (*or* névé) A stage in the transformation of fresh snow to glacier ice. Compaction and recrystallization of the snow increases its density and it becomes firn at a relative density of 0.5. Under further compaction firn may be transformed to glacier ice, this occurring at a relative density of 0.89–0.90.

Fischer-Dieskau, Dietrich (1925–) German baritone. He is renowned for his performances of *Lieder* and of a wide range of operatic roles.

Fischer-Tropsch reaction The formation of light liquid hydrocarbons by passing a mixture of hydrogen and carbon monoxide over catalysts at around 200°C. The reaction enables synthetic liquid fuels to be produced from coal. It was invented by F. Fischer (1852–1932) and H. Tropsch (1839–1935) in 1925 and was extensively used in Germany during World War II.

fish A cold-blooded aquatic vertebrate belonging to either of the two classes *Chondrichthyes* (*see* cartilaginous fish) or *Osteichthyes* (*see* bony fish), which together comprise over 30 000 species occurring worldwide in seas and fresh waters. They have streamlined bodies with a covering of bony scales, a fin-bearing tail, an anal fin, one or more dorsal fins, and paired lateral, pectoral (anterior) and pelvic (ventral) fins, which are used in swimming. Oxygen is obtained from water by means of gills situated in the wall of the mouth cavity, although a

FISH

gar

thresher shark

sea horse

flying fish

scorpion fish

mangrove ray

dorsal fins

caudal (tail) fin

pectoral fin

anal fin

operculum covering gills

pelvic fin

sea lamprey

puffer

Fison's flounder

common eel

chimaera

Atlantic sturgeon

lungfish

FISH *There are numerous variations on the structure of a typical bony fish (mackerel: centre). In the flying fish, for instance, the pectoral fins are enlarged as wings; in the lungfish they are fleshy, for moving on land; and in the mangrove ray they are flattened, for swimming. The dorsal and anal fins of the scorpion fish are armed with poisonous spines and the tail of the sea horse is prehensile.*

few species can also breathe air (*see* lungfish). The majority of fish are carnivorous, feeding mainly on other fish and invertebrates, although some eat plants. Large numbers of small eggs are laid and are usually fertilized externally. Fish are of major importance as a source of food and other products and for sport.

Fishguard 51 59N 4 59W A port and resort in South Wales, in SW Dyfed, with ferry crossings to Cork and Rosslare in the Republic of Ireland. Population (1981): 4798.

fish hawk. *See* osprey.

fission (biology) A form of asexual reproduction in which an individual splits into two (binary fission) or more (multiple fission) equal parts, each part becoming a new individual. It occurs in a variety of plants, bacteria, protozoa, and some multicellular animals (e.g. corals).

fission (physics). *See* nuclear energy.

fission-track dating A method of dating based on the spontaneous nuclear fission of uranium-238 in the sample. The fissions are recorded as tracks, which are then compared to the tracks formed by inducing fission in the uranium-235 present. A comparison of the numbers of tracks is used as a measure of the age of the sample.

Fitzgerald, Edward (1809–83) British poet. His famous *Rubaiyat of Omar Khayyam* (1859) was a free adaptation of the 12th-century Persian original.

Fitzgerald, Ella (1918–) US Black jazz singer. She became famous with the song "A-tisket, A-tasket" (1938), performed with such musicians as Duke Ellington and Oscar Peterson, and made many albums, including *Hello Love, Duke Ellington's Song Book*, and the *Gershwin Song Books*.

Fitzgerald, F(rancis) Scott (Key) (1896–1940) US novelist. His autobiographical first novel, *This Side of Paradise* (1920), was highly successful. After 1924 Fitzgerald lived chiefly on the French Riviera, where he wrote his masterpiece *The Great Gatsby* (1925). His wife Zelda suffered increasingly from schizophrenia and after 1930 was confined to an asylum. Fitzgerald, plagued by guilt, declined into alcoholism. His other works include *The Beautiful and the Damned* (1922) and *Tender is the Night* (1934). *The Last Tycoon* was left unfinished.

Fitzgerald, Garret (1926–) Irish statesman; prime minister of Ireland (1981–82; 1982–87). He was leader of the Fine Gael party (1977–87). In 1985 he negotiated the controversial Anglo-Irish Agreement.

Fiume. *See* Rijeka.

Five, the A group of 19th-century Russian composers dedicated to the formation of a nationalist musical tradition based on folk music. Led by Mili Balakirev, the other members were Borodin, César Cui, Mussorgski, and Rimsky-Korsakov.

fives A British court game that originated in handball and developed in different forms at three public schools, Eton, Rugby, and Winchester. It is played with gloved hands by two or four players on a three- or four-walled court, each side returning the ball in turn to certain areas of wall.

fjord (*or* fiord) A long narrow sea inlet lying between steep mountain slopes, especially in Norway. Usually U-shaped, fjords are glaciated valleys that have been flooded by the sea. Many are extremely deep, but near their mouths they usually have a considerably shallower bar or threshold.

flag A Eurasian iris, *Iris pseudacorus* (yellow flag), growing in marshes and ditches. Up to 1.2 m high, it has yellow flowers and long bladelike leaves. The sweet flag (*Acorus calamus*) is a perennial herbaceous plant native to Asia and North America and naturalized in Britain, growing at the margins of ponds, rivers, etc. About 1 m high, it has wavy-edged leaves, which smell of tangerines when crushed, and the small yellow flowers are tightly packed on a tapering spikelike spadix. Family: *Araceae*.

flagella Long threadlike structures that project from the surface of a cell and produce lashing or undulating movements, used for locomotion or the production of water currents. Flagella occur in protozoa, motile gametes (usually sperms), lower plants, sponges, and also in bacteria (in a simpler form).

Flagellata (*or* Mastigophora) A class of microscopic single-celled animals (*see* Protozoa) having one or more long flagella for swimming and collecting bacteria, protozoans, and other food particles. Some species (subclass *Phytomastigophora*) possess chlorophyll and other pigments to make food by photosynthesis (*see* Euglena). They may also be classed as algae. Animal-like flagellates (subclass *Zoomastigophora*) include the parasites causing trypanosomiasis and leishmaniasis as well as free-living forms.

flageolet A musical instrument similar to the recorder but with two thumb holes on the underside and a more complex head fitted with a slender ivory mouthpiece containing a sponge to absorb condensation.

flags Emblems of nations, clubs, associations, etc., printed on cloth. The flags of the nations are shown on a coloured plate in the map section.

Flagstad, Kirsten Malfrid (1895–1962) Norwegian soprano, famous for her singing of Wagner roles.

Flamboyant In French gothic architecture, the predominant style during the 15th century. Similar to the earlier English Decorated style, Flamboyant takes its name from its characteristic slender and elaborate curves that wind into flamelike patterns, especially in window tracery. St Maclou, Rouen (begun 1432), is a fine Flamboyant church.

flamboyant tree A tree, *Delonix regia*, also called royal poinciana, flame tree, and peacock flower. It has showy flame-coloured flowers with long protruding stamens. Native to Madagascar, it is widely planted in the tropics for shade and ornament. Family: *Leguminosae*.

flamenco A type of Spanish music originating in Andalusia, typically consisting of a song accompanied by dancing, in which the men perform intricate toe and heel tapping steps (*zapateados*) and the women rely on graceful hand and body movements. It was developed by gipsies and shows signs of Moorish influence. Flamenco guitar playing employs a different technique from that of the "classical" guitar, including a percussive effect obtained by tapping the body of the guitar with the fingers.

flame tree One of several unrelated trees with flame-coloured showy flowers. The name is most commonly applied to *Brachychiton acerifolium* (or *Sterculia acerifolia*), a deciduous Australian tree that bears masses of small scarlet bell-like flowers on leafless branches. It may also refer to the flamboyant tree.

flamingo A wading bird belonging to a family (*Phoenicopteridae*; 4 species) occurring in large flocks on saltwater lakes in warm regions of the world. Flamingos have a long neck, a broad wingspan, and white plumage, tinged with pink. They separate algae, diatoms, small molluscs, etc., from mud using their bills, which are lined with sievelike filters. Order: *Ciconiiformes* (herons, storks, etc.).

FLAMENCO   *Spanish dancers in traditional costume.*

Flaminius, Gaius   (d. 217 BC) Roman popular leader. An advocate of the plebeians' rights, he often challenged or disregarded senatorial authority. In 220, as consul, he built the Flaminian Way, Rome's road to N Italy. Elected in 217 as leader against Hannibal, he was defeated and killed at Trasimene.

Flamsteed, John   (1646–1719) English astronomer, who established, with the permission of Charles II, a national observatory at Greenwich and was appointed the first astronomer royal in 1675. His star catalogue gave the positions of more than 3000 stars.

Flanders   A historic region in Europe, in the SW of the Low Countries. It now comprises the provinces of East Flanders and West Flanders in Belgium and parts of N France and the Netherlands. In the middle ages Flanders formed an autonomous region ruled by the Counts of Flanders and after the 12th century it became a major industrial and commercial centre, its cloth being especially important. The scene of many battles during its history, there was heavy fighting here in both World Wars. During World War II the Battle of Flanders (10 May–2 June, 1940) saw the German attack on Holland, Belgium, and France, which resulted in the Allied withdrawal from Dunkirk.

flash point   The lowest temperature at which an inflammable liquid (generally a hydrocarbon) produces enough vapour to ignite on the application of a small flame under specified conditions. Flash points are useful for setting safety standards.

flatfish   Any carnivorous bony fish of the order *Pleuronectiformes* (about 600 species), including many important food fishes, such as halibut, plaice, sole, and turbot. They have a laterally flattened body fringed with dorsal and anal fins. Both eyes occur on the same side of the head and they lie on their "blind" side, usually on sandy or muddy bottoms of coastal waters; the upper surface is coloured to blend with their surroundings. In the larval stage one eye migrates over the head to lie near the other.

flat racing   A form of horse racing in which the horses are not required to jump obstacles. Flat races are usually run over distances between 0.8 km (0.5 mi) and 2.4 km (1.5 mi). Thoroughbred horses are used, mainly as two- and three-year-olds. Weight handicaps are allotted in most races. The most prestigious races are the English Classics, the US Triple Crown, and the French Prix de l'Arc de Triomphe.

flatworm   A flat-bodied wormlike animal of the invertebrate phylum *Platyhelminthes* (9000 species). Some flatworms are free-living (planarians) but the majority are parasitic (*see* fluke; tapeworm). They range in size from 1 mm to 15 m. Many are hermaphrodite.

Flaubert, Gustave   (1821–80) French novelist. His first novel, *Madame Bovary* (1856), was controversially explicit. Other major works include *Salammbô* (1862), *L'Éducation sentimentale* (1870), *La Tentation de Saint Antoine* (1874), and the brilliant short stories in *Trois contes* (1877).

flax   A herbaceous plant of the genus *Linum* (230 species), mostly of the N hemisphere. Cultivated flax (*L. usitatissimum*) is an annual with narrow leaves and blue flowers. Its stem fibres are used to make linen, fine writing paper, and cigarette paper. The seeds contain linseed oil. Flax is cultivated throughout Europe. Family: *Linaceae.*

flea   A small wingless insect belonging to the widely distributed order *Siphonaptera* (about 1600 species). Fleas are bloodsucking parasites of birds and mammals. Their legs are modified for jumping. Fleas have irritating bites and change hosts frequently, acting as carriers of some serious diseases. Two important and widely distributed species are the human flea (*Pulex irritans*) and the oriental rat flea (*Xenopsylla cheopis*), which transmits bubonic plague and typhus to man.

Flémalle, Master of   (c. 1378–1444) One of the founders (with the van Eyck brothers) of the Flemish school of painting. He is usually identified as Robert Campin. His works display the careful realistic rendering of details from everyday life that characterizes the Flemish school as a whole.

Fleming, Sir Alexander   (1881–1955) British microbiologist, who discovered the antibiotic penicillin. In 1928 Fleming noticed that a mould contaminating a bacterial culture had destroyed the bacteria in its vicinity. He identified the mould but could not isolate or identify the antibiotic. This was later achieved by Lord Florey and Sir Ernst Chain, with whom Fleming shared the 1945 Nobel Prize. Fleming also discovered lysozyme.

Fleming, Ian (Lancaster)   (1908–64) British author and journalist, famous for his creation of the archetypal secret agent, James Bond, in 12 novels and 7 short stories, most of them filmed.

Fleming, Sir John Ambrose   (1849–1945) British electrical engineer, who constructed the first rectifying diode in 1904. His invention greatly stimulated the development of radio and led to the invention of the triode two years later by Lee De Forest (1873–1961).

Flemings   Inhabitants of N and W Belgium who speak Flemish, a dialect of Dutch known by them as Vlaams. They number approximately 5 500 000. Like the Dutch they are descended from the Salic Franks, a Germanic people, who settled the area during the 3rd and 4th centuries AD. They retain a cultural identity distinct from that of French-speaking Belgians (*see* Walloons).

FLORENCE *The 13th-century cathedral with Brunelleschi's dome.*

fleur-de-lys A heraldic device, which has three everted petals, resembling the bearded iris. It was the coat of arms of the French monarchy from the middle ages.

Flinders Range A mountain range in E South Australia, extending N from Gulf St Vincent.

flint A variety of chalcedony. It is grey to black, is dense and tough, and breaks with a conchoidal (curved) fracture, leaving sharp edges (hence its use by Stone Age man for tools and weapons). It occurs in nodules in chalk along the bedding planes and as pebbles in river gravels and beach material.

flint glass A durable, brilliant, and highly refractive glass. Also known as lead glass and crystal glass, it is used in high-quality glassware and also in lenses and prisms since it absorbs very little light.

FLN. *See* Front de Libération nationale.

Flodden, Battle of (9 September, 1513) The battle in which the English under Thomas Howard, Earl of Surrey (1443–1524), defeated the Scots under James IV at Flodden Edge, Northumberland. The Scots had invaded England after allying with France against Henry VIII.

Florence (Italian name: Firenze) 43 47N 11 15E A city in Italy, the capital of Tuscany on the River Arno. The principal industry is tourism. Its many famous buildings include the 13th-century cathedral of Sta Maria del Fiore, the campanile of Giotto, the baptistery, and many churches (including Sta Maria Novella and Sta Croce). The Ponte Vecchio (1345) across the River Arno connects the Uffizi gallery to the Palazzo Pitti (now an art gallery). Art treasures in Florence include works by Michelangelo, Donatello, Masaccio, Giotto, Fra Angelico, Botticelli, Raphael, Titian, and Rubens. *History*: an early Roman colony, it had developed into an important centre of trade and industry by the 12th century. It was torn by the struggles between the Guelfs and Ghibellines (13th and 14th centuries) but flourished financially and culturally (14th–16th centuries). The rule of the Medici family began in 1434 and continued almost uninterrupted for three centuries. Following a period of Austrian rule, Florence became part of the new kingdom of Italy in 1861 and was the provisional capital (1865–71). Population (1986): 425 835.

Florey, Howard Walter, Baron (1898–1968) Australian pathologist, who, working with Sir Ernst Chain, isolated and purified the antibiotic penicillin, first discovered by Sir Alexander Fleming in 1928. Florey and Chain developed techniques for producing the pure drug in large quantities. In 1941 they conducted the first clinical trials, in which penicillin proved very effective in combating bacterial infections. Florey shared the 1945 Nobel Prize with Chain and Fleming.

floribunda. *See* rose.

Florida A state in the far SE of the USA, between the Atlantic Ocean and the Gulf of Mexico. It is predominantly a low-lying peninsula with many lakes and rivers. Tourism, based on its subtropical climate, is the most important industry, with many popular resorts, such as Miami Beach and Palm Beach. The John F. Kennedy Space Center is at Cape Canaveral. Florida produces some 75% of the USA's citrus fruits, as well as large quantities of vegetables. *History*: following its exploration by the Spanish, it was ceded to the British in 1763 but returned to Spain after the American Revolution. It passed to the USA in 1819, becoming a state in 1845. It was a supporter of the Confederate cause during the US Civil War. Area: 151 670 sq km (58 560 sq mi). Population (1986 est): 11 675 000. Capital: Tallahassee.

Florida Keys A chain of small islands in the USA, separated from the S coast of Florida by Florida Bay. It includes the islands of Key West and Key Largo and extends for over 160 km (100 mi). The islands are linked by the Overseas Highway, a complex of roads and 42 bridges.

flotsam, jetsam, and lagan Goods cast into the sea that respectively remain afloat, sink, or would sink but have attached to them a buoy, which keeps them afloat. Unless claimed by the owner, they belong to the Crown.

flounder A common name for any flatfish or for certain species. An example is *Platichthys flesus*, which lives in European coastal and fresh waters. It has a greenish or brownish mottled upper surface and is an important food and game fish.

flour The powdered grain of wheat or other cereals, used in baking, chiefly bread. When the two proteins in wheat, glutenin and gliadin, are mixed with water they form gluten, which permits the dough to expand and retain the carbon dioxide resulting from fermentation of the yeast in bread dough. Different types of flour are made by varying the percentage of flour separated from the wheat. The principal commercial flours are whole wheat (100%), wholemeal and stoneground (92%), wheatmeal (80–90%), and white flours (70–72%). Whole wheat and wholemeal flour retain more of the bran (the outer skin of the wheat grain) and have more iron and calcium than white flour, and so are favoured by nutritionists. They are also a good daily source of dietary fibre. Flour with a high gluten content (strong flour) is best when yeast is called for, as in dough for bread. A softer flour with a lower gluten content (fine flour) is used for cakes, shortbread, etc. Plain flour is all-purpose, with a moderate gluten content. Self-raising flour is plain flour with the addition of raising agents.

flower The reproductive organ of flowering plants (angiosperms), which is essential for the production of seeds and fruits. It is made up of the perianth (petals and sepals) and the sexual organs—the stamens producing pollen (male gametes) and the carpels containing the female gametes. The petals and sepals serve to protect the sexual organs and—in flowers pollinated by animals—are brightly coloured, scented, and secrete nectar to attract insects and birds. Wind-pollinated flowers are typically small and inconspicuous and may lack a perianth.

flowering currant An ornamental garden shrub, *Ribes sanguineum*, native to North America. Its drooping spikes of pink tubular flowers appear before the maple-shaped leaves. The fruit is a blue-black berry. The shrub has an odour of blackcurrants. Family: *Grossulariaceae* (*see* currant).

flowering quince. See japonica.

flowering rush A perennial freshwater plant, *Butomus umbellatus*, native to Eurasia but common throughout N temperate regions: it is a popular garden plant. It has long tapering leaves and an umbrella-shaped cluster of pinkish flowers at the tip of a long stalk. Family: *Butomaceae*.

flowerpecker A songbird belonging to a family (*Dicaeidae*; 55 species) occurring in S Asia and Australasia. Flowerpeckers feed on berries and nectar, thereby dispersing seeds and pollinating flowers.

fluidics The use of jets of fluid in a circuit to carry out electronic functions. Fluidic circuits can resist much higher temperatures than electronic circuits and are also unaffected by ionizing radiation and magnetic fields. They therefore have uses in nuclear reactors and spacecraft. They are also used as delay lines since they respond much more slowly than electronic circuits.

fluidization The process of supporting very fine solid particles in a stream of gas so that the combination of solid and fluid behaves like a liquid. The process is used, for example, in transporting coal dust.

fluid mechanics The study of the mechanical properties of fluids. Hydrostatics is concerned with the study of fluids at rest and hydrodynamics (*or* fluid dynamics) with fluids that are flowing. Hydraulics deals with the practical applications of these sciences. Two important aspects of hydrodynamics are the conservation of energy in fluid flow and the distinction between streamline and turbulent flow. *See also* aerodynamics; Reynolds number.

fluke A parasitic flatworm of the class *Trematoda* (over 6000 species). Typically leaf-shaped, some are elongated to fit the body cavities they inhabit. Monogenetic flukes have a single host and are generally external parasites of fishes; the digenetic flukes have life cycles involving up to four different hosts and are mainly internal parasites of vertebrates, passing early larval stages in various invertebrates.

fluorescence. See luminescence.

fluorescent lamp A lamp that uses fluorescence (*see* luminescence) as its source of light. It consists of a glass tube containing a low pressure gas, such as mercury vapour. As a current passes through the gas, collisions between the electrons and atoms of the gas excite the atoms, which emit ultraviolet radiation when they return to the ground state. The radiation strikes a phosphor coating on the inner surface of the tube, causing the phosphor to fluoresce emitting visible light.

fluoridation The addition of fluoride (usually sodium fluoride) to drinking water to reduce dental caries (tooth decay), especially in children. The fluoride combines with apatite—the chief constituent of tooth enamel—to form fluoroapatite, which has a greater resistance to bacterial decay. The recommended level is one part of

fluoride per million. In the UK the decision to implement this recommendation rests with local authorities.

fluorine (F) A highly reactive pale-yellow halogen gas, the most electronegative element known. It was first isolated by H. Moissan in 1886 and occurs naturally in volcanic gases and as fluorite (CaF_2) and cryolite (Na_3AlF_6). It is prepared by electrolysis of potassium hydrogen fluoride (KHF_2) solution in dry hydrofluoric acid (HF). The gas uranium hexafluoride (UF_6) allows separation of the fissile ^{235}U isotope from ^{238}U by gaseous diffusion. Hydrofluoric acid is used to etch glass. Fluorocarbons are chemically unreactive and have many important uses. *See also* fluoridation. At no 9; at wt 18.9984; mp $-219.62°C$; bp $-188.14°C$.

fluorite (*or* fluorspar) A mineral consisting of calcium fluoride, white, green, or yellow in colour. It occurs in hydrothermal veins, often in ore deposits, and in some igneous rocks. Most fluorite is used as a flux in iron and steel making; it is also used as a source of fluorine for manufacturing hydrofluoric acid and in the ceramic- and optical-glass industries. Blue John is a deep blue or purple variety used for ornamental purposes.

fluorocarbons Synthetic compounds of carbon and fluorine (sometimes also containing atoms of other halogens). They are extremely resistant to chemical attack, even at very high temperatures, and are nontoxic and nonflammable. They are used as refrigerants, anaesthetics, heat-transfer agents, and high-temperature lubricants. The fluoroanalogue of polythene, polytetrafluoroethylene (Teflon), is a useful plastic in corrosive environments and has a very low coefficient of friction. Its stability at high temperatures enables it to be used for nonstick coatings in cooking utensils. **Chlorofluorocarbons** (CFCs), containing both fluorine and chlorine, have been much used as propellants for aerosols, although they are opposed on environmental grounds as photochemical reactions in the upper atmosphere may lead to depletion of the ozone layer, which blocks harmful ultraviolet radiation.

fluorspar. See fluorite.

flute A woodwind instrument of ancient origin, existing in many different cultures. The modern side-blown flute (in which a column of air is made to vibrate by blowing across an elliptical mouth hole) and the recorder are members of the same family. Originally made of wood, most flutes are now metal. The modern orchestral flute is about 0.6 m (2 ft) long and has a range of three octaves above middle C.

flux (physics) The net amount of a directional quantity passing through a surface area at right angles to the surface. The concept of flux is used to describe phenomena that involve forces or the flow of energy, such as electric flux, magnetic flux, and luminous flux.

fly An insect belonging to the order *Diptera* (over 85 000 species)—the so-called true, or two-winged, flies—of great economic importance in transmitting disease. The adults have only two wings (the front pair), the hind pair being reduced to balancing organs. The mouthparts are adapted for piercing or sucking, and most species feed on plant juices or suck the blood of mammals. The larvae—often called maggots—are typically scavengers on plant and animal refuse or parasites of pest status. Bloodsucking species, such as mosquitoes and tsetse flies, may transmit such diseases as malaria, sleeping sickness, and yellow fever. The order also includes the houseflies, blowflies, craneflies, and horse flies.

The name fly is also used for various flying insects of other orders: the alderfly, caddis fly, damselfly, firefly, and mayfly are examples.

fly agaric A poisonous mushroom, *Amanita muscaria*, found in woodlands, especially of birch and conifers. Its cap is scarlet or orange-red with white scales and the white stalk has a membranous collar beneath the cap. Fly agaric is seldom fatal. It was formerly used as a fly killer, hence its name.

flycatcher A small active songbird belonging to an Old World family (*Muscicapidae*; 378 species) and feeding on insects, typically caught in flight. They have small bills surrounded by stiff bristles and delicate legs used only for perching. The typical flycatchers are dull coloured and include the grey-and-brown European spotted flycatcher (*Muscicapa striata*) and the black-and-white pied flycatcher (*Ficedula hypoleuca*). The tropical blue flycatchers and paradise flycatchers are beautifully coloured and ornamented. *Compare* tyrant flycatcher.

FLYING DOCTOR SERVICE *One of a small team of expert surgeons who is also an experienced pilot.*

Flying Doctor Service of Australia, Royal A scheme begun in 1928 at Cloncurry, Queensland, to transport doctors to patients in remote areas. The development of a Morse radio transmitter-receiver facilitated long-range consultation and emergency treatment. The service, which is free, is financed by state governments, subscriptions from outposts, and charges levied for messages. Similar schemes are run in Canada and East Africa.

Flying Dutchman In sailors' lore, a ghost ship haunting the sea around the Cape of Good Hope. Its captain, driven back from the Cape by a storm, is supposed to have sworn a blasphemous oath to round it or be forever damned. The story inspired Wagner's opera (1843) of the same name.

flying fish A fish of the family *Exocoetidae* (about 40 species). Flying fish swim just below the surface in warm oceanic waters. If disturbed they launch themselves from the water by rapidly beating the tail and glide through the air using large winglike pectoral fins.

flying fox A fruit bat belonging to the genus *Pteropus* (51 species), ranging from Africa to Australia. Flying foxes have foxlike heads and a wingspan of up to 1.5 m.

flying lemur. *See* colugo.

flying lizard A lizard belonging to the genus *Draco* (15 species) of SE Asia, having large folds of skin between the legs supported by ribs that are spread out when the lizard jumps from a tree. They have greenish bodies and brightly coloured "wings." Family: *Agamidae* (agamas).

flying saucer. *See* unidentified flying objects.

flying snake A slender diurnal arboreal snake belonging to the genus *Chrysopelea* (3 species), occurring in S Asia and the East Indies. They can glide short distances by launching themselves in the air and flattening their belly scales. Family: *Colubridae*.

flying squirrel A nocturnal squirrel of the subfamily *Petauristinae* (37 species), occurring in SE Asia, North America, and Eurasia. Flying squirrels have a flap of loose skin from elbow to knee that is stretched tight by extending the legs, enabling them to glide from branch to branch.

Flynn, Errol (1909–59) Australian actor. He played the handsome adventurous hero in such Hollywood films as *Captain Blood* (1935), *Gentleman Jim* (1942), and (as John Barrymore) *Too Much Too Soon* (1958). His private life was candidly recounted in two autobiographies.

flytrap. *See* Venus flytrap.

f-number The ratio of the focal length of a camera lens to the diameter of the shutter opening (aperture). For example, f-8 means that the focal length is eight times the aperture. The smaller the f-number, the greater the illumination of the film.

Foch, Ferdinand (1851–1929) French marshal. At the outbreak of World War I he commanded the Ninth Army and was largely responsible for halting the German advance at the Marne and for the Allied victory at Ypres (1915). After the Somme offensive (1916), he became chief of the general staff (1917). He returned to action in 1918 and as Allied commander in chief forced the Germans back to the Rhine, effecting their defeat.

foetus. *See* fetus.

fog A cloud near the ground surface, within which visibility is reduced to less than 1 km (0.6 mi). Fog is the result of the condensation of water vapour on tiny particles in the lower layers of air, usually through the cooling of air to below its dew point; it is most likely to occur with light wind conditions and a clear sky at night. There is a greater incidence in industrial areas.

föhn A warm dry wind that descends down the leeward side of mountains. It is a frequent occurrence in the Alps (where the name originated), the Rocky Mountains (where it is known as the **chinook**), and the Andes. In winter it can cause extremely rapid thaws of lying snow, resulting in avalanches.

Fokine, Michel (Mikhail F.; 1880–1942) Russian ballet dancer and choreographer. From 1909 he worked with Diaghilev's Ballets Russes in Paris, for which he choreographed such revolutionary ballets as *The Firebird* (1910) and *Petrushka* (1911). He became a naturalized US citizen in 1932.

fold A buckling of sedimentary rock strata produced by compressional forces acting on it. Large-scale folding produces mountain ranges; this occurs where two continental plates collide (*see* plate tectonics) and the sediment along their margins is compressed and folded. A simple upfold is called an anticline and a downfold, a syncline; however, most folds are much more complex.

folic acid. *See* vitamin B complex.

Folies-Bergère A Parisian variety theatre opened in 1869 and celebrated chiefly for its elaborate revues featuring dancing girls and striptease acts.

folk dance A form of dance developed by country people, usually for their own amusement. Folk dances derive from ancient ritual dances used in religious worship and to invoke the fertility of the land (the original purpose of the maypole dance). They have greatly influenced other forms of dances, notably court dancing, 18th- and 19th-century ballroom dances (such as the waltz and polka), and ballet. In England the most popular types are country dancing and the Morris dance.

FOLK DANCE *Morris dancers.*

Folkestone 51 5N 1 11E A resort and port in SE England, in Kent. Population (1983 est): 44 200.

folklore The social, material, and oral culture of primitive societies. The social culture includes festivals, dances, and religious rites; the material culture comprises architecture and arts and crafts; the oral culture includes songs, legends, proverbs, and riddles.

folk music Song or dance music developed from a communal aural tradition, e.g. Irish ballads and cowboy songs. The melody and words of folksongs are often changed by a succession of performances. Folk music is characterized by modal melody and simple forms, such as dances, lullabies, work songs, and love ballads.

follicle-stimulating hormone. *See* gonadotrophin.

Fonda, Henry (1905–82) US film actor and director, associated particularly with the portrayal of men of solid integrity, notably in *The Grapes of Wrath* (1940). Other films include *War and Peace* (1956), *Twelve Angry Men* (1957), which he directed, and *On Golden Pond* (1981), which earned him his first Oscar and also starred his daughter **Jane Fonda** (1937–). Her other films include *Klute* (1971), *Julia* (1977), and *Agnes of God* (1985).

Fontainebleau 48 24N 2 42E A town in N central France, in the Seine-et-Marne department. The surrounding forest inspired the Barbizon school of painters. The 16th century Royal Palace was largely built by Francis I. Fontainebleau was the headquarters of NATO from 1954 to 1966. Population (1982): 18 753.

Fonteyn, Dame Margot (Margaret Hookham; 1919–) British ballet dancer. She was a member of the Sadler's Wells company and the Royal Ballet from 1934 to 1959 and often performed in partnership with Rudolf Nureyev.

Fonthill Abbey An architecturally influential country house near Bath in Wiltshire, designed (1796–1807) in the gothic revival style by James Wyatt (1747–1813) for William Beckford (?1760–1844). The tower collapsed in 1827 and the rest was demolished soon after.

food additives Substances added to food to alter its taste, texture, appearance, keeping qualities, or other properties. Although additives can reduce the risk of food poisoning, consumer resistance to them has grown following recent reports of their toxic, carcinogenic, or allergic effects. In the UK prepacked and processed foods must list their ingredients, including any additives. About 280 of these currently have an 'E' number, meaning that they have been approved for use in the EC. Additives without an E number must be listed by name.

Food and Agriculture Organization (FAO) A specialized agency of the United Nations constituted in 1945 to coordinate international efforts to raise levels of nutrition and food production and to improve the management of forests. The headquarters are in Rome.

food chain A series of living organisms associated in a feeding relationship: each animal feeds on the one below it in the series. Most commonly, green plants are at the base of a food chain. They are eaten by herbivores, which in turn may be consumed by carnivores. Parasites are also part of the chain, and different food chains are often interconnected to form a **food web**. Other food chains are based on decomposers—organisms that feed on dead organic remains. See p. 274.

food poisoning An acute illness arising from eating contaminated food. Vomiting and diarrhoea are the usual symptoms. *Salmonella* is the bacterium that most commonly causes it; symptoms begin 12–24 hours after eating the food. Patients usually recover within a few days. Another kind of food poisoning is due to a toxin (poison) produced by staphylococci: symptoms occur within one to three hours of taking the food. *Clostridium* bacteria may also cause food poisoning, the most severe form of which is botulism. *See also* Listeria.

fool's gold. *See* pyrite.

foot-and-mouth disease An infectious virus disease affecting cattle, sheep, goats, pigs, and many wild animals. Symptoms, which appear 1–15 days after infection, include fever and blisters in the mouth and on the foot with consequent excessive salivation and lameness. Recovery occurs in 95% of cases but production of offspring and milk yield in females is adversely affected. The disease must be notifed to the authorities in many countries. Infected animals and contacts are usually slaughtered and movement of animals restricted. Vaccination is routine where the disease is endemic.

football A field game played throughout the world, the object of which is to score goals with an inflated ball. The modern games evolved during the 19th century.

American football is played with an oval ball on a field marked out as a gridiron. There are 22 players on the field at any one time, but groups of differently specialized players are used in different phases of the game. The teams toss to decide which is to kick off, which gives possession to the other team. The game progresses in downs, or periods when the offensive team is advancing the ball towards the goal by passing or running with it. A down ends with a successful tackle or missed pass. The team has four downs in which to advance the ball 10 yd

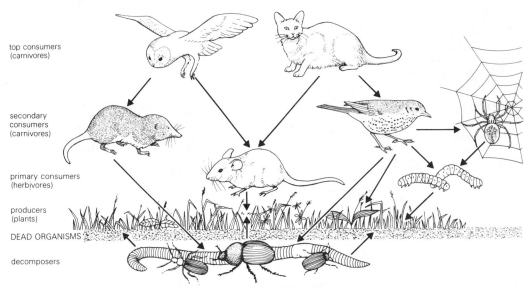

top consumers
(carnivores)

secondary
consumers
(carnivores)

primary consumers
(herbivores)

producers
(plants)

DEAD ORGANISMS

decomposers

FOOD CHAIN *The feeding relationships between some plants and animals of a meadow habitat are simplified in this food web; in practice many more links and various other organisms are involved.*

(9 m). If it fails, the other team is given possession, having the chance to substitute offensive for defensive players. If the 10 yd is covered, the team maintains possession of the ball. A touchdown, in which the ball is taken across the opponents' goal line, scores six points; a conversion after a touchdown, in which the ball is taken over the goal line again from scrimmage or is kicked between the goalposts scores respectively two points or one point; a field goal (kicked from anywhere on the field) scores three points. Players must wear protective clothing.

Association football (*or* soccer) dates back to the founding in England of the Football Association (1863). It is an 11-a-side game played with a spherical ball weighing 14–16 oz (396–453 g) and having a circumference of 27–28 in (69–71 cm). The traditional positions of the players are: goalkeeper; right and left back; right, centre, and left half-back; outside right, inside right, centre forward, inside left, and outside left. These positions have now become very flexible, and a modern line-up consists simply of strikers, midfield players, and defenders. The teams toss for the first kick (the kick-off), following which the teams compete for the ball, trying to kick or head it into the opponents' goal. Only the goalkeeper may use his hands, and then only in his penalty area. Played all over the world, the game is governed internationally by the Fédération internationale de Football association.

Australian Rules is a fast 18-a-side game played with an oval ball measuring 22.75 by 29.5 in (57.2 by 73.6 cm), with which players may run as long as they bounce it every 9 m (10 yd). The ball must be punched instead of thrown (as it is in rugby football). There are four goalposts without crossbars at each end. A goal, kicked between the two inner posts, scores six points; a behind, kicked between an inner and an outer post, scores one point.

Canadian football is similar to American football but is played with 12-a-side teams on a larger field and has slightly different scoring and rules.

Rugby football uses an oval ball that is kicked or passed by hand. The game was first played at Rugby School, England, according to tradition in 1823. In 1871 the Rugby Football Union was formed, but its ban on professionalism led in 1893 to the secession of the Rugby League (then called the Northern Union); there are therefore two types of rugby. Rugby Union football (*or* rugger) is a 15-a-side amateur game played throughout the world. The ball is 11–11.25 in (27.9–28.6 cm) long. A try, in which the ball is touched down behind the opponents' goal line, is worth four points; a goal (a try "converted" by kicking the ball over the crossbar of the goalposts), a further two points; a penalty goal, resulting from a kick awarded as a penalty against the opposing team, three points; and a drop goal, from the field, three points. A scrum, in which the forwards of both teams battle for the ball in a tight mass, is used to restart the game after minor infringements. For more serious infringements a penalty kick is given to the opposing side. Rugby League football is a 13-a-side game with slightly different rules and scoring in which professionalism is allowed; it is played mainly in N England.

Football League An English association football competition for professional teams. It was created in the N in 1888 to help finance professional clubs by providing a systematic series of matches, as the Football Association Challenge Cup series did not. The Second Division was added in 1892 with a system of promotion and relegation between the divisions soon after; the Third Division was added in 1920 and the Fourth in 1958. Similar leagues exist in many other countries.

FOOTBALL

American football

Association football

Australian Rules

Rugby Union football

FOOTBALL   *Dimensions of pitches.*

football pools A system of gambling involving postal betting on the results of football matches. First appearing in the UK in 1923, they are now controlled by a few companies registered under the Betting, Gaming and Lotteries Act (1963). The stake money is pooled, some 30% of which is available as prize money (30% goes in running costs and 40% in government duty). The most popular pool is now the Treble Chance, in which competitors attempt to predict eight games that will result in a draw. From August to April British matches are used and from May to July the pools rely on Australian matches.

Foraminifera An order of small single-celled animals (Protozoa) found on the sea bed or as part of the plankton. They form tiny calcareous often multichambered shells from which they extend fine branching pseudopodia to trap small protozoans and algae. Class: *Sarcodina*. *See also* Globigerina.

force The agency that changes either the speed or the direction of motion of a body (symbol: F). It is a vector quantity defined as the product of the mass of the body and the acceleration produced on it. Force is measured in newtons. *See also* centripetal force; Coriolis force.

Ford, Ford Madox (Ford Hermann Hueffer; 1873–1939) British novelist, grandson of the Pre-Raphaelite artist Ford Madox Brown. Among his 80 or more novels and books of criticism and memoirs are the novels *The Good Soldier* (1915) and *Parade's End* (1924–28), a tetralogy. He founded and edited the *English Review* (1908).

Ford, Gerald R(udolph) (1913–) US statesman; Republican president (1974–77) following Nixon's resignation.

HENRY FORD *Seen with his son Edsel in 1904.*

Ford, Henry (1863–1947) US car manufacturer. The Ford Motor Company was founded in 1903 and in 1912 Ford introduced the assembly line to manufacture the famous Model T, 15 million of which had been mass-produced by 1928.

Foreign and Commonwealth Office The UK government department that deals with foreign and commonwealth affairs and is responsible for presenting and promoting the interests of the UK abroad; it was formed in 1968 by an amalgamation of the Foreign Office and the Commonwealth Office and is headed by the secretary of state for foreign and commonwealth affairs.

Foreign Legion A French military force formed in 1831 to serve in France's African colonies. Its recruits are international but its officers are usually French. The headquarters are at Aubagne, near Marseille, with units in Corsica and Djibouti.

forest An area of land covered largely with trees and undergrowth. Over 20% of world land area is forest, both natural and artificially planted, making forests a vital part of the global ecosystem as major suppliers of oxygen as well as timber. They also provide habitats for wildlife.

The species of trees growing depends mainly on climate. Northern coniferous forests consist largely of pine, spruce, and firs and provide softwood for paper pulp, furniture, construction, etc. In more temperate regions forests consist primarily of mixed deciduous trees, especially oak, ash, elm, beech, sycamore, and other hardwoods, used mainly in furniture. In Mediterranean climates, the trees are adapted to hot dry summers and include the evergreen oaks. Broad-leaved evergreen trees are also found in New Zealand and South America, together with southern conifers. Tropical forests are characterized by a great diversity of species, usually of tall evergreen trees, with many climbing vines and epiphytes. The major tropical rain forests are in the Amazon and Orinoco river basins, with others in Africa and SE Asia. In neighbouring regions of lower and more seasonal rainfall, an open savanna forest predominates, consisting of scattered deciduous trees.

Forestry, the cultivation and management of forests, is of major economic importance. In the UK, forestry is controlled by the Forestry Commission (established in 1919), which is now responsible for the production of most home-grown softwoods.

Forester, C(ecil) S(cott) (1899–1966) British historical novelist who created Horatio Hornblower, a British naval officer of Napoleonic times, in a series of novels, beginning with *The Happy Return* (1937).

forget-me-not An annual or perennial herb of the genus *Myosotis* (50 species), of temperate regions. It has long spikes of small flowers, usually blue with white centres. Several species are grown as garden flowers. Family: *Boraginaceae*.

Forman, Miloš (1932–) Czech film director. His films, which include *The Fireman's Ball* (1967), are noted for their blend of humour and social criticism. In 1968 he went to the USA, where he made *Taking Off* (1970) and *One Flew over the Cuckoo's Nest* (1975).

formic acid (*or* methanoic acid; HCOOH) A colourless corrosive liquid fatty acid with a pungent smell. It is used in textile finishing and chemical manufacture. Formic acid occurs naturally in nettles and insects. Its name comes from the Latin *formica*, ant, whose sting is due to the secretion of formic acid.

Formosa. *See* Taiwan.

Forster, E(dward) M(organ) (1879–1970) British novelist. His fiction and social criticism stress the importance of human affection and the need to cultivate both the intellect and the imagination. His novels include *Where Angels Fear to Tread* (1905), *The Longest Journey* (1907), *A Room with a View* (1908), *Howard's End* (1910), and *A Passage to India* (1924).

Forsythia A genus of shrubs (about 7 species), native to E Europe and Asia and widely grown as garden ornamentals. The masses of four-petalled yellow flowers appear before the leaves. The slender stems make the plants suitable for wall shrubs and hedges. The most common garden forsythia is the hybrid *F.* × *intermedia*. Family: *Oleaceae* (olive family).

Forth, River A river in SE Scotland, rising on the NE slopes of Ben Lomond and flowing 104 km (65 mi) E through Stirling to Alloa. The river then expands into the **Firth of Forth** (an inlet of the North Sea) extending 82 km (51 mi) in length and 31 km (19 mi) wide at its mouth. It is spanned by the cantilever iron Forth Rail Bridge (designed in the 1880s by Benjamin Baker) and a road bridge (1964).

RIVER FORTH *The 19th-century rail bridge in front of the 20th-century road bridge.*

Fort Knox 37 54N 85 59W A military base in the USA, in N Kentucky. Established in 1917, it is the site of the US Depository, which contains US gold reserves. Population (1980): 31 055.

Fort Lamy. *See* N'djamena.

Fortran (*for*mula *tran*slation) A computer-programming language, widely used among scientists and engineers.

Fort Sumter. *See* Charleston.

Fortuna The Roman goddess of fortune and good luck. She was usually portrayed standing on a ball or wheel, indicating her mutability, and holding a cornucopia from which she distributes her favours. She is identical with Tyche.

Fort Worth 32 45N 97 20W A city in the USA, in NE Texas near Dallas, centre of the N Texas industrial area. Population (1980): 385 141.

Forty-five Rebellion. *See* Jacobites.

forum A Roman marketplace, similar to the Greek agora. The forum was the civic centre of the town, containing all the main temples and public buildings.

Fosse Way A Roman road from Exeter through Cirencester to Lincoln. It marked the frontier in the first phase of the Roman conquest of Britain (c. 47 AD). Its characteristically straight course is now followed partly by the modern A429.

fossil The remains or traces of a plant or animal that lived in the past, usually preserved in sedimentary rock. It may be the whole or part of the organism itself that is preserved, usually chemically altered; alternatively it

may have dissolved away leaving an impression (mould), which preserves its exact shape, or a cast, when it has been replaced exactly by mineral matter. Examples of fossils are whole mammoths preserved in ice, insects preserved in amber, and coal (the carbonized remains of extinct swamp plants). Trace fossils include excrement, burrows, or fossil tracks. The study of fossils is called palaeontology.

fossil fuels The mineral fuels coal, oil, and natural gas that occur in rock formations. They were formed by the deposition millions of years ago of the remains of vegetation (coal) and living organisms (oil and gas), which were buried under subsequent deposition and later subjected to heat and pressure. Fossil fuels supply a large proportion of our current energy needs, but the reserves are finite.

Foucault pendulum A very long pendulum with a heavy bob, capable of oscillating for a long period. It demonstrates the earth's rotation since, as it swings, its plane of oscillation slowly rotates. At a latitude λ, the number of hours for a complete rotation is given by $24/\sin \lambda$. It was invented by Jean Foucault (1819–68) and first demonstrated in 1851 in Paris.

Fountains Abbey A ruined Cistercian abbey near Ripon, Yorkshire. Founded in 1132 it became the leading Cistercian community in England and had great wealth prior to its dissolution (1539) at the Reformation.

Fourier, Jean Baptiste Joseph, Baron (1768–1830) French mathematician and physicist, noted for his method of expanding a periodic function in terms of sine and cosine waves, now known as **Fourier analysis**.

Four Noble Truths The fundamental doctrine of Buddhism, set forth by Gautama in the first discourse at Benares. The Truths are: existence is characterized by suffering; the cause of suffering is craving; to end craving is to end suffering; the way to achieve this is the Eightfold Path.

four o'clock plant A bushy perennial herb, *Mirabilis jalapa*, native to tropical America but widely grown as an ornamental. It bears clusters of red, pink, white, yellow, or streaked flowers, which are tubular with a wide flared mouth and open in the late afternoon. Family: *Nyctaginaceae*.

fowl, domestic A domesticated form of the red jungle fowl, *Gallus gallus*, native to Asian forests. It was first domesticated about 4000 years ago as a religious and sacrificial animal and was used by the Romans for food. Since the 19th century, a large number of breeds and varieties have been selected for size, resistance to disease, egg production, etc.

Fowles, John (1926–) British novelist, whose works treat philosophical, psychological, and social themes in a rich and often fantastic manner. His novels include *The Collector* (1963), *The Magus* (1966), and *The French Lieutenant's Woman* (1969), which have been filmed. Other books include *A Maggot* (1985) and the short stories *The Ebony Tower* (1974).

fowl pest An infectious virus disease affecting domestic fowl and certain other birds. Symptoms arise 4–11 days after infection and include a fall in egg production (in laying birds), loss of appetite, lethargy, laboured breathing through a gaping beak, and nasal discharge. In the UK any outbreak must be reported. Vaccination confers immunity after 10–14 days.

fox A carnivorous mammal belonging to the dog family (*Canidae*). Foxes have pointed ears, short legs, and

FOSSIL

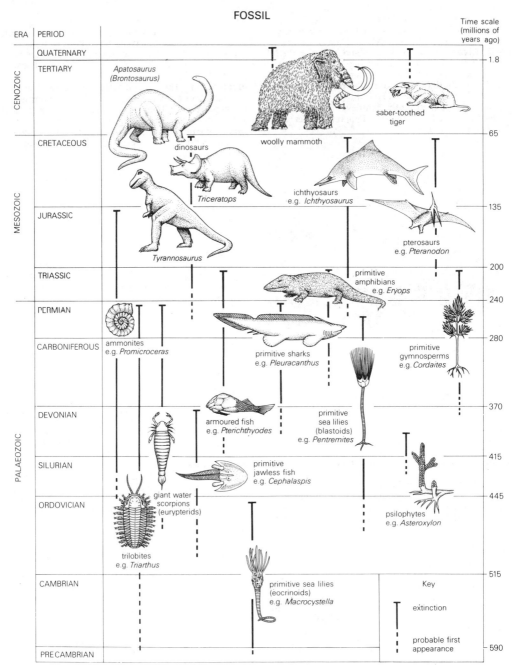

ERA	PERIOD		Time scale (millions of years ago)

Apatosaurus
(Brontosaurus)

saber-toothed
tiger

dinosaurs

woolly mammoth

Triceratops

ichthyosaurs
e.g. Ichthyosaurus

Tyrannosaurus

pterosaurs
e.g. Pteranodon

primitive
amphibians
e.g. Eryops

ammonites
e.g. Promicroceras

primitive sharks
e.g. Pleuracanthus

primitive
gymnosperms
e.g. Cordaites

armoured fish
e.g. Pterichthyodes

primitive
sea lilies
(blastoids)
e.g. Pentremites

primitive
jawless fish
e.g. Cephalaspis

giant water
scorpions
(eurypterids)

psilophytes
e.g. Asteroxylon

trilobites
e.g. Triarthus

primitive sea lilies
(eocrinoids)
e.g. Macrocystella

Key

extinction

probable first
appearance

ERA: CENOZOIC, MESOZOIC, PALAEOZOIC

PERIOD: QUATERNARY, TERTIARY, CRETACEOUS, JURASSIC, TRIASSIC, PERMIAN, CARBONIFEROUS, DEVONIAN, SILURIAN, ORDOVICIAN, CAMBRIAN, PRECAMBRIAN

Time scale: 1.8, 65, 135, 200, 240, 280, 370, 415, 445, 515, 590

FOSSIL   Some extinct animals and plants from past geological ages.

large bushy tails. Generally nocturnal, they are solitary stealthy hunters. The most familiar is the red fox (*Vulpes vulpes*), found in forest and woodland and now venturing into suburban gardens. Some species are specialized for life in difficult habitats, such as the Arctic fox and the fennec. Chief genera: *Vulpes* (9 species), *Dusicyon* (South American foxes; 8 species).

Fox, Charles James (1749–1806) British Whig politician; the first British foreign secretary (1782). He entered parliament (1768) as a supporter of Lord North but opposed North's American policy. Fox resigned following George III's appointment of the Earl of Shelburne (1737–1805) in succession to Rockingham and joined North in a coalition that briefly took office under the Duke of Portland (1738–1809) in 1783. Fox supported the French Revolution, over which issue many Whigs joined the Tories, and in 1798 he was dismissed from the privy council for opposing war with Revolutionary France.

Fox, George (1624–91) English religious leader, founder of the Quakers. A Puritan by upbringing, Fox became dissatisfied with the formalism of established Christianity and the state's control of the church. In 1646 he had a personal revelation and thereafter preached a gospel of love, stressing the immediate guidance of the Holy Spirit. He was frequently imprisoned for his beliefs.

foxglove A herbaceous plant of the genus *Digitalis*, especially *D. purpurea*, a biennial herb native to W Europe but naturalized elsewhere. Foxgloves have large grey-green leaves and tall spikes of drooping bell-shaped flowers, purple, yellow, or white in colour. The dried leaves contain digitalis. Family: *Scrophulariaceae*.

foxhound A dog belonging to one of two breeds used for foxhunting. The English foxhound is more strongly built than the American foxhound. In both, the short coat is a combination of black, tan, and white. Height: 56–63 cm.

foxhunting A sport in which huntsmen on horseback pursue a fox with a pack of 20 to 30 foxhounds, which hunt their quarry by scent. It has been fully organized in the UK since the 18th century. The hunt officials, who are traditionally dressed in scarlet coats, are the master of foxhounds, who directs the hounds, and one or more whippers-in, who help to control them. Mounted followers (the field) accompany the hunt. Hunting has many detractors (notably the League against Cruel Sports) and Oscar Wilde described it as "the unspeakable in pursuit of the uneatable".

fox terrier A breed of dog, either smooth-haired or wire-haired, developed in England for hunting foxes and badgers. It is sturdy with a broad tapering muzzle and small drooping ears. The coat is mainly white with black and tan markings. Height: 37–39 cm.

fracture The breaking of a bone. This usually occurs as a result of injury but it may happen very easily in bones diseased with cancer or osteoporosis (pathological fracture). In a simple fracture the ends of the broken bone are not displaced; in a compound fracture the broken bone pierces the skin. Fractures are treated by aligning the ends of the broken bone and immobilizing them. Healing will result quickly. Sometimes, however, it is necessary to pin fractures surgically.

Fragonard, Jean Honoré (1732–1806) French rococo painter whose light-hearted and delicately erotic subjects include *The Swing* and *The Progress of Love*.

Dutch influence can be seen in a number of his landscapes and portraits.

JEAN HONORÉ FRAGONARD *Detail from* The Swing *(1768–69) in the Wallace Collection, London.*

France, Anatole (Jacques Anatole François Thibault; 1844–1924) French novelist, whose books are noted for their erudition, scepticism, and elegance. His intervention in the Dreyfus case (1897) marked the beginning of his commitment to socialism and, during his final years, communism. In such novels as *L'Île des pingouins* (1909) and *Les Dieux ont soif* (1913) his view of mankind is deeply pessimistic. He was awarded the Nobel Prize in 1921.

France, Republic of A country in W Europe, bordering on the English Channel in the N, the Atlantic Ocean in the W, and the Mediterranean Sea in the S. It includes the island of Corsica and several overseas regions (Martinique, Guadeloupe, and French Guiana). Overseas territories include French Polynesia and New Caledonia. Fertile lowlands cover most of the N and W of France, rising to the Pyrenees in the S, the Massif Central in the SE, and the Vosges, Jura, and Alps in the E. The principal rivers are the Seine, the Loire, and the Rhône. *Economy*: agriculture is important, especially animal products; the wine industry is a major source of revenue. There have been large-scale developments in the industrial sector since World War II. *History*: France today approximates the ancient region of Gaul, which was conquered by Julius Caesar in the 1st century BC. It became part of the Roman Empire and in the 1st century AD Christianity was introduced to the provinces into which Gaul was divided. From the 3rd to the 5th centuries, it was overrun by German tribes, including the Goths, Vandals, and Franks (from whom the name France is derived). The Frankish kingdom reached its peak under Charlemagne (reigned 768–814) and his Carolingian dynasty continued to rule in France until 987, when Hugh Capet became the first Capetian king. During the 10th century Norsemen (Vikings) established themselves in what became Normandy and in 1066 invaded England. The claims of English kings to French territory were realized on a large scale by the Angevins and consequent conflict between France and England culminated in the Hundred Years' War (1337–1453), as a result of which the English were expelled from all of France, except Calais. The Capetians were succeeded by the Valois dynasty (1328–1589), a period that saw the beginning of France's long rivalry with Spain for hegemony in Europe. During the Wars of Religion the first Bourbon, Henry IV, came to the throne (1589). The first half of the 17th century was dominated by Cardinal de Richelieu and his protégé and successor as chief minister, Cardinal Mazarin (1602–61). They were responsible for France replacing Spain, after the Thirty Years' War, as the supreme European power (1659). During the reign (1643–1715) of Louis XIV France reached the zenith of its power and brilliance. Decline, however, began before his death and gathered speed in the following decades. The disastrous Seven Years' War forced France to recognize British supremacy in North America and India and the political reaction and economic incompetence of the later Bourbon kings precipitated the French Revolution in 1789. The First Republic was proclaimed (1792) and Louis XVI was guillotined (1793) in spite of the military opposition of the major European powers (*see* Revolutionary and Napoleonic Wars). In 1799 Napoleon Bonaparte overthrew the Directory, becoming first consul and, in 1804, emperor. By 1808 he had brought most of continental Europe under his sway but in 1815 he was finally defeated at Waterloo and exiled. The Bourbons were restored until 1830, when the July Revolution raised Louis Philippe to the throne. Overthrown in the Revolution of 1848, the monarchy was replaced by the Second Republic of which Louis Napoleon became president; in 1852 he proclaimed himself emperor as Napoleon III. During the Second Empire France underwent the beginnings of industrialization but its prosperity was not sufficient to achieve victory in the Franco-Prussian War, in which Napoleon's ignominious leadership led to his overthrow (1870). The subsequent Third Republic lasted until 1940, in spite of World War I and political dissension. After the outbreak of World War II France fell to Germany and a pro-German government was established at Vichy, while de Gaulle led the Free French resistance in London. In 1944 France was liberated by the Allies and de Gaulle established a provisional government that gave way (1946) to the Fourth Republic. The immediate postwar period was overshadowed by war in Indochina and by the crisis in Algeria that precipitated the fall of the Fourth Republic (1958). De Gaulle was recalled from retirement and, as president of the Fifth Republic, instituted firm government. In May, 1968, however, the Republic was shaken by serious revolts among students and a wave of strikes and in 1969 he resigned. Gaullist principles nevertheless continued to influence government under his successors Pompidou and Giscard d'Estaing. Mitterrand's election (1981) made him the first socialist to hold the office of president in 35 years; proportional representation was introduced for subsequent elections. Official language: French. Official currency: franc of 100 centimes. Area: 543 814 sq km (209 912 sq mi). Population (1987): 55 623 000. Capital: Paris. Main port: Marseille.

Francis Ferdinand (1863–1914) Archduke of Austria and heir apparent to his uncle, Emperor Francis Joseph. His assassination (28 June, 1914) by a Serbian nationalist at Sarajevo precipitated World War I.

Francis Joseph (1830–1916) Emperor of Austria (1848–1916) and King of Hungary (1867–1916). His long reign saw the rise of national tensions in the Empire, which led to the establishment of the Dual Monarchy of Austria-Hungary, under which Austria and Hungary coexisted as equal partners under the Austrian Crown. He was defeated in the Austro-Prussian War of 1866 but in 1879 he allied with the recently formed German Empire and in 1882 with Italy, forming the Triple Alliance. His ultimatum to Serbia, following the assassination by a Serbian nationalist of his nephew, Archduke Francis Ferdinand (1914), led to World War I.

Francis of Assisi, St (Giovanni di Bernardone; c. 1182–1226) Italian friar and founder of the Franciscans, born in Assisi. He renounced his worldly life in 1205 to live in poverty and devote himself to prayer and charitable works. Gaining followers, he founded his order in 1209. He travelled throughout Spain, the Holy Land, and Egypt. A profoundly humble man, in paintings he is often portrayed in the countryside among animals and birds. He received the stigmata in 1224 and was canonized in 1228. Feast day: 4 Oct.

Francis Xavier, St (1506–52) Spanish Jesuit missionary. While studying in Paris (1523–34) he met St Ignatius of Loyola and helped him found the Jesuit order. From 1541 he worked in the Indies, India, and Japan, establishing missions and making many converts. Feast day: 3 Dec.

Franciscans An order of friars founded in 1209 by St Francis of Assisi. His rule was devised to impose both personal and corporate poverty on the order's members. The expanding order found complete poverty practically difficult, and a schism ensued in the early 14th century regarding how strictly the rule should be followed. The order survived, however, and has remained an important missionary and charitable branch of the Roman Catholic Church.

francium (Fr) The heaviest alkali metal, a very unstable radioactive element discovered in 1939 by Perey. The longest-lived isotope ^{223}Fr has a half-life of 22 minutes; traces of the element exist in nature. At no 87; at wt (223).

Franck, César Auguste (1822–90) Belgian composer, organist, and teacher, who settled in Paris in 1834. Franck was influenced by Bach and evolved a highly chromatic form of harmony. He also developed "cyclic form," the use of the same theme in more than one movement of a work. His compositions include *Symphonic Variations* (for piano and orchestra; 1885), a symphony (1886–88), a violin sonata (1886), and a string quartet (1889).

Franco, Francisco (1892–1975) Spanish general and statesman; dictator from 1939 until his death. He became chief of the General Staff in 1935 and on 18 July, 1936, staged a military uprising against the Republican Government of Manuel Azaña (1880–1940) that precipitated the Spanish Civil War. In October, 1936, he became head of state in the Nationalist Zone and commander in chief of the rebel forces. By 1939, with help from Hitler and Mussolini, he had defeated the Republican forces and become the absolute leader of Spain. Franco's government, in which the National Movement (*see* Falange Española) was the only political party, remained sympathetic to Hitler but maintained a neutral position throughout World War II. Spain was excluded from the newly formed UN in 1945 but its isolation was broken during the Cold War, when Franco's anticommunism made him a more attractive ally. Although his government achieved considerable economic advance for Spain, especially in the 1960s, he operated a ruthless dictatorship that tolerated no opposition. The country's move to democracy came under his successor, King Juan Carlos.

Franco-Prussian War (1870–71) A war between France and Prussia. Fearing Bismarck's proposals to make a relative of William I of Prussia the king of Spain, France declared war. Napoleon III and his army were soon defeated at the battle of Sedan but French resistance continued. Napoleon was deposed and the Third Republic was established. The Treaty of Frankfurt imposed a huge indemnity on France, which ceded Alsace and Lorraine to the newly established German Empire; France was left economically weakened and politically divided.

frangipani A tropical American tree, *Plumeria rubra*, cultivated throughout the tropics. It has tapering long-stalked leaves and round clusters of fragrant pink, reddish-purple, white, or yellow flowers, used to make perfume. Family: *Apocynaceae*.

Frank, Anne (1929–45) German Jewish girl, who died in a German concentration camp. Her diary became a symbol of Jewish resistance and courage following its publication in 1947. She wrote it while hiding from the Nazis in Amsterdam in 1942–43.

Frankfurt am Main 50 06N 8 41E A city in central West Germany, in Hessen on the River Main. A major banking and commercial centre, it is famed for its trade fairs, especially the annual book fair. It was the seat of the imperial elections (9th to 18th centuries) and coronations (1562–1792) of the Holy Roman emperors and the original home of the Rothschilds. Population (1986): 593 400.

frankincense (*or* olibanum) An aromatic gum resin obtained chiefly from trees of the genus *Boswellia*, especially *B. carteri*, which grows in the Middle East. It smells of balsam when heated, and burns brightly giving off a fragrant odour. Frankincense has been known since ancient Egyptian times and is still used as an incense, in fumigants, and in perfumes.

BENJAMIN FRANKLIN *An experiment (1752) with a kite to prove that lightning is an electric discharge.*

Franklin, Benjamin (1706–90) US diplomat, scientist, and author. His experiments with static electricity, especially the famous episode in which he flew a kite during a thunderstorm, established the electrical nature of thunderstorms and led him to invent the lightning

conductor. In the disputes that led to the American Revolution he represented Pennsylvania's case to Britain (1757–62, 1766–75) and as a member of the Continental Congress helped frame the Declaration of Independence (1775). Famous as a diplomat in Paris (1776–85), he enlisted French help for the colonies and later negotiated peace with Britain (1783).

Franks A Germanic people, who invaded Roman Gaul from the Rhineland between the 3rd and 5th centuries AD. One of the Frankish tribes, the Salian Franks, gained control of most of Gaul under their ruler Clovis (d. 511) and were converted to Christianity. The Frankish state was ruled by the Merovingian dynasty (named after Clovis' grandfather, Merovech) until its replacement by the Carolingians (named after Charlemagne) in 751. The Carolingian empire lasted until its division in 843. The western Frankish kingdom was the nucleus of France.

Franz Josef Land (Russian name: Zemlya Frantsa Iosifa) A Soviet archipelago of about 85 icebound islands in the N Barents Sea. They were discovered in 1873 by Austrians and annexed by the Soviet Union in 1926. Total area: about 20 700 sq km (79 905 sq mi).

Fraser, (John) Malcolm (1930–) Australian statesman; Liberal prime minister (1975–83).

Fraser, Peter (1884–1950) British-born New Zealand statesman; Labour prime minister (1940–49). He influenced Allied strategy in the Pacific during World War II and helped to establish the UN (1945).

Fraser River A river in W Canada, the chief river of British Columbia. Rising near Mount Robson, it flows rapidly through mountain gorges and eventually empties into the Strait of Georgia near Vancouver. Length: 1370 km (850 mi).

fraud In law, making a false representation, by words or conduct or by withholding facts where there is a duty to disclose them, in order to obtain a material advantage. To prove fraud it is necessary to show that a false representation was made (1) knowingly, (2) without belief in its truth, or (3) recklessly, without concern whether it was true or not.

Frazer, Sir James George (1854–1941) British anthropologist, mythologist, and writer. Frazer's major work was *The Golden Bough* (first edition 1890). The results of his work were far-reaching, influencing people outside the anthropological field.

Frederick (I) Barbarossa (c. 1123–90) Holy Roman Emperor (1152–90; crowned 1155). He was engaged in a long struggle with the papacy and was excommunicated in 1160. His warring against the Lombard cities was ultimately unsuccessful; they regained their independence in 1183. He failed to subdue his powerful cousin, Henry the Lion (?1129–95), but established his authority in Poland, Hungary, Bohemia, and Burgundy.

Frederick II (1194–1250) Holy Roman Emperor (1220–50) and, as Frederick I, King of Sicily (1198–1250). As leader of the fifth Crusade (1228–29) he captured Jerusalem but remained an opponent of papal policy and was excommunicated three times (1227, 1239, 1245). He was a man of wide learning but neglected the government of his possessions.

Frederick (II) the Great (1712–86) King of Prussia (1740–86), who made Prussia a major European power. He liberalized the Prussian legal code and introduced economic and social reforms that reinvigorated Prussian society and institutions. His conquest of Silesia (1740)

FREDERICK (II) THE GREAT *Playing the flute at Sans Souci.*

gave rise to the War of the Austrian Succession (1740–48), after which his possession of the region was confirmed. His victory in the Seven Years' War (1756–63) confirmed the military supremacy of Prussia, both in Germany and in Europe.

freehold. *See* cstate.

freemasonry A secret society for men, which declares itself to be based on brotherly love, faith, and charity. It probably developed from the medieval stonemasons' guilds. In its modern form freemasonry dates from the establishment (1717) in England of the Grand Lodge, to which over 8000 private lodges are now affiliated. During the 18th century masonry spread to America and the colonies as well as to continental Europe. Its ceremonies, which are allegorical and illustrated by symbols, demand a vow of secrecy as well as a belief in God and are based on Old Testament anecdotes and moralities. Opposition to masonry orginated with a papal bull (1738) excommunicating masons, since when Roman Catholics have never accepted its principles or its secrecy. In France and some other European countries it assumed a political character and was condemned by governments. It is banned in E Europe.

Freesia A genus of ornamental South African plants (20 species), cultivated commercially, especially as a source of cut flowers. Growing from corms, they have sword-shaped leaves and clusters of funnel-shaped lemon-scented flowers of various colours. Most cultivated varieties are hybrids derived from *F. refracta* (with yellowish flowers) and *F. armstrongii* (rose-purple flowers). Family: *Iridaceae*.

freestyle wrestling. *See* wrestling.

Freetown 8 20N 13 05W The capital and main port of Sierra Leone, on the Atlantic coast. It was founded in the late 18th century as a refuge for freed slaves and was capital of British West Africa (1808–74), becoming the capital of Sierra Leone in 1961. Population (1985): 469 776.

free verse Poetry without regular metre or form and depending on the rhythms and patterns of natural speech. The original French term, *vers libre*, was coined during the 1880s by poets who wished to emphasize rhythm as the essential principle of poetic form.

free will In philosophy and theology, the ability of man to choose his own destiny, as opposed to the idea that everything that happens to him is inevitable. Philosophers are concerned to discover what the presuppositions and implications of free will are, compared to those of determinism. They are also concerned to discover to what extent free will and determinism can be compatible. In a theistic context, determinism is replaced by predestination, the view that all events, including human choice, are fixed by the will of God.

freeze drying A method of drying foods for preservation in which the food is rapidly frozen under very low pressure. Any water present freezes and then sublimes under the low pressure.

freezing The preservation of food by keeping it frozen, thus arresting the development of the microorganisms responsible for the decay of the food. Home freezers keep food at a temperature of about $-18°C$ ($-0.4°F$). On thawing, the deterioration process restarts. Most foods are well preserved by freezing, with little loss in nutritional value but some with a high water content within the cells of the food, such as strawberries and cucumbers, become soggy after freezing as a result of damage to the cell structure by ice formation. Most vegetables are blanched (boiled for 2–4 minutes) before freezing to arrest the action of enzymes. It is the residual enzymic action that determines the recommended storage time.

Frege, Gottlob (1848–1925) German mathematician and logician. He extended Boole's work on symbolic logic by using logical symbols not already used in mathematics (symbols for *or*, *if-then*, etc.). This is now standard practice in logic.

Fremantle 32 07S 115 44E A major seaport in Western Australia, SW of Perth at the mouth of the Swan River. Kwinana, an important industrial complex with oil and nickel refineries and bulk-grain facilities, is nearby. Population (1986): 24 010.

French A Romance language spoken by 45 million people in France, and extensively in Canada, Belgium, Switzerland, and elsewhere. It is the official language of 21 countries. Standard French, based upon the Parisian dialect known as Francien, has been France's official administrative language since 1539. It has replaced most northern dialects, known collectively as *langue d'oïl*, and has superseded the Occitan dialects of S France, known as *langue d'oc* (*see* Provençal). During the 17th century the Académie Française and the publication of a standard dictionary (1680) quickly stabilized the language. French grammar has been simplified from Latin and the phonology has greatly altered. There are no noun case declensions and the verb is conjugated for three persons.

French bean An annual herb, *Phaseolus vulgaris*, also called kidney bean, probably native to South America but widely cultivated. It has large heart-shaped leaves and white pealike flowers. Both dwarf and twining varieties are grown for their beans, usually eaten in the pod. Family: *Leguminosae*. *See also* haricot bean.

French Community An association of states, comprising France and its former colonies, established by the new Fifth Republic after a constitutional referendum (1958). In addition to France it includes Guadeloupe, Guiana, Martinique, Mayotte, La Réunion, St Pierre and Miquelon, Southern and Antarctic Territories, French Polynesia, New Caledonia, and Wallis and Futuna.

French Equatorial Africa   A former federation of French territories in W central Africa comprising (1910–59) the present-day independent states of the Central African Republic, Chad, Congo (People's Republic of), and Gabon.

French Guiana   A French overseas region on the NE coast of South America. A narrow fertile coastal belt rises to a mountainous interior, which is covered in dense forest rich in valuable timber. *History*: Europeans in search of Eldorado explored the region from the early 16th century, but it was not settled until the 17th century, when the French, Dutch, Portuguese, and English competed for possession. In 1817 it was finally obtained by the French, who established penal colonies, including the notorious one on Devil's Island, in the territory. The French Guianese have had full French citizenship since 1848. Area: about 91 000 sq km (34 740 sq mi). Population (1981 est): 66 400. Capital: Cayenne.

French horn   An orchestral brass instrument, which evolved from the hunting horn. It consists of a long narrow coiled tube with a wide bell and a cup-shaped mouthpiece. In the 18th century crooks of tubing of different length were inserted to enable it to play in a variety of keys. In the 19th century valves were fitted giving the horn in F a complete range of about three octaves above B below the bass stave. It is a transposing instrument, its music being written a fifth higher than it sounds.

French Polynesia   A French overseas territory in the S Pacific Ocean consisting of several island groups. The most important of these are the Gambier Islands, the Society Archipelago, the Tuamotu Archipelago, the Tubuai Islands, and the Marquesas Islands.   Area: about 4000 sq km (1500 sq mi). Population (1987): 183 000. Capital: Papeete.

French Republican calendar   The calendar adopted (1793) in France during the French Revolution and retained until 1806, when the Gregorian calendar was reintroduced. The year began on 22 Sept (the date in 1792 when the Republic came into being) and had 365 days divided into 12 months of 30 days each. The remaining 5 days were festivals, an extra one being added in a leap year. Each month was divided into 3 periods of 10 days and was renamed.

French Revolution   The overthrow of the French monarchy as a reaction to the corrupt, feudal, and incompetent government of the Bourbon kings. In 1789 Louis XVI was forced to summon the States General but its Third Estate, opposing aristocratic attempts to dominate proceedings, formed its own National Assembly. Riots followed, the Bastille was stormed, the king was mobbed at Versailles, and the Assembly (from July the Constituent Assembly) promulgated the Declaration of the Rights of Man. Feudalism was abolished and in September, 1791, a new constitution was accepted by the king following his thwarted attempt to flee France (the flight to Varennes). However, his continuing uncooperativeness fostered the growing republicanism of what became the Legislative Assembly (October, 1791) and then the National Convention (September, 1792). The Convention proclaimed a republic and in January, 1793, Louis was executed. The moderate Girondins, discredited by France's war reverses (*see* Revolutionary and Napoleonic Wars), were now ousted by the Jacobins and power passed to the Committee of Public Safety. Under Robespierre the Committee conducted a Reign of Ter-

ror in which thousands of suspected antirevolutionaries were executed. His extremism, however, brought his downfall (1794) and led to the establishment of the Directory (1795), which struggled for four years with economic crises until Napoleon's coup d'état (1799) brought the Revolution to an end.

French Somaliland.   *See* Djibouti, Republic of.

French Southern and Antarctic Territories   A French territory (since 1955) comprising Adélie Land in Antarctica with the islands of Amsterdam and St Paul and the Kerguelen and Crozet archipelagos in the Indian Ocean.

French Sudan.   *See* Mali, Republic of.

French West Africa   The former French territories in West Africa comprising (1895–1958) the present-day independent countries of Benin, Guinea, Côte d'Ivoire, Niger, and Senegal.

frequency   The number of cycles completed by a vibrating system in unit time, usually one second (symbol: ν or f). The unit of frequency is the hertz. The angular frequency, ω, is related to the frequency by the equation $\omega = 2\pi f$ and is measured in radians per second.

frequency modulation.   *See* modulation.

fresco   A classical and Renaissance method of wall decoration in which pure pigments dissolved in water were applied to the wet lime-plastered surface of a wall, producing a chemical reaction that made the colours a permanent part of the wall. Up to about 1500 the design was sketched freehand onto the rough plaster surface. Separate areas of the sketch were then filled in with fine smooth plaster and detailed colour was applied in layers of different pigments. Subsequently the cartoon, as used by Michelangelo, Raphael, Holbein, and others, allowed for more complicated premeditated design. The composition was drawn on sheets of paper, later applied to the wall, and the design pricked through with a stylus or with charcoal dust forced through the stylus piercings. Fresco painting was revived in the 20th century by the Mexican muralists Orozco and Rivera.

SIGMUND FREUD

Freud, Sigmund   (1856–1939) Austrian psychiatrist and pioneer of psychoanalysis. Freud studied medicine and, in 1882, joined the staff of a psychiatric clinic in Vienna. An interest in hypnosis developed through his collaboration with Josef Breuer (1842–1925) and Jean-

Martin Charcot (1825–93). Following the publication with Breuer of *Studies in Hysteria* (1895), Freud evolved his theory that neuroses were rooted in suppressed sexual desires and sexual experiences of childhood. In *The Interpretation of Dreams* (1899), he analysed the content of dreams in terms of unconscious desires. His emphasis on the sexual origin of mental disorders aroused great controversy. In 1902 Freud established a circle in Vienna, which later (1910) became the International Psycho-Analytical Society. However, many of its members, including Carl Jung and Alfred Adler, resigned over disagreements. Freud left Vienna in 1938, following the Nazi invasion, joining his son in London. His other books include *The Psychopathology of Everyday Life* (1904), *Totem and Taboo* (1913), and *Beyond the Pleasure Principle* (1920).

Freyja (*or* Freya) The Norse goddess of love and fertility, the sister of Frey, the god of sunshine, rain, and fertility. She is the Norse counterpart of Venus and is the leader of the Valkyries. In some sources she is identified with Frigga.

friction A force exerted at the boundary between two solids or fluids that retards motion between them. In solid friction a distinction is drawn between sliding friction and rolling friction. Sliding friction is further divided into dynamic friction, defined as the minimum force needed to keep a body sliding, and static friction, defined as the minimum force needed to move a stationary body. The latter is slightly greater than the former. In rolling friction the force of resistance is less than in sliding friction as the rolling body moves up the side of a depression made in the stationary body. This accounts for the effectiveness of wheels and ball bearings. The coefficient of friction is defined as the ratio of the frictional force to the perpendicular reaction between the surfaces. Friction is caused primarily by the two surfaces interlocking at the microscopic level. It is reduced by the use of lubricants, such as grease or graphite.

Friedman, Milton (1912–) US economist, known for his theories on monetary supply, which contradict those of Keynes. His published work, which argues for the free market economy, includes *A Theory of the Consumption Function* (1957) and *Capitalism and Freedom* (1962). He won the 1976 Nobel Prize.

Friendly Islands. *See* Tonga, Kingdom of.

friendly societies Voluntary mutual-aid associations the members of which regularly contribute money to central funds that provide financial assistance in times of need caused by illness, old age, or death. First formed in the 17th century, the societies enjoyed their greatest popularity in the 19th century and inspired many other self-help and insurance schemes, including the UK National Insurance Act (1911).

Friends of the Earth A British environmental pressure group. Established in 1971, it is organized into 250 local groups in the UK, which campaign on environmental issues through demonstrations, public meetings, and parliamentary legislation. Targets have included motorway projects, commercial whaling, and industrial pollution (including nuclear power plants). The organization also has branches in 25 countries, directed from the Netherlands.

Friesian cattle A breed of black-and-white cattle originating from the province of Friesland in the Netherlands. They were exported to North America by early settlers and there developed as Holstein-Friesians.

They are high-yielding milk producers and crosses, especially with a Charolais or Hereford bull, give good beef.

frigate bird A seabird belonging to the genus *Fregata* and family *Fregatidae* (5 species), occurring in tropical and subtropical oceanic regions, also called man-of-war bird because it often steals food from other birds in mid-air. 80–115 cm long, frigate birds have narrow wings spanning up to 2.3 m, a long hooked bill, and a forked tail. Males are glossy black and develop an inflatable red throat sac in the breeding season; females are brownish black with white underparts. Order: *Pelecaniformes* (gannets, pelicans, etc.).

Frigga (*or* Frigg) The Norse goddess of married love and the hearth, the wife of Odin. In some legends she is identified with Freyja; her name is preserved in *Friday*.

Frisch, Otto Robert (1904–79) Austrian-born physicist, nephew of Lise Meitner, with whom he worked in Copenhagen on nuclear fission. During World War II he worked at Los Alamos on the atom bomb. In 1947 he became professor of physics at Cambridge University.

Frisian A West Germanic language formerly spoken along the North Sea coastal region of Holland as far as Schleswig in Germany. It is now principally confined to Friesland province in Holland and certain offshore islands including Heligoland. It is the language most closely related to English. The Frisians were a seafaring and commercial people before turning to dairy and beef farming.

Frisian Islands A chain of islands in the North Sea extending along the coast of, and politically divided between, the Netherlands, West Germany, and SW Denmark. The chain comprises three main groups: the West, North, and East Frisian Islands.

fritillary (botany) A bulbous perennial plant of the genus *Fritillaria* (80 species), mostly native to N temperate regions. The leaves are narrow and the bell-shaped flowers droop from slender stalks. The European snake's head (*F. meleagris*) has reddish-purple chequered flowers. The crown imperial (*F. imperialis*), native to N India, has a cluster of pendant red flowers at the top of a tall (120 cm) stem, topped by a tuft of leaves. Both species are popular garden plants. Family: *Liliaceae*.

fritillary (zoology) A nymphalid butterfly, usually brown or orange marked with black. Chief genera: *Boloria, Melitaea*.

Friuli-Venezia Giulia A region in the extreme NE of Italy. It was formed in 1947, incorporating Trieste in 1954, and is semiautonomous. It consists of mountains along the N border with Austria and a coastal plain in the S. There is farming throughout the region. Area: 7850 sq km (3031 sq mi). Population (1985 est): 1 214 557. Capital: Trieste.

Froebel, Friedrich Wilhelm August (1782–1852) German pioneer of nursery education. He applied the concept of harmonious growth to the development of children in *The Education of Man* (1826). His view that children should spend time together in creative play led him to found the first kindergarten (1837) at Blankenburg.

frog A tail-less amphibian of the family *Ranidae*, which includes bullfrogs, hairy frogs, and leopard frogs. Many other so-called frogs, such as tree frogs, are actually toads. The European frog (*Rana temporaria*) grows to 10 cm. Greenish-brown with black markings, it spends most of its life on land, feeding on insects, and only returns to water to breed. Order: *Anura*.

froghopper A small jumping insect belonging to the family *Cercopidae* (about 2000 species). Froghoppers feed on plant juices, sometimes becoming pests. Eggs are laid on stems or roots and the nymphs remain stationary until adult. They often protect themselves against predators and desiccation with a cover of white froth ("cuckoo spit"), produced by blowing air mixed with fluid from the anus through a valve in the abdomen. For this reason they are often known as cuckoo-spit insects and spittlebugs. Order: *Hemiptera.*

front In meteorology, the interface between two air masses of different thermal characteristics and origins. Where the air masses converge the warm air, being lighter, rises and slopes over the cold air. Distinctive weather phenomena are associated with fronts, particularly the development of depressions, and they are very important in short-term weather forecasting.

Front de Libération nationale (FLN) An Algerian nationalist group that organized the war of independence against France (1954–62). Formed in 1954, the FLN began a campaign of terrorism and sabotage. In 1956 it organized itself like a government, sending diplomatic missions abroad, and in 1958 set up a provisional government in Tunis. In 1962 the French under Gen de Gaulle agreed to Algerian independence and when Ben Bella (1916–) became president in 1963 the FLN became Algeria's sole political party.

frost A weather condition that occurs when the temperature falls below 0°C (32°F). It is recognized by the icy deposit that forms but if the air is very dry this will not occur. In weather forecasting grades of severity of frost are distinguished as slight (−0.1 to −3.5°C), moderate (−3.6 to −6.4°C), severe (−6.5 to −11.5°C), and very severe (below −11.5°C). A distinction is made between ground frost, measured at grass level, and air frost, measured at a height of 1.4 m (4 ft).

Frost, Robert Lee (1874–1963) US poet. He became famous with the publication of *A Boy's Will* (1913) and *North of Boston* (1914). His work, which is often pastoral, has a dark undercurrent of anxiety and suffering.

frostbite Damage to part of the body, usually a hand or foot, resulting from exposure to extreme cold. The blood vessels to the affected limb constrict so that little blood (and therefore essential oxygen) reaches the skin, nerves, and muscles. This may lead to loss of sensation, ulcers, and eventually gangrene, necessitating amputation. Initial treatment is gently to warm the affected part.

fructose A simple sugar (monosaccharide) that is sweeter than sucrose and present in green leaves, fruits, and honey.

fruit The fertilized ovary of a flower, which contains the seed (or seeds) and may incorporate other parts of the flower (e.g. the receptacle in strawberries, the bracts in pineapples). The variation in the structure of fruits reflects the different means they have evolved to ensure dispersal of the seeds, which is essential to prevent overcrowding and enable the plant to spread and colonize new habitats. Fleshy fruits, for example, are usually eaten by animals, the seeds passing out with their faeces. Animals can also carry hooked or sticky fruits on their bodies. Seeds dispersed by wind are usually very light: they are either forcibly ejected from their fruits, for example from the capsule of poppy and the pods of leguminous plants, or they remain attached to the fruit, which can itself remain airborne for considerable dis-

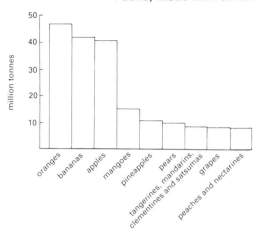

FRUIT *World production of fruit (1988).*

tances, for example the winged fruits of sycamores and ash trees. Some fruits are distributed by water: coconut fruits can be transported several hundred miles by sea. The word fruit is popularly restricted to the fleshy edible fruits, many of which are of economic importance to man: **fruit farming** constitutes an important branch of commercial horticulture.

fruit bat A vegetarian bat belonging to the family *Pteropidae* and suborder *Megachiroptera* (150 species). Fruit bats occur in tropical and subtropical regions of the Old World. They are typically larger than insect-eating bats and have better vision; only one genus (*Rousettus*, 13 species) uses echolocation. Most eat fruit although some feed on flowers or nectar. *See also* flying fox.

fruit fly A fly belonging to the family *Trypetidae* (1200 species)–the true fruit flies. (Insects of the family *Drosophilidae* are known as small fruit flies: *see* Drosophila.) True fruit flies have spotted or banded wings and the larvae of many species feed on fruit, often causing serious damage. For example, the Mediterranean fruit fly (*Ceratitis capitata*) is a pest of almost all succulent fruits.

Frunze (name until 1925: Pishpek) 42 53N 74 46E A city in the SW Soviet Union, the capital of Kirghiz SSR on the River Chu. Industries developed rapidly after World War II and include the manufacture of agricultural machinery, textiles, food, and tobacco products. Population (1985 est): 604 000.

Fry, Christopher (C. Harris; 1907–) British dramatist. His verse plays include *A Phoenix Too Frequent* (1946), *The Lady's Not for Burning* (1948), and *Venus Observed* (1950).

Fry, Roger (Eliot) (1866–1934) British painter and art critic. He is best known for his influential writings on art, e.g. *Vision and Design* (1920), and artists, e.g. *Bellini* (1899) and *Cézanne* (1927).

Fuchs, Klaus Emil Julian (1911–) British physicist and spy, born in Germany. During World War II he worked on atomic bomb research in Britain and in 1950 was tried and found guilty of having passed secret information to the Soviet Union since 1943. He was released from prison in 1959 and emigrated to East Germany.

Fuchs, Sir Vivian (Ernest) (1908–) British explorer. He led the Commonwealth Trans-Antarctic Expedition: with help from Sir Edmund Hillary he covered and surveyed 3500 km (2173 mi) between 24 November, 1957, and 2 March, 1958. He was director of the Falkland Islands Survey (British Antarctic Survey from 1962) from 1947 to 1950 and from 1960 until 1973.

Fuchsia A genus of shrubs and herbs (100 species) mostly native to tropical America and widely cultivated as ornamentals. The plants range from creeping forms, bushes, and small trees to epiphytes. They have deeppink, red, or purple drooping flowers all along the branches; each flower has four long flaring coloured sepals surrounding the shorter petals, below which the stamens and stigma protrude. Most cultivated forms are varieties of *F. magellanica*, *F. coccinea*, and *F. arborescens* or hybrids between them. Family: *Onagraceae* (willowherb family).

Fucus. See wrack.

fuel cell A device that converts the energy of a chemical reaction directly into an electric current. In the simplest type oxygen and hydrogen are fed through two separate porous nickel plates into an electrolytic solution. The gases combine to form water and thus set up a potential difference between the two plates. Fuel cells are distinguished from accumulators in that the latter need to be recharged and do not consume their chemicals. Fuel cells provide a clean source of power but are rather bulky. They may have uses in electric road vehicles and in space vehicles.

fuel injection The pumping of fuel in the form of a spray directly into the cylinders of an internal-combustion engine. This is necessary in the case of continuous-combustion engines, such as rocket motors and gas turbines. In Diesel engines fuel injection is also used and in some petrol engines it replaces the normal carburettor as it gives a more even fuel distribution in the combustion chamber.

fugue A piece of polyphonic music, generally having three or four parts (*or* voices), in which each part enters in turn with a statement of the main theme (*or* subject). After stating the subject each voice continues with the secondary theme (*or* counter-subject). Fugues are not composed to strict patterns; episodes in different tonalities are often interspersed with subsequent groups of entries of the voices. At the climax the voices are overlapped in close succession (*stretto*).

Fujiwara The most illustrious of Japan's noble families, with considerable political and economic power, notably between the 9th and 12th centuries.

Fujiyama (English name: Mount Fuji) 35 23N 138 42E The highest mountain in Japan, it is a dormant volcano in S central Honshu. Long regarded as a symbol of Japan, it has a symmetrical snow-capped (Oct-May) cone and a Shinto shrine. Height: 3776 m (12 388 ft).

Fukuoka 33 39N 130 21E A port in Japan in N Kyushu on Hakata Bay. An ancient commercial centre, Kublai Khan was twice defeated here (1274, 1281). Kyushu University was established in 1910. Industries include textiles and shipbuilding. Population (1987): 1 182 000.

Fulani A Muslim people scattered over a large area of W Africa from Lake Chad to the Atlantic coast. They are a mixed Negroid and, probably, Berber racial type. Their language, known as Fulfulde (*or* Fula), belongs to the Atlantic division of the Niger-Congo family. Their

social and cultural patterns are varied, reflecting influences from surrounding peoples. In N Nigeria many adopted the Hausa language and culture and, as a result of religious wars (1804–10), established a Muslim empire in which they were the ruling elite.

FUJIYAMA

Fuller, Richard Buckminster (1895–1983) US inventor and architect. One of Fuller's main concerns was making the best use of energy sources. His Dymaxion house (1928) and car (1933; improved version 1943) were designed to reduce waste and environmental pollution. His chief contribution was the geodesic dome, a lightweight and cheap structure of mutually supporting interlocking rods that can span large areas.

Fuller, Roy (Broadbent) (1912–) British poet and novelist. His early poetry was concerned with social and political themes; his more recent volumes, including *Buff* (1965) and *New Poems* (1968), are more personal and philosophical. He has published several novels, notably *Image of a Society* (1956).

fuller's earth A nonplastic clay rich in montmorillonite, with the property of absorbing and decolorizing oil and grease. It was formerly used for whitening and removing the grease from fleeces (fulling). It is still used in the textile industry and in refining fats and oils.

fulmar A maritime North Atlantic bird, *Fulmarus glacialis*. It is about 46 cm long and dark grey above with white underparts. Family: *Procellariidae* (petrels).

Funchal 32 40N 15 55W The capital of the Madeira Islands, on the S coast of Madeira, and a popular tourist resort. Population (1984): 44 111.

functionalism (architecture) A doctrine principally associated with the international style. Its main tenet is that the more fitted to its purpose a building is, the more beautiful it will be. Developed under Louis Sullivan in the 1890s, the doctrine's most vocal advocate was Le Corbusier. Functionalism led to a very severe style, lacking in all ornamentation and idiosyncracy. Its dominance faded after 1930.

fundamental constants Any of several constants that frequently appear in physical equations. The term is often reserved for five constants: the velocity of light (c), Planck's constant (h), the charge (e) and mass (m_e) of the electron, and the fine structure constant (α). The latter is defined as $e^2/2hc\varepsilon_0$, where ε_0 is the electric constant; its value is approximately 1/137 and it is a measure of the strength of the electromagnetic interaction. These constants may be regarded as fundamental in that their values determine the magnitude of many physical effects. Other constants sometimes taken as fundamental include the electric constant, the magnetic constant, Avogadro's number, the Boltzmann constant, and the gravitational constant.

fundamental interactions The basic forces that occur in nature. *See* electromagnetic interaction; gravitational interaction; strong interaction; weak interaction.

fundamentalism A religious movement among some US Protestants arising after World War I. It insisted on the completely literal truth of the Bible, of the New Testament miracles, and of such traditional teachings as the Virgin Birth and bodily resurrection of Christ. It rejected any scientific knowledge, such as the theory of evolution, which conflicted with a literal reading of the Bible.

Fundy, Bay of An inlet of the Atlantic Ocean in SE Canada, between Nova Scotia and New Brunswick. Long and narrow, it has tides up to 20 m (66 ft) high, from which electricity is generated.

FUNGI *Giant puffballs.*

fungi Unicellular or multicellular organisms belonging to the group *Mycota* (about 50 000 known species), usually regarded as plants and including mushrooms, mildews, moulds, yeasts, etc. All fungi lack chlorophyll and therefore (unlike green plants) cannot manufacture their own food by photosynthesis. Some are saprophytes, feeding on dead organic matter by means of digestive enzymes; others are parasites of plants or animals. The body of most fungi consists of a network of branching threadlike structures (hyphae), forming a mycelium. Sexual reproduction results in the formation of spores, which may be produced in a specialized structure called a fruiting body: this is the visible part of mushrooms, puffballs, etc. Other fungi consist of single cells, which can reproduce asexually by simple division into two daughter cells. Fungi are distributed worldwide in terrestrial, freshwater, and marine habitats. Some live in the soil and play a vital role in bringing about decomposition of dead organic matter. Other fungi (e.g. *Penicillium* and *Streptomyces*) are of great importance as a source of antibiotics. Many parasitic fungi cause disease in animals and man (*see* infection) or in plants (e.g. the smuts and rusts), while some saprophytes are destructive to timber (*see* dry rot). Some fungi form associations with other plants, most notably with algae to form lichens.

Furies. *See* Erinyes.

furlong A unit of length equal to 220 yards ($\frac{1}{8}$ mile), used in horseracing.

Furness A peninsula in NW England, in Cumbria between the Irish Sea and Morecambe Bay. Chief town: Barrow-in-Furness.

furze. *See* gorse.

Fushun 41 51N 123 53E A city in NE China, in Liaoning province. Its oil, steel, and chemical industries are based on its oil-shale and vast coal deposits. Aluminium production is also important. Population (1986): 1 240 000.

fusion (physics). *See* nuclear energy.

Futuna Islands. *See* Wallis and Futuna.

Fuzhou (Fu-chou *or* Foochow) 26 10N 119 20E A port in SE China, the capital of Fujian province on the Min delta. An ancient capital, it was the centre of foreign trade from the 10th to the 19th centuries. Population (1986): 1 190 000.

Fylingdales The site of an early-warning radar station in NE England, in North Yorkshire, built to give warning of nuclear attack.

Fyns (German name: Fünen) The second largest Danish island, situated between the Little Belt and the Great Belt. Fishing is important and its fertile soil supports cereal growing, dairy farming, and cattle rearing. Area: 3481 sq km (1344 sq mi). Population (1987): 453 483.

G

gabbro A dark-coloured coarse-grained basic igneous rock formed by the crystallization at depth of basalt magma. Calcic plagioclase feldspar, clinopyroxene, and olivine are the main constituents.

Gaberones. *See* Gaborone.

Gable, Clark (1901–60) US film actor. He established his popularity during the 1930s, when he played many tough masculine roles. His films include *It Hap-* *pened One Night* (1934), *Gone with the Wind* (1939), and *The Misfits* (1961).

Gabon, Republic of An equatorial country in West Africa. The population is mainly Fang. *Economy*: almost three-quarters of the land is forested and timber was formerly the most important resource. Now, however, its vast mineral wealth forms the basis of the economy. Agriculture consists chiefly of subsistence farming.

History: trading posts were set up by the Portuguese in the late 15th century and the area later became a centre of the slave trade. Settled by the French in the mid-19th century, it became part of French Equatorial Africa in 1910. It gained internal self-government in 1958 and became independent in 1960. A one-party political system was instituted in 1967; in the 1980s the opposition was led by an underground group known as the *morena*. President: Omar Bongo (Albert Bernard B.; 1935–). Official language: French; Bantu languages are widely spoken. Official currency: CFA (Communauté financière africaine) franc of 100 centimes. Area: 267 000 sq km (103 089 sq mi). Population (1987): 1 224 000. Capital and main port: Libreville.

gaboon viper A highly venomous puff adder, *Bitis gabonica*, occurring in African rain forests. Up to 2 m long, it has hornlike projections on its snout and is patterned with buff, brown, and purple rectangles and triangles. It feeds on small vertebrates.

Gaborone (former name: Gaberones) 24 45S 25 55E The capital of Botswana. The seat of government was transferred here from Mafeking in 1965. Population (1986): 96 000.

Gaddafi, Moammar al- (*or* Qaddafi; 1942–) Libyan colonel and statesman. In 1969 he led a revolt that overthrew the Libyan monarchy and in 1970 became chairman of the Revolutionary Command Council. His Arab nationalist and Islamic socialist policies have led to a reorganization of Libyan society and an active foreign policy.

Gaddi, Taddeo (c. 1300–?1366) Florentine painter, who was the pupil and assistant of Giotto. His works include the *Life of the Virgin* (Baroncelli Chapel, Sta Croce, Florence). His son **Agnolo Gaddi** (c. 1350–96), painted the *Story of the True Cross* in Sta Croce and the *Life of the Virgin* (Duomo, Prato).

gadolinium (Gd) A lanthanide element named after the Finnish chemist J. Gadolin (1760–1852). It is used in television-tube phosphors. At no 64; at wt 157.25;´mp 1313°C; bp 3233°C.

Gadsden Purchase (1853) About 77 700 sq km (30 000 sq mi) of land in what are now New Mexico and Arizona, bought by the USA from Mexico for $10 million. The purchase was named after its negotiator, James Gadsden (1788–1858).

Gaea (*or* Gaia) A Greek goddess personifying the earth. The wife and mother of Uranus (Heaven), by whom she bore the Titans, the Cyclops, and the Gigantes, she incited the revolt of the Titans against him.

Gaelic A language of the Goidelic group of Celtic languages. Irish Gaelic is spoken in Ireland as a first language by approximately 100 000 people and as a second language by around 700 000. Scottish Gaelic (*or* Erse), which is spoken in NW Scotland, is an offshoot of Irish Gaelic.

Gagarin, Yuri Alekseevich (1934–68) Soviet cosmonaut, who on 12 April, 1961, became the first person to orbit the earth reaching a height of about 301 km (187 mi). He died when a plane he was testing crashed.

Gaia. *See* Gaea.

Gainsborough, Thomas (1727–88) British portrait and landscape painter, born in Sudbury, Suffolk. The elegant style of Van Dyck is reflected in Gainsborough's *Countess Howe* (Kenwood House, London) and the *Blue Boy* (San Marino, California) while his landscapes were influenced by Ruisdael, Meindert Hobbema (1638–

1709), and later by Rubens, particularly the *Harvest Wagon* (Barber Institute, Birmingham). After 1774 he successfully rivalled Reynolds; in his later years he painted idyllic rustic scenes, the so-called fancy pictures.

Gaitskell, Hugh (Todd Naylor) (1906–63) British politician; leader of the Labour Party (1955–63). After defeat in the 1959 general election, Gaitskell unsuccessfully attempted to change the constitution. At the 1960 party conference his "Fight, and fight, and fight again" speech against unilateral nuclear disarmament reunited the party.

galago. *See* bushbaby.

Galahad In Arthurian legend, the son of Lancelot and Elaine. As the most perfect exemplar of knighthood, he was (in many romances) the only knight to succeed in the quest of the Holy Grail.

galangal A flavouring obtained from the rhizomes of a Chinese perennial herb, *Alpinia officinarum*. The plant grows to a height of 6 m, with pink, yellow, or white fragrant flowers. Family: *Zingiberaceae*.

GALÁPAGOS *A giant tortoise.*

Galápagos Islands (Spanish name: Archipiélago de Colón) An archipelago in the Pacific Ocean, W of Ecuador. It consists of 12 main islands and several smaller ones, all of volcanic origin. Visited by Charles Darwin in 1835, the islands contain many endemic species, including the Galápagos giant tortoise (*Testude elephantopus*), up to 1.5 m long and weighing up to 150 kg Area: 7428 sq km (2868 sq mi). Population (1986 est): 8000.

Galatea **1.** In Greek legend, a nymph who loved the shepherd Acis and was loved by Polyphemus. When Acis was killed by his rival she turned him into a river. **2.** The name of a statue that came to life in answer to the prayers of Pygmalion.

galaxies Huge assemblies of stars, gas, and dust, bound together by gravitational interactions. **Spiral galaxies** are large flattened systems with spiral arms containing much interstellar gas and dust from which stars can form. Spirals have a mass of 10^{10} to 10^{11} solar masses. **Elliptical galaxies** are actually spheroidal with no clear internal structure. They vary greatly in size and mass, the largest giant ellipticals exceeding 10^{12} solar masses. **Irregular galaxies** have no definite shape and are relatively small, with a high content of interstellar matter.

Galaxy (*or* Milky Way system)   The spiral galaxy to which the sun belongs. It contains about a hundred thousand million (10^{11}) stars. Most lie in its two spiral arms, the sun lying about 33 000 light years from the centre. Light cannot penetrate the dust in the innermost regions of the Galaxy but radio, infrared, and X-ray observations have shown complex phenomena to be occurring, possibly arising from the presence of a black hole at the galactic centre.

Galbraith, John Kenneth   (1908–)   US economist and diplomat. His works in the Keynesian tradition include *The Affluent Society* (1958), and *Economics and the Public Purpose* (1973).

Galen   (129–c. 199 AD) Greek physician and scholar, whose ideas dominated medicine until the Renaissance. Galen showed the importance of the spinal cord in muscle activity, the role of the ureter in kidney and bladder function, and that arteries carry blood rather than air despite holding mistaken views on blood circulation. Galen also wrote on philosophy, law, and mathematics.

galena   The principal ore of lead. It is a grey soft metallic mineral, found as cubic crystals of lead sulphide in hydrothermal veins and as replacement deposits in limestones. Galena ore bodies usually contain silver.

Galicia   **1.** A medieval kingdom in NW Spain. Colonized by the Visigoths, it became a subkingdom of Castile in the late 11th century. **2.** A province in E Europe, divided between Poland and the Soviet Union after World War II.

Galilean satellites   The four largest satellites of Jupiter–Io, Europa, Ganymede, and Callisto–discovered by Galileo (1610) and studied in detail by the US Voyager probes (1979). Io is the most active volcanic body known in the solar system.

Galilee   A district of N Israel, bordering the River Jordan, associated with the early ministry of Jesus Christ, Crusader battles, and Jewish settlement after the fall of Jerusalem (70 AD). Zionist settlements, begun in 1892, became part of Israel in 1949.

Galilee, Sea of (Sea of Tiberias; Lake of Gennesaret; Lake Kinneret)   A lake in NE Israel. It is fed mainly by and drained by the River Jordan; its surface is 209 m (686 ft) below sea level. It was the scene of many episodes in the life of Christ. Area: 166 sq km (64 sq mi).

Galileo Galilei   (1564–1642) Italian mathematician, physicist, and astronomer. Born in Pisa, legend has it that he demonstrated that the rate of fall of a body is independent of its mass by dropping weights from the Leaning Tower of Pisa. He is also reputed to have worked out that the period of a pendulum is independent of its amplitude by watching a swinging chandelier in Pisa Cathedral. In 1609 Galileo designed a telescope and used it to discover sunspots and Jupiter's satellites. His book *Dialogue on Two World Systems* (1632) denounced the Ptolemaic system of astronomy in favour of Copernicus' system. As the Roman Catholic Church had condemned Copernicus' work in 1616, Galileo was forced by the Inquisition to recant his views and placed under house arrest for the rest of his life.

gall   A swelling or excrescence on plants caused by abnormal proliferation of cells due to mechanical injury or attack by insects, mites, fungi, bacteria, or viruses. Some galls are self-limiting, including the oak apples caused by the gall wasp, while others are tumorous.

Galla   A people of Ethiopia numbering about 10 million and making up about 40% of the Ethiopian popula-

tion. They were originally nomads who spread from the SE region during the 16th century. Their language belongs to the Hamito-Semitic family.

GALILEO GALILEI

gall bladder   A saclike organ (7–10 cm long) that receives and stores bile (formerly called gall) formed by the liver. The gall bladder is connected to the liver by the hepatic ducts and to the intestine by the common bile duct. Crystallization of bile components forms gallstones, which may block the bile duct or cause gall bladder infections (cholecystitis) and may necessitate surgical removal of the gall bladder (cholecystectomy).

Gallic Wars   (58–51 BC) The campaigns in which Julius Caesar annexed Transalpine Gaul (France). Caesar's intervention in Gallic intertribal warfare was prompted by concern for Italian security. NE Gaul was pacified by 57 BC and the tribes along the Atlantic coast by 56 BC. In 52 Caesar defeated the tribes of central Gaul, led by Vercingetorix. Caesar's own account of the Gallic Wars has survived.

gallinule   A bird belonging to the family *Rallidae* (rails). Gallinules are widely distributed, occurring on semistagnant water edged by dense vegetation, and commonly have blue, green, or purple plumage for camouflage. They are 30–45 cm long and have long slender toes enabling them to run over floating vegetation. *See also* moorhen.

Gallipoli (Turkish name: Gelibolu)   40 25N 26 41E   A seaport in Turkey, on the NE coast of the Dardanelles. Strategically important for the defence of Istanbul, the town had to be rebuilt after the Gallipoli campaign (*see* World War I). Population (1980): 14 721.

gallium (Ga)   A metallic element with a low melting point and high boiling point, discovered in 1875 by Lecoq de Boisbaudran. **Gallium arsenide** (GaAs) is a semiconductor that is widely used in electronic devices, particularly the field-effect transistor and the Gunn diode. At no 31; at wt 69.72; mp 29.78°C; bp 2403°C.

gallon   An Imperial unit of volume equal to the volume occupied by ten pounds of distilled water under precisely defined conditions. The US gallon is equal to 0.832 68 British gallons.

Galloway. *See* Dumfries and Galloway Region.

gallstones. *See* gall bladder.

gall wasp A small wasp (6–8 mm long), also called gallfly, belonging to the family *Cynipidae*. Gall wasps lay their eggs in plant tissues, particularly oak trees and rose plants, which respond by producing galls.

Galsworthy, John (1867–1933) British novelist and dramatist. *The Man of Property* (1906) began the famous novel series *The Forsyte Saga*, chronicling the decline of a rich English family. His plays, include *The Silver Box* (1906) and *Strife* (1909).

galvanized steel Steel coated with zinc to prevent corrosion. The zinc may be deposited by electroplating the steel in molten zinc, spraying with molten zinc, or by coating it with zinc powder and heating it.

galvanometer An instrument for measuring small electric currents, named after the Italian physician Luigi Galvani (1737–98). The moving-coil galvanometer consists of a coil of wire suspended in a magnetic field. A current passing through the coil causes it to rotate until balanced by the opposing torsion in the suspending thread. The angle of rotation is used to measure the current. In the moving-magnet instrument the magnet is suspended in the earth's magnetic field and deflection is caused by a current passing through the surrounding coil.

Galway (Irish name: Contae Na Gaillimhe) A county in the W Republic of Ireland, in Connacht. Low lying E of Lough Carrib, it rises to Connemara (an area of moors and bogs) in the W. Offshore islands include the Aran Islands. Cattle and sheep rearing are important. Area: 5939 sq km (2293 sq mi). Population (1986): 17 180. County town: Galway.

Galway, James (1939–) Irish flautist. The composer Rodrigo wrote his *Concierto pastorale* (for flute and orchestra; 1978) for him.

VASCO DA GAMA

Gama, Vasco da (c. 1469–1524) Portuguese navigator. In 1497, he departed with three ships to continue the search by Bartolomeu Dias (c. 1450–c. 1500) for the route to India. He rounded the Cape of Good Hope and crossed to Calicut (1498). Received with hostility by the Indians, he withdrew. In 1502 da Gama was sent out on a punitive expedition to establish Portugal's influence in the Indian Ocean, returning to Portugal with considera-

ble amounts of booty. Some 20 years later he went back to India as Portuguese viceroy and died there.

Gambia, Republic of The A country in West Africa, surrounded by Senegalese territory. Swamps along the River Gambia give way to savanna. The majority of the inhabitants are Mandingo. *Economy*: overwhelmingly agricultural, producing groundnuts and rice. In 1988 it agreed a free-trade zone with Senegal. Tourism is being encouraged. *History*: in the 15th century the mouth of the River Gambia was explored by the Portuguese, and in 1661 the English established a trading settlement on James Island. The area was administered by the British from 1807 until achieving independence in 1965, becoming a republic within the British Commonwealth in 1970. Close ties with Senegal were reinforced with the formation of the Senegambia Confederation in 1982. President: Sir Dawda Jawara. Official language: English. Official currency: dalasi of 100 butut. Area: 10 689 sq km (4125 sq mi). Population (1986 est): 698 817. Capital and main port: Banjul.

Gambia, River A river in West Africa. Rising in Guinea, it flows NW through Senegal and The Gambia to the Atlantic Ocean. Length: 1126 km (700 mi).

Gambier Islands 23 10S 135 00W A group of coral islands in the S Pacific Ocean, in French Polynesia. They have been used for French nuclear tests. Area: 30 sq km (11 sq mi). Population (1977): 556. Chief settlement: Rikitea.

gamboge (*or* camboge) A hard brittle gum resin obtained from various SE Asian trees of the genus *Garcinia*. It is orange to brown in colour and turns bright yellow when powdered. Artists use gamboge as a pigment and to colour varnishes. In medicine and veterinary medicine it is used as a strong purgative.

gamete A reproductive cell—either male or female—produced in the sex organs of plants or animals and containing half the number of chromosomes present in a body (somatic) cell. On fertilization the new individual therefore has a complete set of chromosomes, half from each parent. The female gamete (*see* egg) is large and immotile and contains abundant cytoplasm, while the male gamete (*see* sperm) is motile, with little cytoplasm.

game theory The branch of mathematics that seeks to analyse and solve problems arising in economic, business, or military situations on the assumption that each participant adopts strategies that will maximize gain (payoff) and minimize loss, as in playing a game. Worked out originally by John von Neumann and Oskar Morganstern (1907–), it was successfully used in World War II in an analysis of submarine warfare.

gametophyte. *See* alternation of generations.

gamma globulin. *See* globulin.

gamma radiation Highly energetic electromagnetic radiation emitted by certain radioactive substances as a result of transitions of nucleons from a higher to a lower energy level and when an elementary particle and its antiparticle annihilate each other. The wavelength of gamma radiation is between 10^{-10} and 10^{-14} metre.

Ganda A Bantu people of the region W and N of Lake Victoria. They are agriculturalists, whose staple crop is bananas. The largest tribe in Uganda, they were formerly ruled by a king (Kabaka) in their own kingdom of Buganda.

Gandhi, Indira (1917–84) Indian stateswoman; prime minister (1966–77; 1980–84). Daughter of Jawaharlal Nehru, she succeeded Lal Bahadur Shastri as prime minister. In 1975 she was accused of electoral malpractices and threatened with the loss of her seat. She was defeated in the elections of 1977 by Morarji Desai but returned to power in 1980. In the wake of sectarian violence, she was assassinated in 1984 by Sikh members of her bodyguard. Her elder son **Rajiv Gandhi** (1942–) succeeded her as prime minister (1984–89).

GANDHI *The Mahatma at the spinning wheel.*

Gandhi, Mohandas Karamchand (1869–1948) Indian nationalist leader. Mahatma ("Great Soul") Gandhi was born in W India and went to England in 1888 to study law. In 1893 he moved to South Africa to practise law and became a champion of the rights of the Indian community, introducing a policy of noncooperation with the civil authorities (satyagraha), which he utilized after his return to India (1914). There he became leader of the Indian National Congress. Following imprisonment (1922–24) for civil disobedience, Gandhi campaigned against the degradation of untouchables and encouraged the development of Indian craft industries. In 1930 he walked from Ahmedabad to the sea, where he distilled salt from sea water in protest against the government's salt monopoly, and was again imprisoned. In 1932 he undertook his first "fast unto death," against the government's attitude to untouchables. During World War II Gandhi had to reconcile Indian support for Britain with his own policy of nonviolence and his belief in an independent India. In 1942 the British Government offered India complete independence after the war in exchange for cooperation in winning it. In reply Gandhi demanded that the British should withdraw immediately from India. The British responded by gaoling Gandhi and the other Congress leaders until 1944.

Gandhi played a crucial part in the independence talks and finally accepted the establishment of Pakistan. When violence broke out in Bengal, Gandhi undertook a fast in an attempt to halt the conflict. His advocacy of friendship between Hindus and Muslims caused resentment among Hindu fanatics, one of whom (Nathuram Godse) assassinated him. Ghandi, never a member of the cabinet, was for many years regarded as both a saint and the supreme Indian leader.

Gandzha. *See* Kirovabad.

Ganesa One of the principle Hindu deities, portrayed as having an elephant's head on a human body. His father Shiva beheaded him, but then replaced his human head with that of the first creature he found.

Ganges, River (*or* Ganga) The great river of N India. Formed by headstreams in the Himalayas, it flows E across the Ganges plain to the Brahmaputra River, thereafter continuing as the River Padma, which empties into the Bay of Bengal by way of the largest delta in the world. It is the Hindus' most sacred river. Length: 2507 km (1557 mi).

Gang of Four. *See* Jiang Qing.

gangrene Death of tissues, most commonly those of a limb. This usually results from narrowing of the blood vessels of the legs by atherosclerosis or because of diabetes. If the tissues become infected the condition is called wet gangrene. Treatment is aimed at improving the blood flow to the limbs by surgery or by rest; in advanced cases amputation may be necessary.

gannet A seabird belonging to the family *Sulidae*, distributed worldwide. (Tropical members of the family are called boobies.) The North Atlantic gannet (*Sula bassana*), also called solan goose, reaches 90 cm in length. It is white with black wingtips and has a stout bill and a wedge-shaped tail. Gannets feed on fish and nest in dense colonies on rocky islands and cliffs. Order: *Pelecaniformes* (cormorants, pelicans, etc.).

Ganymede (astronomy). *See* Galilean satellites.

Ganymede (mythology) In Greek legend, a Trojan prince of great beauty carried off by Zeus to be his cupbearer in exchange for some immortal horses or a golden vine.

Gaoxiong (*or* Kao-hsiung; Japanese name: Takao) 22 36N 120 17E A city in SW Taiwan, the second largest on the island and its leading port. Under Japanese occupation (1895–1945) it became an important naval base. Population (1986): 1 300 000.

gar A freshwater bony fish, also called garpike, belonging to a family (*Lepisosteidae*; 7 species) found in North and Central America. Gars have a slender body, up to 3.5 m long, and feed mainly on smaller fish. Order: *Semionotiformes*.

Garbo, Greta (Greta Gustafson; 1905–90) Swedish actress. Her aloof beauty contributed much to her portrayal of tragic heroines in such films as *Grand Hotel* (1932), *Anna Karenina* (1935), and *Camille* (1936). As a comedienne she excelled in *Ninotchka* (1939).

García Lorca, Federico (1898–1936) Spanish poet and dramatist. He won international fame with *Gipsy Ballads* (1928), noted for their original imagery. His masterpiece is the trilogy of folk tragedies *Blood Wedding* (1933), *Yerma* (1934), and *The House of Bernarda Alba* (1936). He was shot by Nationalist partisans in the Spanish Civil War.

Garda, Lake (Latin name: Lacus Benacus) A lake in central N Italy. Sheltered on the N by the Alps, it has a temperate climate that attracts holidaymakers. Area: 370 sq km (143 sq mi).

Gardenia A genus of ornamental shrubs and trees (60–100 species) native to tropical and subtropical Africa and Asia. Many are richly scented and used in perfumes and tea. *G. jasminoides* is a popular pot plant. Family: *Rubiaceae* (madder family).

JUDY GARLAND *The 16-year-old actress in* The Wizard of Oz *(1939)*.

garfish. *See* needlefish.

Garibaldi, Giuseppe (1807–82) Italian soldier, a hero of the movement for Italian unification (*see* Risorgimento). Influenced by Mazzini, he joined an attempted republican revolution in Sardinia-Piedmont (1834) and was forced to flee to South America. He returned to Italy to join the Revolution of 1848, fighting the Austrians and play a leading part in the unsuccessful defence of Rome against the French. Following another period of exile, he gave his support to the unification movement led by Cavour and Victor Emmanuel II of Sardinia-Piedmont. In 1860 he set out from Genoa on the Expedition of a Thousand, achieving the conquest of Sicily and Naples and their incorporation in the new kingdom of Italy. He also fought for the French in the Franco-Prussian War (1870–71).

Garland, Judy (Frances Gumm; 1922–69) US singer and film actress. She began her career at the age of five in vaudeville. Her films included *The Wizard of Oz* (1939), *Meet Me in St Louis* (1944), and *A Star is Born* (1954). Although an unhappy private life interfered with her career, she maintained her reputation as a superstar. Her daughter **Liza Minnelli** (1946–) is also a singer and actress. She is best known for her starring roles in *Cabaret* (1972) and *Arthur* (1981).

garlic A widely cultivated perennial herb, *Allium sativum*, native to Asia and naturalized in S Europe and North America. Its leafless flower stem grows to a height of 60 cm. The bulb has a pungent aroma and taste and is a classic flavouring agent in cooking.

garnet A group of minerals with varying compositions. Garnets occur chiefly in metamorphic rocks. They are used as abrasives and flawless crystals are semiprecious stones. Birthstone for January.

Garonne, River A river in SW France. Rising in the central Pyrenees, it enters the Atlantic Ocean by the Gironde estuary. Length: 580 km (360 mi).

garpike. *See* gar.

Garrick, David (1717–79) English actor. He went to London with Samuel Johnson in 1737 and began his long theatrical career with a highly acclaimed performance as Richard III in 1741. As manager of the Drury Lane Theatre from 1747 to 1776, he introduced innovations in production, lighting, and scenery.

Garter, Order of the A British order of knighthood, traditionally founded by Edward III in 1348 and comprising chiefly the sovereign and 25 knights companions. Its motto is *Honi soit qui mal y pense* (The shame be his who thinks badly of it), supposedly the words of Edward III on tying to his leg a garter dropped by a lady at a banquet. The motto is inscribed on the dark blue garter worn by the knights of the order on the left leg below the knee. The order's chapel is St George's Chapel, Windsor.

Gascony A former duchy of SW France. After Roman rule Gascony was conquered by the Visigoths and then by the Franks. It fell to Aquitaine in 1052 and came under English control in the 12th century. It was regained by the French at the end of the Hundred Years' War (1453).

gases Substances that distribute themselves evenly throughout a closed container. The behaviour of a gas under variations of temperature, pressure, and volume is fairly accurately described by the gas laws and the kinetic theory of gases.

Gaskell, Elizabeth Cleghorn (1810–65) British novelist. In 1832 she married a Unitarian minister and settled in Manchester, the industrial setting of her first novel, *Mary Barton* (1848). Her other novels include *Cranford* (1853) and *North and South* (1855). She also wrote the first biography of her friend Charlotte Brontë (1857).

gas laws Relationships between the thermodynamic temperature (T), pressure (p), and volume (V) of a gas. The simplest laws are Boyle's law ($p \propto 1/V$) and Charles's law ($V \propto T$), which are combined in the ideal gas equation: $pV = nRT$, where R is the gas constant, which has the value 8.314 J K^{-1} mol^{-1}, and n is the number of moles present. However, no real gas obeys this equation exactly. Most later gas laws are modifications of this equation. *See* Van der Waals equation.

gastric juice A mixture of hydrochloric acid, protein-digesting enzymes, and mucus secreted by glands in the mucous membrane lining the stomach.

gastric ulcer. *See* peptic ulcer.

gastroenteritis Infection of the stomach and intestines. Gastroenteritis is characterized by diarrhoea and vomiting and usually occurs in areas where hygiene is poor. It is particularly dangerous in babies.

gastropod A single-shelled mollusc belonging to the class *Gastropoda* (about 40 000 species), including snails and slugs, limpets, and sea hares. Measuring 0.1–20 cm in length, gastropods occupy terrestrial, freshwater, and marine habitats. They move by undulating the muscular foot and have two pairs of retractable sensory head tentacles, one pair bearing simple eyes. They feed by scraping plant or animal matter with a rasping tongue (radula). Most gastropods have internal fertilization: the mating individuals may be of separate sexes or hermaphrodite.

gas turbine A form of internal-combustion engine consisting of a turbine in which the power to drive the blades is provided by hot gas. It consists of a compressor, a combustion chamber, and the turbine. Atmospheric air is fed under pressure from the compressor to the combustion chambers, where a fuel, such as natural gas, paraffin, or oil, is burnt; the hot gases then drive the turbine, which in turn drives the compressor. Power is supplied either in the form of thrust from a jet or rotation of the turbine shaft.

GATT. *See* General Agreement on Tariffs and Trade.

Gatwick 51 08N 0 11W A village in SE England, 43 km (27 mi) S of London, in Surrey. It is the site of one of London's two subsidiary airports.

GAUGUIN *Detail from* Nevermore *(1897; Courtauld Institute, London).*

Gauguin, Paul (1848–1903) French postimpressionist painter. After five years at sea he became a stockbroker (1871), painting as a hobby. He became a fulltime painter in 1883 and developed a style called synthetism in such paintings as *Vision after the Sermon* (National Gallery, Edinburgh). He visited Martinique in 1887 and stayed with Van Gogh in Arles in 1888. Seeking the inspiration of a primitive civilization, he moved to Tahiti (1891), where the symbolism in such paintings as *Nevermore* (Courtauld Institute, London) was influenced by native superstitions.

Gaul An ancient region of Europe. It was divided by the Romans into Transalpine Gaul (the area bound by the Rhine, Alps, and Pyrenees) and Cisalpine Gaul (N Italy). Transalpine Gaul was settled from about 1500 BC by Celtic tribes, who inhabited Cisalpine Gaul after around 500 BC. Subsequent Gallic expansion southwards brought conflict with Rome, which the Gauls sacked in 390. In 121 the Romans annexed S Transalpine Gaul, which they called Gallia Narbonensis, and between 58 and 50 Caesar subdued the rest of Gaul, finally crushing the Gallic tribal leader Vercingetorix at Alesia. Gaul was extensively romanized and prospered until the barbarian invasions in the 5th century.

gaur The largest of the wild cattle, *Bos gaurus*, of hilly forests in S Asia. Up to 200 cm high at the shoulder, bulls can weigh up to 1 tonne. Gaurs are dark brown with white socks and both sexes have horns.

Gauss, Karl Friedrich (1777–1855) German mathematician, regarded as one of the greatest mathematicians of all time. He influenced all aspects of mathematics and much of physics. His greatest contributions were in the fields of probability theory, number theory, complex numbers, algebra, and electricity and magnetism.

Gautier, Théophile (1811–72) French Romantic poet and critic. Influenced by Victor Hugo, his early writings include *Poésies* (1830) and *Les Jeunes-France* (1833). The brief lyrical poems in *Émaux et camées*

(1852) embody his belief in the value of art for its own sake. He wrote much criticism and travelled widely.

gavial (*or* gharial) A long-snouted reptile, *Gavialis gangeticus*, occurring in N Indian rivers and sacred to Hindus. 4–5 m long, it has long slender sharp-toothed jaws, which it sweeps from side to side to catch fish. It is the only member of its family (*Gavialidae*). Order: *Crocodilia* (*see* crocodile).

Gawain In Arthurian legend, a knight of the Round Table, the nephew of King Arthur and the son of King Lot of Norway and the Orkneys. He was known for his purity and courage.

Gay, John (1685–1732) British poet and dramatist. A friend of Pope, Swift, and other members of the Scriblerus Club, his *Fables* (1727, 1738) were the most successful of his satirical poems. *The Beggar's Opera* (1728) is a parody of fashionable Italian opera.

Gaya 24 48N 85 00E A city in NE India, in Bihar. A centre of Hindu pilgrimage, it is situated 10 km (6 mi) S of Buddh Gaya, which is sacred to Buddhists. Population (1981): 344 941.

Gay-Lussac, Joseph Louis (1778–1850) French chemist and physicist. He discovered boron (1808) and the law that gases combine in a simple ratio by volume (**Gay-Lussac's law**). He also discovered Charles' law independently of Charles and published his results first.

Gaza Strip A strip of coastal territory, 50 km (30 mi) long, on the SE corner of the Mediterranean Sea. Following the Arab-Israeli War of 1948–49, it was the only part of Palestine held by Egypt. Held by the Israelis for a short time in 1956–57, it was taken by them again in 1967. Under the Camp David agreement (1979), eventual self-government for the area was planned. The Gaza Strip suffers from extreme overpopulation by Palestine refugees; there were violent protests against the Israeli occupation in the 1980s. Agriculture is the chief pursuit, especially the growing of citrus fruit. Population (1988): 635 000, including North Sinai.

gazelle A slender antelope of the genus *Gazella* (about 12 species), of Africa and Asia. 50–90 cm high at the shoulder, gazelles are distinguished from other antelopes by horizontal stripes on the face. In most species both sexes have horns, which are generally lyreshaped with a forward-pointing tip.

GBE. *See* Order of the British Empire.

Gdańsk (German name: Danzig) 54 22N 18 41E A port in N Poland. It is an industrial centre with metallurgy, chemicals, and food processing. Closure of the Lenin shipyard was announced in 1988. *History*: It was under Prussian control (1793–1807 and 1814–1919), becoming a free city under the League of Nations in 1919. In 1939 it was annexed by Germany; the city was returned to Poland in 1945. Population (1985): 467 000.

GDP (gross domestic product). *See* gross national product.

Gdynia 54 31N 18 30E A port in N Poland. Originally a fishing village, it became Poland's main shipbuilding centre and naval base. Population (1985): 243 000.

gean. *See* cherry.

gecko A slender long-tailed nocturnal lizard belonging to the widely distributed family *Gekkonidae* (650 species), found in a wide range of habitats. 3–35 cm long, many geckos have fleshy toe pads covered with microscopic hooks enabling them to cling to smooth surfaces. They feed on insects and have well-developed vocal cords. The tokay (*Gekko gecko*) of E Asia is a large arboreal gecko.

GEIGER COUNTER *A device for detecting radio-activity.*

Geelong 38 10S 144 26E A city and major port in Australia, in S Victoria. Wool, wheat, and oil are the principal exports. Population (1986): 139 792.

gegenschein (German: counterglow) A very faint glow in the night sky that can sometimes be seen on the ecliptic in a direction directly opposite the sun's position. It is part of the zodiacal light.

Geiger counter A device that detects and counts ionizing radiation and particles. Essentially it consists of a metal cylinder containing low-pressure gas and a wire anode. Ionizing particles passing into the tube through a window at one end induce discharges, which can be counted by a suitable circuit. Named after the German physicist Hans Geiger (1882–1945).

geisha A Japanese woman whose profession is to entertain men in a restaurant. Geishas, who are not prostitutes, sing and dance or engage their clients in conversation.

gel. *See* colloid.

gelada A large Old World monkey, *Theropithecus gelada*, of Ethiopian mountains. 120–150 cm long including the tufted tail (70–80 cm), it has a cape of dark-brown hair with two bare patches on the chest and lives in large groups, feeding on roots, leaves, and fruit.

gelatin A protein derived from bones and skins. In solution it forms a reversible gel that becomes fluid as the temperature rises and solidifies on cooling. It is widely used in the food industry, in drug preparations, and in photographic emulsions.

Geldof, Bob (1952–) Irish rock musician Born in Dublin, Geldof made several successful recordings with the Boomtown Rats before becoming involved in fund raising for the starving in Africa in 1984. His efforts, culminating in a massive concert held simultaneously in the UK and the USA in 1985, generated widespread support and unprecedented donations to charity. He received an honorary knighthood in 1986.

gelignite A high explosive consisting of nitroglycerin, cellulose nitrate, potassium nitrate, and woodpulp.

Gell-Mann, Murray (1929–) US physicist, who won the 1969 Nobel Prize for his work on elementary particles. In 1953 he introduced the concept of strange-

ness to account for the absence of certain expected interactions. He also formulated the theory of unitary symmetry and the concept of quarks (*see also* particle physics).

Gemini (Latin: Twins) A conspicuous constellation in the N sky near Orion, lying on the zodiac between Cancer and Taurus. The brightest stars are Pollux and Castor.

gemsbok. *See* oryx.

gene A unit of the hereditary material of an organism that provides the genetic information necessary to fulfil a single function. The term was first coined by W. L. Johannsen (1857–1927) in 1909.

Genes were initially conceived as a string of beads comprising the chromosome. However, with the discovery of the structure of DNA and the molecular basis of heredity, a gene is now regarded as being a functional unit (cistron) corresponding to a specific sequence of the genetic code.

General Agreement on Tariffs and Trade (GATT) A set of trade agreements, in operation from January, 1948, establishing procedures and tariffs for international trading. Signatories agree to favourable tariffs between members and the reduction of trade restrictions, on condition that home producers do not suffer losses as a result. There are more than 80 member countries. The secretariat of GATT, which is a specialized agency of the United Nations, is in Geneva.

General Strike (1926) A national stoppage of work by members of Britain's major industries, lasting from 3 to 12 May. The General Strike began when the Trades Union Council (TUC) called out its members in support of the miners, who had refused to accept a reduction in wages. The government under Stanley Baldwin kept essential services going and nine days later the TUC called off the Strike.

GENERAL STRIKE *Walking to work.*

Genesis The first book of the Bible, traditionally ascribed to Moses and introducing the concept of the covenant between the Israelites and God. It recounts the creation of the universe and of man, the fall of Adam, the Flood, and the scattering of the nations at Babel. The remainder of the book focuses on the lives of Abraham, Isaac, Jacob, and Joseph.

genet   A carnivorous mammal of the genus *Genetta* (9 species) of Africa and Europe. Genets range from the 50-cm Abyssinian genet (*G. abyssinica*) to the 100-cm African giant genet (*G. victoriae*). They have retractile claws, long tails (up to 50 cm), foxlike heads, and pale fur with dark spots or stripes. Genets are nocturnal, preying on birds and small mammals. Family: *Viverridae*.

genetic code   The means by which information for the organization and function of living cells is carried by DNA and RNA molecules. Evidence for the nature of the genetic code was provided in the 1960s by the work of Crick, M. W. Nirenberg (1927–), Har Gobind Khorana (1922–), and others. They found that the basic symbol of the code was a sequence of three consecutive bases of the DNA molecule.

genetic engineering   Alteration of the genetic constitution of organisms, usually bacteria, in order to obtain gene products beneficial to man. Typically, a sequence of desirable genes is inserted into the DNA of a host bacterium. This altered DNA (*or* recombinant DNA) then directs the bacterial cell to synthesize the desired gene product (for example, insulin).

GENGHIS KHAN   *Detail from a 15th-century Persian miniature of the Mongol emperor with his court.*

genetic fingerprinting   A recently developed identification technique based on DNA examination. DNA is extracted from sample cells (e.g. from blood or semen) and broken into fragments using enzymes. These fragments, containing the genetic code unique to each individual, are compared with fragments obtained from a blood sample of the test subject. In 1987 the technique was used for the first time in the UK as forensic evidence.

genetics   The study of heredity and variation in living organisms. The science of genetics is founded on the work of Gregor Mendel. In the early 20th century chromosomes and their genes were established as the carriers of information determining inheritable characteristics, and with the discovery of the structure of DNA in 1953, the molecular basis of genetics was revealed. Genetics is important in plant and animal breeding and in understanding inherited diseases. *See also* genetic engineering.

Geneva   (French name: Genève; German name: Genf) 46 13N 6 09E A city in SW Switzerland. It is a cultural and commercial centre, banking and international finance being particularly important. It is the base of many international organizations including the Interna-

tional Red Cross and the World Health Organization. *History*: originally a prehistoric lake dwelling, it was later a Roman city. It became the centre of the Calvinist Reformation and a refuge for persecuted Protestants. Population (1985): 159 900.

Geneva Bible   An English translation of the Bible published in 1560 by Puritan exiles in Geneva. It is also called the Breeches Bible because of the use of the word in the translation of Genesis 3.7.

Geneva Conventions   International agreements covering the care and protection of noncombatants and wounded troops in wartime. Inspired by the establishment of the International Red Cross, the agreements also cover assistance for forces at sea, the treatment of prisoners of war, and the protection of civilians.

Genghis Khan   (c. 1162–1227) The founder of the Mongol empire. Originally called Tamujin, he adopted the title Genghis Khan (Emperor of All) in 1206 after uniting the nomadic Mongol tribes of the Siberian steppes and destroying Tatar power. Organizing his horsemen into highly mobile squadrons called *ordus* (hence "hordes"), he breached the Great Wall and captured Peking but failed to conquer China completely. Advancing westwards, Genghis crushed resistance in Afghanistan, Persia, and S Russia. After his death his son Ogadai (1185–1241) executed the empire's organization.

Gennesaret, Lake of.   *See* Galilee, Sea of.

Genoa (Italian name: Genova)   44 24N 08 56E A port in NW Italy. A major maritime city during the middle ages, Genoa is Italy's chief port and a major industrial centre. Population (1986): 727 427.

Gent.   *See* Ghent.

gentian   A herbaceous plant of the widely distributed genus *Gentiana* (about 400 species), which includes many alpine perennials. The blue flowers usually form a bell or funnel with spreading lobes. The fruit of most species is a capsule. Family: *Gentianaceae*.

Gentile da Fabriano   (Niccolo di Giovanni di Massio; c. 1370–1427) Florentine painter of the international gothic style. His fresco cycles for the Doge's Palace, Venice, and the Lateran Basilica, Rome, have perished. The *Adoration of the Magi* (Uffizi) shows his rich style.

geocentric system.   *See* Ptolemaic system.

geochemistry   The study of the chemical composition of the earth. It involves estimating the absolute and relative abundance of the constituent elements and their isotopes, as well as their distribution and migration in the various geochemical environments (lithosphere, atmosphere, biosphere, hydrosphere) and in the rocks and minerals that make up the earth.

geochronology   The study of dating geological events, rocks, sediments, and organic remains. Absolute dating involves radioactive dating techniques giving an actual date BP (before present). Relative dating establishes the order of geological events in relation to each other, using fossil correlation, pollen analysis, archaeological evidence, etc.

Geoffrey of Monmouth   (c. 1100–54) English chronicler. His major work, *Historia Regum Britanniae*, was the main source for the whole body of medieval European literature concerned with the Arthurian legend.

geography   The study of the features of the earth's surface, together with their spatial distribution and interrelationships, as man's environment. Modern geography was founded as a discipline in the early 19th century by the German scholars Humboldt and Ritter.

Geography is now divided between the physical and social sciences. Physical geography includes geomorphology (the study of the landforms of the earth), biogeography (the study of soils and the distribution of animals and plants), and climatology (*see* climate). The main branches of human geography are historical geography (studying spatial change in an area over a period of time, economic geography, urban geography, and political geography.

geological time scale A time scale covering the whole of the earth's history. The largest divisions are eras (Palaeozoic, Mesozoic, and Cenozoic); these are subdivided into periods and the Tertiary and Quaternary periods are further subdivided into epochs; epochs consist of several ages, and ages can be divided into chrons. A number of eras together is an eon. The stratomeric standard scale refers to the bodies of rocks formed in these time intervals; the corresponding terms are group (era), system (period), series (epoch), stage (age), and chronozone (chron).

geology The study of the earth: its origin, history, structure, composition, and the natural processes acting on it. The branches of geology are historical (including geochronology, stratigraphy, and palaeontology); physical (including geomorphology, geophysics, petrology, mineralogy, crystallography, and geochemistry); and economic, involving the distribution and occurrence of the economically important rocks and minerals, such as petroleum.

geomagnetic field The earth's magnetic field, causing a compass needle to align north–south. It is believed to be caused by the liquid-iron core acting as a dynamo resulting from the convection currents moving in it. The magnetic poles do not coincide with the geographic poles, and their positions vary with time. Complete reversals of the earth's magnetic field have occurred in the past. The three **magnetic elements** of the earth's field are the magnetic dip, the magnetic declination, and the horizontal field strength.

geometrid moth A moth of the family *Geometridae*, occurring in Europe, Asia, and North America. The name is derived from the looping method of locomotion of the caterpillars, which are known as inch worms, loopers, or measuring worms. The adults, known as pugs, umbers, carpet moths, etc., have slender bodies, a weak flight, and camouflaging coloration.

geometry A branch of mathematics concerned with the properties of space and shapes. In Euclidean geometry the space corresponds to common ideas of physical space and the shapes are idealizations of the common shapes that occur in real life. Other branches of geometry include non-Euclidean geometry, Riemannian geometry, and analytic geometry. *See also* topology.

geophysics The study of the physical forces acting on and within the earth. Important branches of geophysics are seismology, geomagnetism, vulcanology, natural radioactivity, and the earth's rotation and gravitational field.

George I (1660–1727) The first Hanoverian King of Great Britain and Ireland (1714–27) and Elector of Hanover (1698–1727). He divorced his wife for infidelity (1694) and imprisoned her for 32 years. A successful soldier and a shrewd diplomat, he was none the less unpopular in Britain because he seemed to subordinate British to Hanoverian interests. He never learnt English and left government to his Whig ministers.

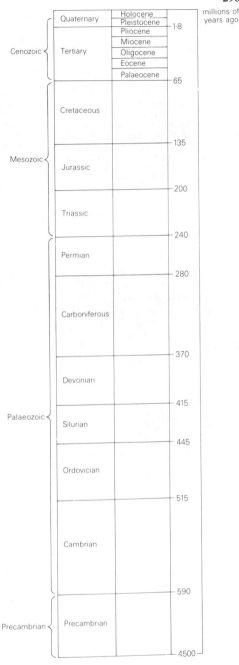

			millions of years ago
Cenozoic	Quaternary	Holocene	
		Pleistocene	1·8
		Pliocene	
	Tertiary	Miocene	
		Oligocene	
		Eocene	
		Palaeocene	65
Mesozoic	Cretaceous		
			135
	Jurassic		
			200
	Triassic		
			240
Palaeozoic	Permian		
			280
	Carboniferous		
			370
	Devonian		
			415
	Silurian		
			445
	Ordovician		
			515
	Cambrian		
			590
Precambrian	Precambrian		
			4500

GEOLOGICAL TIME SCALE

George II (1683–1760) King of Great Britain and Ireland and Elector of Hanover (1727–69). His reliance on such ministers as Sir Robert Walpole influenced the development of constitutional monarchy. In the War of Austrian Succession he fought at Dettingen (1743), the last British king to appear in battle. He was a patron of musicians, notably Handel.

George III (1738–1820) King of Great Britain and Ireland (1760–1820) and Elector (1760–1815) and King (1815–20) of Hanover. He shared with Lord North the blame for the loss of the American colonies but was more astute in backing William Pitt the Younger as prime minister (1783–1801). He was permanently insane by 1811, after which the Prince of Wales (later George IV) acted as regent (*see also* Regency style).

GEORGE IV *An engraving of the king by James Gillray entitled* A Voluptiary under the Horrors of Digestion.

George IV (1762–1830) King of the United Kingdom and of Hanover (1820–30). He secretly married a Roman Catholic, Maria Fitzherbert, in 1785 but the marriage was invalid and in 1795 he married Caroline of Brunswick. George's dissipation and extravagance and his heartless treatment of his wife undermined the prestige of the monarchy.

George V (1865–1936) King of the United Kingdom (1910–36), second son of Edward VII, whose heir he became on the death (1892) of his elder brother Albert Victor. In 1893 George married Mary of Teck.

George VI (1895–1952) King of the United Kingdom (1936–52). Second son of George V, he succeeded to the throne when Edward VIII abdicated. He married (1923) Lady Elizabeth Bowes-Lyon (*see* Elizabeth the Queen Mother).

George, St The patron saint of England and of soldiers. His cult was brought to England by Crusaders returning from Palestine, where he was believed to have been martyred during Emperor Diocletian's rule. In art he is usually portrayed slaying a dragon, a legend that probably derives from the Pegasus myth. Feast day: 23 April.

George Cross The highest British decoration for civilian bravery, awarded since 1940. A silver cross superscribed *For Gallantry*, its recipients include the island of Malta (1942). The **George Medal**, the second highest decoration for civilian bravery, was also instituted in 1940.

Georgetown (*or* Penang) 5 26N 100 16E A city in NW Peninsular Malaysia, the capital of Penang state. It is now Malaysia's chief port. Population (1980): 250 578.

Georgetown 6 46N 58 10W The capital and main port of Guyana. Founded by the British in 1781, it was later occupied by the French and the Dutch. Population (1985 est): 200 000.

Georgia A state on the SE coast of the USA. It can be divided into two physical regions: the Appalachian Mountains in the N and a coastal plain with forests and swamps in the S. Agriculture is important; poultry has replaced cotton as the major item and Georgia is a leading producer of peanuts. *History*: named after George II, it was founded in 1732. Settlement of the state expanded after the American Revolution; a supporter of the Confederate cause in the US Civil War, it suffered considerable damage during Gen Sherman's March to the Sea (1864). During the 20th century it has suffered from a decline in the cotton industry and troubled race relations. Area: 152 488 sq km (58 876 sq mi). Population (1986 est): 6 104 000. Capital: Atlanta.

Georgian The language spoken by the Georgian peoples of the USSR Turkey, and Iran. It belongs to the Kartvelian or South Caucasian group and is written in a script derived from Aramaic with Greek influences and has a literature dating from the 5th century AD. It is the official language of the Georgian SSR.

Georgian style A style of British architecture prevalent during the reigns of George I to George IV (1714–1830). The period was subject to several different influences but was dominated by Palladianism and neoclassicism. Georgian architecture was characterized by the symmetrical use of twelve-paned sash windows and the restrained use of classical features.

geostationary orbit. *See* communications satellite.

geothermal energy Heat produced in the earth's interior. Volcanoes, geysers, and hot springs are all sources of geothermal energy, although only the latter two provide convenient energy sources. It currently supplies about 0.1% of the world's energy requirements.

geranium A herbaceous plant of the genus *Pelargonium* (250 species), most species of which are native to South Africa. They have showy flowers, usually red or pink. Most horticultural geraniums are hybrids. Family: *Geraniaceae*.

Horticultural geraniums should be distinguished from related plants of the genus *Geranium* (*see* cranesbill).

gerbil A small rodent belonging to the subfamily *Gerbillinae* (over 100 species) of Africa and Asia, also called jird and sand rat. Ranging in size from 5–20 cm, gerbils have long hind legs. They spend the day in underground burrows, feeding at night on seeds and roots. Chief genera: *Gerbillus, Tatera*; family: *Cricetidae*.

geriatrics The medical specialty that deals with the diseases and problems of old age. The aim is to restore as much function as possible, by encouraging patients to engage in suitable activities with the aid of physiotherapy and occupational therapy.

German A language of the West Germanic language group. It is the official language of Germany and Austria and one of the four official languages of Switzerland. High German, the official and written form, developed from dialects of the highland areas of Germany and Austria. Old High German was spoken before 1100 AD when Middle High German, based on Upper German dialects, became the standard form. Modern High German developed from the 16th-century dialect of Luther. Low German exists only in a spoken form in N Germany and is derived from Old Saxon and Middle Low German speech.

Germanic languages A subgroup of the Indo-European language group. There are three recognized subgroups: East Germanic, North Germanic, and West Germanic. The first of these is now extinct. North Germanic covers the Scandinavian languages, West Germanic includes modern English and German among its descendants as well as Dutch (Netherlandic) and Frisian. All three branches can be traced back to an unrecorded Proto-Germanic language, which has been reconstructed by philologists by comparing and tracing back similar modern languages.

germanium (Ge) A brittle grey-white metalloid, discovered by C. A. Winkler (1838–1904) in 1886. Like gallium it is present in coal and is concentrated in chimney soot as well as in the flue dusts of zinc smelters, from which it is obtained commercially. The element is a semiconductor and its most important uses are in the electronics industry. At no 32; at wt 72.59; mp 937.4°C; bp 2830°C.

German measles A common contagious disease of children and young adults caused by a virus. Known medically as rubella, it is a mild infection producing a pink rash and a sore throat. If a woman is infected in pregnancy she may give birth to a malformed child.

German shepherd dog (or Alsatian) A breed of large dog originating in Germany. It has a coarse coat that can range in colour from white to black but is often black and tan. German shepherds are used as working dogs, as guard dogs, and as guide dogs for the blind. Height: 61–66 cm (dogs); 56–61 cm (bitches).

Germany A country in central Europe, now comprising (see below) the German Democratic Republic (East Germany) and the Federal Republic of Germany (West Germany). The region was occupied by German tribes from about 500 BC and came repeatedly into conflict with the Romans from the 2nd century BC. Overrun by the Huns in the 4th and 5th centuries, the area was dominated by the Franks from the 6th century and was christianized in the late-7th to 8th centuries. After the failure of the Frankish dynasty the German kings became nominally elective but medieval Germany was in practice ruled by a series of hereditary dynasties claiming the title of Holy Roman Emperor. In the 13th century the first Habsburg emperor was elected and from the 15th century the imperial title remained almost continuously in the family. In the later middle ages the power of the princes was challenged by the Hanseatic League. The 16th and 17th centuries were dominated by religious strife, following Luther's inception of the Reformation at Wittenberg in 1520. The religious conflict was not resolved until the conclusion (1648) of the Thirty Years' War. In the 17th century the Hohenzollern Electors of Brandenburg acquired Prussia, which became the dominant German state and, under Frederick (II) the Great, a major European power. In 1806 the Holy Roman Empire was brought to an end by Napoleon, who formed the Confederation of the Rhine in its place. The post-Napoleonic German confederation was dominated by Austria and Prussia and in 1834 the latter was the moving influence behind the formation of the Zollverein (customs union). Prussian power increased further with victory in the Austro-Prussian War (1866), and in the Franco-Prussian War (1870–71). In 1871 Bismarck achieved his cherished ambition of creating a German

Empire. The late 19th and early 20th centuries saw rapid industrialization, an aggressive armaments programme, and the rise of Germany as a colonial power, especially in Africa; its international aspirations were a major cause of World War I. Defeated in 1918, the Empire came to an end (1919) and was replaced by the Weimar Republic, which was plagued by the economic difficulties that facilitated Hitler's rise to power in the early 1930s. His aggressive foreign policy and attempts to establish a new German empire by an unprecedented ruthlessness precipitated World War II. Following Germany's defeat the country was divided into British, French, Soviet, and US zones before the subsequent formation of the two separate states, the German Democratic Republic and the Federal Republic of Germany.

German Democratic Republic (GDR; German name: Deutsche Demokratische Republik) The N part of the country, which borders on the Baltic Sea. The Harz Mountains rise in the W, the Thuringian Forest in the SW, and the Erzgebirge in the SE. The main rivers are the Elbe and the Oder. *Economy*: highly industrialized. Almost all industry is state-owned. The main mineral resource is lignite, which supplies over half of the country's basic energy. It has two nuclear power stations. Oil and coal are supplied by the Soviet Union. The agricultural sector, which is organized in collectives and state farms, is gradually declining in importance. *History*: formed from the Soviet-occupied zone of Germany following World War II, it was given a provisional constitution as the German Democratic Republic in 1949, becoming independent in 1954. The early years of economic austerity and curbs on civil liberties led to much discontent; the flow of refugees to West Germany continued until 1961, when the Berlin Wall was erected. Low living standards and the government's refusal to consider liberal reform led to mass protests in 1989 and the departure of thousands of refugees to the West. Erich Honecker was replaced as head of state by Egon Krenz; when the reform process remained slow he too resigned and East Germany's first non-Communist government was sworn in, with Hans Modrow as prime minister. Free access was allowed through the Berlin Wall and union with West Germany was discussed. East Germany is a member of COMECON and in 1973 was admitted to the UN as a separate state. Head of state: Manfred Gerlach. Official language: German. Official currency: (GDR) Mark of 100 Pfennige. Area: 108 178 sq km (41 757 sq mi). Population (1986): 16 639 877. Capital: East Berlin. Chief port: Rostock.

Germany, Federal Republic of (German name: Bundesrepublik Deutschland) For administrative purposes, West Germany is divided into 11 *Länder* (German *Land*, state). Extensive plains in the N, which border on the North Sea, rise to a central hilly area with the peaks of the Alps in the extreme S. The chief rivers are the Rhine, Danube, Ems, Weser, and Elbe. *Economy*: rapid reconstruction, particularly of the industrial sector, followed World War II. Considerable mineral resources include coal, iron ore, lead and zinc, and potash. Although the agricultural sector has declined in importance, there is a considerable amount of forestry and an important wine industry. Tourism is an important source of revenue. *History*: formed from the British-, French-, and US-occupied zones following World War II, it became fully independent in 1955. The capital was transferred to Bonn although West Berlin remained a part of the Federal Republic. In the postwar years it enjoyed a spectacular economic recovery making it the most prosperous country in W Europe. Federal President: Richard von Weizsächer (1920–   ). Chancellor: Helmut Kohl. Official language: German. Official currency: Deutsche Mark of 100 Pfennige. Area: 248 620 sq km (95 989 sq mi). Population (1986): 61 066 000. Capital: Bonn. Main port: Hamburg.

germination   The process by which an embryo plant within a seed is transformed into a recognizable plant with roots, stem, and leaves. Water, warmth, and oxygen stimulate germination, which begins with the emergence of the root (radicle) and is followed by the shoot (plumule). Energy for the process is provided by the cotyledons (seed leaves), which either remain below ground (hypogeal germination, as in the broad bean) or form the first leaves of the seedling (epigeal germination, as in the marrow).

Gershwin, George   (Jacob Gershvin; 1898–1937) US composer and songwriter. He wrote many songs for musical shows and films, his jazz-inspired orchestral works include *Rhapsody in Blue* (1924) and *An American in Paris* (1928). The opera *Porgy and Bess* (1935) is still widely performed. His brother **Ira Gershwin** (1896–1983) wrote the lyrics to many of his songs.

GESTALT   *According to the gestalt state of the observer this image is either a vase or two faces in profile.*

Gestalt psychology   A school of psychology that originated in Germany in the early 20th century: Wolfgang Köhler (1887–1967) and Kurt Koffka (1886–1941) were its founders. It regards mental processes as wholes (gestalts) that cannot be analysed into smaller components. According to this theory, when something is learned the individual's entire perception of the environment has been changed.

Gestapo   (German: *Geheime Staatspolizei*, secret state police). The Nazi secret police, formed under Göring and administered from 1936 by the SS. The two organizations were responsible for carrying out the atrocities perpetrated by the Germans in Europe.

Getty, J(ean) Paul   (1892–1976) US businessman, who lived in the UK. He made his fortune in oil, becoming a millionaire at the age of 22. He founded the J. Paul Getty Museum at Malibu, California.

Gettysburg, Battle of   (1–3 July, 1863) The most significant battle of the US Civil War, fought in S central Pennsylvania as part of the Confederacy's second invasion of the North. After three days of fighting the Confederates withdrew; the North lost 23 000 men and the South 25 000. The **Gettysburg Address**, one of the shortest and most famous of modern speeches, was delivered (19 November, 1863) by President Abraham Lincoln at Gettysburg battlefield.

geysers   Jets of hot water and steam issuing intermittently from holes in the earth's crust, some reaching heights of up to 70 m. Geysers are found in volcanically active or recently active regions. They occur when water from deep within the crust becomes superheated and suddenly boils. Cones of sinter (deposits of silica) frequently build up around the vents of geysers.

Ghana, Republic of   A country in West Africa, on the Gulf of Guinea. Coastal plains rise to undulating country around Accra, and, in the centre, the basin of the River Volta rises to plateaus, especially in the N and W. The inhabitants are chiefly of Black Sudanese stock but there are a large number of tribal units. *Economy*: chiefly agricultural. The main cash crop is cocoa, of which Ghana is the world's chief producer. Gold and diamonds are mined, as well as manganese, bauxite, and limestone. Hydroelectricity is being developed and oil was found offshore in 1978. *History*: from the middle ages several small kingdoms flourished in what is now Ghana. In 1472 the Portuguese and subsequently other Europeans set up trading posts in the region, which they called the Gold Coast. The area became the British colony of the Gold Coast in 1874. In 1957, together with the British part of Togo, it became independent, its new name, Ghana, being that of a medieval N African empire. In 1960 it became a republic within the British Commonwealth; since when there have been several successful military coups, in the last of which (1981) Fl Lt Jerry Rawlings (1942–   ) came to power. The expulsion from Nigeria of one million Ghanaians in 1982 created a national emergency. Official language: English. Official currency: cedi of 100 pesawas. Area: 238 305 sq km (92 010 sq mi). Population (1985): 13 004 000. Capital: Accra. Main port: Takoradi.

gharial.   *See* gavial.

Ghats   Two mountain ranges lying along the W and E coasts of India. The **Western Ghats**, which extend about 1500 km (932 mi) from N of Bombay to Cape Comorin, rise to 2693 m (8840 ft). They have dense natural vegetation and are used for tea planting. The **Eastern Ghats** extend about 1400 km (880 mi) from near Cuttack to the Nilgiri Hills.

Ghent   (Flemish name: Gent; French name: Gand) 51 02N 3 42E A city in Belgium, at the confluence of the canalized Rivers Scheldt and Lys. One of Belgium's oldest cities, it is a major port and the country's textile centre. Population (1987): 233 856.

gherkin   A trailing West Indian vine, *Cucumis anguria*. It is cultivated for its prickly edible fruit, 2.5–7.5 cm long, used when immature for pickling. Family: *Cucurbitaceae* (gourd family).

Ghibellines.   *See* Guelfs and Ghibellines.

Ghiberti, Lorenzo   (c. 1378–1455) Florentine Renaissance sculptor. Ghiberti made his name as a sculptor in 1402, when he won the competition for the bronze relief sculptures for the north doors of the Baptistry of the Florentine Duomo. Finished in 1424, these New Testament scenes, mainly in the international gothic style, were followed by Old Testament scenes in the Gates of

Paradise (1425–52). Simultaneously he wrote *I commentarii*, which included histories of ancient and early Renaissance art and an autobiography. His other works include three statues of saints (1416–25) for Orsanmichele.

Ghirlandaio, Domenico (Domenico di Tommaso Bigordi; 1449–94) Florentine painter of the early Renaissance. From 1481 to 1482 he worked on a fresco in the Sistine Chapel but his major undertaking was the fresco cycle (1486–90) in Sta Maria Novella, Florence. The tenderly painted *Old Man and Boy* (Louvre) is a fine example of his portraiture.

Giacometti, Alberto (1901–66) Swiss sculptor and painter. He was influenced initially by cubism and primitive art and later by surrealism, particularly in his abstract construction of sticks, glass, wire, etc., entitled *The Palace at 4 am* (New York). After breaking with surrealism in 1935, he developed a unique figure style.

Giambologna (Giovanni da Bologna *or* Jean de Boulogne; 1529–1608) Italian mannerist sculptor of Flemish birth. Working from 1557 in Florence, where he was patronized by the Medici, he produced fountains, religious sculptures, and small bronze statues. His works include *Samson and a Philistine* (1567; Victoria and Albert Museum).

Giant's Causeway 55 14N 6 32W A promontory in N Northern Ireland, in Antrim. It consists of several thousand closely packed basaltic columns, mainly hexagonal in shape, formed by an outpouring of lava into the sea. According to legend it was built as a bridge for the giants to cross between Ireland and Scotland.

giant star A large very luminous star that has a very tenuous atmosphere but a dense core. It is in a late stage of evolution, having exhausted the normal source of energy in its core (hydrogen), and must derive energy from other nuclear fusion reactions. *See also* red giant.

gibberellins A group of organic compounds that stimulate plant growth. First isolated from the fungus *Gibberella fujikuroi*, over 30 gibberellins are now known. They stimulate the growth of leaves, stems, flowers, and fruit and break the dormancy of seeds and tubers.

gibbon A small ape belonging to the genus *Hylobates* (7 species), of S Asia. 45–65 cm long, they have long arms and hooked fingers used to swing through trees. They live in family groups, feeding chiefly on fruit and leaves, and have a whooping call. Family: *Hylobatidae*. *See also* siamang.

Gibbon, Edward (1737–94) British historian. His ironic treatment of Christianity in his monumental *The History of the Decline and Fall of the Roman Empire* (1776–88) aroused contemporary controversy, but its epic scope and dignity of style ensured its survival.

Gibbons, Grinling (1648–1721) English wood carver and sculptor, born in Rotterdam. Patronized by Charles II and subsequent British monarchs, he produced decorative carvings of flowers, fruit, etc. His best-known works are the choir stalls and organ screen in St Paul's Cathedral.

Gibbons, Orlando (1583–1625) English composer, organist, and virginalist. Of his madrigals, "The Silver Swan" is the best known. He also wrote church music and string fantasias and contributed pieces to *Parthenia* (1611), the first anthology of keyboard music to be printed in England.

Gibbs, Josiah Willard (1839–1903) US physicist. Gibbs founded chemical thermodynamics, which is

largely based on the function known as the Gibbs free energy. He is also known for his phase rule, relating the number of parameters that can be varied in a system of more than one phase.

GRINLING GIBBONS *Detail of a choir stall in St Paul's Cathedral, London.*

Gibraltar A British crown colony occupying a peninsula at the southern tip of Spain. The isthmus that links it to the Spanish mainland rises sharply to the 427 m (1400 ft) limestone Rock of Gibraltar. The population is mainly of Spanish, Genoese, and Portugese descent. *Economy*: British defence expenditure together with tourist earnings and fees for services to shipping form the basis of its economy. *History*: settled by the Moors in 711 AD, the Rock of Gibraltar was taken by Castile in 1462, becoming part of united Spain. It was captured in 1704 by the British to whom it was formally ceded by the Treaty of Utrecht (1713). The colony became an important British naval base. Claims to Gibraltar have long been made by Spain but a UN proposal to end British occupation was defeated in a referendum in 1967. In 1969 Spain closed its frontier with Gibraltar leading to the subsequent import of Moroccan labour. The border was reopened in 1985. Official languages: English and Spanish. Official currency: Gibraltar pound of 100 pence. Area: 6.5 sq km (2.5 sq mi). Population (1987 est): 29 000.

Gibraltar, Strait of A strait between Gibraltar and Africa, joining the Atlantic Ocean and the Mediterranean Sea. It narrows to 13 km (8 mi) and is of great strategic importance.

Gibson Desert A desert in central Western Australia. It consists of a vast arid area of active sand dunes and desert grass. Area: 220 000 sq km (85 000 sq mi).

Gide, André (1869–1951) French novelist and critic. Much of his work is semiautobiographical, reflecting his homosexuality and consequent conflict with conventional morality. In 1895 he married his cousin Madeleine Rondeaux, the inspiration of two short works, *The Immoralist* (1902) and *Strait Is the Gate* (1909). His longer novels are *The Vatican Cellars* (1914) and *The Counterfeiters* (1926). His *Journal*, which he kept from 1885 until his death, is a major work of literary autobiography. He won the Nobel Prize in 1947.

Gielgud, Sir (Arthur) John (1904–) British actor. He is noted for his distinguished speaking voice and for his many fine performances in Shakespearean productions. His *Hamlet*, first performed in 1929, received especial acclaim.

Gigantes In Greek mythology, the giant sons of Uranus (Heaven) and Gaea (Earth), whose rebellion against the Olympian gods was defeated with the help of Heracles. They were subsequently associated with earthquakes and volcanoes.

Gijón 43 32N 5 40W A port in NW Spain, on the Bay of Biscay. Its many ancient buildings include Roman baths and medieval palaces.   Population (1981): 255 969.

Gilbert, William (1544–1603) English physicist and physician to Elizabeth I. His *De magnete* (1600) listed many experimental observations concerning magnets, including the discovery of magnetic dip. He was the first English scientist to accept the ideas of Copernicus and coined such terms as *electricity* and *magnetic pole.*

W. S. GILBERT *Programme (from the 1890s) for* Princess Ida *by Gilbert and Sullivan.*

Gilbert, Sir William Schwenk (1836–1911) British comic dramatist. He wrote comic verses, published as *Bab Ballads* (1869), while studying law. In 1870 he met Arthur Sullivan, the composer for whom he wrote the libretti for 14 popular operas.

Gilbert Islands. *See* Kiribati, Republic of.

Gillespie, Dizzy (John Birks G.; 1917–) US Black jazz trumpeter, band leader, and composer, who was one of the originators of bop. His recordings include *Groovin' High* and *Hot vs Cool.*

gills The respiratory organs of aquatic animals: specialized thin-walled regions of the body surface through which dissolved oxygen is taken into the blood and carbon dioxide released into the water. The gills of fish lie in gill slits on each side of the gullet. The gills of molluscs and fanworms are ciliated and trap food particles in the respiratory currents. The external gills of amphibian larvae (tadpoles) are feathery structures projecting from the body wall.

gilt-edged security A UK government fixed-interest stock. Some, such as Consols, are irredeemable (no date is stipulated for the return of the capital); others are redeemable at par on a specified date. Short-term gilts ("shorts") are redeemable within 5 years, "mediums" in 5–15 years, and "longs" in over 15 years. The price of

gilts depends upon prevailing interest rates. Most gilts are issued in units of £100 (the par value).

gin A spirit distilled usually from grain flavoured with juniper berries (the name is derived from the Dutch *jenever*, juniper). Gin is almost pure alcohol, with little flavour. It is generally drunk with tonic water, vermouth, fruit juice, etc.

ginger A perennial herbaceous plant, *Zingiber officinale*, native to SE Asia and widely grown in the tropics for its pungent underground stems (rhizomes), used as a spice, food, and flavouring and in medicine. The plants are sterile, and propagation is by cuttings from the rootstocks. Family: *Zingiberaceae.*

ginkgo A deciduous gymnosperm tree, *Ginkgo biloba*, also called maidenhair tree, that is the sole living representative of a group of trees that flourished in the Carboniferous period (370–280 million years ago). Growing to a height of 30 m, it has fleshy yellow fruits containing edible kernels. The ginkgo is native to China and widely planted for ornament. Family: *Ginkgoaceae.*

ginseng An extract of the forked roots of either of two herbs, *Panax quinquefolium* or *P. schinseng*, used as a stimulant drug in the Far East and to make aromatic bitters. It is said to have aphrodisiac and life-prolonging properties. Family: *Araliaceae* (ivy family).

Giorgione (c. 1477–1510) Italian painter of the Venetian school. He trained under Giovanni Bellini and worked with Titian. Most of his paintings are small-scale secular pictures, including the *Tempest* (Accademia, Venice), notable for its atmospheric landscape. *The Sleeping Venus* (Gemäldegalerie, Dresden), and *The Three Philosophers* (Kunsthistorisches Museum, Vienna) show the dreamlike mood of his paintings. His portraits, e.g. *Laura* (Vienna), influenced many Venetian painters. He probably died of the plague.

Giotto (Giotto di Bondone; c. 1266–1337) Italian painter and architect, who laid the foundation for Renaissance painting. The fresco cycle of St Francis, in the upper church of S Francesco, Assisi, is thought to be an early work. He painted the innovative frescoes of scenes from the lives of Joachim and Anne and the Virgin and Christ in the Arena Chapel, Padua, and frescoes in Sta Croce, Florence. In 1334 he became architect of the city

GIOTTO Joachim and Anna *(detail; Arena Chapel, Padua).*

and surveyor of Florence Cathedral, for which he designed the campanile.

Gipsies A wandering people found on most continents. The name "Gipsy" is derived from "Egyptian," but they probably originated in India. One group is thought to have migrated through Egypt and North Africa and another through Europe reaching NW Europe during the 15th and 16th centuries. They live largely by seasonal work, itinerant trade, and fortune telling. They have been persecuted frequently, half a million being killed by the Nazis during World War II. Their native language is Romany.

Gir A breed of zebu cattle originating from the Gir forest of W India. They have domed foreheads with backward-curving horns and long ears and are yellowish red to black in colour. Traditionally a dairy breed, they are also used for draught purposes.

giraffe A hoofed mammal, *Giraffa camelopardalis*, of tropical African grasslands. Measuring 3 m at the shoulder, with a neck 2.5 m long, giraffes are marked with reddish-brown blotches on a buff-coloured background. They feed on leaves; both sexes have permanent skin-covered horns. Family: *Giraffidae*.

Girl Guides Association An association founded by Robert and (his sister) Agnes Baden Powell in 1910 to encourage the physical, mental, and spiritual development of girls. The three classes of members are Brownie Guides (for girls aged between 7 and 10), Guides (10–15), and Ranger Guides (14–20). Its counterpart for boys is the Scout Association.

giro A low-cost system for transferring money. It originated in Austria in 1883 and the British National Giro was set up by the Post Office in 1968, becoming independent in 1988 as Girobank PLC. All accounts are held at the Giro Centre (in Bootle, Lancashire), which transfers money from one account to another on receipt of a completed form. Bank giro operates similarly, but accounts are held at bank branches.

Gironde, River An estuary in SW France, on the Bay of Biscay. Formed by the confluence of the Rivers Garonne and Dordogne near Bordeaux, it is used by ocean-going vessels. Length: 72 km (45 mi).

Giscard d'Estaing, Valéry (1926–) French statesman; president (1974–81). Founder of the Independent Republican Party, his attempts at liberal reform were thwarted by his party's dependence on Gaullist support.

Gish, Lillian (1899–) US actress, who began her career as a child actress on stage with her sister **Dorothy Gish** (1898–1968). Both acted for D. W. Griffith in early silent films, including *The Birth of a Nation* (1916) and *Intolerance* (1916). Lillian's later films include *Duel in the Sun* (1946) and *The Night of the Hunter* (1955).

Giulio Romano (Giulio Pippi; c. 1499–1546) Italian mannerist painter and architect (*see* mannerism). He was the pupil of Raphael, whom he assisted in the decoration of the Vatican apartments and the Villa Farnesina. In 1524 he settled in Mantua, where he designed and decorated the Palazzo del Tè, notable for its Room of the Giants, completely covered with illusionistic frescoes.

Giza, El (*or* al-Jizah) 30 01N 31 12E A city in N Egypt, forming a suburb of Cairo. Nearby are the great pyramids of Khafre, Khufu, and Menkaure and the Sphinx. Population (1985): 1 608 000.

glacier A mass of ice and firn of limited width lying chiefly, or completely, on land and moving downslope from its source. **Cirque glaciers** are contained in depressions on mountain slopes or valley heads. **Valley glaciers** are contained within pre-existing valleys, originating either from cirque glaciers or from an icesheet. The longest of these is the Lambert Glacier, 400 km (250 mi) long. Where a glacier emerges from a valley onto a lowland area, a lobe-shaped **piedmont glacier** results; an example is the Malaspina Glacier in Alaska. **Glaciation** is the action of glacier ice on the land surface. The main landforms resulting from glaciation are either erosional or depositional. Erosional features include U-shaped valleys and cirques. Those of depositional origin include glacial drift and till. When water is also involved term fluvioglacial is used; fluvioglacial deposits include eskers and kames.

gladiators The slaves, prisoners of war, condemned criminals, or volunteers who fought to the death in amphitheatres for the entertainment of the ancient Roman people. Gladiatorial combats began as a feature of funeral games but their popularity was soon so great that statesmen sponsored shows to enhance their political prestige.

Gladiolus A genus of ornamental perennial herbaceous plants (300 species), native to Europe, Africa, and the Mediterranean regions and widely cultivated. Growing from a corm, the flowering stem reaches a height of 1.2 m, with funnel-shaped flowers. Principal garden forms are *G. cardinalis*, *G. primulinus*, *G. psittacinus*, *G. purpurea-auratus*, and *G. saundersii*. Family: *Iridaceae*.

WILLIAM GLADSTONE *Detail from a photograph taken during his last premiership.*

Gladstone, W(illiam) E(wart) (1809–98) British statesman; Liberal prime minister (1868–74, 1880–85, 1886, 1892–94). Elected to parliament in 1832, he was initially a Tory and supported the Peelites in the repeal of the Corn Laws, after which the Peelites joined the Whigs (shortly to be termed Liberals). As chancellor of the exchequer (1852–55, 1859–66) Gladstone reduced tariffs and government expenditure. His first ministry disestablished the Irish Church (1869) and introduced the Education Act (1870), the first Irish Land Act (1870), and the Ballot Act (introducing secret ballots). Defeated in the 1874 election, he resigned the Liberal leadership. He again became an MP and prime minister in 1880. His second ministry achieved a second Irish Land Act (1881) and further parliamentary reform (1884) but its failure to save Gordon from Khartoum led to Gladstone's resignation. His last ministries followed his conversion to Irish Home Rule but both his Home Rule bills were rejected (1886, 1893). An impressive speaker, Gladstone with his Conservative opponent Disraeli dominated British politics in the late 19th century.

gland   An organ or group of cells that is specialized for synthesizing a specific chemical substance (secretion) from constituents of the blood and releasing its secretion for use by the body. Man and higher animals have two kinds of glands. The endocrine glands lack ducts and release their secretions (hormones) directly into the bloodstream. The exocrine glands have ducts through which their products are secreted. Exocrine glands include the salivary glands, the sweat and sebaceous glands in the skin, and the pancreatic cells that secrete digestive enzymes. Plants also have glands, which secrete latex, resin, nectar, tannin, etc.

glanders   A highly contagious disease of horses, donkeys, and related animals caused by the bacterium *Pfeifferella mallei*, which can also infect other animals and man. Slaughter of infected animals is compulsory in most countries.

glandular fever (*or* infectious mononucleosis)   An infection characterized by fatigue, sore throat, headache, muscular pain, and enlarged lymph nodes. Most common in children and young adults, it is caused by the Epstein–Barr virus, which can be transmitted in saliva (for example during kissing). Treatment is with bed rest and painkillers.

Glasgow   55 53N 4 15W The largest city in Scotland, the administrative centre of Strathclyde Region on the River Clyde. An important port, Glasgow has a long tradition of shipbuilding. *History*: Glasgow's wealth grew rapidly through trade after the union with England (1707), especially in tobacco and sugar from the New World, and through industry in the industrial revolution. Population (1985 est): 733 794.

glasnost   A policy of increased freedom in social and cultural matters introduced in the Soviet Union by Mikhail Gorbachov in 1986. A Russian word meaning openness, *glasnost* was adopted in conjunction with *perestroika* (meaning progress), which heralded a new (though still limited) flexibility in the economy of the USSR, and facilitated the improvement of relations with the West.

GLASTONBURY   *Ruins of an early Benedictine abbey.*

glass   A translucent and usually transparent noncrystalline substance that behaves as a solid although it has many of the properties of a liquid. Glass itself was known in the 3rd millennium BC but glassblowing was not invented until about 100 BC (in Syria) and windows were not in use until about 100 AD. Ordinary soda glass, used for windows, etc., consists of silica (sand), sodium carbonate, and calcium carbonate (limestone). Flint glass, used for crystal glassware, contains silica, potassium carbonate, potassium nitrate, and lead oxide. Heat-resistant glass also contains borates and alumina; optical glass contains additional elements to control the refractive index and other optical properties. Blown glass is melted and blown inside a mould until it fills the mould. Flint glass is usually blown by hand. Pressed glass is made by pressing the molten glass into a mould. Plate glass, for windows, etc., is now made by floating a rolled sheet of glass on molten tin. *See also* fibreglass.

glass snake   A legless lizard belonging to the genus *Ophisaurus*, occurring in Europe, S and E Asia, N Africa, and North America. Glass snakes feed on insects, lizards, mice, and birds' eggs. Unlike true snakes, they have ears, eyelids, and rigid jaws. When attacked, they shed their tail. Family: *Anguidae*.

glasswort (*or* marsh samphire)   An annual or perennial plant of the genus *Salicornia* (at least 7 species), native to European salt marshes. It was once used in glass-making as a source of soda. Family: *Chenopodiaceae*.

Glastonbury   51 09N 2 43W A market town in SW England, in Somerset. Here by tradition Joseph of Arimathea founded England's first church and King Arthur is said to be buried. Population (1981): 6773.

glaucoma   An eye disease caused by raised pressure inside the eye. Acute glaucoma is often caused by a sudden block to the drainage of the watery fluid (aqueous humour) inside the eye. It leads to pain and disturbed vision, which will result in blindness without urgent treatment. Chronic glaucoma—one of the commonest causes of blindness—comes on slowly and painlessly.

Glazunov, Aleksandr Konstantinovich   (1865–1936) Russian composer and a pupil of Rimsky-Korsakov. Glazunov's works, which were influenced by Wagner and Liszt rather than by Russian musical nationalism, included eight symphonies, concertos, ballets, and string quartets.

Glencoe   A glen in W Scotland, in the Highland Region. It was the scene of the massacre of the Macdonalds by the Campbells and English (1692).

Glendower, Owen   (Welsh name: Owain Glyndwr; c. 1359–c. 1416) Welsh rebel. Allying with Henry IV's opponents, Glendower controlled most of Wales by 1404 but was subsequently defeated and turned to guerrilla warfare. He disappeared in 1416.

Glenn, John   (1921–   ) US astronaut and politician, who on 20 February, 1962, became the first American to orbit the earth. He became a US senator in 1974.

gliders   Light fixed-wing engineless aircraft, sometimes called sailplanes. They are launched into the air by a winch or catapult or by being towed by a car or powered aircraft. Once airborne a glider is lifted by warm air currents. The height record is 14.1 km (P. F. Bikle; 1961) and the distance record 1460.8 km (H. W. Grosse; 1972). Pioneered by Otto Lilienthal, gliders were used by the Wright brothers in designing their powered aircraft. Gliders were also used in World War II notably in the ill-fated Arnhem expedition. Since the 1920s gliding has been a popular sport, controlled in the UK by the British Gliding Association (1924). *See also* hang-gliding.

Glinka, Mikhail Ivanovich (1804–57) Russian composer. He composed the first truly Russian opera *Ivan Susanin* (*A Life for the Tsar*; 1836), piano music, songs, and a second opera *Russlan and Ludmilla* (1842).

global warming. *See* greenhouse effect.

globe artichoke. *See* artichoke.

globefish. *See* puffer.

Globe Theatre An Elizabethan theatre, in Southwark, in which most of Shakespeare's plays were first produced. A cylindrical wooden building open to the sky, it was built in 1599, burnt down in 1613, rebuilt in 1614, and finally demolished in 1644. Its remains were rediscovered in 1989.

globe thistle A stout perennial thistle of the genus *Echinops* (about 15 species), of central and S Europe. 50–200 cm high, it has large spherical flower heads.

Globigerina A genus of protozoan animals that are common components of marine plankton. Ranging in size from 0.3 to 2 mm, their chalky skeletons are a major constituent of the grey mud on some sea beds, forming globigerina ooze. Order: *Foraminifera*.

globulin A type of protein that is generally insoluble in water. Serum (gamma) globulins of the blood include the immunoglobulins (antibodies), which are manufactured by the animal to combat infections. Newborn mammals receive these immunoglobulins in maternal milk. Other globulins occur in eggs, nuts, and seeds.

glockenspiel (German: bell play) A tuned percussion instrument having a keyboard-like arrangement of steel bars played with two small hammers. The notes of its two-and-a-half-octave compass above bottom G of the bass stave sound two octaves higher.

Glomma, River (Norwegian name: Glåma) A river in SE Norway and the longest river in Scandinavia. Length: 588 km (365 mi).

Glorious Revolution (1688) The overthrow of James II of England and the establishment of his daughter Mary and her husband William of Orange on the throne. The opposition to James' pro-Catholic and absolutist policies requested William's armed intervention; James panicked and, offering no resistance, fled to France. As William III and Mary II, the joint monarchs accepted the Bill of Rights.

glottis. *See* larynx.

Gloucester 51 53N 2 14W A market town in W England, the administrative centre of Gloucestershire on the River Severn. First developed under the Romans (Glevum) it is noted for its cathedral. Population (1983 est): 92 200.

Gloucestershire A county of W England, bordering Wales. It consists of three regions: the Cotswold Hills, the Severn Valley, and the Forest of Dean. It is predominantly agricultural. Area: 2638 sq km (1019 sq mi). Population (1986 est): 517 100. Administrative centre: Gloucester.

glowworm. *See* firefly.

gloxinia An ornamental herb, *Sinningia speciosa*, native to Brazil. Gloxinias have large bell-shaped velvety flowers. New plants can regenerate from the base of the leafstalks. Family: *Gesneriaceae*.

Gluck, Christoph Willibald (1714–87) German composer. He reformed opera seria and composed the operas *Orfeo ed Euridice* (1762) and *Alceste* (1767). He also composed over 40 dramatic works.

glucose (*or* dextrose) A simple sugar ($C_6H_{12}O_6$) and an essential substance in the carbohydrate metabolism of living organisms. Carbohydrates (such as starch and glycogen) in food or tissue reserves are broken down to glucose, which is easily transported to cells where it undergoes glycolysis. Organisms can also manufacture glucose from fats and proteins. Glucose levels in blood are regulated by the hormones insulin and glucagon.

gluten A protein mixture derived from wheat. In bread making, dough rises because the gluten in wheat flour expands, trapping the carbon dioxide bubbles in an elastic network. The properties of gluten vary according to the mixture of the proteins. *See also* coeliac disease.

glutton. *See* wolverine.

glycerol (*or* glycerine; $CH_2OHCHOHCH_2OH$) A colourless syrupy liquid with a sweet taste. It is made from fats and oils or by fermentation and is used in explosives, cosmetics, and antifreeze solutions.

glycogen A starchlike carbohydrate found in animal tissues as a reserve energy source. It consists of branched chains of glucose molecules: when required to provide energy, glycogen is broken down to glucose under the influence of hormones.

glycolysis The sequence of chemical reactions occurring in most living cells by which glucose is partially broken down to provide usable energy in the form of ATP. Glycolysis can take place in the presence or absence of oxygen but only a small amount of the available energy is released, the major proportion being released via the Krebs cycle.

Glyndebourne An estate near Lewes, in East Sussex, home of an annual international festival of opera. The opera house was built by John Christie (1882–1962), who founded the Glyndebourne Festival in 1934 for his wife, the opera singer Audrey Mildmay (1900–53).

GMT. *See* Greenwich Mean Time.

gnat Any of the smaller delicate species of two-winged flies, the males of which fly in dancing swarms. The term is applied to the less virulent mosquitoes and phantom gnats (family *Culicidae*), winter gnats (family *Trichoceridae*), fungus gnats (family *Mycetophilidae*), craneflies (family *Tipulidae*), and several others.

gneiss A coarse-grained metamorphic rock consisting predominantly of bands of quartz and feldspar alternating with bands of micas and amphiboles. Gneisses are formed during regional metamorphism; those derived from igneous rocks are termed **orthogneiss**, those from sedimentary rocks **paragneiss**.

Gnosticism A religious movement that flourished in the early Christian era. It contained elements of pagan thought but is most fully recorded as a group of heretical Christian sects. The Gnostics' defining characteristic was their belief in *gnosis* (Greek: knowledge)—a special revelation from God to initiates, which would ensure their salvation. They interpreted Christ (whose humanity they denied) as being sent to rescue particles of spirit (souls) entrapped in matter. Gnosticism influenced Manichaeism and several medieval heresies.

GNP. *See* gross national product.

gnu A large ungainly antelope belonging to the genus *Connochaetes* (2 species), also called wildebeest, of African plains. The brindled gnu (*C. taurinus*) grows to 140 cm high at the shoulder and is blue-grey with a long black mane, black facial tufts, and a black-tufted tail.

GNU   *The brindled gnu.*

The smaller white-tailed gnu (*C. gnou*) has a long white tail and is very rare.

Goa, Daman, and Diu.   *See* Daman and Diu; Goa.

Goa   The 25th state of India, formerly part of Goa, Daman, and Diu Union Territory. A Portuguese overseas territory from 1510 until annexed by India in 1961, it has many fine examples of Portuguese colonial architecture, including the church in which St Francis Xavier is buried. Area: 3496 sq km (1363 sq mi). Population (1981): 1 007 749.

goat   A hoofed ruminant mammal belonging to the genus *Capra* (5 species). Related to sheep, goats are 60–85 cm tall at the shoulder and have hollow horns; males have a scent gland beneath the tail and a beard. Wild goats, found in mountainous regions of Eurasia, live in herds. Goats were first domesticated over 10 000 years ago and are still used to provide milk, meat, and hides in many semiarid regions. Family: *Bovidae. See also* ibex; markhor.

goat moth   A large moth, *Cossus cossus*, of Europe, Asia, and N Africa. Mottled grey and brown, it has a wingspan of 70 mm. The reddish caterpillar bores under the bark of trees and emits a characteristic strong odour.

Gobelins, Manufacture nationale des   A French state-controlled tapestry factory, founded in Paris as a dyeworks in the 15th century by Jean and Philibert Gobelin. Manufacturing tapestries from 1529, it was incorporated by Henry IV in 1607. Since 1826 carpets have also been made here.

Gobi Desert   A vast desert of SE Mongolia and N China. On a plateau 900–1500 m (2950–4920 ft) high, it is rocky with salt marshes and streams that disappear into the sand. It is rich in prehistoric remains. Area: about 1 295 000 sq km (500 000 sq mi).

goby   A fish of the suborder *Gobioidei* (over 800 species), especially the family *Gobiidae* (true gobies). True gobies have smooth elongated bodies, two dorsal fins, and a suction disc formed from fused pelvic fins. Most are 5–10 cm long, although *Pandaka pygmaea* of the Philippines is the smallest known vertebrate at under 13 mm long. They are found chiefly in tropical coastal regions. Order: *Perciformes.*

Godard, Jean-Luc   (1930–   ) French film director, a member of the New Wave. His films are characterized by experimental narrative and editing techniques and by

his Marxist political convictions; they include *Week-End* (1967), *Tout va bien* (1972), and *Je Vous Salue, Marie* (1985).

Godavari, River   A river in central India. Rising in the Western Ghats, it flows ESE to the Bay of Bengal. It is sacred to the Hindus. Length: 1500 km (900 mi).

Godesberg (*or* Bad Godesberg)   50 41N 7 10E A spa in W West Germany, in North Rhine-Westphalia on the River Rhine; since 1968 a district of Bonn.

Godiva, Lady   (d. ?1080) The English woman who, according to the chronicler Roger of Wendover (d. 1236), rode naked through the market place of Coventry in order to persuade her husband Leofric, Earl of Mercia, to reduce his taxes on the town. The story was later embellished with a Peeping Tom who, ignoring Godiva's request that the townspeople remain indoors, was struck blind.

Godthåb.   *See* Nuuk.

Godunov, Boris (Fedorovich)   (c. 1551–1605) Russian statesman and tsar (1598–1605). Godunov rose to power under Ivan the Terrible and became regent for Fyodor I, whose younger brother and heir, Dimitrii, Godunov may have murdered in 1591. After Fyodor's death (1598), Godunov was elected tsar. His authority was challenged by the first False Dimitrii, a pretender who succeeded Godunov.

Godwin Austen, Mount.   *See* K2.

godwit   A long-legged long-billed migratory bird belonging to a genus (*Limosa*; 4 species) that breeds in N Eurasia and North America. The black-tailed godwit (*L. limosa*) is 40 cm long and has a distinctive black-banded white tail. Family: *Scolopacidae* (plovers, sandpipers, etc.).

Goebbels, (Paul) Joseph   (1897–1945) German Nazi politician. Appointed minister of propaganda by Hitler in 1933, he established a vast machine for the control of public information, the arts, cinema, and theatre, all of which he manipulated with a cynical disregard for truth. He committed suicide with his wife after taking the lives of his six children during the collapse of the Third Reich.

JOHANN WOLFGANG VON GOETHE

Goethe, Johann Wolfgang von   (1749–1832) German poet, scholar, and statesman. His discovery of Shakespeare inspired him to write an epic drama, *Götz* *von Berlichingen* (1773) while the autobiographical novel *The Sorrows of Young Werther* (1774) won him international fame. In 1775 he settled at the court of the Duke of Saxe-Weimar, whom he served as prime minister until 1785. At Weimar he fell in love with Charlotte von Stein, who inspired some of his greatest lyric poetry. A visit to Italy (1786–88) made him an enthusiastic advocate of classicism, influencing such plays as *Iphigenia on Tauris* (1787) and *Torquato Tasso* (1790). After the novel *Wilhelm Meister's Apprentice Years* (1795–96) he published the first part of his greatest work *Faust* (1808), a poetic drama of the aspirations of man. He published *Wilhelm Meister's Journeyman Years* in 1829 and the second part of *Faust* he completed shortly before his death.

Gog and Magog In Revelation and other books of the Bible, attendant powers of Satan. In British folklore they appear as the survivors of a race of giants destroyed by Brutus, the legendary founder of Britain. A famous pair of statues depicting them are located in the Guildhall, London.

Gogol, Nikolai Vasilievich (1809–52) Russian novelist and dramatist. Early ambitions to become a poet and an actor and to emigrate all failed, but two volumes of stories based on his Ukrainian childhood won him acclaim from Pushkin and other leading writers. To escape the controversy aroused by his satirical play *The Government Inspector* (1836) he went to Rome, where he wrote his best-known work, *Dead Souls* (1842), a grotesque lampoon of Russian feudalism. In his last years he became a depressive and a religious maniac.

Goiânia 16 43S 49 18W A city in central Brazil, the capital of Goiás state. Founded in 1933 to replace the old capital, it serves a cattle-raising and coffee-growing area. Population (1985): 928 046.

Goidelic languages. *See* Celtic languages.

goitre Swelling in the neck caused by enlargement of the thyroid gland. A goitre is called simple if the thyroid is functioning normally; this occurs in areas where iodine is deficient in the water supply and it may occur sporadically in adolescent girls. A goitre may also be seen when the thyroid is overactive or underactive (*see* cretinism).

Golan Heights A range of hills in SW Syria, under Israeli administration. They are of great strategic importance; Israeli forces stormed the heights in June, 1967, when most of the local populace fled. Jewish settlements have since been established.

gold (Au) A soft dense yellow metal valued since ancient times. It occurs in nature as the element and in compounds with tellurium, in rock veins and alluvial deposits. The metal is the most malleable and ductile known. It alloys with other metals, is a good conductor of heat and electricity, and is chemically unreactive. The major uses for the element are for jewellery, electrical contacts, and as a currency standard (*see* gold standard). Purity is measured in carats. At no 79; at wt 196.967; mp 1064.43°C; bp 2966°C.

Gold Coast The name applied to the coastal zone in West Africa between Axim and the River Volta on the Gulf of Guinea. An important source of gold, it formed part of the British colony of Gold Coast (present-day Ghana).

goldcrest A tiny agile songbird, *Regulus regulus*, occurring chiefly in coniferous woodland of N Europe and Asia and feeding on insects and spiders. It is about 9 cm

long and has a yellow-green plumage and an orange crest. Family: *Muscicapidae* (Old World flycatchers).

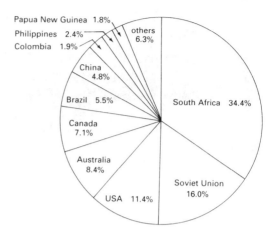

GOLD *World production of gold (1988).*

golden eagle A large dark-brown eagle, *Aquila chrysaetos*, occurring in mountainous regions of North America and Eurasia. It is 70–85 cm long and has a wingspan of up to 230 cm; they catch small mammals and gamebirds.

goldeneye A diving duck, *Bucephala clangula*, that breeds in N Eurasia and winters in more southerly regions. It is 41–45 cm long and males are black and white with a greenish head and a circular white patch on the cheek; females are grey with white markings and a brown head.

GOLDEN FLEECE *The Emperor Maximilian I wearing the chain of the order.*

Golden Fleece The fleece of a sacred winged ram, the recovery of which was the goal of Jason and the Argonauts. Athamas, King of Thebes, had two sons, Prhixus and Helle, by his first wife Nephele. His second wife, Ino, hated her stepsons and plotted their death. They escaped across the sea on the golden ram and, having reached Colchis, sacrificed the ram to Zeus and hung the fleece in a grove sacred to Ares, where it was guarded by a dragon. The **Order of the Golden Fleece** was founded in 1430 by Philip the Good, taking as its badge Jason's fleece. After Burgundy was united with the Habsburg empire (1477), the order became confined to Austria and Spain.

Golden Horn (Turkish name: Haliç)   An inlet of the Bosporus in NW Turkey. It is 7 km (4.5 mi) long and serves as Istanbul's harbour.

golden retriever   A large strongly built breed of dog whose ancestors possibly included labradors, setters, and spaniels. The dense water-resistant wavy coat is gold or cream; they are used as gun dogs, guide dogs, etc. Height: 56–61 cm (dogs); 51–56 cm (bitches).

goldenrod   A perennial herb of the genus *Solidago* (about 120 species), up to 2.5 m tall and mostly native to North America. The stem bears small yellow flowers. Canadian goldenrod (*S. canadensis*) is often grown as a garden ornamental. Family: *Compositae*.

goldfinch   A Eurasian finch, *Carduelis carduelis*. About 12 cm long, it has a brown back, black wings with a broad yellow stripe, black-and-white tail and head, and a red face. It uses its pointed bill to extract seeds from thistles and dandelions and flocks of goldfinches (called charms) are commonly seen on farmland.

goldfish   A freshwater fish, *Carassius auratus*, also called golden carp, of E Asian origin but introduced elsewhere as an ornamental fish. In its natural state it is greenish brown or grey and up to 30 cm long. However, the breeding of abnormal specimens has produced over 125 varieties often with a red-gold coloration. It requires cold well-oxygenated water and is omnivorous.

Golding, Sir William   (1911–   ) British novelist. His best-known novel, *Lord of the Flies* (1954), concerns a group of schoolboys who are isolated on a desert island and revert to savagery. His other novels include *Pincher Martin* (1956), *The Spire* (1964), *Rites of Passage* (1980), which won the 1980 Booker prize, *The Paper Men* (1984), *Close Quarters* (1987), and *Fire Down Below*

(1989). He was awarded the Nobel Prize in 1983.

Goldsmith, Oliver   (1730–74) Anglo-Irish writer. Born in Ireland, he arrived penniless in London in 1756. A friend of Johnson and Boswell, he was inarticulate in conversation and a compulsive gambler. His best-known works are the poem *The Deserted Village* (1770), the novel *The Vicar of Wakefield* (1776), and the play *She Stoops to Conquer* (1773).

gold standard   A monetary system in which paper money was convertible on demand into gold. Rates of exchange between currencies were fixed by their values in gold. In classical economics imbalances in international trade were rectified automatically by the gold standard. A country in deficit would have depleted gold reserves and would therefore reduce its money supply. The resulting fall in demand would reduce imports and the lowering of prices would boost exports, thus rectifying the deficit. It was finally abandoned in 1931. *See also* International Monetary Fund.

Goldwyn, Samuel   (S. Goldfish; 1882–1974) US film producer, born in Poland. In 1916 he cofounded Goldwyn Pictures, a production company that became Metro-Goldwyn-Mayer (MGM) in 1924. His many successful films as an independent producer include *Wuthering Heights* (1939) and *Guys and Dolls* (1955).

golem   In medieval Jewish folklore, an image or automaton that can be brought to life by a charm. They were supposed to have been used as servants by rabbis. The word originally referred to anything incomplete or embryonic.

golf   A club-and-ball game for two or four players played on a golf course. It almost certainly originated in Scotland. A standard course is usually between 4572 m (5000 yd) and 6400 m (7000 yd) and is divided into 18 holes (9 on a small course), each of which is between 90 m (100 yd) and 540 m (600 yd) long. A "hole" comprises the flat starting point, called the "tee," a strip of mown grass about 27–90 m (30–100 yd) wide, called the "fairway," and a smooth putting green. On the green is the

GOLF   *Irons are numbered according to the angle of the face; the greater the angle of inclination, the higher the ball is hit into the air. Thus a good player, under normal conditions, knows the range of each iron. The Number One wood (driver) is used from the tee for the maximum distance and the putter is used on the green.*

actual hole, which has a diameter of 10.8 cm (4.25 in). There are also obstacles around the course, such as trees, ditches, and sand bunkers. The object of the game is to hit the rubber-cored ball from each tee into each hole with as few strokes as possible ("par" for a hole is the standard number of strokes needed by a first-class player; one stroke less than par is called a "birdie," and an "eagle" is two strokes less). To achieve this a player has a set of clubs of which there are three basic types: woods, irons, and putters.

Golgi apparatus (*or* Golgi complex) A structure present in the cytoplasm of nearly all cells, composed of stacks of flattened sacs bounded by membranes and associated with vesicles. Discovered by Camillo Golgi (1843–1926), it is thought to function in the synthesis and concentration of certain materials, especially secretory products, which are then packaged into the vesicles and transported within the cell.

Golgotha. *See* Calvary.

goliath beetle A large beetle belonging to the group of flower chafers. The African goliath beetle (*Goliathus giganteus*) has the largest body of all the insects, about 96 mm in length. It is white with black stripes and brown wing cases. The larvae are found in rotten logs.

goliath frog The largest known living frog, *Rana goliath*, which grows up to 35 cm long. This rare shy frog inhabits deep river pools in Africa.

Gomułka, Władysław (1905–82) Polish statesman. Gomułka was secretary general of the Polish Workers' Party from 1945 until 1948, when his criticism of the Soviet Union led to his imprisonment (1951–54). Following the Poznan Riots, Gomułka became first secretary of the Party. In 1970 he resigned after demonstrations over price increases.

gomuti A palm tree, *Arenga pinnata* (or *A. saccharifera*), also called sugar palm, occurring in SE Asia. The sap yields palm sugar and the fermented juice (palm wine) is distilled to produce arrack. A form of sago is obtained from the pith and the leaf fibres are used to make cord, ropes, etc.

gonadotrophin One of several hormones that control the activity of the testes and ovaries (the gonads) in mammals. The pituitary gland produces three gonadotrophins: luteinizing hormone (LH), which stimulates ovulation and oestrogen production by the ovaries and the production of androgens by the testes; follicle-stimulating hormone (FSH), which promotes ovulation and sperm production; and prolactin, which triggers lactation. LH and FSH are glycoproteins and are usually released together. Human chorionic gonadotrophin (HCG) is produced by the placenta, reaching a peak level in the urine in early pregnancy. Gonadotrophins are also used in fertility drugs.

Goncourt, Edmond de (1822–96) French writer, who collaborated with his brother **Jules de Goncourt** (1830–70) on art criticism, social histories, and novels, most notably *Germinie Lacerteux* (1864) and *Madame Gervaisais* (1869). They are best known for their *Journal*, a lively record of French literary life, and for Edmond's legacy, the Académie Goncourt, which awards France's most prestigious annual literary prize, the **Prix Goncourt**.

Gondwanaland The supercontinent in the S hemisphere believed to have existed prior to 200 million years ago, when the drift of the continents to their present positions began. It probably consisted of South America,

Africa, Australia, Antarctica, Arabia, and India. *See also* Laurasia.

gonorrhoea An acute venereal infection caused by a bacterium (the gonococcus). Symptoms in men are discharge from the penis and a burning pain on passing urine. Women may have vaginal discharge and pain on urinating. Gonorrhoea can be treated with penicillin.

Gooch, Graham Alan (1953–) British cricketer. An outstanding batsman, he played for Essex (1975–), captaining the side (1986–87), and captained England (1988; 1989–).

Good Friday The Friday before Easter, when Christ's crucifixion is commemorated. It is a fast day, and in the Roman Catholic Church the Mass is not celebrated. In the Anglican Church Holy Communion is rarely held, although provided for in the Book of Common Prayer.

Good Hope, Cape of. *See* Cape of Good Hope.

Goodwin Sands A range of dangerous sandbanks off the SE coast of England, in the Strait of Dover. At low tide large areas of sand are exposed.

goose A large long-necked waterbird belonging to the family *Anatidae* (ducks, geese, and swans), occurring in the N hemisphere. Geese have short bills and webbed feet. They chiefly feed on grass, grain, roots, etc., and are highly migratory, flying in characteristic V-formations and honking loudly in flight. The several breeds of domesticated goose are probably descended from the greylag goose. Genera: *Anser* (grey geese), *Branta* (black geese); order: *Anseriformes*. *See also* Canada goose.

gooseberry A fruit bush of the genus *Ribes*, especially *R. uva-crispa* (or *R. grossularia*), which is widely cultivated in the Old World for its hairy prickly-coated edible berries. Family: *Grossulariaceae*.

goosefish. *See* anglerfish.

gopher. *See* souslik.

MIKHAIL GORBACHOV

Gorbachov, Mikhail Sergeevich (1931–) Soviet statesman; general secretary of the Soviet Communist Party (1985–) and president (1988–). As general secretary he began a radical programme of political and economic reform (*see* glasnost). In 1987 he signed a major arms limitation treaty with the USA; in 1989 he introduced the new Congress of People's Deputies and in 1990 under his leadership the Communist Party voted to give up its monopoly of power.

Gordian knot A knot binding the yoke and beam of the chariot of Gordius, a legendary king of Phrygia. According to legend, whoever could unloose the knot would become the ruler of Asia. In 333 BC Alexander the Great is said to have cut the knot with his sword.

Gordon, Charles George (1833–85) British general. Gordon served in the Crimean War and then in China and Egypt. From 1877 to 1880 he was British governor of the Sudan; in 1884 he returned to the Sudan to evacuate Europeans and Egyptians, following al Mahdi's revolt. Gordon was besieged for ten months in Khartoum, which was taken two days before a relief force arrived. Gordon himself was murdered.

Gordon Riots (1780) Anti-Roman Catholic riots in London fomented by Lord George Gordon (1751–93), who opposed the Roman Catholic Relief Act (1778). The riots were crushed; Gordon was arrested but acquitted of treason.

Gorgon In Greek legend, an underworld monster. Hesiod refers to three Gorgons, the sisters Stheno, Euryale, and Medusa. They were usually portrayed as winged females with snakes for hair and boars' tusks for teeth.

gorilla The largest living ape, *Gorilla gorilla*, of tropical African forests. Male gorillas can grow to 1.8 m with a weight of 300 kg. They walk on their feet and knuckles, feeding on plant stems and fruit. Troops are led by a dominant adult male and are generally not aggressive. Three races are recognized: the rare shaggy mountain gorilla and two lowland forms.

Göring, Hermann Wilhelm (1893–1946) German Nazi politician. He served in the air force in World War I and became a Nazi in 1922, taking command of Hitler's Brownshirts. He became president of the Reichstag in 1932. When Hitler came to power in 1933, Göring was appointed air minister of Germany and prime minister of Prussia. He established the Gestapo and probably engineered the Reichstag fire (1933). He directed the development of the Luftwaffe and in 1936 was given charge of mobilizing the economy for war. Hitler declared Göring his successor in 1939 but expelled him from the party shortly before the Nazi collapse. Condemned to hang at Nuremburg, he committed suicide before the execution could take place.

Gorki, Maksim (Aleksei Maksimovich Peshkov; 1868–1936) Russian novelist. His early life is recounted in his trilogy *Childhood* (1913–14), *In the World* (1915–16), and *My Universities* (1923). He established his literary reputation with romantic short stories and followed these with several novels and plays, including *Mother* (1906) and *The Lower Depths* (1906). He lived in exile from 1906 to 1913 and again from 1921 to 1928. He then returned to Russia, becoming an exponent of Stalinism.

Gorkii (Gorki *or* Gorky; name until 1932: Nizhnii Novgorod) 56 20N 44 00E A city in the central Soviet Union, on the Rivers Oka and Volga. It is one of the country's most important industrial cities. The city was renamed in 1932 in honour of the writer Maksim Gorki. Population (1987): 1 425 000.

Gorlovka 48 17N 38 05E A city in the SW Soviet Union, in the Ukrainian SSR in the Donets Basin. It is one of the largest coalmining and industrial centres of the area. Population (1987): 345 000.

gorse (*or* furze) A spiny shrub, *Ulex europaeus*, up to 4 m high, with bright-yellow sweet-scented flowers. The fruit is a black hairy pod that splits open explosively to release the seeds. Gorse is native to grassy areas and heaths throughout Europe and has been introduced elsewhere. Family: *Leguminosae*.

goshawk A large powerful hawk, *Accipiter gentilis*, ranging throughout forests of the N hemisphere and formerly used in falconry. It is 60 cm long with a wingspan of 130 cm and grey plumage. It feeds chiefly on birds.

Gospels (Old English: good news) The four New Testament accounts of Christ's life, ascribed to Matthew, Mark, Luke, and John. The first three are known as the Synoptic Gospels, since they report approximately the same synopsis of the events. Material that is not found in Mark but is common to Matthew and Luke is believed to derive from a single lost source, known as Q. The fourth Gospel, John, may presuppose a knowledge of the Synoptic Gospels.

Gossaert, Jan (c. 1478–c. 1532) Flemish painter, whose popular surname, Mabuse, derives from his birthplace Maubeuge. As one of the first Flemish artists to work in the Italian Renaissance style, he painted sculptural nudes against Italian architectural backgrounds, e.g. *Neptune and Amphitrite* (Berlin). As a portraitist he was noted for his expressive treatment of hands.

Göteborg (English name: Gothenburg) 57 45N 12 00E An important ice-free port in SW Sweden, at the mouth of the River Göta. Sweden's second largest city, it expanded with the opening of the Göta Canal (1832). Population (1986): 429 339.

Gothenburg. *See* Göteborg.

gothic art and architecture The styles flourishing in Europe from the mid-12th to the end of the 15th centuries. "Gothic" originated as a derisory term used by Renaissance artists, who blamed the destruction of classical art on the Goths who invaded the Roman Empire. The gothic is most closely associated with church architecture, the hallmarks of gothic design being the rib and shaft ceiling, the pointed arch, and the flying buttress. It was initiated in France in such edifices as the cathedrals of Notre-Dame (begun 1163), Chartres (begun c. 1194), Reims (begun 1211), etc. In England it has been subdivided into three phases: Early English (c. 1200–c. 1300; e.g. Lincoln Cathedral), Decorated (c. 1300–70; e.g. Exeter Cathedral), and Perpendicular (c. 1370–1540; e.g. Winchester Cathedral). Stained glass was only fully developed in the gothic period, while gothic sculpture mirrored the architecture it adorned, renouncing its early naturalism for a stylized elegance. In painting, the early gothic manifested itself chiefly in manuscript illumination. Its full flowering in panel and manuscript painting came with the international gothic style of the early 15th century. The style was also the foundation of the **gothic revival** of the 19th century, as utilized in such buildings as Fonthill Abbey, the Houses of Parliament, and the Law Courts in London. See p. 310.

gothic novel An English genre, popular in the late 18th and early 19th centuries, characterized by a prevailing atmosphere of mystery and terror and pseudomedieval–"gothic"–settings. Examples include Horace Walpole's *Castle of Otranto* (1765), Ann Radcliffe's *The Mysteries of Udolpho* (1794), and Matthew Gregory Lewis' *The Monk* (1796).

Goths Germanic peoples who originated in Scandinavia (Gotland) and had moved into the Ukraine by the end of the 2nd century AD. Shortly afterwards they invaded the Roman Empire N of the Danube and expanded into the Balkans. Converted to Arian Christianity in the mid-4th century, their empire was soon destroyed by the Huns and their two groups, the Ostrogoths and Visigoths, separated.

Early English   Decorated

Perpendicular

GOTHIC ART AND ARCHITECTURE *In England the three phases of gothic architecture are characterized by distinctive window designs.*

Gotland (Gothland *or* Gottland) The largest of the Swedish islands, in the Baltic Sea. Long disputed between Denmark and Sweden, it was finally ceded to Sweden in 1645. Area: 3140 sq km (1225 sq mi). Population (1986 est): 56 174, including associated islands. Capital: Visby.

Göttingen 51 32N 9 57E A city in E West Germany. With its famous university and the Max Planck Association for the furtherance of science, it is a noted educational centre. Population (1987): 133 700.

Gounod, Charles François (1818–93) French composer. His most successful works were the operas *Faust* (1852–59) and *Romeo and Juliet* (1864). Towards the end of his life he composed much sacred music.

gourami One of several freshwater tropical labyrinth fishes, especially *Osphronemus goramy*. It has a brown or grey oval body, up to 60 cm long, and a filamentous ray extending from each pelvic fin.

gourd The fruit of certain plants of the family *Cucurbitaceae*, especially the white-flowered bottle

gourd (*Lagenaria siceraria*). Other gourds are grown as ornamentals. The dishcloth gourd is used as a bath sponge and the snake gourd is grown for food.

gout Sudden attacks of arthritis caused by the presence of uric acid crystals in the joints. The big toe is most commonly affected, becoming hot, red, and very painful. Gout is commonest in older men and tends to recur; if not treated it may lead to damage to the joint.

Gower Peninsula A peninsula in South Wales, in West Glamorgan. The National Trust owns some of the picturesque S and W.

Goya (y Lucientes), Francesco (Jose) de (1746–1828) Spanish painter. After studying in Italy, he settled in Madrid (1775), where he painted gay scenes of Spanish life for the royal tapestry factory. As court painter from 1789 he produced realistic unflattering portraits of the royal family. He became deaf in 1792, and his works grew pessimistic, as in his etchings of *Los Caprichos* and *The Disasters of War*. Among his best-known paintings are *Maja Clothed*, *The Shootings of 3 May 1808*, and the so-called black paintings, such as *Satan Devouring His Children* (all Prado).

Goyen, Jan Josephszoon van (1596–1656) Dutch landscape painter and etcher. His landscapes were characterized by large expanses of sky and near-monochrome colours.

Gozzoli, Benozzo (Benozzo di Lese; 1420–97) Florentine painter. His major works are the frescoes of the *Journey of the Magi* (Palazzo Medici-Riccardi, Florence), which are noted for their detailed landscapes, and portraits of his contemporaries.

Grace, W(illiam) G(ilbert) (1848–1915) British cricketer, who captained England in 13 Test matches. In his long career (1865–1908) he scored 54 896 runs, including 126 centuries, took 2876 wickets, and held 877 catches.

THE THREE GRACES *Botticelli's* Primavera *(detail; Uffizi, Florence).*

Graces In Greek mythology, the three daughters of Zeus and Hera, representing beauty, grace, and charm. They were named Aglaia, Euphrosyne, and Thalia.

gradient A measure of the inclination of a slope, often expressed as the rise in height divided by the length of the slope, i.e. the sine of the angle of the slope. Mathematically, however, the gradient is the ratio of the vertical rise to the horizontal distance covered, i.e. the tangent of the angle. In calculus the gradient is the slope of the tangent at any point on a curve in a Cartesian coordinate system. If the curve is represented by the function f (x), then the gradient is the first derivative of $f(x)$.

Graf, Steffi (1969–) West German tennis player. Her victories include the Wimbledon singles championship in 1988 and 1989; in 1988 she became the fourth woman to complete a grand slam of the four major singles championships.

grafting 1. (horticulture) The transfer of part of one plant, usually a shoot or a bud, onto another plant. It is used as a means of vegetative propagation, particularly for fruit trees and roses. The cambium (a region of actively dividing cells) of the transplanted piece (the scion) is aligned with that of the recipient plant (the stock): the wound tissue thus formed binds the graft together. 2. (surgery). *See* transplantation.

Graham, Billy (1918–) US evangelist. His association with prominent personalities and carefully staged meetings, in which the audience are invited to "take a decision for Christ," have attracted very large crowds.

Graham, Martha (1893–) US ballet dancer and choreographer. Her ballets include *Primitive Mysteries* (1931), *Circe* (1963), and *Acts of Light* (1981).

KENNETH GRAHAME *Mole entertains Rat, from* Wind in the Willows; *an illustration by Arthur Rackham.*

Grahame, Kenneth (1859–1932) British writer. His best-known book is the children's classic, *The Wind in the Willows* (1908), adapted as a play, *Toad of Toad Hall* (1929), by A. A. Milne.

Graham Land A mountainous peninsula in Antarctica, comprising part of British Antarctic Territory.

Grahamstown (Afrikaans name: Grahamstad) 33 19S 26 32E A town in South Africa, in SE Cape Province. It was the focus of British settlement in 1820. Population (1985 est): 75 000.

Graiae In Greek legend, three goddesses personifying old age, the sisters and protectors of the Gorgons. They shared one eye and one tooth. Perseus stole the eye in order to take the Gorgons by surprise.

Grainger, Percy Aldridge (1882–1961) Australian-born composer and pianist. Grainger was a friend of Grieg and Delius and studied and recorded English folksong. His compositions include *Shepherds' Hey* (1913),

and *Harvest Hymn* (1933), as well as the "clog dance" *Handel in the Strand* (1913).

gram (g) A unit of mass equal to 1/1000 of a kilogram.

grammar schools Secondary schools in the UK providing a largely academic education for children aged 12 to 18. The original grammar schools, established in the middle ages, were preparatory institutions for university or for jobs in which a knowledge of Latin was essential. After World War II, with the growing demand for academic excellence, grammar schools were compelled to restrict entry to those passing the eleven-plus examination. Most grammar schools have been replaced by comprehensive schools; those that remain select by a twelve-plus examination.

gramophone. *See* recording of sound.

Grampian Region An administrative region in NE Scotland, created under local government reorganization in 1975. It consists of fertile lowlands in the NE rising to the Cairngorm and Grampian Mountains in the SW. Agriculture, tourism, and fishing are important. Area: 8708 sq km (3361 sq mi). Population (1986 est): 502 850. Administrative centre: Aberdeen.

Grampians A range of mountains in central Scotland, mainly in the Grampian and Tayside Regions. Its chief summits include Ben Nevis at 1343 m (4406 ft) and Ben Macdhui at 1309 m (4296 ft).

Grampians A mountain range in Australia. It extends SW from Victoria, reaching 1166 m (3827 ft) at Mount William.

grampus A small toothed whale, *Grampus griseus*, of warm and temperate waters, also called Risso's dolphin. About 3.7 m long, dark-grey with a pale belly, grampuses migrate towards the Poles in summer and the equator in winter.

Granada 37 10N 3 35W A city in S Spain, in Andalusia. Formerly the capital of the kingdom of Granada, it includes many Moorish buildings (notably the Alhambra). Population (1981): 262 182.

granadilla. *See* passionflower.

Granados, Enrique (1867–1916) Spanish composer and pianist. He and his wife were drowned during World War I when HMS *Sussex* was torpedoed. Granados is best remembered for the piano pieces entitled *Goyescas* (1911), inspired by Goya.

Gran Chaco A vast plain in South America. It was the cause of the Chaco War between Paraguay and Bolivia (1932–35). Area: 780 000 sq km (300 000 sq mi).

Grand Banks A section of the North American continental shelf in the N Atlantic, an important fishing ground. Area: about 1 280 000 sq km (494 000 sq mi).

Grand Canal (Chinese name: Da Yunhe) A canal in E China, the longest in the world, extending about 1600 km (1000 mi) N–S from Peking to Wuhan.

Grand Canyon A vast gorge in the USA, in Arizona on the Colorado River. It became the **Grand Canyon National Park** in 1919. Length: 451 km (280 mi). Width: 6–29 km (4–18 mi). Greatest depth: 1.5 km (1 mi).

Grand Coulee Dam A large gravity dam on the Columbia River in Washington (USA). It is 1272 m long at its crest, 108 m high, and has a reservoir capacity of 11 600 million cubic metres.

Grande Dixence Dam A gravity dam on the River Dixence (Switzerland). Until 1970 it was the tallest dam in the world (284 m high).

Grand Guignol A type of sensational drama that

flourished in Paris in the late 19th century. The term derives from the name of a theatre at which these plays were performed, and from Guignol, a stock character in French puppet shows.

grand mal. *See* epilepsy.

Grand National Steeplechase The world's most famous steeplechase, run in March at Aintree near Liverpool (England) over 30 assorted obstacles. It was first run in 1839.

granite A coarse-grained plutonic rock of acid composition resulting from the high silica content. Granites contain quartz, feldspar (usually alkali), and mafic (dark-coloured) minerals, usually muscovite and biotite (micas). Most granites crystallize from magma in igneous intrusions known as batholiths, but some are produced by the action of granitic fluids rising from great depths.

Gran Paradiso 45 33N 7 17E The highest mountain in Italy, in the Alps. Height: 4061 m (13 323 ft).

CARY GRANT *With Eva Marie Saint in Hitchcock's* North by Northwest *(1959)*.

Grant, Cary (Archibald Leach; 1904–86) US film actor, born in England. He established his reputation in such films as *Holiday* (1938) and *The Philadelphia Story* (1940). His films for Alfred Hitchcock include *To Catch a Thief* (1955) and *North By Northwest* (1959).

Grant, Ulysses S(impson) (1822–85) US general and statesman; Republican president (1869–77). As supreme commander of the Federal armies (1864–65) he defeated the Confederates by battering them into submission. The consequently great losses to his own side earned him the nickname Grant the Butcher. As president, he acquiesced in Reconstruction attempts to enfranchise Blacks, fought inflation, and unsuccessfully planned to annex the Dominican Republic. Subsequently he became so poor that he had to sell his swords and war souvenirs.

grape The fruit of vines of the genus *Vitis* (about 60 species), especially *V. vinifera*, native to N Asia but cultivated throughout Mediterranean regions. The fruit is green, red, or blue-black and used to make wine, brandy, and liqueurs or eaten fresh or dried (as raisins, sultanas, and currants).

grapefruit A tree, *Citrus paradisi*, 6–12 m high, cultivated in the tropics and subtropics. Its fleshy yellow-skinned fruits, 10–15 cm in diameter, are eaten fresh,

tinned, or crushed to make beverages. *See* Citrus.

grape hyacinth A perennial herbaceous plant of the genus *Muscari* (50 species), mostly native to the Mediterranean region and widely grown as spring-blooming garden bulbs. The blue, pink, or white flowers are borne at the tip of a stalk, up to 15 cm high. Family: *Liliaceae*.

graphite An iron-grey to black form of pure carbon, found in many metamorphic rocks. It occurs in a laminar or massive form. It is soft, flaky, and greasy to the touch. Graphite is used for making metallurgical crucibles, as a lubricant, in paint, rubber, and pencil leads, in batteries and for other electrical purposes, and as a moderator in nuclear reactors. It has often been called plumbago or black lead, since it was formerly mistaken for lead.

Grappelli, Stephane (1908–) French jazz violinist. A member of the Hot Club de France (1934–39), he has recorded with Earl Hines and Yehudi Menuhin among others.

graptolite A small colonial marine animal belonging to the extinct class *Graptolithina*. Their fossils occur in rocks of the Upper Cambrian to Carboniferous periods, about 420–250 million years ago.

grass A monocotyledonous annual or perennial herbaceous plant belonging to the family *Poaceae* (or *Gramineae*; 6000–10 000 species), distributed worldwide. The leaves consist of a basal sheath and a long narrow blade. The flowering stems (culms) bear inconspicuous flowers. The single-seeded fruit (the grain) is known as a caryopsis, with the ovary wall (pericarp) and seed coat fused. Many species are important in agriculture (*see* cereals; sugar cane).

Grass, Günter (1927–) German novelist, poet, and political activist. His first novel, *The Tin Drum* (1959) established him as a moral spokesman for his generation. His other works include the play *The Plebeians Rehearse the Uprising* (1966) and the novels *Dog Years* (1963), *The Meeting at Telgte* (1981), and *The Rat* (1986).

STEPHANE GRAPPELLI

grassfinch A songbird belonging to a subfamily of weaverfinches, occurring chiefly in Australasia. About 10 cm long, grassfinches have long tails and stout bills.

grasshopper A jumping insect belonging to the family *Acrididae* (about 5000 species). 24–110 mm long, both sexes produce sound by rubbing the hind legs against the front wings. Some species can fly, (*see* locust). Grasshoppers feed on low vegetation and the females lay eggs in the soil. Order: *Orthoptera*.

grass monkey A small African guenon monkey, *Cercopithecus aethiops*, inhabiting wooded regions. The West African green monkey, the East African grivet monkey, and the South African vervet or blue monkey are all local races of grass monkey.

grass snake A nonvenomous snake, *Natrix natrix*, also called water snake, occurring throughout Europe. 75–95 cm long, it has a green back with two rows of black spots, vertical black bars along its sides, and a yellow neck patch. Its prey includes fish and small mammals. Family: *Colubridae*.

grass tree A woody plant of the genus *Xanthorrhoea* (about 5 species), native to E Australia. They often have palmlike stems, 5 m tall, that end in a tuft of rigid grasslike leaves, from which extend flower spikes. A red or yellow resin, used for varnishes, exudes from the bases of old leaves. Family: *Xanthorrhoeaceae*.

Gravenhage, 's. *See* Hague, The.

ROBERT GRAVES

Graves, Robert (Ranke) (1895–1985) British poet, critic, and novelist. *Goodbye to All That* (1929) recounts his experiences in World War I. His other writings include poems, *I Claudius* (1934), *Claudius the God* (1934), and *The White Goddess* (1948).

Gravettian A culture of the Upper Palaeolithic, succeeding the Aurignacian in W Europe. Named after the cave at La Gravette in the Dordogne (SW France), the Gravettian is characterized by small pointed stone blades (Gravette points) and dates from between 26 000 and 20 000 BC. The well-known small female figurines called Venuses are of Gravettian origin. The term Eastern Gravettian is applied to similar material from sites in Russia and E Europe. *Compare* Périgordian.

gravitation An attractive force that occurs between all bodies that possess mass. It was first described by Sir Isaac Newton in a law stating that the force between two bodies is directly proportional to the product of their masses and inversely proportional to the square of the distance between them. The constant of proportionality

is called the universal **gravitational constant**, G, which has the value 6.673×10^{-11} newton metre squared per kilogram squared. Gravitation is now more accurately described by the general theory of relativity.

gravitational collapse The sudden collapse of the core of a star when thermonuclear fusion ceases. The star's internal gas pressure can no longer support the weight of the star and the initial result may be a supernova explosion. The gravitational pull of the remains of the star causes it to contract, producing a white dwarf, neutron star, or black hole.

gravitational interaction One of the four kinds of interaction that occur between elementary particles (*see* particle physics) and by far the weakest (about 10^{40} times weaker than the electromagnetic interaction). The interaction occurs between all particles with mass and can be explained as the exchange of virtual particles called gravitons.

gray (Gy) The SI unit of absorbed dose of ionizing radiation equal to the energy in joules absorbed by one kilogram of irradiated material.

Gray, Thomas (1716–71) British poet. His most famous poem is *Elegy Written in a Country Churchyard* (1751), a classical meditation on the graves of the villagers of Stoke Poges, Buckinghamshire.

grayling A troutlike fish of the genus *Thymallus*, sometimes placed in a distinct family (*Thymallidae*). Graylings have a silvery-purple body, up to 50 cm long, with a sail-like dorsal fin, and live in fresh waters of Eurasia and N North America, feeding on aquatic insects. They are important food and game fish. Family: *Salmonidae*.

Gray's Inn. *See* Inns of Court.

Graz 47 05N 15 22E The second largest city in Austria, the capital of Styria. Its historical buildings include a cathedral (1438–62) and a clock tower (1561). Population (1981): 243 166.

Great Artesian Basin An artesian basin of E Australia. The largest area of artesian water in the world, it extends S from Queensland into South Australia and New South Wales. Area: 1 750 000 sq km (676 250 sq mi).

Great Barrier Reef The largest coral reef in the world, off NE Australia. 2012 km (1250 mi) long, its exotic plant and animal life makes it popular with tourists.

Great Basin A large semiarid area in the USA. It extends over most of Nevada, Utah, and parts of California and Oregon.

Great Bear. *See* Ursa Major.

Great Bear Lake A lake in N Canada, on the Arctic Circle. Frozen eight months of the year, it is the fourth largest lake in North America. Area: 31 792 sq km (12 275 sq mi).

Great Britain England, Scotland, and Wales, including those adjacent islands governed from the mainland (i.e. excluding the Isle of Man and the Channel Islands). The term was introduced as early as 1603. Area: 229 523 sq km (88 619 sq mi). Population (1986 est): 55 196 400.

great circle A circle that is the intersection on the surface of a sphere of a plane passing through the centre of that sphere. On the earth, each meridian of longitude is half of a great circle; the equator is the only parallel of latitude that is a great circle.

Great Dane A breed of large dog originating in Germany, where they were developed for hunting boar. The short sleek coat can be golden, black, streaked brown, blue-grey, or white with black patches. Height: 76 cm minimum (dogs); 71 cm minimum (bitches).

GREBE   *The great crested grebe.*

Great Dividing Range (Great Divide *or* Eastern Highlands)   The E highlands of Australia. It extends for about 3700 km (2300 mi) from Cape York Peninsula to the Grampians of Victoria, reaching 2230 m (7316 ft) at Mount Kosciusko.

Greater Antilles   The four largest West Indian islands, in the N Caribbean Sea, comprising Cuba, Hispaniola, Jamaica, and Puerto Rico.

Greater Manchester   A metropolitan county of NW England, created in 1974 from SE Lancashire and parts of NE Cheshire and SW Yorkshire. Area: 1285 sq km (496 sq mi). Population (1986 est): 2 579 500. Administrative centre: Manchester.

Great Exhibition   (1851) A display of the products of industrial Britain and Europe, planned by Prince Albert and held in the Crystal Palace in Hyde Park, London. It contained about 13 000 exhibits.

Great Glen (*or* Glen More)   A rift valley extending across N Scotland from Fort William to Inverness. The Caledonian Canal was constructed along its length.

Great Lakes   Five large lakes along the US-Canadian border: Lakes Superior, Michigan, Huron, Erie, and Ontario. The world's largest freshwater surface, they form part of the St Lawrence Seaway.

Great Ouse River (*or* R. Ouse)   A river in E England, rising in Northamptonshire and flowing NE to the Wash. Length: 257 km (160 mi).

Great Plains   An extensive area in North America. It consists of plains extending from the Mackenzie River Delta in Canada to the Rio Grande in the S. Length: about 4828 km (3000 mi). Average width: about 644 km (400 mi).

Great Rift Valley (*or* East African Rift System)   An extensive rift valley in the Middle East and East Africa. It extends from the Jordan Valley in Syria along the Red Sea into Ethiopia and through Kenya, Tanzania, and

Malawi into Mozambique. Length: about 6400 km (4000 mi).

Great Salt Lake   A salt lake in the USA, in NW Utah in the Great Basin. Its area has fluctuated from less than 2500 sq km (1000 sq mi) to over 5000 sq km (2000 sq mi).

Great Sandy Desert   A desert of N Western Australia. It stretches SE from the Indian Ocean to the Gibson Desert. Area: 415 000 sq km (160 000 sq mi).

Great Schism   (1378–1417) The split in the Roman Catholic Church following the election of two rival popes to succeed Gregory XI. When Urban VI determined to reform the College of Cardinals, they responded by electing an antipope at Avignon, Clement VII. The Schism was ended by the Council of Constance (1414–18) and the election of Martin V in 1417.

Great Trek   The movement from the mid-1830s to mid-1840s of Dutch settlers (Afrikaners) in South Africa northwards from the Cape. The so-called Voortrekkers, under such leaders as Andries Pretorius (1799–1853), moved away from British rule at the Cape in search of more farmland that they could administer themselves. They established the republics of the Transvaal and the Orange Free State.

Great Victoria Desert   A desert of Western and South Australia. It consists of a vast region of sand hills and salt marshes. Area: 323 750 sq km (125 000 sq mi).

Great Wall of China   A medieval defensive fortification in N China. Stretching from the Yellow Sea N of Peking nearly 2400 km (1500 mi) inland, it is the world's largest building achievement. Originally begun in 214 BC as a defence against nomads, it was rebuilt of stone in the 15th and 16th centuries. It is about 9 m (30 ft) high, with numerous watch towers along its length.

Great Zimbabwe   The largest of the ruined Bantu royal centres in Zimbabwe. The word *zimbabwe* is derived from the Bantu for "revered houses." Great Zimbabwe reached its zenith in the late 14th century and traces of widespread trade, based on local gold, have been discovered, including Chinese pottery. Parts of the so-called Elliptical Building (a compound enclosing now vanished huts) stand 10.5 m (35 ft) high.

grebe   A bird belonging to a primitive family (*Podicipitidae*; 21 species) occurring in rivers and lakes worldwide. Grebes have short wings, a very small tail, and partially webbed feet. They feed chiefly on fish and aquatic invertebrates. Grebes are grey, black, or brown, usually with white underparts, and in the breeding season many have brightly coloured erectile crests and ear tufts. Order: *Podicipediformes. See also* dabchick.

Greece, Republic of (Greek name: Ellás)   A country in SE Europe, occupying the S section of the Balkan Peninsula. Numerous islands, lie to the S, E, and W; the largest is Crete. *Economy*: since the early 1970s industry has replaced agriculture as the mainstay of the economy. Mineral resources, including lignite, bauxite, and iron ore, have been intensively exploited The principal crops include wheat, barley, maize, tobacco, sugar beet, tomatoes, and dried and fresh fruits. Tourism is also important. *History*: the centuries following the collapse of the Mycenaean civilization (c. 1200 BC) saw the rise of the Greek city states and establishment of Greek colonies overseas. The 5th century was dominated by the abortive attempt of the Persians to annex Greece and the Peloponnesian War between rival Athens and Sparta. Sparta's subsequent supremacy in Greece lasted until its defeat by Thebes in 371. Greece fell to Philip of

GREAT WALL OF CHINA

Macedon in 338 and was incorporated in the empire of his son Alexander the Great. Following Alexander's death (323), the Greek city states repeatedly attempted to assert their independence until the last Macedonian War (171–168) allowed Rome to dominate Greece. Roman rule lasted until 395 AD, when Greece became part of the Byzantine (Eastern Roman) Empire, centred on Constantinople. In the middle ages Greece was subject to invasions by the Franks, Normans, and the Latin Crusaders. In the early 14th century Byzantium reasserted its control over the area but by 1460 control had passed to the Ottoman Turks. Apart from a Venetian occupation (1686–1715), Greece remained under Ottoman rule until achieving independence in 1829. In 1832 the Greek Crown was offered to a Bavarian prince, who became Otto I (1815–67); after his deposition in 1862 a Danish prince became king as George I (1845–1913). Greek demands for Crete led to a disastrous war with Turkey in 1897, but in the Balkan Wars (1912–13) Greece gained the island together with territory in Thrace and Macedonia. In 1917 Greece entered World War I on the Allied side and the immediate postwar period saw renewed conflict with Turkey, in which Greece lost Smyrna. In 1924 Greece became a republic, which lasted until George II was restored in 1935. In World War II an unsuccessful Italian invasion (1940) was followed by the German occupation (1941–44), after which civil war lasted until 1949. The 1950s were dominated by the question of union with Cyprus. A military coup (1967) deposed Constantine II and led to a succession of military governments. A new constitution (1975) saw the reintroduction of democratic government. Greece became a member of the EC in 1981. In 1989, after indecisive elections, Xenophon Zelotas became head of a coalition government. Head of state: President Christos Sartzetakis. Official language: Greek. Official religion: Greek Orthodox. Official currency: drachma of 100 lepta. Area: 131 986 sq km (50 960 sq mi). Population (1988 est): 10 018 000. Capital: Athens. Main port: Piraeus.

Greek language An Indo-European language spoken chiefly in Greece and the E Mediterranean islands. Well documented since the 14th century BC (*see* Linear B), ancient Greek was a highly complex inflected language. It had many dialect forms, the main groupings being Ionic (E Greece and Asia Minor), Aeolic (Boeotia and Thessaly), and Doric (the Peloponnese). From Ionic developed the Attic dialect, centred on Athens, which became the chief literary language of classical Greece. When the Greek city states lost their independence (4th century BC), their dialects gave way to a new common dialect (*koine*), which became the language of Hellenistic Greece and the New Testament. Modern Greek has two widely differing forms: the classically based Katharevusa (purified tongue) used in official publications, and Demotic, the living language of speech, poetry, and fiction.

Greek Orthodox Church Strictly, the Orthodox Church in Greece, although the term is often applied to the Orthodox Churches as a whole, to distinguish them from the Latin Church of the West. The Church in Greece dates from the 1st century and St Paul's activities, especially at Corinth. Under the patriarchate of Constantinople Greece was, from the acceptance of Christianity by Constantine, one of the main Christian centres. It is now a self-governing Church, the see of Athens holding a primacy of honour after the separation from the patriarchate of Constantinople in 1833.

Greek-Persian Wars An intermittent conflict between the Greeks and Persians. Persian encroachment on Greek territory began in 499 BC, when the Greek cities of Ionia revolted against their Persian overlords and were crushed by Darius I. In 490 the Persians were defeated by a small force of Athenians at Marathon. Darius died in 486 and in 480 Xerxes I crossed the Hellespont with a large force. The Greeks and Persians fought at Thermopylae, where the Spartans (under Leonidas I) heroically held the pass. Xerxes now attacked Attica and Athens was evacuated. At the battle of Salamis the Persians were defeated by the Greek fleet commanded by Themistocles and were again defeated at Plataea (479). Intermittent warfare continued until 449, when the Persians abandoned hope of annexing Greece.

green algae Algae of the division *Chlorophyta* (about 6000 species), which are bright green, owing to the predominance of the green pigment chlorophyll. Green algae range from simple unicellular plants, for example *Chlamydomonas*, to complex seaweeds. They are aquatic (mainly freshwater) or terrestrial in moist areas. Reproduction can be sexual or asexual.

green belt A zone of open, mostly agricultural, land surrounding a town to prevent it from spreading. Sir Ebenezer Howard's garden cities of the early 1900s provided the first practical examples; in 1935 the London County Council initiated the steps towards a London green belt that were realized in the Green Belt Act (1938) and the Town and Country Planning Act (1947). Since the 1950s planners have favoured a selective approach.

Greene, (Henry) Graham (1904–) British novelist. He was converted to Roman Catholicism in 1927, and an intense concern with questions of morality is central to many of his novels, including *Brighton Rock* (1938), *The Power and the Glory* (1940), *The Human Factor* (1978), *Monsignor Quixote* (1982), and *The Captain and the Enemy* (1988). He also wrote a number of literary thrillers, including *The Ministry of Fear* (1943), *The Third Man* (1950), and *Our Man in Havana* (1958).

greenfinch A Eurasian finch, *Carduelis chloris*, about 14 cm long with an olive-green body and a pale bill. The male has a bright yellow-green breast and both sexes show bright-yellow wing flashes in flight.

greenfly. *See* aphid.

greengage A bush or small tree, *Prunus italica*, related to the plum, probably native to Asia Minor and widely cultivated. It bears round green fruits, which are used in preserves and for canning.

Greenham Common A US airbase near Newbury in England, designated as the first UK site for cruise missiles. A protest peace camp set up in 1981 by women, who organized demonstrations of up to 30 000 people, failed to prevent the deployment of the missiles in 1983: Closure of the base was announced in 1990.

greenhouse effect An atmospheric effect in which some of the energy of ultraviolet radiation and visible light from the sun is retained by the earth as heat. The radiation is transmitted through the atmosphere to the earth's surface, where it is reradiated as longer wavelength infrared radiation. The atmosphere only partially transmits the infrared back into space and so a heating effect occurs. The phenomenon takes its name from a greenhouse, in which a similar effect occurs. Concern has been expressed about the resultant global warming.

Greenland (Danish name: Grønland; Greenlandic name: Kalaallit Nunaat) A large island off NE North America. Lying chiefly within the Arctic Circle, it is largely covered by a vast ice cap. Many glaciers emerge from this, including the Humboldt Glacier, breaking off to form large icebergs along the coast. Eskimos form about 80% of the population, the remainder being chiefly Danish. *Economy*: fishing is the chief occupation. Whaling and seal hunting have declined. Sheep are reared in the SW. Lead and zinc have been exploited since the early 1970s; uranium is also present. *History:* in about 986 AD the Norwegian Eric the Red discovered the island, which he named Greenland to attract settlers. Norse colonies on the island disappeared during the 15th century. A Danish colony from 1721, Greenland became an integral part of Denmark in 1953. In 1979 it gained self-government under Danish sovereignty. Prime minister: Jonathan Motzfeldt (1939–). Official language: Greenland Eskimo. Official currency: Danish krone of 100 øre. Area: 2 175 600 sq km (840 000 sq mi). Population (1987): 53 733. Capital: Nuuk.

Greenland Sea An extension of the Arctic Ocean, between Greenland, Svalbard, and Iceland. Covered by drifting ice, it links with the Atlantic Ocean.

green monkey disease An acute, often fatal, viral infection first described in Marburg, West Germany, and therefore sometimes called Marburg disease. It occurs in vervet monkeys and may be transmitted to man.

Green Party A British political party, founded in 1973 as the Ecology Party. Dedicated to protecting the environment and the interests of humanity, the party attracted growing support in the 1980s, prompting other political parties to adopt "green" attitudes. Similar parties have achieved greater power elsewhere in Europe.

GREENPEACE *Challenging the dumping of nuclear waste in the sea.*

Greenpeace movement An international environmental pressure group founded in 1971. It campaigns primarily against nuclear power, dumping nuclear waste, and commercial whaling and sealing. Its use of direct action has sometimes led to confrontation.

Green Revolution. *See* agriculture; arable farming.

green turtle A large brown-green marine turtle, *Chelonia mydas*, which is used to make turtle soup. Up to 1 m long and weighing up to 140 kg, they occur in warm Atlantic coastal waters feeding on marine algae and migrate to lay their eggs on Central American beaches.

Greenwich A borough of E Greater London, on the S bank of the River Thames. The first Renaissance building in England, the Queen's House designed by Inigo Jones (1616), was completed in 1637. The Greenwich Royal Hospital, designed by Wren, became the Royal Naval College in 1873. Wren also designed the original Royal Greenwich Observatory. The tea clipper *Cutty Sark* and Sir Francis Chichester's *Gipsy Moth IV* are at Greenwich Pier. Population (1986 est): 217 800.

Greenwich Mean Time (GMT) The local time at Greenwich, London, located on the 0° meridian (*see* longitude), from which the standard times of different areas of the globe are calculated, 15° longitude representing one hour in time. In 1986 it was succeeded by Coordinated Universal Time.

Greenwich Village A residential section of New York City (USA), in Manhattan. It became a favourite haunt of authors and artists early in the 20th century.

Gregorian calendar. *See* calendar.

Gregorian chant The official liturgical plainchant of the Roman Catholic Church as codified during the papacy of Gregory I (590–604 AD). It consists of single unaccompanied melodic lines sung to flexible rhythms.

Gregory I, St (c. 540–604 AD) Pope (590–604), known as Gregory the Great. As pope he made peace with the Lombards and limited imperial authority over the Church. He reformed the papal states and sponsored Augustine (of Canterbury) in his mission to convert England. He also introduced the use of Gregorian chant into the liturgy. Feast day: 3 September.

Gregory VII, St (Hildebrand; c. 1021–85) Pope (1073–85). He asserted the independence of the Church from lay control but created considerable opposition, especially in France and Germany, where Emperor Henry IV declared his deposition (1076). He in turn excommunicated Henry and released his subjects from allegiance. Henry submitted to Gregory at Canossa (1077) but then appointed Wibert, Archbishop of Ravenna, antipope (1080), invaded Italy, and captured Rome (1084). Gregory was rescued by Norman troops but was nevertheless forced to flee. Feast day: 25 May.

Grenada, State of An island country in the West Indies, in the Windward Islands. It also includes some of the Grenadine Islands. The majority of the population is of mixed European and Indian descent. *Economy*: largely agricultural, the chief products are cocoa, bananas, citrus fruits, sugar, and nutmeg (the main export). *History*: discovered by Columbus in 1493, it was colonized by the French and ceded to the British in 1763. In 1974 it became an independent state within the British Commonwealth. In March, 1979, the government of Sir Eric Gairy (1922–   ) was overthrown in a nearly bloodless coup led by Maurice Bishop (1944–83). Following an uprising in 1983, during which Bishop was killed, the USA invaded the country and democratic government was restored. Prime minister: Ben Jones. Official language: English. Official currency: East Caribbean dollar of 100 cents. Area: 344 sq km (133 sq mi). Population (1987 est): 92 000. Capital: St George's.

Grenadine Islands A chain of West Indian islets, extending for about 100 km (60 mi) between St Vincent and Grenada and administratively divided between the two.

Grenoble 45 11N 5 43E A city in SE France. The capital of the Dauphiné until 1341, it is the principal tourist centre of the French Alps. Population (1982): 159 503.

Grey, Lady Jane (1537–54) Queen of England for nine days (1553) and the great-granddaughter of Henry VII. The Duke of Northumberland had her proclaimed queen when Edward VI died but Mary, the rightful heiress, had popular support and Jane abdicated. She was executed for treason with her husband Lord Guildford Dudley, Northumberland's son.

greyhound An ancient breed of dog used for hare coursing and racing. It has a slender deep-chested streamlined body with long legs and a long muscular neck. The short smooth coat can be of various colours. Greyhounds can reach speeds of up to 70 km per hour. Height: 71–76 cm (dogs); 68–71 cm (bitches).

greylag goose A grazing goose, *Anser anser*, occurring in N and E Europe and central Asia. 75–87 cm long, it has a heavy orange bill and is dark grey above with pale wings, a finely barred neck, and pink legs.

greywacke (*or* graywacke) A dark-coloured sedimentary rock with sand-sized angular rock particles in a finer matrix. Greywackes display a wide range of sedimentary structures and are commonly found in geosynclines.

Grieg, Edvard Hagerup (1843–1907) Norwegian composer. The influence of Norwegian folk music is apparent in many of his works, which include the *Lyric Pieces* (1867–1901), a very popular piano concerto (1868), incidental music to Ibsen's play *Peer Gynt* (1876), chamber music, and many songs.

griffin A mythological creature with the head and wings of an eagle, the body of a lion, and often a serpent's tail. It is common in many ancient eastern mythologies.

Griffith, D(avid) W(ark) (1875–1948) US film director: the most influential pioneer of the cinema in the USA. His major films include *The Birth of a Nation* (1915), *Intolerance* (1916), *Broken Blossoms* (1919), and *Isn't Life Wonderful* (1924).

griffon (dog) A breed of toy dog originating in Belgium and of terrier ancestry. It has a square compact body, a docked tail, and a large head covered with long coarse hair. The coat may be red, black, or black and tan. Weight: 2–5 kg.

griffon vulture One of the largest Old World vultures, *Gyps fulvus*. It is 100 cm long and occurs in mountainous regions of S Europe, South Africa, and Asia. It is grey-brown with darker wingtips and a white head and ruff.

Grimm Two brothers, German philologists and folklorists. After early work on medieval German texts, **Jakob Grimm** (1785–1863) and **Wilhelm Grimm** (1786–1859) set about collecting German folktales, published in 1812–14 as *Kinder- und Hausmärchen*. The *Deutsche Grammatik* (1819, 1822) contains observations on the regularity of sound changes in Indo-European languages, known as **Grimm's law**. Their *Deutsches Wörterbuch* is a historical and descriptive German dictionary.

Grimsby 53 35N 0 05W A seaport in NE England, in Humberside. Formerly a major fishing port, other industries have now been introduced. Population (1985): 95 000.

grizzly bear. *See* brown bear.

Grodno 53 40N 23 50E A port in the W central Soviet Union. Possessed by Lithuania and then by Poland, it includes a medieval castle and a 16th-century palace. Population (1987): 263 000.

LADY JANE GREY *Detail of a painting attributed to Master John, c. 1545.*

Gromyko, Andrei (1909–89) Soviet diplomat; foreign minister (1957–85) and president of the Soviet Union (1985–88). He was a major influence on Soviet foreign policy for over forty years.

Groningen A province in the Netherlands, bordering on the North Sea. Low lying and fertile, it is intensively cultivated. Area: 2350 sq km (900 sq mi). Population (1987): 558 378. Capital: Groningen.

Gropius, Walter (1883–1969) German architect, one of the pioneers of the international modern style of architecture. His first major building, a factory at Alfeld (1911) is a very early example of the new style. As director of the Bauhaus (1919–28) he was able to influence all aspects of contemporary design. The rise of Nazi power forced him to move to America where he continued to design buildings.

Grossglockner 47 05N 12 44E The highest mountain in Austria, in the Alps. The Grossglockner Road (built 1930–35) crosses it, rising to 2576 m (7852 ft). Height: 3797 m (12 457 ft).

gross national product (GNP) A measure of the total annual output of a country, including net income from abroad. GNP can be calculated in three ways: based on income, output, or expenditure. All incomes accruing to residents of the country as a result of economic activity (excluding, for instance, pensions) can be summed. On the basis of output, the value added to a product at each stage of production can be summed. Alternatively the expenditure on consumption products can be calculated. **Gross domestic product** (GDP) is GNP excluding net income from abroad and gives some indication of the strength of domestic industry. **Net national product** makes a provision for depreciation, i.e. the using up of the country's capital stock.

ground beetle A heavily armoured long-legged beetle belonging to a family (*Carabidae*; 25 000 species) that is particularly common in temperate regions. Ground beetles are dark in colour or have a metallic sheen and are from 2 to 85 mm long. Most are nocturnal; the adults and most larvae are active carnivores, preying on insects, slugs, and snails. *See also* bombardier beetle.

ground elder A perennial herbaceous plant, *Aegopodium podagraria*, also called goutweed, bishop's weed, or herb Gerard, common in Europe on waste ground and as a garden weed. 49–100 cm tall, it has small white flowers. The leaves may be eaten as a salad or vegetable. Family: *Umbelliferae*.

groundhog. *See* marmot.

groundnut The fruit of *Arachis hypogea*, also called peanut or earthnut, native to tropical South America but widely cultivated in the tropics. The plant is an erect or creeping annual, 30–45 cm high, with yellow flowers. After fertilization the pod ripens underground. The pod contains one to three seeds (the nuts), which are highly nutritious. Family: *Leguminosae*.

grouper One of several sedentary food and game fish of the family *Serranidae* (*see* sea bass), especially the genera *Epinephelus* and *Mycteroperca*, widely distributed in warm seas. Groupers have a dull-green or brown heavy body, up to or exceeding 2 m long, and a large mouth. Some are poisonous when consumed.

group therapy A form of psychotherapy in which several patients meet together to understand and overcome their problems, usually with the help of a therapist. Sometimes the aim is to increase patients' insight, sometimes to teach social skills, sometimes to act out distressing events, and sometimes to provide support in overcoming a common problem (such as alcoholism).

GROUNDNUT *Pyramids of stored groundnuts in Nigeria.*

grouse A fowl-like game bird, 30–88 cm long, belonging to a family (*Tetraonidae*; about 18 species) of the N hemisphere. Grouse are mostly ground-living, with short round wings, a short strong bill, and feathered legs. They are noted for their spectacular courtship displays (called *leks*). The family includes the black grouse, red grouse, and capercaillie of N Europe; the ptarmigans; and the North American ruffed grouse (*Bonasa umbellus*) and sage grouse. In Britain the grouse-shooting season is from 12 Aug to 10 Dec. Order: *Galliformes*.

growth hormone (*or* somatotrophin) A protein hormone that promotes the metabolic processes involved in growth of bone and muscle. It is secreted by the pituitary gland and stimulates protein synthesis, mobilizes fat reserves, increases glucose levels in the blood, and affects mineral metabolism. Lack of growth hormone in children causes dwarfism.

Grozny 43 21N 45 42E A city in the S Soviet Union. It is one of the country's richest oil-producing areas. Population (1987): 404 000.

Grünewald, Matthias (Mathis Gothardt; d. 1528) German painter. His favourite subject was the crucifixion, as in the *Isenheim Altarpiece* (Colmar, France), noted for its dazzling colour. His style influenced 20th-century German expressionists (*see* expressionism).

grunt A small food fish, belonging to the family *Pomadasyidae* (about 75 species), that can produce piglike grunts. It has a colourful elongated body and a large mouth; it occurs in the warm and tropical coastal waters. Order: *Perciformes*.

Guadalajara 20 30N 103 20W The second largest city in Mexico, at an altitude of 1650 m (5413 ft). Founded by the Spanish (1530), it is a communications centre across the Sierra Madre Occidental. Population (1980): 2 244 715.

Guadalajara 40 37N 3 10W A town in NE Spain Its palace was virtually destroyed during the Spanish Civil War but has since been restored. Population (1981): 56 922.

Guadalcanal 9 30S 160 00E The largest of the Solomon Islands, in the S Pacific Ocean. During World War II the first major US offensive against the Japanese took place here (1942–43). Area: 6475 sq km (2500 sq mi). Population (1987 est): 71 300. Chief settlement: Honiara.

Guadalquivir, River The main river of S Spain. It flows WSW to the Gulf of Cádiz and is navigable to Seville by oceangoing vessels. Length: 560 km (348 mi).

Guadalupe Hidalgo (name from 1931 until 1971: Gustavo A. Madero) 19 29N 99 07W A city in central Mexico, a NE suburb of Mexico City. The Basilica of the Virgin of Guadalupe, which was built after an Indian convert reported seeing a vision of the Virgin Mary here in 1531, is a famous place of pilgrimage. The Treaty of Guadalupe Hidalgo, which ended the Mexican War, was signed here. Population (1980): 370 524.

Guadeloupe A French overseas region in the West Indies, in the E Caribbean Sea. It comprises two main islands, Grande Terre and Basse Terre, together with the island dependencies of Marie Galante, La Désirade, Îles des Saintes, St Barthélemy, and the N part of St Martin. The economy is based on agriculture; sugar cane is the chief crop. Area: 1702 sq km (657 sq mi). Population (1987 est): 335 300. Capital: Basse-Terre.

guaiacum A small evergreen tree of the genus *Guaiacum*, especially *G. officinale* of tropical America, also called lignum vitae. It has blue flowers, yellow fruits, and hard wood, used to make bowling balls. The resin is distilled for medicinal use. Family: *Zygophyllaceae*.

Guam 13 30N 144 40E An island and US unincorporated territory in the West Pacific Ocean, the largest of the Mariana Islands. Spanish from 1565 to 1898, it was occupied by the Japanese (1941–44). It is a major naval and air base, especially important during the Vietnam War. Area: 450 sq km (210 sq mi). Population (1984 est): 115 756. Capital: Agaña.

Guangzhou. *See* Canton.

GUANO *Deposits on the Ballestas Islands off Peru.*

guano The accumulated excrement of certain animals, especially seabirds, seals, and bats. It contains 10–18% nitrogen, 8–12% phosphoric acid, and 2–3% potash, according to the age and origin of the deposit. It has been widely used as a fertilizer.

Guantánamo 20 09N 75 14W A city in SE Cuba, N of Guantánamo Bay. It is the centre of an agricultural area producing sugar cane and coffee. Population (1986 est): 174 400.

Guarani A group of South American Indian peoples of Paraguay and neighbouring areas of Brazil and Argentina who speak languages of the Tupian group. Few now retain their original culture, based on hunting and maize cultivation, warfare, and cannibalism.

Guardi, Francesco (1712–93) Venetian painter, who sometimes collaborated with his elder brother, **Giovanni Antonio Guardi** (1699–1760). His souvenir views of Venice were sometimes copied from Canaletto but they are distinguished by their romantic style and impressionistic technique.

Guardian Angels A US vigilante organization founded in the 1980s to patrol New York's underground railway and elsewhere to deter violent crime. Members, who wear red berets and white sweatshirts, receive basic training in unarmed combat; a London branch was launched in 1989.

Guarini, Guarino (1624–83) Italian baroque architect, philosopher, and mathematician. Although influenced by Francesco Borromini (1599–1667), his work shows great originality and technical skill. Probably his most successful building is the church of S Lorenzo, Turin (1668–87).

Guarneri An Italian family of violin makers, famous in the 17th and 18th centuries. **Andrea Guarneri** (d. 1698) was a pupil (with Stradivari) of Amati in Cremona. Andrea's grandson **Giuseppe Guarneri** (1698–1744), known as "del Gesù," was the most famous member of the family; influenced by the makers of the Brescian school, he signed his violins "Guarnerius."

Guatemala, Republic of A country in Central America, on the Pacific Ocean, with a small outlet on the Caribbean Sea. Tropical forests rise to a central mountainous region, containing a fertile plateau. About half the population are Maya Quiché Indians and most of the rest are of mixed Spanish and Indian descent. *Economy*: mainly agricultural. Since the 1950s a new system of land development has been introduced, largely on a cooperative basis. The main crops are coffee, sugar, bananas, and cotton, which are the principal exports. Minerals include zinc and lead concentrates, and nickel mining is being introduced. Oil was discovered in 1974. *History*: there is extensive archaeological evidence of pre-Spanish civilizations, especially that of the Maya, and, from the 12th century, the Aztecs. From 1524 to 1821 the area was part of the Spanish captaincy general of Guatemala, which included most of Central America. It formed the nucleus of the Central American Federation until 1839, when it became independent. In recent years periods of democratic government have alternated with military dictatorships, accompanied by political unrest. In 1976 it suffered a serious earthquake. Guatemala claims Belize. Official language: Spanish. Official religion: Roman Catholic. Official currency: quetzal of 100 centavos. Area: 108 889 sq km (42 042 sq mi). Population (1987 est): 8 990 000. Capital: Guatemala City. Main port: Puerto Barrios.

Guatemala City 14 38N 90 22W The capital of Guatemala. Founded in 1776, it was the capital of the captaincy general of Guatemala and later of the Central American Federation. Population (1983 est): 1 300 000.

guava A tropical American tree, *Psidium guajava*, about 10 m tall. Its white flowers develop into yellow pear-shaped fruits containing many small seeds. Guava fruits, rich in vitamin C, are used to make jam and jelly, stewed for desserts, or canned. Family: *Myrtaceae* (myrtle family).

Guayaquil (*or* Santiago de Guayaquil) 2 13S 79 54W The largest city and chief port of Ecuador, on the River Guayas. Population (1987): 1 572 615.

gudgeon A freshwater shoaling fish, *Gobio gobio*, related to carp, found in Europe and N Asia. It has a slender greenish or greyish body, up to about 20 cm long, with a row of blackish spots along each side and a pair of barbels at the corners of the mouth. It is used as food and bait.

guelder rose A small tree or shrub, *Viburnum opulus*, 4–5 m high, found throughout Eurasia. It has clusters of flowers, 5–10 cm across, in which the outer flowers are large and sterile and the inner ones are small and fertile. The fruits are red translucent berries. The cultivated form is called snowball tree. Family: *Caprifoliaceae* (honeysuckle family).

Guelfs and Ghibellines The propapal and proimperial factions respectively in medieval Germany and Italy. Commencing in a German struggle between rival claimants to the Holy Roman Empire, the Guelfs (named after Welf, the family name) and Ghibellines (after Waiblingen, a Hohenstaufen castle), their conflict acquired an Italian context because of papal opposition to the Hohenstaufen. The Italian city states were led by Florence (Guelf) and Pisa (Ghibelline).

guenon An Old World monkey belonging to the genus *Cercopithecus* (10 species), of African forests. They are 83–160 cm long including the tail (50–88 cm) and move in troops, feeding on leaves, fruits, insects, and snails. The mona monkey (*C. mona*) is a strikingly marked guenon. *See also* grass monkey.

Guercino (Giovanni Francesco Barbieri; 1591–1666) Italian painter. His masterpiece, the ceiling frescos in the Casino Ludovisi, Rome, commissioned by Pope Gregory XV in 1621, were influenced by the Carracci. While in Rome (1621–23) he also painted the *Burial of St Petronilla* (Capitoline Museum, Rome), which his later work never equalled.

OTTO VON GUERICKE *The Magdeburg hemispheres.*

Guericke, Otto von (1602–86) German physicist, renowned for his investigation of vacuums. In 1650 he invented the air pump, which he used to perform a series of experiments culminating in a demonstration in which two teams of horses failed to separate a pair of large hemispheres (called the Magdeburg hemispheres after

his home town) placed together and evacuated. When air was admitted to the hemispheres they fell apart on their own.

Guernica 43 19N 2 40W A historic Basque town in N Spain, on the Bay of Biscay. During the Spanish Civil War it was virtually destroyed by German planes supporting the Nationalists on 27 April, 1937. This is depicted in a painting by Picasso. Population (1981): 17 836.

Guernsey 49 27N 2 35W The second largest of the Channel Islands, in the English Channel. It is low lying in the N and hilly in the S with rugged coastal cliffs. Agriculture and horticulture are important, especially dairy farming (the Guernsey breed of cattle originated here). Guernsey is also popular as a tourist resort. Area: 63 sq km (24.5 sq mi). Population (1986): 55 482. Capital: St Peter Port.

Guevara, Che (Ernesto G.; 1928–67) Argentine revolutionary and theorist of guerrilla warfare, who became the hero of left–wing youth in the 1960s. A doctor by training, he joined Castro's invasion of Cuba (1956) and became one of his chief lieutenants. After Castro's victory, Che Guevara influenced Cuba's procommunist foreign relations and directed the land-reform policies. In 1967 he was killed while attempting to instigate a revolt in Bolivia.

guide dogs Dogs that are specially selected and trained to guide the blind. The first training schools were established in Germany (1911–18) and the British Guide Dog Association was founded in 1931. Among the most suitable breeds for the four-month training course are German Shepherd dogs (Alsatians), Labradors, and golden retrievers.

Guildford 51 14N 0 35W A city in SE England, in Surrey on the River Wey. A market and residential town, its buildings include Guildford Cathedral (founded in 1936). Population (1981): 56 652.

guilds (*or* gilds) Associations formed in medieval Europe to further their members' common purposes. Originally religious or social in character, the first such guilds are recorded in the 9th century. Merchant guilds were created in many towns in the 11th century to organize local trade and became a powerful force in local government. Craft guilds, confined to specific crafts or trades, were formed from the 12th century. The livery companies of London are descended from the craft guilds.

guillemot A bird, *Uria aalge*, occurring in coastal regions of the N hemisphere. It is 40 cm long and has a dark-brown plumage with a white belly and wing stripe and a slender bill, feeding on fish, shellfish, and worms. The eggs are shaped so that they do not roll off the cliff ledges where they are laid. Family *Alcidae* (auks).

guillotine A device with which a person may be beheaded. It consists of two vertical posts and a horizontal knife that is dropped onto the victim's neck. Invented by Joseph Ignace Guillotin (1738–1814), it was introduced in France in 1792, during the French Revolution.

Guinea, Gulf of A large inlet of the E Atlantic Ocean, bordering on the Guinea Coast of West Africa.

Guinea, Republic of A country on the coast of West Africa. A coastal plain, partly swamp, rises steeply to plateaus and mountains. The population is mainly Fulani and Mandingo. *Economy*: chiefly agricultural, now largely collectivized. The chief crops are rice and palm oil and nuts, as well as coffee, peanuts, and fruits. Livestock is also important. The principal mineral resources are diamonds, iron ore, and bauxite (alumina is the principal export). *History*: the N formed part of Ghana from the 5th to the 8th centuries AD and of the Mali empire in the 16th century. In 1849 the French established a protectorate over part of Guinea, which became part of French West Africa in 1895. In 1958 French Guinea became an independent republic. In recent years accusations have been made of violations of human rights. The army took over in 1984 on the death of President Ahmed Sekon Touré. President: Col Lansana Conté. Official language: French and the languages of eight ethnic groups. Official currency: syli of 100 cauris. Area: 245 857 sq km (95 000 sq mi). Population (1987 est): 6 339 000. Capital and main port: Conakry.

Guinea-Bissau, Republic of (name until 1974: Portuguese Guinea) A small country on the coast of West Africa. It consists chiefly of a coastal plain rising to savanna-covered plateau inland. Most of the population are Fulani, Mandyako, and Mandingo. *Economy*: chiefly agricultural, the principal crops being groundnuts (the main export), rice, palm oil, and nuts. Bauxite deposits have also been discovered. *History*: explored by the Portuguese in the mid-15th century, the area became a centre of the slave trade. It became a Portuguese colony in 1879 and an overseas province of Portugal in 1951. In 1974 it became an independent republic. After a coup in 1980, constitutional rule returned in 1984, with Maj João Bernardo Vieira as elected head of state. Official language: Portuguese; Crioulo is widely spoken. Official currency: Guinea-Bissau peso of 100 centavos. Area: 36 125 sq km (13 948 sq mi). Population (1987 est): 935 000. Capital: Bissau.

Guinea Coast The coastlands of West Africa extending from Gambia to Gabon.

guinea fowl A bird belonging to an African family (*Numididae*; 7–10 species). About 50 cm long, domesticated guinea fowl are descended from the helmet guinea fowl (*Numida meleagris*), which has a large bony crest, a bare face with red and blue wattles, and a grey white-spotted plumage. Guinea fowl scratch for seeds and insects, especially termites. Order: *Galliformes* (pheasants, turkeys, etc.).

guinea pig A domesticated rodent, *Cavia porcellus*, descended from the cavy. Guinea pigs were originally bred for food but are now popular as pets. They should be fed on grain, roots, green food, and hay.

guinea worm A parasitic nematode worm, *Dracunculus medinensis*, that is a serious parasite of man in Africa, India, and the Middle East. The larvae are carried by water fleas (genus *Cyclops*) often present in drinking water. When swallowed by the human host, they burrow into the tissues and grow to maturity: the females reach a length of up to 120 cm, causing ulcers on the feet and legs.

Guinevere In Arthurian legend, the wife of King Arthur and lover of Lancelot. Malory's *Morte d'Arthur* (1485) describes her abduction by Modred and her adulterous love for Lancelot.

Guinness, Sir Alec (1914–) British actor. He established his reputation as a stage actor in repertory in the late 1930s and played Hamlet in modern dress in 1938. His films include *Oliver Twist* (1948), *Kind Hearts and Coronets* (1949), and *The Bridge on the River Kwai* (1957).

guitar A plucked stringed instrument of Moorish origin, which came to Europe via Spain. The modern Span-ish guitar has a flat back, a round sound hole, a fretted fingerboard, and six strings tuned chiefly in fourths. It has a range of over three octaves from the E below the bass stave. Music for it is written an octave higher than it sounds.

ALEC GUINNESS

Guiyang (*or* Kuei-yang) 26 35N 106 40E A city in S China, the capital of Guizhou province. Population (1986): 1 380 000.

Gujarat A state in W India, on the Arabian Sea SE of Pakistan. Lowlands merge into hills in the S and E and into marshes in the NW. Cotton, tobacco, peanuts, and other crops are raised. *History*: a flourishing area under Muslim princes (13th–17th centuries), Gujarat was conquered by the Maratha in the 18th century before passing to Britain. Area: 195 984 sq km (75 650 sq mi). Population (1984): 34 085 799. Capital: Gandhinagar.

Gujarati An Indo-Aryan language spoken by 20 million people in Gujarat and Maharashtra in India. It is related to Rajasthani, uses a modified Devanagari script, and has a long literary tradition.

Gulf States The nations situated on the Persian Gulf. They are Oman, the United Arab Emirates, Qatar, Bahrein, Saudi Arabia, Kuwait, Iraq, and Iran. They comprise the world's major oil-producing area.

Gulf Stream One of the major ocean currents of the world, flowing from the Florida Strait parallel to the North American coast as far as the Newfoundland banks. It bears NE across the Atlantic as the North Atlantic Drift, branching into two main directions, one flowing N towards Spitsbergen and the other flowing S to form the Canary Current. The warm water benefits the climate of NW Europe. See p.322.

Gulf War (1980–88) An indecisive conflict in the Persian Gulf, between Iran and Iraq. The war began when Iraqi forces invaded Iran shortly after the Iranian revolution in pursuit of claims over border territory. A war of attrition developed, costing both sides much in manpower and financial and material resources. The conflict also saw the use of toxic gas (by Iraq), the bombing of major cities, and missile attacks on international shipping in the Gulf.

gulfweed Tropical brown algae, also called rockweed or sea holly, of the genus *Sargassum*, especially *S.*

natans, which forms huge free-floating masses of seaweed in the Sargasso Sea.

GULF STREAM

gull A seabird belonging to the subfamily *Larinae* (about 40 species), ranging throughout the world's coastal regions and also found inland. Up to 75 cm long, gulls are well built and have long pointed wings and a strong slightly hooked bill. Gulls are typically grey and white, often with dark markings. Some gulls feed on fish but most are scavengers. Family: *Laridae* (gulls and terns); order: *Charadriiformes* (gulls, plovers, etc.).

gullet. *See* oesophagus.

gums Adhesive substances exuded by plants. They are odourless tasteless amorphous carbohydrates that form either clear liquid solutions or gelatinous mixtures with water. **Gum arabic** (*or* gum acacia) is obtained from trees of the genus *Acacia*. **Gum tragacanth** is extracted from shrubs of the genus *Astragalus*.

gum tree A tree of the genus *Eucalyptus* (about 600 species), so called because the whole tree is rich in resin and aromatic oils.

gun metal A type of bronze containing about 90% copper and sometimes a little zinc, originally used for making cannons. Admiralty gun metal (88% copper, 10% tin, 2% zinc) is used in shipbuilding.

gunnel An eel-like fish of the family *Pholididae* (about 8 species), found in N Atlantic and N Pacific coastal waters, feeding on invertebrates. The rock gunnel (*Pholis gunnellus*), also called butterfish, is 30 cm long and brownish with 9–13 black spots along the dorsal fin. Order: *Perciformes*.

gunpowder An explosive mixture of saltpetre (potassium nitrate), sulphur, and powdered charcoal. Invented by the Chinese many centuries before its description by Roger Bacon in the 13th century it has had a profound effect on human conflict.

Gunpowder Plot. *See* Fawkes, Guy.

Gunter's chain. *See* chain.

Guomindang (*or* Kuomintang) The National People's Party of Taiwan (Republic of China). Organized in 1912 from Sun Yat-sen's Alliance Society, it formed an alliance with the new Chinese Communist Party (CCP) in 1924. Following Sun's death (1925), the Guomindang was led by Chiang Kai-shek and with the CCP had gained control of most of China by 1926. A break between the two parties (1927) led to civil war until Japanese conquests in China (*see* Sino-Japanese Wars) necessitated renewed cooperation in 1937. After Japan's defeat (1945), civil war was resumed until a communist victory in 1949 drove the Guomindang into exile in Taiwan.

guppy A freshwater fish, *Lebistes reticulatus*, native to N South America and the West Indies. Male guppies are up to 4 cm long and brightly coloured. Females produce live young at monthly intervals. Guppies are popular aquarium fish. Family: *Cyprinodontidae*.

Gurdjieff, George Ivanovitch (1873–1943) Russian occultist, who established a teaching centre near Paris in the 1920s. Part mystic, part bon viveur, and reputedly part charlatan, this enigmatic man had a considerable following, including P. D. Ouspensky, whose books have outlived Gurdjieff's own *All and Everything*, *Beelzebub's Tales to his Grandson*.

Gurkhas Soldiers of Nepalese origin who have served in the British Army since 1815. The name derives from that of the ruling dynasty of Nepal.

gurnard A carnivorous bottom-dwelling fish, also called sea robin, belonging to a family (*Triglidae*; about 40 species) found in temperate and tropical seas. It has a tapering body, up to 70 cm long, a large armoured head, and produces sound by vibrating its swim bladder. The flying gurnards belong to the family *Dactylopteridae*. Order: *Scorpaeniformes*.

guru In Hinduism, a venerated spiritual teacher who personally instructs and guides the disciple. In Tibetan Buddhism the guru embodies the Buddha himself and is correspondingly revered. In Sikhism, guru is the title of the first ten patriarchs (*see* Nanak).

JOHANN GUTENBERG *An early printing press.*

Gutenberg, Johann (c. 1400–c. 1468) German printer, who invented the method of printing with movable metal type. In 1448 he received the financial backing of Johann Fust (1400–66) and by 1455 had produced his great 42-line Bible (the Gutenberg Bible). Fust successfully sued Gutenberg in 1455 for the repayment of his loan and the impoverished Gutenberg was forced to relinquish his machinery.

gutta percha A brownish leathery material obtained from the latex of various trees of the family *Sapotaceae*, especially those of the SE Asian genus *Palaquium*. It was once extensively used, for example as an electrical insulator, but it has now largely been replaced by synthetics.

Guyana, Cooperative Republic of (name until 1966: British Guiana) A country in the NE of South America, on the Atlantic Ocean. Narrow fertile coastal plains give way to higher undulating areas. Most of the population is of African and East Indian descent. *Economy*: agriculture is important, the main crops being rice and sugar. The most important minerals were formerly gold and diamonds, but these have now been overtaken by bauxite. *History*: the coast was first explored by the Spanish in 1499 and settlements were founded by the Dutch in the 17th century. The area became a British colony, as British Guiana, in 1831. In 1961 it gained internal self-government. In 1966, as Guyana, it became independent within the British Commonwealth. It is also a member of CARICOM. The Marxist Cooperative Republic was formed in 1970. President: Desmond Hoyte. Prime minister: Hamilton Green. Official language: English. Official currency: Guyana dollar of 100 cents. Area: 210 000 sq km (83 000 sq mi). Population (1987): 812 000. Capital and main port: Georgetown.

Gwalior 26 12N 78 09E A city in India, in Madhya Pradesh. It developed around its impressive fortress, which is believed to date from the 6th century AD. Population (1981): 560 000.

Gwent A county of SE Wales, on the English border. It was created under local government reorganization in 1974. It is generally hilly and is drained by the Rivers Wye, Usk, Monnow, Ebbw, and Rhymney. There are varied agricultural and industrial activities. Area: 1376 sq km (532 sq mi). Population (1986 est): 441 800. Administrative centre: Newport.

Gwyn, Nell (1650–87) English actress. Originally an orange seller in Drury Lane, she achieved fame as an actress and became Charles II's mistress, bearing him two sons. "Let not poor Nellie starve," are said to have been his last words.

Gwynedd A county of NW Wales, bordering on the Irish Sea. It was created under local government reorganization in 1974. It is predominantly mountainous rising to 1086 m (3563 ft) in Snowdon. Area: 3868 sq km (1493 sq mi). Population (1986 est): 234 600. Administrative centre: Caernarfon.

gymnosperms A group of plants, most of which are trees, forming one of the two classes of seed-bearing plants (*compare* angiosperm). Their sole consistent characteristic is that their seeds are borne naked, often on cone scales. The principal orders are *Coniferales* (*see* conifer), *Ginkgoales* (*see* ginkgo), *Cycadales* (*see* cycad), *Gnetales* (e.g. welwitschia), and several extinct orders, including the *Pteridospermales* (*see* seed fern) and the *Cordaitales*.

gymnure An insectivorous mammal belonging to the family *Erinaceidae* of SE Asia, also called hairy hedgehog. There are four species, including the moon rat.

Short-legged and flat-footed, 15–60 cm long, they live in thick undergrowth and hunt mainly at night.

gynaecology The branch of medicine and surgery concerned with diseases of women and girls, particularly those affecting the reproductive system. **Obstetrics** deals with the care of women during pregnancy, childbirth, and the period immediately after delivery.

Gypsies. *See* Gipsies.

Gypsophila A genus of slender annual or perennial herbs (about 120 species), native to the Mediterranean area. Up to 1.5 m high, they have white or pink flowers. Family: *Caryophyllaceae* (pink family).

NELL GWYN *Detail from a portrait (c. 1675) from the studio of Peter Lely.*

gypsum A colourless or white mineral consisting of hydrated calcium sulphate found in clays, shales, and limestones. Rock gypsum is often red-stained, granular, and found in layers. Gypsite is impure and earthy, occurring as surface deposits. Alabaster is a pure compact fine-grained translucent form. Satin-spar is fibrous and silky. Selenite occurs as transparent crystals in clays and mudstones. Gypsum is used in the manufacture of cement, rubber, paper, plaster of Paris, and blackboard chalk.

gypsy moth A moth, *Lymantria dispar*, distributed throughout the N hemisphere. Males are brownish grey and females white. The larvae, which feed on a variety of trees, are a serious pest. *See also* tussock moth.

gyrfalcon The largest falcon, *Falco rusticolus*, which breeds in N Eurasia, North America, and mountainous regions of Asia. It is 60 cm long and its plumage varies from pure white speckled with black to dark grey with dense black barring. It hunts for hares, rodents, and ground-dwelling birds.

gyrocompass. *See* compass.

H

Haakon VII (1872–1957) The first King of Norway (1905–57) following the restoration of Norwegian independence. In 1896 he married Maud (d. 1938), the daughter of Edward VII of the UK. His refusal to abdicate during the German occupation (1940–45) encouraged Norwegian resistance.

Haarlem 52 23N 4 38E A city in the W Netherlands, the capital of North Holland province. It is a major trade centre for bulbs and is noted for its Frans Hals museum and its fine cathedral. Population (1987): 149 099.

habeas corpus (Latin: have the body) A remedy against unlawful confinement, which takes the form of a writ ordering the person alleged to have unlawful custody of a prisoner to produce him before the court issuing the writ and to submit to whatever the court directs. The writ may be used to test the legality of imprisonment but not to appeal against a lawful conviction or sentence.

Haber-Bosch process A method for the bulk production of ammonia from nitrogen and hydrogen. The pure gases are passed over an iron catalyst at about 500°C and a pressure of 500 atmospheres. The process was devised by Fritz Haber (1868–1934) and adapted by Carl Bosch (1874–1940).

Habsburgs (or Hapsburgs) The most prominent European royal dynasty from the 15th to 20th centuries. The family originated in Switzerland in the 10th century. In 1273 Rudolph I (1218–91) was elected Holy Roman Emperor and consolidated his family's possession of Austria, Carniola, and Styria. The Habsburgs held the imperial title again from 1438 to 1740 and from 1745 to 1806. In 1516 Charles V inherited the Spanish Crown, adding Spain with its European and American possessions to the Habsburg domains. He left the Spanish Crown to his son, Philip II, and his Austrian possessions to his brother, Ferdinand I (1503–64). The Spanish branch ruled until 1700; the Austrian Habsburgs became emperors of Austria in 1804 and of Austria-Hungary in 1867, which they ruled until the end of World War I.

hadal zone. See abyssal zone.

haddock A carnivorous food fish, *Melanogrammus aeglefinus*, related to cod, that usually occurs in shoals near the bottom of N Atlantic coastal waters. It is up to 1 m long, grey or brown above and silvery below, with two anal and three dorsal fins. It is eaten both fresh and smoked.

Hades (or Pluto) The Greek god of the dead; also the name of the underworld he ruled. He was the brother of Zeus and Poseidon and husband of Persephone, whom he abducted. The souls of the dead were ferried to Hades across the River Styx by Charon.

Hadrian (76–138 AD) Roman emperor (117–38). He was admitted to the imperial household as Trajan's ward in 85 and had a successful military career. On Trajan's death he became emperor and from 120 to 131 toured the provinces. His foreign policy was generally defensive (he sponsored the building of Hadrian's Wall in Britain) but he subdued a Jewish revolt (132–35) with considerable severity. From 131 until his death he lived in Rome.

Hadrian IV. *See* Adrian IV.

Hadrian's Wall A Roman frontier defence work. Begun in 122 AD, it was the N frontier of Roman Britain for 250 years. Designed to contain the Scottish tribes, it stretched 120 km (85 mi) from Tyne to Solway. It eventually comprised ditch, stone and turf wall (incorporating forts and signalling turrets), road system, and "vallum" (earthworks delimiting the military area). Substantial portions still stand.

hadron Any elementary particle that takes part in strong interactions. The group thus includes all baryons and mesons but not leptons or the photon. *See* particle physics.

haematite (*or* hematite) The principal ore of iron, ferric oxide, varying in colour from red to grey to black. It contains over 70% iron. It occurs either in crystalline form (specular iron ore) or in massive form.

haematology The study of blood and its diseases. This medical specialty is concerned particularly with treating leukaemias, haemophilia, and rare kinds of anaemia.

haemoglobin The substance, contained within the red blood cells (*see* erythrocyte), that is responsible for the colour of blood. In humans haemoglobin consists of a protein (globin) combined with an iron-containing pigment (haem). Haem combines with oxygen to form oxyhaemoglobin, which gives arterial blood its bright-red colour and is the means by which oxygen is transported around the body. Oxygen is released at the tissues and the pigment acquires a bluish tinge, responsible for the bluish-red colour of venous blood.

haemophilia A hereditary disease in which the blood does not clot properly due to absence of one of the clotting factors. The disease is almost entirely restricted to boys but is transmitted through the mother. If an affected person (a haemophiliac) cuts himself seriously he may bleed to death without appropriate plasma transfusions.

haemorrhoids (*or* piles) Swollen (varicose) veins in the anal canal, which may enlarge sufficiently to hang down outside the anus. Piles may cause bleeding from the anus and itchiness; in severe cases they may need to be surgically removed or injected with a sclerosing agent, which makes them shrivel up.

Ha-er-bin (English name: Harbin) 45 45N 126 41E A port in NE China, the capital of Heilongjiang province on the Songhua River. A trading and industrial centre, it was a haven for refugees from the Russian Revolution (1917). Population (1986): 2 630 000.

hafnium (Hf) A dense ductile metal, first detected in zircon ($ZrSiO_4$) in 1923 and named after the Latin (Hafnia) for Copenhagen, where it was discovered. It is chemically similar to zirconium. The capacity of hafnium to absorb neutrons is used to control nuclear reactors, especially in submarines. Its compounds include the chloride ($HfCl_4$) and other halides, the oxide (HfO_2), the carbide (HfC), and the nitride (Hf_3N_4). At no 72; at wt 178.49; mp 2150°C; bp 5400°C.

HADRIAN'S WALL   *One of the largest Roman remains in the UK.*

Haganah (Hebrew: defence)   The irregular organization of the early Jewish settlers in Palestine established in 1920 to counteract the attacks of the Palestinian Arabs. After the partition of Palestine in 1947, the Haganah became the defence force of the Jewish state, and in 1948 the national army of the state of Israel.

hagfish   A fishlike vertebrate, 40–80 cm long, sometimes called slime eel, belonging to a family (*Myxinidae*; about 20 species) of cyclostomes. They occur on or near the sea bottom in cold regions and feed on dead or dying fish. Hagfishes are initially hermaphrodites but develop either male or female sex organs.

RIDER HAGGARD   *E. K. Johnson's illustration (1886) for* She.

Haggard, Sir H(enry) Rider   (1856–1925) British adventure novelist. His five years in government service in South Africa provided the background of his first novel, *King Solomon's Mines* (1885), reflecting his own liberal views. Of his many later romances, *She* (1887) is the best known.

haggis   A traditional Scottish meat dish, eaten especially on Burns' Night (25 Jan). Haggis is made from minced sheep's heart, liver, and lungs with onion, oatmeal, suet, and seasonings, all stuffed into a bag made from the sheep's stomach.

Hague, The (Dutch name: 's Gravenhage *or* Den Haag) 52 05N 4 16E The seat of government of the Netherlands and capital of South Holland province. It became the seat of the States General of the seven United Provinces of the Netherlands in the 16th century. It is the residence of the court and the International Court of Justice is located here. Notable buildings include the 13th-century Binnenhof, in which the government is housed. It is chiefly a commercial and residential centre with some light industry. Population (1987): 445 127.

Hahn, Otto   ((1879–1968) German chemist and physicist. With Lise Meitner he discovered protactinium in 1918. He continued to work with Meitner until she was forced to leave Germany in 1938. Together they discovered the process of nuclear fission. In 1944 he was awarded the Nobel Prize for Chemistry.

Hahnemann, Samuel Christian Friedrich   (1755–1843) German physician and founder of homeopathy. Hahnemann's methods aroused controversy among his contemporaries and he was forced to leave his practice in Leipzig, eventually settling in Paris.

hahnium (Ha; element 105)   An artificial transuranic element, synthesized in the USA in 1970 by bombarding californium-249 with nitrogen-15 in a particle accelerator and possibly also in the Soviet Union in 1967 by a different method. Named after Otto Hahn. At no 105; at wt (260).

Haifa   32 49N 34 59E A town in NE Israel, on the Mediterranean coast by Mount Carmel. It was the scene of fighting in the 1948–49 Arab-Israeli conflict and has since developed into a manufacturing town. Population (1986): 223 400.

Haig, Douglas, 1st Earl   (1861–1928) British field marshal. Commander of the first army corps in France and later commander in chief of the British Expeditionary Force during World War I, he was criticized for the appalling losses of the Somme and Passchendaele campaigns. Under the supreme command of Foch, Haig directed the final victorious assault on the Hindenburg line.

hail   The approximately spherical ice pellets that fall from cumulonimbus clouds. They originate as small ice particles around which layers of ice freeze as the ice pellets fall or are uplifted within a cloud. Hailstorms occur most frequently in the continental interiors of temperate latitudes.

Haile Selassie I (1892–1975) Emperor of Ethiopia (1930–36, 1941–74). In 1936 Haile Selassie fled to England after the invasion by the Italians, but was restored to the throne by the Allies in 1941. He did much to modernize Ethiopia and was a prominent figure in international affairs before his deposition by a military coup.

Hailsham, Quintin McGarel Hogg, Baron (1907–) British lawyer and Conservative politician; Lord Chancellor (1970–74, 1979–87). From 1959 to 1963 he was minister for science and technology. In 1950 he succeeded his father **Douglas McGarel Hogg, 1st Viscount Hailsham** (1872–1950), Lord Chancellor (1928–29, 1935–38), but disclaimed his viscountcy in 1963, when he made an unsuccessful bid for the Conservative Party leadership. In 1970 he became a life peer.

Hainan Island A Chinese island, the largest in the South China Sea, apart from Taiwan, and separated from the mainland by **Hainan Strait**. Sparsely populated, it is one of China's least developed regions. Rubber and timber are produced and iron ore and other minerals are mined. Area: 33 991 sq km (13 124 sq mi). Population (1956 est): 2 700 000. Capital: Haikou.

Hainaut (Flemish name: Henegouwen; French name: Hainault) A province in SW Belgium, bordering on France. It contains important coalfields and industries include iron and steel processing. Area: 3997 sq km (1466 sq mi). Population (1986): 1 274 034. Capital: Mons.

FRANS HALS   *Detail from* The Laughing Cavalier.

hairy frog A frog, *Astylosternus robustus*, of Cameroon. In the breeding season the skin on the sides and thighs of male frogs develops hairlike filaments, containing many blood vessels, that assist in breathing.

Haiti, Republic of A country in the Caribbean Sea, occupying the W third of the island of Hispaniola. Much of the country is mountainous and forested, with fertile plains lying between the three main mountain ranges. The majority of the population is of African descent. *Economy*: mainly agricultural, mostly organized in small farms. The main crops are coffee (the principal export), sugar, rice, bananas, and sisal. *History*: the island was discovered by Columbus in 1492 and became a Spanish colony. The E part was ceded to France in 1697, becoming the most prosperous of the French colonies, and the remainder was temporarily ceded between 1795

and 1809. In 1804, under Gen Jean Jacques Dessalines (c. 1758–1806), Haiti gained its independence; a period of unrest was followed by union with the rest of the island (1822–44). For most of the time since it has been a republic; after a series of coups Dr François Duvalier came to power in 1957 and was succeeded in 1971 by his son, Jean-Claude Duvalier. In 1986 Duvalier's brutal regime fell in a military coup. After two more coups in 1988 Brig-Gen Prosper Avril became president. Official language: French; Creole is widely spoken. Offical religion: Roman Catholic. Area: 27 750 sq km (10 700 sq mi). Population (1988 est): 6 096 000. Capital and main port: Port-au-Prince.

Haitink, Bernard (1929–) Dutch conductor. He was appointed permanent conductor of the Amsterdam Concertgebouw Orchestra in 1964 and conductor of the London Philharmonic Orchestra in 1967. He became music director of Glyndebourne (1978) and Covent Garden (1986).

hake A food fish, of the genus *Merluccius*, that is related to cod and occurs off European, African, and American coasts. Its elongated body, up to about 1 m long, is dark grey above and lighter below, with two dorsal fins.

Halab. *See* Aleppo.

Haldane, Richard Burdon, 1st Viscount (1856–1928) British army reformer. A Liberal MP (1885–1911) until becoming a peer, he was secretary for war from 1905 to 1912. He formed the Territorial Force (*see* Territorial Army) and facilitated the mobilization of the British Expeditionary Force at the outbreak of World War I. Becoming Lord Chancellor in 1912 he was dismissed in 1915 because of accusations that he was pro-German. He also wrote a study of the philosophical implications of relativity, *The Reign of Relativity* (1921) and helped to found the London School of Economics (1895). His brother **John Scott Haldane** (1860–1936) was a physiologist, noted for his investigations of human respiration. Haldane established that the rate of breathing was regulated according to the concentration of carbon dioxide in the blood. He also improved mine safety by demonstrating the toxic effects of carbon monoxide. J. S. Haldane's son **John Burdon Sanderson Haldane** (1892–1964) was a geneticist and Marxist philosopher, who contributed to many aspects of biology, including evolution and population genetics.

half-life The time taken for half the atoms in a sample of a radioactive isotope to decay. It is therefore a measure of the activity of an isotope. A very active isotope may have a half-life of only a millionth of a second, whereas some more stable isotopes have half-lives of millions of years.

halibut A flatfish of the genus *Hippoglossus*, especially *H. hippoglossus*—a large food fish, up to about 2 m long, found in N Atlantic coastal waters. The eyed (right) side is brown or dark green with mottling. Family: *Pleuronectidae*.
Other halibuts include the Greenland halibut and the California halibut, which belong to the family *Bothidae*.

Haliç. *See* Golden Horn.

Halifax 53 44N 1 52W A town in N England, in West Yorkshire on the River Calder. Halifax has a strong wool textile tradition going back to the 13th century. Carpets, woollens, and worsteds are manufactured as well as machinery. Population (1981): 87 488.

Halifax 44 38N 63 35W A city and major port in E Canada, the capital of Nova Scotia on the Atlantic

Ocean. Founded as a British naval base (1749), it dominates the cultural life, commerce, and industry of the Maritime Provinces. Its industries include shipbuilding, oil refining, steel, and food processing. Population (1986): 113 577.

Hall, Sir Peter (1930–) British theatre director. He was director of the Royal Shakespeare Company from 1960 to 1968 and director of the National Theatre Company from 1973 to 1988.

Halle 51 30N 11 59E A city in SW East Germany, on the River Saale. The birthplace of Handel, Halle has many fine old buildings. Its diverse industries include sugar refining and coalmining. Population (1986): 234 768.

Hallé, Sir Charles (Karl Hallé; 1819–1895) German conductor and pianist. He settled in Britain in 1848 and in 1857 established a series of concerts in Manchester, for which he founded and conducted the **Hallé Orchestra**. *See also* Barbirolli, Sir John.

Hall effect If a conductor carrying an electric current is placed in a transverse magnetic field, an electric field appears across the material, perpendicular to both the current and the magnetic field. The charges flowing in the material are displaced to one side thus creating a potential difference. Named after Edwin H. Hall (1855–1938).

Halley, Edmund (1656–1742) British astronomer, who was appointed professor of geometry at Oxford University in 1703. He was the first to realize that comets have periodic orbits. In 1705 he identified a particular comet, now known as **Halley's comet**, as having a period of 76 years (appearing 1986, 2062, etc.). He also discovered that stars have a proper motion of their own (1718) and was appointed astronomer royal to succeed Flamsteed (1720).

hallmarks A set of marks stamped onto gold or silver objects manufactured in the UK, as a guarantee of purity. Each article has up to five marks: the mark of the assay office, an assay mark to indicate quality, a date mark, the sovereign's head (between 1784 and 1890), and the maker's mark. Gold articles also have a mark to indicate their purity in carats.

Hallowe'en Oct 31, the eve of All Saints' Day. The name is a contraction of All Hallows (hallowed or holy) Eve. In pre-Christian Britain, 31 Oct was the eve of New Year, when the souls of the dead were thought to revisit their homes. Customs include the shaping of a demon's face from a hollow turnip or pumpkin, in which a candle is then placed.

hallucination A vivid but false perception of something that is not really there. Any sense can be affected. It may be a result of mental illness, especially psychosis, when the commonest forms are hearing voices and seeing frightening visions. It can also be caused by drugs, epilepsy, disease of the brain, and sensory deprivation. Transient hallucinations can be experienced by normal people.

hallucinogens Drugs that produce hallucinations due to their stimulant action on the brain. Such drugs are also described as psychedelic. Hallucinogens, which include cannabis and LSD, tend to lead to some form of drug dependence.

halogens The elements forming group VII of the periodic table: fluorine, chlorine, bromine, iodine, and astatine. In chemical reactions they tend to form negative ions or covalent bonds and they have a valence of 1. All

are reactive, particularly fluorine and chlorine. They produce salts on contact with metals ("halogen" means salt-yielding) and react with other nonmetals and many organic compounds.

A typical hallmark, from an article assayed in London in 1796.

London   Birmingham
A leopard's head introduced   *An anchor introduced*
in 1300 (crowned between   *in 1773.*
1478 and 1821).

Sheffield   Glasgow
The crown introduced in   *A tree embellished with*
1773.   *bell, bird, and fish,*
                                               introduced in 1681.

Edinburgh   Dublin
The castle introduced in mid- *The crowned harp*
16th century. The thistle was   *introduced in mid-17th*
introduced in 1759.   *century. In 1731 the*
                                               figure of Hibernia was
                                               added.

marks of some other halls

Chester   Newcastle-on-Tyne   York

Norwich   Exeter

HALLMARKS *A set of typical hallmarks and the marks of the different assay offices.*

Hals, Frans (c. 1581–1666) Dutch painter of portraits and scenes of everyday life. He was born in Antwerp but worked mainly in Haarlem. Apart from his *Laughing Cavalier* (1624; Wallace Collection, London), he is best known for his group portraits. Later works include *Lady-Governors of the Almshouse at Haarlem* (1664; Frans Hals Museum, Haarlem), influenced by Rembrandt.

hamadryas A small baboon, *Papio hamadryas*, of NE Africa and Saudi Arabia. 100–140 cm long including the tail (40–60 cm), hamadryas baboons have a long silvery-brown mane, pinkish face, and red buttocks and live in groups with a complex social structure. They were sacred animals to the ancient Egyptians.

Hamburg 53 33N 10 00E A city in N West Germany, on the Rivers Elbe and Alster. A major port and the largest city in West Germany, it is also an important cultural centre, with a university (1919), art gallery, and opera house (1678). Its many industries include shipbuilding, engineering, and food processing. *History:* its alliance with Lübeck (1241) became the basis of the Hanseatic League. It was a trading centre from the middle ages and the first German stock exchange was established here (1558). It was severely bombed during World War II. Population (1986): 1 575 700.

Hamelin (German name: Hameln) 52 06N 9 21E A town in N West Germany, in Lower Saxony on the River Weser. The Ratcatcher's House (1602–03) is associated with the legendary Pied Piper. Manufactures include carpets and chemicals. Population (1984): 56 000.

Hamilcar Barca (died c. 229 BC) Carthaginian general and Hannibal's father. Commander in Sicily during the first Punic War, he negotiated peace in 241. After suppressing rebellious mercenaries in Carthage, he invaded Spain. He was drowned after the siege of Helice.

Hamilton 43 15N 79 50W A city and port in central Canada, in S Ontario on Lake Ontario. Canada's main centre of heavy industry, it is particularly important for iron and steel, motor vehicles, machinery, chemicals, and electrical goods. Population (1986): 306 728.

Hamilton 37 46S 175 18E A city in New Zealand, in N North Island on the Waikato River. It is the most important inland centre and serves a pastoral and lumbering region. The University of Waikato was established in 1964. Population (1987): 169 000.

Hamilton, Emma (c. 1761–1815) The mistress of Horatio Nelson. She was the mistress of Charles Greville (1749–1809) and then of his uncle Sir William Hamilton (1730–1803), whom she married in 1791. She met Nelson in 1793; they became lovers and in 1801 their daughter Horatia (d. 1881) was born. After Nelson's death (1805), Lady Emma squandered her inheritance and fled to Calais (1814), where she died.

Hamito-Semitic languages A language family spoken in N Africa and S Asia. More appropriately known as Afro-Asiatic, it has five branches that descend from an ancestor language, Proto-Hamito-Semitic, which was spoken between the 6th and 8th millenniums BC. The five branches are Egyptian, Berber, Cushitic, Semitic, and Chadic.

Hammarskjöld, Dag (Hjalmar Agne Carl) (1905–61) Swedish international civil servant; the son of Hjalmar Hammarskjöld (1862–1953), who was a prime minister of Sweden (1914–17). As deputy foreign minister (1951–53) he headed the Swedish delegation to the UN and in 1953 became secretary general of the UN. He dealt with the Suez crisis (1956) and the civil war arising from the grant of independence to the Congo (1960). He was killed in a plane crash and awarded the Nobel Peace Prize posthumously in 1961.

hammerhead shark A shark of the family *Sphyrnidae*, found in warm and temperate salt waters. Up to 4.5 m long, the head is flattened and extended laterally into two hammer- or spade-shaped lobes, which bear the eyes and nostrils. They feed primarily on fish but may attack other animals, including man.

Hammerstein II, Oscar (1895–1960) US lyricist and librettist. With Richard Rodgers he wrote *Oklahoma!* (1943), *Carousel* (1945), *South Pacific* (1949), *The King and I* (1951), and *The Sound of Music* (1959).

hammer throw A field event for men in athletics. The hammer is an iron or brass sphere weighing 16 lb (7.26 kg) attached to a wire handle and grip. It is thrown with both hands within a circle 7 ft (2.13 m) in diameter. World record: 86.74 m (1986) by Yuri Sedykh (Soviet Union).

Hammett, Dashiell (1894–1961) US novelist. He worked as a private detective for eight years before writing his first detective stories. His novels, the realistic and economical style of which influenced Raymond Chandler and other detective-story writers, include *The Maltese Falcon* (1930) and *The Thin Man* (1932).

HAMPTON COURT   *The 16th-century west front with the Great Gatehouse.*

Hampshire A county of S central England, bordering on the English Channel. It consists mainly of gently undulating lowlands, rising to chalk downlands in the N and E. The chief rivers, the Test and Itchen, drain into the Solent, which separates the Isle of Wight from the mainland. It is predominantly agricultural with dairy and arable farming. Industries, centred on Southampton, include shipbuilding and oil refining and there are important naval bases at Portsmouth and Gosport. Tourism is important in the New Forest and coastal resorts. Area: 3772 sq km (1456 sq mi). Population (1986 est): 1 527 700. Administrative centre: Winchester.

Hampton, Lionel (1913–   ) US Black jazz band leader and vibraphone player, who played with Benny Goodman before forming his own orchestra in 1940. Hampton was the first jazz musician to popularize the vibraphone; one of his biggest successes was the record *Flyin' Home* (1942).

Hampton Court A Tudor and Stuart palace on the River Thames near London. Built by Cardinal Wolsey, it was given in the 1520s to Henry VIII, who made substantial alterations; in the 1690s Wren began a further rebuilding project for William III. The palace is now open to the public; it was damaged by fire in 1986.

hamster A small rodent of the family *Cricetidae*. The common hamster (*Cricetus cricetus*), native to Europe and W Asia, has a red-brown coat with white patches on the flanks, neck, and cheek. It feeds on seeds and grains. The golden hamster (*Mesocricetus auratus*) is a domestic pet and all are thought to have descended from a single family found at Aleppo, Syria, in 1930.

Han (206 BC–220 AD) A Chinese dynasty founded by the general Liu Bang (*or* Liu Pang; 256–195 BC), who overthrew the preceding Qin dynasty. The power of the Han was consolidated by the emperor, Wu Di (*or* Wu Ti; 157–87 BC; reigned 140–87), who completed the conquest of a vast empire. Chinese export of silk increased, and a vast canal-building programme was started. Paper was invented by the Han Chinese, who also produced early forms of porcelain. The programme of expansion led to financial difficulties that enabled Wang Mang to usurp the throne in 8 AD. The Han dynasty was subsequently restored for a second period, known as the Later Han (23–220 AD).

Hancock, Tony (Anthony John H; 1924–68) British comedian, best known for his radio series of the 1950s, *Hancock's Half Hour*. He also appeared on television and in several films.

Handel, George Frederick (1685–1759) German composer. He studied in Halle and travelled to Italy, where he became famous as a harpsichordist and as a master of the Italianate style of composition. In 1710 he became kapellmeister to the Elector of Hanover but did not return there after visiting England in 1712. Handel became musical director to James Brydges, first duke of Chandos (1673–1744), in 1718. He subsequently became music master to the family of the Prince of Wales and director of the Royal Academy of Music on its foundation in 1720. His Italian operas were successfully produced in London; from 1739 he turned from opera to oratorio, producing such masterpieces as *Saul* (1739), *Israel in Egypt* (1739), and *Messiah* (1742), which maintained his public popularity. In 1751, however, he began to be afflicted with loss of sight and eventually became completely blind, although he continued to compose. His mastery of composition is reflected in the range of his works, which include the *Water Music* (1717), *Music for the Royal Fireworks* (1749), concerti grossi, sonatas, organ concertos, harpsichord suites, and anthems. He was buried in Westminster Abbey.

Hangchow. *See* Hangzhou.

HANG-GLIDING

hang-gliding Unpowered flight in a hang-glider, consisting of a large bat-shaped cloth wing on a light metal framework from which the pilot hangs in a harness, holding a horizontal control bar. In flight, the wing fills to form an aerofoil (*see* aeronautics). The first hang-glider was built by Otto Lilienthal, but the prototype for modern design was the sail-wing invented by Frances Rogallo (1912–   ). Hang-gliding became popular in the late 1960s. A powered hang-glider was first used to

cross the English Channel in 1979.

Hanging Gardens of Babylon Ancient gardens in the palace of Nebuchadnezzar II (604–562 BC) on the E side of Babylon. One of the Seven Wonders of the World, they were built on top of stone arches and watered from the Euphrates by a complicated mechanical system.

Hangzhou (Hang-chou *or* Hangchow) 30 18N 120 07E A city in E China, the capital of Zhejiang province on Hangzhou Bay, an inlet of the East China Sea. It was the capital (1132–1276) of the Southern Song dynasty. A picturesque tourist centre, its varied industries include silk production. Population (1986): 1 250 000.

Hankou (*or* Hankow). *See* Wuhan.

Hannibal (247–c. 183 BC) Carthaginian general. Appointed commander in Spain in 221, he deliberately provoked the second Punic War with Rome. In 218 he crossed the Alps in winter, losing about 10 000 of his 35 000 men. For two years he devastated Italy, but lost ground in the face of Fabius' guerrilla tactics. Recalled to defend Carthage after Scipio Africanus' invasion of Africa, Hannibal was defeated at Zama (202). Suspected of rebellion, he was forced to flee Roman retribution. He committed suicide to avoid capture.

Hanoi 20 57N 105 55E The capital of Vietnam, situated in the NE of the country on the Red River. The capital of the Vietnamese empire from the 11th until the 17th centuries, it was occupied by the French in 1873 and became the capital of French Indochina. Following the Japanese occupation in World War II, it became the capital of the Democratic Republic of Vietnam. Many ancient buildings in the Vietnamese quarter remain, together with several imposing buildings in the European quarter built by the French. Population (1983 est): 2 674 400.

Hanover (German name: Hannover) 52 23N 9 44E A city in N West Germany, the capital of Lower Saxony on the River Leine. It is a transshipment port and a commercial and industrial centre, where an important industrial fair is held annually. After the destruction of World War II it was largely rebuilt; the Leine Palace (founded 1636) is now the *Land* parliament building. Hanover's manufactures include machinery, rubber, textiles, and motor vehicles. *History*: in 1638 Hanover became the capital of the future electorate and kingdom of Hanover. In 1714 Elector George Louis became George I of Great Britain (*see* Settlement, Act of). He is buried in Hanover. The Kings of Great Britain were Electors (later Kings) of Hanover until 1837. Population (1986): 506 400.

Hansard The official reports of debates in the UK parliament. The name, which was officially adopted in 1943, is that of the family that first printed the reports: **Luke Hansard** (1752–1828) and his son **Thomas Curson Hansard** (1776–1833). The Stationery Office published Hansard from 1890.

Hanseatic League An association of N German trading towns (the Hanse) formed in the 13th century to protect their economic interests overseas. By the mid-14th century, the League, comprising some hundred towns, had become a powerful corporate body and conducted a number of trade wars with Denmark and England. The rise of the non-German Baltic states and changing trade routes contributed to the League's declining influence. It was finally dissolved in 1669.

Hanukka A Jewish festival, commemorating the revolt of the Maccabees. It falls in midwinter and is celebrated by lighting of lamps or candles.

Hanuman In Hindu mythology, a monkey god and one of the principal characters in the *Ramayana*. There are numerous temples dedicated to him in both India and Japan.

Hanyang. *See* Wuhan.

Hapsburgs. *See* Habsburgs.

hara-kiri The honourable way of death for Japanese samurai who wished to avoid shame or demonstrate sincerity. In its strict form it involved ceremoniously cutting one's stomach open with a dagger before decapitation by the single blow of another samurai's sword. It is still sometimes practised by Japanese suicides, although it is now illegal.

Harare (Name until 1982: Salisbury) 17 50 S 31 02 E The capital of Zimbabwe, on a plateau in the NE. Founded in 1890, it was the capital of the Federation of Rhodesia and Nyasaland (1935–63). It has two cathedrals and is the centre of a tobacco-growing area. Population (1983): 681 000.

Harbin. *See* Ha-er-bin.

harbour seal The common seal, *Phoca vitulina*, of coastal Pacific and Atlantic waters. Up to 1.8 m long, with a blotchy grey coat, harbour seals inhabit sandbanks and river estuaries, feeding on fish. Family: *Phocidae*.

Hardanger Fjord A fjord in SW Norway, S of Bergen, penetrating inland from the North Sea for 110 km (68 mi).

Hardecanute (*or* Harthacanute; c. 1019–42) The last Danish King of England (1040–42), succeeding his illegitimate half-brother Harold I Harefoot, and King of Denmark (1035–42). He razed Worcester after a riot against his tax collectors.

Hardie, J(ames) Keir (1856–1915) British politician, who was an important figure in the early parliamentary Labour Party. Born in Scotland, he became a coalminer at the age of ten. He founded the Scottish Parliamentary Labour Party in 1888 and, as an Independent Socialist MP (1892–95), he helped to found (1893) the Independent Labour Party. Again an MP (1900–15), he became chairman (1906) of the future Labour Party. He was an ardent pacifist.

Hardy, Thomas (1840–1928) British novelist and poet. His major novels, which include *The Return of the Native* (1878), *The Mayor of Casterbridge* (1886), and *Tess of the D'Urbervilles* (1891), are tragic tales set in his native Dorset (called "Wessex" in the novels). After the public outrage caused by the alleged immorality of *Jude the Obscure* (1895) he published only verse, beginning with *Wessex Poems* (1898), and an epic drama, *The Dynasts* (1903–08). He was awarded the OM in 1910.

hare A mammal belonging to the widely distributed family *Leporidae* (which also includes the rabbits). Hares are typically larger than rabbits and have long black-tipped ears. They live and breed in the open and are mainly nocturnal, feeding on grass and bark. Chief genus: *Lepus* (about 26 species); order: *Lagomorpha*.

harebell A herbaceous perennial plant, *Campanula rotundifolia*, of N temperate regions, growing to a height of 60 cm. It has rounded leaves and blue bell-shaped flowers. Family: *Campanulaceae*.

Hare Krishna movement (Sanskrit: hail Krishna) An international religious community, the International

Society for Krishna Consciousness (ISKCON), founded in New York in 1966 on Hindu principles by an Indian, Swami Prabhupada (1895–1977). Members are strict vegetarians; gambling, extramarital sex, and the use of drugs are prohibited. They dress in saffron linen robes and the men have shaved heads.

THOMAS HARDY

Hargreaves, James (d. 1778) English inventor, who around 1764 invented the spinning jenny, a machine with which several threads could be spun simultaneously. After local spinners, believing that their jobs were threatened, broke up his machines, Hargreaves set up (1768) a small mill in Nottingham.

haricot bean A variety of French bean (*Phaseolus vulgaris*) grown in warm climates. The seeds, are either brown or light-coloured and are used for making baked beans.

Harlech 52 52N 4 07W A historic town in NW Wales, in Gwynedd on Cardigan Bay. It is a resort with a famous ruined castle. Population (1986 est): 1110.

Harlem 40 49N 73 57W A residential district of New York City, USA, in Manhattan. It is a political and social focus for Blacks.

Harlequin A stock character of the commedia dell'arte. Harlequin began as a comic and covetous servant but developed into the lover of Columbine and the central comic figure of the harlequinade, dressed in a bright diamond-patterned costume, masked, and carrying a wooden club.

Harlow 51 47N 0 08E A town in SE England, in Essex. It is a new town, developed since 1947, with light industries (surgical and scientific instruments, electronics, glass). Population (1981): 79 253.

harmonica The mouth organ: the smallest member of the reed-organ family; its invention is attributed to Sir Charles Wheatstone (1802–75) in 1829. Notes and chords are obtained by blowing or sucking rows of parallel reeds. The instrument's main exponent is Larry Adler (1914–   ).

harmonium A keyboard instrument of the reed organ family, patented in 1848 by Alexandre Debain (1809–77) in Paris. It is a free reed instrument, the air being blown by a bellows activated by foot pedals. It may have several stops (*see* organ).

harmony In music, the combining of notes into chords, so that they are heard simultaneously. Before about 1650 composers made use of polyphony; between about 1650 and about 1900 (the **harmonic period**) a system of harmony evolved based on diatonic chords (*see* scale). Such chords consist of three notes sounded simultaneously; a note of the scale of the tonality of the composition and the notes a third and a fifth above it. The constituent notes of any chord can be rearranged to provide variety. A **harmonic progression** consists of a particular sequence of chords, especially one leading (*or* modulating) into another tonality. In the early years of the 20th century Schoenberg first adopted atonality and later invented serialism as a substitute for traditional harmony. Debussy developed novel harmonic practices, such as harmonizing melodies with chords from unrelated tonalities; other composers of the 20th century have made use of a wide range of harmonic styles.

Harold I Harefoot (d. 1040) Danish King of England (1037–40). The illegitimate son of Canute, he became king while Hardecanute, Canute's legitimate son, was preoccupied in Denmark. Before Hardecanute could oust him, Harold died.

Harold II (c. 1022–66) The last Anglo-Saxon King of England (1066), reputedly designated heir by the dying Edward the Confessor. After becoming king, he crushed the forces of his brother Tostig (d. 1066) and Harold III Hardraade of Norway (1015–66) at Stamford Bridge (1066). Harold was killed in the battle of Hastings by the army of William the Conqueror.

harp A plucked stringed instrument of ancient origin, consisting of an open frame with strings of varying length and tension. The modern orchestral harp is triangular in shape with about 45 strings stretched between the soundbox and the neck. The pillar contains a mechanism that enables the player to raise each string by one or two semitones by means of pedals at the base. It gives the harp a full chromatic range of six and a half octaves from the B below the bass stave.

Harples In Greek mythology, malicious spirits who carried off their victims to their deaths. They were later portrayed as rapacious birds with ugly women's faces.

harpsichord A keyboard instrument with strings plucked by quills, rather than hit by hammers (*see* spinet; virginals; *compare* clavichord; piano). In the 16th, 17th, and 18th centuries it was an instrument of great importance. The tone can be changed by the addition of stops, which sound strings an octave below or above the note depressed.

harquebus (*or* arquebus). *See* musket.

harrier (bird) A slender long-legged hawk belonging to a widely distributed genus (*Circus*). Harriers are about 50 cm long and are usually brown with a small bill and a long tail. They fly low over fields and marshes, searching for frogs, mice, snakes, and insects.

Harris. *See* Lewis with Harris.

Harrogate 54 00N 1 33W A residential town and spa in N England, in North Yorkshire. It is a holiday resort and an important centre for conferences and trade fairs. Population (1987 est): 69 270.

hartebeest A long-faced antelope, *Alcephalus busephalus*, of African plains. About 120 cm high at the shoulder, hartebeests are slender fast-running animals, ranging in colour from dark chestnut to fawn; their horns are generally lyre-shaped.

Hartford 41 45N 72 42W A city in the USA, the capital of Connecticut. Trinity College (1823) and the law and insurance schools of the University of Connecticut are situated here. A commercial, industrial, and financial centre, Hartford is one of the leading insurance centres in the world. Population (1980): 136 392.

Hartlepool 54 41N 1 13W A port in NE England, in Cleveland. Originally an old fishing port and medieval walled town, Hartlepool's main industries are engineering, clothing manufacture, and timber working. Population (1983 est): 93 400.

Hartnell, Sir Norman (1901–79) British fashion designer. He designed new uniforms for the WRAC and for Red Cross nurses and was appointed official dressmaker to Queen Elizabeth II and Elizabeth the Queen Mother. He was knighted in 1977.

Harvard classification system A system, introduced in the 1890s by astronomers at the Harvard Col-

HAROLD II *Being crowned at Westminster (detail from Bayeux tapestry).*

lege Observatory (USA), by which stars are classified according to features in their spectra. The stars are grouped into seven major spectral types: O, B, A, F, G, K, and M, in order of decreasing temperature. There are 10 subdivisions for each spectral type, indicated by a digit (0–9) placed after the letter. Stars of one spectral type can be further classified into supergiants, giants, etc., according to their luminosity. *See also* Hertz-sprung-Russell diagram.

Harvard University The oldest university in the USA (founded 1636), located at Cambridge, Massachusetts. It is named after the clergyman John Harvard (1607–38). The associated women's college, Radcliffe College, dates from 1879.

harvestman An arachnid, also called harvest spider, belonging to the order *Opiliones* (or *Phalangida*; 2200 species), found in tropical and temperate regions. It has an undivided body, 1–22 mm long, and very long delicate legs. It is found in fields, woods, and buildings, feeding on insects and plant materials.

harvest mite A mite, also called chigger and scrub mite, belonging to the genus *Trombicula*. Its larvae are parasitic on vertebrates, including man, feeding on skin and causing inflammation.

WILLIAM HARVEY *An illustration for his book on the circulation of the blood.*

Harvey, William (1578–1657) English physician and anatomist, who discovered the circulation of the blood. Harvey studied under the great anatomist Fabricius ab Aquapendente (1537–1619) and later became physician to James I and Charles I. His findings, published in *On the Motion of the Heart and Blood in Animals* (1628), aroused controversy, but by his death the circulation of blood was generally accepted.

Harwich 51 57N 1 17E A seaport in E England, in Essex on the estuary of the Rivers Stour and Orwell. It has passenger services to Scandinavia and the Continent. Population (1981): 15 076.

Haryana A state in N India, mostly in the fertile Upper Ganges plain. Predominantly rural, it produces wheat, other grains, cotton, sugar cane, and oilseeds. There is some light industry, including textiles, agricultural implements, and sugar refining. Area: 44 222 sq km (17 070 sq mi). Population (1981): 12 850 902. Capital: Chandigarh.

Harz Mountains A mountain range extending about 90 km (56 mi) across the East German-West German border W of Halle. They are the northernmost range of the European mountain system. The highest peak is the Brocken.

Hashemites The Arab descendants of the prophet Mohammed, including the fourth caliph Ali (c. 600–67) and the line of hereditary emirs of Mecca. King Hussein of Jordan is a modern representative of the line.

hashish. *See* cannabis.

Hasidism A Jewish religious movement, founded by the Ba'al Shem Tov (c. 1700–60). Essentially a blend of kabbalah and popular pietism, Hasidism spread, against strong opposition, throughout the Jewish communities of E Europe in the 18th and 19th centuries. Most of the Hasidic communities in Europe were wiped out during the holocaust, but Hasidism still thrives in North America and Israel.

Hassan II (1929–) King of Morocco (1961–). Educated in France, Hassan maintains autocratic rule in Morocco. He introduced some reforms in 1971 following an attempted coup; he has also pressed Morocco's claim to the Western Sahara.

Hastings 50 51N 0 36E A resort town on the S coast of England, in East Sussex. Formerly the chief of the Cinque Ports, it has a ruined castle built by William the Conqueror. Population (1981): 74 803.

Hastings, Battle of (14 October, 1066) The battle between the Normans and the English at Senlac Hill (*see* Battle), near Hastings, in which William, Duke of Normandy, claiming the English throne, defeated Harold II of England. Both sides suffered heavy losses but the death of Harold allowed William to conquer England (*see* Norman conquest) and become its king.

hatchetfish A carnivorous hatchet-shaped fish, up to 10 cm long, belonging to one of two unrelated groups. Deepsea hatchetfish (family *Sternoptychidae*; 15 species) are related to salmon and occur in warm and temperate waters. The freshwater or flying hatchetfish (family *Gasteropelecidae*; about 9 species) of South America are related to carp.

Hathaway, Anne (c. 1556–1623) The wife of William Shakespeare. She was born at Shottery, near Stratford. She married Shakespeare in 1582 and bore him three children. Her cottage may still be seen near Stratford.

Haughey, Charles (1925–) Irish statesman; prime minister of Ireland (1979–81, 1982, and 1987–). He has been president of the Fianna Fáil party since 1979 and has served in several ministerial posts.

Hauraki Gulf A large inlet of the South Pacific Ocean, in New Zealand on the E coast of North Island. Waitemata Harbour, on which stands Auckland, is situated in the SW. Area: about 2290 sq km (884 sq mi).

Hausa A people of NW Nigeria and S Niger, numbering about nine million. Their language belongs to the Chadic subgroup of the Hamito-Semitic family, but has absorbed many Arabic words and influences. It is an official language of Nigeria and a second language in much of West Africa. The Hausa are mainly Muslim. The economy is based on the cultivation of maize, millet, sorghum, and other crops. Cities, such as Kano, date from precolonial times but most Hausa live in small rural settlements.

Havana (Spanish name: La Habana) 23 00N 82 30W The capital of Cuba, a port in the NW. It exports sugar, cotton, and tobacco. The university was founded in

1728. *History*: the original settlement was on the S coast, but the inhabitants moved to the city's present site in 1519. It became the capital of Cuba in the late 16th century. It has an excellent natural harbour. Population (1986 est): 2 014 800.

Havel, Václav (1936–) Czech dramatist; president of Czechoslovakia (1989–). The author of such plays as *Largo Desolato* (1984) and *Temptation* (1985), he was imprisoned (1979–83) for involvement in the dissident Charter 77 movement, but in 1989 took a leading role in the Civil Forum reform movement, being elected president on the resignation of the Communists.

Hawaii (former name: Sandwich Islands) A state in the USA, occupying a chain of over 20 volcanic islands in the central Pacific Ocean. These include the islands of Hawaii (the largest), Maui, Oahu, Kauai, and Molokai. Its population is ethnically diverse. Manufactures include oil and chemical products, steel, textiles, and food. Agriculture is important, the main crops being sugar and pineapples. The principal industry, however, is tourism. There are many US military bases. *History*: first discovered by Capt Cook in 1778, Hawaii remained a kingdom until becoming a republic in 1893. It was annexed by the USA in 1894 and became a territory in 1900. The Japanese attack on Pearl Harbor in 1941 precipitated the entry of the USA into World War II. Hawaii became a state in 1959. Area: 16 641 sq km (6425 sq mi). Population (1986 est): 1 062 000. Capital: Honolulu.

hawfinch A large finch, *Coccothraustes cocothraustes*, of Eurasia and N Africa. 18 cm long, it has a reddish-brown plumage with paler underparts, black-and-white wings, and a massive bill.

Haw-Haw, Lord. *See* Joyce, William.

hawk A bird of prey belonging to a widely distributed family (*Accipitridae*; 205 species) that includes buzzards, eagles, harriers, kites, and vultures. Hawks have down-curved pointed bills, powerful gripping feet, and good eyesight. They usually nest in trees or crags. Order: *Falconiformes*. *Compare* falcon. *See also* falconry.

Hawke, Robert (James Lee) (1929–) Australian statesman; Labour prime minister (1983–). A trade unionist, he was formerly president of the Australian Council of Trade Unions (1970–80).

Hawkesbury River A river in SE Australia, rising in the Great Dividing Range in New South Wales and flowing generally NE to enter the Tasman Sea at Broken Bay. Length: 472 km (293 mi).

Hawking, Stephen William (1942–) British physicist. He has described the particle emission of black holes (1974) and shown that general relativity supports the big-bang theory. His publications include the best-selling *A Brief History of Time* (1987).

Hawkins, Sir John (1532–95) English navigator. In 1562 he became the first English slave trader, transporting slaves from West Africa to the Spanish West Indies. In 1577 he became treasurer of the navy; he died at Puerto Rico on an expedition with Drake. His son **Sir Richard Hawkins** (c. 1562–1622) served against the Armada and in a subsequent expedition was seized by the Spanish and imprisoned (1594–1602). His *Observations in His Voyage into the South Sea* (1622) influenced Charles Kingsley's *Westward Ho!* (1855).

hawk moth A moth belonging to the widespread family *Sphingidae* (about 1000 species), also called sphinx moth or hummingbird moth. They have large bodies with relatively small wings (spanning 5–20 cm), which

they beat rapidly, hovering over flowers and sipping nectar through their long proboscis.

hawksbill turtle A small sea turtle, *Eretmochelys imbricata*, found in warm waters worldwide. It has hooked jaws, feeds on algae, fish, and invertebrates, and is usually 40–55 cm long. Its shell is the tortoiseshell used to make combs, etc.

HAWKSMOOR *St Anne's, Limehouse; an interior view from the gallery.*

Hawksmoor, Nicholas (1661–1736) English baroque architect. Hawksmoor was trained by Wren and collaborated with Vanbrugh at Blenheim Palace and Castle Howard. His finest individual work was at Easton Neston (1702), All Souls', Oxford (1729), and St Anne's, Limehouse (1714).

hawthorn A thorny shrub or tree of the N temperate genus *Crataegus* (about 200 species). Hawthorns have lobed leaves, white flowers, and yellow, black, or red fruits. The common hawthorn, or may (*C. monogyna*), is found in hedgerows and thickets in Europe and the Mediterranean. Up to 10 m high, it has red fruits (haws).

Haydn, Franz Joseph (1732–1809) Austrian composer, born in Rohrau. He became a cathedral chorister in Vienna at the age of eight and subsequently worked as a freelance musician and music teacher. In 1761 he became kapellmeister to the Esterházy family, a post he held for the rest of his life. In 1791 and 1794 he visited London and wrote his last 12 symphonies, which include the *Oxford* and *London* symphonies. Haydn's compositions include piano sonatas, piano trios, string quartets, masses, concertos, 104 symphonies, operas, and the oratorios *The Creation* (1798) and *The Seasons* (1801).

hay fever An allergy to pollen, which leads to sneezing, a streaming nose, and inflamed eyes. Treatment is by desensitization, with antihistamines or, in severe cases, with steroids.

hazel A hardy shrub or tree of the N temperate genus *Corylus* (15 species), cultivated since ancient times for its edible nuts, also called cob nuts. The leaves are rounded and toothed. The male flowers are attractive yellow catkins; each female flower develops into a nut. The best-known species is the European hazel (*C. avellana*), up to 12 m high. Family: *Betulaceae* (birch family) or *Corylaceae*.

Hazlitt, William (1778–1830) British critic and essayist. The son of a Unitarian minister, he studied art and philosophy before becoming a journalist. Hazlitt held independent opinions in politics and literary matters and expressed them in a style notable for its brilliant invective. His best-known collections of essays and lectures are *Lectures on the English Poets* (1818) and *The Spirit of the Age* (1825).

Healey, Denis (Winston) (1917–) British Labour politician; chancellor of the exchequer (1974–79). He was secretary of the Labour Party's international department from 1945 until entering parliament in 1952 and from 1964 to 1970 was defence minister. He was deputy leader of the Labour Party (1981–83).

hearing aid A device used by the partially deaf to increase the loudness of sounds. Most simple is the ear trumpet, which by its conical shape increases the sound pressure at the ear. Modern hearing aids are electronic, consisting of a microphone, an amplifier, and an earphone, or make use of electronic implants.

Hearst, William Randolph (1863–1951) US newspaper proprietor. Beginning with the *San Francisco Examiner* and the New York *Morning Journal*, he built up a vast newspaper empire whose commercial success was based on popular sensationalism.

heart A four-chambered muscular organ that pumps blood around the body. Two chambers—the left and right atria—dilate to receive oxygen-rich blood from the lungs and oxygen-depleted blood from the rest of the body, respectively (this is called diastole). Contraction of the heart (called systole) starts in the atria, forcing blood into the two ventricles. The left ventricle then contracts to force blood into a large artery—the aorta, which leads from the heart and feeds all the other arteries. The right ventricle pumps blood into the pulmonary artery and to the lungs, where it receives oxygen. Valves between the atria and ventricles and at the arterial exits of the heart prevent the backflow of blood. The rhythm of the heartbeat is maintained by the electrical activity of a group of specialized cells within the heart (*see* pacemaker). The muscle of the heart is supplied with blood by the coronary arteries. Atherosclerosis of these arteries may lead to a heart attack (*see* coronary heart disease; myocardial infarction). *See also* circulation of the blood.

heartsease. *See* pansy.

heat The form of energy that is transferred from one body or region to another at a lower temperature. The amount of heat gained or lost by a body is equal to the product of its heat capacity and the temperature through which it rises or falls. Heat is transferred by conduction, convection, or radiation (*see* heat transfer). Heat is measured in joules, but older units, such as calories and British thermal units, are still sometimes used.

heat capacity The amount of heat needed to raise the temperature of a body through one kelvin. It is measured in joules per kelvin. For a gas, the heat capacity may be measured under conditions of either constant pressure or constant volume. *See also* specific heat capacity.

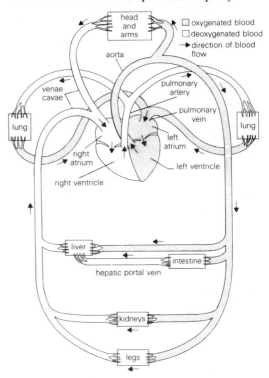

HEART *In man and other mammals the right and left chambers of the heart are completely separate from each other. This ensures that oxygenated and deoxygenated blood do not mix and enables oxygen-depleted blood to receive a fresh supply of oxygen from the lungs before circulating to the rest of the body.*

heat death of universe A hypothetical final state of the universe in which its entropy is at a maximum and no heat is available to do work. In any closed system the total entropy can never decrease during any process. Thus the entropy of the universe will eventually reach a maximum value and when that happens all matter will be totally disordered and at a uniform temperature. This assumes that the universe can be treated as a closed system.

heath An evergreen shrub or tree of the genus *Erica* (about 500 species) of Europe and Africa (about 470 species are native to South Africa). Heaths have spikes of bell-shaped or tubular flowers, white, pink, purple, or yellow in colour. Dwarf heaths are abundant on acid peaty soils, such as moorlands. There are many cultivated varieties, which are popular in rock gardens. Some tree heaths grow to a height of 6 m. Family: *Ericaceae*.

Heath, Edward (Richard George) (1916–) British statesman; Conservative prime minister (1970–74), who took the UK into the EC (1973). He entered parliament in 1950 and assumed cabinet office as minister of labour in 1959. He was Lord Privy Seal (1960–63) and secretary of state for industry (1963–64) and in

1965 succeeded Douglas-Home as leader of the Conservative Party. His Industrial Relations Act (1971) was badly received by the trade unions and his government was twice challenged by miners' strikes. Defeated in both the elections of 1974 (February, October), in 1975 he relinquished the party leadership to Margaret Thatcher. He is an enthusiastic yachtsman and musician.

heather (*or* ling) An evergreen shrub, *Calluna vulgaris*, up to 60 cm high, with scaly leaves and clusters of pale-purple bell-shaped flowers. It grows—often with heath—on acid soils of heaths, moors, and bogs throughout Europe and in parts of N Africa and North America. Family: *Ericaceae*.

Heathrow (*or* London Airport) 51 28N 0 27W The chief air terminal for the UK, in the Greater London borough of Hounslow. Opened to passengers in 1946, it has an underground railway connection from central London (since 1977).

heat pump A device that extracts heat from one substance at a low temperature and supplies it to another substance at a higher temperature, consuming energy in the process. Heat pumps are used to extract the low temperature heat from rivers, etc., for space- and water-heating units. *See also* refrigeration.

heatstroke A rise in body temperature associated with dehydration and exhaustion, caused by overexposure to high temperatures. The emergency treatment is to cool the patient down with water or fans.

heat transfer The transference of energy between two bodies or regions by virtue of the difference in temperatures between them. The three methods of transference are: convection, conduction, and radiation. In convection the heat is transferred by a hotter region flowing into a colder region. In conduction, on the other hand, the heat is transferred by direct contact without any apparent relative motion. In radiation the heat is transferred by means of either infrared radiation or microwave radiation. Radiation is the only method of transferring heat through a vacuum.

heat treatment The process of heating a metal to a temperature below its melting point and then cooling it in order to change its physical properties. Metals are made up of tiny crystals (grains). Their hardness, strength, and ductility is determined by the concentration and distribution of irregularities (dislocations) in the crystal lattice. Heating creates and redistributes dislocations, relieving any internal stresses that have built up. This makes the metal softer and more ductile; a process known as annealing. Dislocation movement is restricted by the boundaries between grains and by the presence of impurities, which make the metal harder and less ductile. Because both the impurity distribution and the grain structure are affected by heating and the rate of cooling, so also is the metal's strength. In steel manufacture, rapid cooling (quenching) by immersion in water or oil hardens the steel, leaving it brittle. Slow cooling makes it soft and ductile.

heaven In Christian belief, the abode of God in which the souls of the virtuous will be rewarded with everlasting life. The iconography of heaven is based upon the Book of Revelation. (*compare* hell). Analogous concepts exist in other major religions.

heavy water Deuterium oxide (D_2O), the form of water containing the isotope of hydrogen with mass number 2. It is chemically less reactive than normal water and has a relative density of 1.1; its boiling point is 101.42°C. It is present to an extent of 1 part in 5000 in natural water and it is used as a moderator and coolant in some nuclear reactors.

Hebrew A Semitic language. It is written from right to left in an alphabet of 22 letters, all consonants, with vowels indicated by subscript and superscript diacritical marks. The oldest and best-known works of Hebrew literature are those preserved in the Bible (Old Testament). Hebrew continued to be a literary language throughout the middle ages, with a particularly rich poetic tradition, besides prose writing. In the late 19th century Hebrew was revived as a spoken language, particularly in Russia and Palestine. In 1948 it became an official language of Israel.

HEBRIDES *Crofts on North Uist.*

Hebrides, the A group of about 500 islands off the W coast of Scotland. The islands are subdivided into the Inner and Outer Hebrides, separated by the Minch. The chief islands of the Outer Hebrides include Lewis with Harris and the Uists; those of the Inner Hebrides include Skye, Mull, Islay, and Jura. The main occupations are stock rearing, fishing, and crofting. Harris tweed is produced, especially in the Uists.

Hebron (Arabic name: Al Khalil) 31 32N 35 06E A town in the S of the West Bank of the River Jordan. It is one of the oldest continuously inhabited cities in the world and is revered by both Jews and Muslims as the burial place of Abraham. Population (1984 est): 75 000.

Hecate A primitive Greek fertility goddess and a ruler of the underworld. She was associated with witchcraft and magic and was worshipped at crossroads. She accompanied Demeter in her search for Persephone.

hectare (ha) A unit of area in the metric system equal to 100 ares or 10 000 square metres. 1 ha = 2.471 acres.

Hector In Greek legend, the eldest son of Priam, King of Troy, and the chief Trojan warrior. He was the husband of Andromache. He fought Ajax in single combat, killed Patroclus, and was killed in revenge by Achilles.

Hecuba In Greek legend, the wife of Priam, King of Troy, and mother of Hector. She was captured by the Greeks after the fall of Troy.

hedgehog A nocturnal prickly-coated insectivorous mammal belonging to the subfamily *Erinaceinae* (15 species), of Africa, Europe, and Asia. The European hedgehog (*Erinaceus europaeus*) grows up to 30 cm long and has brown and cream spines and soft grey-brown underfur. It feeds on worms, beetles, slugs, and snails. Family: *Erinaceidae*.

hedge sparrow. *See* dunnock.

hedonism The ethical theory holding that pleasure is the greatest good. Varying definitions of pleasure distinguished the classical hedonistic schools. Utilitarianism is the most important modern form of hedonism. *Compare* Epicureanism.

Hegel, Georg Wilhelm Friedrich (1770–1831) German philosopher, one of the greatest and most influential thinkers of the 19th century. His first major work, *The Phenomenology of Mind*, was published in 1807, the *Encyclopedia of the Philosophical Sciences* in 1817, and *The Philosophy of Right* in 1821. Besides these major works, he left voluminous lecture notes on history, religion, and aesthetics. He became an eminent and respected figure, collecting disciples, appointments, and decorations.

Heidegger, Martin (1889–1976) German philosopher. His main philosophical work was *Sein und Zeit* (*Being and Time*; 1927). As rector of Freiburg University (1933–34) he supported Hitler and this association, together with logical flaws in his work, has damaged his reputation.

Heidelberg 49 25N 08 42E A city in SW West Germany, in Baden-Württemberg on the River Neckar. A tourist centre, it has a ruined castle (mainly 16th–17th centuries) and the oldest university in Germany (1386). Its varied manufactures include printing presses, cigars, and electrical appliances. *History*: the capital of the Palatinate until 1685, it was devastated during the Thirty Years' War and later by the French. During the 19th century it was the student centre of Germany. In 1952 it became the European headquarters of the US army. Population (1986): 135 800.

Heifetz, Jascha (1901–87) Russian-born US violinist. A child prodigy, he entered the St Petersburg conservatoire in 1910, and at the age of 12 began a worldwide career. He commissioned important works for the violin, including Walton's violin concerto.

Heisenberg, Werner Karl (1901–76) German physicist, who, with Schrödinger, was the main architect of quantum mechanics. In 1927 Heisenberg created a mathematical system, known as matrix mechanics, to explain the structure of the hydrogen atom. In the same year he put forward the theory known as the Heisenberg uncertainty principle, for which he was awarded the Nobel Prize in 1932. During World War II Heisenberg was in charge of Germany's unsuccessful attempts to make an atom bomb at the Max Planck Institute in Berlin. After the war he became director of the Max Planck Institute for Physics in Göttingen.

Heisenberg uncertainty principle If a simultaneous measurement is made of the position and momentum of a particle, there is always an uncertainty in the values obtained. The product of the uncertainties is of the same order as Planck's constant. A similar uncertainty exists with the simultaneous measurement of energy and time. The uncertainty, which is only important at subatomic levels, arises because the act of observing the system interferes with it in an unpredictable way. Named after Werner Heisenberg.

Hejaz (Name from 1981: Western Province) A province in Saudi Arabia, bordering on the Red Sea. Its coastal plain supports some agriculture; income is also derived from pilgrims to Mecca and Medina. The largest town is Jidda. Hejaz, formerly independent, joined Najd in a dual kingdom in 1926, and both became part of Saudi Arabia in 1932. Area: about 350 000 sq km (135 107 sq mi). Population (1985 est): 3 043 189.

Hel In Norse mythology, the underworld; also called Nifleheim. It is also the name of the goddess of death and ruler of the underworld.

Helen In Greek legend, the daughter of Zeus and Leda, famed for her supreme beauty. She married Menelaus, King of Sparta, but later fled to Troy with Paris, thus precipitating the Trojan War.

Helena, St (c. 248–c. 328 AD) Roman empress, mother of Constantine the Great. A Christian from 313, she made a pilgrimage to the Holy Land (c. 326), where she founded several churches and, according to tradition, rediscovered the cross used at the crucifixion. Feast day: 18 Aug. Emblem: the cross.

Helgoland (*or* Heligoland) 54 09N 7 52E A West German island in the North Sea, in the North Frisian group. Ceded to Britain in 1814, it was transferred to Germany in 1890 and was a major German naval base during both World Wars. Area: about 150 ha (380 acres).

HELICOPTER *A rescue operation.*

helicopter An aircraft that obtains both its lift and its thrust from aerofoils (rotors) rotating about a vertical axis (*compare* autogiro). The first successful helicopter was made in 1939 by Igor Sikorsky in the USA. A helicopter using a single rotor requires an anti-torque tail propeller and some models also use a vertical propeller for forward thrust. Helicopters can rise and drop vertically, hover, and move backwards, forwards, and sideways by control of the pitch of the rotors. First used in World War II, helicopters have since been developed for rescue services, police observation, and urban passenger services.

Heliopolis An ancient Egyptian city near present-day Cairo dedicated to the cult of the sun god Re. Cleopatra's Needles came from here.

Helios The Greek sun god, usually represented as a charioteer driving the sun across the sky each day. In later legends he was identified with Hyperion or Apollo.

heliotrope A herb or shrub of the genus *Heliotropium* (220 species), found in tropical and temperate regions and having heads of blue or white flowers. Many horticultural varieties of the cherry-pie plant (*H. peruvianum*) and *H. corymbosa* are used as bedding plants in cooler climates. Family: *Boraginaceae*.

helium (He) The lightest noble gas, first detected in 1868 by Janssen (1838–1904) as an unexpected line in the spectrum of the sun. The term is derived from Greek *helios*, sun. Helium was discovered on earth in 1895 in the uranium mineral, clevite, as a radioactive decay product (*see* radioactivity). It is used for filling balloons, as a gas shield in arc welding, and to replace nitrogen in the breathing mixture used by divers. Helium has the lowest melting point of any element. At no 2; at wt 4.0026; mp $-272.2°C$; bp $-268.9°C$.

helium dating A method of dating rocks, minerals, and fossils that utilizes the production of helium in the form of alpha particles during the radioactive decay of uranium-235, uranium-238, or thorium-232. The amount of helium trapped in the sample may be used to measure its age.

hell In Christian belief, the place in which the souls of the wicked are imprisoned in everlasting torment. The concept of hell as a dark and fiery pit derives from the Book of Revelation. Some Christians insist upon the physical reality of hellfire; others consider it a metaphor for the misery of being deprived forever of the vision of God. *Compare* purgatory.

hellebore A poisonous perennial herb of the genus *Helleborus* (20 species), of Europe and W Asia. The stinking hellebore (*H. foetidus*) grows to a height of 30–50 cm and bears clusters of cup-shaped purple-edged green flowers. Family: *Ranunculaceae. See also* Christmas rose.

Hellen In Greek mythology, the grandson of Prometheus and eponymous ancestor of the Greeks, who called themselves the Hellenes and their country Hellas. The four subgroups of the Hellenes, the Aeolians, Dorians, Ionians, and Achaeans, were named after his sons and grandsons.

Hellenistic age The period, between the death of Alexander the Great of Macedon (323 BC) and the accession of the Roman emperor Augustus (27 BC), when Greek culture spread throughout the Mediterranean. In the Hellenistic period Alexandria in Egypt was the major commercial city and centre of intellectual life, including scholarly literature and grandiose art, Epicureanism, Neoplatonism, Stoic philosophy, Gnosticism, and Christianity. The Koine, common Greek, was the universal language.

Hellespont. *See* Dardanelles.

Hellman, Lillian (1905–84) US dramatist. Her plays, often concerning political themes, include *The Little Foxes* (1939) and *The Searching Wind* (1944). Her

volumes of memoirs include *An Unfinished Woman* (1969), *Pentimento* (1973), and *Scoundrel Time* (1976).

Helmand, River (R. Helmund *or* R. Hilmand) The longest river in Afghanistan. Rising in the E of the country, it flows generally SW then N to enter the marshy lake of Halmun Helmand on the Afghan-Iranian border. Length: 1400 km (870 mi).

Helmholtz, Hermann Ludwig Ferdinand von (1821–94) German physicist and physiologist, who made contributions to many fields of science. In physiology his main interest was the sense organs, developing T. Young's theory of colour vision (now known as the Young-Helmholtz theory). This work was published in his *Physiological Optics* (1856). He played a considerable part in the development of thermodynamics, especially in formulating the concept of free energy.

Heloise. *See* Abelard, Peter.

Helpmann, Sir Robert (1909–86) Australian ballet dancer, choreographer, and actor. He went to England in 1933 and worked mainly with Sadler's Wells Ballet until 1950. He became artistic director of the Australian Ballet in 1955. His ballets include *Comus* (1942) and *Hamlet* (1942).

Helsingfors. *See* Helsinki.

Helsingør (*or* Elsinore) 56 03N 12 38E A seaport in Denmark, in NE Sjælland situated on the Sound opposite Hälsingborg in Sweden. It contains the fortress of Kronborg (1580), famous as the scene of Shakespeare's play *Hamlet*. Population (1987): 56 618.

Helsinki (Swedish name: Helsingfors) 60 13N 24 55E The capital of Finland, a port in the S on the Gulf of Finland. It is the country's commercial and administrative centre; industries include metals, textiles, food processing, and paper. Its famous buildings include the 18th-century cathedral; the city is also renowned for its 20th-century architecture. *History*: founded by Gustavus I Vasa of Sweden in 1550, it replaced Turku as capital of Finland (then under Russian rule) in 1812. Population (1986): 487 581.

Helvetii. *See* Switzerland, Confederation of.

Hemel Hempstead 51 46N 0 28W A market town in SE England, in Hertfordshire. Designated a new town in 1946, the principal industries include light engineering (aircraft components, scientific, electronic, and photographic equipment), paper, and pyrotechnics. Population (1981): 76 776.

Hemichordata A phylum of marine invertebrate animals (about 100 species), found in coastal sand or mud and on the sea bed. The gill slits and nervous system show similarities with those of chordates—hence their name. The group comprises the acornworms and the pterobranchs (class *Pterobranchia*).

Hemingway, Ernest (1899–1961) US novelist. After World War I he joined the American expatriate community in Paris. His first successful novel was *The Sun Also Rises* (1926). In his short stories and his later novels, including *For Whom the Bell Tolls* (1940), about the Spanish Civil War, and *The Old Man and the Sea* (1952), he celebrated the virtues of courage and stoicism in a forceful economical style. Other works include *A Farewell to Arms* (1929), *To Have and Have Not* (1937), and *Islands in the Stream* (1970). He won the Nobel Prize in 1954. Subject to severe depressions after leaving his home in Cuba in 1960, he committed suicide. See p. 338.

ERNEST HEMINGWAY *As a war correspondent (1944).*

hemiplegia. *See* paralysis.

Hemiptera An order of insects (about 50 000 species) —the true bugs—having piercing mouthparts for sucking the juices from plants or animals. The suborder *Heteroptera* includes the plant bugs and the water bugs. The forewings of these insects have both a leathery and a membranous region. The suborder *Homoptera*, including the froghoppers, aphids, cicadas, and scale insects, are all plant feeders and have uniform front wings.

hemlock 1. A poisonous biennial plant, *Conium maculatum*, native to Europe, W Asia, and N Africa. It grows in damp places to a height of 2 m and has branching purple-spotted stems that bear much divided leaves and clusters of tiny white flowers. Family: *Umbelliferae*. **2.** A coniferous tree of the genus *Tsuga* (15 species), native to S and E Asia and North America. The narrow bladelike leaves are grouped in two rows along the stems and the cones are brown and egg-shaped. Family: *Pinaceae*.

hemp An annual herb, *Cannabis sativa*, native to central Asia. It grows to a height of 5 m and bears small yellow flowers. Hemp is cultivated in many temperate regions for its fibre. The flowers, bark, twigs, and leaves contain a narcotic resin (*see* cannabis). Family: *Moraceae*.

Henbury Craters A group of 13 meteoric craters in the central Australian desert near Henbury. The three largest are believed to have been formed by explosions and the others by impact.

henequen A perennial herbaceous plant, *Agave fourcroydes*, native to Mexico and cultivated for its leaf fibres called Yucatan (or Cuban) sisal. The plant stems grow to an average height of 90 cm, each plant yielding 25 leaves annually from 5 to 16 years after planting. The fibres are made into twines used in agriculture, shipping, and rope. Family: *Agavaceae*.

Hengist and Horsa Legendary leaders of the first Anglo-Saxon settlers in Britain. According to the Anglo-Saxon Chronicle (late 9th century AD) Horsa was killed in 455 AD and his brother Hengist ruled over Kent from 455 to 488.

Henley-on-Thames 51 32N 0 56W A town in S central England, in Oxfordshire on the River Thames. It is chiefly a residential and recreational town with an annual Regatta (first held in 1839). Population (1984 est): 10 976.

henna A shrub, *Lawsonia inermis*, occurring in Egypt, India, and the Middle East. Up to 2 m high, it has fragrant white-and-yellow flowers. The leaves are powdered and used for tinting the hair a reddish colour. Family: *Lythraceae*.

henry (H) The SI unit of inductance equal to the inductance of a closed circuit such that a rate of change of current of one ampere per second produces an induced e.m.f. of one volt. Named after the US physicist Joseph Henry (1797–1878).

Henry I (1069–1135) King of England (1100–35); the youngest son of William (I) the Conqueror. Henry became king on the death of his brother William Rufus, successfully defending his throne against the claims of his eldest brother Robert II Curthose, Duke of Normandy. In England his reign is notable for important legal and administrative reforms, especially in the Exchequer. Abroad Henry waged several campaigns against Louis VI of France (1081–1137; reigned 1108–37), Fulk V, Count of Anjou (1092–1143), and Norman rebels.

Henry II (1133–89) King of England (1154–89); the son of Matilda and Geoffrey of Anjou and the grandson of Henry I. Henry succeeded Stephen. Married (1152) to Eleanor of Aquitaine, he ruled an empire that stretched from the River Tweed to the Pyrenees. In spite of frequent hostilities and his quarrel with Thomas Becket, Henry maintained control over his possessions until shortly before his death. His judicial and administrative reforms were of great constitutional importance.

Henry II (1519–59) King of France (1547–59); the husband from 1533 of Catherine de' Medici. He concluded war against the Emperor Charles V at Cateau-Cambrésis (1559). An ardent Roman Catholic, he began the systematic persecution of Huguenots, which ultimately led to the Wars of Religion.

Henry III (1207–72) King of England (1216–72), succeeding his father John. Hubert de Burgh (d. 1243) controlled the government from 1119 to 1232 and Henry's personal government began in 1234. Baronial discontent simmered, boiling over in 1258; reforms—the Provisions of Oxford—were agreed upon but then renounced by Henry. Simon de Montfort led a rebellion against the king (*see* Barons' Wars), which was defeated after initial success.

Henry III (1551–89) King of France (1574–89) during the Wars of Religion. Elected King of Poland in 1573, he abandoned that country on succeeding to the French throne. In France he allied with the Huguenot Henry of Navarre (the future Henry IV). He was assassinated while besieging Paris.

Henry IV (1366–1413) King of England (1399–1413); the eldest son of John of Gaunt. As Henry Bolingbroke, he seized the throne from Richard II. In the early years of his reign Henry faced considerable opposition from Richard's supporters and from the Welsh. Successful in defeating his enemies, the costs of these wars and resultant taxation led to protracted struggles between king and parliament for control of royal expenditure.

Henry IV (1553–1610) The first Bourbon King of France (1589–1610), who restored peace and prosperity following the Wars of Religion. A Protestant, he succeeded his mother to the throne of Navarre in 1572. Shortly afterwards he married Charles IX's sister Margaret of Valois (1553–1615) and was forced to renounce his religion. In 1576 he escaped and became a Huguenot (Protestant) leader in the Wars of Religion. His succession to the throne was secured in 1594, when he became a Roman Catholic; in 1598 he granted the Huguenots freedom of worship by the Edict of Nantes.

HENRY VIII   *An engraving (detail) by T. A. Dean done in 1824 after a painting from a cartoon by Holbein.*

Henry V (1387–1422) King of England (1413–22); the eldest son of Henry IV. He vigorously resumed the Hundred Years' War, his first campaign culminating in the battle of Agincourt (1415); by 1420, in alliance with Burgundy, he controlled much of N France. He married Catherine of Valois and gained recognition (1420) as the heir of her father Charles VI.

Henry VI (1421–71) King of England (1422–61, 1470–71), succeeding his father Henry V. He married Margaret of Anjou in 1445. His inability to govern led to bitter struggles that culminated in the Wars of the Roses. Deposed and imprisoned by the Yorkists (1461), he was briefly restored to power (1470–71). A notable patron of learning, he founded Eton College (1440) and King's College, Cambridge (1447).

Henry VII (1457–1509) King of England (1485–1509). As Henry Tudor, Earl of Richmond, he defeated Richard III at Bosworth (1485) and his marriage (1486) to Richard's niece Elizabeth of York (1465–1503) united the Houses of Lancaster and York, effectively ending the Wars of the Roses. His domestic rule was noted for its harsh financial exactions, efficient royal administration, and growing prosperity. His foreign policy temporarily put an end to war with France.

Henry VIII (1491–1547) King of England (1509–47), who initiated the English Reformation. In 1512 he joined a European alliance against France and in the same year his army thwarted a Scottish invasion at Flodden. His desire to make England a notable European power was pursued from 1515 by his Lord Chancellor, Cardinal Wolsey. From 1527 Henry was preoccupied by his wish to divorce Catherine of Aragon and marry Anne Boleyn. He blamed Catherine's failure to produce a son on the canonical prohibition against marrying one's brother's widow and sought a papal annulment. Only in 1533, after Thomas Cromwell had initiated the legislation that made the English Church, under Henry's supreme headship, independent of Rome, could the king

marry Anne. In 1536 Anne was executed for adultery; Henry then married Jane Seymour, who died shortly after giving birth to the future Edward VI (1537). His marriage to Anne of Cleves was short lived, ending in divorce; shortly afterwards Henry married Catherine Howard, who was executed in 1542, and finally, in 1543, Catherine Parr, who outlived him. Henry's last years were dominated by war with France and Scotland and his attempts to hold back the forces of Protestantism.

Henry, O. (William Sidney Porter; 1862–1910) US short-story writer. He adopted his pseudonym while serving a prison sentence for embezzlement. He subsequently worked in New York, where he published *Cabbages and Kings* (1904), the first of many volumes of short stories.

Henry the Navigator (1394–1460) Portuguese patron of explorers; the fourth son of John I. He won a military reputation at the capture of Ceuta (1415) in N Africa. Becoming governor of the Algarve (1419) he set up a school of navigation at Sagres and inspired and sponsored explorers. Under his auspices Madeira, the Azores, and the Cape Verde Islands were colonized, the W coast of Africa was explored, and many trading stations were established.

hepatitis Inflammation of the liver, most commonly caused by viruses. The two main types are infectious hepatitis, usually contracted by ingesting the virus from food or drink, and serum hepatitis, contracted mainly from dirty hypodermic needles or blood products. The patient usually has a fever, loses his appetite, and later becomes jaundiced. Hepatitis usually resolves without specific treatment.

Hepburn, Katharine (1909–) US actress. She made several films with Spencer Tracy, and her other films include *The Philadelphia Story* (1940), *The African Queen* (1952), *The Lion in Winter* (1968), and *On Golden Pond* (1981).

HEPPLEWHITE   *Designs for chairs (1789).*

Hepplewhite, George (d. 1786) British furniture designer and cabinetmaker, who established a business in London. His neoclassical furniture is a simplified and more functional version of the designs of Robert Adam, with whom he sometimes collaborated. Usually in inlaid mahogany or satinwood, it is characterized by straight tapering legs and heart- or oval-shaped chairbacks filled with openwork designs.

heptathlon An athletic competition for women, consisting of seven events over two days. They are the 100 m hurdle, high jump, shot put, 200 m sprint, long jump, javelin throw, and 800 m sprint.

Hepworth, Dame Barbara (1903–75) British sculptor. She studied in Leeds and at the Royal College of Art. A friend of Henry Moore, she was also influenced by Brancusi and Arp. Her abstract carving in wood and stone developed after *Pierced Form* (1931), creating massive shapes broken by holes with wires stretched across their openings. She received the DBE in 1965.

Hera In Greek mythology, the daughter of Cronus and Rhea and the sister and wife of Zeus. She was jealous of Zeus' mistresses but gave support to Jason and Achilles. She was worshipped as a goddess of women and marriage. She is identified with the Roman Juno.

Heracles (*or* Hercules) A Greek legendary hero, famed for his strength and courage. He was the son of Zeus and Alcmene. After killing his wife and children in a fit of madness, he performed the Twelve Labours in expiation: he killed the Nemean lion and the Hydra of Lerna, captured the Hind of Ceryneia and the Boar of Erymanthus, cleaned the Augean stables, chased away the Stymphalian birds, captured the Cretan bull and the horses of Diomedes, stole the girdle of Hippolyte, captured the oxen of Geryon, stole the apples of the Hesperides, and finally captured and bound Cerberus in Hades.

Herakleion. *See* Iráklion.

heraldry A system of pictorial devices on shields originally used to identify individuals when wearing armour. Personal devices on shields are of great antiquity but in the early 12th century armorial devices became hereditary in Europe. They were also used as seals. Coats of arms are also granted to institutions. In England heraldry is controlled by the College of Arms. The Court of the Lord Lyon has a similar function in Scotland. Coats of arms comprise the shield, a helmet surmounted by a crest, a mantling (stylized drapery behind the shield), a wreath, and a motto. The shield bears the heraldic signs (charges), which have ancient fixed meanings. From these herals can determine genealogy and status.

herbs and spices The fresh or dried parts of aromatic or pungent plants used in food, drink, medicine, and perfumery. Herbs are generally the leaves of plants growing in temperate zones. Common culinary herbs are basil, bay leaves, marjoram, mint, parsley, and thyme. Spices generally grow in hot countries; they were formerly a valuable trade commodity. Spices are usually dried and may be obtained from the root (e.g. ginger), bark (e.g. cinnamon), flower (e.g. clove), seed pod (e.g. chilli), or, most commonly, from the seed itself (e.g. coriander, cumin, pepper).

Hercegovina. *See* Bosnia and Hercegovina.

Herculaneum An ancient Italian city near Naples in Italy. It was destroyed by the same eruption as Pompeii (79 AD). Entombment beneath solidified volcanic mud makes excavation there very difficult.

Hercules. *See* Heracles.

hercules beetle A giant green and black beetle, *Dynastes herculeus*, occurring in Central and South America. The male may reach a length of 15 cm, nearly two-thirds of which is taken up by an enormous pair of horns, extending from the thorax and head. Family: *Scarabeidae* (*see* scarab beetle).

Hereford 52 04N 2 43W A city in W England, in Hereford and Worcester on the River Wye. Situated in an important agricultural area, Hereford deals mainly in agricultural produce, manufacturing cider, beer, leather goods, and chemicals. It has given its name to a famous breed of beef cattle, which are large and stocky with red coats and white faces. The cathedral, begun in 1079, contains one of the oldest maps (*Mappa Mundi*) in the world (about 1314). Population (1981): 47 652.

Hereford and Worcester A county of W England, bordering Wales. It was created in 1974 from the former counties of Herefordshire and Worcestershire. It consists chiefly of two lowland plains, separated by the Malvern Hills, with the Black Mountains in the W. The chief rivers are the Wye in the W and the Severn in the E. It is predominantly agricultural, with hop production, soft fruit and vegetables grown in the Vale of Evesham, and Hereford cattle. Industries include engineering, chemicals, and food processing. Salt is produced near Droitwich. Area: 3927 sq km (1516 sq mi). Population (1986 est): 654 500. Administrative centre: Worcester.

Herefordshire A former county of W England. Under local government reorganization in 1974 it became part of the new county of Hereford and Worcester.

Herero A group of Bantu-speaking peoples of SW Africa, Botswana, and Angola. They are traditionally cat-

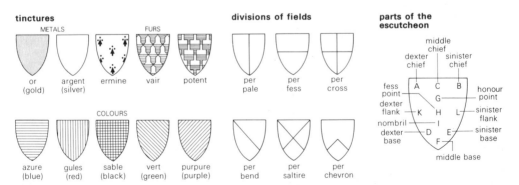

HERALDRY *The terminology of heraldry, of which a few terms are illustrated, reveals the science's French origins.*

tle, sheep, and goat herders but some adopted agriculture after European contact. Their social organization is based on the common principle of counting descent in the male line for some purposes and in the female line for others.

Hereward the Wake (11th century) Anglo-Saxon thegn, who led a raid on Peterborough Abbey (1070) as a protest against William I's appointment of a Norman abbot. He and other disaffected Anglo-Saxon nobles took refuge on the Isle of Ely until its capture by William (1071).

hermaphrodite (*or* bisexual) A plant or animal possessing both male and female reproductive organs. Such organisms may show cross- or self-fertilization: the latter method is particularly common when the opportunity of finding a mate is remote. True hermaphroditism rarely occurs in humans. More common is **pseudohermaphroditism**, in which an individual develops secondary characteristics appropriate to the opposite sex (e.g breasts in a man), due to hormone imbalance.

Hermes In Greek mythology, the messenger and herald of the gods and the guide of travellers. He was regarded as the god of riches and good luck, the protector of merchants and thieves, and the god of dreams. He was usually portrayed as an athletic youth wearing a cap and winged sandals and carrying a golden staff. He was the son of Zeus and Maia. He is identified with the Roman Mercury.

hermit crab A crab with a soft unprotected abdomen, belonging to the worldwide families *Paguridae* and *Coenobitidae*. It lives in portable hollow objects, such as snail shells, for protection. Hermit crabs are found in sandy or muddy-bottomed waters and occasionally on land and in trees. Tribe: *Anomura*.

hernia The protrusion of an organ or tissue through a weak spot in the wall that normally contains it. The most common types are the inguinal hernia (popularly called a rupture), which is a swelling in the groin caused by the protrusion of the abdominal contents, and the hiatus hernia, in which part of the stomach protrudes into the chest cavity. Hernias should usually be surgically repaired or they may become painful and cut off from their blood supply (strangulated).

Hero and Leander Legendary lovers whose story was recounted by the Greek poet Musaeus (4th or 5th century AD). Hero was a priestess of Aphrodite at Sestos and Leander swam to her each night across the Hellespont from Abydos. After a stormy night Hero found her lover's drowned body and in despair drowned herself.

Herod (I) the Great (c. 73–4 BC) King of Judaea (37–4); the son of Antipater the Idumaean (d. 43 BC). Supported by Mark Antony, he became the Romans' king in Judaea. A Jew of Arab origins, he retained power by control of the religious establishment and rigorous suppression of opposition. Shortly before his death he ordered the massacre of the infants of Bethlehem.

Herod Agrippa I (c. 10 BC–44 AD) King of Judaea (41–44); the grandson of Herod the Great. He was educated at the Roman imperial court after the execution of his father by Herod the Great. He intrigued in imperial family politics and helped Emperor Claudius to power, for which he was made King of Judaea. He was a popular ruler but persecuted Christians.

Herod Agrippa II (died c. 100 AD) King of Chalcis (50–c. 100) in S Lebanon; the son of Herod Agrippa I. He attempted to prevent the Jewish rebellion of 66, during which his troops fought on the Roman side, and helped to take Jerusalem in 70.

Herod Antipas (21 BC–39 AD) Tetrarch (governor) of Galilee (4–39 AD) after the partition of the realm of his father Herod the Great. He divorced his wife to marry his niece Herodias, for which he was censured by John the Baptist. Herodias persuaded her daughter Salome to ask for John's head in return for dancing at Antipas' birthday celebration and John was executed. Jesus Christ was brought before Antipas after his arrest, but Antipas returned him to Pontius Pilate of Judaea without passing judgment.

Herodotus (c. 484–c. 425 BC) Greek historian. Born at Halicarnassus, he was exiled for political reasons and moved to Samos. He subsequently moved to Athens and then to the Athenian colony of Thurii in S Italy, where he died. He was the first historian to subject his material to critical evaluation and research. His narrative account of the wars between Greece and Persia in nine books contained much incidental information gathered on his travels.

heroin (*or* diamorphine) A pain-killing drug with a stronger action and fewer side effects than morphine, from which it is made. Heroin is used to alleviate the suffering of terminal illness. Because the regular use of heroin readily leads to physical dependence its use in medicine has been restricted.

heron A wading bird belonging to a subfamily (*Ardeinae*; 60 species) occurring on lakes and rivers worldwide, especially in the tropics. 75–150 cm long, herons have a slim body, longish legs, broad wings, and a grey, blue, greenish, white, purple, or reddish plumage. Herons hunt by seizing fish and insects with the long pointed bill. Family: *Ardeidae* (herons and bitterns). *See also* egret.

herpes A virus that causes chickenpox, shingles, and cold sores. Herpes zoster causes chickenpox in children and shingles in adults. Herpes simplex causes cold sores. Herpes simplex II causes the sexually transmitted genital herpes, which produces painful blisters in the genital area.

Herrick, Robert (1591–1674) English poet. A friend of Jonson and other members of London literary society, he was ordained (1623) after graduating from Cambridge and served as rector of Dean Prior, Devonshire, from 1630 to 1646 and again after the Restoration. The majority of his secular and religious poems, collected in *Hesperides* (1648), are short lyrics influenced by classical models.

herring An important food fish, *Clupea harengus*, found mainly in cold waters of the N Atlantic and the North Sea. It has a slender silvery blue-green body, up to about 40 cm long, with a single short dorsal fin and swims in large shoals, feeding on plankton. A related species (*C. pallasi*) occurs in the N Pacific. Many other small silvery fish of the family *Clupeidae* are called herring. Herrings have long been fished in N Europe, where they are eaten fresh, pickled, and smoked. In the UK, smoked herring are known as kippers, and are produced mainly in Scotland. Order: *Clupeiformes*. *See also* whitebait.

herring gull A large grey and white gull, *Larus argentatus*, occurring around coasts in the N hemisphere. It is omnivorous and is commonly seen scavenging at refuse tips. Adults are 57 cm long and have pink legs and a yellow bill with a red spot on the lower mandible.

THOR HEYERDAHL *The raft used on the Kon-Tiki expedition (1947).*

Hertford 51 48N 0 05W A market town in SE England, the administrative centre of Hertfordshire on the River Lea. Industries include printing, flour milling, brewing, and brush manufacturing. Population (1981): 21 412.

Hertfordshire A county of S England, bordering on Greater London. It lies mainly in the Lower Thames Basin rising to the Chiltern Hills in the NW and is drained by the Rivers Lea, Stort, and Colne. The chief agricultural activity is arable farming, producing barley for the brewing industry. Dairy farming, market gardening, and horticulture are also important. Industries include paper and printing at Watford, and tanning. Area: 1634 sq km (632 sq mi). Population (1986 est): 985 700. Administrative centre: Hertford.

hertz (Hz) The SI unit of frequency equal to one cycle per second. Named after Heinrich Hertz.

Hertz, Heinrich Rudolf (1857–94) German physicist, who first produced and detected radio waves (1888). Maxwell's equations had predicted the existence of electromagnetic radiation over a wide spectrum of frequencies but, until Hertz's discovery, radio-frequency radiation was unknown. The unit of frequency is named after him.

Hertzog, James Barry Munnik (1866–1942) South African statesman; prime minister of the Union of South Africa (1924–39). In the second Boer War he led the Orange Free State forces. He formed the Afrikaner Nationalist Party in 1914 in opposition to Botha, becoming prime minister in 1924. In 1933 he formed a coalition government with Smuts but resigned in 1939. With Malan he then revived the Nationalist Party but retired in 1940.

Hertzsprung-Russell diagram A graphic representation of the classification of stars according to spectral type (*see* Harvard classification system) and brightness —usually absolute magnitude. The stars are not uniformly distributed. Most lie on a diagonal band, the main sequence, the brightest stars of which are spectral types O and B and the faintest are M stars. The somewhat brighter giant stars, the even brighter supergiants, and the faint white dwarfs fall into their own distinct groupings and are at later stages of evolution. The diagram was originally produced, independently, in 1911 by E. Hertzsprung (1873–1967) and in 1913 by H. N. Russell (1897–1957).

Herzl, Theodor (1860–1904) Hungarian-born journalist and playwright, who founded the movement to establish a Jewish nation (*see* Zionism). A world congress of Zionists in Basle (1897), at which the World Zionist Organization was established, elected Herzl as the first president.

Hesperides (Greek: daughters of evening) In Greek mythology, three nymphs who guarded the sacred golden apples of Hera in a garden in the far west. The apples were stolen by Heracles, with the help of Atlas, as one of his Twelve Labours.

Hess, Rudolf (1894–1987) German Nazi politician. Hess joined the Nazi Party in 1920, becoming deputy party leader (1933). After his unsuccessful secret mission to Scotland to negotiate a separate peace with Britain (1941) he was imprisoned until 1946, when he was convicted at the Nuremberg war trials and sent to Spandau prison, where he eventually committed suicide.

Hesse (German name: Hessen) A *Land* in central West Germany. Formed in 1945, it consists of the former duchies of Hesse-Darmstadt and Nassau. Hilly and forested, it is chiefly agricultural, producing potatoes, sugar beet, and wheat. Industry, concentrated in the S, includes publishing and the manufacture of machinery and chemicals. Iron ore, salt, and coal are mined. Area: 21 112 sq km (8150 sq mi). Population (1986): 5 531 300. Capital: Wiesbaden.

Hesse, Hermann (1877–1962) German novelist and poet. He worked as a bookseller until publication of his first novel, *Peter Camenzind* (1904). His early themes of art and self-knowledge were later extended by his interest in Indian mysticism and Jungian psychology, reflected in *Siddharta* (1922). His other major novels are *Steppenwolf* (1927) and *Narziss und Goldmund* (1930). After publication of his last novel, *The Glass Bead Game* (1943), he was awarded a Nobel Prize (1946). From 1911 until his death he lived in Switzerland.

Heyerdahl, Thor (1914–) Norwegian ethnologist, who led the *Kon-Tiki* expedition (1947). The *Kon-Tiki* was a balsawood raft that Heyerdahl built and sailed from the Pacific coast of South America to Polynesia to show that the pre-Incan inhabitants of Peru might thus have migrated to Polynesia. In 1969–70 he attempted to cross the Atlantic Ocean from Morocco to South America in a papyrus boat—the *Ra*; he reached Barbados, showing the possibility of Egyptian influence on the Precolumbian civilization of America.

Hiawatha The legendary chief of the Onondaga tribe of American Indians, who was said to have formed the Iroquois League. His story is the subject of Longfellow's *Song of Hiawatha* (1855).

hibernation A state of dormancy in winter experienced by many fish, amphibians, reptiles, and mammals of temperate and Arctic regions: it is an adaption to avoid death by heat loss, freezing, or food scarcity. Hibernation involves a period of sleep during which the body temperature drops almost to that of the surroundings, the body processes are slowed, and the hibernator lives on a reserve of body fat until it awakens in the spring.

HIGHLAND DRESS *Highland dancers in traditional dress.*

Hibiscus A genus of tropical and subtropical herbs, shrubs, and trees (about 150 species). Two popular cultivated shrubs, up to 3 m high, are the Chinese *H. rosa-sinensis* (rose of China), which has red, pink, or yellow flowers, and the Syrian *H. syriacus* (rose of Sharon), which has pink, blue, or white flowers. The genus also includes plants cultivated for their food value (*see* okra) and for their fibre. Family: *Malvaceae.*

Hick, Graeme (Ashley) British cricketer, born in Zimbabwe. He has played for Zimbabwe (1983–84) and Worcestershire (1984–) and in 1986 became the youngest player to score 2000 runs in a season. In 1988 he achieved the second highest score (405 not out) ever made in England.

hickory A tree of the genus *Carya* (20 species), native to E North America and Asia and cultivated for timber, nuts, and ornament. They grow to 30 m and have compound leaves consisting of paired leaflets. Commercially important species are the shagbark (*C. ovata*) and the pecan (*C. illinoensis*). Family: *Juglandaceae.*

eye	to fly	old age

HIEROGLYPHICS *A picture was used to represent objects, related ideas, and sounds.*

hieroglyphics Originally, an Egyptian system of picture writing in use from about 3000 BC to 300 AD; the term now denotes any pictographic or ideographic writing system. The Egyptians used hieroglyphics largely for monumental inscriptions. The characters are careful reproductions of people, animals, and objects and represent either the objects they portray or the sounds that are featured in the pronunciation of the referent.

hi-fi. *See* high-fidelity sound systems.

Higgins, Alex (1949–) Northern Irish snooker player, known as "Hurricane" Higgins. He won the world professional championship in 1972 and 1982.

high-fidelity sound systems (*or* hi-fi) Systems of recording and reproducing sound in which the quality of the reproduced sound is as close as possible to that of the original source. A typical reproducing system consists of a record player or cassette player, a stereophonic amplifier, and two loudspeakers. To achieve true high fidelity, total distortion in such a system must be less than 2%, the frequency response must be constant between 20 and 20 000 hertz, and the system must be able to reproduce stereophonic or quadraphonic recordings.

high jump A field event in athletics in which jumpers compete to clear a horizontal bar. A competitor is allowed three attempts at a height and is eliminated if he fails to clear it. World records: men: 2.44 m (1989) by Javier Sotomayor (Cuba); women 2.09 m (1987) by Stefka Kostadinova (Bulgaria).

Highland dress The traditional male costume (since the 17th century) of the Scottish Highlands. It consists of the kilt (a wrapover skirt pleated at the back) and the plaid (a cloak worn over one shoulder). Accessories include the sporran (a goatskin pouch), cap, kilt pin, and dagger (worn in the right sock). Highland dress was banned for civilian wear (1746–82) following the Jacobite rebellions. **Tartan,** the material used for the kilt and plaid, is a woollen cloth woven into a design of large-meshed cross stripes. The tradition of each clan having its own tartan probably dates from the 17th century.

Highland Games Scottish athletics meetings, usually professional, held in the Highlands. Events include standard track and field events as well as such Scottish sports as caber tossing, and there are also competitions in highland dancing and playing the bagpipes. The Braemar Games can be traced back to the 8th century AD.

Highland Region An administrative region in N Scotland, created in 1975 from the N part of Argyll, Caithness, Inverness, Nairn, Ross and Cromarty, and Sutherland. The region consists chiefly of glaciated highlands divided from NE to SW by the fault valley, Great Glen, and includes part of the Inner Hebrides. Sheep farming is the main agricultural activity. Industries associated with North Sea oil have developed and aluminium smelting, pulp and paper production, and distilling are all important. Tourism is a major source of revenue. Area: 25 425 sq km (9814 sq mi). Population (1986 est): 200 764. Administrative centre: Inverness.

High Wycombe 51 38N 0 46W A town in SE England, in Buckinghamshire. It has a long tradition of furniture making and also produces paper, precision instruments, and clothing. Hughenden Manor was the home of Disraeli. Population (1981): 60 516.

Hildebrand. *See* Gregory VII, St.

Hildesheim 52 09N 9 58E A city in NE West Germany, in Lower Saxony. The 11th-century cathedral survived World War II. Roman silver plate was found nearby in 1868. Its manufactures include machinery, textiles, and carpets. Population (1986): 100 700.

Hillary, Sir Edmund (Percival) (1919–) New Zealand mountaineer and explorer. In 1953 he and Tenzing Norgay were the first to reach the summit of Mount Everest, for which achievement he was knighted. He was New Zealand High Commissioner in Delhi (1984–89).

Hilliard, Nicholas (1547–1619) English portrait miniaturist, born in Exeter. Like his father, he trained as

HILLIARD *Miniature of* Unknown Man Against a Background of Flames.

a jeweller, later becoming court painter to Elizabeth I and James I. Many of his portraits are in the royal collection at Windsor Castle. In his *Treatise on the Art of Limning* (c. 1600), he describes his style and technique of painting miniatures. *Unknown Man Against a Background of Flames* (Victoria and Albert Museum, London) is typical of his best work.

Hilton, James (1900–54) British novelist. His two most popular novels are *Lost Horizon* (1933), set in the Tibetan monastery of Shangri-La, and *Goodbye, Mr Chips* (1934). From 1935 he worked as a scriptwriter in Hollywood.

Himachal Pradesh A state in NW India, in the W Himalayas beside Tibet's border. Long part of the Punjab, it was formed by the combination of various hill states (1948). Most of the inhabitants are Pahari-speaking Hindus who farm grains, potatoes, maize, and livestock. The forests yield timber and bamboo. Area: 55 673 sq km (21 490 sq mi). Population (1981): 4 237 569. Capital: Simla.

Himalayas A vast mountain system, the highest in the world, structurally the southern edge of the great plateau of central Asia. They extend about 2400 km (1550 mi) along the N Indian border, reaching 8848 m (29 028 ft) at Mount Everest. The region is disputed by China, India, and Pakistan.

Himmler, Heinrich (1900–45) German Nazi politician, infamous for his direction of the SS. He joined the Nazi Party in 1925 and became head of the SS in 1929. From 1936 he also directed the Gestapo and supervised the extermination of Jews in E Europe. After the Nazi collapse he was captured and committed suicide.

Hindemith, Paul (1895–1963) German composer and viola player. He studied in Frankfurt am Main, where he led the opera orchestra (1915–23). His music was banned by the Nazis in 1933; he moved to Turkey and in 1939 went to the USA. His early works were highly dissonant; he later evolved his own system of tonal harmony. Many of his compositions are neoclassical in character (*see* neoclassicism); they include the opera *Cardillac* (1926), the ballet *Nobilissima Visione* (1938), many concertos, instrumental sonatas, and much *Gebrauchsmusik* (German: utility music).

Hindenburg, Paul von Beneckendorff und von (1847–1934) German general, who was recalled from retirement at the outbreak of World War I and with Erich Ludendorff (1865–1937) won a great victory at Tannenberg (1914). In 1916 Hindenburg became commander in chief and directed the German retreat to the **Hindenburg line** (fortified defence on the Western Front). He became president of Germany in 1925 and was re-elected in 1932.

Hindi The national language of India and the most widely spoken, having approximately 134 million speakers. It is an Indo-Aryan language, showing strong Sanskrit influence in its written form but with a much simpler grammar. The standard form, written in Devanagari script, is based on the Khari Boli dialect of Delhi.

Hinduism The religious beliefs and institutions of about 400 million inhabitants of India and parts of neighbouring countries. The complex result of about 5000 years of continuous cultural development, it includes a number of extremely diverse traditional beliefs and practices and has influenced and been influenced by younger religions, including Buddhism, Jainism, Christianity, Islam, and Sikhism. One of its central concepts is that the necessary result of one's actions in life leads to reincarnation at a higher or lower level of life (*see* karma). The goal of the religion is to find a release from the cycle of rebirth and to return to the ultimate unchanging reality, Brahman. Release may be sought through good works, devotion to a particular god, such as the popular deity Krishna, or through various types of meditation and asceticism (e.g. samadhi, yoga). The principle gods are Brahma, Vishnu, and Shiva, together known as the Trimurti. Popular devotion consists mainly of temple worship and the celebration of numerous festivals. The great Hindu texts, the *Mahabharata* and the *Ramayana*, were composed in the 4th century BC. *See also* Vedanta.

Hindustani An Indo-Aryan language that originated in the dialect of the Delhi district. The Moguls and the British promoted its use as a lingua franca throughout India. Urdu and Hindi are the literary forms developed from it.

hip The part of the body where the legs are joined to the trunk. The skeleton of the hip consists of the pelvis and the part of the spine (the sacrum) to which it is attached. The hip joint—the articulation between the pelvis and femur (thigh bone)—is a common site for arthritis: in severe cases the whole joint may be replaced by an artificial one or pins or other devices may be inserted into the damaged parts.

Hipparchus (c. 190–c. 120 BC) Greek astronomer, born in Nicaea. He produced the first accurate map of over 1000 stars, indicating their positions by means of latitude and longitude. He also discovered the precession of the equinoxes and accurately measured the distance to the moon by parallax. In mathematics he invented trigonometry by constructing a table of the ratios of the sides of right-angle triangles.

Hippocrates (c. 460–c. 377 BC) Greek physician and founder of the Hippocratic school of medicine, which greatly influenced medical science until the 18th century. Hippocrates seems to have been a prominent physician, who travelled widely in Greece and Asia Minor. His followers believed that health was governed by the balance of four body fluids, or humours: phlegm, blood, black bile, and yellow bile. The Hippocratic Oath, taken by medical students, was probably not written by Hippocrates.

hippopotamus A large hoofed mammal, *Hippopotamus amphibius*, of tropical Africa. About 150 cm high at the shoulder and weighing around 3.5 tonnes, hippos have virtually naked dark-brown skin and continuously growing tusks up to 60 cm long. They spend the day in rivers or waterholes, emerging at night to graze on surrounding pasture. Herds usually number 10–15 individuals. Family: *Hippopotamidae*. *See also* pygmy hippopotamus.

Hirohito (1901–89) Emperor of Japan (1926–89), having previously been regent for five years after his father Yoshihito (1879–1926) had been declared insane. He married (1924) Princess Nagako Kuai. Ruling as divine emperor until Japan's defeat in World War II, he became no more than a constitutional monarch under the 1946 constitution. He also wrote several books on marine biology.

HIROSHIMA *The Peace Memorial Park commemorating the destruction of the city.*

Hiroshima 34 23N 132 27E A city in Japan, in SW Honshu on the delta of the River Ota. A former military base and important seaport, it was largely destroyed (6 August, 1945) by the first atomic bomb to be used in warfare; over 130 000 people were killed or injured. Many leading architects helped design the rapid rebuilding of the city and it is now a major industrial centre. An international conference is held here annually to oppose nuclear weapons. Population (1985): 1 044 000.

Hispaniola The second largest West Indian island, in the Greater Antilles. It is politically divided between the Dominican Republic and the Republic of Haiti. Area: 18 703 sq km (29 418 sq mi).

histamine An amine, derived from the amino acid histidine, that is released from body tissues after injury or in an allergic reaction, such as asthma or hay fever. It dilates blood vessels, producing inflammation; contracts smooth muscle, which in the lungs leads to breathing difficulties; and stimulates the secretion of gastric juice. Its effects can be counteracted with antihistamine drugs.

histology The study of tissues. Originally histology was limited to the study of tissues by light microscopy, but the development of such techniques as electron microscopy, immunofluorescence, and autoradiography

has enabled the details of subcellular structure to be revealed. *See also* cytology.

history The story of the past. The student of history discovers, examines, and interprets the records of past human societies. Records of events are found in the inscriptions of the ancient Egyptians but history as a literary activity is generally regarded as beginning with the ancient Greeks, among whom Herodotus, Thucydides, and Xenophon were outstanding. Notable Roman historians include Sallust, Cicero, Livy, and Tacitus. Early Christian history writing (historiography) was influenced by Jewish historians, such as Josephus (c. 38–c. 100). Medieval historiography consisted largely of chronicles, such as those of Bede, Matthew Paris, and Jean Froissart (1337–c. 1400); the later middle ages were influenced by Byzantine historians, including Anna Comnena (1083–?1148). The classical interests of early Renaissance scholars (*see* humanism) led to a new concern for textual criticism, which led to the outstanding work of Machiavelli and Francesco Guicciardini (1483–1540) in the early 16th century. Their critical approach to sources was continued by 17th-century historians but the 18th-century Enlightenment enlarged the interests of historians to include a more fundamental study of the pattern of change in human societies. This concern is reflected in the work of the 18th-century British historian Edward Gibbon. In the 19th century, under the influence of such German historians as Leopold von Ranke (1795–1886) and Theodor Mommsen (1817–1903), history was established as an academic discipline in the universities. Outstanding British historians of the 19th century included William Stubbs, Macaulay, and Carlyle. The scope of historiography has greatly widened in the 20th century under the influence of sociology, anthropology, and psychiatry, and new techniques, such as the use of computers to analyse statistics, have been introduced.

Hitchcock, Sir Alfred (1899–1980) British film director. He worked almost exclusively in Hollywood from 1940. He specialized in sophisticated thrillers, using calculated cinematic effects to create an atmosphere of tension and suspense. His films include *Notorious* (1946), *Strangers on a Train* (1951), *Psycho* (1960), and *The Birds* (1963).

Hitler, Adolf (1889–1945) German dictator. Born in Austria, he won the Iron Cross in World War I. In 1919 he joined the German Workers' Party, which was renamed the National Socialist (abbreviated to Nazi) Party in 1920. He became its president in 1921 and two years later staged an abortive coup–the Munich Putsch –against the Bavarian Government. During a brief imprisonment he wrote most of *Mein Kampf* (*My Struggle*), setting out his political philosophy, based on a notion of the innate superiority of the Aryan race, the culpability of the Jews for Germany's defeat in World War I, and a violent anticommunism. In the economic crisis of the late 1920s and early 1930s Hitler's powers of oratory and his propaganda machine brought the Nazis increasing support. In 1933 Hitler was offered the chancellorship by Hindenburg, the German president. He gained a majority in the subsequent elections (in coalition with the Nationalists); following Hindenburg's death in 1934 he assumed the title of Führer (leader). He proceeded to crush his opponents, institute his fanatical persecution of the Jews by the establishment of concentration camps, and launch a massive rearmament programme.

He lent support to Mussolini in Italy and Franco in Spain, precipitating World War II by invading Austria (1938) and Czechoslovakia and Poland (1939). As his dreams of world domination collapsed with the Third Reich in the face of Allied victory, he committed suicide with Eva Braun (whom he had married shortly before) in the bunker of the chancellory in Berlin.

Hittites An Indo-European people who appeared in Anatolia around the beginnning of the second millennium BC. By 1340 BC they had emerged as a major power, conquering much of Anatolia and also Syria. In their polytheistic religion, their king was believed to be the representative of god on earth and became a god himself on death. The society was feudal in organization and also upheld the institution of slavery. Their language is extinct, but is known from cuneiform tablets and inscriptions.

hives. *See* urticaria.

HMSO. *See* Stationery Office, Her Majesty's.

hoatzin A primitive bird, *Opisthocomus hoazin*, that occurs in tropical South American swamps. It is 65 cm long and has a small head with a wispy crest and a long tail. Its plumage is streaked brown with yellowish underparts and it feeds chiefly on flowers and fruit. It is the only member of its family (*Opisthocomidae*). Order: *Galliformes* (pheasants, turkeys, etc.).

Hobart 42 54S 147 18E A city in Australia, the capital and chief port of Tasmania on the Derwent River estuary. Industries include zinc refining and food processing; the chief exports are apples, wool, timber, and dairy produce. The University of Tasmania was established here in 1890. Population (1986): 175 082.

Hobbes, Thomas (1588–1679) English political philosopher. Hobbes was a vigorous proponent of scientific materialism, particularly with regard to human nature. His interests lay in mathematics, geography, and the classics until the breakdown of English political and social order in the 1640s inspired him to devise his own political theory. *Leviathan* (1651) argues that because people are inherently selfish they need to be ruled by an absolute sovereign, whose function is to enforce public order.

Hobbs, Jack (Sir John Berry H.; 1882–1963) British cricketer. The world's greatest batsman between Grace and Bradman, he played for Surrey and for England in 61 Test matches. During his career (1905–34) he scored 61 237 runs and 197 centuries (98 made after the age of 40). He was the first cricketer to be knighted (1953).

Ho Chi Minh (Nguyen That Thanh; 1890–1969) Vietnamese statesman, who led Vietnam in its struggle for independence from the French. As a young man he lived in France (1917–23), where in 1920 he joined the French Communist Party. In 1924 he went to communist-controlled Canton, where he formed the Association of Young Vietnamese Revolutionaries (Thanh Nien), the forerunner of the Indochinese Communist Party (1930). Returning to Vietnam in 1941, he formed the Viet Minh, which waged the long and ultimately victorious colonial war against the French (1945–54; *see* Indochina). According to the Geneva Accords, which Ho Chi Minh attended, Vietnam was divided on either side of the 17th parallel into North Vietnam, of which Ho became president, and South Vietnam. In 1959 he extended support to the Viet Cong guerrilla movement in the South (*see also* Vietnam War) with the aim of Vietnamese unification, achieved after his death.

Ho Chi Minh City (name until 1976: Saigon) 10 46N 106 43E A city in S Vietnam, on the River Saigon. It is the major commercial and industrial centre of the S, with shipbuilding, metalworking, textile, and chemical industries. *History*: an ancient Khmer town, it was the capital of Cochinchina and then of French Indochina (1887–1902). During the Vietnam War it was the capital of South Vietnam. Population (1985): 3 500 000.

HOCKEY *The dimensions of the pitch.*

hockey An 11-a-side field game for men and women, the object of which is to score goals. It has been played in various forms for at least 4000 years. A team comprises a goalkeeper, two full-backs, three half-backs, and five forwards, each of whom carries a curved stick for hitting the ball. Play is started with a bully-off, in which two opposing players cross their sticks and tap the ground three times, and proceeds by players dribbling the ball with the stick and hitting it along the ground or through the air. *See also* ice hockey.

Hockney, David (1937–) British painter, printmaker, and draughtsman, born in Bradford. After studying at the Royal College of Art (1959–62), he travelled widely in the USA, where he developed his realistic but witty style, his favourite subjects being figure studies and aquatic themes. He has also designed stage sets and illustrated books.

Hoffman, Dustin (1937–) US film actor. He made his reputation in the films *The Graduate* (1967) and *Midnight Cowboy* (1969). He won Oscars for his performances in *Kramer vs Kramer* (1980) and *Rain Man* (1989). His other films include *Lenny* (1974) and *Tootsie* (1983).

Hogarth, William (1697–1764) British painter and engraver. He established his reputation with the paintings and engravings of *A Harlot's Progress* (1731–32). He excelled in moralizing social satires in such narrative

WILLIAM HOGARTH *Portrait attributed to J. A. Rouquet (National Portrait Gallery, London).*

series as *A Rake's Progress, Industry and Idleness, Gin Lane,* and the paintings of *Marriage à la Mode* (Tate Gallery), works that led him to campaign for an Engraving Copyright Act (the so-called Hogarth's Act, 1734). The naturalism and vivacity of *Captain Coram* (Foundling Hospital, London) and *Hogarth's Servants* (National Gallery, London) were influential. His artistic theories are expressed in his treatise *The Analysis of Beauty* (1753).

Hogg, Quintin. *See* Hailsham, Quintin McGarel Hogg, Baron.

hogweed A biennial herb, *Heracleum sphondylium,* also called cow parsnip, native to Eurasia and N Africa and introduced to North America. Up to 2 m high, it has hollow ridged stems, divided leaves, and umbrella-like clusters of white or pinkish flowers. The giant hogweed (*H. mantegazzianum*) may reach a height of 3.5 m and is grown as an ornamental. Family: *Umbelliferae.*

Hokkaido (former name: Yezo) The second largest and northernmost of the four main islands of Japan, separated from Honshu by the Tsugaru Strait and from the Soviet island of Sakhalin by La Perouse Strait. Mountainous, volcanic, and forested, with a relatively cool climate, it is popular for winter sports. It has a sizable aboriginal population and the N is largely uninhabited. Main industries are coalmining, agriculture, and fishing. *History:* the Japanese began to settle on the island in the 16th century but did not develop it seriously until after 1868. It became administratively autonomous in 1885. Area: 78 508 sq km (30 312 sq mi). Population (1985): 5 679 000. Capital: Sapporo.

Holbein the Younger, Hans (c. 1497–1543) German painter, born in Augsburg. In 1515 he settled in Basle, where he designed woodcuts of the *Dance of Death.* Settling in England in 1532, he painted portraits of merchants before becoming court painter and designer to Henry VIII (1536). His portrait of Henry VIII in a wall painting (destroyed) for Whitehall Palace became the prototype for other paintings of the king. He was also commissioned to paint Henry's prospective wives, *Christina, Duchess of Milan* (National Gallery, London) and *Anne of Cleves* (Louvre) and established a thriving portrait-painting business, e.g. *The Ambassadors* (Na-

tional Gallery, London). His father **Hans Holbein the Elder** (c. 1465–1524) was also a painter; he painted the *S Sebastian Altar* (Alte Pinakothek, Munich).

hole. *See* semiconductor.

Holiday, Billie (Eleanor Gough McKay; 1915–59) US Black jazz singer, known as "Lady Day." She was discovered in Harlem by Benny Goodman and made her first recording in 1933. She subsequently sang with the bands of Count Basie and Artie Shaw. Addiction to heroin caused her death.

holistic medicine An approach to therapy in which all the physical, mental, and social aspects of the patient's life are taken into account in understanding and curing his disease, as opposed to merely treating his symptoms. A basic tenet of—and often used as a synonym for—alternative medicine, the principle is gaining acceptance among orthodox practitioners.

Holland The low-lying NW region of the Netherlands, now comprising the provinces of North Holland and South Holland. A county of the Holy Roman Empire from the 12th century, Holland came under Burgundy in the 15th century and then (1500) under the Habsburgs. Prominent in the 16th-century Revolt of the Netherlands against Spanish Habsburg rule, Holland became the chief province of the independent United Provinces of the Netherlands. When the kingdom of the Netherlands was established in 1814, its importance diminished. Nevertheless the whole country is still commonly called Holland.

holly A tree or shrub of the widely distributed genus *Ilex* (300 species). The evergreen English holly (*I. aquifolium*) grows to a height of 15 m and has spiny lustrous dark-green leaves and small white flowers; the female flowers develop into red berries. It is widely cultivated for hedging and used for Christmas decorations. Family: *Aquifoliaceae. See also* maté.

Holly, Buddy (Charles Hardin Holley; 1936–59) US rock and roll singer and guitarist. With The Crickets, he recorded such songs as "That'll Be The Day" (1957) and "Peggy Sue" (1957); he died in an air crash.

hollyhock A perennial herb, *Althaea rosea,* native to China but widely cultivated. Up to 3 m high, it bears large white, yellow, or red flowers. Family: *Malvaceae.*

Hollywood 34 00N 118 15W A NW suburb of Los Angeles, in California in the USA. Founded in the 1880s, it is the centre of the US film industry.

holmium (Ho) A metallic lanthanide element, discovered in 1879 by P. T. Cleve (1840–1905) and named after his native city, Stockholm. Holmium occurs in rare-earth minerals, such as monazite ($CePO_4$). It forms an oxide (Ho_2O_3) and halides (HoX_3), but has few uses. At no 67; at wt 164.9304; mp 1474°C; bp 2695°C.

holocaust The extermination of European Jews by the Nazis (1939–45). Some six million Jews from many countries, two-thirds of European Jewry, were killed in Auschwitz and other concentration camps.

Holocene epoch The present, or Recent, epoch in geological time, including the last 10 000 years from the end of the Pleistocene. It is sometimes called the Postglacial, although some authorities consider it to be only an interglacial phase of the Pleistocene. At the beginning of the Holocene the general rise in sea level resulting from melting ice isolated Britain from the rest of Europe.

holography A method of producing a stereoscopic image without using a camera. A monochromatic beam of coherent radiation from a laser is split into two using a

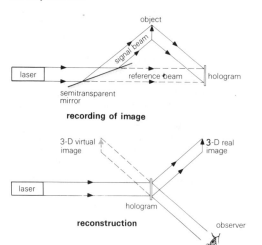

recording of image

reconstruction

HOLOGRAPHY *A three-dimensional image formed by two beams of light is recorded as an interference pattern on a single plate. The two images, giving a 3-D effect, are reconstructed by shining a similar beam through the hologram.*

semitransparent mirror; one beam falls directly onto a photographic film or plate and the other is reflected by the subject onto the film. The two beams form interference patterns on the film, which is called a hologram. To reconstruct the image, light of the same wavelength from a laser is shone onto the hologram. The interference pattern on the hologram diffracts the beam and splits it into two parts. One part gives a real two-dimensional image and the other a virtual three-dimensional image.

Holst, Gustav (Theodore) (1874–1934) British composer and teacher. Having studied composition at the Royal College of Music, he taught at the Royal College of Music, Morley College, and St Paul's Girls' School, for whose string orchestra he wrote the *St Paul's Suite* (1913). His interest in oriental philosophy inspired the chamber opera *Savitri* (1908) and other works. Among his most famous compositions are the choral work *The Hymn of Jesus* (1917), the tone poem *Egdon Heath* (1927), and the orchestral suite *The Planets* (1914–16).

Holy Grail In medieval legend and romance, a vessel or dish having supernatural power. Originally the grail may have had some significance in pre-Christian Celtic mythology; but by the 12th century it was associated with the chalice used by Christ at the Last Supper and later given to Joseph of Arimathea, who received the blood of Christ in it at the crucifixion. Chrétien de Troyes combined the grail legend with the Arthurian legend, and the knightly quest for the Holy Grail is a dominant theme in many Arthurian romances. According to a passage in William of Malmesbury (c. 1090–c. 1143), Joseph brought the Holy Grail to Glastonbury.

Holyhead 53 20N 4 38W A port and resort in North Wales in Anglesey, Gwynedd, on Holy Island. It has steamer services to Dun Laoghaire in the Republic of Ireland. Population (1981): 10 467.

Holy Island (*or* Lindisfarne) 55 41N 1 48W An island, in NE England off the NE coast of Northumberland. Its monastery was founded by St Aidan (635 AD); St Cuthbert was a bishop here (685–87).

holy orders In Christian Churches, specifically those accepting episcopacy, the ranks of bishop, priest, etc., conferred by a bishop. They are traditionally divided into major and minor orders, the former being the ranks of bishop, priest, deacon, and (in the Roman Church) subdeacon. Holy orders are considered a sacrament by the Orthodox and Roman Catholic Churches.

Holy Roman Empire The successor to the western Roman Empire of antiquity. The institution dates from 800, when Charlemagne was crowned emperor of the West by Pope Leo III. Its territory came to comprise much of W and central Europe, being centred on Germany and Austria and including areas of E France and N Italy. After the failure of Charlemagne's Carolingian dynasty the imperial title passed (962) to the German kings, who retained it until the Empire's abolition in 1806. Between the 11th and 13th centuries the emperors vied with the popes for dominance in Europe (*see* Guelfs and Ghibellines), a conflict from which the Empire emerged much weakened. It was further undermined by the Protestant Reformation in the 16th century, the Thirty Years' War in the 17th century, and the rise of Prussia and was finally broken by Napoleon's conquest of imperial territories in the early 19th century.

Holyrood House A palace in Edinburgh, which is the Scottish residence of the British monarch. A medieval building, it was substantially modified in the classical style from 1671 onwards by Sir William Bruce (d. 1710).

Holy Spirit (*or* Holy Ghost) In Christian theology, the third person of the Trinity, coequal and of one substance with the Father and the Son. Old Testament references to the spirit of God are given a more specific application in the New Testament Gospels; in St John's Gospel the Holy Spirit is seen as the "Paraclete" or Comforter; in Acts, the descent of the Holy Spirit upon the Apostles is described. In art, the Holy Spirit is usually symbolized by a dove.

Home of the Hirsel, Alec Douglas-Home, Baron (Alexander Frederick D.-H.; 1903–) British statesman; Conservative prime minister (1963–64). He was an MP (1931–45, 1950–51) before becoming the 14th Earl of Home. He was foreign secretary (1960–63) and then succeeded Macmillan as prime minister, renouncing his peerages. Following the Conservative electoral defeat (1964) he resigned the party leadership (1965). He received a life peerage in 1974.

homeopathy The system of treating illness developed by Samuel Hahnemann at the end of the 18th century and based on the principle of "like cures like." To treat a particular disease homeopathists prescribe small doses of a drug that in larger quantities would cause the symptoms of the disease in a healthy person.

Homer (8th century BC) Greek epic poet, presumed author of the *Iliad* and *Odyssey*. He is believed to have lived in Ionia in Asia Minor and according to legend was blind. The *Iliad* concerns the Trojan War, and its basic tragic theme is enlivened by the variety and human sympathy of its individual episodes. The *Odyssey* relates the various adventures of Odysseus during his voyage home from the Trojan War to his kingdom of Ithaca. Both poems have had a profound influence on western culture.

Home Rule An Irish political movement to repeal the Act of Union with Britain and give Ireland a legislature responsible for domestic affairs. Founded in 1870, the

Home Rule movement achieved parliamentary prominence under the leadership of Parnell from 1880. The Home Rule bills of 1886 and 1893 were defeated; in 1914 the third Home Rule bill was passed but suspended for the duration of the war. A modified act was passed in 1920 providing separate parliaments for northern and southern Ireland. This was accepted by the north but rejected by the south, which in 1922 gained dominion status as the Irish Free State.

homing instinct. *See* migration, animal.

hominid A member of the *Hominidae* family of primates, to which man belongs. Besides man, there are no surviving hominids: the others are known only from fossil remains. The *Hominidae* include the genera *Ramapithecus*, *Australopithecus*, and *Homo*.

Homo A genus of *hominids characterized by a large cranial capacity, erect posture, bipedal gait, a thumb capable of a precision grip, and the ability to make and use tools. The genus includes the species *Homo* (or *Pithecanthropus*) *erectus*, which may have been ancestral to modern man. This species first appeared more than one million years ago. *Neanderthal man also belongs to the genus *Homo*, as does *Cro-Magnon man, who was probably an early form of the species *Homo sapiens* (modern man). *See also* Australopithecus. See p. 350.

homosexuality Sexual attraction or relations between persons of the same sex. It is known as lesbianism when the persons involved are females. Homosexuality is an ancient and widespread phenomenon; related phenomena are bisexuality (when an individual is attracted by people of both sexes), transsexuality, and transvestism. Many European countries have in recent years liberalized their laws concerning homosexuality.

Honduras, Republic of A country in Central America, with a N coastline on the Caribbean Sea and a short S one on the Pacific Ocean. Narrow coastal plains rise to mountainous country, dissected by river valleys. The majority of the population is of mixed Indian and Spanish descent. *Economy*: mainly agricultural, the chief crops are bananas and coffee (the principal exports). Almost half the land is forested, with valuable hardwoods and pine. Fishing is important, especially shrimps for export. The considerable mineral resources include gold, silver, lead, tin and zinc, and mercury. *History*: the area was a centre of Mayan culture from the 4th to the 9th centuries AD and was later occupied by the Lenca Indians. Discovered by Columbus in 1502, it became part of the Spanish captaincy general of Guatemala. It gained independence from Spain in 1821 and then formed part of the Central American Federation (1823–38). Honduras has suffered much internal unrest as well as a long conflict with Guatemala and, more recently, with El Salvador. In 1972 Gen Oswaldo López (1921–) seized power in a bloodless coup but was overthrown in 1975. Military rule continued under Col Juan Melgar Castro (1931–), who was deposed (1978) by a military junta headed by Gen Paz García (1932–). Military rule was ended in 1982 when Dr Roberto Suazo Córdova took office; he was succeeded as president in 1986 by José Azcona Hoya. Official language: Spanish. Official currency: lempira of 100 centavos. Area: 112 088 sq km (43 227 sq mi). Population (1986 est): 4 300 000. Capital: Tegucigalpa.

Honegger, Arthur (1892–1955) French composer, born in Switzerland. He was a pupil of Widor and d'Indy and one of Les Six. He developed his own polyphonic and dissonant style. His compositions include five symphonies, the stage works *King David* (1921) and *Joan of Arc at the Stake* (1934–35), chamber music, and piano music.

honesty A herbaceous plant of the European genus *Lunaria* (3 species). Up to 1 m high, it is often grown in gardens for its papery seed heads. *L. annua* has white to purple flowers while *L. variegata* has crimson flowers and variegated foliage. Family: *Cruciferae*.

honey A sweet thick yellow syrup collected from the honeycomb of bee hives. Bees suck nectar from flowers and empty it into the cells of their hives, where they convert the sugar it contains from sucrose into dextrose and laevulose. Honey consists of about 70% sugars, 18% water, and small amounts of minerals, pollen, and wax.

honey badger. *See* ratel.

honeybee A social bee, *Apis mellifera*, also called hive bee. Native to Europe, it is reared worldwide for its honey and beeswax. Honeybees have large colonies with 50 000–80 000 workers during the summer and a well-defined caste system. Workers attend to nest building, food gathering, and brood care; they use dances to communicate the location of food sources to other colony members. The queen lays her eggs in wax chambers (cells). Larvae hatching from fertilized eggs and fed on protein-rich "royal jelly" throughout their development become queens. New colonies are formed by a swarm of workers led by the old queen (*compare* bumblebee); a young queen continues the established colony. Family: *Apidae*.

honeyeater An arboreal songbird belonging to a family (*Meliphagidae*; 160 species) occurring chiefly in SE Asia and Australasia. They are 10 to 35 cm long and have a drab plumage with wattles or naked patches on the face. The slender bill is down-curved and the long extensible tongue has a central trough, through which nectar is drunk, and a brushlike tip for collecting pollen and small insects.

honeysuckle A shrub or twining plant of the genus *Lonicera* (100 species). The common European honeysuckle (*L. periclymenum*), also called woodbine, is a trailing shrub with clusters of tubular yellowish flowers. Some species are cultivated as ornamentals, including the fragrant climbing honeysuckle (*L. japonica*). Family: *Caprifoliaceae*.

Hong Kong A British crown colony lying off the S coast of China. It consists of the island of Hong Kong, the mainland peninsula of Jiulong, the New Territories, and Stonecutters Island. Much of the land is steep and barren. The majority of the population is Chinese. *Economy*: owing to its strategic position and fine natural harbour, it is an important entrepôt port and banking centre. Much of China's foreign trade passes through Hong Kong. The export of manufactured goods has become increasingly important since World War II and the textile and clothing industry accounts for over half the total domestic exports. Electronics and plastics are also important and there is some heavy industry. *History*: the island was ceded to Britain by China at the end of the first Opium War (1842) and Kowloon was added in 1860. In 1898 the New Territories were granted on a 99-year lease. Hong Kong was occupied by the Japanese during World War II. The return of the colony to Chinese control in 1997 was agreed between Britain and China in 1984. Recent years have seen a big influx of refugees from Vietnam (boat people) and the first forci-

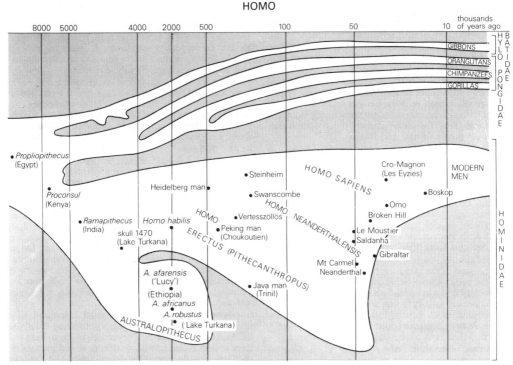

HOMO

evolution of Homo sapiens *The picture of man's evolution is constantly changing as new fossil evidence comes to light. The fossil* Propliopithecus *represents the apparent divergence of the gibbons (Hylobatidae), great apes (Pongidae), and humans (Hominidae) from the monkeys, but palaentologists are still debating many of the other classifications and relationships shown on this chart.*

sites of important discoveries of fossil Hominidae

HONG KONG

ble repatriations. Official language: English; Cantonese is widely spoken. Official currency: Hong Kong dollar of 100 cents. Area: 1031 sq km (398 sq mi). Population (1987): 5 550 000. Capital and main port: Victoria.

Honolulu 21 19N 157 50W A city in the USA, the capital of Hawaii on SE Oahu in the central Pacific Ocean. It is the site of three universities and of Iolani Palace, the former royal residence. Pearl Harbor is still an important naval base. Population (1986): 372 330.

Honshu The largest of the four main islands of Japan, situated between the Pacific Ocean and the Sea of Japan. It is mountainous, volcanic, and prone to earthquakes. The historic centre of Japan, it has been the site of its capital since earliest times. Most of Japan's major ports and cities are here, although agriculture is also very important; rice, fruit, cotton, and tea are grown. Mineral wealth includes oil, zinc, and copper. The traditional industry is silk but the many modern industries include shipbuilding, iron and steel, chemicals, and textiles. Area: 230 448 sq km (88 976 sq mi). Population (1985): 96 687 700. Chief town: Tokyo.

Hooch, Pieter de (1629–c. 1684) Dutch painter, born in Rotterdam. Working in Delft, Leiden, and Amsterdam, he excelled in small paintings, such as *The Pantry* (Rijksmuseum, Amsterdam), depicting household tasks in courtyards or dark interiors.

Hood, Samuel, 1st Viscount (1724–1816) British admiral, who achieved eminence in the American Revolution, when he defeated the French off Dominica (1782). In the French Revolutionary Wars he captured Toulon (1793) and destroyed the defences of Corsica (1794).

Hood, Thomas (1799–1845) British poet. He followed his successful *Odes and Addresses* (1825) with further volumes of humorous verse, and also wrote serious poems of social and political protest, such as *The Song of the Shirt* (1843).

Hooke, Robert (1635–1703) British physicist and instrument maker. In 1660 he discovered **Hooke's law**, which states that for an elastic body, the stress is directly proportioned to the strain. Many of his microscope studies were published in *Micrographia* (1665). Appointed a city surveyor after the Fire of London, he designed several buildings, including the College of Physicians.

Hook of Holland (Dutch name: Hoek van Holland) 51 59N 4 07E A port in the SW Netherlands, in South Holland province at the North Sea end of the Nieuwe Waterweg (New Waterway). A ferry service operates from here to Harwich, England.

hookworm A parasitic nematode worm inhabiting the intestine of animals and man. About 1 cm long, hookworms attach themselves to the gut lining and feed by sucking blood and body fluids. The two main species infecting man are *Necator americanus*, of the southern USA and Africa, and the Eurasian *Ancylostoma duodenale*.

hoopoe A bird, *Upupa epops*, of S Eurasia and Africa. 28 cm long, it has a pink-brown plumage with black and white barred wings, a long tail, and a long black-tipped crest. It feeds on insects and larvae with its long downcurved bill. It is the only member of its family (*Upupidae*). Order: *Coraciformes* (hornbills, kingfishers, etc.).

Hoover, Herbert (Clark) (1874–1964) US statesman; Republican president (1929–33). As secretary of commerce (1921–29) he was chairman of commissions that initiated construction of the Hoover Dam (named after him) and the St Lawrence Seaway.

hop A perennial climbing herb, *Humulus lupus*. Native to Eurasia, where it grows to a length of 3–6 m in hedges and thickets, it is widely cultivated for its pale yellow-green female flowers ("cones"), which are used in brewing to flavour beer. Family: *Cannabiaceae*.

Hope, Bob (Leslie Townes Hope; 1903–) US comedian, born in Britain. He starred in a number of popular films during the 1940s, including *Road to Zanzibar* (1941) and other "Road" films in which he partnered Bing Crosby. He gave many performances for US troops both in and after World War II; he has also acted as compère of the Academy Award presentations.

Hopkins, Gerard Manley (1844–89) British poet. He was converted to Roman Catholicism in 1866 and ordained as a Jesuit priest in 1877. In verse of daring originality he rejected conventional metres in favour of a flexible "sprung rhythm." "The Wreck of the Deutschland" and "The Windhover" are among his best-known poems, which were published posthumously in 1918.

Horace (Quintus Horatius Flaccus; 65–8 BC) Roman poet. Although he was reduced to poverty after fighting for Brutus in the Civil War, he became a leading poet under the emperor Augustus and acquired a farm near Rome, celebrated in his poetry. His *Odes* and his more informal *Satires* and verse *Epistles* vividly portray contemporary Roman society.

hormone A substance that is secreted into the blood in small quantities to cause a response in a specific target organ or tissue of the body. Hormones are produced and secreted by endocrine glands and by specialized nerve cells (*see* neurohormone) under the control of the nervous system or in response to changes in the chemical composition of the blood. Hormones regulate short-term physiological processes, such as digestion, and long-term changes, such as those associated with growth and reproduction; they also help to maintain a constant internal environment in the body. The following are some of the more important hormones now known in man: ACTH, gonadotrophin, growth hormone, and prolactin (secreted by the pituitary); corticosteroids, aldosterone, and adrenaline (from the adrenal glands); androgens and oestrogens (from the sex glands); thyroid hormone (from the thyroid gland); insulin and glucagon (from the pancreas). Chemically, most hormones are proteins or steroids. The study of hormones is called endocrinology.

hornbeam A tree of the genus *Carpinus* (26 species), of N temperate regions. The common Eurasian hornbeam (*C. betulus*) has smooth grey bark, oval pointed leaves with prominent veins, and small nuts with conspicuous winged bracts. It is planted for ornament and for its hard fine-grained timber. Family: *Corylaceae*.

hornbill A bird belonging to a family (*Bucerotidae*; 45 species) occurring in Old World tropical regions. 38–150 cm long, hornbills are characterized by a huge bill, often bearing a large bony "helmet," and feed on fruit and berries. Order: *Coraciiformes* (kingfishers, etc.).

hornblende A mineral of the amphibole group, which occurs widely in igneous and metamorphic rocks. It consists mainly of silicates of sodium, calcium, magnesium, and iron. It is black or greenish black and occurs in crystalline or massive form.

hornet A social wasp, *Vespa crabro*, that is common throughout Europe and has spread to North America and elsewhere. 35 mm long, it is tawny-yellow with brown markings and nests in hollow trees. It feeds chiefly on insects, nectar, and fruit juices and its painful sting can be dangerous to man.
Members of the genera *Dolichorespula*, *Paravespula*, and *Vespula* may also be known as hornets.

hornpipe A traditional British dance, originally accompanied by a wooden pipe. It retains its popularity with sailors as it requires no partners and little space. Like the jigs and reels to which it is related, it was often danced in clogs.

horoscope. *See* astrology.

Horowitz, Vladimir (1904–89) Russian pianist. He settled in the USA in 1940. Horowitz excelled in Russian music and in his own transcriptions. He twice made a a triumphant return to the concert platform after periods of illness during 1936–39 and 1953–65.

horse A hoofed mammal, *Equus caballus*, domesticated worldwide for pack and draught work, riding, and sport. The earliest horse is believed to have been eohippus, which is thought to have originated in North America and spread to Asia. Successive larger forms evolved, in which the central toe became enlarged as the hoof; these horses developed from forest browsers to become grazing animals of the plains.
The many breeds of modern horse are commonly grouped into ponies, light horses, and draught horses. They range in size from the tiny Falabella to the massive Shire horse and are measured in hands (1 hand = 4 in = 10.16 cm) to the top of the shoulders (withers). According to breed, horses mature at 3½–5 years of age and the lifespan is usually 20–35 years. Mares have a gestation period of 11 months, producing usually a single foal. Horses belong to the family *Equidae*, which also includes asses and zebras.

horse chestnut A broad spreading tree, *Aesculus hippocastanum*, native to SE Europe and widely planted as an ornamental. It grows to a height of 25 m, producing large compound leaves and white flowers; the green spiny fruits ripen to release large brown shiny seeds (conkers). Family: *Hippocastanaceae*.

horse fly A stout-bodied fly of the genus *Tabanus* (the term is also used loosely for the other genera—*Chrysops* (deerflies) and *Haematopota* (cleg flies)—of the family *Tabanidae*; 2500 species). Male horse flies feed on nectar but the females are bloodsuckers and inflict painful bites

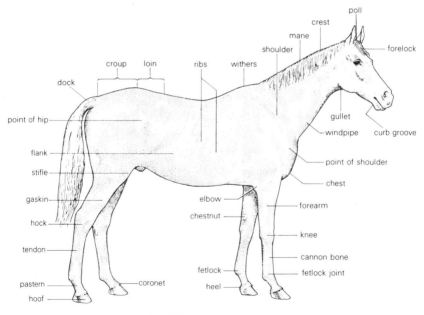

points of the horse

on man, horses, cattle, etc. A few species transmit diseases, such as tularemia and anthrax.

horsepower (hp)   A unit of power equal to 550 footpounds per second. It was devised by James Watt, who found that a strong horse could raise a weight of 150 pounds 4 feet in 1 second. *See also* watt.

horseradish   A perennial herb, *Armóracia rusticana*, probably native to SE Europe and W Asia and widely cultivated. Growing to a height of 125 cm, it has fleshy pungent roots from which horseradish sauce is made and it bears small white flowers. Family: *Cruciferae*.

horseshoe crab   A large nocturnal marine arthropod (up to 50 cm long), also called king crab, belonging to the subclass *Xiphosura*. The two living genera, *Limulus* and *Tachypleus*, are found in shallow waters on the E coasts of North America and Asia respectively. They have a hinged body covered by a brown horseshoe-shaped carapace and a long tail spine. They can swim but usually burrow in sand, feeding on worms and thin-shelled molluscs. Class: *Meristomata*.

horticulture   The cultivation of vegetables (also known as market gardening) and fruit for food and of trees, shrubs, and other plants for ornament. Horticulture is now both a popular domestic pastime and an important commercial activity. Higher-yielding and more disease-resistant plant varieties, increased mechanization, the use of new cultivation techniques, and the application of fertilizers and pesticides have all contributed to improved productivity and quality.

Horus   The Egyptian sun-god, usually portrayed as a falcon or with a falcon's head. He was the son of Osiris and Isis. The pharaohs were conceived as the incarnations of Horus as earthly ruler and added the god's name to their titles.

hospice movement   A movement that provides care for the terminally ill. Hospices specialize in easing the physical and mental distress of the patients and providing support for their families. Most modern hospices are modelled on St Christopher's hospice, founded in London in 1967 by Dame Cicely Saunders.

hospital   An institution providing diagnostic and therapeutic services for the sick on a residential (in-patient) or nonresidential (out-patient) basis. In the ancient world such medical services as existed were provided by religious organizations. In Europe in the middle ages many institutions for the care of the sick were founded by monastic orders and later, during the Crusades, by orders of knighthood. St Bartholomew's (1123) and St Thomas's (1207) in London date back to this period. In the UK, during the 18th and 19th centuries, many new voluntary hospitals were founded by philanthropists and staffed by doctors who gave their services free. Municipal hospitals with paid medical staff arose alongside the voluntary hospitals; both systems were nationalized by the National Health Service Act (1946). Since then all National Health hospitals have provided free services for all who want them, although some have a small number of paybeds. In 1988 plans for "self-governing" hospitals offering services to both the NHS and the private sector were announced. *See also* National Health Service.

Hospitallers (Order of the Hospital of St John of Jerusalem)   A religious order of knighthood that began as a hospital for pilgrims to Jerusalem (c. 1070) and during the Crusades took on a military function. Immensely wealthy, the Hospitallers were the great rivals of the

Templars. After the fall of Acre (1291) they established themselves in Cyprus, Rhodes, and finally Malta.

Hosta   A genus of perennial herbaceous plants (10 species), native to China and Japan and widely planted in gardens. They are grown chiefly for their often variegated foliage–but they also produce attractive spikes of purplish or white funnel-shaped flowers. Family: *Liliaceae*.

hot spring   A spring from which hot water flows continuously from deep within the earth's crust. Like geysers, hot springs normally occur in areas that are (or have recently been) volcanically active. A distinction is sometimes made between hot springs (at a temperature above that of the human body) and *thermal springs* (above the mean annual temperature of the place where they emerge).

Hotspur.   *See* Percy, Sir Henry.

HOUDINI   *With a canister from which he would escape under water.*

Houdini, Harry   (Erich Weiss; 1874–1926) US magician. His ability to escape from handcuffs, straitjackets, and locked containers, even when under water, gained him an international reputation. He wrote articles and books on magic and was deeply interested in spiritualism.

Hounslow   A borough of W Greater London, bordering on the River Thames in the S. Created in 1965 from parts of Middlesex, it contains Hounslow Heath, a former haunt of highwaymen. Population (1983 est): 200 900.

housefly   A dull-grey fly, *Musca domestica*, that is a worldwide household pest. The adult is 5–7 mm long, with mouthparts used for sucking up organic liquids of all kinds. Through the contamination of food it spreads many serious diseases, such as typhoid, tuberculosis, and dysentery. Family: *Muscidae*.

Houston   29 45N 95 25W A city in the USA, the main port in Texas. Founded in 1836, it is named after the Texan leader Sam(uel) Houston (1793–1863). It expanded rapidly following the building of a canal (1912–14), linking it to the Gulf of Mexico, and the development of coastal oilfields. Today it is one of the world's major oil and petrochemical centres; other industries include shipbuilding and the manufacture of steel. The

Lyndon B. Johnson Space Center is nearby. Population (1986): 1 728 910.

hovercraft (*or* air-cushion vehicle) A shiplike vehicle equipped with powerful horizontal blowers capable of lifting it off a surface so that it rides on a cushion of air, which is contained within a rubber skirt. It can navigate on almost any kind of surface and is moved forward at high speed by vertical propellers. The first hovercraft was built by Christopher Cockerell in 1959. Hovercraft are used as ferries between England and France and elsewhere.

hoverfly A fly, also called a flowerfly or syrphid fly, belonging to the family *Syrphidae* (about 4000 species). Many species are black and yellow, resembling bees and wasps, but they do not sting. The larvae of many hoverflies are scavengers in decaying organic matter or the nests of ants, termites, or bees.

Howard, Catherine (c. 1520–42) The fifth wife (1540–42) of Henry VIII of England. She was beheaded for treason when Henry learnt of her premarital love affairs.

Howard, Sir Ebenezer (1850–1928) British theorist of town planning. His book *Garden Cities of Tomorrow*, first published under this title in 1902, propounds his concept of ideal spacious suburbs. This was first realized in the planning of Letchworth (1903), Lutyens' design for Hampstead (1908), and Welwyn Garden City (1920). His ideas continue to be influential.

Howard, Henry. *See* Wyatt, Sir Thomas.

Howard, John (c. 1726–90) English prison reformer. Horrified by conditions in Bedford gaol, which he in-spected while high sheriff of Bedfordshire, Howard campaigned for sanitary improvements and wages for gaolers. An act of 1774 achieved his aims. The **Howard League for Penal Reform**, founded in 1866 as the Howard Association, was named after him.

Howard, Leslie (Leslie Howard Stainer; 1890–1943) British actor of Hungarian descent. He became famous for his performances as the romantic leading man in both British and US films, including *The Scarlet Pimpernel* (1935), *Pygmalion* (1938), and *Gone with the Wind* (1939). He was killed when the aeroplane in which he was travelling was shot down by German aircraft.

Howard, Trevor (1916–88) British actor. After working in the theatre in the 1930s he concentrated on films, including *Brief Encounter* (1946), *The Third Man* (1949), *Mutiny on the Bounty* (1962), *Ryan's Daughter* (1970), *Conduct Unbecoming* (1975), and *White Mischief* (1987).

Howe, Sir (Richard Edward) Geoffrey (1926–) British Conservative politician; chancellor of the ex-chequer (1979–83); foreign secretary (1983–89). In 1989 he assumed the unofficial post of deputy prime minister and became President of the Council and Leader of the House of Commons.

howitzer A low-velocity artillery firearm with a shorter barrel and a larger bore than a gun but a smaller bore and longer barrel than a mortar. They are often mounted on carriages that enable them to fire either flat gun-type trajectories or arched mortar-type trajectories. They were widely used in World War I. The word comes from the Dutch *houwitzer*, catapult.

howler monkey A large monkey belonging to the genus *Alouatta* (6 species), of Central and South American forests. Howlers are 115–180 cm long including the tail (58–91 cm) and are named after their loud voices. They have beards over their enlarged throats, prehensile tails,

and live in groups of up to 40 individuals. Family: *Cebidae*.

Hoya. *See* waxplant.

Hoyle, Sir Fred (1915–) British astronomer, who with H. Bondi (1919–) and T. Gold (1920–) proposed the steady-state theory of the universe. His other theoretical studies have mainly been concerned with stellar evolution. He is also one of the foremost of today's science writers and a notable science-fiction writer.

Hsi-an. *See* Xi An.

Hsi Chiang. *See* Xi Jiang.

Hsiung-nu. *See* Xiong Nu.

Huancayo 12 05S 75 12W A city in W Peru, the chief commercial centre of the central Andes. It has a cathedral and a university (1962). Population (1981): 321 549.

Huang Hai. *See* Yellow Sea.

Huang Ho. *See* Yellow River.

Hubble constant (H_o) The rate at which the velocity of expansion of the universe changes with distance. It relates the recessional velocity, V, of a distant galaxy to its distance, D. Hubble's law, proposed in 1929 by the US astronomer Edwin Hubble (1889–1953), states that recessional velocity and distance are directly proportional: $V = H_o D$.

Hubli 15 20N 75 14E A city in India, in Karnataka. Together with Dharwar, it forms one of the state's most populous areas. Industries include cotton and newspapers. Population (1981): 526 000.

Huddersfield 58 39N 1 47W A town in N England, in West Yorkshire at the confluence of the Rivers Colne and Holme. One of the major wool textile towns of West Yorkshire, Huddersfield produces various fabrics and has important engineering and metalworking industries. Population (1988 est): 121 830.

Hudson, Henry (d. 1611) English navigator. In 1607 he sailed in search of the Northeast Passage to China, reaching Spitzbergen. He tried again, unsuccessfully, in 1608. On a third voyage, under the auspices of the Dutch East India Company, he sailed some 240 km (150 mi) down what came to be called the Hudson River. His fourth voyage (1610–11), in the *Discovery*, took him to what is now Hudson Bay, where his men mutinied and cast him adrift.

Hudson Bay A huge shallow oceanic bay in N central Canada, linked to the Atlantic Ocean by Hudson Strait and to the Arctic Ocean by Foxe Channel. Frozen during winter, in summer it carries grain ships from W Canada to Europe.

Hudson River A river in the NE USA, flowing from the Adirondack Mountains to New York Bay, where it forms part of New York Harbor. An important commercial waterway, it is linked by canals with the Great Lakes and the St Lawrence Seaway. Length: 492 km (306 mi).

Hudson's Bay Company A fur-trading company, formed in 1670, that was given settlement and trading rights in Canada. The company engaged in bitter rivalry with the Northwest Company from the 1780s until 1821, when they were united under the name of the Hudson's Bay Company. In 1870 it sold its territories to Canada but remained a major fur-trading agency with headquarters in London.

Hue 16 28N 107 35E An ancient city in central Vietnam, on the Huong estuary. A commercial centre, Hue has textile, timber, and cement industries. *History*: a Chinese military stronghold from about 200 BC, Hue later fell to Champa and after 1635 was the capital of An-nam and after 1802 of the short-lived Vietnamese em-pire. It suffered heavily during the Vietnam War. Popu-lation (latest est): 165 865.

Hughes, Howard (Robard) (1905–76) US aviator, film producer, and entrepreneur. After founding the Hughes Aircraft Company he broke the landplane speed record in 1935, reaching a speed of 352 mph. His films include *Hell's Angels* (1930), *Scarface* (1932), and *The Outlaw* (1944). From 1950 until his death he lived in se-clusion.

VICTOR HUGO

Hughes, Ted (1930–) British poet. His first vol-ume, *The Hawk in the Rain* (1957), contained many po-ems concerned with the natural world written in a force-ful energetic style. The poems in *Crow* (1970) and subsequent volumes are characterized by increased vio-lence of language and subject matter. He became poet laureate in 1984.

Hugo, Victor (Marie) (1802–85) French poet, dram-atist, and novelist. After several early novels and volumes of poetry, his leadership of the Romantic move-ment was confirmed by the success of his drama *Hernani* (1831). During the 1840s he became increasingly in-volved in republican politics and, after the coup d'état by the future Napoleon III in 1851, he went into exile in the Channel Islands until 1870. His later major works included *Les Contemplations* (1856), a volume of poems, and the novel *Les Misérables* (1862).

Huguenots French Protestants. Their name is de-rived from the Swiss-German *Eidgenoss*, confederate. The Huguenots, chiefly followers of John Calvin, were soon an influential national minority. The rivalry of their leaders with the prominent Roman Catholic Guise family gave rise to the Wars of Religion (1562–94). The Edict of Nantes (1598) guaranteed the Huguenots free-dom of worship but after the revocation of the Edict (1685) over 250 000 Huguenots emigrated.

Hull (official name: Kingston-upon-Hull) 53 45N 0 20W A city and port in NE England, the administra-tive centre of Humberside, situated on the Humber estu-ary. An important fishing port, Hull has vast docks and serves as a port for much of the North and Midlands, with passenger services to the Continent. Its industries include paints, chemicals, and engineering, as well as fish-related industries. Population (1981): 268 302.

humanism 1. The intellectual movement that formed the inspiration and the basis of Renaissance culture. Humanist scholars based their programme upon the rediscovery and study of classical Greek and Roman au-thors, which had been initiated in Italy by such men as Petrarch and Boccaccio. They turned away from the the-ological bias of their forerunners and concentrated in-stead upon human achievements. Erasmus was the greatest N European humanist. 2. A 20th-century philo-sophical viewpoint that is based on a policy of atheism, holding religion to be an outmoded superstition unwor-thy of serious consideration.

human rights Privileges claimed or enjoyed by a human being simply by virtue of being human. The con-cept developed from Roman ideas of "natural law" en-tailing "natural rights" to 20th-century liberal accep-tance of the idea that human beings should have certain equal civil, political, and economic rights. The UN Uni-versal Declaration of Human Rights (1948), itself not a legally binding code, has spawned various subsequent agreements, such as the Covenants on Civil and Political Rights and on Economic, Social, and Cultural Rights (1966), which have been accepted as binding by 35 states.

Humber An estuary in N England, flowing from the confluence of the Rivers Ouse and Trent to the North Sea past the ports of Hull, Immingham, and Grimsby. The **Humber Bridge** (opened 1981) is the world's longest single-span suspension bridge, with a main span of 1410 m (4626 ft). Length: 64 km (40 mi).

Humberside A county in NE England, bordering on the North Sea. It was created in 1974 from N Lincoln-shire and parts of the East and West Ridings of York-shire. It is a rich agricultural region producing cereals, root crops, and livestock. There are important fishing industries at Hull and Grimsby. Other industrial activi-ties include iron and steel manufacture and petrochemi-cals. Area: 3512 sq km (1356 sq mi). Population (1986 est): 848 500. Administrative centre: Hull.

Humboldt Current (*or* Peru Current) An ocean cur-rent constituting part of the South Pacific oceanic circu-lation system. It flows N off the Peruvian coast of South America. It is a cold current rich in plankton and the fish that feed on them, giving rise to Peru's prosperous fish-ing industry.

Humboldt Glacier The largest known glacier in the N hemisphere, in NW Greenland. At its end in Kane Basin it is 100 km (60 mi) wide and 91 m (300 ft) high.

Hume, David (1711–76) Scottish philosopher and historian. In *A Treatise of Human Nature* (1739–40) he developed his influential distinction between impression and ideas, claiming that impressions have more force than ideas. For Hume almost nothing about existence was demonstrable; regarding the existence of God, his position throughout his numerous works is an incisive agnosticism. Although an empiricist like Locke and Berkeley, Hume modified problematic aspects of their philosophies in favour of psychological explanations. Hume's *History of England* (1754–62) was a bestseller for many years.

humidity A measure of the amount of water vapour in the atmosphere. Absolute humidity is the mass of water vapour in unit volume of air, measured in kilograms per cubic metre. Relative humidity is the ratio of the abso-lute humidity at a given temperature to the maximum humidity without precipitation at the same temperature, usually expressed as a percentage.

hummingbird A brightly coloured bird belonging to a New World family (*Trochilidae*; 320 species). Hummingbirds are 5.5–20 cm long and have a slender often downcurved bill and a brush-tipped tongue for feeding on nectar and small insects. Hummingbirds can hover, fly backwards, and produce a humming noise by the rapid vibration of their wings during flight. Order: *Apodiformes* (swifts, etc.).

Humperdinck, Engelbert (1854–1921) German composer. He assisted Wagner with the score of *Parsifal* in 1880–81. Of his many operas only *Hänsel und Gretel* (1893) is still popular: it blends German folklore with Wagnerian operatic techniques.

humus The black organic matter in soil resulting from the decomposition of dead plants and animals (humification). It is rich in such elements as carbon, nitrogen, phosphorus, and sulphur, which are useful in maintaining soil fertility and hence in promoting plant growth. Humus also improves water absorption and workability of the soil.

Hundred Years' War (1337–1453) A war between England and France. It was precipitated by Edward III's claim to the French throne. The Treaty of Brétigny (1360) recognized initial English successes at Sluys (1340), Crécy (1346), and Poitiers (1356) but thereafter the war was waged intermittently with frequent truces. Henry V of England achieved recognition as heir to the French throne after his victory at Agincourt (1415), but the more vigorous French prosecution of the war (inspired by Joan of Arc) reversed his triumph and by 1453 England had been expelled from all French territory except Calais.

Hungarian A language of the Finno-Ugric branch of the Uralic family. It is spoken by 14 million people mainly in Hungary, where it is the official language, and in Czechoslovakia, Romania, and Yugoslavia. It uses a modified Latin alphabet and has borrowed many words from surrounding languages. *See also* Magyars.

Hungary, People's Republic of (Hungarian name: Magyar Népköztársasag) A country in central Europe. It lies mainly in the basin of the middle Danube, which forms the NW boundary with Czechoslovakia before running N–S across the centre of the country. To the E of the Danube lies the Great Hungarian Plain; to the W an undulating plain rises to some low hills in the SW and in the NW to the hilly Bakony Forest. The people are mainly Magyars, with minorities of Germans, Slovaks, and others. *Economy*: agriculture is now organized collectively; the main crops are wheat and maize as well as fruit and vegetables. The only mineral resource of significance is bauxite. Oil and natural gas have been found but most supplies come by pipeline from the Soviet Union. All industry is nationalized and there has been considerable expansion since World War II. Since 1968 there has been a new system of economic planning, aiming at a certain amount of decentralization and encouragement of individual initiative, while still maintaining overall state control. *History*: the Magyars reached the Danube area in the 9th century AD and settled there. In the 11th century St Stephen I converted the country to Christianity and became the first Hungarian king. After a long period of dynastic struggles and threats from foreign powers, Hungary was conquered by the Turks in 1526 and in the 17th century it became part of the Habs-

burg Empire. In 1867 Hungary gained internal self-government as part of the Dual Monarchy of Austria-Hungary. In 1918 Hungary became a republic but, after a short period of communist rule, a constitutional monarchy was formed. After World War II it became a republic again and in 1949 the communists gained control. In 1956 an anti-Stalinist uprising was crushed by Soviet forces. Recent reforms have included legalization of opposition parties. In 1989 the Communist Party was reformed as the Hungarian Socialist Party, which promised free elections. Official language: Hungarian (Magyar). Official currency: forint of 100 fillér. Area: 93 035 sq km (35 911 sq mi). Population (1987): 10 622 000. Capital: Budapest.

Huns Nomadic peoples, originating in Mongolia, who overran much of SE Europe in the late-4th and 5th centuries, overthrowing the Ostrogoths and then invading the Roman Empire. United under Attila, the Huns invaded Greece, Gaul, and finally Italy (452). The death of Attila (453) fragmented their empire and they were defeated by a coalition of tribes at Nedao (455).

Hunt, William Holman (1827–1910) British painter. He helped found the Pre-Raphaelite Brotherhood. His symbolic but technically realistic paintings include *The Light of the World* (Keble College, Oxford) and *The Scapegoat* (Port Sunlight), inspired by a visit to Syria and Palestine (1854).

Huntingdon 52 20N 0 12W A town in E England, in Cambridgeshire on the Great Ouse River. A market town with printing, brewing, and knitwear industries, Huntingdon is the birthplace of Oliver Cromwell. Population (1981): 17 477, with Godmanchester.

Hurd, Douglas (Richard) (1930–) British Conservative politician; foreign secretary (1989–). After service overseas with the Foreign Office, he became an MP in 1974, Secretary of State for Northern Ireland (1984–85), and home secretary (1985–89). He is also known as a writer of political thrillers.

hurdling A track event in athletics in which sprinters jump ten hurdles in the course of a race. Distances are 110 m and 400 m for men and 100 m for women. For the 110 m the height of the hurdles is 106.7 cm (3.5 ft), for the 400 m it is 91.4 cm (3 ft), and for the 100 m 84 cm (2.75 ft). Racers are not normally disqualified for knocking hurdles over.

hurdy-gurdy A stringed instrument sounded by a rosined wheel, turned by the right hand, and stopped by a set of keys played by the left hand; there are also two drone strings. It was very popular in medieval times and survives as a folk instrument in parts of Europe.

hurling (or hurley) An Irish 15-a-side stick-and-ball field game similar to hockey, over 3000 years old. The ball is hit or carried through the air with a broad-bladed curved stick, the hurley (Gaelic word: *caman*), and may be caught in the hand. A goal, hit under the crossbar, scores three points; a hit between the posts but above the bar scores one.

Huron, Lake The second largest of the Great Lakes in North America, situated between the USA and Canada. It is an important shipping route carrying iron ore, coal, grain, and oil. Area: 59 570 sq km (23 000 sq mi).

hurricane 1. A tropical cyclone with surface-wind speeds in excess of 64 knots (32.7 m per second) that occurs around the Caribbean Sea and Gulf of Mexico. The centre (eye) of a hurricane is an area of light winds around which strong winds, cloud, and rain bands spi-

HURRICANE *Damaged houses in Belize.*

ral. **2.** Any wind reaching force 12 on the Beaufort scale (in excess of 64 knots or 32.7 metres per second).

husky One of several breeds of compact sturdy deep-chested dogs used for pulling sledges in Arctic regions. The Siberian husky has small erect ears, a long muzzle, and a brushlike tail curved over the back. The dense double-layered coat provides insulation against the severe climate. Height: 51–63 cm. *See also* Samoyed.

hussars Light-cavalry regiments originating in Hungary in the 15th century. Most European armies have used hussars for reconnaissance and raids. Their uniform included the characteristic dolman, a cloak worn hanging from the left shoulder. The name hussar has now been adopted by some armoured units.

Hussein (ibn Talal) (1935–) King of Jordan (1952–). He became king following the deposition because of mental illness of his father Talal. Hussein led Jordan into the 1967 Arab-Israeli War. In 1970 he ruthlessly crushed al-Fatah guerrillas but in 1974, under pressure from other Arab countries, accepted the claims of the Palestine Liberation Organization to the West Bank of the River Jordan. In 1989 he allowed the first elections for 22 years.

Hussites The followers of the Bohemian heretic, Jan Hus (1372–1415). They demanded a reformed national Church with a vernacular liturgy. In spite of crusades led by the Holy Roman Emperor Sigismund, the Hussites remained undefeated until a compromise was reached at the Council of Basle in 1433. The moderate Utraquists gained many of their demands and survived until the 17th century.

Huston, John (1906–87) US film director. He began his career as a scriptwriter. His first film as director was *The Maltese Falcon* (1941), and subsequent films included *The Treasure of the Sierra Madre* (1948), for which he wrote the script and in which he also acted, *The African Queen* (1951), *The Misfits* (1960), *Annie* (1982), and *Prizzi's Honour* (1985).

Huxley, Thomas Henry (1825–95) British biologist, whose impact spanned both biology and philosophy. Huxley developed his interest in natural history while serving as a ship's surgeon in the Far East. After valuable work in palaeontology Huxley held numerous public posts and was instrumental in bringing enlightened change to educational methods. From 1880 onwards he challenged orthodox theology and coined the term agnosticism to describe his own position. Three of his grandsons achieved fame in the fields of science and literature. **Sir Julian Huxley** (1887–1975) was a zoologist and scientific administrator, who also made valuable contributions to the philosophy of science. He was involved in the improvement of the London Zoo at Regent's Park and was appointed first director general of UNESCO (1946–48). His brother **Aldous Huxley** (1894–1964) was a novelist and writer. His witty satirical novels *Antic Hay* (1923) and *Point Counter Point* (1928) were followed by *Brave New World* (1932) and *Eyeless in Gaza* (1936). His later essays explore such subjects as mysticism and the use of drugs. **Sir Andrew Fielding Huxley** (1917–), half-brother to Sir Julian and Aldous, is a biologist noted for his researches into the mechanisms of nerve-impulse conduction and muscle contraction. Huxley and his collaborator A. L. Hodgkin (1914–) shared a Nobel Prize (1963) with Sir John Eccles (1903–). He was awarded the OM in 1983.

Huygens, Christiaan (1629–95) Dutch astronomer and physicist, who discovered Saturn's rings in 1656. He also built the first pendulum clock and designed an arrangement of lenses called a Huygens eyepiece. He devised a wave theory of light to explain double refraction.

hyacinth A perennial herbaceous plant of the genus *Hyacinthus* (about 30 species), native to the Mediterranean region and tropical Africa and widely planted as ornamental garden and pot plants. Growing from bulbs, the plants have a dense head of bell-shaped flowers, varying from white to deep purple, and slender leaves. The common garden hyacinths are derived from *H. orientalis.* Family: *Liliaceae.*

hybrid The offspring resulting from the mating of two unrelated individuals. The hybrid offspring often shows greater general fitness than either of the two parents, a phenomenon called hybrid vigour (or heterosis). This is commonly used by plant breeders to produce a generation of crop plants giving higher yields and showing improved resistance to disease.

Hyderabad 17 22N 78 26E One of the largest cities in India, the capital of Andhra Pradesh situated on the River Musi. Formerly the capital of the princely state of Hyderabad, it was founded in 1590 by the Muslim Qutb Shahi sultans. An educational centre, Hyderabad is the site of Osmania University (1918), an agricultural university, and several research institutes. There has been considerable industrial growth in recent years. The chief manufactures include bus and railway equipment, textiles, and pharmaceutical goods. Population (1981): 2 528 000.

Hydra In Greek legend, a monster with many heads who grew two more whenever one was cut off. It was killed by Heracles.

Hydra A widely distributed genus of solitary freshwater invertebrate animals belonging to an order (*Hydroida*) of coelenterates. They are flexible polyps, 10–30 mm long, with the mouth at the top surrounded by 6–10 tentacles. Hydras are usually attached to stones, sticks, or aquatic vegetation and feed on small animals. Class: *Hydrozoa.*

Hydrangea A genus of shrubs (about 80 species) native to Asia and North and South America, including several popular ornamentals. The showy heads of white, pink, or blue flowers may be sterile and sometimes change colour according to the acidity or alkalinity of the soil. Family: *Hydrangeaceae*.

hydraulics The study of the applications of hydrostatics and hydrodynamics to design problems. In civil engineering it is used to study the flow of water in pipes, rivers, canals, etc., especially with reference to the construction of dams, reservoirs, and hydroelectric power stations. In mechanical engineering, applications include the design of machinery involving fluids, such as hydraulic presses, turbines, propellers, etc. Hydraulics is concerned with the bulk properties of fluids, such as density, viscosity, elasticity, and surface tension, rather than their molecular properties.

hydrocarbons Compounds containing carbon and hydrogen. The saturated hydrocarbons are classified as alkanes. Unsaturated hydrocarbons include the alkenes and alkynes. Aromatic hydrocarbons include benzene and its many derivatives.

hydrochloric acid A solution in water of the colourless pungent gas hydrogen chloride (HCl). It is made by the action of sulphuric acid on salt or by the direct recombination of hydrogen and chlorine from the electrolysis of sea water. It is very soluble in water and forms a strong acid. Concentrated hydrochloric acid contains about 40% HCl by weight and is a clear fuming corrosive liquid. The acid in the human stomach is dilute hydrochloric acid (0.4%).

hydroelectric power Electricity generation using the energy of falling water. The water turns a turbine connected to an alternator, generating electricity with an efficiency of over 90% at full load and generally over 60% at quarter-load. Water is led through pipes from high-level natural or artificial reservoirs to the power station. The higher the reservoir, the less water is needed for the same power output. Hydroelectric power is, therefore, a cheap power source in mountainous areas with high rainfall. In pumped storage stations, electricity is stored by using it to drive pumps that raise the water to a high-level reservoir. In times of high demand this water is run back through the turbines. Hydroelectric power stations can have an output of 10 000 megawatts but in the UK most produce less than 100 MW.

hydrofoil A ship the hull of which is raised out of the water by foils as its speed increases. The foils provide lift in much the same way as an aerofoil; once the hull is clear of the water the drag is greatly reduced and the speed can be increased far above that of a normal ship of the same size and weight. The first hydrofoil was built in 1906 by Enrico Fortanini (1848–1930). Modern craft use a large V-shaped foil, to provide stability in turns or in rough seas, or small totally submerged foils, which support the hull on streamlined struts. Propulsion is by propeller or by pumped-water jet. Hydrofoils of 150 tonnes are in use in many parts of the world, including cross-Channel service.

hydrogen (H) The lightest of all gases, recognized as an element by Cavendish in 1766 and named by Lavoisier after water (Greek *hudro*, water). Hydrogen makes up about three-quarters of the mass of the universe. It is the simplest element, its nuclei consisting of one proton. Heavier elements are formed by nuclear fusion (*see* nuclear energy) from hydrogen in stars. The heavier isotope of hydrogen, deuterium (D *or* ^{2}H), occurs as about one part in 6000 of ordinary hydrogen. Tritium (^{3}H) also occurs but is unstable. As well as the gaseous element

(H_2) and water (H_2O), hydrogen occurs in organic compounds and in all inorganic acids and alkalis. The gas itself is used as a fuel for rockets, in welding, for filling balloons, and in chemical manufacture. It combines (explosively if in the right proportions) with oxygen to form water and can be obtained from water by electrolysis. Liquid hydrogen is used for experiments in low-temperature physics. At no 1; at wt 1.00797; mp −259.14°C; bp −252.87°C. hydrogen bomb. *See* nuclear weapons.

HYDROLOGY *The hydrological cycle.*

hydrology The science that studies the occurrence and movement of water on and over the surface of the earth. The **hydrological cycle** is the cyclic movement of water from the sea to the atmosphere and back, via precipitation, streams, and rivers. The main processes with which hydrology is concerned are precipitation, evaporation and transpiration, stream flow, and groundwater flow. It has many important applications, such as flood control and the supply of water for domestic and industrial purposes, irrigation, and hydroelectric power.

hydrophobia. *See* rabies.

hydroponics The cultivation of plants in a liquid nutrient solution instead of soil. A carefully prepared aqueous solution of all the nutrients required for healthy growth is used, usually in conjunction with an inert medium, such as sand or gravel, which provides support for the plant-root system. On a small scale, the solution is simply poured over the substrate and excess allowed to drain into containers for re-use. On a commercial scale, this is done by an automatic pumping system in which the solution is monitored to maintain nutrient levels and acidity.

hyena (*or* hyaena) A carnivorous mammal of the family *Hyaenidae*. There are three species: the African spotted hyena (*Crocuta crocuta*); the Asian striped hyena (*Hyaena hyaena*); and the brown hyena (*H. brunnea*) of South Africa, also called strandwolf. Hyenas are doglike in appearance, up to 1.5 m long including the tail, and stand about 90 cm high at the shoulder. They hunt in packs, feeding on carrion and killing young or sick animals.

hygrometer An instrument that measures the relative humidity of the atmosphere. In mechanical hygrometers, a material (usually human hair) is used, the length of which varies with the humidity; the variations being transformed into the movement of a pointer along a scale. In the wet-and-dry bulb hygrometer, two thermometers are placed side by side, one having its bulb covered by a moist cloth. The cooling caused by the evaporation from this wet bulb depends on the atmospheric moisture and thus the difference between the two thermometer readings can be related by standard tables to the relative humidity.

Hymenoptera A large worldwide order of insects (over 100 000 species) including the ants, sawflies, ichneumons, wasps, and bees. Many species show a high degree of social organization. Typically they have two pairs of membranous wings and the first segment of the abdomen is constricted to form a "waist." A tubular egg-laying structure (ovipositor) is generally present and in higher groups is modified for sawing, piercing, or stinging. The larvae (except the sawflies) are legless and have well-developed heads. The males develop from unfertilized eggs. Many species are of benefit to man because they pollinate flowering plants and prey on or parasitize insect pests.

hymn A song of praise in honour of a deity or saint, often in a metrical verse form. Hymns have been an important part of Christian congregational worship since the end of the 4th century. During the middle ages polyphonic settings became common but after the Reformation Lutheran chorales became the basis of the German and English hymn traditions. Famous hymn writers include Martin Luther, Charles Wesley, and Isaac Watts.

hyperbola The curve, or pair of curves, formed by a conic section and defined in Cartesian coordinates (*see* coordinate systems) by the equation $x^2/a^2 - y^2/b^2 = 1$, where a and b are constants. Its two parts have a common axis and are separated by a minimum distance $2a$ along this axis. As it goes out to infinity, the curve becomes increasingly close to two straight lines, called asymptotes.

hyperbolic functions A set of mathematical functions written sinh x, cosh x, tanh x, and their inverses csch x, sech x, and coth x respectively. Sinh x is defined as $\frac{1}{2}(e^x - e^{-x})$, where e is the base of natural logarithms; cosh x is $\frac{1}{2}(e^x + e^{-x})$, and tanh x is sinh x/cosh x. Hyperbolic functions are defined by analogy with the trigonometric functions sin x, etc., and are so named because they are related to the hyperbola in much the same way as the trigonometric functions are related to the circle.

hypermetropia. *See* longsightedness.

hypertension High blood pressure. This is a common condition, which can be caused by kidney disease, hormonal disorders, and some congenital diseases; for most cases, however, no cause can be found. Usually there are no symptoms, with the consequent danger that untreated hypertension may lead to heart failure, kidney failure, cerebral haemorrhage, and blindness. *See* beta blocker; diuretics.

hypnosis The production of a trance state by means of firm suggestion, with the cooperation of the subject. People who have been deeply hypnotized can carry out instructions that would not be possible in a normal waking state. First used for therapeutic purposes by Mesmer in the 18th century, it was developed (and given the name hypnosis) by James Braid (1795–1860) in the 19th century. By the turn of the century it was established as a means of treating certain psychiatric disorders (especially those of psychosomatic origin); it has, however, always been regarded as somewhat disreputable.

hypothalamus A part of the brain, surrounding the lower part of the third ventricle, that is an important coordinating centre for the functions of the autonomic nervous system. It is particularly involved with the control of body temperature, with regulating how much is eaten and drunk, and with the emotions. It also releases neurohormones affecting other organs, especially the pituitary gland.

hypothermia Lowering of the body temperature. This is most commonly seen in old people and young babies—whose body temperature is less well controlled—if they are living in poorly heated rooms. If the body temperature falls very low severe internal changes may occur, but otherwise gentle warming will help the patient to recover.

hyrax An African mammal belonging to the order *Hyracoidea* (6 species), also called cony. 30–60 cm long, hyraxes are related to ungulates (hooved mammals), having hooflike toes and a two-chambered stomach for digesting their vegetable diet. They are nimble and live in small colonies in trees or among rocks, being most active at twilight.

hyssop A perennial herbaceous plant, *Hyssopus officinalis*, native to S Europe, Asia, and Morocco. It is grown elsewhere as a garden ornamental and was formerly cultivated as a medicinal herb. Growing to a height of 60 cm, it has whorls of violet-blue flowers along the stem. Family: *Labiatae*.

hysterectomy The surgical removal of the womb. A subtotal hysterectomy involves removing the body of the womb but leaving the neck (cervix); in total hysterectomy (or panhysterectomy) the entire womb is removed. It is most commonly performed when the womb contains large fibroids—benign tumours that cause heavy menstrual periods. Other conditions that may require hysterectomy include cancer of the womb or the presence of precancerous cells in the cervix. The operation is usually performed through an incision made in the abdominal wall: it invariably precludes subsequent pregnancy but does not affect sexual activity.

hysteresis Any of several physical phenomena in which an induced effect lags behind the inducing cause. The term is most often applied to magnetic hysteresis in which the magnetic induction produced in a ferromagnetic material lags behind the magnetic field.

hysteria A neurotic condition of emotional instability and immaturity in which patients are vulnerable to suggestion and develop physical symptoms. Hysterical symptoms are unconsciously adopted by the individual because they bring some gain. The symptoms may be of "conversion hysteria," characterized by physical symptoms, such as paralysis; or of "dissociative hysteria," with changes in thinking, such as multiple personality. Treatment is usually by psychotherapy.

I

iamb A metrical foot consisting of an unstressed syllable (or in verse based on quantity, a short syllable) followed by a stressed (or long) syllable. Developed by the ancient Greeks, it is the commonest type in English poetry.

Ibadan 7 23N 3 56E The second largest city in Nigeria. It is an important industrial and administrative centre. Population (1983 est): 1 060 000.

Iberian Peninsula A peninsula in SW Europe, occupied by Portugal and Spain. It is separated from the rest of Europe by the Pyrenees and its flora and fauna are similar to those of N Africa. Area: 593 250 sq km (229 054 sq mi).

Iberians A Bronze Age people of S and E Spain in the 1st millennium BC. Their non-Indo-European language, which was displaced by Latin, is known from a variety of inscriptions on stone and other materials. The economic basis was agriculture, mining, and metalworking. The Iberians lost their identity by cultural assimilation to the Celts in Roman times.

IBEX

ibex A rare wild goat, *Capra ibex*, of Eurasian and N African mountains. About 85 cm high at the shoulder, ibexes have backward-curving horns up to 65 cm long and their coat is brownish-grey with variable markings.

ibis A long-necked wading bird belonging to the subfamily *Threskiornithinae* (20 species), distributed worldwide in warm regions. 55–75 cm long, ibises have a characteristic slender downcurved bill, and unfeathered face or head and neck. Family: *Threskiornithidae* (ibises and spoonbills); order: *Ciconiiformes* (herons, storks, etc.).

Ibiza (Iviza *or* Ivica) One of the Balearic islands. A popular tourist centre; exports include almonds, dried figs, apricots, and salt. Area: 541 sq km (209 sq mi). Population (1986): 45 000. Chief town: Ibiza.

Ibn Saud (c. 1880–1953) The first King of Saudi Arabia (1932–53). With the military help of al-Ikhwan, he extended his territory from the Sultanate of Najd, which he reconquered in 1902, to encompass much of Arabia by 1924, when he took Hejaz.

Ibo (*or* Igbo) A people of SE Nigeria who speak Igbo, a language of the Kwa subgroup of the Niger-Congo family. Subsistence cultivators of yams, cassava, and taro, they traditionally lived in scattered small holdings or village clusters of patrilineal kin headed by the eldest male descendant of the founder. *See also* Biafra.

Ibsen, Henrik (1828–1906) Norwegian playwright and poet, the founder of modern prose drama. From 1864 to 1891 he lived in Italy and Germany, with occasional visits to Norway. His fame as a dramatist grew with *Brand* (1865) and *Peer Gynt* (1867). In his next several plays he turned to the presentation of social issues: women's emancipation in *A Doll's House* (1879), inherited disease and guilt in *Ghosts* (1881), and public corruption in *An Enemy of the People* (1882). Subsequent works, such as *The Wild Duck* (1884) and *Hedda Gabler* (1890), dealt with the problems of individuals. In his last plays, *The Master Builder* (1892), *John Gabriel Borkman* (1896), and *When We Dead Awaken* (1899), he turned to the treatment of autobiographical themes in a symbolic manner.

Icarus (astronomy) A very small (about 1 km diameter) minor planet with the smallest known perihelion (0.19 astronomical units). It passed only 600 000 km from earth in 1968.

Icarus (mythology). *See* Daedalus.

Ice Age A period in the earth's history when ice spread towards the equator with a general lowering of temperatures. The most recent of these was the Pleistocene epoch ending about 10 000 years ago, during which four major ice advances occurred. Other ice ages occurred in Permo-Carboniferous times about 250 million years ago and in Pre-Cambrian times about 500 million years ago. Between 1550 and 1850 the **Little Ice Age** occurred, with a significant lowering of temperatures in the N hemisphere.

iceberg A large mass of ice in the sea that has originated on land. Many result from the breaking off of ice from glaciers. In the N hemisphere icebergs originate chiefly from Greenland, in the S hemisphere most break off from the Antarctic ice.

ice hockey A six-a-side team game played with stick and puck on a rink. It derives from field hockey and was first played by Englishmen on the frozen Kingston Harbour, Ontario (c. 1860). Canada is the true home of the game, but it is widely played in the USA, the Soviet Union, Sweden, Czechoslovakia, West Germany, and Finland.

Iceland, Republic of (Icelandic name: Island) An island country in the N Atlantic, just S of the Arctic Circle, off the SE coast of Greenland. It consists mainly of an uninhabited plateau of volcanoes, lava fields, and glaciers; most of the population live around the deeply indented coast. *Economy*: the main exports are fish

products and aluminium. Hydroelectricity and geothermal power (from geysers and thermal springs) are important sources of energy. *History*: the Vikings reached
Iceland about 874 AD and by the 10th century it had
become an independent state with its own parliament,
the Althing, considered to be the oldest in the world. In
1264 it came under Norwegian rule and, with Norway,
passed to the Danish Crown in 1381. In 1918 it became
an independent state under the Danish Crown, attaining
full independence as a republic in 1944. Official language: Icelandic. Official religion: Evangelical Lutheranism. Official currency: króna of 100 aurar (100 old
króna = 1 new Króna introduced 1981). Area:
103 000 sq km (39 758 sq mi). Population (1986):
244 009. Capital and main port: Reykjavik.

Icelandic A North Germanic language of the Western Scandinavian subgroup, developed from Old Norse.
It is the official language of Iceland.

Iceni A British tribe that inhabited the area that is
now Norfolk and Suffolk. Under Boadicea (60 AD) their
revolt against Roman rule was brutally suppressed.

ice plant A succulent annual or biennial plant, *Cry-
ophytum crystallinum*, that is covered in glistening papil-
lae and has long prostrate stems reaching 75 cm. Native
to South Africa, it is widely grown as a garden or pot
plant. Family: *Aizoaceae*.

ICE HOCKEY *The dimensions of the rink.*

ICON *The archangel Michael (14th century).*

ice skating The recreation and sport of sliding over
ice on steel-bladed skates. The main forms of the sport
are speed skating (racing) and two events judged on style
–figure skating (set exercises followed by a freestyle performance to music, either singly or in pairs) and ice
dancing (a combination of dancing and pairs figure skating). *See also* ice hockey.

ichneumon An insect, also called ichneumon fly and
ichneumon wasp, belonging to a family (*Ichneumonidae*;
about 40 000 species) occurring in Europe, North
America, and elsewhere. About 12 mm long, ichneumons resemble wasps but have longer antennae. They
are parasitic upon other insects thereby controlling
many insect pests. Order: *Hymenoptera*.

ichthyosaur An extinct dolphin-like marine reptile
that lived through much of the Mesozoic era but was
most abundant in the Jurassic period (200–135 million
years ago). 1–12 m long, it had broad flexible paddles, a
large tail fin, and a triangular dorsal fin.

icon A painted or mosaic image of Christ or a saint,
peculiar to the Byzantine and Orthodox churches. Unlike other paintings, icons have undergone little stylistic
development and are characterized by a symbolic rather
than realistic approach to colour, perspective, etc.

Iconium. *See* Konya.

id In psychoanalysis, the part of the unconscious mind
that is governed by irrational instinctive forces, such as
libido and aggression. These forces seek immediate (actual or symbolic) relief and the id is therefore said to be
ruled by the pleasure principle and not by reality or logic. *See also* ego; superego.

Idaho A state in the NW USA, dominated by the N
Rocky Mountains. It is primarily agricultural producing
potatoes, wheat, and sugar beet along with beef cattle
and sheep. Rich in minerals, Idaho is a leading US producer of silver and antimony. *History*: first settled in the
early 19th century, it became a state in 1890. Area:
216 412 sq km (83 557 sq mi). Population (1986 est):
1 003 000. Capital: Boise.

ide. *See* orfe.

idealism Any philosophical doctrine that equates reality with mind, spirit, person, soul, thought, or, as in
Plato, archetypal ideas. Philosophers who have held various idealist views include Berkeley, Kant, and Hegel.

ideographic writing systems (*or* ideography) Writing systems in which each concept is represented by a symbol. All ideographic systems were probably derived from pictographic writing systems, stylized representations of abstract concepts being added to the list of symbols. Languages such as Chinese still use ideographic writing systems.

igloo A temporary dome-shaped dwelling made from blocks of snow by Eskimos of the region between the Mackenzie River delta and Labrador in N Canada. The blocks are cut with a long knife and the joints filled with snow. The igloo is entered by a low and narrow semi-cylindrical passageway about three metres long.

Ignatius Loyola, St (1491–1556) Spanish founder of the Jesuits. His interest in religion dated from 1521, after reading the life of Christ while convalescing from a war wound. After visiting the Holy Land (1523), he studied in Spain and in Paris. There, in 1534 he made vows of poverty, chastity, and obedience, with St Francis Xavier and other followers. He was ordained in 1537 and then moved to Rome, where he founded the Society of Jesus with the approval of Pope Paul III in 1540. His *Spiritual Exercises* (1548) has had lasting influence on the Roman Catholic Church. Feast day: 31 July.

igneous rock One of the three major categories of rock (*compare* metamorphic rock; sedimentary rock) consisting mostly of crystalline rocks cooled directly from magma. That cooled at the surface forms extrusive rocks—volcanic lavas with small crystals because they have cooled rapidly. Some extrusive rocks, such as obsidian, are like glass. Igneous rocks cooled at depth are called intrusive or plutonic. They have larger crystals, granite being a common example. A third category contains the hypabyssal rocks, cooled in dykes or sills at intermediate depth and usually having intermediate crystal sizes, for example dolerite. Silica is the dominant chemical constituent of igneous rocks.

iguana A lizard belonging to the predominantly New World family *Iguanidae* (700 species), comprising desert-dwelling, arboreal, and amphibious species. The green common iguana (*Iguana iguana*) reaches a length of 1.8 m including the long tail (about 1.3 m) and has a short spiny crest along the back; males have a dewlap beneath the throat. They feed on vegetation and are excellent swimmers. The marine iguana (*Amblyrhynchus cristatus*) of the Galapagos is the only lizard that feeds in the sea. *See also* basilisk.

Iguanodon A large dinosaur that lived in the Jurassic and Cretaceous periods (200–65 million years ago). It stood on powerful hind legs about 5 m tall and measured 11 m from its head to the tip of its heavy balancing tail. Iguanodons were herbivorous, tearing off leaves with their tongues and cutting them with bladelike teeth. Order: *Ornithischia*.

Île-de-France A former province in N France, surrounding Paris and enclosed by the Rivers Seine, Marne, Beuvronne, Thève, and Oise. It was made a dukedom during the 9th century AD. Following the French Revolution it was divided into departments.

Illinois A group of Algonkian-speaking North American Indian tribes of Wisconsin, Illinois, Missouri, and Iowa. Their villages were of rush-mat-covered dwellings, each housing several families. Men hunted forest game and prairie bison; women cultivated maize and corn. The Illinois were much reduced in population through wars with other tribes and eventually dispersed from their territory.

Illinois A state in the USA, in the Midwest. It consists largely of flat prairies crossed by the Illinois and Kaskaskia Rivers. Approximately half its population is concentrated in the Chicago metropolitan area, the area to the S being predominantly rural. Illinois is a major producer of soya beans, maize, corn, pork, beef, and dairy products. Manufacturing and coalmining are also important. *History*: the first Europeans to visit Illinois were the French in the 17th century. It formed part of the French province of Louisiana but was ceded to Britain (1763). It came under US control (1783), becoming a territory in 1809 and a state in 1818. Area: 146 075 sq km (56 400 sq mi). Population (1986 est): 11 553 000. Capital: Springfield.

ILLUMINATED MANUSCRIPTS *A monastic scribe at work (detail from a 15th-century manuscript).*

illuminated manuscripts Manuscripts of gospels, books of hours, prayers, etc., decorated with designs in watercolour and frequently gold leaf. The art was first practised by monastic scribes in the early middle ages, as in the 8th-century Book of Kells. The Duke of Berry's book of hours by the de Limburg brothers (active c. 1400–c. 1416) is an outstanding example of late medieval illumination.

Illyria The Adriatic coastal region W of the Balkans. Inhabited from the 10th century BC by warlike tribes, Illyria constantly harassed Macedonia and Epirus. Piratical raids in the Adriatic provoked Roman intervention from 228 BC; Illyria became the Roman province of Illyricum in 167 BC.

Iloilo 10 41N 122 33E A port in the central Philippines, in SE Panay. The island's commercial centre, it exports sugar and rice. Population (1980): 244 827.

Ilorin 8 32N 4 34E A city in W Nigeria. It is an important local trading centre. Population (1983 est): 343 900.

Ilyushin, Sergei Vladimirovich (1894–1977) Soviet aircraft designer. He first became known for the Il-2 Stormovik dive bomber; he later worked on commercial aircraft, designing the jet airliner Il-62.

imaginary number. *See* complex numbers.

Imagism A literary movement begun in Britain in 1912, dedicated to composing poetry characterized by the concise expression of pure visual images. It derived from the criticism of T. E. Hulme (1883–1917). *Des Imagistes* (1914), an anthology edited by Ezra Pound, included poems by Richard Aldington, Hilda Doolittle (H. D.), John Gould Fletcher, and Amy Lowell.

Immaculate Conception   A dogma of the Roman Catholic Church stating that the Virgin Mary was conceived free from original sin. It was opposed by prominent theologians, such as St Bonaventure and St Thomas Aquinas but was promulgated as dogma in 1854 by Pope Pius IX.

immunity   In medicine, resistance to infection, usually that specifically acquired due to the presence of antibodies. Newborn babies have a temporary passive immunity from antibodies transferred from the mother's blood through the placenta. Active immunity is produced when an individual forms his (or her) own antibodies after exposure to an antigen, such as occurs following an infection. There are two different kinds of immune response produced by antibodies. Cell-mediated immunity is due to activity of the T-lymphocytes (produced by or dependent on the thymus), which produce cells with antibody bound to their surface. They are responsible for such reactions as graft rejection. Humoral immunity is produced by the B-lymphocytes, (probably formed by lymphatic tissue in the gut), which produce cells that release free antibody into the blood.

Immunization is the production of immunity by artificial means. This may be achieved by injecting antibodies against specific diseases (e.g. tetanus and diphtheria), providing temporary passive immunity, or by vaccination to produce active immunity.

immunology   The study of the biological processes by which the body reacts to foreign substances. Immunologists are also concerned with disorders of the immune system, including allergy and autoimmunity.

immunosuppression   The condition in which the immunity of the body is reduced. This can occur in various diseases (e.g. leukaemia and severe infections) or it may be deliberately induced by certain drugs (e.g. azathioprine and cyclophosphamide). Immunosuppressive drugs are administered after transplant surgery and are also used to treat rheumatoid arthritis and other conditions associated with autoimmunity.

impala   A common antelope, *Aepyceros melampus*, of central and S African savanna. About 100 cm high at the shoulder, impalas have a red-brown coat and white underparts; males have lyre-shaped ridged horns. Impalas are known for their agile springing leaps.

Impatiens   A genus of annual and perennial herbaceous plants (about 700 species), widely distributed in temperate and tropical regions. The genus includes touch-me-not (*I. noli-tangere*) and various cultivated species, such as the red-flowered garden balsam (*I. balsamina*) and busy Lizzies. Family: *Balsaminaceae*.

impeachment   A prosecution brought by the House of Commons as prosecutor and tried by the House of Lords as judge, especially against a minister of the Crown for a serious public offence. In the USA impeachments are brought by the House of Representatives and tried by the Senate.

impedance   A measure of the ability of a circuit to resist the flow of an alternating current. It is given by $Z = R + iX$, where Z is the impedance, R is the resistance, and X is the reactance. Impedance and reactance are measured in ohms.

Imperial War Museum   A British museum founded in 1917 to house collections of military equipment, uniforms, insignia, and art, relating mainly to the two World Wars. It occupies what was formerly Bedlam (the Bethlehem Royal Hospital) in S London.

IMPRESSIONISM   *Detail from a Pissarro (1872; Louvre).*

impressionism   A French art movement that flourished from the late 1860s to the late 1880s. Its name was derived from Monet's painting *Impression: Sunrise* (1872; Musée Marmottan, Paris), shown at the first of the eight impressionist exhibitions (1874, 1876, 1877, 1879, 1880, 1881, 1882, 1886). The leading impressionists were Monet, Pissarro, Sisley, and Renoir. The impressionists aimed to capture fleeting effects of light and weather with dabs of bright colour and a minimum of drawing.

imprinting   In ethology, a rapid and irreversible form of learning that takes place in some animals in the first hours of life. This type of behaviour was first described by Konrad Lorenz.

Incarnation   A central tenet of Christian belief, that the second person of the Trinity took human form and became man. Although in other religions gods temporarily appear in human form (i.e. a theophany), in Christianity the union of the divine and human in Christ is permanent and the integrity of both the divine and human natures is maintained. The doctrine is stated in the opening of the Gospel of St John and in St Paul's Epistle to the Colossians.

Incas   A Quechua-speaking South American Indian people of the Peruvian Andes. From their capital of Cuzco, they established, during the 15th century, an empire extending from Ecuador to central Chile. It was destroyed in the 16th century by the Spaniards. *See also* Machu Picchu.

incense   A mixture of gums and spices (especially gum benzoin) that is burnt for its aroma (*see also* frankincense). It was employed in pagan rituals in ancient Egypt, Greece, and Rome as well as in Judaic ritual and was a valued trade commodity. In the Book of Revelation it is a symbol of the prayers of saints and has been used in Christian worship since the 6th century AD.

incest   Proscribed sexual relations between close kin. The most common and universal prohibitions apply to members of the same nuclear family, such as relations between parents and children and between brothers and sisters. These taboos, founded in folklore, have a sound basis in genetics (unfavourable recessive genes can become dominant when consanguineous relatives breed). However, folklore is not always a reliable guide to what constitutes consanguinity, as in the case of taboos forbidding marriage between a man and his mother-in-law. *See also* child abuse.

Inchcape Rock. *See* Bell Rock.

Inchŏn 37 30N 126 38E A city in NW South Korea, Seoul's main seaport on the Yellow Sea. A UN attack here (1950) during the Korean War halted the North Korean invasion. Population (1980): 1 084 730.

incunabula Books printed during the infancy of modern printing (before 1500) after the invention of movable type by Gutenberg. N European incunabula have a heavy type design known as black letter; Italian books have a more elegant roman typeface.

Independence Day The national holiday in the USA that marks the adoption of the Declaration of Independence by the Continental Congress on 4 July, 1776.

independent school A UK school that is not funded by central government or a local authority. The main groups are the public schools (for 13–17 year olds), the preparatory schools ("prep" schools; 8–13 year olds), and the independent primary schools ("pre-prep" schools; 5–7).

indexation. *See* price index.

INDIA *The distribution of major language groups in the Indian subcontinent.*

India, Republic of (Hindi name: Bharat) A country in S Asia, the seventh largest in the world and the second most populous. Bordering on Pakistan, China, Nepal, Bhutan, and Burma, it comprises 25 states and 7 Union Territories. The Himalayas, in which the River Ganges rises, form a natural barrier to the N. Central India consists of a plateau (the Deccan), flanked by the mountains of the Western and Eastern Ghats. N of this lies the Indo-Gangetic plain, with the Thar Desert in the W. The

lennium before the invading Aryans established theirs (c. 1500 BC) between the Indus and the Ganges. From this civilization Hinduism emerged as India's dominant religion. The Mauryan Empire followed (c. 320 BC– c. 185 BC), which unified most of India. The 4th–6th centuries AD saw a flowering of Hindu culture in the N under the Gupta dynasty. Muslim raids on the N culminated in the establishment of a Muslim sultanate based on Delhi (1129), under which much of India was again unified. A later Muslim invasion resulted in the magnificent Mogul Empire (established 1526). At this time Europeans were also arriving. The British East India Company fought with French traders in the 18th century for a monopoly as the Mogul Empire declined. With Robert Clive's victory at Plassey (1757), the British established their supremacy and power shifted from the East India Company to the British Government. The Indian economy suffered under British trading arrangements, provoking social and political unrest. After the Indian Mutiny (1857–59) reforms were introduced, including the transfer of the East India Company's administrative powers to the India Office, represented by a viceroy and provincial governors. Subsequent reforms allowed greater Indian involvement in government, and in 1919 a parliament was created. However, the nationalist movement (*see* Indian National Congress) became increasingly forceful in its demand for home rule and, under Mahatma Gandhi, pursued a policy of civil disobedience. Independence was finally achieved in 1947 on condition that a separate Muslim state should be established. The creation of Pakistan (1947) was followed by violence and war between the two countries over Kashmir. Trouble between Hindus and Muslims erupted again in 1965 and 1971 (*see also* Bangladesh). India, which became a sovereign state in 1950, has been consolidated by the incorporation of former French and Portuguese territories (1956 and 1961) and Sikkim (1975). Indira Gandhi (prime minister 1966–77, 1980–84) suppressed a militant Sikh movement, advocating autonomy for the Punjab, in 1984. Later that year she was assassinated by Sikhs in her bodyguard; she was succeeded by her son, Rajiv Gandhi. After elections in 1989, Vishwanath Pratap Singh (1931–) became prime minister. Official languages: Hindi and English. Official currency: Indian rupee of 100 paise. Area: 3 287 590 sq km (1 269 072 sq mi), including Jammu and Kashmir. Population (1986): 783 940 000. Capital: New Delhi.

Indiana A state in the USA, forming part of the Mississippi Basin. It is largely undulating prairie with glacial lakes in the N. Agriculture is important in the central population comprises many ethnic and cultural groups and about 1600 languages and dialects are spoken. The chief religions are Hinduism (83% of the population) and Islam (11%). The caste system still survives, although untouchability has been abolished. *Economy*: 70% of the workforce is engaged in agriculture, with rice, pulses, and cereals as the main food crops; tea, jute, cotton, and tobacco are also important. Food supplies are, however, inadequate for the country's needs. Mineral resources include iron ore, manganese, bauxite, mica, and ilmenite. Coal is mined, oil is produced from the Arabian Sea, and India also has nuclear power. India is the world's tenth greatest industrial power. Chief exports are cotton goods, tea, leather, iron ore, and jute. *History*: the Indus Valley was the site of a civilization for a milplain, the major crops being soya beans, maize, wheat, and vegetables; pigs are the primary livestock. Coal and building stone are also exploited. It is a transport centre with the Ohio River linking Indiana with the Mississippi River. *History*: explored by the French in the 17th century, the area was ceded to Britain in 1763, passing to the USA in 1783. Increased settlement followed the defeat of the Indians (1794) and Indiana became a state in 1816. Area: 93 993 sq km (36 291 sq mi). Population (1986 est): 5 503 000. Capital: Indianapolis.

Indianapolis 39 45N 86 10W A city in the USA, the capital of Indiana. It is the scene of annual speedway races, including the **Indianapolis 500**, first held in 1911. Population (1986 est): 719 820.

Indian corn. *See* maize.

Indian languages Languages of widely differing origins spoken in the Indian subcontinent. The two major language families to be found are the Indo-European and the Dravidian. On the NW borders of India, Baluchi and Pashto, members of the Iranian subgroup of the Indo-European family, are spoken. Most of the other Indo-European languages of India are of the Indo-Aryan subgroup. This includes the lingua franca Hindustani; Hindi, the official national language; Rajasthani, Punjabi, Gujarati, and Sindhi in the west; and Bengali and Bihari in the east; and Kashmiri. Most of S India is covered by the Dravidian language family. In addition to these two large families, there are scattered languages of the Munda group in the NE, and languages of Sino-Tibetan origins are spoken in the Himalayas.

INDIAN MUTINY *Sepoys attack a European bungalow at Meerut (1857).*

Indian Mutiny (1857–59) A revolt of about 35 000 sepoys (Indian soldiers in the service of the British East India Company), which developed into a bloody Anglo-Indian War. It began with a massacre of Europeans at Meerut in May, 1857, following which the mutineers captured Delhi. The sepoys then rose in many other N Indian towns and were joined by local princes. Extensive British reinforcements were able under Colin Campbell (1792–1863) to regain Delhi in Sept and relieve besieged Lucknow in Nov; by July, 1858, the revolt had largely been contained.

Indian National Congress The political party, founded in 1885, that governed India after the declaration of independence in 1947. After 1917, chiefly under

the guidance of Mahatma Gandhi, it advocated non-cooperation with the British and in World War II refused to support Britain without being promised Indian independence. The party was led by Jawarhalal Nehru from 1951 to 1964, by Lal Bahadur Shastri (1904–66) until 1966, and then by Mrs Indira Gandhi until her assassination in 1984, when the leadership passed to her son Rajiv Gandhi.

Indian Ocean The world's third largest ocean, extending between Asia, Africa, Australia, and Antarctica. Lying mainly in the S hemisphere, most is within the tropical and temperate zones. The ocean floor is extremely rich in minerals.

indicator A substance used to indicate through changes in colour, fluorescence, etc., the presence of another substance or the completion of a chemical reaction. Indicators are usually weak organic acids or bases that yield ions of a different colour to the unionized molecule. For example, litmus is red in the presence of acids but blue in the presence of alkalis.

indium (In) A soft silvery metal, named after the bright indigo line in its spectrum. It is used in making transistors, rectifiers, thermistors, and alloys of low melting point. At no 49; at wt 114.82; mp 156.6°C; bp 1450°C.

Indochina The area of SE Asia comprising present-day Burma, Thailand, Malaya, Vietnam, Cambodia, and Laos. During the 19th century the French established control over the region, forming (1887) the Union of Indochina. Its capital was Saigon (now Ho Chi Minh City). During World War II the Japanese occupied all Indochina (1941). Following Japan's defeat, fighting broke out between nationalists (*see* Viet Minh) and the French, bitter conflict continuing until 1954, when the Geneva Conference ended French control of Indochina (*see also* Dien Bien Phu).

Indo-European languages The largest language family of the world, sometimes called Indo-Germanic. They are spoken throughout Europe as well as in India, Iran, and in parts of the Soviet Union, and the family is generally thought to include the following subgroups: Germanic; Italic; Indo-Iranian; Celtic; Baltic; Slavic (*see* Slavonic); Albanian; Greek; Armenian; Tocharian; and Anatolian.

Indonesia, Republic of (name from 1798 until 1945: Dutch East Indies) A country in SE Asia, consisting of a series of islands extending E–W for some 5150 km (3200 mi) in the Pacific and Indian Oceans. The main islands are Sumatra, Java and Madura, Bali, Sulawesi, Lombok, the Moluccas, and Timor together with part of Borneo (Kalimantan), and Irian Jaya (the W half of New Guinea). Most of the islands are volcanic. Its ethnically diverse population belongs mainly to the Malaysian race. The Chinese are the largest nonindigenous group. *Economy*: although rich in natural resources, it is a mainly agrarian economy of which the staple crop is rice; cash crops include rubber, palm oil, copra, sugar cane, and coffee. The main exports include oil, timber, sand, and rubber. *History*: in the middle ages kingdoms and empires flourished. In the 16th century it was occupied successively by the Portuguese, the British, and the Dutch, and from 1602 to 1798 it was ruled by the Dutch East India Company. It became a colony of the Netherlands and, after Japanese occupation during World War II, declared itself a republic in 1945 under the leadership of Dr Sukarno. The country was formally granted independence in 1949–50. Under Sukarno Irian Jaya was incorporated in 1963 and there was confrontation with Malaysia (1963–66). A military coup in 1966 under the leadership of Gen Suharto established a harsh military dictatorship; left-wing elements were virtually eliminated. Separatist movements have continued in Irian Jaya and East Timor, which was formally incorporated as a province in 1976. Official language: Bahasa Indonesia. Official currency: rupiah of 100 sen. Area: 1 903 650 sq km (735 000 sq mi). Population (1987): 172 250 000. Capital and main port: Jakarta.

Indore 22 42N 75 54E A city in India, in Madhya Pradesh. Formerly the capital of the princely state of Indore, it is an important trading centre. Population (1981): 827 000.

Indra The principal Hindu deity of the Vedic period, god of war and storm, who slew the dragon Vritra, releasing the fertile water and light necessary to create the universe. He is portrayed as wielding a thunderbolt.

indri The largest Madagascan woolly lemur, *Indri indri*. Up to 70 cm long, it is grey and black, with long hind legs, a short tail, and a doglike head. It lives in treetops, eating leaves, and has a loud howling cry. Family: *Indriidae*.

induction (electromagnetism). *See* electromagnetic induction.

induction (logic) The process of making an empirical generalization by observing particular instances of its operation. The conclusion goes beyond the facts, since not all possible instances can be examined. From induction predictions can be made but they are always liable to falsification.

indulgences In the Roman Catholic Church, remissions of the temporal penalties incurred for sins already forgiven by God in the sacrament of penance. The practice of indulgences arose in the early Church when confessors and those about to be martyred were permitted to intercede for penitents and so mitigate the discipline imposed on them. During the later middle ages, indulgences came to command a financial value, which led to widespread abuse and was one of the chief causes of Luther's attack on the Church at the Reformation. Their sale was prohibited in 1567.

Indus, River A river in S central Asia, one of the longest in the world. Rising in SW Tibet in the Himalayas, it flows NW through Kashmir, then SSW across Pakistan to its large delta near Karachi on the Arabian Sea. Its main tributary is the Panjnad. The Indus Valley contained one of the earliest organized cultures, which lasted from about 2500 until 1700 BC. Length: 2900 km (1800 mi).

industrial revolution The name given to the process of change that transformed Britain and then other countries from agricultural to industrial economies. The industrial revolution began about 1750 when the agricultural revolution was well under way. Inventions were made in the textile industry by such men as James Hargreaves, Richard Arkwright, and Samuel Crompton, which made the production of cloth much faster and the yarn produced of better quality. These new machines necessitated the building of factories to house them, at first near rivers for water power and then, when the steam engine was invented, near coalfields. Industrial towns sprang up, where living and working conditions were pitiable, but the current belief in laissez-faire meant little was done to interfere with the progress of industrial growth. Advances were also made in the production of iron, especially by Henry Cort (1740–1800), and in communications. The canals were extended and from about 1830 railways were built. By the mid-19th century British industrial methods had spread to continental Europe and the USA, laying the foundations for further progress in the 20th century.

inert gases. *See* noble gases.

inertia A property of a body that causes it to resist changes in its velocity or, if stationary, to resist motion. When the body resists changes in its linear motion its mass is a measurement of its inertia (*see* mass and weight). When it resists changes in rotation about an axis its inertia is given by its moment of inertia.

inertial guidance A means of guiding a missile or submarine without communicating with its destination or point of departure. It consists of a set of three gyroscopes, with their axes mounted mutually perpendicular to each other, connected to a computer. The gyroscopes provide a frame of reference, which enables the computer to adjust the controls to steer a preset course.

INDUSTRIAL REVOLUTION *Cotton weaving by power loom (c. 1835).*

infallibility A dogma of the Roman Catholic Church promulgated at the first Vatican Council (1870). It stated that the pope cannot err in defining the Church's teaching in matters of faith and morals when speaking *ex cathedra* (Latin: from the throne), i.e. when intending to make such a pronouncement.

infection Illness caused by microorganisms, including bacteria, viruses, fungi, and protozoa. Examples of bacterial infections are diphtheria, pneumonia, and whooping cough. Viruses cause influenza, measles, and smallpox (among others); malaria and sleeping sickness result from protozoan infection, and fungi cause ringworm. Infectious diseases are the commonest cause of sickness and−except in modern industrial societies−have always been the main cause of death. Methods of transmission include direct contact with an infected person, contact with a human or animal carrier or contaminated objects, and contact with infected droplets produced by coughing and sneezing. Antibiotics are active against a wide range of organisms, but as yet there are few effective drugs for viral diseases (*see* vaccination).

inferiority complex An unconscious belief, first described by Alfred Adler, that one is severely inadequate in some particular way. This leads to defensive behaviour and often to an overcompensation, such as open aggressiveness.

infinity In mathematics, a quantity larger than any that can be specified. The symbols $+\infty$ and $-\infty$ are read as "plus infinity" and "minus infinity" respectively. They indicate infinitely large positive and negative values. $x \rightarrow +\infty$ means that the value of a variable quantity, x, continues to increase and has no maximum.

inflation A general sustained increase in prices resulting from excessive demand for goods (demand-pull inflation), increased pricing by sellers in the absence of increased demand (cost-push inflation), or an expansion of the money supply (monetary inflation). **Deflation** is the opposite process and causes a reduction in both output and employment. Deflation in the 1930s has been followed in the postwar years by a protracted period of inflation. Remedies have varied according to the importance ascribed to each contributory factor: control of wages and prices (prices and incomes policy), increased taxation, control of interest rates, reduced government spending, and a controlled money supply have been among current policies. *Compare* depression.

inflorescence The arrangement of a group of flowers borne on the same main stalk, of which there are two basic types. In a racemose (or indefinite) inflorescence the tip of the main stem continues to grow and flowers arise below it. Examples are the raceme (e.g. foxglove) and the spike (e.g. wheat). A cymose (or definite) inflorescence, or cyme, is one in which a flower is produced at the tip of the main stem, which then ceases to grow. Growth is continued either by one lateral bud below the tip, to produce a monochasium (e.g. buttercup), or by a pair of buds, giving a dichasium (e.g. stitchwort).

information theory The mathematical theory of communication, involving analysis of the information content of messages and the processes used in their transmission, reception, storage, and retrieval. Statistical concepts, such as probability, are used to assess the extra information (redundancy) necessary to compensate for spurious signals (noise) occurring during communication. The bit is the basic unit of information and the channel capacity is a measure of the ability of the

transmission medium, e.g. a telegraph line, to carry information.

infrared radiation Electromagnetic radiation with wavelengths between about 750 nanometres and 1 millimetre. In the electromagnetic spectrum it lies between the red end of visible light and microwaves. It was discovered in 1800 by William Herschel (1738−1822).

infrared telescope A reflecting telescope for detecting and studying infrared radiation from astronomical sources. Semiconductor detectors are used, and these (and in some cases the telescope optics) must be cooled to very low temperatures. Infrared telescopes are normally sited at high altitudes to reduce infrared absorption by the atmosphere or are carried on satellites.

infrasonics The study of sound waves with a frequency below the threshold of human hearing, i.e. below about 20 hertz. They are produced naturally by earthquakes and tidal waves.

INGRES *Detail from a self-portrait (1804; Musée Condé, Chantilly).*

Ingres, Jean-Auguste-Dominique (1780−1867) French painter. His three paintings of the Rivière family (Louvre) established him as a skilled portraitist. Many of his historical and mythological paintings aroused criticism but his *Vow of Louis XIII* (Cathedral, Montauban) established him as an opponent of Romanticism. He is noted for his nudes, e.g. *Valpinçon Bather* (Louvre); his draughtsmanship influenced Degas and Picasso.

inheritance tax A UK tax introduced in 1986 to replace capital-transfer tax. The first £118,000 of an inheritance is tax-free, thereafter a flat rate of 40% is applied. The tax on lifetime gifts was replaced with a tapered charge on gifts made within seven years of death.

initiation rites Rituals performed on the transition from childhood to adult status or on joining certain professions or associations. During this period adolescents among primitive peoples are often educated in the duties of adulthood. Circumcision may be practised at this time.

initiative. *See* referendum and initiative.

ink A coloured fluid for writing or printing. Ordinary permanent blue-black writing ink contains ferrous sulphate, mineral organic acid, and other dyes. Coloured inks contain only synthetic dyes, while washable inks use water-soluble synthetic dyes. Marking ink is a mixture of inorganic and organic salts. Indian ink is a black waterproof ink containing carbon black and shellac. Printing ink consists of pigments suspended in linseed oil, resins, and solvents. Ballpoint pen ink consists of synthetic dye dissolved in organic liquids with a resinous binder.

Ink cap A mushroom belonging to the genus *Coprinus*, the gills of which are digested after release of the spores to form an inky fluid that drips from the cap. The common ink cap (*C. atramentarius*) grows at the base of trees and shrubs, and has a pale brownish-grey cap, 3–7 cm high, and a whitish stalk.

Inkerman, Battle of (5 November, 1854) A decisive battle of the Crimean War, in which the French and British defeated the Russians at Inkerman, near Sevastopol. The Russians lost about 12 000 men, the British, about 2 500, and the French, about 1 000.

Inland Sea A shallow section of the NW Pacific Ocean between the Japanese islands of Honshu, Shikoku, and Kyushu.

Inner Temple. *See* Inns of Court.

Innsbruck 47 17N 11 25E A city in W Austria, the capital of the Tirol on the River Inn. It is a popular tourist and winter-sports centre. Population (1981): 117 287.

Inns of Court Assocations with the exclusive right to confer the rank or degree of barrister-at-law, known as "calling to the Bar." For the English bar, the Inns are the Honourable Societies of Lincoln's Inn (established 1310), Middle Temple (1340), Inner Temple (1340), and Gray's Inn (1357). Most barristers' offices (known as chambers) in London are in one of the Inns.

Inorganic chemistry. *See* chemistry.

Inquisition (*or* Holy Office) An institution of the medieval and early modern Church designed to combat heresy and moral offences. Formally instituted (1231) by Pope Gregory IX (c. 1148–1241), it attempted to place all control of heresy in papal hands. The use of torture was authorized in 1252 and trials were held in secrecy; fines and various penances were imposed on those who confessed, while those who refused were imprisoned or executed by burning. Almost entirely confined to S Europe, the Inquisition was revived in Spain in 1478 against apostate Jews, Muslims, and, later, Protestants. The growth of Protestantism also led to the establishment (1542) of a Roman Inquisition by Pope Paul III. In 1965 the Holy Office was renamed the Sacred Congregation for the Doctrine of the Faith; it is now concerned with maintaining Roman Catholic discipline.

INRI Abbreviation for *Iesus Nazarenus Rex Iudeorum* (Jesus of Nazareth King of the Jews). According to St John (19.19–20) this inscription, written in Hebrew, Greek, and Latin, was placed by order of Pilate on the cross upon which Jesus was crucified.

Insanity In law (although not a legal term), defect of reason caused by disease of the mind, making a person not responsible for his acts. A person is presumed sane until the contrary is proved. If a jury finds an accused person committed an act as charged but was insane, it must return a verdict of not guilty by reason of insanity. According to **M'Naghten's Rules** an accused person is insane if he was unaware of the nature or quality of his act or did not know it was morally wrong. Insanity may affect a person's capacity to make binding contracts or a will or his fitness to stand trial.

Insect An invertebrate animal, 0.2–350 mm long, belonging to the largest class in the animal kingdom (*Insecta*; about a million known species). Insects occur throughout the world and account for 83% of all animal life. An insect's body is divided into three sections: the head, which bears a pair of antennae; the thorax, with three pairs of legs and typically two pairs of wings; and the abdomen. With biting or sucking mouthparts they feed on almost all plant or animal materials. The majority of insects lay eggs, which go through a series of changes (metamorphosis) to reach the adult stage. Insects play an important role in nature as predators, parasites, scavengers, and as prey, but can also spread disease. Others are useful in pollinating crops or killing insect pests and some produce useful substances, such as honey, beeswax, and silk. Phylum: *Arthropoda*.

Insecticides Substances used to kill insects by chemical action. Previously, strong inorganic poisons, such as arsenic compounds and cyanides, were used but these were also toxic to humans and livestock. Synthetic organic substances, beginning with DDT in 1945, are now widely used. **Contact insecticides** are applied directly to the insects, while **residual insecticides** are sprayed on surfaces that the insects touch. Problems of insect immunity and environmental pollution have encouraged research into alternative methods involving biological control.

Insectivora The order of mammals, comprising about 375 species, that includes shrews, tenrecs, hedgehogs, moles and desmans, golden moles, and solenodons. Feeding mainly on invertebrates, insectivores are fairly primitive mammals with narrow snouts and sharp simple teeth. Frequently nocturnal, insectivores are found in nearly all regions; they are absent from the Poles and Australasia.

insectivorous plant. *See* carnivorous plant.

Instinct 1. A complex pattern of behaviour, the form of which is determined by heredity and is therefore characteristic of all individuals of the same species. Although the behaviour may be released and modified by environmental stimuli, its basic pattern does not depend on the experience of the individual. Birdsong and the complex behaviour of social insects (such as bees) are striking examples. **2.** An innate drive, such as hunger or sex, that urges the individual towards a particular goal.

insulin A protein hormone that is secreted by the islets of Langerhans in the pancreas. It stimulates the uptake of glucose and amino acids from the blood by the tissues and the formation of glycogen. Insulin was first isolated in 1921 by Banting and Best and its amino acid composition and three-dimensional structure were revealed by Frederick Sanger (1918–) and Dorothy Hodgkin (1910–). A deficiency of insulin causes the symptoms of diabetes mellitus.

Insurance A method of providing monetary compensation for a misfortune or loss that may not occur. Events that must occur at some time, such as death, are provided for by assurance. In the UK and some other countries insurance against unemployment, sickness, and retirement is provided by the government (*see* National Insurance). Other types of insurance are undertaken either by insurance companies or by Lloyd's. The public does not deal directly with the underwriters (insurers) but arranges to cover a risk through an insurance broker, who works for a commission. The cost to the insured of covering the risk (premium) is calculated by the insurer's actuary on the basis of the probability of the risk occurring.

INSECT

silverfish

swallowtail butterfly

cranefly

hoverfly

mayfly

springtail

earwig

hawthorn shield bug

aphid

damselfly

ocelli (simple eyes)

head

thorax

forewing

hindwing

compound eye

abdomen

antenna

mandible

hind leg

foreleg

middle leg

lacewing

scorpion fly

leaf beetle

flea

termite

green bush cricket

mantis

bumblebee

ant

stick insect

sucking louse

American cockroach

INSECT *The structure of a typical insect (centre), with representatives from all the principal insect orders.*

Intaglio The production of a sunken image, especially in metal or stone, by etching or engraving. It is used in sculpture, gems, and seals, and for making the plates for gravure printing.

Integrated circuit (IC) A solid-state semiconductor circuit contained in a single wafer of semiconductor. ICs are made by a process of etching and diffusing a pattern of impurities into the semiconductor surface, forming tiny p-n junctions, which make up individual diodes, transistors, etc. Since the 1970s computers have been used to make ICs smaller and more complex. A silicon chip (*or* microchip) is covered with circuits, and computer-controlled microscopic probes search out the best points for connections for each specific device.

Intelligence The ability to reason and to profit by experience. An individual's level of intelligence is determined by a complex interaction between his heredity and environment; Jean Piaget (1896–1980) greatly contributed to present-day understanding of intellectual development. The first **intelligence tests** were devised by Alfred Binet (1857–1911) in 1905. An individual's performance in a test is represented by his **intelligence quotient** (IQ). Tests are constructed so that the average IQ is 100 and over 95% of the population come between 70 and 130. However, it is now widely thought that true intelligence can be expressed only through speech and writing (and is therefore inaccessible to testing).

Intelligence service The government department responsible for obtaining information about the military and economic capabilities and political intentions of another country (intelligence) or for thwarting the attempts of a foreign country to obtain such information for itself (counterintelligence). Intelligence services existed in antiquity and the first known treatise on the subject is Sun Tzu's *The Art of War* (c. 400 BC). Elizabeth I of England had a notable intelligence service, as did Cardinal de Richelieu in 17th-century France and Frederick the Great in 18th-century Prussia. The first specifically military service was established in France during the Napoleonic Wars, which the British countered (1808) with the Peninsular Corps of Guides in Spain. A similar corps was set up (1855) during the Crimean War. The subsequent Intelligence Department was active in the second Boer War (1899–1902). In 1909 and 1912 respectively the army general staff's Directorate of Military Operations organized MO-5 (counterintelligence) and MO-6 (intelligence), which soon became MI(Military Intelligence)-5 (the Security Service) and MI-6 (the Secret Intelligence Service). Elsewhere, the best-known intelligence services are the Central Intelligence Agency, the Federal Bureau of Investigation (counterintelligence), and the National Security Agency (dealing with cryptology) in the USA and the KGB in the Soviet Union.

Intelsat. *See* communications satellite.

Inter-American Development Bank An international bank founded in 1959 to provide assistance for developing countries in Latin America and the Caribbean by making loans at very low interest rates.

Interest The amount of money charged by a lender to a borrower for the use of a loan. The principal (P) is the amount on which interest is calculated; the term (t), the length of time in years for which the money is lent; and the interest rate (r), the annual rate of return per 100 units of principal. In simple interest, the principal each year is the sum originally lent. The lender is paid $Prt/100$ in interest and repaid P after t years. In compound interest, the interest each year is not paid to the lender but is added to the principal, so that the principal for the next year becomes $P + r/100$. After t years the lender is paid $P(1 + r/100)^t$.

Interference A wave phenomenon in which two waves combine either to reinforce each other or to cancel each other out, depending on their relative phases. The pattern of light and dark strips so produced is called an **interference pattern** (*or* interference fringe). Interference was discovered in 1801 by Thomas Young and provided strong evidence for the wave theory of light.

An **interferometer** is used to produce interference patterns, mainly for the accurate measurement of wavelengths.

Interferon A protein that appears in the plasma during viral infections: it is released from infected cells and inhibits the growth of the viruses. Interferon plays an important role in immunity because it can enter uninfected cells and render them immune to all viral infections. It was discovered in 1957 by a British virologist, Alick Isaacs (1921–67).

Internal-combustion engine A heat engine in which fuel is burnt inside the engine, rather than in a separate furnace (*see* steam engine). This category includes all piston engines, jet engines, and rockets. The first practical internal-combustion engine was patented by N. Otto in 1876. The modern petrol engine, used to power most road vehicles, has a compression ratio of 8 or 9 to 1, which requires special fuels (*see* tetraethyl lead) to avoid knocking. A simpler but less efficient variety of the petrol engine is the two-stroke, which is used where low power is required. The main alternative to the petrol engine is the oil engine, based on a cycle invented by the German engineer Rudolf Diesel (1858–1913). In this case the compression ratio has to be 15 or 16 to 1, making the engine considerably heavier and more expensive than the petrol engine. The problem of vibration is overcome to some extent in the Wankel engine. The gas turbine uses continuous combustion and with a compression ratio of up to 30:1 can reach a working temperature of 1200 °C. It is therefore more efficient and creates less pollution than piston engines. Jet engines based on the gas turbine are used widely in aircraft.

International An association of national socialist or labour parties formed to promote socialism or communism. The **First International** was founded in London in 1864 as the International Working Men's Association. Karl Marx soon assumed its leadership and its first congress was held in Geneva in 1866. Although the First International was successful in disseminating socialist ideas among workers, it failed to make any political changes. Its last meeting was held in 1876 in Philadelphia.

The **Second International** was founded in Paris in 1889; its headquarters were in Brussels. Its leaders included Ramsay MacDonald. At the outbreak of World War I, the organization collapsed because of division between pro- and anti-war groups. A postwar attempt to revive it failed.

The **Labour and Socialist International** was founded in Vienna in 1921; its goal was to create a socialist commonwealth. It has been called the "second and a half International" because it was composed of those out of sympathy with the Second and Third Internationals. It came to an end following Hitler's invasions in W Europe in 1939.

The **Third International** (*or* Comintern), an organization of world Communist Parties, was founded by Lenin in March, 1919, to encourage worldwide proletariat revolution. Throughout its existence it was influenced by the power struggles within the Soviet party leadership. Stalin dissolved the International in 1943.

The **Fourth International** was founded by Trotsky in Mexico City in 1937 in opposition to Stalin and the Third International. It held its first conference in France in 1938.

The **Socialist International** was founded in 1951 as an association of socialist parties that believe in parliamentary democracy and oppose communism. Its headquarters are in London.

INTERNAL-COMBUSTION ENGINE *Estimates of cost, weight, and pollution for various types of internal-combustion engine compared to a steam engine.*

International Bank for Reconstruction and Development (IBRD)   A specialized agency of the United Nations, known as the World Bank, with headquarters in Washington, DC. It finances development in member countries by making loans to governments or under government guarantee. It was set up by the 1944 Bretton Woods agreements.

International Brigades   A volunteer army recruited during the Spanish Civil War (1936–39) by the Comintern to aid the Republicans against Franco. Comprising at its largest some 20 000 volunteers, of which about 60% were communists, it was disbanded in 1938.

International Civil Aviation Organization (ICAO) A specialized agency of the United Nations established in 1947 to promote high operating standards and fair competition among international airlines. It has its headquarters in Montreal.

International Court of Justice   The judicial body set up by the UN to pass judgment on disputes between states. The court, which normally sits at The Hague, comprises 15 judges, each from a different state, elected by the UN General Assembly. Judgments of the court are enforced by application to the UN Security Council.

International Date Line   A line following the 180° meridian, deviating to avoid some land areas. The date immediately E of the line is one day earlier than to the W.

Internationale   The national anthem of the Soviet Union until 1944, composed by P. Degeyter (1848–1932).

International Labour Organisation (ILO)   A specialized agency of the United Nations dedicated to the improvement of working conditions and living standards. It was first convened in 1919, affiliated to the League of Nations, and its headquarters are in Geneva.

international law   The rules that determine the legal relationship between independent states (public), or the method of resolving disputes between individuals concerning transactions to which two or more legal systems may be relevant, as when a contract made in one country is to be performed in another (private). Public international law, also called the law of nations and administered by the International Court of Justice, is based on: (1) natural law, being laws recognized by civilized nations; (2) agreements between states, i.e. conventions; (3) customs followed in practice; and, to a lesser extent (4) the writings and opinions of respected jurists. Private international law, also called conflict of laws, determines the laws of which country should apply.

International Monetary Fund (IMF)   A specialized agency of the United Nations, with headquarters in Washington, DC, set up by the 1944 Bretton Woods agreements to stabilize exchange rates and facilitate international trade.

International Organization for Standardization (ISO)   An organization, situated in Geneva, for establishing and controlling international scientific, industrial, and commercial standards of measurement and design. It was founded in 1946.

International Phonetic Alphabet (IPA)   An augmented Roman alphabet, developed by the International Phonetic Association in the late 19th century. It attempts to symbolize, on phonetic principles, every sound used in human language.

international style   The predominant architectural style of the 20th century. Originating in W Europe and the USA with such architects as Gropius, Wright, Behrens, and Le Corbusier, the style evolved from the new tastes, materials, and advanced technology produced by industrialization. It is characterized by the use of concrete, often roughcast, cubic forms, and a functional asymmetry.

International Union for the Conservation of Nature.   *See* endangered species.

Interpol (*Inter*national Criminal *Pol*ice Organization) An association of about 120 national police forces formed in 1923 to provide a means of international cooperation in the prevention of crime. Its major concerns are the exchange of police information and the arrest of those who are the subject of an extradition order.

Interregnum.   *See* Commonwealth.

intestine   The part of the digestive tract, in the abdomen, that extends from the stomach to the anus. The small intestine, which includes the duodenum, jejunum, and ileum, is the principal site of digestion and absorption of food. The large intestine consists of the colon, caecum, rectum, and anus. It is largely concerned with the absorption of water from digested food and the formation of faeces, which are expelled from the anus.

intra-uterine device (IUD).   *See* contraception.

introversion (*or* intraversion)   A quality of personality characterized by interest in oneself rather than in the outside world: it is the opposite of extroversion. Introverts are reflective and highly susceptible to permanent conditioning.

intrusive rock. *See* igneous rock.

Invar An alloy of iron with 36% nickel, which expands by only 0.9 mm per km for each centigrade degree temperature rise. It was discovered in 1896 and since then has been used for accurate measuring tapes and chronometer parts.

Inverness 57 27N 4 15W A city in N Scotland, the administrative centre of the Highland Region, at the head of the Moray Firth. It has a 19th-century cathedral and castle. Population (1981): 39 736.

invertebrate Any animal without a backbone. Invertebrates include the protochordates—animals that possess a rodlike skeletal notochord. The term is seldom employed in taxonomic systems.

investment company (*or* investment trust) A company that buys and sells securities to make profits for its shareholders. The company has a fixed capital and its shares are bought and sold on the stock exchange. In the USA it is called a closed-end investment company. *Compare* unit trust.

in vitro fertilization. *See* test-tube baby.

Io (Greek legend) A priestess of Hera, loved by Zeus, who transformed her into a heifer to protect her from discovery. Hera ordered Argus, a herdsman with eyes covering his entire body, to guard her, but she escaped with the help of Hermes and was finally restored to Zeus in Egypt.

iodine (I) A purple-black lustrous solid halogen that evaporates slowly at room temperature to give a purple gas. It was discovered in 1811 by B. Courtois (1777–1838). It is insoluble in water but dissolves readily in organic solvents, such as chloroform ($CHCl_3$) or carbon tetrachloride (CCl_4), to give pink-purple solutions. Potassium iodide (KI) is widely used in photography. The radioactive isotope ^{131}I, with a half-life of 8.1 days, is produced in nuclear reactors. Tincture of iodine is used as an antiseptic. At no 53; at wt 126.904; mp 113.5°C; bp 184.35°C.

ion An atom or group of atoms that has lost or gained one or more electrons and consequently has an electric charge. Positively and negatively charged ions are called **cations** and **anions** respectively. The sign and magnitude of the charge is indicated by a superscript, as in the potassium ion, K^+, or the doubly charged sulphate ion, SO_4^{2-}. Many compounds (electrovalent compounds) are combinations of positive and negative ions; sodium chloride, for example is formed from sodium ions (Na^+) and chloride ions (Cl^-). *See also* chemical bond; ionization.

Iona 56 19N 6 25W A small sparsely populated island in NW Scotland, in the Inner Hebrides. St Columba landed here in 563 AD, establishing a monastery that became the centre of the Celtic Church. Area: 854 ha (2112 acres).

Ionesco, Eugène (1912–) French dramatist, born in Romania. He inaugurated the Theatre of the Absurd with his first play, *The Bald Prima Donna* (1950). His later plays include *The Lesson* (1951), *Rhinoceros* (1960), and *Man With Bags* (1977).

Ionia In antiquity, the central W coast of Asia Minor and the adjacent islands, settled by Greeks about 1000 BC. Between the 8th and 6th centuries BC Miletus, Samos, Ephesus, and other Ionian cities led Greece in trade, colonization, and culture. After 550 BC Ionia passed under the domination of Lydia and later Persia.

IONA *The 13th-century abbey. Two Celtic crosses can be seen in the foreground.*

Ionian Islands A group of Greek islands in the Ionian Sea, including Páxos, Lévkas, Ithaca, and Cephalonia. They belonged to Britain from the Treaty of Paris (1815) until 1864, when they were ceded to Greece. Total area: 2307 sq km (891 sq mi). Population (1981): 182 651.

Ionic order. *See* orders of architecture.

ionization The process of producing ions from neutral atoms or molecules, by solvation (surrounding of an ion by polar solvent molecules), heating (thermal ionization), or bombardment with particles or radiation. The minimum energy required to ionize an atom A (i.e. A → $A^+ + e^-$) is called its **ionization potential**, which is usually measured in electronvolts.

ionization chamber An instrument used for measuring the intensity of ionizing radiation. It consists of a gas-filled chamber containing two electrodes with a large potential difference between them. The Geiger counter is an example of an ionization chamber.

ionizing radiation Any radiation that ionizes the atoms or molecules of the matter through which it passes. It may consist of particles (such as electrons) or it may be electromagnetic radiation (*see* ultraviolet radiation; X-rays; gamma radiation). Ionizing radiation occurs naturally in cosmic rays and is emitted by radioactive substances. It is also produced artificially in X-ray machines, particle accelerators, nuclear reactors, etc.

ionosphere A region of the upper atmosphere that reflects short radio waves, enabling transmissions to be made round the curved surface of the earth by sky waves. The gases in the ionosphere are ionized by absorption of radiation from the sun. Its existence was suggested in 1902 by A. E. Kennelly (1861–1939) and independently by O. Heaviside (1850–1925). Sir Edward Appleton (1892–1925) provided proof by bouncing radio waves off the different layers of the ionosphere, which vary in behaviour with the position of the sun and with the sunspot cycle. The ionization of the D region, at between 50 and 90 kilometres altitude, disappears during the day. The E region is 90 to 160 kilometres high and the F region (sometimes called the Appleton layer) is from 160 up to about 400 kilometres.

Iowa A state in the USA, in the Midwest. The land rises slowly from the Mississippi Valley, with higher land in the NW. Iowa is predominantly an agricultural state, famed for its livestock, particularly pigs. Major crops are corn, oats, soya beans, and other fodder crops. There is also some mining for portland cement and gypsum. *History*: explored by the Frenchmen Louis Jolliet (1645–1700) and Jacques Marquette (1637–75) in 1673, it formed part of the Louisiana Purchase (1803) by the USA. It became a territory (1838) and then a state (1846). Area: 145 790 sq km (56 290 sq mi). Population (1986 est): 2 851 000. Capital: Des Moines.

ipecacuanha A South American herbaceous plant, *Uragoga ipecacuanha*, cultivated in the tropics for its root, which yields medicinal alkaloids used as an expectorant and emetic. Family: *Rubiaceae*.

Iphigenia In Greek legend, the eldest daughter of Agamemnon and Clytemnestra. At the beginning of the Trojan War, Agamemnon was told that Artemis demanded the sacrifice of his daughter before his fleet could sail to Troy. He was about to comply when Artemis took pity on Iphigenia and transported her to Tauris, where she became a priestess of Artemis.

Ipoh 4 36N 101 02E A city in NW Peninsular Malaysia, the capital of Perak state. The tinmining centre of Malaysia, it has noted Chinese rock temples. Population (1980): 300 727.

Ipswich 52 04N 1 10E A town in SE England, the administrative centre of Suffolk at the head of the Orwell estuary. It is a port with engineering, printing, brewing, flour-milling, plastics, fertilizers, tobacco, and textile industries. Cardinal Wolsey was born here. Population (1982 est): 120 908.

IRA. *See* Irish Republican Army.

Iráklion (*or* Herakleion; Italian name: Candia) 32 20N 25 08E The chief port of the Greek island of Crete, on the N coast. It possesses many Venetian fortifications, and is a tourist centre. Exports include raisins, grapes, and olive oil. Population (1981): 101 634.

Iran, Islamic Republic of (name until 1935: Persia) A country in the Middle East lying between the Caspian Sea and the Persian Gulf. Its central plateau, containing deserts and marshes, is surrounded by mountains. The population is mainly Persian with groups of Turks, Kurds, Armenians, Arabs, and such tribes as the Bakhtyari. *Economy*: agriculture supports 75% of the population, although lack of rain hampers productivity. Wheat, rice, tobacco, fruit, sugar beet, and tea are grown; sheep and goats are kept. The main oilfields are in the Zagros Mountains, where oil was first discovered (1908). Other minerals include coal, copper, iron ore, lead, natural gas, and precious stones. Oil revenues have been used to diversify the economy; to this end many capital goods, such as machinery, are imported. *History*: the Caspian coast and the plateau are among the earliest centres of civilization. Early Persian dynasties include the Achaemenians and the Sasanians (*see also* Greek-Persian Wars). Arab domination, which established Islam in the area, was followed by that of the Turks and Mongols before the Persian Safavid dynasty (1502–1736) came into power. Following a period of great prosperity (1587–1629) Persia again declined, encroached on by Uzbeks, Arabs, Afghans, Turks, and Russians. The next great dynasty, the Kajar dynasty (1794–1925),

IRAN *The Islamic Revolution encourages women to return to the chuddar.*

was marked largely by rivalry for domination between Britain and Russia. Repressive rule provoked opposition that was intensified by resentment against the concessions granted to Britain and Russia. The Shah was forced to grant a constitution and National Assembly (the Majlis; 1906); his successor disbanded this and was then deposed (1909). Further disorders brought Reza Khan to power (1921), from 1925 as Reza Shah Pahlavi. Under his virtual dictatorship order returned and the country was westernized; he was forced to abdicate in favour of his son Mohammed Reza Pahlavi (1941). In 1945 the Soviet Union supported an Azerbaidzhan and Kurdish revolt to gain oil concessions (later withdrawn). Oil was also a major issue for the militant National Front movement, which nationalized the oil industry (1951); the British responded with a blockade. The Shah's reform programme, which included in 1963 the enfranchisement of women, the redistribution of land, and compulsory education, led to riots and harsh repression. By 1978 different opposition groups had united under the exiled Muslim leader Ayatollah Ruholla Khomeini. The Shah left the country in 1979, later dying in exile (1980), and Ayatollah Khomeini took over the government in the so-called Islamic Revolution, which established a strict Muslim regime. War with Iraq broke out in September, 1980 (*see* Gulf War). President: Ali Akbar Hashemi Rafsanjani. Official language: Persian (Farsi). Official currency: Iranian rial of 100 dinars. Area: 1 648 000 sq km (636 160 sq mi). Population (1987): 49 700 000. Capital: Tehran.

Iranian languages A subgroup of the Indo-Iranian language family. Iranian languages are spoken in Iran, Afghanistan, Turkey, and parts of the Caucasus and are closely related to Sanskrit. Modern Iranian languages include Persian, Kurdish, Pashto, and Ossetic.

Iraq, Republic of A country in the Middle East, bordering on the Persian Gulf. The SE consists of an alluvial plain around the delta of the Rivers Tigris and Euphrates. The W is a vast desert while the N is mountainous. The population is about 90% Muslim divided evenly between Shiite and Sunnite sects. The Kurds, who live in the NE, form about 15–20% of the population. *Econo-*

my: mainly agricultural, the chief crops being wheat, barley, rice, maize, sorghum, sesame, dates, and cotton. The main industry is oil (first discovered at Kirkuk in 1927) and Iraq is a member of OPEC. *History*: as Mesopotamia, Iraq was the site of the world's first civilization. It was conquered by Arabia and became Muslim in the 7th century AD and was part of the Ottoman Empire from 1534 until World War I, when UK troops expelled the Turks. As a British mandate (1920–32), Iraq became a kingdom (1921). From this period on it has been politically unstable; the monarchy was overthrown in 1958. Since the 1960s the Kurds have been in intermittent rebellion and there has been opposition to the socialist government (in power since 1968) from Muslims and communists. In 1980, following a build up of tensions, war broke out against Iran (*see* Gulf War). President: Sadam Hussein (1935–). Official language: Arabic. Official currency: Iraqi dinar of 1000 fils. Area: 438 446 sq km (169 248 sq mi). Capital: Baghdad. Population (1987): 17 093 000.

Ireland The second largest island in the British Isles, separated from Great Britain by the North Channel, the Irish Sea, and St George's Channel. It consists of a central lowland area of fertile plains, bogs, and moorland, rising to hills and mountains in the N and S. Since 1920 Ireland has been politically divided, the NE part forming Northern Ireland in the UK and the remainder comprising the Republic of Ireland. *History*: Ireland was invaded in the 4th century BC by the Celts. The country came to be divided into the five tribal kingdoms (the Five Fifths) of Ulster, Meath, Leinster, Munster, and Connaught. In the 5th century the country was converted to Christianity—a process in which St Patrick was the outstanding figure. The 9th and 10th centuries saw Viking invasions; in the mid-12th century Ireland was invaded by the Norman conquerors of England and Henry II gained the allegiance of the Irish kings. English law and administration were introduced in the 13th century and an Irish parliament (composed of the Anglo-Irish and subordinate to the English Crown) began to meet. However, English rule was restricted to the area around Dublin (called the Pale) until the 16th century. Revolts, inspired in part by Roman Catholic opposition to the Reformation, were suppressed and the Plantation of Ire-

IRELAND *The Battle of the Boyne (1690), at which William of Orange defeated James II.*

IRELAND *De Valera takes the salute at a rally of the Fianna Fáil (1932).*

land by English and later by Scottish settlers was begun in Ulster. Irish resistance continued, culminating in the rebellion of 1641, which was not suppressed until Oliver Cromwell's notorious expedition in 1649–50. The subsequent redistribution of the rebels' land among English colonists established the economic and political ascendancy of the Protestant minority in Ireland. It was strengthened by the Restoration settlement, which extended Protestant landholdings, and by William of Orange's defeat (1690) of the Irish supporters of the deposed Catholic king, James II. In the 18th century Ireland's subservience to England came to be opposed by many Irish Protestants and in 1782, under the leadership of Henry Grattan, the Irish parliament obtained legislative independence. However, the abortive rebellion of 1798 by the Society of United Irishmen persuaded Pitt the Younger of the need for the complete union of Britain and Ireland (1800; *see* Union, Acts of). It also convinced him of the need for Catholic emancipation, which was not fully obtained until 1829. Attempts by the Young Ireland group to repeal the Act of Union failed, and nationalist agitation was taken up after the Irish (potato) famine first, abortively, by the Fenians and then by the Home Rule movement. While the Land League pursued agrarian reform with some success, Home Rule, in spite of Gladstone's conversion to the cause, was delayed. Following the proclamation of an Irish republic by Sinn Fein (1919) and virtual civil war Britain proposed partition (1920), with the establishment of separate parliaments in the predominantly Protestant NE and Catholic S and W. The formula was unacceptable to the Republicans and in 1921 the Irish Free State, with dominion status, came into being. The NE (Northern Ireland) immediately withdrew, accepting self-government within the UK.

Northern Ireland The province comprises the six counties of Antrim, Armagh, Down, Fermanagh, Londonderry, and Tyrone. *Economy*: since the 1950s, the traditional industries of shipbuilding and linen manufacture as well as agriculture have declined and there has been expansion of the service sector. *History*: the Government of Ireland Act (1920) established a parliament, which met at Stormont Castle in Belfast and had legislative responsibility for most matters other than foreign affairs. Some 17 MPs are returned to the UK parliament. The Protestant majority in Northern Ireland predominantly supports the union with Great Britain, while many of the Roman Catholic minority seek union with the Republic of Ireland. Violent conflict broke out between the two groups in 1969, since when the British army has maintained a peacekeeping force in Northern Ireland. Terrorist activities in Ireland and Great Britain led to the imposition (1972) of direct rule of Northern Ireland by the UK parliament. Bombings and shootings, both by the IRA and Protestant paramilitary groups, continue. The Anglo-Irish Agreement (1985) allowed the Republic a say in Northern Irish affairs. Area: 14 121 sq km (5452 sq mi). Population (1986 est): 1 566 800. Capital: Belfast.

Republic of Ireland (Irish name: Éire) The country is administratively divided into 26 counties. *Economy*: predominantly agricultural, cattle rearing being of major importance. Dairy farming is also extensively practised. Arable crops include barley, wheat, oats, potatoes, and sugar beet. Tourism is the second major source of revenue. Peat is extensively cut as a fuel for power stations and as a household fuel. In 1977 Europe's largest lead-zinc mines were opened at Navan. *History*: Republican opposition to partition continued immediately after the establishment of the Irish Free State but was quelled by 1923. In 1932 De Valera, leader of Fianna Fáil, became prime minister and, in 1937, introduced a new constitution by which the Irish Free State was renamed Éire. In 1949 a coalition took the country, as the Republic of Ireland, out of the British Commonwealth. Since 1969 Irish politics have been dominated by the conflict in Northern Ireland. In 1973 Ireland became a member of the EC. President: Patrick Hillery (1923–). Prime minister: Charles Haughey. Official languages: Irish and English. Chief religion: Roman Catholic. Official currency: punt of 100 pence. Area: 68 893 sq km(26 599 sq mi). Population(1987): 3 700 000. Capital and main port: Dublin.

Ireland, John Nicholson (1879–1962) British composer. His works include *The Forgotten Rite* (for orchestra; 1913) and *Sarnia* (for piano; 1941), which were inspired by the Channel Islands.

iridium (Ir) A hard brittle metal, discovered in 1803 by C. Tennant (1768–1838), in the residue left after dissolving platinum in aqua regia. Its salts are highly coloured, whence its name (Latin *iris*, rainbow). It is used as a hardening agent for platinum and in electrical contacts. At no 77; at wt 192.22; mp 2410°C; bp 4130°C.

iris (anatomy) The muscular tissue in the eye that surrounds the pupil and is situated immediately in front of the lens: it is responsible for eye colour. Reflex contraction of the muscles in the iris cause it to become smaller in dim light (which enlarges the pupil and allows more light to enter the eye) and larger in bright light (thus decreasing the size of the pupil).

Iris (botany) A genus of perennial herbaceous plants (about 300 species), native to N temperate regions and widely planted in gardens. Irises grow from bulbs or rhizomes (underground stems) and their flowers can be three or more colours. Family: *Iridaceae. See also* flag.

Iris (mythology) The Greek goddess of the rainbow and messenger of the gods, especially of Hera. She is portrayed as carrying a herald's staff and often bearing water that could put perjurers to sleep.

Irish Republican Army (IRA) A militant organization established in 1919. It fought a successful war against British forces (1919–21) but the subsequent partition treaty was rejected by many IRA members, who continued to press for an all-Ireland republic. A bombing campaign against England in 1939 and an "offensive" against Northern Ireland (1956–62) both failed. The present troubles began in 1968. In 1969 both the IRA and Sinn Féin, to which many IRA members belong, split into the Officials, desiring a socialist 32-county republic, and the Provisionals, concerned only with expelling the British from the North. Recent campaigns by the IRA have included the murder of Lord Mountbatten (1979), bombings in London, and the attempted assassination of the British prime minister in Brighton (1984). The Irish National Liberation Army (INLA) is a breakaway terrorist group.

Irish Republican Brotherhood. *See* Fenians.

Irish Sea A section of the Atlantic, separating England, Scotland, and Wales from Ireland. Area: about 100 000 sq km (40 000 sq mi). Maximum width: 240 km (149 mi).

Irish wolfhound An ancient breed of large hunting dog originating in Ireland. It has a powerful body and a long narrow head with small ears. The rough wiry coat can be grey, brindle, red, black, white, or fawn. Height: 78 cm minimum (dogs); 71 cm minimum (bitches).

Irkutsk 52 18N 104 15E A city in the S Soviet Union. It is the industrial, cultural, and educational centre of E Siberia. Population (1987): 609 000.

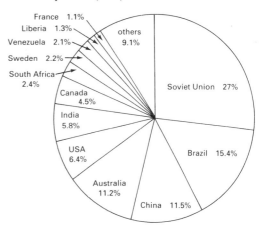

IRON *World production of iron ore (1988).*

iron (Fe) A metallic transition element that has been known and used since prehistoric times. It is the fourth most abundant element in the earth's crust, occurring in the ores haematite (Fe_2O_3), magnetite (Fe_3O_4), and siderite ($FeCO_3$). It is obtained from its ores by smelting in a blast furnace to give pig iron, which is then converted into cast iron, wrought iron, or steel. Iron has two important valence states forming iron II (ferrous) and iron III (ferric) compounds. Common compounds include the sulphates ($FeSO_4$ and $Fe_2(SO_4)_3$), chlorides ($FeCl_2$, $FeCl_3$), and oxides (FeO, Fe_3O_4, Fe_2O_3). Iron is vital to animal life owing to its presence in haemoglobin. Studies suggest that the earth has an iron-nickel core. At no 26;

at wt 55.847; mp 1535°C; bp 2750°C. *See also* ferromagnetism.

Iron Age   The cultural phase during which iron replaced bronze metal technology (*see* Bronze Age). Despite spasmodic earlier use of meteoric iron, it was not until about 1500 BC that iron-working techniques were perfected by the Hittites. It was used in Hallstatt Europe in the 7th century BC. The Chinese were both forging and casting iron about 500 BC, preceding Europe by about 1700 years in casting.

Iron Curtain   The ideological differences that divided the democratic and communist countries after World War II. The term was first used by Winston Churchill in 1946 but was regarded as largely defunct after 1989, when liberal reforms were introduced in many E European states.

Iroquois   North American Indian tribes of the NE region, who spoke the Iroquois language belonging to the Iroquois Caddoan family. They were cultivators and hunters, organized into matrilineal clans. The Mohawk, Oneida, Onondaga, Cayuga, and Seneca tribes formed the **Iroquois League** during the 16th century, which was allied with the British in wars against the French and, except for the Oneida and Tuscarora (members of the League from 1715), against the colonists in the American Revolution (1775–83).

Irrawaddy River   The chief river in Burma, flowing SSW across the country. It enters the Andaman Sea through a swampy delta. Length: 2010 km (1250 mi).

Irving, Sir Henry   (John Henry Brodribb; 1838–1905) British actor and manager. He established his reputation in London during the early 1870s and remained the leading actor of the London stage for the next 30 years. From 1878 to 1902 he was manager of the Lyceum Theatre, where, with Ellen Terry as his leading lady, he acted in a notable series of Shakespearean productions.

Isabella (I) the Catholic   (1451–1504) Queen of Castile (1474–1504). Her marriage (1469) to Ferdinand of Aragon united the two major Spanish kingdoms. The introduction of the Inquisition (1480) and the expulsion of the Jews (1492) were largely due to Isabella's influence. *See also* Ferdinand V and II.

Isabella II   (1830–1904) Queen of Spain (1833–68). Her succession was only secured in 1839, after the first Carlist War. Her governments became increasingly unpopular and she was deposed.

Ischia, Island of   40 44N 13 57E A volcanic island in Italy, in the Bay of Naples. Area: 47 sq km (18 sq mi). Population (1985): 26 000. Chief town: Ischia.

Ise   34 29N 136 41E A city in Japan, in S Honshu. It is the site of Japan's most sacred Shinto shrines. Population (1982 est): 106 453.

Isfahan (*or* Esfahan)   32 41N 51 41E A town in central Iran. It has some fine examples of Persian architecture, including the 17th-century royal mosque. Population (1986): 1 001 248.

Isherwood, Christopher   (1904–86) British novelist. His experiences while teaching in Berlin in the 1930s are described in the novel *Mr Norris Changes Trains* (1935) and in the stories *Goodbye to Berlin* (1939), featuring the memorable Sally Bowles, portrayed in the film *Cabaret* (1968). He collaborated with his friend W. H. Auden on several plays. His other works include the novels *Down There on a Visit* (1962) and *A Single Man* (1964).

Ishtar   The supreme Babylonian and Assyrian god-

dess, the daughter of the sky god Anu or of the moon god Sin. She combined aspects of a beneficent mother goddess and fierce goddess of war and fertility. She descended to the underworld in search of her lover Tammuz.

Isidore of Seville, St   (c. 560–636 AD) Spanish churchman. Archbishop of Seville from about 600, he is famous for his encyclopedia of knowledge, the *Etymologiae*, which was much used by medieval scholars. Feast day: 4 April.

Isis   An Egyptian goddess, the sister and wife of Osiris, whose dismembered body she magically restored to life, and mother of Horus. She was usually portrayed as holding the child Horus and wearing on her head the solar disc and a cow's horns, the same attributes as Hathor.

ISLAM   *The characteristic attitude of prayer.*

Islam (Arabic: submission to God)   A major world religion, which originated in Arabia in the 7th century AD. The essential creed of Islam, whose adherents are called Muslims, is that there is one God, Allah, and that Mohammed is his prophet. The revelations received by Mohammed are recorded in the Koran, which is the basis of Islamic belief and practice and the source of a complex legal and social system (*see also* Islamic law). Five fundamental duties are incumbent upon the individual Muslim: expression of belief in Allah and in the prophethood of Mohammed; observance at set times of five daily prayers, which are recited facing towards Mecca; fasting during the month of Ramadan; payment of a special tax for charitable purposes; and performance of the pilgrimage to Mecca at least once, if means permit. The main sects are the Sunnites (*or* Sunni) and the Shiites (*or* Shiah). There are an estimated 450 million Muslims.

Islamabad   33 40N 73 08E The capital of Pakistan, situated in the N of the country. The site was chosen in 1959 and construction began in 1961. Population (1981): 201 000.

Islamic law   The sacred law of Islam, *shari'ah*, prescribes not only religious duties (*see* Islam) but covers every aspect of the life of a Muslim. Its basic principles were elaborated in the 9th century AD. The law covers marriage, divorce, and inheritance; it forbids usury, the depiction of living beings, the drinking of alcohol, the eating of pork, etc., and prescribes penalties and punishments for crimes. In modern times most Muslim states have adopted secular legal systems at least in part and especially with regard to criminal, financial, and property law.

Islay An island in the Atlantic Ocean, off the W coast of Scotland. Area: 606 sq km (234 sq mi). Population (1981): 3792.

Ismaili A Shiite Muslim sect. In the 8th century AD a group of Shiites recognized Ismail the son of Jafar al-Sadiq as imam, while the rest of the Shiites supported his brother Musa. The Ismaili Fatimids ruled in Egypt and N Africa until 1171, contesting control of the Muslim world with the Abbasid dynasty of Baghdad. Today the best-known Ismaili sect is that headed by the Aga Khan.

ISO. *See* International Organization for Standardization.

Isocrates (436–338 BC) Athenian teacher of rhetoric and political pamphleteer. His appeals to successive military leaders to unite the feuding Greek states against Persia culminated in the *Philippus* (346 BC), addressed to Philip of Macedon.

Isomers Chemical compounds that have the same molecular formulae but different arrangements of atoms. In **structural isomerism** the molecules have different molecular structures. Thus, ethanol (C_2H_5OH) and dimethyl ether (CH_3OCH_3) both have the molecular formula C_2H_6O, although they are different compounds. Another form occurs when functional groups appear at different positions in the molecule. In **stereoisomerism** the isomers differ in their spatial arrangements. **Cis-transisomerism** occurs as a result of the positioning of groups in a planar molecule. Since rotation cannot occur about a double bond it is possible to have two isomers in organic compounds containing double bonds: one with groups on the same side of the bond (the cis isomer) and the other with groups on opposite sides of the bond (trans isomer). Another form of stereoisomerism is **optical isomerism**, in which the two isomeric forms of the molecule are asymmetric and differ in that one molecule is a mirror image of the other; these are optically active, i.e. they rotate polarized light passed through their solutions. Isomers of all types have different physical properties and, to a greater or lesser extent, different chemical properties. In some cases isomers can exist in equilibrium (**tautomerism**).

Isopoda A widely distributed order of crustaceans (4000 species). The group includes the most successful terrestrial crustacean—the woodlouse—as well as aquatic forms. Isopods have oval flattened bodies, covered by armour-like plates, and—usually—seven pairs of walking legs. The young develop within a brood pouch on the female.

isoprene ($CH_2:C(CH_3)CH:CH_2$) A colourless volatile liquid. It is made from chemicals extracted from oil, coal, or tar and is used to make synthetic rubber. Natural rubber consists mainly of a polymer of isoprene. *See also* polymerization.

isotherm A line on a map joining points of equal temperature. Corrections are usually made to compensate for the effect of altitude on temperature.

isothermal process Any process that occurs without a change in the temperature of a system (*compare* adiabatic process).

isotopes Atoms of the same element that contain equal numbers of protons but different numbers of neutrons in their nuclei. They have identical chemical properties but different physical properties. An isotope is indicated by combining its nucleon number and its name or symbol in various ways, for example uranium-235, U-235, ^{235}U. All naturally occurring elements are mixtures of isotopes.

isotopic spin (*or* isospin) A quantum number used to distinguish between elementary particles (*see* particle physics) having the same properties, except that of electric charge. Different charge states of the same particle (e.g. the nucleon) are regarded as having different orientations in a fictitious "isotopic space."

ISRAEL *A visitor to the Holocaust Remembrance Museum, Yad WaShem.*

Israel, State of A country in the Middle East, bordering on the Mediterranean Sea. There are mountains in the N, a narrow coastal plain in the W, and the Negev Desert in the S. The River Jordan flowing through the Great Rift Valley forms part of the E border. The population consists largely of Jews who have immigrated since 1948. Many Palestinian Arabs left the area when Israel was created but some have since returned. Some 3% of the population live in *kibbutzim* (*see* kibbutz) and about 5% live in *moshavim. Economy*: both industrial and agricultural output has increased rapidly since 1948, boosted by investments and gifts of capital from abroad. There are resources of copper ore and phosphates; potash and bromine from the Dead Sea are also exploited. Fishing and tourism are also important. 6% of the work force is employed in agriculture, which depends heavily on artificial irrigation. *History*: Israel's history prior to 1948 is that of Palestine, in which Jewish Zionists had demanded the creation of a Jewish state since the late 19th century. According to a UN recommendation. Palestine was to be divided into a Jewish state, an Arab state, and a small internationally administered zone around Jerusalem. As soon as the state of Israel was proclaimed following British withdrawal (1948), however, Arab forces invaded; by early 1949 Israeli forces had not only repulsed them but had gained control of 75% of Palestine, while the rest had been annexed by Jordan (the West Bank of the River Jordan) and Egypt (the Gaza Strip). Jerusalem was divided between Jews and Arabs. In 1956, Israeli forces occupied the Gaza Strip and the Sinai Peninsula. In the Six Day War (1967) Israel defeated Egypt, Syria, and Jordan and again occupied the Gaza Strip and the Sinai Peninsula as well as the

Golan Heights, the West Bank, and the Arab sector of Jerusalem. A peace agreement with Egypt after the Yom Kippur War (1973; in which the Israelis were taken unawares by Egyptian forces on the Day of Atonement –Yom Kippur), was finally achieved in 1979 at the Camp David talks, following which Israel withdrew from Sinai (1980–82). In 1982 Israel invaded Lebanon and forced the Palestinian Liberation Organization to leave West Beirut, withdrawing in 1985. Israel has recently been criticized for its treatment of Palestinians living in Israeli-occupied territories. Head of state: President Chaim Herzog (1918–). Prime minister: Yitzhak Shamir. Official languages: Hebrew and Arabic. Official currency: Israeli shekel of 100 new agorot. Area: 20 770 sq km (8018 sq mi). Population (1987 est): 4 399 000. Capital: Jerusalem. Main port: Haifa.

Issus, Battle of (333 BC) The battle in which Alexander the Great of Macedon defeated an enormous Persian army under Darius III, which was caught in a narrow pass and outmanoeuvred.

Istanbul (*or* Stamboul) 41 02N 28 57E A city in W Turkey, on both sides of the Bosporus. There are many ancient buildings in the city, including the mainly 6th-century Hagia Sophia (originally a church and now a museum), the Blue Mosque, and the Topkapi Palace (the former sultans' harem). It is a major port and industrial centre. *History*: ancient Byzantium was renamed Constantinople in 330, when the emperor Constantine I declared it the capital of the Eastern Roman Empire. It was the capital of the Byzantine Empire until its capture by the Ottoman Turks in 1453, although it had been held by Crusaders from 1204 to 1261. The Ottomans made it the capital of their empire in 1457; it was officially renamed Istanbul in 1926. Population (1985): 5 494 916.

Istria A peninsula in NW Yugoslavia. Passing to Italy at the end of World War I, it was ceded to Yugoslavia (1947) except for the Territory of Trieste, which was divided between Italy and Yugoslavia in 1954.

Italian A language of the Romance family spoken in Italy. The standard literary and official form is based upon the Tuscan dialect of Florence.

Italian East Africa. *See* Somaliland.

Italic languages A subgroup of the Indo-European language family spoken in central and NE Italy in the thousand years before the rise of Rome. A parent of modern Romance languages, this group comprised four related dialects: Latin, Faliscan, Osco-Umbrian, and Venetic. At the beginning of the 1st millennium BC Osco-Umbrian was the most widely spoken, but with the growth of Roman civilization, Latin replaced it.

italic script A style of handwriting adopted in 15th-century Italy by papal scribes and later (c. 1500) adapted for printing. Italic cursive letters eliminate unnecessary lifts of the pen, permitting rapid legible handwriting. *In print its characteristic sloped letters, such as those used in this sentence, are used mainly for display, emphasis, or to indicate that a word is in a foreign language.*

Italy, Republic of A country in S Europe, occupying a peninsula bordered by the Tyrrhenian Sea (W), the Ionian Sea (S), and the Adriatic Sea (E). The principal offshore islands are Sicily and Sardinia. Except for small coastal areas and the Po Valley in the N, the country is generally rugged and mountainous. The main rivers are the Po, Tiber, Arno, and Adige. *Economy*: agriculture is still important, the main crops being wheat, maize, grapes, and olives. Industry, however, has expanded

ITALY *The leaning tower of Pisa is one of many famous Italian buildings.*

considerably since World War II. The wine industry is growing in importance. Mineral resources are not large and Italy is heavily dependent on imported fossil fuels. Tourism is an important source of revenue. *History*: pre-Roman Italy was inhabited from the 7th century BC by the Etruscans in the N, Italics and Latins in central Italy, and Greek colonists in the southern mainland and Sicily. By 275 BC most of the peninsula had come under the rule of Rome (*see* Roman Republic). As the western Roman Empire declined from the 4th century AD, Italy was invaded by a succession of barbarian tribes, including the Visigoths and the Vandals. The last Roman emperor was deposed in 476 by the German king, Odoacer, who in 493 was in turn overthrown by the Ostrogoths. They were expelled in the early 6th century by the Eastern (Byzantine) Roman Empire, which was then threatened from the mid-6th century by successive invasions by the Lombards and the Franks, a period that also saw the origins of the pope's temporal power (*see* papal states). The Muslims invaded the S in the 9th and 10th centuries, Magyars, the N in the 10th century, and Normans, the S in the 11th century. The claim of the German kings to rule Italy was established in 962, when Otto the Great was crowned Holy Roman Emperor in Rome. The conflict from the 11th century between successive popes and emperors over the investiture controversy embroiled the Italian city states (notably Milan, Pisa, Genoa, Venice, and Florence), which in the 12th century were further divided by the struggle between Guelfs and Ghibellines. Many of the Italian cities came to be dominated by single families, such as the Visconti and then the Sforza in Milan and the Medici in Florence, who during the Renaissance were often outstanding patrons of culture and learning. Following the French invasion of Italy in 1494 Italy became the scene of conflict between France and Spain and from the 16th to early 18th centuries was largely dominated by the latter. During the 18th century control passed to Austria until 1796, when Italy was conquered by Napoleon. After the restoration of Austrian rule the movement for independence and unification (the Risorgimento) developed. By 1861, under the leadership of Victor Emmanuel II of Sardinia-Piedmont and his chief minister Cavour, aided by Garibaldi in the S, the Austrians had been expelled and the kingdom of Italy proclaimed with Victor Emmanuel as its first king. In the late 19th century Italy acquired a colonial empire, notably in East Africa. In 1915 Italy entered World War I on the side of the Allies. The postwar rise of fascism brought Mussolini to power in 1922. In 1936 he conquered Ethiopia and in 1939, Albania. In 1940, Mussolini took Italy into World War II on Germany's side. The Allied conquest of Sicily (1943) brought Mussolini's fall and in 1946 Umberto II abdicated. Since the establishment of the Republic there have been nearly 50 governments, plagued by a stagnating economy, widespread corruption, and lawlessness exacerbated by such groups as the Red Brigades. Italy was a founder member of the EC. President: Francesco Cossiga (1929–). Official language: Italian. Official religion: Roman Catholic. Official currency: lira of 100 centesimi. Area: 301 425 sq km (116 350 sq mi). Population (1988 est): 57 373 000. Capital: Rome. Main port: Genoa.

itch mite   A parasitic mite, *Sarcoptes scabei*, that produces scabies in man and mange in domestic animals. The female burrows into the skin, where it lays eggs and causes irritation. Family: *Sarcoptidae*.

IUCN   (International Union for the Conservation of Nature). *See* endangered species.

Ivan (III) the Great   (1440–1505) Grand Prince of Muscovy (1462–1505). Ivan greatly expanded Muscovite territory and ended Russian subordination to the Tatars. In 1497 he introduced a new legal code. Ivan married (1472) Zoë Palaeologus (d. 1503), the niece of the last Byzantine emperor, and adopted the Byzantine two-headed eagle in his arms.

Ivan (IV) the Terrible   (1530–84) Grand Prince of Muscovy (1533–84), who was crowned tsar in 1547. Ivan reformed the legal code and local administration (1555), conquered Kazan and Astrakhan, and established commercial relations with England. After 1560 his reign was marred by his brutality: thousands were executed and in a fit of rage Ivan murdered his son (1581). The effects of his tyranny were aggravated by the financial strains resulting from the abortive Livonian War (1558–82).

Ives, Charles (Edward)   (1874–1954) US composer.

Noted for his musical inventiveness, he composed more than 500 works. His second piano sonata, subtitled *Concord, Mass* (1909–15), was inspired by US writers associated with the town of Concord. One of his best-known works is *Central Park in the Dark* (1898–1907).

ivory   The close-grained white tissue forming the tusks of elephants, walruses, and narwhals and the teeth of hippos. So-called fossil ivory is obtained from mammoths. Ivory carving is a very ancient art; objects from France date to Palaeolithic times and fine examples survive from Egyptian, Minoan, Mycenaean, Assyrian, Greek, and Roman civilizations. In Europe ivory plaques with relief carving were important during the early middle ages for small religious icons, book covers, caskets, etc. India, SE Asia, China, and Japan have ancient traditions of skilled ivory carving. American Eskimo carvings in walrus ivory are greatly prized by connoisseurs. In 1989 many countries agreed to a ban on ivory imports to help to conserve the African elephant from poachers. Poaching for ivory has reduced the numbers of the African elephant from 1.3 million in 1979 to only 600 000 in 1989. The black rhino is also threatened in a similar way.

Ivory Coast, Republic of.   *See* Côte d'Ivoire.

ivy   An evergreen woody climbing plant, *Hedera helix*, that has glossy leaves, aerial roots (with which it clings to supports), greenish-yellow flowers, and small round fruits ripening from green to black. Native to Europe and W Asia, it is widely cultivated. Family: *Araliaceae*.

Ivy League   A group of universities in the NE USA of high prestige. They include Harvard, Yale, and Princeton and are all members of an athletic conference for intercollegiate sports known as the Ivy League (founded 1870s).

Iwo Jima   24 47N 141 19E   A Japanese island in the W Pacific Ocean, the largest of the Volcano Islands. Captured by US forces in 1945, it was returned in 1968. Sulphur and sugar are produced. Area: 20 sq km (8 sq mi).

Izmir   (former name: Smyrna)   38 25N 27 10E A port in W Turkey, on the Aegean Sea. Much was destroyed by fire in 1922, the rebuilt town being a modern commercial centre. Population (1985): 1 489 817.

J

Jabalpur (*or* Jubbulpore)   23 10N 79 59E A city in India, in Madhya Pradesh. It is an important railway junction and industrial centre. Population (1981): 758 000.

Jacana   A waterbird belonging to a family (*Jacanidae*; 7 species) occurring in tropical regions worldwide, also called lily trotter. Jacanas are characterized by long legs with elongated toes and claws, which enable them to run over floating vegetation. 25–32 cm long, they are commonly reddish to dark-brown in colour. Order: *Charadriiformes* (gulls, plovers, etc.).

Jacaranda   A genus of trees and shrubs (50 species) of South and Central America and the West Indies, often grown as ornamentals. *J. mimosifolia*, up to 15 m tall, and blue or violet tubular flowers. Some species yield valuable timber. Family: *Bignoniaceae*.

jackal   A carnivorous mammal of the genus *Canis*, found in Asia and Africa. Jackals are closely related to dogs and have pricked ears and bushy tails. The African black-backed jackal (*C. mesomeles*) is up to 110 cm long including the tail (25–33 cm) and often hunts in packs for carrion. The African side-striped jackal (*C. adustus*) is smaller and shyer.

jackdaw   An intelligent Eurasian crow, *Corvus monedula*, about 32 cm long, having a black plumage with a grey nape, an erectile crest, and pale-blue eyes. Often found in colonies, jackdaws feed on insects, grain, and carrion.

Jack Russell terrier   A breed of dog developed in England from the fox terrier by the Rev John Russell (1795–1883) for flushing foxes from earth. It has a stocky body and a strong muscular head. The short coat is white, black, and tan. Height: up to 38 cm.

Jackson 32 20N 90 11W A city in the USA, the capital of Mississippi. Founded in 1821, it was virtually destroyed by Gen Sherman in 1863. Population (1986 est): 208 440.

GLENDA JACKSON *As Elizabeth I.*

Jackson, Glenda (1936–) British actress. She has acted in many Royal Shakespeare Company stage productions, but first achieved popular success as Elizabeth I in a television series (1971). Her films include *Women in Love* (1969), *A Touch of Class* (1972), *Hedda* (1976), *Stevie* (1978), and *Turtle Diary* (1985); in 1986 she returned to the stage in *The House of Bernarda Alba*.

Jackson, Michael (1958–) US pop singer, who established himself as a solo star in the 1980s after successes in the 1970s with his brothers, as the Jackson Five. His solo albums include *Thriller* (1982) and *Bad* (1987).

Jackson, Stonewall (Thomas Jonathan J.; 1824–63) US Confederate general in the Civil War. In the first battle of Bull Run, he and his brigade were described as standing "like a stone wall" in the face of the Federal advance. Jackson was a master of rapid tactical movement, shown particularly in the Shenandoah valley campaign (1862). His untimely accidental death at Chancellorsville left a gap in the Confederate command.

Jack the Ripper An unidentified murderer who killed and mutilated at least six prostitutes in the East End of London in late 1888. One recent theory suggests that he was Vassily Konovalov, a Russian who committed similar murders in Paris and St Petersburg.

Jacobites Supporters of the exiled Stuart king, James II (Latin name: Jacobus), and his descendants. Between 1688, when the Glorious Revolution overthrew James II, and 1745, the Jacobites (mainly Roman Catholics and/or Tories), were the rallying point for opposition to the Hanoverian monarchs. Two Jacobite rebellions, in 1715 (the "15 Rebellion" led by James Edward Stuart, the Old Pretender) and 1745 (the "45 Rebellion" led by Charles Edward Stuart, the Young Pretender), were suppressed and thereafter the movement disintegrated.

Jacob's ladder A perennial herb, *Polemonium caeruleum*, native of Eurasia and widely cultivated as a garden flower. Growing to a height of 90 cm, it has bright-blue flowers. Family: *Polemoniaceae*.

jade A hard semiprecious stone, usually green, consisting of either the rare jadeite, $NaAlSi_2O_6$, or the more common nephrite, $Ca_2(Mg,Fe)_5Si_8O_{22}(OH,F)_2$. It has been used for carved ornaments and jewellery since prehistoric times.

Jaffa. *See* Tel Aviv-Jaffa.

Jagannatha A Hindu deity in some contexts synonymous with Krishna. Devotees have been known to throw themselves under the massive chariot on which his idol is annually wheeled during a festival at Puri, in Orissa, and from which the term "juggernaut" is derived.

Jagger, Mick *See* Rolling Stones.

jaguar The largest New World cat, *Panthera onca*, found in the southern USA and Central and South America. Up to 2.5 m long including the tail (70–90 cm), it has dark rosette-shaped spots on its yellow coat. Jaguars inhabit forest and scrub and hunt peccaries, turtles, fish, and capybaras and may attack domestic livestock.

jaguarundi A weasel-like cat, *Felis yagouaroundi*, of Central and South America. Up to 110 cm long, it stands only 28 cm high at the shoulder. It has a red or grey coat, long tail, and small ears. In addition to birds, jaguarundis eat various fruits.

Jainism The religion of between two and three million Indians, followers of Mahavira (?599–527 BC). Founded in the 6th century BC, Jainism stresses ahimsa, asceticism, and meditation. Right belief, knowledge, and conduct are the means of release from the perpetual round of rebirth caused by karma. This release is possible only for monks; the laity aim only for a better rebirth. Jainism is atheistic, although lesser spirits and demons proliferate.

Jaipur 26 53N 75 50E A city in India, the capital of Rajasthan. It has many fine buildings built in pink sandstone and is famous for its enamel work and jewellery, textile printing, and stone, marble, and ivory carving. Population (1981 est): 1 004 669.

Jakarta (*or* Djakarta; name until 1949: Batavia) 6 09S 106 49E The capital of Indonesia, in NW Java. It became a commercial centre as the base of the Dutch East India Company. Population (1985): 7 829 000.

jalap A climbing plant *Ipomoea purga*, of Mexico and South America, that has crimson flowers. The dried tubers yield a resin that is used medicinally as a laxative. Family: *Convolvulaceae*.

Jamaica, State of An island country in the Caribbean Sea, off the S coast of Cuba. A high plateau is crossed by the Blue Mountains, which reach 2255 m (7400 ft). The population is mainly of African and mixed African and European descent. *Economy*: sugar, bauxite, and tourism form the basis. Recent industrial developments include the construction of an oil refinery with Mexican aid. *History*: discovered by Columbus in 1494, it was occupied by the Spanish, who exterminated the original Arawak inhabitants. Captured by the British in 1655, it became a colony and a centre of the slave trade. Self-government was introduced in 1944 and in 1962 Jamaica became an independent state within the British Commonwealth. There has been considerable political unrest in recent years: a state of emergency existed in 1976–77 following riots. Jamaica is a member of the OAS and CARICOM. Prime minister: Michael Manley. Official language: English. Official currency: Jamaican dollar of 100 cents. Area: 10 991 sq km (4244 sq mi). Population (1987 est): 2 300 000. Capital and main port: Kingston.

James I (1394–1437) King of the Scots (1406–37), whose actual rule began on his release (1424) from English imprisonment. He strengthened royal authority at the expense of the nobles and extended royal control over the administration of justice and commerce. He was assassinated by a group of disaffected nobles. He is believed to be the author of the poem "The Kingis Quair" ("The King's Book").

James I (1566–1625) The first Stuart King of England and Ireland (1603–25) and, as James VI, King of the Scots (1567–1625). He succeeded to the Scottish throne after the abdication of his mother Mary, Queen of Scots. As king he reasserted royal authority against the nobility and, less successfully, the Presbyterians. In 1589 he married Anne of Denmark. In England, James encountered opposition from his parliaments (1604–10, the 1614 "Addled" Parliament, 1621–22) and was also unpopular for his choice of favourites and for his attempts to obtain a Spanish marriage for his son. One of the great achievements of his reign was the publication (1611) of the King James Version of the Bible.

James II (1430–60) King of the Scots (1437–60). He established his authority over rival factions and continued the extension of royal control and justice begun by his father James I. He was killed while besieging the English at Roxburgh Castle.

JAMES I OF ENGLAND   *Detail of a portrait (1621) by Daniel Mytens.*

James II (1633–1701) King of England, Scotland, and Ireland (1685–88). The second son of Charles I, James (as Duke of York) escaped to Holland (1648) after his father's defeat in the Civil War and during the 1650s fought for the French and then the Spanish. In 1659 he married the daughter of the Earl of Clarendon, Anne Hyde (1637–71), by whom he had two daughters (later Queens Mary II and Anne). In about 1669 he became a Roman Catholic: consequent attempts to exclude him from the succession failed and in 1685 he became king. The Protestant rebellion of the Duke of Monmouth was suppressed, Roman Catholics were admitted to public office, and religious freedom for all denominations was announced (1687). In 1688 James prosecuted the Archbishop of Canterbury and six bishops who refused to proclaim religious toleration from the pulpit but lost the case. This defeat and the threat of a Roman Catholic succession with the birth of a son (*see*

James Edward Stuart, the Old Pretender) to his second wife, Mary of Modena (1658–1718), precipitated the Glorious Revolution. James was forced to flee and his subsequent attempt to regain the Crown from Ireland failed with his defeat by William III's forces at the Boyne (1690) and Aughrim (1691). He died an exile in France.

James III (1452–88) King of the Scots (1460–88). Until 1469 Scotland was ruled by a regency and his personal rule was marked by baronial revolts. He was killed after defeat by rebel barons near Stirling.

James IV (1473–1513) King of the Scots (1488–1513). In 1503 he married Margaret Tudor. He defeated the rebels who had killed his father James III, procuring internal stability and respect for the monarchy. Recurrent hostility with England culminated in the invasion of Northumberland (1513) and his defeat and death, with most of his nobles, at Flodden.

James V (1512–42) King of the Scots (1513–42). During his minority (1513–28) Scotland was controlled by rival pro-French and pro-English factions. He died shortly after the failure of an invasion of England and was succeeded by his daughter Mary, Queen of Scots.

James VI (King of the Scots).   *See* James I (King of England).

James, Henry (1843–1916) US novelist and critic. He spent much of his childhood in Europe, becoming a British citizen in 1915. His novel *Roderick Hudson* (1875) introduced the theme of Americans confronting European culture that recurred in many of his novels, such as *The Portrait of a Lady* (1881), although he occasionally returned to strictly American settings, as in *Washington Square* (1881) and *The Bostonians* (1886). He wrote more than a hundred shorter works of fiction, of which *The Turn of the Screw* (1898) is perhaps the best known. In his later novels, *The Wings of the Dove* (1902), *The Ambassadors* (1903), and *The Golden Bowl* (1904), action is subordinated to a searching psychological analysis rendered in a highly elaborate style. He was an influential critic and also wrote several plays. His brother **William James** (1842–1910) was a psychologist and philosopher, who developed the theory of pragmatism in ethics. He held that a theory was only true in so far as it successfully helped to solve problems. Religious and moral beliefs were treated in the same nondogmatic way, especially in his influential *Varieties of Religious Experience* (1902) and *The Meaning of Truth* (1909).

James, Jesse (Woodson) (1847–92) US outlaw. After fighting with southern guerrilla groups during the Civil War he formed the James gang and by 1867 was robbing banks, stagecoaches, and trains in his native Missouri and surrounding states. He was shot and killed by Robert Ford, a James gang member who claimed the $10 000 reward offered by the state of Missouri.

James Edward Stuart, the Old Pretender (1688–1766) The son of James II, the deposed Roman Catholic King of England. In exile, he was urged by his supporters, known as Jacobites, to claim the English throne. After their invasion of Scotland failed in 1715, James abandoned his claim and lived in permanent exile in Rome.

Jammu and Kashmir A state in N India, forming part of the disputed area of Kashmir. Area: 100 569 sq km (38 820 sq mi). Population (1981): 5 981 600. Capital: Jammu (winter); Srinagar (summer).

Jamshedpur 22 47N 86 12E A city in India, in Bihar. Founded in 1907 by the industrialist Dorabji Jamsetji

Tata, it is the site of India's principal iron and steel works. Population (1981): 670 000.

Janáček, Leoš (1854–1928) Czech composer. He was over 60 before he gained wide recognition as a composer. In his vocal works he attempted to reproduce natural speech rhythms; he was also influenced by folk music. His works include the operas *Jenufa* (1894–1903), *The Excursions of Mr Broucek* (1908–17), and *The Makropulos Case* (1923–25), two string quartets, and the *Glagolitic Mass* (1926).

Jansenism A movement in the Roman Catholic Church in the 17th and 18th centuries based on the teaching of Cornelius Jansen (1585–1638). Stressing the more rigorously predestinarian aspects of St Augustine's teaching, it brought the Jansenists into conflict with the Jesuits and was condemned by the Church. Among other points, Jansenists argued that the efficacy of the sacraments depended on the moral character of the recipient. One of the most famous Jansenists was Pascal.

Jansky, Karl Guthe (1905–50) US radio engineer, who discovered a source of radio waves outside the solar system (1932), while investigating static interference. Jansky's discovery led to the science of radio astronomy.

Janus The Roman god of doors, thresholds, and beginnings, after whom the month January is named. He is usually portrayed as having two heads facing forwards and backwards.

JAPAN *One of the foremost manufacturers of high-tech products.*

Japan (Japanese name: Nippon *or* Nihon) A country in E Asia, consisting of a series of islands lying between the Pacific Ocean and the Sea of Japan. The four main islands are Honshu, Kyushu, Hokkaido, and Shikoku. Much of the land is mountainous, with the highest mountain, Fujiyama, rising to 3778 m (12 399 ft). The population is of mixed Malay, Manchu, and Korean descent; the original inhabitants, the Ainu, survive in small numbers on Hokkaido. *Economy*: during the past two decades Japan has developed into a highly industrialized country, manufacturing electronic goods, motor vehicles, and petrochemicals. Mineral resources are on the whole sparse. Agriculture is intensive and, although rice is still the main crop, there have been efforts to diversify with such crops as wheat, barley, and soya beans. There is considerable timber production. Japan is also one of the world's leading fishing nations. *History*: about 200

BC the country was united under the Yamato dynasty. Their religion formed the basis of Shinto and Japanese emperors were regarded as divine descendants of the sun goddess. From 1186 AD real power was in the hands of the military shoguns until Emperor Mutsuhito (1852–1912) regained power for the House of Yamato in 1867. 1871 saw the end of Hoken Seido (the feudal system) and from the mid-19th century the country was opened up to western communications and ideas. It expanded colonially, especially in successful wars against China and Russia, and it occupied several Asian countries. It fought against the Allies in World War II and surrendered after the dropping of atomic bombs on Hiroshima and Nagasaki in 1945. By a new constitution of 1947 the emperor renounced his former claim to divinity and became a constitutional monarch. The Liberal Democratic Party has been in power since 1955. Head of state: Emperor Akihito. Prime minister: Toshiki Kaifu. Official language: Japanese. Official currency: yen of 100 sen and 1000 rin. Area: 372 480 sq km (143 777 sq mi). Population (1987 est): 122 053 000. Capital: Tokyo. Main port: Yokohama.

Japan, Sea of A section of the NW Pacific Ocean between Japan and the Asian mainland.

Japanese The language of the people of Japan. Its relationship to other languages is uncertain but it is probably related to Korean. It is polysyllabic and usually stresses all syllables equally. There are many dialects; the standard form is based on the speech of Tokyo. Japanese writing systems are complex. In about the 5th century the Japanese adopted Chinese ideographic characters (*kanji*), which have both Chinese-like (*on*) and native Japanese (*kun*) pronunciations. About 2000 *kanji* are now used. In about the 9th century the Japanese supplemented the *kanji* by deriving from them two phonetic syllabaries, of 48 symbols each, called *hiragana* and *katakana*. *Hiragana* is mainly used for suffixes and grammatical functions and for words for which there are no *kanji*. *Katakana* is mainly used for foreign names, loanwords, and scientific words.

Japanese cedar A conifer, *Cryptomeria japonica*, native to China and Japan, where it is an important timber tree reaching a height of 55 m; elsewhere it is grown for ornament and rarely exceeds 35 m. Japanese cedar has globular spiny cones, 2 cm across. Family: *Taxodiaceae*.

Japanese maple A maple tree, *Acer palmatum*, up to 13 m tall, the 5–11 lobed leaves of which turn scarlet in autumn. Native to Japan, it is a popular ornamental in many cultivated varieties, including purple-leaved and dwarf types. They require shelter in cooler climates.

japonica A shrub or tree of the genus *Chaenomeles* (or *Cydonia*), native to Japan but widely cultivated as an ornamental. Flowering quince (*C. japonica*) and Japanese quince (*C. speciosa*) are the most popular species. These have clusters of scarlet five-petalled flowers, 5 cm across. The apple-like fruit is used in marmalade and jelly. Family: *Rosaceae*.

Japurá, River A river in NW South America, rising in SW Colombia and flowing generally SE to join the River Amazon in Brazil. Length: 2800 km (1750 mi).

Jaruzelski, Wojciech (1923–) Polish general and statesman; prime minister (1981–85); first secretary of the Polish Communist Party (1981–89); president (1989–). Coming to power to halt the liberal reforms obtained by the independent trade union Solidarity, he instituted martial law (1981–83), detained Lech Walesa and other union leaders (1981–82), and dissolved Solidarity (1982), but remained head of state after Solidarity's triumph in 1989.

jasmine A shrub of the genus *Jasminum* (about 300 species), native to tropical and subtropical regions and widely cultivated. Many species yield an essential oil used in perfumery. Two species suitable for temperate gardens are the common jasmine (*J. officinalis*) from S Asia, up to 6 m tall with fragrant white flowers, and the Chinese winter jasmine (*J. nudiflorum*), 3–6 m tall, with yellow flowers. Family: *Oleaceae*.

Jason A legendary Greek hero, heir to the throne of Iolcos in Thessaly. Sent by his uncle, the usurper Pelias, to fetch the Golden Fleece, he and the Argonauts underwent many adventures before finally recovering the Fleece from Colchis with the help of Medea. After many years of wandering he died at Corinth.

jasper An impure variety of chalcedony, usually red or reddish brown. It is slightly translucent and is regarded as a semiprecious stone. It is an abundant mineral, occurring in veins and in cavities in volcanic rocks.

jaundice Yellowing of the skin and whites of the eyes due to the presence of bile pigments. Jaundice may result if there is excessive breakdown of red blood cells, as in haemolytic anaemia, or in disease of the liver, such as hepatitis, or blockage of the bile duct by gallstones.

Java An Indonesian island, the smallest of the Greater Sunda Islands. Its chain of volcanic mountains has formed exceptionally fertile soil, and many rivers feed its intensive wet-rice agriculture. Other food crops, sugar cane, and kapok are grown and forest products include teak. Indonesia's administrative and industrial centre, Java is heavily overpopulated. *History*: Indian colonies in the early centuries AD developed into Hindu and Buddhist kingdoms, with Hindu-Javanese culture reaching its height in the 14th century. The Dutch East India Company was centred here from 1619. Many died during anticommunist purges (1965–67). Area: 132 174 sq km (51 032 sq mi). Population (1980): 91 269 528, with Madura. Capital: Jakarta.

javelin throw A field event in athletics in which a spearlike javelin is thrown as far as possible. The men's javelin is 2.6–2.7 m (8.5–8.9 ft) long and weighs 800 g (1.8 lb). The women's measures 2.2–2.3 m (7.2–7.5 ft) and weighs a minimum of 600 g (1.3 lb). It is thrown with one hand, over the shoulder, after a run-up of approximately 36 m (120 ft), and the metal head must hit the ground first. Each competitor has six tries. World records: men: 87.66 m (1987) by Jan Zelezny (Czechoslovakia); women: 80.00 m (1988) by Petra Felke (East Germany).

Jawara, Sir Dawda (1924–) Gambian statesman; president (1970–). A Muslim, he became prime minister in 1962, in which post he led his country to independence in 1965. When The Gambia became a republic in 1970 Jawara became president.

jay A crow, *Garrulus glandarius*, of Eurasia and N Africa. It is about 34 cm long and brownish pink, with a black tail, white rump, black-barred blue wing patches, and a black-and-white erectile crest. Jays are found mainly in woodland, feeding on insects and larvae in summer and storing seeds for winter food.

Jayawardene, J(unius) R(ichard) (1906–) Sri Lankan statesman; prime minister (1977–78) and then president (1978–89). He became a significant politician in the years before Ceylon (Sri Lanka from 1972) obtained independence in 1948.

Jedda. *See* Jiddah.

THOMAS JEFFERSON

Jefferson, Thomas (1743–1826) US statesman; the third president (1801–09) of the USA. A lawyer, Jefferson was elected a delegate to the second Continental Congress in 1775 and was the chief author of the Declaration of Independence. Jefferson served as governor of Virginia (1779–81), minister to France (1785–89), secretary of state (1789–93), and vice president (1797–1801) under John Adams. During Jefferson's two terms as president, he approved the Louisiana Purchase (1803) and encouraged US neutrality in the Napoleonic Wars. Both he and John Adams died on 4 July, 1826, the 50th anniversary of American independence.

Jefferson City 38 33N 92 10W A city in the USA, the capital of Missouri on the Missouri River. Population (1980): 33 619.

Jeffreys of Wem, George, 1st Baron (c. 1645–89) English judge. A staunch supporter of the Crown, he became a leading prosecutor of suspected traitors following the Popish Plot and, in 1685, James II's Lord Chancellor. He is notorious for the harsh punishments and death sentences that he imposed during the Bloody Assizes, which followed Monmouth's rebellion (1685). He was executed after the downfall of James II.

Jehovah. *See* Yahweh.

Jehovah's Witnesses A religious movement, first known as Bible Students, organized in the early 1870s by Charles Taze Russell (1852–1916) in Philadelphia. From 1884 the Watch Tower Bible and Tract Society was their legal publishing group. Jehovah's Witnesses accept the Bible as their sole authority, worshipping the Creator, Jehovah, and acknowledging Jesus Christ to be God's son and spokesman. They look for the end of wickedness and of the present world order in the near future. They believe that 144 000, the Christian congregation, will rule with Jesus Christ in his heavenly kingdom over the rest of obedient mankind, who will live on a paradise earth. Following the example of the first Christians, they do not engage in politics and are conscientious objectors.

jellyfish A free-swimming aquatic invertebrate animal belonging to a class (*Scyphozoa*; about 200 species) of coelenterates. The translucent gelatinous body, 1.5–2000 mm in diameter, is bell- or umbrella-shaped, with a central tubular projection that hangs down and bears the mouth. Jellyfish occur in all oceans and usually propel themselves through the water by contracting muscles around the edge of the bell. Stinging tentacles are used to capture and paralyse prey. The term jellyfish is also used for the free-swimming sexual form of any other coelenterate (*see* medusa).

Jena and Auerstädt, Battles of (14 October, 1806) Simultaneous battles in which Napoleon defeated the Prussians. Auerstädt and Jena broke Prussia as a military power and left Russia to face Napoleon alone. Prussia remained in the orbit of the French Empire until 1813, when it rejoined the alliance against Napoleon.

Jenner, Edward (1749–1823) British physician, who developed the first effective vaccine–against smallpox. Jenner noticed that people who caught the mild disease cowpox never contracted smallpox. In 1796 he inoculated a small boy with cowpox and, two months later, with smallpox. The boy did not get smallpox. Jenner published his findings in 1798 after which vaccination became a widespread protective measure.

jerboa A small hopping rodent belonging to the family *Dipodidae* (25 species) of Asian and N African deserts, also called desert rat. Jerboas are 4–15 cm long and have kangaroo-like hind feet, a long balancing tail, and sandy fur. They emerge at night from their burrows to feed on seeds.

Jerez de la Frontera 36 41N 6 08W A city in SW Spain, in Andalusia. It is renowned for its wine industry and gave its name to sherry. Population (1981): 176 238.

Jericho 31 52N 35 27E A village in the Jordan Valley (Israel), on the Israeli-occupied West Bank. The nearby site of the old city was excavated by Kathleen Kenyon (1906–78), revealing one of the earliest known towns (before 8000 BC); of the Bronze Age city attacked by Joshua (Joshua 6) nothing remains. The ruins of the palace, Khirbat al-Mafjar, built (739–44 AD) by the Umayyad caliph Hisham (d. 743) can still be seen.

Jerome, St (c. 342–420 AD) Italian biblical scholar; Doctor of the Church and author of the Vulgate Bible, the first Latin translation of the Bible from the Hebrew. After a period as a hermit, he was ordained by St Paulinus of Nola in Antioch. A secretary to Pope Damasus I, he later settled in Bethlehem, where he established a monastery. Feast day: 30 Sept.

Jersey 49 13N 2 07W The largest of the Channel Islands, in the English Channel. Colonized from Normandy in the 11th century, French influence remains strong and French is the official language. It consists chiefly of a plateau incised by deep valleys. Agriculture, particularly dairy farming, is important and the famous Jersey cattle are bred for export. Tourism is also a major source of income. Area: 116 sq km (45 sq mi). Population (1986): 80 212. Capital: St Helier.

Jerusalem (Arabic name: El Quds) 31 47N 35 13E The capital of Israel, in the Judaea Heights between the Mediterranean and the Dead Sea. Jerusalem is a religious centre for three world religions: Christianity, Judaism, and Islam. The modern city spreads to the W of the Old City, which is walled (1537–40) and contains most of the religious shrines, including the Western (Wailing) Wall (part of the retaining wall of the second Jewish Temple, consecrated 515 BC), the Dome of the Rock (691 AD; Islamic), and the Church of the Holy Sepulchre, (begun 335 AD on the traditional site of Christ's crucifixion). *History*: Jerusalem was conquered by King David in 1005 BC; it became the capital of Judah in 930 BC. Nebuchadnezzar, King of Babylon, destroyed the city in 586 BC, when the Jewish inhabitants were exiled to Babylon. In 538 BC, 40 000 Jews returned to the city, whose walls were rebuilt under Nehemiah in 445 BC. It was occupied by Alexander the Great (4th century BC) and the Romans (63 BC), under whose fifth procurator, Pontius Pilate, Jesus was put to death. Occupation by the Turks was succeeded by the establishment of the Kingdom of Jerusalem, a feudal state created in 1099 following conquest by the Crusaders. It was enlarged in the early 12th century by Baldwin I (c. 1058–1118) and his successors, but fell to Saladin in 1187. The Turks took the city again in 1517 and held it until 1917, when it became a British mandate, until 1948. Jerusalem was then divided between the new state of Israel, of which it became the capital (1950), and Jordan. Israel occupied the whole city in June, 1967. Population (1986): 468 900.

Jerusalem artichoke A North American perennial herb, *Helianthus tuberosus*, that grows to a height of 2 m, and has edible tubers up to 10 cm long. They bloom only in hot summers. Family: *Compositae*.

Jesuits Members of the Society of Jesus, an order founded by St Ignatius Loyola in 1533 to propagate the Roman Catholic faith. In addition to vows of chastity, poverty, and obedience, Jesuits were sworn to go wherever the pope might send them. They became one of the dominant forces of the Counter-Reformation and played a prominent role in missions to the New World and the East. Their power eventually brought them into conflict with civil authorities throughout Europe, and in 1773 Pope Clement XIV suppressed the order. Reinstated in 1814, the order is now active worldwide and is noted for its schools and universities.

Jesus (c. 6 BC–c. 30 AD) The founder of Christianity; called by his followers the Messiah or Christ (Greek *khristos*, anointed one). According to the New Testament, Jesus was born at Bethlehem in the last years of the reign of Herod the Great; he was the son of the Virgin Mary, of Nazareth, who belonged to the tribe of Judah and the family of David. Mary's husband, Joseph, was a carpenter. Jesus was baptized in about 27 AD by John the Baptist and began his public ministry in Galilee, preaching largely in parables. His teaching, summarized in the Sermon on the Mount (Matthew 5–7), emphasized the approaching kingdom of God, the need for repentance, and the importance of charity, faith, and humility. Miracles were attributed to him, including healing and miraculously feeding a multitude of 5000. The beginnings of a movement are evident in Galilee when Jesus summoned his disciples, traditionally 12 in number, instructing them to preach the imminence of the Kingdom of God. Accompanied by his disciples he travelled to Jerusalem for Passover, apparently aware of the serious opposition that awaited him. There, after betrayal by Judas, he was arrested and condemned to death by the Jewish tribunal, the Sanhedrin, for claiming to be the Messiah. He was executed according to Roman law as a criminal by order of Pontius Pilate. In the New Testament his death is presented as the fulfilment of a divine purpose, made clear to the disciples at the resurrection (on the next day but one after the crucifixion) and by a number of appearances to individuals and groups of disciples. His ascension into heaven is said to have occurred 40 days after the resurrection.

JET ENGINE   *(a) The principle: equal pressure from the expanding gas inside the engine meets equal resistance except rearwards. The result is a forward thrust. The lower the outside pressure, the greater the thrust. (b) The turbojet, used for subsonic and supersonic flight (especially with reheat). (c) The turbofan, used for subsonic flight: cool air, compressed by the fan, bypasses the engine and mixes with the hot jet.*

jet engine   A form of gas turbine (*see also* internal-combustion engine) in which part of the fuel energy drives a turbine, which in turn drives a compressor to increase the pressure of the air required for combustion, and part is used as a high-velocity jet to provide thrust to drive an aircraft. The jet engine was patented in 1930 by Sir Frank Whittle, the first practical Whittle engine powering a Gloster aircraft in 1941. Thrust in these engines is equal to the mass of the gas produced multiplied by its acceleration and is due to the pressure of the expanding gas on the engine itself rather than on the air through which it is flying. It is therefore more efficient at higher altitudes, where the atmosphere is thinner. Early postwar commercial aircraft used a turboprop engine, in which a propeller is driven by the turbine shaft. For greater speed and economy the turboprop has now been replaced by the turbojet (with reheat) or the turbofan. At over twice the speed of sound (Mach 2), the forward pressure of the air is sufficient for the compressor, and therefore the turbine, to be dispensed with. The resulting engine is called a ramjet. The drawback of the ramjet is that it needs a rocket-assisted take-off. Turboshaft en-

gines, similar to the turboprop, are used in helicopters, ships, etc. *See also* rockets.

Jews   A predominantly Semitic people, claiming descent from the ancient Israelites and practising Judaism. They inhabited Israel until the Babylonian exile, returning in 1948. During the intervening 25 centuries they were dispersed (*see* diaspora) throughout the world and there are now communities in most countries (*see* Ashkenazim; Sephardim). Under Persian, Greek, and Roman rule the Jews gradually evolved a system of communal administration that enabled them to survive as minority communities through many centuries of Christian and Muslim domination, despite frequent persecution. Since the late 18th century they have achieved acceptance in most countries, although the German slaughter of six million Jews in Europe (*see* holocaust) is one of the ugliest episodes in human history. It did, however, provide the Zionist claim for a national home for the Jews with unanswerable force (*see* Zionism).

Jhelum, River   A river in India and Pakistan, the most westerly of the five rivers of the Punjab. Rising in Kashmir it flows generally SSW to join the River Chenab. Length: about 720 km (450 mi).

Jiang Jing Guo.   *See* Chiang Kai-shek.

Jiang Qing.   *See* Mao Tse-tung.

Jiddah (*or* Jedda)   21 30N 39 10E A town in Saudi Arabia, on the Red Sea coast. It is a modern industrial city and the chief port for Muslim pilgrims to Mecca. Population (1983): 1 500 000.

Jimmu   The legendary first ruler of Japan. According to the oldest Japanese writings, Jimmu was descended from the sun-goddess Amaterasu and embarked upon the unification of Japan in 660 BC. This legend, intended to glorify the imperial dynasty, anticipated its true establishment by about seven centuries.

jimsonweed.   *See* thorn apple.

Jinan (Chi-nan *or* Tsinan)   36 41N 117 00E A city in E China, the capital of Shandong province. A city since the 8th century BC, it is a cultural centre. Population (1986): 1 430 000.

jinja   A Shinto shrine dedicated to a deity or nature spirit, situated in a place of exceptional natural beauty. It consists of three parts: the *haiden*, a hall where the laity pray and worship; the *heiden*, where religious ceremonies are performed; and the *honden*, the main inner sanctuary usually accessible only to priests. Before the jinja is a sacred gateway.

Jinnah, Mohammed Ali   (1876–1948) Indian statesman, who was largely responsible for the creation of Pakistan. Born in Karachi, he studied law in England. As a member of the Muslim League and the Indian National Congress he championed Hindu-Muslim unity until 1930, when he resigned from the Congress in opposition to Gandhi's policies. He was president of the League in 1916 and 1920 and from 1934. He advocated a separate state for Indian Muslims, which was achieved with the creation in 1947 of Pakistan, of which he was the first governor general.

Jiulong (*or* Kowloon)   22 20N 114 15E A port in SE China, on the Jiulong peninsula, opposite Hong Kong island and part of the British colony (ceded 1860). Population (1971): 716 272.

Joan of Arc, St   (French name: Jeanne d'Arc; c. 1412–31) French patriot, known as the Maid of Orléans, whose courageous military and moral leadership against the English invaders led to a reversal of French fortunes in the Hundred Years' War. Of peasant origin, she claimed to have been told by Saints Michael, Catherine, and Margaret that it was her divine mission to expel the English from France and enable Charles VII to be crowned. She persuaded Charles to allow her to lead an army to relieve the besieged city of Orléans. Her success resulted in Charles' coronation at Rheims (July, 1429). Other victories followed but she failed to recapture Paris and was subsequently seized by the Burgundians, who sold her to their English allies. They tried her and burned her as a heretic. She was canonized in 1920.

Jocasta. *See* Oedipus.

Jodhpur 26 18N 73 08E A city in India, in Rajasthan. The city is noted for its handicraft industries, such as ivory carvings and lacquerware. It also gave its name to a style of riding breeches that were introduced into Britain during the 19th century. Population (1981): 494 000.

JODRELL BANK

Jodrell Bank The site, near Macclesfield, Cheshire (UK), of the Nuffield Radio Astronomy Laboratories of Manchester University. The principal instrument is the 76.2 m (250 ft) fully steerable radio-telescope dish.

Jogjakarta (*or* Yogyakarta) 7 48S 110 24E A city in Indonesia, in S Java. It was the capital of the 1945–49 Indonesian Republic. A cultural centre, it is rich in Buddhist monuments, notably the temple of Borobudur. Population (1980): 398 727.

Johannesburg 26 10S 28 02E The largest city in South Africa, in the Transvaal. It was founded in 1886 following the discovery of gold in the area. During the second Boer War it was taken by the British (1900). Today it is a major industrial, commercial, and banking centre containing the South African Stock Exchange (1887). Linked to the city is the complex of towns known as Soweto, inhabited by Black Africans. Population (1983): 1 713 000.

John (1167–1216) King of England (1199–1216), nicknamed John Lackland; the youngest son of Henry II, he succeeded his brother Richard I. His reign saw the renewal of war with Philip II Augustus of France, to whom he had lost several continental possessions, including Normandy, by 1205. Struggles with Pope Innocent III over John's objection to the election of Stephen Langton (c. 1150–1228) as Archbishop of Canterbury led to the imposition of an interdict over England (1208) and the king's excommunication (1212). He came into conflict with his barons and was forced to sign the Magna Carta at Runnymede. His subsequent repudiation of the Charter led to the first Barons' War (1215–17).

John (II) the Good (1319–64) King of France (1350–64), who was taken prisoner by the English at the battle of Poitiers (1356) during the Hundred Years' War. He remained in captivity in London, where he was forced to sign the unfavourable Treaty of Brétigny. Released in 1360, he was unable to raise the ransom demanded by the English and was forced to return to London, where he died.

John XXIII (Angelo Roncalli; 1881–1963) Pope (1958–1963). Elected at the age of 77, John was the most popular and innovative pope of modern times. In 1962 he summoned the second Vatican Council. His best-known encyclical, *Pacem in Terris* (*Peace on Earth*; 1963), advocated reconciliation between the western democracies and eastern communist countries.

John, Augustus (Edwin) (1878–1961) British painter, born in Wales. A flamboyantly unconventional character, he travelled widely, often in Gipsy style. His strongly characterized portraits of contemporaries, such as James Joyce and T. E. Lawrence, are indebted to tradition. His sister **Gwen John** (1876–1939) was also a painter.

John, Elton (Reginald Kenneth Dwight; 1947–) British rock pianist and singer, who became popular with such songs as "Rocket Man" and "Daniel."

John Dory (*or* dory) A fish of the family *Zeidae*, found worldwide in moderately deep marine waters. It has a round narrow body with deep sides, each having a black spot surrounded by a yellow ring, and spiny-rayed fins extended into filaments. *Zeus faber*, up to 90 cm long, is a food fish of the Atlantic and Mediterranean. Order: *Zeiformes*.

John of Gaunt (1340–99) The fourth son of Edward III of England; Duke of Lancaster from 1362. After a distinguished career in the Hundred Years' War he assumed an increasingly important role in domestic government. Never popular, John, who supported Wycliffe and the Lollards, was opposed by William of Wykeham (1324–1404). From 1386 to 1389 he attempted without success to realize his claim, through his second wife Constance, to Castile. In 1396 he married his mistress Catherine Swynford, and in 1397 their descendants were legitimized but excluded from the royal succession. They included Margaret Beaufort (1443–1509), the mother of Henry VII.

John O'Groats 58 39N 3 02W A village at the NE tip of Scotland, site of the house of John de Groot, a 16th-century Dutch immigrant. John O'Groats is 970 km (603 mi) in a straight line from Land's End, Cornwall.

John Paul II (Karol Wojtyła; 1920–) Pope (1978–). A Pole, he is the first non-Italian pope since 1522. He has outspokenly defended the Church in communist countries, especially in Poland. His uncompromising position on contraception, abortion, homosexuality, and a celibate clergy has led to considerable opposition. In 1981 he survived an assassination attempt. He succeeded **John Paul I** (Albino Luciani; 1912–78; reigned August–September, 1978), who took the names of his two predecessors, John XXIII and Paul VI.

AMY JOHNSON

Johnson, Amy (1903–41) British aviator. She established several long-distance records with her solo flights to Australia in 1930, to Tokyo in 1932, and to the Cape of Good Hope and back in 1936. In 1932 she married Jim Mollison (1905–59), another pilot, with whom she flew the Atlantic in 1936. She was killed in an air crash near London.

Johnson, Lyndon Baines (1908–73) US statesman; Democratic president (1963–69). A Texan, he succeeded to the presidency after Kennedy's assassination. His Great Society programme initiated broad social reform. He became unpopular for increasing US military involvement in the Vietnam War.

Johnson, Samuel (1709–84) British poet, critic, and lexicographer. He left Oxford without taking a degree, married a wealthy widow in 1735, and went to London in 1737. His early publications include a biography of his friend the poet Richard Savage (1744) and a long didactic poem, *The Vanity of Human Wishes* (1749). From 1750 to 1752 he produced the weekly *Rambler* almost single handed. His *Dictionary* appeared in 1755 after nine years' work and was well received, but he still relied on hackwork for money, writing *Rasselas* (1759) in a week to pay for his mother's funeral. His last major works were an edition of Shakespeare (1765) and his *Lives of the Poets* (1779–81). From the early 1760s he enjoyed the security of a pension and the friendship of Reynolds, Goldsmith, Burke, and other men of letters, including his biographer Boswell. His last years were clouded by the deaths of friends and his estrangement from his companion, Mrs Thrale.

John the Baptist, St In the New Testament, the son of a priest, Zacharias, and Elizabeth, a relative of the Virgin Mary. He began in about 27 AD preaching on the banks of the River Jordan, urging repentance and baptism because of the imminent approach of the Kingdom of God (Matthew 3.2). He baptized Christ, recognizing him as the Messiah. He was beheaded by Herod Antipas, at the request of Salome, for denouncing his second marriage to Herodias. Feast days: 24 June (birth); 29 Aug (beheading).

Johore A swampy forested state in S Peninsular Malaysia. Chief products are rubber, copra, pineapples, palm oil, tin, and bauxite. Area: 18 958 sq km (7330 sq mi). Population (1980): 1 601 504. Capital: Johore Baharu.

joint The point at which two or more bones are connected to each other. There are three broad categories. Immovable joints include the sutures between the bones of the skull. Slightly movable joints include those connecting the individual bones of the spine. Freely movable joints (diarthrodial, or synovial, joints) include the hinge joints at the knee and elbow, the ball-and-socket joints at the hip and shoulder, and the gliding joints at the wrist and ankle. The bone ends at movable joints are covered by cartilage and enveloped in a tough capsule thickened in parts to form ligaments. The inside of the capsule is lined by synovial membrane, which secretes a lubricating fluid.

Joliot-Curie, Frédéric and Irène. *See* Curie, Marie.

Jolson, Al (Asa Yoelson; 1886–1950) US popular singer and songwriter, born in Russia. He became famous for his blacked-up face and the song "Mammy." In 1927 he appeared in the first full-length sound film *The Jazz Singer.*

Jones, Inigo (1573–1652) English classical architect. One of the first Englishmen to study architecture in Italy, Jones was particularly influenced by Palladio in his two best-known buildings, the Queen's House, Greenwich (1616–35), and the Banqueting Hall, Whitehall (1619–22). His career effectively ended with the outbreak of the Civil War in 1642, and his style only became strongly influential in England in the 18th century. With Ben Jonson, he also designed numerous court masques. See p. 388.

jonquil. *See* Narcissus.

Jonson, Ben (1572–1637) English dramatist and poet. In *Every Man in His Humour* (1598) he introduced the "comedy of humours," each character being driven by a particular obsession. Other major satirical plays include *Volpone* (1606), *The Alchemist* (1610), and *Bartholomew Fair* (1614). In collaboration with Inigo Jones he produced many court masques. He also published two collections of poems and translations and influenced a number of younger poets known as "the Tribe of Ben."

Joplin, Scott (1868–1917) US Black pianist and composer of ragtime music. Joplin is remembered for such rags as "Maple Leaf Rag" and "The Entertainer." His ragtime operas *A Guest of Honour* (1903), now lost, and *Treemonisha* (1907) were failures and Joplin died in an asylum in poverty.

Jordaens, Jakob (1593–1678) Flemish painter. Although he painted numerous religious altarpieces, influenced by Rubens, he is best known for his allegorical scenes of merrymaking peasants, such as *The King Drinks* (Brussels).

Jordan, Hashemite Kingdom of A country in the Middle East. It is mainly desert but more fertile in the W and N, where the population is concentrated. The people are Arab, and most are Sunnite Muslims, with Christian and other minorities. *Economy*: Jordan's major industries are the extraction and some processing of phosphates, which are exported from Aqaba. Agriculture is concentrated in the irrigated Jordan Valley. Produce includes cereals, vegetables, wool, and such fruit as melons and olives. *History*: the area that is now Jordan appears to have flourished in the Bronze Age and was part of the Roman Empire by 64 BC. It was controlled by Arabs from the 7th century, Crusaders in the 11th and 12th centuries, and Turks from the 16th century until

INIGO JONES   *His Palladian church, St Paul, Covent Garden, built 1631–33.*

1916, when the part E of the River Jordan was named Transjordan and a League of Nations mandate for its control was given to the UK. It became independent in 1946. In the Arab-Israeli War of 1948–49, Jordan overran the West Bank, but it was occupied by Israel in the Six-Day War of 1967. There followed further bloodshed in the civil war of 1970–71 and the Arab-Israeli War of 1973. Jordan has recognized the Palestine Liberation Organization's right to govern the West Bank. Martial law, imposed in 1967, was lifted in 1989 after riots. King Hussein succeeded to the throne in 1952. Prime minister: Mudar Badran. Official language: Arabic. Official currency: Jordanian dinar of 1000 fils. Area: about 97 740 sq km (37 738 sq mi), including the West Bank. Population (1988 est): 3 958 000, including the West Bank. Capital: Amman.

Jordan, River   A river in the Middle East. It rises in Syria and Lebanon and flows due S through the Sea of Galilee, finally entering the Dead Sea. It forms for some of its course part of the border between Israel and Jordan. Length: 320 km (199 mi).

Joseph, St   In the New Testament, the husband of the Virgin Mary. He was a devout Jew belonging to the line of David but worked humbly as a carpenter. He was dead by the time of the crucifixion. Feast day: 19 March.

Joséphine   (1763–1814) The wife (1796–1809) of Napoleon Bonaparte and Empress of the French from 1804. Her first husband was Alexandre, Vicomte de Beauharnais (1760–94), who was guillotined in the French Revolution. She presided over a brilliant court until divorced by Napoleon because of their childlessness.

Joseph of Arimathea, St   In the New Testament, a man described as a councillor. He asked Pontius Pilate for the body of Christ after the crucifixion and arranged for its burial on the same day. According to medieval legend, he came to England after the crucifixion, bringing with him the Holy Grail, and built the first English church, at Glastonbury. Feast day: 17 March.

Joshua tree   A treelike plant, *Yucca brevifolia*, native to desert regions of the SW USA. Growing to a height of more than 10 m, its branching stem can assume unusual shapes. It has stiff sword-shaped leaves and bears waxy white flowers.

Josquin des Prez   (c. 1450–1521) Flemish composer. A pupil of Ockeghem, he served at the courts of Milan, Ferrara, and Rome. His compositions were either elaborately contrapuntal or expressively homophonic; they include masses, motets, and chansons.

Jotunheimen   A mountain range in S central Norway. It rises to 2472 m (8110 ft) at Glittertinden, the highest mountain in the country.

joule (J)   The SI unit of work or energy equal to the work done when the point of application of a force of one newton moves through a distance of one metre. Named after James Joule.

Joule, James Prescott   (1818–89) British physicist, who performed a series of experiments during the 1840s to determine the mechanical equivalent of heat. His work greatly contributed towards Helmholtz's formulation of the law of conservation of energy. He also investigated the heating effect of an electric current, stating in **Joule's law** that the heat produced is equal to the product of the resistance, the square of the current, and the time for which it flows. With Lord Kelvin he discovered the fall in temperature that occurs when a gas expands adiabatically (the **Joule-Kelvin effect**). The unit of energy is named after him.

Joyce, James   (1882–1941) Irish novelist and poet. Accompanied by Nora Barnacle (whom he did not marry until 1931), he left Ireland in 1904, living first in Trieste (until 1915) and later in Zurich during World War I and Paris (1920–40). *Dubliners* (1914), a volume of short stories, was followed by the semiautobiographical novel *Portrait of the Artist as a Young Man* (1916). In 1922 he published *Ulysses*, a stream-of-consciousness epic portraying a single day in the lives of several Dubliners. He carried linguistic experiment to further extremes in *Finnegans Wake* (1939), a dream recounted in puns and word play. Joyce died in Zurich.

Joyce, William   (1906–46) Nazi broadcaster, known as Lord Haw-Haw. Born in the USA, he broadcast Nazi propaganda to Britain throughout World War II and was subsequently tried as a British subject for treason and executed.

JAMES JOYCE   *Detail of painting by J. E. Blanche (1935).*

JP.   *See* justice of the peace.
Juan Carlos   (1938–   ) King of Spain (1975–   ). The grandson of Alfonso XIII, he was designated heir to the throne by Francisco Franco and became king when he died, presiding over Spain's peaceful transition to democracy. In 1962 he married Sophia (1938–   ), daughter of King Paul of Greece.
Juárez.   *See* Ciudad Juárez.
Juárez, Benito (Pablo)   (1806–72) Mexican statesman, who was the first Indian president of Mexico (1861–65, 1867–72). He won popularity by nationalizing ecclesiastical property and led the successful opposition (1864–67) to the French invasion.
Juba, River   A river in East Africa. Rising in S central Ethiopia, it flows S across Somalia to the Indian Ocean. Length: 1660 km (1030 mi).
Jubbulpore.   *See* Jabalpur.
Judaea   The southern division of ancient Palestine. The Old Testament kingdom of Judah survived Syrian, Assyrian, and Philistine attacks following Solomon's death but came to an end after conquest by Nebuchadnezzar II of Babylon, when its capital, Jerusalem, was destroyed (586 BC) and the Jews were exiled. Judaea came next under Persian domination, when the Jews were allowed to return and rebuild Jerusalem, but under the Seleucids Antiochus IV Epiphanes' desecration of the temple in 167 BC instigated the Maccabees' revolt. Judaea achieved a shortlived independence until the Roman conquest in 63 BC. After years of unrest the Roman province of Syria absorbed it in 135 AD.
Judaism   The religion of the Jews. Its fundamental tenet is belief in a single, eternal God, who created the world and desires its welfare. Judaism's most sacred text is the Torah. There is no agreement as to when Judaism began. Tradition attaches importance to the early figures of Abraham and Moses, but many of the characteristic ideas and institutions emerged during the Babylonian exile and the period of the Second Temple. After the destruction of the temple the rabbis codified the traditional teachings (*see* Midrash; Mishnah; Talmud), and in the middle ages philosophy and the kabbalah exerted a great influence. The modern enlightenment undermined traditional values and gave rise to several conflicting movements. Orthodox Judaism asserts the

supernatural authority of Torah and right behaviour (halakhah), which is challenged by Reform Judaism. Conservative Judaism and Reconstructionism support a compromise between these extreme views.
Judas tree   A shrub or small tree of the genus *Cercis* (7 species), also called redbud, native to S Europe, Asia, and North America, and cultivated for ornament. The pinkish-red clusters of flowers appear before the heart-shaped leaves have opened. The name is used particularly for *C. siliquastrum*, from which Judas Iscariot is said to have hanged himself. Family: *Leguminosae.*
judge   An officer who decides legal disputes and passes sentence on offenders. In England and Wales judges try cases in the House of Lords (the Lords of Appeal in Ordinary, or law lords), the Court of Appeal (the Lords Justices), the High Court of Justice (high-court judges), the Crown Court (high-court judges and circuit judges), and County Courts (circuit judges). A judge is appointed by the Crown on the recommendation of the Lord Chancellor (*see* Lord Chief Justice; Master of the Rolls) and must be a barrister (or a solicitor) of at least ten years' standing. (A part-time recorder, who must also be a solicitor or barrister of ten years' standing, may be appointed to serve in the Crown Court; a justice of the peace or stipendiary magistrate serves in Magistrates' Courts.) *See also* courts of law.

JUDO   *Jigoro Kano, the founder of the sport.*

judo   An international form of wrestling developed from jujitsu in Japan by Jigoro Kano (1860–1938). Contestants wear kimonos and coloured belts to indicate their proficiency. The five *kyu* (pupil) grades wear white, orange, green, blue, or brown belts in order of increasing skill, the 12 *dan* (master) grades all wear black belts. Contests take place on a mat 9 m (30 ft) square and usually last two to ten minutes. The contestants score points by executing prescribed throws, ground holds, and locks. *See also* martial arts.
Juggernaut.   *See* Jagannatha.
Jugoslavia.   *See* Yugoslavia, Socialist Federal Republic of.
jujitsu (Japanese name: *yawara*)   The form of self-defence, usually unarmed, used by the Japanese samurai. The object was to disable, cripple, or kill an opponent by using his own momentum and strength against him. Judo, aikido, and karate developed from it.

jujube A small thorny tree of the genus *Zizyphus* that produces sweet edible fruit. *Z. jujuba*, native to China, has been widely introduced to other hot dry regions. It grows up to a height of 9 m and has small yellow flowers. Family: *Rhamnaceae*. *See also* crown of thorns.

Juliana (1909–) Queen of the Netherlands (1948–80) following the abdication of her mother Wilhelmina. In 1937 she married Prince Bernhard von Lippe-Biesterfeld (1911–). In 1980 Queen Juliana abdicated in favour of her eldest daughter Beatrix.

Julian calendar. *See* calendar.

Jumna, River (R Jamuna *or* R Yamuna) A river in N India. Rising in Uttar Pradesh, it flows S and SE to the River Ganges near Allahabad. Length: 1385 km (860 mi).

Juneau 58 20N 134 20W A city in the USA, the capital of Alaska. A supply centre for a fur-trading and mining region, it is also an ice-free port. Population (1983 est): 26 000.

June beetle A brown beetle, also called May beetle or June bug, belonging to a genus (*Phyllophaga*) of chafers. 12–25 mm long, June beetles are commonly seen during early summer evenings, and can be serious pests.

Jung, Carl Gustav (1875–1961) Swiss psychiatrist and pioneer psychoanalyst. Jung collaborated with Sigmund Freud until, in 1912, their differences became irreconcilable. Jung originated the concept of introvert and extrovert personalities and made valuable studies of mental disorders, including schizophrenia. In his major work, *Psychology of the Unconscious* (1912), Jung regarded the unconscious part of the mind as containing both the personal experiences of the individual and common inherited cultural experiences (*see* collective unconscious). Jung later applied his theories to historical studies of religion and to dreams.

Jungfrau 46 33N 7 58E A mountain peak in S central Switzerland, in the Bernese Oberland. Height: 4158 m (13 632 ft).

jungle fowl An Asian forest bird belonging to the genus *Gallus* (4 species). The males have a large fleshy comb and wattles at the sides of the bill and, in the breeding season, fight fiercely using their sharp leg spurs. The red jungle fowl (*Gallus gallus*) is the ancestor of the domestic fowl. Family: *Phasianidae* (fowl and pheasants).

juniper A coniferous tree or shrub of the genus *Juniperus* (60 species), widely distributed in the N hemisphere. Male and female flowers grow on separate trees. The common juniper (*J. communis*) is native to N Europe, North America, and SW Asia; it rarely exceeds 4 m in height and is often planted for ornament. The cones are used for flavouring gin and foods, as a source of oil, and as a diuretic. Family: *Cupressaceae*.

Juno (mythology) A principal Roman goddess, the wife of Jupiter. She was concerned with all aspects of women's life and is usually portrayed as a matronly figure. She was identified with the Greek Hera.

Jupiter (astronomy) The largest and most massive planet, orbiting the sun every 11.86 years at a mean distance of 778.3 million km. Its rapid axial rotation (in less than 10 hours) has produced a nonspherical shape: equatorial diameter 142 800 km, polar diameter 135 500 km. In a telescope light and dark bands of clouds are visible, together with spots and streaks. Jupiter is composed mainly (99%) of hydrogen and helium (in the ratio 82:17). Ammonia, methane, and other compounds are

JUPITER *Montage of Voyager photographs showing the planet and its four Galilean satellites.*

present in the cloud layers. The planetary interior is liquid hydrogen with possibly a small rocky core. Jupiter radiates heat and is also a source of radio waves. It has a magnetic field and radiation belts of great intensity. The planet has 16 known satellites, including the four large Galilean satellites, and a satellite ring of rocks, discovered in 1979.

Jupiter (mythology) The principal Roman god, identified with the Greek Zeus. Originally a sky god, he controlled the weather and used the thunderbolt as his weapon. His temple on the Capitoline hill was the principal Roman religious structure.

Jura Mountains A mountain range in E France and NW Switzerland. It extends along the border in a NE–SW arc, rising to 1723 m (5653 ft) at Crêt de la Neige.

Jurassic period A geological period of the Mesozoic era, between about 200 and 135 million years ago, following the Triassic and preceding the Cretaceous periods. The dinosaurs and other reptiles flourished and diversified in this period. Fossils of the earliest birds and mammals have also been found in Jurassic rocks.

Juruá, Rio A river in South America, rising in E central Peru and through NW Brazil to the River Amazon. Length: 1900 km (1200 mi).

jury A body of people, usually 12, who have taken an oath to decide questions of fact arising in a court case (now usually a criminal case but occasionally a civil case) according to the evidence before them. To qualify for jury service a person must be a registered elector between 18 and 70 years old and resident in the UK for at least 5 years since the age of 13.
Persons ineligible for jury service are members of the judiciary and anyone involved in administering justice, the clergy, and the mentally ill. Others (MPs, medical personnel, etc.) have a right to be excused from jury service, while those who have received certain types of convictions are disqualified. Before being empanelled, jurors may be "challenged" (rejected) for various reasons by either side in a court case. They may claim compensation for loss of income while serving and are also paid travel expenses and subsistence. By the Criminal Justice Act (1967) a majority verdict (normally ten to two) was permitted in criminal trials and the Courts Act (1971)

permitted similar verdicts in civil proceedings in the High Court.

justice of the peace (JP)   An unpaid magistrate appointed by the Lord Chancellor to keep the peace within a county, with statutory power to try summarily certain cases in a Magistrates' Court and to commit other more serious cases for trial by a higher court.

Justinian Code.   *See* Roman law.

jute   Either of two Indian annual plants, *Corchorus capsularis* or *C. olitorius*, cultivated in India, Pakistan, and Thailand for their fibres. Growing to a height of 3 m, they have small yellow flowers. The stems are cut, soaked in water, and beaten to remove the fibres, which are processed into cloth, etc. There are many grades,

used for ropes, sacks, carpet backings, hessian, and tarpaulin. Family: *Tiliaceae*.

Jutes   A Germanic people, probably from Jutland, who invaded Britain together with the Angles and Saxons in the 5th century AD. The Jutes settled in what are now Kent, the Isle of Wight, and Hampshire.

Jutland (Danish name: Jylland)   A peninsula in N Europe, between the North Sea, the Skagerrak, the Kattegat, and the Little Belt. It is occupied by the continental part of Denmark and part of the West German *Land* of Schleswig-Holstein. The Battle of Jutland (1916) was a major naval engagement in World War I.

Jylland.   *See* Jutland.

K

K2 (*or* Mt Godwin Austen)   35 53N 76 32E The second highest mountain in the world (after Mount Everest), in N Pakistan in the Karakoram Range. As it was the second peak to be measured in the range it was given the symbol, K2. The summit was first reached on 31 July, 1954, by an Italian team. Height: 8611 m (28 250 ft).

kabbalah (Hebrew: tradition)   An esoteric Jewish theosophical system. The classical kabbalistic text is the *Zohar* (*Book of Splendour*), written in Aramaic in 13th-century Spain, but the kabbalah has much older roots. It has strong connections with gnosticism and also with magical practices. An important 16th-century kabbalistic school flourished at Safed, in Galilee, around Isaac Luria (1534–72), and Christian interpretations of the kabbalah blended with Neoplatonism in the 16th and 17th centuries.

Kabuki   A form of Japanese popular theatre that developed from the aristocratic No theatre during the 17th century. The earliest notable dramatist was Chikamatsu Monzaemon (1653–1724). The plays are performed with musical accompaniment on a wide revolving stage and emphasize visual effects and acting skills.

Kabul   34 30N 69 10E The capital of Afghanistan, situated in the NE of the country at an altitude of 1830 m (6000 ft). It was capital of the Mogul Empire (1504–1738), becoming capital of Afghanistan in 1773. Population (1984): 1 179 341.

Kaffirs   The former name for the Pondo and Xhosa peoples of the E Cape Province of South Africa, with whom the advancing White settlers fought a series of wars (the Cape Frontier Wars) in the late 18th and 19th centuries.

Kafirs   A people of the Hindu Kush mountains of Afghanistan and Pakistan, who speak a Dardic language. Their name (Arabic *kafir*: infidel) was acquired from their Muslim neighbours on account of their traditional religion.

Kafka, Franz   (1883–1924) Czech writer. Born in Prague (then in Bohemia), the son of German Jewish parents, he wrote fantasies and parables that portray the individual isolated in an incomprehensible and uneasy environment. Most of his work was published posthumously, against his instructions, by his friend Max Brod. Among his best-known writings are the stories *Meta-*

KABUKI   *The interior of a theatre, from a print by Utagawa Toyokuni.*

morphosis (1912) and *In the Penal Settlement* (1919) and the novels *The Trial* (1925) and *The Castle* (1926).

Kafue River   A river in Zambia, rising on the Zaïre frontier and flowing S and E to the Zambezi River. Length: 966 km (600 mi). The **Kafue Dam** (1972) provides about two-thirds of Zambia's hydroelectric power.

Kagoshima   31 37N 130 32E A port in Japan, in S Kyushu. It was the site of Francis Xavier's landing in Japan (1549). Population (1985): 530 000.

Kaikoura Ranges   Twin mountain ranges in New Zealand, comprising the Inland and the Seaward Kaikouras. They extend SW–NE in NE South Island, reaching 2885 m (9465 ft) at Tapuaenuku in the Inland Kaikouras.

Kalahari Desert   A semiarid area in S Africa, chiefly in Botswana. It is sparsely inhabited by nomadic Bushmen, and although its few rivers are generally dry there is some vegetation. Area: about 250 000 sq km (96 505 sq mi).

Kalanchoe   A genus of small tropical shrubs (over 100 species). They are popular house plants. Most flower in winter, having white, red, yellow, or pink flowers. Family: *Crassulaceae.*

kale   A variety of cabbage, also called borecole, grown for its large edible leaves, which are used as a winter vegetable and as livestock food.

Kalgan.   *See* Zhangjiakou.

Kali   In Hindu mythology, the goddess of death. The wife of Shiva in her destructive aspect, she is represented as a hideous four-armed black woman.

Kalimantan   The Indonesian part of Borneo, comprising the SE two-thirds of the island. It is little developed, but its dense forests provide valuable timber. Small-scale agriculture includes the growing of rice, tobacco, sugar cane, coffee, and rubber. Since Indonesian independence in 1949 separatism against the Java-based government has remained strong with active guerrilla activity. Area: 550 203 sq km (212 388 sq mi). Population (1980): 6 723 086. Chief towns: Banjarmasin and Pontianak.

Kaluga   54 31N 36 16E A port in the central Soviet Union, on the River Oka. Population (1987 est): 307 000.

Kama   In Hindu mythology, the god of love. He is the son of Shiva and his popular epithet of Ananga (bodiless) derives from his having been reduced to ashes by a glance from his father's eye when Kama playfully shot his arrows at him.

Kama, River   A river in the E Soviet Union, rising in the Ural Mountains and flowing mainly SW to the River Volga. Length: 2030 km (1260 mi).

Kamakura   35 19N 139 33E A city in Japan, in SE Honshu. A former Japanese capital (1192–1333), it is, noted for its shrines and for its bronze Buddha, 13 m (43 ft) high. Population (1986 est): 175 975.

Kamchatka   A peninsula in the extreme E Soviet Union. It is about 1200 km (746 mi) long and separates the Sea of Okhotsk from the Bering Sea. Area: about 270 000 sq km (104 225 sq mi).

Kamet, Mount   30 55N 79 36E A mountain in N India, in the Himalayas. It was first climbed in 1931. Height: 7756 m (25 446 ft).

Kamikaze   A Japanese aircraft crashed deliberately by its pilot into its target. Such suicide missions were first flown at the battle of Leyte Gulf (1944) in World War II; at Okinawa (1945) some 3000 sorties sunk 21 US

ships. Kamikaze means divine wind and refers to the typhoon that scattered Kublai Khan's invasion fleet in 1281.

Kampala   0 20N 32 30E The capital of Uganda, N of Lake Victoria. Founded by the British in the late 19th century, it became the capital in 1962. Population (1980 est): 458 423.

Kampuchea, Democratic.   *See* Cambodia.

Kananga   (name until 1966: Luluabourg)   5 53S 22 26E A city in central Zaïre, on the River Lulua. It serves an agricultural and diamond-producing area. Population (1984): 290 898.

Kanazawa   36 35N 136 38E A city in Japan, in central Honshu. It is renowned for its landscape garden. Population (1985): 430 000.

Kanchenjunga, Mount.   *See* Kangchenjunga, Mount.

Kandahar   (*or* Qandahar)   31 36N 65 47E A city in S Afghanistan. Situated on main routes to central Asia and India, it is built on the site of several ancient cities. Population (1984 est): 203 177.

Kandinsky, Wassily   (1866–1944) Russian expressionist painter and art theorist. He painted the first purely abstract pictures in European art (c. 1911). These are characterized by freely applied paint and dazzling colours, from which he drew analogies to music in his book *Concerning the Spiritual in Art* (1911). He was a founder of the Neue Kunstlervereinigung (1909) and Der Blaue Reiter (1911) and taught at the Bauhaus school, where his style became more geometrical.

Kandy   7 17N 80 40E A city in central Sri Lanka. Capital of the kingdom of Kandy from 1480 until 1815, when it was occupied by the British, it has a Buddhist temple, Dalada Malagawa. Population (1985): 140 000.

KANGAROO   *The red kangaroo, with its powerful back legs, can travel at 50 km per hour.*

kangaroo   The largest marsupial mammal. There are two species, the red kangaroo (*Macropus rufus*) of Australia and the grey kangaroo (*M. kanguru*) of Australia and Tasmania. Red kangaroos can reach a height of 2 m and a weight of 90 kg. Kangaroos have short front legs and long hind legs and feet: they travel by a succession of leaps. Family: *Macropodidae. See also* wallaby.

Kangchenjunga, Mount   (*or* Mt Kanchenjunga) 27 44N 88 11E The third highest mountain in the world (after Mount Everest and K2), on the Sikkim (India)–Nepal border in the Himalayas. It was first climbed in 1955. Height: 8598 m (28 208 ft).

Kano 12 00N 8 31E A city in N Nigeria. It was an important trade centre for caravans crossing the Sahara. Population (1983): 487 100.

Kanpur (former name: Cawnpore) 26 27N 80 14E A city in India, in Uttar Pradesh. Ceded to the British East India Company (1801), it became an important British frontier station and during the Indian Mutiny was the scene (1857) of a massacre of British soldiers. Population (1981): 1 688 000.

Kansas A state in the centre of the USA. It consists mainly of undulating prairie. Its large mineral resources include oil, natural gas, coal, sand and gravel. Kansas is the USA's main wheat-growing area; other crops include sorghum grains and hay. *History*: first explored by the Spanish in the 16th century, it was claimed by the French (1682) and formed part of the Louisiana Purchase (1803). It became a state (1861) and the arrival of the railway in the late 1860s and 1870s brought many cattlemen. The Mennonites introduced wheat into the area (1874). Area: 213 063 sq km (82 264 sq mi). Population (1986 est): 2 461 000. Capital: Topeka.

Kansas City. 39 05N 94 37W A city in the USA, in Missouri. Settled in 1821, it expanded rapidly with the arrival of the railways in the mid-18th century. Population (1986): 441 170.

Kant, Immanuel (1724–1804) German philosopher. His early works, notably *Theory of the Heavens* (1755), sought to examine metaphysics in the light of the work of Newton and Leibniz. Acquaintance with Hume's empiricism, however, initiated his so-called "critical period" in which he evolved his doctrine of transcendental idealism. In the famous *Critique of Pure Reason* (1781) he explored the limitations of reason by which mankind interprets experience. The *Critique of Judgment* (1790) deals with aesthetic and teleological judgments. Reason makes experience possible by imposing upon the raw data supplied by the senses the forms of understanding. Kant identified 12 of these basic forms (which he called "categories"). He maintained that there was an absolute moral law and called the obligation to obey this moral law the "categorical imperative."

Kao-hsiung. *See* Gaoxiong.

Kapil Dev (Kapil Dev Ramlal Nikhanj; 1959–) Indian cricketer, who has played for Haryana, Northamptonshire, Worcestershire, and India (1978–). He was the second player to score 3000 runs and take 300 wickets in Test matches, he also captained India (1983–84).

Kapitza, Peter Leonidovich (1894–1984) Soviet physicist, who worked with Rutherford on high transient magnetic fields. Returning to the Soviet Union in 1934 he transferred his attention to low-temperature physics, which led him to the discovery of superfluid helium (1941). For this work he was awarded the 1978 Nobel Prize.

kapok The fine silky hairs covering the seeds of the silk-cotton tree (*Ceiba pentandra*), which are used for stuffing mattresses, etc. The tree is native to tropical America and widely cultivated in the tropics. Growing to 35 m, it has large buttresses at the base of the trunk and white or red flowers. Family: *Bombacaceae*.

Karachi 24 51N 67 02E The largest city and chief seaport in Pakistan, situated on the Arabian Sea just NW of the Indus delta. It became the capital of Pakistan (1947) following partition. The removal of the capital to Islamabad (1959) and the building of new satellite towns has eased overcrowding by refugees. Population (1981): 5 103 000.

KAPIL DEV

Karaganda 49 53N 73 07E A city in the SW Soviet Union. Founded in 1857, Karaganda grew rapidly as the Karaganda coal basin was exploited. Today it is one of the largest producers of bituminous coal in the Soviet Union. Population (1987): 633 000.

Karajan, Herbert von (1908–89) Austrian conductor. Musical director of the Vienna State Opera (1957–64), he founded the Salzburg Easter Festival in 1967 and conducted the Berlin Philharmonic Orchestra from 1955.

Karakoram Range A mountain range mainly in SW China, NE Pakistan, and NW India. It extends about 450 km (280 mi) between the Pamirs and the Himalayas and includes K2, the second highest mountain in the world. In 1978 the **Karakoram Highway** was opened connecting China with Pakistan over the Khunjerab Pass, 4933 m (16 188 ft) high.

karakul A breed of sheep originating in central Asia. The young lambs bear a coat of fine tightly curled black wool, known as Persian lamb.

Kara Kum A desert in the SW Soviet Union, between the Caspian Sea and the River Amu Darya. Area: about 300 000 sq km (115 806 sq mi).

karate An oriental form of unarmed combat that was systematized in Okinawa in the 17th century and spread to Japan in the 1920s, where it absorbed elements of ju-jitsu. Breath-control techniques as well as philosophical attitudes, such as the necessity of mental calm, were taken from Zen Buddhism. The aim is to focus the body's total muscular power in one instant. Hands, feet, elbows, etc., are toughened in stylized training sequences against padded or wooden blocks. In actual fights, however, which last two or three minutes, blows are stopped short before impact. As in judo, grades are distinguished by coloured belts and points are awarded in combat. *See also* martial arts.

Karelian Isthmus A land bridge in the NW Soviet Union, connecting Finland with the Soviet Union to which it was ceded in 1944. It is 40–113 km (25–70 mi) wide and 145 km (90 mi) long and its principal cities are Leningrad and Vyborg.

Kariba, Lake A reservoir in Zambia and Zimbabwe. It is formed by the Zambezi River above the **Kariba Dam** (completed 1959) and generates hydroelectric power. Length: 282 km (175 mi).

Karl-Marx-Stadt (name until 1953: Chemnitz) 50 49N 12 50E A city in S East Germany, on the River Chemnitz. A textile centre since the 14th century, it became famous for machine construction in the 19th century. Population (1986): 314 437.

Karloff, Boris (William Pratt; 1887–1969) British film actor. Following his great success as the monster in *Frankenstein* (1931), he was typecast in sinister roles in many horror films.

Karlsruhe 49 00N 8 24E A city in SW West Germany, in Baden-Württemberg. The capital of the former *Land* of Baden, it is the site of the federal court of justice and has a harbour on the Rhine. Population (1986): 267 000.

karma (Sanskrit: action) The sum of all human actions, which according to Hinduism and Jainism are passed from one individual existence to the next and determine the nature of the individual's rebirth. In Buddhism, karma is associated with mental and physical elements passed on in the cycle of rebirth until the personal self is annihilated in attaining nirvana.

Karnak 25 44N 32 39E A village near Thebes (Upper Egypt), the site of the huge temple of Amon, built (c. 1320–1237 BC) mainly by the pharaohs Seti I (reigned 1313–1292) and Ramses II. *See also* Luxor.

Karpov, Anatoly (1951–) Soviet chess player, who became an International Grandmaster at 19 and subsequently world champion (1975). He successfully defended his title against Victor Korchnoi (1931–) in 1978 and 1981 but lost it to Gary Kasparov in 1985.

karri A tree, *Eucalyptus diversicolor*, native to SW Australia and cultivated elsewhere. It grows to a height of over 35 m in moist areas and produces excellent timber.

karting (*or* go-karting) A form of motor racing that originated in the USA in the 1950s. A kart usually has a tubular chassis, no body or suspension system, and a single driving seat. It has a maximum wheelbase of 50 in (1.27 m) and is usually powered by a single-cylinder two-stroke engine. Most karts are capable of about 160 km per hour (100 mph).

Kasai, River A river in central Africa. Rising in Angola, it flows N into Zaïre to join the Zaïre River. It forms part of the Angola–Zaïre border. Length: 2100 km (1300 mi).

KARPOV *Gary Kasparov playing Anatoly Karpov (left); World Championships, 1986.*

Kashmir The northernmost region of the Indian subcontinent, bordered by China to the NE and Afghanistan to the NW. The S Jammu lowlands rise into the Himalaya and Karakoram Mountains. Rice, other grains, silk, cotton, fruits, and sheep are farmed. Embroidery and other crafts help tourism to thrive. *History*: most Kashmiris became Muslims in the 14th century but in the 19th century Hindu princes won power under British control; violence between Muslims and Hindus continues to the present day. Britain's withdrawal (1947) was followed by fighting between India and Pakistan and resulted in the partition of the region. Pakistan rules 78 932 sq km (30 468 sq mi) of the W and barren N. China occupies 42 735 sq km (16 496 sq mi) in the E. The remainder forms the Indian state of Jammu and Kashmir. Area (all Kashmir): 222 236 sq km (85 783 sq mi).

Kasparov, Gary (Gary Weinstein; 1963–) Soviet chess player, youngest-ever world champion. He won the world championship in 1985 at the age of 22 when he beat Karpov.

Kassel 51 18N 9 30E A city in E West Germany, in Hessen. Notable buildings include the Orangery Palace (1701–11). Population (1986): 184 200.

Kathiawar Peninsula A peninsula in W India, in Gujarat, 190 km (118 mi) square, projecting into the Arabian Sea between the Gulfs of Kutch and Cambay.

Kathmandu (*or* Katmandu) 27 42N 85 19E The capital of Nepal, near the confluence of the Rivers Baghmati and Vishnumati. Founded in the 8th century AD, it possesses numerous historical buildings and is the site of several religious festivals. Population (1982 est): 195 260.

Katmai, Mount An active volcano in the USA, in S Alaska. Following its violent eruption in 1912, the Valley of Ten Thousand Smokes was formed. Height: 2100 m (7000 ft). Depth of crater: 1130 m (3700 ft). Width of crater: about 4 km (2.5 mi).

Katowice (former name (1953–56): Stalinograd) 50 15N 18 59E A city in S central Poland. It is an important industrial centre within the Upper Silesia coalfield. Population (1982): 366 000.

ORKNEYS
Kirkwall

SHETLANDS
Lerwick

Stornaway

WESTERN
ISLES

ATLANTIC
OCEAN

North
Sea

HIGHLAND
Inverness

GRAMPIAN
Aberdeen

TAYSIDE
Dundee
Cupar
FIFE

SCOTLAND

CENTRAL
Stirling
Edinburgh
Glasgow
LOTHIAN

STRATHCLYDE

Newtown
St. Boswells

BORDERS

NORTHERN
IRELAND

DONEGAL
Lifford

DERRY
TYRONE
ANTRIM
Belfast

FERMANAGH
ARMAGH
DOWN
Monaghan
MONAGHAN

DUMFRIES &
GALLOWAY
Dumfries

NORTHUMBERLAND
Newcastle-upon-Tyne (also headquarters for Northumberland)
TYNE & WEAR

Carlisle

Durham
DURHAM
CLEVELAND
Middlesbrough

CUMBRIA

Northallerton

ISLE
OF
MAN
Douglas

NORTH YORKSHIRE

ENGLAND

Sligo
SLIGO
Carrick-on-
Shannon
Cavan

MAYO
Castlebar
ROSCOMMON
Roscommon

LEITRIM

CAVEN
Cavan
LONGFORD
Longford
Mullingar
WEST MEATH

Dundalk
LOUTH

Naven
MEATH

Dublin
DUBLIN
KILDARE
Naas

HUMBERSIDE
Kingston upon Hull

LANCASHIRE
Preston
WEST
YORKS.
Wakefield
Barnsley
S. YORKS.

G.M.
Manchester

Liverpool
MERSYSIDE

Lincoln
LINCOLNSHIRE

GALWAY
Galway

Tullamore
OFFALY
Port Laoise
LAOISE

Caernarfon

Mold
Chester
CHESHIRE

DERBYSHIRE
Matlock
NOTTS.
Nottingham

GWYNEDD
CLWYD

STAFFS

REPUBLIC
OF
IRELAND

CLARE
Ennis

Kilkenny
KILKENNY
Carlow
CARLOW

Wicklow
WICKLOW

Shrewsbury
SHROPSHIRE

POWYS

Stafford
W.M.
Birmingham

LEICS.
Leicester

NORFOLK
Norwich

Limerick
LIMERICK
TIPPERARY
Clonmel

Wexford
WEXFORD

Llandrindod
Wells

Warwick
WARWICK

NORTHANTS.
Northampton

CAMBS.
Cambridge

SUFFOLK
Ipswich

Tralee

KERRY
CORK
Cork

Waterford
WATERFORD

DYFED
Carmarthen

Worcester
HEREFORD & WORC.

Gloucester
GLOS.

Oxford
OXON.

Bedford
BEDS.
Hertford
HERTS.

ESSEX
Chelmsford

WALES

GWENT

W.G.
M.G.
S.G.
Cardiff
(also headquarters for M.G.)
Swansea

Newport
Bristol
AVON.

Aylesbury
BUCKS.

BERKS.
Reading

Kingston
upon Thames
SURREY

GREATER
LONDON

Maidstone
KENT

Trowbridge
WILTS.

HAMPSHIRE
Winchester

WEST SUSSEX
Chichester

EAST SUSSEX
Lewes

SOMERSET
Taunton

DORSET
Dorchester

Newport
ISLE OF
WIGHT

DEVON
Exeter

CORNWALL
Truro

Isles of
Scilly

English Channel

FRANCE

20 0 20 40 60 80 Kilometres

International Boundary
National Boundaries
County/Regional Boundaries
Historic counties in
Northern Ireland

• Administrative Headquarters
G.M. Greater Manchester
W.M. West Midlands

W.G. West Glamorgan
M.G. Mid Glamorgan
S.G. South Glamorgan

© Macmillan Publishers Ltd., 1985. Revised 1990.

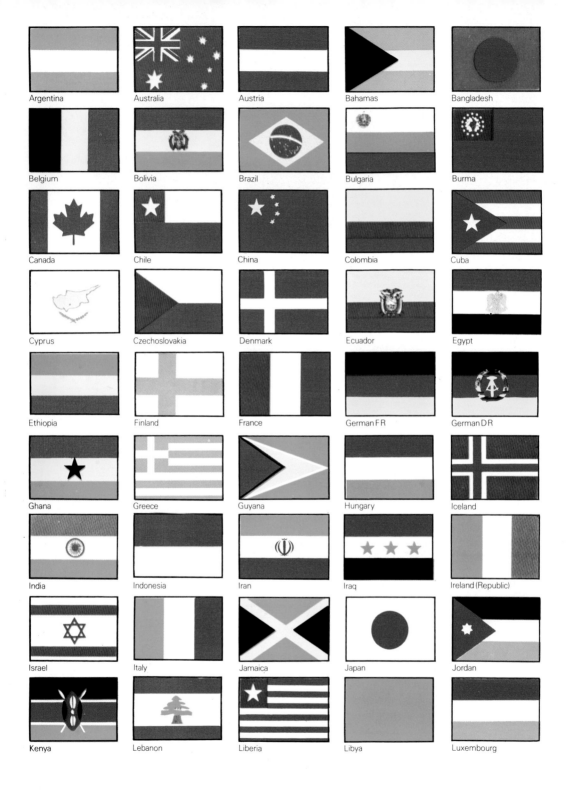

Argentina

Australia

Austria

Bahamas

Bangladesh

Belgium

Bolivia

Brazil

Bulgaria

Burma

Canada

Chile

China

Colombia

Cuba

Cyprus

Czechoslovakia

Denmark

Ecuador

Egypt

Ethiopia

Finland

France

German F R

German D R

Ghana

Greece

Guyana

Hungary

Iceland

India

Indonesia

Iran

Iraq

Ireland (Republic)

Israel

Italy

Jamaica

Japan

Jordan

Kenya

Lebanon

Liberia

Libya

Luxembourg

Malaysia

Malta

Mexico

Morocco

Netherlands

New Zealand

Nigeria

Norway

Pakistan

Philippines

Poland

Portugal

Saudi Arabia

Sierra Leone

Singapore

South Africa

Spain

Sri Lanka

Sweden

Switzerland

Taiwan

Tanzania

Thailand

Trinidad

Turkey

Uganda

USSR

UK

USA

Uruguay

Venezuela

Vietnam

Yugoslavia

Zaire

Zambia

Flags of some recently independent countries and international organizations

Dominica

Fiji

Saint Lucia

St Vincent

Seychelles

Suriname

Zimbabwe

NATO

Olympics

UN

Scale at the Equator
1000   0   1000   2000   3000 Kilometres

International Boundary —
Capital City ▪
Other Town ○

Abbreviations

ALB.	Albania	LEB.	Lebanon
Aust.	Australia	*N.Z.*	New Zealand
AUST.	Austria	*Nor.*	Norway
BEL.	Belgium	P.D.R.YEMEN	People's Democratic Republic of the Yemen
COMM.	Commonwealth		
CZECH.	Czechoslovakia	REP.	Republic
Den.	Denmark	SW.	Switzerland
DOM.REP.	Dominican Republic	U.A.E.	United Arab Emirates
Fr.	France	*(U.K.)*	United Kingdom
FR.GUIANA	French Guiana	*U.S.A.*	United States of America
HOND.	Honduras	YEMEN A.R.	Yemen Arab Republic
HUNG.	Hungary	ZIMB.	Zimbabwe
ISR.	Israel		

© Macmillan Publishers Ltd., 1985. Revised 1990.

ARCTIC OCEAN

Severnaya
Zemlya

New Siberian Is.

Barents
Sea

Novaya
Zemlya

Murmansk

North C.

Helsinki

olm Leningrad

Verkhoyansk

Arctic Circle

Bering Str.

Moscow

Perm Sverdlovsk

UNION OF SOVIET SOCIALIST REPUBLICS

Okhotsk

Bering

Sea

To Anchorage

Kiev

Rostov

Omsk

Novosibirsk

2 816

Irkutsk

L. Baykal

1 529

Kamchatka

Sakhalin

Aleutian Is.

5 584

MANIA

ULGARIA

Istanbul

Ankara

TURKEY

Baku

Tashkent

L. Balkhash

Aral
Sea

Ulan Bator

MONGOLIA

2 012

Harbin

Kuril Is.

Vladivostok

6 888

To Vancouver

Black Sea

CYPRUS LEB SYRIA Baghdad

Tehran

AFGHANISTAN

Islamabad

CHINA

Shenyang

NORTH
KOREA

Beijing Pyongyang

690

Seoul
SOUTH

Tokyo

JAPAN

7 300

To San Francisco

ISR Damascus

Cairo

JORDAN IRAQ Basra

EGYPT

Kabul

IRAN

KUWAIT

Lahore

Nanjing

Chongqing

Wuhan

Osaka

Shanghai

PACIFIC

5 451

3 203

To Honolulu

SAUDI

Riyadh

QATAR

PAKISTAN

Delhi

NEPAL

Karachi

TIBET

BHUTAN

2 482

3 010

BANGLA-
DESH

Calcutta

T'ai-pei

TAIWAN

OCEAN

Tropic of Cancer

ARABIA

Makkah

U.A.E

Muscat

INDIA

2 624

2 189

Hanoi

Hong Kong
(U.K.)

3 203

OMAN

BURMA

Rangoon

Bombay

Hainan

4 989

Wake I.
(U.S.A.)

To Honolulu

3 718

Khartoum

P.D.R.
YEMEN

YEMEN
A.R.

Aden

Arabian Sea

Madras

Bay of
Bengal

Andaman and Nicobar
Is. (India)

THAILAND

Bangkok

VIETNAM

KAMPUCHEA

South
China Sea

Manila

Quezon City

PHILIPPINES

7 660

Mariana Is.
(U.S.A.)

Marshall Is.
(U.S.A.)

SUDAN

DJIBOUTI Djibouti

ETHIOPIA

Socotra
(P.D.R.Yemen)

Lakshadweep
(India)

Ho Chi
Minh City

Caroline Is.
(U.S.A.)

Addis Ababa

SOMALIA

Colombo

SRI LANKA

2 576

W. MALAYSIA

Kuala Lumpur

BRUNEI

MALAYSIA

SABAH

2 881

ui

Kampala

KENYA

Nairobi

MALDIVES

SINGAPORE

SARAWAK

Kalimantan

Equator

RWANDA
BURUNDI

AIRE

TANZANIA

Dodoma Dar es Salaam

SEYCHELLES

COMOROS

INDIAN OCEAN

2 145

Sumatra

Jakarta

Java

INDONESIA

Sulawesi

6 070

Irian Jaya PAPUA
NEW
GUINEA

Port Moresby

SOLOMON IS.

ZAMBIA

usaka Lilongwe

MOZAMBIQUE

Harare

ZIMB.

Antananarivo

MADAGASCAR

MAURITIUS

Réunion
(Fr.)

9 092

Cocos Is.
(Aust.)

5 021

Christmas I.
(Aust.)

Timor

Darwin

Coral
Sea

VANUATU

New Caledonia
(Fr.)

To Fiji

SWANA

ne

teria

OF
TH
CA

Town

Maputo

SWAZILAND

LESOTHO

Durban

9 357

9 036

Tropic of Capricorn

Perth

Fremantle

2 177

AUSTRALIA

Alice Springs

Adelaide

Melbourne

Murray

Darling

Brisbane

Sydney

Canberra

3 186

Norfolk I.
(Aust.)

2 050

Auckland

To Panama

NEW

ZEALAND

Wellington

Christchurch

Tasmania

Hobart

Kerguelen I.
(Fr.)

Antipodes
(N.Z.)

30 East of Greenwich

East of Greenwich

60

90

120

150

180

FINLAND

NORWAY
Bergen
Hardanger
Vidda
Oslo
Stavanger

SWEDEN
Uppsala
Stockholm
Norrköping
Göteborg
Vänern
Vättern
Scotland
Öland
Gotland

Shetland Is.

Orkney Is.
Thurso
Hebrides
Inverness
Aberdeen
SCOTLAND
Grampians
Perth
Dundee
Firth of Forth

North Sea

DENMARK
Jylland
Århus
Esbjerg
Fyn
Odense
Schleswig
Sjælland
Copenhagen
Helsingborg
Malmö
Ålborg

SOVIET
UNION

Baltic Sea
Kaliningrad
Bornholm
Rügen
Stralsund
Rostock
Gdansk
Szczecin

UNITED KINGDOM
Glasgow
Edinburgh
Newcastle
Carlisle
N. IRELAND
Belfast
I. of Man
Isle
Anglesey
Leeds
Hull
Liverpool
Manchester
Sheffield
WALES
Birmingham
ENGLAND
Cardiff
London
Bristol
Southampton
Portsmouth
Plymouth
I. of Wight
Dover
Strait of Dover
Calais
Boulogne

REP. OF
IRELAND
Galway
Dublin
Limerick
Wexford
Cork

Donegal B.

Irish
Sea

St. George's Channel

Bristol Channel

Isles of Scilly

English Channel

Channel Is.

Ushant I.

Cherbourg
Dieppe
Le Havre
Rouen
Caen
Amiens
Reims
Paris

EAST
GERMANY
Lübeck
Hamburg
Bremen
Hanover
Berlin
Magdeburg
Frankfurt
Poznań
Lódź
Warsaw
Wroclaw
Kraków

POLAND

Frisian Islands
Groningen
Osnabrück
IJsselmeer
Amsterdam
The Hague
Rotterdam
NETHERLANDS
Arnhem
Münster
Dortmund
Essen
Düsseldorf
Köln (Cologne)
Bonn
Leipzig
Dresden
GERMANY
Karl Marx Stadt
Prague
Ostrava
Brno
CZECHOSLOVAKIA
Bratislava
Vienna

Ghent
Brussels
Antwerp
Lille
Dunkirk
BELGIUM
Aachen
Liège
LUX.
Mainz
Frankfurt
Mannheim
Nuremberg
Regensburg
Linz

NORTH SEA

Rennes
Le Mans
Orléans

FRANCE

Brest

Nantes

Tours

Troyes
Dijon
Nancy
Metz
Strasbourg
WEST
Karlsruhe
Stuttgart
Augsburg
Munich
Salzburg
Innsbruck
AUSTRIA
Dotomites
Graz
Klagenfurt
Vosges
Schwarzwald
Mulhouse
Basle
Zürich
CZECH.
Lucerne
Bern
Geneva
Lausanne
SWITZERLAND
Trento
Trieste
Rijeka
Zagreb

HUNGARY
Budapest

YUGOSLAVIA

Bay of
Biscay

Bordeaux
Périgueux
Limoges
Clermont
Ferrand
St Étienne
Lyons Mt. Blanc 4807m
Mt. Cenis 2082m
Grenoble
Turin
Milan
Genoa
Brescia
Verona
Padua
Venice
Reggio
Parma
Bologna
Ravenna
SAN
MARINO
San Marino
Ancona
Dinaric Alps
Sarajevo
Dubrovnik
Dalmatian Is.

Adriatic Sea

La Coruña
Vigo
Gijón
Bilbao
Cantabrian Mts.
S. Sebastián
Biarritz
Bayonne
Pyrenees
Pic d'Aneto
3404m
ANDORRA
Toulouse
Perpignan
Nîmes
Montpellier
Avignon
Marseilles
MONACO
Monte Carlo
Nice
Cannes
Toulon
Gulf of Lions
Livorno
Florence
Pisa
Elba
Corsica
Ajaccio
Ligurian Sea
ITALY
Rome

PORTUGAL
Porto
Douro
Oviedo
Valladolid
Guadarrama
Zaragoza
Madrid
SPAIN
Sierra de
Toledo
Tagus
Barcelona
Menorca
Mallorca
Palma
Ibiza
Balearic Is.
Sardinia
Cagliari
Naples
Salerno
Bari
Brindisi
Taranto
Gulf
of
Taranto

Lisbon
Badajoz
Guadiana
Sierra Morena
Córdoba
Valencia
Júcar
Alicante
Murcia
Cartagena

Tyrrhenian
Sea

Faro
Seville
Jerez
Granada
Sa. Nevada
Málaga
Almería

Cádiz
Gibraltar (U.K.)
Str. of Gibraltar
Tangier

Algiers
Constantine
Annaba

Tunis
MALTA

Palermo
Marsala
Sicily
Catania
Messina
Reggio
Str. of Messina
Sicilian Channel

Mediterranean Sea

MOROCCO

West of Greenwich   East of Greenwich

ALGERIA

TUNISIA

	Metres		Metres		Metres		Metres		
	3 200		400		Land below Sea Level		4 000	International Boundaries	■	Capital Cities
	1 600		200		1 000			Internal Boundaries	◉	Important Towns
	800		0		2 000			Main Roads	○	Other Towns
								Railways	✈	Airports
								Mountain Peaks ▲		

50 0 50 100 150 200 Kilometres

Metres	
6 400	
3 200	
1 600	
800	
400	
200	
0	
Land below Sea Level	
1 000	
2 000	
4 000	
8 000	

200 0   400   800   1 200   1 600 Kilometres

━━━━ International Boundaries

╍╍╍╍ European Turkey Boundary

╍·╍·╍ European USSR Boundary

──── Railways

▪ Capital Cities

● Major Towns

○ Other Towns

▲ Mountain Peaks

Population (in millions) of
South and East Asia 1989

World	5 162·4
China	1 110·8
India	813·4
Indonesia	178·5
Japan	123·3
Bangladesh	112·3
Pakistan	109·7
Vietnam	64·8
Philippines	59·7
Thailand	54·8
S. Korea	44·1
Burma	40·1
N. Korea	22·4
Taiwan	19·3
Nepal	18·1
Sri Lanka	17·2
Malaysia	17·0

1 giant represents 500 million people

1 man represents 10 million people

© Macmillan Publishers Ltd., 1985. Revised 1990.

ATLANTIC OCEAN

PORTUGAL
FRANCE
ROMANIA
SPAIN
Corsica
ITALY
YUGOSLAVIA
BULGARIA
ALBANIA
GREECE
Sardinia
TURKEY
Black Sea
SOVIET UNION
Caspian Sea

Tangier
Algiers
Oran
Constantine
Tunis
Sicily
MALTA
5005m
Crete
CYPRUS
SYRIA
IRAN
Rabat
Casablanca
Fès
Atlas Mts.
TUNISIA
Tripoli
LEBANON
ISRAEL
Port Said
IRAQ
Madeira (Port.)
MOROCCO
Marrakech
Mt Toubkal 4165m
Touggourt
Benghazi
Alexandria
Qattara
Depression
Cairo
JORDAN
KUWAIT
Persian Gulf
QATAR
U.A.E.
Canary Is. (Sp.)
Suez
ARAB
REPUBLIC
OF EGYPT
Aswan
High Dam
L. Nasser
SAUDI
ARABIA

El Aaiún
WESTERN
SAHARA
(SADR)
Zouirat
Tropic of Cancer
ALGERIA
LIBYA
Ahaggar
Mts.
Ghat
Libyan
Desert
Nubian
Desert
Port Sudan
YEMEN
PDR
S   a   h   a   r   a
Tibesti

Nouakchott
MAURITANIA
MALI
NIGER
CHAD
Khartoum
Massawa
YEMEN
AR
Socotra
(P.D.R.)

Timbuktu
Niger
SENEGAL
Dakar
Kayes
Bamako
Niamey
Sokoto
Kano
Maiduguri
N'Djaména
Nyala
SUDAN
Asmara
Ras Dashan
4620m
DJIBOUTI
Djibouti
Somali
Peninsula
Banjul
THE GAMBIA
Ouagadougou
Kaduna
Ethiopian
Highlands
Addis Ababa
GUINEA
BISSAU
Bissau
GUINEA
Kankan
BURKINA
FASO
Kaduna
Kainji
Dam
NIGERIA
CENTRAL
AFRICAN REPUBLIC
Wau
Bahr el Arab
White Nile
ETHIOPIA
SOMALIA

Conakry
Freetown
SIERRA LEONE
CÔTE
D'IVOIRE
GHANA
TOGO
REP. OF BENIN
Ibadan
Enugu
CAMEROON
Cameroon 4070m
Bangui
Mogadishu
Monrovia
LIBERIA
Yamoussoukro
Abidjan
Lomé
Accra
Porto
Novo
Lagos
Port Harcourt
Malabo
Douala
Yaoundé
Gulf of Guinea
+5 212m
EQU.
GUINEA
SÃO TOMÉ
and PRÍNCIPE
Equator
Libreville
PEOPLE'S
REP.
OF THE
CONGO
GABON
REPUBLIC
OF
ZAÏRE
UGANDA
Mt. Elgon 4321m
Kisangani
Kampala
Mt
Stanley
RWANDA
BURUNDI
Mwanza
KENYA
Mt Kenya
5 200m
Nairobi
Mt. Kilimanjaro
5895m
Mombasa
Arusha
Pemba
INDIAN
OCEAN
5 340m
Pointe Noire
CABINDA
Brazzaville
Kinshasa
Kigoma
Dodoma
Zanzibar
Dar es Salaam
Ascension
(U.K.)
Luanda
Malanje
TANZANIA
L. Rukwa
Aldabra Is.
ATLANTIC
OCEAN
Benguela
ANGOLA
Lubumbashi
Ndola
Muchinga Mts.
MALAWI
Lilongwe
COMOROS
Moçambique
St. Helena
(U.K.)
+6 050m
Mossâmedes
ZAMBIA
Lusaka
L. Kariba
Harare
MOZAMBIQUE
Beira
Antananarivo
MADAGASCAR
NAMIBIA
Bulawayo
ZIMBABWE
Walvis Bay
Namib
Desert
Windhoek
BOTSWANA
Kalahari
Desert
Gaborone
Pretoria
Johannesburg
Maputo
Lüderitz
SWAZILAND
+5 457m
Tropic of Capricorn
Kimberley
LESOTHO
REP. OF
SOUTH AFRICA
Great Karoo
Drakensberg
+3 480m
Durban
INDIAN
OCEAN
Cape Town
Port Elizabeth
C. of Good Hope

20   West of Greenwich   East of Greenwich   10   20   30   40   50

	Metres		Metres		Metres		Metres			
200 0 200 400 600 800 Kilometres		3 200		400		Land below Sea Level		4 000	— International Boundaries	■ Capital Cities
		1600		200		1000			— Railways	● Major Towns
		800		0		2 000			⌐ Dams	○ Other Towns
									+ Sea Depths	
									▲ Mountain Peaks	

© Macmillan Publishers Ltd., 1980. Revised 1990.

Population of the Soviet Union and Europe (in millions) 1989

Soviet Union	289.3		Netherlands	14.7
West Germany	60.4		Hungary	10.7
Italy	57.5		Portugal	10.5
United Kingdom	56.2		Greece	10.0
France	55.3		Belgium	9.9
Spain	39.5		Bulgaria	9.2
Poland	38.3		Sweden	8.3
Yugoslavia	23.8		Austria	7.5
Romania	23.7		Switzerland	6.4
East Germany	16.9		Denmark	5.1
Czechoslovakia	15.8		Finland	5.0
			Norway	4.2
			Ireland	3.8
			Albania	3.3

(European countries below 1 million are not included)

1 giant represents 50 million people
1 man represents 1 million people

International Boundaries
Capital Cities
Major Towns
Other Towns
Major Roads
Major Railways
Mountain Peaks
Sea Depths
European Soviet Boundary

Metres
6 400
3 200
1600
800
400
200
0 Land below Sea Level
1 000
2 000
4 000
8 000

Scale / Legend

50 0 50 100 200 300 Kilometres

Projection: Bonne's Equal Area

Metres		Metres	
	1 600		200
	800		2 000
	400		6 000
	200		8 000
	0		

International Boundaries
Main Roads
Railways
Tunnels
Airports
Airfields
Capital Cities
Important Towns
Other Towns
▲ Mountain Peaks
Swamps

Map labels

U.S.S.R.

Bikin
Lesozavodsk
Sikhote Alin
Yuzhno-Sakhalinsk
Korsakov
Sakhalin (U.S.S.R.)
Aniva Bay
Sea of Okhotsk
La Perouse Str.
Ussuriysk
Plastum
Olga
Khanka
Rebun
Rishiri
Wakkanai
Tokiwa
Mombetsu
Abashiri
Kunashiri
CHINA
Vladivostok
Nakhodka
Hokkaido
Mayoro
Asahigawa
Asahi 2290m
Dake
Nemuro
Fushan
Penchi
Najin
Unggi
Chongjin
Kambo Ho 2539m
Kilchu
Okushiri
Otaru
Sapporo
Hidaka Ra.
Obihiro
Kushiro
Muroran
Uchiura Bay
C. Erimo
Hakodate
Tsugaru Channel
Ishikari Bay
Anju
Sinuiju
NORTH KOREA
Hamhung
Nangnim Sanmaek
Aomori
Hachinohe
Hirosaki
Yonghung
Hungnam
Akita
Morioka
Kitakami Ra.
Pyongyang
Chinnampo
Wonsan
Sakata
Shinjo
Ishinomaki
Haeju
Chunchon
Taebaek Range
Yamagata
Sendai
Kangnung
Seoul
Wonju
Sado
Niigata
Honshu
Inchon
Suwon
Nagaoka
Fukushima
Koriyama
JAPAN
Iwaki
Hitachi
SOUTH KOREA
Chongju
Andong
Oki Shoto
Takaoka
Toyama
Utsunomiya
Mito
Taejon
Pohang
Fukui
Matsumoto
Nagano
Maebashi
Kanazawa
Kunsan
Chonju
Wakasa Bay
C. Suzu
Toyama Bay
Urawa
Tokyo
Choshi
Ulsan
L. Biwa
Gifu
Kofu
Fujiyama 3776m
Yokohama
Kwangju
Taegu
Chinju
Matsue
Tottori
Kyoto
Nagoya
Numazu
Yokosuka
Masan
Pusan
Chugoku Ra.
Okayama
Yokkaichi
Toyohashi
Shizuoka
C. Najima
Mokpo
Tsushima
Kobe
Osaka
Ise Bay
Hamamatsu
Yellow Sea
G. of Korea
Korea Archipelago
Shimono
Hiroshima
Takamatsu
Sakai
Ise
Kure
Wakayama
Cheju
Shimonoseki
Ube
Himeji
Tokushima
Shingu
Kitakyushu
Yawatahama
Matsuyama
Kochi
Cheju-Do
Retto
Fukuoka
Kurume
Oita
Shikoku
Nakadori Shima
Sasebo
Omuta
Kumamoto
C. Muroto
Fukue Shima
Nagasaki
Goto
Shimo
Kyushu
C. Ashizuri
Bungo Sea
Miyazaki
Miyakonojo
East China Sea
Kagoshima
Kagoshima Bay
Osumi Is.
PACIFIC OCEAN
Amamioshima
Tokunoshima
Ryukyu Is. (Jap)
Okinawa
Naha

Sea of Japan

East of Greenwich

Inset: Tokyo & Yokohama

Fukuoka
Warabi
Narageyama
Kashiwa
Niiza
Asaka
Hatogaya
Soka
Matsudo
Kiyose
Itabashi
Kawaguchi
Ichikawa
Yachiyo
Kodaira
Kurume
Tanashi
Musashino
Funabashi 27m
Narashino
Koganei
Fuchu
Mitaka
Nakano
Sumida
Koenji
Komae
Meguro
Shinagawa
Chiba
Tokyo
Chofu
Setagaya
Machida
Yamato
Kawasaki
Tokyo Bay
Ichihara
Fujisawa
Yokohama
Naka
Kisarazu
Sodegaura
Fukuta
Kamakura
Hayama
Zushi
Yokosuka
Kimitsu
243m
353m
Futtsu
Miura

Urban Areas
Industrial Areas
Wooded Areas
Recreation Areas

City Boundaries
Arterial Roads
Other Roads
Marsh
Railways
Airport

5 0 5 10 15 20 Kilometres

Area of Countries (% of total area)

Uruguay
Suriname
Guyana
French
Guiana
Peru
Paraguay
Ecuador
Colombia
Chile

Venezuela
Argentina
Bolivia
Brazil

Gross Domestic Product per person 1988

Million US Dollars

	500	1 000	1 500	2 000	2 500	3 000
Argentina						
Bolivia						
Brazil						
Chile						
Colombia						
Ecuador						
French Guiana						
Guyana						
Paraguay						
Peru						
Suriname						
Uruguay						
Venezuela						

Population (in millions) of South America 1989

Brazil	147·4	†††††††††††††††
Argentina	32·4	†††
Colombia	31·2	†††
Peru	21·8	††
Venezuela	19·2	††††††††††
Chile	12·8	††
Ecuador	10·5	†
Bolivia	7·1	†††††††
Paraguay	4·1	†††
Uruguay	3·1	†††
Guyana	1·0	†
Suriname	0·4	•
French Guiana	0·1	•

1 giant represents 10 million people

1 man represents 1 million people

1 dot represents less than 500,000 people

Kattegat   A strait between Denmark and Sweden linking the Skagerrak with the Baltic Sea. Length: about 240 km (149 mi).

Katyn Massacre   The execution during World War II of 4250 Polish officers in the Katyn forest, near Smolensk in the Soviet Union. The bodies of the Poles, who had been interned by the Russians following the Soviet occupation of Polish territory in 1939, were discovered by the Germans in 1943. The Russians denied responsibility but the weight of evidence points to Soviet accountability.

Kauffmann, Angelica   (1741–1807) Swiss painter. In England (1765–81) she painted portraits influenced by Reynolds and was employed on decorative work in country houses designed by Robert and James Adam.

Kaunas   (Russian name: Kovno)   54 52N 23 55E A port in the Soviet Union, at the confluence of the Rivers Neman and Viliya. It was held successively by Lithuania, Poland, and Russia before becoming (1918) the capital of independent Lithuania; it was occupied by German forces during World War II. Population (1987): 417 000.

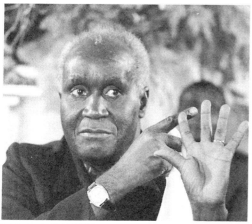

KENNETH KAUNDA

Kaunda, Kenneth (David)   (1924–)   Zambian statesman; president (1964–). In 1958 he founded the militant Zambia African National Congress and was imprisoned for subversion. On his release in 1960 he became president of the United National Independence Party, which took Northern Rhodesia to independence as Zambia in 1964.

kauri pine   A coniferous tree, *Agathis australis*, from New Zealand. Growing to a height of 46 m, it has spherical cones, 5–8 cm in diameter. It yields a resin (kauri copal or gum) used in making varnishes. Its timber is used for building purposes. Family: *Araucariaceae*.

kava   A shrub, *Piper methysticum*, of the Pacific Islands and Australia, the ground and fermented roots of which are made into a narcotic drink. The roots are also chewed, and continued use produces inflammation and ulcers of the mouth. It has been used medicinally and as a local anaesthetic. Family: *Piperaceae*.

Kawasaki   35 32N 139 41E A city in Japan, in SE Honshu, part of the Tokyo-Yokohama industrial complex. Population (1985): 1 089 000.

Kazan   (*or* Kasan)   53 45N 49 10E A city in the E Soviet Union, since 1920 the capital of the Tatar ASSR. *History*: founded in the 14th century by the Tatars, it became the capital of an independent khanate and was captured (1552) by Ivan the Terrible. Its trade and industry developed during the 19th century. Lenin and Tolstoi studied at Kazan's university (1804). Population (1987): 1 068 000.

Kazan, Elia   (E. Kazanjoglous; 1909–)   US stage and film director and novelist, born in Turkey of Greek parentage. He helped to found the Actors' Studio in 1947. For the stage he directed *The Skin of Our Teeth* (1942), *A Streetcar Named Desire* (1947), *Death of a Salesman* (1949), and other outstanding plays. His films include *Viva Zapata* (1952), *On the Waterfront* (1954), *East of Eden* (1955), and *The Arrangement* (1969), which is based on his own novel.

KBE.   See Order of the British Empire.

Kean, Edmund   (c. 1787–1833)   British actor. He was particularly successful as Shylock in *The Merchant of Venice*, his first London success in 1814, Richard III, Macbeth, Iago in *Othello*, and Barabas in Marlowe's *The Jew of Malta*, all roles suited to his passionate style of acting.

Keaton, Buster   (Joseph Francis K.; 1895–1966)   US comedian of silent films. He developed his character of the unsmiling and resilient clown in a series of classic silent comedies, including *The Navigator* (1924), *The General* (1926), and *The Cameraman* (1928).

Keats, John   (1795–1821)   British poet. Despite the failure of his first volume, *Poems* (1817), which contained the sonnet "On First Looking into Chapman's Homer," and the savage criticism directed at his second, *Endymion* (1818), Keats persisted and between 1819 and 1820 wrote most of his best-known poems. His short life was dogged by tragedies, especially the death of his brother from tuberculosis in 1818 and his unrequited love for Fanny Brawne. Such poems as *La Belle Dame Sans Merci*, *The Eve of Saint Agnes*, and the great odes ("To a Nightingale," "On a Grecian Urn," etc.), all published in 1820, eventually established his reputation. He died in Rome in search of a cure for his tuberculosis and was buried there.

Kebnekaise   A mountain range in N Sweden. It rises to 2123 m (6965 ft) at Kebnekaise Sydtopp, the highest mountain in Sweden.

Keeling Islands.   *See* Cocos Islands.

Keeshond   A breed of dog traditionally used by the Dutch as barge dogs. It has a compact body with a fox-like face and a long thick grey coat with black-tipped hairs. The tail is carried over the back and a dense ruff surrounds the neck. Height: 43–45 cm.

Keflavík   64 01N 22 35W A town and fishing port in SW Iceland. It has a NATO air base. Population (1986): 6993.

Keitel, Wilhelm   (1882–1946)   German field marshal, who was Hitler's chief military adviser throughout World War II. In 1945 in Berlin he confirmed the German surrender. He was hanged for war crimes.

Kekulé von Stradonitz, (Friedrich) August   (1829–96) German chemist, whose main interest was in valence. He was the first chemist to establish the valence of the elements and to introduce the notion of single, double, and triple bonds. He went on to deduce the structural formulae of many organic molecules, including that of benzene (**Kekulé formula**), which he claimed to have thought of in 1865 while dozing on a bus. *See also* aromatic compound.

Kelantan A state in central Peninsular Malaysia, bordering on Thailand. Rice is grown on the NE coastal plain, and rubber, copra, and minerals are produced. Area: 14 931 sq km (5765 sq mi). Population (1980): 877 575. Capital: Kota Baharu.

BOOK OF KELLS

Kells (Irish name: Ceanánnus Mór) 54 48N 6 14W A market town in the Republic of Ireland, in Co Meath. A monastery was founded here in the 6th century AD by St Columba in which *The Book of Kells*, an 8th-century illuminated manuscript of the Gospels, is reputed to have been written. Population (1981): 2623.

Kelly, Grace (1929–82) US film actress. Her films include *High Noon* (1952), *The Country Girl* (1955), *To Catch a Thief* (1955), and *High Society* (1956). She retired from acting when she married Prince Rainier III of Monaco in 1956. She died following a road accident.

Kelly, Ned (1855–80) Australian outlaw. He and his brother Dan formed a gang in 1878 that became notorious for its daring robberies in Victoria and New South Wales. He was captured and hanged in 1880 after a gunfight with the police in which the other gang members were killed.

kelp A large brown seaweed belonging to the order *Laminariales* (about 30 genera), found in cold seas, usually below the level of low tide. The giant kelp *Macrocystis*, of the E Pacific coast, reaches a length of 65 m. Its branching fronds are kept afloat by air bladders. The name kelp is also used for the ashes of seaweed, from which potassium and sodium salts and iodine were once obtained.

kelpie A breed of short-haired dog developed in Australia from the Border Collie and used for herding sheep and cattle. Named after a champion sheepdog of the 1870s, the kelpie has a long muzzle and pricked ears. The coat may be black or red (with or without tan), fawn, chocolate, or smoke-blue. Height: 43–50 cm.

kelvin (K) The SI unit of thermodynamic temperature equal to 1/273.16 of the thermodynamic temperature of the triple point of water. Named after Lord Kelvin.

Kelvin, William Thomson, 1st Baron (1824–1907) Scottish physicist. Kelvin was the first physicist to take notice of Joule's work. The two physicists then worked together, discovering the Joule-Kelvin effect; both also made great contributions to the new science of thermodynamics. In 1848 Kelvin postulated that there is a temperature at which the motions of particles cease and their energies become zero. He called this temperature absolute zero and suggested a scale of temperature, now known as the Kelvin scale, in which the zero point is absolute zero. In 1852 he suggested that a heat pump was a feasible device. During the 1860s he worked on the electrical properties of cables in conjunction with the laying of the first transatlantic cable in 1866. The unit of temperature (*see* kelvin) is named after him.

Kempis, Thomas à. *See* Thomas à Kempis.

Kendal 54 20N 2 45W A town in NW England, in Cumbria, called the Gateway to the Lakes. Catherine Parr was born in the Norman castle. Population (1981): 23 411.

kendo A Japanese martial art deriving from samurai sword fighting. Combatants using bamboo staffs or wooden swords try to deliver blows on specified target areas of each other's bodies. Two hits constitute a win.

Kendrew, Sir John Cowdery (1917–) British biochemist, who shared the 1962 Nobel Prize for Chemistry with Max Perutz for his discovery of the structure of the myoglobin molecule. Kendrew used the technique of X-ray diffraction, analysing his results with a computer.

Keneally, Thomas Michael (1935–) Australian writer. He published 16 novels before writing *Schindler's Ark* (1982), which won the 1982 Booker McConnell Prize. His other works include *The Chant of Jimmie Blacksmith* (1972), *Confederates* (1979), *A Family Madness* (1985), and *The Playmaker* (1987).

Kennedy, Cape. *See* Canaveral, Cape.

JOHN F. KENNEDY

Kennedy, Joseph Patrick (1888–1969) US businessman and diplomat. He had five daughters and four sons, three of whom entered public life. **Joseph Patrick Kennedy, Jr** (1915–44), a naval pilot, was killed in World War II. **John Fitzgerald Kennedy** (1917–63), a Democrat, was the first Roman Catholic president of the USA (1961–63). His liberal domestic polices—the so-called New Frontier—involved tax and social reforms and an extension of racial integration. He also established the Peace Corps. Abroad, he presided over the Bay of Pigs invasion (1961) and confronted the Soviet

Union over its installation of missile bases in Cuba (1962). In 1963 he negotiated the Nuclear Test-Ban Treaty. Kennedy's presidency also saw the beginning of US military involvement in Vietnam. He was assassinated in Dallas, apparently by Lee Harvey Oswald. In 1953 he married Jacqueline Bouvier (1929–   ), who became the wife of Aristotle Onassis in 1968. **Robert Francis Kennedy** (1925–68), attorney general (1961–64) and then a senator (1965–68), campaigned for the Democratic presidential nomination in 1968, during which he too was assassinated. **Edward Moore Kennedy** (1932–   ) is a lawyer and Democratic Senator.

Kennelly, Arthur Edwin.   *See* ionosphere.

Kenneth I MacAlpine   (died c. 858) King of the Scots of Dalriada (c. 844–c. 858). He formed the kingdom of Alba, the foundation of modern Scotland.

Kent   A county of SE England, bordering on the English Channel and Greater London. It consists chiefly of undulating lowlands, crossed by the North Downs from W to E, and rising to'the Weald in the SW. Often called the Garden of England, it is the country's leading fruit and hop-growing area. Area: 3730 sq km (1440 sq mi). Population (1986 est): 1 500 900. Administrative centre: Maidstone.

Kentucky   A state in the central USA, lying to the E of the Mississippi River. It consists of the Appalachian Mountains in the E, the Bluegrass region in the centre, an undulating plain in the W, and the basins of the Tennessee and Ohio Rivers in the SW. It is an important coalmining state and also produces petroleum and natural gas. Local timber is used in the furniture and wood industries. Agricultural products include tobacco, corn, hay, soya beans, cattle, sheep, and pigs. It is also an important region for the breeding of thoroughbred horses. *History*: Daniel Boone explored the area (1769) and after rapid settlement it became a state (1792). Area: 104 623 sq km (40 395 sq mi). Population (1986 est): 3 728 000. Capital: Frankfort.

Kenya, Mount   0 10S 37 30E An extinct volcano in Kenya, the second highest mountain in Africa. Height: 5200 m (17 058 ft).

Kenya, Republic of   A country in East Africa, on the Indian Ocean. The land rises gradually from the coast to the highlands of the interior reaching heights of over 5000 m (17 000 ft). Most of the inhabitants are Africans, including Kikuyu, Luo, Masai, and Kamba. *Economy*: The chief cash crops are coffee, tea, sisal, and pineapples; livestock rearing and dairy farming are also important. Forestry is being developed and mineral resources include soda ash, gold, limestone, and salt. Wildlife reserves include the huge Tsavo National Park. *History*: some of the earliest known fossil hominid remains have been found in the region by the Leakey family. The coastal area was settled by the Arabs from the 7th century AD and was controlled by the Portuguese during the 16th and 17th centuries. It became a British protectorate (East Africa Protectorate) in 1895 and a colony in 1920. In the 1950s independence movements led to the Mau Mau revolt. Kenya gained independence in 1963 and in 1964 became a republic within the British Commonwealth, with Jomo Kenyatta as its first president. President: Daniel Arap Moi (1924–   ). Official languages: Swahili and English. Official currency: Kenya shilling of 100 cents. Area: 582 600 sq km (224 960 mi). Population (1988 est): 23 000 000. Capital: Nairobi. Main port: Mombasa.

Kenyatta, Jomo   (c. 1891–1978) Kenyan statesman; president (1964–78). Son of a poor farmer, he became (1947) president of the Kenya African Union and in 1953 was imprisoned for seven years by the colonial government for his part in the Mau Mau rebellion (complicity in which he always denied). While in gaol he was elected leader of the Kenya African National Union (1960), which achieved Kenya's independence in 1963. Kenyatta was prime minister before becoming president of a one-party state.

Kepler, Johannes   (1571–1630) German astronomer, who was one of the first supporters of Copernicus' heliocentric theory of the solar system. Kepler used Tycho Brahe's observations to deduce the shape of planetary orbits, discovering that they were elliptical. He published this discovery, the first of **Kepler's laws**, together with his second law, stating that orbital velocity decreases with distance from the sun, in *Astronomia Nova* (1609). In 1619 he published his third law relating a planet's year to its distance from the sun. In 1610 he received a telescope built by Galileo, which he used to observe Jupiter. In 1611 he constructed an improved version, now known as a Keplerian telescope.

Kerala   A state in SW India. Tropical, beautiful, and poor, it is India's most densely populated state. Rice, tea, coffee, pepper, rubber, nuts, and fruit are farmed. Fishing is also important. *History*: Malayalam-speaking Kerala has traded with the Near and Far East since ancient times, flourishing in the 9th and 10th centuries. Area: 38 855 sq km (14 998 sq mi). Population (1981): 25 403 217. Capital: Trivandrum.

keratin   An insoluble fibrous protein that is the major constituent of hair, nails, feathers, beaks, horns, and scales. Keratin is also found in the skin.

Kerguelen Islands   49 30S 69 30E An archipelago in the S Indian Ocean, in the French Southern and Antarctic Territories. Kerguelen Island, the largest, is the site of several scientific bases. Area: 7215 sq km (2786 sq mi).

Kérkira (*or* Kérkyra).   *See* Corfu.

Kermanshah.   *See* Bakhtaran.

kermes   A scale insect of the genus *Kermes*, especially *K. ilices* of Europe and W Asia, formerly used to produce a red dye. They feed on the small evergreen kermes oak (*Quercus coccifera*), which is native to S Europe, N Africa, and W Asia.

Kern, Jerome (David)   (1885–1945) US composer of musical comedies, the most famous of which was *Show Boat* (1927), written in collaboration with Oscar Hammerstein II. Two of his best-known songs are "Smoke Gets in Your Eyes", and "Ol' Man River"; he also wrote much film music after 1939.

kerosene.   *See* paraffin.

Kerouac, Jack   (1922–69) US novelist. He was a leading figure of the Beat movement, of which his novel *On the Road* (1957) was a seminal work. Other works include *Big Sur* (1962) and *Desolation Angels* (1965).

Kerr effects   Two effects concerned with optical changes produced by magnetic or electric fields. In the magneto-optical effect, plane-polarized light is slightly elliptically polarized when reflected by the pole of an electromagnet. In the electro-optical effect, the plane of polarization of a beam of light is rotated when passed through certain liquids or solids across which a potential difference is applied. This effect is utilized in the **Kerr cell**, which is used as a high-speed shutter and to modulate laser beams. Named after the discoverer John Kerr (1824–1907).

Kerry (Irish name: Chiarraighe)   A county in the SW Republic of Ireland. It rises in the S to Macgillycuddy's Reeks and contains the famous Lakes of Killarney. The chief occupations are fishing, farming, and tourism. Area: 4701 sq km (1815 sq mi). Population (1986): 123 922. County town: Tralee.

Kesselring, Albert (1885–1960) German general, who commanded the Luftwaffe in the invasions of Poland (1939) and France (1940) and in the battle of Britain (1940). In 1943 he became commander of land and air forces in Italy and in 1945 on the Western Front. His death sentence as a war criminal was commuted to life imprisonment and he was released in 1952.

kestrel   A small falcon characterized by a long tail and the ability to hover before diving on its prey. The common kestrel (*Falco tinnunculus*), 32 cm long, is widespread in Eurasia and Africa and hunts small rodents, birds, and insects. The female has a brown streaked plumage; the male is blue-grey with black-streaked pale-brown underparts, a black-tipped tail, and a black eye stripe.

Keswick   54 37N 3 08W A town in NW England, in Cumbria. It is one of the main tourist centres of the Lake District. Population (1985 est): 5000.

ketone   A class of organic chemicals having the general formula RCOR′, where R and R′ are hydrocarbon groups. Ketones are prepared by the oxidation of secondary alcohols. Acetone (dimethyl ketone) is a common example.

Kew Gardens   The Royal Gardens at Kew, near Richmond, Surrey, which occupy land once owned by the royal family. The first botanic garden was created there in 1759, by Augusta (d. 1772), Princess of Wales, and in the late 18th and early 19th centuries Kew became internationally famous. Between 1848 and 1876 William (1785–1865) and Joseph (1817–1911) Hooker founded the Museum of Economic Botany, the Library, Herbarium, and Jodrell Laboratory.

key.   *See* tonality.

Keynes, John Maynard, 1st Baron   (1883–1946) British economist. After attending the Versailles peace conference Keynes published *The Economic Conse-*

quences of the Peace (1919), which attacked the war reparations imposed on Germany. In his greatest work, *General Theory of Employment, Interest and Money* (1936), he argued that unemployment can only be alleviated by increased public spending.

KGB (Committee of State Security)   The Soviet secret police concerned with internal security and intelligence. It was founded in 1954, after the fall of Beria, and replaced the more brutal MGB (Ministry of State Security; 1946–53), which itself replaced the NKVD (People's Commisariat of Internal Affairs; 1934–46).

Khabarovsk   48 32N 135 08E A port in the E Soviet Union, on the River Amur. Situated on the Trans-Siberian Railway, it is an important transport centre. Population (1987): 591 000.

Khachaturian, Aram Ilich   (1903–78) Soviet composer. His music was deeply influenced by Caucasian folk music. His compositions include concertos for piano (1936) and violin (1940) and the famous ballets *Gayaneh* (1942) and *Spartacus* (1954).

Kharkov   50 00N 36 15E A city in the S Soviet Union. It was almost totally destroyed in World War II. Today, it is the third largest railway junction in the country. Population (1987): 1 587 000.

Khartoum (*or* al-Khurtum)   15 40N 32 52E The capital of the Sudan, at the confluence of the Blue and the White Nile Rivers. In 1885 Gordon was besieged and killed here and the town destroyed by the forces of the Mahdi (*see* Mahdi, al-) but was recaptured by Anglo-Egyptian forces in 1898. It has several cathedrals and two mosques. Population (1983): 476 218.

Khazars   A Turkic people who inhabited the lower Volga basin from the 7th to 13th centuries. Noted for their laws, tolerance, and cosmopolitanism, the Khazars embraced Judaism in the 8th century. Slavonic and nomadic Turkic invaders brought the downfall of the Khazars in the 11th century. Itil, near modern Astrakhan, was their capital.

Khmer   A people of Cambodia, Thailand, and Vietnam who speak the Khmer language, one of the Austro-Asiatic languages. They are rice cultivators and fishers, living in village communities headed by an elected chief. Their religion is Theravada Buddhism. The Khmer empire was founded in 616 AD and between the 9th and

KEW GARDENS   *The Palm House, built (1844–48) by Decimus Burton and Richard Turner.*

13th centuries Khmer kings presided over the advanced civilization that was responsible for the great stone buildings of Angkor. The name Khmer was later adopted by the the communist Khmer Rouge movement (*see* Cambodia).

Khoisan The racial grouping comprising the Hottentot and Bushmen people of S Africa. The Khoisan languages are noted for their click sounds. Formerly widespread S of the Zambezi River, the Khoisan tribes have been decimated by Bantu and European encroachments since 1700. The Hottentots were nomads, herding sheep and cattle. They were divided into clans, each with its own territory and chief. The Bushmen were traditionally hunters and gatherers, but most are now farm workers.

Khomeini, Ayatollah Ruholla (1902–89) Iranian Shiite Muslim leader (ayatollah). Following the overthrow of the shah (1979) he returned from 16 years of exile to lead the so-called Islamic Revolution.

Khrushchev, Nikita S(ergeevich) (1894–1971) Soviet statesman; first secretary of the Soviet Communist Party (1953–64) and prime minister (1958–64). Khrushchev was a close associate of Stalin and emerged victorious from the power struggle that followed his death. In 1956 Khrushchev began a programme of destalinization, which gave rise to revolts in other communist countries. Owing to the failure of his economic policies and his unsuccessful foreign policy, notably his attempt to install missiles in Cuba (1962), he was ousted by Brezhnev and Kosygin.

Khufu (*or* Cheops) King of Egypt (c. 2600 BC) of the 4th dynasty; the father of Khafre (reigned c. 2550 BC). He built the Great Pyramid at Giza, which took 20 years to construct.

Khyber Pass (Khaybar Pass *or* Khaibar Pass) 34 06N 71 05E A mountain pass in the Hindu Kush, connecting Afghanistan with Pakistan. Rising to 1072 m (3518 ft), it is of strategic importance.

kibbutz An Israeli collective settlement in which land and property are owned or leased by all its members and work and meals are organized collectively. About 3% of the population live in *kibbutzim*. A **moshav** is a smallholders' cooperative in which machinery alone is shared. About 5% of the Israeli population live in *moshavim*.

Kicking Horse Pass A pass through the Canadian Rocky Mountains, NW of Banff. It is the highest point on the Canadian Pacific Railway. Height: 1627 m (5339 ft).

Kidderminster 52 23N 2 14W A market town in W central England, in Hereford and Worcester. It is famous for carpet manufacture, begun in 1735. Population (1981): 51 261.

kidneys The two organs of excretion in vertebrate animals and man, which also regulate the amount of salt and water in the blood. The human kidneys are bean-shaped, each about 12 cm long and weighing about 150 g, and situated on either side of the spine below the diaphragm. They contain millions of tubules, the outer parts of which filter water and dissolved substances from blood supplied by the renal artery. Most of the water and some substances are reabsorbed back into the blood further down the tubules: the remaining fluid (*see* urine) passes on to the bladder. If one kidney ceases to function or is removed the other will enlarge and take over its function. Removal of both kidneys requires the use of an artificial kidney machine (*see* dialysis) unless a suitable donor kidney is available for transplantation.

Kiel 54 20N 10 08E A city in NE West Germany, the capital of Schleswig-Holstein. A Baltic port, it was the chief naval port of Germany by the late 19th century. It has a 13th-century palace, restored after World War II. It is linked to the North Sea by the Kiel Canal. Population (1986): 244 700.

Kierkegaard, Søren (1813–55) Danish philosopher. Although critical of Hegel, particularly in *The Concept of Irony* (1841), he remained under his influence. Much of his work is poetic and paradoxical even in its titles, for example *Either-Or* (1843) and *Concluding Unscientific Postscript* (1846). Suspicious of both science and the established Church, he saw man as existing in isolation and relating only to God.

Kiev 50 28N 30 29E A city in the SW Soviet Union. It is the third largest city in the country and a major economic and cultural centre. Its opera and ballet companies have a worldwide reputation. Outstanding buildings include the 11th-century St Sophia cathedral and the Golden Gate of Kiev. *History*: Kiev, "the mother of cities," was probably founded in the 6th or 7th century AD. Recurrent Tatar attacks virtually destroyed the city, which subsequently passed to Lithuania. Russian rule was established in the 17th century. After the Russian Revolution Kiev became the capital of the short-lived Ukrainian republic and in 1934, the capital of the Ukrainian SSR. In World War II the city was occupied, after a long siege, by the Germans and thousands of its inhabitants were massacred. Population (1987): 2 554 000.

Kikuyu A Bantu-speaking tribe of Kenya. They cultivate cereals and sweet potatoes and keep livestock, particularly cattle. Small groups of patrilineal kin occupy scattered homesteads of conical-shaped huts. Age grades are an important basis of social organization, boys being initiated by circumcision. Political authority is held by a council of members of the senior age grade. The largest tribe in Kenya, the Kikuyu were deeply involved in the Mau Mau movement.

Kildare (Irish name: Contae Chill Dara) A county in the E Republic of Ireland. It consists chiefly of a low-lying plain containing part of the Bog of Allen and the Curragh, an area noted for its racehorse breeding. Cattle rearing and arable farming are also important. Area: 1694 sq km (654 sq mi). Population (1986): 116 015. County town: Naas.

Kilimanjaro, Mount 3 02S 37 20E A volcanic mountain in Tanzania, the highest mountain in Africa. It has two peaks: Kibo at 5895 m (19 340 ft), and Mawenzi at 5273 m (17 300 ft).

Kilkenny (Irish name: Contae Chill Choinnigh) A county in the SE Republic of Ireland. Agriculture is the chief occupation. Area: 2062 sq km (796 sq mi). Population (1986): 73 094. County town: Kilkenny.

Killarney (Irish name: Cill Airne) 52 03N 9 30W A town in the Republic of Ireland in Co Kerry. A tourist centre near the three Lakes of Killarney, it is famous for its scenery. Population (1981): 7693.

killer whale A large toothed whale, *Orcinus orca*, common in Pacific and Antarctic waters but found in all other oceans. Up to 9 m long, killer whales are black above and pure white beneath, with an erect dorsal fin. They are notorious for their voracious appetites. Like

KILLER WHALE   *Killer whales are known for their spectacular jumps.*

other dolphins, they are intelligent and trainable in captivity. Family: *Delphinidae* (dolphins).

Killiecrankie, Pass of   56 43N 3 40W A pass in the Grampian Mountains, Scotland, in Tayside Region. It was the scene of a massacre of William III's troops by Jacobite Highlanders (1689).

killifish   One of several small elongated fish, also called egg-laying top minnows, belonging to the family *Cyprinodontidae*, especially the genus *Fundulus*. Killifish occur chiefly in tropical America, Africa, and Asia and feed on plant or animal material. Up to 15 cm long, many are brightly coloured and kept as aquarium fish. Similar related fish are the live-bearing top minnows of the family *Poeciliidae*. Order: *Atheriniformes*.

Kilmarnock   55 37N 4 30W An industrial town in SW Scotland, in Strathclyde Region. The Burns museum contains many of his manuscripts. Population (1981): 52 080.

kilogram (kg)   The SI unit of mass equal to the mass of the platinum-iridium prototype kept at the International Bureau of Weights and Measures near Paris.

kiloton   A measure of the explosive power of a nuclear weapon. It is equivalent to an explosion of 1000 tons of trinitrotoluene (TNT).

kilowatt-hour (kW-hr)   A unit of energy used in charging for electricity. It is equal to the work done by a power of 1000 watts in 1 hour.

kilt.   *See* Highland dress.

Kimberley   28 45S 24 46E A city in South Africa, in N Cape Province. It was founded (1871) following the discovery of diamonds and is today the world's largest diamond centre. The Kimberley Open Mine, 1.6 km (1 mi) in circumference, was closed in 1915. Population (1980): 144 923.

Kimberleys.   *See* Western Australia.

Kim Il Sung   (Kim Song Ju; 1912–   ) North Korean statesman; prime minister (1948–72) and then president (1972–   ). He became leader of the Soviet-dominated N in 1945: in 1950 he ordered the invasion of South Korea in an unsuccessful attempt to reunite Korea (*see* Korean War).

kinetic energy   Energy possessed by a body by virtue of its motion. If the body, mass m, is moving in a straight line with velocity v, its kinetic energy is $\frac{1}{2}mv^2$. If it is

rotating its rotational kinetic energy is $\frac{1}{2}I\omega^2$, where I is its moment of inertia and ω its angular velocity.

kinetic theory   A theory developed in the 19th century, largely by Joule and Maxwell, in which the behaviour of gases is explained by regarding them as consisting of tiny dimensionless particles in constant random motion. Collisions, either between the particles or between the particles and the walls of the container, are assumed to be perfectly elastic. The theory explains the pressure of a gas as being due to collisions between the particles and the walls, its temperature as a measure of the *average* kinetic energy of the particles.

King, Jr, Martin Luther   (1929–68) US Black civil-rights leader. An outstanding orator, he followed principles of nonviolent resistance in organizing demonstrations against racial inequality and won the Nobel Peace Prize in 1964. He was assassinated in Memphis, Tennessee, by James Earl Ray.

King Charles spaniel   A breed of spaniel having a compact body, short legs, a short neck, and a large head with a short upturned nose. There are four colour varieties: Blenheim, ruby, tricolour, and black and tan, the last being associated with King Charles II. Weight: 3.5–6 kg; height: about 25 cm. The Cavalier King Charles spaniel is lighter bodied, with longer legs and a longer muzzle. Weight: 5–8 kg; height: about 30 cm.

king crab.   *See* horseshoe crab.

kingcup.   *See* marsh marigold.

kingfisher   A bird belonging to a family (*Alcedinidae*; 85 species) divided into two subfamilies: the *Alcedininae* are narrow-billed and live near water, feeding on small fish; the *Dacetoninae* are broad-billed insectivorous birds not closely associated with water. Kingfishers are 12–45 cm long, with a bright plumage and often brightly coloured bills and usually nest in burrows in banks. Order: *Coraciiformes* (hornbills, kingfishers, etc.).

King James Version   The Authorized Version of the English Bible that appeared in 1611 under the patronage of James I. It was based on the earlier Bishops' Bible (1568), but the translators also consulted and made use of the Geneva Bible and the Douai Bible. It was much indebted to the translations of William Tyndale (c. 1494–1536).

MARTIN LUTHER KING

Kingsley, Charles (1819–79) British clergyman and writer. In many works, such as *Alton Locke* (1850), he championed various social reforms. His works include the popular children's book *The Water Babies* (1863).

King's Lynn (Lynn *or* Lynn Regis) 52 45N 0 24E A historic market town in E England, in Norfolk. Its importance as a port has declined since the middle ages. Population (1981): 33 340.

Kingston 17 58N 76 48W The capital and main port of Jamaica, in the SE. Founded in 1692, it became the capital in 1872. In the early 20th century it suffered from hurricanes and an earthquake. Population (1983 est): 100 637.

Kingston 44 14N 76 30W A city and port in central Canada, in SE Ontario. Founded as a fort (1673), it has Canada's Royal Military College. Population (1981): 52 616.

Kingstown 13 12N 61 14W A port in SW St Vincent, in the West Indies. Exports include bananas, copra, arrowroot, and cotton. Population (1984 est): 32 600.

kinkajou A nocturnal arboreal mammal, *Potos flavus*, of Central and South American forests. Up to 110 cm long including the tail (40–55 cm), it has a soft golden-brown coat, small ears, and a prehensile tail. An agile climber, it feeds mainly on fruit and honey. Family: *Procyonidae* (*see* raccoon).

Kinneret, Lake. *See* Galilee, Sea of.

NEIL KINNOCK *With his wife Glenys.*

Kinnock, Neil (Gordon) (1942–) British Labour politician. He became a member of the National Executive Committee of the Labour Party in 1978 and Labour leader (1983–) following Michael Foot's resignation.

Kinshasa (name until 1966: Léopoldville) 4 18S 15 18E The capital of Zaïre, on the Zaïre River. It has a long history of human settlement and was occupied by the Humbu when Stanley discovered it in the late 19th century. Population (1985): 2 778 281.

Kintyre A peninsula in W Scotland, in Strathclyde Region between the Atlantic Ocean and the Firth of Clyde. The **Mull of Kintyre** headland forms its most southerly point.

Kipling, (Joseph) Rudyard (1865–1936) British writer and poet. Born in Bombay, he was educated in England, returning to India in 1882 to work as a journalist. After returning to England in 1888, he made his reputation with *Barrack Room Ballads and Other Verses* (1892). From 1892 to 1896 he lived in New England, where he wrote *The Jungle Books* (1894, 1895). *Kim* (1901) is the last novel he wrote with an Indian setting. Among his many other works are *Just So Stories* (1902) and *Puck of Pook's Hill* (1906), both for children. He won the Nobel Prize in 1907.

kipper. *See* herring.

Kirchhoff, Gustav Robert (1824–87) German physicist. Working with Robert Bunsen, he invented the technique of spectroscopy and discovered caesium and rubidium in 1861. Kirchoff, working alone, also discovered several elements in the sun, by investigating the solar spectrum. He is also known for **Kirchhoff's laws**, relating to electrical networks.

Kiribati, Republic of (name until 1979: Gilbert Islands) A country in the S Pacific Ocean comprising the Gilbert Islands, the Phoenix Islands, and some of the Line Islands together with Ocean Island. The majority of the inhabitants are Micronesians. *Economy*: chiefly fishing and subsistence agriculture. Ocean Island is rich in phosphates, which, with copra, are the chief exports. *History*: a centre for sperm whale hunting in the 19th century and part of the British protectorate of the Gilbert and Ellice Islands from 1892, they became a colony in 1915. Links with Ellice Islands (*see* Tuvalu, State of) were severed in 1975 and they became independent in 1979 as the Republic of Kiribati. President: Ieremia Tabai. Official languages: English and Gilbertese. Official currency: Australian dollar of 100 cents. Area: 861 sq km (332 sq mi). Population (1987): 66 250. Capital and main port: Tarawa.

Kiritimati. *See* Christmas Island.

Kirkcaldy 56 07N 3 10W A town in E central Scotland, in Fife Region. It is the birthplace of Adam Smith. Population (1981): 46 314.

Kirkwall 58 59N 2 58W A town in NE Scotland, the administrative centre of the island authority of Orkney, on the island of Mainland. Population (1985): 6000.

Kirov (name from 1780 until 1934: Vyatka) 58 38N 49 38E A port in the Soviet Union, on the River Vyatka. Founded in 1181, it was renamed after S. M. Kirov (1888–1934). Population (1987): 421 000.

Kirovabad (name until 1813 and from 1920 until 1935: Gandzha; name from 1813 until 1920: Yelisavetpol) 40 39N 46 20E A city in the S Soviet Union. A medieval commercial centre, it is now important for industry. Population (1987): 270 000.

Kirov Ballet A Soviet ballet company based at the Kirov State Theatre of Opera and Ballet in Leningrad. The theatre was renamed in honour of the politician S. M. Kirov (1888–1934) in 1935. Some of the Kirov's leading dancers, including Rudolf Nureyev, Natalia Makarova (1940–), and Mikhail Baryshnikov (1948–), have earned international reputations.

Kirovograd (name until 1924: Yelisavetgrad; name from 1924 until 1936: Zinoviyevsk) 48 31N 32 15E A city in the SW Soviet Union. It is a major agricultural centre. Population (1987): 269 000.

kirsch (*or* kirschwasser) A spirit distilled from fermented liquor of wild cherries (German *Kirsch*, cherry). It is drunk neat or used in cooking.

Kisangani (name until 1966: Stanleyville) 0 33S 25 14E A riverport in NE Zaïre, on the Zaïre River. It is an agricultural centre. Population (1984): 282 650.

Kish A city of ancient Sumer, near Babylon. Kish was the pre-eminent centre of civilization until eclipsed by Ur (c. 2600 BC). Excavated between 1923 and 1933, its site has produced the earliest known example of writing —pictograms dating to soon after 3500 BC.

Kishinev (Romanian name: Chişinău) 47 00N 28 50E A city in the SW Soviet Union. Founded in the 15th century, it was under Romanian rule (1918–40). Population (1987): 663 000.

Kissinger, Henry (Alfred) (1923–) US diplomat and political scientist; secretary of state (1973–76). Appointed adviser to President Nixon (1969), Kissinger and Le Duc Tho (1911–) were jointly awarded the Nobel Peace Prize (1973) for helping to negotiate an end to the Vietnam War. Under President Ford he became well known for his flying-shuttle style of diplomacy while negotiating a truce between Syria and Israel (1974).

Kitakyushu 33 52N 130 49E A city in Japan, on the Shimonoseki Strait. Formed in 1963 from the cities of Wakamatsu, Yawata, Tobata, Kokura, and Moji, it is one of Japan's leading trade and deepsea fishing ports. Population (1985): 1 056 000.

LORD KITCHENER *The famous World War I recruiting poster.*

Kitchener of Khartoum, Horatio Herbert, 1st Earl (1850–1916) British field marshal. Appointed commander in chief of the Egyptian army in 1892, by 1898, with the battle of Omdurman, he had reconquered the Sudan, becoming its governor general (1899). In the second Boer War he suppressed the guerrillas by a scorched-earth policy and the internment of civilians in concentration camps. In 1914, as war secretary, his recruitment campaign was highly successful. He was drowned on his way to Archangel.

kite A hawk belonging to the subfamily *Milvinae*, which occurs throughout the world, most commonly in warm regions. Typically reddish brown and 52–57 cm long, kites have long narrow wings, a long often forked tail, and a narrow bill and feed on insects, small mammals, and reptiles; some are scavengers.

kittiwake A North Atlantic gull, *Rissa tridactyla*, that is adapted for nesting on narrow cliff ledges. It is 40 cm long and has a white plumage with black-tipped grey wings, short black legs, dark eyes, and a yellow bill. It feeds at sea on fish and offal, going ashore only to breed.

Kitwe 12 48S 28 14E A town in N central Zambia. It is the chief commercial, industrial, and communications centre of the Copperbelt. Population (1980 est): 341 000.

kiwi (bird) A secretive flightless bird belonging to a family (*Apterygidae*; 3 species) occurring in forested regions of New Zealand. 25–40 cm long, kiwis have tiny wings hidden in coarse grey-brown plumage and strong legs with large claws. Kiwis are nocturnal and have weak eyes but well-developed hearing; the long bill is used to probe the soil for worms, insect larvae, etc. Order: *Apterygiformes*.

kiwi (plant) A Chinese climbing shrub, *Actinidia chinensis*, also called Chinese gooseberry. It has white or yellow flowers and an edible rough-skinned fruit, up to 5 cm long. Family: *Actinidiaceae*.

Klagenfurt 46 38N 14 20E A city in S Austria, the capital of Carinthia. It has a cathedral (1578–91) and is a tourist centre. Population (1981): 86 221.

Klaipeda (German name: Memel) 55 43N 21 07E A port in the W Soviet Union, on the Baltic Sea. It has been occupied at various times by Prussia, France, Lithuania, and Germany. Population (1987): 201 000.

Klee, Paul (1879–1940) Swiss painter and etcher. Working initially as an etcher, influenced by Beardsley and Goya, he became associated with Der Blaue Reiter and taught at the Bauhaus school of design (1920–33). Inspired by a visit to Tunisia (1914), he produced small watercolours in brilliant colours; after 1919 he used oils, incorporating signs and hieroglyphs to create a fantasy world influenced by children's art.

Klein, Melanie (1882–1960) Austrian psychiatrist, who moved to England in 1926. She is noted for her psychoanalytical studies of children, which were influenced by Sigmund Freud and his associates.

Klein bottle In topology, a surface that has no edges and only one side. It is made by putting the small end of a tapering tube through the side of the tube, stretching it, and joining it to the large end. It was discovered by the German mathematician Christian Felix Klein (1849–1925).

Klemperer, Otto (1885–1973) German conductor. He became conductor of the German Opera in Prague on the recommendation of Mahler in 1907. Expelled by the Nazis in 1933, he was principal conductor of the Philharmonia Orchestra from 1959 until his death and is particularly remembered for performances of Beethoven.

Klondike The valley of the Klondike River in NW Canada, in the central Yukon, where gold was discovered in 1896. The subsequent gold rush opened up the Yukon, although the population dwindled when the gold started to run out (1900).

KLEIN BOTTLE *A solid with no edges and only one side.*

KNOTS

overhand knot *This is used either to make a knob in a rope or as the basis for another knot.*

reef knot *A non-slip knot for joining ropes of similar thickness.*

quick release knot *A tug on a will quickly unfasten this knot.*

surgeon's knot *The extra twist in the first part of the knot prevents it from slipping loose while the second part is tied.*

Hunter's bend *A strong, easily tied knot invented in 1978 by Dr Edward Hunter.*

bowline *A knot to form a non-slip loop.*

running bowline *A knot for making a running noose.*

sheepshank *A means of temporarily shortening a rope.*

sheet bend *A knot for securely joining two ropes of different thickness.*

double sheet bend *This follows the same principles as the sheet bend.*

fisherman's knot *Used especially for joining lengths of fishing gut.*

carrick bend *A knot well suited to tying heavy ropes together.*

clove hitch *A simple knot for attaching a rope to a ring, rail, etc.*

round turn and two half hitches *Used for similar purposes as the clove hitch, this knot does not easily work loose.*

anchor bend *A secure means of attaching a cable to an anchor.*

rolling hitch *A quickly made and quickly unfastened knot for attaching a rope to a rail or another, standing rope.*

klystron An electronic device used to generate or amplify microwaves. It consists of a sealed evacuated tube in which a steady beam of electrons from an electron gun is alternately accelerated and retarded by high-frequency radio waves (velocity modulation) as it passes through a cavity. The resultant radio-frequency pulses are picked up at a second cavity, either as a voltage oscillation or, if connected to a waveguide, as electromagnetic waves. The second cavity can be tuned to the input frequency or a harmonic of it. *See also* magnetron.

Kneller, Sir Godfrey (1646–1723) Portrait painter of German birth. He worked successively for Charles II, William III, Queen Anne, and George I, and founded the first English academy of painting (1711). His portraits of the Whig Kit Cat Club (c. 1702–17; National Portrait Gallery), established a standard British portrait type.

Knock A village in the Republic of Ireland, in Co Mayo. Visions of the Virgin Mary were allegedly seen here, the first in 1879, and it has become a place of pilgrimage with its own airport.

Knossos The principal city of Minoan Crete, near present-day Heraklion. It was occupied between about 2500 and 1200 BC. Excavated and reconstructed (1899–1935) by Sir Arthur Evans, the Palace of Minos was luxurious and sophisticated. About 1450 BC the palace was burnt down.

knot (bird) A short-legged bird, *Calidris canutus*, that breeds in Arctic tundra and winters on southern coasts. 25 cm long, it has a short black bill and its plumage is mottled grey in winter and reddish in summer. In winter, knots probe mud and sand for snails, worms, and crabs. Family: *Scolopacidae* (sandpipers, snipe, etc.).

knot (unit) A unit of speed, used for ships and aircraft, equal to 1 nautical mile per hour (1.15 miles per hour).

knots Fastenings formed by looping and tying pieces of rope, cord, etc. The mathematical theory of knots, a branch of topology, was developed mainly in the 20th century, and draws on matrix theory, algebra, and geometry. A simple closed curve in space may be knotted in various ways, each with specific topological properties. See p. 403.

Knox, John (c. 1514–72) Scottish Protestant reformer. In 1547 he joined the Protestants who had murdered Cardinal Beaton in revenge for Wishart's execution in St Andrew's Castle. The castle was stormed by the French, who imprisoned Knox as a galley slave. After his release (1549) he became a chaplain to Edward VI in England and contributed to the revision of the Second Book of Common Prayer. On Queen Mary's accession he escaped to the Continent, where he met Calvin in Geneva. Returning to Scotland in 1559, he became its leading reformer. In 1560 the Scottish parliament adopted the *Confession of Faith* that Knox had compiled. His *First Book of Discipline* (1561) outlined a structure for the reformed Church of Scotland.

Knox-Johnston, Robin (William Robert Patrick K.-J.; 1939–) British yachtsman; the first person to sail alone around the world nonstop (1968–69). In 1981 he set the British transatlantic sailing record (11 days 7 hours 45 mins).

Knoxville 36 00N 83 57W A city in the USA, in Tennessee. It is an inland port and agricultural trading centre. Population (1986 est): 173 210.

koala An arboreal marsupial, *Phascolarctus cinereus*, of E Australia. About 60 cm high, koalas have thick greyish fur, tufted ears, a small tail, and long claws. Each adult eats more than 1 kg of eucalyptus leaves every day. The pouch opens towards the female's tail–unusual in herbivorous marsupials. Family: *Phalangeridae*.

kob An African antelope, *Kobus kob*, also called Buffon's kob. Males are about 90 cm high at the shoulder; females are smaller. The coat ranges from orange to nearly black, with white markings on the face, legs, and belly and a black stripe down the foreleg.

Kobe 34 40N 135 12E A major port in Japan, on Osaka Bay. It forms the W end of the Osaka-Kobe industrial area. Population (1985): 1 411 000.

Koblenz (English name: Coblenz) 50 21N 7 36E A city in W West Germany, at the confluence of the Rivers Rhine and Moselle. The seat of Frankish kings during the 6th century AD, it was annexed by France in 1798, passing to Prussia in 1815. Notable buildings include the Ehrenbreitstein fortress (c. 1000) and the birthplace of Metternich. Population (1986): 110 600.

Köchel, Ludwig von (1800–77) Austrian naturalist and musical bibliographer. He compiled a thematic catalogue of Mozart's works, which was published in 1862; a work is referred to by a **Köchel number**, consisting of the letter K followed by the catalogue number.

Kodály, Zoltan (1882–1967) Hungarian composer. In collaboration with Bartók he collected Hungarian peasant songs, which influenced his style of composition. He achieved international recognition with his *Psalmus Hungaricus* (1923); other works include the opera *Háry János* (1926) and *Dances of Galanta* (1933).

Kodiak bear. *See* brown bear.

Koestler, Arthur (1905–83) British writer, born in Hungary. His novel *Darkness at Noon* (1940) called on his own experience as a prisoner in the Spanish Civil War. His other novels include *Thieves in the Night* (1946) and *The Call Girls* (1972). His nonfiction was concerned with politics (*The Yogi and the Commissar*, 1945), scientific creativity (*The Sleepwalkers*, 1959; *The Act of Creation*, 1964; *The Ghost in the Machine*, 1967), and parapsychology. He and his wife committed suicide when his Parkinson's disease and cancer became unbearable.

Koh-i-noor A famous diamond of 108 carats owned by the Mogul dynasty until the Shah of Iran looted it from Delhi (1739). It became Crown property in 1849, when Britain annexed the Punjab. It was set in the coronation crown of George VI's consort, Queen Elizabeth.

Kohl, Helmut (1930–) West German statesman; chancellor (1982–). A Christian Democrat, he led the opposition in the Bundestag (1976–82). In 1989 he led discussions about possible reunification of East and West Germany.

kohlrabi A variety of cabbage, sometimes called turnip-rooted cabbage. The green or purple stem base, which swells like a turnip, is used as a vegetable.

Kokoschka, Oskar (1886–1980) Austrian expressionist painter and writer (*see* expressionism). After World War I he taught at the Dresden Academy, later painting landscapes and city views, particularly of London, where he lived (1938–53). From 1953 he lived and worked in Switzerland.

kola (*or* cola) Either of two trees, *Cola nitida* or *C. acuminata*, native to West Africa and widely grown in the tropics, that produce **kola nuts**. These are rich in caffeine and chewed in Africa and the West Indies for their stimulating effects. Family: *Sterculiaceae*.

KOH-I-NOOR *The diamond is set in the coronation crown of Queen Elizabeth.*

Kolyma, River A river in the NE Soviet Union. Rising in NE Siberia, it flows mainly NE to the East Siberian Sea. Length: 2600 km (1615 mi).

Kommunizma, Pik. *See* Communism Peak.

Komodo dragon A rare monitor lizard, *Varanus komodoensis*, which, at 3 m long and weighing 135 kg, is the largest living lizard. It has a stout neck and body, a long powerful tail, and short strong legs and is powerful enough to kill a man. Komodo dragons feed mainly on carrion but also eat smaller monitors. They occur only on Komodo Island and some of the Lesser Sunda Islands of Indonesia.

KOMSOMOL (All-Union Leninist Communist League of Youth) A Soviet youth organization. Organized in 1918, its members fought in the civil war (1918–21). In 1922 it became a social organization to promote communist ideology.

Konakry. *See* Conakry.

Konoe Fumimaro, Prince (1891–1945) Japanese noble, who was prime minister three times. His first cabinet (1937–39) escalated the conflict with China; his second (1940–41) took Japan into alliance in World War II with Germany and Italy; and his third (1941) made the decision to attack the USA. After Japan's surrender he committed suicide.

Kon-Tiki The name given by Thor Heyerdahl to the balsawood raft on which, between 28 April and 7 August, 1947, he and five companions travelled the 5000 miles between Peru and the Tuamotu islands near Tahiti to demonstrate that ancient peoples of South America could have reached Polynesia. Kon-Tiki was an older name for the Inca creator god, Viracocha, allegedly known in Polynesia as Tiki.

Konya (ancient name: Iconium) 37 51N 32 30E A town in SW central Turkey. It is the centre of the Whirling Dervish sect and was the capital of the Seljuq kingdom of Rum. Population (1985): 438 859.

kookaburra A large grey-brown Australian kingfisher, *Dacelo novaeguineae*, also called laughing jackass because of its chuckling call. 43 cm long, it is arboreal and pounces on snakes, lizards, insects, and small rodents from a perch.

Koran (*or* Quran) The sacred scripture of Islam. According to tradition, the divine revelations given to Mo-

hammed (d. 632 AD) were preserved by his followers and collected as the Koran under the third caliph, Uthman (d. 656). The Koran is one of the main sources of the comprehensive system of Islamic law. Muslims believe that the revelations exist complete in a heavenly book, which contains all that has happened and will happen.

Korda, Sir Alexander (Sandor Kellner; 1893–1956) British film producer and director, born in Hungary. He greatly boosted the British film industry during the 1930s and 1940s with a series of extravagant productions, including *The Private Life of Henry VIII* (1932), *The Scarlet Pimpernel* (1934), and *Anna Karenina* (1948).

kore (Greek: maiden) In archaic Greek sculpture, a draped standing female figure, derived originally (c. 650 BC) from Egyptian models. During the next two centuries the drapery, pose, and expression became increasingly naturalistic. *Compare* kouros.

Korea A country in NE Asia, occupying a peninsula between the Sea of Japan and the Yellow Sea, now divided (*see* below) into the Democratic Republic of Korea (North Korea) and the Republic of Korea (South Korea). Plains in the W rise to mountains in the N and E. Both North and South Koreans are ethnically related to the Mongoloid race. The country long had ties with China but in 1905 became a Japanese protectorate, coming formally under Japanese rule in 1910. In 1945 the Allies divided Korea at the thirty-eighth parallel. The communist Democratic People's Republic of Korea under Kim Il Sung was established in the Soviet-occupied N and the Republic of Korea under Syngman Rhee, in the US-occupied S (1948). Soviet and US troops had withdrawn by 1949 and in 1950 the Korean War broke out between North and South Korea, ending in 1953 with the country still divided.

Korea, Democratic People's Republic of (Korean name: Chosŏn) The division of Korea left the North with almost all the country's mineral wealth and a large proportion of the industries, which had been developed by the Japanese. After the Korean War reconstruction proceeded rapidly. The rather sparse agricultural land was collectivized in the 1950s; mechanization has greatly increased production. President: Kim Il Sung. Official language: Korean. Official currency: won of 100 jun. Area: 122 370 sq km (47 225 sq mi). Population (1986 est): 20 550 000. Capital: P'yŏngyang.

Korea, Republic of (Korean name: Han Kook) The repressive government led by the first president of South Korea, Syngman Rhee, was ended by a military coup in 1961, followed by the rise to power of Gen Park Chung Hee (1917–79), who was assassinated in 1979. US aid has led to the development of a strong industrial sector. President: Roh Tae Woo. Official language: Korean. Official currency: won of 100 chon. Area: 98 447 sq km (38 002 sq mi). Population (1987 est): 41 826 706. Capital: Seoul. Main port: Pusan.

Korean The language of the people of Korea. It is probably distantly related to Japanese. The standard form is based on the dialect of Seoul. It is written in a phonetic script called onmun, devised in the mid-15th century to replace the Chinese characters in use before then.

Korean War (1950–53) An indecisive conflict between communist North Korea and noncommunist South Korea. When North Korean troops crossed the thirty-eighth parallel in 1950 16 member nations of the

KOREAN WAR *Refugees near Inchon; young and old indiscriminately suffer the consequences of conflict between ideologies that barely concern them.*

UN sent troops, under the supreme command of the US general, Douglas MacArthur, to support South Korea. The North Koreans were joined by Chinese Communist troops. An armistice was eventually signed on 27 July, 1953, by which time some five million people had died.

Kosciusko, Mount 36 28S 148 17E The highest mountain in Australia, in SE New South Wales in the Snowy Mountains. Height: 2230 m (7316 ft).

Kosovo An autonomous region of Yugoslavia. Part of the republic of Serbia, it has a majority ethnic Albanian population, which since the late 1980s has called for unity with Albania.

Kosygin, Aleksei Nikolaevich (1904–80) Soviet statesman; prime minister (1964–80). He became prime minister after Khrushchev's fall, initially sharing power with Brezhnev, but had less influence in the late 1960s.

koto A Japanese stringed instrument of the zither family. The narrow 2-metre sound board has 13 strings, which the player, sitting on his heels, plucks with plectra.

kouros (Greek: youth) In archaic Greek sculpture, a nude standing male figure, often more than life-size, derived (c. 650 BC) from Egyptian models. The modelling became increasingly naturalistic. *Compare* kore.

Koussevitsky, Sergei (1874–1951) Russian conductor and composer. He left Russia in 1920 to work in Paris and subsequently in the USA, where he directed the Boston Symphony Orchestra from 1924 to 1949. He founded the Koussevitsky Music Foundation.

Kovno. *See* Kaunas.

Kowloon. *See* Jiulong.

Kozhikode (former name: Calicut) 11 15N 75 45E A seaport on the W coast of India, in Kerala. Formerly famous as a cotton-manufacturing centre (Calicut gave

its name to calico), it was visited by Vasco da Gama (1498) and in 1664 the British East India Company established a trading post here. Population (1981): 394 447.

Kra, Isthmus of The neck of the Malay Peninsula connecting it to the Asian mainland. It is occupied by Burma and Thailand and is 64 km (40 mi) across at its narrowest point.

krait A highly venomous snake belonging to the genus *Bungarus* (12 species) occurring in S Asia. Kraits are usually patterned with blue-and-white or black-and-yellow bands; they prey chiefly on other snakes. The common blue krait (*B. caeruleus*) of India and China is 1.5 m long and its venom can be fatal to humans. Family: *Elapidae* (cobras, mambas, coral snakes).

Kraków (*or* Cracow) 50 03N 19 55E The third largest city in Poland, on the River Vistula. It was the capital of Poland from 1305 to 1609 and remains famous as a cultural centre. Notable buildings include the cathedral (14th century). Population (1985): 716 000.

Krasnodar (name until 1920: Ekaterinodar) 45 02N 39 00E A city in the SW Soviet Union, on the River Kuban. It is the centre of an agricultural region. Population (1987): 623 000.

Krasnoyarsk 56 05N 92 46E A city in the E Soviet Union, on the River Yenisei. It developed greatly after the discovery of gold in the region in the 19th century. Population (1987): 899 000.

Krebs cycle (citric acid cycle *or* tricarboxylic acid cycle) The sequence of chemical reactions, taking place in the mitochondria of cells. Named after its principal discoverer, Sir Hans Krebs (1900–81), the cycle involves the conversion of acetyl coenzyme A, derived from the carbohydrates, proteins, and fats of food, into hydrogen atoms or electrons, from which usable energy in the form of ATP is produced by the cytochrome electron transport chain. Intermediate products are used for the manufacture of carbohydrates, lipids, and proteins by cells.

Krefeld 51 20N 6 32E A city in NW West Germany, on the River Rhine. It was the site of a Prussian victory (1758) during the Seven Years' War. Population (1986): 216 700.

Kreisler, Fritz (1875–1962) Austrian violinist. A child prodigy, he frequently played his own compositions, written in the style of older composers and (until 1935) ascribed to them.

Kremenchug 49 03N 33 25E A city in the SW Soviet Union, on the River Dnepr. It has a large hydroelectric station. Population (1984): 222 000.

Kremlin The citadel of any Russian city, now referring usually to that of Moscow. Built in 1156 but continually extended, it contains the Cathedral of the Assumption (1475–79), the Cathedral of the Annunciation (1484–89), the Great Kremlin Palace (1838–49), etc. Except for the period between 1712 and 1918 it has served continually as the seat of the Russian government and is now also a museum of Russian architecture.

krill Shrimplike marine crustaceans, 8–60 mm long, of the order *Euphausiacea* (82 species). Periodically krill swarms occur in certain regions, becoming an important source of food for fishes, birds, and especially baleen whales.

Krishna A popular Hindu deity, the eighth incarnation of Vishnu. In the *Bhagavadgita* he is revealed as the creator, sustainer, and destroyer of the universe (*see* Trimurti). Elsewhere he is worshipped as a fertility god. He is commonly represented as a beautiful youth with bluish skin wearing a crown of peacock feathers. *See also* Jagannatha.

STANLEY KUBRICK   *On the set of* A Clockwork Orange.

Krishna Menon.   *See* Menon, Krishna.

Krivoi Rog   47 55N 33 24E A city in the SW Soviet Union. Founded by the Cossacks in the 17th century, it is now an important ironmining centre. Population (1984): 680 000.

Kronstadt Rebellion   (1921) An uprising among Soviet sailors in Kronstadt. The sailors, who had supported the Bolsheviks in the Russian Revolution, demanded economic reforms and an end to Bolshevik political domination.

Kruger, (Stephanus Johannes) Paul(us)   (1825–1904) Afrikaner statesman; president (1883–1902) of the South African Republic (Transvaal). A farmer of Dutch descent, Kruger settled with his parents in the Transvaal after taking part in the Great Trek. He led the struggle to regain independence for the Transvaal from the British, achieved in 1881, after the first Boer War. As president he resisted Uitlander (British immigrant) demands for political equality with the Afrikaner, a policy that led to the second Boer War (1899–1902).

Kruger National Park   A game and plant reserve in NE South Africa, adjacent to the border with Mozambique. Area: about 21 000 sq km (8106 sq mi).

krugerrand   A South African coin containing one troy ounce of gold, minted since 1967. It has never been a true currency coin and was minted to enable investors to escape restrictions on the private ownership of gold.

Krupp   A German family of arms manufacturers. Under **Arndt Krupp** (d. 1624), the family settled in Essen, where in 1811 **Friedrich Krupp** (1787–1826) established a steel factory. His son **Alfred Krupp** (1812–87) diversified the family business into arms manufacture. Under Alfred's son-in-law **Gustav Krupp von Bohlen und Halbach** (1870–1950), the company developed Big Bertha, the World War I artillery piece named after Gustav's wife **Bertha Krupp** (1886–1957). Their son **Alfried Krupp** (1907–67) developed Gustav's ties with the Nazis, employed slave labour, and was imprisoned for war crimes.

krypton (Kr)   A noble gas discovered in 1898 by Sir William Ramsay and M. W. Travers (1872–1961), in

the residue left after boiling liquid air. Compounds include the fluoride KrF_2 and some clathrates. It is used for filling some fluorescent light bulbs; the metre was (1960–83) defined in terms of the wavelength of a transition of one of its isotopes. At no 36; at wt 83 80; mp 156.6°C; bp –152.2°C.

Kuala Lumpur   3 10N 101 40E The capital of Malaysia, in central Peninsular Malaysia. It became capital of the Federated Malay States in 1895. Formerly also capital of the state of Selangor, it became a federal territory in 1974. Population (1980): 937 875.

Kuang-chou.   *See* Canton.

Kuban, River   A river in the S central Soviet Union. Rising in the Caucasus Mountains, it flows NW to the Sea of Azov. Length: 906 km (563 mi).

Kublai Khan   (1215–94) Emperor of China (1279–94), who founded the Yuan dynasty. Genghis Khan's grandson, Kublai established himself (1259) as chief of the Mongols after years of conflict with his brother Mangu (d. 1259). The acknowledged ruler of all China from 1279, he administered from Peking an empire extending from the River Danube to the East China Sea. More humane than his predecessors, he opened up communications with Europe, largely through Marco Polo. However, his preoccupation with China and attempts to conquer SE Asia weakened the rest of the empire.

Kubrick, Stanley   (1928–   ) US film writer, director, and producer. His films, mainly satirical and highly imaginative, include *Lolita* (1962), *2001: A Space Odyssey* (1968), *A Clockwork Orange* (1971), and *The Shining* (1980).

kudu   A large antelope, *Tragelaphus strepsiceros*, of African bush regions. About 130 cm high at the shoulder, kudus are red-brown with thin white vertical stripes on the flanks. Males have long corkscrew-shaped horns. The lesser kudu (*T. imberbis*) is smaller and found only in NE Africa.

Kuei-yang.   *See* Guiyang.

Kufah   A town 145 km (90 mi) S of Baghdad, in Iraq. Founded as an Arab garrison town in 638 AD, it is now an archaeological site. Its suburb of Najaf is the burial place of Ali and a flourishing centre of Shiite Islam.

KUBLAI KHAN   *Marco Polo offering papal letters to Kublai Khan in 1271 (from a 14th-century manuscript).*

Kuibyshev (name until 1935: Samara) 53 10N 50 10E A port in the SW central Soviet Union, on the River Volga. Population (1981 est): 1 238 000.

Ku Klux Klan (KKK) A US secret society active against the Blacks. It originated in Tennessee after the Civil War to deter newly enfranchised Blacks from voting. Klansmen in white cloaks and hoods, burning fiery crosses, killed Blacks and destroyed their property. It was revived in 1915 and again in the 1950s in the South in response to the civil-rights movement. The Un-American Activities Committee investigated its leaders in 1965, but it remains active against several minority groups.

Kumamoto 32 50N 130 42E A city in Japan, on the River Shira. One of the strongest centres in feudal Japan, it has a 17th-century castle. Population (1980): 526 000.

Kumasi 6 45N 1 35W The second largest city in Ghana. Formerly the capital of Ashanti, it was taken by the British in 1874. Population (1970): 351 629.

kumquat A shrubby plant of the genus *Fortunella* (6 species), of E and SE Asia, with fruits resembling small oranges. They are mainly used for pickling and preserves. Family: *Rutaceae.*

kung fu An ancient Chinese form of combat, mainly for self-defence. Among the other martial arts it is most closely related to karate, which possibly developed from it. In the second half of the 20th century the *wing chun* style has become particularly well known.

Kunlun Mountains A mountain system in W China, separating Tibet from the Tarim Basin. It extends 1600 km (1000 mi) E–W, reaching 7723 m (25 378 ft) at Ulugh Muztagh.

Kunming 25 04N 102 41E A city in S China, the capital of Yunnan province. It is noted for its Ming bronze temple. Population (1970 est): 1 700 000.

Kuomintang. *See* Guomindang.

Kura, River A river in W Asia. Rising in NE Turkey, it flows N into the Soviet Union, to the Caspian Sea. Length: 1515 km (941 mi).

kurchatovium (Ku) An artificial transuranic element and the first transactinide. It was first detected by Soviet scientists in 1964 and named after the Soviet physicist I. V. Kurchatov (1903–60). The claim is disputed by US scientists, who proposed the name **rutherfordium** (Rf) after Lord Rutherford, following their independent synthesis. At no 104.

Kurdistan An area in the Middle East inhabited by Kurds, comprising parts of SE Turkey, N Syria, N Iraq, and NW Iran, including the Iranian province of Kordestan. The Turkish part includes a plateau that supports some agriculture, the remainder being mainly mountainous. The area was split at the end of World War I. Area: 192 000 sq km (74 600 sq mi).

Kurds The major population group in Kurdistan. Their language, Kurdish, is one of the Iranian languages and is written in either a modified Arabic or a modified Cyrillic script. The Kurds grow cereals and cotton and are now mostly detribalized but a few nomadic groups still exist. They are Muslims but do not restrict their women to the same extent as other Islamic peoples. Nationalistic rebellions in the 19th and 20th centuries have led to reprisals, especially in Turkey (1925), Iraq, and Iran.

Kurgan 55 30N 65 20E A city in the W central Soviet Union, on the River Tobol. Population (1984): 339 000.

Kuria Muria Islands A group of five islands off the coast of Oman, in the Arabian Sea. Area: 72 sq km (28 sq mi).

Kuril Islands A Soviet chain of 56 islands extending 1200 km (746 mi) NE–SW between Kamchatka (Soviet Union) and Hokkaido (Japan). Discovered in 1634 by the Dutch, the islands were Japanese until seized by the Soviet Union in 1945. The largest are Paramushir, Urup, Iturup, and Kunashir. There are hot springs and 38 active volcanoes. Parallel to the chain, about 200 km (124 mi) to the E, is the **Kuril Trench**, which has a maximum depth of 10 542 m (34 587 ft). Total area: about 15 600 sq km (6022 sq mi).

Kurosawa Akira (1910–) Japanese film director. His best-known films are action costume dramas such as *Rashomon* (1950) and *Seven Samurai* (1954). His literary adaptations include *Throne of Blood* (1957) and *Ran* (1985) (from Shakespeare's *Macbeth* and *King Lear*, respectively).

Kursk 51 45N 36 14E A city in the W central Soviet Union. Population (1984): 413 000.

Kutch, Rann of An area of salt waste in central W India, near the border with S Pakistan. It consists of the Great Rann in the N and the Little Rann in the SE. Total area: about 23 000 sq km (8878 sq mi).

Kuwait 29 20N 48 00E The capital of the sheikdom of Kuwait, on the Persian Gulf. The traditional Islamic town has developed into a modern metropolis with the development of the oil industry. Population (1980): 60 525.

Kuwait, State of A country in the Middle East, in Arabia situated at the head of the Persian Gulf. The country is sandy and barren and has a harsh climate. The inhabitants are predominantly Arab, although about half are foreigners, and the Kuwaitis are mainly Sunnite or Shiite Muslim. *Economy*: Kuwait is one of the largest oil producers in the world and has one of the highest per capita incomes. Kuwait is a member of OPEC. *History*: Kuwait was originally settled in the early 18th century by nomads from the Arabian interior, who established a sheikdom in 1756. In 1899, to counter German and Ottoman expansionism, Kuwait gave Britain control over its foreign affairs and on the outbreak of World War I it became a British protectorate. Oil was discovered in 1938 and transformed the Kuwaiti economy after World War II. On gaining independence in 1961, Kuwait had to request troops from Britain to avert annexation by Iraq but soon after became accepted as a sovereign state. Head of state: Sheik Jabir al-Ahmad al-Jabir as-Sabah (1928–). Prime minister: Sheik Saad al-Abdullah as-Salim as-Sabah. Official language: Arabic. Official currency: Kuwait dinar of 1000 fils. Area: 24 286 sq km (9375 sq mi). Population (1983): 1 652 000. Capital: Kuwait.

Kwangju 35 07N 126 52E A city in SW South Korea. Population (1980): 727 627.

kwashiorkor Severe protein deficiency in children under five years. **Marasmus** is deficiency of not only protein but also of carbohydrate and fat. Kwashiorkor, which develops in babies soon after they are weaned, occurs in poor countries where the diet does not contain sufficient protein (the name derives from a Ghanaian word). The children fail to grow, are apathetic, have swollen stomachs and ankles, sparse hair, diarrhoea, and enlarged livers. The slightest infection is usually fatal but the children recover rapidly with a good diet.

Kyoto 35 2N 135 45E A city in Japan, in S Honshu. It has been a leading cultural centre since early times, when it was the Japanese capital (794–1192 AD) and the old imperial palace and ancient Buddhist temples still remain. Population (1980): 1 473 000.

Kyprianou, Spyros (1932–) Cypriot statesman; president (1977–). When Cyprus became independent in 1960 he was appointed minister of justice and then foreign minister (1960–72).

Kyushu The southernmost of the four main islands of Japan. Mountainous and volcanic, it has hot springs and a subtropical climate and is the most densely populated of the Japanese islands. There is a large rice-growing area in the NW, while heavy industry is centred on the N coalfield. Area: 35 659 sq km (13 768 sq mi). Population (1970): 12 496 433. Chief cities: Kitakyushu, Fukuoka, and Nagasaki.

Kyzyl Kum A desert in the W central S Soviet Union, lying between the Rivers Amu Darya and Syr Darya. Area: about 300 000 sq km (115 806 sq mi).

KWASHIORKOR *A victim of kwashiorkor and marasmus in Ethiopia.*

L

Labiatae A family of herbaceous plants and shrubs (about 3500 species), widely distributed but particularly abundant in the Mediterranean region. They typically have square stems, hairy simple leaves, and clusters of tubular two-lipped flowers. Many of the plants are aromatic and yield useful oils (lavender, rosemary, etc.) and many are used as culinary herbs (marjoram, mint, sage, thyme, etc.).

Labor Party The Australian democratic socialist party, formed in New South Wales in 1891. It first held federal office in the period 1904–16, and subsequently 1929–31, 1939–49, and 1972–75 under Gough Whitlam, and from 1983 under Bob Hawke.

Labour Day The day on which the labour movement is celebrated. In 1889, the Second International declared an international labour holiday on May Day. In Britain, Labour Day was the first Sunday in May until 1977, when the first Monday of the month was declared a public holiday.

Labour Party The democratic socialist party in the UK. The party was formed in 1900 as the Labour Representation Committee, being renamed the Labour Party in 1906. Its origins lie in the trades-union movement of the 19th century, and the trade unions continue to provide over three-quarters of its funds. The Fabian Society was also a powerful influence on its formation and political beliefs. In 1922 the Labour Party replaced the divided Liberal Party as one of the two major UK parties (*compare* Conservative Party) and in 1924 and 1929–31 Labour formed a minority government under Ramsay MacDonald. It was not until after World War II, when under Clement Attlee the party won a huge majority in the general election of 1945, that it was able to introduce radical policies. In office from 1945 to 1951, the Labour administration undertook widespread nationalization and set up a comprehensive system of social security.

The party was in office again from 1964 to 1970 and from 1974 to 1979, under Harold Wilson (1964–76) and then James Callaghan. The present leader, from 1983, is Neil Kinnock. *See also* Social Democratic Party.

Labrador (*or* Coast of Labrador) A district of NE Canada, on the Atlantic Ocean. Although the coast has belonged to Newfoundland for several centuries, the interior was finally awarded to Newfoundland in 1927. Labrador is mostly a rolling swampy plateau within the Canadian Shield. Generally barren except for forested river valleys, it has vast reserves of high-grade iron ore, which are being mined. Its hydroelectric potential is enormous. Area: 258 185 sq km (99 685 sq mi). Population (1976): 33 052. *See also* Churchill Falls.

Labrador Current A major ocean current of the N Atlantic, flowing S from the polar seas down the W coast of Greenland and past Newfoundland, until it meets the Gulf Stream and, being cold and dense, sinks beneath it. The Labrador Current carries icebergs S and is a cause of frequent fogs in the region of Newfoundland.

Labrador retriever A breed of dog originating in Newfoundland and brought to Britain by fishermen in the early 19th century. It is solidly built, about 56 cm high, with a tapering otter-like tail and a short dense water-resistant coat, usually black or yellow-brown.

laburnum A tree of the genus *Laburnum*, especially *L. anagyroides*, which is native to mountainous regions of central Europe and widely grown for ornament. Up to 7 m high, its leaves each consist of three dark-green leaflets. The bright-yellow flowers grow in hanging clusters and produce slender brown pods. All parts of the plant are poisonous, especially the seeds. Family: *Leguminosae*.

labyrinth fish A small elongated laterally compressed fish of the family *Anabantidae* (about 70 species), found in fresh waters of tropical Asia and Africa. They have an accessory respiratory organ (labyrinth) with which they obtain oxygen from air gulped at the surface—of benefit in poorly oxygenated water. Some species are popular aquarium fish. Order: *Perciformes. See also* fighting fish; gourami.

LACE *Late 17th-century* Point de France.

lace An ornamental network of threads of silk, linen, etc., used mainly for dress collars, cuffs, altar cloths, etc. Needlepoint lace, originating in Italy in the early 16th century, is made with a needle on parchment or fabric. Pillow or bobbin lace, reputedly invented by Barbara Uttmann (b. 1514) in Saxony, is formed by twisting threads around pins stuck in a pillow. The best work was done in Italy, Flanders, France, and England in the 17th and 18th centuries, famous types of lace being Brussels, Valenciennes, Mechlin, and Honiton. Lace making as an art declined in the 19th century after machine manufacture was introduced.

lacewing An insect belonging to one of several families of the suborder *Plannipennia*. Lacewings have delicate net-veined wings and are carnivorous, with biting mouthparts. Green lacewings (*Chrysopidae*), also called golden-eyed lacewings, are about 10 mm long and occur worldwide near vegetation. Eggs are laid individually on hairlike stalks and the larvae feed on aphids, scale insects, etc. The brown lacewings (*Hemerobiidae*) are smaller and often have spotted wings. Order: *Neuroptera*.

Lachlan River A river in SE Australia, in New South Wales. Rising in the Great Dividing Range it flows generally NW to join the Murrumbidgee River. Length: 1483 km (922 mi).

La Coruña (*or* Corunna) 43 22N 8 24W A port in NW Spain, in Galicia on the Atlantic Ocean. The Spanish Armada sailed from here on 26 July, 1588, and in 1589 the city was sacked by Sir Francis Drake. It is an important fishing centre. Population (1986): 239 505.

lacquer tree A tree, *Rhus vernicifera*, of SE Asia, also called varnish tree. Up to 30 m tall, it has compound leaves, which turn red in autumn. Japanese lacquer is obtained from the milky resin that oozes from cuts in the bark. Family: *Anacardiaceae*.

lacrosse A 10-a-side field game (12 for women) played with a ball and a long-handled stick (the crosse), which has a triangular head with a raw-hide strung pock-

et for catching, throwing, and picking up the ball. Of North American Indian origin, it is played mainly in the USA, Canada, Britain, and Australia. The object is to score goals by running with the ball and passing it. Each team consists of a goalkeeper, three defensive players, three attackmen, and three midfielders. Tackling and striking an opponent's stick to dislodge the ball are allowed, and protective clothing is worn.

lactation The secretion of milk from the breasts or mammary glands. In women lactation is controlled by hormones released from the ovary, placenta, and pituitary gland (*see* prolactin) and starts shortly after childbirth, in response to the sucking action of the baby at the nipple: it will continue for as long as the baby is breastfed. A protein-rich fluid called colostrum is secreted in the first few days of lactation, before the milk has been produced. It contains antibodies that give the baby temporary immunity to disease.

Ladakh Range A mountain range mainly in NW India, extending about 370 km (230 mi) between the Karakoram Range and the Himalayas and rising to over 6000 m (19 685 ft).

Ladino A Romance language originally spoken by Sephardic Jews in Spain but taken by them after their exile in 1492 to the Balkans, the Near East, N Africa, Greece,

The optimum dimensions of the women's ground, although the game is played with no boundaries.

The dimensions of the men's ground.

LACROSSE

and Turkey. It is an old form of Castilian Spanish mixed with Hebrew elements and written in Hebrew characters.

Ladoga, Lake A lake in the NW Soviet Union in the RSFSR, the largest lake in Europe. It discharges via the River Neva into the Gulf of Finland. Area: about 17 700 sq km (6836 sq mi).

ladybird beetle A small round beetle, 8–10 mm long, that belongs to the widely distributed family *Coccinellidae* (5000 species). Most species are red or yellow with black spots and are of great benefit to man. Both the larvae and adults feed on a variety of plant pests, including aphids, scale insects, mealybugs, and whiteflies.

Lady Day The Christian feast of the Annunciation of the Virgin Mary. Celebrated on 25 March, it began the calendar year in England from 1155 to 1752 and is still a quarter day.

Ladysmith 28 34S 29 47E A town in South Africa, in NW Natal. Founded in 1850, it was besieged for four months (1899–1900) by the Boers during the second Boer War. Population (1985): 43 200.

lady's slipper A terrestrial orchid, *Cypripedium calceolus*, native to N Europe and Asia. Up to 45 cm high, it has broad leaves and the flowers are grouped singly or in twos and threes. Each flower has small twisted red-brown petals and an inflated yellow slipper-like lip. The lady's slipper is nearly extinct in Britain. *See also* slipper orchid.

Lafayette, Marie Joseph Gilbert Motier, Marquis de (1757–1834) French general and politician, prominent at the beginning of the French Revolution. His early career was distinguished by his military successes (1777–79, 1780–82) against the British in the American Revolution. In France as a representative in the States General, he presented the Declaration of the Rights of Man (1789) and after the storming of the Bastille he became commander of the new National Guard. In 1792 the rising power of the radicals threatened his life and he gave himself up to France's enemy, Austria. Lafayette was also prominent in the July Revolution (1830), which overthrew Charles X.

Lagomorpha A world-wide order of mammals (66 species) comprising pikas, rabbits, and hares. Lagomorphs have teeth similar to rodents, with four continuously growing incisors. They are vegetarians and eat their own faecal pellets, thus obtaining the maximum value from their food.

Lagos 6 27N 3 28E The capital and main port of Nigeria, on Lagos Island on the Bight of Benin. First settled by Yoruba fishermen in the 17th century, it became the centre of the Portuguese slave trade in West Africa and was ceded to Britain in 1861. One of Africa's largest cities, it is an important commercial and industrial centre. Population (1983 est): 1 097 000.

Lahore 31 34N 74 22E The second largest city in Pakistan, near the River Ravi, founded about the 7th century AD. Traditionally the chief city of the Punjab, Lahore is situated close to the Indian border and has been the scene of much bloodshed and violence. It is a major railway, commercial, and political centre and the headquarters of the Muslim League. The famous Shalimar gardens lie to the E of the city. Population (1981): 2 922 000.

Laing, R(onald) D(avid) (1927–89) British psychiatrist. He was best known for regarding schizophrenia as a defensive façade and madness as a journey of self-real-

ization (*The Divided Self*, 1960). *The Politics of Experience* (1967) and his views on family life (*Sanity, Madness and the Family*, 1965 and *The Politics of the Family*, 1971) aroused controversy. His poetry includes *Knots* (1970).

laissez-faire The economic theory that governments should not interfere with market forces based on self-interest and the profit motive. The concept, originating in France, was advocated by Adam Smith and widely accepted until the beginning of the 19th century. By then the growth of capitalism had exposed its principal weaknesses: the rise of monopolies, the grossly inequitable distribution of wealth, and the exploitation of labour. In western economies, laissez-faire policies have now been largely abandoned for mixed economies.

Lake District (*or* Lakeland) An area in NW England, in Cumbria, a national park since 1951. It consists of a high dome incised by a radial system of glaciated valleys, many of which contain ribbon lakes including Derwentwater, Ullswater, and Windermere. High mountains rise between the valleys, the highest being Scafell Pike and Helvellyn. A major tourist area, hill walking, rock climbing, and water sports are all popular. Other traditional occupations include hill farming, forestry, and quarrying. Area: about 1813 sq km (700 sq mi).

Lakshmi In Hinduism, the goddess of wealth and happiness, the benign aspect of Shakti, the supreme goddess. As the wife of Vishnu she appears in various forms according to his several incarnations. Many festivals are held in her honour (*see* Diwali). Lakshmi is also revered by the Jains.

LALIQUE   *Glass car mascot.*

Lalique, René (1860–1945) French Art Nouveau jeweller and glassmaker.

lamaism *See* Tibetan Buddhism.

Lamarck, Jean-Baptiste de Monet, Chevalier de (1744–1829) French naturalist, noted for his speculations about the evolution of living things, particularly his theory of the inheritance of acquired characteristics (*see* Lamarckism), published 1809. Lamarck also worked on a system of classification for invertebrate animals, published in his *Histoire naturelle des animaux sans vertèbres* (7 vols, 1815–22).

Lamarckism The first theory of evolution as proposed by Jean-Baptiste Lamarck in 1809, based on his concept of the inheritance of acquired characteristics. He suggested that an organism develops structural changes during its lifetime as an adaptation to its particular environment and that these features are then inherited by successive generations through sexual reproduction. A classic example of these acquired characteristics are the forelegs and neck of a giraffe, which he believed became longer through its habit of browsing on tall trees. This now discredited theory has been rejected in favour of Darwin's theory of evolution.

Lamartine, Alphonse de (1790–1869) French poet, one of the major figures of the Romantic movement. He established his reputation with *Méditations poétiques* (1820). In the 1830s he became an active political champion of republican ideals and was briefly head of the provisional government after the Revolution of 1848. His other major works include the narrative poems *Jocelyn* (1836) and *La Chute d'un ange* (1836).

Lamb, Charles (1775–1834) British essayist and critic. He collaborated with his sister Mary on *Tales from Shakespeare* (1807), a children's book. He is best remembered for his *Essays of Elia* (1822).

Lambaréné 0 41S 10 13E A town in W Gabon, on an island in the River Ogooué. Its hospital (1913) was founded by the missionary Albert Schweitzer. Population (latest est): 26 257.

lambert A unit of luminance equal to the luminance of a surface that emits one lumen per square centimetre. Named after J. H. Lambert (1728–77).

Lambert, Constant (1905–51) British composer and conductor. Diaghilev commissioned his ballet *Romeo and Juliet* (1925–26) and he was musical director of the Sadler's Wells from 1928 to 1947. His most famous composition is the choral work *Rio Grande* (1929).

LAMBETH CONFERENCES *Held at Lambeth Palace, rebuilt 1828–34.*

Lambeth Conferences Assemblies normally convened every ten years under the chairmanship of the Archbishop of Canterbury at Lambeth Palace, London, to which all bishops of the Anglican Church are invited. The first was held in 1867. Although their decisions have no binding power, the conferences are important indications of the Anglican episcopate's views and policies.

laminar flow Fluid flow in which the particles move in parallel layers. A fluid moving slowly along a horizontal straight pipe flows in this way. Above a certain velocity, given by the Reynolds number, the layers no longer remain parallel and the flow becomes turbulent.

lammergeier A large vulture, *Gypaetus barbatus*, also called bearded vulture because of the long bristles on its chin. It is over 1 m long with a wingspan of 3 m and occurs in mountainous regions of S Europe, central Asia, and E Africa. It is brown with tawny underparts and a black-and-white face.

lamprey A fishlike vertebrate belonging to a family (*Petromyzonidae*; about 22 species) of cyclostomes. Lampreys have an eel-like body with one or two dorsal fins and seven pairs of gill slits. They occur in fresh or salt water and many are parasitic on fish, attaching themselves with a circular sucking mouth and feeding on the blood and flesh.

lamp shell. *See* Brachiopoda.

Lanark 55 41N 3 48W A town in S central Scotland, in Strathclyde Region; now part of Clydesdale. Nearby New Lanark, founded as a cotton-spinning centre in 1784 by David Dale and Richard Arkwright, is well known for the social experiments carried out there by Robert Owen.

Lancashire A county of NW England, bordering on the Irish Sea. It consists of lowlands in the W rising to the high level plateaus of the Pennines in the E, with the chief river, the Ribble, flowing SW to the Irish Sea. The lowlands are important agricultural regions. Industry is based chiefly on textiles (cotton manufacturing being of major importance until recently), mining, and engineering. Tourism is important in the coastal towns of Blackpool, Southport, and Morecambe. Central Lancs New Town (1970) comprising Preston, Fulwood, Bamber Bridge, Leyland, and Chorley is the new county focus. Area: 3043 sq km (8191 sq mi). Population (1986 est): 1 380 700. Administrative centre: Preston.

Lancaster 54 03N 2 48W A town in NW England, in Lancashire on the River Lune, superseded by Preston as the administrative centre of Lancashire. The castle, partly 13th-century and enlarged by Elizabeth I, stands on the site of a Roman garrison. Its university was founded in 1964. Population (1981): 46 321.

Lancaster A ruling dynasty of England descended from Edmund, the second son of Henry III, who was created Earl of Lancaster in 1267. In 1361 the title passed by marriage to the third son of Edward III, John of Gaunt. His son seized the throne from Richard II and ruled (1399–1413) as Henry IV. He was succeeded by Henry V, whose son Henry VI led the Lancastrians against the Yorkists (*see* York) in the Wars of the Roses (1455–85), in which their emblem was a red rose. Following Henry VI's death (1471) the royal dynasty came to an end.

Lancaster, Duchy of A territory with its own courts and administration created in 1267 by Henry III for his son Edmund (1245–96). After the last Duke of Lancaster became Henry IV in 1399 the Duchy was attached to the Crown, retaining its own jurisdiction. The Crown continues to hold the Duchy's revenues and the chancellor of the Duchy of Lancaster is usually a member of the cabinet.

lancelet. *See* amphioxus.

Lancelot In Arthurian legend, a knight of the Round Table. While a child he was kidnapped by the Lady of the Lake, who educated him and later sent him to serve King Arthur. He was a celebrated warrior but failed in the quest of the Holy Grail because of his adulterous love for Guinevere.

lancers Originally foot soldiers armed with a lance, they subsequently became cavalrymen belonging to one of the regiments called lancers, both on the continent and in the UK. The name is retained in some armoured regiments.

Lanchester, Frederick, William (1868–1946) British engineer, who built the first British car in 1896. He formed the Lanchester Engine Company producing high-quality vehicles.

Lanchow. *See* Lanzhou.

Land. *See* Germany, Federal Republic of.

Land, Edwin Herbert (1909–) US inventor of Polaroid, who set up the Polaroid Corporation in 1937 for its manufacture. He also invented the Polaroid Land Camera in 1947, in which pictures are printed inside the camera.

landau A four-wheeled coach drawn by two or four horses. Landaus have fully collapsible tops and are still used in European royal processions.

land crab A large square-bodied crab of the tropical family *Gecarcinidae*, specialized for a terrestrial existence. It feeds on plant and animal materials. *Cardiosoma guanhumi*, 11 cm across the back, is found in the West Indies and S North America. Tribe: *Brachyura*.

landlord and tenant The relationship arising from a grant (lease) of exclusive possession of land by a landlord to a tenant for a fixed period and, usually, for a regular payment of rent. The relationship is defined by a contract, which is contained in the lease or, for short terms, in a tenancy agreement.

Land Registry, HM An official registry of titles to land, established in 1862. This simplifies conveyancing when the property is sold: by searching in the Registry, outstanding leases, mortgages, etc., may be discovered. Not all land in the UK is yet subject to compulsory registration.

SIR EDWIN LANDSEER *Detail of a painting by John Ballantyne; at work (c. 1865) on one of his lions.*

Landseer, Sir Edwin Henry (1802–73) British artist. He achieved success, particularly with Queen Victoria, with his sentimental animal and Highland subjects,

notably *Dignity and Impudence*. He sculptured the four bronze lions in Trafalgar Square.

Land's End 50 03N 5 44W The extreme western point of England. A granite headland in Cornwall, it lies at a distance of 970 km (603 mi) from John o'Groats at the N tip of Scotland. The southernmost point of England is the Lizard nearby.

Lang, Fritz (1890–1976) German film director. The best known of a number of influential silent films are *Dr Mabuse the Gambler* (1922), *Metropolis* (1926), and *M* (1931). He went to Hollywood in 1933, where he made commercially successful thrillers and westerns.

Lange, David Russell (1942–) New Zealand politician; Labour prime minister (1984–89).

Langtry, Lillie (Emilie Charlotte le Breton; 1853–1929) British actress, known as the Jersey Lily. Having married a wealthy husband she proved that high social position was not incompatible with an acting career. She was noted for her beauty and was an intimate friend of the Prince of Wales, later Edward VII.

languages, classification of The division of languages into groups. There are three methods of classification. The first method is that of geographical or political division, in which languages are grouped together according to the continent or country in which they occur. Examples of the former include Indian languages and European languages. The latter is represented by the similar but politically distinct languages Swedish, Danish, and Norwegian. Such divisions do not always follow the genetic relationships that exist between languages. This relationship forms the basis for the second method of classification, which maps the historical development from one form of the language to another, as in the relation between Old English and modern English. Further back both these and other languages can be traced to their common Indo-European ancestor. The third possible method of classification is on typological evidence, which depends on the grammatical structure of the language. The original three classes were devised by W. von Humboldt (1767–1835): analytic (or isolating), agglutinative, and inflecting languages. English is an analytic language. **Analytic languages** show little variation in the forms of words but rely on strict word order to express grammatical relations. In **agglutinative languages** (e.g. Turkish) words have the capacity to be split up into individual components with separate grammatical roles. In **inflecting languages** (e.g. Latin, Sanskrit) words are characteristically built up of a root plus a component (morpheme) that represents several different grammatical categories.

Languedoc A former province in S France, on the Gulf of Lions. Its name derived from *langue d'oc*, the language of its inhabitants (*see* Provençal). It is now incorporated chiefly into the planning region of **Languedoc-Roussillon.** Area: 27 447 sq km (10 595 sq mi). Population (1986 est): 2 011 900. See p. 414.

langur A leaf-eating Old World monkey of tropical Asia. The largest is the hanuman, or entellus langur (*Presbytis entellus*), 75 cm long with a 95-cm tail. The douc langur (*Pygathrix nemaeus*) of Vietnam is mainly grey with white forearms and is now an endangered species. Chief genera: *Presbytis* (14 species), *Rhinopithecus* (4 species).

lanolin A purified wax extracted from wool. It is a mixture of cholesterol and other sterols, aliphatic alcohols, and esters. Because it is easily absorbed by the skin,

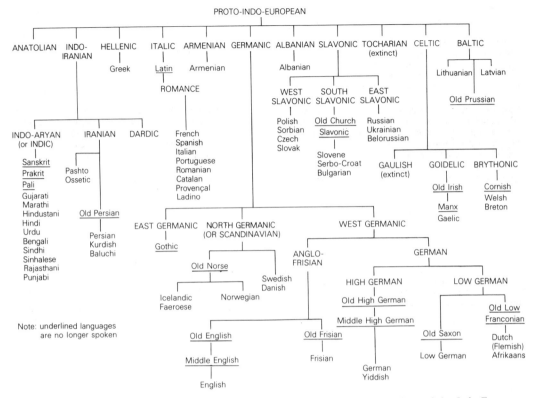

CLASSIFICATION OF LANGUAGES *A simplified family tree shows the relationships of the Indo-European languages, spoken by about half the world's population.*

lanolin is used as a base for creams, soaps, and other skin preparations.

lantern fish A deepsea bony fish belonging to the family *Myctophidae* (about 150 species). Lantern fish have large mouths and eyes and numerous light-producing organs on the head, underside, and base of the tail. Order: *Myctophiformes.*

lanthanides (*or* rare-earth metals) A group of 15 transition-metal elements, atomic numbers 57–71, which all have remarkably similar physical and chemical properties as a result of their electronic structures. They occur together in monazite and other minerals. They are used as catalysts in the petroleum industry, in iron alloys and permanent magnets, and in glass polishes. The **rare earths** are the oxides of these metals.

lanthanum (La) The first of the series of lanthanides. At no 57; at wt 138.9055; mp 921°C; bp 3457°C.

Lanzhou (Lan-chou *or* Lanchow) 36 01N 103 45E A city in N China, the capital of Gansu province at the confluence of the Yellow and Wei Rivers. It is an ancient trade and communications centre and is now an industrial centre. Population (1986): 1 350 000.

Laocoon In Greek legend, a Trojan priest of Apollo who warned against accepting the Greek gift of the Trojan Horse. He and his two sons were killed by sea serpents sent by Apollo, and the Trojans then opened their gates to the wooden horse.

Laoighis (*or* Leix; former name: Queen's County) A county in the E central Republic of Ireland, in Leinster. Predominantly low lying with bogs and drained chiefly by the Rivers Barrow and Nore, it rises to mountains in the NW. Agriculture is the main occupation. Area: 1719 sq km (664 sq mi). Population (1986): 53 270. County town: Portlaoise.

Laos, People's Democratic Republic of A landlocked country in SE Asia, between Vietnam and Thailand. Except for the valley of the River Mekong along its western border, the country is mountainous and forested. Over half the population are Lao (descendants of the Thai) and there are minorities of Vietnamese, Chinese, and others. *Economy*: predominantly agricultural. The valuable mineral resources (tin, iron ore, gold, and copper) have yet to be fully exploited. There is little industry. *History*: the origins of the area as a nation date from the 14th century. European contacts were initiated in the 17th century and in 1893 Laos became a French protectorate. After Japanese occupation, 1941–45, the French returned, 1946, and a constitutional monarchy was formed in 1947. In 1949 Laos became independent within the French Union. In 1953 civil war, which was to last for 20 years, broke out between the government (supported by the USA and by Thai mercenaries) and the communist-led Pathet Lao movement (supported by the North Vietnamese). In 1974 a provisional coalition government was formed, but following the collapse of the South Vietnamese the Pathet Lao gained power (December, 1975) and the People's Democratic Republic of Laos was formed. President: Phoumi Vongvichit. Prime minister: Kaysone Phoumvihan (1920–). Official language: Laotian; French is widely spoken. Official currency: kip of 100 at. Area: 235 700 sq km (91 000 sq mi). Population (1987 est): 4 322 000. Capital: Vientiane.

LAOCOON *Marble by Hagesandros, Athenodoros, and Polydoros of Rhodes (c. 25 BC; Vatican museum).*

Lao Zi (*or* Lao Tzu; ?6th century BC) The founder of Taoism. A shadowy, possibly legendary, figure, he was eventually deified. His purpose, propounded mainly in books compiled about 300 years after his likely date of death, was to reach harmony with the *Tao* (way) by dwelling on the beauty of nature, by being self-sufficient, and by desiring nothing.

La Paz 16 30S 68 00W The administrative capital of Bolivia, situated in the W of the country. At an altitude of 3577 m (11 735 ft), it is the world's highest capital. Founded by the Spanish in 1548, it became the seat of government in 1898. Population (1985): 992 600. *See also* Sucre.

lapis lazuli A blue semiprecious stone composed mainly of the sulphur-rich mineral lazurite. It is formed by the metamorphism of limestone. It often contains specks or threads of yellow iron pyrites. Lapis lazuli has been mined in Afghanistan for over 6000 years. The pigment ultramarine was formerly made by grinding up lapis lazuli.

Laplace, Pierre Simon, Marquis de (1749–1827) French mathematician and astronomer. Laplace worked with J. L. Lagrange (1736–1813) on the effects, known as perturbations, of the small gravitational forces that planets exert on each other. They deduced that the perturbations have a minimal effect, thus proving the stability of the solar system. In the published account of their results, *Mécanique céleste* (1799–1825), Laplace speculated that the solar system was formed from a condensing rotating cloud of gas.

Lapland (*or* Lappland) A vast region in N Europe, inhabited by the Lapps and extending across northern parts of Norway, Sweden, Finland, and into the extreme NW of the Soviet Union. Lying mainly within the Arctic Circle, it consists of tundra in the N, mountains in the W, and forests in the S; there are many lakes and rivers. For many centuries the Lapps were reduced to virtual slavery by their more powerful neighbours. Subsistence farming, fishing, trapping, and hunting are the principal occupations and reindeer are a particularly important source of income. There are rich deposits of iron ore in Swedish Lapland.

Lapps A people of N Scandinavia and the Kola peninsula of the Soviet Union. They speak a Finno-Ugric language, which differs from the related Finnish and Estonian mainly in its sound system. There are three major Lapp dialects.

lapwing A Eurasian plover, *Vanellus vanellus*, also called peewit and green plover. It occurs commonly on farmland, where it feeds on harmful insects. 28 cm long, it has a greenish-black and white plumage and a long crest.

larch A deciduous conifer of the genus *Larix* (10 species), native to the cooler regions of the N hemisphere. Larches have needles growing in bunches on short spurs and produce small woody cones. The common European larch (*L. decidua*), from the mountains of central Europe, is widely cultivated both for timber and ornament. It reaches a height of 40 m. The Japanese larch (*L. kaempferi*) is commonly grown on plantations. Family: *Pinaceae*.

Lares and Penates Roman household gods. The Lares were originally gods of cultivated land who were worshipped at crossroads and boundaries. The Penates were gods of the storeroom. Together with the Manes, they were later worshipped in private homes as guardian spirits of the family, household, and state.

Large White A breed of pig originating in Yorkshire, England, also called the Yorkshire. Relatively large-framed, Large Whites are white-skinned with a sparse coat of fine hair. They are extensively used for bacon production.

lark A slender long-winged songbird belonging to a family (*Alaudidae*; 75 species) found mainly in mudflats, marshes, grasslands, and deserts of the Old World and characterized by a beautiful song. Larks commonly have a brown or buff streaked plumage that often matches the local soil colour. They have long slender bills and feed on seeds and insects. *See also* skylark.

Larkin, Philip (1922–85) British poet. His volumes include *The Whitsun Weddings* (1964) and *High Windows* (1974). He edited *The Oxford Book of Twentieth Century English Verse* (1973).

Larne 54 51N 5 49W A port in Northern Ireland, in Co Antrim at the entrance to Lough Larne. Larne is a tourist centre and has the shortest searoute between Ireland and Britain (Stranraer). Population (1981): 18 222.

La Rochefoucauld, François, Duc de (1613–80) French moralist. He was born into an ancient aristocratic family and played an active part in intrigues against

Richelieu. Thereafter he lived in retirement, writing his *Mémoires* (1664) and compiling his celebrated *Maximes* (1665), a collection of cynical epigrammatic observations on human conduct.

larva The immature form of many animals, which hatches from the egg and often differs in appearance from the adult form. Larvae usually avoid competing for food, etc., with the adults by occupying a different habitat or adopting a different lifestyle. For example, adult barnacles, which are sessile, produce motile larvae, whose role is distribution of the species. Other larvae, such as caterpillars and maggots, are responsible for gathering food reserves for the production of a fully formed adult, whose primary function is to breed. *See also* tadpole.

Larwood, Harold (1904–) British cricketer, who played for Nottinghamshire and England. Larwood was a fast bowler who was at the centre of the bodyline controversy during the 1932–33 tour of Australia.

larynx An organ, situated at the front of the neck above the windpipe (*see* trachea), that contains the **vocal cords**. The larynx contains several cartilages (one of which—the thyroid cartilage—forms the Adam's apple) bound together by muscles and ligaments. Within are the two vocal cords: folds of tissue separated by a narrow slit (glottis). The vocal cords modify the flow of exhaled air through the glottis to produce the sounds of speech, song, etc.

La Scala The principal Italian opera house, opened in Milan in 1776. It is noted for its varied repertoire and attained its highest reputation under Arturo Toscanini, director 1898–1907 and 1921–31.

Lascaux Upper Palaeolithic cave site in the Dordogne (France), discovered in 1940. Lascaux contains rock paintings and engravings of horses, oxen, red deer, and other animals, dating from about 18 000 BC. Deterioration of the paintings caused the cave to be closed again (1963).

Lasdun, Sir Denys (1914–) British architect, whose most important works are East Anglia University (1963) and, in London, the National Theatre (1968–76) and the School of African and Oriental Studies (1970–73).

LASER *The solid-state ruby laser.*

laser (*l*ight *a*mplification by *s*timulated *e*mission of *r*adiation) A device that produces a beam of high-intensity coherent monochromatic radiation (light, infrared, or ultraviolet). Stimulated emission is the emission of a photon when an atomic electron falls from a higher

energy level to a lower level as a result of being stimulated by another photon of the same frequency. In the laser large numbers of electrons are "pumped" into a higher energy level, an effect called population inversion, and then stimulated to produce a high-intensity beam. Laser beams have been produced from solids, liquids, and gases. The simplest type is the ruby laser, consisting of a cylinder of ruby, silvered at one end and partially silvered at the other. A flash lamp is used to excite chromium ions in the ruby to a high energy level. When the ions fall back to their ground state photons are emitted. These photons collide with other excited ions producing radiation of the same wavelength (monochromatic) and the same phase (coherent), which is reflected up and down the ruby crystal and emerges as a narrow beam from the partially silvered end. Lasers are used in surgery, in holography, and in scientific research.

Las Palmas 28 08N 15 27W The largest city in the Canary Islands, the capital of Las Palmas province in Gran Canaria. It is a popular resort. Population (1981): 366 454.

La Spezia 44 07N 9 48E A port and resort in Italy, in Liguria on the Gulf of Spezia. It is a major naval base, with the largest harbour in Italy. Population (1986): 108 937.

Lassa fever A severe virus disease occurring in West Africa and first described in 1969 in Lassa, a village in Nigeria. It is a rare and often fatal disease that is transmitted to man by certain species of rat.

Las Vegas 36 10N 115 12W A city in the USA, in SE Nevada. Founded in 1855, it grew rapidly after construction of the nearby Hoover Dam. It is famous for its nightclubs and the Strip (a row of luxury hotels and gambling casinos). Population (1986 est): 201 300.

La Tène The second phase of the European Iron Age, succeeding Hallstatt from the 5th century BC. Named after the site at La Tène (Switzerland), this recognizably Celtic culture spread throughout Europe, coming into contact with the civilizations of Greece and Rome. Aristocratic chariot burials replaced wagon burials and the geometric patterns of Hallstatt metalwork were superseded by the intricate curvilinear designs of Celtic art. By the 1st century BC Roman expansionism effectively ended coherent La Tène culture. *See also* Celts.

latent heat The amount of heat absorbed or released by a substance when it undergoes a change of state. For example, a liquid absorbs heat (**latent heat of vaporization**) from its surroundings on evaporation, since energy is needed to overcome the forces of attraction between the molecules as the liquid expands into a gas. Similarly a solid absorbs heat (**latent heat of fusion**) when it melts. The heat absorbed or released per unit mass of substance is called the **specific latent heat**.

Lateran Councils Five ecumenical councils of the Roman Catholic Church convened in the Lateran Palace, Rome, in 1123, 1139, 1179, 1215, and 1512–17. The council of 1215, attended by most major European ecclesiastical and secular powers, proclaimed the fifth Crusade (1217–21) and was enormously influential in its formulations of doctrine and Church organization and law.

Lateran Treaty (1929) An agreement between the Italian government of Mussolini and the Vatican. The Vatican City state was created and the papacy abandoned its claims to the former papal states.

Latimeria. *See* coelacanth.

Latin language An Italic Indo-European language, the ancestor of modern Romance languages. First spoken on the plain of Latium near Rome, Latin spread throughout the Mediterranean world as Roman power expanded. An inflected and syntactically complex language, written Latin developed contemporaneously with conversational Latin, although the latter, with its freer syntax and vocabulary, remained less static than the formal language. Colloquial Vulgar Latin used prepositions and conjunctions freely to replace inflected forms and had a simpler word order; it became the Latin of the provinces, contributing to the early development of the Romance languages. As the western Roman Empire's official language, Latin was used in W Europe for religious, literary, and scholarly works until the middle ages.

equator   parallels of latitude   meridians of longitude
Greenwich Meridian

The latitude of P is given by the angle α. In this case it would be α° N. The latitude of R is β° S. The longitude of P is given by the angle x. In this case it would be x° W. R has a longitude y° E.

LATITUDE AND LONGITUDE

latitude and longitude Imaginary lines on the earth's surface, enabling any point to be defined in terms of two angles. **Parallels of latitude** are circles drawn round the earth parallel to the equator; their diameters diminish as they approach the Poles. These parallels are specified by the angle subtended at the centre of the earth by the arc formed between a point on the parallel and the equator. All points on the equator therefore have a latitude of 0°, while the North Pole has a latitude of 90° N and the South Pole of 90° S. Parallels of latitude 1° apart are separated on the earth's surface by about 100 km (63 mi).
Meridians of longitude are half great circles passing through both Poles; they cross parallels of latitude at right angles. In 1884 the meridian through Greenwich, near London, was selected as the prime meridian and given the designation 0°. Other meridians are defined by the angle between the plane of the meridian and the plane of the prime meridian, specifying whether it is E or W of the prime meridian. At the equator meridians 1° apart are separated by about 112 km (70 mi).
latitudinarianism An attitude originating with certain 17th-century Anglican clergymen, who deprecated sectarian squabbles over Church government and forms of ritual and considered such matters unimportant in comparison with personal piety and practical morality. Latitudinarian principles characterized the Cambridge Platonists. Between the 1690s and the rise of the Oxford Movement in the 1830s latitudinarianism was the predominant tendency in the Church of England.

Latter-Day Saints, Church of Jesus Christ of. *See* Mormons.

Latvian A language belonging to the E division of the Baltic languages division of the Indo-European family, spoken by about two million Latvians. Most live in the Latvian SSR, where Latvian is the official language. Also known as Lettish, it is closely related to Lithuanian. It is written in a Latin alphabet.

Laud, William (1573–1645) Anglican churchman, with the Earl of Strafford (1593–1641) the chief adviser to Charles I immediately before the Civil War. Appointed Archbishop of Canterbury (1633–45), he supported Charles I's personal rule and his attempt to enforce liturgical uniformity among both Roman Catholics and Puritans. His pressure on the Scots to accept the Book of Common Prayer led to the Bishops' Wars and paved the way for the Civil War and his own downfall. He was impeached for high treason by the Long Parliament in 1640 and executed.

laudanum. *See* opium.

Lauder, Sir Harry (Hugh MacLennan; 1870–1950) Scots singer and famous music-hall comedian. His most famous songs included "I Love a Lassie" and "Roamin' in the Gloamin'."

laughing jackass. *See* kookaburra.

Laughton, Charles (1899–1962) British actor. His international reputation was based on his numerous films, which included *The Private Life of Henry VIII* (1933), *Mutiny on the Bounty* (1935), and *Rembrandt* (1936).

Launceston 41 25S 147 07E A city and port in Australia, in N Tasmania situated at the confluence of the North and South Esk Rivers. Population (1986): 88 486.

Laurasia The supercontinent of the N hemisphere that is believed to have existed prior to 200 million years ago, when the drift of the continents to their present positions began. It probably consisted of Greenland, Europe, Asia (excluding India), and North America. *See also* Gondwanaland.

laurel One of several unrelated aromatic shrubs or small trees with attractive evergreen leaves. The so-called true laurels (genus *Laurus*) include the bay tree. Other laurels include the ornamental cherry laurel (*Prunus laurasocerasus*), the spotted laurels (genus *Aucuba*; family *Cornaceae*), and the mountain laurel (*Kalmia latifolia*; family *Ericaceae*). The spurge laurel is a species of *Daphne*.

Laurel and Hardy US film comedians. **Stan Laurel** (Arthur Stanley Jefferson; 1890–1965), the thin member of the team and originator of the gags, was born in Britain. He joined with **Oliver Hardy** (1892–1957), who played the fat partner, in 1926. They made numerous films in the 1920s and 1930s, including *The Music Box* (1932) and *Way Out West* (1937). See p. 418.

Laurentian Shield. *See* shield.

Lausanne 46 32N 6 39E A city and resort in W Switzerland, on the N shore of Lake Geneva. A cultural and intellectual centre, Lausanne is the seat of the Swiss Supreme Court and the headquarters of the International Olympic Committee. Population (1985 est): 125 000.

Lausanne, Conferences of 1. (1922–23) A conference between the Allied Powers and Turkey that modified the post-World War I Treaty of Sèvres (1920): Turkey regained territory from Greece and the Allies recognized Turkey's right to control its own affairs. **2.** (1932) A conference between the UK, France, Belgium, and Italy, which ended the payment by Germany of World War I reparations.

LAUREL AND HARDY   *In* Tit for Tat *(1935).*

lava Magma that has reached the earth's surface through volcanic vents and from which the volatile material has escaped, either molten or cooled and solidified. Basic lavas tend to be liquid and flow over large areas, while acid lavas are viscous.

Laval, Pierre (1883–1945) French statesman. A socialist, Laval was prime minister in 1930, 1931, 1932, 1935, and 1936. After the collapse of France (1940) in World War II, he joined Marshal Pétain's Vichy government, became increasingly powerful, and with the support of Germany gained the virtual leadership of the Vichy government in 1942. After the liberation of France (1944) he was tried and executed for his collaboration with Germany during the occupation.

lavender A small shrub of the genus *Lavandula* (about 8 species), especially *L. vera* and *L. angustifolia* (or *L. officinalis*). 30–80 cm high, it has aromatic narrow grey-green leaves and long-stemmed spikes of small mauve or violet flowers. Native to the Mediterranean area, it is widely cultivated for its flowers, which retain their fragrance when dried, and for its oil, which is used in perfumes. Family: *Labiatae.*

laver A red seaweed of the genus *Porphyra*, found growing at the high tide mark in both hemispheres. It has wide irregular membranous fronds, which are edible: in the British Isles they are fried and known as laverbread (*or* sloke).

Lavoisier, Antoine Laurent (1743–94) French chemist. He became wealthy by investing in a private tax-collecting company. This enabled him to build a large laboratory where he discovered in 1778 that air consists of a mixture of two gases, which he called oxygen and nitrogen. He then went on to study the role of oxygen in combustion, finally disposing of the phlogiston theory. Lavoisier also discovered the law of conservation of mass and devised the modern method of naming compounds. Lavoisier was arrested and guillotined during the French Revolution for his involvement with the tax-collecting company.

law The body of rules that govern and regulate the relationship between one state and another (*see* international law), a state and its citizens (public law), and one

person and another when the state is not directly involved (*see* civil law). Two great legal systems are dominant in the western world: Roman law, as used in most countries of continental Europe and South America, and English law. The laws of England, which are enforceable by judicial process, can be divided into: (1) the common law, based on judicial decisions, as opposed to law enacted by parliament; (2) equity, the principles originally applied by the Court of Chancery; and (3) statute law, embodied in specific Acts of Parliament. *See also* courts of law; criminal law.

Law, (Andrew) Bonar (1858–1923) British statesman; Conservative prime minister (1922–23). He fostered the revolt against Asquith's coalition and in the subsequent coalition led by Lloyd George became chancellor of the exchequer. He became prime minister after Lloyd George's resignation.

Lawrence, D(avid) H(erbert) (1885–1930) British novelist, poet, and painter. He published his first novel, *The White Peacock*, in 1911. The semiautobiographical *Sons and Lovers* (1913) established his reputation. In 1912 he eloped with Frieda Weekley. Their extensive travels provided material for the novels *Kangaroo* (1923), reflecting a stay in Australia, and *The Plumed Serpent* (1926), set in Mexico. Lawrence explored marital and sexual relations in *The Rainbow* (1915) and *Women in Love* (1921); he treated this subject in more explicit detail in *Lady Chatterley's Lover* (privately printed, Florence, 1928). The novel was not published in Britain in its unexpurgated form until 1961, after a long trial.

Lawrence, Ernest Orlando (1901–58) US physicist, who in 1930 designed and built the first cyclotron, a type of particle accelerator. For his invention he received the Nobel Prize in 1939.

Lawrence, Gertrude (1898–1952) British actress. She performed in many revues and was especially successful in Noel Coward's *Private Lives* (1930) and *Tonight at 8.30* (1935–36).

T. E. LAWRENCE   *Drawing by Augustus John (1919).*

Lawrence, T(homas) E(dward) (1888–1935) British soldier and writer, known as Lawrence of Arabia. After the outbreak of World War I he worked for army intelligence in N Africa. In 1916 he joined the Arab revolt against the Turks, leading the Arab guerrillas triumphantly into Damascus in October, 1918. His exploits, which brought him almost legendary fame, were recounted in his book *The Seven Pillars of Wisdom* (subscription edition, 1926).

lawrencium (Lr) A synthetic transuranic element discovered in 1961 and named after E. O. Lawrence. At no 103; at wt (257).

Lawson, Nigel (1932–) British Conservative politician; chancellor of the exchequer (1983–89). He became an MP in 1974 and was secretary of state for energy (1981–83).

laxatives (*or* purgatives) Drugs used to treat constipation. Such laxatives as magnesium sulphate (Epsom salts) mix with the faeces and cause them to retain water, which increases their bulk and makes them easier to pass. Irritant laxatives, such as castor oil, senna, and cascara, stimulate the bowel directly. Another group, which includes bran, both lubricates the faeces and increases their bulk.

L-dopa (*or* levodopa) A drug used to treat parkinsonism, which is caused by a deficiency of dopamine (a chemical secreted at nerve endings when an impulse passes) in the brain. L-dopa is converted to this compound in the brain.

Leacock, Stephen (Butler) (1869–1944) English-born Canadian humorist. *Literary Lapses* (1910) and *Nonsense Novels* (1911) were the first of over 30 popular humorous books.

lead (Pb) A dense soft bluish-grey metal, occurring in nature chiefly as the sulphide galena (PbS). The metal is very resistant to corrosion and is used in plumbing (although it is now being replaced by plastics). It is also used to shield X-rays, as ammunition, in crystal glass (as lead oxide), and as an antiknock (as tetraethyl lead; $(C_2H_5)_4Pb$). Most lead salts are insoluble. At no 82; at wt 207.19; mp 327.50°C; bp 1740°C.

Leadbelly (Huddie Ledbetter; 1888–1949) US Black folksinger and songwriter.

leaf An outgrowth from the stem of a plant in which most of the green pigment chlorophyll, used for photosynthesis, is concentrated. Foliage leaves have a large surface area for absorbing light, and they contain pores (stomata) through which exchange of gases and water occurs. They may be simple or compound (composed of a number of leaflets) and with a branching vein system (in dicotyledons) or parallel veins (in monocotyledons). The spines of cacti and the thorns of gorse are modified leaves.

leaf beetle A beetle belonging to a large family (*Chrysomelidae*; 26 000 species) occurring in tropical and temperate regions. Leaf beetles are generally small and brightly coloured. Both the adults and larvae feed on leaves and flowers. Leaf beetles have a wide range of habits; many are serious pests, including the Colorado potato beetle.

leafcutter bee A solitary bee, about 10 mm long, belonging to a genus (*Megachile*) of the family *Megachilidae*. It nests in rotten wood and soil, lining the chamber and egg cells with pieces of leaf cut with its strong jaws.

leaf insect A plant-eating insect belonging to the family *Phyllidae*. It is excellently camouflaged against foliage, having a broad leaflike body and wings and leaflike flaps on the legs.

League of Nations An international organization created (1920) after World War I with the purpose of

achieving world peace. The USA's failure to ratify the Treaty of Versailles meant its exclusion from the League. The League failed to deal effectively with the aggression during the 1930s of Japan in China, Italy in Ethiopia (in which the League's use of sanctions was ineffectual), and Germany, which withdrew from the League in 1933. The UN superseded the League after World War II.

Leakey, Louis Seymour Bazett (1903–72) Kenyan palaeontologist. His work at Olduvai Gorge uncovered evidence for man's early evolution, notably the *Zinjanthropus* skull dating from 1.75 million years ago. In 1974 his wife **Mary Leakey** (1913–) unearthed hominid remains at Laetolil (N Tanzania) dating back 3.75 million years. Their son **Richard Leakey** (1944–) has made fossil finds around Lake Turkana (N Kenya) and is director of Kenya's wildlife department.

Lean, Sir David (1908–) British film director. His early films in collaboration with Noel Coward include *In Which we Serve* (1942), *Blithe Spirit* (1945), and *Brief Encounter* (1946). Adaptations of Charles Dickens' *Great Expectations* (1946) and *Oliver Twist* (1947) were followed by the classic *The Bridge on the River Kwai* (1957). Later films include *Lawrence of Arabia* (1962), *Dr Zhivago* (1965), and *A Passage to India* (1984).

Leander. *See* Hero and Leander.

leap year. *See* calendar.

Lear, Edward (1812–88) British artist and poet, noted for his four books of nonsense verse for children, beginning with *The Book of Nonsense* (1846). He also popularized a form of the limerick.

leaf arrangements on the stem

types of simple leaf

types of compound leaf

LEAF *The type and arrangement of the leaves are characteristic for a particular species of plant. For example, the pear has alternate ovate leaves; the horse chestnut has opposite palmate leaves.*

leasehold. *See* estate.

leather Specially treated animal skin, chiefly that of domesticated animals, such as cows, sheep, goats, and pigs. The skin is first stripped of the fleshy inner and hairy outer layers and then tanned by steeping it in tannin, a preservative, or using chromium salts. Various finishing processes include rubbing to bring out the grain, as in Morocco leather (goatskin); dyeing; oiling; lacquering for patent leather; and sueding to raise a nap. Leather is strong, versatile, flexible, waterproof, and permeable to air. Uses range from industrial parts and saddles to clothing and bookbindings.

leatherback turtle The largest living turtle, *Dermochelys coriacea*, found worldwide. Up to 2.1 m long with a weight of 540 kg, it has no horny external shell and its bones are buried in a ridged leathery brown-black skin. It is a strong swimmer and feeds on marine invertebrates, especially large jellyfish.

Lebanon A country in the Middle East, on the E coast of the Mediterranean Sea. It contains two mountain ranges extending N–S separated by the Beqaa Valley. The population is mixed, having Arab, Phoenician, Crusader, and Greek origins. Roughly half are Christian and half Muslim; political and official posts are rigorously divided between the two religions. Until the civil war of 1975–76, international trade, banking, and insurance were the major sources of income. *History*: Lebanon was an early convert to Christianity but in the 7th century broke away from the rest of the Church and was invaded by Muslims. Lebanon was held by the Mamelukes during the 14th and 15th centuries and by the Ottoman Turks from the early 16th century to 1918. France, having invaded Lebanon in 1861 to stop the massacres of Christians by Druses, was given the mandate over Greater Lebanon after World War I. Lebanon became independent in 1941, although France retained control until 1945. Lebanon did not fight in the 1967 and 1973 Arab-Israeli Wars, but Israel has made raids across the border to eliminate Palestinian guerrillas. In 1975, civil war broke out between Christians and Muslims, which after 19 months was brought to an end by a Syrian-backed Arab Deterrent Force but unrest continued, especially in the S. In 1982 Israel invaded S Lebanon, clashing with Syrian forces in the Beqaa Valley and, after besieging Beirut, forced the Palestine Liberation Organization to leave. Bashir Gemayel (1947–82), the president-elect, was killed in a bomb explosion and his brother, Amin Gemayel (1942–) succeeded him. Violence continued with the United Nations Interim Force in Lebanon (UNIFIL) suffering casualties (1983). Israel withdrew her forces in 1985 leaving UNIFIL to maintain peace between the Israeli-armed Christians, the Muslims, Druses, and Palestinian guerrillas. Since 1986 various groups have taken foreign hostages. In 1987 Syrian troops moved into Beirut but violence continued. Indecisive presidential elections in 1988 resulted in the establishment of rival Christian and Muslim governments. A new Muslim president, René Mouawad, was elected in 1989 but then assassinated. He was succeeded by Elias Hrawi (1925–). Militant Christian opposition continued under Gen Michel Aoun. Official language: Arabic. Official currency: Lebanese pound of 100 piastres. Area: 10 173 sq km (3927 sq mi). Population (1987): 2 762 000. Capital: Beirut.

Le Carré, John (David Cornwell; 1931–) British novelist. He served in the foreign service in Germany (1961–64). His novels *The Spy Who Came in from the Cold* (1963), *Tinker, Tailor, Soldier, Spy* (1974), *Smiley's People* (1980), *The Little Drummer Girl* (1983), and *A Perfect Spy* (1986) are realistic studies of the world of espionage.

Le Corbusier (Charles-Édouard Jeanneret; 1887–1965) French architect, born in Switzerland, whose buildings and writings have been extremely influential. Until World War II he pioneered a rational form of design, especially with his villas at Garches (1927) and Poissy (1929). Afterwards he became more individual, for example at his extraordinary chapel at Ronchamp (1950). He was also concerned with town planning (e.g. Chandigarh, 1950s) and large-scale housing projects (L'Unité, Marseilles, 1945).

Leda In Greek myth, the wife of Tyndareus, King of Sparta, and mother, either by her husband or by Zeus, of Clytemnestra, Helen, and Castor and Pollux. Helen was born from an egg after Zeus had visited Leda as a swan.

Lee, Robert E(dward) (1807–70) US Confederate commander in the Civil War. *See* Civil War, US.

leech A carnivorous aquatic annelid worm of the class *Hirudinea* (about 300 species). Leeches inhabit fresh and salt water throughout the world and also occur in wet soil and cloud forest. They have one sucker around the mouth and a second at the rear. Leeches can move by "looping," using their suckers. Most feed on the blood of animals and man, using piercing mouthparts.

Leeds 53 50N 1 35W A city in N England, the largest city in West Yorkshire on the River Aire. Its main industries are clothing, textiles, printing, engineering, chemicals, and leather goods. Population (1981): 448 528.

leek A hardy biennial plant, *Allium porrum*, native to SW Asia and E Mediterranean regions and widely grown in Europe as a vegetable. The bulb is hardly differentiated from the stem, which bears long broad leaves. The stems and leaves are eaten in the first year, before flowering. The leek is the emblem of Wales.

Leeuwenhoek, Antonie van (1632–1723) Dutch scientist, noted for his microscopic studies of living organisms. He was the first to describe protozoa, bacteria, and spermatozoa and he also made observations of yeasts, red blood cells, and blood capillaries. Leeuwenhoek also traced the life histories of various animals, including the flea, ant, and weevil.

Leeward Islands 1. A West Indian group of islands in the Lesser Antilles, in the Caribbean Sea extending SE from Puerto Rico to the Windward Islands. **2.** A former British colony in the West Indies (1871–1956), comprising Antigua, St Kitts-Nevis-Anguilla, Montserrat, and the British Virgin Islands. **3.** A group of islands in French Polynesia, in the Society Islands in the S Pacific Ocean.

legionnaires' disease An acute severe pneumonia, caused by the bacterium *Legionella pneumophila*, first described in 1976 after an outbreak among US legionnaires in Philadelphia. Over 30 people died in Stafford, England, as a result of an outbreak in 1985. The treatment is with the antibiotic erythromycin. The route of transmission is often air-conditioning systems.

Legion of Honour A French order of knighthood, established by Napoleon in 1802. It has five ranks, to which foreigners are admitted. Its grand master is the president of France.

Leguminosae A worldwide family of herbs, shrubs, and trees (about 7000 species), which includes many im-

LE CORBUSIER *The Assembly Building at Chandigarh.*

portant crop plants, such as peas, beans, clovers, and alfalfa. They all have compound leaves and the fruit is a pod containing a single row of seeds. Both pods and seeds are rich in protein. Most species possess root nodules that contain nitrogen-fixing bacteria and leguminous crops replenish nitrogen in the soil (*see* nitrogen cycle).

Lehár, Franz (Ferencz L.; 1870–1948) Hungarian composer, noted for the composition of operettas, of which *The Merry Widow* (1905) was his greatest success.

Le Havre 49 30N 0 06E A port in N France, in the Seine-Maritime department on the English Channel at the mouth of the River Seine. There is a transatlantic cargo service and a car-ferry service to England. Population (1982): 198 700.

Leibniz, Gottfried Wilhelm (1646–1716) German philosopher and mathematician. He put forward a coherent philosophy, which is summarized in his two philosophical books, *New Essays on the Human Understanding* (c. 1705) and *Theodicy* (1710), and numerous essays. Leibniz' best-known doctrine is that the universe consists of an infinite set of independent substances (monads) in each of which a life force is present. In creating the world, God took account of the wishes of monads and this led to a rational harmony in the "best of all possible worlds". His claim to have invented the calculus was disputed by Newton.

Leicester 52 38N 1 05W A city in central England, the administrative centre of Leicestershire. Lying on the Fosse Way, Leicester has many Roman remains. Parts of the Norman castle also remain. Population (1983 est): 282 300.

Leicester, Robert Dudley, Earl of (c. 1532–88) English courtier; the fifth son of the Duke of Northumberland. Elizabeth I made him Master of the Horse (1558) and then a privy councillor (1559). It was rumoured that he might marry the queen after the death of his wife Amy Robsart (c. 1532–60). His incompetent command (1585–87) of an English force in support of the Revolt of the Netherlands against Spain led to his recall but he retained Elizabeth's favour until his death.

Leicestershire A county in the East Midlands of England. The River Soar, flowing N, separates Charnwood Forest from the uplands of the E. Its fertile

soil makes it an important agricultural county. Hosiery is the staple industry. Area: 2553 sq km (986 sq mi). Population (1986 est): 875 000. Administrative centre: Leicester.

Leiden (English name: Leyden) 52 10N 4 30E A city in the W Netherlands, in South Holland province. Its university was founded in 1575. During the 17th and 18th centuries it was an artistic and educational centre. Population (1987): 106 808.

Leif Eriksson (11th century) Icelandic explorer; the son of Eric the Red (late 10th century). He was converted to Christianity and on his way to promote the faith in Greenland, missed his course and became the first European to reach America (perhaps Newfoundland or Nova Scotia). His story is told in Icelandic sagas.

Leigh, Vivien (Vivien Hartley; 1913–67) British actress. In the theatre, she played many leading Shakespearean roles, frequently appearing with Laurence Olivier, her husband from, 1937 to 1960. Her films include *Gone with the Wind* (1939) and *A Streetcar Named Desire* (1951).

Leinster A province in the SE Republic of Ireland. It consists of the counties of Carlow, Dublin, Kildare, Kilkenny, Laoighis, Longford, Louth, Meath, Offaly, Westmeath, Wexford, and Wicklow. It incorporates the ancient kingdoms of Meath and Leinster. Area: 19 632 sq km (7580 sq mi). Population (1986): 1 851 134.

Leipzig 51 20N 12 21E A city in S East Germany, near the confluence of the Rivers Elster, Pleisse, and Parthe. Leipzig is the country's second largest city and a major industrial and commercial centre. International trade fairs are held here and it is a musical centre. The university was founded in 1409. In 1989 it was the scene of mass demonstrations in favour of political reform. Population (1986): 552 133.

Leitrim A county in the NW Republic of Ireland, in Connacht bordering on Donegal Bay. Mainly hilly, descending to lowlands in the S, it contains several lakes, notably Lough Allen. Area: 1525 sq km (589 sq mi). Population (1986): 27 000. County town: Carrick-on-Shannon.

Leix. *See* Laoighis.

Lely, Sir Peter (Pieter van der Faes; 1618–80) Portrait painter, born in Germany of Dutch parents. He settled in London (1641), where he was patronized by Charles I and later Cromwell. As court painter to Charles II from 1661, he produced his best-known works, including his *Windsor Beauties*.

LENIN   *With Stalin (right) in 1922.*

Le Mans   48 00N 0 12E A city in NW France, the capital of the Sarthe department. Its many historical buildings include the cathedral (11th–15th centuries). The Le Mans Grand Prix, a 24-hour motor race, is held here annually. Population (1982): 150 331.

lemming   A rodent belonging to the subfamily *Microtini* (which also includes voles), found in northern regions of Asia, America, and Europe. They are 7.5–15 cm long and have long thick fur. When their food of grass, berries, and roots is abundant, they breed at a great rate. When food is scarce they migrate southwards, often in large swarms crossing swamps, rivers, and other obstacles; they sometimes drown through exhaustion. Chief genera: *Dicrostonyx* (collared lemmings; 4 species), *Lemmus* (true lemmings; 4 species). Family *Cricetidae*.

lemon   A small tree or shrub, *Citrus limon*, probably native to the E Mediterranean but widely cultivated in subtropical climates for its fruit. Its fragrant white flowers produce oval fruits with thick yellow skin and acid-tasting pulp rich in vitamin C. The juice is used in cookery and as a drink. Family: *Rutaceae*.

lemon sole   A flatfish, *Microstomus kitt*, found in the NE Atlantic and North Sea. Its upper side is red-brown or yellow-brown with light or dark marbling. It is an important food fish. Family: *Pleuronectidae*.

lemur   A small prosimian primate belonging to the family *Lemuridae* (16 species), found only in Madagascar and neighbouring islands. Lemurs are mostly arboreal and nocturnal and often live in groups. The ring-tailed lemur (*Lemur catta*) is 70–95 cm long including the tail (40–50 cm) and is mainly terrestrial. Dwarf lemurs (subfamily *Cheirogaleinae*) are only 25–50 cm long including the tail (12–25 cm).

Lena, River   The longest river in the Soviet Union. Rising in S Siberia, W of Lake Baikal, it flows mainly NE to the Laptev Sea. Its large delta is frozen for about nine months of the year. Length: 4271 km (2653 mi).

Lendl, Ivan   (1960–   ) Czech tennis player. He has won all the major Open championships except Wimbledon, being beaten in the final in 1986 and 1987.

Lenin, Vladimir Ilich   (V. I. Ulyanov; 1870–1924) Russian revolutionary and first leader of communist Russia. In 1893 Lenin, a Marxist, joined a revolutionary group in St Petersburg (subsequently renamed Leningrad), where he practised as a lawyer. In 1895 he was imprisoned and in 1897 exiled to Siberia, where he married (1898) Nadezhda Krupskaya, a fellow Marxist. In 1902 he published *What Is to Be Done?*, in which he emphasized the role of the party in effecting revolution. This emphasis led to a split in the Russian Social Democratic Workers' Party between the Bolsheviks under Lenin and the Mensheviks. After the failure of the Revolution of 1905, Lenin again went into exile, settling in Zurich in 1914, where he wrote *Imperialism, the Highest Stage of Capitalism* (1917). In April, 1917, after the outbreak of the Russian Revolution, Lenin returned to Russia. Calling for the transfer of power from the Provisional Government to the soviets (workers' councils), he was forced to flee to Finland. Lenin returned in October to lead the Bolshevik revolution, which overthrew the Provisional Government and established the ruling Soviet of People's Commissars under Lenin's chairmanship. He made peace with Germany and then led the revolutionaries to victory against the Whites in the civil war (1918–20). He founded (1919) the Third International and initiated far-reaching social reforms. He also introduced the New Economic Policy (1921), which permitted a modicum of free enterprise. A series of strokes from 1922 led to his premature death.

Leningrad   (name from 1703 until 1914: St Petersburg; name from 1914 until 1924: Petrograd)   59 55N 30 25E The second largest city in the Soviet Union and the capital of the Leningrad autonomous region (*oblast*), at the head of the Gulf of Finland on the River Neva. It is a major industrial and commercial centre and its port, although frozen between January and April, is one of the largest in the world. The most notable buildings include the Peter-Paul Fortress, the Winter Palace, and the Gostiny Dvor. *History*: the city was founded (1703) by Peter the Great and was the capital of Russia from 1712 until 1918, replacing Archangel as Russia's main seaport. In the late 19th century it developed as an important industrial centre. In 1905 a general strike took place and on Bloody Sunday (9 January, 1905) more than a thousand people were killed in a march on the Winter Palace. Leningrad was also prominent in the 1917 revolution (*see* Russian Revolution). During World War II the city withstood a siege by the Germans (8 September, 1941–27 January, 1944), in which nearly a million people perished. Population (1987): 4 948 000.

Leninism   Developments in the theory of scientific socialism (*see* Marxism) by V. I. Lenin. His theory of imperialism is an account of the final stage of capitalism, in which it dominates the entire world, decisive control resting with finance capital (banks) as opposed to industrial capital. Because of the worldwide nature of capitalism, socialist revolution becomes possible even in economically underdeveloped countries, the "weak link" of imperialism. According to his theory of the revolutionary party, the most conscious element of the proletariat provides the leadership for the rest of the working class and the peasantry in organizing the overthrow of the capitalist class.

Lenin Peak   39 21N 73 01E The second highest mountain in the Soviet Union, in the Trans-Altai range. Height: 7134 m (23 406 ft).

lens A piece of transparent material, usually glass, quartz, or plastic, used for directing and focusing beams of light. The surfaces of a lens have a constant curvature; if both sides curve outwards at the middle the lens is called convex, if they curve inwards it is concave. The image formed by a lens may be real, in which case the rays converge to the image point (a converging lens), or virtual, in which the rays diverge from the image point (a diverging lens). The focal length of a lens is the distance from the lens at which a parallel beam of light is brought to a focus.

Lent The Christian period of fasting and penance preceding Easter. Beginning on Ash Wednesday, the Lenten fast covers 40 days, in emulation of Christ's 40 days in the wilderness (Matthew 4.2). Since the Reformation the rules of fasting have been generally relaxed in both Roman Catholic and Protestant Churches.

lentil An annual herb, *Lens culinaris*, native to the Near East but widely cultivated. Each pod produces 1–2 flat round green or reddish seeds, which are rich in protein and can be dried and stored for use in soups, stews, etc. Family: *Leguminosae*.

Lenz's law The direction of an induced current in a conductor is such as to oppose the cause of the induction. For example, a current induced by a conductor cutting the lines of flux of a magnetic field would produce a magnetic field of its own, which would oppose the original magnetic field. Named after Heinrich Lenz (1804–65).

LEONARDO DA VINCI *The* Mona Lisa *(detail).*

Leonardo da Vinci (1452–1519) Italian artistic and scientific genius of the Renaissance. He trained in Florence under Verrocchio and painted the *Adoration of the Magi* (1481). In 1482 he became painter, engineer, and

designer to Duke Ludovico Sforza in Milan, where he painted the fresco of the *Last Supper* and the first version of the *Virgin of the Rocks*. His promised equestrian sculpture glorifying the Duke was never cast but the studies of horses for the project have survived. After the French invasion of Milan (1499), he returned to Florence, becoming military engineer and architect (1502) to Cesare Borgia. Paintings in this period include the *Battle of Anghiari*, *The Virgin and Child with St John the Baptist and St Anne*, and the *Mona Lisa*. Some of his paintings were left unfinished and others, because of his experimental techniques, failed to survive. After working again in Milan (1506–13) and in Rome (1513–15), he was invited by Francis I to France (1516), where he died. His notebooks reveal his wide range of interests, including anatomy, botany, geology, hydraulics, and mechanics.

Leoncavallo, Ruggiero (1858–1919) Italian composer of operas. Only *I Pagliacci* (1892) has met with continuing success, although he composed over 15, including a trilogy on Italian historical subjects and, a year after Puccini, his own *La Bohème* (1897).

leopard A large spotted cat, *Panthera pardus*, found throughout Africa and most of Asia. Leopards are slender, up to 2.1 m long including the 90-cm tail, having a yellow coat spotted with black rosettes. Colour variations, such as the panther, sometimes occur. Leopards are solitary and nocturnal.

leopard lily A perennial herbaceous plant, *Belamcanda chinensis*, native to E Asia and widely planted as a garden ornamental. Growing over 1 m tall from an underground stem (rhizome), it has sword-shaped leaves, orange-spotted red flowers, and blackberry-like clusters of seeds. Family: *Iridaceae*.
The name is also given to several other garden flowers, including the snake's head fritillary.

leopard seal A solitary Antarctic seal, *Hydrurga leptonyx*, of the pack ice. Leopard seals are fast agile hunters, feeding mainly on penguins. Grey, with dark spots and blotches, females grow to 3.7 m and males to 3.2 m. Family: *Phocidae*.

Leopold I (1790–1865) The first King of the Belgians (1831–65). He defended Belgium against William III of the Netherlands, who refused to recognize Belgian independence until 1838. A leading diplomat in Europe, at home he encouraged educational and economic reforms. He was briefly (1816–17) married to Charlotte (1796–1817), the daughter of George IV of Great Britain.

Leopold III (1901–83) King of the Belgians (1934–51). He surrendered to the Germans in World War II, provoking opposition to his return to Belgium in 1945 and forcing his abdication in favour of his son Baudouin.

Léopoldville. *See* Kinshasa.

Lepanto, Battle of (7 October, 1571) A naval battle off Lepanto, Greece, in which the Holy League routed the Ottoman navy, which was threatening to dominate the Mediterranean. The Christian force was commanded by John of Austria (1545–78). About 10 000 Christian galley slaves were freed.

Lepidoptera. *See* butterflies and moths.

leprosy A chronic disease, occurring almost entirely in tropical countries, caused by the bacterium *Mycobacterium leprae* (which is related to the tuberculosis bacillus). Leprosy is contracted only after close personal contact with an infected person. In the lepromatous form of

LEPROSY *Mother Teresa in her leprosy hospital in Calcutta.*

the disease lumps appear on the skin, which—together with the nerves—becomes thickened and progressively destroyed, resulting in deformity. Tuberculoid leprosy usually produces only discoloured patches on the skin associated with loss of sensation in the affected areas. There are now potent drugs—sulphones—available to cure the disease.

lepton A group of elementary particles, consisting of the electron, muon, tau particle, neutrinos, and their antiparticles. They take part only in the weak and electromagnetic interactions; together with quarks and photons they are thought to be the only truly elementary particles. *See* particle physics.

Lermontov, Mikhail (1814–41) Russian poet and novelist. His early Romantic poetry was greatly influenced by Byron. As an army officer and an observer of high society he developed the cynical attitudes expressed in his novel *A Hero of Our Time* (1840).

Lerner, Alan Jay (1918–86) US lyricist and librettist, who collaborated with the composer Frederick Loewe in the musicals *Brigadoon* (1947), *My Fair Lady* (1956), and *Camelot* (1960). Lerner also wrote the film scripts for *An American in Paris* (1951) and *Gigi* (1958).

lesbianism. *See* homosexuality.

Lesbos A Greek island in the E Aegean Sea, situated close to the mainland of Turkey. Settled about 1000 BC, it is associated with the development of Greek lyric poetry (especially through the work of Alcaeus and Sappho). Lesbos was a member of the Delian League. Area: 1630 sq km (629 sq mi). Population (1981): 104 620. Chief town: Mytilene.

Lesotho, Kingdom of (name until 1966: Basutoland) A small mountainous country in SE Africa, enclosed by South Africa. Most of the inhabitants are Sotho. *History*: in 1868, following warfare with the Orange Free State, Basutoland came under British protection and came under direct British administration in 1884. In 1910 it was placed under the authority of the British High Commission in South Africa and in 1966 became an independent kingdom within the Commonwealth under King Moshoeshoe II (1939–), who remained head of state following a military coup in 1986. Official languages: Sesotho and English. Official currency:

Loti of 100 lisente. Area: 30 340 sq km (11 716 sq mi). Population (1987 est): 1 626 500. Capital: Maseru.

Lesseps, Ferdinand de (1805–94) French diplomat, who supervised the construction of the Suez Canal, which was completed in 1869. A subsequent project to construct the Panama Canal ended in disaster when Lesseps was prosecuted for embezzling funds.

Lesser Antilles (former name: Caribbees) A West Indian group of islands, comprising a chain extending from Puerto Rico to the N coast of Venezuela. They include the Leeward and Windward Islands, Barbados, Trinidad and Tobago, and the Netherlands Antilles.

Lessing, Doris (1919–) British novelist. Born in Iran and brought up in Rhodesia, she came to England in 1949. Political and social themes predominate in her fiction, notably the sequence of five novels entitled *Children of Violence* (1952–69) and *The Golden Notebook* (1962). Later novels include *Memoirs of a Survivor* (1974), *The Good Terrorist* (1985), and *The Fifth Child* (1988).

Leto In Greek mythology, a daughter of the Titans loved by Zeus. She gave birth to Apollo and Artemis.

Lettish. *See* Latvian.

lettuce An annual herb, *Lactuca sativa*, probably from the Near East and widely cultivated as a salad plant. It has a tight rosette of juicy leaves, rich in vitamin A, and is usually eaten fresh. Cos lettuce has long crisp leaves and oval heads while cabbage lettuce has round or flattened heads and often curly leaves. Family: *Compositae*.

leucocyte (*or* white blood cell) A colourless blood cell, up to 0.02 mm in diameter, of which there are normally 4000–11 000 per cubic millimetre of blood. There are several kinds, all involved in the body's defence mechanisms. Granulocytes and monocytes ingest and feed on bacteria and other microorganisms that cause infection (*see also* phagocyte). The lymphocytes are involved with the production of antibodies.

leucotomy The surgical operation of interrupting the course of white nerve fibres within the brain. It is performed to relieve uncontrollable pain or emotional tension in very severe and intractable psychiatric illnesses, such as severe depression. The original form of the operation—prefrontal leucotomy (*or* lobotomy)—had serious complications. Modern procedures make selective lesions and side effects are uncommon.

leukaemia A disease in which the blood contains an abnormally large number of white blood cells (*see* leucocyte) that do not function properly. Leukaemia is a type of cancer of the blood-forming tissues. Leukaemias may be acute or chronic, depending on the rate of progression of the disease. They are also classified according to the type of white cell affected. For example acute lymphocytic leukaemia (affecting the lymphocytes) occurs most commonly in children and young adults; it can now often be controlled by means of radiotherapy or cytotoxic drugs. Chronic leukaemias occur more often in old people and may not need any treatment.

Levellers An extremist English Puritan sect, active 1647–49. Led by the pamphleteer John Lilburne (c.1614–57), they campaigned for a written constitution, radical extension of the franchise, and abolition of the monarchy and of other social distinctions (hence their name).

Leven, Loch A lake in Scotland, in SE Tayside Region. It has seven islands, on one of which Mary, Queen of Scots, was imprisoned (1567–68). Length: 6 km (3.7 mi). Width: 4 km (2.5 mi).

Lévi-Strauss, Claude (1908–) French anthropologist, the founder of structural anthropology. His works include *The Elementary Structures of Kinship* (1949), *Structural Anthropology* (1958), and *From Honey to Ashes* (1967).

Lewes 50 52N 0 01E A market town in SE England, the administrative centre of East Sussex, on the River Ouse. At the battle of Lewes (1264) Henry III was defeated by the rebel barons under Simon de Montfort. Glyndebourne is nearby. Population (1981): 77 507.

Lewis, C. Day. *See* Day Lewis, C(ecil).

Lewis, C(live) S(taples) (1898–1963) British scholar and writer. He wrote science-fiction including *Out of the Silent Planet* (1938), children's books chronicling the land of Narnia, and works on religious themes, notably *The Problem of Pain* (1940), *The Screwtape Letters* (1942) and *Mere Christianity* (1952).

Lewis, (Harry) Sinclair (1885–1951) US novelist noted for his social satires, which include *Main Street* (1920), *Babbitt* (1922), *Arrowsmith* (1925), and *Elmer Gantry* (1927). He won the 1930 Nobel Prize.

WYNDHAM LEWIS *From an ink and wash self-portrait executed in 1932.*

Lewis, (Percy) Wyndham (1882–1957) British novelist and painter. In many polemical works and brilliant satirical novels, which include *The Apes of God* (1930) and the trilogy *The Human Age* (1928–55), he sustained a continual attack on the liberal cultural establishment. He helped found the art movement vorticism.

Lewis and Clark expedition (1804–06) A journey of exploration across the American continent by Meriwether Lewis (1774–1809) and William Clark (1770–1838). They ascended the Missouri, crossed the Rockies,

and went down the Columbia River to the Pacific, exploring the Yellowstone River on the return journey. Promoted by Thomas Jefferson, the expedition established the US claim to the Louisiana Purchase.

Lewis with Harris The largest island of the Outer Hebrides, separated from the coast of NW Scotland by the Minch. Lewis in the N is linked with Harris by a narrow isthmus. It is famous for its Harris tweed. Area: 2134 sq km (824 sq mi). Population (1981): 23 390. Chief town: Stornoway.

lexicography The compilation of dictionaries. Dictionaries can be monolingual (dealing with only one language) or bi- or multi-lingual (giving equivalents of words in other languages). Monolingual dictionaries differ in the style and fullness of the definitions and in the audience for which they are intended (e.g. for native speakers or foreign learners). Some list definitions of a word in historical order while others list definitions in order of current usage. Almost all dictionaries contain information about spelling and meaning; many also offer guidance on pronunciation, usage, inflected forms of words, etymology, etc. The most famous English dictionaries are Samuel Johnson's *Dictionary* (1755) and the *Oxford English Dictionary on Historical Principles* (1884–1928; chief editor Sir James Murray). The best-known American dictionary is Noah Webster's *American Dictionary of the English Language* (1828).

Leyden. *See* Leiden.

Lhasa 29 41N 91 10E A city in W China, the capital of Tibet. As the traditional centre of Tibetan Buddhism, it is the site of many temples, monasteries, and of the Potala, the former palace of the Dalai Lama, the priest-ruler. Since the Chinese occupation (1951) many Tibetans have fled, including the Dalai Lama following the 1959 uprising, while much Chinese immigration has taken place. Population (1982 est): 110 000.

libel. *See* defamation.

Liberal Democrats. *See* Social and Liberal Democratic Party.

Liberal Party (Australia) A conservative political party, formed in 1944. A Liberal-Country Party (*see* National Country Party) coalition won the election of 1949 and under the leadership successively of Robert Menzies, Harold Holt (1908–67), John Gorton (1911–), and William McMahon held office until 1972. Under Malcolm Fraser the Liberals again held power from 1975 to 1983.

Liberal Party (UK) A political party that grew out of the Whig party. The heyday of the party was from the mid-19th century to World War I, under the prime ministers Gladstone, Campbell-Bannerman, Asquith, and Lloyd George. Conflict between Asquith and Lloyd George led to a split in the party after World War I, and in 1922 the Labour Party replaced the Liberals as the official opposition. The party forged a political alliance with the newly-formed Social Democratic Party in 1981 and merged with it to become the Social and Liberal Democratic Party in 1988.

Liberia, Republic of A country in West Africa, on the Atlantic Ocean. Coastal plains rise to higher ground inland and to mountains in the N; much of the land is covered with tropical rainforest. Most of the population belongs to indigenous tribes, including the Kpelle, Bassa, and Kru, with a minority who are descended from American slaves. *Economy*: agriculture is extensive, the main food crops being rice and cassava. The main cash crop is rubber, some of it grown under concession to US companies. Foreign investment in other areas includes the exploitation of Liberia's rich mineral resources, which form the basis of the country's economy, especially high-grade iron ore and diamonds. Ships are easily registered in Liberia and, with many foreign vessels, its merchant fleet is the largest in the world. *History*: it was founded in 1822 by the American Colonization Society as a settlement for freed American slaves. In 1847 it became the Free and Independent Republic of Liberia with a constitution based on that of the USA. It has had considerable US aid, and from the 1920s the Firestone Company, developing rubber resources, played an important part in the economy, as have many other foreign companies. Liberia also has close economic ties with Sierra Leone. In 1980 the president Dr William R. Tolbert, Jr (1913–80), was assassinated in a military coup led by Master Sergeant Samuel Doe, who was elected president in 1985. Official language: English. Official currency: Liberian dollar of 100 cents. Area: 111 400 sq km (43 000 sq mi). Population (1987 est): 2 500 000. Capital and main port: Monrovia.

Library of Congress The national library of the USA founded in 1800. First housed in the Capitol, it was moved to its present site in Washington in 1897. It contains over 60 million items, and its system of classification is widely used in academic libraries.

libretto (Italian: little book) The text of an opera or operetta. Dramatists whose plays have been used as libretti include von Hofmannsthal (1874–1929), Maeterlinck, and Oscar Wilde. Wagner and Berlioz wrote their own libretti. Notable partnerships between librettists and composers include da Ponte (1749–1838) and Mozart, Boito and Verdi, and Gilbert and Sullivan.

Libreville 0 25N 9 25E The capital of Gabon, a port in the NW on the Gabon Estuary. It was founded by the French in the 19th century, when freed slaves were sent there. Population (1985 est): 350 000.

Librium. *See* benzodiazepines.

Libya (official name: Great Socialist People's Libyan Arab Jamahiriya) A country in N Africa, on the Mediterranean Sea. It consists chiefly of desert, with a narrow coastal plain, rising to the Tibesti Mountains along its southern border and is divided into the three main areas (provinces until 1963) of Cyrenaica, Tripolitania, and Fezzan. The population is mainly of Berber and Arabic origin. *Economy*: between 1955 and 1970 major deposits of oil were discovered, notably at Zelten (1959). Libya is now one of the world's major oil producers and exporters. Subsistence agriculture is important, livestock farming being the main agricultural occupation, nomadic in the S. *History*: during the 16th century the area came under Turkish domination and in 1912 was annexed by Italy. It was the scene of heavy fighting in World War II; the French occupied Fezzan and the British occupied Cyrenaica and Tripolitania. In 1951 the United Kingdom of Libya was formed from the federation of these three areas and the Emir of Cyrenaica, Mohammed Idris Al-Senussi (1889–1983), became its first king. He was deposed in a coup led by Col Moammar al-Gaddafi in 1969 and Libya was proclaimed a republic. The Revolutionary Command Council was established to rule the country. In 1973 Gaddafi introduced a cultural revolution based on Islamic principles. Since 1969 Libya has been firmly aligned against Israel and has been accused of using terrorist methods abroad. In 1986 Libyan ter-

rorist activity precipitated raids on Libyan cities by US jets. Official language: Arabic; English and Italian are also spoken. Official currency: Libyan dinar of 1000 millemes. Area: 1 759 540 sq km (679 216 sq mi). Population (1987 est): 3 883 000. Capital: Tripoli.

lichee. *See* litchi.

lichens A large group of plants (*Lichenes*; about 15 000 species) consisting of two components, an alga and a fungus, in a mutually beneficial association. Millions of algal cells (the phycobiont) are interwoven with fungal filaments (the mycobiont) to form the lichen body (a thallus), which may be crusty, scaly, leafy, or stalked and shrublike in appearance. Lichens occur in almost all areas of the world, mainly on tree trunks, rocks, and soil, and can survive in extremely harsh conditions. They normally reproduce asexually by fragmentation, budding, or by producing special structures (soredia), consisting of a few algal cells enmeshed with fungal threads.

Liechtenstein, Principality of A small country in central Europe, between Switzerland and Austria. Mountains rise from the Rhine Valley to heights of over 2500 m (8000 ft). *Economy*: farming, and, since World War II, light industry. Tourism and the sale of postage stamps are also important. *History:* the principality was formed from the union of the counties of Vaduz and Schellenberg in 1719 and was part of the Holy Roman Empire until 1806. It formed a customs union with Switzerland in 1923. Head of state: Prince Hans Adam (1945–). Head of government: Hans Brunhart. Official language: German. Official religion: Roman Catholic. Official currency: Swiss franc of 100 centimes (*or* Rappen). Area: 160 sq km (62 sq mi). Population (1986): 28 000. Capital: Vaduz.

LIFEBOAT *The RNLI Fraserburgh lifeboat* City of Edinburgh.

lie detector An instrument designed to detect whether a person is lying by measuring such factors as blood pressure, respiration rate, skin conductivity, and pulse rate. A sudden change in these factors in a person being questioned is taken to indicate that he is under stress and may be telling a lie. Lie detectors are not usually accepted in a court of law.

Liège (Flemish name: Luik) 50 38N 5 35E An industrial city in E Belgium, on the River Meuse. It has many old churches, including St Martin's (692 AD). Population (1987 est): 200 891.

life The property that enables a living organism to assimilate nonliving materials from its environment and use them to increase its size and complexity (the process of growth), to repair its existing tissues, and to produce new independent organisms that also possess the properties of life (the process of reproduction). *See also* animal; plant.

Life on earth is thought to have originated between 4500 and 3000 million years ago. The atmosphere then consisted chiefly of methane, hydrogen, ammonia, and water vapour, from which simple organic molecules (such as amino acids, proteins, and fatty acids) were formed as a result of energy supplied by solar radiation, lightning, and volcanic activity. The first cells may have arisen spontaneously as simple envelopes of protein and fat molecules. However, the crucial steps towards life would probably have been the inclusion in such a cell of both the enzyme molecules necessary to perform primitive fermentations and the nucleic acid molecules, such as RNA and DNA, capable of directing the metabolic processes of the cell and of self replication, i.e. passing on this information to succeeding generations. In the course of time increasingly efficient biochemical pathways evolved, including the process of photosynthesis in the first simple green plants. This led to the gradual build-up of oxygen in the atmosphere, which started about 2000 million years ago; by about 400 million years ago the ozone layer in the upper atmosphere was sufficiently dense to shield the land from harmful ultraviolet radiation, enabling plants and animals to survive. With increasing oxygen levels, aerobic respiration—the most efficient method of energy utilization—was adopted by most living organisms.

lifeboat **1.** In the UK, a powerful motorboat, especially designed to right itself in the event of capsize and equipped with safety devices, used by the Royal National Lifeboat Institution (RNLI) as an emergency vessel in the event of a disaster near the shore. **2.** A boat carried aboard a ship, used for accommodating passengers and crew if the ship has to be abandoned.

Liffey, River A river in the E Republic of Ireland, rising in the Wicklow Mountains and flowing mainly W and NE through Dublin to Dublin Bay. Length: 80 km (50 mi).

ligament A strong fibrous tissue that joins one bone to another at a joint. Ligaments are flexible but inelastic: they increase the stability of the joint and limit its movements to certain directions. Unusual stresses on a joint often damage ("pull") a ligament, as occurs in a "twisted" ankle.

light The form of electromagnetic radiation to which the eye is sensitive. It forms the part of the electromagnetic spectrum from 740 nanometres (red light) to 400 nanometres (blue light), white light consisting of a mixture of all the colours of the visible spectrum. Newton supported a corpuscular theory of light in which a luminous body was believed to emit particles of light. This theory adequately explained reflection and geometric optics but failed to explain interference and polarized light. The wave theory, supported in the 19th century by Augustin Fresnel (1788–1827) and Jean Foucault (1819–68), adequately explains these phenomena and achieved a mathematical basis when Maxwell showed that light is a form of electromagnetic radiation. The wave theory, however, does not explain the photoelectric effect and Einstein reverted to a form of the corpuscular theory in using the quantum theory to postulate that in some cases light is best regarded as consisting of energy quanta called photons. The present view, expressing Bohr's concept of complementarity, is that both electromagnetic theory and quantum theory are needed to explain light. *See also* velocity of light.

light-emitting diode. *See* semiconductor diode.

lighthouse A tall structure, built on a coastal promontory or cape or on an island at sea, equipped with a powerful beacon, visible at some distance, to mark an obstruction or other hazard. Modern lighthouses are also equipped with radio beacons. Both light and radio signals are emitted in a unique pattern to enable vessels to identify the lighthouse producing them.

LIGHTNING   *Cloud to ground forked lightning.*

lightning An electrical discharge in the atmosphere caused by the build up of electrical charges in a cloud. The potential difference causing the discharge may be as high as one thousand million volts. The electricity then discharges itself in a lightning flash, which may be between the cloud and the ground or, much more commonly, between two clouds or parts of a cloud. Thunder is the noise made by the discharge or its reverberations. *See also* ball lightning.

lightning conductor An earthed conducting rod placed at the top of buildings, etc., to protect them from damage by lightning. It acts by providing a low-resistance path to earth for the lightning current.

light year A unit of distance, used in astronomy, equal to the distance travelled by light in one year. 1 light year = 9.46×10^{15} metres or 5.88×10^{12} miles.

lignin A complex chemical deposited in plant cell walls to add extra strength and support. It is the main constituent of wood cells, allowing the trunk to support the heavy crown of leaves and branches.

lignum vitae Wood from trees of the genus *Guaiacum*, especially *G. officinale*, a tropical evergreen of the New World. Lignum vitae is hard, dense, greenish-brown, and rich in fat (making it waterproof). It was formerly thought to have medicinal properties: its name (from the Latin) means "wood of life." Family: *Zygophyllaceae.*

Liguria A region in NW Italy. It consists of a narrow strip of land between the Apennines and Maritime Alps in the N and the Gulf of Genoa in the S. Industry and tourism are both important, the region more or less corresponding to the Italian Riviera. Area: 5415 sq km (2091 sq mi). Population (1986 est): 1 758 961. Capital: Genoa.

Ligurian Sea A section of the NW Mediterranean Sea, between Italy (N of Elba) and Corsica.

lilac A deciduous bush or small tree of the genus *Syringa* (30 species), especially *S. vulgaris*, native to temperate Eurasia and often grown as a garden ornamental. It has dense terminal clusters of white, purple, or pink tubular fragrant flowers with four flaring lobes. Family: *Oleaceae.*

Liliaceae A family of monocotyledonous plants (about 250 species), mostly herbaceous and native to temperate and subtropical regions. They usually grow from bulbs or rhizomes to produce six-lobed flowers and three-chambered capsular fruits. The family includes many popular garden plants, including the lilies, tulip, and hyacinth. A few are economically important, for example *Asparagus.* Some authorities include related plants, such as the onion, leek, etc., (*see* Allium), *Agave*, and *Yucca.*

Lille 50 39N 3 05E A city in N France, the capital of the Nord department on the River Deûle. It is at the centre of a large industrial complex. Population (1983): 189 500.

Lillee, Dennis Keith (1949–) Australian cricketer. A fast bowler, he took 355 Test wickets. He retired in 1984.

Lillie, Beatrice (Constance Sylvia Munston, Lady Peel; 1898–1989) British actress, born in Canada, best known for her performances in revues and cabaret.

Lilongwe 13 58S 33 49E The capital of Malawi since 1975. Population (1985 est): 186 800.

lily A perennial herbaceous plant of the genus *Lilium* (80–100 species), native to N temperate regions and widely grown for ornament. Lilies grow from bulbs to produce leafy stems with terminal clusters of showy flowers, usually with backward-curving petals. Some popular species are the tiger lily (*L. tigrinum*), from China and Japan, 60–120 cm high with purple-spotted golden flowers; the Eurasian Madonna lily (*L. candida*), 60–120 cm high with pure-white flowers; and the turk's-cap or martagon lily (*L. martagon*), also from Eurasia, 90–150 cm high, the purplish-pink flowers of which are marked with darker spots. There are numerous varieties and hybrids of these and other species. Family: *Liliaceae.*
The name is also applied to numerous other unrelated plants, such as the arum lily, day lily, and leopard lily.

lily-of-the-valley A fragrant perennial herbaceous plant, *Convallaria majalis*, native to Eurasia and E North America and a popular garden plant. Growing from creeping underground stems (rhizomes), its stem bears a cluster of white bell-shaped flowers. Family: *Liliaceae.*

Lima 12 06S 77 03W The capital of Peru, situated in the E of the country near its Pacific port of Callao. Founded by Pizarro in 1535, it became the main base of Spanish power in Peru. Notable buildings include the 16th-century cathedral and university. Lima has expanded rapidly in recent years and now has considerable industry. Population (1983): 5 258 600.

lima bean A herb, *Phaseolus lunatus*, also called butter bean or Madagascar bean, native to South America but widely cultivated in the tropics and subtropics as a source of protein. It is easily stored when dry. Family: *Leguminosae.*

Limassol 34 40N 33 03E A town in Cyprus, on the S coast. It is the island's second largest town and a major port. Population (1986 est): 113 600.

Limburg 1. A former duchy in W Europe, divided in 1839 between Belgium and the Netherlands. 2. (French name: Limbourg) A province in NE Belgium, bordering on the Netherlands. The N is an industrial region with rich coalfields. The S is chiefly agricultural. Area: 2422 sq km (935 sq mi). Population (1986 est): 734 382. Capital: Hasselt. 3. A province in the SE Netherlands. Coalmining has declined in recent years. Agriculture is varied. Area: 2208 sq km (852 sq mi). Population (1987 est): 1 091 553. Capital: Maastricht.

lime (botany) 1. A large deciduous tree of the genus *Tilia* (about 30 species), also called linden. Growing to a height of 30 m, it has toothed heart-shaped leaves and fragrant pale-yellow flowers that hang in small clusters on a long winged stalk. The small round fruits remain attached to the papery wing when shed. Family: *Tiliaceae.* 2. A tree, *Citrus aurantifolia*, growing to a height of about 4 m and cultivated in the tropics for its fruit. Lime fruits have a thick greenish-yellow skin and acid-tasting pulp; the juice is used to flavour food and drinks.

lime (chemistry) Calcium oxide (*or* quicklime; CaO), calcium hydroxide (*or* slaked lime; Ca(OH)$_2$), or, loosely, calcium salts in general. Ca(OH)$_2$ is prepared by reacting CaO with water and is used in cement. CaO is used in making paper, as a flux in steel manufacture, and in softening water.

limerick A short form of comic and usually bawdy verse having five lines of three or two feet and usually rhyming aabba, as in:
There was a young lady of Lynn
Who was so uncommonly thin
That when she essayed
To drink lemonade,
She slipped through the straw and fell in.
The form, the origin of which is uncertain, was popularized by Edward Lear in the 19th century.

Limerick 52 40N 8 38W A port in the Republic of Ireland, the county town of Co Limerick on the Shannon estuary. Population (1981): 75 520.

Limerick A county in the SW Republic of Ireland, in Munster bordering on the River Shannon estuary. It consists chiefly of lowlands rising to hills in the S. Dairy farming is important. Area: 2686 sq km (1037 sq mi). Population (1986): 164 204. County town: Limerick.

limestone A common sedimentary rock consisting largely of carbonates, especially calcium carbonate (calcite) or dolomite. Most limestones were deposited in the sea in warm clear water, but some limestones were formed in fresh water. Organic limestones, including chalk, consist of fossil skeletal material. Precipitated limestones include evaporites and oolites (spherically grained calcite). Clastic limestones consist of fragments of pre-existing limestones. Marble is metamorphosed limestone. Limestone is used as a building stone, in the manufacture of cement and glass, for agricultural lime, for road metal, and as a flux in smelting.

limitation, statutes of The Acts of Parliament that specify a time (period of limitation) within which legal proceedings must be started by any person seeking to enforce a right; failing this, the right of action is barred.

limited liability The restriction of a shareholder's obligation to meet company debts in the event of its insolvency. The Companies Act allows the formation of corporations the liability of whose shareholders is restricted either to the nominal amount of their shares ("company limited by shares") or to the amount that they have respectively undertaken to contribute if the company is wound up ("company limited by guarantee").

Limoges 45 50N 1 15E A city in W France, the capital of the Haute-Vienne department on the River Vienne. The centre of the French porcelain industry, it has Roman remains and a cathedral (13th–16th centuries). Population (1982): 144 082.

limpet A marine gastropod mollusc with a flattened shell and powerful muscular foot for clinging to rocks and other surfaces. The true limpets (superfamily *Patellacea*; about 400 species) are oval-shaped and up to 10 cm long whereas the keyhole limpets (superfamily *Fissurellacea*; several hundred species) have an opening in the shell for expelling wastes and tend to be smaller.

Limpopo River A river in SE Africa. Rising as the Crocodile River in the Witwatersrand, South Africa, it flows generally NE through Mozambique, to the Indian Ocean, forming part of the border between the Transvaal and Botswana. Length: 1770 km (1100 mi).

There was an Old Man with a nose, who said, "If you choose to suppose
That my nose is too long, you are certainly wrong!"
That remarkable man with a nose.

LIMERICK *An illustration from Lear's* Book of Nonsense.

Lincoln 53 14N 0 33W A city in E central England, the administrative centre of Lincolnshire on the River Witham. The British settlement became Lindum Colonia under the Romans, at the intersection of the im-

portant routeways Fosse Way and Ermine Street. The castle was begun in 1068 and the cathedral in 1075. Population (1983 est): 78 000.

Lincoln, Abraham (1809–65) US statesman; Republican president (1861–65). Lincoln became, in 1847,

ABRAHAM LINCOLN *The US president being shot at by John Wilkes Booth in Ford's Theatre, Washington DC.*

member of Congress for Illinois. Holding long-standing convictions against slavery, he opposed its extension to the new western states and in 1856 joined the newly formed antislavery Republican Party. Elected president on the slavery issue just before the outbreak of the Civil War, in 1863 Lincoln proclaimed the freedom of slaves in the South (the Emancipation Proclamation) and gave his famous Gettysburg Address recalling the principles of equality established by America's founding fathers. He oversaw the 13th amendment prohibiting slavery (1865) and advocated magnanimous Reconstruction measures but was assassinated a few days after the South surrendered.

Lincolnshire A county in E England, bordering on the North Sea. It is generally low lying, including part of the Fens, with the Lincolnshire Edge (a limestone escarpment) in the W and the Lincolnshire Wolds in the E. It is mainly agricultural producing arable crops and livestock; horticulture is also important. Area: 5885 sq km (2272 sq mi). Population (1983 est): 554 300. Administrative centre: Lincoln.

Lincoln's Inn. *See* Inns of Court.

Lind, Jenny (1820–87) Swedish soprano, known as "the Swedish nightingale." She performed in ópera and on the concert platform.

Lindbergh, Charles A(ugustus) (1902–74) US aviator who made the first solo nonstop flight across the Atlantic Ocean, from New York to Paris (1927), in the monoplane *Spirit of St Louis*. His two-year-old son was kidnapped and murdered in 1932.

Lindemann, Frederick Alexander, 1st Viscount Cherwell (1886–1957) German-born British physicist, who became Churchill's scientific adviser in World War II. Criticized for advocating mass bombing of civilians, Lindemann was highly praised by Churchill, who made him paymaster-general (1951–53).

linden. *See* lime.

Lindisfarne. *See* Holy Island.

Lindwall, Raymond Russell (1921–) Australian cricketer. A fast bowler, he took 228 wickets in 61 Test matches (1946–59).

Linear A A syllabic script used (c. 1700–1450 BC) to write the lost language of the Minoan civilization of Crete. It evolved from a pictographic script. Known from fewer than 400 inscriptions, it is still undeciphered, but, like its successor, Linear B, was mainly used on clay tablets to record inventories.

linear accelerator An accelerator in which charged elementary particles are repeatedly accelerated along a long straight tube by a radio-frequency electric field. In modern linear accelerators the field is supplied by the electric component of a travelling radio wave in a waveguide. The particles are confined in the tube by a series of magnetic lenses, which focus the beam. The maximum energy attained by a linear accelerator is about 10 GeV for electrons and 2 GeV for protons.

LINEAR B   *A clay tablet from Knossos, Crete (c. 1400 BC; British Museum).*

Linear B A syllabic script apparently adapted (c. 1450–1400 BC) from Linear A by the invading Mycenaeans at Knossos to write their own language. In 1952 Michael Ventris (1922–56) deciphered this language as an early form of Greek. Several thousand Linear B clay tablets, mainly inventories, survive from Knossos, Pylos, and elsewhere, dating between about 1400 and 1100 BC.

linear motor A form of electric induction motor in which the stator and the rotor are linear instead of cylindrical and parallel instead of coaxial. The development of linear motors as a method of traction for monorail intercity trains has been proposed by E. R. Laithwaite (1921–). In this arrangement one winding would be in the train and the other on the single rail, thus obviating the need for rotating parts.

linen A fabric manufactured from flax (*Linum usitatissimum*), probably the first textile of plant origin. Flax growing was brought to Britain by the Romans and in the 16th century a flourishing trade grew up, especially in Scotland and Northern Ireland. Greatly reduced by the 18th-century expansion of the cotton trade, and even more so by the advent of man-made fibres, these strong absorbent fibres now constitute less than 2% of world fibre production.

line of force. *See* field.

linguistics The scientific study of language. Modern linguistics has three main branches, corresponding to the three main components of language: semantics, grammar, and phonetics. Various specialized interests exist within the field of linguistics. **Comparative linguistics** compares languages either to establish the history of and relationships among related languages (e.g. the Indo-European family) or to test theories about linguistic universals by comparing unrelated languages (*see also* etymology). The main contribution of **structural linguistics**, which developed in the early 20th century, was to free linguistics from the historical and comparative approach, viewing language as a unique relational structure. **Sociolinguistics** deals with social aspects of language, including such matters as how language affects and reflects the role and status of individuals within the community, attitudes to dialect and "correctness," linguistic taboos and preferences, bilingualism, etc. **Psycholinguistics** is the comparatively recent branch of linguistics that deals with psychological aspects of language, including how children acquire language, how language is stored in and generated by the brain, the relationship between meaning and memory, etc.

Linnaeus, Carolus (Carl Linné; 1707–78) Swedish botanist, who established the principles for naming and classifying plants and animals. As a result of his botanical studies, Linnaeus proposed a system for classifying plants based on their flower parts. He published *Systema naturae* in 1735 followed by *Genera plantarum* (1737) and *Species plantarum* (1753). In his system, Linnaeus defined each type of plant by two names: a generic name and a specific name (*see* binomial nomenclature). Furthermore he grouped related genera into classes and combined related classes into orders. Linnaeus also applied his system to the animal kingdom.

linnet A small Eurasian finch, *Acanthis cannabina*, occurring in dry open regions, where it feeds on the seeds of common weed plants. The female has a dull brown-streaked plumage; the male has a crimson crown and breast, a greyish head, and a red-brown back with darker wings and tail. Male linnets have a beautiful flutelike voice.

linseed The flat oval seed of cultivated flax, which is a source of linseed oil, used in paints, inks, varnishes, oilcloth, and sailcloth. The crushed seed residues form linseed meal, an important protein feed for ruminants and pigs.

Linz 48 19N 14 18E The third largest city in Austria, the capital of Upper Austria on the River Danube. Its many historical buildings include two 13th-century baroque churches. Population (1983 est): 199 910.

lion A large carnivorous mammal *Panthera leo*, one of the big cats. Lions are found mainly in Africa (there are a few in India). They are heavily built with sandy-coloured coats: the shaggy-maned males grow to 2.8 m while females lack a mane and are more lightly built. Both sexes have a thin tail with a tuft at the end. Lions inhabit grasslands, living in groups (prides).

Lions, Gulf of An inlet of the NW Mediterranean Sea, on the coast of central S France between Marseille and the Spanish border.

Lipchitz, Jacques (1891–1973) Lithuanian cubist sculptor, who lived in Paris from 1909 and New York after 1941.

lipids A group of compounds, generally insoluble in water but soluble in organic solvents, that includes fats, oils, waxes, phospholipids, sphingolipids, and steroids. Fats and oils function as energy reserves in plants and animals and form a major source of dietary energy in animals. Phospholipids are important structural components of cell membranes, and sphingolipids are found predominantly in nerve tissues. Steroids have many important derivatives, including cholesterol, bile salts, and certain hormones. Lipids often occur in association with proteins as lipoproteins.

Lipizzaner A breed of horse long associated with the Spanish Riding School in Vienna, where they are trained for spectacular displays. It is named after the stud founded by Archduke Charles at Lipizza, near Trieste, in 1580. The Lipizzaner has a short back, strong hindquarters, a powerful neck, and a small head. Born black, they mature to a grey colour. Height: 1.47–1.52 m.

Lippershey, Hans (died c. 1619) Dutch lens grinder, who built the first telescope. News of it eventually reached Galileo, who built his own telescope.

Lippi, Fra Filippo (c. 1406–69) An early Renaissance Florentine painter, who was a Carmelite monk from 1421 to about 1432. He was patronized by the Medici but his greatest works are his fresco decorations for the choir of Prato Cathedral (1452–64), showing scenes from the lives of St John the Baptist and St Stephen. He is also noted for his idealized Madonnas. He abducted and later married a nun, Lucrezia Buti; their son, **Filippino Lippi** (1457–1504), was also a painter.

liquefaction of gases Gases are liquefied in several ways. If the temperature of the gas is below its critical temperature (*see* critical state), it can be liquefied simply by compressing it. If the critical temperature is too low for this, the cascade process can be used. In this a gas with a high critical temperature is first liquefied by compression and then allowed to cool by evaporation under reduced pressure. This gas cools a second gas below its critical temperature, so that it in turn can be liquefied, evaporated, and cooled still further. Thus the temperature is reduced in stages. Other methods include cooling

by the Joule-Kelvin effect and cooling by adiabatic expansion in which a compressed gas is cooled by performing external work.

Liquefied Petroleum Gas (LPG) Propane, propene, butane, butene, or a mixture of any of these. LPG is a product of oil refining and is also produced from natural gas. Most of the LPG produced is sold for heating or used as a raw material for chemical manufacture.

liquid crystal A substance exhibiting some liquid properties, especially fluidity, and some crystalline properties, in that large clusters of molecules are aligned in parallel formations. As liquid crystals change their reflectivity when an electric potential is applied to them, they are used in electronic digital displays.

liquids A state of matter between that of gases and the solid state. Liquids assume the shape of a container in the same way as gases but being incompressible do not expand to fill the container. Intermolecular forces are considerably stronger than in gases but weaker than in solids. Molecules are only maintained in an orderly arrangement by intermolecular forces over relatively small groups of molecules.

liquorice A perennial herb, *Glycyrrhiza glabra*, native to S Europe but cultivated throughout warm temperate regions. It bears clusters of blue flowers and long flat pods and its sweet roots, up to 1 m long, are a source of flavouring. Family: *Leguminosae*.

Lisbon (Portuguese name: Lisboa) 38 44N 9 08W The capital of Portugal, in the SW on the River Tagus. The country's chief seaport, it has one of the finest harbours in Europe. Lisbon is also a major industrial and commercial centre. Historic buildings include the Tower of Belém and the Jerónimos Monastery; its university was founded in 1290. *History*: a settlement from very early times, it was an organized community under the Roman Empire. It was captured by the Portuguese in the 12th century and became their capital in 1256. It flourished in the 15th and 16th centuries, the great age of Portuguese exploration and colonization, but later suffered a decline. In 1755 it was almost totally destroyed by an earthquake. It has expanded considerably in the 20th century and in 1966 one of the world's longest suspension bridges was opened across the River Tagus. Population (1985 est): 827 800.

Lister, Joseph, 1st Baron (1827–1912) British surgeon, who pioneered antiseptic techniques in surgery. In 1865, while surgeon at Glasgow Royal Infirmary, Lister realized the significance of Pasteur's germ theory of disease in trying to prevent the infection of wounds following surgery. Lister devised a means of eliminating contamination and introduced carbolic acid as an antiseptic to dress wounds. His antiseptic procedures eventually became standard practice in hospitals everywhere.

Listeria A genus of rod-shaped bacteria. The single species, *L. monocytogenes*, is a parasite of warm-blooded animals. On transmission to man, especially through eating unpasteurized cheese or yogurt, it may cause **listeriosis**, with symptoms ranging from mild food poisoning to meningitis; in pregnant women it usually results in termination of the pregnancy.

Liszt, Franz (Ferencz L.; 1811–86) Hungarian pianist and composer, considered the greatest performer of his time. As a composer he invented the symphonic poem and made use of advanced harmonies and original forms. His compositions include much piano music (including a sonata in B minor and operatic paraphrases),

JOSEPH LISTER *Using his carbolic spray to reduce infection; his students used to say "Let us spray".*

the *Faust Symphony* (1854–57) and *Dante Symphony* (1855–56), and the symphonic poem *Les Préludes* (1854).

litchi (lychee *or* lichee) A Chinese tree, *Litchi chinensis*, cultivated in the tropics and subtropics for its fruits. The fruit is almost globular with a warty deep-pink rind and is borne in branched clusters. The white translucent watery flesh has a sweet acid flavour and encloses a single large brown seed. Family: *Sapindaceae*.

lithium (Li) The lightest metal (relative density 0.534), discovered by Arfvedson in 1817. It is an alkali metal. It occurs in nature in various minerals as well as in brine, from which it is extracted commercially by electrolysis of the molten chloride (LiCl). The metal has the highest specific heat capacity of any solid element. It is corrosive, combustible, and reacts with water. Because of its efficiency in reflecting neutrons, lithium has important applications as a blanketing material in both the hydrogen bomb and proposed thermonuclear reactors. It forms salts, like the other alkali metals, and the hydride LiH. At no 3; at wt 6.941; mp 180.54°C; bp 1347°C.

lithography. *See* printing.

Lithuanian A language belonging to the E division of the Baltic languages division of the Indo-European family, spoken in the Lithuanian SSR, where it is the official language. Lithuanian is closely related to Latvian. It is written in a Latin alphabet.

Lithuanian Soviet Socialist Republic (*or* Lithuania) A constituent republic in the NW Soviet Union, on the Baltic Sea. Most of Lithuania comprises a central lowland and is a particularly fertile region, with forests and peat reserves. Lithuanians comprise about 80% of the population. *History*: one of the largest states in medieval Europe, in the 14th century Lithuania united with Poland under the Jagiellon dynasty, passing after the partition of Poland in the 18th century to Russia. It became independent in 1918 but was incorporated into the Soviet Union as an SSR in 1940. It was occupied by Germany during World War II, during which the large Jewish minority was virtually exterminated. In recent years it has pressed for independence from the USSR. Area: 65 200 sq km (25 170 sq mi). Population (1986): 3 603 000. Capital: Vilnius.

litmus A soluble compound obtained from certain lichens. Litmus turns red in an acid solution and blue in an alkaline solution. It is therefore used as an indicator, often in the form of **litmus paper**, strips of paper impregnated with litmus.

litre A unit of volume in the metric system formerly defined as the volume of one kilogram of pure water under specified conditions. This definition still applies for purposes of the UK Weights and Measures Act (1963), but in SI units the litre is a special name for the cubic decimetre.

Little Bighorn, Battle of the (25 June, 1876) The battle fought on the S bank of the Little Bighorn River in which Gen Custer and his men were massacred by Sioux Indians led by Crazy Horse (?1849–77) and Sitting Bull (Custer's Last Stand). It was one of the battles fought to seize the American West for White settlement.

liver A large glandular organ, weighing 1.2–1.6 kg, situated in the upper right region of the abdomen, just below the diaphragm. The liver has many important functions concerned with the utilization of absorbed foods. It converts excess glucose into glycogen, which it stores and reconverts into glucose when required; it breaks down excess amino acids into urea; and it stores and metabolizes fats. The liver forms and secretes bile, which contains the breakdown products of worn-out red blood cells, and synthesizes blood-clotting factors, plasma proteins, and—in the fetus—red blood cells. It also breaks down (detoxifies) poisonous substances, including alcohol.

liver fluke A parasitic flatworm that inhabits the bile duct of sheep, cattle, and man. The common liver fluke (*Fasciola hepatica*) passes its larval stages in a marshland snail before infecting grazing animals (or, rarely, man). The Chinese liver fluke (*Opisthorchus sinensis*), 1–2 cm long, passes two larval stages in a freshwater snail and fish before maturing in a human host.

Liverpool 53 25N 2 55W A major city in NW England, the administrative centre of Merseyside, on the estuary of the River Mersey. It is the UK's second most important port but has recently suffered industrial decline. It is linked with Birkenhead and Wallasey on the Wirral Peninsula by two tunnels under the Mersey. Notable buildings include the Royal Liver Building (1910) at the Pier Head, St George's Hall (1854), and the Roman Catholic cathedral constructed (1962–67) in a modern design. *History*: originally trading with Ireland, Liverpool grew rapidly in the 18th and 19th centuries as a result of trade with the Americas and the industrialization of S Lancashire. Britain's first wet dock was built here in 1709. Liverpool developed also as a cultural centre, with the Walker Art Gallery (built 1876), the Royal Liverpool Philharmonic Orchestra, and the Tate Gallery (opened 1988). Population (1984 est): 497 300.

liverwort A bryophyte plant of the class *Hepaticae* (10 000 species), found growing on moist soil, rocks, trees, etc. There are two groups: leafy liverworts, in which the plant body is differentiated into stems and leaves; and thallose liverworts, which have a flat lobed liverlike body (thallus). The liverwort plant is the gamete-producing phase (gametophyte) and gives rise to a capsule, the spore-producing phase (sporophyte).

livery companies Descendants of the medieval craft guilds, so called because of the distinctive dress (livery) worn by their members on ceremonial occasions. Some occupy notable buildings in the City of London and some, such as the Mercers, Haberdashers, and Merchant Taylors, have educational interests. In 1878 the livery companies joined the Corporation of the City of London in setting up the City and Guilds of London Institute to promote technical education.

livestock farming The maintenance and management of domesticated animals for the production of milk, meat, eggs, fibres, skins, etc. Modern improvements in livestock breeds and husbandry techniques have enabled dramatic increases to be made in productivity, nutrition and disease control being essential aspects of management.

Cattle produce milk and beef. Under European conditions, a cow may breed at any time of the year. The gestation period is about 9 months, followed by about 10 months of lactation and a 2-month dry period before calving again. A cow is known as a heifer until her second lactation. Heifers are reared either for beef or as dairy replacements and bull calves are generally castrated and reared for beef, being known as bullocks or

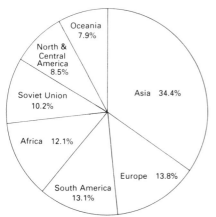

LIVESTOCK FARMING *Distribution of the world's livestock (1988; cattle, sheep, pigs, horses, asses, and mules).*

steers. Age at slaughter is generally about 18 months. Calves for veal are slaughtered at about 14 weeks.

Sheep are farmed worldwide for meat and wool (and in some countries for milk), often grazing on poor mountainous or arid pastures. Under European conditions, the one or two lambs per ewe are born in early spring. Males are castrated and reared for slaughter at weights of 20–45 kg. Selected females are reared as replacement ewes. Each sheep yields 2–5 kg of wool.

Pigs in modern intensive systems are housed under controlled conditions. Young females (gilts) are first mated at 7–8 months. Following the gestation period of 115 days, an average of 7–9 piglets are born per litter. Pork pigs are slaughtered at 40–50 kg, those reared for bacon at 80–100 kg.

Poultry are now kept indoors in an artificially controlled environment. Chicks are hatched artificially, the female birds starting to lay after about 20 weeks and producing about 250 eggs per year. Laying flocks are kept in "batteries" of cages with 3–5 birds per cage, feeding, cleaning, and egg collection being automatic. Table birds are fed ad lib and reach a weight of around 2 kg in 8–12 weeks. Turkeys are also reared for meat under intensive conditions.

Livingstone, David (1813–73) Scottish missionary and explorer of Africa, qualified as a physician. He traced long stretches of the Zambezi, Shire, and Rovuma Rivers, and discovered Lake Ngami (1849), the Victoria Falls (1855), and Lake Nyasa (now Malawi). During an attempt to trace the source of the Nile (1866–73) his famous encounter with Sir Henry Morton Stanley occurred.

Livy (Titus Livius; 59 BC–17 AD) Roman historian, noted for his monumental history of Rome from its legendary foundation to the death of Drusus in 9 BC. Only 35 of the original 142 books survive.

lizard A reptile belonging to the suborder *Sauria* (3000 species), occurring worldwide but most abundant in tropical regions. They are mainly terrestrial with cylindrical or narrow scaly long-tailed bodies, some with limbs reduced or absent (*see* glass snake; skink), and of-

ten with crests, spines, and frills. They range in size from the smallest geckos to the Komodo dragon. Lizards lay leathery-shelled eggs although certain species of colder regions and many skinks bear live young.

Ljubljana (German name: Laibach) 46 04N 14 30E A city in NW Yugoslavia, the capital of Slovenia. Under foreign rule until 1918, it is the centre of Slovene culture. It was largely destroyed by an earthquake in 1895. Population (1983 est): 326 467.

llama A hoofed mammal, *Lama glama*, of S and W South America. Up to 120 cm high at the shoulder, llamas are sure-footed, nimble, and hardy, with thick warm coats. They are now only found in the domesticated state, being used for meat, wool, and as pack animals. Family: *Camelidae* (camels, etc.).

llanos The treeless grasslands of South America that cover about 570 000 sq km (220 000 sq mi) of central Venezuela and N Colombia. Drained by the River Orinoco and its tributaries, the llanos are traditionally a cattle-rearing region but the discovery of oil in the 1930s led to considerable population growth and economic development.

Llewellyn, Richard (R. D. V. L. Lloyd; 1907–83) Welsh novelist, whose works include *How Green Was My Valley* (1939) and the sequel *Up, Into the Singing Mountains* (1960).

Lloyd, Chris(tine). *See* Evert, Chris.

Lloyd, Clive Hubert (1944–) West Indian cricketer, who played for Lancashire (1968–86), captaining the side (1981–84; 1986). A batsman, he captained his country's team (1974–78; 1979–85) in 74 tests. He retired in 1986.

Lloyd, Harold (1893–1971) US film comedian. He appeared as a dogged little man in numerous early silent comedies, most of them characterized by his use of dangerous stunts. His films include *Just Nuts* (1915), *Safety Last* (1923), and *The Freshman* (1925).

Lloyd, Marie (Matilda Wood; 1870–1922) British music-hall entertainer. Her songs, characterized by cockney humour, include "Oh! Mr Porter" and "A Little of What You Fancy."

Lloyd George, David, 1st Earl (1863–1945) British statesman; Liberal prime minister (1916–22). Born in Manchester of Welsh parents, he entered parliament in 1890 and gained a reputation for radicalism as a Welsh nationalist and a supporter of the Afrikaners in the second Boer War (1899–1902). As chancellor of the exchequer (1908–15), he is best known for the so-called People's Budget (1909). This proposed higher death duties, a land value tax, and a supertax; the rejection of this budget by the House of Lords led ultimately to the 1911 Parliament Act, which removed the Lords' veto power. Lloyd George also introduced old-age pensions (1908) and national insurance (1911). In World War I he served as minister of munitions (1915–16) and secretary for war (1916) before succeeding Asquith as prime minister. After the war he continued to lead a coalition government increasingly dominated by the Conservatives. He was criticized for negotiating with Irish militants in the establishment of the Irish Free State (1921) and his government fell when Britain came close to war with the Turkish nationalists. He resigned his parliamentary seat in 1945 on being created an earl.

Lloyd's An association of insurance underwriters named after the 17th-century London coffee house, owned by Edward Lloyd, where underwriters used to

LLOYD'S   *Richard Rogers' new building (1986).*

meet. Lloyd's was incorporated by Act of Parliament in 1871. The corporation itself does not underwrite insurance business, which is all undertaken by syndicates of private underwriters, who are wholly responsible for losses. There are over 6000 underwriters, none of whom are permitted to deal with the public, all insurance policies with the public being transacted by Lloyd's insurance brokers. **Lloyd's Register of Shipping** is an organization formed by Lloyd's to inspect and list all oceangoing vessels over 100 tonnes. The *Register*, published annually, gives up-to-date reports on these ships as a result of periodic checks by Lloyd's surveyors. Lloyd's also publishes *Lloyd's List and Shipping Gazette*, giving shipping news for insurance purposes.

Lloyd Webber, Andrew   (1948–) British composer. His musicals, usually with lyrics by Tim Rice (1944–), include *Joseph and the Amazing Technicolour Dreamcoat* (1968), *Jesus Christ Superstar* (1970), *Evita* (1978), *Cats* (1981), *The Phantom of the Opera* (1986), and *Aspects of Love* (1988).

Llywelyn ap Gruffudd   (d. 1282) The only native Prince of Wales (1258–82) to be recognized as such by England. He aided the English barons against Henry III (1263–67) and refused homage to Edward I (1276), who forced Llywelyn into submission. Llywelyn was killed in another revolt.

loach   A small freshwater bony fish of the family *Cobitidae* (over 200 species), found mainly in Asia, but also in Europe and N Africa. Loaches feed at night on bottom-dwelling invertebrates detected by the three to six pairs of barbels around the mouth. Order: *Cypriniformes*.

Lobelia   A genus of annual and perennial herbs (about 250 species), found in most warm and temperate regions.

The flowers are tubular, with a two-lobed upper lip and a larger three-lobed lower lip. Ornamental species, called cardinal flowers, are usually blue or red. Family: *Lobeliaceae*.

lobotomy.   *See* leucotomy.

lobster   A large marine crustacean of the section *Macrura* that has a long abdomen ending in a tailfan. True lobsters (family *Homaridae*) have segmented bodies, a pair of pincers, four pairs of walking legs, and several pairs of swimming legs (swimmerets). They live on the ocean bottom, feeding on seaweed and animals. Many species are commercially important as food, for example *Homarus vulgaris* and *H. americanus*. Order: *Decapoda*.

local government   The administration of a locality. In the UK local government has developed from the Anglo-Saxon division of the country into shires, hundreds, and boroughs but only became systematized in the 19th century. The Municipal Corporation Act (1835) established 178 municipal councils, elected by ratepayers, which in the following decades grew in number and took over a wide range of responsibilities, including the police and public health. County councils were established in 1888. In 1894 the work of local government was distributed by the creation of borough and urban district councils in urban areas and parish councils in rural areas. The Local Government Act (1972) divided England and Wales into 53 counties. These are divided into districts, and they in turn into parishes or, in Wales, communities. District councils are responsible for a number of important services, including education, housing, and refuse collection. A similar system was established in Scotland in 1973 but in Northern Ireland local government is in the hands of 26 district councils. Local-government spending is financed by rates, rent, borrowing, and central-government grants. *See also* poll tax.

Locarno Pact   (1925) A series of treaties between Germany, France, Belgium, Poland, Czechoslovakia, the UK, and Italy, signed in the Swiss town of Locarno. The most important was an agreement between France, Germany, and Belgium, guaranteed by the UK and Italy, to maintain the borders between Germany and France and Belgium respectively and the demilitarized zone of the Rhineland. The latter was violated by Hitler in 1936.

Locke, John   (1632–1704) English philosopher. His greatest work, the *Essay concerning Human Understanding* (1690), reveals him as a pioneer of empiricism. It maintains, contrary to received tradition, that every one of our ideas comes from sense impressions. Locke's two works *Of Government* (1690) were enormously influential in moulding modern concepts of liberal democracy. He dismissed any divine right to kingship and advocated liberal government.

lockjaw.   *See* tetanus.

locomotive   An engine that draws a train on a railway. The first locomotives, designed by Trevithick and Stephenson, were driven by steam engines and steam dominated the railways until the end of World War II. Thousands of steam locomotives are still in use throughout the world. However, the steam engine has a low efficiency (about 8% in a locomotive, which does not use a condenser), it takes a long time to become operational while steam is raised, it uses an awkward and dirty solid fuel (which it has to pull with it in a tender immediately behind the engine), and it creates pollution. For these

LOCOMOTIVE *Stephenson's "Rocket" was the first locomotive to combine a multi-tubular boiler and a blast pipe. It ran on the earliest public railway, between Stockton and Darlington (NE England), in 1829.*

reasons steam locomotives have largely been replaced in the industrial countries by electric, Diesel-electric, or Diesel trains, all of which have efficiencies of about 22%.

Where the traffic justifies the cost of installing overhead wires or a conductor rail, electric trains are usually preferred, as it is more efficient to generate electricity centrally than in the locomotive. Series-wound direct-current motors are the most widely used, with rectification in the locomotive when the supply is alternating current. When Diesel engines are used, these are either coupled hydraulically to the wheels, using a hydraulic torque converter (or fluid flywheel) and a gearbox, or to an electric generator or alternator, which produces current to power electric motors that drive the wheels. The first Diesel-electric train was used in Sweden in 1912 and the first Diesel-hydraulic in Germany a year later. Because the Diesel provides a very low torque at low speeds, it cannot be used without a hydraulic coupling, but even these units are usually restricted to small trains. *See also* magnetic levitation.

locust (botany) An evergreen Mediterranean tree, *Ceratonia siliqua*, also called carob tree. 12–15 m in height, it produces leathery pods containing a sweet edible pulp and small flat beans. The black locust (*Robinia pseudoacacia*), also called false acacia, is a North American tree widely cultivated for ornament. Up to 24 m tall, it has deeply ridged dark-brown bark, hanging clusters of white flowers, and black pods. Family: *Leguminosae*.

locust (zoology) A grasshopper that, when environmental conditions are favourable, undergoes sporadic increases in population size to form huge swarms, which migrate long distances and devour all the crops and other vegetation on which they settle. Economically important species include the migratory locust (*Locusta migratoria*), about 55 mm long, found throughout Africa and S Eurasia and eastward to Australia and New Zealand; and the desert locust (*Schistocerca gregaria*), occurring from N Africa to the Punjab.

lodestone. *See* magnetite.

Lodge, David (John) (1935–) British novelist. His comic novels lampooning academic life include *Changing Places* (1975), *Small World* (1984), and *Nice Work* (1988).

Łódź 51·49N 19·28E The second largest city in Poland. It developed during the 19th century and is now a leading industrial centre. Population (1985): 849 000.

loess A deposit consisting of wind-born dust from desert or vegetation-free areas at the margins of ice sheets. In Europe loess occurs in Germany, Belgium, and NE France. Deep well-drained soils develop from loess.

Loewe, Frederick (1904–88) Austrian composer of musical comedies, resident in the USA after 1924. He is famous for such musicals as *Brigadoon* (1947), *Paint Your Wagon* (1950), *My Fair Lady* (1956), *Gigi* (1958), and *Camelot* (1960), written with Alan Lerner.

Logan, Mount 60·31N 140·22W The highest mountain in Canada, in SW Yukon in the St Elias Mountains. Height: 6050 m (19 850 ft).

loganberry A bramble-like shrub that is a cross between a raspberry and a blackberry. It bears red fleshy berries, used for preserves, puddings, and wine. It is named after James H. Logan (1841–1928), who first grew it (in California) in 1881. Family: *Rosaceae*.

logarithms A mathematical function used to facilitate multiplication and division. Based on the law that $a^x \times a^y = a^{x+y}$, two numbers p and q can be multiplied together by writing them in the form $p = a^x$ and $q = a^y$ and then adding together the values of x and y (the exponents). x is called the logarithm of p to the base a, i.e. $x = \log_a p$. Pocket calculators have obviated the need for logarithms as a method of computation but they remain useful mathematical functions.

logic In the widest sense, the science of reasoned argument. As a mental discipline, it is concerned not so much with the application of argument in specific instances as with the general rules covering the construction of valid inferences. Aristotle was the first to make a systematic study of the principles governing rational discourse (also called syllogism). His works were the sourcebooks for medieval logicians. After the Renaissance philosophers became increasingly aware of limitations in the Aristotelian approach. Leibniz, for instance, was worried by the difference between the logical and grammatical structure of sentences; two grammatically identical sentences may be very different logically. Rules must therefore be found to formalize ordinary language in such a way as to make plain its underlying logical structure, before further rules for the construction of valid arguments can be drawn up. Since the 19th century formulation of such rules has become mainly the province of mathematicians. Boole and Gottlob Frege (1848–1925) were important pioneers in what is now called "mathematical logic" to differentiate it from the wider still current sense. Russell, whose work had important repercussions for set theory, called "logic . . . the youth of mathematics, and mathematics . . . the manhood of logic."

logical positivism A philosophical movement that arose from the Vienna Circle in the 1920s. Influenced by Ernst Mach (1838–1916) and Wittgenstein, it insisted that philosophy should be scientific, regarding it as an analytical (rather than a speculative) activity, the purpose of which was clarification of thought. Any assertion claiming to be factual has meaning only if its truth (or falsity) can be empirically tested. Metaphysical propositions and those of aesthetics and religion are consequently meaningless. A secondary goal of logical positivism was the analysis and unification of scientific terminology.

Lohengrin In Arthurian legend, the son of Percival (Parzival). He champions a young noblewoman, Elsa of Brabant, whom he agrees to marry on condition that she does not enquire into his origins. When her curiosity overcomes her, he is taken back by his swan guide to the castle of the Holy Grail, whence he came. The story was adapted by Wagner in the opera *Lohengrin* (1850).

Loire, River The longest river in France. Rising in the Cévennes Mountains, it flows mainly W to the Bay of Biscay at St Nazaire, passing through Orléans, Tours, and Nantes. Its tributaries include the Allier, Vienne, and Maine. The Loire Valley is renowned for its vineyards and chateaux (Amboise, Blois, Chambord, Chaumont, Chenonceaux). It is linked by canal with the River Seine. Length: 1020 km (634 mi).

Loki In Norse mythology, a mischief-making giant with the ability to change his shape and sex, who lived among the gods until imprisoned in a cave for the murder of Balder. His offspring—Hel, the goddess of death, Jörmungandr, the evil serpent surrounding the earth, and Fenris, the wolf—are among the forces of evil, which he leads against the gods at doomsday (Ragnarök).

Lollards The followers of the English reformer Wycliffe. Until his retirement from Oxford in 1378, the preaching of his doctrines was largely confined to the University. Thereafter his teachings were taken up by nonacademics, including merchants, lesser clergy, and a few members of Richard II's court. Henry IV's reign saw considerable repression of the Lollards culminating in the defeat in 1414 of the rebellion led by Sir John Oldcastle (c. 1378–1417). The movement then went underground and became increasingly proletarian. Many of its tenets were adopted by the early Protestants.

Lombardo, Pietro (c. 1438–1515) Italian sculptor and architect. Lombardo worked mainly in Venice, where he was the leading sculptor of his generation. He was frequently assisted by his two sons **Antonio Lombardo** (c. 1458–c. 1516) and **Tullio Lombardo** (c. 1460–1532).

Lombardy A region in N Italy, consisting mainly of mountains in the N and lowlands in the S. It is Italy's most industrialized region. Area: 23 834 sq km (9191 sq mi). Population (1986 est): 8 876 787. Capital: Milan.

Lomond, Loch The largest lake in Scotland, in E Strathclyde Region. Length: about 38 km (24 mi). Width: 8 km (5 mi).

London (Latin name: Londinium) 51 30N 0 10W The capital of the UK, in SE England on the River Thames. One of the six largest cities in the world, it comprises a succession of village communities.
London's financial hub is its original nucleus, the **City of London**, roughly a square mile on the N bank of the Thames between Blackfriars Bridge and Tower Bridge. London's **East End**, centring on the borough of Tower Hamlets, has long provided a home for successive immigrant groups. The **West End** comprises the district around Oxford Street (constructed in the 19th century) and is the city's shopping and entertainment centre. London's cultural life is outstanding, with a large number of art galleries, museums, theatres, concert halls, and educational institutions.
Economy: the City of London is one of the world's greatest banking, commodity, shipping, and insurance centres: the Bank of England is to be found in Threadneedle Street with the Stock Exchange nearby, while Lloyd's is in Lime Street. London's commercial development depended to a large extent on its port. However, apart from Tilbury Docks, most of its port area has now been redeveloped for residential and commercial purposes.
History: the Romans built London at the highest point at which the Thames could be forded and at the river's tidal limit—on what was later Cornhill and Ludgate Hill. During the reign of William the Conqueror the famous White Tower (*see* Tower of London) was built. London prospered in the middle ages and both the Church and the guilds sponsored exceptional building programmes. Westminster Abbey dates from the 11th century, being largely rebuilt in the 13th century, when Southwark Cathedral was begun. To the 15th century belong the Guildhall and Lambeth Palace and to the 16th century, when London began to extend westwards, St James' Palace. The early Stuart period witnessed the great work of Inigo Jones, notably the Queen's House at Greenwich (1617–35) and the Banqueting Hall in Whitehall (1619–22). London's population was decimated by the Plague (1665) and much of its fabric was destroyed in the Fire of the following year. The greatest loss—Old St Paul's—was replaced by Wren, who was responsible for much of the work of reconstruction, including 49 new parish churches in the City. Many of London's finest squares were built in the late 17th and early 18th centuries; the early 19th century witnessed the work of Nash: Regent's Park and the terraces around it. The 19th century produced the Palace of Westminster, the Law Courts, and such railway stations as St Pancras. London, especially the City and the East End, was seriously damaged by bomb attacks during World War II and subsequent rebuilding has consisted largely of high-rise offices and flats, including the Barbican (1973) and the National Westminster building (1977), which at 183 m (600 ft) is the tallest building in London. Recent development, including an airport and light railway, has been concentrated on the old docklands area. Area: 1580 sq km (610 sq mi). Population (1986): 6 775 200.

London, Jack (1876–1916) US novelist, best known for *The Call of the Wild* (1903). His other novels include *White Fang* (1906) and *Martin Eden* (1909).

London Bridge A bridge spanning the River Thames from the City of London to the borough of Southwark. Bridges on this site date back to Roman times. The stone bridge built between 1176 and 1209 had a drawbridge and was surmounted by shops and houses. It was replaced by a new bridge in the 1820s, designed by John Rennie (1761–1821). The present bridge was completed in 1973.

Londonderry (Derry) 55 00N 7 19W A city and port in Northern Ireland, the county town of Co Londonderry on the River Foyle. The City of London Corporation was granted Londonderry and the Irish Society established (1610) to administer it. In a famous siege (1688–89) it held out for 105 days against the forces of James II. Population (1981): 62 697.

Long Beach 33 47N 118 06W A city and port in the USA, in California on San Pedro Bay. It is a major tourist centre. Population (1986 est): 396 280.

longbow A bow of straight-grained yew used from about 1400 to about 1600. Originally Welsh, longbows were up to 1.8 m (6 ft) long and could fire a 110 cm (37 in) arrow capable of piercing chainmail and some plate armour at 183 m (200 yd) every 10 seconds.

Longfellow, Henry Wadsworth (1807–82) US poet. He achieved enormous popularity with such narrative

LONDON *A view in 1616 of the first stone London Bridge. The gatehouse (foreground) bears the heads of traitors.*

poems as *Evangeline* (1847) and *The Song of Hiawatha* (1855).

Longford (Irish name: Longphort) A county in the N central Republic of Ireland, in Leinster, chiefly low lying with areas of bog. Area: 1043 sq km (403 sq mi). Population (1986): 31 491. County town: Longford.

Long Island An island in the USA, in New York state separated from the mainland by Long Island Sound. Chiefly residential with many resorts, it contains the New York City boroughs of Brooklyn and Queens and the international John F. Kennedy Airport. Area: 4462 sq km (1723 sq mi).

longitude. *See* latitude and longitude.

long jump A field event in athletics. Competitors sprint up a runway and leap into a sandpit from a take-off board. The competitor who makes the longest jump in three or six tries is the winner. World records: men: 8.9 m (1968) by Robert Beamon (USA); women: 7.52 m (1988) by Galina Chistyakova (Soviet Union).

Longleat An English country house near Warminster, in Wiltshire, owned by the Marquess of Bath. Dating from 1572, Longleat typifies the Elizabethan style of architecture. The house and its grounds, originally laid out by Capability Brown and now containing a lion safari park, are open to the public.

Long Parliament (1640–60) The parliament that was summoned by Charles I of England following his defeat in the second Bishops' War. In 1640 it impeached the king's ministers, the Earl of Strafford (1593–1641) and Archbishop Laud, in 1641 expressed its grievances against Charles in the Grand Remonstrance, and in 1642 assumed control of the militia. Charles' rejection of its demands for reform (Nineteen Propositions) precipitated the outbreak of the Civil War. Its power declined as that of the New Model Army increased and in 1648 it was purged of its moderate members. The remaining Rump Parliament was dismissed in 1653 by Oliver Cromwell, who established the Protectorate. The Rump was reinstated in 1659 and the full membership of the Long Parliament was restored by Gen Monck (1608–70) in 1660. Shortly afterwards it dissolved itself, being replaced by the Convention Parliament, which effected the Restoration.

longship A large sailing vessel equipped with a bank of oars on each side. Longships were used by Scandinavian maritime peoples until the mid-18th century. They had square sails and very high prows and were steered by a long tiller attached to a large rudder.

longsightedness (*or* hypermetropia) Inability to see close objects clearly, because the lens of the eye focuses light to a point behind the retina (light-sensitive layer). This is less common than shortsightedness among young people, but, owing to changes in the lens with age, many people need glasses for reading by the time they are 50. This type of longsightedness is known as **presbyopia**.

loofah The fibrous skeleton of the fruit of the tropical dishcloth gourd, or vegetable sponge (genus *Luffa* (6 species), especially *L. cylindrica*). These vines produce cucumber-like fruits, about 30 cm long. When mature, the pulp and seeds are removed leaving a dense network of fibrous conducting tissue, which is used as a bath sponge, dish washer, and industrial filter. Family: *Cucurbitaceae*.

loom. *See* weaving.

looper. *See* geometrid moth.

loquat A small evergreen tree *Eriobotrya japonica*, native to China and Japan but cultivated in Mediterranean countries for its edible fruit. Family: *Rosaceae*.

Lorca, Federico García. *See* García Lorca, Federico.

Lord Chief Justice The presiding judge of the Queen's Bench Division of the High Court of Justice and the Criminal Division of the Court of Appeal; he is second in the judicial hierarchy to the Lord Chancellor. The present incumbent (since 1980) is Geoffrey Dawson, Baron Lane (1918–   ).

Lord Lyon King of Arms The highest authority in the deciding of heraldic matters in Scotland. Originally a herald in the 14th century, the Lord Lyon now heads four heralds and two pursuivants at the Lyon Office where, since 1677, all claims to arms must be registered. Also a judge, the Lord Lyon has jurisdiction over issues of clan chieftainship and pedigrees.

Lords, House of. *See* parliament.

Lord's cricket ground The cricket ground owned by the Marylebone Cricket Club and situated in St John's Wood, London. It was founded by Thomas Lord (1757–

1832) in Dorset Square and was moved to its present site in 1814. It has been the home of the Middlesex County Cricket Club since 1877.

Loren, Sophia (S. Scicoloni; 1934–) Italian film actress. Her films include *Two Women* (1961), *The Millionairess* (1961), *Marriage Italian Style* (1964), and *The Cassandra Crossing* (1977).

KONRAD LORENZ

Lorenz, Konrad (1903–89) Austrian zoologist, who was one of the founders of modern ethology (the study of animal behaviour). In the 1930s Lorenz identified the phenomenon of imprinting in young chicks. He was concerned with determining the elements of behaviour, how they were stimulated, their development in an individual, and their evolutionary significance. Lorenz wrote several popular books about his work, including *King Solomon's Ring* (1949) and *Man Meets Dog* (1950). He also applied his theories to the human species, with controversial implications (*On Aggression*, 1963). He was awarded a Nobel Prize (1973) with Karl von Frisch (1886–1982) and Niko Tinbergen (1907–88).

loris A nocturnal Asian prosimian primate belonging to the subfamily *Lorisinae* (5 species). Lorises are 20–35 cm long with almost no tail and very large dark eyes. They are generally slow-moving and arboreal. Family: *Lorisidae. See also* potto.

Lorraine A planning region and former province in NE France, bordering on Belgium, Luxembourg, and West Germany. Its valuable iron-ore deposits are the largest in Europe outside Sweden and the Soviet Union. Disputed between France and the Habsburgs, it was finally incorporated into France, as a province, in 1766. Following the Franco-Prussian War (1871) part of Lorraine (now Moselle department) was lost to Germany and united with Alsace to form the imperial territory of Alsace-Lorraine. Area: 23 540 sq km (9087 sq mi). Population (1986 est): 2 313 200.

lory A small brightly coloured parrot belonging to the subfamily *Loriinae* (62 species), occurring in Australia, New Guinea, and Polynesia. Lories have a slender bill with a brush-tipped tongue and feed on pollen and nectar.

Los Alamos 28 54N 103 00W A town in the USA, in New Mexico. Chosen by the US government (1942) for atomic research, the first atom bombs were made here

during World War II. The H-bomb was later developed here by the scientific laboratory of the University of California. Government control of Los Alamos ended in 1962. Population (1980): 11 039.

Los Angeles 34 00N 118 15W A city and seaport in the USA, in S California on the Pacific coast, founded in 1781 by Franciscan missionaries. It comprises a large industrial and urban complex, with the second largest population in the USA. It is the centre of the US film industry. Industrial pollution, augmented by the high density of cars (Los Angeles has no public transport), is a serious problem. Population (1986 est): 3 259 300.

Los Angeles, Victoria de (1923–) Spanish soprano. She established herself as a popular prima donna, particularly in the title roles of Massenet's *Manon Lescaut* and Puccini's *Madame Butterfly*.

Lothian Region An administrative region in SE Scotland, created in 1975 from the counties of East Lothian, Midlothian, and West Lothian. It consists of lowlands bordering on the Firth of Forth in the N and rising gently to the S. The fertile lowlands are important agriculturally. Area: 1756 sq km (677 sq mi). Population (1986 est): 741 910. Administrative centre: Edinburgh.

Lotto, Lorenzo (c. 1480–1556) Venetian painter. He travelled extensively but, unable to compete with Titian's success, worked chiefly in Bergamo. He is noted for his altarpieces, e.g. the *Crucifixion* (Monte San Giusto, Bergamo), and the psychological insight of such portraits as *A Young Man* (Kunsthistorisches Museum, Vienna), and *Andrea Odoni* (Hampton Court).

lotus Any of several different water plants. The sacred lotus of ancient Egypt was probably *Nymphaea lotus*, a sweet-scented white night-flowering water lily with broad petals, or *N. caerulea*, a blue-flowered species. The sacred Indian lotus, *Nelumbo nucifera* (family *Nelumbaceae*), has roselike pink flowers and edible seeds, called lotus nuts. The genus *Lotus* contains about 70 species of herbs, including the birdsfoot trefoils.

loudspeaker A device for converting electrical signals into sound. It usually consists of a small coil fixed to the centre of a movable diaphragm or cone. The coil lies between the poles of a strong magnet. An audio-frequency electrical signal fed to the coil creates a varying magnetic field, which interacts with the steady field in the gap. This causes the coil, and the attached cone, to vibrate and produce sound waves of the same frequencies as the electrical signal. Generally, larger cones give a better response at low frequencies and the smaller cones are best at high frequencies; for the best results two or more different-sized cones are therefore used, either in the same or in separate cabinets. The loudspeaker cabinet can act as a sound baffle and improve the frequency response.

Louis (I) the Pious (778–840 AD) Emperor of the West (813–40); son of Charlemagne. He fostered Christianity but imperial unity was undermined by his rebellious sons and after his death the Empire was partitioned.

Louis (VII) le Jeune (c. 1120–80) King of France (1137–80). He was engaged in a bitter struggle with Henry II of England between 1152, when Henry acquired Aquitaine through his marriage to Louis' former wife Eleanor of Aquitaine, until 1174.

Louis VIII (1187–1226) King of France (1223–26), known as the Lionheart. He was offered the English throne by King John's baronial opponents but his invasion of England was defeated in 1217.

Louis IX, St (1214–70) King of France (1226–70), regarded as the model medieval Christian king. After defeating Henry III of England (1242) he set out as leader of the sixth Crusade (1248), during which he was captured by the Egyptians. On his return to France he introduced administrative reforms and fostered learning and the arts. He died on a Crusade in Tunisia and was canonized in 1297.

Louis XI (1423–83) King of France (1461–83), who united most of France under his rule and in 1477 finally defeated Charles the Bold of Burgundy. He extended royal authority over the church and encouraged commerce, gaining the support of the middle classes.

Louis XII (1462–1515) King of France (1498–1515). His reign was dominated by the wars that his father Charles VIII had initiated in Italy.

Louis XIII (1601–43) King of France (1610–43), whose reign was dominated by his chief minister Cardinal de Richelieu. He was the son of the assassinated Henry IV and of Marie de' Medici (1573–1642), who was regent during his minority. In 1617 he exiled Marie from court but mother and son were later reconciled by Richelieu, her adviser, who in 1624 became Louis' chief minister. The king defeated two Huguenot uprisings (1622, 1628).

LOUIS XIV   *The Sun King in all his glory.*

Louis XIV (1638–1715) King of France (1643–1715), known as the Sun King because of the splendour of his reign. His minority was dominated by Cardinal Mazarin (1602–61), after whose death Louis allowed no single minister to dominate. He was a firm advocate of the divine right of kings and is remembered for his protesta-

tion *L'état c'est moi* (I am the state). His patronage of artists, including the writers Molière and Racine, enhanced the magnificence of his court. In 1660 he married Maria Theresa (1638–83), the daughter of Philip IV of Spain. His mistresses included Mme de Montespan (1641–1707) and then Mme de Maintenon (c. 1635–1719), whom he secretly married after Maria Theresa's death. Abroad, France became the dominant power in Europe during Louis' reign, although the many wars in which he involved France left it economically weak. France was further weakened by Louis' revocation (1685) of the Edict of Nantes, ending toleration of Protestants and driving many of France's most productive citizens into exile. His reign was nevertheless one of incomparable brilliance.

The **Louis Quartorze style** of late 17th-century interior design was developed in a deliberate attempt by Louis XIV and his designers to establish a French national idiom. The formal baroque furniture was sumptuously gilded or veneered for such regal settings as Versailles.

Louis XV (1710–74) King of France (1715–74), whose weak rule discredited the Crown and contributed to the outbreak of the French Revolution of 1789. His early reign was dominated by Cardinal Fleury (1653–1743), after whose death Louis' indecisiveness and the influence of his mistresses, especially Mme de Pompadour and, later, Mme Du Barry, fostered faction and intrigue. The loss of almost all France's colonies in the Seven Years' War (1756–63) increased his unpopularity, which hasty judicial and financial reforms at the end of his reign did nothing to alleviate.

The **Louis Quinze style** of French interior decoration and furnishing lasted from about 1723 until Louis' death. A sophisticated and informal style, it was a reaction to the formal baroque pomp of Louis XIV's court. *See also* rococo.

Louis XVI (1754–93) King of France (1774–93), who was guillotined during the French Revolution. The opposition of Louis' wife Marie Antoinette and the aristocracy thwarted the attempted reforms of his ministers Turgot (1727–81) and Necker (1732–1804). The consequent economic crisis forced the king to summon (1789) the States General, the disaffected Third Estate of which precipitated revolution. The royal family was confined to the Tuileries Palace from which they attempted to flee in 1791, reaching Varennes. Brought back to the Tuileries, Louis was deposed after it had been stormed by the Paris mob. In 1793 he and his wife were guillotined.

The **Louis Seize style**, a neoclassical French style of furnishing, came into fashion after Louis XVI's accession. It was characterized by rejection of the rococo with straight lines replacing curves and a continuing tendency towards lightness and utility. After the French Revolution (1789–99) this style remained in vogue for some time.

Louis XVII (1785–95) King of France in name (1793–95) following the execution of his father Louis XVI during the French Revolution. He died in prison.

Louis XVIII (1755–1824) King of France, in name from 1795, following the death in prison of his nephew Louis XVII, and in fact from 1814, following the overthrow of Napoleon. He fled Paris when Napoleon returned from Elba, being restored with diminished prestige after Waterloo (1815). His attempts to be a moderate constitutional monarch were thwarted by the ultraroyalists.

Louis, Joe (Joseph Louis Barrow; 1914–81) US boxer, called the Brown Bomber, who was world heavyweight champion from 1937 to 1948, when he retired.

Louisiana A state in the S USA, on the Gulf of Mexico. Chiefly low lying, it is crossed by the Mississippi
River, the delta of which dominates the coastal lowlands
in the S. The state produces chemicals and petrochemicals, paper and food products. Oil is exploited throughout the state and there are major deposits of natural gas,
sulphur, and salt. New Orleans and Baton Rouge are
important ports and tourism is a growing industry. Its
favourable climate and fertile soils make it an important
agricultural state. *History*: although discovered by the
Spanish, it was claimed for France and named after Louis XIV in 1682. It was ceded to Spain (1762) but was
restored to France (1800). It was acquired by the USA as
part of the Louisiana Purchase (1803), becoming a state
in 1812. Area: 125 675 sq km (48 523 sq mi). Population
(1985 est): 4 481 000. Capital: Baton Rouge.

Louisiana Purchase (1803) About 2 144 250 sq km
(828 000 sq mi) of land between the Mississippi River
and the Rocky Mountains, purchased by the USA from
France for $27,267,622. The purchase doubled the size
of the USA and established US dominance in North
America.

Louis Philippe (1773–1850) King of the French
(1830–48), the son of the Duke of Orléans. He supported the French Revolution until 1793, when he deserted to the Austrians. He joined the liberal opposition
to the restored Louis XVIII and came to the throne after
the July Revolution had ousted Louis' successor Charles
X. Styled King of the French rather than of France and
described by Thiers as the Citizen King, Louis Philippe
relied on the support of the middle class. His initial mod-
eration turned to repression in the face of the many rebellions against his rule and he abdicated in the Revolution of 1848.

Lourdes 43 06N 0 02W A town in SW France, in the
Hautes-Pyrénées department situated at the foot of the
Pyrenees. It is a major pilgrimage centre for Roman
Catholics (*see* Bernadette of Lourdes). Population
(1982): 17 619.

Lourenço Marques. *See* Maputo.

louse A wingless insect parasitic on warm-blooded
animals. The sucking lice (order *Anoplura*; 225 species)
suck the blood of mammals. They have hairy flattened
bodies, 0.5–6 mm long, and claws for attachment to the
host. One of the most important species is the human
louse (*Pediculus humanus*), of which there are two varieties—the head louse (*P. humanus capitis*) and the body
louse (*P. humanus humanus*). Both are transmitted by
direct contact and lay their eggs ("nits") on hair or clothing. Body lice are carriers of typhus and related diseases.
Biting lice (order *Mallophaga*; 2600 species) resemble
sucking lice but have biting mouthparts for feeding on
the skin, feathers, etc., of birds—their principal hosts.

Louth (Irish name: Contae Lughbhaidh) The smallest
county in the Republic of Ireland, in Leinster bordering
on the Irish Sea. It is chiefly low lying. Agriculture is
important. Area: 821 sq km (317 sq mi). Population
(1986): 91 698. County town: Dundalk.

Louvre The national museum of France containing
the art collection of the French kings and housed in the
former royal palace and Tuileries palace in Paris. It was
opened to the public in 1793.

LOUVRE *The* Venus de Milo *(Aphrodite from Melos);*
2nd century BC.

lovage A perennial herb, *Ligusticum scoticum*, that
has large compound leaves with pairs of divided toothed
leaflets and clusters of greenish-white flowers. It is native to Europe and used as a pot herb and salad plant.
Family: *Umbelliferae*.

lovebird A small brightly coloured parrot belonging
to a genus (*Agapornis*; 9 species) occurring in Africa and
Madagascar. Lovebirds typically have a short tail, a red
bill, and a prominent eye ring. They often feed in large
flocks and may damage crops. They are popular
cagebirds.

Lovelace, Richard (1618–57) English Cavalier poet.
One of his best-known poems is "To Althea, from Prison." *Lucasta* (1649) contains most of his best lyrics.

love-lies-bleeding. *See* Amaranthus.

Lower California (Spanish name: Baja California) A
peninsula in NW Mexico, between the Gulf of California and the Pacific Ocean. It is chiefly mountainous and
arid. There are important mineral deposits. Length:
1223 km (760 mi).

Lowry, L(awrence) S(tephen) (1887–1976) British
painter, born in Manchester. His most characteristic
works have bleak industrial landscapes and towns
dotted with matchstick figures.

Lozi A Bantu-speaking people of Zambia, also known
as Barotse. They are cereal cultivators on the fertile
flood plain of the upper Zambezi, but hunting and
animal husbandry are also important. Political authority
is vested in a divine king and subordinate queen who
rule from separate northern and southern capitals.

LPG. *See* Liquefied Petroleum Gas.

LSD (lysergic acid diethylamide) A drug that—in very
small doses—produces hallucinations, altered sensory

perception, and a sense of happiness and relaxation or, in some people, fear and anxiety. Long-term use of LSD can cause a schizophrenia-like illness.

Lualaba, River A river in SE Zaïre, the headstream of the Zaïre River. Rising in the Shaba region, it flows N to join the River Luvua and becomes the Zaïre River at the Boyoma Falls. Length: 1800 km (1100 mi).

Luanda 8 58S 13 09E The capital of Angola, a port in the NW on the Atlantic Ocean. Founded by the Portuguese in 1575, it became a centre of the slave trade to Brazil. Oil was discovered nearby in 1955 and a refinery was established. Population (1988): 960 000.

Lübeck 53 52N 10 40E A city in NE West Germany, in Schleswig-Holstein on the Trave estuary. A leading city of the Hanseatic League, it has a cathedral (1173) and city hall (13th–15th centuries). It is West Germany's largest Baltic port. Population (1986): 209 800.

Lubitsch, Ernst (1892–1947) US film director, born in Germany. Following the success of *Madame Dubarry* (1919), a historical romance, he went to Hollywood, where he made a series of sophisticated comedies during the 1920s and 1930s. These include *Forbidden Paradise* (1924), *Bluebeard's Eighth Wife* (1938), and *Ninotchka* (1939).

Lubumbashi (name until 1966: Elizabethville) 11 30S 27 31E A city in SE Zaïre. Founded in 1910 as a coppermining settlement, it is the industrial centre of an important mining area. Population (1984): 543 268.

lucerne. *See* alfalfa.

Lucifer In Christian tradition, the leader of the angels expelled from heaven for rebelling against God. Known thereafter as Satan (Hebrew: adversary) or the Devil, he presides over the souls condemned to torment in hell. He is identified with the serpent that tempted Eve (Genesis 3.1–6) and the great red dragon cast out of heaven by Michael (Revelation 12.3–9). The exact nature of Lucifer's sin was much debated; the commonest view is that his sin was pride.

L. S. LOWRY The Pond *(1950; Tate Gallery, London).*

Lucknow 26 50N 80 54E A city in India, the capital of Uttar Pradesh. Capital of the nawabs of Oudh (1775–1856), it has many notable buildings. The British Residency was besieged in 1857 during the Indian Mutiny. Population (1981 est): 1 006 943.

Lucretius (Titus Lucretius Carus; c. 95–c. 55 BC) Roman philosopher and poet. His single work, *De rerum natura*, expounds the philosophy of Epicurus, including his atomic theory of phenomena and the belief that the soul was material (and mortal).

Lucullus, Lucius Licinius (died c. 57 BC) Roman general. After service with Sulla, he successfully conducted the third war against Mithridates (120–63 BC) until his troops mutinied. Lucullus retired to private life and luxury.

Lüda (*or* Lü-ta) 38 53N 121 37E A port complex in NE China, at the end of the Liaodong Peninsula. It comprises the two cities **Lüshun** (English name: Port Arthur) and **Dalian** (*or* Ta-lien; English name: Dairen). Lüshun, a major naval base from 1878, was the base of the Russian Pacific fleet during the Russian occupation (1898–1905). The Russians began the construction of the commercial port at Dalian, completed under Japanese occupation (1905–45). Population (1983 est): 4 500 000.

Luddites A group of Nottingham frameworkers, named after their probably mythical leader, Ned Ludd, who destroyed labour-saving machinery in 1811. Luddism, which spread to other parts of industrial England, showed the hostility to the new machines that were taking the men's livelihood from them. It was severely repressed.

Luftwaffe The German air force. The Luftwaffe, which fought in World War I, was further developed by Göring in the 1930s. In World War II it was involved in the Blitzkreig but was defeated in the battle of Britain.

Lugansk. *See* Voroshilovgrad.

Lugus One of the principal Celtic gods. In Ireland he was called Lug and was skilled in many fields. His Welsh counterpart was Lleu Llaw Gyffes (skilful hand).

lugworm A burrowing annelid worm, *Arenicola marina*, of Atlantic shores. Up to 40 cm long, lugworms have about 20 segments, with tufts of red gills on all but the last few. They feed on organic material in the mud, leaving casts of egested mud on the surface. Class: *Polychaeta*.

Luik. *See* Liège.

Luluabourg. *See* Kananga.

lumen (lm) The SI unit of luminous flux equal to the light emitted per second in a cone of one steradian solid angle by a point source of one candela.

luminescence The emission of light by a substance for any reason except high temperature. It occurs as a result of the emission of a photon by an atom of the substance when it decays from an excited state to its ground state. The atom may be excited by absorbing a photon (photoluminescence), colliding with an electron (electroluminescence), etc. If the luminescence stops as soon as the exciting source is removed, it is known as fluorescence; if it persists for longer than 10^{-8} seconds it is called phosphorescence.

luminosity The intrinsic brightness of an object, such as a star, equal to the total energy radiated per second from the object. A star's luminosity increases both with surface temperature and with surface area: the hotter and larger a star, the greater its luminosity. Stellar luminosity, is related (logarithmically) to absolute magnitude.

luminous flux The rate of flow of light energy, taking into account the sensitivity of the observer or detector to the different wavelengths. For example, the human eye is most sensitive to the colour green. Luminous flux is measured in lumens.

luminous intensity The amount of light emitted per second by a point source per unit solid angle in a specified direction. It is measured in candela.

lumpsucker A slow-moving carnivorous bony fish, also called lumpfish, belonging to the family *Cyclopteridae*, found in cold northern seas.. They have a thickset body, sometimes studded with bony tubercles, a cleft dorsal fin, and a ventral sucking disc formed from fused pelvic fins. *Cyclopterus lumpus* is the largest species, reaching 60 cm long. The roe is used as a substitute for caviar. Order: *Scorpaeniformes*.

Lüneburg 53 15N 10 24E A spa in NE West Germany, in Lower Saxony. There are many fine medieval buildings. **Lüneburg Heath** was the site of the surrender of German troops to Montgomery in 1945 at the end of World War II. Population (1985 est): 61 000.

lungfish A freshwater bony fish belonging to the order *Dipnoi*, now reduced to six species including *Lepidosiren paradoxa* of South America, *Protopterus annectens* of Africa, and the Australian *Neoceratodus forsteri*. Lungfish have slender bodies, narrow paired fins, and tapering tails. Their swim bladders are modified for breathing air, an adaptation for droughts, when some make burrows in the bottom mud, leaving air vents above the mouth. They re-emerge in the rainy season to feed and spawn.

lungs The respiratory organs of many air-breathing animals and man. The human lungs are situated within the rib cage on either side of the heart. Each lung is enclosed by a smooth moist membrane (the pleura), which permits it to expand without friction, and contains many tiny thin-walled air sacs (alveoli), through which exchange of oxygen and carbon dioxide take place during breathing (*see* respiration). Air to the lungs passes through the trachea (windpipe) to the two main airways (bronchi), which subdivide into progressively smaller branches that terminate (as respiratory bronchioles) in the alveoli. Diseases affecting the lungs and airways include virus infections, bronchitis, and cancer.

Lupercalia An ancient Roman festival of purification and fertility held annually on 15 Feb. After performing sacrifices, priests carrying whips of goat hide made a circuit of the Palatine. Women struck by their whips were ensured fertility. The ceremony was suppressed in 494 AD by Pope Gelasius.

lupin An annual or perennial herb of the genus *Lupinus* (about 200 species), native to the N hemisphere and widely cultivated for ornament. They have compound leaves with radiating leaflets and dense spikes of flowers. Family: *Leguminosae*.

lupus A skin disease of which there are two forms. Used alone, the term usually refers to **lupus vulgaris**, a tuberculous infection of the skin, which is now readily cured by drugs. **Lupus erythematosus** (LE) is a disease in which inflammation of tissues is brought about by the body's own antibodies. LE can be controlled with steroid drugs.

Lusaka 15 03S 28 30E The capital of Zambia, lying on the Tanzam Railway. It became the capital of Northern Rhodesia in 1935 and of Zambia on independence in 1964. The centre of an important agricultural region, it has expanded rapidly. Population (1980): 538 469.

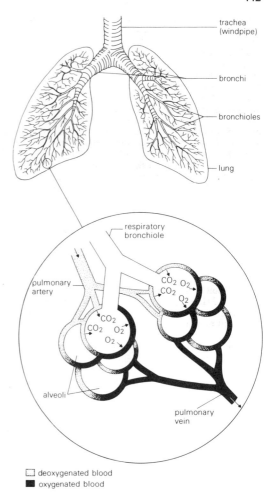

deoxygenated blood
oxygenated blood

LUNGS *The air passages in the lungs terminate in millions of tiny air sacs (alveoli), into which blood from the pulmonary artery releases its carbon dioxide. Inhaled oxygen in the alveoli is absorbed by the blood, which is carried back to the heart by the pulmonary vein.*

Lüshun. *See* Lüda.

Lü-ta. *See* Lüda.

lute A plucked stringed instrument of Moorish origin. The European lute, popular during the 15th, 16th, and 17th centuries, had a body in the shape of a half pear, six or more courses of double strings and a fretted fingerboard. The lute was used chiefly as a solo instrument and to accompany singers; it has been revived in the 20th century.

luteinizing hormone. *See* gonadotrophin.

lutetium (Lu) The heaviest lanthanide element named by its discoverer, G. Urbain (1872–1938) after his native Paris (Latin: *Lutetia*). It was formerly known as **cassiopeium**. At no 71; at wt 174.97; mp 1663°C; bp 3395°C.

Luther, Martin (1483–1546) German Protestant reformer, founder of Lutheranism. An Augustinian monk and from 1507 a priest, he became professor of theology at Wittenberg University in 1511. After experiencing a personal revelation he came to believe that salvation could be attained by faith alone. Several visits to Rome convinced him of the corruption of the papacy, the Dominican monk Johann Tetzel (c.1465–1519), who sold indulgences on behalf of papal funds, being a particular target for his hostility. In 1517 he nailed his 95 theses against this practice to the church door at Wittenberg. He disobeyed the papal summons to Rome (1518) and further attacked the papal system in his writings. His public burning of a papal bull condemning his theses and writings resulted in his excommunication in 1521. He appeared before Charles V's imperial diet (legislative assembly) at Worms but refused to recant and was declared an outlaw. While in hiding at Wartburg, under the protection of the Elector of Saxony, he completed a German translation of the New Testament. In 1522 he returned openly to Wittenberg, where he led the reform of its church. His original intention was reform not schism, but with the Augsburg Confession (1530) a separate Protestant church emerged. Subsequently the leadership of the German Reformation was gradually taken over by Philip Melanchthon (1497–1560).

Lutheranism The belief and practice of the Protestant Churches that derive from the teaching of Martin Luther, especially as formulated in the Augsburg Confession (1530). There is a wide divergence in matters of belief among Lutherans. Essentially Scripture is taken to be the only rule of faith and conservative Lutherans accept Luther's basic doctrine that redemption is only through faith in Christ. Lutheranism is the national faith in all Scandinavian countries, is the principal Protestant Church in Germany, and is also strong in North America. There are 80 million Lutherans world wide.

Lutine bell The ship's bell taken from the *Lutine* (sank 1799) and that now hangs at Lloyd's and is rung when news arrives of a ship previously posted "missing, fate unknown."

Luton 51 53N 0 25W A town in SE England, in Bedfordshire. It has an important motor-vehicle industry. Nearby is Luton Airport. Population (1985 est): 165 000.

Lutuli, Albert (John Mvumbi) (1898–1967) South African Black leader, whose advocacy of nonviolent opposition to racial discrimination won him the Nobel Peace Prize in 1960. A Zulu chief, in 1952 he became president of the African National Congress.

Lutyens, Sir Edwin Landseer (1869–1944) British architect. Known as the last English designer of country houses, he also designed the central square of Hampstead Garden Suburb (1908–10) and the Cenotaph (1919–20) but his most spectacular commission was the layout and viceregal palace of New Delhi (1912–30). His daughter, **Elisabeth Lutyens** (1906–83), a composer, adopted serialism as a basis for composition.

lux (lx) The SI unit of intensity of illumination equal to the illumination resulting from a flux of one lumen falling on an area of one square metre.

Luxembourg A province in SE Belgium, bordering on the Grand Duchy of Luxembourg and France. The Ardennes is a tourist area. Area: 4416 sq km (1705 sq mi). Population (1986 est): 225 563. Capital: Arlon.

Luxembourg, Grand Duchy of A small country in central Europe, between France and Germany. The generally undulating S with its wide valleys rises to the rugged uplands of the Ardennes Plateau in the N. *Economy*: predominantly industrial, the manufacture of iron and steel is especially important although considerable economic diversification has taken place. Agriculture remains important. The city of Luxembourg is an important international centre with the headquarters of the European Parliament and the European Coal and Steel Community. *History*: with the Netherlands and Belgium it formed part of the so-called Low Countries. It became a grand duchy in 1815 under the Dutch Crown. In 1830 it joined the Belgian revolt against the Netherlands, W Luxembourg joining independent Belgium and the E forming part of the Netherlands until obtaining independence in 1867. In 1921 it formed an economic union with Belgium and in 1948 both joined with the Netherlands to form the Benelux Economic Union. Luxembourg is now a member of the EC. Head of state: Grand Duke Jean (1921–). Head of Government: Jacques Santer. Official languages: Luxembourgish, French, and German. Official currency: Luxembourg franc of 100 centimes. Area: 2586 sq km (999 sq mi). Population (1987 est): 369 500. Capital: Luxembourg.

Luxor (*or* El Aksur) 25 40N 32 38E A town in central Egypt, on the River Nile. It occupies the S part of the ancient city of Thebes and has numerous ruins and tombs. Population (1985): 137 300. See p. 444.

Luzon A volcanic island in the N Philippines, the largest and most important. Largely mountainous, its central fertile plain is a major grain growing area with rice terraces to the N. Most industry is concentrated around Manila. Area: 108 378 sq km (41 845 sq mi). Population (1980): 23 900 796. Chief town: Manila.

Lvov 49 50N 24 00E A city in the Soviet Union, in the W Ukrainian SSR. It is a major industrial and cultural centre. Under Austrian rule from 1772, it was ceded to Poland after World War I and to the Soviet Union in 1939. Population (1987): 767 000.

Lyceum The gardens and gymnasium in ancient Athens in which Aristotle lectured and which gave their name to the school and research foundation that he established there in about 335 BC. The name is now applied particularly to Aristotle's philosophical doctrines.

lychee. *See* litchi.

Lydia In antiquity, a region of W Asia Minor with its capital at Sardis. Its last native king, Croesus (ruled 560–546 BC), enriched by Lydia's alluvial gold, controlled Anatolia eastwards to the River Halys, until his defeat by Cyrus the Great (d. 529 BC). The Lydians invented coined money (c. 700 BC).

Lyle, Sandy (1958–) British golfer, who became the first British player to win the US Masters event (1988). His other successes have included the Open Championship in 1985.

lymph A clear colourless fluid, consisting of water and dissolved substances, that is contained in a network of vessels called the **lymphatic system**. It is derived from blood and bathes the cells, supplying them with nutrients and absorbing their waste products, before passing into the lymphatic vessels. Here the lymph passes through a series of small swellings called **lymph nodes**, which filter out bacteria and other foreign particles, before draining into the main lymphatic vessels in the neck. These two vessels are connected to veins in the neck and so drain the lymph back into the bloodstream.

The lymph nodes, which also produce lymphocytes (a type of white blood cell), sometimes become enlarged during infections. The lymphatic system is one of the routes by which cancer is spread.

lymphocyte. *See* leucocyte.

LUXOR   *Ruins of the Temple of Amenhotep III.*

lymphoma Cancer of the lymph nodes. There are several different types but the most common is Hodgkin's disease, which can now often be controlled by chemotherapy.

lynx A short-tailed cat, *Felis lynx*, that inhabits forests of Eurasia and North America. Lynxes are about 1 m long with faintly spotted yellow-brown thick fur; their ears are tipped with black tufts. They hunt at night, usually for small mammals.

Lyon 45 46N 4 50E The third largest city in France, the capital of the Rhône department at the confluence of the Rivers Rhône and Saône. Notable buildings include the cathedral (12th–15th centuries). The focal point of road and rail routes, Lyon is an important financial centre and has been a leading textile centre since the 15th century. Population (1982): 418 476.

lyre An ancient plucked string instrument. It consists of a sound box with two symmetrical arms supporting a cross piece from which strings are stretched to a bridge on the belly.

lyrebird A primitive ground-dwelling passerine bird belonging to a family (*Menuridae*; 2 species) restricted to

forests of E Australia. The male superb lyrebird (*Menura superba*) is brown with grey underparts. Its magnificent tail is spread out into a lyre shape during the courtship display, which is performed on a mound of mud and debris. All lyrebirds sing loudly and are excellent mimics.

Lysander (d. 395 BC) Spartan general and politician. He commanded the fleets that defeated the Athenians at Notium (407) and Aegospotami (405) towards the end of the Peloponnesian War.

Lysenko, Trofim Denisovich (1898–1976) Soviet biologist, who had a damaging influence on Soviet biology. He endorsed Lamarck's discredited theory of evolution through inheritance of acquired characteristics. This led him to attack Mendelian genetics and the chromosome theory of inheritance, which, in the 1930s, were widely accepted elsewhere. With the backing of Stalin, Lysenko's influence grew, and by 1948, Soviet scientific opposition to his views had been stifled. Lysenko's influence was eclipsed after Stalin's death.

lysergic acid diethylamide. *See* LSD.

lysosome A membrane-bounded structure occurring in large numbers in nearly all animal cells and containing enzymes responsible for the breakdown of materials both within and outside the cell. Functions of lysosomes include the destruction of bacteria in white blood cells.

LYNX

M

Mabinogion, the A collection of eleven medieval Welsh folktales. Drawing on Celtic, Norman, and French legends, it was compiled in the 14th century and contains the earliest known Arthurian romance, *Culhwch and Olwen* (c. 1100).

Mabuse. *See* Gossaert, Jan.

Macao (Portuguese name: Macáu; Chinese name: Aomen) 22 13N 113 36E A Portuguese-administered free port in S China, across the Zhu estuary from Hong

Kong. The population is mainly Chinese. Chief industries are textiles and fishing. *History*: it was a major trading centre until the 19th century. Immigration of refugees from Communist China was stopped after procommunist riots (1966–67). Sovereignty will pass to China in 1999. Area: 16 sq km (6 sq mi). Population (1986 est): 426 400.

macaque An Old World monkey belonging to the genus *Macaca* (12 species), found mainly in the forests of S

Asia. 35–78 cm long, macaques have short legs and areas of hard bare skin on the rump. They are mainly terrestrial, feeding on plant and animal matter. *See also* Barbary ape; rhesus monkey.

MacArthur, Douglas (1880–1964) US general. One of the outstanding strategists of World War II, he commanded the occupation of Japan (1945–51) and then commanded the UN forces in the Korean War. His advocacy of active operations against China was contrary to US policy and President Harry S. Truman dismissed him (1951).

Macassar. *See* Ujung Pandang.

Macaulay, Thomas Babington, 1st Baron (1800–59) British essayist and historian. He was a leading contributor to the *Edinburgh Review* and had a long career in parliament. His Whig sympathies are evident in his immensely successful *History of England* (5 vols, 1849–61).

macaw A large brightly coloured parrot belonging to one of two genera (*Ara* and *Anodorhynchos*), ranging from Mexico to Paraguay. Up to 100 cm long, macaws have a characteristically long loose tail and a huge hooked bill.

Macbeth (d. 1057) King of Scots (1040–57), after killing Duncan I in battle at Bothnagowan. He was killed by Duncan's son Malcolm.

Maccabees The name applied loosely to the Hasmonean dynasty, founded in Jerusalem by Judas Maccabee (d. 161 BC) after a revolt against Syrian (Seleucid) rule. It continued until the capture of Jerusalem by the Romans in 63 BC. In Christian usage it is applied to seven young brothers martyred during the revolt. In 1895 it was revived in the name of a Jewish athletics organization, Maccabi, the World Union of which was formed in 1921.
The **Books of Maccabees** are four books of the Apocrypha.

McCarthy, Joseph R(aymond) (1908–57) US Republican senator, who led Senate investigations of supposed communists during the Cold War. His claim to have the names of communist infiltrators into the State Department was not proved and in 1954 his anticommunist witchhunt—commonly known as McCarthyism—came to an end.

Macclesfield 53 16N 2 07W A town in N England, in Cheshire on the W edge of the Pennines. Traditionally a centre of the silk industry, it also produces textile machinery, paper, and plastics. Population (1981): 46 832.

McCullers, Carson (1917–67) US novelist and playwright. Her novels, which include *The Heart Is a Lonely Hunter* (1940) and *A Member of the Wedding* (1946), are set in her native South and describe a grotesque and violent world. Other works include *The Ballad of the Sad Café* (1951) and *Clock Without Hands* (1961).

MacDiarmid, Hugh (Christopher Murray Grieve; 1892–1978) Scottish poet. Active both as a nationalist and Marxist, he virtually created the "Scottish Renaissance" in literature. His early poetry, notably in *A Drunk Man Looks at the Thistle* (1926), was written in a Scots language drawn from regional dialects and Middle Scots writers. A number of later poems, however, are written in English.

MacDonald, (James) Ramsay (1866–1937) British statesman; the first Labour prime minister (1924, 1929–31, 1931–35). He joined the Independent Labour Party in 1894. Elected an MP (1906) he became leader of the

parliamentary Labour Party (1911) but resigned in opposition to World War I (1914). Re-elected to parliament in 1922 he again led the Labour Party, becoming prime minister in 1924. His minority government was defeated after a vote of no confidence in his administration. His 1929–31 government was broadened into a coalition (1931–35) that was increasingly dominated by the Conservatives.

mace. *See* nutmeg.

Macedonia The central region of the Balkans. Inhabited from Neolithic times, Macedonia was settled by many migrating northern tribes. About 640 BC Perdiccas I became the first ruler of the kingdom of Macedon. Philip II (359–336 BC) quelled the warlike tribes and founded Macedon's military and economic power, which under his son Alexander the Great was extended to the East. After defeat (168 BC) in the Macedonian Wars, Macedonia became a Roman province (146). The region is now divided between S Yugoslavia (a constituent republic), N Greece, and SW Bulgaria.

McEnroe, John (Patrick, Jr) (1959–) US tennis player. He won the US singles title in 1979, 1980, 1981, and 1984. An intense competitor noted for his tempestuous court behaviour, he became Wimbledon singles champion in 1981, 1983, and 1984.

Macgillicuddy's Reeks A mountain range in the Republic of Ireland, in Co Kerry. It extends W of the Lakes of Killarney, reaching 1041 m (3414 ft) at Carrantuohill.

Machiavelli, Niccolò (1469–1527) Italian political theorist. He served the Florentine republic as statesman and diplomat from 1498 to 1512, when the restoration of the Medici family forced him into exile. In *The Prince* (1532), written in 1513, he argued that all means are permissible in the realization of a stable state.

Mach number The ratio of the velocity of a body in a fluid to the velocity of sound in that fluid. The velocity is said to be supersonic if the Mach number is greater than one. If it exceeds five the velocity is said to be hypersonic. Named after the Austrian physicist Ernst Mach (1838–1916).

Machu Picchu A well-preserved Inca town in the Urubamba valley (Peru), discovered in 1911. Sited on a precipitous ridge, Machu Picchu is flanked by extensive agricultural terraces. It contains a central plaza, royal palace, and sun temple, all built of polygonal dressed stone blocks. See p. 446.

Macías Nguema. *See* Equatorial Guinea, Republic of.

McIndoe, Sir Archibald Hector (1900–60) New Zealand surgeon, who pioneered techniques in plastic surgery. He is particularly noted for his work in Britain with badly burnt RAF airmen during World War II.

Macintosh, Charles (1766–1843) Scottish chemist, who invented the waterproof garment known as the "mackintosh." He made his discovery in 1823 by noting that rubber dissolved in naphtha could be used to stick together two pieces of cloth, producing a waterproof layer between them. He also patented a steel-making process (1825).

McKenna, Siobhán (1923–86) Irish actress. She acted at the Abbey Theatre, Dublin, from 1943 to 1946 and made her London debut in 1947. She was particularly successful in the roles of St Joan in G. B. Shaw's play and of Pegeen in Synge's *The Playboy of the Western World*.

MACHU PICCHU *The name of the mountain; the name of the ruined Inca town is unknown.*

Mackenzie, Sir (Edward Montague) Compton (1883–1972) British novelist. His early novels include the semiautobiographical *Sinister Street* (1913). His later work includes several volumes of memoirs and many humorous novels, notably *Whisky Galore* (1947).

Mackenzie River The longest river in Canada, flowing from Great Slave Lake in the North West Territories W and NNW to an extensive delta on the Beaufort Sea. Navigable in summer, it carries oil and minerals from the Arctic Ocean to S Canada. Length: 1705 km (1065 mi).

mackerel An important food and game fish belonging to the genus *Scomber*, related to tuna. Mackerels live in shoals in tropical and temperate oceans, feeding on fish and invertebrates. They have a streamlined body, two dorsal fins, and a forked tail. The common Atlantic mackerel (*S. scombrus*), about 30 cm long, is marked with black and green bands above and is silvery-white below.

McKinley, Mount A mountain in the USA, in S central Alaska in the Alaska Range. The highest peak in North America, it was first successfully climbed in 1913 by the US explorer, Hudson Stuck (1863–1920). Height: 6194 m (20 320 ft).

Maclean, Donald (1913–83) British Foreign Office official and Soviet secret agent. He fled to Russia in company with Guy Burgess (1911–63) in 1951. In 1979 it was revealed that Anthony Blunt (1907–83), a distinguished art historian, was implicated in the affair.

McMahon, William (1908–88) Australian statesman; prime minister (1971–72) of a coalition of Liberal and Country Parties. He became Liberal deputy leader in 1966 and minister for foreign affairs in 1969.

Macmillan, Daniel (1813–57) Scottish bookseller and publisher, who with his brother **Alexander Macmillan** (1818–96) founded (1843) Macmillan and Company, which became one of the world's largest publishing houses. Apprenticed to a bookseller in Scotland in 1824, Daniel opened his own shop in Cambridge (1843).

Macmillan, (Maurice) Harold, 1st Earl of Stockton (1894–1986) British statesman; Conservative prime minister (1957–63). The grandson of Daniel Macmillan, he was MP for Stockton (1924–29; 1931–45) and for Bromley (1945–64). 1931. In 1951 he became a successful minister of housing and local government and then minister of defence (1954) and foreign secretary (1955). As chancellor of the exchequer (1955–57) he introduced Premium Bonds (1957). He succeeded Sir Anthony Eden as prime minister. His "wind of change" speech in Africa in 1958 marked his government's support of independence for African states; he is also remembered for his speech during the 1959 election asserting "you've never had it so good." His second ministry suffered a major blow when de Gaulle frustrated Britain's attempt to join the EEC (1963). However, he improved relations with the USA and helped to achieve the Nuclear Test-Ban Treaty (1963). Macmillan became chancellor of Oxford University in 1960, was awarded the OM in 1976, and was granted an earldom in 1984. He became chancellor of Oxford University in 1960.

MacNeice, Louis (1907–63) Irish-born British poet. He published his first volume of poetry, *Blind Fireworks*, in 1929. Among his other volumes are *Autumn Journal* (1939), *The Burning Perch* (1963), and a distinguished collection of plays for radio, *The Dark Tower* (1947).

Mâcon 46 18N 4 50E A town in E France, the capital of the Saône-et-Loire department on the River Saône. An important trading centre for Burgundy wines, its manufactures include textiles, vats, and agricultural machinery. Population (1983): 39 000.

McQueen, Steve (1930–80) US film actor. Following his success in *The Magnificent Seven* (1960) he was usually associated with the roles of tough laconic heroes. His later films include *Bullitt* (1968) and *Papillon* (1973).

HAROLD MACMILLAN *Photographed by Patrick Lichfield on his 90th birthday.*

Madagascar, Democratic Republic of (name until 1975: Malagasy Republic) An island country in the Indian Ocean, off the SE coast of Africa. A narrow coastal plain in the E and a broader one in the W rise to central highlands. Most of the inhabitants are Merina, Betsimisaraka, and Betsileo, all speaking Austronesian dialects. *Economy*: chiefly agricultural: the main crops include rice and manioc as well as coffee, sugar, and spices, the main exports. Minerals include graphite, chrome, and ilmenite. Industry, previously based mainly on food processing and tobacco, now includes metals, plastics, paper, and oil refining. *History*: settled by Indonesians from the 1st century AD and by Muslim traders from Africa from the 8th century, it remained a native kingdom until the late 19th century, when the French laid claim to Madagascar and established a protectorate (1896). It became a French overseas territory in 1946 and a republic within the French Community in 1958, gaining full independence in 1960. In 1975 Madagascar became a democratic republic, with Lt Cdr Didier Ratsiraka (1936–   ) as its first president. Official languages: Malagasy and French. Official currency: Malagasy franc of 100 centimes. Area: 587 041 sq km (229 233 sq mi). Population (1987 est): 10 568 000. Capital: Antananarivo. Main port: Toamasina.

madder   A perennial herb of the genus *Rubia* (about 38 species), especially *R. tinctorum*, native to Eurasia. It has trailing stems with narrow leaves, small yellow flowers, and blackish berry-like fruits. A red dye is extracted from the roots. Family: *Rubiaceae*.

Madeira Islands (*or* Funchal Islands)   A Portuguese archipelago in the Atlantic Ocean, about 640 km (398 mi) off the coast of Morocco. It comprises the inhabited islands of Madeira and Porto Santo and two uninhabited island groups. Madeira, the largest and most important island, is densely vegetated. Its products include basketwork, fruit (such as mangoes), sugar, and the famous Madeira wine. Area: 777 sq km (300 sq mi). Population (1986 est): 269 500. Capital: Funchal.

Madras   13 05N 80 18N A city and major seaport in India, the capital of Tamil Nadu on the Coromandel Coast. Founded (1639) by the British East India Company, the city developed around Fort St George, which is the site of the first English church built in India (1678–80). An important industrial centre, Madras manufactures cars, bicycles, and cement and its chief exports are leather, iron ore, and cotton textiles. Population (1981 est): 4 276 635.

Madrid   40 27N 3 42W The capital of Spain, situated on a high plateau in the centre of the country on the River Manzanares. Its industries include the manufacture of leather goods, textiles, chemicals, engineering, glassware, and porcelain and the processing of agricultural products. A cultural centre, Madrid possesses a university, notable art galleries, and the national library (founded in 1712). Fine buildings include the former royal palace and the 17th-century cathedral. *History*: Madrid was captured from the Moors in 1083 by Alfonso VI. Philip II established it as the capital in 1561. In the Spanish Civil War Madrid was a Republican stronghold until it fell to the Nationalists in March, 1939. Population (1986 est): 3 053 101.

madrigal   A secular polyphonic composition (*see* polyphony) for voices, often a setting of a love poem. In 14th-century Florence, Landini wrote madrigals for voices and instruments. The Italian madrigal of the 16th and 17th centuries developed as an aristocratic art form in the complex compositions of Marenzio, Monteverdi, and Gesualdo. The English school (Byrd, Morley, Weelkes, etc.) wrote in a simpler style.

Maeander, River.   *See* Menderes, River.

Maes, Nicolas   (*or* N. Maas; 1634–93) Dutch painter of domestic scenes and portraits, born in Dordrecht. Initially influenced by his teacher Rembrandt, in such paintings as *Girl at the Window* (c. 1655; Rijksmuseum, Amsterdam), he later adopted the style of Flemish portraiture.

Maeterlinck, Maurice   (1862–1949) Belgian poet and dramatist. Having established his reputation as a poet he became the leading dramatist of the Symbolist movement with such plays as *Pelléas et Mélisande* (1892). He also wrote several philosophical and mystical prose works. He won the Nobel Prize in 1911.

Mafeking   (*or* Mafikeng)   25 53S 25 39E A town in South Africa, in Bophutha Tswana. It was besieged for 217 days by Boers during the second Boer War (1899–1902) but was held by Col Baden-Powell until relieved. It was the capital of the protectorate of Bechuanaland (now Botswana) until 1965. Population (1980): 6775.

Mafia   A criminal organization that originated as a secret society in 13th-century Sicily. The word (meaning "swank") was coined in the 19th century, when the Mafia was employed by the great landowners of Sicily to manage their estates. By extortion, "protection," ransom, and blackmail, the Mafia formed an organization so powerful that it virtually ruled Sicily. Italian emigrants took the Mafia to the USA in the early 20th century, where as Cosa Nostra (Our Affair), it has flourished.

Magdalenian   A culture of the Upper Palaeolithic, succeeding the Solutrean in W Europe. Named after La Madeleine cave in the Dordogne (SW France), the Magdalenian is marked by an abundance of bone and antler tools. Dating from about 15 000 to 10 000 BC, it was the heyday of prehistoric art with magnificent cave paintings (e.g. at Altamira).

Magdeburg   52 8N 11 35E A city in W East Germany, on the River Elbe. It achieved fame in the middle ages for its judicial system, the "Magdeburg Law," which was used as a model by many other European cities. It was also a leading member of the Hanseatic League. An important inland port, its industries include iron, oil and sugar refining, chemicals, and textiles. Population (1986): 288 798.

Magellan, Ferdinand   (c. 1480–1521) Portuguese explorer. He undertook many expeditions to India and Africa for Portugal between 1505 and 1516. In 1519, under Spanish patronage, he set off to seek a passage W to the Moluccas. Late in 1520 the expedition sailed through the Strait of Magellan, which separates the mainland of South America from Tierra del Fuego. In the spring of 1521 they reached the East Indies, where Magellan was killed. Only one ship returned to Spain, thus completing the first circumnavigation of the world. See p. 448.

Maggiore, Lake   (Latin name: Lacus Verbanus)   A long narrow lake in Italy and Switzerland. Sheltered from the N by the Alps, it enjoys a mild climate: the holiday resorts at its edge include Locarno, in Switzerland. Area: 212 sq km (82 sq mi).

Magi   1. In antiquity, the priests of Zoroaster, renowned for their astronomical knowledge (*see* Zoroastrianism). 2. The sages who came from the East, following a star, to worship the infant Christ at Bethlehem (Matthew 2.1–12). Early Christian tradition gave them the title of kings and the names of Caspar, Melchior, and Balthazar; they became the patron saints of Cologne.

Symbolic significance was ascribed to their gifts: gold (kingship), frankincense (divinity), and myrrh (death).

FERDINAND MAGELLAN *Allegorical engraving (c. 1592) of the explorer at sea.*

magic A system of beliefs and practices by which it is believed that man may control the natural and supernatural forces that affect his life. Generally regarded as "superstition" in industrial societies, magic plays an important social role in many preindustrial societies. Its practitioners may rank next to the chief in prestige and authority, being credited with the ability to communicate with good and evil spirits.

Maginot line Fortifications built (1929–38) to protect the E frontier of France. They were named after André Maginot (1877–1932), French minister of war (1929–32), who authorized its construction.

magistrate An officer who administers the law. In England magistrates are either justices of the peace or stipendiary magistrates, who are appointed to try cases in some metropolitan Magistrates' Courts, have wider powers than justices, and are salaried.

maglev. *See* magnetic levitation.

magma Molten rock lying beneath the earth's surface, either in the crust or upper mantle. It may rise to the surface through volcanic fissures and be extruded as lava; if it solidifies under ground it forms intrusive igneous rock. Magma is a hot largely silicate liquid, containing dissolved gases and sometimes suspended crystals.

Magna Carta (1215) The Great Charter that was sealed at Runnymede by King John of England in response to baronial unrest. The Charter defined the barons' feudal obligations to the monarch and confirmed the liberties of the English Church. Of the four extant originals, two are in the British Library, one is in Salisbury Cathedral, and one is in Lincoln Cathedral.

magnesium (Mg) A light silvery-white reactive metal, first isolated by Sir Humphry Davy in 1808. Magnesium is the eighth most common element in the earth's crust and is a major constituent of the earth's mantle. It is extracted by electrolysis of magnesium chloride ($MgCl_2$), which is obtained from sea water and is responsible for the stickiness of unrefined table salt, since magnesium chloride is deliquescent. Magnesium forms many other ionic salts, such as the sulphate ($MgSO_4$; Epsom salts), the carbonate ($MgCO_3$; magnesite), the oxide (MgO), the nitrate ($Mg(NO_3)_2$), and the hydroxide ($Mg(OH)_2$; milk of magnesia). It also plays a central role in plant life, occurring in chlorophyll. It has important commercial uses when alloyed with aluminium. At no 12; at wt 24.312; mp 648.8°C; bp 1090°C.

magnet A body that has an appreciable external magnetic field (*see also* magnetism). Every magnet has two distinct areas around which the field is greatest—called the north and south poles. If two magnets are brought together, the like poles repel each other and the opposite poles attract each other. Ferromagnetic materials (*see* ferromagnetism) are attracted to magnets because the magnet induces a field in the material in line with its own field. **Permanent magnets** are made of ferromagnetic materials and retain their magnetism unless they are heated above a certain temperature or are demagnetized by a strong opposing field. **Electromagnets** only function when an electric current flows through their coils.

magnetic constant (μ_0) A constant frequently occurring in magnetic equations in SI units. Also known as the permeability of free space, its value is $4\pi \times 10^{-7}$ henry per metre. It is related to the electric constant (ε_0) by $\mu_0\varepsilon_0 = 1/c^2$, where c is the velocity of light.

magnetic declination (*or* magnetic variation) The angle between geographical north and the horizontal component of the geomagnetic field at the same point.

magnetic dip The angle formed between the horizon and a compass allowed to swing freely in the vertical plane. It thus indicates the direction of the vertical component of the geomagnetic field.

magnetic domain. *See* ferromagnetism.

magnetic field The concept, devised by Faraday, to explain the action-at-a-distance forces produced by a magnet. The magnet is thought of as being surrounded by a field of force, within which its magnetic properties are effective. The strength and direction of the field is indicated by the lines of force that join the magnet's north and south poles. These lines of force can be seen if a card is laid over a magnet and iron filings sprinkled onto the card; when the card is tapped, the filings congregate along the lines of force. A wire carrying an electric current is also surrounded by a magnetic field, with concentric lines of force. An electromagnet usually consists of a coil of wire, in which the lines of force run through the centre of the coil and around its circumference. *See also* electromagnetic field.

magnetic levitation (maglev) A magnetic method of raising a vehicle above its tracks to provide almost frictionless propulsion. Starting on normal wheels, the train levitates above its elevated track as it gathers speed as a result of the interaction between superconducting magnets buried in the track and those in the base of each coach. Forward propulsion is by linear motor.

magnetic tape. *See* tape recorder.

magnetism A phenomenon in which one body can exert a force on another body with which it is not in contact (action at a distance). The space in which such a force exists is called a magnetic field. Stationary charged particles are surrounded by an electric field; when these charged particles move or spin, an associated effect, the magnetic field, is created. The behaviour of materials when placed in such a field depends on how the spinning electrons inside its atoms align themselves. *See also* ferrimagnetism; ferromagnetism; paramagnetism.

magnetite (*or* lodestone) A black magnetic mineral, a form of iron oxide (Fe_3O_4). It often has distinct north and south magnetic poles and was known around 500 BC for its use as a compass. It is one of the ores from which iron is extracted.

magneto An alternating-current electric generator that uses a permanent magnet, rather than an electromagnet, to create the magnetic field. It usually consists of one or more conducting coils rotating between a number of pairs of magnetic poles. The induced voltage has a frequency equal to the number of magnets times the speed of rotation of the coils. It is used in some small internal-combustion engines to produce the ignition spark.

magnetohydrodynamics (MHD) A method of generating electricity in which current carriers in a fluid are forced by an external magnetic field to flow between electrodes placed in the fluid. Usually the fluid is a hot ionized gas or plasma in which the current carriers are electrons. The electron concentration is increased by adding substances of low ionization potential (e.g. sodium or potassium salts) to the flame.

magnetomotive force (mmf) A measure of the magnetic effect of an electric current in a coil. It is analogous to electromotive force and is measured in ampere-turns, being dependent on the number of turns in the coil.

magnetosphere A region surrounding a planet in which charged particles are controlled by the magnetic field of the planet rather than by the interplanetary magnetic field carried by the solar wind. Its shape arises from the interaction between solar wind and planetary magnetic field. The earth's magnetosphere, which includes the Van Allen radiation belts, extends 60 000 km from the sunward side of the planet but is drawn out to a much greater extent on the opposite side.

magnetostriction The mechanical deformation of a ferromagnetic material (*see* ferromagnetism) when it is subjected to a magnetic field.

magnetron An electronic device used to generate and amplify microwaves. It consists of a sealed evacuated tube containing a central cylindrical cathode (source of electrons) inside a cylindrical anode to which electrons are drawn by an electrostatic field. A steady magnetic field applied along the axis of the tube deflects the electrons from their radial path and, if strong enough, will cause them to rotate around the cathode setting up microwave-frequency oscillations. It is widely used in radar generators.

magnification In optical systems, the ratio of the width of an object to the width of its image, both being measured perpendicular to the axis of the system. For a single lens this reduces to the ratio of the distances of the image and the object from the lens when the image is in focus. For optical instruments the magnification is defined as the ratio of the size of the image on the retina produced by an object with and without the instrument.

magnitude A measure of the brightness of stars and other astronomical objects. An object's **apparent magnitude** is its brightness as observed from earth and depends primarily on its luminosity and its distance. An object's **absolute magnitude** is its apparent magnitude if it lay at a distance of 10 parsecs (32.616 light years). Both apparent and absolute magnitude are measured at various specific wavebands in the visible, ultraviolet, and infrared regions of the electromagnetic spectrum.

Magnolia A genus of evergreen or deciduous shrubs and trees (35 species), native to North America and Asia and widely grown as ornamentals. Up to 45 m high, they have large simple leaves and big showy white, yellow, greenish, or pink flowers. These produce papery cone-like structures containing winged fruits. Family: *Magnoliaceae*.

magpie A noisy black-and-white crow, *Pica pica*, occurring in Eurasia, NW Africa, and W North America. 44 cm long, it has a long wedge-shaped tail. Magpies are omnivorous and notorious predators of eggs and nestlings; they are also attracted to bright objects. The name is also given to Australian songbirds of the family *Cracticidae*, which includes the currawongs.

RENÉ MAGRITTE The Future of Statues (*c. 1937; Tate Gallery, London*).

Magritte, René (1898–1967) Belgian surrealist painter. Initially a wallpaper designer and commercial artist, he became associated with the Paris surrealists (*see* surrealism) in the late 1920s.

Magyars The largest ethnic group in Hungary. They originated from mixed Ugric and Turkic stock, who migrated from Siberia during the 5th century and reached their present location during the late 9th century. Today they are chiefly peasant farmers. *See also* Hungarian.

Maharashtra A state in W central India, on the Arabian Sea. Rising from its coastal plain eastwards over the Western Ghats, it lies mostly on the Deccan plateau. Cotton, millet, wheat, and rice are farmed. The second most industrialized state, it produces cotton textiles, chemicals, machinery, and oil products. Bauxite, manganese, and iron ore are mined. Area: 307 762 sq km (118 796 sq mi). Population (1981): 62 693 898. Capital: Bombay.

Mahayana (Sanskrit: Great Vehicle) The school of Buddhism dominant in Tibet, Mongolia, China, Korea, and Japan. More evolved, adaptable, and less conservative and academic than the rival school, the Theravada, the Mahayana teaching differs from it primarily in promulgating the ideal of the Bodhisattva – the one who, having gained enlightenment, remains in the world in order to help other beings to their release.

Mahdi, al- (Arabic: the guided one) In Islamic tradition, a messianic leader who will appear shortly before the end of the world and, for a few years, restore justice and religion. According to some Shiite Muslims, the 12th imam (9th century AD), who is now hidden, will return as the Mahdi. The best-known claimant to the title was the Sudanese leader **Muhammad Ahmad** (1844–85). After a religious experience, he proclaimed himself the Mahdi and led an uprising against the Egyptian Government. In 1885, after a ten-month siege, he captured Khartoum, which was defended by General Gordon.

mahjong An ancient Chinese game. It is usually played by 4 people using 2 dice and 136 tiles of bone, ivory, or plastic. 108 of the tiles are arranged in 3 suits: circles, bamboos, and characters. There are also four each of red, white, and green dragons and four each of east, south, west, and north winds. The tiles are built into a square of four walls, symbolizing a walled city.

Mahler, Gustav (1860–1911) Austrian composer and conductor. He directed the Viennese Court Opera from 1897–1907. In 1909 he became conductor of the New York Philharmonic Society, but met resistance to his advocacy of modern music. His nine large-scale symphonies (and uncompleted tenth) were written during brief vacations. The second (*Resurrection Symphony*), third, fourth, and eighth (*Symphony of a Thousand*) employ vocal soloists. He also wrote song cycles.

mahogany An evergreen tree of the genus *Swietenia* (7 species), native to tropical America and the West Indies and widely cultivated for timber. Up to about 20 m high, it has large compound leaves, greenish-yellow flower clusters, and fruit capsules containing winged seeds. *S. macrophylla* and *S. mahagoni* are the most important species: their hard red-brown wood is highly valued for furniture. Family: *Meliaceae*.

Mahonia A genus of evergreen shrubs (70 species), native to N temperate regions and often grown as ornamentals. They have leaves with paired, sometimes spiky, leaflets, and bunches of yellow or orange flowers that produce berries. Family: *Berberidaceae*.

maidenhair fern An ornamental fern of the genus *Adiantum* (about 200 species), especially *A. capillus-veneris*, found worldwide in moist warm places. From a creeping rhizome arise delicate brown or black stalks, about 2.5–30 cm high, bearing fan-shaped green leaflets. Clusters of spore capsules (sori) are situated on the leaf margins, which are folded onto the underside. Family: *Adiantaceae*.

maidenhair tree. *See* ginkgo.

Maidstone 51 17N 0 32E A town in SE England, the administrative centre of Kent on the River Medway. It is an ancient town and the centre of an important fruit- and hop-growing region. There are brewing, paper, cement, confectionery, and engineering industries. Population (1983 est): 71 800.

Mailer, Norman (1923–) US novelist and journalist. He established his reputation with the World War II novel *The Naked and the Dead* (1948). His concern with American society, which provided the themes for novels such as *An American Dream* (1965), is more directly expressed in later works, such as *The Armies of the Night*

(1968) and *The Executioner's Song* (1979), both of which were awarded a Pulitzer Prize. More recent works include *Ancient Evenings* (1983), *Tough Guys Don't Dance* (1984), and *Why Are We In Vietnam* (1988).

Main, River A river in central West Germany, flowing generally W through Frankfurt to join the River Rhine at Mainz. It is linked by canal with the River Danube. Length: 515 km (320 mi).

Maine A coastal state in the extreme NE USA. The largest of the New England states, it consists of uplands in the W and NW and lowlands along the deeply indented coast in the E. Four-fifths of the state is forested. It is the most sparsely populated state E of the Mississippi. Manufacturing is most important and the major products are paper and pulp, leather goods, food, timber, and textiles. An area of considerable mineral wealth, limestone, building stone, sand, and gravel are exploited. The state's major agricultural products are potatoes, poultry, dairying, apples, and beef. *History*: although claimed by both Britain and France, it became a British possession (1763). It entered the Union as part of Massachusetts (1788) and later became a separate state (1820). Area: 86 027 sq km (33 215 sq mi). Population (1980): 1 124 660. Capital: Augusta.

Mainland 1. (*or* Pomona) The largest of the Orkney Islands, divided into two main parts by Kirkwall Bay and Scapa Flow. Area: 492 sq km (190 sq mi). Population (1971): 6502. Chief town: Kirkwall. 2. The largest of the Shetland Islands. Area: about 583 sq km (225 sq mi). Population (1986): 19 236. Chief town: Lerwick.

main sequence. *See* Hertzsprung-Russell diagram.

Mainz (French name: Mayence) 50 00N 8 16E A city and port in SW West Germany, the capital of Rhineland-Palatinate at the confluence of the Rivers Rhine and Main. Originally a Celtic settlement, it was the first German archbishopric and in the 15th century Gutenberg set up his printing press here. It is a wine-trading centre with varied industries. Population (1986): 188 500.

MAHJONG *Players in Hong Kong.*

maize An annual cereal grass, *Zea mays*, also called Indian corn, sweet corn, or corn, native to the New World and widely cultivated in tropical and subtropical regions. 1–4.5 m high, it bears a tassel of male flowers at the top of the stem and spikes of female flowers in the leaf axils; these develop into cobs, each comprising long parallel rows of grains. Maize is used as a vegetable, in breakfast cereals, flour, and livestock feed and for the extraction of corn oil. It is the third most important cereal crop (after wheat and rice), the USA being the chief producing country.

Major, John (1943–) British Conservative politician; chancellor of the exchequer (1989–). Entering parliament in 1979, he served as minister of state for social security (1986–87), chief secretary to the Treasury (1987–89), and foreign secretary (July–Oct 1989).

Majorca (Spanish name: Mallorca) A Spanish island in the Mediterranean Sea, the largest of the Balearic Islands. The chief occupations are agriculture and tourism; cereals, legumes, oranges, olives, and figs are produced and marble is quarried. Area: 3639 sq km (1465 sq mi). Population (1981): 561 215. Capital: Palma.

Makarios III (Mikhail Khristodolou Mouskos; 1913–77) Cypriot churchman and statesman; archbishop of the Orthodox Church of Cyprus (1950–77) and president of Cyprus (1960–74, 1974–77). In 1956 he was deported to the Seychelles by the British because of his support for Greek-Cypriot union. He subsequently abandoned this aim.

Makassar. *See* Ujung Pandang.

Malabar Coast (*or* Malabar) The W coast of India from Goa in the N to Cape Comorin in the S. In 1498 Vasco da Gama landed here. The shore is fringed by coconut palms; inland there are lagoons and paddy fields.

Malabo (name until 1973: Santa Isabel) 3 45W 8 48E The capital of Equatorial Guinea, a port in the N of the island of Bioko (formerly Macias Nguema), founded by the British in 1827. Population (1986): 10 000.

Malacca 02 14N 102 14E A historic port in W Peninsular Malaysia, the capital of Malacca state. It was colonized successively by the Portuguese, Dutch, and British after 1511. Population (1980): 88 073.

Malacca A state in W Peninsular Malaysia, on the Strait of Malacca. Consisting chiefly of a low-lying coastal plain, it produces rice, rubber, copra, tin, and bauxite. Area: 1650 sq km (637 sq mi). Population (1980): 453 153. Capital: Malacca.

malachite An ore of copper consisting of hydrated copper carbonate, $Cu_2(OH)_2CO_3$. It is bright green and is found in deposits of copper minerals. It occurs in massive form, often with a smooth surface.

Málaga 36 43N 4 25W A city in S Spain, in Andalusia on the Mediterranean Sea. Founded by the Phoenicians (12th century BC), it passed successively to the Romans, the Visigoths, and the Moors, before falling to Ferdinand and Isabella in 1487. A major tourist centre and port, it exports olives, almonds, and dried fruits. Population (1986 est): 566 480.

Malagasy Republic. *See* Madagascar, Democratic Republic of.

Malamud, Bernard (1914–86) US novelist. With such witty and ironic novels as *The Assistant* (1957) and *A New Life* (1961) he built a reputation as a skilful chronicler of Jewish characters and themes. His other works include the novels *The Tenants* (1971) and *God's Grace* (1982).

malaria An infectious disease caused by protozoa of the genus *Plasmodium*. Malaria is transmitted by the female *Anopheles* mosquito, which lives only in the tropics. There are four species of *Plasmodium* that infect man and cause different types of malaria. Malignant tertian

MALARIA *The mosquito transmits the disease by puncturing the skin.*

malaria (caused by *P. falciparum*) is the most severe; benign tertian malaria (caused by *P. vivax*) is less often fatal but there are repeated attacks. The parasites invade the red blood cells and cause them to burst. There is always fever and there may also be fits, diarrhoea, shock, and jaundice. There are drugs (such as chloroquine) to treat and prevent the disease, but malaria remains a major cause of death and ill health in the tropics.

Malawi, Republic of (name until 1963: Nyasaland) A country in SE Africa, between Tanzania, Zambia, and Mozambique. Lake Malawi lies at its E border and the land consists mainly of high plateaus reaching heights of over 3000 m (9800 ft). The majority of the population is Bantu. *Economy*: chiefly agricultural. The main subsistence crop is maize, and cash crops include tobacco, tea, sugar, and groundnuts, which are the chief exports. Mineral resources are sparse. *History*: the area was visited by the Portuguese in the 17th century and, after Livingstone's exploration, became a British protectorate in 1891. In 1953 it was joined with Northern and Southern Rhodesia to form the Federation of Rhodesia and Nyasaland. Nyasaland became independent in 1964. In 1966 it became a republic within the British Commonwealth with Dr Hastings Banda (c.1906–) as its first president. Official languages: Chichewa and English. Official currency, since 1971: kwacha of 199 tambala. Area: 94 079 sq km (36 324 sq mi). Population (1985 est): 7 058 800. Capital: Lilongwe.

Malay A language of the Indonesian branch of the Austronesian family spoken in SE Asia and Indonesia. The dialect of the S Malay peninsula is the basis of standard Malay. It can be written in Roman or Arabic script. The Malay people probably migrated to this area from China between 2500 and 1500 BC. Since the 15th century Islam has been the accepted religion, but vestiges of former Hinduism survive.

Malay Archipelago (former name: East Indies) An island group in SE Asia, the largest in the world. It lies between the Pacific and Indian Oceans and between the Asian and Australian continents. It comprises the Indonesian, Malaysian, and Philippine islands; New Guinea is sometimes included.

Malaysia, Federation of A country in SE Asia, consisting of the 11 states of Peninsular Malaysia (formerly the Federation of Malaya) and the states of Sabah and Sarawak in N Borneo. Peninsular Malaysia consists of coastal plains rising to mountains in the interior. Most of the inhabitants are Malays and Chinese. *Economy*: Malaysia is a major exporter of rubber, tin, and palm oil. Agriculture is the chief occupation; besides the cash crops of rubber and palms, rice (the chief food crop) is extensively produced. Considerable quantities of timber are produced; fishing is also important. Minerals exploited include tin, iron ore, bauxite, ilmenite, and gold. *History*: from the 9th to the 14th centuries the Srivijaya empire dominated the area. In the 14th century it was overrun by Hindu Javanese and in about 1400 Malacca was established as an Islamic centre. In 1511 the port was taken by the Portuguese and in 1641 by the Dutch. British interest in the Malay states began in the 18th century and increased with the opening of the Suez Canal. Following occupation by the Japanese during World War II, the Federation of Malaya was established (1948). Malaya became independent in 1957 and in 1963 part of the federal state of Malaysia. There has been considerable unrest in recent years caused mainly by Chinese resentment of Malay dominance in the government. Supreme head of state: Sultan Mahmood Iskandar. Prime minister: Datuk Seri Mahathir Muhammed. Official language: Bahasa Malaysia. Official religion: Islam. Official currency: ringgit of 100 cents. Area: 329 749 sq km (127 289 sq mi). Population (1987 est): 16 527 000. Capital: Kuala Lumpur. Main port: Georgetown.

Malcolm III (c. 1031–93) King of the Scots (1057–93). He became king after killing Macbeth, the murderer of his father Duncan I (d. 1040; reigned 1034–40). He became a vassal of William the Conqueror (1072) and was murdered during the last of frequent raids into N England.

Malcolm X (1925–65) US militant Black leader. Formerly a member of the Black Muslims, he founded the rival militant Organization of Afro-American Unity (1964), which supported violent means of achieving racial equality. He was assassinated while addressing a rally.

Maldives, Republic of (Divehi name: Divehi Raajje; name until 1969: Maldive Islands) A small country in the Indian Ocean, to the SW of Sri Lanka. It consists of a large number of small coral islands, grouped in atolls, of which just over 200 are inhabited. Most of the population is of mixed Indian, Sinhalese, and Arabic descent. *Economy*: coconuts, along with fish, are the main export. Other sources of revenue are shipping, tourism, and copra production. *History*: formerly a dependency of Ceylon, the islands were officially under British protection from 1887 to 1965. They were ruled by an elected sultan until 1968, when they became a republic. The Republic of Maldives became a special member of the Commonwealth of Nations in 1982. Head of state: President Maumoon Abdul Gayoon (1937–   ). Official language: Divehi. Official religion: Islam. Official currency: Maldivian rufiyaa of 100 laari. Area: 298 sq km (115 sq mi). Population (1988 est): 195 000. Capital and main port: Malé.

Mali, Republic of (name until 1959: French Sudan) A large landlocked country in West Africa. It consists largely of desert, the flood plains of the River Niger providing most of the fertile land. The majority of the population are Bambara, Fulani, and Senufo. *Economy*:

chiefly subsistence agriculture, especially livestock, including cattle, camels, and sheep. The main crops are rice, millet, cassava, cotton, and groundnuts. River fishing is important and dried and smoked fish, together with cattle and groundnuts, are the main exports. Industry is based mainly on the processing of food and hides and skins. Mineral reserves of bauxite, uranium, and oil are present but only salt and small quantities of gold are exploited. *History*: from the 4th century AD the area was occupied by successive empires, including those of Ghana, Mali, and Gao. In the late 19th century it was conquered by the French and, as French Sudan, it became part of French West Africa. It achieved internal self-government as part of the French Community in 1958 and became a fully independent republic in 1960. In 1968 the government was overthrown in a military coup led by Lt Moussa Traoré (1936–   ), who became president in 1969. Official language: French. Official currency: Mali franc of 100 centimes. Area: 1 204 021 sq km (464 752 sq mi). Population (1987 est): 8 730 000. Capital: Bamako.

mallard A dabbling duck, *Anas platyrhynchos*, common on ponds and lakes in the N hemisphere. About 55 cm long, females are mottled brown and males greyish with a green head, white collar, reddish breast, black rump, a curly tail, and a broad yellow bill. Both sexes have a purple wing speculum.

Mallarmé, Stéphane (1842–98) French poet. He became a major figure of the Symbolist movement, believing that the function of poetry was to evoke the ideal essences that lay behind the world of actual appearances. His best-known works include *Hérodiade* (1864) and *L'Après-midi d'un faune* (1865).

Mallorca. *See* Majorca.

mallow A herbaceous plant of the genus *Malva* (30 species), native to N temperate regions. Mallows, which may be creeping or erect, grow up to 90 cm tall. They have hairy lobed leaves and five-petalled flowers, which are usually purple, pink, or white. The tree mallow (*Lavatera arborea*) is a shrublike biennial, up to 3 m high, with rose-purple flowers. Family: *Malvaceae*. *See also* marsh mallow.

Malmö 55 38N 12 57E A city and port in S Sweden, on the Sound opposite Copenhagen. It was a prominent trade and shipping centre in the middle ages. Malmö's varied industries include shipbuilding, textiles, and food processing. Population (1986): 230 056.

Malory, Sir Thomas (?1400–1471) English writer. He was the author of *Morte d'Arthur* (c. 1469), a narrative in 21 books of the legendary court of King Arthur, drawn mostly from French sources. The work was printed by Caxton in 1485. Malory's identity remains uncertain, but he was probably a Warwickshire knight who had fought in France, became an MP in 1445, and was several times imprisoned.

Malraux, André (1901–76) French novelist and essayist. His career included active service with communist revolutionaries in China in the 1920s, with the Republican forces in the Spanish Civil War, and with the French Resistance in World War II. His novels, which deal with the issues involved in these conflicts, include *Man's Estate* (1933) and *Days of Hope* (1938). He also wrote on art and produced a volume of memoirs, *Antimémoires* (1967).

Malta, Republic of A small country in the Mediterranean Sea, to the S of Sicily comprising the two main islands of Malta and Gozo and several islets. *Economy*: Malta was previously heavily dependent on foreign military bases. The naval dockyards have been converted to commercial use and port facilities are being developed; shipbuilding and repair are important. There is some agriculture, both crops and livestock, and fishing. Tourism is an important source of revenue. Exports include clothing, textiles, machinery, and food. *History*: occupied successively by the Phoenicians, Greeks, Carthaginians, and Romans, the island was conquered by the Arabs in 870 AD. In 1090 it was united with Sicily and in 1530 was granted to the Knights Hospitallers. In 1798 the island was occupied by the French and then by the British, to whom it was formally ceded in 1814. As a crown colony it became an important naval and air base. Malta became fully independent in 1964; in 1974 under Dom Mintoff it became a republic within the British Commonwealth. President: Censu Tabone (1914–   ). Prime minister: Dr Fenech Adami. Official languages: Maltese and English; Italian is widely spoken. Official religion: Roman Catholic. Official currency: Maltese pound of 100 cents and 1000 mils. Area: 316 sq km (122 sq mi). Population (1986 est): 343 334. Capital and main port: Valletta.

Malthus, Thomas Robert (1766–1834) British clergyman and economist, famous for his population theories. In his *Essay on the Principle of Population* (*First Essay*, 1798; *Second Essay*, 1803) Malthus argued that mankind is doomed to remain at near-starvation level as growth in food production, which increases at an arithmetical rate, is negated by the geometrical increase in population.

Maluku. *See* Moluccas.

Malvern 52 05N 2 20W A town in W central England, in Hereford and Worcester, consisting of Great Malvern and several villages incorporating the name. Lying on the E slopes of the Malvern Hills, it is a spa town with a famous public school (Malvern College, founded 1863). Population (1981): 30 187.

Malvinas, Islas. *See* Falkland Islands.

mamba A large agile highly venomous snake belonging to the African genus *Dendroaspis* (4–5 species). The aggressive black mamba (*D. polylepis*) is 4.3 m long, lives in open rocky regions, and preys on birds and small mammals. The smaller arboreal green mamba (*D. angusticeps*) reaches a length of 2.7 m. Mambas are egg-laying snakes. Family: *Elapidae* (cobras, mambas, coral snakes).

mammal A warm-blooded animal belonging to the class *Mammalia* (about 4250 species). The evolution of· mammals from reptiles involved the development of a temperature-regulation system with an insulating layer of fur and sweat glands in the skin for cooling. This enabled mammals to become highly active, with well-developed sense organs and brains, and to colonize cold climates. The survival of the young was improved by the evolution of mammary glands, and in placental mammals a specialized nourishing membrane (the placenta) in the uterus (womb).
The majority of modern mammalian species are terrestrial, ranging in size from tiny shrews to the elephant. However, bats are flying mammals and whales have adapted to a wholly marine existence. See pp. 454–455.

mammary gland The gland in female mammals that secretes milk. Believed to have evolved from sweat glands, there are one or more pairs on the ventral (under) side of the body. The number of glands is related to the number of young produced at one birth. Each gland consists of branching ducts leading from milk-secreting cells and opening to the exterior through a nipple. In the most primitive mammals (*Monotremata*) there are no nipples and the milk is secreted directly onto the body surface. *See also* lactation.

mammoth An extinct elephant belonging to the genus *Mammuthus*, whose remains have been found in India, Europe, and North America. Of the four types known, the imperial mammoth (*M. imperator*) was the largest, 4.5 m at the shoulder. The woolly mammoth (*M. primigenius*) had thick body hair and tusks up to 2.5 m long.

Man, Isle of An island in the Irish Sea, between England and Ireland. It has been a British Crown possession since 1828 but is virtually self-governing with its own parliament, the Court of Tynwald. It consists of central hills rising to 620 m (2034 ft) at Snaefell, with lowlands in the N and S. Tourism is the main source of revenue; attractions include its mild climate, scenery, and the famous annual Tourist Trophy (TT) motorcycle races. Its agriculture is varied; sheep and cattle are raised and produce includes cereals, turnips, and potatoes. *History*: originally inhabited by Celts, the derivative Manx language survived in common usage until the 19th century. The island became a dependency of Norway in the 9th century AD and was ceded to Scotland (1266), coming under English control after 1406. Area: 588 sq km (227 sq mi). Population (1986): 55 482. Capital: Douglas.

Managua 12 06N 86 18W The capital of Nicaragua, on the S shore of Lake Managua. Formerly an Indian settlement, it became capital in 1857. It suffered severe damage from earthquakes in 1931 and 1972 and from the civil war (1979). Population (1985): 682 111.

manatee A herbivorous aquatic mammal belonging to the genus *Trichechus* (3 species), of warm Atlantic waters and coastal rivers of Africa and America. Up to 4.5 m long, manatees have a rounded body with tail fin and flippers and a squarish snout. The American manatee (*T. manatus*) of Florida feeds mainly at night. Family: *Trichechidae*; order: *Sirenia*. *See also* dugong.

Manaus (*or* Manáos) 3 06S 60 00W A city in NW Brazil, the capital of Amazonas state on the Rio Negro. Founded in 1660, it became the centre of the rubber boom (1890–1920). It remains the chief inland port of the Amazon basin and is accessible to oceangoing steamers. Exports include rubber, brazil nuts, timber, and other forest products. Population (1980): 613 098.

Manawatu River A river in New Zealand, in SW North Island flowing generally W and SW to the Tasman Sea NE of Wellington. The surrounding plain is one of New Zealand's most productive farming areas. Length: 182 km (113 mi).

Manchester 53 30N 2 15W A city in NW England, the administrative centre of Greater Manchester, situated on the River Irwell and forming part of a large conurbation. Linked with the Mersey estuary by the Manchester Ship Canal (opened 1894), it is an important port as well as England's second largest commercial centre (banking, insurance). Industries include chemicals, engineering, clothing, printing, paper, rubber, food products, and electrical goods. It has well-known art galleries, the Hallé Orchestra, the University of Manchester (1851), and the national newspaper the *Guardian* (founded as the *Manchester Guardian* in 1821). The 15th-

MAMMAL

tundra and arctic

temperate forest

tropical grassland

tropical forest

Norway lemming

reindeer

musk ox

polar bear

Arctic fox

European flying squirrel

lynx

elk

North American porcupine

wolf

springbok

chacma baboon

spotted hyena

African mongoose

lion

clouded leopard

common opossum

colobus monkey

bongo

Philippine tarsier

fruit bat

MAMMAL *This large and diverse group of animals has succeeded in colonizing almost every available habitat on earth, even the most inhospitable. Representative mammals are shown from eight of the world's major habitats (the animals depicted in each habitat are not necessarily from the same geographical region).*

455

MAMMAL

temperate grassland

American bison

prairie dog

Eurasian hedgehog

saiga antelope

giant anteater

fresh water

beaver

American mink

muskrat

giant otter

desert

Arabian camel

addax

kangaroo rat

fennec fox

red kangaroo

salt water

Florida manatee

blue whale

bottlenose dolphin

walrus

harbour seal

century parish church became Manchester Cathedral in 1847. *History*: the Roman fort of Mancunium, Manchester developed as a regional market place for raw wool and flax and finished pieces. From the mid-18th century onwards it became the world's main cotton-manufacturing town. Its rapid growth led to industrial discontent and political agitation (*see* Peterloo Massacre). It also nurtured the basic principles of economic and political liberalism, embodied in the **Manchester School** (a group of political economists, the most famous being John Bright (1811–89) and Richard Cobden (1804–65)). Population (1985): 451 000.

Manchuria A region in NE China bordering on the Soviet Union, roughly comprising the provinces of Heilongjiang, Jilin, and Liaoning. It is mountainous in the E and W with a large central fertile plain, which is a major industrial and agricultural area. Products include timber, minerals, such as coal and iron, and fish. *History*: the area was for centuries inhabited and fought over by the Manchu, Mongols, and Chinese. Their power struggles resulted in empires established over China by the Mongols (1279–1368; *see* Yuan) and Manchus (1644–1912; *see* Qing). In the late 19th century it was dominated by Russia (1898–1904) and then by Japan (1905–45). In 1931, following the Mukden Incident (*see* Shenyang), Japanese forces invaded Manchuria and established the puppet state of Manchukuo. After 1945 the area received much aid from the Soviet Union until the 1960s, when the break between China and the Soviet Union took place. Since then military forces have been massed along the border. Area: about 1 300 000 sq km (502 000 sq mi).

Mandalay 21 57 96 04E A city in Burma, on the Irrawaddy River. The last capital of the Burmese kingdom, it fell to the British in 1885. It has numerous monasteries, temples, and pagodas and is the site of a university (1964). Mandalay is the principal commercial centre of Upper Burma. Population (1983): 417 266.

mandarin (fruit). *See* tangerine.

mandarin (official) A Chinese bureaucrat, whose appointment to salaried posts in the civil service was by examination. Mandarins occupied a privileged position in society and spoke the Mandarin dialect of Chinese, which in its standard, Peking, form is now spoken by 70% of the population.

Mandela, Nelson (Rolihlahla) (1918–) Black South African lawyer, who practised law in Johannesburg and is active in the African National Congress. He was acquitted of treason in 1961 but retried (1963–64) and sentenced to life imprisonment. His wife, **Winnie Mandela** (1934–), is also active in South African politics and campaigned tirelessly for her husband's release, which was finally achieved in 1990.

mandolin A plucked musical instrument, generally having four double courses of wire strings tuned in the same way as the violin. It is played with a plectrum, using a tremolo effect to sustain longer notes. It is used in informal music making and more rarely as a solo or orchestral instrument.

mandrake A herb of the genus *Mandragora*, especially *M. officinarum*, native to Europe. It has large simple leaves, white flowers, and a thick forked root, which was formerly believed to have healing and aphrodisiac properties. Family: *Solanaceae*.

mandrill A large Old World monkey, *Mandrillus*

sphinx, of West African coastal forests. They are 66–84 cm long including the tail (5–7.5 cm), with red and blue muzzle and buttocks and shaggy yellow-brown hair. They live in small family groups and forage for plants and insects.

Manet, Edouard (1832–83) French painter, born in Paris. By 1860 he was painting contemporary scenes, but throughout his career he remained indebted to the Old Masters, particularly to Velázquez and Hals. He exhibited mainly at the Paris Salon, where such paintings as *Olympia* and *Déjeuner sur l'herbe* (both Louvre) became targets for considerable scorn and derision. In the 1870s he adopted the technique of the impressionists. Such paintings as *The Balcony* (Louvre) and *The Luncheon* (Neue Staatsgaleries, Munich) anticipate 20th-century painting by making brushwork, colour, and design more important than the subject matter.

manganese (Mn) A hard grey brittle transition element that resembles iron, first isolated in 1774 by J. G. Gahn (1745–1818). It occurs in nature in many minerals, especially pyrolusite (MnO_2) and rhodochrosite ($MnCO_3$), in addition to the extensive deposits of manganese nodules discovered on the deep ocean floors. It is extracted by reduction of the oxide, with magnesium or aluminium, or by electrolysis. The metal is used in many alloys, particularly in steel, in which manganese improves the strength and hardness. Manganese forms compounds in a number of different valence states: for example MnO, Mn_3O_4, MnO_2. The permanganate ion (MnO_4^-) is a well-known oxidizing agent. At no 25; at wt 54.9380; mp 1244°C; bp 1962°C.

mange A contagious skin disease, caused by mites, that can affect domestic livestock, pets, and man (*see* scabies). The parasites bite or burrow into the skin causing hair loss, scaly dry skin, pimples, blisters, and intense itching. Treatment is with a suitable insecticide, such as gamma benzene hexachloride.

mangel-wurzel. *See* beet.

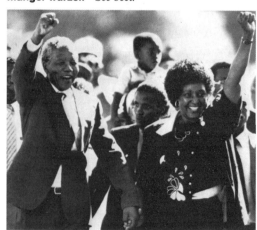

NELSON MANDELA *On his release from prison.*

mango A large evergreen tropical tree, *Mangifera indica*, native to SE Asia but cultivated throughout the tropics for its fruit. Growing 15–18 m high, it has long narrow leaves and pinkish flowers. The oblong fruit, up to 2.3 kg in weight, has a green, yellow, or reddish skin and contains a stony seed, surrounded by juicy orange edible flesh that has a spicy flavour. Family: *Anacardiaceae*.

mangroves Shrubs and trees forming dense thickets and low forests on coastal mudflats, salt marshes, and estuaries throughout the tropics. Many are evergreen, with shiny leathery leaves and aerial supporting (prop) roots. The main species are the common or red mangrove (*Rhizophora mangle*), the black mangrove (*Avicennia nitida*), and *Sonneratia* species.

Manhattan. *See* New York.

Manichaeism A religion influenced by both Gnosticism and Christianity. It originated in Persia (c. 230 AD), spread throughout Asia and the Roman Empire, and survived in Chinese Turkistan until the 13th century. Its founder, Mani (c. 216–c. 276), was martyred by the adherents of Zoroastrianism. Fundamental to his creed was the belief that matter is entirely evil, but within each individual is imprisoned a soul, which is a spark of the divine light.

Manila 14 30N 121 12E The capital and main port of the Philippines, on Manila Bay in Luzon. Founded by the Spanish in 1571, it suffered several foreign occupations over the centuries and the old town was destroyed in World War II. The official capital was transferred to Quezon City on the outskirts (1948–76). An educational centre, it has over 20 universities, including the University of Santo Tomas founded in 1611. It has one of the finest harbours in the world and is also an important industrial centre; its industries include textiles, pharmaceuticals, and food processing. Population (1984 est): 1 728 441.

manioc. *See* cassava.

Manitoba A province of central Canada, in the centre of North America. Although it is one of the Prairie Provinces, only the SW is true prairie. Further to the NE lies the Red River Valley and three large lakes (Winnipeg, Winnipegosis, and Manitoba) with extensive forests in the N. Manitoba's economy is based on large mechanized farms producing grains and livestock. Forests, fisheries, and hydroelectricity are also important. Manitoba produces copper, gold, zinc, silver, nickel, and oil. Greater Winnipeg contains over half the population. *History*: originally exploited for furs, Manitoba first attracted dispossessed Scots Highlanders as settlers (1812). Acquisition of the area by Canada (1869) provoked the Riel Rebellion (1869–70), an uprising of French-speaking halfbreeds (Métis). Manitoba became a province in 1870. Area: 548 495 sq km (211 774 sq mi). Population (1986): 1 063 016. Capital: Winnipeg.

Mann, Thomas (1875–1955) German novelist. Art and the artist are his main themes, in the novella *Death in Venice* (1912), *The Magic Mountain* (1924), and *Doctor Faustus* (1947), a novel about a modern composer of genius. His other works include *Joseph and His Brothers* (1933–44), a series of four novels based on the biblical story of Joseph, and the picaresque *Felix Krull* (1954). Mann opposed Nazism and was forced to emigrate to the USA in the 1930s. He was awarded a Nobel Prize in 1929.

mannerism An art movement dominant in Italy from about 1520 to 1600. Mannerism developed out of the Renaissance style, some of its characteristics being evident in the late work of Raphael and Michelangelo. It aimed to surpass the Renaissance style in virtuosity and emotional impact. In painting this led to a distortion of scale, an elongation of form, and dissonance of colour. Leading mannerist painters were Pontormo, Parmigianino, Vasari, and Bronzino.

Mannheim 49 30N 8 28E A city in SW West Germany, in Baden-Württemberg at the confluence of the Rivers Rhine and Neckar. It was the seat of the Electors Palatine (1720–98) and has a notable baroque castle. It is a major port with an oil refinery and its manufactures include motor vehicles and agricultural machinery. Population (1986): 295 500.

mannikin A waxbill of the genus *Lonchura* (30 species) occurring in Africa, S Asia, and Australasia. Mannikins are typically small (about 11 cm long) and brown or black with paler underparts.

manometer An instrument for measuring pressure differences. The simplest form consists of a U-shaped tube containing mercury, one arm of which is connected to a source of pressure and the other is open. The difference in height of the liquid in the arms is a measure of the pressure difference.

manor The most common unit of agrarian organization in medieval Europe, introduced into England by the Normans. The manor was essentially the lord's landed estate, usually consisting of the lord's own farm (the demesne), and land let out to peasant tenants, chiefly villeins, who worked for the demesne and were legally dependent upon their lord.

Manpower Services Commission (MSC). *See* Training Agency.

Mansell, Nigel (1954–) British racing driver. Since winning the European Grand Prix in 1985 he has been Britain's top Formula One driver.

Mansfield, Katherine (Kathleen Mansfield Beauchamp; 1888–1923) New Zealand short-story writer.

Long Neck *(1532–40; Palazzo Pitti, Florence)* by *Parmigianino*.

She came to Europe in 1908 and published her first collection of stories in 1911. *Bliss* (1920) and *The Garden Party* (1922) contain her best-known stories, often compared in stylistic subtlety to those of Chekhov.

manslaughter The crime of killing a person either (1) accidentally by an unlawful act or by culpable negligence or (2) in the heat of passion, after provocation. The second case is closely related to murder, and is possible only if there is no evidence of premeditation.

manta ray A ray fish, also called devil ray or devil fish, of the family *Mobulidae*. 60–660 cm long, they swim near the surface of warm-temperate and tropical waters, feeding on plankton and small animals swept into the mouth by hornlike feeding fins projecting from the front of the head.

Mantegna, Andrea (c. 1431–1506) Italian Renaissance painter and engraver, born near Vicenza. His marriage (1453) to the daughter of Jacopo Bellini connected him with the Venetian school. As court painter to the Duke of Mantua from 1459, he painted nine panels depicting *The Triumph of Caesar* Hampton Court, London. His fresco decorations for the bridal chamber of the ducal palace include portraits of members of the Mantuan court and an illusionistic ceiling, which anticipates the baroque.

mantis An insect belonging to the family *Mantidae* (2000 species), found in tropical and warm temperate regions. Up to 125 mm long, mantids blend with the surrounding vegetation and are voracious carnivores, using their forelegs to capture insects and other small animals. The "praying" position held by the forelegs at rest accounts for the name praying mantis, applied in particular to *Mantis religiosa*. Order: *Dictyoptera*.

Mantua (Italian name: Mantova) 45 10N 10 47E A city in N Italy, in Lombardy on the River Mincio. It has several notable buildings, including a cathedral (10th–18th centuries) and a 14th-century castle. An important tourist centre, Mantua's industries also include tanning, printing, and sugar refining. Population (1983 est): 60 468.

Manx An extinct language of the Goidelic branch of the Celtic family. An offshoot of Irish Gaelic, it was spoken on the Isle of Man until the 19th century.

Manx cat A breed of short-haired tailless cat from the Isle of Man. The Manx has a short body with deep flanks and a large head.

Maoism The theories developed by Mao Tse-tung. Mao's strategy for revolution in China gave central importance to peasant armies rather than to the action of the industrial working class in urban centres. Similarly, on a world scale, he believed that the socialist revolutions would develop first in the underdeveloped countries rather than in advanced capitalist countries (*compare* Marxism).

Maori A Polynesian people of New Zealand, who make up about 10% of the population. They trace their origins to migrants, probably from the Cook Islands, who came in canoes around 1350. They were an agricultural people who lived mainly in the North Island in large fortified villages of timber dwellings. The traditional arts of wood carving and dancing still survive but urbanization and Christianization have largely destroyed the Maoris' way of life.

Mao Tse-tung (*or* Mao Ze Dong; 1893–1976) Chinese communist statesman. Born into a peasant family,

he was a Marxist by 1920 and helped to form the Chinese Communist Party (CCP) in 1921. In 1931 he became chairman of the Jiangxi Soviet. Forced to evacuate Jiangxi in 1934, Mao led the communist forces on the Long March. His arrival in Yan'an in 1935 marked his emergence as a leader of the CCP. Following the defeat of Japan in the Sino-Japanese War of 1937–45, civil war was resumed, ending in communist victory. In 1949 Mao, as chairman of the Communist Party, proclaimed the establishment of the People's Republic of China. Mao's political writings formed the theoretical basis of the new government and led to the founding of communes and the Great Leap Forward. He stepped down as chairman in 1958, but reappeared with greater standing during the Cultural Revolution.

maple A shrub or tree of the genus *Acer* (over 200 species), widespread in N temperate regions and often grown for timber and ornament. Growing 6–35 m high, maples usually bear lobed leaves, which turn yellow, orange, or red in autumn, and small yellow or greenish flowers, which give rise to paired winged fruits (samaras). The sugar maple (*A. saccharum*) of E North America is the source of maple sugar. Family: *Aceraceae*.

map projection The representation of the curved surface of the earth on a plane surface. The parallels of latitude and meridians of longitude (*see* latitude and longitude) are represented as a network of intersecting lines. It is not possible to produce a projection of the earth's surface without some distortion of area, shape, or direction. In the conical projection the globe is projected onto a cone with its point above either the North or the South Pole. In the cylindrical projection the globe is projected onto a cylinder touching the equator; the Mercator projection is of this type. Part of the globe is projected upon a plane from any point of vision in the azimuthal projection.

Maputo (name ˙until 1975: Lourenço Marques) 25 58S 32 35E The capital and chief port of Mozambique, on Delagoe Bay. It became the capital of Portuguese East Africa in 1907. A major East African port, its exports include minerals from South Africa, Swaziland, and Zimbabwe. Population (1986): 882 800.

marabou A large African stork, *Leptoptilus crumeniferus*. It is 150 cm tall with a wingspan of 2.6 m and has a grey-and-white plumage, a bare black-spotted pink head and neck with a pendulous inflatable throat pouch, and a huge straight pointed bill.

Maracaibo 10 44N 71 37W The second largest city in Venezuela, a port on the NW shore of Lake Maracaibo. Its economic importance is based on oil production; industries include petrochemicals. Population (1987 est): 1 124 432.

Marajó Island (Portuguese: Ilka de Marajó) The world's largest fluvial island, in NE Brazil in the Amazon delta. Area: 38 610 sq km (15 444 sq mi).

marasmus. *See* kwashiorkor.

Marat, Jean Paul (1743–93) French politician, journalist, and physician. He devoted himself to radical journalism during the French Revolution, becoming editor of *L'Ami du peuple*. Elected to the National Convention in 1792, he was murdered by Charlotte Corday (1768–93), a member of the Girondins, whom Marat had helped to overthrow (1793).

marathon A long-distance running race over 42 195 m (26 mi 385 vd). The marathon derives its name from

MAO TSE-TUNG *A typical poster of the Cultural Revolution (1966).*

the story of a soldier who ran from the battlefield of Marathon to Athens with news of the Greek victory. As different courses vary, there is no official world record; the fastest time is 2 hours 6 minutes 50 seconds (1988) by Belanyeh Dinsamo (Ethiopia).

Marathon, Battle of (490 BC) The battle during the Greek-Persian Wars in which the Athenians under Miltiades defeated the Persians. Phidippides was sent to summon Spartan help but the Spartans arrived too late.

marble A rock consisting of metamorphosed limestone, although the term is used of any rock, particularly limestone, that can be cut and polished for ornamental use. Pure marble is white recrystallized calcite, but impurities, such as dolomite, silica, or clay minerals result in variations of colour. Certain quarries in Greece and Italy have been producing large quantities of marble since pre-Christian times.

Marburg disease. *See* green monkey disease.

marcasite A pale bronze mineral form of pyrite. It occurs as nodules in sedimentary rocks as a replacement mineral. Marcasite jewellery is sometimes pyrite but more often polished steel or white metal.

MARCONI *In the wireless room of his yacht* Elettra.

Marceau, Marcel (1923–) French mime. He began to study mime in 1946, gradually developing the original character Bip, a white-faced clown. As well as giving solo performances, he formed his own company.

Marcellus, Marcus Claudius (d. 208 BC) Roman general in the second Punic War. Chosen to check Hannibal's advance through Italy, he captured Syracuse and harassed the Carthaginian armies in S Italy.

Marches The border areas of England and Wales, conquered between 1067 and 1238 by vassals of the English kings. The so-called **marcher lords** enjoyed enormous powers until the union of Wales and England in the 1530s.

Marciano, Rocky (Rocco Francis Marchegiano; 1923–69) US boxer. He took the world heavyweight championship from Joe Walcott in 1952 and retired undefeated in 1956, after 6 defences. Unbeaten in his 49 professional fights, a record among world heavyweight champions, he was killed in an aircrash.

Marconi, Guglielmo (1874–1937) Italian electrical engineer, who invented, independently of Aleksandr Popov (1859–1905), communication by radio. On reading about the discovery of radio waves, Marconi built a device that would convert them into electrical signals. He then experimented with transmitting and receiving radio waves over increasing distances until, in 1901, he succeeded in transmitting a signal across the Atlantic Ocean. He shared the Nobel Prize for Physics in 1909.

Marcos, Ferdinand E(dralin) (1917–89) Philippine statesman; president (1965–86). Threatened by civil unrest, in 1972 he declared martial law and assumed dictatorial powers. The murder in 1983 of opposition leader Begnino Aquino Jr, with alleged government complicity, caused further unrest that culminated in a popular uprising in 1986 when Marcos was forced to go into exile. In 1988 he and his wife Imelda were charged in the US courts with embezzlement and fraud. He was succeeded as president by Aquino's widow Corazón.

Marcus Aurelius (121–180 AD) Roman emperor (161–180), in association with Lucius Verus (130–169) from 161 and alone from 169. Although he is known as the philosopher emperor on account of his *Meditations* (12 books of aphorisms in the Stoic tradition), his rule was active.

Marcuse, Herbert (1898–1979) German-born US thinker. His radical anti-authoritarian philosophy evolved from the Frankfurt School of social research. Marcuse attacked both western positivism and orthodox Marxism. His books include *The Ethics of Revolution* (1966) and *Counter-Revolution and Revolt* (1973).

Marduk The supreme god in Babylonian mythology. He created order out of the universe after defeating the sea dragon Tiamat and the forces of chaos. This victory was celebrated in a festival at the start of each year.

Marengo, Battle of (14 June, 1800) A battle, fought 5 km (3 mi) SE of Alessandria, in Napoleon's Italian campaign (*see* Revolutionary and Napoleonic Wars). Napoleon was surprised by the Austrians with his forces divided and only the timely arrival of reinforcements made French victory possible.

Margaret (Rose) (1930–) Princess of the United Kingdom; the younger daughter of George VI and sister of Elizabeth II, she is tenth in succession to the throne. In 1960 she married Antony Armstrong-Jones (later Lord Snowdon); they were divorced in 1978. Their children are David, Viscount Linley (1961–), and Lady Sarah Armstrong-Jones (1964–).

Margaret of Anjou (1430–82) The wife (1445–71) of Henry VI of England; their marriage constituted an attempt to cement peace between England and France during the Wars of the Roses, in which she was one of the most formidable Lancastrian leaders. She was captured and imprisoned after the Lancastrian defeat in the battle of Tewkesbury (1471). After her husband's death she returned to France (1476).

Margaret Tudor (1489–1541) Regent of Scotland (1513–14) for her son James V. The elder daughter of Henry VII of England and the wife of James IV of the Scots (d. 1513), she was ousted from the regency by the English but continued to play an active role in politics until 1534.

margarine A butter substitute that does not contain dairy-product fat. A type of margarine was first produced in France in 1869 from beef tallow. However, vegetable oils were only able to be used extensively after 1910, when a hydrogenation process was developed to solidify the liquid vegetable oils by adding hydrogen to saturate some of the unsaturated fatty-acid residues in the oils. In modern margarine, pasteurized fat-free milk powder is emulsified with water and such refined vegetable oils as soya-bean oil, groundnut oil, and palm-kernel oil. Vitamins A and D are also added. Soft margarines contain only lightly hydrogenated oils, retaining a large part of their unsaturated nature.

margay A spotted cat, *Felis wiedi* of Central and South America. It is 90 cm long including the tail (30 cm), and is found in forests and brush, hunting small mammals and reptiles in trees and on the ground.

Margrethe II (1940–) Queen of Denmark (1972–), who succeeded her father Frederick IX after the Danish constitution had been altered to permit the accession of a woman to the throne. In 1967 she married a French diplomat Henri de Laborde de Monpezat (Prince Henrik; 1934–); they have two sons, Prince Frederick (1968–) and Prince Joachim (1969–).

marguerite A perennial herb, *Chrysanthemum frutescens*, also called Paris daisy, native to the Canary Isles. Each stem bears a large daisy-like flower. The name is also applied to the oxeye daisy. *See also* Chrysanthemum.

Mari An ancient city on the middle Euphrates River in Syria. Commanding major trade routes, Mari throve during the early Sumerian period (*see* Sumer) and under the rule of Akkad (c. 2300 BC). Its archive of 25 000 cuneiform tablets throws light on contemporary diplomacy, administration, and trade.

Mariana Islands (*or* Ladrone Islands) A group of mountainous islands in the W Pacific Ocean, comprising the US unincorporated territory of Guam and the US commonwealth territory of the Northern Marianas. Strategically important, they include the islands of Tinian and Saipan. Discovered in 1521, the islands were colonized by Spanish Jesuits after 1668. Sugar cane, coffee, and coconuts are produced. Area: 958 sq km (370 sq mi). Population (1984 est): 135 391. Administrative centre: Garapan, on Saipan.

Marianas Trench A deep trench in the earth's crust in the W Pacific; it is the greatest known ocean depth (11 033 m). It marks the site of a plate margin (*see* plate tectonics), where one plate is being submerged beneath another.

Mount Everest 8848 m (29 028 ft)

sea level

Marianas Trench 11 033 m (36 198 ft)

MARIANAS TRENCH

Maria Theresa (1717–80) Archduchess of Austria (1740–80). Her father Emperor Charles VI issued the Pragmatic Sanction (1713) to enable Maria Theresa, as a woman, to succeed to his Austrian territories. Her accession nevertheless precipitated the War of the Austrian Succession (1740–48). Under the influence of Count von Kaunitz (1711–94), Maria Theresa substituted her English alliance with a French coalition but in the subsequent Seven Years' War (1756–63) Austria suffered resounding defeat. At home she combined absolutism with a measure of reform.

Maribor (German name: Marburg) 46 35N 15 40E A town in N Yugoslavia, in Slovenia on the River Drava. A former Habsburg trading centre, it is now one of Yugoslavia's largest industrial centres. Population (1981): 185 699.

Marie Antoinette (1755–93) The wife of Louis XVI of France, whose uncompromising attitude to the French Revolution contributed to the overthrow of the monarchy. The daughter of Emperor Francis I and Maria Theresa, she married the dauphin Louis in 1770. Her extravagance and alleged immorality contributed to the unpopularity of the Crown. After the overthrow of the monarchy and Louis' execution, she was herself guillotined.

marigold One of several annual herbaceous plants of the family *Compositae*, popular as garden ornamentals. The pot marigold (*Calendula officinalis*), native to S Europe, bears orange or yellow flowers. The African and French marigolds (genus *Tagetes*) have single or double flowers with large outer florets; there are several dwarf varieties. *See also* marsh marigold.

marihuana. *See* cannabis.

Mariner probes A series of highly successful US planetary probes. Mariners 2 and 5 approached Venus in 1962 and 1967, while Mariner 10 flew past Venus in 1974 and then three times past Mercury in 1974–75. Mariners 4 (1965), 6 and 7 (1969), and 9 (1971–72) investigated Mars, with Mariner 9 going into Martian orbit. Mariners 11 and 12 were renamed the Voyager probes. Mariners 1, 3, and 8 did not achieve their missions.

Maritain, Jacques (1882–1973) French Roman Catholic thinker. He was interested in applying St Thomas Aquinas' methods to contemporary social problems. *Les Degrés du savoir* (1932) treats mystical, metaphysical, and scientific knowledge as complementary.

Maritime Alps (French name: Alpes Maritimes) A range of mountains in SE France and NW Italy, running about 130 km (81 mi) along the border and constituting the southernmost arm of the Alps. It reaches 3297 m (10 817 ft) at Punta Argentera.

maritime law The branch of law relating to ships and shipping. The Romans, borrowing from the customs of Rhodes, imposed a code in the Mediterranean that was international and uniform in character. This uniformity was preserved until 17th-century nationalism gave rise to various individual codes. The English **Admiralty Court,** established in the 14th century, developed very broad powers in deciding questions of commercial law, but in the 17th century was restricted to matters "done upon the sea." Today the Admiralty Court is mainly concerned with cases involving salvage and collisions at sea. A certain international uniformity has been achieved by the Comité maritime international (CMI), in which 31 member states have agreed and ratified a number of maritime conventions.

Maritime Provinces (Maritimes *or* Atlantic Provinces) The easternmost provinces of Canada, on the Atlantic coast and the Gulf of St Lawrence. They consist of New Brunswick, Nova Scotia, Prince Edward Island, and usually Newfoundland and lie in the Appalachian Highlands.

marjoram One of several aromatic perennial herbs or small shrubs of the Eurasian genera *Origanum* (about 13 species) or *Majorana* (about 4 species). Wild marjoram (*O. vulgaris*), is a hairy plant, 30–80 cm tall, bearing clusters of small tubular pinkish-purple flowers. Sweet marjoram (*M. hortensis*), is widely cultivated for its aromatic leaves and flowers, which are used as culinary flavouring. Family: *Labiatae*.

Mark, St A New Testament evangelist, traditionally the author of the second Gospel. A cousin of Barnabas, he went with him and Paul on their first mission. Subsequently he seems to have assisted Paul in Rome, where he also acted as interpreter for Peter. He was believed to have founded the Church in Alexandria and is also associated with Venice, of which he is patron saint. Feast day: 25 April.

Mark Antony (Marcus Antonius; c. 83–31 BC) Roman general and statesman. Following Julius Caesar's assassination, Antony came into conflict with Octavian (*see* Augustus) but they were later reconciled and formed the second Triumvirate with Lepidus (43). In 42 Antony defeated his opponents, Brutus and Cassius, at Philippi. In 37 Antony abandoned his wife Octavia (Octavian's sister) to live with Cleopatra in Egypt. In 32 the Senate declared war on Egypt and Antony was defeated at Actium. Both he and Cleopatra committed suicide.

market gardening. *See* horticulture.

markhor A large wild goat, *Capra falconeri*, of the Himalayas. Over 100 cm tall at the shoulder, markhors are red-brown in summer and grey in winter and have massive corkscrew-like horns.

Markova, Dame Alicia (Lilian Alicia Marks; 1910–) British ballet dancer. She joined Diaghilev's Ballets Russes in 1925 and the Vic-Wells Ballet in 1931. Her dancing was noted for its lightness and delicacy, particularly evident in her performances in *Giselle*, *Swan Lake*, and *Les Sylphides*.

marl A calcareous clay that is soft and plastic when wet; consolidated marl is usually called marlstone. Marls are deposited in water, either fresh or marine. Marls and marlstones are used in the manufacture of cement.

Marlborough, John Churchill, 1st Duke of (1650–1722) British general. He suppressed Monmouth's rebellion against James II (1685) but subsequently supported the Glorious Revolution (1688) against James. As commander in chief in the War of the Spanish Succession, he won the great victories of Blenheim (1704), Ramillies (1706), Oudenaarde (1708), and Malplaquet (1709). A Whig, his political importance owed much to the influence of his wife **Sarah Churchill** (*born* Jennings; 1660–1744), a confidante of Queen Anne. Following Sarah's fall from favour, he was charged with embezzlement and dismissed (1711). *See also* Blenheim Palace.

marlin A large game fish, also called spearfish, belonging to the genus *Tetrapturus* (or *Makaira*). It has an elongated body, up to 2.5 m long, a cylindrical spearlike snout, and a long rigid dorsal fin. Marlins are fast swimmers, occurring in all seas. Family: *Istiophoridae*; order: *Perciformes*.

Marlowe, Christopher (1564–93) English dramatist and poet. His involvement in secret political activity while a student at Cambridge may have had some bearing on his death in a tavern fight in Deptford. His development of blank verse and dramatic characterization in his plays, which include *Tamburlaine the Great* (written about 1587) and *Faustus* (probably 1592), prepared the way for the achievements of Shakespeare.

Marmara, Sea of A sea lying between European and Asian Turkey and between the Bosporus and the Dardanelles. In it lies the island of Marmara, where marble and granite have long been quarried. Area: 11 474 sq km (4429 sq mi).

MARMOSET

marmoset A small South American monkey belonging to the genus *Callithrix* (9 species), with claws instead of fingernails. Marmosets are 20–90 cm long including the tail (10–38 cm) and have silky fur, often strikingly marked, and long balancing tails. They feed on fruit, insects, eggs, and small birds. Family: *Callithricidae*.

marmot A large ground squirrel belonging to the genus *Marmota* (8 species), also called groundhog, of Europe, Asia, and North America. Marmots are 30–60 cm long and inhabit mountainous or hilly country. The woodchuck (*M. monax*) lives in North American woodlands.

Marne, River A river in NE France. Rising on the Plateau de Langres, it flows N and W to join the River Seine near Paris. Linked by canal to the Rivers Rhine, Rhône, and Aisne, it was the scene of two unsuccessful German offensives during World War I (1914, 1918). Length: 525 km (326 mi).

Marquesas Islands A group of 12 volcanic islands in the S Pacific Ocean, in French Polynesia (annexed 1842). Nuku Hiva is the largest. Mountainous and fertile, the islands export copra, cotton, and vanilla. Area: 1287 sq km (497 sq mi). Population (1984): 6548. Capital: Atuona on Hiva Oa.

Marrakech (*or* Marrakesh) 31 49N 8 00W The second largest city in Morocco. Founded in 1062, it was for a time the capital of the Moorish kingdom of Morocco. It is an important commercial centre, producing carpets and leather goods. Population (1982): 439 728.

marram grass A coarse perennial grass of the genus *Ammophila* (2 species), also called beach grass or sand reed, which grows on sandy coasts of temperate Europe, North America, and N Africa. About 1 m high, it has spikelike leaves and tough scaly underground stems, which can spread over large areas. It is used to stabilize sand dunes.

marrow (botany) A trailing or climbing vine, *Cucurbita pepo*, probably native to the Americas and including several varieties widely cultivated as vegetable crops. Marrows bear yellow or orange cup-shaped flowers and large elongated fleshy fruits, which have orange, green, or yellow skins. Family: *Cucurbitaceae. See also* courgette.

marrow (zoology) The soft tissue contained in the central cavities of bones. In early life the marrow of all bones is engaged in the manufacture of blood cells: it is called red marrow. In adult life the marrow of the limb bones becomes filled with fat cells and ceases to function: this is yellow marrow.

Marryat, Captain Frederick (1792–1848) British novelist. His novels based on his long naval career include *Mr Midshipman Easy* (1836) and *Masterman Ready* (1841). He also wrote children's books, notably *The Children of the New Forest* (1847).

Mars (astronomy) The fourth planet from the sun, orbiting the sun every 687 days at a mean distance of 227.9 million km. Its diameter is 6794 km and its period of axial rotation 24 hours 37 minutes 23 seconds. It has two small satellites. The Martian atmosphere is 95% carbon dioxide and is very thin (surface pressure 7 millibars). The dry reddish dust-covered surface is heavily cratered in the S hemisphere while N regions show signs of earlier volcanic activity.

Mars (mythology) The Roman war god, the son of Juno. He was identified with the Greek Ares and is usually portrayed as an armed warrior. Originally a god of agriculture, he was later worshipped at Rome as a major deity and protector of the city.

Marsala (ancient name: Lilybaeum) 37 48N 12 27E A port in Italy, in W Sicily. Founded in 397 BC as a Carthaginian stronghold, it has ancient remains and a baroque cathedral. Marsala wine, grain, and salt are exported. Population (1981 est): 79 093.

Marseillaise, La The French national anthem, written in 1792, by Claude Rouget de l'Isle (1760–1836). It was originally a patriotic song entitled "Le Chant de guerre de l'armée du Rhin". It was taken up by a group of republican soldiers from Marseille, who were prominent in the storming of the Tuileries, and became the revolutionary anthem.

Marseille (English name: Marseilles) 43 18N 5 22E The principal seaport in France, the capital of the Bouches-du-Rhône department. Founded about 600 BC, it was destroyed by the Arabs in the 9th century AD, redeveloped during the Crusades, and came under the French Crown in 1481. Most industry is associated with its large world trade and includes oil refining at Fos. Population (1982): 878 689.

Marshall, George C(atlett) (1880–1959) US general and statesman. As army chief of staff (1939–45) he organized the build-up of US forces, contributing greatly to the Allied victory. As secretary of state (1947–49) he devised the **Marshall Plan**, or European Recovery Programme, in which the USA undertook to provide economic aid to Europe after World War II. For this he won a Nobel Peace Prize (1953).

marsh gas. *See* methane.

marsh mallow A stout perennial herb, *Althaea officinalis*, of marshy coastal areas of Eurasia. 60–90 cm high, it has lobed leaves and flesh-coloured flowers. The fleshy roots yield a mucilage that was formerly used to make marshmallows (spongy sweets). Family: *Malvaceae*.

marsh marigold A stout perennial herb, *Caltha palustris*, also called kingcup, growing in marshes and wet woods throughout arctic and temperate Eurasia and North America. It has erect or prostrate stems, up to 80 cm long, bearing round leaves and bright golden flowers. Family: *Ranunculaceae*.

Marston Moor, Battle of (2 July, 1644) The battle in the English Civil War in which the parliamentarians and the Scots decisively defeated the royalists at Marston Moor, W of York. The parliamentary victory destroyed the king's hold on N England.

marsupial A primitive mammal belonging to the order *Marsupialia* (176 species). Most marsupials are found in Australia and New Guinea and include the kangaroos, bandicoots, and phalangers. The only New World marsupials are the opossums.
Marsupials have relatively small brains and they lack a placenta. Young marsupials, which are born in a very immature state, complete their development in a pouch of skin on the mother's belly surrounding the teat, from which they are fed until fully formed.

Martello towers Fortifications containing cannon built in S Britain, Ireland, and Guernsey from 1804 to 1812. The towers were intended to check the potential invasion of Britain by Napoleon—which never materialized. They were named after the single tower mounting cannon at Mortella Point, Corsica.

marten A carnivorous mammal belonging to the genus *Martes* (8 species), of Eurasian and North American forests. Up to 90 cm long including the tail (15–30 cm), martens are arboreal agile hunters with dark lustrous fur. The two European species are the pine marten and the smaller stone marten (*M. foina*). The fur of the

American marten (*M. americana*) is called American sable. Family: *Mustelidae*.

MARSUPIAL   *A brush-tailed phalanger (possum) in its mother's pouch.*

martensite   The hard brittle form of steel produced after rapid quenching in heat treatment. When steel is heated to red heat (750°C), the carbon in it forms a solid solution in the iron. On quenching the carbon is frozen into this configuration and the crystal structure of the steel has internal strains, which cause its hardness. Named after Adolph Martens (1850–1914).

martial arts   Styles of armed and unarmed combat developed in the East. The Japanese forms, such as karate, judo, and sumo, derive largely from the fighting skills of the samurai. Since the late 19th century they have become forms of sport, as has the Chinese style, kung fu. *See also* Bushido.

martin   A bird belonging to the swallow family (*Hirundidae*; 78 species). The widely distributed brown sand martin (*Riparia riparia*) is about 12 cm long and has white underparts with a brown breast band. It nests in colonies in tunnels excavated in sand or clay banks. The black-and-white Old World house martin (*Delichon urbica*), about 13 cm long, commonly nests beneath the eaves of houses.

Martin, Pierre-Émile   (1824–1915) French engineer, who invented the Siemens-Martin process of producing steel. In this process Martin employed the open-hearth furnace developed in 1856 by Sir William Siemens (1823–83) but adopted his own steel-producing process, which utilized pig iron and scrap steel.

Martin, St   (c. 316–97 AD) A patron saint of France; Bishop of Tours (372–97). A soldier in the imperial army, he later settled at Poitiers and nearby founded the first monastery in Gaul. His military cloak, part of which he reputedly gave to a naked beggar, has become a symbol of charity. Feast day: 11 Nov.

Martinique   A French overseas region in the West Indies, in the Windward Islands of the Lesser Antilles. It consists of a mountainous island of volcanic origin. Agriculture is of importance, the chief exports being sugar, bananas, and rum. *History*: colonized by the French in 1635, it became a French overseas department in 1946. Area: 1090 sq km (420 sq mi). Population (1987 est): 328 500. Capital: Fort-de-France.

Martinmas   The feast of St Martin (11 Nov), traditionally the date for slaughtering livestock to be salted as winter food. Fairs, at which servants could be hired, were also held at Martinmas, and in Scotland it is a quarter day recognized in common law.

Martinů, Bohuslav   (1890–1959) Czech composer. During World War II he settled in the USA. Largely self-taught, he composed many works, including symphonies, concertos, the ballet *La Revue de cuisine* (1927), and the opera *Julietta* (1936–37).

Marvell, Andrew   (1621–78) English poet. He was employed as tutor by Cromwell and Fairfax and as secretary by Milton. From 1659 until his death he served as MP for Hull. He published several satires and pamphlets attacking religious intolerance and government corruption. His poems, noted for their combination of intelligent argument and lyricism, include "To his Coy Mistress" and "The Garden".

Marx, Karl (Heinrich)   (1818–83) German philosopher, economist, and revolutionary. In 1842 Marx became the editor of a radical paper; after its suppression he left Germany and spent the rest of his life in exile. In Paris he met Friedrich Engels, who later collaborated in many of Marx's writings and provided him with substantial financial support. While in Brussels, Marx's association with a group of German handicraftsmen led to *The Communist Manifesto* (1848). In 1849 Marx moved to London, where he remained for the rest of his life, publishing *A Contribution to the Critique of Political Economy* (1859) and other works. Following the establishment of the International Working Men's Association in 1864, Marx devoted many years to the affairs of the First International. The first volume of *Das Kapital* was published in 1867. *See also* Marxism.

Marx brothers   A US family of comic film actors: **Chico** (Leonard M.; 1886–1961), **Harpo** (Adolph M.; 1888–1964), **Groucho** (Julius M.; 1890–1977), and, until 1933, **Zeppo** (Herbert M.; 1901–79). Their film comedies included *Horse Feathers* (1932), *Duck Soup* (1933), and *A Night at the Opera* (1935). The team disbanded in 1949.

MARX BROTHERS   *(From the top) Harpo, Chico, and Groucho.*

Marxism   The theory of scientific socialism introduced by Marx and Engels, which explains the origin, historical development, and demise of the capitalist economic system. It relies heavily on the philosophy of Hegel (*see* dialectical materialism). Marxism developed the theory of proletarian revolution. The transition to a socialist and eventually a classless society would involve the violent overthrow of the state power of the bourgeois class. The working class would have to establish its own state power, which would be more democratic because it would be the rule of the majority of the population. As classes gradually disappeared, however, state power would also wither away. The classless society of the future would allow the fullest developments of individuals through social cooperation. Since World War I many different versions of Marxism have been expounded (*see also* communism).

Mary I (1516–58) Queen of England and Ireland (1553–58), succeeding her younger half-brother Edward VI. The daughter of Henry VIII and Catherine of Aragon, Mary became queen after the failure of a conspiracy to place Lady Jane Grey on the throne. Her singleminded aim was to restore Roman Catholicism in England: Edward's Protestant legislation was repealed and in 1554 the heresy laws were reintroduced, resulting in almost 300 deaths at the stake and the queen's nickname, Bloody Mary. Her marriage (1554) to Philip II of Spain led to England's entanglement in Philip's foreign policy and the loss in 1558 of its last possession on the Continent, Calais.

Mary II (1662–94) Queen of England, Scotland, and Ireland (1689–94), joint monarch with her husband William III. Daughter of James II, she was brought up as a Protestant and came to the throne after the enforced abdication of her Roman Catholic father during the Glorious Revolution.

Mary, Queen of Scots (1542–87) The daughter of James V and the French noblewoman Mary of Guise (1515–60); she succeeded to the throne shortly after her birth. From 1547 Mary, a Roman Catholic, lived at the French court, where in 1558 she married the dauphin (later Francis II). After Francis' death (1561) Mary returned to Scotland and in 1565 married, unpopularly, her cousin Lord Darnley. In 1566 she gave birth to the future James VI (James I of England). In 1567 Darnley was murdered by Bothwell, who subsequently married Mary. A rebellion of Scottish nobles defeated Mary and Bothwell at Carberry Hill (1567) and Mary was forced to abdicate in favour of her son. Fleeing to England, where her claim to the English succession had long been an embarrassment to Elizabeth I, she was held prisoner for the rest of her life. She became the focus of a series of plots against Elizabeth and was finally tried for complicity in the conspiracy of Anthony Babington (1561–86) and executed.

Mary, the Virgin In the New Testament, the mother of Jesus Christ. The fullest accounts of Mary are contained in the birth stories in Luke and Matthew. John (19.25) reports that she was present at the crucifixion. Luke records the Annunciation; her betrothal to Joseph; her meeting with her cousin Elizabeth; and her song of praise (the Magnificat) when Elizabeth had greeted her as the mother of the Lord. The Gospels also state that she was a virgin. Mary's Immaculate conception has been recognized as a dogma of the Roman Catholic Church since 1854 and the belief that she was taken into heaven (the Bodily Assumption) was defined as doctrine in 1950.

Mary Magdalene, St In the New Testament, the first person to see Jesus after the resurrection. Jesus cured her of possession by evil spirits. She aided his work in Galilee and was present at the crucifixion and burial. Medieval scholars associated her with the repentant prostitute who annointed Jesus' feet, mentioned in Luke's Gospel. Feast day: 22 July. Emblem: an ointment jar.

Maryland A state on the E seaboard of the USA. It consists of the Atlantic Coastal Plain, split by Chesapeake Bay into a low flat plain in the E and uplands in the W, and an area of higher ground, part of the Alleghenies in the N and W. Manufacturing is important, with primary metals, metal products, food processing, transportation and electrical equipment, printing and publishing, and textiles. The state's farmers produce livestock, poultry, dairy products, corn, tobacco, soya beans, and vegetables. *History*: one of the 13 original colonies, it was first settled by the English. It was named after Henrietta Maria, wife of Charles I. Area: 27 394 sq km (10 577 sq mi). Population (1986 est): 4 463 000. Capital: Annapolis. Chief port: Baltimore.

Marylebone Cricket Club (MCC) A cricket club founded in London in 1787. Its headquarters are at Lord's Cricket Ground. The MCC became the leading authority on the laws of cricket and was responsible for the control of English cricket until 1969, when this became the responsibility of the Cricket Council.

MARY ROSE   *A special crane used in reconstructing the raised hull.*

Mary Rose A Tudor warship (Henry VIII's flagship), which sank in 1545 in Portsmouth Harbour while sailing into battle. The wreck was positively identified in 1971. The ship's contents, most of which were remarkably preserved, were raised during the following ten years and the hull itself was lifted in 1982 and placed in dry-dock in Portsmouth. The Mary Rose Trust, of which the Prince of Wales is president, was formed in 1979.

Masaccio (Tommaso di Giovanni di Simone Guidi; 1401–28) Florentine painter of the early Renaissance. He collaborated with Masolino (1383–?1447) on the *Madonna and Child with St Anne* (Uffizi) and other works. His independent paintings include the *Trinity* (Sta Maria Novella, Florence). Masaccio initiated the use of linear perspective and a single light source in painting.

Masada 31 19N 35 21E A precipitous rocky hilltop near the W shore of the Dead Sea, in S Israel. The site of one of Herod the Great's fortified palaces, it was later a centre of the Essene sect and a stronghold of the Jews in their revolt against Rome (66 AD). In the last action of the war (73 AD) the defenders committed mass suicide rather than surrender. The site is an Israeli national monument.

Masai A Nilotic people of Kenya and Tanzania who speak a Sudanic language. They are nomads with little centralized political organization. Milk and blood from cattle form an important part of their diet, the blood being drawn from a vein in the animal's neck without killing it. Tall and active, the Masai highly value courage in their warriors.

Masaryk, Tomáš (Garrigue) (1850–1937) Czechoslovak statesman, who was one of the founders of Czechoslovakia. In Paris, during World War I, he and Beneš founded the Czechoslovak National Council. When Austria-Hungary fell in November, 1918, Masaryk was elected Czechoslovakia's first president; he was re-elected in 1920, 1927, and 1934.

Mascagni, Pietro (1863–1945) Italian opera composer. His fame rests chiefly on his one-act opera *Cavalleria Rusticana* (1889), written as an entry for a competition in which it won first prize.

Masefield, John (1878–1967) British poet. Having served briefly in the merchant navy, he captured the fascination of the sea in his first volume, *Salt-Water Ballads* (1902). He also wrote narrative poems, such as *Reynard the Fox* (1919), and several adventure novels, including *Sard Harker* (1924) and *Odtaa* (1926). He became poet laureate in 1930.

maser (*m*icrowave *a*mplification by *s*timulated *e*mission of *r*adiation) A device that works on the same principle as the laser, the radiation produced being in the microwave region instead of in the visible spectrum. Masers are used as oscillators and amplifiers.

Maseru 29 19S 27 29E The capital of Lesotho, near the South African border. It was founded in 1869. The University of Botswana, Lesotho, and Swaziland was established nearby in 1966. Population (1986): 109 382.

masochism Sexual pleasure obtained from the experience of pain. The condition is named after an Austrian writer, Leopold von Sacher-Masoch (1835–95), whose novels depict it. It is often associated with a pathologically strong need to be humiliated by and submissive to one's sexual partner.

mason bee A solitary bee belonging to the genus *Osmia* and related genera, occurring in Europe, Africa, and elsewhere. It builds nests of soil cemented together with saliva in hollows in wood or stones. Family: *Megachilidae*.

Mason-Dixon line A line drawn in 1767 by two surveyors, Charles Mason and Jeremiah Dixon, to settle the conflict over borders between Pennsylvania and Maryland. Until the Civil War it also represented the division between southern proslavery and northern free states. It has remained a symbolic boundary between the North and South.

masque A form of dramatic court entertainment popular in England during the late 16th and early 17th centuries. It consisted of a combination of verse, dance, and music, usually with a slight dramatic plot based on a mythological theme. The form was perfected in the collaborations of Ben Jonson and Inigo Jones.

mass (physics). *See* mass and weight.

Mass (religion). *See* Eucharist.

Massachusetts A state on the NE coast of the USA, in New England. The uplands in the W, which are cut N–S by the Connecticut River, are separated from the lowlands of the Atlantic Coastal Plain and Cape Cod Peninsula. A major manufacturing state, its industries produce electrical and communications equipment, instruments, chemicals, textiles, and metal and food products. Boston is an important financial and service centre. Its farmers produce dairy products, eggs, poultry, cranberries, and horticultural goods. Massachusetts is an important centre in the educational and cultural life of the USA. *History*: one of the 13 original colonies, the arrival of the Pilgrim Fathers (1620) heralded major settlement. It was a centre for opposition to British colonial policy leading to the American Revolution and became prominent following statehood (1788). Area: 21 386 sq km (8257 sq mi). Population (1984 est): 5 741 000. Capital: Boston.

Massachusetts Institute of Technology (MIT) A university in the USA, situated at Cambridge, Massachusetts. Founded in 1861 at Boston, it moved to its present site in 1916. It is world famous for scientific education and research.

mass action, law of The rate of a chemical reaction for a uniform system at constant temperature varies as the concentration of each reacting substance, raised to the power equal to the number of molecules of the substance appearing in the balanced equation. Thus, for the reaction $2H_2 + O_2 = 2H_2O$ the speed of the forward reaction is proportional to the concentration of O_2 (written $[O_2]$) and to $[H_2]^2$; the reverse reaction depends on $[H_2O]^2$.

mass and weight Two physical quantities used to express the extent to which a substance is present; they are sometimes confused. The mass of a body was defined by Newton as the ratio of a force applied to the body to the acceleration it produces. This is now called the **inertial mass**. **Gravitational mass** is defined in terms of the gravitational force between two bodies in accordance with Newton's law of gravitation. Lóránt Eotvos (1848–1919) showed experimentally that inertial mass and gravitational mass are equal.

Weight is proportional to gravitational mass, being the force by which an object is attracted to the earth. It is therefore equal to the product of the mass and the acceleration of free fall (i.e. $W = mg$). Thus, the weight of a body may vary according to its position; the mass is a constant.

mass defect The difference between the total mass of the constituent protons and neutrons in an atomic nucleus and the mass of the nucleus. This defect is equal to the binding energy of the nucleus.

mass-energy equation. *See* relativity.

Massenet, Jules (1842–1912) French composer. He studied at the Paris conservatoire and won the Prix de Rome in 1863. Massenet wrote 27 operas, of which *Manon* (1884) and *Werther* (1892) are still performed today.

Massey, William Ferguson (1856–1925) New Zealand statesman; prime minister (1912–25). He entered parliament in 1894 and became (1903) leader of the Conservative opposition, which in 1909 he named the Reform Party. His administration, in coalition (1915–19) with the Liberals during World War I, supported agrarian interests.

Massif Central A plateau area in S central France. Generally considered to be that area over 300 m (984 ft) high, it rises to 1885 m (6188 ft) at Puy de Sancy. The central N area is also known as the Auvergne and the SE rim as the Cévennes. There is dairy and arable farming as well as heavy industry. Area: about 90 000 sq km (34 742 sq mi).

Massine, Léonide (Leonid Miassin; 1896–1979) Russian ballet dancer and choreographer. He choreographed for many companies, notably the Ballet Russe de Monte Carlo. Most controversial were his innovatory symphonic ballets *Les Présages* (1933) and *Symphonie Fantastique* (1936).

mass number (*or* nucleon number) The total number of protons and neutrons in the nucleus of an atom.

mastectomy Surgical removal of a breast, usually for the treatment of breast cancer. In a partial mastectomy (or lumpectomy) only the tumour is removed, while in a total mastectomy the entire breast is removed. A radical mastectomy involves removal of the breast together with the lymph nodes in the armpit and the chest muscles associated with it.

Master of the Queen's (*or* King's) **Music** An English court post established in the reign of Charles I. It is now an honorary position held by a composer who may be called upon to write music for ceremonial occasions. The present holder is Malcolm Williamson (since 1975).

Master of the Rolls The presiding judge of the Civil Division of the Court of Appeal. The office originated as the guardian of all charters, patents, etc., entered upon parchment rolls. Judicial adviser to the Lord Chancellor, the Master of the Rolls became a full judge in 1729 and a member of the Court of Appeal in 1881. As his legal responsibilities increased he became less involved in record-keeping.

mastic An evergreen shrub, *Pistacia lentiscus*, up to 1.8 m high, native to the Mediterranean region. An aromatic yellowish-green resin obtained from the bark is used to make varnishes and as an adhesive. Family: *Anacardiaceae*. The name is also applied to other resin-yielding trees.

mastiff An ancient Eurasian breed of large dog long used as a guard dog and for bull- and bear-baiting. It is powerfully built with a large head and a short deep muzzle. The short smooth coat may be apricot, silver, or fawn; the muzzle, ears, and nose are black. Height: 76 cm (dogs); 69 cm (bitches). *See also* bull mastiff.

mastodon An extinct elephant that originated in Africa 34 million years ago and spread throughout Europe, Asia, and America. Early mastodons were small and had two pairs of tusks; later forms were larger. The American mastodons survived until about 8000 years ago.

Mastroianni, Marcello (1924–) Italian actor. He became one of the best-known international film stars of the 1960s, a representative European leading man. He appeared in Visconti's *White Nights* (1957), Fellini's *La dolce vita* (1960), and Antonioni's *La notte* (1961); more recent films include *Blowout* (1973) and *Ginger and Fred* (1985).

Matabeleland An area in W Zimbabwe, between the Limpopo and Zambezi Rivers. It was named after the Ndebele tribe. Consisting chiefly of plains, the area has gold deposits. Area: 181 605 sq km (70 118 sq mi).

MATA HARI

Mata Hari (Margaretha Geertruida Zelle; 1876–1917) Dutch courtesan and secret agent. She lived in Indonesia with her husband, a Dutch colonial officer, from 1897 to 1902. She became a professional dancer in Paris in 1905 and probably worked for both French and German intelligence services. She was executed by the French in 1917.

matchlock. *See* musket.

maté The dried leaves of a holly shrub or tree, *Ilex paraguariensis*, native to Paraguay and Brazil. They are roasted, powdered, and infused with water to make a stimulating greenish tealike beverage.

materialism In classical metaphysics, materialism is the doctrine of Democritus and Leucippus (5th century BC) that everything in the universe is matter or stuff. By contrast Plato sought to establish the existence of some incorporeal objects and Aristotle believed that the soul was immaterial. Marx's economic materialism was developed by Lenin in dialectical materialism. In all these senses materialism is a metaphysical doctrine. More popularly, the term has also been used to signify worldly outlooks and behaviour.

mathematics The logical study of numerical and spatial relationships. It is usually divided into pure and applied mathematics. In pure mathematics the general theoretical principles are studied, often in abstract. Its branches are arithmetic, algebra, calculus, geometry, and trigonometry. The ancient Egyptians, Sumerians, and Chinese were all using a form of abacus to carry out calculations for thousands of years before the Christian era. But it was not until the 9th century AD that al-Khwarizmi introduced the idea of writing down calculations. The Venetian mathematicians of the 11th and 12th centuries were largely responsible for the introduction of these methods to the West. However, the application of mathematics to the physical sciences was largely a 16th-century development inspired by Galileo. It was from this development that applied mathematics grew. It is now largely concerned with mechanics and statistics. *See also* new maths.

Matilda (*or* Maud; 1102–67) The daughter of Henry I of England, who designated her his heir. On his death (1135), his nephew Stephen seized the throne and Matilda invaded England (1139) inaugurating a period of inconclusive civil war. She captured Normandy and in 1152 the Treaty of Wallingford recognized her son Henry as Stephen's heir.

Matisse, Henri (1869–1954) French painter and sculptor. Matisse initiated fauvism in the early 1900s with his boldly patterned and vibrantly coloured still lifes, portraits, and nudes, notably the controversial *Woman with the Hat* (1905). He was also inspired by Islamic art. A stained glass design for the Dominican chapel at Vence (S France) was among his last works.

Ma-tsu. *See* Mazu.

Matsuyama 33 50N 132 47E A port in Japan, in NW Shikoku on the Inland Sea. It is an agricultural and industrial centre, with a university (1949). Population (1985): 427 000.

Matterhorn (French name: Mont Cervin; Italian name: Monte Cervino) 45 59N 7 39E A mountain in Europe, on the Swiss-Italian border in the Alps near Zermatt. First climbed in 1865 by the British mountaineer, Edward Whymper, it is conspicuous because of its striking pyramidal shape. Height: 4478 m (14 692 ft).

Matthew, St In the New Testament, one of the 12 Apostles. He was a tax collector until he became a follower of Jesus. According to tradition, he preached in Judaea, Ethiopia, and Persia and suffered martyrdom. Feast day: 21 Sept. Emblem: a man with wings. **The Gospel according to St Matthew** is generally believed to have been written sometime after St Mark's Gospel, from which it drew material.

Maud. *See* Matilda.

Maugham, W(illiam) Somerset (1874–1965) British novelist and dramatist. Born in Paris, he studied and qualified in medicine but abandoned it after the success of his first novel, *Liza of Lambeth* (1896). His later fiction includes *Of Human Bondage* (1915), *The Moon and Sixpence* (1919), *Cakes and Ale* (1930), and *The Razor's Edge* (1944). He wrote popular comedies of manners, such as *The Circle* (1921), and many short stories with Far Eastern or other exotic settings.

Mau Mau A secret organization among the Kikuyu people of Kenya, which led a revolt (1952–57) against the British colonial government. Secret oaths were administered to participants, who committed appalling atrocities against Whites and uncooperating Blacks. Jomo Kenyatta was thought to be a Mau Mau leader.

Maundy Thursday The Thursday before Good Friday. Its name derives from Latin *mandatum*, commandment, and its traditional foot-washing and almsgiving ceremonies originated at the Last Supper (John 13). The British sovereign's annual distribution of special Maundy money is a survival of these rites.

Maupassant, Guy de (1850–93) French short-story writer and novelist. Introduced into literary circles by Flaubert, he joined Zola's group of naturalist writers (*see* Naturalism). Following the phenomenal success of "Boule de Suif" (1880), he wrote about 300 short stories and 6 novels, including *Une Vie* (1883) and *Bel-Ami* (1885). He suffered from syphilis and died in an asylum.

Mauriac, François (1885–1970) French novelist. His novels, which include *Thérèse Desqueyroux* (1927) and *Le Noeud de vipères* (1933), characteristically portray the conflict between worldly passions and religion in provincial marital and family relationships. He also wrote plays and polemical criticism and journalism. He won the Nobel Prize in 1952.

Mauritania, Islamic Republic of (French name: Mauritanie; Arabic name: Muritaniyah) A country in West Africa, with a coastline on the Atlantic Ocean. The N part is desert while the S is mainly fertile. Most of the inhabitants are Arabs and Berbers with a Negro population, mainly Fulani, in the S. *Economy*: chiefly agricultural. Livestock, especially cattle, are particularly important and the main crops are millet, sorghum, beans, and rice. Fishing is important and fish processing is one of the main industries. Iron ore and copper are exploited. *History*: dominated by Muslim Berber tribes from about 100 AD, the coast was visited by the Portuguese in the 15th century and by the Dutch, English, and French in the 17th century. The area became a French protectorate in 1903 and a colony in 1920 achieving internal self-government within the French Community in 1958. It subsequently joined the Arab League and the Arab Common Market. In 1976, with Morocco, it took over Western Sahara, prompting guerrilla attacks from the Polisario, the Western Saharan independence movement. In 1979 Mauritania withdrew from all but the southern tip of Western Sahara. Its third president, Lt Col Khouna Ould Kaydalla (1940–   ), was ousted in a coup in 1984. President: Moauya Ould Sidi-Ahmad Iaya. Official language: French; Arabic, known as Hassaniya, is widely spoken. Official religion: Islam. Official currency: ouguiya of 5 khoums. Area: 1 030 700 sq km (397 850 sq mi). Population (1987 est): 2 015 000. Capital and main port: Nouakchott.

Mauritius An island country in the Indian Ocean, about 800 km (500 mi) to the E of Madagascar. It is mainly hilly and subject to tropical cyclones. The majority of the population are of Indian descent. *Economy*: it is dependent primarily on sugar production; sugar accounting for 90% of its total exports. Fishing is being developed and industry is being encouraged. *History*: the island was settled by the Dutch in 1598. In 1715 it came under French rule as Île de France and in 1814 it was ceded to Britain. After riots in 1968 it became independent within the British Commonwealth. Official languages: English and French; Creole is widely spoken. Official currency: Mauritius rupee of 100 cents. Area: 1843 sq km (720 sq mi). Population (1987 est): 1 041 000. Capital and main port: Port Louis.

maxwell The unit of magnetic flux in the c.g.s. system equal to the flux through one square centimetre perpendicular to a field of one gauss. Named after James Clerk Maxwell.

Maxwell, James Clerk (1831–79) Scottish physicist, who achieved the unification of electricity, magnetism, and light into one set of equations (known as **Maxwell's equations**). These equations, first published in their final form in 1873, enabled Faraday's lines of force to be treated mathematically by introducing the concept of the electromagnetic field. Maxwell observed that the field radiated outwards from an oscillating electric charge at the speed of light, which led him to identify light as a form of electromagnetic radiation. Maxwell also made important advances in the kinetic theory of gases by introducing Maxwell-Boltzmann statistics, developed independently by Ludwig Boltzmann (1844–1906).

may. *See* hawthorn.

Maya An American Indian people of Yucatán (Mexico) Guatemala, and Belize. There are a number of languages in the Totonac-Mayan language family (*see*

MAYFLOWER *The Pilgrim Fathers landing in America (1620).*

Mesoamerican languages). Today the Maya live mainly in farming villages, but between 300 and 900 AD they had established an advanced civilization. They developed hieroglyphic writing and had considerable knowledge of astronomy and mathematics. Their elaborate ritual and ceremonial life was centred on such sites as Chichén Itzá and Tikal, where large pyramid temples were constructed for the worship of the sun, moon, and rain gods.

Mayence. *See* Mainz.

Mayer, Louis B. (1885–1957) US film producer, born in Russia. With Samuel Goldwyn in 1924 he founded the Metro-Goldwyn-Mayer (MGM) production company, whose films were largely determined by his personal taste for lavish but uncontroversial entertainment.

Mayflower The ship that carried the Pilgrim Fathers to America. The *Mayflower* reached Plymouth (Massachusetts) in December, 1620. There, the Pilgrims drew up the **Mayflower Compact**, which based their government on the will of the colonists, not the English Crown.

mayfly A slender insect of the order *Ephemeroptera* (1500 species), found near fresh water. Up to 40 mm long, mayflies are usually brown or yellow with two unequal pairs of membranous wings. The adults only live long enough to mate and lay eggs. The aquatic nymphs feed on plant debris and algae.

Mayo (Irish name: Contae Mhuigheo) A county in the W Republic of Ireland, in Connacht bordering on the Atlantic Ocean. Mountainous in the W, it contains several large lakes. Cattle, sheep, and pigs are raised and potatoes and oats are grown. Area: 5397 sq km (2084 sq mi). Population (1986): 115 016. County town: Castlebar.

mayor The chief officer of a municipal council. In the UK a mayor or mayoress is the chairman or chairwoman of a district council having borough status. The mayor's counterpart in Scotland is called a provost. The mayor of the City of London and certain other cities is called a **Lord Mayor** (Lord Provost in Scotland).

Mazu (*or* Ma-tsu) 26 10N 119 59E A Taiwanese island in the East China Sea. It is near the Chinese mainland, from which it was bombed in 1958, causing an international incident. Area: 44 sq km (17 sq mi). Population (1982 est): 8199.

Mbabane 26 30S 31 30E The capital of Swaziland, in the Mdimba Mountains. Tourism is important and nearby is a large iron mine. Population (1984 est): 23 109.

MBE. *See* Order of the British Empire.

Mc–. Names beginning Mc are listed under Mac.

MCC. *See* Marylebone Cricket Club.

mead An alcoholic drink of fermented honey and water. The honey is dissolved in water and boiled with spices. When cool, after brewer's yeast has been added, the mead ferments in barrel. It was drunk in Anglo-Saxon England and, called hydromel, by the ancient Romans.

meadowsweet A perennial herb, *Filipendula* (or *Spiraea*) *ulmaria*, common in damp places throughout temperate Eurasia. 60–120 cm high, it has large compound leaves, and small creamy-white fragrant flowers. An oil distilled from the flower buds is used in perfumes. Family: *Rosaceae*.

mealworm. *See* darkling beetle.

mean life (*or* lifetime) The average time for which a radioactive isotope, elementary particle, or other unstable state exists before decaying. *See* radioactivity.

measles A highly infectious viral disease, which usually affects children. After an incubation period of about two weeks the child becomes irritable and fevered and has a running nose and inflamed eyes. Two or three days later a rash appears on the head and face and spreads over the body. Usually the child recovers after a week. *Compare* German measles.

Meath (Irish name: Contae na Midhe) A county in the E Republic of Ireland, in Leinster bordering on the Irish Sea. Consisting chiefly of fertile glacial drifts it is important for agriculture; cattle are fattened and oats and potatoes grown. Area: 2338 sq km (903 sq mi). Population (1986): 103 762. County town: Trim.

MECCA *The court of the Al-Haram Mosque in the centre of the city, showing the black stone of the Kabaa.*

Mecca (Arabic name: Makkah) 21 26N 39 49E A city in W Saudi Arabia, in a narrow valley surrounded by barren hills. Every Muslim is expected to visit Mecca at least once in his lifetime; nonbelievers are not allowed to enter the city. It has been a holy city since ancient times, but was also the birthplace of Mohammed (c. 570). Population (1980 est): 550 000.

mechanics The study of the motion of bodies and systems and the forces acting on them. The subject is traditionally divided into statics, the study of bodies in equilibrium, and dynamics, the study of forces that affect the motion of bodies. Dynamics is further divided into kinetics, the effects of forces and their moments on motion, and kinematics, the study of velocity, acceleration, etc., without regard to the forces causing them. Aristotelian (*see* Aristotle) mechanics was based on the erroneous concept that a force is required to maintain motion. Newtonian mechanics recognizes that once a body is moving a force is required to stop it but no force is needed to keep it moving. The more general relativistic mechanics is applicable to systems moving at speeds comparable to that of light (it reduces to Newtonian mechanics at velocities that are small compared to that of light). Fluid mechanics is the application of mechanical principles to fluids, both stationary (hydrostatics) and flowing (hydrodynamics).

Medawar, Sir Peter Brian (1915–87) British immunologist, noted for his investigation of the development of the immune system in embryonic and young animals, including the phenomenon of acquired immunological tolerance to foreign tissue grafts. Medawar shared the 1960 Nobel Prize with Sir Macfarlane Burnet.

Medea In Greek legend, a sorceress, the daughter of King Aeetes of Colchis and niece of Circe. She helped Jason steal the Golden Fleece. When Jason deserted her for Glauce, daughter of the Corinthian King Creon, she killed Glauce, Creon, and her own two children.

Media An ancient region SW of the Caspian Sea settled by seminomadic tribes of Medes. Between the 8th and 6th centuries BC they began to unite against Assyria and in 612 destroyed Nineveh and overthrew the Assyrian empire.

median 1. The line joining the vertex of a triangle to the midpoint of the opposite side. 2. The middle value of a set of numbers arranged in order of magnitude. For example, the median of 2, 3, 3, 4, 5 is 3.

MEDICI *Lorenzo the Magnificent (detail).*

Medici A family that dominated Florence from 1434 to 1737 (as grand dukes from 1532). The Medici, who were merchants and bankers, dominated the government of Florence in the 15th century by manipulating elections to the key magistracies. The family's power was established by **Cosimo de' Medici** (1389–1464), who also initiated the Medici tradition of artistic patronage. His son **Piero de' Medici** (1416–69) succeeded to his position, which then passed to **Lorenzo the Magnificent** (1449–92). An outstanding patron of Renaissance artists (Botticelli, Ghirlandaio, Michelangelo) and scholars (Ficino, Pico della Mirandola, Politian), Lorenzo tended to neglect the family business, which declined in the late 15th century. He was succeeded by his son **Piero de' Medici** (1472–1503), who was forced to flee Florence in a revolt incited by Savonarola. Piero's brother **Giovanni de' Medici** (1475–1521) was restored to Florence in 1512, a year before he became Pope Leo X (1513–21). **Alessandro de' Medici** (1511–37) became the first Duke of Florence; subsequent grand dukes included **Cosimo I** (1519–74), **Francesco I** (1541–87), and **Ferdinando I** (1549–1609).

Medina (Arabic name: Al Madinah) 24 30N 39 35E A city in W Saudi Arabia, N of Mecca. The tomb of Mohammed is in the mosque at Medina, the second most holy Muslim city after Mecca. Date-packing supplements the city's income from pilgrims, and the Islamic University was founded in 1961. Population (1980 est): 290 000.

Mediterranean Sea An almost landlocked sea extending between Africa and Europe to Asia. It connects with the Atlantic Ocean at Gibraltar, the Black Sea via the Sea of Marmara, and the Red Sea via the Suez Canal. Fed continuously by the Atlantic and to a lesser extent by the Black Sea, it is saltier and warmer than the oceans; pollution is a serious problem. Tidal variation is insignificant.

medlar A thorny shrub or tree, *Mespilus germanica*, native to SE Europe and central Asia and cultivated for its fruit. Growing to a height of 6 m, it bears oblong toothed leaves and white five-petalled flowers. The globular brownish fruit has an opening at the top through which the five seed chambers can be seen. Medlars are eaten when partly decayed and have a pleasant acid taste; they can also be made into jelly. Family: *Rosaceae*.

medulla oblongata. *See* brain.

medusa The free-swimming sexual form that occurs during the life cycle of many animals of the phylum *Coelenterata*. Medusae resemble small jellyfish and have separate sexes, releasing eggs and sperm into the water. The ciliated larvae settle and develop into the sedentary asexual forms (*see* polyp). *See also* coelenterate.

Medusa In Greek mythology, the only mortal Gorgon. Athena, angered by her love affair with Poseidon, made her hair into serpents and her face so ugly that all who saw it were turned to stone. She later sent Perseus to behead her. From her blood sprang Pegasus and Chrysaor, her children by Poseidon.

Medway, River A river in SE England. Rising in Sussex, it flows N and E through Kent to join the River Thames by a long estuary. It passes through Tonbridge, Maidstone, Rochester, Chatham, and Gillingham. Length: 113 km (70 mi).

Meegeren, Hans van (1889–1947) Dutch painter, notorious for his Vermeer forgeries. He successfully misled the art world, notably with works such as *Christ at Emmaus*, bought by the Boymans Museum, Rotterdam, as an early Vermeer painting. In 1945 he was arrested as a Nazi collaborator, confessed his deceptions, was imprisoned, and died in poverty.

meerkat A small carnivorous mammal, *Suricata suricata*, also called suricate, of South African grasslands. It is about 60 cm long including the tail (17–25 cm), and lives in shallow burrows. Meerkats feed on insects, grubs, reptiles, birds, and small mammals. Family: *Viverridae*.

Meerut 29 00N 77 42E A city in India, in Uttar Pradesh. The scene of the first uprising (1857) of the Indian Mutiny, Meerut is an important army headquarters and has diverse industries. Population (1981): 538 000.

megalith (Greek: large stone) A large stone particularly favoured for building monuments in the Neolithic and Bronze Age. Megaliths could be placed singly, in lines, or in simple or complex circles as at Stonehenge. Megaliths were also used for tombs and temples in Malta, Egypt, and elsewhere.

megapode A bird belonging to a family (*Megapodidae*; 12 species) ranging from Australia to Malaysia. 48–68 cm long, megapodes are fowl-like and ground-dwelling with brownish plumage and build a large nest mound in which the eggs are incubated by the heat of fermenting plant material, the sun's rays, or volcanic heat. Order: *Galliformes* (pheasants, turkeys, etc.). *See also* brush turkey.

Megatherium A genus of extinct giant ground sloths that lived in North and South America about a million years ago. *Megatherium* was about the size of a modern elephant and probably ate leaves.

megaton A measure of the explosive power of a nuclear weapon. It is equivalent to an explosion of one million tons of trinitrotoluene (TNT).

Megiddo An ancient site in N Israel. Continuously occupied between about 3000 and 350 BC, Megiddo was strategically positioned on the route between Egypt and Syria and was the scene of many battles. Megiddo is identified with the biblical Armageddon (Revelation 16.16).

meiosis The process by which the nucleus of a germ cell divides prior to the formation of gametes (such as sperm, pollen, or eggs). Meiosis consists of two successive divisions during which one cell with the normal duplicate (diploid) set of chromosomes gives rise to four cells each with only one chromosome of each type (haploid). Meiosis differs from mitosis in that the chromosomes of each pair become closely associated, enabling the interchange of genetic material between maternal and paternal chromosomes. There is no duplication of chromosomes between the two divisions of meiosis.

Meir, Golda (1898–1978) Israeli stateswoman, born in Russia; prime minister (1969–74). A founder member of the Israeli Workers' Party (Mapai) she was its secretary general (1966–68). She was minister of labour (1949–56) and minister of foreign affairs (1956–66) before becoming prime minister. She was committed to the establishment of peace in the Middle East.

Meissen porcelain The first hard-paste porcelain made in Europe following discovery (1709) in Dresden of the technique by the alchemist J. F. Böttger (1682–1719) under the patronage of the Elector of Saxony. The manufacture moved to Meissen, a town on the River Elbe and now in East Germany, in 1710. There followed extensive ranges of domestic ware, figures, chinoiseries, small boxes, seals, and painted ornaments.

Meitner, Lise (1878–1968) Austrian physicist. She

worked with Otto Hahn in Berlin (1907–38); together they discovered protactinium (1918) and caused the first fission of a uranium atom by neutron bombardment (1934). Expelled by the Nazis, she moved to Stockholm, becoming a Swedish citizen in 1949.

Mekong, River A major SE Asian river, rising in Tibet and flowing generally SE through China, Laos, Kampuchea, and Vietnam to the South China Sea. The extensive delta is one of the greatest Asian rice-growing areas. Length: about 4025 km (2500 mi).

Melanesia A division of Oceania in the SW Pacific Ocean, consisting of an arc of volcanic and coral islands NE of Australia. It includes the Bismarck Archipelago, the Solomon, Admiralty, and D'Entrecasteaux Islands, Vanuatu Republic, New Caledonia, and Fiji. *See also* Micronesia; Polynesia.

Melanesians The people of the Melanesian islands. The term also covers similar peoples of New Guinea, though these are also often known as Papuan. They are of Oceanic Negroid race and speak languages of the Austronesian family. The Melanesians cultivate yams, taro, and sweet potatoes and live in small, usually dispersed, homesteads. In coastal areas fishing is important.

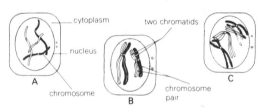

prophase I *The four chromosomes appear as thin threads (A), which form pairs (B). Each chromosome divides into two chromatids and exchange of genetic material occurs between the chromatids of each pair (C).*

metaphase I *The chromosomes of each pair separate from each other and move to opposite poles of the spindle.*

metaphase II *Two new spindles form and the chromatids of each group separate from each other.*

telophase II *Four new nuclei form, each containing two chromosomes.*

MEIOSIS *The formation of four egg or sperm cells from one parent cell takes place in two divisions, each of which is divided into several phases. Only four phases are shown here.*

melanin A pigment, varying from brown-black to yellow, that occurs in hair, skin, feathers, and scales. Derived from the amino acid tyrosine, its presence in the skin helps protect underlying tissues from damage by sunlight. Melanin is also responsible for colouring the iris of the eye.

melanoma A form of cancer, mainly affecting the skin, that arises in the cells producing the pigment melanin. Most melanomas develop from an existing mole, and excessive exposure to sunlight is known to be a contributory factor.

Melba, Dame Nellie (Helen Porter Armstrong; 1861–1931) Australian soprano. She made her debut in 1887 as Gilda in Verdi's opera *Rigoletto*. Her worldwide career culminated in a number of farewell performances in 1926.

Melbourne 37 45S 144 58E The second largest city of Australia, the capital of Victoria on Port Phillip Bay. It is a major commercial centre. Port Melbourne is sited 4 km (2.5 mi) away, on the mouth of the Yarra River; exports include wool, scrap metal, and dairy products. The chief industries are heavy engineering, food processing, and the manufacture of textiles and clothes. A cultural centre, Melbourne possesses three universities and the new Arts Centre of Victoria. The Melbourne Cricket Ground, founded in 1853, is world famous. *History*: founded in 1835, it developed rapidly following the 1851 gold rush. It was the capital of the Commonwealth of Australia from 1901 until 1927. Population (1986): 2 832 893.

Melbourne, William Lamb, 2nd Viscount (1779–1848) British statesman; Whig prime minister (1834, 1835–41). He was chief secretary for Ireland (1827–28) and then home secretary (1830–34), when he dealt harshly with the Tolpuddle Martyrs. During his second ministry his attempted resignation (1839) precipitated Victoria's Bedchamber Crisis. In 1805 he married Lady Caroline Ponsonby (1785–1828). As **Lady Caroline Lamb**, she had a love affair with Lord Byron (1812–13); because of her increasing mental instability, she separated from Lord Melbourne in 1825.

melon An annual tropical African vine, *Cucumis melo*, widely cultivated for its fruits. Melon plants have hairy leaves, yellow or orange cup-shaped flowers, and round or oval fruits, up to 4 kg in weight, with tough skins and sweet juicy flesh surrounding a core of seeds. Varieties include the muskmelon, with a net-veined skin and pinkish flesh; the honeydew melon, with smooth skin and light-green flesh; and the canteloupe, with rough warty skin and orange flesh. Family: *Cucurbitaceae*. *See also* watermelon.

Melos (*or* Mílos) A Greek island in the Aegean Sea, one of the Cyclades. The famous statue, the *Venus de Milo*, was discovered here in 1820. Area: 150 sq km (58 sq mi). Population (1981): 4554.

Melville, Herman (1819–91) US novelist. In 1841 he joined the crew of a whaler; his experiences in the South Seas form the raw material of his works. His masterpiece, *Moby Dick* (1851), is a narrative about whaling with an underlying philosophical theme on the nature of evil. *Billy Budd*, published in 1924 after his death, formed the basis of a libretto for an opera by Benjamin Britten.

Memel. *See* Klaipeda.

memory The recollection of experiences from the past. Three processes are required: registration, in which

an experience is received into the mind; retention, in which a permanent memory trace, or engram, is preserved in the brain; and recall, in which a particular memory is brought back into consciousness. Short-term memories are forgotten with the passage of time unless they are registered in the long-term memory. Failure of memory (*see* amnesia) is a common consequence of diseases of the brain. An abnormally good memory (hypermnesia) can sometimes be produced by hypnosis.

memory, computer The part of a computer that stores information. It usually refers to the computer's internal store, in which the programs and data are held; this is under the direct control of the central processing unit. In large computers, a high-speed buffer store holds information in active use by the central processing unit, while longer-term storage is provided by the slower main store.

Solid-state electronic memory devices operate at very high speeds and are used for the internal memory. Magnetic tapes and disks form the external memory.

Memphis 35 10N 90 00W A city and port in the USA, in Tennessee situated above the Mississippi River. It is a major cotton, timber, and livestock market and its manufactures include textiles and chemicals. Memphis is associated with W. C. Handy, the composer of the blues. Population (1986 est): 652 640.

Memphis An ancient city of Lower Egypt, S of modern Cairo. Memphis was founded as the capital of all Egypt after its unification by Menes (c. 3100 BC), remaining the capital until supplanted by Thebes (c. 1570 BC). The necropolis of Saqqarah and the pyramids and sphinx at Giza formed part of its extensive complex of monuments.

MENAI STRAIT *Telford's bridge photographed c. 1880.*

Menai Strait A channel separating the island of Anglesey from the mainland of NW Wales. It is crossed by a notable suspension bridge designed by Thomas Telford (1819–26). The Britannia railway bridge, built by Robert Stevenson (1850) and seriously damaged by fire in 1970, has been rebuilt.

Menander (c. 341–c. 290 BC) Greek dramatist. The most celebrated dramatist of the New Comedy, he wrote sophisticated comedies on romantic and domestic themes with strongly individualized characters. His single surviving complete play is the *Dyscolus*.

Mendel, Gregor Johann (1822–84) Austrian botanist, who discovered the fundamental principles governing the inheritance of characters in living things (*see* genetics). Mendel was a monk with a scientific education. In 1856 he began to inbreed lines of pea plants to study the characters of tallness and dwarfness. Mendel concluded that such characteristics were determined by factors of inheritance (now called alleles of the gene) that were contributed equally by both parents and that sorted themselves among the offspring according to simple statistical rules. He summarized these findings in his Law of Independence Segregation and Law of Independent Assortment (Mendel's laws). Mendel reported his findings in 1865 but his achievement was not appreciated until the rediscovery of his work by C. E. Correns (1864–1933), Hugo de Vries (1848–1935), and E. von Tschermak (1871–1962) in 1900.

mendelevium (Md) A synthetic element, first produced in 1955 by Ghiorso and others, by bombarding einsteinium with helium ions; it is named after the chemist Mendeleyev. At no 101; at wt (256).

Mendeleyev, Dimitrii Ivanovich (1834–1907) Russian chemist, who was professor at St Petersburg (now Leningrad) from 1866 to 1890. In 1869 he succeeded in arranging the elements in order of increasing atomic weights so that those with similar properties were grouped together (*see* periodic table).

Mendelssohn, Felix (Jacob Ludwig Felix Mendelssohn-Bartholdy; 1809–47) German composer. A child prodigy, his overture to *A Midsummer Night's Dream* (1826) demonstrated his precocious brilliance. In 1836 he became conductor of the Leipzig Gewandhaus orchestra and subsequently founded the Leipzig conservatoire. His compositions include five symphonies, overtures, the oratorios *St Paul* (1836) and *Elijah* (1846), chamber music, and piano music.

Menderes, River (ancient name: R. Maeander; Turkish name: Büyük Menderes) A winding river in W Turkey, flowing WSW into the Aegean Sea. Its ancient name gave rise to the term meander. Length: 400 km (249 mi).

Mendip Hills (*or* Mendips) A range of limestone hills in SW England, in Somerset. It extends NW–SE between Axbridge and the Frome Valley, reaching 325 m (1068 ft) at Blackdown. Its many limestone features include Cheddar Gorge and the caves of Cheddar and Wookey Hole.

Mendoza 32 48S 68 52W A city in W Argentina. It is the commercial centre of an irrigated area specializing in wine production. Population (1980): 597 000.

Menelaus A legendary Spartan king and husband of Helen. He served under his brother Agamemnon in the Trojan War and after the fall of Troy won Helen back.

Menelik II (1844–1913) Emperor of Ethiopia (1889–1913). He greatly expanded Ethiopia, limited the power of the nobility, and modernized the administration.

Mengele, Josef (1894–?1979) German medical scientist who became notorious for atrocities committed in the Nazi concentration camp at Auschwitz. Known as "the Angel of Death", he was camp doctor at Auschwitz from 1943 to 1945 and was subsequently held responsible for the deaths of 400 000 people, mostly Jews, many of whom died in bizarre medical experiments. In 1985 a body was exhumed in Brazil and identified as his.

meningitis Inflammation of the meninges—the membranes that surround the brain. This is usually caused by bacteria or viruses and occurs most commonly in chil-

dren. Symptoms include headache, vomiting, stiff neck, intolerance to light, tiredness, irritability, and fits. Treatment for bacterial meningitis is with antibiotics and the patient usually recovers rapidly. Viral meningitis is often mild but may have serious effects. Before modern drugs were developed, tuberculous meningitis was always fatal.

Menon, Krishna (Vengalil Krishnan Krishna Menon; 1896–1974) Indian diplomat. He was secretary of the India League from 1929 and a major figure in the campaign for Indian independence. After this was achieved in 1947 he became high commissioner for India to the UK and a member of the Indian legislature; he was a delegate at the UN (1952–62) and defence minister (1957–62).

menopause The change of life: the time in a woman's life when the menstrual periods become irregular and finally cease because egg cells are no longer produced by the ovaries. The menopause can occur at any age between the late 30s and late 50s. Some women may experience symptoms, including flushing ("hot flushes"), palpitations, and irritability, due to reduced secretion of oestrogens.

Menorca. *See* Minorca.

Menotti, Gian Carlo (1911–) Italian-born US composer. Among his compositions are the operas *The Medium* (1946) and *The Saint of Bleecker Street* (1954), which both won a Pulitzer Prize, and the television opera *Amahl and the Night Visitors* (1951). In 1958 he founded the Spoleto Festival.

Mensheviks One of the two factions into which the Russian Social Democratic Workers' Party split in 1903 in London. Unlike the rival Bolsheviks, the Mensheviks (meaning those in the minority) believed in a large and loosely organized party. They supported Russia's participation in World War I and were prominent in the Russian Revolution until the Bolsheviks seized power in October, 1917. They were finally suppressed in 1922.

menstruation The monthly discharge of blood and fragments of womb lining from the vagina. This is part of the **menstrual cycle**—the sequence of events, occurring in women from puberty to the menopause, by which an egg cell is released from the ovary. Menstruation is the stage at which the egg cell (with blood, etc.) is expelled from the womb if conception has not occurred. Ovulation occurs at around the middle of the cycle.

menthol ($C_{10}H_{20}O$) A white crystalline solid. It is a constituent of peppermint oil and is responsible for the characteristic smell of the mint plant, but can also be prepared synthetically. Menthol is used as an analgesic and in flavouring for sweets and cigarettes.

Menuhin, Sir Yehudi (1916–) British violinist, of Russo-Jewish parentage. A pupil of Georges Enesco, he became famous in boyhood. From 1959 to 1968 Menuhin was director of the Bath Festival, where he also participated as a conductor. He founded the Yehudi Menuhin School for musically gifted children in 1963.

Menzies, Sir Robert Gordon (1894–1978) Australian statesman; prime minister as leader of the United Australia Party (1939–41) and then of the Liberal Party (1949–66). He was attorney general (1934–39) before becoming prime minister. He resigned in 1941 and formed the Liberal Party in 1944. As Liberal prime minister he increased US influence in Australian affairs and was strongly anticommunist. Loyal to the British Commonwealth, he became Lord Warden of the Cinque Ports in 1965.

Mercator, Gerardus (Gerhard Kremer; 1512–94) Flemish geographer, best known for the Mercator projection. Prosecuted for heresy in 1544, he emigrated to Protestant Germany in 1552, where he was appointed cartographer to the Duke of Cleves. The **Mercator projection** first used in 1569, is a cylindrical map projection. The parallels of latitude are represented as being straight lines of equal length to the equator. The meridians are equally spaced and intersect at right angles. The correct ratio between latitude and longitude is maintained by increasing the distance between the parallels away from the equator causing increased distortion towards the Poles.

merchant banks Financial institutions that became acceptance houses as a result of their foreign trading as merchants. They are now involved in a variety of other businesses, including: the issue, placing, and underwriting of shares and debentures for firms; the issue of long-term loans for governments and institutions abroad; advising on the investment of funds and the management of portfolios; advising on and managing takeover bids; and dealings in foreign exchange.

Mercia A kingdom of Anglo-Saxon England. The Mercians were Angles and their territory embraced most of central England south of the Humber between Wales and East Anglia. Mercia achieved pre-eminence under Offa (757–96); thereafter it declined and was merged in the 9th century into a united England under Wessex.

Mercouri, Melina (1925–) Greek actress and politician; minister of culture and science (1981–85); minister of culture, youth, and sports (1985–). Her best-known films include *Never on Sunday* (1960) and *Topkapi* (1964). She campaigned in exile against the military junta (1967–74).

mercury (botany) An annual or perennial herb of the genus *Mercurialis* (8 species), native to Eurasia and N Africa. The perennial dog's mercury (*M. perennis*) of woodland areas has an evil smell and is poisonous to grazing animals. Growing 15–40 cm high, it has large toothed leaves and small green flowers. The annual mercury (*M. annua*) occurs on wasteland and as a garden weed. Family: *Euphorbiaceae*.

mercury (Hg) The only common metal that is liquid at room temperature (it has a high relative density of 13.546). It occurs chiefly as the sulphide cinnabar (HgS), from which mercury is obtained simply by heating in a current of air. It is used in thermometers, barometers, and batteries and as an amalgam in dentistry. Compounds include the oxide (HgO), mercurous and mercuric chlorides (Hg_2Cl_2, $HgCl_2$), and the explosive mercury fulminate ($Hg(ONC)_2$), which is widely used as a detonator. Mercury and its compounds are highly poisonous and are only slowly excreted by the human body. At no 80; at wt 200.59; mp $-38.87°C$; bp $356.58°C$.

Mercury (astronomy) The innermost and second smallest (4880 km diameter) planet, orbiting the sun every 88 days at a mean distance of 57.9 million km. Its long period of axial rotation, 58.6 days, is two-thirds of its orbital period. Like the moon, Mercury exhibits phases. Its surface is heavily cratered, with intervening lava-flooded plains. It has only a very tenuous atmosphere, mainly helium and argon.

Mercury (mythology) The Roman god of merchants and commerce and patron of astronomy. He is usually portrayed as holding a purse, and also with a cap, winged sandals, and staff, the attributes of the Greek Hermes, with whom he was identified.

Meredith, George (1828–1909) British poet and novelist. His long poem *Modern Love* (1862) was partly based on his unhappy marriage to Mary Ellen Nicholls, daughter of Thomas Love Peacock. His novels include *The Egoist* (1879) and *The Tragic Comedians* (1880).

merganser A duck belonging to a genus (*Mergus*) of the N hemisphere, also called sawbill. 40–57 cm long, mergansers have a long serrated bill for feeding on worms, fish, and eels. Males have a dark-green double-crested head, a chestnut breast, and a grey-and-white back; females are brown with a white wing bar.

Mérida 20 59N 89 39W A city in E Mexico. It is the commercial and industrial centre for an agricultural area specializing in henequen (a fibre) production. It has a 16th-century cathedral and is the site of the University of Yucatán (refounded 1922). Population (1984 est): 285 000.

meridian. *See* latitude and longitude.

Merino A breed of sheep from Spain, noted for its long thick high-quality white fleece. Merinos have been exported to many parts of the world, especially Australia.

meristem An area of actively dividing plant cells responsible for growth in the plant. The main meristematic regions in dicotyledon plants are the shoot tip and root tip (apical meristems) and the cambium (lateral meristem).

merlin A small falcon, *Falco columbarius*, occurring in moorland and heathland regions of the N hemisphere. The female is 32 cm long and is dark brown with heavily streaked underparts; the male is 26 cm long and has a grey-blue back and tail.

MERLIN *Standing behind Arthur as he pulls Excalibur from the stone; from a 13th-century manuscript.*

Merlin In Arthurian legend, the wizard who counsels and assists Arthur and his father, Uther Pendragon. There are various accounts of Merlin's life in Geoffrey of Monmouth and later writers. He helped Uther to win Igraine, Arthur's mother, made the Round Table, cared for Arthur as a child, and armed him with the sword Excalibur.

mermaid A legendary creature whose form is that of a beautiful woman above the waist and a fish below. A mermaid's male counterpart is called a **merman**.

Merovingians The first Frankish ruling dynasty (*see* Franks). It was founded by Merovech, King of the Salian Franks, in the mid-5th century AD. His grandson Clovis (reigned 481–511) greatly extended Merovingian possessions and the kingdom reached its zenith in the mid-6th century. The last Merovingian king, Childeric III, was deposed in 751 by the Carolingian Pepin the Short.

Mersey, River A river in NW England. Formed by the confluence of the Rivers Goyt and Tame at Stockport, it flows W to enter the Irish Sea by way of a 26 km (16 mi) long estuary, with the ocean ports of Liverpool and Birkenhead on its banks. Length: 113 km (70 mi).

Merseyside A metropolitan county of NW England, created in 1974 from SW Lancashire and NW Cheshire. It comprises the districts of Sefton, Liverpool, St Helens, Knowsley, and Wirral. Area: 648 sq km (250 sq mi). Population (1986 est): 1 467 600. Administrative centre: Liverpool.

Merthyr Tydfil (Welsh name: Merthyr Tudful) 51 46N 3 23W A town in South Wales, in Mid Glamorgan on the River Taff. Formerly a world iron and steel centre based on the surrounding coalfields, the main industries are now light and electrical engineering. Population (1982 est): 60 000.

mescaline A hallucinogenic drug obtained from the peyote cactus of Mexico, where it was once widely used in religious ceremonies. Mescaline does not cause serious dependence and the hallucinations are mostly visual.

Mesembryanthemum. *See* fig marigold.

MESMER *Seen treating his patients using Mesmer's tub.*

Mesmer, Franz Anton (1734–1815) German physician, who claimed to cure diseases by correcting the flow of "animal magnetism" in his patients' bodies. Investigation of "mesmerism" concluded that any cures were due to the powers of suggestion, but Mesmer's claims stimulated serious study of hypnosis.

Mesoamerican languages A geographical classification of the languages spoken by the American Indian peoples of Mexico, Guatemala, Honduras, Belize, El Salvador, and Nicaragua. It includes around 70 lan-

guages belonging to a number of families, such as the Uto-Aztecan, Otomangean, and Tarascan.

Mesolithic The middle division of the Stone Age, especially in N Europe, where a distinct cultural stage, the Maglemosian, intervened between the last ice age and the evolution of farming communities. Generally, the Mesolithic is characterized by production of microliths (very minute stone tools), which were hafted into wooden, bone, or other handles.

mesons A group of unstable elementary particles (lifetimes between 10^{-8} and 10^{-15} second) that are classified as hadrons; each meson is believed to consist of a quark-antiquark pair (*see* particle physics).

Mesopotamia The region between the Rivers Tigris and Euphrates. The Sumerians settled in S Mesopotamia about 4000 BC: they established the world's first civilization and founded city states, such as Ur, Kish, and Uruk. Babylon became Mesopotamia's capital under Hammurabi (d. 1750 BC). After his death Mesopotamia was overrun successively by Kassites, Assyrians, and Persians.

Mesozoic era The geological era following the Palaeozoic and preceding the Cenozoic. It contains the Triassic, Jurassic, and Cretaceous periods, and lasted from about 240 to 65 million years ago. The reptiles were at their greatest development during this era but became extinct before the end of it.

Messerschmitt, Willy (1898–1978) German aircraft designer. He is best known for his World War II military planes, particularly the Me-109 fighter (1935) and the Me-262, the first jet fighter.

Messiaen, Olivier (1908–) French composer, organist, and teacher. In 1931 he was appointed organist of La Trinité in Paris. His works, heavily influenced by Catholic mysticism and eastern music, include *La Nativité du Seigneur* (1935), the symphony *Turangalîla* (1948), *La Transfiguration* (for chorus and orchestra; 1965–69), and the opera *St Francis d'Assise* (1986).

Messina 38 13N 15 33E A port in Italy, in NE Sicily on the Strait of Messina. Successively occupied by Greeks, Carthaginians, Mamertines, Romans, Saracens, Normans, and Spaniards, in 1860 it became the last city in Sicily to be made part of a united Italy. Its manufactures include macaroni, chemicals, and soap. Population (1986): 268 896.

metabolism The sum of the processes and chemical reactions that occur in living organisms in order to maintain life. It can be divided into two components. **Anabolism** involves building up the tissues and organs of the body using simple substances, such as amino acids, simple sugars, etc., to construct the proteins, carbohydrates, and fats of which they are made. These processes require energy, which is provided by the oxidation of nutrients or the body's own food reserves. Oxidation and all other processes involving the chemical breakdown of substances with the production of waste products are known collectively as **catabolism**. Basal metabolism is the energy required to maintain vital functions (e.g. respiration, circulation) with the body at rest. It is measured by estimating the amount of heat produced by the body and is controlled by hormones from the thyroid gland.

metal An element that is usually a hard crystalline solid, a good conductor of heat and electricity, and forms a salt and hydrogen when reacted with an acid. Not all metals have these properties, however: mercury is a liquid at normal temperatures and sodium is soft. The most important are the heavy metals (iron, copper, lead, and zinc) used in engineering and the rarer heavy metals (nickel, chromium, tungsten, etc.) used in alloys. Other important metals are the noble metals (gold, silver, and platinum), and the light metals (aluminium and magnesium). Chemically important metals include the alkali metals (sodium, potassium, and lithium), the alkaline-earth metals (calcium, barium, etc.), and the rare-earth metals (*see* lanthanides). Uranium is important in the nuclear power industry (*see* nuclear energy). Most metals occur in the earth's crust in the combined state and have to be mined before being extracted from their ores (*see* metallurgy).

metallography The study of the crystalline structure of metals. It includes various techniques and is used to test the quality of steel after heat treatment. Usually a small sample is taken from a batch and polished before being examined under a microscope for cracks, impurities, or holes. The polished surface may also be treated chemically to show up the different constituents of an alloy or to highlight cracks. The technique of X-ray diffraction developed by Max von Laue (1879–1960) is used to examine metallic crystals.

metalloids Elements displaying the physical and chemical properties both of metals and nonmetals. Examples of metalloids are arsenic and germanium, which both have metallic and nonmetallic allotropes. They may form positive ions as well as covalently bonded compounds. The metalloid elements are often semiconductors.

metallurgy The science and technology of producing metals. It includes the extraction of metals from their ores, alloying to form materials with specific properties, and heat treatment to improve their properties.

metamorphic rock One of the three major rock categories (*compare* igneous rock; sedimentary rock) consisting of rocks produced by the alteration of existing rocks by heat, pressure, and chemically active fluids. Contact (*or* thermal) metamorphism occurs around igneous intrusions and results from heat alone. Regional metamorphism results from the heat and pressure created by crustal deformation. Dislocation metamorphism results from localized mechanical deformation, as along fault planes. Metamorphic rocks often form upland masses. Marble is a metamorphic rock formed from recrystallized limestone.

metamorphosis The process in animals by which a larva changes into an adult. This radical change of internal and external body structures may be gradual or abrupt. Certain insects, such as dragonflies, undergo incomplete metamorphosis, during which successive stages (known as nymphs) become increasingly like the adult through a series of moults. In complete metamorphosis, seen in such insects as butterflies and houseflies, the larva passes into a quiescent pupal stage, during which the adult tissues are developed. Metamorphosis also occurs in amphibians (*see* frog). The process in insects and amphibians is controlled by hormones.

metaphysical poets A group of 17th-century English poets whose work was characterized by intellectual wit and ingenuity, especially in their use of elaborate figures of speech. The leading poet was John Donne, and his successors included George Herbert (1593–1633), Henry Vaughan (c. 1622–95), Andrew Marvell, and Abraham Cowley (1618–67). They frequently employed colloquial speech rhythms in both their secular and their religious verse.

metaphysics The study of existence or being in general. The term derives from the title given to a group of Aristotle's writings. The status of metaphysics has been much debated; Kant thought this kind of investigation impossible because our minds can only cope with the phenomenal world or the world of appearances and Ayer used the word as a pejorative term to indicate the meaninglessness of much traditional philosophy. However, metaphysics is still held to be one of the main divisions of philosophy.

Metazoa A subkingdom of animals whose bodies consist of many cells differentiated and coordinated to perform specialized functions. The Metazoa includes all animals except the single-celled Protozoa and the Parazoa (*see* sponge).

metempsychosis. *See* reincarnation.

meteor A streak of light seen in the night sky when a **meteoroid**–an interplanetary rock or dust particle enters and burns up in the earth's atmosphere. A decaying comet gradually produces a **meteor stream** of meteoroids around its orbit. When the earth passes through a meteor stream, an often spectacular **meteor shower** is observed. A **meteorite** is a large piece of interplanetary debris (mass usually over 100 kg) that falls to the earth's surface. Meteorite composition is either principally iron or stone, or an intermediate mixture.

meteorology The study of the physics, chemistry, and movements of the atmosphere and its interactions with the ground surface. The troposphere and stratosphere, the lower layers of the atmosphere in which most weather phenomena occur, are the chief focuses of meteorology. **Weather** is the state of atmospheric conditions (including temperature, sunshine, wind, clouds, and precipitation) at a particular place and time. A **weather forecast** is a prediction of what weather conditions will be over a stated future period; it is made by studying weather maps, especially those obtained from satellites. Weather forecasts are essential to shipping and aviation and are of use to many other bodies, as well as to farmers. See p. 476. *See also* climate.

methane (CH_4) A colourless odourless flammable gas that is the main constituent of natural gas. It is the simplest member of the alkane series and is used as a fuel and a source of other chemicals. Methane is produced in nature by the decay of vegetable matter under water, rising in bubbles from marshes as **marsh gas**. Coal gas also contains methane. Recently the generation of methane from sewage has been investigated as an alternative energy source. It burns with a clear blue flame.

methanol (methyl alcohol *or* wood alcohol; CH_3OH) A colourless poisonous flammable liquid. Originally produced by distillation of wood, it is now usually made from hydrogen and carbon monoxide by high-pressure catalysis. It is used as a solvent, antifreeze, and a raw material for making other chemicals. *See also* methylated spirits.

Methodism The Christian denomination that developed out of the religious practices advocated by the Wesley brothers. Methodism evolved its own church organization during the 1790s. The supreme decision-making body is the Conference; local societies (congregations) are highly organized and pastoral and missionary work are major concerns. Methodism in the USA accounts for 80% of all Methodists.

weather conditions

• rain	✳ snow	⌒ dew
𝟿 drizzle	▲ hail	≡ fog
▽ showers	△ ice pellets	⊼ thunderstorm

weather map   *The numbers at the stations show temperature (0°C). Isobars show atmospheric pressure in millibars.*

cloud cover

○	clear
◐	1 okta
◑	2
◑	3
◐	4
◕	5
●	6
◗	7
●	8
⊗	sky obscured (1 okta = ⅛ of the sky)

wind

The arrow points in the direction from which the wind is blowing.

knots

◎	calm
○—	1–2
○—⟍	3–7
○—⟋	8–12
○—⟍⟋	13–17
○—⫽	18–22
○—⫽⟋	23–27
○—⫻	28–32
○—⫻⟋	33–37
○—⫼	38–42
○—⫼⟋	43–47
○—▲	48–52

fronts

▼▼▼ **cold front**   *boundary between overtaking cold air mass and warm air mass.*

‿‿‿ **warm front**   *boundary between overtaking warm air mass and cold air mass.*

▼‿▼‿ **stationary**   *boundary between air masses of similar temperature.*

▲▲▲ **occluded**   *line where a cold front overtakes a warm front.*

METEOROLOGY   *Internationally agreed symbols are used throughout the world by meteorological stations to represent current weather conditions. These are plotted on weather maps from which forecasts can be made.*

methyl alcohol.   *See methanol.*

methylated spirits   A form of ethanol (ethyl alcohol) that has been made unsuitable for drinking by the addition of about 9.5% of methanol (methyl alcohol), about 0.5% of pyridine, and a methyl violet dye. In this form it has many household uses, especially as a fuel for spirit burners. Industrial methylated spirits (IMS) consists of ethanol with about 5% of methanol and no pyridine. It is used as a solvent for varnishes, etc.

metre (m)   The unit of length in the metric system. Originally defined in 1791 as one ten-millionth of the length of the quadrant of the earth's meridian through Paris, it was redefined in 1927 as the distance between two marks on a platinum-iridium bar. It is now defined (General Conference on Weights and Measures, 1983) as the length of the path travelled by light in a vacuum in 1/299 792 458 second, which replaces the 1960 definition based on the emission of a krypton lamp.

metre (poetry)   The rhythmic pattern of a line of verse measured in terms of basic metrical units or feet. In accentual verse, as in English, a foot consists of various arrangements of stressed (') and unstressed (˘) syllables. In classical Greek and Latin verse, the quantity or length rather than the stress of syllables determines the foot. In English the most common feet are the iamb (˘ '), the trochee (' ˘), the anapaest (˘˘ '), the dactyl (' ˘˘), and the spondee (' '). Most traditional poetic forms, such as the sonnet, are written according to strict metrical patterns.

metric system   A system of measurement based on the decimal system. First suggested in 1585, it was not given formal acceptance until 1795, when a French law provided definitions for the metre, are, stere, litre, and gram. However, this form of the metric system was not widely used, even in France, until the third decade of the 19th century; during this period it was also adopted by most European countries. Although the metric system was authorized in the UK in 1864, British reluctance to abandon its own "Imperial units" did not weaken until 1963, when the Imperial yard and pound were given legal definitions in terms of metric units. The **Metrication Board**, set up in 1969, was disbanded in April 1980, metrication proceeding thereafter on a voluntary basis. For scientific purposes, former metric systems (such as the c.g.s. system) have been replaced by SI units.

metronome A small device consisting of a pendulum with a small sliding weight on it, which can be regulated to make the pendulum beat at a desired number of beats per minute. The most common type is the clockwork metronome invented by J. N. Maelzel (1770–1838); electric metronomes also exist. Metronome markings are often given in musical scores to indicate the exact speed of the music.

Metropolitan Museum of Art The principal museum in New York City and one of the most important in the world. Founded in 1870, it was opened in its present premises in Central Park in 1880. Its enormous collection comprises paintings, drawings, sculptures, ceramics, furniture, etc., from many periods and countries, including China, ancient Egypt, Greece, and Rome.

Metropolitan Opera Association The principal US opera company, founded in New York in 1883. Enrico Caruso (1873–1921) sang regularly with the company from 1904 to 1921. The company occupied the Metropolitan Opera House until 1966, when it moved into the Lincoln Centre for the Performing Arts, the original building being demolished.

Metternich, Klemens Wenzel Nepomuk Lothar, Fürst von (1773–1859) Austrian statesman, the leading figure in European diplomacy from the fall of Napoleon (1815) until the Revolutions of 1848. As foreign minister (1809–48) he sought to maintain the balance of power in Europe, supporting dynastic monarchies and suppressing liberalism. His policies dominated the Congresses of Vienna (1814–15), Aix-la-Chapelle (1818), Troppau (1820), Laibach (1821), and Verona (1822).

Meuse, River (Dutch and Flemish name: Maas) A river in W Europe. Rising in NE France and flowing mainly N past Liège in Belgium and Maastricht in the S Netherlands, it enters the North Sea at the Rhine Delta. It was the scene of heavy fighting in World War I (1914) and World War II (1940). Length: 926 km (575 mi).

Mexican War (1846–48) The war between Mexico and the USA over disputed border territory. Military operations began when Gen Zachary Taylor invaded New Mexico and ended with the fall of Mexico City (1847). Peace was concluded with the Treaty of Guadalupe-Hidalgo.

Mexico, United States of A country in North America between the Gulf of Mexico and the Pacific Ocean. Narrow coastal plains rise to high mountain ranges in the interior. Much of the N is arid with tropical forest in the S, especially in the Yucatán Peninsula in the SE. Most of the population is of mixed Indian and Spanish descent. *Economy:* Mexico now ranks among the world's main oil-producing countries. Its first nuclear power station started up in 1988. It also has large reserves of natural gas and there are substantial deposits of uranium. Other minerals extracted include iron ore, zinc, sulphur, silver, and copper, and Mexico is the world's largest producer of fluorite and graphite. Agriculture remains relatively underdeveloped. Maize is the main food crop; cash crops include cotton, sugar, coffee, and fruit and vegetables, as well as sisal in Yucatán. Fishing has been developed considerably and important catches include sardines, shrimps, and oysters. Tourism is an important source of foreign currency. *History:* Mexico was the site of the Mayan civilization from the 2nd to the 13th centuries AD, and between the 8th and the 12th centuries the Toltecs flourished. The 14th century saw the rise of the Aztecs. The Aztecs were conquered by the Spanish under Cortés in 1521 and Mexico became part of the viceroyalty of New Spain. The struggle for independence from Spain was achieved in 1821. A turbulent period dominated by Santa Anna (1794–1876) was followed by the Mexican War (1846–48), in which territory was lost to the USA. The Mexican Revolution culminated in the constitution of 1917, the democratic goals of which have been the declared aims of subsequent governments. Mexico is now a one-party state dominated by the Party of Institutionalized Revolution (PRI). Economic pressures in the 1980s have led to high inflation, devaluation of the peso, and austerity measures. Mexico is a member of the OAS. President: Carlos Salinas de Gortari (1948–   ). Official language: Spanish; Indian languages, especially Nahuatl, are widely spoken. Official currency: Mexican peso of 100 centavos. Area: 1 967 183 sq km (761 530 sq mi). Population (1987 est): 76 000 000. Capital: Mexico City. Main port: Veracruz.

Mexico City (Spanish name: Ciudad de México) 19 25N 99 10W The capital of Mexico, in the S of the high central plateau at a height of 2380 m (7800 ft), surrounded by mountains. The 14th-century Aztec city of Tenochtitlán was destroyed by Cortés in 1521. A new Spanish city was built on the site and it rapidly became the most important in the New World. It was captured by the USA and then by France in the 19th century and in the 20th century was the centre of several revolutions. It now has considerable industry. It is the site of the National Autonomous University of Mexico (founded in 1551), the national library, the museum, and the Palace of Fine Arts Theatre. In 1985 the city and surrounding areas were devastated by an earthquake. It suffers atmospheric pollution. Population (1985): 15 667 000.

mezzo-soprano. *See* soprano.

Miami 25 45N 80 15W A city and port in the USA, in Florida on Biscayne Bay. A major tourist resort and retirement centre, it grew during the Florida land boom of the 1920s. It is famous for its citrus fruit and winter vegetables. Industries include aircraft repairing, sponge fisheries, clothing, and concrete. Population (1986 est): 371 975.

micas A group of common rock-forming silicate minerals with a layered structure and complex composition. Muscovite, $K_2Al_4(Si_6Al_2)O_{20}(OH,F)_4$, is a white mica and economically the most important; it occurs in granitic rocks (often pegmatites), gneisses, and schists. The other principal micas are phlogopite (amber), biotite (dark), paragonite, margarite, zinnwaldite, and lepidolite (a source of lithium). Since it is a good insulator and can withstand high temperatures, mica has many electrical uses and is used for furnace windows.

Michaelmas daisy. *See* Aster.

Michelangelo Buonarroti (1475–1564) Italian sculptor, painter, architect, and poet. Working in Rome from 1496 until 1501, he produced his first major sculptures, notably the *Pietà* (St Peter's, Rome). This was fol-

MICHELANGELO *A figure from the ceiling of the Sistine Chapel.*

lowed (1501–05) by his work in Florence, including *David* (Accademia, Florence) and the painting of the *Holy Family* (Uffizi). The celebrated Sistine Chapel ceiling (1508–12), in the Vatican, established his reputation as the greatest painter of his day. Returning to Florence (1516), Michelangelo became the architect and sculptor of the Medici funerary chapel (1520–34) in S Lorenzo and he also designed the Laurentian Library. These architectural projects and the fresco of the *Last Judgment* (1534–41) for the Sistine Chapel were his first major works in the new mannerist style (*see* mannerism). In his last years he worked mainly as an architect, becoming in 1547 chief architect of St Peter's, Rome, in which capacity he designed its great dome.

Michelson, Albert Abraham (1852–1931) US physicist, born in Germany. He designed a highly accurate interferometer known as the Michelson interferometer and used it to measure precisely the speed of light. He also used it in the **Michelson-Morley experiment**, performed with the US chemist E. W. Morley (1838–1923) in 1881 in an attempt to demonstrate the existence of the luminiferous ether by measuring the earth's velocity relative to it. The negative result led to the downfall of the ether theory and was explained by Einstein's theory of relativity in 1905.

Michigan A state in the N central USA, bordered largely by water (Lakes Superior, Huron, Michigan, Erie, and St Clair). It is divided by the Straits of Mackinac into the Lower Peninsula in the S and the Upper Peninsula in the N. Most of Michigan's population and industry is concentrated in the Lower Peninsula. Manufacturing is very important, especially the production of motor vehicles at Detroit; other industries include machinery, iron and steel, and chemicals. It has large mineral reserves of gypsum, calcium, and magnesium compounds, natural gas and oil. *History*: explored by the French in the 17th century, it remained under French control until it was acquired by the British (1763) as part of Canada. It came under American control (1783), becoming a state in 1837. Area: 150 779 sq km (58 216 sq mi). Population (1986 est): 9 145 000. Capital: Lansing.

Michigan, Lake The third largest of the Great Lakes in North America, wholly in the USA. It is linked with Lake Huron via the Straits of Mackinac; Chicago is on its S bank. Area: 58 000 sq km (22 400 sq mi).

microbiology The study of microorganisms, or microbes—organisms that are invisible to the naked eye, including bacteria, small fungi (e.g. yeasts and moulds), algae, protozoa, and viruses. Microorganisms bring about decomposition and the recycling of nutrients. They are vital to numerous industries, including brewing, baking, dairying, and food processing, and they have revolutionized medical treatment with the discovery of antibiotics. Some microorganisms cause disease in plants, animals, and man (*see* infection).

microchip. *See* integrated circuit.

microcomputers Small sophisticated computers designed for a single user and often for a specific application. The central processing unit is a microprocessor.

microcopy A greatly reduced photographic copy of a printed page, drawing, or other image. **Microfilm** is a strip of standard-width film containing microcopies. It was introduced in the 1920s for use in banks and is now widely used for compact storage and ready reference to documents. Special enlarging viewers can rapidly wind the film to the correct page. **Microfiche** is a similar system on cards holding a single film negative, with even greater reduction of the pictures. The viewers often have a printer attached to reproduce paper copies.

microlight aircraft A small powered aircraft of minimal weight. These aircraft were developed in the 1980s, when such models as the British Optica were considered for traffic monitoring and other roles. Some models can be folded up for ease of transport.

micrometer An instrument for measuring small lengths with great accuracy. The object to be measured is held between the jaws of a C-shaped metal piece, one jaw of which can be adjusted by a screw. The screw is turned by rotating a drum with a vernier scale marked on it, from which the required dimension can be read.

Micronesia, Federated States of An island country in the W Pacific Ocean, consisting of 607 islands E of the Philippines. A former Trust Territory, it was founded in 1986 and is divided into the states of Kosrae, Pohnpei, Truk, and Yap. Land area: 702 sq km (271 sq mi). Population (1988): 86 094.

microphone A device that converts sound into electrical signals. A telephone mouthpiece usually consists of a carbon microphone in which the sound waves exert a varying pressure on carbon granules, so varying their electrical resistance. In capacitor microphones, used in music recording, a diaphragm forms one plate of a capacitor, across which the sound waves produce a fluctuating potential difference. Crystal microphones rely on the piezoelectric effect. Ribbon microphones have a highly directional response. They consist of a thin strip of aluminium alloy in a strong magnetic field.

microprocessor The central processing unit of a microcomputer. Its development was made possible in the

1970s by advances in solid-state electronics, in particular the design of integrated circuits of such complexity that all the main calculating functions can be carried out by a single silicon chip (*see* integrated circuit).

MICROSCOPE   *Bacteria on a pinhead as seen by an electron microscope.*

microscope   An optical instrument used for producing a magnified image of a small object. There are several distinct types, the most common being the compound microscope, which contains an objective lens system and an eyepiece system. It was invented in 1609 by a Dutch spectacle maker Zacharias Janssen (1580–c. 1638) and his father, but Robert Hooke gave the first extensive description of its use in biology in his *Micrographia* (1665). In a compound microscope the objective produces a real magnified image, which is further magnified by the eyepiece. The magnification, which may be up to a thousand, is limited by the resolving power of the lenses; the smallest detail capable of resolution by an optical microscope is about 0.2 micrometre. This can be increased by using an oil-immersion lens (*see also* ultramicroscope). Still higher magnifications are obtained by using shorter wavelength radiations as in the electron microscope.

microwave background radiation.   *See* big-bang theory.

microwaves   Electromagnetic radiation with wavelengths between 1 and 300 millimetres, lying between infrared rays and radio waves in the electromagnetic spectrum. They are used in radar and **microwave heating**. This method is used in the rapid cooking of food as the radiation penetrates to the interior of the food. The microwave photon is the same order of magnitude as the vibrational energy of atoms and molecules and therefore heats the interior directly, rather than by conduction from the surface. Microwaves are generated by such devices as magnetrons and klystrons.

Midas   In Greek legend, a king of Phrygia whose wish that everything he touched be turned to gold was granted by Dionysus in gratitude for his hospitality to the satyr Silenus. In another legend, Midas was asked to judge between the music of Pan and Apollo and chose the former. Apollo punished his tactlessness by changing his ears into those of an ass.

middle ages   The period of European history that is generally regarded as commencing in the 5th century

with the fall of the western Roman Empire and ending with the Renaissance. This period begins with the creation of the barbarian kingdoms, which developed into the nation states of W Europe. In Church history, the period covers the rise to supremacy of the Roman Catholic Church. Socially and economically the period saw the rising power of the great landed magnates and the creation of a feudal society, while urban growth and the development of trade reached unprecedented heights.

Middlesbrough   54 35N 1 14W A town in NE England, the administrative centre of Cleveland on the Tees estuary. Local iron ore and local coking coal gave Middlesbrough early industrial advantages. Iron and steel, chemicals, constructional engineering, and shipbuilding are major industries. Population (1983 est): 148 400.

Middle Temple.   *See* Inns of Court.

midge   A small fly, also called a nonbiting midge, belonging to the family *Chironomidae* (over 2000 species). It resembles a mosquito but is harmless. Midges are found near fresh water, often in large swarms. The wormlike aquatic larvae are often red.

The term is also applied loosely to similar but unrelated flies.

Mid Glamorgan   A county of SE Wales. It was created in 1974 from central Glamorgan and a small part of Breconshire and Monmouthshire. It consists of uplands dissected by the deep parallel valleys of the Rivers Taff, Rhymney, and Ogmore. There is sheep farming on the uplands. Coalmining remains an important activity in the inner valleys but the traditional iron industry has been replaced by light industry. Area: 1019 sq km (393 sq mi). Population (1986 est): 534 500. Administrative centre: Cardiff.

Midlands   A collective term for the central counties of England. The area includes the counties of Derbyshire, Leicestershire, Northamptonshire, and Nottinghamshire, which are frequently referred to as the **East Midlands**, and the counties of Staffordshire, Warwickshire, Hereford and Worcester, and the metropolitan county of West Midlands, which comprise the **West Midlands**.

Midlothian   A former county (once called Edinburghshire) of SE Scotland. Under local government reorganization in 1975 its boundaries were adjusted to form a district of the same name, in Lothian Region.

Midrash   (Hebrew: enquiry, exposition)   Exposition of the Bible, and more particularly a book consisting of such exposition. There are many Midrashim, mostly dating from the early middle ages, and they are a valuable source for the religious ideas of the Jews of the time. The Talmuds also contain a great deal of Midrash.

Mies van der Rohe, Ludwig   (1886–1969) German architect. A pioneering architect of the 1920s and 1930s, Mies first achieved fame with his glass skyscrapers (1919–21). However, his most influential building was the glass, steel, and marble German pavilion at the Barcelona international exhibition (1929). In 1937 he moved to the USA, where he designed such buildings as the Illinois Institute of Technology (1939) and the Seagram building, New York (1958). See p. 480.

migraine   Recurrent headaches, usually affecting one side of the head and thought to be caused by contraction and then dilation of the arteries in the brain. The attacks are often preceded by blurring of vision and flickering lights (called an aura). During the headache itself vomiting commonly occurs.

MIES VAN DER ROHE *The Seagram Building in New York.*

migration, animal The periodic movement of animal populations between one region and another, usually associated with seasonal climatic changes or breeding cycles. Migration is best known among birds, but the phenomenon is seen in many other animals, including fish (notably salmon), butterflies, bats, lemmings, and whales. The mechanism of navigation and homing is not completely understood. In birds it seems to involve sighting of visible landmarks, as well as a compass sense, using the sun or the stars as bearings. Other animals are thought to use similar methods.

Míkonos (*or* Mykonos) A Greek island in the S Aegean Sea, one of the Cyclades. It is popular with tourists and is noted for having a large number of churches. Area: 90 sq km (35 sq mi). Population (1981): 5503.

Milan (Italian name: Milano; Latin name: Mediolanum) 45 28N 9 12E A city in N Italy, the capital of Lombardy on the River Olona. Milan is the focal point of rail and road routes and is the chief commercial and industrial centre of Italy. Its manufactures include motor vehicles, machinery, silk and other textiles, and chemicals and it is a major publishing centre. Milan has a gothic cathedral (duomo), the Brera Palace (containing the city's chief art collection), and the opera house of La Scala. *History*: founded by the Gauls about 600 BC, it was captured by the Romans in 222. After the 12th century it enjoyed considerable economic prosperity. Having fallen to Spain in 1535, it was under Austrian rule (1713–96) and in 1797 Napoleon made it capital of the Cisalpine Republic (1797) and capital of the kingdom of Italy (1805–14). Population (1986): 1 495 260.

mildew Any fungus that grows as dense filaments forming visible white patches. Many fungal diseases of plants are called mildews: powdery mildews are infestations by fungi of the order *Peronosporales*, while downy mildews are due to infection by fungi of the family *Erysiphaceae*.

mile A unit of length traditionally used in the UK and USA. A statute mile is equal to 1760 yards. A nautical mile (UK) is equal to 6080 feet; a nautical mile (international) is equal to 1852 metres (6076.12 ft). The unit is based on the Roman mile of 1000 paces.

Miletus An ancient Greek city in Ionia, founded about 1000 BC. Commercially active from Italy to Egypt, Miletus exemplified Ionian energy and enterprise. Milesians were prominent among the 6th-century Ionian thinkers, and even after destruction by Persia (494 BC) Miletus remained commercially important until its harbours silted up.

Milhaud, Darius (1892–1974) French composer, a member of Les Six. He made use of polytonality and jazz in many of his compositions. With Jean Cocteau he wrote the ballets *Le Boeuf sur le toit* (1919) and *Le Train bleu* (1924); with Paul Claudel he wrote the opera *Christophe Colomb* (1928). His other works include 12 symphonies, 15 string quartets, concertos, and Jewish liturgical music.

Militant Tendency A faction within the Labour Party advocating Trotskyist policies, which emerged in the 1970s around the newspaper *Militant*. It attracted notoriety after 1979 in the controversy over reform of the party. In 1982 it was judged to have broken the rules for groups within the party and was banned.

milk A fluid secreted by the mammary glands of mammals to feed their young. Cows' milk consists typically of about 87% water, 3.6% fat, 3.3% protein, 4.7% lactose (milk sugar), small quantities of minerals (mainly calcium and phosphorus), and vitamins (mainly vitamins A and B). (Human milk, in contrast, contains less protein and more lactose.) Milk forms a well-balanced and highly nutritious food. In the UK most milk is sold, after pasteurization, in bottles or cartons, with daily doorstep deliveries. Sterilized and UHT (ultraheat-treated) milk both have a longer shelf-life. *See also* dairy products.

milkweed A herb of the genus *Asclepias* (120 species), native to North America and often grown in the tropics and subtropics for ornament. Up to 1.2 m high, it bears umbrella-shaped clusters of orange, purple, pink, or red flowers and yields a milky latex. Family: *Asclepiadaceae*.

Milky Way The diffuse band of light that is seen, on a clear moonless night, stretching across the sky. It is composed of innumerable stars that are too faint to be seen individually. They lie around the sun in the flattened and densely populated disc of our Galaxy.

Mill, John Stuart (1806–73) British economist and philosopher. His *Principles of Political Economy* (1848) is little more than a restatement of the ideas of Adam Smith and Ricardo. *On Liberty* (1859) shows that he was concerned for the rights of the individual, and he believed strongly in the equality of the sexes, publishing his views in *Subjection of Women* (1869). A prolific journalist, he edited the *London Review* during the period 1835–40.

Millais, Sir John Everett (1829–96) British painter. He was one of the founders of the Pre-Raphaelite Brotherhood, the principles of which he applied to his best paintings, notably the controversial *Christ in the House of His Parents* (1850) and *Ophelia* (1852; both Tate Gallery). After abandoning Pre-Raphaelitism in the 1860s, he painted more popular and sentimental works, such as *Bubbles* (1886), a portrait of his grandson.

Miller, Arthur (1915–) US dramatist. As a Jewish liberal intellectual he has played an active role in political life. His plays include *All My Sons* (1947), *Death of a Salesman* (1947), which won a Pulitzer Prize, *The Crucible* (1953), concerning the Salem witch trials of the 1690s, and *After the Fall* (1964), which is in part a portrait of his late wife Marilyn Monroe.

Miller, Glenn (1904–44) US jazz trombonist, band leader, and composer of the popular songs "Moonlight Serenade" and "In the Mood." Miller's band, assembled in 1938, recorded many hit swing tunes and entertained the troops during World War II.

millet One of various grasses or their seeds, cultivated in Asia and Africa as a cereal crop and in parts of Europe and North America chiefly as a pasture grass and fodder crop. It grows 30–130 cm high and the flowers form spikes or branched clusters. Common or broomcorn millet (*Panicum miliaceum*) is used for poultry feed or for flour milling. Pearl millet (*Pennisetum glaucum*) is grown as a food grain, Italian millet (*Setaria italica*) as a grain crop, and Japanese millet (*Echinochloa crus-galli* var. *frumentacea*) mainly for fodder. A variety of sorghum (durra) is also known as millet.

Millet, Jean François (1814–75) French painter of peasant origin. He studied in Cherbourg and in Paris under Paul Delaroche (1797–1859), achieving acclaim in 1844. After settling in Barbizon (1849), he became associated with the Barbizon school and painted melancholy and sometimes sentimental agricultural scenes, notably *The Gleaners* (1857) and *The Angelus* (1859; both Louvre).

millibar. *See* bar.

MILLIPEDE

millipede A slow-moving arthropod of the widely distributed class *Diplopoda* (about 8000 species). Its slender cylindrical body, 2–280 mm long, is covered by a calcareous cuticle and consists of 20–100 segments, most of which bear two pairs of legs (*compare* centipede). Millipedes live in dark humid places as scavengers of dead plant and animal materials. In defence they secrete a toxic fluid containing cyanide and iodine.

Milne, A(lan) A(lexander) (1882–1956) British novelist and dramatist. He is best known for his books for and about his son Christopher Robin. These include two collections of verse and two books about toy animals, *Winnie-the-Pooh* (1926) and *The House at Pooh Corner* (1928).

Miltiades (c. 550–489 BC) Athenian general and statesman. Sent to govern the Thracian peninsula in Athenian interests, he ruled as tyrant and fought with Darius I of Persia (c. 558–486 BC) in Scythia. Appointed a general in 490, he devised the strategy by which the Greeks decisively defeated the Persians at the battle of Marathon.

Milton, John (1608–74) English poet. His early works include the poems *L'Allegro* and *Il Penseroso* (1632), the masque *Comus* (1633), and the elegy *Lycidas* (1637). During the 1640s and 1650s he actively supported the Puritan revolution and wrote many polemical pamphlets, notably *Areopagitica* (1644), a defence of free speech. In 1649 he was appointed Latin Secretary to the Council of State, but his eyesight began to fail and he had become totally blind by 1652. After the Restoration he retired from public life to write his great epic poem *Paradise Lost* (1667), its sequel *Paradise Regained* (1677), and the dramatic poem *Samson Agonistes* (1671).

Milton Keynes 52 02N 0 42W A town in S England, in Buckinghamshire. Developed since 1967 as a new town around the old village of Milton Keynes, it is the headquarters of the Open University (1969) and has varied light industries. Population (1983 est): 146 000.

Milwaukee 43 03N 87 56W A city and port in the USA, in Wisconsin on Lake Michigan. The state's largest city and a major shipping centre, Milwaukee is a leading producer of heavy machinery, electrical equipment, and diesel and petrol engines. Population (1986 est): 605 090.

mime Acting without words by physical gestures alone. It was practised in ancient Greek and Roman drama and was an important constituent of the commedia dell'arte in the 16th century. Exponents of modern mime include Jean-Louis Barrault (1910–) and Marcel Marceau.

mimesis (Greek: imitation) A philosophical concept introduced by Aristotle in the *Poetics*. He argues that imitation is the basis of all the arts but they differ as to the means they use and the objects they imitate. Imitation in the arts does not refer to a simple realistic rendering of detail but to the poet's (or artist's) ability to select and present his material so as to express essential truth.

mimicry The phenomenon of two or more organisms (commonly different species) resembling each other closely, which confers an advantage–usually protection –to one or both of them. In **Batesian mimicry**, named after H. W. Bates (1825–92), a poisonous or inedible species (the model) has a conspicuous coloration, which acts as a warning to predators. This coloration is adopted by a harmless edible species (the mimic), which derives protection against the same predators. In **Müllerian mimicry**, first described by the German naturalist Fritz Müller (1821–97), two or more species–all inedible–have the same warning coloration. After a predator has associated this pattern with an inedible species it will learn not to select similarly coloured species.

Mimosa A genus of trees, shrubs, and herbs (450–500 species), mostly native to tropical and subtropical America. They have feathery compound leaves and fluffy round catkins of yellow flowers. The genus includes the sensitive plants, *M. pudica* and *M. sensitiva*. Florists' mimosas are species of *Acacia* (*see* wattle). Family: *Leguminosae*.

Mind (National Association for Mental Health) A voluntary British organization founded in 1946 to provide for the needs of the mentally ill and handicapped. It has 130 local associations and campaigns for better services for the mentally ill, runs advice centres, and encourages an understanding of mental illness.

Mindanao An island in the S Philippines, the second, largest. Hemp, maize, pineapples, timber, nickel, and gold are the chief products. Its Muslim population has resisted Spanish, US, and now Philippine rule. Area: 101 919 sq km (39 351 sq mi). Population (1987 est): 13 093 000. Chief towns: Davao and Zamboanga.

minerals Naturally occurring substances of definite chemical composition (although this may vary within limits). Some consist of a single element but most are compounds of at least two. Strictly defined, minerals are solid (except native mercury) and are inorganically formed, although the constituents of organic limestones, for instance, are considered minerals. The term is used loosely for any naturally occurring material that is of economic value. Almost all true minerals are crystalline; a few, such as opal, are amorphous. Minerals are identified by the following properties: crystal system (e.g. cubic) and habit or form (e.g. fibrous), hardness (*see* Mohs' scale), relative density, lustre (e.g. metallic), colour, streak (colour when finely divided), cleavage, and fracture. Rocks are composed of mixtures of minerals.

Minerva A Roman goddess originally of the arts and crafts of wisdom, later identified with the Greek Athena. As goddess of war she almost equalled Mars.

minesweeper A vessel equipped to cut the cables of floating mines. Partially submerged cables are towed through a minefield so that the cable, passing under the mines, cuts their anchor chains, allowing the mines to float so that they can be detonated by gunfire. Mines laid on the seabed are detected by a submersible minefinder.

MING *A flask (15th century) in underglaze blue.*

Ming (1368–1644) A native Chinese dynasty, which succeeded the Mongol Yuan dynasty. It was founded by Hong-wu (1328–98), the first of 17 Ming emperors. The Ming provided an era of stable government personally controlled by the emperor. Painting and pottery, especially blue and white porcelain, flourished under the Ming.

miniature painting The art of painting on a very small scale, using watercolour on a vellum, card, or ivory base. The medieval Persian and Indian miniatures are the first great examples of the art. In Europe it flourished in the form of oval, circular, and occasionally rectangular portraits from the 16th to mid-19th centuries. There it developed from the medieval art of manuscript illumination and Renaissance portrait medals. Nicholas Hilliard was the first major specialist of the art in England. Other famous British miniaturists were Isaac Oliver (?1556–1617), Samuel Cooper (1609–72), and Richard Cosway (1742–1821).

minicomputer A small computer, especially one that fits into a single cabinet. Compared with a large mainframe computer it is slower, has a smaller memory, and is considerably cheaper. The term is no longer used specifically and predates the more usual word, microcomputer, for a small personal device.

minimal art An abstract style of painting and sculpture developed in New York in the late 1960s. In reaction against the personal character of action painting, it aims to eliminate artistic self-expression by reducing creativity to a minimum. This has been achieved by using simple hard-edged geometrical shapes and unmodulated vibrant colours. Leading minimalists include the painters Kenneth Noland (1924–   ) and Frank Stella (1936–   ) and the sculptor Carl André (1935–   ).

minivet An Asian songbird of the genus *Pericrocotus* (10 species), occurring in forests, where it hunts for insects in small flocks. Male minivets, about 17 cm long, have a black-and-red plumage; the females are yellowish grey. Family: *Campephagidae* (cuckoo-shrikes and minivets).

mink A small carnivorous mammal belonging to the genus *Mustela* (weasels, stoats, etc.), prized for its fur. The American mink (*M. vison*) is the largest species (about 70 cm long) and has the most valuable fur. They are nocturnal, semi-aquatic, and prey on fish, rodents, and waterfowl. Family: *Mustelidae*.

Minneapolis 45 00N 93 15W A city in the USA, in Minnesota on the Mississippi River. Adjacent to St Paul, the Twin Cities comprise the commercial, industrial, and financial centre of a large grain and cattle area; flour milling is the main industry. The University of Minnesota was established here in 1851. Population (1986 est): 356 840.

Minnelli, Liza. *See* Garland, Judy.

Minnesota A state in the USA, bordering on Canada in the N and Lake Superior in the NE. It consists of rolling prairies rising to the heavily forested Superior Highlands in the N and contains many lakes. Manufacturing industries (especially food processing) now form the most important sector of the economy, but mining remains important. Agriculture produces maize and soya beans. *History*: part of the Louisiana Purchase in 1803, it became a state in 1858. During the 1880s many Scandinavians settled in Minnesota. Area: 217 736 sq km (84 068 sq mi). Population (1986 est): 4 214 013. Capital: St Paul.

minnow One of several fish of the family *Cyprinidae*, especially *Phoxinus phoxinus*, found in clear fresh waters of Europe and N Asia. Its slim body is usually about 7.5 cm long, has small scales, and ranges in colour from gold to green. Order: *Cypriniformes*. The name is also applied to various other small fish.

Minoan civilization The civilization of Bronze Age Crete, named by Sir Arthur Evans after the legendary

MINOAN CIVILIZATION *Detail of the* Blue Ladies Fresco *(c. 1600 BC) from the Palace of Minos at Knossos.*

King Minos. The most advanced Aegean civilization, the Minoan arose after 2500 BC. It is conventionally divided into three phases: Early (2500–2000), Middle (2000–1700), and Late (1700–1400). During the Middle Minoan period palace building at Knossos, Mallia, and Phaistos attests Crete's growing wealth. Around 1700 these structures were replaced by grander ones, the centres of power in a marine empire covering the S Aegean. A catastrophic eruption on Thera (c. 1450) may have ended Minoan prosperity, although this is a subject of controversy. Three scripts were used: hieroglyphics (c. 1900–1700), Linear A (c. 1700–1450), and Linear B (c. 1450–1400).

Minorca (Spanish name: Menorca) A Spanish island in the Mediterranean Sea, the second largest of the Balearic Islands. It is generally low lying and dry and agriculture is limited. Shoe manufacture is important and it has an expanding tourist industry. Area: 702 sq km (271 sq mi). Population (1985): 55 500. Chief town: Mahón.

minor planet (*or* asteroid) A small nonluminous rocky body that orbits a star. Over 100 000 orbit the sun, mostly (probably 95%) in a main belt between the orbits of Mars and Jupiter, 2.17–3.3 astronomical units from the sun. The smallest minor planets are less than 1 km across with only about 200 exceeding 100 km: the largest is Ceres (1003 km). They are probably debris from collisions of bodies that formed between Mars and Jupiter.

Minos A legendary king of Crete, son of Zeus and Europa. Although usually regarded as a good ruler, the Athenians portrayed him as a tyrant, who exacted an annual tribute of seven youths and seven maidens who were fed to the Minotaur.

Minotaur In Greek legend, a Cretan monster with a bull's head and a man's body. It was the offspring of Pasiphae, wife of Minos, and a bull with which Poseidon had caused her to become enamoured. Theseus killed it with the help of Ariadne.

Minsk 53 51N 27 30E A city in the W Soviet Union, the capital of the Belorussian SSR. Dating from at least the 11th century, it came under Lithuanian and then Po-

lish rule; it was restored to Russia in 1793. It was virtually destroyed in World War II. Its varied industries include machine and vehicle manufacturing, textiles, and food processing. Population (1987): 1 543 000.

mint An aromatic perennial herb of the genus *Mentha* (about 25 species), native to Eurasia and Australia and widely distributed throughout temperate and subtropical regions. It has creeping roots from which arise square stems, bearing simple toothed leaves and terminal clusters of purple, pink, or white flowers. Many species are grown for their fragrance or as culinary herbs, especially peppermint and spearmint. Family: *Labiatae*.

Mint. *See* Royal Mint.

Mintoff, Dom(inic) (1916–) Maltese statesman; Labour prime minister (1955–58, 1971–84). He was an active proponent of Maltese independence.

Miocene epoch. *See* Tertiary period.

Mir A continuing series of manned Soviet space stations first launched into earth orbit in 1986. The first permanently manned space station, it is a refinement of the Salyut station.

Mirabeau, Honoré Gabriel Riquetti, Comte de (1749–91) French statesman. In 1789 he was elected to the States General, championing the cause of the Third Estate at the outbreak of the Revolution. However, he was out of sympathy with the growing republicanism, advocating the establishment of a constitutional monarchy on the British model, and came under increasing attack from the extremist Jacobins.

miracle plays Medieval European dramas based on religious themes. In England, they flourished particularly in the 14th and early 15th centuries. A distinction between mystery plays (based on episodes in the Bible) and miracle plays (based on the lives of saints) is often made with regard to French examples of the genre. Originally performed in churches, they became increasingly secular in form and content and were eventually performed on mobile stages in public marketplaces.

Miró, Joan (1893–1983) Surrealist painter, born in Barcelona. He moved to Paris (1919) and began painting in a childlike style. His "savage" paintings, expressed the horrors of the Spanish Civil War; his *Constellations* were painted (during World War II) with his characteristic amoebic shapes intertwined with threadlike lines.

mirrors Devices for reflecting light, usually consisting of a sheet of glass with one surface silvered. A plane mirror, in which the sheet is flat, forms a laterally inverted virtual image. Spherical mirrors, concave or convex, magnify or reduce the image. To avoid spherical aberration, parabolic mirrors are used in reflecting telescopes.

miscarriage. *See* abortion.

Mishnah (Hebrew: instruction) An early code of Jewish law. Written in Hebrew, it is traditionally thought to have been based on earlier compilations and edited in Palestine by the ethnarch Judah I in the early 3rd century AD. It consists of halakhah on a wide range of subjects, derived partly from biblical law as interpreted by the early rabbis (called *Tannaim*) and partly from customs that had grown up over a long period of time. *See also* Talmud.

Mississippi A state in the S central USA, on the Gulf of Mexico. Mainly low lying, it consists of the cotton-producing alluvial plain of the Mississippi River in the W, extensive swamps in the SW, and low hills in the E and NE. The predominantly rural population has a large Black community. Still an important agricultural state, its main products are cotton, soya beans, poultry, eggs, and livestock. Ship construction and repair, timber and paper products, textiles, chemicals, and food processing are important industries. Petroleum is the main mineral but natural gas, clay, and sand and gravel are also exploited. Mississippi remains, however, one of the country's poorest states. *History*: explored by the Spanish, it was later claimed for France and was ceded to Britain (1763). Colonization followed and the area came under US control (1783). Made a state in 1817, it became a leading cotton producer and slave state until the US Civil War. Area: 123 584 sq km (47 716 sq mi). Population (1985 est): 2 656 600. Capital: Jackson.

Mississippian period. *See* Carboniferous period.

Mississippi River A river in the central USA, the second longest river in North America. Rising in N Minnesota, it flows generally S into the Gulf of Mexico, through several channels (known as the Passes). Famous for its steamboats, it is now one of the world's busiest commercial waterways, with major ports at St Louis and New Orleans. Length: 3780 km (2348 mi).

Missolonghi (Modern Greek name: Mesolóngion) A town in W Greece, on the Gulf of Patras. It is famous for its defence against the Turks during the War of Greek Independence (1821–29). Population (1981): 10 164.

Missouri A state in the central USA, lying immediately W of the Mississippi River. It is divided by the Missouri River into fertile prairies and rolling hills in the N and W and the hills of the Ozark plateau in the S. Manufacturing dominates the economy, with transport and aerospace equipment, food processing, chemicals, and printing and publishing. The leading lead producer in the USA, it also exploits barytes, iron ore, and zinc deposits. Agriculture is diversified producing livestock and dairy products, soya beans, corn, wheat, cotton, and sorghum grains. *History*: explored by the French from Canada and claimed for France (1682), it was ceded to Spain (1783) before returning to France in 1800. It formed part of the Louisiana Purchase (1803) by the USA, becoming a state in 1821. Area: 180 486 sq km (69 686 sq mi). Population (1986 est): 5 066 000. Capital: Jefferson City.

Missouri River A river in the central USA, the longest river in North America and chief tributary of the Mississippi River. Rising in the Rocky Mountains, it flows N and E through Montana, then SE across North and South Dakota before joining the Mississippi at St Louis. Length: 4367 km (2714 mi).

mistle thrush A heavily built thrush, *Turdus viscivorus*, of Eurasia and NW Africa. It is about 28 cm long and has a greyish-brown upper plumage with a thickly speckled yellowish breast and white underwings. It feeds on berries (especially mistletoe—hence its name), snails, and worms.

mistletoe A semiparasitic evergreen shrub of the temperate and tropical family *Loranthaceae* (1300 species), growing on the branches of many trees. The Eurasian mistletoe (*Viscum album*) occurs mainly on apple trees, poplars, willows, and hawthorns. It has rootlike suckers and woody branching stems, 60–90 cm long, bearing oval leathery leaves and yellow flowers. The female flowers give rise to white berries.

Mistletoe was once believed by the Druids to have magic powers and medicinal properties and is a traditional Christmas decoration.

MISTLETOE *The Eurasian variety growing on a poplar tree.*

mistral A cold dry northerly wind that is funnelled down the Rhône Valley in S France to the Mediterranean Sea.

mite A tiny arachnid (up to 6 mm long) comprising —with the ticks—the worldwide order *Acarina* (or *Acari*; over 20 000 species). It has an unsegmented body and eight bristly legs. Mites occur in a wide range of habitats, including soil, stored foods, water, and plants; some are parasitic on animals. They may transmit diseases (including typhus). *See also* harvest mite; itch mite; spider mite.

Mithraism A mystery religion that worshipped Mithra, the Persian god of the sun who represented justice and goodness. It spread through Asia Minor, finally reaching Rome in about 68 BC. Here Mithra was known as Mithras and was worshipped widely among Roman soldiers. He was regarded as the eternal enemy of evil, whose sacrifice of a bull symbolized the regeneration of life. Mithraism rivalled Christianity until its decline in the 3rd century AD.

mitochondria Granular rod-shaped structures that occur in the cytoplasm of nearly all cells. They contain various enzymes that function in cellular respiration and the metabolism of fat, glycogen, proteins, etc., to produce energy. Therefore in very active cells (i.e. those requiring more energy), such as heart muscle, mitochondria are large and numerous.

mitosis The process by which the nucleus of a somatic cell (i.e. any cell that is not a germ cell) duplicates itself exactly, producing two daughter nuclei with chromosomes that are identical to those of the parent nucleus. This nuclear division involves the separation of the two chromatids of each chromosome, which move apart to form two groups at opposite ends of the cell. In the final phase each group becomes enclosed in a new nuclear membrane. After this the cytoplasm usually divides to form two new cells. Mitosis occurs in most animals and plants during the normal growth and repair of tissues. *Compare* meiosis.

Mitterrand, François (Maurice) (1916–) French socialist politician; president (1981–). He was president of a democratic-socialist union (1965–68) and in 1971 assumed leadership of the newly unified Socialist Party. After two unsuccessful runs for the French presidency (1965, 1974), in 1981 he became the first socialist president in 35 years.

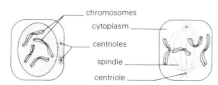

prophase *The genetic material becomes visible in the form of chromosomes and the nuclear membrane disappears.*

metaphase *The chromosomes become attached to the equator of a fibrous spindle.*

anaphase *The two chromatids of each chromosome move to opposite poles of the spindle.*

telophase *Nuclear membranes form around the two groups of chromatids, which become less distinct.*

MITOSIS *Division of the nucleus of an animal cell takes place in four phases, which grade into each other.*

Mizoram A state (since 1986) in NE India, in tropical hills between Bangladesh and Burma. Its largely Christian tribes are subsistence farmers of rice, sugar, and potatoes. Area: 21 230 sq km (8195 sq mi). Population (1981): 487 774. Capital: Aijal.

m.k.s. system A system of metric units based on the metre, kilogram, and second. It has now been replaced for scientific purposes by SI units.

M'Naghten's Rules. *See* insanity.

Mnemosyne In Greek mythology, a daughter of the Titans Uranus and Gaea. She is the personification of memory. After sleeping with Zeus for nine consecutive nights she gave birth to the Muses.

moa An extinct flightless bird belonging to an order (*Dinornithiformes*; about 25 species) that occurred in New Zealand. Moas were 60–300 cm tall and had a small head, a long neck, and long stout legs. They were fast runners but were hunted by early Polynesian settlers.

Moabites A highly civilized Semitic tribe living E of the Dead Sea from the late 14th century BC. They successfully rebelled against Israelite occupation in the 9th century BC. In 582 BC, according to Josephus, they were conquered by the Babylonians.

Mobutu, Sese Seko (Joseph Désiré M.; 1930–) Zaïrese statesman; president (1970–), having come to power in 1965 in a coup. In 1967 he founded the country's only political party—the Popular Movement of the Revolution—and the stability of his authoritarian government is fostered by his personal cult, Mobutuism.

Moçambique. *See* Mozambique, People's Republic of.

mockingbird A songbird that belongs to an American family (*Mimidae*; 30 species) and is noted for its ability to mimic sounds. Mockingbirds live on or near the ground, feeding on insects and fruit. The common mockingbird (*Mimus polyglottus*), which ranges from S Canada to S Mexico, is about 25 cm long with a grey plumage and white wing bars.

mock orange A shrub, also called syringa, belonging to the genus *Philadelphus* (75 species), native to N temperate regions and commonly cultivated for ornament. They have simple leaves and fragrant white flowers resembling orange blossom. *P. coronarius* is the only native European species. Family: *Philadelphaceae*.

Modena (ancient name: Mutina) 44 39N 10 55E A city in N Italy, in Emilia-Romagna. Ruled by the Este family (1288–1860), it has an 11th-century romanesque cathedral, several palaces, and an ancient university (1175). The centre of a rich agricultural area, its industries include agricultural engineering, textiles, and motor vehicles. Population (1986): 176 880.

modes Musical scales derived from ancient Greek music, on which European music was based up to the 16th century. Each mode consists of a different pattern of the five tones and two semitones of the octave; the patterns can be clearly demonstrated using the white notes of the piano keyboard. Two of the most common modes were the Ionian (C-C) and the Aeolian (A-A), which became the basis of the major and minor scales.

Modigliani, Amedeo (1884–1920) Italian painter and sculptor. His mature work, executed in Paris (1906–20), was influenced by Cézanne and Brancusi and, in its angular and elongated character, by Negro masks. From 1909 to 1915 he worked chiefly on sculptures; from 1915 until his death he painted many nudes and portraits.

modulation A method of carrying information (the signal) on an electromagnetic wave or an oscillating electric current. In **amplitude modulation** (AM) the amplitude of a carrier wave is changed according to the magnitude of the signal. This is used in medium-wave sound broadcasting in which audio-frequencies (50–20 000 hertz) are carried on radio waves with a frequency of about one megahertz. In **frequency modulation** (FM) the frequency of the carrier wave is changed within a small bandwidth of the reference frequency. FM is used in VHF radio (about 100 megahertz). Its main advantage over AM is its better signal-to-noise ratio. In **pulse modulation** the carrier is a series of pulses. It is used in digital equipment, such as computers, and in telegraphy and telemetry. A continuous signal alters the height in pulse-amplitude modulation, the width in pulse-duration modulation, or the time between pulses in pulse-position modulation. Pulse-code modulation uses a coded pattern of pulses to carry the signal, e.g. in Morse code.

Mogadishu (*or* Mogadiscio) 2 01N 45 25E The capital and main port of Somalia, on the Indian Ocean. It was founded as an Arab settlement in the 10th century and sold to Italy in 1905 becoming the capital of Italian Somaliland. Population (1987 est): 1 000 000.

Moguls An Indian Muslim dynasty, descended from the Mongol leader Genghis Khan, that ruled from 1526 until 1858. Its founder was Babur (reigned 1526–30); he and the first 5 of his 18 successors are known as the Great Moguls, and by the time of Aurangzeb (1658–1707) the Empire spread from the far N to the far S of India. During the late 17th and the 18th centuries Mogul power declined; the last emperor, Bahadur Shah II

MOGULS *An early 16th-century Mogul holding a portrait of his father.*

(reigned 1837–58), was deposed after the Indian Mutiny.

mohair A wool-like fabric or yarn manufactured from the hair of Angora goats. Warm, light, and durable and frequently blended with wool, silk, or cotton, mohair is used for lightweight suiting, upholstery, and knitwear.

Mohammed (*or* Muhammad; c. 570–632 AD) According to Muslims, the last of the prophets and preacher of Islam to the Arabs. Mohammed is said to have been born in Mecca. In 610 he received revelations from God and called upon his pagan fellow townsmen to prepare for the Last Day and to repent. The Meccans rejected him and in 622 he fled from Mecca to Yathrib, where he established the first Muslim community and began to spread Islam. By 629 the Muslims in Yathrib, now called Medina, were strong enough to defeat the Meccans and obtained control of Mecca. By the time of Mohammed's death, Islam had begun to spread throughout Arabia. Mohammed's revelations were collected after his death to form the Koran.

Mohammed Reza Pahlavi (1918–80) Shah of Iran (1941–79). He became shah when the Allies forced his father Reza Shah Pahlavi, to abdicate in World War II. In 1979 civil war forced him into exile and an Islamic republic was established in Iran under the leadership of Ayatollah Khomeini.

Mohawk An Iroquoian-speaking American Indian tribe of New York state. They were one of the five tribes that formed the league of the Iroquois, said to have been founded by the Mohawk chief Hiawatha.

Mohican An Algonkian-speaking American Indian tribe of New England. Primarily cultivators, they lived in fortified communities or in enclosed villages, but were displaced by wars with the Mohawks.

Mohorovičić discontinuity The boundary between the earth's crust and upper mantle, marked by a sudden increase in velocity in seismic waves as the denser mantle is reached. It lies at a depth of 33–35 km (20–22 mi) beneath the continents and 5–10 km (3–6 mi) beneath the oceans. It is named after the Croatian scientist, Andrija Mohorovičić (1857–1936), who discovered it in 1909.

Mohs' scale A scale of hardness of minerals named after the mineralogist Friedrich Mohs (1773–1839). The ten standard minerals in the scale, in ascending order of hardness, are: 1. talc, 2. gypsum, 3. calcite, 4. fluorite, 5. apatite, 6. orthoclase feldspar, 7. quartz, 8. topaz, 9. corundum, and 10. diamond. Each can be scratched by any mineral higher up the scale, and other minerals can be assigned numbers in the scale according to which materials will scratch them.

Mojave Desert (*or* Mohave Desert) A desert area in the USA, in S California. It comprises part of the Great Basin. Area: 38 850 sq km (15 000 sq mi).

Moji. *See* Kitakyushu.

Moldavia A former principality in SE Europe. It was occupied by the Mongols in the 13th century, becoming independent in the 14th century. It became an Ottoman vassal state in the 16th century. In 1859 Moldavia and Walachia formed Romania. Russian Moldavia became the Moldavian Soviet Socialist Republic in 1940.

mole (medicine) An area of darkly pigmented skin, known medically as a naevus. *See also* melanoma.

mole (metrology; symbol mol) The SI unit of amount of substance equal to the amount of substance that contains the same number of entities as there are atoms in 0.012 kg of carbon-12. One mol of any substance contains $6.022\ 52 \times 10^{23}$ entities (*see* Avogadro). The entities may be atoms, molecules, ions, electrons, etc.

mole (zoology) A burrowing mammal belonging to the family *Talpidae*, of Europe, Asia, and North America. The common Eurasian mole (*Talpa europaea*) is about 14 cm long including its small bristly tail. It is thickset, with velvety-black fur, and has long-clawed digging forefeet. Moles make an extensive system of underground tunnels, feeding on earthworms. They are practically blind above ground. Order: *Insectivora*. *See also* desman.

molecular biology The scientific discipline that deals with the molecular basis of living processes. Molecular biology involves both biochemistry and biophysics: its growth since the 1930s has been made possible by the development of such techniques as chromatography, electron microscopy, and X-ray diffraction, which have revealed the structures of biologically important molecules, such as DNA, RNA, and enzymes.

molecule The smallest portion of a compound that can exist independently and retain its properties. The atoms that make up a molecule are either bonded together covalently, e.g. CO_2, or electrovalently, e.g. NaCl. However, in crystalline substances the bonds extend throughout the whole crystal structure and the molecule has only a notional existence. In covalent gases and liquids, however, the molecule actually exists as a small group of atoms. **Molecular weight** (*or* relative molecular mass) is the ratio of the average mass per molecule to one-twelfth of the mass of a carbon-12 atom.

Molière (Jean-Baptiste Poquelin; 1622–73) French dramatist, the father of modern French comedy. He toured the provinces with his theatrical company from 1645 to 1658. His plays include *Tartuffe* (1664), *Le Misanthrope* (1666), *L'Avare* (1668), and *Le Malade imaginaire* (1673). His ridicule of hypocrisy and his vigorous satire of contemporary manners and types brought him into constant conflict with the religious authorities. He frequently acted in his own productions.

mollusc An invertebrate animal belonging to the phylum *Mollusca* (about 100 000 species). Molluscs occupy marine, freshwater, and terrestrial habitats, being especially common on rocky coasts. They have a soft unsegmented body with a muscular foot, variously modified for crawling, burrowing, or swimming, and a thin dorsal mantle that secretes a shell of one, two, or eight parts. The shell is usually external, as in snails, but it may be internal, as in cuttlefish, or absent, as in slugs. Most molluscs are herbivorous with some carnivorous and scavenging species. *See also* bivalve; cephalopod; gastropod.

MOLOCH

moloch A grotesque desert-dwelling Australian lizard, *Moloch horridus*, also called thorny devil. Its yellow-and-brown body is covered in thorny spines, which provide good camouflage. Ants are its chief food. Family: *Agamidae*.

Moloch A Semitic god whose worship was characterized by the sacrificial burning of children. There are several biblical references to his worship by the Israelites during the period of the Kings (c. 961–c. 562 BC).

Molotov. *See* Perm.

Molotov, Vyacheslav Mikhailovich (V. M. Scriabin; 1890–1986) Soviet statesman. As prime minister (1930–41) and foreign minister (1939–49, 1953–56), Molotov signed the Soviet-German nonaggression treaty in 1939; after the German invasion in 1941, he negotiated alliances with the Allies. His subsequent attitude to the West contributed to the Cold War. The **Molotov cocktail**, named after him, is an incendiary hand grenade.

Moluccas (*or* Maluku) An Indonesian group of islands between Sulawesi and West Irian. It includes the islands of Ambon, Halmahera, and Ceram. Mountainous and volcanic, most are fertile and humid. The indigenous population fishes, hunts, and collects sago; spices, fish, and copra are exported. *History*: before the Portuguese arrival (1512), the islands were ruled by Muslims and known as the Spice Islands. Dutch control was established in the 19th century. With Indonesian independence (1949) the S Moluccas fought to secede but were subjugated by the new government (1950–56). Area: about 74 504 sq km (28 766 sq mi). Population (1980): 1 411 006. Chief town: Ambon.

molybdenum (Mo) A very hard silvery-grey metal of high melting point, it was first prepared in 1782 by P. J. Hjelm (1746–1813). It occurs in nature as molyb-

denite (MoS_2) and as wulfenite (lead molybdenate; $PbMoO_4$). It is extracted by the reduction of molybdenum trioxide (MoO_3). Molybdenum is used in high-temperature filaments and as an alloying agent in the production of high-strength steels. At no 42; at wt 95.94; mp 2617°C; bp 4612°C.

Mombasa 4 04S 39 40E A port in Kenya, on an island in an inlet of the Indian Ocean. It was an important port for Arab traders and was taken in the 16th and 17th centuries by the Portuguese. The modern deepwater port at Kilindini handles most of Kenya's trade; industries include oil refining. Population (1984 est): 481 000.

moment The product of a force and its perpendicular distance from the axis about which it acts. A moment produces a turning effect and is sometimes called a torque. The inertia of a body to a torque is called its **moment of inertia**. This quantity is equal to mr^2 for a single mass (m) rotating about an axis at a distance r from the axis. The moment of inertia of a system of masses is equal to the sum of these products.

momentum The linear momentum of a body is the product of its mass and its linear velocity. The angular momentum of a body is the product of its moment of inertia and its angular velocity. During any process the total momentum of the system always remains constant (the law of conservation of momentum).

Mona. *See* Anglesey.

Monaco, Principality of A small country on the Mediterranean Sea, an enclave within French territory. It consists of three principal localities: the business district around the ports, Monte Carlo, and the capital Monaco. *Economy*: the main sources of revenue are tourism and the sale of postage stamps. *History*: ruled by the house of Grimaldi since 1297, it has been under French protection since 1641. Head of state: Prince Rainier III. Official language: French; Monégasque, a mixture of French and Italian, is also spoken. Official currency: French franc of 100 centimes. Area: 189 hectares (467 acres). Population (1985): 28 000.

Monaghan (Irish name: Contae Mhuineachain) A county in the NE Republic of Ireland, in Ulster bordering on Northern Ireland. It is generally low lying and undulating. Agricultural produce includes oats and potatoes; cattle rearing and dairy farming are also important. Area: 1551 sq km (499 sq mi). Population (1986): 52 332. County town: Monaghan.

mona monkey. *See* guenon.

monarch A widespread American butterfly, *Danaus plexippus*. Light brown with black borders and white dots, the adults migrate southwards for the winter. In spring they move north, breeding on the way. The caterpillars are green with black and yellow bands and feed on milkweed. Family: *Danaidae*.

monazite A rare-earth mineral of composition $(Ce,La,Y,Th)PO_4$ and yellow to reddish-brown colour, found as an accessory in acid igneous rocks and as placer deposits. Monazite is usually obtained as a by-product of titanium and zircon mining; it is the most common source of the rare earths.

Mönchengladbach (*or* München Gladbach) 51 12N 6 25E A city in NW West Germany, in North Rhine-Westphalia. It is the centre of the German textile industry and headquarters of the NATO forces in N central Europe. Population (1986): 254 700.

Mond, Ludwig (1839–1909) German industrial chemist, who lived in Britain from 1862. He discovered nickel carbonyl and its application to the extraction of platinum from its ores, a method now known as the **Mond process**.

Mondrian, Piet (Pieter Cornelis Mondriaan; 1872–1944) Dutch painter. While in Paris (1912–14) he came under the influence of cubism. His first abstract compositions (1917) used only horizontal and vertical lines, primary colours, and black and white. During this period he helped to launch the art movement of de Stijl. After 1919 his style, known as neoplasticism, influenced the Bauhaus school.

Monet, Claude (1840–1926) French impressionist painter. Initially influenced by the Barbizon school, in the late 1860s he developed the impressionist technique in views of Paris and in the 1870s in boating scenes at Argenteuil. He excelled in his series of the same scenes painted at different times of day, e.g. *Gare St Lazare*, *Haystacks*, *Rouen Cathedral*, and the *Poplars*, the last of which anticipates abstract art.

monetarism A revision of old-established economic theories that rivals Keynesianism. Monetarism's most celebrated proponent is the US economist Milton Friedman. Monetarists regard responsible regulation of the money supply as essential to the wellbeing of the economy, advocating a gentle expansion of the money supply at roughly the rate of growth of the economy. Monetarists blame inflation on overexpansion of the money supply.

MONEY *An Athenian tetradrachm (known as an "owl") struck c. 486 BC.*

money A medium of exchange. To be an efficient medium of exchange, money should be divisible (for small transactions), have a high value-to-weight ratio, and be not easily counterfeited. Money also functions as means of credit and a store of wealth, for which purposes its value must remain stable. Money was reputedly invented by the Lydians in the 7th century BC. It originally took the form of something intrinsically valuable (such as a precious metal) but, so long as it is generally acceptable, this is not necessary. Indeed, most money is now in the form of paper.

The total stock of money in the economy is known as the **money supply**. In the UK two definitions of the money supply are used: the narrow M1 (essentially, the total amount of cash and current accounts) and the broad M3

(essentially, the total amount of cash plus both current and deposit accounts).

money spider A tiny spider of the family *Liniphiidae* (over 250 species). It has a reddish or black body and occurs in fields, etc. Money spiders build sheetlike webs on vegetation to which they cling upside down, waiting to catch insects that drop onto the web.

moneywort A perennial herb, *Lysimachia nummularia*, also called creeping jenny, native to damp places in Europe. It has a creeping stem, up to 60 cm long, shiny heart-shaped leaves, and yellow flowers. Family: *Primulaceae*.

Mongolian languages A group of languages that, together with Turkic and Manchu-Tungus, constitute the Altaic language family. Western Mongolian languages are spoken in parts of the Soviet Union, the Mongolian People's Republic, and Afghanistan; Eastern Mongolian is spoken in China and the Mongolian People's Republic. There are more than three million speakers of these languages, the majority of which remain unwritten.

mongolism. *See* Down's syndrome.

Mongoloid The racial grouping comprising the populations of E Asia and the Arctic region of North America. They are characterized by medium skin pigmentation, the epicanthic fold of the upper eyelid, straight coarse black hair, a rather flat face with high cheekbones, and slight facial and body hair.

Mongols An Asiatic people united in the early 13th century by Genghis Khan, who built up an empire that encompassed much of central Asia. The Mongols ruled China as the Yuan dynasty until 1368. They were subsequently confined to the area approximating to the present-day Mongolian People's Republic.

mongoose A carnivorous mammal belonging to the family *Viverridae*, found in warm regions of the Mediterranean, Africa, and Asia. There are about 40 species, ranging in size from 50 to 100 cm including the long tapering furry tail (25–50 cm), with short legs, small ears, and long coarse grey-brown fur. Mongooses are renowned for catching snakes and rats and also eat eggs, small mammals, frogs, and birds. Chief genera: *Galidictis, Herpestes, Helogale*.

monitor lizard A lizard belonging to the Old World family *Varanidae* (30 species), occurring in tropical and subtropical regions. 0.2–3 m long, monitors have an elongated body and well-developed legs. They feed on mammals, snakes, lizards, eggs, and carrion. *See also* Komodo dragon.

monkey A tree-dwelling primate. Monkeys are 20–110 cm long and most have a long balancing tail of up to 100 cm used in climbing, although some are tailless. Agile and intelligent, they have fingernails and an opposable thumb enabling manual dexterity. Most monkeys are omnivorous but they prefer fruit, nuts, and other vegetation. *See also* New World monkey; Old World monkey.

monkey puzzle A coniferous tree, *Araucaria araucana*, also called Chile pine, native to Chile and Argentina and widely grown as an ornamental. Up to 30 m high, it has whorled horizontal branches covered with leathery prickly overlapping leaves, 3–4 cm long. The globular spiny cones break up to release large edible seeds. Family: *Araucariaceae*.

monkfish A shark belonging to the family *Squatinidae*. It has a broad flattened head, an elongated tapering body, winglike pectoral fins, two dorsal fins, and no anal fin. Monkfish occur in tropical and temperate seas and feed on bottom-dwelling fish, molluscs, and crustaceans. A species of anglerfish, *Lophius piscatorius*, is also called monkfish.

MARILYN MONROE *With Arthur Miller.*

monkshood. *See* aconite.

Monmouth, James Scott, Duke of (1649–85) The illegitimate son of Charles II of England and Lucy Walter (d. 1658), who led the Monmouth rebellion against his uncle James II. A focus of the opposition to the succession of the Roman Catholic James, he was banished (1684) after being implicated in the Rye House Plot. After James' accession (1685), Monmouth landed at Lyme Regis to raise a rebellion and was defeated at Sedgemoor, captured, and beheaded.

Monmouthshire A former county of SE Wales. In 1974 it became part of Mid Glamorgan, South Glamorgan, and Gwent.

monoclonal antibody A type of pure antibody that can be produced artificially in large quantities and used, for example, to distinguish the major blood groups. Mouse lymphocytes producing the required antibody are fused with mouse cancer cells; the resulting hybrid cells multiply rapidly and all produce the same type of antibody as their parent lymphocytes.

monocotyledons The smaller of the two main groups of flowering plants, which includes the palms, bananas, orchids, grasses, lilies, and many garden bulbs and corms (*compare* dicotyledons). Monocots have a single seed leaf (cotyledon) in the embryo. Typically the flower parts are in threes (or multiples of three) and the leaves have parallel veins. *See also* angiosperm.

monomer A simple molecule or group of atoms forming a repeated unit in a dimer (two molecules), trimer (three molecules), or polymer (*see* polymerization).

monopoly An industry in which the market is supplied by one supplier. The monopolist can obtain a high profit by restricting supply and demanding a high price. In the public sector of a mixed economy monopolies for the supply of public services are commonplace. In the private sector they are usually restricted by legislation. In the UK the **Monopolies Commission**, the duties of which are set out in the Fair Trading Act (1973), conducts investigations into monopolies and mergers.

monorail A railway using a single rail, either from which to suspend a carriage or over which a carriage is straddled. The former type was first used in 1884, consisting of an electrically driven truck running on a single rail from which was suspended a load-carrying car (called a **telpher**). The latter type has been demonstrated at Birmingham's National Exhibition Centre, using magnetic levitation. Monorail systems are expensive to instal.

monosaccharide (*or* simple sugar) A carbohydrate consisting of a single sugar unit and possessing either a keto group (C=O) or an aldehyde group (CHO). Monosaccharides are classified according to the number of carbon atoms they possess–the most common being pentoses (with five) and hexoses (with six)–and they can exist as either straight-chain or ring-shaped structures. The most widely occurring are glucose and fructose.

monotreme A primitive mammal of the order *Monotremata*, found only in Australia and New Guinea. Monotremes have a single vent for passing urine, faeces, and eggs or sperm. They lay eggs, suckling their young after these hatch. The only living monotremes are the echidnas and duck-billed platypus.

Monroe, James (1758–1831) US statesman; president (1817–25). He was minister to France (1794–96) and Britain (1803–07) before becoming secretary of state (1811). His two peaceful terms as president saw the opening of the West and the acquisition of Spanish Florida. The **Monroe Doctrine** (1823) warned European powers not to intervene in the Americas.

Monroe, Marilyn (Norma Jean Baker *or* Mortenson; 1926–62) US film actress. Promoted as a sex symbol, in such films as *Niagara* (1952) and *Gentlemen Prefer Blondes* (1953), she later developed a real acting talent and ability as a comedienne. Her third husband was Arthur Miller, and her last film appearance was in *The Misfits* (1961), which he wrote. She died from an overdose of barbiturates.

Monrovia 6 20N 10 46W The capital and main port of Liberia, on the Atlantic Ocean. Founded in 1822 as a settlement for freed slaves, it was named after President Monroe of the USA. The University of Liberia was founded in 1851. Population (1985): 500 000.

monsoon A seasonal large-scale reversal of winds in the tropics, resulting chiefly from the differential heating of the land and oceans. The term is now commonly applied to the rainfall that accompanies the wind reversals, especially in S Asia (April to September).

Montaigne, Michel de (1533–92) French essayist. In 1568 he resigned his position as magistrate in Bordeaux and began composing his *Essais*. In 1580 he travelled extensively in Europe and was mayor of Bordeaux from 1581 to 1585. His *Essais*, which inaugurated a new literary genre, expressed his mature humanistic philosophy and constitute a moving self-portrait. They were published in two editions in 1580 and 1588, and a posthumous edition incorporated his final revisions.

Montana The fourth largest state in the USA, bordering on Canada. It is mountainous and forested in the W, with the rolling grasslands of the Great Plains in the E. Its economy is predominantly agricultural, cattle ranching and wheat production being of greatest importance. Other crops include barley and sugar beet. It possesses important mineral resources, notably copper (at Butte) and coal. There are several Indian reservations within the state. *History*: it formed part of the Louisiana Purchase in 1803. During the mid-19th century a gold rush caused an influx of immigrants. During the Indian wars the battle of Little Bighorn (Custer's Last Stand) took place (1876). Area: 377 070 sq km (145 587 sq mi). Population (1986 est): 819 000. Capital: Helena.

Mont Blanc (Italian name: Monte Bianco) 45 50N 6 52E The highest mountain in the Alps, on the French–Italian border. It was first climbed in 1786. A road tunnel (1958–62) beneath it, 12 km (7.5 mi) long, connects the two countries. Height: 4807 m (15 771 ft).

montbretia A perennial herb, *Crocosmia crocosmiflora* (a hybrid between *C. pottsii* and *C. aurea*), native to South Africa but naturalized in Europe and often grown as a garden ornamental. Up to 1 m high, it has long stiff sword-shaped leaves and orange-red funnel-shaped flowers. The name is also applied to the similar and related flowering herbs of the South African genus *Montbretia* (or *Tritonia*). Family: *Iridaceae*.

Monte Bello Islands 20 30S 115 30E A group of uninhabited coral islands in the Indian Ocean, off the W coast of Western Australia. They were used for testing British nuclear weapons in 1952 and 1956.

Monte Carlo 43 44N 7 25E A resort in the principality of Monaco, on the Riviera. It is famous for its casino, motor rally, and other cultural and sporting events. Population (1985): 12 000.

Monterrey 25 40N 100 20W The third largest city in Mexico. Founded in 1579, it has many notable buildings. Monterrey is a major industrial centre specializing in metallurgy. Population (1980): 1 916 472.

Montessori system A system of education for young children devised by the Italian doctor Maria Montessori (1870–1952). It places emphasis on development of the senses and envisages a limited role for the teacher as the child learns by itself through the use of didactic materials.

Monteverdi, Claudio (1567–1643) Italian composer. From 1613 until his death he was maestro di cappella at St Mark's Cathedral, Venice. Monteverdi was the first great composer of opera; enlarging the orchestra, he employed a new range of instrumental effects and made use of an innovatory harmonic style to achieve dramatic effects. His works include the operas *Orfeo* (1607) and *The Coronation of Poppea* (1642), a set of *Vespers* (1610), and many madrigals.

Montevideo 34 55S 56 10W The capital and main port of Uruguay, in the S on the Río de la Plata. Founded in 1726 by the Spanish, it became capital of Uruguay in 1828. In the 20th century it has developed rapidly, as both an industrial and a communications centre, and it is now one of South America's largest cities. Population (1985 est): 1 246 000.

Montezuma II (1466–c. 1520) The last Aztec Emperor of Mexico (1502–20). During his reign his empire was weakened by tribal warfare, which enabled the Spaniards, led by Hernán Cortés, to establish themselves in Mexico.

Montfort, Simon de, Earl of Leicester (c. 1208–65) English statesman, born in Normandy. After serving Henry III of England in Gascony, he joined the antiroyalist faction that demanded greater control of the government, becoming the barons' leader in the subsequent Barons' War. Initially successful, he became virtual ruler of England, summoning a parliament in 1265. In the same year, however, he was defeated and killed at Evesham.

MONTGOLFIER *The first passenger-carrying ascent, October 1783.*

Montgolfier, Jacques-Étienne (1745–99) French balloonist, who with his brother **Joseph-Michel Montgolfier** (1740–1810) invented the hot-air balloon, which was publicly launched in 1782. A much larger balloon, which rose 2000 m, was demonstrated in June 1783 and in October a series of passenger-carrying ascents were made. The Montgolfiers' experiments aroused enormous interest in flying.

Montgomery of Alamein, Bernard Law, 1st Viscount (1887–1976) British field marshal. In World War II he became commander of the Eighth Army (1942) and after the battle of Alamein drove Rommel back to Tunis and surrender (1943). Having played a major role in the invasion of Italy (1943), he became chief of land forces in the 1944 Normandy invasion. He helped plan the Arnhem disaster (September, 1944), but pushed back the subsequent German offensive, receiving Germany's surrender. After the war he was chief of the imperial general staff (1946–48) and deputy commander of NATO forces (1951–58).

month The time taken by the moon to complete one revolution around the earth. The complicated motion of the moon requires the starting and finishing points of the revolution to be specified. The length of the month depends on the choice of reference point. The **sidereal month**, of 27.32 days, is measured with reference to the background stars. The **synodic month**, of 29.53 days, is measured between two identical phases of the moon.

Montpellier 43 36N 3 53E A city in S France, the capital of the Hérault department. A Huguenot stronghold, it was besieged and captured by Louis XIII in 1622. Montpellier trades in wine and brandy and has numerous manufacturing industries. Population (1982): 201 067.

Montreal   45 30N 73 36W A city and port in E Canada, in Quebec on Montreal Island at the junction of the Ottawa and St Lawrence Rivers. Canada's largest city, it is also the greatest transportation, trade, and manufacturing centre. Its many industries include oil refining, meat packing, brewing and distilling, food processing, textiles, and aircraft. Housing four universities, Montreal is a forum for politics, broadcasting, theatre, film, and publishing. Two-thirds of the population is French-speaking. *History*: founded as Ville-Marie (1642), Montreal quickly became a commercial centre. Captured by Britain (1760), it acquired an English-speaking merchant community that has dominated Quebec's economy ever since. Population (1986): 1 015 420.

Montserrat   A British crown colony comprising one of the Leeward Islands, in the Caribbean Sea to the SE of Puerto Rico. It is largely mountainous with active volcanoes. *Economy*: chiefly agricultural, the main crops are cotton, coconuts, and fruit and vegetables, which with cattle are the main exports. *History*: discovered by Columbus in 1493, it was colonized by the Irish in the 17th century. Formerly administratively joined to the Leeward Islands, it became a separate colony in 1960. In 1989 it was devastated by Hurricane Hugo. Official language: English. Official currency: East Caribbean dollar of 100 cents. Area: 106 sq km (40 sq mi). Population (1985): 11 852. Capital: Plymouth.

Mont St Michel   48 38N 1 30W A granite islet in NW France, in the Manche department in the Bay of St Michel. The islet is connected to the mainland by a causeway. It is about 78 m (256 ft) high and is crowned by a Benedictine monastery (founded 966 AD).

Monument.   *See* Fire of London.

moon   The natural satellite of the earth. The moon orbits the earth every 27.32 days at a mean distance of 384 400 km, keeping more or less the same face (the nearside) towards the earth. As it revolves, different phases can be seen from earth, together with up to two or three lunar eclipses per year. The moon is only 81 times less massive than the earth and has a diameter of 3476 km.

The major surface features are the light-coloured highlands and the much darker lava plains—the maria. The surface is heavily cratered with roughly circular walled depressions produced by impacting bodies from space. The extremely tenuous atmosphere exposes the surface to considerable temperature extremes ($-180°C$ to $+110°C$). The first landing on the moon was made by Neil Armstrong and Edwin Aldrin on 20 July, 1969. *See* Apollo moon programme.

moonfish   A deep-bodied fish, also called opah, belonging to the genus *Lampris* and family *Lamprididae*, widely distributed in warm seas. Up to 2 m long, its body is coloured blue above, rose-pink below, and is spotted with white; the fins are scarlet. Order: *Lampridiformes*.

Moonies.   *See* Unification Church.

Moore, G(eorge) E(dward)   (1873–1958) British philosopher. Moore's work centred around language and the analysis of its meaning. His books include *Principia Ethica* (1903) and *Ethics* (1912). He was professor of mental philosophy and logic at Cambridge (1925–39) and editor of the journal *Mind* (1921–47).

Moore, Henry   (1898–1986) British sculptor. His fasci-

nation with primitive African and Mexican art moulded the development of his two characteristic themes: mother and child sculptures and reclining figures. The latter, a lifelong preoccupation, reached its apogee in the sculpture for UNESCO in Paris (1956–57). After devoting himself to abstract work in the 1930s, Moore reverted to the humanist tradition in the early 1940s with his celebrated drawings of sleeping figures in air-raid shelters.

HENRY MOORE

moorhen   A grey-brown to black waterbird, *Gallinula chloropus*, also called common gallinule and waterhen, occurring worldwide except for Australia. It is 32 cm long and has a red bill and forehead and a white patch beneath the tail. It breeds in thick vegetation near ponds and marshes and feeds on seeds, water plants, and aquatic invertebrates. Family: *Rallidae* (rails, etc.).

Moors   The conventional European name for the Arab and Berber inhabitants of NW Africa and, by extension, for the 8th-century Muslim conquerors of the Iberian peninsula. The Moors were the dominant power in Spain until the 11th century. A highly civilized people, they played a major role in transmitting classical science and philosophy to W Europe.

moose.   *See* elk.

moped.   *See* motorcycles.

Moral Rearmament (MRA)   An evangelical movement founded by a US evangelist and former Lutheran pastor, Frank Nathan Daniel Buchman (1878–1961), in the 1920s. It initially received most support at Oxford University and was called the Oxford Group until 1938. It seeks the regeneration of national and individual spirituality through conversion, God's personal guidance, and living in purity, unselfishness, honesty, and love.

Moravia (Czech name: Morava; German name: Mähren)   An area and former province (1918–49) of central Czechoslovakia. Lying chiefly in the basin of the River Morava, it rises in the N to the Sudeten Mountains and in the E to the Carpathian Mountains. It contains important mineral deposits, including coal and iron ore. *History*: settled by Slavic tribes in the late 8th century AD, it formed the centre of an important medieval kingdom (Great Moravia). It became part of the Republic of Czechoslovakia in 1918. Chief town: Brno.

Moravia, Alberto   (Alberto Pincherle; 1907–) Italian novelist. His early novels criticized fascism and the corrupt middle-class society that allowed it to flourish. His later works, which include *The Woman of Rome* (1947), *The Lie* (1966), and *Erotic Tales* (1985) concern themes of social alienation and the futility of sexual relationships. His literary and political essays are collected in *Man As an End* (1963).

moray eel   A thick-bodied eel of the family *Muraenidae* (over 80 species). Up to 1.5 m long, it is brightly coloured and lacks pectoral fins. Moray eels live in rock crevices and reefs of warm and tropical seas.

Moray Firth   An inlet of the North Sea in NE Scotland, extending SW from a line between Tarbat Ness in the Highland Region and Burghead in Grampian Region. Length: about 56 km (35 mi).

More, Sir Thomas   (1477–1535) English lawyer, scholar, and saint. He joined Henry VIII's Privy Council in 1518 and succeeded Wolsey as chancellor in 1529. He resigned the chancellorship in 1532 in opposition to Henry's assumption of the supreme headship of the English Church. In 1534 More was imprisoned after refusing to swear to the new Act of Succession. He was brought to trial for treason in 1535, convicted on false evidence, and beheaded. His best-known scholarly work is *Utopia* (1516).

morel   A fungus belonging to the genus *Morchella*. Morels are typically club-shaped with the surface of the cap pitted like a honeycomb. The edible common morel (*M. esculenta*) has a yellowish-brown cap, 4–8 cm high, and a stout whitish stalk. Class: *Ascomycetes*.

Morgan, John Pierpont   (1837–1913) US financier, who founded (1895) J. P. Morgan and Co, one of the most powerful banking corporations in the USA. During the 1880s he reorganized many foundering railway companies and later financed such consolidations as the US Steel Corporation and General Electric. His son **John Pierpont Morgan, Jr** (1867–1943) succeeded him and helped to organize the credit requirements of the Allies in World War I.

Morgan le Fay   In Arthurian legend, an evil sorceress who plotted the overthrow of her brother King Arthur. According to Malory's *Morte d'Arthur* (1485) she betrayed Guinevere's adultery to Arthur. However, in the earlier *Vita Merlini* (c. 1150) by Geoffrey of Monmouth she is a benevolent figure.

Moriscos   Muslims forced to profess Christianity in Spain. Many Muslims continued to live in Spain after the formerly Muslim areas came under Christian rule and by the 15th century they were forced to become Christians or go into exile. Many chose to remain in Spain while privately remaining Muslims and eventually the government ordered their expulsion. Between 1609 and 1614 about 500 000 Moriscos were forced into exile, settling mainly in Africa.

Morley, Thomas   (1557–1603) English composer, music printer, organist of St Paul's Cathedral, and member of the Chapel Royal. A pupil of Byrd, he wrote madrigals, canzonets, songs, church music, and the textbook *A Plaine and Easie Introduction to Practicall Musicke* (1597).

Mormons   Adherents of the Christian sect that is formally called the Church of Jesus Christ of Latter-Day Saints, founded in 1830 by Joseph Smith in New York state. Smith claimed to have discovered golden tablets that contained the sacred Book of Mormon. After Smith's murder by a mob, the persecuted Mormons moved W under Brigham Young, establishing their headquarters at Salt Lake, Utah, in 1847. Mormons have no professional clergy, reject infant baptism, abstain from alcohol and other stimulants, and run educational and missionary programmes.

morning glory   A trailing or twining plant of the genus *Ipomoea*, native to tropical America and Australia and cultivated for its beautiful flowers. The leaves are often heart-shaped and the trumpet-shaped flowers, up to 12 cm across, are deep blue, purple, pink, or white. Popular species are *I. purpurea* and *I. alba* (the moonflower). The seeds of certain varieties contain hallucinogens. Family: *Convolvulaceae*.

Moro, Aldo   (1916–1978) Italian statesman; Christian Democratic prime minister (1963–68, 1974–76) and foreign minister (1965–66, 1969–72, 1973–74). In 1976 he was instrumental in gaining communist support for the minority Christian Democratic government. In 1978 he was kidnapped and then murdered by the Red Brigades.

Morocco, Kingdom of   A country in NW Africa, bordering on the Atlantic Ocean and Mediterranean Sea. The Atlas Mountains crossing the centre of the country separate the Atlantic coastal area from the Sahara. The population is mainly of Berber and Arabic origin. *Economy*: the chief occupations are agriculture and mining. Wheat, barley, maize, and citrus fruits are grown; livestock, especially sheep and goats, is also important. Morocco is a leading exporter of phosphates; other mineral resources are iron ore, coal, lead, zinc, cobalt, and manganese. Industries include food processing, textiles, and traditional handicraft industries; a major phosphoric acid plant has been developed. There is a thriving fishing industry, sardines and tuna being the chief catch. It is also a popular tourist centre. *History*: part of the Roman province of Mauretania, it fell to the Vandals in the 5th century AD. Its strategic importance was recognized by the European powers in the 19th century, French and Spanish interests conflicting with those of Germany. In the early 20th century Morocco was partitioned into French and Spanish protectorates (1912) and the international zone of Tangier (1923). In 1956 the protectorates were relinquished and Morocco became a sultanate, later a kingdom (1957) under King Mohammed V; his son, Hassan II, acceded to the throne in 1961. Prime minister: Azeddine Laraki (1919–   ). Official religion: Islam. Official language: Arabic. Official currency: dirham of 100 centimes. Area: 458 730 sq km (144 078 sq mi). Population (1987 est): 23 000 000. Capital: Rabat.

morphine   A narcotic analgesic drug obtained from opium and used in medicine for the relief of severe pain. Its depressant effect on the brain accounts for the pain-killing properties; in high doses it also inhibits the breathing and cough centres. Morphine is an addictive drug and readily leads to severe physical dependence.

morphology   (biology) The study of the form and structure of plants, animals, and microorganisms. Anatomy is often used synonymously with morphology but in the former the emphasis is on the gross and microscopic structure of organs and parts.

Morris, Desmond John   (1928–   ) British zoologist, noted for his popularization of biology, especially in his books on human behaviour. *The Naked Ape* (1967), *The Human Zoo* (1969), and *Manwatching* (1977) all set out to prove that human beings are still subject to the basic laws of animal behaviour.

Morris, William (1834–96) British designer, artist, and poet. Associated with the Pre-Raphaelite Brotherhood, he later started a firm of decorators and designers (1861). He designed stained glass, carpets, and furniture, and his wallpaper designs are still used. His Kelmscott Press, founded in 1890, influenced book design and printing generally. He was also one of the founders of British socialism.

Morris dance A ritual English folk dance performed by groups of white-clad men wearing bells and often carrying sticks or handkerchiefs. A common theme is fertility through death and rebirth. Similar dances are found throughout Europe, India, and the Americas, often featuring animal characters or the black-faced Morisco (Moor), whence the name Morris is thought to derive.

Morse, Samuel Finley Breese (1791–1872) US inventor, who erected the first telegraph line, between Washington and Baltimore (1844). Messages were sent by **Morse code**, a system in which each letter of the alphabet and number has a characteristic sequence of dots and dashes (short and long pulses).

mortar (building material) A mixture of sand, hydrated lime, and Portland cement, used to bind together building bricks, etc. It is applied wet as a paste, which sets to a durable solid.

mortar (weapon) A short-barrelled muzzle-loading artillery piece with a low-velocity high-angled trajectory. In World War II the largest Allied mortar had a calibre of 4.2 inches (107 mm), the German version being 8.3 inches (210 mm) with six barrels. Mortars are principally used to fire high-explosive and smoke bombs.

letters

A	·—	N	—·
B	—···	O	———
C	—·—·	P	·——·
D	—··	Q	——·—
E	·	R	·—·
F	··—·	S	···
G	——·	T	—
H	····	U	··—
I	··	V	···—
J	·———	W	·——
K	—·—	X	—··—
L	·—··	Y	—·——
M	——	Z	——··

numbers   punctuation marks

1	·————	·	·—·—·—
2	··———	,	——··——
3	···——	:	———···
4	····—	?	··——··
5	·····	'	·————·
6	—····	-	—····—
7	——···	/	—··—·
8	———··	(or)	—··—·—
9	————·	"	·—··—·
0	—————		

MORSE CODE

mortgage Rights in property (usually land, buildings, etc.) given by a borrower (mortgagor) to a lender (mortgagee) as security for a loan. In the UK building socie-

ties lend money for house purchase in return for a legal charge on the property, which gives them the right to sell it to recover their debt if the borrower defaults. When all the money borrowed and the interest due under the mortgage have been repaid, it is redeemed.

WILLIAM MORRIS *Printed cotton designed c. 1884.*

Mortimer, John Clifford (1923–) British barrister and playwright. He was called to the bar in 1948 and is best known for the televised tales of Horace Rumpole, a fictional barrister. The first of his many plays was *The Dock Brief* (1958); he scripted the television adaptation of *Brideshead Revisited* and wrote the novels *Paradise Postponed* (1985) and *Summer's Lease* (1988).

Morton, Jelly Roll (Ferdinand Joseph La Menthe; 1885–1941) US Black jazz pianist and composer, who made recordings in the 1920s with the group Morton's Red Hot Peppers. Claiming that he "invented jazz in 1902," his reputation has been the subject of controversy.

mosaic A picture or ornamental design made from small coloured cubes of glass, stone, tile, etc. Mosaics were common in ancient Greece, where they were principally used for floors and made from coloured pebbles. During the Roman Empire mosaics of glass became popular for wall and vault decoration, a development that reached its peak in the early Christian churches in Byzantium and Italy. The 6th-century decorations in S Vitale, in Ravenna, are among the most famous mosaics of the middle ages.

Moscow (Russian name: Moskva) 55 45N 37 42E The capital of the Soviet Union and of the Moscow autonomous region (*oblast*), in the RSFSR on the River Moskva. It is the economic and political centre of the Soviet Union and an important transportation centre. Industries include heavy engineering, cars, textiles, electronics, chemicals, publishing, and food processing. The city is based on a radial plan; the Kremlin (citadel) and Red Square are at its heart. The Kremlin, triangular in shape, encloses a number of notable ecclesiastical buildings. Red Square is the traditional setting for military parades and demonstrations. Moscow is a major cultural centre; its many educational institutions include the University of Moscow (1755) and the Academy of Sciences of the USSR. Other famous institutions include the Bolshoi Theatre of Opera and Ballet (1780), the Moscow Art Theatre, and the Moscow State Circus. *History*: first documented in 1147, settlement actually dates back to prehistoric times. By the beginning of the 13th century it was the centre of the Muscovy principality and became the seat of the Russian Church containing the Kremlin (1326). The city was invaded by Napoleon (1812) and the ensuing fire destroyed much of the city. In March, 1918, it became the capital of the RSFSR and following the arrival of Lenin and other communist leaders (1922) the capital of the Soviet Union. Development resumed after World War II, since when Moscow has developed an important tourist industry. Population (1987): 8 815 000.

Moselle, River (German name: R. Mosel) A river in W Europe, flowing N from NE France to join the River Rhine at Koblenz. It forms part of the border between West Germany and Luxembourg. Its valley is one of the main wine-growing areas of West Germany. Length: 547 km (340 mi).

Moses In the Old Testament, the lawgiver of Israel, who led the people from slavery in Egypt (Exodus) and brought them close to the Promised Land. As a child in Egypt (according to the Old Testament), Moses was saved from the slaughter of all Hebrew male children ordered by Pharaoh by being hidden in bulrushes on the Nile. On Mt Sinai he was given the Ten Commandments by Jehovah. He died at the age of 120.

Moses, Grandma (Anna Mary Robertson M.; 1860–1961) US primitive painter, born in Greenwich, New York (*see* primitivism). Entirely self-taught, she only turned seriously to painting at the age of 67. She specialized in naive and nostalgic scenes of farm life.

Mosley, Sir Oswald Ernald (1896–1980) British fascist. He was a Conservative MP (1918–22), an Independent MP (1922–24), and then a Labour MP (1924, 1926–31), serving as chancellor of the Duchy of Lancaster (1929–30). In 1932 he established the British Union of Fascists, which incited antisemitic violence, especially in the East End of London. In World War II he was interned (1940–43) and in 1948 founded the Union Movement.

mosque A Muslim place of worship. It evolved in various styles from a simple rectangular building, such as the first mosque built by Mohammed at Medina in 622 AD. Prayers are said in a large covered area on the side facing Mecca, the direction being indicated by a niche (*mihrab*) in the wall. Mosques are often domed and have minarets (tall slender towers). The mosque has traditionally been the centre of Muslim life, intellectual and social as well as religious.

mosquito A small fly belonging to a family (*Culicidae*; about 2500 species) of almost worldwide distribution, being especially abundant in the tropics. It has long legs, elongated mouthparts, and a long slender abdomen. In most species the males feed on plant juices, while the females bite and suck the blood of mammals, often transmitting serious human and animal diseases. The three important genera are *Anopheles*, *Aedes*, and *Culex* (including the common gnat, *C. pipiens*).

moss A bryophyte plant of the class *Musci* (or *Bryopsida*; about 15 000 species), growing worldwide on moist soil, trees, rocks, etc. The moss plant is differentiated into stems and leaves and produces sex cells (gametes), which give rise to a spore capsule that grows from the

plant on a long stalk. *Sphagnum*, responsible for peat formation, is the only economically important moss. The name is also applied to several unrelated plants, for example Spanish moss.

moss animal. *See* Bryozoa.

Mössbauer effect The emission of a gamma ray (*see* gamma radiation) by an excited nucleus in a solid. Generally such an emission causes the nucleus to recoil, thus reducing the energy of the gamma ray. In the Mössbauer effect the recoil is distributed throughout the solid. The gamma ray therefore loses no energy and may then raise other nuclei into the same excited state. It was discovered by the German physicist Rudolph Mössbauer (1929–) and enables the structure of nuclei and molecules to be examined.

moss pink. *See* Phlox.

motet A polyphonic composition (*see* polyphony) for voices, generally unaccompanied. In the medieval motet the fundamental tenor (holding) part was based on a slow-moving plainchant or popular song while the upper triplex (treble) and motetus (worded) parts had a different text and a quicker rhythm. The 16th-century motet with Latin text, used during church services but not a part of the liturgy, is found in its purest form in the works of Palestrina. Since the 17th century the word has been used to describe a serious but not necessarily religious choral work.

mother-of-pearl. *See* pearl.

moths. *See* butterflies and moths.

motmot A bird of the tropical American family *Motmotidae* (8 species). 16–50 cm long, motmots have short rounded wings, short legs, and long tails with elongated central feathers. The bill is broad and serrated and the plumage is green, blue, brown, and black. Motmots live in forests and prey on insects, spiders, worms, etc. Order: *Coraciiformes* (kingfishers, etc.).

motorcycle racing Racing single-seater motorcycles or sidecar combinations, in classes according to engine capacity. In **road racing**, run usually on special circuits, the main classes are 125, 250, 350, and 500 cc. World championships are awarded according to points won in Grand Prix and other races, such as the Tourist Trophy (TT) races on the Isle of Man (first held in 1907). **Motorcycle trials** are usually events in which a cross-country course has to be completed within a certain time, with points lost for stopping, touching the ground, etc. **Motocross** (or scrambling) takes place on a circuit marked out across rough country. *See also* drag racing.

motorcycles Two-wheeled engine-powered vehicles. The concept of a steam-powered bicycle was first realized by S. H. Roper in the USA in the 1860s. However, the true forerunner of the modern motorcycle was Gottlieb Daimler's 1885 bicycle powered by an Otto four-stroke engine. The first production model was Hildebrand and Wolfmüller's 1894 *Pétrolette*. By 1900 there were some 11 000 motorcycles in France and by the start of World War I over 100 000 were registered in the UK. During the war, motorcycles were extensively used by both sides. The interwar period—the great era of the motorcycle—saw the development of many classic designs: the Harley-Davidson in the USA; the Brough Superior, Triumph Speed Twin, and Ariel Square Four in the UK; and the German DKW two-stroke and BMW four-stroke. All these were in military use in World War II. During and after the war some innovations were made but the basic design remained unchanged. In the 1950s

1860s S.H. Roper Velocipede *One of the earliest steam-powered cycles, this machine survives in the Smithsonian Institute, Washington, USA.*

1885 Daimler *The forerunner of the modern motorcycle, it had a wooden frame, iron tyres, and a 264 cc four-stroke engine.*

1894 Hildebrand and Wolfmüller "Pétrolette" *The first production motor cycle, it had direct rearwheel drive, pneumatic tyres, and a 1488 cc engine. Production was ten machines a day.*

1917 Harley-Davidson *This 989 cc Vee-twin chaindrive machine had the first twist-grip throttle control.*

1930 Brough Superior *Built from 1919 to 1940 this Rolls Royce of motorcycles had a 980 cc Vee-twin JAP engine. Only 3000 were ever made.*

1938 Triumph 500 cc Speed Twin *Capable of over 100 mph, it was widely used by the police.*

1949 Ariel Square Four *The compact arrangement of the four cylinders gave the machine its name. It had telescopic front forks and a sprung rear wheel.*

1988 Honda Goldwing Aspencade *A Japanese tourer with a flat four 1182 cc engine, 5-speed gearbox, drive shaft, and transistorized ignition.*

and 1960s interest in motorcycles in Europe and the USA declined; the motor scooter, a low-powered Italian-originated version of the motorcycle, and the moped, an engine-assisted bicycle, acquired some popularity. In the 1970s, the Japanese, exploiting the closure of European factories, developed a whole new range of motorcycles, based on European designs.

motor racing Racing in cars, from family saloons at club level to highly specialized Grand Prix vehicles. Early races, such as the 1895 race from Paris to Bordeaux and back, were held on roads, but since 1903 they have usually been held on closed-circuit courses, the first of which in England was Brooklands (1907) in Surrey. The most prestigious form of racing is Grand Prix (Formula One) racing, for which specially built single-seater vehicles are raced by professional drivers for manufacturers or private owners. The Drivers' World Championship (instituted in 1950) is awarded according to points won in certain Formula One races. **Sports-car racing** is for production-type or modified sports cars; the most famous sports-car race is the Le Mans 24 Hours. **Autocross** races are amateur races over grass, while **rallycross** is a similar but more professional form, with races held on circuits that are half grass and half tarmac. *See also* drag racing; karting.

mouflon A wild sheep, *Ovis musimon*, native to Corsica and Sardinia and introduced to other parts of Europe and to North America. Mouflons are about 65 cm high at the shoulder and males have large curved horns, a distinctive rump patch, and a white saddle on the back.

mould Any fungus that forms a fine woolly mass growing on food, clothing, etc. Examples are the bread mould and species of *Aspergillus* and *Penicillium*. *See also* slime moulds.

mountain. *See* orogeny.

mountain ash A tree, *Sorbus aucuparia*, also called rowan, native to temperate Eurasia and commonly cultivated as an ornamental. Up to 15 m high, it has long leaves with numerous paired leaflets and large clusters of small cream flowers, which give rise to bright-scarlet berries with a bitter acid taste, used to make wine and jelly. The similar and related American species is *S. americana*. Family: *Rosaceae*.

mountain lion. *See* cougar.

Mountbatten of Burma, Louis, 1st Earl (1900–79) British admiral and colonial administrator; son of Prince Louis of Battenberg (1854–1921) and of Princess Victoria of Hesse-Darmstadt, the granddaughter of Queen Victoria. In World War II he was supreme Allied commander in SE Asia (1943–45), retaking Burma. As viceroy of India (1947) he presided over the transfer of power to India and Pakistan and was then governor general of India (1947–48). He was subsequently commander in chief of the Mediterranean fleet (1952–54) and first sea lord (1955–59), becoming an admiral in 1956. He died in Ireland, the victim of an IRA bomb.

Mounties. *See* Royal Canadian Mounted Police.

Mount of Olives The highest point in a small range of four summits situated just E of Jerusalem. It features in the Old and New Testaments. Its W slope was the site of the Garden of Gethsemane. According to the Acts of the Apostles (1.2–12), Christ ascended to heaven from the Mount of Olives.

Mount Rushmore National Memorial The gigantic sculpture of the heads of four US presidents—Washington, Jefferson, Lincoln, and Theodore Roosevelt—carved (1927–41) to the design of the sculptor Gutzon Borglum (1871–1941) on the NE cliffs of Mount Rushmore, South Dakota. Each head is about 18 m (60 ft) high.

mouse A rodent belonging to the suborder *Myomorpha*. The house mouse (*Mus musculus*) is common in buildings worldwide. Greyish brown, it is 14–16 cm long including its tail (7–8 cm) and feeds on a variety of foods, from sugar and grain to oil-based paints and putty.

Most mice—together with the rats—are grouped into the subfamilies *Murinae* of the Old World and *Cricetinae* of the New World (which also includes hamsters). There are separate subfamilies for African tree mice (*Dendromurinae*; 7 species), jumping mice (*Zapodinae*; 3 species), dormice, and other small groups.

mouse deer. *See* chevrotain.

Mousterian A stone-tool industry of the Middle Palaeolithic, associated with Neanderthal man. Named after caves at Le Moustier in the Dordogne (SW France), the Mousterian occurs, with variants, throughout Eurasia from France to China and in N Africa. Spanning roughly the period of 70 000 to 35 000 BC, it is characterized by a wide variety of hand axes, scrapers, points, and blades.

mouthbrooder A fish belonging to one of several genera of cichlid fishes. The eggs are carried in the mouth of the parent, usually the female, until they hatch. Chief genera: *Tilapia*; *Haplochromis*; *Pelmatochromis*. Other mouthbrooders include certain fighting fish, catfish, and cardinal fish.

mouth organ. *See* harmonica.

Mozambique, People's Republic of (Portuguese name: Moçambique) A country in S East Africa, bordering on the Indian Ocean. Extensive coastal plains rise to plateaus inland with mountains reaching over 2000 m (6500 ft). The chief rivers, notably the Zambezi and Limpopo, flow E and provide both irrigation and hydroelectric power. Most of the population is African, mainly Bantu. *Economy*: chiefly agricultural, the staple food crops being rice and maize. The main cash crops of cashew nuts, cotton, and sugar are also the principal exports. Industry is based largely on food processing and textiles. Mineral resources, including natural gas and high-grade iron ore, are largely unexploited except for coal and bauxite. *History*: the N coast was settled by Arabs from the 10th century and was explored by Vasco da Gama in 1498, becoming a Portuguese colony in the early 16th century. In 1951 it became an overseas province of Portugal. From 1963 FRELIMO (Frente de Libertaçao de Moçambique) waged a guerrilla campaign that achieved the establishment (1975) of an independent socialist republic under Samora Machel (1933–86). The South African-backed Mozambique National Resistance (MNR) has applied military pressure in Mozambique with raids on guerrillas in Maputo. Samora Machel died in an air crash in 1986. President: Joaquin Chissano (1939–). Official language: Portuguese; the main African language is Makua Lomwe. Official currency: Mozambique escudo of 100 centavos. Area: 784 961 sq km (303 070 sq mi). Population (1987 est): 14 543 000. Capital and main port: Maputo.

Mozart, Wolfgang Amadeus (1756–91) Austrian composer, born in Salzburg, the son of the violinist and composer Leopold Mozart (1719–87). Mozart exhibited extraordinary musical talent at the age of four; in 1762

MOZART　*Aged 7 years, with his father and sister.*

his father took him on a tour of Germany and to Paris and London, where he received adulation for his abilities. After a period of unhappy service with the Archbishop of Salzburg (1779–81) he settled in Vienna as a freelance musician and teacher, composing such masterpieces as the operas *The Marriage of Figaro* (1786) and *Don Giovanni* (1787). Mozart achieved a fusion of the Germanic and Italianate styles of composition and his immense productivity enriched almost every musical genre. He composed 49 symphonies, over 40 concertos, 6 string quintets, 26 string quartets, numerous divertimenti, piano sonatas, violin sonatas, and much other music. Some of his finest works, such as the operas *Così fan tutte* (1790) and *The Magic Flute* (1791) and the *Jupiter* symphony (1788), were written in the last years of his life. *See also* Köchel, Ludwig von.

Mubarak, (Mohammed) Hosni (Said) (1928–) Egyptian statesman; president (1981–). A general, he commanded (1972–75) the Egyptian air force in the Yom Kippur War (1973). He became vice president to Anwar Sadat in 1975 and succeeded him on his assassination. A cautious conservative, he has contained inflation and improved relations with the USA and Arab countries.

mucous membrane A moist membrane that lines the digestive and respiratory tracts and the nasal sinuses. It is a type of epithelium containing cells that secrete **mucus**, a slimy substance that protects its surface and –in the digestive tract–also lubricates the passage of food and faeces. In the bronchi the mucus traps particles that are inhaled with air.

Mudéjars (Arabic: vassal) The Muslims (*see* Moors) of Spain who had, by the 13th century, become subject to Christian rule during the reconquest of the Iberian peninsula. Many were of mixed Berber and Spanish descent and continued to preserve their Islamic religion and customs. They created an architectural style notable for its ornamental brickwork and use of ceramic tiling. Many examples survive in Castile and Aragon.

mudskipper A fish of the subfamily *Periophthalminae*, especially the genus *Periophthalmus*, found in swamps, estuaries, and mud flats of Africa, Polynesia, and Australia. Mudskippers have an elongated

body, up to 30 cm long, a blunt head, and dorsally protruding eyes. They are able to climb and walk over land using their limblike pectoral fins. Family: *Gobiidae* (*see* goby).

Mugabe, Robert (Gabriel) (1925–) Zimbabwe statesman; prime minister (1980–87); president (1987–). He helped found the Zimbabwe African National Union (ZANU) in 1963 and, after ten years' (1964–74) detention in Rhodesia, formed the Patriotic Front (PF) with Joshua Nkomo, leader of the Zimbabwe African People's Union (ZAPU). They waged guerrilla warfare against the governments of Ian Smith and then Bishop Muzorewa until agreeing to disarm (*see* Zimbabwe). His party's election victory (1980) brought Mugabe the leadership of newly independent Zimbabwe.

Muhammad. *See* Mohammed.

Muhammad Ahmad. *See* Mahdi, al-.

Muir, Edwin (1887–1959) Scottish poet. Born in Orkney, he moved to Glasgow in 1901 and to London in 1919. During the 1930s he and his wife Willa moved to Prague, where they translated the novels of Franz Kafka. His reputation as a poet was established with *The Voyage* (1946) and *The Labyrinth* (1949). His *Autobiography* (1954) contains much of his best prose.

mujahidin. *See* Afghanistan.

Mukden. *See* Shenyang.

mulberry A tree of the genus *Morus* (12 species), native to N temperate and subtropical regions. The black mulberry (*M. nigra*) is the species most commonly cultivated for its fruit. About 12 m high, it has toothed heart-shaped leaves and round green flower clusters (catkins). The female flowers give rise to a blackberry-like fruit, which is used in jellies, desserts, etc. The leaves of the white mulberry (*M. alba*) are the staple food of silkworms. Family: *Moraceae*.

mule The sterile offspring of a female horse and a male ass. Mules are useful pack and draught animals, being hardy, sure-footed, and strong but smaller than a horse.

Mull An island off the W coast of Scotland, in the Inner Hebrides. It is chiefly mountainous; some sheep and cattle are raised. Other occupations include fishing, forestry, and tourism. Area: 909 sq km (351 sq mi). Population (1981): 2605. Chief town: Tobermory.

mullein A biennial or perennial herb of the genus *Verbascum* (about 300 species), native to N temperate Eurasia. The biennial common mullein (*V. thapsus*), also called Aaron's rod, occurs in dry limy regions. 0.6–2 m tall, it bears large woolly leaves and pale-yellow flowers. Some species, including the European dark mullein (*V. nigrum*), are grown as garden plants. Family: *Scrophulariaceae*.

mullet A food fish, also called grey mullet, belonging to the genus *Mugil* (about 70 species), found in temperate and tropical coastal waters and estuaries. It has a slender silvery-green or grey large-scaled body, 30–90 cm long, with two dorsal fins. Family: *Mugilidae*; order: *Perciformes*. *See also* red mullet.

multiple sclerosis A chronic and usually progressive disease of the nervous system in which the fatty sheaths that surround the nerves in the brain or spinal cord are destroyed. The disease is also called disseminated sclerosis, as its effects are disseminated in different parts of the body. It usually begins in young adults, and the commonest initial symptoms are sudden severe blurring of the vision or weakness in one limb. Later the disease returns, causing permanent handicap.

mummers' play An English folk drama based on the legend of St George and the Seven Champions of Christendom; it was a dumb show (*mummer*, from Middle English *mum*, silent), traditionally enacted on Christmas Day by masked performers.

mummy A human or animal body prepared and embalmed for burial according to ancient Egyptian religious practice. The internal organs were extracted and sealed in Canopic jars and the body was desiccated by packing in dry natron, anointed, and encased in linen bandages.

mumps An acute virus infection that usually occurs in children. After an incubation period of 12 to 20 days the child develops headache and fever; later, the parotid salivary glands (situated under the ear) become tender and swollen. The disease is usually mild and resolves rapidly. In adult male patients the infection may spread to the testicles, which may occasionally lead to sterility.

Munch, Edvard (1863–1944) Norwegian painter and printmaker, who was a major influence on 20th-century German expressionism. His symbolic paintings of love, death, and despair, including the famous *Cry* (1893; Nasjonalgalleriet, Oslo), reflect the pessimism caused by family tragedy.

München. *See* Munich.

München Gladbach. *See* Mönchengladbach.

Münchhausen, Karl Friedrich, Freiherr von (1720–97) German soldier famous as a raconteur. His hyperbolic accounts of his feats passed into legend and were the subject of a series of adventure tales, *The Adventures of Baron Munchhausen* (1793), written by R. E. Raspe (1737–94).

mung bean A bean plant, *Phaseolus aureus*, also known as green gram, native to India and cultivated in tropical and subtropical regions chiefly as a vegetable crop. The slender pods contain up to 15 small edible seeds, which can be dried and stored or germinated in the dark to produce bean sprouts. Family: *Leguminosae*.

Munich (German name: München) 48 08N 11 35E A city in S West Germany, the capital of Bavaria on the River Isar. It has a 15th-century cathedral and many baroque and rococo buildings. It is also noted for its annual Oktoberfest (beer festival). A centre of commerce, industry, and tourism, its manufactures include precision instruments, electrical goods, chemicals, and beer. *History*: Munich was from 1255 the residence and from 1506 the capital of the Dukes of Bavaria (from 1806 Kings). The Nazi movement began here in the 1920s. Population (1986): 1 269 400.

Munich Agreement (1938) The settlement, resulting from the conference between Neville Chamberlain (UK), Daladier (France), Hitler (Germany), and Mussolini (Italy), that recognized Hitler's territorial claims to the Sudetenland. Described by Chamberlain as achieving "peace in our time," it was followed in March, 1939, by Hitler's invasion of Czechoslovakia and in Sept by World War II.

Munro, Hector Hugh. *See* Saki.

Münster 51 58N 7 37E A city and port in NW West Germany, in North Rhine-Westphalia on the Dortmund-Ems Canal. It was an important member of the Hanseatic League and the capital of the former province of Westphalia. It has a 13th-century cathedral and a university (1773). Service industries provide employment for most of the workforce. Population (1986): 268 900.

Munster A province and ancient kingdom of the SW Republic of Ireland. It consists of the counties of Clare, Cork, Kerry, Limerick, Tipperary, and Waterford. Area: 24 125 sq km (9315 sq mi). Population (1986): 1 019 694.

Munthe, Axel (1857–1949) Swedish physician and author. Munthe practised in Paris and Rome before retiring to Capri, where he built the Villa San Michele. *The Story of San Michele* (1929) described his early life and the building of the villa. It has been translated into 44 languages and remains a bestseller.

muntjac A small deer belonging to the subfamily *Muntiacinae* (6 species), occurring in forests of Asia, Sumatra, Java, and Borneo. The Indian muntjac (*Muntiacus muntjak*), also called barking deer or rib-faced deer, is 55 cm high at the shoulder with short unbranched antlers and short sharp fangs. Muntjacs are mainly solitary and nocturnal.

muon A negatively charged unstable elementary particle (lifetime 2×10^{-6} second; mass 207 times that of the electron) that decays into an electron and two neutrinos. It has a corresponding antiparticle. It was originally thought to be a meson (and was called the mu-meson) but is now classified as a lepton. *See* particle physics.

mural painting The decoration of walls and ceilings by such varied techniques as encaustic, tempera, and fresco painting. Renaissance painters often used perspective and architecture in their murals to create the illusion that the painted walls or ceilings were space extensions of the real architecture. Mural painting was revived during the 20th century, principally by the Mexican painters Rivera, Orozco, and Siqueiros, who used it to reach a wider public with their social and political subject matter.

Murdoch, Dame Iris (1919–) British novelist. Born in Dublin, she studied and taught philosophy at Oxford. Her novels are elaborate and witty explorations of human relationships. They include *The Bell* (1958), *A Severed Head* (1961), *The Sea, the Sea* (1978), for which she won the Booker Prize, *The Good Apprentice* (1985), *The Book and the Brotherhood* (1987), and *The Message to the Planet* (1989).

murex A gastropod mollusc belonging to the family *Muricidae* (about 1000 species), mainly of tropical seas. Murex shells are elaborately ornamented with spines and frills; the snail feeds on other molluscs by drilling holes in their shells and extracting the flesh with its long proboscis.

Murillo, Bartolomé Esteban (1617–82) Spanish painter. He spent most of his life in Seville, working for the religious orders and helping to found the Spanish Academy (1660), of which he became first president. After abandoning his early realism, he painted urchins and religious scenes in an idealized style influenced by Rubens and the Venetians.

Murmansk 68 59N 33 08E A port in the NW Soviet Union, in the RSFSR on the Kola inlet of the Barents Sea. Its ice-free harbour is an important fishing base. Population (1987): 432 000.

Murray, Sir James (Augustus Henry) (1837–1915) British lexicographer. After joining the Philological Society and editing some early English texts, he was in 1878 appointed editor of the *New English Dictionary on Historical Principles* (later called the *Oxford English Dictionary*), to which he devoted the rest of his life.

499

music hall

MURAL PAINTING *A mural (detail) by Diego Rivera depicting the history of Mexico.*

Murray River The chief river in Australia. Rising near Mount Koscuisko, in New South Wales, it flows generally W and S forming the boundary between Victoria and New South Wales. It enters Encounter Bay on the Indian Ocean through Lake Alexandrina. The main tributaries are the Darling and Murrumbidgee Rivers; it also receives water from the Snowy Mountains hydroelectric scheme. Length: 2590 km (1609 mi).

Murrumbidgee River A river in SE Australia, rising in the Eastern Highlands in New South Wales and flowing through the Australian Capital Territory before entering the Murray River. Length: 1690 km (1050 mi).

Murry, John Middleton (1889–1957) British literary critic. He edited the literary magazines *Athenaeum* (1919–21) and *Adelphi* (1923–48). His many books include studies of Keats (1925, 1930, 1949) and Blake (1933) as well as an autobiography, *Between Two Worlds* (1935).

Muscat 23 37N 58 38E The capital of Oman, on the Gulf of Oman. Most port traffic is now handled at Matrah to the NW. There is an oil terminal to the W. Population (1982 est): 80 000.

Muscat and Oman. *See* Oman, Sultanate of.

muscle Tissue that is specialized to contract, producing movement or tension in the body. It contains long spindle-shaped cells (muscle fibres) that convert chemical energy (*see* ATP) into mechanical energy. Most of the body's musculature consists of voluntary muscle, which is consciously controlled via the central nervous system. It is also known as skeletal muscle (because it is attached to the bones) and striated (or striped) muscle (because of its banded appearance under the microscope). Individual muscles are made up of bundles of fibres enclosed in a strong fibrous sheath and attached to bones by tendons. Involuntary muscle occurs in the walls of hollow organs, such as blood vessels, intestines, and the bladder. It is responsible for movements not under conscious control and is regulated by the autonomic nervous system. Cardiac muscle is a special type of muscle found only in the heart: its rhythmic contractions produce the heartbeat.

muscovite. *See* micas.

muscular dystrophy A group of chronic and progressive disorders characterized by wasting and weakening of the muscle fibres. The disease is inherited and the commonest type, Duchenne muscular dystrophy, affects predominantly boys. There is no specific treatment but physiotherapy and orthopaedic measures can help.

Muses In Greek mythology, the nine patrons of the arts and sciences, daughters of Zeus and Mnemosyne. Calliope was the muse of epic poetry; Clio, history; Euterpe, flute playing and music; Erato, love poetry and hymns; Terpsichore, dancing; Melpomene, tragedy; Thalia, comedy; Polyhymnia, song and mime; and Urania, astronomy.

mushroom The umbrella-shaped spore-forming body produced by many fungi. (Sometimes the word toadstool is used for those species that are inedible or poisonous, mushroom being restricted to the edible species.) It consists of an erect stem (stipe) and a cap, which may be flat, conical, spherical, or cylindrical and has numerous radiating gills on its undersurface in which the spores are produced. The well-known edible mushrooms belong to the genus *Agaricus*; they have a smooth white or scaly brown cap with gills that become deep brown at maturity.

musical instruments Devices used to produce music. In the orchestra musical instruments are grouped into families. The stringed instruments (*or* strings) include the violin, viola, cello, double bass, and harp (*see also* piano). The wind instruments are divided into the woodwind (flute, clarinet, oboe, and bassoon) and brass (horn, trumpet, trombone, and tuba). The percussion instruments include the triangle, cymbals, xylophone, timpani, and other instruments. Many instruments are used chiefly in jazz or pop (e.g. guitar, vibraphone, and maracas) while others, such as the Indian sitar, feature predominantly in the music of particular countries.

music hall A type of popular entertainment featuring a variety of performers including singers, dancers, comedians, and conjurors. It attained its greatest popularity in 19th-century England, and declined in the 1920s and 1930s with the rise of the cinema and the radio. Notable music-hall performers were Marie Lloyd, Vesta Tilley, Harry Lauder, and Gracie Fields. The US equivalent is known as vaudeville. Celebrated vaudeville performers include W. C. Fields and Will Rodgers (1879–1935).

range of some musical instruments

MUSICAL INSTRUMENTS

musk (botany) A perennial plant, *Mimulus moschatus*, native to North America and grown as an ornamental for its musky fragrance. 20–60 cm tall, it has oval leaves and tubular yellow flowers. The name is also applied to several other plants with a musky odour including the musk mallow (*Malva moschata*) and musk rose (*Rosa moschata*).

musk deer A small solitary deer, *Moschus moschiferus*, found in mountain forests of central Asia. Musk deer are about 60 cm high at the shoulder with long hind legs; males have no antlers but grow long fangs. The secretion of their musk gland is used in the manufacture of perfumes.

musket A smoothbore firearm fired from the shoulder. The earliest form, known as a harquebus (*or* arquebus) evolved in the 15th century as the first hand-held form of the cannon. In the second half of the 16th century a Spanish general invented a heavy shoulder weapon with a sufficiently large charge to penetrate armour. This musket still relied on the matchlock, it was not until the mid-17th century that wheellocks and flintlocks were adopted for military use. The next landmark in the development of the musket was the percussion cap at the beginning of the 19th century, which led to the breech-loading musket with cartridge and percussion-cap ammunition. Muskets were superseded by rifles in the mid-19th century.

musk ox A large hoofed mammal, *Ovibos moschatus*, inhabiting the Arctic tundra of North America. About 150 cm high at the shoulder, musk oxen have long dark shaggy hair and prominent curved horns. Bulls have a strong musky scent in the rutting season. Family: *Bovidae*.

muskrat A large North American water vole, *Ondatra zibethica*, also called musquash. It grows up to 35 cm long, excluding its black hairless tail, and its soft glossy coat is used in the fur trade. Muskrats inhabit marshland and feed on water plants, mussels, and crayfish. Family: *Cricetidae*.

muslin A smooth delicately woven cotton fabric. Originally made in Mosul in Mesopotamia (hence its name), it is used for dresses and curtains. In the USA coarser cotton fabrics used for shirts and sheeting are also called muslins.

musquash. *See* muskrat.

mussel A bivalve mollusc belonging either to the family *Mytilidae* (marine mussels) or the superfamily *Unionacea* (freshwater mussels). Marine mussels have wedge-shaped shells measuring 5–15 cm. The edible mussel (*Mytilus edulis*) is an important seafood. Freshwater mussels inhabit ponds, lakes, and streams.

Musset, Alfred de (1810–57) French poet and dramatist, one of the major figures of the Romantic movement. He published his first volume of poetry, *Contes d'Espagne et d'Italie*, at the age of 20. His autobiographical *La Confession d'un enfant du siècle* (1836) includes an account of his love affair with George Sand.

Mussolini, Benito (Amilcare Andrea) (1883–1945) Italian fascist dictator. Initially an ardent socialist, his support of Italian participation in World War I led to his expulsion from the Socialist Party (1915). In 1919 he formed the Fasci di combattimento (Blackshirts) in Milan and came to power following the March on Rome (1922). He was prime minister until the murder of Giacomo Matteotti persuaded him to establish (1924–29) a dictatorship. As *duce* ("leader") his policies initially impressed the Italian people. However, his expansionist foreign policy, especially his alliance with Hitler, brought him increasing unpopularity. In 1939 he annexed Albania and after the outbreak of World War II he declared war on France and Britain (June, 1940). The Italian war effort was disastrous; following the Allied invasion of Sicily, Mussolini was forced to resign (July, 1943). Rescued by the Germans to head a new fascist republic in N Italy, he was subsequently captured and shot by Italian partisans.

Mussorgski, Modest Petrovich (1839–81) Russian composer. An army officer and civil servant, he had little formal training. His masterpieces are the opera *Boris Godunov* (1868–72), the piano work *Pictures at an Exhibition* (1874), and the orchestral tone poem *A Night on the Bare Mountain* (1860–66).

mustang The wild horse of North America. Mustangs are descended from the domesticated European stock of Spanish settlers and have become tough and small in the harsh conditions. Many were caught and tamed by cowboys and Indians, including the Mustang tribe.

mustard Any of various annual herbs of the genus *Brassica* and closely related genera, native to Europe and W Asia and cultivated chiefly for their seeds—source of the condiment mustard. They have deeply lobed leaves and terminal clusters of yellow flowers. The leaves may be used as fodder, fertilizer, vegetables, or herbs. The main species are the white or yellow mustard, *Sinapis alba* (or *B. hirta*), black or brown mustard (*B. nigra*), and Indian mustard (*B. juncea*).

mutation A change in the hereditary material (*see* DNA) of an organism, which results in an altered physical characteristic. A mutation in a germ cell is inherited by subsequent generations of offspring; a change in any other cell (somatic cell) affects only those cells produced by division of the mutated cell. Gene mutations result from a change in the bases of the DNA molecule; chromosome mutations may be due to the addition or subtraction of bases and can usually be seen under a microscope. Both types of mutation affect the genetic code and hence the corresponding function of the genes.

Very occasionally, mutations occur spontaneously and at random. They can also be induced by certain chemicals, ionizing radiation (such as X-rays), and by ultraviolet light. Most nonlethal mutations are of no benefit to the organism, but they do provide an important source of genetic variation in the population on which natural selection can act, which eventually results in the evolution of new species.

MYCENAE *The entrance to the citadel of Mycenae is by the Lion Gate, between walls of Cyclopean stonework.*

mute swan An Old World swan, *Cygnus olor*, found in marshy areas and estuaries and, as a semidomesticated ornamental bird, on rivers and lakes. It is 160 cm long and has a long neck, white plumage, black legs, and an orange bill with a black base. It is less vocal than other swans.

mutualism. *See* symbiosis.

Muzorewa, Bishop Abel (Tendekayi) (1925–) Zimbabwe statesman and bishop of the Methodist Church. One-time president of the African National Congress and the All Africa Conference of Churches, Muzorewa negotiated a new constitution with Ian Smith's government in 1978 and headed a nominally Black government in Zimbabwe until 1980.

MX missile A US nuclear strategic missile with a range of 9650 km (6000 mi). Carrying 10 warheads, the MX missile was developed in response to the vulnerability of the concrete underground silos in which other ICBMs are housed. The MX missile can be launched from ships, aircraft, submarines, mobile land launchers, or from specially reinforced silos.

Myanmar, Union of. *See* Burma, Socialist Republic of the Union of.

Mycenae An ancient citadel in the Peloponnese (S Greece). Famed in legend as the home of Agamemnon, Mycenae attained its zenith between 1600 and 1200 BC. Massive fortifications attest Mycenae's military readiness and exquisite bronze, gold, and silver articles from its royal graves indicate affluence.

Mycenaean civilization The civilization of Bronze Age Greece. It developed after about 1650 BC in mainland centres, such as Mycenae and Pylos, and after 1450 BC its influence extended to Crete. The Mycenaeans were a warrior aristocracy. They spoke a form of Greek, used Linear B script, and lived in palaces decorated with frescoes and equipped with luxury goods. About 1200 BC the palaces were destroyed, but Mycenaean culture survived until about 1100 BC.

mycology The branch of biology dealing with the study of fungi. Mycology was established as a separate

discipline in the early 19th century, when the Swedish botanist Elias Fries (1794–1878) published the first scientifically based classification of the fungi (1821–32).

mynah A songbird belonging to a genus (*Acridotheres*) native to SE Asia. Mynahs usually have a dark plumage with bright wattles on the face. They feed chiefly on the ground and eat the insects found on cattle. The common mynah (*A. tristis*) has become a pest in some regions. The popular cagebird that mimics human speech is a related species, the hill mynah (*Graculus religiosa*). Family: *Sturnidae* (starlings).

myocardial infarction Death of part of the heart muscle: the cause of what is popularly described as a heart attack. This usually results from atherosclerosis. The patient usually experiences sudden severe central chest pain, which may spread to the neck and arms and is usually accompanied by sweating and nausea.

myopia. *See* shortsightedness.

Myron (5th century BC) Athenian sculptor. His *Discus-Thrower* and *Marsyas*, described by ancient critics, are known through Roman copies.

myrrh An aromatic yellow to red gum resin obtained from small tropical thorny trees of the genus *Commifera*, especially *C. myrrha*, *C. molmol*, and *C. abyssinica*, native to Africa and SW Asia. It is used in incense, perfumes, cosmetics, dentistry, and pharmaceuticals. Family: *Commiphoraceae*.

myrtle An evergreen shrub of the genus *Myrtus* (over 100 species). The common myrtle (*M. communis*), native to the Mediterranean area and W Asia, may grow to a height of 5 m. It has aromatic dark-green shiny leaves, fragrant five-petalled white flowers, and blue-black berries. Its oil is used in perfumery. Family: *Myrtaceae*. Other plants known as myrtle include the sweet gale.

Mysore 12 18N 76 37E A city in India, in Karnataka. Industries include textiles, chemicals, and food processing and it has a university (1916). Population (1981): 476 000.

mystery plays. *See* miracle plays.

mysticism Belief in a type of religious experience in which the individual claims to achieve immediate knowledge of or temporary union with God. Mysticism is an element in most theistic traditions. The usual preliminary is strict asceticism. St Francis of Assisi, St Teresa of Avila, and Julian of Norwich (c. 1342–c, 1413) are among the many famous Christian mystics. Official Church attitudes have alternated between regarding mysticism as a special spiritual grace and suspecting it of verging on Gnosticism, pantheism, or Neoplatonism.

mythology Imaginative poetic stories, traditions, etc., concerning religious beliefs, gods, and supernatural and heroic human beings. Mythology often involves a cosmogony—an attempted explanation of the origin of the universe, of mankind, or of a particular race or culture. The term also refers to the formal study of such stories, traditions, etc. Anthropology and psychoanalysis have thrown new light on the function of myths. Among primitive peoples they serve to provide an explanation or justification for social institutions. They also appear to embody universal values or patterns with regard to human psychology. The mythologies of particular cultures have provided the material of much of the world's great literature and art.

myxomatosis An infectious disease of rabbits and hares that is caused by a virus. Symptoms include swollen eyes, nose, and muzzle, closed eyelids, and fever. The disease, which is usually fatal, was introduced to the UK and Australia during the 1950s as a pest-control measure.

N

NAGA

Nabis (Hebrew: *prophets*) A group of French artists formed in Paris in 1888. The leading members—Paul Sérusier (1863–1927), Maurice Denis (1870–1943), Bonnard, and Édouard Vuillard (1868–1940)—were united by their admiration for Gauguin and Japanese prints. They disbanded in 1899.

Nabokov, Vladimir (1899–1977) US novelist. He achieved popular success with *Lolita* (1955), whose academic antihero lusts after young girls. His other novels include *The Defence* (1930), one of several originally written in Russian, *Pale Fire* (1962), and *Ada* (1969).

nacre. *See* pearl.

Na-Dené languages An American Indian language group. It includes the Athabascan, Tlingit, Haida, and Eyak subgroups.

nadir. *See* zenith.

naga In Hindu mythology, one of a race of minor serpent deities. Vishnu is often portrayed sleeping on the naga Sesha, and there is a Buddhist legend of a naga raising the Buddha on its coils above a flood sent to prevent his attaining enlightenment. Nagas are depicted as half-snake and half-human, as many-headed cobras, or in human form posed beneath a canopy of cobras.

Nagasaki 32 45N 129 52E A port in Japan, in W Kyushu. On 9 August, 1945, the second atomic bomb was dropped on Nagasaki, killing or wounding about 75 000 people. Population (1985): 449 000.

Nagorno-Karabakh An autonomous region (*oblast*) in the SW Soviet Union, in the Azerbaidzhan SSR. Formed in 1923, its population comprises Christian Armenians (76%) and Moslem Azerbaidzhanis. It has metal and mineral deposits but is chiefly agricultural. Since 1988 the Armenians' agitation for union with Armenia has increasingly destabilized the region. Area:

4400 sq km (1700 sq mi). Population (1986): 177 000. Capital: Stepanakert.

Nagoya 35 8N 136 53E A port in Japan, in SE Honshu. The fourth largest city in the country, it was rebuilt after bombing in 1945. Population (1987): 2 138 000.

Nagpur 21 10N 79 12E A city in India, in Maharashtra. Founded in the early 18th century, it fell under British control in 1853. Population (1981 est): 1 297 977.

Nagy, Imre (1896–1958) Hungarian statesman, who led the revolutionary government of 1956. As prime minister (1953–55) Nagy promised numerous reforms. Opposed by Hungary's Stalinists, he was demoted and in 1956 expelled from the Communist Party. In the subsequent Hungarian Revolution Nagy again became prime minister but was executed by the Soviets.

Nahuatl The most widely used American Indian language of the Uto-Aztecan family, spoken in Mexico. It was the language of the Aztecs and Toltecs. The Nahua people are slash-and-burn cultivators, growing maize, beans, tomatoes, and chilis.

Naipaul, Sir V(idiadhur) S(urajprasad) (1932–) British novelist, born in the West Indies. A witty ironic tone characterizes such early novels as *A House for Mr Biswas* (1961). Later novels include *In a Free State* (1971) and *The Enigma of Arrival* (1987).

Nairobi 1 17S 36 50E The capital of Kenya, situated just S of the equator. It is the trading centre of a fertile agricultural region. Population (1985 est): 827 800.

Namib Desert A desert chiefly in W Namibia, extending some 1600 km (994 mi) along the Atlantic coast. It is almost devoid of population.

Namibia (name until 1968: South West Africa) A country in SW Africa. The narrow coastal plains of the Namib Desert rise to the central plateau, with the Kalahari Desert to the N. The majority of the population is African, the largest group being the Ovambo. *Economy*: chiefly subsistence agriculture. Fishing is important, especially for pilchards. Rich mineral resources include diamonds (the main export), copper, lead, zinc, tin, vanadium, and uranium. *History*: a German protectorate from 1884, during World War I it surrendered (1915) to South Africa, which administered South West Africa under a League of Nations mandate. In 1966 South Africa refused to acknowledge that the mandate was at an end and was condemned by both the UN and the South West Africa People's Organization (SWAPO) for illegally occupying the territory. In 1985 South Africa installed an interim administration in Namibia as a first step towards granting independence (achieved in 1990). President: Sam Nujoma. Official languages: Afrikaans and English. Official currency: South African rand of 100 cents. Area: 824 269 sq km (318 261 sq mi). Population (1986 est): 1 184 000. Capital: Windhoek. Main port: Walvis Bay.

Nanak (1469–1539) Indian founder of Sikhism. Born near Lahore, he settled finally in Kartarpur, where he attracted a large community of disciples. His teachings are contained in a number of hymns.

Nancy 48 42N 6 12E A town in NE France, on the River Meurthe. The former capital of the Dukes of Lorraine, it passed to France in 1766. Population (1982): 99 307.

Nanjing (Nan-ching *or* Nanking) 32 05N 118 55E A port in E China, on the Yangtze River. An ancient cultural centre, it was the centre of the Taiping Rebellion (1851–64). Population (1986 est): 2 250 000.

Nansen, Fridtjof (1861–1930) Norwegian explorer, zoologist, and statesman. In 1888 he led an expedition across the Greenland icefield and in 1893, in the *Fram*, set sail across the Arctic. In 1895, with F. J. Johansen (1867–1923), he left the ship and reached 18 14N, the nearest point to the North Pole then attained. He subsequently contributed greatly to the League of Nations and pioneered the **Nansen passport**, an identification card for displaced persons (1922). He won the Nobel Peace Prize (1923).

Nantes 47 14N 1 35W A major port in W France, on the Loire estuary. Its commercial importance dates back to Roman times and it was here that the **Edict of Nantes,** guaranteeing religious toleration, was signed in 1598. Population (1982): 247 227.

Nantucket An island in the USA, off SE Massachusetts. A former whaling centre, it is now chiefly a resort. Length: 24 km (15 mi). Width: 5 km (3 mi).

napalm An inexpensive jelly consisting of a mixture of the aluminium salts of *na*pathenic acid and *palm*itic acid used to thicken petrol so that it can be used in incendiary bombs and flame-throwers. It was used in World War II, the Korean War, and in Vietnam.

naphthalene ($C_{10}H_8$) A white crystalline aromatic hydrocarbon that occurs in coal tar. **Naphthol** ($C_{10}H_7OH$) is the hydroxy derivative. It consists of two isomers; the most important, beta-naphthol, is used in antioxidants for rubbers and dyes and in drugs.

Napier 39 29S 176 58E A port in New Zealand, in E North Island. It is the most important centre of New Zealand's wool trade. Population (1985): 50 100.

Napier, John (1550–1617) Scottish mathematician, who invented logarithms. In 1614 he published a table of logarithms to the base e, now known as Napierian logarithms. Napier also produced an elementary calculating machine, known as **Napier's bones**.

Naples (Italian name: Napoli; ancient name: Neapolis) 40 50N 14 15E A city in S Italy, overlooking the Bay of Naples. It is an important port and a centre of tourism. Its many historic buildings include medieval castles, a gothic cathedral (13th–14th centuries), the 17th-century Royal Palace, and the university (1224). *History*: founded by Greek colonists about 600 BC, it fell to Rome in 326. It was under Byzantine rule (6th–8th centuries AD) and in 1139 it became part of the Norman kingdom of Sicily. Following the revolt known as the Sicilian Vespers (1282), the Italian peninsula S of the Papal States became known as the kingdom of Naples (with Naples as its capital) until it fell to Garibaldi (1860) and was united with the rest of Italy (*see also* Sicily). From this time Naples lagged economically behind the N, resulting in considerable poverty. The city was badly damaged during World War II. Population (1986): 1 204 211.

Napoleon I (1769–1821) Emperor of the French (1804–15). Born Napoleon Bonaparte in Corsica, he became an artillery officer and rose to prominence in 1795,

NAPOLEON I *Detail of David's portrait (1821; Versailles) of the emperor crossing the Alps.*

when he turned the guns of the Paris garrison on a mob. Shortly afterwards he married Josephine de Beauharnais and was appointed to command the French army in Italy (*see* Revolutionary and Napoleonic Wars). His Italian campaign (1796–97) brought the conquest of Milan and Mantua. Napoleon then obtained the Directory's support for his plan to break British imperial power by conquering Egypt and India. In Egypt his great victory of the Pyramids was undermined by Nelson's annihilation of a French fleet at the Battle of the Nile (1798) and in 1799 he returned unobtrusively to France. In the coup d'état of 18 Brumaire (9–10 November, 1799) he became first consul; in 1802 he became consul for life and in 1804 had himself proclaimed emperor.

His outstanding domestic achievement was the *Code Napoléon*, but Napoleon achieved immortality with his exploits abroad. In 1802 he negotiated both the Treaty of Lunéville, which marked his defeat of the Austrians at Marengo, and the Treaty of Amiens with the British. Despite the disaster at Trafalgar (1805), which forced him to abandon his plan for the invasion of Britain, his land victories, especially at Austerlitz (1805), Jena (1806), and Friedland (1806), drew almost every continental power within the French orbit.

However, an attempt to break the British by blockade (the Continental System) failed and the protracted Peninsular War (1808–14) drained French resources. In 1812 Napoleon invaded Russia with half a million men, of whom nearly 400 000 died in the brutal Russian winter. In 1813 Europe rose against Napoleon, inflicting a massive defeat at Leipzig that forced his abdication and subsequent exile to Elba. In 1815, however, he returned to France and attempted in the Hundred Days to regain his former greatness. He suffered a decisive defeat at Waterloo and spent the remainder of his life on the island of St Helena. Napoleon's claim to the French Crown was pursued after his death by the son of his second marriage, to Marie Louise of Austria (*see* Napoleon II), and then by his nephew, Emperor Napoleon III.

Napoleon II (1811–32) The title accorded by supporters of the Bonapartist claim to the French throne to the son of Napoleon I and Empress Marie Louise. At birth entitled King of Rome, he was brought up, after his father's fall (1814), in Austria, with the title Duke of Reichstadt.

Napoleon III (1808–73) Emperor of the French (1852–70); nephew of Napoleon I. Napoleon used the prestige of his name to win the presidential election after the Revolution of 1848. By a coup d'état at the end of 1851, he dissolved the legislative assembly and a, a year later, declared himself emperor. His domestic policies fostered industry and transformed Paris. Abroad, his diplomacy embroiled France in the Crimean War (1854–56), in war against the Austrians in Italy (1859), and in a desultory conflict in Mexico (1861–67). Finally, his aggressive stance towards Bismarck helped to cause the Franco-Prussian War, in which the Second Empire was destroyed and Napoleon was driven into exile.

Napoleonic Code. *See* Code Napoléon.

Napoleonic Wars. *See* Revolutionary and Napoleonic Wars.

Narayan, R(asipuram) K(rishnaswamy) (1906–) Indian novelist and short-story writer. Writing in English and setting his stories in imaginary Malgudi, Narayan drew upon his experiences as a teacher for his first novel, *Swami and Friends* (1935). Later works include *The Man-Eater of Malgudi* (1961) and *Under the Banyan Tree* (1985).

Narcissus (botany) A genus of perennial herbaceous plants (about 40 species), native to Eurasia and N Africa and widely planted in gardens and parks. Growing from bulbs, they produce erect flower stalks, usually up to 30 cm high. The daffodils (*N. pseudonarcissus*) have large solitary yellow flowers with trumpet-shaped crowns; the sweet-scented jonquils (*N. jonquilla*) have smaller pale-yellow flowers with small cuplike crowns; and the poet's narcissus (*N. poeticus*) has solitary flowers with white petals surrounding an orange-tipped crown. Family: *Amaryllidaceae*.

Narcissus (Greek mythology) A beautiful youth who was punished for rejecting the love of the nymph Echo by being made to fall in love with his own reflection in a pool. He died and was transformed into a flower.

narcotics Drugs that cause stupor or sleep and relieve pain by depressing activity of the brain. The term is used particularly for opium and its derivatives (opiates), including morphine and codeine. Synthetic narcotics include heroin, methadone, and pethidine.

Narraganset An Algonkian-speaking North American Indian people of Rhode Island. In 1675, after wars with White settlers, they were dispersed.

Narragansett Bay A bay in the USA, in SE Rhode Island state. It contains many islands including Rhode Island, Prudence Island, and Conanicut Island.

narwhal A gregarious Arctic toothed whale, *Monodon monoceros*, up to 5 m long and feeding on fish and squid. Male narwhals have a long straight spirally twisted tusk

that grows to a length of 3 m; its function is unknown. Family: *Monodontidae*.

NASA (National Aeronautics and Space Administration) The US civilian agency, formed in 1958, that is responsible for all nonmilitary aspects of the US space programme. Its major projects have included the manned Apollo moon programme, Skylab, reusable space shuttles, and successful planetary probes.

Naseby, Battle of (14 June, 1645) The battle in the English Civil War that decided Charles I's defeat. The New Model Army under Fairfax and Oliver Cromwell routed Prince Rupert's royalist forces at Naseby, near Market Harborough, Leicestershire.

Nash, John (1752–1835) British architect of the Regency period. Under the patronage of the Prince of Wales (later George IV), Nash redeveloped parts of London, laying out Marylebone Park (later called Regent's Park) as a formal park surrounded by curved terraces of houses with stucco façades. Regent's Street (1825) was designed to link the park with Westminster. Nash's colonnades were removed later but his All Souls, Langham Place, remains. In London Nash also built Carlton House Terrace (1833), laid out Trafalgar Square and St James's Park (1829), and redesigned Buckingham Palace with the triumphal Marble Arch (1828) as its gateway (it was moved to its present position in 1851). In Brighton he redesigned the Royal Pavilion as an oriental fantasy.

PAUL NASH *Detail from* Totes Meer (*Dead Sea; Tate Gallery, London*) *painted 1940–41.*

Nash, Paul (1889–1946) British painter. He became known for his symbolic war landscapes during World Wars I and II, the finest example being *Totes Meer* (1940–41; Tate Gallery). Nash was also a leading member of Unit One (1933), a group of artists dedicated to promoting modern art. His brother **John Nash** (1893–1977) produced fine watercolour landscapes and botanical illustrations.

Nash, Sir Walter (1882–1968) New Zealand statesman; Labour prime minister (1957–60). Born in Britain, he introduced successful anti-Depression policies while minister of finance (1934–49).

Nashville 36 10N 86 50W A city in the USA, the capital of Tennessee. Founded in 1779, it is a centre of country and western music. Population (1986 est): 473 670.

Nasik   20 00N 73 52E A city in India, in Maharashtra. It is a major Hindu pilgrimage centre. Population (1981): 429 000.

Nassau   25 2N 77 25W The capital of the Bahamas, a port on New Providence Island. Built in 1729, it is an important tourist centre. Population (1982 est): 135 000.

Nasser, Gamal Abdel   (1918–70) Egyptian statesman; prime minister (1954–56) and president (1956–70). An army officer, he helped to found the nationalist Free Officers group, which overthrew the monarchy in 1952. He became prime minister and then president of the Republic of Egypt (United Arab Republic from 1958). His nationalization of the Suez Canal led to an unsuccessful Israeli and Anglo-French attack on Egypt (1956).

nasturtium   An annual garden plant of the genus *Tropaeolum* (90 species), also called Indian cress, native to Central and South America. It has orange, yellow, pink, or red flowers. *T. majus* is the most popular ornamental species. Family: *Tropaeolaceae*.

Natal   5 46S 35 15W A port in NE Brazil, near the mouth of the Rio Potengi. The chief exports are sugar, cotton, and carnauba wax. Population (1985): 512 241.

Natal   The smallest province in South Africa. The land rises sharply from the Indian Ocean in the E to the Drakensberg Mountains in the W. Along the coast sugar cane is the major crop and inland pine, eucalyptus, and wattle plantations supply the timber and paper industries. Durban is the main industrial centre and port. Coal is the chief mineral. *History*: the Boers attempted to establish a republic in Natal (1838) but this was annexed by Britain in 1843 and with additions became a province of the Union of South Africa (1910). Area: 86 967 sq km (33 578 sq mi). Population (1985): 2 145 018. Capital: Pietermaritzburg.

Natchez   A Muskogean-speaking North American Indian tribe of the Lower Mississippi. They were cultivators who, like the Creeks, built mound temples and worshipped the sun.

National Aeronautics and Space Administration. *See* NASA.

National Country Party.   *See* National Party.

National Curriculum   The curriculum of subjects taught in state schools in England and Wales. Established by the Education Reform Act 1988, it requires that all children between the ages of 5 and 16 study three core subjects (English, mathematics, and science) and seven foundation subjects (art, design and technology, geography, history, music, physical education, and –from the age of 11–a foreign language). Children are assessed formally in each subject at the ages of 7, 11, 14, and 16.

national debt   The money that a government borrows; together with the revenue from taxation it makes up the government's income. In the UK, the funded debt consists of money that the government does not have to repay on a fixed date; it makes up about 10% of the national debt. The unfunded debt consists of the floating debt (e.g. treasury bills), gilt-edged securities, and such small savings as Savings Bonds. Money borrowed as unfunded debt has to be repaid on a fixed date.

National Front   An extreme right-wing political party in the UK, formed in 1966. One of its central platforms is the repatriation of all immigrant groups.

National Gallery   An art gallery in Trafalgar Square (London), containing the largest collection of paintings in the UK. Founded for the nation in 1824, it was housed in Pall Mall until William Wilkins (1778–1839) built the present premises (1832–38). The National Gallery has aimed to collect paintings of every leading school and period (except the modern) in Europe.

National Health Service   (NHS) A comprehensive medical service in the UK, financed primarily by taxation. The National Health Service Act (1946), implemented in 1948, covered all aspects of health care except that of the school child and the worker. Complaints during the late 1950s and 1960s that the structure and policies of the NHS did not facilitate medical advance led to substantial reorganization of the Service in 1974 and again in 1982. In England and Wales overall responsibility lies with the minister for health. Administration is based on a system of Regional Health Authorities (RHAs) and District Health Authorities (DHAs). In Scotland and Northern Ireland responsibility lies with the appropriate secretary of state and administration with Area Health Boards.

National Insurance   A UK insurance scheme providing funds to pay for the National Health Service and social security benefits. Contributions from employees, employers, the self-employed, and the government are paid into the National Insurance Fund, from which the benefits (including unemployment, sickness, maternity, and child benefits as well as retirement pensions) are paid. Under the State Earnings-Related Pension Scheme (SERPS) of 1978, contributions to retirement pensions are related to earnings, and pensions are index-linked. Persons may contract out of SERPS and contribute to approved occupational or personal pension schemes.

nationalization   The policy of taking into public ownership industries that were formerly privately owned. Nationalization is the aim of socialism. In the UK after World War II, Attlee's Labour government (1945–51) nationalized those industries in which competition appeared wasteful and those war-damaged enterprises needing huge injections of capital (e.g. coal, railways). Several industries were returned to the private sector in the 1980s by the Conservatives.

National Party, Australian   An Australian political party, founded in 1919 as the Country Party, to represent the interests of farmers. It has held office only in coalition with the Liberal Party. It was formerly the National Country Party.

National Portrait Gallery   An art gallery in London founded in 1856 to house portraits that are authentic likenesses of famous personalities in British history. The main gallery is in St Martin's Place, adjacent to the National Gallery, and there are annexes in Carlton House Terrace and at Montacute House, Somerset.

National Socialist German Workers' Party.   *See* Nazi Party.

National Society for the Prevention of Cruelty to Children   (NSPCC) A British charity, incorporated in 1884, that investigates reports of cruelty to or neglect of children. It handles 30 000 cases a year.

National Theatre Company.   *See* Royal National Theatre Company.

National Trust   An independent charity in the UK, founded in 1895, that acquires and preserves country houses, castles, gardens, and places of interest or natural beauty. Properties bequeathed to the Trust are exempt from capital-transfer tax but must be self-supporting or accompanied by an endowment.

NATO. *See* North Atlantic Treaty Organization.

NATTERJACK *Now an endangered species.*

natterjack A short-legged European toad, *Bufo calamita*. About 7 cm long when fully grown, the natterjack has a yellow stripe down its back. If alarmed, it raises its inflated body on its hind legs to appear larger to the enemy.

natural gas A naturally occurring mixture of gaseous hydrocarbons consisting mainly of methane with smaller amounts of heavier hydrocarbons. It is obtained from underground reservoirs, often associated with oil deposits. Like oil it originates in the bacterial decomposition of animal matter. It also contains nonhydrocarbon impurities, the most important being helium, which is extracted commercially.

Natural History Museum. *See* British Museum.

Naturalism A literary and artistic movement of the late 19th century characterized by the use of realistic techniques to express the philosophical belief that all phenomena can be explained by natural or material causes. It was influenced by the biological theories of Darwin, the philosophy of Comte, and the deterministic theories of the historian Hippolyte Taine (1828–93). Its literary manifesto was *Le Roman expérimentale* (1880) by Zola.

natural selection. *See* Darwinism.

Nauru, Republic of (*or* Naoero; former name: Pleasant Island) A small country in the central Pacific Ocean, NE of Australia comprising a coral island. The small population consists mainly of Naurians and other Pacific islanders. *Economy*: based entirely on the mining of phosphates, the only export. *History*: discovered by the British in 1798, it was under British mandate from 1920 to 1947, when it came under the joint trusteeship of Australia, New Zealand, and the UK. In 1968 it became an independent republic and a special member of the British Commonwealth. President: Hammer DeRoburt (1922–   ). Official language: English. Official currency: Australian dollar. Area: 21 sq km (8 sq mi). Population (1987 est): 8100. Capital and main port: Yaren.

nautical mile. *See* mile.

nautilus One of several cephalopod molluscs with external shells. The pearly nautiluses (genus *Nautilus*; 3 species) live near the bottom of the Pacific and Indian Oceans. Up to 20 cm across, they have 60–90 tentacles surrounding a horny beak and live in the outermost chamber of their flat coiled shells. The others serve as buoyancy chambers. The paper nautilus (*Argonauta argo*) is found in the Atlantic and Pacific Oceans. The female, 20 cm long, secretes from one of its tentacles a papery boat-shaped shell in which the eggs develop. The male is much smaller (about 2 cm long).

Navajo A North American Indian Athabascan-speaking people of New Mexico, Arizona, and Utah. Like their relatives, the Apache, they migrated from the far north, probably during the 17th century. They are farmers and herders and now the most numerous North American Indian tribe.

Navarino, Battle of (20 October, 1827) A naval battle during the War of Greek Independence. French, Russian, and British ships destroyed an Ottoman-Egyptian fleet in the Bay of Navarinou in the Peloponnese. This was the last fleet action fought wholly under sail.

Navarre A former kingdom in N Spain, corresponding to the present-day Spanish province of Navarre and part of the French department of Basses-Pyrénées. S Navarre was conquered by Ferdinand the Catholic of Aragon in 1512 and united with Castile in 1515. French Navarre passed to the French Crown in 1589.

Navigation Acts A series of Acts originally to foster English shipping (1382, 1485, 1540) but subsequently to protect England's colonial trade, especially against its Dutch rivals. The Acts were repealed in 1849.

Navratilova, Martina (1956–   ) Czech-born tennis player who defected to the USA in 1975. She was Wimbledon singles champion 1978–79, 1982–87, and doubles champion 1976, 1979, 1981–86. She also holds a record of 74 consecutive wins.

Náxos A Greek island in the S Aegean Sea, the largest in the Cyclades. Náxos is traditionally the place where Theseus abandoned Ariadne. Area: 438 sq km (169 sq mi). Population (1981): 14 037. Chief town: Náxos.

Nazareth 32 41N 35 16E A town in N Israel, between Haifa and the Sea of Galilee. The city's many churches commemorate its associations with the early life of Jesus Christ. Population (1982 est): 44 900.

Nazi Party (*N*ationalsoz*i*alistische Deutsche Arbeiterpartei) The National Socialist German Workers' Party, founded in 1919 as the German Workers' Party and led from 1921 until 1945 by Adolf Hitler. *See also* fascism.

N'djamena (name until 1973: Fort Lamy) The capital of Chad, a port in the SW. It was founded by the French in 1900. Population (1985): 511 700.

Ndola 13 00S 28 39E A city in N Zambia, near the Zaïre border. It is an important commercial centre for the Copperbelt. Population (1980 est): 323 000.

Neagh, Lough A lake in Northern Ireland, divided between Co Antrim, Co Armagh, and Co Tyrone. It is the largest lake in the British Isles. Area: 388 sq km (150 sq mi).

Neanderthal man An extinct hominid race that inhabited Europe and the adjacent areas of Africa and Asia between about 115 000 and 40 000 years ago. Characterized by heavy brow ridges, receding forehead, heavy protruding jaw, and robust bone structure, Neanderthal man nonetheless had a large cranial capacity and upright posture. They were cave-dwelling hunters; their status as a distinct species (*Homo neanderthalensis*) is now questioned (*see* Homo).

Nebraska   A state in the N central USA, lying W of the Missouri River. Part of the Central Lowlands cover the eastern third of the state, with the higher Great Plains in the W. Traditionally an agricultural state, it is still a leading producer of cattle, corn, and wheat. Most of the population is situated in the industrial E. *History*: explored by the French and Spanish, it formed part of the Louisiana Purchase (1803). It became a state in 1867. Area: 200 018 sq km (77 227 sq mi). Population (1985 est): 1 605 574. Capital: Lincoln.

Nebuchadnezzar II   (*or* Nebuchadrezzar; c. 630–562 BC) King of Babylon (605–562). Nebuchadnezzar extended Babylonian power in Elam, N Syria, and S Asia Minor. He captured Jerusalem in 597 and again in 586, when he destroyed the city and forced the Jews into exile.

NEBULA   *"Horsehead" nebula in Orion.*

nebula   A cloud of interstellar gas and dust that becomes visible for one of three reasons. In an **emission nebula** the gas is ionized by ultraviolet radiation and light (predominantly red and green) is emitted. In a **reflection nebula** light from a nearby star is reflected in all directions by dust in the cloud, thus illuminating the cloud. The dust in a **dark nebula** reduces the amount of light passing through it (by absorption and scattering) and a dark region is seen against a brighter background.

nectar   A sugary solution produced by glandular structures (nectaries) in animal-pollinated flowers. Nectar attracts insects, birds, or bats to the flower and encourages pollination as the animal collects nectar from different sources.

nectarine.   *See* peach.

needlefish   A carnivorous fish, also called garfish, belonging to the family *Belonidae* (about 60 species), that occurs in tropical and warm-temperate seas. It has a slender silvery-blue or green body, up to 1.2 m long, with elongated jaws and numerous sharp teeth. Species include the European garfish (*Belone belone*). Order: *Atheriniformes.*

Needles, the   50 39N 1 34W A group of chalk rocks in S England, off the W coast of the Isle of Wight. A lighthouse stands on the most westerly rock.

Nefertiti   (died c. 1346 BC) The cousin and chief wife of Akhenaton (1379–1362 BC) of Egypt. Her portrait bust is perhaps the best-known work of Egyptian art.

Negev   A desert in S Israel. In recent years large areas have been irrigated by pipeline from the River Jordan. Area: about 12 000 sq km (4632 sq mi).

Negro, Río   1. (Portuguese name: Rio Negro) A river in NE South America. Rising in E Colombia as the Guainía, it joins the River Amazon about 16 km (10 mi) below Manaus. Length: about 2250 km (1400 mi). 2. A river in S Argentina, rising in the Andes and flowing generally SE to the Atlantic Ocean. Length: 1014 km (630 mi).

Negros   A volcanic island in the central Philippines. The chief industry is sugar production. Area: 13 670 sq km (5278 sq mi). Population (1980): 2 749 700. Chief town: Bacolod.

Nehru, Jawaharlal   (1889–1964) Indian statesman; the first prime minister of independent India (1947–64). He was elected president of the Indian National Congress in 1929 in succession to his father Motilal Nehru (1861–1931). Between 1921 and 1945 he served nine prison sentences for participating in the movement of noncooperation against the British. After World War II he helped negotiate independent India. As premier, he carried through many social reforms and maintained a policy of nonalignment with foreign powers. His daughter was Indira Gandhi.

Neisse, River   1. (*or* Glatzer Neisse; Polish name: Nysa) A river in SW Poland, flowing NE to the River Oder. Length: 244 km (159 mi). 2. (*or* Lusatian Neisse) A river rising in NW Czechoslovakia and flowing mainly N to the River Oder in Poland. Length: 225 km (140 mi).

nekton   An ecological division of aquatic animals that includes all those swimming actively in the open waters of a sea or lake (*compare* plankton). The nekton includes fishes, squids, turtles, seals, and whales.

Nelson   41 18S 173 17E A port and resort in New Zealand, in N South Island. Population (1987 est): 44 900.

Nelson, Horatio, Viscount   (1758–1805) British admiral. At the outbreak of the French Revolutionary Wars he was given command of the *Agamemnon* in the

NELSON   *Detail of a painting (c. 1800) by William Beechey.*

Mediterranean. In 1794, at Calvi, he lost the sight in his right eye but went on to play an important part in the victory off Cape St Vincent (1797), for which he was knighted. Shortly afterwards he lost his right arm in action but in 1798 he destroyed France's naval power in the Mediterranean by his great victory in the battle of the Nile. Nelson spent the following year in Naples, where, although married, he fell in love with Emma, Lady Hamilton. Returning to England in 1800, Nelson, now Baron Nelson of the Nile, was given command in the Baltic and was responsible for the victory at Copenhagen (1801); he was created a viscount on his return. In 1803 he became commander in the Mediterranean. He blockaded Toulon for 18 months but in 1805 the French escaped; the ensuing chase culminated in the battle of Trafalgar (1805). Nelson directed this British triumph from aboard the *Victory* but was himself mortally wounded.

Neman, River (*or* R. Nyeman)   A river in the W Soviet Union. It flows mainly NW to the Baltic Sea. Length: 937 km (582 mi).

nematode   A spindle-shaped colourless worm, also called roundworm, belonging to the phylum *Nematoda* (over 10 000 species). Nematodes live almost everywhere in soil, fresh water, and the sea. Some are parasites of plants or animals; others feed on dead organic matter. *See also* eelworm; filaria; guinea worm; hookworm; pinworm.

Nemertina.   *See* ribbonworm.

Nemesia   A genus of annual herbs native to South Africa. They are up to 30 cm tall, with showy white, yellow, red, pink, or purple two-lipped flowers. Family: *Scrophulariaceae.*

Nemesis   In Greek mythology, a goddess personifying the gods' anger at and punishment of human arrogance or hubris.

Nennius   (9th century AD) Welsh antiquary. He is traditionally held to be the author of *Historia Britonum*, a summary of the early history of Britain.

neoclassicism   **1.** In art and architecture, a style dominant in Europe from the late 18th to mid-19th centuries. Although essentially a revival of classical art and architecture, it was distinguished from similar revivals by its new scientific approach to the recreation of the past. This was largely stimulated by archaeological discoveries at Pompeii, Herculaneum, and elsewhere. Key figures in the early development of neoclassicism were the art historian Johann Winckelmann (1717–68) and Giambattista Piranesi (1720–78). Early neoclassical painters included Jacques Louis David (1748–1825) and Ingres. Other leading neoclassicists were the sculptors Antonio Canova (1757–1822) and Bertel Thorvaldsen (1768–1844) and the architects Robert Adam and Jacques Soufflot (1713–80). *See also* Empire style. **2.** A style of composition originating in the 1920s.

neodymium (Nd)   A lanthanide element, occurring in the mineral monazite. It is used with lanthanum in misch metal and, as the oxide (Nd_2O_3), together with praseodymium, to produce special dark glasses used in welding goggles. At no 60; at wt 144.24; mp 1021°C; bp 3068°C.

Neolithic   The final division of the Stone Age. It is characterized by the development of the earliest settled agricultural communities and increasing domestication of animals (*see* Jericho). Although man still used only stone tools and weapons, he evolved improved techniques of grinding stone and the invention of pottery facilitated food storage and preparation.

neon (Ne)   A noble gas present in very small amounts in the earth's atmosphere, discovered in 1898 by Ramsay and M. W. Travers (1872–1961) by fractional distillation of liquid air. It is commonly used in advertising signs and voltage indicator lamps. At no 10; at wt 20.179; mp −248.67°C; bp −246.048°C.

Neoplatonism   The philosophy, formulated principally by Plotinus that emphasizes an eternal world of order, goodness, and beauty, of which material existence is a weak and unsatisfactory copy. The chief influences were Plato's *Symposium* and the *Phaedo.*

neoteny   The condition in which larval characteristics persist in an animal when it reaches sexual maturity. The axolotl is a neotenous salamander that rarely assumes the typical adult form under natural conditions. Neotony is also known in certain primitive marine chordates.

Nepal, Kingdom of   A landlocked country in the Himalayas, between China (Tibet) and India. Most of the country consists of a series of mountain ranges, with some of the world's highest peaks, including Mount Everest, along its northern border. Its predominantly Hindu population is of Mongoloid stock, the Gurkhas having been the dominant group since 1769. *Economy*: chiefly agricultural, the main crops are rice, maize, millet, and wheat. Mineral resources are sparse. Tourism is an important source of revenue. *History*: the independent principalities that comprised the region in the middle ages were conquered by the Gurkhas in the 18th century and Nepal was subsequently ruled by the Shah family and then by the Rana, who continue to reign. Head of state: King Birendra Bir Bikram Shah Dev. Prime minister: Marich Man Singh Shrestha. Official language: Nepali. Official currency: Nepalese rupee of 100 paisa. Area: 141 400 sq km (54 600 sq mi). Population (1987 est): 17 567 000. Capital: Kathmandu.

nephritis (*or* Bright's disease)   Inflammation of the kidneys. It may result from infection, as in pyelitis, or from a disorder of the body's system that affects the kidneys (called glomerulonephritis), which causes protein, cells, and blood to appear in the urine and swelling of the body tissues (*see* oedema).

Neptune (astronomy)   The most distant giant planet, orbiting the sun every 165 years at a mean distance of 4497 million km. It is smaller (48 600 km in diameter) and more massive (17.2 earth masses) than Uranus, but is thought to be almost identical to it in structure. It has eight satellites. Discovered in 1846 by J. G. Galle, it was visited by Voyager 2 in 1989.

Neptune (mythology)   The principal Roman sea god, identified with the Greek Poseidon. He is usually portrayed holding a trident and riding a dolphin.

neptunium (Np)   The first synthetic transuranic element, produced in 1940 at Berkeley, USA, by bombarding uranium with neutrons. It is available in small quantities in nuclear reactors and forms halides (for example NpF_3, $NpCl_4$) and oxides (for example NpO_2). At no 93; at wt 237.0482; mp 640°C; bp 3902°C.

Neri, St Philip   (1515–95) Italian mystic, who founded the Congregation of the Oratory. Over the nave of the Church of San Girolamo he built an oratory to hold religious meetings and concerts of sacred music, from which both the name of Neri's order and the word *oratorio* derive. Feast day: 26 May.

NEPTUNE   *The mythological sea god.*

Nero (Claudius Caesar) (37–68 AD) Roman emperor (54–68), notorious for his cruelty. His early reign was dominated by his mother Agrippina the Younger, Seneca, and Sextus Afranius Burrus but by 62 Nero had thrown off these influences: Agrippina was murdered (59), Burrus died, perhaps by poison (62), and Seneca retired (62). Also in 62, he murdered his wife Octavia in order to marry Poppaea, who herself died in 65 after being kicked by her husband. A conspiracy to assassinate him, after which Seneca was forced to kill himself, failed in 65. In 68, however, revolts in Gaul, Spain, and Africa and the mutiny of his palace guard precipitated his suicide.

nerve. *See* neurone.

nerve gases War gases that inhibit the transmission of impulses from nerve to nerve or muscle. Death results from paralysis of the diaphragm leading to asphyxiation. Most nerve gases are derivatives of phosphoric acid. *See* chemical warfare.

Nervi, Pier Luigi (1891–1979) Italian engineer and architect, famous for his inventive use of reinforced concrete. In 1949 he designed the great exhibition hall in Turin and in 1953 was one of the architects of the UNESCO building in Paris.

nervous system The network of nervous tissue in the body. This comprises the central nervous system (CNS), i.e. the brain and spinal cord, and the peripheral nervous system. The latter includes the cranial and spinal nerves with their ganglia and the autonomic nervous system (ANS). The ANS controls unconscious body functions, such as digestion and heartbeat, and is coordinated by the hypothalamus. The nervous system is chiefly responsible for communication both within the body and between the body and its surroundings. Incoming information passes along sensory neurones to the brain, where it is analysed and compared with memory; nerve impulses then leave the central nervous system along motor nerves.

Ness, Loch A deep lake in N Scotland, in the Highland Region in the Great Glen. The sight of a monster (the **Loch Ness monster**) has frequently been reported. Length: 36 km (22 mi). Depth: 229 m (754 ft).

netball A seven-a-side court game adapted from basketball. The court is 100 × 50 ft (30.5 × 15.25 m), divided into three equal zones. The goal is a net mounted 10 ft (3.05 m) above the ground. The game is played by throwing the ball; players may not run with it.

Netherlandic A subgroup of the Western Germanic languages. It is spoken in Holland and Belgium, where it is called Dutch and Flemish respectively. It is the parent language of Afrikaans.

Netherlands, Kingdom of A country in NW Europe, on the North Sea. It is almost entirely flat except for some low hills in the SE, and considerable areas of land have been reclaimed from the sea. *Economy*: highly developed industries include oil and gas, chemicals, electronics, printing, metals, and food processing. Agriculture is highly mechanized and market gardening is important. *History*: until 1581 the Netherlands formed with present-day Belgium and Luxembourg the region often referred to as the Low Countries. It was under Roman occupation from the 1st century BC to the 4th century AD. It was then overrun by German tribes. After the partition of the Frankish empire in 843 the region was called Lotharingia. The following centuries saw the rise of powerful principalities, notably the bishopric of Utrecht and the counties of Holland and Guelders, which ultimately came under the influence of Burgundy and Spain. In 1581, during the Revolt of the Netherlands, the seven northern provinces—Holland, Zeeland, Utrecht, Overijssel, Gröningen, Drenthe, and Friesland—proclaimed their independence as the United Provinces of the Netherlands under the leadership of William the Silent. War with Spain continued intermittently until, at the conclusion of the Thirty Years' War, Spain recognized the independence of the Dutch Republic in the Peace of Westphalia (1648). In the 17th century the Netherlands reached a peak of prosperity and international prestige, forming a considerable overseas empire. In 1795, however, it fell to Revolutionary France and in 1806 Napoleon made his brother Louis Bonaparte King of Holland. Following Napoleon's defeat the former Dutch Republic was reunited with the southern provinces to form the Kingdom of the Netherlands (1814). In 1830 the S revolted against the union, forming Belgium (1831), and in 1867 Luxembourg became an independent state. The Netherlands remained neutral in World War I but in World War II was occupied by Germany (1940–45). In 1948 the Netherlands joined with Belgium and Luxembourg to form the Benelux economic union; it was a founder member of the EC. The immediate postwar period was dominated by the Dutch colony of Indonesia's fight for independence. In 1980 Queen Juliana abdicated and was succeeded as head of state by her daughter Princess Beatrix. Prime minister: Ruud Lubbers (1939–   ). Official language: Dutch. Official currency: guilder of 100 cents. Area: 41 160 sq km (15 892 sq mi). Population (1987 est): 14 615 125. Capitals: Amsterdam (legal and administrative); The Hague (seat of government). Main port: Rotterdam.

Netherlands Antilles (Dutch name: Nederlandse Antillen) Two groups of West Indian islands in the Lesser Antilles, in the Caribbean Sea some 800 km (497 mi) apart. The S group lies off N Venezuela and consists of Curaçao, Aruba, and Bonaire; the N group (geographically part of the Leeward Islands) consists of St Eustatius, Saba, and the S part of St Martin. Under Dutch control since the 17th century, the islands became self-governing in 1954. The economy is based chiefly on oil refining. Area: 996 sq km (390 sq mi). Population (1987): 176 000. Capital: Willemstad.

nettle An annual or perennial herb of the genus *Urtica* (about 30 species), found in temperate regions worldwide. Up to 1.5 m in height, it may have stinging hairs. Family: *Urticaceae*. Dead nettles are annual or perennial herbs of the genus *Lamium* (about 40 species), occurring in Europe, temperate Asia, and N Africa. Family: *Labiatae*.

nettle rash. *See* urticaria.

Neuchâtel (German name: Neuenburg) 47 00N 6 56E A city in W Switzerland, on Lake Neuchâtel. Industries include watchmaking and chocolate production. Population (1984 est): 31 800.

Neumann, John von (1903–57) US mathematician, born in Hungary. He invented game theory and set quantum theory upon a rigorous mathematical basis.

neurohormone A chemical (*see* hormone) that is secreted by nerve cells and modifies the function of other organs in the body. The hypothalamus, for example, releases several hormones that cause the pituitary gland to secrete its own hormones, the kidney to retain water in the body, and the breast to produce milk.

neurology The study of the structure (neuroanatomy), function (neurophysiology), and diseases (neuropathology) of the nervous system. A neurologist specializes in the diagnosis and treatment of nervous diseases.

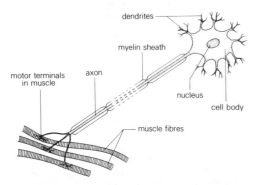

NEURONE *When a nerve impulse transmitted down the axon of a neurone reaches the motor terminals in muscle fibres, the muscle is stimulated to contract.*

neurone (*or* nerve cell) The functioning unit of the nervous system. A neurone consists of a cell body, containing the nucleus; small irregular branching processes called dendrites; and a single long nerve fibre, or axon, which may be ensheathed by layers of fatty material (myelin) and either makes contact with other neurones at synapses or ends at muscle fibres or gland cells. When a neurone is stimulated from outside or by another neurone, a nerve impulse is transmitted electrochemically down the axon. Bundles of nerve fibres are bound together to form **nerves**, which transmit impulses from sense organs to the brain or spinal cord (sensory nerves) or outwards from the central nervous system to a muscle or gland (motor nerves).

Neuroptera An order of slender carnivorous insects (4500 species) with long antennae and two similar pairs of net-veined wings. The order includes the alderflies,

snakeflies, and dobsonflies (suborder *Megaloptera*) and the lacewings and antlions (suborder *Plannipennia*).

neurosis A mental illness in which insight is retained but there is a disordered way of behaving or thinking that causes suffering to the patient (*compare* psychosis). The symptoms include a pathologically severe emotional state, as in anxiety or depression; distressing behaviour and thoughts, as in phobias or obsessions; and physical complaints, as in hysteria. A neurosis with psychological symptoms is known as a **psychoneurosis**. Treatment can include tranquillizers, psychotherapy, and behaviour therapy.

neutrinos A group of three elementary particles and their antiparticles. They are classified as leptons, have no charge, and are probably massless. One type of neutrino is associated with the electron, one with the muon, and one with the tau particle.

neutron An elementary particle that is a constituent of all atomic nuclei except hydrogen–1. It has no electric charge and its mass is slightly greater than that of the proton. Inside the nucleus the neutron is stable but when free it decays, with a mean life of 12 minutes, by the weak interaction to a proton, an electron, and an antineutrino (*see* beta decay). The neutron was discovered by Chadwick in 1932. *See also* particle physics.

neutron bomb. *See* nuclear weapons.

neutron star A star that has undergone gravitational collapse to the extent that most of the protons and electrons making up its constituent atoms have coalesced into neutrons. The density is extremely high (about 10^{17} kg m^{-3}) and the pressure exerted by the densely packed neutrons can support the star against further contraction. Neutron stars are thought to form when the mass of the stellar core remaining after a supernova exceeds about 1.4 times the sun's mass. *See also* pulsar.

Nevada One of the mountain states in the W USA. Lying almost wholly within the Great Basin, most of the state consists of a vast plateau with several mountain ranges. Most of its population and manufacturing industry is located in the two main cities of Las Vegas and Reno. Tourism is by far the most important industry. *History*: ceded by Mexico to the USA in 1848, it became a state (1864) during a mining boom (1860–80). Area: 286 297 sq km (110 540 sq mi). Population (1986 est): 1 007 850. Capital: Carson City.

Nevis. *See* Kitts-Nevis.

Newark 40 44N 74 11W A city in the USA, in New Jersey on Newark Bay. Founded in 1666, it attracted several inventors, whose developments included patent leather (1818), malleable cast iron (1826), the first photographic film (1888), and electrical measuring instruments (1888). Population (1986): 316 300.

New Britain A volcanic island in the SW Pacific Ocean, in Papua New Guinea, the largest of the Bismarck Archipelago. Copra and some minerals are exported. Area: 36 520 sq km (14 100 sq mi). Population (1987 est): 268 400. Chief town: Rabaul.

New Brunswick A province of E Canada, on the Gulf of St Lawrence. Heavily forested, it consists of rugged uplands with fertile river valleys. There is some mixed farming and fishing is important along the Bay of Fundy. Lead, zinc, and some copper are mined at Bathurst. *History*: settlement by French peasants ended shortly after Britain's control of the coastal areas was confirmed in 1713. Colonization from Britain and New England followed, and New Brunswick became a separate colony (1784). It was a founding member of the Dominion of Canada (1867). Area: 72 092 sq km (27 835 sq mi). Population (1986): 709 442; approximately 30% are French speaking. Capital: Fredericton.

New Caledonia (French name: Nouvelle Calédonie) A French island in the SW Pacific Ocean. Together with its dependencies (the Isle of Pines, the Loyalty Islands, and others) it forms a French overseas territory. The main industries are nickel mining and processing and meat preserving. Violence in the 1980s led to a referendum (1988) on the issue of independence; the result favoured reconsideration of New Caledonia's status in 1998. Area: 19 103 sq km (7374 sq mi), including dependencies. Population (1987): 153 500. Capital: Nouméa.

Newcastle 32 55S 151 46E A city in Australia, in New South Wales. Iron and steel industries are important. In 1989 it was hit by Australia's first fatal earthquake, killing 12 people. Population (1985): 300 000.

Newcastle, Thomas Pelham-Holles, 1st Duke of (1693–1768) British statesman; Whig prime minister (1754–56, 1757–62). He resigned as prime minister in 1756 because of early reverses in the Seven Years' War but returned in 1757 with foreign affairs in the hands of Pitt the Elder. His brother **Henry Pelham** (1696–1754) was prime minister (1743–54).

Newcastle upon Tyne 54 59N 1 35W A city in NE England, on the River Tyne. It is the principal port and commercial and cultural centre of NE England. *History*: founded as a Roman settlement (Pons Aelius), Newcastle was the site of George Stephenson's iron works, established in 1823. Population (1981): 192 454.

NEWCOMEN *An engraving (1717) of his engine.*

Newcomen, Thomas (1663–1729) English blacksmith, who in 1712 constructed an early steam engine. It was based on Thomas Savery's engine and was widely used for pumping water out of mines.

New Deal (1933–41) Legislation introduced by the US president, F. D. Roosevelt, to ameliorate the effects of the Depression and to initiate social and economic reforms. Emergency legislation enabled sound banks to reopen and regulated credit, currency, and foreign exchange; the gold standard was abandoned and the dollar devalued. Loans on crops, credit, and refinancing of debts and mortgages supported farmers, while the un-

employed were helped by direct relief and civil-works programmes.

New England An area in the extreme NE USA, bordering on the Atlantic Ocean. It consists of the states of Maine, New Hampshire, Vermont, Massachusetts, Rhode Island, and Connecticut. Explored and named by Capt John Smith (1614), it was first settled by the Puritans (1620). Area: about 164 000 sq km (63 300 sq mi).

New England A district of Australia, in New South Wales. Predominantly agricultural, it occupies the N Tableland between the Moonbi Range and the Queensland border.

New Forest A woodland area in S England, in Hampshire. Originally an ancient hunting forest, it is a popular tourist area, noted for its breed of small ponies. Area: 336 sq km (130 sq mi).

Newfoundland A province of E Canada, consisting of the sparsely populated Coast of Labrador on the Atlantic Ocean and the triangular island of Newfoundland. Pulp and paper has replaced the declining fisheries as the major industry. *History*: discovered by John Cabot (1497), Newfoundland won representative government (1832) and developed steadily until World War I, when it became a dominion. In 1927 it won possession of Labrador's interior and in 1949 became the newest Canadian province. Area: 370 485 sq km (143 044 sq mi). Population (1986): 568 349. Capital: St John's.

Newfoundland dog A breed of working dog originating in Newfoundland. The heavy dense black, brown, or black-and-white coat enables them to withstand icy water. Height: 71 cm (dogs); 66 cm (bitches).

New France The French colonies in E Canada. From about 1600 French trading posts extended along the St Lawrence River to the Great Lakes. France lost these colonies to Britain in the Seven Years' War (1756–63).

New Guinea An island in the SW Pacific Ocean, separated from Australia by the Torres Strait. It consists of the Indonesian province of West Irian in the W and Papua New Guinea in the E. Mountainous and forested, it is largely undeveloped and is famed for its unique species of butterflies and birds. Its linguistically diverse tribal population consists of Melanesian, Negrito, and Papuan ethnic groups. *History*: known to Europeans from 1511, the island was colonized by the Dutch in the 18th century. The W part became part of Indonesia in 1963. The SE was colonized by Britain and the NE by Germany in the late 19th century. Area: 775 213 sq km (299 310 sq mi).

New Hampshire A state in the NE USA, in New England. It is generally hilly, with many lakes. Manufacturing is the principal source of employment. Tourism is the other major industry. *History*: one of the 13 original colonies, it was first settled by English colonists about 1627, becoming a royal province in 1679. One of the first states to declare its independence, it became a state in 1788. Area: 24 097 sq km (9304 sq mi). Population (1985 est): 998 000. Capital: Concord.

New Haven 41 18N 72 55W A city and seaport in the USA, in Connecticut on Long Island Sound. It is best known as the site of Yale University (1701). Population (1980): 126 109.

New Hebrides. *See* Vanuatu Republic.

New Jersey A state in the NE USA, on the mid-Atlantic coast. The Kittatinny Mountains extend across the NW corner of the state, SE of which lies a belt of lowland containing most of New Jersey's major cities. One of the most highly urbanized and densely populated states, it is a major industrial centre. Agriculture is also well developed. Its beaches, forests, and mountain regions form the basis of a thriving tourist industry. *History*: one of the original 13 colonies, it was first settled by the Dutch in the 1620s, coming under British control in 1664. It became a state in 1787. Area: 20 295 sq km (7836 sq mi). Population (1985 est): 7 562 000. Capital: Trenton.

Newman, John Henry, Cardinal (1801–90) British churchman and a leader of the Oxford Movement, until his conversion to Roman Catholicism (1845). He wrote many tracts, including the controversial *Tract 90*, which argued that the Thirty-Nine Articles were not incompatible with Roman Catholicism. In Rome (1846) he joined the Oratorians and later established his own Oratorian congregation at Edgbaston. He was made a cardinal in 1879.

Newman, Paul (1925–) US film actor and political activist. He has frequently played the roles of cynical and witty heroes, notably in *Hud* (1963), *Butch Cassidy and the Sundance Kid* (1969), and *The Sting* (1973); among his other films are *Slap Shot* (1977), *The Verdict* (1982), and *The Color of Money* (1986).

Newmarket 52 15N 0 25E A market town in E England, in Suffolk. It is the centre of British horse racing. Population (1981): 16 235.

new maths A method of teaching mathematics and presenting mathematical relationships that incorporate some of the concepts of formal logic. Set theory and vectors, for example, are sometimes taught at an early stage in school mathematics in the UK and form part of the logical basis of further learning.

New Mexico One of the mountain states in the SW USA. There are three main physical regions: a flat tableland in the E, a central mountainous region cut N–S by the Valley of the Rio Grande, and a region of mountains and plains in the W. Its oil and natural-gas deposits are important. Problems of irrigation are mitigated by the Rio Grande and the Pecos rivers. Tourism is an important source of revenue. *History*: a Spanish possession from the 16th century, it was under Mexican rule when it was annexed by the USA in 1848. Following a period of Indian wars and land disputes, it became a state (1912). Area: 315 113 sq km (121 666 sq mi). Population (1987 est): 1 500 000. Capital: Santa Fe.

New Model Army The parliamentary army formed in 1645 during the English Civil War. Organized by Sir Thomas Fairfax (1612–71), its core comprised the forces of the Eastern Association led by Oliver Cromwell. It wielded increasing political power after its success at Naseby (1645). In 1650 Cromwell became its commander in chief.

New Netherland A Dutch colony in North America. Established in 1613, the colony was centred on New Amsterdam, which after its conquest by the English (1664) was renamed New York.

New Orleans 30 00N 90 03W A city and major port in the USA, in Louisiana. It is one of the leading commercial and industrial centres of the South. The Vieux Carré (French Quarter) has many historic buildings. The famous Mardi Gras festival is held here annually. *History*: founded in 1718, New Orleans became the capital of the French colonial region of Louisiana before passing to Spain in 1763. It returned briefly to France in 1803

but passed to the USA in the same year. Jazz had its origins among the Black musicians of New Orleans during the late 19th century. Population (1986): 554 500.

New Plymouth 39 03S 174 04E A port in New Zealand, in W North Island. New Zealand's chief natural gas field is nearby, at Kapuni. Population (1987): 47 400.

Newport 50 42N 1 18W A market town and port in S England, the chief town of the Isle of Wight. Nearby are Carisbrooke Castle and Parkhurst Prison. Population (1981): 23 570.

Newport (Welsh name: Casnewydd ar Wysg) 51 35N 3 00W A port in South Wales, the administrative centre of Gwent. Its parish church became the cathedral for the Monmouth diocese in 1921. Population (1983): 130 200.

New Siberian Islands (Russian name: Novosïbirskiye Ostrova) A Soviet archipelago off the N coast, between the Laptev Sea and the East Siberian Sea. There is no permanent population. Total area: 35 100 sq km (13 549 sq mi), including the Lyakhov Islands.

New South Wales A state of SE Australia, bordering on the Pacific Ocean. It consists of extensive plains in the W, separated from the narrow coastal belt by the Great Dividing Range with the Snowy Mountains and part of the Australian Alps in the SE. Agricultural products include beef cattle, cereals, fruit and vegetables, wool, and dairy produce. Fishing and forestry are also important. Minerals extracted include coal, silver, lead, zinc, and copper. Over half the population live in Sydney, where most of the industries are located. Area: 801 428 sq km (309 433 sq mi). Population (1986): 5 401 881. Capital: Sydney.

newt A salamander belonging to a family (*Salamandridae*) occurring in Europe, Asia, and North America. The European smooth newt (*Triturus vulgaris*) is greenish brown with dark-brown spots and has a black-spotted orange belly. It grows to a length of 10 cm (including a 5 cm tail). Newts live mainly on land, hibernating under stones in winter and returning to water to breed in spring. The European fire salamander (*Salamandra salamandra*) bears live young and produces a poisonous skin secretion when harmed.

New Testament The 27 books that constitute the second major division of the Christian Bible. Written in Greek, the New Testament has four divisions: the four Gospels (Matthew, Mark, Luke, and John); the Acts of the Apostles; the Epistles, mainly written by St Paul; and the Book of Revelation. It was written between about 50 and 100 AD.

newton (N) The SI unit of force defined as the force required to give a mass of one kilogram an acceleration of one metre per second per second. Named after Sir Isaac Newton.

Newton, Sir Isaac (1642–1727) British physicist and mathematician. His first discovery was the law of gravitation, apocryphally inspired by the realization that an apple falling from a tree is attracted by the same force that holds the moon in orbit. Gravitation required a precise definition of force, this Newton also supplied in his laws of motion (*see* Newtonian mechanics). Newton's second major work was the invention of the calculus; Leibniz and Newton bickered unbecomingly for some years as to who had the idea first. His third contribution was in optics: he recognized that white light is a mixture of coloured lights, which can be separated by refraction. His incorrect belief that this effect could not be correct-

ISAAC NEWTON *A portrait attributed to John Vanderbank (c. 1726; National Portrait Gallery).*

ed, when it occurs as the chromatic aberration of a lens, inspired him to invent the reflecting telescope. Newton's principal publications were *Philosophiae naturalis principia mathematica* (1686–87) and *Optics* (1704), which held that light is a corpuscular phenomenon. He also reformed the coinage when he was Master of the Mint (1699–1727) and was president of the Royal Society from 1703 until his death.

Newtonian mechanics The branch of mechanics concerned with systems in which the results of quantum theory and the theory of relativity can be ignored. It is based on Newton's three laws of motion. The first law states that a body remains at rest or moves with constant velocity in a straight line unless acted upon by a force. The second law states that the acceleration (a) of a body is proportional to the force (f) causing it. The constant of proportionality is the mass (m) of the body: $f = ma$. The third law states that the action of a force always produces a reaction in the body. The reaction is of equal magnitude but opposite in direction to the action.

Newton's rings A series of light and dark rings formed in a plano-convex lens if monochromatic light is shone onto the lens when it rests on a plane mirror. First observed by Newton, they are caused by interference between light reflected by the mirror and light reflected at the curved surface of the lens.

New World A name for the American continent, used especially by early emigrants from Europe and in describing the geographical distribution of plants and animals. *Compare* Old World.

New World monkey A monkey native to the Americas. There are two families: the *Cebidae* (37 species) including uakaris, sakis, titis, howlers, capuchins, squirrel monkeys, spider monkeys, woolly monkeys, and the douroucouli; and the *Callithricidae* (33 species) containing marmosets and tamarins.

New York A state in the NE USA. It is basically an upland region, dissected by the valleys of the Mohawk and Hudson Rivers. New York is the chief manufacturing state in the USA. The presence of New York City also makes it the commercial, financial, and cultural centre of the nation. The most important agricultural activity is dairying. *History*: one of the 13 original colonies, it was first settled by the Dutch in the early 17th

century. It became an English colony in 1664 and later played a prominent role in the American Revolution. Area: 128 402 sq km (49 576 sq mi). Population (1985 est): 17 783 000. Capital: Albany.

New York 40 45N 74 00W The largest city in the USA, situated in New York state at the mouth of the Hudson River. Divided into five boroughs–Manhattan, Brooklyn, the Bronx, Queens, and Richmond (coextensive with Staten Island), it is the nation's leading seaport. As one of the world's financial centres (*see* Wall Street), it is the site of many large corporations and the New York and American Stock Exchanges. Its most notable features include Central Park, the fashionable shops of Fifth Avenue, the Statue of Liberty, Times Square, Greenwich Village, the Brooklyn Bridge (1883), Rockefeller Center, St Patrick's Cathedral (1858–79), and a large number of skyscrapers, such as the Empire State Building (1931), the World Trade Center (1973), and the United Nations Headquarters (1951). As well as the famous Broadway theatre district, there are numerous museums, art galleries, and libraries. *History*: on 3 September, 1609, Henry Hudson sailed into New York Bay and his glowing reports attracted its founding Dutch colonists, who arrived in 1620. In 1625 New Amsterdam, situated at the S tip of Manhattan, became the capital of the newly established colony of New Netherland and the following year the whole island of Manhattan was bought from the Indians for the equivalent of $24. In 1664 the city was captured by the English for the Duke of York and promptly renamed. From 1789 until 1790 it was the first capital of the USA. The opening of the Erie Canal in 1825 ensured its pre-eminence as a commercial city and seaport. Early in the 20th century the arrival of millions of European immigrants supplied New York with limitless cheap labour. During the mid-1970s New York was narrowly saved from bankruptcy by emergency loans. Population (1986): 7 262 700.

New Zealand, Dominion of A country in the Pacific Ocean, to the SE of Australia. It consists of North Island and South Island, together with several smaller islands. Most of the population is of British descent with a large Maori minority. *Economy*: the main basis of the economy is livestock rearing, especially sheep farming. Mineral resources include coal, gold, limestone and silica sand. *History*: from about the 14th century the islands were inhabited by the Maoris, a Polynesian people. The first European to discover New Zealand was Tasman in 1642, who called it Staten Land, later changed to Nieuw Zealand; in 1769 the coast was explored by Cook. During the early part of the 19th century it was used as a whaling and trading base. By the Treaty of Waitangi in 1840 the Maori chiefs ceded sovereignty to Britain and a colony was established. After two wars with the Maoris over land rights, peace was reached in 1871. New Zealand was made a dominion in 1907 and became fully independent by the Statute of Westminster in 1931. Since World War II New Zealand has played an increasing role in international affairs, especially in the Far East. Its economy has suffered from the recent world recession and efforts to curb inflation have included a prices and wages policy. In 1985 relations with the USA became strained when the new Labour government prohibited nuclear vessels from entering New Zealand waters. Prime minister: Geoffrey Palmer. Official language: English. Official currency: New Zealand dollar of 100 cents. Area: 268 704 sq km (103 719 sq mi). Population (1987 est): 3 300 000. Capital: Wellington. Main port: Auckland.

Nguni A division of the Bantu-speaking peoples of S Africa. It includes the Swazi, Xhosa, and Zulu.

NIAGARA FALLS

Niagara Falls Two waterfalls on the US–Canadian border, on the Niagara River. The American Falls, 51 m (167 ft) high and 300 m (1000 ft) wide, are straight while the Horseshoe Falls (Canada), 49 m (162 ft) high and 790 m (2600 ft) wide, are curved.

Niamey 13 32N 2 05E The capital (since 1926) of Niger, on the River Niger. Population (1983): 399 100.

Nicaea, Councils of Two ecumenical councils of the Christian Church held at Nicaea, now Iznik (Turkey). **1.** (325) The council that was summoned by the Byzantine emperor Constantine to establish Church unity and suppress Arianism. The Nicene Creed was the major doctrinal formulation. **2.** (787) The council that was summoned by the Byzantine empress Irene to condemn iconoclasm. It approved a formula for restoring the veneration of icons.

Nicaragua, Republic of A country in Central America between the Caribbean Sea and the Pacific Ocean. Swamp and dense tropical forest on the Caribbean coast, and a broader plain with lakes to the W rise to a central mountain range. The population is mainly of mixed Indian and Spanish descent. *Economy*: chiefly agricultural, the main crops are maize, rice, cotton, coffee, and sugar. Minerals include gold, silver, and copper. Oil and gas deposits are being explored. *History*: sighted by Columbus in 1502, it was colonized by Spain from 1522, becoming part of the captaincy general of Guatemala. It broke away from Spain in 1821 and formed part of the Central American Federation until 1838, when Nicaragua became a republic. From 1933 the government was dominated by the Somoza family, opposition to which culminated in a civil war that forced (1979) the resignation of the president, Gen Anastasio Somoza (1925–80). The victorious Sandinista National Liberation Front (FSLN) under Daniel Ortega instituted socialist policies. Accusing the Sandinistas of supplying arms to the rebels in El Salvador, the USA supported an army of 'Contras' until 1989; in 1990 Violeta Chamorro, heading the UNO coalition party, won a free election against Ortega. Nicaragua is a member of the OAS

and the Central American Common Market. Official language: Spanish. Official currency: córdoba of 100 centavos. Area: 148 000 sq km (57 143 sq mi). Population (1987 est): 3 500 000. Capital: Managua. Main ports: Corinto and Bluefields.

Nice 43 42N 7 16E A city in SE France, the capital of the Alpes-Maritimes department. Ceded by Sardinia to France in 1860, it is one of the leading resorts of the French Riviera. Population (1982): 338 486.

Nicene Creed The statement of Christian belief accepted as orthodox by the first Council of Nicaea (325). The Nicene Creed used in the Eucharist service of Orthodox, Roman Catholic, and Protestant Churches is a version of this creed.

Nicholas I (1796–1855) Emperor of Russia (1825–55), notorious as an autocrat. Nicholas' accession was followed by the Dekabrist revolt, which hardened his conservatism. His ambitions in the Balkans precipitated the Crimean War.

Nicholas II (1868–1918) The last Emperor of Russia (1894–1917). Nicholas' ambition in Asia led to the unpopular Russo-Japanese War, which in turn precipitated the Revolution of 1905. Forced to accept the establishment of a representative assembly, Nicholas nevertheless continued attempts to rule autocratically. In 1915 he took supreme command of Russian forces in World War I, leaving Russia to the mismanagement of the Empress Alexandra and Rasputin. Following the Russian Revolution in 1917, Nicholas was forced to abdicate (March). He and his family were imprisoned by the Bolsheviks and executed at Ekaterinburg (now Sverdlovsk).

Nicholas, St (4th century AD) The patron saint of Russia, sailors, and children. He is thought to have been Bishop of Myra in Asia Minor. Legends telling of his gifts of gold to three poor girls for their dowries gave rise to the practice of exchanging gifts on his feast day, 6 Dec. As he is also identified with the legendary Santa Claus this now happens on 25 Dec in most countries.

Nicholson, Ben (1894–1982) British artist. Some of his best abstract works were produced in the 1930s, while a member of the British art group Unit One (*see* Nash, Paul). These include white-painted plaster reliefs of rectangles combined with circles.

JACK NICKLAUS

Nicholson, Jack (1937–) US film actor. After success in *Easy Rider* (1969), he became a leading star. His films include *One Flew Over the Cuckoo's Nest* (1976), *Prizzi's Honour* (1985), and *Batman* (1989). He won an Oscar for *Terms of Endearment* (1983).

nickel (Ni) A hard silvery metal similar to iron, discovered in 1751 by A. F. Cronstedt (1722–65). It occurs in nature chiefly as pentlandite, NiS, and pyrrhotite, (Fe,Ni)S. It is chemically similar to cobalt and copper, and forms a green oxide (NiO), the chloride ($NiCl_2$), the sulphate ($NiSO_4$), and other compounds. It is used widely in alloys, such as stainless steel, and in coinage. At no 28; at wt 58.71; mp 1453°C; bp 2732°C.

Nicklaus, Jack William (1940–) US golfer, who has won more major championships than any other. His titles since 1959 include five Masters championships.

Nicobar Islands. *See* Andaman and Nicobar Islands.

Nicopolis, Battle of (25 September, 1396) The battle in which a coalition of Crusaders under Emperor Sigismund were decisively defeated by the Turks under Sultan Bayezid I (1347–1403; reigned 1389–1403).

Nicosia (Greek name: Leukosía; Turkish name: Lefkosa) The capital of Cyprus, on the River Pedieas. Originally known as Ledra it has been successively under Byzantine, Venetian, Turkish, and British control. It possesses many old buildings, including the Cathedral of St Sophia (completed 1325). Population (1986 est): 163 700.

Nicotiana A genus of poisonous herbs (over 100 species), native to Central and South America and Australia. 30–300 cm in height, they bear large funnel- or bell-shaped flowers. Many species are cultivated for ornament and certain species are grown commercially for tobacco. Family: *Solanaceae*.

nicotine ($C_{10}H_{14}N_2$) A toxic colourless oily liquid alkaloid that rapidly turns brown on exposure to air. It is obtained from the dried leaves of the tobacco plant and is present in small quantities in cigarettes. It is also used as an insecticide.

nicotinic acid. *See* vitamin B complex.

Nielsen, Carl (August) (1865–1931) Danish composer and conductor. Nielsen developed the principle of progressive tonality in his six symphonies, of which the fourth, entitled *The Inextinguishable* (1914–16), and the fifth (1922) are the best known.

Niemeyer, Oscar (1907–) Brazilian architect. A disciple of Le Corbusier, Niemeyer has made a major contribution to the development of modern architecture in Brazil. His designs for Brasília include the president's palace (1959) and the cathedral (1964).

Niemöller, Martin (1892–1984) German Lutheran pastor and Protestant leader. A U-boat commander in World War I, he became head of the Pastors' Emergency League, which became the Confessing Church, and opposed the nazification of the Church in Germany. In 1937 he was sent to a concentration camp, where he remained until the end of the war.

Nietzsche, Friedrich (1844–1900) German philosopher. His first book, *The Birth of Tragedy* (1872), argued that Wagnerian opera was the successor to Greek drama. Nietzsche rejected Christianity and argued that the "will to power" was the crucial human characteristic. In *Thus Spake Zarathustra* (1883–92), he eulogizes the man who is free, titanic, and powerful, an ideal adopted by the Nazis for the Aryan superman. After 1889 he was permanently insane.

Nifleheim. *See* Hel.

Niger, Republic of A large landlocked country in West Africa, lying mainly in the Sahara. Approximately half the population are Hausa, with large porportions of Zerma, Songhai, and Fulani. *Economy*: agriculture, particularly livestock raising, is important. Mineral resources include salt, natron, tin, and uranium. The main exports are uranium, groundnuts, and livestock. *History*: occupied by France (1883–99), it became a territory of French West Africa in 1904. It won independence in 1960. President: Col Ali Seybou. Official language: French. Official currency: CFA (Communauté financière africaine) franc of 100 centimes. Area: 1 186 408 sq km (458 075 sq mi). Population (1987 est): 6 608 000. Capital: Niamey.

Niger, River The third longest river in Africa. Rising in the S highlands of Guinea, it flows NE and then SE to the Gulf of Guinea. Length: 4183 km (2600 mi).

Niger-Congo languages An African language family spoken in central and S Africa. It is subdivided into six groups: the West Atlantic languages; the Mande languages; the Voltaic languages; the Kwa languages; the Benue-Congo group, which includes the Bantu languages; and the Adamawa-Eastern group.

Nigeria, Federal Republic of A large country in West Africa, on the Gulf of Guinea. Mangrove swamps along the coast give way to tropical rain forest inland rising to open savanna-covered plateaus, with mountains in the E reaching heights of over 2000 m (6000 ft). The inhabitants are mainly Hausa and Fulani in the N, Yoruba in the W, and Ibo in the E. *Economy*: oil production accounts for about 90% of exports although production has declined in recent years; Nigeria is a member of OPEC and the world's eighth largest producer. There are also important reserves of natural gas, tin, coal, iron ore, and columbite. Agriculture is still important; the main cash crops are groundnuts and cotton in the N and palms, coconut, and rubber in the S. *History*: in the middle ages there were highly developed kingdoms in the area, such as those of the Hausa in the N and the Yoruba (e.g. Oyo, Benin) in the SW; the Ibo occupied the SE. The coast was explored in the 15th century by the Portuguese, who developed the slave trade, in which the Dutch and English also participated. In 1861 Lagos was annexed by Britain and in 1886 the Royal Niger Company was incorporated to further British interests. By 1906, the British were in control of Nigeria, which was divided into the protectorate of Northern Nigeria and the colony (of Lagos) and protectorate of Southern Nigeria. These were united in 1914. Nigeria became a federation in 1954, gained independence in 1960, and became a republic within the Commonwealth in 1963. In 1967 the eastern region withdrew to form the Republic of Biafra under Lt Col Odumegwu Ojukwu's (1933–) leadership. Civil war followed, lasting until Biafra's surrender in 1970. In 1985, in the most recent of a series of coups, Maj Gen Ibrahim Babagandi came to power. Official currency: naira of 100 kobo. Area: 923 773 sq km (356 669 sq mi). Population (1988 est): 105 000 000. Capital and main port: Lagos.

nightingale A plump woodland bird, *Luscinia megarhynchos*, that winters in tropical Africa and breeds in S Europe and Asia Minor during the summer. It is about 16 cm long with reddish-brown plumage and pale underparts and feeds on ground insects and spiders.

Nightingales are noted for their beautiful song. Family: *Turdidae* (thrushes).

Nightingale, Florence (1820–1910) British hospital reformer and founder of the nursing profession. On the

FLORENCE NIGHTINGALE *Detail of photograph by H. Heving, taken c. 1857.*

outbreak of the Crimean War, in 1854, she volunteered to lead a party of nurses to work in the military hospitals. She set about transforming the appalling conditions, earning herself the title Lady with the Lamp from her patients. In 1860, she established the Nightingale School for Nurses at St Thomas's Hospital—the first of its kind.

nightjar A nocturnal bird belonging to a subfamily (*Caprimulginae*; 60–70 species) occurring in most temperate and tropical regions, also called goatsucker. About 30 cm long, nightjars have a soft mottled grey, brown, and rufous plumage and a long tail. Its short bill has a wide gape surrounded by long sensitive bristles enabling it to catch insects in flight. Family: *Caprimulgidae*; order: *Caprimulgiformes* (frogmouths, nightjars, etc.).

nightshade One of several plants of the family *Solanaceae*. The most notorious is deadly nightshade (or belladonna). The **woody nightshade**, or bittersweet (*Solanum dulcamara*), is a scrambling shrubby perennial, up to 2 m tall, of Eurasia and N Africa. The red berries are poisonous. The **black nightshade** (*S. nigrum*) is an annual, up to 50 cm high. It has poisonous black berries. The unrelated **enchanter's nightshade** (*Circaea lutetiana*), of Eurasia, is a herbaceous perennial of shady places. Up to 60 cm tall, it has a terminal spike of tiny white flowers. Family: *Onagraceae*.

nihilism A view that rejects all traditional values and institutions. Turgenev invented the label in *Fathers and Sons* (1861) for the philosophy of the character of Basarov. The political expression of nihilism is anarchism.

Niigata 37 58N 139 2E A city in Japan, in NW Honshu. It is the main port for the Sea of Japan. Population (1985): 476 000.

Nijinsky, Vaslav (1890–1950) Russian ballet dancer. In 1909 he joined Diaghilev's company in Paris, and quickly achieved an international reputation. Michel Fokine created *Petrushka*, *Scheherazade*, and other bal-

lets for him, and from 1913 he also began to choreograph. He retired in 1919 suffering from schizophrenia.

Nijmegen, Treaties of (1678–79) The peace treaties between France and, respectively, the Netherlands (1678), Spain (1678), and the Holy Roman Empire (1679) that ended the third Dutch War.

Nikolaev 46 57N 32 00E A port in the Soviet Union, at the confluence of the Rivers Bug and Ingul. Long a naval base, it has important shipbuilding industries. Population (1987): 501 000.

Nile, Battle of the (1 August, 1798) A naval battle in which the British, under Nelson, defeated the French during Napoleon's invasion of Egypt (*see* Revolutionary and Napoleonic Wars). This engagement gave Britain control of the Mediterranean.

Nile, River A river in N Africa, the longest river in the world. The longest of its three main tributaries, the White Nile, rises in Burundi and flows N through Lake Victoria and Lake Mobutu. At Khartoum it is joined by the Blue Nile (which rises in the Ethiopian highlands) and later by the River Atbara before flowing through a broad delta into the Mediterranean Sea. The Nile's annual floodwaters have supported cultivation on its floodplains since ancient times. Vast dams have also been constructed, including the Aswan Dam and Aswan High Dam. Length: 6741 km (4187 mi).

Nilo-Saharan languages A widely varied family of African languages. It includes the Nilotic languages of the Chari-Nile group, such as Dinka and Nuer.

nimbostratus A form of cloud common in temperate latitudes. Dark grey and solid in appearance it has a low base but may show extensive vertical development. Precipitation of snow or rain is often prolonged although not usually heavy.

Nîmes 43 50N 4 21E A city in S France, the capital of the Gard department. An important Roman settlement, it was a Protestant stronghold (16th–17th centuries). Population (1982): 129 924.

Nimrod A legendary biblical figure described in Genesis as a mighty hunter. He founded a Mesopotamian kingdom that included the cities of Babel, Erech, and Akkad and is credited with building the cities of Nineveh and Kalhu (modern Nimrud).

Nimrud An Assyrian capital (ancient Kalhu) near Mosul (Iraq). Founded about 1250 BC it was destroyed by the Medes in 612 BC. Excavations (1845–51) by Sir Austen Layard (1817–94) of the 9th-century city yielded gigantic sculptures and cuneiform tablets. *See also* Nineveh.

Nineveh An Assyrian capital (modern Kuyunjik) near Mosul (Iraq). Nineveh was made cocapital with Nimrud by Sennacherib (c. 700 BC). The Medes sacked it in 612 BC. Sir Austen Layard's great find here was the library of Ashurbanipal.

Ningbo (*or* Ning-po) 29 54N 121 33E A river port in E China, in Zhejiang province. Important for overseas trade (5th–9th centuries), it was also a religious centre. Population (1986 est): 1 020 000.

Niobe In Greek mythology, the daughter of Tantalus and wife of the King of Thebes. After her many children were killed by Apollo and Artemis, she was changed by Zeus into a stone column or statue, the face of which was said continually to shed tears.

niobium (Nb) A soft ductile white metal, discovered in 1801. It was formerly known as columbium in the USA. Niobium is used in specialist alloys in spacecraft, and at low temperatures it has superconducting properties. Its compounds include the white oxide (Nb_2O_5) and the volatile fluoride and chloride (NbF_5, $NbCl_5$). At no 41; at wt 92.9064; mp 2468 $\pm$ 10°C; bp 4742°C.

NIMRUD *Winged bulls guard the gateway to the Palace.*

nipa A small palm tree, *Nipa fruticans*, of brackish waters and estuaries of SE Asia. It has a creeping trunk and large feathery foliage, which is used for thatching and basket making.

Nippur A city of ancient Sumer (modern Niffer in central Iraq). From about 2600 BC it was Sumer's chief religious centre.

nirvana The supreme goal of Buddhism, in which liberation from the limitations of existence and rebirth are attained through the extinction of desire. In Hinduism nirvana also means spiritual release in the sense of freedom from reincarnation or union with God or the Absolute.

Niš 43 20N 21 54E A city in E Yugoslavia, in Serbia. For five centuries to 1877 it was a centre for Serbian resistance to Turkish control. Population (1981): 230 711.

Nishinomiya 34 44N 135 22E A city in Japan, in S Honshu. It is traditionally known for its *sake* (a Japanese rice wine). Population (1985): 421 000.

Niterói 22 54S 43 06W A city in SE Brazil, opposite the city of Rio de Janeiro. It is a popular resort. Population (1985): 442 706.

nitric acid (HNO_3) A fuming corrosive liquid made by the oxidation of ammonia by air in the presence of a platinum catalyst or the action of sulphuric acid on sodium or potassium nitrate. It is used in the manufacture of fertilizers and explosives.

nitrocellulose. *See* cellulose nitrate.

nitrogen (N) A colourless odourless gas, discovered by D. Rutherford (1749–1819) in 1772. It makes up 78% of the earth's atmosphere by volume. The element exists as diatomic molecules (N_2) bonded very strongly together. It forms a range of chemical compounds including ammonia (NH_3), the oxides (N_2O, NO, N_2O_3, NO_2, N_2O_5), nitric acid (HNO_3), and many nitrates (for example $NaNO_3$). Liquid nitrogen has a wide range of cryogenic applications. Ammonia (NH_3) and nitrates are of great importance as fertilizers. At no 7; at wt 14.0067; mp –290.86°C; bp –195.8°C.

nitrogen cycle The sequence of processes by which nitrogen and its compounds are utilized in nature. Nitrogen gas in the air is converted (fixed) to ammonia by certain soil bacteria and fertilizer manufacturers (*see* nitrogen fixation). Nitrifying bacteria in the roots of leguminous plants convert ammonia to nitrites and then to nitrates, which are used by plants to manufacture amino acids. When animals eat plants some of this nitrogenous plant material is incorporated into animal tissues. Nitrogenous excretory products and dead organic matter decompose to produce ammonia, so completing the cycle.

nitrogen fixation The conversion of atmospheric nitrogen gas into nitrogen compounds. The process occurs naturally by the action of bacteria in the roots of leguminous plants (*see* nitrogen cycle). Industrial methods of fixing nitrogen are of immense importance in the manufacture of nitrogen fertilizers.

nitroglycerin ($C_3H_5(NO_3)_3$) A yellow oily highly explosive liquid. It is used as an explosive either alone or as dynamite or gelignite.

Niven, David (1909–83) British film actor. His early films include *The Prisoner of Zenda* (1937) and *Wuthering Heights* (1939), and he later appeared in many stylish comedies and action films, including *Separate Tables* (1958) and *Candleshoe* (1977). He published two highly successful volumes of autobiography, *The Moon's a Balloon* (1972) and *Bring on the Empty Horses* (1975).

Nixon, Richard Milhous (1913–) US statesman; Republican president (1969–74). A Californian-born lawyer, he contributed to McCarthy's anticommunist investigations and was Eisenhower's vice president from 1953 until 1960, when he became the Republican presidential candidate. As president he reduced US troop commitments abroad and in 1973 ended US military involvement in Vietnam. In 1972 he paid a successful visit to the People's Republic of China. Participation in illegal efforts to ensure re-election in 1972 and the subse-

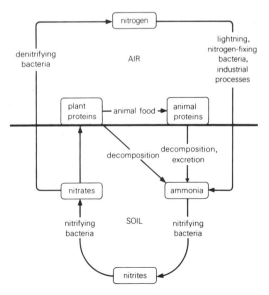

NITROGEN CYCLE

	1986	1987	1988	1989
Physics	Ernst Ruska Gerd Binning Heinrich Roher	Alex Muller Georg Bednorz	Leon Lederman Melvin Schwartz Jack Steinberger	Hans Dehmelt Wolfgang Paulm Norman Ramsey
Chemistry	Dudley Herschbach Yuan Tseh Lee John Polanyi	Donald Cram Jean-Marie Lehn Charles Pedersen	Johann Deisenhofer Robert Huber Hartmut Michel	Sidney Altman Thomas Cech
Medicine	Stanley Cohen Rita Levi-Montalcini	Susumu Tonegawa	James Black	Michael Bishop Harold Varmus
Literature	Wole Soyinka	Joseph Brodsky	Naguib Mahfouz	Camilo José Cela
Peace	Elie Wiesel	Oscar Arias Sánchez	United Nations peace-keeping forces	Dalai Lama
Economics	James Buchanan	Robert M. Solow	Maurice Allais	T. Haavelmo

NOBEL   *Recent prizewinners.*

quent cover-up attempt led to the Watergate scandal. Under threat of impeachment he became the first president to resign office. President Ford granted him a free pardon after succeeding him as president.

Nizhnii Novgorod. *See* Gorkii.

Nizhnii Tagil 58 00N 59 58E A city in the Soviet Union, on the E slopes of the Ural Mountains. Its metallurgical industries arise from the surrounding ironmining region. Population (1987 est): 427 000.

Nkomo, Joshua (1917–) Zimbabwean politician. Nkomo became president of the Zimbabwe African People's Union (ZAPU) in 1961. With headquarters in Zambia, it allied with Robert Mugabe's Zimbabwe African National Union (ZANU) in 1976 to form the Patriotic Front (PF) against the government of Ian Smith in Rhodesia (*see also* Zimbabwe). Nkomo later served as a minister in Mugabe's government.

Nkrumah, Kwame (1909–72) Ghanaian statesman; prime minister (1957–60) and then president (1960–66). He formed (1949) the Convention People's Party, which with a policy of noncooperation with the British took the Gold Coast to independence as Ghana in 1957. Nkrumah was deposed by a military coup while visiting China in 1966.

No A form of Japanese theatre. It is performed with a minimum of scenery and properties and is characterized by the use of dance, mime, and masks. The acting is highly stylized.

Nobel, Alfred Bernhard (1833–96) Swedish chemist and businessman. From his invention of dynamite (1866) and a smokeless gunpowder (1889) and his exploitation of the Baku oilfields he amassed a considerable fortune, leaving £1.75 million as a foundation for the **Nobel Prizes.**

nobelium (No) A synthetic transuranic element discovered in 1957 by bombarding curium with carbon ions in an accelerator. Five isotopes with short half-lives have been discovered. Named after Alfred Nobel. At no 102; at wt (255).

noble gases (*or* inert gases) The elements forming group O of the periodic table: helium, neon, argon, krypton, xenon, and radon. All are colourless odourless tasteless gases, which are slightly soluble in water. They are inert chemically owing to their filled outer electron shells, although complexes of xenon and krypton have recently been isolated (e.g. XeF_4).

Noctiluca A genus of minute single-celled animals found in coastal waters throughout the world. They have a single flagellum that wafts food particles towards the mouth, and are luminescent. Class: *Flagellata*.

noctule An insect-eating bat, *Nyctalus noctula*, of Eurasia. About 12 cm long, it has bright-chestnut fur and long narrow wings. Noctules hibernate only from Dec to Jan. Family: *Vespertilionidae*.

Nolan, Sir Sidney (1917–) Australian painter. He is internationally known for his paintings of Australian historical figures, such as Ned Kelly, and landscapes of the outback.

Nonconformists In its original early-17th-century sense, the term referred to members of the Church of England who did not conform with its rituals. After the Act of Uniformity (1662), the term's scope widened to include members of dissenting Protestant sects, such as the Quakers and Methodists.

Nootka A North American Indian people of the NW Pacific coast region who speak a Wakashan language. They were traditionally hunters, fishers, and expert whale catchers, using large canoes and harpoons.

noradrenaline (*or* norepinephrine) A hormone that is secreted by the central core (medulla) of the adrenal glands. It is a catecholamine, structurally similar to adrenaline but produces different effects in certain target organs, especially the heart, the rate of which it decreases. Noradrenaline is stored by cells of the sympathetic nervous system and subsequently released by nerve endings to excite adjacent nerves in the transmission of impulses. In the hypothalamus it is thought to inhibit transmission of impulses.

Nore, the A sandbank in SE England, at the mouth of the River Thames. A naval mutiny occurred near here (1797).

Norfolk 36 54N 76 18W A seaport in the USA, in Virginia on Hampton Roads. Founded in 1682, it suffered considerable damage in the American Revolution and the US Civil War. Population (1986): 274 800.

NORMAN CONQUEST *The doorway (c. 1140) of the Norman Church at Kilpeck near Hereford.*

Norfolk A county of E England, in East Anglia. It is mainly low lying, with fens in the W and the Norfolk Broads in the E. It is mainly agricultural. Tourism is important. Area: 2763 sq km (1067 sq mi). Population (1986 est): 727 800. Administrative centre: Norwich.

Norfolk, Thomas Howard, 3rd Duke of (1473–1554) English statesman. He became president of the privy council in 1529 and in 1536 suppressed the Pilgrimage of Grace. He lost power after Catherine Howard's execution (1542) and was imprisoned (1546–53) for involvement in the treason (1546) of his son Henry Howard, Earl of Surrey (1517–47). Surrey's son **Thomas Howard, 4th Duke of Norfolk** (1538–72) was imprisoned (1559–60) by Elizabeth I for planning to marry Mary, Queen of Scots. He subsequently plotted against Elizabeth and was executed.

Norfolk Island 29 05S 167 59E A mountainous Australian island in the SW Pacific Ocean, formerly a British penal colony. Area: 36 sq km (14 sq mi). Population (1986): 1977. Chief town: Kingston.

Norman conquest (1066–72) The conquest of England by William, Duke of Normandy (*see* William the Conqueror). After defeating Harold II at the battle of Hastings (1066), William captured London and was crowned. English risings were suppressed by 1070 and with the defeat of the Scots in 1072 the conquest was complete. The English lay and ecclesiastical aristocracy was replaced by Normans and other continentals and feudalism was introduced. Latin became the language of government and Norman French, the literary language; Norman influence was also felt in church architecture.

Normandy (French name: Normandie) A former province in N France, on the English Channel. *History*: during the medieval period Normandy flourished as a major state. William II, Duke of Normandy, conquered England (1066) to become William I of England. Disputed between England and France during the following centuries, it finally reverted to France in 1449. During World War II it suffered severe damage.

Normans Viking settlers in N France (later Normandy) whose rule, under their leader Rollo, was formally recognized (911) by Charles the Simple (879–929; reigned 898–923). By the end of the 11th century they had also conquered England (*see* Norman conquest) and much of S Italy and Sicily and had established crusading states in the E, besides gaining a foothold in Wales and Scotland. Noted for their military inventiveness, they adopted and adapted existing administrative practices in countries they conquered with great success.

Norrköping 58 35N 16 10E A port in SE Sweden, on an inlet of the Baltic Sea. Population (1986): 118 801.

North, Frederick, Lord (1732–92) British statesman; prime minister (1770–82). As prime minister, he was criticized for precipitating the American Revolution (1775–83), and eventually resigned.

North American Indian languages A geographical classification of the languages of the indigenous peoples of North America. It is estimated that these languages originally numbered about 300. Edward Sapir (1884–1939) arranged them into six phyla (1929): Eskimo-Aleut; Algonkian-Wakashan; Na-Dené; Penutian; Hokan-Siouan; and Aztec-Tanoan.

North American Indians A group of peoples of North America, mistakenly believed to be inhabitants of the Indian subcontinent when first discovered by Columbus. In common with other American Indians, they are probably descended from migrants who arrived from Asia some 20 000 years ago. Their traditional cultures range from that of warlike primitive hunters and gatherers to peaceful subsistence cultivators. Social organization is usually based on kinship and depends upon a complex tribal system.

Northampton 52 14N 0 54W A town in England. Administrative centre of Northamptonshire, it is a centre of the footwear industry. Population (1984 est): 163 000.

Northamptonshire (*or* Northants) A county in the East Midlands of England. It is predominantly agricultural. Area: 2367 sq km 915 sq mi). Population (1986 est): 554 400. Administrative centre: Northampton.

North Atlantic Treaty Organization (NATO) An alliance formed in 1949 by Belgium, Canada, Denmark, France, Iceland, Italy, Luxembourg, the Netherlands, Norway, Portugal, the UK, and the USA; Greece and Turkey joined in 1952, West Germany in 1955, and Spain in 1982. All member states are bound to protect any member against attack. Its secretariat headquarters is in Brussels and its military headquarters near Mons.

North Borneo. *See* Sabah.

North Carolina A state in the USA, on the S Atlantic coast. The extensive coastal plain stretches westwards to the Piedmont Plateau and the Appalachian Mountains in the E. It is heavily populated and the leading industrial state in the South. *History*: one of the 13 original colonies, it shares its early history with South Carolina. It was made a separate colony in 1713 and it became a state in 1789. It was a supporter of the Confederate cause in the US Civil War. Area: 136 197 sq km (52 586 sq mi). Population (1986 est): 6 331 000. Capital: Raleigh.

North Dakota A state in the N central USA. It comprises three main physical regions: the Red River Valley along the E border, the Central Lowlands just W of this strip, and the Great Plains in the SW. Agriculture and mining are the two principal economic activities. *History*: early attempts to settle were made by Scottish and Irish families at Pembina in 1812. It formed part of the territory of Dakota from 1861 until 1889 when it was made a separate state. Area: 183 022 sq km (70 665 sq mi). Population (1986 est): 679 000. Capital: Bismarck.

Northeast Caucasian languages A group of about 25 languages of the NE region of the Caucasus, also called the Nakho-Dagestanian family. Chechen, the most important, is part of the Nakh subdivision.

Northeast Passage (Russian name: Severny Morskoy Put) The sea route along the N Eurasian coast, kept open in summer by Soviet icebreakers. It was first traversed by the Swedish explorer, Niels Nordenskjöld (1878–79). *See also* Northwest Passage.

Northern Ireland. *See* Ireland.

Northern Territory An administrative division of N central Australia. It consists chiefly of a plateau with Arnhem Land in the N and the Macdonnell Ranges in the S. SW of Alice Springs and close to the geographical centre of the continent stands Ayers Rock. The main agricultural activity is the rearing of beef cattle. Minerals are important, especially uranium, iron ore, manganese, copper, gold, and bauxite. In 1978 the Northern Territory became an independent state, although the federal government retained control over uranium. Area: 1 346 200 sq km (519 770 sq mi). Population (1986 est): 154 000. Capital: Darwin.

Northern War, Great (1700–21) The war fought for Baltic supremacy between Russia, Denmark, and Poland, on one side, and Sweden, on the other. After the death of Charles XII of Sweden (1718), the war between Denmark, Poland, and Sweden was ended by the Treaties of Stockholm (1719–20). The Treaty of Nystad (1721) between Russia and Sweden marked Russia's emergence as the major Baltic power.

North Island The most northerly of the two principal islands of New Zealand, separated from South Island by Cook Strait. Area: 114 729 sq km (44 281 sq mi). Population (1986): 2 438 249.

NORTH SEA *Oil rig in the Forties oilfield.*

North Sea A section of the Atlantic Ocean in NW Europe, between the British Isles and the continent N of the Strait of Dover. The entire floor is part of the continental shelf, with an average depth of about 300 m (914 ft). Recent exploitation of North Sea oil and natural-gas finds have increased its economic importance.

North Star. *See* Polaris.

Northumberland The northernmost county of England. It consists of a coastal plain rising to the Cheviot Hills in the N and the Pennines in the W. There are outstanding Roman remains, notably Hadrian's Wall. The main agricultural activity is sheep farming. Area: 5033 sq km (1944 sq mi). Population (1986 est): 301 000. Administrative centre: Newcastle-upon-Tyne.

Northumberland, John Dudley, Duke of (1502–53) English statesman, who was virtual ruler of England (1549–53) under Edward VI. He replaced the Duke of Somerset as head of the regency council in 1549, securing his execution in 1552. In 1553 he married his son Guildford Dudley to Lady Jane Grey, whom he persuaded the king to name as his heir. On Edward's death Jane was proclaimed queen but lack of support forced Northumberland's surrender to Mary (I) and he was executed.

Northumbria A kingdom of Anglo-Saxon England north of the Humber. Northumbria became politically pre-eminent in England in the 7th century under Edwin, Saint Oswald, and Oswiu (d. 670). Northumbrian scholarship was also unrivalled, boasting such great names as Bede and Alcuin (c. 735–804 AD). By 829, however, Northumbria had recognized the overlordship of Wessex and in the late 9th century its unity was destroyed by the Danes.

Northwest Caucasian languages A group of languages of the NW region of the Caucasus, also called the Abkhazo-Adyghian family. It includes Abkhaz, Abaza, Adyghian, Kabardian (Circassian), and Ubykh.

North-West Frontier Province A province in NW Pakistan, SE of Afghanistan. Its Pathan inhabitants mostly herd livestock or cultivate grains, fruit, sugar cane, and tobacco. Over the centuries several great powers have sought to control the province, but it has usually remained semiautonomous because of its rugged terrain and fierce inhabitants. Area: 74 522 sq km (28 773 sq mi). Population (1985): 12 287 000. Capital: Peshawar.

Northwest Passage The sea route along the coast of North America, between the Atlantic and Pacific Oceans. It was first traversed by Roald Amundsen (1903–06). *See also* Northeast Passage.

Northwest Territories A territory of N Canada, stretching from 60°N to the North Pole. One of the most sparsely populated areas in the world, two-thirds of the people are Indians and Eskimos. Rich in mineral resources, the economy is dominated by the mining industry. At present, the territory's vast oil reserves are being explored. Area: 3 246 389 sq km (1 253 432 sq mi). Population (1986): 51 384. Capital: Yellowknife.

North Yorkshire. A county in N England. The Pennines rise to the W of the Vale of York, while the Cleveland Hills, North York Moors, and Tabular Hills rise to the E. It is chiefly agricultural. There is some industrial activity in the larger towns, such as York. Coal is mined from a new field centred on Selby (opened 1983). Tourism is centred on Harrogate and Scarborough. Area: 8321 sq km (3213 sq mi). Population (1986 est): 699 800. Administrative centre: Northallerton.

Norway, Kingdom of (Norwegian name: Norge) A country in N Europe occupying the W part of the Scandinavian Peninsula. It is largely mountainous, reaching heights of almost 2500 m (8000 ft), with a heavily indented coastline. Glaciers and forests cover approximately one-quarter of the country. The archipelago of Svalbard and Jan Meyen Island are also part of Norway together with the dependencies of Bouvet Island, Peter I Island, and Queen Maud Land. *Economy*: abundant hydroelectric power has enabled Norway to develop as an industrial nation. Norway is also one of the world's great fishing nations. Revenues from tourism are important. Minerals include iron ore, limestone, coal, copper, zinc, and lead. *History*: its early history was dominated by the Vikings. The many local chieftains were not subjected to a single ruler until the reign of Harold I Haarfager (died c. 930). Christianity was introduced in the 10th century. During the reign (1204–63) of Haakon IV Haakonsson Norway acquired Iceland and Greenland and in the 14th century, under Margaret, was united with Sweden and Denmark. Sweden broke free in 1523 but Norway remained under Danish domination until 1814, when it was united with Sweden, while maintaining internal self-government. Only in 1907 was full independence achieved. Norway declared its neutrality in both World Wars but from 1940 to 1944 was occupied by the Germans, who established a government under Quisling. Abandoning isolationism after World War II, Norway joined the UN and NATO. In 1972 Norwegians rejected membership of the EC in a referendum. In common with other Scandinavian countries Norway has a highly developed social-welfare system. Head of state: Olav V. Prime minister: Jan Peter Syse. Official language: Norwegian. Official religion: Evangelical Lutheran. Official currency: krone of 100 øre. Area: 323 886 sq km (125 053 sq mi). Population (1987): 4 174 005. Capital and main port: Oslo.

Norwegian A North Germanic language of the West Scandinavian division, spoken in Norway. There are two distinct forms known as Dano-Norwegian (Bokmål or Riksmål) and New Norwegian (Nynorsk or Landsmål).

Norwegian Antarctic Territory The area in Antarctica claimed by Norway, lying S of latitude 60°S and between longitudes 20°W and 45°E. It consists of the end of Coats Land, Queen Maud Land, and islands.

Norwich 52 38N 1 18E A city in E England, the administrative centre of Norfolk. Towards the end of the 16th century many weavers from the Netherlands settled in the city and it became a major textile centre. Population (1981): 122 270.

nose The organ of smell, which is also an entrance to the respiratory tract. It leads to the nasal cavity, which is lined by mucous membrane, extends back to the pharynx and windpipe, and is connected to the air sinuses of the skull. Hairs in the nostrils filter particles from inhaled air, which is further cleaned, warmed, and moistened in the nasal cavity. The membrane at the top of the nasal cavity contains olfactory cells, which are sensitive to different smells and are connected to the brain via the olfactory nerve.

Nostradamus (Michel de Notredame; 1503–66) French physician and astrologer, who became famous with his publication of *Centuries* (1555–58), in which he made a number of prophecies in the form of rhyming quatrains. His prophecies are obscure and open to various interpretations.

notochord A flexible skeletal rod that runs along the length of the body in the embryos of all animals of the phylum Chordata (including vertebrates). In primitive chordates, such as the lancelets and lampreys, the notochord remains the main axial support.

Notre-Dame de Paris The gothic cathedral built (1163–1345) on the Île de la Cité, Paris, to replace two earlier churches. The nave, choir, and west front were completed by 1204; the innovatory flying buttresses and

NOTRE-DAME *A view from the southeast showing the flying buttresses.*

the great rose windows are notable features. Damaged during the French Revolution, Notre-Dame was fully restored (1845–64) by Eugène Viollet-le-Duc (1814–79).

Nottingham 52 58N 1 10W A city in N central England, the administrative centre of Nottinghamshire. Charles I raised his standard here in 1642 at the outbreak of the Civil War. Notable buildings include the "Trip to Jerusalem," reputed to be the oldest inn in England. It was once famous for its lace. Population (1981): 271 080.

Nottinghamshire A county in the East Midlands of England. It consists mainly of lowlands, crossed by the River Trent, with the Pennine uplands in the W and Sherwood Forest (famous for the Robin Hood legend) in the SW. Agriculture is important with arable and dairy farming, orchards, and market gardening. It contains important coalfields. Area: 2164 sq km (835 sq mi). Population (1986 est): 1 006 400. Administrative centre: Nottingham.

Nouakchott 18 09N 15 58W The capital of Mauritania, in the W near the Atlantic coast. A small village until the 1950s, it was developed as the capital after independence in 1960. Population (1985 est): 500 000.

Nouméa 22 16S 166 26E The capital of New Caledonia. A port, it exports nickel, chrome, manganese, and iron. Population (1983): 60 112.

nova A binary star that suddenly increases in brightness by perhaps 10 000 times or more and then fades over months or years, usually to its original brightness. Nova eruptions occur in close binary systems comprising a white dwarf with a nearby companion star that is expanding and is losing matter to the white dwarf.

Nova Scotia A province of E Canada. It consists of a peninsula protruding into the Atlantic Ocean and Cape Breton Island. Mostly rolling hills and valleys, Nova Scotia was originally covered by mixed forest but has been largely replanted with conifers. Coal output is down significantly, but Nova Scotia also mines gypsum, salt, and copper. Agriculture includes dairying, mixed farming, livestock, and fruit. *History*: from the first colonization (1605), Britain and France contested the area, Britain eventually gaining possession (confirmed by the Treaty of Paris in 1763). Since joining Canada (1867), its economy has lagged. Area: 52 841 sq km (20 402 sq mi). Population (1986): 873 199. Capital: Halifax.

Novello, Ivor (David Ivor Davies; 1893–1951) British composer, dramatist, and actor. He composed the World War I song "Keep the Home Fires Burning," and is best known for his series of romantic musicals including *Careless Rapture* (1936) and *The Dancing Years* (1939).

Novosibirsk 55 04N 83 05E A city in the central Soviet Union, on the River Ob and the Trans-Siberian Railway. It is the most important economic centre in Siberia. Population (1987): 1 423 000.

NSPCC. *See* National Society for the Prevention of Cruelty to Children.

Nu, U (*or* Thakin Nu; 1907–) Burmese statesman; prime minister (1948–56, 1957–58, 1960–62). He became prime minister on independence and re-emerged as leader of the opposition in 1988.

Nubia A region of NE Africa, between Aswan (Egypt) and Khartoum (Sudan). Much of Nubia is now drowned by Lake Nasser. From about 2000 BC the Egyptians gradually occupied Nubia, which they called Cush. As Egyptian power waned, Nubian kings, based at Napata and Meroë, became influential, even dominating Egypt itself (c. 730–670). Their independent culture lasted until the 4th century AD.

Nubian Desert A desert in the NE Sudan, between the River Nile and the Red Sea. It consists of a sandstone plateau with peaks of up to 2259 m (7411 ft). Area: about 400 000 sq km (154 408 sq mi).

nuclear energy The energy evolved by nuclear fission or nuclear fusion. The energy is liberated in fission when a heavy atomic nucleus, such as uranium, splits into two or more parts, the total mass of the parts being less than the mass of the original nucleus. This difference in mass is equivalent to the binding energy of the nucleus and most of it is converted into the kinetic energy of the components formed in the reaction. In a fusion reaction, two light nuclei, such as hydrogen, combine to form a stable nucleus, such as helium; with light nuclei the nucleus formed has a lower mass than the sum of the component nuclei, again energy is released. In the case of fission, when a nucleus of uranium-235 is struck by a neutron, a U-236 nucleus is formed, which immediately splits into two roughly equal parts. Two or three neutrons are produced at the same time. As these neutrons can cause further fissions, a chain reaction builds up and a lump of U-235 will disintegrate almost instantaneously with enormous explosive power, provided that it is in excess of the critical mass (*see* nuclear weapons). In nuclear power stations the fission reaction is harnessed to produce heat at a controlled rate (to raise steam to drive a turbine). They use natural uranium, which contains only 0.7% of the fissionable U-235 isotope, nearly all of the rest being the isotope U-238. The U-238 isotope absorbs the fast-moving neutrons emitted by the fission of U-235 and prevents a chain reaction from occurring in natural uranium. There are, however, two ways of producing a chain reaction. One is to use a moderator to slow down the fast neutrons so that they are not absorbed by U-238 nuclei (*see* thermal reactor). The other is to enrich the natural uranium with extra quantities of U-235 (or plutonium-239) so that there are sufficient neutrons to sustain the chain reaction in spite of absorption by U-238 (*see* fast reactor). Most present commer-

cial reactors are thermal, although the fast reactor is under development.

The fusion process is the basis of the hydrogen bomb (*see* nuclear weapons; thermonuclear reactor).

nuclear fission. *See* fast reactor; nuclear energy; nuclear power; nuclear weapons; thermal reactor.

nuclear fusion. *See* nuclear energy; nuclear weapons; thermonuclear reactor.

nuclear power The generation of electricity using nuclear energy. The nuclear industry has expanded rapidly over the last 30 years; in 1988 it provided 30% of Europe's electricity (e.g. 70% in France and 19% in the UK), 19.5% of US electricity, and 25% of Japan's. However, the disaster (1986) at Chernobyl caused concern over nuclear safety, leading several countries to postpone nuclear expansion. The unique Soviet design of the Chernobyl reactor, using a single shell building, is now considered unsafe, unlike the US water-cooled reactors using double-walled buildings, which prevented disaster at Three Mile Island in 1979. In addition to safety fears, the price of nuclear-generated electricity, taking into account high decommissioning costs, has seemed to make it uncompetitive with fossil fuels, especially in the UK, where privatization of power has made it a sensitive issue. Nuclear power is still important, however, in view of diminishing fossil fuel reserves and the global warming they cause (*see* greenhouse effect). *See also* fast reactor; thermal reactor; thermonuclear reactor.

nuclear reactor A device for producing nuclear energy in a usable form. *See* fast reactor; nuclear power; thermal reactor; thermonuclear reactor.

Nuclear Test-Ban Treaty (1963) A treaty banning nuclear testing by its signatories on the ground, in the atmosphere, in space, and under water. The signatories were the Soviet Union, the UK, and the USA; many other countries agreed to adhere to the treaty.

nuclear waste *See* radioactive waste.

nuclear weapons Missiles, bombs, shells, or land mines that use fission or fusion of nuclear material (*see* nuclear energy) yielding enormous quantities of heat, light, blast, and radiation. The first **atomic bomb** (*or* fission bomb), manufactured by the USA in World War II, was dropped on Hiroshima in 1945. It consisted of two small masses of uranium-235 forced together by a chemical explosion to form a supercritical mass, in which an uncontrolled chain reaction occurred. The bomb had an explosive power equivalent to 20 000 tons of TNT. Later models used plutonium-239 to even greater effect.

The **hydrogen bomb** (fusion bomb *or* thermonuclear bomb) consists of an atom bomb surrounded by a layer of hydrogenous material, such as lithium deuteride. The atom bomb creates the necessary temperature (about 100 000 000°C) needed to ignite the fusion reaction (*see* thermonuclear reactor). Hydrogen bombs have an explosive power measured in tens of megatons (millions of tons) of TNT. The first hydrogen bomb was exploded by US scientists on Eniwetok Atoll in 1952.

The **neutron bomb** (*or* enhanced radiation bomb) is a nuclear weapon designed to maximize neutron radiation. It is lethal to all forms of life but, having reduced blast, leaves buildings, etc., relatively undamaged.

nucleic acids Organic compounds, found in the cells of all living organisms, that consist of a mixture of nitrogenous bases (purines and pyrimidines), phosphoric acid, and a pentose sugar. The sugar is ribose in the ribonucleic acids (*see* RNA) and deoxyribose in the deoxy-

NUCLEAR ENERGY

nuclear fission

neutron

U-235 atom

fission products

neutrons

nuclear fuel cycle

uranium purification

enriched uranium

uranium oxide fuel

uranium metal fuel

thermal nuclear power stations

irradiated fuel reprocessing

recovered uranium

plutonium for fast reactors

radioactive waste

Magnox reactor

control rods

concrete shield

carbon dioxide coolant

steam generator

fuel elements

electricity generating plant

steel pressure vessel

graphite moderator

advanced gas-cooled reactor (AGR)

carbon dioxide coolant

control rods

concrete pressure vessel

steam generator

graphite moderator

fuel elements

pressurized-water reactor (PWR)

control rods

pressuriser

steam generator

light water coolant

steel pressure vessel

fuel elements

concrete shield

fast reactor

hot sodium

control rods

reactor jacket

primary vessel

fuel elements

steam generator

intermediate heat exchanger

cool sodium

NUCLEAR ENERGY   *Natural uranium metal fuel clad in Magnox (magnesium alloy) is used in Magnox thermal reactors. Enriched uranium dioxide pellets clad in steel are used in AGR and PWR fuel elements. Plutonium for fast reactors and recycled enriched uranium is obtained by reprocessing spent fuel from thermal reactors. The electricity generating plant is similar with all reactor types.*

ribonucleic acids (*see* DNA). Nucleic acids store genetic information in living organisms and interpret that information in protein synthesis. *See also* nucleoprotein.

nucleolus A small dense body, one or more of which can be seen within the nucleus of a nondividing cell. It contains RNA and protein and is involved in the synthesis of ribosomes.

nucleon A collective name for a proton or neutron. *See also* mass number.

nucleoprotein A compound consisting of a nucleic acid associated with one or more proteins. The nucleoprotein of cell nuclei—the chromosomes—consists of DNA and proteins, mainly histones; cytoplasmic nucleoproteins—the ribosomes—are ribonucleoproteins comprising some 60% protein and 40% RNA. Viruses also consist of nucleoprotein.

nucleus (biology) A large granular component of nearly all cells. It is usually spherical or ovoid in shape and is surrounded by a nuclear membrane, which is perforated with pores to allow exchange of materials between the nucleus and cytoplasm. The nucleus contains the chromosomes, made up of the hereditary material (DNA), and is therefore essential for the control and regulation of cellular activities, such as growth and metabolism. During cell division the chromosomes are involved in the transfer of hereditary information (*see* meiosis; mitosis).

nucleus (physics) The central core of the atom (*see* atomic theory) discovered by Lord Rutherford in 1911. All nuclei consist of protons and neutrons (jointly called nucleons), except for hydrogen, which consists of a single proton. The constituent nucleons are held together by the strong interaction. The number of protons in the nucleus determines its charge and atomic number; the number of neutrons (in addition to the number of protons) determines the mass number and the isotope. **Nuclear physics** is the study of the structure and reactions of the nucleus. *See also* particle physics.

Nuffield, William Richard Morris, 1st Viscount (1877–1963) British car manufacturer and philanthropist. He established a car factory in Cowley, near Oxford, which in 1913 produced the first Morris Oxford, soon followed by the Morris Cowley. He founded Nuffield College, Oxford, the Nuffield Trust, and the Nuffield Foundation.

Nuku'alofa 21 09S 175 14W The capital of Tonga in the S Pacific, in N Tongatabu. It is the site of the Royal Palace (1865–67) and Royal Tombs. Population (1986): 28 899.

Nullarbor Plain A plain of SW South Australia and SE Western Australia, bordering on the Great Australian Bight. It consists of a treeless arid plateau. Area: 260 000 sq km (100 000 sq mi).

numbat A rat-sized marsupial, *Myrmecobius fasciatus*, of SW Australia, also called marsupial (*or* banded) anteater. It is slender and rust-coloured, with white stripes across the back and a long tail, and it feeds on ants and termites with its long sticky tongue. Numbats have no pouch. Family: *Dasyuridae*.

number theory The study of the properties of numbers. It includes various theorems about prime numbers, many of which are unproved but apparently true, and the study of Diophantine equations (named after the 3rd-century Greek mathematician Diophantus of Alexandria), i.e. equations that have only integer solutions. Fermat's last theorem deals with the solution of one of

these equations and is a famous unproved theorem. It now includes analytic number theory, originated by Leonhard Euler (1707–83) in 1742; geometric number theory, which uses such geometrical methods of analysis as Cartesian coordinates (*see* coordinate systems), vectors, and matrices; and probabilistic number theory, based on probability theory.

Numidia An ancient kingdom of N Africa, W of Carthage. Its Berber population was nomadic until Masinissa (c. 240–149 BC) promoted agriculture and urbanization. After supporting Pompey against Julius Caesar (46 BC), Numidia lost its monarchy and became part of the Roman province of Africa.

numismatics (*or* coin collecting) Collecting and studying coins, medals, or banknotes as a hobby or as a form of historical research. Coins in good condition are a form of investment, the best being "proof" coins, struck especially for sale to collectors.

nunatak A rock peak protruding above the surface of an ice sheet.

Nuneaton 52 32N 1 28W A town in central England, in Warwickshire. Its name refers to the 12th-century Benedictine nunnery. Population (1984 est): 72 000.

Nuremberg (German name: Nürnberg) 49 27N 11 05E A city in SE West Germany, in Bavaria. It was severely bombed during World War II. *History*: it became the centre of the German Renaissance, when the mastersingers' contests were held here. It was the site of the Nazi Party congresses (1933–38) and the war-crime trials following World War II. Population (1986): 466 500.

Nureyev, Rudolf (1938–) Russian ballet dancer. He danced with the Leningrad Kirov Ballet from 1958 until 1961, when he defected from Russia. In 1962 he joined the Royal Ballet, where he partnered Margot Fonteyn in such ballets as *Giselle* and *Swan Lake*. Since 1983 he has been artistic director of the Paris Opéra Ballet. His films include *Exposed* (1982).

nurse shark A shark, *Ginglymostoma cirratum*, that occurs in warm shallow waters of the Atlantic Ocean. Yellow-brown or grey-brown and up to 4.2 m long, it is considered dangerous to man only when provoked. Family: *Orectolobidae*.

Nusa Tenggara (former name: Lesser Sunda Islands) A volcanic Indonesian island group E of Java, the chief islands being Bali, Lombok, Sumbawa, Sumba, Flores, and Timor. Area: 73 144 sq km (28 241 sq mi). Population (1986 est): 6 156 600.

nut Loosely, any edible nonsucculent fruit, including the peanut and brazil nut. Botanically, a nut is a large dry fruit containing a single seed that is not released from the fruit at maturity. An example is the chestnut.

nutcracker A songbird of the genus *Nucifraga* found in coniferous forests of E Europe and Asia. The common nutcracker (*N. caryocatactes*) is dark brown speckled with white, about 32 cm long, and cracks open pine cones with its sharp bill to extract the seeds. Family: *Corvidae* (crows, jays, magpies).

nuthatch A small stocky bird belonging to a family (*Sittidae*: 30 species) occurring everywhere except South America and New Zealand. Nuthatches have long straight bills, for hammering open nuts, and long-clawed toes, for running up and down tree trunks in search of insects. The European nuthatch (*Sitta europaea*), about 14 cm long, has a blue-grey upper plumage with paler underparts and a black eyestripe.

nutmeg A fragrant tropical evergreen tree, *Myristica fragrans*, native to Indonesia but widely cultivated in SE Asia and the West Indies. Growing to 20 m high, it has tiny male and female flowers borne on separate trees. The yellow fleshy fruit, about 3 cm across, splits when ripe to expose the seed, which has a red fleshy covering (aril). The dried aril (mace) and whole or ground seeds (nutmeg) are used as spices. Family: *Myristicaceae*.

NUREMBERG *Prisoners in the dock at the war-crime trials (1946).*

nutria. *See* coypu.

Nuuk (name until 1979: Godthåb) 64 10N 51 40W The capital of Greenland, a port at the mouth of Godthåb Fjord. Population (1981): 9423.

nyala An antelope, *Tragelaphus angasi*, of SW Africa. About 100 cm high at the shoulder, nyalas are shy and nocturnal and have spiral-shaped horns and a greyish-brown coat with vertical white stripes on the flanks. The mountain nyala (*T. buxtoni*) lives in mountainous regions of S Ethiopia.

Nyasaland. *See* Malawi, Republic of.

Nyeman, River. *See* Neman, River.

Nyerere, Julius (Kambarage) (1922–) Tanzanian statesman; president (1962–85). In 1954 Nyerere formed the Tanganyika African National Union, which led the fight for independence (achieved in 1960). He became chief minister (1960), prime minister (1961), and then president of Tanganyika, which was renamed Tanzania in 1964 after union with Zanzibar. He was instrumental in the overthrow of Amin in Uganda in 1979.

nylon A synthetic material with a translucent creamy white appearance, widely used both in fibre form and in solid blocks because of its lightness, toughness, and elasticity. It is made by polymerization of diamine with fatty acid or by polymerizing a single monomer, in both cases to form a polyamide. Nylon is used to make small engineering components and is also spun and woven into fabrics for clothing, etc., and can be coloured with pigments. Introduced commercially in 1938, nylon was the first truly synthetic fibre.

nymph A stage in the life cycle of insects that show incomplete metamorphosis, including dragonflies, grasshoppers, and bugs. The egg hatches into a nymph, which undergoes a series of moults to form a line of nymphs that show increasing similarity to the adult.

nymphalid butterfly A butterfly belonging to the widely distributed family *Nymphalidae*, also called brush-footed butterfly. Nymphalids are characterized by small hairy forelegs, useless for walking. Many, including the migratory red admiral and painted lady, are strong fast fliers.

nymphs In Greek mythology, female spirits of nature, often portrayed as youthful and amorous dancers or musicians. The several classes of nymphs associated with particular natural phenomena include the dryads, the naiads, and the nereids.

Nyoro A Bantu-speaking people of the western lakes region of Uganda. They were traditionally divided into the Bito clan from whom the hereditary paramount chief (Mukama) always came, the aristocratic Huma pastoralists, and the subordinate Iru cultivators. They are a patrilineal people who live in small scattered settlements.

Nysa, River. *See* Neisse, River.

Nyx (Latin name: Nox) A Greek goddess, the personification of night. She lived in Tartarus, from which she emerged as Hemera, the goddess of day.

O

Oahu A US island in Hawaii, the most populous and the administrative centre. The Japanese attack on Pearl Harbor (1941) was decisive in bringing the USA into World War II. Area: 1584 sq km (608 sq mi). Population (1986 est): 816 700. Chief town: Honolulu.

oak A deciduous or evergreen tree or shrub of the genus *Quercus* (over 800 species), found in N temperate and subtropical regions. The simple leaves usually have lobed or toothed margins and the yellow male catkins and tiny green female flowers are borne on the same tree. The fruit—an acorn—is a hard oval nut partly enclosed by a round cup. Often 30–40 m high, many species are important timber trees, especially the common or pedunculate oak (*Q. robur*) and the durmast oak (both Eurasian). Several are planted for ornament, including the Eurasian Turkey oak (*Q. cerris*) and the Mediterranean holm oak. Family: *Fagaceae*.

Oaks A flat race for three-year-old fillies only, run over the Derby course (2.4 km; 1.5 mi) at Epsom, three days after the Derby in early June. One of the English Classics, it was first run in 1779 and was named after the 12th Earl of Derby's hunting lodge.

oarfish A fish of the genus *Regalecus*, especially *R. glesne*, found in all seas. It has a long silvery ribbon-like body, up to 9 m long, a long red dorsal fin that extends forwards to form a crest, long red oarlike pelvic fins situated near the pectoral fins, and no anal or tail fins. Family: *Trachipteridae* (ribbonfishes).

OAS. *See* Organisation de l'Armée secrète; Organization of American States.

oasis An area within a desert where water is available for vegetation and human use. It may consist of a single small spring around which palms grow or be an extensive area where the water table is at or near the ground surface.

Oates, Lawrence Edward Grace (1880–1912) British explorer and a member of R. F. Scott's expedition to the Antarctic (1910–12). After reaching the Pole Oates, fearing that his lameness (resulting from frostbite) might hinder the already struggling expedition on the return journey, walked out into the blizzard to die. His gallant act, related in Scott's diaries, failed to save his companions.

Oates, Titus. *See* Popish Plot.

oats Annual grasses belonging to the genus *Avena* (10 species), native to temperate regions. The common oat (*A. sativa*) was first cultivated in Europe and is grown widely in cool temperate regions. The grain is used as a livestock feed, especially for horses, and for oatmeal, breakfast cereals, etc. The straw is used for livestock fodder and bedding. Wild oats, especially *A. fatua*, can be a serious weed in cereal crops.

OAU. *See* Organization of African Unity.

Ob, River A river in the N central Soviet Union, flowing N from the Altai Mountains to the **Gulf of Ob** on the Kara Sea. One of the world's largest rivers, its drainage basin covers an area of about 2 930 000 sq km (1 131 000 sq mi). Length: 3682 km (2287 mi).

CAPT OATES *Seen here with Cecil Meares (left), in a detail from a photograph taken by H. Ponting in 1911.*

OBE. *See* Order of the British Empire.

Oberammergau 47 35N 11 07E A town in S West Germany, in the Bavarian Alps. It is noted for its passion play, performed every ten years following a vow made by the villagers (1633) when they were saved from the plague. Population (1980 est): 4900.

oboe A woodwind instrument with a double reed, made in three jointed sections and having a conical bore and small belled end. It derives from the ancient shawm. It has a range of about three octaves above the B flat below middle C and because of its constant pitch usually gives the A to which other orchestral instruments tune.

Obote, (Apollo) Milton (1925–) Ugandan statesman; prime minister (1962–66) and president (1966–71, 1980–85). On independence he became prime minister and in 1966 deposed Mutesa II of Buganda (1924–69). Overthrown by Amin in 1971, he was re-elected in 1980 but deposed in a military coup in 1985.

O'Brien, Edna (1936–) Irish author. Her novels include *The Country Girls* (1960), *The Lonely Girls* (1962; filmed as *The Girl With Green Eyes*, 1965), *Casualties of Peace* (1966), *Night* (1972), *The Dazzle* (1981), *Returning* (1982), and *The High Road* (1988).

obsidian A black glassy volcanic rock with a conchoidal fracture. It is of rhyolitic composition and is formed by the rapid cooling of acid lava.

obstetrics. *See* gynaecology.

O'Casey, Sean (1880–1964) Irish dramatist and nationalist. His early realistic tragicomedies include *The Shadow of a Gunman* (1923) and *Juno and the Paycock* (1924). His later work includes *The Silver Tassie* (1929), *Red Roses for Me* (1943), *The Bishop's Bonfire* (1955), and *The Drums of Father Ned* (1958).

Occitan. *See* Provençal.

occultation The temporary disappearance of one astronomical body behind another, as when the moon passes in front of and obscures a star. *See also* eclipse.

occupational therapy The ancillary medical specialty concerned with restoring the physical and mental health of the sick and disabled. The occupational therapist plays an important role in keeping long-stay hospital patients interested and usefully occupied, in helping them gain confidence to return to work, and in training disabled persons for new employment. *See also* geriatrics.

Oceania The islands of the Pacific Ocean, usually taken to exclude Japan, Indonesia, Taiwan, the Philippines, and the Aleutian Islands, but often including Australasia.

Ocean Island (*or* Banaba) 00 52S 169 35E An island in the SW Pacific Ocean, in Kiribati. Rich deposits of phosphate were mined to exhaustion by the UK, 1900–1979. Resettled on Rabi Island in Fiji during World War II, the Banabans are demanding independence from the government of Kiribati. Area: about 5 sq km (2 sq mi). Population (1985): 189.

oceanography The study of the oceans, particularly their origin, structure, and form, the relief and sediments of the sea floor, the flora and fauna they contain, and the properties of sea water, waves, currents, and tides.

oceans The large areas of water (excluding lakes and seas) covering about 70% of the earth's surface. The oceans are the Pacific (covering about one-third of the world), Atlantic, Indian, and Arctic; the Southern Ocean (waters south of 40°S) is sometimes distinguished. Major structural features are the continental margins (continental shelf and slope), mid-ocean ridges, ocean basins, and trenches. See p. 528.

ocelot A cat, *Felis* (*Panthera*) *pardalis*, of Central and South American forests. 100–150 cm long including the tail (30–50 cm), it has a black-spotted buff coat with stripes on the legs. It frequently hunts by night.

Ockham's Razor The metaphysical principle, associated with the English medieval philosopher William of Ockham (c. 1285–1349), that "Entities should not be multiplied unnecessarily." In analysing a problem one should always choose the hypothesis that makes the least number of assumptions; only indispensible concepts are real.

octane number A measure of the extent to which a fuel causes knocking in a petrol engine. It is the percentage by volume of *iso*-octane (C_8H_{18}) in a mixture of *iso*-octane and *n*-heptane (C_7H_{16}), which has the same knocking characteristics as the fuel under specified conditions.

Octavia (d. 11 BC) The sister of Emperor Augustus, who married her to Mark Antony (40) to seal their reconciliation. Antony divorced her in 32, when he returned to Egypt and Cleopatra.

Octavian. *See* Augustus.

octopus An eight-armed cephalopod mollusc belonging to the genus *Octopus*, found in most oceans. The common octopus (*O. vulgaris*) has a pair of well-developed eyes, a ring of tentacles around its horny beak, and a saclike body. Octopuses feed mainly on crabs and lobsters and may eject a cloud of ink when alarmed. Family: *Octopodidae*; order: *Octopoda*.

Oder, River A river in E Europe. Rising in the Oder Mountains of Czechoslovakia, it flows N and W through Poland and enters the Baltic Sea at Szczecin. Linked by canals to both E and W Europe, it is of great commercial importance. Length: 886 km (551 mi).

Oder-Neisse Line The boundary between Germany and Poland, following the River Oder and Neisse. Confirmed by the Allies at the Potsdam Conference (1945) at the end of World War II, it was recognized by East Germany and Poland in 1950 but not by West Germany until 1970.

Odessa 46 30N 30 46E A port and industrial centre in the Soviet Union, in the S Ukrainian SSR on the Black Sea. Founded in the 14th century as a Tatar fortress, it passed to Russia in 1791 and became a naval base. It was the scene in the Revolution of 1905 of the mutiny on the *Potemkin*. Population (1987 est): 1 141 000.

Odin The principal god of the Teutonic peoples, the husband of Frigga and, according to some legends, the father of Thor. Also known as Woden and Wotan, he was the god of war, learning, and poetry and possessed great magical powers. He was the protector of slain heroes, who were brought to Valhalla by his servants the Valkyries.

Odysseus (*or* Ulysses) A legendary Greek king of Ithaca and hero of Homer's *Odyssey*, notable for his cunning. His many adventures during his voyage home from the Trojan War included encounters with the Cyclops Polyphemus, the enchantress Circe, and the goddess Calypso, with whom he lived for eight years. Having reached Ithaca, he was reunited with his faithful wife Penelope after killing her suitors with the help of his son Telemachus.

OECD. *See* Organization for Economic Cooperation and Development.

oedema The accumulation of fluid in body tissues, leading to swelling, popularly known as dropsy. There are many causes of oedema, including heart failure, kidney failure, liver failure, and malnutrition. Diuretic drugs can usually resolve oedema by causing the patient to pass more urine.

Oedipus In Greek legend, a king of Thebes who unwittingly fulfilled the prophecy of the oracle at Delphi that he would kill his father and marry his mother. He was brought up by Polybus, King of Corinth. He killed his true father, Laius, in a roadside quarrel, and after winning the throne of Thebes by solving the riddle of the sphinx he married his mother, the widowed Jocasta. When they discovered the truth, Jocasta committed suicide and Oedipus blinded himself and went into exile.

Oedipus complex The unconscious sexual feelings of a boy for his mother, which are accompanied by aggressive feelings for his father. According to psychoanalysis this is a normal desire, made unconscious by repression. The female equivalent (in which a girl desires her father) is called the **Electra complex**.

Oersted, Hans Christian (1777–1851) Danish physicist. He discovered the magnetic effect of an electric current and thus established the relationship between electricity and magnetism.

oesophagus The gullet: a muscular tube, about 25 cm long, running from the pharynx at the back of the mouth to the stomach. Contractions of the oesophagus propel swallowed food towards the stomach: the food is lubricated with mucus secreted by the walls of the oesophagus.

oestrogens A group of steroid hormones that function principally as female sex hormones. The most im-

OCEANS

diving petrel

sea surface

crabeater seal

plankton

anchovies

ocean bonito

southern
bluefin tuna

Portuguese
man-of-war

humpback whale

1000 m (3300 ft)

hatchetfish

giant squid

oarfish

3000 m (10 000 ft)

anglerfish

deep-sea
jellyfish

abyssal
sea cucumber

deep-sea
shrimp

brittle star

OCEANS *A selection of animals and plants found at different depths of the ocean.*

portant oestrogens in mammals are oestradiol and oestrone. Produced by the ovaries, they promote the development of the reproductive organs and secondary sexual characteristics (such as enlargement of breasts) at puberty and regulate the changes of the menstrual cycle. Oestrogens are also produced by the placenta, adrenal glands, and testes. Synthetic oestrogens are used to treat menstrual and menopausal disorders; they are also constituents of oral contraceptives.

oestrus The period of "heat" in the sexual cycle of female mammals, when the female will attract males and permit copulation. It corresponds to the time of ovulation, so that mating is most likely to result in pregnancy.

Offa (d. 796) King of Mercia (757–96) and overlord of all England S of the Humber. He accepted greater papal control of the Church, introduced a new currency, and devised a code of laws. **Offa's Dyke**, an earthwork dividing England from Wales, built c. 784–c. 796, marks the frontier established by his wars with the Welsh.

Offaly (Irish name: Uabh Failghe) A county in the central Republic of Ireland, in Leinster bordered in the W by the River Shannon. Area: 2000 sq km (770 sq mi). Population (1986): 59 806. County town: Tullamore.

Offenbach, Jacques (J. Eberst; 1819–80) German composer of French adoption. He wrote a series of popular operettas, including *Orpheus in the Underworld* (1858), *La Belle Hélène* (1864), and *La Vie Parisienne* (1866). He also composed one grand opera, *The Tales of Hoffman* (produced posthumously; 1881).

Ogaden, the A semidesert area in E Ethiopia, enclosed by Somalia except to the W. The nomadic inhabitants are chiefly Muslim Somalis and in the 1960s a claim to the area by Somalia provoked border clashes. Somalia invaded the Ogaden in 1977 but withdrew in 1978. Guerrilla fighting has continued.

O'Higgins, Bernardo (?1778–1842) Chilean national hero of Irish descent, who fought with José de San Martin against Spain and liberated Chile. He was made dictator of the country in 1817 but his wide-ranging reforms created much resentment and he was deposed.

Ohio A state in the USA, in the Midwest situated to the S of Lake Erie. The flat or rolling land of W Ohio gives way in the E to the hill and valley region of the Appalachian Plateau. A major industrial state, it lies at the centre of the most industrialized area of the USA and is strategically located near many rich markets. Agriculture is important, especially livestock. Ceded to Britain in 1763 and to the USA in 1783, it became a state in 1802. Area: 106 764 sq km (41 222 sq mi). Population (1985 est): 10 744 000. Capital: Columbus.

Ohio River A river in the USA flowing mainly SW from Pittsburgh in W Pennsylvania to join the Mississippi (in Illinois) as its main E tributary. Length: 1577 km (980 mi).

ohm (Ω) The SI unit of electrical resistance equal to the resistance between two points on a conductor when a potential difference of one volt between the points produces a current of one ampere. Named after Georg Ohm.

Ohm, Georg Simon (1787–1854) German physicist, who discovered in 1827 that the current flowing through a wire (or circuit element) is directly proportional to the potential difference between its ends (**Ohm's law**). The constant of proportionality is the resistance of the wire or element. The unit of resistance is named after him.

oil There are three types of oil: lipids (*see* fats and oils), essential oils, and mineral oil. Petroleum (*or* rock oil) is the thick greenish mineral oil that occurs in permeable underground rock. It consists mainly of hydrocarbons derived from the remains of living organisms deposited many millions of years ago with rock-forming sediments. Under the effects of heat and pressure this organic material passed through a number of chemical and physical changes ending up as droplets of petroleum, which migrated through porous rocks and fissures to become trapped in large underground reservoirs, often floating on a layer of water and held under pressure beneath a layer of natural gas (mostly methane). The modern oil industry began when oil was discovered in Pennsylvania in 1859 and has grown with the development of the internal-combustion engine, which is entirely dependent on it as a fuel. Once the presence of oil has been detected and its extent determined, the oil well is made by drilling through the rock; a specially prepared

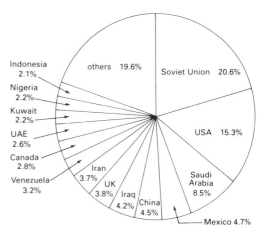

OIL *World crude petroleum production (1988).*

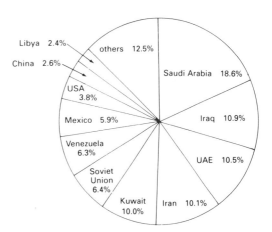

OIL *World crude petroleum reserves (1988).*

mud is pumped through the hollow bit to collect the debris, which is forced back up the shaft around the drilling bit. Drilling for oil below the sea is achieved in a similar manner, except that the drilling rig has to be supported on a base, which has legs sunk into the sea bed.

Petroleum has no uses in its crude form and has to be refined by fractional distillation (i.e. separating the components according to their boiling points) before it is of commercial value. Natural gas is widely used as a substitute for coal gas. Products made by blending the distillation fractions include aviation spirit, petrol, kerosene, Diesel oil, lubricating oil, paraffin wax, and petroleum jelly. Catalytic reforming is used to make a number of valuable chemicals (petrochemicals), which are required to manufacture detergents, plastics, fibres, fertilizers, drugs, etc.

The price, conservation, and political significance of oil are extremely controversial issues. In 1961 the Organization of Petroleum Exporting Countries (OPEC) was set up to protect producing countries from exploitation. Its advent ended the era of cheap energy and prices for petroleum products rose sharply during the ensuing decade. In 1974 the International Energy Agency (IEA) was established to protect consumers.

oil palm A palm tree, *Elaeis guineensis*, native to tropical West Africa and cultivated in Africa, Indonesia, Malaysia, and tropical America as the source of palm oil. The small fleshy fruits contain a white kernel within a hard black shell. Palm oil is extracted from the pulp and kernel and used in making soaps, margarine, lubricants, etc. The residual meal from the kernels is a valuable livestock feed.

oilseeds Oil-bearing seeds of plants from which the edible oil is extracted for making margarine, soaps, etc. Examples include rapeseed, cottonseed, groundnuts, and soya beans. The oil is obtained from the seeds by expelling it under pressure or by extracting it using a solvent; the **oilcake** remaining after most of the oil has been removed is widely used as animal feed.

Oistrakh, David (1908–75) Russian violinist. He played frequently in the West, and was well known for his performances of Brahms, Tchaikovsky, and Prokofiev violin concertos. His son and pupil, the violinist **Igor Oistrakh** (1931–), often gave joint recitals with him and has also conducted.

Ojibwa A North American Indian people of the Great Lakes region, who speak a language of the Algonkian family. They are also known as Chippewa.

okapi A hoofed mammal, *Okapia johnstoni*, of central African rain forests. Okapis have a dark-brown coat with horizontal black and white stripes on the legs and rump. The smaller male has short bony backward-pointing horns. Family: *Giraffidae* (giraffes).

Okeechobee, Lake A large freshwater lake in the USA, in S Florida. It drains into the Atlantic Ocean through the Everglades. Area: 1813 sq km (700 sq mi).

Okinawa A mountainous Japanese island, the main one of the Ryukyu group. Captured by the USA in World War II, it was returned to Japan in 1972, the USA retaining military bases there. Area: 1176 sq km (454 sq mi). Population (1986 est): 1 190 000. Capital: Naha.

Oklahoma A state in the S central USA with a diverse landscape of hills and plains. An oil-rich state, agriculture (especially cattle) remains a major source of reve-

nue. Most industry is located around Oklahoma City and Tulsa (one of the world's leading oil centres). Oklahoma formed part of the Louisiana Purchase in 1803. It was reserved as Indian territory (1828) but after the US Civil War White settlement began and it became a state in 1907. Area: 181 089 sq km (69 919 sq mi). Population (1986 est): 3 305 000. Capital: Oklahoma City.

Oklahoma City 35 28N 97 33W A city in the USA, the capital of Oklahoma on the North Canadian River. Founded in 1889, it expanded rapidly following the discovery of oil (1920s). Today it is a commercial, industrial, and distribution centre for an oil-producing and agricultural area. Population (1986 est): 445 300.

okra An annual African herb, *Hibiscus esculentus*, also called lady's fingers or gumbo, widely cultivated in the tropics and subtropics. It has five-petalled yellow flowers with a crimson centre and edible pods. The seeds are a coffee substitute. Family: *Malvaceae*.

Olaf V (1903–) King of Norway (1957–). A talented sportsman, he took part as a yachtsman in the 1928 Olympic Games. In 1929 he married Princess Märtha of Sweden (1901–54) and his heir is his son Prince Harald (1937–).

Old Catholics Christian Churches from several European countries that separated from the Roman Catholic Church at various times and in 1932 entered into communion with the Church of England. They comprise the Church of Utrecht (1724), the Old Catholic Churches of Germany, Switzerland, and Austria (1870), the National Polish Church (established 1897), and the Yugoslav Old Catholic Church (1924).

Old English sheepdog A breed of working dog originating in England. It has a characteristic ambling gait and a long dense shaggy coat that may be grey or blue-grey with white markings. Height: 55–66 cm.

Old Norse A North Germanic language formerly spoken in Iceland and Norway (c. 1150–c. 1350). It was closely related to the contemporary speech of Denmark and Sweden. From this group the modern Scandinavian languages are derived.

Old Sarum. *See* Salisbury.

Old Testament The collection of 39 books constituting the sacred scriptures of Judaism. Together with the New Testament they also form the first of the two major divisions of the Christian Bible. The title derives from the Latin word for covenant and refers to the pact between God and Israel. The books claim to cover the period from the creation of the universe and man (Adam) to about 400 BC. They are traditionally divided into three parts: the Law or Torah, the first five books, traditionally ascribed to Moses and often called the Pentateuch; the Prophets, bearing the names of individual prophets and containing much historical information; and the Writings or Hagiographa, the latest books admitted to the Hebrew Old Testament (c. 100 AD).

Olduvai Gorge A site in N Tanzania yielding an important sequence of Lower Palaeolithic fossils and tools, many found by the Leakey family.

Old Vic A London theatre built in 1818 and named the Royal Victoria in 1833. It became famous for music hall and, after Lilian Baylis (1874–1937) became manager in 1912, for productions of Shakespeare. It was the temporary home of the National Theatre Company (1963–76). Since 1982 it has been owned by the Canadian entrepreneur Ed(win) Mirvish (1914–), with Jonathan Miller (1934–) as artistic director.

OLDUVAI GORGE *Richard Leakey working at the site.*

Old World A name for Europe, Africa, and Asia, used especially by early emigrants from Europe. *Compare* New World.

Old World monkey A monkey belonging to the family *Cercopithecidae* (58 species), native to Africa or Asia. There are both terrestrial and arboreal species, active mainly by day and either omnivorous or vegetarian. They inhabit forest, savannah, swamps, and rocks. *See also* baboon; guenon; langur; macaque.

oleander A poisonous evergreen shrub, *Nerium oleander*, also called rosebay, native to the Mediterranean region and widely cultivated in warm regions for its attractive flowers. Up to 7 m high, it has long narrow leaves, clusters of white, pink, or purplish five-petalled flowers (up to 7.5 cm across), and dangling pods. Family: *Apocynaceae*.

oleaster A shrub or tree, *Elaeagnus angustifolia*, found throughout S Europe. It has silvery foliage and small fragrant yellowish flowers. The edible olive-shaped yellowish fruits have a silvery scaly coat. Family: *Elaeagnaceae*.

olefines. *See* alkenes.

Oligocene epoch. *See* Tertiary period.

olive An evergreen tree, *Olea europaea*, native to W Asia but cultivated throughout Mediterranean and subtropical regions for its fruits. It has a gnarled grey trunk, lance-shaped leathery grey-green leaves, and fleshy oval berries containing a hard stone. Unripe green olives and ripe black olives are usually pickled for use in hors d'oeuvres and other dishes. **Olive oil**, pressed from the fruit, is one of the finest edible oils. It is also used in making soaps, cosmetics, and textiles. Family: *Oleaceae*.

Olives, Mount of (*or* Olivet) 31 47N 35 15E A hill to the E of the old city of Jerusalem. Near its foot is the Garden of Gethsemane, the scene of the betrayal of Christ (Mark 14.26–50) and it is the traditional site of Christ's Ascension (Acts 1.2–12).

Olivier, Laurence (Kerr), Baron (1907–89) British actor. He played many Shakespearean roles while with the Old Vic Theatre Company, 1937–1949, and a number of outstanding modern roles, including Archie Rice in *The Entertainer* (1957). His films include the Shakespeare adaptations *Henry V* (1944), *Hamlet*

(1948), and *Richard III* (1956). While director of the National Theatre Company (1961–73), he played many leading roles. His second marriage to Vivien Leigh ended in divorce; in 1961 he married Joan Plowright (1929–).

olivine A group of greenish rock-forming silicate minerals, with a conchoidal fracture, that occur in igneous rocks. Peridot is a pale green gem variety. Olivine may be a major constituent of the earth's upper mantle.

Olympia A sanctuary of Zeus, established about 1000 BC in the NW Peloponnese, in W Greece. From 776 BC until at least 261 AD it was the venue of the Olympic Games. The temple of Zeus in the Altis (sacred grove), which later held Phidias' famous statue, was completed in 457 BC. The sanctuary was closed by the Christian Emperor Theodosius (390 AD).

Olympic Games A quadrennial international amateur sports contest. The modern games derive from the ancient Greek athletic festival held at Olympia. They were revived at Athens in 1896. The Winter Olympics were first held in 1924. The Games are governed by the International Olympic Committee, a self-elected international body. Although officially a contest between individuals, hosted by a particular city, the Games are often seen as a competition between countries; they have recently been disrupted by international political tensions, with a US boycott of the Moscow games in 1980, and an East bloc boycott of the Los Angeles games in 1984. Both blocs attended the 1988 Seoul games.

1896	Athens	1952	Helsinki
1900	Paris	1956	Melbourne
1904	St Louis	1960	Rome
1908	London	1964	Tokyo
1912	Stockholm	1968	Mexico City
1920	Antwerp	1972	Munich
1924	Paris	1976	Montreal
1928	Amsterdam	1980	Moscow
1932	Los Angeles	1984	Los Angeles
1936	Berlin	1988	Seoul
1948	London	1992	Barcelona

WINTER OLYMPICS

1924	Chamonix	1964	Innsbruck
1928	St Moritz	1968	Grenoble
1932	Lake Placid	1972	Sapporo
1936	Garmisch-Partenkirchen	1976	Innsbruck
1948	St Moritz	1980	Lake Placid
1952	Oslo	1984	Sarajevo
1956	Cortina d'Ampezzo	1988	Calgary
1960	Squaw Valley	1992	Albertville

OLYMPIC GAMES *Venues since 1896.*

Olympus, Mount 40 05N 22 21E A group of mountains in NE central Greece, held in ancient times to be the home of the gods. Highest point: 2917 m (9570 ft).

Om In Indian religions, the greatest of the mantras or mystical sounds embodying spiritual power. In Sanskrit *Om* comprises three sounds *A, U, M* (the vowels being equivalent to *O*), which represent the three Vedic scriptures, the three worlds (earth, atmosphere, heaven), the Trimurti or some other triple, and ultimately the essence of the universe.

OM. *See* Order of Merit.

Oman, Sultanate of (name until 1970: Muscat and Oman) A country in the Middle East, in E Arabia. It is mainly flat with coastal mountains in the N. The majority of the population is Arab, Ibadhi Muslim by religion, nomadic, and illiterate. Oil, which has been extracted since 1967, accounts for about 90% of the country's revenue. Oman was settled by the Portuguese, Dutch, and English in the 16th century. Since the 19th century Britain has been influential. It supported the present sultan's overthrow of his father in 1970 and has helped fight the guerrillas in Dhofar. Head of State: Sultan Qaboos ibn Sa'id. Official language: Arabic. Official currency: Rial Omani of 1000 baiza. Area: 300 000 sq km (120 000 sq mi). Population (1987): 1 200 000. Capital: Muscat.

Omar (or Umar)   (d. 644 AD) The second caliph (634–44), regarded by Islam as the founder of the Muslim state. Omar continued the Muslim conquests and in 638 visited Jerusalem after its capture. He was murdered.

'Omar Khayyam   (?1048–?1122) Persian poet, mathematician, and astronomer. His poems, characterized by an agnostic and hedonistic philosophy, were written in the form of ruba'is (quatrains). The free translation of 75 of them by Edward Fitzgerald in 1859 became widely popular; more recent translations have also been made.

Omayyads.   See Umayyads.

ombudsman   A person appointed to investigate grievances against maladministration. The post originated in Sweden in 1809. In the UK an ombudsman (the parliamentary commissioner for administration) was first appointed in 1967 to investigate complaints against central government departments; complaints against health authorities are investigated by Health Service Commissioners, appointed since 1973; there have been ombudsmen for local government since 1974.

Omdurman   15 37N 32 29E A city in the Sudan, on the River Nile. The Mahdi made it his capital in 1885 but his successor, the Khalifa, was defeated by Anglo-Egyptian forces under Lord Kitchener in the battle of Omdurman (1898). Population (1983): 526 287.

Omsk   55 00N 73 22E A port in the Soviet Union, in the W central RSFSR at the confluence of the Rivers Irtysh and Om. It is also on the Trans-Siberian Railway. Population (1987): 1 134 000.

Onassis, Aristotle Socrates   (1906–75) Greek businessman, who owned one of the largest independent shipping lines in the world and during the 1950s became one of the first to construct supertankers. In 1968 he married Jacqueline Kennedy, his second wife, after a long relationship with Maria Callas.

oncogene   A gene responsible for turning a normal cell into a cancerous cell. Several viruses (called oncogenic viruses) are known to carry oncogenes; when such a virus infects a host cell the oncogene directly transforms it into a cancer cell without altering the host cell's genes.

Onega, Lake   A lake in the NW Soviet Union, the second largest in Europe. It forms part of the water route from the Gulf of Finland to the White Sea. Area: 9887 sq km (3817 sq mi).

O'Neill, Eugene   (1888–1953) US dramatist. His plays include Beyond the Horizon (1920), Emperor Jones (1920), Anna Christie (1921), Mourning Becomes Electra (1931), The Iceman Cometh (1946), and Long Day's Journey into Night (1956). He won the Nobel Prize in 1936.

One Thousand Guineas   A flat race for three-year-old fillies only, run each spring at Newmarket over the Rowley Mile course. It was the last of the English Classics to be instituted (1814).

onion   A hardy herbaceous perennial plant, Allium cepa, probably native to central or W Asia but now cultivated worldwide, mainly in temperate regions, for its edible bulb. The mature plant has a long leafless stalk, which bears a round head of small white flowers, and six long slender leaves growing directly from the bulb. Immature bulbs, together with their leaves, are eaten raw in salads, etc.: these are spring onions. Family: Liliaceae.

Ontario   The second largest province of Canada, stretching from the Great Lakes N to Hudson Bay. It lies mainly on the mineral-rich Canadian Shield, a rocky forested plateau with many lakes and rivers. Most of the population live in the fertile lowlands near the S Great Lakes, dominated by the highly industrialized belt stretching from Toronto to Windsor. Manufacturing and mining are both important. Penetrated by French explorers and fur traders in the 17th century, Ontario became British (1763) and was settled by expatriate Americans loyal to Britain after the American Revolution. Area: 891 194 sq km (344 090 sq mi). Population (1985 est): 9 100 000. Capital: Toronto.

Ontario, Lake   A lake in E North America, the smallest and easternmost of the Great Lakes. It is fed by the Niagara River and empties into the St Lawrence River. Area: 18 941 sq km (7313 sq mi).

ontogeny.   See phylogeny.

ontology   The branch of philosophy that deals with the theory of being. Ontological theories may assert that only minds exist (extreme idealism), or that only physical objects do (see materialism).

onyx   A semiprecious stone consisting of a variety of chalcedony characterized by straight parallel bands, often distinctly coloured. Onyx occurs in the lower part of steam cavities in igneous rocks.

oolite   A variety of limestone consisting mainly of beds of ooliths, spherical concretions of calcite accumulated in concentric layers around a nucleus (for example a grain of sand or fragment of a shell). Although most oolites are calcareous, oolitic ironstones also occur.

opah.   See moonfish.

opal   A semiprecious stone consisting of a hydrous amorphous variety of silica. The precious variety, used as a gem, shows a characteristic internal play of colours (opalescence) resulting from internal reflection and refraction of light. It occurs in cavities in many rocks, deposited by percolating silica-bearing water.

Op art   A form of abstract art, developed in the 1950s and 1960s, that exploits optical techniques to produce dramatic effects, such as the illusion of movement. Violent colour contrasts and subtly distorted patterns are commonly used. Notable exponents include Victor Vasarely (1908–   ) and Bridget Riley (1931–   ).

OPEC.   See Organization of Petroleum Exporting Countries.

Open College   A nonresidential educational institution in the UK, established in 1987. It provides openlearning courses for vocational and technical qualifications, supported by radio and television programmes.

open-hearth process   A technique for making steel from pig iron, scrap steel, and iron ore, developed in the 1850s. The process uses gaseous fuel, which is preheated by the exhaust gases from the furnace. The molten metal lies in a pool at the bottom or hearth of the furnace.

Open University (OU)   A nonresidential university in the UK, established in 1969 to provide further education on a part-time basis for adults by means of correspondence courses and radio and television programmes, supported by a tutor-counselling service at regional centres throughout the country. It is open to anyone regardless of previous qualifications, age, or school attended. The first courses started in 1971. More recently the OU has moved into nondegree forms of continuing education.

OP ART *Bridget Riley's* Hesitate *(1964).*

opera A staged dramatic work in which all or most of the text is set to music. Opera originated in Florence in the early 17th century as the result of attempts to revive Greek tragedy and to reproduce its musical elements. These became the aria, recitative, and chorus of operatic convention. The earliest opera still in the modern repertory is Monteverdi's *Orfeo* (1607). Opera seria is the Italian style of opera developed by such composers as Scarlatti and Handel and characterized by a heroic or mythological plot. Opera buffa is a form of comic opera containing some spoken dialogue. It developed in the early 18th century and was originally performed between the acts of opera seria. At the end of the 18th century Mozart perfected opera buffa. In the early 19th century the influence of Romanticism gave rise to the works of Weber and Meyerbeer, while the Italian bel canto tradition was maintained by Bellini, Rossini, and Donizetti. In the mid-19th century the musical and dramatic elements of opera were integrated by Wagner in his opera cycle *Der Ring des Nibelungen* (1869–76) and his subsequent operas. Verdi extended the emotional and dramatic range of Italian opera. The realism of Bizet's *Carmen* (1875) influenced Leoncavallo, Mascagni, and Puccini. In the 20th century a wide variety of operatic styles have flourished, including the dramatic realism of Janáček and the neoclassicism of Stravinsky. Richard Strauss's operas were greatly influenced by Wagner. Other important operatic composers of the 20th century include Prokofiev, Britten, Henze, and Tippett.

ophthalmology The medical specialty concerned with the study, diagnosis, and treatment of diseases of the eye. Ophthalmologists are doctors specializing in this. **Optometry** is the assessment and correction of visual defects, and opticians are not doctors: ophthalmic opticians both test eyesight and prescribe suitable lenses; dispensing opticians make and fit glasses.

opium The dried juice obtained from the seed capsule of the opium poppy, *Papaver somniferum*, an annual cultivated in N temperate and subtropical regions. Opium is extracted from the latex of the plant, which exudes from notches made in the half-ripened capsule. A narcotic drug, opium has been used for centuries in medicine for the relief of pain. Although still sometimes given in the form of laudanum (tincture of opium), its main legitimate uses today include the extraction of its active ingredients—morphine (first isolated in 1803), codeine, papaverine, etc.—and preparation of their derivatives (e.g. heroin). Because opium causes drug dependence and overdosage can be fatal, its preparation and use are strictly controlled. (Illegal trading continues however.) India and Turkey are the main opium-producing countries.

Opium Wars **1.** (1839–42) The war between Britain and China precipitated by the confiscation by the Chinese Government of British opium stores in Canton and the murder of a Chinese by British sailors. The British victory led to five treaty ports being opened to British trade and residence. **2.** (1856–60) The war between Britain and France, on one side, and China. Its immediate cause was the boarding of the British *Arrow* by Chinese officials. The allied victory opened further ports to western trade and led to the legalization of opium.

Oporto 41 09N 8 37W The second largest city in Portugal, on the River Douro near the Atlantic coast. Built on terraces, it has many tall granite houses and a modernized 13th-century cathedral. It is famous for the export (chiefly to Britain) of its port wine. Population (1985): 344 500.

opossum A New World marsupial belonging to the family *Didelphidae* (65 species). Opossums are the only marsupials outside Australasia. The common, or Virginian, opossum (*Didelphys marsupialis*) is cat-sized, with a large pouch containing up to 16 teats.

Oppenheimer, J. Robert (1904–67) US physicist, who contributed to quantum mechanics and particle physics. In 1943 he was put in charge of the development of the atom bomb at Los Alamos, New Mexico. After the war he opposed the development of the hydrogen bomb and was labelled a security risk by Senator Joseph McCarthy's committee.

opposition An alignment of two celestial bodies in the solar system, usually the sun and a planet, that occurs when they lie directly opposite each other in the sky. The angle planet-earth-sun is then 180°.

optical activity The rotation of the plane of polarization of plane polarized light as it passes through certain solutions and crystals. The angle through which the plane is rotated is directly proportional to the path length of the light in the substance and, in the case of a solution, to its concentration. If the plane is rotated clockwise (looking at the oncoming light) the substance is said to be dextrorotatory. Laevorotatory substances rotate the plane anticlockwise.

optics The branch of physics concerned with light and vision. Optics is divided into two major branches: geometrical optics studies the geometry of light rays as they pass through an optical system; physical optics concerns light's properties (e.g. diffraction, interference, and polarization) and its interaction with matter (e.g. in refraction, scattering, and absorption).

Opuntia. *See* prickly pear.

orache An annual branching herb or small shrub of the genus *Atriplex* (about 100 species), occurring worldwide on sea shores and waste land. The leaves are narrow or triangular and, in some species, may be used as a vegetable. Family: *Chenopodiaceae.*

ORACLE *Ancient theatre and Temple of Apollo at Delphi.*

oracle A response given by a deity, usually through the medium of a priest or priestess, to an individual's inquiry; also, the sacred place at which such responses were sought. Although occurring in Egyptian and other ancient civilizations, the best-known oracles were those of classical Greece, especially the oracle of Apollo at Delphi.

Oracle. *See* teletext.

oral contraceptive A hormonal drug—usually a mixture of an oestrogen and a synthetic progesterone—taken in the form of tablets ("the Pill") by women to prevent conception. Oral contraceptives act by preventing the monthly release of an egg cell from the ovary. They may cause depression, high blood pressure, weight gain, and in rare cases thrombosis.

Oran 35 45N 0 38W A port in Algeria, on the Mediterranean Sea. Under intermittent Spanish occupation from the 16th to the 18th centuries, it was occupied by France from 1831 until Algerian independence (1962). Population (1987 est): 500 000.

orange One of several small evergreen trees or shrubs of the genus *Citrus*, native to SE Asia but cultivated throughout the tropics and subtropics. They have thick oval shiny leaves and clusters of fragrant white flowers. The globular fruit has a dimpled orange or yellow rind and a juicy pulp, rich in sugars, acids, and vitamin C. Fruit of the sweet orange (*C. sinensis*) is eaten fresh while that of the Seville orange (*C. aurantium*) is used to make marmalade. Oranges are also used in soft drinks and confectionery. Family: *Rutaceae. See also* tangerine.

Orange The ruling dynasty of the Netherlands since 1815. In the 16th century the Princes of Orange, in S France, married into the House of Nassau. William the Silent (1533–84), Prince of Orange-Nassau, led the Revolt of the Netherlands against Spain. He and his descendants (one of whom became William III of England) were stadholders (chief magistrates) of the United Provinces of the Netherlands until its collapse in 1795.

In 1815 the family were restored as monarchs of the newly established kingdom of the Netherlands.

Orange Free State An inland province in South Africa, consisting mainly of the undulating plain of the Highveld. Agriculture is the leading economic activity. Mining has developed recently; diamonds, gold, uranium, and coal are produced. The province has a strong Afrikaner culture. First settled by Voortrekkers in the early 19th century, the area was under British rule from 1848 until an independent Orange Free State was recognized in 1854. It joined the Union of South Africa in 1910. Area: 129 152 sq km (49 886 sq mi). Population (1987): 1 863 327. Capital: Bloemfontein.

Orange Order An Irish sectarian society, named after William III of England (previously William of Orange), pledged to maintain the Protestant succession. Formed in 1795, following William's defeat of the Roman Catholic former king James II, it provided the backbone of Ulster resistance to the Home Rule movement and is the embodiment of Protestant Unionism.

Orange River A river in SW Africa. Rising in NE Lesotho, it flows mainly W across the South African plateau to the Atlantic Ocean. The largest river in South Africa, it forms part of the border between South Africa and Namibia. In 1963 the **Orange River Project** was begun to provide, through a series of dams, irrigation and hydroelectric power. Length: 2093 km (1300 mi).

orang-utan A long-armed great ape, *Pongo pygmaeus*, of Borneo and Sumatra. Orang-utans grow up to 120 cm tall, have long coarse reddish-brown hair, and are mainly vegetarian. They are the only great apes outside Africa.

oratorio A musical composition, usually on a religious subject, for soloists, chorus, and orchestra. The name derives from the Oratory of St Philip Neri in 16th-century Rome where semidramatized versions of biblical stories were performed with musical accompaniment. Among notable oratorios are the *St Matthew* and *St John Passions* of J. S. Bach, Handel's *Messiah*, Haydn's *The Creation*, Mendelssohn's *Elijah*, Elgar's *Dream of Gerontius*, and Tippett's *A Child of Our Time.*

orbital An atomic orbital is the region around the nucleus in which there is an appreciable probability that an electron will be found. Each orbital has a fixed energy and a shape determined by three quantum numbers, one (n) indicating the most probable distance of the electron from the nucleus, one (l) giving its angular momentum, and one (m) giving the orientation of the orbital if it is not spherical. In the formation of a covalent bond between two atoms, a molecular orbital containing two electrons is formed. *See also* wave mechanics.

orchid A herbaceous perennial plant of the family *Orchidaceae* (about 20 000 species), found worldwide, especially in damp tropical regions. Most temperate orchids grow normally in the soil; while tropical orchids tend to grow nonparasitically on trees (i.e. as epiphytes) and form pseudobulbs (storage organs) at the base of the stem. Each flower consists of three petal-like sepals and three petals—the lowest (labellum) being very distinctive. The one or two stamens and stigma are fused to form a central column that bears pollen grains grouped into masses (pollinia), which are transferred to other flowers by insects. The flowers of many species are adapted to receive only a particular species of insect; examples are the bee, fly, and spider orchids (genus *Ophrys*). Many orchids are cultivated for ornament (*see*

Cymbidium; slipper orchid); one genus–*Vanilla*–is of commercial importance as the source of vanilla flavouring.

Order In Council A command or direction issued by the queen with the advice of the Privy Council, although in fact it is issued only with the advice of the cabinet. Apart from the Crown's inherent right (royal prerogative) to issue Orders, for example declarations of war, some Acts of Parliament (statutes) authorize them to give legal force to administrative regulations made by government departments. Only Orders authorized by act of parliament can make or alter the law.

Order of Merit (OM) A British order of chivalry, instituted in 1902. It comprises the sovereign and not more than 24 men and women of great eminence.

Order of the British Empire, The Most Excellent A British order of knighthood, instituted in 1917 and having five classes: Knights or Dames Grand Cross (GBE); Knights or Dames Commanders (KBE or DBE); Commanders (CBE); Officers (OBE); and Members (MBE).

orders of architecture The fundamental elements of classical architecture (*see illustration at* architecture), comprising five main types of supportive column–Doric, Tuscan, Ionic, Corinthian, and Composite. The column was developed by the Greeks and Romans to such an extent that the proportions between its constituent parts determined the proportions of the entire building. Each order usually consists of four main parts, the base, shaft, capital, and entablature, these having individual shapes and types of decoration.

Ordnance Survey The official map-making body of the UK. Established in 1791, following the mapping of Scotland (1726–90), it published its first map in 1801. Maps ranging from the large-scale 1:1250 (used for major urban areas) to the small-scale 1:1 000 000 (covering the entire UK in two parts) have since been produced. The original scale to be used, the 1:63 360 (1 in:1 mi) was converted to the metric scale of 1:50 000 in the 1970s and remains the most widely used scale. The First Series of the 1:50 000 was completed in 1976 and is gradually being replaced by a Second Series with redrawn maps. *See also* digital mapping.

Ordovician period A geological period of the Lower Palaeozoic era, between the Cambrian and Silurian periods. It lasted from about 515 to 445 million years ago. It is divided into the Upper and Lower Ordovician.

ore A rock body or mineral deposit from which one or more useful materials, usually metals, can be economically extracted. The gangue is the waste material left when the desired mineral has been extracted.

oregano An aromatic perennial herb, *Origanum vulgare*, native to the Mediterranean and W Asia. The dried leaves and flowers are used as a culinary flavouring and the plant is a source of essential oils. Family: *Labiatae*.

Oregon A state in the USA, on the NW Pacific coast. The Cascade Range extends N–S dividing the state between the valleys of the W and the dry plateau areas of the E. The economy is based predominantly on agriculture and forestry. Oregon is the nation's leading timber state and approximately half its area is forested; the Douglas fir is especially important. Oregon became a state in 1859, following considerable migration of White settlers from the Midwest during the 19th century. Area: 251 180 sq km (96 981 sq mi). Population (1986 est): 2 698 000. Capital: Salem.

OREGON *19th-century settlers on the Oregon trail.*

Orestes In Greek legend, the son of Agamemnon, King of Mycenae, and Clytemnestra. Encouraged by his sister Electra, he avenged his father's murder by killing his mother and her lover Aegisthus.

orfe A carnivorous food and game fish, *Idus idus*, also called ide, found in rivers and lakes of Europe and NW Asia. Its stout elongated body, 30–50 cm long, is blue-grey or blackish with a silvery belly. The golden orfe is a reddish-gold variety. Family: *Cyprinidae*; order: *Cypriniformes*.

Orff, Carl (1895–1982) German composer, teacher, conductor, and editor. He developed a monodic style of composition characterized by lively rhythms; his best-known work is the oratorio *Carmina Burana* (1935–36).

organ A musical wind instrument of early origin. The modern organ consists of a large number of graduated pipes, some of which contain reeds, fitted over a wind chest and blown by manual or electric bellows. The pipes are made to sound by depressing keys or pedals. Each pipe sounds one note, but groups of duplicate pipes, called stops, can be made to sound together or successively. Different stops have different tone colours, many of which resemble orchestral instruments. An organ console may have as many as five or more keyboards, as well as pedals. Each keyboard has a separate range of stops and different characteristics. The action linking keys and pipes consists of a series of rods called a tracker action or wires conveying electrical impulses. The modern **electronic organ** consists of a series of electronic oscillators to produce notes, which are then amplified.

organic chemistry. *See* chemistry.

organic farming. *See* fertilizers.

Organisation de l'Armée secrète (OAS) An organization of French settlers in Algeria opposed to Algerian independence from France. The OAS was established in 1961 and led by General Raoul Salan (1899–   ). Its campaign of terrorism in Algeria and France included the attempted assassination in September, 1961, of the French president, de Gaulle, who by March, 1962, had reached agreement with the Algerian nationalists (*see* Front de Libération nationale). Salan was captured (imprisoned 1962–68) and the OAS collapsed.

Organization for Economic Cooperation and Development (OECD) An international organization founded in 1961 to further world trade and coordinate aid to developing countries. It succeeded the organization set up in 1948 to coordinate the Marshall Plan for European economic recovery after World War II. The headquarters are in Paris.

Organization of African Unity (OAU) An intergovernmental organization of independent African countries. It was founded in 1963 to provide a forum for discussion of political and economic problems affecting African states and to formulate joint policies.

Organization of American States (OAS) A body founded in 1948 to foster mutual understanding and cooperation between American republics and collective security. It is based on the principle of the Monroe Doctrine, which discouraged European intervention in the Americas. Cuba was expelled in 1962.

Organization of Central American States An international organization founded in 1951. Its members include Costa Rica, El Salvador, Guatemala, Honduras, and Nicaragua, and its headquarters are in Guatemala City. Its aim is to promote social, cultural, and economic development through joint action.

Organization of Petroleum Exporting Countries (OPEC) An organization founded in 1960 to represent the interests of the 11 chief oil-exporting nations (Abu Dhabi, Algeria, Indonesia, Iran, Iraq, Kuwait, Libya, Nigeria, Qatar, Saudi Arabia, and Venezuela) in dealings with the major oil companies. In 1973 OPEC doubled its share in the receipts from oil exported; it has continued to control the price of oil.

organ-pipe cactus A tall branching columnar cactus, of the genus *Lemacrocereus* or *Cereus*, especially *L. thurberi*, which resembles a candelabra and is found in deserts of the S USA and Mexico.

orienteering A navigational sport, held over rugged country, that originated in Sweden in 1918 and is designed to test both intellectual and athletic ability. Using a map and compass, competitors run round a series of control points in a prescribed sequence.

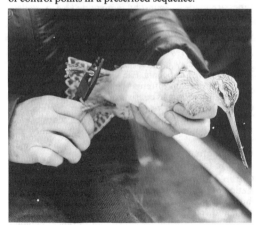

ORNITHOLOGY *Bird ringing.*

origin of life. *See* life.

Orinoco, River The third largest river system in South America. Rising in S Venezuela, it flows in an arc forming part of the Venezuela–Colombia border before entering the Atlantic Ocean via an extensive delta region. Drainage basin area: 940 000 sq km (365 000 sq mi). Length: about 2575 km (1600 mi).

oriole A songbird belonging to an Old World family (*Oriolidae*; 28 species) occurring mainly in tropical forests. Orioles generally have a black-and-yellow plumage, measure 18–30 cm, and feed on fruit and insects. The golden oriole (*Oriolus oriolus*) is the only species reaching Europe. American orioles belong to the family *Icteridae* (87 species). They usually have a black plumage with red, yellow, or brown markings.

Orion A very conspicuous constellation that can be seen from most parts of the world. The brightest stars, Rigel and Betelgeuse, lie at opposite corners of a quadrilateral of stars with Bellatrix and Saiph at the other corners. Inside the quadrilateral three 2nd-magnitude stars form **Orion's Belt**, S of which lies the **Orion nebula**.

Orkney Islands (*or* Orkneys) A group of about 70 islands off the N coast of Scotland, separated from the mainland by the Pentland Firth. The chief ones are Mainland (Pomona), South Ronaldsay, Westray, Sanday, and Hoy. The population is of Scandinavian descent, reflecting the Islands' long connections with Norway and Denmark. It became an island authority in 1975. Agriculture is of major importance within the Islands' economy. It serves as a base for the exploitation of North Sea oil with a pipeline from the Piper field. Area: 974 sq km (376 sq mi). Population (1986 est): 19 266. Administrative centre: Kirkwall.

Orléans 47 54N 1 54E A city in N France, the capital of the Loiret department on the River Loire. In 1429, during the Hundred Years' War, the strategically important city was delivered from the English by Joan of Arc. Its cathedral, which was destroyed by the Huguenots in 1568, was rebuilt in the 17th century. The focal point of road and rail routes, Orléans has an extensive trade in wine, brandy, and agricultural produce. Population (1982): 105 589.

Orléans, Louis Philippe Joseph, Duc d' (1747–93) French revolutionary. A cousin of Louis XVI of France, he nevertheless supported the dissident Third Estate at the beginning of the French Revolution, joining the radical Jacobins in 1791. He was executed after his son (later King Louis Philippe) had joined the Austrian coalition against France.

ormolu (French: *d'or moulu*, powdered gold) Ornamental gilded bronze used as embellishment on furniture, especially French 18th- and 19th-century furniture.

Ornithischia An order of herbivorous dinosaurs that lived in the Jurassic and Cretaceous periods (200–65 million years ago). They had hip bones arranged like those of birds (the name means "bird hips") and a horny beak at the front of the jaw (teeth were present only at the rear). Some were bipedal while others evolved to become quadrupedal and heavily armoured. There were both amphibious and terrestrial forms. *See* Iguanodon; Stegosaurus; Triceratops.

ornithology The study of birds. Ornithology is a popular pastime as well as a branch of zoology; the records of bird spottings made by amateur ornithologists can be valuable in helping to determine the ecology and behaviour of bird populations. Recovery of rings used in bird-ringing experiments provides information regarding the dispersion and migration of birds. Many species are protected by legislation, and bird sanctuaries have been established.

orogeny A period of mountain building. Several major orogenies have occurred in the earth's geological history, major ones since the Precambrian including the Caledonian (in the Lower Palaeozoic) and the Alpine (in the Tertiary). **Orogenesis** is the process of mountain building, including folding, faulting, and thrusting, resulting from the collision of two continents, which compresses the sediment between them into mountain chains (*see* plate tectonics).

Orpheus A legendary Greek poet and musician, the son of the muse Calliope by either Apollo or Oeagrus, King of Thrace. After sailing with the Argonauts he married Eurydice. After her death, he descended to Hades to recover her. Persephone, charmed by his playing on the lyre, released Eurydice but Orpheus lost her when he disobeyed the gods' command not to look back at her. He was murdered by the Maenads, followers of Dionysus.

orrisroot The fragrant rhizome (underground stem) of several European plants of the genus *Iris*. It is dried and ground for use in perfumes and medicines.

Ortega y Gasset, José (1883–1955) Spanish philosopher and writer, best known for his book *La rebelión de las masas* (1930).

orthoclase An alkali potassium feldspar, $KAlSi_3O_8$, found in acid igneous rocks and in many metamorphic rocks. It is white, pink, or greenish grey, and is softer than quartz, with a duller lustre. Commercially orthoclase is frequently obtained from pegmatites; it is used in the manufacture of glass, ceramic glazes, and enamels.

orthodontics. *See* dentistry.

Orthodox Church The federation of self-governing Churches historically associated with the eastern part of the Roman Empire and separated from the Latin Church since 1054; also called the Eastern Orthodox Church. The four ancient patriarchs of Orthodoxy are of Constantinople (which has primacy of honour), Alexandria, Antioch, and Jerusalem; in addition there are patriarchs of Moscow, Georgia, Serbia, Bulgaria, and Romania. Independent Orthodox Churches exist in Greece, Cyprus, Albania, Czechoslovakia, and Poland. There are numerous congregations in other countries, many established by Russian immigrants after the Revolution. Government is by bishops, who must be unmarried, priests, and deacons, who play an important liturgical role. The Orthodox Church claims the authority of apostolic succession and regards itself as the one true Church, accepting as doctrine only the Nicene Creed. Its worship is sacramental and centred on the Eucharist and the ancient liturgies of St John Chrysostom and St Basil, which are always solemnly celebrated and sung without accompaniment. The veneration of icons is a distinctive feature of Orthodox worship; statues and other three-dimensional images are forbidden. Easter is the main feast of the Church year. *See also* Greek Orthodox Church; Russian Orthodox Church.

orthopaedics The medical specialty concerned with treating deformities caused by disease of and injury to the bones and joints. This includes the use of surgery (especially for artificial hip joints), manipulation, traction, etc., in correcting deformities and fractures, together with rehabilitation of patients.

Orthoptera A mainly tropical order of generally large stout-bodied insects (15 000 species), including the grasshoppers and crickets. The hind legs are enlarged and specialized for jumping and the large blunt head has biting jaws for feeding on vegetation. Few species are good fliers. Many species produce sounds by rubbing one part of the body against another (stridulation).

ortolan A Eurasian bunting, *Emberiza hortulana*, about 16 cm long, having a brown-streaked plumage with a yellow throat and pinkish belly. Large numbers are trapped as table delicacies on their autumn migration to N Africa and the Middle East.

Orton, Joe (Kingsley) (1933–67) British dramatist, whose black comedies on themes of sexual perversion and corruption included *Loot* (1966) and *What the Butler Saw* (1969). A homosexual, he was murdered by his lover.

Orwell, George (Eric Blair; 1903–50) British novelist, born in India. His works include *Down and Out in Paris and London* (1933), *The Road to Wigan Pier* (1937), *Homage to Catalonia* (1936), *Animal Farm* (1945), and *Nineteen Eighty Four* (1949).

oryx A desert antelope, *Oryx gazella*, which comprises two races, beisa and gemsbok, of S and E Africa. Oryxes have long slender straight horns and are greyish brown with black markings on the face and legs. The Arabian oryx (*O. leucoryx*) and the N African scimitar-horned oryx (*O. tao*) are both endangered species.

Osaka 34 40N 135 30E A port in Japan, in SW Honshu on the Yodo delta. The third largest city in Japan, it was a leading commercial centre by the 17th century. It is also a cultural centre. Together with Kobe, Kyoto, and several small cities it forms the important **Osaka-Kobe** industrial area. Population (1985): 2 636 000.

Osborne, John (1929–) British dramatist, one of the original Angry Young Men, best known for his play *Look Back in Anger* (1956). His criticism of contemporary Britain continued in such plays as *The Entertainer* (1957), *A Patriot for Me* (1965), and *West of Suez* (1971). Other plays include *Luther* (1960), *Inadmissible Evidence* (1964), and *The Hotel in Amsterdam* (1967).

Osborne House A country house near Cowes, on the Isle of Wight, built for Queen Victoria in 1845 to a design by Prince Albert. It was one of her favourite residences and she died there in 1901.

Oscar. *See* Academy of Motion Picture Arts and Sciences.

oscilloscope. *See* cathode-ray oscilloscope.

osier A small willow tree, *Salix viminalis*, with flexible hairy branches used in basket making. Osiers are found in marshy areas throughout central and S Eurasia.

Osiris The Egyptian god of the dead, the brother and husband of Isis; as the father of Horus (the sun), he was also the god of renewal and rebirth. He was killed by his evil brother Set. After Isis had magically reconstructed his body, he became ruler of the underworld. Dead pharaohs became identified with Osiris. See p. 538.

Oslo (former name (1877–1925): Kristiania) 59 56N 10 54E The capital and main port of Norway, situated in the SE at the head of Oslo Fjord. It is the financial and industrial centre of Norway and is also a cultural centre. Founded in the 11th century, Oslo became capital in 1299 and developed into an important trading post under the influence of the Hanseatic League. Population (1987): 451 099.

osmiridium A naturally occurring alloy consisting mainly of osmium and iridium. It is hard and resistant to wear.

OSIRIS *The third innermost coffin of Tutankhamen, made of gold, portrays the pharoah as Osiris.*

osmium (Os) An extremely hard bluish-silver metal of the platinum group. It is one of the densest elements known (relative density 22.6). Its major use is in the production of hard alloys with other noble metals, for pen nibs and electrical contacts. At no 76; at wt 190.2; mp $3045 \pm 20°C$; bp $5027 \pm 100°C$.

osmosis The passage of a solvent from a less concentrated into a more concentrated solution through a semipermeable membrane (one allowing the passage of solvent, but not solute, molecules). Osmosis stops if the pressure of the more concentrated solution exceeds that of the less concentrated solution by an amount known as the **osmotic pressure** between them. In living organisms the solvent is water and osmosis plays an important role in effecting the distribution of water in plants and animals, causing water to pass into and out of cells.

osprey A large hawk, *Pandion haliaetus*, also called fish hawk, occurring worldwide (except in South America) around coasts and inland waters. It is 65 cm long and its plumage is brown above and white below. It feeds mostly on pike and trout, caught in its talons, which are covered in rough spikes to help grasp prey.

Ostend 1 13N 2 55E A seaport and coast in NW Belgium, on the North Sea. Ostend is the headquarters of the country's fishing fleet and maintains a cross-Channel ferry service to Dover, England. Population (1987 est): 68 318.

osteoarthritis A disease of the joints, mainly back, hips, and knees, in which their internal surfaces are rubbed away and they become swollen and painful. This becomes increasingly common as people age. Drugs can reduce the pain as can surgically installed artificial hips and knees. *See also* arthritis.

osteopathy A system of healing by manipulation and massage, based on the theory that nearly all diseases are due to the displacement of bones, especially the bones of the spine. Osteopathy is undoubtedly of use in treating dislocations, fractures, and disorders of the joint, but it is not legally recognized as a branch of orthodox medicine.

Ostia A town of ancient Rome, at the mouth of the River Tiber. A major naval base under the Republic, its prosperity was greatest in the 2nd century AD, when it was an important commercial centre.

ostrich A fast-running flightless African bird, *Struthio camelus*, occurring in open grassland and semi-desert regions. It is the largest living bird. Males may reach 2.5 m tall and are black with white wing and tail plumes; females are smaller and mainly brown. Ostriches have a long almost naked neck, a small head, and a ducklike bill used to feed on plant material. Order: *Struthioniformes*.

Ostrogoths A branch of the Goths, forced W of the River Dniester by the Huns (375 AD). In the 6th century they frequently invaded N Italy and captured much of the Balkans. Between 493 and 526 Theodoric (c. 445–526), their leader, ruled Italy. The Roman Empire, subsequently destroyed the Ostrogoths (562).

Oswald, Saint (c. 605–41) King of Northumbria (634–41) after defeating and killing the Welsh king, Cadwallader. He restored Christianity in Northumbria with the help of St Aidan. Oswald was killed in battle by Penda. Feast day: 5 Aug.

Oświęcim (German name: Auschwitz) 50 02N 19 11E A town in S Poland, site of a notorious Nazi concentration camp during World War II. Population (1982 est): 45 200.

Ottawa 45 25N 75 43W The capital of Canada, in SE Ontario on the Ottawa River. It is two-thirds English speaking and one-third French speaking. Founded in the early 19th century as a lumbering centre, it became national capital in 1867. Population (1986): 300 763.

Ottawa River A river in central Canada, rising in W Quebec and flowing W, then SE down the Ontario-Quebec border to join the St Lawrence River, as its chief tributary, at Montreal. It is linked with Lake Ontario by the Rideau Canal. Length: 1120 km (696 mi).

otter A semi-aquatic carnivorous mammal belonging to the subfamily *Lutrinae* (18 species), distributed worldwide except in Polar regions, Australasia, and Madagascar. Otters have a cylindrical body with waterproof fur, short legs, partially webbed feet, and a thick tapering tail. The Eurasian otter (*Lutra lutra*) is about 1.2 m long. Chief genera: *Lutra, Paraonyx*; family: *Mustelidae. See also* sea otter.

otterhound A breed of dog once used to hunt otters. It is a strongly built powerful swimmer with large webbed feet and a large head with long drooping ears. Otterhounds have a dense water-resistant undercoat and a long shaggy outer coat.

Otto (I) the Great (912–73 AD) Holy Roman Emperor (936–73; crowned 962). He subdued his rebellious vassals, defeated a Hungarian invasion at the great victory of Lechfeld (955), and extended his influence into Italy.

Otto, Nikolaus August (1832–91) German engineer, who in 1876 devised the four-stroke cycle, known as the Otto cycle, for the internal-combustion engine.

His engine made the development of the motor car possible.

OTTER

Ottoman Empire A Turkish Muslim empire ruling large parts of the Middle East as well as territories in Europe from the 14th to the 20th centuries. Its capital was Istanbul (formerly Constantinople) and its rulers descendants of its founder Osman I (c. 1258–c. 1326). Originating around 1300 as a small Turkish state in Asia Minor, in 1453 the Ottomans captured Constantinople and destroyed the Eastern Roman (Byzantine) Empire. Ottoman power culminated in the 16th century with the conquest of Egypt and Syria (1517) and, under Suleiman the Magnificent, Hungary (1529) and territories in the Middle East and N Africa. From the 17th century the Empire declined. In World War I the Ottomans supported Germany and defeat brought the loss of territories outside Asia Minor. The subsequent nationalist revolution of Kemal Atatürk replaced the Ottoman Empire with the state of Turkey (1922).

Ouagadougou 12 25N 1 30W The capital of Burkina Faso, founded in the 11th century as the centre of a Mossi empire. Population (1985 est): 375 000.

Oudry, Jean-Baptiste (1686–1755) French rococo painter and tapestry designer, head of the Beauvais (1734) and Gobelin (1736) tapestry works. His illustrations to La Fontaine's *Fables* are particularly well known.

ounce. *See* snow leopard.

Ouse, River The name of several rivers in England, including: **1.** A river in NE England, flowing mainly NE through Yorkshire to join the River Trent, forming the Humber estuary. Length: 92 km (57 mi). **2.** A river in S England, flowing E and S across the South Downs to the English Channel at Newhaven. Length: 48 km (30 mi). *See also* Great Ouse River.

ouzel. *See* ring ouzel.

Oval, the A cricket ground at Kennington, London, and the headquarters of the Surrey County Cricket Club. First used for cricket in 1845, the final Test match of an English series always takes place here.

ovary **1.** The organ of female animals in which the egg cells (ova) are produced. In mammals (including women) there are two ovaries close to the openings of the Fallopian tubes, which lead to the uterus (womb). They produce both eggs and steroid hormones (*see* oestrogens; progesterone) in a regular cycle (*see* menstruation). **2.** The part of a flower that contains the ovules. It is situated at the base of the carpel(s) and becomes the fruit wall after fertilization.

Ovett, Steve (1955–) British middle-distance runner. He was a gold medallist in the 800 m event at the 1980 Olympic Games and in the 5000 m events in the 1986 Commonwealth games.

Ovid (Publius Ovidius Naso; 43 BC–17 AD) Roman poet. His poems include the *Amores* and the *Ars amatoria*, on his characteristic theme of love. His greatest work, the *Metamorphoses*, is a poem in 15 books including mythological and historical tales. In 8 AD he was exiled by the emperor Augustus to the Black Sea.

ovule The structure within the ovary of a flower that contains an egg cell and nutritive tissue. After fertilization it develops into the seed containing the embryo.

ovum. *See* egg.

Owen, Dr David (Anthony Llewellyn) (1938–) British Social Democrat politician. He entered parliament as a Labour member (1966) and was foreign secretary (1977–79). A cofounder of the Social Democratic Party (SDP), he became leader in 1983 but resigned in 1987 when the party voted to merge with the Liberals; in 1988 he revived a reduced SDP.

Owen, Wilfred (1893–1918) British poet. His poetry written during World War I includes "Strange Meeting" and "Anthem for Doomed Youth." He was killed in action. His friend Siegfried Sassoon edited his *Poems* (1920).

Owens, Jesse (John Cleveland O.; 1913–80) US athlete. In 1935 he set six world records in 45 minutes (in the long jump, 100 yards, 220 yards, 220 metres, 220 yards hurdles, and 220 metres hurdles). At the Berlin Olympics (1936) he won four gold medals; this success of a Black athlete was inconsistent with the racist theories of Hitler.

JESSE OWENS *In the 1984 Olympic Games, held in Los Angeles, in the last lap of the run bringing the flame from Olympus, the torch was carried by Jesse Owens's granddaughter and Jim Thorpe's grandson.*

owl A nocturnal bird of prey belonging to an order (*Strigiformes*) of worldwide distribution. There are two families: *Strigidae* (typical owls) and *Tytonidae* (barn and bay owls). Owls have a large head with large forward facing eyes surrounded by a facial disc of radiating feathers, soft plumage, usually brown and patterned, and a short sharp hooked bill. Owls hunt mammals, birds, and insects. They range in size from 16 cm (pygmy owls; genus *Glaucidium*) to 70 cm (eagle owls; genus *Bubo*). *See* barn owl; tawny owl.

ox. *See* cattle.

oxalic acid (*or* ethanedioic acid; $(COOH)_2$) A colourless poisonous soluble crystalline solid. Potassium and sodium salts are found in plants. Oxalic acid is used as a metal cleaner and for bleaching textiles and leather.

oxeye daisy A perennial herb, *Chrysanthemum leucanthemum*, also called moon daisy or marguerite, found in grassland and wasteland throughout Europe. It has large solitary flower heads with long white rays surrounding a yellow central disc. Family: *Compositae*.

OXFAM A British charity founded in 1942, and registered in 1948 as the Oxford Committee for Famine Relief. Its purpose is to relieve suffering, throughout the world, caused by natural calamity or lack of resources. Its long-term projects include medical, social, and economic research and training schemes.

Oxford 51 46N 1 15W A city in S central England, the administrative centre of Oxfordshire on the Rivers Thames and Cherwell. Oxford is famous as a centre of learning (*see* Oxford, University of). In the Civil War Oxford was the royalist headquarters. The college buildings dominate the centre of the city but there is considerable industrial development, particularly the huge motor-car works at Cowley. It has one of the world's greatest libraries (the Bodleian Library, 1602). Population (1983 est): 116 000.

Oxford, Provisions of (1258) The scheme of constitutional reform imposed upon Henry III by his barons at Oxford following their opposition to excessive taxation. His repudiation of the Provisions (1261) led to the Barons' War.

OXFORD UNIVERSITY *The Great Quadrangle, All Souls.*

Oxford, University of One of the oldest universities in Europe, dating from the 12th century. It is organized as a federation of colleges, which are governed by their own teaching staff ("Fellows"). The University is responsible for organizing a lecture programme, maintaining the large libraries (such as the Bodleian Library), providing all laboratories, and conducting examinations. The first college, University College, was founded

in 1249. Other notable colleges include All Souls (founded 1438), Christ Church (founded in 1546 by Cardinal Wolsey), and Lady Margaret Hall (founded 1878), which was the first women's college.

Oxford Group. *See* Moral Rearmament.

Oxford Movement A movement within the Church of England in the 19th century aimed at emphasizing the Catholic principles on which it rested. Led by Newman, John Keble (1792–1866), Edward Pusey (1800–82), and James Froude (1818–94) of Oxford University, it was initiated in 1833 and greatly invigorated Anglicanism. *See also* Anglo-Catholicism.

Oxfordshire A county in the South Midlands of England. It consists mainly of a broad vale, crossed by the River Thames, with the Chiltern Hills in the SE and the Cotswold Hills in the NW. It is chiefly agricultural. Area: 2611 sq km (1008 sq mi). Population (1986 est): 574 700. Administrative centre: Oxford.

oxidation and reduction Oxidation is the chemical combination of a substance with oxygen. An example is the combustion of carbon to carbon dioxide: $C + O_2 \rightarrow CO_2$. The converse process, removal of oxygen, is known as reduction; an example is the reduction of iron oxide to iron: $Fe_2O_3 + 3C \rightarrow 2Fe + 3CO$. Reduction also refers to reaction with hydrogen and oxidation to removal of hydrogen. More generally, an oxidation reaction is one involving loss of electrons and a reduction reaction is one in which electrons are gained. Usually oxidation and reduction reactions occur together. Thus, in the reaction of ferric ions (Fe^{3+}) with stannous ions (Sn^{2+}), the ferric ions are reduced to ferrous ions (Fe^{2+}) and the stannous ions oxidized to stannic ions (Sn^{4+}). Reactions of this type are called **redox reactions**.

oxidation number (*or* oxidation state) The number of electrons that would have to be added to an atom to neutralize it. Thus Na^+, Cl^-, and He have oxidation numbers of 1, -1, and 0, respectively. Rules have been developed for assigning oxidation numbers to covalently bound atoms depending on the electric charge that the atom would have if the molecule ionized.

oxpecker An African songbird, genus *Buphagus*, that feeds on ticks and maggots pecked from the hides of cattle and game animals. Family: *Sturnidae* (starlings).

oxygen (O) A colourless odourless gas discovered by J. Priestley. The element exists in two forms—the diatomic molecule (O_2), which constitutes 21% of the earth's atmosphere, and trace amounts of the highly reactive triatomic allotrope, ozone. Oxygen is very reactive and forms oxides with most elements. In addition to its vital importance for plants and animals, its major use is in the production of steel in blast furnaces. It is obtained by the distillation of liquid air. At no 8; at wt 15.9994; mp $-218.4°C$; bp $-182.96°C$.

oxygen cycle The process by which oxygen—present in the atmosphere or dissolved in water—is taken in by plants and animals for use in respiration (intercellular combustion of food materials to provide energy) and released into the environment as a waste product, mostly in the form of free oxygen (by plants in photosynthesis). Oxygen is often combined in organic and inorganic compounds, which may also be considered as part of the cycle. *See also* carbon cycle; nitrogen cycle.

oyster A sedentary bivalve mollusc belonging to the family *Ostreidae* (true osyters), of temperate and warm seas. The lower plate (valve) of the shell is larger and flatter than the upper valve; they are held together by an elastic ligament and powerful muscles. Edible oysters are cultivated for their white flesh; pearl oysters (family *Aviculidae*) are cultivated for their pearls, which they make by coating a grain of sand lodged inside their shell with calcareous material.

oystercatcher A black or black-and-white wading bird belonging to a family (*Haematopodidae*; 4 species) occurring in temperate and tropical coastal regions. 40–50 cm long, oystercatchers have a long or flattened orange-red bill specialized for opening bivalve molluscs and probing in mud for worms and crustaceans. Order: *Charadriiformes*.

ozone (O_3) A pale blue gaseous form of oxygen, formed by passing an electrical discharge through oxygen (O_2). Ozone is a poisonous unstable gas. It is used as an oxidizing agent, for example in water purification. It is present in small amounts in the atmosphere, mostly in the **ozone layer**, which forms 10–50 km (6–30 mi) above the earth's surface as a result of dissociation by solar ultraviolet radiation of molecular oxygen into single atoms, some of which then combine with undissociated oxygen molecules. The ozone layer absorbs in the 230–320 nm waveband, protecting the earth from dangerous excessive ultraviolet radiation. In the 1980s holes in the ozone layer were detected over both poles, prompting the EC to undertake to cease to use harmful fluorocarbons by the year 2000 and individual governments to make similar decisions. *See also* greenhouse effect.

P

pacemaker A small section of specialized heart muscle that initiates heartbeat. It is situated in the right atrium and contracts spontaneously: the impulse to contract is transmitted from the pacemaker to both atria and then to the ventricles. If the pacemaker ceases to function (heart block) it may be replaced by a battery-operated device that stimulates the heart to contract.

Pacific Islands, Trust Territory of the A former UN trust territory administered by the USA. It comprised the Marshall Islands, the Federated States of Micronesia, the Mariana Islands (until 1978), and Belau. Taken by Japan from Germany (1914), the islands were captured by the USA in World War II (1944). The trusteeship was established in 1947 and dissolved in 1987.

Pacific Ocean The world's largest and deepest ocean, covering a third of its surface. It extends between Asia, Australia, Antarctica, and America. It reaches its maximum depth in the Marianas Trench. The S and E have a uniform climate with steady winds, but the W is known for its typhoons, which cause coastal flooding. The Pacific has some diurnal and mixed tides, while Tahitian tides follow the sun and not the moon.

Padang 1 00S 100 21E A port in Indonesia, in W Sumatra. An early Dutch settlement, it flourished when railways were built in the 19th century. It exports coal, cement, coffee, copra, and rubber. Population (1980): 480 922.

Paderewski, Ignacy (Jan) (1860–1941) Polish pianist, composer, and statesman. He achieved an international reputation as a performer and composed a piano concerto and many solo pieces. He was the first prime minister (1919) of newly independent Poland but resigned after ten months to return to his musical career.

Padua (Italian name: Padova) 45 24N 11 53E A city in NE Italy, near Venice. An important city in Roman and Renaissance times, it has several notable buildings; in front of the Basilica of St Anthony stands Donatello's equestrian statue of Gattamelata. Machinery and textiles are produced. Population (1986): 225 769.

paediatrics The medical specialty concerned with the problems and illnesses of infants and children from birth to adolescence. Paediatricians must have a detailed knowledge of obstetrics, genetics, and psychology. Their work includes the management of handicaps at home

Chinese   Japanese

PAGODA   *The exuberantly curving roofs of the typical multi-storeyed Chinese pagoda contrast with the more restrained Japanese form.*

and in school as well as the treatment and prevention of childhood diseases.

Paestum The Roman name for Posidonia, a colony of Sybaris founded about 600 BC on the SW coast of Italy. Paestum is famed for the three great Doric temples the remains of which still stand there. Named after the Greek sea god Poseidon, it was conquered by Rome in 273 BC.

Pagalu. *See* Equatorial Guinea, Republic of.

Paganini, Niccolò (1782–1840) Italian virtuoso violinist. After an adventurous youth he toured Europe, astonishing audiences with his techniques. He composed six violin concertos, showpieces for violin, including a set of variations on the G string, and 24 caprices.

pagoda A Buddhist shrine in the form of a tower for

housing relics of the Buddha. Pagodas originated in India, where their standardized form of a basic unit repeated vertically in diminishing sizes was evolved. From India the pagoda spread to Sri Lanka, SE Asia, China, and Japan.

paint A finely powdered insoluble pigment suspended in a binding medium; on application to a surface the volatile components of the binding medium evaporate, the drying oils oxidize, and the resins polymerize, leaving a decorative or protective skin. The binding medium consists of a drying oil (e.g. linseed oil or tung oil), a resin (rosin or a synthetic alkyd), a thinner (turpentine, benzene, etc.), and a drier (e.g. lead linoleate) to accelerate film formation. Water-based emulsion paints consist of emulsions of a synthetic resin in water.

painted lady An orange, black, and white butterfly, *Vanessa cardui*, of worldwide distribution. It cannot survive cold winters but migrates from warmer regions each year. The caterpillars feed mainly on thistles and nettles.

Paisley 55 50N 4 26W A town in W central Scotland, in Strathclyde Region near Glasgow. Famous for shawls in the 19th century, Paisley's textile industry is still important. The abstract design used for the shawls is still known as **paisley pattern**. Dyeing, bleaching, engineering, and starch and cornflour manufacturing are also important. Population (1981): 84 789.

Paisley, Ian (1926–) Northern Irish politician. A minister of the Free Presbyterian Church of Ulster from 1946, he was a Protestant Unionist MP in the Northern Irish parliament (1970–72) before becoming (1974–85; 1986–) a Democratic Unionist MP in the House of Commons. He has been an MEP since 1979.

Pakistan, Islamic Republic of A country in S Asia, bordering on Iran, Afghanistan, China, and India. The W is mountainous and the E has areas of desert, while the River Indus rises in the Himalayas in the N and flows S to the Arabian Sea. The population is a mixture of many Asian and Middle Eastern racial groups. 97% of the population is Muslim. *Economy*: mainly agricultural, producing chiefly rice, wheat, sugar cane, and cotton. Although industry employs only 14% of the workforce, Pakistan has become a major exporter of cotton and cotton yarn and cloth. Chemical fertilizers, cement, sugar, and handicrafts are also produced, and a steel industry is being developed. Fishing is increasingly important. Resources include coal, iron ore, copper, limestone, oil, and large quantities of natural gas. *History*: the history of Pakistan is that of India until 1947, when it was created to satisfy the Muslim League's demand for a separate state for the Muslim minority. It consisted then of two separate areas; West Pakistan comprised Baluchistan, the Northwest Frontier, West Punjab (now Punjab province), and Sind, while East Pakistan was formed from East Bengal. The most serious problem has been the unification of Pakistan's diverse population groups. The unifying force of the common religion has not been able to contain demands for regional autonomy and increased democracy. Thus each of Pakistan's three constitutions (1956, 1962, 1973) has been replaced by martial law. The electoral victory in East Pakistan of the Awami League (1970), which demanded regional autonomy, led to its secession as Bangladesh (1971). On 30 January, 1972, Pakistan withdrew from the British Commonwealth. More unrest followed the 1977 elections, which led finally to a military coup led by Gen Zia ul-Haq. Demonstrations and riots followed when the former prime minister, Zulfikar Ali Bhutto, was executed

for conspiracy to murder (1979). Zia became president in 1978; after he died in an air crash in 1988 Bhutto's daughter Benazir Bhutto became prime minister. She brought Pakistan back into the Commonwealth in 1989. Official language: Urdu. Official currency: Pakistan rupee of 100 paise. Area (excluding Jammu and Kashmir): 803 943 sq km (310 322 sq mi). Population (1987 est): 102 200 000. Capital: Islamabad.

Palace of Westminster The British parliamentary buildings in Westminster, London, containing the House of Commons and the House of Lords (*see* parliament). It is also known as the Houses of Parliament. A royal palace of medieval construction until the 16th century, when it assumed its present function, it was largely burnt down in 1834, only the Great Hall surviving. It was rebuilt in the gothic revival style by Barry and Pugin. *See also* Big Ben.

Palaeocene epoch. *See* Tertiary period.

Palaeolithic The earliest division of the Stone Age. It extends roughly from the emergence of man to the end of the last ice age. The Palaeolithic has three phases: Lower, beginning as much as 3 500 000 years ago and characterized by pebble-tool manufacture; Middle, beginning about 70 000 years ago and associated with Neanderthal man; and Upper, beginning about 40 000 years ago and associated with Cro-Magnon man.

palaeomagnetism The history of the earth's magnetic field (*see* geomagnetic field) as determined from the remanent magnetism of rocks. The study assumes that the principal component of igneous and sedimentary rocks' magnetism was determined at or near the time at which the rocks were formed. Palaeomagnetism provides evidence for continental drift (*see* plate tectonics) and the movement of the magnetic poles.

palaeontology The study of ancient organisms from their fossil remains in the rocks. Fossils are used to correlate bodies of rock and establish their stratigraphic relationships with each other; this field is called biostratigraphy. The study of ancient microscopic organisms is called **micropalaeontology** and the fossils are known as microfossils.

Palaeozoic era The era of geological time between the Precambrian and the Mesozoic, lasting from about 590 to 240 million years ago. It is divided into the Lower Palaeozoic, which contains the Cambrian, Ordovician, and Silurian periods, and the Upper Palaeozoic, containing the Devonian, Carboniferous, and Permian. It is the first era of Phanerozoic time.

palate The roof of the mouth, which is divided into two parts. The soft palate at the back of the mouth is composed of mucous membrane and prevents food passing into the nose during swallowing. The hard palate, further forward, is composed of two fused halves made up of the palatine bone and part of the maxillary (upper jaw) bones.

Palatinate Two regions of West Germany: the Lower (*or* Rhenish) Palatinate is now in Rheinland-Pfalz, Baden-Württemberg, and Hessen and the Upper Palatinate is now in Bavaria. In 1156 the title of count palatine was bestowed by Emperor Frederick I on his half-brother Conrad, whose territories included what later became the Rhenish Palatinate. When, in 1214, it passed to the Wittelsbach family, their lands in Bavaria became the Upper Palatinate. From 1356 the counts palatine were electors of Holy Roman Emperors. The two Palatinates were separated from 1648 until 1777 but in the early

19th century the Lower Palatinate was divided between France and various German states and the Upper Palatinate passed to Bavaria.

Palau   *See* Belau.

PALLADIANISM   *Chiswick House (begun 1725), designed by Lord Burlington for his own use.*

Palermo   38 08N 13 23E A port in Italy, the capital of Sicily. Founded by the Phoenicians in the 8th century BC, it first established itself as chief town of the island under the Arabs (9th–11th centuries). Its many notable buildings include the gothic cathedral and the Norman palace. It has shipbuilding and textile industries. Population (1986): 723 732.

Palestine (*or* Holy Land)   A historic area in the Middle East, consisting of the area between the Mediterranean Sea and the River Jordan. It now comprises Israel and territories belonging to Jordan and Egypt. Sacred to Jews, Christians, and Muslims alike, the area has been much fought over. Towards the end of the 2nd millennium BC it was settled by the Hebrew people, and in about 1000 BC a Hebrew kingdom was founded by Saul. Following the reign of Solomon it was split into Israel, later conquered by the Assyrians, and Judah (*see* Judaea), later conquered by the Babylonians. From the late 4th century AD many Jews left Palestine, which became a centre first for Christian and later for Muslim pilgrimage (following Arab conquest in 636 AD). Christianity was reinstated in the area by the conquest of the Crusaders (1099 until the 13th century). After a period of Egyptian rule it fell to the Ottoman Turks (1516), who ruled it until World War I. From the mid-19th century Jews returned from the Diaspora to settle in Palestine. The late 19th century saw the beginning of Zionism and in 1909 Tel Aviv, the first new Jewish city, was founded. In 1918 Palestine was captured by the British, who supported the Jewish demand for a Jewish nation in Palestine. This provoked unrest and terrorism among the Arab population, who felt increasingly threatened by Jewish immigration. In 1947 the problem was referred to the UN, which decided to divide Palestine into two separate states, Jewish and Arab. As this was accepted by the Jews but not the Arabs, Britain renounced its mandate in 1948. The state of Israel was then proclaimed and immediately attacked by the surrounding Arab countries. They were repulsed but the rest of Palestine was divided between Jordan and Egypt. In 1988 a new Palestinian state was declared by the PLO, but was not recognized by Israel. *See also* West Bank.

Palestine Liberation Organization (PLO)   An organization of various Palestinian groups opposed to Israel. The PLO is under the leadership of Yassir Arafat's al-Fatah. Terrorist actions carried out by the PLO include the murder of 11 Israeli athletes at the Munich Olympics (1972). In 1982 PLO forces were expelled from Lebanon when Israel invaded. PLO groups that remained subsequently became involved in conflict with other factions within the country. In 1988 the PLO set up a parliament in exile (in Tunis) for the newly declared state of Palestine.

Palestrina, Giovanni Pierluigi da   (?1525–94) Italian composer. He spent most of his life in Rome, as chorister, choirmaster, or maestro at churches including St Peter's. One of the greatest masters of polyphony, he composed 93 masses, 179 motets, and other pieces.

Palladio, Andrea   (1508–80) Italian architect, born in Padua. Palladio is famous for developing the architectural style now known as Palladianism; based on classical Roman public architecture, it was introduced into England in the early 17th century by Inigo Jones. Trained as a stonemason, Palladio's first job was the remodelling of the basilica in Vicenza (begun 1549) and from that emerged a hugely successful career. He produced villas, palaces, and churches, the most famous being S Giorgio Maggiore in Venice (begun 1566).

palladium (Pd)   A silvery-white noble metal of the platinum group, discovered by W. H. Wollaston (1766–1828) in 1803, and named after the asteroid Pallas. Palladium readily absorbs hydrogen and is used as a catalyst for hydrogenation reactions; it is alloyed with gold to form white gold. At no 46; at wt 106.4; mp 1552°C; bp 3140°C.

Pallas Athena.   *See* Athena.

palm   A monocotyledonous plant of the family *Palmae* (or *Arecaceae*; about 2500 species), occurring in tropical and subtropical regions. 1 to 60 m in height, palms typically have an unbranched trunk crowned with a cluster of very large leaves, which are pleated and fan-shaped or feather-like. The flowers are usually grouped into large clusters and give rise to berries or drupes (stone fruits). Palms are commercially important as a source of food (*see* coconut; date; sago), oil (*see* oil palm), wax, fibres, and building materials.

Palma (*or* Palma de Mallorca)   39 35N 2 39E The capital of the Spanish Balearic Islands, in Majorca on the Mediterranean Sea. Its historic buildings include the gothic cathedral (1230–1601) and the 14th-century Bellver Castle. Noted as a tourist resort, it is also a port and commercial centre; industries include textiles, footwear, and crafts. Population (1986 est): 295 351.

palm civet   A mammal of the family *Viverridae* that is smaller than the true civets and more omnivorous than the genets. Most palm civets are Asian (the two-spotted palm civet (*Nandinia binotata*) is the only African species). The masked palm civet (*Paguma larvata*) of SE Asia is up to 140 cm long including the tail (50–65 cm) and is mainly arboreal, feeding on fruit, insects, and some vertebrates.

Palmer, Samuel   (1805–81) British landscape painter and etcher. His best landscapes, often moonlit and either in sepia or watercolour, were painted during his association (1826–35) with a group of painters in Shoreham, who shared Palmer's admiration for William Blake.

Palmerston, Henry John Temple, 3rd Viscount (1784–1865) British statesman; foreign secretary (1830–34, 1835–41, 1846–51) and Liberal prime minister (1855–58, 1859–65). He entered parliament in 1807 as a Tory, serving as secretary for war from 1809 to 1828, but by 1830 he had joined the Whigs (later Liberals). His markedly nationalistic foreign policy sought to defend constitutional states and prevent a Franco-Russian combination. As prime minister Palmerston supported the Confederacy in the US Civil War but was dissuaded by his colleagues from actively involving Britain.

palmyra A palm tree, *Borassus flabellier*, cultivated in India and Sri Lanka. The timber is used for construction and the leaves are used for thatch and made into a type of paper. The sugary sap from the flower heads is fermented to give palm wine and the kernels of the fruits are eaten.

Palmyra (*or* Tadmor) 34 36N 38 15E An ancient Syrian desert city on the route of the E–W caravan trade in the 2nd and 3rd centuries AD. The ruins of the ancient city include the remains of the Temple of Bel (Palmyra's chief deity). Inscriptions in the Palmyric alphabet provide important information on Palmyra's trade.

Palomar, Mount A mountain in the USA, in California. It is the site of the Mount Palomar Observatory. Its 508 cm (200 in) reflecting telescope is among the largest in the world. Height: 1870 m (6140 ft).

Palomino A horse that has a yellow or golden coat and a white or silver mane and tail. Palominos are often Arabs or American Quarter horses but may be of any light saddle-horse breed. They are recognized as a colour breed in the USA but do not breed true.

Pamirs (*or* Pamir) A mountainous area of central Asia, situated mainly in the Tadzhik SSR of the Soviet Union. It consists of a complex of high ranges, with the Tian Shan in the N, the Kunlun and Karakoram in the E, and the Hindu Kush in the W. Its highest point in the Soviet Union is Mount Communism, at 7495 m (24 590 ft). In China it reaches 7719 m (25 326 ft) at Kungur.

Pampas The flat treeless plains of Argentina. They are of major agricultural importance in the E, producing wheat, corn, and beef in particular.

pampas grass A perennial grass of the genus *Cortaderia*, native to South America and widely cultivated as an ornamental. *C. argentea* grows in dense clumps, with leaves up to 2 m long and flowering stems exceeding 3 m in length. The flowers form silvery-white plumes.

Pamplona 42 49N 1 39W A city in NE Spain, in the Basque Provinces. It has a cathedral and holds a renowned fiesta (during which bulls are driven through the streets to the bullring). It is an agricultural centre and its industries include traditional crafts and chemicals. Population (1986 est): 184 340.

Pan The Greek god of shepherds and their flocks, the son of Hermes. He is usually portrayed with the legs, ears, and horns of a goat. He lived in the mountains and was associated especially with Arcadia, where he played his pipes (*see* panpipes).

Panama, Republic of A country in Central America, occupying the Isthmus of Panama. Narrow coastal plains rise to volcanic mountains. The population is largely of mixed Indian, European, and African descent. *Economy*: considerable revenue comes from receipts from the Panama Canal and from international capital. The main agricultural products are bananas, rice, sugar,

and maize and fishing (especially for shrimps) is growing in importance. Industries include oil refining, cement production, and paper and food processing. *History*: discovered by Columbus in 1502 and soon colonized by the Spanish. Panama later became part of the viceroyalty of Peru and then of New Granada. In 1821 it became part of newly independent Colombia, from which it broke free in 1903 after a revolution supported by the USA. A military coup in 1968 brought Gen Omar Torrijos (1929–81) to power; in 1978 he retired as head of state. In 1981 Gen Manuel Noriega (1938–) took over effective control. His alleged involvement in drug-dealing and refusal to relinquish power prompted the USA to send in a military task force (1989), which brought him to the USA to stand trial on drug charges. Guillermo Endara was installed as the new president. Official language: Spanish. Official currency: balboa of 100 centésimos. Area: 78 046 sq km (30 134 sq mi). Population (1987 est): 2 277 000. Capital and main port: Panama City.

Panama Canal A canal across the Isthmus of Panama connecting the Atlantic and Pacific Oceans. Some 82 km (51 mi) long, it was begun by the French Panama Canal Company under Ferdinand de Lesseps. In 1903 the USA acquired the construction rights from Panama and the canal was opened in 1914. The USA also acquired sovereignty in perpetuity over the **Panama Canal Zone**, a region extending 5 km (3 mi) on either side of the canal. In 1978 two treaties provided for Panamanian sovereignty over the canal and the Zone by 2000 but reserved for the USA a perpetual right to keep the canal open. Area: 1676 sq km (647 sq mi). Population (1976): 44 000.

Panama City 5 58N 79 31W The capital of Panama. Founded by the Spanish in 1519 on the site of an Indian fishing village, it was destroyed in 1671 and rebuilt two years later 8 km (5 mi) to the SW. It became capital of the newly independent Panama in 1904. The University of Panama was founded in 1935 and that of Santa Maria de la Antigua in 1965. Population (1987): 439 996.

pancreas A gland, about 15 cm long, situated in the abdomen behind the stomach. When food passes into the intestine the pancreas secretes several digestive enzymes that drain into the intestine through the pancreatic duct. In addition, small clusters of cells (called islets of Langerhans) scattered throughout the pancreas secrete the hormones insulin and glucagon.

panda A bearlike mammal of the family *Procyonidae*. The giant panda (*Ailuropoda melanoleuca*) is rare; it lives in the cold bamboo forests of central China, feeding on young bamboo shoots. Giant pandas are up to 1.6 m long and have bold black and white markings.
The red panda (*Ailurus fulgens*), also called the lesser panda, lives in the forests of the Himalayas and W China. 80–110 cm long including the bushy tail (30–50 cm), it is dark red-brown with black markings on its white face. It feeds on roots, nuts, lichens, and bamboo shoots.

Pandanus. *See* screw pine.

Pandora In Greek mythology, the first woman, fashioned by Hephaestus and invented by Zeus. She married Epimetheus, brother of Prometheus. Her dowry was a box, which, when opened, released all the varieties of evil and retained only hope.

pangolin An armoured mammal belonging to the genus *Manis* and order *Pholidota* (7 species), of Africa and S Asia, also called scaly anteater. 30–80 cm long with long prehensile tails, pangolins are covered on their backs with overlapping horny scales. Toothless, with a long sticky tongue, they feed at night on ants and termites.

PANKHURST *Emmeline and Christabel in prison uniform (1908).*

Pankhurst, Emmeline (1858–1928) British suffragette, who founded, in Manchester, the Women's Social and Political Union (1903). Imprisoned several times, she underwent hunger strikes and forcible feeding. During World War I, she encouraged the industrial recruitment of women. Her daughters **Dame Christabel Pankhurst** (1880–1958) and **Sylvia Pankhurst** (1882–1960) were also suffragettes.

panpipes (*or* syrinx) An ancient musical instrument consisting of a row of small graduated pipes bound together. According to Greek legend it was invented by Pan, who pursued the nymph Syrinx. When she was changed into a reed by Apollo, Pan made the instrument from the reed stem.

pansy A popular annual or perennial garden plant that is a hybrid of the wild pansy (*Viola tricolor*), developed in the early 19th century. There are now many varieties, up to 20 cm high, with (usually) yellow, orange, purple, brown, or white flowers. The wild pansy, or heartsease, found throughout Eurasia, has small flowers coloured purple, yellow, and white. Family: *Violaceae*. *See also* violet.

pantheism Any belief or doctrine presenting the natural world, including man, as part of the divine. Pantheism is a predominant tendency in Hinduism but is frowned on by orthodox Christianity.

Pantheon **1.** A temple dedicated to the worship of many gods. The most famous is that in Rome begun in 27 BC but rebuilt about 118 AD. A circular design topped by a huge concrete dome, in 609 AD it became the Church of Sta Maria Rotonda. **2.** A building honouring the famous. The best known is that in Paris designed by Jacques Soufflot (1713–80) in 1759.

panther A colour variety of leopard that has a great deal of black pigmentation. Panthers can occur among a litter of normally spotted leopards.

pantomime A British form of dramatic entertainment for children, traditionally performed at Christmas. Although the word also refers to several other dramatic forms, such as mime plays and dumbshows, children's pantomime developed during the 19th century from the harlequinade (*see* Harlequin). Based on fairy tales, pantomimes include popular songs and slapstick comedy. The principal boy is traditionally played by a girl, and the dame, a comic old woman, by a man.

papain. *See* papaw.

papal states The central Italian states under papal sovereignty between 756 and 1870. They included parts of Emilia-Romagna, Marche, Umbria, and Lazio. They were a major obstacle to the 19th-century movement for Italian unification (*see* Risorgimento) but were finally annexed in 1870. The popes refused to recognize their loss of temporal power until the Lateran Treaty (1929) established the Vatican City as an independent papal state.

papaw (*or* papaya) A small tropical American tree, *Carica papaya*, cultivated throughout the tropics. About 7.5 m tall, it has lobed toothed leaves and fragrant creamy-white flowers. The yellowish fruit resembles an elongated melon: its succulent pinkish or orange flesh encloses a mass of seeds. The fruits are eaten fresh, boiled, and in preserves or pickles and are a commercial source of the enzyme papain, used as a meat tenderizer. Family: *Caricaceae*.

Papeete 17 32S 149 34W The capital of French Polynesia, in NW Tahiti. A tourist centre, it is a stop on many Pacific routes. Population (1983): 62 735.

paper A substance in sheet form made from the pulped cellulose fibres of wood, grass, cotton, etc., and used for writing and printing on, wrapping, cleaning, etc. The Chinese invented paper (c. 2nd century BC). Foreign competition meant a slow start to British paper making, the first successful mill being set up about 1589. All early paper was handmade; a machine for making paper in a continuous roll was not invented until 1798, in France. Brought to England in 1803 by Henry Fourdrinier (1766–1854), this machine picked up the pulp on a travelling wire mesh and shook it until the fibres were interlaced and the water drained off, before passing it through pressing and drying rollers. The **pulp** for papermaking is obtained chiefly from wood, but also from esparto grass and rags (for strong durable high-quality paper), and increasingly from recycled wastepaper.

papilloma A harmless tumour that grows from the surface of the skin or from the lining of a hollow organ, for example the bladder, womb, or lungs. Warts and polyps are types of papilloma.

paprika. *See* Capsicum.

Papua New Guinea, Independent State of A country in the Pacific Ocean, E of Indonesia. It consists of the E part of New Guinea and several islands, including the Bismarck Archipelago, the N part of the Solomon Islands, and the Admiralty Islands. Most of the population are Melanesians. *Economy*: subsistence agriculture and the growing of cash crops, such as coconuts, cocoa, coffee, and rubber, are the chief occupations. The chief mineral resource and export is copper. Other exports include gold, coffee, cocoa, timber, and copra. *History*: the SE part of the island of New Guinea was annexed by Queensland in 1883, becoming a British colony in 1888, known as the Territory of Papua. The NE part came under Australian rule in 1914 as the Trust Territory of New Guinea. In 1921 the two territories including their islands were merged, later becoming a UN Trusteeship under Australia. It was renamed Papua New Guinea in 1971, achieved self-government in 1973, and became fully independent in 1975. Prime minister: Rabbie Namaliu. Official language: English; Pidgin is widely spoken. Official currency: kina of 100 toea. Area: 462 840 sq km (178 656 sq mi). Population (1987 est): 3 480 000. Capital and main port: Port Moresby.

papyrus An aquatic reedlike plant, *Cyperus papyrus*, up to 3 m tall, originally cultivated in the Nile delta of Egypt and now growing wild in parts of Africa and in Syria. It was used by the ancient Egyptians to make paper, and also for rope, mats, sails, and shoes. The pith was a common food. Family: *Cyperaceae*.

parabola The curve, formed by a conic section, in which the distance from a fixed point (focus) and a fixed line (directrix) are equal. In Cartesian coordinates a standard form of its equation is $y^2 = 4ax$, for a parabola that is symmetrical about the x-axis and cuts it at the origin (vertex).

Paracelsus (Theophrastus Bombastus von Hohenheim; 1493–1541) Swiss physician, whose radical ideas influenced the development of medicine during the Renaissance. He stressed the importance of chemical compounds in treating disease, refuted the notion that mental illness was caused by demons, and linked goitre with minerals in drinking water.

paraffin 1. (*or* kerosene) A mixture of hydrocarbons that boil in the range 150–300°C and have a relative density of 0.78–0.83. It is obtained from crude oil by distillation and is used as a fuel for domestic heating and for aircraft. 2. *See* alkanes.

paraffin wax A wax obtained during the refining of crude oil. Fully refined, it is a white tasteless solid (mp 50–60°C) consisting of higher alkanes; it is extensively used in the manufacture of waxed papers, candles, and polishes.

PARAGUAY *The presidential (Lopez) palace, Asunción.*

Paraguay, Republic of A landlocked country in the centre of South America. It is divided by the River Paraguay into two zones: an area of fertile plains and hills to the E and the semidesert of the Gran Chaco to the W. The great majority of the population is of mixed Spanish and Guaraní Indian descent. *Economy*: chiefly agricultural, livestock rearing is of particular importance. Meat packing is one of the main industries. Exports include meat, cotton, oilseed, and timber. The main crops are cotton, soya beans, cassava, and sugar cane. Hydroelec-

tricity is being developed, especially for the export of power to neighbouring countries. *History*: explored and colonized by the Spanish in the 16th century, it became independent of Spain in 1811, and in 1814 José Gaspar Rodríguez de Francia (1766–1840) was elected dictator. The population suffered great losses in the War of the Triple Alliance (1865–70) against Brazil, Argentina, and Uruguay and again in the Chaco War (1932–35) with Bolivia. In 1954 Gen Alfredo Stroessner (1912–) seized power and became president; he was overthrown in a coup in 1989. Paraguay is a member of the OAS and LAFTA. President: Andrés Rodríguez. Official language: Spanish; the majority speak Guaraní. Official currency: guaraní of 100 céntimos. Area: 406 752 sq km (157 042 sq mi). Population (1987): 3 897 000. Capital and main (river) port: Asunción.

Paraguayan War. *See* Triple Alliance, War of the.

parakeet A small seed-eating parrot characterized by a long tapering tail and a predominantly green plumage and found especially in SE Asia and Australia. Brightly coloured species are popular as cagebirds. *See also* budgerigar; rosella.

paralysis Failure of a muscle or a group of muscles to work. This is most commonly caused by damage to the nerve (and its connections) supplying the muscle, as resulting from injury or infection (*see* poliomyelitis), but it may also be due to failure of the nerve impulse to be transmitted to the muscle (as in myasthenia gravis) or by wasting of the muscle (as in muscular dystrophy). A stroke causes damage to the part of the brain that controls movement and commonly results in **hemiplegia**, in which one half of the body and face becomes paralysed. **Paraplegia** (paralysed legs) results from injury to the spinal cord. **Quadriplegia** (paralysed legs and arms) results when the spinal cord is damaged close to the brain.

paramagnetism A form of magnetism caused by the presence in atoms or molecules of electrons with unpaired spins. The atom or molecule therefore acts like a tiny magnet (*see* ferromagnetism). In the presence of an external magnetic field these microscopic magnets tend to align with the field, reinforcing it. The effect is destroyed by random thermal motion and, except at low temperatures and high field strengths, the permeability (a measure of the extent of alignment) is inversely proportional to the temperature.

Paramaribo 5 52N 55 14W The capital and main port of Suriname, in the N on the River Suriname. Founded by the French (1540), it was later under English and then Dutch rule. The University of Suriname was founded in 1968. Population (1986): 77 558.

Paraná, Rio (Spanish name: Río Paraná) A river in South America. Formed by the confluence of the Rio Grande and Rio Paranaíba in SE central Brazil, it flows generally S for 2900 km (1800 mi) to join the River Uruguay and form the Río de la Plata. The Itaipu Dam, the world's largest dam, which is sited at Foz do Iguaçu near the Paraguayan border, was opened in 1982.

paranoia A mental disorder in which the patient is governed by a rigid system of irrational beliefs (delusions). The sufferer may believe that he is being persecuted by others, or that he is overwhelmingly important. The condition can result from schizophrenia, alcoholism, or manic-depressive psychosis.

paraplegia. *See* paralysis.

Paraquat $(C_9H_{20}N_2(SO_4)_2)$ The trade name for a yellow water-soluble solid that is used as a weedkiller.

Highly toxic, it concentrates in the lungs and also causes kidney damage.

parasite An organism living in or on another organism of a different species (called the host), from which it obtains food and protection: the relationship may or may not be harmful to the host. Many parasites have complex life cycles, with one or more intermediate hosts (of different species) supporting the parasite in the immature stages of its development. The study of parasites –**parasitology**–is of great importance in medicine since many parasites, such as bacteria, ticks, and fleas, either cause or transmit disease. Many plants are either partly or completely parasitic: mistletoe is a partial parasite.

parathyroid glands Two pairs of small endocrine glands lying immediately behind the thyroid gland. These glands secrete **parathyroid hormone** in response to a reduction in the level of calcium in the blood. This hormone causes the release of calcium from the bones and its transfer to the blood. Deficiency of parathyroid hormone results in muscle spasms and cramps (tetany).

parchment Animal skin, usually of the goat, sheep, or calf, treated for writing on. It derives its name from Pergamum, where in the 2nd century BC improved methods of treating skins were developed. It was used for manuscripts and early bound books. More delicate skin from young animals is called vellum. *See also* leather.

Paris 48 52N 2 18E The capital of France and a department of the Paris Region, situated in the N of the country on the River Seine. The administrative, commercial, and cultural centre of France, Paris is also an important industrial base, and many international organizations, including UNESCO, have their headquarters here. At the heart of the city, the Île de la Cité contains the cathedral of Notre-Dame. On the Left Bank lie Montparnasse and the Latin Quarter, which is known for its associations with writers and artists. On the Right Bank stands the Palais du Louvre, one of the world's most important museums. Further W is a series of radiating boulevards meeting at the Place Charles de Gaulle. The Champs Élysées runs from the Arc de Triomphe at the centre of the Place Charles de Gaulle to the Place de la Concorde. Further N lies Montmartre, dominated by the Basilica of the Sacré Coeur (1919). To the S of the Seine stands the Eiffel Tower, built for an exhibition in 1898. *History*: the earliest known settlement was on the Île de la Cité in Roman times. In the 6th century Clovis made it the capital of his Frankish kingdom but it later suffered attacks from Vikings. It regained importance as the capital under the Capetians. Since the storming of the Bastille (1789), heralding the beginning of the French Revolution, it has been the scene of many revolts, such as the July Revolution and the Revolution of 1848. Population (1982): 2 176 243.

Paris In Greek legend, a son of Priam and Hecuba. His abduction of Helen with the help of Aphrodite caused the Trojan War, during which he killed Achilles and was himself killed by Philoctetes. *See also* Eris.

parity In physics, the concept of left- and right-handedness. According to the law of conservation of parity, no fundamental distinction exists between left and right. In 1957 this principle was shown to be violated in weak interactions. For example, when a neutron decays the electron produced is always left-polarized (i.e. spins in a direction opposite to that of its motion), whereas if parity was conserved there would be equal numbers of left- and right-polarized electrons. This lack

of parity provides a fundamental distinction between left and right. The parity of elementary particles is expressed as a quantum number.

MUNGO PARK *Surprised by a lion in Africa; an illustration from his book.*

Park, Mungo (1771–c. 1806) Scottish explorer. In 1795–96 he ascended the Niger from the mouth of the River Gambia, crossed the Sénégal Basin, and was imprisoned by Arabs. His *Travels in the Interior Districts of Africa* (1797) related his adventures. In 1805, under government patronage and with 40 companions, he resumed his exploration. The expedition was attacked by Africans and Park died.

Parker, Charlie (Christopher) (1920–55) US Black jazz saxophonist and composer, known as "Bird" or "Yardbird." With Dizzy Gillespie he originated the bop style of jazz and appeared with a number of bands.

Parkinson, (Cyril) Northcote (1909–) British author, historian, and journalist. While professor of history at the University of Malaya (1950–58), he wrote *Parkinson's Law* (1958), a study of business administration containing the aphorism that work expands to fill the time allotted to it. His other books include *The Law and the Profits* (1960), *Big Business* (1974), and *The Guernseyman* (1982).

parkinsonism (*or* Parkinson's disease) A chronic disease affecting the part of the brain controlling voluntary movement, first described in 1817 by a British physician, James Parkinson (1755–1824). Sometimes the disease may result from infection, side effects of drugs, or injury, but usually no cause is apparent. The symptoms are tremor of the hands and mouth, stiffness, and difficulty in initiating movements. It is treated with drugs, including L-dopa, or surgery.

parliament The legislative assembly of a country. In the UK parliament is the supreme legislature; it consists of the sovereign, the House of Lords, and the House of Commons; its seat is the Palace of Westminster. Parliament developed in the 13th century from the Curia Regis (King's Court), in which the monarch consulted with his barons. In 1213, 1254, and 1258 representatives of the shires were also summoned to attend parliament and in 1265 the parliament summoned by Simon de Montfort included borough representatives–the origins of the House of Commons. By the reign of Edward III (1327–77) Lords and Commons, meeting separately, were recognized constituents of government. Parliament's conflict with James I and Charles I led to the Civil War (1642–51) and the establishment of republican government under Oliver Cromwell. Following the Restoration of the monarchy in 1660, the attempts of James II to rule arbitrarily led to the Glorious Revolution (1688), which achieved the beginning of parliamentary ascendancy over the Crown. The 18th century saw the emergence of party politics and of a prime minister and the development of cabinet government.

The House of Lords has over 1000 members (*see* peerage). Its speaker is the Lord Chancellor. The House of Commons has (1985) 650 members of parliament (MPs), each representing a geographical constituency, and is regulated by the Speaker of the House of Commons. Parliamentary legislation is introduced in the form of private or public bills. After a first reading a bill will be printed and then debated in a second reading. It is then referred to a committee by which it may be amended. Its amendments are considered by the whole house and it then receives a third reading after which it is sent to the other house, where it goes through a similar procedure. After passing both houses the bill receives the royal assent and becomes an Act of Parliament.

parliamentary commissioner for administration. *See* ombudsman.

Parma   44 48N 10 19E A city in N Italy, in Emilia-Romagna. Dating from Roman times, it became an important cultural centre in the middle ages. Its university was established in 1222 and it has a romanesque cathedral and a 16th-century palace. The centre of an agricultural district, Parma's industries include the manufacture of Parmesan cheese, perfume, fertilizers, and glass. Population (1986): 175 842.

Parnassus, Mount   (Modern Greek name: Parnassós) 38 32N 22 41E A mountain in S central Greece, held in ancient times as sacred to the god Apollo and the Muses. Height: 2457 m (8061 ft).

Parnell, Charles Stewart   (1846–91) Irish politician, who in 1880 became the leader of the Home Rule party in the British House of Commons. Parnell, an MP from 1875, reconciled constitutional and radical forces and enjoyed widespread popular support in Ireland. He allied his party with the Liberals in 1886, when Gladstone introduced the Home Rule bill. Parnell remained a dominant political figure until 1890.

Parr, Catherine   (1512–48) The sixth wife (1543–47) of Henry VIII of England. After Henry's death, she married (1547) Thomas, Baron Seymour of Sudeley (d. 1549).

parrot   A bird belonging to the family (*Psittacidae*; 300 species) occurring worldwide in warm regions. 10–100 cm long, parrots have a compact body, a short neck, and strong rounded wings. The plumage is typically brightly coloured and the short stout hooked bill is used to open nuts and to feed on fruits and seeds. Most are arboreal and excellent climbers, having clawed feet with rough scaly toes. They have a harsh screaming voice. Order: *Psittaciformes. See also* cockatoo; lory; lovebird; macaw; parakeet.

parrot fish   A fish, also called parrot wrasse, belonging to the family *Scaridae* found among tropical reefs. The teeth are fused to form a hard beak, which is used to feed on coral, molluscs, and seaweed. Order: *Perciformes*.

Parry, Sir (Charles) Hubert (Hastings)   (1848–1918) British composer of operatic, orchestral, choral, chamber, and solo works, the best known of which is the song *Jerusalem* (1916). He was the director of the Royal College of Music (1894–1918) and professor of music at Oxford University (1900–08).

parsec   A unit of distance, used in astronomy, corresponding to a parallax of one second of arc. 1 parsec = 3.26 light-years or 3.084×10^{16} metres.

Parseeism   The religion of the descendants of Persians who fled their country in the 8th century AD to avoid persecution following the Arab conquest. Mostly located in Bombay, Madras, Calcutta, and Karachi, they continue to practise Zoroastrianism in two sectarian forms.

parsley   A fragrant biennial herb, *Petroselinum crispum*, native to the Mediterranean region but widely cultivated. The compound leaves have an aromatic flavour. They are used fresh or dried in fish and meat dishes, soups, garnishes, and bouquets garnis. The flowering stems, up to 1 m high, bear yellowish flowers. Family: *Umbelliferae*.

parsnip   A hairy strong-smelling biennial plant, *Pastinaca sativa*, native to Eurasia and widely cultivated for its large starchy white taproot, which is eaten as a vegetable or used as cattle feed. The leaves consist of paired lobed toothed leaflets on a long furrowed stalk and the clusters of tiny yellow flowers are borne on stems up to 150 cm high. Family: *Umbelliferae*.

parthenogenesis   A method of reproduction in which the egg develops without fertilization to produce an individual usually identical to the parent. It occurs commonly among lower plants and animals, particularly aphids, ants, bees, and wasps.

PARTHENON

Parthenon   A temple on the hill of the Acropolis in Athens dedicated to the goddess Athena. Built between 447 and 432 BC, it represents the summit of classical Greek architecture. Its rectangular colonnaded exterior of Doric columns originally contained a walled chamber with Phidias' gold and ivory statue of Athena. In the 5th century AD it became a Christian church and in the 15th century a mosque. It blew up during a bombardment by the Venetians in 1687. *See also* Elgin Marbles.

Parthia The region S of the Caspian Sea approximating to present-day Khorasan (NE Iran). Inhabited by seminomadic tribes, Parthia controlled a great empire from about 250 BC to 224 AD with its capital at Ctesiphon. Parthia's famous cavalry and mounted archers overwhelmed Crassus' army in a humiliating defeat at Carrhae in 53 BC. In 224 AD the Parthian empire was conquered by the Sasanians of Persia.

particle physics The study of elementary particles and their interactions. The existence of the electron (J. J. Thomson; 1898) and the discovery of the proton (Rutherford; 1914) made it clear that the atom had an internal structure. When the neutron was discovered (Chadwick; 1932), it appeared that the whole universe was constructed of just these three particles. The outstanding problem was the nature of the force that held neutrons and protons together in the atomic nucleus. The only two fundamental forces known at that time were the gravitational force and the electromagnetic (em) force: the gravitational force was too weak to account for the great stability of the nucleus and the em force had no effect on the electrically uncharged neutron.

In 1935 Yukawa suggested that there might be in nature a short-lived particle (later called the meson) that jumped between protons and neutrons and held them together. This concept of exchange forces and the subsequent discovery of short-lived particles led to intensive research into particle physics throughout the world (*see* accelerators). By the 1960s some 200 "elementary" particles had been identified and it became clear that there were four basic types of force; in addition to gravitational and em forces there were strong interactions (100 times more powerful than em forces) and weak interactions (10^{10} weaker than em forces). There are now believed to be two classes of particles: leptons (the electron, muon, tau particle, and neutrinos), which interact by the em or the weak forces and have no apparent internal structure; and hadrons (including the proton, neutron, pion, etc.), which interact by the strong interaction and do appear to have an internal structure.

The current model of the hadron is based on Murray Gell-Mann's concept of the quark, introduced in 1963. In this model, hadrons themselves are divided into two classes: baryons, which decay into protons; and mesons, which decay into leptons and photons or into proton pairs. Baryons consist of three quarks and mesons consist of a quark-antiquark pair. Thus all the matter in the universe is now seen as being made of leptons and quarks. Quark theory is fairly elaborate; quarks have fractional electronic charges ($+2/3$ or $-1/3$ of the electronic charge) and come in six "flavours" called up (u; $+2/3$), down (d; $-1/3$), charmed (c; $+2/3$), strange (s; $-1/3$), top (t; $+2/3$), and bottom (b; $-1/3$). For each flavour there is an equivalent antiquark (ū, d̄, etc.). The proton consists of uud ($2/3 + 2/3 - 1/3 = 1$) and the neutron consists of udd ($2/3 - 1/3 - 1/3 = 0$).

In this limited form quark theory conflicted with the Pauli exclusion principle and it therefore became necessary to introduce the concept of "colour." Thus each flavour of quark can have one of the three colours red, yellow, or blue, with antiquarks having the corresponding anticolours. "Colour" in this sense has no connection with visual colour but the analogy is useful. All hadrons are regarded as white and baryons must consist of a red, a blue, and a yellow (since these visual colours produce white); mesons consist of a quark of any colour and its corresponding anticolour. *See also* antimatter; charm; quantum number; strangeness.

partridge A small gamebird native to the Old World but widely introduced elsewhere. Partridges are 25–40 cm long and have rounded bodies with short rounded wings. The European partridge (*Perdix perdix*) is a common farmland bird and has a greyish plumage with a red face and tail. Family: *Phasianidae* (pheasants, quail, partridges).

pascal (Pa) The SI unit of pressure equal to one newton per square metre. Named after Blaise Pascal.

Pascal, Blaise (1623–62) French mathematician, physicist, and theologian. He invented Pascal's triangle for calculating the coefficients of a binomial expansion. He also made discoveries in fluid mechanics, notably that the pressure in a fluid is everywhere equal (**Pascal's principle**). In 1641 he invented the first calculating machine. At the age of 31 he had a mystical experience; in the same year he became a Jansenist and his *Lettres provinciales* (1656–57) defended Jansenism against the Jesuits. His greatest work was *Pensées sur la religion* (1669), a poetical and metaphysical treatise on human nature.

Passchendaele. *See* World War I.

passerine bird A bird belonging to the order *Passeriformes*, which includes over half (about 5100) of all bird species. Passerines—the perching birds—are characterized by their feet, which are specialized for gripping branches, and stems. They are the most highly evolved birds and occur in almost every habitat, although few live or feed in water. There are both migratory and sedentary species.

The order is divided into four major groups (suborders): *Eurylaimi* (broadbills); *Tyranni* (includes manakins, ovenbirds, pittas, and tyrant flycatchers); *Menurae* (lyrebirds and scrubbirds); and—the largest and most advanced group—*Oscines* (*see* songbird).

passionflower A climbing plant of the genus *Passiflora* (500 species), native chiefly to tropical and subtropical America and cultivated for ornament. The leaves may be simple or deeply lobed; some are modified as tendrils. The distinctive flowers each consist of a cup-shaped base with five coloured sepals and petals at its upper edge surmounted by a coloured fringe. The fruit is a berry or capsule, which in some species (e.g. *P. quadrangularis*) is edible (passionfruits *or* granadillas). Family: *Passifloraceae*.

Passion plays Religious dramas concerning the crucifixion and resurrection of Christ. They were performed on Good Friday throughout medieval Europe. The Passion play at Oberammergau in West Germany has been performed every ten years since 1634.

Passover (Hebrew word: *Pesah*) One of the three biblical pilgrimage festivals (the others are Weeks and Tabernacles). It commemorates the Exodus from Egypt and also incorporates a spring harvest festival. In Judaism, it is celebrated for seven or eight days, beginning on the eve of the first day with a formal meal. In Christianity it has been replaced by Easter.

Pasternak, Boris (1890–1960) Russian poet and novelist. He published several volumes of Symbolist poetry between 1917 and 1923. His epic novel *Dr Zhivago* was banned in Russia but became internationally successful after its publication in Italy in 1957. Under severe political pressure, he declined the Nobel Prize in 1958.

LOUIS PASTEUR *Women bringing their children for vaccination in the streets of Paris.*

Pasteur, Louis (1822–95) French chemist and microbiologist, who made great advances in the prevention and treatment of diseases caused by microorganisms. In 1854 Pasteur was appointed dean of the faculty of sciences at Lille University. He found that fermentation was caused by microorganisms and that by excluding these, souring or decay could be prevented (*see* pasteurization). Although partially paralysed in 1868, Pasteur's interest in germs and disease directed his attention to anthrax. By 1881 he had devised a means of safely inducing immunity to the disease by injecting a vaccine of heat-treated (attenuated) live anthrax bacilli. Pasteur also produced a vaccine for chicken cholera and an effective rabies vaccine. The Pasteur Institute was founded in 1888 to treat rabies and has since developed into a world centre for biological research.

pasteurization Heat treatment used to destroy the microorganisms in milk. The method involves heating milk for 30 minutes at 60°C, which kills the tuberculosis bacteria without damaging the milk protein. This process is named after Louis Pasteur.

Patagonia A geographic area of S South America in Argentina and Chile, extending S of the River Colorado to the Strait of Magellan. It consists chiefly of an arid plateau rising to the Andes. Sheep raising is the principal economic activity. It contains the major oilfield of Comodoro Rivadavia and the Río Turbio coalfield. Area: about 777 000 sq km (300 000 sq mi).

pathology The branch of medicine concerned with the study of disease and disease processes in order to understand their causes and nature. The specialty originated in the mid-19th century, with the work of Virchow, Pasteur, and Koch on the bacterial cause of disease, but it was not until the beginning of the 20th century that the knowledge gained in the laboratory was applied to the treatment and prevention of disease in patients. Examples of early work in the science of clinical pathology include Schick's test for diphtheria and Wasserman's test for syphilis. Chemical pathology developed notably with the work of Banting and Best on the importance of insulin in diabetes and contributions from such haematologists as Landsteiner in the discovery of the blood groups. Today pathology includes studies of the chemistry of blood, urine, faeces, and diseased tissue, together with the use of X-rays and many other investigative techniques.

Patna 25 37N 85 12E A city in India, the capital of Bihar on the River Ganges. It was founded in 1541 on the former site of Pataliputra, ancient capital of the Maurya and Gupta empires. Population (1981): 916 000.

Patras (*or* Pátrai) 38 14N 21 44E A port in W Greece, in the N Peloponnese on the Gulf of Patras. The War of Greek Independence began here in 1821. Exports include currants, sultanas, tobacco, and olive oil. Population (1981): 141 529.

patricians The hereditary aristocracy of ancient Rome. Originally the sole holders of political and religious offices, the patricians were gradually forced during Republican times to admit plebeians to political offices and their privileged position was eroded.

Patrick, St (c. 390–c. 460 AD) The patron saint of Ireland. A local chief's slave in Antrim, he later escaped to Gaul, finally returning to Ireland as a missionary. He established an archiepiscopal see at Armagh and by the time of his death had firmly established Christianity in Ireland. His only certain works are a spiritual autobiography, the *Confession*, and the *Epistle to Coroticus*. Feast day: 17 March. Emblems: snakes and shamrock.

Patton, George S(mith) (1885–1945) US general. In World War II he commanded the Seventh Army in Sicily (1943) and then the Third Army in France. He breached the German defences in Normandy and led a spectacular advance to the Moselle. In the Ardennes he cleared the W bank of the Rhine, crossed it, and encircled the Ruhr.

Paul VI (Giovanni Battista Montini; 1897–1978) Pope (1963–78). Succeeding John XXIII, Paul continued his predecessor's policies of reform, reconvening the second Vatican Council after his election.

Paul, St (c. 3–c. 64 AD) Christian Apostle, born Saul of Tarsus, who spread Christianity among the Gentiles; the 13 Epistles attributed to him form a major part of the New Testament. The son of a Pharisee and a Roman citizen, he was initially anti-Christian, having participated in the martyrdom of St Stephen. While travelling to Damascus, he had a vision that led to his conversion to Christianity. He began his activity as an Apostle in Damascus, later joining the other Apostles in Jerusalem. His important missionary work consisted of three journeys in which he travelled to Cyprus, Asia Minor, Macedonia, Greece, Ephesus, and elsewhere. Arrested by Roman soldiers on his return to Jerusalem, he eventually appealed to Caesar and, as a Roman citizen, was taken to Rome for trial. He was imprisoned for two years; here the New Testament account (in Acts) ends. Feast day: 29 June.

Pauli, Wolfgang (1900–58) US physicist, born in Austria, who in 1925 formulated the Pauli exclusion principle, that no two fermions may exist in the same state, for which he received the 1945 Nobel Prize. In 1931 he postulated that some of the energy of a beta decay was carried away by massless particles, which Fermi named neutrinos.

Pauling, Linus Carl (1901–) US chemist, who originated and developed important concepts concerning the structure of molecules. Successfully using new analytical techniques, Pauling elucidated the nature of chemical bonding in both simple and complex molecules, publishing *The Nature of the Chemical Bond* in

1939. He received the Nobel Prize for Chemistry (1954) for his research and the Nobel Peace Prize (1962) for his pacifist stance against the use of nuclear weapons.

Pavarotti, Luciano (1935–) Italian operatic tenor. He made his debut at La Scala, Milan, in 1966 and at the Metropolitan Opera in New York in 1968. He specializes in the works of Bellini, Verdi, and Puccini.

Pavlov, Ivan Petrovich (1849–1936) Russian physiologist, noted for his studies of digestion and his demonstration of the conditioned reflex. Pavlov showed how heartbeat is regulated by the vagus nerve and how eating stimulates secretion of digestive juices by the stomach. He extended his theories of reflex behaviour to cover aspects of human behaviour, such as learning. He was awarded the 1907 Nobel Prize.

Pavlova, Anna (1885–1931) Russian ballet dancer. She joined Diaghilev's company in Paris in 1909, and from 1914 she devoted her career to international tours with her own company. She created the chief role in *Les Sylphides* and was especially associated with *Le Cygne*, choreographed for her by Fokine in 1907.

Paxton, Sir Joseph (1801–65) British architect. Initially a gardener, Paxton experimented with new techniques of construction in building greenhouses at Chatsworth. This experience culminated in the design of the revolutionary Crystal Palace for the Great Exhibition of 1851.

pea An annual herb of the genus *Pisum* (about 6 species), native to the Mediterranean area and W Asia, especially the widely cultivated *P. sativum*. The leaves consist of paired oval leaflets and have curling tendrils used for climbing. The edible round seeds are contained in an elongated pod and are an important source of protein for man and livestock. Family: *Leguminosae*.

Peace River A river in W Canada, whose headstreams (Finlay and Parsnip Rivers) rise in the British Columbia Rockies. Flowing generally NE across the N Alberta plains, it empties into the Slave River. It is mostly navigable and is also tapped for hydroelectricity. Its valley is fertile farmland, with important oil and timber reserves. Length: 1923 km (1195 mi), including Finlay River.

peach A small tree, *Prunus persica*, probably native to China but widely cultivated in Mediterranean and warm temperate regions. Up to 6 m high, it has toothed glossy green leaves and pink flowers. The round fleshy fruit (a drupe) has thin velvety skin, yellowish with a crimson tinge. The sweet white or yellow flesh encloses a wrinkled stone. Peaches are eaten fresh, canned, or in preserves. Nectarines (*P. persica* var. *nectarina*) are varieties with smooth-skinned fruits. Family: *Rosaceae*.

peacock. *See* peafowl.

Peacock, Thomas Love (1785–1866) British satirical novelist. He worked for the East India Company from 1819 to 1856 and was a close friend of Shelley. His seven novels, which include *Nightmare Abbey* (1818) and *Gryll Grange* (1860), satirize contemporary fashions and ideas.

peacock butterfly A common Eurasian nymphalid butterfly, *Inachis io*. The adults are brownish purple with a bright eyespot on each wing. They fly from early spring well into summer. The black spiny caterpillars feed on stinging nettles.

peafowl An Old World gamebird belonging to a genus (*Pavo*; 2 species) native to lowland forests of India and SE Asia. Peafowl are 75 cm long and the female (peahen) has a green-brown plumage; males (peacocks) have elaborate lacy tails, 150 cm long, the feathers of which are tipped by blue-and-bronze markings and raised over the body during display. Family: *Phasianidae* (pheasants, partridges, etc.); order: *Galliformes* (pheasants, turkeys, etc.).

Peak District A hilly area in N central England, in Derbyshire, at the S end of the Pennines. It reaches 727 m (2385 ft) at Kinder Scout and contains many limestone caves.

Peake, Mervyn (1911–68) British novelist. His trilogy of novels, *Titus Groan* (1946), *Gormenghast* (1950), and *Titus Alone* (1959), is a modern gothic fantasy whose bizarre horrors parallel those of the real world. *Selected Poems* (1972) was published posthumously.

peanut. *See* groundnut.

pear A tree of the genus *Pyrus* (about 20 species), native to temperate Eurasia. The numerous cultivated varieties of orchard and garden pears are derived from *P. communis*. Up to 13 m high, it has oval leaves and white flowers. The fruit, which narrows towards the stalk, has

SIR JOSEPH PAXTON *The Crystal Palace, Hyde Park, 1851.*

sweet gritty flesh; it is eaten fresh or canned. The wood is used for furniture making. Family: *Rosaceae*.

pearl A natural calcareous concretion formed around a foreign body in certain bivalve molluscs popularly

PEARL   *Embedded in an oyster.*

known as pearl oysters or pearl mussels. Used for jewellery since earliest times, pearls are usually white or bluish grey and of globular, oval, pear-shaped, or irregular form. It consists of concentric films of nacre, consisting of aragonite, which also forms the smooth lustrous lining (mother-of-pearl) in the shells of pearl-bearing molluscs. Cultured pearls are beads of mother-of-pearl artificially inserted into the mollusc, where they are left for three to five years. Birthstone for June.

Pearl Harbor An inlet of the Pacific Ocean in the USA, in Hawaii on Oahu Island. On 7 December, 1941, the Japanese launched an air attack on US military installations in Hawaii. This action precipitated US involvement in World War II. It is now a naval shipyard, supply centre, and submarine base.

Pears, Sir Peter (1910–86) British tenor. He was well known for his performances of Bach and Schubert and was closely associated with the music of his friend Britten.

Pearson, Lester B(owles) (1897–1972) Canadian statesman and diplomat; Liberal prime minister (1963–68). Ambassador to the USA (1945–46), chairman of NATO (1951), and delegate to the UN, Pearson played a key role in settling the Suez crisis (1956), which earned him the Nobel Peace Prize in 1957.

Peary Land An area in N Greenland, between Victoria Fjord and the Greenland Sea. It is the most northerly land area in the world and was named after the Arctic explorer, Robert E. Peary (1856–1920), who first explored it in 1892.

Peasants' Revolt (1381) The only major popular revolt in England during the middle ages. It was occasioned by heavy poll taxes and reflected a general discontent with government policies. The peasants, led by Wat Tyler and John Ball (d. 1381), marched on London. They achieved initial success, but the revolt soon collapsed and its supporters were ruthlessly suppressed.

peat Partially decomposed dark-brown or black plant debris laid down in waterlogged conditions in temperate or cold climates. The remains of *Sphagnum* (peat or bog

moss) are important constituents. Peat is the starting point for coal formation and is itself used as a fuel.

pecan. *See* hickory.

peccary A small gregarious hoofed mammal belonging to the genus *Tayassu* (2 species) of South and Central American forests. Resembling a pig, the collared peccary (*T. tajacu*) is dark grey with a light stripe from chest to shoulder and grows to a length of 90 cm. It has two pairs of short tusks. The white-lipped peccary (*T. albirostris*) is darker and larger and has a white patch on the snout. Both are omnivorous. Family: *Tayassuidae*.

pectin A carbohydrate found combined with cellulose in the cell walls of plants. Ripening fruits change any other pectic compounds present into jelly-like pectin—an essential ingredient for the gelling of jam.

Peel, Sir Robert (1788–1850) British statesman; Conservative prime minister (1834–35, 1841–46). Elected to parliament in 1809, he was twice home secretary (1822–27, 1828–30), introducing prison and criminal-law reforms and founding the Metropolitan Police (1829). In the Tamworth manifesto (1834), a speech to his constituents, he stated a programme of reform that clearly identified the Conservative Party. He is best remembered for the repeal of the Corn Laws (1846).

peepul. *See* bo tree.

peerage In the UK and Ireland, the temporal hereditary noblity and the life peers, comprising (since 1876) the Lords of Appeal in Ordinary and (since 1958) those created in recognition of public service. The five ranks of the hereditary peerage are, in descending order, duke, marquess, earl, viscount, and baron. A life peer has the rank of baron. All peers are permitted to sit in the House of Lords.

peewit. *See* lapwing.

Pegasus (Greek mythology) A winged horse that sprang from the blood of Medusa. It carried the legendary hero Bellerophon in his battles. It became a constellation and the bearer of thunderbolts for Zeus.

PEKING   *A soldier stands guard in front of the Gate of Heavenly Peace after the massacre in Tiananmen Square (June 1989).*

Peking (Chinese name: Beijing *or* Pei-ching)   39 55N 116 25E The capital of the People's Republic of China, an administratively autonomous city situated in the NE of the country in Hobei province. The city has expanded considerably since 1949 and there has been rapid development of industries. *History*: the site has a long history of human habitation. As Ta-tu, it first became the capital (of N China) under the Yuan dynasty in 1272. The capital was later moved to Nanjing, returning to Peking (1420) under the third Ming emperor. In 1928 the Nationalist (Guomindang) government moved the capital to Nanjing. Peking became the capital of the People's Republic of China in 1949. In 1989 thousands of students demonstrating for reform were massacred in Tiananmen Square. Population (1986 est): 5 860 000.

Pekingese An ancient breed of toy dog originating in China and brought to the West by British forces who sacked the Imperial Palace, Peking, in 1860. The Pekingese has a long straight coat forming a luxuriant mane on the shoulders and a black short-muzzled face. Height: 15–23 cm.

Peking man A type of fossil hominid belonging to the species *Homo erectus* and represented by skeletal remains found at Chou-K'ou-Tien (*or* Zhou kou tian) cave near Peking. Formerly known as *Sinanthropus*, Peking man lived during the middle Pleistocene period (c. 500 000 years ago).

Pelagius (c. 360–c. 420 AD) The originator of the heretical Christian doctrine known as Pelagianism. He rejected original sin and predestination, believing in man's free will and inherent capacity for good.

Pelargonium. *See* geranium.

Pelé (Edson Arantes do Nascimento; 1940–) Brazilian Association footballer. The greatest inside forward of his time, he became a world star at 17 when Brazil first won the World Cup (1958). He scored over 1300 goals.

Pelham, Henry. *See* Newcastle, Thomas Pelham-Holles, 1st Duke of.

pelican A large waterbird belonging to a family (*Pelecanidae*; 7 species) occurring on lakes, rivers, and coasts of temperate and tropical regions. 125–180 cm long, pelicans have short legs, a short tail, and very large wings. Their long straight pointed bills have a distensible pouch underneath, in which fish are held before being swallowed. Order: *Pelecaniformes* (gannets, pelicans, etc.).

pellagra A disease caused by deficiency of nicotinic acid (*see* vitamin B complex). It occurs mainly in poor countries in people whose diet consists predominantly of maize. The disease causes dermatitis, diarrhoea, and delirium or depression.

Peloponnese (Modern Greek name: Pelopónnesos) The S peninsula of Greece, joined to central Greece by the Isthmus of Corinth. It includes the towns of Corinth, Patrás (the chief port), and Sparta. Area: 21 637 sq km (8354 sq mi). Population (1981): 1 012 528.

Peloponnesian War (431–404 BC) The conflict between Athens and Sparta and their allies, in which Sparta was finally victorious. Sparta's superior infantry invaded Athens in 431 while Athens, under Pericles, attacked at sea. In 415 Athens led by Alcibiades set out to conquer Sicily, which retaliated with Spartan help and destroyed the Athenian fleet (413). The war continued until Sparta under Lysander besieged Athens, which then surrendered (404).

Peltier effect. *See* thermoelectric effects.

pelvis A basin-like structure composed of the hip bones and lower part of the spine. It protects the soft organs of the lower abdomen and provides attachment for the bones and muscles of the legs.

Penal Laws (1571, 1581, 1593) A series of Acts passed during the reign of Elizabeth I to punish those (recusants), especially Roman Catholics, who refused to attend Church of England services. Recusants were fined, imprisoned, banished, or executed and suffered civil disabilities, such as loss of property. The Laws were repealed in 1829 (*see* Catholic emancipation). *See also* Test Acts.

Penang A state in NW Peninsular Malaysia, on the Strait of Malacca, consisting of Penang island and Province Wellesley on the mainland. The island was the first British settlement in Malaya. The main products are rice, rubber, and tin. Area: 1031 sq km (398 sq mi). Population (1985 est): 1 049 282. Capital: Georgetown.

Penates. *See* Lares and Penates.

pendulum A device in which a mass (the bob) swings freely about a fixed point with a constant period. In the ideal simple pendulum the bob is connected to the fixed point by a length (l) of weightless string, wire, etc. Its period is $2\pi(l/g)^{1/2}$, where g is the acceleration of free fall, and is independent of the mass of the bob. Pendulums are used to regulate a clock mechanism and in instruments that determine the value of g.

Penelope In Homer's *Odyssey*, the wife of Odysseus. During her husband's absence she put off her many suitors by saying that she must first make a shroud for her father-in-law Laertes. Each night she unravelled what she had woven by day.

penguin A flightless black-and-white seabird belonging to a family (*Spheniscidae*; 14–18 species) occurring on cold coasts of the S hemisphere. Penguins are adapted for aquatic life, having wings reduced to narrow flippers giving fast propulsion. 40–120 cm long, they have dense plumage enabling them to tolerate extreme cold. Order: *Sphenisciformes*. *See also* emperor penguin; fairy penguin.

penicillins A group of antibiotics. The first penicillin was discovered in the mould *Penicillium notatum*, in 1929, by Sir Alexander Fleming but was not used to treat infections in man until 1941. Some penicillins must be injected (e.g. benzylpenicillin); others can be taken by mouth (e.g. phenoxymethylpenicillin). Semisynthetic penicillins (e.g. flucloxacillin, methicillin) are effective against infections resistant to naturally occurring penicillins. Penicillins can cause severe allergic reactions in susceptible patients.

Peninsular War (1808–14) That part of the Napoleonic Wars fought in Spain and Portugal. The French took Portugal in 1807 and in 1808 Napoleon's brother, Joseph Bonaparte (1768–1844), replaced Ferdinand VII as King of Spain. Popular revolts broke out and turned into a vicious guerrilla war. British troops under the command of the Duke of Wellington eventually liberated the Peninsula.

penis The male copulatory organ of mammals, some reptiles, and a few birds. In man (and other mammals) it contains a tube (urethra) through which both semen and urine can be discharged. Erectile tissue making up the bulk of the penis becomes engorged with blood during sexual excitement. The corresponding part in women is the **clitoris**, a small erectile mass of tissue situated in front of the urinary opening.

Pen-ki. *See* Benxi.

Penn, William (1644–1718) English Quaker and founder of Pennsylvania, son of Admiral Sir William Penn (1621–70). He joined the Quakers in 1664. In 1668 he was imprisoned in the Tower, where he wrote *No Cross, No Crown* (1669), a classic of Quaker practice. From 1682 he was involved in the establishment of Quaker settlements in America, including Pennsylvania.

Pennines (*or* Pennine Chain) An upland range in N England. It extends from the Cheviot Hills in the N to the valley of the River Trent in the S. Sometimes known as the "backbone of England" it is the watershed of the chief rivers in N England. It rises to 893 m (2930 ft) at Cross Fell.

Pennsylvania A state in the E USA, dominated by the uplands of the Appalachian Plateau. It is a leading iron and steel producer and provides nearly all the country's hard coal. Oil has long been important and the world's first oil well was drilled near Titusville in 1859. Dairy farming predominates in the NE, while the fertile lands of the SE yield cereals, fruit, and vegetables. *History*: one of the 13 original colonies, the first European settlers, the Swedes, were soon dispossessed by the Dutch (1655). In 1681 the area was given to William Penn by Charles II of England as a haven for Quakers. It became a state in 1787. Area: 117 412 sq km (45 333 sq mi). Population (1986 est): 11 889 000. Capital: Harrisburg.

Pennsylvanian period. *See* Carboniferous period.

PENTAGON *In Washington, DC; an aerial view.*

Pentagon The headquarters of the US Defense Department, a massive five-sided building in Virginia built (1941–43) during World War II. It houses all three services and is the largest office building in the world, extending over 14 hectares (34 acres).

pentathlon An athletic competition comprising five events, the winner being the competitor with the highest total. It originated in an Olympic contest instituted in 708 BC. The current women's version, an Olympic event since 1964, consists of the 100 m hurdles, shot put, high jump, long jump, and 800 m run. The men's pentathlon has been replaced in major competitions by the decathlon. The **modern pentathlon** is a sporting competition comprising five events: a 5000 m cross-country ride (on horseback), fencing, pistol shooting, a 300 m swim, and a 4000 m cross-country run. It was first included in the Olympic Games in 1912.

Pentecost. *See* Whit Sunday.

Pentecostal Churches A Christian movement originating in revivalist meetings in the USA in 1906. In Pentecostal assemblies people seek spiritual renewal through baptism by the Holy Spirit, as took place on the first Pentecost (Acts 2.1–4).

pentlandite The principal ore mineral of nickel, (Ni,Fe)S, found in association with pyrrhotite and chalcopyrite in basic and ultrabasic igneous rocks. It is mined in Canada, Australia, and the Soviet Union.

peony A large perennial herb or shrub of the genus *Paeonia* (33 species) of N temperate regions, often cultivated for its showy flowers. It has large glossy leaves and solitary white, pink, crimson, or yellow flowers, about 10 cm across, with incurving petals and a fleshy central disc. The fruit is a large leathery pod containing black seeds. Family: *Paeoniaceae*.

People's Liberation Army (PLA) The military forces of the People's Republic of China. The name was adopted by Chinese communist troops during the civil war of the 1930s and 1940s. Since Liberation (1949) the PLA has exercised considerable power in Chinese communist politics.

Pepin the Short (d. 768 AD) King of the Franks (751–68) after overthrowing the Merovingians. Founder of the Carolingian dynasty, Pepin checked Lombard expansion and in 756 presented Pope Stephen II with the nucleus of the papal states.

pepper A condiment derived from a perennial climbing vine, *Piper nigrum*, native to India. Up to 10 m high, it bears chains of up to 50 inconspicuous flowers that form berry-like fruits (or peppercorns), about 5 mm in diameter. Family: *Piperaceae*.
The fleshy red and green peppers are the fruits of *Capsicum* species.

peppered moth A European geometrid moth, *Biston betularia*, the typical form of which has a similar coloration to the lichen-encrusted tree bark on which it rests. During the past century a dark form, var. *carbonaria*, has become common in sooty industrial areas.

peppermint A perennial herb, *Mentha × piperata*: a hybrid between water mint (*M. aquatica*) and spearmint. It has smooth dark-green leaves and reddish-lilac flowers and is the source of oil of peppermint, used as a flavouring.

pepsin A protein-digesting enzyme found in gastric juice. The inactive form, pepsinogen, is secreted by glands in the stomach wall and converted to pepsin by the hydrochloric acid in the stomach. Pepsin is a powerful coagulant of milk.

peptic ulcer An inflamed eroded area in the wall of the stomach (**gastric ulcer**) or, more commonly, the duodenum (**duodenal ulcer**). Ulcers are more common in people who secrete excessive amounts of stomach acid. They may cause abdominal pain, nausea, and vomiting. Serious complications occur when the ulcer bleeds or perforates (bursts).

peptide A chemical compound comprising a chain of two or more amino acids linked by peptide bonds (–NH–CO–) formed between the carboxyl and amino groups of adjacent amino acids. Polypeptides, containing between three and several hundred amino acids, are the constituents of proteins. Some peptides are important as hormones and as antibiotics.

Pepys, Samuel (1633–1703) English diarist. He was secretary to the Admiralty (1669–88), an MP, and presi-

SAMUEL PEPYS *Detail of a painting by John Hayls, executed in 1666.*

dent of the Royal Society. His *Diary*, which extends from 1660 to 1669 and includes descriptions of the Restoration, the Plague, and the Fire of London, was written in code.

perch One of two species of freshwater food and game fish belonging to the genus *Perca*. The common perch (*P. fluviatilis*) of Eurasia has a deep elongated body, usually about 25 cm long, and is greenish in colour, with dark vertical bars on its sides and a spiny first dorsal fin. Perch usually live in shoals, feeding on fish and invertebrates. Family: *Percidae*; order: *Perciformes*. See *also* sea bass.

Percy, Sir Henry (1364–1403) English rebel, called Hotspur. Together with his father, Henry, 1st Earl of Northumberland (1342–1408), he led the most serious revolt against Henry IV, whom they had helped to the throne in 1399. He appears in Shakespeare's *Henry IV*, Part I.

peregrine falcon A large powerful falcon, *Falco peregrinus*, occurring in rocky coastal regions worldwide. It is 33–48 cm long and has long pointed wings and a long tail. The male is blue-grey with black-barred white underparts; females are browner. It feeds mainly on ducks, shorebirds, and mammals.

Pereira 4 47N 75 46W A city in W Colombia. An agricultural trading centre, it has coffee-processing, brewing, and clothing industries. Population (1985): 301 715.

perennials Plants that can live for many years. In herbaceous perennials aerial parts die down each winter and the plants survive in the form of underground organs (rhizomes, bulbs, corms, etc.). Woody perennials have woody stems, which overwinter above ground.

Peres, Shimon (1923–) Israeli statesman, prime minister (1984–86); foreign minister (1986–88); finance minister (1988–). Born in Poland, Peres emigrated to Palestine in 1934. He became head of the navy in 1948 and was defence minister from 1974 to 1977. When a coalition government was formed in 1984, he became Labour prime minister under a special power-sharing agreement with Yitzhak Shamir.

perestroika. See glasnost.

Pérez de Cuéllar, Javier (1920–) Peruvian diplomat; UN secretary-general (1982–). A respected negotiator, he sought peaceful solutions to the Falklands conflict, the Gulf War, and other crises.

Pergamum An ancient city of W Asia Minor. After about 230 BC it became capital of a powerful Hellenistic kingdom. Pergamum became rich largely from parchment and luxury textiles mass-produced by slave labour. The last king bequeathed his realm to Rome (133 BC).

Pericles (c, 495–429 BC) Athenian statesman, who presided over Athens' golden age. Pericles became leader of the democratic party in 461 and secured power shortly afterwards. He dominated Athens until 430 by virtue of his outstanding oratory and leadership and his reputation for honesty. Under Pericles, Athens asserted its leadership of the Delian League and revolts among its members were suppressed. By 431, rivalry between Athens and Sparta had led to the outbreak of the Peloponnesian War. The effectiveness of Pericles' strategy was undermined by the plague of 430 and Pericles briefly lost office. He died shortly after his reinstatement.

peridotite An ultrabasic coarse-grained igneous rock consisting mainly of olivine. The earth's mantle is sometimes called the peridotite shell. Peridotites occur beneath many mountains and islands.

perigee The point in the orbit of the moon or of an artificial satellite around the earth at which the body is nearest the earth. *Compare* apogee.

Perigordian A culture of the Upper Palaeolithic. Perigordian is the preferred French designation for the pre-Solutrean industries in W Europe, excluding the typologically different Aurignacian. Upper Perigordian is approximately equatable with Gravettian.

Périgueux 45 12N 0 44E A town in SW France, the capital of the Dordogne department. It is renowned for its *pâte de foie gras,* truffles, and wine. Manufactures include hardware and chemicals. Population (1982): 35 392.

perihelion The point in the orbit of a body around the sun at which the body is nearest the sun. The earth is at perihelion on 3 Jan. *Compare* aphelion.

period. See geological time scale; periodic table.

periodic table A tabular arrangement of the chemical elements in order of increasing atomic number, such that physical and chemical similarities are displayed. The earliest version was devised in 1871 by D. Mendeleyev, who predicted the existence of several elements from gaps in the table. The rows across the table are known as periods and the columns as groups. The elements in a group all have a similar configuration of outer electrons and therefore show similar chemical behaviour. Across each period, atoms are electropositive (form positive ions) to the left and electronegative to the right. Atomic theory explains this behaviour using the concept of electron shells, corresponding to different energy levels of the atomic electrons. Atoms combine in order to form complete outer shells. The shells are built up by filling the lower energy states (inner shells) first. The first shell takes two electrons, and the second, eight. In larger atoms, the inner electrons screen the outer electrons from the nucleus, resulting in a more complex shell-filling sequence. The short periods are from lithium (Li) to neon (Ne) and from sodium (Na) to argon (Ar). The noble gases in column 0 have complete outer shells and are generally chemically inactive. See p. 556.

periodontal disease Disease of the gums and other structures surrounding the teeth, formerly known as pyorrhoea. Caused by the action of bacteria on food debris

1A	2A	3B	4B	5B	6B	7B		8		1B	2B	3A	4A	5A	6A	7A	0
1 H																	2 He
3 Li	4 Be											5 B	6 C	7 N	8 O	9 F	10 Ne
11 Na	12 Mg				←		TRANSITION ELEMENTS				→	13 Al	14 Si	15 P	16 S	17 Cl	18 Ar
19 K	20 Ca	21 Sc	22 Ti	23 V	24 Cr	25 Mn	26 Fe	27 Co	28 Ni	29 Cu	30 Zn	31 Ga	32 Ge	33 As	34 Se	35 Br	36 Kr
37 Rb	38 Sr	39 Y	40 Zr	41 Nb	42 Mo	43 Tc	44 Ru	45 Rh	46 Pd	47 Ag	48 Cd	49 In	50 Sn	51 Sb	52 Te	53 I	54 Xe
55 Cs	56 Ba	57† La	72 Hf	73 Ta	74 W	75 Re	76 Os	77 Ir	78 Pt	79 Au	80 Hg	81 Tl	82 Pb	83 Bi	84 Po	85 At	86 Rn
87 Fr	88 Ra	89‡ Ac															

† Lanthanides	57 La	58 Ce	59 Pr	60 Nd	61 Pm	62 Sm	63 Eu	64 Gd	65 Tb	66 Dy	67 Ho	68 Er	69 Tm	70 Yb	71 Lu
‡ Actinides	89 Ac	90 Th	91 Pa	92 U	93 Np	94 Pu	95 Am	96 Cm	97 Bk	98 Cf	99 Es	100 Fm	101 Md	102 No	103 Lr

PERIODIC TABLE

that forms a hard deposit (tartar) in the spaces between the gums and teeth, it results in swelling and bleeding of the gums: eventually—if untreated—the teeth become loose and fall out. Periodontal disease is the major cause of tooth loss in adults: it may be prevented (and the early stages treated) by regular brushing, scaling, and polishing, to remove the tartar. Advanced cases require surgery.

periscope An optical device consisting, typically, of a tube in which mirrors or prisms are arranged so that light passing through an aperture at right angles to the tube is reflected through the length of the tube to emerge at an aperture at the other end also at right angles to the tube. Extendible periscopes are used by submerged submarines to see above the surface of the water.

Perissodactyla An order of hoofed mammals (16 species) that includes horses, tapirs, and rhinoceroses. The name—meaning odd-toed—reflects the fact that the weight of the body is carried mainly by the central (third) digit of the foot. They are herbivorous, but have only a single stomach, which is less efficient than the digestive system of ruminants. *Compare* Artiodactyla.

peritonitis Inflammation of the peritoneum—the membrane that lines the abdominal cavity. This results from the bursting of an abdominal organ (such as the appendix) or of a peptic ulcer. Alternatively it may result from bacterial infection. An operation is essential to repair the perforated organ and cleanse the abdomen; antibiotics are also given.

periwinkle (botany) An evergreen creeping shrub or perennial herb of the genus *Vinca* (5 species), native to Europe and W Asia. The attractive solitary flowers are blue or white and the fruit is usually a long capsule. They are cultivated as ornamentals: *V. major* is an important species. Family: *Apocynaceae.*

periwinkle (zoology) A gastropod mollusc belonging to the family *Littorinidae*, also called winkle. The common edible winkle (*Littorina littorea*) of European seashores is about 2 cm high and has a dark-green rounded shell with a pointed spire and grazes on algae.

Perkin, Sir William Henry (1838–1907) British chemist, who in 1856 synthesized the first artificial dye, aniline purple. The following year he built a factory to manufacture the dye but he later returned to chemical research and the synthesis of many compounds.

Perm (name from 1940 until 1957: Molotov) 58 01N 56 10E A port in the Soviet Union, in the W RSFSR on the River Kama. Its varied industries include engineering, chemical manufacturing, and oil refining. The Permian period was first identified here. Population (1987): 1 075 000.

permafrost The permanent freezing of the ground, sometimes to great depths, in areas bordering on ice sheets. During the summer season the top layer of soil may thaw and become marshy, while the frozen ground below remains an impermeable barrier.

permeability, magnetic (μ) A measure of the response of a material to a magnetic field equal to the ratio of the magnetic flux induced in the material to the applied magnetic field strength. The relative permeability, μ_r, is the ratio of μ in the medium to that in a vacuum, μ_0 (*see* magnetic constant). Paramagnetic materials have a μ_r greater than unity because they reinforce the magnetic field. Ferromagnetic materials can have a μ_r as high as 100 000. Diamagnetic materials have a μ_r of less than one.

Permian period The last geological period of the Palaeozoic era, between the Carboniferous and Triassic periods, lasting from about 280 to 240 million years ago. The period was marked by an increasingly dry climate that continued into the Triassic, and the two periods are often linked together as the Permo-Triassic.

permittivity (ε) The absolute permittivity of a medium is the ratio of the electric displacement to the electric field at the same point. The absolute permittivity of free space is called the electric constant. The relative permittivity (or dielectric constant) $ε_r$ of a capacitor is the ratio of its capacitance with a specified dielectric between the plates to its capacitance with free space between the plates.

Pernambuco. *See* Recife.

JUAN PERÓN *With his wife Evita.*

Perón, Juan (Domingo) (1895–1974) Argentine statesman; president (1946–55, 1973–74). Elected in 1946 after winning popular support as head of the labour secretariat, his position was strengthened by the popularity of his second wife, **Evita Perón** (María Eva Duarte de P.; 1919–52), who was idolized by the poor for her charitable work. After her death, support for Perón waned and he was deposed. He was re-elected president in 1973.

Perpendicular The style of gothic architecture predominant in England between about 1370 and the mid-16th century. The name derives from the panel-like effect of the window design, with its pronounced vertical mullions broken regularly by horizontal divisions. King's College chapel, Cambridge (1446–1515) and St George's chapel, Windsor (begun 1481) are masterpieces of the Perpendicular style.

Perpignan 42 42N 2 54E A city in S France, the capital of the Pyrénées-Orientales department situated near the Spanish border. The capital of the former province of Roussillon in the 17th century, it has a gothic cathedral and a 13th-century castle. Perpignan is a tourist and commercial centre, trading in wine, fruit, and vegetables. Population (1982): 113 646.

Persephone (Roman name: Proserpine) Greek goddess of the underworld, daughter of Zeus and Demeter. She was abducted by Hades, who made her queen of the underworld. Zeus allowed her to spend part of each year on earth, symbolizing the regeneration of natural life in the spring.

Persepolis An ancient Persian city in Fars province, Iran. Darius I (reigned 522–486 BC) planned Persepolis as the ceremonial capital of his empire and its wealth

and splendour were legendary. Alexander the Great destroyed Persepolis in 330 BC.

Perseus (Greek mythology) The son of Zeus and Danae. One of the greatest Greek heroes, he beheaded the Medusa with the help of Athena, who gave him a mirror to avoid looking at the Gorgon and being turned to stone. He married Andromeda, daughter of the Ethiopian king.

Pershing missile A US army two-stage solid-fuelled nuclear surface-to-surface missile launched from mobile launcher vehicles and having a range of 740 km (460 mi). Several improved versions of the missile have been produced; Pershing II missiles were deployed in Europe in 1984. It is named after Gen J. J. Pershing (1860–1948).

Persia. *See* Iran.

Persian cat A domesticated cat, also called a Longhair, having a long flowing coat with a ruff or frill around the neck. The coat may be of any colour, although the Blue Persian is most popular.

Persian Gulf An arm of the Arabian Sea, extending some 950 km (590 mi) NW beyond the Gulf of Oman. The large offshore oil deposits are exploited by the surrounding Gulf States. Area: 233 000 sq km (89 942 sq mi).

Persian Wars. *See* Greek–Persian Wars.

persimmon A tree of the genus *Diospyros* that produces edible fruits. These are the Japanese persimmon (*D. kaki*), the American persimmon (*D. virginiana*), and the Asian date plum (*D. lotus*). They have dark-green oval leaves and produce round orange, yellow, or red fruits, 5–8 cm across. Persimmons are eaten fresh, cooked, or candied. Family: *Ebenaceae*.

Perspex (polymethyl methacrylate) A colourless transparent thermoplastic material made by polymerization of methyl methacrylate. It can be extruded and moulded and coloured, for use in light fittings, aircraft parts, and car parts. It is widely used as an unbreakable substitute for glass.

perspiration. *See* sweat.

Perth 56 24N 3 28W A city in E Scotland, in Tayside Region on the River Tay. It was an early capital of Scotland. There are dyeing, textiles, whisky distilling, and carpet industries and it is a popular tourist centre. Population (1984 est): 41 654.

Peru, Republic of A country in the NW of South America, on the Pacific Ocean. Narrow coastal plains rise to the Andes, reaching heights of over 6500 m (21 000 ft). The land descends again to the tropical forests of the Amazon basin. Most of the population is of Indian or mixed Indian and European descent. *Economy*: Peru is one of the world's leading fishing countries, the main product being fishmeal. Agriculture is important, and the main crops include maize, rice, sugar cane, cotton, and coffee. Livestock is particularly important to the economy, especially the production of wool. Rich mineral resources include copper, silver, lead, zinc, and iron; oil has been discovered in considerable quantities. With its relics of ancient civilizations, Peru has a valuable tourist trade. The main exports include minerals and metals and fishmeal. *History*: Peru's precolonial history encompasses the civilization of the Chimú and that of the Incas, who were conquered by the Spanish under Pizarro in 1533. Peru was the last of Spain's American colonies to declare its independence (1821) and the Spanish were finally defeated in 1824. Political stability was achieved by Gen Ramón Castilla (1797–1867) who developed Peru's economy. However, the country's prosperity was undermined by the War of the Pacific (1879–83). Since World War II the country has witnessed a series of coups, most recently in 1975. In 1980, in Peru's first general elections to be held in 17 years, Fernando Belaúnde Terry was elected president; in 1985 he was replaced by Alan Garcia Pérez (1949–   ). Peru is a member of the OAS and LAFTA. Official languages: Spanish and Quechua; Aymará is also widely spoken. Official currency: inti of 1000 soles. Area: 1 285 215 sq km (496 093 sq mi). Population (1987 est): 20 727 000. Capital: Lima. Main port: Callao.

PERUGIA *The Maggiore Fountain on the south side of the 14th-century cathedral.*

Perugia 43 07N 12 23E A city in Italy, the capital of Umbria. Originally an Etruscan city, it has 13th-century city walls, a 14th-century cathedral, and a university (1200). Perugia is an agricultural trading centre and its manufactures include furniture and textiles. Population (1986): 146 713.

Perutz, Max Ferdinand (1914–   ) British chemist, born in Austria, who developed X-ray diffraction to determine the molecular structure of haemoglobin. For this work he shared a Nobel Prize (1962) with J. C. Kendrew.

Peshawar 34 01N 71 40E A city in N Pakistan, situated at the E end of the Khyber Pass. It is one of the oldest cities in Pakistan. Industries include textiles, shoes, and pottery. Population (1981): 555 000.

Pestalozzi, Johann Heinrich (1746–1827) Swiss educationalist, pioneer of mass education. His book *Wie Gertrud ihre Kinder lehrt* (1801) reflected his ideas on the intuitive method of education. Pestalozzi's work is commemorated in the **Pestalozzi International Children's Villages**, the first of which was established in 1946 for war orphans at Trogen (Switzerland). A second international village was established in 1958 at Sedlescombe, East Sussex, in the UK.

Pétain, (Henri) Philippe (1856–1951) French general and statesman. In World War I he distinguished himself at the defence of Verdun (1916), becoming marshal of France (1918). In World War II, when France was on the verge of defeat (1940), Pétain became prime minister. In June, 1940, he signed an armistice with Hitler that allowed for a third of France to remain unoc-

cupied by Germany. Pétain was sentenced to death in August, 1945, for collaboration but was reprieved.

Peter (I) the Great (1672–1725) Tsar (1682–1721) and then Emperor (1721–25) of Russia, who established Russia as a major European power. Peter travelled in W Europe in the late 1690s, acquiring knowledge of western technology. He instituted many reforms in government and administration, trade and industry, and in the army. In the Great Northern War (1700–21), he acquired Livonia, Estonia, and also Ingria, where in 1703 he founded St Petersburg (now Leningrad). He campaigned less successfully against the Turks (1710–13) but gained territory in the Caspian region from war with Persia (1722–23).

Peter, St In the New Testament, one of the 12 Apostles. He was a fisherman until called by Jesus. Although his faith often wavered, notably at the crucifixion, when he denied Christ three times, Peter was named as the rock upon which the Church was to be built. He was also entrusted with the "keys of the Kingdom of Heaven" (Matthew 16.19)—hence his symbol of two crossed keys. After Christ's death, he dominated the Christian community for 15 years, undertaking missionary work despite imprisonment. Feast day: 29 June.

Peterborough 52 35N 0 15W A city in E central England, in Cambridgeshire on the River Nene. The cathedral (begun in the 12th century) contains the tomb of Catherine of Aragon. Designated a new town in 1967, it is an important marketing centre for the surrounding agricultural area. Population (1985 est): 138 500.

Peterloo Massacre (1819) The name given, by analogy with the battle of Waterloo, to the violent dispersal of a political meeting held in St Peter's Fields, Manchester. A peaceful crowd had gathered to hear Henry Hunt (1773–1835) speak on parliamentary reform. The magistrates called in local troops, the cavalry were ordered to charge, and 11 people were killed.

Peterson, Oscar Emmanuel (1925–   ) Canadian Black jazz pianist, who has played with many leading jazz musicians as well as with his own trio. His many recordings include *The Gershwin Song Book* and *Peterson Plays Basie.*

petition of right The procedure by which a person formerly petitioned against the English Crown for the restoration of property that the Crown had taken possession of, or for damages for breach of contract. This method of claiming against the Crown, dating back to the reign of Edward I, has been replaced by ordinary court actions under the Crown Proceedings Act (1947). The **Petition of Right** (1628) was a parliamentary declaration accepted by Charles I. It made illegal imprisonment without trial, taxation without parliamentary approval, and the billeting of soldiers on private individuals.

petit mal. *See* epilepsy.

Petra An ancient town in S Jordan. It was the capital of the Nabataeans, nomadic Arabs who settled along the caravan routes from Arabia to the Mediterranean. Petra was a great trading centre from the 3rd century BC. It was incorporated in the Roman Empire in 106 AD and was superseded by Palmyra in the 2nd century. Accessible only through a narrow gorge, Petra is renowned for its rock-cut temples and dwellings.

Petrarch (Francesco Petrarca; 1304–74) Italian poet. He travelled widely in Europe and in 1341 was crowned as poet laureate in Rome. His humanist works of scholarship anticipated the Renaissance in their combination of classical learning and Christian faith. His other works include *Secretum meum*, and *Africa*, but he is remembered chiefly for the *Canzoniere*, a series of love poems addressed to Laura.

petrel   A marine bird belonging to a widely distributed family (*Procellariidae*; 55 species) characterized by a musky smell, thick plumage, webbed feet, and a hooked bill with long tubular nostrils. 27–90 cm long, petrels feed on fish and molluscs. Diving petrels belong to a family (*Pelecanoididae*; 5 species) occurring in the S hemisphere; they are 16–25 cm long and feed mostly on crustaceans. Order: *Procellariiformes. See also* fulmar; prion; shearwater; storm petrel.

petrochemicals.   *See* oil.

Petrograd.   *See* Leningrad.

petroleum.   *See* oil.

petrology   The study of rocks, including their formation, structure, texture, and mineral and chemical composition. **Petrogenesis** is the origin or mode of formation of rocks; **petrography** is the description and classification of rocks from hand specimens or thin sections.

Petunia   A genus of tropical American herbs (about 40 species), cultivated for their showy funnel-shaped flowers. Ornamental species include *P. integrifolia*, with pink, blue, or purple flowers, the white-flowered *P. axillaris*, and hybrids between them. Family: *Solanaceae*.

pewter   An alloy of tin with lead or copper, antimony, and bismuth. It was formerly used for plates, spoons, and other utensils but now only beer mugs are made from it.

PETRA   *The rock-cut Treasury, El Khazneh.*

PHARAOH   *The pharaoh's double crown, combining the red crown of Lower Egypt with the white crown of Upper Egypt, symbolized the unification of the two lands (c. 3100 BC).*

peyote   A blue-green cactus, *Lophophora williamsii*, also called mescal, native to Mexico and the SW USA. It bears white to pink flowering heads, which, when dried, are known as "mescal buttons." They contain the alkaloid mescaline, which produces hallucinations when chewed.

pH   A measure of the acidity or alkalinity of a solution, equal to the logarithm to the base 10 of the reciprocal of the number of moles per litre of hydrogen ions it contains. In neutral solutions, therefore, the hydrogen ion concentration is 10^{-7} and the pH is consequently 7. In acid solutions the pH is less than 7; alkaline solutions have pH values greater than 7. The pH scale is logarithmic; for example, a solution with a pH of 2 is ten times more acidic than one with a pH of 1. *See also* acids and bases.

Phaedra   In Greek mythology, the daughter of Minos and Pasiphaë and the wife of Theseus. She fell in love with her stepson Hippolytus. When he rejected her, she hanged herself.

phagocyte   A cell that engulfs and then digests particles from its surroundings: this process is called phagocytosis. Many protozoans are phagocytic, but the word specifically refers to certain white blood cells that protect the body by engulfing bacteria and other foreign particles.

phalanger   A small herbivorous marsupial of the family *Phalangeridae* (48 species), occurring in woodlands of Australia and New Guinea. They are adapted for climbing trees, having strong claws and prehensile tails. The family includes the cuscuses, flying phalangers, honey mouse, koalas, and possums.

phalarope   A lightly built migratory shorebird belonging to a family (*Phalaropodidae*; 3 species) in which the female courts the male, which rears the young. 20–25 cm long, phalaropes have a slim neck, lobed toes, and a grey and red-brown plumage. Two species breed in the Arctic and one inland in North America.

pharaoh   The title of ancient Egyptian rulers. The word derives via Hebrew from the Egyptian for great house. The royal cobra, the sun god Ra's symbol, signified divinity; pharaoh represented Ra reigning on earth. The first dynasty, or line of pharaohs, was founded about 3200 BC.

Pharisees   An ancient Jewish religious and political party. The party originated in the 2nd century BC and vied for political influence with the Sadducees. In the Gospels they are frequently criticized by Jesus, although his own teachings are very close to theirs.

pharmacology   The study of the action of drugs on living organisms. Pharmacologists examine the uptake of drugs after administration, their subsequent effects, their unwanted side effects, the interaction between different drugs, etc. **Pharmacy** is the science concerned with the preparation, manufacture, packaging, quality, and supply of medicinal drugs. The practice of pharmacy should conform to the standards laid down in the official **pharmacopoeia**, a government-approved list giving details of the manufacture, dosage, uses, and characteristics of drugs.

Pharos of Alexandria An ancient lighthouse, one of the Seven Wonders of the World. Built in about 280 BC by Sostratus of Cnidos for Ptolemy II of Egypt, it was over 135 m (440 ft) high. It was demolished in the 13th century AD.

Pharsalus, Battle of (48 BC) The decisive encounter near present-day Fársala (Greece) in the Roman civil war, in which Julius Caesar defeated Pompey. Pompey's defeat opened the way to Caesar's dictatorship.

pharynx The muscular tract, lined with mucous membrane, between the back of the mouth and oesophagus (gullet) and larynx. It acts as a passageway for food and it also conducts air from the nasal cavity to the larynx and windpipe. Inflammation of the pharynx (pharyngitis) is a common cause of a sore throat.

phase (astronomy) The fraction of the face of the moon or a planet that is illuminated at a particular time in its orbit. Lunar phases vary from new moon (unilluminated) through a waxing crescent, first quarter, a waxing gibbous moon, to full moon, followed by a waning gibbous moon, last quarter, a waning crescent, and the next new moon.

phase (physics) **1.** The fraction of its whole cycle that a periodically varying system has completed. For example, two alternating currents of the same frequency are **in phase** if they reach their maximum values at the same instant. In an electricity-supply system there are usually three phases. **2.** Any portion of a system that is physically distinct, is homogeneous throughout, and can be mechanically separated from other phases. For example, a salt solution is a one-phase system, whereas a mixture of ice and water is a two-phase system.

pheasant A long-tailed gamebird belonging to an Old World subfamily (*Phasianinae*; 50 species) occurring in open or woodland regions. Pheasants have short rounded wings, a short bill, and strong claws for scratching up grain, roots, and grubs. Males are brightly coloured, with bright fleshy wattles, large leg spurs, and long tail feathers. Family: *Phasianidae* (pheasants, quail, partridges); order: *Galliformes* (pheasants, turkeys, etc.). *See also* tragopan.

phenobarbitone. *See* barbiturates.

phenols A class of organic compounds with the general formula ROH, in which the –OH group is linked directly to a carbon atom in an aromatic ring. The simplest example, phenol itself (or **carbolic acid**), C_6H_5OH, is a white deliquescent solid used as a disinfectant and in the production of drugs, weedkillers, and synthetic resins.

phenylketonuria A genetic disease that leads to mental deficiency if untreated. Patients are unable to metabolize the amino acid phenylalanine, which is a normal constituent of diet; the amino acid and its derivatives accumulate in the body and prevent proper mental development. Phenylketonuria can now be easily detected at birth by a routine test. Babies with the disease need a special diet that contains little phenylalanine, which should be maintained until adolescence.

pheromone A chemical substance produced by animals to communicate with others of the same species.

PHEROMONE *The antennae of this moth contain scent receptors for detecting pheromones.*

The best-known pheromones are the sex attractants secreted by moths to attract mates. Pheromones are also used by ants to lay trails and by mammals to mark out territories.

Phidias (c. 490–c. 417 BC) Athenian sculptor, one of the most influential artists of his time. Phidias designed and supervised the sculptures of the Parthenon (*see* Elgin Marbles). His works included two famous chryselephantine statues: Athena in the Parthenon and Zeus at Olympia.

Phidippides (5th century BC) Greek runner who ran 241 km (150 mi) from Athens to Sparta in two days to ask for help against the Persians before the battle of Marathon in 490 BC. The modern marathon race derives from this feat.

Philadelphia 40 00N 75 10W A city in the USA, situated on the Delaware River in Pennsylvania at the junction of the Schuylkill River. Founded in 1681 by the Quaker, William Penn, it has many historic buildings, including Independence Hall (1732–59), where the Declaration of Independence was adopted. It is the USA's fourth largest city and has the world's largest freshwater port. Industries include oil refining, textiles, and shipbuilding. Population (1986): 1 642 900.

Philadelphus. *See* mock orange.

Philip (II) of Macedon (382–336 BC) King of Macedon (359–336), who founded the Macedonian empire. Philip unified Macedonia, expanded the economy, and trained a professional army. Despite the resolute opposition of Demosthenes at Athens, the Greeks were defeated at the battle of Chaeronea (338). Philip planned to lead a combined force against Persia but he was assassinated.

Philip II Augustus (1165–1223) King of France (1179–1223), who destroyed the Angevin empire of the English kings. He waged war with Henry II (1187–89), Richard Lionheart (1194–99), and John; he took Normandy in 1204, followed by Maine, Touraine, and Anjou (1204–05), and in 1214 defeated an English-imperial alliance at Bouvines.

Philip II (1527–98) King of Spain (1556–98). He married Mary I of England in 1554. Philip faced the Revolt of the Netherlands and the Turkish threat in the Mediterranean, suppressed the Moriscos, launched the Spanish Armada against Protestant England (1588), and intervened in the French Wars of Religion against the Huguenots.

Philip V (1683–1746) The first Bourbon King of Spain (1700–24, 1724–46). The grandson of Louis XIV of France, his accession instigated the War of the Spanish Succession. He abdicated in 1724 in favour of his son Luis (1707–24) but returned to the throne when Luis died.

Philip, Prince, Duke of Edinburgh (1921–) The husband (from 1947) of Elizabeth II of the United Kingdom. A descendant of Queen Victoria and the son of Prince Andrew of Greece, he assumed the name Mountbatten in 1947, when he took British citizenship. In 1956 he introduced the **Duke of Edinburgh's Award Scheme** to encourage the leisure activities of young people between the ages of 14 and 25.

Philip, St In the New Testament, one of the 12 Apostles. In medieval art he is symbolized by loaves because of his participation in the miracle of the loaves and fishes. Feast day: 11 May.

Philippi, Battle of (42 BC) The battle in which Mark Antony and Octavian (later Emperor Augustus) defeated Brutus and Cassius Longinus in the Roman civil war.

Philippines, Republic of the A country in SE Asia, consisting of an archipelago of over 7000 islands between the Pacific Ocean and the South China Sea. There are few extensive lowlands, most of the larger islands, being mountainous and volcanic. Most of the inhabitants are Filipinos. *Economy*: based principally on agriculture, forestry, and fishing. The production of the staple crops of rice and maize and the main cash crops (sugar, coconuts, bananas, and pineapples) is concentrated around the central plain of Luzon. The country has a wide range of metallic minerals, including copper, gold, iron ore, manganese, molybdenum, zinc, lead, and silver. Forests cover over half the land, providing gums and resins, bamboo, and dyes in addition to good-quality hardwoods. The main industries are food processing, textiles, wood processing, and oil refining. *History*: colonized by Spain in 1565, the islands were ceded to the USA in 1898 following the Spanish-American War. They became an independent republic in 1946. Following the election of President Marcos in 1965 rapid economic development and a greatly improved infrastructure brought increased prosperity to the Philippines. During the early 1970s growing communist guerrilla activity in the N and a Muslim separatist movement in the S led to the declaration of martial law (1972). Although martial law was lifted in 1981, unrest increased when the exiled opposition leader Benigno S. Aquino was assassinated on his return to Manila in 1983. After elections in early 1986, Marcos went into exile and Corazon Aquino, widow of Benigno Aquino, became president. Official languages: Pilipino and English. Official currency: Philippine peso of 100 centavos. Area: 300 000 sq km (115 830 sq mi). Population (1987 est): 57 360 000. Capital and main port: Manila.

Philippopoli. *See* Plovdiv.

Philistines A non-Semitic people, who were driven from Egypt about 1200 BC and settled in Canaan; the region took the name Palestine from its new settlers. A

warlike seafaring people, without cultural pretensions (hence the derogatory word philistine), they were largely absorbed into the kingdom of Israel under King David about 1000 BC.

Philodendron A genus of woody, usually climbing, plants (275 species), native to tropical America. They have oval, oblong, arrow-shaped, or heart-shaped leaves, and they cling to trees or other supports by means of aerial roots growing from their stems. Cultivated as ornamental house plants for their foliage, *P. andreanum* and *P. erubescens* are among the most popular species. Family: *Araceae*.

philosopher's stone A hypothetical substance sought by alchemists for its ability to turn less valuable minerals into gold. In alchemical literature it is also called the elixir, the tincture, and of other names. It was sometimes credited with the power of curing all diseases and of making its possessors immortal. *See* alchemy.

phloem Plant tissue specialized to transport synthesized foods, mainly sugars, around the plant. It consists principally of tubelike cells that lack nuclei, the end of one cell being linked to the next by means of a porous wall (sieve plate). The cells are controlled by small neighbouring cells, known as companion cells.

phlogiston theory An 18th-century theory of combustion based on the belief that all combustible substances contain phlogiston, which is liberated when the substance is heated, leaving calx or ash. The more combustible the substance, the more phlogiston it contains. The theory was finally overthrown in the late 18th century by A. Lavoisier, who correctly explained combustion in terms of oxidation.

Phlox A genus of ornamental herbs (about 65 species), mostly native to North America. The flowers have five white, pink, red, or purple spreading petals. The creeping phlox, or moss pink (*P. subulata*), forms carpets of flowers in rock gardens. *P. drummondii* is the source of most garden varieties. Family: *Polemoniaceae*.

Phnom Penh (*or* Pnom Penh; Cambodian name: Phnum Pénh) 11 35N 104 55E The capital of Cambodia, a port at the head of the Mekong delta. The capital since about 1432, it is now the site of the royal palace, many museums and pagodas, and several universities. The country's commercial centre, its industries include textiles and food processing. Population (1983 est): 500 000.

phobia A pathologically strong fear of a particular situation or thing. The main kinds are agoraphobia, which is fear of public places and open spaces; claustrophobia (fear of enclosed places); specific phobias of individual things, such as sharp knives; social phobias of encountering people; and animal phobias, as of spiders, rats, or snakes. Phobias are sometimes learned after a frightening incident, sometimes acquired in childhood from other people, and sometimes result from depression.

Phoenicia A group of city states on the coastal plain of Syria N of ancient Canaan. Semitic peoples settled here sometime before 1800 BC and after about 1000 BC they became outstanding navigators and merchants, establishing trading posts all over the E Mediterranean and beyond. Their major cities were Tyre, Sidon, and Byblos. The Phoenician alphabet was the ancestor of all western alphabets. Phoenicia was attacked by Alexander the Great (332 BC), becoming part of the Hellenistic and later the Roman Empires. See p. 562.

PHOENICIA *From their homeland along the E Mediterranean shore (modern Lebanon and Syria) the Phoenicians traded throughout the Mediterranean and beyond and established many settlements.*

phoenix A fabulous bird associated with sun worship, especially in Egypt, and representing resurrection and immortality. It was like an eagle in size and shape, had red and golden plumage, and lived for 500 years. The dying phoenix was consumed by fire in a nest of aromatic materials and from its ashes a new bird arose.

Phoenix 33 30N 112 03W A city in the USA, the capital of Arizona on the Salt River. The state's largest city, the commercial centre for a cotton and farming region, its industries include the manufacture of aircraft and textiles. Population (1986 est): 881 640.

phonetics The study of the production and perception of sounds in languages. Sounds are classified in terms of the way in which they are produced by the speech organs. The study of the system of sounds within any given language is called **phonology** and the selected individual sounds are called phonemes. Phonetics also includes the study of stress and intonation.

phosphorescence. *See* luminescence.

phosphorus (P) A nonmetallic solid element discovered by H. Brand (died c. 1692) in 1669. It exists in at least four forms: white (α and β), red, and black. White phosphorus is a waxy solid, which ignites spontaneously in air to form the pentoxide (P_2O_5). Red phosphorus, a more stable allotrope, is formed when white phosphorus is heated to 400°C; it is used in matches. Black phosphorus is also stable and forms when white phosphorus is heated to 200–300°C. Phosphorus exists in nature chiefly as the mineral apatite ($Ca_3(PO_4)_2$), from which the element is obtained, either by reduction with carbon or reaction with silica at high temperatures. Phosphates are used extensively as fertilizers (mainly as "superphosphate"—calcium hydrogen phosphate) but find other uses in detergents, water softeners, and specialist glasses. Some organo-phosphorus compounds are extremely toxic and are used as nerve gases. At no 15; at wt 30.9738; mp (white) 44.1°C; bp (white) 280°C.

photocell (*or* photoelectric cell) A device that makes use of a photoelectric effect to measure or detect light or other electromagnetic radiation. In the photoemissive cell, a photosensitive cathode emits electrons when it is illuminated; these photoelectrons constitute a current when they flow to the positive anode of the cell. In solid-state devices the light changes the behaviour of a p–n junction (as in the photodiode), creating a potential difference by the photovoltaic effect. In the conductivity cell, the resistance of a substance, such as selenium, changes when light falls on it as a result of photoconductivity. Photocells are widely used in light-operated controls, such as fire alarms; they are also used in solar cells (*see* solar power) and photographic light meters.

photoemissive cell *Illumination releases electrons from the cathode.*

photovoltaic cell *Illumination creates a potential difference at a p-n semiconductor junction.*

photoconductivity cell *Illumination increases the conductivity of a semiconductor, such as selenium.*

PHOTOCELL

photocopying machine A device that prints copies of documents, drawings, etc., from an optical image. The most common technique is a dry electrostatic process known as xerography. A pattern of electric charge is induced by light falling on a layer of semiconductor material on a conducting surface. Toner powder is sprayed or rolled onto this material, so that it sticks to the highly charged areas. The image so formed is printed onto charged paper, where it is fixed by heating to produce the final copy.

photoelectric effects A number of effects in which electromagnetic radiation interacts with matter, frequently with the emission of electrons. These effects include photoconductivity, the photovoltaic effect, and the Compton effect and the Auger effect. The frequency of the radiation (f) has to be such that the energy of the photon (hf, where h is Planck's constant) is sufficient to liberate the electron. For solids, the minimum energy required is called the work function; for free atoms or molecules it is equal to the first ionization potential, the effect then being known as photoionization. For most substances, an ultraviolet frequency is needed to eject an electron, but for some metals, such as caesium, visible light is sufficient. *See* photocell.

photography The recording of images on sensitized material, by means of visible light, X-rays, or other radiation, and the subsequent chemical processing. The first photograph was taken in 1826 by Joseph Nicéphore Niépce (d. 1833). In 1839, Daguerre introduced the daguerrotype, a positive image of milky white on a silver background, produced directly from silver iodide emulsion on plates exposed inside a simple camera. Modern photography involves a negative made by the development of film coated with silver salts. The positive picture is obtained by shining light through the negative onto light-sensitive paper with a coating similar to that on the original film. Lenses can be used to enlarge or reduce the size of the final image on the print. Transparencies, for use with a slide projector, may also be made. Film is usually developed and printed in a darkroom by dipping it in baths of chemicals. Polaroid photography, however, produces positive pictures directly from the camera in one stage. This system was invented by Edwin Land in 1947 and is used for instant pictures for security passes, laboratory records, etc.

photoluminescence. *See* luminescence.

photolysis The breaking of a chemical bond by absorbed electromagnetic radiation. The photon energy of the radiation must exceed the bond energy, and photolytic reactions can be produced by light, ultraviolet radiation, and X-rays. Examples occur in photosynthesis, suntan, and photography. **Flash photolysis** is a technique for identifying and studying unstable reaction intermediates. The intermediates are produced in a gas by an intense brief flash of light, and their reactions are followed by spectroscopy.

photometry The branch of physics concerned with measuring quantities related to the intensity of light. If the intensity is measured in terms of the energy of the light, they are known as radiant quantities. They may also be measured in terms of their visual effect; they are then known as luminous quantities.

photon The quantum of electromagnetic radiation, having an energy hf, where h is the Planck constant and f is the frequency of the radiation. It may also be regarded as an elementary particle with spin 1 and zero mass that travels at the speed of light.

photosphere The boundary between the atmosphere of a star and its much denser interior. The sun's photosphere is several hundred kilometres thick. Almost all the energy emitted by the sun is radiated from the photosphere. Its temperature falls from about 6000°C at the

convective zone to about 4000°C where the photosphere merges with the chromosphere. *See also* sunspots.

photosynthesis The means by which plants and certain bacteria produce carbohydrates from carbon dioxide and a hydrogen source. The energy for the process is provided by light absorbed by the green pigment chlorophyll, which is contained in the chloroplasts. Plants use water (H_2O) as the hydrogen source and release its oxygen as a by-product. Photosynthesis comprises two sets of reactions. One set, which requires light, produces energy-storing and reducing compounds; the other reactions use these compounds to add hydrogen atoms to carbon dioxide and make carbohydrates. The overall reactions can be summarized by the equation $6CO_2 + 6H_2O \rightarrow C_6H_{12}O_6 + 6O_2$.

Phrygia The central and W areas of Asia Minor inhabited after the Hittite empire collapsed (12th century BC) by Thracian migrants. The shortlived Phrygian kingdom, centred on its capital Gordium, reached its peak in the late 8th century. The legendary Midas was King of Phrygia. The Phrygians are reputed to have invented embroidery.

phylloxera A plant-eating insect belonging to the family *Phylloxeridae*, closely related to the aphids. The grape, or vine, phylloxera (*Phylloxera vitifoliae* or *Viteus vitifolii*) is a notorious pest of grapevines. The insect forms galls on the leaves and roots, which damage the plant. The grape phylloxera almost destroyed the wine industry in France in the 19th century.

phylogeny The history of the evolution of a species or other group of organisms. By studying the fossil record, comparative anatomy, embryology, biochemistry, and geographical distribution of the groups involved, one can establish the probable lines of descent and degrees of relationship between broad groups of plants or animals to produce a phylogenetic tree. Phylogeny forms the basis for the classification of organisms (*see* taxonomy). It should be distinguished from **ontogeny**, which is the succession of developmental stages through which an individual organism passes during its lifetime. *See also* biogenetic law.

phylum A major unit of classification for animals (*see* taxonomy). Organisms belonging to the same phylum share basic features but are divided into classes, orders, genera, and species according to their supposed degrees of relationship. In most plant-classification systems the equivalent term is division.

physics The study of the interrelationship between matter and energy, without reference to chemical change. Traditionally the subject was divided into the study of mechanics, electricity and magnetism, heat and thermodynamics, optics, and acoustics. More modern aspects of the subject include quantum mechanics, relativity, nuclear physics, particle physics, solid-state physics, and astrophysics.

physiology The study of the functioning of living organisms and their constituent parts. Physiology is closely linked with both anatomy (the study of structure) and biochemistry (the chemical reactions that play a vital role in many physiological processes).

pi In mathematics, the ratio of the circumference of a circle to its diameter, denoted by the Greek letter π. It was proved to be an irrational number by J. H. Lambert (1728–77) and transcendental by F. Lindemann (1852–1939). Its value is 3.14159 ....

Piaf, Edith (Edith Giovanna Gassion; 1915–63) French cabaret and music-hall singer. Originally a street singer, her small size earned her the nickname "piaf" (French slang: sparrow). Her songs include "Je ne regrette rien" and "La Vie en rose".

piano A musical instrument consisting of a number of wire strings stretched over a metal frame, which are hit by felt-covered wooden hammers operated by a keyboard. The piano was invented by Bartolommeo Cristofori (1655–1731) in the early 18th century; the name derives from the Italian *pianoforte*, soft-loud, referring to the variation in volume obtainable on the piano in contrast to the earlier clavichord and harpsichord. In the modern instrument the frame is either horizontal, as in the **grand piano**, or vertical, as in the **upright piano**. The piano has a compass of seven and a quarter octaves and the largest repertory of any instrument.

Picardy (French name: Picardie) A planning region and former province in N France. It was incorporated into France in 1477 by Louis XI of France. During World War I it was the scene of heavy fighting. Area: 19 411 sq km (7493 sq mi). Population (1986 est): 1 774 000.

PICASSO *Seen here, aged 87, among some of his paintings.*

Picasso, Pablo (1881–1973) Spanish artist, born in Malaga. Picasso trained in Barcelona but worked chiefly in Paris after 1900. Although his most popular paintings are those of his blue (1901–04) and rose (1905–08) periods, his most original work began with *Les Demoiselles d'Avignon* (1907), influenced by Cézanne and African sculpture, and resulted in his development of cubism with Braque. One of his major works, *Guernica* (1937), is a horrific depiction of the destruction of the Basque capital during the Spanish Civil War.

Piccard A family of Swiss scientists and explorers. **Auguste Piccard** (1884–1962) and his twin **Jean-Félix Piccard** (1884–1963) pioneered the scientific study of the stratosphere in balloons, reaching a height of 16 940 metres in 1932. In 1948 Auguste designed a bathyscaphe, using it to explore the sea depths. His son **Jacques Piccard** (1927–   ) collaborated with his father in designing bathyscaphes and reached a depth of 10 917 metres in 1960.

piccolo A woodwind instrument, the smallest and shrillest member of the flute family. It is pitched an oc-

tave higher than the flute and its music is written an octave lower than it sounds. It is used in the orchestra and in the military band.

picketing The act of employees or their union representatives in attending at their place of work to persuade others not to work in furtherance of a trade dispute. **Primary picketing** (in which the employer is the immediate party to the dispute) is not wrongful if carried out peacefully. **Secondary picketing** (in which the employer is not directly concerned in the dispute) is not always wrong. Employees may, for example, picket their employer, who is a supplier of the employer in the dispute. **Flying pickets** are pickets that are ready to move at a moment's notice to a plant at which they are not employed, and have no immunity from legal action. Flying and secondary picketing caused considerable industrial unrest in the UK in the miners' strike of 1984–85.

pick-up A device that converts information stored in a gramophone record into an electrical signal. In a record player, the pick-up cartridge, usually a removable assembly, consists of a stylus and a transducer. The stylus is forced to vibrate by the undulations in the record groove. The transducer responds electrically to these vibrations. The most common types of transducer use the piezoelectric effect or electromagnetic induction.

Picts (painted people) The Roman name (referring to their tattoos) for all Scottish tribes living N of the Antonine Wall. Perpetually hostile to the Romans, the Picts had forced them to withdraw behind Hadrian's Wall by 200 AD, and remained independent until Kenneth I MacAlpine unified S Scotland in the 9th century.

piddock A burrowing bivalve mollusc belonging to the family *Pholadidae*, of cold and temperate seas. Piddocks are adapted for boring into rock, having shells with serrated cutting edges. They can damage concrete breakwaters, sea walls, and wharves.

Piedmont (Italian name: Piemonte) A region in NW Italy. Associated with the House of Savoy since the early 11th century, it became the nucleus of Italian unification in the mid-19th century. It consists of the upper Po Valley, bordered by the Alps in the N and W and the Apennines in the S. Manufacturing is important, with engineering and steel centred on Turin; other industries include textiles, chemicals, rubber, and food products. Agriculture is also important, producing rice, cereals, wine, and dairy products. Area: 25 400 sq km (9807 sq mi). Population (1985 est): 4 389 430. Capital: Turin.

Piero della Francesca (c. 1420–92) Italian Renaissance painter. *The Baptism of Christ* (National Gallery, London) shows his monumental figure style. He frequently worked at the court of Urbino, where he painted the double portrait of the duke and his wife in profile (Uffizi). His lifelong interest in perspective is reflected in his fresco cycle *The Legend of the True Cross*, painted for the church of S Francesco, Arezzo, and in his treatise *On Perspective in Painting*.

Pietermaritzburg 29 36S 30 24E A city in South Africa, the capital of Natal. It was founded by Boers (1838) and named after their leaders, Piet Retief and Gert Maritz, massacred by the Zulus. It is the centre of a rich farming area. Population (1986): 133 809.

piezoelectric effect The production of electric charges on the opposite faces of certain asymmetric crystals when they are compressed or expanded. The charges are of equal magnitude but opposite in sign on the two faces, the sign on each face depending on whether the crystal is expanded or compressed. Such piezoelectric crystals include quartz and Rochelle salt. In the converse effect a voltage applied across a piezoelectric crystal causes it to expand or contract. The effect is used in the piezoelectric oscillator, the crystal microphone, and the piezoelectric loudspeaker.

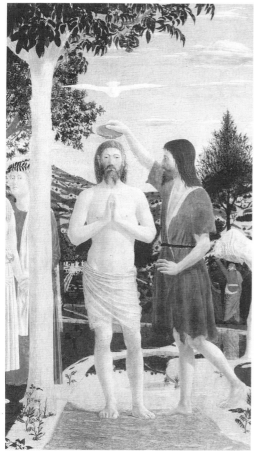

PIERO DELLA FRANCESCA *Detail from* The Baptism of Christ *(National Gallery, London) painted c. 1439.*

pig A hoofed mammal belonging to the Old World family *Suidae* (8 species). Also called hogs or swine, pigs have a stocky body with short legs, a short neck, and a large head with a long cylindrical snout used for digging up roots, seeds, small animals, etc., from soil. Modern breeds are reared for pork and bacon (*see* livestock farming). Other members of the pig family include the babirusa and wart hog. *See also* peccary.

pigeon A bird belonging to a family (*Columbidae*; 300 species) occurring worldwide except in the coldest regions; the smaller long-tailed forms are called doves. 17–75 cm long, pigeons have soft plumage, a plump body, a small head, short bill and legs, and a characteristic cooing call. Pigeons feed mainly on seeds and other plant material. They are often fast fliers and some are highly migratory, domesticated breeds being used as messengers and for racing. Order: *Columbiformes* (pigeons and sandgrouse). *See also* wood pigeon.

Piggott, Lester Keith (1935–) British jockey, who rode his first winner at the age of 12 (1948). Champion jockey eleven times and Derby winner a record nine times, he rode over 4349 winners. He became a trainer in 1985, having won a record 29 classics, but was gaoled (1987–88) for tax evasion.

pig iron The type of iron produced by blast furnaces, and used as the first stage in steel making. It has a high carbon content (about 4% by weight) and contains impurities, including some slag, which make it brittle. *See also* cast iron.

pigmies. *See* Pygmies.

pika A small mammal belonging to the genus *Ochotona* (14 species), of Asia and North America, also called mouse hare, cony, and rock rabbit. 12.5–30 cm long and resembling large short-tailed mice, pikas live in cold rocky areas above the tree line. Family: *Ochotonidae*; order: *Lagomorpha*.

pike (fish) A freshwater fish of the genus *Esox* found in temperate regions of Eurasia and America. It has a broad flat snout, and a large mouth with strong teeth. It feeds voraciously on fish and other animals. The common pike (*E. lucius*) is olive-grey above with silvery underparts and pale spots. Family: *Esocidae*; order: *Salmoniformes*.

pikeperch One of several food and game fish related to perch, especially members of the genera *Lucioperca* and *Stizostedion*, found in Europe and North America. The European pikeperch or zander (*L. lucioperca*) has a slender elongated body, 0.5–1 m long, with greenish or greyish mottling. It is carnivorous, feeding mainly on other fish.

Pilate, Pontius (1st century AD) Roman governor. As procurator of Judaea and Samaria (26–36) he condemned Christ to death but, according to the New Testament Gospels, did so reluctantly, fearing the outcome of any other course. He came into frequent conflict with the Jews and was finally dismissed for his cruel suppression of a Samaritan rebellion.

Pilbara. *See* Western Australia.

pilchard An important food fish, *Sardina pilchardus*, related to the herring and sprat, that occurs in abundance in the Mediterranean, E Atlantic, and English Channel. Its slender body, 25–35 cm long, is bluish green above and whitish below and it swims in large shoals feeding on crustaceans and fish eggs. Pilchards up to one year old are called sardines. Pilchards are eaten fresh and tinned.

piles. *See* haemorrhoids.

Pilgrimage of Grace (1536) A revolt in N England against the government of Henry VIII. The rebels were united by their opposition to the recent Reformation legislation and the dissolution of the monasteries as well as by economic grievances. Under Robert Ashe (c. 1500–37) they seized York but were persuaded to surrender. However, some 230 men, including Ashe, were executed.

Pilgrim Fathers The 102 English colonists who established the first settlement in New England in 1620. They included 35 Puritans, escaping persecution in England, and sailed in the *Mayflower* to New Plymouth, Massachusetts.

Pill, the. *See* oral contraceptive.

Pillars of Hercules Two promontories at the entrance to the Mediterranean Sea, known in ancient times as Calpe (modern Gibraltar) and Abyla (modern Jebel Musa, at Ceuta, Morocco). According to one legend, the promontories were joined until Heracles tore them apart.

pilot fish A fish, *Naucrates ductor*, that has a pale-blue elongated body marked with dark vertical bands. It is found in warm and tropical seas, accompanying ships and large fish, especially sharks, to feed on parasites and scraps of food. Family: *Carangidae*; order: *Perciformes*.

Piltdown man Skeletal remains once thought to be those of a fossil hominid, found on Piltdown Common, near Lewes (England), in 1912. In 1953–54 the "find" was shown to be a hoax or fraud.

pimento. *See* allspice.

pimpernel A slender annual or perennial herb of the genus *Anagallis* (about 20 species), found in Eurasia, Africa, and America, especially the annual scarlet pimpernel (*A. arvensis*). Growing 5–30 cm tall, pimpernels have simple leaves and small red, pink, blue, or white bell-shaped flowers. The fruit is a capsule, which opens by a round lid. The yellow pimpernel (*Lysimachia nemorum*) belongs to a closely related genus. Family: *Primulaceae*.

Pindar (518–438 BC) Greek poet. Of his 17 books of choral lyrics only 4 survive. These contain Epinician Odes written in honour of victors of athletic games and noted for their exalted style and deep religious feeling.

pine A coniferous tree of the genus *Pinus* (about 80 species), widely distributed in the N hemisphere. Pines have long slender needles and hanging cones made up of overlapping woody scales. Pines are important softwoods: the timber is easily worked and yields turpentine, tar, pitch, and other resinous products. Commercially important and widely planted species include the Scots pine (*P. sylvestris*), of N and W Europe and Asia, up to 40 m high and the maritime pine (*P. pinaster*), of W Mediterranean regions and N Africa, up to 35 m high. These and other species are also planted for shelter and ornament and some species have edible seeds (*see* stone pine). Family: *Pinaceae*. *See also* bristlecone pine.
A number of other unrelated conifers are called pines, including species of *Araucaria*, the cypress pine, and the kauri pine.

pineal gland A small gland within the brain. In some lower animals, for example certain lizards, it is receptive to light and is visible externally as a third eye (pineal eye); in man its function is unknown, although it may help to regulate the onset of puberty.

pineapple A perennial herbaceous plant, *Ananas comosus*, native to tropical and subtropical America and cultivated in many warm and tropical regions for its fruit. It reaches a height of 1 m. Purplish flowers occur at the centre of a rosette of leaves and—with their bracts —fuse to form the composite fruit, which ripens 5–6 months after flowering begins and can weigh up to 10 kg. The major producing countries are the Hawaiian Islands, Brazil, Mexico, Cuba, and the Philippines. Family: *Bromeliaceae*.

pine marten A European carnivorous mammal, *Martes martes*. About 70 cm long, it inhabits dense evergreen forests, preying on squirrels, birds, insects, and eggs. As with other martens, the female has a litter (2–5 cubs) only every second year.

Pinero, Sir Arthur Wing (1855–1934) British dramatist. His early plays, which included *The Magistrate* (1885) and *Dandy Dick* (1887), were hugely successful farces. His later plays, notably *The Second Mrs Tanqueray* (1893), were more serious treatments of contemporary social problems.

pink One of several usually perennial herbaceous plants derived from *Dianthus plumarius* and often grown as fragrant garden ornamentals. They have long slender leaves and showy white, pink, or red flowers, often with fringed petals. Family: *Caryophyllaceae*.

Pinochet, Augusto (1915–) Chilean general and head of state (1973–). He led a military coup that overthrew Salvador Allende and became the head of a repressive military junta. Electoral defeat in 1988 meant he must relinquish office within 15 months.

pintail A duck, *Anas acuta*, occurring in the N hemisphere, that breeds on inland waters and winters in coastal areas. The male has a dark-brown head and neck with a white band down the neck, grey flanks, and long black central tail feathers. Females have mottled brown plumage and both sexes have a blue-grey bill.

Pinter, Harold (1930–) British dramatist. In his plays, which include *The Birthday Party* (1958), *The Caretaker* (1960), *The Homecoming* (1965), *Old Times* (1971), *Betrayed* (1978), *Family Voices* (1981), and *Mountain Language* (1988), he uses elliptical dialogue to evoke an atmosphere of tension and ambiguity. He has also written film scripts and directed plays.

pinto A horse whose coat consists of sharply defined patches of white and a darker colour—either black (piebald pattern) or brown, bay, dun, or roan (skewbald pattern). Pintos were commonly used by American Indians. Height: 1.42 m minimum (14 hands).

pinworm A slender parasitic nematode worm, *Enterobius vermicularis*, also called seatworm or threadworm. Up to 1 cm long, pinworms are white and inhabit the human intestine; they are common in Europe and America. Female worms migrate to the anus to lay thousands of eggs, causing itching, especially at night.

Pinyin. *See* Chinese.

pion A group of three elementary particles (*see* particle physics) classified as mesons (symbol: π). The charged pions (π^+ and π^-) have a mass of 139.6 MeV, the neutral pion (π°) a mass of 136 MeV. The strong interaction can be represented by the exchange of virtual pions between particles (*see* virtual particle).

pipal. *See* bo tree.

Piper, John (1903–) British painter and writer. He painted abstract works in the 1930s and was an official war artist in World War II. He is best known for his watercolours and aquatints of architecture. He has also designed stained glass, notably for Coventry Cathedral, and stage sets including those for Benjamin Britten's *Death in Venice* (1973).

pipistrelle A small insect-eating bat belonging to the genus *Pipistrellus* (50 species) with a worldwide distribution. The Eurasian pipistrelle (*P. pipistrellus*) is about 3.5 cm long with a 20-cm wingspan. Pipistrelles have a prehensile tail, used when crawling into crevices to roost. Family: *Vespertilionidae*.

pipit A small insectivorous songbird of the genus *Anthus* (30 species), 14–16 cm long with a brown-streaked plumage and paler speckled underparts. The meadow pipit (*A. pratensis*) occurs on moors and downs in Britain. The water pipit (*A. spinoletta*) inhabits the high mountains of Eurasia and North America; it is also found in coastal regions, when it is known as the rock pipit. Family: *Motacillidae* (wagtails and pipits).

JOHN PIPER *Part of the Benjamin Britten memorial window in Aldeburgh Church, Suffolk.*

Piraeus (Modern Greek name: Piraiévs) 37 57N 23 42E The chief port of Greece, SW of Athens on the Saronic Gulf. It was founded during the 5th century BC as the port of Athens. Industries include shipbuilding, oil refining, and chemicals. Its exports include wine and olive oil. Population (1981): 196 389.

Pirandello, Luigi (1867–1936) Italian dramatist and novelist. His writing was greatly influenced by life with his insane wife. He gained international success with his plays exploring the nature of reality and illusion, notably *Six Characters in Search of an Author* (1921) and *Henry IV* (1922). His other works include the novel *The Late Mattia Pascal* (1904) and the critical study *Humour* (1908). He won the Nobel Prize in 1934.

piranha A freshwater fish, also called caribe and piraya, belonging to a genus (*Serrasalmus*) found in South America. It has a deep body, ranging from silver to black in colour, strong jaws, and razor-sharp teeth. Piranhas swim in groups and feed voraciously on other fish; they will also attack larger animals, including man. Family: *Characidae*.

Pisa 43 43N 10 24E A city in Italy, in Tuscany on the River Arno. Dating from Etruscan times, it developed into a thriving maritime republic (11th–12th centuries) but declined in importance after it fell to the Florentines in 1509. A popular tourist centre, the most famous of its buildings is the Leaning Tower of Pisa, which is 59 m (194 ft) high and about 5 m (17 ft) out of perpendicular. Machinery, textiles, bicycles, and glass are manufactured. Population (1986): 104 384.

Pisano, Nicola (c. 1220–c. 1278) Italian sculptor. He initiated the revival of antique Roman forms that led eventually to Renaissance sculpture, beginning with his pulpit in the Baptistry, Pisa. Later works reveal the co-operation of his son **Giovanni Pisano** (c. 1250–1314). Giovanni introduced French gothic elements into his sculptures for the façade of Siena Cathedral.

Pissarro, Camille (1830–1903) French impressionist painter, born in the West Indies. Chiefly influenced by Corot, he was more interested in landscape structure than the other impressionists. He is noted for his encour-

agement of younger painters, especially Cézanne and Gauguin. In the 1880s he experimented with pointillism.

pistachio A small aromatic tree, *Pistacia vera*, native to central Eurasia and widely cultivated in Mediterranean regions for its edible green kernels ("nuts"). Growing 7–10 m high, it has compound leaves and drooping spikes of small male and female flowers. The oval white fruits, 1.5–2 cm long, often split to expose the kernels, which are used as dessert nuts and for decorating and flavouring confectionery, cakes, etc. Family: *Anacardiaceae*.

pistil The part of a flower consisting of the female reproductive organs. It consists of one or more carpels, which may be united into a single structure. Some plants, such as the cucumber, have separate male and female flowers: the latter are described as pistillate.

pistol A short-range small arm that can be used with one hand. Pistols are divided into two classes: the revolver and the automatic. The first successful revolver was the Colt of 1835, in which a magazine chamber revolves behind a single barrel. The first automatics (1893) combined a box magazine in the butt with a recoil loading action. The Luger 9 mm automatic went into service with the German navy in 1904. Both revolvers and automatics are still in military and police use throughout the world.

Pitcairn Islands A small island group in the central S Pacific Ocean, a British dependent territory, consisting of Pitcairn Island and three uninhabited islands. Subsistence agriculture is the chief occupation. Pitcairn Island was occupied in 1790 by mutineers from the *Bounty* and women from Tahiti. By 1856 the island was overpopulated and the inhabitants were moved to Norfolk Island; some later returned. Area: 4.6 sq km (1.75 sq mi). Population (1987): 59. Sole town: Adamstown.

17th-century English wheellock pistol.

18th-century Scottish flintlock with ram's-horn butt.

Colt 45 revolver first produced in 1873 and still in use.

Colt 45 automatic.

PISTOL

pitch (chemistry) A black or dark-brown residue resulting from the partial evaporation or fractional distillation of coal tars or tar products. The term is sometimes used for the residue obtained from petroleum distillation (bitumen) or for the naturally occurring petroleum residue (asphalt). Bitumen is a mixture of heavy hydrocarbons with a high proportion of free carbon. It is used as a binding agent (it is the main constituent of road tars), as a protective coating in bituminous paints, in roofing felts, and as a fuel.

pitchblende The chief ore of uranium, a massive form of uraninite, UO_2, a black radioactive mineral found in hydrothermal veins and as an accessory mineral in acid igneous rocks.

pitcher plant Any carnivorous plant with pitcher-shaped leaves, belonging mainly to the families *Nepenthaceae* and *Sarraceniaceae*. The pitcher is often brightly coloured and secretes nectar to attract insects, which often fall inside and drown in the digestive juices at the bottom of the pitcher.

Pitman, Sir Isaac. *See* shorthand.

pitot tube A type of anemometer for measuring the velocity of a fluid, invented by Henri Pitot (1695–1771). It consists of an L-shaped tube placed in the moving fluid; the vertical limb of the tube has an opening facing into the flow. The difference in pressure between the interior of the tube and the surroundings enables the velocity of the fluid to be calculated. The device is used to measure the velocity of liquids, aircraft airspeeds, etc.

Pittsburgh 40 26N 80 00W A city in the USA, in Pennsylvania at the confluence of the Allegheny and Monongahela Rivers, which here form the Ohio River. It is the site of several colleges and universities, including the University of Pittsburgh (1787) and the famous Carnegie Institute. Pittsburgh has grown as a major centre of the steel industry and is the country's largest inland port. Other manufactures include machinery, petroleum, coal, glass, and chemicals. Population (1986): 387 490.

WILLIAM PITT THE YOUNGER *Caricature (1805) depicting Pitt and Napoleon carving up Europe.*

Pitt the Elder, William, 1st Earl of Chatham (1708–78) British statesman, known as the Great Commoner. Entering parliament in 1735 as MP for the pocket borough of Old Sarum, he established a reputation as an outstanding orator. In 1756 he became secretary of state and leader of the House of Commons but was dismissed in 1757 and then recalled to form a ministry with Newcastle. In charge of foreign affairs, he was largely responsible for British victory in the Seven Years' War, reorganizing the militia and navy and rallying public opinion.

His second son **William Pitt the Younger** (1759–1806) was twice prime minister (1783–1801, 1804–06), the youngest in British history. As prime minister he inherited an enormous public debt, which he reduced by a fiscal policy influenced by Adam Smith. He also reformed the Indian administration. Pitt negotiated the first (1793) and second (1798) coalitions against France (*see* Revolutionary and Napoleonic Wars) and resolved the crisis caused by the Irish rebellion in 1798 by union of Britain and Ireland in 1800. His second ministry was marked by an alliance with Russia, Sweden, and Austria against Napoleon, which collapsed shortly before his death in office.

pituitary gland A small endocrine gland, about 12 mm by 8 mm, lying within the skull close to the centre of the head. The anterior (front) lobe produces growth hormone, prolactin, and hormones that regulate the function of other glands. The posterior (back) lobe is a downgrowth from the hypothalamus and stores various neurohormones that are synthesized in this part of the brain. Neural control of the entire endocrine system is effected from the pituitary gland.

Pius V, St (Michele Ghislieri; 1504–72) Pope (1566–72). A Dominican friar, he enforced the decrees of the Council of Trent and expanded the activities of the Inquisition. He excommunicated the Protestant Elizabeth I of England in 1570. He was canonized in 1712. Feast day: 6 May.

Pius IX (Giovanni Maria Mastai-Ferretti; 1792–1878) Pope (1846–78). At first sympathetic to liberal and nationalist movements, he abandoned radicalism for reaction after the Revolution of 1848, in which he fled Rome. He refused to acknowledge the newly established kingdom of Italy, into which Rome was incorporated in 1870. He defined the Immaculate Conception (1854) and papal infallibility (1869–70).

Pizarro, Francisco (c. 1475–1541) Spanish conquistador. In the 1520s he explored the NW coast of South America. In 1531 he crossed the Andes to Cajamarca, where he treacherously murdered the Inca king, Atahuallpa. Over the next nine years he consolidated the Spanish conquest of the Inca empire, founding Lima in 1535.

PK. *See* telekinesis.

placenta 1. An organ formed within the womb of mammals and other viviparous animals during pregnancy, composed of fetal and maternal tissues. Via the placenta the fetus receives nutrients, oxygen, and antibodies from the mother's blood and its waste products are absorbed into the mother's circulation. The fetus is attached to the placenta by the umbilical cord. **2.** A tissue in plants that connects the ovules (later the seeds) to the ovary (later the fruit wall).

plague An infectious disease caused by the bacterium *Pasteurella pestis*, which is transmitted to man by rat fleas. There are three forms of the disease, the most common of which is bubonic plague, in which fever, vomiting, and headache are accompanied by swollen inflamed lymph nodes (buboes). Epidemics of plague afflicted Europe throughout the middle ages, the Black Death of 1348 being the most devastating. The **Great Plague of London** (1665–66) claimed an estimated 70 000 lives.

Today plague is usually restricted to areas of poor sanitation in tropical countries.

plaice A commercially important flatfish, *Pleuronectes platessa*, that occurs in the N North Atlantic and British coastal waters. It is usually 25–40 cm long and is coloured brown with bright-red or orange spots above and white beneath.

Plaid Cymru A political party, founded in 1925, dedicated to the achievement of Welsh independence from the UK. The party won its first parliamentary seat in 1966; by 1989 it had three seats. It received a setback in 1979 when devolution was rejected in a referendum by the Welsh electorate.

Planck, Max Karl Ernst Ludwig (1858–1947) German physicist; the originator of quantum theory. Planck solved the problem of black-body radiation by assuming that the radiation was emitted in discrete amounts called quanta, the magnitude of a quantum being the product of the frequency of the radiation and a constant, now known as the Planck constant. For this work he received the Nobel Prize in 1918. His eldest son, **Erwin Planck** (1914–44) was executed for his involvement in the plot to assassinate Hitler.

Planck's radiation law Electromagnetic radiation is emitted from and absorbed by matter in discrete amounts (quanta) known as photons. The energy (E) of a photon is related to the frequency (f) of the radiation by the equation $E = hf$, where h is known as **Planck's constant** (which has the value $6.626\ 196 \times 10^{-34}$ J s). Max Planck discovered the law (1900) while investigating the distribution of wavelengths of the radiation emitted by a black body. It forms the basis of the quantum theory.

planet A celestial body that moves around a star and shines by light reflected from its surface. The only known planets are those orbiting the sun (solar system): there are nine major planets and numerous minor planets. The major planets in order from the sun are Mercury, Venus, earth, and Mars (the **terrestrial planets**), Jupiter, Saturn, Uranus, and Neptune (the **giant planets**) and, usually outermost, Pluto.

plane tree A large tree of the genus *Platanus* (10 species), native to the N hemisphere and often grown for shade and ornament. Up to 50 m tall, the trees have patchy peeling bark, large lobed leaves, and separate round clusters (catkins) of male and female flowers: the female flowers give rise to bristly round fruits. The London plane (*P. × acerifolia*) is a hybrid between the Oriental plane (*P. orientalis*) and North American buttonwood (*P. occidentalis*). The timber is a valuable hardwood used in carpentry. Family: *Platanaceae*.

plankton Minute or microscopic animals (zooplankton) and plants (phytoplankton) that float and drift in the open waters of a sea or lake. The phytoplankton carry out photosynthesis in the surface waters. The zooplankton include protozoa, small crustaceans, and larvae. Plankton are of great ecological and economic importance as a food source for fish and whales.

plant A living organism belonging to the kingdom *Plantae*, of which there are some 400 000 or so species. Plants are typically immobile and most manufacture their own food from simple inorganic nutrients by photosynthesis, trapping the energy required for the process in the green pigment chlorophyll. Plant cells have rigid cell walls, providing support, and growth occurs from specialized zones of tissue (*see* meristem), continuously

or periodically throughout life. Plants lack specialized sense organs and a nervous system; response to external stimuli is usually slow and often permanent. Green plants are the primary source of food and oxygen for all animals. See p.570, 571.

Plantagenet The surname of the Angevin, Lancastrian, and Yorkist Kings of England (1154–1485). They were descended from Queen Matilda and Geoffrey Martel, Count of Anjou (d. 1151), who was nicknamed Plantagenet because he wore a sprig of broom (*plante genêt*) in his cap. The name was not formally adopted until the 15th century.

Plantagenet, Richard, Duke of York. *See* York, Richard Plantagenet, 3rd Duke of.

plantain 1. An annual or perennial herb of the genus *Plantago* (about 50 species), occurring in temperate regions and on mountains in the tropics, often as a troublesome weed. Plantains have a basal rosette of simple leaves from which arises a stalk bearing a dense terminal head of inconspicuous green, white, yellow, or brown flowers with protruding stamens. Family: *Plantaginaceae*. **2.** *See* banana.

plasma (anatomy) The fluid constituent of blood, in which the blood cells are suspended. Plasma consists of a solution of various salts, sugars, etc., and contains numerous proteins, including those involved in blood clotting and the immunological response to infection (i.e. antibodies). It is obtained by centrifuging unclotted blood. *Compare* serum.

plasma (physics) A gas the atoms of which have been completely ionized. Sometimes called the fourth state of matter, plasmas occur at enormously high temperatures and are also created in thermonuclear reactors.

Plasmodium A genus of parasitic single-celled animals (*see* Protozoa) that cause malaria in man. *Plasmodium* undergoes the sexual phase of its development in bloodsucking mosquitoes of the genus *Anopheles*, through which it is transmitted to man. Four species cause different forms of malaria: *P. falciparum, P. vivax, P. malariae*, and *P. ovale*. Class: *Sporozoa*.

plaster A paste used to give a smooth hard coating to ceilings, walls, etc. A number of formulations are in use, the traditional one being a mixture of lime, sand, and water, which hardens in air owing to drying and reaction with atmospheric carbon dioxide.

plaster of Paris A hydrated form of calcium sulphate ($CaSO_4 . \frac{1}{2}H_2O$) made by partial dehydration of gypsum by heating. When mixed with water it sets into a hard mass by formation of the dihydrate ($CaSO_4 . 2H_2O$). It is used for casts for broken limbs and for modelling.

plastics Synthetic materials that consist of polymers, which are moulded during manufacture. Plastics are made from synthetic resins. **Thermosetting plastics** harden on heating to give a rigid product that cannot then be softened. Polyurethanes, polyesters, and epoxy resins all form thermosetting plastics. **Thermoplastic materials** soften when heated and harden again when cooled. These include derivatives of cellulose and polythene, and other polymers, which contain a reactive double bond.

The first synthetic material was Celluloid, made in 1870 from cotton and camphor. This highly inflammable substance was replaced during World War I by cellulose acetate and casein products. These materials were all based on naturally occurring large molecules. The first polymers to be made by joining together smaller mole-

PLANT

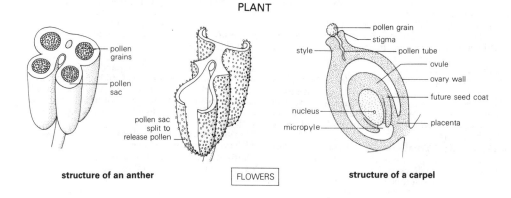

structure of an anther

FLOWERS

structure of a carpel

STEMS

transverse section of a dicotyledon stem

section of a woody stem showing four seasons' growth

ROOTS

section of the tip of a root

LEAVES

transverse section of a leaf

detail of stomata

broad category	major groups (usually divisions)	important classes	representative members
ALGAE	Chlorophyta Chrysophyta Phaeophyta Rhodophyta		green algae (*Spirogyra*, sea lettuce, etc.) yellow-green algae, diatoms brown algae (wracks, kelps, etc.) red algae
FUNGI	Myxomycophyta Eumycophyta	Phycomycetes Ascomycetes Basidiomycetes	slime fungi (clubroot, etc.) pin mold *Penicillium, Aspergillus* mushrooms, puffballs, bracket fungi
MOSSES and LIVERWORTS	Bryophyta	Hepaticae Musci	liverworts (e.g. *Pellia*) mosses (e.g. *Sphagnum*)
VASCULAR PLANTS (TRACHEOPHYTES)	Pteridophyta	Lycopsida Sphenopsida Pteropsida	clubmosses horsetails ferns
	Spermatophyta (seed plants)	Gymnospermae	cycads, *Ginkgo*, conifers (pines. larches, spruces, etc.)
		Angiospermae	monocotyledons (grasses, palms, orchids, lilies, etc.), dicotyledons (most trees and flowering plants)

PLANT *A simplified classification of the plant kingdom.*

cules were the phenol-formaldehyde resins (trade name Bakelite) invented in 1908 by Leo Baekeland (1863–1944). Since then a vast number of different resins have been synthesized.

Plata, Río de la (English name: River Plate) The estuary of the Río Paraná and the River Uruguay, on the Atlantic coast of SE South America between Uruguay and Argentina. Montevideo, the capital of Uruguay, lies on the N shore and Buenos Aires, the capital of Argentina, is situated on the S shore. A naval battle was fought off its mouth in 1939 (*see* World War II). Length: 275 km (171 mi). Width (at mouth): 225 km (140 mi).

platelet A small particle, 0.001–0.002 mm in diameter, produced by the bone marrow and found in the blood. Platelets are essential for blood clotting, accumulating in large numbers at the site of an injured blood vessel. There are normally 150 000 to 400 000 platelets per cubic millimetre of blood.

plate tectonics The theory, developed mainly in the 1960s, that the earth's crust is divided into rigid plates (oceanic, continental, or a combination of both), which move about the earth's surface at rates of 1–9 cm per annum. At constructive plate margins new oceanic crust is created where two plates are moving apart and magma rises to fill the gap; this occurs at midocean ridges. At destructive plate margins two plates collide and one dips beneath the other, producing deep-sea trenches. Where two continental plates collide, mountain chains are formed.

Plath, Sylvia (1932–63) US poet and writer. In 1956 she married the British poet Ted Hughes, whom she had met at Cambridge University. The disciplined poems of her first volume, *The Colossus* (1960), contrast with the anguished poems of *Ariel* (1965), published two years after her suicide. She also wrote a novel, *The Bell Jar* (1966). Her journals (Pulitzer Prize; 1982) were published posthumously.

platinum (Pt) A precious silver-white noble metal. It is malleable, ductile, and has a high melting point. Platinum is found in nature in nickel ore. It can absorb large quantities of hydrogen and is used as a catalyst, particularly in contact process for making sulphuric acid. It is also used in thermocouple wires and in jewellery. Although unreactive, platinum also forms other compounds, including the hexafluoride (PtF_6), one of the most powerful oxidizing agents known. At no 78; at wt 195.09; mp 1772°C; bp 3827 ± 100°C.

Plato (429–347 BC) Greek philosopher. An Athenian nobleman, he became a devoted follower of Socrates, after whose death he travelled widely. In 387 he returned to Athens and founded his Academy, to which he devoted the rest of his life. Some of Plato's poetry and all his prose works survive. Apart from 13 possibly spurious letters and the *Apology*, which purports to be Socrates' defence of himself before his judges, they are dramatic dialogues of outstanding literary merit. The early ones illustrate Socrates' character and philosophical methods. The *Phaedo*, *Symposium*, and *Republic* of Plato's middle period develop Plato's mature views on such topics as metaphysics, love, and government, notably his theory of ideas (Forms), the perfect spiritual entities or prototypes of which the physical world is a feeble and imperfect copy.

Platyhelminthes. *See* flatworm.

platypus. *See* duck-billed platypus.

plebeians Romans other than the privileged patricians. At first without civil rights, in 493–92 the plebeians forced the Senate to appoint their own tribunes and an assembly. During the subsequent two centuries of conflict, the plebeians gradually gained admission to all Roman offices.

Plélade, La A group of seven French writers in the 16th century who sought to liberate French poetry from medieval tradition. Their principles, deriving from the study of Greek, Latin, and Italian literature, were expounded in *Défense et illustration de la langue française* (1549) by Joachim du Bellay (1522–60), and their innovations included the introduction of the sonnet, the ode, and the alexandrine. Led by Pierre de Ronsard (1524–85), the group included du Bellay, J.-A. de Baïf (1532–89), Étienne Jodelle (c. 1532–73), Rémy Belleau (c. 1528–77), Pontus de Tyard (c. 1522–1605), and Jacques Peletier (1517–82) or Jean Dorat (1508–88).

Pleiades A young open star cluster in the constellation Taurus that contains several hundred stars, of which six are clearly visible to the naked eye. They were named after the seven daughters of Atlas, who were changed by the gods into stars while being pursued by Orion.

Pleistocene epoch The epoch of geological time between the Pliocene and the Holocene, at the beginning of the Quaternary period. It lasted from about 1.8 million to 10 000 years ago. It is often called the Ice Age because during this time the earth experienced great fluctuations in temperature. Fossils from the Pleistocene include horses, pigs, and elephants.

plesiosaur A widely distributed marine reptile of the Jurassic and Cretaceous periods (200–65 million years ago). Up to about 12 m long, plesiosaurs had broad turtle-like bodies with paddle-like limbs, a long flexible neck, and jaws armed with sharp teeth used to catch fish.

pleurisy Inflammation of the pleura—the membrane that covers the lungs and lines the chest cavity. The commonest cause of pleurisy is bacterial or viral infection. The patient will often have a fever, a pain in the chest that is worse on coughing or taking a deep breath, and a cough.

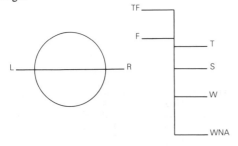

PLIMSOLL LINE *The lines and letters mark the waterline under various conditions. TF = fresh water in the tropics; F = fresh water; T = salt in the tropics; S = salt water in the summer; W = salt water in the winter; WNA = winter in the N Atlantic. LR represents Lloyd's Register.*

Plimsoll line A series of lines painted on the outside of a cargo ship's hull showing the various safe levels to which the ship can be loaded. The measure was introduced in the UK as a result of the Merchant Shipping Act (1876) at the instigation of the MP Samuel Plimsoll (1824–98).

Pliny the Elder (Gaius Plinius Secundus; 23–79 AD) Roman scholar, whose universal encyclopedia, *Natural History*, was a major source of scientific knowledge until the 17th century. During his military career, Pliny assembled material from numerous sources on a wide range of disciplines, including astrology, geography, agriculture, medicine, zoology, and botany. He finally

completed this work of 37 volumes in 77 AD. His nephew and adopted son **Pliny the Younger** (Gaius Plinius Caecilius Secundus; c. 61–c. 113 AD) held various administrative posts and was a prominent legal orator. His ten volumes of private letters constitute an intimate unofficial history of his time.

Pliocene epoch. *See* Tertiary period.

PLO. *See* Palestine Liberation Organization.

Plotinus (205–70 AD) Greek philosopher and founder of Neoplatonism. Born in Egypt, he studied at Alexandria, and finally settled in Rome. Developing Plato's mysticism, he taught that the immaterial impersonal indescribable "One" is the ground of all existence and value. From it emanate successively mind, soul, and nature. By rejecting material nature and cultivating the intellect man may briefly become mystically united with the One.

Plovdiv (former name: Philippopoli) 42 08N 24 45E A city in S central Bulgaria, on the River Maritsa. Bulgaria's second largest city, its industries include food processing and carpet manufacture. Population (1985): 342 201.

plover A bird belonging to a widely distributed family (*Charadriidae*; 56 species) occurring in open regions and along shores. Plovers have brown or grey plumage, often mottled, with white underparts. They feed on insects and other small invertebrates and nest on the ground. Order: *Charadriiformes* (gulls, plovers, etc.). *See also* lapwing.

plum A small tree, *Prunus domestica*—a natural hybrid between the blackthorn and the cherry plum (*P. cerasifera*), native to SW Asia and cultivated in most Mediterranean and N temperate regions for its fruit. It has oval toothed leaves and white flowers. The fruit is round or oval and has a dark-red to blue-black skin (when ripe), enclosing a sweet greenish-yellow pulp and a central oval stony seed. Plums are eaten fresh, cooked in desserts, canned, or dried as prunes. Family: *Rosaceae*. *See also* damson.

plumbago. *See* graphite.

Plumbago A genus of herbaceous plants, shrubs, and climbers (12 species), native to warm regions and including a number of ornamentals. They have simple leaves and terminal clusters of white, blue, violet, pink, or red flowers. *P. auriculata*, with pale-blue flowers, and *P. rosea*, with red flowers, are popular greenhouse plants. Some species are used for medicinal purposes. Family: *Plumbaginaceae*.

Plutarch (c. 46–c. 120 AD) Greek biographer and essayist. He was a citizen of both Athens and Rome and a priest of Delphi. His *Parallel Lives* consists of biographies of 23 pairs of Greek and Roman statesmen and soldiers. The *Moralia* contain 83 essays on ethical, scientific, and literary topics.

Pluto (astronomy) The smallest and usually outermost planet, orbiting the sun every 248 years at a mean distance of 5900 million km. Pluto was discovered in 1930 but little was known about it until its satellite was discovered in 1978. It is a very cold low-density body about 3000 km in diameter.

Pluto (mythology). *See* Hades.

plutonic rock. *See* igneous rock.

plutonium (Pu) An important synthetic transuranic element discovered in 1940. Trace quantities exist in natural uranium ores. It is produced in large quantities in nuclear reactors by beta-decay from uranium-239. Plutonium is fissile and was used in the atomic bomb dropped on Nagasaki in 1945 (*see* nuclear weapons). It forms oxides (PuO, PuO_2), halides (for example PuF_3), and other compounds. It is used in fast reactors and small power units for spacecraft. At no 94; at wt (244); mp 641°C; bp 3235°C.

Plymouth 50 23N 4 10W A port in SW England, in Devon on Plymouth Sound between the Tamar and Plym estuaries. On Plymouth Hoe Drake is reputed to have finished his game of bowls while the Spanish Armada approached and the *Mayflower* embarked from here for America in 1620 (*see* Pilgrim Fathers). Plymouth is an important naval base with associated marine industries. More recent industries include the manufacture of clothing, radio equipment, and processed foods. Population (1981): 243 895.

Plymouth Brethren An austere Protestant sect founded at Plymouth in 1830 by a former Anglican priest, J. N. Darby (1800–82). The Brethren have strict standards of behaviour and shun many secular trades and professions. Small groups exist throughout the world, often as active missionaries.

pneumoconiosis Chronic lung disease caused by inhaling dust, most commonly coal dust (causing coalworkers' pneumoconiosis) and silica (causing silicosis). Considerable coal dust may be taken into the lungs without causing much damage, but later progressive massive fibrosis may develop. *See also* asbestosis.

pneumonia Inflammation of the lungs, most commonly caused by infection. Pneumonia may arise in only one lobe of the lung (lobar pneumonia) or in patches in both lungs (bronchopneumonia). The infective organisms may be streptococci, viruses, tubercle bacilli, or other organisms, such as mycoplasmas. The patient has a fever, cough, and pain in the chest and may be breathless.

Po, River (Latin name: Padus) The longest river in Italy rising in the Cottian Alps and flowing mainly ENE through Turin to enter the Adriatic Sea by way of a large delta in the E. The Po Valley is the most fertile and economically important region in Italy. Length: 652 km (405 mi).

pochard A large-headed duck, *Aythya ferina*, occurring in temperate inland waters of Eurasia. It has grey legs and a grey-blue bill; males have a reddish head, black breast, and grey body; females are brown. It feeds on water plants and small aquatic invertebrates.

pocket gopher A rodent belonging to the subfamily *Geomyinae* (39 species), of North and Central America. They inhabit open dry country, where they dig extensive burrows, and feed on roots, seeds, insects, and mice. Their large cheek pouches have an outside opening like a pocket.

podzol A type of soil typical of many cool temperate humid zones especially with coniferous vegetation, as in the taiga of the Soviet Union and North America. It is characterized by an ashen-coloured upper layer (A horizon) and an underlying layer (B horizon) of redeposition humus and iron, which may develop into an impermeable pan.

Poe, Edgar Allan (1809–49) US poet, short-story writer, and critic. After publishing two volumes of poetry (1827, 1829), he began to contribute to and work for literary magazines. Among his many prose tales and horror stories are "The Fall of the House of Usher" (1839), "The Black Cat" (1843), and the first ever detec-

EDGAR ALLEN POE

tive story, "The Murders in the Rue Morgue" (1841). His best-known poems are "The Raven" (1845) and *The Bells* (1849) and his most influential critical work is "The Philosophy of Composition" (1846).

poet laureate A title bestowed by the British monarch on a contemporary poet, whose traditional duties include the writing of commemorative odes on important public occasions. The first official poet laureate was John Dryden, who served from 1668 to 1688, and his most recent successors include C. Day Lewis (1968–72), John Betjeman (1972–84), and Ted Hughes (1984–).

Poincaré, Raymond (1860–1934) French statesman; president (1913–20) and prime minister (1912–13, 1922–24, 1926–29). His foreign policy aimed to prevent French isolation in the face of possible German aggression. His postwar economic policy brought a period of stability to France. His cousin **Jules Henri Poincaré** (1854–1912) was a mathematician, regarded by some as the last universal mathematician. A gifted writer, Poincaré wrote important treatises on the nature of mathematical creativity, emphasizing its intuitional aspects.

poinsettia An ornamental shrub, *Euphorbia pulcherrima*, native to Mexico and tropical America and a popular pot plant at Christmas in Europe and North America. It has simple dark-green leaves and clusters of tiny greenish-yellow flowers surrounded by large scarlet bracts, up to 14 cm long, which resemble petals. Family: *Euphorbiaceae*.

pointer A breed of sporting dog originating in England and named after its habit of pointing its nose towards game. It is lithely built with a long tapering tail, a long muzzle, and drooping ears. The short smooth coat is white combined with yellow, orange, liver, or black. Height: 63–68 cm (dogs); 61–66 cm (bitches).

pointillism A style of painting using dots of pure colour. The pointillists applied primary colours to the canvas in dots and allowed the colours to be mixed by the eye. It was developed by Seurat in France in the 1880s.

point-to-point. *See* steeplechase.

Poisson, Siméon Dénis (1781–1840) French mathematician. He made important contributions to the mathematical theory of electricity, magnetism, and mechanics. His work on electricity led him in 1837 to discover Poisson's equation, which describes the electric field created by an arbitrary charge density. Poisson's distribution is widely used in probability calculations and **Poisson's ratio** (the ratio of the lateral strain to the longitudinal strain in a stretched wire) is used by engineers in studying the elongation of structural members.

Poland, People's Republic of A country in N Europe, on the Baltic Sea. Extensive plains in the N rise to the Carpathian Mountains in the S, which reach heights of over 2500 m (8000 ft). Approximately 70% of the inhabitants are Roman Catholic. *Economy*: Poland remains one of the world's leading agricultural nations. The chief crops are rye, wheat, oats, sugar beet, and potatoes. Its mineral wealth includes rich deposits of copper and sulphur and natural gas has been found as well as some oil. An important shipbuilding nation, Poland's industries include textiles, engineering, steel, cement, chemicals, and food products. *History*: Poland first appeared as a separate state in the 10th century, which also saw the introduction of Christianity. From the 14th to 16th centuries its power was extended under the Jagiellon dynasty. Foreign intervention in the 18th century culminated in partition by Russia, Austria, and Prussia (in 1772, 1793, and 1795), and at the Congress of Vienna in 1815 the Congress Kingdom of Poland was created under the Russian Crown. After the defeat of the Central Powers in World War I independence was declared. In 1939 Poland was invaded by Germany. Polish resistance to Germany contributed to the Allied victory, and in 1945 Poland was occupied by the Russians. The first postwar elections, in 1948, brought a communist-controlled government to power under Gomułka. Unrest in 1970 led to his enforced resignation and he was succeeded by Edward Gierek (1913–   ). Gierek was dismissed in 1980 and succeeded by Stanisław Kania, who resigned (1981) to be replaced by Gen Wojciech Jaruzelski. In December, 1981, the independent trade union Solidarity, led by Lech Wałesa (1943–   ), was outlawed and martial law was declared. Martial law was lifted in 1983 but unrest continued, often expressed through the church. In 1989 Solidarity was relegalized and allowed to contest a general election; it won all but two of the seats contested and led the new government. Prime minister: Tadeusz Mazowiecki. Official language: Polish. Official currency: złoty of 100 groszy. Area: 312 677 sq km (120 624 sq mi). Population (1987): 37 572 000. Capital: Warsaw. Main port: Gdańsk.

Polanski, Roman (1933–   ) Polish film director, born in Paris. After 1961 he worked in Britain and the USA. His films include *Repulsion* (1965), *Rosemary's Baby* (1968), *The Tenant* (1976), and *Tess* (1979).

polar bear A white bear, *Thalarctos maritimus*, living on the shores of the Arctic Ocean. Up to 2.5 m long and weighing 500–700 kg (depending on the season), polar bears prey on seals, fish, and birds.

Polaris (*or* North Star) A remote cream supergiant, apparent magnitude 2.0 and about 650 light years distant, that is the brightest star in the constellation Ursa Minor. It is the present pole star, lying about 1° from the N celestial pole. It is a Cepheid variable and is the primary component of a multiple star.

Polaris missile A US navy two-stage solid-fuelled nuclear strategic missile launched from a submarine and having a range of 4500 km (2800 m). Travelling at speeds of over mach 10, some versions (Poseidon) are capable of delivering 10 separately guided 15-kiloton warheads. When fired from below the surface, the missile is ejected from the vessel by compressed gas, its rocket firing at the surface. Firing is by two-key control, linked directly to Washington.

polarized light Light in which the direction of vibration is restricted. In ordinary light (and other types of electromagnetic radiation) the transverse vibrations of the electric and magnetic fields are at right angles to each other in all possible planes. In **plane-polarized light** the vibrations of the electric field are confined to one plane and the magnetic field to one at right angles to it. Plane-polarized light can be produced by reflection at a certain angle (*see* Brewster's law) or by passing light through such doubly refracting substances as Polaroid (a plastic sheet impregnated with tiny crystals of a dichroic substance orientated parallel to each other). **Circularly** and **elliptically polarized light** occur when the electric vector describes a circle or an ellipse round the direction of the light beam.

polder An area of low-lying land reclaimed from the sea or other water, often for agricultural purposes. Polders are usually formed by constructing dykes around the area, which is then drained. The most notable polders are those of Holland, next to the IJsselmeer.

polecat A carnivorous mammal, *Mustela putorius*, found in woods and grassland throughout Europe, Asia, and N Africa. About 50 cm long, it has a dark-brown coat with yellowish patches on the face and ears. Polecats are nocturnal, foraging for rodents and insects. They eject a pungent fluid when alarmed. Family: *Mustelidae* (weasels, etc.). *See also* ferret.

Poles, North and South The most northerly and southerly points of the earth's surface and the ends of the earth's axis, about which it rotates. The magnetic north and south poles are the points to which a magnetic compass needle points and where the lines of force of the earth's magnetic field are vertical. They do not coincide with the geographical poles and their positions slowly change. *See also* Arctic Circle; Antarctica.

pole star Either of two bright stars that are nearest the N or S celestial pole. The poles are not fixed in position but, owing to precession of the earth's axis, trace out two circles in the sky over a period of 25 800 years. There is thus a sequence of stars that slowly, in turn, become the N or S pole star. *See also* Polaris.

pole vault A field event for men in athletics, in which competitors use a fibreglass pole to lever themselves over a horizontal bar. A competitor is allowed three tries at each height. The height is increased until only one competitor is left. World record: 6.06 m (1988) by Sergei Bubka (Soviet Union).

poliomyelitis A viral infection of the central nervous system that may result in muscle paralysis. It was formerly known as infantile paralysis, because children were most commonly affected. In most cases the infection is mild, but sometimes a more severe illness develops, which may lead to severe pain in the limbs followed by permanent paralysis. A vaccine is available that gives complete protection (*see* Sabin vaccine; Salk vaccine).

Polish (*or* Lekhitic) A West Slavonic language spoken in Poland and closely related to Czech, Slovak, and Sorbian. It is written in a Latin alphabet and the standard form is based on the dialect of Poznań.

polka A Bohemian folk dance in 2/4 time, which became a ballroom dance in 19th-century Europe and rivalled the waltz in popularity. It is characterized by three steps and a hop.

pollen The male gametes of seed plants, which are produced in the stamens of flowering plants and in the male cones of conifers and other gymnosperms. To ensure fertilization, the pollen must be transferred to the stigma (in flowering plants) or the female cone (in conifers)—the process of **pollination**. Many flowers are cross-pollinated, i.e. the pollen from one plant is deposited on the stigma of another of the same species by means of animal carriers (usually insects), wind, or water. Some flowers are self-pollinated, the pollen being transferred from the anthers to the stigma of the same plant: the stamens are usually bent over the stigma to assist the process. After pollination, a pollen tube grows down from the pollen grain into the pistil of the pollinated flower until it reaches the ovule. Two pollen nuclei travel down this tube: one fertilizes the egg cell, which develops into the embryo plant in the seed; the other fuses with a nucleus in the ovule to become food for the seed.

Pollock, Jackson (1912–56) US painter. Early in his career he was influenced by surrealism. By 1947 he had developed an abstract style (*see* action painting) to express feelings and unconscious thoughts through the act of painting itself. He dripped paints onto very large canvases to form patterns of interweaving lines.

poll tax A levy on individuals (*poll*, head), regardless of means. First levied regularly in England in 1377, it was a direct cause of the Peasants' Revolt in 1381 and was abolished in 1698. It replaced domestic rates in Scotland in 1989 and in the rest of the UK in 1990. In the USA the poll tax as a voting qualification was abused as a means of disenfranchising Blacks and was constitutionally banned.

pollution The addition to the environment of substances that cannot be rendered harmless by normal biological processes. Modern industrial and agricultural activities have led to pollution by either man-made toxic substances (such as pesticides and fertilizers) or by the overproduction of naturally occurring substances (such as carbon dioxide gas). Current problems include the disposal of radioactive wastes; increasing amounts of heavy metals (such as lead) in the atmosphere; atmospheric pollution by carbon dioxide, carbon monoxide, etc.; the disposal of human refuse and sewage; and unacceptable noise levels. *See also* acid rain; greenhouse effect; ozone.

polo A four-a-side stick-and-ball game, in which the players are mounted on specially bred ponies. It was played in Persia by 600 BC and was rediscovered by British officers in India in the 19th century. The riders use long sticks with mallet heads to hit a solid wooden ball, with the object of scoring goals. A game consists of up to eight seven-minute periods, or "chukkas," after each of which mounts are changed.

Polo, Marco (c. 1254–1324) Venetian traveller. His father and uncle travelled to Peking in 1271 at the request of the Mongol emperor, Kublai Khan, taking Marco with them. Having learned Mongolian, he entered Kublai's service, conducting missions as far as S India, until leaving China in 1292. He subsequently fought for the Venetians against the Genoese and was captured. In prison (1296–98) he dictated an account of his travels.

polonium (Po) A highly radioactive element discovered in 1898 by Marie Curie in minute amounts in pitchblende. It is 5000 times as radioactive as radium and liberates considerable amounts of heat. Polonium has 27 isotopes, more than any other element. It is used in compact radiation and thermoelectric power sources. At no 84; at wt (209); mp 254°C; bp 962°C.

POLO *The dimensions of the ground. If the side lines are boarded, the width is 160 yd (146.4 m) and there is a safety area extending 10 yd (9 m) beyond each side line and 30 yd (27 m) beyond each goal line.*

poltergeist A noisy, mischievous, and frequently destructive invisible agent that persecutes the occupants of a house, most commonly by throwing or moving objects. Famous poltergeist hauntings have included the 20th-century Borley Rectory phenomena.

polyanthus A hardy perennial, *Primula × polyanthus*, derived from a cross between the common primrose and the cowslip. There are many varieties, with yellow, brown, blue, or red flowers. *See also* Primula.

polyesters Synthetic resins or plastics that are polymers of esters. Saturated polyesters (those with no double bonds), made by a condensation reaction, are widely used in such synthetic fibres as Dacron and Terylene. Unsaturated polyesters are used as resins to make thermosetting plastics.

Polygonum A genus of annual or perennial herbs (about 75 species), found worldwide. 10 to 200 cm in height, they bear simple leaves and small white or pink flowers. Family: *Polygonaceae*.

polymerization The chemical combination of simpler molecules (monomers) to form long chain molecules (**polymers**) of repeating units. In **addition polymerization**, the monomers simply add together and no other compound is formed. Polythene is made from ethylene in this way. In **condensation polymerization**, water, alcohol, or some other small molecule is formed in the reaction, as in the production of nylon.

polymethyl methacrylate. *See* Perspex.

polymorphism In biology, the functional or structural variation between two or more members of a species, determined by differences in either genetic constitution, environmental conditions, or both. It is a widespread phenomenon in animals and plants. In **transient polymorphism** two different forms exist together temporarily, while one form is replacing the other; in **balanced polymorphism** the different forms continue to coexist.

Polynesia A division of Oceania in the S and central Pacific Ocean. The volcanic and coral islands include those of French Polynesia, Hawaii, Samoa, Tonga, Tuvalu, Kiribati, and the Line and Cook Islands. *See also* Melanesia; Micronesia.

Polynesian The people of the Pacific islands contained within the roughly triangular area between and including Hawaii, New Zealand, and Easter Island. They are seafarers, with considerable skill in navigation. Fishing and cultivating are also important. The Polynesian languages belong to the Oceanic branch of the Austronesian family and include Samoan, Maori, Tongan, Tahitian, and Hawaiian.

polyp (biology) A sedentary form that occurs during the life cycle of many animals of the phylum *Coelenterata*. It has a cylindrical stalklike body attached at the base, with the mouth at the free end surrounded by tentacles bearing stinging cells (nematocysts). Polyps occur singly or in colonies; colonial polyps are modified for different functions, such as feeding, reproduction, and protection.

polyp (*or* polypus) (medicine) A growth that has a narrow base or stalk. Polyps may occur in the bowel, the nose, the womb, the larynx, and other sites. They often cause obstruction or infection and some forms may become cancerous.

polypeptide. *See* peptide.

polyphony (Greek: many voices) Music that consists of a horizontal combination of melodic strands rather than a series of vertical chords. The high point of the polyphonic style was reached in the 16th century with Palestrina's church music, the Italian madrigal, the English madrigal, and the church music of Tallis and Byrd. *See* counterpoint; harmony; modes.

polypropylene A thermoplastic material made by polymerization of propylene (CH_2:$CHCH_3$). It is similar to high-density polythene but stronger, lighter, and more rigid. Polypropylene products, such as beer crates, luggage, and hinges, are injection moulded. Fibres, which are used to make sacks and carpet backings, are made by extrusion.

polysaccharide A carbohydrate comprising chains of between three and several thousand linked monosaccharide units. Polysaccharides, such as starch, glycogen, and cellulose, are important as energy reserves and structural components of plants and animals.

polytechnics Institutes of higher education concentrating on courses with vocational relevance while maintaining high academic standards. The first polytechnic was established in Paris in 1794 to provide technical training for artillery and engineering officers. The development of the polytechnic movement in the UK began with the establishment of the Regent Street Polytechnic in 1880. During the period 1969–73 some 30 educational institutions in England and Wales were formally designated polytechnics. Degrees, comparable to university standards, were awarded by the Council for National Academic Awards (CNAA) until 1987, when polytechnics began to award their own degrees.

polytetrafluoroethene (PTFE) A synthetic material produced by the polymerization of tetrafluoroethylene (F_2C:CF_2). It can withstand temperatures of up to 400°C and has a very slippery surface. PTFE is used to coat nonstick cooking utensils and in gaskets, bearings, and electrical insulation. It is sold under the tradenames Teflon and Fluon.

polythene (polyethylene) A white translucent thermoplastic material made by polymerization of ethylene. **Low-density polythene** is made at high pressure and is a soft material used for flexible pipes, sheets, and bags. **High-density polythene** is made at lower pressures, is more rigid, and softens at a higher temperature. It is used for moulded articles.

polyurethane A synthetic polymer the molecules of which contain the –NH.CO.O– group. Some polyurethanes form thermosetting resins and others, thermoplastic resins. They have a wide range of properties and are used in paints, adhesives, moulded articles, rubbers, lacquers, and foams.

polyvinyl chloride (PVC) A vinyl resin or plastic produced by polymerization of vinyl chloride (chloroethene; CH_2:$CHCl$), a toxic gas. Rigid PVC products are made by moulding. The addition of a plasticizer produces flexible PVC. PVC is tough, nonflammable, and a good electrical insulator.

pomegranate A shrub or small tree, *Punica granatum*, native to W Asia and widely cultivated in the tropics and subtropics for its fruit. 5–7 m tall, it has narrow pointed leaves and orange-red flowers. The large round fruit has a thick leathery yellowish-reddish skin and contains several chambers, each containing many seeds coated with a pinkish acid-sweet juicy pulp. Pomegranates are eaten fresh or used in beverages or wines. The seeds are used in preserves and syrups. Family: *Punicaceae*.

Pomeranian A breed of toy dog, developed in Pomerania, a region of NE Europe now divided between Poland and E Germany. Its ancestors are thought to have been Scandinavian sledge dogs. The Pomeranian has a compact body and foxlike head with small erect ears. The short undercoat is covered by a long straight outercoat and the fluffy tail is held over the back. The coat may be any recognized colour, including white, black, brown, or reddish. Height: 14–18 cm.

Pomona (Orkneys). *See* Mainland.

Pompadour, Mme de (Jeanne Antoinette Poisson, Marquise de P.; 1721–64) The mistress of Louis XV, who exerted considerable political influence from 1745 until her death. She influenced the negotiation of an Austrian alliance against Prussia and was blamed for French defeats in the subsequent Seven Years' War. She was a notable patron of artists and scholars.

Pompeii An ancient city near Naples, in Italy. It was buried four to six metres deep under volcanic ash by the eruption of Mount Vesuvius (79 AD) and rediscovered in 1748. Pompeii provides unparalleled evidence for daily life in Roman times: buildings, with extensive wall paintings and graffiti; food and wooden furniture, preserved by the ash; and personal possessions abandoned by the fleeing inhabitants.

Pompey (Gnaeus Pompeius; 106–48 BC) Roman general and statesman, called Pompeius Magnus (Pompey the Great). In 60 he joined Julius Caesar and Crassus in the first Triumvirate, marrying Caesar's daughter Julia (d. 54) in 59, but in 50 he supported the Senate's demand for Caesar to resign his armies. In the civil war that followed Pompey was defeated by Caesar at Pharsalus (48) and fled to Egypt, where he was murdered.

Pompidou, Georges (Jean Raymond) (1911–74) French statesman; prime minister (1962–68) and president (1969–74). He served under de Gaulle during World War II and was his personal assistant in 1958–59, when he helped draft the constitution of the Fifth Republic. He negotiated a settlement with the Algerians (1961) and with the students in the revolt of May, 1968.

POMPEII *Gate leading to the forum with Mount Vesuvius in the background.*

Pondicherry A Union Territory in SE India, on the Coromandel Coast. Founded by the French in 1674, it was their chief settlement in India until transferred to Indian administration in 1954. Rice and millet are the chief products. Area: 479 sq km (185 sq mi). Population (1981 est): 604 136. Capital: Pondicherry.

pondweed A usually perennial aquatic herb of the genus *Potamogeton* (100 species), found worldwide in fresh water. It has submerged or floating oblong or pointed leaves and tiny greenish flowers. Family: *Potamogetonaceae.*
The Canadian pondweed (*Elodea canadensis*) has submerged stems, up to 3 m long, with whorls of narrow backward-curving dark-green leaves. Native to North America, it is naturalized in Europe. Family: *Hydrocharitaceae.*

Ponte Vecchio A bridge over the River Arno in Florence. Topped by buildings, it was designed by Taddeo Gaddi and finished in 1345. It was a highly advanced structure for its period.

Pontianak 0 05S 109 16E A port in Indonesia, in W Kalimantan on the Kapuas delta. Formerly Borneo's main gold town, its chief industries are shipbuilding and rubber, palm oil, sugar, and timber processing. Population (1980): 304 778.

pontoon (*or* vingt-et-un) A card game in which the objective is to score 21, counting court cards as 10 and the ace as 1 or 11. One card is dealt to each player, who puts up a stake accordingly; a second card is then dealt. Players then have the option of "sticking" (keeping the cards they have), buying another card face down, or "twisting" (accepting another card face up at no cost). Hands scoring more than 21 lose their stakes (go "bust"). The winner is the player with the score nearest to 21. Players scoring exactly 21 win double their stakes. *See also* blackjack.

pony A horse that does not exceed 1.47 m (14½ hands) in height at maturity, measured from the top of the shoulders (withers). The many modern breeds of pony are thought to have developed from one or two original types. Ponies have traditionally been used by man as pack animals and for riding. Today, they are especially popular as children's mounts and for pony trekking.

poodle A breed of dog of uncertain origins but long associated with France and Germany. The poodle is an active intelligent dog with a long straight muzzle, drooping ears, and a docked tail. The dense coat was originally clipped to enable them to swim and retrieve in water. The miniature poodle and toy poodle are derivative breeds of the standard poodle. Height: 38 cm minimum (standard); 28–38 cm (miniature); under 28 cm (toy).

Poona (*or* Pune) 18 34N 73 58E A city in India, in Maharashtra. Capital of the Marathas in the late 18th century, it was taken by the British in 1817. A commercial, manufacturing, and military centre, it has cotton textiles, rubber, paper, and munitions industries. Population (1981 est): 1 685 266.

Poor Laws The laws that governed assistance to the poor in Britain. From the 16th century parishes were responsible for providing for their poor and from 1572 levied a rate for poor relief. The Poor Law Amendment Act of 1834 abolished such outdoor relief and those seeking assistance had to enter a workhouse. The Poor Law system was not abolished until 1947. *See also* social security.

Pope, Alexander (1688–1744) British poet. He established his reputation as a poet of biting wit and skill, especially in his masterly use of the heroic couplet, with *An Essay on Criticism* (1711) and the mock epic *The Rape of the Lock* (1712–14). His other works include translations of Homer's *Iliad* (1715–20) and *Odyssey* (1725–26), the mock epic *The Dunciad* (1728; revised 1742–43), the philosophical poem *An Essay on Man* (1733–34), and poems modelled on the satires of Horace.

PONTE VECCHIO

Popish Plot (1678) A conspiracy invented by Titus Oates (1649–1705) and Israel Tonge. They alleged the existence of a plot to assassinate Charles II and place his Roman Catholic brother, James, on the throne. The anti-Catholic passions Oates and Tonge thus aroused led to the execution of 35 suspects and the exclusion of Catholics from parliament (*see* Test Acts).

poplar A shrub or tree of the genus *Populus* (about 30 species), native to N temperate regions and grown for wood pulp, shade, and ornament. Up to 40 m tall, the trees may have a broad spreading crown, as in the European black poplar (*P. nigra*), or a tall slender one, as in the Lombardy poplar (*P. nigra* var. *italica*). The poplar has oval, triangular, or heart-shaped leaves and drooping catkins. The seeds have tufts of silky white hairs. Family: *Salicaceae. See also* aspen.

poppy An annual, biennial, or perennial plant of the genus *Papaver* (about 120 species), native mainly to the N hemisphere and often grown for ornament. It yields a milky sap (latex) and bears large lobed or divided leaves and showy white, pink, or red flowers with 4–6 petals surrounding a dense whorl of stamens. The fruit is a capsule with pores through which the seeds are dispersed. Species include the corn poppy and opium poppy. Family: *Papaveraceae. See also* Welsh poppy.

porbeagle A mackerel shark, *Lamna nasus*, commonly called the Atlantic mackerel shark, that lives mainly in N temperate shallow waters. It has a dark-blue robust body, 1.5–3 m long, with a white belly and feeds principally on shoals of fish, especially mackerel.

porcelain White vitrified ceramic evolved by Chinese potters about 900 AD. It was not invented but developed out of stoneware pottery. There are three kinds of porcelain: hard-paste or true porcelain, soft-paste or artificial, and English bone china. Hard-paste porcelain consists of china clay (kaolin) and fusible feldspathic rock (petuntse) finely mixed and fired to about 1400°C. This forms a translucent white resonant vitreous body, which is usually glazed with pure petuntse during the firing. Soft-paste porcelain differs from hard-paste in that the clay or kaolin is mixed with an artificial flux, such as sand with lime, flint, soda, etc. The mixture is fired at about 1100°C and the glaze, usually of glass, is applied in a second firing at about 1000°C. Bone porcelain is an 18th-century English invention using bone ash as a flux.

porcupine A large herbivorous spiny rodent belonging to either of the families *Erethizontidae* (New World porcupines; 11 species) or *Hystricidae* (Old World porcupines; 15 species). American porcupines tend to be arboreal and have prehensile tails. The North American porcupine (*Erethizon dorsatum*) is about 75 cm long and grows a soft winter coat that almost conceals its covering of quills. Old World porcupines are mainly ground-dwelling. The Indian crested porcupine (*Hystrix indica*) grows to 1 m in length and may have spines 35 cm long. Porcupines respond to a threat by turning their backs and raising their spines.

porgy. *See* sea bream.

porphyria A group of genetic disorders in which there is an accumulation in the body of one or more porphyrins—precursors of the red blood pigment—due to an enzyme defect. The disease affects the digestive tract, causing abdominal pain, vomiting, and diarrhoea; the nervous system, causing psychotic disorder, epilepsy, and weakness; the circulatory system, causing high blood pressure; and the skin, causing photosensitivity.

porphyry An igneous rock, usually hypabyssal, containing numerous large crystals called phenocrysts set in a finer-grained, or sometimes glassy, groundmass. The term porphyry is often given with the name of the prophyritic mineral, for example quartz porphyry.

porpoise A small toothed whale belonging to the family *Phocoenidae* (7 species), of coastal waters. The common, or harbour, porpoise (*Phocoena phocoena*) of the N Atlantic and Pacific, has a rounded body, tapering towards the tail, blue-grey above and pale grey beneath. It feeds on fish, squid, and crustaceans.

port A fortified usually dessert wine from Oporto (N Portugal). The grapes grown on the Douro hillsides are trodden in stone presses. Fermentation is halted by adding brandy. Subsequently the wine is taken to the lodges near Oporto, where it matures in wood.

Port-au-Prince 18 40N 72 20W The capital of Haiti, a port in the SW on the Gulf of Gonaïves. Its main exports are coffee and sugar. The University of Haiti was founded here in 1944. Population (1987): 472 895.

Porter, Cole (Albert) (1893–1964) US composer of musical comedies and popular songs. He wrote a series of musicals, including *The Gay Divorcee* (1932), *Anything Goes* (1934), *Kiss Me Kate* (1948), and *Can Can* (1953). His songs included "Night and Day" and "Begin the Beguine."

Portland, Isle of A peninsula in S England, in Dorset connected to the mainland by Chesil Bank. It contains Portland Castle, built by Henry VIII (1520). The Portland stone quarried here has been used in many London buildings, notably St Paul's Cathedral.

Port Louis 20 10S 57 30E The capital of Mauritius, in the NW of the island. Founded in about 1736, it is the site of two cathedrals. Sugar is exported. Population (1986): 138 482.

Pôrto Alegre 30 03S 51 10W A city in S Brazil, the capital of Rio Grande do Sul state on the Lagôa (Lagoon) dos Patos. It is a major commercial and industrial centre; industries are chiefly related to agriculture and include meat processing, tanning, and the manufacture of textiles. It is the seat of two universities. Population (1985): 1 275 483.

Port-of-Spain 10 38N 61 31W The capital and main port of Trinidad and Tobago since 1783, on the W coast of Trinidad. Notable buildings include the Anglican and Roman Catholic cathedrals. Petroleum products, sugar, and rum are among the main exports. Population (1986 est): 57 400.

Porto Novo 6 30N 2 47E The capital of Benin, on the Gulf of Guinea. A former centre of the slave trade with the Portuguese, it came under French rule in the late 19th century. Trade includes palm oil and cotton. Population (1982): 208 258.

Port Said (*or* Bur Said) 31 17N 32 18E A major port in Egypt, situated at the Mediterranean entrance to the Suez Canal. Founded in 1859, it became an important fuelling point but suffered from the closure of the Suez Canal (1967–75) and Israeli occupation of the E bank. Population (1985): 374 000.

Portsmouth 50 48N 1 05W A port in S England, in Hampshire at the entrance to Portsmouth Harbour. Notable landmarks include Nelson's flagship HMS *Victory*. The chief naval base in the UK, Portsmouth is also a commercial port. The resort of Southsea is within the district. Population (1981 est): 179 419.

Port Sudan 19 38N 37 07E A port in the Sudan, on the Red Sea. It handles much of the country's trade; exports include cotton, gum arabic, and sesame seeds. It also has an important salt-panning industry. Population (1983): 206 727.

Portugal, Republic of A country in SW Europe, occupying the W section of the Iberian Peninsula and bordering on the Atlantic Ocean. The Madeira Islands are an integral part of Portugal. Coastal plains rise to mountains, reaching 1935 m (6352 ft) in the N. *Economy*: traditionally agricultural, Portugal's principal exports are textiles, clothing, cork, wood products, sardines, and fortified wines. Rich mineral resources include coal, copper pyrites, kaolin, haematite and hydroelectricity is a valuable source of power. *History*: the early history of the region is that of the rest of the Iberian Peninsula (*see* Spain, Kingdom of). Portugal as a distinct Christian territory dates from 868. It became a kingdom in 1139 under Alfonso I (1112–85) and its long alliance with England began in the 14th century. From the 15th century Portuguese explorers opened up new trade routes, allowing for the establishment of an extensive overseas empire. In 1807 Portugal was invaded by the French, who were defeated in the subsequent Peninsular War. A revolution in 1910 overthrew the monarchy and established a republic. A long period of political instability culminated in a military coup in 1926. A prominent role in the new government was played by António Salazar, who became prime minister in 1932. In April, 1974, the government of Salazar's successor, Marcello Caetano (1906–80), was overthrown in a military coup led by Gen Antonio de Spinola (1911–   ), who fell from power later the same year. Constitutional government was restored in 1976. In 1986 Portugal joined the EC. President: Mário Soares (1925–   ). Official language: Portuguese. Official religion: Roman Catholic. Official currency: escudo of 100 centavos. Area: 91 631 sq km (34 861 sq mi). Population (1983 est): 10 008 000. Capital and main port: Lisbon.

Portuguese   A Romance language spoken in Portugal, Galicia (Spain), Brazil, Madeira, and the Azores. Brazilian Portuguese differs slightly in grammar and sound system. A notable characteristic of Portuguese is the use of nasal vowel sounds.

Portuguese Guinea.   *See* Guinea-Bissau, Republic of.

Portuguese man-of-war   A colonial marine invertebrate animal belonging to a genus (*Physalia*) of coelenterates found mainly in warm seas. It has a translucent bladder-like float (pneumatophore), pink, blue, or violet in colour. Attached underneath are polyps bearing stinging tentacles, up to 50 m long, which paralyse fish and other prey. Order: *Siphonophora*; class: *Hydrozoa*.

PORTSMOUTH   *Nelson's flagship* The Victory *in the harbour.*

Poseidon   The Greek god of the sea and earthquakes, brother of Zeus and Hades. His many offspring included Theseus, Polyphemus, and the winged horse Pegasus. He was usually portrayed with a trident and dolphin. He was identified with the Roman Neptune.

positron   The antiparticle of the electron, having the same mass and spin as the electron but opposite electric charge. A positron and an electron annihilate each other on collision, producing two gamma-ray photons.

possum   The most common Australian marsupial, *Trichosurus vulpecula*, also called brush-tailed phalanger. Nocturnal and arboreal, it is cat-sized and has a soft greyish coat and bushy tail. It feeds mainly on buds, leaves, and fruit, and occasionally fledgling birds. The name possum is often used for other members of the family *Phalangeridae*.

POSTIMPRESSIONISM   *Detail of Seurat's* Bathers, Asnières *(1883–84; National Gallery, London).*

postimpressionism   The art of the late 19th-century French painters Cézanne, Seurat, Van Gogh, Gauguin, Toulouse-Lautrec, and their followers whose work developed out of and, to some extent, in reaction to impressionism. The term was coined by the British art critic, Roger Fry.

postmortem.   *See* autopsy.

potassium (K)   A reactive alkali metal discovered by Sir Humphry Davy in 1807. It is a common constituent of the earth's crust; forming feldspars ($KAlSi_3O_8$), clays, and evaporite minerals. The metal is prepared by electrolysis of the molten hydroxide. It is soft, easily cut with a knife, and reacts readily with water, catching fire and liberating hydrogen. It oxidizes rapidly in air and must therefore be stored under oil. The element is highly electropositive and its chemistry is dominated by its ability to form ionic salts (e.g. KCl). Its largest use is in fertilizers, potassium being essential for plant growth. Alloys of potassium and sodium have been proposed as heat transfer media in nuclear reactors, since the lowest melting alloy melts at $-12.3°C$. One of the three isotopes (^{40}K) is radioactive with a half-life of 1.3×10^9 years and is used in potassium-argon dating. The metal and its salts impart a lilac colour to flames. At no 19; at wt 39.102; mp 63.65°C; bp 774°C.

potassium-argon dating   A method of radiometric dating of geological specimens based on the decay of the radioactive isotope potassium-40, which is present to a small extent in all naturally occurring potassium. Its half-life is 1.3×10^9 years and it decays to argon-40;

thus an estimate of the ratio of the two isotopes in a specimen of rock gives an indication of its age.

potato A perennial herbaceous plant, *Solanum tuberosum*, native to the Andes but cultivated throughout the world, especially in temperate regions, as an important vegetable crop. Potatoes were first introduced to England in the late 16th century by Sir Walter Raleigh. The plants grow to a height of 50–100 cm, with compound leaves and clusters of white and purple flowers. The tubers have a thin brownish-white, white, yellow, or pinkish skin and are rich in starch; there are several varieties, up to 1.5 kg in weight, and they are eaten cooked or ground into flour. Family: *Solanaceae*. *See also* sweet potato.

potential, electric A measure of electrical work. The potential at a point in an electric field is one volt when one joule of energy is needed to bring a positive charge of one coulomb to that point from infinity. Usually the potential difference between two points, rather than the absolute potential, is used. *See also* electromotive force.

potential energy Energy stored in a body by virtue of its position or configuration. Thus a body, mass m, at a height h above the ground has a potential energy equal to mgh, where g is the acceleration of free fall, relative to the ground. A compressed spring and an electrically charged body also store potential energy.

Potentilla A genus of mostly perennial herbs (500 species), found mainly in N temperate and arctic regions. It includes several species and hybrids grown as ornamentals. They have erect or creeping stems, 5–70 cm long, bearing compound leaves and yellow, white, or red flowers. The fruit is a group of seedlike achenes. Family: *Rosaceae*.

potholing. *See* speleology.

pot marigold A herb, *Calendula officinalis*, native to S Europe and cultivated in temperate regions as an ornamental. About 30–35 cm tall, it bears simple oblong leaves and yellow or orange daisy-like flowers, often double in cultivated varieties. The fresh petals may be eaten in salads or puddings or are dried and used in medicines. Family: *Compositae*.

Potomac River A river in the E central USA, rising in the Appalachian Mountains of W Virginia and flowing generally NE through Washington, DC, to Chesapeake Bay. Length: 462 km (287 mi).

Potsdam 52 19N 13 15E A city in central East Germany, on the River Havel adjoining Berlin. It was the residence of Prussian kings and German emperors. Notable buildings include the Brandenburg Gate (1770) and the Sanssouci Palace (1745–47). An industrial city, Potsdam has many scientific institutes. After World War II, Truman, Stalin, and Churchill (later Attlee) met here to confirm the conclusions of the Yalta Conference. Population (1986): 140 198.

Potter, Beatrix (1866–1943) British children's writer and illustrator. *The Tale of Peter Rabbit* (1900) was the first of a series of famous children's books concerning the domestic lives of such animals as Jemima Puddle-Duck and Mrs Tittlemouse.

potter wasp A solitary wasp belonging to the genus *Eumerus*, common in North America and Europe. It constructs juglike nests of mud or clay, cemented by saliva and attached to plant stems. A single egg is laid in each nest.

potto A loris, *Perodictus potto*, of African forests. It is about 40 cm long with a short tail, a catlike face, stout legs, and strong grasping hands. Pottos have a row of spines on the neck and shoulders, used for self-defence.

BEATRIX POTTER *Author and sheep breeder, seen here with her prizewinning Herdwick ewe.*

Poulenc, Francis (1899–1963) French composer, a member of Les Six. He produced a wide variety of compositions, including the song cycle *Le Bestiaire* (1919), the operas *Les Mamelles de Tirésias* (1944) and *Les Dialogues des Carmélites* (1953–56), and the ballet *Les Biches* (1923).

Pound, Ezra (1885–1972) US poet and critic. He went to Europe in 1908 and became a dynamic propagandist for modernist literary and artistic movements in London (*see* Imagism; Vorticism). His early poetry included *Aliume Spento* (1908), and the long poems *Homage to Sextus Propertius* (1917) and *Hugh Selwyn Mauberly* (1920). *The Spirit of Romance* (1910) was a collection of literary criticism. He moved to Paris and, in 1924, to Italy, where he worked on the *Cantos* (1925–69).

Poussin, Nicolas (1594–1665) French painter, regarded as one of the greatest exponents of classicism. Poussin lived in Rome from 1624 until his death, apart from two years in France. His representation of religious themes, such as *The Martyrdom of St Erasmus* (1628; Vatican), gave way to an interest in mythology and the Old Testament, for example *The Worship of the Golden Calf* (c. 1635; National Gallery, London). The pure classicism of his second Roman period is exemplified in such landscapes as *Landscape with Diogenes* (1648; Louvre).

powder metallurgy The shaping of metals by pressing powdered metal into blocks, heating (*see* sintering), and then shaping it by stamping. The method is used for working metals, such as platinum and tungsten, that are difficult to shape by other means. It leaves no scrap and is suitable for intricate shapes. Nonmetal additives can be easily included, such as the graphite lubricant in self-lubricating bearings.

Powell, Anthony (1905–) British novelist. His novel sequence *A Dance to the Music of Time* comprises 12 social satires beginning with *A Question of Upbringing* (1951) and ending with *Hearing Secret Harmonies* (1975). He has also written a biography of John Aubrey (1948), four volumes of memoirs, and several plays.

Powell, (John) Enoch (1912–) British politician. He became a Conservative MP in 1950. From 1960 to 1963 he was minister of health, his only cabinet post, and in 1968 was dismissed from Edward Heath's shadow cabinet following a controversial speech against immigration. From October 1974 to June 1987 he was the United Ulster Unionist Council MP for South Down.

power The rate at which a body or system does work. It is measured in watts or horsepower.

power station An electricity generating plant that forms part of the electricity supply system. In **thermal power stations**, heat from the burning of fossil fuels (oil, coal, and gas) or from thermal nuclear reactors is used to generate steam. The steam drives turbines connected to alternating-current generators (turbo-alternators), thus converting heat into electricity. Gas turbines are also used, missing out the steam-generation stage. They are easy to build and flexible to run, but have an efficiency of only about 25%. Sometimes the exhaust gas is used to help generate steam for a steam turbine, in order to increase the station's overall efficiency. Usually in a steam-turbine thermal station about 30 to 40% of the heat is converted to electricity, most of the rest being lost when steam is condensed to water before it is returned to the boilers. **Hydroelectric power stations** are more efficient (up to 90%) and provide a significant proportion of UK electricity supplies. *See also* energy.

Powys A county of E Central Wales, bordering on England. It was formed under local government reorganization in 1974 from Montgomeryshire, Radnorshire, and most of Breconshire. It is generally mountainous, rising to 886 m (2907 ft) in the Brecon Beacons. Agricultural activities include sheep, cattle, dairy, and arable farming. Area: 5077 sq km (1960 sq mi). Population (1986 est): 112 400. Administrative centre: Llandrindod Wells.

Pozsony. *See* Bratislava.

Prado An art gallery in the Prado Avenue, Madrid. Designed originally as a natural-history museum by Juan de Villanueva (1739–1811), the art gallery was founded in 1818 by Ferdinand VII. Most of its collection consists of paintings collected by the Spanish monarchs from the 16th century onwards. It includes works by Velazquez, Goya, El Greco, Titian, and Bosch.

Praetorian Guard The official bodyguard of the Roman emperors created by Augustus in 27 BC. Composed of up to 16 long-serving cohorts (infantry divisions) each of 500–1000 men, and stationed as a single unit in Rome, the Guard and its commanders developed great political influence; as senatorial power diminished emperors came to rely upon Praetorian support for election and in later imperial times the emperor's position and even his life depended on the Guard's favour.

Prague (Czech name: Praha) 50 8N 14 25E The capital of Czechoslovakia, in the centre of the country on the River Vltava. The industrial and commercial centre of Czechoslovakia, its various manufactures include machinery, cars, aircraft, food processing, clothing, and chemicals. Notable buildings include Hradčany Castle and the mainly gothic Cathedral of St Vitus. *History*: in the middle ages it was the seat of the Přemyslid kings of Bohemia. Under Habsburg rule from the 16th century, it was made the capital of newly independent Czechoslovakia in 1918. In 1968 the city was occupied by Soviet troops; in 1989 it witnessed demonstrations in favour of liberal reform. Population (1986): 1 194 000.

prairie dog A large ground squirrel, *Cynomys ludovicanis*, of North America, also called black-tailed prairie marmot. Heavily built animals, about 30 cm long, prairie dogs feed on grass and have been treated as pests by cattle ranchers.

prairies The extensive grasslands of the interior of North America. They occupy a broad N–S belt extending from Alberta and Saskatchewan through the Midwest into Texas, reaching as far W as the Rocky Mountains. Little of the original true prairie now remains, having been extensively ploughed for wheat production. *See also* steppes.

prairie wolf. *See* coyote.

praseodymium (Pr) A lanthanide element, which was separated from its mixture with neodyminium by von Welsbach in 1885. It forms trihalides (for example $PrCl_3$) and an oxide (Pr_2O_3), which is used to give a strong yellow colour to glass. At no 59; at wt 140.9077; mp 931°C; bp 3512°C.

prawn A large shrimplike crustacean (up to 20 cm long), belonging to the suborder *Natantia*. The antennae are longer than the body and a forward projection of the carapace forms a spike (rostrum) between the eyes, bearing six or more teeth. The second pair of appendages are enlarged to form pincers (*compare* shrimp). The common edible prawn (*Leander serratus*) occurs in temperate coastal waters and is 5–8 cm long.

Praxiteles (mid-4th century BC) Athenian sculptor, renowned for his handling of marble. His statue of Hermes, discovered at Olympia in 1877, exemplifies the sensuous grace and repose for which his work was noted.

Precambrian Geological time from the formation of the earth's crust, about 4500 million years ago, to about 590 million years ago when the Palaeozoic era began. Precambrian rocks lie below the Cambrian system. Most are metamorphosed and have undergone one or more Precambrian mountain-building periods as well as later ones. The largest areas of exposed Precambrian rocks are the shield areas.

precession of the equinoxes The gradual westward motion of the equinoxes around the ecliptic in a period of about 25 800 years. It is caused by the precession of the earth's axis of rotation, which results mainly from the gravitational pull of the sun and moon on the equatorial bulge of the nonspherical earth. As the axis precesses, slowly tracing out a cone in the sky, the celestial equator moves relative to the ecliptic. The points of intersection, i.e. the equinoxes, thus continuously change.

predestination In Christian doctrine, God's foreordaining of salvation for certain people. The idea is explicitly propagated by St Paul in the Epistles. It raises enormous problems about the nature of divine justice and the role of the human will and endeavours, problems that Christian philosophers have never satisfactorily solved.

Preminger, Otto (Ludwig) (1906–86) US film director, born in Austria. His films range from literary adaptations to large-scale epics and include *Laura* (1944), *Anatomy of a Murder* (1959), and *Exodus* (1960).

premium bond A UK government security, held in numbered units of one pound, the interest on which is put into a fund and allocated to bond holders by a monthly lottery, as tax-free prizes. The numbers of winning bonds are selected by Electronic Random Number

Indicator Equipment (ERNIE). Premium bonds were introduced in 1956.

preparatory school. *See* independent schools.

Pre-Raphaelite Brotherhood A group including the

PRE-RAPHAELITE BROTHERHOOD The Daydream *(detail; 1880) by Rossetti.*

British painters Dante Gabriel Rossetti, John Everett Millais, and William Holman Hunt, who joined together in 1848 in reaction to the banality of contemporary British painting and its enthusiasm for Raphael. Signing all their works PRB, they sought to emulate Italian painters earlier than Raphael and to paint subjects of a moral or religious character. The PRB had a strong influence on such artists as William Morris and Edward Burne-Jones.

presbyopia. *See* longsightedness.

Presbyterianism A Protestant church organization based on government by elders. These elders determine Church policy through a hierarchical system of presbyteries, synods, and general assemblies. Presbyterianism originated with the 16th-century followers of Calvin. In Scotland the tenets of Presbyterianism were formulated (1560) by Knox and it became the established church in 1696.

Presley, Elvis (Aaron) (1935–77) US popular singer, whose first big hit, "Heartbreak Hotel" (1956), was followed by "Hound Dog" and "Don't Be Cruel." Presley also appeared in numerous films. His death, probably due to drug dependence, made him a cult figure.

Pressburg. *See* Bratislava.

Press Council An organization founded in 1953 to defend the freedom of the press. Funded by newspapers and journalistic bodies, it comprises 18 professional and 18 nonprofessional members and an independent chairman. Among other activities, it considers complaints against newspapers and periodicals.

press gang A band of men employed to force paupers, vagabonds, or criminals into the army or navy. This system of impressment, common throughout the world in the 18th century, ceased when improved pay and conditions in the army and navy increased voluntary recruitment.

pressure Force per unit area. For a liquid, density d, the pressure at a depth h is hdg, where g is the acceleration of free fall. Pressure is usually measured in pascals, millimetres of mercury, or millibars.

pressure gauge An instrument for measuring the pressure of a fluid. Atmospheric pressure is measured with a mercury barometer or an aneroid barometer. Pressures above atmospheric pressure are usually measured with a Bourdon gauge, which consists of a flattened curved tube that tends to straighten under pressure. Low pressures are measured with such vacuum gauges as the McLeod gauge or Pirani gauge.

Preston 53 46N 2 42W A town and port in NW England, the administrative centre of Lancashire on the River Ribble. It has plastics, chemical, motor-vehicle and aircraft construction, and electronics industries as well as the traditional cotton and engineering works. Population (1983 est): 125 000.

Pretender, Old. *See* James Edward Stuart, the Old Pretender.

Pretender, Young. *See* Charles Edward Stuart, the Young Pretender.

Pretoria 25 36S 28 12E The administrative capital of South Africa and the capital of the Transvaal. Founded in 1855, it became the capital of the Union of South Africa in 1910. The University of South Africa was founded here in 1873; other important institutions are the University of Pretoria (1930) and the Onderstepoort Veterinary Research Institute. Its industries include iron and steel processing, engineering, and food processing. Population (1985): 741 300.

ELVIS PRESLEY *In a scene from* King Creole *(1958).*

Priam In Greek legend, the last king of Troy, husband of Hecuba. As an old man he witnessed the deaths of many of his 50 sons in the Trojan War.

Priapus A Greek fertility god associated with gardens, son of Dionysus and Aphrodite. He was usually portrayed as a comic ugly figure with an enormous phallus. The donkey, symbol of lust, was sacrificed to him.

price index　A single figure used to measure the average percentage change in the price of a set of goods over a period of time, taking a base figure of 100 for a specified year. The best-known indexes are the Wholesale Price Index and the Retail Price Index, the latter providing a reliable guide to the cost of living. Some wages, salaries, and costs are **index-linked** (i.e. increase in proportion to a specified price index) to cover the devaluation of money as a result of inflation. **Indexation** is commonly used in agreements that extend over a long period during which inflation is expected to be a significant factor.

prickly pear　A cactus of the genus *Opuntia*, native to North and South America and introduced to Australia and South Africa. It has flat jointed spiny stems bearing large orange or yellow flowers, which give rise to edible pear-shaped fruits. The seeds are used to produce an oil and the shoots are eaten as vegetables or used as animal feed.

Priestley, J(ohn) B(oynton)　(1894–1984) British novelist and dramatist. He first won popular success with his picaresque novel *The Good Companions* (1929). His plays include *An Inspector Calls* (1946), *Dangerous Corner* (1932), *Laburnum Grove* (1933), and several mildly experimental expressionist dramas, including *The Glass Cage* (1957).

Priestley, Joseph　(1733–1804) British chemist and one of the discoverers of oxygen, together with Carl Scheele (1742–86). Priestley, being a firm believer in the phlogiston theory, named his gas dephlogisticated air and first prepared it in 1774 by heating mercuric oxide. In 1778–79 Lavoisier demolished the phlogiston theory and named the gas oxygen. Priestley also produced and studied several other gases, including ammonia, sulphur dioxide, and hydrogen chloride. He invented the method of collecting them over mercury, since some of these gases dissolved in water.

primary colours　The minimum number of colours that, when mixed in the correct proportions, are capable of giving all the other colours in the visible spectrum. When light of three **primary additive colours** (usually red, green, and blue) is mixed in equal intensities, white light results. This principle is used in colour television and colour photography. Any particular colour can also be obtained by subtracting from white light a mixture of three **primary subtractive colours**, usually cyan (blue-green), magenta (purplish red), and yellow, which are complementary to red, green, and blue. Adding pigments of these in equal proportions gives black pigment.

primate　A mammal belonging to the order *Primates* (about 195 species), which includes the prosimians, monkeys, apes, and man. Primates probably evolved from insectivorous climbing creatures like tree shrews and have many adaptations for climbing, including five fingers and five toes with opposable first digits (except in the hind feet of man). They have well-developed sight and hearing and enlarged cerebral hemispheres of the brain.

prime minister　A head of government. In the UK the post developed in the 18th century. Sir Robert Walpole is generally regarded as the first prime minister (1721–42) but the post was not formally recognized until 1905. The prime minister is customarily a member of the House of Commons and is head of government by virtue of being the leader of the dominant political party in the Commons. See table p. 793.

prime number　An integer greater than one that has no integral factors except itself and one; for example 2, 3, 5, 7, 11, 13, 17. Every natural number can be expressed uniquely as a product of prime numbers; for example $1260 = 2^2 \times 3^2 \times 5 \times 7$.

PRIMITIVISM　Tropical Storm with a Tiger *(detail; National Gallery, London) by Henry Rousseau.*

primitivism　In art, the style of untrained artists who ignore or are ignorant of both traditional aesthetic standards and avantgarde trends. Its chief characteristics are meticulous detail, brilliant colours, childlike representation, and faulty perspective. The best known primitive is the French painter Henri Rousseau. Recent primitives include the Yugoslav peasant Ivan Generalič (1914–) and the American Grandma Moses. The term is also sometimes applied to African and Polynesian indigenous art.

primrose　A perennial herbaceous plant, *Primula vulgaris*, growing in woodlands and hedge banks in Europe and N Africa. It has a basal rosette of puckered spoon-shaped leaves, with solitary pale-yellow flowers. Family: *Primulaceae*. *See also* evening primrose.

Primula　A genus of perennial plants (about 500 species), native mainly to N temperate regions and often grown as ornamentals. They have a basal rosette of leaves and five-petalled flowers, red, pink, purple, blue, white, or yellow in colour and usually with a different coloured centre. The fruit is a capsule. The genus also includes the cowslip and primrose. Family: *Primulaceae*.

Prince Edward Island　An island province of E Canada, in the S Gulf of St Lawrence. Its small farms produce potatoes, grains, dairy cattle, and other livestock. Tourism and fishing are also important. *History*: discovered (1534) and colonized (1720) by France, the island was captured (1758) and resettled by Britain. In 1873 it joined Canada. Area: 5657 sq km (2184 sq mi). Population (1986): 126 646. Capital: Charlottetown.

Prince of Wales　A title customarily conferred on the eldest son of the British sovereign. It was a native Welsh title until 1301, when Edward I, following his annexation of Wales, bestowed it on his son, the future Edward II. The present holder of the title is Prince Charles.

Príncipe Island.　*See* São Tomé and Príncipe.

printed circuit　An electronic circuit in which the connections between components are formed by a pattern of conducting film on a board, instead of by wires. The method greatly facilitates mass-production. An insulating board is coated with a conducting material, such as copper, and a protective pattern is deposited on it using photographic techniques. The unprotected metal is then etched away and components are soldered in place.

printing The production of multiple copies of text or pictures, usually on paper. The oldest method, in use in China and Japan before 800 AD, is **letterpress**, in which the raised surfaces of etched, engraved, or cast material are inked and pressed onto the paper. This method was revolutionized by the invention of movable type in the 15th century. Early printing presses were of the hand-operated platen variety in which the type stands on a horizontal surface and the paper is pressed onto it from above. Faster production became possible on the power-driven presses of the 19th century: first the cylinder press, and later the rotary press.

In **lithography**, a method invented by Aloys Senefelder (1771–1834) in 1798, the printing surface is smooth, the printing and nonprinting areas being made grease-receptive and grease-repellent respectively. Greasy ink rolled over the entire area is taken up only by the grease-receptive areas; the ink is then transferred by rolling onto the paper. **Offset printing**, involves an intermediate rubber-covered cylinder that transfers the ink from plate to paper. In **gravure printing**, the small square etched holes (cells) in the copper printing plate are filled with a free-flowing ink, the rest of the plate is wiped clean, and the plate is rolled against the paper, which absorbs the ink out of the cells.

Letterpress and offset lithography are used for almost all types of printing job; gravure is limited to long runs, such as cheap illustrated magazines, postage stamps, and packaging. Direct lithography has been used almost exclusively by artists. In **silk-screen printing** (screen-process printing *or* serigraphy), a piece of taut open-weave silk, metal, or synthetic fabric carries the negative of the desired image in an impervious substance, such as glue; ink is forced through the clear (printing) areas by a squeegee onto the paper, glass, fabric, or other material, behind. It is used for printing posters, electronic circuit boards, labelling on bottles, etc.

Full-colour reproduction is achieved by **colour-process printing**, in which all colours can be produced from combinations of three primary colours—yellow, cyan (blue), and magenta.

prion A petrel belonging to a genus (*Pachyptila*; 4 species) found in Antarctica and nearby islands. Prions have a blue-grey plumage with white underparts. The flattened bill has a fringe of strainers with the floor of the mouth forming a small pouch; it feeds by skimming over the sea and straining out small invertebrates.

prism A piece of glass or other transparent material having parallel polygonal ends, with a number of rectangular surfaces meeting them at right angles. They are used in optical instruments, such as cameras and binoculars, for changing the direction of light, either by refraction or by reflection from their walls. They are also used for splitting light into its component colours as a result of double refraction.

prisons Institutions used for confining convicted criminals (*see* criminal law). In primitive societies, and throughout much of history, prisons were primarily places in which people were held until other punishments could be carried out. It was not until the 18th century that the main purpose of prisons became custodial. The appalling prison conditions at this time led to the reform movements of John Howard and Elizabeth Fry (1780–1845). During the 19th century a massive prison-building programme was carried out in the UK,

letterpress   **lithography**   **gravure**

platen letterpress

cylinder letterpress

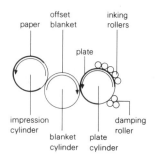

rotary offset lithography

PRINTING   *Principles of three major printing processes and the three major designs of printing press.*

modelled on Pentonville (1842), the structure of which was based on the principle of solitary confinement. Reforms since have changed the emphasis in penal institutions from retribution to correction and rehabilitation. The first "open prison," in which prisoners are permitted some personal freedom, was opened in 1936. *See also* community service; electronic tagging.

PROBOSCIS MONKEY

Pritchett, Sir V(ictor) S(awden) (1900–) British short-story writer and critic. He travelled widely in Europe during the 1920s and has written frequently about Spain. He has published critical works, volumes of stories including *Collected Stories* (1982), and two much acclaimed autobiographical books, *A Cab at the Door* (1968) and *Midnight Oil* (1971).

privatization The sale of a public corporation to the private sector. Margaret Thatcher's Conservative government in the 1980s sold its interests in British Aerospace, Britoil, British Telecom, British Gas, and British Airways, etc., to private investors to increase the efficiency of these organizations and the number of shareholders in the community. *See* nationalization.

privet An evergreen or deciduous shrub or small tree of the genus *Ligustrum* (40–50 species), native to Eurasia and Australia and widely used for ornamental hedges, especially the European common privet (*L. vulgare*). Growing up to about 5 m high, it has simple oval leaves and small creamy flowers, which give rise to black berries. Family: *Oleaceae*.

Privy Council A body advising the British monarch, now having chiefly formal functions. It consists of all cabinet ministers, the Archbishops of Canterbury and York, the speaker of the House of Commons, and senior British and Commonwealth statesmen, who are all addressed as the Right Honourable.

probability The mathematical concept concerned with the effects of chance on an event, experiment, or observation. It originated in 1654, when the mathematicians Pascal and Fermat worked on problems sent to them by a gambler. If an event can occur in n ways and r is the number of ways it can occur in a specified way, then the **mathematical probability** of it occurring in the specified way is r/n. For example, the probability of the number 5 coming up on a six-faced dice in one throw is $1/6$. The probability of a 5 coming up x times in x throws

is obtained by multiplication, i.e. it is $(1/6)^x$. Probabilities are expressed as numbers between 1 (a certainty) and 0 (an impossibility). If an event has occurred n times and failed m times, the **empirical probability** of success in the next trial is $n/(n + m)$. Actuarial tables of life expectancy are based on empirical probabilities.

probation In English law, a court order, given instead of a sentence, requiring an offender to be under the supervision of a probation officer for between 1 and 3 years. Failure to comply with the order makes the offender liable to be sentenced for the original offence.

proboscis monkey A large leaf-eating Old World monkey, *Nasalis larvatus*, of Borneo. Up to 1.5 m tall, proboscis monkeys have a protruding nose and live in groups in forests, feeding on young palm leaves.

Proconsul A genus of extinct apes whose remains have been found in E Africa. They lived 20 million years ago and were probably ground-dwellers but could not stand erect. They were ancestors of modern apes.

productivity The output of goods and services in a factory, country, etc., in relation to inputs (men, machines, land) used to produce them. It is difficult to produce a single measure of productivity, but output per manhour can be used as a rough approximation. Increases in productivity are largely responsible for the large increases in output in western economies since World War II; these increases are probably largely due to increased investment in new machines and the higher levels of education and skill in the workforce. Two causes of low productivity may be distinguished: overmanning, the use of too many men to produce a given level of output, and underproduction, a given number of men producing less output than they should. **Productivity bargaining** is a form of collective bargaining in which wage increases are agreed subject to a corresponding increase in productivity.

progesterone A steroid hormone secreted mainly by the corpus luteum of the mammalian ovary following ovulation. It prepares the womb for implantation of the embryo and maintains this state during pregnancy. Progestogens—synthetic steroids with progesterone-like actions—are constituents of oral contraceptives.

program, computer A series of instructions that controls the operation of a computer. The programs executed by the computer are in a machine code, which has the form of a series of numbers that the device interprets as either instructions or data. Programming languages simplify the programmer's task. Low-level languages are those that resemble closely the logic of the machine; high-level languages, such as Basic, Fortran, Cobol, Algol, and Pascal, use abstract constructs more suited to human thought and are independent of any particular machine. *See also* software.

Prohibition (1919–33) A period during which the manufacture, sale, and transportation of alcoholic drinks were prohibited in the USA by the 18th Amendment to the constitution. The temperance movement, combined with the wartime need to divert grain from distilleries to food manufacture, led to national prohibition. It was repealed by the 21st Amendment.

Prokofiev, Sergei (1891–1953) Soviet composer and pianist. He won the Anton Rubinstein Prize in 1914, playing his first piano concerto. He lived abroad from 1918 to 1933 and in 1948 was officially condemned for "undemocratic tendencies" in his music. His work includes seven symphonies, five piano concertos, two violin concertos, the operas *Love for Three Oranges* (1919), the ballet *Romeo and Juliet* (1935–36), and *Peter and the Wolf* (1936) for speaker and orchestra.

PROMENADE CONCERTS *Enthusiastic audience participation at "the last night of the Proms".*

prolactin A protein hormone, produced by the pituitary gland, that initiates and maintains lactation in mammals. In other animals, it has a variety of functions, being involved in growth and the balance of water and salts, as well as reproduction. *See also* gonadotrophin.

proletariat Originally, the lower class of Rome and other ancient states, the term was later used to refer to the lower class of any community. Marx defined the proletariat as the wage labourers of capitalist economies. *See* Marxism.

promenade concerts Originally, concerts in which the audience was free to walk about, now a series of concerts organized by the BBC, which were started by Henry Wood in 1895 and subsequently taken over by the BBC. These BBC Promenade Concerts (the Proms) have been held in the Royal Albert Hall since the original venue, the Queens Hall, was destroyed by bombs in World War II.

Prometheus (Greek: forethought) In Greek mythology, the son of a Titan and Themis who created man and endowed him with reason. He also stole fire from heaven to give to man. Zeus chained him to a rock in the Caucasus and sent an eagle each day to devour his liver, which grew again by night.

promethium (Pm) A radioactive element, not known on earth but identified by its spectrum in the light from stars, in which it is continuously being formed by nuclear reactions. The most stable isotope has a half-life of 17.7 years. Promethium salts exhibit bluish-green luminescence and can be used in photoelectric cells. It is obtained from nuclear reactors. At no 61; at wt (145); mp about 1080°C.

pronghorn A hoofed mammal, *Antilocapra americana*, resembling an antelope and found in rocky deserts of the W USA. Up to 100 cm high at the shoulder, pronghorns are brown above and white beneath. They have brilliant-white rump hairs used for signalling.

proof spirit. *See* alcohol strength.

propellant 1. A solid or liquid substance used to provide thrust in a rocket engine or gun. Propellants utilize

very fast exothermic chemical reactions to produce large quantities of expanding gas quickly. Generally, they are explosive substances or mixtures. 2. The pressurized inert liquids used to drive an aerosol from its container.

propeller A device for converting the rotation of a shaft into thrust in the direction of its axis. A **marine propeller** has between two and six blades, shaped as part of a helical surface. It acts as a screw, accelerating a column of water rearwards. An **air propeller** (*or* airscrew) has longer thinner blades (usually two or four) and a higher rotational speed. It, too, accelerates a mass of air rearwards thrusting the aircraft forwards.

proportional representation (PR) A voting system that aims to reflect accurately the wishes of the electorate and to ensure that votes for candidates standing for minority parties are not wasted. In the system of PR known as the **single transferable vote** electors indicate their preferences among the candidates by numbering them on their ballot paper. Those candidates who are named as a first choice and who obtain the required quota are elected. First-choice votes for an unsuccessful candidate are then redistributed to second-choice votes for that candidate, and so on. In the **party-list system** electors vote for a party, which is then allocated seats in proportion to its total vote.

Proserpine. *See* Persephone.

prosimian A primate of the suborder *Prosimii* (53 species), including the lemurs, indris, sifakas, lorises, bushbabies, tarsiers, tree shrews, and the aye-aye. Prosimians are mainly arboreal.

Prost, Alain (1955–) French motor racing driver. In 1987 he became the most successful Formula One driver ever, having won 28 Grand Prix races; he won the World Championship in 1985, 1986, and 1989.

prostaglandins Compounds derived from long-chain (essential) fatty acids and found in mammalian body tissues. Their effects include stimulation of contraction in the womb, dilation of blood vessels, and modification of hormonal activity. They are released at sites of inflammation following tissue damage and the pain-relieving properties of such drugs as aspirin are due to their inhibition of prostaglandin synthesis.

prostate gland A gland in men, situated just beneath the bladder. It secretes an alkaline fluid during ejaculation that forms part of the semen. Enlargement of the prostate commonly occurs in elderly men, obstructing the bladder and preventing urination. It is usually treated by surgical removal of the gland (prostatectomy).

protactinium (Pa) A radioactive actinide element, first identified in 1913. It is present in pitchblende as a member of the uranium decay series. The oxide (Pa_2O_5) and iodide (PaI_5) have been produced. The latter decomposes on heating to give the metal. At no 91; at wt (231); mp < 1600°C.

Protea A genus of evergreen shrubs and trees (over 100 species), native to S and central Africa. They have small white, pink, yellow, or orange flowers that are grouped in clusters. The flowers are a national emblem of South Africa. Family: *Proteaceae*.

protected species. *See* endangered species.

Protectorate (1653–59) The period during which England was governed by Oliver Cromwell. The Instrument of Government (1653) vested executive authority in the Lord Protector (Cromwell) and a state council and legislative authority in the Protector and a triennial parliament. The Instrument was modified by the Humble

Petition and Advice (1657), which gave more power to parliament. Cromwell's relations with parliament subsequently deteriorated and he dismissed it in 1658.

protein A complex organic compound that consists of one or more chains of amino acids linked by peptide bonds (-NH-CO-). These chains are variously coiled, wound, and cross-linked to form a three-dimensional molecular structure that determines the biological properties of the protein. Proteins are manufactured by cells according to the genetic information carried in the chromosomes and the specific function of the cell (*see* DNA; RNA). Proteins fulfil many important biological roles: some, including collagen and keratin, are important structural materials of body tissues, while the proteins of muscle—actin and myosin—are responsible for its contractile properties. Proteins vital to the functioning of the body include enzymes, antibodies, and many hormones.

Protestantism The movement for Church reform that arose in the Western Church in the 16th century and led to the establishment of the Reformed Churches. The word derives from the *protestatio* of the dissident reforming minority at the Diet of Speyer (1529). The early leaders of the Reformation—Luther, Calvin, and Ulrich Zwingli (1484–1531)—each promoted his own brand of Protestantism. Under Elizabeth I Protestantism finally became the established religion in England.

There are many doctrinal divisions among Protestants, but all reject a varying number of tenets and practices retained in Catholicism. In general Protestants rely less upon ecclesiastical tradition, believing the Bible to be the sole source of truth. They deny papal authority and admit a variety of forms of Church government. Transubstantiation, purgatory, special veneration of the Virgin Mary, and invocation of saints are all repudiated. The importance of the sacraments is minimized, with only baptism and the Eucharist being accorded widespread acceptance. The preaching and studying of God's word in the Bible is conversely important.

Proteus A Greek sea god who served Poseidon as a shepherd of seals. He had prophetic powers but used his ability to change his form to avoid communicating his knowledge.

proton A positively charged elementary particle classified as a baryon (*see* particle physics). It forms part of all atomic nuclei, a single proton being the nucleus of the hydrogen atom. It is a stable particle, 1836 times heavier than the electron.

protostar An embryonic star that has formed out of a contracting cloud of interstellar gas and dust. It continues to contract, the density and temperature at its centre rising until they are sufficiently high to cause energy-releasing thermonuclear reactions to begin in the central core. The collapse is then halted, and the object becomes a luminous star.

Protozoa A phylum of typically microscopic single-celled organisms (about 30 000 species), usually classified as simple animals and widely distributed in moist and watery places, including mud, soil, fresh waters, and oceans. Protozoans range in size from 0.1 mm to several centimetres. They may have one or several nuclei and a variety of specialized structures, including a contractile vacuole for regulating the water content and cilia or flagella for movement and feeding. The cell may be fairly rigid, with a stiff cell wall (pellicle) or skeletal elements, or flexible and variable. Some protozoans contain pig-

ment and obtain food by photosynthesis in the same way as plants. However, most forms take in dissolved nutrients or solid food particles (detritus, bacteria, etc.). Asexual reproduction is by means of simple division of the parent cell (binary fission) or by budding to form new cells; various forms of sexual reproduction occur, including conjugation. Protozoans can survive dry or adverse conditions by forming resistant cysts or spores. Some are important parasites of man and animals, including species of *Plasmodium*, which cause malaria, and trypanosomes, which cause sleeping sickness. The phylum includes the classes *Sarcodina*, *Ciliata*, *Flagellata*, and *Sporozoa*. See p. 588.

Proust, Joseph-Louis (1754–1826) French chemist, who demonstrated by accurate analysis that compounds always contain fixed proportions of elements. This is now known as the law of definite proportion or sometimes as Proust's law. This work contributed to Dalton's atomic theory.

Proust, Marcel (1871–1922) French novelist. In the 1890s he became a socialite in the most fashionable aristocratic circles in Paris. After the deaths of his parents (1903, 1905), he dedicated his life to writing. In 1912 he financed the publication of the first volume (*Swann's Way*) of what was to become his masterpiece, *Remembrance of Things Past*. The second volume, *Within a Budding Grove* (1919), won the Prix Goncourt; it was followed by *The Guermantes Way* (1920–21) and *Cities of the Plain* (1921–22). Proust managed to complete but not revise the final three volumes before his death. *Remembrance of Things Past* is a detailed portrait of the society that Proust had abandoned, recreated through the involuntary workings of memory. There is a strong autobiographical element in the narration.

Provençal A Romance language, strictly the dialect of Provence, but also used to refer to the dialects of various regions of S France and in this broad sense often called Occitan. These dialects are also collectively described as the *langue d'oc*, in contrast to the *langue d'oïl* spoken in northern and central areas of France (*oc* and *oïl* being the medieval forms for *yes* in these two dialect areas). About nine million people still speak it.

Provence A former province in SE France, bordering on Italy and the Mediterranean Sea. A kingdom during the 9th century AD, it became part of France in 1481 and now forms the modern planning region of **Provence-Côte-d'Azur**. Chiefly mountainous, its fertile river valleys produce grapes, olives, and mulberries. It contains the French Riviera along the S coast. Area: 31 435 sq km (12 134 sq mi). Population (1986 est): 4 058 800.

Prunus A genus of deciduous or evergreen shrubs and trees (over 200 species), mostly native to N temperate regions. It includes the plums, almonds, apricots, peaches, and cherries as well as many ornamental species. They have oval toothed leaves, and white or pink flowers. They produce stone fruits (*see* drupe), often with edible flesh or kernels. Family: *Rosaceae*.

Prussia A former state in N Germany on the NE Baltic coast. Established in the 13th century by the Teutonic Knights, Prussia became a duchy in 1525 under Hohenzollern rule. United with Brandenburg in 1618, it became the most powerful N German state. In the 18th century, under Frederick the Great, Prussia annexed Silesia and parts of Poland and became a major European power. Under Bismarck's ambitious leadership, Prussia defeated Austria and Austria's German allies (1866), ac-

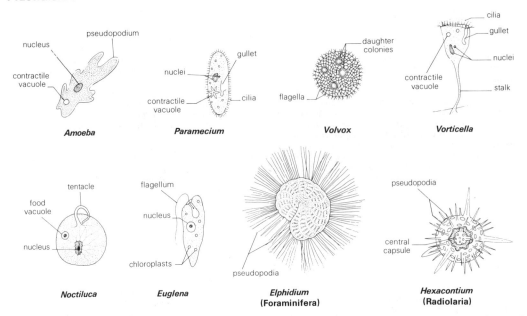

nucleus, pseudopodium, contractile vacuole — **Amoeba**

nuclei, gullet, contractile vacuole, cilia — **Paramecium**

daughter colonies, flagella — **Volvox**

cilia, gullet, nuclei, contractile vacuole, stalk — **Vorticella**

tentacle, food vacuole, nucleus — **Noctiluca**

flagellum, nucleus, chloroplasts — **Euglena**

pseudopodia — **Elphidium (Foraminifera)**

pseudopodia, central capsule — **Hexacontium (Radiolaria)**

PROTOZOA   *Although consisting only of single cells, these primitive animals show a surprising complexity of structure. Many have organs of locomotion (pseudopodia, flagella, or cilia) and some have gullets.*

quiring Schleswig-Holstein and forming the North German Confederation. Following victory in the Franco-Prussian War (1870–71) the German Empire was proclaimed under Prussian leadership. Prussia was abolished by the Allies after World War II.

PRZEWALSKI'S HORSE

Przewalski's horse   The single surviving species of wild horse, *Equus przewalskii*, discovered in Mongolia in about 1880 by the Russian explorer Nicolai Mikhailovich Przewalski (1839–88). It is sturdily built with a short erect dark-brown mane and a dark dorsal stripe. The coat is reddish brown. Height: 1.22–1.42 m (12–14 hands).

psaltery   A medieval musical instrument, a type of zither. It was plucked by the fingers of both hands or by two plectra.

pseudopodium   A temporary extension of the cytoplasm found in some Protozoa and used for locomotion and for engulfing food particles. In *Amoeba*, the pseudopodia are blunt lobular processes but in other protozoa they may be slender, filamentous, or branching.

Psilocybe   A genus of mushrooms growing in soil and dung. The Mexican species *P. mexicana* contains the hallucinogenic compounds psilocin and psilocybin. It was regarded as a sacred mushroom in Mexico and eaten during religious ceremonies. Mushrooms of the liberty cap fungus (*P. semilanceolata*) are common in pastures and lawns, having greyish-brown or olive-green conical caps.

psittacosis (*or* parrot disease)   An infectious illness caused by a microorganism of the *Chlamydia* group, which is caught from birds, particularly parrots. The severity of the disease varies, but usually it causes pneumonia.

psoriasis   A chronic recurring skin disease marked by excessive scaling of the skin. It begins with small red patches covered in scales and may spread extensively. The knees, elbows, lower back, scalp, and nails are most commonly affected.

psychedelic drugs.   *See* hallucinogens.

psychiatry   The study and treatment of mental disorders. A psychiatrist is a medically qualified physician specializing in mental illness. The range of mental disorders includes psychosis, neurosis, psychosomatic disorders, drug dependence, and mental retardation. Within psychiatry there are several specialities, notably child psychiatry, psychotherapy, and geriatric psychiatry (psychogeriatrics).

psychoanalysis A school of psychology and a method of treating mental disorders based upon the teachings of Sigmund Freud (*see also* Adler, Alfred; Jung, Carl). Psychoanalysis stresses the dynamic interplay of unconscious mental forces and the way in which the adult personality is determined by the course of sexual development in childhood. The chief techniques of psychoanalysis are free association and the recall of dreams in the course of intensive psychotherapy, the object being to bring repressed conflicts into consciousness so that they can be resolved. *See also* ego; id; Oedipus complex; repression; superego; unconscious.

psychokinesis. *See* telekinesis.

psychology The scientific study of the behaviour of man and animals. Different schools of psychology use differing methods and theories. These include behaviourism; experimental psychology; Gestalt psychology; associationist psychology; and psychoanalysis. Clinical psychology applies these approaches to the understanding and treatment of mental illness (*see also* psychiatry). Educational psychology studies the ways in which children learn, in order to intervene as problems arise. Occupational psychology studies people in their working environment. *See also* ethology.

psychosis A severe mental illness in which the sufferer loses contact with reality. Organic psychoses are caused by diseases affecting the brain, such as epilepsy, alcoholism, and dementia; functional psychoses have no known physical cause. The major functional psychoses are schizophrenia and manic-depressive psychosis. All psychoses can cause hallucinations, delusions, and altered thought processes.

psychotherapy Psychological methods of treatment for mental disorders. There are many different approaches to psychotherapy, including psychoanalysis and group therapy. In client-centred therapy the therapist refrains from giving any direct advice. Family therapy involves several members of a family meeting together with a therapist to improve their relationships. All these approaches share the goal of helping self-understanding and personal development through the relationship between the client and the therapist. *See also* behaviour therapy; hypnosis.

ptarmigan A grouse, *Lagopus lagopus*, found in Arctic tundra and mountain regions. 35 cm long, it has white wings and a mottled blackish-brown body that changes to white in winter. Its feet are covered with feathers and it feeds on shoots and fruits in summer and on lichens and leaves dug from the snow in winter.

pteridophyte A flowerless perennial vascular plant of the division *Pteridophyta*, which shows a distinct alternation of generations with the asexual spore-bearing (sporophyte) generation predominating. The sporophyte plant consists typically of leaves, stems, and roots and bears spores in special capsules (sporangia), which are often arranged in clusters (sori) on the leaves. Pteridophytes are subdivided into the *Lycopsida* (e.g. clubmosses), *Sphenopsida* (e.g. horsetails), *Psilopsida*, or *Psilotopsida* (mostly extinct), and *Pteropsida* (*see* fern).

pterodactyl. *See* pterosaur.

pterosaur An extinct flying reptile, also called pterodactyl, that lived during the Jurassic and Cretaceous periods (200–65 million years ago). A thin wing membrane stretched from the elongated fourth finger of the fore limb along the body to the knee; a second membrane stretched to the neck. It had long slender hind limbs, probably used to cling, batlike, to rocks and trees. Its light bones and toothless beaked jaw resembled those of modern birds.

Ptolemaic system A theory concerning the motions of the sun, moon, and planets that was originally advanced in Greece in the 3rd century BC and was completed by Ptolemy in the 2nd century AD. It was a geocentric system in which the moon, Mercury, Venus, Sun, Mars, Jupiter, and Saturn moved around the earth. Ptolemy proposed that each orbiting body moved in a small circle (an epicycle) the centre of which moved in a larger circle (a deferent) around the earth. The Ptolemaic system was finally abandoned when the heliocentric system of Copernicus was accepted.

Ptolemy (*or* Claudius Ptolemaeus; 2nd century AD) Egyptian mathematician, astronomer, and geographer. The foremost of his works outlines the Ptolemaic system of astronomy and was known to Arab astronomers by the Greek superlative *Megiste*, which took the Arab form *Almagest*, the name by which it is still known. His other works include *Analemma* and *Planisphaerium* on geometry and *Geographike hyphegesis*.

Ptolemy I Soter (?367–?283 BC) The first Macedonian King of Egypt and founder of the Ptolemaic dynasty. He was a general of Alexander the Great, after whose death he became governor of Egypt. He conquered Palestine, Cyprus, and much of Asia Minor, taking the title of king in 304. He made Alexandria his capital, and wrote a history of Alexander's campaigns.

ptomaines Compounds formed during the bacterial decomposition of proteins in animal and plant tissues. Most are amines, such as diethylamine, putrescine, and cadaverine, and they may be poisonous, although the symptoms ascribed to "ptomaine poisoning" are usually due to bacterial toxins in contaminated food (*see* food poisoning).

public school In the USA the term denotes a school that is not under private ownership or control, whereas in the UK the name refers to a fee-paying school, usually a boarding school. Although traditionally male preserves, most public schools now admit girls, especially at sixth-form level, and a number of well-known independent girls' schools were established in the 19th century; entrance is usually at 13. Any school the headmaster of which is a member of the Headmasters' Conference is now usually regarded as a public school, making the total number about 200, although this includes many of the former direct-grant schools (state-assisted schools that have been gradually phased out and either incorporated into the state system or have become totally independent).

public sector Those parts of the productive and nonproductive sectors of the economy that are financed out of taxation, are under state control, or both. It embraces all the employees and activities of central and local government, public institutions and utilities, and nationalized industries. In the UK most businesses the products and services of which are essential to the life of the community were nationalized after World War II and state ownership of shares in other firms represents a modified form of nationalization. The amount by which the receipts of the public sector, including taxation, fall short of public expenditure constitutes the Public Sector Borrowing Requirement.

Puccini, Giacomo (1858–1924) Italian opera composer. His first major success was *Manon Lescaut* (1893).

The operas that followed established Puccini as the master of the Italian stage and of the *verismo* (Italian: realism) style: *La Bohème* (1896), *Tosca* (1900), and *Madame Butterfly* (1904). An opera on an American subject, *La fanciulla del West* (1910) and the three one-act operas of *Il Trittico* (1918) were less successful; his final masterpiece, *Turandot*, was produced posthumously in 1926.

Pueblo Indians North American Indian tribes of the SW region including the Tewa, Keres, Hopi, and Zuni. Their collective name derives from the Spanish term for their villages—*pueblos*. They began to abandon their hunting existence and adopt their present farming economy about 1600 years ago. They were always extremely peaceful peoples, much given to ritual and ceremonial pursuits. Communities were traditionally governed by a council of the heads of the various secret religious societies. The diversity of Pueblo languages indicates different origins.

Puerto Rico, Commonwealth of (name from 1898 until 1932: Porto Rico) An island and self-governing commonwealth in association with the USA. It is in the West Indies, the smallest and most easterly island in the Greater Antilles. It is largely mountainous, rising over 1200 m (3937 ft) and supports one of the densest populations in the world. *Economy*: industrialization has transformed the economy from a basically agricultural one to a mixed one. Manufacture (chemicals, textiles, plastics, food processing) is the main source of income, while in the agricultural sector income from dairy and livestock farming has overtaken that of sugar, the principal crop. *History*: discovered by Columbus in 1508, it was under Spanish rule for nearly 400 years until ceded to the USA in 1898. Full US citizenship was granted in 1917 and it attained its present status in 1952. In 1976 the New Progressive Party regained governorship and legislative control, led by Carlos Romero Barceló (1932–), who is an advocate of the incorporation of Puerto Rico as a state of the USA. Since 1974, however, there has been growing militant pressure for the independence of Puerto Rico. Official language: Spanish; English is also widely spoken. Official currency: US dollar of 100 cents. Area: 8674 sq km (3349 sq mi). Population (1987): 3 330 000. Capital: San Juan.

puff adder A large stout-bodied highly venomous adder belonging to the genus *Bitis* (8 species), occurring in semiarid areas of Africa and characterized by its habit of hissing loudly and inflating its body in a threatening posture. Puff adders are brown or grey with yellow chevron patterning.

puffball The globular or pear-shaped fruiting body of certain fungi. As it matures, the outer layer cracks and sloughs off; the spongy interior produces powdery spores. The greyish-white giant puffball (*C. giganteum*) occurs in pastures, woodlands, and road verges and may reach over 1 m across. Class: *Basidiomycetes*.

puffer A fish, also called globefish, belonging to the family *Tetraodontidae*, that inflates its body with air or water when disturbed. The tough spiny skin contains a highly toxic chemical (tetraodontoxin), which can be fatal. Puffers live mainly in tropical and subtropical seas, feeding on corals, molluscs, and crustaceans. Order: *Tetraodontiformes*.

puffin A N Atlantic seabird, *Fratercula arctica*. 29 cm long, it is black with a white face and underparts, red legs, and a blue ring around the eye. Its large triangular bill is striped red, yellow, and blue in the breeding season. It feeds at sea on fish and molluscs and breeds in disused rabbit burrows. Family: *Alcidae* (auks).

pug A breed of toy dog originating in China and introduced to Britain from Holland in the 17th century. It is stockily built, and has a wrinkled skin and a large head with a short square muzzle. The short smooth coat can be silver, black, or apricot-fawn with a black mask on the face. Height: 25–28 cm.

PUGIN *The Central Lobby of the Houses of Parliament.*

Pugin, Augustus Welby Northmore (1812–52) British architect and theorist. Pugin was the most vocal exponent of the English gothic revival, particularly in his most influential book, *Contrasts* (1836), which exalted the English Decorated style (late 13th to early 14th centuries) above all other architectural forms. As an architect he was most accomplished at designing churches, such as Nottingham Cathedral (1842). However, he is best known for his collaboration with Barry on the Palace of Westminster, being responsible for the interior design.

Puglia. *See* Apulia.

Pulitzer Prizes Annual awards endowed by the US editor and publisher Joseph Pulitzer (1847–1911) for achievements in journalism and literature. The $1,000 prizes for journalism, and the $500 prizes for literature were first awarded in 1917. Since 1943 a prize for musical composition has also been awarded.

pulsar A celestial object that emits extremely regular pulses of radiation and is almost certainly a rotating neutron star. Pulsars were originally discovered, in 1967, at radio wavelengths. The Crab and Vela pulsars also emit pulses at optical and gamma-ray wavelengths. The pulses arise when a beam of radio waves emitted by the rotating star sweeps past the earth. The radiation (synchrotron radiation) is generated by electrons moving in the star's strong magnetic field; the emission site is still uncertain. Pulsars are thought originate in supernovae.

pulsating stars. *See* variable stars.

puma. *See* cougar.

pumice A volcanic rock derived from acidic lava. It resembles sponge in having many cavities produced by bubbles of gas trapped on rapid solidification. Pumice is light in colour and weight and often floats on water.

pumpkin The fruit of certain varieties of *Cucurbita pepo* and *C. maxima*, small bushes or trailing vines cultivated in North America and Europe. The fruit is large and round, up to 30 kg in weight with a lightly furrowed yellow rind surrounding an edible fleshy pulp and numerous seeds. It is cooked and eaten as a vegetable, in pies, puddings, and soups or used as animal feed. Family: *Cucurbitaceae*.

Punic Wars Three wars between Rome and Carthage, which gave Rome control of the Mediterranean. The first Punic (from the Latin *Punicus*, Carthaginian) War (264–241 BC) was provoked by Roman intervention in Sicily and was marked by the emergence of Roman naval power: its newly built fleet was victorious off the Aegates Insulae (241), which brought the war to an end. The second Punic War (218–201) was instigated by Hannibal's capture (219) of Saguntum, a Roman ally in Spain. His advance into Italy was eventually checked by Fabius Maximus and Scipio Africanus, who defeated Hannibal at Zama (202). Roman fears of a resurgence of Carthaginian power caused the third Punic War (149–146), in which Carthage was destroyed and its territory became the Roman province of Africa.

Punjab A region of the NW Indian subcontinent, in India and Pakistan below the Himalayan foothills on the flat alluvial plain of five Indus tributaries. Hot and dry, it produces grain surpluses with irrigation. Pulses, cotton, sugar cane, oilseeds, fruit, and vegetables are also grown. Industries include textiles, bicycles, electrical and metal goods, machinery, and food products. Its population is 60% Sikh in India's Punjab state, and almost entirely Muslim in Pakistan's Punjab province. *History*: the Punjab was conquered by Muslims (11th century) but eventually became a Sikh stronghold until Britain established control (19th century). On the partition of India and Pakistan (1947), the Punjab was divided on a religious basis. The W section became the Pakistan province of West Punjab (renamed Punjab in 1949), with an area of 205 346 sq km (79 284 sq mi) and its capital at Lahore; its population in 1985 was 53 840 000. The Indian section was reorganized in 1966 on a linguistic basis when the Punjabi-speaking state of Punjab was created, 50 376 sq km (19 445 sq mi), with its capital at Chandigarh; its population in 1981 was 16 669 755.

pupa A stage in the life cycle of certain insects, including flies, butterflies, ants, bees, and beetles, during which complete metamorphosis from larva to adult takes place. The adult emerges by cutting or digesting the pupal case after a period of a few days to several months.

pupil. *See* eye; iris.

Purcell, Henry (1659–95) English composer and organist. In 1677 he was appointed composer to the orchestra of the Chapel Royal and, in 1682, organist there. He wrote keyboard pieces, sonatas, anthems,

songs, cantatas, and much music for the stage, including incidental music for *King Arthur* (1691) and *The Fairy Queen* (1692) and one opera, *Dido and Aeneas* (1689).

purgatory In Roman Catholic doctrine, the state in which souls are purified after death to make them fit for heaven. Masses or prayers for the dead are believed to shorten a soul's purgatorial sufferings. The doctrine of purgatory was officially adopted by the Church in the late 6th century, but at the Reformation the Protestants rejected the concept.

Purim A Jewish festival, commemorating the frustration of an attempt to exterminate the Jews of the Persian Empire (473 BC), as narrated in the book of Esther. It is celebrated on the 14th Adar (Feb–March), with lighthearted festivities and charitable gifts.

purine An organic nitrogenous base ($C_5H_4N_4$) consisting of a two-ringed molecule of carbon and nitrogen atoms. The derivatives adenine and guanine are constituents of the nucleic acids DNA and RNA. Uric acid and caffeine are also purines.

Puritanism A movement among Protestants in 16th- and 17th-century England. The term originally denoted members of the Church of England in Elizabeth I's reign who wished to eliminate elements in the Church's liturgy and hierarchy that were reminiscent of Roman Catholicism. In the 17th century the Puritans, many of them now forming extremist sects (*see* Levellers), became associated with the parliamentary side in the Civil War. After the Act of Uniformity (1662) the term Nonconformists became generally applied to the sects of Puritan origin that survived.

Purple Heart Oldest US military decoration, established as the Badge of Military Merit by George Washington in 1782. Reinstituted in 1932, it is awarded to those wounded in battle. It is a purple heart of cloth, bordered by bronze.

Pusan 35 05N 129 02E A port in SE South Korea, on the Korea Strait, capital of South Kyongsang province and South Korea's second largest city. Its industries include shipbuilding. Population (1985): 3 516 768.

Pushkin, Aleksandr (1799–1837) Russian poet, novelist, and dramatist. In 1820 he was exiled to the southern provinces for his political verse. In exile, he began the epic verse novel *Eugene Onegin* (1833), on which Tchaikovsky based his opera (1877–78). In 1824 he was transferred to NW Russia, where he wrote the historical drama *Boris Godunov* (1831). He returned to Moscow in 1826. During his last years he wrote the epic poem *The Bronze Horseman* (1837) as well as lyrical poetry and several prose works. He was killed in a duel.

puss moth A moth, *Cerura vinula*, of Europe, Asia, and N Africa. The adult has a fat white hairy body with black spots. The caterpillar is green with black markings and when alarmed it presents a grotesque appearance with the head and tail appendages raised up. It feeds on sallow, willow, and poplar.

Puttnam, David (Terence) (1941–) British film producer, who was chairman (1986–87) of Columbia Pictures. His films include *Midnight Express* (1978), *Chariots of Fire* (1981), *The Killing Fields* (1984), and *The Mission* (1986).

PVC. *See* polyvinyl chloride.

Pygmalion In Greek mythology, a legendary king of Cyprus who made an ivory statue and fell in love with it. When he prayed for a wife who would be as beautiful as the statue, Aphrodite gave the statue life.

PYRAMIDS   *At El Giza in Egypt.*

Pygmies   Peoples of the tropical forest region of Africa, who are much smaller in stature than their Bantu neighbours. The males are less than 150 cm (4 ft 11 in) in height. They are nomadic hunters and gatherers, wandering in small and basically patrilineal exogamous bands of around 30 members. They speak various Bantu languages.

pygmy hippopotamus   A small hippopotamus, *Choeropsis liberiensis*, of West African forests. Up to 100 cm high at the shoulder and weighing about 200 kg, pygmy hippos frequent river banks, sleeping during the day and feeding in the forest at night.

P'yŏngyang   39 00N 125 47E The capital of the Democratic People's Republic of (North) Korea, in the NW on the River Taedong. Reputedly the oldest city in Korea, it is a major industrial as well as administrative centre. Population (1981): 1 280 000.

Pyracantha   A genus of thorny evergreen shrubs (about 10 species), known as firethorns, native to SE Eurasia and widely cultivated as garden shrubs. A commonly grown species is *P. coccinea*. It has finely toothed leaves and white or pinkish-yellow flowers. The round scarlet berries may last all winter. Family: *Rosaceae*.

pyralid moth   A moth of the widespread family *Pyralidae*. The adults have generally narrow forewings and broader hindwings. The larvae feed on a variety of substances, including dried stored products. They can be serious economic pests, especially the corn borer, wax moth, and meal moth (*Pyralis farinalis*).

pyramids   Royal funerary monuments in ancient Egypt. The greatest are the pyramids of Khufu, Khafre, and Menkaura (Greek name: Mycerinus) at Giza (built c. 2600–2500 BC), the only survivors of the Seven Wonders of the World. Pyramids were also built in ancient Mexico.

Pyramus and Thisbe   Legendary lovers in a Babylonian story retold by Ovid. The couple were forbidden to marry by their parents but exchanged vows through a chink in the wall between their houses. They arranged a secret meeting. Thisbe arrived first at the meeting place, which was near a mulberry tree; but she was frightened by a lion and fled, dropping her veil. Pyramus, finding her veil and thinking her dead, stabbed himself, and when Thisbe returned she killed herself also. The mulberry tree has borne blood-red fruit ever since. The rustics' farce in Shakespeare's *A Midsummer Night's Dream* is based on this story.

Pyrenean mountain dog (*or* Great Pyrenees)   A breed of large dog, possibly of Asian origin, used in Europe for over 3000 years to guard shepherds and their flocks. They are massively built with drooping ears. The long thick slightly wavy coat is white, with or without grey or brown patches. Height: 71 cm (dogs); 66 cm (bitches).

Pyrenees (French name: Pyrénées; Spanish name: Pirineos)   A mountain range in SW Europe. It extends between the Bay of Biscay in the W and the Mediterranean Sea in the E, forming a barrier between France and Spain. The entire republic of Andorra lies within the range, which rises to 3404 m (11 168 ft) at Pico de Aneto.

pyrethrum   A perennial plant, *Chrysanthemum coccineum* (or *Pyrethrum roseum*), with finely divided leaves and showy red, pink, lilac, or white flowers. It is native to Persia and the Caucasus and widely cultivated for ornament in temperate regions. An insecticide is prepared from its dried flower heads. Family: *Compositae*.

Pyrex   The trade name for a heat-resistant glass containing borosilicate. It is also resistant to many chemicals and is an electrical insulator. Pyrex is used in laboratory glassware, ovenware, and large telescopes.

pyridine (C_6H_5N)   A hygroscopic colourless liquid, with a strong odour, which boils at 115°C. It is a basic aromatic compound with a six-membered heterocyclic molecule, made by passing tetrahydrofurfuryl alcohol and ammonia over a catalyst at 500°C. It is used as an industrial solvent and in the manufacture of various drugs and pesticides.

pyridoxine.   *See* vitamin B complex.

pyrimidine   An organic base ($C_4H_4N_2$) consisting of a six-membered ring of carbon and nitrogen atoms. Its derivatives cytosine, thymine, and uracil are constituents of the nucleic acids RNA and DNA.

pyrite (*or* iron pyrites)   A pale brassy yellow mineral, FeS_2, the most common sulphide mineral. It occurs as an accessory mineral in igneous rocks, in hydrothermal veins, in contact metamorphic rocks, and in sediments laid down in anaerobic conditions. It is usually mined for its sulphur, used for the manufacture of sulphuric acid, or for the gold and copper found in association with it. Because of its colour it has been called fool's gold.

pyroelectricity   The development of opposite electric charges on opposite faces of asymmetric crystals when they are heated. The charges occur on those faces that are responsible for the crystal's asymmetry. Quartz and tourmaline have pyroelectric properties. *See also* piezoelectric effect.

pyrometer   An instrument used for measuring high temperatures. The two most important types are the optical pyrometer and the radiation pyrometer. In the optical pyrometer a filament, heated to a known temperature, is viewed with the hot body in the background. The temperature of the filament is adjusted until it appears to vanish, at which point its temperature is the same as the temperature to be measured. In the radiation pyrometer, radiant heat from the hot body is focused into a thermopile, which develops a potential difference proportional to the temperature.

pyroxenes   A group of ferromagnesian rock-forming silicate minerals. They usually occur in basic and ultrabasic igneous rocks but also in some metamorphosed rocks. Those of orthorhombic crystal structure are orthopyroxenes and those of monoclinic structure are clinopyroxenes. Orthopyroxenes vary in composition between the end-members enstatite ($MgSiO_3$) and orthoferrosilite ($FeSiO_3$). Clinopyroxenes, the larger group, include diopside, hedenbergite, augite, pigeonite, aegirine, jadeite, and spodumene (a source of lithium).

Pyrrhus (319–272 BC) King of Epirus (307–303, 297–272). Having secured his throne (297), Pyrrhus pursued an adventurous policy of expansion but his empire was short-lived: in support of Tarentum against Rome he won victories that cost much in loss of life ("Pyrrhic" victories), and he was forced to withdraw.

pyruvic acid An organic acid ($CH_3COCOOH$). Its anion, pyruvate ($CH_3-CO-COO^-$), is an important intermediate compound in the carbohydrate metabolism of living organisms.

Pythagoras (6th century BC) Greek philosopher and religious leader. Born at Samos, he migrated in about 530 BC to Crotone (S Italy), where he founded a religious society that governed Crotone for many years until its suppression (460–440 BC). Its members followed an ascetic regime aimed at purifying the soul and releasing it from "entombment" in successive bodies. Pythagoras probably discovered the geometrical theorem named after him and certainly discovered the arithmetical ratios governing musical intervals, which led him to interpret the universe in terms of mathematics alone. Pythagoreans were pioneers in several branches of science. *See also* Alcmaeon.

python A large constrictor snake belonging to the Old World subfamily *Pythoninae* (20–25 species), occurring in tropical and temperate regions. Pythons usually live near water and tend to be sluggish, catching prey—which may include goats, pigs, and deer—by ambush. The reticulated python (*Python reticulatus*) is the largest of all constrictors, reaching 10 m in length. Family: *Boidae*.

Q

Qaboos ibn Sa'id (1940–) Sultan of Oman (1970–). He became sultan after deposing, with British support, his reactionary father Sa'id ibn Taymur. With Omani oil revenues Qaboos has initiated modernization programmes.

Qatar, State of A country in the Middle East, in Arabia. The native population is mainly Arab and Wahhabi Sunnite Muslim, but over 80% of workers are immigrants from other countries. *Economy*: oil extraction accounts for over 90% of the national income. Qatar is a member of OPEC. *History*: Qatar relied on Britain for most of the 19th and 20th centuries, becoming a protectorate in 1916; it became independent in 1971. Head of state: Emir Sheik Khalifa bin Hamad Al-Thani (1937–). Official language: Arabic. Official currency: Qatar riyal of 100 dirhams. Area: 11 000 sq km (4246 sq mi). Population (1987): 371 863. Capital: Doha.

Qin (*or* Ch'in; 221–206 BC) The dynasty under which China became a unified empire. The first Qin emperor, Shi Huangdi (*or* Shih Huang Ti; c. 259–210 BC), consolidated his vast conquest by unifying weights, measures, and coinage and by creating one system of writing for the whole empire. It was during the Qin reign that much of the Great Wall of China was built. Excavations in the vicinity of his tomb in the late 1970s revealed several thousand life-size terracotta men and horses. The remains of the Qin capital were discovered in 1985.

Qing (*or* Ch'ing; 1644–1911) A Manchu dynasty, founded by Nurhachi (1559–1626), that ruled China from the fall of the Ming dynasty until 1911. At its height in the 18th century under Qian Long (1711–99), the Qing ruled a vast empire that included Outer Mongolia, Tibet, and Turkistan. Trade and commerce flourished, as did cultural life and learning. Bureaucratic conservatism, however, resisted modernization, corruption became rife, and China suffered a series of defeats by foreign powers (e.g. Opium Wars) as well as internal rebellions (e.g. the Taiping Rebellion) that culminated in the overthrow of the Qing in 1911.

Qingdao (Ch'ing-tao *or* Tsingtao) 36 04N 120 22E A port in E China, in Shandong province on the Yellow Sea. From 1898 to 1922 it was under German and then Japanese control. Population (1986): 1 250 000.

Qom (*or* Qum) 34 39N 50 57E A city in central Iran, S of Tehran. It is the burial place of many Islamic saints. Population (1986): 550 630.

quadratic equation An algebraic equation in which the greatest power of the variable is two. It is usually written in the form $ax^2 + bx + c = 0$, in which the two roots are given by $x = [-b \pm \sqrt{(b^2 - 4ac)}]/2a$. Both of these roots are real numbers when the quantity under the square-root sign is greater than or equal to zero. They are equal when that quantity is zero. If it is less than zero the roots are complex numbers.

quadriplegia. *See* paralysis.

Quadruple Alliances **1.** (1718) The alliance formed by Britain, France, the Holy Roman Emperor, and the Netherlands to maintain the Treaties of Utrecht (1713–14), which had been repudiated by Spain. **2.** (1814) The alliance formed by Britain, Austria, Prussia, and Russia against Napoleon. **3.** (1834) The alliance between Britain, France, Spain, and Portugal that sought to maintain constitutional monarchy in Spain and Portugal.

quail A round-bodied short-tailed gamebird of open grassland and farmland. Old World quail (subfamily *Perdicinae*; 95 species) are 13–20 cm long and characterized by a smooth-edged bill and leg spurs; they are stocky and usually sandy in colour. New World quail (subfamily *Odontophorinae*; 36 species) are up to 30 cm long and have a strong serrated bill, no leg spurs, and are brightly coloured and patterned. Family: *Phasianidae* (pheasants, partridges, and quail).

Quakers The Christian sect, formally known as the Religious Society of Friends, founded in England by George Fox in the late 1640s. They suffered violent persecution for many years and in 1682 William Penn led a colony of Friends to Pennsylvania. In the USA they were leaders in the fight against slavery. The early

QUAKERS   *A Quaker meeting.*

Quakers adopted an unostentatious dress and way of life. They were (and remain) pacifists, refused to take oaths, and rejected the use of titles.

quaking grass An annual or perennial grass of the genus *Briza* (about 20 species), mostly native to South America. Their long slender flower stalks bear spikelets of open flower clusters, which quiver in the wind. *B. media* is native to temperate Eurasia and grows 20–50 cm high.

quango (*qu*asi-*a*utonomous *n*ational *go*vernment *or*ganization) A term that came into use in the UK in the 1970s to describe organizations, such as the Monopolies Commission and the Equal Opportunities Commission, which have been set up by the government as independent bodies but are dependent on the government for their existence. In the USA the acronym stands for "quasi-autonomous non-governmental organization."

quantity theory of money A theory that seeks to explain how the money supply (*see* money) affects the economy. Originally put forward in the 17th century, it has been restated in its modern form by the US economist Milton Friedman. It states that if there is a change in the money supply, either the price level will change or the supply of goods in the economy will alter.

quantum number An integral or half-integral number $(0, \frac{1}{2}, 1, 1\frac{1}{2}, 2, \ldots)$ that gives the possible values of a property of a system according to the quantum theory. For example, in Bohr's atomic theory the angular momentum of an electron moving in orbit round an atomic nucleus can only have the values $nh/2\pi$, where n is a quantum number specifying these values and h is Planck's constant. Bohr's theory has now been replaced by the more versatile wave mechanics, but the concept of quantum numbers is useful in some contexts. It is also used to quantify the properties of elementary particles (*see* particle physics).

quantum theory The theory first developed by Max Planck in 1900 to explain the distribution of wavelengths of electromagnetic radiation emitted by a black body. The experimental observations could only be explained when Planck assumed that the radiation was emitted and absorbed in discrete amounts, which he called quanta. The energy of each quantum has the value hf, where h is a universal constant (now known as the

Planck constant) and f is the frequency of the radiation. Planck's theory was used by Einstein to explain the photoelectric effect and in 1913 by Niels Bohr to explain the spectrum of hydrogen. **Quantum mechanics** is the application of quantum theory to the mechanics of atomic systems; **quantum electrodynamics** is the theory of electromagnetic interactions between elementary particles.

quarantine The period during which a person or animal suspected of carrying an infectious disease is kept in isolation. The term was originally applied to the 40-day period (French: *quarantaine*) during which ships suspected of carrying infected people were prevented from communicating with the shore. The quarantine period is now slightly longer than the incubation period of the disease.

quarks. *See* particle physics.

quarter days In law, days in each quarter of the year on which rent and other dues on land were traditionally paid. In England they are 25 March (Lady Day), 24 June (Midsummer Day), 29 Sept (Michaelmas Day), and 25 Dec (Christmas Day).

quartz The commonest of all minerals, consisting of crystalline silica. It occurs in many rocks, particularly acid igneous rocks (such as granite), many metamorphic rocks (such as gneisses), and in sands and gravels, which form sandstones on consolidation. Pure quartz is colourless and is known as rock crystal; it is used in glassmaking, in jewellery, and (because of its piezoelectric properties) in making electrical oscillators. Some coloured varieties, such as amethyst (violet), rose quartz (pink), and citrine (yellow), are used as gemstones.

quartzite A resistant pale-coloured rock consisting almost wholly of quartz. It is formed by the metamorphism of a pure sandstone.

quasar (*qu*asi-*stellar* object; *or* QSO) A class of celestial objects discovered in 1964–65. They appear as star-like points of light but are each emitting more energy than several hundred giant galaxies. Quasar redshifts are extremely large and indicate that quasars are the most distant and hence the youngest extragalactic objects known. The prodigious energy could result from matter spiralling into a supermassive black hole (maybe 10^9 solar masses) lying at the centre of a galaxy.

Quasimodo, Salvatore (1901–68) Italian poet. His early work, such as *And Suddenly It's Night* (1942), was evocative and private, but after World War II his poetry, as in *Il falso e vero verde* (1956), expressed his active concern for social issues. He won the Nobel Prize in 1959.

Quassia A genus of tropical Asian trees and shrubs (40 species). Bitterwood (*Q. amara*) is an attractive shrub with red flowers. The heartwood is a source of quassiin, used in medicine. Family: *Simaroubaceae*.

Quaternary period The most recent period of geological time, from the end of the Tertiary (about 1.8 million years ago) to the present day. It includes the Pleistocene (Ice Age) and Holocene epochs.

Quathlamba. *See* Drakensberg Mountains.

Quayle, Dan (James Danforth Q.; 1946–) US statesman; Republican vice-president (1989–) under George Bush.

Quebec The largest province of Canada, stretching from the St Lawrence River N to Hudson Bay and Strait. Most of the population lives in the St Lawrence valley. The SE strip of Quebec enters the fertile Appalachian Highlands. The province's highly industrialized economy is based on its abundant natural resources. Asbestos, iron-ore, copper, zinc, gold, and other minerals are mined. Fishing, farming, and tourism are also important. *History*: claimed by France (1534), Quebec or New France was a French colony (1608–1763) until ceded to Britain. French-Canadian culture was preserved after the formation of Canada (1867). Area: 1 356 791 sq km (523 858 sq mi). Population (1986): 6 532 461; over 80% are French speaking. Capital: Quebec. *See also* Montreal.

Quebec 46 50N 71 15W A city and port in E Canada, the capital of Quebec. First settled in 1608, it is strategically located above a sudden narrowing of the St Lawrence River. Quebec was the key to New France until captured by Britain (1759). Most of the workforce is employed by government and service industries. The Plains of Abraham lie to the SW of the city. Population (1986): 164 580.

Quechua The language of the Incas and of the present-day American Indian peoples of the central Andean highlands. The people are nominally Roman Catholic but many pagan beliefs and rituals survive.

Queen Anne style An English architectural and decorative style with some baroque elements, dating from about 1700 to 1715. Beautiful walnut veneered furniture was made, enhanced by the restrained use of herringbone inlays. Chairs became lighter, more comfortable, and invariably had cabriole legs. Plateglass wall mirrors in gilt frames decorated panelled rooms.

Queen Charlotte Islands An archipelago of W Canada, in British Columbia 160 km (100 mi) off the Pacific coast. Mountainous with lush vegetation, the islands are mostly inhabited by Haida Indians engaged in fishing and forestry. Area: 9596 sq km (3705 sq mi). Population (1981): 5884.

Queen Maud Land. *See* Norwegian Antarctic Territory.

Queen's Award An award to industry in the UK, instituted in 1965 and made on the birthday (21 April) of Queen Elizabeth II. Awarded to firms, rather than individuals, it entitles holders to make use of a special emblem for five years.

Queensberry Rules. *See* boxing.

Queen's Counsel (QC) A barrister appointed to senior rank as counsel to the English queen (or king) on the recommendation of the Lord Chancellor. QCs have no special duties to the Crown; they wear a silk gown, sit within the Bar of the court, and take precedence over the "utter barristers" (i.e. the outer barristers, who sit outside the Bar).

Queen's County. *See* Laoighis.

Queensland The second largest state of Australia, situated in the NE. The Great Dividing Range separates the hilly coastlands from the vast inland plain and the Great Barrier Reef runs parallel to the Pacific coast. The area is rich in natural resources, which form the basis of Queensland's rapid economic progress. Coal is the most important mineral. Other minerals include copper, bauxite, lead, silver, and zinc; oil production began in 1964; natural gas is piped to Brisbane. Beef, sugar, and wool are major industries. Another growing industry is tourism. Area: 1 728 000 sq km (667 000 sq mi). Population (1986): 2 587 315. Capital: Brisbane.

quelea A small brown African weaverbird, *Quelea quelea*, about 13 cm long, also called the red-billed dioch. Queleas live in vast colonies: they destroy grain

crops, frequently causing famine, and also damage the trees in which they roost.

Quetta 30 15N 67 00E A city in W central Pakistan, at an altitude of 1650 m (5500 ft). The chief town of Baluchistan, it was badly damaged by an earthquake in 1935. Population (1981): 285 000.

quetzal A Central American bird, *Pharomachus mocinno*, that lives in cloud forests and feeds on fruit, insects, tree frogs, and lizards. The male reaches 1.3 m in length, including its curved ornamental tail feathers; its plumage is iridescent green, red, and white. Family: *Trogonidae* (trogons).

QUETZALCOATL *The plumed serpent from the wall of the temple at Tehotihuacan, Mexico.*

Quetzalcoatl A Mexican wind and fertility god, usually portrayed as a feathered snake. During the Aztec period (14th–16th centuries) he was identified with the planet Venus, symbol of death and resurrection.

Quezon City 14 39N 121 01E A city in the N Philippines, in S Luzon near to Manila. It was the nation's former capital (1948–76). Population (1984): 1 326 000.

quillwort A small perennial pteridophyte plant of the genus *Isoetes* (about 60 species), which grows mainly in swampy cooler regions of N North America and Eurasia. Tufts of stiff spiky quill-like leaves, about 5–18 cm long, grow from a short stout rhizome that bears numerous roots. The common Eurasian quillwort (*I. lacustris*) is aquatic. Class: *Lycopsida* (clubmosses, etc.).

quince A small tree or shrub, *Cydonia vulgaris*, probably native to W Asia but cultivated in temperate regions for its fruit. 4.5–6 m high, it has white or pink flowers, 5 cm across. The pear-shaped fruit is 7.5–10 cm long with a golden-yellow skin and many pips. Family: *Rosaceae*.

quinine The first drug used to treat malaria. Quinine, which is obtained from the bark of *Cinchona* trees, has now been largely replaced by other drugs (e.g. chloroquine), which have fewer side effects and are less toxic. Quinine-like compounds (e.g. quinidine) are used to treat abnormal heart rhythms.

quinone ($O:C_6H_4:O$) An aromatic compound with two hydrogen atoms in the benzene ring replaced by two oxygen atoms. Quinones are used in photography and dye manufacture. They are also found in plants.

quinsy An abscess in the tissue surrounding a tonsil. This arises from infection of the tonsils and may be a complication of tonsillitis. The patient has a sore throat and difficulty in swallowing. Quinsy is sometimes treated by surgical draining of the abscess.

Quisling, Vidkun (Abraham Lauritz Jonsson) (1887–1945) Norwegian army officer and Nazi collaborator, whose name is a synonym for "traitor." After serving as a diplomat, Quisling formed (1933) the fascist National Union Party in Norway. He encouraged the Nazi occupation of Norway (1940), and as "minister president" in the occupation government, sent a thousand Jews to concentration camps. Arrested in 1945, he was found guilty of war crimes and executed.

Quito 0 20S 78 45W The capital of Ecuador, on the slopes of the volcano Pichincha at an altitude of 2850 m (9350 ft). It was the capital of the Inca kingdom of Quito until 1534, when it was captured by the Spanish. It contains many Spanish-colonial churches. Population (1982): 1 110 248.

Qum. *See* Qom.

Qumeran, Khirbat The site on the NW shore of the Dead Sea in Israel, where a Jewish sect called the Essenes lived from about 125 BC to 68 AD. The community produced the Dead Sea Scrolls, found by Bedouin shepherds in 1947 in nearby caves.

R

Ra (*or* Re) The Egyptian sun god and lord of creation, usually portrayed with a falcon's head bearing a solar disc. During the 18th dynasty (1567–1320 BC) he became identified with the Theban god Amon as Amon-Ra.

Rabat (Arabic name: Ribat) 34 00N 6 42W The capital of Morocco, near the Atlantic coast. Founded in the 12th century, it became the capital under the French protectorate in the early 20th century. Population (1984): 556 000.

rabbi A Jewish scholar and religious authority. For a long time the rabbinate was not a salaried office; the title indicated scholarly achievement and legal competence. In modern Jewish communities rabbis are communal leaders, preachers, and pastoral workers.

rabbit A burrowing mammal belonging to the family *Leporidae* (which also includes the hares). The European rabbit (*Oryctolagus cuniculus*) grows to about 45 cm; it has long ears, a short tail, and soft grey-brown fur. Rabbits are gregarious, living in large warrens and feeding on grasses and vegetation. Order: *Lagomorpha*.

Rabelais, François (1483–1553) French satirist. He became a Franciscan and then a Benedictine monk, left the monastery to practise medicine, and visited Italy. His humanist philosophy is expressed in his works of inventive and often coarse comic satire, *Pantagruel* (1532), *Gargantua* (1534), *Tiers Livre* (1546), and *Quart Livre* (1552). The classic English translation of his works is by Sir Thomas Urquhart (1653).

rabies An acute viral infection of the brain that can affect all warm-blooded animals and may be transmitted to man through the bite of an infected animal (usually a dog). Symptoms, which appear after an incubation period of from ten days to two years, include painful spasms of the throat on swallowing. Later, the very sight of water induces convulsions and paralysis (hence the alternative name of the disease—hydrophobia, literally "fear of water") and the patient eventually dies in a coma. Antirabies vaccine and rabies antiserum given to patients immediately after they have been bitten may prevent the infection from developing. In the UK there are strict quarantine regulations for imported domestic animals to prevent the disease from reaching Britain.

raccoon An omnivorous mammal belonging to the genus *Procyon* (7 species), of the Americas. About 1 m long, raccoons are stockily built, with long hind legs and short forelegs. A masklike black patch across the eyes and a striped tail contrast with the thick grey coat. Family: *Procyonidae*; order: *Carnivora*.

Rachmaninov, Sergei (1873–1943) Russian composer, pianist, and conductor. He spent most of the rest of his life (from 1917) in the USA. His works include four operas, three symphonies, four piano concertos (which he also recorded), the *Rhapsody on a Theme of Paganini* (1934), and *The Bells* (1910).

Racine, Jean (1639–99) French dramatist. His major classical verse tragedies, influenced initially by those of Pierre Corneille (1606–84), include *Andromaque* (1667), *Britannicus* (1669), *Bérénice* (1670), and *Phèdre* (1677). In 1677 he retired from the theatre, married a young pious girl, and accepted a post at the court of Louis XIV. His final works were two religious dramas *Esther* (1689) and *Athalie* (1691).

rad The unit of absorbed dose of ionizing radiation in the c.g.s. system equal to an energy absorption of 100 ergs per gram of irradiated material.

radar (*r*adio *d*etection *and r*anging) A method of locating distant objects used in military surveillance, air traffic control, and navigation; it was developed before World War II by a British team led by Sir Robert Watson-Watt. High-frequency (300 to 30 000 megahertz) radio waves are sent out in pulses from a powerful rotating transmitter and are reflected back by any object they encounter. The reflected signal is picked up by a receiver antenna and is used to deflect the electron beam in a cathode-ray tube. The beam scans the screen of the tube by rotating at the same speed as the antenna, so that its angular position indicates the direction of the located object. The distance from the centre of the screen shows the distance away of the object.

radian (rad) The SI unit of plane angle equal to the angle subtended at the centre of a circle by an arc equal in length to the radius of the circle.

radiation The propagation of energy by means of beams of particles or waves. It includes all electromagnetic waves, beams of elementary particles, ions, etc., and sound waves.

radiation sickness Illness caused by exposure to ionizing radiation. Short-term effects include nausea and diarrhoea, while long-term effects include sterility, haemorrhage, loss of hair, and cancer.

primary aerial

secondary aerial

6051 ∨
250
55

BR321
050
25

1500

Key
DR107- callsign
140 — height ×100 in feet
20 — speed ×10 in knots
X — secondary target
0 — primary target

RADAR *The high-frequency pulses sent out by the transmitting aerial are reflected back by the target and displayed on a screen. The typical air-traffic control picture seen here shows East Anglia (only a few of the targets are labelled, for clarity).*

radical A group of atoms in a chemical compound that behaves as a unit in chemical reactions. For example, the methanol molecule (CH_3OH) can be considered as a methyl radical (CH_3.) and a hydroxyl radical (.OH) which is the functional group of alcohols. **Free radicals** are groups existing independently. Because they have unpaired electrons they are usually extremely reactive transient species.

radio The transmission of sound or other information by radio-frequency (3 kilohertz to 300 gigahertz) electromagnetic waves. The use of radio waves for communication was pioneered by Marconi in 1895, although their existence had been postulated by Maxwell in 1873 and demonstrated by Hertz in 1888. See p. 598.

A **radio transmitter** generates a radio-frequency electrical signal (carrier wave) in an oscillator and superimposes the sound signal on it by a modulation process. The composite signal is then fed to an aerial, which transmits electromagnetic waves. Transmission beyond the horizon is made possible by the ionosphere, a layer of the upper atmosphere that reflects radio waves in the long and medium wavebands. Long-wave (30 to 300 kilohertz) and medium-wave (300 to 3000 kilohertz) radio is used for direct (ground-wave) transmission in am-plitude-modulated (AM) sound broadcasting. Short-wave radio is used for AM sound broadcasting over longer distances using the ionosphere (sky waves) and for communication to ships and aircraft. VHF (very high frequency; 30 to 300 megahertz) is used for stereophonic sound broadcasting in frequency modulated (FM) transmissions. Television uses mostly UHF (ultrahigh frequency). Neither VHF nor UHF are reflected by the ionosphere, but can be relayed by communications satellites. All **radio receivers** consist of an aerial, a resonant circuit, a demodulator, an amplification system, and one or more loudspeakers,

radioactive tracer A radioactive isotope used for following the course of a substance during a physical, biological, or chemical process. A nonradioactive isotope in the substance is replaced by a radioactive isotope of the same element, which can then be detected by observing its emitted radiation with, for example, a Geiger counter.

radioactive waste Waste products from nuclear reactors, uranium-processing plants, etc., that have become radioactive. Solid waste is either stored underground or placed in drums weighted with concrete and sunk in deep sea water (there is at present a ban on this).

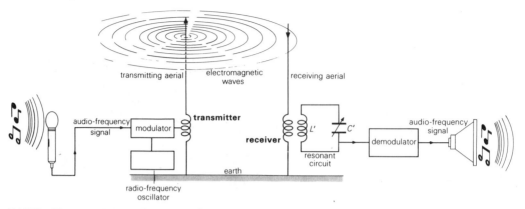

RADIO   *The transmission and reception of sound broadcasts.*

radioactivity   The spontaneous emission of a particle by an atomic nucleus. The emitted particle may be an alpha particle (a helium nucleus consisting of two protons and two neutrons), in which case the process is known as alpha decay; or it may be a beta particle (an electron), when the process is known as beta decay. Highly energetic X-rays (*see* gamma radiation) may also be emitted simultaneously. In both alpha and beta decay the nucleus changes into that of another element. Radioactive decay is a random process and its occurrence for a single nucleus can be neither predicted nor controlled. However, for a large number of nuclei the time taken for a certain fraction of nuclei to decay can be accurately predicted as either its mean life or half-life. These quantities vary from about 10^{-8} second to 10^{10} years depending on the isotope. The phenomenon was first discovered in 1898 by Becquerel in uranium.

radio astronomy   The study of celestial objects by means of the radio waves they emit. This radio emission was first noticed by K. G. Jansky in 1932. It now forms an important branch of astronomy.

radiocarbon dating   A method of estimating the age of a material, such as wood, that was once living. All living things absorb a small proportion of carbon-14 from atmospheric carbon dioxide, however, once dead, the level of carbon-14 falls as a result of beta decay. By measuring the radioactivity of a material, the concentration of carbon-14 and hence its age can be estimated.

radio galaxy   A radio source that lies beyond our Galaxy, is identified with an optical galaxy, and the radio-power output of which greatly exceeds that of a normal galaxy. A massive black hole at the galaxy centre has been postulated as a possible energy source.

radiography   The technique of examining the internal structure of a solid body by passing X-rays or gamma radiation through it to produce an image on a photographic plate or fluorescent screen. Radiography is used in medicine (*see* radiology) and in industry to find structural defects.

radio interferometer.   *See* radio telescope.

radioisotope (*or* radioactive isotope)   An isotope that is radioactive. Radioisotopes are used in the production of nuclear energy, in radiotherapy, as radioactive tracers, and in dating techniques. Some are naturally occurring (those with mass numbers in excess of 208) while others can be made radioactive by neutron bombardment.

Radiolaria   An order of single-celled animals (*see* Protozoa) found chiefly in the sea, as a component of plankton. Radiolarians are typically spherical, 0.1 mm to several millimetres in diameter, with a silicaceous skeleton of radiating spines from which long thin pseudopodia extend to capture food particles. The skeletal remains of dead radiolarians form radiolarian ooze. Class: *Sarcodina.*

radiology   The branch of medicine concerned with the use of radiation in the diagnosis and treatment of disease. A radiologist is a doctor specialized in the interpretation of X-ray photographs and films. *See also* radiotherapy; tomography.

radio source   A celestial object that emits radio waves. The sun and Jupiter are solar-system sources. Other radio sources within our Galaxy are pulsars, supernova remnants, interstellar hydrogen clouds, and the galactic centre. Extragalactic sources include spiral galaxies, radio galaxies, and some quasars.

radio telescope   An instrument for detecting and measuring the radio emissions from celestial radio sources. It consists of an antenna, or system of antennas, the radio-frequency signals of which are carried by wires or waveguides to one or more receivers. The antenna may be a large metal parabolic or spherical dish, usually steerable, that brings radio waves from a radio source to a focus on a secondary antenna. Alternatively simple dipole antennas may be used. The **radio interferometer**, in two separate units, has a very much greater resolving power than a single antenna. The largest single radio telescope dish in the world is that at Arecibo, Puerto Rico; it measures 305 m (1000 ft) across. The best-known radio telescope in the UK is that at Jodrell Bank.

radiotherapy   The use of X-rays and other forms of radiation for treating disease. The radiation may be directed at the target organ from a distance or radioactive needles, wires, pellets, etc., may be implanted in the body. Radiation is used in treating various forms of cancer and overactivity of the thyroid gland.

radish   An annual or biennial herb, *Raphanus sativus*, widely grown for its edible root, which may be red, white, or purple. The plant bears white flowers. Family: *Cruciferae.*

radium (Ra) A metallic element, discovered in pitchblende in 1898 by Pierre and Marie Curie. It is a divalent alkaline-earth element, forming a number of simple salts, such as the chloride ($RaCl_2$). It decays to form the noble gas radon and is used in radiotherapy. At no 88; at wt (226); mp 700°C; bp 1140°C.

radon (Rn) The heaviest noble gas, produced by the decay of radium, thorium, and actinium. It is radioactive, the longest-lived isotope (^{222}Rn) having a half-life of 3.825 days. Like the other noble gases, Rn forms clathrates and fluorides. At no 86; at wt (222); mp −71°C; bp −61.8°C.

Raeder, Erich (1876–1960) German admiral; commander in chief of the navy (1928–43). He rebuilt the German navy in the years before World War II but was dismissed after disagreeing with Hitler over strategy. He was sentenced to life imprisonment for war crimes but was released in 1955.

RAF. *See* Royal Air Force.

raffia (*or* raphia) A palm tree of the genus *Raphia*, especially *R. pedunculata* (or *R. ruffia*), native to Madagascar. Its leaves, up to 20 m long, are composed of 80–100 leaflets from which the fibre is torn in thin strips and dried in the sun. Raffia is woven into mats and baskets and used in horticulture, etc.

Rafflesia A genus of Malaysian parasitic herbs (12 species). The monster plant (*R. arnoldii*) has the world's largest flower—up to 45 cm across and weighing up to 10 kg. It smells of rotten meat and attracts carrion flies, which act as pollinators. The genus was named after Sir Stamford Raffles (1781–1826). Family: *Rafflesiaceae.*

LORD RAGLAN *From an engraving of 1855.*

Raglan, FitzRoy James Henry Somerset, 1st Baron (1788–1855) British field marshal. In 1854 he became commander in the Crimean War and, in spite of success at Inkerman, his strategy was much criticized (*see also* Balaclava, Battle of). The Raglan sleeve is named after him.

Ragnarök In Norse mythology, doomsday, when a catastrophic battle between the gods and the forces of evil will occur. After the defeat of the gods everyone will be destroyed except for Lif and Lifthrasir.

ragtime A precursor of New Orleans style jazz. Ragtime was characterized by syncopation in the melody against a marchlike accompaniment and was popular from the 1890s. Scott Joplin was the first ragtime composer to write down his music.

ragworm A marine annelid worm, *Nereis cultrifera*, also called chainworm, of European coastal waters. 5–10 cm long, ragworms swim by means of paddle-like structures occurring in pairs on each body segment. Most live in burrows in sand or mud or among stones, feeding on dead organisms and detritus. Class: *Polychaeta.*

rail A slender secretive ground-dwelling bird belonging to a widely distributed family (*Rallidae*; about 300 species), occurring mostly in swamps, marshes, and fresh waters. 11–45 cm long, rails have short rounded wings, a short tail, and typically a dull grey or brown plumage, often barred for camouflage. Order: *Gruiformes* (cranes, rails, etc.). *See also* coot; corncrake; gallinule.

rainbow An optical phenomenon consisting of an arc of light across the sky composed of the colours of the spectrum. It is caused by the refraction of sunlight through falling water drops; the larger the drops the stronger the colours.

rain forest. *See* forest.

Rainier III (1923–) Prince of Monaco (1949–). He repudiated the principle of the divine right of kings in a new constitution (1962). In 1956 he married Grace Kelly. Their three children are Prince Albert (1958–), Princess Caroline (1957–), and Princess Stephanie (1965–).

Rajkot 22 18N 70 53E A city in India, in Gujarat. It is a commercial and industrial centre. Population (1981): 444 000.

Rajput A group of clans in N and central India, now numbering about 11 million people. Descended from invading tribes from Central Asia, they were once included within the Ksatriya (warrior) caste of Hindu society. The Rajput states resisted the Muslim invaders, maintaining their independence in Rajasthan. They acknowledged the overlordship of the Moguls in the 16th century, the Marathas in the 18th century, and the British in 1808.

Raleigh, Sir Walter (1554–1618) British explorer and writer; a favourite of Elizabeth I. Unsuccessful in founding (1584–89) a colony in Virginia, he brought back the potato and tobacco plant from America. In 1595–96 he led an expedition to South America, which he described in *The Discoverie of Guiana* (1596), and in 1596 took part in the sack of Cádiz. At James I's accession (1603) he stood trial for treason, but the death sentence was commuted to imprisonment; while in the Tower of London he wrote *The History of the World* (1614). He was released in 1616 to search for gold along the Orinoco but his mission was a failure and after his return he was executed. See p. 600.

Rama The seventh incarnation of Vishnu, appearing as a hero in the epics the *Ramayana* and *Mahabharata*. In the *Upanishads* and elsewhere he appears as a god. He is usually represented holding a bow and arrow and attended by his wife.

Ramadan The ninth month of the Muslim year. It is a time of atonement, and every Muslim is required to observe a strict fast daily from dawn to dusk until the new moon of the next month is visible.

Ramapithecus A genus of fossil hominids that lived during the late Miocene and early Pliocene. They were about the size of a gibbon, possibly walked erect, and may represent the early ancestors of modern man.

SIR WALTER RALEIGH *With his elder son, Wat, in 1602.*

Ramayana (Sanskrit: romance of Rama) Hindu epic poem in seven books. It tells the story of Rama and his devoted wife Sita, her abduction by the demon king Ravana, and Rama's struggle to recover her with the aid of Hanuman.

Rambert, Dame Marie (Cyvia Rabbam, later Miriam Rambach; 1888–1982) British ballet dancer and choreographer, born in Poland. As director of the Carmargo Society, which in 1935 became the Ballet Rambert, she trained and encouraged many young British dancers and choreographers.

Ramblers' Association A British organization founded in 1935 to promote love and care for the countryside. Director: Alan Mattingly.

Rameau, Jean Philippe (1683–1764) French composer. He wrote a *Traité de l'harmonie* (1722), before beginning to compose. His works include chamber, keyboard, and vocal music, as well as 24 operas and opera-ballets, including *Les Indes galantes* (1735) and *Castor et Pollux* (1737).

Ramillies, Battle of (23 May, 1706) The battle in the War of the Spanish Succession in which Marlborough defeated the French 21 km (13 mi) N of Namur. The victory gave much of the Spanish Netherlands to the allies.

Ramsay, Sir William (1852–1916) Scottish chemist, whose work on the noble gases earned him the 1904 Nobel Prize for Chemistry. In 1894, Ramsay, working with Rayleigh, discovered argon. By fractionally distilling argon, Ramsay isolated neon, xenon, and krypton in 1898. In 1895 he had discovered the inert gas, helium, being given off by the mineral cleveite.

Ramses (II) the Great King of Egypt (1304–1237 BC) of the 19th dynasty. His warfare against the Hittites ended in lasting peace around 1284. Ramses also built the temple complex of Abu Simbel. He is probably the pharaoh who oppressed the Israelites.

Rance, River A river in NW France, rising in Brittany and flowing E and N to the Gulf of St Malo. Length: 100 km (62 mi).

Rand, the. *See* Witwatersrand.

Rangoon (name from 1989: Yangon) 16 47N 96 10E The capital of Burma, a port in the S on the River Rangoon. Industry has increased greatly since independence in 1948. *History*: a settlement grew up in very early times around the Shwe Dagon Pagoda, which is the focal point of Burmese religious life. Twice captured by the British in the 19th century, it became the capital of all Burma in 1886. It was badly damaged in World War II. Population (1983): 2 458 712.

Ranunculaceae A family of herbaceous and woody plants (about 1300 species), found all over the world but most abundant in N temperate and Arctic regions. The family includes many garden flowers, such as *Anenome*, *Aquilegia*, *Clematis*, and *Delphinium*, as well as common weeds, e.g. buttercup (genus *Ranunculus*).

Rapanui. *See* Easter Island.

rape (botany) An annual or biennial herb, *Brassica napus* var. *arvensis*, also called oilseed rape or coleseed, that grows to a height of 1 m and has yellow flowers. It is widely cultivated for its seeds, which yield an edible oil. Family: *Cruciferae*.

Raphael (Raffaello Sanzio; 1483–1520) Italian Renaissance painter and architect. He trained in Perugia, where he painted *The Marriage of the Virgin* (Brera, Milan) before moving to Florence in 1504. There, influenced by Leonardo and Michelangelo, he painted numerous Madonnas and also the portraits of Angelo and Maddalena Doni (Palazzo Pitti, Florence). Settling in Rome in 1508, he decorated the papal apartments in the Vatican with frescoes. He painted his patron Pope Julius II (Palazzo Pitti) and the *Sistine Madonna* (Dresden). In 1514 he succeeded Bramante as architect of St Peter's. In 1515 he designed tapestries for the Sistine Chapel. His last work, the *Transfiguration* (Vatican Museum), anticipates mannerism.

RAPHAEL The Miraculous Draught of Fishes *(detail from a cartoon; 1515–16).*

Rarotonga 21 15S 159 45W A mountainous island in the SW Pacific Ocean, the administrative centre of the Cook Islands. Copra and citrus fruit are exported. Area: 67 sq km (26 sq mi). Population (1981): 9530. Chief town: Avarua.

Rashid. *See* Rosetta Stone.

raspberry A prickly woody perennial plant, *Rubus idaeus*, native to Eurasia and North America. Up to 1.5 m high, it produces red sweet fruits. Upright canes grow from basal buds and bear fruit in their first autumn or second summer. Family: *Rosaceae*.

Rasputin, Grigori Yefimovich (c. 1872–1916) Russian mystic, who was a favourite of Emperor Nicholas II and Alexandra. A Siberian peasant, Rasputin's apparent ability to ease the bleeding of the haemophiliac crown prince brought him considerable influence over the royal family. His unpopularity, aggravated by his debauchery, led to his murder by a group of nobles: when poison inexplicably failed he was shot and thrown into the River Neva.

Rastafarians Members of a West Indian religious and political sect, who believe that Ras Tafari Makonnen (Haile Selassie) will arrange for the deliverance of the black races by procuring for them a homeland in Ethiopia. Rastafarian men wear their hair in long matted curls (dreadlocks).

rat A rodent belonging to the suborder *Myomorpha*, distributed worldwide. Typical rats belong to the Old World genus *Rattus* (137 species) The black rat (*R. rattus*), originally Asian, has spread to most regions of the world, living in human habitations and sewers. The brown rat (*R. norvegicus*) is larger, measuring 30–45 cm including its tail (15-20 cm), and tends to live outdoors in burrows. Both species eat a wide variety of plant and animal materials, often causing serious damage and transmitting disease. *See also* mouse.

ratel An omnivorous mammal, *Mellivora capensis*, also called honey badger, of Africa and S Asia. About 70 cm long, grey above and black underneath, it lives in thick woods. Family: *Mustelidae*.

rationalism A philosophical movement stemming from 17th-century attempts to study the universe using reason rather than sense-experience. Descartes, for example, tried to deduce what God's world is like from the axioms of divine existence and goodness. Conflict between the new sciences and religion is reflected in the work of Spinoza, Antoine Arnauld (1612–94), and Leibniz. Kant was called a rationalist in so far as he believed in the possibility of synthetic a priori propositions.

rat kangaroo A marsupial belonging to the subfamily *Potoroinae* (9 species), of Australia (including Tasmania). Two species are commonly known as boodies and two others as potoroos. Measuring 23–44 cm excluding the tail (15–38 cm), rat kangaroos are related to kangaroos and have a narrow ratlike face. They forage at night for grubs and tubers. Family: *Macropodidae*.

rattan The stems of climbing palms of the genus *Calamus* (375 species), native to Old World tropical regions. Up to 130 m long, the stems are used in furniture, matting, etc.

Rattigan, Sir Terence (1911–77) British dramatist. His highly successful plays include upper-class comedies (*French without Tears*, 1936), more ambitious studies of human relationships (*The Deep Blue Sea*, 1952), and studies of historical characters (*Ross*, 1960).

rattlesnake A pit viper belonging to either of two genera, *Sisturus* (2 species) or *Crotalus* (28 species), and characterized by having a rattle composed of loosely connected horny tail segments. Rattlesnakes occur in both North and South America and are 0.3–2.5 m long with dark diamond, hexagonal, or spotted markings on a pale background. *See also* sidewinder.

Ravel, Maurice (1875–1937) French composer of the impressionist school. His works include, for piano, *Pavane pour une infante défunte* (1899), *Valses nobles et sentimentales* (1911), and *Le Tombeau de Couperin* (1914–17), the suite *Gaspard de la nuit* (1908), and two piano concertos; for orchestra, *La Valse* (1920), *Boléro* (1927), and the ballet *Daphnis and Chloe* (1909–12); the opera *L'Enfant et les sortilèges* (1920–25); and many songs.

raven A large glossy black crow, *Corvus corax*, about 63 cm long with a massive bill and a wedge-shaped tail. It feeds on carrion, small animals, seeds, and fruits and often roosts in large colonies. Ravens occur in mountain and moorland regions of the N hemisphere.

RAVENNA *A Byzantine mosaic of Justinian, in the church of S Vitale.*

Ravenna 44 25N 12 12E A city and port in N Italy, connected to the Adriatic Sea by canal. Ravenna was the capital of the western Roman Empire (402–76 AD), of the Ostrogothic kings (476–526), and of the Byzantine exarchate (military governorship) from 584 to 751. It is noted for its mosaics. Population (1986): 136 016.

Ravi, River A river in NW India and Pakistan. Rising in the Himalayas, it flows W and SW to the River Chenab. Length: 724 km (450 mi).

Rawalpindi 33 40N 73 08E A city in N Pakistan. From 1959 until 1969 it acted as the interim capital while the new capital at Islamabad was being built. Population (1981): 982 000.

ray A predominantly marine cartilaginous fish of the worldwide order *Batoidea* (or *Rajiformes*; about 350 species). Rays have a flattened head and body with greatly enlarged winglike pectoral fins; the tapering tail often bears sharp poison spines. Rays are generally bottom-dwelling and feed mainly on fish and invertebrates. Subclass: *Elasmobranchii*.

Ray, Satyajit (1921–) Indian film director. He achieved an international reputation with *Pather Panchali* (1955), *The Unvanquished* (1956), and *The*

World of Apu (1959), a trilogy of films about social change in India; his other films include *Charulata* (1964) and *An Enemy of the People* (1989).

Rayleigh, John William Strutt, 3rd Baron (1842–1919) British physicist. His work on black-body radiation was upset by Planck's discovery of the quantum theory but he did much valuable work in optics, hydrodynamics, and the theory of electrical units. He was awarded the 1904 Nobel Prize for his discovery of argon, in conjunction with Sir William Ramsay.

rayon A textile fibre or fabric made from cellulose. **Viscose rayon** is made by dissolving wood pulp in a mixture of sodium hydroxide and carbon disulphide. The fibres are reconstituted in an acid bath. **Acetate rayon** is made by mixing wood pulp with acetic anhydride, acetic acid, and sulphuric acid to form cellulose acetate, which is then dissolved in a solvent and forced through fine holes to form fibres as the solvent evaporates.

razorbill A black-and-white auk, *Alca torda*, that breeds around N Atlantic coasts and winters in the Mediterranean. 40 cm long, it has a laterally compressed bill. It dives to catch fish, shellfish, and worms.

razor shell A burrowing bivalve mollusc of the family *Solenidae* (about 40 species), also called a jack-knife clam, of Atlantic and Pacific coasts. The common razor (*Ensis siliqua*), about 15 cm long, has a narrow shell with squared ends; its curved foot burrows into sand.

reactance. *See* impedance.

Reading 51 28N 0 59W A town in S England, the administrative centre of Berkshire. It is the headquarters of several industries. Population (1985): 138 000.

Reagan, Ronald (1911–) US statesman; Republican president (1981–89). He achieved fame as a film actor before entering politics. In 1981 he survived an assassination attempt. As president he cut taxes, increased defence spending, and approved the US invasion of Grenada (1983) and CIA operations in Nicaragua, despite Congress opposition. Re-elected in 1984, he agreed the Intermediate Nuclear Forces (INF) Treaty with the Soviet Union in 1987 and, despite early hostility, improved US-Soviet relations after Gorbachov came to power. *See also* Strategic Defence Initiative.

realism 1. The medieval philosophical theory that general terms (called universals) have a real existence, that is that there is some abstract entity that corresponds with the term. Plato and Aristotle were realists in believing that the universe contained universals in addition to particulars. Aquinas and Duns Scotus were leading realists. 2. In modern philosophy, a stance opposed to idealism. Realists, such as G. E. Moore, assert that objects exist independently of being perceived.

real tennis (royal tennis) A racket-and-ball indoor court game, which originated in France in the 12th–13th centuries as *jeu de paume* (game of the palm). It was originally played with the bare hand, the strung racket being developed in about 1500. Many other court games developed from it. The stone floor area is approximately 29 × 10 m (96 × 32 ft). The cloth ball is hit over a central net, as in tennis, but it also bounces off the side walls, as in squash rackets and fives.

Réaumur, René-Antoine Ferchault de (1683–1757) French physicist, whose work on thermometers led him to devise the temperature scale that bears his name. On this scale water freezes at 0° and boils at 80°.

received pronunciation (RP) The pronunciation of English most generally accepted as standard or correct.

The term was coined in 1926 by Daniel Jones (1881–1967) to describe the characteristic accent of the public schools and universities. Historically, it is derived from Middle English spoken in the London area.

recessive gene The allele of a gene the function of which is hidden when the organism concerned is crossed with one carrying a different allele (called the dominant allele) for the same gene.

Recife (*or* Pernambuco) 8 06S 34 53W A port in NE Brazil, on the Atlantic Ocean. It is a major port. Population (1985): 1 289 627.

recombinant DNA. *See* genetic engineering.

Reconstruction (1865–77) The period after the US Civil War in which the defeated Confederate states were brought back into the Union. The new state governments were dominated by Whites prepared to compromise, newly enfranchised Blacks, and northern carpetbaggers, but after the withdrawal of Federal troops in 1877 southerners dedicated to White supremacy were restored to power.

recorder (law). *See* judge.

recorder (music) A woodwind instrument of medieval origin. The recorder is end-blown, through a whistle mouthpiece mounted in a block (*or* fipple). The holes are covered with the fingers; the tone is quieter than that of the flute.

recording of sound A system for storing and reproducing sound. The gramophone record is made by converting the sound into an electrical signal, which is normally temporarily stored on tape. This signal is amplified and used to control a cutter that produces a spiral undulating groove in a master disc. Plastic (vinyl) copies of this are mass-produced for sale. In a record-player, the stylus travels along the groove and reproduces the mechanical vibrations of the cutter. The pick-up then converts these to an electrical signal, which is amplified and fed to a loudspeaker. Many electronic devices are used to ensure that sounds in the frequency range 80–12 000 hertz are reproduced without distortion. Recent innovations include the compact disc, which consists of a specially treated glass disc cut by a high-intensity laser beam and is played back on a compact disc player. Digital audio tape (DAT), which reproduces sound equal in quality to the compact disc and also permits home-recording, makes use of **digital recording** technology. In this the musical signal is sampled, up to 30 000 times per second, and translated into a digital code, which is then transmitted or recorded and reconstituted in the receiver or player. In this way the actual signal suffers no interference or distortion during transmission or in the recording process.

rectifier A device that allows electric current to flow in one direction only; it is generally used to convert alternating current to direct current. Semiconductor diodes have now replaced thermionic valves (diodes) for lower voltage applications. For power supplies of several megawatts, mercury-arc rectifiers are used.

rectum. *See* intestine.

red admiral A butterfly, *Vanessa atalanta*, found throughout Europe, Asia, and North America. The wings are black with red and white markings. Red admirals migrate to northern regions for the summer. The caterpillars feed mainly on stinging nettles. Family: *Nymphalidae*.

red algae Algae of the division *Rhodophyta* (about 3000 species), which are usually red or blue in colour due to the presence of the pigments phycoerythrin (red) or phycocyanin (blue), which mask the green chlorophyll. They range from small unicellular or filamentous forms to branching or sheetlike seaweeds. Reproduction is asexual or sexual.

Red Brigades (Italian name: Brigate Rosse) A group of Italian terrorists formed in 1969 and dedicated to the violent overthrow of capitalist society. They were responsible for the murder of the statesman Aldo Moro in 1978.

Red Cross, International An organization founded by the Geneva Convention of 1864 to provide care for the casualties of war. Inspired by Henri Dunant (1828–1910), its headquarters are in Geneva and its emblem, the red cross, represents the Swiss flag with its colours reversed. Muslim countries have generally adopted the crescent as their emblem. The International Red Cross has twice won the Nobel Peace Prize, in 1917 and 1944.

redcurrant A shrub of the genus *Ribes* (*see* currant), cultivated for its red fruits, which may be made into jellies, jams, etc. Cultivated redcurrants have been derived from *R. rubrum* of Eurasia, *R. sativum* of W Europe, and *R. petraeum* of central and S Europe.

red deer A large reddish-brown deer, *Cervus elaphus*, of European and Asian woodlands. Over 120 cm high at the shoulder, males have spreading branched antlers up to 125 cm long; females are more lightly built. Stags and hinds come together in the autumn for the rut, when mature males compete to gather hinds.

Red Duster The popular name for the British Merchant Navy's Red Ensign—a red flag with the Union Flag in its upper corner nearest the flagstaff. It was authorized in 1674.

ROBERT REDFORD *In* The Sting *(1973)*.

Redford, Robert (1936–   ) US film actor. He co-starred with Paul Newman in *Butch Cassidy and the Sundance Kid* (1969) and *The Sting* (1973). His other films include *The Candidate* (1972), *All the President's Men* (1976), and *Out of Africa* (1986).

red giant A greatly distended cool but very luminous giant star. It is one of the final evolutionary stages of a normal star, attained when its central hydrogen has been converted to helium. As it evolves it may change to a hotter more compact type of giant and then swell back to a red giant.

Redgrave, Sir Michael (1908–85) British Shakespearean actor, who also performed in and directed modern plays. His films included *The Browning Version* (1951) and *The Go-Between* (1971). His daughter **Vanessa Redgrave** (1937–   ) has acted on stage and in films, including *Blow-Up* (1967), *Julia* (1977), and *Comrades* (1987), and is well known for her left-wing political activities, as is his son **Corin Redgrave** (1939–   ), who is an actor. His daughter **Lynn Redgrave** (1944–   ) is also an actress.

red grouse A grouse, *Lagopus lagopus scoticus*, found on moorlands of Great Britain and Ireland, where it is managed as a gamebird. 34–37 cm long, it feeds on ling heather. The male is red-brown with red wattles above the eyes and the female is browner and barred.

Red Guards High-school and university students organized by Mao Tse-tung during the Cultural Revolution The Red Guards destroyed property, humiliated foreign diplomats, and attacked those officials who opposed Mao's policies.

red-hot poker A plant of the African genus *Kniphofia*, cultivated as garden plants. 45–120 cm tall, they have tubular flowers, usually scarlet and/or yellow. Family: *Liliaceae*.

red mullet A fish, also called surmullet or goatfish, belonging to the family *Mullidae* (about 50 species), found usually in shallow warm seas. They have an elongated body, up to 25 cm long, with two long chin barbels. They feed on bottom-dwelling invertebrates. Order: *Perciformes*.

redox reactions. *See* oxidation and reduction.

redpoll A tiny finch, *Acanthis flammea*, about 12 cm long with a brown streaked plumage, a red crown, and a black chin. The male has a red breast in summer. It breeds in the Arctic tundra and high mountains of Europe, migrating to central Europe and the N USA in winter.

Red River (Vietnamese name: Song Hong) The chief river of N Vietnam, rising in S China and flowing SE to the Gulf of Tonkin. Length: 500 km (310 mi).

Red River of the North (*or* Red River) A river in central North America, rising in W Minnesota and flowing N into Canada. Length: 1000 km (621 mi).

red salmon. *See* sockeye salmon.

Red Sea A long narrow arm of the Indian Ocean between Africa and Asia, extending some 2400 km (1491 mi) NNW beyond the Gulf of Aden and the Bab el-Mandeb. In the N, it is connected to the Mediterranean Sea by the Suez Canal. Area: 438 000 sq km (169 076 sq mi).

redshank An Old World sandpiper, *Tringa totanus*, that breeds in cool marshy regions of Eurasia. 30 cm long, it has long reddish legs, a black-tipped red bill, and a brown-grey plumage with a white rump. It winters on mudflats of Africa and Asia, feeding on crustaceans, molluscs, and ragworms.

redshift An overall displacement towards larger wavelengths of the spectral lines of a celestial object. Its astronomical significance was suggested by Edwin Hubble (1889–1953) in 1929, when it was used as the basis of the theory that the universe is expanding (*see* expanding universe). A redshift usually arises from the Doppler effect, that is from recession of a celestial object. It increases as the object's radial velocity increases and for an extragalactic body can be used as a measure of distance. A **gravitational redshift** occurs whenever radiation is emitted by a body.

red squirrel A tree squirrel, *Sciurus vulgaris*, of Eurasia. About 20 cm long with a 20-cm tail, red squirrels have dark glossy red fur and tufted ears. They feed mainly on seeds and nuts.

redstart A small Eurasian thrush of the genus *Phoenicurus*, about 14 cm long with a sharp fine bill. The male European redstart (*P. phoenicurus*) is grey with a russet breast, black throat and face with a white stripe, and a red tail, which it fans out in its courtship display to the yellow and brown female. It is found in woodland and heathland.

reduction. *See* oxidation and reduction.

redwood A coniferous tree, *Sequoia sempervirens*, thought to be the tallest tree in the world and one of the longest lived: a specimen in California is over 111 m tall and some Californian trees are over 2000 years old. Also called coast redwood, it is native to the Pacific coast between Oregon and California and is an important timber tree. It has brown-red fibrous bark and red-brown globular cones, about 2 cm long. Family: *Taxodiaceae*. *See also* sequoia.

reed Any of several species of tall aquatic grasses, especially those of the genus *Phragmites* (2–3 species). The common reed (*P. communis*) has a creeping underground stem (rhizome) and grows worldwide along the margins of marshes, lakes, streams, and fens.

Reed, Sir Carol (1906–76) British film director. His best-known films include *The Fallen Idol* (1948) and *The Third Man* (1949) both with screenplays by Graham Greene. His later films include *The Agony and the Ecstasy* (1965) and *Oliver!* (1968).

reedbuck An African antelope belonging to the genus *Redunca* (3 species). The common reedbuck (*R. arundinium*) grows to 90 cm high at the shoulder and has a stiff grey coat and slender ridged horns and inhabits lush grassland. The bohor reedbuck (*R. redunca*) is smaller and lives in swampy regions, while the gregarious mountain reedbuck (*R. fulvorufula*) lives in hilly areas.

reedling A Eurasian bird, *Panurus biarmicus*, about 16 cm long, also called bearded tit. It lives in reedbeds, feeding on insects and seeds. The plumage is brown with pale underparts: the male has a grey head with a black moustache of feathers. Reedlings belong to the babbler family.

reedmace A widely distributed perennial herbaceous plant, *Typha latifolia*, also called bulrush or cat's-tail, growing in reed swamps. It has an erect stem, 1.5–2.5 m high, bearing cylindrical fruit. There are several other reedmaces of the genus *Typha*. Family: *Typhaceae*.

reed warbler An acrobatic warbler, *Acrocephalus scirpaeus*, about 12 cm long with a reddish-brown plumage, pale underparts, and a pale eyestripe. It winters in SE Africa and breeds in European reedswamps.

referendum and initiative Votes on specific legislation by the whole electorate. In the UK referendums have been held concerning membership of the EC (1975) and devolution for Scotland and Wales (1979). Initiatives are proposals, drafted by a citizen or group of citizens, that by virtue of attaining a requisite number of signatures on a petition are put to the electorate for acceptance or rejection.

reflection The rebounding of a wave of light or other radiation when it strikes a surface. Reflected light obeys two laws: first, the normal (an imaginary line vertical to the surface at the point of impact), the incident ray, and the reflected rays all lie in the same plane; second, the angle between the incident ray and the normal is equal to the angle of reflection. *See also* mirrors.

reflex An automatic and involuntary response by an organism to a change in the environment, which occurs before the brain has had time to convey the necessary information to the muscles involved. *See also* conditioned reflex.

Reform Acts The legislation that reformed the British parliamentary system. The Reform Act of 1832 gave many more people the right to vote, disenfranchised some rotten and pocket boroughs, and gave parliamentary representation to new industrial towns. The 1867 Reform Act gave the vote to many working-class householders for the first time. The 1884 Reform Act made the county franchise the same as that in the towns, thus increasing the electorate to about five million.

REFORMATION   *Martin Luther (detail of portrait by Lucas Cranach; c. 1543).*

Reformation A religious movement in 16th-century Europe that began as an attempt to reform the Roman Catholic Church and ended with the establishment of independent Protestant Churches (*see* Protestantism).

The Reformation began on 31 October, 1517, when Martin Luther nailed his 95 theses on the door of the castle church at Wittenburg. Luther's attack on the sale of indulgences and, subsequently, on papal authority and the sacraments (save baptism and the Eucharist) was condemned by the pope and the Holy Roman Emperor but gained the support of several German princes. The consequent conflict (*see* Charles V) was not resolved until 1555 (*see* Augsburg, Peace of).

In Switzerland, the Reformation was initiated by Ulrich Zwingli (1484–1531) in Zurich in 1520, spreading to Basle, Berne, and also to Geneva, where it was led by John Calvin. In France, where Protestants were called Huguenots, the Reformation became involved in a political struggle for control of the Crown, giving rise to the Wars of Religion, and in the Low Countries it fired the Revolt of the Netherlands against Spanish rule.

In England, the Reformation had three stages. Under Henry VIII papal authority in England was destroyed. Thomas Cromwell's legislation (1529–36) culminated in Henry's divorce from Catherine of Aragon and the Act of Supremacy (1534), which proclaimed the king supreme head of the English Church; in 1536 the dissolution of the monasteries was authorized. Under Edward VI Protestantism was established by the 1552 Book of Common Prayer, the accompanying Acts of Uniformity, and the 42 Articles (1553). Protestantism finally became the established Church of England under Elizabeth I and a new Act of Supremacy was passed (1559). In Scotland, the Reformation was influenced by John Knox and Presbyterianism was established in 1592. *See also* Counter-Reformation.

Reformed Churches. *See* Protestantism.

Reform Judaism A religious movement attempting to adapt traditional Judaism to modern circumstances. It began in Germany in the early 19th century. The first Reform synagogue in England was established in 1840; the Liberal movement (founded 1903) instituted more radical reforms typical of US Reform Judaism. The World Union for Progressive Judaism was founded in London in 1926 (it is now based in Jerusalem). The reforms include abolition of many of the ritual laws, acceptance of modern biblical criticism, vernacular services, and full equality for women.

refraction The bending of a beam of radiation as it passes from one medium onto another. For a light ray the amount by which it is bent depends on the angle of the incident ray and on the refractive indices of the two media, the exact dependence being given by Snell's law. Refraction is caused by the difference in the velocity of the radiation in the two media. The ratio of the velocity of light in the two media is known as the **refractive index**.

refrigeration The process of lowering the temperature inside a closed insulated container. In the domestic refrigerator the method most commonly used is the vapour-compression cycle in which a liquid refrigerant, such as Freon (a compound of chlorine, fluorine, and carbon), is pumped through cooling coils formed into the ice-making compartment. In these coils the refrigerant evaporates, taking the latent heat required to make it into a gas from the surroundings. It is then passed to an electrically driven compressor; after compression it condenses back to liquid, when the absorbed heat is given out (usually at the back of the refrigerator). This cycle is repeated over and over again until the required temperature (about $1-2°C$ in the food chamber and $-15°C$ in the deep-freeze compartment) is achieved. *See also* freezing.

Regency style An English decorative style fashionable from about 1800 to 1830 and influenced by the French Empire style. Dark woods and veneers were popular and were set off by ormolu mounts. Concurrently there was a vogue for oriental motifs (*see* chinoiserie) and some magnificent lacquer was produced, for example for the Prince Regent's Pavilion at Brighton.

regeneration In biology, the regrowth and development of tissues or organs lost through injury, as a normal process (e.g. during moulting), or by any other means. It is particularly well developed in plants and simple animals. Thus, whole plants can regenerate from stem and leaf cuttings and simple animals, such as sponges and planarians, can develop from minute fragments. More complex animals, such as crustaceans, replace lost appendages, while lizards can grow new tails. In mammals regeneration is limited to wound healing and regrowth of peripheral nerve fibres.

Regina 50 30N 104 38W A city in W Canada, the capital of Saskatchewan. Founded in 1882, it has expanded rapidly since 1945. Population (1986): 186 521.

Rehoboam King of Judah (c. 922–915 BC); the son of Solomon. His intransigent attitude to the northern tribes resulted in the secession of Israel under Jeroboam and the disintegration of Solomon's empire.

Reichstag (Imperial Diet) The legislative assembly of the German Empire (1871–1918) and the Weimar Republic (1919–33). Its origins lay in the diet of the Holy Roman Empire. It was divided into an electoral college, a college of princes, and a college of cities. It was revived by Bismarck in 1867 as the representative assembly of the North German Confederation. In 1933 the Reichstag building was burnt out; Nazi allegations of communist responsibility provided an excuse to ban opposition parties.

Reign of Terror (1793–94) The most violent period of the French Revolution. Dominated by Robespierre, the governing Committee of Public Safety authorized severe measures against the Revolution's opponents. About 1400 were summarily guillotined. Public reaction caused Robespierre's downfall and execution in July, 1794.

Reims (*or* Rheims) 49 15N 4 02E A city in NE France, in the Marne department. An important Roman town, it was the scene of the coronations of most of the French kings. The magnificent gothic cathedral was badly damaged in World War I. Population (1983): 178 000.

reincarnation (*or* metempsychosis) The migration of the soul from one body at death and its re-entry into another (human or animal) body. The cycle of reincarnation (*samsara*) is fundamental to Hindu, Buddhist, and Jain conceptions of the world, all spiritual effort being directed towards release (*moksa*) from the cycle. Orthodox Christianity rejected it as contrary to belief in the resurrection of the body.

reindeer A large deer, *Rangifer tarandus*, of European and North American tundra (in America it is called a caribou). About 125 cm high at the shoulder, reindeer have a grey-brown coat and spreading branched antlers. Reindeer feed mainly on lichens (reindeer moss) but also eat dwarf willow and other shrubs.

reindeer moss A grey tufted lichen, *Cladonia rangiferina*, that is very abundant in Arctic regions. Up to 8 cm high, it serves as the major food source for reindeer, moose, musk oxen, etc.

Reinhardt, Django (Jean Baptiste R.; 1910–53) Belgian jazz guitarist of gipsy origin. He injured his hand in a fire at the age of 18 but developed an original guitar technique. From 1934 to 1939 he led the quintet of the Hot Club de France with Stephane Grappelli.

Reith, John Charles Walsham, 1st Baron (1889–1971) British administrator. His severe moral principles greatly influenced the early development of the BBC, of which he was director general from 1927 to 1938. The Reith lectures, broadcast annually, were named in his honour.

relativistic mass The mass of a body that is moving at a velocity comparable to the velocity of light. According to the theory of relativity, if the velocity of the body is v then its mass is $m_0(1 - v^2/c^2)^{-½}$, where c is the velocity of light and m_0 the rest mass (the mass when stationary).

1.

RELATIVITY **1**. *Two cars, A and B, travelling along a motorway. The speed of car A relative to the earth is 90 mph. The speed of car B relative to the earth is 70 mph. The speed of car A relative to car B is 90−70 = 20 mph.* **2**. *Car B is now stationary; its headlight beams are turned on as supercar A passes, travelling at 5000 miles per second. The speed of car B's headlight beam relative to car A is 186 000 miles per second (not 186 000−5000 miles per second). The velocity of light is absolute.*

2.

relativity The first part of the theory, published by Albert Einstein in 1905 and known as the special theory, applies only to motion in which there is no acceleration. Up to this time it was thought that light travelled through a stationary medium, called the ether, at a constant speed and that its speed relative to an observer could be calculated in the same way as the relative speed of any two moving objects. For example, if one car (A) travelling at 90 mph on a motorway overtakes another (B) travelling at 70 mph, the speed of the two cars relative to each other is 20 mph. In talking about relative speeds it is necessary to be precise about what a particular speed is relative to. Car A's speed relative to car B is 20 mph, but relative to the earth it is 90 mph. Relative to the sun it is about 24 million mph. Because two American scientists, Michelson and Morley, had shown that light travelled at the same speed whether measured in the direction of the earth's rotation or at right angles to this direction, Einstein suggested that the restriction about relative motion does not apply to light. It always has the same speed of 2.998×10^8 metres per second (186 000 miles per second), irrespective of the motion of the observer.

In his special theory Einstein suggested that as bodies increase in speed they become shorter and heavier. This effect is only noticeable as the speed of light is approached. An electron travelling at 99% of the speed of light becomes seven times heavier than its mass at rest. Einstein also showed that no body could actually travel at the speed of light itself. If it did it would be infinitely heavy and have zero length.

The increase in mass and decrease in length that a body undergoes when moving at high speeds led Einstein to the conclusion that an energy (E) has a mass (m); they are related by the simple equation $E = mc^2$, where c is the velocity of light. The atom bomb and nuclear energy both depend on this equation.

In the general theory of 1915, Einstein considered accelerated relative motion, especially as it is concerned with gravitation. The gravitational force experienced by a body is treated as a property of space and time, which Einstein suggested was "curved" by the presence of the mass. The observed bending of light rays as they pass close to the sun and the shift of certain lines in the solar spectrum have provided experimental verification of the theory.

relay, electric An electrical switching device in which one circuit is controlled by a separate circuit, often to avoid the danger of direct contact with high-voltage supplies or to reduce the length of high-current cable needed. Relays may involve mechanical movement and an electromagnetic connection between the two circuits or be controlled entirely by solid-state electronic components.

reluctance (*or* magnetic resistance) The ratio of the magnetomotive force in a material to the total magnetic flux induced by it. It is analogous to electrical resistance.

Remarque, Erich Maria (1898–1970) German novelist. Wounded in World War I, he described life in the trenches in *All Quiet on the Western Front* (1929).

Rembrandt (Harmenszoon) van Rijn (1606–69) Dutch painter and etcher. Settling permanently in Amsterdam (1631), he made his name as a portrait painter with *The Anatomy Lesson of Dr Tulp* (1632; The Hague). It was followed by many other portraits, including those of his wife Saskia and culminating in the famous group portrait, *The Nightwatch* (1642; Rijksmuseum, Amsterdam). He also treated dramatic mythological and biblical subjects and excelled as a landscapist. His etchings are among the finest ever produced. He eventually had financial difficulties and became bankrupt.

Remembrance Sunday The day on which the British remember the dead of both World Wars. Since 1956 it has been observed on the second Sunday of November. A two-minute silence marks the time, 11 am, of the signing of the Armistice and wreaths of Flanders poppies are laid at the Cenotaph in Whitehall, London, and at other war memorials.

remora A dark slender elongated fish, 30–90 cm long, belonging to a family (*Echeneidae*; 8–10 species) found in warm marine waters. The dorsal fin is modified to form a flat oval sucking disc on its head by which it attaches itself to various marine animals or ships to feed on scraps of food or the hosts' parasites. Order: *Perciformes*.

Remus. *See* Romulus and Remus.

RENAISSANCE   The Procession of the Magi *(detail of fresco by Benozzo Gozzoli; c. 1459).*

Renaissance (French: rebirth) An intellectual and cultural movement that began in Italy in the 14th century, spread to N Europe, and flourished until the mid-16th century. Fundamental to the Renaissance were the revival of classical learning, art, and architecture and the concept of the dignity of man, which characterized humanism. Great writers of the Italian Renaissance included Petrarch, Dante, Boccaccio, Machiavelli, and Ludovico Ariosto (1474–1533).

The first painter to mirror these new ideals was Giotto. He was followed in the 15th century by Masaccio, Uccello, Piero della Francesca, Mantegna, and others, who introduced the use of linear perspective. The High Renaissance denotes the period between about 1500 and about 1520, when the artists Leonardo da Vinci, Raphael, and Michelangelo were developing the harmony and balance associated with classical art to its highest form.

In sculpture the major figures were Nicola Pisano, Donatello, Ghiberti, Verrocchio, and Michelangelo. In building Brunelleschi was the first to revive the classical use of the orders of architecture. Later architects, such as Donato Bramante (1444–1514), Leon Alberti (1404–72), and Palladio, also revived ancient temples and domed structures.

In the 16th century the Renaissance spread to N Europe, where it manifested itself in the art of Dürer, the scholarship of Erasmus, the plays of Shakespeare, and particularly in the courts of such rulers as Elizabeth I of England.

Reni, Guido (1575–1642) Italian painter. In Rome (c. 1600–14) he established a studio and painted his masterpiece, the ceiling fresco of *Aurora* (Palazzo Rospigliosi). Later, working mainly in Bologna, his highly idealized style became somewhat sentimental.

renin An enzyme, secreted by the kidneys, that breaks down a liver protein to form the peptide angiotensin I. This is converted to angiotensin II, which constricts blood vessels–causing a rise in blood pressure–and increases the secretion of aldosterone from the adrenal glands.

Rennes 48 06N 1 40W A city in NW France, in the Ille-et-Vilaine department. The capital of of Brittany, it was badly damaged by fire in 1720. It is now the main

commercial centre of W France. Population (1983): 195 785.

rennet An extract, prepared from cows' stomachs, that contains the milk-coagulating enzyme rennin. It is used in the manufacture of cheese and junket.

Renoir, Pierre Auguste (1841–1919) French impressionist painter, born in Limoges. He exhibited at the first three impressionist exhibitions but later abandoned impressionism. Increasingly crippled by arthritis, he spent his last years in the south of France, painting many sensuous nudes. His best-known works include *Les Parapluies* (National Gallery, London) and *Le Moulin de la Galette* (Louvre). His son **Jean Renoir** (1894–1979) was a film director whose prewar films include *La Grande Illusion* (1937) and *La Règle du jeu* (1939). During World War II he went to Hollywood but returned to Europe to make *French Can-can* (1955), and other films.

Representatives, House of. See Congress.

repression In psychoanalysis, the process of excluding unacceptable ideas from consciousness. Repressed wishes and thoughts continue to exist in the unconscious mind and may give rise to symptoms. One of the goals of psychoanalytic treatment is to bring repressed material back into conscious awareness so that it can be coped with rationally.

reptile A vertebrate animal belonging to the class *Reptilia* (about 6000 species), which includes crocodiles, turtles, lizards, snakes, and the tuatara. Reptiles, which evolved from amphibians, occur in terrestrial, freshwater, and marine habitats, chiefly in tropical regions. They have a covering of horny scales and are cold-blooded. Fertilization of the egg takes place within the female, unlike fish and most amphibians. The large egg has a leathery shell, enabling it to be laid on land. In some lizards and snakes the eggs are retained inside the female and live young are born. Young reptiles resemble their parents and–unlike amphibians–do not undergo metamorphosis. See p. 608.

Republican Party One of the two major political parties of the USA (*compare* Democratic Party). The name was used by Jefferson's Republican Democrats (formed in 1792), but the modern Republican Party originated in 1854 as an alliance of those opposed to the extension of slavery in the new territories in the W USA. After the

REPTILE

green turtle

terrapin

Komodo dragon

snapping turtle

flying lizard

common chameleon

tuatara

tokay

common iguana

African snake skink

reticulated python

adder

Indian cobra

American alligator

Nile crocodile

Indian gavial

REPTILE *Some representative reptiles.*

election of the first Republican president, Lincoln, in 1860, the Republicans were usually the ascendant party until the 1930s. Recent Republican presidents include Eisenhower, Nixon, Reagan, and Bush.

requiem shark A shark of the family *Carcharhinidae* (over 60 species), found worldwide mainly in warm oceans. 1.5–5.5 m long, they have two dorsal fins and are carnivorous, feeding on fish and invertebrates. Some species, such as the tiger shark, are dangerous to man.

resale price maintenance (rpm) A restrictive trade practice operated by a manufacturer, who prohibits retailers from selling a product below a certain price. The drawbacks of the system are that it prevents price competition between retailers and keeps inefficient retailers in business. In the UK, the Resale Prices Act (1964) forbids rpm unless it can be proved to be in the public interest.

resins Adhesive nonflammable organic polymers, usually insoluble in water but soluble in organic solvents. **Natural resins**, such as rosin and shellac, are exuded by plants and insects. **Synthetic resins** are made by modifying natural polymers or by polymerization of petrochemicals. Thermosetting resins, those that harden on heating, include epoxy and some polyurethane resins. Thermoplastic resins, those that soften on heating, include polythene, polyvinyl chloride, and polypropylene.

resistance The property of all materials, except superconductors (*see* superconductivity), that reduces the flow of electricity through them. It is defined by Ohm's law as the ratio of the potential difference between the ends of a conductor to the current flowing through it (*see also* impedance).

resolving power 1. The ability of a microscope to produce separate images of two neighbouring points; the closer the points, the greater the resolving power of the microscope. The resolving power may be increased by using shorter wavelength radiation (e.g. ultraviolet radiation) or by using very short wavelength electrons (as in the electron microscope). Alternatively the refractive index of the medium between the specimen and the objective lens may be increased, as in the oil-immersion lens. 2. A measure of the ability of a telescope to distinguish detail, usually the smallest angle between two point objects that produces distinct images.

resonance (chemistry) The existence of a compound with a molecular structure intermediate between two or more conventional structures. For example, the polar molecule HCl, can be regarded as a **resonance hybrid** between two structures. One is the covalent molecule H–Cl and the other the ionic compound H^+Cl^-.

resonance (physics) The sympathetic oscillation of a system in response to an external excitation. A wire under tension, for example, will not respond to an external vibration unless the vibration is at the natural frequency of oscillation of the wire. A **resonant circuit** consists of a capacitance in parallel with an inductance. When the capacitor discharges through the inductor an induced emf is produced, which again charges the capacitor (in the opposite sense). The circuit will then continue to oscillate, provided that energy is supplied from an outside source. Such circuits, feeding an aerial, are used in radio transmitters to generate radio-frequency oscillations and in receivers to detect incoming signals.

Respighi, Ottorino (1879–1936) Italian composer. He wrote several operas, the symphonic poems *The Fountains of Rome* (1917) and *The Pines of Rome* (1924),

the orchestral suite *The Birds* (1927), and ballets, including *La Boutique fantasque* (1919).

respiration The process by which an organism takes up oxygen from its environment and discharges carbon dioxide into it. In man and most air-breathing animals the organs through which this takes place are the lungs (aquatic animals use gills; insects use tracheae). Oxygen-depleted blood is pumped from the heart to the air sacs (alveoli) of the lungs, where it receives oxygen (from inhaled air) and releases carbon dioxide (which is exhaled). Oxygen in the blood is carried to the tissues and cells, where it oxidizes foodstuffs to produce energy.

respirator A machine used to maintain breathing in patients whose respiratory muscles are paralysed. The cabinet respirator (iron lung) encloses the patient in a sealed container from the neck down; by lowering the pressure in the cabinet the chest expands and draws air into the lungs. A positive-pressure respirator pumps air at regular intervals into the lungs through a tube placed in the windpipe.

Restoration (1660) The re-establishment of the monarchy in England following the fall of the Protectorate. The Restoration of Charles II, whose father Charles I had been executed (1649) during the Civil War, was engineered by General Monck (1608–70). In April, 1660, the Convention Parliament accepted Charles' Declaration of Breda, in which he promised religious toleration and an amnesty to all but 57 of those who had fought the Crown.

restrictive trade practices Agreements between traders that limit competition in an industry. In the UK, under the Fair Trading Act (1973) restrictive practices are held to be against the public interest unless proved otherwise in the Restrictive Practices Court.

resurrection plant. *See* rose of Jericho.

retina The light-sensitive layer that forms the inner surface of the eye. Light is focused by the lens onto the retina, which contains numerous interconnecting light-sensitive cells (rods and cones) that send signals to the visual centre of the brain via the optic nerve. The rods are responsible for vision in dim light and the cones are sensitive to colour and visual detail. *See also* detached retina.

retriever A large strongly built sporting dog descended from the Labrador and characterized by a "soft" mouth and good swimming ability. The flat-coated retriever has a dense coat while the curly-coated retriever has a coat of small tight curls, indicating possible poodle ancestry. Height: 56–68 cm. *See also* golden retriever.

Reuben, tribe of One of the 12 tribes of Israel, claiming descent from Reuben, the eldest son of Jacob and Leah. The territory allocated to Reuben's people was E of the Dead Sea.

Réunion A volcanic island and French overseas department in the W Indian Ocean, in the Mascarene Islands. It was settled in about 1642 by the French with their African and Indian slaves. Sugar, rum, and molasses are exported. Area: 2512 sq km (970 sq mi). Population (1987 est): 564 600. Capital: Saint-Denis.

Reval. *See* Tallinn.

Revelation, Book of A prophetic book, the last in the New Testament, written perhaps about 90–95 AD by "John the Divine," who is often identified with the apostle John. It consists of seven highly symbolic visions that trace the fortunes of the Christian Church from its inception to the end of the world.

PAUL REVERE *Warning of the coming of the British in arms at the start of the American Revolution.*

Revere, Paul (1735–1818) American silversmith and revolutionary. On 18 April, 1775, he rode out to warn the people of Massachusetts that the British troops were on the march. On the following morning the first shots of the American Revolution were fired on the British at Lexington. Revere's ride is celebrated in a poem by Longfellow.

Revolt of the Netherlands The rebellion against Spanish rule in the Netherlands, inspired by political and economic grievances and resentment at the suppression of Protestantism. The revolt broke out in 1568 but the independence of the United Provinces of the Netherlands was not acknowledged until 1648, when the Peace of Westphalia was signed.

Revolutionary and Napoleonic Wars (1792–1815) A series of European wars precipitated by the French Revolution and Napoleon's ambitions for the conquest of Europe. War broke out as a result of the hostile reaction of Austria and Prussia to the arrest of Louis XVI. Initial French success prompted Britain, the Netherlands, and Spain to close ranks with Austria and Prussia in the first coalition (1793). Hard pressed, France achieved a series of victories. In 1795 Prussia, the Netherlands, and Spain sued for peace and, following Napoleon's first Italian campaign (1796–97), Austria followed suit. French supremacy was thwarted only by British naval strength and Nelson's great victory of the Nile (1798). In 1798–99 the second coalition of Britain, the Ottoman Empire, Naples, Portugal, and Austria was formed but collapsed (1801) in the face of Napoleon's victories, especially at Hohenlinden (1800), and the Revolutionary Wars ended with the uneasy Treaty of Amiens (1802) between Britain and France.

Napoleon's aggression, including his imposition of the Continental System against Britain, led to the resumption of naval war between Britain and France. In 1805 Pitt the Younger negotiated a third coalition against Napoleon, who was defeated by Nelson at Trafalgar. Napoleon now defeated Austria and Russia at Ulm and Austerlitz (1805), Prussia at Jena and Auerstadt (1806), and Russia again at Friedland (1807). With the failure of the Continental System and Wellington's victories in the Peninsular War, Napoleon's dominance diminished. Following his disastrous Russian campaign (1812) the allies

were able to defeat him at Leipzig (1813) and, after his return from exile, at Waterloo (1815). The post-Napoleonic settlement of Europe was decided at the Congress of Vienna.

Revolution of 1905 An insurrection in Russia, an expression of the widespread discontent that culminated in the Russian Revolution of 1917. It began on 22 January, 1905 (Bloody Sunday), when a group of workers marched peacefully on the Winter Palace in St Petersburg and were fired on by troops. The massacre precipitated nationwide strikes, uprisings, and mutinies (including the mutiny on the battleship *Potemkin*). The Revolution was substantially crushed by the end of December.

Revolutions of 1848 A series of revolutions in continental Europe caused by economic distress and liberal agitation. The first revolution broke out in France, where the insurgents overthrew the July Monarchy of Louis Philippe, but a split in their ranks led to the suppression of the Left and the election of Louis Napoleon (later Napoleon III) as president. In the Italian states the revolution formed part of the movement against the Austrian presence in Italy (*see* Risorgimento). In the Austrian Empire revolts in Vienna secured the resignation of Metternich and the summoning of a constituent assembly. In Prussia, Frederick William IV was forced to convene a constituent assembly. By December, however, the revolutions there and in other German states had been suppressed. The revolutions were all quelled but not without some concessions to liberal and nationalist movements.

revolver A short-range small arm having a revolving cylinder containing the rounds behind the barrel. Calibres range from .21 inches to .455 inches. The first successful revolver was the Colt, designed in 1835. *See also* pistol.

Reykjavík 64 10N 21 53W The capital of Iceland, an important fishing port, on Faxa Fjord in the SW. Founded by the Vikings in 874 AD, it became the seat of parliament (the Althing) in 1843 and capital of Iceland in 1918. Population (1986): 91 394.

Reynolds, Sir Joshua (1723–92) British portrait painter. Using the techniques of the Old Masters in such paintings as *Sarah Siddons as the Tragic Muse* (San Marino, California), Reynolds aimed to give portraits the prestige of history paintings. In 1768 he became the first president of the Royal Academy, where he delivered the *Discourses*, which contain his artistic theories. His friends included Dr Johnson and Garrick, both of whom he painted.

Reza Shah Pahlavi (1878–1944) Shah of Iran (1925–41). After leading an army coup in 1921, he deposed Ahmad Shah Qajar (1898–1930) in 1925. As shah himself, Reza aimed at the modernization of Iran. In 1941 Britain and the Soviet Union forced Reza Shah to abdicate in favour of his son Mohammed Reza Pahlavi.

rhea A large flightless bird belonging to a family (*Rheidae*; 3 species) occurring in South America. 120 cm tall, rheas have a brownish plumage and long legs with three toes. They live in flocks, feeding on leaves, roots, seeds, insects, and small vertebrates. Order: *Rheiformes*.

Rhea In Greek religion, a Titan, daughter of Uranus and Gaea. Her consort Cronus swallowed her children, fearing that they would overthrow him. Rhea substituted a stone for one child, Zeus, who eventually overthrew Cronus and forced him to disgorge the other children.

Rhee, Syngman (1875–1965) Korean statesman; president of South Korea (1948–60). He became leader of South Korea in 1945 during the US occupation and as its first president claimed his government's right to rule over all Korea. Popular unrest unseated him in 1960.

Rhelms. *See* Reims.

rhenium (Re) A dense (relative density 21.02) silvery-white transition metal with a very high melting point. The metal is very ductile and is used to alloy with tungsten. Alloys with molybdenum are superconducting. The metal is obtained as a by-product of molybdenum refining. At no 75; at wt 186.2; mp 3180°C; bp 5620°C.

rhesus factor (Rh factor) A blood protein present on the red cells in 83% of the population: the presence or absence of the Rh factor is the basis of the Rh blood group system, people with the factor being described as Rh positive and those without as Rh negative. If a Rh-negative woman has a Rh-positive baby she may produce anti-Rh antibodies that will react against subsequent Rh-positive pregnancies. The affected baby's blood cells may be destroyed by these antibodies, leading to the severe anaemia of haemolytic disease of the newborn. The incidence of this disease has been reduced by taking steps to prevent the formation of maternal anti-Rh antibodies soon after delivery of the first baby.

rhesus monkey A macaque monkey, *Macaca mulatta*, of S Asia, widely used in medical research. In the wild, rhesus monkeys live in large colonies in forests or on hillsides.

rheumatic fever A disease of children that occurs (rarely) after infection with a streptococcus bacterium. The symptoms develop 10–14 days after the original infection (which is usually of the throat) and include fever, aching joints, chorea (involuntary movements), and inflammation of the heart, which—in a few cases—may lead to chronic heart disease. Treatment is with bed rest, penicillin, aspirin, and sometimes steroids.

rheumatism Any condition involving pain in the joints. This may be caused by a simple strain or by rheumatoid arthritis, osteoarthritis, gout, or rheumatic fever.

Rhine, River (German name: Rhein; Dutch name: Rijn) A river in central and W Europe. Rising in SE Switzerland, it flows N along the Swiss-German border, the Franco-German border and into West Germany and the Netherlands before entering the North Sea. The main tributaries are the Rivers Ruhr, Main, Moselle, and Neckar. It is W Europe's main navigable waterway. Length: 1320 km (820 mi).

rhinoceros A large hoofed mammal belonging to the family *Rhinocerotidae* (5 species), of Asia and Africa. Rhinos have a massive virtually naked dark-skinned body with short thick legs, a short neck, and a large head. The Indian rhinoceros (*Rhinoceros unicornis*) has a single horn; all other rhinos have two horns. Rhinos range in size from the large rare African white rhinoceros (*Diceros simus*), up to 2 m high and weighing 3.5 tonnes, to the Sumatran rhinoceros (*Didermocerus sumatrensis*), which is up to 150 cm high and weighs 500–1000 kg. Rhinos are generally solitary grazers. All are now endangered species.

rhinoceros beetle A horned scarab beetle, up to 150 mm long (including the horn). The larvae of most rhinoceros beetles live in rotting wood. *Oryctes rhinoceros* is sometimes a serious pest in oriental coconut groves. *See also* hercules beetle.

RHINOCEROS *The rare white rhinoceros.*

rhizome An underground plant stem producing aerial leaves and shoots. It may extend some distance below ground and can be fleshy (as in the iris) or wiry (as in couch grass). Rhizomes can function both as organs of vegetative reproduction and as overwintering structures.

Rhode Island The smallest state in the USA, indented by Narragansett Bay. One of the New England states, it is the second most densely populated US state. It is highly industrialized and has important naval installations. It is famous for its poultry. *History*: settled in 1636, it was the first colony to declare its independence from Britain. Area: 3144 sq km (1214 sq mi). Population (1986 est): 975 000. Capital: Providence.

Rhode Island Red A breed of domestic fowl developed on Rhode Island farms in the 19th century. It has a deep broad long body with a nearly horizontal back and a slightly curved beak. The plumage is red. Weight: 3.8 kg (cocks); 3.0 kg (hens).

Rhodes (Modern Greek name: Ródhos) A Greek island in the SE Aegean Sea, the largest of the Dodecanese group. It has a mountainous interior with fertile coastal strips, producing cereals, fruit, and wine. Tourism is important. *History*: colonized by Dorians before 1000 BC, Rhodes entered its period of greatest prosperity in the 3rd century BC. It suffered several earthquakes, one of which destroyed the Colossus of Rhodes in 244 BC. It was occupied by the Knights Hospitallers from 1282 until 1528, when it became part of the Ottoman Empire. Conquered by Italy in 1912, it was ceded to Greece in 1947. Area: 1400 sq km (540 sq mi). Population (1981); 40 392. Capital: Rhodes.

Rhodes, Cecil (John) (1853–1902) South African financier and statesman. Born in Britain, he went to South Africa in 1870. In 1888 his company, De Beers Consolidated Mines, bought up the Kimberley mines and in 1889 he gained a charter for the British South Africa Company to develop the territory that in 1895 was named Rhodesia in his honour. He became prime minister of Cape Colony in 1890 but was forced to resign in 1896 over the abortive Jameson raid into the Transvaal. Rhodes endowed 170 Rhodes scholarships at Oxford University for students from the British Empire, the USA, and Germany.

Rhodesia. *See* Zimbabwe.

Rhodesia and Nyasaland, Federation of (*or* Central African Federation) A former (1953–63) federation of the British colony of Southern Rhodesia (now Zimbabwe) and the British protectorates of Northern Rhodesia (now Zambia) and Nyasaland (now Malawi).

Rhodesian ridgeback A breed of hunting dog originating in South Africa, characterized by a ridge of hair along the back. Height: 63–68 cm (dogs); 61–66 cm (bitches).

rhodium (Rh) A metal of the platinum group, discovered in 1803 by W. H. Wollaston (1766–1828). It is a very hard highly reflective metal and is used to plate jewellery and optical instruments. At no 45; at wt 102.905; mp 1966 ± 3°C; bp 3727 ± 100°C.

Rhododendron A genus of small trees and shrubs (about 250 species), mainly of N temperate regions. They have leathery often evergreen leaves, large scaly winter buds, and colourful fragrant bell- or funnel-shaped flowers. Many, including azaleas, are cultivated as ornamentals. Family: *Ericaceae*.

Rhône, River A major river in W Europe. Rising in the Rhône Glacier in Switzerland, it flows through Lake Geneva to enter France, flowing generally SW. Since 1976 the River Rhône has been canalized from Lyon to the Mediterranean Sea. Length 812 km (505 mi).

rhubarb A perennial plant, *Rheum rhaponticum*, possibly of Asian origin, widely cultivated for its juicy red or green leafstalks, up to 1 m high, which are cooked in sugar. The leaves are poisonous. Family: *Polygonaceae*.

rib A curved bone, 12 pairs of which make up the rib cage, enclosing and protecting the heart and lungs. Each rib articulates with the spine, permitting movement of the rib cage during breathing. The other ends of the upper seven ribs (the so-called true ribs) are fixed directly to the breastbone by means of a cartilage. Each of the next three pairs (the "false" ribs) is connected by the cartilage to the rib above it, and the two lowest ribs (the floating ribs) end in the muscles of the body wall.

Ribbentrop, Joachim von (1893–1946) German Nazi politician and diplomat. From 1936 to 1938 he was ambassador to the UK and then became Hitler's foreign minister. He was arrested in 1945 and hanged for war crimes..

ribbonworm A long flat wormlike animal, also called proboscis worm, belonging to the invertebrate phylum *Nemertina* (about 600 species). Ranging in length from 1 mm to 30 m, ribbonworms live in shallow seas, feeding on annelid worms, molluscs, and crustaceans.

Ribeirão Prêto 21 09S 47 48W A city in S Brazil, in São Paulo state. It is the centre of a coffee- and sugar-growing area. Population (1980 est): 300 704.

Ribera, José de (*or* Jusepe R.; 1591–1652) Spanish-born painter and etcher. He settled in Naples (1616), where he was known as Lo Spagnoletto (Little Spaniard). He painted chiefly religious subjects and some everyday life scenes and portraits, the best examples of which are *The Martyrdom of St Bartholomew* (Prado) and *Clubfooted Boy* (Louvre).

riboflavin. *See* vitamin B complex.

ribonucleic acid. *See* RNA.

ribose A simple sugar ($C_5H_{10}O_5$). Ribose and its derivative deoxyribose are important constituents of RNA and DNA respectively.

ribosome A granular particle present in enormous numbers in the cytoplasm of nearly all cells. Ribosomes

are composed of RNA and protein and are the site of protein synthesis.

rice An annual cereal grass, *Oryza sativa*, or its edible grain, probably native to India but widely cultivated throughout tropical, subtropical, and warm temperate regions. Seedlings are generally transplanted to flooded paddy fields, although varieties of upland rice do not require flooding. The field is drained to enable mechanical harvesting. Milling the grain removes either the outer husk alone, resulting in brown rice, or both the husk and the bran layer, resulting in vitamin-B-deficient white rice.

Richard (I) the Lionheart (1157–99) King of England (1189–99); a hero of medieval legend, he spent all but six months of his reign abroad. The third son of Henry II and Eleanor of Aquitaine, he joined the third Crusade in 1189 and conquered Messina and Cyprus before arriving in the Holy Land. His victory at Arsuf gained Joppa (1191). On his way home he was captured in Austria and was only released after payment of an enormous ransom (1194). He died campaigning in France.

RICHARD II *The 10-year-old king; detail from a portrait by an unknown artist.*

Richard II (1367–1400) King of England (1377–99). Succeeding his grandfather Edward III, as a minor, government was largely in the hands of his uncle John of Gaunt. Factional struggles culminated in the banishment in 1398 of Gaunt's son Henry Bolingbroke. He returned in 1399, while Richard was in Ireland, and seized the throne as Henry IV. Richard died shortly afterwards at Pontefract Castle in mysterious circumstances.

Richard III (1452–85) King of England (1483–85). He was the youngest brother of Edward IV, on whose death in 1483 he became protector for Edward V, a minor. After destroying the power of the Woodville faction, Richard imprisoned Edward and his brother and seized the throne. It was, and continues to be, alleged that Richard murdered the boys, who disappeared in August, 1483. As king, he made important administrative and financial reforms but faced considerable opposition, first from Henry Stafford, 2nd Duke of Buckingham (executed in October, 1483), and then from Henry Tudor (subsequently Henry VII), by whom Richard was defeated and killed at Bosworth.

Richard, Cliff (Harry Rodger Webb; 1940–) British pop singer, originally with the rock group the Shadows. He starred in the films *The Young Ones* (1961) and *Summer Holiday* (1962) and the musical *Time* (1986).

Richards, Sir Gordon (1904–86) British jockey, who was champion jockey a record 26 times (1925–53). He rode 4870 winners out of a total of 21 843 mounts (1920–54).

Richardson, Sir Ralph (1902–83) British actor. He established his reputation as an actor of Shakespearean roles while working with the Old Vic Company during the 1930s and 1940s. He also acted in modern plays, such as David Storey's *Home* (1970) and Harold Pinter's *No Man's Land* (1976) and made many films.

Richardson, Samuel (1689–1761) British novelist. His pioneering novel *Pamela* (1740) evolved from a publisher's commission for a book of model letters for inexperienced writers. His acute psychological characterization was further developed in *Clarissa* (1748).

Richelieu, Armand Jean du Plessis, Cardinal de (1585–1642) French statesman, who greatly increased the absolute authority of the Crown and France's power in Europe. He rose to prominence as adviser to Louis XIII's mother Marie de' Medici (1573–1642), becoming Louis' chief minister in 1629. He ruthlessly suppressed the Huguenots and by means of an extensive secret service thwarted a series of aristocratic conspiracies against himself. He directed France with brilliance in the Thirty Years' War and founded the French Academy.

Richmond 37 34N 77 27W A city and port in the USA, the capital of Virginia. Richmond was the capital of the Confederate states during the US Civil War. Population (1986): 217 700.

Richter scale A scale of earthquake magnitude devised in 1935 by C. F. Richter (1900–85). It is a logarithmic scale from 0–9, the largest earthquakes having the highest numbers. The strongest earthquake so far recorded had a Richter scale value of 8.6.

Richthofen, Manfred, Freiherr von (1892–1918) German air ace of World War I, who shot down 80 Allied aircraft before being killed himself in action. His nickname, the Red Baron, referred to the colour of his plane.

rickets A disease of children affecting the bones and caused by vitamin D deficiency. With a poor diet and/or inadequate sunshine the bones become soft and do not grow properly.

rickettsia A minute organism belonging to a group of parasites that cannot reproduce outside the bodies of their hosts. They infect arthropods (especially ticks and mites) and can be transmitted to man, in whom they cause such diseases as typhus and Rocky Mountain spotted fever. All species live within living cells: they are regarded as intermediate between bacteria and viruses. The name derives from the principal genus (*Rickettsia*), which was named after the US pathologist H. T. Ricketts (1871–1910).

Ridgeway A prehistoric trackway in S England. It runs along the scarp of the Berkshire Downs, linking the Avebury region with the Thames.

Rif A Berber people of N Morocco. Most of the 19 tribes speak the Rif dialect of the Berber language but a few speak Arabic. Many are light skinned and have blue or grey eyes. The Rif are Muslims and are renowned for their warrior tradition.

rifle A shoulder small arm with a spiral groove inside its long barrel to make the projectile spin during its trajectory. Invented in the 15th century, the rifle superseded the musket during the 18th and 19th centuries. During the 1880s breech-loading rifles became capable of firing more than one cartridge without reloading. These were the immediate predecessors of the modern repeating rifle. *See also* Browning Automatic Rifle.

riflebird A large bird of paradise having a black plumage with iridescent throat patches and small ornamental plumes. The magnificent riflebird (*Craspedophora magnifica*) is about 30 cm long with a slender curved bill, a glossy green crown, and a purplish throat. The male performs its courtship display on fiercely defended perches.

rift valley A steep-sided valley with a flat floor formed as a result of the valley floor subsiding between two roughly parallel faults. The most notable example is the vast Great Rift Valley in Africa.

Riga 56 53N 24 08E A port in the W Soviet Union, on the Baltic Sea. It is an industrial and cultural centre. *History*: the order of Livonian Knights was founded here in 1201, and in 1282 Riga became a member of the Hanseatic League. It then passed to Poland (1581), to Sweden (1621), and to Russia (1710). It was the capital of independent Latvia (1918–40) and was occupied by the Germans (1941–44) in World War II. Population (1987 est): 900 000.

right ascension An angular distance, analogous to terrestrial longitude, that is used with **declination** to specify the position of an astronomical body on the celestial sphere. It is measured eastwards along the celestial equator from the vernal equinox. Declination is the angular distance of the body N or S of the celestial equator.

Rights of Man and of the Citizen, Declaration of the (1789) The formal expression of the ideals of the French Revolution. Comprising 17 articles, it was drafted by the National Assembly to preface the constitution of 1791. Incorporating Enlightenment theories and both English and American precedents (*see* Bill of Rights), the Declaration asserted that "all men are born free and equal in rights."

right whale A whale of the family *Balaenidae* (5 species), so called because they were the right whales to catch (by whalers). Up to 18 m long and weighing over 20 tonnes, they are large-headed slow-moving plankton feeders.

Rijeka (Italian name: Fiume) 45 20N 14 27E The chief seaport in Yugoslavia, in Croatia on the Adriatic Sea. Made a free port in 1723, it was annexed by Hungary in 1779. In 1919, Gabriele D'Annunzio (1863–1938) led a force to capture it for Italy. It again became a free port in 1920, reverted to Italy in 1924, finally coming to Yugoslavia in 1947. Population (1983): 193 044.

RIJKSMUSEUM   The Syndics of the Cloth Guild *(detail), painted by Rembrandt in 1662.*

Rijksmuseum   A museum and art gallery in Amsterdam, housing the national collection of the Netherlands. It originated in 1808 as the Royal Museum and became the Rijksmuseum in 1817. Its paintings of the Dutch school include the celebrated *Night Watch* by Rembrandt.

Rijswijk, Treaty of   (1697) The treaty that ended the War of the Grand Alliance between France and England, Spain, Austria, and the Netherlands. Louis XIV of France surrendered most of the territories he had conquered, recognized William III as King of England, and granted trading concessions to the Dutch.

Rilke, Rainer Maria   (1875–1926) Austrian poet, born in Prague. Paris is the setting for the meditative prose of *Die Aufzeichnungen des Malte Laurids Brigge* (1910). In his poetry, the mysticism of *Das Stunden-Buch* (1905) develops into a pantheistic celebration of life in the *Duino Elegies* (1923) and the *Sonnets to Orpheus* (1923).

Rimbaud, Arthur   (1854–91) French poet. He was welcomed to Paris in 1871 by Verlaine, with whom he formed a tempestuous relationship that eventually ended in a violent quarrel. His visionary theories about poetry were expressed in *Une Saison en enfer* (1873) and *Les Illuminations* (1886). At the age of 20 he renounced poetry and wandered in Europe and the Near East, eventually becoming a gun-runner in Ethiopia.

Rimini   (Latin name: Ariminium)   44 03N 12 24E A town and resort in Italy, on the N Adriatic coast. It has various Roman and medieval remains. Population (1986): 130 698.

Rimsky-Korsakov, Nikolai   (1844–1908) Russian composer. He was a member of the group of nationalist composers known as the Mighty Five. He wrote 15 operas, including *The Snow Maiden* (1880–81) and *The Golden Cockerel* (1906–07), such orchestral works as *Scheherazade* (1888), chamber music, and songs.

ringlet   A satyrid butterfly characterized by brownish wings marked with small white rings. The larval food plants are mainly grasses. Chief genera: *Aphantopus, Cacnonympha, Erebia.*

ring ouzel   A shy songbird, *Turdus torquatus,* of mountainous regions. The male is black with a broad white crescent around the throat; the female is dark brown with less distinct markings. Family: *Turdidae* (thrushes).

ringworm   A highly infectious disease of the skin, hair, and nails that is caused by various fungi: it is known medically as tinea. Ringworm is usually transmitted by direct contact. The affected area is typically ring-shaped (especially on the scalp). Serious infections are treated with the antibiotic griseofulvin.

Río Bravo.   *See* Rio Grande.

Rio de Janeiro   22 53S 43 17W The chief port in Brazil, the capital of Rio de Janeiro state. Discovered by the Portuguese in 1502, it was the capital of Brazil from 1763 until 1960. It is renowned for its spectacular setting backed by mountains, the most famous of which is the conical Sugar Loaf Mountain. Another famous landmark is the giant figure of Christ standing on the highest peak. It is an important port and trading centre. Population (1985): 5 615 149.

Rio Grande   (Spanish names: Río Bravo; Río Bravo del Norte)   The fifth longest river of North America. Rising in the Rocky Mountains, it forms the entire border between Texas (USA) and Mexico.   Length: 2040 km (1885 mi).

Río Muni.   *See* Equatorial Guinea, Republic of.

Risorgimento   (Italian: resurgence)   The nationalist movement in 19th-century Italy that achieved the country's independence and unification. Secret societies, such as the Carbonari and Young Italy, encouraged Italian patriotism after 1815. In 1859, the Piedmontese prime minister Cavour freed Lombardy and in 1860 Garibaldi surrendered to Piedmont the conquests made in the S by his Expedition of the Thousand. Tuscany, Modena, Parma, Bologna, and Romagna then accepted entry into the kingdom of Italy under the House of Piedmont, proclaimed in 1861. Unification was completed by Italy's annexation of Venetia in 1866 and of the papal states in 1870.

Rivera, Diego   (1886–1957) Mexican mural painter. In Mexico in the 1920s, he revived the old techniques of fresco and encaustic painting. His communist-inspired subject matter made him notorious in the USA.

Riverina   A district of Australia, in S New South Wales. It consists chiefly of flat alluvial plains. Area: 68 658 sq km (26 509 sq mi).

Riviera (French name: Rivière) The narrow Mediterranean coastal belt of France and Italy, extending roughly between Toulon and La Spezia. Its climate, scenery, and beaches have made it a long-standing cosmopolitan resort.

Riyadh 24 39N 46 46E A city in Saudi Arabia, in the centre of the Arabian Peninsula. Riyadh and Mecca are joint capitals of the kingdom. Population (1984 est): 1 000 000.

RNA (or ribonucleic acid) A nucleic acid that is important in the synthesis of proteins by living organisms. In some viruses RNA is the genetic material. Structurally, it is similar to DNA but usually occurs as a single-stranded molecule with the sugar ribose and the base uracil replacing the deoxyribose and thymine of DNA. The genetic code in DNA is transcribed into a strand of messenger (m) RNA and carried to the ribosomes, where it is translated into a particular polypeptide chain. The amino acids making up the protein are brought to their correct positions in the chain by transfer (t) RNA.

roach One of several freshwater fish related to carp, especially *Rutilus rutilus*, a game fish found in N Europe. It has an elongated body, 15–45 cm long, olive-green to grey-green above and silvery white below with reddish fins and red eyes. It lives in shoals, feeding on small animals and plants.

robber crab (or coconut crab) A crab, *Birgus latro*, found on the shores of the SW Pacific and Indian Oceans. It has an extremely large body (about 1 m from head to tail), ranging from violet to brown in colour. It lives in sand burrows during the day, emerging at night to feed on coconuts. Tribe: *Anomura*.

robber fly A predatory fly, also called assassin fly, belonging to a worldwide family (*Asilidae*); over 4000 species) of insect eaters. Some species (e.g. *Asilis crabroniformis*) resemble bees and wasps. Most larvae are herbivorous and live in the soil.

Robert (I) the Bruce (1274–1329) King of the Scots (1306–29). After a long career of rebellion against the English Crown Robert seized the Scottish throne in 1306. Although immediately forced into exile by Edward I of England, on the accession of Edward II he slowly recovered the kingdom, decisively defeating the English forces at Bannockburn (1314).

Robert II (1316–90) The first Stuart King of the Scots (1371–90). He was three times regent of Scotland (jointly 1334–35; alone 1338–41 and 1346–57) while his uncle David II (1324–71) was imprisoned or in exile. His own rule, as an old man, was of little consequence.

Robeson, Paul (1898–1976) US Black actor and singer of Negro spirituals. His stage performances include the title role of Othello, and he actively campaigned for Black civil rights.

Robespierre, Maximilien François Marie Isidore de (1758–94) French revolutionary. A lawyer, Robespierre was elected to the States General in 1789 and became one of the leaders of the radical Jacobins. After the execution of Louis XVI he was instrumental in the overthrow of the Girondins (1793). He subsequently wielded supreme power on the Committee of Public Safety, instituting the Reign of Terror. In 1794 the tide turned against him and his cult of the Supreme Being: he was denounced in the Legislative Assembly and guillotined.

robin A small Eurasian songbird, *Erithacus rubecula*. About 13 cm long it has an olive-brown plumage with an orange-red breast, throat, and forehead and feeds on insects, earthworms, fruit, and seeds. A robin defends its territory fiercely. Family: *Turdidae* (thrushes).

Robin Hood An English outlaw, probably legendary, who figures in a series of medieval ballads. According to the *Lytell Geste of Robyn Hoode* (c. 1495) he killed the evil sheriff of Nottingham, was visited in his forest home by the king, and was subsequently employed in the royal household.

Robinson, Sugar Ray (Walker Smith; 1921–89) US boxer, world welterweight champion (1946–51) and five times middleweight champion (twice in 1951, 1955, 1957, 1958–60). He fought 202 professional bouts, of which he lost only 19.

ROBOTICS *Fitting the rear screen by robot at an Austin-Rover factory.*

robotics The study of automatic machines that are capable of simulating and replacing human activities. Some robotic machines have sensory devices and can make decisions based on a sensory input and a self-programming facility. However, most robots in current industrial use carry out a fixed sequence of computer-controlled operations.

Rob Roy (Robert Macgregor; 1671–1734) Scottish outlaw, whose violent life was romanticized in Sir Walter Scott's novel *Rob Roy* (1818). He embarked on his career of banditry after losing his family fortunes in 1712.

Robson, Dame Flora (1902–84) British actress. She was successful in both comedy, as in *Captain Brassbound's Conversion* (1948), and in serious drama, such as Ibsen's *Ghosts* (1958) and *John Gabriel Borkman* (1963). In her many films she usually played character parts.

Rochester 43 12N 77 37W A city in the USA, in New York state on Lake Ontario. Founded in 1789, its industries include the manufacture of photographic equipment. Population (1986): 235 970.

Rochester 51 24N 0 30E A city and port in SE England, in Kent on the Medway estuary. It was a Roman stronghold. Population (1981): 52 505.

rock (petrology) A solid mixture of minerals forming part of the earth's crust. Rocks are classified according to their formation (*see* igneous rock; metamorphic rock; sedimentary rock), their age (*see* stratigraphy), and their composition. The principal minerals in rocks are the silicates (including silica), carbonates, and oxides. The essential minerals in a rock are those that determine its classification; accessory minerals are those that do not affect its classification. Petrology is the study of rocks.

rock crystal. *See* quartz.

Rockefeller, John D(avison) (1839–1937) US industrialist, who founded the monopolistic oil-refining company, Standard Oil (1870). A philanthropist, he founded the University of Chicago in 1891 and, with his son **John D(avison) Rockefeller, Jr** (1874–1960), established the Rockefeller Institute for Medical Research (now Rockefeller University) in 1901. The latter's nephew **Nelson A(ldrich) Rockefeller** (1908–79) was Gerald Ford's vice-president (1974–77).

rockets Vehicles or missiles powered by jet propulsion that carry their own fuel and oxidizer and can therefore travel both in space and in the atmosphere. Rockets have no lift surfaces (*see* aeronautics), obtaining both lift and thrust from their propulsive jets. Solid-fuel firework rockets were known to the Chinese in the 13th century; the first liquid-fuelled rocket to fly was designed by the American R. H. Goddard (1882–1945) in 1926. This achievement attracted little interest, except in Germany, where the Peenemünde rocket research station was set up. It was here that Werner von Braun produced the V-2 rocket in World War II. Intercontinental ballistic missiles (with nuclear warheads) developed from this model. These rockets, in turn, led to the space rockets that carried man to the moon.

Space rockets are built in stages, a high-thrust vehicle providing lift-off and acceleration into the thinner atmosphere, where this first stage is jettisoned and the second stage takes over. The world's biggest rocket, the US Saturn V, is a three-stage rocket weighing 3000 tonnes fully laden. The first stage burns kerosene and the second and third stages burn liquid hydrogen. Liquid oxygen (lox) is the oxidizer for all stages.

rockrose A small spreading shrub, *Helianthemum chamaecistus*, up to 30 cm high with bright-yellow flowers; it is found in grassland and scrub of Europe and W Asia. Family: *Cistaceae.*

Rocky Mountains (*or* Rockies) The chief mountain system in North America. It extends roughly N–S for about 4800 km (3000 mi) between New Mexico (USA) and the Yukon (Canada), forming the Continental Divide. It rises to 4399 m (14 431 ft) at Mount Elbert.

rococo A style dominant in the fine arts and decorative arts of France between about 1700 and 1750. Developing in reaction to the baroque pomp of the Louis XIV period, it was characterized by curved forms, slender proportions, asymmetry, pastel colours, and a general effect of gaiety and delicacy. Famous rococo artists include the painters Fragonard, Boucher, and Watteau and the sculptor Clodion (1738–1814). The style spread to Austria and Germany, where the leading exponent was the architect Balthazar Neumann (1687–1753). England remained largely untouched by it.

rodent A mammal belonging to the order *Rodentia* (over 1700 species). Rodents are distributed worldwide and occupy a wide range of habitats. They range in size from about 7.5 cm (the smallest mice) to 130 cm (the capybara). Rodents have distinctive teeth. The single pairs of chisel-like incisors in each jaw continue to grow throughout life, as they are worn away by gnawing. There are no second incisor or canine teeth, leaving a gap between the front teeth and cheek teeth. Rodents are divided into three suborders: *Hystricomorpha*

(porcupines, cavies, chinchillas, etc.; 180 species); *Sciuromorpha* (squirrels, beavers, marmots, chipmunks, etc.; 366 species); and *Myomorpha* (rats, mice, lemmings, voles, etc.; 1183 species).

Rodgers, Richard Charles (1902–79) US composer of musical comedies. With the lyricist Lorenz Hart (1895–1943) he wrote such works as *The Girl Friend* (1926) and *Pal Joey* (1940). After Hart's death he collaborated with Oscar Hammerstein II in *Oklahoma* (1943), *The King and I* (1951), and other musicals.

Rodin, Auguste (1840–1917) French sculptor. He produced his first major work, *The Age of Bronze* (1877), after visiting Italy (1875), where he was influenced by the work of Michelangelo and Donatello. *The Burghers of Calais* (1884–86), his nude monument of Victor Hugo, and his dressing-gowned Balzac were all initially rejected. Nevertheless, by 1900 Rodin had established an international reputation, his bronze portrait busts and his marble *The Kiss* (1886; Tate Gallery), being particularly admired. His most personal work, *The Gates of Hell*, was left unfinished at his death.

Rodney, George Brydges, 1st Baron (1719–92) British admiral. He wrecked (1759–60) a French invasion fleet during the Seven Years' War and won victories (1780–82) against the powers that supported the American Revolution. His victory over the French off Dominica (1782) helped Britain to gain favourable terms in the concluding Peace of Versailles (1783).

Rodrigo, Joaquín (1902–   ) Spanish composer, blind since the age of three. His works include the *Concierto de Aranjuez* (for guitar and orchestra; 1940) and *Concierto Pastorale* (for flute and orchestra; 1978).

roe deer A small deer, *Capreolus capreolus*, of temperate Eurasian forests. About 70 cm high, roe deer have a dark-brown winter coat, a red-brown summer coat, and a large white rump patch; males have small antlers. They feed at night on leaves, shoots, and berries.

roentgen A unit of dose of ionizing radiation equal to the dose that produces ions of one sign carrying a charge of 2.58×10^{-4} coulomb in air.

Roentgen, Wilhelm Konrad (1845–1923) German physicist. In 1895 Roentgen was investigating the luminescence that cathode rays produce in certain substances and discovered that the luminescence persisted when the cathode rays themselves were blocked by cardboard. He correctly concluded that some other type of radiation was coming from the cathode-ray tube. He named the radiation X-rays.

Rogation Days Four days in the Christian calendar devoted to prayer and fasting. The Major Rogation is on 25 April and the Minor Rogations are on the three days before Ascension Day. In England beating the parish bounds took place at Rogationtide.

Rogers, Ginger (Virginia McMath; 1911–   ) US actress and singer. During the 1930s she partnered Fred Astaire in film musicals, including *Top Hat* (1935), *Swing Time* (1936), and *Follow the Fleet* (1936).

Rogers, Richard (1933–   ) British architect, born in Italy. With his wife Su he formed Team 4 with Norman and Wendy Foster (until 1967). His buildings include the Pompidou Centre in Paris (1971–77; with Renzo Piano) and Lloyd's in London (1986).

Rolland, Romain (1866–1944) French novelist, dramatist, and essayist. His best-known novel, *Jean Christophe* (1904–12), concerns a German composer. He won the Nobel Prize in 1915.

ROLLING STONES   *The original members in 1966.*

Rolling Stones, the   A British rock group, formed in 1962. Their early hits included "The Last Time" and "Satisfaction". The original members of the group were Mick Jagger (1944–), Keith Richard (1943–), Bill Wyman (1941–), Charlie Watts (1941–), and Brian Jones (1944–69).

Romains, Jules   (Louis Farigoule; 1885–1972) French poet, novelist, and dramatist. He was a leading exponent of the philosophical theory of *unanimisme*. His best-known works are the play *Knock* (1923) and the novel cycle *Les Hommes de bonne volonté* (1932–46).

Roman Catholic Church   The Christian Church of which the pope is the temporal leader. After the split with the Eastern Orthodox Churches (1054), Roman Catholicism was the unchallenged spiritual authority in W Europe. In the early 16th century the rising tide of Protestantism demonstrated the need for urgent reforms within the Church. The Council of Trent (1545–63) has largely determined the present dogmatic, disciplinary, and liturgical character of Roman Catholicism (*see also* Counter-Reformation), although important reforms were initiated by the second Vatican Council. The Church organization is centralized and hierarchical and the pope's decisions are reinforced by the doctrine of infallibility. Other accepted doctrines include transubstantiation and purgatory. The number of the sacraments has been fixed at seven since the 12th century. The cult of the Virgin Mary, which flourished in the middle ages, underwent a major revival in the 19th century. Until the mid-20th century Latin was the sole language of the Mass. Roman Catholicism has spread worldwide due to strenuous missionary efforts since the 16th century (*see* Jesuits) and is the largest Christian denomination. Some modernization of the Church has taken place (the use of the vernacular in the Mass, etc.), although other controversial issues (abortion, contraception, divorce, married priests, etc.) remain to be resolved.

Romance languages   Descendants of the Italic language group, in particular of the spoken form of Latin, called Vulgar Latin. The group consists of modern French, Italian, Spanish, Portuguese, Romanian, Catalan, the Rhaetian (*see* Romansch) group of dialects, Sardinian, and the now extinct Dalmatian. They are classified as a group on the basis of a shared section of basic vocabulary, which originated in the influence of the language of the Roman conquerors of the Mediterranean.

Roman Curia   (Latin: *Curia Romana*) The papal court, comprising the chief judicial and administrative bodies of the Roman Catholic Church. Extensively reformed in 1967 by Pope Paul VI, it consists of three tribunals, which are mainly concerned with judicial matters; five offices, including the Chancery, which issues papal bulls, and the offices of the Palatinate Secretaries; and nine Roman Congregations, which are permanent commissions of cardinals having specific tasks.

Roman Empire   The imperial period of ancient Roman history from 27 BC, when Octavian became emperor as Augustus, until 476 AD. Under imperial government many of the political institutions of the Roman Republic, notably the Senate, continued to function, although Augustus and his successors enjoyed supreme power as *princeps* (chief citizen). Augustus fostered peace and prosperity, which continued, despite outbreaks of rebellion, under the paternalistic rule of the Flavian (69–96 AD: Vespasian, Titus, and Domitian) and Antonine (96–180: Nerva, Trajan, Hadrian, Antoninus Pius, Marcus Aurelius) emperors. Civil war, however, followed the death of Commodus (193). Order was briefly restored by Lucius Septimus Severus (reigned 193–211), who openly acknowledged his dependence on military might. The 3rd century saw a rapid succession of army-nominated emperors, while Rome's frontiers were threatened by the Sasanians and the Goths. Diocletian (reigned 284–305) countered these attacks with the reorganization of the Empire between East (*see* Eastern Roman Empire) and West (293). It was reunited (324) under Constantine the Great, who founded a new imperial capital at Constantinople (*see* Istanbul). Civil war and economic decline followed his death and the western Empire fell prey to barbarian invasions. In 476 the last Roman emperor of the West, Romulus Augustulus (b. ?461), was deposed by the German king Odoacer. The Eastern Roman, or Byzantine, Empire survived until 1453. See p. 618.

Romania, Socialist Republic of   A country in SE Europe, with an E coastline on the Black Sea. The Carpathian Mountains and the Transylvanian Alps separate the plains in the E and S from the Transylvanian plateau in the NW. *Economy*: In agriculture, the main crops are maize, wheat, potatoes, sugar beet, and fruit. Livestock is also important. Minerals include oil and gas, salt, lignite, iron, and copper. Industry produces the main exports. There is a considerable timber industry. *History*: formed in 1861 from the principalities of Moldavia and Walachia, Romania gained independence from the Ottoman Empire in 1878 and in 1881 became a kingdom under Carol I. Romania joined (1916) the Allies in World War I and was occupied by the Germans. In 1918 it obtained Bessarabia, Bukovina, and Transylvania, which it was forced to relinquish to the Axis Powers in 1940. Shortly afterwards Carol II abdicated in favour of his son Michael and Antonescu came to power. He gave Romanian military support to Germany until Soviet forces entered the country and Antonescu's government was overthrown (1944). After World War II a communist-dominated coalition was established (1945) and in 1947 Michael abdicated. Elections in 1948 resulted in a clear communist victory. Romania became increasingly independent of the Soviet Union and resisted pressure for political reform under the Stalinist regime

0   200   400 mi

0   600 km

BRITANNIA
(after 43 AD)

UPPER
GERMANY

NORICUM
UPPER
PANNONIA

GALLIA
BELGICA

GALLIA
LUGDUNENSIS

RHAETIA

LOWER
PANNONIA

BLACK SEA

LESSER ARMENIA

Danube

Lugdunum

AQUITANIA

Alpine
Provinces

GALLIA
NARBONENSIS

ILLYRICUM

MOESIA

ARMENIA

BITHYNIA-PONTUS

ADRIATIC SEA

ITALY

THRACE

GALATIA

Tigris

CAPPADOCIA

HISPANIA
TARRACONENSIS

Rome

MACEDONIA

Pergamum

ASIA

Antioch

CILICIA

SYRIA

Euphrates

LUSITANIA

Actium

Corinth

Ephesus

LYCIA

AEGEAN SEA

ACHAEA

HISPANIA
BAETICA

Baleares
Insulae

SICILY

JUDAEA

ARABIA-PETRAEA

Gades

Carthage

Alexandria

MAURETANIA

AFRICA

CYRENAICA

EGYPT

Nile

—— imperial frontier

.... provincial frontiers

///// client (dependent) states

ROMAN EMPIRE *In 14 AD, at the death of Augustus, Roman rule or influence extended all the way round the Mediterranean.*

of President Nicolae Ceauçescu. In 1989 mass demonstrations in Bucharest, Timisoara, and elsewhere led to many deaths and culminated in a full-scale revolution. Ceauçescu was executed and a new reformist administration installed. President: Ion Iliescu. Prime minister: Petre Roman. Official language: Romanian. Official currency: leu of 100 bani. Area: 237 500 sq km (91 699 sq mi). Population (1986): 22 724 836. Capital: Bucharest. Main port: Conṣtanta.

Romanian A Romance language, spoken in Romania as Daco-Romanian. Other forms are Aromanian or Macedo-Romanian (Greece, Yugoslavia, Albania, and Bulgaria); Megleno-Romanian (N Greece); and Istro-Romanian (Istrian peninsula).

Roman law The body of laws compiled by the Romans, which forms the basis of the civil law of many modern countries throughout the world. Before about 150 BC the laws of the Twelve Tables (450 BC) were elaborated as the *jus civile* (civil law), i.e. the law applicable exclusively to Roman citizens. With increasing interests abroad, another system, the *jus gentium* (law of nations), was also applied by Roman courts. This system of international law derived from the philosophical concept of natural law (i.e. a law common to all men and to nature) and was used in cases involving provincial Roman subjects of different states and in suits between a foreigner or provincial and a Roman citizen. As Roman law developed there arose a number of anomalies, until the Byzantine emperor Justinian I (482–565 AD) sponsored the *Corpus Juris Civilis* (Body of Civil Law) or Justinian Code, published between 529 and 565 AD. This consisted of four parts: (1) the *Codex Constitutionum*, a chrono-

logical collection of the ordinances (*constitutiones*) of the emperors, with all anomalies eliminated; (2) the *Digest*, a collection of statements by jurists on points of law; (3) the *Institutes*, a textbook explaining legal institutions; and (4) the *Novellae* or *Novels*, the new ordinances issued by Justinian after the publication of the *Codex*. The most influential modern codification based on it was the *Code Napoléon*.

Roman numerals The system of numbers used by the Romans, based on letters of the alphabet: $I = 1$, $V = 5$, $X = 10$, $L = 50$, $C = 100$, $D = 500$, and $M = 1000$. Intermediate numbers are given by the sum of a larger number and the smaller number that follows it (e.g. $VI = 6$) or the difference between a larger number and the smaller number that precedes it ($IV = 4$).

Roman Republic (510–27 BC) The period of ancient Roman history between the expulsion of Tarquin the Proud and the proclamation of Augustus as the first Roman emperor. Republican government comprised two chief magistrates (later consuls) elected annually, an increasing number of subordinate magistrates, the Senate, and popular assemblies. Power lay in the hands of the patricians until the plebeians, after two centuries of struggle, achieved access to all state offices.

Roman dominance over the rest of Italy was achieved by the early 3rd century. By the mid-2nd century Cisalpine Gaul had been subdued and the Punic Wars with Carthage brought control of the Mediterranean (146) and Rome's first overseas provinces. Concomitantly, dominance over Greece was achieved and control of much of Asia Minor. In the mid-1st century Caesar completed the conquest of Transalpine Gaul. The Republic was gradually undermined, however, by provincial unrest, which, together with the military ineptness of the Senate in the late 2nd century, brought a series of ambitious army commanders to the fore.

The first of these, Marius (c. 157–86 BC), lost a bloody power struggle to the aristocrat, Sulla, whose dictatorship (83–79) was marked by legislation to strengthen the Senate. This was revoked in 70 by Pompey and Crassus, who ten years later formed the so-called first Triumvirate with Caesar. The death of Crassus (53) and Pompey's intrigues with Caesar's senatorial enemies brought civil war. Caesar's victory and subsequent short-lived dictatorship rang the knell of the Roman Republic, which was finally destroyed by Octavian's defeat of Mark Antony and his assumption of absolute power as Augustus. *See also* Roman Empire.

Romansch A Romance language belonging to the Rhaetian group, spoken in N Italy and in the Rhine Valley in Switzerland.

Romanticism A fundamental development in western art, literature, music, and their related fields of theory in the late 18th and early 19th centuries. Romanticism constituted a reaction against the unquestioned authority of reason and tradition (*see* classicism) and an affirmation of faith in man's innate powers of creativity. Its various manifestations included a passionate concern with the relationship between man and his natural environment and a new interest in the primitive and the irrational. In literature, English Romanticism is usually dated from the publication of *Lyrical Ballads* by Wordsworth and Coleridge in 1798.

Romany The language spoken by gipsies. It is related to Sanskrit and the Indo-Aryan languages of N India but diverged from these about 1000 AD, when the gipsies began their nomadic way of life. Romany has been greatly influenced in vocabulary by the languages spoken in regions the gipsies have passed through, resulting in many different dialects.

Rome (Italian name: Roma) 41 53N 12 33E The capital of Italy, on the River Tiber. It is mainly an administrative and cultural centre and, with the Vatican City within its boundaries, the focal point of the Roman Catholic Church. Relics of classical times include the Forum, the Pantheon, and the Colosseum. There are many ancient churches the origins of which go back to the early Christian era. The Renaissance produced not only many outstanding buildings, such as St Peter's Basilica, but the paintings and sculpture of such artists as Michelangelo and Raphael. *History*: according to legend Rome was founded on the Palatine Hill in 753 BC by Romulus, its first king. Seven kings were followed by the Roman Republic, and the Roman Empire was founded in the 1st century BC. As the Empire declined in the 5th century AD Rome was sacked by Germanic tribes. From the 6th century it regained importance, this time as an ecclesiastical power. In 800 Charlemagne was crowned emperor here. It remained under papal control until 1871, when it became capital of the newly unified Italy. The popes however refused formally to relinquish their temporal power until the Lateran Treaty of 1929, when their jurisdiction was confined to the Vatican City. Mussolini's March on Rome in 1922 marked the beginning of his fascist rule; the city was occupied by the Allies in World War II. Population (1986): 2 815 457.

Rome, Treaties of (1957) Two treaties signed in Rome, which led to the establishment of the European Economic Community and the European Atomic Energy Community.

Rommel, Erwin (1891–1944) German general, known as the Desert Fox. In 1940 he became commander of the Seventh Panzer Division and, in 1941, of the Afrika Corps. In N Africa he was hailed as a liberator by the Arabs and gained the respect of the enemy but in 1943, after his defeat at Alamein (1942), he was recalled and became commander of the Channel defence. His involvement in the attempt to assassinate Hitler in 1944 (*see* Stauffenberg, Claus, Graf von) led to his suicide, under pressure from Hitler.

Romney, George (1734–1802) British portrait painter. He attracted a fashionable clientele and rivalled Reynolds when he moved to London in 1762. He is best known for his numerous portraits of Emma, Lady Hamilton.

Romulus and Remus The legendary founders of Rome, the sons of Mars and Rhea Silvia, daughter of Numitor, King of Alba Longa. Amulius, who had deposed Numitor, threw the twin babies into the Tiber. They were washed ashore and suckled by a she-wolf. They eventually founded Rome at the place where they had been rescued.

rondo A musical form in which a recurring theme alternates with contrasting episodes. In its simplest form it consists of the pattern ABACADA, A being the rondo theme and B, C, and D the episodes.

rook A large blue-black Eurasian crow, *Corvus frugilegus*, about 45 cm long and having a narrow grey bill with pale patches of bare skin at its base. Rooks are highly gregarious and feed on earthworms, larvae, carrion, and grain.

Roosevelt, Franklin D(elano) (1882–1945) US statesman; Democratic president (1933–45). He was paralysed from the waist down by poliomyelitis in 1921 but despite this disability became the only US president to be re-elected three times. He helped US recovery from the Depression with the New Deal relief programmes. After the outbreak of World War II he introduced lend-lease aid to the Allies and, after the Japanese bombing of Pearl Harbor (1941), took the USA into the war. He attended the Tehran and Yalta Conferences but died in office before the conclusion of the war.

Roosevelt, Theodore (1858–1919) US statesman; Republican president (1901–09). A rancher and big-game hunter, he led the Rough Riders (1st Volunteer Cavalry) in the 1898 war with Cuba. As president he introduced his Square Deal programme for social reform. Roosevelt's foreign policy was to "speak softly and carry a big stick." He established US control over the building of the Panama Canal and made the USA a policing power in the Americas.

root (algebra) 1. One of the equal factors of a number. The square root is one of two equal factors; for example $\sqrt{9} = \pm 3$; the rth root of a number n is the number that when raised to the rth power gives n. 2. The solution of an equation, i.e. the values of the variable that will satisfy the equation. *See* quadratic equation.

root (botany) The part of a plant that provides anchorage and enables the uptake of water and nutrients from the soil. Some plants, such as the dandelion, have one main root with smaller branches—a tap root system; others, such as grasses, have a mass of similar-sized roots

−a fibrous root system. Roots can act as food-storage organs, as in the carrot and turnip (tap roots); fibrous roots that become swollen with food are called tuberous roots. Some roots act as supports.

root-mean-square value (*or* rms value)   The square root of the arithmetic average of the squares of a set of numbers; for example the rms of 2, 4, 5, 6 is $[(2^2 + 4^2 + 5^2 + 6^2)/4]^{1/2} = 4\frac{1}{2}$. The rms value is useful in continuous quantities, such as alternating electric current, in which the heating effect is proportional to the current squared.

Roque de los Muchachos Observatory   An international observatory on the island of La Palma in the Canaries at an altitude of 2400 m, set up in the 1980s by Britain, Denmark, Spain (who owns the site), and Sweden.

rorqual   A small-headed fast-moving whalebone whale of the family *Balaenopteridae* (6 species). The common rorqual (*Balaenoptera physalus*), also called fin whale or razorback, grows up to 25 m long; it has a dark back, shading to white underneath, and a small dorsal fin that shows when it is blowing. *See also* blue whale; sei whale.

Rorschach test   A psychological test intended to measure aspects of personality. Devised by the Swiss psychiatrist Hermann Rorschach (1884–1922), it consists of ten inkblots in complex shapes. The way in which the subject describes these pictures suggests his character.

Rosaceae   A cosmopolitan family of trees, shrubs, and herbs (about 2000 species). They include important fruit trees (cherries, apricots, apples, plums, etc.) and ornamentals (notably roses).

Rosario   33 00S 60 40W The second largest city in Argentina, on the Río Paraná. It is an industrial and commercial centre and the terminus of the pampas railways. Population (1980): 935 471.

Roscommon   (Irish name: Ros Comáin)   A county in the N Republic of Ireland, in Connacht. It has many lakes and extensive bogs. Agriculture is the chief occupation. Area: 2463 sq km (951 sq mi). Population (1986): 54 551. County town: Roscommon.

rose   A prickly shrub or climber of the genus *Rosa* (200–250 species), native to N temperate regions but widely cultivated. The flowers are usually white, yellow, pink, or red and the fruits are red, yellow, or black hips, rich in vitamin C, containing many seeds. Modern hybrid roses—usually with double flowers—include the hybrid teas, derived from the tea rose (*R. odorata*), and the floribundas. Wild species include dog rose and sweet briar. Family: *Rosaceae*.

rosella   A brightly coloured parakeet belonging to a genus (*Platycercus*; 7 species) occurring in Australia and New Zealand. 18 cm long, rosellas have a long broad tail, which is usually blue or green edged with white, black shoulders, and distinctive face and throat markings. They are largely ground-dwelling.

rosemary   An evergreen shrub, *Rosmarinus officinalis*, native to the Mediterranean region and W Asia. Up to 2 m high, it has bluish flowers. It is widely cultivated for its oil and for its leaves, which are used as a culinary herb. Family: *Labiatae*.

rose of Jericho   A perennial herb, *Anastatica hierochuntica*, also called resurrection plant, native to W Asia. During the dry season the leaves are shed and the whole plant forms a wickerwork-like ball that is blown

by the wind. When moistened, the plant regains its shape and produces tiny white flowers. Family: *Cruciferae*.

rose of Sharon.   *See* Hibiscus; St John's wort.

Roses, Wars of the   (1455–85) The civil wars between the Houses of Lancaster (the red rose) and York (the white rose) for possession of the English Crown. The Lancastrian Henry VI's incompetent rule resulted in factional struggles led by the Lancastrian Beauforts and Richard Plantagenet, Duke of York, and the Earl of Warwick (the Kingmaker). Open warfare broke out in 1455. York was killed in 1460 and his son seized the Crown in 1461, becoming Edward IV, and crushed the Lancastrians. In 1470–71 Henry VI was briefly restored by disaffected Yorkists but Edward returned after his victory at Tewkesbury and ruled until 1483. He was succeeded by his brother Richard III, whose reign ended with his defeat by Henry (VII) at Bosworth (1485). The remaining Yorkists were finally overcome at Stoke in 1487.

Rosetta Stone   An inscribed stone slab discovered (1799) at Rosetta (Arabic name: Rashid), near Alexandria (Egypt). It carries a decree (196 BC) of Ptolemy V Epiphanes (reigned 205–180) in Egyptian hieroglyphic and demotic, and Greek. The repetition of Ptolemy's name in the different scripts gave Thomas Young the clue to deciphering hieroglyphs.

rosewood   An attractive hardwood, usually dark reddish and often rose-scented, derived from several tropical evergreen trees of the genus *Dalbergia* (family *Leguminosae*). These include Brazilian rosewood, or blackwood (*D. nigra*), used for veneers and cabinetwork; Honduras rosewood (*D. stevensoni*), used for musical instruments; and East Indian rosewood (*D. latifolia*).

Rosh Hashana   (Hebrew: head of the year)   The Jewish New Year festival, celebrated in Sept or Oct. It is regarded as a time of penitence and preparation for Yom Kippur. A ram's horn (*shofar*) is blown in the synagogue.

Rosicrucianism   An esoteric movement for spiritual renewal that originated in Protestant Germany in the early 17th century. Its manifesto traces its source to a fictitious brotherhood founded by a certain Christian Rosenkreuz in 1484. *See also* freemasonry.

rosin   (*or* colophony)   A yellowish resin obtained as a residue from the distillation of turpentine. It is used in varnishes, soaps, soldering flux, and to rub on violin bows.

Ross Dependency   An area in Antarctica claimed by New Zealand (since 1923), lying between longitudes 160°E and 150°W and including the Ross Sea and islands S of latitude 60°S. Area: about 414 400 sq km (160 000 sq mi).

Rossetti, Dante Gabriel   (Gabriel Charles Dante R.; 1828–82) British painter and poet. In 1848 Rossetti joined with John Everett Millais, William Holman Hunt, and other artists to found the Pre-Raphaelite Brotherhood. He founded the shortlived Pre-Raphaelite journal *The Germ* (1850–51) and later published several volumes of poetry and translations, including *Poems* (1870) and *Ballads and Sonnets* (1881). His sister **Christina Georgina Rossetti** (1830–74), a poet, was influenced by the Oxford Movement. *Goblin Market and Other Poems* (1862), her first published volume, gave literary expression to Pre-Raphaelite ideals.

Rossini, Gioacchino Antonio   (1792–1868) Italian composer. He wrote 36 highly successful operas, includ-

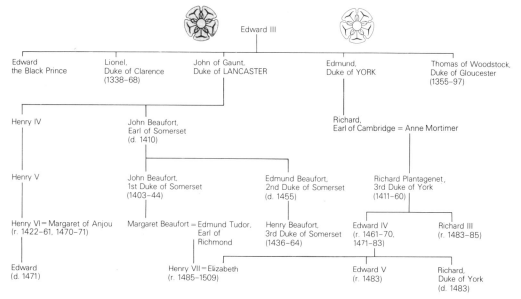

Edward III

Edward
the Black Prince

Lionel,
Duke of Clarence
(1338–68)

John of Gaunt,
Duke of LANCASTER

Edmund,
Duke of YORK

Thomas of Woodstock,
Duke of Gloucester
(1355–97)

Henry IV

John Beaufort,
Earl of Somerset
(d. 1410)

Richard,
Earl of Cambridge = Anne Mortimer

Henry V

John Beaufort,
1st Duke of Somerset
(1403–44)

Edmund Beaufort,
2nd Duke of Somerset
(d. 1455)

Richard Plantagenet,
3rd Duke of York
(1411–60)

Henry VI = Margaret of Anjou
(r. 1422–61, 1470–71)

Margaret Beaufort = Edmund Tudor,
Earl of
Richmond

Henry Beaufort,
3rd Duke of Somerset
(1436–64)

Edward IV
(r. 1461–70,
1471–83)

Richard III
(r. 1483–85)

Edward
(d. 1471)

Henry VII = Elizabeth
(r. 1485–1509)

Edward V
(r. 1483)

Richard,
Duke of York
(d. 1483)

WARS OF THE ROSES *The rival Houses of Lancaster and York.*

ing *Tancredi* (1813), *The Italian Girl in Algiers* (1813), *The Barber of Seville* (1816), *The Thieving Magpie* (1817), and *William Tell* (1829). He also invented a number of recipes, including Tournedos Rossini.

Ross Island 77 40S 168 00E A volcanic island in the W Ross Sea, at the edge of the **Ross Ice Shelf**, a vast mass of permanent ice.

Ross Sea A large inlet of the S Pacific Ocean, in the Antarctic continent between Victoria Land and Byrd Land.

Rostock 54 03N 12 07E A city and Baltic port in N East Germany. Its fine medieval buildings have been restored following damage during World War II. Population (1986): 245 606.

ROSSETTI *This photograph by Lewis Carroll shows the painter (left) and his family.*

Rostov-na-Donu 47 15N 39 45E A port in the S Sovi-

et Union, on the River Don. Its importance owes much to its position on the route from the W to the Caucasus. Population (1987): 1 004 000.

Rostropovich, Mstislav (1927–) Soviet cellist. He left the Soviet Union in 1975 and now lives in London. Prokofiev, Britten, and Shostakovich all wrote cello works for him.

Roth, Philip (1933–) US novelist. Middle-class Jewish themes predominated in his early works including *Portnoy's Complaint* (1969). In later novels, such as *The Anatomy Lesson* (1983) and *The Prague Orgy* (1985), the targets of his satire are more various.

Rothschild, Mayer Amschel (1744–1812) German merchant and banker, whose business in Frankfurt prospered during the Napoleonic Wars, making loans to the various combatants and trading in high-demand goods such as arms, wheat, and cotton. His sons later established branches of the firm in Vienna, London, Naples, and Paris.

rotifer A tiny invertebrate animal belonging to the phylum *Rotifera* (about 2000 species), also called wheel animalcule, found mainly in fresh water. Rotifers vary in shape and range between 0.1 and 0.5 mm in length. Each has a ring of cilia (corona) for wafting food particles into the mouth and providing a means of locomotion in active species.

Rotorua 38 07S 176 17E A spa city in New Zealand, in N North Island. A Maori centre, situated within a volcanic area with hot springs, it has been developed as a health resort. Population (1987): 52 200.

Rotterdam 51 55N 4 29E The chief port and second largest city in the Netherlands, on the New Meuse River. It became important during the 19th century, mainly with the opening of the 35 km (12 mi) long Nieuwe Waterweg (New Waterway) in 1872 linking it to the North Sea. During World War II the city centre was destroyed; this has since been rebuilt with an underground railway. Its buildings include the restored Groote Kerk (Great Church). Population (1987): 572 642.

Rottweiler A breed of working dog developed originally in Rottweil, Germany, with a reputation for aggression. It has a broad round body, a strong neck, and a large head with a deep muzzle. The coarse short coat is black with tan markings. Height: 63–68 cm (dogs); 58–63 cm (bitches).

Rouault, Georges (Henri) (1871–1958) French artist. A major 20th-century religious artist, he executed many paintings of clowns and prostitutes, which expressed his sympathy with social outcasts. As a graphic artist his main achievement was his series of etchings (1916–27), entitled *Miserere* and *Guerre*.

Rouen (Latin name: Rotomagus) 49 26N 1 05E A city and port in NW France, on the River Seine. The ancient capital of Normandy, it was here that Joan of Arc was tried and burned in 1431. Many of its notable buildings, including the cathedral (13th–16th centuries), survived the damage of World War II. Population (1982): 105 083.

rounders A nine-a-side bat-and-ball field game, which is probably the prototype of baseball. The two teams take turns at batting and fielding and a match consists of two innings per team. The hard ball is delivered underarm to each batsman in turn until all are out. The batsmen try to score rounders by hitting it and running round the four bases without being caught or run out.

Roundheads The parliamentary party during the English Civil War. The name referred originally to the short haircuts of the apprentices who demonstrated against the king at Westminster in 1640.

Round Table Conference (1930–32) Three meetings held in London to discuss a form of government acceptable to India. The meetings were attended by representatives of the British Government and of India's major political parties and all its states. The result of the Conference was the Government of India Act of 1935.

roundworm. *See* nematode.

Rousseau, Henri (1844–1910) French painter. From 1886 he exhibited at the Salon des Indépendants but his work, resembling folk art in technique (*see* primitivism), was ridiculed. After 1894, when he exhibited *War* (Louvre), followed by the *Sleeping Gypsy* (1897; New York), he received more serious attention. The childlike quality of his jungle landscapes influenced many 20th-century painters.

Rousseau, Jean Jacques (1712–78) French philosopher and writer. Through his acquaintance with Diderot, Rousseau joined the Encyclopedists. In the *Discourse on the Origin and Foundations of Inequality amongst Men* (1754) he argued that man's perfect nature is spoiled by corrupt society. *Émile* (1762), a novel on education, expanded his views on ideal unfallen human nature. Such political works as *Du contrat social* (1762) found favour with revolutionaries. His romantic outlook inspired Shelley, Byron, and Wordsworth.

rowan. *See* mountain ash.

Rowlandson, Thomas (1756–1827) British caricaturist. Using a reed pen and delicate washes of colour, he produced the satirical *Dr Syntax* series (1812–21) and the *English Dance of Death* (1815–16). He also illustrated books by Smollett, Goldsmith, and Sterne.

Royal Academy An art society in Burlington House, London, that holds annual summer exhibitions of contemporary British art, as well as loan exhibitions of modern artists and the old masters. Founded in 1768, it moved to its present premises in 1867.

Royal Academy of Dramatic Art (RADA) The leading British school of acting, founded in London in 1904 by Sir Herbert Beerbohm Tree. It has received a government subsidy since 1924.

Royal Air Force (RAF) A British armed service formed in 1918 by the amalgamation of the Royal Flying Corps (1912) with the Royal Naval Air Service (1914). It contributed to the final operations on the western front in World War I and played a decisive role in World War II. It is now divided into Strike Command (the operational command), Maintenance Command, and Training Command and is administered by the Air Force Department of the Ministry of Defence. The **Women's Royal Air Force** was formed in 1949 in succession to the Women's Auxiliary Air Force (WAAF) of World War II and the short-lived Women's Royal Air Force (1918–20). *See also* aircraft.

royal antelope The world's smallest antelope, *Neotragus pygmaeus*, of West African forests. 25–30 cm high, it is red-brown with white underparts; males have short spiky horns. They are nocturnal.

Royal Ballet The leading British ballet company and school. Based at the Royal Opera House, Covent Garden, since 1946, it was known as the Sadler's Wells Ballet until 1956. It was founded by Dame Ninette de Valois in 1931.

Royal British Legion An organization for ex-servicemen and women, founded in 1921 largely through the efforts of Douglas Haig. It provides assistance with housing or employment problems and runs homes for the sick and aged. It also manufactures the Flanders poppies sold before Remembrance Sunday.

Royal Canadian Mounted Police (*or* Mounties) Canadian police force. Founded in 1873 as the North West Mounted Police, it has become famous for the efficiency of its members, dressed in their distinctive scarlet tunics, blue breeches, and wide-brimmed hats.

Royal Geographical Society A British learned society, established in 1830 and incorporated in 1859, for the advancement of geographical knowledge. Among other functions it provides grants to expeditions. Two Royal Medals are awarded annually by the Queen to geographers recommended by the Society.

Royal Greenwich Observatory An observatory founded in 1675 by Charles II at Greenwich, London, in a building designed by Sir Christopher Wren. The meridian through Greenwich (0°) was internationally adopted as the prime meridian in 1884. The observatory was based at Herstmonceux, Sussex (1948–86), before its main telescope was moved to the new Roque de los Muchachos Observatory in the Canary Islands; the observatory moved to Cambridge in 1990.

Royal Horticultural Society A society in the UK that exists to further interest in vegetables and ornamental plants. Founded in 1804, it now has its headquarters in Vincent Square, London. The society promotes new varieties and rare plants at various shows, the most famous being the annual Chelsea Flower Show.

Royal Institution One of the first scientific research centres, founded by Benjamin Thompson, Count Rumford, in 1799. Several famous scientists have worked at its premises in Albermarle Street, London, including Davy, Faraday, and Bragg.

ROYAL GREENWICH OBSERVATORY *Wren's original interior.*

royal jelly A thick white mixture of proteins, carbohydrates, minerals, and vitamins that is secreted by worker bees and fed to the larvae. Larvae destined to become queens are fed entirely on royal jelly. *See also* honeybee.

Royal Marines A corps of troops, founded in England in 1664, which serves on land, at sea, or in the air. Their ranks correspond to those of the army but they are administered by the Navy Board. They served in both World Wars, in the Korean War and in Northern Ireland.

Royal Mint The factory in which the UK's coins are made. It was formerly in the Tower of London, moving to Tower Hill in 1811 and to Llantrisant, South Wales, in 1968.

Royal National Lifeboat Institution A voluntary organization, founded in 1824, that operates a 24-hour lifeboat service around British coasts. Each lifeboat has a full-time mechanic but the other crew members are volunteers.

Royal National Theatre Company A British government-subsidized theatre company established as the National Theatre Company in 1963. Laurence Olivier, its first director, was succeeded by Peter Hall in 1973 and Richard Eyre in 1988. The company's new building, designed by Sir Denys Lasdun and opened in 1976, comprises an open-stage theatre called the Olivier, a proscenium-stage theatre called the Lyttleton, and a studio theatre for experimental plays called the Cottesloe. The prefix Royal was added in 1988.

Royal Navy (RN) The senior of Britain's three armed services. Founded in the 9th century by Alfred the Great, the RN emerged as "the wooden walls of England" in the 16th century with such victories as that over the Spanish Armada (1588). The 17th century saw further victories against the Dutch, but little improvement in the lot of the sailors ("Jack Tars"). Mutiny finally broke out at the Nore and Spithead (1797) even as the RN entered its greatest era with a series of victories under Nelson against Napoleonic France. The supreme sea power during the 19th century, the RN fought its last set-piece battle at Jutland (1916) during World War I. The modern RN is probably the most efficient navy in the world and undertakes fishery protection, mine sweeping, and NATO roles.

Royal Opera The leading British opera company, based at the Royal Opera House in Covent Garden. The company acquired its present name in 1969. Conductors with the Royal Opera have included Sir Thomas Beecham, Karl Rankl, and Sir Georg Solti. Chairman: Sir John Sainsbury.

Royal Shakespeare Company (RSC) A British theatre company, founded in 1960 from the company at the Shakespeare Memorial Theatre in Stratford-upon-Avon. Peter Hall, its first director, was succeeded in 1968 by Trevor Nunn, who was joined by Terry Hands in 1978. The company performs Shakespeare and modern plays at Stratford and at the Barbican in London and tours frequently.

Royal Society The oldest and most important scientific society in the UK. It originated in 1645 and was incorporated by royal charter in 1662, early members including Sir Christopher Wren and Samuel Pepys. With the presidency from 1703–27 of Isaac Newton, the Royal Society achieved great standing and financial security. The Society publishes scientific papers in the *Proceedings* and the *Philosophical Transactions*, maintains a large library, disburses grants, and awards medals for scientific achievement.

Royal Society for the Prevention of Cruelty to Animals (RSPCA) A British charity founded in 1824 to investigate reports of cruelty to animals. Funded by voluntary contributions, it has branches in the Commonwealth. Executive director: F. Dixon Ward.

Royal Society for the Protection of Birds (RSPB) A British charity founded in 1889 to protest against the wholesale killing of birds for their plumage. Since then it has promoted the conservation of wild birds throughout Britain. Executive director: Ian Prestt.

Royce, Sir (Frederick) Henry (1863–1933) British car manufacturer, who founded, with the Hon. Charles Rolls (1877–1910), Rolls-Royce Ltd (1906). In 1884 Royce opened an engineering business in Manchester and in 1904 began to build cars, which much impressed Rolls and led to the merger of their businesses. Royce and his team designed many famous cars and the aero-engine that became the Merlin (used in Spitfires and Hurricanes in World War II).

RSC. *See* Royal Shakespeare Company.

RSPB. *See* Royal Society for the Protection of Birds.

RSPCA. *See* Royal Society for the Prevention of Cruelty to Animals.

Ruapehu, Mount 39 18S 175 36E An active volcano in New Zealand, the highest peak in North Island. Height: 2797 m (9175 ft).

Rub' al-Khali The S part of the Arabian Desert, mainly in Saudi Arabia. It constitutes the largest continuous area of sand in the world. Area: about 800 000 sq km (308 815 sq mi).

rubber A synthetic or natural organic polymer that is elastic and tough. The name comes from its ability to erase pencil marks. **Natural rubber**, which consists mainly of polyisoprene–$(CH_2CH:C.CH_3:CH_2)_n$–is made from the latex of the rubber tree (*Hevea brasiliensis*) grown in SE Asia. The rubber is coagulated from latex (using acids) and pressed into sheets. Vulcanization increases its durability. **Synthetic rubbers** are made from petrochemicals (*see* oil). Styrene-butadiene rubber (SBR), now the commonest synthetic rubber, was introduced during World War II. See p. 624.

RUBBER *Latex being extracted in Malaysia.*

rubber plant A tree, *Ficus elastica*, native to India and Malaysia, where it grows to a height of 35 m in forests. Its latex is the source of Assam or India rubber. Family: *Moraceae*.

rubella. *See* German measles.

Rubens, Peter Paul (1577–1640) Flemish painter, who lived chiefly in Antwerp. The greatest of the baroque artists, Rubens first worked for the Mantuan court in Italy (1600–08). Returning to Antwerp, he painted his first major works, *The Raising of the Cross* and *Descent from the Cross* (both Antwerp Cathedral). Many commissions followed, including a cycle for Marie de' Medici (Louvre) and the ceiling of the Banqueting House, Whitehall, for Charles I. His most personal works are his portraits of his family, notably *Helena Fourment with a Fur Cloak* (Kunsthistorisches Museum, Vienna) and such landscapes as *The Château de Steen* (National Gallery, London).

Rubicon A stream in N central Italy, which formed the boundary between Italy and Cisalpine Gaul in the time of the Roman Republic. In 49 BC Julius Caesar precipitated civil war by leading his army across the Rubicon into Italy, an illegal act. Hence *crossing the Rubicon* has come to mean taking an irrevocable step.

rubidium (Rb) A highly electropositive alkali metal, discovered spectroscopically by R. W. Bunsen and G. R. Kirchhoff in 1861. The element is soft and silvery-white. It ignites spontaneously in air and reacts violently with water. The isotope ^{87}Rb is radioactive with a half-life of 5×10^{11} years and is used in rubidium-strontium dating. Rubidium forms ionic salts and four oxides (Rb_2O, Rb_2O_2, Rb_2O_3, RbO_2). At no 37; at wt 85.47; mp 38.89°C; bp 688°C.

rubidium-strontium dating A method of radiometric dating, used mainly for rocks, fossils, etc. It utilizes the fact that naturally occurring rubidium contains about 28% of the radioactive isotope rubidium-87, which undergoes beta decay to strontium-87. Thus by measuring the ratio of rubidium-87 to strontium-87 in the sample, its age may be estimated.

Rubinstein, Artur (1888–1982) Polish-born US pianist. He acquired a worldwide reputation, particularly as a performer of Chopin.

ruby A red transparent variety of corundum, the colour being due to traces of chromium. It is used as a gemstone and in lasers, watches, and other precision instruments. Prior to the 14th century rubies were called carbuncles.

rudd A game fish, *Scardinius erythrophthalmus*, found in fresh waters of Europe and W Asia. It has a stout body, 35–40 cm long, golden- or olive-brown above and silvery white below, deep-red fins, and golden eyes.

Rudolf, Lake. *See* Turkana, Lake.

rue An evergreen shrub, *Ruta graveolens*, also known as herb of grace, native to S Europe. 90 cm high, it has yellow flowers. The leaves yield a bitter oil, once used as a spice and in medicines. Family: *Rutaceae*.

ruff An Old World sandpiper, *Philomachus pugnax*, that breeds in coastal wetlands of N Eurasia and winters on mudflats of South Africa and S Asia. The female (called a reeve) is 25 cm long and has a grey-brown plumage; the larger male has a double crest and a multicoloured collar in the breeding season.

Rugby 52 23N 1 15W A town in the English Midlands, in Warwickshire. According to tradition the game of rugby football originated here in 1823 at the famous public school (1567), which was described in *Tom Brown's Schooldays*. Rugby's industries include engineering and cement. Population (1981): 59 564.

Rügen An East German island in the Baltic Sea, 2.5 km (1.5 mi) off Stralsund, to which it is connected by a road and rail causeway. Area: 926 sq km (358 sq mi). Population (1983): 84 501.

Ruhr, River A river in West Germany, rising in the Sauerland and flowing NW and W to the River Rhine. The Ruhr Valley (German name: Ruhrgebiet) is the centre of the German iron and steel industry. Length: 235 km (146 mi).

Ruisdael, Jacob van (?1628–82) The greatest of Dutch landscape painters. His baroque compositions are noted for their dramatic contrasts of light and shade. *The Jewish Cemetery* (c. 1660) is a striking evocation of human mortality.

rum A colourless spirit distilled from molasses derived from sugar cane. Better-quality rums are aged in oak casks for several years.

Rumania. *See* Romania, Socialist Republic of.

Rumford, Benjamin Thompson, Count (1753–1814) American-born scientist, who spied for the British in the American Revolution. In England he carried out scientific research in ballistics and the theory of heat. Suspected of spying for the French, he left England in 1785 for Paris and then Bavaria, where he became a count of the Holy Roman Empire. In 1795 he returned to England, where he helped to found the Royal Institution (1799).

ruminant A hoofed mammal belonging to the suborder *Ruminantia* (about 175 species), which includes deer, cattle, antelopes, sheep, and goats. Ruminants are characterized by possession of a four-chambered stomach. Ruminants regurgitate their food periodically to "chew the cud," which helps to break up the plant cell walls.

Rump Parliament. *See* Long Parliament.

Rum Rebellion (1808) A rebellion in Australia in which William Bligh, governor of New South Wales, was imprisoned by officers of the New South Wales Corps. It was incited by Bligh's suppression of the rum traffic.

Runcie, Robert Alexander Kennedy (1921–) British churchman; Archbishop of Canterbury (1980–). He was formerly bishop of St Albans (1970–80).

Rundstedt, (Karl Rudolf) Gerd von (1875–1953) German field marshal, who was recalled from retirement at the outbreak of World War II, becoming (1942) commander in chief in France. He was captured in 1945 but his ill health secured his release.

runic alphabet An alphabetical writing system used for Norse and certain other Germanic languages. It originated, probably as a modified version of the Etruscan or the Roman alphabet, in the 2nd or 3rd century AD, and went out of use gradually after the 14th century. The runes were always associated with magical powers.

runner bean A climbing plant, *Phaseolus coccineus*, also known as scarlet runner, native to South America and widely cultivated as an annual vegetable crop. Growing up to 3 m high, it bears usually red flowers, which give rise to bean pods, 20–60 cm long, that are eaten cooked. Family: *Leguminosae. See also* bean.

Runnymede (*or* Runnimede) 51 26N 0 33W A meadow in SE England, on the S bank of the River Thames. The Magna Carta was granted here by King John (1215).

Runyon, Damon (1884–1946) US humorous writer. His stories about New York characters were first collected in *Guys and Dolls* (1932).

Rupert, Prince (1619–82) Cavalry officer, who fought for the Royalists in the Civil War; he was the son of Frederick the Winter King of the Palatinate and Elizabeth, daughter of James I of England. A bold and charismatic leader, he lacked the ability to maintain control when battle commenced. He was defeated at Marston Moor (1644) and Naseby (1645) and after Charles' surrender he was banished from England. He returned at the Restoration (1660) and served as an admiral in the Dutch Wars.

Rupert's Land (*or* Prince Rupert's Land) A region in N and W Canada around Hudson Bay. In 1670 it was granted by Charles II to the Hudson's Bay Company, the first governor of which was Prince Rupert.

rupture. *See* hernia.

rush A grasslike plant of the genus *Juncus* (over 300 species), found worldwide in damp temperate and cold regions. Rushes have tufts of slender rigid stalks, up to about 1 m high, bearing long flat leaves and produce many-seeded capsules. Family: *Juncaceae*. The name is also applied to similar plants, including the bulrush, flowering rush, and woodrush.

Rushdie, Salman (1947–) British novelist, born in India. His first novel, *Grimus* (1975), was followed by the much acclaimed Booker prizewinner *Midnight's Children* (1981), *Shame* (1983), and *The Satanic Verses* (1988), which many Muslims (especially fundamentalists) interpreted as blasphemous; after the Ayatollah Khomeini offered a reward for killing the author, the UK, supported by other EC countries, broke diplomatic relations with Iran.

Ruskin, John (1819–1900) British art and social critic. He wrote *Modern Painters* (1843–60) to defend the paintings of J. M. W. Turner. In *The Stones of Venice* (1851–53) he promoted the gothic style in architecture. In *Unto This Last* (1862) and other volumes of social criticism he denounced materialism and laissez-faire economics. During his last years he became insane.

Russell, Bertrand Arthur William, 3rd Earl (1872–1970) British philosopher, grandson of Lord John Russell (1792–1878). His first major philosophical work, *Principia Mathematica* (1910–13), written with A. N. Whitehead, presented pure mathematics as a de-

BERTRAND RUSSELL   *At a rally (1962) for nuclear disarmament.*

velopment of logic. *Our Knowledge of the External World* (1914) attempted a new approach to epistemology. From his pupil Wittgenstein, he also acquired a lasting interest in language. His prolific writings always stimulated interest, often to his own detriment. He was imprisoned (1918) for his outspoken pacifism and again in 1961 for civil disobedience during the Campaign for Nuclear Disarmament. He was awarded the Nobel Prize for Literature in 1950.

RUSSIAN REVOLUTION   *The February Revolution; an uprising in Petrograd.*

Russell, Ken (1927–) British film director. His major films include *Women in Love* (1969), *Tommy* (1974), and *The Rainbow* (1989) and controversial biographical films, such as *The Music Lovers* (1970), about Tchaikovsky, *Mahler* (1974), *Valentino* (1977), and *Gothic* (1986).

Russia. *See* Soviet Union.

Russian The main language of the Soviet Union, belonging to the East Slavonic family. It is a highly inflected language and is written in the Cyrillic alphabet. The standard form is based on the dialect of Moscow.

Russian Blue A breed of short-haired cat, thought to have been introduced to the UK by Russian sailors. The

Russian Blue has a slender body and a short flat·head with large pointed ears and green eyes. The coat is uniformly blue-grey.

Russian Orthodox Church An offshoot of the Greek Orthodox Church, dating from the baptism of the emperor Vladimir (later St Vladimir) in 988. Since 1328 the metropolitan see has been at Moscow.

Russian Revolution (1917) The revolution between March and November (Old Style February and October), 1917, that established the world's first communist state. It began with the February Revolution, when riots in Petrograd led to the establishment of a provisional government of Duma deputies, which forced Nicholas II to abdicate. The failure of Prince Lvov (1861–1925) and then Aleksandr Kerenski (1881–1970) to end Russia's participation in World War I and to deal with food shortages led to the October (*or* Bolshevik) Revolution, in which Lenin seized power and established the Soviet of People's Commissars. In the subsequent civil war (1918–21) the Red Army was ultimately victorious against the anticommunist White Russians but with the loss of some 100 000 lives. See p. 625.

Russo-Finnish War (*or* Winter War; 1939–40) The war between the Soviet Union and Finland at the beginning of World War II. It was won by the Soviet Union, the aggressor, which gained part of the Karelian Isthmus.

Russo-Japanese War (1904–05) A confrontation arising from conflicting Japanese and Russian interests in Manchuria. In 1904 Japan attacked Port Arthur (now Lüda), which fell in January, 1905. In May a Japanese fleet destroyed Russia's Baltic Fleet in the Tsushima Straits, forcing Russia's surrender.

rust A reddish-brown solid consisting of hydrated iron oxide. Rusting is a special case of corrosion; the mechanism involves the setting up of a cell in which iron is the anode and a metal impurity the cathode. Both water and oxygen must be present for rust to form although the most serious damage, pitting, is always found in an oxygen-free portion of metal.

rust fungi Fungi, belonging to the order *Uredinales*, that are parasites of plants, forming spots, blotches, and pustules on the stems and foliage of their hosts. Several are important pests of cereal crops, including black rust (*Puccinia graminis*) of wheat. Other important wheat rusts include yellow rust (*P. striiformis*) and brown rust (*P. recondita*). Class: *Basidiomycetes*.

Ruth, Babe (George Herman R.; 1895–1948) US baseball player. Known as the "Sultan of Swat", he became the top player of the 1920s.

ruthenium (Ru) A hard metal of the platinum group, first separated in 1844 by K. K. Klaus (1796–1864). It is used to harden platinum and palladium for use in electrical contacts and is a versatile catalyst. The tetroxide (RuO_4) is toxic. The element shows a wide range of valence states. At no 44; at wt 101.07; mp 2310°C; bp 3900°C.

Rutherford, Ernest, 1st Baron (1871–1937) English physicist, born in New Zealand. He made fundamental discoveries concerning the nature of radioactivity, distinguishing between the three types of radiation, which he named alpha, beta, and gamma rays. Working with Hans Geiger (1882–1945) he discovered that alpha radiation consisted of positively charged helium atoms. In 1906, he deduced the existence of a heavy positively charged core in the atom, which he called the nucleus. In

1908, Rutherford received the Nobel Prize for Chemistry. He was made a baron in 1931.

rutherfordium. *See* kurchatovium.

rutile A brown to black form of natural titanium dioxide, TiO_2. It is found in igneous and metamorphic rocks, in veins, and as fibres in quartz, known as Venus' hair.

Rutland A former county in the East Midlands of England. In 1974 it became part of Leicestershire. It was the smallest county in England.

Rwanda, Republic of A small landlocked country in E central Africa. Lake Kivu forms most of its W boundary and the land is chiefly mountainous. Most inhabitants are Bantu-speaking Hutu or Nilotic Tutsi. *Economy*: chiefly subsistence agriculture. The principal cash crop is coffee. Methane gas has been found under Lake Kivu. *History*: a Tutsi kingdom from the 16th century, the area came under German East Africa in 1890. From 1919, it was administered by Belgium as the N part of Ruanda-Urundi. In 1959 the Tutsi kingdom was overthrown by the Hutu, who in 1961 declared Rwanda a republic; independence was recognized by Belgium in 1962. In 1973 Maj Gen Juvénal Habyalimana (1937–) came to power in a bloodless coup; he later became president. Official languages: Kinyarwanda and French. Official currency: Rwanda franc of 100 centimes. Area: 26 330 sq km (10 166 sq mi). Population (1986 est): 6 324 000. Capital: Kigali.

Ryazan 54 37N 39 43E A city in the W central Soviet Union. Founded in 1095, it was the capital of a principality until annexed by Russia in 1521. Population (1987 est): 508 000.

Rybinsk. *See* Andropov.

Ryder, Sue. *See* Cheshire, (Geoffrey) Leonard, Group Capt.

Ryder Cup A biennial golf tournament between members of the British and US Professional Golfers' Associations, first played in 1927. In 1979 the British team was opened to continental golfers.

rye A cereal grass, *Secale cereale*, native to W Asia but widely cultivated in cool temperate and upland regions. 1–2 m high, it bears a terminal spike, 10–15 cm long. The grain is milled to produce a dark-coloured flour, used in making black bread or for livestock feed.

Rye 50 57N 0 44E A town in SE England, in East Sussex. Once a Cinque Port, it is now about 3 km (2 mi) inland from Rye Bay, on the Strait of Dover. Population (1985): 4490.

Ryle, Gilbert (1900–76) British philosopher. His philosophy centred on detailed analysis of mental concepts. *The Concept of Mind* (1949) refuted Descartes' idea of the human being consisting of mind and body ("the ghost in the machine").

Ryle, Sir Martin (1918–84) British astronomer; astronomer royal (1972–84). A pioneer of radio telescopy, his most important work was the development of a technique for studying distant radio sources. In 1974 he shared the Nobel Prize for Physics.

Ryukyu Islands A group of volcanic and coral islands in the W Pacific Ocean, extending almost 650 km (400 mi) from Kyushu to N Taiwan. An independent kingdom until the 14th century, the islands were dominated by the Chinese before becoming a part of Japan (1879). They were under US control (1945–72). Area: 2196 sq km (849 sq mi). Population (1985): 1 179 000. Chief city: Naha (on Okinawa).

S

Saarbrücken 49 15N 6 58E An industrial city in SW West Germany, the capital of Saarland on the River Saar near the French border. It was under French administration 1801–15, 1919–35, 1945–57. Population (1986): 185 100.

Saarinen, Eero (1910–61) Innovative US architect, born in Finland. His most famous building is the Trans World Airlines terminal at Kennedy Airport, New York (1956–62), which has reinforced concrete vaults spreading outwards to suggest flight.

Sabah (former name: North Borneo) A state in Malaysia, in NE Borneo on the South China and Sulu Seas. Forested and mountainous, it is largely undeveloped but timber and rubber are important. It has copper and oil resources. North Borneo was first colonized by the British in 1877, becoming a protectorate in 1882. In 1963 it joined Malaysia under its present name. Area: 76 115 sq km (29 388 sq mi). Population (1985 est): 1 222 718. Capital: Kota Kinabalu.

Sabines The peoples of the scattered hilltop communities NE of ancient Rome. The legendary abduction of the Sabine women by Roman settlers indicates the early interbreeding of Sabines with Romans. Sabine influence on Roman religion was especially strong. They became Roman citizens in 268 BC.

Sabin vaccine A vaccine that prevents poliomyelitis, developed by a US virologist, A. B. Sabin (1906–   ). It contains a weakened polio virus that stimulates the body's defence against polio without causing the disease. Sabin vaccine is given by mouth (often on a sugar lump) in three consecutive doses. *See also* Salk vaccine.

sable A carnivorous mammal, *Martes zibellina*, native to N Eurasia. It is less than 50 cm long and has thicker legs and longer ears than other martens. Its coat is thick, soft, and glossy and is valued as fur (Siberian sable).

sabre-toothed tiger An extinct cat that lived 30 million years ago and became extinct in the Pleistocene epoch (1 million years ago). *Smilodon*, a Pleistocene form, was about the size of a tiger, with very long upper canine teeth used to pierce the thick hide of its prey.

saccharin An organic compound ($C_7H_5NO_3S$) used as a sweetening agent in the food industry and as a sugar substitute. It has about five hundred times the sweetening power of table sugar.

sackbut. *See* trombone.

sacrament In Christian theology, a ritual having a special significance as a visible sign of an inner grace in its participants. The Roman Catholic Church and Orthodox Churches accept seven sacraments: baptism, confirmation, penance, the Eucharist, marriage, ordination, and anointing of the sick (formerly extreme unction). Baptism and the Eucharist are the only commonly accepted sacraments among the Protestant Churches.

Sacramento 38 32N 121 30W A city in the USA, the capital of California on the Sacramento River. Founded in 1839, it grew after the discovery of gold nearby in 1848. Linked by canal (1963) to San Francisco Bay, it is a deepwater port and serves an extensive agricultural area. Population (1986 est): 323 550.

sacred ibis An African ibis, *Threskiornis aethiopica*, that was revered in ancient Egypt. 75 cm long, it is pure white except for dark ornamental plumes on its back, dark wing tips, and a black head, neck, and bill. It feeds in flocks along rivers.

Sadat, Anwar (1918–81) Egyptian statesman; president (1970–81). Sadat was twice vice president (1964–66, 1969–70) before becoming president on Nasser's death. He moved Egypt away from the Soviet Union and towards the USA, under the influence of which he negotiated a peace agreement with Israel in 1979. He shared the 1978 Nobel Peace Prize with Israel's President Begin. He was assassinated (1981) by Islamic extremists.

Sadducees An ancient Jewish religious and political party. They formed a conservative and aristocratic group centring on the priesthood in Jerusalem. With the destruction of the temple the party ceased to exist. *See also* Pharisees.

Sade, Donatien Alphonse François, Marquis de (1740–1814) French novelist. Most of his works of sexual fantasy and perversion, which include *Justine*, *La Philosophie dans le boudoir*, and *Les 120 Journées de Sodome*, were written in the 1780s and 1790s, during his many years of imprisonment for sexual offences. The sexual perversion "sadism," in which sexual pleasure is derived from causing or observing pain, is named after him.

Sadler's Wells Theatre A theatre in London where Lilian Baylis (1874–1937) established an opera and ballet company in 1931. From the 1680s the medicinal wells on the site were exploited and its owner, Mr Sadler, later erected a music hall. In 1753 this became a theatre, which closed (1878) but was restored by Baylis. Since the removal of the Sadler's Wells Opera Company to the London Coliseum in 1969, the theatre has been used by touring companies. The Sadler's Wells Royal Ballet (founded in 1946 as the Sadler's Wells Theatre Ballet) moved to Birmingham in 1990. *See also* English National Opera; Royal Ballet.

SACRED IBIS

safflower An annual herbaceous plant, *Carthamus tinctorius*, native to Asia and Africa. Its flowers yield a red dye. It is cultivated for its seeds, which yield safflower oil, used in paints, varnishes, cooking oils, and margarines. Family: *Compositae*.

saffron The dried orange-yellow stigmas of the saffron crocus (*C. sativa*), used for flavouring and colouring foods and liqueurs and formerly as a fabric dye. The crocus, which has purple flowers, is cultivated mainly in France, Spain, and Italy. About 100 000 flowers are needed to produce 1 kg of saffron.

Sagan, Françoise (Françoise Quoirez; 1935–) French writer. Her best-selling novels include *Bonjour Tristesse* (1954), *Aimez-Vous Brahms?* (1959), *La Femme fardée* (1981), and *With Fondest Regards* (1986).

sagas Heroic prose narratives in Old Norse, the best of which were written down in Iceland in the 12th and 13th centuries. characteristic subject matter was drawn from ancient Scandinavian oral traditions and included fictionalized accounts of the deeds of Norwegian kings, for example *Heimskringla* by Snorri Sturluson (1178–1241), and heroic legends of the pagan past.

sage A perennial herb or shrub, *Salvia officinalis*, native to the Mediterranean region and widely cultivated for its leaves, which are used for flavouring foods. It has blue, pink, or white flowers. *See also* Salvia.

sage grouse A large grouse, *Centrocercus urophasianus*, occurring in sagebrush deserts of western USA. It is 75 cm long and the male has ornamental wattles and a long slender tail, which is fanned out during its courtship display.

sago A starchy food obtained mainly from the Indonesian sago palms (*Metoxylon sagu* and *M. rumphii*), cultivated in Malaysia. It is extracted from the pithy stems.

Sahara The largest desert in the world, covering most of N Africa. The terrain consists chiefly of a plateau with central mountains rising to 3415 m (11 204 ft) and some areas of sand dunes, such as the Libyan Desert in the NE. The vegetation is sparse. Geological evidence shows that the Sahara was once well vegetated and that parts were formerly under the sea. There are large deposits of oil and gas in Algeria and Libya and phosphates in Morocco and Western Sahara. Rainfall is minimal and irregular, but there are numerous scattered oases. Area: about 9 000 000 sq km (3 474 171 sq mi).

saiga A small antelope, *Saiga tatarica*, of Asian deserts and steppes. Saigas are slightly built with a pale woolly coat and a remarkable swollen snout with convoluted nasal tracts, thought to be an adaptation for warming inhaled air or to be related to their keen sense of smell. Males have straight ridged horns. Saigas form large herds to migrate southwards in winter.

Saigon. *See* Ho Chi Minh City.

Saimaa, Lake A lake in SE Finland. It is the primary lake in a system spread over most of S Finland. Area: about 1760 sq km (680 sq mi).

saint In Christian belief, a person characterized by special holiness. In the Roman Catholic Church saints formally admitted to the calendar of saints by canonization can be invoked as intercessors. Protestantism rejects the invocation of saints, although the Church of England's calendar recognizes a number of saints' days.

St Albans 51 46N 0 21W A city in SE England, in Hertfordshire. Across the River Ver stood the important Romano-British town of Verulamium, where the martyrdom of St Alban took place; Roman remains include

a theatre and mosaic pavement. The Benedictine abbey, founded in honour of the saint in 793 AD, was made a cathedral in 1877 and has the second longest nave in Britain.

St Andrews 56 20N 2 48W A resort in E Scotland, in Fife Region on St Andrews Bay. An ancient ecclesiastical centre, its university (1412) is the oldest in Scotland. The famous Royal and Ancient Golf Club was founded here in 1754. Population (1985 est): 16 000.

St Bartholomew's Day Massacre The slaughter of Huguenots that began on 24 August, 1572, in Paris. The massacre was ordered by Charles IX of France under the influence of his mother, Catherine de' Medici. Some 3000 Huguenots died in Paris and many more were murdered in the provinces.

St Basil's Cathedral The cathedral of the Russian Orthodox Church in Moscow built between 1554 and 1560 for Ivan the Terrible. It is named after the Russian saint, who was buried there at the end of the 16th century.

St Bernard A breed of large working dog developed in Europe from Asian ancestors and employed as a rescue dog by the hospice of St Bernard in the Swiss Alps since the 17th century. It is massively built, having a large head with drooping ears. The coat is white marked with red-brown or brindle. Height: 65 cm minimum.

St Catherines 43 10N 79 15W A city and port in E Canada, in S Ontario at the entrance to the Welland Ship Canal. Founded in 1790, it is a fruit-farming and industrial centre and houses Brock University (1962). Population (1986): 123 455.

St Christopher. *See* St Kitts-Nevis.

St Croix (*or* Santa Cruz) A West Indian island, the largest of the US Virgin Islands. The economy is based on tourism and agriculture. Area: 207 sq km (80 sq mi). Population (1985): 55 300. Chief town: Christiansted.

Saint-Cyr, École de French military academy founded in 1803 and established in 1808 at Saint-Cyr-l'École, near Versailles. Its buildings were destroyed in World War II and it is now at Coëtquidan, Brittany.

ST DAVID'S *The cathedral.*

St David's 51 54N 5 16W A village in SW Wales in Dyfed, the smallest cathedral city in Britain. The 12th-century cathedral, the largest in Wales, was an important medieval pilgrimage centre for the shrine of St David. Population (1984): 1595.

St Dunstan's (for Men and Women Blinded on War Service) A British organization for the training, settlement, and lifelong care of those blinded in war. It was founded in 1915 by a blind newspaper proprietor, Sir Arthur Pearson (1866–1921).

St Elmo's fire A small electrical discharge, with a luminous appearance, that is associated with stormy weather and seen around the extremities of tall objects, such as the tops of trees and mastheads.

Saint-Exupéry, Antoine de (1900–44) French novelist and aviator. His novels include *Night Flight* (1931) and *Wind, Sand and Stars* (1939). He also wrote a fable for children, *The Little Prince* (1943).

St George's 12 04N 61 44W The capital of Grenada, on the SW coast, both a port and tourist resort. Founded by the French in the 17th century, it was capital of the British Windward Islands from 1885 to 1958. Population (1981): 4788.

St George's Channel A channel between SE Ireland and Wales, linking the Irish Sea with the Atlantic Ocean. Length: about 160 km (100 mi). Maximum width: 145 km (90 mi).

St Helena 15 58S 5 43W A mountainous island in the S Atlantic Ocean, a British dependent territory. Napoleon I was exiled here (1815–21). Area: 122 sq km (47 sq mi). Population (1985): 5895. Capital: Jamestown.

St Helens 53 28N 2 44W A town in NW England, in Merseyside. It has an important glass industry, besides brick and tile manufacturing, engineering, pharmaceutical production, brewing, and, nearby, coalmining. Population (1981): 98 769.

St Helens, Mount 46 12N 122 11W A volcano in the USA, in SW Washington state in the S Cascade Range. Dormant since 1857, the mountain erupted in May, 1980, causing widespread destruction in which more than 50 people died. Height: 2950 m (9677 ft).

St Helier 49 12N 2 07W A market town and resort in the Channel Islands, on the S coast of Jersey. There is a substantial trade in early vegetables and Jersey cattle. Population (1988 est): 82 536.

St James's Palace A royal palace in Pall Mall, in London, built for Henry VIII on the site of an 11th-century hospital. It was the principal London residence of the monarch from 1697, when Whitehall was burnt down, until superseded by Buckingham Palace in 1837. Much of the original building was destroyed by a fire in 1807.

St John River A river in E North America. Rising in Maine, USA, it flows NE to New Brunswick, Canada, and then SE to the Bay of Fundy, where high tides cause the river to reverse its course at the famous Reversing Falls. Length: 673 km (418 mi).

St John's 47 34N 52 41W A city in E Canada, the capital and commercial centre of Newfoundland. Settled in the 16th century, it is located beside a huge protected harbour. Population (1986): 96 216.

St John's wort A perennial herb or shrub, genus *Hypericum* (400 species), found in temperate regions. They have yellow five-petalled flowers with many stamens and many species are cultivated for ornament, including *H. calycinum* (also known as rose of Sharon). Family: *Guttiferae*.

St Kilda 57 49N 8 34W A group of three small mountainous islands off the Scottish mainland, the most westerly of the Outer Hebrides. Evacuated in 1930, they are now a nature reserve. Area: about 16 sq km (6 sq mi).

St Kitts-Nevis, Federation of (*or* St Christopher-Nevis) A country in the West Indies, in the Leeward Islands in the E Caribbean Sea. From 1967 it was a UK associated state consisting of three islands: St Kitts, Nevis, and Anguilla. Anguilla became a separate British dependency in 1980. St Kitts-Nevis became fully independent within the British Commonwealth in 1983. The economy is primarily agricultural, with tourism increasing. Prime minister: Dr Kennedy Simmonds. Area: 262 sq km (101 sq mi). Population (1987 est): 47 000. Capital: Basseterre, on St Kitts.

Saint-Laurent, Yves (1936–) French fashion designer, who trained with Dior and took over his fashion house (1957), opening his own in 1962. He established his reputation as the first designer to produce ready-to-wear clothes for the mass market; he has also produced clothes for men and a range of perfumes.

St Lawrence River A river in North America that belongs to one of the world's greatest water systems, draining the Great Lakes into the Atlantic Ocean. From Lake Ontario it flows NE along the Canadian-US border through the Thousand Islands, a major tourist district. Above Montreal it enters Canada and passes through rapids where hydroelectricity is produced. At Quebec it broadens into a long estuary that gradually merges with the Gulf of St Lawrence, an arm of the Atlantic Ocean and a major fishing ground. The St Lawrence valley is an important agricultural and industrial belt as well as a rail, water, and road corridor. The upper reaches of the river become unnavigable during winter months as does the gulf. Length: Lake Ontario to Quebec 480 km (298 mi); St Louis River headwaters to Anticosti Island 3395 km (2110 mi). *See also* St Lawrence Seaway.

St Lawrence Seaway A navigable waterway in North America through the St Lawrence River and the Great Lakes, completed in 1959. With a season of over eight months, it admits ships of up to 9000 tons.

St Leger A flat race for three-year-old horses, run in September at Doncaster over 2.9 km (1 mi 6½ furlongs). It was the earliest of the English Classics to be established (1776).

St Louis 38 40N 90 15W A city and port in the USA, in Missouri on the Mississippi River. A major centre in the colonization of the West, it is now a large industrial and university large city and an important agricultural market. Population (1986 est): 429 300.

St Lucia An island country in the West Indies, in the Windward Islands in the E Caribbean Sea. It is a mountainous island of volcanic origin. The population is mainly of African descent. The economy is mainly agricultural, with a growing tourist industry. St Lucia became internally self-governing in 1967 and attained full independence within the British Commonwealth in February, 1979. Prime minister: John Compton. Official language: English. Official currency: East Caribbean dollar of 100 cents. Area: 616 sq km (238 sq mi). Population (1987): 143 600. Capital: Castries.

St Mark's Cathedral The cathedral church of Venice since 1807. It was built in the 9th century to house the relics of St Mark but rebuilt in the 11th century after a fire. Designed as a Greek cross surmounted by five domes, it is strongly influenced by Byzantine art and is famous for its opulent mosaic and sculptural decoration.

St Moritz 46 30N 9 51E A resort in SE Switzerland, on St Moritz Lake. A renowned winter-sports centre, its Cresta Run (for bobsleds) dates from 1885. Population (1980): 5900. Altitude: 1822 m (5978 ft).

St Paul 45 00N 93 10W A city in the USA, the capital of Minnesota on the Mississippi River. Adjacent to Minneapolis, the Twin Cities comprise the commercial and industrial centre of an extensive grain and cattle area. Population (1986 est): 263 680.

ST PAUL'S CATHEDRAL *Sir Christopher Wren's double dome is seen in this engraving of 1755.*

St Paul's Cathedral The cathedral of the diocese of London; there have been five cathedrals on this site, the first three of which were Saxon. The present building was designed by Sir Christopher Wren and replaced the Norman structure burnt down in the Great Fire. It features a traditional cruciform plan, a classical two-tiered portico, a great dome, and flanking towers.

St Peter Port 49 27N 2 32W A resort in the Channel Islands, the only town in Guernsey. It has a large protected harbour. Population (1986): 16 085.

St Peter's Basilica The Catholic basilica in the Vatican City, Rome. It dates from the 16th century and replaced the original gothic building. It is the largest church in the world. Its general shape was determined by Donato Bramante (1444–1514), although it was designed together with its enormous dome by Michelangelo. Giacomo da Vignola (1507–73) continued the work and the nave and façade were added by Carlo Maderna (1556–1629). Bernini completed the building in the 17th century.

St Petersburg. *See* Leningrad.

Saint-Saëns, Camille (1835–1921) French composer, conductor, pianist, and organist. His compositions include 12 operas, five symphonies, *The Carnival of the* *Animals* (published posthumously; 1922) for two pianos and orchestra, and five piano concertos.

St Thomas 18 22N 64 57W A West Indian island in the US Virgin Islands, in the Lesser Antilles, once a major sugar producer and slave-trading centre. Tourism is of major importance. Area: 83 sq km (28 sq mi). Population (1985): 52 660. Capital: Charlotte Amalie.

St Vincent, Cape 37 01N 8 59W A promontory in the extreme SW of Portugal, in the Algarve on the Atlantic Ocean. Several naval battles have been fought off the cape, including the British defeat (1797) of the Spanish fleet during the Napoleonic Wars.

St Vincent and the Grenadines A country in the E Caribbean Sea, in the Windward Islands of the Lesser Antilles. It consists of the principal island of St Vincent together with its dependencies of the Grenadine islets. A British possession since 1763 it became fully independent in 1979. It is predominantly agricultural. Prime minister: James Mitchell. Area: 390 sq km (150 sq mi). Population (1987 est): 112 000. Capital: Kingstown.

saithe A food fish, *Pollachius* (or *Gadus*) *virens*, also called coalfish or coley, that is related to cod and lives in shoals in the North Atlantic. About 120 cm long, it is greenish brown above and silvery white below.

saké (*or* rice wine) An alcoholic drink made in Japan from steamed rice, to which a special yeast is added, and slowly fermented. It resembles a light sherry in taste and is served warm.

Sakharov, Andrei Dimitrievich (1921–89) Soviet physicist. After helping to develop the Soviet hydrogen bomb during the 1940s and 1950s he spoke out against nuclear weapons in the 1960s and argued for freedom of speech in the Soviet Union. He was awarded the Nobel Peace Prize in 1975. His exile to Gorkii in 1980 aroused international protest and ended in 1986. In 1989 he was elected to the new Soviet People's Congress of Deputies.

Saki (H(ector) H(ugh) Munro; 1870–1916) British writer. Born in Burma, he settled in London in 1908. He published several volumes of humorous short stories many of which featured his fastidious and snobbish heroes Clovis and Reginald. He was killed in action in World War I.

ANDREI SAKHAROV *Arriving in Moscow on his release from Gorkii (1986).*

Saladin (?1137–93) The leader of the Muslims against the Crusaders in Syria. He obtained control over the Muslim lands in Egypt, of which he became sultan in 1175, and Syria. He then captured the Kingdom of Jerusalem following his great victory over the Crusaders at the battle of Hattin (1187). During the third Crusade he won his legendary reputation as a chivalrous warrior.

Salam, Abdus (1926–) Pakistani physicist, who became professor of physics at Imperial College, London, in 1957. He is also director of the International Centre for Theoretical Physics in Trieste. In 1979 he shared the Nobel Prize with the US physicists Sheldon Glashow (1932–) and Steven Weinberg (1933–) for their work on weak interactions.

Salamanca 40 58N 5 40W A city in central Spain, in Salamanca. During the Peninsular War the battle of Salamanca was fought here on 22 July, 1812, in which Wellington secured a decisive victory over the French. An intellectual centre of Renaissance Europe, Salamanca remains an important cultural centre with a university (founded 1218). Its many notable old buildings include two cathedrals and it has a fine Roman bridge. Population (1986): 152 766.

salamander A tailed amphibian belonging to a widely distributed order (*Urodela* or *Caudata*; about 225 species). Salamanders have short legs and long bodies and move by bending the body from side to side to give as wide a movement as possible for their feet. They usually hide in damp places when not hunting small worms and insects. Their habits range from wholly aquatic to wholly terrestrial. *See also* newt.

Salazar, António de Oliveira (1889–1970) Portuguese dictator. Prime minister from 1932 to 1968, his New State repressed political opposition and fought long colonial wars in Africa, which gravely impeded the country's economic development.

Salerno 40 40N 14 46E A port in Italy, in Campania on the Gulf of Salerno. Founded by the Romans in 197 BC, its medical school flourished in the middle ages. It was the scene of heavy fighting during World War II (1943). Population (1986): 154 848.

Salford 53 30N 2 16W An industrial city in NW England, in Greater Manchester on the River Irwell and the Manchester Ship Canal. The docks for Manchester are here. Population (1981): 98 024.

Salic Law The law of the Salian Franks issued under Clovis in the early 6th century. Owing little to other contemporary law codes or to Roman law, it is concerned with both criminal and civil law. Its importance for later periods lies in its prohibition against women inheriting land. This canon was invoked in France in 1316 and 1321 to prevent a woman from succeeding to the throne and, in 1328, Edward III's claim to the French Crown was rejected on the grounds that his claim was by female descent.

Salieri, Antonio (1750–1825) Italian composer and conductor in Vienna from 1766. His pupils included Beethoven, Schubert, and Liszt. Because of his rivalry with Mozart, he was fancifully credited with having poisoned him.

Salinger, J(erome) D(avid) (1919–) US novelist who achieved success with *The Catcher in the Rye* (1951). Later works include *Franny and Zooey* (1961), *Raise High the Roof Beam, Carpenters* (1963), and *Seymour, An Introduction* (1963).

Salisbury. *See* Harare.

Salisbury 51 05N 1 48W A city in S England, in Wiltshire at the confluence of the Rivers Avon and Wylye.

Nearby is Old Sarum, the site of an Iron Age hill fort with extensive earthworks; settlement here continued until the 13th century, when the cathedral was moved to New Sarum (Salisbury). Old Sarum was the most notorious of the pre-1832 rotten boroughs. Population (1983 est): 40 000.

Salisbury, Robert Cecil, 1st Earl of. *See* Burghley, William Cecil, Lord.

Salisbury, Robert Arthur Talbot Gascoyne-Cecil, 3rd Marquess of (1830–1903) British statesman; Conservative prime minister (1885–86, 1886–92, 1895–1902). Elected an MP in 1853, he became Disraeli's foreign secretary in 1878. As prime minister he served as his own foreign secretary (except in 1886 and 1900–02) and his policy has been characterized as one of "splendid isolation."

saliva The fluid secreted by three pairs of **salivary glands** around the mouth in response to the sight, smell, taste, or thought of food. Its major role is to bind the food particles and to lubricate the mouth and gullet.

Salk vaccine The first antipolio vaccine to be used successfully. It was developed by the US virologist J. E. Salk (1914–) and first used in 1954. It has been replaced by the Sabin vaccine in many countries.

Sallust (Gaius Sallustius Crispus; c. 86–c. 34 BC) Roman politican and historian. Expelled from the Senate for alleged immorality, he supported Julius Caesar in the war against Pompey and became governor of Numidia. He was accused of corruption and extortion and retired from politics in about 44 BC. His best-known works are the monographs *Bellum Catilinae* and *Bellum Jugurthinum*.

salmon One of several fish of the genera *Oncorhynchus* or *Salmo*, especially the Atlantic salmon (*S. salar*)—a valuable food and game fish. It has an elongated body, up to 150 cm long, and two dorsal fins. Salmon live mainly in the sea, feeding on other fish, but migrate into fresh water to spawn. The spawned fish (kelts) either die or return to the sea and spawn in successive years. On hatching the young fish are known as parr once they start feeding. At about two years the coat becomes silver and the fish (smolt) migrate to the sea to reach maturity. After about two to three years they return to their native spawning waters as grilse, guided upstream by their sense of smell. Family: *Salmonidae*; order: *Salmoniformes*.

Salmonella A genus of rod-shaped bacteria that are parasites of animals and man and cause several diseases: *S. typhi* and *S. paratyphi* cause typhoid fever in man while *S. typhimurium* is a common cause of food poisoning.

Salonika. *See* Thessaloniki.

Salop. *See* Shropshire.

salp. *See* tunicate.

salsify A biennial herb, *Tragopogon porrifolius*, native to the Mediterranean region. It is cultivated in temperate regions for its fleshy white root, supposed to taste like oysters when cooked. The plant has long narrow leaves, used in salads, a head of purple flowers surrounded by stiff pointed green sepals. Family: *Compositae*.

salt 1. (sodium chloride; NaCl) The crystalline solid that is used for seasoning and preserving food and is present in sea water and halite, which are its chief sources. It has an important function in the human body and is used in the manufacture of many chemicals, such as soap, fertilizer, and ceramics. 2. Any similar com-

SALT *Salar of Uyuni, 4350 m (12 000) ft) up in the Bolivian Andes.*

pound formed, together with water, when an acid reacts with a base.

Salt Lake City 40 45N 111 55W A city in the USA, the capital of Utah near Great Salt Lake. Founded in 1847 by the Mormons under the leadership of Brigham Young, it is the world headquarters of the Mormon Church. Population (1986 est): 158 440.

saltpetre (potassium nitrate *or* nitre; KNO_3) A white crystalline solid used as a fertilizer, a food preservative, and in gunpowder and fireworks.

saltwort An annual or perennial herb belonging to the widely distributed genus *Salsola* (50 species), found on seashores and salt marshes. They have fleshy spiked leaves. Family: *Chenopodiaceae*.

saluki An ancient breed of hunting dog. It has a slender body with long legs, giving speed and agility, and a small head with a long narrow muzzle. The smooth soft coat can be of various colours. Height: 50–70 cm.

Salvador (*or* Bahia) 12 58S 38 29W A port in NE Brazil, the capital of Bahia state on the Atlantic Ocean. It has a fine natural harbour. Population (1985): 1 811 367.

Salvador. *See* El Salvador, Republic of.

Salvation Army The international Christian organization founded in 1865 in London by William Booth. Run on strictly military lines, its members wear a characteristic uniform on public occasions. It is famous for its social and evangelistic work.

Salvia A genus of perennial herbs and shrubs (about 700 species), widely distributed in temperate and tropical regions. Many are cultivated for ornament, including the Brazilian scarlet sage (*S. splendens*) and the blue-flowered *S. patens*. Common sage is the culinary herb. Family: *Labiatae*.

Salyut A series of manned Soviet space stations first launched into earth orbit in 1971. Crews were conveyed to and from the orbiting laboratory by Soyuz spacecraft. They lived in weightless conditions, sometimes for very long periods, conducting a variety of experiments and observations. The series was eventually superseded by the Mir space stations.

Salzburg 47 54N 13 03E A city in central Austria, the capital of Salzburg. It has many fine buildings. Mozart

was born here and a famous musical event, the Salzburg Festival, is held annually. Population (1981): 139 426.

Samar The third largest island in the Philippines, in the Visayan Islands linked by bridge to Leyte. Its frequent typhoons restrict agriculture; the chief products are rice, coconuts, and hemp. Copper and iron ore are mined. Area: 13 415 sq km (5181 sq mi). Population (1980): 1 200 592. Chief town: Catbalogan.

Samara. *See* Kuibyshev.

Samaria **1.** The central region of ancient Palestine, which became part of the northern kingdom of Israel in the 10th century BC. *See also* Samaritans. **2.** 32 17N 35 12E The capital from the 9th century until its destruction in about 721 BC of the kingdom of Israel. The city was rebuilt in the 1st century AD and renamed Sebaste.

Samaritans **1.** A people of ancient Samaria (now in N Israel), with a religion closely akin to Judaism but much disliked by the Jews. They declined under Muslim rule. **2.** A British telephone service for the suicidal and despairing, started in 1953 by the Rev Chad Varah (1911–) in a London church (St Stephen Walbrook). A nonreligious charity, it offers a nonprofessional, confidential, and anonymous service to anyone in distress through its 186 UK branches. Many overseas branches belong to the associated Befrienders International.

samarium (Sm) A lanthanide element, discovered 1879, that occurs naturally, with other lanthanides, in monazite ($CePO_4$). At no 62; at wt 150.4; mp 1077 ± 5°C; bp 1791°C.

Samarkand 39 40N 66 57E A city in the S central Soviet Union, in the Uzbek SSR. It was the chief junction of the ancient Silk Road between China and the Mediterranean and, conquered by the Arabs in the 8th century, became the Abbasids' capital (9th–10th centuries) and a great Islamic centre. In the 14th century it became the capital of Timur's mighty empire, coming later under the rule of the Uzbek people (16th–19th centuries). The city's remarkable historic buildings include Timur's mausoleum. Population (1987 est): 388 000.

Samoa A chain of volcanic islands in the S central Pacific Ocean. Discovered by the Dutch in the 18th century, the islands were politically divided in 1900 between the USA and Germany. **American Samoa**, comprising the E islands of the chain, is an unincorporated US territory; the chief island os Tutuila. Area: 197 sq km (76 sq mi). Population (1981 est): 33 000. Capital: Pago Pago. **Western Samoa** was a German protectorate until World War I and then under New Zealand control, becoming independent in 1962; the main islands are Savai'i and Upolu. Head of state: HH Malietoa Tanumafili II (1913–). Prime minister: Tofilau Eti Alesana. Official languages: Samoan and English. Official currency: Western Samoa dollar. Area: 2842 sq km (1097 sq mi). Population (1986 est): 163 000. Capital: Apia.

Samoyed (dog) A breed of dog developed in Siberia and used by the Samoyed tribesmen as a sledge dog. It is robustly built with husky-like features; the white or cream coat consists of a short soft undercoat and a long coarse outer coat. Height: 51–56 cm (dogs); 46–51 cm (bitches).

Samoyed (people) A group of Siberian peoples of the tundra and N forest region of the central Soviet Union. They were traditionally nomadic reindeer hunters and fishers, now mainly settled as reindeer breeders. Shamanism dominates their religious life. The five Samoyed languages belong to the Uralic family, only Nenets (*or* Yurak) having a considerable number of speakers.

samurai The provincial warriors who rose to power in Japan in the 11th century. Most became the vassals of *daimyo* (feudal lords). The samurai class was sharply divided from other classes by its superior status and marked distinctions also existed within its own ranks. After the Meiji restoration (1868) the samurai lost their special position but ex-samurai became leaders in various areas of modern Japanese life.

San'a' 15 23N 44 14E The capital of North Yemen, in the centre of the country. Notable buildings include the Great Mosque, where there is a sacred Muslim shrine. Population (1986): 427 185.

SAN ANDREAS FAULT   *An example of a tear fault in which the rocks are being displaced horizontally.*

San Andreas Fault A fault in the earth's crust, 1200 km (750 mi) in length, running along the margin between the Pacific tectonic plate (*see* plate tectonics) and the North American plate in NW California. In 1906 a horizontal displacement between the plates of about 6 metres and a lateral displacement of 1 metre caused an earthquake that devasted San Francisco; in 1989 another earthquake caused further damage to the city. It is named after San Andreas Lake, through which it passes.

San Antonio 29 25N 98 30W A city in the USA, in Texas. Founded in 1718, it was the scene of the Mexican attack on the Alamo (1836) during the Texan revolution. San Antonio has several military bases and is a commer-

cial and industrial centre for a large agricultural region. Population (1986 est): 914 350.

sanctions Penalties imposed for breaking a law, especially international law. First imposed by the League of Nations on Italy following its invasion of Ethiopia, the most recent examples of sanctions are those imposed by UN countries against Rhodesia (now Zimbabwe), following its unilateral declaration of independence in 1965, and those against South Africa (1985).

sand Unconsolidated grains of rock, varying in size from 0.06 to 2.00 mm in diameter. Consolidated sands form sandstones; grits are coarse sandstones with angular grains. Most sands consist principally of quartz, derived from the weathering of quartz-bearing rocks. Sand is used in glass and cement production, and as an abrasive.

Sand, George (Aurore Dupin, Baronne Dudevant; 1804–76) French novelist. Her first book, *Indiana* (1832), the first of an enormous number of successful novels. Among her many lovers were Alfred de Musset and Frédéric Chopin.

sandalwood An evergreen tree belonging to the genus *Santalum* (about 25 species), native to SE Asia and the Pacific Islands. The true sandalwood (*S. album*) is partially parasitic on the roots of other trees. Its white wood is used to make boxes and furniture and, when distilled, yields sweet-scented sandalwood oil. Family: *Santalaceae*.

sand dollar A marine invertebrate animal belonging to an order (*Clypeastroida*) of echinoderms. Its round flat rigid body is covered with small spines and saclike organs (tube feet). Sand dollars live on the sea bed and sift minute food particles from the sand in which they burrow. Class: *Echinoidea*.

sanderling A bird, *Calidris alba*, that nests on Arctic coasts and winters on shores worldwide. 20 cm long, it has a rust-coloured upper plumage, changing to pale-brown in winter, and a long white wing stripe. It feeds on shrimps, sandhoppers, and molluscs with its straight slender bill. Family: *Scolopacidae* (sandpipers).

sand flea. *See* sand hopper.

sandfly A small fly belonging to the widely distributed genus *Phlebotomus*. Sandflies are among the worst pests of the tropics: the bloodsucking females can give a painful bite and several species are carriers of serious human diseases.

The name has also been used for many bloodsucking gnats and midges of sandy places.

sand hopper A small terrestrial jumping crustacean, also called beach hopper and sand or beach flea, belonging to the family *Talitridae*. Its body is laterally flattened and lacks a carapace. During the day it is buried in sand but at night it emerges to feed on organic debris under stones or among seaweed. Order: *Amphipoda*.

Sandhurst 51 02N 0 34E A village in SE England, in Berkshire. The Royal Military Academy (1799) for training officers and the National Army Museum are situated here. Population (1985 est): 17 832.

San Diego 32 45N 117 10W A city in the USA, in California on San Diego Bay. It has a US naval base and large naval air service facilities, and is also an important scientific research centre. Population (1989): 1 086 600.

sand lizard A slender long-tailed European lizard, *Lacerta agilis*, occurring in sandy regions. It has white-centred dark spots along its pale-brown or grey back. Family: *Lacertidae*. See p. 634.

SAND LIZARD

sandpiper A wading bird belonging to a family (*Scolopacidae*; 82 species) occurring chiefly in the N hemisphere, breeding in northerly latitudes and migrating south to winter. Sandpipers typically have long legs, long wings, a mottled brown or grey plumage, which commonly changes colour seasonally, and a long slender bill. They nest in marshy regions or on mud flats. Order: *Charadriiformes* (gulls, plovers, etc.).

Sandringham 52 49N 0 30E A village in E England, in Norfolk. The Sandringham estate was bought by Queen Victoria for the Prince of Wales (later Edward VII) in 1861. Sandringham House remains a royal residence.

sandstone A sedimentary rock consisting of consolidated sand, cemented mainly by calcareous, siliceous, or ferruginous minerals. They may be deposited by wind action in deserts or in shallow seas, estuaries and deltas, and along low-lying coasts by water. Sandstones vary in colour from red to yellow to white according to the presence of other minerals in addition to the quartz.

Sandwich, John Montagu, 4th Earl of (1718–92) British politician; first lord of the admiralty (1748–51, 1771–82). The inadequacy of the navy during the American Revolution was attributed to his corrupt practices. He gave his name to the sandwich, a snack devised to sustain him through round-the-clock gaming.

San Francisco 37 40N 122 25W A city in the USA, in California situated on a peninsula between San Francisco Bay and the Pacific Ocean. It is a major seaport, a financial and insurance centre, and a major cultural centre. Its many famous landmarks include the San Francisco–Oakland Bay Bridge (1936), the Golden Gate Bridge (1937), Chinatown, and the city's cable cars. Founded by the Spanish in 1776, it was captured by the USA (1846) during the Mexican War. It expanded rapidly following the discovery of gold in California (1848) and it was during this period that the first Chinese settled in the city. In 1906 there was movement in the San Andreas Fault, and San Francisco was almost completely destroyed by an earthquake and three-day fire. In 1989 another earthquake resulted in widespread damage and 67 deaths. Population (1986 est): 749 000.

Sanhedrin The highest court of the Jews, which met in Jerusalem. Its composition and its jurisdiction varied with its history. In New Testament times, the high priest was president and its functions were administrative, judicial, and religious.

San José 37 20N 121 55W A city in the USA, in California on the S arm of San Francisco Bay. Founded in 1777, it was the first city in California and state capital (1849–51). Situated in the fertile Santa Clara Valley, it has many food-processing plants and wineries as well as aerospace and electronics industries. Population (1986 est): 712 080.

San José 9 50N 84 02W The capital of Costa Rica, situated in the centre of the country in a high fertile valley. It was founded in 1736; a university was established in 1843. Population (1984): 241 464.

San Juan 18 29N 66 08W The capital and main port of Puerto Rico, in the N. Founded by the Spanish in 1508, it was later attacked by the English and by the Dutch; in 1898 it was captured by the US navy. It has expanded considerably in the 20th century and is now also an industrial and tourist centre. Population (1980): 432 973.

San Marino, Republic of A small independent republic, an enclave in Italian territory, situated on the slopes of the Apennines mountain range, SW of Rimini. Farming, tourism, and the sale of postage stamps are the main sources of income. Dating from the 4th century AD, it was an independent commune by the 12th century. In 1862, the newly established kingdom of Italy guaranteed San Marino's independence and a customs union. Official language: Italian. Official currency: both Italian and Vatican City currencies are in use. Area: 61 sq km (24 sq mi). Population (1987): 22 100. Capital: San Marino.

San Martín, José de (1778–1850) South American soldier and statesman; the national hero of Argentina. After participating in the struggle of Buenos Aires against the Spanish, he raised and trained an army in Argentina (1814–16), which he led across the Andes, and, with Bernardo O'Higgins, defeated the Spanish at Chacabuco (1817) and Maipo (1818), achieving the liberation of Chile. In 1821 he entered Lima, proclaimed the independence of Peru, and became its "protector." He resigned in 1822, after differences with Bolívar.

San Salvador 13 59N 89 18W The capital of El Salvador, situated in the centre of the country. Founded by the Spanish in 1525, it become capital in 1839. It has suffered severe earthquakes, most recently in 1986, and in 1989 witnessed conflict between rebel and government forces. Population (1985): 459 902.

San Sebastián 43 19N 1 59W A seaside resort in N Spain, in the Basque Provinces on the Bay of Biscay. It possesses a cathedral and palace. Population (1986): 175 138.

Sansevieria A genus of herbaceous perennial plants (60 species) native to tropical and S Africa and S Asia. They have a basal rosette of stiff swordlike leaves arising from thick creeping underground stems (rhizomes). *S. trifasciata* var. *laurentii* (mother-in-law's tongue) is a popular house plant with long leaves, striped green and yellow. The leaves of several species yield a fibre used for ropes, mats, etc. Family: *Liliaceae*.

Sanskrit The classical literary language of the Hindu scriptures, belonging to the Indo-Aryan family. From it the Prakrits and modern N Indian languages developed. It was spoken in NW India from 1500 BC, becoming a scholarly language in the 5th century BC, and is still used

SANSKRIT *Detail of a 12th-century palm-leaf manuscript.*

as a sacred language. It is highly complex and is written in the Devanagari script.

Santa Anna, Antonio López de   (1794–1876) Mexican soldier and statesman; president (1833–36) and dictator (1839, 1841–45). Santa Anna dominated Mexican politics from 1823 until driven into exile in 1845. He is best known for his defeat of Texan forces at the Alamo (1836).

Santa Cruz   17 45S 63 14W A city in SE Bolivia. It is the commercial centre for an area producing chiefly sugar cane, rice, and coffee. Industries include the manufacture of cigarettes and sugar refining. Population (1985 est): 441 717.

Santa Isabel.   *See* Malabo.

Santayana, George   (1863–1952) Spanish-born US philosopher and poet. His philosophy was set out in *Realms of Being* (1927–40). His witty and urbane works include *The Sense of Beauty* (1896), *The Life of Reason* (1905–06), *Scepticism and Animal Faith* (1923), and *The Last Puritan* (1935).

Santiago (*or* Santiago de Chile)   33 35S 70 40W The capital of Chile, situated in the centre of the country at the foot of the Andes. It was founded by the Spanish in 1541 and is now a major industrial centre. Population (1985 est): 4 318 305.

Santo Domingo   18 32N 69 50W The capital of the Dominican Republic, a port on the S coast. Founded by Columbus in 1496, it became the capital of the first Spanish colony in the Americas and is the site of the first cathedral (1521) and the first university (1538) in the New World. It became capital of the new Dominican Republic in 1844. Population (1983 est): 1 410 000.

Santos   23 56S 46 22W A city in SE Brazil, in São Paulo state on the Atlantic Ocean. It is the leading coffee port of the world. Population (1985): 461 096.

São Luís   2 34S 44 16W A port in N Brazil, the capital of Maranhão state. The chief exports are babaçu palm products, cotton, sugar, and balsam. It is the site of the University of Maranhão (1966). Population (1985): 564 434.

Saône, River   A river in E France, rising in Lorraine and flowing mainly S to join the River Rhône at Lyons. It is linked by canal to the Rivers Moselle, Rhine, Loire, Seine, and Meuse. Length: 480 km (298 mi).

São Paulo   23 33S 46 39W The largest city in Brazil, the capital of São Paulo state. Founded in 1554, it grew rapidly after 1880 with the development of coffee plantations. Coffee remains important but there has been considerable diversification of industry and it is now the fastest-growing city in Brazil. Population (1985): 10 099 086.

São Tomé and Príncipe, Democratic Republic of   A small island country off the coast of West Africa, in the Gulf of Guinea. An archipelago, it comprises the two main islands with coastal plains rising to volcanic mountains in their interiors, together with two islets. Most of the population is descended from African slaves and southern Europeans. Chiefly agricultural, the main crops are cocoa, copra, palm oil and kernels, and coffee. Discovered by the Portuguese in 1471, the islands came under Portuguese rule in 1522. They became an overseas province in 1951 and gained independence in 1975. President: Dr Manuel Pinto da Costa. Official language: Portuguese. Official currency: dobra of 100 centavos. Area: 964 sq km (372 sq mi). Population (1987 est): 113 000. Capital and main port: São Tomé.

sap   The fluid found in the vascular (conducting) system of plants. It consists of water and minerals, absorbed from the soil and transported through the plant in the xylem, and sugars, made in the leaves and distributed in solution in the phloem.

sapodilla   An evergreen tree, *Achras sapota*, native to Central America but cultivated elsewhere in the tropics. It produces large edible brown rounded fruits, with a juicy pulp surrounding black seeds. Milky latex from the bark is a source of chicle gum, used in chewing gum. Family: *Sapotaceae*.

sapphire   A transparent variety of corundum that may be any colour except red (*see* ruby) due to traces of iron and titanium. It is used as a gemstone and in record-player styluses. Sapphires occur in igneous and metamorphic rocks but most are obtained from detrital gravels.

Sappho   (c. 612–c. 580 BC) Greek lyric poet, contemporary with Alcaeus. Her passionate poetry, which has survived in fragments, was written for her group of female admirers on the island of Lesbos (from which the term "lesbianism" is derived).

Sapporo   43 5N 141 21E A city in Japan, in SW Hokkaido. It is the island's main administrative and educational centre. It is also a ski resort, site of the 1972 winter Olympics. Population (1985): 1 543 000.

saprophyte   An organism that obtains its energy by feeding on dead or decaying tissue. Bacteria and fungi are important saprophytes, using enzymes to break down organic material and release nutrients into the soil, which can be used by plants.

Saragossa.   *See* Zaragoza.

Sarajevo   43 52N 18 26E A city and industrial centre in W central Yugoslavia, the capital of Bosnia and Hercegovina. A centre of resistance to Austrian domination, it was here that the heir apparent of Austria-Hungary, Francis Ferdinand, was assassinated (28 June, 1914), precipitating World War I. Population (1982): 448 500. See p. 636.

Saratoga, Battles of   (19 September and 7 October, 1777) Two battles fought near Saratoga, New York, which formed the turning point of the American Revolution. The second ended with the surrender of Gen Burgoyne to the Americans. The outcome of the battles helped persuade the French to recognize and support the USA.

SARAJEVO *Archduke Francis Ferdinand moments before his assassination.*

Sarawak A state in Malaysia, in NW Borneo on the South China Sea. It has a mountainous forested interior with a swampy coastal plain, where rubber, pepper, sago, and rice are grown. Oil production is of prime importance. It was given in 1841 by the sultan of Brunei to the British explorer James Brooke, the "white rajah". Made a British protectorate in 1888, it was ruled by the Brooke family until World War II, when it was occupied by the Japanese. Ceded to Britain in 1946, it joined Malaysia in 1963. Area: 124 970 sq km (48 250 sq mi). Population (1980): 1 294 753. Capital: Kuching.

sarcoma. *See* cancer.

sardine A young pilchard or any of several species of food fish of the family *Clupeidae*, especially members of the genera *Sardina*, *Sardinops*, and *Sardinella*.

Sardinia The second largest island in the Mediterranean Sea, comprising an autonomous region of Italy. It is largely mountainous. Agriculture is important, especially on the fertile alluvial plain in the SW. Its major industry is mineral production, especially lead, zinc, coal, fluorspar, and sea salt. First settled by the Phoenicians, it was ceded to Savoy by Austria (1720) in exchange for Sicily and formed the kingdom of Sardinia with Piedmont, which formed the basis of a unified Italy. Area: 23 813 sq km (9194 sq mi). Population (1985): 1 643 789. Capital: Cagliari.

Sargasso Sea An elliptical section of the N Atlantic Ocean between latitudes 20°N and 35°N and longitudes 30°W and 70°W. Contained within a current system, it is still and warm. It takes its name from the floating brown seaweed of the genus *Sargassum*, found in it.

Sargent, John Singer (1856–1925) US portrait painter. Working in Paris, London, and the USA, he achieved considerable success with his elegant portraits of celebrities. He also produced remarkable landscape studies of World War I.

Sargent, Sir Malcolm (1895–1967) British conductor and organist. He was chief conductor at the London Promenade Concerts (1957–1967). He was also conductor of the BBC Symphony Orchestra (1950–57).

Sark 49 26N 2 22W The smallest of the four main Channel Islands. It consists of Great Sark and Little Sark, connected by a narrow isthmus. It is governed by a hereditary seigneur or dame in a semifeudal system. Cars are prohibited here. Area: 5 sq km (2 sq mi). Population (1981): 560.

Sarnia 42 57N 82 24W A city and port in E Canada, in SW Ontario at the S end of Lake Huron. It is a major oil refining and petrochemical centre. Population (1981): 47 586.

sarsaparilla An extract of the roots of several perennial climbing or trailing vines of the genus *Smilax*, especially *S. aristolochiaefolia*, cultivated in Central and South America. The dried roots are used as a tonic and as flavouring for medicines and beverages. Family: *Smilacaceae*.

Sartre, Jean-Paul (1905–80) French philosopher, novelist, dramatist, and critic. A leading existentialist, his major works of philosophy include *Being and Nothingness* (1943). His novels include *Nausea* (1938) and the trilogy *The Roads to Freedom* (1945–49). Among his several plays are *The Flies* (1943), *In Camera* (1944), *The Respectable Prostitute* (1946), and *Lucifer and the Lord* (1951).

Sarum. *See* Salisbury.

SAS. *See* Special Air Service.

Saskatchewan A province of W Canada, on the Great Plains. The N is covered by forest with lakes and swamps. The S is open prairie and is one of the world's most important wheatlands. The province is rich in minerals, including uranium, oil, natural gas, potash, zinc, and copper; associated industries are important. Explored in the 17th and 18th centuries, Saskatchewan was first exploited for furs. Agricultural settlement began slowly (1870s) but sped up in the decade before 1914. The area became a province in 1905. Area: 570 269 sq km (220 181 sq mi). Population (1986): 1 009 613. Capital: Regina.

Saskatchewan River A river in W Canada, rising in two separate branches in the Rocky Mountains and flowing generally E through prairie grainlands to unite in central Saskatchewan. The river then continues to Lake Winnipeg. Length: 1940 km (1205 mi).

sassafras A tree, *Sassafras albidum*, native to North America. It bears clusters of yellow flowers and dark-blue berries. The aromatic roots are dried for use in medicines and also yield oil of sassafras, which is used in perfumes and as flavouring for beverages. Family: *Lauraceae*.

Sassoon, Siegfried (1886–1967) British poet and writer. In 1917 his disgust with the progress of World War I led him to make a public refusal to serve, for which he was sent to a military hospital where he met Wilfred Owen. His antiwar poetry appeared in *The Old Huntsman* (1917) and *Counterattack* (1918), and he wrote several volumes of autobiographical war memoirs.

satellite **1.** A celestial body orbiting a planet. The planets of the solar system have at least 50 known satellites, ranging greatly in size. The small bodies comprising the rings of Saturn, Uranus, and Jupiter may also be regarded as satellites. Mercury and Venus have no satellites. Spacecraft have sent back information on various satellites, including the earth's moon, the four large Galilean satellites of Jupiter, Saturn's rings and its largest satellite Titan, and the satellites of Uranus and Neptune. Many small satellites have been discovered by these spacecraft, notably several of Uranus (1986). **2.** A spacecraft that is launched into orbit around the

Planet & Satellite	diameter (km)	distance from primary (1000km)	year of discovery
EARTH			
Moon	3 476	384.40	–
MARS			
Phobos	22	9.38	1877
Deimos	13	23.46	1877
JUPITER			
Metis	40	128	1979
Adrastea	20	129	1979
Amalthea	190	181	1892
Thebe	100	222	1979
Io	3 630	422	1610
Europa	3 140	671	1610
Ganymede	5 260	1 070	1610
Callisto	4 800	1 883	1610
Leda	15	11 094	1974
Himalia	185	11 480	1904
Lysithea	35	11 720	1938
Elara	75	11 737	1905
Ananke	30	21 200	1951
Carme	40	22 600	1938
Pasiphae	50	23 500	1908
Sinope	35	23 700	1914
SATURN			
Atlas	30	138	1980
Prometheus	105	139	1980
Pandora	90	142	1980
Janus	90	151	1966
Epimetheus	120	151	1966
Mimas	390	186	1789
Enceladus	500	238	1789
Tethys	1 060	295	1684
Telesto	30	295	1980
Calypso	25	295	1980
Dione	1 120	377	1684

Planet & Satellite	diameter (km)	distance from primary (1000km)	year of discovery
Helene	30	377	1980
Rhea	1 530	527	1672
Titan	5 150	1 222	1655
Hyperion	290	1 481	1848
Iapetus	1 460	3 561	1671
Phoebe	220	12 952	1898
URANUS			
Cordelia	40	50	1986
Ophelia	50	54	1986
Bianca	50	59	1986
Cressida	60	62	1986
Desdemona	60	63	1986
Juliet	80	64	1986
Portia	90	66	1986
Rosalind	60	70	1986
Belinda	50	75	1986
Puck	170	86	1985
Miranda	480	129	1948
Ariel	1 160	191	1851
Umbriel	1 190	266	1851
Titania	1 610	436	1787
Oberon	1 550	584	1787
NEPTUNE			
1989 N6	50	48	1989
1989 N5	90	50	1989
1989 N3	140	53	1989
1989 N4	160	62	1989
1989 N2	200	74	1989
1989 N1	420	118	1989
Triton	2 720	354	1846
Nereid	340	5 511	1949
PLUTO			
Charon	1 200	19	1978

PLANETARY SATELLITES
earth or enters an orbit around some other solar-system body. It may be a communications satellite, retransmitting radio signals from one location on earth to another. Alternatively, its instruments may gather information from earth or from other celestial objects and transmit it, by radio signals, to ground-based receiving stations. This information is used, for example, in weather forecasting, navigation, scientific and astronomical research, and for military purposes.

Satie, Erik (1866–1925) French composer, well known for his eccentricity. He was influential in turning away from impressionism towards a clear-textured style that admitted humour. His works include the ballet *Parade* (1916), piano pieces, including *Trois Gymnopédies* (1888), *Pièces froides* (1897), and *Trois morceaux en forme de poire* (1903), and many songs.

satinwood A tree, *Chloroxylon swietenia*, native to S India and Sri Lanka. Its wood is valued in cabinetmaking for its fine golden-yellow finish. The wood of certain West Indian species is also known as satinwood. Family: *Meliaceae*.

satsuma. *See* tangerine.

Saturn (astronomy) The second largest planet, orbiting the sun every 29.5 years at a mean distance of 1427 million km. The most oblate planet, its equatorial diameter is 120 000 km. The dominant feature is **Saturn's rings**, lying in the equatorial plane and tilted at 27° to the orbital plane. There are six rings, differing considerably in brightness and width but are all composed of small icy chunks. The overall diameter is almost 600 000 km but the thickness is only a few hundred metres. The main rings, C, B, and A, were discovered in the 17th century. The outermost, A, is separated from the brightest ring, B. Saturn also has at least 20 satellites. Saturn is made up primarily of hydrogen and helium.

Saturn (mythology) The Roman god of agriculture and father of the gods, identified with the Greek Cronus. Various aspects of the Saturnalia, his annual festival held in December, at which presents were exchanged and normal social rules relaxed, were taken over by the Christian festival of Christmas.

saturniid moth A moth belonging to the mainly tropical family *Saturniidae* (about 800 species). They are usually large with a transparent eyespot on each wing. Their cocoons can be a source of silk.

satyrid butterfly A butterfly of the worldwide family *Satyridae*. The wings are mainly brownish with a few or numerous eyespots. The forelegs are rudimentary and the flight weak and fluttering. Satyrids hide when alarmed, folding the forewings inside the camouflaged hindwings.

Satyrs and Sileni In Greek mythology, male fertility spirits of the woods and fields, usually portrayed with goats' legs and pointed ears or horns. Associated with Dionysus, they were typically drunk and lustful. *See also* Silenus.

Saud (1902–69) King of Saudi Arabia (1953–64), son of Ibn Saud. He was deposed and the throne passed to his brother Faisal.

Saudi Arabia, Kingdom of A country in the Middle East comprising most of Arabia, bordering on the Red Sea and the Persian Gulf. In the W a line of mountains runs close to the Red Sea, while the Najd, the central plateau, slopes downwards W–E. In the N and SE are large areas of desert. The population, densest in the SW, is mainly Arab Muslim. About 27% are nomads. *Economy*: based on oil in the Persian Gulf, exploited since 1938. The country, a member of OPEC, is the world's greatest exporter of oil. Income is also derived from pilgrims visiting Mecca, Medina, and Jidda. *History*: the establishment of Saudi Arabia (1932) under Ibn Saud followed the 19th-century struggle by the Saud family to dominate the warring tribes of the peninsula and take overall control from Turkey. Asir was incorporated in 1934. Saudi Arabia became a founding member of the Arab League (1945). Under Ibn Saud's son, Faisal Ibn Abdul Aziz, there was economic development, Faisal using the oil crisis of the early 1970s to increase Saudi holdings in oil operations. The present king, since 1982, is a brother of Faisal, Fahd Ibn Abdul Aziz. Official language: Arabic. Official currency: rial of 100 nilalas. Area: 2 400 000 sq km (927 000 sq mi). Population (1987 est): 12 483 000. Capital: Riyadh. Chief port: Jidda.

Saul In the Old Testament, the first King of Israel, who reigned in the 11th century BC. Son of Kish, he was anointed king by Samuel. He began his reign with a great victory over the Ammonites, followed by many battles against the Philistines. His last years were marked by a growing enmity with David.

Sault Ste Marie 46 32N 84 20W A city in E Canada, in NW Ontario on the St Mary's River opposite Sault Ste Marie, USA. Its canal allows ships to bypass local rapids that provide hydroelectricity. Population (1981): 82 697.

Saunders, Dame Cicely Mary Strode (1918–) British philanthropist. After training as a nurse, in 1967 Cicely Saunders founded St Christopher's Hospice in London for the care of the terminally ill, which specializes in the relief of pain and support for the families. She is also the author of such books as *Care of the Dying* (1960) and *Living with Dying* (1983). *See also* hospice movement.

Saurischia An order of dinosaurs dominant in the Jurassic period (about 195–130 million years ago). They had hip bones like those of modern lizards (the name means "lizard hips") and were mostly bipedal carnivores, although some were quadrupedal herbivores. *See also* Allosaurus; Apatosaurus; Tyrannosaurus.

saury A marine fish, also called skipper, belonging to the family *Scomberesocidae* (about 4 species). It has a long slim body, blue or olive above and golden or silvery below, with beaklike jaws. Sauries occur in large shoals in tropical and temperate surface waters, and are often seen leaping or skipping over the surface to escape predators. Order: *Atheriniformes*.

Savage, Richard (c. 1696–1743) British poet. Although he claimed to be the illegitimate son of an earl, he was of humble origin. He led a disorderly bohemian life and died in a debtors' prison in Bristol. His works include *Sir Thomas Overbury* (1723), a tragedy, and *The Wanderer* (1729), a long poem. He was the subject of a sympathetic biography (1744) by his friend Dr Johnson.

savanna (*or* savannah) The extensive tropical grasslands, bordering on the equatorial rain forests in both the N and S hemispheres. They cover extensive areas in N Australia, Africa, and South America (where they are known as the llanos in Venezuela and Colombia and the campos in Brazil). The vegetation of savannas is dominated by tall grasses, such as elephant grass, interspersed with low often flat-topped trees and bushes. Grazed by herds of hooved animals, savannas are ideal cattle-rearing areas.

Savonarola, Girolamo (1452–98) Italian religious reformer. A Dominican prior in Florence from 1491, he began a crusade against religious and political corruption, centring his attacks on the papacy and the Medici. He became the virtual ruler of Florence when the Medici were expelled by the populace in 1494. Excommunicated in 1497, he was hanged and burned for heresy.

savory A herb belonging to the genus *Satureja*, of warm and temperate regions. Summer savory (*S. hortensis*) is an annual, native to central Europe and Asia. Both the dried leaves and the oil extract are used for flavouring foods. The perennial winter savory (*S. montana*) is also a culinary herb. Family: *Labiatae*.

Savoy An Alpine frontier region of SE France corresponding to the present-day departments of Savoie and Haute-Savoie. Strategically important for its mountain passes, the county of Savoy was founded in 1034. Piedmont was acquired in the 14th century and Sardinia in 1720; Savoyard dukes then took the title King of Sardinia, which in 1748 became the kingdom of Piedmont-Sardinia. Savoy (but not Sardinia) was annexed by France during the Revolutionary Wars but restored in 1815 and Piedmont-Sardinia became the leading spirit in the movement for Italian unification (*see* Risorgimento). Savoy became part of France in 1860, but the House of Savoy ruled the newly formed kingdom of Italy (1861–1946).

sawfly An insect belonging to the widely distributed suborder *Symphyta*. The female possesses a needle-like tubular ovipositor, used to insert eggs into foliage and timber. The larvae, resembling caterpillars, damage trees. Chief families: *Argidae, Siricidae, Cimbicidae, Diprionidae, Tenthredinidae*; order: *Hymenoptera*.

Saxe-Coburg-Gotha The ruling dynasty of a German duchy. The children of Duke Francis Frederick (1750–1806) included Victoria Mary Louisa (1786–1861), who married (1818) Edward, Duke of Kent (their daughter was Queen Victoria); and Ernest I (1806–44), father of Prince Albert, who married Queen Victoria in 1840. The UK royal house was called Saxe-Coburg-Gotha until 1917, when the name Windsor was adopted.

saxifrage A perennial herb belonging to certain genera of the family *Saxifragaceae*, found in cold and temperate regions. The leaves may either form a basal rosette or occur in pairs along the stem and the flowers are white, yellow, purple, or red.

Saxons A Germanic people who, during the 5th century AD, expanded from their Baltic coastal homelands to other areas of N Germany, the coast of Gaul (France), and (with the Angles and Jutes) to Britain. Charlemagne eventually defeated the continental Saxons in the 8th century and converted them to Christianity. *See also* Anglo-Saxons.

Saxony (German name: Sachsen) An ancient NW German duchy. Named after its original inhabitants, the Saxons, it was incorporated into Charlemagne's empire and subsequently became a duchy. In the 13th century Saxony became an electorate and in the 16th and 17th centuries a leading German Protestant state. In 1697 Elector Frederick Augustus I (1670–1733) became King of Poland and Saxony's subsequent involvement in Polish affairs kept it apart from German power struggles until the 19th century. Conquered by Napoleon in 1806, N Saxony was annexed by Prussia in 1815 and in 1866 joined the Prussian-dominated North German Confederation. The remainder of Saxony joined the German Empire in 1871.

saxophone A woodwind instrument with a brass body, keys, and a single reed mouthpiece similar to that of a clarinet. It was invented by the Belgian Adolphe Sax (1814–94) and patented in France in the 1840s. The most common sizes of saxophone are the soprano, alto, tenor, and baritone. They are most commonly used as solo instruments in jazz.

Sayers, Dorothy L(eigh) (1893–1957) British writer, best known for her series of detective novels, beginning with *Whose Body?* (1923), featuring the erudite detective Lord Peter Wimsey.

scabies A contagious skin infection caused by the itch mite, which tunnels and breeds in the skin, causing intense itching. Treatment is by application of benzylbenzoate cream.

scabious An annual or perennial herb belonging to the genus *Scabiosa* (80–100 species), native to the Mediterranean region and temperate parts of Eurasia and Africa. The small scabious (*S. columbaria*) is widely distributed on chalky soils. It has a cluster of small bluish-lilac flowers borne on a long stalk. The field scabious, *S.* (or *Knautia*) *arvensis*, is very similar. Family: *Dipsacaceae*.

Scafell Pike 54 28N 3 12W The highest peak in England, in Cumbria, in the Lake District. Height: 978 m (3210 ft).

scalar quantity A quantity that is represented by magnitude only. Unlike a vector quantity, a scalar quantity has no direction. Examples include mass, time, and speed.

scale (music) An ascending or descending succession of notes, characterized by a fixed succession of intervals between the notes that constitute it. Many thousands of different scales exist; all the major musical traditions are based upon them.
In western music there are three **diatonic scales**: the major scale, the harmonic minor scale, and the melodic minor scale. The octave is divided into 12 notes and any of these scales may be constructed on these notes. The version of the scale produced is associated with a particular tonality. The **chromatic scale** includes all 12 semitones of the octave.

scale insect An insect belonging to the superfamily *Coccoidea* (about 4000 species), abundant in warm and tropical regions. Scale insects are usually small and the females are often legless, wingless, and eyeless and covered by a waxy scale or mass of threads. They become encrusted on plants and suck the juices, often becoming serious pests. Other species are of value by producing shellac, cochineal, and various waxes. Suborder: *Homoptera*; order: *Hemiptera*.

scallop An edible bivalve mollusc belonging to the family *Pectinidae* (about 400 species), of warm and temperate seas. The valves of the shell are broad, flattened, and deeply fluted, and the animal swims by flapping them with a single powerful muscle.

Scandinavian languages A subgroup of the Germanic group of languages consisting of Swedish, Norwegian, Danish, Icelandic, and Faeroese. The first three are similar enough to be mutually intelligible, their separateness being imposed by their history and political boundaries. They all developed from a common Scandinavian ancestor, which originally used the runic alphabet (*see also* Old Norse). This language spread with the Vikings to Iceland, the Faeroes, and to other Baltic and Atlantic islands.

scandium (Sc) The first transition metal, predicted by Mendeleyev and discovered in 1879. It is trivalent, light (relative density 2.989), and has a high melting point. At no 21; at wt 44.956; mp 1541°C; bp 2831°C.

scanner (medicine). See tomography; ultrasonics.

Scapa Flow A section of the Atlantic Ocean off the N coast of Scotland, in the Orkney Islands. It was the main base of the British Grand Fleet in World War I. Following its surrender, the German fleet scuttled itself here (1919). Length: 24 km (15 mi). Width: 13 km (8 mi).

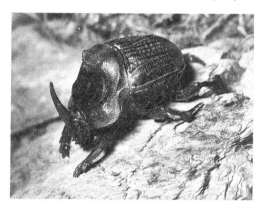

SCARAB BEETLE *This African species is one of the rhinoceros beetles.*

scarab beetle A beetle belonging to the worldwide family *Scarabaeidae* (over 19 000 species). Scarabs show a great variety in size and form: the largest beetles – the goliath and hercules beetles – are scarabs, while other species have developed extraordinary horns (*see* rhinoceros beetle). The family has two main groups – the dung beetles and chafers. Certain dung-rolling beetles, especially *Scarabaeus sacer*, were the sacred scarabs of the ancient Egyptians.

Scarborough 54 17N 0 24W A resort in NE England, on the North Yorkshire coast. The promontory separating the North and South Bays is the site of a prehistoric settlement, a Roman signal station, and a 12th-century castle. There is fishing and tourism. Population (1989 est): 50 908.

Scarlatti, Domenico (1685–1757) Italian composer and noted harpsichordist and organist, working in Lisbon from 1720 and in Madrid from 1729. Besides some operas and church music, he wrote over 600 harpsichord sonatas, many of which were highly innovative. His father **Alessandro Scarlatti** (1660–1725) was also a composer, working chiefly in Rome and Naples. His works include over a hundred operas, 600 chamber cantatas, 200 masses, 12 chamber symphonies, and 14 oratorios.

scarlet fever A highly infectious disease of children caused by streptococcus bacteria. The child develops a sore throat, fever, and headache, and 24–48 hours later a red rash spreads from the chest over the whole body. Before antibiotics scarlet fever killed many children or left them disabled with rheumatic fever, kidney disease, or ear infections; it can now be rapidly cured with penicillin.

Scheldt, River A river in W Europe. Rising in NE France, it flows generally NNE through W Belgium to Antwerp, then NW to the North Sea in the SW Netherlands. Canals connect it to the Rivers Somme, Seine, Sambre, Meuse, and Rhine. Length: 435 km (270 mi).

Schiller, (Johann Christoph) Friedrich (von) (1759–1805) German dramatist, poet, and writer. His first play, *Die Räuber* (1781), typifies the *Sturm und Drang* call for political freedom. With Goethe's encouragement from 1794, Schiller turned from historical and academic studies to produce brilliant dramas: the trilogy *Wallenstein* (1798–99), *Maria Stuart* (1800), *Die Jungfrau von Orleans* (1801), and *Wilhelm Tell* (1804). His nondramatic works include poems and an important essay on aesthetics.

schipperke A breed of dog originating in Flanders and used as a guard dog on barges. It has a stocky tailless body with short legs and a foxlike head with erect ears. The dense coat is usually black and thick around the neck, forming a mane. Height: 30.5–33 cm.

schistosomiasis (*or* bilharziasis) A widespread disease of the tropics caused by blood flukes of the genus *Schistosoma* (or *Bilharzia*). The disease is contracted by bathing in water contaminated by snails, which harbour the larvae of the parasite. The larvae penetrate the skin and—when mature—settle in the blood vessels of the intestine or bladder. Symptoms, caused by the release of eggs by adult flukes, include anaemia, inflammation, and diarrhoea and dysentery (from an intestinal infection), or cystitis and blood in the urine (from a bladder infection). The disease is treated by drugs that destroy the parasite. A vaccine (discovered 1987) is being tested.

schizophrenia A severe mental disorder characterized by disintegration of the processes of thinking, contact with reality, and emotional responsiveness. Delusions and hallucinations are common, especially those that produce the feeling of a loss of personal identity. Modern treatment consists of such drugs as phenothiazines and vigorous psychological and social rehabilitation. *See also* paranoia; psychosis.

Schleswig-Holstein A low-lying *Land* in NE West Germany bordering on the North Sea, the Baltic Sea, and Denmark. During the 19th century Denmark and the Austrian-led German confederacy both laid claim to the two duchies of Schleswig and Holstein. The duchies were eventually annexed to Prussia in 1866, the *Land* being formed in 1949. Area: 15 696 sq km (6059 sq mi). Population (1986): 2 612 700. Capital: Kiel.

Schliemann, Heinrich (1822–90) German archaeologist. After a successful business career, Schliemann retired (1863) to search for Homeric Troy. He excavated Hissarlik on the Asia Minor coast of Turkey, finding ruins of nine successive cities. His spectacular finds at Mycenae (1874–76), Orchomenos in Boeotia (1880), and Tiryns (1884–85) established him as the discoverer of Mycenaean civilization.

Schmidt, Helmut (1918–   ) West German statesman; Social Democratic chancellor (1974–82). Entering Federal politics in 1953, he was Federal minister of defence (1969–72) and for finance (1972–74) before becoming chancellor.

Schmidt telescope A telescope that uses a thin "correcting" lens in front of the spherical primary mirror. It was developed by the Estonian instrument maker Bernard Voldemar Schmidt (1879–1935). It produces very sharp photographic images of celestial objects over a very wide angle of sky.

schnauzer A breed of dog originating in Germany and used as a guard dog. Strongly built with a docked tail, it has a characteristic square muzzle with long sidewhiskers. The wiry coat is black or light grey and brown. Two varieties are the giant schnauzer bred for farm and police work and the miniature schnauzer. Height: 33–35 cm (miniature); 45–48 cm (standard); 54–65 cm (giant).

Schoenberg, Arnold (1874–1951) Austrian-born composer. Forced as a Jew to leave Berlin (1933), he became a US citizen in 1941. His early compositions, in a late Romantic style, include two string quartets and the symphonic poem *Pelleas und Melisande* (1902–03). Later works were characterized by atonality. In 1924 Schoenberg developed the theory and technique of serialism, which he employed in most of his subsequent works, including a violin concerto (1936), a piano concerto (1942), and the unfinished opera *Moses und Aaron* (begun 1932).

scholasticism The intellectual discipline comprising all the philosophical and theological activities pursued in the medieval universities (schools). As the international philosophy of Christendom it respected orthodoxy and was concerned with the philosophies of Plato and Aristotle. For scholastics, such as Abelard and Aquinas, religion was predominant and it was by theology that the selection of problems for study and the scope of scientific enquiry were to be decided.

Schopenhauer, Arthur (1788–1860) German philosopher. He placed emphasis upon the human will as a means to understanding. *The World as Will and Idea* (1818) sets out his principal ideas and pessimistic conclusions. He was distrustful of rationalism and the scientific method, believing that contemplative freedom could be achieved through art.

Schrödinger, Erwin (1887–1961) Austrian physicist, who worked in Dublin, 1940–56. He shared the 1933 Nobel Prize with Dirac for his development of the form of the quantum theory known as wave mechanics.

Schubert, Franz (Peter) (1797–1828) Austrian composer, who achieved little recognition before his premature death. Schubert's melodic genius is evident in his 600 *Lieder*, which include "Death and the Maiden" and "The Trout." Some of his greatest songs are to be found in the song-cycles *Die Schöne Müllerin* (1823) and *Die Winterreise* (1827). His other more large-scale compositions include nine symphonies (of which one is lost and the eighth is unfinished), string quartets, piano trios, an octet, two quintets, piano sonatas, and much choral music.

Schumann, Robert (Alexander) (1810–56) German composer. Almost all his musical compositions up to 1840 were for the piano, including *Kreisleriana* (1838). His works also include four symphonies and many songs. He wrote much as a critic, founding and editing (1835–44) a musical journal. Gradual insanity developed in later life and he died in an asylum.

His wife **Clara Schumann** (1819–96), whom he married in 1840, was a famous pianist, teacher, and composer, and became a great interpreter and editor of her husband's works.

FRANZ SCHUBERT

Schuschnigg, Kurt von (1897–1977) Austrian statesman; chancellor (1934–38). He tried in vain to prevent the Nazi *Anschluss* and was forced to resign, being imprisoned by Hitler throughout World War II. On his release he taught in the USA until 1967, when he returned to Austria.

Schwarzkopf, Elisabeth (1915–) German soprano, especially noted for her interpretation of Mozart and Richard Strauss.

Schweitzer, Albert (1875–1965) Alsatian-born theologian, medical missionary, and organist. From 1913 until his death, Schweitzer practised as a doctor in the hospital he founded in Gabon at the jungle village of Lambaréné. In 1952 he received the Nobel Peace Prize.

Science Museum A museum in South Kensington, London, devoted to the history and development of science, engineering, and industry. Its full name is the British National Museum of Science and Industry. It was separated from the Victoria and Albert Museum in 1909. The National Railway Museum, York, (opened 1975) is an outstation.

scientology A tradename for a religious doctrine followed by the Church of Scientology, founded in 1954 in California by L(afayette) Ron(ald) Hubbard (1911–86). Originally a method of psychotherapy, this doctrine was later presented as a religious philosophy claiming to increase a member's IQ, creativity, etc., until he has realized his full spiritual potential. The Church's methods, particularly its practice of counselling ("auditing") to release adherents from past emotional bonds, have been widely criticized.

Scilly, Isles of (*or* Scillies) A group of about 140 islands and islets in the Atlantic Ocean, off the extreme SW coast of England. Only five are inhabited, namely St Mary's (the largest), Tresco, St Martin's, St Agnes, and Bryher. Their mild climate has been exploited to produce early spring flowers for the UK market. Agriculture is intensive. Area: 16 sq km (6 sq mi). Population (1981): 2628. Chief town: Hugh Town.

sclerosis Stiffening and hardening of the tissues. This is a feature of many diseases. *See* multiple sclerosis; arteriosclerosis; atherosclerosis.

Scofield, (David) Paul (1922–) British actor. His major theatrical roles include Hamlet (1948, 1955), Lear (1962), Prospero (1976), and Othello (1980). His best-known film performance was as Sir Thomas More in *A Man for All Seasons* (1966).

Scone 56 25N 3 24W A parish in E central Scotland, in Tayside Region. It consists of the villages of New Scone and Old Scone, the Pictish and later Scottish capital where most Scottish kings were crowned. The coronation stone was taken from here by Edward I in 1296 and placed in Westminster Abbey. It was removed in 1950 and taken to Arbroath but later recovered.

scops owl A small owl of the mainly tropical genus *Otus*, also called screech owl because of its call. Scops owls are mostly arboreal, with camouflaging plumage resembling bark.

scorpion An arachnid of the order *Scorpionida* (about 800 species), found in warm dry regions. The second pair of appendages form large pincers and the elongated abdomen curls upwards and bears a poisonous sting, which can be fatal to man. They prey at night, mainly on insects and spiders.

scorpion fish A carnivorous fish, often called rockfish or zebra fish, belonging to the family *Scorpaenidae*, found mainly on rocky beds of tropical and temperate coastal waters. It has a stout body, up to 1 m long, a large spiny head, and strong fin spines, which can inflict painful wounds and may be venomous. Order: *Scorpaeniformes*.

scorpion fly An insect of the order *Mecoptera* (400 species), so called because the males of many species curl the abdomen over the body, like a scorpion. Scorpion flies have long legs and antennae and, typically, two similar pairs of net-veined wings. Larvae and adults feed on dead animals and plants.

Scotland A country occupying the N part of Great Britain and comprising a political division of the United Kingdom. Most of the population lives in a narrow lowland belt, which runs E–W across the country and separates the lower hills of the S (including the Tweedsmuir and Cheviot Hills) from the higher mountains of the N (including the Grampian and Cairngorm Mountains). There are many islands off the N and W coasts, including the Hebrides to the W and the Orkneys and Shetlands to the N. The principal rivers are the Clyde, Forth, Tay, and Spey. There are several lochs in the northern mountains, and Lochs Ness and Lochy form the Great Glen (valley) between Fort William and Inverness. Administratively, Scotland is divided into nine regions and three island areas, which replaced the former counties in 1975. *Economy*: the central belt of the country is highly industrialized, based originally on the coal found there. Coal is still mined in Lothian and Fife Regions. Other long-established industries include shipbuilding. Whisky, for which Scotland is internationally famous, is produced in Highland and Grampian Regions. The discovery of oil in the North Sea has led to a boom on the E coast of the country. Agriculture remains important and includes sheep farming in the upland areas, dairying in the SW, beef production in the E and NE lowlands, and market gardening. Forestry is important in the Highlands. Fishing is another source of revenue. *History*: Scotland was never completely subdued by the

Romans, but the barbaric northern tribes were kept N of Hadrian's Wall and, for some 40 years, the more northerly Antonine Wall (from the Forth to the Clyde). The diverse peoples (Picts, Scots, Britons, and Angles) of Scotland gradually united, helped by the spread of Christianity, and Kenneth I MacAlpine (died c. 858) is regarded as their first king. During the middle ages there was recurrent war between England and Scotland. In 1296 Edward I of England declared himself King of Scotland but after his death Robert the Bruce reasserted Scottish independence, which was recognized by England in 1328. The 14th century saw the establishment of a long-standing alliance between France and Scotland and the succession of the Stuart dynasty. Under the influence of John Knox the Scottish Church became Presbyterian (*see* Church of Scotland) during the reign of Mary, Queen of Scots. In 1603 her son James VI succeeded as James I to the throne of England but political union was not established until 1707 (*see* Union, Acts of). After the Hanoverian succession the Stuart cause was kept alive by the Jacobites, who staged two unsuccessful rebellions (1715, 1745) against George I and George II. Rapid industrialization in the 19th century encouraged considerable Irish immigration. Following the parliamentary Reform Act (1832) a tradition for Liberalism was established in Scotland but Labour gained political dominance in the 20th century. Devolution plans were rejected in a referendum in 1979. Area: 78 769 sq km (30 405 sq mi). Population (1986 est): 5 121 000. Capital: Edinburgh.

Scots law   Originally Scots law differed little from English law, but from the beginning of the 16th century there was a tendency to introduce elements of Roman law, especially as embodied in the civil law of France and the Netherlands. This resulted in marked differences from English law, the preservation of which was guaranteed by the Treaty of Union with England in 1707. An example is the Scots law of contract, in which the principle of "consideration" does not have the importance it has in English law. Modern statutes have, however, introduced many new laws that are the same for both countries.

Scott, Sir George Gilbert   (1811–78) British architect. An advocate of the gothic revival style, Scott was a noted designer, restorer of medieval buildings, and author. He renovated many churches and cathedrals, including Westminster Abbey. His original buildings include the Albert Memorial (1864) and St Pancras station (1865). His grandson **Sir Giles Gilbert Scott** (1880–1960) was also an architect. He designed the Anglican Cathedral in Liverpool (begun 1904), the new Bodleian Library, Oxford (1936–46), and the new Waterloo Bridge (1939–45).

Scott, Paul (Mark)   (1920–78) British novelist. He is best known for the "Raj Quartet", a series of novels (1966–75) dealing with the final period of British rule in India, and the novel *Staying On* (1977).

Scott, Robert Falcon   (1868–1912) British explorer and naval officer. He led two expeditions to the Antarctic, 1900–04 and 1910–12. With a party of four he reached the South Pole on 17 January, 1912, only to find that Amundsen had preceded them. Delayed by illness and blizzards they perished only a few miles from safety. His son **Sir Peter Markham Scott** (1909–89) was a noted ornithologist and wildlife painter. In 1946 he

CAPTAIN SCOTT   *Seen writing his diary in the hut at Cape Evans (Antarctic) in 1912.*

founded the Wildfowl Trust (renamed the Wildfowl and Wetlands Trust in 1989) based at Slimbridge, Gloucestershire, for the study and conservation of birds.

Scott, Sir Walter   (1771–1832) Scottish novelist. His early works included a collection of border ballads (1802–03) and the popular narrative poem *The Lay of the Last Minstrel* (1805). *Waverley* (1814) was the first of a series of successful historical novels that included *Old Mortality* (1816) and *The Heart of Midlothian* (1818).

Scottish National Party   (SNP) A political party, founded in 1928, dedicated to achieving Scottish independence from the UK. The party secured 11 seats and 30.4% of the Scottish vote in the 1974 parliamentary election, but after the devolution referendum in 1979 held only two seats in the subsequent general election. After the 1987 election it held three seats.

Scottish terrier   A breed of dog, originally called Aberdeen terrier, used to chase foxes from earth. It is thickset with short legs, a short erect tail, and pricked ears. The long muzzle has characteristically long whiskers and the wiry coat is usually black. Height: 25–28 cm.

Scout Association   An association founded by Robert Baden Powell in 1908 to encourage boys to become enterprising members of society. It includes Cub Scouts (for boys aged 8 to 11), Scouts (11–16), and Venture Scouts (16–29). Girl Scouts were first admitted in 1990. *See also* Girl Guides Association.

scree.   *See* talus.

screech owl.   *See* scops owl.

screw pine   A treelike plant of the genus *Pandanus* (about 150 species), native to the Old World tropics. The name derives from the spiral arrangement of the leaves, which leave scars in a corkscrew spiral when they fall. Stout aerial prop roots grow down from the stem into the ground: the part of the stem below these roots decays, so that the plant is supported entirely by the prop roots. The long stiff leaves are used for matting and weaving. The flowers grow in large heads enclosed in leafy structures (spathes) and the fruits of some species are edible. Family: *Pandanaceae*.

Scriabin, Alexander   (1872–1915) Russian composer and pianist. His mature compositions were characterized by chords built on the interval of the fourth. His works include three symphonies, a piano concerto

(1894), ten piano sonatas, and *Prometheus* or *The Poem of Fire* (1909–10).

scrofula   Ulceration of a lymph node infected with tuberculosis, seen most commonly in the neck. This form of tuberculosis is now uncommon in developed countries. Treatment is with antibiotic drugs and surgery.

scurvy   A disease caused by deficiency of vitamin C (which is present in most fresh fruits and vegetables). In the past scurvy was common among sailors on long voyages, but it is now rarely seen.

Scylla and Charybdis   In Greek mythology, two sea monsters on opposite sides of the Strait of Messina who menaced Odysseus, the Argonauts, and other legendary heroes. Scylla was a monster with six heads and a pack of baying hounds, while Charybdis was a raging whirlpool.

Scyphozoa.   *See* jellyfish.

Scythians   An Indo-European people who temporarily settled in Asia Minor before settling in what is now S Russia in the 6th century BC. The true Scythians, called Royal Scyths, established a kingdom N of the Black Sea. Their skill as horsemen and archers halted Persian and Macedonian invasions but they disappeared from history during the Gothic onslaughts of the 3rd century AD.

SDI.   *See* Strategic Defence Initiative.

sea anemone   A sedentary marine invertebrate animal of a worldwide order (*Actiniaria*; over 1000 species) of coelenterates. It has a soft columnar body (*see* polyp) with a mouth at the top surrounded by rings of tentacles, which—when expanded—give the animal a flower-like appearance. Sea anemones are often found attached to rocks and weeds. They feed mainly on fish and other animals. Class: *Anthozoa*.

sea bass   A carnivorous fish, also called sea perch, of the family *Serranidae* (about 400 species), found mainly in coastal waters of tropical and temperate seas. Its elongated body ranges up to 3.75 m long and varies in colour with the species. They may be active or sedentary and certain species are hermaphrodite while others, such as groupers, are able to change sex. Many are valued food and game fish. Order: *Perciformes*. *See also* bass.

sea bream   A fish, also called porgy, belonging to a family (*Sparidae*; about 400 species) found mainly in shallow waters of tropical and subtropical seas. It has a deep laterally flattened body covered with large scales, a single long dorsal fin, and well-developed teeth. It lives in shoals and feeds by scraping algae and small animals off rocks.

sea cow.   *See* dugong.

sea cucumber   A marine invertebrate animal belonging to a worldwide class (*Holothuroidea*; 1100 species) of echinoderms. At one end of its leathery cucumber-shaped body there is a mouth surrounded by a ring of tentacles. It crawls sluggishly on the sea bottom or burrows in sand or mud.

sea-floor spreading   A concept developed in the 1960s that provides a mechanism for continental drift. Magma rises from the earth's mantle to the surface along midocean ridges (constructive plate margins; *see* plate tectonics), cools to form new oceanic crust, and displaces the older material sideways at an average rate of 4 cm per year. Magnetic reversals recorded in the rocks in approximately symmetrical strips at each side of the midocean ridges provide strong evidence.

sea gooseberry.   *See* ctenophore.

seagull.   *See* gull.

SEA HORSE

sea horse   One of several small bony-plated marine fish of the family *Syngnathidae*, especially the genus *Hippocampus*, that lives in shallow warm waters. The horselike head with its long tubular snout is set at an angle to the body. They use the prehensile tail to cling to seaweed and swim in a vertical position by undulating the dorsal fin. Order: *Gasterosteiformes*.

sea kale   A bushy perennial herb, *Crambe maritima*, found on Atlantic coasts of Europe. It is cultivated for its young edible cabbage-like leaves. Family: *Cruciferae*.

seal   (zoology)   A carnivorous marine mammal belonging to the order *Pinnipedia* (32 species). Seals have a streamlined body with a smooth rounded head and an insulating layer of blubber under the sleek-coated skin. Both pairs of limbs flatten into flippers. They feed mainly on fish and breed on land or ice.
There are two main families: the *Otariidae* (eared seals; 13 species) including fur seals and sealions, which have external ears and can turn their hind flippers forward for walking on land; and the *Phocidae* (true seals; 18 species), which lack external ears and have trailing hind flippers. *See also* walrus.

sea lettuce   A green seaweed of the genus *Ulva*, found mainly between high and low tide levels on most rocky shores. It has broad flat translucent fronds, and grows in bunches. It is rich in iodine and vitamins and is sometimes used in salads and soups.

sea lily.   *See* crinoid.

sealion   A large seal belonging to the family *Otariidae*. Californian sealions (*Zalophus californianus*) of the Californian coast grow to 2 m and live in groups with a definite social hierarchy. Steller's sealion (*Eumetopias jubatus*) is the largest species, growing to over 3 m.

Sealyham terrier   A breed of dog developed (1850–91) on the Sealyham estate, Haverfordwest, Wales, for hunting foxes and badgers. It is sturdily built with short legs, drooping ears, and a short thin tail. White with darker markings, Sealyhams have a soft under coat and a wiry outer coat. Height: 27–30 cm.

sea otter   A marine otter, *Enhydra lutris*, of the N Pacific, living in colonies of up to 90 individuals. Sea otters feed on molluscs, crustaceans, and fish and can crack open shells using a pebble. Once hunted for their valuable fur, they are now a protected species.

Sea Peoples   The seafaring tribes, uncertainly identified, who colonized Asia Minor, the Aegean, and N Africa in the 13th and 12th centuries BC, destroying the Hittite empire. About 1170 they were almost annihilated by Rameses III of Egypt and those that survived scattered.

sea perch.   *See* sea bass.

sea robin.   *See* gurnard.

sea slug   A marine gastropod mollusc of the order *Nudibranchia*. Sea slugs have exposed feathery gills, two pairs of tentacles, and no shell. They browse on sponges, sea anemones, and corals and are often brightly coloured.

sea snake   A venomous fish-eating snake belonging to the family *Hydrophiidae* (50 species) occurring mainly in coastal waters of Australasia and SE Asia. Sea snakes are adapted to an underwater life by having a flattened body with an oarlike tail and valvelike closures in the nostrils. Most produce live young (rather than eggs).

sea squirt.   *See* tunicate.

SEATO.   *See* South East Asia Treaty Organization.

Seattle   47 35N 122 20W A city and port in the USA, in Washington state between the Puget Sound and Lake Washington. A port of entry to the Klondike, it became a boom town with the 1897 Alaska Gold Rush. There are large timber mills and various forest-based industries. Population (1986 est): 486 200.

sea urchin   A marine invertebrate animal, belonging to the class *Echinoidea*, with a typically spherical rigid body covered by long movable spines. Sea urchins live on shores and ocean floors and use a complex feeding apparatus to masticate algae and other organic material scraped off rocks. Phylum: *Echinodermata* (*see* echinoderm).

sea water   The water constituting the world's oceans and seas. It is usually saline, average salinity being about 35 g per kg of sea water. The principal dissolved salts are sodium chloride (2.8%), magnesium chloride (0.4%), and magnesium sulphate (0.2%). Where evaporation is high, salinity is increased, as in the Red Sea. *See also* desalination).

seaweed   Large multicellular red, brown, or green marine algae that are generally found attached to the sea bed, rocks, or other solid structures by rootlike structures called holdfasts. The plants have stemlike stalks and fronds, which may be flat and undivided, threadlike, or branched, sometimes with small air bladders for buoyancy. Seaweeds often occur in dense aggregations along shores. Many are of commercial importance as food (e.g. carrageen, laver, and sea lettuce), as fertilizers, in chemical and pharmaceutical products, etc. *See also* kelp; wrack.

sebaceous glands.   *See* skin.

Sebastian, St   (3rd century AD) Roman martyr, killed by archers. According to tradition, he was an officer of the Praetorian Guards until his Christianity was discovered by Diocletian. Feast day: 20 Jan.

Sebastiano del Piombo   (S. Luciano; c. 1485–1547) Venetian painter. Although he was a pupil of Giovanni Bellini, his early works, notably *St John Chrysostom* (c. 1509; S Giovanni Crisostomo, Venice), were influenced by Giorgione. Moving to Rome in 1511, he painted decorations in the Farnesina with Raphael, whose *Transfiguration* he directly challenged with his *Raising of Lazarus* (1517–19; National Gallery, London). He was also known as a portraitist; his sitters included Christopher Columbus and Pope Clement VII, who appointed

SEBASTIANO DEL PLOMBO   The Raising of Lazarus *(detail)*.

him keeper of the papal seals (*piombi*) in 1531–hence his nickname.

Sebastopol.   *See* Sevastopol.

second   **1.** (s) The SI unit of time equal to the duration of 9 192 631 770 periods of the radiation corresponding to a specified transition of the caesium-133 atom. **2.** A unit of angle equal to one-sixtieth of a minute.

secondary education   Education for adolescent children, aged approximately from 11 to 18. In the UK the Education Act (1944) introduced universal secondary education (compulsory to the age of 15, extended to 16 in 1972). Initially a tripartite system (comprising grammar schools for higher ability pupils, secondary modern schools, and technical schools) was implemented in England and Wales, selection being based upon the eleven-plus examination. This exam has now been largely phased out and a widespread system of comprehensive schools introduced.

secondary emission   The ejection of electrons from the surface of a metal when it is bombarded with charged particles of sufficient energy. When the bombarding particles are themselves electrons, these are known as primary electrons and the ejected electrons are called secondary electrons. The effect is used in such devices as the electron multiplier.

secretary bird   A large long-legged terrestrial bird of prey, *Sagittarius serpentarius*, that lives in dry uplands of Africa. It has a hawklike face and a grey plumage with a long pair of central tail feathers and a black crest of quills behind its head–hence its name. Order: *Falconiformes* (falcons, hawks, etc.).

Sedan, Battle of   (1 September, 1870) The battle in the Franco-Prussian War in which German forces, invading NE France, defeated the army of Napoleon III. This precipitated revolution in Paris and marked the end of the Second Empire.

sedatives   Drugs that relieve restlessness, anxiety, and tension. Most drugs that depress the activity of the nervous system have this effect (including barbiturates and narcotics), but the most widely used sedatives are the minor tranquillizers, for example benzodiazepines.

sedge   A perennial herbaceous grasslike plant of the genus *Carex* (about 2000 species), growing throughout the world, mainly in swampy places. Sedges have solid triangular stems, with long narrow **leaves** and small male and female flowers usually grouped into separate clusters (spikes). Family: *Cyperaceae*.

Sedgemoor, Battle of (6 July, 1685) The battle, SE of Bridgewater, Somerset, in which the forces of James II of England defeated the rebellion of his nephew, the Duke of Monmouth.

sedimentary rock One of the three major categories into which rocks are divided (*compare* igneous rock; metamorphic rock). Sedimentary rocks are deposited mainly under water, usually in approximately horizontal layers (beds). **Clastic sedimentary rocks** are formed from the erosion and deposition of pre-existing rocks and are classified according to the size of the particles: those with sand-grade particles include the sandstones; those with silt- or clay-grade particles include siltstones and mudstones; those with gravel-grade and larger fragments include the breccias, conglomerates, etc. Organically formed sedimentary rocks are derived from the remains of plants and animals, for example limestone and coal. Chemically formed sedimentary rocks result from natural chemical processes and include sedimentary iron ores. Many sedimentary rocks show complex internal structures, formed during or after deposition.

Sedum. *See* stonecrop.

Seebeck effect. *See* thermoelectric effects.

seed The reproductive structure formed after pollination and fertilization in higher plants. In flowering plants (angiosperms) the seed begins to develop after the pollen nucleus has fused with the egg. In gymnosperms (conifers and related plants) the ovule begins dividing before pollination. All seeds contain an embryo and usually a food store, which is mobilized on germination. Angiosperm seeds are surrounded by a seed coat and contained within a fruit; gymnosperm seeds are naked (*see* cone). The development of the "seed habit" has given the higher plants a marked advantage over the ferns, mosses, algae, and fungi. Water is not needed for fertilization, and therefore the plants can colonize arid habitats. In addition, seeds—unlike the spores of lower plants —can survive adverse conditions.

seed fern A fernlike gymnosperm plant belonging to the extinct order *Pteridospermales*, abundant during the Carboniferous and Permian periods (370–240 million years ago). Seed ferns—unlike ferns—produced seeds and were probably the ancestors of plants that evolved into the angiosperms (flowering plants).

Segovia, Andrés (1893–1987) Spanish guitarist, who revived the popularity of the guitar as a concert instrument.

Seine, River A river in N France. Rising on the Plateau de Langres, it flows mainly NW through Paris to the English Channel, S of Le Havre. It is the second longest river in France, linked by canal with the Rivers Somme, Scheldt, Meuse, Rhine, Saône, and Loire. Length: 776 km (482 mi).

seismic belts (*or* seismic zones) The narrow distinct belts on the earth's surface that are subject to frequent earthquakes. They usually follow the line of plate boundaries (*see* plate tectonics), especially along midocean ridges, island arc systems, and major faults.

seismic wave An elastic shock wave emanating from the focus of an earthquake or explosion. When seismic activity is recorded, several types of wave can be identified: longitudinal P (*primae*) waves and transverse S (*secundae*) waves are small rapid vibrations that come directly through the earth's interior in the preliminary tremor of an earthquake. The main earthquake consists of large slow L (*longae*) waves travelling along the surface. The study of seismic waves has provided much of our knowledge of the earth's interior.

SEISMOLOGY *Seismograph in California recording minor tremors.*

seismology The branch of geophysics concerned with the study of earthquakes: their origin, the waves they produce (*see* seismic wave), their effects, their distribution, and their prediction and modification. The instruments used are the **seismograph**, which records the magnitude of the oscillations during an earthquake, and the **seismometer**, which detects and records the motions of the earth in a particular direction (usually used in sets of three).

sei whale A widely distributed rorqual, *Balaenopteris borealis*. Up to 18 m long, it has a dark back, a white belly, and a large dorsal fin.

Selby 53 48N 1 04W A market town in N England, in North Yorkshire on the River Ouse. It has a famous 12th-century abbey church. Industries include the rich Selby coalfield (the first mine went into production in 1983). Population (1981): 107 726.

Selene The Greek moon-goddess, daughter of the Titan Hyperion and sister of Helios (the sun) and Eos (dawn). She became identified with the later Greek goddess Artemis and with the Roman Diana.

selenium (Se) A chemical element that is a member of the sulphur family and exists in several forms, including deep-red crystals, but the commonest allotrope is grey. The element has photovoltaic properties and is used in photocells, light meters, and in photocopying machines. It is a semiconductor and is widely used in rectifiers. At no 34; at wt 78.96; mp 217°C; bp 685°C.

Seleucids A Middle Eastern dynasty of the Hellenistic age (323–27 BC) founded by Seleucus I Nicator (c. 356–280 BC), the Macedonian general who, after Alexander the Great's death, became governor and then ruler (312) of Babylonia. He extended his kingdom to the frontiers of India in the east and then into Syria in the west but his successors failed to maintain his conquests. Antiochus the Great (reigned 223–187) briefly restored Seleucid power in the east but could not prevent Rome's Mediterranean expansion. The empire was further weakened by the revolt of the Maccabees, who were repressed, but the Parthians precipated the final disintegration of the Seleucid empire. In 64 BC Pompey annexed what was left of it to form the Roman province of Syria.

Sellers, Peter (1925–80) British comic actor. He made his name in the 1950s with the BBC radio comedy series *The Goon Show*. His many films include *I'm All Right, Jack* (1959), *The Millionairess* (1961), *Dr Strangelove* (1963), *What's New, Pussycat?* (1965), *The Pink Panther* series (1963–77), and *Being There* (1980).

Selznick, David O(liver) (1902–65) US film producer. In 1936 he formed his own production company and produced *A Star Is Born* (1937) and *Gone with the Wind* (1939) among other films. His later films included *Duel in the Sun* (1946) and *A Farewell to Arms* (1957).

semantics Broadly, the branch of philology concerned with the study of the relationship between words and meanings. Semantics as the study of meaning in individual words is part of linguistics, but there are philosophical problems involved in trying to account for the relationship between words and the objects they refer to, particularly when a theory is extended to cover words that have no concrete referent (e.g. "honesty"). Logical analysis is widely accepted in explaining the aspect of meaning that is a function of grammatical structure, i.e. sentence meaning is seen as a matter of internal relationships among the words, word particles, and phrases involved.

n (1)   b (2)   c (3)   d (4)   u (5)   f (6)   g (7)

h (8)   i (9)   j   k (0)   l   m   n

o   p   q   r   s   t   u

v   w   x   y   z

numerical   message received   end of signal (AR)

SEMAPHORE

semaphore 1. A visual method of communication between ships at sea, used mainly by warships wishing to maintain radio silence, and consisting of a pattern of signalling by the use of two flags, held by a signalman, their relative positions symbolizing an alphabetical or numerical character. 2. A mechanical railway signalling device, consisting of a movable steel arm.

Semarang 6 58S 110 29E A port in Indonesia, in central Java on the Java Sea. A commercial centre with tex-

tile and shipbuilding industries, it exports sugar, rubber, coffee, kapok, and copra. The port is sometimes disrupted by the monsoon. Its university was established in 1960. Population (1984): 1 077 000.

semen. *See* sperm.

semiconductor A crystalline material in which the electrical conductivity increases with temperature and is between that of a conductor and an insulator. The conductivity is also sensitive to minute quantities of impurities in the crystal lattice. Some (donor) impurities increase the number of negative charge carriers (electrons), creating what is known as an n-type semiconductor. Other (acceptor) impurities increase the number of positive charge carriers (holes), creating a p-type semiconductor. The introduction of these impurities is called doping. Solid-state electronic components, such as diodes, transistors, and integrated circuits depend on the properties of junctions between p-type and n-type regions in the same piece of semiconductor crystal (p-n junctions). Metal oxide semiconductor (MOS) devices also use the properties of a thin layer of insulating oxide on the semiconductor surface. The element silicon is now the most widely used semiconducting material.

semiconductor diode A solid-state electronic device with two electrodes. It consists of a single p-n junction (*see* semiconductor). When the p-region is at a more positive voltage than the n-region (forward bias), the current flow increases exponentially as the voltage rises. In reverse bias, very little current flows until a sufficiently high reverse voltage has built up to cause breakdown; the current then increases sharply. The diode is, therefore, commonly used as a rectifier. Semiconductor diodes are also used to generate microwaves by the Gunn effect, to detect light in photocells, and to emit light in low-voltage displays (**light-emitting diodes** LEDs).

Semites A group of peoples, including the Jews and Arabs, said in the Bible to be descended from Shem, Noah's eldest son. The Babylonians, Assyrians, Canaanites, and Phoenicians were ancient Semitic peoples.

Semitic alphabets The earliest known truly alphabetic writing systems, developed among the Semitic peoples of the E Mediterranean around 2000 BC. From them all the major alphabets of today are derived: the south Semitic version gave rise to the modern Amharic script of Ethiopia; from North Semitic were derived Greek (and from Greek came the Roman, Cyrillic, runic, and other alphabets), Phoenician, and Aramaic (from which came the scripts of Hebrew, Arabic, and Devanagari in India).

Semitic languages A subgroup of the Hamito-Semitic language family spoken in a large area of N Africa, extending through Palestine to the SW corner of Asia. The Semitic languages originated in Mesopotamia in the 3rd millennium BC and are recorded in Sumerian cuneiform inscriptions. Although many, including Aramaic, Assyrian, and Babylonian are now extinct, examples of living Semitic languages are Hebrew, modern Arabic, and Maltese.

semolina Fine grains of durum wheat used in the manufacture of pasta and also for making milk puddings.

Senate In ancient Rome, the state council. During Republican times the Senate was largely composed of ex-magistrates and, although its role was primarily to advise the magistrates, it carried much weight, especially in foreign policy, finance, and religion. Under the Empire membership of the Senate became largely hereditary and its chief function was to ratify imperial decisions. *See also* Curia, Roman.

Senate, US. *See* Congress.

Sendai 38 16N 140 52E A city in Japan, in NE Honshu. It is the largest city of N Japan and an important commercial centre. Population (1985 est): 700 000.

Seneca the Elder (Marcus Annaeus Seneca; c. 55 BC–c. 41 AD) Roman rhetorician, born at Córdoba (Spain). Parts of his work on oratory, addressed to his sons, have survived. One of his sons, **Seneca the Younger** (Lucius Annaeus Seneca; c. 4 BC–65 AD), was an author and politician. He was tutor and later chief minister to Nero. Retiring in 64 AD, he was accused of treason and forced to commit suicide. His philosophical writings advocate Stoicism. His nine tragedies, which influenced the Elizabethan dramatists, also survive.

Senegal, Republic of A country in West Africa, on the Atlantic Ocean. The River Senegal forms its N boundary and the River Gambia flows E–W through the country to the border of The Gambia, which forms an enclave within Senegalese territory. Senegal consists chiefly of level plains rising to a dissected plateau in the SE. Most of the population are Wolof, Sere, and Tukolor. *Economy*: chiefly agricultural, the production of groundnuts being dominant. Phosphates, iron ore, and offshore oil and natural gas have been found in significant quantities. *History*: the French extended their control in the mid-19th century over most of the region. The country achieved self-government in 1958 as a member of the French Community and in 1959–60 briefly formed the Federation of Mali with Sudan. Senegal became a separate independent republic in 1960. In 1982 it formed the Senegambia Confederation with The Gambia with each country retaining its independence but having joint defence, foreign, and monetary policies. President: Abdou Diouf (1935–). Official language: French. Official currency: CFA (Communauté financière africaine) franc of 100 centimes. Area: 197 722 sq km (76 320 sq mi). Population (1987): 6 793 000. Capital and main port: Dakar.

senna. *See* Cassia.

sensitive plants. *See* Mimosa.

Seoul 37 30N 127 00E The capital of the Republic of (South) Korea, in the NW on the River Han near the coast. It was the capital of Korea from 1394. Population (1985): 9 645 824.

Sephardim (Hebrew *Sepharad*: Spain) Jews who went to Spain and Portugal in the diaspora. When the Jews were expelled from Spain in 1492 they spread to many parts of the world, preserving their customs and their language, Ladino. The first Jewish settlers in England were Marranos from Spain. In the 17th century the Sephardim came from Holland; they opened their first synagogue in 1657, which was replaced in 1701 by a synagogue in Bevis Marks in the City of London, which is still in use. The term is now sometimes applied, especially in Israel, to all non-Ashkenazim.

septic tank A large tank of steel or concrete sunk in the ground to provide sewage disposal for isolated buildings or small communities. Effluent flows into the tank, the settled sludge being decomposed to a certain extent by bacterial action. The tank must be large enough (minimum 2.7 cu m in the UK) to store the sludge for several months, before emptying.

SEPTIC TANK *The sewage enters low in the tank without disturbing the contents. Purer water separates at the top and sludge forms at the bottom.*

sequoia Either of two Californian coniferous trees, the redwood (*Sequoia sempervirens*), which is the world's tallest tree, or the giant sequoia, *Sequoiadendron giganteum* (formerly *Sequoia gigantea*), also called Wellingtonia. The giant sequoia forms natural forests in California's Sierra Nevada, where some trees are over 3000 years old, with a height of over 80 m and a girth of over 24 m. In Europe it is grown as an ornamental. The redbrown bark is soft and fibrous and the shoots are densely covered with pointed scalelike leaves. Family: *Taxodiaceae*.

seraphim. *See* cherubim and seraphim.

Serbia A constituent republic of Yugoslavia, incorporating the autonomous regions of Vojvodina and Kosovo. It is chiefly mountainous, descending in the N to the basin of the River Danube. Agriculture is of major importance as is mining, especially for copper, antimony, coal, and chrome. *History*: first settled by the Serbs in the 7th century AD, it later came under Turkish control (1389–1804), finally regaining its independence in 1878. It played a major role in events leading up to World War I, Austria accusing Serbia of direct involvement in the assassination of Archduke Francis Ferdinand. In 1918 Serbia became part of the kingdom of Serbs, Croats, and Slovenes, later renamed Yugoslavia. Area: 128 278 sq km (49 528 sq mi). Population (1985 est): 9 600 000. Capital: Belgrade.

Serbo-Croat The language of the Serbs and Croats of Yugoslavia, where it is the most widely spoken language. Serbian and Croatian differ only marginally in terms of vocabulary and not at all in grammar but Serbian is written in Cyrillic and Croatian in Latin script.

serf An unfree peasant of the middle ages. Serfdom was characteristic of the manorial economic system (*see* manor). A serf was bound to the soil he tilled, paying his lord a fee and providing service in return for the use of his land. Serfs had their own homes, plots, and livestock and enjoyed customary rights. While serfdom declined in W Europe in the late middle ages, it was strengthened in E Europe, where it was only abolished in the 19th century.

serialism (*or* twelve-tone music) A method of composing music using all 12 notes of the chromatic scale equally, invented by Arnold Schoenberg in the 1920s. Schoenberg sought an alternative to chromaticism and atonality by using a fixed sequence of 12 notes (called a **series** or tone row) as a source of melody and harmony. The series could be transposed so as to begin on any degree of the scale and could also be inverted and used in a retrograde form. In strict serialism no single note of the row could be repeated until the other 11 had occurred in melody or harmony; Schoenberg himself did not always follow this rule. In place of traditional harmony he developed chords built on fourths.

series The sum of the terms in a sequence, written as $a_1 + a_2 + a_3 + \ldots a_r + \ldots$. The partial sum to the nth term is denoted by S_n. A series is convergent if S_n approaches a particular value as n increases and divergent if it increases without limit. A geometric series has the general form $a + an + an^2 + \ldots$, where a and n are constant. A power series has the general form like a snake's skin. They occur in igneous rocks. Rock consisting mainly of serpentine is sometimes quarried for ornamental stone.

serum The fluid that remains after blood has been allowed to clot. It can be obtained by centrifuging clotted blood and is similar in composition to plasma, except that it lacks the factors, such as fibrinogen, that are involved in blood clotting.

serval A slender long-legged cat, *Felis serval*, of the African bush. It is about 1.25 m long including the tail and has large ears and a spotted coat. Servals hunt birds and small mammals, mainly at night.

service tree A tree, *Sorbus domestica*, about 15 m high, native to S Europe, W Asia, and N Africa and commonly grown for ornament. Related to the mountain ash, it has compound leaves and its small green fruits are used for making wine. Family: *Rosaceae*.

sesame An annual herb, *Sesamum indicum*, cultivated in Central and South America, the Middle East, and SE Asia for its seeds, which are used in confectionery and as food flavouring. An edible oil is extracted from the seeds; the residue is used as cattle feed. Family: *Pedaliaceae*.

Set An Egyptian deity. Originally a sun and sky god, he murdered his brother Osiris and so came to represent all evil. He was killed by Horus, son of Osiris.

setter One of three breeds of sporting dog with a lean deep-chested body and drooping ears. Setters are named after their habit of squatting flat ("setting") after finding game. The English setter has a long white silky coat flecked with darker markings. The heavier Gordon setter, first bred at Gordon Castle, Scotland, is black with chestnut markings, while the Irish, or red, setter has a flat silky chestnut coat. Height: 61–69 cm.

set theory The study, founded by Georg Cantor, of the logical and mathematical laws of sets. A set is a defined collection of objects or elements; for example the set of odd integers between 0 and 10 is 1, 3, 5, 7, 9. The empty or null set has no elements. All sets are contained in the universal set E. The relationships between sets can be illustrated in a Venn diagram, named after the British logician John Venn (1834–1923), or shown by symbols. $a \in A$ means the element a is a member of the set A. $A \subset B$ means set A is contained in set B. $A \cup B$ means

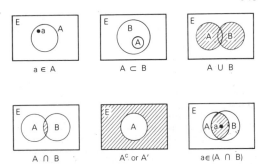

the union of A and B. $A \cap B$ means the intersection of A and B, i.e. those elements in both. A^c or A' is the complement of A, all elements in E but not in A.

SET THEORY *Venn diagrams.*

Settlement, Act of (1701) The Act that established the Hanoverian succession to the English throne. In the absence of heirs to William III or Anne, the Crown was to pass to James I's granddaughter Sophia (1657–1714), Electress of Hanover, or to her Protestant descendants. The Act stipulated that the monarch must be a Protestant and that foreigners must not hold public office or enter parliament. Anne was succeeded by the first Hanoverian king, George I, in 1714.

Seurat, Georges (1859–91) French painter, famous for developing neoimpressionism, popularly called pointillism. Although he finished only seven paintings in this demanding style, for example the famous *Sunday Afternoon on the Island of the Grande Jatte* (1884–86), his work was very influential.

Sevastopol (English name: Sebastopol) 44 36N 33 31E A port in the Soviet Union, in the Crimean *oblast* (region) of the S Ukrainian SSR on the Black Sea. It is a popular seaside resort. Founded in 1783, after Russia's annexation of the Crimea it became an important naval base and, later, a commercial port. It was besieged by the British and French during the Crimean War, falling after 11 months. Population (1987 est): 350 000.

Seven Deadly Sins Pride, covetousness, lust, envy, gluttony, anger, and sloth. The traditional Christian list was already established by the 6th century.

Seventh Day Adventists. *See* adventists.

Seven Weeks' War. *See* Austro-Prussian War.

Seven Wonders of the World The supreme manmade structures of the ancient world. They were the Pyramids of Egypt, the Colossus of Rhodes, the Hanging Gardens of Babylon, the Mausoleum of Halicarnassus, the statue of Zeus at Olympia, the temple of Artemis at Ephesus, and the Pharos of Alexandria. Only the Pyramids have survived.

Seven Years' War (1756–63) The war between Prussia, Britain, and Hanover on one side and France, Austria, Russia, and Spain on the other. The war had two main aspects: the rivalry between Austria and Prussia for domination of Germany and the struggle between France and Britain for overseas supremacy. The war was precipitated by Austria's desire to regain Silesia, lost to Frederick the Great of Prussia in the War of the Austrian Succession, and began with Frederick's invasion of Saxony. Russia's defection (1762) to Prussia enabled Frederick ultimately to emerge victorious and Prussian ascendancy was confirmed by the Peace of Hubertusberg. Overseas, the British despite initial reverses won a series of spectacular victories in India (by Clive) and Canada (by Wolfe). By the Treaty of Paris (1763) Britain was confirmed as the supreme world power.

Severn, River The longest river in the UK, rising in central Wales and flowing NE and E into England, then S to the Bristol Channel. It passes through Welshpool, Shrewsbury, Worcester, Tewkesbury, and Gloucester. It is linked by canal to the Rivers Thames and Trent and is spanned near its estuary by the **Severn Bridge**, a suspension bridge 988 m (3240 ft) long, built in the 1960s. Plans are being drawn up for a tidal barrage to supply up to 6% of the UK's electricity needs. Length: 365 km (227 mi).

Seville 37 24N 5 59W A city and port in SW Spain, in Andalusia on the River Guadalquivir. Now a major industrial centre, it was important during Roman times, thrived under the Moors (711–1248) as a cultural centre, and became a major port in the 16th century. There is a university (founded 1502) and a cathedral (1401–1591). Population (1986): 651 299.

Sèvres porcelain The finest French porcelain, first produced in Vincennes in 1738 and still made. The factory moved to Sèvres near Versailles in 1756. It always enjoyed royal patronage. Early output was soft-paste porcelain but from 1768 hard-paste was made. Products were figures, vases, ornaments, and table services with blue, rose Pompadour, yellow, or green grounds richly gilded for royal taste.

sex chromosome A chromosome that carries the genes for determining the sex of an individual. In humans there are two types of sex chromosomes, called X and Y. The body cells of normal males possess one X and one Y chromosome while those of normal females have two X chromosomes. Human sperm is therefore either "male" or "female" depending on whether it carries an X or a Y chromosome. The sex of the embryo is determined by which type of sperm fertilizes the female egg (which always carries an X chromosome). Abnormal numbers of sex chromosomes cause a range of disabilities, including physical abnormalities, mental retardation, and sterility.

sex hormones Hormones that regulate the growth, development, and functioning of the reproductive organs and determine external sexual characteristics. The major female sex hormones are the oestrogens, progesterone, and prolactin while the androgens are the principal male ones. Their production is regulated by gonadotrophins from the pituitary gland.

sextant An instrument used primarily in navigation for determining latitudes by measuring the angle subtended by some celestial body to the horizon. Thomas Godfrey of Philadelphia and John Hadley of London, working independently, discovered the sextant's principle in 1730. The graduated metal strip, shaped in an arc of the sixth part of a circle, gave the instrument its name. In use the movable index arm is slid along the scale until the image of the reference star as viewed in the half-silvered index mirror is aligned with the horizon. The reading on the scale then indicates the angle subtended.

sexton beetle See burying beetle.

sexually transmitted disease (STD) Any disease transmitted by sexual intercourse, also known as venereal disease. Among the most prevalent STDs today are genital herpes, nonspecific urethritis, hepatitis B, and AIDS; syphilis and gonorrhoea—the former scourges—are now easily treatable with antibiotics.

Seychelles, Republic of A country consisting of 87 widely scattered islands in the W Indian Ocean, NE of Madagascar. The main island is Mahé. Most of the population is of mixed African and European descent. *Economy*: the chief products and exports are copra and cinnamon bark. Tourism is expanding rapidly. *History*: the uninhabited islands became a French colony in the mid-18th century as a spice plantation. Captured by the British in 1794, they became a dependency of Mauritius from 1814 until 1903, when they became a British crown colony. In 1976 the country became an independent republic within the British Commonwealth. President: Albert René (1935–   ). Official languages: English and French; the majority speak Creole. Official currency: Seychelles rupee of 100 cents. Area: 444 sq km (171 sq mi). Population (1987 est): 67 000. Capital and main port: Victoria.

SEXTANT *Angle α measures the angle between horizon and reference arm; β is the angle between index mirror and horizon glass, marked by the angular movement of the index arm along the limb.* $\alpha = 2\beta$, *therefore the graduations on the scale are marked twice the actual angular movement to give the correct altitude.*

Seymour, Jane (c. 1509–37) The third wife (1536–37) of Henry VIII of England. A lady in waiting to both his former wives, Catherine of Aragon and Anne Boleyn, she married Henry 11 days after Anne's execution. Jane was the mother of Edward VI, dying shortly after his birth.

's Gravenhage. See Hague, The.

Shackleton, Sir Ernest Henry (1874–1922) British explorer. He accompanied Scott's expedition of 1901–04 and on his own expedition in 1908–09 nearly reached the South Pole. In an expedition of 1914–16 his ship, the *Endurance*, was marooned but he and his men reached Elephant Island by sledge and boats. With five others he then journeyed 1300 km (800 mi) to find relief. He died on his fourth expedition.

shad A food fish, belonging to a genus (*Alosa*) related to herrings, that occurs in the N Atlantic, Mediterranean, and North Sea. It has one or a succession of black spots along each side and a notch in the upper jaw. They migrate in large shoals to spawn in fresh waters.

Shaffer, Peter (1926–) British dramatist. His plays include *Five-Finger Exercise* (1958), *The Royal Hunt of the Sun* (1964), *Equus* (1973), *Amadeus* (1979), *Yonadab* (1985), and *Lettice and Lovage* (1987). His twin brother **Anthony Shaffer** (1926–) is also a playwright, best known for the thriller *Sleuth* (1970).

Shah Jahan (1592–1666) Emperor of India (1628–58) of the Mogul dynasty; the son of Jahangir (1569–1627). His powerful reign was as ruthless as his means of attaining it; he put his nearest relatives to death in 1628. His passion for fine architecture produced such monuments as the Taj Mahal and the Delhi Red Fort. He was deposed by his son Aurangzeb (1618–1707).

Shah of Iran. *See* Mohammed Reza Pahlavi; Reza Shah Pahlavi.

WILLIAM SHAKESPEARE *An engraving by Martin Droeshout.*

Shakespeare, William (1564–1616) English dramatist, universally recognized as the greatest English writer. Born in Stratford-upon-Avon, he married in 1582 a local girl, Anne Hathaway, by whom he had three children. Soon afterwards he went to London, where he became an actor in the leading theatrical company, the Lord Chamberlain's Men (called the King's Men after 1603). The three parts of *Henry VI* and *Richard III* were his first plays (1589–92). His dramatic poems *Venus and Adonis* (1593) and *The Rape of Lucrece* (1594) were dedicated to his patron Henry Wriothesley, 3rd Earl of Southampton. His *Sonnets* (1609) were probably written at this time. His early comedies (1593–95) were *Love's Labour's Lost*, *The Two Gentlemen of Verona*, and *The Taming of the Shrew*. These were followed (1595–1600) by *A Midsummer Night's Dream*, *The Merchant of Venice*, *Much Ado About Nothing*, *Twelfth Night*, and *As You Like It*. During this period he also wrote his first significant tragedy, *Romeo and Juliet*, as well as *Richard II* and *Julius Caesar*. In 1597 he bought New Place, a large house in Stratford, and later became a shareholder in the Globe Theatre in London and bought other property in London and Stratford. The two parts of *Henry IV* were completed before *Hamlet*, *Othello*, *King Lear*, and *Macbeth*, his major tragedies (1600–06). His final experimental plays included *The Winter's Tale* (c. 1610) and *The Tempest* (c. 1611). In about 1611 he retired to Strat-

ford, where he died. The first collected edition of his works, known as the First Folio and containing 36 plays, was published in 1623. His other plays were: *The Comedy of Errors*, *Titus Andronicus*, *King John*, *Henry V*, *The Merry Wives of Windsor*, *Antony and Cleopatra*, *Coriolanus*, *Troilus and Cressida*, *Measure for Measure*, *All's Well That Ends Well*, *Timon of Athens*, *Pericles*, *Cymbeline*, and, with John Fletcher (1579–1625), *Henry VIII* and *The Two Noble Kinsmen*.

shale A fine-grained sedimentary rock that splits easily along the closely spaced bedding planes as a result of the alignment of the clay mineral particles parallel to the bedding planes. Shales may disintegrate in water. They are softer and lighter than slate, which is a fine-grained metamorphic rock.

shallot A hardy perennial herbaceous plant, *Allium ascalonium*, probably of Asiatic origin. Its small hollow cylindrical leaves are often used for dressing food and in salads. Its small angular bulbs occur in garlic-like clusters and are used for flavouring and pickling. Family: *Liliaceae*.

shamanism The religious beliefs and practices common in certain tribal societies of Asia, such as the Samoyed. The term is also applied to North American Indian practices. The shaman is a tribal priest generally felt to be possessed by a spirit or deity and hence to have supernatural powers. He may also act as the tribal ruler and judge.

Shamir, Yitzhak (1915–) Israeli statesman, born in Poland; prime minister (1983–84, 1986–). He led the Israeli Freedom Fighters (1940–41), served in Israel's secret service (1955–65), and was foreign minister (1980–83, 1984–86). During the coalition government of 1984–88 he had a special power-sharing agreement with Shimon Peres.

shamrock Any of several plants bearing leaves with three leaflets, especially various clovers, black medick (*Medicago lupulina*), and wood sorrel (*Oxalis acetosella*). The shamrock is worn on St Patrick's Day.

Shanghai 31 13N 121 25E An administratively autonomous port in E China, on the Yangtze estuary. The largest city in China, it is its chief port and industrial city. It grew rapidly after it was opened to foreign trade in 1842, coming under British, US, and French rule until World War II. Population (1987 est): 7 330 000.

Shankar, Ravi (1920–) Indian sitar player. He has popularized Indian music in the West.

Shannon, River The longest river in the Republic of Ireland. Rising in NW Co Cavan, it flows S to Limerick and then W to the Atlantic. Length: 386 km (240 mi).

Shari, River. *See* Chari, River.

shari'ah. *See* Islamic law.

Sharjah. *See* United Arab Emirates.

shark A cartilaginous fish belonging to the worldwide order *Selachii* (about 250 species). Ranging in size from the smallest dogfish to the enormous whale shark, they have a torpedo-shaped body with a muscular tail used in swimming, five to seven pairs of gill slits on the sides of the head, and numerous sharp teeth. They are chiefly marine and carnivorous. Subclass: *Elasmobranchii*.

Sharpeville A Black African town in South Africa, in the S Transvaal near Vereeniging. It was the scene of a riot on 21 March, 1960, in which African demonstrators were fired on by the police. Over 60 of the demonstrators were killed and many others wounded. There were riots on the anniversary in 1984 and 1985, when 19 died.

MARY SHELLEY   *Portrait (1841) by R. Rothwell.*

Shaw, George Bernard (1856–1950) Irish dramatist, critic, and man of letters, born in Dublin. He went to London in 1876, becoming a music and drama critic, an active socialist, and one of the founding members of the Fabian Society. He wrote more than 40 plays, the Prefaces indicating at length the social and moral issues involved. *Plays Pleasant and Unpleasant* (1898) included *The Philanderer*, *Mrs Warren's Profession* (on prostitution), and the "pleasant" comedies *Arms and the Man*, *You Never Can Tell*, *Candida*, and *The Man of Destiny*. His *Three Plays for Puritans* (published 1901) comprised *The Devil's Disciple*, *Caesar and Cleopatra*, and *Captain Brassbound's Conversion*. The epic comedy of ideas, *Man and Superman* (1903), was followed by *John Bull's Other Island* (1904), *Major Barbara* (1905), *The Doctor's Dilemma* (1906), *Getting Married* (1908), *Misalliance* (1910), and *Androcles and the Lion* (1913). *Pygmalion* (1913), an outstanding commercial success, was followed by *Heartbreak House* (1917) and the series of plays entitled *Back to Methuselah* (1921). The historical drama *St Joan* (1924) is generally regarded as his greatest work. He also wrote many important prose works. In 1925 he was awarded the Nobel Prize.

Shcherbakov. *See* Rybinsk.

shear stress. *See* stress.

shearwater One of a group of birds (about 15 species) of the oceanic family *Procellariidae*. Shearwaters have a dark plumage (some species have white underparts), long narrow wings, and slender bills; they feed on fish from the sea surface. The great shearwater (*Puffinus gravis*) breeds in the South Atlantic, migrating to spend summer and autumn in the North Atlantic. The Manx shearwater (*P. puffinus*) breeds off British and Mediterranean coasts and winters in E South America and Australia. Order: *Procellariiformes*. *See also* petrel.

Sheba In the Bible, a land corresponding to Sabaea in present-day Yemen (SW Arabia). It was known for its trade in spices and gold. Its most famous monarch was the Queen of Sheba who visited King Solomon in Jerusalem (I Kings 10.1–13).

sheep A hoofed ruminant mammal belonging to the genus *Ovis* (7 species), native to mountainous regions of Eurasia and North America. Related to goats, sheep are generally 75–100 cm tall at the shoulder. They have a compact body with slender legs and a short tail and the coat ranges from white to brown in colour. Males (rams) have large spiralled horns; females (ewes) have smaller less curved horns. There are over 200 breeds of domestic sheep (*O. aries*), which are reared worldwide for meat, wool, and milk (*see* livestock farming). Family: *Bovidae*. *See also* aoudad; bighorn; mouflon.

sheepdog A dog used for handling sheep, such as the collie, German shepherd dog, Old English sheepdog, and Shetland sheepdog, as well as crossbred derivatives.

Sheffield 52 23N 1 30W A city in N England, the largest in South Yorkshire on the River Don. It is world famous for steel, produced here since the mid-18th century. Population (1986): 538 700.

Sheffield plate Articles that are made by fusing a silver coat onto copper, a process discovered in about 1742. Used as a substitute for solid silver, Sheffield-plated articles, usually tableware, followed contemporary silver designs. The process was superseded by electroplating, introduced in the mid-19th century.

shelduck A large duck, *Tadorna tadorna*, found around coasts of W and central Eurasia. It is 65 cm long and has black-and-white plumage with a green head, chestnut shoulders, and a red bill.

shellac A natural thermoplastic resin made from the secretions of the lac insect, *Laccifer lacca*, which is parasitic on certain trees in India and Thailand. Its solution in alcohol is used as a varnish and in lacquers.

Shelley, Percy Bysshe (1792–1822) British poet. He wrote the revolutionary poem *Queen Mab* in 1813 and soon after left for the Continent, where he met Byron. From 1818 until his death he lived in Italy, where he wrote the verse dramas *The Cenci* (1819) and *Prometheus Unbound* (1818–19), the elegy *Adonais* (1821) prompted by the death of Keats, and much lyrical poetry. He was drowned in a sailing accident off the Italian coast. His second wife **Mary Wollstonecraft Shelley** (1797–1851), British novelist, was best-known for her book *Frankenstein: the Modern Prometheus* (1818).

shells The hard casings secreted by some animals to protect themselves or their eggs. The term usually refers to the shells of molluscs, which consist largely of calcium carbonate and come in a wide variety of shapes and sizes. They may be spiralled or flat, with one valve (in gastropods, such as snails) or two (in bivalves, such as mussels). The pearly nautilus has a many chambered shell, which provides buoyancy. See p. 652.

Shelter (National Campaign for the Homeless) A British organization, founded in 1966, to raise funds for housing projects and housing aid centres for the homeless and to campaign for more and better housing.

Shenyang (former name: Mukden) 41 50N 123 26E A city in NE China, on the River Hun, the capital of Liaoning province. China's fourth largest city, it is a major industrial centre. Population (1986 est): 4 200 000.

Shepard, Jr, Allan Bartlett (1923–) US astronaut, who on 5 May, 1961, became the first American in space. His flight, which came 23 days after Gagarin's flight, lasted 15 minutes and reached a height of 185 km.

Sher, Antony (1949–) British actor and writer, born in South Africa. Acclaimed for his Shakespearean roles, he was especially admired as Richard III (1985). His books include two autobiographies and the novel *Middlepost* (1989).

Sheraton, Thomas (1751–1806) British furniture designer, who made his name with the designs in his

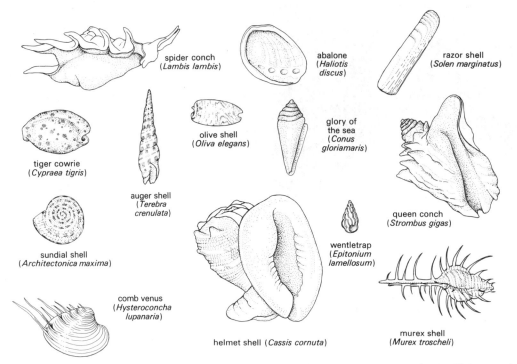

spider conch
(*Lambis lambis*)

abalone
(*Haliotis
discus*)

razor shell
(*Solen marginatus*)

tiger cowrie
(*Cypraea tigris*)

olive shell
(*Oliva elegans*)

glory of
the sea
(*Conus
gloriamaris*)

auger shell
(*Terebra
crenulata*)

sundial shell
(*Architectonica maxima*)

queen conch
(*Strombus gigas*)

wentletrap
(*Epitonium
lamellosum*)

comb venus
(*Hysteroconcha
lupanaria*)

helmet shell (*Cassis cornuta*)

murex shell
(*Murex troscheli*)

SHELLS   *A selection of mollusc shells, drawn to scale (the largest, the helmet shell, is 35 cm long). All these species are marine and several, including the glory of the sea, are collectors' items.*

Cabinet-Maker and Upholsterer's Drawing Book (1791–94). Influenced by Adam and contemporary French styles, these designs were characterized by elegance, delicacy, straight lines, and inlaid decoration.

Sheridan, Richard Brinsley (1751–1816) Anglo-Irish dramatist, who lived in England from childhood. He wrote witty comedies of manners, of which the best known are *The Rivals* (1775) and *School for Scandal* (1777). He was a Whig MP from 1780 to 1812, during which time he was recognized as being one of the great parliamentary orators.

sheriff   An official with administrative and judicial responsibilities in England, Scotland, and the USA. Originating in the 10th century as the king's representative in the shire and at the shire court, the sheriff continued in this role under the Normans, who expanded his judicial competence. The sheriffs' powers were reduced by Henry II and succeeding kings and became little more than ceremonial in the 16th century. Sheriffs in England and Scotland are normally appointed by the Crown to each county. In Scotland sheriffs are also the chief county judges. In the USA they are elected and are the principal law enforcement officers in a county.

Sherpa   A people of Nepal who speak a dialect of Tibetan. They often act as porters for Himalayan expeditions. With Edmund Hillary, the Sherpa Tenzing Norgay reached the summit of Everest in 1953.

sherry   A fortified wine, originally made around Jerez de la Frontera (whence its name) in S Spain. There are two basic types of sherry: fino is a pale dry wine on

which the *flor* (flower or yeast) has developed fully; oloroso is a rich full-bodied wine on which the *flor* is little developed. Other types of sherry are related to these two, for example amontillado is a strong dark derivative of a fino and cream sherry is a heavily sweetened oloroso.

Sherwood Forest   An ancient forest in the Midlands of England, in Nottinghamshire. Once an extensive royal hunting ground, it is now much reduced; it is famous for its associations with Robin Hood.

Shetland Islands (*or* Shetland; official name until 1974: Zetland)   An island authority of about 100 islands in the North Sea, off the N coast of Scotland. The largest islands include Mainland, Yell, and Unst. Shetland is best known for its ponies and knitted goods (especially in the Shetland and Fair Isle patterns). The islands are a base for North Sea oil exploitation with a pipeline from the Brent field. Area: 1427 sq km (551 sq mi). Population (1986 est): 23 580. Administrative centre: Lerwick.

Shetland pony   The smallest British pony breed, native to the Shetland Islands. It has a sturdy compact body with short legs and a relatively large head. The mane and tail are profuse and the coat becomes thick in winter. Height: up to 1.05 m (10½ hands).

Shetland sheepdog (*or* Sheltie)   A breed of dog developed in the Shetland Islands for working sheep. Related to and resembling the collie, it has a soft undercoat and a long outer coat and may be black, brown, or blue-grey, with white and tan markings. Height: about 35 cm.

Shevardnadze, Eduard (1928–) Soviet statesman; minister for foreign affairs (1985–). A protégé of Gorbachov, he has played a key role in arms negotiations with the USA.

shield An extensive rigid block of Precambrian rocks. Shields are the oldest continental regions, frequently of igneous granite or metamorphic gneiss. The shields were once the site of Precambrian mountain belts, although the mountains have been completely eroded. The **Canadian** (*or* Laurentian) **Shield** is the largest, covering several million square kilometres of NE North America.

Shih Huang Ti. *See* Qin.

Shih tzu A breed of small dog originating in Tibet and introduced to the UK in the 1930s. It has a long body with short legs, a short muzzle, and drooping ears. The long straight coat can be of various colours and the plumed tail is held over the back. Height: about 26 cm.

Shiites (*or* Shiah) The general term applied to a number of different Muslim sects, the main body of which is dominant in Iran. The distinctive belief of the Shiites, which differentiates them from the other major Muslim group, the Sunnites, is that Ali, the fourth caliph, is the only legitimate successor of Mohammed. The leader of Islam, the imam, must be a descendant of Ali and has authority in secular and religious matters.

Shikoku The smallest of the four main islands of Japan, separated from Honshu and Kyushu by the Inland Sea. Its population is concentrated on the coastal plains, with industry mainly in the N. Area: 17 759 sq km (6857 sq mi). Population (1985): 4 227 400. Chief cities: Matsuyama and Takamatsu.

shingles An infection caused by the herpes zoster virus, which lodges in nerve cells in the spinal cord. Shingles affects adults who have had chickenpox as children. It usually starts with pain along the course of a sensory nerve, followed by a band of blisters round half of the body or face. The rash usually eventually disappears but the patient may be left with severe neuralgia.

Shinto The native religion of Japan. Shinto is primarily an attitude of nationalistic and aesthetic reverence towards familiar places and traditions, rather than a set of religious beliefs. However, the central themes are the belief in numerous usually amoral *kamis* or nature spirits, together with ancestor worship and an ideal of military chivalry. The two principal *kamis* are the sun-goddess (reputedly mother of the emperor) and her brother the storm-god. The conflict between them expresses the creative and destructive forces of nature. After World War II, Shinto was disestablished as the state religion.

ships Early mariners included the Egyptians, Chinese and Phoenicians. The short broad Phoenician merchant ships of the 13th century BC were propelled by oars and a single square sail to catch the prevailing wind.
The Greeks developed biremes (with two banks of oars) and triremes (with three banks) as warships, especially strengthened for ramming enemy vessels. The Romans also relied on oars, but their larger grain ships had a number of square sails. In the N the double-ended longships of the Vikings were designed to cope with the rough and windy North Sea. Developed in the 8th century AD and propelled by sail and oars, ships of this kind brought William the Conqueror to England. It was not until the 12th century and the stimulus of the Crusades that the art of using sails was sufficiently developed for oars to be dispensed with. Sailing into the wind was originally pioneered by the Chinese in their junks, but it was the Arabs who perfected the lateen sail, which made it a

reliable means of propulsion for large ships. By the 14th century sailing ships were commonplace. The warships of the period had "castles" built at each end to house fighting men, and guns were usually carried on the forecastle. By the end of the 15th century the heavy muzzle-loading cannons were carried in gun ports low in the hull. During this period, too, the single-master with one large heavy sail gave way to the three-master with more manageable small sails and full rigging. During the next 300 years sailing ships developed in many ways, usually with the merchantmen following the innovations in hull design and rigging made by the designers of warships. Sailing ships reached their zenith in the 19th-century clippers, which remained supreme until the steam engine revolutionized seafaring. The first steamer to cross the Atlantic (in April, 1827) was the Dutch *Curaçao* (built 1826), the first British ship to do so (in April, 1838) being Brunel's *Great Western*, a wooden paddle steamer. In the next century the propeller completely replaced the paddle and Parson's steam turbine largely replaced the reciprocating engine. Passenger travel across the Atlantic has now been almost entirely captured by the airlines; modern shipbuilding concentrates on cargo vessels, especially oil tankers.
Warships in the age of steam were largely modelled on the turbine-driven battleship *Dreadnought* (1906), which together with the cruiser, destroyer, frigate, and submarine dominated naval warfare in World War I. By World War II the aircraft carrier had evolved and with its long-range striking power became the supreme weapon of the war at sea. However, the strength of navies is now reckoned in terms of their nuclear-powered submarines armed with long-range missiles. See pp. 654, 655.

Shire horse A breed of draught horse descended from the English warhorse and one of the world's largest horses. It is massively built with characteristic long white hair (called feathering) covering the lower parts of the legs. The coat is grey, bay, or black. Height: about 1.73 m (17 hands).

Shiva The third member of the Hindu trinity, the Trimurti. He is known as the Destroyer, but also represents the principle of generation symbolized by the lingam or phallus. His female counterpart is Parvati, also known in her more ominous aspects as Kali and Durga. He is often portrayed in human form with four arms, a third eye in the centre of the forehead, and sometimes wearing a necklace of skulls. His most famous depiction is as *Nataraja* (king of dancing), his dance symbolizing the cosmic rhythm of creation and destruction. The worship of Shiva is characterized by an asceticism that contrasts with the gentler worship of Vishnu, the other major sect of modern Hinduism.

shock 1. A severe condition resulting from failure of the circulatory system, when the blood supply to the tissues is inadequate. The shock may be caused by failure of the heart to pump sufficiently strongly, for example after a heart attack; by loss of blood fluid, for example through haemorrhage or burns; or by widening of the blood vessels so that there is not enough blood to fill them, for example after injury or during a very severe infection. 2. Injury resulting from electrocution. The extent of the injury depends on the current passing through the body, which is related to the voltage and the skin resistance. As skin resistance is greatly reduced when it is wet, mains voltage (240 V) can cause a lethal

Roman merchantman (c. 100 AD)   *The Romans' need to transport grain from N Africa to Europe encouraged the building of imposing ships up to 180 ft (55 m) long.*

Portuguese caravel (c. 1450)   *Although it was only a little longer than a large rowing boat, the caravel took part in most of the 15th-century voyages of discovery. The lateen sail, derived from Arab examples, enabled it to sail against the prevailing winds.*

Cutty Sark (1869)   *The 19th-century clippers were renowned for their speed and grace. The* Cutty Sark, *built to bring tea from China, was one of the fastest and most consistent sailing ships of its time. It is now permanently moored at Greenwich,* **England.**

Great Britain (1843)   *The second steam ship designed by I. K. Brunel, the* Great Britain *was the first all-iron propeller-driven ship to cross the Atlantic, taking 15 days between Liverpool and New York. Wrecked off the Falkland Islands in 1937, it was* **returned to England in 1970 for restoration.**

Queen Mary (1934)   *In 1938 this British passenger liner captured the Blue Riband for the fastest Atlantic crossing with a time of 3 days 20 hours 42 minutes. In 1967 it was anchored off Long Beach, California, as a tourist attraction.*

oil tanker (1968)   *The largest vessels afloat today, some of these giant ships have a deadweight capacity of over 300 000 tons.*

WARSHIPS

Greek bireme (c. 500 BC) *Propelled during an attack by its two ranks of oars, the bireme was strongly built **around a keel to** support the strain of the ram attached to its bows.*

Viking longship (c. 1000 AD) *The clinker-built, double-ended longship, propelled by oars and sail, was used mainly to transport fighting men.*

medieval nef (c. 1400) *This single-masted vessel had platforms (castles) for fighting men at either end and one on the mast (topcastle) from which missiles could be hurled.*

Victory (1778) *Nelson's flagship at the battle of Trafalgar (1805), the* Victory *carried 100 guns and a crew of 850. It is now preserved at Portsmouth, England.*

Dreadnought (1906) *The design of the British* Dreadnought *became the model for battleships in a period in which a country's naval strength was calculated in terms of how many battleships it possessed. The* Dreadnought *carried ten 12- inch guns, 27 smaller guns, and five underwater torpedo tubes.*

Nautilus (1954) *The first nuclear-powered warship, the US* Nautilus *heralded an era in which naval strength is calculated in terms of nuclear submarines. They are armed with torpedoes and long- and short-range missiles carrying nuclear warheads, all of which can be fired while the vessel is submerged.*

current (about 15 milliamps) to flow through the body if live terminals are touched with wet hands.

Shockley, William Bradfield (1910–89) US physicist, born in England, who shared the 1956 Nobel Prize with John Bardeen and Walter Brattain for their discovery of the transistor while working at the Bell Telephone laboratories in 1948.

shock wave A narrow region of a high pressure in a fluid, created when a fast-moving body passes through the fluid. The waves are propagated outwards from the body and occur, for example, when an aircraft passes through the sound barrier.

shogun A military title held hereditarily by the heads of three families; they were successively the actual rulers of Japan, although the emperors retained formal sovereignty. The shogunate was secured for the Minamoto from the emperor in 1192 after Minamoto Yoritomo's victory over the Taira league. From 1338 to 1573 the Ashikaga family held the title and in 1603 Tokugawa Ieyasu (1542–1616), who claimed Minamoto ancestry, revived it. The last shogun was Tokugawa Keiki (1827–1913; ruled 1867–68).

Sholokhov, Mikhail (1905–84) Soviet novelist. His first major novel (1928–40) was translated in two parts as *And Quiet Flows the Don* and *The Don Flows Home to the Sea*. He won the Nobel Prize in 1965.

shooting Discharging a weapon at a target or at game. The two main categories of **target shooting** for rifles are small bore (.22 calibre) at ranges of 25–200 m (27–219 yd), and full bore (7.62 calibre) at ranges of 200–1200 yd (183–1097 m); full-bore courses are fired from standing, sitting, kneeling, and prone (lying down) positions. Weapons for pistol shooting range from the .177 air pistol to the .45 pistol, with ranges between 10 and 50 yd (9–45 m). In **clay-pigeon shooting** (*or* trap-shooting) clay discs are mechanically flung into the air and fired at with shotguns. In **grouse shooting** (in the UK permitted only from 12 Aug to 10 Dec), **pheasant shooting** (1 Oct to 1 Feb), and **partridge shooting** (1 Sept to 1 Feb) the birds are either driven by a semicircle of beaters towards the shooters in butts (hides) or are flushed out by hunting dogs and beaters for a moving party of shooters.

Shorthorn A breed of cattle originating in NE England and formerly popular for both beef and dairy purposes. Stocky, with short legs, Shorthorns range from red to white with various mottled mixtures. They have been replaced by specialist beef and dairy breeds.

shortsightedness (*or* myopia) Inability to focus on distant objects. This is the commonest kind of visual defect and commonly runs in families: it is due to a slightly misshapen eyeball, in which the light rays are focused in front of the retina (light-sensitive layer). It is corrected by wearing glasses with concave lenses or contact lenses.

Shoshoni A group of North American Indian tribes of the Great Basin region who spoke a language of the Uto-Aztecan family. Some acquired horses and moved onto the Plains, including the Comanche.

Shostakovich, Dmitri (1906–75) Russian composer. His 15 symphonies include the very successful first symphony (1924) and the wartime seventh symphony (*The Leningrad*; 1941). He also composed two concertos each for piano, violin, and cello, 15 string quartets, operas, and much other music.

shot put (*or* putting the shot) A field event in athletics, in which an iron or brass sphere is thrown as far as

possible. It weighs 7.26 kg (16 lb) for men and 4 kg (8.8 lb) for women. It is thrown, or put, one-handed from in front of the shoulder and the putter must stay within a circle 2.1 m (7 ft) in diameter. World records: men 23.06 m (1988) by Ulf Timmermann (East Germany); women: 22.63 m (1987) by Natalya Lisovskaya (USSR).

shoveler duck A duck, *Spatula clypeata*, found in the N hemisphere, having a large bill specialized for feeding on water plants and invertebrates. 50 cm long, it has a pale-blue wing flash; the male has a dark-green head, white breast, and chestnut underparts and the female is brown.

shrew A small insectivorous mammal belonging to the family *Soricidae* (265 species), found all over the world except Australasia and the Polar regions. The dwarf shrew (*Suncus etruscus*) is the smallest mammal in the world, weighing only 2 g and measuring 7–8 cm. Shrews are very active: the common shrew (*Sorex araneus*) eats its own weight in food every 24 hours. Order: *Insectivora*.

Shrewsbury 52 43N 2 45W A town in W central England, the administrative centre of Shropshire on the River Severn and a market town for the surrounding agricultural area. A Roman town, it achieved importance as a gateway to Wales, and a castle was built in 1070. The famous boys' public school was founded here in 1552. Population (1987): 91 900.

shrike A fierce predatory songbird belonging to a family (*Laniidae*; 74 species) occurring in Eurasia, Africa, and North America and also called butcherbird. Shrikes dive on insects and small vertebrates from the air, killing them with their hooked falcon-like bills, often impaling prey on thorns.

shrimp A crustacean, usually 4–8 cm long, belonging to a worldwide suborder (*Natantia*; about 2000 species) that occurs in fresh and salt water. Shrimps have a semi-transparent body with long slender legs (the first pair pincer-like), a fanlike tail, and long whiplike antennae. They feed on small animals or plants. Many species, including the European *Crangon vulgaris*, are commercially important as food. Order: *Decapoda*.

Shropshire (name 1974–80: Salop) A county in the West Midlands of England, bordering on Wales. The River Severn separates the lowlands in the N and E from the uplands in the S and W. During the 18th century it became the main iron-producing county in England; the world's first cast-iron bridge was built at Ironbridge in 1779. It is now chiefly agricultural. Area: 3490 sq km (1348 sq mi). Population (1988 est): 400 800. Administrative centre: Shrewsbury.

Shroud of Turin A relic believed by some to be the linen cloth used to wrap Christ's body for burial. It bears impressions of a human body marked with wounds consonant with Christ's at the crucifixion. It has been kept in Turin since 1578, but there are gaps in its history prior to the 14th century. Carbon dating in 1988 established that it was woven from flax gathered between 1260 and 1390.

Shrove Tuesday The day before the beginning of Lent (*see* Ash Wednesday), so called from the "shriving" (i.e. confession and absolution) of the faithful that was customary before the Lenten season. In many countries carnivals are held and in England pancakes are traditionally eaten—hence the popular name Pancake Day.

sial The earth's continental crust, which is composed of granitic rocks rich in silicon (Si) and aluminium (Al).

It is less dense than the underlying layer of sima and much thicker.

Siam. *See* Thailand.

siamang The largest of the gibbons, *Hylobates syndactylus*, found in Malaya and Sumatra. Up to 90 cm tall, with arms spanning 150 cm, siamangs have a large naked vocal sac on the throat, which expands to give volume to their cries.

Siamese cat A breed of short-haired cat, originating from SE Asia. The Siamese has a slender body, slanted blue eyes, large pointed ears, and a long slim tapering tail. The fur on the body is cream-coloured or off-white, shading into one of several colours (most popularly seal-brown or blue-grey) on the ears, mask, paws, and tail (the "points").

SIAMESE TWINS *The original Siamese twins, Chang and Eng, produced by incomplete separation of a single fertilized egg.*

Siamese twins Identical twins who are fused together, usually at the head or along the trunk. They can sometimes be surgically separated, providing that vital organs are not involved in the point of union. The original Siamese twins, Chang and Eng (1811–74), were born in Siam; they were joined at the hip and remained fused.

Sian. *See* Xi An.

Sibelius, Jean (Johan Julius Christian S.; 1865–1957) Finnish composer. Many of his works have Finnish associations and many were inspired by the epic poem, the *Kalevala*. They include seven symphonies, symphonic poems such as *The Swan of Tuonela* (1893) and *Finlandia* (1899–1900), a violin concerto, and many songs.

Siberia A region in the Soviet Union, chiefly in the RSFSR. Corresponding to N Asia, it is bordered on the W by the Ural Mountains, on the N by the Arctic Ocean, on the E by the Pacific Ocean, and on the S by Mongolia and China. Siberia comprises three geographical areas – the West Siberian Plain, the Central Siberian Plateau, and the Soviet Far East. It is notorious for its long harsh winters. Its outstandingly rich mineral resources include coal and petroleum. Forestry is also important and Siberia's many rivers (notably the Ob, Yenisei, and Lena) are harnessed for hydroelectric power. Russian settlement was intermittent until the building (1891–1905) of the Trans-Siberian Railway. Siberia has long been a place of exile for Russian criminals and political prisoners. Area: about 13 807 037 sq km (5 330 896 sq mi).

Sibyl In Greek and Roman mythology, any of various divinely inspired prophetesses, the most famous of which was the Sibyl of Cumae, near Naples. Three books of these Sibylline prophecies were preserved in the Temple of Jupiter on the Capitoline hill at Rome and were consulted in national emergencies.

Sica, Vittorio De. *See* De Sica, Vittorio.

Sicilian Vespers (1282) The massacre of 2000 French residents of Palermo that began the Sicilian revolt, backed by Pedro III of Aragon (1236–85; reigned 1276–85), against the oppressive regime of the Angevin Charles I. Aragonese control was finally established in 1302 under Pedro's son Frederick II (1272–1337).

Sicily The largest island in the Mediterranean Sea, which together with adjacent islands comprises an autonomous region of Italy. It is separated from the mainland by the Strait of Messina. Sicily is largely mountainous, highest point Mount Etna, and underdeveloped. The mining industry is important, especially oil. *History*: occupied by the Greeks, Carthaginians, Romans, and later the Arabs, in 1060 the Norman conquest of Sicily began. In 1266 Charles I became the first Angevin King of Sicily. The island was conquered by Aragon in 1284 following the revolt (called the Sicilian Vespers) in 1282 against Charles' oppressive regime. In 1734 Don Carlos of Bourbon (later Charles III of Spain) became Charles IV of Naples and Sicily, which formally became the Kingdom of the Two Sicilies in 1815 under Ferdinand I. After conquest by Garibaldi (1860), Sicily was united with the rest of Italy. Since then Sicily's history has been one of trouble and discontent as a result of an ailing economy, widespread poverty, and other forces on the island presenting an obstacle to reform. Area: 25 710 sq km (9927 sq mi), with adjacent islands. Population (1985 est): 5 112 073. Capital: Palermo. *See also* Mafia.

Sickert, Walter Richard (1860–1942) British impressionist painter and etcher, born in Munich of Danish and Irish parentage. His paintings of Venice and Dieppe (1895–1905) and scenes from the music hall and domestic life are distinguishable from French impressionism chiefly by their sombre colours.

sickle-cell disease A condition resulting from the production of an abnormal form of haemoglobin (the pigment of red blood cells). The disease is hereditary and affects only Negroes. When the blood is deprived of oxygen the abnormal haemoglobin crystallizes and distorts the red cells into a sickle shape: these sickle cells are removed from the blood by the spleen, which leads to anaemia. Those less severely affected survive and even tend to have some built-in resistance to malaria.

Siddons, Sarah (*born* Kemble; 1755–1831) English actress, acclaimed at her London debut in 1782 as the leading tragic actress of her time.

sidereal period The time taken by a planet or satellite to return to the same point in its orbit, i.e. to complete one revolution, with reference to the background stars.

sidewinder A small nocturnal rattlesnake, *Crotalus cerastes*, occurring in deserts of the S USA and Mexico, that has a sideways looping method of locomotion enabling it to move quickly over loose sand.

Sidney, Sir Philip (1554–86) English poet and courtier. His works include the prose romance *Arcadia* (1580), the sequence of Petrarchan sonnets, *Astrophel and Stella* (1591), and an important work of critical theory, *The Defence of Poesy* (1595). A gifted linguist, he served as a diplomat in Europe.

Siegfried A hero of Germanic legend, who also appears in early Scandinavian legend as Sigurd. In the Germanic *Nibelungenlied*, Siegfried wins Brunhild for his brother-in-law Gunther, but a quarrel between Brunhild and Siegfried's wife Kriemhild leads to Siegfried's death by treachery. In the Old Norse *Volsungasaga*, Sigurd is betrothed to Brynhild (the Old Norse version of her name) but is tricked (by a magic potion) into forgetting her and marries Gudrun. He then wins Brynhild for his brother-in-law Gunnar; later Brynhild incites Gunnar to kill him. Siegfried is the hero of the last two operas of Wagner's *The Ring of the Nibelung*.

siemens (S) The SI unit of conductance equal to the conductance between two points on a conductor when a potential difference of one volt between the points causes a current of one ampere to flow. Named after the German electrical engineeer Ernst Werner von Siemens (1816–92).

SIENA *The cathedral.*

Siena 43 19N 11 19E A city in central Italy, in Tuscany. Founded by the Etruscans, it was an important commercial and artistic centre in the middle ages. Its many fine buildings include a 13th-century cathedral, a university (1240), and several palaces. Population (1989): 58 354.

Sierra Leone, Republic of A country in West Africa, on the Gulf of Guinea. Coastal plains, fringed by mangrove swamps, rise to higher land in the interior. The majority of the population is African, the main groups being Mende and Temne. *Economy*: chiefly agricultural, with recent development in fishing, forestry, and mining industries. *History*: in 1787 local chiefs ceded to Britain a piece of land along the coast for the settlement of slaves freed in the colonies. In 1896 the region

became a British protectorate, gaining independence within the Commonwealth in 1961. In 1971, following a troubled period, Sierra Leone became a republic. In 1977 one-party government (by the All-People's Congress) was introduced. President: Joseph Saidu Momoh. Official language: English; Krio is widely spoken. Official currency, since 1964: leone of 100 cents. Area: 73 326 sq km (27 925 sq mi). Population (1987 est): 3 666 000. Capital and main port: Freetown.

Sierra Madre The chief mountain system of Mexico. It extends for about 2500 km (1500 mi) SE from the US border, reaching 5699 m (18 697 ft) at Citlaltépetl.

Sierra Nevada A mountain range in the USA. It extends generally NW–SE through California, reaching 4418 m (14 495 ft) at Mount Whitney. It contains the famous Yosemite National Park.

Sierra Nevada A mountain range in S Spain. It rises to 3481 m (11 421 ft) at Mulhacén, the highest point in Spain.

Sihanouk, Norodim, Prince (1923–) King (1941–55) of Cambodia. When the Japanese occupation ended in 1945, Sihanouk, after much opposition, achieved Cambodia's independence from France (1953). Abdicating in 1955, he dominated Cambodian politics as prime minister until 1970, when he was deposed and went into exile in China. Briefly head of state (1975–76), he returned into exile from which he headed a coalition of opposition parties.

sika A deer, *Cervus nippon*, also called Japanese deer, native to S Asia, Japan, and Taiwan and introduced to New Zealand and Europe. Grey-brown in winter and chestnut with white spots in summer, its shoulder height is 70–100 cm. Stags have slender eight-pointed antlers about 80 cm long.

Sikhism The religion of some nine million Indians, mostly inhabiting the Punjab. Founded in the 15th century by the Guru Nanak, Sikhism combines Hindu and Islamic ideas. The Hindu concepts of karma and rebirth are accepted, but the caste system is rejected. Sikhs believe that god is the only reality and that spiritual release can be obtained by taming the ego. The guidance of the guru is essential. The concept of Khalsa, a chosen race of warrior-saints, is central, as are the so-called five Ks: *kangha* (comb); *kacch* (shorts); *kirpan* (sword); *kara* (steel bracelet); and *kes* (uncut hair and beard). The occupation of the Sikh Golden Temple at Amritsar by Indian troops in 1984 led to the assassination a few months later of the Indian prime minister Indira Gandhi by Sikh members of her bodyguard. Violent reprisals against Sikhs followed throughout India.

Sikorski, Władysław (1881–1943) Polish general and statesman. Sikorski was prime minister (1922–23) and then minister of military affairs (1924–25). After Poland's collapse in 1939, he became prime minister of the Polish government-in-exile in London. The circumstances of his death, in an aeroplane crash near Gibraltar, are the subject of a controversial play by Rolf Hochhuth (1933–).

Sikorsky, Igor Ivan (1889–1972) US aeronautical engineer, born in Russia, who invented the helicopter. He produced the S-1 biplane in 1910. After moving to the USA (1919) he completed the first successful helicopter, the VS-300, in 1939.

Silbury Hill A prehistoric mound in S England, near Avebury, Wiltshire. Begun about 2150 BC, it is the largest man-made hill in Europe, standing 40 m (130 ft) high.

Silenus In Greek mythology, an elderly Satyr, companion of the god Dionysus. He was famed for his wisdom and prophetic powers as well as his drunkenness. The Sileni were his fellow nature spirits.

Silesia A region of E central Europe now in Czechoslovakia and Poland. Because of its geographical position, mineral wealth, and industrial potential, Silesia has been disputed territory since the 17th century, when it was claimed by both Austria and Prussia. The seizure of most of it by Prussia was finally recognized by Austria in 1763, after the Seven Years' War. After World War I it was divided between Czechoslovakia, Germany, and Poland and after World War II, between Czechoslovakia and Poland.

silica The mineral silicon dioxide, SiO_2, the most abundant of all minerals. There are three main forms of silica: quartz, tridymite, and cristobalite, the last two occurring in acidic volcanic rocks. Silica content is used to classify igneous rocks. In one scheme the rocks are divided into acidic (over 65% silica), intermediate (52–66% silica), basic (45–52% silica), and ultrabasic (under 45% silica) varieties; these terms do not reflect pH value.

silicon (Si) The second most abundant element in the earth's crust, after oxygen. It is a major constituent of almost all rock-forming minerals (*see* silicate minerals). Pure silicon is of great importance in the electronics industry as a semiconductor. Silicates have been important for centuries as the main constituents of pottery, glasses, and many building materials. Silicon carbide (*see* carborundum) is a widely used abrasive, refractory, and semiconductor. Organic silicon compounds are known as silicones. At no 14; at wt 28.086; mp 1410°C; bp 2355°C.

silicon chip. *See* integrated circuit.

silicones Synthetic polymers consisting of chains of alternating silicon and oxygen atoms, with organic groups attached to the former. Silicones include fluids, greases, rubbers, and resins. All have similar chemical properties: stability to heat, oxidation, many chemicals, and oils. The main applications are in adhesives, paints, elastomers, and waterproofing agents.

silicosis A lung disease caused by prolonged inhalation of silica dust: an occupational disease of stone cut-

ters, quarry workers, etc. The air sacs of the lungs become thickened and scarred, causing breathlessness and coughing. There is no specific treatment so prevention is essential. *See also* pneumoconiosis.

silk The thread produced by the caterpillar of the silkworm moth and the luxury fabric woven from it. The cocoons are unravelled and the filaments from several twisted together; processing this raw silk includes combining these strands and washing away the sticky secretion. China, where silk production was first practised, and Japan are the leading producers of pure silk; wild silk, produced by silkworms that feed on leaves other than mulberry or by uncultivated silkworms, includes a coarser brown Indian silk. Silk is lustrous, elastic, absorbent, and very strong.

silk-cotton tree. *See* kapok.

Silk Road A trade route, 6400 km (4000 mi) long, that connected China with the Mediterranean. It was most used in antiquity, when silk was taken westwards and wool and precious metals eastwards, but was again travelled in the later middle ages, notably by Marco Polo.

silkworm A caterpillar that spins a silken cocoon, especially one that is suitable for commercial silk production. The commonest is the Chinese silkworm (*Bombyx mori*), which feeds on mulberry leaves. The pupae are killed by heat and the silken thread, up to 900 m long, is then unwound. The Japanese oak silkmoth (*Antherea yamanai*) and the Chinese species *A. pernyi* are also used.

silky oak One of two species of Australian trees. *Grevillea robusta*, of E Australia, has fernlike leaves. It is widely cultivated in the tropics as an ornamental or shade tree. The northern silky oak (*Cardwellia sublimis*) has pinkish soft wood and is an important timber tree.

sill A horizontal or near-horizontal sheetlike mass of intrusive igneous rock. Most sills consist of medium-grained hypabyssal rock, the commonest being dolerite.

Sillitoe, Alan (1928–) British novelist, who won immediate success with his first novel, *Saturday Night and Sunday Morning* (1958), and a book of short stories, *The Loneliness of the Long Distance Runner* (1959). His later works include a trilogy of autobiographical novels, ending with *The Open Door* (1989).

silt A fine-grained sedimentary deposit, the rock par-

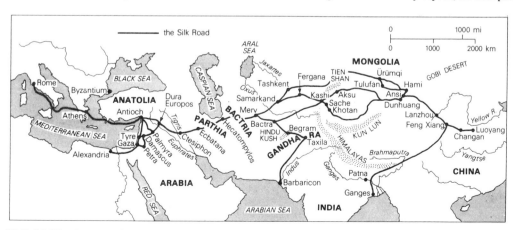

SILK ROAD *Between the 1st century BC and the 3rd century AD Chinese silks travelled westwards to the Mediterranean in exchange for precious metals.*

ticles of which range from 0.002 to 0.06 mm in diameter. Silts consist mainly of clay minerals, with iron oxides and hydroxides and silica. They collect in sheltered marine environments, such as estuaries, making dredging necessary. Consolidated silts form siltstones.

Silurian period A geological period of the Lower Palaeozoic era between the Ordovician and Devonian periods, lasting from about 445 to 415 million years ago. Conditions were mainly marine and the first true fish appeared. The first evidence of land plants also comes from Silurian rocks. The Caledonian period of mountain building reached its peak.

silver (Ag) A metallic element that occurs in nature as the metal, as argentite (Ag_2S), and in lead, zinc, and copper ores. Pure silver has the highest electrical and thermal conductivity known. In air, silver tarnishes forming a coating of the black sulphide (Ag_2S). Sterling silver (92.5% pure) is used for jewellery. Although not a reactive metal, silver forms many compounds including the oxide (Ag_2O), the nitrate ($AgNO_3$), and halides (for example AgCl, AgBr). Silver salts are of great importance in photography since they are light sensitive. At no 47; at wt 107.868; mp 961.93; bp 2212°C.

silverfish A widely distributed primitive wingless insect, *Lepisma saccharina*. One' of the three-pronged bristletails, it is covered with silvery scales and is common in buildings, feeding on starchy materials, including books and fabrics. Family: *Lepismatidae*.

silverplate Any object that is plated with silver rather than being solid silver. The original Sheffield plate was first produced in 1742. In 1840 the advent of electroplating brought silverplated domestic articles to a much wider public. Many silverplated articles are marked EPNS (electroplated nickel silver)—nickel silver itself is an alloy of copper, nickel, and zinc and contains no silver; in this process a layer of silver is electroplated onto the nickel-silver base.

sima The earth's oceanic crust, which is composed of basaltic rocks rich in silica (Si) and magnesium (Mg). It is denser than the sial of the continental crust and is believed to continue beneath it.

Simenon, Georges (1903–89) Belgian novelist. The best known of his several hundred novels feature the Parisian *commissaire de police*, Maigret.

Simon, Paul (1942–) US pop singer. With **Art Garfunkel** (1942–) he wrote songs for the film *The Graduate* (1967) and such albums as *Bridge over Troubled Water* (1970). His solo albums include *Graceland* (1986).

simple harmonic motion Any oscillation performed by a body about some reference point so that the restraining force is directly proportional to its displacement from that point. Examples include a pendulum swinging through a small angle and a vibrating string. The displacement, x, at a time t is represented by the equation $x = A\sin\omega t$, where A is the amplitude (maximum displacement) and ω the angular frequency, which is related to the period of oscillation T by $\omega = 2\pi/T$.

Simplon Pass An alpine pass linking Brig in Switzerland with Iselle in Italy. Built 1800–07 it reaches 2009 m (6590 ft). The **Simplon Tunnel** was, at 20 km (12 mi), the longest rail tunnel in the world until 1979.

Simpson Desert (*or* Arunta Desert) A desert of central Australia, mainly in Northern Territory. Area: about 77 000 sq km (29 723 sq mi).

Sinai A desert peninsula in Egypt, bounded by Israel and the Gulf of Aqaba to the E and the Gulf of Suez and mainland Egypt to the W. Mount Sinai, 2285 m (7497 ft) high, is in the mountain range in the S. The N half of the desert is plateau. The chief resources of the region are manganese and the oil deposits in the W, based on Sudr. Sinai was occupied by Israel in the 1956 and 1967 Arab-Israeli Wars and following the 1973 war Egyptian and Israeli lines were established on either side of a UN buffer zone. Under the 1979 Egyptian-Israeli agreement a large proportion of the area was returned to Egypt with Israeli withdrawal completed in 1982.

FRANK SINATRA *Police restraining fans of the young singer in New York in the 1950s.*

Sinatra, Frank (Francis Albert S.; 1915–) US singer and film actor, who recorded his first hit, "All or Nothing at All," in 1943. His nonsinging role in the film *From Here to Eternity* (1953), earned him an Oscar; he subsequently appeared in such films as *Guys and Dolls* (1955), and *The Manchurian Candidate* (1962). He has remained a popular singer and recorded such hits as "Strangers in the Night" (1966).

Singapore, Republic of A republic in SE Asia, off the S tip of Peninsular Malaysia, consisting of the island of Singapore and over 50 islets. The city of Singapore, located in the S, occupies a substantial part of the island's area. The majority of the diverse population is Chinese with minorities of Malays, Indians, and others. *Economy*: Singapore is the largest port in SE Asia and lies on a major searoute. It is a major commercial centre and in recent years industry has been expanded and diversified, oil refining being important. *History*: although a prosperous commercial centre in the middle ages, the island was largely uninhabited in 1819 when Sir Stamford Raffles established a station of the British East India Company here. In 1824 it was ceded to Britain. During World War II it was occupied by the Japanese, the British defence forces having surrendered in 1942. It became a separate British colony in 1946 and gained its independence in 1959. It joined the Federation of Malaysia on its formation (1963) but broke away in 1965. and formed an independent republic. President: Wee Kim Wee. Prime minister: Lee Kuan Yew (1922–). Official languages: Chinese, English, Malay, and Tamil. Official currency: Singapore dollar of 100 cents. Area: 602 sq km (232 sq mi). Population (1987): 2 616 000.

Singer, Isaac Bashevis (1904–) Polish-born US writer. His novels and stories, written in Yiddish and frequently dramatizing Jewish life in Poland, include *Gimpel the Fool* (1957), *The Slave* (1960), *Shosha* (1978), *Old Love* (1979), and *The King of the Fields* (1989). He won the Nobel Prize in 1978.

Sinhalese The major ethnic group in Sri Lanka. They speak an Indo-Aryan language that has been much influenced by Pali and the Dravidian languages, particularly Tamil. They are descended from migrants from Bengal who colonized Sri Lanka during the 5th century BC. An agricultural people, they base their social organization on caste and practise Theravada Buddhism.

Sinn Féin (Irish: Ourselves) An Irish nationalist party organized by Arthur Griffith in 1905. In 1918, under Éamon De Valera, it won a majority of the Irish seats in the British parliament and achieved the creation of the Irish Free State in 1922. Sinn Féin exists today as the political wing of the republican movement. *See also* Irish Republican Army.

Sino-Japanese Wars **1.** (1894–95) The war between China and Japan resulting from rivalry in Korea. China, heavily defeated, was forced to pay a large indemnity and cede Taiwan, the Pescadores, and the Liaodong peninsula. **2.** (1937–45) The war between China and Japan brought about by Japanese expansion into China in the 1930s. The Japanese had established a puppet state in Manchuria in 1932 but only after internal nationalist-communist cooperation against Japan did full war break out. The Japanese took Shanghai and Nanchang in 1937 and Wuhan and Canton in 1938. Their position remained strong until the USA entered World War II (1941) and gave China assistance. After Japan's surrender (1945) China regained Manchuria, Taiwan, and the Pescadores.

Sino-Tibetan languages A group of languages spoken in E Asia. It includes all the Chinese dialects (which use the same alphabet but differ substantially in sound), the Tibeto-Burman languages (Tibetan, Burmese, and many related languages of the Himalayas), and probably the Tai languages, such as Siamese, Laotian, and Shan. The main characteristic is the monosyllabic nature of the vocabulary of these languages and their use of tonality to differentiate otherwise similar words. They all use word order, not inflection, to determine grammatical relations.

sintering The heating without melting of powdered substance, usually metal or plastic, so that it becomes a solid mass. *See also* powder metallurgy.

Sintra (former name: Cintra) 38 48N 9 22W A town in central Portugal. The many notable buildings include the royal palace (14th–15th centuries) in Moorish and gothic styles. It is a tourist and agricultural centre. Population (1981): 20 574.

sinus A hollow cavity, especially one in a bone. The term usually refers to the air sinuses of the head, which are cavities in the facial bones; all have connections to the nasal cavity and they are susceptible to infection and inflammation (**sinusitis**).

Siouan languages A family of North American Indian languages including Dakota Sioux, Crow, and several others. Most are spoken by Plains tribes.

Sioux A confederation of North American Plains Indian tribes, also known as the Dakota. They fought fiercely against White encroachments upon their territories and defeated Gen Custer at the battle of the Little Bighorn (1876) under their leaders Sitting Bull and Crazy Horse. They were ultimately subdued, one group making a last stand at Wounded Knee (1890).

Sirens In Greek mythology, female creatures, sometimes portrayed with birdlike features, who lured sailors to their island by their singing and then destroyed them. Odysseus saved himself by tying himself to the mast of his ship and filling the ears of his crew with wax. The Argonauts were protected by the superior singing of Orpheus.

sirocco (*or* scirocco) A southerly wind occurring in N Africa, Sicily, and S Italy. Hot and dry on the N African coast, it picks up moisture as it crosses the Mediterranean Sea bringing extensive cloud to S Italy.

sisal A perennial plant, *Agave sisalana*, native to central America and cultivated throughout the tropics for its fibre, which is extracted from the leaves. It is used in shipping, general industry, and agriculture.

siskin A Eurasian finch, *Carduelis spinus*, occurring in N forests and at high altitudes in the south. It is about 12 cm long with a dark yellow-green plumage, paler streaked underparts, bright-yellow wingbars, and in the male a black chin and crown. Siskins feed on small seeds.

Sisley, Alfred (1839–99) Impressionist painter, born in Paris of British parents. In 1862 he met Monet and Renoir and later exhibited with them. In the 1870s he produced some of his best landscapes, for example *Misty Morning*, and three pictures of the *Floods at Port-Marly*.

Sistine Chapel The principal chapel of the Vatican, built for Pope Sixtus V (1473) by Giovanni dei Dolci. It is famous for its Renaissance interior decoration, with murals by Perugino (c. 1450–1523), Botticelli, and Ghirlandaio and the roof and ceiling by Michelangelo.

Sisyphus A legendary Greek king of Corinth. For various offences he was condemned in the underworld eternally to roll a boulder to the top of a hill, from whence it always rolled down again.

sitar An Indian long-necked lute with a resonating body made from a large gourd, seven metal strings stopped against movable arched frets, and a series of sympathetic strings.

Sitting Bull (c. 1834–93) American Sioux Indian chief. Resisting US expansion into the Plains, Sitting Bull led the massacre of Gen Custer and his men at the Little Bighorn (1876). After an amnesty he settled on a Dakota reservation but was killed during further hostilities.

Sitwell, Edith (1887–1964) British poet and writer. A lighthearted aestheticism characterizes her early experimental poetry, especially *Façade* (1923), for which Sir William Walton wrote a musical accompaniment. Her brother **Sir Osbert Sitwell** (1892–1969) wrote poems, short stories, and novels, notably *Before the Bombardment* (1926), but his best-known works are his nostalgic autobiographical memoirs. Both he and his sister rebelled against bourgeois philistinism. They gave encouragement to a number of writers, artists, and musicians.

SI units (Système International d'Unités) An international system of units, based on the m.k.s. system, used for all scientific purposes. It has seven base units (metre, kilogram, second, ampere, kelvin, candela, and mole) and two supplementary units (radian and steradian). All physical quantities are expressed in these units or in derived units consisting of combinations of these units, 17 of which have special names and agreed symbols. Deci-

SLAVERY *Slave auction in Virginia (1856).*

mal multiples of all units are expressed by a set of prefixes, such as kilo-, milli-, and mega-. See p. 794.

Six Day War. *See* Israel.

Skagerrak A channel in N Europe, lying between Denmark and Norway and connecting the Kattegat to the North Sea.

skate A large ray fish belonging to the family *Rajidae* (over 100 species), especially the genus *Raja*. 50–200 cm long, skates have a diamond-shaped flattened body with spiny or thorny structures on the upper surface and often an extremely long snout.

skimmer A black-and-white bird belonging to a family (*Rhynchopidae*; 3 species) occurring chiefly around western Atlantic coasts and African and Asian rivers. The skimmer fishes by flying close to the water, shearing the surface with the lower mandible and snapping the bill shut as soon as a fish is caught.

skin The tissue that covers the body. The outer layer (epidermis) consists of several layers of cells: the outermost layer contains dead cells made of keratin, which are constantly sloughed off and replaced by the deeper layers of continuously dividing cells. The inner layer of skin (dermis) contains connective tissue with blood vessels, sensory nerve endings, sweat glands, sebaceous glands (which secrete an oily substance, sebum, that protects the skin surface), and hair follicles. The skin protects the body from external injury and desiccation, assists in regulating body temperature (e.g. by sweating), and is sensitive to touch, temperature, and pain. The branch of medicine concerned with the diagnosis and treatment of skin disorders is called **dermatology**. Skin grafting is one of the most important and successful transplantation operations.

skink A lizard belonging to the family *Scincidae* (600 species), occurring throughout the tropics and in temperate North America. Skinks are well adapted for burrowing: they have cylindrical streamlined bodies with smooth scales, internal eardrums, a transparent covering over the eye, and often reduced limbs. Many have an elongated tail and move with sideways undulations of the body.

Skinner, Burrhus Frederic (1904–) US psychologist and advocate of behaviourism. Many of Skinner's experiments involved teaching animals (such as rats and

pigeons) by reinforcing the desired action with rewards of food. He developed equipment, including the Skinner box, in order to standardize the teaching of simple actions to small animals and applied his principles to human educational aids. His novel *Walden Two* (1948) describes a utopian society based on his behaviourist principles. His other works include *The Behaviour of Organisms* (1938), *Science and Human Behaviour* (1953), and *Beyond Freedom and Dignity* (1971).

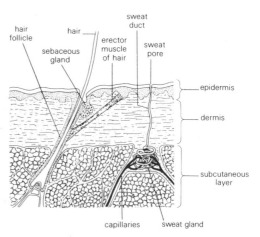

SKIN *A vertical section through the human skin shows its microscopical structure. The subcutaneous layer of fat cells provides insulation.*

Skopje 42 00N 21 28E A city in S Yugoslavia, the capital of Macedonia, on the River Vardar. It was burned down in 1689 to stop a cholera epidemic and almost completely destroyed by an earthquake in 1963. Population (1981): 506 547.

skua A large hook-billed seabird belonging to a family (*Stercorariidae*; 4 species), breeding in Arctic and Antarctic regions and wintering in warmer latitudes.

Skuas are strong fliers and have a dark plumage with two long central tail feathers. They scavenge around seabird colonies, feeding on eggs, chicks, and food scraps. Order: *Charadriiformes* (gulls, plovers, etc.).

skull The skeleton of the head, made up of 22 bones of varying shapes and sizes. The cranium consists of eight flat platelike bones that surround and protect the brain. The remaining 14 bones, including the mandible, form the face: the mandible is the only movable bone in the skull; the rest are connected by immovable joints called sutures. Numerous holes puncture the skull to allow blood vessels and nerves to pass to and from the brain.

skunk A black and white carnivorous mammal of the family *Mustelidae* that is known for its defensive habit of ejecting a foul-smelling fluid. The nine species are found in North, South, and Central America. The nocturnal North American striped skunk (*Mephitis mephitis*) inhabits woodland.

Skye The largest and most northerly island of the Inner Hebrides group, off the W coast of Scotland. Crofting and tourism are important. Area: 1735 sq km (670 sq mi). Population (1985 est): 7500. Chief town: Portree.

Skylab A US manned space station launched into earth orbit in May, 1973, and crewed by three groups of three US astronauts during the period May, 1973, to February, 1974. In a weightless environment, they conducted a variety of experiments and observations (especially of the sun]. Physical and psychological fitness were carefully monitored. Skylab crashlanded in July, 1979, in the Indian Ocean.

skylark A lark, *Alauda arvensis*, occurring in Eurasia and N Africa and noted for its sustained warbling flight song. It is about 17 cm long, with brown plumage, a small crest and a white stripe above the eye.

slander. *See* defamation.

slate A fine-grained rock produced by the low-grade metamorphism of mudstone, siltstone, or other argillaceous sediments. Its perfect cleavage is due to the parallel alignment of crystals of mica and chlorite. Slate is used as a constructional material.

SKYLAB *An astronaut taking a shower (1973).*

slavery The condition in which human beings are owned by others as chattels. In ancient Greece and early Rome captives from conquered lands were the chief source of slaves, who often had special skills, were well treated, and might be freed (manumission). The condition of slaves in later Roman times greatly worsened. Slaving became a lucrative business in the 16th century, when European traders began to transport thousands of Africans to the Americas. By the early 19th century humanitarians, such as William Wilberforce, had begun to attack slavery on moral grounds and it was abolished in all British territories by 1834. In the USA, slavery in the South became one of the causes of the Civil War. In 1863 Abraham Lincoln liberated all slaves in the southern states; in 1865 the Constitution was amended to abolish slavery.

Slavonic languages A subgroup of the Indo-European language family. Native to E Europe and NW Asia, they are often classified into three groups: South Slavonic (languages of Yugoslavia and Bulgaria, including Serbo-Croat, Slovene, Bulgarian, and Macedonian); West Slavonic (languages of Czechoslovakia, Poland, and E Germany, including Czech, Slovak, Sorbian, and Polish); and East Slavonic (Russian, Belorussian, and Ukrainian). All the dialects are linked historically and all developed from a common ancestor, Proto-Slavonic. The peoples who originally settled in these regions migrated from Asia during the second or third millennium BC. The present Slav nations began to emerge around the 5th and 6th centuries AD, when there was further westward movement. Most Slavs speak Russian, many learning it as a second language.

sleep A naturally occurring state of unconsciousness. Orthodox sleep occurs in four stages, which vary in depth. The electrical activity of the brain continues but is more rhythmical than when awake and reacts less to outside stimuli. It is periodically interrupted by paradoxical sleep, in which the eyes move rapidly and the brain is more active, but the muscles are especially relaxed. Paradoxical sleep is particularly associated with dreams. Sleep is biologically necessary and probably helps to control physical growth; individuals' needs vary widely between three and ten hours a night. Insomnia can be caused by changes of routine, anxiety, depression, and by many drugs.

sleeping sickness A disease caused by infection with a protozoan of the genus *Trypanosoma*, which is transmitted by the tsetse fly and occurs only in East, central, and West Africa: it is the African form of trypanosomiasis. Initial symptoms are swelling of the lymph nodes and fever, which persists for several months. The brain is then infected, causing lethargy, weakness, and depression: without treatment the patient dies.

sleepy sickness A highly infectious viral disease of the brain. Known medically as encephalitis lethargica, it is marked by drowsiness leading eventually to coma.

Sligo (Irish name: Contae Shligigh) A county in the NW Republic of Ireland, in Connacht bordering on the Atlantic Ocean. Chiefly hilly, much of the land is devoted to pasture. Area: 1795 sq km (693 sq mi). Population (1986): 55 979. County town: Sligo.

Slim, William Joseph, 1st Viscount (1891–1970) British field marshal. In World War II he became commander of the 14th Army (the "forgotten army") in Burma (1943). After successful operations against the Japanese he became commander in chief of Allied land forces in SE Asia. In 1948 he became chief of the imperial general staff and was then governor general of Australia (1953–60).

slime moulds Organisms belonging to the group *Myxomycophyta*, usually regarded as fungi (since they produce fruiting bodies) but having affinities with the protozoa. The so-called true slime moulds (*Myxomycetes*) are found beneath logs and in other damp places. They consist of slimy sheets of protoplasm that engulf bacteria, wood particles, etc. The cellular slime moulds (*Acrasiales*) are single-celled amoeba-like organisms found in soil. The parasitic slime moulds (*Plasmodiophorales*) live in the tissues of plants.

slipper orchid A terrestrial orchid of the tropical Asian genus *Paphiopedilum* (about 50 species) and the related genera *Cypripedium* and *Phragmipedium*. Popular greenhouse ornamentals, they are characterized by their flowers, which have a pouched slipper-shaped lip and are usually borne singly or in clusters of two or three.

Sloane, Sir Hans (1660–1753) British physician and naturalist, whose collection of books, manuscripts, pictures, etc., formed the nucleus of the British Museum.

sloe. *See* blackthorn.

SLOTH

sloth A primitive arboreal mammal belonging to the family *Bradypodidae* (7 species) of Central and South America, also called ai or unau. 50–65 cm long, sloths are slow-moving and hang upside down from branches, feeding on leaves and fruit. Their greyish-brown fur lies so that rain runs off easily and is often greenish from algae. Order: *Edentata*.

Slough 51 31N 0 36W A town in SE England, in Berkshire. It grew rapidly after a large trading estate was built here in the 1920s and now has a great variety of light industries. Population (1981): 87 005.

Slovak A Western Slavonic language, closely related to Czech, spoken in E Czechoslovakia, where it is an official language. It is written in the Latin alphabet.

Slovakia A mountainous area and former province of E Czechoslovakia. Lying mainly within the Carpathian Mountains, it descends SW to the plains of the Danube Valley. Conquered by the Magyars in the 10th century, Slovakia was part of Hungary until 1918 when it became a province of the Czechoslovak Republic, remaining as such until 1949. Chief town: Bratislava.

Slovenia A constituent republic of N Yugoslavia. It is mountainous and possesses important deposits of coal, mercury, and zinc. Slovenia was chiefly under Habsburg rule from the 14th century until 1918, when it was incorporated into the kingdom of Serbs, Croats, and Slovenes, later renamed Yugoslavia. In 1989, on a wave of nationalism, it voted to give itself the right to secede from Yugoslavia. Area: 20 251 sq km (7819 sq mi). Population (1985 est): 1 930 000. Capital: Ljubljana.

slowworm A legless lizard, *Anguis fragilis*, also called blindworm, occurring in heaths and open woodlands of Europe. It is about 30 cm long, usually brown, grey, or reddish, and feeds on snails, slugs, and other soft-bodied invertebrates. Family: *Anguidae*.

slug A gastropod mollusc of the order *Stylommatophora*, widely distributed in moist terrestrial habitats. Slugs have slimy soft bodies with the shell vestigial or absent. They range in colour from yellow through red-brown to black. Some are carnivorous or scavenging while others feed on soft plant tissues. Subclass: *Pulmonata. Compare* sea slug.

smallage. *See* celery.

smallpox A highly infectious virus disease marked by a skin rash that leaves permanent pitted scars. Smallpox is transmitted by direct contact; the initial symptoms of fever, prostration, severe headache, and backache are followed by the rash on the face and limbs. Secondary infection with staphylococci is often fatal. After a worldwide vaccination programme sponsored by the World Health Organization smallpox was officially declared to have been eradicated in 1979.

smell, sense of. *See* nose.

smelt A slender food fish of the genus *Osmerus* and family *Osmeridae*, occurring in coastal and estuarine waters of Europe and North America. It migrates to fresh water to spawn. The European smelt (*O. eperlanus*), up to about 30 cm long, is greenish grey above and silvery below. Order: *Salmoniformes*.

smelting The extraction of a metal from its ore by heating. The method used depends on the metal, the type of ore, and the melting points of both. The smelting takes place either in a blast furnace (e.g. to extract iron) or a reverberatory furnace (e.g. to extract copper).

Smetana, Bedřich (1824–84) Bohemian composer. In 1859 he joined a group of composers in Prague who were establishing a national opera. *The Brandenburgers in Bohemia* (1862–63) and *The Bartered Bride* (1863–66) were composed for it. In 1874 he became totally deaf but continued to compose, writing the four symphonic poems *Má Vlast* (1874–79) and a string quartet (1876).

Smith, Adam (1723–90) Scottish moral philosopher and political economist. In 1776, he published *An Enquiry into the Nature and Causes of the Wealth of Nations*, an attack on mercantilism that was to become the bible of the free-trade movement. He held that employment, trade, production, and distribution are as much a part of a nation's wealth as its money. An individual allowed to promote his own interests freely within the law often promotes the interests of society as a whole.

Smith, Ian (Douglas) (1919–   ) Prime minister (1964–79) of Rhodesia (now Zimbabwe). An advocate of White supremacy, he demanded full independence for Southern Rhodesia in 1964 but opposed Britain's stipulation that Black majority rule be prepared for. In 1965 he made a unilateral declaration of independence (UDI), maintained until 1976 when he agreed to the principle of Black majority rule.

Smith, Joseph (1805–44) US founder of the Mormons. Smith announced in 1827 his discovery of the sacred *Book of Mormon*, which he claimed he had translated from two gold tablets written by a prophet named Mormon. His new church, founded in Fayette, New York (1830), grew rapidly but attracted considerable opposition. While in jail on charges of conspiracy, Smith was killed by an angry mob. The Mormons migrated westward to Utah under Brigham Young.

Smith, Dame Maggie (1934–   ) British actress. A performer with an exceptional talent for comedy, she appeared in a number of films, including *The Prime of Miss Jean Brodie* (1969), *California Suite* (1979), *A Private Function* (1984), *A Room with a View* (1986), and *The Lonely Passion of Judith Hearne* (1988).

STEVIE SMITH

Smith, Stevie (Florence Margaret S.; 1902–71) British poet, whose deceptively simple poetry blended tenderness, toughness, and humour. The best known of her idiosyncratic novels is *Novel on Yellow Paper* (1936). Her *Collected Poems* (1975) were published posthumously.

Smithsonian Institution A research institution in Washington, DC, founded in 1846 with a bequest from the Englishman James Smithson (1765–1829). It has carried out important scientific work and explorations throughout the world, and administers several important museums, including the National Air and Space Museum and the National Collection of Fine Arts.

smoke tree (*or* smoke bush) One of several species of trees and shrubs having a whitish cloudy appearance at some stage of the season. The American smoke tree (*Cotinus obovatus*) grows to a height of 9 m and has a smoke-like mass of whitish flower heads, as does the Australian smoke bush (*Conospermum stoechadis*). *Rhus cotinus* is the common smoke bush native to the Mediterranean area and parts of Asia.

Smollett, Tobias (George) (1721–71) Scottish writer. His lively picaresque novels include *Roderick Random* (1748), *Peregrine Pickle* (1751), and *Humphry Clinker* (1771).

smooth snake A widespread Eurasian snake, *Coronella austriaca*, that has smooth glossy scales and is brown or reddish with a pale belly and dark spots along its back and tail. Up to 65 cm long, it favours sandy heathlands. Family: *Colubridae*.

smut A disease affecting flowering plants, particularly the cereals and grasses, caused by various basidiomycete fungi of the genus *Ustilago*. Infection is not usually apparent until spore formation, when dark powdery masses of spores are released over the flower head. Stinking smuts, are caused by fungi belonging to the related genus *Tilletia*. Both types are controlled by spraying crops with fungicide and by treating seed before sowing.

Smuts, Jan (Christiaan) (1870–1950) South African statesman and general; prime minister (1919–24, 1939–48). He was a commando leader in the second Boer War (1899–1902) but thereafter worked for reconciliation with Britain. He played an important part in the achievement of responsible government for the Transvaal (1906) and the Union of South Africa (1910), becoming a minister in Louis Botha's government (1910–19) and succeeding him as prime minister, 1919–24. Out of office until 1933, he succeeded Hertzog as prime minister in 1939, advocating South Africa's entry into World War II. His desire to maintain South Africa's links with the British Commonwealth made him unpopular among Afrikaners.

Smyrna. *See* Izmir.

snail A gastropod mollusc with a spirally coiled shell, including terrestrial, freshwater, and marine forms. The common garden snail (*Helix pomatia*) is active at night, feeding on vegetation and sheltering by day in crevices.

snake A legless reptile belonging to the suborder *Serpentes* (about 3000 species), occurring worldwide but especially common in the tropics. Snakes range from 0.12–10 m in length and grow throughout their lives, periodically shedding the skin in one piece. They feed chiefly on other vertebrates, which they swallow whole, having flexible ligaments and joints allowing the two parts of the lower jaw to move apart during swallowing. Prey may be killed by constriction, by engulfing it alive, or by the injection of a potent venom by means of hollow or grooved fangs. The major families are the *Boidae* (pythons, boas, etc.), the *Colubridae* (typical snakes, e.g. the grass snake), the *Elapidae* (cobras, coral snakes, etc.), and the *Viperidae* (vipers, etc.). Order: *Squamata* (lizards and snakes).

Snake River A river in the NW USA. Rising in the Yellowstone National Park in Wyoming, it flows W through Idaho to join the Columbia River in Washington State. Length: 1670 km (1038 mi).

snapdragon. *See* Antirrhinum.

snapper A carnivorous shoaling fish of the family *Lutjanidae* (about 250 species), found in tropical seas. It has an elongated body, a large mouth, and sharp teeth. Some are valuable food fish, especially the red snapper (*Lutjanus blackfordi*); others are poisonous.

Snell's law When a ray of light passes from one medium to another the angle (r) between the refracted ray and a line normal to the interface between the media is related to the angle (i) of the incident ray, also taken to the normal, by the equation $\sin i / \sin r = n$, where n is the relative refractive index of the media (*see* refraction). It is named after the Dutch astronomer Willebrord Snell (1591–1626).

snipe A sandpiper belonging to a subfamily (*Scolopacinae*; 10 species) occurring in wet areas of warm and temperate regions. Snipe have a long flexible bill used to probe for worms, and a barred and striped brown, black, and white plumage. The common snipe (*Gallinago gallinago*) is popular gamebird.

snooker A game, deriving from billiards, that arose among British officers in India (1875). It is played by two players or pairs of players on a billiards table. There are 22 balls: 1 white cue ball, 15 red balls (value 1 point each), and 6 coloured balls—yellow (2 points), green (3), brown (4), blue (5), pink (6), black (7). The object is to pocket a red ball and a coloured ball alternately, each time returning the coloured ball to its prescribed spot on the table. The red balls are not replaced. When all the red balls have been potted the colours are potted.

snow A solid form of precipitation composed of ice crystals or snowflakes. Ice crystals occur when temperatures are well below freezing point; with temperatures nearer to 0°C (32°F) snowflakes develop through the clustering together of crystals.

Snow, C(harles) P(ercy), Baron (1905–80) British novelist and scientist. The moral problems of politics and power are a recurrent theme of his series of novels beginning with *Strangers and Brothers* (1940) and ending with *Last Things* (1970).

snowball tree. *See* guelder rose.

Snowdon 53 04N 4 05W The highest mountain in Wales, in Gwynedd. The surrounding area, **Snowdonia**, was designated a National Park in 1951. Height: 1085 m (3560 ft).

Snowdon, Antony Armstrong-Jones, Earl of (1930–) British photographer. His work includes several television documentaries and photographic books, such as *Venice* (1972). His marriage (1960–78) to Princess Margaret ended in divorce.

snowdrop A small early spring-blooming herbaceous plant of the genus *Galanthus* (about 10 species) native to Europe and W Asia. They grow from bulbs to produce grasslike leaves and slender stems bearing solitary nodding white flowers, tipped with green or yellow. There are over 50 cultivated varieties. *G. nivalis* is the common European snowdrop. Family: *Amaryllidaceae*.

SNOW LEOPARD

snow goose An Arctic goose, *Anser caerulescens*. It is either pure white with black wingtips, pink legs, and a red bill or blue-grey with a white head. Snow geese winter in the southern USA, Japan, and China.

snow leopard A big cat, *Panthera* (or *Uncia*) *uncia*, also called ounce, found in the mountains of central

Asia. It is 1.9 m long, with a thick ash-grey coat marked with dark rosettes.

Snowy Mountains A mountain range in Australia. It lies in New South Wales, and contains Australia's highest mountain, Mount Kosciusko.

snuff A preparation of tobacco and other ingredients that is sniffed rather than smoked. Added ingredients introduce flavour and scent to the mixture.

soaps Salts of fatty acids. Household soap (**hard soap**) is a mixture of sodium stearate, oleate, and palmitate. It is made by the hydrolysis of fats with caustic soda (sodium hydroxide), thus converting the glycerides of stearic, oleic, and palmitic acids into sodium salts and glycerol. **Soft soap** is made with potassium hydroxide instead of sodium hydroxide. Soaps have a cleansing action because they contain negative ions composed of a long hydrocarbon chain (which has an affinity for grease and oil) attached to a carboxyl group (which has an affinity for water). Particles of grease or oil are therefore emulsified in soapy water. *See also* detergents.

soapstone. *See* talc.

Soares, Mario (1924–) Portuguese statesman; prime minister (1976–79; 1983–85); president (1986–). He was a critic of Salazar and lived in exile from 1970 to 1974, when he became foreign minister in the new military government.

Sobers, Gary (Sir Garfield Saint Aubrun S.; 1936–) West Indian cricketer, who captained the West Indies and Nottinghamshire. One of the greatest all-rounders, he played in 93 Test matches, scoring 8032 runs, including 26 centuries, and taking 235 wickets.

Social and Liberal Democratic Party (SLD) A British political party of the centre, established in 1988 when a majority of the Social Democratic Party merged with the Liberal Party. Informally known as the Liberal Democrats, members elected Paddy Ashdown as their first leader.

Social Democratic and Labour Party (SDLP) A British political party, active in Northern Ireland. Founded in 1970, it supports peaceful union with Ireland. Its parliamentary leader is John Hume (1937–).

Social Democratic Party (SDP) A British political party of the centre, formed in 1981 by the "gang of four" labour dissidents: Roy Jenkins, Shirley Williams, Dr David Owen (leader 1983–87; 1988–), and William Rodgers. The SDP formed a political alliance with the Liberal Party in 1981; in 1987, the SDP voted to merge with the Liberals and Owen was replaced by Robert Maclennan. After the majority of the party joined the new Social and Liberal Democratic Party in 1988, Owen relaunched a reduced SDP.

socialism A concept, resulting in diverse political movements, that generally emphasizes cooperation rather than competition. In the early 19th century one sense of the word implied a continuation of liberalism, the emphasis being on reform of the social system to develop liberal values, such as political freedom, and the ending of class privileges. Socialism in a second sense was explicitly contrasted with a competitive individualist form of society; practical cooperation could not be achieved until a society based on private property was replaced by one based on social ownership and control.

In 1848 Marx and Engels laid down the principles of scientific socialism in *The Communist Manifesto* and Marxism became the theoretical basis for most socialist thought. The British Fabian Society (founded 1884) revived a variant of the first sense of the term, which later found political expression in the Labour Party. It was the split in Russia, however, between the revolutionary Bolsheviks and the reformist Mensheviks that led to the decisive distinction between the terms communism and socialism as they are now generally understood, socialists being those who seek change by peaceful reform and communists being those dedicated to change by revolution.

Society Islands   An archipelago in French Polynesia, discovered in 1767. It consists of two mountainous island groups, the **Windward Islands** (including Tahiti and Moorea) and the **Leeward Islands** (including Raiatea and Huahine). The capital of French Polynesia, Papeete, is on Tahiti. Area: 1595 sq km (616 sq mi). Population (1983): 142 129.

Society of Friends.   *See* Quakers.

Society of Jesus.   *See* Jesuits.

sociology   The systematic study of the development, organization, functioning, and classification of human societies. Its growth was stimulated by the rapid industrial and social change in Europe in the early 19th century. It has employed techniques of participant observation, the systematic comparison of different societies, and surveys of social conditions, attitudes, and behaviour. Contemporary sociology is divided into several specialized subdisciplines including demography, political, educational, and urban sociology as well as sociological studies of deviance, religion, and culture.

sockeye salmon   A salmon, *Oncorhynchus nerka*, also called red salmon or blueback, that lives in the N Pacific and spawns in Canadian fresh waters.

Socrates   (c. 469–399 BC) Athenian philosopher, whose ideas, intellect, integrity, and courage are known through his disciples Plato and Xenophon. Socrates diverted philosophy from physical speculations about the universe towards ethics. His insistence upon thorough critical analysis of ethical concepts also marked the beginning of logic. The "Socratic method" of teaching was by eliciting answers from interlocutors to reveal inconsistencies in accepted opinions. His resolute stance against tyranny brought about his trial on charges of atheism and "corrupting the youth," and he was condemned to die by drinking hemlock.

Soddy, Frederick   (1877–1956) British chemist, who worked under Rutherford and Ramsay and went on to win the 1921 Nobel Prize for his discovery of isotopes.

sodium   (Na)   A highly reactive alkali metal, long-recognized in compounds but first isolated as the element by Sir Humphry Davy in 1807. It is obtained commercially by electrolysis of common salt (NaCl). It occurs naturally in some silicate minerals (for example feldspars; $NaAlSi_3O_8$), as well as in salt deposits and in the oceans. The metal is soft, bright, and less dense (relative density 0.97) than water, with which it reacts violently, liberating hydrogen. It is a highly electropositive element, forming many ionic salts of great importance, such as the chloride (common salt; NaCl), the carbonate (soda ash; Na_2CO_3), the bicarbonate (baking-soda; $NaHCO_3$), various phosphates, and the nitrate (NaNO_3). At no 11; at wt 22.9898; mp 97.8°C; bp 882.9°C.

sodium bicarbonate (sodium hydrogen carbonate *or* bicarbonate of soda; $NaHCO_3$)   The white soluble powder that is a constituent of baking powder and is used to make fizzy drinks and as an antacid in medicine.

sodium carbonate (Na_2CO_3)   A white soluble salt. The commercial form (**soda ash**) is a white anhydrous powder and is used in making glass, soap, paper, as well as other chemicals. **Washing soda**, its hydrated form, is a white crystalline solid used as a domestic cleanser and water softener.

sodium hydroxide (*or* caustic soda; NaOH)   A white solid that is strongly alkaline in aqueous solution and is very corrosive to organic tissue. It is used in making rayon, paper, detergents, and other chemicals.

Sodom and Gomorrah   In the Old Testament, two cities of Palestine, known as the "cities of the plain," S of the Dead Sea in the area in which Lot, the nephew of Abraham, settled. According to Genesis (18, 19), they were destroyed by fire and brimstone from heaven because of the utter depravity of their inhabitants.

Sofia   42 40N 23 18E   The capital of Bulgaria, situated on a plateau in the W of the country. Sofia came under the Byzantine Empire in the 6th century and was taken over by the Bulgars in the 9th century. Under Turkish rule from 1382, it was liberated by the Russians in 1878 and became the national capital (1879). Population (1985): 1 114 962.

software   The suite of programs that sets up a computer system for operation, as distinct from the physical equipment (hardware). Software supplied by the computer manufacturer controls various parts of the system and provides facilities for further programming. Additional programs are purchased separately or written by the user. *See also* program, computer.

Sogne Fjord   The longest and deepest fjord in Norway, extending 204 km (127 mi) inland N of Bergen. It is flanked by spectacular mountain scenery.

soil   The mixture of unconsolidated mineral particles, derived from weathered rock, and organic matter (humus), derived from the breakdown of plant tissue by living organisms, that covers much of the earth's land surface and provides a medium for plant growth. Soils are characterized by their texture, which depends on particle sizes (*see* sand; silt; clay), and their structure, which depends on the way the particles are bound into aggregates (e.g. crumbs, granules, flakes, etc.). These are important factors in determining the fertility of the soil, particularly its moisture and air content, susceptibility to leaching (the removal of nutrients to deeper levels by percolating water), and ease of cultivation. Soils are also classified according to their profiles—the arrangement of the layers (horizons) between the ground surface and the bedrock. *See also* chernozem; podzol.

sol.   *See* colloid.

Solanaceae   A family of herbaceous plants and shrubs (about 2000 species), widely distributed but chiefly tropical. Their flowers have five fused sepals and petals. The family includes several commercially important species (e.g. the potato, tomato, pepper, and tobacco) and some ornamentals (e.g. *Petunia*); various other members are poisonous (e.g. the nightshades).

solar cell.   *See* solar power.

solar constant   The total amount of solar energy passing perpendicularly through unit area per unit time at a particular distance from the sun. It is about 1.36 kW m^{-2} at the earth's mean orbital distance.

solar flare   A sudden brightening, within minutes, of areas in the sun's atmosphere, resulting from an explosive release of energetic particles and radiation. Flares often occur above sunspot groups. Large flares affect radio transmission on earth and produce auroras.

solar power   The use of the sun's energy to provide heating or to generate electricity. Solar energy is most

SOLAR POWER   *An experimental car powered by solar cells.*

commonly converted into heat by direct heating of water flowing through special panels on the roof of a building. The temperature rise produced is fairly small but it reduces the energy required from other sources for hot water and space heating. Higher temperatures, sufficient to form steam for electricity generation, are possible using large mirrors to collect and focus the sun's rays. Direct conversion of solar radiation into electrical energy is possible with **solar cells**. These are semiconductor devices sensitive to the photovoltaic effect. The method is used mainly in small-scale specialized applications, for example powering remote monitoring equipment, spacecraft, marine beacons, etc.

solar system   A system comprising the sun and the astronomical bodies gravitationally bound to the sun, that is the nine major planets, their satellites, and the immense numbers of minor planets, comets, and meteoroids. Almost all the mass of the solar system (99.86%) resides in the sun. The planets orbit the sun in the same direction and, with the exception of Pluto, move in paths close to the earth's orbital plane. The solar system formed some 4600 million years ago, following the contraction and subsequent flattening of a rotating cloud of interstellar gas and dust.

solar wind   An almost radial outflow of charged particles discharged from the sun's corona into interplanetary space. The particles, mainly protons and electrons, are moving at speeds between 200 and 900 km per second in the vicinity of the earth's orbit. They interact with the earth's magnetosphere.

solder   An alloy that is melted to form a joint between other metals or, occasionally, nonmetals. The surfaces to be joined are heated by a soldering iron or by a flame, but are not melted. **Soft solder** is usually made of lead and tin and melts in the range 200–250°C. It cannot be used for joints that have to stand up to stress or heat, but is used for making secure electrical connections. **Brazing**, also called **hard soldering**, uses a harder alloy with a higher melting temperature (850–900°C), usually a brass with 60% zinc and 40% copper. **Silver solder** has a slightly lower melting point (630–830°C) than brass, and often contains antimony or other metals but no longer contains silver. Like brazing, its strength makes it useful in engineering applications. A flux of zinc chloride or a resin is applied to the hot surfaces before soldering to clean them and to enable the solder to flow.

sole   An elongated flatfish of the family *Soleidae* (over 100 species), found in temperate and tropical seas. The common European sole (*Solea solea*), also called Dover sole, is a valuable food fish and has a blotchy brown body with a black spot on each pectoral fin. *See also* lemon sole.

solenoid   A coil of wire usually forming a long cylinder. When electric current flows through it a magnetic field is created. This field can be used to move an iron rod placed on its axis. Solenoids are often used to operate mechanical valves attached to the iron rod by switching on or off the current.

Solent, the   A channel between the coast of Hampshire in S England and the Isle of Wight. It is an important shipping route between Southampton and the English Channel.

solicitor   In the UK, a member of the legal profession qualified to give legal advice to clients, to present clients' cases in Magistrates' Courts, County Courts, and (since 1971) to present certain cases in the Crown Court, and to undertake other legal work, such as the transfer of property (conveyancing). They are eligible for appointment as circuit judges and recorders, but are not eligible for the higher judiciary. A barrister must always be instructed through a solicitor.

Solidarity   A Polish trade union. Formed in Gdansk (1980) under a strike settlement agreement and led by Lech Wałesa, Solidarity became a focus of resistance to Jarulzelski's Soviet-dominated government and was outlawed from 1981 until 1989, when it again became legal. In June 1989 the movement triumphed in elections, forming the first non-Communist government in the Communist world.

solid state   One of the four states of matter and that to which all substances, except helium, revert at sufficiently low temperatures. It is distinguished from the other states by being the only one in which matter retains its shape, as a result of the stronger intermolecular forces.

solid-state devices   Electronic devices made with solid semiconductor components. They have no moving parts and depend for their operation on the movement of charges within a crystalline solid. Solid-state devices are compact, robust, and easily mass-produced. *See also* semiconductor diode; transistor.

solmization   A method of teaching sight-singing that eliminates learning to read music notation from the stave. In the tonic sol-fa system the notes of the rising major scale are represented by the syllables doh, ray, me,

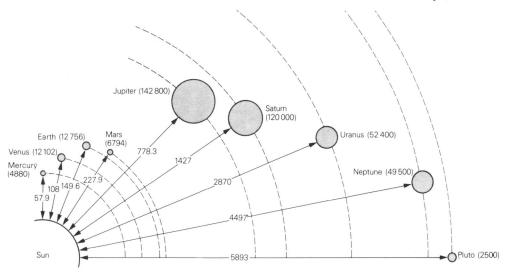

SOLAR SYSTEM   *The planets with their equatorial diameters in kilometres (in brackets after the planet's name) and their distance from the sun in millions of kilometres (not to scale).*

fah, soh, lah, ti, and doh. The system can be applied in any key, and modulation to a different key simply involves shifting doh to another pitch. Vocal exercises on solmization syllables are known by the Italian word *solfeggio*.

Solo.   *See* Surakarta.

Solomon   In the Old Testament, the third King of Israel, son of David and Bathsheba, who reigned in the 10th century BC. During his peaceful reign several foreign alliances were formed (notably with Phoenicia and Egypt), trade and commerce were expanded and the Temple at Jerusalem as well as many palaces were built. To realize his schemes he had to impose heavy taxation and use compulsory labour, which resulted in the revolt of N Israel. He was famous for his wisdom.

Solomon Islands   A country in the Pacific Ocean, E of New Guinea. It consists of numerous small islands, the largest of which are Guadalcanal, Malaita, San Cristobal, New Georgia, Santa Isabel and Choiseul. (Bougainville, however, is part of Papua New Guinea.) The larger islands are mainly forested and mountainous, with some active volcanoes. Most of the population are Melanesian, with Polynesian and Micronesian minorities. The islands were discovered by the Spanish in 1568. The four main islands became a British protectorate in 1893 and others were added in 1898–99. They achieved self-government in 1976 and became independent within the British Commonwealth in 1978. Prime Minister: Solomon Mamaloni. Official language: English. Official currency: Australian dollar of 100 cents. Area: 29 785 sq km (11 500 sq mi). Population (1987): 291 800. 256 000. Capital and main port: Honiara.

Solon   (6th century BC) Athenian statesman, who laid the foundations of Athenian democracy. As archon (c. 594–593), Solon cancelled debts for which land or liberty was the security and introduced a new coinage and weights and measures. He also instituted a new constitution and a more lenient legal code.

solstice   Either of two points on the ecliptic, midway between the equinoxes, at which the sun reaches its greatest angular distance above or below the celestial equator (*see* celestial sphere). In the N hemisphere the sun's northernmost position occurs at the **summer solstice**, usually on 21 June, when daylight hours are at a maximum. Its southernmost position occurs at the **winter solstice**, usually on 22 December, when daylight hours are minimal.

Solti, Sir Georg   (1912–) Hungarian-born naturalized British conductor. He was conductor of the Royal Opera, Covent Garden (1961–71), the Orchestre de Paris (1972–75), the London Philharmonic Orchestra (1979–83), and the Chicago Symphony Orchestra (1969–89).

solution   A homogenous liquid mixture of two or more substances. Solutions, unlike colloids, contain no identifiable particles of different substances. When a solid or gas is dissolved in a liquid, the liquid is known as the solvent and the dissolved material the solute. If the components are all liquid, the one in excess is the solvent.

Solvay process   An industrial process for the production of sodium carbonate. Limestone is first heated strongly to produce calcium oxide and carbon dioxide, which is then passed through brine saturated with ammonia, precipitating sodium hydrogencarbonate ($NaHCO_3$). This, on mild heating, yields sodium carbonate and some carbon dioxide, which is recycled. The ammonia is also recovered. Named after E. Solvay (1833–1922).

solvent abuse   The sniffing of organic solvents in glue, cleaning fluids, aerosols, etc., especially by adolescents. The practice has grown up as an offshoot of the drug culture and is highly dangerous. In the UK there are now restrictions on the sale of materials containing solvents to children.

Solzhenitsyn, Aleksandr   (1918–) Soviet-born novelist. After World War II he was held in prison camps until 1956. In 1974 he left the Soviet Union

SOLZHENITSYN *Receiving an honorary doctorate.*

and now lives in the USA. His major works include *Cancer Ward* (1968), *The First Circle* (1968), and *The Gulag Archipelago* (1974–78). He won the Nobel Prize in 1970.

Somali An E African people occupying Somalia, Djibouti (where they are called Issas), Ethiopia, and NW Kenya. There are many tribes. Some Somalis are nomadic herdsmen while others dwell in towns and along the coast as traders and farmers. Their language belongs to the Cushitic branch of the Hamito-Semitic family.

Somalia (official name: Somali Democratic Republic) A country in East Africa, occupying most of the Horn of Africa between the Gulf of Aden and the Indian Ocean. Coastal plains rise in the N to a high plateau. Most of the inhabitants are nomadic Somalis with minorities of Sab, Bantu, and others. The economy is chiefly agricultural, livestock raising being especially important. Communications are difficult; there are no railways. The region was occupied in the 19th century by the French, British, and Italians (*see* Somaliland). The former British and Italian territories gained independence in 1960 (while the French territory of the Afars and Issas became independent Djibouti in 1977). In 1969, after a military coup, a Supreme Revolutionary Council was established in Somalia under Gen Mohammed Siad Barré (1919–   ). The country has had serious territorial disputes with Ethiopia (*see* Ogaden), which has a considerable Somali population, and has been torn by civil war for several years. Official language: Somali; Arabic, Italian, and English are used extensively. Official religion: Islam. Official currency: Somali shilling of 100 centesemi. Area: 700 000 sq km (270 000 sq mi). Population (1987 est): 6 110 000. Capital and main port: Mogadishu.

Somaliland A region corresponding to present-day Somalia and Djibouti. Between the 7th and 12th centuries AD the coastal region was occupied by Muslim traders while the N was settled from the 10th century by nomadic Somalis. During the 19th century the region was divided between France, Britain, and Italy. Italian Somaliland was united with Ethiopia by Mussolini (1935) and was acquired by Britain in World War II. British Somaliland became independent as Somalia in 1960 and the French territory, Afars and Issàs, as Djibouti in 1977.

somatotrophin. *See* growth hormone.

Somerset A county of SW England, bordering on the Bristol Channel. It consists mainly of a flat plain enclosed by the Quantock Hills and Exmoor in the W, the Blackdown Hills in the S, and the Mendip Hills (containing Cheddar Gorge) in the NE. It is predominantly agricultural; dairy farming is especially important and there is the traditional cider making. Area: 3458 sq km (1335 sq mi). Population (1986 est): 448 900. Administrative centre: Taunton.

Somme, River A river in N France, rising in the Aisne department and flowing mainly W through Amiens and Abbeville to the English Channel. It was the scene of extensive fighting in World War I (1916). Length: 245 km (152 mi).

sonar. *See* echo sounding.

sonata (Italian: sounded, as opposed to *cantata*, sung) A piece of music for one or more instruments. The name has been used of a variety of abstract musical forms. **Sonata form**, the normal structure of the first movement of the classical sonata, was based on the exposition, development, and recapitulation of two contrasting themes. It was applied to the first movement of the symphony and of chamber music compositions as well as the sonata proper. Beethoven and his successors enlarged the formal boundaries of the sonata; Liszt evolved a single-movement form out of the three or four movements of the classical sonata. In the 20th century sonata form has been adapted in a variety of ways,

Sondheim, Stephen (Joshua) (1930–   ) US composer, who studied lyric writing with Oscar Hammerstein. He wrote the lyrics for the musicals *West Side Story* (1957), *A Little Night Music* (1973), and *Sweeney Todd* (1979). The revue *Side by Side by Sondheim* (1976) contains many of his songs.

songbird A passerine bird belonging to the suborder *Oscines* (about 4000 species), in which the vocal organ (syrinx), at the junction of the trachea (windpipe) and bronchi, is highly developed. The flow of air vibrates the vocal membranes; muscles alter their tension and so produce the different notes. Bird song communicates the identity and whereabouts of an individual to other birds and also signals alarm and sexual intentions; it is especially important in birds that feed or migrate in flocks.

sonic boom. *See* sound barrier.

sonnet A poem of 14 lines originating in Italy in the 13th century and introduced into England in the 16th century by Sir Thomas Wyatt. Its two principal variations are the Petrarchan sonnet, usually divided into an octet rhyming *abbaabba* and a sestet rhyming *cdecde*, and the Shakespearean sonnet, usually rhyming *abab cdcd efef gg.*

Soochow. *See* Suzhou.

Sophists The Greek sages of the 5th and early 4th centuries BC who were itinerant experts on various subjects including public speaking, grammar, ethics, literature, mathematics, and elementary physics. In philosophy they tried to explain the phenomenal world. Their educational programme centred on the belief that virtue can be taught. From their opponent Plato, they acquired a bad name as philosophical tricksters.

Sophocles (c. 496–406 BC) Greek dramatist; with Aeschylus and Euripides, one of the three great Athenian tragic dramatists. He developed the more static drama of Aeschylus by introducing a third actor and reducing the role of the chorus. Of his 123 plays, 7 survive, including *Electra*, *Oedipus Rex*, and *Antigone*. He led an active public life, holding several important civil and military administrative posts.

soprano (Italian: upper)   The highest female singing voice. Range: middle C to the C above the treble stave. The **mezzo-soprano** voice lies between the soprano and the contralto. Range: A below middle C to F an octave and a sixth above.

Sorghum   A genus of annual or perennial grasses (about 30 species), native to Africa, especially *S. vulgare*, of which there are several varieties, such as sweet sorghum, durra, and kaffir corn, widely cultivated as cereal crops. They have rigid stalks, sometimes containing a sweet sap, long flat leaves, and terminal flower clusters bearing 800–3000 starch-rich seeds. The seeds are used as grain for making bread, etc., and as a source of edible oil, starch, and sugar. The stalks are used as fodder or sometimes for syrup manufacture.

sorrel   A tall perennial herb, *Rumex acetosa*, common throughout temperate Eurasia and North America. It bears numerous small red flowers. The tangy-tasting leaves are used as a culinary flavouring and in salads. Family: *Polygonaceae*. *See also* wood sorrel.

Sotho   A large group of Bantu-speaking peoples of S Africa. The term applies in a general sense to the peoples of Botswana, Lesotho, and the Transvaal (South Africa), but, more specifically, to one of the four main divisions of these peoples, the Sotho of Lesotho. The other branches are the Tswana, Pedi, and Venda, each with many tribes.

Soto   The largest Japanese school of Zen Buddhism, founded in China in the 9th century AD and brought to Japan in 1227. Soto emphasizes meditation and morality.

sound   A disturbance propagated through a medium by longitudinal waves. Strictly the term applies only to those waves that are audible to the human ear, i.e. with frequencies between about 20 and 20 000 hertz, those with higher frequencies being called ultrasound. Sound is propagated by vibrations of molecules in the medium, producing fronts of compression and rarefaction. Sound waves are longitudinal as the molecules vibrate in the direction of propagation; the speed of sound in air at 0°C is about 332 metres per second (760 mph). The three principal characteristics of a sound are its pitch (the frequency of the wave), loudness (the amplitude of the wave), and timbre (the extent to which it contains harmonics of the fundamental frequency). *See also* acoustics; sound intensity.

sound barrier   An obstacle experienced by subsonic aircraft attempting to fly at or above the speed of sound. Drag increases sharply, lift falls off, and the aircraft becomes difficult to control (*see* aeronautics). At subsonic speeds the pressure waves created by the aircraft as it flies through the air are able to move ahead of the aircraft; at supersonic speeds they cannot escape in a forward direction as the source is moving faster than the pressure waves themselves. Thus shock waves build up on the aircraft's wings and fuselage, creating an apparent barrier to supersonic flight. Many aircraft are now capable of supersonic flight (including Concorde) by greater streamlining, sweptback wings, and more powerful engines. As these aircraft cross the sound barrier a **sonic boom** is heard. This is created by a shock-wave cone with the nose of the aircraft at its vertex. In level flight the intersection of this cone with the ground pro-

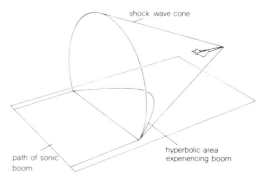

SOUND BARRIER   *As an aircraft passes through the sound barrier the sonic boom is heard along a hyperbolic area on the ground.*

duces a hyperbola at all points along which the boom is heard.

sound intensity   The rate at which sound energy is propagated through a unit area perpendicular to the direction of propagation. It is measured in watts per square metre. The intensities of two sound levels are compared by a unit called the decibel. The intensity of sound is not the same as its loudness, the latter being the magnitude of the sensation produced by the human ear, which is dependent on the frequency of the sound.

Sousa, John Philip   (1854–1933) US composer and bandmaster. He wrote military marches including "The Stars and Stripes Forever," "The Washington Post," and "Liberty Bell" and invented the **sousaphone**, a tuba-like band instrument with a forward-facing bell.

souslik (*or* suslik)   A nocturnal ground squirrel belonging to the genus *Citellus* (34 species), of E Europe, Asia, and North America (where it is sometimes called a gopher). The European souslik (*C. citellus*) is yellowish brown with large eyes and small ears. *See also* chipmunk.

South Africa, Republic of   A country occupying the S tip of Africa. Narrow coastal plains rise to plateaus in the interior, with the Drakensberg mountains in the E. The N is mainly desert. The Limpopo, Molopo, and Orange Rivers mark the N boundary. The Vaal, a tributary of the Orange, is another important river. The majority of the inhabitants are Africans (71%) with White, Coloured, and Asian (mostly Indian) minorities. *Economy*: although South Africa is highly industrialized, agriculture is still important. Rich and varied mineral resources include gold, diamonds, chrome, platinum, uranium, coal, manganese, phosphates, and iron. Well-developed industry includes metals, machinery, chemicals, food processing, and textiles. *History*: Bantu-speaking tribes arrived from the north between 1000 and 1500. The Portuguese under Bartolomeu Dias (c. 1450–c. 1500) first sighted the Cape of Good Hope (1488) but made no permanent settlement there. The Dutch East India Company settlement (1652) at Table Bay (Cape Town) expanded into a colony that spread into the interior. During the Napoleonic Wars Britain acquired the Cape Colony for strategic reasons, a possession confirmed in 1814. In the 1830s increasing numbers of Dutch farmers (or Boers, forebears of the modern

SOUTH AFRICA *The capital, Cape Town, set against the Table Mountain.*

Afrikaners) moved E and N to escape British rule, clashing with the Bantu peoples who were then migrating southwards (*see* Great Trek). The Boers founded two independent republics, the Orange Free State and the Transvaal, but their republic in Natal was soon annexed by the British (1843), who were also expanding the eastern boundaries of the Cape Colony. Kruger's assertion of Boer independence led to war (1880–81), which broke out again (1899–1902) between the Boers and the British (*see* Boer Wars). The need for cooperation led the two former Boer republics and the two British colonies to combine in the Union of South Africa (1910). In both World Wars South Africa, under J. C. Smuts, enthusiastically supported Britain, but in 1948 Smuts was ousted by the anti-British Afrikaner National Party and in 1961 South Africa became a republic outside the British Commonwealth. Since 1910 the treatment of the non-White majority has been the crucial political issue (*see* apartheid) and in 1976 the Transkei became the first independent Bantu Homeland (Bantustan). South Africa has also intervened in Angola (1976) and Namibia, and has supported the White minorities in Zimbabwe and Mozambique. In the face of increasing internal unrest, some non-Whites received limited parliamentary power under a new tricameral constitution instituted in 1984. In 1985 a state of emergency was declared in some areas in response to violent race riots and the USA imposed economic sanctions in protest against apartheid. Continuing unrest led to the replacement in 1989 of P.W. Botha by F.W. de Klerk as president. The African National Congress and the Communist Party were then legalized and ANC leader Nelson Mandela was released after 27 years in prison; other reforms were promised. Official languages: Afrikaans and English. Official currency, since 1959: rand of 100 cents. Area: 1 221 042 sq km (472 359 sq mi). Population (1987): 28 881 000. Capitals: Pretoria (administrative), Bloemfontein (judicial), Cape Town (legislative).

South America The fourth largest continent, lying chiefly in the S of the W hemisphere between the Pacific and Atlantic Oceans. It is linked to the continent of North America by the Isthmus of Panama. An ancient shield occupies much of the NE part of the continent and forms the Brazilian and Guiana Highlands. These are separated by the vast basins of the Orinoco, Amazon, and Paraná–Paraguay river systems. In the extreme W, beyond a series of plains, rise the mountains and high plateaus of the Andes. South America's climate varies considerably, largely because of its length, but much is tropical with vast areas of tropical rainforest (selva). The population consists chiefly of the indigenous Indians, Europeans (especially Spanish and Portuguese), and mestizos together with large numbers of Negroids. *History*: the flourishing kingdoms of South America (such as those of the Incas and Chibchas), were vanquished by the Spanish conquistadors. The entire continent was divided—Portugal taking the NE portion (now Brazil) and Spain the remainder—during the 16th century. With the collapse of the Spanish Empire during the early 19th century, there followed struggles for independence under national leaders, who included Bolívar and San Martín. Large-scale European immigration occurred in the 19th century. During the 20th century the constituent nations have become increasingly industrialized and seen rapid rises in their populations. Area: 17 767 331 sq km (6 858 527 sq mi). Population (1985 est): 263 300 000.

Southampton 50 55N 1 25W A city in S England, in Hampshire on Southampton Water (an inlet of the English Channel). It is the UK's principal passenger port, used by the largest transatlantic liners, and has four tides daily. It is also an industrial centre with a large oil refinery at Fawley on Southampton Water. Population (1981): 204 406.

Southampton, Henry Wriothesley, 3rd Earl of (1573–1624) English courtier, famous as the patron of Shakespeare. He was involved in the Earl of Essex's conspiracy against Elizabeth I (1600), sentenced to death, but pardoned by James I (1603).

South Australia A state of S central Australia, bordering on the Indian Ocean and Great Australian Bight. It consists chiefly of low-lying plains with the Great Victoria Desert in the W, rising in the NW to the Musgrave Ranges and in the SE to the Flinders Range. The only major river is the Murray. Intensive agriculture is restricted to the S. The vineyards of the fertile Barossa Valley are especially important, producing almost half of Australia's wine. Mineral resources include iron ore, coal, large natural gas fields in the N, and opals. Industry is concentrated in Adelaide. Area: 984 377 sq km (380 070 sq mi). Population (1986): 1 345 945. Capital: Adelaide.

South Carolina A state in the SE USA, on the Atlantic coast. Lowlands make up two-thirds of the state rising to uplands in the NW. The large areas of woodland supply the furniture industries and the large textile and clothing industries are based on the region's cotton crop. One of the 13 original colonies, it became separate from North Carolina in 1713 and was the first state to secede from the Union (1860). Area: 80 432 sq km (31 055 sq mi). Population (1986 est): 3 376 000. Capital: Columbia. *See also* Charleston.

South Caucasian languages A group of languages, also known as the Kartvelian languages, spoken by the people of W Transcaucasia and adjacent regions. It includes Georgian, Svan, Mingrelian, and Laz. Only Georgian possesses a literary tradition.

South China Sea A section of the W Pacific Ocean, between SE Asia, Borneo, the Philippines, and Taiwan. A monsoon area, it is heavily fished.

South Dakota One of the Plains states in N central USA. The Missouri River separates the arid Badlands, the Black Hills, and the Great Plains in the W from the flat fertile prairie in the E, which forms the basis of South Dakota's predominantly agrarian economy. Livestock and livestock products are the chief source of revenue. Part of the Louisiana Purchase (1803), the gold rush and land boom of the 1880s brought many settlers and South Dakota became a state in 1889. Area: 199 551 sq km (77 047 sq mi). Population (1986 est): 708 000. Capital: Pierre.

South East Asia Treaty Organization (SEATO) An organization formed to protect SE Asia from possible communist aggression. It was analogous to the North Atlantic Treaty Organization. The treaty was signed in Manila in 1954 by Australia, France, New Zealand, Pakistan, the Philippines, Thailand, the UK, and the USA. Pakistan withdrew in 1973 and the organization was formally ended in 1977.

Southend-on-Sea 51 33N 0 43E A resort in SE England, in Essex on the lower Thames estuary. It is the nearest seaside resort to London, which it also serves as a dormitory town, and has the world's longest pleasure pier. Population (1981): 156 683.

Southern Alps The highest range of mountains in New Zealand. It extends SW–NE through South Island and contains many peaks over 3000 m (10 000 ft), including Mount Cook. Glaciers, fed by the central snowfields, flank the mountains. It is an important wintersports area.

Southern Rhodesia. *See* Zimbabwe, State of.

South Georgia An island in the S Atlantic Ocean, a dependency of the Falkland Islands. King Edward Point is a British Antarctic Survey base. With the Falkland Islands, it was invaded by Argentina (April, 1982) but was soon recaptured. Area: 3755 sq km (1450 sq mi).

South Glamorgan A county of SE Wales, bordering on the Bristol Channel. It was created in 1974 from S Glamorgan and SW Monmouthshire. It consists chiefly of a low undulating plateau (the fertile Vale of Glamorgan), drained by the River Taff. Agriculture is important with industry centred on Barry and Cardiff. Area: 416 sq km (161 sq mi). Population (1986 est): 395 700. Administrative centre: Cardiff.

South Island The larger of the two principal islands of New Zealand, separated from North Island by Cook Strait. It is generally mountainous, including the Southern Alps in the W, with coastal plains.

South Orkney Islands A group of islands within the British Antarctic Territory, in the S Atlantic Ocean, a dependency of the Falkland Islands until 1962. They are also claimed by Argentina.

Southport 53 39N 3 01W A town and resort in NW England, in N Merseyside on the Irish Sea. Its annual flower show is famous and there is a well-known golf course at nearby Birkdale. Population (1981): 89 745.

South Sea Bubble (1720) The collapse of the British market in South Sea stocks that had far-reaching political repercussions. The South Sea Company was founded in 1711 to trade with Spanish America and in 1718 George I became its governor. A boom in South Sea stock was followed by collapse and the subsequent inquiry revealed corruption among ministers and even touched the king. The day was saved by Sir Robert Walpole, who transferred the South Sea stocks to the Bank of England and the East India Company.

South Shields 55 00N 1 25W A port in NE England, in Tyne and Wear on the Tyne estuary opposite North

Shields. Industries include shipbuilding, marine engineering, petrochemicals, and paint manufacture. The first lifeboat was built here (1790). Population (1981): 87 203.

South West Africa. *See* Namibia.

South Yorkshire A metropolitan county of N England, created in 1974 from the S part of the West Riding of Yorkshire and a small part of NE Derbyshire. It comprises the districts of Sheffield, Rotherham, Doncaster, and Barnsley. Agriculture is important on the Pennines in the W and on the lowlands in the E. The main industrial activities are iron and steel, engineering, and coalmining. Area: 1562 sq km (603 sq mi). Population (1986 est): 1 297 900. Administrative centre: Barnsley.

Soutine, Chaim (1893–1943) Lithuanian-born painter, who emigrated to Paris in 1913. Using thickly applied paint, intense colour, and distorted and writhing forms, he was, together with Chagall, the leading representative of French expressionism.

soviet A government council in the Soviet Union. Soviets originated as committees of workers' deputies in the Revolution of 1905 and were again established in the Russian Revolution of 1917. The Supreme Soviet is in theory the supreme organ of government in the Soviet Union; soviets are also elected at the local, provincial, and republican levels. Candidates, one for each deputy, are selected by the Communist Party.

SOVIET UNION   *The May Day parade in Moscow (1989); a huge billboard with portraits of Marx, Engels, and Lenin overlooks a more festive scene than usual.*

Soviet Union (official name: Union of Soviet Socialist Republics) The world's largest country and its third most populous, covering N Eurasia. It is officially a federal state comprising 15 constituent republics: the Armenian, Azerbaidzhan, Belorussian, Estonian, Georgian, Kazakh, Kirghiz, Latvian, Lithuanian, Moldavian, Russian Soviet Federal, Tadzhik, Turkmen, Ukrainian, and Uzbek Soviet Socialist Republics. Administrative subdivisions include 20 Autonomous Soviet Socialist Republics and, within some of these, 8 autonomous regions (Russian *oblast*, region). The area W of the River Yenisei consists of vast plains and depressions, dissected by the Ural Mountains, while the E consists mainly of mountains and plateaus. The mountain belt along the S border includes the Carpathian, Caucasus, Pamir, and Sayan Mountains, the Stanovoi Range, and the Tien Shan. The population includes over a hundred national groups. The most numerous are the Russians, Ukrainians, Uzbeks, Belorussians, Tatars, and Kazakhs. *Economy*: based on the system of state ownership, it is controlled through Gosplan (the State Planning Commission) and Gosbank (the State Bank). It has been directed since 1928 by a series of five-year plans. Its main asset is the country's vast natural resources. The Soviet Union is the world's leading producer of oil, coal, iron ore, cement, and steel; manganese, gold, natural gas, and other minerals are also of major importance. Industry has concentrated on the production of capital goods. Agriculture is organized in a system of state and collective farms, is highly mechanized but not very productive. In 1988 measures were introduced to allow a new system of land leasing. Fishing, forestry, and dependent industries are also important. Largely self-sufficient, it trades little in comparison to its economic strength. *History*: little is known of the region's history until the 8th century AD, when European and Middle Eastern traders began its exploration. Control of the area between the Baltic and Black Seas was established by Scandinavian adventurers by 1000. Dominated by Kiev from the mid-10th to mid-11th centuries, these Varangian principalities submitted (after 1223) to the overrule of the Golden Horde. By the time of the Horde's collapse in the 14th century, Moscow, ruled by Rurik princes, had emerged as a powerful principality, becoming the capital of a united Russia under Ivan the Great in the 15th century. Contact with W Europe was established in the late 17th century by Peter the Great, who also established the Russian bureaucracy and educational system and built a new capital, St Petersburg (present-day Leningrad). By the 19th century Russia had been greatly extended but its bureaucracy had grown unwieldy and oppressive, and its Romanov emperors (tsars) were opposed to any political change. Revolutionary activity began with the Dekabrists' conspiracy, uncovered in 1825, and, although serfdom was abolished in 1861, its abolition was achieved on terms unfavourable to the peasants and served to encourage revolutionaries, a group of whom assassinated Alexander II in 1881. Following the Revolution of 1905, a parliament, the Duma, was established in 1906, but political unrest continued and was aggravated during World War I by military defeat and food shortages. The February and October Revolutions (*see* Russian Revolution) were followed by civil war (1918–22), after which communist control was complete. After Lenin's death (1924) Stalin had emerged as leader by 1928, having ousted Trotsky. Under Stalin, who replaced Lenin's New Economic Policy with five-year plans and collective farms, the Soviet Union (established 1922) became a major industrial power but a totalitarian state, with effective political opposition eliminated during the 1930s by purges. World War II established the Soviet Union as one of the two major superpowers. Relations with the other superpower, the USA, improved after the Cold War, although the Soviet invasion of Afghanistan (1979) provoked US condemnation. Since 1985, when Mikhail Gorbachov came to power, there has been considerable reform, despite internal opposition, with the introduction of *glasnost* and *perestroika* policies. Improved relations with the West facilitated agreement of the Intermediate Nuclear Forces (INF) treaty in 1987. In 1989 a new parliament, the Congress of People's Deputies (with 2250 elected members), was established as a move towards increased democracy, while in 1990 the Communist party voted to renounce its guaranteed right to power. Such liberalization has, however, stimulated unrest in constituent republics. The Soviet Union is a member of COMECON. President and Chairman of the Presidium of the Supreme Soviet: Mikhail Gorbachov. Official language: Russian. Official currency: rouble of 100 kopeks. Area: 22 402 200 sq km (8 647 675 sq mi). Population (1988): 284 500 000. Capital: Moscow.

Soweto 26 10S 28 02E A large urban area in South Africa, in the Transvaal forming a suburb of Johannesburg. It is inhabited by Black Africans and comprises 36 townships, divided into tribal areas. In June, 1976, it was the scene of serious rioting by African students during which over a hundred people died; there were further riots in 1985. Population (1983): 915 872.

soya bean (*or* soybean) An annual plant, *Glycine max*, widely cultivated for its seeds. The many commercial varieties produce clusters of pods, each containing two or three seeds. The ripe seeds contain 35% protein. Soya-bean oil is extracted for use in making margarines, cooking oils, resins, and paints and for many other foods, chemicals, and textiles. The meal residue is an important protein food for livestock and a meat substitute for man. The beans are also eaten whole, ground into flour, and as soy sauce. Family: *Leguminosae*.

Soyinka, Wole (1934–) Nigerian dramatist and poet. His works include the play *The Lion and the Jewel* (1963) and the novels *The Interpreters* (1965), *The Man Died* (1973), and *Aké* (1982). He was imprisoned during the Nigerian civil war (1967–69). He won the 1986 Nobel Prize.

Soyuz. *See* Salyut.

spacecraft A vehicle designed to be launched into space and to function effectively for a considerable period of time in the hostile conditions of space. Unmanned craft include several thousand satellites of diverse functions and numerous planetary probes. Space stations and space shuttles carry crews.

space shuttle One of a series of manned reusable US space transportation systems developed by NASA. First launched in April 1981 it was operational by 1982. It consists of a delta-wing Orbiter that has three powerful rocket engines, a large cargo bay, and living space. It is launched into low earth orbit by rocket propulsion. Satellites and other craft can be launched from the cargo bay. Scientific, technological, and medical experiments are also performed. Having completed its mission (7–30 days), the shuttle enters the earth's atmosphere in a shallow dive and makes an unpowered landing. Flights were suspended following the explosion of the Challenger shuttle (January, 1986) but resumed in 1988. The first reusable Soviet shuttle, Buran, was launched in 1988.

space station A large orbiting spacecraft on which people can live and work in weightless conditions. The first space station was the Soviet Salyut–1, launched in 1971; America's Skylab was orbited in 1973. Both the USSR and the USA are planning larger permanently manned stations. *See also* Mir.

space-time continuum A coordinate system that has four dimensions, three representing physical space and the fourth time. It is used in relativity.

spadefoot toad A nocturnal burrowing toad belonging to a widely distributed family (*Pelobatidae*). Spadefoot toads survive in arid regions by digging themselves deep holes in sand or mud with a special horny structure on the foot.

SPANISH CIVIL WAR *Republican troops behind a barricade of dead horses (1936).*

Spain, Kingdom of A country in SW Europe, occupying over four-fifths of the Iberian Peninsula. The Balearic and Canary Islands are also part of Spain. It consists mainly of a high plateau, rising over 3000 m (10 000 ft) in the Pyrenees in the NE. *Economy*: traditionally agricultural, the industrial sector had begun to predominate by the early 1970s. Tourism is a major source of foreign currency. Forestry, fishing, and wine are important and there are rich mineral resources. *History*: following settlements by Iberians, Celts, Phoenicians, and Greeks, the Carthaginians conquered most of the Iberian peninsula in the 3rd century BC but were expelled by the Romans in the second Punic War (218–201 BC). Christianity was introduced in the 1st century AD and by the 5th century the Romans had given way to German tribes, including the Vandals and then the Visigoths. The Visigothic kingdom collapsed (711) in the face of Muslim invaders, who dominated most of the central and S parts of the peninsula under a series of powerful dynasties. The Reconquest of Muslim Spain was pursued throughout the middle ages by the Christian kingdoms in the N and was completed in 1492 with the conquest of Granada by Ferdinand of Aragon and Isabella of Castile. The union of Spain, begun by the union of Aragon and Castile, was now complete. The year 1492 also saw the expulsion from Spain of the Jews, who were followed after much persecution (1609) by the Muslims; the influence of both peoples on Spanish culture was enormous. The 16th century was Spain's golden age. Overseas exploration led to the formation of an empire in the New World, which brought great wealth to Spain. The country's prestige and power, as well as its possessions, in Europe were furthered by the Habsburg kings Charles I (who as Charles V was also Holy Roman Emperor) and his son Philip II but the latter's reign witnessed the beginnings of decline. The Revolt of the Netherlands against Spanish rule led to the secession (1581) of the northern Dutch provinces and in 1588 Spain suffered the humiliating defeat of the Armada by the English. Following the Thirty Years' War Spain lost to France its position as the leading European power (1659). The death in 1700 of the last Habsburg king (Charles II), without an heir, led to the War of the Spanish Succession (1701–14). This confirmed the Bourbon succession and also deprived Spain of the Spanish Netherlands, Milan, Naples, Sardinia, and Sicily. In the second half of the 18th century Spain's decline was arrested by reform, especially under Charles III, but in 1808 Napoleon established his brother Joseph Bonaparte on the Spanish throne. The Spanish resistance to their French conquerors contributed to the defeat of Napoleon (*see* Peninsular War) and in 1814 the Bourbon Ferdinand III (1716–88) was restored. Carlism and conflict between monarchists and republicans (the latter achieved short-lived victory in 1873–74) dominated the 19th century, during which Spain also lost its last American possessions. It was neutral in World War I, following which Miguel Primo de Rivera (1870–1930) established a military dictatorship that undermined the position of the monarchy. In 1931 Alfonso XIII abdicated and the Second Republic was established. The electoral victory of the Popular Front under Azaña in 1936 precipitated a military revolt led by Gen Franco that became the Spanish Civil War (1936–39). Franco's victory initiated over three decades of Nationalist dictatorship. Following Franco's death in 1975, the monarchy was restored and Juan Carlos de Borbón became king and head of state. The return to a more democratic form of government has since proceeded rapidly. In 1978 provisional regional self-government was granted to Catalonia, Valencia, the Canary Islands, Aragon, Galicia, and the Basque provinces, but terrorist activities by Basque separatists have continued. Spain's first Socialist government in nearly 50 years was elected in 1982 under Felipe González (1942–   ). Spain joined NATO in 1982 and the EC in 1986. Official language: Spanish. Official religion: Roman Catholic. Official currency: peseta of 100 céntimos. Area: 504 879 sq km (194 883 sq mi). Population (1987): 38 832 000. Capital: Madrid. Main port: Barcelona.

spaniel One of several breeds of sporting dogs developed in Britain and thought to have originated in Spain. The English springer spaniel is typical, having a lean compact body, long muzzle, and long drooping ears. It is longer in the leg than the similar cocker spaniel but has the same flat wavy weather-resistant coat. It is generally black and white or liver and white, while the smaller Welsh springer spaniel is always red and white. Height: 51 cm (English springer). *See also* King Charles spaniel.

Spanish A Romance language spoken in Spain, Latin America, the Philippines, and elsewhere by about 308 million people. The standard form is based on the Castilian dialect.

Spanish Civil War (1936–39) The civil war in Spain precipitated by a military revolt on 18 July, 1936, led by the Nationalist Gen Franco, against the Republican Government of Manuel Azaña (1880–1940). By the end of 1936 the Nationalists had gained control of most of W and S Spain, while the Republicans held the urban areas of the E and N, including Madrid, Valencia, Barcelona, and Bilbao. During 1937 the Nationalists, with Italian and German help, failed in their attempt to take Madrid but captured Bilbao. In 1938, in spite of the assistance of the International Brigade and the Soviet Union, the Republican front was broken and early in 1939 Barcelona, Valencia, and then Madrid fell. The Republican cause rallied liberals throughout Europe against fascism.

Spanish moss 1. An epiphytic plant, *Tillandsia usneoides* (or *Dendropogon usneoides*), found in warm regions of America. Its seeds are windblown to trees, where they germinate and grow downwards in large silvery-grey beardlike masses, 6–7.5 m long. It is covered in hairlike scales, which absorb water from the air. Family: *Bromeliaceae*. **2.** A tropical lichen, *Usnea longissima*, which resembles *T. usneoides*.

Spanish Riding School A centre for classical horsemanship in Vienna, originally sited in the Habsburg imperial palace and probably founded in the late 16th century. The purest *haute école* dressage of the 16th and 17th centuries is practised. The white Lipizzaner stallions used here have been bred from horses imported from Spain in the 16th century—hence the title "Spanish."

Spanish Sahara. *See* Western Sahara.

Spanish Succession, War of the (1701–14) The third of the European wars caused by Louis XIV's attempts to increase French power. The immediate cause of conflict was the dispute over the succession to the Spanish throne. Following the death of the childless Charles II, Louis proclaimed the succession of his grandson as Philip V. England felt menaced, and with the Dutch Republic and the Holy Roman Emperor formed an alliance against France in 1701; they were joined by most German states upon the outbreak of general hostilities (1702). Spain, Bavaria, Portugal, and Savoy supported France. The English won a series of brilliant victories under the Duke of Marlborough but pressed for peace in 1712, when a Spanish-Austrian union threatened. The Treaties of Utrecht (1713–14) concluded the war, which marked the end of French expansionism under Louis.

Spark, Muriel (1918–) Scottish novelist, who achieved success with a series of witty satirical novels including *Memento Mori* (1959) and *The Prime of Miss Jean Brodie* (1961). Her later novels include *The Abbess of Crewe* (1974), *The Takeover* (1976), *Territorial Rights* (1979), *Loitering With Intent* (1981), *The Only Problem* (1984), and *A Far Cry from Kensington* (1988).

sparrow A small thick-billed member of the weaverbird family. Sparrows are generally brown and grey in colour, often with black or bright yellow patches. They are mostly tropical Old World species but also occur in Eurasia; the Eurasian house sparrow (*Passer domesticus*) has been introduced to North America, where it is now a pest. Sparrows eat seeds, etc., feeding on the ground. Subfamily: *Passerinae*.

sparrowhawk A small woodland hawk, *Accipiter nisus*, occurring in Eurasia and NW Africa. It has a long tail and short rounded wings and the male (27 cm long) is grey with brown-barred white underparts; females (38 cm long) are brown above. It hunts small birds.

Sparta 37 05N 22 25E In ancient Greece, the capital of Laconia on the River Eurotas in the S Peloponnese. Developing during the 10th century BC, Sparta controlled much of Laconia and Messenia by 700 BC. It became an austere militaristic state, where weaker boys were abandoned at birth and those that survived were subjected from the age of seven to a rigid military training. Its military strength brought conflict in the 5th century with Athens, and ultimate victory (404) in the consequent Peloponnesian War: defeat by the Thebans at Leuctra (371) marked the beginning of Spartan decline. The ancient city was destroyed by the Visigoths in 396 AD.

Spartacus Thracian gladiator, who led a slave revolt against Rome in 73 BC. After defeating the Romans in five separate engagements in Italy, he moved N to Cisalpine Gaul. When his followers refused to disperse, Spartacus marched S again and was defeated by Marcus Licinius Crassus (71). He and his followers were crucified.

Spartina A genus of grasses (16 species), known as cordgrass, found on salt marshes and tidal flats of North America, Europe, and Africa. They have stiff erect stems and yellowish flower spikes. Townsend's cord grass (*S. townsendii*) has been used extensively to help reclaim coastal land.

spastic. *See* cerebral palsy.

Speaker of the House of Commons The presiding officer of the lower chamber of the British parliament. Elected by each new parliament, a Speaker or his deputy regulate with impartiality all the debates and proceedings of the House, except for proceedings in committee.

spearmint An aromatic perennial herb, *Mentha spicata*, native to central and S Europe and widely cultivated as a culinary herb. The oil extract from the leaves is used to flavour sweets, etc. Family: *Labiatae*.

Special Air Service (SAS) A specialist division of the British army, formed in 1942. The unit is highly trained in operations behind enemy lines and is the most secretive of the British forces. Its motto is "Who dares wins."

Special Drawing Rights (SDRs) The rights of member countries of the International Monetary Fund to draw on the fund to finance balance-of-payments deficits. SDRs (unlike normal drawings) do not have to be repaid and therefore form a permanent addition to the drawing country's reserves.

species A unit of classification of animals and plants. Individuals of the same species usually resemble one another closely and can breed among themselves to produce fertile offspring that resemble the parents. Some species are subdivided into subspecies and varieties. Breeds of domestic animals and cultivated varieties of plants have been specially developed by man for economic or other purposes and are all derived from a few wild species. Those originating from the same species can interbreed, despite obvious differences in character. All breeds of domestic dog, for instance, belong to the same species—*Canis familiaris*—and can breed together.

specific gravity. *See* density.

specific heat capacity (*c*) The quantity of heat needed to raise a unit mass of substance by 1 K. It is measured in joules per kelvin per kilogram. For gases, the specific heat capacity at constant pressure (c_p) exceeds that at constant volume (c_v) as heat is required to do work against the surroundings during the expansion.

spectacled bear The only South American bear, *Tremarctos ornatus*, also called Andean bear. It is brownish-black with white circles around the eyes and climbs trees to feed on leaves, nuts, and fruit.

spectacles Lenses worn in frames in front of the eyes to correct defective vision. Convex lenses bend parallel light rays inward; they are used by those unable to focus on close objects (*see* longsightedness). Concave lenses have the opposite effect and are used by those unable to focus on distant objects (*see* shortsightedness). Astigmatism is treated by wearing lenses that produce a compensating distortion of the light rays. Bifocal spectacles have convex lenses consisting of upper and lower parts of different curvatures, for focusing on distant and near objects, respectively: they are worn for presbyopia. *See also* contact lenses.

spectral type. *See* Harvard classification system.

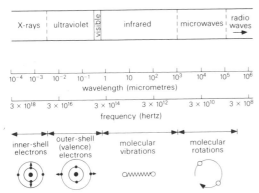

SPECTRUM *Photons in the X-ray region of the spectrum alter the excitation of atomic inner-shell electrons. The ultraviolet and visible photons interact with the outer-shell electrons that participate in chemical reactions. Infrared photons alter the vibrational states of molecules and microwave photons affect molecular rotation.*

spectrum In general, the way in which a particular property of a system is distributed over its components. The visible spectrum, for example, is observed in a rainbow, which shows the distribution of frequencies when sunlight is split up into its components by raindrops. The visible spectrum, however, is only a small part of the electromagnetic spectrum, which ranges from gamma rays to radio waves. **Spectroscopy** is concerned with analysing the emission and absorption of electromagnetic energy by atoms and molecules. Atoms emit and absorb radiation at characteristic frequencies, which show up as lines in their spectrum and can be used to identify particular elements.

speed of light. *See* light.

speed of sound. *See* sound.

speedwell An annual or perennial herbaceous plant of the genus *Veronica* (about 200 species), occurring throughout temperate regions. The flowers are usually blue. The fruit is a flattened heart-shaped capsule. Family: *Scrophulariaceae*.

Speedwriting. *See* shorthand.

Speke, John Hanning (1827–64) British explorer. He accompanied Richard Burton (1821–90) on the expeditions (1855, 1857–58) to discover the source of the Nile. They discovered Lake Tanganyika and then Speke went on alone to discover Lake Victoria, which on a second visit in 1860, accompanied by J. A. Grant (1827–92), he established to be the source of the Nile. Burton disputed Speke's claim.

speleology (*or* spelaeology) The study and exploration of caves and underground water courses. This includes the survey of caves and the study of their formation, plant and animal life (past and present), and geology. Potholing—or descending through potholes into underground drainage passages in order to follow the course of underground streams—is a popular activity.

Spence, Sir Basil (1907–76) British architect, who became internationally known with his design for rebuilding Coventry Cathedral (consecrated 1962). Later buildings included Sussex University and the British Embassy in Rome (completed 1971).

Spencer, Herbert (1820–1903) British philosopher, an influential exponent of laissez-faire. He believed that state intervention limited progress and he developed this idea fully in his popular *The Man versus the State* (1884). Spencer's other writings include works on psychology, ethics, and sociology. He supported Darwin's theory of evolution and applied evolutionary ideas to social development.

Spencer, Sir Stanley (1891–1959) British painter. He is known for his religious subjects, often depicted in the everyday setting of his native village of Cookham, Berkshire.

Spender, Sir Stephen (1909–) British poet and critic. A friend of W. H. Auden, he published left-wing poetry during the 1930s. His later poetry, included in *Collected Poems* (1955) and *The Generous Days* (1971), is more personal. He has also published several volumes of criticism and the novel *The Temple* (1988).

Spenser, Edmund (c. 1552–99) English poet. His major work, *The Faerie Queene*, a long moral allegory in nine-line "Spenserian" stanzas, was dedicated to Elizabeth I and published in six books in 1590 and 1596. His other works include *The Shepheardes Calendar* (1579), the sonnet sequence *Amoretti* (1595) and the *Epithalamion* (1595), celebrating his second marriage.

sperm (*or* spermatozoon) The reproductive cell of male animals, which is formed in the testis and fertilizes an egg cell during sexual reproduction. A sperm usually has a head region, containing the genetic material, and a tail, by means of which it swims to the egg. In man, sperms develop and mature in the testes. At ejaculation they are mixed with secretions from various glands (including the prostate gland) to form semen.

sperm whale A large toothed whale, *Physeter cathodon*, also called cachalot. It is 18 m long, grey-blue above and pale beneath, with tiny flippers and large tail flukes. Family: *Physeteridae*.

Spey, River A fast-flowing river in NE Scotland, flowing mainly NE through the Grampian Mountains to Spey Bay. It is known for its salmon fishing. Length: 172 km (107 mi).

Sphagnum A widely distributed genus of mosses (over 300 species), called bog or peat moss, forming dense raised clumps in bogs and other waterlogged places. Green to dark red in colour, the fine stems bear clusters of threadlike branches, densely clothed with tiny leaves, and globular spore capsules. The ability of the stems and leaves to retain water means that these mosses can drain very wet ground and form bogs. The dead remains form peat. Family: *Sphagnaceae*.

spherical polar coordinates. *See* coordinate systems.

sphinx A mythological creature with a lion's body and a human head, occurring in the art and legends of most ancient Near and Middle Eastern civilizations. The most famous representation is the Great Sphinx at Giza, Egypt, dating from the 3rd millennium BC. In Greek legend, the Sphinx was a female monster that preyed on travellers going to Thebes. She killed those who could not answer her riddle, which was finally solved by Oedipus.

STEVEN SPIELBERG   ET, *the creature from outer space.*

sphygmomanometer   A device for measuring arterial blood pressure. It consists of an inflatable arm cuff connected via a rubber tube to a column of mercury with a graduated scale or an aneroid device. The cuff is inflated until the pulse cannot be detected (using a stethoscope) and then slowly deflated until the systolic and then the diastolic pressure can be recorded as the pulse returns.

Spice Islands.   *See* Moluccas.

spices.   *See* herbs and spices.

spider   An arachnid belonging to the worldwide order *Araneae* (or *Araneida*; over 30 000 species). The body of a spider consists of a cephalothorax and an abdomen separated by a narrow "waist." There are eight walking legs, up to eight eyes, and several pairs of spinnerets, which produce silk used for making webs, egg cocoons, etc. Spiders are predominantly terrestrial and prey mainly on insects, hunting them or trapping them in their webs. The victims are killed with poison-bearing fangs; in a few species the poison is harmful to man. The female is generally larger than the male, which she sometimes kills and eats after mating. *See also* black widow; tarantula; water spider; wolf spider.

spider crab   A marine crab belonging to the widely distributed family *Maiidae*, especially one of the genus *Libinia*. It has a thick rounded body with long spindly legs and generally moves slowly. Most spider crabs are scavengers, especially of dead animals.

spider mite   A red or yellow mite, also called red spider mite, belonging to the family *Tetranychidae*. It sucks plant juices from foliage and fruits and is a serious pest of orchard trees, crops, and house plants.

spider monkey   A monkey belonging to the genus *Ateles* (4 species), of Central and South American forests. Spider monkeys have very long legs and a long prehensile tail, which is capable of supporting their weight. They live in family groups in thick forest, feeding on seeds and leaves. Family: *Cebidae*.

spider plant   A plant of the genus *Chlorophytum*, especially *C. elatum*, native to South Africa and widely grown as a house plant. It has long narrow green and white striped leaves and periodically produces a stem bearing small white flowers or young plantlets. Family: *Liliaceae*.

spiderwort.   *See* Tradescantia.

Spielberg, Steven   (1946–) US film director, whose commercially successful films include *Jaws* (1975), *Close Encounters of the Third Kind* (1977), *ET* (1982), *Gremlins* (1984), *The Color Purple* (1986), and *Empire of the Sun* (1988).

spin   A property possessed by elementary particles as a result of which they possess a constant angular momentum that is independent of their motion. The spin is quantized and labelled by a spin quantum number (symbol: s), which may be integral or half-integral.

spina bifida   A defect, present at birth, in which the backbone fails to fuse properly, leaving the spinal cord and its coverings exposed. Commonly the child has paralysed legs and disordered bladder and bowel function. Intelligence is often normal, but the condition is frequently associated with hydrocephalus. It can be diagnosed during pregnancy (*see* amniocentesis).

spinach   An annual herbaceous plant, *Spinacia oleracea*, native to Asia and widely cultivated as a vegetable. Its edible leaves are rich in iron and vitamins A and C. Family: *Chenopodiaceae*.

spinal cord   An elongated part of the central nervous system, running downwards from the base of the brain and consisting of a core of grey matter (nerve cell bodies) surrounded by white matter (nerve fibres). It is surrounded and protected by the spine and is enclosed in membranes (meninges). It gives off spinal nerves, usually in pairs, and ends in a bundle of nerves supplying the legs and lower part of the body. Through it run the nerve fibres between the brain and the body; injury can therefore cause paralysis and loss of sensation.

spine   In anatomy, the backbone, or vertebral column: a series of small bones (vertebrae) that runs up the centre of the back. The spine encloses and protects the spinal cord, articulates with the skull, ribs, and pelvis, and provides attachment for muscles of the back. There are 26 vertebrae in the adult spine. The vertebrae are connected by tough discs of cartilage (intervertebral discs), which absorb the shock produced by running and other movements.

spinet   A plucked keyboard instrument of the harpsichord family that superseded the virginals in the 17th century. It is wing shaped, the strings (one to each note) being at an angle of 45° to the keyboard.

spinning   The process of converting cleaned and straightened fibres into yarn by twisting overlapping fibres together. Yarn was made originally by drawing out a length of fibre from the mass and attaching it to a vertically hanging stick (spindle) that was weighted to help it spin round. This process was mechanized first by the spinning wheel (in Europe not until the 14th century). The inventions of Hargreaves, Arkwright, and Crompton in the late 18th century industrialized the process. Modern spinning machines produce thousands of metres of yarn every hour. As applied to synthetic fibres, spinning is the extrusion of viscous solutions to form continuous filaments.

Spinoza, Benedict   (*or* Baruch de S.; 1632–77) Dutch philosopher and theologian of Jewish parentage. Influenced by the writings of Descartes, Hobbes, and Giordano Bruno (1548–1600), Spinoza rejected the concepts of the personal nature of God and the immortality of the soul. The Jewish community of his native Amsterdam expelled him in 1656 on account of his unorthodoxy and his *Tractatus Theologico-Politicus*

(1670) was furiously attacked by Christian scholars. The idea of God as the basis of all things was, however, central to his philosophy. His major work, generally known as the *Ethics*, could only be published posthumously in 1677.

Spiraea A genus of shrubs (about 100 species), widely distributed in N temperate regions. Many are cultivated as ornamentals, including the willow spiraea (*S. salcifolia*), which bears dense clusters of small pink flowers. Family: *Rosaceae*.

spirochaete A bacterium belonging to the order *Spirochaetales*. Spirochaetes are corkscrew-shaped and flexible: they swim by means of bending and looping motions, achieved by contraction of a bundle of fibrils within the cell. Some spirochaetes cause diseases, including syphilis and yaws in man.

Spirogyra A genus of green algae, also called mermaid's tresses or pond scum, in the form of threadlike strands of connected cells up to about 30 cm long. Large masses may be found floating near the surface of quiet fresh waters. Reproduction is asexual (by fragmentation) or sexual (*see* conjugation).

Spitsbergen. *See* Svalbard.

spittlebug. *See* froghopper.

spitz One of a group of dog breeds originating in N Eurasia and having a thick coat, small pricked ears, and a brushlike tail carried over the back. The Finnish spitz, bred in Finland as a hunting and guard dog, has a reddish-brown or yellowish-red coat.

spleen A rubbery dark-red organ, about 14 cm long, situated in the abdomen just beneath the lower border of the left side of the rib cage. The spleen assists in the body's defence mechanisms by producing antibodies in newborn babies and by absorbing and digesting bacteria in the bloodstream. It also removes worn-out and abnormal red blood cells and other particles from the circulation. The spleen becomes enlarged in some diseases, including liver disease and severe infections.

Split (Italian name: Spalato) 43 31N 16 28N A port in W Yugoslavia, in Croatia on the Adriatic Sea. The vast 3rd-century AD Palace of Diocletian contains the present-day city centre, including the cathedral, which was Diocletian's mausoleum. It has a university (1974) and diverse industries. Population (1981): 235 922.

Spode porcelain Fine tableware and other porcelain made in the Staffordshire (England) factory started by Josiah Spode I in 1770. The meticulous decoration used transfer printing and painted Japan patterns enhanced by careful gilding.

Spoleto 42 44N 12 44E A town in Italy, in Umbria. Dating from Etruscan times, it has Roman remains and a 12th-century cathedral. Its annual festival of music and drama was founded in 1958 by Gian Carlo Menotti. Population (1985): 37 000.

sponge An aquatic invertebrate animal belonging to the phylum *Porifera* (about 5000 species). Most sponges are marine, found attached to rocks or the sea bed, and measure up to several metres across: they may be treelike, cylindrical, or flat irregular masses. Sponges have an internal skeleton of lime, silica, or a fibrous protein (spongin). Bath sponges are spongin skeletons without the living animals. The simplest type of sponge has a vase-shaped body with a pore at the top and smaller pores in the sides. The inside is lined with special cells, which maintain a flow of water in through the side pores and out at the top. Food particles in the water are ex-

tracted by these cells; other cells in the body wall digest food, secrete the skeleton, and produce eggs and sperm. Fertilized eggs are dispersed in the water current and the free-swimming larvae eventually settle and become new sponges. The animals can also reproduce asexually, by budding or fragmentation.

spoonbill A long-legged wading bird belonging to a subfamily (*Plataleinae*; 6 species) occurring around estuaries, and lakes in tropical and subtropical regions worldwide. 60–80 cm long, spoonbills are usually entirely white, often with a naked head. They feed on fish and crustaceans picked up by sweeping the large spatulate bill from side to side in mud or shallow water. Family: *Threskiornithidae* (ibises and spoonbills); order: *Ciconiiformes* (herons, storks, etc.).

Spooner, William Archibald (1844–1930) British clergyman and academic. A somewhat eccentric Oxford don, Spooner became famous for his frequent transposition of the first letters of words, for example "a well-oiled bicycle" became "a well-boiled icicle." Such a transposition became known as a **Spoonerism**.

SPODE *A pair of Spode urn-shaped pot-pourri vases, c. 1820 (135 mm high).*

spore The small, often single-celled, reproductive unit of plants, protozoa, and bacteria, which may serve either as a rapid means of propagation or as a dormant stage in the life cycle. Spores may be produced sexually or asexually, i.e. fusion of sex cells (gametes) may or may not occur before their formation. In plants exhibiting an alternation of generations spores are formed by the sporophyte following meiosis and give rise to the gametophyte, which produces the sex cells.

sporophyte. *See* alternation of generations.

Sporozoa A phylum of microscopic single-celled animals (*see* Protozoa), all of which are parasites with complex life cycles involving asexual and sexual forms of reproduction. They are often found in the intestinal tracts or blood of animals and form resistant spores or cysts, which can remain dormant until entering a suitable host.

sprat A small food fish, *Clupea (Sprattus) sprattus*, that is similar and related to the herring. It lives in shoals in the E Atlantic, N Mediterranean, and British coastal waters. The young are known as whitebait.

springbok A rare antelope, *Antidorcas marsupialis*, inhabiting arid regions of S Africa. It has a white face with a black line along each side of the muzzle and a patch of white hairs on the rump, which can be flashed as an alarm signal.

Springsteen, Bruce (1949–) US rock singer and guitarist. Born in New Jersey, he built up a huge following with songs describing modern industrial US society and with his energetic live performances; his albums include *Born to Run* (1975), *The River* (1980), and *Nebraska* (1982).

springtail An eyeless wingless insect of the worldwide order *Collembola* (about 3500 species). It has a forked appendage on the abdomen, which is used for jumping.

spruce A coniferous tree of the genus *Picea* (about 50 species), widely distributed in the N hemisphere. Its needles grow in spirals and leave peglike projections on the shoots when they fall. The woody cones hang down from the branches. An important and widely grown timber tree is the Norway spruce (*Picea abies*), from N and central Europe; the timber is known as white wood or deal. Young specimens are used as Christmas trees in Britain. Family: *Pinaceae*.

spurge. *See* Euphorbia.

Sputnik A series of Soviet unmanned satellites, the first of which was the first spacecraft to be launched (4 October, 1957).

Square Deal A programme of economic and social reform intended by Theodore Roosevelt (president 1901–09) to benefit the "plain man" in the USA. It sponsored improved labour conditions, regulations regarding food, and antimonopoly legislation.

square root. *See* root.

squash The fruit of certain plants belonging to the genus *Cucurbita* (15 species), especially *C. maxima*. Native to the New World, squash plants are widely cultivated, producing fleshy edible fruits. They are usually served as a cooked vegetable. Family: *Cucurbitaceae*. *Compare* gourd; pumpkin.

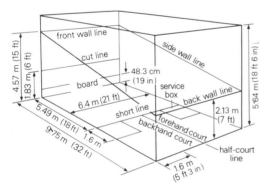

SQUASH RACKETS *The dimensions of the court.*

squash rackets A racket-and-ball game played in a four-walled court. Players hit the ball with the object of making a shot that the opponent cannot return. (When the ball is played it must hit the front wall of the court and may hit any other wall.) The service goes to the winner of the previous point. The British competitive version is a singles game going to nine or sometimes more points and only the server may score.

squid A cephalopod mollusc of the order *Decapoda*. Surrounding the mouth, squids have ten arms bearing suckers; two arms are long tentacles used for capturing prey. Their tapering bodies have fins on either side. Squids feed on fish and molluscs, using a siphon to produce a jet of water to dart forwards. The giant squid (genus *Architeuthis*) can reach 20 m in length.

squint (*or* strabismus) A condition in which both the eyes cannot focus on the same object at the same time. This may be caused by paralysis of one of the nerves moving the eye, in which case the squint is often temporary. Nonparalytic squints are often seen in children and may be corrected.

squirrel A rodent belonging to the family *Sciuridae*, which includes ground squirrels, flying squirrels, and tree squirrels, distributed worldwide. The grey squirrel (*Sciurus carolinensis*), native to North America but now found in most parts of the world, is an agile climber with a long bushy balancing tail. Grey squirrels feed chiefly on nuts, berries, and buds and have become a pest of orchards and gardens. *See also* red squirrel.

Sri Lanka, Democratic Socialist Republic of (name until 1972: Ceylon) An island country in the Indian Ocean, to the E of the S tip of the Indian subcontinent. Broad coastal plains rise to a mountainous area in the S central part of the island. The population consists of two main groups: the Sinhalese, who are mainly Buddhists, and the Tamils, who are chiefly Hindus. *Economy*: predominantly agricultural, the chief activities are the processing and export of tea, rubber, and coconuts. The industrial sector has recently expanded. *History*: in 1505 the Portuguese established settlements in the W and S, which passed to the Dutch in the mid-17th century and to the British in 1796. In 1802 the whole of the island was made a separate crown colony. Following World War II Ceylon became a dominion (1948) within the British Commonwealth and in 1972 Sri Lanka became a republic. Conflict between the Sinhalese and Tamil communities has been a continuing problem and in 1987 an Indian peacekeeping force arrived. Delays in an Indian withdrawal led to the threat of war between the two countries. President: Ranasinghe Premadasa (1924–). Official language: Sinhala. Official currency: Sri Lanka rupee of 100 cents. Area: 65 610 sq km (25 332 sq mi). Population (1987): 16 353 000. Capital: Colombo.

SS (German: *Schutzstaffel*, Defence Squad) The elite Nazi military corps, created in 1925 as Hitler's bodyguard and commanded by Heinrich Himmler from 1929. The SS, or Blackshirts, by the mid-1930s controlled the Nazis' security system, including the Gestapo, concentration camp guards, and the Waffen SS, an elite corps of combat troops in World War II. The activities of the SS were condemned at the Nuremburg trials (1946).

St. Names beginning St are listed under Saint.

Staffordshire A county in the Midlands of England. It consists mainly of gently undulating lowlands rising to moorlands in the N, with the River Trent flowing SE. Agriculture is important, especially dairy farming. Industries are based on the coalfields in the N and include the pottery industry, which became famous during the 18th century, especially through the work of Josiah Wedgwood. Area: 2716 sq km (1049 sq mi). Population (1988 est): 1 032 900. Administrative centre: Stafford.

Staffordshire bull terrier A breed of dog developed from a bulldog-terrier cross as a pit dog. It is stockily built with a broad deep head and a short smooth coat that may be of various colours. Height: 35–40 cm (English).

stag beetle A beetle belonging to a family (*Lucanidae*; about 900 species) occurring mostly in the tropical regions. The males have well-developed mandibles that in many species resemble antlers. They are used during combat with other males. Most stag beetles are black or brown, although tropical species are often more colourful.

staghorn fern A fern of the genus *Platycerium*, which grows upon other plants but is not a parasite. The fronds fork repeatedly into long pointed leaflets, resembling antlers, and the spore capsules are borne on their undersides. The fern, which is native to most warm regions, is cultivated as a pot plant. Family: *Polypodiaceae*.

stainless steel An alloy steel containing up to 20% chromium and 10% nickel. It is corrosion resistant because the oxide that forms on the surface remains intact and protects the metal, unlike other steels in which it flakes off. Stainless steel is used in a wide variety of engineering applications where this property is important, as well as in kitchen utensils.

stalactites and stalagmites Deposits of calcium carbonate in limestone caves; stalactites are conical or cylindrical projections from the cave roof, while stalagmites grow upwards from the floor and are generally more stumpy. They sometimes meet to form a continuous column. They are gradually formed from water containing calcium bicarbonate dripping from the roof. When the water evaporates a solid residue of calcium carbonate is left.

STANLEY   *The meeting with Dr Livingstone.*

Stalin, Joseph (J. Dzhugashvili; 1879–1953) Soviet statesman. Born in Georgia, Stalin (whose adopted name means "man of steel") became a Marxist in the 1890s. In 1903 he joined the Bolsheviks under Lenin and in the years preceding the Russian Revolution (1917) was repeatedly imprisoned and exiled. In 1922 he became general secretary of the Communist Party. After Lenin's death in 1924 Stalin struggled to eliminate his rivals, above all Trotsky, and emerged as supreme dictator in 1929. He abandoned Lenin's New Economic Policy, initiating a series of five-year plans to enforce, with great brutality, the collectivization of industry and agriculture. The 1930s saw the reign of terror, culminating in the great purge, in which Stalin sought to enhance his power by the removal of his real, or imagined, rivals. In

World War II, Stalin became chairman of the Council of People's Commissars and, following Hitler's invasion of the Soviet Union (1941), reversed the German alliance of 1939. He attended Allied conferences at Tehran (1943) and at Yalta and Potsdam (1945). In the postwar years, when Stalin's autocracy intensified, he pursued a foreign policy of imperialism towards the communist countries of E Europe together with unremitting hostility towards the noncommunist world. In recent years many of Stalin's polices have been discredited by the soviet regime.

Stalingrad.   *See* Volgograd.

Stalingrad, Battle of (1942–43) A battle in World War II, in which the German 6th Army under Friedrich Paulus (1890–1957), having entered Stalingrad (now Volgograd), surrendered to the Russians under Zhukov. The Germans lost 200 000 men.

Stalinsk.   *See* Novokuznetsk.

Stamboul.   *See* Istanbul.

stamen The part of a flower that produces the pollen (male gametes). It comprises an anther, a lobed structure consisting of four pollen sacs, borne on a stalk (filament). The pollen develops within the sacs, which split open to release it. In self-pollinated flowers, the stamens open inwards, towards the pistil, but in cross-pollinated flowers they open outwards. *See also* flower.

Stamford Bridge 53 59N 0 55W A village in N England, in Humberside on the River Derwent. Here King Harold defeated his brother Tostig and King Harald of Norway in 1066, three weeks before his own defeat at Hastings by William the Conqueror.

Stamp Act (1765) The first British Act that imposed direct taxes on documents, newspapers, and dice in the American colonies. Parliament was forced by colonial hostility to repeal the Act but asserted its right to impose laws on the colonies (Declaratory Act, 1766), thus aggravating the opposition that led to the American Revolution.

standard deviation.   *See* variance.

Stanislavsky, Konstantin (K. Alekseyev; 1863–1938) Russian actor and theatre director. As director of the Moscow Art Theatre, which he cofounded in 1898, he developed an innovatory style of naturalistic production. His theories about acting, later developed in the USA as "method" acting at the Actors' Studio, emphasized the value of ensemble playing and of the actor's complete identification with the character he played.

Stanley 51 45S 57 56W The capital of the Falkland Islands, in NE East Falkland Island on the Atlantic Ocean. It was the focal point of the Falklands War of 1982. Population (1986 est): 1200.

Stanley, Sir Henry Morton (1841–1904) British explorer and journalist. He went to the USA in 1859, joined the *New York Herald*, and in 1871 was sent to search for David Livingstone in Africa. Having found him at Ujiji, the two men explored Lake Tanganyika together. On a second expedition (1874–77) Stanley followed the Congo River (now Zaïre River) to its mouth. By obtaining Belgian sponsorship for exploration in the Congo he was instrumental in securing Belgian sovereignty over the Congo Free State.

Stanley Falls.   *See* Boyoma Falls.

Stanleyville.   *See* Kisangani.

Stannaries The tinmining district of Cornwall and Devon. Until 1897 the Stannaries held its own courts, which had jurisdiction over tinminers except in such cases as murder or land disputes.

Staphylococcus A genus of spherical bacteria. *S. aureus* is responsible for boils and mastitis, *S. pyogenes* infects wounds, and certain strains cause acute food poisoning.

star A luminous celestial body that is composed of gas and that derives its energy from thermonuclear reactions in its hot dense core. The sun is a typical star: stellar mass usually ranges from about 0.05 to 60 times the sun's mass. The higher the mass, the brighter, hotter, and larger the star and the shorter its life. Young stars evolve from the protostar stage when they begin to generate energy by the thermonuclear fusion of hydrogen to form helium. This continues for some 10^{10} years for stars of solar mass but for only a few million years for the most massive stars. When the hydrogen is exhausted, stars evolve into giant stars, those of near solar mass becoming red giants, and further thermonuclear reactions occur. A low-mass star finally evolves to a white dwarf. More massive stars explode as supernovae. Stars are not distributed uniformly throughout the universe, but are grouped into enormous assemblies, called galaxies, as a result of gravitational forces. The nearest star to the sun is 4.3 light years away.

starch A carbohydrate that is an important storage product of many plants. Chemically it consists of linked glucose units. Starch occurs naturally as white powdery granules that are insoluble in cold water but form a gelatinous solution in hot water. Plants manufacture starch by photosynthesis and it is a major constituent of seeds, fruits, roots, and tubers and a major source of dietary energy for animals and man.

Star Chamber, Court of A court, originating in the king's council of medieval England, that met in the Star Chamber at Westminster Palace. It was concerned chiefly with breaches of the peace. Its misuse by Charles I to enforce his unpopular policies led to its abolition (1641) by the Long Parliament on the eve of the Civil War.

starfish A marine invertebrate animal belonging to a worldwide class (*Asteroidea*; 1800 species) of echinoderms. Its fleshy star-shaped body is covered with a spiny skin and has five or more radiating arms. Starfish occur on shores and ocean floors and move slowly, using saclike tube feet on the underside of the arms. They feed mainly on molluscs, crustaceans, and other invertebrates.

starling A noisy sharp-winged songbird, *Sturnus vulgaris*, having a black plumage speckled with iridescent purple, green, and white. It is a versatile bird, common on farmland, where it probes the soil for insects, and also in cities, where it is a scavenger. It is gregarious and commonly nests in flocks. Family: *Sturnidae*.

star-of-Bethlehem A spring-blooming perennial plant, *Ornithogalum umbellatum*, native to the Mediterranean and grown in gardens. Growing from a bulb, it has clusters of star-shaped white flowers striped with green. Family: *Liliaceae*.

star of David (Hebrew *magen David*; shield of David) A six-pointed star or hexagram, composed of two equilateral triangles. Widely used from antiquity as an ornament or magical sign, it has been regarded since the 17th century as a Jewish symbol, and was imposed on the Jews as a "badge of shame" by the Nazis. In 1897 it was officially adopted as an emblem of Zionism and it now appears on the flag of Israel.

States General In France, the assembly of representatives of the three estates–clergy, nobility, and the Third Estate or commons. It did not meet after 1614 until summoned by Louis XVI in 1789 on the eve of the French Revolution. The Third Estate declared itself a National Assembly, which replaced the States General.

static electricity The effects created by electrical charges at rest. Current electricity is an effect resulting from a flow of electrons; in static electricity electrons from one object are pulled onto another object, usually by rubbing them together, but they do not flow. The effect can be observed with many nonconducting materials, for example a comb passing through dry hair. A force exists between two charged bodies (*see* electric field), attractive if they have opposite charges, repulsive if the charges are similar; the magnitude of the force is given by Coulomb's law.

statics. *See* mechanics.

Stationery Office, Her Majesty's (HMSO) The UK government office that supplies all the stationery, office supplies, office machinery, and printing and binding needed for use in the civil service. HMSO also publishes and sells government publications.

Stations of the Cross A series of 14 pictures or images depicting the final events in the life of Christ, beginning at Pontius Pilate's house, where he was condemned to death, and concluding at the sepulchre. They are usually arranged on the walls of a church and form the basis of a devotion in which prayers are recited as each station is visited in turn. The devotion was popularized in the middle ages by the Franciscans but derived from the early custom of pilgrims who followed the Way of the Cross (Via Dolorosa) in Jerusalem.

statistics The study of methods for collecting and analysing quantitative data. The data measure certain characteristics of a group of people or objects, called the population; usually the whole population cannot be observed, often because it is too large, so data are collected from a representative sample of the population. The sample is analysed and conclusions are inferred about the whole population, using probability theory because the inferences cannot be certain.

Statue of Liberty A statue of a woman 46 m (152 ft) high holding a torch in her raised right hand, on Liberty Island in New York harbour. It was given to the Americans by the French in 1884 to commemorate the French and American Revolutions. Unveiled and dedicated in 1886, it has been a US national monument since 1924.

Stauffenberg, Claus, Graf von (1907–44) German army officer, who attempted to assassinate Hitler in 1944. Stauffenberg served in N Africa, where he was badly wounded. He tried to eliminate Hitler by bombing his headquarters at Rastenburg. He and his fellow conspirators were executed.

steady-state theory A cosmological theory proposed in 1948 by Hermann Bondi (1919–), Hoyle, and T. Gold (1920–) in which the universe is regarded as having always existed in a steady state. The expansion of the universe is compensated by the continuous creation of new matter. On the present evidence this theory has largely been discredited in favour of the big-bang theory.

steam engine A heat engine in which heat from a furnace is used to raise steam, the expansion of which forces a piston to move up and down in a cylinder to provide mechanical energy. A primitive steam engine was in-

beam
piston rod
cylinder
A
superheater
flywheel
C
B
cold
condenser
feedwater
hot flue gases
boiler
steam
water
condenser
furnace

STEAM ENGINE *The principle of a double-action beam engine of the kind patented by James Watt. During the first half of the cycle, valve A opens, steam flows in and pushes the cylinder down, and steam flows out to the condenser through valve C. During the second half of the cycle, B opens and the steam pushes the piston the other way.*

vented in 1698 by a Capt Savery to pump water from mines. In 1711 Newcomen improved on this design but still relied on cooling the cylinder with a jet of water after each stroke. Watt's single-acting steam engine, patented in 1769, was the first to use a separate condenser. Watt went on to invent the double-acting engine, the crank and crosshead mechanism, and the governor. It was largely this engine that created the industrial revolution. The steam engine was the supreme prime mover of railways throughout the world from 1829 (when Stephenson built his first locomotive) until after World War II, when steam was largely replaced by electric and Diesel-electric trains. From the beginning of the 19th century steam engines were also widely used in place of sails in ships. Moreover, it was the steam engine that drove the first electricity generators for public supply. However, the more compact and efficient steam turbine has now replaced the steam engine for this purpose.

steatite. *See* talc.

steel An alloy of iron containing a small carefully controlled proportion of carbon, usually less than 1%. Carbon steels contain principally iron and carbon. Alloy steels have other metals added. Steel products form the basis of modern technology and steel production is therefore a key factor in the world economy. For many engineering products the starting material is **mild steel**, a carbon steel with between 0.2% and 0.8% carbon and sometimes a little manganese or silicon. It can be further improved by heat treatment. Alloy steels, such as stainless steel, are usually more expensive to produce. They are used where special hardness, strength, or corrosion resistance are needed.
Steel is made by smelting iron ore in a blast furnace to produce pig iron, which is added to melted down scrap

iron before being converted by the basic-oxygen process, or formerly by the Bessemer process, the open-hearth furnace, or the electric-arc furnace.

Steel, Sir David (Martin Scott) (1938–) British politician; leader of the Liberal Party (1976–88). He entered parliament in 1964 and succeeded Jeremy Thorpe as Liberal leader. In the 1980s he headed the SDP-Liberal Alliance alongside the SDP leader, David Owen.

steeplechase 1. A form of horse race that grew out of foxhunting, in which horses jump artificial hedges and ditches. Hurdling is a less taxing version over lower lighter fences and shorter distances. Point-to-points are steeplechases for amateur riders. 2. A track event for men in athletics over a 3000 m course that includes 28 hurdles 91 cm (3 ft) high and seven water jumps 3.66 m (12 ft) across per lap. World record: 8 minutes 5.4 seconds (1978) by Henry Rono (Kenya).

Stegosaurus A dinosaur of the late Jurassic period (about 150–135 million years ago). 7 m long and weighing 1.75 tonnes, it had a double row of large triangular plates arranged in pairs along its back. It fed on soft plants. Order: *Ornithischia*.

Steinbeck, John (1902–68) US novelist. The majority of his novels, notably *Of Mice and Men* (1937) and *The Grapes of Wrath* (1939) deal with the social and economic conditions of his native California. *East of Eden* (1952) is the most ambitious of his later novels. He won the Nobel Prize in 1962.

Steiner, Rudolf (1861–1925) Austrian-born philosopher. He aimed in his system of anthroposophy to reintegrate man with the world of the spirit. He founded his first school in 1919 and his teachings are now propagated in over 70 Rudolf Steiner schools, which aim to develop the child's whole personality.

Stendhal (Henri Beyle; 1783–1842) French novelist. His two major novels, *Le Rouge et le noir* (1830) and *La Chartreuse de Parme* (1839), are notable for their blend of romantic vigour with dispassionate and often ironical psychological analysis. He also wrote works of literary, artistic, and musical appreciation.

STEGOSAURUS *It was originally thought that the plates on the back of this dinosaur were erect and probably functioned as weapons. Recent theories, however, postulate a horizontal arrangement of plates, which acted as heat exchangers.*

Stentor A genus of tiny single-celled animals (*see* Protozoa) occurring in fresh water. They are trumpet-shaped, with tracts of hairlike cilia over the body surface, and are often attached by a stalk to the substrate. Class: *Ciliata*.

Stephanotis   A genus of evergreen climbing shrubs (5 species), native to Madagascar, and including some ornamental species. *S. floribunda* is a popular greenhouse plant with small fragrant white waxy flowers. Family: *Asclepiadaceae*.

Stephen   (c. 1097–1154) King of England (1135–54); grandson of William the Conqueror. Stephen seized the throne from Henry I's daughter Matilda, who invaded England in 1139. Civil war followed. In 1152, after much of the country had been ravaged in factional fighting and the royal administration had broken down, Stephen recognized Matilda's son Henry (later Henry II) as heir to the throne.

Stephenson, George   (1781–1848) British engineer, who developed a greatly improved steam locomotive. Stephenson became interested in locomotives in 1813 and two years later built the *Blucher*, which could draw 30 tons of coal at 4 mph. He went on to construct a number of improved models, culminating in his most famous locomotive, the *Rocket*, built in 1829. It carried passengers at a speed of 36 mph on the new Liverpool–Manchester line and stimulated railway development throughout Europe and in North America.

steppes   The midlatitude grasslands of Eurasia extending in a broad belt from the Ukraine to SW Siberia. They correspond to the prairies of North America and consist chiefly of level, virtually treeless, plains.

steradian   (sr)   The SI unit of solid angle equal to a solid angle that encloses a surface on a sphere equal to the square of its radius.

stereophonic sound   Sound reproduction in which two signals are used to give a directional quality. It results in more realistic reproduction than a single signal system (monophonic sound) because the brain distinguishes the direction by assessing the difference between the sound in each ear. For recording, either two directional microphones at right angles in one place or two separated microphones are needed. Playing back requires at least two loudspeakers, one for each signal.

sterility   Inability to produce offspring by sexual reproduction. Sterility, or infertility, in men may be caused by various conditions in which the sperms are deficient in numbers or defective in quality. It may also result from psychological problems causing impotence. In women sterility may be due to disease of the womb, blockage of the Fallopian tubes leading from the ovaries to the womb, or failure of the ovaries to produce egg cells. *See also* sterilization.

sterilization   The surgical technique or any other means used to induce sterility. Surgical sterilization may be performed for contraceptive purposes or when pregnancy would damage the health of the woman. For men, the operation–vasectomy–involves cutting and tying the duct (vas deferens) that conveys sperm from the testicle. In women the Fallopian tubes are clipped or tied (tubal ligation), which prevents the passage of the egg cells to the womb. Neither operation affects sexual desire or the ability to satisfy it. Sterilization should be considered as irreversible. *See also* castration.

sterling   **1.** The currency of the UK. The pound sterling is named after the Norman *steorling*, a coin with a star (*steorra*) on one face. Coins of the realm that comply with the standards laid down from time to time are called sterling. **2.** Sterling silver is a silver alloy containing at least 92.5% silver.

Stern, Isaac   (1920–   )   Russian-born US violinist, taken to the USA as a young child.

Sterne, Laurence   (1713–68) Irish-born British novelist, and clergyman, best known for his eccentric comic novel *Tristram Shandy* (1759).

steroids   A class of organic chemical compounds with a basic structure of three six-membered carbon rings joined to a five-membered ring. Steroids and their hydroxy derivatives (**sterols**) fulfil many biological roles in plants and animals and include the sex hormones, corticosteroids, bile acids, and vitamin D. Cholesterol is an important precursor in the synthesis of many steroids.

stethoscope   An instrument widely used by doctors to listen to sounds within the body. Modern instruments consist of two earpieces joined by two tubes to a head, which is placed on the body. The head usually has a diaphragm (for high-pitched sounds) and a bell (for low-pitched sounds). More sophisticated stethoscopes are fitted with electronic amplification devices.

Stettin.   *See* Szczecin.

Stevenage   51 55N 0 14W A town in SE England, in Hertfordshire. The first of the new towns (1946) to be developed after World War II, it is now an important industrial centre manufacturing aircraft, electrical, and plastic goods. Population (1985 est): 75 700.

Stevenson, Adlai E(wing)   (1900–65) US Democratic politician, governor of Illinois (1949–53). He twice ran for the presidency (1952, 1956) but was defeated on both occasions by Eisenhower. He helped to found the UN, to which he was later US delegate (1961–65).

ROBERT LOUIS STEVENSON   *Detail of a portrait done in 1887 by W. B. Richmond.*

Stevenson, Robert Louis   (1850–94) Scottish novelist. Returning to Scotland from California, he published several books, which remain among the best-known works of fiction in the language: *Treasure Island* (1883), *Kidnapped* (1886), and *The Strange Case of Dr Jekyll and Mr Hyde* (1886). Constantly troubled by respiratory disease, he returned to the USA in 1887. His other works include the novel *The Master of Ballantrae* (1889).

Stewart, James (Maitland)   (1908–   ) US film actor. He established himself as an incorruptible hero with a distinctive drawl in numerous films, including *Mr Smith Goes to Washington* (1939), *Destry Rides Again*

(1939), *The Philadelphia Story* (1940), *The Glenn Miller Story* (1953), *Shenandoah* (1965), and *Airport 77* (1977).

Stewarts. *See* Stuarts.

stick insect An insect belonging to the family *Phasmidae*. It has a twiglike body and long spindly legs and the wings are reduced or absent. Males are rare; the females live in trees or shrubs, producing eggs that drop to the ground and develop without fertilization (*see* parthenogenesis). Order: *Phasmida* (stick and leaf insects).

stickleback A fish of the family *Gasterosteidae* (about 12 species), found in both fresh and salt water in temperate regions of the N hemisphere. Sticklebacks have a row of spines along the back. The male builds a nest for the eggs and guards the young. Order: *Gasterosteiformes*.

stigma The part of the pistil of a flower that is specialized to receive pollen. In insect-pollinated flowers the stigma is sticky, whereas wind-pollinated flowers have large feathery stigmas.

stimulants A large group of drugs that stimulate activity of the nervous system. Caffeine (in tea and coffee) and nicotine (in cigarettes) are stimulants used widely to reduce feelings of tiredness and to improve concentration. Hallucinogens, amphetamine, and cocaine are also stimulants. Stimulants may affect other parts of the body, particularly the heart.

stingray A round or diamond-shaped ray fish belonging to a family (*Dasyatidae*; 89 species) found mainly in warm shallow ocean waters. Most species have a whiplike tail armed with one or more saw-edged venomous spines, which can inflict an intensely painful wound causing paralysis and occasionally death.

stinkhorn A fungus of the order *Phallales*, producing a phallus-shaped fruiting body. This consists of a stout whitish stalk arising from a basal egg-shaped structure and bearing a thimble-shaped cap containing spores. When the spores are ripe the cap produces a strong-smelling secretion that attracts flies, which disperse the spores. Class: *Basidiomycetes*.

Stirling 56 07N 3 57W A town in Scotland, the administrative centre of the Central Region on the River Forth. Once a residence of the Scottish kings, the first Scottish parliament was held here in 1326. The castle occupies a prominent position. Stirling is an important market town. Population (1985 est): 29 238.

stoat A small carnivorous mammal, *Mustela erminea*, of Europe, Asia, and North America. About 35 cm long, with a long sinuous body, flattish head, and short legs, it can be distinguished from a weasel by its black-tipped tail. Stoats prey mainly on rabbits.

stock One of several herbaceous plants of the genus *Matthiola* that are cultivated as ornamentals. Many garden varieties, including ten-week stocks and Brompton stocks, are derived from the European biennial *M. incana*, which has clusters of purple flowers. The night-scented stock (*M. bicornis*) has small lilac flowers that emit their fragrance at night. Family: *Cruciferae*.

stock exchange A market in which securities are bought and sold. The three largest stock exchanges are in London, New York, and Tokyo. A stock exchange is an essential part of the capital market, providing capital for industry and a form of investment for savers. Members of the London Stock Exchange, founded in 1773, were formerly either stockbrokers or stockjobbers, but this distinction ceased to exist with the change in City practices known as the "Big Bang" (October, 1986).

Thereafter the market became a highly computerized free-for-all, in which commissions were negotiable.

Stockhausen, Karlheinz (1928–) German composer. His early works employed serialism but he later rejected traditional forms and techniques, developing a concept of music as a sequence of sound "events" in such works as *Gruppen* (for three orchestras; 1955–57), *Zyklus* (for solo percussionist; 1959), and *Kontra-Punkte* (for ten instruments; 1962). Such works as *Mantra* (for two pianos and percussion; 1970) were influenced by Indian mysticism. Later works include the opera *Donnerstag aus Licht* (1978–80).

Stockholm 59 20N 18 95E The capital of Sweden, built on several islands between Lake Mälar and the Baltic Sea. It is the country's second largest port. The old town contains many buildings erected in the middle ages and in the 16th and 17th centuries. A settlement from very early times, Stockholm became the capital in 1436. Population (1986 est): 183 430.

Stockport 53 25N 2 10W A town in N England, in Greater Manchester on the River Mersey. Traditionally a textile town (particularly for cotton), Stockport also manufactures hats and caps, textile and electrical machinery, paper, plastics, and chemicals. Population (1981): 136 496.

stocks and shares Documents representing money invested in industrial and commercial corporations or loaned to a government. In the UK stocks represent fixed-interest loans made to the government (*see* gilt-edged security), foreign governments, local authorities, or companies (*see* debenture stock). Shares represent equal amounts of capital subscribed to a company in return for membership rights. Ordinary shareholders are the last to receive their dividends, which fluctuate according to the level of profits. They usually have voting rights in the company. Shares in public companies can be bought and sold on a stock exchange. In the USA ordinary shares are called common stock.

Stockton, 1st Earl of. *See* Macmillan (Maurice) Harold.

Stockton-on-Tees 53 34N 1 19W A town in NE England, in Cleveland on the River Tees. The first passenger railway was built from here to Darlington in 1825, and it was once an important port. Population (1981): 154 585.

Stoicism The philosophical school founded about 300 BC in Athens by Zeno of Citium. Stoics believed that God (identified with reason) was the basis of the universe, that human souls were sparks of the divine fire, and that the wise man lived "in harmony with nature." Knowledge of virtue was all-important. Stoicism was subsequently modified to stress the primacy of active virtue and duty. Its doctrines influenced many later thinkers.

Stoke-on-Trent 53 00N 2 10W A city in England, in the N Midlands in Staffordshire, on the River Trent. Formed in 1910 by the amalgamation of five towns, the area is known as the Potteries and is the centre of the British ceramic industry. Population (1981): 252 351.

stomach A muscular sac, just beneath the diaphragm, that opens from the oesophagus (gullet) and leads to the duodenum (part of the small intestine). The stomach secretes gastric juice, containing hydrochloric acid and the enzyme pepsin, which continue the digestion of food that started in the mouth. Release of acid is triggered in response to the presence of food. The churning action of the stomach ensures constant mixing of the food and its secretions.

Stone Age The cultural phase during which man relied on stone, supplemented by wood, bone, or antler, as material for weapons and tools. It is the earliest phase in a system devised (1816) for classifying human technological progress (*compare* Bronze Age; Iron Age). The Stone Age is subdivided into: Old (*see* Palaeolithic), Middle (*see* Mesolithic), and New (*see* Neolithic).

stone bass. *See* wreckfish.

stonechat A small chat, *Saxicola torquata*, occurring in Eurasia and N Africa and feeding chiefly on insects and their larvae. The male has a dark-brown head and back, chestnut underparts, and white rump; the female is a drabber brown. Stonechats favour dry heathland regions.

stonecrop An annual or perennial herb belonging to the genus *Sedum* (600 species), found in N temperate regions and also in Central and South America. They have white, pink, or yellow flowers. Some are popular ornamentals. Family: *Crassulaceae*.

stone curlew A ground-nesting bird belonging to a widely distributed family (*Burhinidae*; 9 species) characterized by thickened tarsal joints, also called thickknee. They are typically nocturnal, feeding on beetles, worms, etc. Order: *Charadriiformes* (gulls, plovers, etc.).

stonefly An insect of the order *Plecoptera* (3000 species), 6–60 mm long with long antennae and two pairs of membranous wings. The short-lived adults rarely feed and are found near fresh water. The aquatic nymphs feed on plants, decaying organic material, or other insects.

Stonehenge A famous megalithic structure on Salisbury Plain in Wiltshire (England). Sarsens and bluestones, the latter brought from S Wales, are set upright in concentric circles and horseshoes the orientation of which suggests one purpose as being sun and moon observation. The alleged "Druid" connection dates only from the 18th century AD. *See also* megalith.

stone pine A pine tree, *Pinus pinea*, native to SW Europe and Asia but planted throughout Mediterranean regions since Roman times for its edible seeds. Up to 30 m high, it has cones about 12.5 cm long.

Stoppard, Tom (1937–) British dramatist, born in Czechoslovakia. He achieved international success with *Rosencrantz and Guildenstern Are Dead* (1967), using characters from Shakespeare's *Hamlet*. In *Jumpers* (1972), *Travesties* (1975), *Night and Day* (1978), *The Real Thing* (1982), and *Hapgood* (1988), he explored philosophical ideas with wit and great verbal facility.

storax A tree or shrub belonging to the genus *Styrax* (130 species), occurring in warm and tropical regions. They have small white flowers and several species are cultivated as ornamentals. The storax used today in cough mixtures, pastilles, etc., is extracted from trees of the genus *Liquidambar* (sweet gums). Family: *Styracaceae*.

Storey, David (1933–) British novelist and dramatist. He achieved literary success with his novel *This Sporting Life* (1960). His later novels include *Pasmore* (1972), *Saville* (1976), and *Present Times* (1984), and his plays include *Home* (1970) and *The March on Russia* (1989).

stork A large bird belonging to a widely distributed family (*Ciconiidae*; 17 species) occurring in warm and

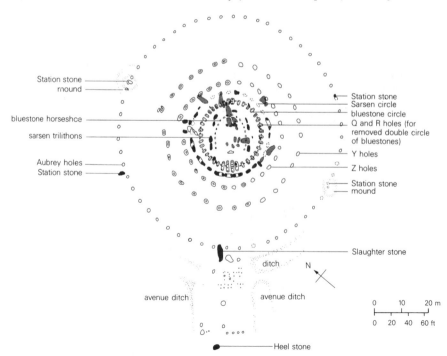

Station stone mound
bluestone horseshoe
sarsen trilithons
Aubrey holes
Station stone

Station stone
Sarsen circle
bluestone circle
Q and R holes (for removed double circle of bluestones)
Y holes
Z holes
Station stone mound

Slaughter stone
ditch   N
avenue ditch   avenue ditch

0   10   20 m
0   20   40   60 ft

Heel stone

STONEHENGE   *The plan reveals features of consecutive building phases that may no longer be visible.*

temperate regions. 60–150 cm tall, storks have long necks, legs, and bill and are white with black markings. They feed chiefly on fish, frogs, molluscs, and insects and build a large nest platform of twigs in a tree or on a rooftop. Order: *Ciconiiformes* (herons, storks, flamingos). *See also* adjutant stork; marabou.

storksbill A herb of the genus *Erodium* (about 90 species) occurring in Eurasia, Australia, and South America. The common storksbill (*E. cicutarium*) grows to a height of 60 cm and has purplish-pink flowers. Family: *Geraniaceae*.

Stormont A castle in Belfast that housed the parliament of Northern Ireland, established in 1921. Following the eruption of violence in the province in 1969, the UK Government reinstituted direct rule from London (1972).

storm petrel A small seabird belonging to a family (*Hydrobatidae*; 20 species) occurring in all oceans. 13–25 cm long, storm petrels have dark-grey or brown plumage, often with paler underparts. Species of southern oceans feed by "walking" on the water with wings outstretched, picking up plankton. Northern species feed by swooping on fish. Order: *Procellariiformes* (petrels).

Stornoway 58 12N 6 23W A port in NW Scotland, on the Isle of Lewis. It is the administrative centre of the Western Isles Islands Area. Population (1989): 8400.

Stourbridge 52 27N 2 09W A town in central England, in the West Midlands on the River Stour. Dr Johnson attended the grammar school (founded 1552). Population (1981): 54 661.

stout. *See* beer and brewing.

Stowe, Harriet Beecher (1811–96) US novelist. *Uncle Tom's Cabin* (1852) greatly stimulated antislavery feeling.

strabismus. *See* squint.

Stradivari, Antonio (?1644–1737) Italian violin maker. He was a pupil of Niccolò Amati. From 1666 he and two of his sons made outstanding violins, violas, and cellos at their workshop in Cremona.

strain In physics, the deformation of a body when it is subjected to a stress. **Longitudinal strain** is the extension per unit length when a body is stretched; **bulk strain** is the volume change per unit volume when a body is compressed; and **shear strain** is an angular measure of deformation.

strangeness A property of matter, expressed as a quantum number (s), postulated to account for the unusually long lifetime of some hadrons. In the quark model (*see* particle physics) strange hadrons contain the strange quark or its antiquark.

Strasbourg (German name: Strassburg) 48 35N 7 45E A city in NE France, on the River Ill. An important inland port, it is famous for its *pâté de foie gras*. *History*: made a free imperial city in the 13th century, it was ceded to France in 1697. Captured by the Germans (1871), it was returned to France after World War I. Population (1983): 252 300.

Strategic Defence Initiative (SDI) A US research project, also known as "star wars", which aims to destroy incoming nuclear missiles in space. Announced by President Reagan at the end of 1984, the programme includes tests of various systems, of which ground-based or satellite-mounted lasers are favoured.

Stratford-on-Avon 52 12N 1 41W A town in central England, in Warwickshire on the River Avon. It is famous as the birthplace of William Shakespeare. The

Royal Shakespeare Theatre (opened in 1932) is devoted mainly to Shakespeare's plays. Population (1986 est): 20 860.

Strathclyde Region An administrative region in W Scotland. It was created under local government reorganization in 1975 It consists of lowlands in the Glasgow area surrounded by highlands and includes offshore islands such as Mull, Arran, and Jura. Agriculture is important on the lowlands. Industries include shipbuilding and coal-mining. Area: 13 856 sq km (5348 sq mi). Population (1986 est): 2 344 585. Administrative centre: Glasgow.

stratigraphy The branch of geology concerned with the formation, composition, sequence in time, and spatial correlation of stratified rocks. **Lithostratigraphy** involves the lithological and spatial relations of rock units. **Biostratigraphy** utilizes fossils in calibrating rock successions. **Chronostratigraphy** studies rock bodies according to the time of their formation (*see* geological time scale).

stratocumulus cloud (Sc) A low type of cloud composed of dark grey globular masses, often forming extensive sheets.

stratosphere. *See* atmosphere.

stratus cloud A low type of cloud forming below 2400 m (7874 ft), having a grey uniform appearance; it may actually occur at ground level as hill fog.

RICHARD STRAUSS

Strauss, Richard (1864–1949) German composer and conductor. Strauss was much influenced by Wagner, whose use of leitmotifs he adopted. From 1887 to 1899 Strauss wrote a series of symphonic poems, including *Death and Transfiguration* (1889), *Till Eulenspiegels lustige Streiche* (1894–95), *Also sprach Zarathustra* (1895–96), *Don Quixote* (1897), and *Ein Heldenleben* (1898). He then turned to opera, writing 15 works, including *Salome* (1905), *Elektra* (1906–08), *Der Rosenkavalier* (1909–10), and *Ariadne auf Naxos* (1912).

Strauss the Younger, Johann (1825–99) Austrian violinist, conductor, and composer. He wrote a great many waltzes, such as "The Blue Danube," "Vienna Blood," and "Tales from the Vienna Woods," as well as polkas and marches. He also wrote 16 operettas, including *Die Fledermaus* (1874), *A Night in Venice* (1883), and *The Gipsy Baron* (1885). His father **Johann Strauss the Elder** (1804–49) composed 152 waltzes as well as quadrilles, marches (including the "Radetzky March"), galops, etc.

Stravinsky, Igor (1882–1971) Russian-born US composer. He became famous with the series of ballet scores commissioned by Diaghilev including *The Firebird* (1910), *Petrushka* (1911), and *The Rite of Spring* (1913), which provoked demonstrations at its premiere and had a strong influence on 20th-century music. Stravinsky subsequently developed a neoclassical style in which he attempted to revive baroque and classical composition in a modern form. Towards the end of his life Stravinsky adopted serialism in such works as *Canticum Sacrum* (1955).

strawberry A perennial herb belonging to the genus *Fragaria* (15 species), native to N temperate regions and widely cultivated for its edible fruit. Most of the commercial varieties are hybrids derived from the European hautbois strawberry (*F. moschata*), the Chilean strawberry (*F. chiloensis*), and the North American scarlet strawberry (*F. virginiana*). The plants are low growing, with white flowers. Family: *Rosaceae*.

strawberry tree. *See* Arbutus.

Streep, Meryl (Mary Louise S.; 1949–) US actress. After appearing in *The Deerhunter* (1978) she became the leading US actress of the 1980s. Her other films include *Kramer vs Kramer* (1980), *The French Lieutenant's Woman* (1981), *Sophie's Choice* (1982), *Out of Africa* (1986), and *A Cry in the Dark* (1989).

Streisand, Barbra (1942–) US singer and actress. She has performed on stage and in film musicals including *Funny Girl* (1968), *Hello Dolly* (1969), *The Way We Were* (1973), *A Star is Born* (1976), and *Yentl* (1983).

Streptococcus A genus of spherical anaerobic bacteria many of which live as parasites in the respiratory and digestive systems of animals and man. *S. pyogenes* causes scarlet fever in man.

streptomycin An antibiotic, obtained from the bacterium *Streptomyces griseus*, that revolutionized the treatment of tuberculosis. It is usually administered (by injection) in combination with other antibiotics.

stress (physics) The force per unit area that causes a deformation (or strain) in a body. **Tensile stress** tends to stretch a body; **bulk stress** tends to compress it; and **shear stress** tends to twist it.

strike A form of industrial action in which a group of employees, usually organized in a trade union (or unions), withdraws its labour in order to achieve its demands. A strike is the last resort in the process of collective bargaining: it may prompt a settlement either because it proves that neither side is bluffing or because the costs involved (in terms of lost pay and profits) force a compromise. As future orders and job security may be jeopardized by a strike, responsible unions only resort to the measure in extreme cases.
An official strike is one that is recognized by a trade union, whereas an unofficial (or wildcat) strike is a walkout organized by shopfloor workers without official union backing. The Trade Union Act (1984) provides for compulsory ballots in connection with strikes and other industrial actions. *See also* picketing.

Strindberg, August (1849–1912) Swedish dramatist and writer. His unhappy childhood and three unsuccessful marriages gave rise to mental instability and a violent hatred of women. This is reflected in the plays *The Father* (1887) and *Miss Julie* (1888), the autobiographical prose work *Confessions of a Fool* (1912), and a study of

mental illness entitled *Inferno* (1897). Other works include the trilogy *To Damascus* (1904), *The Dance of Death* (1900), the symbolistic *Easter* (1901), and *A Dream Play* (1901). His late chamber plays, such as *The Ghost Sonata* (1907), combine irrational elements with realistic settings.

stringed instruments Musical instruments in which notes are produced by the vibration of stretched strings. The strings may be plucked, bowed, plucked mechanically, struck mechanically, or played with hammers.

stroke (*or* apoplexy) Sudden loss of consciousness with weakness or paralysis of one side of the body, caused by interruption of the blood supply to the brain. This may be due to a blood clot in one of the arteries of the brain (*see* embolism; thrombosis) or to the rupture of a blood vessel in the brain (cerebral haemorrhage). With careful nursing and physiotherapy many patients recover completely.

Stromboli An Italian island in the Tyrrhenian Sea, in the Lipari Islands. Its active volcano produces a stream of lava.

strong interaction One of the four basic forces in the universe; it occurs between the class of elementary particles called hadrons (*see* particle physics). It is the strongest of the four (being 100 times stronger than the electromotive interaction) but is effective only over about 10^{-15} metre. It is the force that holds the protons and neutrons together in the nucleus. *Compare* weak interaction.

strontium (Sr) A reactive alkaline-earth metal, discovered by Sir Humphry Davy in 1808 and named after Strontian, a town in Scotland where the carbonate ($SrCO_3$) is found. It also occurs as the sulphate, celestine ($SrSO_4$). It is a highly reactive metal, being more electropositive than calcium and reacting vigorously with water to liberate hydrogen. The isotope ^{90}Sr is produced in nuclear fallout. At no 38; at wt 87.62; mp 769°C; bp 1384°C.

strychnine An alkaloid poison derived from plants of the genus *Strychnos*. It acts on the central nervous system, causing convulsions and ultimately death.

Stuarts (*or* Stewarts) The ruling dynasty of Scotland from 1371 to 1714 and of England from 1603 to 1714. The first Stuart king was Robert II (crowned 1371) of Scotland. The direct male line ended with the death of James V in 1542, when the throne passed to his daughter Mary, Queen of Scots, and following her abdication (1567) to her son James VI, who inherited the English Crown (1603) as James I. He was succeeded by Charles I, Charles II, James II, Mary II (and her husband William III), and Anne (d. 1714). The Crown then passed to the Hanoverians (*see* Settlement, Act of) but the Stuart claim was kept alive by James Edward Stuart the Old Pretender, and his son, Charles Edward Stuart the Young Pretender. The last royal Stuart was Henry Stuart, Cardinal York (d. 1807).

Stubbs, George (1724–1806) British animal painter. He is best known for his horse paintings, such as *Mares and Foals in a Landscape* (Tate Gallery), but he also painted portraits and farming scenes. His meticulous observation of nature reflects his maxim that nature is always superior to art.

sturgeon A bony fish belonging to a family (*Acipenseridae*; about 24 species) found in N temperate waters. Sturgeons have a large sharklike body, up to 8.4 m long, with five longitudinal rows of sharp bony plates, a small ventral mouth, and four sensory barbels. Eggs are laid in fresh water and are commercially important as caviar. *See also* beluga.

GEORGE STUBBS   Mares and Foals in a Landscape *(detail; c. 1760–70).*

Sturm und Drang (German: Storm and Stress) A German literary movement of the late 18th century that anticipated many aspects of Romanticism. Its influence is most notable in the drama, characterized by epic scale and the rejection of structural conventions.

Stuttgart   48 47N 9 12E A city in SW West Germany, on the River Neckar. It became the capital of Württemberg in 1482. It was largely destroyed in World War II. Population (1986): 564 500.

stye   A small abscess at the root of an eyelash. Styes are usually treated with warm compresses to drain the pus.

stylops   A minute insect of the order *Strepsiptera* (about 400 species), which is parasitic on bees and other insects. The grublike female lives permanently inside the host's body; the winged male, often less than 4 mm long, leaves its host to find and fertilize a female.

Styx   In Greek mythology, the main river of Hades across which the souls of the dead were ferried by Charon. It was sometimes personified as the daughter of Oceanus.

sublimation.   In chemistry, the evaporation of a solid without melting. For any substance the liquid phase only occurs within certain limits of temperature and pressure—if the pressure is low enough, heating a solid will result in sublimation. Substances that sublime at atmospheric pressure include carbon dioxide (dry ice) and iodine.

submarine   A warship designed for sustained operation under water. The earliest record of a submarine craft is that developed by Cornelis Drebbel (1572–1634) of Holland in 1620. A more practical model, the "Turtle," was invented by David Bushnell (1742–1824) of Connecticut in 1776, and saw limited use in the American Revolution. Submarines, called **U-boats** (German name: *Unterseeboot*, undersea boat), were first used extensively by the German navy in World War I. They became an important armament in World War II. Modern submarines may be powered by nuclear reactors and can remain submerged for months at a time. These vessels also carry one or more guns mounted on deck, torpedoes

for firing under water, and missiles that can be launched when the submarine is submerged.

substitution reaction   A type of chemical reaction in which one atom or group of atoms is displaced by another. An example is the reaction of methyl chloride (CH_3Cl) with hydroxide ions (OH^-) to give methanol (CH_3OH) and chloride ions (Cl^-). The hydroxide ion, in this case, is referred to as the substituent.

succession   In ecology, the process of continual change that takes place in the composition of a community of organisms occupying a particular habitat from the time of its initial colonization to the establishment of a stable climax community.

Sucre   19 00S 65 15W The capital of Bolivia, in the S at an altitude of 2790 m (9153 ft). It was founded by the Spanish in 1538. The seat of government was moved to La Paz in 1898. Population (1985 est): 86 609.

sucrose (cane sugar *or* beet sugar *or* saccharose)   A carbohydrate consisting chemically of one molecule each of glucose and fructose linked together. It is commercially the most important of the sugars.

Sudan, Republic of the   A large country in NE Africa, bordering on the Red Sea. It consists chiefly of a vast plateau rising to mountains in the S and W. The main rivers are the Blue Nile and White Nile. About half the population are Arabs, and there are minorities of Dinka, Nubians, and others. *Economy*: chiefly agricultural, the main cash crop and export being cotton. Livestock rearing is also important. Forest products include gum arabic. Mineral resources include iron ore, gold, and manganese. *History*: the NE was part of ancient Nubia. The region was Christianized in the 6th century and invaded from the N in the 13th century, after which it was converted to Islam. In 1821 it was conquered by the Egyptians, against whom a revolt under the Mahdi took place in 1881. In 1898 an Anglo-Egyptian force under Kitchener subdued his followers and in 1899 an Anglo-Egyptian condominium was established. In 1956 the Sudan became an independent republic. A coup in 1969 brought Col Jaafar al Nemeiry (1929–) to power. During widespread famine in 1985, Nimeiry was overthrown and civilian rule re-established. A further coup under Brig-Gen Omar Hassan Ahmed el-Bashir reinstated military rule in 1989. Official language: Arabic; English is widely spoken. Official currency: Sudanese pound of 100 piastres and 1000 millièmes. Area: 2 500 000 sq km (967 500 sq mi). Population (1987 est): 25 550 000. Capital: Khartoum. Main port: Port Sudan.

Sudbury   46 30N 81 01W A city in E Canada, in Ontario. Established in 1883, it is one of the world's greatest mining cities. Population (1986): 88 717.

Sudetenland   A mountainous region on the W borders of Czechoslovakia. The Sudetenland, incorporated in Czechoslovakia in 1919, was reoccupied by Germany in 1938. After World War II Czechoslovakia regained the Sudetenland and expelled the Sudeten Germans.

Suez (Arabic name: As-Suways)   29 59N 32 33E A port in Egypt, near the mouth of the Suez Canal. An important refuelling station, it has been rebuilt since the Arab-Israeli War of 1967. Population (1985): 254 000.

Suez Canal   A canal in Egypt connecting the Mediterranean Sea and the Red Sea. Running between Port Said in the N and Suez in the S, it is 165 km (103 mi) long. It was designed by the French engineer Ferdinand de Lesseps and was opened in 1869. In 1888 it became a neutral zone, with Britain the guarantor of its status. In

1956, President Nasser nationalized the canal, provoking an Anglo-French attack on Egypt. However, they withdrew within a few days in the face of international censure. The canal was closed from 1967 to 1975 because of Arab-Israeli hostilities.

Suffolk A county in E England, on the North Sea. It consists of undulating lowlands. It is mainly agricultural, producing cereals and sugar beet, and is noted for its horse breeding. Area: 3800 sq km (1467 sq mi). Population (1986 est): 628 600. Administrative centre: Ipswich.

Suffolk Punch A breed of draught horse originating in Suffolk, England. It has a powerful round body and short thick neck and legs and is always chestnut. Height: about 1.63 m (16 hands).

Sufism (Arabic *sufi*: wearer of a woollen cloak, mystic) A mystical movement arising within Islam in the 8th and 9th centuries AD. The goal of the Sufis was mystical union with God achieved by fervent worship. Later Sufism shows the influence of Neoplatonism and Hindu asceticism.

sugar beet A biennial herb derived from the European sea beet (*Beta vulgaris*). Sugar beet is widely cultivated for the sucrose content of its large roots. Family: *Chenopodiaceae*.

sugar cane A perennial grass of the tropical genus *Saccharum* (5 species), especially *S. officinarum*, which is cultivated for its sugar content. The clumps of stalks (canes), 3–8 m high, may bear dense woolly clusters of female flowers. Usually, the canes are crushed to extract the sugary liquid. This is concentrated and refined to produce table sugar, etc. The remaining liquor (molasses) is used for animal feedstuffs, industrial alcohol, etc. The fibrous residue (bagasse) is used as fuel, cattle feed, etc.

sugars A class of sweet-tasting carbohydrates, classified chemically as monosaccharides or disaccharides. The sugar widely used to sweeten food, drinks, and confectionery is the disaccharide sucrose, derived from sugar cane (11–15% sucrose) and from sugar beet (17% sucrose). Sugar manufacture is believed to have originated in India (Sanskrit *sarkara*, sand) around 3000 BC; it was taken to the New World by Christopher Columbus in 1493. Sucrose is extracted from raw sugar cane by pressure, the extract being crystallized by evaporation. It is extracted from beet by hot water. Raw cane sugar and beet sugar are further refined to produce granulated, caster, icing, and cube sugars. By-products include molasses and sugar-beet pulp, both of which are used in animal feedstuffs.

Suharto (1921–) Indonesian statesman and general; president (1968–). He gained prominence in the struggle for Indonesian independence. He came to power in the gradual overthrow (1965–68) of Sukarno.

Sukarno (1901–70) Indonesian statesman, the first president of Indonesia (1945–65). He helped to found the Indonesian Nationalist Party in 1927 and was Indonesia's leader during the Japanese occupation (1942–45). When Indonesia was declared independent he became president. A military coup deposed him in 1965–66.

Sulawesi (former name: Celebes) An island in Indonesia, off E Borneo. It is mountainous and forested. Area, including adjacent islands: 189 033 sq km (72 986 sq mi). Population (1986 est): 11 803 100. Chief towns: Ujung Pandang and Menado,

SULEIMAN THE MAGNIFICENT   *In Constantinople (from a contemporary engraving).*

Suleiman (I) the Magnificent (?1494–1566) Ottoman sultan (1520–66), under whom the Ottoman Empire reached its peak. Suleiman captured Belgrade in 1521 and Rhodes in 1522. In 1526 he defeated the Hungarians at Mohács and annexed large parts of Hungary. In 1529 he besieged Vienna. In campaigns against Persia he made many conquests and the Ottoman navy, under Barbarossa (d. 1546) and others, controlled the E Mediterranean.

Sulla, Lucius Cornelius (c. 138–78 BC) Roman dictator; an opponent of Gaius Marius (c. 157–86 BC) and Cinna. Enraged because his command against Mithridates (120–63 BC) was transferred to Marius, he stormed Rome (87), forcing Marius and Cinna to flee. Although outlawed when his rivals returned, he successfully concluded the campaign against Mithridates and in 83 invaded Italy. Elected dictator, Sulla butchered his political opponents. After restoring the Senate's constitutional powers, he retired into private life (79).

Sullivan, Sir Arthur (1842–1900) British composer. He is best known for his collaboration with the librettist W. S. Gilbert in such comic operas as *The Pirates of Penzance* (1879), *The Mikado* (1885), and *The Yeomen of the Guard* (1888).

sulphonamides (*or* sulpha drugs) A group of drugs, derived from sulphanilamide, that prevent the growth of bacteria. Sulphonamides are used to treat a wide variety of infections, particularly those of the urinary tract and the eye. Sulphonamides are also combined with trimethoprim, which improves their effectiveness. In some patients sulphonamides may cause severe allergic disorders.

sulphur (S) A yellow nonmetallic solid element, occurring in various crystalline and amorphous forms. Sulphur was known in ancient times as brimstone. It is found near volcanoes and in large deposits associated with oil trapped against salt domes. Extraction is by the Frasch process, in which the sulphur is melted and pumped to the surface. Sulphur reacts readily with many elements to form sulphides, sulphates, and oxides. The oxides SO_2 and SO_3 are acidic gases that dissolve in water to form sulphurous acid (H_2SO_3) and sulphuric acid (H_2SO_4). At no 16; at wt 32.06; mp 113°C; bp 444.6°C.

sulphuric acid (H_2SO_4) A colourless oily liquid that has a great affinity for water and is used as a drying agent. H_2SO_4 is made by the contact process, in which sulphur dioxide is heated and passed through columns of platinized asbestos catalyst to produce sulphur trioxide (SO_3). The SO_3 is then dissolved in water to form H_2SO_4. Adding further SO_3 to H_2SO_4 produces fuming sulphuric acid (oleum; $H_2S_2O_7$), a fuming liquid that forms a crystalline solid on cooling. Sulphuric acid is one of the most important industrial chemicals.

Sulu Archipelago An island group in the SW Philippines. The most important of its 400 islands are Basilan and Jolo. Area: 2815 sq km (1087 sq mi). Population (1980): 555 239. Chief town: Jolo.

sumach (*or* sumac) A tree or shrub of the genus *Rhus* (250 species), native to warm temperate and subtropical regions. The leaves of the Sicilian sumach (*R. coraria*) yield a substance used in tanning and dyeing. Several species are cultivated as garden ornamentals: the stag's-horn sumach (*R. typhina*) of North America grows to a height of 7–12 m and has a crimson or orange autumn foliage. Some species are poisonous and irritate the skin on contact, particularly the American poison ivy and poison sumach (*R. vernix*). Family: *Anacardiaceae. See also* lacquer tree.

Sumatra (*or* Sumatera) The second largest Indonesian island, separated from Peninsular Malaysia by the Strait of Malacca. The mountainous volcanic spine descends in the NE to swamps. It is Indonesia's chief rubber and oil producer. Crops include coffee, tea, and pepper. *History*: the Buddhist kingdom of Sri Vijaya (7th–13th centuries) was based in Palembang. During the 15th century the Islamic influence became dominant, resisting Dutch domination in the N until 1908. Since 1949 there has been considerable separatist activity. Area: 524 097 sq km (202 311 sq mi). Population (1986 est): 19 105 900. Chief towns: Palembang and Medan.

Sumer The area in S Mesopotamia in which the earliest civilization evolved during the 4th millennium BC. The fertile natural environment encouraged settlements that grew into such politically independent cities as Ur. After 2000 BC Sumer was absorbed into Babylonia.

sumo. *See* wrestling.

sun The nearest star, lying at an average distance of 149.6 million km from earth at the centre of the solar system. It has a diameter of 1 392 000 km, a mass of 1.99×10^{30} kg, and rotates on its axis in a mean period of 25.38 days. It is a typical yellow (G2) main-sequence star and is composed primarily (99%) of hydrogen and helium in the approximate ratio 3:1 by mass. In its hot central core, about 400 000 km in diameter, energy is generated by nuclear fusion reactions. The surface, called the photosphere, is the boundary between the opaque outer (convective) zone of the sun's interior and its transparent atmosphere. The atmosphere comprises the chromosphere and the inner and outer corona. There are regions of intense localized magnetic fields on the sun, where sunspots, solar prominences, and solar flares occur. *See also* solar wind.

sun bear A bear, *Helarctos malayanus*, of tropical forests of Asia, Sumatra, and Borneo. It is the smallest bear, (110–140 cm long) and climbs well, hunting for small vertebrates, fruit, and honey.

sunbird An arboreal bird belonging to a tropical family (*Nectariniidae*; 104 species) ranging from Africa to Australasia. Sunbirds are 9–15 cm long and have a brilliant metallic plumage, slender down-curved bills, and long extensible tongues for feeding on nectar.

Sunda Islands An Indonesian group of islands, between the Indian Ocean and South China Sea. It consists of the **Greater Sunda Islands** including Sumatra, Java, Borneo, and Sulawesi and Nusa Tenggara.

Sunderland 54 55N 1 23W A port in NE England, in Tyne and Wear at the mouth of the River Wear. Sunderland has exported coal from the Durham coalfield since the 14th century. Population (1981): 196 152.

sundew A perennial or annual carnivorous plant of the genus *Drosera* (about 100 species), of temperate and tropical regions. Sundews have a basal rosette of leaves covered in sticky reddish gland-tipped hairs, used to trap insects. Family: *Droseraceae.*

sunfish An omnivorous fish of the family *Molidae*, especially *Mola mola*, found in all tropical and temperate seas. It has a disc-shaped laterally flattened body, up to 3 m long, with the tail fin reduced to a wavy frill attached to the triangular dorsal and anal fins. Order: *Tetraodontiformes*. The name is also applied to several carnivorous freshwater food and game fish of the North American family *Centrarchidae*. They have deep laterally flattened bodies, 2.5–80 cm long, and a single long dorsal fin. Order: *Perciformes*.

sunflower A herbaceous plant of the genus *Helianthus*, native to North and South America. *H. annuus* is about 3 m high with yellow flower heads, up to 35 cm in diameter. It is cultivated both for ornament and for its seeds, from which oil is obtained. Perennial sunflowers include *H. salicifolius* and *H. decapetalus*. Family: *Compositae*.

sunn An annual herb, *Crotalaria juncea*, cultivated in India for its stem fibres. It grows to a height of 2–3 m and produces small yellow flowers. The fibres are used for netting, canvas, yarns, and in certain paper products. Family: *Leguminosae*.

Sunnites (*or* Sunni; Arabic *sunna*: custom) The name of the larger of the two main Muslim Sects. In contrast to the Shiite Muslims, the Sunnites accept the first three caliphs as Mohammed's legitimate successors. They are strictly orthodox in their obedience to the Koran. They form the majority party in most Islamic countries except Iran.

sunspots Comparatively dark markings on the sun's photosphere, typically a few thousand kilometres across with the central region being darkest and coolest. They can influence the climate on earth. They are centres of intense localized magnetic fields. The number of sunspots seen in a year, and their mean solar latitude, varies in a cycle of about 11 years, known as the **sunspot cycle**.

sunstroke A form of heatstroke caused by overexposure to the sun. **Sunburn** is damage to the skin resulting from overexposure to the sun's rays. This may vary from slight reddening to large painful blisters.

superconductivity A phenomenon in which the electrical resistance of certain metals vanishes when they are cooled to low temperatures. The temperature at which superconductivity occurs is called the transition temperature and varies for different substances. If a loop of a superconducting substance is cooled to below its transition temperature, a current will flow through the loop indefinitely. Ceramic conductors have now been found that operate at higher temperatures than the metal conductors first used.

supercooling The reduction in the temperature of a liquid below its freezing point without its solidification. The effect can only be achieved by slow and continuous cooling with pure liquids. A supercooled liquid is in a metastable state and any disturbance will cause solidification.

superego In psychoanalysis, the part of the mind that acts as a moral conscience. It was believed by Freud to result from the incorporation of the parent's instructions into a child's mind. *See also* ego; id.

SURFACE TENSION *An upward force at the surface enables a razor blade to float on water.*

superfluid A fluid that exhibits a very high thermal conductivity and virtually no friction at temperatures close to absolute zero. Such a fluid will flow up the sides and out of an open container.

supergiant The largest and most luminous type of star. They evolve from very massive but more compact stars. Rigel, Betelgeuse, and Antares are examples. *See also* giant star.

superheterodyne A system widely used in radio receivers; the incoming radio-frequency signal is combined with a locally generated carrier wave to give an intermediate frequency between radio- and audio-frequency (*see* modulation). The intermediate frequency is easier to amplify than radio-frequency.

Superior, Lake The largest of the Great Lakes in North America, situated between the USA and Canada. The lake is important for shipping. Area: 82 362 sq km (31 800 sq mi).

supernova A cataclysmic stellar explosion, seen as a sudden increase in a star's brightness. Most or all of the star's substance is blown off at high velocity, forming an expanding gas shell—the **supernova remnant**. If the star's core survives, it will most probably end up as a neutron star or black hole. *See also* Crab nebula.

superphosphates Highly active phosphorus-containing fertilizers. Single superphosphate is made by reacting sulphuric acid with insoluble calcium phosphate rock to form calcium sulphate and soluble calcium hydrogen phosphate $Ca(H_2PO_4)_2$. Often the process is carried out under pressure. Triple superphosphate is more concentrated.

Supreme Court of the United States The highest law court in the USA, comprising the chief justice and eight associate justices appointed for life by the president. Its main functions include interpreting and safeguarding the constitution. It also decides disputes between states and between one state and the citizens of another and hears appeals from state and federal courts.

Sur. *See* Tyre.

Surabaja 7 14S 112 45E A port in Indonesia, in E Java. It is Indonesia's second largest city and chief naval base. Population (1985): 2 345 000.

Surakarta (*or* Solo) 7 32S 110 50E A city in Indonesia, in central Java. A cultural centre noted for its shadow plays, it is the site of a sultan's palace (1745). Population (1980): 469 888.

Surat 21 10N 72 54E A city in India, in Gujarat on the River Tapti. It was the Mogul Empire's chief port (16th–17th centuries). It was the headquarters of the East India Company until 1687. Population (1981): 913 000.

surface tension A force occurring on the surface of a liquid that makes it behave as if the surface has an elastic skin. It is caused by forces between the molecules of the liquid: only those at the surface experience forces from below, whereas those in the interior are acted on by intermolecular forces from all sides. Surface tension causes a meniscus to form, liquids to rise up capillary tubes, paper to absorb water, and droplets and bubbles to form. It is defined as the force acting tangentially to the surface on one side of a line of unit length (newtons per metre) or as the work required to produce unit increase in surface area (joules per square metre).

surfactant A substance that lowers the surface tension of a liquid, thus allowing easier penetration and spreading. For this reason they are often known as **wetting agents**. Surfactants are widely used in detergents, emulsifiers, paints, adhesives, inks, etc.

surgeonfish A tropical marine fish, also called tang, belonging to the family *Acanthuridae* (about 100 species). Its deep laterally flattened body, up to about 50 cm long, is often brightly coloured, with a single long dorsal fin, and a sharp bladelike spine on each side of the tail. They feed mainly on algae. Order: *Perciformes*.

Suriname, Republic of (name until 1948: Dutch Guiana) A country on the N coast of South America. Much of the land is covered by tropical forest. The majority of the population is of Indian and mixed descent. *Economy*: based primarily on bauxite, the chief industry is aluminium processing. Fishing is important. *History*: sighted by Columbus in 1498, the first permanent settlement was established by the English in 1650. It was ceded to the Netherlands in 1667. During the Revolutionary and Napoleonic Wars it was again (1799–1802, 1804–16) under British rule. In 1949 it gained a certain measure of self-government, subsequently becoming an autonomous part of the Netherlands (1954) and then an independent republic (1975). In a coup in 1984 Lieut-Col Deysi Bouterse came to power; he restored democracy in 1988. Suriname is a member of the OAS. President: Ramsewak Shankar (1937–). Official language: Dutch; English, Hindustani, and Javanese are widely spoken and the local vernacular, Surinamese, is used as a lingua franca. Official currency: Suriname guilder of 100 cents. Area: 163 265 sq km (63 020 sq mi). Population (1987): 415 000. Capital: Paramaribo.

surrealism A European movement in art and literature of the 1920s and 1930s. Surrealism began as a literary movement, when its leader, the poet André Breton (1896–1966), published the surrealist manifesto in Paris

(1924). It aimed, under the influence of Freud, to embody in art and poetry the irrational forces of dreams and the subconscious mind. The leading surrealists were the poets Louis Aragon (1897–1982) and Paul Eluard (1895–1952) and the painters Ernst, Miró, Dali, Magritte, Paul Delvaux (1897–), and Yves Tanguy (1900–55).

Surrey A county in SE England, bordering on Greater London. The North Downs run E–W across the middle of the county. Although it has developed primarily as a residential area, agriculture is important in the S. Area: 1655 sq km (639 sq mi). Population (1986 est): 1 011 400. Administrative centre: Kingston-upon-Thames.

Surrey, Henry Howard, Earl of. *See* Wyatt, Sir Thomas.

surrogate motherhood. *See* artificial insemination.

Surya In Hindu mythology, the sun-god. He appears as a major deity in the *Vedas* and remained prominent as patron of numerous Hindu royal dynasties.

Susa (*or* Shushan) An ancient city in SW Iran. Occupied since the 4th millennium BC, it was a capital of Elam. Susa's heyday was as administrative capital of the Achaemenian kings of Persia (521–331).

Susquehanna River A river in the E USA. It rises in New York State and flows mainly S to Chesapeake Bay. Length: 715 km (444 mi).

Sussex. *See* West Sussex; East Sussex.

Sutherland, Graham Vivian (1903–80) British artist. He turned to painting in 1935, specializing in disturbing landscapes and scenes of war desolation. Also well known are his *Crucifixion* (1946; St Matthew's, Northampton), his tapestry for Coventry Cathedral, and his portraits, e.g. of Somerset Maugham (Tate Gallery).

Sutherland, Dame Joan (1926–) Australian operatic soprano. She established her reputation at Covent Garden in 1959 in the title role of Donizetti's *Lucia di Lammermoor.*

Sutlej, River A river in India and Pakistan. Rising in SW Tibet, it flows mainly SW across the Punjab plain into Pakistan, where it joins the River Chenab. Length: 1368 km (850 mi).

suttee An ancient Hindu custom of self-immolation of widows on their husbands' funeral pyres. It was officially abolished in India by the British in 1829.

Sutton Coldfield 52 34N 1 48W A town in England, in the West Midlands, a mainly residential suburb of Birmingham. Population (1981): 86 494.

Sutton Hoo The site of a Saxon ship-burial near Woodbridge, in Suffolk (E England). Excavations in 1939 revealed the remnants of a 38-oar boat containing a magnificent treasure hoard. The mound is thought to be a cenotaph to King Raedwald (died c. 625 AD).

Suva 18 08S 178 25E The capital of Fiji, on the S coast of Viti Levu. Its industries include tourism and the production of coconut oil and soap. Population (1986): 69 481.

Suwannee River (*or* Swanee R.) A river in the SE USA, flowing from the Okefenokee Swamp in SE Georgia across Florida to the Gulf of Mexico. Length: 400 km (200 mi).

Suzhou (Su-chou *or* Soochow) 31 21N 120 40E A city in E China, on the Yangtze delta. Famed for its beautiful canals and gardens, it is a centre of culture and the silk industry. Population (1985 est): 611 500.

Svalbard (*or* Spitsbergen) A Norwegian archipelago in the Arctic Ocean. Following disputes over their sovereignty, they were granted to Norway in 1920. Covered largely by icefields and glaciers their major importance is as a source of coal. Area: 62 050 sq km (23 958 sq mi). Population (1976 est): 3495. Chief town: Longyearbyen.

Sverdlovsk (name until 1924: Ekaterinburg) 56 52N 60 35E A city in the central Soviet Union. Nicholas II and his family were executed here in 1918. Population: (1987): 1 331 000.

Swabia (German name: Schwaben) A former region in SW Germany now divided between Germany, Switzerland, and France. Swabia was one of the leading German duchies in the middle ages. Napoleon finally partitioned Swabia among neighbouring states in 1807.

Swahili (*or* Kiswahili) A Bantu language of East Africa and the lingua franca of Tanzania, Kenya, Zaïre, and Uganda. There are three main dialects.

swallow A songbird belonging to a cosmopolitan family (*Hirundidae*; 78 species) of acrobatic fliers that catch insects on the wing. Swallows are 10–22 cm long, with short necks, long pointed wings, short legs, and often forked tails. All temperate swallows migrate to hot climates for the winter. *See also* martin.

SUTTON HOO *Gold shoulder-clasps found in the ship burial.*

swallowtail butterfly A papilionid butterfly having long swallow-like tails on the hindwings. Many species are tropical and brightly coloured, with the sexes often of different colours. The caterpillars give off a strong odour if they are disturbed. Family: *Papilionidae.*

swamp cypress A deciduous conifer, *Taxodium distichum*, also called bald cypress, native to swampy regions of the SE USA and grown for its timber and as an ornamental. In waterlogged soils its roots protrude above the water. Up to 45 m high, it has globular cones, 2.5 cm across. Family: *Taxodiaceae.*

swan A large waterbird belonging to a genus (*Cygnus*; 7–8 species) occurring worldwide on fresh waters or sheltered coasts and estuaries. 100–160 cm long, swans are usually white with black legs and have large feet, a long neck, and a powerful spatulate bill, which they use to feed on underwater plants. Immature swans have a mottled brown plumage. *See also* black swan; mute swan. Family: *Anatidae* (ducks, geese, swans).

Swansea (Welsh name: Abertawe) 51 38N 3 57W A city and port in South Wales, the administrative centre of West Glamorgan. It is the second largest city in

Wales and a major industrial centre. Population (1981): 167 796.

swastika An ancient symbol of uncertain origin, generally held to signify prosperity and creativity. It is a cross, the four arms of which are deflected at right angles either clockwise or anticlockwise. It has been revered by Buddhists, Hindus, Celts, and North American Indians. The Nazis adopted the symbol, mistakenly believing it to be of pure Aryan origins.

Swazi A Bantu-speaking people who occupy Swaziland and adjacent areas of South Africa. They are an agricultural and pastoral people. Polygyny is practised by senior men. Traditionally ancestor worship, witchcraft, and magic were prominent features of religious life.

Swaziland, Kingdom of A small country in SE Africa between South Africa and Mozambique. It consists of three distinct regions. *Economy*: chiefly agricultural, the main food crop being maize. The chief cash crop is sugar. Rich mineral resources include iron ore, asbestos, and coal. *History*: the Swazi occupied the area in the late 18th century. It became a South African protectorate in 1894 and, in 1902, after the Boer War it came under British rule. It became an independent kingdom within the British Commonwealth in 1968. Head of state: King Mswati III. Official languages: Siswati and English. Official currency: emalangeni of 100 lilangeni; South African currency is also legal tender. Area: 17 400 sq km (6705 sq mi). Population (1987): 716 000. Capital: Mbabane.

sweat (*or* perspiration) A watery fluid, consisting mainly of sodium chloride and urea in solution, that is secreted by the sweat glands in the skin. Sweating is a means of excreting nitrogenous waste products, but it is also, and more importantly, a means of temperature regulation.

swede An annual or biennial herbaceous plant, *Brassica napus napobrassica*, growing to a height of 1 m, with yellow flowers. It is cultivated for its fleshy edible taproot; this is eaten as a vegetable and also fed to livestock. Family: *Cruciferae*.

Sweden, Kingdom of (Swedish name: Sverige) A country in N Europe occupying the E part of the Scandinavian peninsula. Undulating land in the S rises to mountains in the N. There are numerous lakes and forests. *Economy*: rich in mineral resources, notably iron ore, which forms the basis of the country's heavy industry and is a major export. The large forests support important pulp and paper industries. There is a thriving fishing industry. Agricultural activities are concentrated in the S. *History*: the area was inhabited from early times by German tribes, the Swedes in the N and the Goths in the S, and its people participated in the exploits of the Vikings. Christianity was introduced in the 9th century. Finland was acquired in the 13th century and the 14th century witnessed the Kalmar Union of Sweden with Denmark and Norway. Independence was achieved in 1523 under Gustavus I Vasa, during whose reign Lutheranism was introduced, and in the 17th century, under Gustavus Adolphus, Sweden emerged from the Thirty Years' War as a major European power, a position undermined by the Great Northern War (1700–21). In 1809, during the Napoleonic Wars, Finland was surrendered to Russia. In 1814 Norway was ceded to Sweden, the two countries remaining united until 1905. Sweden remained neutral in both World Wars, and has a highly developed welfare state. On the accession of Carl XVI Gustaf in 1975 a new constitution reduced the power of the monarchy. When the Social Democrat prime minister Olaf Palme was assassinated in 1986, Ingvar Carlsson (1934–) took his place. Official language: Swedish. Official currency: krona of 100 oere. Area: 411 479 sq km (158 830 sq mi). Population (1987): 8 387 000. Capital and main port: Stockholm.

Swedish A language belonging to the Scandinavian branch of the North Germanic group. It is the official language of Sweden and is spoken by a minority in Finland. The standard literary form is based mainly on the dialect of Stockholm.

sweet briar A stiffly branched prickly fragrant rose, *Rosa rubiginosa* (or *R. eglanteria*), also called eglantine. Found in scrub and chalk grassland across the N hemisphere, it grows to a height of 2 m and has bright-pink flowers.

sweet corn. *See* maize.

sweet pea An annual climbing herb, *Lathyrus odoratus*, native to Sicily and widely cultivated as a garden ornamental. Flower colours include shades of red, purple, blue, white, and yellow. Family: *Leguminosae*.

sweet potato An annual herb, *Ipomoea batatas*, native to tropical America and widely cultivated for its starchy edible tubers (swollen roots), which are reddish-brown with white or orange flesh. Family: *Convolvulaceae*.

sweetsop A small tree, *Annona squamosa*, also called sugar apple, native to tropical America and cultivated for its yellowish-green edible fruits. The yellow flesh is soft and sweet. Family: *Annonaceae*.

sweet william A usually biennial herb, *Dianthus barbatus*, native to S Europe and widely cultivated as a garden ornamental. Growing to a height of 30–70 cm, sweet williams produce flowers of red or pink in the wild but of various shades and patterns in cultivated varieties. Family: *Caryophyllaceae*.

swift A bird belonging to a widely distributed family (*Apodidae*; 75 species). 9–23 cm long, swifts have grey or brown plumage with white markings; a wide slightly curved bill, and forked tail. With scimitar-shaped wings and a high-speed flight they capture insects and even mate and sleep on the wing. Order: *Apodiformes* (swifts, hummingbirds, etc.).

Swift, Jonathan (1667–1745) Anglo-Irish clergyman, poet, and satirist. Born in Dublin, he recounted his life in London in *Journal to Stella* (1710–13). While in England, he wrote the satire *A Tale of a Tub* (1704). In 1714 he returned to Dublin, where he wrote his satirical masterpiece, *Gulliver's Travels* (1726).

swiftlet A small swift belonging to a genus (*Collocalia*; 15–20 species) occurring in SE Asia and Australia. 9–15 cm long, swiftlets use echolocation to navigate in the caves where they nest.

Swinburne, Algernon Charles (1837–1909) British poet. His poetry, especially in the first volume of *Poems and Ballads* (1866), is characterized by sensuous flowing rhythms and imagery. He supported republican movements in Europe and rebelled against conventional British morality.

Swindon 51 34N 1 47W A town in S England, in Wiltshire. It developed around the workshops of the former Great Western Railway. Industries include car manufacture. Population (1985 est): 129 300.

JONATHAN SWIFT *An illustration from* Gulliver's Travels.

swine fever An infectious virus disease of pigs. In young pigs the disease is usually acute, resulting in death. Animals are treated with antiserum and antibiotics to combat secondary infection. In the UK infected animals are slaughtered.

Swithin, St (d. 862) English churchman. He was appointed Bishop of Winchester in 852. His tomb in Winchester Cathedral has become a famous shrine and according to legend the weather conditions on his feast day, 15 July, continue for 40 days.

Switzerland, Confederation of (French name: Suisse; German name: Schweiz; Italian name: Svizzera) A small landlocked country in central Europe. Undulating land in the N rises to the Jura Mountains in the W and the Alps in the S. The majority of the population is German, with large French and Italian minorities. *Economy*: although lacking in mineral wealth, Switzerland owes much of its prosperity to its terrain and central European position. The latter has led to its development as a centre for trade, banking, and insurance, while the magnificent scenery has long been a major tourist attraction. The principal exports are machinery, watches, chemicals, and textiles. *History*: its Celtic inhabitants (the Helvetii) were conquered by the Romans in the 1st century BC and the region was overrun by German tribes in the 5th century AD, becoming part of the Holy Roman Empire in the 10th century. In 1291 Uri, Schwyz, and Nidwalden formed the Everlasting League, which is traditionally regarded as the origin of the Swiss Federation. By 1499 the Federation had achieved virtual independence and in the 16th century became an important centre of the Reformation. In 1648 its independence was formally recognized by the European powers. The French conquered Switzerland in 1798, but after Napoleon's fall (1815) the Congress of Vienna guaranteed Swiss neutrality. Religious conflict led to a modified constitution (1848) by which Switzerland became a unified federal state. It maintained its neutrality through both World Wars and has become the headquarters of many international organizations. Official languages: French, German, Italian, and Romansch. Official currency: Swiss franc of 100 centimes (*or* Rappen). Area: 41 288 sq km (15 941 sq mi). Population (1987): 6 586 000. Capital: Bern.

swordfish A food and game fish, *Xiphias gladius*, related to tuna and found in all tropical and temperate seas. It has an elongated body, up to 4.6 m long, a triangular front dorsal fin, no pelvic fins, and an elongated swordlike snout used to slash at shoaling fish on which it feeds. It is the only member of its family (*Xiphiidae*).

swordtail A tropical freshwater fish of the genus *Xiphophorus*, especially *X. helleri*. It has an elongated body, up to 13 cm long, and males have a long swordlike extension of the lower lobe of the tail fin. Swordtails are naturally green with a red strip on each side, but have been bred in many colours for aquaria. Family: *Poeciliidae*; order: *Atheriniformes*.

Sybaris 39 39N 16 20E A Greek settlement founded about 700 BC in S Italy. Sybarites were famous for their luxurious lives (hence the word sybaritic, meaning pleasure seeking). In 510 and again in 457 Sybaris was destroyed by its neighbour Croton.

sycamore A large maple tree, *Acer pseudoplatanus*, native to central and S Europe and widely grown elsewhere. Up to 30 m tall, it produces winged fruits. The wood is used for violin cases, carvings, and furniture.

SYDNEY *The Harbour Bridge with the Opera House in the background.*

Sydney 33 55S 151 10E The oldest and largest city in Australia, the capital of New South Wales, situated on Port Jackson inlet. It is a commercial, cultural, and financial centre. The N side of Port Jackson is predominantly residential, industry being located to the S. The two shores are connected by Sydney Harbour Bridge (1932), the second largest single span bridge in the world. Cultural centres include the Sydney Opera House (opened 1973). *History*: a penal settlement was established at Port Jackson in 1788. Under the governorship of Lachlan Macquarie (1810–21), it developed into a thriving town. Area: 1735 sq km (670 sq mi). Population (1986 est): 3 430 600.

syenite A range of coarse-grained intrusive rocks (*see* igneous rock) consisting mainly of alkali feldspar or feldspathoids, together with hornblende and biotite.

syllabaries Writing systems in which each symbol represents a syllable in the language rather than a concept (*compare* ideographic writing systems). The only major language using a syllabary today is Japanese.

symbiosis Any close relationship between individuals of two different species of organisms. The term can therefore include parasitism (*see* parasite), commensalism, and inquilinism but is often restricted to—and used synonymously with—**mutualism**, in which both partners (symbionts) benefit from the association. An example of such a symbiotic relationship is provided by a sea anemone (*Adamsia paliata*), which lives attached to the snail shell inhabited by the hermit crab (*Eupagurus prideauxii*). The anemone protects the crab, from which it receives food and transport.

symphonic poem (*or* tone poem) A one-movement orchestral composition based on a literary, dramatic, or pictorial theme. The symphonic poem was invented by Liszt, who composed a series of such works.

symphony An orchestral composition, usually in four movements. The classical symphony evolved in the mid-18th century and was perfected by Haydn and Mozart: the fast first movement was generally in sonata form, the second was slow and expressive, the third a minuet and trio, and the fourth fast. Beethoven extended the formal and emotional range of the symphony, introducing a chorus and soloists in the last movement of his ninth symphony. In the hands of such composers as Bruckner and Mahler the symphony underwent further enlargement: Mahler's eighth symphony (1907) requires a thousand performers. Sibelius developed a concentrated approach to symphonic writing: his seventh symphony (1924) is in one movement. Nielsen, Shostakovich, Vaughan Williams, and others have all developed the symphony in differing ways.

synagogue A Jewish place of worship. The synagogue probably originated during the Babylonian exile as a substitute for the Temple at Jerusalem. In antiquity it was a public meeting place, devoted mainly to the reading and exposition of the Torah. It is now primarily a house of prayer. The principal piece of furniture is the cupboard (Ark) containing the Torah scrolls.

synapse The meeting point between one nerve cell and another (*see* neurone). The nerve impulse, as it arrives at the end of one nerve process, causes a chemical neurotransmitter (e.g. acetylcholine or noradrenaline) to be released. This reaches receptors on the opposite neurone and produces a new nerve impulse.

synchrocyclotron A type of cyclotron in which the frequency of the accelerating electric field can be varied to compensate for the relativistic increase in the mass of the accelerated particles. This enables energies of up to 500 MeV to be obtained.

synchrotron A particle accelerator, similar to the cyclotron, in which protons or electrons are accelerated in a circular path by an alternating electric field. The frequency of the field is synchronized with the energy of the particles to counteract their relativistic increase in mass. Proton energies of several hundred GeV have been attained in these devices.

synchrotron radiation Electromagnetic radiation emitted in certain directions by a charged particle when the presence of a magnetic field confines its motion to a circle. The particle has to be moving at speeds comparable to that of light for a noticeable amount of radiation to be emitted. Therefore a high magnetic field is needed. Such fields are used in synchrotrons.

syncline A trough-shaped fold or downfold in folded rock strata, the strata dipping towards a central axis (*compare* anticline). The youngest rocks occur in the core unless very complex deformation has occurred.

Where the strata dip inwards from all directions the resulting structural feature is called a structural basin.

syndicalism A type of socialism, advocated by Sorel, under which the workers, not the state, would take over the productive resources of industry. Syndicalists were widely influential in Europe from the late 19th century until World War I.

Synge, John Millington (1871–1909) Anglo-Irish dramatist. Most of his plays, which contributed greatly to the Irish Literary Renaissance, were inspired by his experience of life in an isolated Irish community, recorded in *The Aran Islands* (1907). His best-known play, *The Playboy of the Western World* (1907), caused riots at its first performance.

synodic period The average time taken by a planet or satellite to return to the same point in its orbit, relative to the sun, as seen from earth or from the satellite's primary (i.e. the body it orbits). It is therefore the interval between oppositions or between identical phases.

synthesizer A device that can reproduce the sounds of conventional instruments electronically or produce a variety of artificial tones. Electronic oscillators produce a range of signals, which after amplification and appropriate filtering are converted to sound waves. Individual circuits can be plugged in and out by the player, enabling a wide range of sounds to be produced.

syphilis A sexually transmitted disease caused by the spirochaete bacterium *Treponema pallidum*. In primary syphilis chancres (hard ulcers) appear after about 25 days at the site of infection (usually the genitals). Weeks or months later the rash of secondary syphilis occurs. Arthritis, meningitis, and hepatitis may also occur at this stage. Without treatment the tertiary stage of syphilis may appear up to 30 years later and give rise to a variety of symptoms, including large tumour-like masses (gummas) in many organs, heart disease, blindness, and madness and paralysis. Syphilis can be treated with penicillin. The Wasserman test is one of many blood tests available for diagnosing the disease.

Syracuse (Italian name: Siracusa) 37 04N 15 18E A seaport in Italy, in SE Sicily. Founded by Greeks in 734 BC, it became an important cultural centre in the 5th century. In 212 BC Syracuse fell to the Romans after a three-year siege. Ancient remains include a Greek temple, a Roman amphitheatre, and a fortress. Population (1986): 160 750.

Syr Darya, River (ancient name: Jaxartes) A river in the S central Soviet Union, rising in the Tian Shan and flowing mainly W to the Aral Sea. Length: 2900 km (1800 mi).

Syria (official name: Syrian Arab Republic) A country in the Middle East, bordering on the Mediterranean Sea. In the W the Ghab depression runs N–S. To the E of this is steppe and desert with some mountains. The main fertile areas are the coastal strip and the basin of the River Euphrates (*see* Fertile Crescent). The population is predominantly Muslim (mainly Sunnites). *Economy*: largely agricultural. Natural resources include oil, natural gas, phosphates, and salt. Syria has a planned socialist economy; much of its industry is nationalized, and land has been redistributed in favour of the peasants. *History*: before the 20th century Syria, together with Palestine, extended over much of the Middle East. In ancient times the Amorites settled here and later Phoenicia flourished. Islam was introduced by conquering Arabs (c. 640 AD). Under Turkish control from the

11th century, it was the site of battles with the Crusaders. From 1517 until World War I it was part of the Ottoman Empire. In 1920 it became part of a French mandate. Demands for Syrian independence were finally satisfied in 1946. It united briefly with Egypt in the United Arab Republic (1958–61). In 1971 Syria, Libya, and Egypt united loosely in the Federation of Arab Republics. Syria intervened in Lebanon (1975–76), at first as a mediator but later as an active supporter of certain Muslim factions. Syria is a member of the Arab League. President: Lieut Gen Hafiz al-Assad (1928–   ). Prime minister: Mahmoud Zubi. Official language: Arabic. Official currency: Syrian pound of 100 piastres. Area: 185 680 sq km (71 772 sq mi). Population (1987): 10 969 000. Capital: Damascus.

Syriac   A Semitic language based on the dialect of Aramaic spoken in Edessa (now Urfa, SE Turkey). It became an important literary and liturgical language during the 3rd to the 7th centuries AD.

syringa.   *See* lilac; mock orange.

syrinx   The vocal organ of birds, located at the base of the windpipe. Air from the lungs vibrates membranes within a resonating chamber. Muscular tension alters pitch, and the two halves of the syrinx can produce different notes simultaneously.

Syros (Modern Greek name: Síros)   A Greek island in the S Aegean Sea. The chief town, Hermopolis, is the capital of the Cyclades. Area: 85 sq km (33 sq mi). Population (1981): 19 668.

systole.   *See* blood pressure; heart.

Szczecin (German name: Stettin)   53 25N 14 32E A city in the extreme NW of Poland, on the River Oder. It is a major port, the chief export being coal. *History*: it became a member of the Hanseatic League in 1360. Seized by the Swedes (1648) it passed to Prussia in 1720, remaining under German control until being ceded to Poland (1945). It suffered severe damage during World War II. Population (1985): 391 000.

Szilard, Leo   (1898–1964) US physicist, born in Hungary, who in 1934, while working in England, conceived the idea of a self-sustaining nuclear chain reaction. He joined Teller in persuading Einstein to write to Roosevelt to warn him of the possibility that Germany might make an atom bomb first. During World War II he actually worked on the atom bomb, but later pressed for the abolition of all nuclear weapons.

T

tabasco   A hot red pepper or sauce made from the entire fruits of a variety of the South American plant *Capsicum frutescens* and used to flavour soups, stews, curries, etc. Family: *Solanaceae*.

table tennis (*or* Ping-Pong)   An indoor game for two or four players that originated in England in the late 19th century from real tennis. It is played on a table 2.74 m (9 ft) long and 1.52 m (5 ft) wide, divided across its width by a net 15.25 cm (6 in) high. The players hit a resilient small hollow plastic ball with a rubber-faced wooden bat. A point is scored when the opponent fails to return the ball after it has bounced once. Each player serves five consecutive points and the winner of a game is the first to reach 21 points with at least a two-point lead.

Tabriz   38 05N 46 18E A city in NW Iran The most notable buildings are the Blue Mosque (15th century) and the citadel, and Tabriz is famous for its carpets; it is connected by rail to Tehran and the Soviet Union and has an airport. Population (1976): 598 576.

tachometer   An instrument for measuring the speed of rotation of a shaft, such as a revolution counter in a car. Centrifugal tachometers measure the force experienced by rotating masses. Others are electrical or magnetic, measuring electrical current or force generated by a small generator in the instrument.

Tacitus, Cornelius   (c. 55–c. 120 AD) Roman historian. He established his reputation as a public orator in Rome and became consul in 97 AD; in 112–13 he was governor of Asia. In 98 he wrote two historical monographs, *Germania* and *Agricola*, the latter an account of his father-in-law's career. His major works, the *Histories* and the *Annals*, survey Roman history during the periods 69–96 AD and 14–68 AD.

tadpole   The aquatic larva of frogs and toads. The newly hatched tadpole feeds on vegetation but later becomes carnivorous. The external gills of the young tadpole are gradually replaced by internal gills, and after about ten weeks the limbs start to appear, the tail degenerates, the lungs develop, and the circulatory system changes to enable the adult to lead a terrestrial life.

Tadzhiks   An Iranian people of Afghanistan and Soviet Turkistan. They are an agricultural people using irrigation to grow cereal crops and fruit trees. Trade has also been important traditionally because of their position on the caravan routes between China, India, and Persia. They speak a form of Persian and are Muslims.

Taegu   35 52N 128 36E A city in SE South Korea, the capital of North Kyongsang province. An old cultural centre, it has an important textile industry. Population (1980): 1 607 458.

Taft, William Howard   (1857–1930) US statesman; Republican president (1909–13). Taft's conservative presidency was characterized by antitrust legislation and high protective tariffs, which split the Republican vote and lost the 1912 election to the Democrats.

Tagore, Rabindranath   (1861–1941) Indian poet, philosopher, and teacher. Knighted in 1915, he resigned the honour in 1919 as a protest against the Amritsar massacre. He advocated cultural links between the East and the West and won the Nobel Prize for Literature in 1913 after the publication in English of *Gitanjali* (1912), a volume of spiritual poetry. His father **Debendranath Tagore** (1817–1905) established the "Abode of Peace," a retreat in Bengal made famous by his son as an educational centre.

Tagus, River (Portuguese name: Tejo; Spanish name: Tajo)   A river in SW Europe. Rising in E central Spain, it flows NW and then SW to the Atlantic Ocean at Lisbon. Length: 1007 km (626 mi).

Tahiti   The largest of the Society Islands in the S central Pacific Ocean, in French Polynesia. Mountainous and famous for its beauty, it was Gauguin's home for two years (1891–93). Settled by Polynesians in the 14th century, it was first visited by Europeans in 1767. It became French in 1842. Tourism is important, and copra, sugar cane, vanilla, and coffee are exported. Area: 1005 sq km (388 sq mi). Population (1983 est): 116 000. Chief town: Papeete.

Tai Peoples of SE Asia and China who speak a group of related languages probably belonging to the Sino-Tibetan family. They are traditionally rice cultivators and Theravada Buddhists Major groupings are the Thai or Siamese, the Lao, Shan, and Lu.

Taibei. *See* Taipei.

taiga The coniferous forests, composed chiefly of spruces, pines, and firs, in the N hemisphere in subpolar latitudes. It extends from Norway across Sweden, Finland, and the Soviet Union (including Siberia), in Eurasia. The coniferous forests of North America are also known as taiga.

tailorbird A S Asian warbler belonging to the genus *Orthotomus* (9 species), named after its habit of sewing the edges of a large leaf together to form a bag in which the nest is built.

Tainan 23 01N 120 14E A city in SW Taiwan. It is the island's former capital (1683–1891). Population (1985): 633 607.

taipan A small-headed cobra, *Oxyuranus scutellatus*, that occurs in NE Australia and New Guinea. Up to 3.3 m long, it has a ridged brown back and a yellow belly. Its venom contains a blood-clotting agent that is fatal within a few minutes.

Taipei (*or* Taibei) 25 00N 121 32E The capital of Taiwan, in the N of the island. Founded in the 18th century, it was under Japanese occupation (1895–1945) and became the seat of the Nationalist Government (*see* Guomindang) in 1949. Population (1985 est): 2 500 000.

Taiping Rebellion (1851–64) A peasant rebellion in China that seriously undermined the Qing dynasty. In 1851 a Hakka peasant, Hong Xiu Quan, raised an army of rebels and marched N, capturing Nanjing in 1853. They then marched on Peking but imperial forces, and cold weather, drove them back. When Nanjing fell, Hong and his followers committed mass suicide.

Taiwan (Republic of China) An island off the SE coast of mainland China. Together with several nearby islands, including the Penghu Islands and the islands of Jinmen and Mazu, it comprises the Republic of China. Taiwan Island is largely mountainous, and two-thirds of the land is under forest. The people are predominantly Chinese. *Economy*: in recent years the balance of the economy has shifted from agriculture to industry. Iron and steel are important and the large volume of exports also includes television and radio sets, mass-produced plastic goods, chemicals, textiles, sugar, and vegetables. As well as coal, gold, and other minerals, oil, and natural gas have been found, although timber remains the main natural resource. The chief crops are sugar cane, rice, and sweet potatoes. *History*: the island, named Formosa ("beautiful") by the Portuguese, who discovered it in 1590, was ceded by China to Japan in 1897. It surrendered to Gen Chiang Kai-shek in 1945. Following threats by the People's Republic of China the USA undertook in 1955 to protect Taiwan from outside attacks. However, Taiwan's importance in international affairs has diminished, and in 1979 the USA, on establishing diplomatic relations with mainland China, severed those

with Taiwan. Relations with China improved in the 1980s. President: Lee Teng-hui. Official language: Mandarin Chinese. Official currency: new Taiwan dollar of 100 cents. Area: 35 981 sq km (13 892 sq mi). Population (1987): 19 630 000. Capital: Taibei. Main port: Kaohsiung.

Taiyuan 37 50N 112 30E A city in NE China, the capital of Shanxi province. An ancient fortified city, it is a centre of technology, coalmining, and heavy industry. Population (1986): 1 880 000.

TAJ MAHAL *Over 20 000 workmen were employed in the building of the mausoleum (1631–53).*

Taj Mahal The mausoleum in Agra (N India) built (1631–53) for Mumtaz-i-Mahal, wife of the Mogul emperor, Shah Jahan, who is also buried here. Set in formal gardens, the Taj Mahal is built mainly of white marble, delicately carved and inlaid with precious stones.

Tajo, River. *See* Tagus, River.

Takao. *See* Gaoxiong.

talapoin The smallest guenon monkey, *Cercopithecus talapoin*, of central West Africa, also called pygmy guenon. Only 30 cm long, it has slightly webbed fingers and inhabits swampy forests. It has olive-green fur and conspicuously swollen genitals.

talaq An Islamic extra-judicial law of divorce enabling a husband to unilaterally divorce his wife by repudiating her three times. The marriage is then dissolved, unless the husband revokes the pronouncement during the next three months or, if the wife is pregnant, before the child is born.

talc A white or green mineral of hydrated magnesium silicate, $Mg_3(Si_4O_{10})(OH)_2$, with a layered structure. It is soft (hardness 1 on Mohs' scale) and greasy. Soapstone (steatite) is a rock consisting almost wholly of talc. Besides its use as talcum powder, it is used as a filler, lubricant, and soft abrasive.

Ta-lien. *See* Lüda.

talipot palm A palm tree, *Corypha umbraculifera*, cultivated in India and Burma. Its trunk bears fan-shaped leaves up to 5 m in diameter. The pyramid-shaped flower cluster, more than 7 m tall, is the largest in the plant kingdom. The seeds are used for buttons and ornaments and the leaves for matting, fans, and thatching.

Talleyrand (Charles Maurice de Talleyrand-Périgord; 1754–1838) French politician and diplomat. He was foreign minister from 1797 until 1807, and again under the restored Louis XVIII. He represented France at the Congress of Vienna and was ambassador to Great Britain (1830–34).

Tallinn (German name: Reval)   59 22N 24 48E A port in the NW Soviet Union, the capital of the Estonian SSR on Tallinn Bay in the Gulf of Finland. Its varied industries include shipbuilding. A member of the Hanseatic League, it was a prominent trading centre in the middle ages. It was independent Estonia's capital (1918–40). Population (1987): 478 000.

Tallis, Thomas   (c. 1505–85) English composer. He was joint organist of the Chapel Royal with his pupil Byrd. In 1575 he and Byrd produced *Cantiones Sacrae*, a collection of their motets. Tallis' most famous works are *The Lamentations of Jeremiah* and *Spem in Alium*.

Talmud   Two of the most important works of Jewish religious literature: the Babylonian and the Palestinian (or Jerusalem) Talmud. Both Talmuds have the same form: they are written in a mixture of Hebrew and Aramaic and are presented as a commentary (*gemara*) on the Mishnah. They contain records of rabbinic discussions, concentrating especially on halakhah. The rabbis mentioned in the Talmuds are called *Amoraim*; the Palestinian *Amoraim* flourished in the 3rd and 4th centuries AD; the Babylonian *Amoraim* continued to about 500.

tamandua   An insect-eating mammal, *Tamandua tetradactyla*, of Central and South American forests, also called lesser anteater. Almost 1 m long including the long prehensile tail, it is pale in colour and feeds on termites. Family: *Myrmecophagidae*; order: *Edentata*.

tamarin   A South American monkey found in open woodland and forests, closely related to marmosets. Tamarins have tusklike lower canine teeth and feed on fruit, insects, eggs, etc. Chief genera: *Leontocebus* (21 species), *Leontideus* (3 species); family: *Callithricidae*.

tamarind   An evergreen tree, *Tamarindus indica*, cultivated in tropical regions for its fruit. It bears clusters of yellow flowers. The fruit is a plump pod containing seeds and a bitter-sweet pulp, which is used in chutneys, curries, and medicines. Family: *Leguminosae*.

tamarisk   A tree or shrub belonging to the genus *Tamarix* (90 species), native to W and S Europe, central Asia, and India. Tamarisks have small scalelike leaves, feathery clusters of small pink flowers, and deep roots. They have been widely planted to stabilize sand dunes. *T. mannifera* of the Middle East and central Asia exudes a sweet white edible substance (manna) from the stems. The false tamarisks (genus *Myricaria*; 10 species) are native to temperate Eurasia. Family: *Tamaricaceae*.

Tambo, Oliver   (1917–   ) South African politician; president of the African National Congress (1977–   ). A lawyer, he was arrested with Nelson Mandela in 1956, but released a year later. Since 1960 he has directed ANC activities from outside South Africa.

Tamerlane.   *See* Timur.

Tamil   A Dravidian language of S India and Sri Lanka. It is the official language of the state of Tamil Nadu. There are several regional dialects. It is written in a script known as Vattelluttu and there are marked differences between the written and spoken forms. Tamil society, mainly Hindu, is stratified into caste groups.

Tampere   (Swedish name: Tammerfors)   61 32N 23 45E The second largest city in Finland. It has a 20th-century cathedral and a university (1925). Its manufactures include railway rolling stock, textiles, wood pulp, paper, and footwear. Population (1986): 169 994.

Tampico   22 18N 97 52W A port and winter resort in SE Mexico, on the Río Panuco. Oil refining is the chief industry. Population (1980): 267 957.

tanager   A brightly coloured songbird belonging to a family (*Thraupidae*; 222 species) occurring in tropical and subtropical America. Tanagers are 10–20 cm long, plumpish, with a short neck and a conical bill. They live mainly in forests and feed on fruit, nectar, and insects.

Tang   (or T'ang; 618–906 AD) A Chinese dynasty that established an empire extending over much of central Asia and Korea. In Tang times foreign trade was encouraged and many Chinese scientific inventions, such as gunpowder, spread to the West. Arts, especially poetry, flourished, printing was invented, and paper money was used for the first time. In 751 Arab forces recaptured Turkestan and the Tang empire began to disintegrate. Two rebellions finally led to the collapse of the dynasty.

Tanganyika.   *See* Tanzania, United Republic of.

Tanganyika, Lake   A lake in E central Africa, in Zaïre, Burundi, Tanzania, and Zambia. It is drained intermittently to the W by the River Lukuga. Area: about 33 000 sq km (12 738 sq mi).

tangerine   The fruit of a tree, *Citrus reticulata*, also called mandarin, native to SE Asia and cultivated in the S USA and the Mediterranean region. The orange fruit, which peels easily and readily splits into segments, is usually eaten fresh. Many varieties have been developed, including the satsuma and clementine.

Tangier   (or Tangiers)   35 48N 5 45W A port in N Morocco, on a bay on the Strait of Gibraltar. An important Roman town, it was established as an international zone in 1923. Its international status was abolished on Moroccan independence (1956). Its industries include cigarette and textile manufacture, fishing, and market gardening, and it is also a tourist centre. Population (1982): 266 346.

tank   An armour-plated military vehicle, self-propelled on caterpillar tracks and typically armed with a gun (usually turret-mounted) and machine guns. Tanks are classified as main battle tanks (MBTs), for independent operation, and light tanks, for reconnaissance and other specialized uses. Based on a design of Sir Ernest Swinton (1868–1951), they were first used during the Somme offensive in September, 1916. In World War II tank battles across Europe and N Africa replaced the static trench warfare of World War I. Modern tank development has concentrated on improving weapons, armour, and computer-aided navigation and fire control. See p. 700.

tanker   A seagoing vessel equipped with a large cargo tank for transporting liquids, especially oil. The forerunner of the modern tanker was built in 1885; modern **supertankers** with a carrying capacity of 75 000 tonnes were developed after World War II. Ultra-Large Crude Carriers (ULCCs) have deadweights of up to nearly half a million tonnes.

Tannhäuser   (c. 1200–c. 1270) German poet. A Minnesinger several of whose lyrics survive. Wagner's opera is based on the legend of his seduction by Venus, his life of sensuality at her court, and his pilgrimage to seek papal forgiveness.

tannin   (or tannic acid)   One of a group of phenol derivatives present in the bark, leaves, fruits, and galls of many plants. Tannins are used as mordants for many dyes, in tanning leather, and in making ink.

TANK

Mark IV British *Tanks were first successfully used during World War I in the battle of Cambrai in November, 1917. They were designed to be able to cross trenches.*

German Pz III *At the beginning of World War II the German Panzer divisions were based on Pz III tanks, armed with a 50-mm gun and having a maximum speed of 30 mph (48 km per hour).*

Soviet T-34 *The Nazi invasion of the Soviet Union (1941) met resistance from the T-34, then probably the best design in the world. It had a 76.2-mm gun and a top speed of 32 mph (51 km per hour).*

US M-4 *A US design used extensively in World War II was the M-4, known as the "General Sherman." Introduced in 1942, it had a 75-mm gun and a top speed of 24 mph (38 km per hour).*

Soviet T-54 *This main battle tank, with its 100-mm gun, effective use of armour, and road speed of 34 mph (54 km per hour) was the most advanced tank in the world when it appeared in 1954.*

British Challenger *Introduced during the 1980s, this main battle tank is heavily armed with a 120-mm gun, has a top speed of 35 mph (56 km per hour), and is protected by Chobham armour.*

tansy A perennial herb, *Tanacetum* (or *Chrysanthemum*) *vulgare*, native to temperate Eurasia. It has flat-topped clusters of yellow flowers and was formerly cultivated for its aromatic leaves, used for cooking and medicinal purposes. Family: *Compositae*.

tantalum (Ta) A very hard grey dense metallic element, discovered in 1802 by A. K. Ekeberg (1767–1813). It is similar to niobium (Nb) and is difficult to separate from it. Tantalum occurs naturally in the ore columbite ($Fe(Nb,Ta)_2O_6$). It is resistant to chemical attack and is used in alloys, for example in surgical materials for implantation in the body and in incandescent filaments. The oxide (Ta_2O_5) is used in special glass, with high refractive index, for camera lenses. At no 73; at wt 180.948; mp 2996°C; bp 5425 ±100°C.

Tantalus A legendary Greek king of Lydia, son of Zeus and Pluto and father of Niobe and Pelops. In Hades he was punished for certain offences against the gods by being made to stand within reach of water and fruits that moved away whenever he tried to drink or eat.

Tantras A group of Sanskrit religious texts written in India in the 5th century AD. They form the basis of esoteric systems of meditation in both Hinduism and Buddhism. In the **Tantric yoga** of Hinduism, two principles are postulated: Shiva and Shakti, male and female, mind and creative energy. The object of tantric practices is to arouse the female element and ultimately to unite it with the male principle. **Tantric Buddhism** involves an elaborate system of meditation by means of mudras (gestures), mantras (symbolic sounds, and mandalas (diagrams). The imagery of sexual union is the distinctive feature of both systems.

Tanzania, United Republic of A country in East Africa, on the Indian Ocean. It consists of a mainland area (formerly the republic of Tanganyika) and the islands of Zanzibar and Pemba, as well as some smaller islands. The land rises from the coast through plateaus to mountains, especially in the N, with Mount Kilimanjaro at 5950 m (19 520 ft). The majority of the population is African, mainly of Bantu origin. *Economy*: chiefly agricultural, especially subsistence farming. In mainland Tanzania the chief crops are cotton, maize, and cassava. Zanzibar (with Pemba) is the world's largest producer of cloves, with coconuts as the second cash crop. Food crops include rice, bananas, and cassava. Minerals extracted in Tanzania include diamonds, gold, tin, and salt, and coal and iron have been found, as well as offshore gas. The main exports are coffee, cloves, cotton, and diamonds. *History*: important prehistoric remains have been found by the Leakey family. Tanganyika was occupied by the Germans in the 1880s, becoming a German protectorate in 1891. After World War I it was under British rule. It gained independence in 1961 and in 1962 became a republic within the British Commonwealth with Dr Julius K. Nyerere as its first president. In 1964 Tanganyika and Zanzibar joined to form the United Republic of Tanganyika and Zanzibar, now known as Tanzania. In 1967 Nyerere launched a policy of decentralization, which has involved the division of rural areas into cooperative communities (Ujamaas). President: Ali Hassan Mwinyi. Official languages: Swahili and English. Official currency, since 1966: Tanzanian shilling of 100 cents. Area: 945 087 sq km (364 900 sq mi). Population (1987 est): 23 200 000. Capital: Dodoma. Main port: Dar es Salaam.

Taoism Emerging in the 6th century BC, Taoism is one of the two great native Chinese religio-philosophical systems (the other is Confucianism) and a major influence in the development of Chinese culture. The goal of Taoism as a philosophy is joyful, mystical, and practical harmony with the universe. *Yin* (the feminine) balances *yang* (the masculine). *Te* (virtue) and *Ch'i* (energy) represent the power of effortless action accessible to the Taoist. Taoism emphasizes breath control, diet, exercises, sexual continence, and chemical elixirs as a means of achieving immortality. Since the Chinese Cultural Revolution (1966–68) religious Taoism survives mainly in Taiwan. Western interest has been aroused by philosophical Taoism, especially by the *I Ching*, which claims to demonstrate purpose in chance events.

tape recorder A device for recording and playing back sound stored on magnetic tape, which is usually wound into cassettes or cartridges. In recording, the sound is converted to an electrical signal by a microphone, amplified, then fed to an electromagnet in the recording head. The varying field of the magnet leaves a pattern of magnetization in the iron (or sometimes chromium) oxide coating of the tape. To play back, the magnetized tape induces a current in a coil as it passes the reproducing head. The coil current is then amplified and fed to loudspeakers.

tapeworm A parasitic hermaphrodite flatworm of the class *Cestoda* (about 3000 species). Tapeworms range from 20 mm to 15 m in length and anchor themselves inside the intestine of their host by means of hooks and suckers on the head. The body consists of a chain of progressively large segments through which food is absorbed. The terminal segments—full of eggs—are regularly shed, passing out of the host's body to infect a secondary host, where larvae invade muscle tissue. Species infecting man include the beef tapeworm (*Taenia saginata*) and the pork tapeworm (*T. solium*).

tapioca. *See* cassava.

tapir A shy nocturnal hoofed mammal belonging to the genus *Tapirus* (4 species). The largest species is the black and white Malayan tapir (*T. indicus*), reaching about 1 m at the shoulder and weighing up to 350 kg. Other species are brown. All have a large head with a short fleshy snout. Young tapirs are marked with white spots and stripes. Tapirs inhabit forests near water, feeding on leaves and shoots. Family: *Tapiridae*; order: *Perissodactyla*.

tar A thick black semisolid substance of organic origin, especially coaltar obtained when coal is heated to over 1000°C in the absence of air (1 kg of coal yielding about 50 g of tar). Tar can be used as it is, or can be distilled to produce a wide range of organic chemicals including benzene, naphthalene, and anthracene and their derivatives. The substance remaining is called pitch.

Tara 53 34N 6 35W A village in the Republic of Ireland, in Co Meath. The Hill of Tara was the ancient religious and political centre of Ireland and here the early Irish Kings lived and were crowned.

tarantula A large dark hairy spider (up to 75 mm long) of the family *Theraphosidae*, found in tropical America. Many tarantulas live on trees or in burrows in the soil, feeding mainly at night on insects and occasionally frogs, toads, mice, and small birds. Their poisonous bite is painful but not fatal to man. The name was originally given to a wolf spider (*Lycosa tarentula*) of Taranto (Italy).

taro A perennial herbaceous plant, *Colocasia esculenta*, also known as eddo, dasheen, and elephant's ear, native to tropical Asia and widely cultivated in tropical and subtropical areas for its edible tubers. The tubers, which are large, starchy, and spherical, contain more protein than potatoes and are eaten cooked as vegetables or made into puddings or bread. Family: *Araceae*.

TAROT *The Wheel of Fortune, the 10th card of the Greater Arcana, from a pack of French tarot cards.*

tarot A pack of 78 cards used primarily in fortune telling, although they are also the forerunners of modern playing cards. They originated in 14th-century Italy. The original pack is now known as the Greater Arcana; this consists of 22 cards (believed to correspond to the letters of the Hebrew alphabet), 21 numbered cards representing natural elements, vices, and virtues and a "Fool" (the original joker). During the 14th century these were combined with 56 number cards, now known as the Lesser Arcana, in 4 suits: cups, swords, money, and clubs or rods, representing clergy, nobility, merchants, and peasants. Each suit consists of number cards from one to ten and four court cards: king, queen, knave, and knight.

Tarquin the Proud (Tarquinius Superbus) The last King of Rome, who ruled, according to Roman tradition, from 534 to 510 BC. Tarquin is probably a historical figure but many myths evolved to account for the nickname Superbus.

tarragon A perennial herb, *Artemisia dracunculus*, native to central Asia and widely cultivated. It has slender leaves and flowers, which are often dried and used in salads, sauces, pickles, etc. It also yields an essential oil used in cooking and perfumery. Family: *Compositae*.

tarsier A small nocturnal prosimian primate belonging to the genus *Tarsius* (3 species), of Sumatra, Borneo, Celebes, and the Philippines. 22–43 cm long including the naked tail (13–27 cm), tarsiers have enormous eyes, large hairless ears, and gripping pads at the end of their digits. They are mainly arboreal. Family: *Tarsiidae*.

Tarsus 36 52N 34 52E A town in central S Turkey, near Adana. The first known settlement here was Neolithic; it was Assyrian for many centuries and an important town in the Roman and Byzantine Empires. St Paul was born here. Population (1980): 121 074.

tartan. *See* Highland dress.

Tashkent 41 16N 69 13E A city in the S central Soviet Union, the capital of the Uzbek SSR. It is the oldest and largest city of central Asia, being a major communications, industrial, and cultural centre. Textiles, food- and tobacco-processing, and chemical industries are important. *History*: dating from at least the 1st century BC, it fell successively to the Arabs (7th century) and the Turks (12th century). It was captured by Russia in 1865. Population (1987): 2 124 000.

Tasmania An island and the smallest state of Australia, separated from the SE corner of the mainland by Bass Strait. Discovered by the Dutch navigator Abel Tasman (c. 1603–c. 1659) in 1642, it was called Van Dieman's Land, after Tasman's patron, until 1856. Agriculture is important with mixed and dairy farming, sheep rearing, and the cultivation of apples and hops. More than 40% of the island is covered by forest and the export of wood chips to Japan is a significant industry. Large mineral deposits include tin, iron ore, zinc, lead, and copper. Area: 68 332 sq km (26 383 sq mi). Population (1985): 442 111. Capital: Hobart.

Tasmanian devil A carnivorous marsupial, *Sarcophilus harrisi*, now restricted to Tasmania. About 1 m long, it is black with a large head and wide jaws containing doglike teeth. Strong and heavily built, it feeds on wallabies, birds, and lizards and fights ferociously when cornered. Family: *Dasyuridae* (dasyures).

Tasmanian wolf. *See* thylacine.

Tasman Sea A section of the SW Pacific Ocean, lying between SE Australia and Tasmania on the W and New Zealand on the E. Area: about 2 300 000 sq km (900 000 sq mi).

taste. *See* tongue.

Tatars A mainly Muslim people, mainly living in the Tatar ASSR of the Soviet Union, who belong to the NW division of the Turkic-speaking peoples. They traditionally lived by farming and herding. The Tatars are descended from peoples associated with the Mongol empire and the name was often used to refer to all the nomadic Turkic and Mongol peoples of the steppes.

Tate Gallery An art gallery on Millbank, London, housing paintings of the British school and modern foreign paintings and sculpture. It was built in 1897 with the financial support of the sugar merchant and philanthropist Sir Henry Tate (1819–99). Highlights are its Pre-Raphaelite works and paintings by Turner. A new Tate Gallery was opened in Liverpool in 1988.

Tatra Mountains Two mountain ranges in central E Europe: the **High Tatras**, which extend 90 km (56 mi) E–W along the Polish-Czech border and constitute the highest area of the Carpathian Mountains, and, to the S, the **Low Tatras**, which run parallel for some 150 km (93 mi) and rise to 2043 m (6703 ft).

Taunton 51 01N 3 06W A market town in SW England, the administrative centre of Somerset. The Great Hall in the 12th-century castle was the scene of Judge Jeffreys' Bloody Assizes (1685). Textile and leather goods, gloves, aeronautical instruments, and cider are manufactured. Population (1987 est): 53 285.

Taupo, Lake (*or* Taupomoana) The largest lake in New Zealand. It lies on the volcanic plateau of central North Island and is drained by the Waikato River. Area: 616 sq km (238 sq mi).

tautomerism. *See* isomers.

Tavener, John (1944–) British composer, a pupil of Lennox Berkeley. His compositions include the cantata *The Whale* (for reciter, chorus, and orchestra; 1966), *A Celtic Requiem* (1968–69), and the opera *Thérèse* (1979).

Taverner, John (c. 1495–1545) English composer. He became choirmaster at Cardinal College (later renamed Christ Church) Oxford, in 1526. In 1528 he was imprisoned for heresy and left Oxford in 1530. He became a paid agent of Thomas Cromwell and gave up music. He left 28 motets, a *Te Deum*, 8 masses, and some instrumental music.

tawny owl A common owl, *Strix aluco*, occurring in Europe and SE Asia. It has short rounded wings, dark-brown eyes, a mottled brown plumage, and lacks ear tufts.

taxidermy The art of making lifelike zoological models of creatures by preserving their skins and mounting them on suitable dummies. Taxidermy dates from the 17th century; improved technology and the use of plastic body forms have resulted in greater degrees of realism.

taxis The movement of a living organism or cell in response to an external stimulus: the movement is either towards or away from the stimulus, i.e. a positive or negative taxis. **Chemotaxis** is the response to a change in the concentration of a chemical. Many insects, for example, respond chemotactically to the scents emitted by the opposite sex. **Phototaxis** is the response to light: cockroaches are negatively phototactic. *Compare* tropism.

taxonomy The study of the classification and nomenclature of organisms. The principles of taxonomy were established in the 18th century by the work of Linnaeus (*see also* binomial nomenclature). As far as possible, organisms are arranged into a hierarchy of groups (called taxa) based on degrees of relationship (*see* phylogeny). When knowledge of the evolution of a group is lacking, taxonomy is based on structural and other similarities. The basic unit of classification is the species. Related species are grouped into genera, which are arranged into orders and then classes, and finally phyla.

Tay, River The longest river in Scotland, rising in the Grampian Mountains and flowing through Loch Tay. It enters the North Sea through the Firth of Tay. Length: 193 km (120 mi).

Taylor, Elizabeth (1932–) US film actress, born in England. She began her career as a child star, notably in *National Velvet* (1944). Her other films include *Cleopatra* (1962) and *Who's Afraid of Virginia Woolf?* (1966), in both of which she costarred with Richard Burton, to whom she was twice married.

Taylor, Zachary (1784–1850) US statesman and general; president (1849–50). In the Mexican War

(1846–48), he won the victory of Buena Vista although his forces were outnumbered by four to one.

Tayside Region An administrative region in SE Scotland, bordering on the North Sea. It was created under local government reorganization in 1975 from the counties of Angus, most of Perth, and Kinross. The SE lowlands rise NW to the Grampian Mountains. Agricultural produce includes arable crops and soft fruit; dairy and beef cattle are important. Industries include wool products and engineering. Area: 7668 sq km (2959 sq mi). Population (1986): 392 346. Administrative centre: Dundee.

Tbilisi (former name: Tiflis) 41 43N 44 48E A city in the SW Soviet Union, the capital of the Georgian SSR on the River Kura. Engineering and the manufacture of textiles, wine, and food are the principal economic activities. *History*: founded in the mid-5th century, it fell successively to the Persians, Byzantines, Arabs, Mongols, Turks, and, finally, the Russians (1801). Population (1987): 1 194 000.

TCHAIKOVSKY

Tchaikovsky, Peter Ilich (1840–93) Russian composer. He became professor at the Moscow conservatoire in 1866. After the success of his first piano concerto, Tchaikovsky was offered financial support from Nadezhda von Meck (1831–94), a wealthy widow, whom he never met. Among his compositions are six symphonies, including the *Pathétique* (1893), three piano concertos (one unfinished), a violin concerto, string quartets, the opera *Eugene Onegin* (1877–78), and the ballets *Swan Lake* (1876–77) and the *Nutcracker* (1891–92).

tea The dried leaves and shoots of the evergreen shrub or tree, *Camellia sinensis*, which yield a beverage when infused with water. Native to parts of India and China, the tea plant has three major varieties—China, Assam, and Cambodia—and numerous hybrids. The shoots and young leaves are picked by hand and left to wilt before being lightly rolled and dried. The major tea exporters are India and Sri Lanka; most of China's production goes for home consumption. Tea is usually sold in the form of chopped leaves—loose or contained in small porous paper bags (tea bags). Its stimulating effect is due to the caffeine content (about 3.5%); flavour depends on the presence of volatile oils, and tannins are responsible for its colour. Family: *Theaceae*.

teak A tropical tree, *Tectonia grandis*, native to SE Asia and cultivated for its timber. It has small white flowers and fleshy fruits. The aromatic golden-yellow heartwood becomes brown when seasoned and is very hard and durable, being used for furniture, door and window frames, etc. Burma is the major teak exporter. Family: *Verbenaceae*.

teal A small dabbling duck, *Anas crecca*, of the N hemisphere, nesting on marshes and wintering on mud-flats and estuaries. It feeds on water plants and aquatic invertebrates. Drakes are grey and have a chestnut head and a white wing stripe; females are mottled brown and both sexes have a green-and-black wing patch.

tear gas (*or* lachrymator) A substance, generally an atomized liquid rather than a gas, that is used to control crowds by causing acute eye irritation with temporary blindness and copious flow of tears. Chloroacetophenone (Mace) is the best-known example. *See also* chemical warfare.

teasel A biennial herb, *Dipsacus fullonum*, native to Europe, W Asia, and N Africa. The prickly stems grow to a height of 2 m and bear conical heads of blue, purple, or white flowers with stiff hooked bracts. The flower heads of fuller's teasel (*D. fullonum sativus*) were formerly used to tease fabrics. Family: *Dipsacaceae*.

Tebbitt, Norman (Beresford) (1931–) British Conservative politician; chairman of the Conservative Party and Chancellor of the Duchy of Lancaster (1985–87). He served in several ministerial posts, including secretary of state for employment (1981–83) and trade and industry (1983–85).

technetium (Tc) A silvery-grey radioactive element that was the first to be produced artificially. It does not occur naturally on earth but has been observed spectroscopically in a number of stars. It is chemically similar to rhenium and the compound $KTcO_4$ is a remarkable corrosion inhibitor in steels. At no 43; at wt (99); mp 2227°C; bp 4627°C.

tectonics The study of the major structural features of the earth's crust and the processes by which they are constructed. *See also* plate tectonics.

Tedder, Arthur William, 1st Baron (1890–1967) British air marshal. He joined the Royal Flying Corps in 1916. In World War II he was appointed (1940) to command the RAF in the Middle East and then (1943) in the Mediterranean. He became Eisenhower's deputy in 1944 and contributed to the success of the Normandy landings.

Tees, River A river in N England. Rising in the Pennines in Cumbria, it join the North Sea in the Teesmouth estuary at Middlesbrough. **Teesside** is an industrial district on the estuary. Length: 113 km (70 mi).

teeth Hard structures in the mouth, embedded in the jaws, used for biting and chewing food. The human adult (permanent) dentition consists of 32 teeth, including incisors (8), canines (4), premolars (8), and molars (12), which replaces the milk (deciduous) dentition of young children. The third molars (wisdom teeth) do not normally appear until the age of about 20. The crown of a tooth consists of very dense hard enamel (largely apatite) overlying the yellow bonelike dentine, which is slightly spongy and very sensitive to touch, temperature, and pain. The pulp at the centre contains blood vessels and nerve fibres. *See also* dentistry.

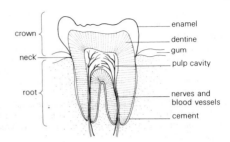

molar tooth *The root of the tooth is anchored into the socket by a bonelike substance, cement.*

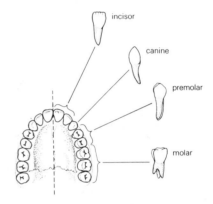

teeth in the adult upper jaw *The incisors and canines are used principally for biting; the premolars and molars are for grinding and chewing. The lower jaw contains the same number and type of teeth.*

TEETH

Tegucigalpa 14 20N 87 12W The capital of Honduras, situated in the centre of the country in a high valley. Founded in 1579, it was an important centre of gold and silver mining. It became the capital in 1824. Population (1985): 571 400.

Tehran (*or* Teheran) 35 40N 51 26E The capital of Iran, in the N centre of the country at the foot of the Elburz Mountains. Tehran is the commercial, industrial, administrative, and cultural centre of the country, with six universities (oldest 1934). It became the capital in 1788 and has been greatly enlarged this century. Population (1986): 6 022 078.

Tehran Conference (1943) The conference in World War II attended by F. D. Roosevelt (USA), Stalin (Soviet Union), and Churchill (UK). Its chief purpose was to coordinate Allied strategy in W and E Europe.

Teilhard de Chardin, Pierre (1881–1955) French Jesuit theologian and palaeontologist. His philosophical books were suppressed by the Roman Catholic Church during his lifetime. In *The Phenomenon of Man* (1955) and *Le Milieu divin* (1957), he maintained that the universe and mankind are in constant evolution towards a perfect state.

Tejo, River. *See* Tagus, River.

Tė Kanawa, Dame Kiri (1944–) New Zealand soprano. She made her major debut in the *Marriage of Figaro* at Covent Garden in 1971. She was made a DBE in 1982.

tektites Small glassy objects, which have been found in certain parts of the earth, often stewn over immense areas. They are apparently composed of rapidly cooled molten material, probably terrestrial in origin and formed during the impact of giant meteorites.

Tel Aviv-Jaffa 32 05N 34 46E A city in central Israel, on the Mediterranean coast. It is the largest city in Israel, and the country's commercial, industrial, and cultural centre. The city's port is at Ashdod, to the S. *History*: Tel Aviv was originally a suburb to the N of Jaffa, founded in 1909 to relieve the overpopulation of ·the Jewish quarter. Following tension between Arabs and Jews, the two towns were separated in 1921. Almost the entire Arab population fled Jaffa on its capture by Jewish forces in 1948, and the two cities were reunited in 1950. Population (1986): 320 300.

telekinesis Apparent change in or movement of material objects, caused by mental effort alone. It is also called psychokinesis (PK). Telekinesis has been evoked to explain levitation and certain poltergeist manifestations.

Telemann, Georg Philipp (1681–1767) German composer. Whilst studying law at Leipzig University he taught himself to play various instruments and to compose. He held musical posts in various cities, including Frankfurt and Hamburg (1721). His output was very large and included operas, oratorios, church music, and .much chamber music.

teleost Any bony fish belonging to the infraclass *Teleostei* (over 20 000 species), which includes nearly all the important food and game fish and many aquarium fish. Teleosts have a symmetrically divided (homocercal) tail fin and an air-filled swim bladder. Most lay eggs on rocks or plants, or freely in the water, although some bear live young. Chief orders: *Clupeiformes* (*see* herring; anchovy), *Salmoniformes* (*see* salmon; trout; pike), *Cypriniformes* (*see* carp), *Gadiformes* (*see* cod; hake), *Perciformes* (*see* perch; mackerel), *Pleuronectiformes* (*see* flatfish); subclass: *Actinopterygii*.

telepathy. *See* extrasensory perception.

telescope An optical instrument that produces a magnified image of distant objects.
.The **refracting telescope** was invented in 1608 by Lippershey in Holland and developed by Galileo as an astronomical instrument a year later. The light in the refracting telescope falls on a converging long-focus .objective lens. The resulting image is then magnified by the short-focus eyepiece to produce the final image. An example is the **Keplerian telescope**. Refractors are also used as terrestrial telescopes, usually containing an additional lens or a prism to cause the inverted image to be seen erect. The first **reflecting telescope** was produced by Newton in 1668. In the reflecting telescope the light from an object is collected by a concave, usually paraboloid, mirror of long focal length. This primary mirror reflects the lights into a secondary optical system, which in turn reflects it into a short-focus eyepice. The eyepiece 'lenses produce a magnified image that can be viewed or photographed. Depending on the secondary optics, reflectors are called **Gregorian, Newtonian, Cassegrain,** or

refractors

Galilean *The simplest practical form of refracting telescope was developed by Galileo in about 1609 from Lippershey's invention.*

Keplerian *Kepler's arrangement produces an inverted image but was much used for astronomical observations in which the inversion did not matter.*

reflectors

Gregorian *James Gregory proposed this design in 1663 but it has had little general application.*

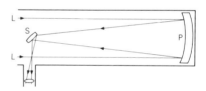

Newtonian *In Newton's 1671 design the secondary mirror is placed at an angle of 45° to the axis of the beam.*

Cassegrain *Widely used, this form was invented by the obscure French astronomer N. Cassegrain in 1672.*

coudé (French: angled) *This arrangement is valuable in larger telescopes as it increases their focal length.*

L = *light rays* P = *primary mirror*
E = *eyepiece* S = *secondary mirror*

TELESCOPE

coudé telescopes. *See also* Schmidt telescope; radio telescope.

teletext An information service in which pages of text are transmitted together with normal television broadcasts for display on a modified domestic television set. The system utilizes two of the unused lines between picture frames. All the stored information, which may be weather reports, news flashes, sports results, etc., is sent ·out continuously in a cycle. The required pages are selected for display by keyboard. The two systems in use in the UK are **Ceefax**, run by the BBC, and **Oracle**, run by the Independent Broadcasting Authority. *See also* viewdata.

television (TV) The broadcasting of pictures and sound by radio waves or electric cable. Television was invented by John Logie Baird in 1926. A television camera converts the picture into an electrical signal. In most of Europe the picture consists of 625 lines made by an electron beam scanning the screen of a cathode-ray tube, 25 such pictures being formed every second. A brightness signal and a synchronization signal (to form the lines and frames of the picture) make up the picture signal, which is used to modulate (*see* modulation) a VHF or UHF carrier wave and is broadcast with the modulated sound carrier wave (which has a slightly different frequency). In colour TV, a colour signal has to be added to the picture signal.

The aerial or dish (for satellite broadcasts) of the TV receiver detects the broadcast radio waves and the picture and sound signals are separated within the receiver. The picture signal is demodulated, and the resulting current is used to control the electron beam in a cathode-ray tube so that the picture is reconstructed.

In a **colour television** camera light from the scene to be televised is filtered into three primary colour components: red, green, and blue. Light of each colour goes to a separate image tube. There are three systems in use for encoding colour picture information for transmission, all of which combine colour and intensity information with sound and synchronization in a similar way to black-and-white television. The colour television receiv-

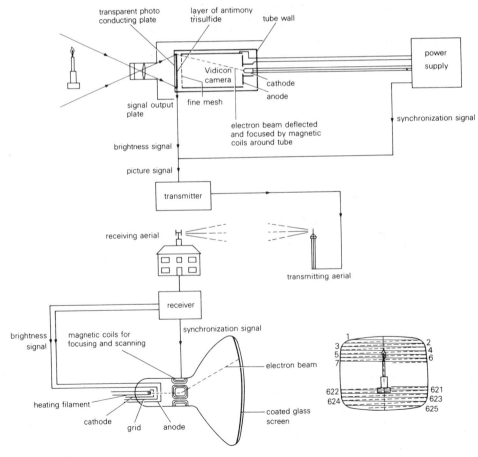

TELEVISION

er splits the signal into red, green, and blue components and applies these to three separate electron guns. The beam from each gun activates a set of phosphor dots of that colour on the screen, thus reconstructing the red, green, and blue components of the picture.

TEMPLARS *Being burnt at the stake, from a 14th-century manuscript.*

Telex A telegraphy system using telephone lines to transmit printed messages from one terminal (the teleprinter) to another. The message is typed onto a keyboard transmitter, which converts the characters into a coded electrical signal for transmission. A printing receiver carries out the reverse process, typing out messages as they arrive. The system is extensively used by commercial and other organizations.

Telford, Thomas (1757–1834) British civil engineer. His suspension bridge over the Menai Strait, completed in 1825, is 177 metres long. Telford also designed some 1500 kilometres of roads, many bridges and aqueducts, and canals. He also designed St Katherine's Dock in London.

Tell, William A Swiss national hero who is first mentioned in a 15th-century chronicle and who, in Schiller's play *Wilhelm Tell* (1804), embodies the Swiss struggle for independence from the Austrian Habsburgs. After refusing to do homage as required by Gessler, the Austrian governor, Tell was ordered to shoot an apple from his son's head with a crossbow at 80 paces. He passed this test and later killed Gessler.

Teller, Edward (1908–) US physicist, born in Hungary. He worked on the fission bomb during World War II and subsequently on the fusion bomb, making a significant contribution to its development. Teller's unfavourable evidence in the Robert Oppenheimer security-clearance hearing lost him some respect amongst scientists.

tellurium (Te) A silvery-white semiconductor of the sulphur group, discovered by Müller von Reichenstein in 1782. The hydride (H_2Te) is volatile and toxic, with a powerful smell of bad eggs. Bismuth telluride (BiTe) is used as an effective thermoelectric cooler. The metal is used in some special alloys and in some semiconducting devices. At no 52; at wt 127.60; mp 449.5 ± 0.3°C; bp 989 ± 3°C.

Telstar. *See* communications satellite.

temperature A physical quantity that is a measure of the average kinetic energy of the constituent particles of a body. It determines the direction in which heat flows when two bodies are in contact, the body with the higher temperature losing heat to that with the lower. The temperature of a body is measured in kelvins, degrees Celsius, or degrees Fahrenheit.

Templars (Poor Knights of Christ and of the Temple of Solomon) A religious order of knighthood founded (c. 1120) in Jerusalem by a group of French knights. The Templars were, with the Hospitallers, the most important military order of the Crusades. Accused of heresy and immorality by Philip IV of France, the Templars were suppressed by the papacy in 1312.

Temple, Shirley (1928–) US film actress. She featured as a child star in many films during the 1930s, including *Little Miss Marker* (1934) and *Heidi* (1937). She won a special Academy Award in 1934. During the 1960s she went into politics and was appointed US ambassador to Ghana in 1974 and to Czechoslovakia in 1989 under her married name, Shirley Temple Black.

Temple of Jerusalem The ancient centre of Jewish religious life. The first Temple was built by King Solomon (c. 950 BC) and destroyed by Nebuchadnezzar in 586 BC. The second Temple was built later in the 6th century BC, restored by the Maccabees and later by Herod the Great, and destroyed by the Romans in 70 AD. An attempt was made to rebuild the Temple under the Roman emperor Julian (362 AD) but it was abandoned. Both temples were built on the same walled platform, known as the Temple Mount; part of the western retaining wall of this structure is the **Western (Wailing) Wall**, still a holy site for Jews. Since 691 AD the Muslim Dome of the Rock has stood on the Temple Mount.

tench An elongated fish, *Tinca tinca*, that is related to carp and occurs in European fresh waters. Its slimy body is greenish or blackish above with lighter undersides. It lives in quiet waters that are rich in vegetation, feeding on small animals and plants.

tendon A strong fibrous cord that joins a muscle to a bone. The tendon fibres merge with the muscle fibres

SHIRLEY TEMPLE *In* Rebecca of Sunnybrook Farm *(1938).* .

TENNIEL   The Mad Hatter's Tea Party *from* Alice in Wonderland.

and extend to the fibrous tissue lining the bone, serving to concentrate the pull of the muscle on a small part of the bone.

Tenerife   28 15N 16 35W A Spanish island in the Atlantic Ocean, the largest of the Canary Islands. Its Pico de Teide mountain is, at 3710 m (12 172 ft), the highest in Spain. Early fruit and vegetables are produced and the island is popular for holidays. Area: 2020 sq km (780 sq mi). Population (1981): 688 273. Chief town: Santa Cruz de Tenerife.

Teniers the Younger, David   (1610–90) Flemish painter. Known chiefly for his peasant scenes, he also made historically valuable copies of the paintings in the collection of Archduke Leopold Wilhelm, whose court painter he became in Brussels in 1651. His father **David Teniers the Elder** (1582–1649) was a painter of religious subjects.

Ten Lost Tribes of Israel   *See* tribes of Israel.

Tennessee   A state in the S central USA. In the E there is an upland region of thickly wooded mountains and in Middle Tennessee an area of upland plateau and rolling hills gives way in the W to an area of lowland plains and swamps situated between the Tennessee and Mississippi Rivers. An agriculturally poor state, its major crops are tobacco, soya beans, and cotton. Beef and dairy products are also important. The leading industries produce chemicals, food products, machinery, and textiles. The state is an important hardwood producer. It is the USA's largest producer of zinc and the extraction of stone is a major source of revenue. *History*: disputed by the English and French in the 17th century, it was under British rule during the American Revolution. The area became a territory in 1790 and a state in 1796. Area: 109 411 sq km (42 244 sq mi). Population (1986 est): 4 803 000. Capital: Nashville.

Tennessee River   A river in SE USA. It follows a U-shaped course from E Tennessee, flowing through NE Alabama before returning across Tennessee to join the Ohio River at Paducah, Kentucky. **The Tennessee Valley Authority**, created in 1933, built dams along the river to control floods, arrest soil erosion, and generate electricity. Length: 1049 km (652 mi).

Tenniel, Sir John   (1820–1914) British cartoonist and book illustrator. He worked for *Punch* from 1851 to 1901 and specialized in humorous political cartoons. His illustrations for *Alice in Wonderland* are his most famous works.

tennis (*or* lawn tennis)   A game for two or four players using rackets to hit a cloth-covered rubber ball on a

TENNIS   *The dimensions of the court. For singles the posts holding the net are moved inside the doubles sidelines. The net is 3 ft (91.4 cm) high at the centre.*

grass or composition (hard) court. It originated in England in the mid-19th century. A match lasts a maximum of five sets for men and three for women and the minimum number of games per set is six. A lead of two games is usually needed to win a set. The scoring system derives from real tennis and a minimum of four points is needed for a game: 15, 30, 40, and game; a lead of two points is also needed to win a game. Players take turns to serve for a game. A player is allowed two attempts to serve into the service court diagonally opposite, alternating courts between points. To win points players must return the ball over the net either before it bounces (volley) or after the first bounce, positioning it so that their opponents cannot return it. The game is immensely popular at all levels of play, from the local club to the All England Championships at Wimbledon. Other highly prized trophies are the Davis Cup and the Wightman cup.

Tennyson, Alfred, Lord (1809–92) British poet. He published two volumes in 1830 and 1832, but he gained general acclaim only with his 1842 volume, which included "Morte d'Arthur." In 1850 he married, became poet laureate, and published *In Memoriam*, a sequence of elegaic lyrics mourning the death of his close friend Arthur Hallam (1811–33). He reinforced his popularity with *Idylls of the King* (1859) and other poems. He accepted a peerage in 1884.

tenor A high adult male singing voice. The word comes from the Latin *tenere*, to hold; in Renaissance polyphonic music the tenor part held the melody on which the music was based. Range: C on the bass stave to C two octaves above.

tenrec An insect-eating mammal belonging to the family *Tenrecidae* (30 species), found only in Madagascar and the Comoro Islands. Tenrecs measure 5–40 cm, some with long tails and some tailless, and generally have a brownish coat of bristly hairs or spines. Most tenrecs live in burrows and are nocturnal, feeding mainly on small invertebrates with some plant material. Order: *Insectivora*.

Tenzing Norgay (c. 1914–86) Sherpa mountaineer, who, with Sir Edmund Hillary, was the first man to reach the summit of Mount Everest (1953). He later became a director at the Himalayan Mountaineering Institute, Darjeeling.

tequila A Mexican spirit made of the fermented juice of an agave plant (*see* Agave), water, and, sometimes, sulphuric acid and yeast. The spirit is distilled twice in potstills then may be aged in casks. It is produced near the town of Tequila.

terbium (Tb) A lanthanide element, discovered in 1843 by C. G. Mosander (1797–1858) and named after the village Ytterby in Sweden. It is obtained from monazite ($CePO_4$), and the brown oxide (Tb_2O_3) is used as a phosphor in colour-television tubes. The metal is silvery-grey and can be cut with a knife. At no 65; at wt 158.92; mp 1356°C; bp 3041.

terebinth A small tree, *Pistacia terebinthus*, native to the Mediterranean region. It has small flowers producing purple fruit and was formerly an important source of turpentine. Family: *Pistaciaceae*.

Teresa, Mother (Agnes Gonxha Bejaxhui; 1910–) Yugoslav nun, who founded the Order of the Missionaries of Charity in Calcutta in 1948. Her nuns work throughout the world helping lepers, cripples, and the aged and dying. In 1971 she received the first Pope John XXIII Peace Prize and in 1979 the Nobel Peace Prize.

Teresa of Ávila, St (1515–82) Spanish Carmelite nun and mystic, who dedicated her life to reforming the Carmelite order. She joined the Carmelites at Ávila in 1533 and in 1555 experienced a spiritual awakening followed by several visions. She founded the Convent of St

Joseph in Ávila in 1562 and later other religious houses with the help of St John of the Cross (1542–91). The mystical side of her life is described in her books, notably *Life* (1562–65), *The Way of Perfection* (after 1565), and *The Interior Castle* (1577).

Teresina 5 09S 42 46W A city in NE Brazil, the capital of Piauí state on the Rio Parnaíba. It is a commercial centre; exports include cattle, hides, cotton, rice, and manioc. Population (1980 est): 348 900.

termite A social insect, also called white ant (although unrelated to the ants), belonging to the mainly tropical order *Isoptera* (2000 species). Termite colonies nest in tunnels and galleries in wood, soil, or earth mounds (termitaria). There are three major castes: winged reproductives, workers, and soldiers. The reproductives found new colonies; the workers construct galleries, feed the colony, and care for the young; while the soldiers are concerned with defence. Termites eat cellulose and are very destructive when they invade houses and attack wood products.

tern A seabird belonging to a subfamily (*Sterninae*; 35–40 species) occurring around coasts and inland waters worldwide. Terns have long wings, short legs, usually a forked tail, and their plumage is white, black-and-white, or almost totally black. They feed on fish and crustaceans and often migrate long distances. Family: *Laridae* (gulls and terns).

terracotta (Italian: baked earth) A fired clay, usually reddish in colour, used to make sculpture, tiles, bricks, containers, etc. Terracotta figurines, often painted, were very common in ancient Greece and Rome. The art was revived during the Renaissance.

terrapin A small edible turtle belonging to the family *Emydidae*, occurring chiefly in the New World. The diamondback terrapin (*Malaclemys terrapin*), which occurs in coastal waters and salt marshes of North America, has diamond-shaped patterns on its dark carapace and is yellow with black speckles underneath. It is regarded as a table delicacy.

terrier One of about 20 breeds of dog characterized by their small compact sturdy build and traditionally used for hunting vermin and rousing foxes and badgers from cover. The Scottish breeds, such as the cairn terrier, Scottish terrier, Skye terrier, and West Highland white terrier, tend to be smaller and longer haired than other terriers.

Territorial Army A British force of volunteers, created as the Territorial Force in 1907 and renamed in 1922. Between 1967 and 1979 it was known as the Territorial Army Volunteer Reserve. Its 84 000 men constitute a pool of trained and equipped reinforcements for the regular army.

Terry, Dame Ellen (Alice) (1847–1928) British actress. A member of a large and talented family of actors, from 1878 to 1898 she acted with Sir Henry Irving at the Lyceum Theatre, achieving particular success in the major Shakespearean roles. Her correspondence with G. B. Shaw was published in 1931.

Tertiary period The first geological period of the Cenozoic era, following the Cretaceous period and preceding the Quaternary. It lasted from about 65 to 1.8 million years ago and contains the Palaeocene, Eocene, Oligocene, Miocene, and Pliocene epochs, in ascending order. Modern invertebrates and mammals evolved and became increasingly abundant; the modern angiosperms became the dominant plants. The Alpine period of mountain formation reached its peak in the Miocene. The climate began to deteriorate in the Oligocene, finally leading to the Ice Age of the Pleistocene.

tesla (T)   The SI unit of magnetic flux density equal to one weber per square metre. Named after Nikola Tesla (1856–1943), US engineer.

Test Acts   1. In England, the Acts stipulating that public office holders must take Holy Communion in the Church of England (1673) and excluding all Roman Catholics except the Duke of York (later James II) from parliament (1678). They were not formally repealed until the mid-19th century. **2.** In Scotland, the Act (1681) that forced all public office holders to declare their belief in Protestantism; it was repealed in 1889.

testis   The organ of male animals in which sperm is produced. In men there is a pair of testes, or testicles, which produce both sperm and sex hormones (*see* androgens). Before birth the testicles descend into the scrotum—a sac of skin outside the abdominal cavity—since sperms require a temperature lower than that of the body to mature. The sperms complete their development in a convoluted tube (epididymis) outside the testis.

testosterone   A steroid hormone—the most important of the androgens—first isolated from bull testes in 1935. Synthetic testosterone has various medical uses, including treatment of certain forms of sterility in men.

test-tube baby   A baby produced by fertilizing the mother's egg cell with sperm from the father in a test tube (*in vitro* fertilization): the fertilized egg is then implanted surgically into the mother's womb. It is a means of overcoming sterility in a woman due to blocked Fallopian tubes or any similar defect. The first test-tube baby was born in July, 1978, and the first from a frozen embryo in 1988. *See also* artificial insemination.

tetanus   A serious disease caused by the bacterium *Clostridium tetani* entering wounds and producing a powerful toxin (poison) that irritates the nerves supplying muscles. After an incubation period of seven–ten days, stiffness, spasm, and rigidity of the muscles affects the jaw (hence the popular name—lockjaw) and spreads to other muscles. The disease can be prevented by completing a full course of antitetanus immunization.

tetra   One of several small brightly coloured freshwater fish of the family *Characidae*, found in South America and Africa and popular for aquaria. Well-known species include the black tetra (*Gymnocorymbus ternetzi*) and silver tetra (*Ctenobrycon spilurus*).

tetracyclines   A group of antibiotics derived from *Streptomyces* bacteria. Tetracyclines are active against a large number of different bacteria. Taken by mouth, they may cause the side effects of diarrhoea, nausea, and discoloration of growing teeth and bones.

tetraethyl lead ($Pb(C_2H_5)_4$)   A colourless poisonous oily liquid. It is made by treating lead-sodium alloys with chloroethane and is added to petrol to prevent knocking in internal-combustion engines. However, lead-free petrol is now being widely promoted to reduce lead pollution of the atmosphere.

Texas   The second largest and the third most populous state in the USA, situated in the SW of the country. It consists of four main physical regions: the West Gulf Coastal Plain in the SE; the Central Lowland; the Great Plains, which extend into New Mexico; and the Trans-Pecos or mountainous area in the W. It leads the nation in the production of oil and natural gas and is also a major producer of sulphur. Oil-related industries dominate the manufacturing sector, the most important being the chemical industry. There is also an important space centre at Houston and Dallas is a major commercial and industrial centre. Texas is a major agricultural region; it produces a variety of crops, especially cotton, sorghum grains, rice, and peanuts and it is a leading livestock producer. *History*: colonized by the Spanish in 1682, the first permanent Anglo-American settlement was established by Stephen F. Austin in 1821. In 1836 the Texans set up a provisional government in opposition to the Mexican dictatorship of Antonio López de Santa Anna and following the heroic defence of the Alamo, the revolutionary army finally defeated Mexican forces. A republic was established and Texas remained independent for almost a decade until annexation by the USA was agreed upon and Texas became a state. Area: 692 402 sq km (267 338 sq mi). Population (1985 est): 16 370 000. Capital: Austin.

Teyte, Dame Maggie   (1888–1976) British soprano. She studied in Paris (1903–07) and became famous for her performances in opera and for her recitals of French songs. She was created a DBE in 1958.

Thackeray, William Makepeace   (1811–63) British novelist. After publishing several early novels in magazines under pseudonyms, he won fame and financial success with *Vanity Fair* (1847–48), which he followed with the semiautobiographical *The History of Pendennis* (1848–50) and the historical novel *Henry Esmond* (1852). In his last years he edited the *Cornhill Magazine* (1860–62).

Thailand, Kingdom of (name until 1939: Siam)   A country in SE Asia, on the Gulf of Thailand. Fertile plains and hills in the S rise to mountains in the N. Most of the population is Thai. *Economy*: the chief food crop is rice, which is also the main export. Forests cover 60% of the land, producing especially teak and rubber in the N and yang in the S. Mineral resources include tin, manganese, antimony, and zinc. Industry is based mainly on textiles and cement. *History*: by the 6th century AD the Thais had reached the area from the N. They conquered the Mons to the S and in succeeding centuries were involved in frequent struggles with the Burmese and Khmers. In the 19th century they lost some territory to the French and the British but remained independent. In 1932 the long-standing absolute monarchy was replaced by a constitutional monarchy, since when civil and military governments have alternated, accompanied by political upheavals and violence. Head of state: King Bhumibol Adulyadej (1927–). Prime minister: Gen Chatichai Choonhaven. Official language: Thai. Official religion: Hinayana Buddhism. Official currency: baht of 100 satang. Area: 514 000 sq km (198 250 sq mi). Population (1987): 53 722 000. Capital and main port: Bangkok.

Thales   (c. 624–547 BC) The first of the Greek speculative scientists, born at Miletus. He used the data from Babylonian astronomers to predict the solar eclipse of 28 May, 585 BC, advised on stellar navigation, and introduced Egyptian methods of land measurement into Greece. He held that all things derive from water and set the Presocratics on their quest for the basic substance of the universe.

thalidomide   A sedative drug that was found to cause severe developmental defects in the fetus when taken during pregnancy. The most common thalidomide-induced abnormality is phocomelia, in which the feet and hands develop normally without corresponding growth of the bones of the arms and legs. Between 1959 and 1962 some 500 deformed babies were born in the UK.

thallium (Tl) A metallic element, discovered spectroscopically by Sir William Crookes in 1861 and named after the Greek *thallos*, a green shoot, because of its bright-green spectral line. The metal is soft and malleable and reacts easily to form numerous salts. It occurs naturally in sulphide ores of lead and zinc and in iron pyrites (FeS_2). At no 81; at wt 204.37; mp 303.5°C; bp $1457 \pm 10°C$.

Thallophyta In some plant classification systems, a subkingdom containing all those plants that lack true stems, leaves, and roots, i.e. the algae, fungi, and lichens. The plant body (a thallus) lacks conducting tissue.

RIVER THAMES *The tidal barrier.*

Thames, River The longest river in England. Rising in the Cotswold Hills near Cirencester, it flows mainly ESE through Oxford, Reading, and London to enter the North Sea at the Nore. A tidal barrier was constructed below London to reduce the danger of flooding. Length: 346 km (215 mi).

Thanet, Isle of 51 22N 1 15E An island in SE England, separated from the Kent mainland by two channels of the River Stour. It contains the resorts of Ramsgate and Margate. Area: 109 sq km (42 sq mi).

Thanksgiving Day A national holiday in the USA, celebrated on the fourth Thursday in November. Thanksgiving Day was originally observed by the Pilgrim Fathers, who in 1621 celebrated their first harvest in North America. It became a national holiday in 1863. It is also celebrated in Canada, on the second Monday in October.

Thant, U (1909–74) Burmese diplomat; secretary general of the UN (1962–72). U Thant helped to resolve the US-Soviet crisis over the Soviet installation of missile bases in Cuba.

Thatcher, Margaret (Hilda) (1925–) British stateswoman; Conservative prime minister (1979–). She entered parliament in 1959 and was appointed minister of pensions and national insurance in 1961. In 1969 she became opposition spokesman on education and was secretary of state for education and science from 1970 to 1974. In 1975 she succeeded Edward Heath as Conservative leader and in 1979 became the first woman prime minister of the UK. In office she increased privatization, cut government spending, and used military force to retain control of the Falkland Islands (1982).

Her government continued following a landslide victory in 1983 and a further victory in 1987. The longest serving UK prime minister of the century, she continued to pursue monetarist policies but the resignation of her chancellor, Nigel Lawson, over her use of a personal adviser and her unwillingness to commit the UK to full participation in the EC, led to an unsuccessful challenge to her leadership in 1989.

Theatre of the Absurd A theatrical genre popularized in the 1960s in which the human condition is presented as absurd. It was applied to the plays of Eugene Ionesco, Samuel Beckett, Arthur Adamov (1908–70), and others, which were characterized by lack of logical form and which use comic effects in developing pessimistic philosophical themes. The influence of Alfred Jarry (1873–1907) and the surrealists is also discernible.

Thebes An ancient city in Upper Egypt and capital of all Egypt (c. 1570–c. 1085 BC). Thebes' power was linked with the supremacy of its god Amon in the Egyptian pantheon.

Thebes 88 19N 23 19E A town in Boeotia, in central Greece. It was founded in Mycenaean times and its legendary history was a favourite theme in Greek drama. Thebes lost influence by supporting the Persians in 480 BC, but briefly became the leading Greek state after defeating the Spartans at Leuctra (371). Population (1981): 18 712.

theft The offence of dishonestly appropriating property belonging to another with the intention of permanently depriving the other person of it. The earlier offence of larceny was until 1827 divided into Grand Larceny and Petty Larceny. It was replaced by theft as defined by the Theft Act (1968).

thegn A person in Anglo-Saxon England who held land from his lord in return for service. The status of thegn (meaning one who serves) was hereditary. The king's thegns, who were the most important thegns, had military and administrative duties and also attended the witan (king's council). Their importance declined in the early 11th century, when the Danish kings introduced their housecarls, and the thegns died out as a clan after the Norman conquest.

MARGARET THATCHER

theism The belief in a personal God as creator and preserver of the universe, who reveals himself by supernatural means to his creatures. Apparently coined (1678) by Ralph Cudworth (1617–88) as an opposite to atheism, theism has been refined in meaning to exclude both pantheism and deism.

Themistocles (c. 528–462 BC) Athenian statesman. Themistocles persuaded Athens to expand its navy (483) and to transfer its port from Phaleron to the more defensible Piraeus. These policies, and his leadership at the battle of Salamis, saved Greece from Persia (480) (*see* Greek-Persian Wars). Themistocles also argued successfully for the fortification of Athens.

theodolite An instrument used in surveying to measure horizontal and vertical angles. It consists of a telescope, with crosshairs in the eyepiece for focusing on the target, that can swivel on horizontal and vertical axes, which pass through two circular scales. It has a spirit level to indicate when the instrument is horizontal.

Theodosius (I) the Great (347–95 AD) Roman emperor in the East (379–94) and sole emperor (394–95). Theodosius allowed the Visigoths independence on Roman territory by a treaty in 382. A devout and orthodox Christian, he imposed Christianity on the Empire in 391, closing pagan temples and forbidding sacrifices.

theology Literally, the study of God. Christian theology includes within its scope the nature of God, his relationship with the universe, his providence regarding man, and the teachings of the Church. Different traditions exist within the Roman Catholic, Orthodox, and Protestant communions, but typical subdivisions of theology are dogmatic, historical, and pastoral theology.

Thérèse, St (Marie Françoise Thérèse Martin; 1873–97) French Carmelite nun, known as the Little Flower of Jesus. She entered the Carmelite convent at Lisieux when only 15 and died there 9 years later of tuberculosis. Her fame rests on her spiritual autobiography, *Histoire d'une âme* (1898). She was canonized in 1925. Feast day: 3 Oct.

thermal reactor A nuclear reactor (*see* nuclear energy) in which natural or enriched uranium is used with a moderator so that the velocities of the emitted neutrons are comparable to the velocities of gas molecules ("thermal" velocities). The reactor core consists of fuel rods made of uranium metal or oxide surrounded by a moderator, the heat of the reaction being removed by a coolant. After leaving the core, the coolant passes to a heat exchanger in which steam is raised. The rate of reaction is controlled by a series of control rods, which can move in and out of the core: the rods contain a neutron-absorbing element, such as boron. Early British reactors (Magnox) used natural uranium; the next generation (advanced gas-cooled reactor) used enriched uranium dioxide and CO_2 as a coolant. The US-designed pressurized-water reactors, using ordinary water as both moderator and coolant, are now widely used.

thermionic valve A device consisting of an evacuated glass or metal tube, into which two or more electrodes are inserted. One heated electrode, the cathode, emits electrons, which are attracted to the positively charged anode, forming an electric current. This current flows in one direction only and can be controlled by the voltage applied at one or more other electrodes (called grids). The **diode valve** was invented in 1904 by Sir John Ambrose Fleming. The **triode valve** with one grid was invented in 1910 by Lee De Forest; it was the first to function as an amplifier. The weak signal fed to the grid produces a stronger signal in the anode circuit. Diode

and triode valves made possible the development of radio transmitters and receivers, although now semiconductor diodes and transistors have replaced them.

thermistor A semiconductor device with an electrical resistance that decreases sharply as temperature increases. It is used in temperature-control circuits and can be calibrated for use as a thermometer.

thermocouple A type of thermometer consisting of an electric circuit formed by two dissimilar metals joined at each end. One junction is exposed to the temperature to be measured, a voltage being generated between it and the other (reference) junction as a result of the temperature difference between them (*see* thermoelectric effects). The output is usually displayed on a galvanometer. Copper-constantan junctions are used up to 500°C and platinum-rhodium alloy up to 1500°C. A **thermopile** consists of several thermocouples connected in series.

thermodynamics The study of heat and its relationship with other forms of energy. Thermodynamics is primarily a statistical subject, thermodynamic quantities, such as temperature and entropy, being dependent on the statistical behaviour of the particles that comprise a system. There are three fundamental laws of thermodynamics. The first law states that the energy of a closed system remains constant during any process. The second law states that heat cannot flow from a cold body to a hot body without the expenditure of external work; or, that the entropy of a closed system can never decrease. The third law states that as the thermodynamic temperature of a system aproaches absolute zero, its entropy aproaches zero. *See* heat death of universe.

thermoelectric effects The effects of changes of temperature on electric circuits or devices. The **Seebeck effect**, named after Johann Seebeck (1770–1831), provides the basis for the thermocouple; it occurs when a circuit has two junctions between dissimilar metals. If the junctions are maintained at different temperatures, a voltage is generated between them. The **Peltier effect**, named after Jean Peltier (1785–1845), is the converse of this. One junction heats up and the other cools down when a steady current flows through such a circuit. In the **Thomson** (*or* Kelvin) **effect**, named after Lord Kelvin, a temperature gradient along a single metal conductor causes a current to flow through it.

thermometer An instrument used for measuring temperature. Thermometers make use of some property of a substance that varies uniformly with temperature, most commonly the expansion of a liquid, such as mercury. A clinical thermometer is a typical mercury-in-glass thermometer; more accurate thermometers use the expansion of a gas, which is much greater than that of a liquid. Other thermometers include the resistance thermometer, which depends on the variation in the resistance of a wire (usually platinum); the bimetallic strip, which makes use of the unequal expansion of two metals welded together; and the thermistor, in which the change in conductivity of a semiconductor is used as a measure of temperature. High temperatures are measured by a pyrometer.

thermonuclear reactor A reactor in which a fusion reaction (*see* nuclear energy) takes place with the controlled release of energy.

A typical fusion reaction is the combination of deuterium and tritium to form helium ($^2_1H + ^3_1H = ^4_2He + n + 17.6$ MeV). To overcome the electromagnetic interaction between nuclei a temperature of about 40 million

deuterium-tritium fusion reaction

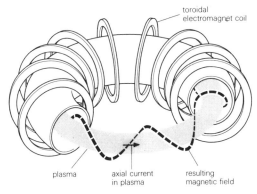

fusion reactor experiment

THERMONUCLEAR REACTOR *The combination of deuterium ($^2_1$H) and tritium ($^3_1$H) in a fusion reaction that forms helium. This is being attempted using a toroidal electromagnet to contain plasma consisting of deuterium and tritium nuclei.*

°C is needed. Containing the plasma (as the high-temperature ionized gas is called) is the problem to be solved. In magnetic containment a high current passed through the plasma creates a magnetic bottle that keeps the plasma away from the containing walls. To produce useful energy at this temperature, the product of the plasma density and the containment time must exceed 10^{14} particle seconds per cm^3. Russian toroidal Tokamak devices have so far only achieved a figure of 10^{12}. Other possible devices include a pellet of fuel exposed to pulses from laser beams.

thermopile. *See* thermocouple.

Thermopylae, Battle of (480 BC) The battle in which the Greeks under the Spartan king, Leonidas (reigned ?490–480), attempted for three days to hold the pass of Thermopylae in E central Greece against the Persians. After the main Greek force had retreated the Spartans and Thespians, surrounded and outnumbered, fought to the death.

Theseus A legendary Greek hero. He freed the Athenians from their annual tribute to Minos by killing the Minotaur of Crete. He extended the rule of Athens

over various Attic communities and was the subject of many legends.

Thessaloníki (English name: Salonika) 40 38N 22 58E The second largest port in Greece, in Macedonia on the Gulf of Salonika. Founded in 315 BC as Thessalonica, it became the capital of Macedonia. It was captured by the Turks (1430) and remained in the Ottoman Empire until ceded to Greece (1913). The port handles about one-third of Greek exports, including chrome, manganese, and agricultural produce. Industries include the manufacture of textiles and food processing. Population (1981): 402 443.

Thessaly (Modern Greek name: Thessalía) A region of E central Greece, bordering on the Aegean Sea. In the 4th century BC it fell to Philip of Macedon. Freed from Macedonian rule by Rome in 196 BC, it was incorporated in the Roman province of Macedonia in 148 BC. It subsequently formed part of the Byzantine Empire, falling to Turkey in the late 14th century AD. It was annexed by Greece in 1881.

thiamine. *See* vitamin B complex.

thiazine An organic compound that has a molecular structure containing a ring of four carbon atoms and two sulphur atoms. Thiazine derivatives are used in such drugs as tranquillizers, antihistamines, and antibiotics, as well as in various dyes.

thiazole (C_3H_3NS) An organic compound that has a molecular structure containing a ring of three carbon atoms, one sulphur atom, and one nitrogen atom. Thiazole derivatives occur in thiamine (vitamin B_1), penicillin, and in numerous synthetic drugs, dyes, and chemicals.

Third Reich (1933–45) The Nazi regime in Germany. The name refers to the Nazi ambition to revive the medieval Holy Roman Empire (the first Reich) and the German Empire (the second Reich; 1871–1918). The Third Reich ended with Germany's defeat in World War II.

Thirty-Nine Articles (1563) The doctrine, together with the Book of Common Prayer, of the Church of England. They were derived from Thomas Cranmer's 42 Articles (1553), which had been revoked by Mary I in re-establishing Roman Catholicism in England. The Articles do not represent a creed; rather they deal with specific points that were matters of controversy and give in broad terms the Anglican position with regard to these points. The clergy of the Church of England are no longer required to subscribe formally to the Articles but only to promise not to teach beliefs that contradict them.

Thirty Years' War (1618–48) The conflict between rival dynastic and religious interests in the Holy Roman Empire that escalated into a major European war. It was caused by the revolt of Protestants in Bohemia against the Counter-Reformation policies of the imperial government at Prague. Although imperial forces defeated the Bohemians in 1620, the revolt spread. With the Edict of Restitution (1629) Emperor Ferdinand II dispossessed many German Protestants. In 1635 France, hoping to contain the power of Spain and the Empire, entered the conflict. The war ended with the Peace of Westphalia (1648), although the Franco-Spanish conflict continued until 1659. The war caused serious economic and demographic reverses in Germany.

Thisbe. *See* Pyramus and Thisbe.

thistle A prickly-leaved herb belonging to one of several genera of the family *Compositae*, especially *Carduus* (120 species), *Cirsium* (120 species), *Carlinus* (20 species), and *Onopordum* (20 species), distributed throughout the N hemisphere. Thistles characteristically have heads of small purple flowers and spiny stems. The perennial creeping thistle (*Cirsium arvense*) grows to a height of 1 m and is a persistent weed. *See also* globe thistle.

Thistle, Order of the A Scottish order of knighthood, probably founded by James III (1451–88); it was revived by James VII (II of England) in 1687. It comprises the sovereign and 16 knights and its motto is *Nemo me impune lacessit* (vernacular: Wha daur meddle wi' me?).

thixotropy A property possessed by certain gels as a result of which they become liquid when stirred and return to a gel-like state when left to stand. Thixotropic gels are used in nondrip paints. Certain types of quicksand are naturally thixotropic.

Thomas, Dylan (1914–53) Welsh poet. Born in Swansea, Wales, he moved to London after the publication of *18 Poems* in 1934 and worked for the BBC. *Deaths and Entrances* (1946) contains many of his best-known poems. In 1949 he returned to Wales, where he wrote his popular radio play *Under Milk Wood* (1954). Alcoholism precipitated his death.

Thomas, St In the New Testament, one of the 12 Apostles. He is known as "Doubting Thomas" because he refused to believe in the resurrection until he had seen and touched Christ. Feast day: 21 Dec.

Thomas à Kempis (Thomas Hemmerken; c. 1380–1471) German spiritual writer and monk. He spent most of his life writing and teaching at the Augustinian convent of Agnietenberg near Zwolle (Netherlands). His fame rests on his devotional treatise, *The Imitation of Christ*.

Thompson, Daley (Francis Morgan T.; 1958–   ) British decathlete. Originally a sprinter, he won the decathlon in the Commonwealth Games in 1978. He won all the decathlons he entered between 1978 and 1987 and two Olympic gold medals (1980 and 1984).

Thomson, Sir Joseph John (1856–1940) British physicist, who discovered the electron. In 1897 he succeeded in deflecting cathode rays by an electric field, thus showing that they consisted of negatively charged particles. He also measured the ratio of their charge to mass and deduced that electrons were about 2000 times lighter than the hydrogen atom. Thomson thought that atoms consist of electrons embedded in a positively charged sphere, a concept that was superseded by Rutherford's model. He was awarded the Nobel Prize in 1906.

Thomson, William. *See* Kelvin, William Thomson, 1st Baron.

Thomson effect (*or* Kelvin effect). *See* thermoelectric effects.

Thor The Teutonic god of thunder, in some legends the son of Odin. He presided over the home and controlled the weather and crops; he was also worshipped as a god of war. His name survives in *Thursday*.

thorax In mammals (including man), the region of the body between the diaphragm and the neck, which contains the lungs and heart and their associated vessels. The skeleton of the thorax is formed by the breastbone at the front, the spine at the back, and the ribs at the sides. In arthropods the thorax is between the head and abdomen.

thorium (Th) A naturally occurring radioactive metal. It is possible that thorium-fuelled nuclear reactors may be developed in the future, since it is more abundant than uranium and does not produce plutonium-239 in appreciable quantities (*see* uranium). Thorium oxide (ThO_2) has one of the highest known melting points (3300°C), which led to its use in gas mantles, as it glows white when heated. At no 90; at wt 232.038; mp 1750°C; bp 3800°C.

DALEY THOMPSON

thorium series One of three naturally occurring series of radioactive decays. The thorium series is headed by thorium-232, which undergoes a series of decays ending with the stable isotope lead-208. *See also* actinium; uranium series.

thorn apple An annual herb, *Datura stramonium*, also called jimsonweed, occurring in N temperate and subtropical regions. It has white trumpet-shaped flowers producing a fruit with a spiny capsule that splits to release the black seeds. All parts of the plant are very poisonous, containing the alkaloids hyoscyamine, hyoscine, and scopolamine. Family: *Solanaceae*.

thornbill A drab-coloured Australian bird belonging to one of three genera, especially *Acanthiza*. The yellow-tailed thornbill (*A. chrysorrhoea*) builds a very long oval nest with several nest chambers. Family: *Muscicapidae* (*see* flycatcher).

Thrace The Balkan region bordered by the Black Sea, the Aegean, Macedonia, and the River Danube. From the 8th century BC Greek cities colonized the coasts, while the independent inland tribes were an easy target for invaders—the Persians in about 516 BC and then Philip II of Macedon in the mid-4th century. Having come under the influence of Rome in 168 BC; it became a Roman province in 46 AD. Famous for its horses and horsemen, and for ecstatic religious rituals, Thrace was traditionally the birthplace of the mysteries and orgiastic rites associated with the worship of Dionysus. It is now divided between Turkey, Greece, and Bulgaria.

threadfin A fish, also called threadfish, belonging to the family *Polynemidae* (about 24 species), that is found along warm seashores. It has a silvery elongated body, and long threadlike pectoral fin rays. Order: *Perciformes*.

threadworm. *See* pinworm.

thrift A perennial herb, *Armeria maritima*, also called sea pink, native to mountains, salt marshes, and sandy coastal regions of N Europe. The flower stem rises from a basal tuft of long narrow grasslike leaves and bears a cluster of rose-pink or white flowers. Family: *Plumbaginaceae*.

thrips A minute insect, also called thunder fly, belonging to the order *Thysanoptera* (about 3000 species). Thrips have dark slender bodies, 0.5–5 mm long, and usually two pairs of narrow fringed wings. Many species suck the juices of flowering plants, often causing serious damage and spreading plant diseases.

thrombosis The formation of a blood clot inside a blood vessel, which often obstructs the flow of blood. Thrombosis is more likely to occur if the blood vessel is damaged or if the blood flow is very slow. The commonest site of thrombosis is in the veins of the legs. This is particularly likely to occur if a person is bedridden for a long time. The clot may become detached and carried to the lungs, causing pulmonary embolism.

Thrombosis can also occur in the arteries supplying the heart (coronary thrombosis), causing a heart attack (*see* myocardial infarction), or the brain, causing stroke.

thrush (bird) A songbird belonging to a family (*Turdidae*; 300 species) found throughout the world but predominantly in Old World regions. Thrushes are slender billed and usually brown–often with speckling or patches of red, yellow, or blue. They feed chiefly on insects and fruit and often have melodious songs, as in the song thrush (*Turdus philomelus*). Northern species are migratory. *See also* blackbird; mistle thrush; ring ouzel.

thrush (disease). *See* candidiasis.

Thucydides (c. 460–c. 400 BC) Greek historian. He served as an Athenian general in the Peloponnesian War but was banished in 424 BC for allowing the Spartan general Brasidas to capture the colony of Amphipolis. His eight-volume *History of the Peloponnesian War* is notable for its political, moral, and psychological analysis of the issues and leaders involved.

Thuja. *See* arbor vitae.

thulium (Tm) The least abundant of the lanthanide elements, discovered in 1879 by P. T. Cleve (1840–1905). Radioactive ^{169}Tm is used in portable X-ray generators. At no 69; at wt 168.934; mp 1545°C; bp 1947°C.

Thurber, James (1894–1961) US humorous writer and cartoonist. An early and continuing contributor to the *New Yorker*, he satirized intellectual fashions and domestic habits with irony and sophistication. His essays and stories are collected in *The Thurber Carnival* (1945) and other volumes.

Thutmose III (d. 1450 BC) King of Egypt (c. 1504–1450) of the 18th dynasty, who ruled Egypt at its most powerful and prosperous. In 1468 he defeated Syrian rebels at Megiddo and in later campaigns advanced beyond the River Euphrates. He organized and supervised the country's complicated administration and was an outstanding athlete and big-game hunter and a patron of art and architecture.

thylacine The largest carnivorous marsupial, *Thylacinus cynocephalus*, also called Tasmanian wolf or tiger and now probably extinct. About 1.5 m long, it resembles a dog with dark stripes across its grey-brown back. Family: *Dasyuridae*.

thyme A small shrub belonging to the genus *Thymus* (about 50 species), native to temperate Eurasia. Garden thyme (*T. vulgaris*) is cultivated for its fragrant leaves, which are dried and used as a culinary herb. An oil extract is used in perfumes and medicines. The common wild thyme (*T. drucei*) has a branching creeping stem and clusters of rose-purple flowers. Family: *Labiatae*.

thymus An organ situated at the base of the neck, above the heart. The thymus grows until puberty, after which it shrinks and ceases to function. During infancy the thymus produces lymphocytes that form the antibodies associated with allergic responses and the rejection of transplanted tissues and organs. *See also* immunity.

thyristor A solid-state electronic device, also called a semiconductor or silicon-controlled rectifier; it consists of four layers of semiconductor forming three p-n junctions. It acts as a switch, blocking the current through two terminals until it has been turned on by a pulse applied to the third terminal. This pulse can be initiated by light or a temperature change. Thyristors can pass currents ranging from milliamperes to several hundred amperes and for many purposes have replaced gas-filled valve relays.

thyroid gland An endocrine gland situated at the base of the neck, in front and on either side of the windpipe. It secretes the hormone thyroxine, which controls the basal metabolism of the body; thyroxine secretion is regulated by thyroid-stimulating hormone, released from the pituitary gland. Because thyroxine production requires iodine, deficiency of iodine causes the thyroid to enlarge in an attempt to produce adequate amounts of the hormone (*see* goitre). *See also* cretinism.

Tiber, River (Italian name: Tevere; Latin name: Tiberis) A river in central Italy, rising in the Apennines of Tuscany and flowing mainly S through Rome to the Tyrrhenian Sea near Ostia. Length: 405 km (252 mi).

Tiberias, Sea of. *See* Galilee, Sea of.

Tiberius (42 BC–37 AD) Roman emperor (14–37 AD). Tiberius was recognized by his stepfather, Emperor Augustus, as his successor in 4 AD. As emperor his policies were unambitious though sound but he faced the Senate's hostility, family intrigue, and military rebellion. He retired to Capri in 26 AD, where he gained a reputation for depravity.

Tibet (Chinese name: Xizang Autonomous Region) An administrative region in W China, bordering on India, Nepal, Bhutan, and Burma. It consists of a high plateau and is surrounded by mountains, including the Himalayas and the Kunlun Mountains. Most agriculture and the country's cities are in the river valleys. The area is rich in minerals. *History*: Buddhism, introduced in the 7th century AD, has exerted a profound influence on Tibetan history. The lamas (priests) of Tibetan Buddhism attained political power in the 13th century. In 1642, the fifth Dalai Lama became ruler of all Tibet. In 1720 the Chinese Qing dynasty established a control over Tibet that lasted until 1911. Independence was declared, but in 1950 Tibet again fell to the Chinese. An uprising in 1959 was brutally suppressed. There have been further riots in the 1980s, leading to the imposition of martial law. Area: 1 221 601 sq km (471 660 sq mi). Population (1985): 1 970 000. Capital: Lhasa.

Tibetan Buddhism (*or* lamaism) A form of Mahayana Buddhism practised in Tibet and Mongolia. Introduced into Tibet in the 7th century AD, it has a complex symbolic literature and monastic discipline. The guru is of prime importance; some are held to be reincarnations of previous lamas. Until 1959, the Dalai Lama was temporal and spiritual head of the state.

tick A parasitic arachnid of the worldwide suborder *Metastigmata* (850 species), which sucks the blood of birds and mammals and may transmit such diseases as typhus and relapsing fever. Its round unsegmented body, up to 30 mm long, bears eight bristly legs. After feeding, the adults drop off the host and lay eggs on the ground. The larvae attach themselves to a suitable victim, feed, then drop off and moult into nymphs, which repeat the procedure. Order: *Acarina* (or *Acari*). *Compare* mite.

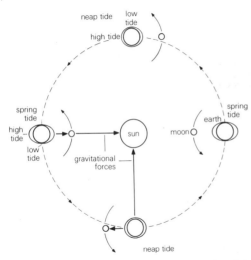

TIDES   *The force of gravity between the earth and the moon pulls the waters of the seas towards the moon, creating high tides once a day. The second daily high tide occurs because the moon pulls the earth itself away from the water on the far side from the moon. Exceptionally high spring tides occur twice monthly when the gravitational force of the moon is in line with that of the sun. The lower neap tides occur when these two forces are at right angles.*

tides The regular rising and falling of seawater resulting from the gravitational attraction between the earth, sun, and moon. Most parts of the world experience semidiurnal tides (occurring twice per tidal day—24 hours 5 minutes). Tidal currents are periodic horizontal flows of water resulting from the rise and fall of the tide. Near the coast they are usually perpendicular to it and reversing, but in the ocean they flow in a rotary manner around a series of nodal points.

Tiepolo, Giovanni Battista (1696–1770) Venetian rococo painter. His early sombre style evolved into the exuberance of his first major frescoes, for the Archbishop's Palace at Udine (1725–29). These were followed by decorations for many N Italian palaces and churches. Abroad he decorated the Residenz Palace, Würzburg (1750–53) and the Royal Palace in Madrid (1762–66).

Tierra del Fuego An archipelago separated from the mainland of S South America by the Strait of Magellan. The W and S belong to Chile, the E to Argentina. Sheep farming and oil production are the principal economic activities. Chief towns: Punta Arenas (Chile); Ushuaia (Argentina).

Tiflis. *See* Tbilisi.

tiger A large cat, *Panthera tigris*. Tigers are usually about 3 m long, but the race of Siberian tigers can reach 4 m. Tigers evolved in Siberia and have spread south to most of Asia; they shed their coat seasonally and shelter from hot sun during the day. They hunt (mainly antelope) at night.

tiger moth A moth belonging to the family *Arctiidae*, occurring in Eurasia, N Africa, and North America. The adults have a stout body and are brightly coloured, often orange and black. The hairy larvae, commonly called woolly bears, are seldom destructive.

tiger shark A large requiem shark, *Galeocerdo cuvieri*, that lives mainly in tropical seas. It has a greyish-brown body, up to about 5.5 m long, patterned with vertical bars and a lighter underside. It eats virtually anything, including mammals, birds, fish, invertebrates, refuse, and man.

Tigris, River A river in SW Asia, rising in SE Turkey and flowing SE through Diyarbakir, along the Turkish-Syrian border, and into Iraq. It joins the River Euphrates to form the Shatt al-Arab. Length: 1850 km (1150 mi).

Tijuana 39 29N 117 10W A city in NW Mexico, on the US border. Tijuana is the main entry point to Mexico from California and is a popular tourist resort. Population (1980): 461 257.

timber wolf A large shaggy-coated wolf of North America, also called the grey wolf. A Texan variety with a rufous coat is called the red wolf.

timbre A quality in the sound of a musical instrument, voice, etc., that distinguishes it from others. Thus a violin and a clarinet sound different even when they are playing the same note. The difference arises because each type of instrument produces different overtones in different strengths when a note is played. The production of overtones is controlled by the way the note is produced (plucking, blowing, etc.) and by the characteristics of the individual instrument.

Timbuktu (French name: Tombouctou) 16 49N 2 59W A town in E central Mali, on the River Niger. It was an important centre on the trans-Saharan caravan route and an Islamic cultural centre (1400–1600). Population (1975): 10 500.

time dilation An effect predicted by Einstein's special theory of relativity. If two observers, A and B, are moving at a velocity v relative to each other, it will appear to A that B's clock will show that time is running more slowly; thus a time t measured on A's clock will be $t(1-v^2/c^2)^{1/2}$ on B's clock, where c is the velocity of light.

Timor An Indonesian island, the largest of the Nusa Tenggara group. Mountainous and dry, it is largely undeveloped. Crops include coffee, coconut, and sandalwood. *History*: in 1859 it was divided between Portugal and Holland. West (Dutch) Timor was included in independent Indonesia (1949). East Timor erupted in civil war in 1975 and was annexed by Indonesia (1976). Area: 39 775 sq km (11 883 sq mi). Chief towns: Kupang and Dili.

Timothy, St In the New Testament, a disciple of Paul, whom he accompanied on many missions. According to tradition he was martyred in Ephesus. Feast day: 6 Feb.

Timur (*or* Tamerlane; c. 1336–1405) Mongol conqueror, a descendant of Genghis Khan. After winning control of Turkestan in central Asia, Timur swept ruthlessly through Mongolia, Persia, Turkey, Russia, and India, leaving death and destruction behind him. Paradoxically, he spared and encouraged all kinds of artists.

tin (Sn) A silvery-white metal known to the ancients. Its principal ore is the oxide cassiterite (SnO_2), often found in alluvial concentrations. The element exists as at least two allotropes–the grey alpha-tin, and beta-tin, which is the common form above 13.2°C. At low temperature beta-tin slowly changes into alpha-tin causing **tin plague**. It is obtained by reduction with coal in a reverberatory furnace. The major use of tin is in tinplate. It alloys with copper to form bronzes and with niobium to give a superconducting composition, which is used in electromagnets. At no 50; at wt 118.69; mp 231.89°C; bp 2270°C.

tinamou A solitary ground-dwelling bird belonging to a family (*Tinamidae*; 50 species) occurring in Central and South America. Well camouflaged with a mottled grey or brown plumage, tinamous have small wings and a very short tail and are poor fliers. They feed on seeds, fruit, and insects.

tineid moth A moth of the widespread family *Tineidae*. The adults are usually small with a golden or silvery sheen and frequently do not feed. The caterpillars feed on a variety of plant and animal matter. *See* clothes moth.

Tintagel 50 40N 4 45W A village and resort in SW England, on the N coast of Cornwall. On the rugged promontory of Tintagel Head are the ruins of Tintagel Castle, reputedly the site of King Arthur's court.

Tintoretto (Jacopo Robusti; 1518–94) Venetian painter, whose nickname, meaning "little dyer," derived from his father's profession of silk dyeing. His three paintings of the *Miracles of St Mark* (1562–66) for the Confraternity of S Marco were followed by his series of the life of Christ (1564–87; Scuola di S Rocco) and his paintings for the Doge's Palace, including the enormous *Paradise*. As a portraitist, he was particularly adept at painting old men, for example *Bearded Man with Fur* (Kunsthistorisches Museum, Vienna).

Tipperary (Irish name: Contae Tiobraid Árann) A county in the S Republic of Ireland, in Munster. It contains part of the Golden Vale (one of the most fertile areas in Ireland) in the SW. Predominantly agricultural, dairy farming is especially important. Area: 4255 sq km (1643 sq mi). Population (1986): 136 504. County town: Clonmel.

Tippett, Sir Michael (1905–   ) British composer. He has written five operas, including *The Midsummer Marriage* (1947–52), *The Knot Garden* (1966–70), *The Mask of Time* (1982), and *New Year* (1989). His other works include four symphonies, four string quartets, three piano sonatas, and the oratorio *A Child of Our Time* (1940). In 1983 he was appointed president of the London College of Music and a member of the OM.

Tirana (Albanian name: Tiranë) 41 20N 19 49E The capital of Albania, situated on a fertile plain in the centre of the country. Founded in the 17th century, it became the capital in 1920. There has been considerable industrial expansion since World War II. Population (1983): 206 000.

Tiresias In Greek legend, a blind Theban seer who lived for seven generations. Oedipus learned from him of his own patricide and incest and Odysseus consulted him in the underworld, where he retained his prophetic powers.

Tirich Mir, Mount 36 18N 71 55E A mountain in NW Pakistan, the highest in the Hindu Kush. Height: 7692 m (25 236 ft).

Tirol (*or* Tyrol) A mountainous federal state in W Austria, bordering on West Germany and Italy. It has an international reputation for winter sports, especially at Kitzbühel, and tourism is important throughout the year. The chief occupations are agriculture and forestry, with some mining and manufacturing industries. Area: 12 648 sq km (4883 sq mi). Population (1986): 605 774. Capital: Innsbruck.

Tissot, James Joseph Jacques (1836–1902) French painter and etcher. After settling in England in the 1870s he became known for his charming scenes of Victorian life, notably *The Ball on Shipboard* (Tate Gallery).

Tisza, River (Slavonic and Romanian name: Tisa) A river in S central Europe. Rising in the Soviet Union, in the W Ukranian SSR, it flows across the Hungarian Plain to join the River Danube below Novi Sad in Yugoslavia. It is a source of irrigation and power, especially in NE Hungary. Length: 980 km (610 mi).

tit A small acrobatic songbird (also called titmouse) belonging to a family (*Paridae*; 65 species) occurring in Eurasia, North America, and Africa. Tits frequent woodlands and gardens, feeding chiefly on insects. Their soft plumage is usually grey or black, often with blue and yellow markings. *See also* blue tit; crested tit.

TITANIC *Setting out on its first and last voyage (1912).*

Titanic A luxury passenger ship that on 14–15 April, 1912, struck an iceberg near Newfoundland on its maiden voyage and sank with the loss of 1513 lives. Because of its special design it was thought to be unsinkable. As a result of the disaster safety rules for ships at sea were drawn up. The wreck of the Titanic was located on the sea bed and photographed in 1985.

titanium (Ti) A relatively light strong transition metal discovered in 1791 by W. Gregor (1761–1817). It occurs in nature in the minerals rutile (TiO_2), ilmenite (Fe-TiO_3), sphene ($CaTiO_3$), and in some iron ores. The dioxide (TiO_2) is used in white paint as it has excellent opacity. The metal is as strong as steel but 45% lighter (relative density 4.54) and 60% heavier than aluminium but twice as strong. It is used in alloys for missiles and aircraft. At no 22; at wt 47.90; mp 1660°C; bp 3287°C.

Titans In Greek mythology, 12 primeval gods and goddesses, the children of Uranus and Gaea. They were Oceanus, Coeus, Crius, Hyperion, Iapetus, Cronus, Thea, Rhea, Themis, Mnemosyne, Phoebe, and Tethys. They were overthrown by Zeus and the Olympian deities.

tithes The tenth part of an income allotted to religious purposes. Originating in the offering of the "first fruits" as a divine sacrifice, tithes were decreed by Mosaic law, which demanded payment in kind from all agricultural produce. Christian ecclesiastical law also enjoined tithes to maintain churches and clergy. Tithes were abolished in Britain in 1936.

Titian (Tiziano Vecellio; c. 1488–1576) Venetian painter of the High Renaissance. He collaborated with Giorgione on frescoes for the façade of the German Exchange (1508). In his *Assumption of the Virgin* (Sta Maria dei Frari) his more monumental style links him with such Florentine painters as Raphael. His greatest works for the Habsburgs, who patronized him from 1530 onwards, were the equestrian portrait of Emperor Charles V at Mühlberg (1548; Prado) and *Philip II* (1550–51; Prado). His mythological works include *Bacchus and Ariadne* (National Gallery, London).

Titicaca, Lake A lake in South America, between Peru and Bolivia, in the Andes. At an altitude of 3809 m (12 497 ft) it is the world's highest lake navigable to large vessels. Area: 8135 sq km (3141 sq mi). Depth: 370 m (1214 ft).

titmouse. *See* tit.

Tito (Josip Broz; 1892–1980) Yugoslav statesman; president 1953–80. Tito was captured by the Russians in World War I and subsequently fought with the Red Army in the Russian civil war. He returned to Yugoslavia in 1920 and joined the Communist Party; in 1937 he became secretary general of the Party. In World War II he led the partisans in resistance to the German occupation, becoming a marshal in 1943. He became Yugoslavia's postwar leader and introduced the policy of decentralization to workers' councils. Following Yugoslavia's expulsion (1948) from the Cominform, Tito successfully maintained his country's independence from Soviet interference, pursuing a foreign policy of nonalignment.

Titus (Flavius Vespasianus) (39–81 AD) Roman emperor (79–81). He fought with his father Vespasian in Judaea and ended the Jewish revolt (70) by capturing Jerusalem. Titus was a popular emperor; when Vesuvius erupted (79), he aided the victims generously. At his death he was deified.

Tivoli 41 58N 12 48E A town in central Italy, in Lazio. A summer resort in Roman times, it possesses the remains of Hadrian's villa and the Renaissance Villa d'Este, with its terraced water gardens. Population (1981 est): 51 528.

Tiw. *See* Tyr.

Tlingit A North American Indian people of the NW Pacific coast in SE Alaska. There were 14 tribes divided into independent matrilineal clans, each headed by a chief. They lived by salmon fishing and hunting. Their language belongs to the Na-Dené group.

TNT (trinitrotoluene; $C_6H_2(NO_2)_3CH_3$) A highly explosive pale yellow crystalline solid. It is prepared from toluene treated with concentrated sulphuric and nitric acids and is used in shells, bombs, etc., and blasting explosives.

toad A tail-less amphibian belonging to a widely distributed order (*Anura*; about 2600 species). Toads have long hind legs and short forelegs; they swim by means of partially webbed feet. They have a long sticky tongue that can extend very rapidly to capture flying insects. *See also* natterjack; tree frog; spadefoot toad.

toadfish A bottom-dwelling carnivorous bony fish of the order *Batachoidiformes* (about 45 species), found mainly in tropical and subtropical seas. It has a heavy brownish body and makes grunting or croaking sounds resembling a toad.

toadstool. *See* mushroom.

tobacco A plant belonging to the genus *Nicotiana*, especially *N. tabacum* and *N. rustica*, which are cultivated for their leaves, used to make cigarettes, cigars, snuff, etc. Commercial tobacco plants grow to a height of 1–3 m and bear pink, white, or greenish flowers. After harvesting, their large sticky leaves are slowly dried and then fermented. The main growing regions are the USA, China, India, and the Soviet Union.
Tobacco contains about 2–4% nicotine, which produces its stimulant and addictive properties. Family: *Solanaceae*.

Tobago Island. *See* Trinidad and Tobago, Republic of.

Tobata. *See* Kitakyushu.

Toc H An interdenominational Christian fellowship open to anyone over the age of 16 and devoted to social service. It was founded in 1915 in Belgium by the Rev P. B. Clayton (1885–1972), a Church of England chaplain, as a military chapel and club; it was named Talbot House in memory of Gilbert Talbot (1891–1915), a British lieutenant, killed in action, who was a member of a prominent Anglican family. Its name derives from army signallers' designations of the initials *T H*.

Togo, Republic of (French name: République Togolaise) A small narrow country in West Africa, on the Gulf of Guinea between Ghana and Benin. The majority of the population is African. *Economy*: chiefly agricultural, food crops consist mainly of cassava, maize, and rice and cash crops include cocoa, coffee, and cotton. Forests produce not only timber but oil palms and dyewoods. There are rich deposits of phosphates, which, with cocoa and coffee, are the main export. Bauxite was found in the 1950s and there is some limestone and iron ore. Industry is being developed, concentrating mainly on food processing, but there is also a large cement plant and a new oil refinery. *History*: settled by the Ewe in the 12th and 13th centuries, the area was raided for slaves from the 17th to 19th centuries. From 1884 to 1914 Togoland was a German protectorate and after World War I it was divided between France and the UK. The French territory gained full independence in 1960. (The British part joined Ghana in 1957.) A coup in 1967 brought Lt Col (later Gen) Etienne Gnassingbe

Eyadéma (1937–) to power. Official language: French. Official currency: CFA (Communauté financière africaine) franc of 100 centimes. Area: 56 000 sq km (21 616 sq mi). Population (1987 est): 3 158 000. Capital and main port: Lomé.

tokay. *See* gecko.

Tokyo 35 40N 139 45E The capital of Japan, in E central Honshu on Tokyo Bay (an inlet of the Pacific). Administratively joined to its port Yokohama and to the industrial centre of Kawasaki, Greater Tokyo is the world's largest city. It has over 100 universities. *History*: the village of Edo was founded in the 12th century. As Tokyo, it replaced Kyoto as imperial capital in 1868. It was badly damaged by an earthquake in 1923 and by bombing during World War II, since when its industrial growth has been dramatic. Population (1986): 8 379 385.

Toledo 41 40N 83 35W A city in the USA, in Ohio on Lake Erie at the mouth of the River Maumee. It is a major Great Lakes port, shipping oil, coal, and farm products. Industrial activities include shipbuilding and oil refining. Population (1986 est): 340 680.

Toledo 39 52N 4 02W A city in central Spain, in New Castile on the River Tagus. It was formerly the capital of Spain. Famous for its swords and knives, it produces metalwork engraved in the Moorish tradition. Population (1982 est): 61 813.

J. R. R. TOLKIEN

Tolkien, J(ohn) R(onald) R(euel) (1892–1973) British scholar and writer. His novel *The Lord of the Rings* (1954–55), in which he created a richly detailed fantasy world, became a bestseller. Related works include *The Hobbit* (1937) and *The Silmarillion* (1977).

Tolpuddle Martyrs Six members of the Friendly Society of Agricultural Labourers of Tolpuddle, Dorset, founded in 1833. The six were unfairly charged with administering unlawful oaths and transported to Australia. They were pardoned in 1836.

Tolstoy, Leo (Nikolaevich), Count (1828–1910) Russian writer and moralist. Following his marriage in 1862 he wrote two novels, *War and Peace* (1865–69), concerning the Napoleonic War, and *Anna Karenina* (1875–77), both acknowledged masterpieces of Russian literature. Around 1879 he underwent a spiritual crisis from which he emerged with a faith in an extreme form of Christian anarchism. He worked and dressed as a peasant, became a vegetarian, espoused total pacifism, repudiated his former literary works, and divided his property among the members of his family.

Toltecs An Indian people who dominated central Mexico between the 10th and 12th centuries AD. Their language, Nahuatl, was also spoken by the Aztecs. A militaristic people, they created an empire and introduced the cult of Quetzalcoatl. The Aztecs destroyed their capital of Tula in the mid-12th century.

tomato An annual plant, *Lycopersicon esculentum*, native to South America and widely cultivated for its fleshy red fruit. In warm temperate regions, tomatoes are grown in fields and are low branching plants; the hothouse tomatoes of cooler regions often grow a single erect fruiting stem. The yellow flowers produce rounded or pear-shaped fruits which are eaten fresh or canned and made into purée, pickles, etc. Family: *Solanaceae*.

Tombouctou. *See* Timbuktu.

tomography The technique, widely used in medicine for diagnostic purposes, of producing an image of a selected plane of the body using X-rays or other forms of radiation. In **computerized tomography** (CT), a ring-shaped X-ray machine (CT scanner) is rotated around the patient and records different planes of the body. The information thus obtained is assembled by the scanner's built-in computer into a three-dimensional representation of the body.

Tomsk 56 30N 85 05E A port in the central Soviet Union, in the RSFSR on the River Tom. Industries include engineering and it has a university (1888). Population (1987): 489 000.

ton An Imperial unit of weight equal to 2240 lb (long ton) or 1016 kilograms. In the USA a unit equal to 2000 lb (short ton) is also used. The metric ton (or **tonne**) is equal to 1000 kilograms.

tonality The presence of a tonal centre or key in a musical composition. Musical compositions from at least the early 17th century to about 1900 are in distinct keys. These are based on individual scales, in which certain notes (the tonic and dominant degrees) form tonal centres to which the music periodically returns. Music in which tonal centres are deliberately avoided exhibits atonality. *See also* serialism.

tone poem. *See* symphonic poem.

Tonga, Kingdom of (*or* Friendly Islands) A country in the SW Pacific Ocean, E of Fiji. It consists of 169 small islands. *Economy*: agricultural, the main products are copra and bananas. Oil has been discovered recently. *History*: under King Taufa'ahau Tupou (George I; 1797–1893) in the 19th century, the civil war between rival dynasties was ended and the islands converted to Christianity. The country became a British protectorate in 1900, and in 1970 became an independent state within the British Commonwealth. Head of State: King Taufa'ahau Tupou IV (1918–). Official languages: Tongan and English. Official currency: pa'anga of 100 seniti. Area: 700 sq km (270 sq mi). Population: (1987) 94 800. Capital: Nuku'alofa.

tongue A muscular organ situated in the floor of the mouth. The root of the tongue is attached by muscles to the U-shaped hyoid bone in the neck. The tongue is the main organ of taste: its surface is covered by taste buds, which detect sweet, sour, salt, and bitter tastes. It also manipulates food during chewing and swallowing and plays an important role in the articulation of speech.

tonic sol-fa. *See* solmization.

tonsils Patches of tissue situated on each side at the back of the mouth. They produce lymphocytes, which protect the body against infection. Inflammation of the tonsils (tonsillitis) may be caused by a variety of infections.

topaz A mineral consisting of a hydrous fluosilicate of aluminium, $Al_2SiO_4(OH,F)_2$. It occurs in acidic igneous rocks, in pegmatites and veins. It is usually colourless or yellow, and when cut and polished it is used as a gemstone. The finest specimens come mainly from the Urals, Brazil, and Ceylon. Birthstone for November.

top minnow. *See* killifish.

topology The branch of geometry concerned with the properties of an object that do not change under homeomorphisms, i.e. when the object is bent, stretched, or shrunk but not torn or deformed so that several points on it are fused. Topology is often called rubber-sheet geometry; it was formerly called analysis situs. One application is in networks in which the topological properties depend on the so-called Euler characteristic, named after Leonhard Euler (1707–83), $V - E + F$, where V is the number of vertices in the network, E the number of edges, and F the number of areas enclosed by the edges.

Torah (Hebrew: instruction) The five books of Moses (Genesis, Exodus, Leviticus, Numbers, and Deuteronomy), which constitute the first of the three divisions of the Hebrew Bible. In Judaism, the term is also applied more widely to the whole body of religious teachings, viewed as the revealed word of God and including both the written and the oral Torah.

Torino. *See* Turin.

TORNADO *Sweeping through Texas.*

tornado A violently rotating column of air, small in diameter, characterized by a funnel-shaped cloud, which may reach ground surface. Wind speeds of up to 200 knots (100 m per second) have been experienced. Occurring over land, tornadoes cause large-scale destruction and are a considerable problem in the central USA and Australia.

Toronto 43 42N 79 25W A city and port in E Canada, the capital of Ontario on Lake Ontario. It is Canada's second largest city, housing a stock exchange and many business headquarters. Its diversified industries include heavy engineering, electrical, chemical, and wood products, foods, clothing, sporting goods, publishing, and films. *History*: established as Upper Canada's capital and military centre (1793), Toronto was scene of the Mackenzie Rebellion (1837) against oligarchic government. It became an industrial and commercial centre with the development of railways (1850s). Population (1981): 559 217.

torpedo (armament) A self-propelled guided underwater missile carrying a high-explosive warhead. They can be launched by ships or aircraft but have been used most successfully by submarines. Designed in 1866 by a British engineer, Robert Whitehead (1823–1905), they were used to sink 25 million tons of Allied shipping in World Wars I and II. Modern torpedos are driven by steam turbines or by battery-powered electric motors and have sophisticated active or passive acoustic homing systems.

torpedo (fish). *See* electric ray.

Torquemada, Tomás de (1420–98) Spanish Dominican friar and Grand Inquisitor. Confessor to Ferdinand and Isabella, he was appointed head of the Spanish Inquisition in 1483. His sentences were extremely harsh and he was responsible for the expulsion of the Jews from Spain in 1492.

Torres Strait A channel between New Guinea and Cape York Peninsula, N Australia, linking the Arafura Sea and Coral Sea. It was discovered (1606) by the Spaniard Luis Vaez de Torres. Width: 145 km (90 mi).

Torricelli, Evangelista (1608–47) Italian physicist. He discovered that the atmosphere exerts a pressure and demonstrated it by showing that it could support a column of mercury in a tube, thus inventing the mercury barometer (1643). He also created the first man-made vacuum in his simple barometer, the space above the mercury still being called a Torricellian vacuum.

tort In law, a civil wrong that constitutes a breach of a duty established by law rather than by contract. It is distinguished from a crime in that it affects the interests of the injured person rather than of the state.

Tortelier, Paul (1914–) French cellist. He won first prize at the Paris conservatoire at the age of 16. After playing in orchestras in the USA he began a career as a soloist, composer, and teacher.

tortoise A slow-moving herbivorous reptile belonging to the family *Testudinidae* (40 species). Tortoises have a protective high-domed shell, tough scaly legs, and range in size from about 10 cm to 1.5 m (*see* Galápagos Islands). Tortoises lay eggs and have long lifespans, reputedly up to 150 years. *Compare* turtle; terrapin.

tortoiseshell butterfly A nymphalid butterfly whose wings are mainly orange with black markings. Tortoiseshells are found in Europe, Asia, and North America. The caterpillars feed mainly on nettles and willows. Chief genera: *Aglais*, *Nymphalis*.

Toscanini, Arturo (1867–1957) Italian conductor. He made his debut in 1886 and subsequently conducted at La Scala, Milan, and at the Metropolitan Opera in New York. From 1937 until his death he conducted the NBC (National Broadcasting Company) Symphony Orchestra.

toucan A noisy forest-dwelling bird belonging to a family (*Ramphastidae*; 37 species) occurring in tropical America. Toucans have huge brightly coloured bills and typically black plumage with a brightly coloured breast. They feed on fruit. Order: *Piciformes* (woodpeckers, etc.).

touchstone A black or grey flintlike stone, formerly used for testing the purity of gold and silver. The metal to be tested and one of known purity are both rubbed with the touchstone and compared. The colour of the marks left indicates the impurities present.

Toulon 43 07N 5 55E A port in SE France, in the Var department on the Mediterranean Sea. Toulon is one of France's principal naval bases and has marine engineering, chemical, oil, and textile industries. Population (1989): 185 000.

Toulouse 43 33N 1 24E A city in S France, the capital of the Haute-Garonne department on the River Garonne. A major commercial and industrial centre, it has aircraft, armaments, chemical, and textile industries. It is also an important agricultural trading centre. Notable buildings include the basilica (11th–13th centuries), the gothic cathedral, and the university (1230). Population (1982): 354 289.

Toulouse-Lautrec, Henri (Marie Raymond) de (1864–1901) French artist. Stunted in growth by a childhood accident, he settled in Paris, where he led an unconventional life among the music halls and cafés of Montmartre. His comic but sympathetic studies of popular entertainers, circus life, and prostitutes in posters, lithographs, and paintings were influenced by Degas and Japanese prints. Characteristic paintings are *At the Moulin Rouge* (Art Institute of Chicago) and *La Toilette* (Louvre).

touraco. *See* turaco.

Tour de France The main Continental professional cycling race. Founded in 1903, the road race lasts three weeks or more and has a maximum length of approximately 4000 km (2480 mi). The race starts in a different town each year but always ends in Paris.

tourmaline A group of minerals composed of complex cyclosilicates containing boron. There are numerous varieties, some being used as gemstones and some for their piezoelectric and polarizing properties. Tourmalines are found in veins and pegmatites, in granite rocks.

Tours 47 23N 0 42E A city in central France, the capital of the Indre-et-Loire department situated between the Rivers Loire and Cher. Notable buildings include the gothic cathedral, the archiepiscopal palace (17th–18th centuries), and the university (1970). Tours is a tourist centre for the Loire Valley and has varied manufacturing industries. Population (1982): 136 483.

Tower Bridge A bridge over the River Thames, next to the Tower of London. Built in 1894 in the gothic style, it has a central portion that lifts to allow large ships to pass through it into the Pool of London.

Tower of London A royal fortress on the N bank of the River Thames, to the E of the City of London. It was begun in the 11th century and added to in subsequent centuries. It was a royal palace until the 17th century and a state prison. It is now a barracks, armoury, and museum, containing the British crown jewels.

TOWER BRIDGE

Townsend, Sue (1946–) British novelist and dramatist. Her novel *The Secret Diary of Adrian Mole* (1982) was immensely popular. Her plays include *The Great Celestial Cow* (1984).

toxaemia The presence of bacterial toxins in the blood. However, the term is most often used to describe a condition affecting pregnant women, formerly thought to be due to toxins but is now known to be caused by hypertension (raised blood pressure).

toxin A poison produced by a living organism. Many microorganisms, including bacteria and fungi, produce toxins. In diphtheria and tetanus the toxin is produced by the bacteria within the infected person; in botulism the toxin is produced in contaminated food. Some toxins are useful: penicillin is a toxin that kills bacteria.

Trabzon (former name: Trebizond) 41 00N 39 43E A port in NE Turkey, on the Black Sea. It was the capital of the Comnenian empire (1204–1461) and has a university (1963). Population (1985): 155 960.

trachea **1.** The windpipe: a tube that conducts air from the larynx to the left and right bronchi, which continue to the lungs. The trachea is lined by mucous membrane and supported by hoops of cartilage in its wall. **2.** One of the air passages in insects, which lead directly to the tissues. Each trachea has an external opening (spiracle) that can be opened and closed.

trachoma An eye disease that occurs in dry poor parts of the world and is caused by a virus-like organism of the genus *Chlamydia*. It is a severe form of conjunctivitis in which the membrane lining the eyelids becomes scarred and shrunken. Trachoma is the world's most common cause of blindness.

Tracy, Spencer (1900–67) US film actor. He began his film career in the 1930s by playing gangsters, but later costarred with Katherine Hepburn in nine films, including *Adam's Rib* (1949) and *Guess Who's Coming to Dinner* (1967). Other notable films include *The Old Man and the Sea* (1958) and *Judgement at Nuremberg* (1961).

trade cycle The repeated cycle of boom, recession, depression, recovery, and boom in an economy. In the UK in the 19th century, the trade cycle displayed remarkable regularity and stability; in the 20th century, it has fluctuated more. The Depression of the 1930s was a severe and protracted world slump followed, after World War II, by a period of boom, interrupted by only minor recessions, which persisted until another depression was entered in the 1970s. The causes of the cycle are uncertain, but it may result from the persistence of erratic shocks to the economy, such as wars, political rises in the prices of essential commodities (such as oil), etc. Many government economic policies attempt to avoid the excesses of the trade cycle.

trademarks Distinctive emblems owned by a manufacturer or trader and applied to his goods to identify them as produced or sold by him. The owner of a trademark has the right to its exclusive use in connection with the goods associated with it. Any trademark can be protected against infringement by legal action and registered trademarks enjoy additional statutory protection.

Tradescantia A genus of flowering plants (about 60 species), native to North and Central America and popular as ornamentals. Varieties of the wandering jew (*T. fluminensis*) are popular house plants, having oval green leaves, tinged with pink or mauve or with silver stripes. Spiderworts, derived from *T. virginiana*, have three-petalled blue, purple, red, or white flowers and grasslike leaves; they are attractive border plants. Family: *Commelinaceae*.

trade union An organization of employees joined together to present a collective front in negotiations with an employer and to provide a measure of security for its members. The origins of trade unions lie in the local clubs of skilled craftsmen in 18th-century Britain. Robert Owen's Grand National Consolidated Trades Union (1834), the first attempt to unite skilled and unskilled workers, collapsed following the transportation of the Tolpuddle Martyrs. In 1851 the first successful national trade union, the Amalgamated Society of Engineers, was formed and in 1868 the Trades Union Congress (TUC) met for the first time. Granted legal status in 1871, trade unions began to be formed by unskilled workers. Unions in the UK finally became politically and financially secure with the passing of the Trade Disputes Act (1906), which prevented employers from suing unions for damages after a strike. The failure of the General Strike (1926) was a blow to the trades union movement in Britain and the consequent Trade Disputes Act (1927) made general strikes illegal. This was repealed by the postwar Labour Government but the position of unions in law is still often a subject of debate, especially with regard to strikes and picketing. National union organizations (such as the TUC) have become important political forces. The first international trade union was the first International (1864); the international trades union movement is now represented by the World Federation of Trade Unions and the International Confederation of Free Trade Unions.

trade winds (*or* tropical easterlies) The predominantly easterly winds that blow in the tropics. They blow from the NE in the N hemisphere and from the SE in the S hemisphere, converging towards the equator.

Trafalgar, Battle of (21 October, 1805) The naval battle in the Napoleonic Wars in which the British under Nelson (in the *Victory*) defeated the French W of Cape Trafalgar, between Cádiz and Gibraltar (SW Spain). The British success, which was tragically marred by Nelson's death in the hour of victory, ended the threat of a French invasion of Britain.

tragacanth. *See* gums.

tragedy A form of drama recounting the fall (usually, the death) of a noble protagonist. The form evolved in ancient Greece from the dithyramb, a choral song, and was fully developed in the plays of Aeschylus, Sophocles, and Euripides. Little tragic drama of worth was then written until the tragedies of Shakespeare and his followers. In 17th-century France the neoclassical tragedies of Racine and Corneille were carefully based on principles derived from Aristotle's *Poetics*. Ibsen and Strindberg in Europe and Eugene O'Neill in the USA contributed to the development of tragic drama in the 19th and 20th centuries.

tragopan A short-tailed pheasant belonging to a genus (*Tragopan*) occurring in wet forests of the Himalayas. Male tragopans have vivid plumage and two erectile blue fleshy "horns" on the head; a fold of skin beneath the bill forms a large bib during display.

Training Agency A statutory body that organizes the British government's employment and training services. Formerly the Manpower Services Commission (MSC), it is subdivided into Adult Employment Training and the Youth Training Scheme (YTS).

tranquillizers A group of drugs used to quieten aggressive, restless, or anxious patients. The major tranquillizers are powerful drugs used in the treatment of schizophrenia and other mental disorders. They include reserpine, the phenothiazines, and the butyrophenones (e.g. haloperidol). Minor tranquillizers, which include the benzodiazepines, are used for the treatment of neuroses and anxiety and can be addictive.

transcendentalism A philosophy that emphasizes the modes of thought and apprehension beyond the world of experience. In the philosophy of Kant, everything beyond man's limited experience is transcendental and essentially unknowable. Human intuitions about time and space and understanding of quality and quantity are vital for experience, but are transcendent in that they do not come from that experience.

TRADE WINDS

transformer A device for converting alternating current from one voltage to another. The input is fed to a primary winding, a coil of wire round a soft iron core, creating an oscillating magnetic field in the core. This field induces a secondary current of the same frequency in the secondary winding wound on the same core. The ratio of primary to secondary voltage is equal to the ratio of the number of turns in the secondary coil to that in the primary. The device is widely used both in electronic circuits and in the transmission and distribution of electric power (*see* electricity supply).

TRANSISTOR

Germanium is a typical semiconductor. The four outer electrons in each of its atoms form covalent bonds with adjacent atoms. In the pure state it acts as an insulator as no electrons are available to carry current.

Arsenic atoms have five outer electrons. Germanium containing arsenic atoms as an impurity can carry current because the fifth electron is available as a carrier. This is an n-type semiconductor because current is carried by negative electrons.

Indium atoms have three outer electrons. Germanium doped with indium therefore has holes in its electronic structure. These can be filled by electrons from neighbouring atoms, creating new holes; this has the effect of positive charge moving through the crystal in the opposite direction to electrons. This is p-type germanium.

In the bipolar junction transistor a piece of p-type material is sandwiched between two n-type pieces, making an n-p-n structure (p-n-p transistors are also used).

In an n-p-n transistor, a negative voltage is applied to one end (the emitter) and a positive to the other (the collector). No current flows, however, because a potential barrier forms at the junction between the emitter and the central region (the base).

If the base region is positively biased, the free electrons in the emitter are attracted to the p-type base and current flows through the thin base to the collector. As the collector current depends on the amount of bias to the base, the device can be used as an amplifier.

In the symbolic representation of a transistor, the direction of the arrow on the emitter indicates current direction and the type of transistor (n-p-n or p-n-p).

TRANSISTOR The operation of the bipolar junction transistor.

transistor A semiconductor device with three or more electrodes. Transistors form the basic elements of electronic amplifiers and logic circuits, often combined with other components in integrated circuits. They were first developed in 1948 by William Shockley and his coworkers at the Bell Telephone Co and now replace thermionic valves in most applications. A **bipolar junction transistor** consists of two junctions between p-type and n-type semiconductors forming either a p-n-p or n-p-n structure. Current is carried across these junctions by both negative and positive charge carriers (electrons and holes). Depending on how it is connected into a circuit, the junction transistor can act as a voltage or current amplifier in much the same way as a triode valve.

Originally, junction transistors were made by alloying the impurity metal onto the semiconductor crystal or by adding impurities as the crystal was being grown. Now the doping is diffused in as a gas, introduced by ion implantation, or, more commonly, achieved by a combined process of etching and diffusion, known as the planar process.

The **field effect transistor** (FET) is a unipolar device, in which current is carried by only one type of charge. There are two types: the junction FET (JFET) has a region of semiconductor of one doping type flanked by two highly doped layers of the opposite type. Current flows parallel to the junctions, between the so-called source and drain electrodes, through a narrow channel between the highly doped regions (the gate); it is controlled by the electric field arising from the gate input voltage, which alters the width of the conducting channel. The JFET is used as a separate component in amplifiers and switches. In the insulated-gate FET (IGFET) the source and drain electrodes are highly doped regions in a substrate of the opposite type. The gate electrode is a conductor separated from the substrate by a thin insulating layer across the surface. The electric field caused by the gate voltage controls the source-drain current on the other side of the insulator. The IGFET is used mainly in metal-oxide semiconductor (MOS) integrated circuits. It is smaller than the equivalent bipolar junction transistor and uses less power. The first plastic transistor was built in 1988. See p. 723.

transition elements A large group of metallic elements, including most of the commonly used metals, the inner electron shells of which are incomplete. The lanthanides and the actinides are sometimes included in this definition. The elements show considerable similarities to their horizontal neighbours in the periodic table. In general, they are hard, brittle, high-melting, and excellent conductors of heat and electricity. They have multiple valencies and form coloured compounds.

Transjordan. *See* Jordan, Hashemite kingdom of.

Transkei, Republic of A small country in South Africa, consisting of three separate areas. Most of the population is Xhosa. *Economy*: chiefly subsistence agriculture, especially livestock, although such cash crops as tea, coffee, and flax are now being developed. *History*: created in 1963, when South Africa granted self-government to the Xhosa nation, as the first of the Bantu Homelands, it became independent in 1976. In 1978, after constant disputes, it broke off diplomatic relations with South Africa. In 1987 a coup brought Maj-Gen Bantu Holomisa to power. President: Tutor Nyangelizwe Vulinolela Ndamase. Official currency: South Af-

rican rand. Area: 43 188 sq km (16 675 sq mi). Population (1985 est): 3 000 000. Capital: Umtata.

transmigration of souls. *See* reincarnation.

transmutation The conversion of one element into another. An early (unfulfilled) aim of alchemy was the transmutation of base metals into gold. Transmutations were achieved in the 20th century by bombarding elements with alpha particles or neutrons.

transpiration The loss of water vapour from the surface of a plant, which occurs primarily through small pores (stomata) in the leaves but also (slowly) through the cuticle of the epidermis. The rate of water loss is controlled by the opening and closing of the stomata, greater loss occurring during the day than at night.

transplantation The surgical implantation of a tissue or organ derived either from another part of the patient's body or from another individual (the donor). Skin grafting is an example of the former: it is used particularly to repair damage and disfigurement caused by burns and other injuries. Transplantation of donor organs requires careful matching of the donor's and recipient's tissues together with the use of drugs that suppress the recipient's immune responses (*see* immunosuppression). The first successful heart transplant operation was performed by Christiaan Barnard in 1967; other organs that have been transplanted include the kidneys, lung, and liver. The first implantation of an artificial heart, made of titanium, took place in 1988.

transportation In law, the practice of sending a convicted criminal to some place outside Britain, usually to one of the colonies, to be kept in hard labour. Transportation dates back to the reign of Elizabeth I; it ceased in the 19th century.

Trans-Siberian Railway The world's longest railway, running 9335 km (5800 mi) from Moscow to Vladivostok. Double track, largely electrified, has replaced the original single track line built between 1891 and 1905. The complete journey with nearly a hundred stops takes nine days.

transubstantiation In Roman Catholic theology, the doctrine that the substance of the elements of bread and wine in the Eucharist is changed at consecration into the substance of the body and blood of Christ. Only the accidents (i.e. the qualities apparent to the senses) of the bread and wine remain.

transuranic elements Elements with higher atomic number than uranium. Apart from traces of neptunium and plutonium, none of them has ever been detected in nature, since no isotopes of sufficient half-life exist; they have been created since 1940 in nuclear reactions. *See also* actinides.

Transvaal The most northerly province in South Africa. Heavily populated in the S, it contains the country's main industrial area, centred on the Witwatersrand; iron, steel, and chemicals are produced. Mineral deposits include gold, diamonds, uranium, coal, chromite, tin, and platinum. It has a well-developed agriculture producing maize, wheat, peanuts, citrus fruit, cotton, and tobacco; sheep and cattle are raised. *History*: originally an Afrikaner republic, it fought in the Boer Wars against Britain (1880–81, 1899–1902). It joined the Union of South Africa in 1910. Area: 283 917 sq km (109 621 sq mi). Population (1985): 7 532 179. Capital: Pretoria.

Transylvania A region of SE Europe, bounded by the Carpathian Mountains and the Transylvanian Alps. Transylvania retained its distinctive character under successive Roman, Magyar, and Hungarian rulers; during the 16th and 17th centuries, it was a self-governing princedom within the Ottoman Empire. Restored to Hungary in 1687, Transylvania became part of Romania after World War I.

trap-door spider A spider, especially one of the family *Ctenizidae*, that constructs a silk-lined burrow in the ground covered by a tight-fitting silk-hinged door. Ctenizids are dull brown, with short stout legs. They occur in tropical and subtropical regions.

Trappists A Roman Catholic monastic order, officially known as the Cistercians of the Strict Observance. It was founded in 1664 at the abbey of La Trappe in Normandy; there are now monasteries in Britain, Ireland, North America, and elsewhere. The order is notable for its austerity, which includes the observance of strict silence.

treason The violation by a citizen of his allegiance to the sovereign or the state. In England, the Statute of Treasons (1352) defined two kinds of treason: high treason, which is punishable by death, is (1) to plot to kill or maim the sovereign; (2) to wage war against him or to join his enemies; (3) to kill his eldest son or heir; (4) to violate his wife, eldest daughter (if unmarried), or heir's wife; (5) to kill the chancellor, or any judge while he or she is performing his or her office. Petty treason, abolished in 1828, was the violation of private allegiance.

treasure trove In law, money or coin, gold, silver plate, or bullion of unknown ownership found hidden in a house or in the ground. In England it belongs to the Crown provided its owner is unknown; if it has been abandoned or lost the finder has the first claim on it after the true owner. The finder of treasure trove is rewarded the value of the property found, unless he conceals it, in which case he is liable to imprisonment.

Treasury The UK government department, established in 1653, that is responsible, with the Bank of England, for the management of the economy and the allocation of the available government money between the spending departments. The prime minister is the first lord of the treasury, but it is run by the chancellor of the exchequer, assisted by the chief secretary to the Treasury and the financial secretary.

Trebizond. *See* Trabzon.

tree A tall perennial woody plant, usually with a single main stem (the trunk) and secondary stems (the branches) arising some distance above ground level. Most tree species are either dicotyledons (angiosperms) – the broad-leaved trees – or conifers (gymnosperms). These are of economic importance as producers of hardwoods and softwoods, respectively. Other groups containing trees are the cycads (gymnosperms), monocotyledons (notably the palms), and the ferns. The conifers and tropical trees are mostly evergreen plants, while broad-leaved trees growing in regions with marked seasonal changes in climate are typically deciduous. The study of the ecology and classification of trees is called **dendrology**. *See also* forest. *See* p. 726.

Tree, Sir Herbert (Draper) Beerbohm (1853–1917) British actor and theatre manager, halfbrother of the writer Max Beerbohm (1872–1956). He was manager of the Haymarket Theatre from 1887 to 1899 and then of Her Majesty's Theatre, where he staged many lavish Shakespearean productions. In 1904 he founded the Royal Academy of Dramatic Art.

treecreeper A small songbird belonging to a family (*Certhiidae*; 5 species) occurring in Europe, Asia, and North America. It has a brownish streaked plumage with pale silvery underparts, long claws, and a slender down-curved bill. The European treecreeper (*Certhia familiaris*) occurs mainly in coniferous woods, where it creeps up tree trunks to probe for small beetles, spiders, woodlice, etc.

tree frog A small toad belonging to a widely distributed family (*Hylidae*; about 500 species). They have adapted to living in trees and have adhesive pads on their toes that enable them to cling to leaves and branches, leaping acrobatically to capture insects.

tree of heaven A tree, *Ailanthus altissima*, native to central Asia and planted elsewhere as an ornamental. Growing to a height of 30 m, it has compound leaves, up to 1 m, composed of paired leaflets. Its flowers form greenish-white clusters; the female flowers produce winged fruits. Family: *Simaroubaceae*.

tree-ring dating. *See* dendrochronology.

tree shrew A primitive prosimian primate belonging to the family *Tupaiidae* (18 species), found in Java, Borneo, Sumatra, the Philippines, and S Asia. The common tree shrew (*Tupaia glis*) is 30–45 cm long including the tail (15–23 cm) and has a slender pointed face. It darts among the branches, feeding on insects, fruit, and seeds.

Trematoda. *See* fluke.

Trent, Council of (1545–63) The 19th general council of the Roman Catholic Church, an expression of the Counter-Reformation, which was summoned by Pope Paul III in its confrontation with Protestantism. It was held in Trento (N Italy). There were three sessions (1545–47, 1551–52, 1562–63), which clarified doctrine and instituted reforms. The Council condemned Luther's doctrine of justification by faith alone and defined transubstantiation.

Trent, River A river in central England. Flowing mainly NE from Staffordshire through Nottingham, it joins the River Ouse to form the Humber estuary. The Midlands' main river, it is linked to the Mersey by the Trent, Mersey, and Grand Union Canals. Length: 270 km (170 mi).

Trento (German name: Trent) 46 04N 11 08E A city in N Italy, the capital of Trentino-Alto Adige on the River Adige. Dating from pre-Roman times, it has a romanesque cathedral (12th-century) and the 16th-century Church of Sta Maria Maggiore, where the Council of Trent met. Population (1987): 100 202.

Trèves. *See* Trier.

Triassic period (*or* Trias) A period of geological time at the beginning of the Mesozoic era, lasting from about 240 to 200 million years ago. The rocks of the period were laid down mainly under continental conditions. The dinosaurs, ichthyosaurs, and plesiosaurs appeared in the Triassic.

tribes of Israel In the Bible, the Hebrew people. The 12 tribes, descended from the sons of Jacob, were Reuben, Simeon, Judah, Issachar, Zebulun, Benjamin, Dan, Naphtali, Gad, Asher, Levi, and Ephraim and Manasseh. These last two were usually counted as one. After the death of Solomon, ten of the tribes broke away from Benjamin and Judah to form the northern kingdom of Israel; they are known as the Ten Lost Tribes of Israel.

tribune In ancient Rome, a plebeian magistrate appointed to protect plebeians' rights. Instituted during the 5th-century political struggles between patricians

TREE

softwoods

Scots pine silver fir Norway spruce European larch

hardwoods

teak common oak English elm blue gum

food trees

crab apple Seville orange walnut cocoa

ornamentals

horse chestnut magnolia silver wattle jacaranda

and plebeians, the tribunes could veto legislative proposals of the Senate or popular assemblies and could themselves propose legislation without senatorial approval.

Triceratops A three-horned dinosaur of the late Cretaceous period (about 100–65 million years ago). 8 m long and weighing 8.5 tonnes, it had an enormous head with one horn on the snout and one over each eye. It also had a large bony neck frill and browsed on tough plants. Order: *Ornithischia*.

Trident missile A US navy three-stage solid-fuelled nuclear strategic missile launched from a submarine and having a range of 7800 km (4800 mi). Designed as a replacement for the Poseidon missile, Trident missiles, first deployed in the early 1980s, are capable of great accuracy at increased distances and carry a new stellar-inertial guidance system.

Trier (French name: Trèves) 49 45N 6 39E A city in SW West Germany, in Rhineland-Palatinate on the River Moselle. Founded by the Emperor Augustus, it has important Roman remains. It is a wine-trading and industrial centre. Population (1975 est): 100 338.

Trieste (Serbo-Croat name: Trst) 45 39N 13 47E A seaport in Italy, the capital of Friuli-Venezia Giulia, situated on the Gulf of Trieste at the head of the Adriatic Sea. An important transit port for central Europe, it has shipyards, oil refineries, and a steel industry. *History*: an important Roman port in the 1st century AD, it passed to Austria in 1382. It expanded rapidly in the 19th century and in 1920 was ceded to Italy. Following World War II it became the capital of the Free Territory of Trieste. In 1954 most of the N of the Territory (including Trieste) passed to Italy and the remainder to Yugoslavia. Population (1980 est): 257 697.

triggerfish A shallow-water fish, belonging to a family (*Balistidae*) related to puffers, that occurs in tropical seas. Its deep laterally flattened body is covered with large scales. The strong spine of the first dorsal fin is erected and locked into position by the second dorsal fin, forming a "trigger" that wedges the fish into crevices.

trigonometry A branch of mathematics founded by Hipparchus in the mid-2nd century BC, concerned originally with the measurement of triangles. The ratios of the lengths of the sides of a right-angled triangle are used to define the sine, cosine, and tangent of one of the angles of the triangle. Trigonometry deals with the properties of these and related functions.

trilobite An extinct marine arthropod belonging to a subphylum (*Trilobita*; over 4000 species) that flourished 500–200 million years ago. Trilobite fossils are abundant in rocks of this period. Its flattened oval body, 10–675 mm long, was divided by two longitudinal furrows into three lobes. The head bore a pair of antennae eyes and each segment of the thorax and tail region carried a pair of forked appendages.

Trimurti The Hindu triad of gods, Brahma, Vishnu, and Shiva, representing the creative, sustaining, and destructive aspects of reality respectively, sometimes portrayed as one body with three heads.

Trinidad and Tobago, Republic of A country off the N coast of South America, consisting of the islands of Trinidad and Tobago. Both are hilly and wooded. Most of the population is of African and East Indian descent. *Economy*: oil and asphalt have replaced cocoa and sugar as the main source of the country's wealth and

reserves of offshore gas have also been discovered. Other industrial developments include aluminium smelting, plastics, electronics, iron and steel, and petrochemicals. It is a member of CARICOM. *History*: Trinidad was inhabited by Arawak and Carib Indians when it was discovered by Columbus in 1498. It was a Spanish colony from the 16th century until 1802, when it was ceded to Britain; it joined with Tobago in 1809. The country became an independent state within the British Commonwealth in 1962. In 1976 it became a republic with the former governor general, Ellis Clarke (1917–), as its first president. Prime minister: George Chambers. Official language: English. Official currency: Trinidad and Tobago dollar of 100 cents. Area: 5128 sq km (1980 sq mi). Population (1983 est): 1 211 000. Capital and main port: Port-of-Spain.

Trinity, the A central doctrine of Christian theology, stating that God is one substance but with three distinct, coequal, and coeternal "persons," the Father, the Son, and the Holy Spirit. The belief is based on a number of passages in the New Testament. It was given a first formal definition by the Council of Nicaea (325).

triode. *See* thermionic valve.

Triple Alliance (1882) An alliance between Germany, Austria-Hungary, and Italy, which with the opposing Triple Entente shaped European diplomacy in the decades before World War I. At the outbreak of war (1914) Italy declared its neutrality, thus breaking the alliance.

Triple Alliance, War of the (*or* Paraguayan War; 1865–70) The war between Paraguay and a coalition of Argentina, Brazil, and Uruguay. Conflict was precipitated by the belligerent diplomacy of Paraguay's dictator, F. S. López (1826–70), towards Argentina, which with Brazil and Uruguay invaded Paraguay. López refused to surrender and following the capture of Asunción in 1868 waged a guerrilla war in the N until taken prisoner in 1870.

Triple Entente An informal combination of France, Russia, and Britain resulting from the Franco-Russian alliance (1893), the Franco-British Entente Cordiale (1904), and the Anglo-Russian agreement (1907). It was formed in opposition to the Triple Alliance.

Tripoli (Arabic name: Tarabulus) 32 58N 13 12E The capital and main port of Libya, on the Mediterranean Sea. Originally founded as Oea by the Phoenicians, it became the capital of Libya on independence in 1951.

TRIGONOMETRY *Definitions of the trigonometric functions sine, cosine, and tangent and of their reciprocals cosecant, secant, and cotangent.*

Exports include fruit and olive oil and it is a transshipment centre. Population (1982): 980 000.

Tripoli (Arabic name: Tarabalus) 34 27N 35 50E A port in NW Lebanon, on the Mediterranean Sea. It was the capital of a Phoenician federation of three other cities. Iraqi oil is brought by pipeline to the refinery here. Population (1985 est): 500 000.

trireme. *See* ships.

Tristan The tragic hero of several medieval romances. After accidentally drinking a magic love potion, he becomes the lover of Iseult (Isolde), who is betrothed to his uncle, King Mark of Cornwall. He later renounces Iseult and goes to Brittany, where he marries the duke's daughter. Dying from a wound, he sends for Iseult; she arrives too late and dies of grief at his side. Of Celtic origin, the legend appeared in a French poem, written in about 1150. Other versions include Gottfried von Strassburg's *Tristan und Isolde*, the source of Wagner's opera. In a 13th-century prose romance the story was incorporated into the Arthurian legend.

Tristan da Cunha 37 15S 12 30W A group of four small islands in the S Atlantic Ocean, a dependency of St Helena. The only settlement, Edinburgh, is on Tristan (the largest island). In 1961 the inhabitants were evacuated to the UK to escape a volcanic eruption but most chose to return in 1963. The economy is based on crawfish canning and postage stamps. Area: about 100 sq km (40 sq mi). Population (1980): 323.

tritium (T *or* ³H) A radioactive isotope of hydrogen, the nucleus of which contains one proton and two neutrons. It does not occur naturally but is produced in nuclear reactors and is used as a radioactive tracer and in nuclear weapons. Tritium decays with a half-life of 12.3 years, emitting beta-rays.

triton shell A gastropod mollusc of the family *Cymatiidae* (about 100 species), occurring mainly in tropical seas. Triton trumpets (genus *Charonia*) grow to 40 cm and have ribbed shells, often with prominent knobs. They feed on molluscs and echinoderms.

triumvirate In Roman affairs, a board of three men officially appointed for special administrative duties. The so-called first Triumvirate (60 BC) of Caesar, Pompey, and Crassus was merely a private arrangement. The triumvirate, or triple dictatorship, of Mark Antony, Lepidus, and Octavian was unique; appointed in 43 BC to maintain public order in Rome, they held office with absolute powers until Lepidus was ousted in 36.

trogon An insectivorous bird belonging to a family (*Trogonidae*; 35 species) occurring in forested regions of Africa, Asia, and America. Trogons have iridescent plumage, which in males is usually dark with a bright red or yellow belly. They have rounded wings, a short curved bill, and a long tail. *See also* quetzal.

Troilus In Greek mythology, a son of King Priam of Troy who was killed by Achilles. The story of his love for Cressida, who deserted him for the Greek Diomedes, first appeared in the *Roman de Troie* by the 12th-century French poet Benoît de Sainte-Maure.

Trojan Horse In Greek legend, a gigantic hollow wooden horse used in the Trojan War. The Trojans hauled it inside their city, believing it to be a gift to Athena, and Greek warriors then emerged from it to open the gates to their army.

Trojan War In Greek legend, a ten years' war waged by the Greeks against Troy after the abduction of Helen

by Paris. Its history, probably based on an actual war fought in the 12th century BC, is related in Homer's *Iliad*. The Greeks were led by Agamemnon and their champions included Achilles, Diomedes, and Odysseus. The chief Trojan warriors were Hector and Paris, sons of King Priam. The war culminated in the capture of Troy by the stratagem of the Trojan Horse.

troll In Scandinavian folklore, originally a gigantic ogre-like creature imagined as guarding treasure, inhabiting a castle, and stalking through the forest at night. In later folklore, trolls were conceived as dwarflike cave- and mountain-dwellers who were skilled craftsmen.

Trollope, Anthony (1815–82) British novelist. He worked for the General Post Office from 1834 until he retired in 1867. He established his reputation with a series of novels, including *Barchester Towers* (1857), set in the imaginary county of Barsetshire with a cast of predominantly clerical characters. A second series of novels, set against a political background, includes *Phineas Finn* (1869) and *The Eustace Diamonds* (1873).

trombone A brass musical instrument, consisting of a cylindrical tube, about 3 m (9 ft) long, turned back upon itself, a cup-shaped mouthpiece, and a flaring bell. By means of a slide and by varying lip pressure, a chromatic range of almost three octaves can be produced. The trombone has been part of the symphony orchestra since the late 18th century and is frequently used in jazz. The old English name for the trombone was the **sackbut**.

Trondheim 63 36N 10 23E A city and seaport in W Norway on Trondheim Fjord. It has a famous cathedral (12th–14th centuries) where Norwegian sovereigns have been crowned since early times and two universities. Its industries include shipbuilding and fishing; the main exports are timber, wood pulp, fish, and metal goods. Population (1987): 134 496.

TROOPING THE COLOUR *The Queen celebrating her official birthday on horseback for the last time.*

trooping the Colour Traditionally, the parade of the British sovereign's flag, or Colour, displayed so that foreign mercenaries would recognize it in battle. It is now a military parade held on the Horse Guards parade ground in Whitehall, London, on the sovereign's official birthday.

tropic bird A white seabird belonging to a family (*Phaethontidae*; 3 species) occurring in tropical and subtropical waters. Tropic birds have black eye and wing

729   **Truman, Harry S.**

markings and are up to 50 cm long excluding the long streamer-like tail feathers. Order: *Pelecaniformes* (cormorants, pelicans, etc.).

tropics The area of the earth's surface lying roughly between the Tropic of Cancer on the 23°30′N parallel of latitude and the Tropic of Capricorn on the 23°30′S parallel.

tropism The growth of a plant or sedentary animal in response to a directional external stimulus: a growth movement towards the stimulus is a positive tropism; the opposite response is a negative tropism. For example, positive **hydrotropism** is growth towards water; negative **geotropism** is growth away from the pull of gravity.

troposphere. *See* atmosphere.

Trotsky, Leon (Lev Bronstein; 1879–1940) Russian revolutionary and Marxist theorist. Trotsky became a Marxist in the 1890s and was imprisoned and exiled for participating in revolutionary activities. He lived in W Europe from 1902 until the Revolution of 1905, when he was again imprisoned and exiled. On the outbreak of the Russian Revolution, he returned to Russia and abandoned his previous Menshevik loyalities to become a Bolshevik. He played a major role in the October Revolution and as war commissar during the civil war (1918–20) directed the Red Army to victory. Under Lenin, Trotsky was Russia's second most powerful man but lost to Stalin the power struggle that followed Lenin's death. *See also* Trotskyism.

Trotskyism The form of Marxism developed by Leon Trotsky, who advocated world revolution in opposition to the view that socialism could be achieved in one country in isolation. Trotskyists believed that the revolution could only be maintained and capitalism defeated by developing the strength and solidarity of the working class throughout the world. To this end Trotsky and his supporters founded the Fourth International in 1937; in 1979 the Fourth International had functioning sections in over 60 countries.

troubadours Provençal poets of the 12th to 14th centuries whose lyric poetry had a profound influence on both the subject matter and form of subsequent European verse. Both poets and composers, the troubadours wrote songs introducing a new concept of love, later labelled courtly love. They developed several poetic genres and verse forms. The earliest troubadour was Guillaume, 9th Duc d'Aquitaine (1071–1127). Other famous troubadours were Vicomte de Hautefort (c. 1140–c. 1207); Arnaut Daniel (c. 1180), who was credited with inventing the *sestina*; and Bernard de Ventadour (late 12th century), in whose lyrics the conventions of courtly love were most clearly developed.

trout One of several predatory fish belonging to the family *Salmonidae*, especially the genus *Salmo*, that are native to the N hemisphere but introduced elsewhere as food and game fish. It has a stout body with a blunt head and varies in colour from blackish to light olive with characteristic black or red spots or X-shaped markings. Trout occur mainly in fresh water. The common European brown trout (*S. trutta*) has a migratory variety called the sea trout. The North American rainbow trout (*S. gairdneri*) is distinguished by a broad purple band along its sides. Order: *Salmoniformes*.

Troy An ancient city in Asia Minor, near the Dardanelles. According to legend, when the Trojan prince Paris abducted Helen, Agamemnon led a Greek army to recover her and captured Troy (*see* Trojan War).

Schliemann's excavations (1870) identified Troy at Hissarlik. Excavations have revealed nine superimposed cities, the seventh of which was contemporary with the legendary siege. *See also* Homer.

Trudeau, Pierre Elliott (1919–) Canadian statesman; Liberal prime minister (1968–79, 1980–84). A French Canadian, he nevertheless opposed French separatism and in 1970 briefly introduced martial law to deal with separatist agitation in Quebec. Defeated in 1979 by Joseph Clark (1939–), he was re-elected in 1980. He retired from office in 1984, and his Liberal party lost the subsequent general election.

Trueman, Fred (Frederick Sewards T.; 1931–) British cricketer, who played for Yorkshire and England. A great fast bowler, he was the first bowler to take 300 Test wickets.

Truffaut, François (1932–84) French film director. He was an influential member of the New Wave. His films, noted for their visual charm and elegance, include *Jules et Jim* (1961), *L'Enfant sauvage* (1970), *Day for Night* (1973), and *Le Dernier Métro* (1980).

TROUBADOURS *Minstrels depicted on a 14th-century French ivory bas-relief.*

truffle A fungus belonging to the order *Tuberales*. Up to 10 cm across, truffles are rounded and occur in chalky soils, usually in association with tree roots. Several species are regarded as delicacies, including the black Périgord truffle (*Tuber melanosporum*) and the white Piedmont truffle (*T. magnatum*), both of France. They are collected in oak woods using trained pigs or dogs. The bluish-black English truffle (*T. aestivum*) is found mainly in beech woods. Class: *Ascomycetes*.

Trujillo 8 06S 79 00W A city in Peru, situated 13 km (8 mi) from its port, Salaverry, on the Pacific coast. Founded in 1535, Trujillo is the commercial centre for an area producing sugar cane and rice. Population (1987): 476 000.

Truman, Harry S. (1884–1972) US statesman; Democratic president (1945–53). One of his earliest acts as president was to order the atomic bombing of Hiroshima and Nagasaki to end the war with Japan. In the **Truman Doctrine** he announced economic and military aid to countries threatened by interference from other states. His administration saw the establishment of the North Atlantic Treaty Organization (1949). In domestic politics his Fair Deal programme promised social reform.

trumpet A brass musical instrument. The modern trumpet consists of a cylindrical tube, 1.5 m (5 ft) long, turned back on itself, a cup-shaped mouthpiece, and a flaring bell. Three valves alter the effective length of the tube; with varying lip pressure the B flat trumpet has a chromatic range of two and a half octaves.

trunkfish A tropical fish, also called boxfish or cowfish, belonging to a family (*Ostraciidae*) related to puffers, that occurs in the Atlantic and Pacific Oceans. Its body is often brightly coloured and encased in a boxlike shell of fused bony plates with spaces for the fins, etc.

Truro 50 16N 5 03W A cathedral city in SW England, the administrative centre of Cornwall. It is a small port and market town, with pottery and biscuit manufacturing. Population (1982): 16 040.

trypsin A digestive enzyme, secreted by the pancreas, that breaks down dietary proteins in the small intestine. It is secreted in an inactive form, which is converted to trypsin by the enzyme enterokinase in the intestine.

tsar The title (derived from the Latin, Caesar) of the rulers of Russia from 1547 to 1721. It was first adopted by Ivan the Terrible and, though commonly used until 1917, was officially replaced with the title Emperor by Peter the Great.

Tsaritsyn. *See* Volgograd.

tsetse fly A fly, 6–16 mm long, belonging to a genus (*Glossina*; 22 species) restricted to tropical Africa. Both sexes bite and suck the blood of mammals; *G. palpalis* transmits sleeping sickness to man and *G. morsitans* transmits nagana to cattle. Family: *Muscidae*.

Tsinan. *See* Jinan.

Tsingtao. *See* Qingdao.

Tuamotu Archipelago A chain of about 80 coral atolls in the S Pacific Ocean, in French Polynesia. Rangiroa is the largest island and Fakarava, the most important economically. French nuclear tests were held here during the 1960s. Mother-of-pearl, phosphate, and copra are produced. Area: 860 sq km (332 sq mi). Population (1983): 11 793. Administrative centre: Apataki atoll.

tuatara A lizard-like reptile, *Sphenodon punctatus*, that is the only living representative of the primitive order *Rhynchocephalia*, which lived 200 million years ago. It is found only on islands off the North Island of New Zealand and has a brown-black to greenish body with a crest of spines running from head to tail; up to 70 cm long, it may live 100 years. Tuataras live in burrows during the day and emerge at night to feed on spiders, insects, and birds' eggs.

tuba A valved brass instrument with a conical bore and low pitch, derived originally from the saxhorn. Various types of tuba exist under a variety of names; the instrument is used in the symphony orchestra as well as in the military band.

tuber A swollen underground plant stem in which carbohydrates (often in the form of starch) are stored. Some tubers, for example potatoes and yams, are important human foods. Tuber-bearing plants may reproduce vegetatively from buds on the tuber, and tuber crops are usually grown from tubers rather than seed.

tuberculin A protein derived from tuberculosis bacilli that have been killed. In the Mantoux test tuberculin is injected into the skin to test whether a person has been in contact with tuberculosis. The appearance of an in-

flamed patch (a positive reaction) indicates previous exposure to the bacilli.

tuberculosis An infectious disease caused by the bacillus *Mycobacterium tuberculosis* (which was first recognized by the bacteriologist Robert Koch (1843–1910) in 1882). In pulmonary tuberculosis the bacillus is inhaled into the lungs, where it forms a primary tubercle that usually heals without trouble. Alternatively the disease may smoulder for months without showing any symptoms. Reactivation of the primary disease, or reinfection, may lead to active tuberculosis ("consumption"), characterized by a cough, fever, lassitude, weight loss, and breathlessness. The TB bacillus can also enter the body through drinking infected cows' milk. Improved environmental conditions, pasteurization of milk, X-ray screening, and BCG vaccinations have all reduced the incidence of TB in developed countries.

tubifex A freshwater annelid worm, also called bloodworm, belonging to the widely distributed family *Tubificidae*. Found along muddy rivers and estuaries, the most common species is the bright-red extremely active *Tubifex tubifex*, up to 85 mm long. Class: *Oligochaeta*.

TUC. *See* trade union.

Tucson 32 15N 110 57W A city and health resort in the USA, in Arizona. Its growth came with the arrival of the Southern Pacific Railroad (1880) and the discovery of silver at nearby Tombstone. Tucson is an industrial centre for the surrounding agricultural and mining district. Population (1986 est): 384 385.

TUDORS *Henry VII, the first Tudor monarch.*

Tudors The ruling dynasty of England from 1485 to 1603. Owen Tudor (c. 1400–61), a Welshman, entered the service of Henry V and married (1422) his widow Catherine of Valois (1401–37). Their eldest son Edmund, Earl of Richmond (c. 1430–56), married Margaret Beaufort (1443–1509), the great-great-granddaughter of Edward III, and their son became the first Tudor monarch, Henry VII. Subsequent Tudor monarchs were Henry VIII, Edward VI, Mary I, and Elizabeth I.

tulip A perennial herbaceous plant of the genus *Tulipa* (about 100 species), native to the Old World but widely cultivated for ornament. Growing from bulbs, most tulips have a solitary bell-shaped flower, with bluish-green leaves clustered at the base of the plant. There are nearly

4000 varieties of garden tulips: the older varieties are descended from *T. gesneriana* and *T. suaveolens*; the newer ones often have *T. kaufmanniana*, *T. greigi*, or *T. fosteriana* as one of the parent species. Family: *Liliaceae*.

tulip tree A tree, *Liriodendron tulipifera*, native to E North America and widely planted for ornament. Reaching a height of 58 m in the wild, it has three-lobed leaves and large tulip-like flowers, greenish white or yellow, produce papery cones containing winged fruits. The wood, known as white wood, is used for furniture, plywood, paper, and boxes. The Chinese tulip tree (*L. chinense*) is similar but smaller. Family: *Magnoliaceae*.

Tull, Jethro (1674–1741) English agriculturist, best known for his invention in 1701 of the seed drill. He made many other innovations in agricultural methods.

Tulsa 36 07N 95 58W A city in the USA, in Oklahoma on the Arkansas River. Oil was discovered in 1901 and today over 800 oil companies have established plants here. Population (1986 est): 373 000.

tumour Any swelling in the body caused by the abnormal proliferation of cells. Tumours that do not spread to other parts of the body (i.e. are noncancerous) are described as benign. They are usually harmless. Tumours that destroy the tissue in which they arise and spread to other parts of the body are described as malignant (*see* cancer).

tuna A carnivorous food and game fish, sometimes called tunny, belonging to a family (*Scombridae*) found in warm seas. Its elongated robust body is generally dark above and silvery below. The large bluefin tuna (*Thunnus thynnus*) reaches 4.3 m in length. Large quantities of tinned tuna are consumed throughout the world. Order: *Perciformes. See also* albacore.

Tunbridge Wells (*or* Royal Tunbridge Wells) 51 08N 0 16E A town in SE England, in Kent. Visited for its medicinal waters since the 17th century, it became a fashionable health resort. Population (1981): 44 821.

tundra The level, virtually treeless, areas in the N hemisphere (in Eurasia and North America) lying between the most northerly region in which trees grow and the polar regions of perpetual snow and ice. Winters are long and severe with brief summers in which temperatures remain below 10°C (50°F); permafrost is a feature. Vegetation includes mosses, lichens, dwarf shrubs, herbaceous perennials, and a few stunted trees.

tungsten (*or* wolfram; W) A grey brittle metal with the highest melting point of any element. It was discovered in 1779 and is obtained from the ores wolframite ($FeWO_4$) and scheelite ($CaWO_4$) by reduction with hydrogen or carbon. It oxidizes readily when heated, forming the oxide WO_3. The metal is used as filaments in electric light bulbs, in television tubes, contact breakers, and X-ray tubes, and in many hard alloys for high-speed cutting tools. Tungsten carbide (WC) is very hard and is used for tipping drill bits. At no 74; at wt 183.85; mp $3410 \pm 20°C$; bp 5660°C.

tunicate A small marine animal belonging to the subphylum *Urochordata* (or *Tunicata*; about 2000 species). Tunicates range from several millimetres to over 30 cm in size. They have a saclike cellulose tunic covering the body; food particles are filtered from water drawn in through a siphon at the top and expelled through a second siphon. The free-swimming tadpole-like larvae show the major characteristics of all Chordata; they subsequently metamorphose to the adult form and lose their chordate features. Sea squirts (class *Ascidacea*) live attached to rocks, etc., singly or in colonies, while the salps (class *Thaliacea*) float in the sea, sometimes as chains of several hundred individuals.

Tunis (Arabic name: Tunus) 36 48N 10 13E The capital of Tunisia, on the Gulf of Tunis. It was developed by the Arabs in the 7th century AD. It came under French rule in the late 19th century, and became the capital on independence in 1956. Industries include chemicals, lead smelting, and textiles. Population (1984): 556 654.

Tunisia, Republic of (Arabic name: al-Jumhuriyah at-Tunisiyah) A small country in N Africa, bordering on the Mediterranean Sea. Its narrow coastal zone extends into desert in the S and rises to uplands in the N. The population is largely Arabic. *Economy*: predominantly agricultural, the chief products include wheat, olive oil, citrus fruits, dates, and wine; livestock, including sheep, cattle, and goats, is also important. Tunisia is one of the world's largest producers of phosphates. Oil reserves were discovered in 1964 and exploitation began in 1972; iron ore and lead are also mined. Manufacturing industry includes oil refining, cement, and steel processing. Fine beaches and notable architecture contribute to Tunisia's popularity with tourists. *History*: first settled by the Phoenicians, it developed into the empire of Carthage and was later absorbed into the Roman Empire. Under the dynasty of the Berber Hafsids (1207–1574) it became powerful. In 1883 it became a French protectorate, gaining independence from France in 1956. Habib Bourguiba was elected president in 1957; he was replaced in a bloodless coup by Zine al-Abidine Ben Ali in 1987. Official religion: Islam. Official language: Arabic; French is widely spoken. Official currency: Tunisian dinar of 1000 millimes. Area: 164 150 sq km (63 362 sq mi). Population (1987): 7 636 000. Capital: Tunis.

tunnel effect The passage of an electron or other particle through a potential barrier when, according to classical mechanics, it has insufficient energy to do so. It is explained by wave mechanics on the basis that the electron is not completely localized in space, part of the energy of the associated wave being able to tunnel through the barrier. The effect has a negligible probability in large-scale systems, but a finite probability in microscopic systems. It is made use of in the **tunnel diode**, a semiconductor device that has a negative resistance over part of its operating range.

tunny. *See* tuna.

Tupi A group of South American Indian peoples and languages including the Guarani. They are mainly a tropical rainforest people; they also fish in the rivers and off the coast where their villages are located. Cannibalism was common. Culture varied considerably from one region to another. Religion emphasized nature spirits.

Tupolev, Andrei Niklaievich (1888–1972) Soviet designer of the first supersonic passenger aircraft, the TU-144, tested in 1969. He also designed supersonic bombers, such as the TU-22, and swing-wing bombers. His TU-104, first produced in 1955, was one of the first passenger jet aircraft.

turaco (*or* touraco) A brightly coloured arboreal bird belonging to a family (*Musophagidae*; 18 species) occurring in Africa. Turacos have short rounded wings, a short down-curved bill, and are often crested. Most species have a greenish plumage. Order: *Cuculiformes* (cuckoos and turacos).

overshot water wheel   undershot water wheel   Pelton wheel

Francis turbine   Kaplan turbine   De Laval's impulse steam turbine

multistage steam turbine

TURBINE

turbine A device in which a moving fluid drives a wheel or motor, converting the kinetic energy of the fluid into mechanical energy. In its simplest form it is known as a **water wheel**, which has been in use since ancient times to drive mills, pumps, etc. The principle of the water wheel forms the basis of the hydraulic turbine, used in the generation of hydroelectricity. The Pelton wheel (patented in 1889 by L.A. Pelton) consisting of a ring of buckets or bucket-shaped vanes arranged around the periphery of a wheel, is known as an impulse turbine as it is only the impulse of the water that makes the wheel turn. The Francis turbine (designed in 1849 by J.B. Francis), with its outer ring of stationary guide vanes and inner ring of curved vanes on the surface of one side of the wheel, is a reaction turbine; part of the energy is derived from the impulse of the water and part from the reaction between the water and the blades. The steam-driven turbine was invented in the 1st century AD by the Greek engineer and mathematician Hero of Alexandria. However, the first practical turbine to be

driven by steam was a reaction device with several rows of turbine wheels (enabling the energy of the expanding steam to be utilized in stages) invented in 1884 by the British engineer, Sir Charles Parsons (1854–1931). An impulse turbine using several steam nozzles was invented by Carl de Laval (1845–1913) in the 1890s. Since the beginning of the 20th century steam turbines based on these designs have replaced the steam engine as the prime mover in power stations. *See also* gas turbine.

turbot A flatfish, *Scophthalmus maximus*, that occurs off European shores. It has a broad circular body, up to 1 m long, which is usually light- or grey-brown on the upper (left) side and whitish underneath. It is a valuable food fish. Family: *Bothidae*.

Turgenev, Ivan (1818–83) Russian novelist. His *Sportsman's Sketches* (1852) criticized the Russian social system; later works, such as the novel *Fathers and Sons* (1862) and the long story *The Torrents of Spring* (1872), are noted for their analysis of intellectual and social trends. He also wrote poetry and plays, notably *A Month* *in the Country* (published 1870). A lifelong admirer of western society, he went into self-imposed exile in Baden Baden (1862–70) and Paris (1871–83).

Turin (Italian name: Torino) 45 04N 7 40E A city in NW Italy, the capital of Piedmont on the River Po. Dating from Roman times, it was the first capital (1861–65) of united Italy. Notable buildings include a 15th-century cathedral and a 17th-century palace. It is important for the production of motor vehicles. Other industries include engineering, publishing, and the manufacture of textiles, paper, chocolate, wine, and leather goods. Population (1987): 1 035 565.

Turkana, Lake (name until 1979: Lake Rudolph) A lake in Kenya and Ethiopia. Fish and birds abound here and, since it has no outlet, it has become increasingly saline through evaporation. Significant fossil finds have been made here by Richard Leakey. Area: about 6405 sq km (2473 sq mi).

turkey A large terrestrial bird belonging to a family (*Meleagrididae*; 2 species) native to North and Central American woodlands. Wild turkeys have green-bronze plumage, a warty red neck, and a long fleshy bill ornament and throat wattle. The common turkey (*Meleagra gallopavo*) was brought to Europe in the 16th century and is now farmed for its flesh. Order: *Galliformes* (pheasants, turkeys, etc.).

Turkey, Republic of A country in the Middle East. The large Asian area, Anatolia, lies between the Mediterranean Sea and the Black Sea. The small European area, Thrace, is bordered by Greece and Bulgaria. Anatolia consists of a central semiarid plateau surrounded by mountains. The coastal areas are the most populous. 98% of the population is Muslim. *Economy*: mainly agricultural. Wheat, barley, sugar beet, potatoes, and rice are grown in the interior, and cotton, tobacco, and citrus fruit are grown for export around the coast. Cattle, sheep, and goats are kept for skins, wool, and mohair, which are exported. Copper, chromium, borax, coal, bauxite, and oil are produced. The main industries are steel, cement, textiles, and fertilizers. Turkey is an associate member of the EC. *History*: Anatolia, formerly known as Asia Minor, was dominated by the Seljuqs (1055–1243) and later became the core of the Ottoman Empire (c. 1300–1922). Under Kemal Atatürk, who ruled as a virtual dictator, the new Republic of Turkey (declared 1923) was rapidly westernized. After the death of Kemal (1938) and World War II, Turkey became less stable politically. The Democratic Party came to power in 1950 but grew increasingly reactionary; unrest increased until a military coup took place in 1960. The army again intervened in 1971, when martial law was imposed (until 1973). Violent clashes and economic difficulties continued during the 1970s. Rivalry with Greece over Cyprus almost resulted in war in 1974, when the island was invaded by Turkish troops; relations with the USA were also strained for a time by the invasion of Cyprus. In 1980 a military coup overthrew the government of Suleiman Demeril (1924–   ). President: Turgut Özal. Official language: Turkish; Kurdish and Arabic are also spoken. Official currency: Turkish lira of 100 kurus. Area: 779 452 sq km (330 883 sq mi). Population (1987): 52 845 000. Capital: Ankara.

Turkic languages A group of languages of the Altaic language family, related to Mongolian and Manchu-Tungus. Spoken by more than 66 million people, the languages are spread over a geographical area extending from Turkey to Siberia. Originally written in the Arabic script in the 9th century, the languages are now written in the Cyrillic alphabet in the Soviet Union and in Latin script in Turkey.

Turkish A Turkic language, spoken mainly in Turkey. Since 1929 it has been written in a modified Latin alphabet, replacing Arabic script. Its grammatical system is based on the use of suffixes.

Turkistan (*or* Turkestan) A region of central Asia, now comprising the Xinjiang Uygur AR of the People's Republic of China and the Kazakh, Turkmen, Tadzhik, Kirghiz, and Uzbek SSRs of the Soviet Union. Turkistan has come under many different rulers. The W has been ruled by the Persians from the 6th century BC, Islam from the 7th century AD, and the Russians from the 18th century; the E was long disputed between Chinese dynasties and nomadic tribes.

Turkmen (*or* Turkoman) A people of SW Asia speaking a language that is part of the Turkic language group. The majority live as settled farmers in the Turkmen SSR, but groups in Iran, Afghanistan, E Turkey, N Syria, and N Iraq retain their traditional nomadic existence. They are Sunni Muslims.

Turks and Caicos Islands A British crown colony consisting of a series of over 30 islands in the Atlantic Ocean, to the SE of the Bahamas. The most important are Grand Turk, Grand Caicos, and Salt Cay. Most of the inhabitants are of African descent. *Economy*: mainly based on fishing, with exports of conchs, conch shells, crawfish, salt, and fishmeal. *History*: the islands were discovered by the Spanish in 1512. A dependency of Jamaica (1874–1959), they became a crown colony in 1962 and gained internal self-government in 1976. From 1986 to 1988 they were put under the direct control of the governor following allegations of widespread corruption. Official language: English. Official currency: US dollar of 100 cents. Area: 430 sq km (192 sq mi). Population (1980): 7436. Capital: Grand Turk.

turmeric A perennial herbaceous plant, *Curcuma longa*, native to S India and Indonesia and cultivated for its underground rhizomes. It has narrow leaves and yellow flowers. The rhizomes are boiled and dried in the sun for 5–7 days, then polished and usually sold in ground form. Turmeric is used as a spice in curries, etc., and as a yellow dye. Family: *Zingiberaceae*.

Turner, Joseph Mallord William (1775–1851) British landscape and marine painter. After painting many watercolours, he achieved success in the late 1790s with his landscapes in oil. In 1809 he made the first of several continental tours, which provided him with such scenic subjects as the Alps, Venice, and Rome. While supervising the publication of his *Liber Studiorum* (1807–19), a series of engravings based on his works, his style evolved into a romantic vision of colour, light, and weather anticipating French impressionism. This vision becomes the subject of such late paintings as *Rain, Steam, and Speed* (National Gallery, London) and *Interior at Petworth* (Tate Gallery). See p. 734.

turnip A biennial plant, *Brassica rapa*, probably native to Asia and widely cultivated for its thick fleshy root, which is used as a vegetable. An erect branching stem grows out of the basal leaf rosette and produces bright-yellow flowers. Family: *Cruciferae*.

turnstone A small plover, *Arenaria interpres*, that breeds around Arctic coasts and migrates to the S hemisphere to winter. It has a black-and-brown upper plumage, becoming tortoiseshell in summer, and white underparts. Turnstones have short black bills used to turn over pebbles and shells in search of molluscs, small fish, and sandhoppers.

JOSEPH MALLORD WILLIAM TURNER *Chalk drawing made in 1842. (National Portrait Gallery).*

turpentine An oily liquid extracted from pine resin. Its main constituent is pinene ($C_{10}H_{16}$); it is used as a solvent for paints.

Turpin, Dick (1706–39) British highwayman. He was hanged at York for murder and horse stealing. The story of his ride from London to York on his horse Black Bess, popularized in Harrison Ainsworth's novel *Rookwood* (1834), is probably based on a much older legend.

turquoise An opaque greenish-blue mineral used as a gem. It consists of a basic aluminium phosphate, traces of copper providing the colour. Birthstone for December.

turtle An aquatic reptile belonging to the order *Chelonia*, which also includes tortoises and terrapins. 10–200 cm long, turtles have broad paddle-like flippers and a streamlined shell and occur in most seas. Their diet consists of worms, snails, crustaceans, and fish. Some turtles live in fresh water. *See also* green turtle; leatherback turtle.

turtle dove A small slender dove, *Streptopelia turtur*, occurring in S Europe and N Africa, visiting N Europe in the summer. It has a chequered red-brown back, grey wings, a pink breast, a black-and-white striped neck patch, and a long white-tipped tail. Family: *Columbidae* (pigeons).

Tuscan order. *See* orders of architecture.

Tuscany (Italian name: Toscana) A region in N central Italy, consisting mainly of hills and mountains with coastal lowlands in the W. It is a predominantly agricultural region producing cereals, wines (Chianti), olives, and fruit. The major manufacturing industries are iron, steel, and shipbuilding. Lignite, iron, mercury, salt, borax, and marble are mined. Florence is an important tourist and cultural centre. Area: 22 989 sq km (8876 sq mi). Population (1985 est): 3 571 538. Capital: Florence.

Tussaud, Marie (Marie Grosholtz; 1761–1850) French wax modeller, who went to London in 1802, where she founded the waxworks museum known as Madame Tussaud's.

tussock moth A moth belonging to the family *Lymantriidae*, occurring in both the Old and New Worlds and including the vapourers, tussocks, and gypsy moths. The caterpillars, cocoons, and adults are typically hairy, frequently causing skin irritation and swelling if handled.

Tutankhamen King of Egypt (c. 1361–1352 BC) of the 18th dynasty. Tutankhamen became king at the age of 11. He abandoned Akhenaton's worship of the sun-god Aton, reinstating that of Amon and transferring the capital once more to Thebes. His splendid and elaborate tomb was discovered by Howard Carter (1874–1939) in 1922.

Tutu, Desmond (1931–) South African clergyman, noted for his opposition to apartheid. Ordained in 1960, he became the first black general secretary of the South African Council of Churches in 1978, Anglican Bishop of Johannbesburg in 1984, and Archbishop of Cape Town in 1986. He won the Nobel Peace Prize in 1984.

Tuvalu, State of (name until 1976: Ellice Islands) A small country in the SW Pacific Ocean. It consists of a group of nine islands, the main one being Funafuti. Most of the population is Polynesian. *Economy*: subsistence agriculture and fishing are the chief occupations. The main export is copra. *History*: formerly part of the Gilbert and Ellice Islands colony, it became a separate colony in 1974 and gained independence in 1978. Tuvalu is a member of the Commonwealth of Nations. Prime minister: Dr Tomasi Puapua. Official language: Tuvalu. Official currency: Australian dollar of 100 cents. Area: 24 sq km (9.5 sq mi). Population (1987): 8200. Capital: Funafuti.

DESMOND TUTU

Twain, Mark (Samuel Langhorne Clemens; 1835–1910) US novelist. He worked as a steamboat pilot on the Mississippi before gaining a national reputation for his humorous journalism. He wrote several works based on his early life, notably *Life on the Mississippi* (1883) and his masterpiece *The Adventures of Huckleberry Finn* (1884).

Tweed, River A river in SE Scotland and NE England. Flowing E from the Tweedsmuir Hills to the North Sea at Berwick, it forms part of the border between England and Scotland. Length: 156 km (97 mi).

Twelfth Day. *See* Epiphany.

twelve-tone music. *See* serialism.

twins Two individuals born from the same pregnancy. Identical twins are produced when a fertilized egg splits in two and develops as two fetuses of the same sex. More commonly, nonidentical (or fraternal) twins are produced when two eggs are fertilized at the same time; they may be of different sexes. *See also* Siamese twins.

Two Thousand Guineas A flat race for three-year-old horses, run each spring at Newmarket. One of the English Classics, it was instituted in 1809.

Tyburn A stream in SE England, in London. It now flows underground from Hampstead to the River Thames. The London gallows, known as the Tyburn Tree (1571–1759), stood at the W end of Oxford Street.

Tyler, Wat (d. 1381) English rebel, who led the Peasants' Revolt (1381). He was murdered during negotiations with Richard II at Smithfield.

Tyne, River A river in N England. Flowing E from the SW Cheviot Hills to the North Sea at Tynemouth, it passes through Newcastle, Gateshead, and Jarrow. Length: 48 km (30 mi).

Tyne and Wear A metropolitan county of NE England, created in 1974 from SE Northumberland and NE Durham. It comprises the districts of Newcastle-upon-Tyne, North Tyneside, Gateshead, South Tyneside, and Sunderland. Industries grew up along the River Tyne allied to the large coalfields; in the 19th century the development of the shipyards was especially important. During the Depression of the 1930s it suffered severely. The whole county is now designated a special development area with government financial assistance for firms located in the county. Area: 540 sq km (208 sq mi). Population (1986 est): 1 135 500. Administrative centre: Newcastle upon Tyne.

typewriter A hand-operated machine for producing printed symbols. The first machine was invented in the USA in 1867 but the commercial success of the typewriter began in 1874 with the machines produced by Remington and Sons. This design, with the paper held in a moving platen, remained the basis of the typewriter until the advent of electric golf-ball machines, with a stationary platen, in the early 1960s. More sophisticated machines are now available providing, in conjunction with a microcomputer, proportional spacing and justification. *See* word processor.

typhoid fever An infectious disease of the digestive tract caused by the bacterium *Salmonella typhi*. This disease (and paratyphoid fever) are usually contracted by drinking infected water. The symptoms include fever, headache, cough, loss of appetite, and constipation; a characteristic red rash may appear. If untreated, the patient may develop bowel haemorrhage or perforations.

typhoon A tropical cyclone or hurricane with winds above force 12 on the Beaufort scale occurring in the China Sea and the W Pacific Ocean. The name is derived from a Chinese word meaning great wind.

typhus An infection caused by certain bacteria-like microorganisms (*see* rickettsia), which are transmitted to man by lice, fleas, mites, or ticks. The many different forms of typhus share the symptoms of fever, headache, pains in muscles and joints, delirium, and a rash. Treatment is with tetracycline antibiotics or chloramphenicol.

Tyr (*or*, in Old English, Tiw) In Teutonic mythology, the god of war; with Odin and Thor, he is one of the three main Germanic gods. His name is linguistically related to *Zeus* and survives in *Tuesday*.

Tyrannosaurus A huge bipedal dinosaur that lived in North America during the late Cretaceous period (about 100–65 million years ago). This animal was 15 m long, stood 6.5 m tall, and weighed up to 10 tonnes. It had a massive body with a short thick neck supporting a large head, large muscular hind limbs with clawed feet, and tiny fore legs. It was a carnivore with long dagger-like teeth. Order: *Saurischia.*

tyrant flycatcher A passerine bird belonging to the New World family *Tyrannidae* (365 species), ranging from 9–27 cm in length and generally grey, brown, or olive-coloured with paler underparts. They are typically arboreal and dart out from a perch to seize flying insects. Tyrant flycatchers will attack large birds that enter their breeding territories. *Compare* flycatcher.

Tyre (modern name: Sur) 33 12N 35 11E A port in SW Lebanon, on the Mediterranean Sea. It was important to the Phoenicians for several centuries and was taken by Alexander the Great in 322 BC and by the Romans in 68 BC. The city was long held by the Crusaders but fell to Muslim forces in 1291. Population (1980 est): 14 000.

Tyrol. *See* Tirol.

Tyson, Mike (1966–) US boxer. He became the youngest ever world heavyweight champion in 1986 when he won the World Boxing Championship title. In 1990 he lost the title in a surprise defeat by James Douglas.

U

Ubangi-Shari. *See* Central African Republic.

Uccello, Paolo (P. di Dono; 1397–1475) Florentine painter. His frescoes for Sta Maria Novella, Florence, include the famous *Flood*, which shows his preoccupation with perspective. In the three paintings of the battle of San Romano, he combines a geometric structure with the international gothic style.

Ufa 54 45N 55 58E A city in the W central Soviet Union. Situated in the Ural Mountains, it has oil refineries. Population (1987): 1 092 000.

Uffizi An art gallery in Florence, containing the art treasures of the Medici. Built by Vasari, the Uffizi was opened as a museum in 1765. The major part of its collection comprises Italian Renaissance paintings.

Uganda, Republic of A landlocked country in East Africa. It consists chiefly of a high plateau rising to mountains; a considerable proportion of the total area is occupied by lakes, notably Lake Victoria. The majority of the population is African, especially Ganda. *Economy*: chiefly agricultural, cash crops include coffee tea, tobacco, and cotton; livestock is also important. The chief mineral resource is copper. *History*: the area was dominated by the kingdom of Buganda before becoming a British protectorate in 1894. It became an independent state within the British Commonwealth in 1962 and the following year a republic was established with Obote as prime minister. In 1971 the government was overthrown in a military coup that brought Gen Idi Amin to power. His repressive regime was overthrown in April, 1979, by Ugandan exiles aided by Tanzanian troops. In 1986, in the latest in a series of coups, Yoweri Museveni came to power. Official language: English; Swahili is widely spoken. Official currency, since 1967: Ugandan shilling of 100 cents. Area: 236 860 sq km (91 343 sq mi). Population (1987 est): 16 789 000. Capital: Kampala.

ugli A hybrid cross between a grapefruit and a tangerine. The fruit has brownish-yellow warty skin and orange flesh. It is grown in the West Indies.

Uist Two islands in NW Scotland, in the Outer Hebrides. North Uist is separated from South Uist by the island of Benbecula.

Ujjain 23 11N 75 50E A city in India, in Madhya Pradesh. One of the seven sacred Hindu cities, it is the scene of the 12-yearly bathing festival (Kumbh Mela). Population (1981): 282 000.

Ujung Pandang (Makassar *or* Macassar) 5 09S 119 08E A port in central Indonesia, in SW Sulawesi. Its exports include coffee, copra, and vegetable oils. Population (1980): 709 038.

UKAEA. *See* Atomic Energy Authority.

ukulele A small guitar, patented in Hawaii in 1917. The fingerboard is fretted; the four gut or nylon strings are strummed with fingers or a small plectrum.

Ulan Bator (*or* Ulaanbaatar; former name: Urga) 47 54N 106 52E The capital of the Mongolian People's Republic, situated on a plateau in the N of the country. Built around a monastery, in the 17th century it developed as a centre of trade between China and Japan. It became the capital when Outer Mongolia declared its independence in 1911. Population (1984): 479 500.

Ulbricht, Walter (1893–1973) East German statesman. Ulbricht was the leading architect of the German Democratic Republic after World War II. He was general secretary of the Socialist Unity Party from 1950 and in 1960 became chairman of the newly established council of state. In 1961 he erected the Berlin Wall.

ulcer An inflamed eroded area of skin or mucous membrane. There are many forms of ulcer, one of the most prevalent being peptic ulcers, which affect the stomach and duodenum. Ulcers may also occur in the colon (*see* colitis). Varicose ulcers may develop in the skin of patients with chronic varicose veins.

Ullswater The second largest lake in England, in Cumbria in the Lake District. Length: 12 km (7.5 mi).

Ulm, Battle of (25 September–20 October, 1805) A battle in which Napoleon with 210 000 men defeated 72 000 Austrians in Bavaria.

Ulster A province in the Republic of Ireland and former kingdom of N Ireland. The land passed to the English Crown in 1461. It was partitioned in 1921 to form the six counties of Northern Ireland and the Ulster province of the Republic of Ireland. Area: 8013 sq km (3094 sq mi). Population (1981): 230 159.

Ulster Democratic Unionist Party A British political party, active in Northern Ireland. Its parliamentary leader is Rev Ian Paisley.

Ulster Unionist Party A British political party, active in Northern Ireland. Its parliamentary leader is James Molyneaux (1920–).

ultramicroscope A type of microscope, invented by Richard Zsigmondy (1865–1929) in 1902, used to study colloidal particles in a liquid medium. A beam of light illuminates the particles from the side, the scattered light enabling the movements of the particles to be observed as flashes against a dark background (dark-field illumination).

ULTRASONICS *A routine examination of an unborn baby.*

ultrasonics The study of sound waves the frequencies of which are too high to be audible to the normal human ear, i.e. above about 20 000 hertz. Ultrasound waves may be produced by magnetostriction or by applying a rapidly alternating voltage across a piezoelectric crystal. Ultrasound is widely used in medical diagnosis in place of X-rays.

ultraviolet radiation Electromagnetic radiation the frequency of which lies between that of the violet end of the visible spectrum and X-rays, i.e. between about 380 and 5 nanometres. Ultraviolet radiation is produced during arc discharges and by gas-discharge tubes. It is also produced in large quantities by the sun, although the radiation below 200 nm is absorbed by the ozone layer of the atmosphere.

Ulyanovsk (name until 1924: Simbirsk) 54 19N 48 22E A port in the W central Soviet Union, on the River Volga. It was renamed in honour of Lenin (originally V. I. Ulyanov), who was born here. Population (1987): 589 000.

Ulysses. *See* Odysseus.

Umar. *See* Omar.

Umayyads (*or* Omayyads) The first dynasty of caliphs, which ruled Islam from 661 to 750 AD. The dynasty reached its peak with 'Abd al-Malik (reigned 685–705). The Umayyads were overthrown by a rebellion of discontented Arabs and pious Muslims. In Muslim Spain, an Umayyad, 'Abd ar-Rahman, seized power in 756 and established a dynasty that ruled until 1030.

Umbelliferae A widely distributed family of plants (2850 species), most abundant in N temperate regions. Most species are herbaceous, with tiny flowers. A few species have dome-shaped flower heads. The family includes vegetables, such as the carrot, celery, and parsnip, and many culinary herbs and spices.

Umberto I (1844–1900) King of Italy (1878–1900). He commanded with distinction in the war against the

Austrians (1866). As king he led Italy into the Triple Alliance (1882) and encouraged Italian colonialism in Africa. Two unsuccessful attempts on Umberto's life were followed by his assassination at Monza.

Umberto II (1904–83) The last King of Italy (1946), following the abdication of his father Victor Emmanuel III. He himself was forced to abdicate after a referendum approved the establishment of republican government.

umbilical cord The structure, about 50 cm long, that connects a fetus to the placenta in the womb. It contains three blood vessels (two arteries and one vein) that convey blood to and from the placenta. At birth the umbilical cord is tied off and cut.

Un-American Activities Committee US House of Representatives committee established in 1935 to investigate subversive organizations in the USA. Spurred on by Senator McCarthy, it blacklisted several Hollywood writers and directors and investigated government officials. Public protest resulted in the committee's eventual abolition (1975).

uncertainty principle. *See* Heisenberg uncertainty principle.

undulant fever. *See* brucellosis.

UNESCO. *See* United Nations Educational, Scientific and Cultural Organization.

uniat churches Various churches of Eastern Orthodox Christianity that are in full communion with the Roman Catholic Church. They retain their own traditional liturgies and canon law.

UNICEF. *See* United Nations International Children's Emergency Fund.

UNICORN *From a 15th-century tapestry.*

unicorn A mythical animal resembling a white horse, but with one long straight horn on its forehead. In the middle ages it was symbolically associated with chastity (and thus could be captured only by a virgin) and also with Christ's love of mankind.

Unification Church A religious sect founded in South Korea in 1954 by a millionaire Korean businessman, Sun Myung Moon (1920–   ). The ideology of the cult is summarized in Moon's book, *Divine Principle*, which he claims was revealed to him by Christ in 1936. Absolute obedience is demanded of members ('Moonies'), who spend most of their waking hours earn-

ing money for the organization. Moon was imprisoned for tax evasion in 1984 and released in 1985.

unified field theory A theory that encompasses the four fundamental interactions—strong, weak, electromagnetic, and gravitational—in terms of a single field, analogous to the electromagnetic or gravitational fields. Einstein failed to unify gravitation and electromagnetism, although a measure of unification has been achieved between the weak and electromagnetic fields.

Uniformity, Acts of A series of Acts (1549, 1552, 1559, 1562) that enforced the use of the Book of Common Prayer in England during the Reformation.

Union, Acts of **1.** The Acts (1536–43) uniting England and Wales. They imposed English law and administration on Wales, made English the language of officialdom, and provided for Welsh representation in parliament. **2.** The Act (1707) uniting England and Scotland to form Great Britain. Scotland retained its legal system and Presbyterian Church and was to be represented in parliament by 16 peers and 45 MPs. **3.** The Act (1800) that united Great Britain and Ireland to form (1801) the United Kingdom. It provided for Irish representation in parliament (4 spiritual peers, 28 life peers, 100 MPs).

Union of Soviet Socialist Republics. *See* Soviet Union.

Unitarians A group of Christians who reject the doctrine of the Trinity and the divinity of Christ, believing instead in the single personality of God. Modern Unitarian thought dates from the Reformation, but congregations were first formed in Britain and the USA in the 18th century.

United Arab Emirates (UAE; former name: Trucial States) A federation of seven sheikdoms in the Middle East, in Arabia, comprising Abu Dhabi, Ajman, Dubai, Fujairah, Ras al-Khaimah, Sharjah, and Umm al-Qaiwain. The population is mainly Arab and Sunnite Muslim. The terrain is flat sandy desert. *Economy*: the oil of Abu Dhabi and Dubai is the chief product and export. *History*: the sheikdoms signed several common treaties with Britain from 1820; that of 1892 made them protectorates—the Trucial States. The federation was formed in 1971 (Ras al-Khaimah not joining until 1972) and is a member of OPEC. President: Sheik Zayed bin Sultan al-Nahayan of Abu Dhabi (1918–   ). Prime minister: Sheik Rashid bin Said al-Maktoum. Official language: Arabic. Official currency: UAE dirham of 10 dinars and 1000 fils. Area: 83 650 sq km (32 290 sq mi). Population (1987): 1 856 000. Provisional capital: Abu Dhabi. Chief port: Dubai.

United Arab Republic (UAR) The state created by the union of Egypt and Syria in 1958. Joined by North Yemen in the same year, it collapsed in 1961 but Egypt retained the name until 1971.

United Australia Party (UAP) A political party, comprising the Nationalist Party and ex-members of the Labor Party, that governed Australia from 1931 to 1941. It was dissolved in 1944.

United Kingdom (UK) A country in N Europe, consisting of England, Scotland, Wales, and the province of Northern Ireland (*see* Ireland). The UK does not include the Channel Isles and the Isle of Man, which are direct dependencies of the Crown with their own legislatures and taxation systems. The United Kingdom of Great Britain and Ireland, formed in 1801, became the United Kingdom of Great Britain and Northern Ireland in 1922, following the creation of the Irish Free State. Head of state: Queen Elizabeth II. Prime minister: Margaret Thatcher. Area: 244 014 sq km (94 214 sq mi). Population (1987): 56 878 000. Capital: London.

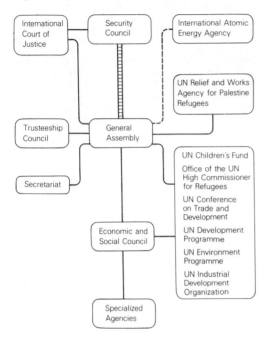

UNITED NATIONS   *The structure of the organization.*

United Nations (UN)   An organization established to maintain international peace and to foster international cooperation in the resolution of economic, social, cultural, and humanitarian problems. The UN was founded on 24 October, 1945 (United Nations Day). There were 51 founder members; most countries are now members of the UN. The headquarters of the UN are in New York. The organization's main deliberative organ is the **General Assembly**. Each member state has one equal vote in the Assembly, which cannot impose its will upon members. The **Security Council** bears the chief responsibility for maintaining international peace. Its permanent members are China, France, the Soviet Union, the UK, and the USA; a further ten members are elected by the General Assembly for two-year terms. Decisions, except on procedure, must be agreed by nine members, including all the permanent members (the so-called veto privilege). In the event of a breach of international peace the Council may commit military forces to re-establish peace. The **Economic and Social Council** (ECOSOC) co-ordinates the economic and social work of the UN. The **Trusteeship Council** is responsible for the one remaining trust territory (Micronesia). The principal judicial organ of the UN is the International Court of Justice. The **Secretariat**, headed by the secretary general (currently Javier Pérez de Cuellar), is responsible for administration.

Other UN bodies are the **United Nations Development Programme** (UNDP), which fosters the economic growth of the developing countries; the **United Nations Conference on Trade and Development** (UNCTAD), which encourages international trade; the **United Nations Industrial Development Organization** (UNIDO), which promotes industrial development; and the **United Nations Environment Programme** (UNEP), which is concerned with the protection of the environment. Other specialized agencies include the Food and Agriculture Organization, International Civil Aviation Organization, International Labour Organisation, International Monetary Fund, International Telecommunication Union, United Nations Educational, Scientific and Cultural Organization, International Bank for Reconstruction and Development, World Health Organization, and the World Meteorological Organization.

United Nations Educational, Scientific and Cultural Organization (UNESCO)   A specialized agency of the United Nations established in 1945 to promote international cooperation in education, science, and culture. Its headquarters are in Paris. Objecting to inefficiency and political bias, the USA withdrew from UNESCO in 1984. The United Kingdom withdrew in 1985.

United Nations High Commissioner for Refugees, Office of the (UNHCR)   A United Nations body established in 1950 to provide international protection for refugees. Its headquarters are in Geneva. It won the Nobel Peace Prize in 1981.

United Nations International Children's Emergency Fund (UNICEF)   A United Nations body established in 1946. It is chiefly concerned with providing health care, education, and improved nutrition to developing countries. Its headquarters are in Geneva. It won the Nobel Peace Prize in 1965.

United Provinces of the Netherlands   The northern provinces of the Netherlands, which united (1579) during the Revolt of the Netherlands against Spain and formed (1581) a self-governing independent federation.

United States of America (USA)   A country in North America, the fourth largest in the world. It is a federal republic comprising 50 states, including Alaska, in the extreme NW of the continent, and Hawaii, in the central Pacific Ocean. The Pacific mountain system and the Rocky Mountains extend N–S in the W with an arid area between, while the Appalachian Mountains extend N–S in the E. In the centre lie vast plains. The population is of mixed ethnic stock, the majority being of European descent. *Economy*: the USA is the world's greatest industrial producer, with a highly diversified economy. Its large resources of minerals and fuels make it the leading producer of natural gas, lead, copper, aluminium, and sulphur and of electrical and nuclear energy. 15% of all exports are agricultural products. Cereals, cotton, and tobacco are the main crops. Main exports include motor vehicles, aircraft, machinery, grain, and chemicals. *History*: extensively explored following its discovery by Columbus in 1492, America was settled from 1565, most successfully by the British. However, during the 18th century conflict developed between local colonial assemblies and their British governors, particularly over taxation. The colonists' confidence in themselves was strengthened by their success in the French and Indian Wars (1754–63) and the 13 colonies finally won independence in the American Revolution (1775–83). The USA was rapidly expanding W at this time and through the Mexican War (1846–48) acquired California; the discovery of gold there (1848) further encouraged settlement in the W. By 1820 conflict was developing between the cotton-growing states of the South (where African slaves had worked since the late 17th century) and the commercial North (where slavery was opposed). This led to the Civil War (1861–65), which ended in victory for the North and the abolition of slavery. It was followed by a period of rapid industrial and economic expansion, while territorial expansion continued with the purchase of Alaska (1867), the annexation of Hawaii (1898), and the Spanish-American War (1898), in which the USA acquired the Philippines, Puerto Rico, Guam, and a measure of control over Cuba. Intervention in Colombia led to the construction of the Panama Canal (opened 1914). The status of the USA as a world power was confirmed by its role in World War I, which it entered reluctantly (1917) because of its policy of isolationism. The 1920s saw another economic boom, which ended in the Depression that followed the Crash of 1929. The USA was again reluctant to enter World War II but was forced to do so by the Japanese bombing of Pearl Harbor in Hawaii (December, 1941). Postwar fear of Soviet expansion resulted in the Marshall Plan (1947), designed to render Europe less susceptible to communism, in the Cold War, and in the harassment of supposed communists at home (*see also* McCarthy, Joseph R.; Un-American Activities Committee). Fear of the spread of communism led also to intervention in Korea (1950–53), Cuba (1961–62), and Vietnam (1961–75). After 1963 relations with the Soviet Union improved and diplomatic relations were established with China in 1979. Interventionist policy continued, however, with the role of the CIA in foreign affairs criticized and investigated (1975–76) following the government's loss of credibility resulting from the Watergate affair (1972–74). Domestic problems since World War II have included race riots in the 1960s and opposition to the Vietnam War. The postwar economic boom was followed by a prolonged decline. Abroad, US troops have intervened in Lebanon (1982), Grenada (1983), in El Salvador in covert operations against the Sandinista regime in Nicaragua, and in Panama (1989). Relations with the USSR were further strained by the Soviet invasion of Afghanistan (1979), and Reagan's Strategic Defence Initiative but subsequently improved under the Soviet president, Gorbachev. There was also considerable tension in US relations with Iran and Libya during the 1980s. President: George Bush. Official language: English. Official currency: US dollar of 100 cents. Area: 9 363 123 sq km (3 614 343 sq mi). Population (1989): 246 900 000. Capital: Washington, DC.

unit trust An organization that uses funds raised by selling "units" to the public to buy and sell securities in order to make profits for distribution to unit holders. Securities are held in the names of trustees, usually banks. The small investor buying unit trusts has the advantages of a professionally managed widespread portfolio. In the USA it is called an open-end investment company. *Compare* investment company.

Universal Decimal Classification (*or* Brussels Classification) A system of library classification developed in 1895 in Brussels. It extends the division of the Dewey Decimal Classification, on which it is based.

Upanishads About 200 prose and verse treatises on metaphysical philosophy, produced as commentaries on the *Vedas* and dating from around 400 BC. They deal with the nature of Brahman and the soul and are reputedly divinely inspired.

Updike, John (Hoyer) (1932–) US novelist and short-story writer. In novels, such as *Rabbit, Run* (1960), *Couples* (1968), *Rabbit Redux* (1972), and *Of the Farm* (1988), he has explored the moral confusions of contemporary US society. His novel *Rabbit is Rich* (1981) won a Pulitzer Prize (1982).

Upper Volta, Republic of. *See* Burkina Faso.

Uppsala 59 55N 17 38E A city in E central Sweden. It is a historic and cultural centre, with Sweden's oldest university (1477), where Linnaeus taught. Population (1988): 161 828.

Ur An ancient city of Sumer (S Iraq). Sir Leonard Woolley's excavations (1922–34) made famous the spectacularly rich royal burials of about 2500 BC and seemed to provide historical evidence for Noah's flood. The leading city in Sumer when it was sacked by barbarians about 2000 BC, Ur was superseded by Babylon.

uraemia The accumulation of urea in the blood due to

UR *The "Standard" of Ur (c. 2500 BC; British Museum, London). It consists of a hollow box, the sides of which depict a king's campaign, decorated with lapis lazuli and red limestone.*

kidney failure. Kidney failure can occur suddenly due to shock, obstruction of both ureters, injury, or acute kidney disease or it may arise slowly due to nephritis or other diseases. The kidneys will often recover after dialysis. In chronic conditions a kidney transplant is preferred.

Ural, River A river in the central Soviet Union, rising in the S Ural Mountains, and flowing S to the Caspian Sea. Length: 2534 km (1575 mi).

Uralic languages A major language family comprising two related groups of languages, the Finno-Ugric and the Samoyedic (*see* Samoyed). The two branches of the Uralic language family have developed into multiple forms covering an extensive area.

Ural Mountains A mountain range in the NW central Soviet Union. It extends 2000 km (1243 mi) N–S from the Kara Sea to the steppes NE of the Caspian Sea. The highest point is Mount Narodnaya, in the N, at 1894 m (6214 ft).

uranium (U) A radioactive metallic element (*see* nuclear energy). Uranium is a silvery-white metal, almost as hard as steel and very dense (relative density 18.95). Uranium has the highest atomic number of the naturally occurring elements. It was first isolated in 1841 by E. Péligot (1811–90), although it had been identified before this in pitchblende. Natural uranium contains three isotopes: ^{238}U (99.283%), ^{235}U (0.711%), and ^{234}U (0.006%). ^{238}U has a half-life of 4.51×10^9 years and is useful in dating rocks, as well as in fuel for fast reactors. ^{235}U is used in thermal reactors. Some reactors use uranium dioxide (UO_2). Other oxides include U_3O_8 and UO_3. At no 92; at wt 238.029; mp 1132°C; bp 3818°C.

uranium-lead dating A group of methods of radiometric dating certain rocks, depending on the decay of the radioactive isotope uranium-238 to lead-206 or of uranium-235 to lead-207.

uranium series One of three naturally occurring series of radioactive decays. The uranium series is headed by uranium-238, which undergoes a series of alpha and beta decays ending with the stable isotope lead-206. *See also* actinium; thorium series.

Uranus (astronomy) A giant planet, orbiting the sun every 84 years (between Saturn and Neptune) at a mean distance of 2870 million km. It is somewhat larger (50 800 km in diameter) than Neptune and exhibits a similar greenish featureless disc in a telescope. In its equatorial plane lie fifteen moons and about twenty rings. Its atmospheric and interior structure are thought to be almost identical to those of Neptune. Uranus was discovered telescopically in 1781 by Sir William Herschel.

Uranus (Greek mythology) The personification of Heaven. He was the son of Gaea (Earth), and his children by her included the Titans and the Cyclops. He was castrated by his son Cronus and his genitals were thrown into the sea, which gave birth to Aphrodite.

Urdu An Indo-Aryan language of N India and Pakistan. Like Hindi it arose from Hindustani. It is written in a modified Arabic script.

urea (*or* carbamide) A white crystalline compound ($CO(NH_2)_2$) derived from ammonia and carbon dioxide. It is widely used as a nitrogen fertilizer, a feed supplement for ruminant animals, and in industry. Urea is also present in urine.

urea-formaldehyde resins Synthetic thermosetting resins that are made by the condensation in aqueous solution of urea and formaldehyde with an ammonia catalyst. Cellulose filler is added to produce a moulding powder. This powder is used to make cups, bathroom fittings, etc.

urethane A white crystalline solid, $CO(NH_2)$ (OC_2H_5), made by heating ethanol with urea nitrate. It is used to manufacture polyurethane foam.

Urga. *See* Ulan Bator.

uric acid A compound ($C_5H_4N_4O_3$) formed during the nitrogen metabolism of animals. In man, raised levels of uric acid in the blood are associated with gout.

urine The fluid that is formed by the kidneys and contains the waste products of metabolism and surplus water and salts. In man the kidneys normally produce 0.9–1.5 l of urine per day.

Urmia, Lake A shallow lake in NW Iran, the largest in the country, lying 1300 m (4265 ft) above sea level. It has no outlet and varies in size. Average area: 5000 sq km (1930 sq mi).

URSA MAJOR *An illustration from an 11th-century Arab manuscript.*

Ursa Major (Latin: Great Bear) A large conspicuous constellation in the N sky. The seven brightest stars form the Plough.

Ursa Minor (Latin: Little Bear) A constellation in the N sky that contains the N celestial pole. The brightest star is Polaris.

Ursula, St A legendary British martyr. According to tradition, she and 11 000 virgins were murdered by the Huns at Cologne while returning from a pilgrimage to Rome in the 3rd or 5th century. Feast day: 21 Oct.

urticaria (*or* hives) An acute or chronic allergic disorder in which itching white raised patches surrounded by red areas appear on the skin: they resemble nettle stings (hence the alternative name—nettle rash). Acute urticaria usually arises from allergy to food or drugs and usually disappears quickly if the cause is removed. Chronic urticaria occurs in young people and its cause is not certain.

Uruguay, Oriental Republic of A country in SE South America. Coastal plains rise to higher ground, especially in the N. Most of the population is of Spanish and Italian descent. *Economy*: the traditional livestock industry was badly affected by the 1974 EC ban on meat imports. The cultivation of wheat, maize, and sorghum has been intensified and the fishing industry has been expanded. The principal industries include food processing, hides and leather, textiles, construction, metallurgy, and rubber. *History*: explored by the Spanish in the 16th century, its early history was one of rivalry between Spanish and Portuguese settlements. In 1776 it became part of the Spanish viceroyalty of the Río de la Plata. Under the leadership of Artigas, Uruguay joined Argentina against Spain but was subsequently fought over by Argentina and Brazil. In 1828, with British help, Uruguay achieved independence. The late 19th century saw considerable immigration from Europe and later the establishment of Latin America's first welfare state. In 1973 the army took over, imposing repressive measures that led to international protests. Military rule officially ended in early 1985. President: Luis Alberto Lacalle. Uruguay is a member of the OAS and LAFTA. Official language: Spanish. Official currency: new Uruguayan peso of 100 centésimos. Area: 186 926 sq km (72 172 sq mi). Population (1987): 3 058 000. Capital and main port: Montevideo.

Uruguay, River (Portuguese name: Rio Uruguai; Spanish name: Río Uruguay) A river in South America. Rising in S Brazil, it flows SW forming the Argentina–Brazil and Argentina–Uruguay borders before joining the Rio Paraná. Length: about 1600 km (1000 mi).

Uruk (biblical name: Erech; modern name: Warka) An ancient city in S Mesopotamia. The site testifies to the beginnings of Sumerian civilization in the 4th millennium BC. Supplanted by Ur (c. 2100), Uruk nevertheless remained inhabited until the early Christian era.

USSR. *See* Soviet Union.

Ussuri River A river in E Asia, rising in the extreme E Soviet Union and forming part of the border with China as it flows N to the River Amur. Length: about 800 km (500 mi).

Ustinov, Peter (Alexander) (1921–) British actor, director, and dramatist of Russian descent. His own plays include *Romanoff and Juliet* (1956) and *Beethoven's Tenth* (1983); his many films include *Death on the Nile* (1978). He has written novels and an autobiography; he is also well known as an impersonator and television personality.

PETER USTINOV   *With David Niven (left) in* Death on the Nile.

MAURICE UTRILLO   La Place du Tertre *(c. 1910; Tate Gallery).*

Utah One of the mountain states in the SW USA. The Wasatch Range of the Rocky Mountains divides the state into two arid regions: the Great Basin, which includes the Great Salt Lake, and the Great Salt Lake Desert in the W and the Colorado Plateau in the E. The raising of livestock is the principal agricultural activity. There are significant deposits of copper, oil, natural gas, and uranium. Scenic attractions make it a popular tourist area. *History*: the persecuted Mormons began major settlements here in 1847 and continue to dominate the life of the state. Ceded to the USA by Mexico in 1848, Utah was finally admitted to the Union in 1896. Area: 219 931 sq km (84 916 sq mi). Population (1985 est): 1 645 000. Capital: Salt Lake City.

uterus. *See* womb.

utilitarianism An ethical doctrine holding that the best action is the one that will result in the greatest happiness and least pain for the greatest number of people. Utilitarianism flourished in Britain from the mid-18th century to the mid-19th century. Hume, Bentham, and James Mill (1773–1836) propounded it and John Stuart Mill defended it.

utopianism A programme of total social and political reform with the object of establishing a perfect society. The term derives from the imaginary state depicted in Thomas More's *Utopia* (1516). Utopian experiments have included the New Lanark community established by Robert Owen (1771–1858). Utopianism advocates a communistic organization of society, but the concomitant authoritarianism reveals that no way has been found of reconciling individual freedom and happiness with social justice.

Utrecht 52 06N 5 07E A city in the central Netherlands. The Union of Utrecht (1579) united the northern provinces of the Netherlands against Spain. The Treaties of Utrecht (1713–14), ending the War of the Spanish Succession, were concluded here. Its notable buildings include the gothic cathedral (14th century). Population (1987): 229 326.

Utrillo, Maurice (1883–1955) French painter. For almost his entire life, he suffered from alcoholism and drug addiction. He specialized in painting street scenes, notably of Montmartre, which are distinguished by their near-monochrome colours and precise drawing.

V

V-2 *The rocket undergoing postwar British trials.*

V-1 A German World War II unguided missile, also called a flying bomb. Powered by an air-breathing type of ramjet, it carried about 2000 pounds (900 kg) of high explosive. Some 8000 were launched against London between June 1944 and March 1945, killing 5500 civilians.

V-2 A German World War II ballistic missile powered by a rocket engine using alcohol and liquid oxygen as fuel. It carried about 2000 pounds (900 kg) of high explosive and had a preset guidance system. Some 4000 were used against Britain and the Low Countries in 1944 and 1945. It became the basis for both US and Soviet postwar rocket design.

Vaal River A river in South Africa, rising in the SE Transvaal. It flows generally W and SW, to join the Orange River and forms part of the Orange Free State–Transvaal border. Length: 1210 km (750 mi).

vaccination (*or* inoculation) The introduction of inactivated or dead disease-causing microorganisms (vaccine) into the body to stimulate the formation of antibodies to these agents (*see also* immunity). The first vaccination (against smallpox) was performed by Edward Jenner in 1798. Vaccines are usually given by injection but some can be administered through skin scratches and some are taken by mouth.

vacuum A region of space that contains no matter. In practice, a perfect vacuum is impossible to obtain. In technical work a soft (*or* low) vacuum goes down to a pressure of 10^{-2} pascal, a hard (*or* high) vacuum is between 10^{-2} and 10^{-7} pascal, and an ultrahigh vacuum is below 10^{-7} pascal. Vacuum technology is used in making cathode-ray tubes, light bulbs, etc., and is used in food preservation.

vacuum flask. *See* Dewar flask.

Vadodara (former name: Baroda) 22 19N 73 14E. A city in India, in Gujarat. The siting of an oil refinery at nearby Kouali has helped to promote Vadodara's industrial growth and its chief products include petrochemicals, cotton textiles, wood, and tobacco. Population

(1981): 744 881.

Vaduz 47 08N 9 32E The capital of Liechtenstein. Its castle (restored 1905–16) is the residence of the ruling prince. Population (1986 est): 4920.

vagina The part of the reproductive tract of women and other female mammals into which the penis is inserted during sexual intercourse. It connects the womb to the exterior and is readily distensible to allow for childbirth.

vagus nerve An important nerve that connects the brain with the throat, larynx, heart, lungs, stomach, and gut. Surgical cutting of a branch of the vagus nerve (**vagotomy**) is sometimes carried out in the treatment of a peptic ulcer.

valence (*or* valency) The combining power of an atom, ion, or radical. It is equal to the number of hydrogen atoms that the atom, ion, or radical can combine with or replace in forming compounds. Many elements have more than one valence. A **valence electron** is an electron in the outer shell of an atom that participates in forming chemical (valence) bonds. *See also* energy band.

Valencia 39 29N 0 24W The third largest city in Spain, on the Guadalaviar estuary. In 1021 it became the capital of the Moorish kingdom of Valencia. El Cid took the city from the Moors in 1094. Its many notable buildings include the cathedral (1262–1482). Population (1981): 751 734.

Valencia 10 14N 67 59W The third largest city in Venezuela. It is the focus of the country's chief agricultural area. Population (1981): 751 734.

Valentine, St (died c. 269) Roman priest and martyr, known as the patron of lovers. The customs practised on his feast day (14 Feb) have no connection with his life.

Valentinian I (d. 375 AD) Western Roman emperor (364–75). He fought campaigns in the north of the Empire, restoring the Rhine frontier and Hadrian's Wall.

Valentino, Rudolf (Rodolpho Guglieml di Valentina d'Antonguolla; 1895–1926) US film actor, born in Italy. His performances in *The Sheik* (1921), *Blood and Sand* (1922), *Son of the Sheik* (1926), and other silent romantic dramas established him as the leading cinema idol of the 1920s.

Valera, Eamon De. *See* De Valera, Eamon.

Valéry, Paul (1871–1945) French poet, essayist, and critic. *Cahiers* (29 vols, 1957–60) is a record of his metaphysical speculations from 1894 until his death. His later poetry in *La Jeune Parque* (1917) and *Charmes* (1922) combines sensuous lyricism with intellectual force.

Valhalla In Teutonic mythology, one of the three homes of Odin. Half of the warriors who die in battle are brought by the Valkyries to Valhalla, where they spend their days in battle and their nights in feasting and listening to songs of their heroic exploits.

Valium. *See* benzodiazepines.

Valkyries In Teutonic mythology, beautiful maidens, who are the personal attendants of Odin. They wear armour and, led by Freyja, ride on horseback over battlefields in order to carry away the slain warriors whom Odin has chosen to live with him in Valhalla.

Valladolid 41 39N 4 45W A city in central Spain, in Old Castile. It was formerly the capital of Castile and León (14th–15th centuries). It has a 16th-century cathedral and contains Cervantes' house; Christopher Columbus died here (1506). Population (1982): 358 629.

Valletta 35 54N 14 32E The capital of Malta. Founded in 1566 by the Knights of St John, it was formerly an important British naval base. Population (1985): 9263.

valley An elongated depression in the earth's surface. Valleys have various origins but the common **V-shaped valley** is formed as the result of erosion by a river. Those that originated through glacial erosion are **U-shaped valleys**, with steep sides and broad floors, often occupied by deep lakes (*see* fjord). *See also* rift valley.

Valley of the Kings The cemetery of the Egyptian pharaohs from about 1580 to about 1085 BC, near Thebes. All the tombs were robbed, except that of Tutankhamen.

Valois The royal dynasty of France from 1328 to 1589. The Hundred Years' War (1337–1453) nearly destroyed Valois power, which was saved by Charles VII (reigned 1422–61). Succeeding rulers, Charles VIII (reigned 1483–98) and Louis XII, waged disastrous wars in Italy, where they opposed the Habsburgs. The last Valois were the victims of rival religious factions at court (*see* Wars of Religion).

Valois, Dame Ninette de. *See* de Valois, Dame Ninette.

Valparaíso 33 05S 71 40W The second largest city in Chile, on the Pacific Ocean. Founded by the Spanish (1536), Valparaíso is a major port. Population (1985 est): 267 025.

value-added tax (VAT) An indirect tax on goods calculated by adding a percentage to the value of a product as it increases at each stage of production; the whole cost of the tax is eventually passed on to the consumer. The tax was introduced in the UK in 1973.

VAMPIRE BAT *Its chisel-like incisor teeth are used to cut the flesh of the victims to cause a flow of blood.*

vampire bat A bat of the family *Desmodontidae* (3 species), of Central and South America. The most common species is *Desmodus rotundus*, 7.5–9 cm long. Vampire bats feed on the blood of mammals or birds. Vampire bats are too small to cause serious blood loss to their host; they do, however, transmit dangerous diseases.

vanadium (V) A transition metal, named after the Norse goddess Vanadis. The metal is isolated by reduction of the trichloride (VCl$_3$) with magnesium or of the pentoxide (V$_2$O$_5$) with calcium. At no 23; at wt 50.942; mp 1890 ± 10°C; bp 3380°C.

Van Allen radiation belts Two regions of charged particles in the earth's magnetosphere. The toroidal inner belt lies 1000–5000 km above the equator; the outer belt lies 15 000–25 000 km above the equator, curving down towards the earth's magnetic poles. The belts were discovered in 1958 by the US physicist James Van Allen (1914–   ).

Vanbrugh, Sir John (1664–1726) English architect, soldier, and playwright. His plays included *The Relapse* (1697) and *The Provok'd Wife* (1697). Vanbrugh was also England's most successful baroque architect. His most impressive buildings were Castle Howard (1699–1726), Blenheim Palace (begun 1705), on which he collaborated with Hawksmoor, and Seton Delaval (begun 1720).

Vancouver 49 13N 123 06W A city and port in W Canada, in British Columbia. Established in 1862 at the S end of the Coast Mountains, Vancouver is the commercial and industrial centre of British Columbia. Population (1986): 431 147.

Vancouver Island A Canadian island off the Pacific coast of British Columbia. Its E coastal plain rises to glaciers and forested mountains. The economy depends on timber, mining, fishing, and tourism. Area: 32 137 sq km (12 408 sq mi). Population (1981): 461 573. Chief town: Victoria.

Vandals A Germanic tribe that during the first four centuries AD migrated southwards from Scandinavia and the S Baltic coast. In 455 they sacked Rome. The devastation they caused gave rise to the term vandalism.

Van de Graaff generator A type of electrostatic generator, invented by the US physicist Robert Jemison Van de Graaff (1901–67), that produces static potentials of millions of volts. Charge from an external source is fed onto a continuously moving belt, which transfers it to the inside of a large hollow conducting sphere. The charge moves to the outer surface of the sphere, leaving the inside neutral and able to collect more charge.

Van der Post, Sir Laurens (1906–   ) South African writer and traveller. His books include *Venture to the Interior* (1952), *The Lost World of the Kalahari* (1958), *The Hunter and the Whale* (1967), and *Testament to the Bushmen* (1984).

Van der Waals' equation A modification of the ideal gas equation, $pV = RT$, where p is the pressure exerted by a gas with volume V and thermodynamic temperature T. R is the gas constant. Van der Waals adjusted V to $(V - b)$ to take account of the volume occupied by the molecules. He also assumed that forces (**Van der Waals' forces**) exist between the molecules and therefore adjusted the pressure term to $(p - a/V^2)$. Both a and b are constant for a particular gas.

van de Velde A family of 17th-century Dutch painters. **Willem van de Velde the Elder** (1611–93) and his eldest son **Willem van de Velde the Younger** (1633–1707) were both marine artists, living in England after 1672. His younger son **Adriaen van de Velde** (1636–72) was a landscape painter. **Esaias van de Velde** (c. 1591–1630), the landscape painter, was probably the brother of Willem van de Velde the Elder. He is best known as the teacher of Jan van Goyen and for such works as *Winter Scene* (National Gallery, London).

Van Dieman's Land. *See* Tasmania.

Van Dyck, Sir Anthony (*or* Vandyke; 1599–1641) Flemish baroque painter. Working chiefly in England, he painted many religious and mythological subjects, although his reputation rests largely on his portraits of the English court. *Charles I on Horseback* (National Gallery, London) and *Thomas Killigrew and Lord Croft* (Windsor Castle) demonstrate the elegance and grandeur of his style.

Vänern, Lake The largest lake in Sweden. It drains into the Kattegat via the River Göta. Area: 5546 sq km (2141 sq mi).

van Eyck, Jan (c. 1390–1441) Flemish painter. He is noted for his realistic portraits, particularly *The Arnolfini Marriage* and *Man in a Red Turban* (both National Gallery, London). He certainly perfected and possibly invented the Flemish technique of oil painting, in which the pigment is mixed with oil and turpentine and applied in thin glazes.

VAN GOGH   *Detail of* Self-portrait with Bandaged Ear.

Van Gogh, Vincent (1853–90) Dutch postimpressionist painter. His early works were chiefly drawings of peasants. On moving to Paris (1886) he briefly adopted the style of impressionism and later of pointillism. In Arles in 1888 he painted his best-known works –orchards, sunflowers, and the local postman and his family–but only one painting was sold during his lifetime. The visit of his friend Gauguin ended in a quarrel during which Van Gogh cut off part of his own left ear. In 1889 he entered a mental asylum at Saint-Rémy. The ominous *Wheatfield with Crows* (Stedelijk Museum, Amsterdam) was painted shortly before his suicide, in Auvers. *See* expressionism.

Vanilla A genus of climbing orchids (about 90 species), native to tropical Asia and America. They have long fleshy stems attached to trees by aerial roots and produce large white and yellow flowers. Several species are cultivated commercially for the flavouring agent vanilla.

Van't Hoff, Jacobus Henricus (1852–1911) Dutch chemist, who pioneered the field of stereoisomerism, showing that the bonds of a carbon atom are arranged in a tetrahedron. This enabled him to explain optical activity in terms of molecular structure. He also contributed to chemical thermodynamics and to the theory of solutions, for which he won the 1901 Nobel Prize.

Vanua Levu A volcanic island in the S Pacific Ocean, the second largest in Fiji. Sugar, copra, and gold are exported. Area: 5535 sq km (2137 sq mi). Chief town: Lambasa.

Vanuatu, Republic of (formerly: New Hebrides) A chain of about 80 forested volcanic islands in the SW Pacific Ocean. Espíritu Santo is the largest island. Discovered by the Portuguese (1606), they were jointly administered by France and the UK (1906–80). In 1980 they became independent as the Vanuatu Republic. Copra, cocoa, coffee, and beef are exported. Area: about 14 760 sq km (5700 sq mi). Population (1987): 141 400. Capital: Vila, on Efate.

Varanasi (*or* Benares)–25 20N 82 00E A city in India, on the River Ganges. A major place of pilgrimage for Hindus, Jains, Sikhs, and Buddhists, it has 5 km (3 mi) of ghats (steps), from which thousands of Hindus bathe in the sacred river. Population (1981): 794 000.

variable stars Stars the brightness of which varies with time. In regular variables the brightness completes a cycle of changes in a period ranging from minutes to years. The brightness variation can be up to several magnitudes. The three major groups are: eclipsing binary stars, cataclysmic variables, and pulsating stars.

variance In a set of numbers, usually measurements, the quantity obtained by summing the squares of the differences between each number and the average value of the set and then dividing by the number of members of the set. Variance and, more often, its square root, called the **standard deviation**, are used to estimate scatter or random error in experimental results.

varicose veins Swollen tortuous veins in the legs caused by malfunctioning of the valves in the veins, which obstructs blood flow. Varicose veins tend to run in families and are commoner in older and fat people, women, and those who are constantly standing.

Varna 43 12N 27 57E A city and port in E Bulgaria, on the Black Sea. Founded in the 6th century BC, it finally passed to Bulgaria in 1878. Population (1982): 295 038.

Varna, Battle of (10 November, 1444) The battle in which the Hungarians were decisively defeated by the Turks. It enabled the Turks to expand further into the Balkans.

varnish A resinous solution in oil or alcohol that dries to form a hard transparent coating on wood, metal, etc. Natural resins include shellac, copal, dammar, and congo. Polyurethane is a particularly durable and chemical-resistant synthetic resin. Polyesters and alkyds are also used.

varnish tree. *See* lacquer tree.

varve dating A technique used in geology and archaeology to give the age of a sediment and to provide information about the climate during which it was formed. Varves are layers of claylike sediment deposited from a melting glacier into a lake. Each varve represents a single year's deposition.

Vasa The ruling dynasty of Sweden (1523–1818) and of Poland (1587–1668) founded by Gustavus I Vasa (1496–1560). The best-known Vasa monarchs in Sweden were Gustavus II Adolphus (1594–1632) and Christina (1626–89).

Vasari, Giorgio (1511–74) Italian painter, architect, and writer. In Florence he painted fresco cycles and built the Uffizi, both works showing his respect for mannerism. However he is best known for his *Lives of the Most Eminent Italian Architects, Painters, and Sculptors*, tracing the history of Renaissance art.

vasectomy. *See* sterilization.

Västerås 59 36N 16 32E A city in central Sweden, on Lake Mälar. An important city in medieval times, it has a 12th-century castle. Population (1986): 117 732.

VAT. *See* value-added tax.

VATICAN CITY *St Peter's Basilica, the largest church in the world.*

Vatican City, State of the A small independent state within the city of Rome, the seat of government of the Roman Catholic Church. It came into being in 1929, when Pius XI signed the Lateran Treaty with Mussolini. The state is governed by a commission appointed by the pope. Supreme pontiff: John Paul II. Official language: Italian. Area: 44 hectares (109 acres). Population (1985 est): 1000.

Vatican Councils **1.** (1869–70) The council that was convoked by Pius IX, resulting in the promulgation of the doctrine of papal infallibility. **2.** (1962–65) The council that was convoked by John XXIII and continued by Paul VI. It established an atmosphere in which progressive critics could freely express their views.

Vaughan Williams, Ralph (1872–1958) British composer. Influenced by English folksong and Tudor music, he developed a modal style that found its full expression in *Fantasia on a Theme by Tallis* (for string orchestra; 1910). His works include nine symphonies, the ballet *Job* (1931), the opera *The Pilgrim's Progress* (1951), and much other orchestral, chamber, and choral music.

vector (mathematics) A quantity that has both magnitude and direction. Examples of vectors include velocity, force, magnetic flux density, etc. A vector needs three numbers (called components) to be defined, each number representing its magnitude in one of three mutually perpendicular directions.

vector (medicine) An organism capable of transmitting a disease-causing organism (pathogen) from one organism to another. Transmission may be accidental or the vector may play a significant role in the life cycle of the pathogen, for example the malarial parasite spends part of its life cycle in the mosquito, which transmits it to man.

Vedanta The various philosophical schools of Hinduism, which derive from the commentaries on the *Vedas*, especially the *Upanishads*, the *Brahmasutras*, and the *Bhagavadgita*. The schools have in common the belief in reincarnation, the truth of the *Vedas*, the law of karma, and the need for spiritual release. Believing Brahman to be the cause of the world, they condemn Buddhism and Jainism.

Vedas (Sanskrit: divine knowledge) The basic Hindu scriptures, written in archaic Sanskrit (Vedic) around 1500 BC. It comprises hymns, invocations, mantras, spells, and rituals, mostly concerning the sacrificial worship of gods representing various natural forces.

Vega A conspicuous white star, apparent magnitude 0.03 and 26.5 light years distant, that is the brightest star in the constellation Lyra.

vegetarianism The practice of abstaining from eating animal flesh for ethical, religious, or nutritional reasons. Some vegetarians will not eat any animal products, including milk, cheese, eggs, etc., and are called **vegans**. Vegetarianism occurs in many religious traditions, including Buddhism, Jainism, and Hinduism, and it was advocated by Pythagoras, Plato, and many other thinkers. Vegetarians, especially vegans, can suffer from anaemia unless their diet includes sufficient vitamin B_{12}.

vein (physiology) A thin-walled blood vessel that carries oxygen-depleted blood from the tissues to the heart. The veins opening directly into the heart are the superior and inferior vena cavae and the pulmonary veins from the lungs, which are unique in carrying oxygenated blood.

Velázquez, Diego Rodriguez de Silva (1599–1660) Spanish painter. Initially he specialized in painting religious subjects and still-lifes, later painting portraits of the royal family and the chief minister Olivares. Other works include his famous *Pope Innocent X* (Rome) and the *Rokeby Venus* (National Gallery, London).

veld (*or* veldt) A tract of open grassland on the plateau of S Africa. It includes the Highveld (over 1500 m), Middleveld (1500–900 m), and Lowveld (below 900 m).

velocity The rate of change of a body's position in a given direction. The speed of a body is not in a specified direction. Velocity is thus a vector quantity and speed is a scalar quantity. **Angular velocity** is the rate of change of a body's motion about an axis. It is measured in radians per second.

Venda, Republic of The smallest country in mainland Africa, within South African territory. Most of the population is Venda. *Economy*: chiefly agricultural. *History*: it was the third Bantu Homeland to be granted full independence from South Africa (1979), but this is not recognized elsewhere in the world. President: Chief Patrick Mphephu (1925–). Official currency: South African rand. Area: 7410 sq km (2861 sq mi). Population (1985 est): 424 000. Capital: Thokoyandou.

venereal disease. *See* sexually transmitted disease.

Venezuela, Republic of A country on the N coast of South America. The plains of the Orinoco basin in the N rise to the Guiana Highlands in the SE, and in the NW the N end of the Andean chain reaches heights of over 5000 m (16 000 ft). Most of the population is of mixed European and Indian descent. *Economy*: based chiefly on oil. Efforts are being made to diversify the economy. Venezuela is also rich in diamonds, gold, zinc, copper, lead, silver, phosphates, manganese, and titanium. Crop growing in the N includes coffee, cocoa, sugar, maize, and rice. *History*: sighted by Columbus in 1498, it was visited in 1499 by Vespucci, who named it Venezuela ("Little Venice") on seeing Indian villages built on stilts over Lake Maracaibo. Spanish settlement began in 1520 and Venezuela remained under Spanish rule until liberated by Bolívar in 1821. It then formed part of Colombia until 1830. Independent Venezuela was ruled by a succession of dictators until the post-World War II period, which has witnessed the development of more democratic governments. Venezuela is a member of the OAS, LAFTA, and OPEC. President: Carlos Andrés Pérez. Official language: Spanish. Official currency: bolívar of 100 céntimos. Area: 912 050 sq km (352 143 sq mi). Population (1985 est): 17 316 740. Capital: Caracas. Main port: Maracaibo.

VENICE   *Gondoliers on the Grand Canal.*

Venice (Italian name: Venezia)   45 26N 12 20E A city in NE Italy. It is a seaport built on over 100 islands in the Lagoon of Venice. Venice is a centre of commerce and tourism and its manufactures include glassware, textiles, and lace. The Grand Canal and about 170 smaller canals provide waterways for water buses (*vaporetti*) and gondolas. Famous bridges include the Rialto Bridge and the Bridge of Sighs. Situated at the centre of Venice is St Mark's Square (Piazza San Marco) overlooked by St Mark's Cathedral, the 15th-century Clock Tower, the Campanile, and the Doge's Palace. The Accademia houses a unique collection of Venetian paintings; the Lido, a seaside resort, is 3 km (2 mi) to the SE. *History*: originally settled by refugees fleeing barbarian invasions (5th century AD onwards), Venice was united under the first doge in 697. It became an independent republic in 1380. Venice is currently endangered by floods, pollution, and subsidence. Population (1986): 331 454.

Venn diagram.   *See* set theory.

ventricle.   *See* brain; heart.

Venturi tube   A device consisting of an open-ended tube with a central constriction, used to measure the rate of flow of a fluid, which can be calculated from the pressure difference between the centre and the ends. It is used to measure the airspeed of aircraft. Invented by G. B. Venturi (1746–1822).

Venus (goddess)   A Roman goddess originally of gardens and fertility who became identified with the Greek Aphrodite as goddess of love. This identification followed the introduction into Rome of the cult of Aphro-

dite of Eryx in Sicily and was further established by the Julian family, who claimed descent from Aeneas, son of Aphrodite.

Venus (planet)   The second planet in order from the sun, orbiting the sun every 225 days at an average distance of 108 million km. It is 12 102 km in diameter and has an extremely long period of axial rotation (243 days). It can be one of the most brilliant objects in the sky, reaching a magnitude of −4.4, and like the moon exhibits phases. Its surface is totally obscured by dense swirling yellowish clouds of sulphuric acid droplets and sulphur particles. The atmosphere is primarily (98%) carbon dioxide. Planetary probes have shown that the surface temperature is a hostile 470°C and the surface atmospheric pressure is about 90 times that of earth.

Venus flytrap   A carnivorous plant, *Dionaea muscipula*, native to the eastern USA. The upper part of each leaf is hinged at the midrib and an alighting insect triggers the leaf to snap shut, thus trapping the prey. Family: *Droseraceae*.

Venus's girdle   A marine invertebrate animal, *Cestum veneris*, belonging to an order (*Cestida*) of ctenophores. Its transparent ribbon-like body is about 5 cm wide and 1 m or more long. It occurs in the Mediterranean Sea and Atlantic Ocean.

Veracruz (*or* Veracruz Llave)   19 11N 96 10W A major port in E Mexico, on the Gulf of Mexico. Population (1980): 305 456.

Verbena   A genus of herbaceous plants or dwarf shrubs (about 250 species), chiefly native to North and South America. Lemon verbena (*Lippia citriodora*) is a related shrub from tropical America, the leaves of which yield an oil used in perfumery. Family: *Verbenaceae*.

Verde, Cape (French name: Cap Vert)   14 43N 17 33W The westernmost point of Africa, in Senegal, consisting of a promontory extending into the Atlantic Ocean.

Verdi, Giuseppe   (1813–1901) Italian composer of operas. His first mature work was *Rigoletto* (1851); this was quickly followed in 1853 with *La Traviata* and *Il Trovatore*. In 1869 he wrote *Aida* (1871). His last works were the *Requiem* (1874) and the operas *Otello* (1887) and *Falstaff* (1893).

verdigris   A green copper acetate used as a paint pigment. The term is also applied to the green coating, consisting of copper sulphate or carbonate, that forms on copper roofs, etc.

Verdun   49 10N 5 24E A town in NE France, on the River Meuse. It was the scene of a major battle in 1916 (*see* World War I). Population (1982): 24 120.

Verlaine, Paul   (1844–96) French poet. His tempestuous relationship with Rimbaud, who influenced his experimental *Romances sans paroles* (1874), resulted in the break-up of his marriage, and in 1873 he was imprisoned for shooting and wounding Rimbaud. After the publication of *Les Poètes maudits* (1884), Verlaine was the acknowledged leader of the Symbolist poets.

Vermeer, Jan   (1632–75) Dutch painter, who spent his entire life in Delft. His best-known paintings of everyday scenes include *The Milkmaid* (Rijksmuseum, Amsterdam), *The Lacemaker* (Louvre), and *Allegory of Painting* (Kunsthistorisches Museum, Vienna), showing himself at work. See p. 751.

vermiculite   A clay mineral with the property of expanding up to 22 times its original thickness on heating.

Vermiculite results from the hydrothermal alteration of biotite and the intrusion of acid magma into basic rock.

vermilion Red mercuric sulphide (HgS). It sublimes readily on heating and occurs naturally as the mineral cinnabar. It is used as a pigment.

Vermont A state in the NE USA, in New England. The extensively forested Green Mountains run N–S through the centre of the state. Small manufacturing industries, mining, and tourism are important. The state's farmers produce dairy products, hay, potatoes, corn, and maple syrup. *History*: settled by the British in 1724, it declared its independence in 1777 and joined the Union in 1791. Area: 24 887 sq km (9609 sq mi). Population (1986 est): 541 000. Capital: Montpelier.

Verne, Jules (1828–1905) French writer. Verne's *Voyages extraordinaires* introduced such technological marvels as the submarine, space travel, and television. They included *Journey to the Centre of the Earth* (1864) and *Twenty Thousand Leagues Under the Sea* (1873). Other stories included *Around the World in Eighty Days* (1873).

VERNIER SCALE *An auxiliary scale used to measure accurately to two places of decimals.*

Vernier scale A device for measuring subdivisions of a scale, such as those on a pair of calipers. The auxiliary Vernier scale is divided so that ten of its subdivisions correspond to nine of those on the main scale. Named after Pierre Vernier (1580–1637).

Verona 45 26N 11 00E A city in N Italy, on the River Adige. A tourist centre, it possesses a Roman amphitheatre, a 12th-century cathedral, and the medieval Castelvecchio. Population (1986): 259 151.

Veronese, Paolo (P. Caliari; 1528–88) Italian paint-er of the Venetian school. In the Villa Barbaro at Maser, designed by Palladio, he painted illusionistic landscapes, mythological scenes, and portraits. His religious works, for example *Marriage at Cana* (Louvre), were often pretexts for depicting contemporary banquets in impressive architectural settings.

Veronica. *See* speedwell.

Verrocchio, Andrea del (Andrea del Cione; c. 1435–88) Florentine Renaissance sculptor, painter, and goldsmith. Verrocchio's best-known sculpture is the equestrian monument of Bartolommeo Colleoni in the Campo SS Giovanni e Paolo, Venice.

verruca. *See* wart.

Versailles 48 48N 2 08E A town in N central France. Versailles is chiefly famed for its baroque palace, the residence of the French kings from 1678 to 1769. Historic events enacted at the palace include Britain's recognition of American independence (1783), the crowning (1871) of William I as German emperor, and the signing of the **Treaty of Versailles** (1919), which imposed reparations on Germany after World War I and established the League of Nations. Population (1982): 95 240.

vertebra. *See* spine.

Vertebrata (*or* Craniata) A subphylum of animals that includes the fish, amphibians, reptiles, birds, and mammals. They are characterized by a backbone consisting of interlocking vertebrae, which forms the main support for the body and protects the nerve cord (spinal cord). Phylum: *Chordata*.

vervet. *See* grass monkey.

Verwoerd, Hendrik Frensch (1901–66) South African statesman; prime minister (1958–66). He took South Africa out of the Commonwealth in 1960. He was assassinated in parliament in Cape Town.

Vesalius, Andreas (1514–64) Flemish anatomist, whose major work, *The Seven Books on the Structure of the Human Body* (1543), contained some of the first accurate descriptions of human anatomy.

Vespasian (9–79 AD) Roman emperor (69–79). Vespasian's decisive policies brought an end to civil war and he increased taxes and reformed the army. He was deified after his death.

Vespucci, Amerigo (1454–1512) Italian navigator, after whom America is named. In 1499 he explored the

VERSAILLES *The west front of the Palace.*

NE coast of South America.

Vesta (goddess) The Roman goddess of the hearth, identified with the Greek Hestia. She was worshipped in private households, and her annual festival, the Vestalia, was held in June. The **Vestal Virgins**, her priestesses, tended the eternal fire at her shrine in Rome.

Vesuvius 40 49N 14 26E A volcano in S central Italy, near Naples. In 79 AD it engulfed Herculaneum and Pompeii; the last eruption was in 1944. Average height: 1220 m (4003 ft).

vetch A climbing or trailing annual or perennial herb of the genus *Vicia* (about 150 species), native to N temperate regions and South America. Some species are grown as fodder crops. Family: *Leguminosae*.

Vibrio A genus of freshwater and marine bacteria. They are rod-shaped, either straight or curved, and swim by means of whiplike flagella. *V. cholerae* causes cholera in man.

Viburnum A genus of shrubs and small trees (about 200 species), mostly native to N temperate regions. They have white or pink flowers. Many are grown as ornamentals, including the snowball tree (*see* guelder rose) and laurustinus. Family: *Caprifoliaceae*.

Vicenza 45 33N 11 33E A city in NE Italy. It was the home of the 16th-century architect Andrea Palladio. Population (1986): 110 449.

Vichy 46 07N 3 25E A spa in central France, on the River Allier. From 1940 until 1944, it was the seat of the French government of Marshal Pétain. Its waters, which were known to the Romans, are bottled and exported worldwide. Population (1982): 30 554.

Victor Emmanuel II (1820–78) King of Italy (1861–78). Victor Emmanuel fought the Austrians, supported Cavour, and coordinated with Garibaldi in the campaign that freed S Italy. As King of Italy he acquired Venetia (1866) and Rome (1870), which he made the Italian capital.

Victor Emmanuel III (1869–1947) King of Italy (1900–46) following the assassination of his father Umberto I. He acquiesced in Mussolini's seizure of power (1922) and after Mussolini's fall (1943) relinquished his powers to his son Umberto II.

Victoria A state of SE Australia. It consists of central uplands, descending to plains in the N and S. Gippsland is a noted dairying area. cattle production is now concentrated in S Victoria. Brown coal is mined in Central Gippsland and gas and oil are piped from the Bass Strait. Industry is concentrated on Melbourne. Area: 227 600 sq km (87 884 sq mi). Population (1987 est): 4 188 300. Capital: Melbourne.

Victoria 22 16N 114 13E The capital of Hong Kong, situated on the N of the island. Population (1981): 590 771.

Victoria (1819–1901) Queen of the United Kingdom (1837–1901). The daughter of George III's fourth son Edward, Duke of Kent (1767–1820), Victoria succeeded her uncle William IV. In 1840 she married her cousin Prince Albert of Saxe-Coburg-Gotha; they had nine children. Albert's death in 1861 was a severe blow to Victoria and she resolved thereafter to act exactly as he would have wished. She had an exalted view of the monarch's role in government, failing to appreciate the limitations of constitutional monarchy. Her refusal to dismiss her Whig ladies of the bedchamber when the Tory, Robert Peel, was attempting to form a ministry caused the Bedchamber Crisis (1839) and to Palmerston she insisted that no policy should be modified once she had approved it. Her close friendship with Disraeli, who made her Empress of India (1876), contrasted with her strained relations with his rival Gladstone. In the last years of her reign, especially after her Golden Jubilee (1887), she enjoyed enormous popularity.

Victoria, Lake (*or* Victoria Nyanza) The largest lake in Africa, in Uganda, Tanzania, and Kenya. It was discovered for Europeans in 1858 by Speke. Area: 69 485 sq km (26 826 sq mi).

Victoria and Albert Museum A London museum founded in 1853 to house examples of applied arts of all periods and cultures. Originally at Marlborough House, it moved to South Kensington in 1857.

Victoria Cross (VC) The highest British decoration for "bravery . . . in the presence of the enemy." Instituted by Queen Victoria in 1856, VCs were formerly cast from the metal of Russian guns taken during the Crimean War (1854–56).

QUEEN VICTORIA *With the three kings who succeeded her; (from the left) George V, Edward VII, and Edward VIII.*

Victoria Falls 17 55S 25 52E A waterfall in the Zambezi River on the border of Zimbabwe and Zambia. The river drops as much as 128 m (420 ft), and then flows through a narrow gorge known as the **Boiling Pot**.

vicuna A hoofed mammal, *Vicugna vicugna*, of high Andean plateaus. Resembling a small camel, the vicuna is 75 cm high and has a tawny-brown coat with a white bib and underparts. Aggressively territorial, they are valued for their wool. Family: *Camelidae* (camels, etc.).

video recording The storage of a television programme on magnetic tape. Because the demodulated video (vision) signal can have frequencies in the megahertz range, the signal is recorded diagonally on the tape (each diagonal line representing one line of the picture) and the tape is run slowly over a drum on which the recording and reading heads rotate at high speeds. Video discs include those in which the signal can be retrieved by a laser system.

Vienna (German name: Wien) 48 12N 16 20E The capital of Austria, on the River Danube. With its musical and theatrical life, its museums, and parks, it is a popular tourist attraction. Trade and industry, however, form the basis of the economy. Most of the chief buildings lie on or within the Ringstrasse, the boulevard built in 1857 to replace the old city ramparts. *History*: seat of the Habsburgs (1278–1918) and residence of the Holy Roman Emperor (1558–1806), Vienna became an important cultural centre in the 18th and 19th centuries, having associations with Haydn, Mozart, Beethoven, Schubert, and the Strauss family. It suffered considerable damage during World War II and was jointly occupied by the Allied Powers (1945–55). Population (1987): 1 506 201.

Vienna, Congress of (1814–15) A conference of European powers that met following the fall of Napoleon. Its Final Act created a kingdom of the Netherlands, a German confederation of 39 states, Lombardy-Venetia subject to Austria, and the Congress Kingdom of Poland. Legitimate monarchs were restored in Spain, Naples, Piedmont, Tuscany, and Modena, and Louis XVIII was confirmed as King of France.

Vienna Circle The group of scientific philosophers who developed the doctrine of logical positivism (*or* logical empiricism). Founded by Moritz Schlick (1882–1936) in 1924, the Vienna Circle flourished until 1939. Members included Carnap, Kurt Gödel (1906–78), and Otto Neurath (1882–1945). *See also* Ayer, Sir Alfred (Jules).

Vienne, River A river in W central France, flowing mainly NNW to the River Loire. Length: 354 km (220 mi).

Vientiane 18 06N 102 30E The capital of Laos, a port on the River Mekong. Founded in the 13th century, it came under Siamese control in the 18th century and was destroyed (1828) following a revolt against Siamese rule. It became capital of the French protectorate of Laos in the late 19th century. Population (1984 est): 120 000.

Viet Cong Communist guerrillas who fought in the Vietnam War (1954–75). In 1960 they established the National Liberation Front, which amalgamated the various groups opposed to the South Vietnamese Government.

Viet Minh The Vietnam League for Independence, formed in 1941 by Ho Chi Minh to create an independent Vietnamese republic. After World War II, the Viet Minh played a prominent role in the Indochina war against France (1946–54).

Vietnam, Socialist Republic of A country in SE Asia, occupying the E part of the Indochina peninsula. Fertile coastal lowlands rise to forested plateaus and mountains, the most populated areas being around the Mekong delta in the S and the Red River delta in the N. The inhabitants are mainly Vietnamese, with minorities of Chinese and others. *Economy*: agriculture remains the most important sector. Teak and bamboo are the chief forest products and fishing is also important. Industrial developments have been concentrated mainly in the N. The principal exports are coal, rubber, wood, tea, spices,

and coffee. *History*: the northern kingdom of Nam Viet was conquered in 111 BC by the Chinese. In 939 AD it broke free and resisted further Chinese invasions until the 15th century, when it was again briefly occupied. Its southward expansion culminated in the establishment (1802) of a united Vietnamese empire, which lasted until the establishment of the Union of Indochina by the French (1887). Vietnam was occupied by the Japanese in World War II. France's refusal in 1945 to recognize Ho Chi Minh's government led to war (1946–54) after which, following defeat at Dien Bien Phu, the French withdrew. The Geneva Conference (1954) divided Vietnam along the seventeenth parallel into communist North Vietnam and noncommunist South Vietnam, between which civil war ensued. In 1961 the USA extended assistance to the South and remained involved in the conflict until 1973 (*see* Vietnam War). In 1976, the victorious North proclaimed the reunited Socialist Republic of Vietnam. A deterioration of Sino-Vietnamese relations led to Vietnam's invasion of Cambodia (December, 1978–January, 1979) and increased reliance on the Soviet Union. The Chinese invasion of Vietnam (February–March, 1979) led to a massive increase in the number of refugees, known as the Boat People, attempting to leave Vietnam by small craft across the South China Sea. In 1989 Vietnamese troops withdrew from Cambodia. President: Vo Chi Cong (1914–). Official language: Vietnamese. Official currency: dong of 100 hao. Area: 329 466 sq km (127 180 sq mi). Population (1987): 62 468 000. Capital: Hanoi. Main port: Haiphong.

VIETNAM WAR *Children fleeing from a napalm strike; South Vietnam, 1972.*

Vietnam War (1954–75) The war between communist North Vietnam and South Vietnam, the latter aided from 1961 by the USA. It resulted in communist victory and the union (1976) of North and South Vietnam. Some 900 000 Viet Cong and North Vietnamese, 50 000 Americans, and some 400 000 South Vietnamese died in the war. *See also* Indochina.

viewdata An information storage and retrieval system in which pages of text are transmitted as coded signals along telephone wires and displayed on a domestic television receiver. The user has direct access to a central computer store via a keyboard, and there is therefore no delay in response.

Vigo 42 15N 8 44W A port and naval base in NW Spain, on the Atlantic coast. In 1702 an English-Dutch fleet sank a Spanish treasure fleet here. Population (1981): 258 724.

Vijayawada (former name: Bezwada) 16 34N 80 40E A city in India, on the River Krishna. Industries include engineering and rice milling. Population (1981): 545 000.

Viking probes Two identical US spacecraft that went into orbit around Mars in 1976. The Lander sections landed on the surface in July and September and performed various experiments. The Orbiter sections took extensive measurements and photographs of Mars' surface and two satellites.

Vikings Scandinavian sea warriors active from the late 8th to the mid-11th centuries. They established important settlements in the British Isles (especially at York and Dublin), where an Anglo-Danish dynasty was founded (1016) by Canute, and in Normandy. They also established settlements in the E Baltic, Vinland, and Greenland. Viking literature (the sagas) and art are noted for their vitality.

Villa, Pancho (Francesco V.; 1878–1923) Mexican revolutionary. Villa supported successive revolts against Mexican governments and came to dominate the north with an irregular army. In 1916 he raided Texas and New Mexico. After an agreement with the Mexican Government in 1920, he disbanded his army. He was later assassinated.

Villa-Lobos, Heitor (1887–1959) Brazilian composer. He toured Brazil collecting folksongs and in 1945 founded the Brazilian Academy of Music. His vast output includes 12 symphonies, *Bachianas Brasileiras* (1930–45), *Rudepoema* (1921–26) for piano, and the ballet *Uirapurú* (1917).

Villanovan The earliest Iron Age culture of N Italy, named after the site of Villanova near Bologna. Emerging in the 9th century BC Villanovan culture is characterized by sophisticated metalworking.

villein The unfree peasant of medieval Europe, holding land from the lord of the manor in return for labour. Many villeins acquired written titles to their holdings following the Peasants' Revolt.

Villeneuve, Pierre (1763–1806) French admiral during the Napoleonic Wars. He was defeated by Nelson at Trafalgar (1805) and taken prisoner. After his release he committed suicide.

Villon, François (1431–?1463) French poet. He led a life of vagrancy and crime and was condemned to be hanged in 1463 but was banished instead. The ballades and other poems in his *Lais* and *Grand Testament* are characterized by compassion, irony, and a fascination with death and decay.

Vilnius (Polish name: Wilno) 54 40N 25 19E A city in the W Soviet Union, on the River Neris. *History*: it was Gediminas' capital in the 14th century. It was ceded to Russia in 1795. After World War I it was given to newly independent Lithuania but was seized by Poland in 1922. Restored to Lithuania in 1940, it then became part of the Soviet Union. The Germans occupied Vilnius in World War II, when its large Jewish population was virtually exterminated. Population (1987): 566 000.

Vimy. *See* World War I.

vinegar A dilute solution of acetic acid, produced from soured wine, beer (malt vinegar), or other dilute alcoholic liquids. It is used in salad dressings, preserving, etc.

vingt-et-un. *See* pontoon.

Vinland The Viking name for the area of NE America, probably Newfoundland, discovered, explored, and briefly settled by Leif Eriksson (c. 1000). The area was possibly visited a decade earlier by Bjarni Herjolfsson.

vinyl resins. *See* polyvinyl chloride.

viol A bowed stringed instrument, common from the 15th until the early 18th centuries, when it was eclipsed by the violin. Viols have six strings, tuned mainly in fourths, a shallow bridge, gut frets on the fingerboard, sloping shoulders, and flat backs. They are held between the knees when played and the bow is held in an underhand grip. The bass viol acquired the name **viola da gamba** from the Italian *gamba*, leg.

viola A musical instrument of the violin family. It is similar to the violin, although larger in size, having thicker strings and a heavier bow. It has a range of over four octaves from the C below middle C; its strings are tuned C, G, D, A.

violet A perennial herb of the genus *Viola*, up to 40 cm tall, whose solitary flowers are usually blue, purple, or white. The sweet-scented garden violets are derived from the Eurasian sweet violet (*V. odorata*). The dog violet (*V. canina*) is another common species, and the genus also includes the pansies. Family: *Violaceae*.

VIOLIN *Making the instrument requires great skill and patience.*

violin A bowed string instrument, the soprano member of the family that includes the viola, cello, and double bass. It has four strings tuned in fifths (G, D, A, E), an arched bridge, and a smooth fingerboard. It has a range of over four octaves from the G below middle C. The violin is played with a bow strung with horsehair; the strings can also be plucked. The design of the violin was perfected by the Amati, Guarneri, and Stradivari families in Italy between the mid-16th and early 18th centuries.

violoncello. *See* cello.

viper A venomous snake, belonging to the family *Viperidae* (150 species), that has long erectile fangs. 0.3–3 m long, vipers feed on small animals. Most give birth to live young. Old World vipers (subfamily *Viperinae*) are stout-bodied and broad-headed and mostly ground-dwelling. New World vipers (subfamily *Crotalinae*) are known as pit vipers.

Virgil (Publius Vergilius Maro; 70–19 BC) Roman poet. Reacting against the troubled political background, he described in his *Eclogues* (42–37 BC) an idealized pastoral landscape. His more practical vision of Italy in the *Georgics* (36–29 BC) is informed by his passionate interest in agriculture. During his final years he worked on the *Aeneid*, a national epic in 12 books describing the wanderings of Aeneas, the founding of Rome, and extolling the Julian dynasty and Augustus. He died of fever after returning from a voyage to Greece. The supreme poet of imperial Rome, Virgil became the object of superstitious reverence to later generations.

virginals A keyboard instrument of the 16th and 17th centuries, the earliest and simplest form of the harpsichord. Often made in the form of a box, which could be set on the table, the strings (one to each note) run parallel to the keyboard.

Virginia A state on the mid-Atlantic coast of the USA. The low-lying coastal plain rises to the forested Appalachian Mountains in the W. The principal industries are chemicals and tobacco processing. Fishing, tourism, and mining are also significant. The state produces tobacco, hay, corn, apples, and peaches. *History*: one of the 13 original colonies, it was named after Elizabeth I of England, the Virgin Queen. It became a state in 1788. Area: 105 716 sq km (40 817 sq mi). Population (1986 est): 5 787 000. Capital: Richmond.

Virginia creeper A climbing shrub, also called woodbine, of the genus *Parthenocissus*, especially *P. tricuspidata* of SE Asia and *P. quinquefolia* of North America. It clings by means of branched tendrils. Family: *Vitaceae*.

Virgin Islands A West Indian group of approximately one hundred small islands and cays in the Lesser Antilles. **The British Virgin Islands** consist of about 40 islands, the largest being Tortola. They became a British crown colony in 1956. Area: 153 sq km (59 sq mi). Population (1980): 12 034. Capital: Road Town. **The Virgin Islands of the United States** consist of three main islands, the largest being St Croix, and about 50 smaller ones. They were purchased from Denmark in 1917. Area: 344 sq km (133 sq mi). Population (1985): 110 800. Capital: Charlotte Amalie.

Virgo (Latin: Virgin) A large equatorial constellation that lies on the zodiac between Libra and Leo. The brightest star is Spica. The constellation contains the **Virgo cluster** of galaxies, which contains over 2500 members.

virtual particle A short-lived particle that is used in quantum mechanics to represent the interaction between stable particles. In quantum mechanics the electromagnetic interaction would be represented by the exchange of virtual photons between them. The strong interaction is represented by the exchange of virtual pions, the weak interaction by the exchange of intermediate vector bosons, and the gravitational interaction by the exchange of virtual gravitons.

virus A minute noncellular particle that can reproduce only in living cells. Viruses consist of a core of nucleic acid (either DNA or RNA), surrounded by a protein coat (capsule) and, in some types, a lipid-containing envelope. Viruses alternate between an inert virion stage and an infective stage, in which the capsule binds to the host cell and the viral nucleic acid (containing its genes) enters the cell and directs the components of the host cell to assemble replica viruses. These are finally liberated, often with damage to or death of the host cell. Viruses are responsible for a wide range of diseases in plants and animals.

viscacha A gregarious South American rodent, *Lagostomus maximus*, related to chinchillas. Over 50 cm in length, viscachas live in warrens of 12–15 burrows. They are nocturnal and feed on grasses, roots, and seeds. Family: *Chinchillidae*.

Visconti, Luchino (1906–76) Italian film director. Born into a noble family, he became a committed Marxist. His late films especially are characterized by elaborate and formal visual composition. They include *The Leopard* (1963), *The Damned* (1970), and *Death in Venice* (1971). He also directed many opera and drama productions.

viscosity A measure of the degree to which a fluid resists a deforming force. Viscosity is defined by Newton's law of viscosity: if two layers of a fluid, area A and distance x apart, flow with a relative velocity v, there is a force between them equal to vAv/x. v is called the coefficient of viscosity. Viscosity is measured in newton seconds per square metre. The **kinematic viscosity** is the coefficient of viscosity divided by the density of the fluid.

Vishakhapatnam 17 42N 83 24E A city in India, on the Bay of Bengal. An important port, India's first steamer was launched here in 1948. Population (1981): 594 000.

VIRGINALS A Young Woman Standing at a Virginal *(detail) by Vermeer (National Gallery).*

Vishnu The second member of the Hindu trinity, the Trimurti. He is known as the Preserver and is married to Lakshmi. He has ten avatars or manifestations, the most famous of which are Rama and Krishna. He is often portrayed as lying asleep on a seven-headed snake.

Visigoths A branch of the Goths. Forced by the Huns across the Danube (376 AD), they destroyed a Roman army at Adrianople (378) and, under Alaric I (c. 370–410 AD), sacked Rome in 410.

Vistula, River (Polish name: Wisła) The longest river of Poland, rising in the Carpathian Mountains and flowing N and NW to enter the Baltic Sea near Gdańsk. Length: 1090 km (677 mi).

vitamin An organic compound, other than a protein, fat or carbohydrate, that is required in small amounts by living organisms for normal growth and maintenance of life. Vitamins function as coenzymes in many metabolic reactions.

vitamin A (*or* retinol) A fat-soluble vitamin and an essential constituent of the visual pigments of the eyes. It also functions in the maintenance of healthy mucous membranes. Sources include liver, fish-liver oils, and egg yolk.

vitamin B complex A group of water-soluble vitamins that are all constituents of coenzymes involved in metabolic reactions. Thiamine (B_1) occurs in cereal grains, beans, peas, and pork. Deficiency leads to beriberi. Riboflavin (B_2) is found in yeast, liver, milk, and green leafy plants. Nicotinamide (nicotinic acid *or* niacin) can be synthesized from the amino acid tryptophan; liver is a rich source of the vitamin and milk and eggs of tryptophan. Vitamin B_6 (pyridoxine) is widely distributed in yeast, liver, milk, beans, and cereal grains. Also common in many foods are pantothenic acid, a constituent of coenzyme A; biotin, which is synthesized by intestinal bacteria; and choline, a precursor of acetylcholine (which transmits nervous impulses). Folic acid and vitamin B_{12} (cyanocobalamin) can be synthesized by intestinal bacteria. Liver is a good source of vitamin B_{12}.

vitamin C (*or* ascorbic acid) A water-soluble compound that is required especially for the maintenance of healthy connective tissue. It cannot be synthesized by man and certain animals. Fruit and vegetables, especially citrus fruits, are good sources. Deficiency of vitamin C leads to scurvy.

vitamin D A fat-soluble vitamin consisting of several related compounds (sterols), principally cholecalciferol (D_3) and ergocalciferol (D_2). Vitamin D is important in calcium and phosphorus metabolism. Vitamin D_3 is produced by the action of sunlight on skin. Fish and fish-liver oils are the main natural sources, while vitamin D_2 is added to margarine. Deficiency in infants causes rickets.

vitamin E A vitamin consisting of a group of related compounds that function as biological antioxidants. The most potent form of vitamin E is alpha-tocopherol, found in green leafy plants, cereal grains, and eggs.

vitamin K A vitamin consisting of a group of quinone-based compounds that are necessary for the formation of prothrombin, important in blood clotting. Vitamin K occurs in vegetables, cereals, and egg yolk and can be synthesized by intestinal bacteria.

Viti Levu The largest Fijian island, in the S Pacific Ocean. Mount Victoria rises to 1302 m (4341 ft). Sugar, pineapples, cotton, and rice are produced. Area: 10 386 sq km (4010 sq mi). Chief settlement: Suva.

Vitoria 42 51N 2 40W A city in N Spain. Wellington defeated the French here (1813). Population (1981): 192 773.

Vitruvius (Marcus Vitruvius Pollio; 1st century BC) Roman architect and military engineer. His *De architectura* describes all aspects of Roman architecture. It strongly influenced architects in Renaissance Italy.

Vivaldi, Antonio (1678–1741) Italian composer and violinist. Besides operas and sacred music, Vivaldi wrote over 450 concertos for a wide range of solo instruments, including a set of four violin concertos entitled *The Four Seasons*.

VOLCANOES *Mount St Helens, Oregon, extinct for 123 years, suddenly erupted in 1980.*

Viverridae A family of mammals of the order *Carnivora*. The 82 species include the genets, civets, linsangs, and mongooses. Viverrids typically have a long body and tail and short legs.

viviparity A reproductive process in animals in which the embryo develops within the maternal body. Viviparity occurs in most mammals—the embryos being nourished through the placenta—and in some snakes, lizards, and sharks.

vivisection The use of live animals for experiments. Many animals are used worldwide to determine the effects of drugs, cosmetics, food additives, and other chemicals on living organisms. They are also used in medical and biological research. In the UK experimenters are licensed by the Home Office. Alternatives to live animals include the use of test-tube (*in vitro*) techniques, tissue cultures, and computer-based mathematical models.

Vladivostok 43 09N 131 53E A port of the SE Soviet Union, on the Sea of Japan. It is the terminus of the Trans-Siberian Railway and a major Soviet naval base. Population (1987): 615 000.

Vltava, River A river in Czechoslovakia, rising in the Forest of Bohemia and flowing mainly SE then N to join the River Elbe. Length: 434 km (270 mi).

vocal cords. *See* larynx.

vodka A spirit distilled from potatoes, rye, barley, or malt, usually in E Europe. Being colourless and without a distinctive flavour, vodka is used in many mixed drinks.

voiceprint A graphic record of the sounds produced during speech. The record shows the range of frequencies and harmonics produced and can be used to identify any individual voice.

volcanoes Vents or fissures in the earth's surface through which magma rises from the earth's interior and erupts lava, gases, and pyroclastic material. Basaltic lava tends to produce gently sloping cones, the lava flowing over a wide area, whereas the more viscous acid lava produces a steeper-sided cone. Volcanic cones are often topped by craters, created by volcanic explosions. The world's highest volcano (extinct) is Aconcagua (6959 m) in the Andes.

Volcano Islands A group of three small volcanic Japanese islands in the W Pacific Ocean. They were under US administration (1951–68). Sulphur and sugar are produced. Area: about 28 sq km (11 sq mi).

vole A small short-tailed rodent belonging to the subfamily *Microtinae*. Voles are found in Europe, Asia, and North America and range in size from 7 to 35 cm. They have blunt noses and their cheek teeth grow continuously. The common field voles (genus *Microtus*; 42 species) eat nearly their own weight in seeds, roots, and leaves every 24 hours. Family: *Cricetidae*.

Volga, River A river in the W Soviet Union, the longest river in Europe. Rising in the Valdai Range, it flows mainly E and S to the Caspian Sea. Length: 3690 km (2293 mi).

Volgograd (name until 1925: Tsaritsyn; name from 1925 until 1961: Stalingrad) 48 45N 44 30E A city in the Soviet Union, on the River Volga. It has been rapidly redeveloped since World War II (*see* Stalingrad, Battle of). Population (1987): 988 000.

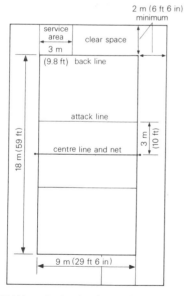

VOLLEYBALL *The height of the ceiling is a minimum of 7 m (23 ft). The top of the net is 2.43 m (8 ft) above the floor for men or 2.24 m (7ft 4 in) for women.*

volleyball A six-a-side court game invented in the USA in 1895, in which an inflated ball is hit with the hands or arms. After the service each team is allowed to

hit the ball three times before it crosses the net. A rally ends when the ball touches the ground or is not returned correctly. A game goes to 15 points and a 2-point lead is required to win.

volt (V) The SI unit of potential, potential difference, or electromotive force equal to the potential difference between two points on a conductor carrying a steady current of one ampere when the power dissipated is one watt. Named after the Italian physicist Alessandro Volta (1745–1827).

Volta, River A river in West Africa. Its headstreams, the Black Volta and White Volta Rivers, join in N central Ghana to form the River Volta, which then flows S to enter the Bight of Benin. Length: 480 km (300 mi).

Voltaire (François-Marie Arouet; 1694–1778) French man of letters, philosopher, scientist, and moralist, whose versatile work epitomizes the age of Enlightenment. He conducted a lifelong campaign against injustice and intolerance. His voluminous writings include the satirical and philosophical fable *Candide* (1759), *Traité de la tolérance* (1763), the *Dictionnaire philosophique* (1764), and histories of Peter the Great and Louis XV.

voltmeter A device for measuring voltage. In the direct-current moving-coil voltmeter the magnetic force on a coil in a magnetic field is used to deflect a needle, the high impedance needed being provided by a high resistance in series with the coil. Cathode-ray oscilloscopes and digital voltmeters are used for both direct and alternating current.

Volturno, River A river in S central Italy, flowing SE and SW to the Tyrrhenian Sea. In 1860 it was the scene of a battle in which Garibaldi defeated the Neapolitans (*see* Risorgimento). Length: 175 km (109 mi).

Voluntary Service Overseas (VSO) A British organization founded in 1958 by Alexander Dickson (1914–) to send skilled volunteers at the request of overseas governments to work as teachers and doctors or on agricultural, industrial, or business schemes. Director: Neil Mackintosh.

Volvox A genus of freshwater single-celled organisms that live in hollow spherical colonies of 500–50 000 individuals, which are linked together by cytoplasm. New colonies are formed asexually or by sexual reproduction. *Volvox* is regarded by some authorities as an alga (it contains the green pigment chlorophyll) and by others as a protozoan of the class *Flagellata*.

von Braun, Wernher (1912–77) US rocket engineer, born in Germany. He was director of the German Rocket Test Centre at Peenemünde during World War II, when the V-2 rocket was built. After the war von Braun worked on US space rockets (*see* rockets).

voodoo Magical and animistic cults of West African origin, practised in the Caribbean and in parts of South America. Trances induced by spirit possession are central to voodoo ritual. Other elements in the nocturnal rites are animal sacrifice, drum beating, dancing, and debased elements of Roman Catholic liturgy.

Voronezh 51 40N 39 13E A city in the central Soviet Union. It is at the centre of an agricultural region. Population (1987): 872 000.

Voroshilovgrad (name until 1935: Lugansk) 48 35N 39 20E A city in the SW Soviet Union. It lies in the coal-producing Donets Basin and has iron, steel, and chemical industries. Population (1987): 509 000.

Vorster, Balthazar Johannes (1915–83) South African statesman; prime minister (1966–78) and briefly president (1978). Vorster was known for his strict enforcement of racial policies. He retired during investigations of financial irregularities.

Vorticella A genus of microscopic aquatic single-celled animals. 0.05–0.15 mm long, they are bell-shaped and attached to the substrate by a long coiled contractile stalk.

VORTICISM *The Vorticists in 1915; Ezra Pound (seated left) and Wyndham Lewis (centre) dominate.*

Vorticism A British art movement inaugurated in 1913 by Wyndham Lewis. It called for an art expressing the advanced technology and pace of modern life. Its journal, *Blast*, included contributions from Ezra Pound and T. S. Eliot. The sculptors Henri Gaudier-Brzeska

(1891–1915) and Epstein were also associated with the movement.

Vosges A range of mountains in NE France. It extends roughly N–S to the W of the River Rhine, rising to 1423 m (4672 ft).

Voyager probes Two US planetary probes launched in 1977. Voyager 1 approached Jupiter in 1979 then flew towards Saturn, which it reached in 1980. Voyager 2 flew past Jupiter in 1979, Saturn in 1981, Uranus in 1986, and reached Neptune in August, 1989.

VSO. *See* Voluntary Service Overseas.

Vulcan The Roman god of fire. He became patron of smiths and metalworkers after his identification with the Greek Hephaestus, whose myths he assumed.

Vulcanite (*or* Ebonite) A hard black insulating material made by heating rubber with sulphur.

vulcanization A process in which sticky natural rubber is made into a harder useful material by heating it with sulphur. Vulcanization involves the formation of sulphur bridges (–S–S–) between the polymer chains. An inert filler is incorporated at the same time.

Vulgate The Latin translation of the Bible made by St Jerome in the 4th century AD. It is the oldest surviving translation of the whole Bible. It was adopted by the Council of Trent (1546) as the official version of the Roman Catholic Church.

vulture A large carrion-eating bird belonging to the order *Falconiformes*. 60–100 cm long with a wingspan of up to 270 cm, vultures have a fleshy naked head. New World vultures (family *Cathartidae*; 6 species) have a slender hooked bill, large feet, and are voiceless. *See also* condor. Old World vultures (subfamily *Aegypiinae*; 20 species) are widely distributed in open temperate and tropical regions except Australia. They have a feathered ruff at the base of the neck. Family: *Accipitridae* (hawks and eagles). *See also* griffon vulture; lammergeier.

W

Waddington, David (Charles) (1929–) British Conservative politician; home secretary (1989–). He was government chief whip (1987–89).

Wade-Giles system. *See* Chinese.

wadi A normally dry valley in a desert area. It will occasionally contain water following the infrequent violent downpours of rain that occur in these areas.

Wagner, (Wilhelm) Richard (1813–83) German composer. His early operas *Rienzi* (1842) and *The Flying Dutchman* (1843) led to his appointment as conductor at the Dresden opera house. In 1845 his opera *Tannhäuser* was successfully performed there but in 1848, after the failure of the May uprising, Wagner fled to Zürich, where he began the operatic cycle *Der Ring des Nibelungen*, an epic treatment of German mythology. Wagner developed the use of leitmotifs in order to achieve an integration of music and drama in opera. During the composition of the *Ring*, he fell in love with Mathilde Wesendonck (1828–1902), who inspired the opera *Tristan und Isolde*. Wagner later eloped with Cosima von Bülow (1837–1930), Liszt's daughter, whom he married in 1870. In 1868 he produced his comic opera *Die Meis-*

RICHARD WAGNER *Photographed in 1865.*

tersinger von Nürnberg and continued work on the *Ring*, raising money to build a theatre in Bayreuth for the first performance of the cycle (1876). His last opera, *Parsifal*, was produced in Bayreuth in 1882.

Wagram, Battle of (5–6 July, 1809) The battle in which Napoleon finally defeated the Austrians. Fought NE of Vienna, Wagram witnessed the largest recorded concentration of field artillery.

wagtail A fine-billed songbird noted for its constantly bobbing tail. The pied wagtail (*Motacilla alba*) is black, grey, and white, about 18 cm long, and commonly occurs near houses. The larger grey wagtail (*M. cinerea*) lives near streams, catching flying insects. The yellow wagtail (*M. flava*) visits Britain in the summer. Family: *Motacillidae* (wagtails and pipits).

Waikato River The longest river in New Zealand, in North Island. Rising in Mount Ruapehu, it flows NW to the Tasman Sea. Length: 350 km (220 mi).

Waitangi, Treaty of (1840) A treaty between the British Government and 46 Maori chiefs in New Zealand, which gave the Maori full rights and confirmed their possession of their lands. Its infringement by settlers led to the Maori Wars.

Wakamatsu. *See* Kitakyushu.

Wakashan languages A group of North American Indian languages of the NW Pacific coast, including Nootka and Kwakiutl.

Wakefield 53 42N 1 29W A city in N England, the administrative centre of West Yorkshire on the River Calder. A battle was fought here in 1460 during the Wars of the Roses. Population (1988 est): 75 750.

Walachia (*or* Wallachia) A principality in SE Europe. Founded in 1290, it was a Hungarian fief until 1330. In the late 14th century it came under Turkish domination. In 1859 Walachia united with Moldavia to form Romania, independent from 1878.

Walcheren An island in the SW Netherlands, in the Scheldt estuary. Protected from the sea by dykes, it produces sugar beet and vegetables. Area: 212 sq km (82 sq mi). Chief towns: Flushing and Middelburg.

Waldheim, Kurt (1918–) Austrian diplomat; secretary general of the UN (1972–81), president of Austria (1986–). He became president despite controversy over his war record as a Nazi army officer.

Wales (Welsh name: Cymru) A principality in the W of Great Britain, comprising a political division of the United Kingdom. It is bordered by England to the E, the Irish Sea to the N, St George's Channel to the W, and the Bristol Channel to the S. Much of the country is covered by hills and mountains. The Isle of Anglesey lies off the NW coast. The country has been divided into eight counties since April, 1974. Most of the population lives in the valleys and coastal plains of the S and along the coastal strip in the N. *Economy*: the valleys and coastal plain in the S are highly industrialized, based originally on the coal found there. Wales also accounts for about half the UK's production of steel sheet and almost all its production of tinplate. The Royal Mint is now situated at Llantrisant and, among other activities, vehicle manufacture is carried out. Milford Haven, in the far SW, is used for the importing of oil, which has given rise to oil refining and associated petrochemical industries here and near Swansea. Tourism, forestry, and sheep rearing are also important. *History*: the Celts living in Wales were little affected by the Roman occupation and were christianized in the 3rd century AD. King Offa of Mercia

built a great dyke (8th century) stretching from sea to sea, providing a frontier behind which the Welsh kingdoms were contained. Temporary unity was achieved by Hywel the Good (d. 950) but the country's subsequent disunity enabled Edward I of England to defeat Llywelyn ap Gruffud (d. 1282) and establish English supremacy. Owen Glendower's revolt in the early 14th century was also crushed and English rule was formalized with the Acts of Union (1536–43). Wales adopted Protestantism in the 16th century and has been a centre of Nonconformity since the 18th century. The early 19th century was characterized by rural overpopulation and near famine, and Wales also suffered during the Depression of the 1930s. Welsh nationalism has been a powerful force in recent years, although devolution plans were rejected in a referendum in 1979. Area: 20 767 sq km (8016 sq mi). Population (1986 est): 2 821 000. Capital: Cardiff.

Wałesa, Lech (1943–) Polish trade unionist. An electrician at Gdansk shipyard, he became leader of the independent trade union Solidarity from its establishment (1980). He was awarded the 1983 Nobel Peace Prize for his efforts to ensure workers' rights and played a key role in forming a Solidarity-led government in 1989.

walking (*or* race walking) In athletics, a form of racing in which a particular gait is used; the advancing foot must touch the ground before the other leaves it.

wallaby A herbivorous marsupial belonging to the kangaroo family (*Macropodidae*). Hare wallabies (genus *Lagorchestes*; 3 species) are the smallest, measuring up to 90 cm in length. Rock wallabies (genus *Petrogale*; 6 species) have rough-soled feet for negotiating rocky ground. Scrub wallabies (genus *Protemnodon*; about 11 species) inhabit brush or open forest.

Wallace, Alfred Russel (1823–1913) British naturalist, who formulated a theory of evolution by natural selection independently of Charles Darwin. Wallace spent eight years (1854–62) assembling evidence in the Malay Archipelago, sending his conclusions to Darwin in England. He also proposed an imaginary line (**Wallace's line**) dividing the fauna of Asia and Australia.

Wallace Collection An art museum in Manchester Square, London. The collection, which was given to the nation in 1897, was formed by the 4th Marquess of Hertford and his half-brother Sir Richard Wallace (1818–90). It includes 18th-century French paintings and furniture, armour, and *The Laughing Cavalier* by Hals.

Wallachia. *See* Walachia.

wallcreeper A Eurasian songbird, *Tichodroma muraria*, about 17 cm long and having a grey plumage with broad black wings patched with red. It climbs rock faces clinging with its sharp claws and probing crevices for insects. Family: *Sittidae* (nuthatches).

Wallenberg, Raoul (1912–) Swedish diplomat. Sent to Hungary in 1944 as a special envoy, he helped thousands of Jews to escape the Nazis, issuing them with Swedish passports. While visiting Budapest in 1945 he was arrested by the Soviet authorities and disappeared. Although some supporters believe he is still alive, it is probable that he was shot in Moscow's Lubianka prison in 1947.

Waller, (Thomas) Fats (1904–1943) US Black jazz musician and songwriter. An exceptional pianist, his own compositions, included "Honeysuckle Rose" and "Ain't Misbehavin'".

wallflower An annual or perennial herb of the genera *Cheiranthus* (about 10 species), native to Eurasia and North America, or *Erysimum* (about 80 species), native to Eurasia. Wallflowers have orange, yellow, red, or brown flowers. Many varieties of *C. cheiri* are cultivated as garden ornamentals. The Siberian wallflower (*E. × marshallii*) has brilliant orange or yellow flowers. Family: *Cruciferae*.

Wallis, Sir Barnes (Neville) (1887–1979) British aeronautical engineer. He designed the airship R100 and geodetic constructions, which he used in his Wellington bomber. He also invented the swing-wing aircraft but is best known for his invention in 1943 of the bouncing bomb.

Wallis and Futuna A French overseas territory in the SW Pacific Ocean comprising two small groups of islands. The chief of the **Wallis Islands** is Uvéa, while the **Futuna Islands** (*or* Îles de Horne) consist of Futuna and Alofi. Copra and timber are produced. Area: 275 sq km (106 sq mi). Population (1984 est): 13 000. Capital: Matautu, on Uvéa.

Walloons The French-speaking inhabitants of Belgium, living mainly in the S and E of the country. They are descended from the northernmost group of Franks who adopted the Romance speech. *Compare* Flemings.

Wall Street The centre of the financial district in New York City, in which the New York Stock Exchange is situated. Wall Street, often known as the Street, is synonymous with the stock exchange.

walnut A tree of the genus *Juglans* (about 17 species), especially the Eurasian species *J. regia*, which produces the best quality nuts. Up to 30 m tall, it has grey deeply furrowed bark. The plum-sized green fruits each contain an edible kernel enclosed in a wrinkled pale-brown shell. The whole fruits may be eaten pickled. The timber of this species and of the American black walnut (*J. nigra*) is valued for furniture. Family: *Juglandaceae*.

Walpole, Sir Hugh (Seymour) (1884–1941) British novelist. Born in New Zealand, he wrote *The Dark Forest* (1916), set in Russia, *The Cathedral* (1922), and a four-volume family saga, *The Herries Chronicle* (1930–33).

Walpole, Sir Robert, 1st Earl of Orford (1676–1745) British statesman, regarded as the first prime minister (1721–42). He became a Whig MP in 1700 and was secretary for war (1708–10) and treasurer of the navy (1710–11). In 1712 he was impeached for corruption but came back into the government in 1715 as first lord of the treasury and chancellor of the exchequer. Again losing office in 1717, he became paymaster general in 1770, and after his effective handling of the South Sea Bubble again became (1721) first lord of the treasury and chancellor of the exchequer. His power was supreme after he had secured the dismissal of John Carteret (1690–1763) in 1724 and the resignation of Charles Townshend (1674–1738) in 1730. Conflict with Spain led to the War of Jenkins' Ear and Walpole was forced to resign. His fourth son **Horace Walpole, 4th Earl of Orford** (1717–97) was a writer. Strawberry Hill, his villa at Twickenham, became a showpiece of the gothic architectural revival. He wrote the popular gothic novel, *The Castle of Otranto* (1765) and numerous letters.

walrus A large seal, *Odobenus rosmarus*, of coastal Arctic waters. Males are up to 3.7 m long and weigh about 1400 kg. Walruses have tusks–elongated upper canine teeth up to 1 m long–used in digging for molluscs and for fighting and display. Family: *Odobenidae*.

Walsall 52 35N 1 58W An industrial town in central England, in the West Midlands. Population (1981): 178 900.

Walter, Bruno (B. W. Schlesinger; 1876–1962) German conductor. He conducted the first performance of Mahler's *Das Lied von der Erde* in 1911.

Walton, Ernest Thomas Sinton (1903–) Irish physicist, who shared the 1951 Nobel Prize with Sir John Cockcroft for their invention in 1929 of the first particle accelerator.

Walton, Izaak (1593–1683) English writer. His best-known work is *The Compleat Angler* (1653), an entertaining treatise on fishing. He also wrote biographies of John Donne (1640), George Herbert (1670), and other churchmen.

HORACE WALPOLE   *Strawberry Hill, his gothic villa.*

Walton, Sir William (Turner) (1902–83) British composer. He first became well known through *Façade* (1922), a setting of poems by Edith Sitwell. Later works include two symphonies (1932–35, 1960), the opera *Troilus and Cressida* (1954), concertos for viola (1929), violin (1939), and cello (1957), the oratorio *Belshazzar's Feast* (1931), and music for Laurence Olivier's films of Shakespeare's *Hamlet*, *Henry V*, and *Richard III*.

wandering Jew. *See* Tradescantia.

Wankel engine A four-stroke rotary internal-combustion engine. It consists of a triangular-shaped rotating piston, with outward curved sides and rounded corners. This rotates in an oval-shaped chamber, slightly narrowed in the middle, which has inlet and exhaust ports and a sparking plug. The small number of moving parts and the lack of vibration are the chief advantages of this engine, but gas leakage has been the principal problem. It was invented by the German engineer Felix Wankel (1902–88).

wapentake Any of the medieval administrative subdivisions into which the parts of England settled by the Danes (*see* Danelaw) were divided. They corresponded to the hundreds found in the rest of England.

waratah A much-branched Australian shrub, *Telopea speciosissima*: the floral emblem of New South Wales. Up to 2 m tall, it has crimson or scarlet flowers. The fruit is a leathery capsule containing winged seeds. Family: *Proteaceae*.

Warbeck, Perkin (c. 1474–99) Flemish-born impostor, the focus of a Yorkist plot against Henry VII of England. Pretending to be the Duke of York (presumed murdered in 1483) he landed in Cornwall in 1497 but he and his 6000 followers fled in the face of Henry's troops. Captured at Beaulieu, he was hanged.

warble fly A parasitic fly belonging to the family *Oestridae*, widespread in Europe and North America. *Hypoderma boris* and *H. lineatum* attack cattle: eggs are laid on the legs and the larvae burrow into the tissue. When mature the larvae leave the host and pupate in the ground.

warbler A small songbird belonging to a family (*Sylviidae*; 400 species) widely distributed in Old World regions. 9–25 cm in length, warblers have slender bills, soft thick plumage, and feed on insects and berries. They are usually drab brown or olive in colour. *See* blackcap; chiffchaff; reed warbler; whitethroat.

Ward, Sir Joseph George (1856–1930) New Zealand statesman; Liberal (1906–12) and United Party (1928–30) prime minister. He advocated greater unity within the British Empire in foreign affairs and led the Liberals in the coalition government (1915–19) under W. F. Massey, before becoming leader of the United Party.

WANKEL ENGINE *The rotary piston draws the fuel mixture through the inlet port into chamber A. At the same time the gas drawn into chamber B in the previous third of a cycle is compressed and ignited to drive the piston round. Meanwhile, the gas in chamber C is discharged through the outlet port.*

Wardrobe A royal administrative department in medieval England. Originally the room in which the king kept his clothes and jewels, it became a government department in the late 12th century. Closely controlled by the king, it was used by Henry III to counterbalance the Exchequer. It declined in importance during the 14th century.

Warhol, Andy (Andrew Warhola; 1926–87) US pop artist and film producer. He achieved notoriety in the early 1960s with paintings of soup cans and portraits of film stars made with the silk-screen printing technique. His controversial films include *The Chelsea Girls* (1966).

War of 1812 (1812–14) The war declared on Britain by the USA in response to Britain's impressment of sailors from US ships and its blockade on US shipping during the Napoleonic Wars. The USA was also incensed by British assistance to Indians harassing NW settlements. The war was inconclusive but helped forge US unity.

ANDY WARHOL *With one of his architectural sketches.*

War of Independence, American. *See* American Revolution.

Warrington 53 24N 2 37W A town in NW England, in Cheshire. It was designated a new town in 1968. Population (1989 est): 188 000.

Warrumbungle Range A mountain range of Australia. It lies in N New South Wales and contains the Breadknife, a rock 90 m (300 ft) high but only 1.5 m (5 ft) wide.

Warsaw (Polish name: Warszawa) 52 15N 21 00W The capital of Poland, on the River Vistula. It became the capital in 1611. It was occupied by Russia in 1794 and later by France and Prussia. After German occupation in World War I, it became the capital again when independence was achieved (1918). During the German occupation of the city in World War II, a ghetto was established (1940) for 400 000 Jews and in February, 1943, the survivors (about 100 000) staged an uprising, after which they were put to death. After the war much of the old town was faithfully reconstructed. It is now an important industrial and communications centre. Population (1985): 1 649 000.

Warsaw Pact (*or* Warsaw Treaty Organization) A military treaty signed in 1955 by the Soviet Union, Albania (until 1968), Bulgaria, Czechoslovakia, East Germany, Hungary, Poland, and Romania. It was formed as a communist counterpart to NATO.

Wars of Religion (1562–98) French civil wars arising out of the struggle of the Huguenots (French Protestants) for religious liberty and the rivalry between Protestants and Roman Catholic nobles. The wars ended in the victory of the Huguenot leader Henry of Navarre, who issued the Edict of Nantes in 1598, giving the Huguenots religious freedom.

wart (*or* verruca) A small leathery growth on the skin, caused by viruses. Warts are commonest in children and usually appear on the hands and on the soles of the feet. They appear suddenly and may disappear without treatment. Persistent warts can be treated by cauterization, freezing, or with drugs (such as podophylline).

warthog A wild pig, *Phocochoerus aethiopicus*, of tropical African woodland. Short-legged, with a large head, bulging eyes, and long curved tusks, warthogs grow to about 75 cm high. They are grey-brown with sparse body hair and feed during the day on roots, grass, etc.

Warwick 52 17N 1 34W A town in central England, the administrative centre of Warwickshire on the River Avon. It is a historic town with a 14th-century castle. Population (1981): 21 936.

Warwick, Richard Neville, Earl of (1428–71) English statesman, known as the Kingmaker. A supporter of the Yorkists in the Wars of the Roses, he was responsible for the seizure of the Crown in 1461 by Edward, Duke of York (Edward IV). In 1470, he changed sides and briefly restored Henry VI to the throne. After the Lancastrians were routed (1471), he was killed, at Barnet.

Warwickshire A county in the Midlands of England. It consists mainly of undulating countryside, drained to the SW by the River Avon. It is predominantly agricultural. Area: 1981 sq km (765 sq mi). Population (1987 est): 484 200. Administrative centre: Warwick.

Wash, the A shallow inlet of the North Sea, in E England between Lincolnshire and Norfolk. Length: about 30 km (19 mi). Width: 24 km (15 mi).

Washington One of the Pacific states in NW USA. Mountains ring the state, including Mount St Helens, and the Columbia Basin covers much of the central area. The state's major manufacturing industry is the construction of aircraft. Attempts to diversify the economy have led to a growing tourist industry and significant mineral extraction, especially of gold, silver, and uranium. *History*: the British Hudson Bay Company dominated the area until the 1840s. In 1846 the boundary between Washington and Canada was agreed and the state (1889) was named after George Washington. Area: 176 616 sq km (68 192 sq mi). Population (1985 est): 4 409 000. Capital: Olympia.

Washington, DC 38 55N 77 00W The capital of the USA, in the E on the Potomac River. Coextensive with the District of Columbia, it is the centre of the government of the USA. Its many notable landmarks include the Washington Monument, the Lincoln Memorial, the Capitol, the White House, the Pentagon, the Library of Congress, the Smithsonian Institution, and the Vietnam Veterans Memorial. *History*: its location was chosen by George Washington and approved by Congress in 1790. Planned by the French engineer, Pierre L'Enfant (1754–1825), its first constructions date from 1793. Population (1986 est): 626 000.

Washington, George (1732–99) US statesman and general; the first president of the USA (1789–97). Washington gained a high military reputation in the French and Indian War before becoming a leading opponent of British rule. On the outbreak of the American Revolution (1775–83) he was appointed commander in chief of the American forces. After winning the final victory at Yorktown (1781), Washington presided over the Constitutional Convention (1787) and was unanimously elected president.

wasp A stinging insect, 6–40 mm long, belonging to the order *Hymenoptera*. The common European wasps (genus *Vespula*) are typical social wasps, forming colonies that consist of a queen, males, and workers. The adults feed on nectar, ripe fruit, insects, etc. New colonies are established by young fertilized queens—the only

individuals to survive the winter. Certain parasitic wasps lay their eggs in the nests of other wasps. Solitary wasps (family *Sphecidae*) lay their eggs in individual nests. *See also* gall wasp; hornet; potter wasp.

Wasserman, August von (1866–1925) German bacteriologist, who invented the Wasserman test for detecting syphilis. Wasserman also developed a test for tuberculosis and an antitoxin against diphtheria.

watch A timepiece small enough to be worn by a person. Watches first came into use in the 16th century with the invention by Peter Henlein (1480–1542) of the mainspring. Based on a verge escapement, watches were then bulky devices worn on the girdle. The invention of the balance spring (claimed by both Hooke and Huygens) in 1675 converted the watch into a more functional article that could be concealed in the pocket. By the 18th century pocket watches had attained a high degree of accuracy. At the beginning of the 20th century wrist watches were introduced. Between the wars wrist watches became smaller and cheaper or boasted such features as rust and shock resistance, luminous dials, or self-winding mechanisms. In the early 1950s the first electromagnetic watches were developed (powered by tiny batteries), but it was not until the late 1960s that the first electronic watch appeared. In the 1970s quartz watches were developed without moving parts: this is the solid-state digital watch in which the dial and hands are replaced by a digital display. This can be made so small that some digital wrist watches incorporate several additional functions as well as a tiny calculator.

water (H_2O) A colourless odourless tasteless liquid consisting of eight parts of oxygen to two parts of hydrogen by weight. Water covers 72% of the earth's surface and is found in all living matter, in minerals, and as a small but important constituent of the atmosphere. The solid form of water (ice) is less dense (916.8 kg/m^3) than the liquid at 0°C (999.84 kg/m^3), which is why ice floats and frozen water pipes burst. The maximum density (999.97 kg/m^3) occurs at 3.98°C, unlike most liquids in which the maximum density occurs at the melting point. The molecules of water are polar, i.e. they have a positive electric charge at one end and a negative at the other. This makes it an excellent solvent.

water beetle A beetle of the family *Dytiscidae*—the so-called true water beetles. The name is also used loosely for any aquatic beetle, including the whirligig beetles (family *Cyrinidae*); the water scavenging beetles (family *Hydrophilidae*); and the crawling water beetles (family *Haliplidae*).

water boatman A water bug belonging to the cosmopolitan family *Corixidae* (over 300 species). It has a flattened boat-shaped body with fringed oarlike hind legs and feeds on plant debris and algae, scooped up by the spoon-shaped front legs.

waterbuck A large African antelope, *Kobus ellipsiprymnus*. About 130 cm high at the shoulder, waterbucks have a long wiry brown coat with a white rump patch and long spreading horns.

water buffalo A large buffalo, *Bubalus bubalis*, also called Asiatic buffalo or carabao, found wild in swampy land of SE Asia and widely domesticated throughout Asia. Up to 180 cm at the shoulder and heavily built, water buffaloes are grey-black with long backward-curving horns. Domestic breeds are used for milk and as draught animals.

verge escapement

balance wheel and lever escapement

quartz-crystal watch *A crystal of quartz (Q) uses the piezoelectric effect accurately to control the frequency of an oscillating electronic circuit consisting of a capacitor (C) and inductance (L).*

digital watch

WATCH   *Early watches used the verge escapement of clocks. The balance wheel and lever escapement dominated watch design until the quartz crystal and digital watch emerged in the 20th century.*

water bug An insect of the suborder *Heteroptera* (*see* Hemiptera) that lives in or on fresh or brackish water. True water bugs include the backswimmer and water boatman. The surface water bugs include the pond skater (*Gerridae*), water cricket (*Vellidae*), and water measurer (*Hydrometridae*).

water chestnut An annual aquatic plant of the genus *Trapa*, especially the Eurasian species *T. natans*, which has floating leaves, feathery submerged leaves, and small white flowers. The hard spiny dark-grey fruit, up to 5 cm across, contains edible seeds. Family: *Trapaceae*. The Chinese water chestnut is the edible tuber of an E Asian sedge, *Eleocharis tuberosa*. Family: *Cyperaceae*.

watercress Either of two perennial herbs, *Nasturtium officinale* or *N. microphyllum* × *officinale*, native to Eurasia and widely cultivated for the peppery young shoots, which are used in salads. Watercress grows submerged or floating in streams or on mud. Family: *Cruciferae*.

water flea A small freshwater crustacean of the suborder *Cladocera* (about 430 species). Its compact body, usually 1–3 mm long, is covered, behind the head, by a laterally flattened transparent carapace, which encloses 4–6 pairs of appendages. Common genera: *Daphnia*, *Leptodora*; subclass: *Branchiopoda*.

Waterford (Irish name: Port Lairge)   52 15N 7 06W A city and port in the SE Republic of Ireland, the county

town of Co Waterford. It has Protestant and Roman Catholic cathedrals and is famous for its glass making. Population (1986): 39 516.

Waterford (Irish name: Contae Port Lairge)   A county in the S Republic of Ireland. Chiefly hilly, it is drained by the Rivers Blackwater and Suir. The traditional glass-making industry is of note. Area: 1838 sq km (710 sq mi). Population (1986): 91 098. County town: Waterford.

water gas A mixture of equal amounts of hydrogen and carbon monoxide made by passing steam over red hot coke: $H_2O + C \rightleftharpoons H_2 + CO$. The mixture is a useful fuel gas. Water gas can be made in conjunction with an exothermic reaction–that between air and carbon: $O_2 + 4N_2 + 2C \rightleftharpoons 2CO + 4N_2$. The mixture of carbon monoxide and nitrogen is called **producer gas**. It has a lower calorific value than water gas. The heating value of water gas can be improved by passing it through petroleum while hot (carburetting)

Watergate A building complex in Washington, DC, that gave its name to a political scandal leading to the resignation of the Republican president, Richard Nixon. The *Washington Post* exposed the involvement of presidential officials during the 1972 presidential election in a burglary of the headquarters of the Democratic Party at the Watergate, and in subsequent arrangements (the "coverup") to buy off the convicted burglars. Following the prosecution of top White House staff, Nixon resigned under the threat of impeachment (1974).

water glass (*or* sodium silicate) A mixture of silicates with the general chemical formula xNa$_2$O.ySiO$_2$, forming a clear viscous solution in water. It is made by fusing sodium carbonate and sand (silica) in an electric furnace and is used in making silica gel, detergents, and textiles.

Waterhouse, Alfred (1830–1905) British architect of the gothic revival. His early work was done in Manchester and included the Assize Court (1859; demolished 1959) and the Town Hall (1868). In London he built the romanesque Natural History Museum (1881) and the now demolished gothic redbrick St Paul's School (1885) and City and Guilds College (1879).

water lily An annual or perennial freshwater plant of the family *Nymphaeaceae* (75 species), native to temperate and tropical regions. Water lilies have round waxcoated leaves floating on the water surface and borne on long central stalks arising from creeping stems buried in the mud below. The large showy flowers are cup-shaped, usually white, yellow, pink, red, blue, or purple in colour. *See also* lotus.

Waterloo, Battle of (18 June, 1815) The battle in which Napoleon Bonaparte was finally defeated by British, Dutch, Belgian, and German forces commanded by Wellington and the Prussians under von Blücher. Napoleon caught Wellington 5 km (3 mi) S of the village of Waterloo (Belgium) in isolation from the Prussians and attempted to smash his army by a direct offensive. However, British lines held until the Prussians arrived, when a concerted charge brought victory.

watermark A distinctive mark produced in paper during manufacture by making it slightly thinner in some places than in others. In handmade paper, the watermark is formed by the wires in the bottom of the mould. In machine-made paper the mark is put in by a roller.

watermelon The fruit of an annual climbing plant, *Citrullus vulgaris*, native to Africa but widely cultivated. The plant produces large oval fruits, up to 25 cm across, with a shiny dark-green rind and red, yellow, or white flesh, which is juicy and sweet-flavoured. Family: *Cucurbitaceae*. *See also* melon.

water polo A ball game played seven-a-side (with four substitutes), usually in a swimming pool. It originated in England in the 1870s, with players riding floating barrels to resemble horses and hitting the ball with paddles; in the modern game players swim.

water rat A large aquatic rodent belonging to the subfamily *Hydromyinae* (13 species) found in Australia, New Guinea, and the Philippines. The Australian water rat (*Hydromys chrysogaster*) is about 35 cm long and has otter-like fur and a white-tipped tail. Family: *Muridae*. Water voles and muskrats are also known as water rats.

water snake. *See* grass snake.

water spider A European freshwater spider, *Argyroneta aquatica*, that lives under water in a bell-shaped structure constructed from silk and plant material and filled with bubbles of air. It feeds inside on small animals. The male (15 mm long) is–usually–larger than the female (10 mm long).

waterspout A funnel-shaped cloud extending from the base of a cumulonimbus cloud to the surface of the sea. It is a small-scale intense low-pressure system, characterized by intense rotating winds.

WATER POLO *The dimensions of the field of play. The water must be at least 1 m deep.*

water table The upper level of the water that has percolated into the ground and become trapped in permeable rocks. The level varies with topography and rainfall. *See also* artesian well.

WATER TABLE

water vole A large vole, *Arvicola terristris*, of Europe and Asia. 15–20 cm long, they are heavily built with light-brown to black fur. Water voles burrow into river banks and feed on aquatic vegetation.

water wheel. *See* turbine.

Watford 51 40N 0 25W A town in SE England, in Hertfordshire. In addition to some local industry, it is a dormitory town for London. Population (1986): 76 500.

Watling Street The Roman road that traversed Britain from London to Wroxeter, with a branch to the legionary fortress at Chester.

Watson, James Dewey (1928–) US geneticist, who (with Francis Crick) proposed a model for the molecular structure of DNA (1953). Watson later investigated aspects of the genetic code. He received a Nobel Prize (1962) with Crick and Maurice Wilkins.

Watson, John Broadus (1878–1958) US psychologist and founder of the US school of behaviourism. Watson declared that speculations about animal behaviour should be based entirely on observations made under laboratory conditions. In *Psychology from the Standpoint of the Behaviourist* (1919), Watson applied his principles to human behaviour.

Watson-Watt, Sir Robert Alexander (1892–1973) Scottish physicist, who pioneered the development of radar. In 1935 the British Government put him in charge of a research team, which enabled radar to be used by the Allies in World War II ahead of the Axis powers.

watt (W) The SI unit of power equal to one joule per second. In electrical terms it is the energy per second expended by a current of one ampere flowing between points on a conductor between which there is a potential difference of one volt. Named after James Watt.

Watt, James (1736–1819) British engineer, whose development of the steam engine contributed to the industrial revolution. He realized that the Newcomen engine could be made more efficient if the steam was condensed in a separate chamber. Watt's steam engine, completed in 1769, soon replaced the Newcomen engine. By 1800 some 500 stationary Watt engines were in use. He later invented the centrifugal governor. Watt devised the unit "horsepower" and the metric unit of power is named after him.

Watteau, (Jean) Antoine (1684–1721) French rococo painter. Despite his early death from tuberculosis, he achieved fame with his charming *fêtes galantes* (scenes of gallantry) and paintings of comedians, notably *L'Embarquement pour l'île de Cythère* and the portrait of the clown *Gilles* (both Louvre).

wattle Any of various Australian trees and shrubs, especially those of the genus *Acacia*, used for fencing, turnery, etc. The commonest are the black wattle (*A. binervata*), the golden or green wattle (*A. pycnantha*), and the silver wattle (*A. dealbata*), which has globular yellow flower heads and is used by florists under the name of mimosa.

wattmeter An instrument for measuring electrical power. The most common type has two conducting coils connected in series, one fixed and one movable. The magnetic forces between them produce a deflection of the movable coil proportional to the square of the current, which is in turn proportional to the power.

Waugh, Evelyn (Arthur St John) (1903–66) British novelist. With *Decline and Fall* (1928) and other novels, including *Vile Bodies* (1930), *A Handful of Dust* (1934), and *The Loved One* (1948), he established his reputation as a brilliant social satirist. After his conversion to Roman Catholicism in 1930, religious themes played an increasing part in his novels, especially in *Brideshead Revisited* (1945). Later novels include his war trilogy—*Men at Arms* (1952), *Officers and Gentlemen* (1955), and *Unconditional Surrender* (1961). Evelyn's son **Auberon Waugh** (1939–) is a novelist and journalist. Among his novels is *Consider the Lilies* (1968).

wave Any periodic change in a property of a system that is propagated through a medium (or through space). Waves are classified according to the curve produced when their magnitude is plotted against time on a graph. If the wave is shaped like a sine curve, it is known as a sine (*or* sinusoidal) wave. Examples include electromag-

netic waves and sound waves. A wave is characterized by amplitude, the maximum displacement of the wave; wavelength; and frequency. The wave may propagate energy, in which case it is known as a travelling wave, or it may not, when it is known as a standing or stationary wave.

waveguide A hollow conductor for transmitting microwaves over short distances. The waveguide is usually filled with air but occasionally some other dielectric is used.

wavelength The distance between successive peaks (or troughs) of a wave. It is equal to the velocity of the wave divided by its frequency.

EVELYN WAUGH *A photograph of the writer by Cecil Beaton.*

Wavell, Archibald Percival, 1st Earl (1883–1950) British field marshal. After service in World War I he became Allenby's chief of staff in Palestine. In World War II, as commander in chief in the Middle East, he defeated the Italians in N and East Africa. After the failure of his offensive against Rommel in June, 1941, he was transferred to SE Asia, where he was again replaced after failing to halt the Japanese advance. He was viceroy of India from 1943 to 1947.

wave mechanics A branch of quantum theory in which elementary particles are treated as de Broglie waves. Systems of particles are described by a wave equation, known as the Schrödinger equation. The solutions of this equation give the allowed values of the energy of each particle (eigenvalues) and the associated wave functions (eigenfunctions); the wave functions provide a measure of the probability that each particle will appear at different points in space. The theory, first proposed by de Broglie, was developed by Erwin Schrödinger.

wave power The use of the energy of wave motion in the sea to generate electricity. Wave-power generators of various types have been developed, the best known being the "nodding-duck" type, which consists of a string of floats that bob up and down in the waves. The bobbing motion turns a generator. It is estimated that there are between 50 and 100 kilowatts of power per metre in the waves off the coast of Britain, a total of 120 gigawatts over all the suitable sites.

wax A smooth substance of low melting point (40–80°C) obtained from plants (e.g. carnauba wax) or animals (e.g. beeswax, lanolin) or made synthetically. They consist of esters of higher fatty acids than are found in fats, usually with monohydric alcohols. Mineral waxes include paraffin wax, which is obtained from the distillation of petroleum. Waxes are used in making polishes, candles, mouldings, etc., and in modelling.

waxbill A bird of the weaverfinch family having a stout waxy-red conical bill. Most waxbills inhabit open grassy regions of Africa. They are 7.5 to 15 cm long and typically grey or brown with red, yellow, or brown markings and fine barring on the wings. Many waxbills rear the nestlings of the whydahs, which lay their eggs in waxbills' nests.

waxplant An evergreen climbing plant, *Hoya carnosa*, native to China and Australia. It produces clusters of large fragrant waxy white flowers with pink centres and is cultivated as an ornamental. Family: *Asclepiadaceae*.

waxwing A broad-billed fruit-eating songbird, *Bombycilla garrulus*, occurring in N coniferous forests and birch woods, sometimes migrating south in hard winters. It has a soft plumage, liver-coloured above with a reddish crest, a yellow-banded tail, and a black throat and eyestripe. The red tips of the flight feathers resemble sealing wax. Family: *Bombycillidae* (9 species).

Wayland (*or* Weland) In Teutonic mythology, a skilled smith. He was captured and lamed by a Swedish king, Nidudr, who kept him on an island, where he was forced to practise his metalworking for the king. Wayland secretly murdered the king's sons, made ornaments of their skulls, eyes, and teeth, raped the king's daughter, and then revealed all to Nidudr before escaping. In England his forge, "Wayland's Smithy," is associated with an ancient site near White Horse Hill on the Berkshire Downs.

Wayne, John (Marion Michael Morrison; 1907–79) US film actor. Following his success in *Stagecoach* (1939) he played the tough hero of numerous classic westerns including *Red River* (1948), *Rio Bravo* (1959), and *True Grit* (1969).

weak interaction One of the four fundamental interactions between elementary particles (*see* particle physics). The weak interaction is about 10^{10} times weaker than the electromagnetic interaction. It is believed to be generated by the exchange of virtual particles known as intermediate vector bosons.

weasel A small carnivorous mammal, *Mustela nivalis*, of Europe, Asia, N Africa, and New Zealand. Growing to about 25 cm long, it is long-bodied and short-legged, bright red-brown above with white underparts. Weasels feed on rats, mice, and voles. They swim well but do not climb. Family: *Mustelidae*.

weather. *See* meteorology.

weaverbird A small songbird belonging to a mainly tropical Old World family (*Ploceidae*; 132 species). Most species build elaborate domed nests. The communal nest of the sociable weaver (*Philetairus socius*) houses 20–30 pairs of birds. Weavers are seed eaters with stout conical bills and variously coloured plumage. *See also* sparrow; quelea.

weaverfinch A small finchlike seed-eating songbird belonging to a family (*Estrildidae*; 108 species) occurring in tropical regions of Africa, SE Asia, and Australasia. Weaverfinches have large conical bills and are usually brightly coloured. *See* grassfinch; mannikin; waxbill; zebra finch.

weaving The process of interlacing two or more yarns at right angles to produce a fabric. The equipment used

is called a loom, which is first set up with a series of longitudinal threads (warp). In plain weave, alternate warp threads are raised and lowered by means of wires or cords (heddles) to allow the crosswire threads (weft), wound onto a bobbin (shuttle), to pass between them. Different kinds of weave, such as twill and herringbone, are made by altering the pattern of interlacing. Power looms were invented by Edmund Cartwright in 1786.

Webb, Sidney (James), Baron Passfield (1859–1947) British economist and socialist. He helped to organize the Fabian Society in 1884 and was one of the founders of the London School of Economics (1895). He initiated many educational reforms while he was a member of the London County Council (1892–1910) and, after entering parliament in 1922, held important government posts. His wife **Beatrice (Potter) Webb** (1858–1943), collaborated with him on a number of books, including *The History of Trade Unionism* (1894) and *Industrial Democracy* (1897).

weber (Wb) The SI unit of magnetic flux equal to the flux linking a circuit of one turn that produces an electromotive force of one volt when reduced uniformly to zero in one second. Named after Wilhelm Weber (1804–91).

Weber, Carl Maria von (1786–1826) German composer. His most successful opera, *Der Freischütz* (1821), based on a German fairy story, was the first opera in the German Romantic tradition.

Webern, Anton von (1883–1945) Austrian composer. He was killed by an American soldier during the occupation of Vienna. His compositions, which employ the technique of serialism, include a concerto for nine instruments (1934) and a string quartet (1938).

Webster, John (c. 1580–c. 1625) English dramatist. Little is known of his life. His major plays are *The White Devil* (1612) and *The Duchess of Malfi* (c. 1613). The plays are distinguished by their poetic intensity and psychological insight.

Weddell Sea A large inlet of the S Atlantic Ocean in Antarctica, between the Antarctic Peninsula and Coats Land. It is named after the British explorer James Weddell (1787–1834).

Wedgwood, Josiah (1730–95) British potter, industrialist, and writer. Trained under his brother Thomas, he opened his own factory at Burslem, Staffordshire (England). In 1769 he opened a new factory (Etruria), where he also built a village for his workmen, displaying his interest in social welfare. Employing such leading artists as John Flaxman (1755–1826), Wedgwood popularized the neoclassical taste in pottery. His high-quality ceramics, **Wedgwood ware**, perfected creamware and developed basalt and jasperware; they also brought transfer printing to Staffordshire.

weevil A beetle, also called a snout beetle, belonging to the largest family (*Curculionidae*; about 60 000 species) in the animal kingdom. Most weevils are small (less than 6 mm) and their mouthparts are at the tip of a beaklike rostrum, which can sometimes exceed the body length. Many species are serious pests.

Weigela A genus of E Asian flowering shrubs (12 species), including several ornamentals, often called Japanese honeysuckles. Up to 4 m high, they have white to red flowers, about 3.5 cm long. Family: *Caprifoliaceae*.

weight. *See* mass and weight.

weight lifting A sport in which men and women compete to lift weighted barbells. In the most common form of competition contestants make three attempts in each of two styles, the snatch and the clean and jerk.

WEDGWOOD *His copy of the Portland Vase in jasperware (c. 1790).*

Weil, Simone (1909–43) French mystic and philosopher. An active socialist in the 1930s, she served in a nonmilitary capacity in the Spanish Civil War. After a mystical experience she became a convinced Roman Catholic, although she refused baptism. During World War II she worked for the Free French Resistance in London. Her writings on spiritual and social themes, published posthumously, include *Waiting for God* (1951) and *The Need for Roots* (1952).

Weill, Kurt (1900–50) German composer. His collaboration with Bertolt Brecht began with the opera *The Rise and Fall of the City of Mahagonny* (1927), a satirical portrayal of American life. Their most famous work was *The Threepenny Opera* (1928), a modernistic version of *The Beggar's Opera* (*see* Gay, John).

Weimar 50 59N 11 15E A city in SW East Germany, on the River Ilm. It was the capital of the grand duchy of Saxe-Weimar-Eisenach (1815–1918). In 1919 the German National Assembly met in the city and drew up the constitution of the new Weimar Republic. Population (1983 est): 63 900.

Weimaraner (*or* Weimeraner) A breed of dog developed in Weimar, Germany, for hunting and retrieving game. It is a lithe dog with drooping ears and a short slender tail. The short sleek coat is silver-grey or mouse-grey. Height: 61–69 cm (dogs); 56–64 cm (bitches).

Weimar Republic The government of Germany from 1919 to 1933. Named after the town in which the new German constitution was formulated, the Republic faced constant crises and was finally overthrown by Hitler.

Weismann, August Friedrich Leopold (1834–1914) German biologist, who (in 1883) proposed that heredity was based upon the transfer, from generation to generation, of a substance—germ plasm—with a definite molecular constitution. Weismann is now regarded as one of the founders of modern genetics.

Weizmann, Chaim (Azriel) (1874–1952) Israeli statesman; the first president of Israel (1949–52). A leader of the English Zionist movement, his discovery (1916) of a manufacturing process for the production of acetone, which contributed to the British war effort, fa-

cilitated the negotiations that led to the Balfour Declaration (1917). His moderate policies as president (1920–31, 1935–46) of the World Zionist Movement played an important part in the establishment of Israel in 1948.

Welland Ship Canal A canal in S central Canada, in S Ontario bypassing Niagara Falls. Part of the St Lawrence Seaway, it links Lake Erie to Lake Ontario. Length: 45 km (28 mi).

Welles, (George) Orson (1915–85) US film actor and director. After establishing his reputation as a theatre and radio producer he went to Hollywood in 1940. His first film, *Citizen Kane* (1941), became one of the most famous of all time. His other films include *The Magnificent Ambersons* (1942), *Macbeth* (1948), *The Trial* (1962), and *Chimes at Midnight* (1966). As a film actor he is best remembered for *The Third Man* (1949).

Wellington 41 17S 174 47E The capital of New Zealand, a port in S North Island. It became the seat of central government in 1865 and is now the commercial and communications centre of New Zealand. Population (1983 est): 342 500.

Wellington, Arthur Wellesley, 1st Duke of (1769–1852) British general and statesman, known as the Iron Duke; prime minister (1828–30). Born in Dublin, he went to India in 1799, where he held command against Tipu Sahib (1749–99) and became governor of Mysore. In the Napoleonic Wars he was responsible for victory (1814) in the Peninsular War and commanded at Waterloo (1815), where he and Marshal Blücher (1742–1819) finally defeated Napoleon. He served in Lord Liverpool's Tory government and represented Britain at the Congresses of Aix-la-Chapelle (1818) and Verona (1822). As prime minister he supported Catholic eman-

DUKE OF WELLINGTON *Addressing the House of Lords.*

cipation and persuaded George IV to accept the bill of 1829. Wellington's opposition to parliamentary reform brought about his resignation under pressure. Under Peel he served as foreign secretary (1834–35) and was commander in chief of the British army from 1827 to 1828 and again from 1842 to 1852. His home at Apsley House, Piccadilly (London) is now the Wellington Museum.

Wellingtonia. *See* sequoia.

Wells, Henry (1805–78) US businessman, who with **William Fargo** (1818–81) and others founded Wells, Fargo and Company (1852). An express business, it carried mail to and from the newly developed West. It also controlled banks and later ran a stagecoach service.

Wells, H(erbert) G(eorge) (1866–1946) British novelist. He won literary success with *The Time Machine* (1895) and other science-fiction novels and with a series of comic social novels, including *Kipps* (1905) and *The History of Mr Polly* (1910). A member of the Fabian Society, he engaged in frequent controversy with G. B. Shaw. He wrote distinguished theoretical works, including *The Outline of History* (1920) and *The Shape of Things to Come* (1933).

wels A large nocturnal predatory catfish, *Silurus glanis*, also called waller, found in fresh waters of Europe and W Asia. Up to 4.5 m long, it has three pairs of barbels, a long anal fin, and is usually mottled olive-green to blue-black with a paler belly.

Welsh Nationalist Party. *See* Plaid Cymru.

Welsh pony One of two breeds of pony originating in Wales. The Welsh Mountain pony, used for riding and draught work, has a compact muscular body with short strong legs and a profuse mane and tail. The larger Welsh riding pony is a popular children's mount. Both may be any solid colour. Height: Mountain pony: up to 1.22 m (12 hands); riding pony: up to 1.37 m (13½ hands).

Welsh poppy A perennial herbaceous plant, *Mecanopsis cambrica*, up to 38 cm tall and found in damp regions of W Europe. It bears solitary yellow flowers, up to 7.5 cm across.

welwitschia An unusual gymnosperm plant, *Welwitschia mirabilis*, confined to the deserts of SW Africa. The very short stem bears two strap-shaped waxy leaves, up to 1 m long. The small conelike flowers produce winged seeds. Individual plants may live for more than a hundred years. Order: *Gnetales*.

Welwyn Garden City 51 48N 0 13W A town in SE England, in Hertfordshire. Founded in 1919 by Sir Ebenezer Howard, it became a new town in 1948. Population (1981): 40 496.

Wenceslas, St (d. 929 AD) Duke of Bohemia (?924–29), famous for his piety. Wenceslas' unpopular submission to the German king Henry the Fowler gave rise to a conspiracy of nobles, who incited Wenceslas' brother to assassinate him. He became Bohemia's patron saint.

wentletrap A gastropod mollusc of the worldwide family *Epitoniidae* (about 200 species). 2–10 cm long, wentletraps have shells with long spires; that of the precious wentletrap (*Epitonium scalare*) is prized by collectors. They can produce a purple substance used as a dye.

werewolf In folklore, a man who becomes a wolf by night and preys on humans. Some werewolves, who have no power over their condition because it is hereditary or the result of a spell or another werewolf's bite, only

WEREWOLF *Reports of werewolves were particularly common in 16th-century France.*

change form during a full moon, a transformation known as lycanthropy. Belief in werewolves is worldwide and of ancient origin.

wergild The sum payable as compensation in Anglo–Saxon England to the family of a slain man by his assassin or the latter's kin. The amount was regulated according to the status and nationality of the victim.

Weser, River A river in N West Germany. It flows NW from Münden to the North Sea. Length: 477 km (296 mi).

Wesker, Arnold (1932–) British dramatist. He wrote a successful trilogy of plays reflecting his socialist beliefs: *Chicken Soup with Barley* (1958), *Roots* (1959), and *I'm Talking about Jerusalem* (1960). Later plays include *Chips with Everything* (1962), *The Merchant* (1978), and *Shoeshine* (1988).

Wesley, John (1703–91) British religious leader, founder of Methodism. As a student, Wesley was one of a group nicknamed "Methodists," who sought to live disciplined religious lives. His younger brother **Charles Wesley** (1707–88) was also a member. The brothers, both ordained, sailed to Georgia as missionaries in 1735, but returned disillusioned in 1738. In the same year both experienced a spiritual awakening while attending meetings of the Moravians as a result of which they toured the country preaching a message of repentance, faith, and love. They did not intend to form a new denomination, the Wesleyan Methodist Church being organized only after their death. John travelled the country on horseback preaching thousands of sermons. Charles was the author of many well-known hymns.

Wessex The kingdom of the West Saxons, under which Anglo-Saxon England was united in the 9th century. Egbert, King of Wessex (802–39), destroyed Mercian ascendancy in 825 and made possible the subsequent union of England under Alfred the Great.

West, Mae (1892–1980) US actress. Her unashamedly sensual performances established her as an international sex symbol during the 1930s. Her films, many of which she wrote, include *She Done Him Wrong* (1933), *I'm No Angel* (1933), and *My Little Chickadee* (1939).

West, Dame Rebecca (Cicely Isabel Fairfield, 1892–1983) British novelist and journalist. She was the author of several novels, including *The Thinking Reed* (1936) and *The Birds Fall Down* (1966). Her political journalism includes *The Meaning of Treason* (1949).

West Atlantic languages A subgroup of the Niger-Congo family, spoken in Guinea and Senegal. It includes the languages Wolof and Fulani.

West Bank A territory in the Middle East, on the W bank of the River Jordan. It comprises the hills of Judaea and Samaria and part of Jerusalem. Formerly part of Palestine, it was left in Arab hands after partition (1948), became part of Jordan following the ceasefire of 1949, and was occupied by Israeli forces in 1967. Israel has since been under pressure to withdraw and allow an autonomous Palestinian state to be set up. In the Camp David agreement (1978) proposals were put forward for future negotiations leading to the setting up of a self-governing authority in the West Bank. In 1988 Jordan relinquished claims to the area and the PLO declared a Palestinian state, unrecognized by Israel. Area: about 6000 sq km (2320 sq mi).

West Bromwich 52 31N 1 59W An industrial town in central England, in the West Midlands. Population (1981): 154 930.

westerlies The chief winds blowing between 30° and 70° latitude. In the N hemisphere winds blow mainly from the SW and in the S hemisphere, from the NW.

Western Australia The largest state of Australia, bordering on the Indian Ocean, Timor Sea, and Great Australian Bight. It is mainly an arid undulating plateau with the Great Sandy Desert, the Gibson Desert, and the Great Victoria Desert in the interior. In the SW is the Darling Range. In the N the broken edge of the plateau is marked by the Kimberleys. Agricultural activities include dairy farming, lumbering, and the cultivation of citrus fruits, wheat, and vines in the extreme SW. Mineral resources include bauxite, nickel, oil, gold, and huge deposits of ferrous minerals. Industry is located chiefly around Perth. Area: 2 527 621 sq km (975 920 sq mi). Population (1986): 1 440 607. Capital: Perth.

Western European Union An organization formed in 1955 by the UK, Belgium, France, Italy, Luxembourg, the Netherlands, and West Germany to coordinate defence policy and to cooperate in political and other spheres. Portugal and Spain joined in 1988.

Western Isles Islands Area An administrative area of NW Scotland consisting of the Outer Hebrides (*see*

Hebrides, the). Area: 2901 sq km (1120 sq mi). Population (1986 est): 31 494. Administrative centre: Stornoway.

Western Sahara (name until 1975: Spanish Sahara) A territory in NW Africa, bordering on the Atlantic Ocean, Mauritania, and Morocco. It consists chiefly of desert. *History*: in 1884 Spain claimed a protectorate over the S coastal zone of Río de Oro and in 1958 Spanish Sahara became a province of Spain with its capital at El Aaiún. In 1976 the province was partitioned between Mauritania and Morocco. Since then the Polisario Front, a guerrilla organization seeking to establish an independent Saharan Arab Democratic Republic, has been supported by Algeria. Morocco occupied the S Western Sahara when Mauritania withdrew in 1979. Area: 266 000 sq km (102 680 sq mi). Population (1986 est): 180 000.

Western (Wailing) Wall. *See* Temple of Jerusalem.

West Germany. *See* Germany.

West Glamorgan A county of South Wales, bordering on the Bristol Channel. It was created in 1974 from W Glamorgan. The uplands of the South Wales coalfield descend in the SW to the Gower Peninsula. Area: 815 sq km (315 sq mi). Population (1986 est): 363 400. Administrative centre: Swansea.

West Indies An archipelago extending for over 2400 km (1500 mi) from Florida to Venezuela enclosing the Caribbean Sea. It is often subdivided into the Greater Antilles, the Lesser Antilles, and the Bahamas. The islands are chiefly of volcanic origin but some are composed of coral. Hurricanes occur frequently. The West Indian people are of mixed origin but the descendants of African slaves form the largest group. The original Arawak and Carib Indians have virtually disappeared. *Economy*: sugar-cane cultivation has been of importance since the beginning of colonization. Many islands also grow tobacco, bananas, spices, or coffee. Mineral deposits include asphalt and bauxite. *History*: Columbus discovered the archipelago in 1492 and named it in the belief that he had found the west route to India. The Spanish, who were the first Europeans to settle, introduced the cultivation of sugar and imported African slaves to work the plantations. The slave trade was maintained until the 19th century. Following the collapse of the Federation of the West Indies (1958–62), the noncolonial status of associated state within the British Commonwealth was adopted by Antigua, Dominica, Grenada, St Kitts-Nevis-Anguilla, and St Lucia in 1967 and St Vincent in 1969. Grenada became independent in 1974, Dominica in 1978, St Lucia and St Vincent in 1979, and St Kitts-Nevis in 1983. Area: over 235 000 sq km (91 000 sq mi).

Westmeath (Irish name: Contae Na Hiarmhidhe) A county in the central Republic of Ireland. Predominantly low lying with areas of bog, much of the land is under pasture. Area: 1764 sq km (681 sq mi). Population (1986): 63 306. County town: Mullingar.

West Midlands A metropolitan county in the West Midlands of England, created in 1974 from SE Staffordshire, NW Warwickshire, and part of NE Worcestershire. Area: 899 sq km (347 sq mi). Population (1986 est): 2 632 300. Administrative centre: Birmingham.

Westminster, City of A borough of central Greater London, on the N bank of the River Thames. It was created in 1965 from the former metropolitan boroughs of

Westminster, Paddington, and St Marylebone. The heart of London's West End, it contains many famous theatres, restaurants, and shops. Included among its historic buildings are Buckingham Palace, the Palace of Westminster, and Westminster Abbey. It also contains St James's Park, Green Park, Hyde Park, and Regent's Park. Population (1986 est): 176 100.

Westminster, Statutes of 1. (1275, 1285, 1290) Legislation initiated by Edward I of England. The first Statute dealt principally with criminal law and procedures for the improvement of royal justice while the second dealt with rights of inheritance. The Statute of 1290 prohibited subinfeudation of land (i.e. the granting of portions of a knight's estate), which had occasioned considerable loss of feudal dues. 2. (1931) The Statute that established the Commonwealth of Nations.

WESTMINSTER ABBEY *The Coronation Chair incorporating the Stone of Scone.*

Westminster Abbey A historic abbey church at Westminster, London. The present building, begun (1245) by Henry III, replaces one dedicated (1065) by Edward the Confessor, whose shrine the abbey still houses. Since William I, every English monarch (except Edward V and Edward VIII) has been crowned in Westminster Abbey and many are buried there in magnificent tombs. The Coronation Chair, first used in 1307, incorporates the Stone of Scone, captured by Edward I from the Scots in 1296. Other notable features include Poets' Corner, where Chaucer, Spenser, Dryden, Tennyson, Dickens, Browning, Kipling, and many others are buried or have memorials.

Westphalia A region of NW Germany, approximating to present-day Nordrhein-Westfalen. By the 12th

century Westphalia comprised many small principalities and in the 18th century came largely under Prussian control. During the period 1807–13 Prussian Westphalian territories became the kingdom of Westphalia. The Congress of Vienna (1815) restored most of Westphalia to Prussia.

Westphalia, Peace of (1648) The agreements, negotiated in Osnabrück and Münster (Westphalia), that ended the Thirty Years' War. The peace marked the end of the supremacy in Europe of the Holy Roman Empire. It recognized the sovereignity of the German states, the Swiss Confederation, and the Netherlands, and granted W Pomerania to Sweden. Lutherans, Calvinists, and Roman Catholics were given equal rights.

West Point 41 23N 73 58W A military reservation in the USA, in New York state. It is the site of the United States Military Academy (1802).

West Sussex A county of S England, formerly part of Sussex, bordering on the English Channel. It is mainly low lying, rising in the S to the South Downs. It is predominantly agricultural. Tourism is important in the coastal resorts. Area: 2016 sq km (779 sq mi). Population (1989): 714 100. Administrative centre: Chichester.

West Virginia A state in the E central USA. It consists of a ridge and valley region (the Great Appalachian Valley) in the E and the Appalachian Plateau. Although predominantly a rural state, manufacturing and mining (especially of coal) are important. *History*: originally part of Virginia, it joined the Union as a separate State in 1863. Area: 62 628 sq km (24 181 sq mi). Population (1985 est): 1 936 000. Capital: Charleston.

West Yorkshire A metropolitan county of NE England, created in 1974 from the W part of the West Riding of Yorkshire. Coalmining and wool textiles are important. Area: 2039 sq km (787 sq mi). Population (1986 est): 2 053 100. Administrative centre: Wakefield.

wet rot The decay that affects timber with a relatively high moisture content, caused by the cellar fungus (*Coniophora cerebella*) and characterized by the formation of a dark surface mass. Treatment is by drying affected timbers. *Compare* dry rot.

Wexford (Irish name: Contae Loch Garman) A county in the SE Republic of Ireland. It was the first Irish county to be colonized from England (1169). Lowlands rise to mountains in the W. Area: 2352 sq km (908 sq mi). Population (1986): 102 456. County town: Wexford.

Weyden, Rogier van der (c. 1400–64) Flemish painter of portraits and religious altarpieces. The influence of the Master of Flémalle is evident in *The Deposition* (Prado). In 1450 he visited Italy and paintings from this period, for example the *Entombment* (Uffizi), show Italian influences.

Weymouth 50 36N 2 28W A town in S England, on the coast of Dorset. It is a resort and port with ferries to the Channel Islands and Cherbourg. Population (1985 est): 57 400, with Melcombe Regis.

whale A large marine mammal belonging to the order *Cetacea*. Whales have no hind limbs; their forelimbs are flippers and their tails are horizontally flattened to form a pair of flukes. They breathe through a blowhole on top of the head. Whales are insulated by a thick layer of blubber under the skin. The whalebone whales (*Mysticetae*; 12 species)—including the rorquals, blue whale, and right whales—are large and slow-moving and feed on krill. Toothed whales (*Odontocetae*; 80 species)—including the dolphins, narwhal, and sperm whale—are smaller and more agile. They feed on fish and squid and are often gregarious. *See also* whaling.

whaling The hunting of whales for their carcasses. Modern whaling fleets comprise a mother factory ship and a fleet of small hunter vessels equipped with harpoon guns and winches. The carcasses are a source of meat, fats, oils, and other chemicals. Whaling has depleted whale populations to the point that some species are in danger of extinction. The International Whaling Commission has called for a complete ban on commercial whaling.

WHALING *The threat of extinction has brought about the industry's decline.*

Whangarei 35 43S 174 20E A city in New Zealand, in North Island. It is the site of New Zealand's only oil refinery (1964). Population (1987): 43 600.

wheat A cereal grass belonging to the genus *Triticum*, native to W Asia but widely cultivated. With the exception of einkorn (*T. monococcum*), most commercial wheats are hybrids with the genus *Aegilops*. The stems, up to 1 m high, each bear a cylindrical head of up to a hundred flower clusters. The grain of bread wheat (*T. aestivum*) is milled to produce flour. Hard or durum wheat (*T. durum*) is used to make pasta and semolina. Surplus grain, bran, etc., is fed to livestock. Wheat is also a commercial source of alcohol, dextrose, gluten, malt, and starch.

wheel animalcule. *See* rotifer.

Wheeler, Sir (Robert Eric) Mortimer (1890–1976) British archaeologist. Wheeler's skill in interpreting archaeological strata was renowned. He excavated Romano-British sites, including Maiden Castle.

wheel of life. *See* Bhavachakra.

whelk A gastropod mollusc of the family *Buccinidae* (over 400 species), of warm and cold seas. 4–12 cm long, whelks feed on molluscs and worms. The common northern whelk (*Buccinum undatum*), 5 cm long, has a drab yellow-brown shell and edible flesh. Tropical species are more colourful.

whidah. *See* whydah.

Whigs Members of a British political group that became the Liberal Party after about 1868. Originally an abusive Scottish name for a horsethief, it was later applied to one who wished to exclude the Roman Catholic Duke of York (later James II) from the succession. The Whigs dominated politics in the first half of the 18th century. Identifying with industrialist, Nonconformist, and reforming interests, they became the Liberal Party under Gladstone.

whimbrel A curlew, *Numenius phaeopus*, that breeds on Arctic tundra and winters in Africa, South America, and S Asia. 40 cm long, it has a streaked brown plumage and a dark crown with a pale central stripe. It feeds on insects, spiders, worms, and snails.

whinchat A migratory chat, *Saxicola rubetra*, common on open farmland. It winters in Africa and breeds in Eurasia, feeding on flies and moths. The male has a streaked brown plumage, pale chestnut breast, white wingbars, and a white eyestripe; the female is duller.

whip In the UK, an official of a political party responsible for ensuring that the party's MPs vote according to its leadership's policies. The term also refers to the summons to vote sent by whips to MPs, a crucial summons being underlined three times (three-line whip).

whipbird A shy songbird belonging to the Australian genus *Psophodes* (2 species). They are about 25 cm long with a dark-green plumage, and feed on insects among scrub and undergrowth. The eastern whipbird (*P. olivaceus*) has a long whistling call ended by a whipcrack sound. Family: *Muscicapidae*.

whippet A breed of dog developed in England during the 19th century from terrier and greyhound stock and used for coursing and racing. It has a slender streamlined build. The fine short coat can be any mixture of colours. Height: 46 cm (dogs); 43 cm (bitches).

whip snake A slender arboreal snake belonging to the genus *Zamenis* (5 species). The common European speckled grey whip snake (*Z. gemonensis*) feeds on other snakes and lizards. The green whip snakes (genus *Dryophis*; 8 species) occur in tropical Asia and Australasia. Family: *Colubridae*.

whirligig A dark shiny water beetle belonging to the widely distributed family *Gyrinidae* (about 700 species). It spins around on the surface of still or slow-moving fresh water, feeding on insects or other small animals. If disturbed, whirligig beetles exude a foul-smelling milky liquid.

whirlwind A small revolving column of air, which whirls around a low-pressure centre produced by local heating and convectional uprising. It may pick up small pieces of debris and dust and in desert areas may cause sandstorms.

whisky A spirit distilled from malted barley or other grain. The word comes from the Gaelic *uisgebeatha*, water of life. The milled grain is mixed with water to form a mash, which must be converted to sugar before fermentation; the resulting alcoholic liquid is distilled and then aged in the cask for at least three years.

Whistler, James (Abbott) McNeill (1834–1903) US painter. He specialized in portraits and landscapes dominated by one or two colours, the best known being *The Artist's Mother* (Louvre) and *Nocturne in Blue and Gold* (Tate Gallery). In 1877 Ruskin described one of Whistler's works as "flinging a pot of paint in the public's face" and was sued for libel (1878). Whistler was also famous as a wit.

Whitbread Book of the Year Award Britain's richest literary award, with £23,000 for the winner. Announced in 1985, it is open to both fiction and non-fiction, but the author must live in the UK. The prize is administered by the Booksellers Association of Great Britain. Winners have been Kazuo Ishiguro (*An Artist of the Floating World*; 1987), Paul Sayer (*The Comforts of Madness*; 1988), and Richard Holmes (*Coleridge, Early Visions*; 1989).

Whitby, Synod of (663 AD) A council convened at Whitby by King Oswy of Northumbria to decide whether to adopt Roman or Celtic Church usages in Britain. The Roman view triumphed and the English Church was brought into line with the Continent.

White, Patrick (1912–) Australian novelist. He explored the national consciousness in his epic novels *The Tree of Man* (1955) and *Voss* (1957). His other works include *A Fringe of Leaves* (1976) and *Netherwood* (1983). He won the Nobel Prize in 1973.

white ant. *See* termite.

whitebait The young of herrings, sprats, and sometimes silversides. They are highly valued as food.

whitebeam A tree, *Sorbus aria*, up to 15 m tall and found mainly in S and central Europe. Swedish whitebeam (*S.* × *intermedia*), a hybrid between whitebeam and mountain ash, is often planted in parks. Family: *Rosaceae*.

white dwarf A very small faint low-mass star (less than 1.44 solar masses) that has undergone gravitational collapse following exhaustion of its nuclear fuel. Electrons are stripped from the constituent atoms, and it is the pressure exerted by these densely packed electrons that eventually halts the star's contraction. The density is then 10^7–10^{11} kg m^{-3}.

whitefish A slender fish, belonging to a genus (*Coregonus*) related to trout, that occurs mainly in deep northern lakes and rivers of Europe, Asia, and North America. It has a small mouth, minute teeth, and a covering of large silvery scales. Whitefish feed on insects and other small animals.

white fly A small winged insect of the mainly tropical family *Aleyrodidae*. 2–3 mm long, it is covered with a mealy white powder and resembles a minute moth. White flies suck plant juices and exude honeydew on which a black mould grows, often damaging crops. Suborder: *Homoptera*; order *Hemiptera*.

Whitehall A street in Westminster, London, where many government offices are located; the name is often applied to the civil service. The Cenotaph is also in Whitehall.

WHITE HOUSE *The colonnaded north portico was added in the 1820s.*

Whitehead, A(lfred) N(orth) (1861–1947) British philosopher and mathematician. Whitehead's first major work, the *Principia Mathematica* (1910–13), was written with Bertrand Russell. In *Principles of Natural Knowledge* (1919) and *The Concept of Nature* (1920), he explored the relationships between concepts and sense perception.

White Horse, Vale of the A valley in S England, in Oxfordshire. Its name derives from the Uffington White Horse, the figure of a horse 110 m (361 ft) long cut in the chalk of the Berkshire Downs.

White House The official residence of the president of the USA. In Washington, DC, the building was burnt (1814) by the British during the War of 1812 but was subsequently restored, being painted white to hide the smoke stains.

Whitelaw, William (Stephen Ian), 1st Viscount (1918–) British Conservative politician; leader of the House of Lords (1983–88). He was leader of the House of Commons (1970–72), secretary of state for Northern Ireland (1972–73), for employment (1973–74), and home secretary (1979–83).

White Russians The Russians who fought against the Soviet Red Army in the civil war (1917–21) that followed the Russian Revolution. The name derives from that of the royalist opponents to the French Revolution, called Whites because they adopted the white flag of the French Bourbon dynasty.

White Sea (Russian name: Beloye More) A gulf of the Arctic Ocean in the NW Soviet Union. It gives access to Archangel and Kandalaksha.

white shark A dangerous man-eating mackerel shark, *Carcharodon carcharias*, that occurs in tropical and temperate seas. Its heavy body, up to 11 m long, is grey-brown to slate-blue with light-grey undersides.

whitethroat An Old World warbler, *Sylvia communis*, that breeds in N Eurasia and winters in central Africa. It is about 14 cm long. The male is russet brown with a greyish head and white throat and performs a tumbling courtship display in flight. The female is a duller brown.

white whale A small Arctic toothed whale, *Delphinapterus leucas*, also called beluga. Young white whales are blue-grey, but change to white as they mature. About 4.5 m long with a rounded head, they feed mainly on fish. Family: *Monodontidae*.

whiting A marine food and game fish belonging to the genus *Gadus* (or *Merlangius*) especially *M. merlangus* found in shallow European waters. It has a slender body, up to 70 cm long, which is olive, sandy, or bluish above and silvery white below, and three dorsal and two anal fins.

Whitlam, (Edward) Gough (1916–) Australian statesman; Labor prime minister (1972–75). He ended conscription, relaxed rules on immigration, and tried to lessen US influence. In 1975, after Malcolm Fraser had blocked government finance bills, Whitlam was dismissed by the governor, Sir John Kerr (1914–).

Whitman, Walt (1819–92) US poet. He expressed his democratic idealism in *Leaves of Grass* (1855), revised and enlarged in nine editions during his lifetime. During the Civil War he nursed wounded soliders. His later works include the prose *Democratic Vistas* (1871).

Whit Sunday (*or* Pentecost) The seventh Sunday after Easter, a Christian festival commemorating the descent of the Holy Spirit on the Apostles on the 50th day after Easter (Acts 2.1). Whit Sunday became a time for baptisms, hence its name ("White" Sunday), referring to the white baptismal robes.

Whittington, Dick (Richard W.; d. 1423) English merchant, who was three times Lord Mayor of London (1397–98, 1406–07, 1419–20). The legend of Whittington and his cat dates from the early 17th century.

Whittle, Sir Frank (1907–) British aeronautical engineer who designed and flew the first British jet aircraft. The engine was fitted into a specially constructed Gloster E28/39; its maiden flight took place on 15 May, 1941.

WHO. *See* World Health Organization.

whooping cough A respiratory infection of children caused by the bacterium *Bordetella pertussis*. After an incubation period of 7–14 days, the child develops a cough, a nasal discharge, and low fever, followed by paroxysms of coughing accompanied by a characteristic whooping sound. A vaccine is available but its use is controversial, since rare cases of brain damage in immunized children have been attributed to it.

whooping crane A rare bird, *Grus americana*, that breeds in NW Canada and winters in SE Texas: 150 cm tall with a wingspan of 210 cm, it has a white plumage with black-tipped wings, black legs, and a bare red face and has a loud whooping call. Family: *Gruidae* (cranes).

whortleberry. *See* bilberry.

whydah (*or* whidah) A small weaverbird belonging to the genus *Vidua* (11 species), also called widowbird and occurring in open grassy regions of Africa. The males have long tail feathers used in the courtship display and the females lay their eggs in the nests of waxbills, which rear their young.

Wichita 37 43N 97 20W A city in the USA, in Kansas. Founded in 1864, it is the state's largest city. Population (1986 est): 288 070.

Wicklow (Irish name: Contae Chill Mhantáin) A county in the E Republic of Ireland. Fertile lowlands rise to the central Wicklow Mountains. Agriculture is the chief occupation. Area: 2025 sq km (782 sq mi). Population (1986): 94 492. County town: Wicklow.

Wien. *See* Vienna.

Wiener, Norbert (1894–1964) US mathematician. A child prodigy, Wiener developed an interest in the mathematics of information and communication, which he called cybernetics. After World War II, during which he worked on anti-aircraft guns, Wiener spent the rest of his life writing about the social problems resulting from automation.

Wiesbaden 50 05N 8 15E A spa city in SW West Germany, on the River Rhine. Its hot saline springs have made it a popular resort since Roman times. Population (1986): 266 700.

Wigan 53 33N 2 38W A town in NW England, in Greater Manchester. It is an industrial and market town in a coalmining area. Population (1981): 79 535.

wigeon A fast-flying duck, *Anas penelope*, that breeds in N Eurasia and winters as far south as Africa and S Asia. 45 cm long, males have a chestnut head with a yellowish crown and grey back, while females are brown with a white belly and white shoulders.

Wight, Isle of (Latin name: Vectis) 50 40N 1 15W An island and county in S England, separated from the mainland by the Solent and Spithead. It consists chiefly of undulating chalk downs with the Needles off the W coast. Tourism is important. The annual Cowes Regatta

Week is famous. Area: 380 sq km (147 sq mi). Population (1989): 132 000. Administrative centre: Newport.

Wightman Cup An annual tennis competition between British and US women's teams, instituted in 1923. The trophy was donated by the US player Hazel Hotchkiss (who later became Mrs George Wightman; 1886–1974).

Wigner, Eugene Paul (1902–) US physicist, born in Hungary, who worked out the theory of neutron absorption by nuclei and discovered that solids change their size under radiation (Wigner effect). He won a share of the 1963 Nobel Prize for his work on nuclear physics.

Wilberforce, William (1759–1833) British philanthropist. As an MP (1780–1825) he led the parliamentary campaign to abolish the slave trade (achieved in 1807) and then to emancipate existing slaves (achieved a month after his death).

wildcat A cat, *Felis sylvestris*, of Europe and W Asia. About 75 cm long, it has a bushy rounded tail and thick striped coat. Wildcats inhabit dense woodland and breed once a year. They may interbreed with domestic cats.

OSCAR WILDE

Wilde, Oscar (Fingal O'Flahertie Wills W.; 1854–1900) British dramatist and poet, born in Dublin. He dazzled London society with his wit and became a leading figure of the Aesthetic movement. His works include *Poems* (1881), a novel *The Picture of Dorian Gray* (1891), and a series of brilliant social comedies: *Lady Windermere's Fan* (1892), *A Woman of No Importance* (1893), *An Ideal Husband* (1895), and *The Importance of Being Earnest* (1895). Socially and financially ruined by a trial in 1895 arising from his homosexual relationship with Lord Alfred Douglas (1870–1945), he was imprisoned for two years. In exile in France he produced his best-known poem, *The Ballad of Reading Gaol* (1898).

wildebeest. *See* gnu.

Wilder, Billy (Samuel W.; 1906–) US film director, born in Austria. His films include *The Lost Weekend* (1945), *Sunset Boulevard* (1950), *Some Like It Hot* (1959), and *Front Page* (1974).

Wilder, Thornton (1897–1975) US novelist and dramatist. His best-known plays are *Our Town* (1938) and *The Skin of Our Teeth* (1942), and his novels include *The Bridge of San Luis Rey* (1927).

Wilhelmina (1880–1962) Queen of the Netherlands (1890–1948), who encouraged Dutch resistance in World War II. She abdicated in favour of her daughter Juliana.

Wilhelmshaven 53 32N 8 07E A seaport in NW West Germany, on the North Sea. It was founded in 1869 as the main Prussian (later German) naval base. Population (1984 est): 98 200.

Wilkes, John (1725–97) British journalist and politician. He was a member of the Hellfire Club of debauchees and founded the weekly *North Briton*, in which he attacked George III's ministers. The famous issue No 45 (1763) accused the government of lying in the king's speech and Wilkes was arrested for libel. Outlawed in 1764 and three times expelled from the House of Commons he was at last permitted to take his seat in 1774.

Wilkins, Maurice Hugh Frederick (1916–) New Zealand physicist, who worked on the atom bomb during World War II. After the war, he assisted James Watson and Francis Crick in determining the structure of DNA. These three scientists shared the 1962 Nobel Prize.

Willemstad 12 12N 68 56W The capital and main port of the Netherlands Antilles, on the SE coast of Curaçao. Population (1983): 50 000.

WILLIAM THE CONQUEROR *Detail from a French 13th-century manuscript.*

William (I) the Conqueror (c. 1028–1087) Duke of Normandy (1035–87) and the first Norman King of England (1066–87). He claimed to have been named by Edward the Confessor as heir to the English throne. When Harold II succeeded Edward, William invaded England, defeated and killed his rival at the battle of Hastings, and became king. His administration relied upon Norman and other foreign personnel, especially his Archbishop of Canterbury, Lanfranc (c. 1010–89). In 1085 William commissioned the Domesday Book.

William (I) the Lion (1143–1214) King of the Scots (1165–1214). After his capture in a revolt against Henry II of England in 1174, he became a vassal of the English throne. On Henry's death in 1189 he regained independence for his kingdom in return for a payment to Richard I.

William (I) the Silent (1533–84) The leader of the Revolt of the Netherlands against Spanish rule. When open revolt broke out in 1568, William soon emerged as its leader and in 1576 succeeded in uniting the Roman Catholic provinces in the south with the Protestant north. This union was short lived, however, and in 1579 the northern provinces declared independence with William as their first stadholder (chief magistrate). He was assassinated by a Spanish agent.

William II Rufus (c. 1056–1100) King of England (1087–1100), succeeding his father William the Conqueror. His harsh rule aroused baronial and ecclesiastical opposition, notably from Anselm. He made several attempts to recover Normandy from his elder brother Robert (d. 1134) and was killed by an arrow while hunting in the New Forest.

William III (1650–1702) King of England (1689–1702) and Stadholder (chief magistrate) of the United Provinces (1672–1702), known as William of Orange. Grandson of Charles I of England and son of William II, Prince of Orange (1626–50), in 1677 he married James II of England's daughter Mary. In 1688 he was invited by the opposition to his father-in-law to invade England and in 1689 was proclaimed joint sovereign with his wife, Mary II (*see* Glorious Revolution). William defeated the former king at the Boyne in 1690. On the Continent he was successful in the War of the Grand Alliance (1689–97) against France.

William IV (1765–1837) King of England and Hanover (1830–37), known as the Sailor King or Silly Billy. He served in the Royal Navy from 1778 to 1790. He had ten illegitimate children by the Irish actress Dorothea Jordan before marrying (1818) Adelaide of Saxe-Meiningen (1792–1849). William was succeeded in England by his niece Victoria and in Hanover by his brother Ernest Augustus (1771–1851).

William and Mary style An English derivative (1689–1702) of the Louis XIV style of furniture. The cabriole leg was a typical innovation replacing the preceding twist turned legs. Rich gilding was common and some important furniture was made of cast silver. Cabinet furniture was finely veneered with marquetry or lacquered and gilded.

William of Ockham. *See* Ockham's Razor.

William of Orange. *See* William III (King of England).

William of Wykeham (1324–1404) English churchman and statesman. Bishop of Winchester from 1366 and Lord Chancellor (1367–71, 1389–91), he founded New College, Oxford (1379), and Winchester College (1382).

Williams, John (1941–) Australian guitarist, living in the UK. A virtuoso of the classical guitar, he also composes and performs music influenced by pop and jazz.

Williams, Tennessee (1911–83) US dramatist. *The Glass Menagerie* (1945), his first major success, introduced his recurrent themes of family tensions and sexual frustration, which were treated with increasing violence in *A Streetcar Named Desire* (1947) and *Cat on a Hot Tin Roof* (1955).

Williamson, Malcolm (1931–) Australian composer, living in the UK since 1953. His works include an organ concerto (1961), the operas *Our Man in Havana* (1963) and *The Violins of St Jacques* (1966), *Mass of Christ the King* (1977), and seven symphonies.

willow A tree or shrub of the genus *Salix* (about 300 species), native to temperate and arctic regions. Male and female catkins are borne on separate trees and open before the leaves. Willows are common in wet places and some are grown as ornamentals, especially the weeping willow (*S. babylonica*), with its slender drooping branches, and the bay willow (*S. pentandra*). Family: *Salicaceae. See also* osier.

willow pattern A chinoiserie pattern attributed to Thomas Minton and introduced about 1780. The elements are a willow tree, pagoda, figures on a river bridge, and two flying birds in an elaborate border.

Wilson, Sir Angus (1913–) British novelist. His satirical novels and collections of short stories include *Hemlock and After* (1952), *Anglo-Saxon Attitudes* (1956), *No Laughing Matter* (1967), *Setting the World on Fire* (1980), and *The Collected Stories of Angus Wilson* (1987).

Wilson, Charles Thomson Rees (1869–1959) British physicist, who won the 1927 Nobel Prize for his invention of the Wilson cloud chamber. He discovered that moisture condensed in the presence of ions and, when X-rays and radioactivity were discovered, applied his discoveries to invent the cloud chamber.

Wilson, (James) Harold, Baron (1916–) British statesman; Labour prime minister (1964–70, 1974–76). He was economic assistant to the war cabinet secretariat (1940–41) and to the mines department (1941–43) and then director of economics and statistics at the ministry of fuel and power (1943–44). After World War II he became an MP (1945) and president of the Board of Trade in 1947. He succeeded Gaitskill as Labour leader in 1963 and achieved electoral victory in 1964. His statutory incomes policy and plans for industrial-relations reform were unpopular and he lost the 1970 election. His second ministry saw the renegotiation of the UK's terms of membership of the EC, which was confirmed by a referendum in 1975. In 1976 Wilson unexpectedly resigned. He was made a life peer in 1983.

Wilson, (Thomas) Woodrow (1856–1924) US statesman; Democratic president (1913–21). In his first term as president he introduced progressive reforms. In World War I, Wilson declared war on Germany (1917) in response to its unrestricted submarine campaign. Wilson's Fourteen Points (1918) proposed a basis on which peace might be settled and contained a plan for a League of Nations that was incorporated into the Treaty of Versailles.

Wiltshire A county of S England. It consists of a rolling chalk plateau, bordered by lowlands in the NW and SE. It is predominantly agricultural. Prehistoric sites include Stonehenge and Avebury. Area: 3481 sq km (1344 sq mi). Population (1989 est): 564 000. Administrative centre: Trowbridge.

Winchester 51 04N 1 19W A city in S England, the administrative centre of Hampshire. As capital of Saxon Wessex, it rivalled London. The cathedral, built in the 11th century on earlier Saxon foundations, contains many royal tombs. Winchester College (1382), founded by William of Wykeham, is England's oldest public school. Population (1985 est): 35 500.

Windermere The largest lake in England, in Cumbria in the Lake District. The lake is extensively used for watersports. Length: 17 km (10.5 mi).

Windhoek 22 34S 17 06E The capital of Namibia. It is the centre of the world's karakul (Persian lamb) skin industry. Population (1983): 105 100.

windmills Machines that enable useful work to be obtained from wind power. The wind turns a set of vanes or sails mounted on a horizontal shaft, the rotation of which is transmitted by gearing to working machinery. Windmills had appeared by 1150 in NE Europe and were used for grinding corn, pumping water, and powering light industry. Two common designs were the Dutch mill, in which only the sails and the conical roof moved to catch the wind, and the German post mill, in which the whole millhouse rotated around a central supporting pole. The modern metal windmill with multiple-bladed sails is found world wide in rural areas. *See* wind power.

wind power The use of wind energy to generate electricity. Because of the world shortage of conventional energy resources, wind-power generators (aerogenerators), like other alternative energy sources, have now become more attractive economically. Some advantages of wind power are that it is free from pollution, uses no fuel, and the times of peak output are likely to coincide with peak demand. There are several different designs of aerogenerator: some with a horizontal axis and blades like the familiar windmill; some with specially shaped aerofoil blades rotating on a vertical axis. About 12 wind turbines in the UK are feeding the national grid, mainly using Atlantic winds on the W coast. By 2005 1% of UK energy may be provided by wind power.

Windsor 51 29N 0 38W A town in SE England, in Berkshire on the River Thames. Windsor Castle, a royal residence, dominates the town. Population (1986): 31 225.

Windsor, House of The name of Britain's royal family from 1917, when it replaced that of House of Saxe-Coburg-Gotha, of which Prince Albert had been a member. In 1960 Elizabeth II declared that those of her descendants in the male line who were not princes or princesses would take the surname Mountbatten-Windsor. See p. 772.

Windsor Castle A royal residence in Windsor, Berkshire. It was begun by William the Conqueror as a stockaded earthwork. Many additions were made by subsequent monarchs, notably the keep by Henry III, St George's Chapel, an example of the Perpendicular style, by Edward IV, and the Albert Memorial Chapel (so called by Queen Victoria) by Henry VII. Many monarchs are buried in these chapels.

Windward Islands (Spanish name: Islas de Barlovento) A West Indian group of islands forming part of the S Lesser Antilles. They comprise the islands of Martinique, St Lucia, St Vincent, the N Grenadines, and Grenada.

wine An alcoholic drink made from fermented grape juice. The grapes are first crushed, traditionally by treading, now generally by machine. This process brings the yeast on the grapeskins, visible as the "bloom," into contact with the sugar in the juice, which it then converts into ethanol (ethyl alcohol). Depending upon when the fermentation is stopped, the resulting wine is dry, medium, or sweet. Table wines contain about 9–13% alcohol. Fortified wines (e.g. port, sherry) contain about 16–23% alcohol. The bubbles in sparkling wines are caused by a secondary fermentation in the bottle (*see also* champagne). Red wines are made from whole grapes; for white wines the grapeskins are removed at an early stage in production. True rosé wines are made from the grenache grape, from which the skins are removed before the juice is deeply stained by them. The variety of grape, the soil of the vineyard, and the local climate govern a wine's quality. The appellation "vintage" is now used to designate a wine of outstanding quality.

Wingate, Orde Charles (1903–44) British soldier, who led the Chindits. A Zionist, he organized Jewish guerrillas in Palestine (1936–39). In World War II, after taking Addis Ababa from the Italians (1941), he formed the Chindits to disrupt communications behind the Japanese lines in Burma. He was killed in an aircrash.

Winnipeg 49 53N 97 10W A city in W Canada, capital of Manitoba. Established as a fur-trading post (1806), it expanded with the growth of farming and the arrival of the railway (1881) from E Canada. Population (1986): 594 551.

Winnipeg, Lake A lake in W Canada, in S Manitoba. Emptying into Hudson Bay, it drains much of the Canadian prairies. Area: 24 514 sq km (9465 sq mi).

wintergreen An evergreen creeping perennial herb or small shrub of the family *Pyrolaceae* (about 35 species), found in N temperate and arctic regions. The flowers are white or pale-pink and the fruit is a capsule. Oil of wintergreen comes from the leaves of the winterberry (*Gaultheria procumbens*), a North American shrub, whereas the common wintergreen (*Pyrola minor*) is a herb of Eurasia and North America.

Winterhalter, Franz Xaver (1806–73) German painter and lithographer, famous for his portraits of European royalty. His sitters included King Louis Philippe and Napoleon III as well as Queen Victoria.

Winter War. *See* Russo-Finnish War.

wireworm. *See* click beetle.

Wirral Peninsula A peninsula in NW England, in Merseyside and Cheshire. Chiefly low-lying, it serves mainly as a residential area for Liverpool.

Wisconsin A state in the N central USA. The Central Lowlands give way in the N to the Superior Upland, which contains many forests and lakes. Manufacturing is the state's major economic activity. *History*: ceded to the USA by the British in 1783, large-scale immigration in the 1820s led to its organization as a territory (1836) and it became a state in 1848. Area: 145 438 sq km (56 154 sq mi). Population (1987 est): 4 794 792. Capital: Madison.

wisent. *See* bison.

Wisteria A genus of twining usually woody vines (10 species), native to E Asia and North America and grown as ornamentals, especially *W. floribunda* from Japan, which may reach a height of 30 m. Family: *Leguminosae*.

witan A body of 30 to 40 high-ranking laymen and ecclesiastics, which advised Anglo-Saxon kings on such major policy matters as foreign policy and taxation. It met only at the king's will and had no fixed procedure.

witchcraft The supposed manipulation of natural events by persons using supernatural means. In Europe the biblical injunction "Thou shalt not suffer a witch to live" sanctioned widespread persecution. Social and religious upheavals in the 16th and 17th centuries brought an upsurge in witch hunts; the famous outbreak at Salem, Massachusetts (1692), is a paradigm case of witch hysteria. Witches were accused of worshipping the devil at nocturnal orgies (sabbaths), of keeping evil spirits (familiars), and of killing livestock, wrecking crops, and causing barrenness, impotence, and fits. Many tradi-

HOUSE OF WINDSOR

Champagne　　Bordeaux　　Burgundy　　Alsatian white

WINE *The major French wine-producing regions and some standard bottle shapes.*

tional African communities hold witchcraft accountable for similarly inexplicable misfortunes.

witch hazel A shrub or small tree of the genus *Hamamelis* (6 species), native to E Asia and North America, especially the American *H. virginiana*, which is the source of witch-hazel lotion used in pharmacy. This and several other species are often grown as ornamentals. Family: *Hamamelidaceae*.

Wittenberg 53 00N 11 41E A town in central East Germany, on the River Elbe. The Reformation began here on 31 October, 1517, when Martin Luther nailed his 95 theses to the door of All Saints Church. Population (1983 est): 54 043.

Wittgenstein, Ludwig (1889–1951) Austrian philosopher. His two major works are the *Tractatus Logicophilosophicus* (1921) and the posthumously published *Philosophical Investigations* (1953). In his earlier work he developed the "picture theory" of language—words represent things by established conventions—but later he considered actual usage to be more important than set convention.

Witwatersrand (*or* the Rand) A ridge of hills in NE South Africa. It extends about 160 km (99 mi) chiefly W of Johannesburg. It has been worked for gold since the 1880s.

woad A branching perennial or biennial herb, *Isatis tinctoria*, native to central and S Europe. Formerly cultivated for the blue dye extracted from its crushed leaves, it is now rare. Up to 120 cm tall, it has tiny yellow flowers. Family: *Cruciferae*.

Wodehouse, Sir P(elham) G(renville) (1881–1975) British-born writer, who became a US citizen in 1955. In his many comic novels featuring Bertie Wooster and his manservant Jeeves, including *The Inimitable Jeeves* (1923) and *The Code of the Woosters* (1938), he portrayed an English upper-class society fixed forever in the 1920s.

Woden. *See* Odin.

wolf A wild dog, *Canis lupus*, of Eurasia and North America. Wolves are 140–190 cm long including the tail (30–55 cm). They live in packs of 5–30 and feed mainly on mice, fish, and carrion but also attack deer. Mating is often for life. Wolves in colder climates are generally larger and shaggier. There is an almost white N Siberian race, while the Indian pale-footed wolf is small and grey. *See also* timber wolf.

Wolf, Hugo (1860–1903) Austrian composer. He died insane. He wrote 300 *Lieder*, the opera *Der Corregidor* (1895), and an *Italian Serenade* for string quartet.

Wolfe, James (1727–59) British soldier. He distinguished himself against the Jacobites in the 1740s and after the outbreak of the Seven Years' War was sent to Canada. He excelled in the capture of Louisberg (1758) and in the following year he besieged the Marquis de Montcalm (1712–59) in Quebec. His forces scaled the undefended Heights of Abraham and a pitched battle ensued in which both commanders were killed. The British victory established their supremacy in Canada.

wolfhound. *See* borzoi; Irish wolfhound.

Wolfit, Sir Donald (1902–68) British actor and manager. He acted all the major Shakespearean roles, receiving especial acclaim for his Lear, first performed in 1943.

wolfram. *See* tungsten.

wolframite The principal ore of tungsten, consisting of ferrous tungstate, $(Fe,Mn)WO_4$. It is brown, black, grey, or reddish in colour and is found particularly in quartz veins associated with granitic rocks.

P. G. WODEHOUSE *Known as "Plum" to his friends.*

Wolfram von Eschenbach (c. 1170–c. 1220) German poet. His great romance, *Parzifal* (c. 1212), is the first German work to use the story of the Holy Grail and is the basis of Wagner's opera.

wolf spider A spider, also called hunting spider, belonging to a widespread family (*Lycosidae*; over 175 species). Wolf spiders, up to 25 mm long, are dark brown with long stout legs and are usually active at night, hunting prey rather than trapping it in webs. The female carries the eggs and young.

Wollongong, Greater 34 25S 150 52E A city in Australia, in New South Wales. It includes the towns of Wollongong, Bulli, and Port Kembla. Population (1985 est): 237 600.

MARY WOLLSTONECRAFT *Detail of a portrait by J. Opie.*

Wollstonecraft, Mary (1759–97) British writer. In 1797 she married the social philosopher William Godwin (1756–1836). Her best-known work is *A Vindication of the Rights of Women* (1792), which argued for equal opportunities for all in education. She died giving birth to her daughter Mary, who married Shelley.

Wolsey, Thomas, Cardinal (c. 1475–1530) English churchman and statesman; Lord Chancellor (1515–29) under Henry VIII. As chancellor he interfered unsuccessfully in the conflict between Francis I of France and Emperor Charles V. Wolsey's attempts to raise taxes to pay for his foreign policy encountered violent opposition. He fell from power after failing to persuade the pope to permit Henry to divorce Catherine of Aragon and died on his way to face trial in London.

Wolverhampton 52 36N 2 08W A town in central England, in the West Midlands. Metalworking and engineering are the principal industries. Population (1984): 254 000.

wolverine A carnivorous mammal, *Gulo gulo*, also called glutton, inhabiting northern evergreen forests of Europe, Asia, and America. It is heavily built, about 1 m long and weighing about 25 kg, and hunts lemmings and hares. Family: *Mustelidae*.

womb (*or* uterus) The part of a woman's reproductive tract in which the fetus develops. The womb is a hollow muscular organ, connected by the vagina to the outside and to the ovaries by the Fallopian tubes. In a nonpregnant woman the lining of the womb is shed at monthly intervals (*see* menstruation). During childbirth the womb, which is greatly enlarged (about 30 cm long), undergoes strong contractions to expel the baby.

wombat A bearlike marsupial belonging to the family *Phascolomidae* (2–3 species), of Australia (including Tasmania). The coarse-haired wombat (*Phascolomis ursinus*) is about 1 m long and has strong claws, which it uses for tunnelling. It feeds on grass, roots, and tree bark.

Women's Institutes, National Federation of A British organization founded in 1915 to develop the quality, chiefly through further education, of rural life for women. Local institutes meet monthly to hear talks on a wide range of subjects.

Women's Royal Voluntary Service A British organization founded in 1938 as the Women's Voluntary Service (WVS). Its members perform many voluntary welfare services, including Meals on Wheels.

wood The hard tissue of the stems and branches of trees and shrubs, beneath the bark, consisting of xylem cells strengthened with deposits of lignin. The central part of the trunk—heartwood—consists of dead xylem. Conifers are referred to as softwoods because the xylem is porous; broad-leaved (angiosperm) trees, which are called hardwoods, contain more fibres and are therefore stronger (*see* timber).

Wood A family of English architects, known for their contribution to town planning and urban classical architecture. They mainly worked in Bath, which **John Wood the Elder** (1704–54) began to develop in the late 1720s. His work was continued by his son **John Wood the Younger** (1728–81), who designed the famous Royal Crescent (1767–75) and the Assembly Rooms (1769–71).

Wood, Sir Henry (Joseph) (1869–1944) British conductor. He is remembered for the London Promenade concerts, which he established at the Queen's Hall, London, and which continued at the Albert Hall after the Queen's Hall was bombed in World War II.

woodbine. *See* honeysuckle; Virginia creeper.

woodchuck. *See* marmot.

woodcock A Eurasian gamebird, *Scolopax rusticola*, occurring in dense damp woodland and generally active at night. It has a stocky body, 34 cm long, and a russet plumage with a dark-barred head and underparts and a white-tipped tail. Woodcocks have long bills and feed on worms and insect larvae. Males perform a slow display flight (called roding) during courtship. Family: *Scolopacidae* (sandpipers, snipe).

woodcut A relief printing technique. The design is drawn on the surface of a block of wood, all the undrawn parts being cut away. The design is then transferred to paper by pressing the inked block onto the paper. The woodcut was used in China (c. 5th century AD) for textile design but its history in Europe dates from the 14th century. Leading 16th-century German artists, such as Dürer and Holbein, used the medium to supreme effect.

wood engraving A technique of printing images, refined in the 18th century by Thomas Bewick. The surface of the woodblock is cut away to leave raised areas which, when treated with ink, will appear dark when printed, in contrast to the white line of the incised areas.

woodlouse A terrestrial crustacean of the suborder *Oniscoidea*, found in damp shady places under stones, logs, etc. Woodlice have a body covering of armour-like plates. A common species is the pill bug or woodlouse (*Armadillidium vulgare*), about 17 mm long, which rolls into a ball when disturbed. Common genera: *Oniscus, Porcellio*; order: *Isopoda*.

woodpecker A bird belonging to a family (*Picidae*; about 220 species) occurring worldwide except Madagascar, Australia, and New Zealand. 9–57 cm long, woodpeckers have multicoloured plumage, often barred or spotted. Most are exclusively arboreal, chiselling through bark with their long straight bills in search of insects.

wood pigeon A large Eurasian pigeon, *Columba palumbus*, which is a serious pest on farmland. 40 cm long, it has a predominantly grey plumage with a black-tipped tail, brownish back and wings, white wing patches, and a green, purple, and white neck patch.

wood sorrel A herbaceous plant of the genus *Oxalis* (about 800 species), of temperate and tropical regions, especially *O. acetosella*, of Europe. This species has solitary white flowers. Some species, including the vegetable oca (*O. tuberosa*), have edible tubers. Family: *Oxalidaceae*.

woodwasp A sawfly belonging to the families *Xiphydriidae* (Europe and North America), *Sytexidae* (North America), or *Orussidae* (worldwide). *Xiphydriidae* larvae bore into deciduous trees. *Sytexidae* are restricted to the incense cedar tree. *Orussidae* larvae are external parasites on wood-dwelling beetle larvae.

woodwind instruments Blown musical instruments in which a column of air is made to vibrate either by blowing across a mouth·hole, as in the flute, or by making a single or a double reed vibrate, as in the oboe, bassoon, clarinet, and saxophone.

woodworm A wood-boring beetle of the genus *Anobium*, especially the furniture beetle (*A. punctatum*), 5 mm long, which damages furniture and old buildings. The larvae bore into wood and emerge when adult. Family: *Anobiidae*.

wool Fibres obtained from the fleeces of domestic sheep. Elastic, resilient, and absorbent, it is also an excellent insulator. Merino wool is the best in quality. Wools from the 26 British breeds vary widely, while New Zealand sheep are crossbreeds of merino and British. The wool of Asian sheep and mountain breeds is used chiefly for carpets. Since World War II synthetic fibres have been mixed with wool.

Woolf, (Adeline) Virginia (*born* Stephen; 1882–1941) British novelist; a central figure of the Bloomsbury group. Her novels include *Mrs Dalloway* (1925), *To the Lighthouse* (1927), and *The Waves* (1931). Her fantasy *Orlando* (1928) caused a considerable impression. She also wrote biographies and criticism, including a series of essays entitled *The Common Reader* (1925–32). She committed suicide by drowning. Her husband **Leonard (Sidney) Woolf** (1880–1969), whom she married in 1912 and with whom she founded the Hogarth Press in 1917, was literary editor of the *Nation* (1923–30) and wrote five volumes of autobiography (1960–69).

Woolley, Sir Leonard (1880–1960) British archaeologist. He worked at Carchemish and Tell el-Amarna but is famous chiefly for his brilliant excavations at Ur (1922–34).

woolly bear. *See* tiger moth.

woolly rhinoceros A rhinoceros belonging to the extinct genus *Coelodonta*, which inhabited Eurasia and North Africa during the Pleistocene epoch (2.5 million to 10 000 years ago). Well-preserved specimens show that it was a large shaggy-coated animal with two horns.

woolsack A large red cushion, stuffed with wool, that is the seat of the Lord Chancellor when acting as speaker of the House of Lords. It is supposed to have been placed there in the middle ages, when the wool trade was important.

VIRGINIA WOOLF *A photograph taken in 1902.*

Woomera 31 11S 136 54E A town in central South Australia. It was the site of the Long Range Weapons Establishment and a launching base for space satellites. Population (1984): 1800.

Worcester 52 11N 2 13W A city in W central England, the administrative centre of Hereford and Worcester on the River Severn. The cathedral, begun in 1084, is mainly 14th-century. At the battle of Worcester (1651) Charles II was defeated by Cromwell. It is famous for its porcelain. Population (1987): 79 900.

word processor A form of computerized typewriter enabling documents, letters, etc., to be created, edited, printed, and stored. A typical word processor consists of a keyboard, visual-display unit, a disk backing store, and a high-quality printer.

Wordsworth, William (1770–1850) British poet. Born in Cumberland, he became an enthusiastic republican during a visit to Revolutionary France (1791–92). In 1795 he met S. T. Coleridge, with whom he collaborated on *Lyrical Ballads* (1798), a seminal work of the Romantic movement. In 1799 he settled in the Lake District, where, cared for by his wife Mary and his sister Dorothy, he wrote his masterpiece, a verse autobiography entitled *The Prelude* (completed 1805; published 1850).

work The product of a force and the distance through which it causes a body to move in the direction of the force. Work, like energy, is measured in joules.

workhouses Institutions set up in the 17th century in Britain and elsewhere to provide employment and shelter for paupers. However, the 1834 Poor Law Amendment Act made it necessary for anyone seeking assistance to enter a workhouse, which because of their inhuman rules soon became dreaded places.

Working Men's Club and Institute Union A club founded in 1862 and now having over 4000 affiliated clubs throughout the UK. The Working Men's Clubs provide educational and recreational facilities.

World Bank. *See* International Bank for Reconstruction and Development.

World Council of Churches An organization of more than 200 Protestant and Orthodox churches. A product of the ecumenical movement, it was founded at Amsterdam in 1948, with headquarters in Geneva.

World Health Organization (WHO) A specialized agency of the United Nations established in 1948. WHO supports programmes to eradicate diseases, carries out and finances epidemiological research, trains health workers, strengthens national health services, and has established international health regulations; it also provides aid in emergencies. Its headquarters are in Geneva.

World Meterological Organization (WMO) A specialized agency of the United Nations established in 1951 with the aim of standardizing international meteorological observations and improving the exchange of weather information. Its headquarters are in Geneva.

WORLD WAR I *The Eastern Front.*

World War I (1914–18) The Great War between the Allied Powers including countries of the British Empire, France, Russia, Belgium, Japan, Serbia, Italy (from May, 1915), Portugal (from March, 1916), Romania (from August, 1916), the USA (from April, 1917), and Greece (from July, 1917) on one side, and the Central Powers, including Germany, Austria-Hungary, Turkey (from November, 1914), and Bulgaria (from October, 1915) on the other. Its causes included fear of the German Empire's European and colonial ambitions; tensions among European powers were expressed by the formation of the Triple Alliance and of the Triple Entente. The immediate cause of the war lay in the conflict

of interests between Russia and Austria-Hungary in the Balkans. On 28 June, 1914, the heir to the Austro-Hungarian throne, Archduke Francis Ferdinand, was assassinated at Sarajevo by a Serbian nationalist and on 28 July Austria-Hungary, with German support, declared war on Serbia. On 29 July Russia mobilized its forces in support of Serbia; on 1 August Germany declared war on Russia and on 3 August, upon France. Germany's invasion of Belgium brought the UK into the war at midnight on 4 August.

Western Front: German strategy at the start of the war was based on the Schlieffen plan. The German forces under von Moltke advanced rapidly through Belgium until they were forced by the British Expeditionary Force (BEF) and the French under Joffre, at the first battle of the Marne (5–9 Sept), to retreat across the River Aisne. Germany's effort to reach the Channel was thwarted at the first battle of Ypres (12 Oct–11 Nov) and the combatants settled to futile trench warfare. 1915 saw inconclusive battles at Neuve-Chapelle (March), again at Ypres (April–May), where the Germans used poison gas for the first time, and at Loos (Sept). On 21 February, 1916, the Germans launched a crippling attack on the French at Verdun but on 1 July Haig, who had succeeded Sir John French as commander of the BEF, opened the crucial battle of the Somme, during which tanks were used (by the British) for the first time; the Allies lost some 600 000 men and the Germans, about 650 000. In early 1917 the Germans under Ludendorff withdrew behind the Hindenburg line; in April Haig took Vimy Ridge (with the loss of 132 000 men); but the French campaign in Champagne was disastrous and command passed to Pétain. With the USA (incensed by German submarine warfare) now participating, on 31 July Britain launched the third battle of Ypres and by 6 November had taken Passchendaele (with 245 000 British losses). In the spring of 1918 Germany thrust a bulge in the Allied line, which Foch was able to wipe out at the second battle of the Marne. In September the Hindenburg line was broken by Haig between Saint Quentin and Cambrai. By October Germany was suing for peace.

Eastern Front: in August, 1914, the Russians advanced into E Prussia but were defeated at Tannenburg. When late in 1914 Turkey attacked Russia in the Caucasus Mountains, the Allies launched the **Gallipoli campaign**, fought mainly by Australian and New Zealand forces (*see* ANZAC). It failed to break through the Dardanelles and by January, 1916, the Allies had withdrawn. Germany's offensive in the summer of 1915 secured Poland, most of Lithuania, and Serbia. Meanwhile, the Allies landed at Salonika, the ensuing **Macedonian campaign** continuing until Bulgaria capitulated in September, 1918. The failure of the Allies to relieve Russia led to its collapse following the Russian Revolution (March, 1917).

Middle East: the **Mesopotamian campaign**, intended to protect oil installations, was launched on 6 November, 1914. However, the Allies failed to take Baghdad (November, 1915) and in April, 1916, they lost Kut al-Amara to the Turks. In February, 1917, it was retaken and, in March, Baghdad fell. Meanwhile the Allies had invaded Palestine and, aided by the Arab revolt, Allenby took Jerusalem in December, 1917; his victory at Megiddo (September, 1918) and capture of Damascus and Aleppo finally crushed the Turks.

Italy: the Italian front was maintained along the River Isonzo through 11 battles until 1917, when the Italians were defeated by Austria-Hungary at Caporetto (Oct-Nov). In October, 1918, Austria-Hungary was defeated at Vittorio-Veneto and in November capitulated.

War at sea and in the air: at **sea** the larger British navy was dominant in the North Sea. Although defeated off Coronel in November, 1914, victory in December off the Falkland Islands facilitated the capture of the German colonies in Africa and the Pacific by September, 1916. German raids on the English coast were repudiated by Beatty's victory at Dogger Bank in January, 1915. The indecisive battle of Jutland (31 May 1916) was the only engagement between the main fleets. The real threat to the Allies at sea came from the German U-boats, which sunk some 6000 ships, including the *Lusitania*, in the course of the war. World War I was the first war in which **aircraft** were used: in 1915 the German Zeppelins began to attack British cities and in 1917 German aircraft were also thus employed. Some air combat took place on the Western and Eastern Fronts and towards the end of the war the newly established Royal Air Force was bombing German cities.

Conclusion: with the defeat of the Turks and Bulgarians in September, 1918, and of Germany on the Western Front and Austria-Hungary in Italy in October, revolt broke out in Germany. On 9 November the German emperor, William II, fled and on 11 November Germany signed the armistice. On 18 January, 1919, the Allies met at the Paris Peace Conference to determine the peace settlement, which was signed by Germany (the Treaty of Versailles) on 28 June. The Allies lost some 5 million lives (of which 3 million were French and Russian) in the war and the Central Powers, some 3.5 million (of which 3 million were German and Austro-Hungarian). 21 million combatants were wounded.

World War II (1939–45) The war between the Allied Powers, including countries of the Commonwealth, France, the Soviet Union (from June, 1941), the USA (from December, 1941), and China (from December, 1941) on one side, and the Axis Powers, including Germany, Italy (from June, 1940), and Japan (from December, 1941) on the other. The war was caused by the failure of the Paris Peace Conference and by the territorial ambitions of Nazi Germany under Adolf Hitler. In March, 1938, Germany annexed Austria (*see* Anschluss) and in September, following the Munich Agreement, the Sudetenland. In March, 1939, Hitler occupied the rest of Czechoslovakia. On 23 May Hitler came to an agreement with Mussolini's Italy, which in April had conquered Albania. Hitler's and Stalin's nonaggression pact followed on 23 August and Britain, France, and Poland made an agreement of mutual assistance on 25 Aug. On 1 September Germany invaded Poland and two days later Britain and France declared war on Germany.

Western Europe (1939–41): by 27 September Poland had succumbed to the German Blitzkreig. The Soviet invasion of Finland (*see* Russo-Finnish War) brought Finnish capitulation by March, 1940, and in April Germany invaded Denmark and Norway. The Allied failure in Scandinavia led to Neville Chamberlain's resignation and on 10 May, the day that Germany invaded Belgium and the Netherlands, Churchill became Britain's prime minister. The German advance outflanked the Maginot line and split the Allied forces; on 26 May an Allied evacuation from the Continent was ordered. Between 29

May and 4 June, some 338 226 Allied troops were rescued from Dunkirk. On 22 June Pétain signed the French armistice with Germany, following which French resistance to the Axis Powers was directed by de Gaulle from London, where he organized the Free French.

Britain now faced an imminent German invasion. In August and September, 1940, the German Luftwaffe attacked SE England and then London in a series of daytime raids. In October German bombing was carried out at night and extended to other British cities. The Luftwaffe failed to cripple the RAF and by the end of October the so-called battle of Britain had been won by the RAF under Dowding. The RAF lost 915 aircraft in the conflict and the Luftwaffe some 1733.

Africa and the Middle East (1940–43): in September, 1940, Italy advanced from Libya into Egypt but was forced to retreat by Wavell's troops. By 6 February, 1941, the Allies had captured 113 000 Italian soldiers but their success was undermined by the arrival in N Africa of Rommel and the German Afrika Corps. In March Wavell's force was weakened by the dispatch of troops to aid Greece (Yugoslavia and Greece fell in April, and Crete in May) and retreated to the Egyptian border.

In November Auchinleck (who had replaced Wavell in July) launched an offensive against Rommel but by January, 1942, had been forced to take up a defensive position at El-Alamein, inside the Egyptian frontier. In August Auchinleck was replaced by Alexander and Montgomery became commander of the Eighth Army. In the decisive battle of Alamein (23 Oct–4 Nov) Montgomery defeated Rommel, forcing his retreat along the N African coast. On 8 November an Anglo-US force under Eisenhower landed on the coast of French N Africa. The French under Darlan surrendered and the Allies advanced through Tunisia to meet (7 April, 1943) with Montgomery's Eighth Army. On 7 May the Allies took Bizerta and Tunis and on 13 May the Axis forces surrendered (some 248 000 troops were captured).

In **East Africa**, Wavell had taken Addis Ababa from the Italians in April, 1941, and had secured Ethiopia and British Somaliland (captured by Italy in August, 1940), by May. In the **Middle East**, in April Britain occupied Iraq, by June Lebanon and Syria were in Allied hands, and in August the Allies gained control of Iran.

Italy (1943–45): on 10 July, 1943, Alexander's army group (the Eighth under Montgomery and the US Fifth Army), under the supreme command of Eisenhower, landed in Sicily. On 25 July Mussolini fell and on 3 Sept the Italian armistice was signed and the Allies landed on the Italian mainland. The Germans held back the Allies at the Ortona-Garigliano line until an Allied offensive, launched on 12 May, 1944, succeeded in breaking through to Rome (4 June). Bologna and then Milan were taken in April, 1945, and on 2 May Trieste fell.

Eastern Front (1941–45): Germany, with Finland, Hungary, and Romania, invaded the Soviet Union on 22 June, 1941. The Axis forces took the Crimea and the Ukraine in the S, besieged Leningrad in the N, and by November were in sight of Moscow. The Soviets staged an effective counterattack in the winter of 1941–42 but Germany retaliated in June and by August the battle of Stalingrad had begun. Following this heroic Soviet victory, the Germans launched a new offensive in July but were gradually forced back until expelled from Soviet

WORLD WAR II   *The development of the Western Front after the Allied D-day invasion of Normandy.*

soil in August, 1944. On 23 August the Soviet Union secured a Romanian armistice and on 19 Sept, a Finnish armistice. Also in September Bulgaria declared war on Germany and the Germans evacuated Greece. On 5 October Belgrade fell following collaboration between the Red Army and Tito's Partisans. In October Soviet troops invaded Germany and in January, 1945, launched a final offensive, taking Poland, Austria, and Hungary and entering Czechoslovakia. Berlin fell on 2 May, shortly after Hitler's suicide.

Western Front (1944–45): on 6 June, 1944, D-Day, the Allied invasion of Normandy began under Eisenhower. The RAF Bomber Command, which had previously been bombing German cities, had prepared the way with strategic bombing and by 2 July one million US and British troops had landed. The British under Montgomery took Caen and US troops, after capturing St Lô (July), invaded Brittany. The Canadians took Falaise on 17 August, shortly after US and French troops had landed in the South of France from the Mediterranean. On 25 August Paris fell to the Allies, who now advanced into the Ruhr.

At the battle of Arnhem in September, however, air-

borne troops were withdrawn after sustaining heavy losses. In December the Germans launched a counteroffensive (the battle of the Bulge) in the Ardennes region of S Belgium. US troops forced the Germans to retreat in January, 1945, and the final Allied offensive was launched. The Rhine was crossed in March and by 1 April the Ruhr was encircled. On 4 May, Montgomery accepted the surrender of German forces in NW Germany, Holland, and Denmark at Lüneburg Heath. On 7 May the Germans signed a general surrender at Reims, which was ratified two days later in Berlin.

War at sea: The battle for control of the sea routes, known as the **battle of the Atlantic**, was fought from December, 1939, when the German *Graf Spee* inflicted considerable damage on HMS *Exeter* in the battle of the River Plate in the S Atlantic. In November, 1940, a successful naval air attack was launched on Taranto and in March, 1941, at Cape Matapan the British Mediterranean fleet thwarted an Italian attempt to prevent the transfer of British troops from Egypt to Greece. In May occurred the famous sinking of the *Hood* by the *Bismarck* and, three days later, of the *Bismarck* by the *Dorsetshire*. However, as in World War I, the major threat was posed by the German U-boats. These reached their height of effectiveness early in 1943 but by the summer, partly owing to the introduction of Allied escort carriers, 37 U-boats had been sunk and the battle of the Atlantic was over.

Asia (1941–45): the Japanese attack on Pearl Harbor on 7 December, 1941, initiated a truly "world" war. On 10 December Germany and Italy declared war on the USA and the second Sino-Japanese War became part of the wider conflict.

Japan invaded Malaya on 8 December and captured Hong Kong (25 Dec), Manila (3 January, 1942), and Singapore (15 Feb). The Dutch East Indies fell on 10 March and the Philippines and Burma in May. However, the US naval and air victories of the Coral Sea (4–8 May), Midway Island (4–6 June), and Guadalcanal (Aug) then halted Japan's eastward expansion. In October, 1944, the Japanese fleet was decisively defeated at Leyte Gulf and the Allied conquest of Manila (February, 1945), the Philippines (June), and Borneo (May-June) followed. Burma, where Lord Mountbatten had become supreme commander, SE Asia, in August, 1943, was reconquered by the 14th ("forgotten") Army under Slim (January–May, 1945). Japanese resistance was finally ended by the atomic bombing on 6 and 9 August respectively of Hiroshima and Nagasaki, and Japan formally surrendered on 14 August.

Conclusion: in May, 1945, with the fall of Berlin, the war in Europe was over. The postwar settlement was decided at the Potsdam Conference in July and August (*see also* Tehran Conference; Yalta Conference).

In the course of the war Germany lost some 3.5 million combatants and 780 000 civilians. In contrast the UK lost 92 673 civilians; some 264 443 combatants died. The Soviet Union lost 11 million combatants and 7 million civilians; the Japanese 1.3 million and 672 000 respectively; and the USA, 292 131 and 6000. In addition some 5.7 million Jews died in Nazi concentration camps.

World Wide Fund for Nature An international organization dedicated to the conservation of endangered species and their natural habitats. Founded in 1961 as the World Wildlife Fund (WWF), it has financed projects both in Britain and abroad. The international president is HRH the Duke of Edinburgh.

worm A soft-bodied elongated invertebrate. The term is applied to members of several different groups, especially earthworms and various parasitic species, and sometimes the larvae of insects. *See also* annelid worm; flatworm; nematode; ribbon worm.

Worms 49 38N 8 23E A town in SW West Germany, on the River Rhine. Heavily bombed during World War II, it has an 11th-century cathedral and synagogue (1034). *History*: in the 5th century AD it was the capital of Burgundy. Among the imperial diets (assemblies) held here was that of 1521 at which Luther refused to recant. It was annexed by France in 1797 and passed to Hesse-Darmstadt in 1815. Population (1984): 73 000.

wormwood An aromatic herb or shrub of the worldwide genus *Artemisia* (about 200 species), especially *A. absinthium*, which is found in grasslands of the N hemisphere and is the source of absinthe. Up to 80 cm high, it has small yellow flowers. Family: *Compositae*.

Worthing 50 48N 0 23W A resort in S England, on the West Sussex coast. Nearby on the South Downs is the neolithic Cissbury Ring. Population (1985 est): 93 400.

Wotan. *See* Odin.

Wounded Knee The site in SW South Dakota (USA) of the last confrontation (29 December, 1890) between the Indians and US troops. Fearing an uprising among the discontented Sioux, troops killed over 200 men, women, and children at Wounded Knee creek. In 1973 two Indians were killed when the American Indian Movement occupied the village of Wounded Knee in protest against government Indian policies.

wrack A large brown seaweed of the order *Fucales*, found almost worldwide on rocky shores. Leathery branching fronds arise from a circular rootlike anchor (holdfast), often bearing air bladders to aid flotation. Examples are bladderwrack (*Fucus vesiculosus*) and serrated wrack (*F. serratus*).

wrasse A fish of the family *Labridae* (300 species) found near rocks or coral reefs in shallow tropical and temperate seas. It has a slender often brilliantly coloured body, 5–200 cm long, long dorsal and anal fins, and thick lips. They are known for their elaborate courtship and nesting behaviour. Order: *Perciformes*.

wreckfish A carnivorous fish, *Polyprion americanus*, also called stone bass, found in Mediterranean and Atlantic offshore waters. It has a deep heavy body, up to 2 m long, dark brown above and yellowish below, a large head, and a jutting lower jaw. Family: *Serranidae*; order: *Perciformes*.

wren A small brown bird belonging to a family (*Troglodytidae*; 63 species) found chiefly in South America. Wrens are 9–22 cm long with sharp slender bills and short cocked tails. The only Eurasian species, *Troglodytes troglodytes*, is about 10 cm long and has a reddish-brown plumage with barring on the wings and tail. The name is also given to the families *Maluridae* (Australian wrens) and *Xenicidae* (New Zealand wrens).

Wren, Sir Christopher (1632–1723) English architect and scientist. He was a founder member of the Royal Society and later its president (1680–82). His first architectural designs were for Pembroke College chapel, Cambridge (1663), and the Sheldonian Theatre, Oxford (1664). Within days of the Fire of London Wren produced a new plan for the whole City, incorporating spacious avenues and piazzas. The plan was rejected but Wren was commissioned to rebuild 51 City churches and some 36 company halls. Basing many of his designs for the churches on Vitruvius' Roman basilica, Wren showed enormous ingenuity in fitting his buildings into the old irregular sites. His design for St Paul's Cathedral was accepted, after many modifications, in 1675. His later buildings include the Greenwich Hospital (begun in 1694) and additions to Hampton Court (1698).

wrestling A form of unarmed combat, in which two people attempt to throw and hold each other down. It first became an Olympic sport in 704 BC. In **Graeco-Roman wrestling** holds on the body below the waist and the use of legs to hold or trip are not allowed. They are, however, allowed in **freestyle wrestling**. In both styles a wrestler wins a match by securing a fall (throwing his opponent onto his back and pinning both shoulders to the mat for one second) or by accumulating the most points according to a complex scoring system. **Sambo wrestling** originated in the Soviet Union. **Sumo** is the highly popular Japanese style in which the wrestlers, usually weighing around 130 kg (20 stone), attempt to force each other out of the ring. *See also* judo.

FRANK LLOYD WRIGHT *Interior of the Guggen-heim Museum, New York.*

Wrexham   53 03N 3 00W A town in North Wales, in Clwyd. It is a market town and coalmining centre. Population (1983 est): 40 357.

Wright, Frank Lloyd   (1869–1959) US architect. He first demonstrated his originality in a series of Chicago houses between 1900 and 1909, the most famous being the Robie house (1909). Later buildings include the Johnson Wax factory at Racine, Wisconsin (1936–39), Taliesin West (1938), his winter home in the Arizona desert, and the Guggenheim Museum (1959).

Wright, Orville   (1871–1948) US aviator, who with his brother **Wilbur Wright** (1867–1912) is usually considered to have made the first powered and controlled flights (17 December, 1903). They took place near Kitty Hawk, North Carolina, and in the second, lasting about a minute, the aircraft flew 250 metres.

Wrocław   (German name: Breslau)   51 05N 17 00E A city in SW Poland, on the River Oder. Founded during the 10th century, it suffered severe damage in World War II under siege from the Soviet armies (1945). Population (1985): 636 000.

wrought iron   An almost pure form of iron, often with less than 0.1% carbon. It was originally produced by re-peatedly hammering and folding hot pig iron to squeeze out the impurities. The puddling process has now super-seded hand working.

Wuhan   30 35N 114 19E A port in E central China, at the confluence of the Yangtze and Han Rivers. Formed by the amalgamation (1950) of the ancient cities of Hankou (*or* Hankow), Hanyang, and Wuchang, it is the commercial and industrial centre of central China. Population (1986): 3 400 000.

Wu-hsi.   *See* Wuxi.

Wuppertal   51 05N 7 10E A city in NW West Germany, in the Ruhr. It was formed in 1929 from six towns, including Elberfeld, and was heavily bombed in World War II. Population (1989): 380 000.

Würzburg   49 48N 9 57E A city in S West Germany, on the River Main. The former episcopal residence (1720–44), containing frescoes by Tiepolo, was damaged in World War II but later restored.   Population (1986): 127 500.

Wuxi   (*or* Wu-hsi)   31 35N 120 19E A city in E China, on the Grand Canal. A major grain market since the 7th century AD, it is also an industrial centre. Population (1987 est): 696 300.

Wyatt, Sir Thomas   (1503–42) English poet.   With Henry Howard, Earl of Surrey (1517–47) he introduced Italian verse forms and metres, notably the Petrarchan sonnet, into English poetry. 96 of his poems, together with 40 by Surrey, were included in *Tottel's Miscellany* (1557).

Wycherley, William   (1640–1716) English dramatist. He wrote four comedies, notably *The Country Wife* (1675) and *The Plain Dealer* (1676), adapted from Molière's *Le Misanthrope*. His plays are more fiercely satirical than those of his fellow Restoration dramatists.

Wycliffe, John   (c. 1329–84) English religious reformer. He made increasingly radical criticisms of the Church, resulting in his condemnation as a heretic. He attacked the doctrine of transubstantiation and emphasized the importance of the Bible, of which he supervised the first English translation from the Latin. Wycliffe's adherents, the Lollards, were forerunners of English Protestantism.

Wye, River   A river in E Wales and W England. Flowing mainly SE from Plynlimmon it joins the River Severn near Chepstow. Length: 210 km (130 mi).

Wyoming   One of the mountain states in the NW USA. Its natural resources include oil, natural gas, uranium, coal, trona, bentonite clay, and iron ore. Livestock production dominates farming. Tourism is significant with such attractions as the Yellowstone National Park. *History*: part of the territory acquired from France by the Louisiana Purchase (1803), the arrival of the Union Pacific Railway (1867–69) brought settlement in the S and the area became a state in 1890. Area: 253 596 sq km (97 914 sq mi). Population (1986 est): 485 111. Capital: Cheyenne.

X

xenon   (Xe)   A noble gas, present in the atmosphere and discovered in 1898 by Sir William Ramsay and M. W. Travers (1872–1961), in the residue of distilled liquid air. The first noble gas compounds were discovered by N. Bartlett (1932–), by reacting xenon with dioxygenyl platinum hexafluoride ($O_2^+ PtF_6^-$) to form $Xe^+ PtF_6^-$. Xenon is used in special lamps and the radioactive isotope ^{133}Xe is produced in nuclear reactors. It is a "poison," i.e. a neutron absorber, and is a crucial factor in the control of the chain reaction (*see* nuclear energy). At no 54; at wt 131.3; mp $-111.9°C$; bp $-107°C$.

Xenophon (c. 430–c. 354 BC) Greek historian and soldier. He was born in Athens and became a disciple of Socrates. In 410 he successfully led a group of 10 000 Greek mercenaries in a heroic retreat through the hostile Persian Empire to the Black Sea, after their former commander, Cyrus, was killed in battle. This feat formed the subject of his best-known work, the *Anabasis*. He later served in the Spartan army under King Aegesilaus. He wrote numerous other works, including *Memorabilia*, *Apology*, and *Symposium*, which deal with Socrates.

xerography. *See* photocopying machine.

xerophyte A plant that lives in a hot dry climate and is adapted for conserving water. Cacti, for example, often have spiny leaves (to prevent water loss) and green succulent stems (in which water is stored). A **xeromorph** is a plant that shows some of the features of xerophytes but may not live in desert areas.

Xerxes I (d. 465 BC) King of Persia (486–465). Having brutally repressed revolts in Egypt, he invaded Greece (*see* Greek-Persian Wars) in 480. However, defeat at Salamis (480), Plataea and Mycale (479), and the consequent revolt of the Asiatic Greeks forced him to withdraw. This tyrannous ruler and compulsive builder was assassinated in a court intrigue.

Xhosa A Bantu people of the Transkei (South Africa). Many Xhosa are migrant labourers in other areas of South Africa. Their language employs click sounds borrowed from the Khoisan languages.

Xi An (Hsi-an *or* Sian) 34 16N 108 54E A city in central China, on the Wei Ho (River). It contains many Tang pagodas and a noted museum. *History*: as a Tang capital (618–906 AD) it attracted many Buddhist, Muslim, and Christian missionaries. After 1935 it was a Guomindang (Nationalist) base. It is now an industrial centre. Population (1986): 2 330 000.

Xi Jiang (*or* Hsi Chiang) The most important river in S China, rising in Yunnan province and flowing E to form the densely populated Canton delta and the Zhu Jiang. Length: about 1900 km (1200 mi).

Xingu, River (Portuguese name: Rio Xingu) A river in central Brazil, rising on the Mato Grosso plateau and flowing generally N to enter the Amazon delta. Length: 1932 km (1200 mi).

Xiong Nu (*or* Hsiung-nu) Turkish and Mongol tribes on the N and NW borders of China, which threatened Chinese security from about 500 BC. The Chinese attempted to control the Xiong Nu by building the Great Wall of China, marrying their daughters to Xiong Nu leaders, and trading with them.

X-ray diffraction The diffraction of X-rays when they strike a crystal. The angle through which the X-rays are diffracted depends on the spacing between the different planes in the crystal in a manner given by Bragg's law. The technique is used in studying crystal structure.

X-rays Electromagnetic radiation lying between ultraviolet radiation and gamma rays in the electromagnetic spectrum. X-rays may have wavelengths between 10^{-9} metre and 10^{-11} metre. Discovered by Wilhelm

X-RAYS *The first radiograph of a human body (from Roentgen's original plate). The keys in his pocket and his suspenders are clearly visible.*

Roentgen in 1895, they are produced when heavy metal atoms are struck by sufficiently energetic electrons, as in an **X-ray tube**. The electrons in an X-ray tube are produced by a heated cathode in an evacuated tube and accelerated to the heavy-metal anode by an electric field. The collisions knock inner electrons from the atoms, X-rays being emitted when the vacancy is filled by outer electrons. X-rays cause ionization in gases and penetrate matter. X-rays have many uses in medical diagnosis, radiotherapy, structural analysis, and the study of crystals (X-ray diffraction), etc.

xylem A plant tissue specialized for the transport of water and salts. The main cells are tubelike, with their walls strengthened by deposits of lignin. In trees and shrubs the lignin deposits eventually block the tubes completely: this tissue forms wood, and new secondary xylem is produced.

xylene (*or* dimethyl benzene; $C_6H_4(CH_3)_2$) A colourless toxic flammable liquid consisting of a mixture of three isomers. It is obtained by fractional distillation of petroleum and is used as an aviation fuel and as a solvent.

xylophone   A pitched percussion instrument, consisting of a frame on which wooden bars in the pattern of a keyboard are fixed, each with a tubular metal resonator beneath it. It is played with two sticks. Orchestral xylophones usually have a compass of three octaves.

Y

Yahweh   The conjectural pronunciation of one of the Hebrew names of God. The name YHWH (the Tetragrammaton or "four-letter" name) occurs often in the Bible; out of reverence it was traditionally not pronounced except by the high priest when he entered the Holy of Holies. "Jehovah" represents another attempt to pronounce this name.

yak   A shaggy-coated wild ox, *Bos grunniens*, inhabiting mountain pastures of central Asia. Yaks have long been domesticated for draught purposes and milk; their dung is used as fuel. Wild yaks, up to 2 m high with long upward-curving horns, are larger than domestic yaks and are always black.

Yale University   One of the oldest universities in the USA (founded 1701), situated at New Haven, Connecticut. It is named after Elihu Yale (1648–1721), who donated his books to the college.

Yalta Conference   (1945) The conference, held at the Black Sea port of Yalta, towards the end of World War II attended by F. D. Roosevelt (USA), Stalin (Soviet Union), and Churchill (UK). They agreed upon the postwar occupation of Germany and decided that German surrender must be unconditional.

yam   A twining herbaceous plant of the genus *Dioscorea*, cultivated in wet tropical regions for its edible tubers. Tubers can reach a length of 2.6 m and a weight of 45 kg; species commonly cultivated are *D. alata* (white yam), *D. rotundata* (white guinea yam), *D. batatas* (Chinese yam), and *D. cayenensis* (yellow yam). Family: *Dioscoreaceae*.

Yamasaki, Minoru   (1912–86) US architect. His earliest buildings, such as Missouri's St Louis airport (1953–55), were remarkable for their simple but dramatic elegance. However, later works, such as the World Trade Center in New York (1970–77), employed controversial pseudo-Gothic elements.

Yamoussoukro   6 49N 5 17W The capital of Côte d'Ivoire. Yamoussoukro was chosen as an inland replacement for the old capital of Abidjan in 1983. It includes the largest basilica in the world, completed in 1989. Population (1989 est): 100 000.

Yang, Chen Ning   (1922–) US physicist, born in China, who shared the 1957 Nobel Prize with his countryman Tsung-Dao Lee for the theoretical work suggesting that parity would not be conserved in the weak interaction. This was quickly confirmed by observations of beta decay.

Yangon.   *See* Rangoon.

Yangtze River   (Chinese name: Chang Jiang *or* Ch'ang Chiang)   The longest river in China and the third longest in the world. Rising in a remote mountain range on the Tibetan borders, it flows E to the East China Sea via an extensive delta. The Yangtze is one of China's main transport routes. Length: 6380 km (3964 mi).

Yaoundé   (*or* Yaunde)   3 51N 11 31E The capital of Cameroon. Founded in 1888, it has been capital of Cameroon since 1922 (except during World War II). Population (1985 est): 583 500.

yard   An Imperial unit of length originally defined as the distance between two gold plugs on a bronze bar. In 1963 the yard was redefined as 0.9144 metre (*see* metric system).

Yarmouth   (*or* Great Yarmouth)   52 37N 1 44E A resort and port in E England, in Norfolk. Once a major herring-fishing port, it is now a base for North Sea gas and oil. Population (1981): 48 273.

Yawata.   *See* Kitakyushu.

yaws   A chronic tropical disease caused by a spirochaete bacterium, *Treponema pertenue*. It occurs mostly among poor children and is spread by skin contact. After an incubation period of three to four weeks a growth appears on the thighs or buttocks; later, multiple growths appear all over the skin. If not treated the disease can be very disfiguring. Treatment with penicillin is highly effective.

year   The time taken by the earth to complete one revolution around the sun. This is equal to the period of the sun's apparent motion around the ecliptic. The **tropical year**, of 365.2422 days, is the interval between two successive passages of the sun through the vernal equinox. The **sidereal year**, of 365.2564 days, refers to successive passages of the sun through a point relative to the background stars. These periods differ because of the precession of the equinoxes. *See also* calendar.

yeast   A single-celled fungus that is capable of fermenting carbohydrates and that reproduces asexually by budding new cells from its surface. Typical yeasts belong to the family *Saccharomycetaceae*. Strains of *Saccharomyces cerevisiae* are widely used to cause fermentation in baking, brewing, etc. Yeast extracts are used as a food for their high vitamin B content. Class: *Ascomycetes*.

Yeats, William Butler   (1865–1939) Irish poet and dramatist. His best-known poems, many of which appeared in *The Tower* (1928) and *The Winding Stair* (1929), included tragic meditations on personal and political themes. Among them are 'Easter, 1916', 'The Second Coming', and 'Sailing to Byzantium'. He was an admirer of Maud Gonne (1866–1953), Irish actress and nationalist, and with Lady Gregory (1852–1932) in 1904 he founded the Abbey Theatre, Dublin, for which he wrote many plays. He was a senator of the Irish Free State (1922–28) and won the Nobel Prize in 1923. His brother **Jack Butler Yeats** (1871–1957) was a noted Irish painter.

yellow fever   An acute viral infection transmitted by female mosquitoes of the genus *Aëdes*, which occur in tropical rain forests. After an incubation period of 3–14 days the patient develops a fever with aching muscles. In severe cases the virus affects the liver causing jaundice (hence the name), the kidneys, and the heart; death may result from liver or heart failure. There is no specific treatment but two kinds of vaccine can prevent it.

W. B. YEATS

yellow-green algae Algae of the division *Chrysophyta* (about 6000 species), which are yellow-green to brown in colour. Most are unicellular or colonial and they form a major constituent of plankton (*see also* diatoms). Most reproduce asexually by spores.

yellowhammer A Eurasian bunting, *Emberiza citrinella*, that occurs on farmland and roadsides, where it feeds on grain and seeds. About 16 cm long, the male has a bright-yellow head and underparts, chestnut rump, and a brown-streaked back; females are less colourful.

Yellow River (Chinese name: Huang He *or* Huang Ho) A river in China, rising in the W and flowing roughly E to enter the Gulf of Chihli via a fertile delta. Its diversion as a measure against the Japanese invasion (1938) resulted in the death of 900 000 people. Length: about 4350 km (2700 mi).

Yellow Sea (Chinese name: Huang Hai) A large shallow inlet of the W Pacific Ocean, bordered by China and Korea. It is so called because of the yellowish silt deposited by the Chinese rivers.

Yellowstone National Park The largest national park in the USA, chiefly in NW Wyoming but extending into S Montana and E Idaho. Its many active geysers include Old Faithful. Area: 8956 sq km (3458 sq mi).

Yellowstone River A river in the W USA, rising in NW Wyoming and flowing N through the Yellowstone National Park then E to join the Missouri River. Length: 1080 km (671 mi).

Yemen, People's Democratic Republic of (*or* South Yemen; name until 1970: People's Republic of Southern Yemen) A country in the Middle East, in S Arabia bordering on the Gulf of Aden and the Arabian Sea. It includes the islands of Kamaran in the Red Sea, Perim Island, Socotra, and the Kuria Maria Islands. Mountains dissected by wadis rise from the narrow coastal plain; the N and E are desert. The mainly Arab population is largely Sunnite Muslim. *Economy*: mainly agricultural. Cotton is the main crop. Sardine fishing is important; mineral deposits are not yet exploited. Industry consists chiefly of an oil refinery and a little light industry in Aden. The economy suffered badly from the closure of the Suez Canal (1967–75). Aid is received main-

ly from China and the Soviet Union. *History*: ruled by the imams (priest-kings) of Yemen, the area (excluding Aden) was nominally part of the Ottoman Empire from the 16th century to 1918. Aden was captured from the Turks in 1839 and occupied by the British East India Company. The British also made protectorate treaties with other local rulers (1886–1914), finally uniting them under Aden Protectorate (1937). In 1963 Aden and ten others formed the Federation of South Arabia. This collapsed in 1967 and South Yemen became independent. Its history has been marked chiefly by border disputes with Oman (until 1976) and with North Yemen. In 1986 an outbreak of violence in Aden forced foreigners to evacuate the area and brought Haider Abu Bakr al Attas to power as president. Official currency: South Yemen dinar of 1000 fils. Official language: Arabic. Area: about 336 870 sq km (130 066 sq mi). Population (1987 est): 2 278 000. Capital: Aden.

Yemen Arab Republic (*or* North Yemen) A country in the Middle East in SW Arabia, bordering on the Red Sea. It consists of a narrow dry W coastal plain, central mountains (the wettest and most fertile in Arabia), and E desert. The Arab population is Muslim, either Sunnite or Zaidi. *Economy*: mainly agricultural; cotton, coffee, cereals, vegetables, fruit, and the narcotic qat are the chief crops and livestock are kept. Salt is mined and handicrafts are important. North Yemen receives money from Yemeni workers abroad and relies on foreign aid. *History*: rule by a Muslim imam (priest-king) originated in the 9th century and lasted until 1962, although from 1520 until 1918 the area was nominally part of the Ottoman Empire. North Yemen joined the Arab League (1945) and the UN (1947) and was loosely allied

YELLOWSTONE NATIONAL PARK   *The geyser* Old Faithful, *which regularly erupts every hour.*

with Egypt and Syria (1958–61) in the United Arab Republic. Civil war (1962–70) ended with the recognition of a republican regime. Successive heads of state were assassinated in 1977 and 1978. Moves were made towards uniting the two Yemens following the border clashes of 1967–72, 1978, and 1989. President: Lt Col Ali Abdullah Saleh (1942–). Official currency: riyal of 100 rial. Area: 195 000 sq km (73 300 sq mi). Population (1987 est): 6 533 265. Capital: San'a. Chief port: Hodeida.

Yenisei, River A river in the central Soviet Union, rising in the Sayan Mountains and flowing N to **Yenisei Bay** on the Kara Sea. Length: about 4000 km (2485 mi).

Yeomen of the Guard The bodyguard of the British sovereign established by Henry VII in 1485. Their last appearance in battle was at Dettingen in 1743. Known as Beefeaters because of their magnificent physiques, they wear a red and gold uniform.

Yerevan (Russian name: Erevan) 40 10N 44 31E A city in the SW Soviet Union, capital of the Armenian SSR. It dates from at least the 7th century AD. Long disputed by Persia and Turkey, it was ceded to Russia in 1828. Population (1987): 1 168 000.

Yeti. See Abominable Snowman.

Yevtushenko, Yevgenii (1933–) Soviet poet. His implicit criticism of the Soviet authorities in such poems as *Babi Yar* (1961) gained him wide popularity among both Soviet and western readers. He has given many poetry readings in Europe and the USA. In 1989 he was elected to the Congress of People's Deputies.

yew A coniferous tree or shrub of the genus *Taxus* (10 species), native to the N hemisphere. Male and female flowers, which produce bright-red berries, grow on separate trees. The berries are sweet-tasting and attractive to birds, but the seeds and leaves are poisonous. The most widespread species is the common yew (*T. baccata*), of Europe, SW Asia, and N Africa. Family: *Taxaceae*.

Yezo. See Hokkaido.

Yggdrasill In Norse mythology, an evergreen ash tree embracing the whole universe. Its three roots join the underworld, the land of giants, and the home of the gods (Asgard). The maypole and the Christmas tree are possibly symbolic derivatives of Yggdrasill.

Yiddish A language used by Ashkenazim (East European) Jews and based on a dialect of High German. It emerged during the 9th century and has absorbed many Slavonic and other influences. It is written in the Hebrew alphabet. After the holocaust it yielded its place as the principal literary language of the Jews to Hebrew.

yield point The point at which a body becomes permanently deformed when subjected to a sufficiently large stress. Below the yield point the body is elastic, above the yield point it becomes plastic.

YIN AND YANG *The symbols are interlocked and each contains a tiny portion of the other.*

yin and yang Contrasting but complementary principles at the root of traditional Chinese cosmology. Yin is the negative feminine mode, associated with the earth, darkness, and passivity. Yang is the positive dynamic principle of masculine energy associated with heaven and light.

ylang-ylang A slender evergreen tropical Asian tree, *Cananga odorata*, also called perfume tree. It bears fragrant stalked greenish-yellow flowers throughout the year. An oil distilled from the flowers is used in perfumery, cosmetics, and soaps. Family: *Annonaceae*.

YMCA. See Young Men's Christian Association.

yoga The principles and practice of self-training that permeates all Indian philosophical traditions. Traces of it exist from the Indus Valley civilization. The methods used include physical control and meditative techniques. Physical control is stressed in Hindu yoga; in the Buddhist practice contemplative methods predominate; in Jainism asceticism is emphasized. Usually the aim is a state of release and liberation from the material world.

yogurt. See dairy products.

Yogyakarta. See Jogjakarta.

Yokohama 35 28N 139 28E A port and second largest city of Japan, in SE Honshu. Together with Tokyo it forms Japan's greatest urban area. *History*: it grew rapidly after 1859, but was almost destroyed by the 1923 earthquake and bombed during World War II. Population (1985): 2 993 000.

Yokosuka 35 18N 139 39E A port in Japan, in SE Honshu on Tokyo Bay. William Adams (d. 1620), the first Englishman to visit Japan (1600), is buried here. It has a major naval base and its chief industry is shipbuilding. Population (1985): 427 000.

Yom Kippur (Hebrew: Day of Atonement) A Jewish holy day, falling nine days after Rosh Hashanah. It is a day of penitence and cleansing from sin and is marked by 24 hours' total fast.

Yom Kippur War. See Israel.

Yonkers 40 56N 73 54W A city in the USA, in New York state on the Hudson River. Population (1986 est): 186 080.

York (Latin name: Eboracum) 53 58N 1 05W A city in N England, in North Yorkshire on the River Ouse. It was the principal Roman garrison in Britain and was for long regarded as the northern capital. The cathedral (Minster), seat of the Archbishop of York, was begun in 1154. It was damaged by fire in 1984. The medieval walls and four city gateways remain. The National Railway Museum opened in 1975 and the Jorvik Viking Centre in 1984. Population (1981): 99 787.

York A ruling dynasty of England descended from Edmund, Duke of York (1342–1402), the fourth son of Edward III. Richard Plantaganet, Duke of York, led the Yorkist opposition to Henry VI in the Wars of the Roses (1455–85), in which the Yorkist emblem was the white rose. His son Edward IV, established the royal dynasty. After the brief rule of his son Edward V and the overthrow of Richard III (1485) the Crown passed to Henry VII, the first Tudor monarch, who married Edward IV's daughter Elizabeth.

York, Archbishop of The second of the two archbishops of England and head of the northern province of the Church of England. York became an archiepiscopal see in 735 AD. Controversy between Canterbury and York regarding primacy was settled by Pope Innocent II

(1352–62), with precedence given to the Archbishop of Canterbury, called Primate of All England, while the Archbishop of York was styled Primate of England. He ranks next to the Lord Chancellor. Recent archbishops are: (93rd) (Frederick) Donald Coggan (1961–74); (94th) Stuart (Yarworth), Baron Blanch (1974–83); (95th) John Habgood (1983–   ).

DUKE OF YORK *With the Duchess at the Royal Windsor Horse Show.*

York, Prince Andrew, Duke of (1960–   ) Second son of Elizabeth II and fourth in succession to the throne. A helicopter pilot in the Royal Navy, he married Miss Sarah Fergusson in July 1986; their daughter, Princess Beatrice, was born in 1988.

York, Richard Plantagenet, 3rd Duke of (1411–60) English magnate. His claim to the throne against Henry VI resulted in the outbreak of the Wars of the Roses in 1455. He was killed in a skirmish at Wakefield. His sons became Edward IV and Richard III.

Yorkshire A former county in NE England. It was reorganized in 1974 to form the counties of North Yorkshire and Humberside and the metropolitan counties of West Yorkshire and South Yorkshire.

Yorkshire terrier A breed of toy dog developed in N England during the 19th century. It is small and compact with a very long straight coat that trails on the ground. This is black at birth but matures to steel-blue with tan on the head and chest. Height: 20–23 cm.

Yosemite National Park A national park in the USA, in central California. The scenic Yosemite Valley contains the world's three largest monoliths of exposed granite. Its many lakes, rivers, and waterfalls include the Yosemite Falls. Area: 3061 sq km (1182 sq mi).

Young, Brigham (1801–1877) US Mormon leader, who succeeded Joseph Smith. A former Methodist, Young joined the new church in 1832. After Smith's death he led the major migration to Salt Lake City, Utah (1846–47).

Young, Thomas (1773–1829) British physician and physicist. He identified astigmatism and described the ciliary muscles of the eye. He demonstrated the interference of light and suggested a wave theory of light in opposition to Newton's corpuscular theory. As a result of his work on the elasticity of materials, the ratio of stress to strain is known as Young's modulus. Also an Egyptologist, he helped decipher the Rosetta Stone.

Young Men's Christian Association (YMCA) A Christian organization for young men and, since 1971, for young women, founded in 1844 by George Williams (1821–1905). Its aim is to encourage Christian morality and qualities of leadership.

Young's modulus. *See* elastic modulus.

Young Women's Christian Association (YWCA) A Christian organization for women (to which men may now also belong). Founded in 1855 by Emma Robarts and Mary Jane Kinnaird to promote unity among Christians and understanding between different faiths.

Youth Hostels Association (YHA) A British organization, founded in 1930, to promote a greater understanding of the countryside, especially by providing hostels where young people of limited means may stay. There are over 250 hostels in England and Wales.

Youth Training Scheme (YTS). *See* Training Agency.

Ypres (Flemish name: Ieper) 50 51N 2 53E A town in W Belgium, on the River Yperlee. Its many medieval buildings were almost completely destroyed during World War I. Population (1985 est): 35 000.

ytterbium (Yb) A lanthanide element, named after Ytterby in Sweden. It forms trivalent compounds, including the oxide (Yb_2O_3) and trihalides (for example $YbCl_3$). At no 70; at wt 173.04; mp 819°C; bp 1194°C.

yttrium (Y) A lanthanide element, discovered in 1794 by J. Gadolin (1760–1852). It is widely used as the oxide (Y_2O_3) to make red television-tube phosphors. At no 39; at wt 88.906; mp 1522 ± 8°C; bp 3338°C.

Yuan (1279–1368) A Mongol dynasty that ruled China after overthrowing the Song dynasty. The first and strongest Mongol ruler was Kublai Khan, who held the empire together by military force.

Yucatán A peninsula of Central America, chiefly in SE Mexico but extending into Belize and Guatemala, separating the Gulf of Mexico from the Caribbean Sea. It was a centre of Maya civilization. Area: about 181 300 sq km (70 00 sq mi).

Yucca A genus of succulent plants (about 40 species), native to S North America and varying in height from small shrubs to 15-m-high trees. Most are stemless and have a rosette of stiff sword-shaped leaves crowded on a stout trunk. The waxy white bell-shaped flowers are pollinated by female yucca moths (genus *Pronuba*). Several species are cultivated as ornamentals, including Adam's needle (*Y. filamentosa*) and Spanish dagger (*Y. gloriosa*). Family: *Agavaceae. See also* Joshua tree.

Yugoslavia, Socialist Federal Republic of (Serbo-Croat name: Jugoslavia) A country in SE Europe, on the Adriatic Sea. Fertile plains in the NE rise to mountains in the S and W. The Serbs and the Croats make up the majority of the population. *Economy*: agriculture is organized in cooperatives. Livestock is especially important and the principal crops are wheat, maize, sugar beet, sunflowers, and potatoes. There is a thriving wine industry and forestry and fishing are important sources of revenue. Rich mineral resources include coal, iron ore, copper, and lead, and some oil is produced. Development of heavy and light industry has been rapid since World War II and there is a growing tourist industry. *History*: Yugoslavia was so named in 1927 but was formed in 1918 as the kingdom of the Serbs, Croats, and Slovenes by the federation of Serbia, Montenegro, Croatia, Slovenia, and Bosnia-Herzegovina. Alexander I assumed absolute power in 1929 and was assassinated by

Croatian nationalists in 1934. In World War II Yugoslavia was occupied by the Germans and Peter II fled to London. Internal resistance became divided between the Chetniks and the Partisans. After the war the Partisans' leader Tito became head of a communist government. Since 1948 Yugoslavia has preserved a policy of nonalignment in foreign affairs. Since Tito's death a new premier is chosen each year. In the late 1980s there was increasing ethnic unrest in Serbia and elsewhere and Slovenia threatened to secede from Yugoslavia. In 1990 the Communist Party gave up its monopoly of power and free elections were promised. Official languages: all national languages, with Serbo-Croat serving as the lingua franca. Official currency: dinar of 100 para. Area: 255 804 sq km (98 725 sq mi). Population (1987): 23 433 000. Capital: Belgrade. Main port: Rijeka.

Yukawa, Hideki (1907–81) Japanese physicist, who postulated (1935) that the strong interaction could be accounted for by the exchange of virtual particles. He calculated the mass of the particle involved. Confirmation came in 1947, when Cecil Powell (1903–69) discovered the pion. Yukawa won a Nobel Prize in 1949.

Yukon A territory of NW Canada, on the Beaufort Sea. It is covered by tundra in the N. Poor soils and low precipitation produce only sparse vegetation, except in S valleys. The population is concentrated on the central plateau, where silver, lead, zinc, copper, and asbestos are mined. There is some lumbering and tourism. The Yukon was first opened up by the Klondike gold rush (1897–99). Area: 531 844 sq km (205 345 sq mi). Population (1986 est): 26 166. Capital: Whitehorse.

Yukon River A river in NW North America. Rising in NW Canada, it flows N through Alaska, USA, then SW into the Bering Sea. Length: 3185 km (1979 mi).

YWCA. *See* Young Women's Christian Association.

Z

Zagreb 45 48N 15 58E The second largest city of Yugoslavia, on the River Sava. A cultural centre of the Croats since the 16th century, it possesses a gothic cathedral. Population (1981): 1 174 512.

Zagros Mountains A mountain system in W Iran, extending 1600 km (994 mi) NW–SE between the Soviet border and the Strait of Hormuz. It rises to 4811 m (15 784 ft) at Sabalan.

Zaïre, Republic of (name from 1960 until 1971: Congo) A large country in central equatorial Africa, with a short coastline on the Atlantic Ocean. The central part of the country is dominated by a vast plateau, rising to the Ruwenzori Mountains in the SE. Most of the population is African, the largest groups being Luba, Mongo, and Kongo. *Economy*: efforts are being made to increase agricultural production, which has fallen in recent years through droughts and political unrest. The chief cash crops are coffee, cotton, palm oil, and rubber. Zaïre has rich and varied mineral resources, principally copper (the chief export) from the Shaba mines, and is the world's chief producer of industrial diamonds and cobalt. Other minerals include manganese, zinc, and uranium and oil has been found offshore (exploited since 1975). Zaïre is estimated to have about 50% of Africa's total potential hydroelectric capacity. The rivers, especially the Zaïre River, are also important for transport. *History*: when the Portuguese penetrated the region in the late 15th century it was dominated by the kingdom of the Kongo. In the late 19th century it was explored by Livingstone and, under Belgian auspices, by Stanley. Leopold II of the Belgians established personal rule over the Congo Free State, which was recognized by the European powers at the Conference of Berlin (1884–85). In 1908 it was annexed by Belgium, becoming the colony of the Belgian Congo. Independence was obtained in 1960, as the Republic of the Congo. The almost immediate secession of Katanga province under Tshombe resulted in civil war in which the UN intervened (an international force remained in the country until 1964). In 1965 Mobutu Sese Seko seized power and in 1971 the Congo was renamed Zaïre. In 1977 and again in 1978 an inva-sion force entered Shaba (formerly Katanga) province from Angola, in unsuccessful attempts to topple Mobutu, and on the second occasion the massacre of Europeans in Kolwezi brought French and Belgian forces to Zaïre. In 1978 Zaïre became a one-party state. Official language: French. Official currency, since 1967: zaïre of 100 makuta. Area: 2 345 409 sq km (895 348 sq mi). Population (1987 est): 31 780 000. Capital: Kinshasa. Main port: Matadi.

Zaïre River (former name: Congo R.) The second longest river in Africa. Its source is disputed, one headstream being the River Lualaba and the other the River Chambezi (later the River Luvua). Below the confluence it flows N, being known as the Lualaba until the Boyoma Falls, where it becomes the Zaïre River. It flows generally W then SW to enter the Atlantic Ocean at Boma. The Zaïre River is an important potential source of hydroelectric power with the construction of dams in the 1970s. Length: 4820 km (3000 mi).

zaltys A green snake that was a symbol of wealth and fertility in the Baltic region in ancient times. Households often kept a zaltys and it was believed that misfortune would befall anyone who killed one.

Zambezi River A river in S Africa. Rising in NW Zambia, it flows generally S through E Angola before re-entering Zambia and curving E along the Caprivi Strip frontier of Namibia. It then forms the Zambia–Zimbabwe border, the Victoria Falls and Kariba Dam being located along this course, before flowing SE to enter the Indian Ocean. It has a drainage area of about 1 347 000 sq km (520 000 sq mi). Length: 2740 km (1700 mi).

Zambia, Republic of (name until 1964: Northern Rhodesia) A landlocked country in S central Africa. It consists chiefly of low undulating plateaus and is drained along its southern border by the Zambezi River; other main rivers are the Kafue and Luangwa. The population is largely Bantu, with small minorities of Europeans, Asians, and Chinese. *Economy*: copper accounts for about 96% of the total mineral production and comes mainly from the Copperbelt. Lead and zinc from Kabwe are also important, some coal is mined, and there are extensive iron-ore deposits, as yet unexploited. Agriculture is a major occupation; the chief subsistence crop is maize. Cash crops include tobacco, groundnuts, cotton, and sugar. Livestock and forestry are also important. *History*: the area had already been occupied by Bantu peoples when it was raided by Arab slave traders in the 18th century. In the 19th century British missionaries, notably Livingstone, paved the way for Cecil Rhodes, who incorporated the region into a territory named Rhodesia in his honour and administered by the British South Africa Company. Constituted as Northern Rhodesia in 1911, it became a British protectorate in 1924. It formed part of the Federation of Rhodesia and Nyasaland (1953–63), obtaining internal self-government and, shortly afterwards, full independence within the British Commonwealth as the Republic of Zambia (1964). Kaunda has been president since independence. In 1972 a new constitution led to one-party (the United National Independence Party) rule. Official language: English. Official currency, since 1968: kwacha of 100 ngwee. Area: 752 262 sq km (290 586 sq mi). Population (1987 est): 7 120 000. Capital: Lusaka.

Zanzibar An island in Tanzania, off the NE coast of the mainland. It came under Arab influence early on in its history and was, together with Pemba, a sultanate from 1856 to 1964. It was under British rule from 1890 until it became independent within the British Commonwealth in 1963. In 1964 the Sultan was exiled and Zanzibar united with Tanganyika to form Tanzania. It exports mainly cloves and copra. Area: 1658 sq km (640 sq mi). Population (1985 est): 571 000. Chief town: Zanzibar.

EMILIANO ZAPATA

Zapata, Emiliano (?1877–1919) Mexican revolutionary, who championed the cause of agrarian reform against the president Porfirio Díaz (1830–1915) and succeeding governments. By late 1911 he controlled the state of Morelos, where he carried out land reforms, chasing out the estate owners and dividing their land amongst the peasants. In 1919 he was tricked into an ambush and assassinated.

Zaporozhye (name until 1921: Aleksandrovsk) 47 50N 35 10E A city in the SW Soviet Union, on the River Dnepr. A large hydroelectric station, built here in the

years 1927–32, was destroyed in World War II but subsequently rebuilt. Population (1987): 875 000.

Zapotecs An American Indian people of the Oaxaca valleys (S Mexico). Their traditional culture, emerging about 300 AD, developed into one of the classic Mesoamerican Indian civilizations. Monte Alban, their chief city, declined under pressure from the Mixtecs (c. 900–50).

Zaragoza (English name: Saragossa) 41 39N 0 54W A city in NE Spain, in Aragon on the River Ebro. During the Peninsular War it heroically resisted a French siege until about 50 000 of its defenders had died (1808–09). It has two cathedrals and a university (founded 1533). An industrial centre, Zaragoza produces paper and wine. Population (1981): 590 750.

Zarathustra. *See* Zoroaster.

Zealots A Jewish political party of the 1st century AD. They were bitterly opposed to Roman rule in Judaea, and played a leading part in the revolt of 66 AD. Their last stronghold, Masada, fell in 73. After the war their influence in Judaea was minimal but they may have been responsible for the further revolts in Egypt, Libya, and Cyprus in 115 AD.

zebra An African wild horse having characteristic black and white stripes covering part or all of the body. There are three races of the plains zebra (*Equus burchelli*), distinguished by the extent and nature of their stripes. The mountain zebra (*E. zebra*) has very bold stripes and a dewlap on the throat, while Grévy's zebra (*E. grevyi*) is the largest species, standing over 1.5 m at the shoulder with narrow stripes.

zebra finch An Australian grassfinch, *Taeniopyga castanotis*, occurring in large flocks in the interior grasslands. It has a red bill and the males are grey above with white underparts, reddish flanks, red-brown ear patches, and black-and-white barred throat, breast, and tail. Zebra finches are popular cagebirds and have been selectively bred to produce a white form with the black-and-white barring.

zebra fish A tropical freshwater fish, *Brachydanio rerio*, also called zebra danio, found in E India and popular in aquaria. It has a shiny blue body, up to 4.5 cm long, with four longitudinal yellowish gold stripes along its sides. *See also* scorpion fish.

zebu The domestic cattle of Asia and Africa, *Bos indicus*, also called Brahmin (*or* Brahman). Larger and leaner than western cattle, zebus have a distinctive hump over the shoulders, a large dewlap under the throat, and long horns. Zebus are no longer found in the wild and have been exported to hot countries for their heat tolerance and insect resistance in crosses with beef breeds.

Zeebrugge 51 20N 3 13E A small port in NW Belgium, on the North Sea, connected by ship canal (1907) to Bruges. A German submarine base in World War I, the canal was blocked by British naval forces in 1918. In 1987 the British ferry *Herald of Free Enterprise* capsized here, with the loss of 193 lives.

Zeeman, Pieter (1865–1943) Dutch physicist, who discovered (1886) the splitting of the spectral lines of a substance when placed in a magnetic field (**Zeeman effect**). It is caused by changes in the energy levels of the electrons of the emitting atoms as a result of interaction between the magnetic moment of the orbit and the external field. For this discovery he shared the 1902 Nobel Prize with Hendrik Lorentz (1853–1928).

Zeffirelli, G. Franco (1923–) Italian director and stage designer. Having started as an actor under the direction of Visconti, he went on to direct film versions of *The Taming of the Shrew* (1966) and *Romeo and Juliet* (1968). Other films include *Jesus of Nazareth* (1975), *La Traviata* (1983), and *Otello* (1986). He has worked on numerous operas at Covent Garden, Glyndebourne, the Metropolitan, New York, and in Italy. His many stage productions include *Othello* (Stratford-upon-Avon, 1961) *Hamlet* (Old Vic, 1964), and *Filumena* (1977).

Zen Buddhism (Japanese *Zen*, meditation) In China and Japan, a Buddhist school emphasizing the transmission of enlightenment from master to disciple without reliance on the scriptures. It derives from the teaching of Bodhidharma, who came to China in 520 AD. The two major sects, Soto and Rinzai, stress meditation and the use of logical paradoxes (*koans*) respectively, in order to confound the rational mind so that transcendental wisdom can arise and the disciple can realize his own Buddha-nature. Much of Japanese and Chinese art, music, and literature, as well as calligraphy, the tea ceremony, the martial arts, etc., express the spontaneous Zen attitude to life. Recently Zen has gained followers in the West, where its opposition to rationalism has popular appeal.

zenith The point in the sky lying directly above an observer and 90° from all points on his horizon. The (unobservable) point diametrically opposite the zenith is the **nadir**.

Zenobia (3rd century AD) The wife of Odaenathus of Palmyra, whom she may have murdered (267) and whom she succeeded as regent for their son. Zenobia occupied Syria, Egypt, and much of Asia Minor before the Roman emperor Aurelian (c. 215–275 AD) defeated and captured her in 272. She enjoyed a reputation for beauty and intelligence.

Zeno of Citium (c. 335–262 BC) Greek philosopher, who was born in Cyprus of Phoenician stock, came to Athens in 313 BC, and attended lectures at Plato's Academy. He was influenced by various philosophical schools, including the Cynics, before evolving his own doctrine of Stoicism.

Zeno of Elea (born c. 490 BC) Greek philosopher. Zeno's paradoxes, supporting the doctrines of the Greek philosopher Parmenides (c. 510–c. 450 BC) that reality is indivisible and reason is at variance with the senses, are the first dialectic arguments, eliciting contradictory conclusions from an opponent's hypotheses. These paradoxes include: Achilles and the tortoise–if space is infinitely divisible, once Achilles has given the tortoise a start he cannot overtake it, for whenever he arrives where the tortoise was it has already moved on; the flying arrow–if space is divisible into finite parts, a moving arrow at each moment of its flight is opposite a particular piece of ground and therefore stationary.

zeolites A group of complex silicate minerals containing loosely held water. They are divided into three groups: fibrous (natrolite, mesolite, scolecite), platy (heulandite, stilbite), and equant (harmatome, chabazite). Most occur in cavities in basic volcanic rocks. They are usually colourless or white and are relatively soft. Because of their property of base exchange they were used as water softeners before the introduction of artificial substitutes. They are also used as molecular sieves in the petroleum industry and as drying agents.

Zeppelins. *See* airships.

Zetland. *See* Shetland Islands.

Zeus The Greek sky and weather god, the supreme deity, identified with the Roman Jupiter. He was the son of Cronus and Rhea, and brother of Poseidon and Hades. His defeat of Cronus and the Titans represents the triumph of the Olympian deities over their predecessors. His offspring included Athena, Apollo, and Dionysus and from his many love affairs, which excited the jealousy of his wife, Hera, were produced numerous other divine and semidivine children. He was usually portrayed as a bearded man, with thunderbolts and the eagle as his attributes.

Zeus, statue of The chryselephantine statue designed by the Greek sculptor Phidias in about 430 BC for the temple of Zeus at Olympia. One of the Seven Wonders of the World, it was 12 m (40 ft) high and covered with jewels and gold. It was destroyed in the 5th century AD.

Zhangjiakou (*or* Chang-chia-k'ou; Mongolian name: Kalgan) 40 51N 114 59E A city in NE China, in Hebei province near the Great Wall. It was historically important for defence against and trade with the Mongols and is the site of two forts (1429, 1613). Population (1980 est): 1 094 000.

Zhengzhou (*or* Cheng-chou) 34 35N 113 38E A city in E China, the capital of Henan province. An old administrative centre, it has many industries developed since 1949. Population (1986): 1 590 000.

Zhou (?1027–221 BC) The earliest Chinese dynasty of which there is accurate knowledge. The dynasty was founded in the area now called Shenxi after the Zhou ruler, Wu Wang, had annihilated the armies of the preceding Shang dynasty and set up a system of government under feudal rulers. These undermined Zhou authority in the so-called Warring States period (481–221), after which the Qin emerged to unite China. Under the Zhou human sacrifice was abolished and the Chinese idea of ancestor worship came into being. The late Zhou was also the great period of Chinese philosophy, when Taoist and Confucian thought first emerged.

Zhukov, Georgi Konstantinovich (1896–1974) Soviet marshal. An armoured-warfare expert, he became chief of the army general staff (1941). He planned or commanded almost every major Soviet military operation in World War II, including the Soviet occupation force in Germany. Under Khrushchev he became defence minister and then a member of the presidium of the Communist Party.

Ziegfeld, Florenz (1867–1932) US theatrical producer. His lavish revues were modelled on the Folies-Bergère. *The Ziegfeld Follies*, billed as "An American Institution," appeared annually from 1907 until his death. Using the slogan, "Glorifying the American Girl," he created such hits as *Sally* (1920), *Show Boat* (1927), and *Bitter Sweet* (1929). He also launched Will Rogers, W. C. Fields, Eddie Cantor, and others on their careers.

Ziegler, Karl (1898–1973) German chemist, who shared the 1963 Nobel Prize with Giulio Natta (1903–) for their work on plastics and polymers. Ziegler showed that certain organometallic compounds (**Ziegler catalysts**) would catalyze the polymerization of ethylene giving unbranched polymers that were tougher and had a higher melting point than those previously obtainable.

ZIGGURAT   *An imaginary view of the Tower of Babel.*

ziggurat   An ancient Mesopotamian brick-built temple tower. Ziggurats were constructed of rectangular terraces of diminishing size, generally with a shrine for the god on top. They existed in every major Sumerian, Babylonian, and Assyrian centre, the one at Babylon being the probable original of the Tower of Babel.

ZIMBABWE   *Robert Mugabe.*

Zimbabwe, State of (name until 1979: Rhodesia)   A landlocked country in SE Africa. It is bounded in the N by the Zambezi River and in the S by the Limpopo River. Much of the land consists of plateau, generally over 1000 m (3300 ft), with extensive areas of savanna. The majority of the population is Bantu with small minorities of Europeans, Asians, and others. *Economy*: agriculture is important, but the imposing of economic sanctions (1965–79) has changed its emphasis. The production of tobacco has declined and a diversification to cotton and cattle has taken place; other cash crops include sugar, tea, and citrus fruit. The chief subsistence crops are maize, millet, and groundnuts. Forestry and fishing are important with fish farming on Lake Kariba. Zimbabwe has rich mineral resources including copper, asbestos, gold, chrome, and nickel, but it has no oil

reserves. Industry is expanding. *History*: ruins at Great Zimbabwe attest the existence of a medieval Bantu civilization in the region. In 1837 its Mashona inhabitants were conquered by the Matabele and later in the 19th century it was explored by European missionaries, notably David Livingstone. In 1889 Cecil Rhodes obtained a charter for the British South Africa Company, which conquered the Matabele and their territory, named Rhodesia (1895) in Rhodes' honour. In 1911 it was divided into Northern Rhodesia (now Zambia) and Southern Rhodesia, the latter becoming a self-governing British colony in 1922. In 1953 the two parts of Rhodesia were reunited in the Federation of Rhodesia and Nyasaland, and after its dissolution in 1963 the Whites demanded independence for Southern Rhodesia (Rhodesia from 1964). The UK's refusal to permit independence without a guarantee of majority rule led the prime minister Ian Smith to issue a unilateral declaration of independence (UDI) in 1965. Both the UK and the UN imposed economic sanctions but these proved fruitless. In 1970 Rhodesia declared itself a republic. In 1974 the Rhodesian government opened negotiations with the leaders of the Zimbabwe African People's Union (ZAPU) and the Zimbabwe African National Union (ZANU), which had pursued guerrilla activities since the 1960s. Smith failed to negotiate an agreement with the Black nationalists, who remained divided under the umbrella of the African National Council (ANC). In 1978, following the intervention of the US secretary of state Kissinger (1976) and the UK (1977), agreement was reached between Smith and the ANC on a transitional government leading to Black majority rule. However, the failure of the subsequent government under Muzorewa to obtain the support of the Patriotic Front led to agreement at the 1979 Commonwealth Conference to hold an all-party conference to achieve internal unity. Following this conference (1979–80), Lord Soames (1920–87) was appointed governor to oversee the disarming of guerrillas, the holding of elections (which Robert Mugabe won), and the granting of independence to Zimbabwe as a member of the Commonwealth (1980). In 1987 ZAPU and ZANU were unified and Mugabe became president of a one-party state. Official language: English; the most important African languages are Ndebele and Shona. Official currency, since 1979: Zimbabwe dollar of 100 cents. Area: 390 622 sq km (150 820 sq mi). Population (1987 est): 8 640 000. Capital: Harare (formerly Salisbury).

zinc (Zn)   A bluish-white metal known in antiquity in India and the Middle East. It occurs in nature principally in the ores calamine ($ZnCO_3$), zincite (ZnO), and zinc blende (ZnS). Zinc is widely used to make galvanized steel and forms a number of useful low-melting alloys, including brass. The sulphide (ZnS) is a phosphor and is used in making television screens and fluorescent tubes. Zinc oxide (ZnO) is widely used as a pigment and in medicines, batteries, cosmetics, plastics, and other products. Trace amounts of zinc are also important for growth in animals, including human beings. At no 30; at wt 65.37; mp 419.58°C; bp 907°C.

zincite   A minor ore of zinc, consisting of zinc oxide. It is often found in association with sphalerite and probably results from the alteration of sphalerite. It usually contains some manganese.

Zinnia   A genus of herbs and shrubs (about 15 species), mostly native to North America. They have stiff hairy stems, oval to heart-shaped leaves, and daisy-like flower heads with yellow or brownish central disc florets and variously coloured ray florets. Cultivated zinnias are hybrids derived from the Mexican species *Z. elegans*. They have double flowers, about 11 cm across, and most are half-hardy annuals. Family: *Compositae*.

Zinoviev, Grigori Yevseevich (1883–1936) Soviet politician. Zinoviev became a member of the politburo (1918) and chairman of the Comintern (1919) but was expelled from the Communist Party in 1927. In 1935 he was accused of complicity in the murder of Sergei Kirov (1888–1934) and was executed. A letter allegedly written by Zinoviev, in which the British Communist Party was urged to revolt, contributed to the defeat of the Labour Government in 1924.

Zion (*or* Sion) A stronghold (II Samuel 5.6–7) on the SE hill of Jerusalem, captured by David, who made it the centre of his capital (Jerusalem). Another name for Jerusalem, it is also described throughout the Old Testament as the place in which God dwells and reigns. In the New Testament and in later Christian writings, it symbolizes heaven.

Zionism A Jewish nationalist movement. It emerged during the 19th century on a tide of European antisemitism and was formally established at the First Zionist Congress (Basle, 1897). The Congress defined its political aim as the establishment of a Jewish national home in Palestine; the World Zionist Organization was set up, with Theodor Herzl as its first president. Jewish immigration into Palestine (*aliyah*) was encouraged, especially through the Jewish National Fund (founded 1901) and the Jewish Agency for Palestine (1929). It was also supported by the Balfour Declaration, facilitated by Chaim Weizmann's relationship with the British government. After World War II, the holocaust provided Zionism with an unanswerable case. Since the establishment of Israel in 1948 the Zionist movement has continued to foster *aliyah* and support for and interest in Israel.

zircon A mineral consisting of zirconium silicate, found as an accessory mineral in intermediate and acid igneous rocks. It is usually colourless or yellowish. Gem varieties include hyacinth (red) and jargoon (colourless or smoky grey). It is the chief ore of zirconium and is used as a refractory material.

zirconium (Zr) A grey high-melting-point transition metal, isolated by J. J. Berzelius in 1824. It occurs in nature as zircon (zirconium silicate; $ZrSiO_4$), which is used as a gemstone. The dioxide (zirconia; ZrO_2) has a high melting point (2715°C) and is used as a refractory and crucible material. The metal is used in cladding fuel elements in nuclear reactors. At no 40; at wt 91.22; mp 1852°C; bp 4377°C.

zither A plucked stringed instrument of ancient origin, consisting of a flat resonating box fitted with 30 to 40 strings, approximately 5 of which lie across a fretted fingerboard for playing the melody. The rest are used for playing accompanying chords. It is particularly popular in Bavaria and the Tirol.

zodiac A zone of the heavens extending about 8° on either side of the ecliptic. Within it lies the apparent annual path of the sun, as seen from the earth, and the orbits of the moon, and major planets, apart from Pluto. The 12 constellations in the zodiac are known as "signs" or "houses" to astrologers, who believe them capable of stamping their individual dispositions upon those born under their influence (*see* astrology). The 12 signs and their astrologically effective dates (different from their

ZODIAC *The signs of the zodiac from* De astrorum scientia *by Leopold of Austria (Augsburg, 1489).*

astronomical periods on account of precession) are: Aries, the Ram 21 Mar–19 Apr; Taurus, the Bull 20 Apr–20 May; Gemini, the Twins 21 May–21 June; Cancer, the Crab 22 June–22 July; Leo, the Lion 23 July–22 Aug; Virgo, the Virgin 23 Aug–22 Sept; Libra, the Scales 23 Sept–23 Oct; Scorpio, the Scorpion 24 Oct–21 Nov; Sagittarius, the Archer 22 Nov–21 Dec; Capricornus, the Goat 22 Dec–19 Jan; Aquarius, the Water-carrier 20 Jan–18 Feb; and Pisces, the Fish 19 Feb–20 Mar.

zodiacal light A faint glow that is visible in the western sky just after sunset and the eastern sky just before sunrise, especially in the tropics. It can be seen along the direction of the ecliptic, tapering upwards from the horizon to an altitude of perhaps 20°. It is sunlight reflected from interplanetary dust particles.

Zog I (1895–1961) King of Albania (1928–39). Zog was proclaimed king after serving as prime minister (1922–24) and president (1925–28). He let Albania fall under Italian economic domination and when Mussolini invaded Albania (1939), he fled into exile.

Zohar (Hebrew: splendour) The classical text of the kabbalah. Written in Aramaic, it purports to be a mystical commentary on the Torah and a collection of theosophical discussions dating from the time of the Mishnah. It was actually written about 1280 by the Spanish kabbalist Moses de Leon, although it contains some later additions.

Zola, Émile (1840–1902) French novelist. He worked as a journalist and a clerk in a publishing firm until the success of his first major novel, *Thérèse Raquin* (1867). He then dedicated himself to a literary career, conceiving the plan for the series of 20 novels entitled *Les*

Rougon-Macquart (1871–93). *L'Assommoir* (1877) describes the effects of drink on the disintegration of a working-class family. *Nana* (1880), concerning a girl from the slums, *Germinal* (1885), about a mining community, and *La Terre* (1887), concerning the life of peasants, are among his outstanding novels. He fled to England after defending Dreyfus in an open letter, *J'accuse* (1898), but was welcomed back as a hero after Dreyfus had been cleared of the charges against him.

Zollverein A customs union of 18 German states formed under Prussian dominance in 1834. By 1867 all German states except Hamburg and Bremen had joined. This commercial union helped pave the way for German unification under Prussian leadership (1871).

zoogeography The study of the geographical distribution of animals. It is based mainly on the work of A. R. Wallace (with later modifications), who divided the world into a number of zoogeographical regions, each with a distinctive fauna. The present-day distribution of animals reflects both their evolutionary history and the movements of the land masses in past geological ages (*see* continental drift). Thus the concentration of marsupials in the Australasian region is explained by the fact that the separation of Australia from the Asian mainland coincided with the evolutionary radiation of this group. The Australian marsupials therefore avoided competing with the more efficient placental mammals, which subsequently evolved on the mainland.

zoology The branch of biological sciences specializing in the scientific study of animals. This includes their classification, anatomy, physiology, ecology, behaviour, evolution, etc. The importance of animals as food producers, pests, etc., in relation to man makes many aspects of zoology economically significant. *See also* entomology; ornithology.

Zoroaster (*or* Zarathustra; c. 628–c. 551 BC) Iranian prophet, founder of Zoroastrianism. Probably born near Tehran, he is believed to have been a priest in the ancient polytheistic religion when he received a vision of Ahura Mazda, who exhorted him to preach a new faith based on his worship. Zoroaster introduced reforms, abolishing orgiastic rituals, although animal sacrifice and the ancient fire cult continued to be practised. The teachings attributed to him are preserved in the Gathas (hymns) in the Avesta.

Zoroastrianism The pre-Islamic dualistic religion of Persia founded by Zoroaster, surviving there in some areas and in India among the Parsees (*see* Parseeism). It recognizes two principles, good and evil, as personified by Ahura Mazda and Ahriman. Ahura Mazda will eventually triumph, resurrecting the dead and creating a paradise on earth, presaged by the return of Zoroaster. Procreation and life are extolled, but death defiles—hence the custom of exposing corpses to be devoured by vultures.

Zuccarelli, Francesco (1702–88) Italian painter. He worked chiefly in Venice (after 1732) and in England (1752–62, 1765–71). A founding member of the Royal Academy and a favourite painter of George III, he specialized in picturesque landscapes.

Zuccari Two Italian painters, born at Sant' Angelo in Vado. Both leading figures in Roman mannerism, **Taddeo Zuccari** (1529–66) is known for his frescoes, while his brother and pupil **Federico Zuccari** (c. 1540–1609)

ZOOGEOGRAPHY *The world can be divided into six regions according to the distribution of its animals. Since some animals are less fixed in their habitats than others and may be found in more than one region, the divisions between the regions are somewhat arbitrary. For example, Wallace's line, separating the Oriental and Australasian regions, has since been modified.*

was also an art theorist. Federico painted Elizabeth I in England (1575) and decorated the dome of the Duomo, Florence, and the high altar in the Escorial.

zucchini. *See* courgette.

Zuider Zee A former inlet of the SE North Sea, within the Netherlands. The N part, the Waddenzee, is separated from the S part (now the IJsselmeer) by a huge dam (completed 1932).

Zululand An area of South Africa, in NE Natal. The home of the Zulu people, it became a powerful state during the 1820s under their king Shaka (c. 1787–1828). Following conflict with the Boers the Zulus, under Cetshwayo (c. 1826–84), were defeated by the British (1879) and Zululand was incorporated into Natal in 1897. It comprises part of the Bantu Homeland of KwaZulu.

Zulus A Bantu people of Natal (South Africa). They are traditionally cattle herders and cattle are still a prestige possession. Polygyny is practised by important men.

In the 19th century under Shaka (c. 1787–1828), the Zulus conquered an extensive empire until eventually defeated in wars with the Europeans. Their highly efficient military organization was based on the age-set system; warriors could not marry until they attained a certain grade. Ancestor worship and witchcraft were prominent in their religious beliefs and the king had important ritual functions. Today, many Zulus are migrant labourers.

Zürich 47 23N 8 33E The largest city in Switzerland, on Lake Zürich. It is the commercial and industrial centre of Switzerland. Zürich's Alpine setting has contributed to the rise of its tourist industry. The Romans occupied the site in the 1st century BC. During the middle ages it became the most important Swiss town and joined the Swiss confederation in 1351. A leading centre of the Reformation, Zürich became a refuge for those persecuted in the Counter-Reformation. Population (1985): 351 500.

zygote. *See* fertilization.

PRIME MINISTERS

GREAT BRITAIN (from 1721)

Name	Sovereign	Term
Robert Walpole	George I, II	1721-42
Spencer Compton, Earl of Wilmington	George II	1742-43
Henry Pelham	George II	1743-54
Thomas Pelham-Holles, Duke of Newcastle	George II	1754-56
William Cavendish, Duke of Devonshire	George II	1756-57
Thomas Pelham-Holles, Duke of Newcastle	George II, III	1757-62
John Stuart, Earl of Bute	George III	1762-63
George Grenville	George III	1763-65
Charles Watson-Wentworth, Marquis of Rockingham	George III	1765-66
William Pitt, Earl of Chatham	George III	1766-68
Augustus Henry Fitzroy, Duke of Grafton	George III	1768-70
Frederick North	George III	1770-82
Charles Watson-Wentworth, Marquis of Rockingham	George III	1782
William Petty, Earl of Shelburne	George III	1782-83
William Henry Cavendish Bentinck, Duke of Portland	George III	1783
William Pitt (son of Earl of Chatham)	George III	1783-1801
Henry Addington	George III	1801-04
William Pitt	George III	1804-06
William Wyndham Grenville, Baron Grenville	George III	1806-07
William Bentinck, Duke of Portland	George III	1807-09
Spencer Perceval	George III	1809-12
Robert Banks Jenkinson, Earl of Liverpool	George III, IV	1812-27
George Canning	George IV	1827
Frederick John Robinson, Viscount Goderich	George IV	1827-28
Arthur Wellesley, Duke of Wellington	George IV, William IV	1828-30
Charles Grey, Earl Grey	William IV	1830-34
William Lamb, Viscount Melbourne	William IV	1834
Robert Peel	William IV	1834-35
William Lamb, Viscount Melbourne	William IV, Victoria	1835-41
Robert Peel	Victoria	1841-46
John Russell	Victoria	1846-52
Edward George Geoffrey Smith Stanley, Earl of Derby	Victoria	1852
George Hamilton Gordon, Earl of Aberdeen	Victoria	1852-55
Henry John Temple, Viscount Palmerston	Victoria	1855-58
Edward Stanley, Earl of Derby	Victoria	1858-59
Henry Temple, Viscount Palmerston	Victoria	1859-65
John Russell, Earl Russell	Victoria	1865-66
Edward Stanley, Earl of Derby	Victoria	1866-68
Benjamin Disraeli	Victoria	1868
William Ewart Gladstone	Victoria	1868-74
Benjamin Disraeli, Earl (1876) of Beaconsfield	Victoria	1874-80
William Ewart Gladstone	Victoria	1880-85
Robert A. T. Gascoyne-Cecil, Marquis of Salisbury	Victoria	1885-86
William Ewart Gladstone	Victoria	1886
Robert Gascoyne-Cecil, Marquis of Salisbury	Victoria	1886-92
William Ewart Gladstone	Victoria	1892-94
Archibald Philip Primrose, Earl of Rosebery	Victoria	1894-95
Robert Gascoyne-Cecil, Marquis of Salisbury	Victoria, Edward VII	1895-1902
Arthur James Balfour	Edward VII	1902-05
Henry Campbell-Bannerman	Edward VII	1905-08
Herbert Henry Asquith	Edward VII, George V	1908-16
David Lloyd George	George V	1916-22
Andrew Bonar Law	George V	1922-23
Stanley Baldwin	George V	1923-24
James Ramsay MacDonald	George V	1924
Stanley Baldwin	George V	1924-29
James Ramsay MacDonald	George V	1929-35
Stanley Baldwin	George V, Edward VIII, George VI	1935-37
Neville Chamberlain	George VI	1937-40
Winston Churchill	George VI	1940-45
Clement Richard Attlee	George VI	1945-51
Winston Churchill	George VI, Elizabeth II	1951-55
Anthony Eden	Elizabeth II	1955-57
Harold Macmillan	Elizabeth II	1957-63
Alec Douglas-Home	Elizabeth II	1963-64
Harold Wilson	Elizabeth II	1964-70
Edward Heath	Elizabeth II	1970-74
Harold Wilson	Elizabeth II	1974-76
James Callaghan	Elizabeth II	1976-79
Margaret Thatcher	Elizabeth II	1979-

AUSTRALIA

Edmund Barton	1901-03	
Alfred Deakin	1903-04	
John C. Watson	1904	
George Houstoun Reid	1904-05	
Alfred Deakin	1905-08	
Andrew Fisher	1908-09	
Alfred Deakin	1909-10	
Andrew Fisher	1910-13	
Joseph Cook	1913-14	
Andrew Fisher	1914-15	
William M. Hughes	1915-23	
Stanley M. Bruce	1923-29	
James H. Scullin	1929-31	
Joseph A. Lyons	1932-39	
Robert Gordon Menzies	1939-41	
Arthur William Fadden	1941	
John Curtin	1941-45	
Joseph Benedict Chifley	1945-49	
Robert Gordon Menzies	1949-66	
Harold Edward Holt	1966-67	
John Grey Gorton	1968-71	
William McMahon	1971-72	
Gough Whitlam	1972-75	
J. Malcolm Fraser	1975-83	
Robert Hawke	1983-	

CANADA

John A. Macdonald	1867-73
Alexander Mackenzie	1873-78
John A. Macdonald	1878-91
John J. C. Abbott	1891-92
John S. D. Thompson	1892-94
Mackenzie Bowell	1894-96
Charles Tupper	1896
Wilfrid Laurier	1896-1911
Robert L. Borden	1911-20
Arthur Meighen	1920-21
W. L. Mackenzie King	1921-26
Arthur Meighen	1926
W. L. Mackenzie King	1926-30
Richard B. Bennett	1930-35
W. L. Mackenzie King	1935-48
Louis Stephen St. Laurent	1948-57
John George Diefenbaker	1957-63
Lester B. Pearson	1963-68
Pierre Elliott Trudeau	1968-79
Joseph Clark	1979-80
Pierre Elliott Trudeau	1980-84
John Turner	1984
Brian Mulroney	1984-

NEW ZEALAND

Henry Sewell	1856
William Fox	1856
Edward William Stafford	1856-61
William Fox	1861-62
Alfred Domett	1862-63
Frederick Whitaker	1863-64
Frederick Aloysius Weld	1864-65
Edward William Stafford	1865-69
William Fox	1869-72
Edward William Stafford	1872
George Marsden Waterhouse	1872-73
William Fox	1873
Julius Vogel	1873-75
Daniel Pollen	1875-76
Julius Vogel	1876
Harry Albert Atkinson	1876-77
George Grey	1877-79
John Hall	1879-82
Frederick Whitaker	1882-83
Harry Albert Atkinson	1883-84
Robert Stout	1884
Harry Albert Atkinson	1884
Robert Stout	1884-87
Harry Albert Atkinson	1887-91
John Ballance	1891-93
Richard John Seddon	1893-1906
William Hall-Jones	1906
Joseph George Ward	1906-12
Thomas Mackenzie	1912
William Ferguson Massey	1912-25
Francis Henry Dillon Bell	1925
Joseph Gordon Coates	1925-28
Joseph George Ward	1928-30
George William Forbes	1930-35
Michael J. Savage	1935-40
Peter Fraser	1940-49
Sidney G. Holland	1949-57
Walter Nash	1957-60
Keith J. Holyoake	1960-72
John R. Marshall	1972
Norman Kirk	1972-74
Wallace Rowling	1974-75
Robert D. Muldoon	1975-84
David Lange	1984-89
Geoffrey Palmer	1989-

UNITS OF MEASUREMENT

SI units (Système International d'Unités) are now widely used throughout the world, especially for scientific purposes. SI units are metric units, based on the metre, kilogram, and second.

The base units are:

quantity	SI unit	symbol
length	metre	m
mass	kilogram	k
time	second	s
current	ampere	A
temperature	kelvin	K
luminous intensity	candela	c
amount of substance	mole	mol
plane angle	radian	rad
solid angle	steradian	sr

The derived units with special names are:

quantity	SI unit	symbol
frequency	hertz	Hz
energy	joule	J
force	newton	N
power	watt	W
pressure	pascal	Pa
electric charge	coulomb	C
potential difference	volt	V
electric resistance	ohm	Ω
electric conductance	siemens	S
electric capacitance	farad	F
magnetic flux	weber	Wb
inductance	henry	H
magnetic flux density	tesla	T
luminous flux	lumen	lm
illuminance	lux	lx
absorbed dose	gray	Gy

SI units are used in decimal multiples, e.g. 1 km = 1000 metres, often written 10^3 m ($1 \times 10^3 = 10 \times 10 \times 10 = 1000$); 1 cm = 1/100 of a metre, often written 10^{-2} m ($1 \times 10^{-2} = 1 \div (10 \times 10) = 1/100$). The following prefixes are used:

submultiple	prefix	symbol	multiple	prefix	symbol
10^{-1}	deci-	d	10^1	deca-	da
10^{-2}	centi-	c	10^2	hecto-	h
10^{-3}	milli-	m	10^3	kilo-	k
10^{-6}	micro-	μ	10^6	mega-	M
10^{-9}	nano-	n	10^9	giga-	G
10^{-12}	pico-	p	10^{12}	tera-	T
10^{-15}	femto-	f	10^{15}	peta-	P
10^{-18}	atto-	a	10^{18}	exa-	E

These prefixes are used with all SI units.

length
SI base unit: metre
Imperial units: inch, foot, yard, mile

1 cm = 0.3937 in	1 in = 2.54 cm
1 m = 3.2808 ft = 1.09361 yds	1 ft = 0.3048 m
1 km = 0.62137 mile	1 mile = 1.60934 km

Examples
The radius of an electron is about 3 femtometres (3×10^{-15} m).
The distance between the sun and its nearest neighbour (Proxima Centauri) is about 40 petametres (4×10^{16} m).

mass
SI base unit: kilogram
Imperial units: ounce, pound, ton

1 g = 0.03527 oz	1 oz = 28.3495 g
1 kg = 2.20462 lb	1 lb = 0.45359 kg
1 tonne (1000 kg) = 0.9842 ton	1 ton = 1.01605 tonnes

Examples
The mass of a carbon atom is about 20 millionths of an attogram (2×10^{-23} g).
The mass of the earth is about six thousand million exagrams (6×10^{27} g).

time
SI base unit: second
Other units: minute, hour, day, year

Examples
The time between collisions of oxygen molecules at $0°C$ (760 mmHg) is about 0.2 nanosecond (2×10^{-10} s).
The earth was created about ten thousand teraseconds ago (10^{16} s).

temperature
SI base unit: kelvin (K)
Other units: degree Celsius (centigrade), degree Fahrenheit

1 kelvin = $1°C$
1 kelvin = $1.8°F$

Examples
Absolute zero is a temperature of 0 kelvin.
The temperature inside the hottest stars is about 1 gigakelvin (10^9 K).

energy
SI unit: joule (J)
Other units: calorie, British thermal unit

1 joule = 0.2388 cal	1 cal = 4.1868 joules
1000 joules = 0.9478 Btu	1 Btu = 1055.06 joules

Examples
The energy released by a single disintegrating uranium atom is 40 picojoules (4×10^{-11} J).
The Hiroshima atom bomb released 84 terajoules (8.4×10^{13} J).